The Compact Bedford Introduction to Drama

FOURTH EDITION

Lee A. Jacobus
University of Connecticut

BEDFORD / ST. MARTIN'S   BOSTON ◆ NEW YORK

This book is dedicated to James O. Barnhill.

For Bedford/St.Martin's
Developmental Editor: Maura Shea
Production Editor: Bridget Leahy
Production Supervisor: Dennis Conroy
Director of Marketing: Karen Melton
Editorial Assistant: Tracey Lynne Finch
Production Assistant: Thomas Crehan
Copyeditor: Rosemary Winfield
Text Design: Claire Seng-Niemoeller
Cover Design: Hannus Design Associates
Cover Photo: From the Cottesloe Theatre/Royal National Theatre (London) 1997
   production of *Othello*. Photograph by Donald Cooper/Photostage.
Composition: Stratford Publishing Services
Printing and Binding: RR Donnelley & Sons Company

President: Charles H. Christensen
Editorial Director: Joan E. Feinberg
Editor in Chief: Karen S. Henry
Director of Editing, Design, and Production: Marcia Cohen
Managing Editor: Elizabeth M. Schaaf

Library of Congress Control Number: 00–190745

For information, write: Bedford/St. Martin's, 75 Arlington Street, Boston, MA 02116 (617-399-4000)

ISBN: 0–312–25595–0

Acknowledgments

Greek Drama

Figure 1. The Theater of Epidauros, Greece. CORBIS/Michael Nicholson.
Figure 2. Theater at Epidauros from *The Theatre of Dionysus in Athens* by Arthur Wallace Pickard-Cambridge. Reprinted by permission of Oxford University Press.

Acknowledgments and copyrights are continued at the back of the book on pages 963–65, which constitute an extension of the copyright page. It is a violation of the law to reproduce these selections by any means whatsoever without the written permission of the copyright holder.

Preface for Instructors

The Compact Bedford Introduction to Drama, Fourth Edition, owes its existence to the continual demand for a briefer (and less expensive) collection of plays than the longer edition provides — but with historical and critical material essential for a full understanding of different ages of drama. Instructors in many theater and literature programs convinced us that although a shorter version of *The Bedford Introduction to Drama* should be concise, it should not ignore the problems of performance, issues concerning drama criticism, and the needs of instructors who want their students to write intelligently about drama.

As a result of this demand, *The Compact Bedford Introduction to Drama* has all the features of the longer edition, but with only twenty-six plays. Nonetheless, it affords the most comprehensive collection available in a compact edition of drama. The book incorporates a number of features that distinguish it from other compact introductions to drama. Most notably it presents two major playwrights in greater than usual depth, with two plays by Sophocles and two by William Shakespeare. Fifty-one commentaries by playwrights, directors, actors, reviewers, and critics, a cultural casebook, thorough biographical and critical introductions, brief performance histories, and photographs of landmark productions accompany these and all the plays in the book and offer drama students a unique opportunity to study and write about major figures in the development of drama.

Even when it appears most timeless, all drama (like, of course, all literature) is a product of language, an era, and a complex range of political, social, and ethnic influences. *The Compact Bedford Introduction to Drama* offers a succinct but thorough history of Western drama. A general introduction gives an overview of the great ages of drama, the major genres and elements, and the cultural value of drama. Throughout the book, introductions to significant periods of drama, the playwrights, and the plays focus on the cultural contexts of the works and on their stage history. Timelines following the introduction to each dramatic period present important developments in theater history in their appropriate political, social, and cultural contexts.

The Compact Bedford Introduction to Drama is also a complete resource book for the beginning student of drama. In the general introduction, a discussion of the elements of drama defines the important terms and concepts and demonstrates these concepts in action, drawing its examples from Lady

Gregory's one-act play, *The Rising of the Moon*. Nearly every play is accompanied by one or more striking theater photographs, and the plays by playwrights treated in depth are illustrated by photo essays often featuring more than one production to help students understand the plays as texts to be interpreted through performance.

Writing about Drama, the first appendix, shows students possible approaches to commenting on dramatic literature and points the way to developing ideas that can result in probing critical essays. From prewriting to outlining and drafting, the process of writing about drama is illustrated by reference to Lady Gregory's play, and a sample essay on the play provides one example of drama criticism. Especially useful for assignments involving attendance at theater productions, the section on How to Write a Review analyzes professional reviews and offers suggestions for students writing reviews. The second appendix, the Glossary of Dramatic Terms, defines concepts and terms clearly and concisely. When these terms are first introduced and defined in the text, they appear in small capital letters.

The Selected Bibliography, a third appendix, includes a list of reference works for the major periods of drama, the playwrights, and the plays by the two playwrights treated in depth. The cited general references, histories, biographies, critical studies, journal articles, reviews, and collections of plays are especially useful for research in drama.

While the book presents the plays as texts to be read, a fourth appendix, the Selected List of Film, Video, and Audiocassette Resources, reinforces the element of performance. This list, accompanied by a list of distributors, can help instructors and students find an illuminating treatment of the plays in performance.

New to This Edition
New Plays and Commentaries

Eight plays are new to this edition; among them are William Shakespeare's *Othello*, Oscar Wilde's *The Importance of Being Earnest*, Susan Glaspell's *Trifles*, Bertolt Brecht's *Mother Courage*, and Yasmina Reza's *"Art."* Also new to this edition are seventeen of fifty-one commentaries that provide a variety of ways for students to think about a play — from the perspective of a critic, a reviewer, an actor, a director, and a playwright.

The fourth edition continues the tradition of offering a strong representation of multicultural and women playwrights and representing them with their most significant works, including *Trifles* by Susan Glaspell, *A Raisin in the Sun* by Lorraine Hansberry, *Fences* by August Wilson, *"Art"* by Yasmina Reza, and *How I Learned to Drive* by Paula Vogel.

New Cultural Casebook

A cultural casebook on "The Issue of Race and *Othello*" enables students to think critically about the play by examining its cultural contexts pertaining to the issue of race. The casebook is comprised of an introduction to the topic followed by selected documents — including travel accounts, letters, and essays — that reveal what Shakespeare and his audience knew about "Moors" and how this knowledge might have influenced their perception of the play. The documents are accompanied by visuals that lend further insight on the subject.

More Performance Photographs and Enhanced Design

Significantly more theater photographs (twenty-seven are new) of important productions help students visualize the plays in performance. Illuminating theater diagrams and photographs have been added to the historical introductions. New portraits accompany each playwright who is represented by multiple plays. The new larger trim size and opaque paper enhance the quality of the reproductions.

Companion Web Site and Video Library

The new companion Web site at www.bedfordstmartins.com/jacobus helps students succeed in the course with study questions, writing suggestions, and Web assignments to accompany each play; annotated research links for the plays and playwrights in the book; and links to online reviews, important repertory theaters around the country, and internship opportunities. Sample syllabi and assignment ideas are offered for instructors.

A selection of videotapes of plays in the book is available from the Bedford/St. Martin's video library to qualified adopters.

Acknowledgments

I would like to thank first the large number of teachers of drama who shared suggestions for inclusion and encouragement for the first three editions of *The Bedford Introduction to Drama*. In the first edition: Jeff Glauner, Park College; Susan Smith, University of Pittsburgh; and Jordan Miller, University of Rhode Island. Second, I am grateful to those who read the introductions and commentaries in the first edition and who gave me the advantage of their knowledge and wisdom. G. Jennifer Wilson, University of California, Los Angeles; William Carroll, Boston University; Ronald Bryden, Graduate Centre for the Study of Drama, University of Toronto; Robert Dial, University of Akron; Jonnie Guerra, Mount Vernon College; and John Timpane, Lafayette College, were all unhesitating in offering suggestions and improvements.

For the second edition, experts in specific historical periods examined the introductions for accuracy and comprehensiveness. Each of the introductions was revised with their suggestions in mind. These reviewers were Michael Cadden, Princeton University; Mary Coogan, University of Colorado, Boulder; Anthony Graham-White, University of Illinois, Chicago; C. Fenno Hoffman; Robert D. Hume, Pennsylvania State University; Paul G. Reeve, University of Houston, University Park; Laurence Senelick, Tufts University; and Timothy Wiles, Indiana University, Bloomington.

I am also grateful to Keith Hull of the University of Wyoming for the warmth of his response to the book. Especially helpful in preparing the second edition were Elias Abdou, Community College of Allegheny, Pittsburgh; Robert E. Aldridge, Kirkwood Community College; Katya Amato, Portland State University; Keith Appler, University of Illinois, Urbana; Nora Bicki, University of Illinois, Champaign; Reverend Doctor Nadean Bishop, Eastern Michigan University; François Bonneville, State University of New York, Albany; Michael Boudreau, University of Illinois, Urbana; David Bratt, Winona State University; Marianne Cooley, University of Houston, University Park; Walter Creed, University of Hawaii, Manoa; Mary Beth Culp, Marymount College; Merilee Cunningham, University of Houston; Joan D'Antoni, University of Louisville;

Wayne G. Deahl, Eastern Wyoming College; Charlotte Doctor, Los Angeles Pierce College; Janet Dow, Western Connecticut State University; Jerry D. Eisenhour, Eastern Illinois University; Fred M. Fetrow, United States Naval Academy; Jane E. Fisher, Canisius College; Charles Frey, University of Washington; Robert W. Funk, Eastern Illinois University; Stephen R. Grecco, Pennsylvania State University; L. W. Harrison, Santa Rosa Junior College; Dave Hartley, Central Florida Community College; Andrew Jay Hoffman, Central Connecticut State University; Claudia L. Johnson, Marquette University; Ellen Redding Kaler, University of Kansas; Harvey Kassebaum, Cuyahoga Community College; Dorothy Louise, Franklin and Marshall College; Annette McGregor, Purdue University; Jack Mahoney, Vincennes University; James Marlow, Southeastern Massachusetts University; Christy Minadeo, Eastern Michigan University; Carol A. Moore, Louisiana State University; Roark Mulligan, University of Oregon; Eric Pederson, Butler County Community College; M. Bernice Pepke, Manatee Community College; Patrick Quade, Saint Olaf College; Carol Replogle, Loyola University, Chicago; William Reynolds, Hope College; Mark Rocha, California State University, Northridge; Matthew C. Roudane, Georgia State University; Dolores J. Sarafinski, Gannon University; Carol Scklenica, Marquette University; Rodney Simard, California State University, San Bernardino; James Stephens, Marquette University; Jeannie B. Thomas, University of Oregon; Gregory Ulmer, Kearney State College; Susan Vick, Worcester Polytechnic Institute; Linda Wells, Boston University; Keith Welsh, Webster University; Virginia West, Franklin and Marshall College; Paul Wood, Villanova University; and J. S. Wszalek, James Madison University.

For the third edition, Samuel Abel of Dartmouth College reviewed the historical material for accuracy and offered a number of very useful suggestions that I incorporated into the text. I am grateful for his help and for the response of those who offered suggestions and advice for improving the book, especially Cora Agatucci, Central Oregon Community College; Joan D'Antoni, University of Louisville; Harold J. Baxter, Trinity International University; Irene Blakely, Northland College; Cynthia Bowers, Loyola University, Chicago; Jody D. Brown, Ferrum College; Mark Browning, Johnson County Community College; William D. Buckley, Indiana University NW; William J. Campbell, SUNY College of Technology at Delhi; Heather S. Collins, Mott Community College; Ruth Contrell, New Mexico State University; Kenneth Cox, Oklahoma State University; Judith P. Cronk, Oklahoma State University; Marsha Cummins, Bronx Community College; James D. Cunningham, Florida Southern College; Tom DeSpain, Chemeketa Community College; Dexter Roger Dixon, University of Arkansas; Nancy Eddy, Indiana University–Purdue University at Indianapolis; Tom Empy, Casper College; Shawn Paul Evans, University of Tennessee at Chattanooga; Harry Feiner, Queens College; Monika Fischer, University of Oregon; James Fisher, Wabash College; Kay Forston, Phillips University; John E. Hallwas, Western Illinois University; Wilma Hahn Hasse, Mitchell University; David Henry, El Paso Community College; Kirsten F. Herdd, Eastern Michigan University; D. E. Jukes, Community College of Allegheny County; E. Kahn, Lehigh University; Jackson Kesler, Western Kentucky University; Lawrence Kinsman, New Hampshire College; Terry A. Klenk, Santa Fe Community College; Marcia K. Morrison, Genesee Community College; Eva Patton, Fordham University; Richard Pettergill, University of Illinois at Chicago; David Pinner, Colgate University; Joseph Rice, University of Cincinnati; Deborah A. Ring, Case Western Reserve University; Hans H. Rudnick, Southern Illinois University; Samuel Schuman, University of North Carolina; William O. Scott, University of Kansas; Rita Smilkstein, North Seattle Community College; Gerald F. Snelson, Frostburg State University; N. J. Stanley, Agnes Scott College; Catherine Stevenson, University of Hartford; John S. Terhes, Chemeketa Community College; Charles Trainor, Siena College; Anita J. Turpin, Roanoke College; Joy Walsh, Butler County Community College; Gladdy White, Notre Dame College; Celeste Wiggins, Ursuline College; Salaam Yousif, California State University; and Ruth Zielke, Concordia College.

For the fourth edition, I am grateful to those who offered suggestions and advice for the book, especially David Adamson, University of North Carolina, Chapel Hill; Joan Angelis, Woodbury University; Karen C. Blansfield, University of North Carolina, Chapel Hill; Stephen F. Bloom, Emmanuel College; Cathy A. Brookshire, James Madison University; Barbara Clayton, University of Wisconsin, Madison; John J. Conlon, University of Massachusetts, Boston; Heath A. Diehl, Bowling Green State University; Richard Donnelly, University of Notre Dame; Joseph Fahey, Ohio State University; John E. R. Friedenberg, Wake Forest University; Stanton B. Garner Jr., University of Tennessee; Anthony Graham-White, University of Illinois at Chicago; Leigh Harbin, Angelo State University; Jim Hauser, William Patterson University; Don Haynes, Robert Morris College; Gregory Kable, University of North Carolina, Chapel Hill; Theresa M. Kenosa, Lincoln Land Community College; Sonya Lancaster, University of Kansas; Charlotte Langford, Pima Community College; Sandee McGlaun, Ohio State University; Deborah Montuori, Shippensburg University; Joan Navarre, Marquette University; Susan Sanders, Northern Essex Community College; Helen Scheck, University of Albany; Joel Shatzky, SUNY College at Cortland; Michelle L. Stie, University of Kansas; James Symmons, Penn State University, Media; George Wead, James Madison University; Janet S. Wolf, SUNY College at Cortland; and Tom Zimmerman, Washtenaw Community College.

For this compact fourth edition, I am especially grateful to those who offered specific suggestions and advice for improving *The Compact Bedford Introduction to Drama*, Second Edition, especially Ann Bliss, Western Oregon University; Ray Dolley, University of North Carolina, Chapel Hill; Richard E. Donnelly, University of Notre Dame; Tom Isbell, University of Minnesota, Duluth; Walter H. Johnson, Cumberland County College; Margaret Thomas Kelso, Humboldt State University; James Reynolds, Eastern Michigan University; C. Warren Robertson, East Tennessee State University; and Mary Beth Tallon, Marquette University.

I am indebted to many talented people who, were they in a drama, could constitute a crowd scene, and yet each played an indispensable solo role in making this book a reality. Martha Friedman did the photo research and secured permissions in outstanding fashion. Virginia Creedon cleared the text permissions in record time. Ed Kahn researched performance histories and located many commentaries. Julie Parker assisted him. Valerie Smith updated the Selected Bibliography and, with Amanda Nelson, wrote the study questions, writing suggestions, and Web assignments for the Web site. Joanne Diaz expanded and updated the timelines, updated the list of audiovisual materials, and checked controversial dates and facts throughout the book. Jon Rossini of Duke University provided the excellent gloss notes for the phrases of Calò dialect in Luis Valdez's *Zoot Suit*.

A number of colleagues at the University of Connecticut were generous with their time — both in talking about the plays they love and teach and in talking about how they should be presented in a text such as this. Among them are Brenda Murphy, Thomas Jambeck, and Jack Manning, all of whom teach drama regularly. I also wish to thank Michael Meyer and Regina Barreca, with whom my discussions of literature have been an ongoing delight for more than a decade.

I owe a very special debt of gratitude to the people at Bedford/St. Martin's who worked behind the scenes to produce this book. In preparation for this revision, editorial assistants Amanda Bristow and Nicole Simonsen contacted users of earlier editions, solicited their suggestions and opinions, and collated their responses. Tracey Finch provided invaluable editorial assistance throughout the book's development, including numerous hours of library research and profoundly helpful manuscript preparation. The production editor, Bridget Leahy, who worked on earlier versions of this book, kept the production on schedule and made the process seem effortless. Production supervisor Dennis Conroy and managing editor Elizabeth Schaaf watched over the project carefully, keeping everything going smoothly throughout. Thomas Crehan, production assistant, helped meet the deadlines. The copyeditor, Rosemary Winfield; the book's designer, Claire Seng-Niemoeller; and proofreaders Janet Cocker and Jocelyn Hummelsine all worked together to make the book both accurate and pleasant to read. Art director Donna Dennison and junior designer Zenobia Rivetna made the cover dynamic and inviting. Project manager/copywriter Pelle Cass oversaw the design, production, and distribution of the brochure. Web master Jen Lesar took care in the design and production of the Web site, one of the special features of this edition.

As always, I owe an immense debt of gratitude to the guidance and intelligence of the publishers, Charles Christensen and Joan Feinberg, who stand not just as pillars of publishing but as staunch friends for whom this book has a special meaning. They are smart, imaginative, and inspirational. Karen Henry, my editor for the first three editions of this book, has become a standard-bearer but is also a person of warmth, with an affection for the art of drama and a passion for getting it right. She kept her hand in this edition and remains a beacon for my work. Finally, I must single out my current editor, Maura Shea, who is the most amazing "go-to" editor I have worked with. She worked closely with me on every stage of this project, from selection of photos to selection of plays, from innovations in design to development of casebooks. Her enthusiasm and her intelligence in relation to the development of drama have been powerful elements in making this edition new and vigorous. She has my total respect and admiration because she represents everything that the term *editorial excellence* implies.

Lee A. Jacobus
University of Connecticut, Storrs

Contents

Appendices

Introduction: Thinking about Drama

What Is Drama?

DRAMA is the art of representing for the pleasure of others events that happened or that we imagine happening. The primary ingredients of drama are characters, represented by players; action, described by gestures and movement; thought, implied by dialogue, words, and action; spectacle, represented by scenery, music, and costume; and, finally, audiences, who respond to this complex mixture.

When we are in the theater, we see the actors, hear the lines, are aware of the setting, and sense the theatrical community of which we are a part. Even when reading a play, we should imagine actors speaking lines and visualize a setting in which those lines are spoken. Drama is an experience in which we participate on many levels simultaneously. On one level, we may believe that what we see is really happening; on another level, we know it is only make-believe. On one level we may be amused, but on another level we realize that serious statements about our society are being made. Drama both entertains and instructs.

When Aristotle wrote about drama in the *Poetics,* a work providing one of the earliest and most influential theories of drama, he began by explaining it as the imitation of an action (MIMESIS). Those analyzing his work have interpreted this statement in several ways. One interpretation is that drama imitates life. On the surface, such an observation may seem simple, even obvious. But on reflection we begin to find complex significance in his comment. The drama of the Greeks, for example, with its intense mythic structure, its formidable speeches, and its profound actions, often seems larger than life or other than life. Yet we recognize characters saying words that we ourselves are capable of saying, doing things that we ourselves might do. The great Greek tragedies are certainly lifelike and certainly offer literary mirrors in which we can examine human nature. And the same is true of Greek comedies.

The relationship between drama and life has always been subtle and complex. In some plays, such as Luigi Pirandello's *Six Characters in Search of an Author,* it is one of the central issues. We begin our reading or viewing of most plays knowing that the dramatic experience is not absolutely real in the sense that, for example, the actor playing Hamlet does not truly die or truly see a ghost or truly frighten his mother. The play imitates those imagined actions,

1

but when done properly it is realistic enough to make us fear, if only for a moment, that they could be real.

We see significance in the actions Hamlet imitates; his actions help us live our own lives more deeply, more intensely, because they give us insight into the possibilities of life. We are all restricted to living this life as ourselves; drama is one art form that helps us realize the potential of life, for both the good and the bad. In an important sense, we can share the experience of a character such as Hamlet when he soliloquizes over the question of whether it is better to die than to live in a world filled with sin and crime.

Drama and Ritual

Such imaginative participation is only a part of what we derive from drama. In its origins, drama may have evolved from ancient Egyptian and Greek rituals, ceremonies that were performed the same way again and again and were thought to have a propitious effect on the relationship between the people and their gods.

In ancient Egypt some religious rituals evolved into repeated passion plays, such as those celebrating Isis and Osiris at the festivals of Heb-Seb in Abydos some three thousand years ago. Greek drama was first performed during yearly religious celebrations dedicated to the god Dionysus. The early Greek playwrights, such as Sophocles in *Oedipus Rex* and *Antigone,* emphasized the interaction between the will of the gods and the will of human beings, often pitting the truths of men and women against the truths of the gods.

The rebirth of drama in the Middle Ages — after the fall of Rome and the loss of classical artistic traditions — took place first in monasteries, then later in the cathedrals of Europe. It evolved from medieval religious ceremonies that helped the faithful understand more about their own moral predicament. *Everyman,* a late play in the medieval theater (it was written about 1500), concerns itself with the central issue of reward and punishment after this life because the soul is immortal.

Drama: The Illusion of Reality

From the beginning, drama has had the capacity to hold up an illusion of reality like the reflection in a mirror: we take the reality for granted while recognizing that it is nonetheless illusory. As we have seen, Aristotle described DRAMATIC ILLUSION as an imitation of an action. But unlike the reflection in a mirror, the action of most drama is not drawn from our actual experience of life but from our potential or imagined experience. In the great Greek drama, the illusion includes the narratives of ancient myths that were thought to offer profound illumination. The interpretation of the myths by the Greek playwrights over a two-hundred-year period helped the Greek people participate in the myths, understand them, and apply their values to their daily lives.

Different ages have had different approaches to representing reality onstage. Greek actors spoke in verse and wore masks. The staging consisted of very little setting and no special costumes except for some comedies and satyr plays. Medieval drama was sometimes acted on pushwagons and carts, but the special machinery developed to suggest hellfire and the presence of devils was said to be so realistic as to be frightening. Elizabethan audiences were accustomed to actors who spoke directly to the crowds at their feet near the apron of the stage. All Elizabethan plays were done in essentially contemporary clothing, often with no more scenery than the suggestion of it in the spoken descriptions of the players. The actors recited their lines in verse, except when the author had a particular reason to use prose — for example, to imply that the speaker was of low social station. Yet Elizabethans reported that their theater was much like life itself.

In Shakespeare's *A Midsummer Night's Dream,* fairies, enchantments, an ass's head on the shoulders of a man — all these are presented as illusions, and we accept them. They inform the audience — in Shakespeare's day and in modern times — not by showing us ourselves in a mirror but by demonstrating that even fantastic realities have significance for us.

Certainly *A Midsummer Night's Dream* gives us insight into the profound range of human emotions. We learn about the pains of rejection when we see Helena longing for Demetrius, who in turn longs for Hermia. We learn about jealousy and possessiveness when we see Oberon cast a spell on his wife, Titania, over a dispute concerning a changeling. And we learn, too, about the worldly ambitions of the "rude mechanicals" who themselves put on a play whose reality they fear might frighten their audience. They solve the problem by reminding their audience that it is only a play and that they need not fear that reality will spoil their pleasure.

In modern drama the dramatic illusion of reality includes not just the shape of an action, the events, and the characters but also the details of everyday life. When the action changes locale, the setting changes as well. Some contemporary playwrights make an effort to re-create a reality close to the one we live in. Some modern plays, like August Wilson's *Fences,* make a precise representation of reality a primary purpose, shaping the tone of the language to reflect the way modern people speak, re-creating contemporary reality in the setting, language, and other elements of the drama.

But describing a play as an illusion of reality in no way means that it represents the precise reality that we take for granted in our everyday experience. Rather, drama ranges widely and explores multiple realities, some of which may seem very close to our own and some of which may seem improbably removed from our everyday experience.

Seeing a Play Onstage

For an audience, drama is one of the most powerful artistic experiences. When we speak about participating in drama, we mean that as a member of the audience we become a part of the action that unfolds. This is a mysterious phenomenon.

When we see a play today, we are usually seated in a darkened theater looking at a lighted stage. In ages past, this contrast was not the norm. Greek plays took place outdoors during the morning and the afternoon; most Elizabethan plays were staged outdoors in the afternoon; in the Renaissance, some plays began to be staged indoors with ingenious systems of lighting that involved candles and reflectors. In the early nineteenth century most theaters used gaslight onstage; electricity took over in the later part of the century, and its use has grown increasingly complex. In most large theaters today computerized lighting boards have replaced Renaissance candles.

Sitting in the darkness has made the experience of seeing Greek and Eliza-bethan plays much different for us than it was for the original audiences. We do not worry about being seen by the "right people" or about studying the quality of the audience, as people did during the Restoration in the late seven-teenth century. The darkness isolates us from all except those who sit adjacent to us. Yet we instantly respond when others in the audience laugh, when they gasp, when they shift restlessly. We recognize in those moments that we are part of a larger community drawn together by theater and that we are all involved in the dramatic experience.

Theaters and Their Effect

Different kinds of theaters make differing demands on actors and audiences. Despite its huge size, the open ARENA style theater of the early Greeks brought the audience into a special kind of intimacy with the actors. The players came very close to the first rows of seats, and the acoustics permitted even a whisper onstage to be audible in the far seats. The Greek theater also imparted a sense of formality to the occasion of drama. For one thing, its regularity and circu-larity was accompanied by a relatively rigid seating plan. The officials and nobility sat in special seats. Then each section of the theater was given over to specific families, with the edges of the seating area devoted to travelers and strangers to the town. One knew one's place in the Greek theater. Its regularity gave the community a sense of order.

Medieval theater also gave its audiences a sense of community, both when it used playing areas called *mansions* inside and outside the churches and when it used wagons wheeled about in processions in the streets or outside the city walls. That the medieval theater repeated the same cycles of plays again and again for about two hundred years, to the delight of many European communi-ties, tells us something about the stability of those communities. Their drama was integrated with their religion, and both helped them express their sense of belonging to the church and the community.

In some medieval performances the actors came into the audience, breaking the sense of distance or the illusion of separation. It is difficult for us to know how much participation and involvement in the action the medieval audience felt. Modern audiences have responded very well to productions of medieval plays such as *The Second Shepherds' Play, Noah's Flood,* and *Everyman,* and we have every reason to think that medieval audiences enjoyed their dramas immensely. The guilds that performed them took pride in making their plays as exciting and involving as possible.

The Elizabethan playhouse was a wooden structure providing an enclosed space around a courtyard open to the sky. A covered stage thrust into the courtyard. As in the Greek theater, the audience was arranged somewhat by social station. Around the stage, which was about five feet off the ground, stood the groundlings, those who paid least for their entrance. Then in covered galleries in the building itself sat patrons who paid extra for a seat. The effect of the enclosed structure was of a small, contained world. Actors were in the habit of speaking directly to members of the audience, and the audience rarely kept a polite silence. It was a busy, humming theater that generated intimacy and involvement between actors and audience.

The proscenium stage of the nineteenth and twentieth centuries distanced the audience from the play, providing a clear frame (the PROSCENIUM) behind which the performers acted out their scenes. This detachment was especially effective for plays that demanded a high degree of realism because the effect of the proscenium is to make the audience feel that it is witnessing the action as a silent observer, looking in as if through an imaginary fourth wall on a living room or other intimate space in which the action takes place. The proscenium arch gives the illusion that the actors are in a world of their own, unaware of the audience's presence.

In the twentieth century some of the virtues of the Greek arena theater, or THEATER IN THE ROUND, were rediscovered. In an effort to close the distance between audience and players, Antonin Artaud, the French actor and director, developed in the 1920s and 1930s a concept called the *theater of cruelty*. Using theater in the round, Artaud robbed the audience of the comfort of watching a distant stage and pressed his actors into the space of the viewers. His purpose was to force theatergoers to deal with the primary issues of the drama by stripping them of the security of darkness and anonymity. Theaters in Russia and Britain developed similar spaces in the 1930s and 1940s, and since the 1950s the Arena Theater in Washington, D.C., and the Circle in the Square in New York have continued the tradition.

Twenty-first-century theater is eclectic. It uses thrust, arena, proscenium, and every other kind of stage already described. Some contemporary theater also converts nontheatrical space, such as warehouses or city streets, into space for performance.

Reading a Play

Reading a play is a different experience from seeing it enacted. For one thing, readers do not have the benefit of the interpretations made by a director, actors, and scene designers in presenting a performance. These interpretations are all critical judgments based on a director's ideas of how the play should be presented and on actors' insights into the meaning of the play.

A reading of a play produces an interpretation that remains in our heads and is not translated to the stage. The dramatic effect of the staging is lost to us unless we make a genuine effort to visualize it and to understand its contribution to the dramatic experience. For a fuller experience of the drama when reading plays, one should keep in mind the historical period and the conventions of staging that are appropriate to the period and that are specified by the playwright.

Some plays were prepared by their authors for reading as well as for staging, as evident in plays whose stage directions supply information that would be unavailable to an audience, such as the color of the characters' eyes, characters' secret motives, and other such details. Occasionally, stage directions, such as those of Bernard Shaw and Tennessee Williams, are written in a poetic prose that can be appreciated only by a reader.

It is not a certainty that seeing a play will produce an experience more "true" to the play's meaning than reading it. Every act of reading silently or speaking the lines aloud is an act of interpretation. No one can say which is the best interpretation. Each has its own merits, and the ideal is probably to read and see any play.

The Great Ages of Drama

Certain historical periods have produced great plays and great playwrights, although why some periods generate more dramatic activity than others is still a matter of conjecture for scholars examining the social, historical, and religious conditions of the times. Each of the great ages of drama has affected the way plays are written, acted, and staged in successive ages. In every age, drama borrows important elements from each earlier period.

Greek Drama

The Greeks of the fifth century B.C. are credited with the first masterful dramatic age, which lasted from the birth of Aeschylus (c. 525 B.C.) to the death of Aristophanes (c. 385 B.C.). Their theaters were supported by public funds, and the playwrights competed for prizes during the great festivals of Dionysus. Sometimes as many as ten to fifteen thousand people sat in the theaters and watched with a sense of delight and awe as the actors played out their tales.

Theater was extremely important to the Greeks as a way of interpreting their relationships with their gods and of reinforcing their sense of community. The fifth-century B.C. audience, mostly wealthy citizens, came early in the morning and spent the entire day in the theater. Drama for the Greeks was not mere escapism or entertainment, not a frill or a luxury. Connected as it was with religious festivals, it was a cultural necessity.

Sophocles' plays *Oedipus Rex* and *Antigone* are examples of the powerful tragedies that have transfixed audiences for centuries. Euripides, slightly younger than Sophocles, was also a prize-winning tragedian. His *Trojan Women, Alcestis, Medea, Bacchae,* and *Elektra* [*Electra*] are still performed and still exert an influence on today's drama. The same is true of Aeschylus, who was slightly older than both and whose *Agamemnon, The Libation Bearers, The Eumenides* (known collectively as the *Oresteia*), and *Prometheus Bound* have all been among the most lasting of plays.

In addition to such great tragedians, the Greeks also produced the important comedians Aristophanes and Menander (late fourth century B.C.), whose work has been plundered for plays as diverse as a Shakespeare comedy and a Broadway musical. Aristophanes' *Lysistrata,* in which the Athenian and Spartan women agree to withhold sex from their husbands until the men promise to stop making war, is a powerful social comedy. Menander produced a more subtle type of comedy that made the culture laugh at itself. Both styles of comedy are the staple of popular entertainment even today. Menander's social comedies were the basis of the comedy of manners, in which society's ways of behavior are criticized. The comedy of manners is exemplified in William Congreve's eighteenth-century *The Way of the World* and Molière's *The Misanthrope.*

Roman Drama

The Romans became aware of Greek drama in the third century B.C. and began to import Greek actors and playwrights. Because of many social and cultural differences between the societies, however, drama never took a central role in the life of the average Roman. Seneca, who is now viewed as Rome's most important tragedian, almost certainly wrote his plays to be read rather than to be seen onstage.

Roman comedy produced two great playwrights, Plautus and Terence, who helped develop the STOCK (or type) CHARACTER, such as the skinflint or the prude. Plautus was the great Roman comedian in the tradition of Menander's comedy of manners. Plautus's best-known plays are *The Braggart Warrior* and

The Twin Menaechmi; and during the Renaissance, when all European school-children read Latin, his works were favorites.

Terence's work was praised during the Middle Ages and the Renaissance as being smoother, more elegant, and more polished and refined than Plautus's. In his own age Terence was less admired by the general populace but more admired by connoisseurs of drama. His best-known plays — *The Woman of Andros, Phormio,* and *The Brothers* — are rarely performed today.

Drama took its place beside many other forms of entertainment in Roman culture — sports events, gladiator battles to the death, chariot races, the slaughter of wild beasts, and sacrifices of Christians and others to animals. The Roman public, when it did attend plays, enjoyed farces and relatively coarse humor. The audiences for Plautus and Terence, aristocratic in taste, may not have represented the cross-section of the community that was typical of Greek audiences.

Medieval Drama

After the fall of Rome and the spread of the Goths and Visigoths across southern Europe in the fifth century, Europe experienced a total breakdown of the strong central government Rome had provided. When Rome fell, Greek and Roman culture virtually disappeared. The great classical texts went largely unread until the end of the medieval period in the fourteenth and fifteenth centuries; however, expressions of culture, including art forms such as drama, did not entirely disappear. During the medieval period the church's power and influence grew extensively, and it tried to fill the gap left by the demise of the Roman empire. The church became a focus of both religious and secular activity for people all over Europe.

After almost five centuries of relative inactivity, European drama was reborn in religious ceremonies in monasteries. It moved inside churches, then out of doors by the twelfth century, perhaps because its own demands outgrew its circumstances. Drama had become more than an adjunct of the religious ceremonies that had spawned it.

One reason that the medieval European communities regarded their drama so highly is that it expressed many of their concerns and values. The age was highly religious; in addition, the people who produced the plays were members of guilds whose personal pride was represented in their work. Their plays came to be called MYSTERY PLAYS because the trade that each guild represented was a special skill — a mystery to the average person. Of course, the pun on religious mystery was understood by most audiences.

Many of these plays told stories drawn from the Bible. The tales of Noah's Ark, Abraham and Isaac, and Samson and Delilah all had dramatic potential, and the mystery plays capitalized on that potential, as did plays on the life and crucifixion of Christ. Among mystery plays, *The Second Shepherds' Play* and *Abraham and Isaac* are still performed regularly.

Most mystery plays were gathered into groups of plays called CYCLES dramatizing incidents from the Bible, among other sources. They were usually performed outdoors, at times on movable wagons that doubled as stages. The audience either moved from wagon to wagon to see each play in a cycle, or the wagons moved among the audience.

By the fifteenth and sixteenth centuries, another form of play developed that was not associated with cycles or with the guilds. These were the MORALITY

PLAYS, and their purpose was to touch on larger contemporary issues that had a moral overtone. *Everyman,* the best known of the morality plays, was performed in many nations in various languages.

Renaissance Drama

The revival of learning in the Renaissance, beginning in Italy in the fourteenth century, had considerable effect on drama because classical Greek and Roman plays were discovered and studied. In the academies in Italy, some experiments in re-creating Greek and Roman plays introduced music into drama. New theaters, such as Teatro Olympico in Vicenza (1579), were built to produce these plays; they allow us to see how the Renaissance reconceived the classical stage. Some of these experiments developed into modern opera. The late medieval traditions of the Italian theater's COMMEDIA DELL'ARTE, a stylized improvisational slapstick comedy performed by actors' guilds, began to move outside Italy into other European nations. The commedia's stock characters, Harlequins and Pulcinellas, began to appear in many countries in Europe.

Elizabethan and Jacobean (named for King James I, who succeeded Elizabeth and reigned from 1603 to 1625) drama developed most fully during the fifty years from approximately 1590 to 1640. Audiences poured into the playhouses eager for plays about history and for the great tragedies of Christopher Marlowe, such as *Doctor Faustus,* and of Shakespeare, including *Macbeth, Hamlet, Othello, Julius Caesar,* and *King Lear.* But there were others as well: Middleton and Rowley's *The Changeling,* Cyril Tourneur's *Revenger's Tragedy,* and John Webster's *The White Devil* and his sensational *The Duchess of Malfi.*

The great comedies of the age came mostly from the pen of William Shakespeare: *A Midsummer Night's Dream, The Comedy of Errors, As You Like It, Much Ado about Nothing, The Taming of the Shrew,* and *Twelfth Night.* Many of these plays derived from Italian originals, usually novellas or popular poems and sometimes comedies. But Shakespeare, of course, elevated and vastly improved everything he borrowed.

Ben Jonson, a playwright who was significantly influenced by the classical writers, was also well represented on the Elizabethan stage, with *Volpone, The Alchemist, Everyman in His Humour, Bartholomew Fair,* and other durable comedies. Jonson is also important for his contributions to the MASQUE, an aristocratic entertainment that featured music, dance, and fantastic costuming. His *Masque of Blacknesse* was performed in the royal court with the queen as a performer.

The Elizabethan stage sometimes grew bloody, with playwrights and audiences showing a passion for tragedies that, like *Hamlet,* centered on revenge and often ended with most of the characters meeting a premature death. Elizabethan plays also show considerable variety, with many plays detailing the history of English kings and, therefore, the history of England. It was a theater of powerful effect, and contemporary diaries indicate that the audiences delighted in it. Theaters also flourished in Spain in this period, producing Lope de Vega (1562–1635), who may have written as many as seventeen hundred plays.

Vega's immediate successor, Pedro Calderón de la Barca (1600–1681), is sometimes considered to be more polished in style, but also more stiffly aristocratic in appeal. He wrote fewer plays than Vega, but still produced an amazing body of work. He is said to have written at least 111 dramas and seventy or eighty *auto sacramentales,* the Spanish equivalent of religious morality plays designed for special religious ceremonies. Calderón is best known for *La vida es sueño (Life Is a Dream),* which is still performed today.

Theaters in Shakespeare's day were built outside city limits in seamy neighborhoods near brothels and bear-baiting pits, where chained bears were set upon by large dogs for the crowd's amusement. Happily, the theaters' business was good; the plays were constructed of remarkable language that seems to have fascinated all social classes, since all flocked to the theater by the thousands.

Late Seventeenth- and Eighteenth-Century Drama

After the Puritan reign in England from 1642 (when the theaters were closed) to 1660, during which dramatic productions were almost nonexistent, the theater was suddenly revived. In 1660 Prince Charles, sent to France by his father during the English Civil War, was invited back to be king, thus beginning what was known in England as the Restoration. It was a gay, exciting period in stark contrast to the gray Puritan era. During the period new indoor theaters modeled on those in France were built, and a new generation of actors and actresses (women took part in plays for the first time in England) came forth to participate in the dramatic revival.

Since the mid-1600s, French writers, interpreting Aristotle's description of Greek drama, had leaned toward development of a classical theater, which was supposed to observe the "unities" of time, place, and action: a play had one plot and one setting and covered the action of one day. In 1637 Pierre Corneille wrote *Le Cid,* using relatively modern Spanish history as his theme and following certain classical techniques. Jean-Baptiste Racine was Corneille's successor, and his plays became even more classical by centering on classical topics. His work includes *Andromache, Britannicus,* and, possibly his best play, *Phaedra.* Racine retired from the stage at the end of the century, but he left a powerful legacy of classicism that reached well into the eighteenth century.

Molière, an actor and producer, was the best comedian of seventeenth-century France. Among his plays, *The Misanthrope* and several others are still produced regularly in the West. Molière was classical in his way, borrowing ancient comedy's technique of using type, or stock, characters in his social satires.

Among the important playwrights of the new generation were Aphra Behn, the first professional English female writer, whose play *The Rover* was one of the most popular plays of the late seventeenth century, and William Congreve, whose best-known play, *The Way of the World,* is often still produced. The latter is a lively comedy that aimed to chasten as well as entertain Congreve's audiences.

The eighteenth century saw the tradition of the comedy of manners continued in Richard Brinsley Sheridan's *School for Scandal* and Oliver Goldsmith's *She Stoops to Conquer.* The drama of this period focuses on social manners, and much of it is SATIRE — that is, drama that offers mild criticism of society and holds society up to comic ridicule. But underlying that ridicule is the relatively noble motive of reforming society. We can see some of that motive at work in the plays of Molière and Congreve.

During much of the eighteenth century, theater in France centered on the court and was controlled by a small coterie of snobbish people. The situation in England was not quite the same, although the audiences were snobbish and socially conscious. They went to the theater to be seen, and they often went in claques — groups of like-minded patrons who applauded or booed together to express their views. Theater was important, but attendance at it was like a material possession, something to be displayed for others to admire.

Nineteenth-Century Drama through the Turn of the Century

English playwrights alone produced more than thirty thousand plays during the nineteenth century. Most of the plays were sentimental, melodramatic, and dominated by a few very powerful actors, stars who often overwhelmed the works written for them. The audiences were quite different from those of the seventeenth and eighteenth centuries. The upwardly mobile urban middle classes and the moneyed factory and mill owners who had benefited economically from the industrial revolution demanded a drama that would entertain them.

The new audiences were not especially well educated, nor were they interested in plays that were intellectually demanding. Instead, they wanted escapist and sentimental entertainment that was easy to respond to and did not challenge their basic values. Revivals of old plays and adaptations of Shakespeare were also common in the age, with great stars like Edmund Kean, Sir Henry Irving, Edwin Forrest, Edwin Booth, and William Macready using the plays as platforms for overwhelming, and sometimes overbearing, performances. Thrillers were especially popular, as were historical plays and melodramatic plays featuring a helpless heroine.

As an antidote to such a diet, the new Realist movement in literature, marked by the achievements of French novelists Émile Zola and Gustave Flaubert, finally struck the stage in the 1870s and 1880s in plays by August Strindberg and Henrik Ibsen. Revolutionizing Western drama, these Scandinavians forced their audiences to pay attention to important issues and deeper psychological concerns than earlier audiences had done.

Strindberg's *Miss Julie,* a psychological study, challenged social complacency based on class and social differences. Ibsen's *A Doll House* was a blow struck for feminism, but it did not amuse all audiences. Some were horrified at the thought that Nora Helmer was to be taken as seriously as her husband. Such a view was heretical, but it was also thrilling for a newly awakened European conscience. Those intellectuals and writers who responded positively to Ibsen, including Bernard Shaw, acted as the new conscience and began a move that soon transformed drama. Feminism is also a theme, but perhaps less directly, of Ibsen's *Hedda Gabler,* the story of a woman whose frustration at being cast into an inferior role contributes toward a destructive — and ultimately self-destructive — impulse. Both plays are acted in a physical setting that seems to be as ordinary as a nineteenth-century sitting room, with characters as small — and yet as large — as the people who watched them.

The Russian Anton Chekhov's plays *Three Sisters, Uncle Vanya,* and *The Cherry Orchard,* written at the turn of the twentieth century, are realistic as well, but they are also patient examinations of character rather than primarily problem plays — like Ibsen's successful dramas *Ghosts* and *The Master Builder.* Chekhov is aware of social change in Russia, especially the changes that revealed a hitherto repressed class of peasants evolving into landowners and merchants. *The Cherry Orchard* is suffused with an overpowering sense of inevitability through which Chekhov depicts the conflict between the necessity for change and a nostalgia for the past. The comedies of Oscar Wilde, such as *Lady Windermere's Fan* and *The Importance of Being Ernest,* poked fun at the foibles of the upper classes. Amusing as they are, their satirical quality constitutes social criticism.

These plays introduced a modern realism of a kind that was rare in earlier drama. Melodrama of the nineteenth century was especially satisfying to mass audiences because the good characters were very good, the bad characters were very bad, and justice was meted out at the end. But it is difficult in Chekhov to be sure who the heroes and villains are. Nothing is as clear-cut in these plays as it is in popular melodramas. Instead, Chekhov's plays are as complicated as life itself. Such difficulties of distinction have become the norm of the most important drama of the twentieth century.

Drama in the Early and Mid-Twentieth Century

The drama of the early twentieth century nurtured the seeds of nineteenth-century realism into bloom, but sometimes this drama experimented with audience expectations. Eugene O'Neill's *Desire under the Elms* is a tragedy that features the ordinary citizen rather than the noble. This play focuses on New England farmers as tragic characters. Arthur Miller's *Death of a Salesman* invokes a sense of dreadful inevitability within the world of the commercial salesman, the ordinary man. As in many other twentieth-century tragedies, the point is that the life of the ordinary man can be as tragic as Oedipus's life.

Luigi Pirandello experiments with reality in *Six Characters in Search of an Author,* a play that has a distinctly absurd quality, since it expects us to accept the notion that the characters on the stage are waiting for an author to put them into a play. Pirandello plays with our sense of illusion and of expectation and realism to such an extent that he forces us to reexamine our concepts of reality.

Bertolt Brecht's *Mother Courage,* an example of what the playwright called EPIC DRAMA, explores war from a complex series of viewpoints. On the one hand Courage is a powerful figure who has been seen as a model of endurance, but Brecht also wanted his audience to see that Courage brings on much of her own suffering by trying to profit from war. The sole act of self-sacrifice in the play comes at the end, when Kattrin beats her drum to warn villagers of the approach of a destroying army. Brecht produced the play early in World War II as a protest. Playwrights around the world responded to events such as World War I, the Communist revolution, and the Great Depression by writing plays that no longer permitted audiences to sit comfortably and securely in darkened theaters. Brecht and other playwrights instead came out to get their audiences, to make them feel and think, to make them realize their true condition.

Samuel Beckett's dramatic career began with *Waiting for Godot,* which audiences interpreted as an examination of humans' eternal vigilance for the revelation of God or of some transcendent meaning in their lives. In the play, Godot never comes, yet the characters do not give up hope. *Endgame*'s characters seem to be awaiting the end of the world: in the 1950s the shadow of nuclear extinction cast by the cold war dominated most people's imagination.

Tennessee Williams examines a physically and psychically frail young woman's withdrawal from life in *The Glass Menagerie.* The play derives from personal experience: Williams's sister was such a woman. Personal experience may also inform his *Cat on a Hot Tin Roof,* which portrays themes of homosexuality and marital sexual tension — themes that were not openly discussed in contemporary American theater except in veiled mythic terms, in the manner, for example, of O'Neill's *Desire under the Elms.*

Nigerian playwright Wole Soyinka, who won the Nobel Prize for literature in 1986, portrays the complex intersection of a person's past and the present in his play *The Strong Breed,* set in an African village reminiscent of the Greek *polis.* Indeed, he has experimented with Greek tragic forms in *The Bacchae of Euripides,* which is also set in Africa. Soyinka's insights into the nature of culture and drama provide us with a new way of reflecting on drama's power in our lives.

Modern dramatists from the turn of the century to the Korean War explored in many different directions and developed new approaches to themes of dramatic illusion as well as to questions concerning the relationship of an audience to the stage and the players.

Contemporary Drama

As we begin the twenty-first century, the stage is vibrant. Although the commercial theaters in England and America are beset by high costs, they are producing remarkable plays. In Latin America, Germany, and France, the theater is active and exciting. Poland produced unusual experimental drama in the 1960s that is still performed today. The former Soviet Union, too, produced a number of plays that have been given a worldwide currency.

The hallmark of many of these plays has been experimentalism. Caryl Churchill's *Cloud Nine* confounds expectations by having a wife played by a man, a black servant played by a white, and a son, Edward, played by a woman. Because the play is about colonial exploitation, these experiments heighten the audience's awareness of central themes.

Sam Shepard, well known as an actor, was for many years among the most experimental playwrights living in New York's Greenwich Village. *True West* begins as a relatively straightforward play about Austin and Lee, two brothers, but quickly reveals the drama that lies beneath the surface. Lee has arrived to steal his mother's television set but ends by stealing something of his brother's personality.

In *'night, Mother,* Marsha Norman portrays two women whose lives are constricted, limited, and painful. Thelma, the mother, is desperately trying to keep Jessie, her daughter, from committing suicide. The structure of the play is traditional, but the material is highly controversial. The people in these modern plays have been given a bad deal and have given themselves a bad deal, and the drama compels us both to examine characters from whom we might otherwise turn away and to confront what those characters represent in our own lives.

Not all modern theater is experimental, however. August Wilson's *Fences* shows us the pain of life at the lower end of the economic ladder and in a form that is recognizably realistic and plausible. The play is set in the 1950s and focuses on Troy Maxon, a black man, and his relationship with his son and his wife. Tenement life is one subject of the play, but the most important subject is the courage it takes to keep going after tasting defeat. The entire drama develops within the bounds of conventional nineteenth-century realism.

Suzan-Lori Parks is a highly experimental playwright, generally forsaking the structure of the conventional realistic drama. Her *The Death of the Last*

Black Man in the Whole Entire World, like its title, is blissfully excessive. She employs some of Brecht's techniques by structuring the play in "panels"— brief, intense scenes that connect imaginatively. Tony Kushner employs similar techniques in *Angels in America.* Its brilliantly staged scenes are filled with emotional intensity and the audience is carried on waves of imaginative speculation on America's history as well as on America's present. Anna Deavere Smith brings an interesting experimentation to a logical conclusion: she writes and performs her work, assuming the parts of multiple characters of every race and gender. Her *Twilight in Los Angeles: 1992,* an example of PERFORMANCE ART, is a form of drama becoming popular in many parts of the world. Laurie Anderson, Karen Finley, and Eric Bogosian are a few of the best-known performance artists. Experimentation is probably at the heart of the work of many playwrights, although it still does not please mainstream audiences on the scale of traditional drama.

The most celebrated of contemporary playwrights seem to mix experimental and conventional dramatic techniques. Martin McDonagh, a young Irish playwright, examines the past in plays such as *The Beauty Queen of Leenane* and *The Cripple of Inishmaan,* both set in mid-twentieth century Ireland. He successfully combines the techniques of John Millington Synge with the melodramatic techniques of an even earlier Irish playwright, Dion Boucicault, who was popular in the 1860s. Yasmina Reza, author of *Art,* has characters speak directly to the audience while remaining engaged in the action, which takes place in one extended act of several scenes. Paula Vogel's plays frequently interrupt the dramatic action with asides, but they are also imaginatively structured so that time feels fluid and the action moves in emotionally significant sweeps. *The Baltimore Waltz,* derived from Vogel's experience of watching her brother die of AIDS, brings humor to a tragic situation. Similarly, *How I Learned to Drive,* which sensitively treats the subject of sexual molestation in families, also has comic moments. In *Cloud Tectonics,* José Rivera, one of the more experimental of contemporary dramatists, plays with time and reality in ways that surprise and excite audiences. The theater in our time experiments with a wide range of techniques to which audiences respond positively.

Genres of Drama
Tragedy

Drama since the great age of the Greeks has taken several different forms. As we have seen, tragedies were one genre that pleased Greek audiences, and comedies pleased the Romans. In later ages, a blend of the comic and the tragic produced a hybrid genre: tragicomedy. In our time, unless a play is modeled on the Greek or Shakespearean tragedies, as is O'Neill's *Desire under the Elms,* it is usually considered tragicomic rather than tragic. Our age still enjoys the kind of comedy that people laugh at, although most plays that are strictly comedy are frothy, temporarily entertaining, and not lasting.

TRAGEDY demands a specific worldview. Aristotle, in his *Poetics,* points out that the tragic hero or heroine should be noble of birth, perhaps a king like Oedipus or a princess like Antigone. This has often been interpreted to mean that the tragic hero or heroine should be more magnanimous, more daring, larger in spirit than the average person.

Modern tragedies have rediscovered tragic principles, and while O'Neill and Miller rely on Aristotle's precepts, they have shown that in a modern society shorn of the distinctions between noble and peasant it is possible for audiences to see the greatness in all classes. This has given us a new way of orienting ourselves to the concept of fate; to HAMARTIA, the wrong act that leads people to a tragic end; and to the hero's or heroine's relationship to the social order.

Aristotle suggested that plot was the heart and soul of tragedy and that character came second. But most older tragedies take the name of the tragic hero or heroine as their title; this signifies the importance that dramatists invested in their tragic characters. Yet they also heeded Aristotle's stipulation that tragic action should have one plot rather than the double or triple plots that often characterize comedies. (Shakespeare was soundly criticized in the eighteenth century for breaking this rule in his tragedies.) And they paid attention to the concept of PERIPETEIA, which specifies that the progress of the tragic characters sometimes leads them to a reversal: they get what they want, but what they want turns out to be destructive. Aristotle especially valued a plot in which the reversal takes place simultaneously with the recognition of the truth, or the shift from ignorance to awareness, as it does in Sophocles' *Oedipus Rex*.

Playwrights in the seventeenth and eighteenth centuries in France were especially interested in following classical precepts. They were certain that Greek tragedy and Roman comedy were the epitome of excellence in drama. They interpreted Aristotle's discussion of dramatic integrity to be a set of rules governing dramatic form. These became known as the dramatic UNITIES specifying one plot, a single action that takes place in one day in a single setting. The neoclassical reinterpretation of the unities was probably much stricter than Aristotle intended.

Comedy

Two kinds of comedy developed among the ancient Greeks: OLD COMEDY, which resembles FARCE (light drama characterized by broad satirical comedy and an improbable plot) and often pokes fun at individuals with social and political power, and NEW COMEDY, which is a more refined commentary on the condition of society.

Old Comedy survives in the masterful works of Aristophanes, such as *Lysistrata*, while New Comedy hearkens back to the lost plays of Menander and resurfaces in plays such as Molière's *The Misanthrope*. Molière uses humor but mixes it with a serious level of social commentary. Modern COMEDY OF MANNERS studies and sometimes ridicules modern society as in Oscar Wilde's *The Importance of Being Earnest*.

Comedy is not always funny. Chekhov thought *The Cherry Orchard* was a comedy, while his producer, the great Konstantin Stanislavsky, who trained actors to interpret his lines and who acted in other Chekhov plays, thought it was a tragedy. The argument may have centered on the ultimate effect of the play on its audiences, but it may also have centered on the question of laughter. There are laughs in *The Cherry Orchard,* but they usually come at the expense of a character or a social group. This is true, as well, of Samuel Beckett's *Endgame.* We may laugh, but we also know that the play is at heart very serious.

Tragicomedy

Since the early seventeenth century, serious plays have been called TRAGICOMEDIES when they do not adhere strictly to the structure of tragedy, which emphasizes the nobility of the hero or heroine, fate, the wrong action of the hero or heroine, and a resolution that includes death, exile, or a similar end.

Many serious plays have these qualities, but they also have some of the qualities of comedy: a commentary on society, raucous behavior that draws laughs, and a relatively happy ending. Yet their darkness is such that we can hardly feel comfortable regarding them as comedies.

Plays such as Sam Shepard's *True West* and Lorraine Hansberry's *A Raisin in the Sun* can be considered tragicomedy. Indeed, the modern temperament has especially relied on the mixture of comic and tragic elements for its most serious plays. Eugene O'Neill, Tennessee Williams, Harold Pinter, Marsha Norman, and Caryl Churchill have all been masters of tragicomedy.

In contemporary drama tragicomedy takes several forms. One is the play whose seriousness is relieved by comic moments; another is a play whose comic structure absorbs a tragic moment and continues to express affirmation. Yet another is the dark comedy whose sardonic humor leaves us wondering how we can laugh at something that is ultimately frightening. This is the case with some absurdist comedies, which insist that there is no meaning in events other than the meaning we invent for ourselves. Pinter's *Betrayal* and Beckett's *Endgame* are such plays. They are funny yet sardonic, and when we laugh we do so uneasily.

Other genres of drama exist, although they are generally versions of tragedy, comedy, and tragicomedy. Improvisational theater, in which actors use no scripts and may switch roles at any moment, defies generic description. Musical comedies and operas are dramatic entertainments that have established their own genres related in some ways to the standard genres of drama.

Genre distinctions are useful primarily because they establish expectations in the minds of audiences with theatrical experience. Tragedies and comedies make different demands on an audience. According to Marsha Norman's explanation of the "rules" of drama, you have to know in a play just what is at stake. Understanding the principles that have developed over the centuries to create the genres of drama helps us know what is at stake.

Elements of Drama

All plays share some basic elements with which playwrights and producers work: plots, characters, settings, dialogue, movement, and themes. In addition, many modern plays pay close attention to lighting, costuming, and props. When we respond to a play, we observe the elements of drama in action together, and the total experience is rich, complex, and subtle. Occasionally, we respond primarily to an individual element — the theme or characterization, for instance — but that is rare. Our awareness of the elements of drama is most useful when we are thinking analytically about a play and the way it affects us.

For the sake of discussion, we will consider the way the basic elements of drama function in Lady Gregory's one-act play *The Rising of the Moon* (which follows this section). It has all the elements we expect from drama, and it is both a brief and a very successful play.

Plot

PLOT is a term for the action of a drama. Plot implies that the ACTION has a shape and form that will ultimately prove satisfying to the audience. Generally, a carefully plotted play begins with EXPOSITION, an explanation of what happened before the play began and of how the characters arrived at their present situation. The play then continues, using SUSPENSE to build tension in the audience and in the characters and to develop further the pattern of RISING ACTION. The audience wonders what is going to happen, sees the characters set in motion, and then watches as certain questions implied by the drama are answered one by one. The action achieves its greatest tension as it moves to a point of CLIMAX, when a revelation is experienced, usually by the chief characters. Once the climax has been reached, the plot continues, sometimes very briefly, in a pattern of FALLING ACTION as the drama reaches its conclusion and the characters understand their circumstances and themselves better than they did at the beginning of the play.

The function of plot is to give action a form that helps us understand elements of the drama in relation to one another. Plays can have several interrelated plots or only one. Lady Gregory's *The Rising of the Moon* has one very simple plot: a police sergeant is sent out with two policemen to make sure a political rebel does not escape from the area. The effect of the single plot is that the entire play focuses intensely on the interaction between the rebel, disguised as a ballad singer, and the sergeant. The sergeant meets the rebel, listens to him sing ballads, and then recognizes in him certain qualities they share. The audience wonders if a reward of one hundred pounds will encourage the sergeant to arrest the ballad singer or if, instead, the ballad singer's sense that his cause is just will convince the sergeant to let him go. The climax of the action occurs when the sergeant's two policemen return, as the ballad singer hides behind a barrel, and ask if the sergeant has seen any signs of the rebel. Not until that moment does the audience know for sure what the sergeant will do. When he gives his answer, the falling action begins.

Plots depend on CONFLICT between characters, and in *The Rising of the Moon* the conflict is very deep. It is built into the characters themselves, but it is also part of the institution of law that the sergeant serves and the ongoing struggle for justice that the ballad singer serves. This conflict, still evident today, was a very significant national issue in Ireland when the play was first produced in Dublin in 1907.

Lady Gregory works subtly with the conflict between the sergeant and the ballad singer, showing that although they are on completely opposite sides of the law — and of the important political issues — they are more alike than they are different. The ballad singer begins to sing the "Granuaile," a revolutionary song about England's unlawful dominance over Ireland through seven centuries; when he leaves out a line, the sergeant supplies it. In that action the sergeant reveals that, although he is paid by the English to keep law and order, his roots lie with the Irish people. By his knowledge of the revolutionary songs he reveals his sympathies.

Characterization

Lady Gregory has effectively joined CHARACTER and conflict in *The Rising of the Moon:* as the conflict is revealed, the characters of the sergeant and the ballad singer are also revealed. At first the sergeant seems eager to get the reward, and he acts bossy with Policeman X and Policeman B. And when he first meets the ballad singer he seems demanding and policemanlike. It is only when he begins to sense who the ballad singer really is that he changes and reveals a deep, sympathetic streak.

Lady Gregory, in a note to the play, said that in Ireland when the play was first produced, those who wanted Ireland to become part of England were incensed to see a policeman portrayed so as to show his sympathies with rebels. Those who wished Ireland to become a separate nation from England were equally shocked to see a policeman portrayed so sympathetically.

The sergeant and the ballad singer are both major characters in the play, but it is not clear that either is the villain or the hero. When the play begins, the sergeant seems to be the hero because he represents the law and the ballad singer appears to be the villain because he has escaped from prison. But as the action develops, those characterizations change. What replaces them is an awareness of the complications that underlie the relationship between the law and the lawbreaker in some circumstances. This is part of the point of Lady Gregory's play.

Lady Gregory has given a very detailed portrait of both main characters, although in a one-act play she does not have enough space to be absolutely thorough in developing them. Yet we get an understanding of the personal ambitions of each character, and we understand both their relationship to Ireland and their particular allegiances as individuals. They speak with each other in enough detail to show that they understand each other, and when the ballad singer hides behind the barrel at the approach of the other two policemen, he indicates that he trusts the sergeant not to reveal him.

Policeman X and Policeman B are only sketched in. Yet their presence is important. It is with them that the sergeant reveals his official personality, and it is their presence at the end that represents the most important threat to the security of the ballad singer. We know, though, little or nothing about them personally. They are characters who are functionaries, a little like Rosencrantz and Guildenstern in *Hamlet,* but without the differentiating characterizations that Shakespeare was able to give minor players in his full-length play.

The plays in this collection have some of the most remarkable characters ever created in literature. Tragedy usually demands complex characters, such as Oedipus, Antigone, Medea, Hamlet, and Willy Loman. We come to know them through their own words, through their interaction with other characters, through their expression of feelings, through their decisions, and through their presence onstage depicted in movement and gesture.

Characters in tragicomedies are individualized and complexly portrayed, such as Madame Ranevskaya in *The Cherry Orchard,* Hedda Gabler, Miss Julie, and Nora Helmer in *A Doll House.* But just as effective in certain kinds of drama are characters drawn as types, such as Alceste, the misanthrope in Molière's play, and Everyman in medieval drama.

In many plays we see that the entire shape of the action derives from the characters, from their strengths and weaknesses. In such plays we do not feel that the action lies outside the characters and that they must live through an arbitrary sequence of events. Instead we feel that they create their own opportunities and problems.

Setting

The SETTING of a play includes many things. First, it refers to the time and place in which the action occurs. Second, it refers to the scenery, the physical elements that appear onstage to vivify the author's stage directions. In Lady Gregory's play, we have a dock with barrels to suggest the locale and darkness to suggest night. These are important details that influence the emotional reaction of the audience.

Some plays make use of very elaborate settings, as does August Wilson's *Fences,* which is produced with a detailed tenement backyard onstage. Others make use of simple settings, such as the empty stage of Pirandello's *Six Characters in Search of an Author.*

Lady Gregory's setting derives from her inspiration for the play. She visited the quays — places where boats dock and leave with goods — as a young girl and imagined how someone might escape from the nearby prison and make his getaway "under a load of kelp" in one of the ships. The quay represents the meeting of the land and water, and it represents the getaway, the possibility of freedom. The barrel is a symbol of trade, and the sergeant and the ballad singer sit on its top and trade the words of a revolutionary song with each other.

The title of the play refers to another element of the setting: the moonlight. The night protects the ballad singer, and it permits the sergeant to bend his sworn principles a bit. The rising of the moon, as a rebel song suggests, signifies a change in society, the time when "the small shall rise up and the big shall fall down." Lady Gregory uses these elements in the play in a very effective way, interrelating them so that their significance becomes increasingly apparent as the play progresses.

Dialogue

Plays depend for their unfolding on dialogue. The DIALOGUE is the verbal exchanges between the characters. Since there is no description or commentary on the action, as there is in most novels, the dialogue must tell the whole story. Fine playwrights have developed ways of revealing character, advancing action, and introducing themes by a highly efficient use of dialogue.

Dialogue is spoken by one character to another, who then responds. But sometimes, as in Shakespeare's *Hamlet,* a character delivers a SOLILOQUY, in which he or she speaks onstage to him- or herself. Ordinarily, such speeches take on importance because they are thought to be especially true. Characters, when they speak to each other, may well wish to deceive, but generally when they speak to themselves, they have no reason to say anything but the truth.

In *The Rising of the Moon* Lady Gregory has written an unusual form of dialogue that reveals a regional way of speech. Lady Gregory was Anglo-Irish, but she lived in the west of Ireland and was familiar with the speech patterns that the characters in this play would have used. She has been recognized for her ability to re-create the speech of the rural Irish, and passages such as the following are meant to reveal the peculiarities of the rhythms and syntax of English as it was spoken in Ireland at the turn of the century:

> SERGEANT: Is he as bad as that?
> MAN: He is then.
> SERGEANT: Do you tell me so?

Lady Gregory makes a considerable effort to create dialogue that is rich in local color as well as in spirit. John Millington Synge, another Irish playwright, whose dialogue in *Playboy of the Western World* is also an effort to re-create the sounds and rhythms of rural Irish speech, once said: "In a good play every speech should be as fully flavored as a nut or apple, and such speeches cannot be written by anyone who works among people who have shut their lips on poetry." Lady Gregory, who produced the plays of Synge at the Abbey Theatre in Dublin, would certainly agree, as her dialogue in *The Rising of the Moon* amply shows.

Music

Lady Gregory introduces another dramatic element: music. In *The Rising of the Moon* the music is integral to the plot because it allows the ballad singer, by omitting a line of a rebel song, gradually to expose the sergeant's sympathies with the rebel cause. The sergeant is at first mindful of his duty and insists that the balladeer stop, but eventually he is captivated by the music. As the ballad singer continues, he sings a song containing the title of the play, and the audience or reader realizes that the title exposes the play's rebel sympathies.

Movement

We as readers or witnesses are energized by the movement of the characters in a play. As we read, stage directions inform us where the characters are, when they move, how they move, and perhaps even what the significance of their movement is. In modern plays the author may give many directions for the action; in earlier plays stage directions are few and often supplemented by those of a modern editor. In performance the movements that you see may well have been invented by the director, although the text of a play often requires certain actions, as in the ghost scene and final dueling scene in *Hamlet*. In some kinds of drama, such as musical comedy and Greek drama, part of the action may be danced.

Lady Gregory moves the ballad singer and the sergeant in telling ways. They move physically closer to one another as they become closer in their thinking. Their movement seems to pivot around the barrel, and in one of the most charming moments of the play, they meet each other's eyes when the ballad singer sits on the barrel and comments on the way the sergeant is pacing back and forth. They then both sit on the barrel, facing in opposite directions, and share a pipe between them, almost as a peace offering.

Theme

The theme of a play is its message, its central concerns — in short, what it is about. It is by no means a simple thing to decide what the theme of a play is, and many plays contain several rather than just a single theme. Often, the search for a theme tempts us to oversimplify and to reduce a complex play to a relatively simple catchphrase.

Sophocles' *Antigone* focuses on the conflict between human law and the law of the gods when following both sets of laws seems to be impossible. Antigone wishes to honor the gods by burying her brother, but the law of Kreon decrees that he shall have no burial, since her brother is technically a traitor to the state. Similar themes are present in other Greek plays. *Hamlet* has many themes. On a very elementary level, the main theme of *Hamlet* is revenge. This is played out in the obligation of a son to avenge the murder of a father, even when the murderer is a kinsman. Another theme centers on corruption in the state of Denmark.

Lady Gregory's play has revolution as one theme. The rising of the moon is a sign for "the rising" or revolution of the people against their English oppressors. The sergeant is an especially English emblem of oppression because the police were established by an Englishman, Robert Peele. At one point the balladeer suggests a song, "The Peeler and the Goat," but rejects it because in slang a peeler is a policeman.

Another important theme in *The Rising of the Moon* is that of unity among the Irish people. The sergeant seems to be at an opposite pole from the ballad singer when the play opens. He is posting signs announcing a reward that he could well use, since he is a family man. But as the play proceeds, the sergeant moves closer in thought to the Irish people, represented by the rebel, the ballad singer.

If concerned that readers and viewers will miss their thematic intentions, playwrights sometimes reveal these in one or two speeches. Usually, a careful reader or viewer has already divined the theme, and the speeches are intrusive. But Lady Gregory is able to introduce thematic material in certain moments of dialogue, as in this comment by the sergeant, revealing that the police are necessary to prevent a revolution:

> SERGEANT: Well, we have to do our duty in the force. Haven't we the whole country depending on us to keep law and order? It's those that are down would be up and those that are up would be down, if it wasn't for us.

But the thematic material in *The Rising of the Moon* is spread evenly throughout, as is the case in most good plays.

In every play, the elements of drama will work differently, sometimes giving us the feeling that character is dominant over theme, or plot over character, or setting over both. Ordinarily, critics feel that character, plot, and theme are the most important elements of drama, while setting, dialogue, music, and movement come next. But in the best of dramas each has its importance and each balances the others. The plays in this collection strive for that harmony; most achieve it memorably.

Lady Gregory

Isabella Augusta Persse (1852–1932) was born in the west of Ireland. Her family was known as "ascendancy stock"— that is, it was educated, wealthy, and Protestant living in a land that was largely uneducated, poverty-ridden, and Roman Catholic. A gulf existed between the rich ascendancy families, who lived in great houses with considerable style, partaking in lavish hunts and balls, and the impoverished Irish, who lived in one-room straw-roofed homes and worked the soil with primitive tools.

Lady Gregory took a strong interest in the Irish language, stimulated in part by a nurse who often spoke the language to her when she was a child. Her nurse was an important source of Irish folklore and a contact with the people who lived in the modest cottages around her family estate. It was extraordinary for any wealthy Protestant to pay attention to the language or the life of the poor laborers of the west of Ireland. Yet these are the very people who figure most importantly in the plays that Lady Gregory wrote in later life.

Isabella Persse met Sir William Gregory when she was on a family trip to Nice and Rome. They were actually neighbors in Ireland, but only slightly acquainted. He was also of Irish ascendancy stock and had been a governor of Ceylon. They were married the following year, when she was twenty-eight and he was sixty-three. Their marriage was apparently quite successful, and in 1881, their son, Robert Gregory, was born. They used the family home, Coole Park, as a retreat for short periods, but most of their time was spent traveling and living in London, where Sir William was a trustee of the National Gallery of Art. W. B. Yeats, Bernard Shaw, and numerous other important literary figures spent time in Coole Park and its beautiful great house in the early part of the twentieth century.

Lady Gregory led a relatively conventional life until Sir William Gregory died in 1892. According to the laws of that time, the estate passed to her son, so she anticipated a life of relatively modest circumstances. In the process of finishing Sir William's memoirs, she found herself to be a gifted writer. She used some of her spare time to learn Irish well enough to talk with the old cottagers in the hills, where she went to gather folklore and old songs. Although W. B. Yeats and others had collected volumes of Irish stories and poems, they did not know Irish well enough to authenticate what they heard. Lady Gregory published her Kiltartan tales (she had dubbed her neighborhood Kiltartan) as a way of preserving the rapidly disappearing myths and stories that were still told around the hearth as a matter of course in rural Ireland.

She was already an accomplished writer when she met W. B. Yeats in 1894. Their meeting was of immense importance for the history of drama, since they decided to forge their complementary talents and abilities to create an Irish theater. Their discussions included certain Irish neighbors, among them Edward Martyn, a Catholic whose early plays were very successful. They also talked with Dr. Douglas Hyde, a mythographer and linguist and the first president of modern Ireland. Another neighbor who took part, the flamboyant George Moore, was a well-established novelist and playwright.

The group's first plays — Yeats's *The Countess Cathleen* and Martyn's *The Heather Field* — were performed on May 8 and 9, 1899, under the auspices of the Irish Literary Theatre in Dublin at the Ancient Concert Rooms. Dedicated to producing plays by Irish playwrights on Irish themes, the Irish Literary Theatre became an immediate success. The greatest problem the founders faced was finding more plays. Lady Gregory tried her own hand and discovered herself, at age fifty, to be a playwright.

Her ear for people's speech was unusually good — good enough that she was able to give the great poet Yeats lessons in dialogue and to help him prepare his own plays for the stage. She collaborated with Yeats on *The Pot of Broth* in 1902, the year she wrote her first plays, *The Jackdaw* and *A Losing Game*. Her first produced play, *Twenty-Five,* was put on in 1903. By 1904 the group had rented the historic Abbey Theatre. Some of her plays were quite popular and were successful even in later revivals: *Spreading the News* (1904); *Kincora* and *The White Cockade* (1905); and *Hyacinth Halvey, The Doctor in Spite of Himself, The Gaol Gate,* and *The Canavans* (all 1906). In the next year, there were troubles at the Abbey over John Millington Synge's *Playboy of the Western World.* The middle-class audience resented the portrait of the Irish peasants as people who would celebrate a self-confessed father-killer, even though he had not actually done the "gallous deed." Lady Gregory faced down a rioting audience who were protesting what she felt was excellent drama.

In 1918 her son, a World War I pilot, was shot down over Italy. The years that followed were to some extent years of struggle. Lady Gregory managed the Abbey Theatre, directed its affairs, and developed new playwrights, among them Sean O'Casey. During the Irish Civil War (1920–1922), she was physically threatened, and eventually her family home, Roxborough, was burned. In 1926, after discovering that she had cancer, she made arrangements to sell Coole Park to the government with the agreement that she could remain there for life. She died in 1932, the writer of a large number of satisfying plays and the prime mover in developing one of the century's most important literary theaters.

THE RISING
OF THE MOON

One of Lady Gregory's shortest but most popular plays, *The Rising of the Moon* is openly political in its themes. Lady Gregory had been writing plays only a short time, and she had been directing the Irish Literary Theatre when it became the Abbey Theatre Company and produced this play in 1907. Her interest in Irish politics developed, she said, when she was going through the papers of a distant relative of her husband. That man had been in the Castle, the offices of the English authorities given the task of ruling Ireland from Dublin. She said that the underhanded dealings revealed in those papers convinced her that Ireland should be a nation apart from England if justice were ever to be done.

In 1907 the question of union with England or separation and nationhood was on everyone's lips. Ireland was calm, and the people in Dublin were relatively prosperous and by no means readying for a fight or a revolution. Yet there had been a tradition of risings against the English dating back to the Elizabethan age and earlier. In 1907 the average Irish person believed that revolution was a thing of the past; actually, it was less than ten years in the future. Certain organizations had been developing, notably the widespread Gaelic League and the less-known Sinn Féin (We Ourselves), to promote Irish lore, language, and culture. English was the dominant language in Ireland, since it was the language of commerce, but it tended to obliterate the Irish culture. Lady Gregory's work with the Abbey Theatre, which was making one of the age's most important contributions to Irish culture, thus coincided with growing interest in the rest of Ireland in rediscovering its literary past.

The title *The Rising of the Moon* comes from a popular old rebel song that pointed to the rising of the moon as the signal for the rising of peoples against oppression. The main characters of the play represent the two opposing forces in Ireland: freedom and independence, personified by the ballad singer ("a Ragged Man"); and law and order, represented by the sergeant. The ballad singer is aligned with those who want to change the social structure of Ireland so that the people now on the bottom will be on top. The sergeant's job is to preserve the status quo and avoid such a turning of the tables.

In an important way, the sergeant and the ballad singer represent the two alternatives that face the modern Irish — now as in the past. One alternative is to accept the power of the English and be in their pay, like the sergeant; one would then be well fed and capable of supporting a family. The other alternative is to follow the revolutionary path of the ballad singer and risk prison, scorn, and impoverishment. The ballad singer is a ragged man because he has been totally reduced in circumstances by his political choices.

For Lady Gregory, this play was a serious political statement. She and W. B. Yeats — both aristocratic Protestant Irish — were sympathetic to the Irish revolutionary causes. They each wrote plays that struck a revolutionary note during this period. Neither truly expected a revolution; when the Easter Uprising of 1916 was put down with considerable loss of life and immense destruction of central Dublin, Yeats lamented that his plays may have sent some young men to their deaths.

It is possible that if either Yeats or Lady Gregory had thought there would be a revolution they would not have written such plays. They opposed violence, but it was clear to some that violence was the only means by which Ireland would be made into a separate nation.

The success of *The Rising of the Moon* lies in Lady Gregory's exceptional ear for dialogue. She captures the way people speak, and she also manages to draw the characters of the sergeant and ballad singer so as to gain our sympathies for both. In a remarkably economic fashion she dramatizes the problem of politics in Ireland, characterizing the two polarities and revealing some of the complexities that face anyone who tries to understand them.

Lady Gregory (1852–1932)
THE RISING OF THE MOON

1907

Persons

SERGEANT   POLICEMAN B
POLICEMAN X   A RAGGED MAN

Scene: *Side of a quay in a seaport town. Some posts and chains. A large barrel. Enter three policemen. Moonlight.*

(*Sergeant, who is older than the others, crosses the stage to right and looks down steps. The others put down a pastepot and unroll a bundle of placards.*)

POLICEMAN B: I think this would be a good place to put up a notice. (*He points to barrel.*)

POLICEMAN X: Better ask him. (*Calls to Sergeant.*) Will this be a good place for a placard?

(*No answer.*)

POLICEMAN B: Will we put up a notice here on the barrel?

(*No answer.*)

SERGEANT: There's a flight of steps here that leads to the water. This is a place that should be minded well. If he got down here, his friends might have a boat to meet him; they might send it in here from outside.

POLICEMAN B: Would the barrel be a good place to put a notice up?

SERGEANT: It might; you can put it there.

(*They paste the notice up.*)

SERGEANT (*reading it*): Dark hair — dark eyes, smooth face, height five feet five — there's not much to take hold of in that — It's a pity I had no chance of seeing him before he broke out of jail. They say he's a wonder, that it's he makes all the plans for the whole organization. There isn't another man in Ireland would have broken jail the way he did. He must have some friends among the jailers.

POLICEMAN B: A hundred pounds is little enough for the Government to offer for him. You may be sure any man in the force that takes him will get promotion.

SERGEANT: I'll mind this place myself. I wouldn't wonder at all if he came this way. He might come slipping along there (*points to side of quay*), and his friends might be waiting for him there (*points down steps*), and once he got away it's little chance we'd have of finding him; it's maybe under a load of kelp he'd be in a fishing boat, and not one to help a married man that wants it to the reward.

POLICEMAN X: And if we get him itself, nothing but abuse on our heads for it from the people, and maybe from our own relations.

SERGEANT: Well, we have to do our duty in the force. Haven't we the whole country depending on us to keep law and order? It's those that are down would be up and those that are up would be down, if it wasn't for us. Well, hurry on, you have plenty of other places to placard yet, and come back here then to me. You can take the lantern. Don't be too long now. It's very lonesome here with nothing but the moon.

POLICEMAN B: It's a pity we can't stop with you. The Government should have brought more police into the town, with *him* in jail, and at assize° time too. Well, good luck to your watch.

(*They go out.*)

SERGEANT (*walks up and down once or twice and looks at placard*): A hundred pounds and promotion sure. There must be a great deal of spending in a hundred pounds. It's a pity some honest man not to be better of that.

(*A Ragged Man appears at left and tries to slip past. Sergeant suddenly turns.*)

SERGEANT: Where are you going?
MAN: I'm a poor ballad-singer, your honor. I thought to sell some of these (*holds out bundle of ballads*) to the sailors.

(*He goes on.*)

SERGEANT: Stop! Didn't I tell you to stop? You can't go on there.
MAN: Oh, very well. It's a hard thing to be poor. All the world's against the poor!
SERGEANT: Who are you?
MAN: You'd be as wise as myself if I told you, but I don't mind. I'm one Jimmy Walsh, a ballad-singer.
SERGEANT: Jimmy Walsh? I don't know that name.
MAN: Ah, sure, they know it well enough in Ennis. Were you ever in Ennis, sergeant?
SERGEANT: What brought you here?
MAN: Sure, it's to the assizes I came, thinking I might make a few shillings here or there. It's in the one train with the judges I came.
SERGEANT: Well, if you came so far, you may as well go farther, for you'll walk out of this.
MAN: I will, I will; I'll just go on where I was going.

(*Goes toward steps.*)

SERGEANT: Come back from those steps; no one has leave to pass down them tonight.
MAN: I'll just sit on the top of the steps till I see will some sailor buy a ballad off me that would give me my supper. They do be late going back to the ship. It's often I saw them in Cork carried down the quay in a handcart.
SERGEANT: Move on, I tell you. I won't have anyone lingering about the quay tonight.
MAN: Well, I'll go. It's the poor have the hard life! Maybe yourself might like one, sergeant. Here's a good sheet now. (*Turns one over.*) "Content and a pipe"— that's not much. "The Peeler and the goat"— you wouldn't like that. "Johnny Hart"— that's a lovely song.
SERGEANT: Move on.
MAN: Ah, wait till you hear it. (*Sings.*)

assize: Judicial inquest.

There was a rich farmer's daughter lived near the
 town of Ross;
She courted a Highland soldier, his name was
 Johnny Hart;
Says the mother to her daughter, "I'll go distracted
 mad
If you marry that Highland soldier dressed up in
 Highland plaid."
SERGEANT: Stop that noise.

(*Man wraps up his ballads and shuffles toward the steps.*)

SERGEANT: Where are you going?
MAN: Sure you told me to be going, and I am going.
SERGEANT: Don't be a fool. I didn't tell you to go that way; I told you to go back to the town.
MAN: Back to the town, is it?
SERGEANT (*taking him by the shoulder and shoving him before him*): Here, I'll show you the way. Be off with you. What are you stopping for?
MAN (*who has been keeping his eye on the notice, points to it*): I think I know what you're waiting for, sergeant.
SERGEANT: What's that to you?
MAN: And I know well the man you're waiting for — I know him well — I'll be going.

(*He shuffles on.*)

SERGEANT: You know him? Come back here. What sort is he?
MAN: Come back is it, sergeant? Do you want to have me killed?
SERGEANT: Why do you say that?
MAN: Never mind. I'm going. I wouldn't be in your shoes if the reward was ten times as much. (*Goes on off stage to left.*) Not if it was ten times as much.
SERGEANT (*rushing after him*): Come back here, come back. (*Drags him back.*) What sort is he? Where did you see him?
MAN: I saw him in my own place, in the County Clare. I tell you you wouldn't like to be looking at him. You'd be afraid to be in the one place with him. There isn't a weapon he doesn't know the use of, and as to strength, his muscles are as hard as that board (*slaps barrel*).
SERGEANT: Is he as bad as that?
MAN: He is then.
SERGEANT: Do you tell me so?
MAN: There was a poor man in our place, a sergeant from Ballyvaughan. — It was with a lump of stone he did it.
SERGEANT: I never heard of that.
MAN: And you wouldn't, sergeant. It's not everything that happens gets into the papers. And there was a policeman in plain clothes, too. . . . It is in Limerick he was. . . . It was after the time of the attack on the police barrack at Kilmallock. . . . Moonlight . . . just like this . . . waterside. . . . Nothing was known for certain.

SERGEANT: Do you say so? It's a terrible county to belong to.

MAN: That's so, indeed! You might be standing there, looking out that way, thinking you saw him coming up this side of the quay (*points*), and he might be coming up this other side (*points*), and he'd be on you before you knew where you were.

SERGEANT: It's a whole troop of police they ought to put here to stop a man like that.

MAN: But if you'd like me to stop with you, I could be looking down this side. I could be sitting up here on this barrel.

SERGEANT: And you know him well, too?

MAN: I'd know him a mile off, sergeant.

SERGEANT: But you wouldn't want to share the reward?

MAN: Is it a poor man like me, that has to be going the roads and singing in fairs, to have the name on him that he took a reward? But you don't want me. I'll be safer in the town.

SERGEANT: Well, you can stop.

MAN (*getting up on barrel*): All right, sergeant. I wonder, now, you're not tired out, sergeant, walking up and down the way you are.

SERGEANT: If I'm tired I'm used to it.

MAN: You might have hard work before you tonight yet. Take it easy while you can. There's plenty of room up here on the barrel, and you see farther when you're higher up.

SERGEANT: Maybe so. (*Gets up beside him on barrel, facing right. They sit back to back, looking different ways.*) You made me feel a bit queer with the way you talked.

MAN: Give me a match, sergeant (*he gives it and man lights pipe*); take a draw yourself? It'll quiet you. Wait now till I give you a light, but you needn't turn round. Don't take your eye off the quay for the life of you.

SERGEANT: Never fear, I won't. (*Lights pipe. They both smoke.*) Indeed it's a hard thing to be in the force, out at night and no thanks for it, for all the danger we're in. And it's little we get but abuse from the people, and no choice but to obey our orders, and never asked when a man is sent into danger, if you are a married man with a family.

MAN (*sings*): As through the hills I walked to view the hills and shamrock plain,
    I stood awhile where nature smiles to view the rocks and streams,
    On a matron fair I fixed my eyes beneath a fertile vale,
    And she sang her song it was on the wrong of poor old Granuaile.

SERGEANT: Stop that; that's no song to be singing in these times.

MAN: Ah, sergeant, I was only singing to keep my heart up. It sinks when I think of him. To think of us two sitting here, and he creeping up the quay, maybe, to get to us.

SERGEANT: Are you keeping a good lookout?

MAN: I am; and for no reward too. Amn't I the foolish man? But when I saw a man in trouble, I never could help trying to get him out of it. What's that? Did something hit me?

(*Rubs his heart.*)

SERGEANT (*patting him on the shoulder*): You will get your reward in heaven.

MAN: I know that, I know that, sergeant, but life is precious.

SERGEANT: Well, you can sing if it gives you more courage.

MAN (*sings*): Her head was bare, her hands and feet with iron bands were bound,
    Her pensive strain and plaintive wail mingles with the evening gale,
    And the song she sang with mournful air, I am old Granuaile.
    Her lips so sweet that monarchs kissed . . .

SERGEANT: That's not it. . . . "Her gown she wore was stained with gore." . . . That's it — you missed that.

MAN: You're right, sergeant, so it is; I missed it. (*Repeats line.*) But to think of a man like you knowing a song like that.

SERGEANT: There's many a thing a man might know and might not have any wish for.

MAN: Now, I daresay, sergeant, in your youth, you used to be sitting up on a wall, the way you are sitting up on this barrel now, and the other lads beside you, and you singing "Granuaile"? . . .

SERGEANT: I did then.

MAN: And the "Shan Van Vocht"? . . .

SERGEANT: I did then.

MAN: And the "Green on the Cape"?

SERGEANT: That was one of them.

MAN: And maybe the man you are watching for tonight used to be sitting on the wall, when he was young, and singing those same songs. . . . It's a queer world. . . .

SERGEANT: Whisht! . . . I think I see something coming. . . . It's only a dog.

MAN: And isn't it a queer world? . . . Maybe it's one of the boys you used to be singing with that time you will be arresting today or tomorrow, and sending into the dock. . . .

SERGEANT: That's true indeed.

MAN: And maybe one night, after you had been singing, if the other boys had told you some plan they had, some plan to free the country, you might have joined with them . . . and maybe it is you might be in trouble now.

SERGEANT: Well, who knows but I might? I had a great spirit in those days.

MAN: It's a queer world, sergeant, and it's little any mother knows when she sees her child creeping on the floor what might happen to it before it has gone through its life, or who will be who in the end.

SERGEANT: That's a queer thought now, and a true thought. Wait now till I think it out. . . . If it wasn't for the sense I have, and for my wife and family, and for me joining the force the time I did, it might be myself now would be after breaking jail and hiding in the dark, and it might be him that's hiding in the dark and that got out of jail would be sitting up here where I am on this barrel. . . . And it might be myself would be creeping up trying to make my escape from himself, and it might be himself would be keeping the law, and myself would be breaking it, and myself would be trying to put a bullet in his head, or to take up a lump of stone the way you said he did . . . no, that myself did. . . . Oh! (*Gasps. After a pause.*) What's that? (*Grasps man's arm.*)

MAN (*jumps off barrel and listens, looking out over water*): It's nothing, sergeant.

SERGEANT: I thought it might be a boat. I had a notion there might be friends of his coming about the quays with a boat.

MAN: Sergeant, I am thinking it was with the people you were, and not with the law you were, when you were a young man.

SERGEANT: Well, if I was foolish then, that time's gone.

MAN: Maybe, sergeant, it comes into your head sometimes, in spite of your belt and your tunic, that it might have been as well for you to have followed Granuaile.

SERGEANT: It's no business of yours what I think.

MAN: Maybe, sergeant, you'll be on the side of the country yet.

SERGEANT (*gets off barrel*): Don't talk to me like that. I have my duties and I know them. (*Looks round.*) That was a boat; I hear the oars.

(*Goes to the steps and looks down.*)

MAN (*sings*): O, then, tell me, Shawn O'Farrell,
    Where the gathering is to be.
In the old spot by the river
    Right well known to you and me!

SERGEANT: Stop that! Stop that, I tell you!

MAN (*sings louder*): One word more, for signal token,
    Whistle up the marching tune,
With your pike upon your shoulder,
    At the Rising of the Moon.

SERGEANT: If you don't stop that, I'll arrest you.

(*A whistle from below answers, repeating the air.*)

SERGEANT: That's a signal. (*Stands between him and steps.*) You must not pass this way. . . . Step farther back. . . . Who are you? You are no ballad-singer.

MAN: You needn't ask who I am; that placard will tell you. (*Points to placard.*)

SERGEANT: You are the man I am looking for.

MAN (*takes off hat and wig. Sergeant seizes them*): I am. There's a hundred pounds on my head. There is a friend of mine below in a boat. He knows a safe place to bring me to.

SERGEANT (*looking still at hat and wig*): It's a pity! It's a pity. You deceived me. You deceived me well.

MAN: I am a friend of Granuaile. There is a hundred pounds on my head.

SERGEANT: It's a pity, it's a pity!

MAN: Will you let me pass, or must I make you let me?

SERGEANT: I am in the force. I will not let you pass.

MAN: I thought to do it with my tongue. (*Puts hand in breast.*) What is that?

VOICE OF POLICEMAN X (*outside*): Here, this is where we left him.

SERGEANT: It's my comrades coming.

MAN: You won't betray me . . . the friend of Granuaile. (*Slips behind barrel.*)

VOICE OF POLICEMAN B: That was the last of the placards.

POLICEMAN X (*as they come in*): If he makes his escape it won't be unknown he'll make it.

(*Sergeant puts hat and wig behind his back.*)

POLICEMAN B: Did anyone come this way?

SERGEANT (*after a pause*): No one.

POLICEMAN B: No one at all?

SERGEANT: No one at all.

POLICEMAN B: We had no orders to go back to the station; we can stop along with you.

SERGEANT: I don't want you. There is nothing for you to do here.

POLICEMAN B: You bade us to come back here and keep watch with you.

SERGEANT: I'd sooner be alone. Would any man come this way and you making all that talk? It is better the place to be quiet.

POLICEMAN B: Well, we'll leave you the lantern anyhow.

(*Hands it to him.*)

SERGEANT: I don't want it. Bring it with you.

POLICEMAN B: You might want it. There are clouds coming up and you have the darkness of the night before you yet. I'll leave it over here on the barrel. (*Goes to barrel.*)

SERGEANT: Bring it with you, I tell you. No more talk.

POLICEMAN B: Well, I thought it might be a comfort to you. I often think when I have it in my hand and can be flashing it about into every dark corner (*doing so*) that it's the same as being beside the fire at home, and the bits of bogwood blazing up now and again.

(*Flashes it about, now on the barrel, now on Sergeant.*)

SERGEANT (*furious*): Be off the two of you, yourselves and your lantern!

(*They go out. Man comes from behind barrel. He and Sergeant stand looking at one another.*)

SERGEANT: What are you waiting for?

MAN: For my hat, of course, and my wig. You wouldn't wish me to get my death of cold?

(*Sergeant gives them.*)

MAN (*going toward steps*): Well, good night, comrade, and thank you. You did me a good turn tonight, and I'm obliged to you. Maybe I'll be able to do as much for you when the small rise up and the big fall down . . . when we all change places at the Rising (*waves his hand and disappears*) of the Moon.

SERGEANT (*turning his back to audience and reading placard*): A hundred pounds reward! A hundred pounds! (*Turns toward audience.*) I wonder, now, am I as great a fool as I think I am?

Greek Drama

Origins of Greek Drama

Because our historical knowledge of Greek drama is limited by the available contemporary commentaries and by partial archaeological remains — in the form of ruined theaters — we do not know when Greek theater began or what its original impulses were. Our best information points to 534 B.C. as the beginning of the formal competitions among playwrights for coveted prizes that continued to be awarded for several centuries. Thespis, credited as the first tragedy writer, seems to have changed the nature of the form by stepping out of the chorus and taking a solo part. But the origin of *tragedy*, which translates in Greek as "goat-song" or "song for the sacrificial goat," is obscure. One theory is that tragedy may have developed from the rites of rural cults that sacrificed a she-goat at some Dionysian festivals or from masked animal dances at certain cult celebrations.

One source that may well have influenced the Greeks was the Egyptian civilization of the first millennium B.C. Egyptian culture was fully formed, brilliant, and complex. And while Egyptologists do not credit it with having a formal theater, certain ceremonies, repeated annually at major festivals, seem to have counterparts in later Greek rituals and drama. The most important and most impressive Egyptian ritual, described by some scholars as a passion play, concerned the dramatic story of Isis and Osiris and the treachery of Osiris's brother Set.

The closest Greek counterpart to Osiris was DIONYSUS, who inspired orgiastic celebrations that found their way into early Greek drama. Dionysus was an agricultural deity, the Greek god of wine and the symbol of life-giving power. In several myths he, like Osiris, was ritually killed and dismembered and his parts scattered through the land. These myths paralleled the agricultural cycle of death and disintegration during the winter, followed by cultivation and rebirth in the spring, and reinforced the Greeks' understanding of the meaning of birth, life, and death.

Drama developed in ancient Greece in close connection with the Dionysia, religious celebrations dedicated to Dionysus. Four Dionysiac celebrations were held each winter in Athens beginning at the grape harvest and culminating during the first wine tastings: the Rural Dionysia in December, the Lenaia in January, the Anthesteria in February, and the City Dionysia in March. Except for the Anthesteria, the festivals featured drama contests among playwrights, and some of the works performed in those competitions have endured through the centuries. Theories that connect the origins of drama with religion hypothesize that one function of the religious festivals within which the drama competitions took place was the ritual attempt to guarantee fertility and the growth of the crops, on which the society depended.

The CITY DIONYSIA, the most lavish of the festivals, lasted from five to seven days. It was open to non-Athenians and therefore offered Athenians the opportunity to show off their wealth, their glorious history, and their heroes, who were often honored in parades the day before the plays began. There is some question about what was presented on each day. Two days were probably taken up with dithyrambic contests among the ten tribes of Athens. Generally each tribe presented two choruses — one of men and one of boys — each singing a narrative lyric called a DITHYRAMB. A prize was awarded the best performers. Three days were devoted to contests among tragedians, most of whom worked for half the year on three tragedies and a SATYR PLAY, an erotic piece of comic relief that ended the day's performance. A tragedian's three plays sometimes shared related themes or myths, but often they did not. The tragedians wrote the plays, trained and rehearsed the actors, composed music, and created setting, dances, costumes, and masks. After 486 B.C. the first comedy competition was held, when five and later three comedies were also presented during the festival. The performances were paid for by wealthy Athenians as part of their civic duty. The great Greek plays thus were not commercial enterprises but an important part of civic and religious festivals.

Judges chosen by lottery awarded prizes, usually basing their decisions on the merits of the dramas. First prize went to the tragedian whose four plays were most powerful and most beautifully conceived.

The Greeks and Their Gods

The great achievement of Greek religion was the humanizing of their gods. Apollo, Zeus, Aphrodite, Athena, and Bacchus had recognizable emotions and pleasures. The Greeks built temples to their gods and made offerings at appropriate times to avoid catastrophe and bad luck. But the Greeks had no official religious text, no system of religious belief that they all followed, and few ethical teachings derived from religion. The impression we have today is that Greeks' efforts to define and know the gods were shaped by great artists such as Phidias, who sculpted Zeus at Olympia; Homer, who portrayed the gods in *The Iliad* and *The Odyssey;* and the great Greek playwrights, who sometimes revealed the actions of the gods. Our present knowledge of Greek gods resides in the literary and artistic remains of Greek culture.

Fortunately for us, most Greek drama was associated with important celebrations designed to honor Greek gods. We would not, however, call this drama religious in nature — as we characterize the medieval drama designated to celebrate Christian holidays. What we learn from Greek drama is that the gods can favor individual humans for reasons of their own. And likewise, the gods can choose to punish individual humans. To some extent Greek drama is designed to explain the divine approach to favor and disfavor.

The Greek Stage

At the center of the Greek theater was the ORCHESTRA, where the chorus sang and danced (*orches* is derived from the Greek for "dancing place"). The audience, sometimes numbering fifteen thousand, sat in rising rows on three sides of the orchestra. The steep sides of a hill formed a natural amphitheater for Greek audiences. Eventually, on the rim of the orchestra, an oblong building called the SKENE, or scene house, developed as a space for the actors and a background for the action. The term PROSKENION was sometimes used to refer to a raised stage added in later times in front of the *skene* where the actors performed. The theater at Epidaurus (Figures 1 and 2) was a model for the Greek theater plan.

Greek theaters were widely dispersed from Greece to present-day Turkey, to Sicily, and even to southern France. Wherever the Greeks developed new colonies and city-states, they built theaters. In many of the surviving theaters the acoustics are so fine that a human voice onstage can be heard from any seat in the theater.

Perhaps the most spectacular theatrical device used by the Greek playwrights, the MEKANE ("machine"), was implemented onstage by means of elaborate booms or derricks. Actors were lowered onto the stage to enact the roles of Olympian gods intervening in the affairs of humans. Some commentators, such as Aristotle (384–322 B.C.), felt that the *mekane* should be used only if the intercession of deities was in keeping with the character of the play. The last of the great Greek tragedians, Euripides (c. 485–c. 406 B.C.), used the device in almost half of his tragedies. In *Medea* Euripides uses the *mekane* to lift Medea to the roof of the *skene* and into her dragon chariot as a means of resolving the play's conflict. At the end of the play Medea is beyond her persecutors' reach and is headed for safety in another country. Modern dramatists use a version of this, called *deus ex machina,* literally, "the god from the machine," when they rescue characters at the last moment by improbable accidents or strokes of luck. Usually, these are unsatisfying means of solving dramatic problems.

Genres of Greek Drama
Tragedy

Greek tragedy focused on a person of noble birth who in some cases had risen to a great height and then fell precipitately. Tragedies showed humans at the mercy of MOIRA, their fate, which they only partly understood. One objective of Greek drama was to have the audience experience a CATHARSIS, which Aristotle describes as a purging or purifying of the emotions of pity and fear. According to the Greeks, these are emotions that a person associates with the fall of someone in a high social station, such as a king or queen. A central character, or PROTAGONIST, of noble birth was therefore an essential element for the playwright striving to evoke catharsis in an audience. Twentieth-century experiments with tragic figures who are ordinary people, such as Arthur Miller's *Death of a Salesman,* as masterful as they are, would not have made sense to the Greeks. For the Greeks, tragedy could befall only the great.

The modern critic Kenneth Burke identified a pattern for Greek tragedies. The tragic figure — for whom the play is usually named — experiences three stages of development: purpose, passion, and perception. The play begins with a purpose, such as finding the source of the plague in *Oedipus Rex.* Then, as the path becomes tangled and events unfold, the tragic figure begins an

Figure 1. The theater at Epidaurus, Greece, looking east. This is the best preserved (and now restored) Greek theater. Built in the fourth century B.C. by Polykleitos the Younger and approximately 124 feet in diameter, it seats twelve thousand people and remains in use today with excellent acoustics.

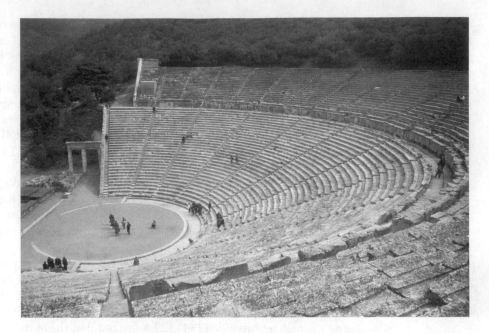

Figure 2. Theater at Epidaurus.

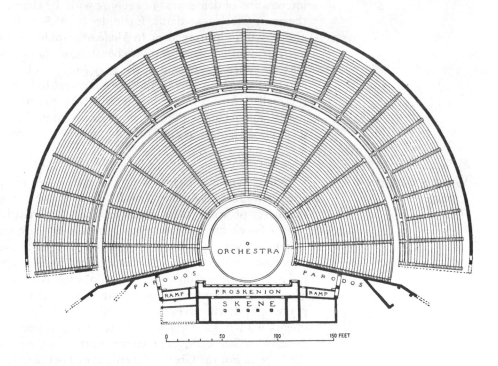

extensive process of soul-searching and suffers an inner agony — the passion. The perception of the truth involves a fate that the tragic figure would rather not face. It might be death or, as in *Oedipus Rex,* exile. It always involves separation from the human community. For the Greeks, that was the greatest punishment.

According to Aristotle, the tragic hero's perception of the truth was the most intense moment in the drama. He called it ANAGNORISIS, or recognition. When it came at the same moment that the tragic figure's fortunes reversed — the PERIPETEIA — Aristotle felt that the tragedy was most fulfilling for the audience. This is the case in *Oedipus Rex*. Aristotle's comments in his *Poetics* on the structure and effect of *Oedipus Rex* remain the most significant critical observations made by a contemporary on Greek theater. (See the excerpt from the *Poetics* on p. 65.)

The Structure of Greek Tragedies. The earliest tragedies seem to have developed from the emotional, intense dithyrambs sung by Athenian choruses. The CHORUS in most tragedies numbered twelve or fifteen men. They usually represented the citizenry in the drama. They dressed simply, and their song was sometimes sung in unison, sometimes delivered by the chorus leader. Originally, there were no actors separate from the chorus.

According to legend, Thespis (sixth century B.C.) was the first actor — the first to step from the chorus to act in dialogue with it — thus creating the AGON, or dramatic confrontation. He won the first prize for tragedy in 532 B.C. As the only actor, he took several parts, wearing MASKS to distinguish the different characters. One actor was the norm in tragedies until Aeschylus (525–456 B.C.), the first important Greek tragedian whose work survives, introduced a second actor, and then Sophocles (c. 496–c. 406 B.C.) added a third. (Only comedy used more: four actors.)

Like the actors, the members of the chorus wore masks. At first the masks were simple, but they became more ornate, often trimmed with hair and decorated with details that established the gender, age, or station of each character. The chorus and all the actors were male.

Eventually the structure of the plays became elaborated into a series of alternations between the characters' dialogue and the choral odes, with each speaking part developing the action or responding to it. Often crucial information furthering the action came from the mouth of a messenger, as in *Oedipus Rex*. The tragedies were structured in three parts: the PROLOGUE established the conflict; the episodes or agons developed the dramatic relationships between characters; and the EXODOS concluded the action. Between these sections the chorus performed different songs: PARODOS while moving onto the stage and STASIMA while standing still. In some plays the chorus sang choral ODES called the STROPHE as it moved from right to left. It sang the ANTISTROPHE while moving back to the right. The actors' episodes consisted of dialogue with each other and with the chorus. The scholar Bernhard Zimmerman has plotted the structure of *Oedipus Rex* in this fashion:

Prologue: Dialogue with Oedipus, the Priests, and Kreon establishing that the plague afflicting Thebes will cease when Laios's murderer is found.

Parodos: The opening hymn of the Chorus appealing to the gods.

First Episode: Oedipus seeks the murderer; Teiresias says it is Oedipus.

First Stasimon: The Chorus supports Oedipus, disbelieving Teiresias.

Second Episode: Oedipus accuses Kreon of being in league with Teiresias and the real murderer. Iokaste pleads for Kreon and tells the oracle of Oedipus's birth and of the death of Laios at the fork of a road. Oedipus sends for the eyewitness of the murder.

Second Stasimon: The Chorus, in a song, grows agitated for Oedipus.

Third Episode: The messenger from Oedipus's "hometown" tells him that his adoptive father has died and is not his real father. Iokaste guesses the truth and Oedipus becomes deeply worried.

Third Stasimon: The Chorus delivers a reassuring, hopeful song.

Fourth Episode: Oedipus, the Shepherd, and the Messenger confront the facts and Oedipus experiences the turning point of the play: he realizes he is the murderer he seeks.

Fourth Stasimon: The Chorus sings of the illusion of human happiness.

Exodos: Iokaste kills herself; Oedipus puts out his eyes; the Chorus and Kreon try to decide the best future action.

As this brief structural outline of *Oedipus Rex* demonstrates, the chorus assumed an important part in the tragedies. In Aeschylus's *Agamemnon* it represents the elders of the community. In Sophocles' *Oedipus Rex* it is a group of concerned citizens who give Oedipus advice and make demands on him. In *Antigone* the chorus consists of men loyal to the state. In Euripides' *Medea* the chorus is a group of the important women of Corinth.

Satyr Plays

The drama competitions held regularly from 534 B.C. consisted usually of the work of three playwrights who each produced three tragedies and one satyr play, a form of comic relief. In a satyr play, the chorus dressed as satyrs, comic half-beast, half-man figures who cavorted with a PHALLUS, a mock penis, and engaged in riotous, almost slapstick antics. The characters were not psychologically developed, as they were in tragedy; the situations were not socially instructive, as they were in comedy. Rough-hewn and lighthearted, the satyr plays may have been a necessary antidote to the intensity of the tragedies.

Only one satyr play survives, perhaps an indication that the form was not as highly valued as tragedy. In Euripides' *Cyclops,* based on Odysseus's confrontation with the one-eyed giant who dined on a number of his men, Odysseus outwits the giant with the aid of a well-filled wineskin. The powers of Bacchus (Dionysus) are often alluded to, and drunkenness is a prime ingredient. The play is witty, entertaining, and brief. It might well have been the perfect way to end an otherwise serious drama festival.

Comedy

No coherent Greek theories on comedy have come down to us. (Aristotle is said to have written a lost treatise on comedy.) In the *Poetics,* Aristotle points out that comedy shows people from a lower social order than the nobility, who are the main figures in tragedy.

The two greatest Greek comic writers were Aristophanes (c. 448–c. 385 B.C.), whose *Lysistrata* appears in this collection, and Menander (c. 342–c. 291 B.C.). The first was a master of OLD COMEDY (which lasted from c. 486 to c. 400 B.C.), in which individuals — sometimes well known to the audience — could be attacked personally. The nature of the humor was often ribald, coarse, and brassy, but, according to Aristotle, it was not vicious. Physical devices onstage, such as the erect phalluses beneath the men's garments in *Lysistrata,* accompanied ribald lines, and Athenian audiences were mightily entertained. Comedy appears to have provided release, but for entirely different emotions than those evoked by tragedy.

The Old Comedy of Aristophanes concentrated on buffoonery and farce. Although we know little about it, a form known as MIDDLE COMEDY seems to have flourished from approximately 400 to 320 B.C. Our evidence is from statuettes of players that indicate a more realistic portrayal of character and thus a less broad and grotesque form of comedy than in some of the plays of Aristophanes. The NEW COMEDY of Menander and others whose work is now lost provided a less ribald humor that centered on the shortcomings of the middle classes. Although Menander enjoyed a great reputation in his own time and was highly regarded by Roman playwrights much later, very little of his work has survived. He is said to have written a few more than one hundred plays, but only one, *The Grouch,* survives intact. Twenty-three of his plays existed in a manuscript in Constantinople in the sixteenth century, but nothing of that volume seems to have survived. We know a number of titles, such as *The Lady from Andros, The Flatterer,* and *The Suspicious Man.* And we know that the Romans pilfered liberally from his plays. Beyond that we know little.

Menander's New Comedy concentrated on social manners. Instead of attacking individuals, as Aristophanes frequently did, Menander was more likely to attack a vice, such as vanity, or to portray the foibles of a social class. He aimed at his own middle class and established the pattern of parents or guardians struggling, usually over the issue of marriage, against the wishes of their children. The children ordinarily foil their parents' wishes, frequently with the help of an acerbic slave who provides the comedy with most of its humor. This pattern has proved so durable that it is used virtually every day in modern situation comedies on television.

Both Old and New Comedy have influenced theater from the time of the Greeks to the present. The nineteenth-century comedy of Oscar Wilde (in this collection) is an example of New Comedy, while the Marx Brothers' movies are examples of Old Comedy.

The Great Age of Greek Drama

The fifth century B.C. was not only the great creative age of Athenian theater but also the age of Athenian power in Greek politics. By the beginning of the century, Greece dominated trade in the Mediterranean and therefore in many of the major civilized urban centers of the world. The most important threat to Greek power came from the Persians, living to the east. After the Persians attacked in 490, Greek city-states such as Athens formed the Delian League to defend themselves, pouring their funds into the treasury at Delos. When the Persians threatened again in 483 B.C., Themistocles (525?–460? B.C.), Athenian soldier and statesman, realized he could not win a battle on land. By skillful political moves he managed to create a powerful navy. When the Persians attacked Athens in 480 B.C., Themistocles left a small rear guard to defend the Acropolis, the city's religious fortress. The Persians took the fortress, burned everything, and were lured by a clever ruse to Salamis, where they thought that a puny Athenian navy was making a getaway. Once the Persians set sail for

Salamis, Themistocles turned on them and revealed a powerful fighting force that defeated the Persians once and for all.

In the years immediately following, Athens overstated its role in the Persian defeat and assumed an air of imperial importance. It appropriated the gold in the Delian League treasury, using it to rebuild the Acropolis beginning in 448 B.C. The great Greek general and leader Pericles (495?–429? B.C.) chose his friend Phidias to supervise the construction of the Parthenon and the other main buildings that are on the Acropolis even today. The threat of Athenian domination seems to have triggered the Peloponnesian Wars (432–406 B.C.), which pitted the Spartan alliance against the Athenian alliance. Athens eventually lost the war and its democratic government.

The events of these years — dominated by interminable wars, threats of a return to tyranny, cultural instability — are coterminous with the great flourishing of Greek art, drama, and philosophy. The geniuses of Greek drama cluster in the period dating from the birth of Aeschylus (c. 525 B.C.) to the death of the philosopher Socrates (399 B.C.). Aeschylus wrote *The Persians* (472 B.C.); *Seven against Thebes* (467 B.C.); and the *Oresteia* (458 B.C.), a trilogy centering on Orestes and consisting of *Agamemnon, The Libation Bearers,* and *The Eumenides. The Suppliants* and *Prometheus Bound* are of uncertain dates.

Aeschylus's introduction of a second actor made it possible to intensify the dramatic value of each *agon,* the confrontation between ANTAGONISTS. He is also notable for giving minor characters, such as the watchman who opens *Agamemnon,* both dimension and depth. Aeschylus's *Oresteia,* the only surviving trilogy, tells of the death of Agamemnon and the efforts of his son Orestes to avenge that death.

Sophocles (c. 496–c. 406 B.C.) and Euripides (c. 485–406 B.C.) learned from Aeschylus and from each other since they were all sometimes rivals. In addition to *Oedipus Rex* (c. 429 B.C.), Sophocles is known today for *Ajax* (c. 442 B.C.), *Philoctetes* (c. 409 B.C.), *Oedipus at Colonus* (406 B.C.), and *Electra* (date uncertain).

Euripides, the last of the great tragedians, may have written as many as ninety-two plays. Of the nineteen that survive, the best known are *Alcestis* (438 B.C.), *Medea* (431 B.C.), *Electra* (date uncertain), *The Trojan Women* (415 B.C.), and *The Bacchae* (produced in 405 B.C.). He is especially noteworthy for his portrayal of women and for his experimental approach to theater.

These three tragedians, along with Aristophanes, provide us with insight into the Greek dramatic imagination. They also reveal something of our common humanity, since their achievement — lost though it was for many centuries — shapes our current dramatic practice. The Greeks give us not only the beginnings of drama but the basis of drama. We build on it today whenever a play is written, whenever we witness a play.

Greek Drama Timeline

DATE	THEATER	POLITICAL	SOCIAL/CULTURAL
1000–800 B.C.			Classic paganism is in full bloom in Greece.
			Temple of Hera, oldest surviving temple in Olympia, Greece, is built.
			9th c.: Age of the Homeric epic; *The Illiad, The Odyssey*
800–700		First Messenian War: Sparta gains power in Greece.	Choral and dramatic music develops.
			Hesiod, poet whose *Works and Days* classified the five ages of mankind: Golden (peaceful), Silver (less happy), Bronze (art and warfare), Heroic (Trojan War), and Iron (the present)
			776: First Olympian festival (predecessor of the modern Olympic games). Only one event is featured: a footrace of approximately 200 meters.
700–600		First written laws of Athens are recorded by Draco.	Sappho of Lesbos, Greek poet
			Archilochus, Greek lyricist and author of fables
			Construction of the Acropolis begins in Athens.
600–500	**534:** First contest for best tragedy is held in Athens as part of the annual City Dionysia, a major religious festival. The winning playwright (and actor) is Thespis.	**594:** Solon's law allows for the Council of Four Hundred and various reforms pertaining to land ownership and civil liberties.	The influence of the oracle at Delphi and its priestess is at its height.
	c. 501: Satyr plays are added to the City Dionysia play competition. Each playwright now has to present a trilogy of tragedies and a satyr play.	**c. 525–459:** Themistocles, Athenian statesman and naval commander, builds a Greek navy and fortifications.	The theater of Delphi is built.
			c. 582–507: Pythagoras, philosopher, mathematician, and musical theorist
			Public libraries in Athens
		525–405: Persians conquer Egypt.	**c. 563–483:** Siddartha, founder of Buddhism, begins his religious journey in 534.
			c. 520–438: Pindar, Greek musician and poet
500–400	**487–486:** Comedy is introduced as a dramatic form in the City Dionysia.	**500–449:** Persian Wars	**c. 460–370:** Hippocrates, Greek physician who did much to separate medicine from superstition.
	c. 471: Aeschylus introduces the second actor in the performance of tragedy at the City Dionysia.	**494:** King Darius of Persia annexes all of Greece.	**485–424:** Herodotus, a Greek historian, writes the history of the Persian Wars.
		490: Athenians defeat the Persians in the Battle of Marathon.	

Greek Drama Timeline (continued)

DATE	THEATER	POLITICAL	SOCIAL/CULTURAL
500–400 B.C. (continued)	c. 468: Sophocles is credited with introducing the third actor in the performance of tragedies at the City Dionysia. 458: First performance of Aeschylus's trilogy the *Oresteia* at the City Dionysia 458: *Skene,* or scene house, is introduced in Greek theater. c. 441: First performance of Sophocles' *Antigone* at the City Dionysia c. 430–425: First performance of Sophocles' *Oedipus Rex* at the City Dionysia 411: First performance of Aristophanes' *Lysistrata*	480: At the Battle of Thermopylae, the Spartans defeat the Persians. 479: Xerxes, son of Darius, returns to Persia; the Persian Wars end. 462–429: Periclean Athens 431: The Peloponnesian War begins; Athens is defeated in 404. Thucydides records the events in his history *The Peloponnesian War.*	460–370: Democritus, Greek philosopher who believed that all living things are composed of atoms 438: The Parthenon is completed.
400–300	400–c. 320: Era of Middle Comedy, which concentrates on more accurately portraying daily life rather than the more fantastic plots of Old Comedy (Aristophanes) 336–300: Era of New Comedy. Menander and others move further away from Aristophanes; stock characters are common. 335–323: Aristotle writes *Poetics.*	395: The Corinthian War begins. Athens joins with Corinth, Thebes, and Argos to attack Sparta. Athens emerges from the ten-year war as a partially restored power. 332: Alexander the Great conquers Egypt. 321: Alexander the Great dies of a fever at age thirty-three. His successors divide the empire into Macedon, Egypt, and the Seleucid empire.	399: Socrates is tried and executed for corrupting the youth of Athens. 373: Plato writes *Republic.* 340–271: Epicurus, Greek philosopher who believed in pleasure, spontaneity, and freedom of will 320–330: Hellenistic period of Greek art 307: The museum and library of Alexandria are begun under Ptolemy Soter.
300–100	277: Artists of Dionysis, a performing artists' guild, is formed.		275–195: Eratosthenes, Greek scientist, suggests that the earth moves around the sun and makes close estimates of the earth's circumference.
100 B.C.– 300 A.D.		100 B.C.–1 A.D.: Alexandria is the Mediterranean center of culture and commerce.	
300–400 A.D.			346–395: The Roman emperor Theodosius forbids the celebration of Olympic games in Greece.

Sophocles

Sophocles (c. 496–c. 406 B.C.) won more prizes than any other tragedian in the Greek drama competitions, and he never came in lower than second place. His first victory was against the grand old master Aeschylus in 468 B.C. Sophocles' last plays, which he wrote in his eighties, were among his greatest. We have fragments of some ninety plays or poems and seven complete tragedies, while records suggest that his output numbered something over a hundred twenty plays.

Sophocles lived in interesting times. He would have recalled the first defeat of the Persians in 490 B.C., when the news came by a messenger who had run twenty-six miles from Marathon to Athens. In his adolescence, Athens achieved its astonishing and decisive victory over the Persians at Salamis. His popularity as a tragedian and as a statesman coincided with the development of an imperial attitude in Athens. Athenian society honored the greatness of men like Aeschylus, Sophocles, Euripides, the historian Herodotus, and all the politicians and artists that Pericles drew to Athens for its rebuilding. It was a golden age shadowed by war.

Sophocles was both sociable and religious, serving as the priest of several religious cults. He was also a man of action, popular enough to be elected as one of Athens's twelve generals; he participated with Pericles in the Samian War (440–439 B.C.). His plays — especially *Antigone* (441 B.C.), which preceded his election to generalship — often have deep political concerns. One of his primary themes concerns the relation of the individual to the *polis,* the state itself. Since the Greeks valued the individual and at the same time regarded the *polis* as a sacred bulwark against a return to barbarism, conflicts between the individual and the *polis* were immensely painful.

When Sophocles began writing, he broke with an old tradition. From the time of Thespis (mid-sixth century B.C.), each playwright acted in his own plays. Aeschylus probably did so, but it is on record that Sophocles' voice was not strong enough to permit him to take a part in his plays. He played the lyre well enough to appear onstage, and he participated in a game of ball in one of his plays, but he did not appear as an actor. He also introduced innovations in the structure of his plays by changing the size of the chorus to fifteen and by adding painted scenery, more props, and a third actor to the two that Aeschylus and other tragedians had used. Sophocles wrote some of his plays with specific actors in mind, much as Shakespeare, Molière, and many other first-rank playwrights have done.

Sophocles was versed in the epics of Homer. Some of his plays derive from the *Iliad* or the *Odyssey,* although Sophocles always adapted the material of others to his own purposes. His nickname was the Attic Bee because he could investigate wonderful pieces of literature and always return with a useful idea. The approach he took to the structure of the play, measuring the effect of the rising action of complication and then ensuring that the moment of recognition occurred at the same time the falling action began, was recognized as a supremely elegant skill. Nowhere is this illustrated with more completeness than in *Oedipus Rex*.

Bust of Sophocles. The
Capitoline Museum, Rome.

The plays of Aeschylus, powerful though they are, do not have the same delicacy of construction as do Sophocles'. They are forceful but, in terms of structure, somewhat simpler. The structure of the plays of Euripides, Sophocles' successor, was never as fully worked out; and when Aristotle discussed the nature of tragedy in his *Poetics*, it was to Sophocles he turned for a model, not to the other two master playwrights of the genre.

Besides the Oedipus plays, Sophocles' other surviving plays are *Philoctetes, Ajax, Trachiniae,* and *Elektra*.

OEDIPUS REX

Oedipus Rex is one of three plays by Sophocles that treat the fate of Oedipus and his children. The plays were written over a period of thirty years: *Antigone* (first produced in 441 B.C.), *Oedipus Rex* (produced approximately fifteen years later, between 430 and 427 B.C.), and *Oedipus at Colonus* (produced in 401 B.C., after Sophocles' death). When these plays are produced together today, they are usually given in an order that follows the events of Oedipus's and Antigone's lives — *Oedipus Rex, Oedipus at Colonus,* and *Antigone* — almost like the trilogies that Athenian audiences often viewed in the early years of the drama competitions. In fact, they were never a unified trilogy, and one of Sophocles' distinctions is that he did not present as trilogies plays that were thematically related, as poets before him had done.

The original narratives of the Oedipus plays were known to Sophocles' audience — with the possible exception of the story of Antigone — and one of the special pleasures for the audience watching the action of *Oedipus Rex* was that they knew the outcome. They watched for the steps, the choices, that led Oedipus to his fate.

Oedipus Rex is the story of a noble man who seeks knowledge that in the end destroys him. His greatness is measured in part by the fact that the gods have prophesied his fate: the gods do not take interest in insignificant men. Before the action of the play begins, Oedipus has set out to discover whether he is truly the son of Polybos and Merope, the people who have reared him. He learns from the oracle of Apollo at Delphi, the most powerful interpreter of the voice and the will of the gods, that he will kill his father and marry his mother. His response is overwhelmingly human: he has seen his *moira,* his fate, and he cannot accept it. His reaction is to do everything he can, including leaving his homeland as quickly as possible, to avoid the possibility of killing Polybos and marrying Merope.

The Greek audience would have known that Oedipus was a descendant of Kadmos, founder of Thebes, who had sown the dragon teeth that produced the Spartoi (the sown men). Legend determined that the rulership of Thebes would be in dispute, with fraternal rivalry resembling that of the Spartoi, who fought and killed each other. This bloody legacy follows Oedipus, but it also reaches into all the plays of the trilogy. For example, in *Antigone* we learn that Antigone's brothers Polyneices and Eteocles killed each other in the shadow of the city walls. Thus, the fate Oedipus attempts to avoid actually dooms most of the characters in the three plays, including his true father, Laios, and his daughter Antigone.

Sophocles develops the drama in terms of IRONY — the disjunction between what seems to be true and what is true. Knowing the outcome of the action, the audience savors the ironic moments from the beginning of the play to the end. Oedipus flees his homeland to avoid fulfilling the prophecy, only to run headlong into the fate foretold by the oracle. He unwittingly returns to his original home, Thebes, and to his parents, murdering Laios, his true father, at a crossroads on the way and marrying Iokaste, his true mother, and becoming king of Thebes. The blind seer Teiresias warns Oedipus not to pursue the truth, but, in human fashion, Oedipus refuses to heed Teiresias's warnings. When the complete truth becomes clear to Oedipus, he physically blinds himself in horror and expiation. Like the blind Teiresias, Oedipus must now look inward for the truth, without the distractions of surface experiences.

The belief that the moral health of the ruler directly affected the security of the *polis* was widespread in Athenian Greece. Indeed, the Athenians regarded their state as fragile — like a human being whose health, physical and moral, could change suddenly. Because the Greeks were concerned for the well-being of their state, the *polis* often figures in the tragedies. The Sophoclean Oedipus trilogy is usually called the Theban plays, a nomenclature that reminds us that the story of Oedipus can be read as the story of an individual or as the story of a state.

Oedipus Rex examines the tension between and interdependence of the individual and the state. The agricultural and ritual basis of the Dionysian festivals — in which Greek drama developed — underscores the importance the Greeks attached to the individual's dependence on the state that feeds him and on the proper ways of doing things. This could be planting and harvesting or worshiping the gods or living as part of a political entity.

The underlying conflict in the play is political. The political relationship of human beings to the gods, the arbiters of their fate, is dramatized in Oedipus's relationship with the seer Teiresias. If he had his way, Oedipus might disregard Teiresias entirely. But Oedipus cannot command everything, even as ruler. His incomplete knowledge, despite his wisdom, is symptomatic of the limitations of every individual.

The contrast of Oedipus and Kreon, Iokaste's brother, is one of political style. Oedipus is a fully developed character who reveals himself as sympathetic but willful. He acts on his misunderstanding of the prophecy without reconsulting the oracle. He marries Iokaste and blinds himself without reconsulting the oracle. Kreon, who is much less complicated, never acts without consulting the oracle and thoughtfully reflecting on the oracle's message. Oedipus sometimes behaves tyrannically, and he appears eager for power. Kreon takes power only when forced to do so.

The depth of Sophocles' character development was unmatched, except by his contemporary Euripides, for almost two thousand years. Sophocles' drama is one of psychological development. His audiences saw Oedipus as a model for human greatness but also as a model for the human capacity to fall from a great height. The play is about the limits of human knowledge; it is also about the limits and frailty of human happiness.

Oedipus Rex in Performance

Oedipus Rex has enjoyed great popularity since its first performance. The Greeks, who originally restricted their plays to one performance, eventually began to revive plays of the masters. *Oedipus* was one of the most popular. In modern times, performance has been almost constant since the seventeenth century. Great dramatists have produced it in their own adaptations — Corneille (1659), John Dryden (1679), Voltaire (1718), William Butler Yeats (1923), and Jean Cocteau (1931) — proving the durability of the themes and the adaptability of the play. The early American performances (beginning in 1881) were in Greek but soon gave way to English. Modern versions have been both very traditional, such as those developed by the Royal Shakespeare Company in the 1970s, and experimental, such as that of Peter Brook (1968). Brook's production began with a huge golden cube reflecting brilliant light like the sun and ended with the ritual unveiling of a giant phallus. John Gielgud played Oedipus and Irene Worth, all in black, played Iokaste. Currently, Greek companies perform the play regularly in the theater of Dionysus in Athens as well as in Epidaurus and elsewhere.

Sophocles (c. 496–c. 406 B.C.)

OEDIPUS REX

TRANSLATED BY DUDLEY FITTS AND ROBERT FITZGERALD

c. 430 B.C.

Characters

OEDIPUS, *King of Thebes, supposed son of Polybos and Merope, King and Queen of Corinth*

IOKASTE, *wife of Oedipus and widow of the late King Laios*

KREON, *brother of Iokaste, a prince of Thebes*

TEIRESIAS, *a blind seer who serves Apollo*

PRIEST

MESSENGER, *from Corinth*

SHEPHERD, *former servant of Laios*

SECOND MESSENGER, *from the palace*

CHORUS OF THEBAN ELDERS

CHORAGOS, *leader of the Chorus*

ANTIGONE *and* ISMENE, *young daughters of Oedipus and Iokaste. They appear in the Exodos but do not speak.*

SUPPLIANTS, GUARDS, SERVANTS

The Scene: *Before the palace of Oedipus, King of Thebes. A central door and two lateral doors open onto a platform which runs the length of the facade. On the platform, right and left, are altars; and three steps lead down into the orchestra, or chorus-ground. At the beginning of the action these steps are crowded by suppliants who have brought branches and chaplets of olive leaves and who sit in various attitudes of despair. Oedipus enters.*

PROLOGUE°

OEDIPUS: My children, generations of the living
  In the line of Kadmos,° nursed at his ancient hearth:
  Why have you strewn yourselves before these altars
  In supplication, with your boughs and garlands?
5 The breath of incense rises from the city
  With a sound of prayer and lamentation.
               Children,
  I would not have you speak through messengers,
  And therefore I have come myself to hear you —
  I, Oedipus, who bear the famous name.
  (*To a Priest.*) You, there, since you are eldest in the
10   company,
  Speak for them all, tell me what preys upon you,
  Whether you come in dread, or crave some blessing:

Prologue: Portion of the play explaining the background and current action. **2. Kadmos:** Founder of Thebes.

Tell me, and never doubt that I will help you
In every way I can; I should be heartless
Were I not moved to find you suppliant here.   15
PRIEST: Great Oedipus, O powerful king of Thebes!
  You see how all the ages of our people
  Cling to your altar steps: here are boys
  Who can barely stand alone, and here are priests
  By weight of age, as I am a priest of God,   20
  And young men chosen from those yet unmarried;
  As for the others, all that multitude,
  They wait with olive chaplets in the squares,
  At the two shrines of Pallas,° and where Apollo°
  Speaks in the glowing embers.
               Your own eyes   25
  Must tell you: Thebes is tossed on a murdering sea
  And can not lift her head from the death surge.
  A rust consumes the buds and fruits of the earth;
  The herds are sick; children die unborn,
  And labor is vain. The god of plague and pyre   30
  Raids like detestable lightning through the city,
  And all the house of Kadmos is laid waste,
  All emptied, and all darkened: Death alone
  Battens upon the misery of Thebes.

You are not one of the immortal gods, we know;   35
  Yet we have come to you to make our prayer
  As to the man surest in mortal ways
  And wisest in the ways of God. You saved us
  From the Sphinx,° that flinty singer, and the tribute
  We paid to her so long; yet you were never   40
  Better informed than we, nor could we teach you:
  A god's touch, it seems, enabled you to help us.

Therefore, O mighty power, we turn to you:
  Find us our safety, find us a remedy,
  Whether by counsel of the gods or of men.   45
  A king of wisdom tested in the past
  Can act in a time of troubles, and act well.
  Noblest of men, restore
  Life to your city! Think how all men call you
  Liberator for your boldness long ago;   50
  Ah, when your years of kingship are remembered,

---

24. Pallas: Pallas Athene, daughter of Zeus and goddess of wisdom. **Apollo:** Son of Zeus and god of the sun, of light and truth. **39. Sphinx:** A winged monster with the body of a lion and the face of a woman, the Sphinx had tormented Thebes with her riddle, killing those who could not solve it. When Oedipus solved the riddle, the Sphinx killed herself.

Let them not say *We rose, but later fell* —
Keep the State from going down in the storm!
Once, years ago, with happy augury,
55   You brought us fortune; be the same again!
No man questions your power to rule the land:
But rule over men, not over a dead city!
Ships are only hulls, high walls are nothing,
When no life moves in the empty passageways.
60   OEDIPUS: Poor children! You may be sure I know
All that you longed for in your coming here.
I know that you are deathly sick; and yet,
Sick as you are, not one is as sick as I.
Each of you suffers in himself alone
65   His anguish, not another's; but my spirit
Groans for the city, for myself, for you.

I was not sleeping, you are not waking me.
No, I have been in tears for a long while
And in my restless thought walked many ways.
70   In all my search I found one remedy,
And I have adopted it: I have sent Kreon,
Son of Menoikeus, brother of the queen,
To Delphi,° Apollo's place of revelation,
To learn there, if he can,
75   What act or pledge of mine may save the city.
I have counted the days, and now, this very day,
I am troubled, for he has overstayed his time.
What is he doing? He has been gone too long.
Yet whenever he comes back, I should do ill
80   Not to take any action the god orders.
PRIEST: It is a timely promise. At this instant
They tell me Kreon is here.
OEDIPUS: O Lord Apollo!
May his news be fair as his face is radiant!
PRIEST: Good news, I gather! he is crowned with bay,
The chaplet is thick with berries.
85   OEDIPUS: We shall soon know;
He is near enough to hear us now.   (*Enter Kreon.*)
O prince:
Brother: son of Menoikeus:
What answer do you bring us from the god?
KREON: A strong one. I can tell you, great afflictions
90   Will turn out well, if they are taken well.
OEDIPUS: What was the oracle? These vague words
Leave me still hanging between hope and fear.
KREON: Is it your pleasure to hear me with all these
Gathered around us? I am prepared to speak,
But should we not go in?
95   OEDIPUS: Speak to them all,
It is for them I suffer, more than for myself.
KREON: Then I will tell you what I heard at Delphi.
In plain words
The god commands us to expel from the land of
Thebes
100   An old defilement we are sheltering.

73. **Delphi:** Site of the oracle, source of religious authority and
prophecy, under the protection of Apollo.

It is a deathly thing, beyond cure;
We must not let it feed upon us longer.
OEDIPUS: What defilement? How shall we rid ourselves
of it?
KREON: By exile or death, blood for blood. It was
Murder that brought the plague-wind on the city.   105
OEDIPUS: Murder of whom? Surely the god has named
him?
KREON: My Lord: Laios once ruled this land,
Before you came to govern us.
OEDIPUS: I know;
I learned of him from others; I never saw him.
KREON: He was murdered; and Apollo commands us
now   110
To take revenge upon whoever killed him.
OEDIPUS: Upon whom? Where are they? Where shall
we find a clue
To solve that crime, after so many years?
KREON: Here in this land, he said. Search reveals
Things that escape an inattentive man.   115
OEDIPUS: Tell me: Was Laios murdered in his house,
Or in the fields, or in some foreign country?
KREON: He said he planned to make a pilgrimage.
He did not come home again.
OEDIPUS: And was there no one,
No witness, no companion, to tell what happened?   120
KREON: They were all killed but one, and he got away
So frightened that he could remember one thing
only.
OEDIPUS: What was that one thing? One may be the
key
To everything, if we resolve to use it.
KREON: He said that a band of highwaymen attacked
them,   125
Outnumbered them, and overwhelmed the king.
OEDIPUS: Strange, that a highwayman should be so
daring —
Unless some faction here bribed him to do it.
KREON: We thought of that. But after Laios' death
New troubles arose and we had no avenger.   130
OEDIPUS: What troubles could prevent your hunting
down the killers?
KREON: The riddling Sphinx's song
Made us deaf to all mysteries but her own.
OEDIPUS: Then once more I must bring what is dark to
light.
It is most fitting that Apollo shows,   135
As you do, this compunction for the dead.
You shall see how I stand by you, as I should,
Avenging this country and the god as well,
And not as though it were for some distant friend,
But for my own sake, to be rid of evil.   140
Whoever killed King Laios might — who knows? —
Lay violent hands even on me — and soon.
I act for the murdered king in my own interest.

Come, then, my children: leave the altar steps,
Lift up your olive boughs!
One of you go   145

And summon the people of Kadmos to gather here.
I will do all that I can; you may tell them that.
                                        (*Exit a Page.*)
So, with the help of God,
We shall be saved — or else indeed we are lost.
150 PRIEST: Let us rise, children. It was for this we came,
And now the king has promised it.
Phoibos° has sent us an oracle; may he descend
Himself to save us and drive out the plague.

(*Exeunt*° *Oedipus and Kreon into the palace by the central door. The Priest and the Suppliants disperse right and left. After a short pause the Chorus enters the orchestra.*)

PARADOS° • *Strophe*° *1*

CHORUS: What is God singing in his profound
Delphi of gold and shadow?
What oracle for Thebes, the Sunwhipped city?
Fear unjoints me, the roots of my heart tremble.
Now I remember, O Healer, your power, and
5   wonder:
Will you send doom like a sudden cloud, or weave it
Like nightfall of the past?
Speak to me, tell me, O
Child of golden Hope, immortal Voice.

Antistrophe° *1*

Let me pray to Athene, the immortal daughter of
10   Zeus,
And to Artemis° her sister
Who keeps her famous throne in the market ring,
And to Apollo, archer from distant heaven —
O gods, descend! Like three streams leap against
15 The fires of our grief, the fires of darkness;
Be swift to bring us rest!
As in the old time from the brilliant house
Of air you stepped to save us, come again!

Strophe 2

Now our afflictions have no end,
20 Now all our stricken host lies down
And no man fights off death with his mind;
The noble plowland bears no grain,
And groaning mothers can not bear —
See, how our lives like birds take wing,

Like sparks that fly when a fire soars,   25
To the shore of the god of evening.

Antistrophe 2

The plague burns on, it is pitiless,
Though pallid children laden with death
Lie unwept in the stony ways,
And old gray women by every path   30
Flock to the strand about the altars
There to strike their breasts and cry
Worship of Phoibos in wailing prayers:
Be kind, God's golden child!

Strophe 3

There are no swords in this attack by fire,   35
No shields, but we are ringed with cries.
Send the besieger plunging from our homes
Into the vast sea-room of the Atlantic
Or into the waves that foam eastward of Thrace —
For the day ravages what the night spares —   40
Destroy our enemy, lord of the thunder!
Let him be riven by lightning from heaven!

Antistrophe 3

Phoibos Apollo, stretch the sun's bowstring,
That golden cord, until it sing for us,
Flashing arrows in heaven!
                    Artemis, Huntress,   45
Race with flaring lights upon our mountains!
O scarlet god,° O golden banded brow,
O Theban Bacchos in a storm of Maenads,°

(*Enter Oedipus, center.*)

Whirl upon Death, that all the Undying hate!
Come with blinding torches, come in joy!   50

SCENE 1

OEDIPUS: Is this your prayer? It may be answered.
    Come,
Listen to me, act as the crisis demands,
And you shall have relief from all these evils.

Until now I was a stranger to this tale,
As I had been a stranger to the crime.   5
Could I track down the murderer without a clue?
But now, friends,
As one who became a citizen after the murder,

---

152. Phoibos: Apollo.   **154.** [S.D.] *Exeunt:* Latin for "they go out."   **Parados:** The song or ode chanted by the Chorus on their entry.   **Strophe:** Song sung by the Chorus as they danced from stage right to stage left.   **Antistrophe:** Song sung by the Chorus following the Strophe, as they danced back from stage left to stage right.   **11. Artemis:** The huntress, daughter of Zeus, twin sister of Apollo.

47. scarlet god: Bacchus, god of wine and revelry; also called Dionysus.   **48. Maenads:** Female worshipers of Bacchus (Dionysus).

I make this proclamation to all Thebans:
If any man knows by whose hand Laios, son of
10   Labdakos,
Met his death, I direct that man to tell me everything,
No matter what he fears for having so long
      withheld it.
Let it stand as promised that no further trouble
Will come to him, but he may leave the land in safety.
Moreover: If anyone knows the murderer to be
15   foreign,
Let him not keep silent: he shall have his reward
      from me.
However, if he does conceal it; if any man
Fearing for his friend or for himself disobeys this
      edict,
Hear what I propose to do:

20 I solemnly forbid the people of this country,
Where power and throne are mine, ever to receive
      that man
Or speak to him, no matter who he is, or let him
Join in sacrifice, lustration, or in prayer.
I decree that he be driven from every house,
25 Being, as he is, corruption itself to us: the Delphic
Voice of Apollo has pronounced this revelation.
Thus I associate myself with the oracle
And take the side of the murdered king.

As for the criminal, I pray to God —
30 Whether it be a lurking thief, or one of a number —
I pray that that man's life be consumed in evil and
      wretchedness.
And as for me, this curse applies no less
If it should turn out that the culprit is my guest here,
Sharing my hearth.
               You have heard the penalty.
35 I lay it on you now to attend to this
For my sake, for Apollo's, for the sick
Sterile city that heaven has abandoned.
Suppose the oracle had given you no command:
Should this defilement go uncleansed for ever?
40 You should have found the murderer: your king,
A noble king, had been destroyed!
                    Now I,
Having the power that he held before me,
Having his bed, begetting children there
Upon his wife, as he would have, had he lived —
45 Their son would have been my children's brother,
If Laios had had luck in fatherhood!
(And now his bad fortune has struck him down) —
I say I take the son's part, just as though
I were his son, to press the fight for him
50 And see it won! I'll find the hand that brought
Death to Labdakos' and Polydoros' child,
Heir of Kadmos' and Agenor's line.°

51–52. **Labdakos, Polydoros, Kadmos, and Agenor:** Father, grandfather, great-grandfather, and great-great-grandfather of Laios.

And as for those who fail me,
May the gods deny them the fruit of the earth,
Fruit of the womb, and may they rot utterly!   55
Let them be wretched as we are wretched, and
      worse!

For you, for loyal Thebans, and for all
Who find my actions right, I pray the favor
Of justice, and of all the immortal gods.
CHORAGOS: Since I am under oath, my lord, I swear   60
I did not do the murder, I can not name
The murderer. Phoibos ordained the search;
Why did he not say who the culprit was?
OEDIPUS: An honest question. But no man in the world
Can make the gods do more than the gods will.   65
CHORAGOS: There is an alternative, I think —
OEDIPUS: Tell me.
Any or all, you must not fail to tell me.
CHORAGOS: A lord clairvoyant to the lord Apollo,
As we all know, is the skilled Teiresias.
One might learn much about this from him, Oedipus.   70
OEDIPUS: I am not wasting time:
Kreon spoke of this, and I have sent for him —
Twice, in fact; it is strange that he is not here.
CHORAGOS: The other matter — that old report —
      seems useless.
OEDIPUS: What was that? I am interested in all reports.   75
CHORAGOS: The king was said to have been killed by
      highwaymen.
OEDIPUS: I know. But we have no witnesses to that.
CHORAGOS: If the killer can feel a particle of dread,
Your curse will bring him out of hiding!
OEDIPUS: No.
The man who dared that act will fear no curse.   80

(*Enter the blind seer Teiresias, led by a Page.*)

CHORAGOS: But there is one man who may detect the
      criminal.
This is Teiresias, this is the holy prophet
In whom, alone of all men, truth was born.
OEDIPUS: Teiresias: seer: student of mysteries,
Of all that's taught and all that no man tells,   85
Secrets of Heaven and secrets of the earth:
Blind though you are, you know the city lies
Sick with plague; and from this plague, my lord,
We find that you alone can guard or save us.

Possibly you did not hear the messengers?   90
Apollo, when we sent to him,
Sent us back word that this great pestilence
Would lift, but only if we established clearly
The identity of those who murdered Laios.
They must be killed or exiled.
                      Can you use   95
Birdflight° or any art of divination
To purify yourself, and Thebes, and me

96. **Birdflight:** Prophets used the flight of birds to predict the future.

From this contagion? We are in your hands.
There is no fairer duty
100   Than that of helping others in distress.
TEIRESIAS: How dreadful knowledge of the truth can be
When there's no help in truth! I knew this well,
But did not act on it; else I should not have come.
OEDIPUS: What is troubling you? Why are your eyes so
cold?
105 TEIRESIAS: Let me go home. Bear your own fate, and I'll
Bear mine. It is better so: trust what I say.
OEDIPUS: What you say is ungracious and unhelpful
To your native country. Do not refuse to speak.
TEIRESIAS: When it comes to speech, your own is
neither temperate
110   Nor opportune. I wish to be more prudent.
OEDIPUS: In God's name, we all beg you —
TEIRESIAS: You are all ignorant.
No; I will never tell you what I know.
Now it is my misery; then, it would be yours.
OEDIPUS: What! You do know something, and will not
tell us?
115   You would betray us all and wreck the State?
TEIRESIAS: I do not intend to torture myself, or you.
Why persist in asking? You will not persuade me.
OEDIPUS: What a wicked old man you are! You'd try a
stone's
Patience! Out with it! Have you no feeling at all?
120 TEIRESIAS: You call me unfeeling. If you could only see
The nature of your own feelings . . .
OEDIPUS: Why,
Who would not feel as I do? Who could endure
Your arrogance toward the city?
TEIRESIAS: What does it matter?
Whether I speak or not, it is bound to come.
OEDIPUS: Then, if "it" is bound to come, you are
125   bound to tell me.
TEIRESIAS: No, I will not go on. Rage as you please.
OEDIPUS: Rage? Why not!
                        And I'll tell you what I think:
You planned it, you had it done, you all but
Killed him with your own hands: if you had eyes,
130   I'd say the crime was yours, and yours alone.
TEIRESIAS: So? I charge you, then,
Abide by the proclamation you have made:
From this day forth
Never speak again to these men or to me;
135   You yourself are the pollution of this country.
OEDIPUS: You dare say that! Can you possibly think
you have
Some way of going free, after such insolence?
TEIRESIAS: I have gone free. It is the truth sustains me.
OEDIPUS: Who taught you shamelessness? It was not
your craft.
TEIRESIAS: You did. You made me speak. I did not
140   want to.
OEDIPUS: Speak what? Let me hear it again more
clearly.
TEIRESIAS: Was it not clear before? Are you tempting
me?

OEDIPUS: I did not understand it. Say it again.
TEIRESIAS: I say that you are the murderer whom you
seek.
OEDIPUS: Now twice you have spat out infamy.
You'll pay for it!   145
TEIRESIAS: Would you care for more? Do you wish to
be really angry?
OEDIPUS: Say what you will. Whatever you say is
worthless.
TEIRESIAS: I say you live in hideous shame with those
Most dear to you. You can not see the evil.
OEDIPUS: Can you go on babbling like this for ever?   150
TEIRESIAS: I can, if there is power in truth.
OEDIPUS: There is:
But not for you, not for you,
You sightless, witless, senseless, mad old man!
TEIRESIAS: You are the madman. There is no one here
Who will not curse you soon, as you curse me.   155
OEDIPUS: You child of total night! I would not touch
you;
Neither would any man who sees the sun.
TEIRESIAS: True: it is not from you my fate will come.
That lies within Apollo's competence,
As it is his concern.
OEDIPUS: Tell me, who made   160
These fine discoveries? Kreon? or someone else?
TEIRESIAS: Kreon is no threat. You weave your own
doom.
OEDIPUS: Wealth, power, craft of statemanship!
Kingly position, everywhere admired!
What savage envy is stored up against these,   165
If Kreon, whom I trusted, Kreon my friend,
For this great office which the city once
Put in my hands unsought — if for this power
Kreon desires in secret to destroy me!

He has bought this decrepit fortune-teller, this   170
Collector of dirty pennies, this prophet fraud —
Why, he is no more clairvoyant than I am!
                              Tell us:
Has your mystic mummery ever approached the
truth?
When that hellcat the Sphinx was performing here,   175
What help were you to these people?
Her magic was not for the first man who came along:
It demanded a real exorcist. Your birds —
What good were they? or the gods, for the matter of
that?
But I came by,
Oedipus, the simple man, who knows nothing —   180
I thought it out for myself, no birds helped me!
And this is the man you think you can destroy,
That you may be close to Kreon when he's king!
Well, you and your friend Kreon, it seems to me,
Will suffer most. If you were not an old man,   185
You would have paid already for your plot.
CHORAGOS: We can not see that his words or yours
Have been spoken except in anger, Oedipus,
And of anger we have no need. How to accomplish

And that bridal-descant of yours — you'll know it
then,
The song they sang when you came here to Thebes
And found your misguided berthing.
All this, and more, that you can not guess at now, 210
Will bring you to yourself among your children.

Be angry, then. Curse Kreon. Curse my words.
I tell you, no man that walks upon the earth
Shall be rooted out more horribly than you.
OEDIPUS: Am I to bear this from him? — Damnation 215
Take you! Out of this place! Out of my sight!
TEIRESIAS: I would not have come at all if you had not
asked me.
OEDIPUS: Could I have told that you'd talk nonsense,
that
You'd come here to make a fool of yourself, and of
me?
TEIRESIAS: A fool? Your parents thought me sane
enough. 220
OEDIPUS: My parents again! — Wait: who were my
parents?
TEIRESIAS: This day will give you a father, and break
your heart.
OEDIPUS: Your infantile riddles! Your damned
abracadabra!
TEIRESIAS: You were a great man once at solving riddles.
OEDIPUS: Mock me with that if you like; you will find
it true. 225
TEIRESIAS: It was true enough. It brought about your
ruin.
OEDIPUS: But if it saved this town?
TEIRESIAS (to the Page):   Boy, give me your hand.
OEDIPUS: Yes, boy; lead him away.
                              — While you are here
We can do nothing. Go; leave us in peace. 230
TEIRESIAS: I will go when I have said what I have to say.
How can you hurt me? And I tell you again:
The man you have been looking for all this time,
The damned man, the murderer of Laios,
That man is in Thebes. To your mind he is
foreign-born, 235
But it will soon be shown that he is a Theban,
A revelation that will fail to please.
                              A blind man,
Who has his eyes now; a penniless man, who is rich
now;
And he will go tapping the strange earth with his staff.
To the children with whom he lives now he will be 240
Brother and father — the very same; to her
Who bore him, son and husband — the very same
Who came to his father's bed, wet with his father's
blood.
Enough. Go think that over.
If later you find error in what I have said, 245
You may say that I have no skill in prophecy.

190   The god's will best: that is what most concerns us.
        TEIRESIAS: You are a king. But where argument's
                concerned
        I am your man, as much a king as you.
        I am not your servant, but Apollo's.
        I have no need of Kreon or Kreon's name.

195   Listen to me. You mock my blindness, do you?
        But I say that you, with both your eyes, are blind:
        You can not see the wretchedness of your life,
        Nor in whose house you live, no, nor with whom.
        Who are your father and mother? Can you tell me?
200   You do not even know the blind wrongs
                That you have done them, on earth and in the world
                        below.
        But the double lash of your parents' curse will whip
                you
        Out of this land some day, with only night
        Upon your precious eyes.
205   Your cries then — where will they not be heard?
        What fastness of Kithairon° will not echo them?

206. Kithairon: The mountain where Oedipus was abandoned
as an infant.

(*Exit Teiresias, led by his Page.
Oedipus goes into the palace.*)

48

FAR LEFT: Le Clanche Du Rand as Iokaste in Donald Sutherland and Robert Loper's production of *Oedipus Rex* at the 1975 Oregon Shakespeare Festival in Ashland. RIGHT: Philip L. Jones as the Shepherd. (Photos by Henry S. Kranzler.) BELOW: Franz Mertz's design for a 1952 production of *Oedipus Rex* directed by G. R. Sellner at Darmstadt Landestheater.

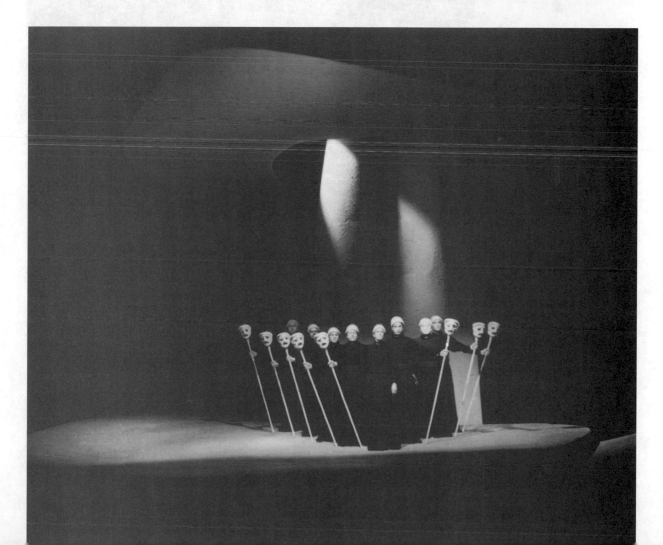

ODE° 1 • *Strophe 1*

CHORUS: The Delphic stone of prophecies
    Remembers ancient regicide
    And a still bloody hand.
    That killer's hour of flight has come.
5   He must be stronger than riderless
    Coursers of untiring wind,
    For the son of Zeus° armed with his father's thunder
    Leaps in lightning after him;
    And the Furies° hold his track, the sad Furies.

Ode: Song sung by the Chorus. **7. son of Zeus:** Apollo.
9. Furies: Spirits called on to avenge crimes, especially against kin.

Antistrophe 1

Holy Parnassos'° peak of snow   10
Flashes and blinds that secret man,
That all shall hunt him down:
Though he may roam the forest shade
Like a bull gone wild from pasture
To rage through glooms of stone.   15
Doom comes down on him; flight will not avail him;
For the world's heart calls him desolate,
And the immortal voices follow, for ever follow.

10. Parnassos: Mountain sacred to Apollo.

Josef Svoboda's stage design for M. Machacek's 1963 production of *Oedipus Rex* in Prague.

Strophe 2

But now a wilder thing is heard
From the old man skilled at hearing Fate in the
20   wing-beat of a bird.
Bewildered as a blown bird, my soul hovers and can
          not find
Foothold in this debate, or any reason or rest of
          mind.
But no man ever brought — none can bring
Proof of strife between Thebes' royal house,
25   Labdakos' line, and the son of Polybos;°
And never until now has any man brought word
Of Laios' dark death staining Oedipus the King.

Antistrophe 2

Divine Zeus and Apollo hold
Perfect intelligence alone of all tales ever told;
And well though this diviner works, he works in his
30   own night;
No man can judge that rough unknown or trust in
          second sight,
For wisdom changes hands among the wise.
Shall I believe my great lord criminal
At a raging word that a blind old man let fall?
I saw him, when the carrion woman° faced him of
35   old,
Prove his heroic mind. These evil words are lies.

SCENE 2

KREON: Men of Thebes:
I am told that heavy accusations
Have been brought against me by King Oedipus.

I am not the kind of man to bear this tamely.

5   If in these present difficulties
He holds me accountable for any harm to him
Through anything I have said or done — why, then,
I do not value life in this dishonor.
It is not as though this rumor touched upon
10   Some private indiscretion. The matter is grave.
The fact is that I am being called disloyal
To the State, to my fellow citizens, to my friends.
CHORAGOS: He may have spoken in anger, not from his
          mind.
KREON: But did you not hear him say I was the one
15   Who seduced the old prophet into lying?
CHORAGOS: The thing was said; I do not know how
          seriously.
KREON: But you were watching him! Were his eyes
          steady?

25. **Polybos:** King who adopted Oedipus.   35. **woman:** The
Sphinx.

Did he look like a man in his right mind?
CHORAGOS: I do not know.
I can not judge the behavior of great men.
But here is the king himself.

(Enter Oedipus.)

OEDIPUS: So you dared come back.   20
Why? How brazen of you to come to my house,
You murderer!
                    Do you think I do not know
That you plotted to kill me, plotted to steal my
          throne?
Tell me, in God's name: am I coward, a fool,
That you should dream you could accomplish this?   25
A fool who could not see your slippery game?
A coward, not to fight back when I saw it?
You are the fool, Kreon, are you not? hoping
Without support or friends to get a throne?
Thrones may be won or bought: you could do
          neither.   30
KREON: Now listen to me. You have talked; let me talk,
          too.
You can not judge unless you know the facts.
OEDIPUS: You speak well: there is one fact; but I find it
          hard
To learn from the deadliest enemy I have.
KREON: That above all I must dispute with you.   35
OEDIPUS: That above all I will not hear you deny.
KREON: If you think there is anything good in being
          stubborn
Against all reason, then I say you are wrong.
OEDIPUS: If you think a man can sin against his own
          kind
And not be punished for it, I say you are mad.   40
KREON: I agree. But tell me: what have I done to
          you?
OEDIPUS: You advised me to send for that wizard,
          did you not?
KREON: I did. I should do it again.
OEDIPUS: Very well. Now tell me:
How long has it been since Laios —
KREON: What of Laios?
OEDIPUS: Since he vanished in that onset by the road?   45
KREON: It was long ago, a long time.
OEDIPUS: And this prophet,
Was he practicing here then?
KREON: He was; and with honor,
          as now.
OEDIPUS: Did he speak of me at that time?
KREON: He never did,
At least, not when I was present.
OEDIPUS: But . . . the enquiry?
I suppose you held one?
KREON: We did, but we learned nothing.   50
OEDIPUS: Why did the prophet not speak against me
          then?
KREON: I do not know; and I am the kind of man
Who holds his tongue when he has no facts to
          go on.

OEDIPUS: There's one fact that you know, and you
    could tell it.
KREON: What fact is that? If I know it, you shall
55   have it.
OEDIPUS: If he were not involved with you, he could
    not say
    That it was I who murdered Laios.
KREON: If he says that, you are the one that knows
    it! —
    But now it is my turn to question you.
60 OEDIPUS: Put your questions. I am no murderer.
KREON: First, then: You married my sister?
OEDIPUS: I married your sister.
KREON: And you rule the kingdom equally with her?
OEDIPUS: Everything that she wants she has from me.
KREON: And I am the third, equal to both of you?
65 OEDIPUS: That is why I call you a bad friend.
KREON: No. Reason it out, as I have done.
    Think of this first: would any sane man prefer
    Power, with all a king's anxieties,
    To that same power and the grace of sleep?
70   Certainly not I.
    I have never longed for the king's power — only his
    rights.
    Would any wise man differ from me in this?
    As matters stand, I have my way in everything
    With your consent, and no responsibilities.
75   If I were king, I should be a slave to policy.
    How could I desire a scepter more
    Than what is now mine — untroubled influence?
    No, I have not gone mad; I need no honors,
    Except those with the perquisites I have now.
80   I am welcome everywhere; every man salutes me,
    And those who want your favor seek my ear,
    Since I know how to manage what they ask.
    Should I exchange this ease for that anxiety?
    Besides, no sober mind is treasonable.
85   I hate anarchy
    And never would deal with any man who likes it.
    Test what I have said. Go to the priestess
    At Delphi, ask if I quoted her correctly.
    And as for this other thing: if I am found
90   Guilty of treason with Teiresias,
    Then sentence me to death. You have my word
    It is a sentence I should cast my vote for —
    But not without evidence!
                   You do wrong
    When you take good men for bad, bad men for
    good.
95   A true friend thrown aside — why, life itself
    Is not more precious!
                 In time you will know this well:
    For time, and time alone, will show the just man,
    Though scoundrels are discovered in a day.
CHORAGOS: This is well said, and a prudent man
    would ponder it.
100   Judgments too quickly formed are dangerous.
OEDIPUS: But is he not quick in his duplicity?
    And shall I not be quick to parry him?

Would you have me stand still, hold my peace,
    and let
    This man win everything, through my inaction?
KREON: And you want — what is it, then? To banish
    me?   105
OEDIPUS: No, not exile. It is your death I want,
    So that all the world may see what treason means.
KREON: You will persist, then? You will not believe
    me?
OEDIPUS: How can I believe you?
KREON: Then you are a fool.
OEDIPUS: To save myself?
KREON: In justice, think of me.   110
OEDIPUS: You are evil incarnate.
KREON: But suppose that you are wrong?
OEDIPUS: Still I must rule.
KREON: But not if you rule badly.
OEDIPUS: O city, city!
KREON: It is my city, too!
CHORAGOS: Now, my lords, be still. I see the queen,
    Iokaste, coming from her palace chambers;   115
    And it is time she came, for the sake of you both.
    This dreadful quarrel can be resolved through her.

(*Enter Iokaste.*)

IOKASTE: Poor foolish men, what wicked din is this?
    With Thebes sick to death, is it not shameful
    That you should take some private quarrel up?   120
    (*To Oedipus.*) Come into the house.
                    — And you, Kreon, go now:
    Let us have no more of this tumult over nothing.
KREON: Nothing? No, sister: what your husband plans
    for me
    Is one of two great evils: exile or death.
OEDIPUS: He is right.
           Why, woman I have caught him squarely 125
    Plotting against my life.
KREON: No! Let me die
    Accurst if ever I have wished you harm!
IOKASTE: Ah, believe it, Oedipus!
    In the name of the gods, respect this oath of his
    For my sake, for the sake of these people here! 130

Strophe 1

CHORAGOS: Open your mind to her, my lord. Be ruled
    by her, I beg you!
OEDIPUS: What would you have me do?
CHORAGOS: Respect Kreon's word. He has never
    spoken like a fool,
    And now he has sworn an oath.
OEDIPUS: You know what you ask?
CHORAGOS: I do.
OEDIPUS: Speak on, then.
CHORAGOS: A friend so sworn should not be baited so, 135
    In blind malice, and without final proof.
OEDIPUS: You are aware, I hope, that what you say
    Means death for me, or exile at the least.

Strophe 2

CHORAGOS: No, I swear by Helios, first in heaven!
140   May I die friendless and accurst,
        The worst of deaths, if ever I meant that!
        It is the withering fields
        That hurt my sick heart:
        Must we bear all these ills,
145   And now your bad blood as well?
    OEDIPUS: Then let him go. And let me die, if I must,
        Or be driven by him in shame from the land of
            Thebes.
        It is your unhappiness, and not his talk,
        That touches me.
                            As for him —
150   Wherever he goes, hatred will follow him.
    KREON: Ugly in yielding, as you were ugly in rage!
        Natures like yours chiefly torment themselves.
    OEDIPUS: Can you not go? Can you not leave me?
    KREON: I can.
        You do not know me; but the city knows me,
155   And in its eyes I am just, if not in yours.

                                        (*Exit Kreon.*)

Antistrophe 1

CHORAGOS: Lady Iokaste, did you not ask the King to
        go to his chambers?
    IOKASTE: First tell me what has happened.
    CHORAGOS: There was suspicion without evidence; yet
        it rankled
        As even false charges will.
    IOKASTE: On both sides?
    CHORAGOS: On both.
160 IOKASTE: But what was said?
    CHORAGOS: Oh let it rest, let it be done with!
        Have we not suffered enough?
    OEDIPUS: You see to what your decency has brought
        you:
        You have made difficulties where my heart saw
            none.

Antistrophe 2

CHORAGOS: Oedipus, it is not once only I have told
165   you —
        You must know I should count myself
            unwise
        To the point of madness, should I now forsake
            you —
            You, under whose hand,
                In the storm of another time,
170   Our dear land sailed out free.
        But now stand fast at the helm!
    IOKASTE: In God's name, Oedipus, inform your wife as
        well:
        Why are you so set in this hard anger?

OEDIPUS: I will tell you, for none of these men deserves
        My confidence as you do. It is Kreon's work,   175
        His treachery, his plotting against me.
    IOKASTE: Go on, if you can make this clear to me.
    OEDIPUS: He charges me with the murder of Laios.
    IOKASTE: Has he some knowledge? Or does he speak
        from hearsay?
    OEDIPUS: He would not commit himself to such a
        charge,   180
        But he has brought in that damnable soothsayer
        To tell his story.
    IOKASTE: Set your mind at rest.
        If it is a question of soothsayers, I tell you
        That you will find no man whose craft gives
            knowledge
        Of the unknowable.
                            Here is my proof: 185
        An oracle was reported to Laios once
        (I will not say from Phoibos himself, but from
        His appointed ministers, at any rate)
        That his doom would be death at the hands of his
            own son —
        His son, born of his flesh and of mine!   190

        Now, you remember the story: Laios was killed
        By marauding strangers where three highways meet;
        But his child had not been three days in this world
        Before the king had pierced the baby's ankles
        And left him to die on a lonely mountainside.   195

        Thus, Apollo never caused that child
        To kill his father, and it was not Laios' fate
        To die at the hands of his son, as he had feared.
        This is what prophets and prophecies are worth!
        Have no dread of them.
                                It is God himself   200
        Who can show us what he wills, in his own way.
    OEDIPUS: How strange a shadowy memory crossed my
        mind,
        Just now while you were speaking; it chilled my
        heart.
    IOKASTE: What do you mean? What memory do you
        speak of?
    OEDIPUS: If I understand you, Laios was killed   205
        At a place where three roads meet.
    IOKASTE: So it was said;
        We have no later story.
    OEDIPUS: Where did it happen?
    IOKASTE: Phokis, it is called: at a place where the
        Theban Way
        Divides into the roads toward Delphi and Daulia.
    OEDIPUS: When?
    IOKASTE: We had the news not long before you came 210
        And proved the right to your succession here.
    OEDIPUS: Ah, what net has God been weaving for me?
    IOKASTE: Oedipus! Why does this trouble you?
    OEDIPUS: Do not ask me yet.
        First, tell me how Laios looked, and tell me
        How old he was.

215 IOKASTE: He was tall, his hair just touched
        With white; his form was not unlike your own.
    OEDIPUS: I think that I myself may be accurst
        By my own ignorant edict.
    IOKASTE: You speak strangely.
        It makes me tremble to look at you, my king.
220 OEDIPUS: I am not sure that the blind man can not see.
        But I should know better if you were to tell me —
    IOKASTE: Anything — though I dread to hear you ask
        it.
    OEDIPUS: Was the king lightly escorted, or did he ride
        With a large company, as a ruler should?
    IOKASTE: There were five men with him in all: one was
225   a herald;
        And a single chariot, which he was driving.
    OEDIPUS: Alas, that makes it plain enough!
                                    But who —
    Who told you how it happened?
    IOKASTE: A household servant,
        The only one to escape.
    OEDIPUS: And is he still
        A servant of ours?
230 IOKASTE: No; for when he came back at last
        And found you enthroned in the place of the dead
            king,
        He came to me, touched my hand with his, and
            begged
        That I would send him away to the frontier district
        Where only the shepherds go —
235   As far away from the city as I could send him.
        I granted his prayer; for although the man was a
            slave,
        He had earned more than this favor at my hands.
    OEDIPUS: Can he be called back quickly?
    IOKASTE: Easily.
        But why?
240 OEDIPUS: I have taken too much upon myself
        Without enquiry; therefore I wish to consult him.
    IOKASTE: Then he shall come.
                        But am I not one also
        To whom you might confide these fears of yours?
    OEDIPUS: That is your right; it will not be denied you,
245   Now least of all; for I have reached a pitch
        Of wild foreboding. Is there anyone
        To whom I should sooner speak?

        Polybos of Corinth is my father.
        My mother is a Dorian: Merope.
250   I grew up chief among the men of Corinth
        Until a strange thing happened —
        Not worth my passion, it may be, but strange.
        At a feast, a drunken man maundering in his cups
        Cries out that I am not my father's son!
255   I contained myself that night, though I felt anger
        And a sinking heart. The next day I visited
        My father and mother, and questioned them. They
            stormed,
        Calling it all the slanderous rant of a fool;
        And this relieved me. Yet the suspicion

Remained always aching in my mind;   260
I knew there was talk; I could not rest;
And finally, saying nothing to my parents,
I went to the shrine at Delphi.

The god dismissed my question without reply;
He spoke of other things.
                    Some were clear,   265
Full of wretchedness, dreadful, unbearable:
As, that I should lie with my own mother, breed
Children from whom all men would turn their
    eyes;
And that I should be my father's murderer.

I heard all this, and fled. And from that day   270
Corinth to me was only in the stars
Descending in that quarter of the sky,
As I wandered farther and farther on my way
To a land where I should never see the evil
Sung by the oracle. And I came to this country   275
Where, so you say, King Laios was killed.

I will tell you all that happened there, my lady.
There were three highways
Coming together at a place I passed;
And there a herald came towards me, and a chariot   280
Drawn by horses, with a man such as you describe
Seated in it. The groom leading the horses
Forced me off the road at his lord's command;
But as this charioteer lurched over towards me
I struck him in my rage. The old man saw me   285
And brought his double goad down upon my head
As I came abreast.
                He was paid back, and more!
Swinging my club in this right hand I knocked him
Out of his car, and he rolled on the ground.
                                I killed him.

I killed them all.   290
Now if that stranger and Laios were — kin,
Where is a man more miserable than I?
More hated by the gods? Citizen and alien alike
Must never shelter me or speak to me —
I must be shunned by all.
                        And I myself   295
Pronounced this malediction upon myself!

Think of it: I have touched you with these hands,
These hands that killed your husband. What
    defilement!

Am I all evil, then? It must be so,
Since I must flee from Thebes, yet never again   300
See my own countrymen, my own country,
For fear of joining my mother in marriage
And killing Polybos, my father.
                            Ah,
If I was created so, born to this fate,
Who could deny the savagery of God?   305

O holy majesty of heavenly powers!
May I never see that day! Never!
Rather let me vanish from the race of men
Than know the abomination destined me!

310 CHORAGOS: We too, my lord, have felt dismay at this.
But there is hope: you have yet to hear the shepherd.
OEDIPUS: Indeed, I fear no other hope is left me.
IOKASTE: What do you hope from him when he comes?
OEDIPUS: This much:
If his account of the murder tallies with yours,
Then I am cleared.
315 IOKASTE: What was it that I said
Of such importance?
OEDIPUS: Why, "marauders," you said,
Killed the king, according to this man's story.
If he maintains that still, if there were several,
Clearly the guilt is not mine: I was alone.
320 But if he says one man, singlehanded, did it,
Then the evidence all points to me.
IOKASTE: You may be sure that he said there were
several;
And can he call back that story now? He can not.
The whole city heard it as plainly as I.
325 But suppose he alters some detail of it:
He can not ever show that Laios' death
Fulfilled the oracle: for Apollo said
My child was doomed to kill him; and my child —
Poor baby! — it was my child that died first.

330 No. From now on, where oracles are concerned,
I would not waste a second thought on any.
OEDIPUS: You may be right.
                              But come: let someone go
For the shepherd at once. This matter must be
settled.
IOKASTE: I will send for him.
335 I would not wish to cross you in anything,
And surely not in this. — Let us go in.
                              (*Exeunt into the palace.*)

ODE 2 • *Strophe 1*

CHORUS: Let me be reverent in the ways of right,
Lowly the paths I journey on;
Let all my words and actions keep
The laws of the pure universe
5 From highest Heaven handed down.
For Heaven is their bright nurse,
Those generations of the realms of light;
Ah, never of mortal kind were they begot,
Nor are they slaves of memory, lost in sleep:
10 Their Father is greater than Time, and ages not.

Antistrophe 1

The tyrant is a child of Pride
Who drinks from his great sickening cup

Recklessness and vanity,
Until from his high crest headlong
He plummets to the dust of hope.   15
That strong man is not strong.
But let no fair ambition be denied;
May God protect the wrestler for the State
In government, in comely policy,
Who will fear God, and on his ordinance wait.   20

Strophe 2

Haughtiness and the high hand of disdain
Tempt and outrage God's holy law;
And any mortal who dares hold
No immortal Power in awe
Will be caught up in a net of pain: 25
The price for which his levity is sold.
Let each man take due earnings, then,
And keep his hands from holy things,
And from blasphemy stand apart —
Else the crackling blast of heaven   30
Blows on his head, and on his desperate heart.
Though fools will honor impious men,
In their cities no tragic poet sings.

Antistrophe 2

Shall we lose faith in Delphi's obscurities,
We who have heard the world's core   35
Discredited, and the sacred wood
Of Zeus at Elis praised no more?
The deeds and the strange prophecies
Must make a pattern yet to be understood.
Zeus, if indeed you are lord of all,   40
Throned in light over night and day,
Mirror this in your endless mind:
Our masters call the oracle
Words on the wind, and the Delphic vision blind!
Their hearts no longer know Apollo,   45
And reverence for the gods has died away.

SCENE 3

(*Enter Iokaste.*)

IOKASTE: Princes of Thebes, it has occurred to me
To visit the altars of the gods, bearing
These branches as a suppliant, and this incense.
Our king is not himself: his noble soul
Is overwrought with fantasies of dread,   5
Else he would consider
The new prophecies in the light of the old.
He will listen to any voice that speaks disaster,
And my advice goes for nothing. (*She approaches
the altar, right.*)
                    To you, then, Apollo,

10   Lycean lord, since you are nearest, I turn in prayer
      Receive these offerings, and grant us deliverance
      From defilement. Our hearts are heavy with fear
      When we see our leader distracted, as helpless
          sailors
      Are terrified by the confusion of their helmsman.

(*Enter Messenger.*)

15   MESSENGER: Friends, no doubt you can direct me:
      Where shall I find the house of Oedipus,
      Or, better still, where is the king himself?
      CHORAGOS: It is this very place, stranger; he is inside.
      This is his wife and mother of his children.
20   MESSENGER: I wish her happiness in a happy house,
      Blest in all the fulfillment of her marriage.
      IOKASTE: I wish as much for you: your courtesy
      Deserves a like good fortune. But now, tell me:
      Why have you come? What have you to say to us?
      MESSENGER: Good news, my lady, for your house and
25   your husband.
      IOKASTE: What news? Who sent you here?
      MESSENGER: I am from Corinth.
      The news I bring ought to mean joy for you,
      Though it may be you will find some grief in it.
      IOKASTE: What is it? How can it touch us in both
          ways?
      MESSENGER: The word is that the people of the
30   Isthmus
      Intend to call Oedipus to be their king.
      IOKASTE: But old King Polybos — is he not reigning
          still?
      MESSENGER: No. Death holds him in his sepulchre.
      IOKASTE: What are you saying? Polybos is dead?
      MESSENGER: If I am not telling the truth, may I die
35   myself.
      IOKASTE (*to a Maidservant*): Go in, go quickly; tell this
          to your master.
      O riddlers of God's will, where are you now!
      This was the man whom Oedipus, long ago,
      Feared so, fled so, in dread of destroying him —
40   But it was another fate by which he died.

(*Enter Oedipus, center.*)

      OEDIPUS: Dearest Iokaste, why have you sent for me?
      IOKASTE: Listen to what this man says, and then tell
          me
      What has become of the solemn prophecies.
      OEDIPUS: Who is this man? What is his news for me?
      IOKASTE: He has come from Corinth to announce your
45   father's death!
      OEDIPUS: Is it true, stranger? Tell me in your own
          words.
      MESSENGER: I can not say it more clearly: the king is
          dead.
      OEDIPUS: Was it by treason? Or by an attack of
          illness?
      MESSENGER: A little thing brings old men to their rest.
      OEDIPUS: It was sickness, then?
50   MESSENGER: Yes, and his many years.

OEDIPUS: Ah!
      Why should a man respect the Pythian hearth,° or
      Give heed to the birds that jangle above his head?
      They prophesied that I should kill Polybos,
      Kill my own father; but he is dead and buried,   55
      And I am here — I never touched him, never,
      Unless he died of grief for my departure,
      And thus, in a sense, through me. No. Polybos
      Has packed the oracles off with him underground.
      They are empty words.
IOKASTE: Had I not told you so?   60
OEDIPUS: You had; it was my faint heart that betrayed
      me.
IOKASTE: From now on never think of those things
      again.
OEDIPUS: And yet — must I not fear my mother's bed?
IOKASTE: Why should anyone in this world be afraid
      Since Fate rules us and nothing can be foreseen?   65
      A man should live only for the present day.

      Have no more fear of sleeping with your mother:
      How many men, in dreams, have lain with their
          mothers!
      No reasonable man is troubled by such things.
OEDIPUS: That is true, only —   70
      If only my mother were not still alive!
      But she is alive. I can not help my dread.
IOKASTE: Yet this news of your father's death is
      wonderful.
OEDIPUS: Wonderful. But I fear the living woman.
MESSENGER: Tell me, who is this woman that you fear?   75
OEDIPUS: It is Merope, man; the wife of King Polybos.
MESSENGER: Merope? Why should you be afraid of
      her?
OEDIPUS: An oracle of the gods, a dreadful saying.
MESSENGER: Can you tell me about it or are you sworn
      to silence?
OEDIPUS: I can tell you, and I will.   80
      Apollo said through his prophet that I was the man
      Who should marry his own mother, shed his father's
          blood
      With his own hands. And so, for all these years
      I have kept clear of Corinth, and no harm has
          come —
      Though it would have been sweet to see my parents
          again.   85
MESSENGER: And is this the fear that drove you out of
      Corinth?
OEDIPUS: Would you have me kill my father?
MESSENGER: As for that
      You must be reassured by the news I gave you.
OEDIPUS: If you could reassure me, I would reward
      you.
MESSENGER: I had that in mind, I will confess: I   90
      thought
      I could count on you when you returned to Corinth.
OEDIPUS: No: I will never go near my parents again.

52. **Pythian hearth:** Delphi.

MESSENGER: Ah, son, you still do not know what you
    are doing —
OEDIPUS: What do you mean? In the name of God tell
    me!
MESSENGER: — If these are your reasons for not going
95   home.
OEDIPUS: I tell you, I fear the oracle may come true.
MESSENGER: And guilt may come upon you through
    your parents?
OEDIPUS: That is the dread that is always in my heart.
MESSENGER: Can you not see that all your fears are
    groundless?
100 OEDIPUS: Groundless? Am I not my parents' son?
MESSENGER: Polybos was not your father.
OEDIPUS: Not my father?
MESSENGER: No more your father than the man
    speaking to you.
OEDIPUS: But you are nothing to me!
MESSENGER: Neither was he.
OEDIPUS: Then why did he call me son?
MESSENGER: I will tell you:
105   Long ago he had you from my hands, as a gift.
OEDIPUS: Then how could he love me so, if I was not
    his?
MESSENGER: He had no children, and his heart turned
    to you.
OEDIPUS: What of you? Did you buy me? Did you find
    me by chance?
MESSENGER: I came upon you in the woody vales of
    Kithairon.
OEDIPUS: And what were you doing there?
110 MESSENGER: Tending my flocks.
OEDIPUS: A wandering shepherd?
MESSENGER: But your savior, son, that day.
OEDIPUS: From what did you save me?
MESSENGER: Your ankles should tell you that.
OEDIPUS: Ah, stranger, why do you speak of that
    childhood pain?
MESSENGER: I pulled the skewer that pinned your feet
    together.
OEDIPUS: I have had the mark as long as I can
115   remember.
MESSENGER: That was why you were given the name°
    you bear.
OEDIPUS: God! Was it my father or my mother who
    did it?
    Tell me!
MESSENGER: I do not know. The man who gave you
    to me
    Can tell you better than I.
120 OEDIPUS: It was not you that found me, but another?
MESSENGER: It was another shepherd gave you to me.
OEDIPUS: Who was he? Can you tell me who he was?
MESSENGER: I think he was said to be one of Laios'
    people.
OEDIPUS: You mean the Laios who was king here years
    ago?

116. name: "Oedipus" literally means swollen foot.

MESSENGER: Yes; King Laios; and the man was one of
    his herdsmen.   125
OEDIPUS: Is he still alive? Can I see him?
MESSENGER: These men here
    Know best about such things.
OEDIPUS: Does anyone here
    Know this shepherd that he is talking about?
    Have you seen him in the fields, or in the town?
    If you have, tell me. It is time things were made
    plain.   130
CHORAGOS: I think the man he means is that same
    shepherd
    You have already asked to see. Iokaste perhaps
    Could tell you something.
OEDIPUS: Do you know anything
    About him, Lady? Is he the man we have
    summoned?
    Is that the man this shepherd means?
IOKASTE: Why think of him? 135
    Forget this herdsman. Forget it all.
    This talk is a waste of time.
OEDIPUS: How can you say that,
    When the clues to my true birth are in my hands?
IOKASTE: For God's love, let us have no more
    questioning!
    Is your life nothing to you?   140
    My own is pain enough for me to bear.
OEDIPUS: You need not worry. Suppose my mother a
    slave,
    And born of slaves: no baseness can touch you.
IOKASTE: Listen to me, I beg you: do not do this thing!
OEDIPUS: I will not listen; the truth must be made
    known.   145
IOKASTE: Everything that I say is for your own good!
OEDIPUS: My own good
    Snaps my patience, then; I want none of it.
IOKASTE: You are fatally wrong! May you never learn
    who you are!
OEDIPUS: Go, one of you, and bring the shepherd here.
    Let us leave this woman to brag of her royal name. 150
IOKASTE: Ah, miserable!
    That is the only word I have for you now.
    That is the only word I can ever have.
                           (*Exit into the palace.*)
CHORAGOS: Why has she left us, Oedipus? Why has
    she gone
    In such a passion of sorrow? I fear this silence: 155
    Something dreadful may come of it.
OEDIPUS: Let it come!
    However base my birth, I must know about it.
    The Queen, like a woman, is perhaps ashamed
    To think of my low origin. But I
    Am a child of Luck, I can not be dishonored. 160
    Luck is my mother; the passing months, my
    brothers,
    Have seen me rich and poor.
                        If this is so,
    How could I wish that I were someone else?
    How could I not be glad to know my birth?

ODE 3 • Strophe

CHORUS: If ever the coming time were known
    To my heart's pondering,
    Kithairon, now by Heaven I see the torches
    At the festival of the next full moon
5   And see the dance, and hear the choir sing
    A grace to your gentle shade:
    Mountain where Oedipus was found,
    O mountain guard of a noble race!
    May the god° who heals us lend his aid,
10   And let that glory come to pass
    For our king's cradling-ground.

Antistrophe

    Of the nymphs that flower beyond the years,
    Who bore you,° royal child,
    To Pan° of the hills or the timberline Apollo,
15   Cold in delight where the upland clears,
    Or Hermes° for whom Kyllene's° heights are piled?
    Or flushed as evening cloud,
    Great Dionysos,° roamer of mountains,
    He — was it he who found you there,
20   And caught you up in his own proud
    Arms from the sweet god-ravisher
    Who laughed by the Muses'° fountains?

SCENE 4

OEDIPUS: Sirs: though I do not know the man,
    I think I see him coming, this shepherd we want:
    He is old, like our friend here, and the men
    Bringing him seem to be servants of my house.
5   But you can tell, if you have ever seen him.

(*Enter Shepherd escorted by Servants.*)

CHORAGOS: I know him, he was Laios' man. You can
    trust him.
OEDIPUS: Tell me first, you from Corinth: is this the
    shepherd
    We were discussing?
MESSENGER: This is the very man.
OEDIPUS (*to Shepherd*): Come here. No, look at me.
    You must answer
10   Everything I ask. — You belonged to Laios?

---

9. **god:** Apollo.　**13. Who bore you:** The Chorus is asking if Oedipus is the son of an immortal nymph and a god: Pan, Apollo, Hermes, or Dionysus. **14. Pan:** God of nature, forests, flocks, and shepherds, depicted as half-man and half-goat. **16. Hermes:** Son of Zeus, messenger of the gods. **Kyllene:** Mountain reputed to be the birthplace of Hermes; also the center of a cult to Hermes.　**18. Dionysos:** (Dionysus) God of wine around whom wild, orgiastic rituals developed; also called Bacchus. **22. Muses:** Nine sister goddesses who presided over poetry and music, art and sciences.

SHEPHERD: Yes: born his slave, brought up in his
    house.
OEDIPUS: Tell me: what kind of work did you do for
    him?
SHEPHERD: I was a shepherd of his, most of my life.
OEDIPUS: Where mainly did you go for pasturage?
SHEPHERD: Sometimes Kithairon, sometimes the hills
    near-by.   15
OEDIPUS: Do you remember ever seeing this man out
    there?
SHEPHERD: What would he be doing there? This man?
OEDIPUS: This man standing here. Have you ever seen
    him before?
SHEPHERD: No. At least, not to my recollection.
MESSENGER: And that is not strange, my lord. But I'll
    refresh   20
    His memory: he must remember when we two
    Spent three whole seasons together, March to
    September,
    On Kithairon or thereabouts. He had two flocks;
    I had one. Each autumn I'd drive mine home
    And he would go back with his to Laios'
    sheepfold. —   25
    Is this not true, just as I have described it?
SHEPHERD: True, yes; but it was all so long ago.
MESSENGER: Well, then: do you remember, back in
    those days,
    That you gave me a baby boy to bring up as my
    own?
SHEPHERD: What if I did? What are you trying to say?   30
MESSENGER: King Oedipus was once that little child.
SHEPHERD: Damn you, hold your tongue!
OEDIPUS: No more of that!
    It is your tongue needs watching, not this man's.
SHEPHERD: My king, my master, what is it I have done
    wrong?
OEDIPUS: You have not answered his question about
    the boy.   35
SHEPHERD: He does not know . . . He is only making
    trouble . . .
OEDIPUS: Come, speak plainly, or it will go hard with
    you.
SHEPHERD: In God's name, do not torture an old man!
OEDIPUS: Come here, one of you; bind his arms behind
    him.
SHEPHERD: Unhappy king! What more do you wish to
    learn?   40
OEDIPUS: Did you give this man the child he speaks of?
SHEPHERD: I did.
    And I would to God I had died that very day.
OEDIPUS: You will die now unless you speak the truth.
SHEPHERD: Yet if I speak the truth, I am worse than
    dead.
OEDIPUS (*to Attendant*): He intends to draw it out,
    apparently —   45
SHEPHERD: No! I have told you already that I gave him
    the boy.
OEDIPUS: Where did you get him? From your house?
    From somewhere else?

The Shepherd (Oliver Cliff) tells Oedipus (Kenneth Welsh) the truth about his birth in the Guthrie Theater Company's 1973 production directed by Michael Langham.

SHEPHERD: Not from mine, no. A man gave him
    to me.
OEDIPUS: Is that man here? Whose house did he
    belong to?
SHEPHERD: For God's love, my king, do not ask me any
50   more!
OEDIPUS: You are a dead man if I have to ask you
    again.
SHEPHERD: Then . . . Then the child was from the
    palace of Laios.
OEDIPUS: A slave child? or a child of his own line?
SHEPHERD: Ah, I am on the brink of dreadful speech!
55 OEDIPUS: And I of dreadful hearing. Yet I must hear.
SHEPHERD: If you must be told, then . . .
                 They said it was Laios' child;
  But it is your wife who can tell you about that.
OEDIPUS: My wife — Did she give it to you?
SHEPHERD: My lord, she did.
OEDIPUS: Do you know why?
SHEPHERD: I was told to get rid of it.
OEDIPUS: Oh heartless mother!
60 SHEPHERD: But in dread of prophecies . . .
OEDIPUS: Tell me.
SHEPHERD: It was said that the boy would kill
    his own father.
OEDIPUS: Then why did you give him over to this old
    man?
SHEPHERD: I pitied the baby, my king,
  And I thought that this man would take him far
    away
  To his own country.
65   He saved him — but for what a fate!
  For if you are what this man says you are,
  No man living is more wretched than Oedipus.
OEDIPUS: Ah God!
  It was true!
      All the prophecies!
            — Now,
70 O Light, may I look on you for the last time!
I, Oedipus,
Oedipus, damned in his birth, in his marriage
    damned,
Damned in the blood he shed with his own hand!

(*He rushes into the palace.*)

ODE 4 • *Strophe 1*

CHORUS: Alas for the seed of men.
  What measure shall I give these generations
  That breathe on the void and are void
  And exist and do not exist?
5 Who bears more weight of joy
  Than mass of sunlight shifting in images,
  Or who shall make his thought stay on
  That down time drifts away?
  Your splendor is all fallen.
10 O naked brow of wrath and tears,

O change of Oedipus!
I who saw your days call no man blest —
Your great days like ghosts gone.

Antistrophe 1

That mind was a strong bow.
Deep, how deep you drew it then, hard archer,   15
At a dim fearful range,
And brought dear glory down!
You overcame the stranger° —
The virgin with her hooking lion claws —
And though death sang, stood like a tower   20
To make pale Thebes take heart.
Fortress against our sorrow!
True king, giver of laws,
Majestic Oedipus!
No prince in Thebes had ever such renown,   25
No prince won such grace of power.

Strophe 2

And now of all men ever known
Most pitiful is this man's story:
His fortunes are most changed; his state
Fallen to a low slave's   30
Ground under bitter fate.
O Oedipus, most royal one!
The great door° that expelled you to the light
Gave at night — ah, gave night to your glory:
As to the father, to the fathering son.   35
All understood too late.
How could that queen whom Laios won,
The garden that he harrowed at his height,
Be silent when that act was done?

Antistrophe 2

But all eyes fail before time's eye,   40
All actions come to justice there.
Though never willed, though far down the deep
    past,
Your bed, your dread sirings,
Are brought to book at last.
Child by Laios doomed to die,   45
Then doomed to lose that fortunate little death,
Would God you never took breath in this air
That with my wailing lips I take to cry:
For I weep the world's outcast.
I was blind, and now I can tell why:
Asleep, for you had given ease of breath
To Thebes, while the false years went by.   50

---

18. stranger: The Sphinx.   **33. door:** Iokaste's womb.

EXODOS°

(*Enter, from the palace, Second Messenger.*)

SECOND MESSENGER: Elders of Thebes, most honored
    in this land,
    What horrors are yours to see and hear, what
      weight
    Of sorrow to be endured, if, true to your birth,
    You venerate the line of Labdakos!
5   I think neither Istros nor Phasis, those great rivers,
    Could purify this place of all the evil
    It shelters now, or soon must bring to light —
    Evil not done unconsciously, but willed.

    The greatest griefs are those we cause ourselves.
CHORAGOS: Surely, friend, we have grief enough
10   already;
    What new sorrow do you mean?
SECOND MESSENGER: The queen is dead.
CHORAGOS: O miserable queen! But at whose hand?
SECOND MESSENGER: Her own.
    The full horror of what happened you can not
      know,
    For you did not see it; but I, who did, will tell you
15   As clearly as I can how she met her death.

    When she had left us,
    In passionate silence, passing through the court,
    She ran to her apartment in the house,
    Her hair clutched by the fingers of both hands.
    She closed the doors behind her; then, by that bed
20   Where long ago the fatal son was conceived —
    That son who should bring about his father's
      death —
    We heard her call upon Laios, dead so many years,
    And heard her wail for the double fruit of her
      marriage,
25   A husband by her husband, children by her child.

    Exactly how she died I do not know:
    For Oedipus burst in moaning and would not let us
    Keep vigil to the end: it was by him
    As he stormed about the room that our eyes were
      caught.
    From one to another of us he went, begging a
30   sword,
    Hunting the wife who was not his wife, the mother
    Whose womb had carried his own children and
      himself.
    I do not know: it was none of us aided him,
    But surely one of the gods was in control!
35   For with a dreadful cry
    He hurled his weight, as though wrenched out of
      himself,
    At the twin doors: the bolts gave, and he rushed in.
    And there we saw her hanging, her body swaying

Exodos: Final scene.

From the cruel cord she had noosed about her neck.
A great sob broke from him, heartbreaking to hear,   40
As he loosed the rope and lowered her to the
    ground.

I would blot out from my mind what happened
    next!
For the king ripped from her gown the golden
    brooches
That were her ornament, and raised them, and
    plunged them down
Straight into his own eyeballs, crying, "No more,   45
No more shall you look on the misery about me,
The horrors of my own doing! Too long you have
    known
The faces of those whom I should never have seen,
Too long been blind to those for whom I was
    searching!
From this hour, go in darkness!" And as he spoke,   50
He struck at his eyes — not once, but many times;
And the blood spattered his beard,
Bursting from his ruined sockets like red hail.

So from the unhappiness of two this evil has sprung,
A curse on the man and woman alike. The old   55
Happiness of the house of Labdakos
Was happiness enough: where is it today?
It is all wailing and ruin, disgrace, death — all
The misery of mankind that has a name —
And it is wholly and for ever theirs.   60
CHORAGOS: Is he in agony still? Is there no rest for
    him?
SECOND MESSENGER: He is calling for someone to open
    the doors wide
So that all the children of Kadmos may look upon
His father's murderer, his mother's — no,
I can not say it!
              And then he will leave Thebes,   65
Self-exiled, in order that the curse
Which he himself pronounced may depart from the
    house.
He is weak, and there is none to lead him,
So terrible is his suffering.
              But you will see:
Look, the doors are opening; in a moment   70
You will see a thing that would crush a heart of
    stone.

(*The central door is opened; Oedipus, blinded, is led in.*)

CHORAGOS: Dreadful indeed for men to see.
    Never have my own eyes
    Looked on a sight so full of fear.

Oedipus!   75
What madness came upon you, what demon
Leaped on your life with heavier
Punishment than a mortal man can bear?
No: I can not even
Look at you, poor ruined one.   80

And I would speak, question, ponder,
If I were able. No.
You make me shudder.
OEDIPUS: God. God.
85   Is there a sorrow greater?
Where shall I find harbor in this world?
My voice is hurled far on a dark wind.
What has God done to me?
CHORAGOS: Too terrible to think of, or to see.

Strophe 1

90 OEDIPUS: O cloud of night,
Never to be turned away: night coming on,
I can not tell how: night like a shroud!
My fair winds brought me here.
                              O God. Again
The pain of the spikes where I had sight,
95   The flooding pain
Of memory, never to be gouged out.
CHORAGOS: This is not strange.
You suffer it all twice over, remorse in pain,
Pain in remorse.

Antistrophe 1

100 OEDIPUS: Ah dear friend
Are you faithful even yet, you alone?
Are you still standing near me, will you stay here,
Patient, to care for the blind?
                              The blind man!
Yet even blind I know who it is attends me,
105   By the voice's tone —
Though my new darkness hide the comforter.
CHORAGOS: Oh fearful act!
What god was it drove you to rake black
Night across your eyes?

Strophe 2

110 OEDIPUS: Apollo. Apollo. Dear
Children, the god was Apollo.
He brought my sick, sick fate upon me.
But the blinding hand was my own!
How could I bear to see
115   When all my sight was horror everywhere?
CHORAGOS: Everywhere; that is true.
OEDIPUS: And now what is left?
Images? Love? A greeting even,
Sweet to the senses? Is there anything?
120   Ah, no, friends: lead me away.
Lead me away from Thebes.
                              Lead the great wreck
And hell of Oedipus, whom the gods hate.
CHORAGOS: Your misery, you are not blind to that.
Would God you had never found it out!

Antistrophe 2

OEDIPUS: Death take the man who unbound   125
My feet on that hillside
And delivered me from death to life! What life?
If only I had died,
This weight of monstrous doom
Could not have dragged me and my darlings down.   130
CHORAGOS: I would have wished the same.
OEDIPUS: Oh never to have come here
With my father's blood upon me! Never
To have been the man they call his mother's husband!
Oh accurst! Oh child of evil,   135
To have entered that wretched bed —
                              the selfsame one!
More primal than sin itself, this fell to me.
CHORAGOS: I do not know what words to offer you.
You were better dead than alive and blind.
OEDIPUS: Do not counsel me any more. This
      punishment   140
That I have laid upon myself is just.
If I had eyes,
I do not know how I could bear the sight
Of my father, when I came to the house of Death,
Or my mother: for I have sinned against them both 145
So vilely that I could not make my peace
By strangling my own life.
                  Or do you think my children,
Born as they were born, would be sweet to my eyes?
Ah never, never! Nor this town with its high walls,
Nor the holy images of the gods.
                              For I,   150
Thrice miserable! — Oedipus, noblest of all the line
Of Kadmos, have condemned myself to enjoy
These things no more, by my own malediction
Expelling that man whom the gods declared
To be a defilement in the house of Laios.   155
After exposing the rankness of my own guilt,
How could I look men frankly in the eyes?
No, I swear it,
If I could have stifled my hearing at its source,
I would have done it and made all this body   160
A tight cell of misery, blank to light and sound:
So I should have been safe in my dark mind
Beyond external evil.
                      Ah Kithairon!
Why did you shelter me? When I was cast upon you,
Why did I not die? Then I should never   165
Have shown the world my execrable birth.

Ah Polybos! Corinth, city that I believed
The ancient seat of my ancestors: how fair
I seemed, your child! And all the while this evil
Was cancerous within me!
                      For I am sick   170
In my own being, sick in my origin.
O three roads, dark ravine, woodland and way
Where three roads met; you, drinking my father's
      blood,

My own blood, spilled by my own hand: can you remember
175 The unspeakable things I did there, and the things
I went on from there to do?
                                      O marriage, marriage!
The act that engendered me, and again the act
Performed by the son in the same bed —
                                      Ah, the net
Of incest, mingling fathers, brothers, sons,
180 With brides, wives, mothers: the last evil
That can be known by men: no tongue can say
How evil!
            No. For the love of God, conceal me
Somewhere far from Thebes; or kill me; or hurl me
Into the sea, away from men's eyes for ever.

185 Come, lead me. You need nor fear to touch me.
Of all men, I alone can bear this guilt.

(*Enter Kreon.*)

CHORAGOS: Kreon is here now. As to what you ask,
He may decide the course to take. He only
Is left to protect the city in your place.
OEDIPUS: Alas, how can I speak to him? What right have I
190 have I
To beg his courtesy whom I have deeply wronged?
KREON: I have not come to mock you, Oedipus,
Or to reproach you, either.
(*To Attendants.*)   — You, standing there:
If you have lost all respect for man's dignity,
195 At least respect the flame of Lord Helios:°
Do not allow this pollution to show itself
Openly here, an affront to the earth
And Heaven's rain and the light of day. No, take him
Into the house as quickly as you can.
200 For it is proper
That only the close kindred see his grief.
OEDIPUS: I pray you in God's name, since your courtesy
Ignores my dark expectation, visiting
With mercy this man of all men most execrable:
205 Give me what I ask — for your good, not for mine.
KREON: And what is it that you turn to me begging for?
OEDIPUS: Drive me out of this country as quickly as may be
To a place where no human voice can ever greet me.
KREON: I should have done that before now — only,
210 God's will had not been wholly revealed to me.
OEDIPUS: But his command is plain: the parricide
Must be destroyed. I am that evil man.
KREON: That is the sense of it, yes; but as things are,
We had best discover clearly what is to be done.
215 OEDIPUS: You would learn more about a man like me?
KREON: You are ready now to listen to the god.

---

195. Lord Helios: The sun god.

OEDIPUS: I will listen. But it is to you
That I must turn for help. I beg you, hear me.

The woman is there —
Give her whatever funeral you think proper: 220
She is your sister.
                — But let me go, Kreon!
Let me purge my father's Thebes of the pollution
Of my living here, and go out to the wild hills,
To Kithairon, that has won such fame with me,
The tomb my mother and father appointed for me,   225
And let me die there, as they willed I should.
And yet I know
Death will not ever come to me through sickness
Or in any natural way: I have been preserved
For some unthinkable fate. But let that be.   230

As for my sons, you need not care for them.
They are men, they will find some way to live.
But my poor daughters, who have shared my table,
Who never before have been parted from their
    father —
Take care of them, Kreon; do this for me.   235

And will you let me touch them with my hands
A last time, and let us weep together?
Be kind, my lord,
Great prince, be kind!
                Could I but touch them,
They would be mine again, as when I had my eyes.   240

(*Enter Antigone and Ismene, attended.*)

Ah, God!
Is it my dearest children I hear weeping?
Has Kreon pitied me and sent my daughters?
KREON: Yes, Oedipus: I knew that they were dear to you
In the old days, and know you must love them still.   245
OEDIPUS: May God bless you for this — and be a friendlier
Guardian to you than he has been to me!

Children, where are you?
Come quickly to my hands: they are your brother's —
Hands that have brought your father's once clear eyes   250
To this way of seeing —
                Ah dearest ones,
I had neither sight nor knowledge then, your father
By the woman who was the source of his own life!
And I weep for you — having no strength to see you — ,
I weep for you when I think of the bitterness   255
That men will visit upon you all your lives.
What homes, what festivals can you attend
Without being forced to depart again in tears?
And when you come to marriageable age,

260 Where is the man, my daughters, who would dare
Risk the bane that lies on all my children?
Is there any evil wanting? Your father killed
His father; sowed the womb of her who bore him;
Engendered you at the fount of his own existence!
That is what they will say of you.

265   Then, whom
Can you ever marry? There are no bridegrooms for
   you,
And your lives must wither away in sterile
   dreaming.

O Kreon, son of Menoikeus!
You are the only father my daughters have,
270 Since we, their parents, are both of us gone for ever.
They are your own blood: you will not let them
Fall into beggary and loneliness;
You will keep them from the miseries that are mine!
Take pity on them; see, they are only children,
275 Friendless except for you. Promise me this,
Great prince, and give me your hand in token of it.

(Kreon clasps his right hand.)

Children:
I could say much, if you could understand me,
But as it is, I have only this prayer for you:
280 Live where you can, be as happy as you can —
Happier, please God, than God has made your
   father.
KREON: Enough. You have wept enough. Now go
   within.

OEDIPUS: I must, but it is hard.
KREON: Time eases all things.
OEDIPUS: You know my mind, then?
KREON: Say what you desire.
OEDIPUS: Send me from Thebes!
KREON: God grant that I may!   285
OEDIPUS: But since God hates me . . .
KREON: No, he will grant your wish.
OEDIPUS: You promise?
KREON: I can not speak beyond my knowledge.
OEDIPUS: Then lead me in.
KREON: Come now, and leave your children.   290
OEDIPUS: No! Do not take them from me!
KREON: Think no longer
That you are in command here, but rather think
How, when you were, you served your own
   destruction.

*(Exeunt into the house all but
the Chorus; the Choragos
chants directly to the audience.)*

CHORAGOS: Men of Thebes: look upon Oedipus.

This is the king who solved the famous riddle   295
And towered up, most powerful of men.
No mortal eyes but looked on him with envy,
Yet in the end ruin swept over him.

Let every man in mankind's frailty
Consider his last day; and let none   300
Presume on his good fortune until he find
Life, at his death, a memory without pain.

COMMENTARIES

Critical comment on the plays of Sophocles has been rich and various and has spanned the centuries. We are especially fortunate to have a commentary from the great age of Greek thought a century after Sophocles himself flourished. In *Oedipus Rex* Sophocles gave the philosopher Aristotle a perfect drama on which to build a theory of tragedy, and Aristotle's observations have remained the most influential comments made on drama in the West. In some ways they have established the function, limits, and purposes of drama. In the twentieth century, for instance, when Bertolt Brecht tried to create a new theory of the drama, he specifically described his ideas as an alternative to Aristotelian notions.

Although not a critic, Sigmund Freud saw in the Oedipus myth as interpreted by Sophocles a basic psychological phenomenon experienced by all people in their infancy. This "Oedipus complex" is now well established in psychology and in the popular imagination.

The extraordinary range of commentary on the Oedipus story is demonstrated nowhere more amazingly than in Claude Lévi-Strauss's structural reading of the myth, both in Sophocles' version and in other versions. Lévi-Strauss shows that a pattern emerges when certain actions in the play are placed side by side. If he is correct, his theory offers a way to interpret myths and to see why they were valued so highly by the Greeks in their drama.

Aristotle (384–322 B.C.)
POETICS: COMEDY AND EPIC AND TRAGEDY   c. 334–323 B.C.

TRANSLATED BY GERALD F. ELSE

Aristotle was Plato's most brilliant student and the heir of his teaching mantle. He remained with Plato for twenty years and then began his own school, called the Lyceum. His extant work consists mainly of his lectures, which were recorded by his students and carefully preserved. Called his treatises, they have greatly influenced later thought and deal with almost every branch of philosophy, science, and the arts. His Poetics remains, more than two thousand years later, a document of immense importance for literary criticism. Although sometimes ambiguous, difficult, and unfinished, it provides insight into the theoretical basis of Greek tragedy and comedy, and it helps us see that the drama was significant enough in intellectual life to warrant an examination by the best Greek minds.

Comedy

Comedy is, as we said it was, an imitation of persons who are inferior; not, however, going all the way to full villainy, but imitating the ugly, of which the ludicrous is one part. The ludicrous, that is, is a failing or a piece of ugliness which causes no pain or destruction; thus, to go on farther, the comic mask° is something ugly and distorted but painless.

Now the stages of development of tragedy, and the men who were responsible for them, have not escaped notice but comedy did escape notice in the beginning because it was not taken seriously. (In fact it was late in its history that the presiding magistrate officially "granted a chorus" to the comic poets; until then they were volunteers.) Thus comedy already possessed certain defining characteristics when the first "comic poets," so-called, appear in the record. Who gave it masks, or prologues, or troupes of actors and all that sort of thing is not known. The composing of plots came originally from Sicily; of the Athenian poets, Crates° was the first to abandon the lampooning mode and compose arguments, that is, plots, of a general nature.

---

the comic mask: Actors in Greek drama wore masks behind which they spoke their lines. The masks were made individually for each character.

Crates: Greek actor and playwright (fl. 470 B.C.), credited by Aristotle with developing Greek comedy into a fully plotted, credible form. Aristophanes (c. 448–c. 385 B.C.), another Greek comic playwright, says that Crates was the first to portray a drunkard onstage.

Epic and Tragedy

Well, then, epic poetry followed in the wake of tragedy up to the point of being a (1) good-sized (2) imitation (3) in verse (4) of people who are to be taken seriously; but in its having its verse unmixed with any other and being narrative in character, there they differ. Further, so far as its length is concerned, tragedy tries as hard as it can to exist during a single daylight period, or to vary but little, while the epic is not limited in its time and so differs in that respect. Yet originally they used to do this in tragedies just as much as they did in epic poems.

The constituent elements are partly identical and partly limited to tragedy. Hence anybody who knows about good and bad tragedy knows about epic also; for the elements that the epic possesses appertain to tragedy as well, but those of tragedy are not all found in the epic.

Tragedy and Its Six Constituent Elements

Our discussions of imitative poetry in hexameters,° and of comedy, will come later; at present let us deal with tragedy, recovering from what has been said so far the definition of its essential nature, as it was in development. Tragedy, then, is a process of imitating an action which has serious implications, is complete, and possesses magnitude; by means of language which has been made sensuously attractive, with each of its varieties found separately in the parts; enacted by the persons themselves and not presented through narrative; through a course of pity and fear completing the purification of tragic acts which have those emotional characteristics. By "language made sensuously attractive" I mean language that has rhythm and melody, and by "its varieties found separately" I mean the fact that certain parts of the play are carried on through spoken verses alone and others the other way around, through song.

Now first of all, since they perform the imitation through action (by acting it), the adornment of their visual appearance will perforce constitute some part of the making of tragedy; and song-composition and verbal expression also, for those are the media in which they perform the imitation. By "verbal expression" I mean the actual composition of the verses, and by "song-composition" something whose meaning is entirely clear.

Next, since it is an imitation of an action and is enacted by certain people who are performing the action, and since those people must necessarily have certain traits both of character and thought (for it is thanks to these two factors that we speak of people's actions also as having a defined character, and it is in accordance with their actions that all either succeed or fail); and since the imitation of the action is the plot, for by "plot" I mean here the structuring of the events, and by the "characters" that in accordance with which we say that the persons who are acting have a defined moral character, and by "thought" all the passages in which they attempt to prove some thesis or set forth an opinion — it follows of necessity, then, that tragedy as a whole has just six constituent elements, in relation to the essence that makes it a distinct species; and they are plot, characters, verbal expression, thought, visual adornment, and song-composition. For the elements by which they imitate are two (i.e., verbal expression and song-composition), the manner in which they imitate is one (visual adornment), the things they imitate are three (plot,

---

hexameters: The first known metrical form for classical verse. Each line had six metrical feet, some of which were prescribed in advance. It is the meter used for epic poetry and for poetry designed to teach a lesson. The form has sometimes been used in comparatively modern poetry but rarely with success except in French.

characters, thought), and there is nothing more beyond these. These then are the constituent forms they use.

The Relative Importance of the Six Elements

The greatest of these elements is the structuring of the incidents. For tragedy is an imitation not of men but of a life, an action, and they have moral quality in accordance with their characters but are happy or unhappy in accordance with their actions; hence they are not active in order to imitate their characters, but they include the characters along with the actions for the sake of the latter. Thus the structure of events, the plot, is the goal of tragedy, and the goal is the greatest thing of all.

Again: a tragedy cannot exist without a plot, but it can without characters: thus the tragedies of most of our modern poets are devoid of character, and in general many poets are like that; so also with the relationship between Zeuxis and Polygnotus,° among the painters: Polygnotus is a good portrayer of character, while Zeuxis's painting has no dimension of character at all.

Again: if one strings end to end speeches that are expressive of character and carefully worked in thought and expression, he still will not achieve the result which we said was the aim of tragedy; the job will be done much better by a tragedy that is more deficient in these other respects but has a plot, a structure of events. It is much the same case as with painting: the most beautiful pigments smeared on at random will not give as much pleasure as a black-and-white outline picture. Besides, the most powerful means tragedy has for swaying our feelings, namely the peripeties and recognitions,° are elements of plot.

Again: an indicative sign is that those who are beginning a poetic career manage to hit the mark in verbal expression and character portrayal sooner than they do in plot construction; and the same is true of practically all the earliest poets.

So plot is the basic principle, the heart and soul, as it were, of tragedy, and the characters come second: [. . .] it is the imitation of an action and imitates the persons primarily for the sake of their action.

Third in rank is thought. This is the ability to state the issues and appropriate points pertaining to a given topic, an ability which springs from the arts of politics and rhetoric; in fact the earlier poets made their characters talk "politically," the present-day poets rhetorically. But "character" is that kind of utterance which clearly reveals the bent of a man's moral choice (hence there is no character in that class of utterances in which there is nothing at all that the speaker is choosing or rejecting), while "thought" is the passages in which they try to prove that something is so or not so, or state some general principle.

Fourth is the verbal expression of the speeches. I mean by this the same thing that was said earlier, that the "verbal expression" is the conveyance of thought through language: a statement which has the same meaning whether one says "verses" or "speeches."

Zeuxis and Polygnotus: Zeuxis (fl. 420–390 B.C.) developed a method of painting in which the figures were rounded and apparently three-dimensional. Thus, he was an illusionistic painter, imitating life in a realistic style. Polygnotus (c. 470–440 B.C.) was famous as a painter, and his works were on the Acropolis as well as at Delphi. His draftsmanship was especially praised.

peripeties and recognitions: The turning about of fortune and the recognition on the part of the tragic hero of the truth. This is, for Aristotle, a critical moment in the drama, especially if both events happen simultaneously, as they do in *Oedipus Rex*. It is quite possible for these moments to happen apart from one another.

The song-composition of the remaining parts is the greatest of the sensuous attractions, and the visual adornment of the dramatic persons can have a strong emotional effect but is the least artistic element, the least connected with the poetic art; in fact the force of tragedy can be felt even without benefit of public performance and actors, while for the production of the visual effect the property man's art is even more decisive than that of the poets.

General Principles of the
Tragic Plot

With these distinctions out of the way, let us next discuss what the structuring of the events should be like, since this is both the basic and the most important element in the tragic art. We have established, then, that tragedy is an imitation of an action which is complete and whole and has some magnitude (for there is also such a thing as a whole that has no magnitude). "Whole" is that which has beginning, middle, and end. "Beginning" is that which does not necessarily follow on something else, but after it something else naturally is or happens; "end," the other way around, is that which naturally follows on something else, either necessarily or for the most part, but nothing else after it; and "middle" that which naturally follows on something else and something else on it. So, then, well constructed plots should neither begin nor end at any chance point but follow the guidelines just laid down.

Furthermore, since the beautiful, whether a living creature or anything that is composed of parts, should not only have these in a fixed order to one another but also possess a definite size which does not depend on chance — for beauty depends on size and order; hence neither can a very tiny creature turn out to be beautiful (since our perception of it grows blurred as it approaches the period of imperceptibility) nor an excessively huge one (for then it cannot all be perceived at once and so its unity and wholeness are lost), if for example there were a creature a thousand miles long — so, just as in the case of living creatures they must have some size, but one that can be taken in a single view, so with plots: they should have length, but such that they are easy to remember. As to a limit of the length, the one is determined by the tragic competitions and the ordinary span of attention. (If they had to compete with a hundred tragedies they would compete by the water clock, as they say used to be done [?].) But the limit fixed by the very nature of the case is: the longer the plot, up to the point of still being perspicuous as a whole, the finer it is so far as size is concerned; or to put it in general terms, the length in which, with things happening in unbroken sequence, a shift takes place either probably or necessarily from bad to good fortune or from good to bad — that is an acceptable norm of length.

But a plot is not unified, as some people think, simply because it has to do with a single person. A large, indeed an indefinite number of things can happen to a given individual, some of which go to constitute no unified event; and in the same way there can be many acts of a given individual from which no single action emerges. Hence it seems clear that those poets are wrong who have composed *Heracleïds, Theseïds,* and the like. They think that since Heracles was a single person it follows that the plot will be single too. But Homer, superior as he is in all other respects, appears to have grasped this point well also, thanks either to art or nature, for in composing an *Odyssey* he did not incorporate into it everything that happened to the hero, for example how he was wounded on Mt. Parnassus° or how he

Mt. Parnassus: A mountain in central Greece traditionally sacred to Apollo. In legend, Odysseus was wounded there, but the point Aristotle is making is that the writer of epics need not include every detail of his hero's life in a given work. Homer, in writing the *Odyssey,* was working with a hero, Odysseus, whose story had been legendary long before he began writing.

feigned madness at the muster, neither of which events, by happening, made it at all necessary or probable that the other should happen. Instead, he composed the *Odyssey* — and the *Iliad* similarly — around a unified action of the kind we have been talking about.

A poetic imitation, then, ought to be unified in the same way as a single imitation in any other mimetic field, by having a single object: since the plot is an imitation of an action, the latter ought to be both unified and complete, and the component events ought to be so firmly compacted that if any one of them is shifted to another place, or removed, the whole is loosened up and dislocated; for an element whose addition or subtraction makes no perceptible extra difference is not really a part of the whole.

From what has been said it is also clear that the poet's job is not to report what has happened but what is likely to happen: that is, what is capable of happening according to the rule of probability or necessity. Thus the difference between the historian and the poet is not in their utterances being in verse or prose (it would be quite possible for Herodotus's work to be translated into verse, and it would not be any the less a history with verse than it is without it); the difference lies in the fact that the historian speaks of what has happened, the poet of the kind of thing that *can* happen. Hence also poetry is a more philosophical and serious business than history; for poetry speaks more of universals, history of particulars. "Universal" in this case is what kind of person is likely to do or say certain kinds of things, according to probability or necessity; that is what poetry aims at, although it gives its persons particular names afterward; while the "particular" is what Alcibiades did or what happened to him.

In the field of comedy this point has been grasped: our comic poets construct their plots on the basis of general probabilities and then assign names to the persons quite arbitrarily, instead of dealing with individuals as the old iambic poets° did. But in tragedy they still cling to the historically given names. The reason is that what is possible is persuasive; so what has not happened we are not yet ready to believe is possible, while what has happened is, we feel, obviously possible: for it would not have happened if it were impossible. Nevertheless, it is a fact that even in our tragedies, in some cases only one or two of the names are traditional, the rest being invented, and in some others none at all. It is so, for example, in Agathon's *Antheus* — the names in it are as fictional as the events — and it gives no less pleasure because of that. Hence the poets ought not to cling at all costs to the traditional plots, around which our tragedies are constructed. And in fact it is absurd to go searching for this kind of authentication, since even the familiar names are familiar to only a few in the audience and yet give the same kind of pleasure to all.

So from these considerations it is evident that the poet should be a maker of his plots more than of his verses, insofar as he is a poet by virtue of his imitations and what he imitates is actions. Hence even if it happens that he puts something that has actually taken place into poetry, he is none the less a poet; for there is nothing to prevent some of the things that have happened from being the kind of things that can happen, and that is the sense in which he is their maker.

old iambic poets: Aristotle may be referring to Archilochus (fl. 650 B.C.) and the iambic style he developed. The iamb is a metrical foot of two syllables, a short and a long syllable, and was the most popular metrical style before the time of Aristotle. "Dealing with individuals" implies using figures already known to the audience rather than figures whose names can be arbitrarily assigned because no one knows who they are.

*Simple and Complex
Plots*

Among simple plots and actions the episodic are the worst. By "episodic" plot I mean one in which there is no probability or necessity for the order in which the episodes follow one another. Such structures are composed by the bad poets because they are bad poets, but by the good poets because of the actors: in composing contest pieces for them, and stretching out the plot beyond its capacity, they are forced frequently to dislocate the sequence.

Furthermore, since the tragic imitation is not only of a complete action but also of events that are fearful and pathetic,° and these come about best when they come about contrary to one's expectation yet logically, one following from the other; that way they will be more productive of wonder than if they happen merely at random, by chance — because even among chance occurrences the ones people consider most marvelous are those that seem to have come about as if on purpose: for example the way the statue of Mitys at Argos killed the man who had been the cause of Mitys's death, by falling on him while he was attending the festival; it stands to reason, people think, that such things don't happen by chance — so plots of that sort cannot fail to be artistically superior.

Some plots are simple, others are complex; indeed the actions of which the plots are imitations already fall into these two categories. By "simple" action I mean one the development of which being continuous and unified in the manner stated above, the reversal comes without peripety or recognition, and by "complex" action one in which the reversal is continuous but with recognition or peripety or both. And these developments must grow out of the very structure of the plot itself, in such a way that on the basis of what has happened previously this particular outcome follows either by necessity or in accordance with probability; for there is a great difference in whether these events happen because of those or merely after them.

"Peripety" is a shift of what is being undertaken to the opposite in the way previously stated, and that in accordance with probability or necessity as we have just been saying; as for example in the *Oedipus* the man who has come, thinking that he will reassure Oedipus, that is, relieve him of his fear with respect to his mother, by revealing who he once was, brings about the opposite; and in the *Lynceus,* as he (Lynceus) is being led away with every prospect of being executed, and Danaus pursuing him with every prospect of doing the executing, it comes about as a result of the other things that have happened in the play that *he* is executed and Lynceus is saved. And "recognition" is, as indeed the name indicates, a shift from ignorance to awareness, pointing in the direction either of close blood ties or of hostility, of people who have previously been in a clearly marked state of happiness or unhappiness.

The finest recognition is one that happens at the same time as a peripety, as is the case with the one in the *Oedipus*. Naturally, there are also other kinds of recognition: it is possible for one to take place in the prescribed manner in relation to inanimate objects and chance occurrences, and it is possible to recognize whether a person has acted or not acted. But the form that is most integrally a part of the plot, the action, is the one aforesaid; for that kind of recognition combined with peripety will excite either pity or fear (and these are the kinds of action of which tragedy is

---

fearful and pathetic: Aristotle said that tragedy should evoke two emotions: terror and pity. The terror results from our realizing that what is happening to the hero might just as easily happen to us; the pity results from our human sympathy with a fellow sufferer. Therefore, the fearful and pathetic represent significant emotions appropriate to our witnessing drama.

an imitation according to our definition), because both good and bad fortune will also be most likely to follow that kind of event. Since, further, the recognition is a recognition of persons, some are of one person by the other one only (when it is already known who the "other one" is), but sometimes it is necessary for both persons to go through a recognition, as for example Iphigenia is recognized by her brother° through the sending of the letter, but of him by Iphigenia another recognition is required.

These then are two elements of plot: peripety and recognition; third is the *pathos*. Of these, peripety and recognition have been discussed; a *pathos* is a destructive or painful act, such as deaths on stage, paroxysms of pain, woundings, and all that sort of thing.

Sigmund Freud (1856–1939)
THE OEDIPUS COMPLEX   *1900–1930°*

TRANSLATED BY JAMES STRACHEY

Sigmund Freud is the most celebrated psychiatrist of the twentieth century and the father of psychoanalytic theory. His researches into the unconscious changed the way we think about the human mind, and his explorations into the symbolic meaning of dreams have been widely regarded as a breakthrough in connecting the meaning of world myth to personal life.

In his Interpretation of Dreams *he turned to Sophocles' drama and developed his theories of the Oedipus complex: the desire to kill one parent and marry the other may be rooted in the deepest natural psychological development of the individual. The following passage provides insight not only into a psychological state that all humans may share but also into the way in which a man of Freud's temperament read and interpreted a great piece of literature. Like Sophocles himself, Freud believed that the myth underlying* Oedipus Rex *has a meaning and importance for all human beings.*

In my experience, which is already extensive, the chief part in the mental lives of all children who later become psychoneurotics is played by their parents. Being in love with the one parent and hating the other are among the essential constituents of the stock of psychical impulses which is formed at that time and which is of such importance in determining the symptoms of the later neurosis. It is not my belief, however, that psychoneurotics differ sharply in this respect from other human beings who remain normal — that they are able, that is, to create something absolutely new and peculiar to themselves. It is far more probable — and this is confirmed by occasional observations on normal children — that they are only distinguished by exhibiting on a magnified scale feelings of love and hatred to their parents which occur less obviously and less intensely in the minds of most children.

---

her brother: Orestes is Iphigenia's brother. Aristotle may be referring to a lost play.
   1900–1930: *Interpretation of Dreams* was first published in 1900 and updated regularly by Freud through eight editions. This passage is taken from the eighth edition, published in 1930.

This discovery is confirmed by a legend that has come down to us from classical antiquity: a legend whose profound and universal power to move can only be understood if the hypothesis I have put forward in regard to the psychology of children has an equally universal validity. What I have in mind is the legend of King Oedipus and Sophocles' drama which bears his name.

Oedipus, son of Laïus, King of Thebes, and of Jocasta, was exposed [to the elements and left to die] as an infant because an oracle had warned Laïus that the still unborn child would be his father's murderer. The child was rescued and grew up as a prince in an alien court, until, in doubts as to his origin, he too questioned the oracle and was warned to avoid his home since he was destined to murder his father and take his mother in marriage. On the road leading away from what he believed was his home, he met King Laïus and slew him in a sudden quarrel. He came next to Thebes and solved the riddle set him by the Sphinx who barred his way. Out of gratitude the Thebans made him their king and gave him Jocasta's hand in marriage. He reigned long in peace and honor, and she who, unknown to him, was his mother bore him two sons and two daughters. Then at last a plague broke out and the Thebans made inquiry once more of the oracle. It is at this point that Sophocles' tragedy opens. The messengers bring back the reply that the plague will cease when the murderer of Laïus has been driven from the land.

> But he, where is he? Where shall now be read
> The fading record of this ancient guilt?[1]

The action of the play consists in nothing other than the process of revealing, with cunning delays and ever-mounting excitement — a process that can be likened to the work of a psychoanalysis — that Oedipus himself is the murderer of Laïus, but further that he is the son of the murdered man and of Jocasta. Appalled at the abomination which he has unwittingly perpetrated, Oedipus blinds himself and forsakes his home. The oracle has been fulfilled.

Oedipus Rex is what is known as a tragedy of destiny. Its tragic effect is said to lie in the contrast between the supreme will of the gods and the vain attempts of mankind to escape the evil that threatens them. The lesson which, it is said, the deeply moved spectator should learn from the tragedy is submission to the divine will and realization of his own impotence. Modern dramatists have accordingly tried to achieve a similar tragic effect by weaving the same contrast into a plot invented by themselves. But the spectators have looked on unmoved while a curse or an oracle was fulfilled in spite of all the efforts of some innocent man: later tragedies of destiny have failed in their effect.

If *Oedipus Rex* moves a modern audience no less than it did the contemporary Greek one, the explanation can only be that its effect does not lie in the contrast between destiny and human will, but is to be looked for in the particular nature of the material on which that contrast is exemplified. There must be something which makes a voice within us ready to recognize the compelling force of destiny in the *Oedipus,* while we can dismiss as merely arbitrary such dispositions as are laid down in [Grillparzer's] *Die Ahnfrau* or other modern tragedies of destiny. And a factor of this kind is in fact involved in the story of King Oedipus. His destiny moves us

---

[1]Lewis Campbell's translation (1883), lines 108ff [Dudley Fitts and Robert Fitzgerald, *Sophocles: The Oedipus Cycle, an English Version* (Harcourt Brace & Company, 1949), Prologue, lines 112–13].

only because it might have been ours — because the oracle laid the same curse upon us before our birth as upon him. It is the fate of all of us, perhaps, to direct our first sexual impulse toward our mother and our first hatred and our first murderous wish against our father. Our dreams convince us that that is so. King Oedipus, who slew his father Laïus and married his mother Jocasta, merely shows us the fulfillment of our own childhood wishes. But, more fortunate than he, we have meanwhile succeeded, in so far as we have not become psychoneurotics, in detaching our sexual impulses from our mothers and in forgetting our jealousy of our fathers. Here is one in whom these primeval wishes of our childhood have been fulfilled, and we shrink back from him with the whole force of the repression by which those wishes have since that time been held down within us. While the poet, as he unravels the past, brings to light the guilt of Oedipus, he is at the same time compelling us to recognize our own inner minds, in which those same impulses, though suppressed, are still to be found. The contrast with which the closing Chorus leaves us confronted —

> . . . Fix on Oedipus your eyes,
> Who resolved the dark enigma, noblest champion and most wise.
> Like a star his envied fortune mounted beaming far and wide:
> Now he sinks in seas of anguish, whelmed beneath a raging tide . . .[2]

— strikes as a warning at ourselves and our pride, at us who since our childhood have grown so wise and so mighty in our own eyes. Like Oedipus, we live in ignorance of these wishes, repugnant to morality, which have been forced upon us by Nature, and after their revelation we may all of us well seek to close our eyes to the scenes of our childhood.[3]

There is an unmistakable indication in the text of Sophocles' tragedy itself that the legend of Oedipus sprang from some primeval dream material which had as its content the distressing disturbance of a child's relation to his parents owing to the first stirrings of sexuality. At a point when Oedipus, though he is not yet enlightened, has begun to feel troubled by his recollection of the oracle, Jocasta consoles him by referring to a dream which many people dream, though, as she thinks, it has no meaning:

> Many a man ere now in dreams hath lain
> With her who bare him. He hath least annoy
> Who with such omens troubleth not his mind.[4]

Today, just as then, many men dream of having sexual relations with their mothers, and speak of the fact with indignation and astonishment. It is clearly the key to the tragedy and the complement to the dream of the dreamer's father being dead. The story of Oedipus is the reaction of the imagination to these two typical dreams.

[2]Lewis Campbell's translation, lines 1524ff [Fitts and Fitzgerald, antistrophe 2, lines 292–96].

[3][Footnote added by Freud in 1914 edition.] None of the findings of psychoanalytic research has provoked such embittered denials, such fierce opposition — or such amusing contortions — on the part of critics as this indication of the childhood impulses toward incest which persist in the unconscious. An attempt has even been made recently to make out, in the face of all experience, that the incest should only be taken as "symbolic." — Ferenczi (1912) has proposed an ingenious "overinterpretation" of the Oedipus myth, based on a passage in one of Schopenhauer's letters. [Added 1919.] Later studies have shown that the "Oedipus complex," which was touched upon for the first time in the above paragraphs in the Interpretation of Dreams, throws a light of undreamt-of importance on the history of the human race and the evolution of religion and morality.

[4]Lewis Campbell's translation, lines 982ff [Fitts and Fitzgerald, scene 3, lines 67–69].

And just as these dreams, when dreamt by adults, are accompanied by feelings of repulsion, so too the legend must include horror and self-punishment. Its further modification originates once again in a misconceived secondary revision of the material, which has sought to exploit it for theological purposes. . . . The attempt to harmonize divine omnipotence with human responsibility must naturally fail in connection with this subject matter just as with any other.

Claude Lévi-Strauss (b. 1908)
FROM *THE STRUCTURAL STUDY OF MYTH*   1955

Claude Lévi-Strauss is one of a handful of modern anthropologists whose interests span the range of thought, culture, and understanding. His work has been of immense influence on French intellectual life and, by extension, on the intellectual life of modern times. His works include Triste Tropiques *(translated as* A World on the Wane*), about his own experiences as an anthropologist;* Structural Anthropology, *about the ways in which the study of anthropology implies a study of the structure of thought; and* Mythologies, *a four-volume summation of his thought. The excerpt that follows is structuralist in scope in that it attempts to understand the myth of Oedipus by examining the patterns of repetition in the original narrative. By setting up a grid, Lévi-Strauss begins to sort out the implications of the myth and to seek a meaning that is not necessarily apparent in the chronological order of the narrative. He examines the myth diachronically — across the lines of time — and thereby sees a new range of implications, which he treats as the structural implications of the myth. His reading is complex, suggesting that the Oedipus myth is a vegetation myth explaining the origins of mankind. Lévi-Strauss gives us a new way to interpret the significance of literary myths.*

The time has come to give a concrete example of the method we propose. We will use the Oedipus myth which has the advantage of being well known to everybody and for which no preliminary explanation is therefore needed. By doing so, I am well aware that the Oedipus myth has only reached us under late forms and through literary transfigurations concerned more with esthetic and moral preoccupations than with religious or ritual ones, whatever these may have been. But as will be shown later, this apparently unsatisfactory situation will strengthen our demonstration rather than weaken it.

The myth will be treated as would be an orchestra score perversely presented as a unilinear series and where our task is to reestablish the correct disposition. As if, for instance, we were confronted with a sequence of the type: 1,2,4,7,8,2,3,4,6,8,1,4,5,7,8,1,2,5,7,3,4,5,6,8 . . . , the assignment being to put all the 1's together, all the 2's, the 3's, etc.; the result is a chart:

$$
\begin{array}{cccccc}
1 & 2 & 4 & & 7 & 8 \\
 & 2 & 3 & 4 & 6 & 8 \\
1 & & 4 & 5 & 7 & 8 \\
1 & 2 & & 5 & 7 & \\
 & 3 & 4 & 5 & & \\
 & & & & 6 & 8 \\
\end{array}
$$

We will attempt to perform the same kind of operation on the Oedipus myth, trying out several dispositions. [. . .] Let us suppose, for the sake of argument, that the best arrangement is the following (although it might certainly be improved by the help of a specialist in Greek mythology):

Kadmos seeks his sister Europa ravished by Zeus.			
		Kadmos kills the dragon.	
	The Spartoi kill each other.		
			Labdacos (Laios's father) = *lame* (?).
	Oedipus kills his father Laios.		Laios (Oedipus's father) = *left-sided* (?).
		Oedipus kills the Sphinx.	
Oedipus marries his mother Jocasta.			
	Eteocles kills his brother Polyneices.		Oedipus = *swollen-foot* (?).
Antigone buries her brother Polyneices despite prohibition.			

Thus, we find ourselves confronted with four vertical columns each of which includes several relations belonging to the same bundle. Were we to *tell* the myth, we would disregard the columns and read the rows from left to right and from top to bottom. But if we want to *understand* the myth, then we will have to disregard one half of the diachronic° dimension (top to bottom) and read from left to right, column after column, each one being considered as a unit.

All the relations belonging to the same column exhibit one common feature which it is our task to unravel. For instance, all the events grouped in the first column on the left have something to do with blood relations which are overemphasized, i.e., are subject to a more intimate treatment than they should be. Let us say, then, that the first column has as its common feature the *overrating of blood relations*. It is obvious that the second column expresses the same thing, but inverted: *underrating of blood relations*. The third column refers to monsters being slain. As to the fourth, a word of clarification is needed. The remarkable connotation of the

diachronic: Not ordered linearly in time but through time.

surnames in Oedipus's father-line has often been noticed. However, linguists usually disregard it, since to them the only way to define the meaning of a term is to investigate all the contexts in which it appears, and personal names, precisely because they are used as such, are not accompanied by any context. With the method we propose to follow the objection disappears since the myth itself provides its own context. The meaningful fact is no longer to be looked for in the eventual sense of each name, but in the fact that all the names have a common feature: i.e., that they may eventually mean something and that all these hypothetical meanings (which may well remain hypothetical) exhibit a common feature, namely they refer to *difficulties to walk and to behave straight*.

What is then the relationship between the two columns on the right? Column three refers to monsters. The dragon is a chthonian° being which has to be killed in order that mankind be born from the earth; the Sphinx is a monster unwilling to permit men to live. The last unit reproduces the first one which has to do with the *autochthonous*° origin of mankind. Since the monsters are overcome by men, we may thus say that the common feature of the third column is *the denial of the autochthonous origin of man*.

This immediately helps us to understand the meaning of the fourth column. In mythology it is a universal character of men born from the earth that at the moment they emerge from the depth, they either cannot walk or do it clumsily. This is the case of the chthonian beings in the mythology of the Pueblo: Masauwu, who leads the emergence, and the chthonian Shumaikoli are lame ("bleeding-foot," "sore-foot"). The same happens to the Koskimo of the Kwakiutl after they have been swallowed by the chthonian monster, Tsiakish: when they returned to the surface of the earth "they limped forward or tripped sideways." Then the common feature of the fourth column is: *the persistence of the autochthonous origin of man*. It follows that column four is to column three as column one is to column two. The inability to connect two kinds of relationships is overcome (or rather replaced) by the positive statement that contradictory relationships are identical inasmuch as they are both self-contradictory in a similar way. Although this is still a provisional formulation of the structure of mythical thought, it is sufficient at this stage.

Turning back to the Oedipus myth, we may now see what it means. The myth has to do with the inability, for a culture which holds the belief that mankind is autochthonous [. . .] to find a satisfactory transition between this theory and the knowledge that human beings are actually born from the union of man and woman. Although the problem obviously cannot be solved, the Oedipus myth provides a kind of logical tool which, to phrase it coarsely, replaces the original problem: born from one or born from two? born from different or born from same? By a correlation of this type, the overrating of blood relations is to the underrating of blood relations as the attempt to escape autochthony is to the impossibility to succeed in it. Although experience contradicts theory, social life verifies the cosmology by its similarity of structure. Hence cosmology is true.

Two remarks should be made at this stage.

In order to interpret the myth, we were able to leave aside a point which has until now worried the specialists, namely, that in the earlier (Homeric) versions of

---

chthonian: From the underworld.
autochthonous: Native, aboriginal; in this case, born of the earth.

the Oedipus myth, some basic elements are lacking, such as Jocasta killing herself and Oedipus piercing his own eyes. These events do not alter the substance of the myth although they can easily be integrated, the first one as a new case of auto-destruction (column three) while the second is another case of crippledness (column four). At the same time there is something significant in these additions since the shift from foot to head is to be correlated with the shift from: autochthonous origin negated to: self-destruction.

Thus, our method eliminates a problem which has been so far one of the main obstacles to the progress of mythological studies, namely, the quest for the *true* version, or the *earlier* one. On the contrary, we define the myth as consisting of all its versions; to put it otherwise: a myth remains the same as long as it is felt as such. A striking example is offered by the fact that our interpretation may take into account, and is certainly applicable to, the Freudian use of the Oedipus myth. Although the Freudian problem has ceased to be that of autochthony *versus* bisexual reproduction, it is still the problem of understanding how *one* can be born from *two*: how is it that we do not have only one procreator, but a mother plus a father? Therefore, not only Sophocles, but Freud himself, should be included among the recorded versions of the Oedipus myth on a par with earlier or seemingly more "authentic" versions.

ANTIGONE

Antigone was Sophocles' thirty-second play, produced in March 441 B.C., when he was in his mid-fifties. It draws a powerful response from its audience partly because it portrays the conflict between two proud, willful people: Antigone, a daughter of Oedipus and Iokaste, and Kreon, Iokaste's brother and the king of Thebes. Its original success was due in part to its portrayal of the individual's struggle against a tyrannical king. After enjoying thirty years of peace with its archrival Sparta, Athens was moving slowly toward war; and the memory of previous tyrants — both good, like Peisistratus, and bad, like his son Hippias — remained in the minds of Sophocles' audience.

It has never been easy to determine which of the two main characters is correct. Kreon's portrayal as a tyrant content to take up the state as his private property tells us that he is not to be fully trusted. At the same time, Antigone knows that the social mores of Thebes imply that a citizen must obey the ruler. Antigone's great courage makes the audience feel sympathy and admiration for her. She is a martyr to her beliefs, an ancient Joan of Arc.

The main conflict in *Antigone* centers on a distinction between law and justice, the conflict between a human law and a higher law. Kreon, the uncle of Antigone and Ismene, has made a decree: Polyneices, the brother of Antigone and Ismene, was guilty not only of killing his brother Eteocles but also of attacking the state and, like all traitors, will be denied a proper burial. When the action of the play begins, Antigone is determined to give her brother the burial that ancient tradition and her religious beliefs demand.

The opening dialogue with Ismene clarifies the important distinction between human law and the higher law on which Antigone says she must act. Ismene declares simply that she cannot go against the law of the citizens. Kreon has been willful in establishing the law, but it is nonetheless the law. Antigone, knowing full well the consequences of defying Kreon, nonetheless acts on her principles.

The complex conflict between Antigone and Kreon occurs on the level of citizen and ruler and is affected on the personal level by the relationship between Haimon, Kreon's son, and his intended bride, Antigone. The antagonism between Kreon and Haimon begins slowly, as Haimon appears to yield to the will of his father, but culminates in Haimon's ultimate rejection of his father by choosing to join Antigone in death.

When Teiresias reveals a prophecy of death and punishment and begs Kreon, for the sake of the suffering Thebes, to rescind his decree and give Polyneices a proper burial, Kreon willfully continues to heed his own declarations rather than oracular wisdom or the pleas of others.

By the time Kreon accepts Teiresias's prophecy, it is too late: he has lost his son, and his wife has killed herself. Power not only has corrupted Kreon but also has taken from him the people about whom he cared most. He emerges as an unyielding tyrant, guilty of making some of the same mistakes that haunted Oedipus.

Antigone emerges as a heroine who presses forward in the full conviction that she is right. She must honor her dead brother at all costs. Even if she must break the law of the state, she must answer to what she regards as a higher law. As she says early in the play, she has "dared the crime of piety." Yet she has within her the complexity of all humans: she in one sense acts in the knowledge that she is right but in another dares Kreon to punish her. She challenges Kreon so boldly that her every move forces the proud Kreon to harden his position and set in motion the ultimate tragedy — the loss of all he holds dear. This is yet one more tragic irony in the Theban trilogy.

Antigone in Performance

Since the eighteenth century *Antigone* has been produced in Europe and the Western Hemisphere in more or less its original form and in various adaptations and rewritings. Jean Cocteau combined his version with music by Arthur Honegger in 1930. It was rewritten and produced by Walter Hasenclever in 1917 as a protest against the First World War and then in 1944 by Jean Anouilh as a protest against Nazi occupation of Paris during World War II (see the excerpt on p. 98). The Royal Shakespeare Company produced *Antigone* along with all the surviving Greek tragedies in 1980. Bertolt Brecht's production of *Antigone* in 1948 introduced a Gestapo officer and Nazi brutality. Athol Fugard's *The Island* (1973) features a remarkable production of *Antigone* as a play within a play, produced by convicts in a South African island jail as a Christmas entertainment for their jailers and specially invited white guests. Fugard found, as have so many other adapters and producers, that the political power of *Antigone* leaps out for virtually all contemporary audiences. Janusz Glowacki, a Polish playwright, produced *Antigone in New York* at the Arena Stage in Washington in March 1993. Inspired by both Sophocles and Beckett, it is set in Tompkins Square Park in New York. The action centers on a homeless Puerto Rican woman's efforts to bury a homeless man in the park. The action of the play demonstrates the durability of *Antigone*'s basic concept — that a decent burial is an essential vestige of humanity.

Sophocles (c. 496–c. 406 B.C.)

ANTIGONE   *441 B.C.*

TRANSLATED BY DUDLEY FITTS AND ROBERT FITZGERALD

Characters

ANTIGONE, } *daughters of Oedipus*
ISMENE,
EURYDICE, *wife of Kreon*
KREON, *King of Thebes*
HAIMON, *son of Kreon*
TEIRESIAS, *a blind seer*
A SENTRY
A MESSENGER
CHORUS

Scene: *Before the palace of Kreon, King of Thebes. A central double door, and two lateral doors. A platform extends the length of the facade, and from this platform three steps lead down into the orchestra, or chorus-ground.*

Time: *Dawn of the day after the repulse of the Argive army from the assault on Thebes.*

PROLOGUE°

(*Antigone and Ismene enter from the central door of the palace.*)

ANTIGONE: Ismene, dear sister,
    You would think that we had already suffered enough
    For the curse on Oedipus.°

Prologue: Portion of the play explaining the background and current action.   **3. curse on Oedipus:** Oedipus, king of Thebes and the father of Antigone and Ismene, was abandoned by his parents as an infant after the oracle foretold that he would one day kill his father and marry his mother. Rescued by a shepherd and raised by the king of Corinth, Oedipus returned years later to Thebes and unknowingly lived out the oracle's prophecy by killing Laios and marrying Iokaste. After his two sons, Eteocles and Polyneices, killed each other in combat, the throne went to Kreon, Iokaste's brother.

    I cannot imagine any grief
That you and I have not gone through. And now —   5
Have they told you of the new decree of our King
    Kreon?
ISMENE: I have heard nothing: I know
    That two sisters lost two brothers, a double death
    In a single hour; and I know that the Argive army
    Fled in the night; but beyond this, nothing.   10
ANTIGONE: I thought so. And that is why I wanted
    you
    To come out here with me. There is something we
    must do.
ISMENE: Why do you speak so strangely?
ANTIGONE: Listen, Ismene:
    Kreon buried our brother Eteocles   15
    With military honors, gave him a soldier's funeral,
    And it was right that he should; but Polyneices,
    Who fought as bravely and died as miserably, —
    They say that Kreon has sworn
    No one shall bury him, no one mourn for him,   20
    But his body must lie in the fields, a sweet treasure
    For carrion birds to find as they search for food.
    That is what they say, and our good Kreon is
    coming here
    To announce it publicly; and the penalty —
    Stoning to death in the public square!
                    There it is,   25
    And now you can prove what you are:
    A true sister, or a traitor to your family.
ISMENE: Antigone, you are mad! What could I possibly
    do?
ANTIGONE: You must decide whether you will help me
    or not.
ISMENE: I do not understand you. Help you in what?   30
ANTIGONE: Ismene, I am going to bury him. Will you
    come?
ISMENE: Bury him! You have just said the new law
    forbids it.
ANTIGONE: He is my brother. And he is your brother,
    too.

ISMENE: But think of the danger! Think what Kreon
     will do!
ANTIGONE: Kreon is not strong enough to stand in my
35   way.
ISMENE: Ah sister!
     Oedipus died, everyone hating him
     For what his own search brought to light, his eyes
     Ripped out by his own hand; and Iocaste died,
40   His mother and wife at once: she twisted the cords
     That strangled her life; and our two brothers died,
     Each killed by the other's sword. And we are left:
     But oh, Antigone,
     Think how much more terrible than these
     Our own death would be if we should go against
45   Kreon
     And do what he has forbidden! We are only
        women,
     We cannot fight with men, Antigone!
     The law is strong, we must give in to the law
     In this thing, and in worse. I beg the Dead
50   To forgive me, but I am helpless: I must yield
     To those in authority. And I think it is dangerous
        business
     To be always meddling.
ANTIGONE: If that is what you think,
     I should not want you, even if you asked to come.
     You have made your choice, you can be what you
        want to be.
55   But I will bury him; and if I must die,
     I say that this crime is holy: I shall lie down
     With him in death, and I shall be as dear
     To him as he to me.
                         It is the dead,
     Not the living, who make the longest demands:
     We die for ever . . .
60   You may do as you like,
     Since apparently the laws of the gods mean nothing
        to you.
ISMENE: They mean a great deal to me; but I have no
        strength
     To break laws that were made for the public good.
ANTIGONE: That must be your excuse, I suppose. But as
        for me,
     I will bury the brother I love.
65 ISMENE: Antigone,
     I am so afraid for you!
ANTIGONE: You need not be:
     You have yourself to consider, after all.
ISMENE: But no one must hear of this, you must tell no
        one!
     I will keep it a secret, I promise!
ANTIGONE: O tell it! Tell everyone!
70   Think how they'll hate you when it all comes out
     If they learn that you knew about it all the time!
ISMENE: So fiery! You should be cold with fear.
ANTIGONE: Perhaps. But I am doing only what I must.
ISMENE: But can you do it? I say that you cannot.
75 ANTIGONE: Very well: when my strength gives out,
     I shall do no more.

ISMENE: Impossible things should not be tried at all.
ANTIGONE: Go away, Ismene:
     I shall be hating you soon, and the dead will too,
     For your words are hateful. Leave me my foolish
        plan: 80
     I am not afraid of the danger; if it means death,
     It will not be the worst of deaths — death without
        honor.
ISMENE: Go then, if you feel that you must.
     You are unwise,
     But a loyal friend indeed to those who love you.   85

(*Exit into the palace. Antigone goes off, left. Enter the
Chorus.*)

PARODOS° • *Strophe*° 1

CHORUS: Now the long blade of the sun, lying
     Level east to west, touches with glory
     Thebes of the Seven Gates. Open, unlidded
     Eye of golden day! O marching light
     Across the eddy and rush of Dirce's stream,°   5
     Striking the white shields of the enemy
     Thrown headlong backward from the blaze of
        morning!
CHORAGOS:° Polyneices their commander
     Roused them with windy phrases,
     He the wild eagle screaming   10
     Insults above our land,
     His wings their shields of snow,
     His crest their marshalled helms.

Antistrophe° 1

CHORUS: Against our seven gates in a yawning ring
     The famished spears came onward in the night;   15
     But before his jaws were sated with our blood,
     Or pinefire took the garland of our towers,
     He was thrown back, and as he turned, great
        Thebes —
     No tender victim for his noisy power —
     Rose like a dragon behind him, shouting war.   20
CHORAGOS: For God hates utterly
     The bray of bragging tongues;
     And when he beheld their smiling,
     Their swagger of golden helms,
     The frown of his thunder blasted   25
     Their first man from our walls.

Parodos: The song or ode chanted by the Chorus on its entry.
Strophe: Song sung by the Chorus as it danced from stage right
to stage left.   **5. Dirce's stream:** River near Thebes.   **8. Choragos:** Leader of the Chorus.   **Antistrophe:** Song sung by the
Chorus following the Strophe, as it danced back from stage left
to stage right.

Antigone (Martha Henry)
reassures Ismene in the
Repertory Theatre of Lincoln
Center production of *Antigone*
at the Vivian Beaumont
Theatre, directed by John
Hirsch in 1971.

Strophe 2

CHORUS: We heard his shout of triumph high in the air
    Turn to a scream; far out in a flaming arc
    He fell with his windy torch, and the earth struck
       him.
30   And others storming in fury no less than his
    Found shock of death in the dusty joy of battle.
CHORAGOS: Seven captains at seven gates
    Yielded their clanging arms to the god
    That bends the battle-line and breaks it.
35   These two only, brothers in blood,

Face to face in matchless rage,
Mirroring each the other's death
Clashed in long combat.

Antistrophe 2

CHORUS: But now in the beautiful morning of victory
    Let Thebes of the many chariots sing for joy!   40
    With hearts for dancing we'll take leave of war:
    Our temples shall be sweet with hymns of praise,
    And the long nights shall echo with our chorus.

SCENE 1

CHORAGOS: But now at last our new King is coming:
    Kreon of Thebes, Menoikeus' son.
    In this auspicious dawn of his reign
    What are the new complexities
5   That shifting Fate has woven for him?
    What is his counsel? Why has he summoned
    The old men to hear him?

(*Enter Kreon from the palace, center. He addresses the
Chorus from the top step.*)

KREON: Gentlemen: I have the honor to inform you that
    our Ship of State, which recent storms have threat-
10   ened to destroy, has come safely to harbor at last,
    guided by the merciful wisdom of Heaven. I have
    summoned you here this morning because I know
    that I can depend upon you: your devotion to King
    Laios was absolute; you never hesitated in your duty
15   to our late ruler Oedipus; and when Oedipus died,
your loyalty was transferred to his children. Unfortunately, as you know, his two sons, the princes Eteocles and Polyneices, have killed each other in battle;
and I, as the next in blood, have succeeded to the full
power of the throne.   20

    I am aware, of course, that no Ruler can expect
complete loyalty from his subjects until he has been
tested in office. Nevertheless, I say to you at the very
outset that I have nothing but contempt for the kind
of Governor who is afraid, for whatever reason, to   25
follow the course that he knows is best for the State;
and as for the man who sets private friendship above
the public welfare, — I have no use for him, either. I
call God to witness that if I saw my country headed
for ruin, I should not be afraid to speak out plainly;   30
and I need hardly remind you that I would never
have any dealings with an enemy of the people. No
one values friendship more highly than I; but we
must remember that friends made at the risk of
wrecking our Ship are not real friends at all.   35

Kreon (Philip Bosco), Antigone, and Haimon (David Birney).

These are my principles, at any rate, and that is
why I have made the following decision concerning
the sons of Oedipus: Eteocles, who died as a man
should die, fighting for his country, is to be buried
40 with full military honors, with all the ceremony that
is usual when the greatest heroes die; but his brother
Polyneices, who broke his exile to come back with
fire and sword against his native city and the shrines
of his fathers' gods, whose one idea was to spill
45 the blood of his blood and sell his own people into
slavery — Polyneices, I say, is to have no burial: no
man is to touch him or say the least prayer for
him; he shall lie on the plain, unburied; and the birds
and the scavenging dogs can do with him whatever
50 they like.

    This is my command, and you can see the wisdom
behind it. As long as I am King, no traitor is going to
be honored with the loyal man. But whoever shows
by word and deed that he is on the side of the
55 State, — he shall have my respect while he is living
and my reverence when he is dead.

CHORAGOS: If that is your will, Kreon son of
    Menoikeus,
You have the right to enforce it: we are yours.

KREON: That is my will. Take care that you do your
    part.

CHORAGOS: We are old men: let the younger ones carry
60   it out.

KREON: I do not mean that: the sentries have been
    appointed.

CHORAGOS: Then what is it that you would have us do?

KREON: You will give no support to whoever breaks
    this law.

CHORAGOS: Only a crazy man is in love with death!

65 KREON: And death it is; yet money talks, and the wisest
    Have sometimes been known to count a few coins
    too many.

(*Enter Sentry from left.*)

SENTRY: I'll not say that I'm out of breath from running,
    King, because every time I stopped to think about
    what I have to tell you, I felt like going back. And all
70   the time a voice kept saying, "You fool, don't you
    know you're walking straight into trouble?"; and
    then another voice: "Yes, but if you let somebody
    else get the news to Kreon first, it will be even worse
    than that for you!" But good sense won out, at least I
75   hope it was good sense, and here I am with a story
    that makes no sense at all; but I'll tell it anyhow,
    because, as they say, what's going to happen's going
    to happen and —

KREON: Come to the point. What have you to say?

80 SENTRY: I did not do it. I did not see who did it.
    You must not punish me for what someone else has
    done.

KREON: A comprehensive defense! More effective,
    perhaps,
If I knew its purpose. Come: what is it?

SENTRY: A dreadful thing . . . I don't know how to put
    it —

KREON: Out with it!

SENTRY: Well, then;   85
    The dead man —

                    Polyneices —

(*Pause. The Sentry is overcome, fumbles for words.
Kreon waits impassively.*)

                      out there —
                           someone, —
    New dust on the slimy flesh!

(*Pause. No sign from Kreon.*)

    Someone has given it burial that way, and
    Gone . . .

(*Long pause. Kreon finally speaks with deadly control.*)

KREON: And the man who dared do this?

SENTRY: I swear I
    Do not know! You must believe me!
                        Listen: 90
    The ground was dry, not a sign of digging, no,
    Not a wheeltrack in the dust, no trace of anyone.
    It was when they relieved us this morning: and one
      of them,
    The corporal, pointed to it.
                      There it was,
    The strangest —
               Look: 95
    The body, just mounded over with light dust: you
      see?
    Not buried really, but as if they'd covered it
    Just enough for the ghost's peace. And no sign
    Of dogs or any wild animal that had been there.

    And then what a scene there was! Every man of us   100
    Accusing the other: we all proved the other man
      did it.
    We all had proof that we could not have done it.
    We were ready to take hot iron in our hands,
    Walk through fire, swear by all the gods,
    It was not I!   105
    I do not know who it was, but it was not I!

(*Kreon's rage has been mounting steadily, but the Sentry
is too intent upon his story to notice it.*)

    And then, when this came to nothing, someone said
    A thing that silenced us and made us stare
    Down at the ground: you had to be told the news,
    And one of us had to do it! We threw the dice,   110
    And the bad luck fell to me. So here I am,
    No happier to be here than you are to have me:
    Nobody likes the man who brings bad news.

CHORAGOS: I have been wondering, King: can it be that
    the gods have done this?

KREON (*furiously*): Stop!   115
    Must you doddering wrecks

Go out of your heads entirely? "The gods"!
Intolerable!
The gods favor this corpse? Why? How had he
    served them?
120 Tried to loot their temples, burn their images,
Yes, and the whole State, and its laws with it!
Is it your senile opinion that the gods love to honor
    bad men?
A pious thought! —
                            No, from the very beginning
There have been those who have whispered
    together,
Stiff-necked anarchists, putting their heads
125 together,
Scheming against me in alleys. These are the men,
And they have bribed my own guard to do this
    thing.
(*Sententiously.*) Money!
There's nothing in the world so demoralizing as
    money.
130 Down go your cities,
Homes gone, men gone, honest hearts corrupted,
Crookedness of all kinds, and all for money!
(*To Sentry.*)   But you —
I swear by God and by the throne of God,
The man who has done this thing shall pay for it!
135 Find that man, bring him here to me, or your death
Will be the least of your problems: I'll string you up
Alive, and there will be certain ways to make you
Discover your employer before you die;
And the process may teach you a lesson you seem to
    have missed:
140 The dearest profit is sometimes all too dear:
That depends on the source. Do you understand
    me?
A fortune won is often misfortune.
SENTRY: King, may I speak?
KREON: Your very voice distresses me.
SENTRY: Are you sure that it is my voice, and not your
    conscience?
145 KREON: By God, he wants to analyze me now!
SENTRY: It is not what I say, but what has been done,
    that hurts you.
KREON: You talk too much.
SENTRY: Maybe; but I've done nothing.
KREON: Sold your soul for some silver: that's all you've
    done.
SENTRY: How dreadful it is when the right judge judges
    wrong!
150 KREON: Your figures of speech
May entertain you now; but unless you bring me the
    man,
You will get little profit from them in the end.
                                (*Exit Kreon into the palace.*)
SENTRY: "Bring me the man"— !
I'd like nothing better than bringing him the man!
But bring him or not, you have seen the last of me
155 here.
At any rate, I am safe!   (*Exit Sentry.*)

ODE° 1 • *Strophe 1*

CHORUS: Numberless are the world's wonders, but
    none
    More wonderful than man; the stormgray sea
    Yields to his prows, the huge crests bear him high;
    Earth, holy and inexhaustible, is graven
    With shining furrows where his plows have gone   5
    Year after year, the timeless labor of stallions.

Antistrophe 1

    The lightboned birds and beasts that cling to cover,
    The lithe fish lighting their reaches of dim water,
    All are taken, tamed in the net of his mind;
    The lion on the hill, the wild horse windy-maned,   10
    Resign to him; and his blunt yoke has broken
    The sultry shoulders of the mountain bull.

Strophe 2

    Words also, and thought as rapid as air,
    He fashions to his good use; statecraft is his
    And his the skill that deflects the arrows of snow, 15
    The spears of winter rain: from every wind
    He has made himself secure — from all but one:
    In the late wind of death he cannot stand.

Antistrophe 2

    O clear intelligence, force beyond all measure!
    O fate of man, working both good and evil!   20
    When the laws are kept, how proudly his city stands!
    When the laws are broken, what of his city then?
    Never may the anarchic man find rest at my hearth,
    Never be it said that my thoughts are his thoughts.

SCENE 2

(*Reenter Sentry leading Antigone.*)

CHORAGOS: What does this mean? Surely this captive
    woman
    Is the Princess, Antigone. Why should she be taken?
SENTRY: Here is the one who did it! We caught her
    In the very act of burying him. — Where is Kreon?
CHORAGOS: Just coming from the house.

(*Enter Kreon, center.*)

KREON: What has happened?   5
    Why have you come back so soon?
SENTRY (*expansively*):   O King,

Ode: Song sung by the Chorus.

A man should never be too sure of anything:
I would have sworn
That you'd not see me here again: your anger
Frightened me so, and the things you threatened me
10   with;
But how could I tell then
That I'd be able to solve the case so soon?
No dice-throwing this time: I was only too glad to
        come!
Here is this woman. She is the guilty one:
15   We found her trying to bury him.
Take her, then; question her; judge her as you will.
I am through with the whole thing now, and glad of
        it.
KREON: But this is Antigone! Why have you brought
        her here?
SENTRY: She was burying him, I tell you!
KREON (*severely*):   Is this the truth?
20 SENTRY: I saw her with my own eyes. Can I say more?
KREON: The details: come, tell me quickly!
SENTRY: It was like this:
After those terrible threats of yours, King,
We went back and brushed the dust away from the
        body.
The flesh was soft by now, and stinking,
25   So we sat on a hill to windward and kept guard.
No napping this time! We kept each other awake.
But nothing happened until the white round sun
Whirled in the center of the round sky over us:
Then, suddenly,
A storm of dust roared up from the earth, and the
30   sky
Went out, the plain vanished with all its trees
In the stinging dark. We closed our eyes and
        endured it.
The whirlwind lasted a long time, but it passed;
And then we looked, and there was Antigone!
35 I have seen
A mother bird come back to a stripped nest, heard
Her crying bitterly a broken note or two
For the young ones stolen. Just so, when this girl
Found the bare corpse, and all her love's work
        wasted,
40 She wept, and cried on heaven to damn the hands
That had done this thing.
                      And then she brought more dust
And sprinkled wine three times for her brother's
        ghost.
We ran and took her at once. She was not afraid,
Not even when we charged her with what she had
        done.
She denied nothing.
45   And this was a comfort to me,
And some uneasiness: for it is a good thing
To escape from death, but it is no great pleasure
To bring death to a friend.
                      Yet I always say
There is nothing so comfortable as your own safe
        skin!

KREON (*slowly, dangerously*): And you, Antigone,   50
You with your head hanging, — do you confess this
        thing?
ANTIGONE: I do. I deny nothing.
KREON (*to Sentry*):   You may go.
                              (*Exit Sentry.*)
(*To Antigone.*) Tell me, tell me briefly:
Had you heard my proclamation touching this
        matter?
ANTIGONE: It was public. Could I help hearing it?   55
KREON: And yet you dared defy the law.
ANTIGONE: I dared.
It was not God's proclamation. That final Justice
That rules the world below makes no such laws.

Your edict, King, was strong,
But all your strength is weakness itself against   60
The immortal unrecorded laws of God.
They are not merely now: they were, and shall be,
Operative for ever, beyond man utterly.

I knew I must die, even without your decree:
I am only mortal. And if I must die   65
Now, before it is my time to die,
Surely this is no hardship: can anyone
Living, as I live, with evil all about me,
Think Death less than a friend? This death of mine
Is of no importance; but if I had left my brother   70
Lying in death unburied, I should have suffered.
Now I do not.
                You smile at me. Ah Kreon,
Think me a fool, if you like; but it may well be
That a fool convicts me of folly.
CHORAGOS: Like father, like daughter: both headstrong,
        deaf to reason!   75
She has never learned to yield.
KREON: She has much to learn.
The inflexible heart breaks first, the toughest iron
Cracks first, and the wildest horses bend their necks
At the pull of the smallest curb.
                              Pride? In a slave?
This girl is guilty of a double insolence,   80
Breaking the given laws and boasting of it.
Who is the man here,
She or I, if this crime goes unpunished?
Sister's child, or more than sister's child,
Or closer yet in blood — she and her sister   85
Win bitter death for this!
(*To Servants.*)   Go, some of you,
Arrest Ismene. I accuse her equally.
Bring her: you will find her sniffling in the house
        there.

Her mind's a traitor: crimes kept in the dark
Cry for light, and the guardian brain shudders;   90
But how much worse than this
Is brazen boasting of barefaced anarchy!
ANTIGONE: Kreon, what more do you want than my
        death?

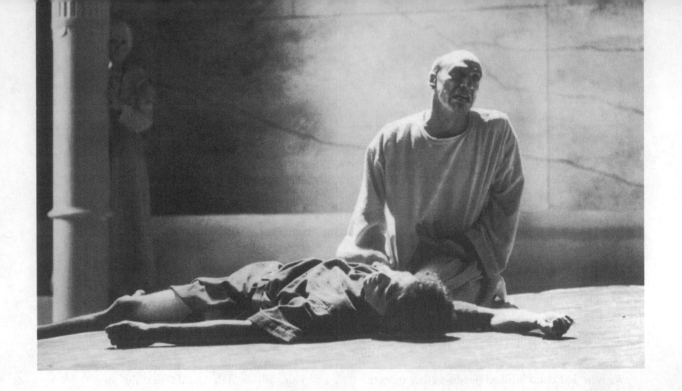

TOP: Kreon (F. Murray
Abraham) in a scene from the
1982 New York Shakespeare
Festival production directed by
Joseph Chaikin. RIGHT:
Antigone (Lisa Banes)
steadfastly admitting her guilt.

The Chorus urges Kreon to change his decree before it is too late.

KREON: Nothing.
    That gives me everything.
ANTIGONE: Then I beg you: kill me.
95 This talking is a great weariness: your words
    Are distasteful to me, and I am sure that mine
    Seem so to you. And yet they should not seem so:
    I should have praise and honor for what I have
        done.
    All these men here would praise me
100 Were their lips not frozen shut with fear of you.
    (*Bitterly.*) Ah the good fortune of kings,
    Licensed to say and do whatever they please!
KREON: You are alone here in that opinion.
ANTIGONE: No, they are with me. But they keep their
        tongues in leash.
105 KREON: Maybe. But you are guilty, and they are not.
ANTIGONE: There is no guilt in reverence for the dead.
KREON: But Eteocles — was he not your brother too?

ANTIGONE: My brother too.
KREON: And you insult his memory?
ANTIGONE (*softly*): The dead man would not say that I
        insult it.
KREON: He would: for you honor a traitor as much as
        him.   110
ANTIGONE: His own brother, traitor or not, and equal
        in blood.
KREON: He made war on his country. Eteocles defended
        it.
ANTIGONE: Nevertheless, there are honors due all the
        dead.
KREON: But not the same for the wicked as for the
        just.
ANTIGONE: Ah Kreon, Kreon,   115
    Which of us can say what the gods hold wicked?
KREON: An enemy is an enemy, even dead.
ANTIGONE: It is my nature to join in love, not hate.

KREON (*finally losing patience*): Go join them then; if
      you must have your love,
120   Find it in hell!
CHORAGOS: But see, Ismene comes:

(*Enter Ismene, guarded.*)

      Those tears are sisterly, the cloud
      That shadows her eyes rains down gentle sorrow.
KREON: You too, Ismene,
125   Snake in my ordered house, sucking my blood
      Stealthily — and all the time I never knew
      That these two sisters were aiming at my throne!
                                                    Ismene,
      Do you confess your share in this crime, or deny it?
      Answer me.
130 ISMENE: Yes, if she will let me say so. I am guilty.
ANTIGONE (*coldly*): No, Ismene. You have no right to
      say so.
      You would not help me, and I will not have you
      help me.
ISMENE: But now I know what you meant; and I am
      here
      To join you, to take my share of punishment.
ANTIGONE: The dead man and the gods who rule the
      dead
135   Know whose act this was. Words are not friends.
ISMENE: Do you refuse me, Antigone? I want to die
      with you:
      I too have a duty that I must discharge to the dead.
ANTIGONE: You shall not lessen my death by sharing it.
140 ISMENE: What do I care for life when you are dead?
ANTIGONE: Ask Kreon. You're always hanging on his
      opinions.
ISMENE: You are laughing at me. Why, Antigone?
ANTIGONE: It's a joyless laughter, Ismene.
ISMENE: But can I do nothing?
ANTIGONE: Yes. Save yourself. I shall not envy you.
      There are those who will praise you; I shall have
145   honor, too.
ISMENE: But we are equally guilty!
ANTIGONE: No more, Ismene.
      You are alive, but I belong to Death.
KREON (*to the Chorus*): Gentlemen, I beg you to
      observe these girls:
      One has just now lost her mind; the other,
150   It seems, has never had a mind at all.
ISMENE: Grief teaches the steadiest minds to waver,
      King.
KREON: Yours certainly did, when you assumed guilt
      with the guilty!
ISMENE: But how could I go on living without her?
KREON: You are.
      She is already dead.
ISMENE: But your own son's bride!
KREON: There are places enough for him to push his
155   plow.
      I want no wicked women for my sons!
ISMENE: O dearest Haimon, how your father wrongs
      you!

KREON: I've had enough of your childish talk of
      marriage!
CHORAGOS: Do you really intend to steal this girl from
      your son?
KREON: No; Death will do that for me.
CHORAGOS: Then she must die?   160
KREON (*ironically*): You dazzle me.
                          — But enough of this talk!
      (*To Guards.*) You, there, take them away and guard
      them well:
      For they are but women, and even brave men run
      When they see Death coming.
            (*Exeunt° Ismene, Antigone, and Guards.*)

ODE 2 • Strophe 1

CHORUS: Fortunate is the man who has never tasted
      God's vengeance!
      Where once the anger of heaven has struck, that
      house is shaken
      For ever: damnation rises behind each child
      Like a wave cresting out of the black northeast,
      When the long darkness under sea roars up   5
      And bursts drumming death upon the windwhipped
      sand.

Antistrophe 1

      I have seen this gathering sorrow from time long
      past
      Loom upon Oedipus' children: generation from
      generation
      Takes the compulsive rage of the enemy god.
      So lately this last flower of Oedipus' line   10
      Drank the sunlight! but now a passionate word
      And a handful of dust have closed up all its beauty.

Strophe 2

      What mortal arrogance
      Transcends the wrath of Zeus?
      Sleep cannot lull him nor the effortless long months 15
      Of the timeless gods: but he is young for ever,
      And his house is the shining day of high Olympos.
          All that is and shall be,
          And all the past, is his.
      No pride on earth is free of the curse of heaven.   20

Antistrophe 2

      The straying dreams of men
          May bring them ghosts of joy:
      But as they drowse, the waking embers burn them;

165. [S.D.] *Exeunt:* Latin for "they go out."

Or they walk with fixed eyes, as blind men walk.
25   But the ancient wisdom speaks for our own time:
        Fate works most for woe
        With Folly's fairest show.
     Man's little pleasure is the spring of sorrow.

SCENE 3

CHORAGOS: But here is Haimon, King, the last of all
        your sons.
     Is it grief for Antigone that brings him here,
     And bitterness at being robbed of his bride?

(*Enter Haimon.*)

KREON: We shall soon see, and no need of diviners.
                                                — Son,
5   You have heard my final judgment on that girl:
     Have you come here hating me, or have you come
     With deference and with love, whatever I do?
HAIMON: I am your son, father. You are my guide.
     You make things clear for me, and I obey you.
     No marriage means more to me than your
10   continuing wisdom.
KREON: Good. That is the way to behave: subordinate
     Everything else, my son, to your father's will.
     This is what a man prays for, that he may get
     Sons attentive and dutiful in his house,
15   Each one hating his father's enemies,
     Honoring his father's friends. But if his sons
     Fail him, if they turn out unprofitably,
     What has he fathered but trouble for himself
     And amusement for the malicious?
                                So you are right
20   Not to lose your head over this woman.
     Your pleasure with her would soon grow cold,
        Haimon,
     And then you'd have a hellcat in bed and
        elsewhere.
     Let her find her husband in Hell!
     Of all the people in this city, only she
25   Has had contempt for my law and broken it.

     Do you want me to show myself weak before the
        people?
     Or to break my sworn word? No, and I will not.
     The woman dies.
     I suppose she'll plead "family ties." Well, let her.
30   If I permit my own family to rebel,
     How shall I earn the world's obedience?
     Show me the man who keeps his house in hand,
     He's fit for public authority.
                                I'll have no dealings
     With lawbreakers, critics of the government:
35   Whoever is chosen to govern should be obeyed —
     Must be obeyed, in all things, great and small,
     Just and unjust! O Haimon,
     The man who knows how to obey, and that man
        only,

Knows how to give commands when the time
        comes.
     You can depend on him, no matter how fast   40
     The spears come: he's a good soldier, he'll stick it
        out.
     Anarchy, anarchy! Show me a greater evil!
     This is why cities tumble and the great houses rain
        down,
     This is what scatters armies!
     No, no: good lives are made so by discipline.   45
     We keep the laws then, and the lawmakers,
     And no woman shall seduce us. If we must lose,
     Let's lose to a man, at least! Is a woman stronger
        than we?
CHORAGOS: Unless time has rusted my wits,
     What you say, King, is said with point and dignity. 50
HAIMON (*boyishly earnest*): Father:
     Reason is God's crowning gift to man, and you are
        right
     To warn me against losing mine. I cannot say —
     I hope that I shall never want to say! — that you
     Have reasoned badly. Yet there are other men   55
     Who can reason, too; and their opinions might be
        helpful.
     You are not in a position to know everything
     That people say or do, or what they feel:
     Your temper terrifies — everyone
     Will tell you only what you like to hear.   60
     But I, at any rate, can listen; and I have heard them
     Muttering and whispering in the dark about this girl.
     They say no woman has ever, so unreasonably,
     Died so shameful a death for a generous act:
     "She covered her brother's body. Is this indecent?   65
     She kept him from dogs and vultures. Is this a
        crime?
     Death? — She should have all the honor that we can
        give her!"

     This is the way they talk out there in the city.
     You must believe me:
     Nothing is closer to me than your happiness.   70
     What could be closer? Must not any son
     Value his father's fortune as his father does his?
     I beg you, do not be unchangeable:
     Do not believe that you alone can be right.
     The man who thinks that,   75
     The man who maintains that only he has the power
     To reason correctly, the gift to speak, the soul —
     A man like that, when you know him, turns out
        empty.
     It is not reason never to yield to reason!

     In flood time you can see how some trees bend,   80
     And because they bend, even their twigs are safe,
     While stubborn trees are torn up, roots and all.
     And the same thing happens in sailing:
     Make your sheet fast, never slacken, — and over
        you go,
     Head over heels and under: and there's your voyage. 85

Forget you are angry! Let yourself be moved!
I know I am young; but please let me say this:
The ideal condition
Would be, I admit, that men should be right by
    instinct;
90   But since we are all too likely to go astray,
The reasonable thing is to learn from those who can
    teach.
CHORAGOS: You will do well to listen to him, King,
If what he says is sensible. And you, Haimon,
Must listen to your father. — Both speak well.
KREON: You consider it right for a man of my years
95   and experience
To go to school to a boy?
HAIMON: It is not right
If I am wrong. But if I am young, and right,
What does my age matter?
KREON: You think it right to stand up for an anarchist?
100 HAIMON: Not at all. I pay no respect to criminals.
KREON: Then she is not a criminal?
HAIMON: The City would deny it, to a man.
KREON: And the City proposes to teach me how to rule?
HAIMON: Ah. Who is it that's talking like a boy now?
KREON: My voice is the one voice giving orders in this
105   City!
HAIMON: It is no City if it takes orders from one voice.
KREON: The State is the King!
HAIMON: Yes, if the State is a desert.

(*Pause.*)

KREON: This boy, it seems, has sold out to a woman.
HAIMON: If you are a woman: my concern is only for
        you.
KREON: So? Your "concern"! In a public brawl with
110   your father!
HAIMON: How about you, in a public brawl with
        justice?
KREON: With justice, when all that I do is within my
        rights?
HAIMON: You have no right to trample on God's right.
KREON (*completely out of control*): Fool, adolescent
        fool! Taken in by a woman!
115 HAIMON: You'll never see me taken in by anything vile.
KREON: Every word you say is for her!
HAIMON (*quietly, darkly*):   And for you.
    And for me. And for the gods under the earth.
KREON: You'll never marry her while she lives.
HAIMON: Then she must die. — But her death will
        cause another.
120 KREON: Another?
        Have you lost your senses? Is this an open threat?
HAIMON: There is no threat in speaking to emptiness.
KREON: I swear you'll regret this superior tone of
        yours!
        You are the empty one!
HAIMON: If you were not my father,
125   I'd say you were perverse.
KREON: You girl-struck fool, don't play at words with
        me!

HAIMON: I am sorry. You prefer silence.
KREON: Now, by God —
I swear, by all the gods in heaven above us,
You'll watch it, I swear you shall!
(*To the Servants.*)   Bring her out!
Bring the woman out! Let her die before his eyes!   130
Here, this instant, with her bridegroom beside her!
HAIMON: Not here, no; she will not die here, King.
And you will never see my face again.
Go on raving as long as you've a friend to endure
        you.   (*Exit Haimon.*)
CHORAGOS: Gone, gone.   135
Kreon, a young man in a rage is dangerous!
KREON: Let him do, or dream to do, more than a man
        can.
He shall not save these girls from death.
CHORAGOS: These girls?
You have sentenced them both?
KREON: No, you are right.
I will not kill the one whose hands are clean.   140
CHORAGOS: But Antigone?
KREON (*somberly*):   I will carry her far away
Out there in the wilderness, and lock her
Living in a vault of stone. She shall have food,
As the custom is, to absolve the State of her death.
And there let her pray to the gods of hell: 145
They are her only gods:
Perhaps they will show her an escape from death,
Or she may learn,
                        though late,
That piety shown the dead is pity in vain.
                                        (*Exit Kreon.*)

ODE 3 • *Strophe*

CHORUS: Love, unconquerable
    Waster of rich men, keeper
    Of warm lights and all-night vigil
    In the soft face of a girl:
    Sea-wanderer, forest-visitor!   5
    Even the pure Immortals cannot escape you,
    And mortal man, in his one day's dusk,
    Trembles before your glory.

Antistrophe

    Surely you swerve upon ruin
    The just man's consenting heart,   10
    As here you have made bright anger
    Strike between father and son —
    And none has conquered but Love!
    A girl's glance working the will of heaven:
    Pleasure to her alone who mocks us,   15
    Merciless Aphrodite.°

16. **Aphrodite:** Goddess of love and beauty.

SCENE 4

CHORAGOS (*as Antigone enters guarded*): But I can no
longer stand in awe of this,
Nor, seeing what I see, keep back my tears.
Here is Antigone, passing to that chamber
Where all find sleep at last.

Strophe 1

5 ANTIGONE: Look upon me, friends, and pity me
Turning back at the night's edge to say
Good-by to the sun that shines for me no longer;
Now sleepy Death
Summons me down to Acheron,° that cold shore:
10 There is no bridesong there, nor any music.
CHORUS: Yet not unpraised, not without a kind of
honor,
You walk at last into the underworld
Untouched by sickness, broken by no sword.
What woman has ever found your way to death?

Antistrophe 1

15 ANTIGONE: How often I have heard the story of Niobe,°
Tantalos' wretched daughter, how the stone
Clung fast about her, ivy-close: and they say
The rain falls endlessly
And sifting soft snow; her tears are never done.
20 I feel the loneliness of her death in mine.
CHORUS: But she was born of heaven, and you
Are woman, woman-born. If her death is yours,
A mortal woman's, is this not for you
Glory in our world and in the world beyond?

Strophe 2

25 ANTIGONE: You laugh at me. Ah, friends, friends,
Can you not wait until I am dead? O Thebes,
O men many-charioted, in love with Fortune,
Dear springs of Dirce, sacred Theban grove,
Be witnesses for me, denied all pity,
30 Unjustly judged! and think a word of love
For her whose path turns
Under dark earth, where there are no more tears.
CHORUS: You have passed beyond human daring and
come at last
Into a place of stone where Justice sits.
35 I cannot tell
What shape of your father's guilt appears in this.

9. **Acheron:** River in Hades, domain of the dead.   15. **Niobe:**
When Niobe's many children (up to twenty in some accounts)
were slain in punishment for their mother's boastfulness, Niobe
was turned into a stone on Mount Sipylus. Her tears became
the mountain's streams.

Antistrophe 2

ANTIGONE: You have touched it at last: that bridal bed
Unspeakable, horror of son and mother mingling:
Their crime, infection of all our family!
O Oedipus, father and brother!   40
Your marriage strikes from the grave to murder
mine.
I have been a stranger here in my own land:
All my life
The blasphemy of my birth has followed me.
CHORUS: Reverence is a virtue, but strength   45
Lives in established law: that must prevail.
You have made your choice,
Your death is the doing of your conscious hand.

Epode°

ANTIGONE: Then let me go, since all your words are
bitter,
And the very light of the sun is cold to me.   50
Lead me to my vigil, where I must have
Neither love nor lamentation; no song, but silence.

(*Kreon interrupts impatiently.*)

KREON: If dirges and planned lamentations could put
off death,
Men would be singing for ever.
(*To the Servants.*)   Take her, go!
You know your orders: take her to the vault   55
And leave her alone there. And if she lives or dies,
That's her affair, not ours: our hands are clean.
ANTIGONE: O tomb, vaulted bride-bed in eternal rock,
Soon I shall be with my own again
Where Persephone° welcomes the thin ghosts
underground: 60
And I shall see my father again, and you, mother,
And dearest Polyneices —
dearest indeed
To me, since it was my hand
That washed him clean and poured the ritual wine:
And my reward is death before my time!   65

And yet, as men's hearts know, I have done no
wrong,
I have not sinned before God. Or if I have,
I shall know the truth in death. But if the guilt
Lies upon Kreon who judged me, then, I pray,
May his punishment equal my own.
CHORAGOS: O passionate heart, 70
Unyielding, tormented still by the same winds!
KREON: Her guards shall have good cause to regret
their delaying.
ANTIGONE: Ah! That voice is like the voice of death!

Epode: Song sung by the Chorus while standing still after
singing the strophe and antistrophe.   60. **Persephone:** Abducted by Pluto, god of the underworld, to be his queen.

KREON: I can give you no reason to think you are
      mistaken.
75 ANTIGONE: Thebes, and you my fathers' gods,
      And rulers of Thebes, you see me now, the last
      Unhappy daughter of a line of kings,
      Your kings, led away to death. You will remember
      What things I suffer, and at what men's hands,
80   Because I would not transgress the laws of heaven.
      (*To the Guards, simply.*) Come: let us wait no
         longer.   (*Exit Antigone, left, guarded.*)

ODE 4 • *Strophe 1*

CHORUS: All Danae's beauty was locked away
      In a brazen cell where the sunlight could not come:
      A small room still as any grave, enclosed her.
      Yet she was a princess too,
5   And Zeus in a rain of gold poured love upon her.°
      O child, child,
      No power in wealth or war
      Or tough sea-blackened ships
      Can prevail against untiring Destiny!

Antistrophe 1

10   And Dryas's son° also, that furious king,
      Bore the god's prisoning anger for his pride:
      Sealed up by Dionysos in deaf stone,
      His madness died among echoes.
      So at the last he learned what dreadful power
15   His tongue had mocked:
      For he had profaned the revels,
      And fired the wrath of the nine
      Implacable Sisters° that love the sound of the flute.

Strophe 2

      And old men tell a half-remembered tale
20   Of horror° where a dark ledge splits the sea
      And a double surf beats on the gray shores:
      How a king's new woman, sick
      With hatred for the queen he had imprisoned,
      Ripped out his two sons' eyes with her bloody
         hands

1–5. **All Danae's beauty . . . poured love upon her:** Locked
away to prevent the fulfillment of a prophecy that she would
bear a son who would kill her father, Danae was nonetheless
impregnated by Zeus, who came to her in a shower of gold.
The prophecy was fulfilled by the son that came of their union.
10. Dryas's son: King Lycurgus of Thrace, whom Dionysus,
god of wine, caused to be stricken with madness.   **18. Sisters:**
The Muses, nine sister goddesses who presided over poetry and
music, arts and sciences.   **19–20. half-remembered tale of horror:** The second wife of King Phineas blinded the sons of his
first wife, Cleopatra, whom Phineas had imprisoned in a cave.

      While grinning Ares° watched the shuttle plunge   25
      Four times: four blind wounds crying for revenge,

Antistrophe 2

      Crying, tears and blood mingled. — Piteously born,
      Those sons whose mother was of heavenly birth!
      Her father was the god of the North Wind
      And she was cradled by gales,   30
      She raced with young colts on the glittering hills
      And walked untrammeled in the open light:
      But in her marriage deathless Fate found means
      To build a tomb like yours for all her joy.

SCENE 5

(*Enter blind Teiresias, led by a boy. The opening speeches
of Teiresias should be in singsong contrast to the realistic lines of Kreon.*)

TEIRESIAS: This is the way the blind man comes,
      Princes, Princes,
      Lockstep, two heads lit by the eyes of one.
KREON: What new thing have you to tell us, old
      Teiresias?
TEIRESIAS: I have much to tell you: listen to the prophet,
      Kreon.
KREON: I am not aware that I have ever failed to listen.   5
TEIRESIAS: Then you have done wisely, King, and ruled
      well.
KREON: I admit my debt to you. But what have you to
      say?
TEIRESIAS: This, Kreon: you stand once more on the
      edge of fate.
KREON: What do you mean? Your words are a kind of
      dread.
TEIRESIAS: Listen, Kreon: 10
      I was sitting in my chair of augury, at the place
      Where the birds gather about me. They were all a-
         chatter,
      As is their habit, when suddenly I heard
      A strange note in their jangling, a scream, a
      Whirring fury; I knew that they were fighting,   15
      Tearing each other, dying
      In a whirlwind of wings clashing. And I was afraid.
      I began the rites of burnt-offering at the altar
      But Hephaistos° failed me: instead of bright flame,
      There was only the sputtering slime of the fat
         thigh-flesh   20
      Melting: the entrails dissolved in gray smoke,
      The bare bone burst from the welter. And no blaze!

      This was a sign from heaven. My boy described it,
      Seeing for me as I see for others.
      I tell you, Kreon, you yourself have brought   25

25. **Ares:** God of war.   **Scene 5, 9. Hephaistos:** God of fire.

This new calamity upon us. Our hearths and altars
Are stained with the corruption of dogs and carrion
    birds
That glut themselves on the corpse of Oedipus's son.
The gods are deaf when we pray to them, their fire
30 Recoils from our offering, their birds of omen
Have no cry of comfort, for they are gorged
With the thick blood of the dead.
                            O my son,
These are no trifles! Think: all men make mistakes,
But a good man yields when he knows his course is
    wrong,
35 And repairs the evil. The only crime is pride.

Give in to the dead man, then: do not fight with a
    corpse —
What glory is it to kill a man who is dead?
Think, I beg you:
It is for your own good that I speak as I do.
40 You should be able to yield for your own good.
KREON: It seems that prophets have made me their
    especial province.
All my life long
I have been a kind of butt for the dull arrows
Of doddering fortune-tellers!
                        No, Teiresias:
45 If your birds — if the great eagles of God himself
Should carry him stinking bit by bit to heaven,
I would not yield. I am not afraid of pollution:
No man can defile the gods.
                        Do what you will,
Go into business, make money, speculate
50 In India gold or that synthetic gold from Sardis,
Get rich otherwise than by my consent to bury him.
Teiresias, it is a sorry thing when a wise man
Sells his wisdom, lets out his words for hire!
TEIRESIAS: Ah Kreon! Is there no man left in the
    world —
KREON: To do what? — Come, let's have the
55   aphorism!
TEIRESIAS: No man who knows that wisdom outweighs
    any wealth?
KREON: As surely as bribes are baser than any
    baseness.
TEIRESIAS: You are sick, Kreon! You are deathly sick!
KREON: As you say: it is not my place to challenge a
    prophet.
60 TEIRESIAS: Yet you have said my prophecy is for sale.
KREON: The generation of prophets has always loved
    gold.
TEIRESIAS: The generation of kings has always loved
    brass.
KREON: You forget yourself! You are speaking to your
    King.
TEIRESIAS: I know it. You are a king because of me.
65 KREON: You have a certain skill; but you have sold out.
TEIRESIAS: King, you will drive me to words that —
KREON: Say them, say them!
Only remember: I will not pay you for them.

TEIRESIAS: No, you will find them too costly.
KREON: No doubt. Speak:
Whatever you say, you will not change my will.
TEIRESIAS: Then take this, and take it to heart!   70
The time is not far off when you shall pay back
Corpse for corpse, flesh of your own flesh.
You have thrust the child of this world into living
    night,
You have kept from the gods below the child that is
    theirs:
The one in a grave before her death, the other,   75
Dead, denied the grave. This is your crime:
And the Furies° and the dark gods of Hell
Are swift with terrible punishment for you.

Do you want to buy me now, Kreon?

                            Not many days,
And your house will be full of men and women
    weeping,   80
And curses will be hurled at you from far
Cities grieving for sons unburied, left to rot
Before the walls of Thebes.

These are my arrows, Kreon: they are all for you.

(*To Boy.*) But come, child: lead me home.   85
Let him waste his fine anger upon younger men.
Maybe he will learn at last
To control a wiser tongue in a better head.

                            (*Exit Teiresias.*)

CHORAGOS: The old man has gone, King, but his
    words
Remain to plague us. I am old, too,   90
But I cannot remember that he was ever false.
KREON: That is true. . . . It troubles me.
Oh it is hard to give in! but it is worse
To risk everything for stubborn pride.
CHORAGOS: Kreon: take my advice.
KREON: What shall I do?   95
CHORAGOS: Go quickly: free Antigone from her
    vault
And build a tomb for the body of Polyneices.
KREON: You would have me do this!
CHORAGOS: Kreon, yes!
And it must be done at once: God moves
Swiftly to cancel the folly of stubborn men.   100
KREON: It is hard to deny the heart! But I
Will do it: I will not fight with destiny.
CHORAGOS: You must go yourself, you cannot leave it
    to others.
KREON: I will go.
                    — Bring axes, servants:
Come with me to the tomb. I buried her, I   105

---

77. **Furies:** Spirits called on to avenge crimes, especially those
against kin.

Will set her free.
                    Oh quickly!
My mind misgives —
The laws of the gods are mighty, and a man must
      serve them
To the last day of his life!   (*Exit Kreon.*)

PAEAN° • *Strophe 1*

CHORAGOS: God of many names
CHORUS: O Iacchos
                                        son
   of Kadmeian Semele
                         O born of the Thunder!
   Guardian of the West
                         Regent
   of Eleusis' plain
                     O Prince of maenad Thebes
5   and the Dragon Field by rippling Ismenos:°

Antistrophe 1

CHORAGOS: God of many names
CHORUS: the flame of torches
      flares on our hills
                         the nymphs of Iacchos
   dance at the spring of Castalia:°
   from the vine-close mountain
                              come ah come in ivy:
10   *Evohe evohe!*° sings through the streets of Thebes

Strophe 2

CHORAGOS: God of many names
CHORUS: Iacchos of Thebes
      heavenly Child
                     of Semele bride of the Thunderer!
   The shadow of plague is upon us:
                                   come
   with clement feet
                     oh come from Parnasos
   down the long slopes
                         across the lamenting water
15

Paean: A song of praise or prayer.   **1–5. God of many names . . . rippling Ismenos:** The following is a litany of names for Dionysus (Iacchos): he was son of Zeus ("Thunder") and Semele; he was honored in secret rites at Eleusis; and he was worshiped by the Maenads of Thebes. Kadmos, Semele's father, sowed dragon's teeth in a field beside the river Ismenos from which sprang warriors who became the first Thebans.   **8. spring of Castalia:** A spring on Mount Parnassus used by priestesses of Dionysus in rites of purification.   **10.** *Evohe evohe!*: Cry of the Maenads to Dionysus.

Antistrophe 2

CHORAGOS: Io Fire! Chorister of the throbbing stars!
   O purest among the voices of the night!
   Thou son of God, blaze for us!
CHORUS: Come with choric rapture of circling Maenads
   Who cry *Io Iacche!*°
                 God of many names!   20

EXODOS°

(*Enter Messenger from left.*)

MESSENGER: Men of the line of Kadmos, you who live
   Near Amphion's citadel,°
                        I cannot say
   Of any condition of human life "This is fixed,
   This is clearly good, or bad." Fate raises up,
   And Fate casts down the happy and unhappy alike: 5
   No man can foretell his Fate.
                        Take the case of Kreon:
   Kreon was happy once, as I count happiness:
   Victorious in battle, sole governor of the land,
   Fortunate father of children nobly born.
   And now it has all gone from him! Who can say   10
   That a man is still alive when his life's joy fails?
   He is a walking dead man. Grant him rich,
   Let him live like a king in his great house:
   If his pleasure is gone, I would not give
   So much as the shadow of smoke for all he owns.   15
CHORAGOS: Your words hint at sorrow: what is your
      news for us?
MESSENGER: They are dead. The living are guilty of
      their death.
CHORAGOS: Who is guilty? Who is dead? Speak!
MESSENGER: Haimon.
   Haimon is dead; and the hand that killed him
   Is his own hand.
CHORAGOS: His father's? or his own?   20
MESSENGER: His own, driven mad by the murder his
      father had done.
CHORAGOS: Teiresias, Teiresias, how clearly you saw it
      all!
MESSENGER: This is my news: you must draw what
      conclusions you can from it.
CHORAGOS: But look: Eurydice, our Queen:
   Has she overheard us?   25

(*Enter Eurydice from the palace, center.*)

EURYDICE: I have heard something, friends:
   As I was unlocking the gate of Pallas'° shrine,
   For I needed her help today, I heard a voice
   Telling of some new sorrow. And I fainted

20. *Io Iacche!*: Ritual cry.   **Exodos:** Final scene.   **2. Amphion's citadel:** A name for Thebes.   **27. Pallas:** Pallas Athene, goddess of wisdom.

30   There at the temple with all my maidens about me.
        But speak again: whatever it is, I can bear it:
        Grief and I are no strangers.
MESSENGER: Dearest Lady,
        I will tell you plainly all that I have seen.
        I shall not try to comfort you: what is the use,
35   Since comfort could lie only in what is not true?
        The truth is always best.
                                I went with Kreon
        To the outer plain where Polyneices was lying,
        No friend to pity him, his body shredded by dogs.
        We made our prayers in that place to Hecate
40   And Pluto,° that they would be merciful. And we
                bathed
        The corpse with holy water, and we brought
        Fresh-broken branches to burn what was left of it,
        And upon the urn we heaped up a towering barrow
        Of the earth of his own land.
                                When we were done, we ran
        To the vault where Antigone lay on her couch of
45   stone.
        One of the servants had gone ahead,
        And while he was yet far off he heard a voice
        Grieving within the chamber, and he came back
        And told Kreon. And as the King went closer,
50   The air was full of wailing, the words lost,
        And he begged us to make all haste. "Am I a
                prophet?"
        He said, weeping, "And must I walk this road,
        The saddest of all that I have gone before?
        My son's voice calls me on. Oh quickly, quickly!
55   Look through the crevice there, and tell me
        If it is Haimon, or some deception of the gods!"

        We obeyed; and in the cavern's farthest corner
        We saw her lying:
        She had made a noose of her fine linen veil
60   And hanged herself. Haimon lay beside her,
        His arms about her waist, lamenting her,
        His love lost under ground, crying out
        That his father had stolen her away from him.

        When Kreon saw him the tears rushed to his eyes
        And he called to him: "What have you done, child?
65   speak to me.
        What are you thinking that makes your eyes so
                strange?
        O my son, my son, I come to you on my knees!"
        But Haimon spat in his face. He said not a word,
        Staring —
                And suddenly drew his sword
        And lunged. Kreon shrank back, the blade missed;
70   and the boy,
        Desperate against himself, drove it half its length

39–40. Hecate and Pluto: Goddess of witchcraft and sorcery
and King of Hades, the underworld.

        Into his own side, and fell. And as he died
        He gathered Antigone close in his arms again,
        Choking, his blood bright red on her white cheek.
        And now he lies dead with the dead, and she is his   75
        At last, his bride in the house of the dead.

                        (*Exit Eurydice into the palace.*)

CHORAGOS: She has left us without a word. What can
        this mean?
MESSENGER: It troubles me, too; yet she knows what is
        best,
        Her grief is too great for public lamentation,
        And doubtless she has gone to her chamber to
                weep   80
        For her dead son, leading her maidens in his dirge.

(*Pause.*)

CHORAGOS: It may be so: but I fear this deep silence.
MESSENGER: I will see what she is doing. I will go in.

                        (*Exit Messenger into the palace.*)

(*Enter Kreon with attendants, bearing Haimon's body.*)

CHORAGOS: But here is the king himself: oh look at
        him,
        Bearing his own damnation in his arms.   85
KREON: Nothing you say can touch me any more.
        My own blind heart has brought me
        From darkness to final darkness. Here you see
        The father murdering, the murdered son —
        And all my civic wisdom!   90

        Haimon my son, so young, so young to die,
        I was the fool, not you; and you died for me.
CHORAGOS: That is the truth; but you were late in
        learning it.
KREON: This truth is hard to bear. Surely a god
        Has crushed me beneath the hugest weight of
                heaven,   95
        And driven me headlong a barbaric way
        To trample out the thing I held most dear.

        The pains that men will take to come to pain!

(*Enter Messenger from the palace.*)

MESSENGER: The burden you carry in your hands is
        heavy,
        But it is not all: you will find more in your house.   100
KREON: What burden worse than this shall I find there?
MESSENGER: The Queen is dead.
KREON: O port of death, deaf world,
        Is there no pity for me? And you, Angel of evil,
        I was dead, and your words are death again.   105
        Is it true, boy? Can it be true?
        Is my wife dead? Has death bred death?
MESSENGER: You can see for yourself.

(*The doors are opened and the body of Eurydice is disclosed within.*)

KREON: Oh pity!
110   All true, all true, and more than I can bear!
   O my wife, my son!
MESSENGER: She stood before the altar, and her heart
   Welcomed the knife her own hand guided,
   And a great cry burst from her lips for Megareus°
     dead,
115   And for Haimon dead, her sons; and her last breath
   Was a curse for their father, the murderer of her sons.
   And she fell, and the dark flowed in through her
     closing eyes.
KREON: O God, I am sick with fear.
   Are there no swords here? Has no one a blow for
     me?
MESSENGER: Her curse is upon you for the deaths of
120   both.
KREON: It is right that it should be. I alone am guilty.
   I know it, and I say it. Lead me in,
   Quickly, friends.
   I have neither life nor substance. Lead me in.

---

114. **Megareus:** Son of Kreon and brother of Haimon, Megareus sacrificed himself in the unsuccessful attack upon Thebes, believing that his death was necessary to save Thebes.

CHORAGOS: You are right, if there can be right in so
   much wrong.   125
   The briefest way is best in a world of sorrow.
KREON: Let it come,
   Let death come quickly, and be kind to me.
   I would not ever see the sun again.
CHORAGOS: All that will come when it will; but we,
   meanwhile,   130
   Have much to do. Leave the future to itself.
KREON: All my heart was in that prayer!
CHORAGOS: Then do not pray any more: the sky is deaf.
KREON: Lead me away. I have been rash and foolish.
   I have killed my son and my wife.   135
   I look for comfort; my comfort lies here dead.
   Whatever my hands have touched has come to
     nothing.
   Fate has brought all my pride to a thought of dust.

(*As Kreon is being led into the house, the Choragos advances and speaks directly to the audience.*)

CHORAGOS: There is no happiness where there is no
   wisdom;
   No wisdom but in submission to the gods.   140
   Big words are always punished,
   And proud men in old age learn to be wise.

COMMENTARIES

    Oliver Taplin's emphasis on the audience's emotional state during the performance of a Greek tragedy brings us back to the seminal comments of Aristotle. Tragedies were noted for their capacity to invoke pity and fear in the audience. Taplin helps us understand how an audience's emotional response can clarify our critical view of tragedy.

    Jean Anouilh, a major French playwright in the mid-twentieth century, wrote a version of *Antigone* during the Nazi occupation of Paris and much of France. The political content of the play takes on interesting meaning in light of his experience. The excerpt that appears here offers a modern interpretation of the struggle between Antigone and Kreon.

Oliver Taplin (b. 1943)
EMOTION AND MEANING IN GREEK TRAGEDY   1983

Scholar Oliver Taplin focuses on one of Aristotle's concerns in his commentary on tragedy: the emotions aroused by drama. Taplin explores the argument that devalues an emotional response to tragedy, and then he considers the proposition that "tragedy is essentially the emotional experience of its audience."

It seems to me, then, that Gorgias° is right that tragedy is essentially the *emotional experience of its audience.* Whatever it tells us about the world is conveyed by means of these emotions. Plato agreed with Gorgias in this, but he disapproved of the process and regarded it as harmful. Aristotle agreed with him too, but, contrary to Plato, regarded it as beneficial and salutary. Plato's objection was that such emotions are not the province of the highest part of the soul, the intellectual part. This is the forefather of the error made by so many later critics who have not acknowledged the centrality of emotion in the communication of tragedy. They think that if tragedy is essentially an emotional experience, it must be *solely* that; and they think this because they assume that strong emotion is necessarily in opposition to thought, that the psychic activities are mutually exclusive. But is this right? Understanding, reason, learning, moral discrimination; these things are not, in my experience, incompatible with emotion (nor presumably in the experience of Gorgias and Aristotle): What is incompatible is cold insensibility. Whether or not emotion is inimical to such intellectual processes depends on the *circumstances in which it is aroused.*

The characteristic tragic emotions — pity, horror, fascination, indignation, and so forth — are felt in many other situations besides in the theater. Above all we suffer them in the face of the misfortunes of real life, of course. What distinguishes the experience of a great tragedy? For one thing, as already remarked, we feel for the fortunes of people who have no direct personal relation to us: While this does not decrease the intensity of the emotion, it affords us some distance and perspective. We can feel and at the same time observe from outside. But does this distinguish tragedy from other "contrived" emotional experiences (most of them tending to the anti-intellectual), for example an animal hunt, a football match, an encounter group, reading a thriller, or watching a horror movie? Well, the experience of tragedy is by no means a random series of sensations. Our emotional involvement has perspective and context at the same time, and not just in retrospect. Thus the events of the tragedy are in an ordered *sequence,* a sequence which gives shape and comprehensibility to what we feel. And, most important of all, the affairs of the characters which move us are given a moral setting which is argued and explored in the play. They act and suffer within situations of moral conflict, or social, intellectual, and theological conflict. The quality of the tragedy depends *both* on its power to arouse our emotions *and* on the setting of those emotions in a sequence of moral and intellectual complications which is set out and examined. Tragedy evokes our feelings for others, like much else; but it is distinguished by the order and significance it imparts to suffering. So if the audience is not moved, then the tragedy,

Gorgias: Greek orator and rhetorician (c. 483–376 B.C.).

however intellectual, is a total failure: If its passions are aroused, but in a thoughtless, amorphous way, then it is merely a bad tragedy, sensational, melodramatic.

Thus it is that our emotions in the theater, far from driving out thought and meaning, are indivisible from them: They are simultaneous and mutually dependent. The experience of tragedy can achieve this coherence in a way that the emotional experiences of real life generally cannot because they are too close, too cluttered with detail and partiality, to be seen in perspective. Tragedy makes us feel that we understand life in its tragic aspects. We have the sense that we can better sympathize with and cope with suffering, misfortune, and waste. It is this sense of understanding (not isolated pearls of wisdom) that is the "message" of a tragedy, that the great playwright imparts. This is well put in T. S. Eliot's essay "Shakespeare and the Stoicism of Seneca," where he argues that it is the quality of the emotional expression rather than the quality of the philosophy which makes literature great, which makes it "strong, true and informative . . . useful and beneficial in the sense in which poetry is useful and beneficial." "All great poetry," Eliot° writes, "gives the illusion of a view of life . . . for every precise emotion tends towards intellectual formulation."

T. S. Eliot: Poet and critic (1888–1965).

Jean Anouilh (1910–1987)
FROM *ANTIGONE*   *1942*

TRANSLATED BY LEWIS GALANTIÈRE

Jean Anouilh began writing plays in 1931. Some of his best-known works, in addition to Antigone, *are* Eurydice *(1941),* Orestes *(1942),* Medea *(1946),* Ring Round the Moon *(1947),* The Waltz of the Toreadors *(1951), and* The Lark *(1952), which is about Joan of Arc. Anouilh wrote* Antigone *in 1942 in occupied Paris and produced it with his wife in the title role in February 1944, when the Nazis controlled most of Europe. Kreon (spelled Creon in this excerpt) is more willing to compromise in Anouilh's version of the play, and for that reason some critics saw the play as pro-Nazi. But Anouilh's sympathies were with Antigone, who represented the anti-Nazi view of the Parisian Resistance. Throughout its early run, the play was an inspiration to the patriotic French.*

This excerpt begins when Ismene returns to accept some of the responsibility for Polyneices' burial and continues through the confrontation of Haimon (Haemon in this excerpt) and Kreon to the end of the play.

(*Ismene enters through arch.*)

ISMENE (*distraught*): Antigone!
ANTIGONE (*turns to Ismene*): You, too? What do you want?
ISMENE: Oh, forgive me, Antigone. I've come back. I'll be brave. I'll go with you now.
ANTIGONE: Where will you go with me?
ISMENE (*to Creon*): Creon! If you kill her, you'll have to kill me too.
ANTIGONE: Oh, no, Ismene. Not a bit of it. I die alone. You don't think I'm going to let you die with me after what I've been through? You don't deserve it.

ISMENE: If you die, I don't want to live. I don't want to be left behind, alone.

ANTIGONE: You chose life and I chose death. Now stop blubbering. You had your chance to come with me in the black night, creeping on your hands and knees. You had your chance to claw up the earth with your nails, as I did; to get yourself caught like a thief, as I did. And you refused it.

ISMENE: Not anymore. I'll do it alone tonight.

ANTIGONE (*turns round toward Creon*): You hear that, Creon? The thing is catching! Who knows but that lots of people will catch the disease from me! What are you waiting for? Call in your guards! Come on, Creon! Show a little courage! It only hurts for a minute! Come on, cook!

CREON (*turns toward arch and calls*): Guard!

(*Guards enter through arch.*)

ANTIGONE (*in a great cry of relief*): At last, Creon!

(*Chorus enters through left arch.*)

CREON (*to the Guards*): Take her away! (*Creon goes up on top step.*)

(*Guards grasp Antigone by her arms, turn and hustle her toward the arch, right, and exeunt.° Ismene mimes horror, backs away toward the arch, left, then turns and runs out through the arch. A long pause, as Creon moves slowly downstage.*)

CHORUS (*Behind Creon. Speaks in a deliberate voice*): You are out of your mind, Creon. What have you done?

CREON (*his back to Chorus*): She had to die.

CHORUS: You must not let Antigone die. We shall carry the scar of her death for centuries.

CREON: She insisted. No man on earth was strong enough to dissuade her. Death was her purpose, whether she knew it or not. Polynices was a mere pretext. When she had to give up that pretext, she found another one — that life and happiness were tawdry things and not worth possessing. She was bent upon only one thing: to reject life and to die.

CHORUS: She is a mere child, Creon.

CREON: What do you want me to do for her? Condemn her to live?

HAEMON (*calls from offstage*): Father! (*Haemon enters through arch, right. Creon turns toward him.*)

CREON: Haemon, forget Antigone. Forget her, my dearest boy.

HAEMON: How can you talk like that?

CREON (*grasps Haemon by the hands*): I did everything I could to save her, Haemon. I used every argument. I swear I did. The girl doesn't love you. She could have gone on living for you; but she refused. She wanted it this way; she wanted to die.

HAEMON: Father! The guards are dragging Antigone away! You've got to stop them! (*He breaks away from Creon.*)

CREON (*looks away from Haemon*): I can't stop them. It's too late. Antigone has spoken. The story is all over Thebes. I cannot save her now.

CHORUS: Creon, you must find a way. Lock her up. Say that she has gone out of her mind.

CREON: Everybody will know it isn't so. The nation will say that I am making an exception of her because my son loves her. I cannot.

CHORUS: You can still gain time and get her out of Thebes.

CREON: The mob already knows the truth. It is howling for her blood. I can do nothing.

HAEMON: But, Father, you are master in Thebes!

CREON: I am master under the law. Not above the law.

HAEMON: You cannot let Antigone be taken from me. I am your son!

CREON: I cannot do anything else, my poor boy. She must die and you must live.

HAEMON: Live, you say! Live a life without Antigone? A life in which I am to go on admiring you as you busy yourself about your kingdom, make your persuasive

exeunt: Latin for "they go out."

speeches, strike your attitudes? Not without Antigone. I love Antigone. I will not live without Antigone!

CREON: Haemon — you will have to resign yourself to life without Antigone. (*He moves to left of Haemon.*) Sooner or later there comes a day of sorrow in each man's life when he must cease to be a child and take up the burden of manhood. That day has come for you.

HAEMON (*backs away a step*): That giant strength, that courage. That massive god who used to pick me up in his arms and shelter me from shadows and monsters — was that you, Father? Was it of you I stood in awe? Was that man you?

CREON: For God's sake, Haemon, do not judge me! Not you, too!

HAEMON (*pleading now*): This is all a bad dream, Father. You are not yourself. It isn't true that we have been backed up against a wall, forced to surrender. We don't have to say *yes* to this terrible thing. You are still king. You are still the father I revered. You have no right to desert me, to shrink into nothingness. The world will be too bare, I shall be too alone in the world, if you force me to disown you.

CREON: The world *is* bare, Haemon, and you *are* alone. You must cease to think your father all-powerful. Look straight at me. See your father as he is. That is what it means to grow up and be a man.

HAEMON (*stares at Creon for a moment*): I tell you that I will not live without Antigone. (*Turns and goes quickly out through arch.*)

CHORUS: Creon, the boy will go mad.

CREON: Poor boy! He loves her.

CHORUS: Creon, the boy is wounded to death.

CREON: We are all wounded to death.

(*First Guard enters through arch, right, followed by Second and Third Guards pulling Antigone along with them.*)

FIRST GUARD: Sir, the people are crowding into the palace!

ANTIGONE: Creon, I don't want to see their faces. I don't want to hear them howl. You are going to kill me; let that be enough. I want to be alone until it is over.

CREON: Empty the palace! Guards at the gates!

(*Creon quickly crosses toward the arch; exit. Two Guards release Antigone; exeunt behind Creon. Chorus goes out through arch, left. The lighting dims so that only the area about the table is lighted. The cyclorama° is covered with a dark blue color. The scene is intended to suggest a prison cell, filled with shadows and dimly lit. Antigone moves to stool and sits. The First Guard stands upstage. He watches Antigone, and as she sits, he begins pacing slowly downstage, then upstage. A pause.*)

ANTIGONE (*turns and looks at the Guard*): It's you, is it?

GUARD: What do you mean, me?

ANTIGONE: The last human face that I shall see. (*A pause as they look at each other, then Guard paces upstage, turns, and crosses behind table.*) Was it you that arrested me this morning?

GUARD: Yes, that was me.

ANTIGONE: You hurt me. There was no need for you to hurt me. Did I act as if I was trying to escape?

GUARD: Come on now, Miss. It was my business to bring you in. I did it. (*A pause. He paces to and fro upstage. Only the sound of his boots is heard.*)

ANTIGONE: How old are you?

GUARD: Thirty-nine.

ANTIGONE: Have you any children?

GUARD: Yes. Two.

ANTIGONE: Do you love your children?

GUARD: What's that got to do with you? (*A pause. He paces upstage and downstage.*)

ANTIGONE: How long have you been in the Guard?

---

cyclorama: Curved cloth or wall forming the back of many modern stage settings.

GUARD: Since the war. I was in the army. Sergeant. Then I joined the Guard.

ANTIGONE: Does one have to have been an army sergeant to get into the Guard?

GUARD: Supposed to be. Either that or on special detail. But when they make you a guard, you lose your stripes.

ANTIGONE (*murmurs*): I see.

GUARD: Yes. Of course, if you're a guard, everybody knows you're something special; they know you're an old N.C.O.° Take pay, for instance. When you're a guard you get your pay, and on top of that you get six months' extra pay, to make sure you don't lose anything by not being a sergeant anymore. And of course you do better than that. You get a house, coal, rations, extras for the wife and kids. If you've got two kids, like me, you draw better than a sergeant.

ANTIGONE (*barely audible*): I see.

GUARD: That's why sergeants, now, they don't like guards. Maybe you noticed they try to make out they're better than us? Promotion, that's what it is. In the army, anybody can get promoted. All you need is good conduct. Now in the Guard, it's slow, and you have to know your business — like how to make out a report and the like of that. But when you're an N.C.O. in the Guard, you've got something that even a sergeant major ain't got. For instance —

ANTIGONE (*breaking him off*): Listen.

GUARD: Yes, Miss.

ANTIGONE: I'm going to die soon.

(*The Guard looks at her for a moment, then turns and moves away.*)

GUARD: For instance, people have a lot of respect for guards, they have. A guard may be a soldier, but he's kind of in the civil service, too.

ANTIGONE: Do you think it hurts to die?

GUARD: How would I know? Of course, if somebody sticks a saber in your guts and turns it round, it hurts.

ANTIGONE: How are they going to put me to death?

GUARD: Well, I'll tell you. I heard the proclamation all right. Wait a minute. How did it go now? (*He stares into space and recites from memory.*) "In order that our fair city shall not be pol-luted with her sinful blood, she shall be im-mured — immured." That means, they shove you in a cave and wall up the cave.

ANTIGONE: Alive?

GUARD: Yes. . . . (*He moves away a few steps.*)

ANTIGONE (*murmurs*): O tomb! O bridal bed! Alone! (*Antigone sits there, a tiny figure in the middle of the stage. You would say she felt a little chilly. She wraps her arms round herself.*)

GUARD: Yes! Outside the southeast gate of the town. In the Cave of Hades. In broad daylight. Some detail, eh, for them that's on the job! First they thought maybe it was a job for the army. Now it looks like it's going to be the Guard. There's an outfit for you! Nothing the Guard can't do. No wonder the army's jealous.

ANTIGONE: A pair of animals.

GUARD: What do you mean, a pair of animals?

ANTIGONE: When the winds blow cold, all they need do is to press close against one another. I am all alone.

GUARD: Is there anything you want? I can send out for it, you know.

ANTIGONE: You are very kind. (*A pause. Antigone looks up at the Guard.*) Yes, there is something I want. I want you to give someone a letter from me, when I am dead.

GUARD: How's that again? A letter?

ANTIGONE: Yes, I want to write a letter; and I want you to give it to someone for me.

GUARD (*straightens up*): Now, wait a minute. Take it easy. It's as much as my job is worth to go handing out letters from prisoners.

ANTIGONE (*removes a ring from her finger and holds it out toward him*): I'll give you this ring if you will do it.

N.C.O.: Noncommissioned officer, usually of a subordinate rank such as sergeant.

GUARD: Is it gold? (*He takes the ring from her.*)

ANTIGONE: Yes, it is gold.

GUARD (*shakes his head*): Uh-uh. No can do. Suppose they go through my pockets. I might get six months for a thing like that. (*He stares at the ring, then glances off right to make sure that he is not being watched.*) Listen, tell you what I'll do. You tell me what you want to say, and I'll write it down in my book. Then, afterwards, I'll tear out the pages and give them to the party, see? If it's in my handwriting, it's all right.

ANTIGONE (*winces*): In your handwriting? (*She shudders slightly.*) No. That would be awful. The poor darling! In your handwriting.

GUARD (*offers back the ring*): O.K. It's no skin off my nose.

ANTIGONE (*quickly*): Of course, of course. No, keep the ring. But hurry. Time is getting short. Where is your notebook? (*The Guard pockets the ring, takes his notebook and pencil from his pocket, puts his foot up on chair, and rests the notebook on his knee, licks his pencil.*) Ready? (*He nods.*) Write, now. "My darling . . ."

GUARD (*writes as he mutters*): The boyfriend, eh?

ANTIGONE: "My darling. I wanted to die, and perhaps you will not love me anymore . . ."

GUARD (*mutters as he writes*): ". . . will not love me anymore."

ANTIGONE: "Creon was right. It is terrible to die."

GUARD (*repeats as he writes*): ". . . terrible to die."

ANTIGONE: "And I don't even know what I am dying for. I am afraid . . ."

GUARD (*looks at her*): Wait a minute! How fast do you think I can write?

ANTIGONE (*takes hold of herself*): Where are you?

GUARD (*reads from his notebook*): "And I don't even know what I am dying for."

ANTIGONE: No. Scratch that out. Nobody must know that. They have no right to know. It's as if they saw me naked and touched me, after I was dead. Scratch it all out. Just write: "Forgive me."

GUARD (*looks at Antigone*): I cut out everything you said there at the end, and I put down, "Forgive me"?

ANTIGONE: Yes. "Forgive me, my darling. You would all have been so happy except for Antigone. I love you."

GUARD (*finishes the letter*): ". . . I love you." (*He looks at her.*) Is that all?

ANTIGONE: That's all.

GUARD (*straightens up, looks at notebook*): Damn funny letter.

ANTIGONE: I know.

GUARD (*looks at her*): Who is it to? (*A sudden roll of drums begins and continues until after Antigone's exit. The First Guard pockets the notebook and shouts at Antigone.*) O.K. That's enough out of you! Come on!

(*At the sound of the drum roll, Second and Third Guards enter through the arch. Antigone rises. Guards seize her and exeunt with her. The lighting moves up to suggest late afternoon. Chorus enters.*)

CHORUS: And now it is Creon's turn.

(*Messenger runs through the arch, right.*)

MESSENGER: The Queen . . . the Queen! Where is the Queen?

CHORUS: What do you want with the Queen? What have you to tell the Queen?

MESSENGER: News to break her heart. Antigone had just been thrust into the cave. They hadn't finished heaving the last block of stone into place when Creon and the rest heard a sudden moaning from the tomb. A hush fell over us all, for it was not the voice of Antigone. It was Haemon's voice that came forth from the tomb. Everybody looked at Creon; and he howled like a man demented: "Take away the stones! Take away the stones!" The slaves leaped at the wall of stones, and Creon worked with them, sweating and tearing at the blocks with his bleeding hands. Finally a narrow opening was forced, and into it slipped the smallest guard.

Antigone had hanged herself by the cord of her robe, by the red and golden twisted cord of her robe. The cord was round her neck like a child's collar. Haemon was on his knees, holding her in his arms and moaning, his face buried in her robe. More stones were removed, and Creon went into the tomb. He tried to raise Haemon to his feet. I could hear him begging Haemon to rise to his feet. Haemon was deaf to his father's voice, till suddenly he stood up of his own accord, his eyes dark and burning. Anguish was in his face, but it was the face of a little boy. He stared at his father. Then suddenly he struck him — hard; and he drew his sword. Creon leaped out of range. Haemon went on staring at him, his eyes full of contempt — a glance that was like a knife, and that Creon couldn't escape. The King stood trembling in the far corner of the tomb, and Haemon went on staring. Then, without a word, he stabbed himself and lay down beside Antigone, embracing her in a great pool of blood.

(*A pause as Creon and Page enter through arch on the Messenger's last words. Chorus and the Messenger both turn to look at Creon; then exit the Messenger through curtain.*)

CREON: I have had them laid out side by side. They are together at last, and at peace. Two lovers on the morrow of their bridal. Their work is done.

CHORUS: But not yours, Creon. You have still one thing to learn. Eurydice, the Queen, your wife —

CREON: A good woman. Always busy with her garden, her preserves, her sweaters — those sweaters she never stopped knitting for the poor. Strange, how the poor never stop needing sweaters. One would almost think that was all they needed.

CHORUS: The poor in Thebes are going to be cold this winter, Creon. When the Queen was told of her son's death, she waited carefully until she had finished her row, then put down her knitting calmly — as she did everything. She went up to her room, her lavender-scented room, with its embroidered doilies and its pictures framed in plush; and there, Creon, she cut her throat. She is laid out now in one of those two old-fashioned twin beds, exactly where you went to her one night when she was still a maiden. Her smile is still the same, scarcely a shade more melancholy. And if it were not for that great red blot on the bed linen by her neck, one might think she was asleep.

CREON (*in a dull voice*): She, too. They are all asleep. (*Pause.*) It must be good to sleep.

CHORUS: And now you are alone, Creon.

CREON: Yes, all alone. (*To Page.*) My lad.

PAGE: Sir?

CREON: Listen to me. They don't know it, but the truth is, the work is there to be done, and a man can't fold his arms and refuse to do it. They say it's dirty work. But if we didn't do it, who would?

PAGE: I don't know, sir.

CREON: Of course you don't. You'll be lucky if you never find out. In a hurry to grow up, aren't you?

PAGE: Oh, yes, sir.

CREON: I shouldn't be if I were you. Never grow up if you can help it. (*He is lost in thought as the hour chimes.*) What time is it?

PAGE: Five o clock, sir.

CREON: What have we on at five o'clock?

PAGE: Cabinet meeting, sir.

CREON: Cabinet meeting. Then we had better go along to it.

(*Exeunt Creon and Page slowly through arch, left, and Chorus moves downstage.*)

CHORUS: And there we are. It is quite true that if it had not been for Antigone they would all have been at peace. But that is over now. And they are all at peace. All those who were meant to die have died: those who believed one thing, those who believed the contrary thing, and even those who believed nothing at all, yet were caught up in the web without knowing why. All dead: stiff, useless, rotting. And those who have survived will now begin quietly to forget the dead: they won't remember who was who or which was which. It is all over. Antigone is calm tonight, and we shall never know the name of the fever that consumed her. She has played her part.

(*Three Guards enter, resume their places on steps as at the rise of the curtain, and begin to play cards.*)

A great melancholy wave of peace now settles down upon Thebes, upon the empty palace, upon Creon, who can now begin to wait for his own death. Only the guards are left, and none of this matters to them. It's no skin off their noses. They go on playing cards.

(*Chorus walks toward the arch, left, as the curtain falls.*)

Aristophanes

The best known of the Greek comic playwrights, Aristophanes (c. 448–c. 385 B.C.) lived through some of the most difficult times in Athenian history. He watched Athenian democracy fade and decay as factionalism and war took their toll on the strength of the city-state. By the time he died, Athens was caught up in a fierce struggle between supporters of democracy and supporters of oligarchy, government by a small group of leaders.

Aristophanes' plays are democratic in that they appealed to sophisticated and unsophisticated theatergoers alike. Skilled at complex wordplay, he also enjoyed spirited and rowdy comedy. Since his plays were often sharply critical of Athenian policies, his ability to make people laugh was essential to conveying his message. He was a practitioner of what we now call Old Comedy, an irreverent form that ridiculed and insulted prominent people and important institutions. By Aristophanes' time, Old Comedy had become fiercely satirical, especially concerning political matters. Because Aristophanes held strong opinions, he found satire an ideal form for his talents.

Of his more than thirty known plays, only eleven survive. They come from three main periods in his life, beginning, according to legend, when he was a young man, in 427 B.C. *The Acharnians* (425 B.C.), from his first period, focuses on the theme of peace. Dicaeopolis (whose name means "honest" or "good citizen") decides to make a separate peace after the Spartans have ravaged the Acharnian vineyards. The Acharnians vow revenge, but Dicaeopolis explains that peace must begin as an individual decision. Aristophanes saw war as a corporate venture; peacemaking was easier for an individual than for a group or a nation.

The Acharnians was followed by *The Peace* in 421 B.C., just before Sparta and Athens signed a treaty, and it seems clearly to have been written in support of the Athenian peace party, whose power had been growing from the time of *The Acharnians* and whose cause had been aided by that play.

His second period was also dominated by the problems of war. Athens's ill-fated expedition to Sicily in violation of the Treaty of Nicias lies thematically beneath the surface of *The Birds* (414 B.C.), in which some citizens build Cloud-Cuckoo-Land to come between the world of humans and the world of the gods. *Lysistrata* (411 B.C.) is also from this period; its frank antiwar theme is related to the Sicilian wars and to the ultimately devastating Peloponnesian Wars. These were wars fought by Greek city-states in the areas south of Athens, the Peloponneus. The states had voluntarily contributed money to arm and support Athens against the Persians in 480 B.C. — resulting in the Athenian victory at Salamis. The states later became angry when Pericles, the Athenian leader, demanded that they continue giving contributions, much of which he used to fund the rebuilding of the Akropolis and other civic projects in Athens.

The other Greek city-states felt that Athens was becoming imperialistic and was overreaching itself. War broke out between the city-states in 431 B.C. and lasted for nearly thirty years. These struggles and the difficulties of conducting a costly, long-distance war in Sicily combined eventually to exhaust the Athenian resources of men and funds. Soundly defeated in 405 B.C., Athens surrendered to Sparta in 404. Aristophanes lived to see the Spartan ships at rest in the harbors of Athens's chief port, the Piraeus. And he saw, too, the destruction of the walls of the city, leaving it essentially defenseless.

Aristophanes' third and final period, from 393 B.C. to his death, includes *The Ecclesiazusae* (c. 392 B.C.) (translated as "The Women in Government"), in which women dress as men, find their way into parliament, and pass a new constitution. It is a highly topical play that points to the current situation in Athens and the people's general discontent and anxiety. The last part of *The Plutus,* written five years later, is an allegory about the god of wealth, who is eventually encouraged to make the just wealthy and the unjust poor.

Among the best known of Aristophanes' plays are several whose names refer to the disguises or costumes of the chorus, among them *The Knights, The Wasps,* and *The Frogs. The Frogs* (405 B.C.) is especially interesting for its focus on literary issues. It features a contest in the underworld between Aeschylus, who had been dead more than fifty years, and Euripides, who had just died at a relatively young age. Aristophanes uses the contest to make many enlightening comments about Greek tragedy and the skills of the two authors.

Even in his last period Aristophanes was an innovative force in theater. His last surviving play virtually does away with the chorus as an important character in the action. His later plays resemble modern comedies partly because the chorus does not intrude in the action. His genius helped shape later developments in comedy.

LYSISTRATA

At the time *Lysistrata* was written (411 B.C.), Athens had had a steady diet of war for more than twenty years. Political groups were actively trying to persuade Athenian leaders to discontinue the policies that had alienated Athens from the other city-states that were once its supporters in the Delian League, the group that had funded Athens's struggle against the Persian threat. Aristophanes opposed the imperialist attitudes that conflicted with the democratic spirit of only a generation earlier.

Lysistrata makes it clear that war is the central business of the nation at that time. No sooner is one campaign ended than another begins. The men encountered by the heroine Lysistrata (whose name means "disband the army") on the Acropolis — men who guard the national security and the national treasury — are old and decrepit. The young men are in the field. As Kalonike tells Lysistrata, her man has been away for five months. Such separations were common, and these women are fed up. Lysistrata has gathered the discontented women together to propose a scheme to bring peace and negotiate a treaty.

The scheme is preposterous, but, typical of Old Comedy, its very outrageousness is its source of strength. In time, the idea begins to seem almost reasonable: Lysistrata asks the women to refuse to engage in sex with their husbands until the men stop making war. The women also seize the Acropolis and hold the treasury hostage. Without the national treasury there can be no war. And because they are confident of getting the support of the larger community of women in other nations — who suffer as they do — they do not fear the consequences of their acts.

In amusing scenes generated by this situation Aristophanes pokes fun at both sexes. We hear the gossipy conversation of the women, all of whom arrive late to Lysistrata's meeting. The men are dependent, helpless, ineffectual, and cannot resist the takeover. When the truth begins to settle in, the men solicit their wives' attention with enormous erections protruding beneath their gowns, one example of the exaggerated visual humor Aristophanes counted on. The double meanings in the conversations are also a great source of humor.

The wonderful scene (3) between Myrrhine and her husband Kinesias is predicated on the agony of the husband whose wife constantly promises, and then reneges, to build his sexual excitement to a fever pitch. It is no wonder that Lysistrata can eventually bring the men to sign any treaties she wants.

This heterosexual hilarity is also balanced by a number of homosexual allusions. Kleisthenes, possibly a bisexual Athenian, stands ready to relieve some of the men's sexual discomfort, while Lysistrata admits that if the men do not capitulate, the women will have to satisfy their own needs. Such frankness is typical of Athenian comedy.

Women dominate the action of the play, although we must remember that male actors played women's roles. The women see the stupidity and waste of the war and devise a plan that will end it. Observing that they are the ones who suffer most from the effects of war, the women also note that they pay their taxes in babies. The suffering of women had been a major theme in the tragedies of Euripides, and everyone in Aristophanes' audience would have understood Lysistrata's motivation. The idea that a woman should keep her place is expressed by several characters. And since Athenian audiences would have agreed that women should not meddle in war or government, Aristophanes offered them a fantasy that challenged them on many levels.

Aristophanes praises Lysistrata's ingenuity and her perseverance. When the other women want to give up the plan because of their own sexual needs, she holds firm. She demands that they stand by their resolve. The picture of a strong, independent, intelligent, and capable woman obviously pleased the Athenians because they permitted this play to be performed more than once — an unusual practice. Lysistrata became a recognizable and admirable character in Athenian life.

The following translation of *Lysistrata* has several interesting features. It is comprised of scenes, a division not made in the original Greek. The strophe and antistrophe are speeches given by the chorus, probably moving first in one direction and then in the opposite. Instead of having a chorus of elders, as in *Antigone,* Aristophanes uses two choruses — one of men and one of women — that are truly representative of the people: they are as divided and antagonistic as Sophocles' chorus is united and wise. The KORYPHAIOS (leader) of the men's chorus speaks alone, often in opposition to the koryphaios of the women's chorus.

The rhyming patterns of some of the songs are approximated in English, and the sense of dialect is maintained in the speech of Lampito, who represents a kind of country bumpkin. She is very muscular from the workouts that she and all other Spartans engaged in; Aristophanes reveals certain Athenian prejudices toward the Spartans in the scene where Lampito is taunted for her physique.

Lysistrata in Performance

Lysistrata has enjoyed and still enjoys numerous productions, both on college and commercial stages. Because it is a bawdy play, it has sometimes run into trouble. In 1932 the New York police shut down a performance and sent out a warrant for the arrest of "Arthur" Aristophanes. In 1959 Dudley Fitts's translation (used here) was performed at the Phoenix Theater in New York with "women . . . wearing simulated breasts, tipped with sequins, and the ruttish old men stripped down to union suits." Hunter College's 1968 production used rock music, hippie beads, and headbands. Less controversial productions include the first modern version, by Maurice Donnay in Paris (1892), in which Lysistrata takes a general as a lover. The Moscow Art Theater produced a highly acclaimed version in 1923 and brought it to the United States in 1925. That version, modified by Gilbert Seldes (published in book form with illustrations by Picasso), was produced throughout the 1930s. All-black versions of the play have been staged several times since 1938. *Lysistrata* ranks among the favorites of classical drama.

Aristophanes c. 448–c. 385 B.C.)

LYSISTRATA   *411 B.C.*

TRANSLATED BY DUDLEY FITTS

Persons Represented

LYSISTRATA,
KALONIKE, } *Athenian women*
MYRRHINE,
LAMPITO, *a Spartan woman*
CHORUS
COMMISSIONER
KINESIAS, *husband of Myrrhine*
SPARTAN HERALD
SPARTAN AMBASSADOR
A SENTRY
[BABY SON OF KENESIAS
STRATYLLIS
SPARTANS
ATHENIANS]

Scene: *Athens. First, a public square; later, beneath the walls of the Akropolis;° later, a courtyard within the Akropolis.*

Akropolis: Fortress of Athens, sacred to the goddess Athena.

PROLOGUE°

(*Athens; a public square; early morning; Lysistrata alone.*)

LYSISTRATA: If someone had invited them to a
            festival —
    of Bacchos,° say; or to Pan's° shrine, or to
            Aphrodite's°
    over at Kolias — , you couldn't get through the
            streets,
    what with the drums and the dancing. But now,
    not a woman in sight!
                            Except — oh, yes!   5

(*Enter Kalonike.*)

Prologue: Portion of the play explaining the background and current action.   **2. Bacchos:** (Bacchus) God of wine and the object of wild, orgiastic ritual and celebration; also called Dionysus.   **Pan:** God of nature, forests, flocks, and shepherds, depicted as half-man and half-goat. Pan was considered playful and lecherous.   **Aphrodite:** Goddess of love.

Here's one of my neighbors, at last. Good
    morning, Kalonike.
KALONIKE: Good morning, Lysistrata.
                                 Darling,
    don't frown so! You'll ruin your face!
LYSISTRATA: Never mind my face.
    Kalonike,
    the way we women behave! Really, I don't blame
10   the men
    for what they say about us.
KALONIKE: No; I imagine they're right.
LYSISTRATA: For example: I call a meeting
    to think out a most important matter — and
      what happens?
    The women all stay in bed!
KALONIKE: Oh, they'll be along.
15   It's hard to get away, you know: a husband, a cook,
    a child . . . Home life can be *so* demanding!
LYSISTRATA: What I have in mind is even more
      demanding.
KALONIKE: Tell me: what is it?
LYSISTRATA: It's big.
KALONIKE: Goodness! *How* big?
LYSISTRATA: Big enough for all of us.
KALONIKE: But we're not all here!
LYSISTRATA: We would be, if *that's* what was up!
20   No, Kalonike,
    this is something I've been turning over for nights,
    long sleepless nights.
KALONIKE: It must be getting worn down, then,
    if you've spent so much time on it.
LYSISTRATA: Worn down or not,
    it comes to this: Only we women can save Greece!
KALONIKE: Only we women? Poor Greece!
25 LYSISTRATA: Just the same,
    it's up to us. First, we must liquidate
    the Peloponnesians —
KALONIKE: Fun, fun!
LYSISTRATA: — and then the Boiotians.°
KALONIKE: Oh! But not those heavenly eels!
LYSISTRATA: You needn't worry.
    I'm not talking about eels. — But here's the point:
30   If we can get the women from those places —
    all those Boiotians and Peloponnesians —
    to join us women here, why, we can save all Greece!
KALONIKE: But dearest Lysistrata!
    How can women do a thing so austere, so
35   political? We belong at home. Our only armor's
    our perfumes, our saffron dresses and
    our pretty little shoes!
LYSISTRATA: Exactly. Those
    transparent dresses, the saffron, the perfume, those
      pretty shoes —
KALONIKE: Oh?
LYSISTRATA: Not a single man would lift
    his spear —

---

27. **Boiotians:** Crude-mannered inhabitants of Boiotia, which
was noted for its seafood.

KALONIKE: I'll send my dress to the dyer's tomorrow!
LYSISTRATA: — or grab a shield —
KALONIKE: The sweetest little negligee —   40
LYSISTRATA: — or haul out his sword.
KALONIKE: I know where
    I can buy the dreamiest sandals!
LYSISTRATA: Well, so you see. Now, shouldn't
    the women have come?
KALONIKE: Come? They should have *flown*!
LYSISTRATA: Athenians are always late.
                   But imagine!
    There's no one here from the South Shore, or from
      Salamis.   45
KALONIKE: Things are hard over in Salamis, I swear.
    They have to get going at dawn.
LYSISTRATA: And nobody from Acharnai.
    I thought they'd be here hours ago.
KALONIKE: Well, you'll get
    that awful Theagenes woman: she'll be
    a sheet or so in the wind.
                  But look!   50
    Someone at last! Can you see who they are?

(*Enter Myrrhine and other women.*)

LYSISTRATA: They're from Anagyros.
KALONIKE: They certainly are.
    You'd know them anywhere, by the scent.
MYRRHINE: Sorry to be late, Lysistrata.
                 Oh come,
    don't scowl so. Say something!
LYSISTRATA: My dear Myrrhine,   55
    what is there to say? After all,
    you've been pretty casual about the whole thing.
MYRRHINE: Couldn't find
    my girdle in the dark, that's all.
                  But what *is*
    "the whole thing"?
KALONIKE: No, we've got to wait
    for those Boiotians and Peloponnesians.   60
LYSISTRATA: That's more like it. — But, look!
    Here's Lampito!

(*Enter Lampito with women from Sparta.*)

LYSISTRATA: Darling Lampito,
    how pretty you are today! What a nice color!
    Goodness, you look as though you could strangle a
      bull!   65
LAMPITO: Ah think Ah could! It's the work-out
    in the gym every day; and, of co'se that dance of ahs
    where y' kick yo' own tail.
KALONIKE: What an adorable figure!
LAMPITO: Lawdy, when y' touch me lahk that,
    Ah feel lahk a heifer at the altar!
LYSISTRATA: And this young lady?   70
    Where is she from?
LAMPITO: Boiotia. Social-Register type.
LYSISTRATA: Ah. "Boiotia of the fertile plain."
KALONIKE: And if you look,
    you'll find the fertile plain has just been mowed.

LYSISTRATA: And this lady?

LAMPITO: Hagh, wahd, handsome.
75 She comes from Korinth.

KALONIKE: High and wide's the word for it.

LAMPITO: Which one of you
called this heah meeting, and why?

LYSISTRATA: I did.

LAMPITO: Well, then, tell us:
What's up?

MYRRHINE: Yes, darling, what *is* on your mind, after
all?

LYSISTRATA: I'll tell you. — But first, one little question.

MYRRHINE: Well?

LYSISTRATA: It's your husbands. Fathers of your
80   children. Doesn't it bother you
that they're always off with the Army? I'll stake my
life,
not one of you has a man in the house this minute!

KALONIKE: Mine's been in Thrace the last five months,
keeping an eye
on that General.

MYRRHINE: Mine's been in Pylos for seven.

LAMPITO: And mahn,
85 whenever he gets a *dis*charge, he goes raht back
with that li'l ole shield of his, and enlists again!

LYSISTRATA: And not the ghost of a lover to be found!
From the very day the war began —
those Milesians!
I could skin them alive!
— I've not seen so much, even,
90 as one of those leather consolation prizes. —
But there! What's important is: If I've found a way
to end the war, are you with me?

MYRRHINE: I should *say* so!
Even if I have to pawn my best dress and
drink up the proceeds.

KALONIKE: Me, too! Even if they split me
right up the middle, like a flounder.

95 LAMPITO: Ah'm shorely with you.
Ah'd crawl up Taygetos° on mah knees
if that'd bring peace.

LYSISTRATA: All right, then; here it is:
Women! Sisters!
If we really want our men to make peace,
we must be ready to give up —

100 MYRRHINE: Give up what?
Quick, tell us!

LYSISTRATA: But *will* you?

MYRRHINE: We will, even if it kills us.

LYSISTRATA: Then we must give up going to bed with
our men.

(*Long silence.*)

Oh? So now you're sorry? Won't look at me?
Doubtful? Pale? All teary-eyed?
But come: be frank with me.
Will you do it, or not? Well? Will you do it?

96. **Taygetos:** A mountain range.

MYRRHINE: I couldn't. No. 105
Let the war go on.

KALONIKE: Nor I. Let the war go on.

LYSISTRATA: You, you little flounder,
ready to be split up the middle?

KALONIKE: Lysistrata, no!
I'd walk through fire for you — you *know* I
would! — but don't
ask us to give up *that*! Why, there's nothing like it! 110

LYSISTRATA: And you?

BOIOTIAN: No. I must say *I'd* rather walk
through fire.

LYSISTRATA: What an utterly perverted sex we women
are!
No wonder poets write tragedies about us.
There's only one thing we can think of.
But you from Sparta:
if you stand by me, we may win yet! Will you? 115
It means so much!

LAMPITO: Ah sweah, it means *too* much!
By the Two Goddesses,° it does! Asking a girl
to sleep — Heaven knows how long! — in a great
big bed
with nobody there but herself! But Ah'll stay with
you!
Peace comes first!

LYSISTRATA: Spoken like a true Spartan! 120

KALONIKE: But if —
oh dear!
— if we give up what you tell us to,
will there *be* any peace?

LYSISTRATA: Why, mercy, of course there will!
We'll just sit snug in our very thinnest gowns,
perfumed and powdered from top to bottom, and
those men
simply won't stand still! And when we say No, 125
they'll go out of their minds! And there's your peace.
You can take my word for it.

LAMPITO: Ah seem to remember
that Colonel Menelaos threw his sword away
when he saw Helen's breast all bare.°

KALONIKE: But, goodness me!
What if they just get up and leave us?

LYSISTRATA: In that case 130
we'll have to fall back on ourselves, I suppose.
But they won't.

KALONIKE: I must say that's not much help. But
what if they drag us into the bedroom?

LYSISTRATA: Hang on to the door.

KALONIKE: What if they slap us?

LYSISTRATA: If they do, you'd better give in.
But be sulky about it. Do I have to teach you how? 135

117. **Two Goddesses:** A woman's oath referring to Demeter, the earth goddess, and her daughter Persephone, who was associated with seasonal cycles of fertility. **128–29. Colonel Menelaos . . . Helen's breast:** Helen, wife of King Menelaos of Sparta, was abducted by Paris and taken to Troy. The incident led to the Trojan War.

You know there's no fun for men when they have to
      force you.
There are millions of ways of getting them to see
      reason.
Don't you worry: a man
doesn't like it unless the girl cooperates.

140 KALONIKE: I suppose so. Oh, all right. We'll go along.
LAMPITO: Ah imagine us Spahtans can arrange a peace.
      But you
Athenians! Why, you're just war-mongerers!
LYSISTRATA: Leave that to me.
I know how to make them listen.
LAMPITO: Ah don't see how.
After all, they've got their boats; and there's lots of
      money
piled up in the Akropolis.

145 LYSISTRATA: The Akropolis? Darling,
we're taking over the Akropolis today!
That's the older women's job. All the rest of us
are going to the Citadel to sacrifice — you
      understand me?
And once there, we're in for good!
LAMPITO: Whee! Up the rebels!
Ah can see you're a good strate*egist.*

150 LYSISTRATA: Well, then, Lampito,
what we have to do now is take a solemn oath.
LAMPITO: Say it. We'll sweah.
LYSISTRATA: This is it.
      — But where's our Inner Guard?
                          — Look. Guard: you see this shield?
Put it down here. Now bring me the victim's
      entrails.
KALONIKE: But the oath?
LYSISTRATA: You remember how in Aischylos'
                                              Seven°
155
they killed a sheep and swore on a shield? Well, then?
KALONIKE: But I don't see how you can swear for
      peace on a shield.
LYSISTRATA: What else do you suggest?
KALONIKE: Why not a white horse?
We could swear by that.
LYSISTRATA: And where will you get a white horse?
KALONIKE: I never thought of that. *What* can we do?
160 LYSISTRATA: I have it!
Let's set this big black wine-bowl on the ground
and pour in a gallon or so of Thasian,° and swear
not to add one drop of water.
LAMPITO: Ah lahk *that* oath!
LYSISTRATA: Bring the bowl and the wine-jug.
KALONIKE: Oh, what a simply *huge* one!
LYSISTRATA: Set it down. Girls, place your hands on the
165   gift-offering.
O Goddess of Persuasion! And thou, O Loving-cup:
Look upon this our sacrifice, and
be gracious!

155. *Seven:* Aeschylus's *Seven against Thebes,* which deals with
the war between the sons of Oedipus for the throne of Thebes.
162. Thasian: Wine from Thasos.

KALONIKE: See the blood spill out. How red and pretty
      it is!
LAMPITO: And Ah must say it smells good.
MYRRHINE: Let me swear first! 170
KALONIKE: No, by Aphrodite, we'll match for it!
LYSISTRATA: Lampito: all of you women: come, touch
      the bowl,
and repeat after me — remember, this is an oath — :
I WILL HAVE NOTHING TO DO WITH MY
      HUSBAND OR MY LOVER
KALONIKE: *I will have nothing to do with my husband*
      or my lover   175
LYSISTRATA: THOUGH HE COME TO ME IN
      PITIABLE CONDITION
KALONIKE: *Though he come to me in pitiable condition*
      (Oh Lysistrata! This is killing me!)
LYSISTRATA: IN MY HOUSE I WILL BE
      UNTOUCHABLE
KALONIKE: *In my house I will be untouchable*   180
LYSISTRATA: IN MY THINNEST SAFFRON SILK
KALONIKE: *In my thinnest saffron silk*
LYSISTRATA: AND MAKE HIM LONG FOR ME.
KALONIKE: *And make him long for me.*
LYSISTRATA: I WILL NOT GIVE MYSELF   185
KALONIKE: *I will not give myself*
LYSISTRATA: AND IF HE CONSTRAINS ME
KALONIKE: *And if he constrains me*
LYSISTRATA: I WILL BE COLD AS ICE AND NEVER
      MOVE
KALONIKE: *I will be cold as ice and never move*   190
LYSISTRATA: I WILL NOT LIFT MY SLIPPERS
      TOWARD THE CEILING
KALONIKE: *I will not lift my slippers toward the ceiling*
LYSISTRATA: OR CROUCH ON ALL FOURS LIKE
      THE LIONESS IN THE CARVING
KALONIKE: *Or crouch on all fours like the lioness in*
      the carving
LYSISTRATA: AND IF I KEEP THIS OATH LET ME
      DRINK FROM THIS BOWL   195
KALONIKE: *And if I keep this oath let me drink from*
      this bowl
LYSISTRATA: IF NOT, LET MY OWN BOWL BE
      FILLED WITH WATER.
KALONIKE: *If not, let my own bowl be filled with*
      water.
LYSISTRATA: You have all sworn?
MYRRHINE: We have.
LYSISTRATA: Then thus
      I sacrifice the victim.

(*Drinks largely.*)

KALONIKE: Save some for us!   200
      Here's to you, darling, and to you, and to you!

(*Loud cries offstage.*)

LAMPITO: What's all *that* whoozy-goozy?
LYSISTRATA: Just what I told you.
The older women have taken the Akropolis.
Now you, Lampito,

rush back to Sparta. We'll take care of things here.
205   Leave
these girls here for hostages.
                                  The rest of you,
up to the Citadel: and mind you push in the bolts.

KALONIKE: But the men? Won't they be after us?

LYSISTRATA: Just you leave
the men to me. There's not fire enough in the world,
210   or threats either, to make me open these doors
except on my own terms.

KALONIKE: I hope not, by Aphrodite!
After all,
we've got a reputation for bitchiness to live up to.
                                          (*Exeunt.*°)

PARODOS:°
CHORAL EPISODE

(*The hillside just under the Akropolis. Enter Chorus of
Old Men with burning torches and braziers; much puffing and coughing.*)

KORYPHAIOS(man):° Forward march, Drakes, old friend:
      never you mind
that damn big log banging hell down on your back.

Strophe° 1

CHORUS(men): There's this to be said for longevity:
      You see things you thought that you'd never see.
5   Look, Strymodoros, who would have thought it?
      We've caught it —
                  the New Femininity!
The wives of our bosom, our board, our bed —
Now, by the gods, they've gone ahead
And taken the Citadel (Heaven knows why!),
10   Profanèd the sacred statuar-y,
                        And barred the doors,
                        The subversive whores!

KORYPHAIOS(m): Shake a leg there, Philurgos, man: the
      Akropolis or bust!
Put the kindling around here. We'll build one
      almighty big
15   bonfire for the whole bunch of bitches, every last one;
and the first we fry will be old Lykon's woman.

Antistrophe° 1

CHORUS(m): They're not going to give me the old horse-
      laugh!

No, by Demeter, they won't pull this off!
      Think of Kleomenes: even he
      Didn't go free
                        till he brought me his stuff.   20
A good man he was, all stinking and shaggy,
Bare as an eel except for the bag he
Covered his rear with. God, what a mess!
Never a bath in six years, I'd guess.
                        Pure Sparta, man!   25
                        He also ran.

KORYPHAIOS(m): That was a siege, friends! Seventeen
      ranks strong
we slept at the Gate. And shall we not do as much
against these women, whom God and Euripides hate?
If we don't, I'll turn in my medals from Marathon.   30

Strophe 2

CHORUS(m): Onward and upward! A little push,
      And we're there.
Ouch, my shoulders! I could wish
      For a pair
Of good strong oxen. Keep your eye   35
      On the fire there, it mustn't die.
            Akh! Akh!
The smoke would make a cadaver cough!

Antistrophe 2

Holy Herakles, a hot spark
      Bit my eye!   40
Damn this hellfire, damn this work!
      So say I.
Onward and upward just the same.
(Laches, remember the Goddess: for shame!)
            Akh! Akh!   45
The smoke would make a cadaver cough!

KORYPHAIOS(m): At last (and let us give suitable thanks
      to God
for his infinite mercies) I have managed to bring
my personal flame to the common goal. It breathes,
      it lives.
Now, gentlemen, let us consider. Shall we insert   50
the torch, say, into the brazier, and thus extract
a kindling brand? And shall we then, do you think,
push on to the gate like valiant sheep? On the whole
      yes.
But I would have you consider this, too: if they —
I refer to the women — should refuse to open,   55
what then? Do we set the doors afire
and smoke them out? At ease, men. Meditate.
Akh, the smoke! Woof! What we really need
is the loan of a general or two from the Samos
      Command.°
At least we've got this lumber off our backs.   60
That's something. And now let's look to our fire.

---

213. [S.D.] *Exeunt:* Latin for "they go out."   **Parodos:** The song
or ode chanted by the Chorus on their entry.   **1. Koryphaios:**
Leader of the Chorus; also called *Choragos.* There are two
Choruses and two Koryphaioi, one male and one female.
Strophe: Song sung by the Chorus as it danced from stage right
to stage left.   **Antistrophe:** Song sung by the Chorus following
the Strophe, as it danced back from stage left to stage right.

59. Samos Command: Headquarters of the Athenian military.

O Pot, brave Brazier, touch my torch with flame!
Victory, Goddess, I invoke thy name!
Strike down these paradigms of female pride
65 And we shall hang our trophies up inside.

(*Enter Chorus of Old Women on the walls of the Akropolis, carrying jars of water.*)

KORYPHAIOS(woman): Smoke, girls, smoke! There's smoke all over the place!
Probably fire, too. Hurry, girls! Fire! Fire!

Strophe 1

CHORUS(women): Nikodike, run!
Or Kalyke's done
70 To a turn, and poor Kritylla's
Smoked like a ham.
                    Damn
These old men! Are we too late?
I nearly died down at the place
Where we fill our jars:
75   Slaves pushing and jostling —
Such a hustling
I never saw in all my days.

Antistrophe 1

But here's water at last.
Haste, sisters, haste!
80 Slosh it on them, slosh it down,
The silly old wrecks!
                    Sex
Almighty! What they want's
A hot bath? Good. Send one down.
Athena of Athens town,
85   Trito-born!° Helm of Gold!
Cripple the old
Firemen! Help us help them drown!

(*The old men capture a woman, Stratyllis.*)

STRATYLLIS: Let me go! Let me go!
KORYPHAIOS(w):   You walking corpses,
have you no shame?
KORYPHAIOS(m):   I wouldn't have believed it!
90 An army of women in the Akropolis!
KORYPHAIOS(w): So we scare you, do we? Grandpa,
you've seen
only our pickets yet!
KORYPHAIOS(m):   Hey, Phaidrias!
Help me with the necks of these jabbering hens!
KORYPHAIOS(w): Down with your pots, girls! We'll need
both hands
if these antiques attack us!
95 KORYPHAIOS(m):   Want your face kicked in?
KORYPHAIOS(w): Want your balls chewed off?

85. **Trito-born:** Athena, goddess of wisdom, was said to have been born near Lake Tritonis in Libya.

KORYPHAIOS(m):   Look out! I've got a stick!
KORYPHAIOS(w): You lay a half-inch of your stick on
Stratyllis,
and you'll never stick again!
KORYPHAIOS(m): Fall apart!
KORYPHAIOS(w):   I'll spit up your guts!
KORYPHAIOS(m):   Euripides! Master!
How well you knew women!
KORYPHAIOS(w):   Listen to him, Rhodippe,   100
up with the pots!
KORYPHAIOS(m):   Demolition of God,
what good are your pots?
KORYPHAIOS(w):   You refugee from the tomb,
what good is your fire?
KORYPHAIOS(m):   Good enough to make a pyre
to barbecue you!
KORYPHAIOS(w):   We'll squizzle your kindling!
KORYPHAIOS(m): You think so?
KORYPHAIOS(w):   Yah! Just hang around a while!   105
KORYPHAIOS(m): Want a touch of my torch?
KORYPHAIOS(w):   It needs a good soaping.
KORYPHAIOS(m): How about you?
KORYPHAIOS(w):   Soap for a senile bridegroom!
KORYPHAIOS(m): Senile? Hold your trap
KORYPHAIOS(w):   Just *you* try to hold it!
KORYPHAIOS(m): The yammer of women!
KORYPHAIOS(w):   Oh is that so?
You're not in the jury room now, you know.   110
KORYPHAIOS(m): Gentlemen, I beg you, burn off that
woman's hair!
KORYPHAIOS(w): Let it come down!

(*They empty their pots on the men.*)

KORYPHAIOS(m): What a way to drown!
KORYPHAIOS(w):   Hot, hey?
KORYPHAIOS(m):   Say, enough!
KORYPHAIOS(w): Dandruff
needs watering. I'll make you   115
nice and fresh.
KORYPHAIOS(m):   For God's sake, you,
hold off!

SCENE 1

(*Enter a Commissioner accompanied by four constables.*)

COMMISSIONER: These degenerate women! What a
racket of little drums,
what a yapping for Adonis° on every house-top!
It's like the time in the Assembly when I was listening
to a speech — out of order, as usual — by that fool
Demostratos,° all about troops for Sicily,°   5
that kind of nonsense —
                    and there was his wife

2. **Adonis:** Fertility god, loved by Aphrodite.   5. **Demostratos:** Athenian orator and politician.   **Sicily:** Reference to the Sicilian Expedition (415–413 B.C.) in which Athens was decisively defeated.

trotting around in circles howling
Alas for Adonis! —
                         and Demostratos insisting
we must draft every last Zakynthian that can walk —
10   and his wife up there on the roof,
drunk as an owl, yowling
Oh weep for Adonis! —
                         and that damned ox Demostratos
mooing away through the rumpus. That's what we
    get
for putting up with this wretched woman-business!
KORYPHAIOS(m): Sir, you haven't heard the half of it.
15   They laughed at us!
Insulted us! They took pitchers of water
and nearly drowned us! We're still wringing out our
    clothes,
for all the world like unhousebroken brats.
COMMISSIONER: Serves you right, by Poseidon!
20   Whose fault is it if these women-folk of ours
get out of hand? We coddle them,
we teach them to be wasteful and loose. You'll see a
    husband
go into a jeweler's. "Look," he'll say,
"jeweler," he'll say, "you remember that gold choker
you made for my wife? Well, she went to a dance
25   last night
and broke the clasp. Now, I've got to go to Salamis,
and can't be bothered. Run over to my house tonight,
will you, and see if you can put it together for her."
Or another one
30   goes to a cobbler — a good strong workman, too,
with an awl that was never meant for child's play.
    "Here,"
he'll tell him, "one of my wife's shoes is pinching
her little toe. Could you come up about noon
and stretch it out for her?"
                         Well, what do you expect?
35   Look at me, for example, I'm a Public Officer,
and it's one of my duties to pay off the sailors.
And where's the money? Up there in the Akropolis!
And those blasted women slam the door in my face!
But what are we waiting for?
                         — Look here, constable,
40   stop sniffing around for a tavern, and get us
some crowbars. We'll force their gates! As a matter
    of fact,
I'll do a little forcing myself.

(*Enter Lysistrata, above, with Myrrhine, Kalonike, and
the Boiotian.*)

LYSISTRATA: No need of forcing.
Here I am, of my own accord. And all this talk
about locked doors — ! We don't need locked doors,
45   but just the least bit of common sense.
COMMISSIONER: Is that so, ma'am!
                         — Where's my constable?
                         — Constable,
arrest that woman, and tie her hands behind her.
LYSISTRATA: If he touches me, I swear by Artemis

there'll be one scamp dropped from the public pay-
    roll tomorrow!
COMMISSIONER: Well, constable? You're not afraid, I
    suppose? Grab her,   50
two of you, around the middle!
KALONIKE: No, by Pandrosos!°
Lay a hand on her, and I'll jump on you so hard
your guts will come out the back door!
COMMISSIONER: That's what *you* think!
Where's the sergeant? — Here, you: tie up that
    trollop first,
the one with the pretty talk!
MYRRHINE: By the Moon-Goddess,°   55
just try! They'll have to scoop you up with a spoon!
COMMISSIONER: Another one!
                         Officer, seize that woman!
                                        I swear
I'll put an end to this riot!
BOIOTIAN: By the Taurian,°
one inch closer, you'll be one screaming bald-head!
COMMISSIONER: Lord, what a mess! And my
    constables seem ineffective.   60
But — women get the best of us? By God, no!
                         — Skythians!°
Close ranks and forward march!
LYSISTRATA: "Forward," indeed!
By the Two Goddesses, what's the sense in *that*?
They're up against four companies of women
armed from top to bottom.
COMMISSIONER: Forward, my Skythians!   65
LYSISTRATA: Forward, yourselves, dear comrades!
You grainlettucebeanseedmarket girls!
You garlicandonionbreadbakery girls!
Give it to 'em! Knock 'em down! Scratch 'em!
Tell 'em what you think of 'em!

(*General melee, the Skythians yield.*)

                         — Ah, that's enough!   70
Sound a retreat: good soldiers don't rob the dead.
COMMISSIONER: A nice day *this* has been for the
    police!
LYSISTRATA: Well, there you are. — Did you really
    think we women
would be driven like slaves? Maybe now you'll admit
that a woman knows something about spirit.
COMMISSIONER: Spirit enough,   75
especially spirits in bottles! Dear Lord Apollo!
KORYPHAIOS(m): Your Honor, there's no use talking to
    them. Words
mean nothing whatever to wild animals like these.
Think of the sousing they gave us! and the water
was not, I believe, of the purest.   80

---

51. Pandrosos: A woman's oath referring to one of the daughters of the founder of Athens.   **55. Moon-Goddess:** Artemis,
goddess of the hunt and of fertility, daughter of Zeus.
58. Taurian: Reference to Artemis, who was said to have been
worshiped in a cult at Taurica Chersonesos.   **61. Skythians:**
Athenian archers.

KORYPHAIOS[(w)]: You shouldn't have come after us. And
    if you try it again,
  you'll be one eye short! — Although, as a matter of
    fact,
  what I like best is just to stay at home and read,
  like a sweet little bride: never hurting a soul, no,
85 never going out. But if you *must* shake hornets' nests,
  look out for the hornets.

Strophe 1

CHORUS[(m)]: Of all the beasts that God hath wrought
    What monster's worse than woman?
  Who shall encompass with his thought
90   Their guile unending? No man.

  They've seized the Heights, the Rock, the Shrine —
    But to what end? I wot not.
  Sure there's some clue to their design!
    Have you the key? I thought not.
KORYPHAIOS[(m)]: We might question them, I suppose.
95   But I warn you, sir,
  don't believe anything you hear! It would be un-
    Athenian
  not to get to the bottom of this plot.
COMMISSIONER: Very well.
  My first question is this: Why, so help you God,
  did you bar the gates of the Akropolis?
LYSISTRATA: Why?
100 To keep the money, of course. No money, no war.
COMMISSIONER: You think that money's the cause of
    war?
LYSISTRATA: I do.
  Money brought about that Peisandros° business
  and all the other attacks on the State. Well and good!
  They'll not get another cent here!
105 COMMISSIONER: And what will you do?
LYSISTRATA: What a question! From now on, we intend
  to control the Treasury.
COMMISSIONER: Control the Treasury!
LYSISTRATA: Why not? Does that seem strange?
    After all,
  we control our household budgets.
COMMISSIONER: But that's different!
LYSISTRATA: "Different"? What do you mean?
110 COMMISSIONER: I mean simply this:
  it's the Treasury that pays for National Defense.
LYSISTRATA: Unnecessary. We propose to abolish war.
COMMISSIONER: Good God. — And National
    Security?
LYSISTRATA: Leave that to us.
COMMISSIONER: You?
LYSISTRATA: Us.
COMMISSIONER: We're done for, then!
115 LYSISTRATA: Never mind.

103. Peisandros: A politician who plotted against the Athenian
democracy.

We women will save you in spite of yourselves.
COMMISSIONER: What nonsense!
LYSISTRATA: If you like. But you must accept it, like it
  or not.
COMMISSIONER: Why, this is downright subversion!
LYSISTRATA: Maybe it is.
  But we're going to save you, Judge.
COMMISSIONER: I don't *want* to be saved.
LYSISTRATA: Tut. The death-wish. All the more reason.   120
COMMISSIONER: But the idea of women bothering
  themselves about peace and war!
LYSISTRATA: Will you listen to me?
COMMISSIONER: Yes. But be brief, or I'll —
LYSISTRATA: This is no time for stupid threats.
COMMISSIONER: By the gods,
  I can't stand any more!
AN OLD WOMAN: Can't stand? Well, well.
COMMISSIONER: That's enough out of you, you old
  buzzard!   125
  Now, Lysistrata: tell me what you're thinking.
LYSISTRATA: Glad to.
            Ever since this war began
  We women have been watching you men, agreeing
    with you,
  keeping our thoughts to ourselves. That doesn't mean
  we were happy: we weren't, for we saw how things
    were going;   130
  but we'd listen to you at dinner
  arguing this way and that.
            — Oh you, and your big
  Top Secrets! —
          And then we'd grin like little patriots
  (though goodness knows we didn't feel like
    grinning) and ask you:
  "Dear, did the Armistice come up in Assembly
    today?"   135
  And you'd say, "None of your business! Pipe
    down!" you'd say.
  And so we would.
AN OLD WOMAN: *I* wouldn't have, by God!
COMMISSIONER: You'd have taken a beating, then!
              — Go on.
LYSISTRATA: Well, we'd be quiet. But then, you know,
  all at once
  you men would think up something worse than ever. 140
  Even *I* could see it was fatal. And, "Darling," I'd say,
  "have you gone completely mad?" And my husband
    would look at me
  and say, "Wife, you've got your weaving to attend
    to.
  Mind your tongue, if you don't want a slap.
  'War's a man's affair!' "°   145
COMMISSIONER: Good words, and well pronounced.
LYSISTRATA: You're a fool if you think so.
           It was hard enough
  to put up with all this banquet-hall strategy.

144–45. 'War's a man's affair!': Quoted from Homer's *Iliad*,
VI, 492, Hector's farewell to his wife, Andromache.

But then we'd hear you out in the public square:
150 "Nobody left for the draft-quota here in Athens?"
    you'd say; and, "No," someone else would say, "not
      a man!"
    And so we women decided to rescue Greece.
    You might as well listen to us now: you'll have to,
      later.
COMMISSIONER: *You* rescue Greece? Absurd.
LYSISTRATA: You're the absurd one.
COMMISSIONER: You expect me to take orders from a
    woman?
155   I'd die first!
LYSISTRATA: Heavens, if that's what's bothering you,
      take my veil,
    here, and wrap it around your poor head.
KALONIKE: Yes
    and you can have my market-basket, too.
    Go home, tighten your girdle, do the washing, mind
160   your beans! "War's
    a woman's affair!"
KORYPHAIOS[w]:   Ground pitchers! Close ranks!

Antistrophe

CHORUS[w]: This is a dance that I know well,
      My knees shall never yield.
    Wobble and creak I may, but still
165   I'll keep the well-fought field.
    Valor and grace march on before,
      Love prods us from behind.
    Our slogan is EXCELSIOR,
      Our watchword SAVE MANKIND.
KORYPHAIOS[w]: Women, remember your grandmothers!
170   Remember
    that little old mother of yours, what a stinger she
      was!
    On, on, never slacken. There's a strong wind astern!
LYSISTRATA: O Eros of delight! O Aphrodite! Kyprian!°
    If ever desire has drenched our breasts or dreamed
    in our thighs, let it work so now on the men of
175   Hellas°
    that they shall tail us through the land, slaves, slaves
    to Woman, Breaker of Armies!
COMMISSIONER: And if we do?
LYSISTRATA: Well, for one thing, we shan't have to
      watch you
    going to market, a spear in one hand, and heaven
      knows
    what in the other.
180 KALONIKE: Nicely said, by Aphrodite!
LYSISTRATA: As things stand now, you're neither men
      nor women.

Armor clanking with kitchen pans and pots —
    You sound like a pack of Korybantes!°
COMMISSIONER: A man must do what a man must do.
LYSISTRATA: So I'm told.
    But to see a General, complete with Gorgon-shield,   185
    jingling along the dock to buy a couple of herrings!
KALONIKE: *I* saw a Captain the other day — lovely
      fellow he was,
    nice curly hair — sitting on his horse; and — can
      you believe it? —
    he'd just bought some soup, and was pouring it into
      his helmet!
    And there was a soldier from Thrace   190
    swishing his lance like something out of Euripides,
    and the poor fruit-store woman got so scared
    that she ran away and let him have his figs free!
COMMISSIONER: All this is beside the point.
                              Will you be so kind
    as to tell me how you mean to save Greece?
LYSISTRATA: Of course.   195
    Nothing could be simpler.
COMMISSIONER: I assure you, I'm all ears.
LYSISTRATA: Do you know anything about weaving?
    Say the yarn gets tangled: we thread it
    this way and that through the skein, up and down,
    until it's free. And it's like that with war.   200
    We'll send our envoys
    up and down, this way and that, all over Greece,
    until it's finished.
COMMISSIONER: Yarn? Thread? Skein?
    Are you out of your mind? I tell you,
    war is a serious business.
LYSISTRATA: So serious   205
    that I'd like to go on talking about weaving.
COMMISSIONER: All right. Go ahead.
LYSISTRATA: The first thing we have to do
    is to wash our yarn, get the dirt out of it.
    You see? Isn't there too much dirt here in Athens?
    You must wash those men away.
                              Then our spoiled wool —   210
    that's like your job-hunters, out for a life
    of no work and big pay. Back to the basket,
    citizens or not, allies or not,
    or friendly immigrants.
                              And your colonies?
    Hanks of wool lost in various places. Pull them   215
    together, weave them into one great whole,
    and our voters are clothed for ever.
COMMISSIONER: It would take a woman
    to reduce state questions to a matter of carding and
      weaving.
LYSISTRATA: You fool! Who were the mothers whose
      sons sailed off
    to fight for Athens in Sicily?

---

173. **Kyprian:** Reference to Aphrodite's association with Cyprus
(Kyprus), a place sacred to her and a center for her worship.
175. **Hellas:** Greece.

183. **Korybantes:** Priestesses of Cybele, a fertility goddess, who
was celebrated in frenzied rituals accompanied by the beating
of cymbals.

220 COMMISSIONER: Enough!
    I beg you, do not call back those memories.
    LYSISTRATA: And then,
    instead of the love that every woman needs,
    we have only our single beds, where we can
       dream
    of our husbands off with the Army.
                           Bad enough for wives!
225 But what about our girls, getting older every day,
    and older, and no kisses?
    COMMISSIONER: Men get older, too.
    LYSISTRATA: Not in the same sense.
                        A soldier's discharged,
    and he may be bald and toothless, yet he'll find
    a pretty young thing to go to bed with.
                                  But a woman!
230 Her beauty is gone with the first gray hair.
    She can spend her time
    consulting the oracles and the fortune-tellers,
    but they'll never send her a husband.
    COMMISSIONER: Still, if a man can rise to the
       occasion —
235 LYSISTRATA: Rise? Rise, yourself!

    (*Furiously.*)

    Go invest in a coffin!
                      You've money enough.
                                   I'll bake you
    a cake for the Underworld.
                        And here's your funeral wreath!

    (*She pours water upon him.*)

    MYRRHINE: And here's another!

    (*More water.*)

    KALONIKE: And here's
       my contribution!

    (*More water.*)

    LYSISTRATA: What are you waiting for?
       All aboard Styx Ferry!
240   Charon's° calling for you!
    It's sailing-time: don't disrupt the schedule!
    COMMISSIONER: The insolence of women! And
       to me!
    No, by God, I'll go back to town and show
    the rest of the Commission what might happen to
       them.   (*Exit Commissioner.*)
    LYSISTRATA: Really, I suppose we should have laid out
245   his corpse
    on the doorstep, in the usual way.
                                  But never mind.
    We'll give him the rites of the dead tomorrow
       morning.

             (*Exit Lysistrata with Myrrhine and Kalonike.*)

240. Charon: The god who ferried the souls of the newly dead
across the river Styx to Hades.

PARABASIS:°
CHORAL EPISODE • Ode° *1*

KORYPHAIOS(m): Sons of Liberty, awake! The day of
       glory is at hand.
CHORUS(m): I smell tyranny afoot, I smell it rising from
       the land.
    I scent a trace of Hippias,° I sniff upon the breeze
    A dismal Spartan hogo that suggests King
          Kleisthenes.°
    Strip, strip for action, brothers!   5
    Our wives, aunts, sisters, mothers
    Have sold us out: the streets are full of godless
       female rages.
    Shall we stand by and let our women confiscate our
       wages?

                                  [Epirrhema° 1]
KORYPHAIOS(m): Gentlemen, it's a disgrace to Athens, a
       disgrace
    to all that Athens stands for, if we allow these
       grandmas   10
    to jabber about spears and shields and making
       friends
    with the Spartans. What's a Spartan? Give me a
       wild wolf
    any day. No. They want the Tyranny back, I
       suppose.
    Are we going to take that? No. Let us look like
    the innocent serpent, but be the flower under it,   15
    as the poet sings. And just to begin with,
    I propose to poke a number of teeth
    down the gullet of that harridan over there.

Antode° *1*

KORYPHAIOS(w): Oh, is that so? When you get home,
       your own mamma won't know you!
CHORUS(w): Who do you think we are, you senile
       bravos? Well, I'll show you.   20
    I bore the sacred vessels in my eighth year,° and at ten
    I was pounding out the barley for Athena Goddess;°
       then

Parabasis: Section of the play in which the author presented his
own views through the Koryphaios directly to the audience.
The parabasis in *Lysistrata* is shorter than those in Aristophanes'
other works and unusual in that the Koryphaios does not
speak directly for the author.   **Ode:** Song sung by the Chorus.
3. Hippias: An Athenian tyrant.   **4. Kleisthenes:** A bisexual
Athenian.   **Epirrhema:** A part of the parabasis spoken by the
Koryphaios following an ode delivered by his or her half of the
Chorus.   **Antode:** Lyric song sung by half of the Chorus in
response to the Ode sung by the other half.   **21. eighth year:**
Young girls between the ages of seven and eleven served in the
temple of Athena in the Akropolis.   **22. pounding out the bar-
ley for Athena Goddess:** At age ten a girl could be chosen to
grind the sacred grain of Athena.

They made me Little Bear
At the Brauronian Fair;°
25   I'd held the Holy Basket° by the time I was of age,
The Blessed Dry Figs had adorned my plump
decolletage.

                                        [Antepirrhema° 1]
KORYPHAIOS(w): A "disgrace to Athens," and I, just at
the moment
I'm giving Athens the best advice she ever had?
Don't I pay taxes to the State? Yes, I pay them
30   in baby boys. And what do you contribute,
you impotent horrors? Nothing but waste: all
our Treasury,° dating back to the Persian Wars,
gone! rifled! And not a penny out of your pockets!
Well, then? Can you cough up an answer to that?
35   Look out for your own gullet, or you'll get a crack
from this old brogan that'll make your teeth see
stars!

Ode 2

CHORUS(m): Oh insolence!
Am I unmanned?
Incontinence!
40   Shall my scarred hand
Strike never a blow
To curb this flow-
ing female curse?

Leipsydrion!°
45   Shall I betray
The laurels won
On that great day?
Come, shake a leg,
Shed old age, beg
50   The years reverse!

                                        [Epirrhema 2]
KORYPHAIOS(m): Give them an inch, and we're done
for! We'll have them
launching boats next and planning naval
strategy,
sailing down on us like so many Artemisias.
Or maybe they have ideas about the cavalry.
55   That's fair enough, women are certainly good
in the saddle. Just look at Mikon's paintings,
all those Amazons wrestling with all those men!
On the whole, a straitjacket's their best uniform.

Antode 2

CHORUS(w): Tangle with me,
And you'll get cramps.   60
Ferocity
's no use now, Gramps!
By the Two,
I'll get through
To you wrecks yet!   65

I'll scramble your eggs,
I'll burn your beans,
With my two legs.
You'll see such scenes
As never yet   70
Your two eyes met.
A curse? You bet!

                                        [Antepirrhema 2]
KORYPHAIOS(w): If Lampito stands by me, and that
delicious Theban girl,
Ismenia — what good are *you*? You and your
seven
Resolutions! Resolutions? Rationing Boiotian eels   75
and making our girls go without them at Hekate's°
Feast!
That was statesmanship! And we'll have to put up
with it
and all the rest of your decrepit legislation
until some patriot — God give him strength! —
grabs you by the neck and kicks you off the Rock.   80

SCENE 2

(*Reenter Lysistrata and her lieutenants.*)

KORYPHAIOS(w) (*tragic tone*): Great Queen, fair
Architect of our emprise,
Why lookst thou on us with foreboding eyes?
LYSISTRATA: The behavior of these idiotic women!
There's something about the female temperament
that I can't bear!
KORYPHAIOS(w):   What in the world do you mean?   5
LYSISTRATA: Exactly what I say.
KORYPHAIOS(w): What dreadful thing has happened?
Come, tell us: we're all your friends.
LYSISTRATA: It isn't easy
to say it; yet, God knows, we can't hush it up.
KORYPHAIOS(w): Well, then? Out with it!
LYSISTRATA: To put it bluntly,   10
we're dying to get laid.
KORYPHAIOS(w):   Almighty God!
LYSISTRATA: Why bring God into it? — No, it's just as
I say.
I can't manage them any longer: they've gone
man-crazy,

---

24. Brauronian Fair: A ritual in the cult of Artemis, who is
associated with wild beasts, in which young girls dressed up as
bears and danced for the goddess.   **25. Holy Basket:** In one
ritual to Athena, young girls carried baskets of objects sacred to
the goddess.   **Antepirrhema:** The speech delivered by the second Koryphaios after the second half of the Chorus had sung
an ode.   **32. Treasury:** Athenian politicians were raiding the
funds that were collected by Athens to finance a war against
Persia.   **44. Leipsydrion:** A place where Athenian patriots had
heroically fought.

76. Hekate: Patron of successful wars, object of a Boiotian cult
(later associated with sorcery).

they're all trying to get out.
                                    Why, look:
15   one of them was sneaking out the back door
over there by Pan's cave; another
was sliding down the walls with rope and tackle;
another was climbing aboard a sparrow, ready to
     take off
for the nearest brothel — I dragged *her* back by the
     hair!
They're all finding some reason to leave.
20   Look there!
There goes another one.
                         — Just a minute, you!
Where are you off to so fast?
FIRST WOMAN: I've got to get home.
I've a lot of Milesian wool, and the worms are
     spoiling it.
LYSISTRATA: Oh bother you and your worms! Get back
     inside!
25   FIRST WOMAN: I'll be back right away, I swear I will.
I just want to get it stretched out on my bed.
LYSISTRATA: You'll do no such thing. You'll stay
     right here.
FIRST WOMAN: And my wool?
You want it ruined?
LYSISTRATA: Yes, for all I care.
SECOND WOMAN: Oh dear! My lovely new flax from
     Amorgos —
I left it at home, all uncarded!
30   LYSISTRATA: Another one!
And all she wants is someone to card her flax.
Get back in there!
SECOND WOMAN: But I swear by the Moon-Goddess
the minute I get it done, I'll be back!
LYSISTRATA: I say No.
If you, why not all the other women as well?
THIRD WOMAN: O Lady Eileithyia!° Radiant goddess!
35   Thou
intercessor for women in childbirth! Stay, I pray thee,
oh stay this parturition. Shall I pollute
a sacred spot?°
LYSISTRATA: And what's the matter with *you*?
THIRD WOMAN: I'm having a baby — any minute now.
LYSISTRATA: But you weren't pregnant yesterday.
40   THIRD WOMAN: Well, I am today.
Let me go home for a midwife, Lysistrata:
there's not much time.
LYSISTRATA: I never heard such nonsense.
What's that bulging under your cloak?
THIRD WOMAN: A little baby boy.
LYSISTRATA: It certainly isn't. But it's something hollow,
45   like a basin or — Why, it's the helmet of Athena!
And you said you were having a baby.
THIRD WOMAN: Well, I am! So there!

---

35. **Eileithyia:** Goddess of childbirth.   37–38. **pollute a sacred spot:** Giving birth on the Akropolis was forbidden because it was sacred ground.

LYSISTRATA: Then why the helmet?
THIRD WOMAN: I was afraid that my pains
might begin here in the Akropolis; and I wanted
to drop my chick into it, just as the dear doves do.
LYSISTRATA: Lies! Evasions! — But at least one thing's
     clear: 50
you can't leave the place before your purification.°
THIRD WOMAN: But I can't stay here in the Akropolis!
     Last night I dreamed
of the Snake.
FIRST WOMAN: And those horrible owls, the noise they
     make!
I can't get a bit of sleep; I'm just about dead.
LYSISTRATA: You useless girls, that's enough: Let's have
     no more lying.   55
Of course you want your men. But don't you imagine
that they want you just as much? I'll give you my
     word,
their nights must be pretty hard.
                                  Just stick it out!
A little patience, that's all, and our battle's won.
I have heard an Oracle. Should you like to hear it?   60
FIRST WOMAN: An Oracle? Yes, tell us!
LYSISTRATA: Here is what it says:
WHEN SWALLOWS SHALL THE HOOPOE SHUN
     AND SPURN HIS HOT DESIRE,
ZEUS WILL PERFECT WHAT THEY'VE BEGUN
     AND SET THE LOWER HIGHER.   65
FIRST WOMAN: Does that mean we'll be on top?
LYSISTRATA: BUT IF THE SWALLOWS SHALL FALL
     OUT
     AND TAKE THE HOOPOE'S BAIT,
A CURSE MUST MARK THEIR HOUR OF
     DOUBT,
     INFAMY SEAL THEIR FATE.   70
THIRD WOMAN: I swear, *that* Oracle's all too clear.
FIRST WOMAN: Oh the dear gods!
LYSISTRATA: Let's not be downhearted, girls. Back to
     our places.
The god has spoken. How can we possibly fail him?

(*Exit Lysistrata with the dissident women.*)

CHORAL EPISODE • *Strophe*

CHORUS[(m)]: I know a little story that I learned way
     back in school
Goes like this:
Once upon a time there was a young man — and no
     fool —
Named Melanion; and his
One aversion was marriage. He loathed the very
     thought.   5
So he ran off to the hills, and in a special grot
Raised a dog, and spent his days
Hunting rabbits. And it says

---

51. **purification:** A ritual cleansing of a woman after childbirth.

That he never never never did come home.
10   It might be called a refuge *from* the womb.
All right,
        all right,
                all right!
We're as bright as young Melanion, and we hate the
    very sight
Of you women!
A MAN: How about a kiss, old lady?
15   A WOMAN: Here's an onion for your eye!
A MAN: A kick in the guts, then?
A WOMAN: Try, old bristle-tail, just try!
A MAN: Yet they say Myronides
    On hands and knees
20   Looked just as shaggy fore and aft as I!

Antistrophe

CHORUS(w): Well, *I* know a little story, and it's just as
    good as yours.
Goes like this:
Once there was a man named Timon — a rough
    diamond, of course,
And that whiskery face of his
Looked like murder in the shrubbery. By God, he
25   was a son
Of the Furies, let me tell you! And what did he do
    but run
From the world and all its ways,
Cursing mankind! And it says
That his choicest execrations as of then
30   Were leveled almost wholly at *old* men.
All right,
        all right,
                all right!
But there's one thing about Timon: he could always
    stand the sight
of us women.
A WOMAN: How about a crack in the jaw, Pop?
35   A MAN: I can take it, Ma — no fear!
A WOMAN: How about a kick in the face?
A MAN: You'd reveal your old caboose?
A WOMAN: What I'd show,
    I'll have you know,
40   Is an instrument you're too far gone to use.

SCENE 3

(*Reenter Lysistrata.*)

LYSISTRATA: Oh, quick, girls, quick! Come here!
A WOMAN: What is it?
LYSISTRATA: A man.
    A man simply bulging with love.
                              O Kyprian Queen,°
    O Paphian, O Kythereian! Hear us and aid us!

2. **Kyprian Queen:** Aphrodite.

A WOMAN: Where is this enemy?
LYSISTRATA: Over there, by Demeter's shrine.
A WOMAN: Damned if he isn't. But who *is* he?
MYRRHINE: My husband.   5
    Kinesias.
LYSISTRATA: Oh then, get busy! Tease him! Undermine
    him!
    Wreck him! Give him everything — kissing, tickling,
        nudging,
    whatever you generally torture him with — : give
        him everything
    except what we swore on the wine we would not
        give.
MYRRHINE: Trust me.
LYSISTRATA: I do. But I'll help you get him started.   10
    The rest of you women, stay back.

(*Enter Kinesias.*)

KINESIAS: Oh God! Oh my God!
    I'm stiff from lack of exercise. All I can do to stand
    up.
LYSISTRATA: Halt! Who are you, approaching our lines?
KINESIAS: Me? I.
LYSISTRATA: A man?
KINESIAS: You have eyes, haven't you?
LYSISTRATA: Go away.   15
KINESIAS: Who says so?
LYSISTRATA: Officer of the Day.
KINESIAS: Officer, I beg you,
    by all the gods at once, bring Myrrhine out.
LYSISTRATA: Myrrhine? And who, my good sir, are
    you?
KINESIAS: Kinesias. Last name's Pennison. Her husband.
LYSISTRATA: Oh, of course. I beg your pardon. We're
    glad to see you.   20
    We've heard so much about you. Dearest Myrrhine
    is always talking about Kinesias — never nibbles an
        egg
    or an apple without saying
    "Here's to Kinesias!"
KINESIAS: Do you really mean it?
LYSISTRATA: I do.
    When we're discussing men, she always says   25
    "Well, after all, there's nobody like Kinesias!"
KINESIAS: Good God. — Well, then, please send her
    down here.
LYSISTRATA: And what do *I* get out of it?
KINESIAS: A standing promise.
LYSISTRATA: I'll take it up with her.
                              (*Exit Lysistrata.*)
KINESIAS: But be quick about it!
    Lord, what's life without a wife? Can't eat. Can't
    sleep.   30
    Every time I go home, the place is so empty, so
    insufferably sad. Love's killing me, Oh,
    hurry!

(*Enter Manes, a slave, with Kinesias's baby; the voice of
Myrrhine is heard offstage.*)

MYRRHINE: But of course I love him! Adore him —
                                                   But no,
   he hates love. No. I won't go down.

(*Enter Myrrhine, above.*)

KINESIAS: Myrrhine!
35   Darlingest Myrrhinette! Come down quick!
MYRRHINE: Certainly not.
KINESIAS: Not? But why, Myrrhine?
MYRRHINE: Why? You don't need me.
KINESIAS: Need you? My God, *look* at me!
MYRRHINE: So long!

(*Turns to go.*)

KINESIAS: Myrrhine, Myrrhine, Myrrhine!
   If not for my sake, for our child!

(*Pinches Baby.*)

                                 — All right, you: pipe up!
BABY: Mummie! Mummie! Mummie!
40   KINESIAS: You hear that?
   Pitiful, I call it. Six days now
   with never a bath; no food; enough to break your
      heart!
MYRRHINE: My darlingest child! What a father *you*
      acquired!
KINESIAS: At least come down for his sake.
MYRRHINE: I suppose I must.
45   Oh, this mother business!   (*Exit.*)
KINESIAS: How pretty she is! And younger!
   The harder she treats me, the more bothered I get.

(*Myrrhine enters, below.*)

MYRRHINE: Dearest child,
   you're as sweet as your father's horrid. Give me a kiss.
KINESIAS: Now don't you see how wrong it was to get
      involved
50   in this scheming League of women? It's bad
   for us both.
MYRRHINE: Keep your hands to yourself!
KINESIAS: But our house
   going to rack and ruin?
MYRRHINE: I don't care.
KINESIAS: And your knitting
   all torn to pieces by the chickens? Don't you care?
MYRRHINE: Not at all.
55   KINESIAS: And our debt to Aphrodite?
   Oh, *won't* you come back?
MYRRHINE: No. — At least, not until you men
   make a treaty and stop this war.
KINESIAS: Why, I suppose
   that might be arranged.
MYRRHINE: Oh? Well, I suppose
   I might come down then. But meanwhile,
   I've sworn not to.
60   KINESIAS: Don't worry. — Now let's have fun.
MYRRHINE: No! Stop it! I said no!
                                 — Although, of course,
   I *do* love you.

KINESIAS: I know you do. Darling Myrrhine:
   come, shall we?
MYRRHINE: Are you out of your mind? In front of the
      child?
KINESIAS: Take him home, Manes.
                           (*Exit Manes with Baby.*)
                           There. He's gone.
                                       Come on!
   There's nothing to stop us now.
MYRRHINE: You devil! But where?   65
KINESIAS: In Pan's cave. What could be snugger than
      that?
MYRRHINE: But my purification before I go back to the
      Citadel?
KINESIAS: Wash in the Klepsydra.°
MYRRHINE: And my oath?
KINESIAS: Leave the oath to me.
   After all, I'm the man.
MYRRHINE: Well . . . if you say so.
                                 I'll go find a bed.
KINESIAS: Oh, bother a bed! The ground's good
      enough for me.   70
MYRRHINE: No. You're a bad man, but you deserve
   something better than dirt.   (*Exit Myrrhine.*)
KINESIAS: What a love she is! And how thoughtful!

(*Reenter Myrrhine.*)

MYRRHINE: Here's your bed.
   Now let me get my clothes off.
                                 But, good horrors!
   We haven't a mattress.
KINESIAS: Oh, forget the mattress!
MYRRHINE: No.
   Just lying on blankets? Too sordid.
KINESIAS: Give me a kiss.   75
MYRRHINE: Just a second.   (*Exit Myrrhine.*)
KINESIAS: I swear, I'll explode!

(*Reenter Myrrhine.*)

MYRRHINE: Here's your mattress.
   I'll just take my dress off.
                                 But look —
   where's our pillow?
KINESIAS: I don't *need* a pillow!
MYRRHINE: Well, *I* do.
                                 (*Exit Myrrhine.*)
KINESIAS: I don't suppose even Herakles°
   would stand for this!

(*Reenter Myrrhine.*)

MYRRHINE: There we are. Ups-a-daisy!   80
KINESIAS: So we are. Well, come to bed.
MYRRHINE: But I wonder:
   is everything ready now?
KINESIAS: I can swear to that. Come, darling!

68. Klepsydra: A water clock beneath the walls of the Akropolis. Kinesias's suggestion borders on blasphemy.   **79. Herakles:**
Greek hero (Hercules) known for his Twelve Labors.

MYRRHINE: Just getting out of my girdle.
                                    But remember, now,
    what you promised about the treaty.
KINESIAS: Yes, yes, yes!
MYRRHINE: But no coverlet!
85 KINESIAS: Damn it, I'll be your coverlet!
MYRRHINE: Be right back.   (*Exit Myrrhine.*)
KINESIAS: This girl and her coverlets
    will be the death of me.

(*Reenter Myrrhine.*)

MYRRHINE: Here we are. Up you go!
KINESIAS: Up? I've been up for ages.
MYRRHINE: Some perfume?
KINESIAS: No, by Apollo!
MYRRHINE: Yes, by Aphrodite!
90   I don't care whether you want it or not.
                                    (*Exit Myrrhine.*)
KINESIAS: For love's sake, hurry!

(*Reenter Myrrhine.*)

MYRRHINE: Here, in your hand. Rub it right in.
KINESIAS: Never cared for perfume.
    And this is particularly strong. Still, here goes.
MYRRHINE: What a nitwit I am! I brought you the
        Rhodian bottle.
95 KINESIAS: Forget it.
MYRRHINE: No trouble at all. You just wait here.
                                    (*Exit Myrrhine.*)
KINESIAS: God damn the man who invented perfume!

(*Reenter Myrrhine.*)

MYRRHINE: At last! The right bottle!
KINESIAS: I've got the rightest bottle of all,
    and it's right here waiting for you.
    Darling, forget everything else. Do come to bed.
MYRRHINE: Just let me get my shoes off.
100   — And, by the way,
    you'll vote for the treaty?
KINESIAS: I'll think about it.
                                    (*Myrrhine runs away.*)
    There! That's done it! The damned woman,
    she gets me all bothered, she half kills me,
    and off she runs! What'll I do? Where
    can I get laid?
105   — And you, little prodding pal,
    who's going to take care of *you*? No, you and I
    had better get down to old Foxdog's Nursing Clinic.
CHORUS[m]: Alas for the woes of man, alas
        Specifically for you.
110   She's brought you to a pretty pass:
        What are you going to do?
    Split, heart! Sag, flesh! Proud spirit, crack!
    Myrrhine's got you on your back.
KINESIAS: The agony, the protraction!
KORYPHAIOS[m]:   Friend,
115   What woman's worth a damn?
    They bitch us all, world without end.
KINESIAS: Yet they're so damned sweet, man!

KORYPHAIOS[m]: Calamitous, that's what I say.
    You should have learned that much today.
CHORUS[m]: O blessed Zeus, roll womankind   120
        Up into one great ball;
    Blast them aloft on a high wind,
        And once there, let them fall.
    Down, down they'll come, the pretty dears,
    And split themselves on our thick spears.   125
                                    (*Exit Kinesias.*)

SCENE 4

(*Enter a Spartan Herald.*)

HERALD: Gentlemen, Ah beg you will be so kind
    as to direct me to the Central Committee.
    Ah have a communication.

(*Reenter Commissioner.*)

COMMISSIONER: Are you a man,
    or a fertility symbol?
HERALD: Ah refuse to answer that question!
    Ah'm a certified herald from Spahta, and Ah've come   5
    to talk about an ahmistice.
COMMISSIONER: Then why
    that spear under your cloak?
HERALD: Ah have no speah!
COMMISSIONER: You don't walk naturally, with your
        tunic
    poked out so. You have a tumor, maybe,
    or a hernia?
HERALD: You lost yo' mahnd, man?
COMMISSIONER: Well,   10
    something's up, I can see that. And I don't like it.
HERALD: Colonel, Ah resent this.
COMMISSIONER: So I see. But what *is* it?
HERALD: A staff
    with a message from Spahta.
COMMISSIONER: Oh, I know about those staffs.
    Well, then, man, speak out: How are things in Sparta?
HERALD: Hahd, Colonel, hahd! We're at a standstill.   15
    Cain't seem to think of anything but women.
COMMISSIONER: How curious! Tell me, do you
        Spartans think
    that maybe Pan's to blame?
HERALD: Pan? No, Lampito and her little naked friends.
    They won't let a man come nigh them.   20
COMMISSIONER: How are you handling it?
HERALD: Losing our mahnds,
    if y' want to know, and walking around hunched over
    lahk men carrying candles in a gale.
    The women have swohn they'll have nothing to do
        with us
    until we get a treaty.
COMMISSIONER: Yes. I know.   25
    It's a general uprising, sir, in all parts of Greece.
    But as for the answer —
                                    Sir: go back to Sparta
    and have them send us your Armistice Commission.

Geraldine James (far left) is Lysistrata in the Old Vic Theatre production in London, 1993.

I'll arrange things in Athens.
                                    And I may say
30   that my standing is good enough to make them listen.
     HERALD: A man after mah own haht! Seh, Ah thank
         you.   (*Exit Herald.*)

CHORAL EPISODE • *Strophe*

CHORUS(m): Oh these women! Where will you find
     A slavering beast that's more unkind?
         Where's a hotter fire?
     Give me a panther, any day.
5   He's not so merciless as they,
         And panthers don't conspire.

Antistrophe

CHORUS(w): We may be hard, you silly old ass,
     But who brought you to this stupid pass?
         You're the ones to blame.
10   Fighting with us, your oldest friends,
     Simply to serve your selfish ends —
         Really, you have no shame!
KORYPHAIOS(m): No, I'm through with women for ever.

KORYPHAIOS(w):   If you say so.
     Still, you might put some clothes on. You look too
         absurd
     standing around naked. Come, get into this cloak.   15
KORYPHAIOS(m): Thank you; you're right. I merely took
         it off
     because I was in such a temper.
KORYPHAIOS(w):   That's much better.
     Now you resemble a man again.
                              Why have you been so horrid?
     And look: there's some sort of insect in your eye.
     Shall I take it out?
KORYPHAIOS(m):   An insect, is it? So that's   20
     what's been bothering me. Lord, yes: take it out!
KORYPHAIOS(w): You might be more polite.
                                    — But, heavens!
     What an enormous mosquito!
KORYPHAIOS(m):   You've saved my life.
     That mosquito was drilling an artesian well
     in my left eye.
KORYPHAIOS(w):   Let me wipe   25
     those tears away. — And now: one little kiss?
KORYPHAIOS(m): No, no kisses.
KORYPHAIOS(w): You're so difficult.
KORYPHAIOS(m): You impossible women! How you do
     get around us!

30   The poet was right: Can't live with you, or without
     you.
   But let's be friends.
   And to celebrate, you might join us in an Ode.

Strophe 1

CHORUS^(m and w): Let it never be said
    That my tongue is malicious:
35   Both by word and by deed
    I would set an example that's noble and gracious.
    We've had sorrow and care
    Till we're sick of the tune.
    Is there anyone here
40   Who would like a small loan?
      My purse is crammed,
      As you'll soon find;
    And you needn't pay me back if the Peace gets signed.

Strophe 2

    I've invited to lunch
45   Some Karystian rips° —
    An esurient bunch,
    But I've ordered a menu to water their lips.
    I can still make soup
    And slaughter a pig.
50   You're all coming, I hope?
    But a bath first, I beg!
      Walk right up
      As though you owned the place,
    And you'll get the front door slammed to in your face.

SCENE 5

(*Enter Spartan Ambassador, with entourage.*)

KORYPHAIOS^(m): The Commission has arrived from
    Sparta.
        How oddly they're walking!
            Gentlemen, welcome to Athens!
    How is life in Lakonia?
AMBASSADOR: Need we discuss that?
    Simply use your eyes.
CHORUS^(m):   The poor man's right:
           What a sight!
5 AMBASSADOR: Words fail me.
    But come, gentlemen, call in your Commissioners,
    and let's get down to a Peace.
CHORAGOS^(m):   The state we're in! Can't bear
    a stitch below the waist. It's a kind of pelvic
    paralysis.

---

45. Karystian rips: The Karystians were allies of Athens but
were scorned for their primitive ways and loose morals.

COMMISSIONER: Won't somebody call Lysistrata? —
                   Gentlemen,
    we're no better off than you.
AMBASSADOR: So I see.   10
A SPARTAN: Seh, do y'all feel a certain strain early in the
    morning?
AN ATHENIAN: I do, sir. It's worse than a strain.
    A few more days, and there's nothing for us but
      Kleisthenes,
    that broken blossom.
CHORAGOS^(m):   But you'd better get dressed again.
    You know these people going around Athens with
      chisels   15
    looking for statues of Hermes.°
ATHENIAN: Sir, you are right.
SPARTAN: He certainly is! Ah'll put mah own clothes
    back on.

(*Enter Athenian Commissioners.*)

COMMISSIONER: Gentlemen from Sparta, welcome.
    This is a sorry business.
SPARTAN (*to one of his own group*): Colonel, we got
      dressed just in time. Ah sweah,
    if they'd seen us the way we were, there'd have been
      a new wah   20
    between the states.
COMMISSIONER: Shall we call the meeting to order?
                   Now, Lakonians,
    what's your proposal?
AMBASSADOR: We propose to consider peace.
COMMISSIONER: Good. That's on our minds, too.
               — Summon Lysistrata.
    We'll never get anywhere without her.
AMBASSADOR: Lysistrata? 25
    Summon Lysis-*any*body! Only, summon!
KORYPHAIOS^(m):   No need to summon:
    here she is, herself.

(*Enter Lysistrata.*)

COMMISSIONER: Lysistrata! Lion of women!
    This is your hour to be
    hard and yielding, outspoken and shy, austere and
    gentle. You see here   30
    the best brains of Hellas (confused, I admit,
    by your devious charming) met as one man
    to turn the future over to you.
LYSISTRATA: That's fair enough,
    unless you men take it into your heads
    to turn to each other instead of to us. But I'd know 35
    soon enough if you did.
             — Where is Reconciliation?
    Go, some of you: bring her here.
               (*Exeunt two women.*)

---

16. statues of Hermes: The usual representation of Hermes was
with an erect phallus. Statues of Hermes were scattered
throughout Athens and were attacked by vandals just before
the Sicilian Expedition.

And now, women,
lead the Spartan delegates to me: not roughly
or insultingly, as our men handle them, but gently,
40   politely, as ladies should. Take them by the hand,
or by anything else if they won't give you their hands.

(*The Spartans are escorted over.*)

There. — The Athenians next, by any convenient
   handle.

(*The Athenians are escorted.*)

Stand there, please. — Now, all of you, listen to me.

(*During the following speech the two women reenter,
carrying an enormous statue of a naked girl; this is
Reconciliation.*)

I'm only a woman, I know; but I've a mind,
45   and, I think, not a bad one: I owe it to my father
and to listening to the local politicians.
So much for that.
                  Now, gentlemen,
since I have you here, I intend to give you a scolding.
We are all Greeks.
50   Must I remind you of Thermopylai,° of Olympia,
of Delphoi? names deep in all our hearts?
Are they not a common heritage?
                      Yet you men
go raiding through the country from both sides,
Greek killing Greek, storming down Greek cities —
55   and all the time the Barbarian across the sea
is waiting for his chance!
               — That's my first point.
AN ATHENIAN: Lord! I can hardly contain myself.
LYSISTRATA: As for you Spartans:
Was it so long ago that Perikleides°
came here to beg our help? I can see him still,
his gray face, his sombre gown. And what did he
60   want?
An army from Athens. All Messene
was hot at your heels, and the sea-god splitting your
   land.
Well, Kimon and his men,
four thousand strong, marched out and saved all
   Sparta.
And what thanks do we get? You come back to
65   murder us.
AN ATHENIAN: They're aggressors, Lysistrata!
A SPARTAN: Ah admit it.
When Ah look at those laigs, Ah sweah Ah'll
   aggress mahself!

---

50. **Thermopylai:** A narrow pass where, in 480 B.C., an army
of three hundred Spartans held out for three days against a superior Persian force.   **58. Perikleides:** Spartan ambassador to
Athens who successfully urged Athenians to aid Sparta in
quelling a rebellion.

LYSISTRATA: And you, Athenians: do you think you're
   blameless?
Remember that bad time when we were helpless,
and an army came from Sparta,   70
and that was the end of the Thessalian menace,
the end of Hippias and his allies.
                  And that was Sparta,
and only Sparta; but for Sparta, we'd be
cringing slaves today, not free Athenians.

(*From this point, the male responses are less to Lysistrata
than to the statue.*)

A SPARTAN: A well shaped speech.
AN ATHENIAN: Certainly it has its points. 75
LYSISTRATA: Why are we fighting each other? With all
   this history
of favors given and taken, what stands in the way
of making peace?
AMBASSADOR: Spahta is ready, ma'am,
so long as we get that place back.
LYSISTRATA: What place, man?
AMBASSADOR: Ah refer to Pylos.
COMMISSIONER: Not a chance, by God! 80
LYSISTRATA: Give it to them, friend.
COMMISSIONER: But — what shall we have to bargain
   with?
LYSISTRATA: Demand something in exchange.
COMMISSIONER: Good idea. — Well, then:
Cockeville first, and the Happy Hills, and the country
between the Legs of Megara.
AMBASSADOR: Mah government objects. 85
LYSISTRATA: Overruled. Why fuss about a pair of legs?

(*General assent. The statue is removed.*)

AN ATHENIAN: I want to get out of these clothes and
   start my plowing.
A SPARTAN: Ah'll fertilize mahn first, by the Heavenly
   Twins!
LYSISTRATA: And so you shall,
once you've made peace. If you are serious,   90
go, both of you, and talk with your allies.
COMMISSIONER: Too much talk already. No, we'll
   stand together.
We've only one end in view. All that we want
is our women; and I speak for our allies.
AMBASSADOR: Mah government concurs.
AN ATHENIAN: So does Karystos. 95
LYSISTRATA: Good. — But before you come inside
to join your wives at supper, you must perform
the usual lustration. Then we'll open
our baskets for you, and all that we have is yours.
But you must promise upright good behavior   100
from this day on. Then each man home with his
   woman!
AN ATHENIAN: Let's get it over with.
A SPARTAN: Lead on. Ah follow.
AN ATHENIAN: Quick as a cat can wink!
             (*Exeunt all but the Choruses.*)

Antistrophe 1

CHORUS(w): Embroideries and
105   Twinkling ornaments and
          Pretty dresses — I hand
   Them all over to you, and with never a qualm.
          They'll be nice for your daughters
          On festival days
110   When the girls bring the Goddess
          The ritual prize.
          Come in, one and all:
          Take what you will.
   I've nothing here so tightly corked that you can't
          make it spill.

Antistrophe 2

115   You may search my house
          But you'll not find
          The least thing of use,
   Unless your two eyes are keener than mine.
          Your numberless brats
120   Are half starved? and your slaves?
          Courage, grandpa! I've lots
          Of grain left, and big loaves.
          I'll fill your guts,
          I'll go the whole hog;
   But if you come too close to me, remember: 'ware
125   the dog!   (*Exeunt Choruses.*)

EXODOS°

(*A Drunken Citizen enters, approaches the gate, and is halted by a sentry.*)

CITIZEN: Open. The. Door.
SENTRY: Now, friend, just shove along!
   — So you want to sit down. If it weren't such an old
        joke,
   I'd tickle your tail with this torch. Just the sort of
        gag
   this audience appreciates.
CITIZEN: I. Stay. Right. Here.
5 SENTRY: Get away from there, or I'll scalp you!
        The gentlemen from Sparta
   are just coming back from dinner.

(*Exit Citizen; the general company reenters; the two Choruses now represent Spartans and Athenians.*)

A SPARTAN: Ah must say,
   Ah never tasted better grub.
AN ATHENIAN: And those Lakonians!
   They're gentlemen, by the Lord! Just goes to show,
   a drink to the wise is sufficient.

Exodos: Final scene.

COMMISSIONER: And why not?   10
   A sober man's an ass.
   Men of Athens, mark my words: the only efficient
   Ambassador's a drunk Ambassador. Is that clear?
   Look: we go to Sparta,
   and when we get there we're dead sober. The result?   15
   Everyone cackling at everyone else. They make
        speeches;
   and even if we understand, we get it all wrong
   when we file our reports in Athens. But today — !
   Everybody's happy. Couldn't tell the difference
   between *Drink to Me Only* and   20
   The Star-Spangled Athens.
                    What's a few lies,
   washed down in good strong drink?

(*Reenter the Drunken Citizen.*)

SENTRY: God almighty,
   he's back again!
CITIZEN: I. Resume. My. Place.
A SPARTAN (*to an Athenian*): Ah beg yo', seh,
   take yo' instrument in yo' hand and play for us.   25
   Ah'm told
   yo' understand the intricacies of the floot?
   Ah'd lahk to execute a song and dance
   in honor of Athens,
                    and, of cohse, of Spahta.
CITIZEN: Toot. On. Your. Flute.   30

(*The following song is a solo — an aria — accompanied by the flute. The Chorus of Spartans begins a slow dance.*)

A SPARTAN: O Memory,
   Let the Muse speak once more
   In my young voice. Sing glory.
   Sing Artemision's shore,
   Where Athens fluttered the Persians. *Alalai,*°   35
   Sing glory, that great
   Victory! Sing also
   Our Leonidas and his men,
   Those wild boars, sweat and blood
   Down in a red drench. Then, then   40
   The barbarians broke, though they had stood
   Numberless as the sands before!

   O Artemis,
   Virgin Goddess, whose darts
   Flash in our forests: approve   45
   This pact of peace and join our hearts,
   From this day on, in love.
   Huntress, descend!
LYSISTRATA: All that will come in time.
                    But now, Lakonians,
   take home your wives. Athenians, take yours.   50
   Each man be kind to his woman; and you, women

35. *Alalai:* War cry.

be equally kind. Never again, pray God,
shall we lose our way in such madness.
KORYPHAIOS^(Athenian):   And now let's dance our joy.

(*From this point the dance becomes general.*)

CHORUS^(Athenian): Dance, you Graces
                              Artemis, dance
    Dance, Phoibos,° Lord of dancing
55   Dance,
    In a scurry of Maenads,° Lord Dionysos
                              Dance, Zeus Thunderer
        Dance, Lady Hera°
    Queen of the sky
                      Dance, dance, all you gods
    Dance witness everlasting of our pact
60 *Evohi Evohe°*
    Dance for the dearest
                      the Bringer of Peace
    Deathless Aphrodite!
COMMISSIONER: Now let us have another song from
    Sparta.
CHORUS^(Spartan): From Taygetos, from Taygetos,
65 Lakonian Muse, come down.

Sing to the Lord Apollo
Who rules Amyklai Town.

Sing Athena of the House of Brass!°
Sing Leda's Twins,° that chivalry
    Resplendent on the shore   70
Of our Eurotas; sing the girls
    That dance along before:
Sparkling in dust their gleaming feet,
    Their hair a Bacchant fire,
And Leda's daughter, thyrsos° raised,   75
    Leads their triumphant choir.

CHORUS^(S and A): *Evohe!*
                      Evohai!
                              Evohe!
                                  We pass
                      Dancing
                              dancing
                                  to greet
Athena of the House of Brass.

---

55. Phoibos: Apollo, god of the sun.   **56. Maenads:** Female worshipers of Bacchus (Dionysus).   **57. Hera:** Wife of Zeus.
60. *Evohi Evohe:* "Come forth! Come forth!" An orgiastic cry associated with rituals of Bacchus.

68. *House of Brass:* Temple to Athena on the Akropolis of Sparta.   **69. Leda's Twins:** Leda, raped by Zeus, bore quadruplets, two daughters (one of whom was Helen) and two sons.
75. thyrsos: A staff twined with ivy and carried by Bacchus and his followers.

COMMENTARY

Brooks Atkinson (1894–1984)
REVIEW OF *LYSISTRATA*   *1930*

> *This 1930 review of* Lysistrata *by the then-reigning* New York Times *reviewer reminds us that the play is racy enough that "members of the constabulary" needed to view it to be sure it would not offend the public's sensibilities. Atkinson's review captures the lively sense of fun manifest in producer Norman Bel Geddes's comedic romp.*

On second thought, the *Lysistrata*, which was put on at the Forty-fourth Street last evening, does not come direct from Athens. Between Aristophanes and us stands Norman Bel Geddes, scene designer extraordinary, who produced this version for the Philadelphia Theatre Association several weeks ago, and whose bountiful scenery now sweeps up toward the flies in a Broadway playhouse. He has designed a magnificent production, imaginative, free, sculptural and colorful, and the concluding bacchanal, when viewed from the rear of the auditorium, is a memorable flow of color and motion.

If *Lysistrata* were *Antigone* or *Electra,* this spacious edifice would be a masterful scene conception for the dignity of groupings and the declamation of Greek tragedy. But *Lysistrata* is horseplay, broader than a Second Avenue burlesque, full of rough-and-tumble, full of bawdry. The comic spirit could dance more freely if Mr. Geddes had spared the picture somewhat and tightened the performance. When he has experienced actors at his command — Violet Kemble Cooper, Ernest Truex, Sydney Greenstreet — Aristophanes triumphs over magnificence of scenery, for good actors know the craft of expression. But the pictorial quality of this *Lysistrata* is no unmixed dispensation for the younger actors. When the performance begins to sprawl, as it still does despite considerable cutting, you suspect that Mr. Geddes's setting is more on the side of the tragedians than the mountebanks.

But that is counsel of perfection, and *Lysistrata* is too hearty a comedy to be stared out of countenance by a promethean artist. Gilbert Seldes has written an English adaptation colloquial enough to be relished, and the sheer artlessness of the slapstick episodes makes them palatable and enjoyable even for the sciolists of Broadway. As everyone must know by this time, *Lysistrata* is the story of the women of Greece who plot to conclude a tedious and ruinous interstate war by abstaining from love until their menfolk have made peace. Soldiers denied the consolations of domesticity grew less Martian and more reasonable politically. [. . .]

Members of the constabulary were present last evening to safeguard the morals of Broadway art patrons. Although the police listened to some of the raciest conversation to be heard outside the marts of commerce, they will be relieved to know that it is tamer than what members of the Philadelphia Theatre Association heard when *Lysistrata* opened in that well-bred metropolis. [. . .]

Although *Lysistrata* is a robust comedy, it is not sophisticated. Instead of cracking jokes, it pummels and grimaces, or splashes jars of water on a parcel of feeble old men. And, although the pace of the performance is slow and uneven, and lacking rhythm, it is a tempo not unsuited to the festival quality of the humors.

Those who expect a neat, brisk show will be disappointed. But those who still like to snort over the earthy japery of elementary comedy will find that the congenial version of *Lysistrata* has laughing matter of rare quality.

Roman Drama

Indigenous Sources

Roman drama has several sources, not all of them well understood. The first and most literary is Greek drama, but among the more curious are the indigenous sources, which are especially difficult to trace. One such source might be the Etruscans, members of an old and obscure civilization in northern Italy that reached its height in the sixth century B.C. and that the Romans eventually absorbed. The Etruscans had developed an improvised song and dance that was very entertaining. The town of Atella provided another indigenous comic tradition known as the ATELLAN FARCE, a very broad and sometimes coarse popular comedy. Such entertainments may have been acted in open spaces or at fairs, probably not on a stage at first.

The Atellan farce is especially interesting for developments in later Roman drama and world drama. The characters in this farce seem to have been STOCK CHARACTERS, characters who are always recognizable and whose antics are predictable. The most common in the Atellan farce are Maccus the clown; Bucco the stupid, and probably fat, clown; Pappus, the foolish or stubborn old man; and the hunchbacked, wily slave Dossennus. At first these pieces of drama were improvised to a repeatable pattern, often involving a master who tries to get his slave to do his bidding but who somehow ends up being made to look the fool by the cunning slave. When the farces began to develop in Rome, they were written down and played onstage.

The concept of the stock character is associated with the masters of Roman comedy, Plautus and Terence, who often adapted Greek plays and made them their own. The braggart warrior (*miles gloriosus*), a stock character on the Roman stage, reappears in modern plays. The miser has been a mainstay in literature since Roman times and probably is best known today as Scrooge in Dickens's *A Christmas Carol* and as *The Miser* of Molière. The parasite was Roman in origin and can be seen today in numerous television situation comedies. Another Roman invention is the use of identical twins for comic effect. Because it permitted a wide range of comic misunderstandings, this device has been used by many playwrights, including Shakespeare in *The Comedy of Errors*. The Roman use of masks made the twins device much easier to employ than it would be in today's productions.

The Greek Influence

According to legend, in 240 B.C., a slave, Livius Andronicus, presented performances of his Latin translations of a Greek tragedy and a Greek comedy, giving the Romans their first real taste of Greek drama and literature. Livius soon earned his freedom, and his literary career became so firmly established that his translations from the Greek were those read in Rome for more than two hundred years. His translation of the *Odyssey* was the standard text through the time of Cicero (first century B.C.).

Roman comedy derived primarily from the New Comedy of Menander, although it could, like Aristophanes' Old Comedy, sometimes be risqué. Comedy was the most well attended and the most performed of Rome's drama. That is not to say that the Romans produced no tragedies. They did, and the influence of Roman tragedy has been as long-lasting as that of comedy. Still, the Roman people preferred to laugh rather than to feel the pity and terror of tragic emotion.

Just as the Greek plays developed in connection with festivals, the Roman plays became associated with games held several times a year. During the games, performances were offered on an average of five to eleven days. The Megalesian Games took place in early April, in honor of the Great Mother, the goddess Cybele, whose temple stood on the Palatine Hill. In late April the Floral Games were held in front of the temple of Flora on the Aventine Hill. The most important were the Roman Games in September and the Plebeian Games in November.

The Greek drama competitions had no counterpart among the Romans, for whom drama was not the primary entertainment during the festivals. Roman playwrights and actors were hired to put on performances to entertain and divert the impatient audiences who could choose among a variety of spectacles, including gladiator fights, chariot races, and animal baiting. The producer had to please the audience or lose his chance to supply more entertainment.

Roman comedies were sometimes revisions or amalgamations of Greek plays. The themes and characters of Roman tragedies also derived from Greek originals. Figuring often in Roman tragedies was the Trojan War; its characters were reworked into new situations and their agonies reinterpreted.

For costumes the actors wore the Greek tunic (called a CHITON) and a long white cloak or mantle called the PALLIUM. Like the Greeks, the Romans wore low shoes, called the SOCK, for comedy, and shoes with an elevated sole, the BUSKIN, for tragedy. For plays that had a totally Roman setting and narrative, the actors wore the Roman toga. Eventually, Roman actors used traditional Greek masks that immediately identified the characters for the audience. (The question of whether the earliest Roman actors wore masks as well has not been resolved.) The younger Roman characters wore black wigs, older characters wore white wigs, and characters representing slaves wore red wigs.

One of the most intriguing questions concerning Roman plays is the importance of music in the drama. In Greek plays the chorus took most of the responsibility for the music, but in Roman drama actors may have sung their lines, so the Roman plays may have resembled musical comedies. The dialogue in some comedies introduces an interlude of flute playing, indicating that there were times with no actor onstage, no spoken words, and no mimed action, but only a musician to entertain the audience.

The Roman Stage

In the third century B.C. the Romans began building wooden stages that could be taken down quickly and moved as necessary. Eventually, they built stone theaters following Greek plans but varying from the Greek model in a number of important respects. They were built on flat ground, rather than on the hillsides as were the Greek theaters. The influence of the Romans' early wooden stage remained in the permanent buildings in several ways. The Roman stage was elevated, and since there was little or no chorus, the orchestra, in which the chorus moved from place to place, was no longer needed. The SCAENA, or background, against which the action took place, was often three stories tall and was proportionally longer than the Greek *skene* (as in Figure 3). This wide but shallow stage was exploited by the playwrights, who often set their plays on a street with various houses, temples, and other buildings along it.

The space in front of the *scaena* was known as the PROSCAENA, from which the PROSCENIUM ARCH, which frames the stage and separates the actors from the audience, developed much later in the Renaissance. The action took place on

Figure 3. Roman theater at Sabratha, Libya. With the *frons scaena* still in good shape, this photograph shows how the Romans modified the basic Greek design.

Figure 4. Theater of Marcellus.

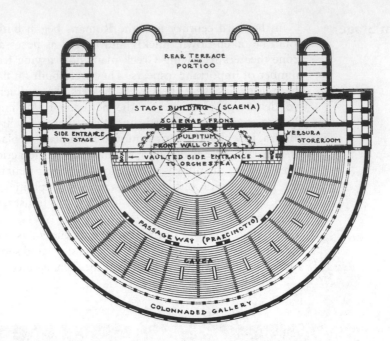

the *pulpitum*, behind the *proscaena*. The potential for the proscenium arch is evident in the plan of the Theater of Marcellus (Figure 4), where the sections to the left and the right of the stage (*pulpitum*) already indicate a separation from the audience.

As in the plan of the Theater of Marcellus, the *frons scaena* (the front wall, or façade) usually had three doors (some had only two), which were ordinarily established as doors of separate buildings, sometimes a temple and the others the homes of chief characters. These doors were active "participants" in the drama; it has been said that the most common line heard in a Roman play is a statement that the door is opening and someone is coming in. The standard Roman play takes great care to justify the entrances and exits of its characters, which may indicate that Roman audiences expected more realism in their comedies than did their Greek counterparts.

The *frons scaena,* the front of the theater, not only was several stories high but also was much more architecturally developed than the *skene* of the Greek theater. The typical Roman architectural devices of multiple arches, columns, and pilasters decorated the *scaena,* giving it a stately appearance. Like the Greek theater, the Roman theater used machinery that permitted actors to be moved through the air and to make entrances from the heavens.

The greatest of the Roman dramatists, Plautus and Terence, would have had their plays produced originally on early wooden stages or on Greek stages. The characteristic Roman theater was not created until the period of the empire, more than a hundred years after their deaths. By that time Seneca could have seen his plays produced in the Roman theater, but they may not ever have been produced in Roman times. His plays may have been closet dramas, designed only to be read.

Roman Drama Timeline

DATE	THEATER	POLITICAL	SOCIAL/CULTURAL
800–600 B.C.			753: Rome is founded.
600–500			6th c.: The Circus Maximus is constructed for chariot races and athletic contests. 509–527: Roman Republic
500–400			450: Roman law is codified in the Twelve Tables.
400–300		390: Rome is rebuilt after a Gallic invasion.	
300–200	3rd c.: Atellan farce, lively improvised scenarios based on domestic life, is imported from southern Italy to Rome. 240: Ludi Romani, a festival in honor of Jupiter, incorporates comedy and tragedy for the first time. The festival, established by the elder Tarquin, Etruscan ruler of Rome, already included chariot races, boxing matches, and other popular entertainments. The plays performed at the festival in 240 are probably translations or imitations of Greek plays. 205–184: Titus Maccius Plautus writes his plays, including *The Twin Menaechmi*.	272: Rome conquers central and southern Italy. 264–241: First Punic War with Carthage 222: Rome conquers northern Italy. 218–201: Second Punic War	c. 300: Roman consul Appius Claudius Crassus builds the Appian Way, which stretches from Rome to Capua. 287: Full equality between plebeians and patricians in Rome
200–100	160: Publius Terentius Afer (Terence) writes *The Brothers*. c. 126–c. 62: Roscius, a popular Roman actor	195: Cato the Elder becomes consul and initiates many reforms in urban development and government representation. 149–146: The Third Punic War. Rome destroys Carthage and Corinth and conquers Greece. 133: Tiberius Gracchus, Roman reformer, is murdered at the instigation of the Senate.	186: Wild animals are exhibited at the Circus Maximus. Contests between wild animals and humans begin shortly hereafter. 106–43: Cicero, Roman orator 105: Gladiatorial contests become part of state festivals.

Roman Drama Timeline (continued)

DATE	THEATER	POLITICAL	SOCIAL/CULTURAL
100 B.C.–1 A.D.		69 B.C.: Cleopatra born. She reigns as queen of Egypt from 51 to 49 and from 48 to her death in 30.	87–54: Catullus, Roman poet
	1st c.: Theaters are built throughout the Roman empire.	60: First Triumvirate (Pompey, Crassus, and Julius Caesar) rules Rome.	70–19: Virgil (P. Virgilius Maro), poet and author of the *Aeneid*
	90: Vitruvius writes *De Architectura*, a treatise on Roman architecture that discusses theater architecture in Greece and Rome.	47: Herod is appointed King of Judea.	47: The library of Ptolemy in Alexandria destroyed by fire; many valuable manuscripts and works of art are lost.
	55: The first permanent stone theater is built in Rome.	45: Julius Caesar is declared dictator by Roman Senate.	46: Julius Caesar stages the first *naumachia* (mock sea battle).
		44: On the Ides of March Caesar is assassinated.	43 B.C.–A.D. 17: Ovid (Publius Ovidius Naso), poet and author of the *Metamorphoses*
		43–28: The Second Triumvirate (Antony, Lepidus, and Octavius) rules Rome.	
		27 B.C.–A.D. 476: Roman empire	22: Roman pantomime, a predecessor of modern ballet, is introduced by Pylades and Bathyllus.
	4 B.C.–A.D. 65: Seneca. Dates for his plays, including *Medea,* are unknown. Seneca commits suicide after suffering a decline in power and influence.	27: Gaius Octavius, Julius Caesar's grand-nephew, becomes the first emperor of the Roman empire, assuming the name Augustus.	19: Horace (65–8 B.C.) writes *Ars Poetica*. 4: Birth of Jesus
1–100		14: Augustus dies, and his stepson Tiberius becomes emperor.	c. 30: Crucifixion of Jesus
		37: Tiberius's grand-nephew Gaius Caesar (Caligula) is named emperor.	
		41: Caligula is assassinated by his own guards; his wife and young daughter are also murdered. Caligula's uncle Claudius is named emperor.	
		54: Claudius is allegedly poisoned by his wife, Julia Agrippina. Claudius's stepson Nero is named emperor.	64: Much of Rome is destroyed by fire. Nero blames the fire on Rome's increasing Christian population and initiates the first large-scale persecution of Christians in Rome.
		68: Nero commits suicide.	79: Mount Vesuvius erupts, destroying Pompeii.
		69: Vespasian is named emperor. He is succeeded by his son Titus.	80: The Colosseum is completed.

Roman Drama Timeline (continued)

DATE	THEATER	POLITICAL	SOCIAL/CULTURAL
100–200	**197–202:** Tertullian writes *De Spectaculis*, denouncing the theater as anti-Christian.	**117:** Hadrian becomes emperor. **120:** Hadrian commissions the building of the Pantheon ("the place of all gods"). **122–126:** Hadrian's Wall is extended across Great Britain. **138:** Hadrian dies and is succeeded by Antonius Pius and then by Marcus Aurelius.	**c. 130–200:** Galen, Roman physicist and pioneer in anatomy and physiology **164–180:** A devastating plague sweeps the Roman empire.
200–300	**c. 300:** Records of earliest religious plays.	Roman citizenship given to every freeborn subject in the empire. Under Roman rule, Carthage regains prominence as a center of culture and commerce. **220:** Goths invade the Balkan Peninsula and Asia Minor. **257:** Goths invade the Black Sea provinces.	
300–400		**313:** Edict of Milan. Emperor Constantine establishes toleration of Christianity. **331:** Emperor Constantine moves the Roman capital from Rome to Constantinople. **360:** Huns invade Europe.	**354–430:** St. Augustine, author of the influential *City of God* and *Confessions* **c. 360:** Scrolls begin to be replaced by books.
400–500		**401–403:** Visigoths invade Italy. **410:** Alaric, king of Visigoths, sacks Rome.	**c. 400:** In part because of the rise of Christianity, state festivals honoring pagan gods cease in Rome. **404:** Gladiatorial contests are abolished. **c. 410:** Experiments with alchemy begin. **523:** Wild animal contests are abolished.

Roman Dramatists
Plautus

All surviving Roman comedy shows the influence of Greek originals. Plautus (254–184 B.C.) is among Rome's most famous playwrights and may have been a member of a troupe that performed Atellan comedy. His middle name is Maccius (a form of Maccus, the clown of the farces), possibly alluding to the role he had habitually played. Tradition has it that he was in the theater for a good while before he began writing comedies. His first plays date from 205 B.C., about thirty-five years after Livius introduced Greek drama to the Romans. No one knows how many plays he wrote, and it has been common to assign many unauthenticated titles to him. About twenty-one plays exist that are thought to be his, the most famous of which are *Amphitryon, The Pot of Gold, The Captives, Curculio, The Braggart Warrior, The Rope,* and *The Twin Menaechmi.*

The last play is probably the best-known Roman comedy. It features Menaechmus from Syracuse, who goes to Epidamnus searching for his lost twin. There he meets people who mistake him for his brother: a cook; a prostitute; Sponge, a typical parasite; and even his brother's wife and father-in-law. The comedy uses all the confusions inherent in mistaken identity.

Plautus (254–184 B.C.)

FROM *THE TWIN MENAECHMI*   *c. 205–184* B.C.

TRANSLATED BY LIONEL CASSON

The Twin Menaechmi was the first ancient play to be translated into a modern language and put on the stage (1486 in Italy). It has been adapted by numerous modern playwrights, including Shakespeare in *The Comedy of Errors* and, more recently, Rodgers and Hart in *The Boys from Syracuse* (1938), a musical that ran on Broadway for 235 performances. *Boys* has been revived numerous times and is still a popular summer theater play. The following scene from the beginning of act III of *The Twin Menaechmi* shows the parasite Sponge mistaking the identity of Menaechmus of Syracuse for that of his friend Menaechmus of Epidamnus. They have a great go-around over a dress in a typical mixup of the kind that originated with Roman comedies and has been popular in farces and comedies ever since.

ACT III

SPONGE: I'm over thirty now, and never have I ever in all those years pulled a more damned fool stunt than the one I pulled today: There was this town meeting, and *I* had to dive in and come up right in the middle of it. While I'm standing there with my mouth open, Menaechmus sneaks off on me. I'll bet he's gone to his girlfriend. Perfectly willing to leave me behind, too!

(*Paces up and down a few times, shaking his head bitterly. Then, in a rage.*) Damn, damn, damn the fellow who first figured out town meetings! All they do is keep a busy man away from his business. Why don't people pick a panel of men of leisure for this kind of thing? Hold a roll call at each meeting and whoever doesn't answer gets fined on the spot. There are plenty of persons around who need only one meal a day; they don't have business hours to keep because they don't go after dinner invitations or give them out. They're the ones to fuss with town meetings and town elections. If that's how things were run, I wouldn't have lost my lunch today. He sure wanted me along, didn't he? I'll go in, anyway. There's still hope of leftovers to soothe my soul. (*He is about to go up to the door when it suddenly swings open and Menaechmus of Syracuse appears, standing on the threshold with a garland, a little askew, on his head; he is holding the dress and listening to Lovey who is chattering at him from inside. Sponge quickly backs off into a corner.*) What's this I see? Menaechmus — and he's leaving, garland and all! The table's been cleared! I sure came in time — in time to walk him home. Well, I'll watch what his game is, and then I'll go and have a word with him.

MENAECHMUS OF SYRACUSE (*to Lovey inside*): Take it easy, will you! I'll have it back to you today in plenty of time, altered and trimmed to perfection. (*Slyly.*) Believe me, you'll say it's not your dress; you won't know it any more.

SPONGE (*to the audience*): He's bringing the dress to the dressmaker. The dining's done, the drinks are down — and Sponge spent the lunch hour outside. God damn it I'm not the man I think I am if I don't get even with him for this, but really even. You just watch. I'll give it to him, I will.

MENAECHMUS OF SYRACUSE (*closing the door and walking downstage; to the audience, jubilantly*): Good god, no one ever expected less — and got more blessings from heaven in one day than me. I dined, I wined, I wenched, and (*holding up the dress*) made off with this to which, from this moment on, she hereby forfeits all right, title, and interest.

SPONGE (*straining his ears, to the audience*): I can't make out what he's saying from back here. Is that full-belly talking about me and my right title and interest?

MENAECHMUS OF SYRACUSE (*to the audience*): She said I stole it from my wife and gave it to her. I saw she was mistaking me for someone else, so I promptly played it as if she and I were having a hot and heavy affair and began to yes her; I agreed right down the line to everything she said. Well, to make a long story short, I never had it so good for so little.

SPONGE (*clenching his fists, to the audience*): I'm going up to him. I'm itching to give him the works. (*Leaves his corner and strides belligerently toward Menaechmus.*)

MENAECHMUS OF SYRACUSE (*to the audience*): Someone coming up to me. Wonder who it is?

SPONGE (*roaring*): Well! You featherweight, you filth, you slime, you disgrace to the human race, you double-crossing good-for-nothing! What did I ever do to you that you had to ruin my life? You sure gave me the slip downtown a little while ago! You killed off the day all right — and held the funeral feast without me. Me who was coheir under the will! Where do you come off to do a thing like that!

MENAECHMUS OF SYRACUSE (*too pleased with life to lose his temper*): Mister, will you please tell me what business you and I have that gives you the right to use language like that to a stranger here, someone you never saw in your life? You hand me that talk and I'll hand you something you won't like.

SPONGE (*dancing with rage*): God damn it, you already have! I know god damned well you have!

MENAECHMUS OF SYRACUSE (*amused and curious*): What's your name, mister?

SPONGE (*as before*): Still making jokes, eh? As if you don't know my name!

MENAECHMUS OF SYRACUSE: So help me, so far as I know, I never heard of you or saw you till this minute. But I know one thing for sure: whoever you are, you'd better behave yourself and stop bothering me.

SPONGE (*taken aback for a minute*): Menaechmus! Wake up!

MENAECHMUS OF SYRACUSE (*genially*): Believe me, to the best of my knowledge, I am awake.

SPONGE: You don't know me?

MENAECHMUS OF SYRACUSE (*as before*): If I did, I wouldn't say I didn't.

SPONGE (*incredulously*): You don't know your own parasite?

MENAECHMUS OF SYRACUSE: Mister, it looks to me as if you've got bats in your belfry.

SPONGE (*shaken, but not convinced*): Tell me this: Didn't you steal that dress there from your wife today and give it to Lovey?

MENAECHMUS OF SYRACUSE: Good god, no! I don't have a wife, I never gave anything to any Lovey, and I never stole any dress. Are you in your right mind?

SPONGE (*aside, groaning*): A dead loss, the whole affair. (*To Menaechmus.*) But you came out of your house wearing the dress! I saw you myself!

MENAECHMUS OF SYRACUSE (*exploding*): Damn you! You think everybody's a pervert just because you are? I was wearing this dress? Is that what you're telling me?

SPONGE: I most certainly am.

MENAECHMUS OF SYRACUSE: Now you go straight to the one place fit for you! No — get yourself to the lunatic asylum; you're stark-raving mad.

SPONGE (*venomously*): God damn it, there's one thing nobody in the world is going to stop me from doing: I'm telling the whole story, exactly what happened, to your wife this minute. All these insults are going to boomerang back on your own head. Believe you me, you'll pay for eating that whole lunch yourself. (*Dashes into the house of Menaechmus of Epidamnus.*)

MENAECHMUS OF SYRACUSE (*throwing his arms wide, to the audience*): What's going on here? Must everyone I lay eyes on play games with me this way? Wait — I hear the door.

(*The door of Lovey's house opens, and one of her maids comes out holding a bracelet. She walks over to Menaechmus and, as he looks on blankly, hands it to him.*)

MAID: Menaechmus, Lovey says would you please do her a big favor and drop this at the jeweler's on your way? She wants you to give him an ounce of gold and have him make the whole bracelet over.

MENAECHMUS OF SYRACUSE (*with alacrity*): Tell her I'll not only take care of this but anything else she wants taken care of. Anything at all. (*He takes the piece and examines it absorbedly.*)

MAID (*watching him curiously, in surprise*): Don't you know what bracelet it is?

MENAECHMUS OF SYRACUSE: Frankly no — except that it's gold.

MAID: It's the one you told us you stole from your wife's jewel box when nobody was looking.

MENAECHMUS OF SYRACUSE (*forgetting himself, in high dudgeon*): I never did anything of the kind!

MAID: You mean you don't remember it? Well, if that's the case, you give it right back!

MENAECHMUS OF SYRACUSE (*after a few seconds of highly histrionic deep thought*): Wait a second. No, I *do* remember it. Of course — this is the one I gave her. Oh, and there's something else: Where are the armlets I gave her at the same time?

MAID (*puzzled*): You never gave her any armlets.

MENAECHMUS OF SYRACUSE (*quickly*): Right you are. This was all I gave her.

MAID: Shall I tell her you'll take care of it?

MENAECHMUS OF SYRACUSE: By all means, tell her. I'll take care of it, all right. I'll see she gets it back the same time she gets the dress back.

MAID (*going up to him and stroking his cheek*): Menaechmus dear, will you do me a favor too? Will you have some earrings made for me? Drop earrings, please; ten grams of gold in each. (*Meaningfully.*) It'll make me *so* glad to see you every time you come to the house.

MENAECHMUS OF SYRACUSE: Sure. (*With elaborate carelessness.*) Just give me the gold. I'll pay for the labor myself.

MAID: Please, you pay for the gold too. I'll make it up to you afterward.

MENAECHMUS OF SYRACUSE: No, you pay for the gold. I'll make it up to *you* afterward. Double.

MAID: I don't have the money.

MENAECHMUS OF SYRACUSE (*with a great air of magnanimity*): Well, any time you get it, you just let me have it.

MAID (*turning to go*): I'm going in now. Anything I can do for you?

MENAECHMUS OF SYRACUSE: Yes. Tell her I'll see to both things — (*sotto voce, to the audience*) that they get sold as quickly as possible for whatever they'll bring. (*As the maid starts walking toward the door.*) Has she gone in yet? (*Hearing a slam.*) Ah, she's in, the door's closed. (*Jubilantly.*) The lord loves me! I've had a helping hand from heaven! (*Suddenly looks about warily.*) But why hang around when I have the time and chance to get away from this (*jerking his thumb at Lovey's house*) pimping parlor here? Menaechmus! Get a move on, hit the road, forward march! I'll take off this garland and toss it to the left here (*doing so*). Then, if anyone tries to follow me, he'll think I went that way. Now I'll go and see if I can find my servant. I want to let him know all the blessings from heaven I've had.

(*He races off, stage right. The stage is now empty.*)

Terence

Terence (c. 190–159 B.C.) is said to have been a North African slave brought to Rome, where his master realized he was unusually intelligent and gifted. After he was freed, Terence took his place in Roman literary life and produced a body of six plays, all of which still exist: *The Woman of Andros, The Self-Tormentor, The Eunuch, Phormio, The Mother-in-Law,* and *The Brothers.* Terence's plays are notable for including a subplot or secondary action — carefully — and for avoiding the technique of addressing the audience directly.

The Romans preferred Plautus's broad farcical humor to Terence's more carefully plotted, elegantly styled plays. Terence borrowed liberally from Greek sources, often more than one for each of his plays, to develop unusually complicated plots. A manager or producer worked with him on all his plays, and the musician who worked with him was a slave, Flaccus. Terence's productive life was relatively short. He died on a trip to Greece, apparently worrying over a piece of missing luggage said to have contained new plays.

Terence's situation was unusual: he had two wealthy Roman patrons who were interested in seeing the best Greek comedy brought to the Romans. Consequently, they paid for his productions and gave him more support than the average comic playwright could have expected. Terence's dramatic skills developed considerably from the beginning to the end of his work, contrasting sharply with the repetitive nature of Plautus's work. Terence was more than a translator, but he wrote at a time when Romans were interested in emulating the Greeks, and his fidelity to Greek originals was one of his strongest recommendations.

Terence (*c. 190–159 B.C.*)
FROM *THE BROTHERS*   *160 B.C.*
TRANSLATED BY ROBERT GRAVES

The ending of *The Brothers,* generally recognized as Terence's masterpiece and certainly the most influential of his plays, has Demea planning a reversal on his brother, Micio. Micio is a good, easygoing bachelor who wishes well for others. Demea has been a stern father to one of his sons, Ctesipho, and has tried to steer him in a direction other than the one Ctesipho wants to follow. Demea has entrusted the upbringing of his second son, Aeschinus, to his lenient brother, Micio. Both sons deceive both brothers and end up with the women they want rather than the women the brothers want for them. Meanwhile, Demea gives up and turns the tables on Micio, engineering his brother's marriage to Aeschinus's mother-in-law. In the process of all this, Demea decides to adopt the gentle, easygoing ways of his brother and to forsake his former stern behavior.

This play was adapted often in the seventeenth century by Marston, Beaumont and Fletcher, and others. Molière relied on it for his *School for Wives*. At least five plays were adapted from it for the eighteenth-century English stage.

FROM ACT V

MICIO (*to Syrus, within*): My brother ordered it,° say ye! Where is he? . . . Hah, Brother, was it you who ordered this?

DEMEA: Yes, that I did! And in this and all things else I'm ready to do whatever may conduce to the uniting, serving, helping, and the joining together of both families.

AESCHINUS (*to Micio*): Pray, Sir, let it be so!

MICIO: Well, I've nothing to say against it.

DEMEA: Truth, 'tis no more than we are obliged to do. For first, she's your son's mother-in-law . . .

MICIO: What then?

DEMEA: A very virtuous and modest woman . . .

MICIO: So they say indeed.

DEMEA: Not weighed down by years . . .

MICIO: Not yet.

DEMEA: But past child-bearing: a lonesome woman whom nobody esteems . . .

MICIO (*aside*): What the Devil is he at?

DEMEA: . . . Therefore you ought to marry her; and you Aeschinus, should do what you can to bring this about.

MICIO: Who? I marry?

DEMEA: Yes, you.

MICIO: I, prithee?

DEMEA: Yes, you I say.

MICIO: Pho, you are fooling us, surely?

DEMEA (*to Aeschinus*): If thou hast any life in thee, persuade him to it.

AESCHINUS: Dear Father . . .

MICIO (*interrupting*): Blockhead! Dost thou take in earnest what he says?

DEMEA: 'Tis in vain to refuse; it can't be avoided.

MICIO: Pho, you are in your dotage!

AESCHINUS: Good Sir, let me win this one favor.

MICIO (*angrily*): Art out of thy wits, let me alone!

DEMEA: Come, come! Hearken for once to what your son says.

MICIO: Haven't ye played the fool enough yet? Shall I at threescore and five marry an old woman who's ready to drop into the grave? This is your wise counsel, is it?

AESCHINUS: Pray, Sir, do; I've promised you shall.

MICIO: You promised, with a mischief! Promise for thyself, thou chit!

DEMEA: Fie, fie! What if he had begged a greater favor from you?

MICIO: As if there were any greater favor than this!

DEMEA: Pray grant his request.

AESCHINUS: Good Sir, be not so hard-hearted.

DEMEA: Pho, promise him for once!

MICIO: Will ye never leave baiting me?

My brother ordered it: Demea ordered the breaking down of a wall to allow the two families to communicate. In this way Demea imitates the good-naturedness of his brother, Micio, and traps him into marrying Aeschinus's mother-in-law.

AESCHINUS: Not till I've prevailed, Sir.

MICIO: Truth, this is downright forcing a man.

DEMEA: Come, Micio, be good-natured and consent.

MICIO: Though this be the most damned, foolish, ridiculous whim, and the most averse to my nature that could possibly be, yet since you are so extremely set upon it, I'll humor ye for once.

AESCHINUS: That is excellent, I'm obliged to ye beyond measure.

DEMEA (*aside*): Well, what's next? . . . What shall I say next? This is as I'd have it. . . . What's more to be done?

(*To Micio.*)

Ho! There's Hegio our poor kinsman, and nearest relation; in truth, we ought in conscience to do something for him.

MICIO: What, pray?

DEMEA: There's a small plot of land in the suburbs, which you farm out — pray let's give him that to live on.

MICIO: A small one, say ye?

DEMEA: Though it were a great one, you might yet give it to him. He has been as good as a father to Pamphila; he's a very honest man, our kinsman, and you couldn't bestow it better. Besides, Brother, there's a certain proverb (none of my own, I assure you) which you so well and wisely made use of: "That age has always this ill effect of making us more worldly, as well as wiser." We should do well to avoid this scandal. 'Tis a true proverb, Brother, and ought to be held in mind.

MICIO: What's all this? . . . Well, so let it be, if he has need of it.

AESCHINUS: Brave Father, I vow!

DEMEA: Now you are my true brother, both in body and soul.

MICIO: I'm glad of it.

DEMEA (*aside, laughing*): I've stabbed him with his own weapons, i'fack!

(*Enter Syrus, with a pick-axe upon his shoulders.*)

SYRUS (*to Demea*): The job is done as ye ordered, Sir.

DEMEA: Thou art an honest lad. . . . And upon my conscience I think Syrus deserves his freedom.

MICIO: He, his freedom? For what exploit?

DEMEA: O, for a thousand.

SYRUS: O dear Mr. Demea, you are a rare gentleman, edad you are! You know I've looked after the young gentlemen from their cradles. I taught them, advised them, and instructed them all I possibly could.

DEMEA: Nothing more evident! Nay, more than that, he catered for them, pimped for them, and in the morning took care of a debauchee for them. These are no ordinary accomplishments, I can assure ye.

SYRUS: Your worship's very merry.

DEMEA: Besides, he was prime mover in buying this music-girl. It was he who managed the whole intrigue, and 'tis no more than justice to reward him, as an encouragement to others! In short, Aeschinus desires the same thing.

MICIO (*to Aeschinus*): Do you desire it too?

AESCHINUS: Yes, if you please, Sir.

MICIO: Since 'tis so, come hither, Syrus! Thou art a free man.

(*Syrus kneels down, Micio lays his hand on his head, and after that gives him a cuff on the ear.*)

SYRUS (*rising up*): Generously done! A thousand thanks to ye all, and to you, Mr. Demea.

DEMEA: I'm well satisfied.

AESCHINUS: And I too.

SYRUS: I won't question it, Sir. But I wish heartily my joy were more complete, that my poor spouse Phrygia might be made as free as I am.

DEMEA: Truth, she's a mighty good woman.

SYRUS: And your grandson's first foster-mother, too.

DEMEA: Faith, in good earnest, if for that, she deserves her freedom before any woman in the world.

MICIO: What! For that simple service?

DEMEA: Yes, indeed! In fine, I'll pay for her freedom myself.

SYRUS: God's blessing light upon your worship, and grant all your wishes.

MICIO: Syrus, thou hast made a good day's work of it.

DEMEA: Besides, Brother, it would be a deed of charity to lend him a little money to set up in business that he may face the world without fear. I undertake that he'll soon repay it.

MICIO: Not a penny-piece!

AESCHINUS: He's a very honest fellow, Sir.

SYRUS: Upon my word, I'll repay you the loan. Do but trust me!

AESCHINUS: Pray do, Sir.

MICIO: I'll consider the matter with care.

DEMEA: He shall pay ye, I'll see to that.

SYRUS (to Demea): Egad, you're the best man alive.

AESCHINUS: And the pleasantest in the world.

MICIO: What's the meaning of this, Brother? How comes this sudden change of humor? Why this gallant squandering and profusion?

DEMEA: I'll tell ye, Brother. These sons of yours don't reckon you a sweet-natured and pleasant man because you live as you should and do what is just and reasonable, but because you fawn upon them, cocker them up, and give them what they'll spend. Now, son Aeschinus, if you are dissatisfied with my course of life, because I wouldn't indulge you in all things, right or wrong, then I'll not trouble my head with you any further. Be free to squander, buy mistresses, and do what you will! But if you wish me to advise ye, and set ye up, and help ye too in matters of which your youth can give ye but little understanding — matters of which you are over-fond, and don't well consider — see, here I'm ready to stand by you.

AESCHINUS: Dear Sir, we commit ourselves wholly to your charge; for you know what's fitting to be done far better than we . . . But what will ye do for my brother Ctesipho?

DEMEA: Why, let him take the music-girl; and so bid adieu to general wenching.

AESCHINUS: That's very reasonable. (To the spectators.) Gentlemen, your favor!

(Exeunt° all.)

[S.D.] *Exeunt:* Latin for "they go out."

Seneca

The surviving Roman plays come from just three hands: Plautus, Terence, and Seneca (4 B.C.–A.D. 65). The comedies of Plautus are raucous, broad, and farcical; those of Terence are polished and carefully structured. Seneca wrote tragedies that were well known to Elizabethans such as Marlowe and Shakespeare, and it is clear that the Elizabethan Age found SENECAN TRAGEDY to be peculiarly suited to its own temperament.

Senecan tragedies were based on either Greek or Roman themes and included murder, bloodthirsty actions (many of which did not occur on stage but were only described), horror of various kinds, ghosts, and long, bombastic speeches. Signs of Senecan influence can be seen in Elizabethan drama, with its taste for many of these devices; plays like *Hamlet* are notable for ending in a pool of blood, with most of the actors lying dead onstage. The theme of revenge was also prized by Seneca and, later, by the Elizabethans.

Not a professional theater person, Seneca was wealthy and learned, a philosopher active in the government of Emperor Nero's Rome. His plays, most of which were adapted from Euripides, were probably written only to be read, as was common at his time, or perhaps recited, although there is no record of their having been performed. The Roman people thirsted for mime and farce but had much less taste for serious plays.

Ten plays attributed to Seneca exist, nine of which are surely his and one of which is only possibly his. His most famous are *Mad Hercules, The Phoenician Women, Medea, Phaedra, Agamemnon, Thyestes,* and *The Trojan Women.*

Seneca (4 B.C.–A.D. 65)
FROM *THYESTES*

TRANSLATED BY ELLA ISABEL HARRIS

Thyestes, probably adapted from the *Oresteia* of Aeschylus, influenced a number of Elizabethan revenge tragedies, such as Shakespeare's *Hamlet.* The story is gruesome even by modern standards. Thyestes seduces his brother Atreus's wife, and Atreus banishes him. When Atreus summons Thyestes to Atreus's home, he goes suspiciously, hoping to be able to see his children. The banquet Atreus holds for Thyestes seems to signal reconciliation between the brothers. But when it is over, Atreus brings in the heads of Thyestes' children, revealing that Thyestes has just eaten their bodies in the feast.

The second scene from act V — before Thyestes is told about the meal he has eaten — follows in its entirety. It shows Thyestes wrestling with himself in a passion of uncertainty. Thyestes' soliloquy is a psychological study of the effects of grief, care, uncertainty, and fear. Seneca's plays have many such soliloquies, and their revelations of complex emotional states deeply impressed the age of Shakespeare.

ACT V • Scene II

(*Thyestes sits alone at the banquet table, half overcome with wine; he tries to sing and be gay, but some premonition of evil weighs upon him.*)

THYESTES (*to himself*): By long grief dulled, put by thy cares, my heart,
    Let fear and sorrow fly and bitter need,
    Companion of thy timorous banishment,
    And shame, hard burden of afflicted souls.
    Whence thou has fallen profits more to know
    Than whither; great is he who with firm step
    Moves on the plain when fallen from the height;
    He who, oppressed by sorrows numberless
    And driven from his realm, with unbent neck
    Carries his burdens, not degenerate
    Or conquered, who stands firm beneath the weight
    Of all his burdens, he is great indeed.
    Now scatter all the clouds of bitter fate,
    Put by all signs of thy unhappy days,
    In happy fortunes show a happy face,
    Forget the old Thyestes. Ah, this vice
    Still follows misery: never to trust

In happy days; though better fortunes come,
Those who have borne afflictions find it hard
To joy in better days. What holds me back,
Forbids me celebrate the festal tide?
What cause of grief, arising causelessly,
Bids me to weep? What art thou that forbids
That I should crown my head with festal wreath?
It does forbid, forbid! Upon my head
The roses languish, and my hair that drips
With ointment rises as with sudden fear,
My face is wet with showers of tears that fall
Unwillingly, and groans break off my song.
Grief loves accustomed tears, the wretched feel
That they must weep. I would be glad to make
Most bitter lamentation, and to wail,
And rend this robe with Tyrian purple dyed.
My mind gives warning of some coming grief,
Presages future ills. The storm that smites
When all the sea is calm weighs heavily
Upon the sailor. Fool! What grief, what storm,
Dost thou conceive? Believe thy brother now.
Be what it may, thou fearest now too late,
Or causelessly. I do not wish to be
Unhappy, but vague terror smites my breast.
No cause is evident and yet my eyes
O'erflow with sudden tears. What can it be,
Or grief, or fear? Or has great pleasure tears?

The surviving Roman plays offer enough variety to give us an idea of what the drama achieved. Like so much of Roman culture, Roman drama rested in the shadow of Greek accomplishments. The Romans were responsible for maintaining the Greek texts, allowing us to see a great deal of their work. Although it may be true that much of the Roman drama that was produced no longer exists, what survives shows variety and high quality.

Medieval Drama

The Role of the Church

The medieval period in Europe (A.D. 476–1500) began with the collapse of Rome, a calamity of such magnitude that the years between then and the beginning of the Crusades in 1095 have been traditionally, if erroneously, called the Dark Ages. Historians used this term to refer to their lack of knowledge about a time in which no great central powers organized society or established patterns of behavior and standards in the arts.

Drama, or at least records of it, all but disappeared. The major institution to profit from the fall of the Roman empire was the Roman Catholic Church, which in the ninth and tenth centuries enjoyed considerable power and influence. Many bishops considered drama a godless activity, a distraction from the piety that the church demanded of its members. During the great age of cathedral building and the great ages of religious painting and religious music — from the seventh century to the thirteenth — drama was not officially approved. Therefore, it is a striking irony that the rebirth of drama in the Western world should have taken place in the heart of the monasteries, developing slowly and inconspicuously until it outgrew its beginnings.

The Church may well have intended nothing more than the simple dramatization of its message. Or it is possible that the people may have craved drama, and the Church's response could have been an attempt to answer their needs. In either event, the Church could never have foreseen the outcome of adding a few moments of drama to the liturgy, the church services. LITURGICAL DRAMA began in the ninth century with TROPES, or embellishments, which were sung during parts of the Mass (the public celebration of the Eucharist). The earliest known example of a trope, called the QUEM QUAERITIS ("Whom seek ye?"), grew out of the Easter Mass and was sung in a monastic settlement in Switzerland called St. Gall:

ANGEL: Whom seek ye in the sepulchre, O ye Christians?
THREE MARYS: Jesus of Nazareth, who was crucified, O ye Angels.
ANGEL: He is not here; he is risen as he has foretold.
    Go, announce that he is risen from the sepulchre.

Some scholars think that in its earliest form this trope was sung by four monks in a dialogue pattern, three monks representing the three Marys at Christ's

145

tomb and the other representing the angel. Tropes like the *Quem Quaeritis* evolved over the years to include a number of participants — monks, nuns, and choirboys in different communities — as the tropes spread from church to church throughout the Continent. These dramatic interpolations never became dramas separate from the Mass itself, although their success and popularity led to experiments with other dramatic sequences centering on moments in the Mass and in the life of Christ. The actors in these pieces did not think of themselves as specialists or professionals; they were simply monks or nuns who belonged to the church. The churchgoers obviously enjoyed the tropes, and more were created, despite the Church's official position on drama.

In the tenth century a nun called Hrotsvitha entertained herself and her fellow nuns with imitations of the Latin dramatist Terence. Although her own subject matter was holy in nature, she realized that Terence was an amusing comic writer with a polished style. She referred to herself as "the strong voice of Gandersheim," her community in Saxony, and said that she had "not hesitated to imitate in my writings a poet whose works are so widely read, my object being to glorify, within the limits of my poor talent, the laudable chastity of Christian virgins." Her plays are very short moral tales, often illustrating moments in the lives of Christian martyred women. As far as is known, these plays do not seem to have gone beyond the nuns' walls; therefore, they had little effect on the drama developing in the period.

Once dramatic scenes were added that took the action outside of the liturgy, it was not long before dramas were being staged outside the church. The Anglo-Norman drama *Adam,* dating from the twelfth century, has explicit stage directions establishing its setting outside the church. The play is to be staged on the west side of the church with a platform extending from the steps. The characters of Adam, Eve, God (called Figura), and the Devil and his assistants are given costumes and extensive dialogue. The dramatic detail in this play implies a considerable development of plot and action, which, despite its theological matter, is plainly too elaborate to be contained within the service of the Mass.

Miracle Plays

Once outside the church, the drama flourished and soon became independent, although its themes continued to be religious and its services were connected with religious festivals. In 1264 Pope Urban IV added to the religious calendar a new, important feast: Corpus Christi, celebrated beginning on the first Thursday after Trinity Sunday, about two months after Easter. The purpose of the feast was to celebrate the doctrine declaring that the body of Christ was real and present in the Host (consecrated bread or wafer) taken by the faithful in the sacrament of Communion.

At first the feast of Corpus Christi was localized in Liège, Belgium. But in the fourteenth and fifteenth centuries it spread through papal decree and became one of the chief feasts of the church. Among other things, it featured a procession and pageant in which the Host was displayed publicly through the streets of a town. Because of the importance and excitement of this feast, entire communities took part in the celebration.

MIRACLE PLAYS on the subject of miracles performed by saints developed late in the twelfth century in both England and on the Continent. Typically, these plays focused on the Virgin Mary and St. Nicholas, both of whom had strong followings (sometimes described as cults) during the medieval period. Mary is often portrayed as helping those in need and danger — often at the last minute. Some of those she saved may have seemed unsavory sinners to a pious audience, but the point was that the saint saved all who truly wished to be saved.

Although they quickly became public entertainments removed from the church building and were popular as Corpus Christi entertainments throughout the fifteenth century, few miracle plays survive in English because King Henry VIII banned them in the middle of the sixteenth century during his reformation of the Church. As a result, they were not performed or preserved.

The craft guilds, professional organizations of workers involved in the same trade — carpenters, wool merchants, and so on — soon began competing with each other in producing plays that could be performed during the feast of Corpus Christi. Most of their plays derived from Bible stories and the life of Christ. Religious guilds, such as the Confrerie of the Passion, produced plays in Paris and elsewhere on the Continent. Because the Bible is silent on many details of Christ's life, some plays invented new material and illuminated dark areas, thereby satisfying the intense curiosity medieval Christians had about events the Bible omitted.

Mystery Plays

The Church did not ignore drama after it left the church buildings. Since the plays had religious subject matter and could be used to teach the Bible and to model Christian behavior, they remained of considerable value to the Church.

First performed by the clergy, these religious plays dramatized the mystery of Christ's Passion. Later the plays were produced by members of craft guilds, and they became known as CRAFT or MYSTERY PLAYS. Beginning in the medieval period, the word *mystery* was used to describe a skill or trade known only to a few who apprenticed and mastered its special techniques; it also referred to religious mysteries.

By the fifteenth century, mystery plays and the feast of Corpus Christi were popular almost everywhere in Europe, and in England certain towns produced exceptionally elaborate cycles with unusually complex and ambitious plays. The CYCLES were groups of plays numbering from twenty-four to forty-eight. Four cycles have been preserved: the Chester, York, Towneley (Wakefield), and N-Town cycles, named for their towns of origin. N-Town plays were a generic version of plays that any town could take and use as its own, although the plays were probably written near Lincoln.

The plays were performed again and again during annual holidays and feasts, and the texts were carefully preserved. Some of the plays, such as *The Fall of Lucifer,* are very short. Others are more elaborate in length and complexity and resemble modern plays: *Noah,* from the Wakefield Cycle, which has been produced regularly in recent history; *The Slaughter of Innocents;* and *The Second Shepherds' Play,* one of the most entertaining mystery plays.

The producers of the plays often had a sense of appropriateness in their choice of subjects. For example, the Water-Drawers guild sponsored *Noah's Flood,* the Butchers (because they sold "flesh") *Temptation, The Woman Taken in Adultery,* and the Shipwrights *The Building of the Ark.*

Among the best-known mystery plays is the somewhat farcical *The Second Shepherds' Play,* which is both funny and serious. It tells of a crafty shepherd named Mak who steals a lamb from his fellow shepherds and takes it home. His wife, Gill, then places it in a cradle and pretends it is her baby. Eventually the shepherds — who suspect Mak from the first — smoke out the fraud and give Mak a blanket-tossing for their trouble. But after they do so, they see a star in the heavens and turn their attention to the birth of baby Jesus, the Lamb of God. They join the Magi and come to pay homage to the Christ Child.

The easy way in which the profane elements of everyday life coexisted with the sacred in medieval times has long interested scholars. *The Second Shepherds' Play* virtually breaks into two parts, the first dedicated to the wickedness of Mak and Gill and the horseplay of the shepherds. But once Mak has had his due reward, the play alters in tone and the sense of devotion to Christian teachings becomes uppermost. The fact that the mystery plays moved away from liturgical Latin and to the vernacular (local) language made such a juxtaposition of sacred and profane much more possible.

The dominance of the guilds in producing mystery plays suggests that guilds enjoyed increasing political power and authority. The guilds grew stronger and more influential — probably at the expense of the Church. Some historians have seen this development as crucial to the growing secularization of the Middle Ages.

Morality Plays

MORALITY PLAYS were never part of any cycle but developed independently as moral tales in the late fourteenth or early fifteenth century on the Continent and in England. They do not illustrate moments in the Bible, nor do they describe the life of Christ or the saints. Instead, they describe the lives of people facing the temptations of the world. The plays are careful to present a warning to the unwary that their souls are always in peril, that the devil is on constant watch, and that people must behave properly if they are to be saved.

One feature of morality plays is their reliance on ALLEGORY, a favorite medieval device. Allegory is the technique of giving abstract ideas or values a physical representation. In morality plays, abstractions such as goodness became characters in the drama. In modern times we sometimes use allegory in art, as when we represent justice as a blindfolded woman. Allegorically, justice should act impartially because she does not "see" any distinctions, such as those of rank or privilege, that characterize most people standing before a judge.

The use of allegory permitted medieval dramatists to personify abstract values such as sloth, greed, daintiness, vanity, strength, and hope by making them characters and placing them onstage in action. The dramatist specified symbols, clothing, and gestures appropriate to these abstract figures, thus helping the audience recognize the ideas the characters represented. The use of allegory was an extremely durable technique that was already established in medieval painting, printed books, and books of emblems, in which, for example, sloth would be shown as a man reclining lazily on a bed or greed would be represented as overwhelmingly fat and vanity as a figure completely absorbed in a mirror.

The central problem in the morality play was the salvation of human beings, represented by an individual's struggle to avoid sin and damnation and achieve salvation in the otherworld. As in *Everyman* (c. 1495), a late-medieval play that is the best known of the morality plays, the subjects were usually abstract battles between certain vices and specific virtues for the possession of the human soul, a theme repeated in the Elizabethan age in Marlowe's *Doctor Faustus*.

In many ways the morality play was a dramatized sermon designed to teach a moral lesson. Marked by high seriousness, it was nevertheless entertaining. Using allegory to represent abstract qualities allowed the didactic playwrights to draw clear-cut lines of moral force: Satan was always bad; angels were always good. The allegories were clear, direct, and apparent to all who witnessed the plays.

We do not have much knowledge of the origins of morality plays. Many of them are lost, but some that remain are occasionally performed: *The Pride of Life,* the earliest extant morality play; *The Castle of Perseverance; Wisdom; Mankind;* and *Everyman* are the best known. They all enjoyed a remarkable popularity in the latter part of the medieval period, all the way up to the early Renaissance.

The Medieval Stage

Relatively little commentary survives about the conventions of medieval staging, and some of it is contradictory. We know that in the earliest years — after the tropes developed into full-blown religious scenes acted inside the cathedrals — certain sections of the church were devoted to specific short plays. These areas of the church became known as MANSIONS; each mansion represented a building or physical place known to the audience. The audience moved from one mansion to another, seeing play after play, absorbing the dramatic representation of the events, characters, and locale associated with each mansion.

The tradition of moving from mansion to mansion inside the church carried over into the performances that took place later outside the church. Instead of mansions, wagons with raised stages provided the playing areas. Usually, the wagons remained stationary and the audience moved from one to another. During the guild cycles the pageants would move; the performers would give their plays at several locales so that many people could see them.

According to medieval descriptions, drawings, and reconstructions, a PAGEANT CART could also be simply a flat surface drawn on wheels that had a wagon next to it; these structures touched on their long side. In some cases a figure could descend from an upper area as if from the clouds, or actors could descend from the pageants onto the audience's level to enact a descent into an underworld. The stage was, then, a raised platform visible to the audience below (Figure 5).

A curtain concealed a space, usually inside or below the wagon, for changing costumes. The actors used costumes and props, sometimes very elaborate and expensive, in an effort to make the drama more impressive. Indeed, between the thirteenth and the sixteenth centuries, a number of theatrical effects were developed to please a large audience. For instance, in the morality and mystery plays the devils were often portrayed as frightening, grotesque, and sometimes even comic figures. They became crowd pleasers. A sensational element was developed in some of the plays in the craft cycles, especially those about the lives of the saints and martyrs, in which there were plenty of chances to portray horrifying tortures.

The prop that seems to have pleased the most audiences was a complex machine known as the MOUTH OF HELL or "Hell mouth," usually a large fish-shaped orifice from which smoke and explosions, fueled by gunpowder, belched constantly. The devils took great delight in stuffing their victims into these maws. According to a contemporary account, one of the machines required seventeen men to operate.

The level of realism achieved by medieval plays was at times startling. In addition to visual realism, medieval plays involved a psychological level of participation on the part of both audience and actor. Sometimes they demanded

Figure 5. Pageant wagon

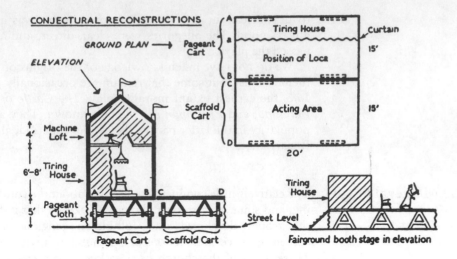

that the actors suffer in accord with the characters they played. Some records attest to characters playing Christ on the cross having to be revived after their hearts stopped, and at least one Judas apparently was hanged just a little too long and had to be resuscitated.

The Actors

In the early days of liturgical drama, the actors in the tropes were monks and choirboys, and in the mystery plays they were drawn from the guilds. At first all the actors were male, but records show that eventually women took important roles.

The demands of more sophisticated plays encouraged the development of a kind of professionalism, although it seems unlikely that players in the cycles could have supported themselves exclusively on their earnings. Special skills became essential for the design and operation of complex stage machines and for the performance of acrobatics that were expected of certain characters, such as devils. As actors developed facility in delivering lines and as writers found ways to incorporate more challenging elements in their plays, a professionalism no doubt arose, even if actors and writers had few opportunities to earn a living on the stage.

By the second half of the sixteenth century, the early Renaissance, groups of wandering actors were producing highly demanding and sophisticated plays, and writers such as Shakespeare were able to join them and make a living. When these professionals secured their own theaters, they had no problems filling them with good drama, with actors, and with an audience.

Dramatic techniques developed in the medieval period were put to good use in the Renaissance theater. For example, the colorful and dramatic devil characters that stalked the mystery plays were transformed into sophisticated villains in Elizabethan drama. The devil Mephistopheles (Mephistophilis) behaves like a smooth Tudor lawyer in Marlowe's *Doctor Faustus;* Iago in *Othello* is suspected of having cloven hooves. Perhaps one important difference is that the Elizabethan devil-villains are truly frightening, since they are so recognizably human in their villainy.

Medieval Drama Timeline

DATE	THEATER	POLITICAL	SOCIAL/CULTURAL
400–500		**476:** The fall of Rome and beginning of the Dark Ages **483–565:** Byzantine Emperor Justinian, author of the Code of Civil Laws	**480–524:** Boëthius, Roman scholar, philosopher, and theologian, is executed for treason.
500–600	**500–1000:** Traveling performers proliferate in Europe.		**570–632:** Muhammed, founder of Islam **590–594:** Devastating plague spreads through Europe and kills half the population.
600–700		Persians take Damascus and Jerusalem.	**636:** Anglo-Saxons are introduced to Christianity. **695:** Jews are persecuted in Spain.
700–800		**768–814:** Charlemagne reigns in France and is crowned Holy Roman Emperor in 800 by Pope Leo III in Rome on Christmas Day. **792:** Beginning of the Viking era in Britain	**c. 710:** Buddhist monasteries in Japan become centers of civilization. **787:** The Council of Nicaea officially rejects iconoclasm.
800–900	**9th c.:** Beginnings of liturgical drama	**843:** Treaty of Verdun divides the Holy Roman Empire into German, French, and Italian kingdoms. **850:** Rurik, a Northman, becomes ruler of Kiev, an important Russian trading post. Trade begins with Constantinople, which remains a commercial and cultural center throughout the Dark Ages.	**c. 800–1000:** *Beowulf,* one of the first long poems written in English **855:** Earliest known attempts at polyphonic music **863:** Cyril and Methodius invent a Slavic alphabet called Cyrillic.
900–1000	**c. 900:** Farces make their first appearance since classical times. **925:** Earliest extant Easter trope **965–975:** Compilation of the *Regularis Concordia* (Monastic Agreement) by Ethelwood, bishop of Winchester, England. The *Regularis Concordia* contains the text of the earliest extant playlet in Europe, with directions for its performance.		**c. 900:** The beginnings of the famous Arabian tales called *A Thousand and One Nights*

Medieval Drama Timeline (continued)

DATE	THEATER	POLITICAL	SOCIAL/CULTURAL
900–1000 (continued)	970: Plays of Hrosvitha, a German nun and the first known female playwright. The six plays are modeled on the comedies of Terence but deal with serious religious matters.	1000: Leif Ericson, possibly the first European to venture to North America	975: Arabic arithmetical notation is brought to Europe by the Arabs. 980–1037: Avicenna (Ibn Sina), Arab physician and philosopher 990: Development of systemic musical notation.
1000–1100		1066: The Normans conquer Britain. 1086: Compilation of the *Domesday Book,* a survey of the British economy, population, and land ownership at that time 1096–1099: First Crusade. Crusaders take Jerusalem from the Arabs.	1054: The Great Schism separates Eastern and Western Churches in Europe. 1079–1142: Peter Abelard, French theologian and philosopher
1100–1200	12th c.: Religious plays are first performed outside churches.	1109–1113: Anglo-French War 1147–1149: Second Crusade. Crusaders lose Jerusalem to the Arabs. 1167–1227: Genghis Khan, founder of Mongol empire 1189-1193: Third Crusade. Crusaders fail to recapture Jerusalem.	c. 1125: Beginnings of French troubadour and trouvère music 1133–1855: St. Bartholomew's Fair, London, England 1167: Oxford University is founded.
1200–1300	1250: *Easter Play of Muri,* beginnings of German drama 1276–1277: French poet Adam de la Halle writes *The Play of the Greenwood,* the oldest extant medieval secular drama.	1202–1204: Fourth Crusade. Crusaders seize Constantinople. 1212: Children's Crusade. Thousands of children are sent as crusaders to Jerusalem; most die or are sold as slaves. 1215: King John of England signs the Magna Carta, guaranteeing habeas corpus, trial by jury, and restrictions on the power of the king. 1224–1227: Anglo-French War 1228: Sixth Crusade 1248: Seventh Crusade	c. 1202: Court jesters appear at European courts. 1225: Guillaume de Lorris writes *Roman de la Rose,* a story of courtly wooing. 1225–1274: Thomas Aquinas, important Scholastic philosopher 1254–1324: Marco Polo, Venetian traveler whose accounts of life in China became famous in the West 1264: First celebration of the feast of Corpus Christi c. 1282: Florence emerges as the leading European city of commerce and finance.

Medieval Drama Timeline (continued)

DATE	THEATER	POLITICAL	SOCIAL/CULTURAL
1300–1400	**14th c.:** Beginnings of *noh* drama in Japan	**1337:** Hundred Years War begins.	**c. 1302:** Dante's *Divine Comedy* **1304–1374:** Petrarch, Italian poet **1347–1351:** The Black Death kills approximately 75 million people throughout Europe. **1360–1400:** *Piers Plowman* and *Sir Gawain and the Green Knight*: achievements of Middle English literature **1387:** Chaucer's *Canterbury Tales*
	c. 1375: *The Second Shepherds' Play,* part of the English Wakefield Cycle **1398–1548:** Confrèrie de la Passion at Paris performs religious plays.		
1400–1500	**c. 1425:** *The Castle of Perseverance,* English morality play **1429:** Plautus's plays are rediscovered in Italy.	**1429:** Joan of Arc's troops resist the British siege of Orleans, an important turning point in the Hundred Years War. **1431:** Joan of Arc is captured and burned as a heretic. **1453:** France wins the Hundred Years War and becomes an important continental power. England abandons the Continent to develop its naval forces. **1481:** Spanish Inquisition	**1400–1455:** Fra Angelico, Italian painter **c. 1406–1469:** Fra Lippo Lippi, Italian painter best known for his frescoes **c. 1430:** Modern English develops from Middle English. **c. 1450:** Gutenberg invents movable type.
	c. 1470: *Pierre Patheline,* most renowned of medieval French farces	**1482–1485:** Reign of Richard III. Richard maintains a company of actors at court, which tours surrounding towns when not needed by His Majesty. **1485–1509:** Reign of Henry VII, first of the Tudor rulers. Like Richard III, Henry maintains a company of actors.	**1485:** Sir Thomas Malory publishes *Le Morte Darthur,* one of the first books printed in England. **1492:** Columbus sets sail across the Atlantic.
	1490: *Corpus Christi* play of Eger, Bohemia **c. 1495:** *Everyman,* best-known English morality play		
1500–1600	**1527:** Henry VII builds a House of Revels in which to stage court entertainments. **1548:** Production of plays is forbidden in Paris. **1558:** Elizabeth I forbids performance of all religious plays.	**1509–1547:** Reign of Henry VII **1534:** Henry VII breaks with the Roman Catholic Church. Drama is used as a political instrument to attack or defend opposing viewpoints. **1558–1603:** Reign of Elizabeth I	**1509:** Pope Clement V resides at Avignon, beginning the Babylonian Captivity, during which Rome is not the papal seat. **1545–1563:** The Council of Trent is convened by the Catholic Church to solidify its control over expressions of Church doctrine. Medieval religious plays are deemed provocative and controversial.

Hrosvitha

The German nun Hrosvitha (also Hroswitha, Roswitha, Hrotsvit, and Hrotsuit) belonged to the Benedictine convent in Gandersheim, founded in 852. Her name translates to "strong voice," a term she uses to describe herself in her writing. Her voice is that of a learned woman, and today it can be heard as a feminist voice in a time and society that were unquestioningly patriarchal.

Hrosvitha is considered not only the earliest German woman poet but the first woman dramatist in Europe. A Saxon noblewoman, she entered the convent c. 959, living with nuns who were themselves of noble birth. The abbey was under the protection of Otto I (912–973), who united a powerful Germany and produced a long-lasting period of peace and development. Otto became the Holy Roman Emperor on February 13, 962. His rule, dubbed the Ottonian Renaissance, favored religion, learning, the arts, and music.

During this period, the abbey at Gandersheim was obligated not to the Church but to the king himself, and Otto eventually released it from his direct governance, permitting it to maintain a law court and to coin money. While such political issues may not have affected Hrosvitha, the fact that the period was one of learning and scholarship was of great importance. Hrosvitha was educated in the liberal arts, beginning with the quadrivium (geometry, arithmetic, music, and astronomy) and continuing with the trivium (grammar, rhetoric, and logic). Her studies were conducted in Latin, the language she used to write her plays. Her education was comparable to that of liberally educated men and of the nuns who lived with her.

Hrosvitha's work is deeply rooted in her religious beliefs. Her religious order meditated on the drama of the lives of Christian saints and especially on their often spectacular martyrdoms. The abbey gave its inhabitants a life of contemplation, removed from the world. But it is also clear that the nuns had the talent, education, and opportunities to write religious tracts and, in the case of Hrosvitha, religious drama. The question of whether Hrosvitha's six plays were actually produced is not settled.

Hrosvitha wrote six plays and several other prose and poetic works. The plays reject the temptations of the world in the name of Christ. In *Gallicanus* the title character is promised the hand of Constantia if he wins a specific battle, but Constantia, daughter of the Christian emperor Constantine, has taken a vow of chastity. Eventually, with the aid of saints, Gallicanus converts to Christianity and becomes a martyr. The conversion of an important Roman is the theme of *Callimachus,* and the conversion theme dominates *Paphnutius* and *Abraham. Sapientia* also emphasizes martyrdom. Sapienta's three daughters, whose names translate as Faith, Hope, and Charity, offer a threat to the stability of Emperor Hadrian's rule. They are tortured brutally but survive without pain until Hadrian beheads them. Eventually Sapientia joins her daughters in heavenly bliss, inspiring the local women who have witnessed the events.

DULCITIUS

Dulcitius is probably the second of Hrosvitha's plays. It was rediscovered in 1494 in an eleventh-century manuscript along with her other dramatic works. Its first printing was in 1501 in an edition with woodcuts by Albrecht Dürer, indicating its importance at the time. The play is plainly didactic and was designed to teach a lesson rather than merely to entertain. The lesson, as in all her plays, is a moral one, urging listeners or readers to live a life of purity and virtue to celebrate the greatness of God. In this sense, Hrosvitha wrote in the medieval literary tradition of Europe. Her plays are fascinating to the modern reader, however, because she purposely emulated the techniques of the Roman playwright Terence.

She chose Terence as her model because his texts were used in education and therefore widely known in Europe. Moreover, they were amusing comedies written with such great style that they were models of elocution. Hrosvitha admits to imitating Terence, but her motives were subversive. She wished to use the eloquent style of Terence not to entertain her audience with secular amusement and charming courtesans but to honor the virtue of chaste virgins who praised God and Christian virtues.

Dulcitius, a jail governor, lusts after the three virgins Agape, Chionia, and Hirenia (Love, Purity, and Peace). Hrosvitha emphasizes his power, but all his worldly power comes to nothing in the face of the virgins' beliefs. In this sense, Hrosvitha celebrates how the apparent weakness of females in her own society can confound the apparent strength of males. Despite his position and power, Dulcitius's lust cannot be satisfied.

Moreover, the three virgins are problematic not only to Dulcitius but to Emperor Diocletian as well. When Agape tells Diocletian that it is dangerous to offend almighty God, Diocletian asks: "Dangerous to whom?" She responds, "To you and to the state you rule." Hrosvitha therefore not only establishes the power of the virgins but of the Christian religion. Astonishingly, this "newfangled religion" threatens Rome itself, which is why Diocletian persecuted Christians so brutally during his reign.

The play's short lines, quick realistic dialogue, and carefully focused interaction are recognizably like Terence's. The present translation uses virgules (/) to indicate the end of lines as they were printed in the original Latin. The broad farcical humor of the "miraculous" scene in which Dulcitius embraces pots and pans in the kitchen thinking they are the three virgins — a scene performed while the virgins watch through the crack in the door — is also in the tradition of Roman comedy.

Despite the three virgins' ultimate martyrdom, the play is a comedy. The soldiers and Dulcitius will end up in "Tartarus," while the virgins "will enter the heavenly bridal chamber of the Eternal King." For the devout canonness Hrosvitha, no ending could be happier.

Dulcitius in Performance

In the opinion of most scholars, the plays of Hrosvitha were not produced but instead read as CLOSET DRAMA. On the other hand, comic scenes such as the one in which Dulcitius blackens his face against the pots and pans have led some theater historians to speculate that the plays were performed by the nuns themselves in the abbey. In any event, _Dulcitius_ would not have had a public audience and may not have influenced other medieval drama. It is, however, a remarkable moment in the history of drama. As Hrosvitha tells us: "I, the strong voice of Gandersheim, have not hesitated to imitate in my writings a poet whose works are so widely read, my object being to glorify, within the limits of my poor talent, the laudable chastity of Christian virgins in that self-same form of composition which has been used to describe the shameless acts of licentious women."

Hrosvitha (c. 935–1000)

DULCITIUS   _c. 965_

THE MARTYRDOM OF THE HOLY VIRGINS AGAPE, CHIONIA, AND HIRENA

TRANSLATED BY K. M. WILSON

[Characters

DIOCLETIAN
AGAPE   WIFE (OF DULCITIUS)
CHIONIA   SISSINUS
HIRENA   SOLDIERS
DULCITIUS   GUARDS]

The martyrdom of the holy virgins° Agape, Chionia, and Hirena, whom, in the silence of the night, Governor Dulcitius secretly visited, desiring to delight in their embrace. But as soon as he entered, / he became demented / and kissed and hugged the pots and pans, mistaking them for the girls until his face and his clothes were soiled with disgusting black dirt. Afterward Count Sissinus, acting on orders, / was given the girls so he might put them to tortures. / He, too, was deluded miraculously / but finally ordered that Agape and Chionia be burnt and Hirena be slain by an arrow.

DIOCLETIAN: The renown of your free and noble descent / and the brightness of your beauty demand / that you be married to one of the foremost men of my court. This will be done according to our command if you deny Christ° and comply by bringing offerings to our gods.°

The martyrdom of the holy virgins: The martyrdom of the three virgins occurred in 290 during Diocletian's persecution of the Christians in Thessalonica.   **5. deny Christ:** Deny the vow of virginity they made in the name of Christ.   **6. our gods:** Gods acknowledged by the Roman empire.

AGAPE: Be free of care, / don't trouble yourself to prepare our wedding / because we cannot be compelled under any duress / to betray Christ's holy name, which we must confess, / nor to stain our virginity.   10

DIOCLETIAN: What madness possesses you? What rage drives you three? /

AGAPE: What signs of our madness do you see? /

DIOCLETIAN: An obvious and great display. /

AGAPE: In what way?   15

DIOCLETIAN: Chiefly in that renouncing the practices of ancient religion / you follow the useless, new-fangled ways of the Christian superstition. /

AGAPE: Heedlessly you offend the majesty of the omnipotent God. That is dangerous . . .   20

DIOCLETIAN: Dangerous to whom?

AGAPE: To you and to the state you rule. /

DIOCLETIAN: She is mad; remove the fool! /

CHIONIA: My sister is not mad; she rightly reprehended your folly.   25

DIOCLETIAN: She rages even more madly; remove her from our sight and arraign the third girl. /

HIRENA: You will find the third, too, a rebel / and resisting you forever. /

DIOCLETIAN: Hirena, although you are younger in birth, / be greater in worth! /   30

HIRENA: Show me, I pray, how?

DIOCLETIAN: Bow your neck to the gods, set an example for your sisters, and be the cause for their freedom!

HIRENA: Let those worship idols, Sire, / who wish to incur God's ire. / But I won't defile my head, anointed   35

with royal unguent by debasing myself at the idols'
feet.

DIOCLETIAN: The worship of gods brings no dishonor /
40   but great honor. /

HIRENA: And what dishonor is more disgraceful, / what
disgrace is any more shameful / than when a slave is
venerated as a master?

DIOCLETIAN: I don't ask you to worship slaves / but the
45   mighty gods of princes and greats. /

HIRENA: Is he not anyone's slave / who, for a price, is up
for sale? /

DIOCLETIAN: For her speech so brazen, / to the tortures
she must be taken. /

50 HIRENA: This is just what we hope for, this is what we
desire, / that for the love of Christ through tortures
we may expire. /

DIOCLETIAN: Let these insolent girls / who defy our
decrees and words / be put in chains and kept in the
55   squalor of prison until Governor Dulcitius can examine them.

DULCITIUS: Bring forth, soldiers, the girls whom you
hold sequestered. /

SOLDIERS: Here they are whom you requested. /

60 DULCITIUS: Wonderful, indeed, how beautiful, how
graceful, how admirable these little girls are!

SOLDIERS: Yes, they are perfectly lovely.

DULCITIUS: I am captivated by their beauty.

SOLDIERS: That is understandable.

65 DULCITIUS: To draw them to my heart, I am eager. /

SOLDIERS: Your success will be meager. /

DULCITIUS: Why?

SOLDIERS: Because they are firm in faith.

DULCITIUS: What if I sway them by flattery? /

70 SOLDIERS: They will despise it utterly. /

DULCITIUS: What if with tortures I frighten them? /

SOLDIERS: Little will it matter to them. /

DULCITIUS: Then what should be done, I wonder? /

SOLDIERS: Carefully you should ponder. /

75 DULCITIUS: Place them under guard in the inner room of
the pantry, where they keep the servants' pots. /

SOLDIERS: Why in that particular spot? /

DULCITIUS: So that I may visit them often at my leisure. /

SOLDIERS: At your pleasure. /

80 DULCITIUS: What do the captives do at this time of
night? /

SOLDIERS: Hymns they recite. /

DULCITIUS: Let us go near. /

SOLDIERS: From afar we hear their tinkling little voices
85   clear. /

DULCITIUS: Stand guard before the door with your
lantern / but I will enter / and satisfy myself in their
longed-for embrace. /

SOLDIERS: Enter. We will guard this place. /

90 AGAPE: What is that noise outside the door? /

HIRENA: That wretched Dulcitius coming to the fore. /

CHIONIA: May God protect us!

AGAPE: Amen.

CHIONIA: What is the meaning of this clash of the pots
and the pans?   95

HIRENA: I will check. / Come here, please, and look
through the crack! /

AGAPE: What is going on?

HIRENA: Look, the fool, the madman base, / he thinks
he is enjoying our embrace. /   100

AGAPE: What is he doing?

HIRENA: Into his lap he pulls the utensils, / he embraces
the pots and the pans, giving them tender kisses. /

CHIONIA: Ridiculous!

HIRENA: His face, his hands, his clothes, are so soiled, so 105
filthy, that with all the soot that clings to him, he
looks like an Ethiopian.

AGAPE: It is only right that he should appear in body the
way he is in his mind: possessed by the Devil.

HIRENA: Wait! He prepares to leave. Let us watch how   110
he is greeted, / and how he is treated / by the soldiers
who wait for him.

SOLDIERS: Who is coming out? / A demon without
doubt. / Or rather, the Devil himself is he; / let us flee! /

DULCITIUS: Soldiers, where are you taking yourselves   115
in flight? / Stay! Wait! Escort me home with your
light! /

SOLDIERS: The voice is our master's tone / but the look
the Devil's own. / Let us not stay! / Let us run away;
the apparition will slay us! /   120

DULCITIUS: I will go to the palace and complain, / and
reveal to the whole court the insults I had to sustain. /

DULCITIUS: Guards, let me into the palace; / I must have
a private audience. /

GUARDS: Who is this vile and detestable monster cov-   125
ered in torn and despicable rags? Let us beat him, /
from the steps let us sweep him; / he must not be
allowed to enter.

DULCITIUS: Alas, alas, what has happened? Am I not
dressed in splendid garments? Don't I look neat and   130
clean? / Yet anyone who looks at my mien / loathes
me as a foul monster. To my wife I shall return, / and
from her learn / what has happened. But there is my
spouse, / with disheveled hair she leaves the house, /
and the whole household follows her in tears.   135

WIFE: Alas, alas, my Lord Dulcitius, what has happened
to you? / You are not sane; the Christians have made
a laughing stock out of you. /

DULCITIUS: Now I know at last. I owe this mockery to
their witchcraft.   140

WIFE: What upsets me so, what makes me more sad, is
that you were ignorant of all that happened to you.

DULCITIUS: I command that those insolent girls be led
forth, / and that they be publicly stripped of all their
clothes, / so that they experience similar mockery in   145
retaliation for ours.

SOLDIERS: We labor in vain; / we sweat without gain. /
Behold, their garments stick to their virginal bodies
like skin, / and he who urged us to strip them snores
in his seat, / and he cannot be awakened from his   150

sleep. / Let us go to the Emperor and report what has happened.

DIOCLETIAN: It grieves me very much / to hear that Governor Dulcitius has been so greatly deluded, / so greatly insulted, / so utterly humiliated. / But these vile young women shall not boast with impunity of having made a mockery of our gods and those who worship them. I shall direct Count Sissinus to take due vengeance.

SISSINUS: Soldiers, where are those insolent girls who are to be tortured?
SOLDIERS: They are kept in prison.
SISSINUS: Leave Hirena there, / bring the others here. /
SOLDIERS: Why do you except the one?
SISSINUS: Sparing her youth. Perchance, she may be converted easier, if she is not intimidated by her sisters' presence. /
SOLDIERS: That makes sense. /

SOLDIERS: Here are the girls whose presence you requested.
SISSINUS: Agape and Chionia, give heed, / and to my council accede! /
AGAPE: We will not give heed. /
SISSINUS: Bring offerings to the gods.
AGAPE: We bring offerings of praise forever / to the true Father eternal, / and to His Son co-eternal, / and also to the Holy Spirit.
SISSINUS: This is not what I bid, / but on pain of penalty prohibit. /
AGAPE: You cannot prohibit it; neither shall we ever sacrifice to demons.
SISSINUS: Cease this hardness of heart, and make your offerings. But if you persist, / then I shall insist / that you be killed according to the Emperor's orders.
CHIONIA: It is only proper that you should obey the orders of your Emperor, whose decrees we disdain, as you know. For if you wait and try to spare us, then you could be rightfully killed.
SISSINUS: Soldiers, do not delay, / take these blaspheming girls away, / and throw them alive into the flames.
SOLDIERS: We shall instantly build the pyre you asked for, and we will cast these girls into the raging fire, and thus we'll put an end to these insults at last. /
AGAPE: O Lord, nothing is impossible for Thee; / even the fire forgets its nature and obeys Thee; / but we are weary of delay; / therefore, dissolve the earthly bonds that hold our souls, we pray, / so that as our earthly bodies die, / our souls may sing your praise in Heaven.
SOLDIERS: Oh, marvel, oh stupendous miracle! Behold their souls are no longer bound to their bodies, / yet no traces of injury can be found; neither their hair, nor their clothes are burnt by the fire, / and their bodies are not at all harmed by the pyre. /
SISSINUS: Bring forth Hirena.

SOLDIERS: Here she is.
SISSINUS: Hirena, tremble at the deaths of your sisters and fear to perish according to their example.

HIRENA: I hope to follow their example and expire, / so with them in Heaven eternal joy I may acquire. /
SISSINUS: Give in, give in to my persuasion. /
HIRENA: I will never yield to evil persuasion. /
SISSINUS: If you don't yield, I shall not give you a quick and easy death, but multiply your sufferings.
HIRENA: The more cruelly I'll be tortured, / the more gloriously I'll be exalted. /
SISSINUS: You fear no tortures, no pain? / What you abhor, I shall ordain. /
HIRENA: Whatever punishment you design, / I will escape with help Divine. /
SISSINUS: To a brothel you will be consigned, / where your body will be shamefully defiled. /
HIRENA: It is better that the body be dirtied with any stain than that the soul be polluted with idolatry.
SISSINUS: If you are so polluted in the company of harlots, you can no longer be counted among the virginal choir.
HIRENA: Lust deserves punishment, but forced compliance the crown. With neither is one considered guilty, / unless the soul consents freely. /
SISSINUS: In vain have I spared her, in vain have I pitied her youth.
SOLDIERS: We knew this before; / for on no possible score / can she be moved to adore our gods, nor can she be broken by terror.
SISSINUS: I shall spare her no longer. /
SOLDIERS: Rightly you ponder. /
SISSINUS: Seize her without mercy, / drag her with cruelty, / and take her in dishonor to the brothel. /
HIRENA: They will not do it. /
SISSINUS: Who can prohibit it? /
HIRENA: He whose foresight rules the world. /
SISSINUS: I shall see . . . /
HIRENA: Sooner than you wish, it will be. /
SISSINUS: Soldiers, be not afraid / of what this blaspheming girl has said. /
SOLDIERS: We are not afraid, / but eagerly follow what you bade. /

SISSINUS: Who are those approaching? How similar they are to the men / to whom we gave Hirena just then. / They are the same. Why are you returning so fast? / Why so out of breath, I ask? /
SOLDIERS: You are the one for whom we look. /
SISSINUS: Where is she whom you just took? /
SOLDIERS: On the peak of the mountain.
SISSINUS: Which one?
SOLDIERS: The one close by. /
SISSINUS: Oh you idiots, dull and blind. / You have completely lost your mind! /
SOLDIERS: Why do you accuse us, / why do you abuse us, / why do you threaten us with menacing voice and face?
SISSINUS: May the gods destroy you!
SOLDIERS: What have we committed? What harm have we done? How have we transgressed against your orders?
SISSINUS: Have I not given the orders that you should take that rebel against the gods to a brothel?

SOLDIERS: Yes, so you did command, / and we were eager to fulfill your demand, / but two strangers intercepted us / saying that you sent them to us / to lead Hirena to the mountain's peak.

270 SISSINUS: That's new to me. /

SOLDIERS: We can see. /

SISSINUS: What were they like? /

SOLDIERS: Splendidly dressed and an awe-inspiring sight. /

275 SISSINUS: Did you follow? /

SOLDIERS: We did so. /

SISSINUS: What did they do? /

SOLDIERS: They placed themselves on Hirena's left and right, / and told us to be forthright / and not to hide

280 from you what happened.

SISSINUS: I see a sole recourse, / that I should mount my horse / and seek out those who so freely made sport with us.

SISSINUS: Hmm, I don't know what to do. I am bewil-

285 dered by the witchcraft of these Christians. I keep going around the mountain and keep finding this track / but I neither know how to proceed nor how to find my way back. /

SOLDIERS: We are all deluded by some intrigue; / we are afflicted with a great fatigue; / if you allow this 290 insane person to stay alive, / then neither you nor we shall survive. /

SISSINUS: Anyone among you, / I don't care which, string a bow, and shoot an arrow, and kill that witch! / 295

SOLDIERS: Rightly so. /

HIRENA: Wretched Sissinus, blush for shame, and proclaim your miserable defeat because without the help of weapons, you cannot overcome a tender little virgin as your foe. / 300

SISSINUS: Whatever the shame that may be mine, I will bear it more easily now because I know for certain that you will die.

HIRENA: This is the greatest joy I can conceive, / but for you this is a cause to grieve, / because you shall 305 be damned in Tartarus° for your cruelty, / while I shall receive the martyr's palm and the crown of virginity; / thus I will enter the heavenly bridal chamber of the Eternal King, to whom are all honor and glory in all eternity. / 310

306. **Tartarus:** Hell.

COMMENTARIES

Marla Carlson
READING HROTSVIT'S TORMENTED BODIES   *1998*

> *In this excerpt from an article that appeared in* Theatre Journal, *Marla Carlson reminds us in this brief treatment of* Dulcitius *that the question of physical beauty can be interpreted in several different ways. In the world of Hrosvitha, the pagan emphasis on the physical body must always be seen in relation to the Christian emphasis on the soul. Carlson sees a gender connection between the two.*

In *The Martyrdom of the Holy Virgins Agape, Chionia, and Hirena,* beauty is a transparent sign of virtue. The play (also known as *Dulcitius*) begins with an ironic contrast: the pagan Emperor Diocletian manifests the rage and madness he attributes to the virgins, while they remain impassive. The girls' bodies function as foci of desire but are themselves free from desire. By contrast, the non-Christian men are represented as desiring subjects, which also means they are *subject* to their bodies. Diocletian wants to direct the disposal of the girls in marriage. Governor Dulcitius wants to use and possess them himself, and his desire produces his downfall. After he is blackened in the kitchen by making love to the pots and pans he mistakes for the virgins, Agape observes that now Dulcitius's body corresponds to his mind. On the other side of the balance, although the physical beauty of the girls is a visible manifestation of their virtue, pagan interpreters misread it as a sign of commodity exchange value, beginning with Diocletian's demand that the girls bring offerings to the Roman gods *in order* to be married well (the last thing they'd want!). But while the signs can be misread, Christian virtue cannot be *degraded*. When Dulcitius orders Agape, Chionia, and Hirena stripped for display, their clothes magically adhere to their bodies and cannot be removed. Hirena is threatened with sexual degradation in a brothel and retorts: "Lust deserves punishment, but forced compliance the crown; neither is one considered guilty, / unless the soul consents freely." All the same, God prevents her body from being defiled, and although Agape and Chionia are thrown into a fire and their souls depart at once, their physical bodies remain unharmed. Death is not a sign of pagan power but of God's grace, and at the final Resurrection, the martyr's beautiful body will again serve as the proper sign of the pure soul. In this play, the body — and in particular, its sexual properties — focuses the conflict between Christian female and pagan male.

Sue-Ellen Case (b. 1942)
RE-VIEWING HROTSVIT

1983

Sue-Ellen Case not only examines the plays of Hrosvitha but actually produced them. She discusses the feminist issues in the plays and explains the symmetry between Hrosvitha's six plays and the six plays of Terence. She demonstrates the significance of the plays of Hrosvitha for a modern audience.

The Plays

Hrotsvit wrote six plays in response to the six plays of Terence. Her project was to change the roles for women on the stage from negative ones to positive ones. However, critics have traditionally ignored this feminist aspect of her project and concentrated on the Christian context for it. A. Daniel Frankforter, in his article "Sexism and the Search for Thematic Structure of the Plays of Hroswitha of Gandersheim," characterizes the critics' misapprehension of Hrotsvit as stemming from "an asexual (male) perspective" which regards Hrotsvit as "a monk of generation" whose "sex is assumed to have little or no significance . . . her choice of women as chief characters is not seen as crucial to interpretation," and therefore "she emerges as a minor eulogist of ordinary Christian heroes."[1] Frankforter opposes this sexist perspective and finds that if Hrotsvit's project is seen as a revision of the roles for women "what emerges from the six plays . . . is a systematic exploration of each of the opportunities for female integrity possible in the social roles permitted women in Hroswitha's world."[2]

A brief description of roles of women in three of Terence's plays elicits some of the basic roles and attendant social issues Hrotsvit revised. *The Girl from Andros* never appears onstage, though her offstage screams during labor are used for comic development of the plot. Only two women appear onstage: a "sloppy drunken

---

[1]A. Daniel Frankforter, "Sexism and the Search for Thematic Structure of the Plays of Hroswitha of Gandersheim," *International Journal of Women's Studies,* vol. 2, no. 3, p. 225.

[2]Frankforter, p. 226.

slut" who is a midwife from Lesbos and a slave girl who is frightened and manipulated by her witty male counterpart, the slave Davus.[3] This Imperial Comedy centers on the relationship between father and son in which women are assets (ingenues from good families) or liabilities (mercenary courtesans) in the son's economy of obedience to his father and the patriarchal social order. *The Self Tormentor* uses the traditional double plot, centering on two father/son relationships. The double plot engineers male rivalry for the possession of women, completing the portrait of patriarchal economy. Luce Irigaray, a pioneer in feminist theories of morphology, described women's position within this economy: "woman is traditionally use-value for man, exchange value among men. Merchandise, then . . . she is never anything more than the scene of more or less rival exchange between two men."[4] In this play, an interesting piece of women's social history emerges to push the plot to its happy ending. One of the fathers had ordered his wife to kill their baby if it were a girl. The wife did not obey (an act perceived as cowardice and infidelity), and now the girl can be used as marriage material to solve the rivalry between the two sons and reconcile them both with their father's wishes.

The Eunuch was Terence's most popular play in Rome. The central issue in the play is one central to several plays by Hrotsvit — rape. A young man sees a girl cross the marketplace (an apt setting) and falls in love with her because of her beauty. In order to gain entrance to her house, he disguises himself as a eunuch and rapes her. The girl's response is never staged, but it is reported that she sits in torn garments and weeps. Nevertheless, because of his love for her, the young man's crime is forgiven, and he gains the girl in marriage. From these three plays, one can summarize the Classical inheritance Hrotsvit received for women on the stage: they are relatively invisible, their responses are rarely dramatized and most often reported by men, they are manipulated as use value among men in the plot situation, and their best possible ending is marriage — with or without consent.

The most striking difference between the plays of Hrotsvit and those of Terence is that in her plays women are at the center of the action and it is their response to male aggression which determines the development of the plot. Hrotsvit places her heroines in the context of objectification, use, and violence but offers them an alternative. The play *Dulcitius* opens with three young women before the Emperor Diocletian and his soldiers. Diocletian declares the patriarchal edict: "The pure and famous race to which you belong and your own rare beauty make it fitting that you should be wedded to the highest in the court." Beauty and high station are the trap of objectification. In spite of the rank and military power which confronts these young girls, they resist, answering that they have vowed to live in chastity. Angered, the emperor sends them to prison and to the charge of Governor Dulcitius. Dulcitius wants them because of their beauty, but the guards tell him they will resist seduction. He responds "Then I shall woo in another fashion — with torture!" The latent relationship in such a patriarchal society between desire and dominance becomes literal. The stage setting reveals the passive position of the women as prisoners and sets up the alliance between desire and privilege in the role of the Governor. However, the internal power of the women's wishes overcomes

---

[3]Constance Carrier and Douglass Parker, *The Complete Comedies of Terence* (New Brunswick: Rutgers University Press, 1974), p. 21.

[4]Luce Irigaray, "This Sex Which Is Not One," in *New French Feminisms* (New York: Schocken Books, 1981), p. 105.

this material one. A spell overcomes Dulcitius as he enters to rape them, and he makes love to pots and pans, thinking they are the women. Hrotsvit has given a stage metaphor to the objectification of women, as objects are substituted for women, particularly objects associated with their domestic labor. The women watch Dulcitius and giggle. In their laughter and his foolishness as a result of their spell-binding power, the women dominate the rapist. The male dramatic perspective has been reversed.

The play *Callimachus* also centers on rape. In the opening scenes, Callimachus tells Drusiana he loves her because of her beauty. Her response is one of incomprehension: "My beauty? What is my beauty to you?" From a woman's point of view, this is a deep, provocative question, but Callimachus answers it in terms of patriarchal economy: "But little now . . . I hope it might be much before long." Drusiana persists in her refusal, telling Callimachus that even though she is married, she has taken the vow of chastity. He responds that he will use all of his skill and strength to trap her — the motor of Classical plots. Instead, Drusiana asks Christ to help her to die, so she may escape her dilemma. Christ complies with her wish immediately. Women have the power to petition and to succeed. Undaunted by her death, Callimachus enters her tomb to rape the corpse. Hrotsvit has dramatized the essence of the passive victim and of the objectification of patriarchal desire. Unlike Terence, who ultimately resolves it as natural, she has staged it as perverse. Callimachus is killed by a heavenly serpent before he can complete the act (nature is on the side of the heroine) and is later resurrected (along with Drusiana) and converted to her world view. In other words, the plot moves in her direction and is moved by her resolve.

The alternative to patriarchal possession is characterized by Hrotsvit as the vow of chastity. Later periods have regarded this vow as ultimate repression rather than as a declaration of independence. Yet Hrotsvit's solution answers a question posed by Irigaray "What if the goods refuse to go to market? What if they maintained among themselves another kind of trade?"[5] Chastity was the choice available to women to remain outside the patriarchal order of desire. In the case of a nun such as Hrotsvit, the removal into a women's community (perhaps the first separatist collectives) brought the opportunity to be educated and to be an educator. Hrotsvit was what Frankforter calls a "career nun."[6] Given her collective context, Hrotsvit may have been the first woman playwright to write for a community of women. Thus, in writing from a woman's point of view for women to watch, she is involved in an entirely new dramatic dynamic. Yet her identity as a nun has traditionally been cited as the cause of elements of suppression rather than liberation in her works. The patriarchal bias of Freudian analysis perceived her profession as oppression. Rosamond Gilder formulated the case simply: "Hrotsvit gives expression to a vein of sadism which is also associated with certain acts of repression." Gilder elaborates on the psychological mechanism: "Hrotsvit obtained a certain release for her emotional suppressions by elaborating these pictures of carnal dangers and the pitfalls of the flesh."[7] Such a Freudian analysis assigns the responsibility for the victimization of women in the plays to Hrotsvit's repressed sexuality and its resultant fantasies rather than to the patriarchal society in which her characters

[5]Irigaray, p. 110.
[6]Frankforter, p. 226.
[7]Rosamond Gilder, *Enter the Actress* (London: Harrap and Co., 1931), pp. 34–35.

were situated. Perhaps the easiest refutation of such an assertion lies in the fact that Hrotsvit did not invent her own plots. Instead, she worked from materials which were considered historical in her time. For example, the martyrdom and rape of the young women in *Dulcitius* was taken from *The Acts of Christian Martyrs*. The story was recorded in the fourth century, based on historical edicts of Diocletian and records of the trial and punishment of the women. Hrotsvit's project was to dramatize the violence against women recorded in these histories and was in no way to record her own fantasies.

Feminine Morphology and Paphnutius

Since this essay is meant to be merely an exploration of the application of feminist critical technique to the work and role of Hrotsvit, this section will illustrate the application of only one feminist theory of form to a single play — *Paphnutius*. The theory is derived from essays by Irigaray, Hélène Cixous (whose work "The Laugh of the Medusa" is now a classic in feminist studies), and Jane Gallop's book on feminism and psychoanalysis.[8] The source of their ideas lies in a feminist reading of the works of Derrida, Lacan, and Foucault. The basic assumption of these authors is that the dominant cultural form is phallocentrism. This means two things: that the dominant form is organized around a concept of centrality and that the phallus is at the center of all dominant morphology. Because of its centric location, the phallus determines a form based upon phallic privilege, phallic exhibition, and a phallic desire to possess. Therefore, the phallocentric form is both clear (exhibited, as in linear, logical development) and closed (self-possessed — as in beginning, middle, and end).

The alternative form found in women's work is described as contiguous. Irigaray describes it as a "nearness," a form "constantly in the process of weaving itself . . . embracing words and yet casting them off," concerned not with clarity, but with what is "touched upon" (p. 103). Cixous calls it "working the in-between" (p. 254), while Gallop describes it as "the register of touching, nearness, presence, immediacy, contact" (p. 30). It can be elliptical rather than illustrative, fragmentary rather than whole, ambiguous rather than clear, and interrupted rather than complete. The stage society within such a form could never be the plain patriarchy of Terence, with its clear line of power from father to son. Rather, it is a complex society of subtle dependencies which manifest themselves in resonances of one another's changes.

This sense of contiguity is the organizing principle, as well as the subject of the opening scene of the play *Paphnutius*. The play opens on the sadness of Father Paphnutius. When asked by his disciples about its cause, he launches into a medieval discourse on the world as harmonic, proceeding from an explanation of the quadrivium, through a Boethian discussion of music to the organizing principle of concord and discord. The organization of all things is contiguous. Paphnutius describes its residence in "not only, as I have told you, in the combination of body and soul, and in the utterance of the voice, now high, now low, but even in the pulsation of the veins and in the proportion of our members." As the scene proceeds, the disciples ask Paphnutius about his sadness. He replies that it is because of the

---

[8]Hélène Cixous, "The Laugh of the Medusa," in Irigaray, *New French Feminisms;* and Jane Gallop, *The Daughter's Seduction: Feminism and Psychoanalysis* (Ithaca: Cornell University Press, 1982).

whore Thais. The rest of the play is concerned with his work to change her relationship to her own sexuality, her residency in a convent in which she practices self-mortification, and Paphnutius's concluding vision of her transfiguration.

The "contempt with which the learned musical Prologue was regarded for over half a century" originated in an assessment of the Scholastic discourse as mediocre medieval philosophy.[9] The "modern disparagement of the Prologue" rests on the perception that it does not work in the overall construction of the drama.[10] There seems to be no connection between the ideas of music and nature, and the sadness in Paphnutius caused by the whore Thais. The ideas in the prologue seem to be abandoned as the story of Thais unfolds. Yet if one replaces the phallocentric model of form with one of contiguity, the play seems to be tightly constructed. Hrotsvit has begun her play with an exposition of the contiguous dependency among parts of the world. A monk in a distant monastery, who has never seen the whore Thais, can find no peace until the concord between her understanding and her sexuality is restored. The inner dynamics of Thais's personality "touches upon" the surrounding world in which she lives. Paphnutius can find no peace until he has removed this woman from the colonized use of her body in the city to her own repossession of it within a convent. Hrotsvit has merely used the most basic ideas in Scholastic discourse to set up her dramatic situation — to provide the intellectual environment for the personal story. Hrotsvit makes no linear transition from the opening scene to the story because her world is contiguous. Her short scenes suggest rather than explicate, "touch upon" each other rather than develop. In this play, she has replaced the objectified, patriarchal intercourse between men and women which she dramatizes in her Roman settings, with the contiguous resonances of sexual concord which exist between Thais and Paphnutius. When the play is approached from a feminist, rather than phallocentric model of form, it seems a masterpiece rather than a mediocre medieval morality story.

Performance

Hrotsvit's plays were not collected for circulation until the sixteenth century. They were not translated into modern Romance languages until the mid-nineteenth century and not into English until the twentieth century. The relative unavailability of her texts made production before the twentieth century improbable. Yet in the twentieth century, it is important to note that productions of her plays were often by women or in times in which women's issues were important to the theater world. A good example of the latter condition is the production history of Hrotsvit's work in London. The first major production of *Paphnutius* was directed by Edith Craig (daughter of Ellen Terry and sister of Gordon) in London in 1914. The production was by the Pioneer Players, a group founded and directed by Edith Craig, with Ellen Terry playing the role of the abbess in the convent in which Thais was confined. The translation was done by Christopher St. John, a *nom de plume* (indicative practice) for Christabel Marshall. Marshall had recently adapted the suffragette play *How the Vote Was Won* in 1909 and the play *The First Actress* in 1911 — an indication that her interest in the text of Hrotsvit probably came from an interest in a woman playwright. Indeed, there was a movement in London the-

---

[9]David Chamberlain, "Musical Learning and Dramatic Action in Hrotsvit's *Pafnutius*," *Studies in Philology*. Fall 1980, p. 319.
[10]Ibid.

ater at that time to be concerned with women's issues — particularly the vote. In 1908, actresses had formed a franchise league to support the suffrage movement, which produced plays about the vote and satires of male chauvinism.[11] The English women did not get the vote until 1928, and the decade of the 1920s was filled with the issue. Within this context, the 1920 production of *Callimachus* at the Art Theatre, the 1924 production of *Paphnutius* at the Maddermarket Theatre, the founding of the Roswitha club in 1926, the new translations by St. John, Waley and Tillyard during the decade, and the cessation of Hrotsvit productions after that decade can be easily understood.

My production of her works in 1982 came as a result of teaching a class on women and theater and becoming familiar with all of the new productions and critical studies evolving from the works of women playwrights and women's theater groups. The first problem in producing Hrotsvit is the obscurity of her name and play titles. The second is the short playing time of her texts. I decided to solve both problems by directing three plays in one evening and creating a title which might attract the Seattle women's community by identifying the plays according to the social roles of their three heroines: "The Virgin (*Dulcitius*), The Whore (*Paphnutius*), and The Desperate One" (*Callimachus*). My choice of production concept was determined by my goal of producing the first woman playwright. In order to emphasize her historical role, I decided to direct the play as a period piece. This introduces another set of difficulties, since the theater has no tradition of staging plays from the early Middle Ages and hence no concept of costumes, sets, or playing style. We took the costumes from mosaics and illuminations around the period and decided on flats, imitating the two-dimensional painting style of the time, with edifices found in Ottonian manuscript illuminations. The playing style was a combination of a classical sense of formal blocking and gestures, combined with intense, personal purpose. A projection screen rose from the back of a steeply raked stage and a processional ramp ran from the front of the stage through the center of the audience. This combination created the feeling of the space in a cathedral. The elevated ramp gave the Saints elevation and dominance. Between the plays, early medieval music was performed. All this allowed a style to emerge which was both an imitation of classical formality and liturgical ceremony.

The context of Christianity and its trappings often created an audience response which was marked in its silent reverence. People seemed afraid to wiggle or whisper. At other times, this same sense turned into an active irreverence, manifested by laughter and something close to jeering. Contemporary staging of a Christian play is complicated to understand. Shakespeare productions have prepared an audience for the Elizabethan world of superstition, and Greek plays have prepared them for the world of pagan mythology, but the relative absence of medieval productions leaves the world of medieval Christianity to be understood by personal opinions about Christianity rather than the sense of it as a historical world view. Thus, for some feminists, the Christianity was seen as offensive and patriarchal. Particularly in these times of the Moral Majority, Hrotsvit's plays seemed to them to be written by an "Uncle Tom" trapped by male values. Many audience members laughed hysterically at the miracles, the voice of God, and the resurrections — seeing them not as stage conventions but as bygone beliefs. Christopher St. John records a similar

[11]Michelene Wandor, *Understudies: Theatre and Sexual Politics* (London: Eyre Methuen, 1981), p. 10.

reaction to the plays in their early London productions, citing a scene in *Callimachus* "Drusiana's prayer that she might die rather than yield to Callimachus was greeted with shouts of laughter" (p. 159). I think the only solution to this problem lies not in the staging concept of such scenes, but in establishing a familiarity with the playwright and her conventions through productions and an acquaintance with her texts in theater history and criticism classes.

For the actors, this problem translates into ways for them to individually understand the dilemma of their characters. The women identified instances of martyrdom and conviction which meant something to them. These ranged from pictures of concentration camp women, which some of the Jewish women brought to rehearsal, to stories of guerrillas in El Salvador or instances of rape victims who resisted. They did not focus so much on religious experiences, as on sexual ones, political ones, or psychological approaches to their own fears and strengths. The men in the cast resisted identifying with the male aggression and cruelty portrayed by many of the characters. When asked to torment one of the young virgins in a flirtatious manner, they insisted they didn't know how. This identification came slowly, through memories of teasing girls in grade school, to early experiences of seduction and sexual aggression. For the men playing Saints, the problem was in giving focus to the women onstage and learning how to respond to the power of the women in a realistic fashion. This involved investigating their own fears of women's power.

For the actors, one of the most difficult aspects of Hrotsvit's work was her contiguous sense of form and her compressed, almost fragmentary sense of a scene. Characters have extremely short speeches of only one or two sentences, compressed into scenes of relatively scant dialogue and often no physical action. Fortunately, recent productions of plays by such authors as Beckett and Kroetz provided the actors with some experience in this style. The method which seemed most useful was to play the entire scene by improvising a long, literal development of its situation and then compress it moment by moment until it played in Hrotsvit's form. One fortunate consequence of this playing style is that the concentration and deliberation required by the actor, made him or her oblivious to the sometimes raucous audience response.

Finally, the response of the critics illustrated an interesting aspect of viewing the plays. Almost all announcements and reviews of the plays included the words "rape" and "necrophilia" in their titles. One critic pointed out that these plays should make contemporary audiences feel less defensive about violence on TV, since it was already popular in the early Middle Ages. The titles are surprising, since neither the rapes nor the necrophilia ever occur. They are the intentions of the male characters but are foiled by heavenly intervention. The preoccupation by critics with these intentions might suggest that they were watching the male characters more than the females, even though it was not the focus of the text nor of the blocking. In fact, given the staging of resurrections and other such miracles, these dramatic intentions seemed minor parts of the staging. Yet they were the focus of critical reviews. This critical reception points out the necessity for a re-viewing of Hrotsvit from a feminist point of view and underlines the sense that her position and its implications in the world of theater is still long overdue.

EVERYMAN

This late medieval play may have origins in northern Europe. A Flemish play, *Elckerlijk* ("Everyman"), dates from c. 1495, and the question of whether the English *Everyman* was translated from it or whether it is a translation of *Everyman* has not been settled. Both plays may have had a common origin in an unknown play. The English *Everyman* was produced frequently in the early years of the sixteenth century. Its drama was largely theological; its purpose, to reform the audience. One indication that entertainment was not the primary goal of this morality play is its lack of the comic moments found in other plays, such as *The Second Shepherds' Play*.

The author of the play may have been a priest. This assumption has long been common because the play has much theological content and offers a moral message of the kind one might expect to hear from the pulpit. The theme of the play is fundamental: the inevitability of death. And for that reason, in part, the play continues to have a universal appeal. Modern productions may not give the audience a suitable medieval chill, but the message of the play is still relevant for everyone.

The medieval reliance on allegory is apparent in the naming of the characters in *Everyman*: Death, Kindred, Cousin, Goods, Knowledge, Strength, Beauty, and Everyman himself. Each character does not just stand for a specific quality; he or she *is* that quality. The allegorical way of thinking derived from the medieval faith that everything in the world had a moral meaning. Morality plays depended on this belief and always articulated setting, characters, and circumstances in terms of their moral value. This was in keeping with the medieval belief that the soul was always in jeopardy and that life was a test of one's moral condition. When Everyman meets a character, the most important information about his or her moral value is communicated instantly in the name of the character. Characters in allegorical plays also reveal themselves through their costumes and props. The character Good Deeds is simply good deeds: there is no need for psychological development because the medieval audience had a full understanding of what good deeds meant and how Good Deeds as a character would behave.

The structure of *Everyman* resembles a journey. Everyman undertakes to see who among all his acquaintances will accompany him on his most important trip: to the grave and the judgment of God Almighty. Seeing life as a journey — or as part of a journey — was especially natural for the medieval mind, which had as models the popular and costly religious pilgrimages to holy shrines and to the Holy Land itself. If life on earth is only part of the journey of the soul, then the morality play helps to put it into clear perspective. This life is not, the play tells us, the most important part of the soul's existence.

At its core, *Everyman* has a profound commercial metaphor: Everyman is called to square accounts with God. The metaphor of accounting appears early in the play, when Everyman talks about his accounts and reckonings as if they appeared in a book that should go with him to heaven. His life will be examined, and if he is found wanting, he will go into the fires of hell. If he has lived profitably from a moral viewpoint, he will enjoy life everlasting. The language of the play is heavily loaded with accounting metaphors that identify it as the product of a society quite unlike that of the Greeks or the Romans. Such metaphors suggest that *Everyman* directs its message to middle-class merchants for whom accounting was a significant concept.

Like many sermons, *Everyman* imparts a lesson that its auditors were expected to heed. Hence the key points of the play are repeated at the end by the Doctor. For moderns, didactic plays are sometimes tedious. For the medieval mind, they represented delightful ways of learning important messages.

Everyman in Performance

Very little is known about early productions of *Everyman*. It was produced in Holland and England for seventy-five years beginning in the mid-fifteenth century. The play disappeared from the stage for centuries, finally resurfacing in 1901 in a production under the auspices of the Elizabethan Stage Society in London, directed by William Poel. Poel designed the costumes and set, directed, and played at first the part of Death, and then when he got older, the part of God. Poel produced *Everyman* many times over the next fifteen years.

The 1901 production was followed by a 1902 revival in New York starring Edith Wynne Matthison and produced by Ben Greet, marking the play's first American performance. Greet continued producing *Everyman* for the next thirty-five years in both England and America.

After seeing Poel's production, Max Reinhardt, the legendary German director, decided to produce *Everyman* in Germany. The Austrian poet and playwright Hugo von Hofmannsthal wrote a new German adaptation, *Jedermann,* for Reinhardt. The adaptation features Everyman as a wealthy burgher, and central to the play is an ornate banquet scene in which Death appears. Hofmannsthal's German adaptation marked a shift in emphasis from the simpler and more personal English *Everyman* to the spectacular *Jedermann* that concentrates on a wealthy man's lustful life and his attempts to get into heaven. *Jedermann* was first produced in Berlin on December 1, 1911. In 1913 Reinhardt produced the play in Salzburg, Austria, at the Salzburg Cathedral square, and except for the years of World War II, Reinhardt's version of *Jedermann* has been performed regularly at the annual Salzburg Festival. The critic Brooks Atkinson found Reinhardt's production "nothing short of miraculous." In a review of Reinhardt's 1927 production, the critic Gilbert Gabriel found *Jedermann,* "crammed with splendors for the eye, largesse of bells and uplifting voices for the ear." A reviewer at the 1936 Salzburg Festival production of *Jedermann* wrote that the play "has everything but simplicity."

The popularity of the Reinhardt productions of *Jedermann* paved the way for numerous productions of *Everyman* over the years. In 1936, during the Great Depression in the United States, the WPA (Works Progress Administration) held special Sunday church performances of *Everyman*. Other notable productions include a 1941 *Everyman* in New York performed by refugee actors from Europe, and a 1955 tour with college casts in New England and California. In 1922 a new English adaptation of the German *Jedermann* by Sir

John Martin-Harvey was presented at Stratford-on-Avon. This production toured to London and New York in 1923. In 1936 Sir John's adaptation was performed at the Hollywood Bowl in California with Peggy Wood and Lionel Braham. Long popular with college and community groups, the play continues to be performed around the world.

Anonymous

EVERYMAN

EDITED BY A. C. CAWLEY

c. 1495

Characters

GOD	KNOWLEDGE
MESSENGER	CONFESSION
DEATH	BEAUTY
EVERYMAN	STRENGTH
FELLOWSHIP	DISCRETION
KINDRED	FIVE WITS
COUSIN	ANGEL
GOODS	DOCTOR
GOOD DEEDS	

Here beginneth a treatise how the high Father of Heaven sendeth Death to summon every creature to come and give account of their lives in this world, and is in manner of a moral play.

MESSENGER: I pray you all give your audience,
    And hear this matter with reverence,
    By figure° a moral play:
    The *Summoning of Everyman* called it is,
5   That of our lives and ending shows
    How transitory we be all day.°
    This matter is wondrous precious,
    But the intent of it is more gracious,
    And sweet to bear away.
10   The story saith: Man, in the beginning
    Look well, and take good heed to the ending,
    Be you never so gay!
    Ye think sin in the beginning full sweet,
    Which in the end causeth the soul to weep,
15   When the body lieth in clay.
    Here shall you see how Fellowship and Jollity,
    Both Strength, Pleasure, and Beauty,
    Will fade from thee as flower in May;
    For ye shall hear how our Heaven King
20   Calleth Everyman to a general reckoning:
    Give audience, and hear what he doth say.
                              (*Exit.*)

---

3. By figure: In form.   **6. all day:** Always.

(*God speaketh.*)

GOD: I perceive, here in my majesty,
    How that all creatures be to me unkind,°
    Living without dread in worldly prosperity:
    Of ghostly sight° the people be so blind,   25
    Drowned in sin, they know me not for their God;
    In worldly riches is all their mind,
    They fear not my righteousness, the sharp rod.
    My law that I showed, when I for them died,
    They forget clean, and shedding of my blood red;   30
    I hanged between two, it cannot be denied;
    To get them life I suffered to be dead;
    I healed their feet, with thorns hurt was my head.
    I could do no more than I did, truly;
    And now I see the people do clean forsake me: 35
    They use the seven deadly sins damnable,
    As pride, covetise, wrath, and lechery
    Now in the world be made commendable;
    And thus they leave of angels the heavenly
        company.
    Every man liveth so after his own pleasure,   40
    And yet of their life they be nothing sure:
    I see the more that I them forbear
    The worse they be from year to year.
    All that liveth appaireth° fast;
    Therefore I will, in all the haste,   45
    Have a reckoning of every man's person;
    For, and° I leave the people thus alone
    In their life and wicked tempests,
    Verily they will become much worse than beasts;
    For now one would by envy another up eat;   50
    Charity they do all clean forget.
    I hoped well that every man
    In my glory should make his mansion,
    And thereto I had them all elect;
    But now I see, like traitors deject,°   55

---

23. unkind: Ungrateful.   **25. ghostly sight:** Spiritual vision.
44. appaireth: Degenerates.   **47. and:** If.   **55. deject:** Abject.

They thank me not for the pleasure that I to them
  meant,
Nor yet for their being that I them have lent.
I proffered the people great multitude of mercy,
And few there be that asketh it heartily.
60 They be so cumbered with worldly riches
That needs on them I must do justice,
On every man living without fear.
Where art thou, Death, thou mighty messenger?

(*Enter Death.*)

DEATH: Almighty God, I am here at your will,
65   Your commandment to fulfill.
GOD: Go thou to Everyman,
And show him, in my name,
A pilgrimage he must on him take,
Which he in no wise may escape;
70 And that he bring with him a sure reckoning
Without delay or any tarrying.
                (*God withdraws.*)
DEATH: Lord, I will in the world go run overall,
And cruelly outsearch both great and small;
Every man will I beset that liveth beastly
75 Out of God's laws, and dreadeth not folly.
He that loveth riches I will strike with my dart,
His sight to blind, and from heaven to depart° —
Except that alms be his good friend —
In hell for to dwell, world without end.
80 Lo, yonder I see Everyman walking.
Full little he thinketh on my coming;
His mind is on fleshly lusts and his treasure,
And great pain it shall cause him to endure
Before the Lord, Heaven King.

(*Enter Everyman.*)

85 Everyman, stand still! Whither art thou going
Thus gaily? Hast thou thy Maker forget?
EVERYMAN: Why askest thou?
Wouldest thou wit?°
DEATH: Yea, sir; I will show you:
90 In great haste I am sent to thee
From God out of his majesty.
EVERYMAN: What, sent to me?
DEATH: Yea, certainly.
Though thou have forget him here,
95 He thinketh on thee in the heavenly sphere,
As, ere we depart, thou shalt know.
EVERYMAN: What desireth God of me?
DEATH: That shall I show thee:
A reckoning he will needs have
100 Without any longer respite.
EVERYMAN: To give a reckoning longer leisure I crave;
This blind matter troubleth my wit.
DEATH: On thee thou must take a long journey;
Therefore thy book of count° with thee thou
  bring,

77. depart: Separate.   88. wit: Know.   104. count: Account.

For turn° again thou cannot by no way. 105
And look thou be sure of thy reckoning,
For before God thou shalt answer, and show
Thy many bad deeds, and good but a few;
How thou hast spent thy life, and in what wise,
Before the chief Lord of paradise. 110
Have ado that we were in that way,°
For, wit thou well, thou shalt make none attorney.°
EVERYMAN: Full unready I am such reckoning to give.
I know thee not. What messenger art thou?
DEATH: I am Death, that no man dreadeth,° 115
For every man I rest,° and no man spareth;
For it is God's commandment
That all to me should be obedient.
EVERYMAN: O Death, thou comest when I had thee
  least in mind!
In thy power it lieth me to save; 120
Yet of my good° will I give thee, if thou will be kind:
Yea, a thousand pound shalt thou have,
And defer this matter till another day.
DEATH: Everyman, it may not be, by no way.
I set not by gold, silver, nor riches, 125
Ne by pope, emperor, king, duke, ne princes;
For, and I would receive gifts great,
All the world I might get;
But my custom is clean contrary.
I give thee no respite. Come hence, and not tarry. 130
EVERYMAN: Alas, shall I have no longer respite?
I may say Death giveth no warning!
To think on thee, it maketh my heart sick,
For all unready is my book of reckoning.
But twelve year and I might have abiding,° 135
My counting-book I would make so clear
That my reckoning I should not need to fear.
Wherefore, Death, I pray thee, for God's mercy,
Spare me till I be provided of remedy.
DEATH: Thee availeth not to cry, weep, and pray; 140
But haste thee lightly that thou were gone that
  journey,°
And prove thy friends if thou can;
For, wit thou well, the tide abideth no man,
And in the world each living creature
For Adam's sin must die of nature.° 145
EVERYMAN: Death, if I should this pilgrimage take,
And my reckoning surely make,
Show me, for saint charity,°
Should I not come again shortly?
DEATH: No, Everyman; and thou be once there, 150
Thou mayst never more come here,
Trust me verily.

105. turn: Return.   111. Have ado . . . that way: Let us see about making that journey.   112. none attorney: No one [your] advocate.   115. no man dreadeth: Fears no man.   116. rest: Arrest.   121. good: Goods.   135. But twelve year . . . abiding: If I could stay for just twelve more years.   141. But haste thee . . . that journey: But set off quickly on your journey.   145. of nature: In the course of nature.   148. for saint charity: In the name of holy charity.

EVERYMAN: O gracious God in the high seat celestial,
 Have mercy on me in this most need!
155 Shall I have no company from this vale terrestrial
 Of mine acquaintance, that way me to lead?
DEATH: Yea, if any be so hardy
 That would go with thee and bear thee company.
 Hie thee that thou were gone to God's magnificence,
160 Thy reckoning to give before his presence.
 What, weenest° thou thy life is given thee,
 And thy worldly goods also?
EVERYMAN: I had wend° so, verily.
DEATH: Nay, nay; it was but lent thee;
165 For as soon as thou art go,
 Another a while shall have it, and then go therefro,
 Even as thou has done.
 Everyman, thou art mad! Thou hast thy wits five,
 And here on earth will not amend thy life;
170 For suddenly I do come.
EVERYMAN: O wretched caitiff,° whither shall I flee,
 That I might scape this endless sorrow?
 Now, gentle Death, spare me till to-morrow,
 That I may amend me
175 With good advisement.
DEATH: Nay, thereto I will not consent,
 Nor no man will I respite;
 But to the heart suddenly I shall smite
 Without any advisement.
180 And now out of thy sight I will me hie;
 See thou make thee ready shortly,
 For thou mayst say this is the day
 That no man living may scape away.

          (*Exit Death.*)

EVERYMAN: Alas, I may well weep with sighs deep!
185 Now have I no manner of company
 To help me in my journey, and me to keep;
 And also my writing is full unready,
 How shall I do now for to excuse me?
 I would to God I had never be get!°
190 To my soul a full great profit it had be;
 For now I fear pains huge and great.
 The time passeth. Lord, help, that all wrought!
 For though I mourn it availeth nought.
 The day passeth, and is almost ago;°
195 I wot not well what for to do.
 To whom were I best my complaint to make?
 What and I to Fellowship thereof spake,
 And showed him of this sudden chance?
 For in him is all mine affiance;°
200 We have in the world so many a day
 Be good friends in sport and play.
 I see him yonder, certainly.
 I trust that he will bear me company;
 Therefore to him will I speak to ease my sorrow.
205 Well met, good Fellowship, and good morrow!

(*Fellowship speaketh.*)

FELLOWSHIP: Everyman, good morrow, by this day!
 Sir, why lookest thou so piteously?
 If any thing be amiss, I pray thee me say,
 That I may help to remedy.
EVERYMAN: Yea, good Fellowship, yea;   210
 I am in great jeopardy.
FELLOWSHIP: My true friend, show to me your mind;
 I will not forsake thee to my life's end,
 In the way of good company.
EVERYMAN: That was well spoken, and lovingly. 215
FELLOWSHIP: Sir, I must needs know your heaviness;°
 I have pity to see you in any distress.
 If any have you wronged, ye shall revenged be,
 Though I on the ground be slain for thee —
 Though that I know before that I should die. 220
EVERYMAN: Verily, Fellowship, gramercy.°
FELLOWSHIP: Tush! by thy thanks I set not a straw.
 Show me your grief, and say no more.
EVERYMAN: If I my heart should to you break,°
 And then you to turn your mind from me, 225
 And would not me comfort when ye hear me speak,
 Then should I ten times sorrier be.
FELLOWSHIP: Sir, I say as I will do indeed.
EVERYMAN: Then be you a good friend at need:
 I have found you true herebefore.   230
FELLOWSHIP: And so ye shall evermore;
 For, in faith, and thou go to hell,
 I will not forsake thee by the way.
EVERYMAN: Ye speak like a good friend; I believe you well.
 I shall deserve° it, and I may.   235
FELLOWSHIP: I speak of no deserving, by this day!
 For he that will say, and nothing do,
 Is not worthy with good company to go;
 Therefore show me the grief of your mind,
 As to your friend most loving and kind. 240
EVERYMAN: I shall show you how it is:
 Commanded I am to go a journey,
 A long way, hard and dangerous,
 And give a strait count, without delay,
 Before the high Judge, Adonai.°   245
 Wherefore, I pray you, bear me company,
 As ye have promised, in this journey.
FELLOWSHIP: That is matter indeed.° Promise is duty;
 But, and I should take such a voyage on me,
 I know it well, it should be to my pain; 250
 Also it maketh me afeard, certain.
 But let us take counsel here as well as we can,
 For your words would fear a strong man.
EVERYMAN: Why, ye said if I had need
 Ye would me never forsake, quick ne dead, 255
 Though it were to hell, truly.

---

161. weenest: Suppose. **163. wend:** Supposed. **171. caitiff:** Captive. **189. be get:** Been born. **194. ago:** Gone. **199. affiance:** Trust.

216. heaviness: Sorrow. **221. gramercy:** Thanks. **224. break:** Open. **235. deserve:** Repay. **245. Adonai:** Hebrew name for God. **248. That is matter indeed:** That is a good reason indeed [for asking me].

FELLOWSHIP: So I said, certainly,
   But such pleasures be set aside, the sooth to say;
   And also, if we took such a journey,
260   When should we come again?
EVERYMAN: Nay, never again, till the day of doom.
FELLOWSHIP: In faith, then will not I come there!
   Who hath you these tidings brought?
EVERYMAN: Indeed, Death was with me here.
265 FELLOWSHIP: Now, by God that all hath bought,°
   If Death were the messenger,
   For no man that is living to-day
   I will not go that loath journey —
   Not for the father that begat me!
270 EVERYMAN: Ye promised otherwise, pardie.°
FELLOWSHIP: I wot well I said so, truly;
   And yet if thou wilt eat, and drink, and make good
      cheer,
   Or haunt to women the lusty company,°
   I would not forsake you while the day is clear,°
275   Trust me verily.
EVERYMAN: Yea, thereto ye would be ready!
   To go to mirth, solace, and play,
   Your mind will sooner apply,
   Than to bear me company in my long journey.
280 FELLOWSHIP: Now, in good faith, I will not that way.
   But and thou will murder, or any man kill,
   In that I will help thee with a good will.
EVERYMAN: O, that is a simple advice indeed.
   Gentle fellow, help me in my necessity!
285   We have loved long, and now I need;
   And now, gentle Fellowship, remember me.
FELLOWSHIP: Whether ye have loved me or no,
   By Saint John, I will not with thee go.
EVERYMAN: Yet, I pray thee, take the labor, and do so
      much for me
290   To bring me forward, for saint charity,
   And comfort me till I come without the town.
FELLOWSHIP: Nay, and thou would give me a new gown,
   I will not a foot with thee go;
   But, and thou had tarried, I would not have left
      thee so.
295   And as now God speed thee in thy journey,
   For from thee I will depart as fast as I may.
EVERYMAN: Whither away, Fellowship? Will thou
      forsake me?
FELLOWSHIP: Yea, by my fay!° To God I betake° thee.
EVERYMAN: Farewell, good Fellowship; for thee my
      heart is sore.
300   Adieu for ever! I shall see thee no more.
FELLOWSHIP: In faith, Everyman, farewell now at the
      ending;
   For you I will remember that parting is mourning.
                     (*Exit Fellowship.*)

265. **bought:** Redeemed.   270. **pardie:** By God.   273. **haunt to women the lusty company:** Frequent the lively company of women.   274. **while the day is clear:** Until daybreak.   298. **fay:** Faith. **betake:** Commend.

EVERYMAN: Alack! shall we thus depart° indeed —
   Ah, Lady, help! — without any more comfort?
   Lo, Fellowship forsaketh me in my most need.   305
   For help in this world whither shall I resort?
   Fellowship herebefore with me would merry make,
   And now little sorrow for me doth he take.
   It is said, "In prosperity men friends may find,
   Which in adversity be full unkind."   310
   Now whither for succor shall I flee,
   Sith° that Fellowship hath forsaken me?
   To my kinsmen I will, truly,
   Praying them to help me in my necessity;
   I believe that they will do so,   315
   For kind will creep where it may not go.°
   I will go say,° for yonder I see them.
   Where be ye now, my friends and kinsmen?

(*Enter Kindred and Cousin.*)

KINDRED: Here be we now at your commandment.
   Cousin, I pray you show us your intent   320
   In any wise, and do not spare.
COUSIN: Yea, Everyman, and to us declare
   If ye be disposed to go anywhither;
   For, wit you well, we will live and die together.
KINDRED: In wealth and woe we will with you hold,   325
   For over his kin a man may be bold.°
EVERYMAN: Gramercy, my friends and kinsmen kind.
   Now shall I show you the grief of my mind:
   I was commanded by a messenger,
   That is a high king's chief officer;   330
   He bade me go a pilgrimage, to my pain,
   And I know well I shall never come again;
   Also I must give a reckoning strait,
   For I have a great enemy° that hath me in wait,°
   Which intendeth me for to hinder.   335
KINDRED: What account is that which ye must render?
   That would I know.
EVERYMAN: Of all my works I must show
   How I have lived and my days spent;
   Also of ill deeds that I have used   340
   In my time, sith life was me lent;
   And of all virtues that I have refused.
   Therefore, I pray you, go thither with me
   To help to make mine account, for saint charity.
COUSIN: What, to go thither? Is that the matter?   345
   Nay, Everyman, I had liefer fast bread and water°
   All this five year and more.
EVERYMAN: Alas, that ever I was bore!
   For now shall I never be merry,
   If that you forsake me.   350

303. **depart:** Part.   312. **Sith:** Since.   316. **for kind will creep where it may not go:** For kinship will creep where it cannot walk; i.e., blood is thicker than water.   317. **say:** Essay, try.   326. **For over his kin . . . may be bold:** For a man may be sure of his kinsfolk.   334. **enemy:** Devil. **hath me in wait:** Has me under observation.   346. **liefer fast bread and water:** Rather fast on bread and water.

KINDRED: Ah, sir, what ye be a merry man!
    Take good heart to you, and make no moan.
    But one thing I warn you, by Saint Anne —
    As for me, ye shall go alone.
355 EVERYMAN: My Cousin, will you not with me go?
COUSIN: No, by our Lady! I have the cramp in my toe.
    Trust not to me, for, so God me speed,
    I will deceive you in your most need.
KINDRED: It availeth not us to tice.°
360   Ye shall have my maid with all my heart;
    She loveth to go to feasts, there to be nice,°
    And to dance, and abroad to start:
    I will give her leave to help you in that journey,
    If that you and she may agree.
EVERYMAN: Now show me the very effect° of your
365   mind:
    Will you go with me, or abide behind?
KINDRED: Abide behind? Yea, that will I, and I may!
    Therefore farewell till another day.
                      (*Exit Kindred.*)
EVERYMAN: How should I be merry or glad?
370   For fair promises men to me make,
    But when I have most need they me forsake.
    I am deceived; that maketh me sad.
COUSIN: Cousin Everyman, farewell now,
    For verily I will not go with you.
375   Also of mine own an unready reckoning
    I have to account; therefore I make tarrying.
    Now God keep thee, for now I go.
                      (*Exit Cousin.*)
EVERYMAN: Ah, Jesus, is all come hereto?
    Lo, fair words maketh fools fain;°
380   They promise, and nothing will do, certain.
    My kinsmen promised me faithfully
    For to abide with me steadfastly,
    And now fast away do they flee:
    Even so Fellowship promised me.
385   What friend were best me of to provide?°
    I lose my time here longer to abide.
    Yet in my mind a thing there is:
    All my life I have loved riches;
    If that my Good° now help me might,
390   He would make my heart full light.
    I will speak to him in this distress —
    Where art thou, my Goods and riches?

(*Goods speaks from a corner.*)

GOODS: Who calleth me? Everyman? What! hast thou
    haste?
    I lie here in corners, trussed and piled so high,
395   And in chests I am locked so fast,
    Also sacked in bags. Thou mayst see with shine eye
    I cannot stir; in packs low I lie.
    What would ye have? Lightly° me say.

EVERYMAN: Come hither, Good, in all the haste thou
    may,
    For of counsel I must desire thee.   400
GOODS: Sir, and ye in the world have sorrow or
    adversity,
    That can I help you to remedy shortly.
EVERYMAN: It is another disease that grieveth me;
    In this world it is not, I tell thee so.
    I am sent for, another way to go,   405
    To give a strait count general
    Before the highest Jupiter of all;
    And all my life I have had joy and pleasure in thee,
    Therefore, I pray thee, go with me;
    For, peradventure, thou mayst before God
    Almighty   410
    My reckoning help to clean and purify;
    For it is said ever among
    That money maketh all right that is wrong.
GOODS: Nay, Everyman, I sing another song.
    I follow no man in such voyages;   415
    For, and I went with thee,
    Thou shouldst fare much the worse for me;
    For because on me thou did set thy mind,
    Thy reckoning I have made blotted and blind,
    That shine account thou cannot make truly;   420
    And that hast thou for the love of me.
EVERYMAN: That would grieve me full sore,
    When I should come to that fearful answer.
    Up, let us go thither together.
GOODS: Nay, not so! I am too brittle, I may not
    endure;   425
    I will follow no man one foot, be ye sure.
EVERYMAN: Alas, I have thee loved, and had great
    pleasure
    All my life-days on good and treasure.
GOODS: That is to thy damnation, without leasing,°
    For my love is contrary to the love everlasting;   430
    But if thou had me loved moderately during,
    As to the poor to give part of me,
    Then shouldst thou not in this dolor be,
    Nor in this great sorrow and care.
EVERYMAN: Lo, now was I deceived ere I was ware,   435
    And all I may wite° misspending of time.
GOODS: What, weenest thou that I am thine?
EVERYMAN: I had wend so.
GOODS: Nay, Everyman, I say no.
    As for a while I was lent thee;   440
    A season thou hast had me in prosperity.
    My condition is man's soul to kill;
    If I save one, a thousand I do spill.°
    Weenest thou that I will follow thee?
    Nay, not from this world, verily.   445
EVERYMAN: I had wend otherwise.
GOODS: Therefore to thy soul Good is a thief;
    For when thou art dead, this is my guise —

---

359. tice: Entice.   **361. nice:** Wanton.   **365. effect:** Tenor.
379. fain: Glad.   **385. me of to provide:** To provide myself with.
389. Good: Goods.   **398. Lightly:** Quickly.

429. without leasing: Without a lie, i.e., truly.   **436. wite:** Blame.
443. spill: Ruin.

Another to deceive in this same wise
450   As I have done thee, and all to his soul's reprief.°
EVERYMAN: O false Good, cursed may thou be,
       Thou traitor to God, that hast deceived me
       And caught me in thy snare!
GOODS: Marry, thou brought thyself in care,
455   Whereof I am glad;
       I must needs laugh, I cannot be sad.
EVERYMAN: Ah, Good, thou hast had long my heartly
          love;
       I gave thee that which should be the Lord's above.
       But wilt thou not go with me indeed?
460   I pray thee truth to say.
GOODS: No, so God me speed!
       Therefore farewell, and have good day.

                                        (*Exit Goods.*)

EVERYMAN: O, to whom shall I make my moan
       For to go with me in that heavy journey?
465   First Fellowship said he would with me gone;
       His words were very pleasant and gay,
       But afterward he left me alone.
       Then spake I to my kinsmen, all in despair,
       And also they gave me words fair;
470   They lacked no fair speaking,
       But all forsook me in the ending.
       Then went I to my Goods, that I loved best,
       In hope to have comfort, but there had I least;
       For my Goods sharply did me tell
475   That he bringeth many into hell.
       Then of myself I was ashamed,
       And so I am worthy to be blamed;
       Thus may I well myself hate.
       Of whom shall I now counsel take?
480   I think that I shall never speed
       Till that I go to my Good Deed.
       But, alas, she is so weak
       That she can neither go nor speak;
       Yet will I venture on her now.
485   My Good Deeds, where be you?

(*Good Deeds speaks from the ground.*)

GOOD DEEDS: Here I lie, cold in the ground;
       Thy sins hath me sore bound,
       That I cannot stir.
EVERYMAN: O Good Deeds, I stand in fear!
490   I must you pray of counsel,
       For help now should come right well.°
GOOD DEEDS: Everyman, I have understanding
       That ye be summoned account to make
       Before Messias, of Jerusalem King;
       And you do by me,° that journey with you will I
495   take.
EVERYMAN: Therefore I come to you, my moan to
          make;
       I pray you that ye will go with me.

GOOD DEEDS: I would full fain, but I cannot stand,
          verily.
EVERYMAN: Why, is there anything on you fall?
GOOD DEEDS: Yea, sir, I may thank you of° all;   500
       If ye had perfectly cheered me,
       Your book of count full ready had be.
       Look, the books of your works and deeds eke!°
       Behold how they lie under the feet,
       To your soul's heaviness.   505
EVERYMAN: Our Lord Jesus help me!
       For one letter here I cannot see.
GOOD DEEDS: There is a blind reckoning in time of
          distress.
EVERYMAN: Good Deeds, I pray you help me in this
          need,
       Or else I am for ever damned indeed;   510
       Therefore help me to make reckoning
       Before the Redeemer of all thing,
       That King is, and was, and ever shall.
GOOD DEEDS: Everyman, I am sorry of your fall,
       And fain would I help you, and I were able.   515
EVERYMAN: Good Deeds, your counsel I pray you
          give me.
GOOD DEEDS: That shall I do verily;
       Though that on my feet I may not go,
       I have a sister that shall with you also,
       Called Knowledge, which shall with you abide,   520
       To help you to make that dreadful reckoning.

(*Enter Knowledge.*)

KNOWLEDGE: Everyman, I will go with thee, and be thy
          guide,
       In thy most need to go by thy side.
EVERYMAN: In good condition I am now in every
          thing,
       And am wholly content with this good thing,   525
       Thanked be God my creator.
GOOD DEEDS: And when she hath brought you there
       Where thou shalt heal thee of thy smart,
       Then go you with your reckoning and your Good
          Deeds together,
       For to make you joyful at heart   530
       Before the blessed Trinity.
EVERYMAN: My Good Deeds, gramercy!
       I am well content, certainly,
       With your words sweet.
KNOWLEDGE: Now go we together lovingly   535
       To Confession, that cleansing river.
EVERYMAN: For joy I weep; I would we were there!
       But, I pray you, give me cognition
       Where dwelleth that holy man, Confession.
KNOWLEDGE: In the house of salvation: 540
       We shall find him in that place,
       That shall us comfort, by God's grace.

(*Knowledge takes Everyman to Confession.*)

---

450. **reprief:** Shame.   491. **should come right well:** Would be
very welcome.   495. **by me:** As I advise.

500. **of:** For.   503. **eke:** Also.

Lo, this is Confession. Kneel down and ask mercy,
For he is in good conceit° with God Almighty.
EVERYMAN: O glorious fountain, that all uncleanness
545   doth clarify,
Wash from me the spots of vice unclean,
That on me no sin may be seen.
I come with Knowledge for my redemption,
Redempt with heart° and full contrition;
550 For I am commanded a pilgrimage to take,
And great accounts before God to make.
Now I pray you, Shrift, mother of salvation,
Help my Good Deeds for my piteous exclamation.
CONFESSION: I know your sorrow well, Everyman.
555 Because with Knowledge ye come to me,
I will you comfort as well as I can,
And a precious jewel I will give thee,
Called penance, voider of adversity;
Therewith shall your body chastised be,
560 With abstinence and perseverance in God's service.
Here shall you receive that scourge of me,
Which is penance strong that ye must endure,
To remember thy Savior was scourged for thee
With sharp scourges, and suffered it patiently;
565 So must thou, ere thou scape that painful pilgrimage.
Knowledge, keep him in this voyage,
And by that time Good Deeds will be with thee.
But in any wise be siker° of mercy,
For your time draweth fast; and° ye will saved be,
570 Ask God mercy, and he will grant truly.
When with the scourge of penance man doth him
      bind,
The oil of forgiveness then shall he find.
EVERYMAN: Thanked be God for his gracious work!
For now I will my penance begin;
575 This hath rejoiced and lighted my heart,
Though the knots be painful and hard within.
KNOWLEDGE: Everyman, look your penance that ye
      fulfill,
What pain that ever it to you be;
And Knowledge shall give you counsel at will
580 How your account ye shall make clearly.
EVERYMAN: O eternal God, O heavenly figure,
O way of righteousness, O goodly vision,
Which descended down in a virgin pure
Because he would every man redeem,
585 Which Adam forfeited by his disobedience:
O blessed Godhead, elect and high divine,
Forgive my grievous offense;
Here I cry thee mercy in this presence.°
O ghostly treasure, O ransomer and redeemer,
590 Of all the world hope and conductor,
Mirror of joy, and founder of mercy,
Which enlumineth heaven and earth thereby,
Hear my clamorous complaint, though it late be;

Receive my prayers, of thy benignity;
Though I be a sinner most abominable,   595
Yet let my name be written in Moses' table.°
O Mary, pray to the Maker of all thing,
Me for to help at my ending;
And save me from the power of my enemy,
For Death assaileth me strongly.   600
And, Lady, that I may by mean of thy prayer
Of your Son's glory to be partner,
By the means of his passion, I it crave;
I beseech you help my soul to save.
Knowledge, give me the scourge of penance;   605
My flesh therewith shall give acquittance:°
I will now begin, if God give me grace.
KNOWLEDGE: Everyman, God give you time and space!
Thus I bequeath you in the hands of our Saviour;
Now may you make your reckoning sure.   610
EVERYMAN: In the name of the Holy Trinity,
My body sore punished shall be:
Take this, body, for the sin of the flesh!

(Scourges himself.)

Also° thou delightest to go gay and fresh,
And in the way of damnation thou did me bring,   615
Therefore suffer now strokes and punishing.
Now of penance I will wade the water clear,
To save me from purgatory, that sharp fire.

(Good Deeds rises from the ground.)

GOOD DEEDS: I thank God, now I can walk and go,
And am delivered of my sickness and woe.   620
Therefore with Everyman I will go, and not spare;
His good works I will help him to declare.
KNOWLEDGE: Now, Everyman, be merry and glad!
Your Good Deeds cometh now; ye may not be sad.
Now is your Good Deeds whole and sound,   625
Going upright upon the ground.
EVERYMAN: My heart is light, and shall be evermore;
Now will I smite° faster than I did before.
GOOD DEEDS: Everyman, pilgrim, my special friend,
Blessed be thou without end;   630
For thee is preparate the eternal glory.
Ye have me made whole and sound,
Therefore I will bide by thee in every stound.°
EVERYMAN: Welcome, my Good Deeds; now I hear thy
      voice,
I weep for very sweetness of love.   635
KNOWLEDGE: Be no more sad, but ever rejoice;
God seeth thy living in his throne above.
Put on this garment to thy behoof,°

---

544. conceit: Esteem. **549. heart:** Heartfelt. **568. siker:** Sure. **569. and:** If. **588. in this presence:** In the presence of this company.

596. Moses' table: Medieval theologians regarded the two tablets given to Moses on Mount Sinai as symbols of baptism and penance. Thus Everyman is asking to be numbered among those who have escaped damnation by doing penance for their sins. **606. acquittance:** Satisfaction (as part of the sacrament of penance). **614. Also:** As. **628. smite:** Strike. **633. stound:** Trial. **638. behoof:** Advantage.

Which is wet with your tears,
640   Or else before God you may it miss,
When ye to your journey's end come shall.
EVERYMAN: Gentle Knowledge, what do ye it call?
KNOWLEDGE: It is a garment of sorrow:
From pain it will you borrow;°
645   Contrition it is,
That geteth forgiveness;
It pleaseth God passing well.
GOOD DEEDS: Everyman, will you wear it for your
    heal?°
EVERYMAN: Now blessed be Jesu, Mary's Son,
650   For now have I on true contrition.
And let us go now without tarrying;
Good Deeds, have we clear our reckoning?
GOOD DEEDS: Yea, indeed, I have it here.
EVERYMAN: Then I trust we need not fear;
655   Now, friends, let us not part in twain.
KNOWLEDGE: Nay, Everyman, that will we not, certain.
GOOD DEEDS: Yet must thou lead with thee
Three persons of great might.
EVERYMAN: Who should they be?
660 GOOD DEEDS: Discretion and Strength they hight,°
And thy Beauty may not abide behind.
KNOWLEDGE: Also ye must call to mind
Your Five Wits as for your counsellors.
GOOD DEEDS: You must have them ready at all hours.
665 EVERYMAN: How shall I get them hither?
KNOWLEDGE: You must call them all together,
And they will hear you incontinent.°
EVERYMAN: My friends, come hither and be present,
Discretion, Strength, my Five Wits, and Beauty.

(*Enter Beauty, Strength, Discretion, and Five Wits.*)

670 BEAUTY: Here at your will we be all ready.
What will ye that we should do?
GOOD DEEDS: That ye would with Everyman go,
And help him in his pilgrimage.
Advise you, will ye with him or not in that voyage?
675 STRENGTH: We will bring him all thither,
To his help and comfort, ye may believe me.
DISCRETION: So will we go with him all together.
EVERYMAN: Almighty God, lofed° may thou be!
I give thee laud that I have hither brought
Strength, Discretion, Beauty, and Five Wits. Lack I
680   nought.
And my Good Deeds, with Knowledge clear,
All be in my company at my will here;
I desire no more to my business.
STRENGTH: And I, Strength, will by you stand in
    distress,
685   Though thou would in battle fight on the ground.
FIVE WITS: And though it were through the world
    round,
We will not depart for sweet ne sour.

BEAUTY: No more will I unto death's hour,
Whatsoever thereof befall.
DISCRETION: Everyman, advise you first of all;   690
Go with a good advisement and deliberation.
We all give you virtuous monition°
That all shall be well.
EVERYMAN: My friends, harken what I will tell:
I pray God reward you in his heavenly sphere.   695
Now harken, all that be here,
For I will make my testament
Here before you all present:
In alms half my good I will give with my hands twain
In the way of charity, with good intent,   700
And the other half still shall remain
In queth,° to be returned there it ought to be.°
This I do in despite of the fiend of hell,
To go quit out of his peril°
Ever after and this day.   705
KNOWLEDGE: Everyman, harken what I say:
Go to priesthood, I you advise,
And receive of him in any wise°
The holy sacrament and ointment together.
Then shortly see ye turn again hither;   710
We will all abide you here.
FIVE WITS: Yea, Everyman, hie you that ye ready were.
There is no emperor, king, duke, ne baron,
That of God hath commission
As hath the least priest in the world being;   715
For of the blessed sacraments pure and benign
He beareth the keys, and thereof hath the cure°
For man's redemption — it is ever sure —
Which God for our soul's medicine
Gave us out of his heart with great pine.°   720
Here in this transitory life, for thee and me,
The blessed sacraments seven there be:
Baptism, confirmation, with priesthood good,
And the sacrament of God's precious flesh and blood,
Marriage, the holy extreme unction, and penance;   725
These seven be good to have in remembrance,
Gracious sacraments of high divinity.
EVERYMAN: Fain would I receive that holy body,
And meekly to my ghostly father I will go.
FIVE WITS: Everyman, that is the best that ye can do.   730
God will you to salvation bring,
For priesthood exceedeth all other thing:
To us Holy Scripture they do teach,
And converteth man from sin heaven to reach;
God hath to them more power given   735
Than to any angel that is in heaven.
With five words° he may consecrate,

---

644. **borrow:** Release.   648. **heal:** Salvation.   660. **hight:** Are
called.   667. **incontinent:** Immediately.   678. **lofed:** Praised.

692. **monition:** Forewarning.   702. **queth:** Bequest. **returned
there it ought to be:** This line probably refers to restitution, that
is, the restoration to its proper owner of unlawfully acquired
property.   704. **quit out of his peril:** Free out of his power.
708. **in any wise:** Without fail.   717. **cure:** Charge.   720. **pine:**
Suffering.   737. **five words:** *Hoc est enim Corpus meum* ("For
this is my body," the words of the consecration of the body of
Christ at Mass).

Scene from the Guthrie Theater
production of *Everyman,* directed by
Robert Benedetti.

God's body in flesh and blood to make,
And handleth his Maker between his hands.
740 The priest bindeth and unbindeth all bands,
Both in earth and in heaven.
Thou ministers all the sacraments seven;
Though we kissed thy feet, thou were worthy;
Thou art surgeon that cureth sin deadly:
745 No remedy we find under God
But all only priesthood.°
Everyman, God gave priests that dignity,

746. But all only priesthood: Except only from the priesthood.

And setteth them in his stead among us to be;
Thus be they above angels in degree.

(*Everyman goes to the priest to receive the last sacraments.*)

KNOWLEDGE: If priests be good, it is so, surely.   750
But when Jesus hanged on the cross with great
  smart,
There he gave out of his blessed heart
The same sacrament in great torment:
He sold them not to us, that Lord omnipotent.
Therefore Saint Peter the apostle doth say   755
That Jesu's curse hath all they

Which God their Savior do buy or sell,
Or they for any money do take or tell.°
Sinful priests giveth the sinners example bad;
Their children sitteth by other men's fires, I have
760   heard;
And some haunteth women's company
With unclean life, as lusts of lechery:
These be with sin made blind.
FIVE WITS: I trust to God no such may we find;
765 Therefore let us priesthood honor,
And follow their doctrine for our souls' succor.
We be their sheep, and they shepherds be
By whom we all be kept in surety.
Peace, for yonder I see Everyman come,
770 Which hath made true satisfaction.
GOOD DEEDS: Methink it is he indeed.

(*Reenter Everyman.*)

EVERYMAN: Now Jesu be your alder speed!°
I have received the sacrament for my redemption,
And then mine extreme unction:
775 Blessed be all they that counselled me to take it!
And now, friends, let us go without longer respite;
I thank God that ye have tarried so long.
Now set each of you on this rood° your hand,
And shortly follow me:
780 I go before there I would be; God be our guide!
STRENGTH: Everyman, we will not from you go
Till ye have done this voyage long.
DISCRETION: I, Discretion, will bide by you also.
KNOWLEDGE: And though this pilgrimage be never so
    strong,°
785 I will never part you fro.
STRENGTH: Everyman, I will be as sure by thee
As ever I did by Judas Maccabee.°

(*Everyman comes to his grave.*)

EVERYMAN: Alas, I am so faint I may not stand;
My limbs under me doth fold.
790 Friends, let us not turn again to this land,
Not for all the world's gold;
For into this cave must I creep
And turn to earth, and there to sleep.
BEAUTY: What, into this grave? Alas!
795 EVERYMAN: Yea, there shall ye consume, more and less.
BEAUTY: And what, should I smother here?
EVERYMAN: Yea, by my faith, and never more appear.
In this world live no more we shall,
But in heaven before the highest Lord of all.

BEAUTY: I cross out all this;° adieu, by Saint John!   800
I take my cap in my lap,° and am gone.
EVERYMAN: What, Beauty, whither will ye?
BEAUTY: Peace, I am deaf; I look not behind me,
Not and thou wouldest give me all the gold in thy
    chest.   (*Exit Beauty.*)
EVERYMAN: Alas, whereto may I trust?   805
Beauty goeth fast away from me;
She promised with me to live and die.
STRENGTH: Everyman, I will thee also forsake and
    deny;
Thy game liketh° me not at all.
EVERYMAN: Why, then, ye will forsake me all?   810
Sweet Strength, tarry a little space.
STRENGTH: Nay, sir, by the rood of grace!
I will hie me from thee fast,
Though thou weep till thy heart to-brast.°
EVERYMAN: Ye would ever bide by me, ye said.   815
STRENGTH: Yea, I have you far enough conveyed.
Ye be old enough, I understand,
Your pilgrimage to take on hand;
I repent me that I hither came.
EVERYMAN: Strength, you to displease I am to blame;   820
Yet promise is debt, this ye well wot.
STRENGTH: In faith, I care not.
Thou art but a fool to complain;
You spend your speech and waste your brain.
Go thrust thee into the ground!   (*Exit Strength.*) 825
EVERYMAN: I had wend surer I should you have found.
He that trusteth in his Strength
She him deceiveth at the length.
Both Strength and Beauty forsaketh me;
Yet they promised me fair and lovingly.   830
DISCRETION: Everyman, I will after Strength be gone;
As for me, I will leave you alone.
EVERYMAN: Why, Discretion, will ye forsake me?
DISCRETION: Yea, in faith, I will go from thee,
For when Strength goeth before   835
I follow after evermore.
EVERYMAN: Yet, I pray thee, for the love of the Trinity,
Look in my grave once piteously.
DISCRETION: Nay, so nigh will I not come;
Farewell, every one!   (*Exit Discretion.*) 840
EVERYMAN: O, all thing faileth, save God alone —
Beauty, Strength, and Discretion;
For when Death bloweth his blast,
They all run from me full fast.
FIVE WITS: Everyman, my leave now of thee I take;   845
I will follow the other, for here I thee forsake.
EVERYMAN: Alas, then may I wail and weep,
For I took you for my best friend.
FIVE WITS: I will no longer thee keep;
Now farewell, and there an end.   850
                    (*Exit Five Wits.*)

755–58. Therefore Saint Peter . . . do take or tell: Reference to the sin of simony, the selling of church offices or benefits. **tell:** Count out, i.e., sell. **772. your alder speed:** The helper of you all. **778. rood:** Cross. **784. strong:** Grievous. **787. Judas Maccabee:** Judas Maccabeus, who overcame Syrian domination and won religious freedom for the Jews in 165 B.C., believed that his strength came not from worldly might but from heaven (1 Maccabees 3:19).

800. I cross out all this: I cancel all this, i.e., my promise to stay with you. **801. I take my cap in my lap:** Doff my cap [so low that it comes] into my lap. **809. liketh:** Pleases. **814. brast:** Break.

EVERYMAN: O Jesu, help! All hath forsaken me.
GOOD DEEDS: Nay, Everyman; I will bide with thee.
   I will not forsake thee indeed;
   Thou shalt find me a good friend at need.
EVERYMAN: Gramercy, Good Deeds! Now may I true
855   friends see.
   They have forsaken me, every one;
   I loved them better than my Good Deeds alone.
   Knowledge, will ye forsake me also?
KNOWLEDGE: Yea, Everyman, when ye to Death shall
     go;
860   But not yet, for no manner of danger.
EVERYMAN: Gramercy, Knowledge, with all my heart.
KNOWLEDGE: Nay, yet I will not from hence depart
   Till I see where ye shall become.
EVERYMAN: Methink, alas, that I must be gone
865 To make my reckoning and my debts pay,
   For I see my time is nigh spent away.
   Take example, all ye that this do hear or see,
   How they that I loved best do forsake me,
   Except my Good Deeds that bideth truly.
870 GOOD DEEDS: All earthly things is but vanity:
   Beauty, Strength, and Discretion do man forsake,
   Foolish friends, and kinsmen, that fair spake —
   All fleeth save Good Deeds, and that am I.
EVERYMAN: Have mercy on me, God most mighty;
   And stand by me, thou mother and maid, holy
875   Mary.
GOOD DEEDS: Fear not; I will speak for thee.
EVERYMAN: Here I cry God mercy.
GOOD DEEDS: Short our end, and minish our pain;
   Let us go and never come again.
880 EVERYMAN: Into thy hands, Lord, my soul I
     commend;
   Receive it, Lord, that it be not lost.
   As thou me boughtest, so me defend,
   And save me from the fiend's boast,
   That I may appear with that blessed host
885 That shall be saved at the day of doom.
   In manus tuas, of mights most
   For ever, *commendo spiritum meum.*°

(He sinks into his grave.)

KNOWLEDGE: Now hath he suffered that we all shall
     endure;
   The Good Deeds shall make all sure.
   Now hath he made ending;   890
   Methinketh that I hear angels sing,
   And make great joy and melody
   Where Everyman's soul received shall be.
ANGEL: Come, excellent elect spouse, to Jesu!
   Hereabove thou shalt go   895
   Because of thy singular virtue.
   Now the soul is taken the body fro,
   Thy reckoning is crystal-clear.
   Now shalt thou into the heavenly sphere,
   Unto the which all ye shall come   900
   That liveth well before the day of doom.

(Enter Doctor.)

DOCTOR: This moral men may have in mind.
   Ye hearers, take it of worth, old and young,
   And forsake Pride, for he deceiveth you in the end;
   And remember Beauty, Five Wits, Strength, and
     Discretion,   905
   They all at the last do every man forsake,
   Save his Good Deeds there doth he take.
   But beware, for and they be small
   Before God, he hath no help at all;
   None excuse may be there for every man.   910
   Alas, how shall he do then?
   For after death amends may no man make,
   For then mercy and pity doth him forsake.
   If his reckoning be not clear when he doth come,
   God will say: *"Ite, maledicti, in ignem eternum."*°   915
   And he that hath his account whole and sound,
   High in heaven he shall be crowned;
   Unto which place God bring us all thither,
   That we may live body and soul together.
   Thereto help the Trinity!   920
   Amen, say ye, for saint charity.

Thus endeth this moral play of Everyman.

886–87. *In manus tuas . . . commendo spiritum meum:* Into your hands, most mighty One for ever, I commend my spirit.

915. *"Ite, maledicti, in ignem eternum":* Depart, ye cursed, into everlasting fire.

Renaissance Drama

Italian Drama

The period following the Middle Ages in Europe, from about the fourteenth to the seventeenth centuries, is known as the *Renaissance,* a term meaning "rebirth." In this period a shift away from medieval values and culture was motivated by a revival of classical learning; advances in physics, astronomy, and the biological sciences; the exploration of the "new world" of the Americas; and political and economic developments. This shift was not abrupt, however; it was gradual, like a thaw. It began in the south, in Italy, in the late 1300s and moved northward through the activities of scholars, travelers, performers, and writers, until it reached England sometime late in the 1400s.

The Renaissance built on medieval culture and at the same time developed a secular understanding of the individual in society that eventually transformed this culture, long dominated by the Roman Catholic Church in many spheres — artistic, intellectual, and political, as well as spiritual. The transformation was influenced by the work of great writers, scholars, philosophers, and scientists such as Desiderius Erasmus (1466?–1536), Niccolò Machiavelli (1469–1527), Nicolaus Copernicus (1473–1543), Francis Bacon (1561–1626), and Galileo Galilei (1564–1642). In addition, the rise in power of the guilds and the increase in wealth of the successful Italian trading states, which produced large and influential families in cities such as Florence, Venice, Milan, and Genoa, contributed to the erosion of the Church's power.

Italian scholars, following classical models, had begun in the last decades of the fourteenth century to center their studies on human achievements. Such studies, known as the humanities, became the chief concern of the most innovative thinkers of the day. Their interests were well served by the rediscovery of ancient Greek philosophical and scientific texts. Although ancient texts had been preserved in monasteries for centuries, knowledge of them was restricted. A new demand for classical texts, fed by the humanists' focus on ancient models as the source of wisdom and by their return to a liberal arts curriculum established by the Greeks, led to the wide dissemination of the works of Plato, Aristotle, Cicero, and important Greek dramatists during the Renaissance. The achievement of the ancients was an inspiration to Renaissance writers and reaffirmed their conviction that a study of the humanities was the key to transforming the old medieval attitudes into a new, dynamic worldview.

Vitruvius and the Rediscovery of Roman Design

Most medieval Italian theater depended on portable stages, but it was clear in the last decades of the fourteenth century that to present the newly rediscovered Roman or Greek plays, something more closely resembling the original Greek theater would be necessary. Fortunately, *The Ten Books of Architecture* (written c. 16–13 B.C.) of the great Roman architect Vitruvius (first century B.C.) was rediscovered in a manuscript in the monastery of St. Gall. It included detailed plans for the Greek-inspired Roman theater.

Using Vitruvius's designs, the Italians began building stages that were raised platforms with a FRONS SCAENA, the flat front wall used in the Roman theater. The earliest Italian woodcuts show the stages to be relatively simple with pillars supporting a roof or cover. Curtains stretched between the pillars permitted the actors to enter and exit. Usually, three "doors" with names over each indicated the houses of specific characters.

The study of Roman architecture eventually produced, in 1584, one of the wonders of the Renaissance, the Olympic Theater (Teatro Olimpico) in Vicenza, designed by the great Renaissance architect Andrea Palladio (1508–1580), whose interpretation of Roman architecture was so compelling that it influenced architecture all over the world (Figure 6). The Olympic Theater, which has been preserved and is still used for performances, has an orchestra, a semicircular seating area, and a multistory frons scaena. But it also has several vistas of streets constructed in three-dimensional forced perspective running backward from the frons scaena.

The Olympic Theater was built with an essentially conservative design that worked well for Roman plays but not for Renaissance plays. It did not inspire new theater designs. In newer theaters, Italian plays had begun to use scenery and painted backdrops that could be changed to suggest a change in location of the action. Carefully painted backdrops were also effective in increasing illusion: one backdrop could immediately locate an action on a city street, while another could help shift the audience imaginatively to a woodland scene. These innovations proved difficult in the Olympic Theater.

The theory of vanishing-point perspective developed by the architect Filippo Brunelleschi (1377–1446) and published by Leon Battista Alberti in *On Painting* in 1435 helped revolutionize the design of flat theatrical backdrops. Earlier Renaissance painters had had no way to establish a firm sense of perspective on a flat surface, so all three-dimensional objects appeared flat; all space in a landscape or cityscape seemed shortened and unreal. The use of a single vanishing point — in which lines were lightly drawn from the edges of the canvas (or theatrical backdrop) so that they met in a single point in the center — made it possible to show buildings, trees, and figures in their proper proportion to one another (Figure 7). For the first time, Renaissance painters could achieve lifelike illusions on a flat surface. On the other hand, three-dimensional scenery was possible in the Olympic Theater — as well as some others — at this time, and the illusion of reality was thus intensified.

The designer Sebastiano Serlio (1475–1554) used the vanishing-point technique, intensified by receding lines of tiles in the floor and on the painted

ABOVE: Figure 6. Designed by Andrea Palladio, the Teatro Olimpico (begun 1579) in Vicenza, Italy, was the first indoor theater of the Renaissance. The scaena's openings produced an illusion of depth. RIGHT: Figure 7. Perspective setting designed by Baldassare Peruzzi (1481–1536).

backdrop. Serlio established all-purpose settings for comedy, tragedy, and satire. The rigidity of the backdrops for comedy and tragedy — both used a piazza, a small town square, ringed by stone buildings — restricted their use. But the setting for satire was rustic: trees, bushes, a couple of cottages. Until the nineteenth century, European theaters were equipped with sets of backdrops and wingpieces derived from his designs.

The most important and long-lasting development of Italian theater design in the mid-1500s was the PROSCENIUM ARCH, a "frame" that surrounds the stage, permitting the audience to look in on the scene, whether in a room or in a town square. The arch lent a finished touch to the theater, separating the action from the audience and distancing the actors. The proscenium arch is common in most theaters today.

Commedia dell'Arte

Renaissance Italy had two traditions of theater. *Commedia erudita* was learned, almost scholarly, in its interests in Roman staging and Roman plays. COMMEDIA DELL'ARTE was less reverent, more slapstick, and generally more popular. It is difficult, however, to say which was more influential on literature over the years. Each made its contribution.

In terms of acting and storytelling, the influence of the commedia dell'arte is almost unparalleled. The term means "comedy performed by professionals." The actors usually had grown up in performing families that made their living touring the countryside, performing at fairs and on feast days. From the early Renaissance through the eighteenth century, the commedia dell'arte entertained all of Europe and influenced comic theater in every nation.

The essence of commedia dell'arte was improvised scripts. A general narrative outline served as a basis, but the speeches were improvised to a degree (with some reliance on set elements and on experience with performing the same role many times). The principal characters were types who soon became familiar all over Europe: Pantalone, the often magisterial but miserly old man; Arlecchino (Harlequin), the cunning clown. Pulcinella, the Punch of Punch and Judy, and Columbina, the innocent *zanni,* began as clowns. They joined a host of other STOCK CHARACTERS such as pedantic lawyers, a braggart captain, and a serving maid. Certain versions of general characters — such as Arlecchino,

who began as a simple *zanno* — became famous and were copied in many countries. When Volpone calls Mosca a "zany" near the end of Ben Jonson's *Volpone,* he reminds his audience that his characters are indebted to the *zanni* in commedia dell'arte. Knowing who the characters were even before the play began was a convenience that Renaissance audiences enjoyed.

The youthful lovers in the commedia did not require masks, but the old men, the *zanni,* and other characters all had masks that identified them and made them look, to modern eyes, rather grotesque. These masks survive today in the carnival, in Venice, where the commedia began. Stock characters thrive in popular comedies everywhere. Molière and, much later, Bernard Shaw depended on them. To a large extent, one of comedy's greatest sources of energy lies in the delight that audiences have always taken in stock characters. Today hardly a situation comedy on television could survive without them.

The staging of commedia dell'arte was simple. It often took place in open air, but sometimes indoors in a more formal theatrical setting. Sometimes performers dispensed with the stage altogether and worked in marketplaces. Their scenarios were farcical crowd pleasers filled with buffoonery. They were based on the LAZZO and the BURLA. The *burla* was the general plot for any given performance. *Lazzi* were comic routines something like Abbott and Costello's "Who's on First?" skit. Abbott and Costello developed their routine for burlesque, a form of comedy popular in the first half of the twentieth century centering on broad gags, routines, and running jokes. *Lazzi* were carefully planned to seem to be spontaneous interruptions of the action. Chevy Chase's trademark pratfall as he enters a scene is a descendant of the sixteenth-century *lazzo.*

Elizabethan Drama

The reign of Queen Elizabeth I (1558–1603) is known as the Elizabethan age in England — a period of discovery and prosperity as well as a period of great achievement in the arts, especially drama. Sir Francis Drake and Sir Walter Raleigh adventured across the Atlantic Ocean to the "New World," and England secured its economic future by defeating the invasion attempt of the Spanish Armada in 1588. England had become Protestant in the 1530s — one reason Catholic Spain felt it needed to subdue the nation.

Elizabethan England, especially after the defeat of the Armada, produced one of the great ages of drama, rivaling the great age of Greece. During this period, playwrights such as Thomas Kyd (1558–1594), Christopher Marlowe (1564–1593), William Shakespeare (1564–1616), Ben Jonson (1572–1637), John Marston (1576–1634), John Fletcher (1579–1625), John Webster (1580?–1625?), Thomas Middleton (1580?–1627), and John Ford (1586–1639) drew crowds by the thousands.

That the Elizabethans enjoyed plays with a moral basis is plain from the fact that so much of the great drama of the late 1500s and early 1600s is moral in character. Still, early Elizabethan plays were less obviously moralistic than the then-popular morality plays. They did not aim specifically to teach a moral lesson, although there are many lessons to be learned from Shakespeare and his contemporaries.

During Shakespeare's youth wandering players put on a number of plays from REPERTORY, their stock of perhaps a dozen current plays they could perform. How many players there were or what their source of plays was, we do not know. Much of what we know comes directly from *Hamlet* and the appearance of the players who perform Hamlet's "Mouse-trap." What we learn there tells us that dramatic styles had developed in the English countryside and that theater was thriving.

The First Professional Companies

Although professional players' groups had long been licensed to perform in France and Italy, until the 1570s professional actors — those who had no other trade — did not enjoy favor in England. Such people could be arrested for vagrancy. The law, however, changed, and actors with royal patronage were permitted to perform. The history of theater changed, too. In 1576 James Burbage (father of the famous star of Shakespeare's plays, Richard Burbage) built the first building made specially for plays in England. It was called The Theatre.

Soon there were other theaters: the Swan, the Globe (Figure 8), the Rose, the Fortune, the Hope. The Globe was large enough to accommodate two to three thousand people. Because these theaters were open-air, they could not be used in winter, but all were extraordinarily successful. Shakespeare, who was part owner of the Globe and, later, of the second indoor Blackfriars Theatre, received money from admission fees and from his role as chief playwright. He became rich enough to retire in splendid style to Stratford, his hometown. Few other Elizabethan actors and playwrights had as much of a financial stake in their work as did Shakespeare.

The Elizabethan Theater

The design of the Elizabethan theater is a matter of some speculation. Many of the plays popular before the theaters were built were performed in a square inn yard, with a balcony above. The audience looked out their windows or stood in the yard. One location of the earliest English drama is the Inns of Court, essentially a college for law students in London, where students staged plays. The audience there would have been learned, bright, and imaginative. Indeed, the first English tragedy, *Gorboduc,* by Thomas Sackville and Thomas Norton, was played indoors at the Inner Temple, one of the Inns of Court, in 1562, before Marlowe and Shakespeare were born.

The shape of the early theaters was often octagonal or circular, like the bear pits in which bears, tied to stakes, were baited by dogs for the amusement of the audience. The stage was raised about five feet from the ground with levels of seating in several galleries. Approximately half the area over the stage was roofed and contained machinery to lower actors from the "heavens"; it was painted blue with stars to simulate the sky. Some stages were approximately twenty-five by forty feet. Doors or curtained openings at the back of the stage served for entrances and exits, and at the back of the stage was a special room for costume changes. The stage may have contained a section that was normally curtained but that opened to reveal an interior, such as a bedroom. The existence of this feature is, however, in considerable dispute.

The Elizabethan Audience

The entrance fee to the theaters was a penny, probably the equivalent of five to ten dollars in today's money. For another penny one could take a seat, probably on a bench, in one of the upper galleries. In some theaters more private spaces were available as well. A great many playgoers were satisfied to stand

Figure 8. A conjectural reconstruction of the Globe Theatre, 1599 to 1613.

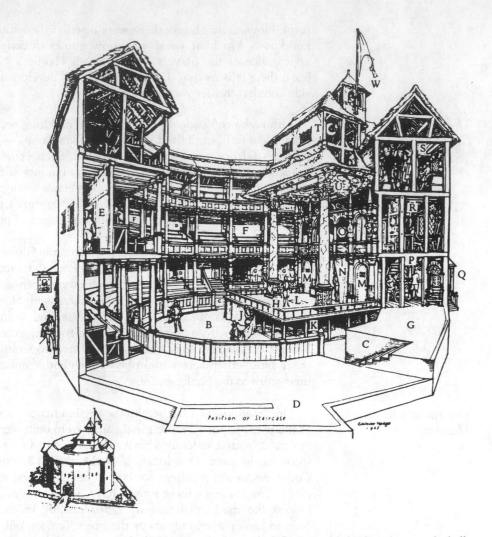

A	Main entrance	L	The stage trap leading down to the hell
B	The yard	M	Stage doors
C	Entrances to lowest gallery	N	Curtained "place behind the stage"
D	Position of entrances to staircase and upper galleries	O	Gallery above the stage, used as required sometimes by musicians, sometimes by spectators, and often as part of the play
E	Corridor serving the different sections of the middle gallery	P	Backstage area (the tiring-house)
F	Middle gallery ("Twopenny Rooms")	Q	Tiring-house door
G	Position of "Gentlemen's Rooms" or "Lords' Rooms"	R	Dressing-rooms
H	The stage	S	Wardrobe and storage
J	The hanging being put up round the stage	T	The hut housing the machine for lowering enthroned gods, etc., to the stage
K	The "hell" under the stage	U	The "heavens"
		W	Hoisting the playhouse flag

around the stage and were thus nicknamed "groundlings." Hamlet calls them the "understanding gentlemen of the ground." The more academic playwrights, Marlowe and Jonson, used the term to mean those who would not perfectly understand the significance of the plays.

Shakespeare and other Elizabethan playwrights expected a widely diverse audience — from coarse to extraordinarily polished. Shakespeare had the gift, as did Marlowe and even Jonson in his comedies, to appeal to them all. Shakespeare's plays were given in public playhouses open to everyone. They were also given in university theaters, as in the case of *Macbeth;* in indoor private theaters; and in royal command performances. Shakespeare's universality reveals itself in his appeal to many different kinds of people.

Female Characters on the English Stage

Because the theater was considered to be morally questionable, women were not allowed to act on English stages. Boys and young men filled the parts of young female characters such as Juliet, Desdemona, and Ophelia. No contemporary commentator makes any complaint about having to put up with a boy playing the part of Juliet or any of Shakespeare's other love interests, such as Desdemona in *Othello,* Ophelia in *Hamlet,* or even Queen Cleopatra. Older women, such as the Nurse in *Romeo and Juliet,* were played by some of the gifted male character actors of the company.

The Masque

The Elizabethan MASQUE was a special entertainment of royalty. It was a celebration that included a rudimentary plot, a great deal of singing and dancing, and magnificent costumes and lighting. Masques were usually performed only once, often to celebrate a royal marriage. Masque audiences participated in the dances and were usually delighted by complex machinery that lifted or lowered characters from the skies. The masque was devised in Italy in the 1570s by Count Giovanni Bardi, founder of the Florentine Camerata, a Renaissance group of theatergoers sponsored by Lorenzo de' Medici.

The geniuses of the masque are generally considered to have been Ben Jonson and Inigo Jones. Jones was the architect whose Banqueting Hall at Whitehall in London, which still stands, provided the setting for most of the great masques of the seventeenth century. Jonson and Jones worked together from 1605 to 1631 to produce a remarkable body of masques that today resemble the bones of a dinosaur: what we read on the page suggests in only the vaguest way what the presentation must have been like when the masques were mounted.

Because of the expenses of costuming and staging, most masques were too costly to be produced more than once. The royal exchequer was frequently burdened in Queen Elizabeth's time; more so after King James took the throne in 1603. Masque costumes were impressive, the scenery astounding, and the effects amazing. In all of this, the words — which are, after all, at the center of Shakespeare's plays as well as other plays of the period — were of least account. As a result of the emphasis on the machinery and designs — the work of Inigo Jones — Jonson abandoned his partnership in a huff, complaining that he could not compete with the scene painters and carpenters.

The value placed on spectacle in the masques tells us something about the taste of the aristocrats, who enjoyed sumptuous foods, clothes, and amusements. Eventually, audiences of the public theaters hungered for spectacle, too.

Their appetite was satisfied by masques inserted in the plays of Marston, Webster, and Shakespeare, whose masque in *The Tempest* is a delightful short tribute to the genre. An added device for achieving spectacular effects onstage was huge storm machines installed in the Globe. Some say that one reason Shakespeare wrote *The Tempest* was to take advantage of the new equipment. Foreign visitors described London theaters as gorgeous places of entertainment far surpassing their own. The quest for more intense spectacle eventually led to disaster in one theater. The Globe actually burned down in 1613 because a cannon in the roof above the stage misfired and brought the house down in real flames.

The royal demand for masques was unaffected. As Francis Bacon said in his essay "On Masques" (1625), "These things are but toys to come amongst such serious observations. But yet, since princes will have such things, it is better they should be graced with elegancy than daubed with cost. Dancing to song is a thing of great state and pleasure."

Spanish Drama

The Spanish developed, independently, a corral, or open theatrical space, resembling the Elizabethan inn yard, in which they produced plays. This development may have been an accident of architecture — because of the widespread need for inns and for places to store horses — that permitted the symmetry of growth of the English Elizabethan and the Spanish Golden Age theaters.

The most important playwright of the Spanish theater was Lope de Vega (1562–1635), who is said to have written twelve hundred plays (seven hundred fifty survive). Many of them are relatively brief, and some resemble the scenarios for the commedia dell'arte. A good number, though, are full-length and impressive works, such as *The Sheep Well, The King, The Greatest Alcalde,* and *The Gardener's Dog.* Pedro Calderón de la Barca (1600–1681) became, on Lope de Vega's death, the reigning Spanish playwright. His *Life Is a Dream* is performed regularly throughout the world. Calderón became a priest in 1651 and wrote religious plays that on rare occasions got him into trouble with the Inquisition, an agency of the church that searched out and punished heresy. He was especially imaginative in his use of stage machinery and especially gifted in producing philosophical and poetic dialogue.

Renaissance Drama Timeline

DATE	THEATER	POLITICAL	SOCIAL/CULTURAL
1300–1400	**1377–1446:** Filippo Brunelleschi, an Italian architect, develops vanishing-point perspective, which allows theatrical scenery to be drawn in realistic proportions.		**1348–1353:** Boccaccio's *Decameron* becomes a model for Italian prose. **c. 1386–1466:** Donatello, Italian painter and major innovator in Renaissance sculpture
1400–1500	**1414:** Rediscovery of Vitruvius's *De Architectura* (90 B.C.) in Italy. After its publication in 1486, the treatise significantly influences the development of staging practices.		**1450:** Florence under the Medici family becomes the center of Renaissance and humanism. **1452–1519:** Leonardo da Vinci, brilliant inventor, architect, musician, and artist **1469–1527:** Niccolò Machiavelli, who writes the political treatise *The Prince* in 1513 and the comedy *Mandragola* between 1513 and 1520 **1473–1543:** Nicolaus Copernicus, founder of modern astronomy
	1495: The Dutch morality play *Elckerlijk* by Peter Dorland van Diest becomes the prototype for the English *Everyman*.	**1494:** The Parliament of Drogheda marks the subservience of Ireland to England.	**1496:** Henry VII commissions Venetian navigator John Cabot (1450–1498) to discover a new trade route to Asia. **1497:** Cabot reaches the east coast of North America. **1497:** Vasco de Gama (c. 1469–1524) rounds the Cape of Good Hope.
1500–1600		**1503:** James IV of Scotland marries Margaret Tudor, daughter of Henry VII.	**1507:** Pope Julius II announces the sale of indulgences to finance the rebuilding of St. Peter's Basilica in Rome. **1509–1564:** John Calvin, Swiss reformer **c. 1509:** A massive slave trade begins in the New World.
	1508: Vernacular drama begins in Italy with Ludovico Ariosto's *The Casket*. **1508:** The Hôtel de Bourgogne, a permanent theater building, opens in Paris.		**1512:** Copernicus's *Commentariolus* states that the earth and other planets turn around the sun. **1514–1564:** Andreas Vesalius, Dutch physician, founder of modern anatomy **1516–1547:** Henry Howard, Earl of Surrey, English poet
	1512: The word *masque* is first used to denote a poetic drama.	**1517:** Martin Luther protests the sale of indulgences by posting his 95 theses on a church door in Wittenberg, Germany, thus launching the Protestant Reformation in Germany.	**1519:** Hernando Cortés enters Tenochtitlán, capital of Mexico; is received by Montezuma, the Aztec ruler; and assumes control of Mexico in 1521.

DATE	THEATER	POLITICAL	SOCIAL/CULTURAL
1500–1600 (continued)	**1550–1650:** Golden Age of Spanish drama. The two principal playwrights are Lope de Vega (1562–1635) and Pedro Calderón de la Barca (1600–1681).	**1534:** Henry VIII (reigned 1509–1547) breaks with the Roman Catholic Church.	**1522:** Luther translates the New Testament into German and translates the Old Testament in 1534.
	1558–1594: Playwright Thomas Kyd, author of *The Spanish Tragedy* (c. 1587)	**1535:** Henry VIII's Act of Supremacy names him head of the Church of England. Sir Thomas More is executed after refusing to comply with the Act.	**1547–1616:** Miguel de Cervantes, author of the novel *Don Quixote* and many plays
	1562: The First English tragedy, *Gorboduc*, is performed at the Inns of Court.	**1547:** Ivan IV (the Terrible) becomes czar of Russia. Moscow is destroyed by fire in the same year.	**c. 1552–1599:** Edmund Spenser, English poet, author of *Faerie Queene*
	1564–1593: Christopher Marlowe, author of *Doctor Faustus* (c. 1588), *Tamburlaine* (1590), and *Edward II* (c. 1592)	**1553–1558:** Reign of Mary I of England. The country returns temporarily to Catholicism.	**1554–1586:** Sir Philip Sidney, poet and soldier, author of *An Apology for Poetry*
	1564–1616: William Shakespeare	**1558–1603:** Reign of Elizabeth I in England. Protestantism becomes the religion of the realm. England emerges as a world power.	**1561–1626:** Francis Bacon, English philosopher and statesman
	c. 1568: Formation of the Italian commedia dell'arte company I Gelosi		**1564–1642:** Galileo Galilei, Italian astronomer
	1572–1637: Playwright Ben Jonson, author of *Volpone* (1605) and *Bartholomew Fair* (1614)	**1570:** Japan opens the port of Nagasaki to trade with the West.	**1571–1630:** Johannes Kepler, German astronomer. His laws accurately describe the revolutions of the planets around the sun.
	1574: The Earl of Leicester's Men, the first important acting troupe in London, is licensed.	**1572:** At the Saint Bartholomew's Day Massacre in France, thousands of Protestants are killed.	**1572–1631:** John Donne, English metaphysic poet
	1575: *Gammer Gurton's Needle*, early English farce, author unknown		
	1576: James Burbage builds The Theatre for the public performance of plays. Blackfriars, London's first private theater, is also built.		
	1577: John Northbrooke publishes *A Treatise against Dicing, Dancing, Plays, and Interludes*, one of several tracts attacking the growing professional theater.		**1577:** *Chronicles of England, Scotland and Ireland* is published by Raphael Holinshed and provides Shakespeare with information for his historical plays.
	1580–1627: Playwright Thomas Middleton, author of *A Chaste Maid in Cheapside* (1630) and *The Changeling* (with William Rowley, 1622)		**1580:** Sir Francis Drake, first Englishman to circumnavigate the globe

Renaissance Drama Timeline (continued)

DATE	THEATER	POLITICAL	SOCIAL/CULTURAL
1500–1600 (continued)	**1584:** Completion of the Teatro Olimpico in Vicenza, Italy, designed by architect Andrea Palladio (1508–1580). **1586?–c. 1640:** Playwright John Ford, author of *'Tis Pity She's a Whore* (1633) **1593:** London theaters are closed because of a plague and open again in 1594. **1595–1596:** Shakespeare's comedy *A Midsummer Night's Dream* **1599:** The Globe Theatre is built in London.	**1587:** The Catholic Mary Stuart, queen of Scotland, is executed in England. **1587–1649:** John Winthrop, first governor of the Massachusetts Bay Colony **1588:** The English fleet defeats the Spanish Armada. **1589:** Henry IV of France, first of the Bourbon line **1589:** Russian czar Boris Godunov separates Moscow's church from that in Constantinople. **1595:** The Dutch begin to colonize the East Indies. **1598:** The Edict of Nantes grants French Huguenots freedom of worship, but is revoked in 1685.	**1583:** Sir Philip Sydney's *Defence of Poesy* argues for literature's importance in teaching morality and virtue. **1596–1650:** René Descartes, French philosopher, mathematician, and scientist
1600–1700	**1600–1601:** Shakespeare's *Hamlet* **1611–1612:** Shakespeare's *The Tempest* **1613:** Fire destroys the Globe Theatre. **1633:** The Oberammergau Passion play is first performed in Germany. **1642:** The English Parliament closes the theaters.	**1603:** Death of Elizabeth I. James VI of Scotland, son of Mary Stuart, becomes James I of England. **1605:** The Gunpowder Plot, an attempt to blow up the English Parliament and James I, is uncovered. **1618–1648:** The Thirty Years War is initiated by a Protestant revolt in Bohemia against the authority of the Holy Roman emperor. **1625:** Death of James I. His son becomes Charles I of England. **1630:** John Winthrop founds Boston. **1642:** Civil war begins in England. **1643:** Louis XIV becomes king of France at age four. **1649:** Charles I is beheaded in England, beginning the Commonwealth and Protectorate. **1648:** The Treaty of Westphalia ends the Thirty Years War.	**1600:** Dutch opticians invent the telescope. **1602:** The Dutch East India Company is established to trade with the Far East. **1606–1669:** Rembrandt van Rijn, greatest master of the Dutch school of painting **1607:** Jamestown, Virginia, the first permanent settlement across the Atlantic, is founded. **1608–1674:** John Milton, English poet, author of *Paradise Lost* **1611:** The King James Bible is published. **1619:** The first slaves from Africa arrive in Virginia. **1620:** The Pilgrims land at Plymouth Rock, Massachusetts. **1626:** Peter Minuit purchases Manhattan Island from native Indian chiefs. **1632–1704:** John Locke, English philosopher, founder of empiricism

William Shakespeare

Despite the fact that Shakespeare wrote some thirty-seven plays, owned part of his theatrical company, acted in plays, and retired a relatively wealthy man in the city of his birth, there is much we do not know about him. His father was a glovemaker with pretensions to being a gentleman; Shakespeare himself had his coat of arms placed on his home, New Place, purchased in part because it was one of the grandest buildings in Stratford. Church records indicate that he was born in April 1564 and died in April 1616, after having been retired from the stage for two or three years. We know that he married Anne Hathaway in 1582, when he was eighteen and she twenty-six; that he had a daughter Susanna and twins, Judith and Hamnet; and that Hamnet, his only son, died at age eleven. He has no direct descendants today.

We know very little about his education. We assume that he went to the local grammar school, since as the son of a burgess he was eligible to attend for free. If he did so, he would have received a very strong education based on rhetoric, logic, and classical literature. He would have been exposed to the

The engraving by Martin Droeshout of William Shakespeare appeared in the First Folio Edition, published in 1623.

192

comedies of Plautus, the tragedies of Seneca, and the poetry of Virgil, Ovid, and a host of other, lesser writers.

A rumor has persisted that he spent some time as a Latin teacher. No evidence exists to suggest that Shakespeare went to a university, although his general learning and knowledge are so extraordinary and broad that generations of scholars have assumed that he may have also gone to the Inns of Court to study law. This cannot be proved, though; thus, some people claim that another person, with considerable university education, must have written his plays. However, no one in the Elizabethan theater had an education of the sort often proposed for Shakespeare. Marlowe and Ben Jonson were the most learned of Elizabethan playwrights, but their work is quite different in character and feeling from that of Shakespeare.

One recent theory about Shakespeare's early years suggests that before going to London to work in theater he belonged to a wandering company of actors much like those who appear in *Hamlet*. It is an ingenious theory and has much to recommend it, among which is explaining how Shakespeare could take the spotlight so quickly as to arouse the anger of more experienced London writers.

Shakespeare did not begin his career writing for the stage but, in the more conventional approach for the age, as a poet. He sought the support of an aristocratic patron, the earl of Southampton. Like many wealthy and polished young courtiers, Southampton felt it a pleasant ornament to sponsor a poet whose works would be dedicated to him. Shakespeare wrote sonnets apparently with Southampton in mind, and, hoping for preferment, the long narrative poems *Venus and Adonis, The Rape of Lucrece,* and *The Phoenix and the Turtle*. However, Southampton eventually decided to become the patron of another poet, John Florio, an Italian who had translated Michel de Montaigne's *Essays*.

Shakespeare's response was to turn to the stage. His first plays were a considerable success: *King Henry VI* in three parts — three full-length plays. Satisfying London's taste for plays that told the history of England's tangled political past, Shakespeare won considerable renown with a lengthy series of plays ranging from *Richard II* through the two parts of *King Henry IV* to *Henry V*. Audiences were delighted; competing playwrights envied him his triumphs. Francis Meres's famous book of the period, *Palladis Tamia: Wit's Treasury,* cites Shakespeare as modern Plautus and Seneca, the best in both comedy and tragedy. Meres says that by 1598 Shakespeare was known for a dozen plays. That his success was firm by this time is demonstrated by his having purchased his large house, New Place, in Stratford in 1597. He could not have done this without financial security.

In the next few years Shakespeare made a number of interesting purchases of property in Stratford; he also made deals with his own theater company to secure the rights to perform in London. These arrangements produced legal records that give us some of the clearest information we have concerning Shakespeare's activities during this period. His company was called the Lord Chamberlain's Men while Queen Elizabeth was alive but was renamed the King's Men by King James in the spring of 1603, less than two months after Elizabeth died. As the King's Men, Shakespeare's company had considerable power and success. Its audience sometimes included King James, as in the first performance of *Macbeth*.

Shakespeare was successful as a writer of histories, comedies, and tragedies. He also wrote in another genre, known as romance. These plays share elements with both comedies and tragedies, and they often depend on supernatural or improbable elements. *Cymbeline, The Winter's Tale,* and *The Tempest* are the best known of Shakespeare's romances. They are late works and have a fascinating complexity.

When Shakespeare died on April 23, 1616, he was buried as a gentleman in the church in which he had been baptized in Stratford-upon-Avon. His will left most of his money and possessions to his two daughters, Judith and Susanna.

A MIDSUMMER NIGHT'S DREAM

A Midsummer Night's Dream (1595–1596) is an early comedy and one of Shakespeare's most beloved works. It is also one of his most imaginative plays, introducing us to the world of fairies and the realm of dreams. Romantic painters, such as Fuseli, have long found in this play a rich store of images that stretch far beyond the limits of the real world of everyday experience.

For Shakespeare the fun of the play is in showing how the world of the fairies intersects with the world of real people, and we can interpret the play as a hint of what would happen if the world of dreams were to cross the world of real experience. The fact that these worlds are more alike than they are different gives Shakespeare the comic basis on which to work. He also finds some new and amusing ways to interpret the device of mistaken identities.

The play is set in Athens, with Duke Theseus about to wed Hippolyta, the queen of the Amazons. Helena and Hermia are young women in love with Demetrius and Lysander, respectively. Demetrius, however, wants to marry Hermia and has the blessing of Hermia's father. Hermia's refusal to follow her father's wishes drives her into the woods, where she is followed by both young men and Helena, who does not want to lose Demetrius.

The four young people find themselves in the world of the fairies, although the humans cannot see the fairies. Puck, an impish sprite, is ordered by Oberon, king of the fairies, to put the juice of a certain flower in Demetrius's eyes so that he will fall in love with Helena. When Puck puts it in Lysander's eyes instead, the plot backfires: Lysander is suddenly in love with Helena, and Hermia is confounded. Oberon has Puck place the same juice in the eyes of Titania, the queen of the fairies, causing her to fall in love with the first creature she sees when she awakes.

That creature is Bottom, the "rude mechanical" (ignorant artisan) whose head has been transformed into an ass's head. Such a trick opens up possibilities for wonderful comic elements. The richness of the illusions that operate onstage constantly draws us to the question of how we ever can know the truth of our own experiences, especially when some of them are dreams whose imaginative power is occasionally overwhelming.

Shakespeare plays here with some of the Aristotelian conventions of the drama, especially Aristotle's view that drama imitates life. One of the great comic devices in *A Midsummer Night's Dream* is the play within a play that Bottom, Quince, Snug, Flute, and Starveling are to put on before Theseus and Hippolyta. They tell the story of Pyramus and Thisby, lovers who lose each other because they misinterpret signs. It is "Merry and tragical! Tedious and brief!" But it is also a wonderful parody of what playwrights — including Shakespeare — often do when operating in the Aristotelian mode. The aim of the play is realism, yet the players are naive and inexperienced in drama; they do their best constantly to remind the audience that it is only a play.

The comic ineptness of the rude mechanicals' play needs no disclaimers of this sort, and the immediate audience — Theseus, Hippolyta, Demetrius, Helena, Lysander, and Hermia — is amused by the ardor of the players. The audience in the theater is also mightily amused at the antics of the mechanicals, which on the surface are simply funny and a wonderful pastiche of artless play-acting.

Beneath the surface, something more serious is going on. Shakespeare is commenting on the entire function of drama in our lives. He constantly reminds us in this play that we are watching an illusion, even an illusion within an illusion, but he also convinces us that illusions teach us a great deal about reality. The real-world setting of *A Midsummer Night's Dream* — Athens — is quite improbable. The mechanicals all have obviously English names and are out of place in an Athenian pastoral setting. The play on the level of Athens is pure fantasy, with even more fantastic goings-on at the level of the fairy world. But fantasy nourishes us. It helps us interpret our own experiences by permitting us to distance ourselves from them and reflect on how they affect others, one of the deepest functions of drama.

As in most comedies, everything turns out exceptionally well. A multiple marriage, one of the delightful conventions of many comedies, ends the drama, and virtually everyone receives what she or he wanted. We are left with a sense of satisfaction because we, too, get our wish about how things should turn out. Puck, one of the greatest of Shakespeare's characters, turns out to be sympathetic and human in his feelings about people. And Bottom, a clown whose origins are certainly Greek and Roman, endears us to him with his generosity and caring toward others. Shakespeare promotes a remarkably warm view of humanity in this play, leaving us with a sense of delight and a glow that is rare even in comedy.

A Midsummer Night's Dream in Performance

A Midsummer Night's Dream has attracted many great directors in modern times, although in the late seventeenth and eighteenth centuries the play was adapted essentially as a vehicle for presenting the world of the fairies. It even became an opera in 1692. Ludwig Tieck engaged Mendelssohn to write incidental music for the play in Berlin in 1843; their production was for many years the most influential post-Shakespearean adaptation. Beerbohm Tree's 1900 production in London's Savoy Theatre included real rabbits and many other highly realistic details; eventually it played to more than 220,000 patrons. After numerous adaptations it was produced by Granville Barker in London from 1912 to 1914 in its original text, and in New York in 1915. The Old Vic's 1954 production was so lavish that it was staged at the Metropolitan Opera House in New York. Peter Brook played down the fairies and explored the play as a study of love. His 1970 production is well remembered for his having placed Oberon and Puck on trapezes set against a stark white background. He also used some costumes and other elements of commedia dell'arte to spark the comedy. (See Barnes's review of the Brook production on p. 233.) The American Repertory Theatre's 1986 Boston production (see photos on pp. 206–07) reflects the approach to staging that the Royal Shakespeare Company has taken in recent years. The themes of love and transformation inspire the players in a way that shows off the brilliance of the play.

A Midsummer's Night Dream has been filmed several times. In 1935 both James Cagney and Mickey Rooney starred in a version that has some charm. In 1968 the Royal Shakespeare Company with Diana Rigg produced a somewhat less interesting film. The most recent version with Kevin Kline, Michelle Pfeiffer, and Stanley Tucci was produced to generally good reviews in 1999.

William Shakespeare (1564–1616)
A MIDSUMMER NIGHT'S DREAM
c. 1596

[Dramatis Personae

THESEUS, *Duke of Athens*
EGEUS, *father to Hermia*
LYSANDER, } *in love with Hermia*
DEMETRIUS,
PHILOSTRATE, *Master of the Revels to Theseus*

QUINCE, *a carpenter*
SNUG, *a joiner*
BOTTOM, *a weaver*
FLUTE, *a bellows-mender*
SNOUT, *a tinker*
STARVELING, *a tailor*

HIPPOLYTA, *Queen of the Amazons, betrothed to Theseus*
HERMIA, *daughter to Egeus, in love with Lysander*

Note: The text of *A Midsummer Night's Dream* has come down to us in different versions — such as the first quarto, the second quarto, and the first Folio. The copy of the text used here is largely drawn from the first quarto. Passages enclosed in square brackets are taken from one of the other versions.

HELENA, *in love with Demetrius*
OBERON, *King of the Fairies*
TITANIA, *Queen of the Fairies*
PUCK, *or Robin Goodfellow*
PEASEBLOSSOM,
COBWEB,
MOTH, } *fairies*
MUSTARDSEED,
Other FAIRIES *attending their king and queen*
ATTENDANTS *on Theseus and Hippolyta*

Scene: *Athens, and a wood near it.*]

{ACT I • *Scene 1*}°

(*Enter Theseus, Hippolyta, [Philostrate,] with others.*)

THESEUS: Now, fair Hippolyta, our nuptial hour
    Draws on apace. Four happy days bring in
    Another moon; but, O, methinks, how slow

I, I. **Location:** The palace of Theseus.

This old moon wanes! She lingers° my desires
5 Like to a step-dame° or a dowager°
Long withering out a young man's revenue.
HIPPOLYTA: Four days will quickly steep themselves in
    night,
Four nights will quickly dream away the time;
And then the moon, like to a silver bow
10 New-bent in heaven, shall behold the night
Of our solemnities.
THESEUS: Go, Philostrate,
Stir up the Athenian youth to merriments,
Awake the pert and nimble spirit of mirth,
Turn melancholy forth to funerals;
15 The pale companion° is not for our pomp.°
                              [*Exit Philostrate.*]
Hippolyta, I woo'd thee with my sword,°
And won thy love doing thee injuries;
But I will wed thee in another key,
With pomp, with triumph,° and with reveling.

(*Enter Egeus and his daughter Hermia, and Lysander,
and Demetrius.*)

20 EGEUS: Happy be Theseus, our renowned Duke!
THESEUS: Thanks, good Egeus. What's the news with
    thee?
EGEUS: Full of vexation come I, with complaint
Against my child, my daughter Hermia.
Stand forth, Demetrius. My noble lord,
25 This man hath my consent to marry her.
Stand forth, Lysander. And, my gracious Duke,
This man hath bewitch'd the bosom of my child.
Thou, thou, Lysander, thou hast given her rhymes
And interchang'd love tokens with my child.
30 Thou hast by moonlight at her window sung
With feigning voice verses of feigning° love,
And stol'n the impression of her fantasy,°
With bracelets of thy hair, rings, gauds,° conceits,°
Knacks,° trifles, nosegays, sweetmeats —
    messengers
35 Of strong prevailment in unhardened youth.
With cunning hast thou filch'd my daughter's heart,
Turn'd her obedience, which is due to me,
To stubborn harshness. And, my gracious Duke,
Be it so she will not here before your Grace
40 Consent to marry with Demetrius,
I beg the ancient privilege of Athens:
As she is mine, I may dispose of her,

Which shall be either to this gentleman
Or to her death, according to our law
Immediately° provided in that case.   45
THESEUS: What say you, Hermia? Be advis'd, fair maid.
To you your father should be as a god —
One that compos'd your beauties, yea, and one
To whom you are but as a form in wax
By him imprinted and within his power   50
To leave° the figure or disfigure° it.
Demetrius is a worthy gentleman.
HERMIA: So is Lysander.
THESEUS: In himself he is;
But in this kind,° wanting° your father's voice,°
The other must be held the worthier.   55
HERMIA: I would my father look'd but with my eyes.
THESEUS: Rather your eyes must with his judgment look.
HERMIA: I do entreat your Grace to pardon me.
I know not by what power I am made bold,
Nor how it may concern° my modesty,   60
In such a presence here to plead my thoughts;
But I beseech your Grace that I may know
The worst that may befall me in this case,
If I refuse to wed Demetrius.
THESEUS: Either to die the death, or to abjure   65
Forever the society of men.
Therefore, fair Hermia, question your desires,
Know of your youth, examine well your blood,°
Whether, if you yield not to your father's choice,
You can endure the livery° of a nun,   70
For aye° to be in shady cloister mew'd,°
To live a barren sister all your life,
Chanting faint hymns to the cold fruitless moon.
Thrice blessed they that master so their blood
To undergo such maiden pilgrimage,   75
But earthlier happy° is the rose distill'd,
Than that which withering on the virgin thorn
Grows, lives, and dies in single blessedness.
HERMIA: So will I grow, so live, so die, my lord,
Ere I will yield my virgin patent° up   80
Unto his lordship, whose unwished yoke
My soul consents not to give sovereignty.
THESEUS: Take time to pause; and, by the next new
    moon —
The sealing-day betwixt my love and me
For everlasting bond of fellowship —   85
Upon that day either prepare to die
For disobedience to your father's will,
Or° else to wed Demetrius, as he would,
Or on Diana's altar° to protest°
For aye austerity and single life.   90

4. **lingers:** Lengthens, protracts. 5. **step-dame:** Stepmother.
dowager: Widow with a jointure or dower [an estate or title
from her deceased husband]. 15. **companion:** Fellow.
pomp: Ceremonial magnificence. 16. **with my sword:** In a
military engagement against the Amazons, when Hippolyta
was taken captive. 19. **triumph:** Public festivity. 31. **feigning:** (1) Counterfeiting, (2) faining, desirous. 32. **And . . .
fantasy:** And made her fall in love with you (imprinting your
image on her imagination) by stealthy and dishonest means.
33. **gauds:** Playthings. **conceits:** Fanciful trifles. 34. **Knacks:**
Knickknacks.

45. **Immediately:** Expressly. 51. **leave:** Leave unaltered. **disfigure:** Obliterate. 54. **kind:** Respect. **wanting
voice:** Approval. 60. **concern:** Befit. 68. **blood:** Passions.
70. **livery:** Habit. 71. **aye:** Ever. **mew'd:** Shut in (said of a
hawk, poultry, etc.). 76. **earthlier happy:** Happier as respects
this world. 80. **patent:** Privilege. 88. **Or:** Either. 89. **Diana's altar:** Diana was a virgin goddess. **protest:** Vow.

DEMETRIUS: Relent, sweet Hermia, and, Lysander, yield
   Thy crazed° title to my certain right.
LYSANDER: You have her father's love, Demetrius;
   Let me have Hermia's. Do you marry him.
95 EGEUS: Scornful Lysander! True, he hath my love,
   And what is mine my love shall render him.
   And she is mine, and all my right of her
   I do estate unto° Demetrius.
LYSANDER: I am, my lord, as well deriv'd° as he,
100   As well possess'd;° my love is more than his;
   My fortunes every way as fairly° rank'd,
   If not with vantage,° as Demetrius';
   And, which is more than all these boasts can be,
   I am belov'd of beauteous Hermia.
105   Why should not I then prosecute my right?
   Demetrius, I'll avouch it to his head,°
   Made love to Nedar's daughter, Helena,
   And won her soul; and she, sweet lady, dotes,
   Devoutly dotes, dotes in idolatry,
110   Upon this spotted° and inconstant man.
THESEUS: I must confess that I have heard so much,
   And with Demetrius thought to have spoke thereof;
   But, being over-full of self-affairs,
   My mind did lose it. But, Demetrius, come,
115   And come, Egeus, you shall go with me;
   I have some private schooling for you both.
   For you, fair Hermia, look you arm° yourself
   To fit your fancies° to your father's will;
   Or else the law of Athens yields you up —
120   Which by no means we may extenuate° —
   To death, or to a vow of single life.
   Come, my Hippolyta. What cheer, my love?
   Demetrius and Egeus, go° along.
   I must employ you in some business
125   Against° our nuptial, and confer with you
   Of something nearly that° concerns yourselves.
EGEUS: With duty and desire we follow you.

       (*Exeunt*° [*all but Lysander and Hermia*].)

LYSANDER: How now, my love, why is your cheek so
   pale?
   How chance the roses there do fade so fast?
130 HERMIA: Belike° for want of rain, which I could well
   Beteem° them from the tempest of my eyes.
LYSANDER: Ay me! For aught that I could ever read,
   Could ever hear by tale or history,
   The course of true love never did run smooth;
135   But either it was different in blood° —

HERMIA: O cross,° too high to be enthrall'd to low!
LYSANDER: Or else misgraffed° in respect of years —
HERMIA: O spite, too old to be engag'd to young!
LYSANDER: Or else it stood upon the choice of
   friends° —
HERMIA: O hell, to choose love by another's eyes!   140
LYSANDER: Or, if there were a sympathy in choice,
   War, death, or sickness did lay siege to it,
   Making it momentany° as a sound,
   Swift as a shadow, short as any dream,
   Brief as the lightning in the collied° night,   145
   That, in a spleen,° unfolds° both heaven and earth,
   And ere a man hath power to say "Behold!"
   The jaws of darkness do devour it up.
   So quick° bright things come to confusion.°
HERMIA: If then true lovers have been ever cross'd,°   150
   It stands as an edict in destiny.
   Then let us teach our trial patience,°
   Because it is a customary cross,
   As due to love as thoughts and dreams and sighs,
   Wishes and tears, poor fancy's° followers.   155
LYSANDER: A good persuasion. Therefore, hear me,
   Hermia.
   I have a widow aunt, a dowager
   Of great revenue, and she hath no child.
   From Athens is her house remote seven leagues;
   And she respects° me as her only son.   160
   There, gentle Hermia, may I marry thee,
   And to that place the sharp Athenian law
   Cannot pursue us. If thou lovest me, then,
   Steal forth thy father's house tomorrow night;
   And in the wood, a league without the town,   165
   Where I did meet thee once with Helena
   To do observance to a morn of May,°
   There will I stay for thee.
HERMIA: My good Lysander!
   I swear to thee, by Cupid's strongest bow,
   By his best arrow with the golden head,°   170
   By the simplicity° of Venus' doves,°
   By that which knitteth souls and prospers loves,
   And by that fire which burn'd the Carthage queen,
   When the false Troyan° under sail was seen,

---

92. **crazed:** Cracked, unsound.   98. **estate unto:** Settle or bestow upon.   99. **deriv'd:** Descended, i.e., "as well born."   100. **possess'd:** Endowed with wealth.   101. **fairly:** Handsomely.   102. **vantage:** Superiority.   106. **head:** Face.   110. **spotted:** Morally stained.   117. **look you arm:** Take care you prepare.   118. **fancies:** Likings, thoughts of love.   120. **extenuate:** Mitigate.   123. **go:** Come.   125. **Against:** In preparation for.   126. **nearly that:** That closely.   127. [s.d.] *Exeunt:* Latin for "they go out."   130. **Belike:** Very likely.   131. **Beteem:** Grant, afford.   135. **blood:** Hereditary station.

136. **cross:** Vexation.   137. **misgraffed:** Ill grafted, badly matched.   139. **friends:** Relatives.   143. **momentany:** Lasting but a moment.   145. **collied:** Blackened (as with coal dust), darkened.   146. **in a spleen:** In a swift impulse in a violent flash. **unfolds:** Discloses.   149. **quick:** Quickly; or, perhaps, living, alive. **confusion:** Ruin.   150. **ever cross'd:** Always thwarted.   152. **teach . . . patience:** Teach ourselves patience in this trial.   155. **fancy's:** Amorous passion's.   160. **respects:** Regards.   167. **do . . . May:** Perform the ceremonies of May Day.   170. **best arrow . . . golden head:** Cupid's best gold-pointed arrows were supposed to induce love, his blunt leaden arrows aversion.   171. **simplicity:** Innocence. **doves:** Those that drew Venus's chariot.   173–74. **by that fire . . . false Troyan:** Dido, Queen of Carthage, immolated herself on a funeral pyre after having been deserted by the Trojan hero Aeneas.

175 By all the vows that ever men have broke,
In number more than ever women spoke,
In that same place thou hast appointed me
Tomorrow truly will I meet with thee.
LYSANDER: Keep promise, love. Look, here comes
Helena.

(*Enter Helena.*)

180 HERMIA: God speed fair° Helena, whither away?
HELENA: Call you me fair? That fair again unsay.
Demetrius loves your fair.° O happy fair!°
Your eyes are lodestars,° and your tongue's sweet air°
More tuneable° than lark to shepherd's ear
185 When wheat is green, when hawthorn buds appear.
Sickness is catching. O, were favor° so,
Yours would I catch, fair Hermia, ere I go;
My ear should catch your voice, my eye your eye,
My tongue should catch your tongue's sweet melody.
190 Were the world mine, Demetrius being bated,°
The rest I'd give to be to you translated.°
O, teach me how you look, and with what art
You sway the motion° of Demetrius' heart.
HERMIA: I frown upon him, yet he loves me still.
HELENA: O that your frowns would teach my smiles
195   such skill!
HERMIA: I give him curses, yet he gives me love.
HELENA: O that my prayers could such affection°
    move!°
HERMIA: The more I hate, the more he follows me.
HELENA: The more I love, the more he hateth me.
200 HERMIA: His folly, Helena, is no fault of mine.
HELENA: None, but your beauty. Would that fault were
    mine!
HERMIA: Take comfort. He no more shall see my face.
Lysander and myself will fly this place.
Before the time I did Lysander see,
205 Seem'd Athens as a paradise to me.
O, then, what graces in my love do dwell,
That he hath turn'd a heaven unto a hell!
LYSANDER: Helen, to you our minds we will unfold.
Tomorrow night, when Phoebe° doth behold
210 Her silver visage in the wat'ry glass,°
Decking with liquid pearl the bladed grass,
A time that lovers' flights doth still° conceal,
Through Athens' gates have we devis'd to steal.
HERMIA: And in the wood, where often you and I
215 Upon faint° primrose beds were wont to lie,
Emptying our bosoms of their counsel° sweet,

There my Lysander and myself shall meet;
And thence from Athens turn away our eyes,
To seek new friends and stranger companies.
Farewell, sweet playfellow. Pray thou for us,   220
And good luck grant thee thy Demetrius!
Keep word, Lysander. We must starve our sight
From lovers' food till morrow deep midnight.
LYSANDER: I will, my Hermia.   (*Exit Hermia.*)
                        Helena, adieu.
As you on him, Demetrius dote on you!   225
                    (*Exit Lysander.*)
HELENA: How happy some o'er other some can be!°
Through Athens I am thought as fair as she.
But what of that? Demetrius thinks not so;
He will not know what all but he do know.
And as he errs, doting on Hermia's eyes,   230
So I, admiring of° his qualities.
Things base and vile, holding no quantity,°
Love can transpose to form and dignity.
Love looks not with the eyes, but with the mind,
And therefore is wing'd Cupid painted blind.   235
Nor hath Love's mind of any judgment taste;°
Wings, and no eyes, figure° unheedy haste.
And therefore is Love said to be a child,
Because in choice he is so oft beguil'd.
As waggish boys in game° themselves forswear,   240
So the boy Love is perjur'd everywhere.
For ere Demetrius look'd on Hermia's eyne,°
He hail'd down oaths that he was only mine;
And when this hail some heat from Hermia felt,
So he dissolv'd, and show'rs of oaths did melt.   245
I will go tell him of fair Hermia's flight.
Then to the wood will he tomorrow night
Pursue her; and for this intelligence°
If I have thanks, it is a dear° expense.°
But herein mean I to enrich my pain,   250
To have his sight thither and back again.   (*Exit.*)

{*Scene II*}°

(*Enter Quince the Carpenter, and Snug the Joiner, and
Bottom the Weaver, and Flute the Bellows-Mender, and
Snout the Tinker, and Starveling the Tailor.*)

QUINCE: Is all our company here?
BOTTOM: You were best to call them generally,° man by
    man, according to the scrip.°

---

180. **fair:** Fair-complexioned (generally regarded by the Elizabethans as more beautiful than dark-complexioned).   182. **your
fair:** Your beauty (even though Hermia is dark-complexioned).
happy fair: Lucky fair one.   183. **lodestars:** Guiding stars.
air: Music.   184. **tuneable:** Tuneful, melodious.   186. **favor:**
Appearance, looks.   190. **bated:** Excepted.   191. **translated:**
Transformed.   193. **motion:** Impulse.   197. **affection:** Passion.
move: Arouse.   209. **Phoebe:** Diana, the moon.   210. **glass:**
Mirror.   212. **still:** Always.   215. **faint:** Pale.   216. **counsel:**
Secret thought.

226. **o'er . . . can be:** Can be in comparison to some others.
231. **admiring of:** Wondering at.   232. **holding no quantity:**
Unsubstantial, unshapely.   236. **Nor . . . taste:** Nor has Love,
which dwells in the fancy or imagination, any *taste* or least
bit of judgment or reason.   237. **figure:** Are a symbol of.
240. **game:** Sport, jest.   242. **eyne:** Eyes (old form of plural).
248. **intelligence:** Information.   249. **dear:** Costly. **a dear
expense:** A trouble worth taking.   I, II. **Location:** Athens.
Quince's house(?).   2. **generally:** Bottom's blunder for *individually.*   3. **scrip:** Script, written list.

QUINCE: Here is the scroll of every man's name which is
5   thought fit, through all Athens, to play in our interlude before the Duke and the Duchess on his
wedding-day at night.

BOTTOM: First, good Peter Quince, say what the play
treats on, then read the names of the actors, and so
10   grow to° a point.

QUINCE: Marry,° our play is "The most lamentable comedy and most cruel death of Pyramus and Thisby."

BOTTOM: A very good piece of work, I assure you, and a
merry. Now, good Peter Quince, call forth your
15   actors by the scroll. Masters, spread yourselves.

QUINCE: Answer as I call you. Nick Bottom, the weaver.

BOTTOM: Ready. Name what part I am for, and proceed.

QUINCE: You, Nick Bottom, are set down for Pyramus.

BOTTOM: What is Pyramus? A lover, or a tyrant?

20   QUINCE: A lover, that kills himself most gallant for love.

BOTTOM: That will ask some tears in the true performing of it. If I do it, let the audience look to their eyes.
I will move storms; I will condole° in some measure.
To the rest — yet my chief humor° is for a tyrant. I
25   could play Ercles° rarely, or a part to tear a cat° in, to
make all split.°
       "The raging rocks
       And shivering shocks
       Shall break the locks
30   Of prison gates;
       And Phibbus' car°
       Shall shine from far
       And make and mar
           The foolish Fates."
35   This was lofty! Now name the rest of the players. This
is Ercles' vein, a tyrant's vein. A lover is more con-
doling.

QUINCE: Francis Flute, the bellows-mender.

FLUTE: Here, Peter Quince.

40   QUINCE: Flute, you must take Thisby on you.

FLUTE: What is Thisby? A wand'ring knight?

QUINCE: It is the lady that Pyramus must love.

FLUTE: Nay, faith, let not me play a woman. I have a
beard coming.

45   QUINCE: That's all one.° You shall play it in a mask, and
you may speak as small° as you will.

BOTTOM: An° I may hide my face, let me play Thisby
too. I'll speak in a monstrous little voice, "Thisne,
Thisne!" "Ah Pyramus, my lover dear! Thy Thisby
50   dear, and lady dear!"

QUINCE: No, no; you must play Pyramus; and, Flute,
you Thisby.

BOTTOM: Well, proceed.

QUINCE: Robin Starveling, the tailor.

STARVELING: Here, Peter Quince.   55

QUINCE: Robin Starveling, you must play Thisby's
mother. Tom Snout, the tinker.

SNOUT: Here, Peter Quince.

QUINCE: You, Pyramus' father; myself, Thisby's father;
Snug, the joiner, you, the lion's part; and I hope here   60
is a play fitted.

SNUG: Have you the lion's part written? Pray you, if it
be, give it me, for I am slow of study.

QUINCE: You may do it extempore, for it is nothing but
roaring.   65

BOTTOM: Let me play the lion too. I will roar that I will
do any man's heart good to hear me. I will roar that I
will make the Duke say, "Let him roar again, let him
roar again."

QUINCE: An you should do it too terribly, you would   70
fright the Duchess and the ladies, that they would
shriek; and that were enough to hang us all.

ALL: That would hang us, every mother's son.

BOTTOM: I grant you, friends, if you should fright the
ladies out of their wits, they would have no more dis- 75
cretion but to hang us; but I will aggravate° my voice
so that I will roar you° as gently as any sucking dove;
I will roar you an 'twere any nightingale.

QUINCE: You can play no part but Pyramus; for Pyramus is a sweet-fac'd man, a proper° man as one shall   80
see in a summer's day, a most lovely gentleman-like
man. Therefore you must needs play Pyramus.

BOTTOM: Well, I will undertake it. What beard were I
best to play it in?

QUINCE: Why, what you will.   85

BOTTOM: I will discharge° it in either your° straw-color
beard, your orange-tawny beard, your purple-in-
grain° beard, or your French-crown-color° beard,
your perfect yellow.

QUINCE: Some of your French crowns° have no hair at   90
all, and then you will play barefac'd. But, masters,
here are your parts. [He distributes parts.] And I am
to entreat you, request you, and desire you, to con°
them by tomorrow night; and meet me in the palace
wood, a mile without the town, by moonlight. There   95
will we rehearse; for if we meet in the city, we shall be
dogg'd with company, and our devices° known. In
the meantime I will draw a bill° of properties, such as
our play wants. I pray you, fail me not.

BOTTOM: We will meet, and there we may rehearse most 100
obscenely° and courageously. Take pains, be perfect;°
adieu.

---

10. grow to: Come to.   11. Marry: A mild oath, originally the
name of the Virgin Mary.   23. condole: Lament, arouse pity.
24. humor: Inclination, whim.   25. Ercles: Hercules (the tradition of ranting came from Seneca's *Hercules Furens*).   tear a
cat: Rant.   26. make all split: Cause a stir, bring the house
down.   31. Phibbus' car: Phoebus's, the sun-god's, chariot.
45. That's all one: It makes no difference.   46. small: High-
pitched.   47. An: If.

76. aggravate: Bottom's blunder for *diminish*.   77. roar you:
Roar for you.   80. proper: Handsome.   86. discharge: Perform.   your: I.e., you know the kind I mean.   87–88. purple-
in-grain: Dyed a very deep red (from *grain*, the name applied to
the dried insect used to make the dye).   88. French-crown-
color: Color of a French crown, a gold coin.   90. crowns:
Heads bald from syphilis, the "French disease."   93. con:
Learn by heart.   97. devices: Plans.   98. bill: List.   101. ob-
scenely: An unintentionally funny blunder, whatever Bottom
meant to say.   perfect: Letter-perfect in memorizing your parts.

QUINCE: At the Duke's oak we meet.
BOTTOM: Enough. Hold, or cut bow-strings.°

(*Exeunt.*)

{*ACT II • Scene 1*}°

(*Enter a Fairy at one door, and Robin Goodfellow [*Puck*] at another.*)

PUCK: How now, spirit! Whither wander you?
FAIRY: Over hill, over dale,
   Thorough° bush, thorough brier,
   Over park, over pale,°
5   Thorough flood, thorough fire,
   I do wander every where,
   Swifter than the moon's sphere;
   And I serve the Fairy Queen,
   To dew her orbs° upon the green.
10   The cowslips tall her pensioners° be.
   In their gold coats spots you see;
   Those be rubies, fairy favors,°
   In those freckles live their savors.°
   I must go seek some dewdrops here
15   And hang a pearl in every cowslip's ear.
   Farewell, thou lob° of spirits; I'll be gone.
   Our Queen and all her elves come here anon.°
PUCK: The King doth keep his revels here tonight.
   Take heed the Queen come not within his sight.
20   For Oberon is passing fell° and wrath,°
   Because that she as her attendant hath
   A lovely boy, stolen from an Indian king;
   She never had so sweet a changeling.°
   And jealous Oberon would have the child
25   Knight of his train, to trace° the forests wild.
   But she perforce° withholds the loved boy,
   Crowns him with flowers and makes him all her joy.
   And now they never meet in grove or green,
   By fountain° clear, or spangled starlight sheen,
30   But they do square,° that all their elves for fear
   Creep into acorn-cups and hide them there.
FAIRY: Either I mistake your shape and making quite,
   Or else you are that shrewd° and knavish sprite°
   Call'd Robin Goodfellow. Are not you he
35   That frights the maidens of the villagery,
   Skim milk, and sometimes labor in the quern,°
   And bootless° make the breathless huswife churn,

And sometime make the drink to bear no barm,°
Mislead night-wanderers, laughing at their harm?
Those that Hobgoblin call you and sweet Puck,   40
You do their work, and they shall have good luck.
Are you not he?
PUCK: Thou speakest aright;
   I am that merry wanderer of the night.
   I jest to Oberon and make him smile
   When I a fat and bean-fed horse beguile,   45
   Neighing in likeness of a filly foal;
   And sometime lurk I in a gossip's° bowl,
   In very likeness of a roasted crab,°
   And when she drinks, against her lips I bob
   And on her withered dewlap° pour the ale.   50
   The wisest aunt,° telling the saddest° tale,
   Sometime for three-foot stool mistaketh me;
   Then slip I from her bum, down topples she,
   And "tailor"° cries, and falls into a cough;
   And then the whole quire° hold their hips and
      laugh,   55
   And waxen° in their mirth and neeze° and swear
   A merrier hour was never wasted there.
   But, room, fairy! Here comes Oberon.
FAIRY: And here my mistress. Would that he were
    gone!

(*Enter [*Oberon*] the King of Fairies at one door, with his train; and [*Titania*] the Queen at another, with hers.*)

OBERON: Ill met by moonlight, proud Titania.   60
TITANIA: What, jealous Oberon? Fairies, skip hence.
   I have forsworn his bed and company.
OBERON: Tarry, rash wanton.° Am not I thy lord?
TITANIA: Then I must be thy lady; but I know
   When thou hast stolen away from fairy land,   65
   And in the shape of Corin° sat all day,
   Playing on pipes of corn° and versing love
   To amorous Phillida.° Why art thou here,
   Come from the farthest steep° of India,
   But that, forsooth, the bouncing Amazon,   70
   Your buskin'd° mistress and your warrior love,
   To Theseus must be wedded, and you come
   To give their bed joy and prosperity.
OBERON: How canst thou thus for shame, Titania,
   Glance at my credit with Hippolyta,°   75
   Knowing I know thy love to Theseus?
   Didst not thou lead him through the glimmering
    night

---

104. Hold . . . bow-strings: An archer's expression not definitely explained, but probably meaning here "keep your promises, or give up the play." II, 1. Location: A wood near Athens. 3. Thorough: Through. 4. pale: Enclosure. 9. orbs: Circles, i.e., fairy rings. 10. pensioners: Retainers, members of the royal bodyguard. 12. favors: Love tokens. 13. savors: Sweet smells. 16. lob: Country bumpkin. 17. anon: At once. 20. passing fell: Exceedingly angry. wrath: Wrathful. 23. changeling: Child exchanged for another by the fairies. 25. trace: Range through. 26. perforce: Forcibly. 29. fountain: Spring. 30. square: Quarrel. 33. shrewd: Mischievous. sprite: Spirit. 36. quern: Handmill. 37. bootless: In vain.

38. barm: Yeast, head on the ale. 47. gossip's: Old woman's. 48. crab: Crab apple. 50. dewlap: Loose skin on neck. 51. aunt: Old woman. saddest: Most serious. 54. tailor: Possibly because she ends up sitting cross-legged on the floor, looking like a tailor. 55. quire: Company. 56. waxen: Increase. neeze: Sneeze. 63. wanton: Headstrong creature. 66, 68. Corin, Phillida: Conventional names of pastoral lovers. 67. corn: Here, oat stalks. 69. steep: Mountain range. 71. buskin'd: Wearing half-boots called buskins. 75. Glance . . . Hippolyta: Make insinuations about my favored relationship with Hippolyta.

From Perigenia,° whom he ravished?
And make him with fair Aegles° break his faith,
80   With Ariadne° and Antiopa?°
TITANIA: These are the forgeries of jealousy;
And never, since the middle summer's spring,°
Met we on hill, in dale, forest, or mead,
By paved° fountain or by rushy° brook,
85   Or in° the beached margent° of the sea,
To dance our ringlets° to the whistling wind,
But with thy brawls thou hast disturb'd our sport.
Therefore the winds, piping to us in vain,
As in revenge, have suck'd up from the sea
90   Contagious° fogs; which falling in the land
Hath every pelting° river made so proud
That they have overborne their continents.°
The ox hath therefore stretch'd his yoke in vain,
The ploughman lost his sweat, and the green corn°
95   Hath rotted ere his youth attain'd a beard;
The fold° stands empty in the drowned field,
And crows are fatted with the murrion° flock;
The nine men's morris° is fill'd up with mud,
And the quaint mazes° in the wanton° green
100   For lack of tread are undistinguishable.
The human mortals want° their winter° here;
No night is now with hymn or carol bless'd.
Therefore° the moon, the governess of floods,
Pale in her anger, washes all the air,
105   That rheumatic diseases° do abound.
And thorough this distemperature° we see
The seasons alter: hoary-headed frosts
Fall in the fresh lap of the crimson rose,
And on old Hiems'° thin and icy crown
110   An odorous chaplet of sweet summer buds
Is, as in mockery, set. The spring, the summer,

78. **Perigenia:** Perigouna, one of Theseus's conquests. (This and the following women are named in Thomas North's translation of Plutarch's *Life of Theseus*.)   79. **Aegles:** Aegle, for whom Theseus deserted Ariadne according to some accounts. 80. **Ariadne:** The daughter of Minos, King of Crete, who helped Theseus escape the labyrinth after killing the Minotaur; later she was abandoned by Theseus.   **Antiopa:** Queen of the Amazons and wife of Theseus; elsewhere identified with Hippolyta, but here thought of as a separate woman.   82. **middle summer's spring:** Beginning of midsummer.   84. **paved:** With pebbled bottom.   **rushy:** Bordered with rushes.   85. **in:** On. **margent:** Edge, border.   86. **ringlets:** Dances in a ring. (See *orbs* in line 9.)   90. **Contagious:** Noxious.   91. **pelting:** Paltry; or striking, moving forcefully.   92. **continents:** Banks that contain them.   94. **corn:** Grain of any kind.   96. **fold:** Pen for sheep or cattle.   97. **murrion:** Having died of the murrain, plague.   98. **nine men's morris:** Portion of the village green marked out in a square for a game played with nine pebbles or pegs.   99. **quaint mazes:** Intricate paths marked out on the village green to be followed rapidly on foot as a kind of contest. **wanton:** Luxuriant.   101. **want:** Lack.   **winter:** Regular winter season; or proper observances of winter, such as the *hymn or carol* in the next line (?).   103. **Therefore:** I.e., as a result of our quarrel.   105. **rheumatic diseases:** Colds, flu, and other respiratory infections.   106. **distemperature:** Disturbance in nature.   109. **Hiems:** The winter god.

The childing° autumn, angry winter, change
Their wonted liveries,° and the mazed° world,
By their increase,° now knows not which is which.
And this same progeny of evils comes   115
From our debate,° from our dissension;
We are their parents and original.°
OBERON: Do you amend it then; it lies in you.
Why should Titania cross her Oberon?
I do but beg a little changeling boy,   120
To be my henchman.°
TITANIA: Set your heart at rest.
The fairy land buys not the child of me.
His mother was a vot'ress° of my order,
And, in the spiced Indian air, by night,
Full often hath she gossip'd by my side,   125
And sat with me on Neptune's yellow sands,
Marking th' embarked traders° on the flood,°
When we have laugh'd to see the sails conceive
And grow big-bellied with the wanton° wind;
Which she, with pretty and with swimming gait, 130
Following — her womb then rich with my young
     squire —
Would imitate, and sail upon the land
To fetch me trifles, and return again,
As from a voyage, rich with merchandise.
But she, being mortal, of that boy did die;   135
And for her sake do I rear up her boy,
And for her sake I will not part with him.
OBERON: How long within this wood intend you stay?
TITANIA: Perchance till after Theseus' wedding-day.
If you will patiently dance in our round°   140
And see our moonlight revels, go with us;
If not, shun me, and I will spare° your haunts.
OBERON: Give me that boy, and I will go with thee.
TITANIA: Not for thy fairy kingdom. Fairies, away!
We shall chide downright, if I longer stay.   145

(*Exeunt [Titania with her train]*.)

OBERON: Well, go thy way. Thou shalt not from° this
     grove
Till I torment thee for this injury.
My gentle Puck, come hither. Thou rememb'rest
Since° once I sat upon a promontory,
And heard a mermaid on a dolphin's back   150
Uttering such dulcet and harmonious breath°
That the rude sea grew civil at her song
And certain stars shot madly from their spheres,
To hear the sea-maid's music.
PUCK: I remember.
OBERON: That very time I saw, but thou couldst not,   155

112. **childing:** Fruitful, pregnant.   113. **wonted liveries:** Usual apparel.   **mazed:** Bewildered.   114. **their increase:** Their yield, what they produce.   116. **debate:** Quarrel.   117. **original:** Origin.   121. **henchman:** Attendant, page.   123. **vot'ress:** Female votary; devotee, worshiper.   127. **traders:** Trading vessels.   **flood:** Flood tide.   129. **wanton:** Sportive.   140. **round:** Circular dance.   142. **spare:** Shun.   146. **from:** Go from. 149. **Since:** When.   151. **breath:** Voice, song.

Flying between the cold moon and the earth,
Cupid all° arm'd. A certain aim he took
At a fair vestal° throned by the west,
And loos'd his love-shaft smartly from his bow,
160   As° it should pierce a hundred thousand hearts;
But I might° see young Cupid's fiery shaft
Quench'd in the chaste beams of the wat'ry moon,
And the imperial vot'ress passed on,
In maiden meditation, fancy-free.°
165   Yet mark'd I where the bolt of Cupid fell:
It fell upon a little western flower,
Before milk-white, now purple with love's wound,
And maidens call it love-in-idleness.°
Fetch me that flow'r; the herb I showed thee once.
170   The juice of it on sleeping eyelids laid
Will make or man or° woman madly dote
Upon the next live creature that it sees.
Fetch me this herb, and be thou here again
Ere the leviathan° can swim a league.
175   PUCK: I'll put a girdle round about the earth
In forty° minutes.   [*Exit.*]
OBERON: Having once this juice,
I'll watch Titania when she is asleep,
And drop the liquor of it in her eyes.
The next thing then she waking looks upon,
180   Be it on lion, bear, or wolf, or bull,
On meddling monkey, or on busy ape,
She shall pursue it with the soul of love.
And ere I take this charm from off her sight,
As I can take it with another herb,
185   I'll make her render up her page to me.
But who comes here? I am invisible,
And I will overhear their conference.

(*Enter Demetrius, Helena following him.*)

DEMETRIUS: I love thee not, therefore pursue me not.
Where is Lysander and fair Hermia?
190   The one I'll slay, the other slayeth me.
Thou told'st me they were stol'n unto this wood;
And here am I, and wode° within this wood,
Because I cannot meet my Hermia.
Hence, get thee gone, and follow me no more.
195   HELENA: You draw me, you hard-hearted adamant;°
But yet you draw not iron, for my heart
Is true as steel. Leave° you your power to draw,
And I shall have no power to follow you.

DEMETRIUS: Do I entice you? Do I speak you fair?°
Or, rather, do I not in plainest truth   200
Tell you I do not nor I cannot love you?
HELENA: And even for that do I love you the more.
I am your spaniel; and, Demetrius,
The more you beat me, I will fawn on you.
Use me but as your spaniel, spurn me, strike me,   205
Neglect me, lose me; only give me leave,
Unworthy as I am, to follow you.
What worser place can I beg in your love —
And yet a place of high respect with me —
Than to be used as you use your dog?   210
DEMETRIUS: Tempt not too much the hatred of my
spirit,
For I am sick when I do look on thee.
HELENA: And I am sick when I look not on you.
DEMETRIUS: You do impeach° your modesty too much
To leave the city and commit yourself   215
Into the hands of one that loves you not,
To trust the opportunity of night
And the ill counsel of a desert° place
With the rich worth of your virginity.
HELENA: Your virtue° is my privilege.° For that°   220
It is not night when I do see your face,
Therefore I think I am not in the night;
Nor doth this wood lack worlds of company,
For you in my respect° are all the world.
Then how can it be said I am alone,   225
When all the world is here to look on me?
DEMETRIUS: I'll run from thee and hide me in the
brakes,°
And leave thee to the mercy of wild beasts.
HELENA: The wildest hath not such a heart as you.
Run when you will, the story shall be chang'd: 230
Apollo flies and Daphne holds the chase,°
The dove pursues the griffin,° the mild hind°
Makes speed to catch the tiger — bootless° speed,
When cowardice pursues and valor flies.
DEMETRIUS: I will not stay° thy questions.° Let me go! 235
Or if thou follow me, do not believe
But I shall do thee mischief in the wood.
HELENA: Ay, in the temple, in the town, the field,
You do me mischief. Fie, Demetrius!
Your wrongs do set a scandal on my sex.   240
We cannot fight for love, as men may do;
We should be woo'd and were not made to woo.
                                        [*Exit Demetrius.*]

---

157. **all:** Fully.   158. **vestal:** Vestal virgin (contains a complimentary allusion to Queen Elizabeth as a votaress of Diana and probably refers to an actual entertainment in her honor at Elvetham in 1591).   160. **As:** As if.   161. **might:** Could.   164. **fancy-free:** Free of love's spell.   168. **love-in-idleness:** Pansy, heartsease.   171. **or . . . or:** Either . . . or.   174. **leviathan:** Sea monster, whale.   176. **forty:** Used indefinitely.   192. **wode:** Mad (pronounced "wood" and often spelled so).   195. **adamant:** Lodestone, magnet (with pun on *hard-hearted*, since adamant was also thought to be the hardest of all stones and was confused with the diamond).   197. **Leave:** Give up.

199. **fair:** Courteously.   214. **impeach:** Call into question.   218. **desert:** Deserted.   220. **virtue:** Goodness or power to attract. **privilege:** Safeguard, warrant. **For that:** Because.   224. **in my respect:** As far as I am concerned.   227. **brakes:** Thickets.   231. **Apollo . . . chase:** In the ancient myth, Daphne fled from Apollo and was saved from rape by being transformed into a laurel tree; here it is the female who *holds the chase*, or pursues, instead of the male.   232. **griffin:** A fabulous monster with the head of an eagle and the body of a lion. **hind:** Female deer.   233. **bootless:** Fruitless.   235. **stay:** Wait for. **questions:** Talk or argument.

I'll follow thee and make a heaven of hell,
To die upon° the hand I love so well.   [*Exit.*]
OBERON: Fare thee well, nymph. Ere he do leave this
245   grove,
Thou shalt fly him and he shall seek thy love.

(*Enter Puck.*)

Hast thou the flower there? Welcome, wanderer.
PUCK: Ay, there it is.   [*Offers the flower.*]
OBERON: I pray thee, give it me.
I know a bank where the wild thyme blows,°
250 Where oxlips° and the nodding violet grows,
Quite over-canopied with luscious woodbine,°
With sweet musk-roses° and with eglantine.°
There sleeps Titania sometime of the night
Lull'd in these flowers with dances and delight;
255 And there the snake throws° her enamel'd skin,
Weed° wide enough to wrap a fairy in.
And with the juice of this I'll streak° her eyes,
And make her full of hateful fantasies.
Take thou some of it, and seek through this grove.
                  [*Gives some love-juice.*]
260 A sweet Athenian lady is in love
With a disdainful youth. Anoint his eyes,
But do it when the next thing he espies
May be the lady. Thou shalt know the man
By the Athenian garments he hath on.
265 Effect it with some care, that he may prove
More fond on° her than she upon her love;
And look thou meet me ere the first cock crow.
PUCK: Fear not, my lord, your servant shall do so.
                     (*Exeunt.*)

{*Scene II*}°

(*Enter Titania, Queen of Fairies, with her train.*)

TITANIA: Come, now a roundel° and a fairy song;
Then, for the third part of a minute, hence —
Some to kill cankers° in the musk-rose buds,
Some war with rere-mice° for their leathern wings,
5 To make my small elves coats, and some keep back
The clamorous owl, that nightly hoots and wonders
At our quaint° spirits. Sing me now asleep.
Then to your offices and let me rest.

(*Fairies sing.*)

FIRST FAIRY: You spotted snakes with double° tongue,
10   Thorny hedgehogs, be not seen;

Newts° and blindworms, do no wrong,
Come not near our fairy queen.
[*Chorus.*] Philomel,° with melody
Sing in our sweet lullaby;
Lulla, lulla, lullaby, lulla, lulla, lullaby.   15
Never harm,
Nor spell nor charm,
Come our lovely lady nigh.
So, good night, with lullaby.
FIRST FAIRY: Weaving spiders, come not here;   20
Hence, you long-legg'd spinners, hence!
Beetles black, approach not near;
Worm nor snail, do no offense.
[*Chorus.*] Philomel, with melody, etc.
SECOND FAIRY: Hence, away! Now all is well.   25
One aloof stand sentinel.

        [*Exeunt Fairies. Titania sleeps.*]

(*Enter Oberon* [*and squeezes the flower on Titania's eye-lids*].)

OBERON: What thou seest when thou dost wake,
Do it for thy true-love take;
Love and languish for his sake.
Be it ounce,° or cat, or bear,   30
Pard,° or boar with bristled hair,
In thy eye that shall appear
When thou wak'st, it is thy dear
Wake when some vile thing is near.   [*Exit.*]

(*Enter Lysander and Hermia.*)

LYSANDER: Fair love, you faint with wand'ring in the
    wood;   35
And to speak troth,° I have forgot our way.
We'll rest us, Hermia, if you think it good,
And tarry for the comfort of the day.
HERMIA: Be 't so, Lysander. Find you out a bed,
For I upon this bank will rest my head.   40
LYSANDER: One turf shall serve as pillow for us both,
One heart, one bed, two bosoms, and one troth.°
HERMIA: Nay, good Lysander; for my sake, my dear,
Lie further off yet, do not lie so near.
LYSANDER: O, take the sense, sweet, of my
    innocence!°   45
Love takes the meaning in love's conference.°
I mean, that my heart unto yours is knit
So that but one heart we can make of it;
Two bosoms interchained with an oath —
So then two bosoms and a single troth.   50

---

244. **upon:** By. 249. **blows:** Blooms. 250. **oxlips:** Flowers resembling cow-slip and primrose. 251. **woodbine:** Honeysuckle. 252. **musk-roses:** A kind of large, sweet-scented rose. **eglantine:** Sweetbriar, another kind of rose. 255. **throws:** Sloughs off, sheds. 256. **Weed:** Garment. 257. **streak:** Anoint, touch gently. 266. **fond on:** Doting on. II, I. **Location:** The wood. 1. **roundel:** Dance in a ring. 3. **cankers:** Cankerworms. 4. **rere-mice:** Bats. 7. **quaint:** Dainty. 9. **double:** Forked.

11. **Newts:** water lizards (considered poisonous, as were blindworms — small snakes with tiny eyes — and spiders). 13. **Philomel:** The nightingale. (Philomela, daughter of King Pandion, was transformed into a nightingale, according to Ovid's *Metamorphoses,* after she had been raped by her sister Procne's husband, Tereus.) 30. **ounce:** Lynx. 31. **Pard:** Leopard. 36. **troth:** Truth. 42. **troth:** Faith, troth-plight. 45. **take . . . innocence:** Interpret my intention as innocent. 46. **Love . . . conference:** When lovers confer, love teaches each lover to interpret the other's meaning lovingly.

Then by your side no bed-room me deny,
For lying so, Hermia, I do not lie.°
HERMIA: Lysander riddles very prettily.
Now much beshrew° my manners and my pride
55 If Hermia meant to say Lysander lied.
But, gentle friend, for love and courtesy
Lie further off, in human° modesty;
Such separation as may well be said
Becomes a virtuous bachelor and a maid,
60 So far be distant; and, good night, sweet friend.
Thy love ne'er alter till thy sweet life end!
LYSANDER: Amen, amen, to that fair prayer, say I,
And then end life when I end loyalty!
Here is my bed. Sleep give thee all his rest!
HERMIA: With half that wish the wisher's eyes be
65   press'd!°
[*They sleep, separated by a short distance.*]

(*Enter Puck.*)

PUCK: Through the forest have I gone,
But Athenian found I none
On whose eyes I might approve°
This flower's force in stirring love.
70 Night and silence. — Who is here?
Weeds of Athens he doth wear.
This is he, my master said,
Despised the Athenian maid;
And here the maiden, sleeping sound,
75 On the dank and dirty ground.
Pretty soul! She durst not lie
Near this lack-love, this kill-courtesy.
Churl, upon thy eyes I throw
All the power this charm doth owe."
[*Applies the love-juice.*]
80 When thou wak'st, let love forbid
Sleep his seat on thy eyelid.
So awake when I am gone,
For I must now to Oberon.   (*Exit.*)

(*Enter Demetrius and Helena, running.*)

HELENA: Stay, though thou kill me, sweet Demetrius.
DEMETRIUS: I charge thee, hence, and do not haunt me
85   thus.
HELENA: O, wilt thou darkling° leave me? Do not so.
DEMETRIUS: Stay, on thy peril!° I alone will go.
[*Exit.*]
HELENA: O, I am out of breath in this fond° chase!
The more my prayer, the lesser is my grace.°
90 Happy is Hermia, wheresoe'er she lies,°
For she hath blessed and attractive eyes.

How came her eyes so bright? Not with salt
   tears;
If so, my eyes are oft'ner wash'd than hers.
No, no, I am as ugly as a bear;
For beasts that meet me run away for fear.   95
Therefore no marvel though Demetrius
Do, as a monster, fly my presence thus.
What wicked and dissembling glass of mine
Made me compare with Hermia's sphery eyne?°
But who is here? Lysander, on the ground?   100
Dead, or asleep? I see no blood, no wound.
Lysander, if you live, good sir, awake.
LYSANDER [*awaking*]: And run through fire I will for
   thy sweet sake.
Transparent° Helena! Nature shows art,
That through thy bosom makes me see thy heart.   105
Where is Demetrius? O, how fit a word
Is that vile name to perish on my sword!
HELENA: Do not say so, Lysander, say not so.
What though he love your Hermia? Lord, what
   though?
Yet Hermia still loves you. Then be content.   110
LYSANDER: Content with Hermia? No! I do repent
The tedious minutes I with her have spent.
Not Hermia but Helena I love.
Who will not change a raven for a dove?
The will of man is by his reason sway'd,   115
And reason says you are the worthier maid.
Things growing are not ripe until their season;
So I, being young, till now ripe not° to reason.
And touching° now the point° of human skill,°
Reason becomes the marshal to my will   120
And leads me to your eyes, where I o'erlook°
Love's stories written in love's richest book.
HELENA: Wherefore was I to this keen mockery born?
When at your hands did I deserve this scorn?
Is 't not enough, is 't not enough, young man,   125
That I did never, no, nor never can,
Deserve a sweet look from Demetrius' eye,
But you must flout my insufficiency?
Good troth,° you do me wrong, good sooth,° you do,
In such disdainful manner me to woo.   130
But fare you well. Perforce I must confess
I thought you lord of° more true gentleness.
O, that a lady, of° one man refus'd,
Should of another therefore be abus'd!°   (*Exit.*)
LYSANDER: She sees not Hermia. Hermia, sleep thou
   there,   135
And never mayst thou come Lysander near!
For as a surfeit of the sweetest things
The deepest loathing to the stomach brings,

52. **lie:** Tell a falsehood (with a riddling pun on *lie,* recline).
54. **beshrew:** Curse (but mildly meant).   57. **human:** Courteous.   65. **With . . . press'd:** May we share your wish, so that your eyes too are *press'd,* closed, in sleep.   68. **approve:** Test.
79. **owe:** Own.   86. **darkling:** In the dark.   87. **on thy peril:** On pain of danger to you if you don't obey me and stay.
88. **fond:** Doting.   89. **my grace:** The favor I obtain.
90. **lies:** Dwells.

99. **sphery eyne:** Eyes as bright as stars in their spheres.
104. **Transparent:** (1) Radiant; (2) able to be seen through.
118. **ripe not:** (Am) not ripened.   119. **touching:** Reaching.
point: Summit. **skill:** Judgment.   121. **o'erlook:** Read.
129. **Good troth, good sooth:** Indeed, truly.   132. **lord of:** Possessor of. **gentleness:** Courtesy.   133. **of:** By.   134. **abus'd:**
Ill treated.

NEAR RIGHT: Oberon instructing Puck in the power of the "little western flower" in the American Repertory Theatre's 1986 production. CENTER: Oberon with Titania upon his shoulder. FAR RIGHT: The rude mechanicals: Moonshine with Lion. BELOW: Kevin Kline, Bottom, and Michelle Pfeiffer, Titania, in a touching moment from the 1999 film, *William Shakespeare's A Midsummer Night's Dream,* directed by Michael Hoffman.

Or as the heresies that men do leave
140 Are hated most of those they did deceive,
So thou, my surfeit and my heresy,
Of all be hated, but the most of me!
And, all my powers, address your love and might
To honor Helen and to be her knight!   (*Exit.*)

HERMIA [*awaking*]: Help me, Lysander, help me! Do
145   thy best
To pluck this crawling serpent from my breast!
Ay me, for pity! What a dream was here!
Lysander, look how I do quake with fear.
Methought a serpent eat° my heart away,
150 And you sat smiling at his cruel prey.°
Lysander! What, remov'd? Lysander! Lord!
What, out of hearing? Gone? No sound, no word?
Alack, where are you? Speak, an if you hear,
Speak, of all loves!° I swoon almost with fear.
155 No? Then I well perceive you are not nigh.
Either death, or you, I'll find immediately.
        (*Exit.* [*Manet*° *Titania lying asleep.*])

149. **eat:** Ate (pronounced "et").   150. **prey:** Act of preying.
154. **of all loves:** For all love's sake.   156. [S.D.] ***Manet:*** Latin
for "she remains."

{*ACT III • Scene 1*}°

(*Enter the Clowns* [*Quince, Snug, Bottom, Flute, Snout,
and Starveling*].)

BOTTOM: Are we all met?
QUINCE: Pat, pat; and here's a marvailes° convenient
    place for our rehearsal. This green plot shall be our
    stage, this hawthorn brake° our tiring-house,° and
    we will do it in action as we will do it before the   5
    Duke.
BOTTOM: Peter Quince?
QUINCE: What sayest thou, bully° Bottom?
BOTTOM: There are things in this comedy of Pyramus
    and Thisby that will never please. First, Pyramus   10
    must draw a sword to kill himself, which the ladies
    cannot abide. How answer you that?
SNOUT: By 'r lakin,° a parlous° fear.

III, 1. **Location:** Scene continues.   2. **marvailes:** Marvelous.
4. **brake:** Thicket.   **tiring-house:** Attiring area, hence backstage.   8. **bully:** Worthy, jolly, fine fellow.   13. **By 'r lakin:** By
our ladykin, the Virgin Mary.   **parlous:** Perilous.

STARVELING: I believe we must leave the killing out,
15   when all is done.°
BOTTOM: Not a whit. I have a device to make all well.
     Write me° a prologue; and let the prologue seem to
     say, we will do no harm with our swords and that
     Pyramus is not kill'd indeed; and, for the more better
20   assurance, tell them that I Pyramus am not Pyramus,
     but Bottom the weaver. This will put them out of
     fear.
QUINCE: Well, we will have such a prologue, and it shall
     be written in eight and six.°
25 BOTTOM: No, make it two more; let it be written in eight
     and eight.
SNOUT: Will not the ladies be afeard of the lion?
STARVELING: I fear it, I promise you.
BOTTOM: Masters, you ought to consider with your-
30   selves, to bring in — God shield us! — a lion among
     ladies,° is a most dreadful thing. For there is not a
     more fearful° wild-fowl than your lion living; and we
     ought to look to 't.
SNOUT: Therefore another prologue must tell he is not a
35   lion.
BOTTOM: Nay, you must name his name, and half his
     face must be seen through the lion's neck, and he
     himself must speak through, saying thus, or to the
     same defect:° "Ladies"— or "Fair ladies — I would
40   wish you"— or "I would request you"— or "I
     would entreat you — not to fear, not to tremble;
     my life for yours.° If you think I come hither as a
     lion, it were pity of my life.° No, I am no such thing,
     I am a man as other men are." And there indeed let
45   him name his name, and tell them plainly he is Snug
     the joiner.
QUINCE: Well, it shall be so. But there is two hard
     things: that is, to bring the moonlight into a cham-
     ber; for, you know, Pyramus and Thisby meet by
50   moonlight.
SNOUT: Doth the moon shine that night we play our play?
BOTTOM: A calendar, a calendar! Look in the almanac.
     Find out moonshine, find out moonshine.
                    [*They consult an almanac.*]
QUINCE: Yes, it doth shine that night.
55 BOTTOM: Why then may you leave a casement of the
     great chamber window, where we play, open, and the
     moon may shine in at the casement.
QUINCE: Ay; or else one must come in with a bush of

thorns° and a lantern, and say he comes to disfigure,°
or to present,° the person of Moonshine. Then there 60
is another thing: we must have a wall in the great
chamber; for Pyramus and Thisby, says the story, did
talk through the chink of a wall.
SNOUT: You can never bring in a wall. What say you,
Bottom?   65
BOTTOM: Some man or other must present Wall. And
let him have some plaster, or some loam, or some
rough-cast° about him, to signify wall; and let him
hold his fingers thus, and through that cranny shall
Pyramus and Thisby whisper.   70
QUINCE: If that may be, then all is well. Come, sit down,
every mother's son, and rehearse your parts. Pyramus, you begin. When you have spoken your speech,
enter into that brake, and so every one according to
his cue.   75

(*Enter Robin [Puck].*)

PUCK: What hempen° home-spuns have we swagg'ring
     here,
     So near the cradle of the Fairy Queen?
     What, a play toward?° I'll be an auditor;°
     An actor too perhaps, if I see cause.
QUINCE: Speak, Pyramus. Thisby, stand forth.   80
BOTTOM: "Thisby, the flowers of odious savors
     sweet,"—
QUINCE: Odors, odors.
BOTTOM: —"Odors savors sweet;
     So hath thy breath, my dearest Thisby dear.
     But hark, a voice! Stay thou but here awhile,   85
     And by and by I will to thee appear."   (*Exit.*)
PUCK: A stranger Pyramus than e'er played here.°
                                                     [*Exit.*]
FLUTE: Must I speak now?
QUINCE: Ay, marry, must you; for you must understand
     he goes but to see a noise that he heard, and is to   90
     come again.
FLUTE: "Most radiant Pyramus, most lily-white of hue,
     Of color like the red rose on triumphant brier,
     Most brisky juvenal° and eke° most lovely Jew,°
     As true as truest horse that yet would never tire.   95
     I'll meet thee, Pyramus, at Ninny's tomb."
QUINCE: "Ninus'° tomb," man. Why, you must not speak
     that yet. That you answer to Pyramus. You speak all

---

15. when all is done: When all is said and done.   **17. Write me:** Write at my suggestion.   **24. eight and six:** Alternate lines of eight and six syllables, a common ballad measure. **30–31. lion among ladies:** A contemporary pamphlet tells how at the christening in 1594 of Prince Henry, eldest son of King James VI of Scotland, later James I of England, a "blackmoor" instead of a lion drew the triumphal chariot, since the lion's presence might have "brought some fear to the nearest." **32. fearful:** Fear-inspiring.   **39. defect:** Bottom's blunder for *effect*.   **42. my life for yours:** I pledge my life to make your lives safe.   **43. it were . . . life:** My life would be endangered.

58–59. bush of thorns: Bundle of thornbush faggots (part of the accoutrements of the man in the moon, according to the popular notions of the time, along with his lantern and his dog). **59. disfigure:** Quince's blunder for *prefigure*. **60. present:** Represent.   **68. rough-cast:** A mixture of lime and gravel used to plaster the outside of buildings.   **76. hempen:** Made of hemp, a rough fiber.   **78. toward:** About to take place.   **auditor:** One who listens, i.e., part of the audience.   **87. here:** In this theater (?).   **94. brisky juvenal:** Brisk youth.   **eke:** Also. **Jew:** Probably an absurd repetition of the first syllable of *juvenal*.   **97. Ninus:** Mythical founder of Nineveh (whose wife, Semiramis, was supposed to have built the walls of Babylon where the story of Pyramus and Thisby takes place).

100 your part at once, cues and all. Pyramus enter. Your
     cue is past; it is, "never tire."
FLUTE: O —"As true as truest horse, that yet would
     never tire."

[*Enter Puck, and Bottom as Pyramus with the ass head.*]°

BOTTOM: "If I were fair,° Thisby, I were° only thine."
QUINCE: O monstrous! O strange! We are haunted.
     Pray, masters! Fly, masters! Help!

     [*Exeunt Quince, Snug, Flute, Snout, and Starveling.*]

105 PUCK: I'll follow you, I'll lead you about a round,°
     Through bog, through bush, through brake,
          through brier.
     Sometime a horse I'll be, sometime a hound,
     A hog, a headless bear, sometime a fire,°
     And neigh, and bark, and grunt, and roar, and burn,
110 Like horse, hound, hog, bear, fire, at every turn.
                                        (*Exit.*)
BOTTOM: Why do they run away? This is a knavery of
     them to make me afeard.

     (*Enter Snout.*)

SNOUT: O Bottom, thou art chang'd! What do I see on
     thee?
115 BOTTOM: What do you see? You see an ass-head of your
     own, do you?   [*Exit Snout.*]

     (*Enter Quince.*)

QUINCE: Bless thee, Bottom, bless thee! Thou art trans-
     lated.°   (*Exit.*)
BOTTOM: I see their knavery. This is to make an ass of
120 me, to fright me, if they could. But I will not stir from
     this place, do what they can. I will walk up and down
     here, and I will sing, that they shall hear I am not
     afraid.   [*Sings.*]
     The woosel cock° so black of hue,
125   With orange-tawny bill,
     The throstle° with his note so true,
          The wren with little quill° —
TITANIA [*awaking*]: What angel wakes me from my
     flow'ry bed?
130 BOTTOM [*sings*]: The finch, the sparrow, and the lark,
          The plain-song° cuckoo grey,
     Whose note full many a man doth mark,
          And dares not answer nay° —
     For, indeed, who would set his wit to so foolish a
     bird? Who would give a bird the lie,° though he cry
135 "cuckoo" never so?°

101. [S.D.] *with the ass head*: This stage direction, taken from
the Folio, presumably refers to a standard stage property.
102. fair: Handsome. were: Would be. 105. about a round:
Roundabout. 108. fire: Will-o'-the-wisp. 117–18. translated:
Transformed. 124. woosel cock: Male ousel or ouzel, black-
bird. 126. throstle: Song thrush. 127. quill: Literally, a reed
pipe; hence, the bird's piping song. 130. plain-song: Singing
a melody without variations. 132. dares . . . nay: Cannot
deny that he is a cuckold. 134. give . . . lie: Call the bird a
liar. 135. never so: Ever so much.

TITANIA: I pray thee, gentle mortal, sing again.
     Mine ear is much enamored of thy note;
     So is mine eye enthrallèd to thy shape;
     And thy fair virtue's force° perforce doth move me
     On the first view to say, to swear, I love thee.   140
BOTTOM: Methinks, mistress, you should have little rea-
     son for that. And yet, to say the truth, reason and
     love keep little company together nowadays. The
     more the pity that some honest neighbors will not
     make them friends. Nay, I can gleek° upon occasion. 145
TITANIA: Thou art as wise as thou art beautiful.
BOTTOM: Not so, neither. But if I had wit enough to get
     out of this wood, I have enough to serve mine own
     turn.°
TITANIA: Out of this wood do not desire to go.   150
     Thou shalt remain here, whether thou wilt or no.
     I am a spirit of no common rate.°
     The summer still° doth tend upon my state;°
     And I do love thee. Therefore, go with me.
     I'll give thee fairies to attend on thee,   155
     And they shall fetch thee jewels from the deep,
     And sing while thou on pressèd flowers dost sleep.
     And I will purge thy mortal grossness so
     That thou shalt like an airy spirit go.
     Peaseblossom, Cobweb, Moth,° and Mustard-
          seed!   160

(*Enter four Fairies [Peaseblossom, Cobweb, Moth, and
Mustardseed].*)

PEASEBLOSSOM: Ready.
COBWEB: And I.
MOTH: And I
MUSTARDSEED: And I.
ALL: Where shall we go?
TITANIA: Be kind and courteous to this gentleman.
     Hop in his walks and gambol in his eyes;
     Feed him with apricocks and dewberries,   165
     With purple grapes, green figs, and mulberries;
     The honey-bags steal from the humble-bees,
     And for night-tapers crop their waxen thighs
     And light them at the fiery glow-worm's eyes,
     To have my love to bed and to arise;   170
     And pluck the wings from painted butterflies
     To fan the moonbeams from his sleeping eyes.
     Nod to him, elves, and do him courtesies.
PEASEBLOSSOM: Hail, mortal!
COBWEB: Hail!   175
MOTH: Hail!
MUSTARDSEED: Hail!
BOTTOM: I cry your worship's mercy, heartily. I beseech
     your worship's name.

139. thy . . . force: The power of your beauty. 145. gleek:
Scoff, jest. 148–49. serve . . . turn: Answer my purpose.
152. rate: Rank, value. 153. still: Ever always. doth . . .
state: Waits upon me as part of my royal retinue. 160. Moth:
Mote, speck. (The two words *moth* and *mote* were pronounced
alike.)

180 COBWEB: Cobweb.
BOTTOM: I shall desire you of more acquaintance, good
    Master Cobweb. If I cut my finger, I shall make bold
    with you.° Your name, honest gentleman?
PEASEBLOSSOM: Peaseblossom.
185 BOTTOM: I pray you, commend me to Mistress Squash,°
    your mother, and to Master Peascod,° your father.
    Good Master Peaseblossom, I shall desire you of more
    acquaintance too. Your name, I beseech you, sir?
MUSTARDSEED: Mustardseed.
190 BOTTOM: Good Master Mustardseed, I know your pa-
    tience° well. That same cowardly, giant-like ox-beef
    hath devour'd many a gentleman of your house. I
    promise you your kindred hath made my eyes water
    ere now. I desire you of more acquaintance, good
195 Master Mustardseed.
TITANIA: Come wait upon him; lead him to my bower.
    The moon methinks looks with a wat'ry eye;
    And when she weeps,° weeps every little flower,
    Lamenting some enforced° chastity.
200 Tie up my lover's tongue, bring him silently.

                                        (*Exeunt.*)

{*Scene II*}°

(*Enter* [*Oberon,*] *King of Fairies.*)

OBERON: I wonder if Titania be awak'd;
    Then, what it was that next came in her eye,
    Which she must dote on in extremity.

([*Enter*] *Robin Goodfellow* [*Puck*].)

    Here comes my messenger. How now, mad spirit?
5   What night-rule° now about this haunted° grove?
PUCK: My mistress with a monster is in love.
    Near to her close° and consecrated bower,
    While she was in her dull° and sleeping hour,
    A crew of patches,° rude mechanicals,°
10 That work for bread upon Athenian stalls,
    Were met together to rehearse a play
    Intended for great Theseus' nuptial day.
    The shallowest thick-skin of that barren sort,°
    Who Pyramus presented,° in their sport
15 Forsook his scene° and ent'red in a brake.
    When I did him at this advantage take,
    An ass's nole° I fixed on his head.

Anon his Thisby must be answered,
And forth my mimic° comes. When they him spy,
As wild geese that the creeping fowler eye,   20
Or russet-pared choughs,° many in sort,°
Rising and cawing at the gun's report,
Sever° themselves and madly sweep the sky,
So, at his sight, away his fellows fly;
And, at our stamp, here o'er and o'er one falls;   25
He murder cries and help from Athens calls.
Their sense thus weak, lost with their fears thus
    strong,
Made senseless things begin to do them wrong,
For briers and thorns at their apparel snatch;
Some, sleeves — some, hats; from yielders all things
    catch.   30
I led them on in this distracted fear
And left sweet Pyramus translated there,
When in that moment, so it came to pass,
Titania wak'd and straightway lov'd an ass.
OBERON: This falls out better than I could devise.   35
    But hast thou yet latch'd° the Athenian's eyes
    With the love-juice, as I did bid thee do?
PUCK: I took him sleeping — that is finish'd too —
    And the Athenian woman by his side,
    That, when he wak'd, of force° she must be ey'd.   40

(*Enter Demetrius and Hermia.*)

OBERON: Stand close. This is the same Athenian.
PUCK: This is the woman, but not this the man.
                            [*They stand aside.*]
DEMETRIUS: O, why rebuke you him that loves you so?
    Lay breath so bitter on your bitter foe.
HERMIA: Now I but chide; but I should use thee worse, 45
    For thou, I fear, hast given me cause to curse.
    If thou hast slain Lysander in his sleep,
    Being o'er shoes in blood, plunge in the deep,
    And kill me too.
    The sun was not so true unto the day   50
    As he to me. Would he have stolen away
    From sleeping Hermia? I'll believe as soon
    This whole° earth may be bor'd and that the moon
    May through the center creep and so displease
    Her brother's° noontide with th' Antipodes.°   55
    It cannot be but thou has murd'red him;
    So should a murderer look, so dead,° so grim.
DEMETRIUS: So should the murdered look, and so
        should I,
    Pierc'd through the heart with your stern cruelty.
    Yet you, the murderer, look as bright, as clear,   60
    As yonder Venus in her glimmering sphere.
HERMIA: What's this to my Lysander? Where is he?
    Ah, good Demetrius, wilt thou give him me?

182–83. If . . . you: Cobwebs were used to stanch bleeding.
185. Squash: Unripe pea pod.   186. Peascod: Ripe pea pod.
190–91. your patience: What you have endured.   198. she
weeps: I.e., she causes dew.   199. enforced: Forced, violated; or, possibly, constrained (since Titania at this moment is
hardly concerned about chastity).   III, II. Location: The
wood.   5. night-rule: Diversion for the night.   haunted:
Much frequented.   7. close: Secret, private.   8. dull: Drowsy.
9. patches: Clowns, fools.   rude mechanicals: Ignorant artisans.   13. barren sort: Stupid company or crew.   14. presented: Acted.   15. scene: Playing area.   17. nole: Noddle,
head.

---

19. mimic: Burlesque actor.   21. russet-paled choughs: Gray-
headed jackdaws.   in sort: In a flock.   23. Sever: Scatter.
36. latch'd: Moistened, anointed.   40. of force: Perforce.
53. whole: Solid.   55. Her brother's: I.e., the sun's.   th' Antip-
odes: The people on the opposite side of the earth.   57. dead:
Deadly, or deathly pale.

DEMETRIUS: I had rather give his carcass to my hounds.
HERMIA: Out dog! Out cur! Thou driv'st me past the
65   bounds
    Of maiden's patience. Hast thou slain him, then?
    Henceforth be never numb'red among men!
    O, once tell true, tell true, even for my sake!
    Durst thou have look'd upon him being awake,
70   And hast thou kill'd him sleeping? O brave touch!°
    Could not a worm,° an adder, do so much?
    An adder did it, for with doubler tongue
    Than thine, thou serpent, never adder stung.
DEMETRIUS: You spend your passion° on a mispris'd
    mood.°
75 I am not guilty of Lysander's blood,
    Nor is he dead, for aught that I can tell.
HERMIA: I pray thee, tell me then that he is well.
DEMETRIUS: An if I could, what should I get
    therefore?
HERMIA: A privilege never to see me more.
80   And from thy hated presence part I so.
    See me no more, whether he be dead or no.
                               (*Exit.*)
DEMETRIUS: There is no following her in this fierce
    vein.
    Here therefore for a while I will remain.
    So sorrow's heaviness doth heavier° grow
85   For debt that bankrupt° sleep doth sorrow owe;
    Which now in some slight measure it will pay,
    If for his tender here I make some stay.°
                  (*Lie down [and sleep].*)
OBERON: What hast thou done? Thou hast mistaken
    quite
    And laid the love-juice on some true-love's sight.
90   Of thy misprision° must perforce ensue
    Some true love turn'd and not a false turn'd true.
PUCK: Then fate o'er-rules, that, one man holding
    troth,°
    A million fail, confounding oath on oath.°
OBERON: About the wood go swifter than the wind,
95   And Helena of Athens look thou find.
    All fancy-sick° she is and pale of cheer°
    With sighs of love, that cost the fresh blood° dear.
    By some illusion see thou bring her here.
    I'll charm his eyes against she do appear.°

PUCK: I go, I go; look how I go   100
    Swifter than arrow from the Tartar's bow.°
                             [*Exit.*]
OBERON: Flower of this purple dye,
    Hit with Cupid's archery.
    Sink in angle of his eye.
           [*Applies love-juice to Demetrius' eyes.*]
    When his love he doth espy,   105
    Let her shine as gloriously
    As the Venus of the sky.
    When thou wak'st, if she be by,
    Beg of her for remedy.

(*Enter Puck.*)

PUCK: Captain of our fairy band,   110
    Helena is here at hand,
    And the youth, mistook by me,
    Pleading for a lover's fee.°
    Shall we their fond pageant° see?
    Lord, what fools these mortals be!   115
OBERON: Stand aside. The noise they make
    Will cause Demetrius to awake.
PUCK: Then will two at once woo one;
    That must needs be sport alone;°
    And those things do best please me   120
    That befall prepost'rously.°
                     [*They stand aside.*]

(*Enter Lysander and Helena.*)

LYSANDER: Why should you think that I should woo in
    scorn?
    Scorn and derision never come in tears.
    Look when° I vow, I weep; and vows so born,
    In their nativity all truth appears.°   125
    How can these things in me seem scorn to you,
    Bearing the badge° of faith, to prove them true?
HELENA: You do advance° your cunning more and
    more.
    When truth kills truth,° O devilish-holy fray!
    These vows are Hermia's. Will you give her o'er?   130
    Weigh oath with oath, and you will nothing weigh.
    Your vows to her and me, put in two scales
    Will even weigh, and both as light as tales.°
LYSANDER: I had no judgment when to her I swore.
HELENA: Nor none, in my mind, now you give her o'er. 135
LYSANDER: Demetrius loves her, and he loves not you.
DEMETRIUS [*awaking*]: O Helen, goddess, nymph,
    perfect, divine!
    To what, my love, shall I compare thine eyne?

---

70. **brave touch:** Noble exploit (said ironically). 71. **worm:** Serpent. 74. **passion:** Violent feelings. **mispris'd mood:** Anger based on misconception. 84. **heavier:** (1) Harder to bear, (2) drowsier. 85. **bankrupt:** Demetrius is saying that his sleepiness adds to the weariness caused by sorrow. 86–87. **Which . . . stay:** To a small extent I will be able to "pay back" and hence find some relief from sorrow, if I pause here a while (*make some stay*) while sleep "tenders" or offers itself by way of paying the debt owed to sorrow. 90. **misprision:** Mistake. 92. **troth:** Faith. 93. **confounding . . . oath:** Invalidating one oath with another. 96. **fancy-sick:** Lovesick. **cheer:** Face. 97. **sighs . . . blood:** An allusion to the physiological theory that each sigh costs the heart a drop of blood. 99. **against . . . appear:** In anticipation of her coming.

101. **Tartar's bow:** Tartars were famed for their skill with the bow. 113. **fee:** Privilege, reward. 114. **fond pageant:** Foolish exhibition. 119. **alone:** Unequaled. 121. **prepost'rously:** Out of the natural order. 124. **Look when:** Whenever. 124–25. **vows . . . appears:** Vows made by one who is weeping give evidence thereby of their sincerity. 127. **badge:** Identifying device such as that worn on servants' livery. 128. **advance:** Carry forward, display. 129. **truth kills truth:** One of Lysander's vows must invalidate the other. 133. **tales:** Lies.

140 Crystal is muddy. O, how ripe in show°
Thy lips, those kissing cherries, tempting grow!
That pure congealed white, high Taurus'° snow,
Fann'd with the eastern wind, turns to a crow°
When thou hold'st up thy hand. O, let me kiss
This princess of pure white, this seal° of bliss!
145 HELENA: O spite! O hell! I see you all are bent
To set against me for your merriment.
If you were civil and knew courtesy,
You would not do me thus much injury.
Can you not hate me, as I know you do,
150 But you must join in souls to mock me too?
If you were men, as men you are in show,
You would not use a gentle lady so —
To vow, and swear, and superpraise° my parts,°
When I am sure you hate me with your hearts.
155 You both are rivals, and love Hermia;
And now both rivals, to mock Helena.
A trim° exploit, a manly enterprise,
To conjure tears up in a poor maid's eyes
With your derision! None of noble sort
160 Would so offend a virgin and extort°
A poor soul's patience, all to make you sport.
LYSANDER: You are unkind, Demetrius. Be not so;
For you love Hermia; this you know I know.
And here, with all good will, with all my heart,
165 In Hermia's love I yield you up my part;
And yours of Helena to me bequeath,
Whom I do love and will do till my death.
HELENA: Never did mockers waste more idle breath.
DEMETRIUS: Lysander, keep thy Hermia; I will none.°
170 If e'er I lov'd her, all that love is gone.
My heart to her but as guest-wise sojourn'd,
And now to Helen is it home return'd.
There to remain.
LYSANDER: Helen, it is not so.
DEMETRIUS: Disparage not the faith thou dost not know,
175 Lest, to thy peril, thou aby° it dear.
Look where thy love comes; yonder is thy dear.

(*Enter Hermia.*)

HERMIA: Dark night, that from the eye his° function
takes,
The ear more quick of apprehension makes;
Wherein it doth impair the seeing sense,
180 It pays the hearing double recompense.
Thou art not by mine eye, Lysander, found;
Mine ear, I thank it, brought me to thy sound.
But why unkindly didst thou leave me so?
LYSANDER: Why should he stay, whom love doth press
to go?

HERMIA: What love could press Lysander from my
side?   185
LYSANDER: Lysander's love, that would not let him
bide,
Fair Helena, who more engilds the night
Than all yon fiery oes° and eyes of light.
Why seek'st thou me? Could not this make thee
know,
The hate I bear thee made me leave thee so?   190
HERMIA: You speak not as you think. It cannot be.
HELENA: Lo, she is one of this confederacy!
Now I perceive they have conjoin'd all three
To fashion this false sport, in spite of me.°
Injurious Hermia, most ungrateful maid!   195
Have you conspir'd, have you with these contriv'd°
To bait° me with this foul derision?
Is all the counsel° that we two have shar'd,
The sisters' vows, the hours that we have spent,
When we have chid the hasty-footed time   200
For parting us — O, is all forgot?
All school-days friendship, childhood innocence?
We, Hermia, like two artificial° gods,
Have with our needles created both one flower,
Both on one sampler, sitting on one cushion,   205
Both warbling of one song, both in one key,
As if our hands, our sides, voices, and minds
Had been incorporate. So we grew together,
Like to a double cherry, seeming parted,
But yet an union in partition;   210
Two lovely° berries molded on one stem;
So, with two seeming bodies, but one heart;
Two of the first, like coats in heraldry,
Due but to one and crowned with one crest.°
And will you rent° our ancient love asunder,   215
To join with men in scorning your poor friend?
It is not friendly, 'tis not maidenly.
Our sex, as well as I, may chide you for it,
Though I alone do feel the injury.
HERMIA: I am amazed at your passionate words.   220
I scorn you not. It seems that you scorn me.
HELENA: Have you not set Lysander, as in scorn,
To follow me and praise my eyes and face?
And made your other love, Demetrius,
Who even but now did spurn me with his foot,   225
To call me goddess, nymph, divine and rare,
Precious, celestial? Wherefore speaks he this
To her he hates? And wherefore doth Lysander
Deny your love, so rich within his soul,
And tender° me, forsooth, affection,   230
But by your setting on, by your consent?

---

139. **show:** Appearance. **141. Taurus:** A lofty mountain
range in Asia Minor. **142. turns to a crow:** Seems black by
contrast. **144. seal:** Pledge. **153. superpraise:** Overpraise.
parts: Qualities. **157. trim:** Pretty, fine (said ironically).
160. extort: Twist, torture. **169. will none:** Wish none of her.
175. aby: Pay for. **177. his:** Its.

188. **oes:** Circles, orbs, stars. **194. in spite of me:** To vex
me. **196. contriv'd:** Plotted. **197. bait:** Torment, as one sets
on dogs to bait a bear. **198. counsel:** Confidential talk.
203. artificial: Skilled in art or creation. **211. lovely:** Loving.
213–14. Two . . . crest: We have two separate bodies, just as a
coat of arms in heraldry can be represented twice on a shield
but surmounted by a single crest. **215. rent:** Rend. **230. tender:** Offer.

What though I be not so in grace° as you,
So hung upon with love, so fortunate,
But miserable most, to love unlov'd?
235 This you should pity rather than despise.
HERMIA: I understand not what you mean by this.
HELENA: Ay, do! Persever, counterfeit sad° looks,
Make mouths° upon° me when I turn my back,
Wink each at other, hold the sweet jest up.
240 This sport, well carried,° shall be chronicled.
If you have any pity, grace, or manners,
You would not make me such an argument.°
But fare ye well. 'Tis partly my own fault,
Which death, or absence, soon shall remedy.
245 LYSANDER: Stay, gentle Helena; hear my excuse,
My love, my life, my soul, fair Helena!
HELENA: O excellent!
HERMIA: Sweet, do not scorn her so.
DEMETRIUS: If she cannot entreat,° I can compel.
LYSANDER: Thou canst compel no more than she
       entreat.
Thy threats have no more strength than her weak
250   prayers.
Helen, I love thee, by my life, I do!
I swear by that which I will lose for thee,
To prove him false that says I love thee not.
DEMETRIUS: I say I love thee more than he can do.
255 LYSANDER: If thou say so, withdraw, and prove it too.
DEMETRIUS: Quick, come!
HERMIA: Lysander, whereto tends all this?
LYSANDER: Away, you Ethiope!°
        [*He tries to break away from Hermia.*]
DEMETRIUS: No, no; he'll
Seem to break loose; take on as you would follow,
But yet come not. You are a tame man, go!
LYSANDER: Hang off,° thou cat, thou burr! Vile thing,
260   let loose,
Or I will shake thee from me like a serpent!
HERMIA: Why are you grown so rude? What change is
       this,
Sweet love?
LYSANDER: Thy love? Out, tawny Tartar, out!
Out, loathed med'cine!° O hated potion, hence!
HERMIA: Do you not jest?
265 HELENA: Yes, sooth,° and so do you.
LYSANDER: Demetrius, I will keep my word with thee.
DEMETRIUS: I would I had your bond, for I perceive
A weak bond° holds you. I'll not trust your word.
LYSANDER: What, should I hurt her, strike her, kill her
       dead?
270 Although I hate her, I'll not harm her so.

232. **grace:** Favor.   237. **sad:** Grave, serious.   238. **mouths:**
Maws, faces, grimaces.   **upon:** At.   240. **carried:** Managed.
242. **argument:** Subject for a jest.   248. **entreat:** Succeed by
entreaty.   257. **Ethiope:** Referring to Hermia's relatively dark
hair and complexion; see also *tawny Tartar* six lines later.
260. **Hang off:** Let go.   264. **med'cine:** Poison.   265. **sooth:**
Truly.   268. **weak bond:** Hermia's arm (with a pun on *bond,*
oath, in the previous line).

HERMIA: What, can you do me greater harm than hate?
Hate me? Wherefore? O me, what news,° my love?
Am not I Hermia? Are not you Lysander?
I am as fair now as I was erewhile.°
Since night you lov'd me; yet since night you left me.   275
Why, then you left me — O, the gods forbid! —
In earnest, shall I say?
LYSANDER: Ay, by my life!
And never did desire to see thee more.
Therefore be out of hope, of question, of doubt;
Be certain, nothing truer. 'Tis no jest   280
That I do hate thee and love Helena.
HERMIA: O me! You juggler! You cankerblossom!°
You thief of love! What, have you come by night
And stol'n my love's heart from him?
HELENA: Fine, i' faith!
Have you no modesty, no maiden shame,   285
No touch of bashfulness? What, will you tear
Impatient answers from my gentle tongue?
Fie, fie! You counterfeit, you puppet,° you!
HERMIA: Puppet? Why so? Ay, that way goes the game.
Now I perceive that she hath made compare   290
Between our statures; she hath urg'd her height,
And with her personage, her tall personage,
Her height, forsooth, she hath prevail'd with him.
And are you grown so high in his esteem,
Because I am so dwarfish and so low?   295
How low am I, thou painted maypole? Speak!
How low am I? I am not yet so low
But that my nails can reach unto thine eyes.
        [*She flails at Helena but is restrained.*]
HELENA: I pray you, though you mock me, gentlemen,
Let her not hurt me. I was never curst;°   300
I have no gift at all in shrewishness;
I am a right° maid for my cowardice.
Let her not strike me. You perhaps may think,
Because she is something° lower than myself,
That I can match her.
HERMIA: Lower! Hark, again!   305
HELENA: Good Hermia, do not be so bitter with me.
I evermore did love you, Hermia,
Did ever keep your counsels, never wrong'd you;
Save that, in love unto Demetrius,
I told him of your stealth° unto this wood.   310
He followed you; for love I followed him.
But he hath chid me hence and threat'ned me
To strike me, spurn me, nay, to kill me too.
And now, so° you will let me quiet go,
To Athens will I bear my folly back   315
And follow you no further. Let me go.
You see how simple and how fond° I am.
HERMIA: Why, get you gone. Who is 't that hinders you?

272. **what news:** What is the matter.   274. **erewhile:** Just now.
282. **cankerblossom:** Worm that destroys the flower bud (?).
288. **puppet:** (1) Counterfeit, (2) dwarfish woman (in reference to Hermia's smaller stature).   300. **curst:** Shrewish.
302. **right:** True.   304. **something:** Somewhat.   310. **stealth:**
Stealing away.   314. **so:** If only.   317. **fond:** Foolish.

HELENA: A foolish heart, that I leave here behind.
HERMIA: What, with Lysander?
320 HELENA: With Demetrius.
LYSANDER: Be not afraid; she shall not harm thee,
      Helena.
DEMETRIUS: No, sir, she shall not, though you take her
      part.
HELENA: O, when she is angry, she is keen and
      shrewd!°
      She was a vixen when she went to school;
325   And though she be but little, she is fierce.
HERMIA: "Little" again! Nothing but "low" and
      "little"!
      Why will you suffer her to flout me thus?
      Let me come to her.
LYSANDER: Get you gone, you dwarf!
      You minimus,° of hind'ring knot-grass° made!
      You bead, you acorn!
330 DEMETRIUS: You are too officious
      In her behalf that scorns your services.
      Let her alone. Speak not of Helena;
      Take not her part. For, if thou dost intend°
      Never so little show of love to her,
      Thou shalt aby° it.
335 LYSANDER: Now she holds me not;
      Now follow, if thou dar'st, to try whose right,
      Of thine or mine, is most in Helena.   [*Exit.*]
DEMETRIUS: Follow? Nay, I'll go with thee, cheek by
      jowl.°

                    [*Exit, following Lysander.*]

HERMIA: You, mistress, all this coil° is 'long of° you.
      Nay, go not back.°
340 HELENA: I will not trust you, I,
      Nor longer stay in your curst company.
      Your hands than mine are quicker for a fray;
      My legs are longer, though, to run away.   [*Exit.*]
HERMIA: I am amaz'd, and know not what to say.
                                              (*Exit.*)
345 OBERON: This is thy negligence. Still thou mistak'st,
      Or else committ'st thy knaveries willfully.
PUCK: Believe me, king of shadows, I mistook.
      Did not you tell me I should know the man
      By the Athenian garments he had on?
350   And so far blameless proves my enterprise
      That I have 'nointed an Athenian's eyes;
      And so far am I glad it so did sort°
      As this their jangling I esteem a sport.
OBERON: Thou see'st these lovers seek a place to fight.
355   Hie therefore, Robin, overcast the night;
      The starry welkin° cover thou anon

With drooping fog as black as Acheron,°
And lead these testy rivals so astray
As° one come not within another's way.
Like to Lysander sometime frame thy tongue,   360
Then stir Demetrius up with bitter wrong;°
And sometime rail thou like Demetrius.
And from each other look thou lead them thus,
Till o'er their brows death-counterfeiting sleep
With leaden legs and batty° wings doth creep.   365
Then crush this herb° into Lysander's eye,

                              [*Gives herb.*]

Whose liquor hath this virtuous° property,
To take from thence all error with his° might
And make his eyeballs roll with wonted° sight.
When they next wake, all this derision°   370
Shall seem a dream and fruitless vision,
And back to Athens shall the lovers wend
With league whose date° till death shall never end.
Whiles I in this affair do thee employ,
I'll to my queen and beg her Indian boy;   375
And then I will her charmed eye release
From monster's view, and all things shall be peace.
PUCK: My fairy lord, this must be done with haste,
For night's swift dragons° cut the clouds full fast,
And yonder shines Aurora's harbinger,°   380
At whose approach, ghosts, wand'ring here and
      there,
Troop home to churchyards. Damned spirits all,
That in crossways and floods have burial,°
Already to their wormy beds are gone.
For fear lest day should look their shames upon,   385
They willfully themselves exile from light
And must for aye° consort with black-brow'd night.
OBERON: But we are spirits of another sort.
I with the Morning's love° have oft made sport,
And, like a forester,° the groves may tread   390
Even till the eastern gate, all fiery-red,
Opening on Neptune with fair blessed beams,
Turns into yellow gold his salt green streams.
But, notwithstanding, haste; make no delay.
We may effect this business yet ere day.   [*Exit.*] 395
PUCK: Up and down, up and down,
      I will lead them up and down,
      I am fear'd in field and town.

---

323. **shrewd:** Shrewish.   329. **minimus:** Diminutive creature.
knot-grass: A weed, an infusion of which was thought to stunt
the growth.   333. **intend:** Give sign of.   335. **aby:** Pay for.
338. **cheek by jowl:** Side by side.   339. **coil:** Turmoil, dissension.
'long of: On account of.   340. **go not back:** Don't retreat. (Hermia is again proposing a fight.)   352. **sort:** Turn out.
356. **welkin:** Sky.

357. **Acheron:** River of Hades (here representing Hades itself).   359. **As:** That.   361. **wrong:** Insults.   365. **batty:** Bat-like.   366. **this herb:** The antidote (mentioned in II, I, 184)
to love-in-idleness.   367. **virtuous:** Efficacious.   368. **his:** Its.
369. **wonted:** Accustomed.   370. **derision:** Laughable business.   373. **date:** Term of existence.   379. **dragons:** Supposed
to be yoked to the car of the goddess of night.   380. **Aurora's
harbinger:** The morning star, precursor of dawn.   383. **crossways . . . burial:** Those who had committed suicide were buried
at crossways, with a stake driven through them; those
drowned, i.e., buried in floods or great waters, were condemned to wander disconsolate for want of burial rites.
387. **for aye:** Forever.   389. **Morning's love:** Cephalus, a beautiful youth beloved by Aurora; or perhaps the goddess of the
dawn herself.   390. **forester:** Keeper of a royal forest.

Goblin, lead them up and down.
400   Here comes one.

(Enter Lysander.)

LYSANDER: Where art thou, proud Demetrius? Speak
     thou now.
PUCK [*mimicking Demetrius*]: Here, villain, drawn°
     and ready. Where art thou?
LYSANDER: I will be with thee straight.°
PUCK: Follow me, then,
     To plainer° ground.
               [*Lysander wanders about, following the voice.*]°

(Enter Demetrius.)

DEMETRIUS: Lysander! Speak again!
405   Thou runaway, thou coward, art thou fled?
     Speak! In some bush? Where dost thou hide thy
          head?
PUCK [*mimicking Lysander*]: Thou coward, art thou
     bragging to the stars,
     Telling the bushes that thou look'st for wars,
     And wilt not come? Come, recreant;° come, thou
          child,
410   I'll whip thee with a rod. He is defil'd
     That draws a sword on thee.
DEMETRIUS: Yea, art thou there?
PUCK: Follow my voice. We'll try° no manhood here.
                              (Exeunt.)

[*Lysander returns.*]

LYSANDER: He goes before me and still dares me on.
     When I come where he calls, then he is gone.
415   The villain is much lighter-heel'd than I.
     I followed fast, but faster he did fly,
     That fallen am I in dark uneven way,
     And here will rest me. [*Lies down.*] Come, thou
          gentle day!
     For if but once thou show me thy gray light,
420   I'll find Demetrius and revenge this spite.   [*Sleeps.*]

([*Enter*] *Robin* [*Puck*] *and Demetrius.*)

PUCK: Ho, ho, ho! Coward, why com'st thou not?
DEMETRIUS: Abide me, if thou dar'st; for well I wot°
     Thou runn'st before me, shifting every place,
     And dar'st not stand nor look me in the face.
     Where art thou now?
425 PUCK: Come hither. I am here.
DEMETRIUS: Nay, then, thou mock'st me. Thou shalt
     buy° this dear,°
     If ever I thy face by daylight see.
     Now, go thy way. Faintness constraineth me

To measure out my length on this cold bed.
By day's approach look to be visited.   430
                    [*Lies down and sleeps.*]

(Enter Helena.)

HELENA: O weary night, O long and tedious night,
     Abate° thy hours! Shine, comforts, from the east,
     That I may back to Athens by daylight,
     From these that my poor company detest;
     And sleep, that sometimes shuts up sorrow's eye,   435
     Steal me awhile from mine own company.
                    [*Lies down and*] *sleep*[s].

PUCK: Yet but three? Come one more;
     Two of both kinds makes up four.
     Here she comes, curst and sad.
     Cupid is a knavish lad,   440
     Thus to make poor females mad.

[*Enter Hermia.*]

HERMIA: Never so weary, never so in woe,
     Bedabbled with the dew and torn with briers,
     I can no further crawl, no further go;
     My legs can keep no pace with my desires.   445
     Here will I rest me till the break of day.
     Heavens shield Lysander, if they mean a fray!
                    [*Lies down and sleeps.*]

PUCK: On the ground
     Sleep sound.
     I'll apply   450
     To your eye,
     Gentle lover, remedy.
               [*Squeezing the juice on Lysander's eyes.*]
     When thou wak'st,
     Thou tak'st   455
     True delight
     In the sight
     Of thy former lady's eye;
     And the country proverb known,
     That every man should take his own,
     In your waking shall be shown: 460
     Jack shall have Jill;
     Nought shall go ill;
     The man shall have his mare again, and all shall be
          well.   [*Exit. Manent the four lovers.*]

{*ACT IV* • *Scene 1*}°

(Enter [*Titania,*] *Queen of Fairies, and* [*Bottom the*]
Clown, and Fairies; and [*Oberon,*] *the King, behind*
them.)

TITANIA: Come, sit thee down upon this flow'ry bed,
     While I thy amiable° cheeks do coy,°
     And stick musk-roses in thy sleek smooth head,

---

402. **drawn:** With drawn sword.   403. **straight:** Immediately.
404. **plainer:** Smoother.   404. [s.d.] *Lysander wanders about*:
It is not clearly necessary that Lysander exit at this point; neither exit nor reentrance is indicated in the early texts.
409. **recreant:** Cowardly wretch.   412. **try:** Test.   422. **wot:**
Know.   426. **buy:** Pay for.   **dear:** Dearly.

432. **Abate:** Lessen, shorten.   IV, I. **Location:** Scene continues.
The four lovers are still asleep onstage.   2. **amiable:** Lovely.
coy: Caress.

And kiss thy fair large ears, my gentle joy.
                                            [*They recline.*]
BOTTOM: Where's Peaseblossom?
PEASEBLOSSOM: Ready.
BOTTOM: Scratch my head, Peaseblossom. Where's
    Mounsieur Cobweb?
COBWEB: Ready.
10 BOTTOM: Mounsieur Cobweb, good mounsieur, get you
    your weapons in your hand, and kill me a red-hipp'd
    humble-bee on the top of a thistle; and, good moun-
    sieur, bring me the honey-bag. Do not fret yourself
    too much in the action, mounsieur; and, good moun-
15 sieur, have a care the honey-bag break not; I would
    be loath to have you overflown with a honey-bag,
    signior. Where's Mounsieur Mustardseed?
MUSTARDSEED: Ready.
BOTTOM: Give me your neaf,° Mounsieur Mustardseed.
20   Pray you, leave your curtsy,° good mounsieur.
MUSTARDSEED: What's your will?

19. **neaf:** Fist.   20. **leave your curtsy:** Put on your hat.

BOTTOM: Nothing, good mounsieur, but to help Cav-
    alery° Cobweb° to scratch. I must to the barber's,
    mounsieur; for methinks I am marvailes hairy about
    the face; and I am such a tender ass, if my hair do but   25
    tickle me, I must scratch.
TITANIA: What, wilt thou hear some music, my sweet
    love?
BOTTOM: I have a reasonable good ear in music. Let's
    have the tongs and the bones.°   30
                            [*Music: tongs, rural music.*]°
TITANIA: Or say, sweet love, what thou desirest to eat.
BOTTOM: Truly, a peck of provender. I could munch your
    good dry oats. Methinks I have a great desire to a
    bottle° of hay. Good hay, sweet hay, hath no fellow.°

22–23. **Cavalery:** Cavalier. Form of address for a gentleman.
23. **Cobweb:** Seemingly an error, since Cobweb has been sent to
bring honey while Peaseblossom has been asked to scratch.
30. **tongs . . . bones:** Instruments for rustic music. (The tongs
were played like a triangle, whereas the bones were held between the fingers and used as clappers.)   [s.d.] *Music . . . music:*
This stage direction is added from the Folio.   34. **bottle:**
Bundle.   **fellow:** Equal.

RIGHT: Elizabeth McGovern as Helena in the 1987 New York Shakespeare festival production of *A Midsummer Night's Dream*, directed by A. J. Antoon.
LEFT: F. Murray Abraham (left) as Bottom, playing Pyramus.

35 TITANIA: I have a venturous fairy that shall seek
    The squirrel's hoard, and fetch thee new nuts.
    BOTTOM: I had rather have a handful or two of dried
    peas. But, I pray you, let none of your people stir me.
    I have an exposition° of sleep come upon me.
40 TITANIA: Sleep thou, and I will wind thee in my arms.
    Fairies, be gone, and be all ways° away.
                              [*Exeunt fairies.*]
    So doth the woodbine the sweet honeysuckle
    Gently entwist; the female ivy so
    Enrings the barky fingers of the elm.
45 Oh, how I love thee! How I dote on thee!
                              [*They sleep.*]

(*Enter Robin Goodfellow [Puck].*)

    OBERON [*advancing*]: Welcome, good Robin. See'st
        thou this sweet sight?
    Her dotage now I do begin to pity.
    For, meeting her of late behind the wood,
    Seeking sweet favors° for this hateful fool,
50 I did upbraid her and fall out with her.
    For she his hairy temples then had rounded
    With coronet of fresh and fragrant flowers;
    And that same dew, which sometime° on the buds

Was wont to swell like round and orient pearls,°
Stood now within the pretty flouriets'° eyes   55
Like tears that did their own disgrace bewail.
When I had at my pleasure taunted her,
And she in mild terms begg'd my patience,
I then did ask of her her changeling child;
Which straight she gave me, and her fairy sent   60
To bear him to my bower in fairy land.
And, now I have the boy, I will undo
This hateful imperfection of her eyes.
And, gentle Puck, take this transformed scalp
From off the head of this Athenian swain,   65
That, he awaking when the other° do,
May all to Athens back again repair,
And think no more of this night's accidents
But as the fierce vexation of a dream.
But first I will release the Fairy Queen.   70
[*Squeezes juice in her eyes.*]
Be as thou wast wont to be;
See as thou wast wont to see.
Dian's bud° o'er Cupid's flower

---

39. exposition: Bottom's word for *disposition*.   **41. all ways:** In all directions.   **49. favors:** I.e., gifts of flowers.   **53. sometime:** Formerly.

54. orient pearls: The most beautiful of all pearls, those coming from the Orient.   **55. flouriets':** Flowerets'.   **66. other:** Others.   **73. Dian's bud:** Perhaps the flower of the *agnus castus* or chaste-tree, supposed to preserve chastity; or perhaps referring simply to Oberon's herb by which he can undo the effects of "Cupid's flower," the love-in-idleness of II, i, 165–68.

Hath such force and blessed power.
75   Now, my Titania, wake you, my sweet queen.
TITANIA [*waking*]: My Oberon! What visions have I
          seen!
     Methought I was enamor'd of an ass.
OBERON: There lies your love.
TITANIA: How came these things to pass?
     O, how mine eyes do loathe his visage now!
80 OBERON: Silence awhile. Robin, take off this head.
     Titania, music call, and strike more dead
     Than common sleep of all these five° the sense.
TITANIA: Music, ho! Music, such as charmeth sleep!
                                              [*Music.*]
PUCK [*removing the ass's head*]: Now, when thou
     wak'st, with thine own fool's eyes peep.
OBERON: Sound, music! Come, my queen, take hands
85   with me,
     And rock the ground whereon these sleepers be.
                                              [*Dance.*]
     Now thou and I are new in amity,
     And will tomorrow midnight solemnly°
     Dance in Duke Theseus' house triumphantly
90   And bless it to all fair prosperity.
     There shall the pairs of faithful lovers be
     Wedded, with Theseus, all in jollity.
PUCK: Fairy King, attend, and mark:
     I do hear the morning lark.
95 OBERON: Then, my queen, in silence sad,°
     Trip we after night's shade.
     We the globe can compass soon,
     Swifter than the wand'ring moon.
TITANIA: Come, my lord, and in our flight
100   Tell me how it came this night
     That I sleeping here was found
     With these mortals on the ground.   (*Exeunt.*)
                                    (*Wind horn* [*within*].)

(*Enter Theseus and all his train;* [*Hippolyta, Egeus*].)

THESEUS: Go, one of you, find out the forester,
     For now our observation° is perform'd;
105   And since we have the vaward° of the day,
     My love shall hear the music of my hounds.
     Uncouple in the western valley; let them go.
     Dispatch, I say, and find the forester.
                              [*Exit an Attendant.*]
     We will, fair queen, up to the mountain's top
110   And mark the musical confusion
     Of hounds and echo in conjunction.
HIPPOLYTA: I was with Hercules and Cadmus° once,
     When in a wood of Crete they bay'd° the bear
     With hounds of Sparta.° Never did I hear

Such gallant chiding; for, besides the groves,   115
The skies, the fountains, every region near
Seem'd all one mutual cry. I never heard
So musical a discord, such sweet thunder.
THESEUS: My hounds are bred out of the Spartan kind,
     So flew'd,° so sanded;° and their heads are hung   120
     With ears that sweep away the morning dew;
     Crook-knee'd, and dewlapp'd° like Thessalian bulls;
     Slow in pursuit, but match'd in mouth like bells,
     Each under each.° A cry° more tuneable°
     Was never holla'd to, nor cheer'd with horn,   125
     In Crete, in Sparta, nor in Thessaly.
     Judge when you hear. [*Sees the sleepers.*] But, soft!
          What nymphs are these?
EGEUS: My lord, this' my daughter here asleep;
     And this, Lysander; this Demetrius is;
     This Helena, old Nedar's Helena.   130
     I wonder of their being here together.
THESEUS: No doubt they rose up early to observe
     The rite of May, and, hearing our intent,
     Came here in grace of our solemnity.°
     But speak, Egeus. Is not this the day   135
     That Hermia should give answer of her choice?
EGEUS: It is, my lord.
THESEUS: Go, bid the huntsmen wake them with their
          horns.
                              [*Exit an Attendant.*]

(*Shout within. Wind horns. They all start up.*)

     Good morrow, friends. Saint Valentine° is past.
     Begin these wood-birds but to couple now?   140
LYSANDER: Pardon, my lord.   [*They kneel.*]
THESEUS: I pray you all, stand up.
     I know you two are rival enemies;
     How comes this gentle concord in the world,
     That hatred is so far from jealousy
     To sleep by hate and fear no enmity?   145
LYSANDER: My lord, I shall reply amazedly,
     Half sleep, half waking; but as yet, I swear,
     I cannot truly say how I came here.
     But, as I think — for truly would I speak,
     And now I do bethink me, so it is —   150
     I came with Hermia hither. Our intent
     Was to be gone from Athens, where° we might,
     Without° the peril of the Athenian law —
EGEUS: Enough, enough, my lord; you have enough.
     I beg the law, the law, upon his head.   155
     They would have stol'n away; they would, Demetrius,

---

82. **these five:** I.e., the four lovers and Bottom.   88. **solemnly:**
Ceremoniously.   95. **sad:** Sober.   104. **observation:** Observance to a morn of May (I, i, 167).   105. **vaward:** Vanguard,
i.e., earliest part.   112. **Cadmus:** Mythical founder of Thebes.
(This story about him is unknown.)   113. **bay'd:** Brought to
bay.   114. **hounds of Sparta:** Breed famous in antiquity for
their hunting skill.

120. **So flew'd:** Similarly having large hanging chaps or fleshy
covering of the jaw.   **sanded:** Of sandy color.   122. **dew-
lapp'd:** Having pendulous folds of skin under the neck.
123–24. **match'd . . . under each:** Harmoniously matched in
their various cries like a set of bells, from treble down to bass.
124. **cry:** Pack of hounds.   **tuneable:** Well tuned, melodious.   134. **solemnity:** Observance of these same rites of May.
139. **Saint Valentine:** Birds were supposed to choose their
mates on St. Valentine's Day.   152. **where:** Wherever; or to
where.   153. **Without:** Outside of, beyond.

Thereby to have defeated you and me,
You of your wife and me of my consent,
Of my consent that she should be your wife.

DEMETRIUS: My lord, fair Helen told me of their
160   stealth,
Of this their purpose hither to this wood,
And I in fury hither followed them,
Fair Helena in fancy following me.
But, my good lord, I wot not by what power —
165 But by some power it is — my love to Hermia,
Melted as the snow, seems to me now
As the remembrance of an idle gaud.°
Which in my childhood I did dote upon;
And all the faith, the virtue of my heart,
170 The object and the pleasure of mine eye,
Is only Helena. To her, my lord,
Was I betroth'd ere I saw Hermia,
But like a sickness did I loathe this food;
But, as in health, come to my natural taste,
175 Now I do wish it, love it, long for it,
And will for evermore be true to it.

THESEUS: Fair lovers, you are fortunately met.
Of this discourse we more will hear anon.
Egeus, I will overbear your will;
180 For in the temple, by and by, with us
These couples shall eternally be knit.
And, for° the morning now is something° worn,
Our purpos'd hunting shall be set aside.
Away with us to Athens. Three and three,
185 We'll hold a feast in great solemnity.
Come, Hippolyta.

                 [*Exeunt Theseus, Hippolyta, Egeus, and train.*]

DEMETRIUS: These things seem small and
      undistinguishable,
Like far-off mountains turned into clouds.

HERMIA: Methinks I see these things with parted° eye,
When every thing seems double.

190 HELENA: So methinks;
And I have found Demetrius like a jewel,
Mine own, and not mine own.°

DEMETRIUS: Are you sure
That we are awake? It seems to me
That yet we sleep, we dream. Do not you think
195 The Duke was here, and bid us follow him?

HERMIA: Yea, and my father.

HELENA: And Hippolyta.

LYSANDER: And he did bid us follow to the temple.

DEMETRIUS: Why, then, we are awake. Let's follow
      him,
And by the way let us recount our dreams.

                                         [*Exeunt.*]

BOTTOM [*awaking*]: When my cue comes, call me, and   200
I will answer. My next is, "Most fair Pyramus."
Heigh-ho! Peter Quince! Flute, the bellows-mender!
Snout, the tinker! Starveling! God's my life, stol'n
hence, and left me asleep! I have had a most rare
vision. I have had a dream, past the wit of man to say   205
what dream it was. Man is but an ass, if he go about°
to expound this dream. Methought I was — there is
no man can tell what. Methought I was — and methought I had — but man is but a patch'd° fool, if he
will offer° to say what me-thought I had. The eye of   210
man hath not heard, the ear of man hath not seen,
man's hand is not able to taste, his tongue to conceive, nor his heart to report, what my dream was. I
will get Peter Quince to write a ballad of this dream.
It shall be call'd "Bottom's Dream," because it hath   215
no bottom; and I will sing it in the latter end of a
play, before the Duke. Peradventure, to make it the
more gracious, I shall sing it at her° death.   [*Exit.*]

{*Scene II*}°

(*Enter Quince, Flute, [Snout, and Starveling].*)

QUINCE: Have you sent to Bottom's house? Is he come
home yet?

STARVELING: He cannot be heard of. Out of doubt he is
transported.°

FLUTE: If he come not, then the play is marr'd. It goes   5
not forward, doth it?

QUINCE: It is not possible. You have not a man in all
Athens able to discharge° Pyramus but he.

FLUTE: No, he hath simply the best wit of any handicraft
man in Athens.   10

QUINCE: Yea, and the best person too; and he is a very
paramour for a sweet voice.

FLUTE: You must say "paragon." A paramour is, God
bless us, a thing of naught.

(*Enter Snug the Joiner.*)

SNUG: Masters, the Duke is coming from the temple,   15
and there is two or three lords and ladies more married. If our sport had gone forward, we had all been
made men.

FLUTE: O sweet bully Bottom! Thus hath he lost sixpence a day° during his life; he could not have scap'd   20
sixpence a day. An the Duke had not given him sixpence a day for playing Pyramus, I'll be hang'd. He
would have deserv'd it. Sixpence a day in Pyramus,
or nothing.

(*Enter Bottom.*)

---

167. idle gaud: Worthless trinket.   **182. for:** Since.   **something:**
Somewhat.   **189. parted:** Improperly focused.   **191–92. like
. . . not mine own:** Like a jewel that one finds by chance and
therefore possesses but cannot certainly consider one's own
property.

206. go about: Attempt.   **209. patch'd:** Wearing motley, i.e.,
a dress of various colors.   **210. offer:** Venture.   **218. her:**
Thisby's (?).   **IV, II. Location:** Athens, Quince's house (?).
4. transported: Carried off by fairies; or, possibly, transformed.
8. discharge: Perform.   **19–20. sixpence a day:** As a royal
pension.

Stage model of the set for Max
Reinhardt's 1913 production of
A Midsummer Night's Dream at
the Deutsches Theater in Berlin.
The design called for an entire
forest to be built on a stage that
revolved as the action shifted.

25 BOTTOM: Where are these lads? Where are these hearts?°
QUINCE: Bottom! O most courageous day! O most
happy hour!
BOTTOM: Masters, I am to discourse wonders.° But ask
me not what; for if I tell you, I am no true Athenian. I
30 will tell you everything, right as it fell out.
QUINCE: Let us hear, sweet Bottom.
BOTTOM: Not a word of° me. All that I will tell you
is, that the Duke hath din'd. Get your apparel together, good strings° to your beards, new ribands° to
35 your pumps, meet presently° at the palace, every man
look o'er his part; for the short and the long is, our
play is preferr'd.° In any case, let Thisby have clean
linen; and let not him that plays the lion pare his
nails, for they shall hang out for the lion's claws. And,
40 most dear actors, eat no onions nor garlic, for we
are to utter sweet breath; and I do not doubt but to
hear them say, it is a sweet comedy. No more words.
Away! go, away!   [*Exeunt.*]

25. **hearts:** Good fellows.   28. **am . . . wonders:** Have wonders
to relate.   32. **of:** Out of.   34. **strings:** To attach the beards.
ribands: Ribbons.   35. **presently:** Immediately.   37. **preferr'd:**
Selected for consideration.

{*ACT V • Scene 1*}°

(*Enter Theseus, Hippolyta, and Philostrate, [Lords, and Attendants].*)

HIPPOLYTA: 'Tis strange, my Theseus, that° these lovers
speak of.
THESEUS: More strange than true. I never may° believe
These antic° fables, nor these fairy toys.°
Lovers and madmen have such seething brains
Such shaping fantasies,° that apprehend   5
More than cool reason ever comprehends.
The lunatic, the lover, and the poet
Are of imagination all compact.°
One sees more devils than vast hell can hold;
That is the madman. The lover, all as frantic,   10
Sees Helen's° beauty in a brow of Egypt.°
The poet's eye, in a fine frenzy rolling,

V, I. **Location:** Athens. The palace of Theseus.   **1. that:** That
which.   **2. may:** Can.   **3. antic:** Strange, grotesque (with
additional punning sense of *antique,* ancient).   **fairy toys:**
Trifling stories about fairies.   **5. fantasies:** Imaginations.
8. compact: Formed, composed.   **11. Helen's:** Of Helen of
Troy, pattern of beauty.   **brow of Egypt:** Face of a gypsy.

Doth glance from heaven to earth, from earth to
   heaven;
And as imagination bodies forth
15 The forms of things unknown, the poet's pen
Turns them to shapes and gives to airy nothing
A local habitation and a name.
Such tricks hath strong imagination
That, if it would but apprehend some joy,
20 It comprehends some bringer° of that joy;
Or in the night, imagining some fear,°
How easy is a bush suppos'd a bear!
HIPPOLYTA: But all the story of the night told over,
And all their minds transfigur'd so together,
25 More witnesseth than fancy's images°
And grows to something of great constancy;°
But, howsoever,° strange and admirable.°

(*Enter lovers: Lysander, Demetrius, Hermia, and Helena.*)

THESEUS: Here come the lovers, full of joy and mirth.
Joy, gentle friends! Joy and fresh days of love
Accompany your hearts!
30 LYSANDER: More than to us
Wait in your royal walks, your board, your bed!
THESEUS: Come now, what masques, what dances shall
   we have,
To wear away this long age of three hours
Between our after-supper and bed-time?
35 Where is our usual manager of mirth?
What revels are in hand? Is there no play,
To ease the anguish of a torturing hour?
Call Philostrate.
PHILOSTRATE: Here, mighty Theseus.
THESEUS: Say, what abridgement° have you for this
   evening?
40 What masque? What music? How shall we beguile
The lazy time, if not with some delight?
PHILOSTRATE: There is a brief° how many sports are
   ripe.
Make choice of which your Highness will see first.
                    [*Giving a paper.*]
THESEUS [*reads*]: "The battle with the Centaurs,° to be
   sung
45 By an Athenian eunuch to the harp."
We'll none of that. That have I told my love,
In glory of my kinsman° Hercules.

[*Reads.*] "The riot of the tipsy Bacchanals,
Tearing the Thracian singer in their rage."°
That is an old device; and it was play'd   50
When I from Thebes came last a conqueror.
[*Reads.*] "The thrice three Muses mourning for the
   death
Of Learning, late deceas'd in beggary."°
That is some satire, keen and critical,
Not sorting with° a nuptial ceremony.   55
[*Reads.*] "A tedious brief scene of young Pyramus
And his love Thisby; very tragical mirth."
Merry and tragical? Tedious and brief?
That is, hot ice and wondrous strange° snow.
How shall we find the concord of this discord?   60
PHILOSTRATE: A play there is, my lord, some ten words
   long,
Which is as brief as I have known a play;
But by ten words, my lord, it is too long,
Which makes it tedious. For in all the play
There is not one word apt, one player fitted.   65
And tragical, my noble lord, it is,
For Pyramus therein doth kill himself.
Which, when I saw rehears'd, I must confess,
Made mine eyes water, but more merry tears
The passion of loud laughter never shed.   70
THESEUS: What are they that do play it?
PHILOSTRATE: Hard-handed men that work in Athens
   here,
Which never labor'd in their minds till now,
And now have toil'd° their unbreathed° memories
With this same play, against° your nuptial.   75
THESEUS: And we will hear it.
PHILOSTRATE: No, my noble lord,
It is not for you. I have heard it over,
And it is nothing, nothing in the world;
Unless you can find sport in their intents,
Extremely stretch'd° and conn'd° with cruel pain, 80
To do you service.
THESEUS: I will hear that play;
For never anything can be amiss'
When simpleness and duty tender it.
Go, bring them in; and take your places, ladies.

[*Philostrate goes to summon the players.*]

HIPPOLYTA: I love not to see wretchedness o'ercharg'd° 85
And duty in his service° perishing.
THESEUS: Why, gentle sweet, you shall see no such thing.

---

20. **bringer:** Source. 21. **fear:** Object of fear. 25. **More . . .
images:** Testifies to something more substantial than mere
imaginings. 26. **constancy:** Certainty. 27. **howsoever:** In
any case. **admirable:** A source of wonder. 39. **abridgement:**
Pastime (to abridge or shorten the evening). 42. **brief:** Short
written statement, list. 44. **"battle . . . Centaurs":** Probably
refers to the battle of the Centaurs and the Lapithae, when the
Centaurs attempted to carry off Hippodamia, bride of Theseus's friend Pirothous. 47. **kinsman:** Plutarch's *Life of Theseus* states that Hercules and Theseus were near-kinsmen.
Theseus is referring to a version of the battle of the Centaurs in
which Hercules was said to be present.

48–49. **"The riot . . . rage":** This was the story of the death of
Orpheus, as told in *Metamorphoses.* 52–53. **"The thrice . . .
beggary":** Possibly an allusion to Spenser's *Teares of the Muses*
(1591), though "satires" deploring the neglect of learning and
the creative arts were common-place. 55. **sorting with:** Befit-
ting. 59. **strange:** Seemingly an error for some adjective that
would contrast with *snow,* just as *hot* contrasts with *ice.*
74. **toil'd:** Taxed. **unbreathed:** Unexercised. 75. **against:**
In preparation for. 80. **stretch'd:** Strained. **conn'd:** Memorized. 85. **wretchedness o'ercharg'd:** Incompetence over-
burdened. 86. **his service:** Its attempt to serve.

HIPPOLYTA: He says they can do nothing in this kind.°
THESEUS: The kinder we, to give them thanks for
    nothing.

90   Our sport shall be to take what they mistake;
    And what poor duty cannot do, noble respect
    Takes it in might, not merit.°
    Where I have come, great clerks° have purposed
    To greet me with premeditated welcomes;
95   Where I have seen them shiver and look pale,
    Make periods in the midst of sentences,
    Throttle their practic'd accent° in their fears,
    And in conclusion dumbly have broke off,
    Not paying me a welcome. Trust me, sweet,
100   Out of this silence yet I pick'd a welcome;
    And in the modesty of fearful duty
    I read as much as from the rattling tongue
    Of saucy and audacious eloquence.
    Love, therefore, and tongue-tied simplicity
105   In least° speak most, to my capacity.°

[*Philostrate returns.*]

PHILOSTRATE: So please your Grace, the Prologue° is
    address'd.°
THESEUS: Let him approach.   [*Flourish of trumpets.*]

(*Enter the Prologue* [*Quince*].)

PROLOGUE: If we offend, it is with our good will.
    That you should think, we come not to offend,
110   But with good will. To show our simple skill,
    That is the true beginning of our end.
    Consider, then, we come but in despite.
    We do not come, as minding° to content you,
    Our true intent is. All for your delight
115   We are not here. That you should here repent you,
    The actors are at hand; and, by their show,
    You shall know all that you are like to know.
THESEUS: This fellow doth not stand upon points.°
LYSANDER: He hath rid his prologue like a rough° colt;
120   he knows not the stop.° A good moral, my lord: it is
not enough to speak, but to speak true.
HIPPOLYTA: Indeed he hath play'd on his prologue like
a child on a recorder;° a sound, but not in government.°
125 THESEUS: His speech was like a tangled chain, nothing°
impair'd, but all disorder'd. Who is next?

---

88. kind: Kind of thing.   92. Takes . . . merit: Values it for the
effort made rather than for the excellence achieved.
93. clerks: Learned men.   97. practic'd accent: Rehearsed
speech; or usual way of speaking.   105. least: Saying least.
to my capacity: In my judgment and understanding.
106. Prologue: Speaker of the prologue.   address'd: Ready.
113. minding: Intending.   118. stand upon points: (1) Heed
niceties or small points, (2) pay attention to punctuation in his
reading. (The humor of Quince's speech is in the blunders of its
punctuation.)   119. rough: Unbroken.   120. stop: (1) The
stopping of a colt by reining it in, (2) punctuation mark.
123. recorder: A wind instrument like a flute.   123–24. government: Control.   125. nothing: Not at all.

(*Enter Pyramus and Thisby, and Wall, and Moonshine,
and Lion.*)

PROLOGUE: Gentles, perchance you wonder at this
    show;
    But wonder on, till truth make all things plain.
    This man is Pyramus, if you would know;
    This beauteous lady Thisby is certain.   130
    This man, with lime and rough-cast, doth present
    Wall, that vile Wall which did these lovers sunder;
    And through Wall's chink, poor souls, they are
      content
    To whisper. At the which let no man wonder.
    This man, with lantern, dog, and bush of thorn,   135
    Presenteth Moonshine; for, if you will know,
    By moonshine did these lovers think no scorn°
    To meet at Ninus' tomb, there, there to woo.
    This grisly beast, which Lion hight° by name,
    The trusty Thisby, coming first by night,   140
    Did scare away, or rather did affright;
    And, as she fled, her mantle she did fall,°
    Which Lion vile with bloody mouth did stain.
    Anon comes Pyramus, sweet youth and tall,°
    And finds his trusty Thisby's mantle slain;   145
    Whereat, with blade, with bloody blameful blade,
    He bravely broach'd° his boiling bloody breast.
    And Thisby, tarrying in mulberry shade,
    His dagger drew, and died. For all the rest,
    Let Lion, Moonshine, Wall, and lovers twain   150
    At large° discourse, while here they do remain.

(*Exeunt Lion, Thisby, and Moonshine.*)

THESEUS: I wonder if the lion be to speak.
DEMETRIUS: No wonder, my lord. One lion may, when
    many asses do.
WALL: In this same interlude it doth befall   155
    That I, one Snout by name, present a wall;
    And such a wall, as I would have you think,
    That had in it a crannied hole or chink,
    Through which the lovers, Pyramus and Thisby,
    Did whisper often very secretly.   160
    This loam, this rough-cast, and this stone doth show
    That I am that same wall; the truth is so.
    And this the cranny is, right and sinister,°
    Through which the fearful lovers are to whisper.
THESEUS: Would you desire lime and hair to speak better?   165
DEMETRIUS: It is the wittiest partition° that ever I heard
    discourse, my lord.

[*Pyramus comes forward.*]

THESEUS: Pyramus draws near the wall. Silence!

---

137. think no scorn: Think it no disgraceful matter.
139. hight: Is called.   142. fall: Let fall.   144. tall: Courageous.   147. broach'd: Stabbed.   151. At large: In full, at
length.   163. right and sinister: The right side of it and the
left (sinister); or running from right to left, horizontally.
166. partition: (1) Wall, (2) section of a learned treatise or
oration.

PYRAMUS: O grim-look'd° night! O night with hue so
   black!
170 O night, which ever art when day is not!
   O night, O night! Alack, alack, alack,
   I fear my Thisby's promise is forgot.
   And thou, O wall, O sweet, O lovely wall,
   That stand'st between her father's ground and mine,
175 Thou wall, O wall, O sweet and lovely wall,
   Show me thy chink, to blink through with mine eyne!

                    [*Wall holds up his fingers.*]

   Thanks, courteous wall. Jove shield thee well for
   this!
   But what see I? No Thisby do I see.
   O wicked wall, through whom I see no bliss!
180 Curs'd be thy stones for thus deceiving me!
THESEUS: The wall, methinks, being sensible,° should
   curse again.
PYRAMUS: No, in truth, sir, he should not. "Deceiving
   me" is Thisby's cue: she is to enter now, and I am to
185 spy her through the wall. You shall see, it will fall pat
   as I told you. Yonder she comes.

(*Enter Thisby.*)

THISBY: O wall, full often hast thou heard my moans,
   For parting my fair Pyramus and me.
   My cherry lips have often kiss'd thy stones,
190 Thy stones with lime and hair knit up in thee.
PYRAMUS: I see a voice. Now will I to the chink,
   To spy an° I can hear my Thisby's face.
   Thisby!
THISBY: My love! Thou art my love, I think.
PYRAMUS: Think what thou wilt, I am thy lover's
195   grace;°
   And, like Limander° am I trusty still.
THISBY: And I like Helen,° till the Fates me kill.
PYRAMUS: Not Shafalus° to Procrus° was so true.
THISBY: As Shafalus to Procrus, I to you.
200 PYRAMUS: O, kiss me through the hole of this vile wall!
THISBY: I kiss the wall's hole, not your lips at all.
PYRAMUS: Wilt thou at Ninny's tomb meet me
   straightway?
THISBY: 'Tide° life, 'tide death, I come without delay.

           [*Exeunt Pyramus and Thisby.*]

WALL: Thus have I, Wall, my part discharged so;
205 And, being done, thus Wall away doth go.   [*Exit.*]
THESEUS: Now is the mural down between the two
   neighbors.
DEMETRIUS: No remedy, my lord, when walls are so
   willful to hear° without warning.°
210 HIPPOLYTA: This is the silliest stuff that ever I heard.

169. **grim-look'd:** Grim-looking.   181. **sensible:** Capable of feeling.   192. **an:** If.   195. **lover's grace:** Gracious lover.   196. **Li-**
mander: Blunder for *Leander.*   197. **Helen:** Blunder for *Hero.*
198. **Shafalus, Procrus:** Blunders for *Cephalus* and *Procris,* also
famous lovers.   203. **'Tide:** Betide, come.   209. **to hear:** As to
hear.   **without warning:** Without warning the parents.

THESEUS: The best in this kind° are but shadows;° and
   the worst are no worse, if imagination amend them.
HIPPOLYTA: It must be your imagination then, and not
   theirs.
THESEUS: If we imagine no worse of them than they of 215
   themselves, they may pass for excellent men. Here
   come two noble beasts in, a man and a lion.

(*Enter Lion and Moonshine.*)

LION: You, ladies, you, whose gentle hearts do fear
   The smallest monstrous mouse that creeps on floor,
   May now perchance both quake and tremble here, 220
   When lion rough in wildest rage doth roar.
   Then know that I, as Snug the joiner, am
   A lion fell,° nor else no lion's dam;
   For, if I should as lion come in strife
   Into this place, 'twere pity on my life. 225
THESEUS: A very gentle beast, and of a good conscience.
DEMETRIUS: The very best at a beast, my lord, that e'er I
   saw.
LYSANDER: This lion is a very fox for his valor.°
THESEUS: True; and a goose for his discretion.° 230
DEMETRIUS: Not so, my lord; for his valor cannot carry
   his discretion; and the fox carries the goose.
THESEUS: His discretion, I am sure, cannot carry his
   valor, for the goose carries not the fox. It is well.
   Leave it to his discretion, and let us listen to the 235
   moon.
MOON: This lanthorn° doth the horned moon present —
DEMETRIUS: He should have worn the horns on his
   head.°
THESEUS: He is no crescent, and his horns are invisible 240
   within the circumference.
MOON: This lanthorn doth the horned moon present;
   Myself the man i' th' moon do seem to be.
THESEUS: This is the greatest error of all the rest. The
   man should be put into the lanthorn. How is it else 245
   the man i' th' moon?
DEMETRIUS: He dares not come there for the° candle;
   for, you see, it is already in snuff.°
HIPPOLYTA: I am aweary of this moon. Would he would
   change! 250
THESEUS: It appears, by his small light of discretion, that
   he is in the wane; but yet, in courtesy, in all reason,
   we must stay the time.
LYSANDER: Proceed, Moon.

211. **in this kind:** Of this sort.   **shadows:** Likenesses, representations.   223. **lion fell:** Fierce lion (with a play on the idea of
lion skin).   229. **is . . . valor:** His valor consists of craftiness
and discretion.   230. **goose . . . discretion:** As discreet as a
goose, that is, more foolish than discreet.   237. **lanthorn:** This
original spelling may suggest a play on the *horn* of which
lanterns were made and also on a cuckold's horns; but the
spelling *lanthorn* is not used consistently for comic effect in this
play or elsewhere. In V, I, 135, for example, the word is *lantern*
in the original.   238–39. **on his head:** As a sign of cuckoldry.
247. **for the:** Because of the.   248. **in snuff:** (1) Offended,
(2) in need of snuffing.

255   MOON: All that I have to say is to tell you that the lanthorn is the moon, I, the man in the moon, this thorn-bush my thorn-bush, and this dog my dog.
DEMETRIUS: Why, all these should be in the lanthorn; for all these are in the moon. But silence! Here comes
260   Thisby.

(*Enter Thisby.*)

THISBY: This is old Ninny's tomb. Where is my love?
LION [*roaring*]: Oh —   [*Thisby runs off.*]
DEMETRIUS: Well roar'd, Lion.
THESEUS: Well run, Thisby.
265   HIPPOLYTA: Well shone, Moon. Truly, the moon shines with a good grace.

[*The Lion shakes Thisby's mantle, and exit.*]

THESEUS: Well mous'd,° Lion.
DEMETRIUS: And then came Pyramus.
LYSANDER: And so the lion vanish'd.

(*Enter Pyramus.*)

PYRAMUS: Sweet Moon, I thank thee for thy sunny
270   beams;
I thank thee, Moon, for shining now so bright;
For, by thy gracious, golden, glittering gleams,
I trust to take of truest Thisby sight.
    But stay, O spite!
275   But mark, poor knight,
What dreadful dole° is here!
    Eyes, do you see?
    How can it be?
O dainty duck! O dear!
280   Thy mantle good,
    What, stain'd with blood!
Approach, ye Furies fell!°
    O Fates, come, come,
    Cut thread and thrum;°
285   Quail,° crush, conclude, and quell!°
THESEUS: This passion, and the death of a dear friend, would go near to make a man look sad.°
HIPPOLYTA: Beshrew my heart, but I pity the man.
PYRAMUS: O wherefore, Nature, didst thou lions frame?
290   Since lion vile hath here deflow'r'd my dear,
Which is — no, no — which was the fairest dame
That liv'd, that lov'd, that lik'd, that look'd with cheer.°
    Come, tears, confound,
    Out, sword, and wound
295   The pap of Pyramus;
    Ay, that left pap,
    Where heart doth hop.   [*Stabs himself.*]
Thus die I, thus, thus, thus.

Now am I dead,
Now am I fled;   300
My soul is in the sky.
    Tongue, lose thy light;
    Moon, take thy flight.   [*Exit Moonshine.*]
Now die, die, die, die, die.   [*Dies.*]
DEMETRIUS: No die, but an ace,° for him; for he is but   305
one.°
LYSANDER: Less than an ace, man; for he is dead, he is nothing.
THESEUS: With the help of a surgeon he might yet recover, and yet prove an ass.°   310
HIPPOLYTA: How chance Moonshine is gone before Thisby comes back and finds her lover?
THESEUS: She will find him by starlight. Here she comes; and her passion ends the play.

[*Enter Thisby.*]

HIPPOLYTA: Methinks she should not use a long one for   315
such a Pyramus. I hope she will be brief.
DEMETRIUS: A mote will turn the balance, which Pyramus, which° Thisby, is the better: he for a man God warr'nt us; she for a woman, God bless us.
LYSANDER: She hath spied him already with those sweet   320
eyes.
DEMETRIUS: And thus she means,° videlicet:°
THISBY: Asleep, my love?
    What, dead, my dove?
O Pyramus, arise!   325
    Speak, speak. Quite dumb?
Dead, dead? A tomb
Must cover thy sweet eyes.
    These lily lips,
    This cherry nose,   330
These yellow cowslip cheeks,
    Are gone, are gone!
    Lovers, make moan.
His eyes were green as leeks.
    O Sisters Three,°   335
    Come, come to me,
With hands as pale as milk;
    Lay them in gore,
    Since you have shore°
With shears his thread of silk.   340
    Tongue, not a word.
    Come, trusty sword,
Come, blade, my breast imbrue!°   [*Stabs herself.*]
    And farewell, friends.
    Thus Thisby ends.   345
Adieu, adieu, adieu.   [*Dies.*]

267. **mous'd:** Shaken.   276. **dole:** Grievous event.   282. **fell:** Fierce.   284. **thread and thrum:** The warp in weaving and the loose end of the warp.   285. **Quail:** Overpower.   **quell:** Kill, destroy.   286–87. **This . . . sad:** If one had other reason to grieve, one might be sad, but not from this absurd portrayal of passion.   292. **cheer:** Countenance.

305. **ace:** The side of the die featuring the single pip, or spot. (The pun is on *die* as a singular of *dice*; Bottom's performance is not worth a whole *die* but rather one single face of it, one small portion.)   306. **one:** (1) An individual person, (2) unique.   310. **ass:** With a pun on *ace*.   317–18. **which . . . which:** Whether . . . or.   322. **means:** Moans, laments.   **videlicet:** To wit.   335. **Sisters Three:** The Fates.   339. **shore:** Shorn.   343. **imbrue:** Stain with blood.

THESEUS: Moonshine and Lion are left to bury the dead.
DEMETRIUS: Ay, and Wall too.
BOTTOM [*starting up*]: No, I assure you; the wall is
350   down that parted their fathers. Will it please you to
see the epilogue, or to hear a Bergomask dance° between two of our company?
THESEUS: No epilogue, I pray you; for your play needs
no excuse. Never excuse; for when the players are all
355   dead, there need none to be blam'd. Marry, if he that
writ it had play'd Pyramus and hang'd himself in
Thisby's garter, it would have been a fine tragedy;
and so it is, truly, and very notably discharg'd. But,
come, your Bergomask. Let your epilogue alone.
                                                    [*A dance.*]
360   The iron tongue of midnight hath told° twelve.
Lovers, to bed; 'tis almost fairy time.
I fear we shall outsleep the coming morn
As much as we this night have overwatch'd.°
This palpable-gross° play hath well beguil'd
365   The heavy° gait of night. Sweet friends, to bed.
A fortnight hold we this solemnity,
In nightly revels and new jollity.   (*Exeunt.*)

(*Enter Puck*)

PUCK: Now the hungry lion roars,
And the wolf behowls the moon;
370   Whilst the heavy ploughman snores,
All with weary task fordone.°
Now the wasted brands° do glow,
Whilst the screech-owl, screeching loud,
Puts the wretch that lies in woe
375   In remembrance of a shroud.
Now it is the time of night
That the graves, all gaping wide,
Every one lets forth his sprite,°
In the churchway paths to glide.
380   And we fairies, that do run
By the triple Hecate's° team
From the presence of the sun,
Following darkness like a dream,
Now are frolic.° Not a mouse
385   Shall disturb this hallowed house.
I am sent with broom before,
To sweep the dust behind° the door.

(*Enter [Oberon and Titania,] King and Queen of Fairies,
with all their train.*)

OBERON: Through the house give glimmering light,
By the dead and drowsy fire;
Every elf and fairy sprite   390
Hop as light as bird from brier;
And this ditty, after me,
Sing, and dance it trippingly.
TITANIA: First, rehearse your song by rote,
To each word a warbling note.   395
Hand in hand, with fairy grace,
Will we sing, and bless this place.
                                    [*Song and dance.*]
OBERON: Now, until the break of day,
Through this house each fairy stray.
To the best bride-bed will we,   400
Which by us shall blessed be;
And the issue there create°
Ever shall be fortunate.
So shall all the couples three
Ever true in loving be;   405
And the blots of Nature's hand
Shall not in their issue stand;
Never mole, hare lip, nor scar,
Nor mark prodigious,° such as are
Despised in nativity,   410
Shall upon their children be.
With this field-dew consecrate,°
Every fairy take his gait,°
And each several° chamber bless,
Through this palace, with sweet peace;   415
And the owner of it blest
Ever shall in safety rest.
Trip away; make no stay;
Meet me all by break of day.

(*Exeunt [Oberon, Titania, and train].*)

PUCK: If we shadows have offended,   420
Think but this, and all is mended,
That you have but slumb'red here°
While these visions did appear.
And this weak and idle theme,
No more yielding but° a dream,   425
Gentles, do not reprehend.
If you pardon, we will mend.
And, as I am an honest Puck,
If we have unearned luck
Now to scape the serpent's tongue,°   430
We will make amends ere long;
Else the Puck a liar call.
So, good night unto you all.
Give me your hands,° if we be friends,
And Robin shall restore amends.   435
[*Exit.*]

351. **Bergomask dance:** A rustic dance named for Bergamo,
a province in the state of Venice.   360. **told:** Counted,
struck ("tolled").   363. **overwatch'd:** Stayed up too late.
364. **palpable-gross:** Obviously crude.   365. **heavy:** Drowsy,
dull.   371. **fordone:** Exhausted.   372. **wasted brands:**
Burned-out logs.   378. **Every . . . sprite:** Every grave lets forth
its ghost.   381. **triple Hecate's:** Hecate ruled in three capacities: as Luna or Cynthia in heaven, as Diana on earth, and as
Proserpina in hell.   384. **frolic:** Merry.   387. **behind:** From
behind. (Robin Goodfellow was a household spirit who helped
good housemaids and punished lazy ones.)

402. **create:** Created.   409. **prodigious:** Monstrous, unnatural.
412. **consecrate:** Consecrated.   413. **take his gait:** Go his way.
414. **several:** Separate.   422. **That . . . here:** That it is a "midsummer night's dream."   425. **No . . . but:** Yielding no more
than.   430. **serpent's tongue:** Hissing.   434. **Give . . . hands:**
Applaud.

COMMENTARIES

Some of the finest critical commentary ever written has been devoted to the works of Shakespeare. From the seventeenth century to the present, critics have taken a considerable interest in the nuances of his work.

In the commentary on *A Midsummer Night's Dream* we find a wide range of responses to the work. Enid Welsford's comments are in a special context, that of the court masque, the rich entertainments that were designed to please royalty. As Welsford explains, *A Midsummer Night's Dream* has many elements of the masque.

In a more specifically feminist observation, critic Linda Bamber shows how assumptions regarding power in a male-female relationship affect our interpretation of the play.

Peter Brook, one of the most notable contemporary directors of Shakespeare and the producer of a landmark production of *A Midsummer Night's Dream* (1970), gives us a director's view of the play. He centers the discussion on love, which in many forms is at the heart of the play. See the review of his production on page 230.

Clive Barnes's review gives us a clear sense of the visual and kinetic details that made Peter Brook's *A Midsummer Night's Dream* one of the most memorable modern stagings of Shakespeare. The use of juggling, acrobats, and trapezes energized the production and underscored the youthful vitality of the characters.

Contemporary reviews of Shakespeare's plays take a very different approach to the plays than do critical studies. The reviewers are concerned first with the actors and their interpretation of the drama. They are then concerned with the director's insights and sense of pacing. In addition to focusing on the title roles, critics also aim to communicate a sense of the dynamics of the production as a whole. Peter Brook's production of *A Midsummer Night's Dream*, for example, was perhaps most startling for its all-white set and backdrop, and for the marvelous scenes staged with principal actors lolling on simple white swings. Critics can give us insight into the staging of the work and the ways in which the staging imparts meaning to the drama.

Enid Welsford (1892–1981)
MASQUE ELEMENTS IN A MIDSUMMER NIGHT'S DREAM   1927

Enid Welsford examines A Midsummer Night's Dream *from the point of view of its masquelike qualities.* Shakespeare's The Tempest *includes a masque and has certain scenic qualities that link it to that tradition, and so does* A Midsummer Night's Dream. *Its fantastic costumes and remarkable fairy population could be considered part of the antimasque, a parody of the masque itself. The antimasque often involved masquers dressed in grotesque animal costumes, making a loud racket, and dancing in erratic and fantastic gestures. Meant originally as a contrast to the magnificence of the masque, the antimasque became a favorite of the less conservative masquers.*

The only character study in *A Midsummer Night's Dream* is to be found in the portrayal of Bottom, Theseus, and perhaps Hippolyta. Even in drawing these characters Shakespeare was evidently influenced by the memory of pageants, complimentary speeches, and entertainments addressed by townspeople and humble folk to the Queen or to the nobility. A glance through Nichols's *Public Progresses* shows what innumerable lengthy speeches, what innumerable disguisings and shows, Elizabeth was obliged to bear with gracious demeanor. Her experiences were similar to those of Theseus:

> Where I have come, great clerks have purposed
> To greet me with premeditated welcomes;
> Where I have seen them shiver and look pale,
> Make periods in the midst of sentences,
> Throttle their practic'd accent in their fears,
> And, in conclusion, dumbly have broke off,
> Not paying me a welcome.

One Sunday afternoon, at Kenilworth Castle, Elizabeth and her court whiled away the time by watching the countrypeople at a Brideale and Morris Dance. Their amused kindly tolerance is just that of Theseus and the lovers toward the Athenian workmen. So that even in the most solid and dramatic parts of his play Shakespeare is only giving an idealized version of courtly and country revels and of the people that played a part in them.

In *A Midsummer Night's Dream* Bottom and his companions serve the same purpose as the antimasque in the courtly revels. It is true that Shakespeare's play was written before Ben Jonson had elaborated and defined the antimasque, but from the first grotesque dances were popular, and the principle of contrast was always latent in the masque. There is, however, a great difference between Jonson's and Shakespeare's management of foil and relief. In the antimasque the transition is sudden and the contrast complete, a method of composition effective enough in spectacle and ballet. But in a play, as Shakespeare well knew, the greatest beauty is gained through contrast when the difference is not obvious and striking, but rises out of a deep though unobtrusive resemblance. This could not be better illustrated than by the picture of Titania winding the ass-headed Bottom in her arms. Why is it that this is a pleasing picture, why is it that the rude mechanicals do not, as a matter of fact, disturb or sully Titania's "close and consecrated bower"? Malvolio° in Bottom's place would be repellent, yet Malvolio, regarded superficially, is less violently contrasted to the Fairy Queen than is Nick Bottom. Bottom with his ass's head is grotesquely hideous, and in ordinary life he is crude, raw, and very stupid. We have no reason to suppose that Malvolio was anything but a well-set-up, proper-looking man, spruce, well dressed, the perfect family butler. His mentality too is of a distinctly higher order than Bottom's. He fills a responsible position with credit, he follows a reasoned line of conduct, he thinks nobly of the soul. Two things alone he lacks (and that is why no self-respecting fey could ever kiss him) — humor and imagination. Malvolio is, therefore, the only character who cannot be included in the final harmony of *Twelfth Night*. Bottom and his fellows did perhaps lack humor (though the interview with the fairies suggests that Bottom had a smack of it), but in its place they possessed unreason. Imagination they did have, of the most simple, primal, childlike kind. It is their artistic ambition that lifts them out of the humdrum world and turns them into Midsummer Dreamers, and we have seen how cunningly Shakespeare extracts from their very stupidity romance and moonshine. But, indeed, grotesqueness and stupidity (of a certain kind) have a kinship with beauty. For these qualities usually imply a measure of spiritual freedom, they lead to at least a temporary relief from the tyranny of reason and from the pressure of the external world. In *A Midsummer Night's Dream* the dominance of the Lord of Misrule is not marked by coarse parody, but by the partial repeal of the laws of cause and effect. By delicate beauty, gentle mockery, and simple romantic foolishness our freedom is gained.

Malvolio: A character in Shakespeare's *Twelfth Night*.

Linda Bamber (b. 1945)
On *A Midsummer Night's Dream*   1982

The question of masculine and feminine is central to A Midsummer Night's Dream. *Much of the action is precipitated by a power struggle between Titania and Oberon, and the young Athenians who rush off to the woods are there because a father has decided to oppose the will of his daughter regarding her marriage. Linda Bamber is a feminist critic interested in examining the centers of power in the play, particularly with an eye for what we accept as the natural order of relationships. She shows that the action of the comedy is essentially tied into questions of gender, which begin to become questions of genre.*

The best example [in Shakespeare] of the relationship between male dominance and the status quo comes in *A Midsummer Night's Dream*, which begins with a rebellion of the feminine against the power of masculine authority. Hermia refuses the man both Aegeus and Theseus order her to marry; her refusal sends us off into the forest, beyond the power of the father and the masculine state. Once in the forest, of course, we find the social situation metaphorically repeated in this world of imagination and nature. The fairy king, Oberon, rules the forest. His rule, too, is troubled by the rebellion of the feminine. Titania has refused to give him her page, the child of a human friend who died in childbirth. But by the end of the story Titania is conquered, the child relinquished, and order restored. Even here the comic upheavals, whether we see them as May games or bad dreams, are associated with an uprising of women. David P. Young has pointed out how firmly this play connects order with masculine dominance and the disruption of order with the rebellion of the feminine:

> It is appropriate that Theseus, as representative of daylight and right reason, should have subdued his bride-to-be to the rule of his masculine will. That is the natural order of things. It is equally appropriate that Oberon, as king of darkness and fantasy, should have lost control of his wife, and that the corresponding natural disorder described by Titania should ensue.[1]

The natural order, the status quo, is for men to rule women. When they fail to do so, we have the exceptional situation, the festive, disruptive, disorderly moment of comedy.

A Midsummer Night's Dream is actually an anomaly among the festive comedies. It is unusual for the forces of the green world to be directed, as they are here, by a masculine figure. Because the green world here is a partial reproduction of the social world, the feminine is reduced to a kind of first cause of the action while a masculine power directs it. In the other festive comedies the feminine Other presides. She does not *command* the forces of the alternative world, as Oberon does, but since she acts in harmony with these forces her will and desire often prevail.

Where are we to bestow our sympathies? On the forces that make for the disruption of the status quo and therefore for the plot? Or on the force that asserts itself against the disruption and reestablishes a workable social order? Of course we cannot choose. We can only say that in comedy we owe our holiday to such forces as the tendency of the feminine to rebel, whereas to the successful reassertion of masculine power we owe our everyday order. Shakespearean comedy endorses both sides. Holiday is, of course, the subject and the analogue of each play; but the plays always end in a return to everyday life. The optimistic reading of Shakespearean comedy says that everyday life is clarified and enriched by our holiday from it; according to the pessimistic reading the temporary subversion of the social order has revealed how much that order excludes, how high a price we pay for it. But whether our return to everyday life is a comfortable one or not, the return itself is the inevitable conclusion to the journey out.

Does this make the comedies sexist? Is the association of women with the disruption of the social order an unconscious and insulting projection? It seems to begin as such; but as the form of Shakespearean comedy develops, the Otherness of the feminine develops into as powerful a force in the drama as the social authority of the masculine Self. For the feminine in Shakespearean comedy begins as a shrew but develops into a comic heroine. The shrew's rebellion directly challenges masculine authority, whereas the comic heroine merely presides over areas of experience to which masculine authority is irrelevant. But the shrew is essentially powerless against the social system, whereas the comic heroine is in alliance with forces that can never be finally overcome. The shrew is defeated by the superior strength,

---

[1]David P. Young, *Something of Great Constancy* (New Haven, CT: Yale UP, 1966), 183.
hegemony: Overriding authority.

physical and social, of a man, or by women who support the status quo. She provokes a battle of the sexes, and the outcome of this battle, from Shakespeare's point of view, is inevitable. The comic heroine, on the other hand, does not fight the system but merely surfaces, again and again, when and where the social system is temporarily subverted. The comic heroine does not actively resist the social and political hegemony° of the men, but as an irresistible version of the Other she successfully competes for our favor with the (masculine) representatives of the social Self. The development of the feminine from the shrew to the comic heroine indicates a certain consciousness on the author's part of sexual politics; and it indicates a desire, at least, to create conditions of sexual equality within the drama even while reflecting the unequal conditions of men and women in the society at large.

Peter Brook (*b. 1925*)
The Play Is the Message . . .   *1987*

When a distinguished director becomes a critic, we have the opportunity to understand a play from the point of view of one who has to make the play work in front of an audience. Brook's production of A Midsummer Night's Dream *was a sensation in England and the United States in 1970. It featured absolutely white lighting, white sets, and actors in swings. Brook had analyzed the play in such a fashion that he saw love as its constant concern, "constantly repeated." He concluded that to present the play, the players must embody the concept of love. They must bring to the play their own realization of the play's themes — even to the point of seeing theater anew, like the mechanicals "who are touching an extraordinary world with the tips of their fingers, a world which transcends their daily experience and which fills them with wonder"— the effect of the love they bring to their task.*

People have often asked me: "What is the theme of *A Midsummer Night's Dream*?" There is only one answer to that question, the same as one would give regarding a cup. The quality of a cup is its cupness. I say this by way of introduction, to show that if I lay so much stress on the dangers involved in trying to define the themes of the *Dream* it is because too many productions, too many attempts at visual interpretation are based on preconceived ideas, as if these had to be illustrated in some way. In my opinion we should first of all try to rediscover the play as a living thing; then we shall be able to analyze our discoveries. Once I have finished working on the play, I can begin to produce my theories. It was fortunate that I did not attempt to do so earlier because the play would not have yielded up its secrets.

At the center of the *Dream*, constantly repeated, we find the word "love." Everything comes back to this, even the structure of the play, even its music. The quality the play demands from its performers is to build up an atmosphere of love during the performance itself, so that this abstract idea — for the word "love" is in itself a complete abstraction — may become palpable. The play presents us with forms of love which become less and less blurred as it goes on. "Love" soon begins to resound like a musical scale and little by little we are introduced to its various modes and tones.

Love is, of course, a theme which touches all men. No one, not even the most hardened, the coldest, or the most despairing, is insensitive to it, even if he does not know what love is. Either his practical experience confirms its existence or he suffers from its absence, which is another way of recognizing that it exists. At every moment the play touches something which concerns everyone.

As this is theater, there must be conflicts, so this play about love is also a play about the opposite of love, love and its opposite force. We are brought to realize that love, liberty, and imagination are closely connected. Right at the beginning of the play, for example, the father in a long speech tries to obstruct his daughter's love and we are surprised that such a character, apparently a secondary role, should have so long a speech — until we discover the real importance of his words. What he says not only reflects a generation gap (a father opposing his daughter's love because he had intended her for someone else), it also explains the reasons for his feeling of suspicion toward the young man whom his daughter loves. He describes him as an individual prone to fantasy, led by his imagination — an unpardonable weakness in the father's eyes.

From this starting point we see, as in any of Shakespeare's plays, a confrontation. Here it is between love and its opposing qualities, between fantasy and solid common sense — caught in an endless series of mirrors. As usual, Shakespeare confuses the issue. If we asked someone's opinion on the father's point of view, he might say, for example, that "The father is in the wrong because he is against freedom of the imagination," a very widespread attitude today.

In this way, for most present-day audiences, the girl's father comes over as the classical father figure who misunderstands young people and their flights of fancy. But later on, we discover surprisingly that he is right, because the imaginative world in which this lover lives causes him to behave in a quite disgusting way toward the very same daughter: as soon as a drop of liquid falls into his eyes, acting as a drug which liberates natural tendencies, he not only jilts her but his love is transformed into violent hate. He uses words which might well be borrowed from *Measure for Measure,* denouncing the girl with the kind of vehemence that, in the Middle Ages, led people to burn one another at the stake. Yet at the end of the play we are once more in agreement with the Duke, who rejects the father in the name of love. The young man has now been transformed.

So we observe this game of love in a psychological and metaphysical context; we hear Titania's assertion that the opposition between herself and Oberon is fundamental, primordial. But Oberon's acts deny this, for he perceives that within their opposition a reconciliation is possible.

The play covers an extraordinarily broad range of universal forces and feelings in a mythical world, which suddenly changes, in the last part, into high society. We find ourselves back in the very real palace: and the same Shakespeare who, a few pages earlier, offered us a scene of pure fantasy between Titania and Oberon, where it would be absurd to ask prosaic questions like "Where does Oberon live?" or "When describing a queen like Titania did Shakespeare wish to express political ideas?," now takes us into a precise social environment. We are present at the meeting point of two worlds, that of the workmen and the court, the world of wealth and elegance, and alleged sensitivity, the world of people who have had the leisure to cultivate fine sentiments and are now shown as insensitive and even disgusting in their superior attitude toward the poor.

At the beginning of the court scene we see our former heroes, who have spent the entire play involved in the theme of love, and would no doubt be quite capable of giving academic lectures on the subject, suddenly finding themselves plunged into a context which has apparently nothing to do with love (with their own love, since all their problems have been solved). Now they are in the context of a relationship with each other and with another social class, and they are at a loss. They do not realize that here too scorn eliminates love.

We see how well Shakespeare has situated everything. Athens in the *Dream* resembles our Athens in the sixties: the workmen, as they state in the first scene, are very much afraid of the authorities; if they commit the slightest error they will be hanged, and there is nothing comical about that. Indeed, they risk hanging as soon as they shed their anonymity. At the same time they are irresistibly attracted by the carrot of "sixpence a day" which will enable them to escape poverty. Yet their real motive is neither glory nor adventure nor money (that is made very clear and should guide the actors who perform this scene). Those simple men who have only ever worked with their hands apply to the use of the imagination exactly the same quality of love which traditionally underlies the relationship between a craftsman and his tools. That is what gives these scenes both their strength and their comic quality. These craftsmen make efforts which are grotesque in one sense because they push awkwardness to its limit, but at another level they set themselves to their task with such love that the meaning of their clumsy efforts changes before our eyes.

The spectators can easily decide to adopt the same attitude as the courtiers: to find all this quite simply ridiculous; to laugh with the complacency of people who quite confidently mock the efforts of others. Yet the audience is invited to take a step back: to feel it cannot quite identify with the court, with people who are too grand and too unkind. Little by little, we come to see that the craftsmen, who behave with little understanding but who approach their new job with love, are discovering theater — an imaginary world for them, toward which they instinctively feel great respect. In fact, the "mechanicals" scene is often misinterpreted because the actors forget to look at theater through innocent eyes, they take a professional actor's views of good or bad acting, and in so doing they diminish the mystery and the sense of magic felt by these amateurs, who are touching an extraordinary world with the tips of their fingers, a world which transcends their daily experience and which fills them with wonder.

We see this quite clearly in the part of the boy who plays the girl, Thisby. At first sight this tough lad is irresistibly absurd, but by degrees, through his love for what he is doing, we discover what more is involved. In our production, the actor playing the part is a professional plumber, who only took to acting a short while ago. He well understands what is involved, what it means to feel this nameless and shapeless kind of love. This boy, himself new to theater, acts the part of someone who is new to theater. Through his conviction and his identification we discover that these awkward craftsmen, without knowing it, are teaching us a lesson — or it might be preferable to say that a lesson is being taught us through them. These craftsmen are able to make the connection between love for their trade and for a completely different task, whereas the courtiers are not capable of linking the love about which they talk so well with their simple role as spectators.

Nonetheless, little by little the courtiers become involved, even touched by the play within the play, and if one follows very closely what is there in the text we see that for a moment the situation is completely transformed. One of the central images of the play is a wall, which, at a given moment, vanishes. Its disappearance, to which Bottom draws our attention, is caused by an act of love. Shakespeare is showing us how love can pervade a situation and act as a transforming force.

The *Dream* touches lightly on the fundamental question of the transformations which may occur if certain things are better understood. It requires us to reflect on the nature of love. All the landscapes of love are thrown into relief, and we are given a particular social context through which the other situations can be measured. Through the subtlety of its language the play removes all kinds of barriers. It is therefore not a play which provokes resistance, or creates disturbance in the usual sense. Rival politicians could sit side by side at a performance of *A Midsummer Night's Dream* and each leave with the impression that the play fits his point of view perfectly. But if they give it a fine, sensitive attention they cannot fail to perceive a world just like their own, more and more riddled with contradictions and, like their own, waiting for that mysterious force, love, without which harmony will never return.

Clive Barnes (b. 1927)
REVIEW OF *A MIDSUMMER NIGHT'S DREAM*   1970

Clive Barnes's review credits the Peter Brook production of A Midsummer Night's Dream *as a landmark. Audiences in Stratford, London, New York, and elsewhere agreed. Brook (b. 1925) emphasized the dramatic spectacle — the sets, costumes, and action — in such a way as to reveal new depths of emotion. The playfulness of the jugglers, acrobats, and those on the trapezes emphasized the joy and youth of the main characters.*

Once in a while, once in a very rare while, a theatrical production arrives that is going to be talked about as long as there is a theater, a production that, for good or ill, is going to exert a major influence on the contemporary stage. Such a production is Peter Brook's staging of Shakespeare's *A Midsummer Night's Dream*, which the Royal Shakespeare Company introduced here tonight.

It is a magnificent production, the most important work yet of the world's most imaginative and inventive director. If Peter Brook had done nothing else but this "Dream" he would have deserved a place in theater history.

Brook has approached the play with a radiant innocence. He has treated the script as if it had just been written and sent to him through the mail. He has staged it with no reference to the past, no reverence for tradition.

He has stripped the play down, asked exactly what it is about. He has forgotten gossamer fairies, sequined eyelids, gauzy veils, and whole forests of Beerbohm-trees.

He sees the play for what it is — an allegory of sensual love, and a magic playground of lost innocence and hidden fears. Love in Shakespeare comes as suddenly as death, and when Shakespeare's people love they are all but consumed with sexual passion.

Brook's first concern is to enchant us — to reveal this magic playground. He has conceived the production as a box of theatrical miracles. It takes place in a pure-white setting. The stage is walled in on three sides and the floor is also white. Ladders lead up the walls and on the top are scaffolds and rostrums from which actors can look down on the playing area like spectators at a bullfight.

The fairy characters — Oberon, Titania, and Puck — are made into acrobats and jugglers. They swing in on trapezes, they amaze us with juggling tricks, Tarzan-like swings across the stage, all the sad deftness of clowns.

Shakespeare's quartet of mingled lovers, now mod kids humming love songs to loosely strummed guitars, are lost in the Venetian woods. The trees are vast metal coils thrown down from the walls on fishing rods, and moving in on unwary lovers like spiraling metallic tendrils. And in this wood of animal desire the noises are not the friendly warblings of fairyland, but the grunts and groans of some primeval jungle.

Sex and sexuality are vital in the play. Oberon and Titania, even when quarreling, kiss with hasty, hungry passion — no shining moon for them — and the lovers seem to be journeying through some inner landscape of their own desires toward maturity.

The sexual relationships — with the wittiest use of phallic symbolism the stage can have ever seen — is stressed between Titania and her Bottom. Yet the carnality of the piece is seen with affectionate tolerance rather than the bitterness the playwright shows in *Troilus and Cressida,* and this tolerance, even playfulness, suffuses the production.

Brook is a magician and he gives us new eyes. Here, for reasons admirably supported by the text, he has Theseus and Hippolyta (that previously rather dull royal couple whose wedding provides the framework for the play) played by the same actors as play Oberon and Titania. At once the play takes on a new and personal dimension. The fairies take on a new humanity, and these human princelings, once so uninteresting, are now endowed with a different mystery, and the gentle, almost sad note on which the play ends has a feeling of human comprehension and godlike compassion to it. It is most moving.

Two other characters take on dual assignments. Philostrate, that court master of ceremonies for Theseus, is also, naturally enough, Puck, and, rather more puzzlingly, Egeus, the angry father of Hermia, whose opposition to her marriage sets off the action, is also Peter Quince, one of the mechanicals. Presumably the purpose is to bring the play within the play more closely into the main structure, for just as Egeus initiates the real action, so Quince initiates the inner play. But it savors of a literary rather than dramatic device.

Puck is the key figure in this version. Looking like a more than usually perky Picasso clown, he bounces through the action with happy amiability, the model of toleration. John Kane plays him delightfully, performing his tricks with a true circus expertise and acting with unaffected delight.

The Theseus/Oberon and Hippolyta/Titania of Alan Howard and Sara Kestelman are special pleasures, and the mechanicals with the terrible tragedy of *Pyramus and Thisbe* are the best I have ever seen, with David Waller's virile Bottom particularly splendid.

But the star of this dream is Peter Brook himself, with his ideas, his theories, and above all his practices. Of course he is helped — first by the samite-white pleasure palace devised by his Los Angeles–based designer, Sally Jacobs, and the richly evocative music and sound score provided by Richard Peaslee. But Mr. Brook is the genius architect of our most substantial pleasure.

He makes it all so fresh and so much fun. After a riotously funny and bawdy courtship of Titania by Bottom, the two leave the stage to, of all wonderful things, Mendelssohn's Wedding March, and all hell breaks loose, with confetti, paper streamers, and Oberon himself flying in urbane mockery across the stage.

And Brook uses everything to hand — he is defiantly eclectic. It is as though he is challenging the world, by saying that there is no such thing as Shakespearean style. If it suits his purpose he will use a little kathakali, a pop song, sparklers borrowed from a toyshop, dramatic candles borrowed from Grotowski. It is all splendid grist to his splendid mill. Shakespeare can be fun, Shakespeare can be immediate, Shakespeare can most richly live.

OTHELLO

Othello was one of Shakespeare's most popular plays, produced frequently in his lifetime and throughout the seventeenth century. Although the date of composition is uncertain, we do know that the earliest recorded production was November 1, 1604, in the old Banqueting Hall at the court of King James I and his wife, Anne of Denmark. This detail is interesting because it coincides with the later production — during the same winter season and at the same theater — of Ben Jonson's *Masque of Blackness,* which was specifically commissioned by Queen Anne so that she could "paint herself black" along with the ladies in her retinue.

There seems to have been a vogue for blackness in England at the time. A great many Moors — the term, as Shakespeare and others of his time use it, means a dark-skinned person from Africa — were living in England at the end of Queen Elizabeth's reign and the beginning of King James's, the period of both performances. Though her government had given Moors "full diplomatic recognition" as a gesture of thanks for their conquest of England's enemy Spain, in 1601 Queen Elizabeth was so alarmed by the number of blacks in England that she appointed a foreign merchant to transport them from the kingdom. In 1604 a delegation of Arabs visited London, and their customs and style caused some stir, both of admiration and concern. While the color black was symbolically associated by white people with the devil and moral turpitude, and the practice of slavery was already advanced, a number of black African noblemen had traveled to England, and some had returned to Africa as translators and intermediaries in trading expeditions.

Aaron, a Moor in Shakespeare's *Titus Andronicus* (1594), was dark-skinned and a villain. Early on, however, Shakespeare represents black characters in other entertainments as noble. He establishes the noble birth and character of Othello, for instance, who tells us, "I am black" (III, iii, 263). The character of Othello, a general of the Venetian forces, derives from an early Italian story by Geraldi Cinthio published in 1566 in Italian and 1584 in French. Shakespeare might have read either one. He adapted the story, adding new characters, reinterpreting the action, and completely reimagining Othello, Desdemona, and Iago.

The setting, Venice, was exotic for Elizabethan audiences, but it was appropriate for establishing a character who was unusual and something of "the other," as, for example, Shylock was in the earlier *Merchant of Venice* (1596–1597). It was especially felicitous a choice of setting for Othello's generalship because the Venetian republic, by law, had to have a foreigner as general of the armies. No one in the play disputes Othello's leadership and soldiership — not even Iago.

While the play makes great use of the contrasts of black and white, light and dark, evening and day, both to establish mood and to imply moral values, the central action is not devoted to issues relative to Othello's race. The opening scenes reveal that Brabantio, Desdemona's father, and Iago, Othello's ensign, are capable of racial slurs. But each speaks out of anger and disappointment. The official governors of Venice never once imply racial inequity, nor do they condone any disrespect for Othello. Indeed, they support him in his marriage once they hear Desdemona indicate her willing choice of Othello as her mate.

The dramatic action centers on Iago's bitter disappointment at having been passed over for promotion in favor of Cassio, whom he regards as an inexperienced boy. Cassio is well enough regarded by Othello and others to end the play as governor of Mauritania, the country in northwest Africa that was settled by Berbers and from which the name Moors is derived. Even if Cassio was preferred because he was the intermediary between Othello and Desdemona, and even though he has the weakness of sometimes being an unsoldierly drunk, he proves more worthy than the villainous Iago, who virtually personifies the devil. At the end of the play, Othello, understanding how terribly he has been betrayed, wishes to look at Iago's foot to see if, like the devil's, it is cleft.

In some productions of the play, Iago almost steals the show. His soliloquies indicating how he will manipulate the characters to achieve his evil ends are so powerful as to chill an audience. He seems to be the force driving the action, while Othello struggles like a fly in the web of his deceit. Yet Othello is the great character in the drama. He rises majestically to deliver some of the greatest speeches Shakespeare ever wrote. Eventually, his initial innocence is replaced by rage and anger. Iago purposely infects Othello with jealousy, implying that his young, new wife Desdemona is dallying with Cassio. He offers "ocular proof" but proof that would not be convincing if Othello were not anxious to be convinced. Iago moves Othello from a contented man — a soldier at peace with himself — to a deracinated jealous husband.

Watching the progress of that action rivets the audience. Seeing how the villain Iago improvises at every turn to take advantage of each opportunity to present false "evidence" fascinates audience and reader alike. Ironically, the symbolism of blackness is reversed in Iago, whose inner soul is dark and hell bound, while Othello is led to commit a heinous crime whose horror he ultimately recognizes. He pays with his own death by his own hand. Our sympathy is with him at the end of the play, despite his moments of frightening anger and horror. He has been used by a lesser man, and what has permitted him to be deceived — as interpreted by some critics — is his essential innocence and goodness.

Among the patterns of imagery in the play, those connected with animals — such as the pig, the barbary horse, and the black ram — support Iago's efforts to emphasize Othello's bestiality. When he claims that Othello and Desdemona are "making the beast with two backs," he wishes to enlist Brabantio's aid in humiliating Othello and perhaps damaging his reputation with the Duke of Venice. The careful manipulation of this imagery helps Iago forward his plan even before he knows what it is.

Othello himself stands as one of the towering figures in Shakespeare's works, challenging actors in his own day and in ours. Desdemona may be faulted for her willfulness in marrying without her father's knowledge or permission — at the time a grave infraction. But the audience forgives her if only because it is obvious that nothing she could have said would have convinced her father to look kindly on Othello as a son-in-law. And while passion is at the core of the play, it may not have been passion alone that caused her to act as she did.

Othello in Performance

The first recorded production of *Othello* was November 1604 at the court of King James. But public performances probably were held at the Globe Theatre sometime that year or the following. Although no reliable performance records are available, we know that the play was produced by Shakespeare's company, The King's Men, both at the Globe in April 1610 and in Oxford in September of the same year. It was performed again in 1629, 1635, and 1636. It was popular in the eighteenth and nineteenth centuries as well as in the twentieth century and is among Shakespeare's most produced plays.

The first Othello was Richard Burbage, Shakespeare's finest actor in one of his finest roles. He wore Elizabethan clothes with no special effort to adopt a Moorish costume. We have no record of his makeup, and the only eyewitness account describes him as a "grieved Moor." However, judging from the tradition maintained up to 1709, when we have a portrait of Othello, we can assume he was played as a black man. The play enjoyed such popularity that it constantly attracted the most gifted actors of the day.

The nineteenth century produced several notable Othellos, but it also saw the beginning of a trend in which Othello became "tawny" rather than black. He became what was then known as a "white Moor." Edmund Kean, the greatest actor of his day, portrayed Othello in this fashion to extraordinary acclaim. The first black actor to play Othello was Ira Aldridge, an American on the London stage in the nineteenth century.

In modern times, two productions stand out as milestones: Paul Robeson's in New York in 1943–1944 and Laurence Olivier's in London in 1964. Robeson was known as a great singer but had performed onstage in Eugene O'Neill's *The Emperor Jones* prior to *Othello*. His physical presence on stage was striking in every way, especially when linked with his commanding voice. Martin Wine describes him as the "outstanding 'romantic' Othello of our time," by which he means a sympathetic and moving Othello. The Broadway production played for more performances than nearly any American production of Shakespeare up to that time. James Earl Jones, who played the role many years later, was in the audience and felt that Robeson's command of the concept of honor was singular and has never been approached since.

Laurence Olivier had himself made up not just as a black man but as a black African. Some critics were impressed by the achievement, but others felt it was still difficult to accept the idea of a white actor in the part. Yet Olivier's version was taut, powerful, and one of his greatest achievements. He took comfort in the fact that Shakespeare wrote the role for a white actor and did not worry over the shift in tradition. Martin Wine described his performance as "the most controversial" performance of our time. Olivier's interpretation was of an egotistical Othello, one who was tormented by neurotic tendencies and even a touch of paranoia. Olivier's Othello was less a man of the Renaissance than a man of modern times.

Most modern productions have made use of effective lighting, emphasizing the opening darkness of the drama. They also make use of simple staging, using archways effectively and suggestions of buildings, ships and sails, and sometimes Moorish architectural details.

William Shakespeare (1564–1616)
OTHELLO THE MOOR OF VENICE

1604

The Names of the Actors

OTHELLO, THE MOOR
BRABANTIO, [*a Venetian senator,*] *father to Desdemona*
CASSIO, *an honorable lieutenant* [*to Othello*]
IAGO, [*Othello's ancient,*] *a villain*
RODERIGO, *a gulled gentleman*
DUKE OF VENICE
SENATORS [*of Venice*]
MONTANO, *governor of Cyprus*
LODOVICO AND GRATIANO, [*kinsmen to Brabantio,*]
   two noble Venetians
SAILORS
CLOWNS
DESDEMONA, *wife to Othello*
EMILIA, *wife to Iago*
BIANCA, *a courtesan*
[MESSENGER, HERALD, OFFICERS, VENETIAN
   GENTLEMEN, MUSICIANS, ATTENDANTS

Scene: Venice and Cyprus]

ACT I • Scene I

A street in Venice.

Enter Roderigo and Iago.

RODERIGO: Tush, never tell me! I take it much
   unkindly
   That thou, Iago, who hast had my purse
   As if the strings were thine, shouldst know of this.°
IAGO: 'Sblood,° but you'll not hear me!
5   If ever I did dream of such a matter,
   Abhor me.
RODERIGO: Thou told'st me thou didst hold him in thy
   hate.
IAGO: Despise me if I do not. Three great ones of the
   city,
   In personal suit to make me his lieutenant,
10   Off-capped to him;° and, by the faith of man,
   I know my price; I am worth no worse a place.
   But he, as loving his own pride and purposes,
   Evades them with a bombast circumstance,°
   Horribly stuffed with epithets of war;
15   [And, in conclusion,]
   Nonsuits° my mediators; for, "Certes," says he,

"I have already chose my officer."
And what was he?
Forsooth, a great arithmetician,°
One Michael Cassio, a Florentine   20
(A fellow almost damned in a fair wife°)
That never set a squadron in the field,
Nor the division of a battle knows
More than a spinster; unless the bookish theoric,
Wherein the togèd consuls can propose   25
As masterly as he. Mere prattle without practice
Is all his soldiership. But he, sir, had th' election;
And I (of whom his eyes had seen the proof
At Rhodes, at Cyprus, and on other grounds
Christian and heathen) must be belee'd and calmed° 30
By debitor and creditor; this counter-caster,°
He, in good time, must his lieutenant be,
And I — God bless the mark! — his Moorship's
   ancient.°
RODERIGO: By heaven, I rather would have been his
   hangman.
IAGO: Why, there's no remedy; 'tis the curse of service. 35
   Preferment goes by letter and affection,°
   And not by old gradation, where each second
   Stood heir to th' first. Now, sir, be judge yourself,
   Whether I in any just term am affined°
   To love the Moor.
RODERIGO: I would not follow him then.   40
IAGO: O, sir, content you;
   I follow him to serve my turn upon him.
   We cannot all be masters, nor all masters
   Cannot be truly followed. You shall mark
   Many a duteous and knee-crooking knave   45
   That, doting on his own obsequious bondage,
   Wears out his time, much like his master's ass,
   For naught but provender; and when he's old,
   cashiered.°
   Whip me such honest knaves! Others there are
   Who, trimmed° in forms and visages of duty,   50
   Keep yet their hearts attending on themselves;
   And, throwing but shows of service on their lords,
   Do well thrive by them, and when they have lined
   their coats,
   Do themselves homage. These fellows have some
   soul;

---

19. arithmetician: Theoretician.   **21. almost . . . wife:** (An obscure allusion; Cassio is unmarried, but see IV, I, 115–16). **30. belee'd and calmed:** Left in the lurch.   **31. counter-caster:** Bookkeeper.   **33. ancient:** Ensign.   **36. affection:** Favoritism. **39. affined:** Obliged.   **48. cashiered:** Turned off.   **50. trimmed:** Dressed up.

I, I. 3. this: I.e., Desdemona's elopement.   **5. 'Sblood:** By God's blood.   **10. him:** I.e., Othello.   **13. a bombast circumstance:** Pompous circumlocution.   **16. Nonsuits:** Rejects.

55   And such a one do I profess myself. For, sir,
        It is as sure as you are Roderigo,
        Were I the Moor, I would not be Iago.
        In following him, I follow but myself;
        Heaven is my judge, not I for love and duty,
60   But seeming so, for my peculiar end;
        For when my outward action doth demonstrate
        The native act and figure of my heart°
        In compliment extern,° 'tis not long after
        But I will wear my heart upon my sleeve
65   For daws to peck at; I am not what I am.
        RODERIGO: What a full fortune does the thick-lips°
            owe°
        If he can carry't thus!
        IAGO: Call up her father,
        Rouse him. Make after him, poison his delight,
        Proclaim him in the streets. Incense his kinsmen,
70   And though he in a fertile climate dwell,
        Plague him with flies; though that his joy be joy,
        Yet throw such changes of vexation on't
        As it may lose some color.
        RODERIGO: Here is her father's house. I'll call aloud.
75   IAGO: Do, with like timorous° accent and dire yell
        As when, by night and negligence, the fire
        Is spied in populous cities.
        RODERIGO: What, ho, Brabantio! Signior Brabantio,
            ho!
        IAGO: Awake! What, ho, Brabantio! Thieves! thieves!
            thieves!
80   Look to your house, your daughter, and your bags!
        Thieves! thieves!

Brabantio at a window.°

        BRABANTIO (*above*): What is the reason of this terrible
            summons?
        What is the matter there?
        RODERIGO: Signior, is all your family within?
        IAGO: Are your doors locked?
85   BRABANTIO: Why, wherefore ask you this?
        IAGO: Zounds, sir, y' are robbed! For shame, put on
            your gown!
        Your heart is burst; you have lost half your soul.
        Even now, now, very now, an old black ram
        Is tupping your white ewe. Arise, arise!
90   Awake the snorting° citizens with the bell.
        Or else the devil will make a grandsire of you.
        Arise, I say!
        BRABANTIO: What, have you lost your wits?
        RODERIGO: Most reverend signior, do you know my
            voice?
95   BRABANTIO: Not I. What are you?
        RODERIGO: My name is Roderigo.

BRABANTIO: The worser welcome!
        I have charged thee not to haunt about my doors.
        In honest plainness thou hast heard me say
        My daughter is not for thee; and now, in madness,
        Being full of supper and distemp'ring draughts,   100
        Upon malicious knavery dost thou come
        To start my quiet.
        RODERIGO: Sir, sir, sir —
        BRABANTIO: But thou must needs be sure
        My spirit and my place have in them power   105
        To make this bitter to thee.
        RODERIGO: Patience, good sir.
        BRABANTIO: What tell'st thou me of robbing? This is
            Venice;
        My house is not a grange.°
        RODERIGO: Most grave Brabantio,
        In simple and pure soul I come to you.
        IAGO: Zounds, sir, you are one of those that will not   110
        serve God if the devil bid you. Because we come to do
        you service, and you think we are ruffians, you'll
        have your daughter covered with a Barbary horse;
        you'll have your nephews° neigh to you; you'll have
        coursers for cousins, and gennets for germans.°   115
        BRABANTIO: What profane wretch art thou?
        IAGO: I am one, sir, that comes to tell you your daughter
        and the Moor are now making the beast with two
        backs.
        BRABANTIO: Thou are a villain.
        IAGO: You are — a senator.   120
        BRABANTIO: This thou shalt answer. I know thee,
            Roderigo.
        RODERIGO: Sir, I will answer anything. But I beseech
            you,
        If't be your pleasure and most wise consent,
        As partly I find it is, that your fair daughter,
        At this odd-even° and dull watch o' th' night,   125
        Transported, with no worse nor better guard
        But with a knave of common hire, a gondolier,
        To the gross clasps of a lascivious Moor —
        If this be known to you, and your allowance,°
        We then have done you bold and saucy wrongs;   130
        But if you know not this, my manners tell me
        We have your wrong rebuke. Do not believe
        That, from the sense° of all civility,
        I thus would play and trifle with your reverence.
        Your daughter, if you have not given her leave,   135
        I say again, hath made a gross revolt,
        Tying her duty, beauty, wit, and fortunes
        In an extravagant and wheeling° stranger
        Of here and everywhere. Straight satisfy yourself.
        If she be in her chamber, or your house,   140
        Let loose on me the justice of the state
        For thus deluding you.

---

62. **The . . . heart:** What I really believe and intend.   63. **compliment extern:** Outward appearance.   66. **thick-lips:** An Elizabethan epithet for blacks, including Moors.   **owe:** Own.
75. **timorous:** Terrifying.   [s.d.] *Brabantio at a window:* (Added from quarto).   90. **snorting:** Snoring.

108. **grange:** Isolated farmhouse.   114. **nephews:** I.e., grandsons.
115. **gennets for germans:** Spanish horses for near kinsmen.
125. **odd-even:** Between night and morning.   129. **allowance:** Approval.   133. **from the sense:** In violation.   138. **extravagant and wheeling:** Expatriate and roving.

BRABANTIO: Strike on the tinder, ho!
　　Give me a taper! Call up all my people!
　　This accident° is not unlike my dream.
145　Belief of it oppresses me already.
　　Light, I say! light!   *Exit* [*above*].
IAGO: Farewell, for I must leave you.
　　It seems not meet, nor wholesome to my place,
　　To be produced — as, if I stay, I shall —
　　Against the Moor. For I do know the state,
150　However this may gall him with some check,°
　　Cannot with safety cast° him; for he's embarked
　　With such loud reason to the Cyprus wars,
　　Which even now stand in act,° that for their souls
　　Another of his fathom° they have none
155　To lead their business; in which regard,
　　Though I do hate him as I do hell-pains,
　　Yet, for necessity of present life,
　　I must show out a flag and sign of love,
　　Which is indeed but sign. That you shall surely find
　　　him,
160　Lead to the Sagittary° the raisèd search;
　　And there will I be with him. So farewell.   *Exit.*

Enter [*below*] *Brabantio in his nightgown,° and Servants
with torches.*

BRABANTIO: It is too true an evil. Gone she is;
　　And what's to come of my despisèd time
　　Is naught but bitterness. Now, Roderigo,
165　Where didst thou see her? — O unhappy girl! —
　　With the Moor, say'st thou? — Who would be a
　　　father? —
　　How didst thou know 'twas she! — O, she deceives
　　　me
　　Past thought! — What said she to you? — Get moe°
　　　tapers!
　　Raise all my kindred! — Are they married, think
　　　you?
170　RODERIGO: Truly I think they are.
BRABANTIO: O heaven! How got she out? O treason of
　　　the blood!
　　Fathers, from hence trust not your daughters' minds
　　By what you see them act. Is there not charms
　　By which the property° of youth and maidhood
175　May be abused? Have you not read, Roderigo,
　　Of some such thing?
RODERIGO: Yes, sir, I have indeed.
BRABANTIO: Call up my brother. — O, would you had
　　　had her! —
　　Some one way, some another. — Do you know
　　Where we may apprehend her and the Moor?
180　RODERIGO: I think I can discover him, if you please
　　To get good guard and go along with me.
BRABANTIO: I pray you lead on. At every house I'll call;

I may command at most. — Get weapons, ho!
And raise some special officers of night. —
On, good Roderigo; I'll deserve° your pains.   185
　　　　　　　　　　　　　　　　　Exeunt.

Scene II

Before the lodgings of Othello.

Enter Othello, Iago, and Attendants with torches.

IAGO: Though in the trade of war I have slain men,
　　Yet do I hold it very stuff o' th' conscience
　　To do no contrived murther. I lack iniquity
　　Sometimes to do me service. Nine or ten times
　　I had thought t' have yerked° him here under the
　　　ribs.   5
OTHELLO: 'Tis better as it is.
IAGO: Nay, but he prated,
　　And spoke such scurvy and provoking terms
　　Against your honor
　　That with the little godliness I have
　　I did full hard forbear him. But I pray you, sir,   10
　　Are you fast° married? Be assured of this,
　　That the magnifico° is much beloved,
　　And hath in his effect a voice potential°
　　As double° as the Duke's. He will divorce you,
　　Or put upon you what restraint and grievance   15
　　The law, with all his might to enforce it on,
　　Will give him cable.
OTHELLO: Let him do his spite.
　　My services which I have done the signiory°
　　Shall out-tongue his complaints. 'Tis yet to
　　　know° —
　　Which, when I know that boasting is an honor,   20
　　I shall promulgate — I fetch my life and being
　　From men of royal siege;° and my demerits°
　　May speak unbonneted to as proud a fortune
　　As this that I have reached.° For know, Iago,
　　But that I love the gentle Desdemona,   25
　　I would not my unhousèd° free condition
　　Put into circumscription and confine
　　For the sea's worth. But look what lights come
　　　yond?
IAGO: Those are the raisèd father and his friends.
　　You were best go in.
OTHELLO: Not I; I must be found.   30
　　My parts, my title, and my perfect soul°
　　Shall manifest me rightly. Is it they?
IAGO: By Janus, I think no.

---

144. **accident:** Occurrence.　150. **check:** Reprimand.　151. **cast:**
Discharge.　153. **stand in act:** Are going on.　154. **fathom:**
Capacity.　160. **Sagittary:** An inn.　[S.D.] *nightgown:* Dress-
ing gown.　168. **moe:** More.　174. **property:** Nature.

185. **deserve:** Show gratitude for.　**I, II. 5. yerked:** Stabbed.
11. **fast:** Securely.　12. **magnifico:** Grandee (Brabantio).
13. **potential:** Powerful.　14. **double:** Doubly influential.
18. **signiory:** Venetian government.　19. **yet to know:** Still
not generally known.　22. **siege:** Rank.　**demrits:** Deserts.
24. **May speak . . . reached:** Are equal, I modestly assert, to
those of Desdemona's family.　26. **unhousèd:** Unrestrained.
31. **perfect soul:** Stainless conscience.

Enter Cassio, with torches, Officers.

OTHELLO: The servants of the Duke, and my
          lieutenant.
35   The goodness of the night upon you, friends!
       What is the news?
CASSIO: The Duke does greet you, general;
       And he requires your haste-post-haste appearance
       Even on the instant.
OTHELLO: What's the matter, think you?
CASSIO: Something from Cyprus, as I may divine.
40   It is a business of some heat. The galleys
       Have sent a dozen sequent° messengers
       This very night at one another's heels,
       And many of the consuls, raised and met,
       Are at the Duke's already. You have been hotly
          called for;
45   When, being not at your lodging to be found,
       The Senate hath sent about three several quests
       To search you out.
OTHELLO: 'Tis well I am found by you.
       I will but spend a word here in the house,
       And go with you.   [*Exit*]
CASSIO: Ancient, what makes he here?
50 IAGO: Faith, he to-night hath boarded a land carack.°
       If it prove lawful prize, he's made for ever.
CASSIO: I do not understand.
IAGO: He's married.
CASSIO: To who?

[*Enter Othello.*]

IAGO: Marry, to — Come, captain, will you go?
OTHELLO: Have
          with you.
CASSIO: Here comes another troop to seek for you.

*Enter Brabantio, Roderigo, and others with lights and
weapons.*

55 IAGO: It is Brabantio. General, be advised.
       He comes to bad intent.
OTHELLO: Holla! stand there!
RODERIGO: Signior, it is the Moor.
BRABANTIO: Down with him, thief!

[*They draw on both sides.*]

IAGO: You, Roderigo! Come, sir, I am for you.
OTHELLO: Keep up° your bright swords, for the dew
       will rust them.
60   Good signior, you shall more command with years
       Than with your weapons.
BRABANTIO: O thou foul thief, where hast thou stowed
          my daughter?
       Damned as thou art, thou hast enchanted her!
       For I'll refer me to all things of sense,
65   If she in chains of magic were not bound,
       Whether a maid so tender, fair, and happy,

So opposite to marriage that she shunned
The wealthy curlèd darlings of our nation,
Would ever have, t' incur a general mock,
Run from her guardage to the sooty bosom   70
Of such a thing as thou — to fear, not to delight.
Judge me the world if 'tis not gross in sense°
That thou hast practiced on her with foul charms,
Abused her delicate youth with drugs or minerals
That weaken motion.° I'll have't disputed on;   75
'Tis probable, and palpable to thinking.
I therefore apprehend and do attach° thee
For an abuser of the world, a practicer
Of arts inhibited and out of warrant.
Lay hold upon him. If he do resist,   80
Subdue him at his peril.
OTHELLO: Hold your hands,
Both you of my inclining and the rest.
Were it my cue to fight, I should have known it
Without a prompter. Where will you that I go
To answer this your charge?
BRABANTIO: To prison, till fit time   85
Of law and course of direct session°
Call thee to answer.
OTHELLO: What if I do obey?
How may the Duke be therewith satisfied,
Whose messengers are here about my side
Upon some present business of the state   90
To bring me to him?
OFFICER: 'Tis true, most worthy signior.
The Duke's in council, and your noble self
I am sure is sent for.
BRABANTIO: How? The Duke in council?
In this time of the night? Bring him away.
Mine's not an idle° cause. The Duke himself,   95
Or any of my brothers of the state,
Cannot but feel this wrong as 'twere their own;
For if such actions may have passage free,
Bondslaves and pagans shall our statesmen be.
                                        Exeunt.

Scene III

The Venetian Senate Chamber.

*Enter Duke and Senators, set at a table, with lights and
Attendants.*

DUKE: There is no composition° in these news
       That gives them credit.
1. SENATOR: Indeed they are disproportioned.
       My letters say a hundred and seven galleys.
DUKE: And mine a hundred forty.
2. SENATOR: And mine two hundred.
       But though they jump° not on a just account —   5

---

41. **sequent:** Consecutive. 50. **carack:** Treasure ship. 59. **Keep
up:** I.e., sheath.

72. **gross in sense:** Obvious. 75. **motion:** Perception. 77. **attach:** Arrest. 86. **direct session:** Regular trial. 95. **idle:** Trifling. I, III. 1. **composition:** Consistency. 5. **jump:** Agree.

As in these cases where the aim° reports
'Tis oft with difference — yet do they all confirm
A Turkish fleet, and bearing up to Cyprus.
DUKE: Nay, it is possible enough to judgment.
10   I do not so secure me° in the error
But the main article° I do approve°
In fearful sense.
SAILOR (*within*):   What, ho! what, ho! what, ho!
OFFICER: A messenger from the galleys.

Enter Sailor.

DUKE: Now, what's the business?
SAILOR: The Turkish preparation makes for Rhodes.
15   So was I bid report here to the state
By Signior Angelo.
DUKE: How say you by this change?
1. SENATOR: This cannot be
By no assay° of reason. 'Tis a pageant
To keep us in false gaze.° When we consider
20   Th' importancy of Cyprus to the Turk,
And let ourselves again but understand
That, as it more concerns the Turk than Rhodes,
So may he with more facile question bear° it,
For that it stands not in such warlike brace,°
25   But altogether lacks th' abilities
That Rhodes is dressed in — if we make thought of
      this,
We must not think the Turk is so unskillful
To leave that latest which concerns him first,
Neglecting an attempt of ease and gain
30   To wake and wage° a danger profitless.
DUKE: Nay, in all confidence, he's not for Rhodes.
OFFICER: Here is more news.

Enter a Messenger.

MESSENGER: The Ottomites, reverend and gracious,
Steering with due course toward the isle of Rhodes,
35   Have there injointed them with an after fleet.
1. SENATOR: Ay, so I thought. How many, as you guess?
MESSENGER: Of thirty sail; and now they do restem°
Their backward course, bearing with frank
      appearance
Their purposes toward Cyprus, Signior Montano,
40   Your trusty and most valiant servitor,
With his free duty recommends you thus,
And prays you to believe him.
DUKE: 'Tis certain then for Cyprus.
Marcus Luccicos,° is not he in town?
45   1. SENATOR: He's now in Florence.
DUKE: Write from us to him; post, post-haste dispatch.
1. SENATOR: Here comes Brabantio and the valiant
      Moor.

6. **aim:** Conjecture.   10. **so secure me:** Take such comfort.
11. **article:** Substance.   **approve:** Accept.   18. **assay:** Test.
19. **in false gaze:** Looking the wrong way.   23. **with . . .
bear:** More easily capture.   24. **brace:** Posture of defense.
30. **wake and wage:** Rouse and risk.   37. **restem:** Steer again.
44. **Marcus Luccicos:** (Presumably a Venetian envoy).

*Enter Brabantio, Othello, Cassio, Iago, Roderigo, and
Officers.*

DUKE: Valiant Othello, we must straight employ you
Against the general enemy Ottoman.

[*To Brabantio.*]

I did not see you. Welcome, gentle signior.   50
We lacked your counsel and your help to-night.
BRABANTIO: So did I yours. Good your grace, pardon
      me.
Neither my place, nor aught I heard of business,
Hath raised me from my bed; nor doth the general
      care
Take hold on me; for my particular grief   55
Is of so floodgate° and o'erbearing nature
That it engluts° and swallows other sorrows,
And it is still itself.
DUKE: Why, what's the matter?
BRABANTIO: My daughter! O, my daughter!
ALL: Dead?
BRABANTIO: Ay, to me.
She is abused, stol'n from me, and corrupted   60
By spells and medicines bought of mountebanks;
For nature so prepost'rously to err,
Being not deficient,° blind, or lame of sense,
Sans witchcraft could not.
DUKE: Whoe'er he be that in this foul proceeding   65
Hath thus beguiled your daughter of herself,
And you of her, the bloody book of law
You shall yourself read in the bitter letter
After your own sense; yea, though our proper° son
Stood in your action.°
BRABANTIO: Humbly I thank your grace.   70
Here is the man — this Moor, whom now, it seems,
Your special mandate for the state affairs
Hath hither brought.
ALL: We are very sorry for't.
DUKE [*to Othello*]: What, in your own part, can you
      say to this?
BRABANTIO: Nothing, but this is so.   75
OTHELLO: Most potent, grave, and reverend signiors,
My very noble, and approved° good masters,
That I have ta'en away this old man's daughter,
It is most true; true I have married her.
The very head and front of my offending   80
Hath this extent, no more. Rude° am I in my
      speech,
And little blessed with the soft phrase of peace;
For since these arms of mine had seven years' pith°
Till now some nine moons wasted, they have used
Their dearest action in the tented field;   85
And little of this great world can I speak
More than pertains to feats of broil and battle;

56. **floodgate:** Torrential.   57. **engluts:** Devours.   63. **deficient:** Feeble-minded.   69. **our proper:** My own.   70. **Stood
in your action:** Were accused by you.   77. **approved:** Tested by
experience.   81. **Rude:** Unpolished.   83. **pith:** Strength.

And therefore little shall I grace my cause
In speaking for myself. Yet, by your gracious
   patience,
90   I will a round° unvarnished tale deliver
Of my whole course of love — what drugs, what
   charms,
What conjuration, and what mighty magic
(For such proceeding am I charged withal)
I won his daughter.
BRABANTIO: A maiden never bold;
95   Of spirit so still and quiet that her motion
Blushed° at herself; and she — in spite of nature,
Of years, of country, credit, everything —
To fall in love with what she feared to look on!
It is a judgment maimed and most imperfect
100   That will confess perfection so could err
Against all rules of nature, and must be driven
To find out practices° of cunning hell
Why this should be. I therefore vouch° again
That with some mixtures pow'rful o'er the blood,°
105   Or with some dram, conjured to this effect,
He wrought upon her.
DUKE: To vouch this is no proof,
Without more certain and more overt test
Than these thin habits° and poor likelihoods
Of modern seeming° do prefer against him.
110   1. SENATOR: But, Othello, speak.
Did you by indirect and forcèd° courses
Subdue and poison this young maid's affections?
Or came it by request, and such fair question°
As soul to soul affordeth?
OTHELLO: I do beseech you,
115   Send for the lady to the Sagittary
And let her speak of me before her father.
If you do find me foul in her report,
The trust, the office, I do hold of you
Not only take away, but let your sentence
Even fall upon my life.
120   DUKE: Fetch Desdemona hither.
OTHELLO: Ancient, conduct them; you best know the
   place.

             Exit [*Iago, with*] *two or three* [*Attendants*].

And till she come, as truly as to heaven
I do confess the vices of my blood,
So justly to your grave ears I'll present
125   How I did thrive in this fair lady's love,
And she in mine.
DUKE: Say it, Othello.
OTHELLO: Her father loved me, oft invited me;
Still° questioned me the story of my life
130   From year to year — the battles, sieges, fortunes

That I have passed.
I ran it through, even from my boyish days
To th' very moment that he bade me tell it.
Wherein I spoke of most disastrous chances,
Of moving accidents by flood and field;   135
Of hairbreadth scapes i' th' imminent deadly
   breach;
Of being taken by the insolent foe
And sold to slavery; of my redemption thence
And portance° in my travels' history;
Wherein of anters° vast and deserts idle,   140
Rough quarries, rocks, and hills whose heads touch
   heaven,
It was my hint° to speak — such was the process;
And of the Cannibals that each other eat,
The Anthropophagi,° and men whose heads
Do grow beneath their shoulders. This to hear   145
Would Desdemona seriously incline;
But still the house affairs would draw her thence;
Which ever as she could with haste dispatch,
She'ld come again, and with a greedy ear
Devour up my discourse. Which I observing,   150
Took once a pliant° hour, and found good means
To draw from her a prayer of earnest heart
That I would all my pilgrimage dilate,°
Whereof by parcels° she had something heard,
But not intentively.° I did consent,   155
And often did beguile her of her tears
When I did speak of some distressful stroke
That my youth suffered. My story being done,
She gave me for my pains a world of sighs.
She swore, i' faith, 'twas strange, 'twas passing
   strange;   160
'Twas pitiful, 'twas wondrous pitiful.
She wished she had not heard it; yet she wished
That heaven had made her such a man. She thanked
   me;
And bade me, if I had a friend that loved her,
I should but teach him how to tell my story,   165
And that would woo her. Upon this hint° I spake.
She loved me for the dangers I had passed,
And I loved her that she did pity them.
This only is the witchcraft I have used.
Here comes the lady. Let her witness it.   170

Enter Desdemona, Iago, Attendants.

DUKE: I think this tale would win my daughter too.
   Good Brabantio,
Take up this mangled matter at the best.
Men do their broken weapons rather use
Than their bare hands.
BRABANTIO: I pray you hear her speak.   175

---

90. **round:** Plain.   95–96. **her motion Blushed:** Her own emotions caused her to blush.   102. **practices:** Plots.   103. **vouch:** Assert.   104. **blood:** Passions.   108. **thin habits:** Slight appearances.   109. **modern seeming:** Everyday supposition. 111. **forcèd:** Violent.   113. **question:** Conversation.   129. **Still:** Continually.

139. **portance:** Behavior.   140. **anters:** Caves.   142. **hint:** Occasion.   144. **Anthropophagi:** Man-eaters.   151. **pliant:** Propitious.   153. **dilate:** Recount in full.   154. **parcels:** Portions.   155. **intentively:** With full attention.   166. **hint:** Opportunity.

If she confess that she was half the wooer,
Destruction on my head if my bad blame
Light on the man! Come hither, gentle mistress.
Do you perceive in all this noble company
Where most you owe obedience?
180 DESDEMONA: My noble father,
I do perceive here a divided duty.
To you I am bound for life and education;°
My life and education° both do learn me
How to respect you: you are the lord of duty;
185 I am hitherto your daughter. But here's my husband;
And so much duty as my mother showed
To you, preferring you before her father,
So much I challenge° that I may profess
Due to the Moor my lord.
BRABANTIO: God be with you! I have done.
190 Please it your grace, on to the state affairs.
I had rather to adopt a child than get° it.
Come hither, Moor.
I here do give thee that with all my heart
Which, but thou hast already, with all my heart
195 I would keep from thee. For your sake,° jewel,
I am glad at soul I have no other child;
For thy escape° would teach me tyranny,
To hang clogs on them. I have done, my lord.
DUKE: Let me speak like yourself° and lay a sentence°
200 Which, as a grise° or step, may help these lovers
[Into your favor.]
When remedies are past, the griefs are ended
By seeing the worst, which late on hopes depended.
To mourn a mischief that is past and gone
205 Is the next way to draw new mischief on.
What cannot be preserved when fortune takes,
Patience her injury a mock'ry makes.
The robbed that smiles steals something from the thief;
He robs himself that spends a bootless grief.
210 BRABANTIO: So let the Turk of Cyprus us beguile:
We lose it not so long as we can smile.
He bears the sentence well that nothing bears
But the free comfort which from thence he hears;
But he bears both the sentence and the sorrow
215 That to pay grief must of poor patience borrow.
These sentences, to sugar, or to gall,
Being strong on both sides, are equivocal.
But words are words. I never yet did hear
That the bruised heart was piercèd through the ear.
220 Beseech you, now to the affairs of state.
DUKE: The Turk with a most mighty preparation makes
for Cyprus. Othello, the fortitude° of the place is best
known to you; and though we have there a substi-
tute of most allowed° sufficiency, yet opinion,° a more

sovereign mistress of effects, throws a more safer   225
voice on you. You must therefore be content to slub-
ber° the gloss of your new fortunes with this more
stubborn and boist'rous expedition.
OTHELLO: The tyrant custom, most grave senators,
Hath made the flinty and steel couch of war   230
My thrice-driven bed of down. I do agnize
A natural and prompt alacrity
I find in hardness;° and do undertake
These present wars against the Ottomites.
Most humbly, therefore, bending to your state,   235
I crave fit disposition for my wife,
Due reference of place, and exhibition,°
With such accommodation and besort°
As levels° with her breeding.
DUKE: If you please,
Be't at her father's.
BRABANTIO: I will not have it so.   240
OTHELLO: Nor I.
DESDEMONA: Nor I. I would not there reside,
To put my father in impatient thoughts
By being in his eye. Most gracious Duke,
To my unfolding lend your prosperous° ear,   245
And let me find a charter in your voice,
T' assist my simpleness.°
DUKE: What would you, Desdemona?
DESDEMONA: That I did love the Moor to live with
        him,
My downright violence, and storm of fortunes,   250
May trumpet to the world. My heart's subdued
Even to the very quality of my lord.
I saw Othello's visage in his mind,
And to his honors and his valiant parts
Did I my soul and fortunes consecrate.   255
So that, dear lords, if I be left behind,
A moth of peace, and he go to the war,
The rites for which I love him are bereft me,
And I a heavy interim shall support
By his dear absence. Let me go with him.   260
OTHELLO: Let her have your voice.
Vouch with me, heaven, I therefore beg it not
To please the palate of my appetite,
Not to comply with heat° — the young affects°
In me defunct — and proper satisfaction;   265
But to be free and bounteous to her mind;
And heaven defend your good souls that you think
I will your serious and great business scant
When she is with me. No, when light-winged toys
Of feathered Cupid seel° with wanton dullness   270
My speculative and officed instruments,°

182. education: Upbringing.   189. challenge: Claim the right.
191. get: Beget.   195. For your sake: Because of you.   197. escape: Escapade.   199. like yourself: As you should.   sentence:
Maxim.   200. grise: Step.   222. fortitude: Fortification.
224. allowed: Acknowledged.   opinion: Public opinion.

227. slubber: Sully.   231–33. agnize . . . hardness: Recognize
in myself a natural and easy response to hardship.   237. exhibition: Allowance of money.   238. besort: Suitable company.
239. levels: Corresponds.   245. prosperous: Favorable.
247. simpleness: Lack of skill.   264. heat: Passions.   young
affects: Tendencies of youth.   270. seel: Blind.   271. My . . .
instruments: My perceptive and responsible faculties.

That° my disports corrupt and taint my business,
Let housewives make a skillet of my helm,
And all indign° and base adversities
275   Make head against my estimation!°
DUKE: Be it as you shall privately determine,
  Either for her stay or going. Th' affair cries haste,
  And speed must answer it.
1. SENATOR: You must away to-night.
OTHELLO: With all my heart.
280 DUKE: At nine i' th' morning here we'll meet again.
  Othello, leave some officer behind,
  And he shall our commission bring to you,
  With such things else of quality and respect
  As doth import° you.
OTHELLO: So please your grace, my ancient;
285   A man he is of honesty and trust
  To his conveyance I assign my wife,
  With what else needful your good grace shall
     think
  To be sent after me.
DUKE: Let it be so.
  Good night to every one.
    [*To Brabantio.*]   And, noble signior,
290 If virtue no delighted° beauty lack,
  Your son-in-law is far more fair than black.
1. SENATOR: Adieu, brave Moor. Use Desdemona well.
BRABANTIO: Look to her, Moor, if thou hast eyes to see:
  She has deceived her father, and may thee.

      Exeunt [*Duke, Senators, Officers, etc.*].

295 OTHELLO: My life upon her faith! — Honest Iago,
  My Desdemona must I leave to thee.
  I prithee let thy wife attend on her,
  And bring them after in the best advantage.°
  Come, Desdemona. I have but an hour
300 Of love, of worldly matters and direction,
  To spend with thee. We must obey the time.

      Exit Moor and Desdemona.

RODERIGO: Iago, —
IAGO: What say'st thou, noble heart?
RODERIGO: What will I do, think'st thou?
305 IAGO: Why, go to bed and sleep.
RODERIGO: I will incontinently° drown myself.
IAGO: If thou dost, I shall never love thee after. Why,
  thou silly gentleman!
RODERIGO: It is silliness to live when to live is torment;
310   and then have we a prescription to die when death is
  our physician.
IAGO: O villainous! I have looked upon the world for
  four times seven years; and since I could distinguish
  betwixt a benefit and an injury, I never found man
315   that knew how to love himself. Ere I would say I

would drown myself for the love of a guinea hen, I
would change my humanity with a baboon.
RODERIGO: What should I do? I confess it is my shame
  to be so fond, but it is not in my virtue to amend it.
IAGO: Virtue? a fig! 'Tis in ourselves that we are thus or 320
  thus. Our bodies are our gardens, to which our wills
  are gardeners; so that if we will plant nettles or sow
  lettuce, set hyssop and weed up thyme, supply it with
  one gender° of herbs or distract it with many —
  either to have it sterile with idleness or manured with 325
  industry — why, the power and corrigible authority°
  of this lies in our wills. If the balance of our lives had
  not one scale of reason to poise° another of sensuality, the blood and baseness° of our natures would
  conduct us to most preposterous conclusions. But we 330
  have reason to cool our raging motions,° our carnal
  strings, our unbitted° lusts; whereof I take this that
  you call love to be a sect or scion.°
RODERIGO: It cannot be.
IAGO: It is merely a lust of the blood and a permission of 335
  the will. Come, be a man! Drown thyself? Drown
  cats and blind puppies! I have professed me thy
  friend, and I confess me knit to thy deserving with
  cables of perdurable toughness. I could never better
  stead thee than now. Put money in thy purse. Follow 340
  thou the wars; defeat thy favor° with an usurped
  beard. I say, put money in thy purse. It cannot be that
  Desdemona should long continue her love to the
  Moor — put money in thy purse — nor he his to her.
  It was a violent commencement in her, and thou shalt 345
  see an answerable sequestration° — put but money
  in thy purse. These Moors are changeable in their
  wills — fill thy purse with money. The food that to
  him now is as luscious as locusts shall be to him
  shortly as bitter as coloquintida.° She must change 350
  for youth: when she is sated with his body, she will
  find the error of her choice. [She must have change,
  she must.] Therefore put money in thy purse. If thou
  wilt needs damn thyself, do it a more delicate way
  than drowning. Make° all the money thou canst. If 355
  sanctimony and a frail vow betwixt an erring° barbarian and a supersubtle Venetian be not too hard
  for my wits and all the tribe of hell, thou shalt enjoy
  her. Therefore make money. A pox of drowning thyself! 'Tis clean out of the way. Seek thou rather to 360
  be hanged in compassing thy joy than to be drowned
  and go without her.
RODERIGO: Wilt thou be fast to my hopes, if I depend on
  the issue?
IAGO: Thou art sure of me. Go, make money. I have told 365
  thee often, and I retell thee again and again, I hate the

---

272. **That:** So that.   274. **indign:** Unworthy.   275. **estimation:** Reputation.   284. **import:** Concern.   290. **delighted:** Delightful.   298. **in the best advantage:** At the best opportunity.   306. **incontinently:** Forthwith.

324. **gender:** Species.   326. **corrigible authority:** Corrective power.   328. **poise:** Counterbalance.   329. **blood and baseness:** Animal instincts.   331. **motions:** Appetites.   332. **unbitted:** Uncontrolled.   333. **sect or scion:** Offshoot, cutting.   341. **defeat thy favor:** Spoil thy appearance.   346. **sequestration:** Estrangement.   350. **coloquintida:** A medicine.   355. **Make:** Raise.   356. **erring:** Wandering.

Moor. My cause is hearted;° thine hath no less rea-
son. Let us be conjunctive in our revenge against him.
If thou canst cuckold him, thou dost thyself a plea-
370 sure, me a sport. There are many events in the womb
of time, which will be delivered. Traverse,° go, pro-
vide thy money! We will have more of this tomorrow.
Adieu.
RODERIGO: Where shall we meet i' th' morning?
375 IAGO: At my lodging.
RODERIGO: I'll be with thee betimes.
IAGO: Go to, farewell — Do you hear, Roderigo?
[RODERIGO: What say you?
IAGO: No more of drowning, do you hear?
380 RODERIGO: I am changed.
IAGO: Go to, farewell. Put money enough in your
    purse.]
RODERIGO: I'll sell all my land.   *Exit.*
IAGO: Thus do I ever make my fool my purse;
    For I mine own gained knowledge should profane
385 If I would time expend with such a snipe°
    But for my sport and profit. I hate the Moor;
    And it is thought abroad that 'twixt my sheets
    H'as done my office. I know not if't be true;
    But I, for mere suspicion in that kind,
390 Will do as if for surety. He holds me well;°
    The better shall my purpose work on him.
    Cassio's a proper man. Let me see now:
    To get his place, and to plume up° my will
    In double knavery — How, how? — Let's see: —
395 After some time, to abuse Othello's ears
    That he is too familiar with his wife.
    He hath a person and a smooth dispose°
    To be suspected — framed to make women false.
    The Moor is of a free° and open nature
400 That thinks men honest that but seem to be so;
    And will as tenderly be led by th' nose
    As asses are.
    I have't! It is engend'red! Hell and night
    Must bring this monstrous birth to the world's light.
                                Exit.

ACT II • *Scene* I

An open place in Cyprus, near the harbor.

Enter Montano and two Gentlemen.

MONTANO: What from the cape can you discern at sea?
1. GENTLEMAN: Nothing at all: it is a high-wrought
    flood.
    I cannot 'twixt the heaven and the main
    Descry a sail.
5 MONTANO: Methinks the wind hath spoke aloud at land;

A fuller blast ne'er shook our battlements.
    If it hath ruffianed so upon the sea,
    What ribs of oak, when mountains melt on them,
    Can hold the mortise?° What shall we hear of this?
2. GENTLEMAN: A segregation° of the Turkish fleet.   10
    For do but stand upon the foaming shore,
    The chidden billow seems to pelt the clouds;
    The wind-shaked surge, with high and monstrous
        mane,
    Seems to cast water on the burning Bear
    And quench the Guards° of th' ever-fixèd pole.°   15
    I never did like molestation° view
    On the enchafèd flood.
MONTANO: If that the Turkish fleet
    Be not ensheltered and embayed, they are drowned;
    It is impossible to bear it out.

Enter a third Gentleman.

3. GENTLEMAN: News, lads! Our wars are done.   20
    The desperate tempest hath so banged the Turks
    That their designment halts.° A noble ship of Venice
    Hath seen a grievous wrack and sufferance°
    On most part of their fleet.
MONTANO: How? Is this true?
3. GENTLEMAN: The ship is here put in,   25
    A Veronesa;° Michael Cassio,
    Lieutenant to the warlike Moor Othello,
    Is come on shore; the Moor himself at sea,
    And is in full commission here for Cyprus.
MONTANO: I am glad on't. 'Tis a worthy governor.   30
3. GENTLEMAN: But his same Cassio, though he speak
    of comfort
    Touching the Turkish loss, yet he looks sadly
    And prays the Moor be safe, for they were parted
    With foul and violent tempest.
MONTANO: Pray heaven he be;
    For I have served him, and the man commands   35
    Like a full soldier. Let's to the seaside, ho!
    As well to see the vessel that's come in
    As to throw out our eyes for brave Othello,
    Even till we make the main and th' aerial blue
    An indistinct regard.°
3. GENTLEMAN: Come, let's do so;   40
    For every minute is expectancy
    Of more arrivance.

Enter Cassio.

CASSIO: Thanks, you the valiant of this warlike isle,
    That so approve the Moor! O, let the heavens
    Give him defense against the elements,   45
    For I have lost him on a dangerous sea!
MONTANO: Is he well shipped?

---

367. **My cause is hearted:** My heart is in it.   371. **Traverse:** Forward march.   385. **snipe:** Fool.   390. **well:** In high regard.
393. **plume up:** Gratify.   397. **dispose:** Manner.   399. **free:**
Frank.

II, I. 9. **hold the mortise:** Hold their joints together.   10. **segregation:** Scattering.   15. **Guards:** Stars near the North Star.
pole: Polestar.   16. **molestation:** Tumult.   22. **designment halts:**
Plan is crippled.   23. **sufferance:** Disaster.   26. **Veronesa:**
Ship furnished by Verona.   40. **An indistinct regard:** Indistinguishable.

CASSIO: His bark is stoutly timbered, and his pilot
    Of very expert and approved allowance;
50   Therefore my hopes, not surfeited to death,°
    Stand in bold cure.°
       (*Within.*)   A sail, a sail, a sail!

Enter a messenger.

CASSIO: What noise?
MESSENGER: The town is empty; on the brow o' th' sea
    Stand ranks of people, and they cry "A sail!"
55 CASSIO: My hopes do shape him for the governor.

A shot.

2. GENTLEMAN: They do discharge their shot of
    courtesy:
    Our friends at least.
CASSIO: I pray you, sir, go forth
    And give us truth who 'tis that is arrived.
2. GENTLEMAN: I shall.   *Exit.*
MONTANO: But, good lieutenant, is your general
60   wived?
CASSIO: Most fortunately. He hath achieved a maid
    That paragons° description and wild fame;
    One that excels the quirks° of blazoning° pens,
    And in th' essential vesture of creation
    Does tire the ingener.°

Enter Second Gentleman.

65   How now? Who has put in?
2. GENTLEMAN: 'Tis one Iago, ancient to the general.
CASSIO: H'as had most favorable and happy speed:
    Tempests themselves, high seas, and howling winds,
    The guttered° rocks and congregated sands,
70   Traitors ensteeped° to clog the guiltless keel,
    As having sense of beauty, do omit
    Their mortal° natures, letting go safely by
    The divine Desdemona.
MONTANO: What is she?
CASSIO: She that I spake of, our great captain's captain,
75   Left in the conduct of the bold Iago,
    Whose footing° here anticipates our thoughts
    A se'nnight's° speed. Great Jove, Othello guard,
    And swell his sail with thine own pow'rful breath,
    That he may bless this bay with his tall ship,
80   Make love's quick pants in Desdemona's arms,
    Give renewed fire to our extincted spirits,
    [And bring all Cyprus comfort!]

*Enter Desdemona, Iago, Roderigo, and Emilia [with
Attendants].*

                O, behold!

---

50. **surfeited to death:** Overindulged. 51. **in bold cure:** A good
chance of fulfillment. 62. **paragons:** Surpasses. 63. **quirks:**
Ingenuities. **blazoning:** Describing. 64–65. **And . . . ingener:**
Merely to describe her as God made her exhausts her praiser.
69. **guttered:** Jagged. 70. **ensteeped:** Submerged. 72. **mortal:** Deadly. 76. **footing:** Landing. 77. **se'nnight's:** Week's.

    The riches of the ship is come on shore!
    You men of Cyprus, let her have your knees.°
    Hail to thee, lady! and the grace of heaven, 85
    Before, behind thee, and on every hand,
    Enwheel thee round!
DESDEMONA: I thank you, valiant Cassio.
    What tidings can you tell me of my lord?
CASSIO: He is not yet arrived; nor know I aught
    But that he's well and will be shortly here. 90
DESDEMONA: O but I fear! How lost you company?
CASSIO: The great contention of the sea and skies
    Parted our fellowship.
       (*Within.*)   A sail, a sail! [*A shot.*]
                      But hark. A sail!
2. GENTLEMAN: They give their greeting to the citadel;
    This likewise is a friend.
CASSIO: See for the news. 95

                 [*Exit Gentleman.*]

    Good ancient, you are welcome.
    [*To Emilia.*]   Welcome, mistress. —
    Let it not gall your patience, good Iago,
    That I extend my manners. 'Tis my breeding
    That gives me this bold show of courtesy.

[*Kisses Emilia.*°]

IAGO: Sir, would she give you so much of her lips 100
    As of her tongue she oft bestows on me,
    You would have enough.
DESDEMONA: Alas, she has no speech!
IAGO: In faith, too much.
    I find it still when I have list to sleep.
    Marry, before your ladyship, I grant, 105
    She puts her tongue a little in her heart
    And chides with thinking.
EMILIA: You have little cause to say so.
IAGO: Come on, come on! You are pictures out of
    doors,
    Bells in your parlors, wildcats in your kitchens, 110
    Saints in your injuries, devils being offended,
    Players in your housewifery,° and housewives° in
    your beds.
DESDEMONA: O, fie upon thee, slanderer!
IAGO: Nay, it is true, or else I am a Turk:
    You rise to play, and go to bed to work. 115
EMILIA: You shall not write my praise.
IAGO: No, let me out.
DESDEMONA: What wouldst thou write of me, if thou
    shouldst praise me?
IAGO: O gentle lady, do not put me to't,
    For I am nothing if not critical.
DESDEMONA: Come on, assay.° — There's one gone to
    the harbor? 120

---

84. **knees:** I.e., kneeling. [S.D.] *Kisses Emilia:* (Kissing was a
common Elizabethan form of social courtesy). 112. **housewifery:** Housekeeping. **housewives:** Hussies. 120. **assay:** Try.

IAGO: Ay, madam.

DESDEMONA: I am not merry; but I do beguile
    The thing I am by seeming otherwise. —
    Come, how wouldst thou praise me?

125 IAGO: I am about it; but indeed my invention
    Comes from my pate as birdlime° does from
        frieze° —
    It plucks out brains and all. But my Muse labors,
    And thus she is delivered:
    If she be fair and wise, fairness and wit —
130   The one's for use, the other useth it.

DESDEMONA: Well praised! How if she be black° and
    witty?

IAGO: If she be black, and thereto have a wit,
    She'll find a white that shall her blackness fit.

DESDEMONA: Worse and worse!

135 EMILIA: How if fair and foolish?

IAGO: She never yet was foolish that was fair,
    For even her folly° helped her to an heir.

DESDEMONA: These are old fond° paradoxes to make
    fools laugh i' th' alehouse. What miserable praise
140   hast thou for her that's foul° and foolish?

IAGO: There's none so foul, and foolish thereunto,
    But does foul pranks which fair and wise ones do.

DESDEMONA: O heavy ignorance! Thou praisest the
    worst best. But what praise couldst thou bestow on a
145   deserving woman indeed — one that in the authority
    of her merit did justly put on the vouch° of very mal-
    ice itself?

IAGO: She that was ever fair, and never proud;
    Had tongue at will, and yet was never loud;
150   Never lacked gold, and yet went never gay;
    Fled from her wish, and yet said "Now I may";
    She that, being ang'red, her revenge being nigh,
    Bade her wrong stay, and her displeasure fly;
    She that in wisdom never was so frail
155   To change the cod's head for the salmon's tail;°
    She that could think, and ne'er disclose her mind;
    See suitors following, and not look behind:
    She was a wight (if ever such wight were) —

DESDEMONA: To do what?

160 IAGO: To suckle fools and chronicle small beer.°

DESDEMONA: O most lame and impotent conclusion!
    Do not learn of him, Emilia, though he be thy hus-
    band. How say you, Cassio? Is he not a most profane
    and liberal° counsellor?

165 CASSIO: He speaks home,° madam. You may relish him
    more in the soldier than in the scholar.

IAGO [*aside*]: He takes her by the palm. Ay, well said,
    whisper! With as little a web as this will I ensnare as

great a fly as Cassio. Ay, smile upon her, do! I will
gyve thee in thine own courtship.° — You say true; 170
'tis so, indeed! — If such tricks as these strip you out
of your lieutenantry, it had been better you had not
kissed your three fingers so oft — which now again
you are most apt to play the sir° in. Very good! well
kissed! an excellent courtesy! 'Tis so, indeed. Yet 175
again your fingers to your lips? Would they were
clyster pipes° for your sake! (*Trumpet within.*) The
Moor! I know his trumpet.

CASSIO: 'Tis truly so.

DESDEMONA: Let's meet him and receive him. 180

CASSIO: Lo, where he comes.

Enter Othello and Attendants.

OTHELLO: O my fair warrior!

DESDEMONA: My dear Othello!

OTHELLO: It gives me wonder great as my content
    To see you here before me. O my soul's joy!
    If after every tempest come such calms, 185
    May the winds blow till they have wakened death!
    And let the laboring bark climb hills of seas
    Olympus-high, and duck again as low
    As hell's from heaven! If it were now to die,
    'Twere now to be most happy;° for I fear 190
    My soul hath her content so absolute
    That not another comfort like to this
    Succeeds in unknown fate.

DESDEMONA: The heavens forbid
    But that our loves and comforts should increase
    Even as our days do grow.

OTHELLO: Amen to that, sweet powers! 195
    I cannot speak enough of this content;
    It stops me here; it is too much of joy.
    And this, and this, the greatest discords be

They kiss.

    That e'er our hearts shall make!

IAGO [*aside*]:   O, you are well
        tuned now!
    But I'll set down° the pegs that make this music, 200
    As honest as I am.

OTHELLO: Come, let us to the castle.
    News, friends! Our wars are done; the Turks are
        drowned.
    How does my old acquaintance of this isle? —
    Honey, you shall be well desired° in Cyprus;
    I have found great love amongst them. O my sweet, 205
    I prattle out of fashion, and I dote
    In mine own comforts. I prithee, good Iago,
    Go to the bay and disembark my coffers.
    Bring thou the master° to the citadel;

---

126. **birdlime:** A sticky paste. **freize:** Rough cloth.
131. **black:** Brunette. 137. **folly:** Wantonness. 138. **fond:**
Foolish. 140. **foul:** Ugly. 146. **put on the vouch:** Compel
the approval. 155. **To . . . tail:** I.e., to exchange the good for
the poor but expensive. 160. **chronicle small beer:** Keep petty
household accounts. 164. **profane and liberal:** Worldly and
licentious. 165. **home:** Bluntly.

170. **gyve . . . courtship:** Manacle you by means of your
courtly manners. 174. **sir:** Courtly gentleman. 177. **clyster
pipes:** Syringes. 190. **happy:** Fortunate. 200. **set down:**
Loosen. 204. **well desired:** Warmly welcomed. 209. **master:**
Ship captain.

Sir Laurence Olivier as Othello and
Maggie Smith as Desdemona in a tense
moment in his National Theatre
production of *Othello* in London, 1964.

John Douglas Thomas as Othello and
Jennifer Mudge Tucker as Desdemona in
the Trinity Repertory production of
Othello, Providence, Rhode Island, 1998.

210 He is a good one, and his worthiness
Does challenge° much respect. — Come,
            Desdemona,
Once more well met at Cyprus.

            Exit Othello [with all but Iago and Roderigo].

IAGO: [*to an Attendant, who goes out*]: Do thou meet
me presently at the harbor. [*To Roderigo.*] Come
215 hither. If thou be'st valiant (as they say base men
being in love have then a nobility in their natures
more than is native to them), list me. The lieutenant
to-night watches on the court of guard.° First, I must
tell thee this: Desdemona is directly in love with him.
220 RODERIGO: With him? Why, 'tis not possible.
IAGO: Lay thy finger thus,° and let thy soul be instructed.
Mark me with what violence she first loved the
Moor, but for bragging and telling her fantastical
lies; and will she love him still for prating? Let not
225 thy discreet heart think it. Her eye must be fed; and
what delight shall she have to look on the devil?
When the blood is made dull with the act of sport,
there should be, again to inflame it, and to give satiety a fresh appetite, loveliness in favor, sympathy in
230 years, manners, and beauties; all which the Moor is
defective in. Now for want of these required conveniences,° her delicate tenderness will find itself
abused, begin to heave the gorge,° disrelish and
abhor the Moor. Very nature will instruct her in it
235 and compel her to some second choice. Now, sir, this
granted — as it is a most pregnant° and unforced
position — who stands so eminent in the degree of
this fortune as Cassio does? A knave very voluble; no
further conscionable° than in putting on the mere
240 form of civil and humane° seeming for the better
compassing of his salt° and most hidden loose affection? Why, none! why, none! A slipper° and subtle
knave; a finder-out of occasions; that has an eye can
stamp and counterfeit advantages, though true advan-
245 tage never present itself; a devilish knave! Besides,
the knave is handsome, young, and hath all those
requisites in him that folly and green minds look
after. A pestilent complete knave! and the woman
hath found him already.
250 RODERIGO: I cannot believe that in her; she's full of
most blessed condition.°
IAGO: Blessed fig's-end! The wine she drinks is made of
grapes. If she had been blessed, she would never have
loved the Moor. Blessed pudding! Didst thou not see
255 her paddle with the palm of his hand? Didst not
mark that?
RODERIGO: Yes, that I did; but that was but courtesy.

IAGO: Lechery, by this hand! an index and obscure
prologue to the history of lust and foul thoughts.
They met so near with their lips that their breaths 260
embraced together. Villainous thoughts, Roderigo!
When these mutualities° so marshal the way, hard at
hand comes the master and main exercise, th' incor-
porate° conclusion. Pish! But, sir, be you ruled by me:
I have brought you from Venice. Watch you to-night; 265
for the command, I'll lay't upon you. Cassio knows
you not. I'll not be far from you: do you find some
occasion to anger Cassio, either by speaking too
loud, or tainting° his discipline, or from what other
course you please which the time shall more favor- 270
ably minister.
RODERIGO: Well.
IAGO: Sir, he's rash and very sudden in choler,° and haply
with his truncheon may strike at you. Provoke him
that he may; for even out of that will I cause these of 275
Cyprus to mutiny; whose qualification° shall come
into no true taste° again but by the displanting of
Cassio. So shall you have a shorter journey to your
desires by the means I shall then have to prefer°
them; and the impediment most profitably removed 280
without the which there were no expectation of our
prosperity.
RODERIGO: I will do this if you can bring it to any
opportunity.
IAGO: I warrant thee. Meet me by and by at the citadel; I 285
must fetch his necessaries ashore. Farewell.
RODERIGO: Adieu.   *Exit.*
IAGO: That Cassio loves her, I do well believe't;
That she loves him, 'tis apt° and of great credit.
The Moor, howbeit that I endure him not, 290
Is of a constant, loving, noble nature,
And I dare think he'll prove to Desdemona
A most dear husband. Now I do love her too;
Not out of absolute lust, though peradventure
I stand accountant° for as great a sin, 295
But partly led to diet° my revenge,
For that I do suspect the lusty Moor
Hath leaped into my seat; the thought whereof
Doth, like a poisonous mineral, gnaw my inwards;
And nothing can or shall content my soul 300
Till I am evened with him, wife for wife;
Or failing so, yet that I put the Moor
At least into a jealousy so strong
That judgment cannot cure. Which thing to do,
If this poor trash of Venice, whom I trash° 305
For° his quick hunting, stand the putting on,°
I'll have our Michael Cassio on the hip,°

---

262. mutualities: Exchanges.   **263–64. incorporate:** Carnal.
269. tainting: Discrediting.   **273. sudden in choler:** Violent in
anger.   **276. qualification:** Appeasement.   **277. true taste:**
Satisfactory state.   **279. prefer:** Advance.   **289. apt:** Probable.
295. accountant: Accountable.   **296. diet:** Feed.   **305. I trash:**
I weight down (in order to keep under control).   **306. For:** In
order to develop.   **stand the putting on:** Responds to my incit-
ing.   **307. on the hip:** At my mercy.

---

211. challenge: Deserve.   **218. court of guard:** Headquarters.
221. thus: I.e., on your lips.   **231–32. conveniences:** Compati-
bilities.   **233. heave the gorge:** Be nauseated.   **236. pregnant:**
Evident.   **239. conscionable:** Conscientious.   **240. humane:**
Polite.   **241. salt:** Lecherous.   **242. slipper:** Slippery.
251. condition: Character.

Abuse him to the Moor in the rank garb°
(For I fear Cassio with my nightcap too),
310   Make the Moor thank me, love me, and reward me
For making him egregiously an ass
And practicing upon° his peace and quiet
Even to madness. 'Tis here, but yet confused:
Knavery's plain face is never seen till used.   *Exit.*

Scene II

A street in Cyprus.

Enter Othello's Herald, with a proclamation.

HERALD: It is Othello's pleasure, our noble and valiant
general, that, upon certain tidings now arrived,
importing the mere perdition° of the Turkish fleet,
every man put himself into triumph; some to dance,
5   some to make bonfires, each man to what sport and
revels his addiction leads him. For, besides these beneficial news, it is the celebration of his nuptial. So
much was his pleasure should be proclaimed. All
offices° are open, and there is full liberty of feasting
10   from the present hour of five till the bell have told
eleven. Heaven bless the isle of Cyprus and our noble
general Othello!   *Exit.*

Scene III

The Cyprian Castle.

Enter Othello, Desdemona, Cassio, and Attendants.

OTHELLO: Good Michael, look you to the guard to-
night.
Let's teach ourselves that honorable stop,
Not to outsport discretion.
CASSIO: Iago hath direction what to do;
5   But not withstanding, with my personal eye
Will I look to't.
OTHELLO: Iago is most honest.
Michael, good night. To-morrow with your earliest
Let me have speech with you.
    [*To Desdemona.*]   Come, my dear love.
The purchase made, the fruits are to ensue;
10   That profit's yet to come 'tween me and you. —
Good night.

            Exit [*Othello with Desdemona and Attendants*].

Enter Iago.

CASSIO: Welcome, Iago. We must to the watch.
IAGO: Not this hour, lieutenant; 'tis not yet ten o' th'
clock. Our general cast° us thus early for the love of

his Desdemona; who let us not therefore blame. He   15
hath not yet made wanton the night with her, and she
is sport for Jove.
CASSIO: She's a most exquisite lady.
IAGO: And, I'll warrant her, full of game.
CASSIO: Indeed, she's a most fresh and delicate creature.   20
IAGO: What an eye she has! Methinks it sounds a parley
to provocation.
CASSIO: An inviting eye; and yet methinks right modest.
IAGO: And when she speaks, is it not an alarum to love?
CASSIO: She is indeed perfection.   25
IAGO: Well, happiness to their sheets! Come, lieutenant,
I have a stoup° of wine, and here without are a brace
of Cyprus gallants that would fain have a measure to
the health of black Othello.
CASSIO: Not to-night, good Iago. I have very poor and   30
unhappy brains for drinking; I could well wish courtesy would invent some other custom of entertain-
ment.
IAGO: O, they are our friends. But one cup! I'll drink for
you.   35
CASSIO: I have drunk but one cup to-night, and that was
craftily qualified° too; and behold what innovation°
it makes here. I am unfortunate in the infirmity and
dare not task my weakness with any more.
IAGO: What, man! 'Tis a night of revels: the gallants de-   40
sire it.
CASSIO: Where are they?
IAGO: Here at the door; I pray you call them in.
CASSIO: I'll do't, but it dislikes me.   *Exit.*
IAGO: If I can fasten but one cup upon him   45
With that which he hath drunk to-night already,
He'll be as full of quarrel and offense
As my young mistress' dog. Now my sick fool
    Roderigo,
Whom love hath turned almost the wrong side out,
To Desdemona hath to-night caroused   50
Potations pottle-deep;° and he's to watch.
Three lads of Cyprus — noble swelling spirits,
That hold their honors in a wary distance,°
The very elements° of this warlike isle —
Have I to-night flustered with flowing cups,   55
And they watch too. Now, 'mongst this flock of
    drunkards
Am I to put our Cassio in some action
That may offend the isle.

Enter Cassio, Montano, and Gentlemen [*; Servants following with wine*].

                        But here they come.
If consequence do but approve my dream,
My boat sails freely, both with wind and stream.   60
CASSIO: 'Fore God, they have given me a rouse° already.

---

308. **rank garb:** Gross manner.   312. **practicing upon:** Plot-
ting against.   II, II. 3. **mere perdition:** Complete destruction.
9. **offices:** Kitchens and storerooms.   II, III. 14. **cast:** Dismissed.

27. **stoup:** Two-quart tankard.   37. **qualified:** Diluted.   **innovation:** Disturbance.   51. **pottle-deep:** Bottoms up.   53. **That
. . . distance:** Very sensitive about their honor.   54. **very elements:** True representatives.   61. **rouse:** Bumper.

MONTANO: Good faith, a little one; not past a pint, as I
   am a soldier.
IAGO: Some wine, ho!
   [*Sings.*]
65   And let me the canakin clink, clink;
   And let me the canakin clink
      A soldier's a man;
      A life's but a span,
   Why then, let a soldier drink.
70   Some wine, boys!
CASSIO: 'Fore God, an excellent song!
IAGO: I learned it in England, where indeed they are most
   potent in potting. Your Dane, your German, and your
   swag-bellied Hollander — Drink, ho! — are nothing
75   to your English.
CASSIO: Is your Englishman so expert in his drinking?
IAGO: Why, he drinks you with facility your Dane dead
   drunk; he sweats not to overthrow your Almain; he
   gives your Hollander a vomit ere the next pottle can
80   be filled.
CASSIO: To the health of our general!
MONTANO: I am for it, lieutenant, and I'll do you
   justice.
IAGO: O sweet England!
   [*Sings.*]
85   King Stephen was a worthy peer;
      His breeches cost him but a crown;
   He held 'em sixpence all too dear,
      With that he called the tailor lown.°
   He was a wight of high renown,
90   And thou art but of low degree.
   'Tis pride that pulls the country down;
      Then take thine auld cloak about thee.
   Some wine, ho!
CASSIO: 'Fore God, this is a more exquisite song than
95   the other.
IAGO: Will you hear't again?
CASSIO: No, for I hold him to be unworthy of his place
   that does those things.° Well, God's above all; and
   there be souls must be saved, and there be souls must
100   not be saved.
IAGO: It's true, good lieutenant.
CASSIO: For mine own part — no offense to the general,
   nor any man of quality — I hope to be saved.
IAGO: And so do I too, lieutenant.
105   CASSIO: Ay but, by your leave, not before me. The lieutenant is to be saved before the ancient. Let's have no
   more of this; let's to our affairs. — God forgive us
   our sins! — Gentlemen, let's look to our business. Do
   not think, gentlemen, I am drunk. This is my ancient;
110   this is my right hand, and this is my left. I am not
   drunk now. I can stand well enough, and I speak well
   enough.
ALL: Excellent well!
CASSIO: Why, very well then. You must not think then
115   that I am drunk.   *Exit.*

88. **lown:** Rascal.   98. **does . . . things:** I.e., behaves in this
fashion.

MONTANO: To th' platform, masters. Come, let's set the
   watch.
IAGO: You see this fellow that is gone before.
   He's a soldier fit to stand by Caesar
   And give direction; and do but see his vice.
   'Tis to his virtue a just equinox,°   120
   The one as long as th' other. 'Tis pity of him.
   I fear the trust Othello puts him in,
   On some odd time of his infirmity,
   Will shake this island.
MONTANO: But is he often thus?
IAGO: 'Tis evermore his prologue to his sleep: 125
   He'll watch the horologe a double set°
   If drink rock not his cradle.
MONTANO: It were well
   The general were put in mind of it.
   Perhaps he sees it not, or his good nature
   Prizes the virtue that appears in Cassio   130
   And looks not on his evils. Is not this true?

Enter Roderigo.

IAGO [*aside to him*]: How now, Roderigo?
   I pray you after the lieutenant, go!   *Exit Roderigo.*
MONTANO: And 'tis great pity that the noble Moor
   Should hazard such a place as his own second   135
   With one of an ingraft° infirmity.
   It were an honest action to say
   So to the Moor.
IAGO: Not I, for this fair island!
   I do love Cassio well and would do much
   To cure him of this evil.
      (*Within:* Help! help!)
                           But hark! What noise?   140

Enter Cassio, driving in Roderigo.

CASSIO: Zounds, you rogue! you rascal!
MONTANO: What's the matter, lieutenant?
CASSIO: A knave to
   teach me my duty?
   I'll beat the knave into a twiggen° bottle.
RODERIGO: Beat me?
CASSIO: Dost thou prate, rogue?

[*Strikes him.*]

MONTANO: Nay, good lieutenant!

[*Stays him.*]

   I pray you, sir, hold your hand.
CASSIO: Let me go, sir,   145
   Or I'll knock you o'er the mazzard.°
MONTANO: Come, come,
   you're drunk!
CASSIO: Drunk?

They fight.

120. **just equinox:** Exact equivalent.   126. **watch . . . set:** Stay
awake twice around the clock.   136. **ingraft:** I.e., ingrained.
143. **twiggen:** Wicker-covered.   146. **mazzard:** Head.

IAGO [*aside to Roderigo*]: Away, I say! Go out and cry
    a mutiny!   *Exit Roderigo.*
    Nay, good lieutenant. God's will, gentlemen!
    Help, ho! — lieutenant — sir — Montano — sir —
150   Help, masters! — Here's a goodly watch indeed!

A bell rung.

    Who's that which rings the bell? Diablo, ho!
    The town will rise.° God's will, lieutenant, hold!
    You'll be shamed for ever.

Enter Othello and Gentlemen with weapons.

OTHELLO: What is the matter here?
MONTANO: Zounds, I bleed still. I am hurt to th' death.

He dies.

155 OTHELLO: Hold for your lives!
IAGO: Hold, hold! Lieutenant — sir — Montano —
    gentlemen!
    Have you forgot all sense of place and duty?
    Hold! The general speaks to you. Hold, for shame!
OTHELLO: Why, how now ho? From whence ariseth
    this?
160   Are we turned Turks, and to ourselves do that
    Which heaven hath forbid the Ottomites?
    For Christian shame put by this barbarous brawl!
    He that stirs next to carve for° his own rage
    Holds his soul light; he dies upon his motion.
165   Silence that dreadful bell! It frights the isle
    From her propriety.° What is the matter, masters?
    Honest Iago, that looks dead with grieving,
    Speak. Who began this? On thy love, I charge thee.
IAGO: I do not know. Friends all, but now, even now,
170   In quarter,° and in terms like bride and groom
    Devesting them for bed; and then, but now —
    As if some planet had unwitted men —
    Swords out, and tilting one at other's breast
    In opposition bloody. I cannot speak
175   Any beginning to this peevish odds,°
    And would in action glorious I had lost
    Those legs that brought me to a part of it!
OTHELLO: How comes it, Michael, you are thus
    forgot?
CASSIO: I pray you pardon me; I cannot speak.
OTHELLO: Worthy Montano, you were wont to be
180   civil;
    The gravity and stillness of your youth
    The world hath noted, and your name is great
    In months of wisest censure.° What's the matter
    That you unlace° your reputation thus
185   And spend your rich opinion° for the name
    Of a night-brawler? Give me answer to it.
MONTANO: Worthy Othello, I am hurt to danger.
    Your officer, Iago, can inform you,

    While I spare speech, which something now
        offends° me,
    Of all that I do know; nor know I aught   190
    By me that's said or done amiss this night,
    Unless self-charity be sometimes a vice,
    And to defend ourselves it be a sin
    When violence assails us.
OTHELLO: Now, by heaven,
    My blood° begins my safer guides to rule,   195
    And passion, having my best judgment collied,°
    Assays° to lead the way. If I once stir
    Or do but lift this arm, the best of you
    Shall sink in my rebuke. Give me to know
    How this foul rout began, who set it on;   200
    And he that is approved in° this offense,
    Though he had twinned with me, both at a birth,
    Shall lose me. What! in a town of war,
    Yet wild, the people's hearts brimful of fear,
    To manage° private and domestic quarrel?   205
    In night, and on the court and guard of safety?
    'Tis monstrous. Iago, who began't?
MONTANO: If partially affined, or leagued in office,°
    Thou dost deliver more or less than truth,
    Thou art no soldier.
IAGO: Touch me not so near.   210
    I had rather have this tongue cut from my mouth
    Than it should do offense to Michael Cassio;
    Yet I persuade myself, to speak the truth
    Shall nothing wrong him. This it is, general.
    Montano and myself being in speech,   215
    There comes a fellow crying out for help,
    And Cassio following him with determined sword
    To execute° upon him. Sir, this gentleman
    Steps in to Cassio and entreats his pause.
    Myself the crying fellow did pursue,   220
    Lest by his clamor — as it so fell out —
    The town might fall in fright. He, swift of foot,
    Outran my purpose; and I returned then rather
    For that I heard the clink and fall of swords,
    And Cassio high in oath;° which till to-night   225
    I ne'er might say before. When I came back —
    For this was brief — I found them close together
    At blow and thrust, even as again they were
    When you yourself did part them.
    More of this matter cannot I report;   230
    But men are men; the best sometimes forget.
    Though Cassio did some little wrong to him,
    As men in rage strike those that wish them best,
    Yet surely Cassio I believe received
    From him that fled some strange indignity,   235
    Which patience could not pass.°

---

152. rise: Grow riotous.   163. carve for: Indulge.   166. propriety: Proper self.   170. quarter: Friendliness.   175. peevish
odds: Childish quarrel.   183. censure: Judgment.   184. un-
lace: Undo.   185. rich opinion: High reputation.

189. offends: Pains.   195. blood: Passion.   196. collied:
Darkened.   197. Assays: Tries.   201. approved in: Proved
guilty of.   205. manage: Carry on.   208. partially . . . office:
Prejudiced by comradeship or official relations.   218. execute:
Work his will.   225. high in oath: Cursing.   236. pass: Pass
over, ignore.

OTHELLO: I know, Iago,
    Thy honesty and love doth mince this matter,
    Making it light to Cassio. Cassio, I love thee;
    But never more be officer of mine.

Enter Desdemona, attended.

240   Look if my gentle love be not raised up!
    I'll make thee an example.
DESDEMONA: What's the matter?
OTHELLO: All's well now, sweeting; come away to bed.

[*To Montano.*]

    Sir, for your hurts, myself will be your surgeon.
    Lead him off.

[*Montano is led off.*]

245   Iago, look with care about the town
    And silence those whom this vile brawl distracted.°
    Come, Desdemona; 'tis the soldiers' life
    To have their balmy slumbers waked with strife.

                        Exit [with all but Iago and Cassio].

IAGO: What, are you hurt, lieutenant?
250 CASSIO: Ay, past all surgery.
IAGO: Marry, God forbid!
CASSIO: Reputation, reputation, reputation! O, I have
    lost my reputation! I have lost the immortal part of
    myself, and what remains is bestial. My reputation,
255   Iago, my reputation!
IAGO: As I am an honest man, I thought you had re-
    ceived some bodily wound. There is more sense in
    that than in reputation. Reputation is an idle and
    most false imposition; oft got without merit and lost
260   without deserving. You have lost no reputation at all
    unless you repute yourself such a loser. What, man!
    there are ways to recover° the general again. You are
    but now cast in his mood° — a punishment more in
    policy than in malice, even so as one would beat his
265   offenseless dog to affright an imperious lion. Sue to
    him again, and he's yours.
CASSIO: I will rather sue to be despised than to deceive
    so good a commander with so slight, so drunken,
    and so indiscreet an officer. Drunk! and speak par-
270   rot!° and squabble! swagger! swear! and discourse
    fustian° with one's own shadow! O thou invisible
    spirit of wine, if thou hast no name to be known by,
    let us call thee devil!
IAGO: What was he that you followed with your sword?
275   What had he done to you?
CASSIO: I know not.
IAGO: Is't possible?
CASSIO: I remember a mass of things, but nothing dis-
    tinctly; a quarrel, but nothing wherefore. O God, that
280   men should put an enemy in their mouths to steal

away their brains! that we should with joy, pleas-
ance, revel, and applause° transform ourselves into
beasts!
IAGO: Why, but you are now well enough. How came   285
    you thus recovered?
CASSIO: It hath pleased the devil drunkenness to give
    place to the devil wrath. One unperfectness shows
    me another, to make me frankly despise myself.
IAGO: Come, you are too severe a moraler. As the time,
    the place, and the condition of this country stands, I   290
    could heartily wish this had not so befall'n; but since
    it is as it is, mend it for your own good.
CASSIO: I will ask him for my place again: he shall tell
    me I am a drunkard! Had I as many mouths as
    Hydra,° such an answer would stop them all. To be   295
    now a sensible man, by and by a fool, and presently a
    beast! O strange! Every inordinate cup is unblest,
    and the ingredient° is a devil.
IAGO: Come, come, good wine is a good familiar crea-
    ture if it be well used. Exclaim no more against it.   300
    And, good lieutenant, I think you think I love you.
CASSIO: I have well approved° it, sir. I drunk!
IAGO: You or any man living may be drunk at some
    time, man. I'll tell you what you shall do. Our gen-
    eral's wife is now the general. I may say so in this   305
    respect, for that he hath devoted and given up him-
    self to the contemplation, mark, and denotement of
    her parts and graces. Confess yourself freely to her;
    importune her help to put you in your place again.
    She is of so free,° so kind, so apt, so blessed a disposi- 310
    tion she holds it a vice in her goodness not to do
    more than she is requested. This broken joint be-
    tween you and her husband entreat her to splinter;°
    and my fortunes against any lay° worth naming, this
    crack of your love shall grow stronger than it was   315
    before.
CASSIO: You advise me well.
IAGO: I protest, in the sincerity of love and honest kind-
    ness.
CASSIO: I think it freely; and betimes in the morning will   320
    I beseech the virtuous Desdemona to undertake for
    me. I am desperate of my fortunes if they check me
    here.
IAGO: You are in the right. Good night, lieutenant; I must
    to the watch.   325
CASSIO: Good night, honest Iago.   *Exit Cassio.*
IAGO: And what's he then that says I play the villain,
    When this advice is free I give and honest,
    Probal° to thinking, and indeed the course
    To win the Moor again? For 'tis most easy   330
    Th' inclining Desdemona to subdue°
    In an honest suit; she's framed as fruitful

---

246. **distracted:** Excited.   262. **recover:** Regain favor with.
263. **in his mood:** Dismissed because of his anger.   269–70. **par-
rot:** Meaningless phrases.   271. **fustian:** Bombastic nonsense.

282. **applause:** Desire to please.   295. **Hydra:** Monster with
many heads.   298. **ingredient:** Contents.   302. **approved:**
Proved.   310. **free:** Bounteous.   313. **splinter:** Bind up with
splints.   314. **lay:** Wager.   329. **Probal:** Probable.   331. **subdue:** Persuade.

As the free elements. And then for her
To win the Moor — were't to renounce his baptism,
335 All seals and symbols of redeemèd sin —
His soul is so enfettered to her love
That she may make, unmake, do what she list,
Even as her appetite shall play the god
With his weak function. How am I then a villain
340 To counsel Cassio to this parallel° course,
Directly to his good? Divinity° of hell!
When devils will the blackest sins put on,°
They do suggest at first with heavenly shows,
As I do now. For whiles this honest fool
345 Plies Desdemona to repair his fortunes,
And she for him pleads strongly to the Moor,
I'll pour this pestilence into his ear,
That she repeals him° for her body's lust;
And by how much she strives to do him good,
350 She shall undo her credit with the Moor.
So will I turn her virtue into pitch,
And out of her own goodness make the net
That shall enmesh them all.

Enter Roderigo.

How, now, Roderigo?
RODERIGO: I do follow here in the chase, not like a
355 hound that hunts, but one that fills up the cry.° My
money is almost spent; I have been to-night exceedingly well cudgelled; and I think the issue will be — I
shall have so much experience for my pains; and so,
with no money at all, and a little more wit, return
360 again to Venice.
IAGO: How poor are they that have not patience!
What wound did ever heal but by degrees?
Thou know'st we work by wit, and not by
witchcraft;
And wit depends on dilatory time.
365 Does't not go well? Cassio hath beaten thee,
And thou by that small hurt hast cashiered Cassio.°
Though other things grow fair against the sun,
Yet fruits that blossom first will first be ripe.
Content thyself awhile. By the mass, 'tis morning!
370 Pleasure and action make the hours seem short.
Retire thee; go where thou art billeted.
Away, I say! Thou shalt know more hereafter.
Nay, get thee gone!   *Exit Roderigo.*
Two things are to be done:
My wife must move for Cassio to her mistress;
375 I'll set her on;
Myself the while to draw the Moor apart
And bring him jump° when he may Cassio find
Soliciting his wife. Ay, that's the way!
Dull no device by coldness and delay.   *Exit.*

---

340. parallel: Corresponding. **341. Divinity:** Theology.
342. put on: Incite. **348. repeals him:** Seeks his recall.
355. cry: Pack. **366. cashiered Cassio:** Maneuvered Cassio's
discharge. **377. jump:** At the exact moment.

ACT III • *Scene I*

Before the chamber of Othello and Desdemona.

Enter Cassio, with Musicians and the Clown.

CASSIO: Masters, play here, I will content° your pains:
Something that's brief; and bid "Good morrow,
general."

[*They play.*]

CLOWN: Why, masters, ha' your instruments been in
Naples,° that they speak i' th' nose thus?
MUSICIAN: How, sir, how?   5
CLOWN: Are these, I pray you, called wind instruments?
MUSICIAN: Ay, marry, are they, sir.
CLOWN: O, thereby hangs a tail.
MUSICIAN: Whereby hangs a tail, sir?
CLOWN: Marry, sir, by many a wind instrument that I   10
know. But, masters, here's money for you; and the
general so likes your music that he desires you, for
love's sake, to make no more noise with it.
MUSICIAN: Well, sir, we will not.
CLOWN: If you have any music that may not be heard,   15
to't again: but, as they say, to hear music the general
does not greatly care.
MUSICIAN: We have none such, sir.
CLOWN: Then put up your pipes in your bag, for I'll
away. Go, vanish into air, away!   20

Exit Musician [with his fellows].

CASSIO: Dost thou hear, my honest friend?
CLOWN: No, I hear not your honest friend. I hear you.
CASSIO: Prithee keep up thy quillets.° There's a poor
piece of gold for thee. If the gentlewoman that at-
tends the general's wife be stirring, tell her there's one   25
Cassio entreats her a little favor of speech. Wilt thou
do this?
CLOWN: She is stirring sir. If she will stir hither, I shall
seem to notify unto her.
CASSIO: [Do, good my friend.]   *Exit Clown.*

Enter Iago.

In happy time,° Iago.   30
IAGO: You have not been abed then?
CASSIO: Why, no; the day had broke
Before we parted. I have made bold, Iago,
To send in to your wife: my suit to her
Is that she will to virtuous Desdemona   35
Procure me some access.
IAGO: I'll send her to you presently;
And I'll devise a mean to draw the Moor
Out of the way, that your converse and
business
May be more free.

III, I. 1. content: Reward.   **4. Naples:** (Notorious for its association with venereal disease).   **23. quillets:** Quips.   **30. In
happy time:** Well met.

CASSIO: I humbly thank you for't.   *Exit* [*Iago*].
40   I never knew
A Florentine° more kind and honest.

Enter Emilia.

EMILIA: Good morrow, good lieutenant. I am sorry
For your displeasure: but all will sure be well.
The general and his wife are talking of it,
45   And she speaks for you stoutly. The Moor replied
That he you hurt is of great fame in Cyprus
And great affinity,° and that in wholesome wisdom
He might not but refuse you; but he protests he
    loves you,
And needs no other suitor but his likings
50   [To take the safest occasion° by the front°]
To bring you in again.
CASSIO: Yet I beseech you,
If you think fit, or that it may be done,
Give me advantage of some brief discourse
With Desdemona alone.
EMILIA: Pray you come in.
55   I will bestow you where you shall have time
To speak your bosom° freely.
CASSIO: I am much bound to you.

                                        Exeunt.

Scene II

The castle.

Enter Othello, Iago, and Gentlemen.

OTHELLO: These letters give, Iago, to the pilot
And by him do my duties to the Senate.
That done, I will be walking on the works;°
Repair there to me.
IAGO: Well, my good lord, I'll do't.
5   OTHELLO: This fortification, gentlemen, shall we see't?
GENTLEMEN: We'll wait upon your lordship.   *Exeunt.*

Scene III

The castle grounds.

Enter Desdemona, Cassio, and Emilia.

DESDEMONA: Be thou assured, good Cassio, I will do
All my abilities in thy behalf.
EMILIA: Good madam, do. I warrant it grieves my
    husband
As if the cause were his.
DESDEMONA: O, that's an honest fellow. Do not doubt,
5   Cassio,

But I will have my lord and you again
As friendly as you were.
CASSIO: Bounteous madam,
Whatever shall become of Michael Cassio,
He's never anything but your true servant.
DESDEMONA: I know't; I thank you. You do love my
    lord;   10
You have known him long; and be you well assured
He shall in strangeness° stand no farther off
Than in a politic distance.°
CASSIO: Ay, but, lady,
That policy may either last so long,
Or feed upon such nice and waterish diet,°   15
Or breed itself so out of circumstance,
That, I being absent, and my place supplied,
My general will forget my love and service.
DESDEMONA: Do not doubt° that; before Emilia here
I give thee warrant of thy place. Assure thee,   20
If I do vow a friendship, I'll perform it
To the last article. My lord shall never rest;
I'll watch him tame° and talk him out of patience;
His bed shall seem a school, his board a shrift;°
I'll intermingle everything he does   25
With Cassio's suit. Therefore be merry, Cassio,
For thy solicitor shall rather die
Than give thy cause away.

Enter Othello and Iago [at a distance].

EMILIA: Madam, here comes my lord.
CASSIO: Madam, I'll take my leave.   30
DESDEMONA: Why, stay, and hear me speak.
CASSIO: Madam, not now: I am very ill at ease,
Unfit for mine own purposes.
DESDEMONA: Well, do your discretion.   *Exit Cassio.*
IAGO: Ha! I like not that.
OTHELLO: What dost thou say?   35
IAGO: Nothing, my lord; or if — I know not what.
OTHELLO: Was not that Cassio parted from my wife?
IAGO: Cassio, my lord? No, sure, I cannot think it,
That he would steal away so guilty-like,
Seeing your coming.
OTHELLO: I do believe 'twas he.   40
DESDEMONA: How now, my lord?
I have been talking with a suitor here,
A man that languishes in your displeasure.
OTHELLO: What is't you mean?
DESDEMONA: Why, your lieutenant, Cassio. Good my
    lord,   45
If I have any grace or power to move you,
His present° reconciliation take;
For if he be not one that truly loves you,
That errs in ignorance, and not in cunning,

---

41. Florentine: I.e., even a Florentine (like Cassio; Iago was a Venetian). **47. affinity:** Family connections. **50. occasion:** Opportunity. **front:** Forelock. **56. your bosom:** Your inmost thoughts. **III, II. 3. works:** Fortifications.

III, III. 12. strangeness: Aloofness. **13. Than . . . distance:** Than wise policy requires. **15. Or . . . diet:** Or be continued for such slight reasons. **19. doubt:** Fear. **23. watch him tame:** Keep him awake until he gives in. **24. shrift:** Confessional. **47. present:** Immediate.

50   I have no judgment in an honest face,
        I prithee call him back.
OTHELLO: Went he hence now?
DESDEMONA: Yes, faith; so humbled
        That he hath left part of his grief with me
        To suffer with him. Good love, call him back.
OTHELLO: Not now, sweet Desdemon; some other
55   time.
DESDEMONA: But shall't be shortly?
OTHELLO: The sooner, sweet, for you.
DESDEMONA: Shall't be to-night at supper?
OTHELLO: No, not to-night.
DESDEMONA: To-morrow dinner then?
OTHELLO: I shall not dine at home;
        I meet the captains at the citadel.
DESDEMONA: Why then, to-morrow night, or Tuesday
60   morn,
        On Tuesday noon or night, or Wednesday morn.
        I prithee name the time, but let it not
        Exceed three days. I' faith, he's penitent;
        And yet his trespass, in our common reason
65   (Save that, they say, the wars must make examples
        Out of their best), is not almost° a fault
        T' incur a private check.° When shall he come?
        Tell me, Othello. I wonder in my soul
        What you could ask me that I should deny
        Or stand so mamm'ring on.° What? Michael
70   Cassio,
        That came a-wooing with you, and so many a
            time,
        When I have spoke of you dispraisingly,
        Hath ta'en your part — to have so much to do
        To bring him in? By'r Lady, I could do much —
OTHELLO: Prithee no more. Let him come when he
75   will!
        I will deny thee nothing.
DESDEMONA: Why, this is not a boon;
        'Tis as I should entreat you wear your gloves,
        Or feed on nourishing dishes, or keep you warm,
        Or sue to you to do a peculiar profit
80   To your own person. Nay, when I have a suit
        Wherein I mean to touch your love indeed,
        It shall be full of poise and difficult weight,
        And fearful° to be granted.
OTHELLO: I will deny thee nothing!
        Whereon I do beseech thee grant me this,
85   To leave me but a little to myself.
DESDEMONA: Shall I deny you? No. Farewell, my lord.
OTHELLO: Farewell, my Desdemon: I'll come to thee
        straight.
DESDEMONA: Emilia, come. — Be as your fancies teach
        you;
        Whate'er you be, I am obedient. *Exit [with Emilia].*
90 OTHELLO: Excellent wretch!° Perdition catch my soul

        But I do love thee! and when I love thee not,
        Chaos is come again.
IAGO: My noble lord —
OTHELLO: What dost thou say, Iago?
IAGO: Did Michael Cassio, when you wooed my lady,
        Know of your love?   95
OTHELLO: He did, from first to last. Why dost thou
        ask?
IAGO: But for a satisfaction of my thought;
        No further harm.
OTHELLO: Why of thy thought, Iago?
IAGO: I did not think he had been acquainted with her.
OTHELLO: O, yes, and went between us° very oft.   100
IAGO: Indeed?
OTHELLO: Indeed? Ay, indeed! Discern'st thou aught in
        that?
        Is he not honest?
IAGO: Honest, my lord?
OTHELLO: Honest. Ay, honest.
IAGO: My lord, for aught I know.
OTHELLO: What dost thou think?
IAGO: Think, my lord?
OTHELLO: Think, my lord?   105
        By heaven, he echoes me,
        As if there were some monster in his thought
        Too hideous to be shown. Thou dost mean
            something:
        I heard thee say even now, thou lik'st not that,
        When Cassio left my wife. What didst not like?   110
        And when I told thee he was of my counsel
        In my whole course of wooing, thou cried'st
            "Indeed?"
        And didst contract and purse thy brow together,
        As if thou then hadst shut up in thy brain
        Some horrible conceit.° If thou dost love me,   115
        Show me thy thought.
IAGO: My lord, you know I love you.
OTHELLO: I think thou dost;
        And, for I know thou'rt full of love and honesty
        And weigh'st thy words before thou giv'st them
            breath,
        Therefore these stops of thine fright me the more; 120
        For such things in a false disloyal knave
        Are tricks of custom; but in a man that's just
        They are close dilations, working from the heart
        That passion cannot rule.°
IAGO: For Michael Cassio,
        I dare be sworn I think that he is honest.   125
OTHELLO: I think so too.
IAGO: Men should be what they seem;
        Or those that be not, would they might seem none!°
OTHELLO: Certain, men should be what they seem.
IAGO: Why then, I think Cassio's an honest man.

---

66. **not almost:** Hardly.   67. **a private check:** Even a private reprimand.   70. **mamm'ring on:** Hesitating about.   83. **fearful:** Dangerous.   90. **wretch:** (A term of endearment).

100. **went . . . us:** (I.e., as messenger).   115. **conceit:** Fancy. 123–24. **close dilations . . . rule:** Secret emotions which well up in spite of restraint.   127. **seem none:** I.e., not pretend to be men when they are really monsters.

130 OTHELLO: Nay, yet there's more in this.
    I prithee speak to me as to thy thinkings,
    As thou dost ruminate, and give thy worst of
        thoughts
    The worst of words.
    IAGO: Good my lord, pardon me:
    Though I am bound to every act of duty,
135 I am not bound to that all slaves are free to.°
    Utter my thoughts? Why, say they are vile and false,
    As where's that palace whereinto foul things
    Sometimes intrude not? Who has a breast so pure
    But some uncleanly apprehensions
140 Keep leets and law days,° and in Sessions sit
    With meditations lawful?
    OTHELLO: Thou dost conspire against thy friend, Iago,
    If thou but think'st him wronged, and mak'st his ear
    A stranger to thy thoughts.
    IAGO: I do beseech you —
145 Though I perchance am vicious in my guess
    (As I confess it is my nature's plague
    To spy into abuses, and oft my jealousy°
    Shapes faults that are not), that your wisdom yet
    From one that so imperfectly conjects°
150 Would take no notice, nor build yourself a trouble
    Out of his scattering and unsure observance.
    It were not for your quiet nor your good,
    Nor for my manhood, honesty, and wisdom,
    To let you know my thoughts.
    OTHELLO: What dost thou mean?
155 IAGO: Good name in man and woman, dear my lord,
    Is the immediate° jewel of their souls.
    Who steals my purse steals trash; 'tis something,
        nothing;
    'Twas mine, 'tis his, and has been slave to
        thousands;
    But he that filches from me my good name
160 Robs me of that which not enriches him
    And makes me poor indeed.
    OTHELLO: By heaven, I'll know thy thoughts!
    IAGO: You cannot, if my heart were in your hand;
    Nor shall not whilst 'tis in my custody.
    OTHELLO: Ha!
165 IAGO: O, beware, my lord, of jealousy!
    It is the green-eyed monster, which doth mock°
    The meat it feeds on. That cuckold lives in bliss
    Who, certain of his fate, loves not his wronger;
    But O, what damnèd minutes tells he o'er
170 Who dotes, yet doubts — suspects, yet strongly loves!
    OTHELLO: O misery!
    IAGO: Poor and content is rich, and rich enough;
    But riches fineless° is as poor as winter
    To him that ever fears he shall be poor.

    Good God, the souls of all my tribe defend   175
    From jealousy!
    OTHELLO: Why, why is this?
    Think'st thou I'ld make a life of jealousy,
    To follow still the changes of the moon
    With fresh suspicions? No! To be once in doubt
    Is once to be resolved. Exchange me for a goat   180
    When I shall turn the business of my soul
    To such exsufflicate and blown° surmises,
    Matching this inference. 'Tis not to make me jealous
    To say my wife is fair, feeds well, loves company,
    Is free of speech, sings, plays, and dances;   185
    Where virtue is, these are more virtuous.
    Nor from mine own weak merits will I draw
    The smallest fear or doubt of her revolt,°
    For she had eyes, and chose me. No, Iago;
    I'll see before I doubt; when I doubt, prove;   190
    And on the proof there is no more but this —
    Away at once with love or jealousy!
    IAGO: I am glad of this; for now I shall have reason
    To show the love and duty that I bear you
    With franker spirit. Therefore, as I am bound,   195
    Receive it from me. I speak not yet of proof.
    Look at your wife; observe her well with Cassio;
    Wear your eyes thus, not jealous nor secure:°
    I would not have your free and noble nature,
    Out of self-bounty,° be abused. Look to't.   200
    I know our country disposition well:
    In Venice they do let God see the pranks
    They dare not show their husbands; their best
        conscience
    Is not to leave't undone, but keep't unknown.
    OTHELLO: Dost thou say so?   205
    IAGO: She did deceive her father, marrying you;
    And when she seemed to shake and fear your looks,
    She loved them most.
    OTHELLO: And so she did.
    IAGO: Why, go to then!
    She that, so young, could give out such a seeming
    To seel° her father's eyes up close as oak° —   210
    He thought 'twas witchcraft — but I am much to
        blame.
    I humbly do beseech you of your pardon
    For too much loving you.
    OTHELLO: I am bound to thee for ever.
    IAGO: I see this hath a little dashed your spirits.
    OTHELLO: Not a jot, not a jot.
    IAGO: I' faith, I fear it has.   215
    I hope you will consider what is spoke
    Comes from my love. But I do see y' are moved.
    I am to pray you not to strain my speech
    To grosser issues° nor to larger reach
    Than to suspicion.   220

---

135. **bound . . . free to:** Bound to tell that which even slaves are allowed to keep to themselves. 140. **leets and law days:** Sittings of the courts. 147. **jealousy:** Suspicion. 149. **conjects:** Conjectures. 156. **immediate:** Nearest the heart. 166. **mock:** Play with, like a cat with mouse. 173. **fineless:** Unlimited.

182. **exsufflicate and blown:** Spat out and flyblown. 188. **revolt:** Unfaithfulness. 198. **secure:** Overconfident. 200. **self-bounty:** Natural goodness. 210. **seel:** Close. **oak:** Oak grain. 219. **To grosser issues:** To mean something more monstrous.

Laurence Fishburne, Othello,
and Kenneth Branagh, Iago, in
Oliver Parker's 1995 film
version of *Othello*.

OTHELLO: I will not.
IAGO: Should you do so, my lord,
  My speech should fall into such vile success°
  As my thoughts aim not at. Cassio's my worthy
    friend —
  My lord, I see y' are moved.
OTHELLO: No, not much moved:
225 I do not think but Desdemona's honest.°
IAGO: Long live she so! and long live you to think so!
OTHELLO: And yet, how nature erring from itself —
IAGO: Ay, there's the point! as (to be bold with you)
  Not to affect many proposèd matches
230 Of her own clime, complexion, and degree,
  Whereto we see in all things nature tends —
  Foh! one may smell in such a will most rank,
  Foul disproportions, thought unnatural —
  But pardon me — I do not in position°
235 Distinctly speak of her; though I may fear
  Her will, recoiling° to her better judgment,
  May fall to match° you with her country forms,
  And happily° repent.
OTHELLO: Farewell, farewell!
  If more thou dost perceive, let me know more.
240 Set on thy wife to observe. Leave me, Iago.
IAGO: My lord, I take my leave.   [*Going.*]
OTHELLO: Why did I marry? This honest creature
    doubtless
  Sees and knows more, much more, than he unfolds.

222. **vile success:** Evil outcome. 225. **honest:** Chaste.
234. **position:** Definite assertion. 236. **recoiling:** Reverting.
237. **fall to match:** Happen to compare. 238. **happily:** Haply,
perhaps.

IAGO [*returns*]: My lord, I would I might entreat your
    honor
  To scan this thing no further: leave it to time.   245
  Although 'tis fit that Cassio have his place,
  For sure he fills it up with great ability,
  Yet, if you please to hold off a while,
  You shall by that perceive him and his means.
  Note if your lady strain his entertainment°   250
  With any strong or vehement importunity;
  Much will be seen in that. In the mean time
  Let me be thought too busy° in my fears
  (As worthy cause I have to fear I am)
  And hold her free,° I do beseech your honor.   255
OTHELLO: Fear not my government.°
IAGO: I once more take my leave.   *Exit.*
OTHELLO: This fellow 's of exceeding honesty,
  And knows all qualities,° with a learned spirit
  Of° human dealings. If I do prove her haggard,°   260
  Though that her jesses° were my dear heartstrings,
  I'd whistle her off and let her down the wind
  To prey at fortune.° Haply, for I am black
  And have not those soft parts of conversation°
  That chamberers° have, or for I am declined   265
  Into the vale of years — yet that's not much —

250. **strain his entertainment:** Urge his recall. 253. **busy:**
Meddlesome. 255. **hold her free:** Consider her guiltless.
256. **government:** Self-control. 259. **qualities:** Natures.
259–60. **learned spirit Of:** Mind informed about. 260. **haggard:** A wild hawk. 261. **jesses:** Thongs for controlling a
hawk. 262–63. **whistle . . . fortune:** Turn her out and let her
take care of herself. 264. **soft . . . conversation:** Ingratiating
manners. 265. **chamberers:** Courtiers.

She's gone. I am abused, and my relief
Must be to loathe her. O curse of marriage,
That we can call these delicate creatures ours,
270   And not their appetites! I had rather be a toad
And live upon the vapor of a dungeon
Than keep a corner in the thing I love
For others' uses. Yet 'tis the plague of great ones;°
Prerogatived° are they less than the base.
275   'Tis destiny unshunnable, like death.
Even then this forkèd plague° is fated to us
When we do quicken.° Look where she comes.

Enter Desdemona and Emilia.

If she be false, O, then heaven mocks itself!
I'll not believe't.
DESDEMONA: How now, my dear Othello?
280   Your dinner, and the generous° islanders
By you invited, do attend your presence.
OTHELLO: I am to blame.
DESDEMONA: Why do you speak so faintly?
Are you not well?
OTHELLO: I have a pain upon my forehead, here.
DESDEMONA: Faith, that's with watching;° 'twill away
285   again.
Let me but bind it hard, within this hour
It will be well.
OTHELLO: Your napkin° is too little;

[*He pushes the handkerchief from him, and it falls unnoticed.*]

Let it° alone. Come, I'll go in with you.
DESDEMONA: I am very sorry that you are not well.

                    Exit [with Othello].

290   EMILIA: I am glad I have found this napkin;
This was her first remembrance from the Moor,
My wayward husband hath a hundred times
Wooed me to steal it; but she so loves the token
(For he conjured her she should ever keep it)
295   That she reserves it evermore about her
To kiss and talk to. I'll have the work ta'en out°
And give't Iago.
What he will do with it heaven knows, not I;
I nothing but to please his fantasy.°

Enter Iago.

300   IAGO: How now? What do you here alone?
EMILIA: Do not you chide; I have a thing for you.
IAGO: A thing for me? It is a common thing —
EMILIA: Ha?
IAGO: To have a foolish wife.

EMILIA: O, is that all? What will you give me now   305
For that same handkerchief?
IAGO: What handkerchief?
EMILIA: What handkerchief!
Why, that the Moor first gave to Desdemona;
That which so often you did bid me steal.
IAGO: Hast stol'n it from her?   310
EMILIA: No, faith; she let it drop by negligence,
And to th' advantage,° I, being here, took't up.
Look, here it is.
IAGO: A good wench! Give it me.
EMILIA: What will you do with't, that you have been so
    earnest
To have me filch it?
IAGO: Why, what is that to you?   315

[*Snatches it.*]

EMILIA: If it be not for some purpose of import,°
Give't me again. Poor lady, she'll run mad
When she shall lack it.
IAGO: Be not acknown on't;° I have use for it.
Go, leave me.   *Exit Emilia.*   320
I will in Cassio's lodgings lose this napkin
And let him find it. Trifles light as air
Are to the jealous confirmations strong
As proofs of holy writ. This may do something.
The Moor already changes with my poison: 325
Dangerous conceits° are in their nature poisons,
Which at the first are scarce found to distaste,
But with a little act upon the blood
Burn like the mines of sulphur.

Enter Othello.

                    I did say so.
Look where he comes! Not poppy nor mandragora,°   330
Nor all the drowsy syrups of the world,
Shall ever med'cine thee to that sweet sleep
Which thou owedst yesterday.
OTHELLO: Ha! ha! false to me?
IAGO: Why, how now, general? No more of that!
OTHELLO: Avaunt! be gone! Thou hast set me on the
    rack.   335
I swear 'tis better to be much abused
Than but to know't a little.
IAGO: How now, my lord?
OTHELLO: What sense had I of her stol'n hours of lust?
I saw't not, thought it not, it harmed not me;
I slept the next night well, fed well, was free° and
    merry;   340
I found not Cassio's kisses on her lips
He that is robbed, not wanting° what is stol'n,
Let him not know't, and he's not robbed at all.
IAGO: I am sorry to hear this.

---

273. **great ones:** Prominent men.   274. **Prerogatived:** Privileged.   276. **forkèd plaque:** I.e., horns of a cuckold.   277. **do
quicken:** Are born.   280. **generous:** Noble.   285. **watching:**
Working late.   287. **napkin:** Handkerchief.   288. **it:** I.e., his
forehead.   296. **work ta'en out:** Pattern copied.   299. **fantasy:** Whim.

312. **to th' advantage:** Opportunely.   316. **import:** Importance.   319. **Be . . . on't:** Do not acknowledge it.   326. **conceits:**
Ideas.   330. **mandragora:** A narcotic.   340. **free:** Carefree.
342. **wanting:** Missing.

345 OTHELLO: I had been happy if the general camp,
      Pioneers° and all, had tasted her sweet body,
      So I had nothing known. O, now for ever
      Farewell the tranquil mind! farewell content!
      Farewell the plumèd troop, and the big° wars
350 That make ambition virtue! O, farewell!
      Farewell the neighing steed and the shrill trump,
      The spirit-stirring drum, th' ear-piercing fife,
      The royal banner, and all quality,
      Pride, pomp, and circumstance° of glorious war!
355 And O you mortal engines° whose rude throats
      Th' immortal Jove's dread clamors counterfeit,°
      Farewell! Othello's occupation's gone!
   IAGO: Is't possible, my lord?
   OTHELLO: Villain, be sure thou prove my love a
         whore!
360 Be sure of it; give me the ocular proof;
      Or, by the worth of mine eternal soul,
      Thou hadst been better have been born a dog
      Than answer my waked wrath!
   IAGO: Is't come to this?
   OTHELLO: Make me to see't; or at the least so prove it
365 That the probation° bear no hinge nor loop
      To hang a doubt on — or woe upon thy life!
   IAGO: My noble lord —
   OTHELLO: If thou dost slander her and torture me,
      Never pray more; abandon all remorse;
370 On horror's head horrors accumulate;
      Do deeds to make heaven weep, all earth amazed;
      For nothing canst thou to damnation add
      Greater than that.
   IAGO: O grace! O heaven forgive me!
      Are you a man? Have you a soul or sense? —
375 God b' wi' you! take mine office. O wretched fool,
      That liv'st to make thine honesty a vice!
      O monstrous world! Take note, take note, O world,
      To be direct and honest is not safe.
      I thank you for this profit;° and from hence
380 I'll love no friend, sith love breeds such offense.
   OTHELLO: Nay, stay. Thou shouldst be honest.
   IAGO: I should be wise; for honesty's a fool
      And loses that it works for.
   OTHELLO: By the world,
      I think my wife be honest, and think she is not;
385 I think that thou art just, and think thou art not.
      I'll have some proof. Her name, that was as fresh
      As Dian's visage, is now begrimed and black
      As mine own face. If there be cords, or knives,
      Poison, or fire, or suffocating streams,
390 I'll not endure it. Would I were satisfied!°
   IAGO: I see, sir, you are eaten up with passion:
      I do repent me that I put it to you.
      You would be satisfied?

   OTHELLO: Would? Nay, I will.
   IAGO: And may; but how? how satisfied, my lord?
      Would you, the supervisor,° grossly gape on?   395
      Behold her topped?
   OTHELLO: Death and damnation! O!
   IAGO: It were a tedious difficulty, I think,
      To bring them to that prospect. Damn them then,
      If ever mortal eyes do see them bolster°
      More than their own! What then? How then?   400
      What shall I say? Where's satisfaction?
      It is impossible you should see this,
      Were they as prime° as goats, as hot as monkeys,
      As salt° as wolves in pride,° and fools as gross
      As ignorance made drunk. But yet, I say,   405
      If imputation and strong circumstances
      Which lead directly to the door of truth
      Will give you satisfaction, you may have't.
   OTHELLO: Give me a living reason she's disloyal.
   IAGO: I do not like the office.   410
      But sith I am ent'red in this cause so far,
      Pricked to't by foolish honesty and love,
      I will go on. I lay with Cassio lately,
      And being troubled with a raging tooth,
      I could not sleep.   415
      There are a kind of men so loose of soul
      That in their sleeps will mutter their affairs.
      One of this kind is Cassio.
      In sleep I heard him say, "Sweet Desdemona,
      Let us be wary, let us hide our loves!"   420
      And then, sir, would he gripe and wring my
         hand,
      Cry "O sweet creature!" and then kiss me hard,
      As if he plucked up kisses by the roots
      That grew upon my lips; then laid his leg
      Over my thigh, and sighed, and kissed, and then   425
      Cried "Cursèd fate that gave thee to the Moor!"
   OTHELLO: O monstrous! monstrous!
   IAGO: Nay, this was but
         his dream.
   OTHELLO: But this denoted a foregone conclusion;°
      'Tis a shrewd doubt,° though it be but a dream.
   IAGO: And this may help to thicken other proofs   430
      That do demonstrate thinly.
   OTHELLO: I'll tear her all to pieces!
   IAGO: Nay, but be wise. Yet we see nothing done;
      She may be honest yet. Tell me but this —
      Have you not sometimes seen a handkerchief
      Spotted with strawberries in your wife's hand?   435
   OTHELLO: I gave her such a one; 'twas my first gift.
   IAGO: I know not that; but such a handkerchief —
      I am sure it was your wife's — did I to-day
      See Cassio wipe his beard with.
   OTHELLO: If it be that —

---

346. **Pioneers:** Sappers, laborers.   349. **big:** Stately.   354. **circumstance:** Pageantry.   355. **mortal engines:** Deadly artillery.
356. **counterfeit:** Imitate.   365. **probation:** Proof.   379. **profit:**
Profitable lesson.   390. **satisfied:** Completely informed.

395. **supervisor:** Spectator.   399. **bolster:** Lie together.
403. **prime:** Lustful.   404. **salt:** Lecherous.   **pride:** Heat.
428. **foregone conclusion:** Previous experience.   429. **a
shrewd doubt:** Cursedly suspicious.

440 IAGO: If it be that, or any that was hers,
    It speaks against her with the other proofs.
    OTHELLO: O, that the slave had forty thousand lives!
    One is too poor, too weak for my revenge.
    Now do I see 'tis true. Look here, Iago:
445 All my fond love thus do I blow to heaven.
    'Tis gone.
    Arise, black vengeance, from the hollow hell!
    Yield up, O love, thy crown and hearted throne
    To tyrannous hate! Swell, bosom, with thy
        fraught,°
    For 'tis of aspics'° tongues!
450 IAGO: Yet be content.
    OTHELLO: O, blood, blood, blood!
    IAGO: Patience, I say. Your mind perhaps may
        change.
    OTHELLO: Never, Iago. Like to the Pontic sea,°
    Whose icy current and compulsive course
455 Ne'er feels retiring ebb, but keeps due on
    To the Propontic and the Hellespont,
    Even so my bloody thoughts, with violent pace,
    Shall ne'er look back, ne'er ebb to humble love,
    Till that a capable° and wide revenge
    Swallow them up.
460 (*He kneels.*)   Now, by yond marble heaven,
    In the due reverence of a sacred vow
    I here engage my words.
    IAGO: Do not rise yet.

    (*Iago kneels.*)

    Witness, you ever-burning lights above,
    You elements that clip° us round about,
465 Witness that here Iago doth give up
    The execution° of his wit,° hands, heart
    To wronged Othello's service! Let him command,
    And to obey shall be in me remorse,°
    What bloody business ever.

    [*They rise.*]

    OTHELLO: I greet thy love,
    Not with vain thanks but with acceptance
470   bounteous,
    And will upon the instant put thee to't.
    Within these three days let me hear thee say
    That Cassio's not alive.
    IAGO: My friend is dead; 'tis done at your request.
475 But let her live.
    OTHELLO: Damn her, lewd minx! O, damn her! damn
        her!
    Come, go with me apart. I will withdraw
    To furnish me with some swift means of death
    For the fair devil. Now art thou my lieutenant.
480 IAGO: I am your own forever.   *Exeunt.*

---

449. **fraught:** Burden.   450. **aspics:** Deadly poisonous snakes.
453. **Pontic sea:** Black Sea.   459. **capable:** All-embracing.
464. **clip:** Encompass.   466. **execution:** Activities. **wit:**
Mind.   468. **remorse:** Pity.

Scene IV

The environs of the castle.

Enter Desdemona, Emilia, and Clown.

DESDEMONA: Do you know, sirrah, where Lieutenant
    Cassio lies?°
CLOWN: I dare not say he lies anywhere.
DESDEMONA: Why, man?
CLOWN: He's a soldier, and for me to say a soldier lies is   5
    stabbing.
DESDEMONA: Go to. Where lodges he?
CLOWN: To tell you where he lodges is to tell you where
    I lie.
DESDEMONA: Can anything be made of this?   10
CLOWN: I know not where he lodges; and for me to
    devise a lodging, and say he lies here or he lies there,
    were to lie in mine own throat.
DESDEMONA: Can you enquire him out, and be edified
    by report?   15
CLOWN: I will catechize the world for him; that is, make
    questions, and by them answer.
DESDEMONA: Seek him, bid him come hither. Tell him I
    have moved° my lord on his behalf and hope all will
    be well.   20
CLOWN: To do this is within the compass of man's wit,
    and therefore I'll attempt the doing of it.   *Exit.*
DESDEMONA: Where should I lose that handkerchief,
    Emilia?
EMILIA: I know not, madam.   25
DESDEMONA: Believe me, I had rather have lost my
        purse
    Full of crusadoes,° and but my noble Moor
    Is true of mind, and made of no such baseness
    As jealous creatures are, it were enough
    To put him to ill thinking.
EMILIA: Is he not jealous?   30
DESDEMONA: Who? he? I think the sun where he was
        born
    Drew all such humors° from him.

Enter Othello.

EMILIA: Look where he comes.
Desdemona: I will not leave him now till Cassio
    Be called to him — How is't with you, my lord?
OTHELLO: Well, my good lady. [*Aside.*] O, hardness to
        dissemble! —   35
    How do you, Desdemona?
DESDEMONA: Well, my good lord.
OTHELLO: Give me your hand. This hand is moist, my
        lady.
DESDEMONA: It yet hath felt no age nor known no
        sorrow.
OTHELLO: This argues fruitfulness and liberal heart.

III, IV. 2. **lies:** Lives, lodges.   19. **moved:** Made proposals to.
27. **crusadoes:** Portuguese gold coins.   32. **humors:** Inclinations.

40   Hot, hot, and moist. This hand of yours requires
      A sequester° from liberty, fasting and prayer,
      Much castigation, exercise devout;
      For here's a young and sweating devil here
      That commonly rebels. 'Tis a good hand,
      A frank one.
45 DESDEMONA: You may, indeed, say so;
      For 'twas that hand that gave away my heart.
      OTHELLO: A liberal hand! The hearts of old gave
         hands;
      But our new heraldry° is hands, not hearts.
      DESDEMONA: I cannot speak of this. Come now, your
         promise!
50 OTHELLO: What promise, chuck?
      DESDEMONA: I have sent to bid Cassio come speak
         with you.
      OTHELLO: I have a salt and sorry rheum° offends me.
         Lend me thy handkerchief.
      DESDEMONA: Here, my lord.
      OTHELLO: That which I gave you.
      DESDEMONA: I have it not about me.
      OTHELLO: Not?
      DESDEMONA: No, faith, my lord.
55 OTHELLO: That's a fault.
      That handkerchief
      Did an Egyptian° to my mother give.
      She was a charmer,° and could almost read
      The thoughts of people. She told her, while she kept
         it,
60   'Twould make her amiable° and subdue my father
      Entirely to her love; but if she lost it
      Or made a gift of it, my father's eye
      Should hold her loathèd, and his spirits should hunt
      After new fancies. She, dying, gave it me,
65   And bid me, when my fate would have me wive,
      To give it her. I did so; and take heed on't;
      Make it a darling like your precious eye.
      To lose't or give't away were such perdition°
      As nothing else could match.
      DESDEMONA: Is't possible?
70 OTHELLO: 'Tis true. There's magic in the web of it.
      A sibyl that had numb'red in the world
      The sun to course two hundred compasses,°
      In her prophetic fury sewed the work;
      The worms were hallowed that did breed the silk;
75   And it was dyed in mummy° which the skillful
      Conserved of maidens' hearts.
      DESDEMONA: I' faith? Is't true?
      OTHELLO: Most veritable. Therefore look to't well.
      DESDEMONA: Then would to God that I had never
         seen't!

41. **sequester:** Removal.   48. **heraldry:** Heraldic symbolism.
52. **salt . . . rheum:** Distressing head cold.   57. **Egyptian:** Gypsy.
58. **charmer:** Sorceress.   60. **amiable:** Lovable.   68. **perdition:** Disaster.   72. **compasses:** Annual rounds.   75. **mummy:** A drug made from mummies.

      OTHELLO: Ha! Wherefore?
      DESDEMONA: Why do you speak so startingly and
         rash?   80
      OTHELLO: Is't lost? Is't gone? Speak, is it out o' th'
         way?
      DESDEMONA: Heaven bless us!
      OTHELLO: Say you?
      DESDEMONA: It is not lost. But what an if it were?
      OTHELLO: How?   85
      DESDEMONA: I say it is not lost.
      OTHELLO: Fetch't, let me see't!
      DESDEMONA: Why, so I can, sir; but I will not now.
         This is a trick to put° me from my suit:
         Pray you let Cassio be received again.
      OTHELLO: Fetch me the handkerchief! My mind
         misgives.   90
      DESDEMONA: Come, come!
         You'll never meet a more sufficient man.
      OTHELLO: The handkerchief!
      [DESDEMONA: I pray talk me of Cassio.
      OTHELLO: The handkerchief!]
      DESDEMONA: A man that all his time°
         Hath founded his good fortunes on your love,   95
         Shared dangers with you —
      OTHELLO: The handkerchief!
      DESDEMONA: I' faith, you are to blame.
      OTHELLO: Zounds!   *Exit Othello.*
      EMILIA: Is not this man jealous?   100
      DESDEMONA: I ne'er saw this before.
         Sure there's some wonder in this
            handkerchief;
         I am most unhappy in the loss of it.
      EMILIA: 'Tis not a year or two shows us a man.
         They are all but stomachs, and we all but food;   105
         They eat us hungerly, and when they are full,
         They belch us.

      Enter Iago and Cassio.

                    Look you — Cassio and my husband!
      IAGO: There is no other way; 'tis she must do't.
         And lo the happiness!° Go and importune her.
      DESDEMONA: How now, good Cassio? What's the news
         with you?   110
      CASSIO: Madam, my former suit. I do beseech you
         That by your virtuous means I may again
         Exist, and be a member of his love
         Whom I with all the office of my heart
         Entirely honor. I would not be delayed.   115
         If my offense be of such mortal kind
         That neither service past, nor present sorrows,
         Nor purposed merit in futurity,
         Can ransom me into his love again,
         But to know so must be my benefit.   120
         So shall I clothe me in a forced content,

88. **put:** Divert.   94. **all . . . time:** During his whole career.
109. **happiness:** Good luck.

And shut myself up in° some other course,
To fortune's alms.
DESDEMONA: Alas, thrice-gentle Cassio!
My advocation° is not now in tune.
125   My lord is not my lord; nor should I know him,
Were he in favor° as in humor altered.
So help me every spirit sanctified
As I have spoken for you all my best
And stood within the blank° of his displeasure
130   For my free speech! You must a while be patient.
What I can do I will; and more I will
Than for myself I dare. Let that suffice you.
IAGO: Is my lord angry?
EMILIA: He went hence but now,
And certainly in strange unquietness.
135   IAGO: Can he be angry? I have seen the cannon
When it hath blown his ranks into the air
And, like the devil, from his very arm
Puffed his own brother — and is he angry?
Something of moment then. I will go meet him.
140   There's matter in't indeed if he be angry.
DESDEMONA: I prithee do so.   *Exit [Iago].*
                    Something sure of state,°
Either from Venice or some unhatched practice°
Made demonstrable here in Cyprus to him,
Hath puddled° his clear spirit; and in such cases
145   Men's natures wrangle with inferior things,
Though great ones are their object. 'Tis even so;
For let our finger ache, and it endues°
Our other, healthful members even to a sense
Of pain. Nay, we must think men are not gods,
150   Nor of them look for such observancy
As fits the bridal. Beshrew me much, Emilia,
I was, unhandsome warrior° as I am,
Arraigning his unkindness with my soul;°
But now I find I had suborned the witness,
155   And he's indicted falsely.
EMILIA: Pray heaven it be state matters, as you
    think,
And no conception nor no jealous toy°
Concerning you.
DESDEMONA: Alas the day! I never gave him cause.
160   EMILIA: But jealous souls will not be answered so;
They are not ever jealous for the cause,
But jealous for they're jealous. 'Tis a monster
Begot upon itself,° born on itself.
DESDEMONA: Heaven keep that monster from Othello's
    mind!

EMILIA: Lady, amen.   165
DESDEMONA: I will go seek him. Cassio, walk here
    about:
If I do find him fit, I'll move your suit
And seek to effect it to my uttermost.
CASSIO: I humbly thank your ladyship.

                    Exeunt Desdemona and Emilia.
Enter Bianca.

BIANCA: Save you, friend Cassio!
CASSIO: What make you from home?   170
How is't with you, my most fair Bianca?
I' faith, sweet love, I was coming to your house.
BIANCA: And I was going to your lodging, Cassio.
What, keep a week away? seven days and nights?
Eightscore eight hours? and lovers' absent hours,   175
More tedious than the dial° eightscore times?
O weary reck'ning!
CASSIO: Pardon me, Bianca:
I have this while with leaden thoughts been pressed;
But I shall in a more continuate° time
Strike off this score of absence. Sweet Bianca,   180

[*Gives her Desdemona's handkerchief.*]

Take me this work out.°
BIANCA: O Cassio, whence came this?
This is some token from a newer friend.
To the felt absence now I feel a cause.
Is't come to this? Well, well.
CASSIO: Go to, woman!
Throw your vile guesses in the devil's teeth,   185
From whence you have them. You are jealous now
That this is from some mistress, some
    remembrance.
No, by my faith, Bianca.
BIANCA: Why, whose is it?
CASSIO: I know not, sweet; I found it in my chamber.
I like the work° well; ere it be demanded,   190
As like enough it will, I'd have it copied.
Take it and do't, and leave me for this time.
BIANCA: Leave you? Wherefore?
CASSIO: I do attend here on the general
And think it no addition, nor my wish,   195
To have him see me womaned.
BIANCA: Why, I pray you?
CASSIO: Not that I love you not.
BIANCA: But that you do not love me!
I pray you bring me on the way a little,
And say if I shall see you soon at night.
CASSIO: 'Tis but a little way that I can bring you,   200
For I attend here; but I'll see you soon.
BIANCA: 'Tis very good. I must be circumstanced.°
                                        Exeunt.

122. **shut myself up in:** Confine myself to.   124. **advocation:**
Advocacy.   126. **favor:** Appearance.   129. **blank:** Bull's-eye
of the target.   141. **state:** Public affairs.   142. **unhatched
practice:** Budding plot.   144. **puddled:** Muddied.   147. **en-
dues:** Brings.   152. **unhandsome warrior:** Inadequate soldier.
153. **Arraigning . . . soul:** Indicting his unkindness before the
bar of my soul.   157. **toy:** Fancy.   163. **Begot . . . itself:** Self-
engendered.

176. **dial:** Clock.   179. **continuate:** Uninterrupted.   181. **Take
. . . out:** Copy this embroidery for me.   190. **work:** Needlework.   202. **circumstanced:** Governed by circumstances.

ACT IV • *Scene 1*

The environs of the castle.

Enter Othello and Iago.

IAGO: Will you think so?
OTHELLO: Think so, Iago?
IAGO: What,
   To kiss in private?
OTHELLO: An unauthorized kiss.
IAGO: Or to be naked with her friend in bed
   An hour or more, not meaning any harm?
5 OTHELLO: Naked in bed, Iago, and not mean harm?
   It is hypocrisy against the devil.°
   They that mean virtuously, and yet do so,
   The devil their virtue tempts, and they tempt
      heaven.
IAGO: So they do nothing, 'tis a venial slip.
10   But if I give my wife a handkerchief —
OTHELLO: What then?
IAGO: Why, then 'tis hers, my lord; and being hers,
   She may, I think, bestow't on any man.
OTHELLO: She is protectress of her honor too;
15   May she give that?
IAGO: Her honor is an essence that's not seen;
   They have it very oft that have it not.
   But for the handkerchief —
OTHELLO: By heaven, I would most gladly have forgot
      it!
20   Thou said'st — O, it comes o'er my memory
   As doth the raven o'er the infected° house,
   Boding to all! — he had my handkerchief.
IAGO: Ay, what of that?
OTHELLO: That's not so good now.
IAGO: What
   If I had said I had seen him do you wrong?
25   Or heard him say — as knaves be such abroad
   Who having, by their own importunate suit,
   Or voluntary dotage of some mistress,
   Convincèd or supplied° them, cannot choose
   But they must blab —
OTHELLO: Hath he said anything?
30 IAGO: He hath, my lord; but be you well assured,
   No more than he'll unswear.
OTHELLO: What hath he said?
IAGO: Faith, that he did — I know not what he did.
OTHELLO: What? what?
IAGO: Lie —
OTHELLO: With her?
35 IAGO: With her, on her; what you will.
OTHELLO: Lie with her? lie on her? — We say lie on
   her when they belie her. — Lie with her! Zounds,
   that's   fulsome. — Handkerchief — confessions —
   handkerchief! — To confess, and be hanged for his

labor — first to be hanged, and then to confess! 40
   I tremble at it. Nature would not invest herself in
   such shadowing passion without some instruction.°
   It is not words that shakes me thus. — Pish! Noses,
   ears, and lips? Is't possible? — Confess? — Handkerchief? — O devil!   45

(Falls in a trance.)

IAGO: Work on,
   My med'cine, work! Thus credulous fools are
      caught,
   And many worthy and chaste dames even thus,
   All guiltless, meet reproach. — What, ho! my lord!
   My lord, I say! Othello!

Enter Cassio.

                         How now, Cassio?   50
CASSIO: What's the matter?
IAGO: My lord is fall'n into an epilepsy.
   This is his second fit; he had one yesterday.
CASSIO: Rub him about the temples.
IAGO: No, forbear.
   The lethargy° must have his quiet course.   55
   If not, he foams at mouth, and by and by
   Breaks out to savage madness. Look, he stirs.
   Do you withdraw yourself a little while.
   He will recover straight. When he is gone,
   I would on great occasion speak with you.   60
                                   [*Exit Cassio.*]
   How is it, general? Have you not hurt your head?
OTHELLO: Dost thou mock me?
IAGO: I mock you? No, by heaven.
   Would you would bear your fortune like a man!
OTHELLO: A hornèd man's° a monster and a beast.
IAGO: There's many a beast then in a populous city, 65
   And many a civil monster.
OTHELLO: Did he confess it?
IAGO: Good sir, be a man.
   Think every bearded fellow that's but yoked
   May draw with you. There's millions now alive
   That nightly lie in those unproper° beds   70
   Which they dare swear peculiar:° your case is better.
   O, 'tis the spite of hell, the fiend's arch-mock,
   To lip a wanton in a secure° couch,
   And to suppose her chaste! No, let me know;
   And knowing what I am, I know what she shall be. 75
OTHELLO: O, thou art wise! 'Tis certain.
IAGO: Stand you
   awhile apart;
   Confine yourself but in a patient list.°
   Whilst you were here, o'erwhelmèd with your
      grief —

IV, I. 6. hypocrisy . . . devil: I.e., feigned sin instead of feigned
virtue.   21. infected: Plague-stricken.   28. Convincèd or supplied: Overcome or gratified.

41–42. Nature . . . instruction: My natural faculties would not
be so overcome by passion without reason.   55. lethargy:
Coma.   64. hornèd man: Cuckold.   70. unproper: Not exclusively their own.   71. peculiar: Exclusively their own.
73. secure: Free from fear of rivalry.   77. in a patient list:
Within the limits of self-control.

A passion most unsuiting such a man —
80 Cassio came hither. I shifted him away
And laid good 'scuse upon your ecstasy,°
Bade him anon return, and here speak with me;
The which he promised. Do but encave° yourself
And mark the fleers, the gibes, and notable scorns
85 That dwell in every region of his face;
For I will make him tell the tale anew —
Where, how, how oft, how long ago, and when
He hath, and is again to cope° your wife.
I say, but mark his gesture. Marry, patience!
90 Or I shall say y'are all in all in spleen,°
And nothing of a man.
OTHELLO: Dost thou hear, Iago?
I will be found most cunning in my patience;
But — dost thou hear? — most bloody.
IAGO: That's not amiss:
But yet keep time in all. Will you withdraw?

[*Othello retires.*]

95 Now will I question Cassio of Bianca,
A huswife° that by selling her desires
Buys herself bread and clothes. It is a creature
That dotes on Cassio, as 'tis the strumpet's plague
To beguile many and be beguiled by one.
100 He, when he hears of her, cannot refrain
From the excess of laughter. Here he comes.

Enter Cassio.

As he shall smile, Othello shall go mad;
And his unbookish° jealousy must conster°
Poor Cassio's smiles, gestures, and light behavior
105 Quite in the wrong. How do you now, lieutenant?
CASSIO: The worser that you give me the addition°
Whose want even kills me.
IAGO: Ply Desdemona well, and you are sure on't.
Now, if this suit lay in Bianca's power,
How quickly should you speed!
110 CASSIO: Alas, poor caitiff!°
OTHELLO: Look how he laughs already!
IAGO: I never knew a woman love man so.
CASSIO: Alas, poor rogue! I think, i' faith, she loves me.
OTHELLO: Now he denies it faintly, and laughs it out.
IAGO: Do you hear, Cassio?
115 OTHELLO: Now he importunes him
To tell it o'er. Go to! Well said, well said!
IAGO: She gives out that you shall marry her.
Do you intend it?
CASSIO: Ha, ha, ha!
120 OTHELLO: Do you triumph, Roman? Do you triumph?
CASSIO: I marry her? What, a customer?° Prithee bear
some charity to my wit; do not think it so unwhole-
some. Ha, ha, ha!

OTHELLO: So, so, so, so! They laugh that win!
IAGO: Faith, the cry goes that you shall marry her.   125
CASSIO: Prithee say true.
IAGO: I am a very villain else.
OTHELLO: Have you scored me?° Well.
CASSIO: This is the monkey's own giving out. She is per-
suaded I will marry her out of her own love and flat-   130
tery, not out of my promise.
OTHELLO: Iago beckons° me; now he begins the story.
CASSIO: She was here even now; she haunts me in every
place. I was t' other day talking on the sea bank with
certain Venetians, and thither comes the bauble,°   135
and, by this hand, she falls me thus about my neck —
OTHELLO: Crying "O dear Cassio!" as it were. His gesture imports it.
CASSIO: So hangs, and lolls, and weeps upon me; so
shakes and pulls me! Ha, ha, ha!   140
OTHELLO: Now he tells how she plucked him to my
chamber. O, I see that nose of yours, but not that dog
I shall throw it to.
CASSIO: Well, I must leave her company.

Enter Bianca.

IAGO: Before me! Look where she comes.   145
CASSIO: 'Tis such another fitchew!° marry, a perfumed
one. What do you mean by this haunting of me?
BIANCA: Let the devil and his dam haunt you! What did
you mean by that same handkerchief you gave me
even now? I was a fine fool to take it. I must take out   150
the whole work? A likely piece of work that you
should find it in your chamber and know not who
left it there! This is some minx's token, and I must
take out the work? There! Give it your hobby-horse.°
Wheresoever you had it, I'll take out no work on't.   155
CASSIO: How now, my sweet Bianca? How now? how
now?
OTHELLO: By heaven, that should be my handkerchief!
BIANCA: An you'll come to supper to-night, you may; an
you will not, come when you are next prepared for.   160
Exit.
IAGO: After her, after her!
CASSIO: Faith, I must; she'll rail in the street else.
IAGO: Will you sup there?
CASSIO: Yes, I intend so.
IAGO: Well, I may chance to see you; for I would very   165
fain speak with you.
CASSIO: Prithee come. Will you?
IAGO: Go to! say no more.   *Exit Cassio.*
OTHELLO [*comes forward*]: How shall I murder him,
Iago?   170
IAGO: Did you perceive how he laughed at his vice?°
OTHELLO: O Iago!
IAGO: And did you see the handkerchief?
OTHELLO: Was that mine?

---

81. ecstasy: Trance.   **83. encave:** Conceal.   **88. cope:** Meet.
90. all in all in spleen: Wholly overcome by your passion.
96. huswife: Hussy.   **103. unbookish:** Uninstructed.   **conster:**
Construe, interpret.   **106. addition:** Title.   **110. caitiff:** Wretch.
121. customer: Prostitute.

128. scored me: Settled my account (?).   **132. beckons:** Signals.   **135. bauble:** Plaything.   **146. fitchew:** Polecat (slang for
whore).   **154. hobby-horse:** Harlot.   **171. vice:** I.e., vicious
conduct.

175 IAGO: Yours, by this hand! And to see how he prizes° the
foolish woman your wife! She gave it him, and he
hath giv'n it his whore.
OTHELLO: I would have him nine years a-killing — A
fine woman! a fair woman! a sweet woman!
180 IAGO: Nay, you must forget that.
OTHELLO: Ay, let her rot, and perish, and be damned tonight; for she shall not live. No, my heart is turned to
stone; I strike it, and it hurts my hand. O, the world
hath not a sweeter creature! She might lie by an
185 emperor's side and command him tasks.
IAGO: Nay, that's not your way.
OTHELLO: Hang her! I do but say what she is. So delicate with her needle! an admirable musician! O, she
will sing the savageness out of a bear! Of so high and
190 plenteous wit and invention° —
IAGO: She's the worse for all this.
OTHELLO: O, a thousand thousand times! And then, of
so gentle a condition!°
IAGO: Ay, too gentle.
195 OTHELLO: Nay, that's certain. But yet the pity of it, Iago!
O Iago, the pity of it, Iago!
IAGO: If you are so fond over her iniquity, give her
patent° to offend; for if it touch not you, it comes
near nobody.
200 OTHELLO: I will chop her into messes! Cuckold me!
IAGO: O, 'tis foul in her.
OTHELLO: With mine officer!
IAGO: That's fouler.
OTHELLO: Get me some poison, Iago, this night. I'll not
205 expostulate with her, lest her body and beauty unpro-
vide° my mind again. This night, Iago!
IAGO: Do it not with poison. Strangle her in her bed,
even the bed she hath contaminated.
OTHELLO: Good, good! The justice of it pleases. Very
210 good!
IAGO: And for Cassio, let me be his undertaker,° you
shall hear more by midnight.
OTHELLO: Excellent good!

A trumpet.

What trumpet is that same?
IAGO: I warrant something from Venice.

Enter Lodovico, Desdemona, and Attendants.

215   'Tis Lodovico.
This comes from the Duke; and see, your wife is
with him.
LODOVICO: God save you, worthy general!
OTHELLO: With all my
heart, sir.
LODOVICO: The Duke and senators of Venice greet
you.

[*Gives him a letter.*]

OTHELLO: I kiss the instrument of their pleasures.

[*Opens the letter and reads.*]

DESDEMONA: And what's the news, good cousin
Lodovico?   220
IAGO: I am very glad to see you, signior.
Welcome to Cyprus.
LODOVICO: I thank you. How does Lieutenant
Cassio?
IAGO: Lives, sir.
DESDEMONA: Cousin, there's fall'n between him and
my lord
An unkind breach; but you shall make all well.   225
OTHELLO: Are you sure of that?
DESDEMONA: My lord?
OTHELLO [*reads*]: "This fail you not to do, as you
will — "
LODOVICO: He did not call; he's busy in the paper.
Is there division 'twixt thy lord and Cassio?   230
DESDEMONA: A most unhappy one. I would do much
T' atone° them, for the love I bear to Cassio.
OTHELLO: Fire and brimstone!
DESDEMONA: My lord?
OTHELLO: Are you wise?
DESDEMONA: What, is he angry?
LODOVICO: May be the letter
moved him;
For, as I think, they do command him home,   235
Deputing Cassio in his government.
DESDEMONA: By my troth, I am glad on't.
OTHELLO: Indeed?
DESDEMONA: My lord?
OTHELLO: I am glad to see you mad.°
DESDEMONA: Why, sweet Othello —
OTHELLO: Devil!

[*Strikes her.*]

DESDEMONA: I have not deserved this.   240
LODOVICO: My lord, this would not be believed in
Venice,
Though I should swear I saw't. 'Tis very much.
Make her amends; she weeps.
OTHELLO: O devil, devil!
If that the earth could teem° with woman's tears,
Each drop she falls would prove a crocodile.°   245
Out of my sight!
DESDEMONA: I will not stay to offend you.
                                          [*Going.*]
LODOVICO: Truly, an obedient lady.
I do beseech your lordship call her back.
OTHELLO: Mistress!
DESDEMONA: My lord?
OTHELLO: What would you with her, sir?   250
LODOVICO: Who? I, my lord?

---

175. prizes: Values. 190. invention: Imagination. 193. condition: Disposition. 198. patent: License. 205. unprovide:
Disarm. 211. be his undertaker: Undertake to deal with him.

232. atone: Reconcile. 238. mad: I.e., waggish. 244. teem:
Breed. 245. crocodile: (Crocodiles were supposed to shed
hypocritical tears to lure men to destruction).

Paul Robeson in the 1930 London production of *Othello*.

Paul Robeson as Othello in the 1943 New York production, directed by Margaret Webster.

OTHELLO: Ay! You did wish that I would make her
    turn.
  Sir, she can turn, and turn, and yet go on
  And turn again; and she can weep, sir, weep;
255 And she's obedient; as you say, obedient,
  Very obedient. — Proceed you in your tears. —
  Concerning this, sir — O well-painted passion!° —
  I am commanded home. — Get you away;
  I'll send for you anon. — Sir, I obey the mandate
260 And will return to Venice. — Hence, avaunt!

                            [Exit Desdemona.]

  Cassio shall have my place. And, sir, to-night
  I do entreat that we may sup together.
  You are welcome, sir, to Cyprus — Goats and
    monkeys!

                                      Exit.

LODOVICO: Is this the noble Moor whom our full
    Senate
265 Call all in all sufficient? Is this the nature
  Whom passion could not shake? whose solid virtue
  The shot of accident nor dart of chance
  Could neither graze nor pierce?
IAGO: He is much changed.
LODOVICO: Are his wits safe? Is he not light of brain?
270 IAGO: He's that he is; I may not breathe my censure.
  What he might be — if what he might he is not —
  I would to heaven he were!
LODOVICO: What, strike his wife?
IAGO: Faith, that was not so well; yet would I knew
  That stroke would prove the worst!
LODOVICO: Is it his use?°
275 Or did the letters work upon his blood
  And new-create this fault?
IAGO: Alas, alas!
  It is not honesty in me to speak
  What I have seen and known. You shall observe
    him,
  And his own courses will denote him so
280 That I may save my speech. Do but go after
  And mark how he continues.
LODOVICO: I am sorry that I am deceived in him.

                                   Exeunt.

Scene II

Within the castle.

Enter Othello and Emilia.

OTHELLO: You have seen nothing then?
EMILIA: Nor ever heard, nor ever did suspect.
OTHELLO: Yes, you have seen Cassio and she together.
EMILIA: But then I saw no harm, and then I heard
5 Each syllable that breath made up between them.
OTHELLO: What, did they never whisper?

257. **passion:** Grief.   274. **use:** Custom.

EMILIA: Never, my lord.
OTHELLO: Nor send you out o' th' way?
EMILIA: Never.
OTHELLO: To fetch her fan, her gloves, her mask, nor
  nothing?
EMILIA: Never, my lord.   10
OTHELLO: That's strange.
EMILIA: I durst, my lord, to wager she is honest,
  Lay down my soul at stake. If you think other,
  Remove your thought; it doth abuse your bosom.°
  If any wretch have put this in your head,   15
  Let heaven requite it with the serpent's curse!°
  For if she be not honest, chaste, and true,
  There's no man happy; the purest of their wives
  Is foul as slander.
OTHELLO: Bid her come hither. Go.

                            Exit Emilia.
  She says enough; yet she's a simple bawd   20
  That cannot say as much. This is a subtle whore,
  A closet lock and key of villainous secrets;
  And yet she'll kneel and pray; I have seen her do't.

Enter Desdemona and Emilia.

DESDEMONA: My lord, what is your will?
OTHELLO: Pray, chuck,
  come hither.
DESDEMONA: What is your pleasure?
OTHELLO: Let me see your eyes. 25
  Look in my face.
DESDEMONA: What horrible fancy's this?
OTHELLO *[to Emilia]*: Some of your function, mistress.
  Leave procreants° alone and shut the door;
  Cough or cry hem if anybody come.
  Your mystery, your mystery!° Nay, dispatch! 30

                            Exit Emilia.

DESDEMONA: Upon my knees, what doth your speech
    import?
  I understand a fury in your words,
  [But not the words.]
OTHELLO: Why, what art thou?
DESDEMONA: Your wife, my lord;
  your true
  And loyal wife.
OTHELLO: Come, swear it, damn thyself; 35
  Lest, being like one of heaven,° the devils
    themselves
  Should fear to seize thee. Therefore be double-
    damned —
  Swear thou art honest.°
DESDEMONA: Heaven doth truly know it.
OTHELLO: Heaven truly knows that thou art false as
  hell.

IV, II. 14. **abuse . . . bosom:** Deceive your heart. 16. **serpent's curse:** (Cf. Genesis 3:14). 28. **procreants:** Mating couples. 30. **mystery:** Trade, occupation. 36. **being . . . heaven:** Looking like an angel. 38. **honest:** Chaste.

DESDEMONA: To whom, my lord? With whom? How
40   am I false?
OTHELLO: Ah, Desdemona! away! away! away!
DESDEMONA: Alas the heavy day! Why do you weep?
   Am I the motive of these tears, my lord?
   If haply you my father do suspect
45   An instrument° of this your calling back,
   Lay not your blame on me. If you have lost him,
   Why, I have lost him too.
OTHELLO: Had it pleased heaven
   To try me with affliction, had they rained
   All kinds of sores and shames on my bare head,
50   Steeped me in poverty to the very lips,
   Given to captivity me and my utmost hopes,
   I should have found in some place of my soul
   A drop of patience. But, alas, to make me
   A fixèd figure for the time of scorn°
55   To point his slow unmoving finger at!
   Yet could I bear that too; well, very well.
   But there where I have garnered up my heart,
   Where either I must live or bear no life,
   The fountain from the which my current runs
60   Or else dries up — to be discarded thence,
   Or keep it as a cistern for foul toads
   To knot and gender in — turn thy complexion
      there,°
   Patience, thou young and rose-lipped cherubin!
   Ay, there look grim as hell!
65 DESDEMONA: I hope my noble lord esteems me honest.
OTHELLO: O, ay; as summer flies are in the shambles,°
   That quicken° even with blowing. O thou weed,
   Who art so lovely fair, and smell'st so sweet,
   That the sense aches at thee, would thou hadst ne'er
      been born!
DESDEMONA: Alas, what ignorant sin have I
70   committed?
OTHELLO: Was this fair paper, this most goodly book,
   Made to write "whore" upon? What committed?
   Committed? O thou public commoner!°
   I should make very forges of my cheeks
75   That would to cinders burn up modesty,
   Did I but speak thy deeds. What committed?
   Heaven stops the nose at it, and the moon winks;°
   The bawdy wind, that kisses all it meets,
   Is hushed within the hollow mine of earth
80   And will not hear it. What committed?
   Impudent strumpet!
DESDEMONA: By heaven, you do me wrong!
OTHELLO: Are not you a strumpet?
DESDEMONA: No, as I am a Christian!
   If to preserve this vessel for my lord
   From any other foul unlawful touch
85   Be not to be a strumpet, I am none.

45. **An instrument:** To be the cause.   54. **time of scorn:** Scornful world.   62. **turn thy complexion there:** Change thy color at that point.   66. **shambles:** Slaughterhouse.   67. **quicken:** Come to life.   73. **commoner:** Harlot.   77. **winks:** Closes her eyes.

OTHELLO: What, not a whore?
DESDEMONA: No, as I shall be saved!
OTHELLO: Is't possible?
DESDEMONA: O, heaven forgive us!
OTHELLO: I cry you mercy° then.
   I took you for that cunning whore of Venice
   That married with Othello. — [*Calling.*] You,
      mistress,   90
   That have the office opposite to Saint Peter
   And keep the gate of hell!

Enter Emilia.

                 You, you, ay, you!
   We have done our course; there's money for your
      pains:
   I pray you turn the key, and keep our counsel. *Exit.*
EMILIA: Alas, what does this gentleman conceive?   95
   How do you, madam? How do you, my good lady?
DESDEMONA: Faith, half asleep.°
EMILIA: Good madam, what's the matter with my lord?
DESDEMONA: With who?
EMILIA: Why, with my lord, madam.   100
DESDEMONA: Who is thy lord?
EMILIA: He that is yours, sweet lady.
DESDEMONA: I have none. Do not talk to me, Emilia.
   I cannot weep; nor answer have I none
   But what should go by water. Prithee to-night
   Lay on my bed my wedding sheets, remember;   105
   And call thy husband hither.
EMILIA: Here's a change indeed!
                       Exit.
DESDEMONA: 'Tis meet I should be used so, very meet.
   How have I been behaved, that he might stick
   The small'st opinion° on my least misuse?°

Enter Iago and Emilia.

IAGO: What is your pleasure, madam? How is't with
   you?   110
DESDEMONA: I cannot tell. Those that do teach young
   babes
   Do it with gentle means and easy tasks:
   He might have chid me so; for, in good faith,
   I am a child to chiding.
IAGO: What is the matter, lady?
EMILIA: Alas, Iago, my lord hath so bewhored her,   115
   Thrown such despite and heavy terms upon her
   As true hearts cannot bear.
DESDEMONA: Am I that name, Iago?
IAGO: What name, fair lady?
DESDEMONA: Such as she said my lord did say I was.
EMILIA: He called her whore. A beggar in his drink   120
   Could not have laid such terms upon his callet.°
IAGO: Why did he so?
DESDEMONA: I do not know; I am sure I am none such.

88. **cry you mercy:** Beg your pardon.   97. **half asleep:** I.e., stunned.   109. **small'st opinion:** Least suspicion.   **least misuse:** Slightest misconduct.   121. **callet:** Whore.

IAGO: Do not weep, do not weep. Alas the day!

125 EMILIA: Hath she forsook so many noble matches,
    Her father and her country, and her friends,
    To be called whore? Would it not make one weep?

DESDEMONA: It is my wretched fortune.

IAGO: Beshrew him for't!
    How comes this trick° upon him?

DESDEMONA: Nay, heaven doth know.

130 EMILIA: I will be hanged if some eternal villain,
    Some busy and insinuating rogue,
    Some cogging, cozening° slave, to get some office,
    Have not devised this slander. I'll be hanged else.

IAGO: Fie, there is no such man! It is impossible.

135 DESDEMONA: If any such there be, heaven pardon him!

EMILIA: A halter pardon him! and hell gnaw his bones!
    Why should he call her whore? Who keeps her
        company?
    What place? what time? what form? what likelihood?
    The Moor 's abused by some most villainous knave,
140 Some base notorious knave, some scurvy fellow.
    O heaven, that such companions° thou 'dst unfold,°
    And put in every honest hand a whip
    To lash the rascals naked through the world
    Even from the east to th' west!

IAGO: Speak within door.°

145 EMILIA: O, fie upon them! Some such squire he was
    That turned your wit the seamy side without
    And made you to suspect me with the Moor.

IAGO: You are a fool. Go to.

DESDEMONA: Alas, Iago,
    What shall I do to win my lord again?
150 Good friend, go to him; for, by this light of heaven,
    I know not how I lost him. Here I kneel:
    If e'er my will did trespass 'gainst his love
    Either in discourse° of thought or actual deed,
    Or that mine eyes, mine ears, or any sense
155 Delighted them in any other form,
    Or that I do not yet, and ever did,
    And ever will (though he do shake me off
    To beggarly divorcement) love him dearly,
    Comfort forswear° me! Unkindness may do much;
160 And his unkindness may defeat° my life,
    But never taint my love. I cannot say "whore."
    It does abhor me now I speak the word;
    To do the act that might the addition earn
    Not the world's mass of vanity could make me.

165 IAGO: I pray you be content. 'Tis but his humor.
    The business of the state does him offense,
    [And he does chide with you.]

DESDEMONA: If 'twere no other —

IAGO: 'Tis but so, I warrant.

[*Trumpets within.*]

Hark how these instruments summon you to supper.
The messengers of Venice stay the meat: 170
Go in, and weep not. All things shall be well.

Exeunt Desdemona and Emilia.

Enter Roderigo.

    How now, Roderigo?

RODERIGO: I do not find that thou deal'st justly with me.

IAGO: What in the contrary?

RODERIGO: Every day thou daff'st me with some   175
    device,° Iago, and rather, as it seems to me now,
    keep'st from me all conveniency° than suppliest me
    with the least advantage of hope. I will indeed no
    longer endure it; nor am I yet persuaded to put up in
    peace what already I have foolishly suffered.   180

IAGO: Will you hear me, Roderigo?

RODERIGO: Faith, I have heard too much; for your
    words and performances are no kin together.

IAGO: You charge me most unjustly.

RODERIGO: With naught but truth. I have wasted myself 185
    out of my means. The jewels you have had from me
    to deliver to Desdemona would half have corrupted a
    votarist.° You have told me she hath received them,
    and returned me expectations and comforts of sud-
    den respect° and acquaintance; but I find none.   190

IAGO: Well, go to; very well.

RODERIGO: Very well! go to! I cannot go to, man; nor
    'tis not very well. By this hand, I say 'tis very scurvy,
    and begin to find myself fopped° in it.

IAGO: Very well.   195

RODERIGO: I tell you 'tis not very well. I will make my-
    self known to Desdemona. If she will return me my
    jewels, I will give over my suit and repent my unlaw-
    ful solicitation; if not, assure yourself I will seek satis-
    faction of you.   200

IAGO: You have said now.

RODERIGO: Ay, and said nothing but what I protest in-
    tendment of doing.

IAGO: Why, now I see there's mettle in thee; and even
    from this instant do build on thee a better opinion   205
    than ever before. Give me thy hand, Roderigo. Thou
    has taken against me a most just exception; but yet I
    protest I have dealt most directly° in thy affair.

RODERIGO: It hath not appeared.

IAGO: I grant indeed it hath not appeared, and your   210
    suspicion is not without wit and judgment. But,
    Roderigo, if thou hast that in thee indeed which I
    have greater reason to believe now than ever, I mean
    purpose, courage, and valor, this night show it. If
    thou the next night following enjoy not Desdemona,   215
    take me from this world with treachery and devise
    engines for° my life.

---

129. trick: Freakish behavior.   132. cogging, cozening: Cheat-
ing, defrauding.   141. companions: Rogues.   unfold: Expose.
144. within door: With restraint.   153. discourse: Course.
159. Comfort forswear: Happiness forsake.   160. defeat: Destroy.

175–76. thou . . . device: You put me off with some trick.
177. conveniency: Favorable opportunities.   188. votarist:
Nun.   190. sudden respect: Immediate notice.   194. fopped:
Duped.   208. directly: Straightforwardly.   217. engines for:
Plots against.

RODERIGO: Well, what is it? Is it within reason and compass?
220 IAGO: Sir, there is especial commission come from Venice to depute Cassio in Othello's place.
RODERIGO: Is that true? Why, then Othello and Desdemona return again to Venice.
IAGO: O, no; he goes into Mauritania and takes away
225 with him the fair Desdemona, unless his abode be lingered here° by some accident; wherein none can be so determinate° as the removing of Cassio.
RODERIGO: How do you mean removing of him?
IAGO: Why, by making him uncapable of Othello's
230 place — knocking out his brains.
RODERIGO: And that you would have me to do?
IAGO: Ay, if you dare do yourself a profit and a right. He sups to-night with a harlotry, and thither will I go to him. He knows not yet of his honorable fortune. If
235 you will watch his going thence, which I will fashion to fall out between twelve and one, you may take him at your pleasure. I will be near to second your attempt, and he shall fall between us. Come, stand not amazed at it, but go along with me. I will show
240 you such a necessity in his death that you shall think yourself bound to put it on him. It is now high supper time, and the night grows to waste. About it!
RODERIGO: I will hear further reason for this.
IAGO: And you shall be satisfied.   *Exeunt.*

Scene III

Within the castle.

Enter Othello, Lodovico, Desdemona, Emilia, and Attendants.

LODOVICO: I do beseech you, sir, trouble yourself no further.
OTHELLO: O, pardon me; 'twill do me good to walk.
LODOVICO: Madam, good night. I humbly thank your ladyship.
DESDEMONA: Your honor is most welcome.
OTHELLO: Will you walk, sir?
5   O, Desdemona —
DESDEMONA: My lord?
OTHELLO: Get you to bed on th' instant; I will be returned forthwith. Dismiss your attendant there. Look't be done.
10 DESDEMONA: I will, my lord.

      Exit [Othello, with Lodovico and Attendants].

EMILIA: How goes it now? He looks gentler than he did.
DESDEMONA: He says he will return incontinent.°

He hath commanded me to go to bed,
And bade me to dismiss you.
EMILIA: Dismiss me?
DESDEMONA: It was his bidding; therefore, good Emilia,   15
Give me my nightly wearing, and adieu.
We must not now displease him.
EMILIA: I would you had never seen him!
DESDEMONA: So would not I. My love doth so approve him
That even his stubbornness,° his checks,° his frowns —   20
Prithee unpin me — have grace and favor in them.
EMILIA: I have laid those sheets you bade me on the bed.
DESDEMONA: All's one. Good faith, how foolish are our minds!
If I do die before thee, prithee shroud me
In one of those same sheets.
EMILIA: Come, come! You talk.   25
DESDEMONA: My mother had a maid called Barbary.
She was in love; and he she loved proved mad°
And did forsake her. She had a song of "Willow";
An old thing 'twas; but it expressed her fortune,
And she died singing it. That song to-night   30
Will not go from my mind; I have much to do
But to go hang my head all at one side
And sing it like poor Barbary. Prithee dispatch.
EMILIA: Shall I go fetch your nightgown?°
DESDEMONA: No, unpin me here.   35
This Lodovico is a proper man.
EMILIA: A very handsome man.
DESDEMONA: He speaks well.
EMILIA: I know a lady in Venice would have walked barefoot to Palestine for a touch of his nether lip.   40
DESDEMONA (*sings*):
      "The poor soul sat sighing by a sycamore tree
      Sing all a green willow;
      Her hand on her bosom, her head on her knee,
      Sing willow, willow, willow.
      The fresh streams ran by her and murmured her moans;   45
      Sing willow, willow, willow;
      Her salt tears fell from her, and soft'ned the stones" —
Lay by these.
      "Sing willow, willow, willow" —
Prithee hie thee;° he'll come anon.   50
      "Sing all a green willow must be my garland.
      Let nobody blame him; his scorn I approve" —
Nay, that's not next. Hark! who is't that knocks?
EMILIA: It's the wind.
DESDEMONA (*sings*):
      "I call my love false love; but what said he then?   55
      Sing willow, willow, willow:

20. **stubbornness:** Roughness. **checks:** Rebukes.   **27. mad:**
Wild, faithless. **34. nightgown:** Dressing gown.   **50. hie thee:**
Hurry.

If I court moe women, you'll couch with moe
   men."
So get thee gone; good night. Mine eyes do itch.
Doth that bode weeping?
EMILIA: 'Tis neither here nor there.
DESDEMONA: I have heard it said so. O, these men,
60 these men!
Dost thou in conscience think — tell me, Emilia —
That there be women do abuse their husbands
In such gross kind?
EMILIA: There be some such, no question.
DESDEMONA: Wouldst thou do such a deed for all the
   world?
EMILIA: Why, would not you?
65 DESDEMONA: No, by this heavenly light!
EMILIA: Nor I neither by this heavenly light.
   I might do't as well i' th' dark.
DESDEMONA: Wouldst thou do such a deed for all the
   world?
70 EMILIA: The world's a huge thing; it is a great price for a
   small vice.
DESDEMONA: In troth, I think thou wouldst not.
EMILIA: In troth, I think I should; and undo't when I had
   done it. Marry, I would not do such a thing for a
75 joint-ring,° nor for measures of lawn, nor for gowns,
   petticoats, nor caps, nor any petty exhibition;° but,
   for all the whole world — 'Ud's pity! who would not
   make her husband a cuckold to make him a monarch? I should venture purgatory for't.
80 DESDEMONA: Beshrew me if I would do such a wrong
   For the whole world.
EMILIA: Why, the wrong is but a wrong i' th' world; and
   having the world for your labor, 'tis a wrong in your
   own world, and you might quickly make it right.
85 DESDEMONA: I do not think there is any such woman.
EMILIA: Yes, a dozen; and as many to th' vantage° as
   Would store° the world they played for.
   But I do think it is their husbands' faults
   If wives do fall. Say that they slack their duties
90 And pour our treasures into foreign laps;
   Or else break out in peevish° jealousies,
   Throwing restraint upon us; or say they strike us,
   Or scant our former having° in despite —
   Why, we have galls;° and though we have some
      grace,
95 Yet have we some revenge. Let husbands know
   Their wives have sense like them. They see, and
      smell,
   And have their palates both for sweet and sour,
   As husbands have. What is it that they do
   When they change us for others? Is it sport?
100 I think it is. And doth affection breed it?
   I think it doth. Is't frailty that thus errs?

It is so too. And have not we affections,
Desires for sport, and frailty, as men have?
Then let them use us well; else let them know,
The ills we do, their ills instruct us so.   105
DESDEMONA: Good night, good night. God me such
   usage° send,
Not to pick bad from bad, but by bad mend!
                              Exeunt.

ACT V • *Scene I*

A street in Cyprus.

Enter Iago and Roderigo.

IAGO: Here, stand behind this bulk;° straight will he
   come.
   Wear thy good rapier bare, and put it home.
   Quick, quick! Fear nothing; I'll be at thy elbow.
   It makes us, or it mars us — think on that,
   And fix most firm thy resolution.   5
RODERIGO: Be near at hand; I may miscarry in't.
IAGO: Here, at thy hand. Be bold, and take thy stand.

[Stands aside.]

RODERIGO: I have no great devotion to the deed,
   And yet he hath given me satisfying reasons.
   'Tis but a man gone. Forth my sword! He dies!   10
IAGO: I have rubbed this young quat° almost to the
      sense,°
   And he grows angry. Now whether he kill Cassio,
   Or Cassio him, or each do kill the other,
   Every way makes my gain. Live Roderigo,
   He calls me to a restitution large   15
   Of gold and jewels that I bobbed° from him
   As gifts to Desdemona.
   It must not be. If Cassio do remain,
   He hath a daily beauty in his life
   That makes me ugly; and besides, the Moor   20
   May unfold me to him; there stand I in much peril.
   No, he must die. Be't so! I hear him coming.

Enter Cassio.

RODERIGO: I know his gait. 'Tis he. Villain, thou diest!

[Makes a pass at Cassio.]

CASSIO: That thrust had been mine enemy indeed
   But that my coat° is better than thou know'st.   25
   I will make proof of thine.

[Draws, and wounds Roderigo.]

RODERIGO: O, I am slain!

   *[Iago darts from concealment behind Cassio,
      wounds him in the leg, and exits.]*

---

75. **joint-ring:** Ring made in separable halves. 76. **exhibition:** Gift. 86. **to th' vantage:** Besides. 87. **store:** Populate.
91. **peevish:** Senseless. 93. **having:** Allowance. 94. **galls:**
Spirits to resent.

106. **usage:** Habits. V, I. 1. **bulk:** Projecting shop-front.
11. **quat:** Pimple. **sense:** Quick. 16. **bobbed:** Swindled.
25. **coat:** Undershirt of mail.

CASSIO: I am maimed for ever. Help, ho! Murder! murder!

[*Falls.*]
Enter Othello.

OTHELLO: The voice of Cassio. Iago keeps his word.
RODERIGO: O, villain that I am!
OTHELLO: It is even so.
30 CASSIO: O, help, ho! light! a surgeon!
OTHELLO: 'Tis he. O brave Iago, honest and just,
    That hast such noble sense of thy friend's wrong!
    Thou teachest me. Minion,° your dear lies dead,
    And your unblest fate hies.° Strumpet, I come.
    Forth of my heart those charms, thine eyes, are
35   blotted.
    Thy bed, lust-stained, shall with lust's blood be
        spotted.   *Exit Othello.*

Enter Lodovico and Gratiano.

CASSIO: What, ho? No watch? No passage?° Murder!
    murder!
GRATIANO: 'Tis some mischance. The cry is very
    direful.
CASSIO: O, help!
40 LODOVICO: Hark!
RODERIGO: O wretched villain!
LODOVICO: Two or three groan. It is a heavy° night.
    These may be counterfeits. Let's think't unsafe
    To come in to the cry without more help.
45 RODERIGO: Nobody come? Then shall I bleed to death.
LODOVICO: Hark!

Enter Iago, with a light.

GRATIANO: Here's one comes in his shirt, with light
    and weapons.
IAGO: Who's there? Whose noise is this that cries on°
    murder?
LODOVICO: We do not know.
IAGO: Did not you hear a cry?
CASSIO: Here, here! For heaven's sake, help me!
IAGO: What's
50   the matter?
GRATIANO: This is Othello's ancient, as I take it.
LODOVICO: The same indeed, a very valiant fellow.
IAGO: What are you here that cry so grievously?
CASSIO: Iago? O, I am spoiled, undone by villains!
55   Give me some help.
IAGO: O me, lieutenant! What villains have done this?
CASSIO: I think that one of them is hereabout
    And cannot make° away.
IAGO: O treacherous villains!

[*To Lodovico and Gratiano.*]

    What are you there? Come in, and give some help.

RODERIGO: O, help me here!   60
CASSIO: That's one of them.
IAGO: O murd'rous slave! O villain!

[*Stabs Roderigo.*]

RODERIGO: O damned Iago! O inhuman dog!
IAGO: Kill men i' th' dark? — Where be these bloody
    thieves? —
    How silent is this town! — Ho! murder! murder! —
    What may you be? Are you of good or evil?   65
LODOVICO: As you shall prove us, praise us.
IAGO: Signior Lodovico?
LODOVICO: He, sir.
IAGO: I cry you mercy. Here's Cassio hurt by villains.
GRATIANO: Cassio?   70
IAGO: How is't, brother?
CASSIO: My leg is cut in two.
IAGO: Marry,° heaven forbid!
    Light, gentlemen. I'll bind it with my shirt.

Enter Bianca.

BIANCA: What is the matter, ho? Who is't that cried?
IAGO: Who is't that cried?   75
BIANCA: O my dear Cassio! my sweet Cassio!
    O Cassio, Cassio, Cassio!
IAGO: O notable strumpet! — Cassio, may you suspect
    Who they should be that have thus mangled you?
CASSIO: No.   80
GRATIANO: I am sorry to find you thus. I have been to
    seek you.
IAGO: Lend me a garter. So. O for a chair°
    To bear him easily hence!
BIANCA: Alas, he faints! O Cassio, Cassio, Cassio!
IAGO: Gentlemen all, I do suspect this trash   85
    To be a party in this injury. —
    Patience a while, good Cassio. — Come, come!
    Lend me a light. Know we this face or no?
    Alas, my friend and my dear countryman
    Roderigo? No — Yes, sure. — O heaven, Roderigo!   90
GRATIANO: What, of Venice?
IAGO: Even he, sir. Did you know him?
GRATIANO: Know him? Ay.
IAGO: Signior Gratiano? I cry your gentle pardon.
    These bloody accidents must excuse my manners
    That so neglected you.
GRATIANO: I am glad to see you.   95
IAGO: How do you, Cassio? — O, a chair, a chair!
GRATIANO: Roderigo?
IAGO: He, he, 'tis he!

[*A chair brought in.*]

    O, that's well said;° the chair.
    Some good man bear him carefully from hence.
    I'll fetch the general's surgeon. [*To Bianca.*] For you,   100
        mistress,

---

33. Minion: Mistress.   **34. hies:** Hurries on.   **37. passage:**
Passersby.   **42. heavy:** Cloudy, dark.   **48. cries on:** Raises the
cry of.   **58. make:** Get.

72. Marry: (From "By Mary").   **82. chair:** Litter.   **99. well
said:** Well done.

Save you your labor. — He that lies slain here,
  Cassio,
Was my dear friend. What malice was between you?
CASSIO: None in the world; nor do I know the man.
IAGO [to Bianca]: What, look you pale? — O, bear him
105 out o' th' air.

               [Cassio and Roderigo are borne off.]

Stay you, good gentlemen. — Look you pale,
  mistress? —
Do you perceive the gastness° of her eye? —
Nay, if you stare, we shall hear more anon.
Behold her well; I pray you look upon her.
110 Do you see, gentlemen? Nay, guiltiness will speak.
Though tongues were out of use.

Enter Emilia.

EMILIA: 'Las, what's the matter? What's the matter,
  husband?
IAGO: Cassio hath here been set on in the dark
  By Roderigo, and fellows that are scaped.
115 He's almost slain, and Roderigo dead.
EMILIA: Alas, good gentlemen! alas, good Cassio!
IAGO: This is the fruits of whoring. Prithee, Emilia,
  Go know of Cassio where he supped to-night.

[*To Bianca.*]

  What, do you shake at that?
BIANCA: He supped at my house; but I therefore shake
120 not.
IAGO: O, did he so? I charge you go with me.
EMILIA: Fie, fie upon thee, strumpet!
BIANCA: I am no strumpet, but of life as honest°
  As you that thus abuse me.
EMILIA: As I? Foh! fie upon thee!
125 IAGO: Kind gentlemen, let's go see poor Cassio dressed.

[*To Bianca.*]

  Come, mistress, you must tell 's another tale.
  Emilia, run you to the citadel
  And tell my lord and lady what hath happed.

                    [*Exit Emilia.*]

  Will you go on afore?   *Exeunt* [*all but Iago*].
               This is the night
130 That either makes me or fordoes° me quite. [*Exit.*]

Scene II

A bedchamber in the castle.

Desdemona [*asleep*] *in her bed. Enter Othello with a light.*

OTHELLO: It is the cause, it is the cause,° my soul.
  Let me not name it to you, you chaste stars!

It is the cause. Yet I'll not shed her blood,
Nor scar that whiter skin of hers than snow,
And smooth as monumental alabaster.   5
Yet she must die, else she'll betray more men.
Put out the light, and then put out the light.
If I quench thee, thou flaming minister,°
I can again thy former light restore,
Should I repent me; but once put out thy light,   10
Thou cunning'st pattern of excelling nature,
I know not where is that Promethean heat°
That can thy light relume.° When I have plucked the
  rose,
I cannot give it vital growth again;
It needs must wither. I'll smell thee on the tree.   15

(*He kisses her.*)

O balmy breath, that dost almost persuade
Justice to break her sword! One more, one more!
Be thus when thou art dead, and I will kill thee,
And love thee after. One more, and that's the last!
So sweet was ne'er so fatal. I must weep,   20
But they are cruel tears. This sorrow's heavenly;
It strikes where it doth love. She wakes.
DESDEMONA: Who's there? Othello?
OTHELLO: Ay, Desdemona.
DESDEMONA: Will you come to bed, my lord?
OTHELLO: Have you prayed to-night, Desdemon?
DESDEMONA: Ay,
  my lord.   25
OTHELLO: If you bethink yourself of any crime°
  Unreconciled as yet to heaven and grace,
  Solicit for it straight.
DESDEMONA: Alack, my lord, what may you mean by
  that?
OTHELLO: Well, do it, and be brief; I will walk by.   30
  I would not kill thy unprepared spirit.
  No, heaven forfend!° I would not kill thy soul.
DESDEMONA: Talk you of killing?
OTHELLO: Ay, I do.
DESDEMONA: Then heaven
  Have mercy on me!
OTHELLO: Amen, with all my heart!
DESDEMONA: If you say so, I hope you will not kill me. 35
OTHELLO: Hum!
DESDEMONA: And yet I fear you; for you're fatal then
  When your eyes roll so. Why I should fear I know
    not,
  Since guiltiness I know not; but yet I feel I fear.
OTHELLO: Think on thy sins.
DESDEMONA: They are loves I bear to you. 40
OTHELLO: Ay, and for that thou diest.
DESDEMONA: That death 's unnatural that kills for
  loving.
  Alas, why gnaw you so your nether lip?
  Some bloody passion shakes your very frame.

---

107. **gastness:** Terror. 123. **honest:** Chaste. 130. **fordoes:**
Destroys. V, II. 1. **cause:** Cause of justice.

8. **minister:** Servant. 12. **Promethean heat:** Divine fire. 13. **re-**
lume: Relight. 26. **crime:** Sin. 32. **forfend:** Forbid.

45   These are portents,° but yet I hope, I hope,
      They do not point on me.
OTHELLO: Peace and be still!
DESDEMONA: I will so. What's the matter?
OTHELLO: That handkerchief which I so loved and
         gave thee
      Thou gav'st to Cassio.
DESDEMONA: No, by my life and soul!
      Send for the man and ask him.
50   OTHELLO: Sweet soul, take heed,
      Take heed of perjury; thou art on thy deathbed.
DESDEMONA: Ay, but not yet to die.
OTHELLO: Yes, presently.°
      Therefore confess thee freely of thy sin;
      For to deny each article with oath
55   Cannot remove nor choke the strong conception°
      That I do groan withal. Thou art to die.
DESDEMONA: Then Lord have mercy on me!
OTHELLO: I say amen.
DESDEMONA: And have you mercy too! I never did
      Offend° you in my life; never loved Cassio
60   But with such general warranty of heaven
      As I might love. I never gave him token.
OTHELLO: By heaven, I saw my handkerchief in's hand!
      O perjured woman! thou dost stone my heart,°
      And mak'st me call what I intend to do
65   A murder, which I thought a sacrifice.
      I saw the handkerchief.
DESDEMONA: He found it then.
      I never gave it him. Send for him hither.
      Let him confess a truth.
OTHELLO: He hath confessed.
DESDEMONA: What, my lord?
OTHELLO: That he hath used thee.
DESDEMONA: How? Unlawfully?
70   OTHELLO: Ay.
DESDEMONA: He will not say so.
OTHELLO: No, his mouth is stopped.
      Honest Iago hath ta'en order° for't.
DESDEMONA: O, my fear interprets. What, is he dead?
OTHELLO: Had all his hairs been lives, my great
         revenge
75   Had stomach for them all.
DESDEMONA: Alas, he is betrayed, and I undone!
OTHELLO: Out, strumpet! Weep'st thou for him to my
         face?
DESDEMONA: O, banish me, my lord, but kill me not!
OTHELLO: Down, strumpet!
80   DESDEMONA: Kill me to-morrow; let me live to-night!
OTHELLO: Nay, if you strive —
DESDEMONA: But half an hour!
OTHELLO: Being done, there is no pause.
DESDEMONA: But while I say one prayer!
OTHELLO: It is too late.

---

45. **portents:** Signs of impending violence.   52. **presently:** At
once.   55. **conception:** Belief.   59. **Offend:** Wrong.   63. **stone
my heart:** Turn my heart to stone.   72. **ta'en order:** Taken
measures.

(*Smothers her.*)

[DESDEMONA: O Lord, Lord, Lord!]

Emilia at the door.

EMILIA (*calls within*): My lord, my lord! What, ho! my
      lord, my lord!   85
OTHELLO: What noise is this? Not dead? not yet quite
         dead?
      I that am cruel am yet merciful;
      I would not have thee linger in thy pain.
      So, so.
EMILIA (*within*): What, ho! my lord, my lord!
OTHELLO: Who's there?   90
EMILIA (*within*): O, good my lord, I would speak a
      word with you!
OTHELLO: Yes, 'tis Emilia. — By and by.° — She's
         dead. —
      'Tis like she comes to speak of Cassio's death.
      The noise was here. Ha! no more moving?
      Still as the grave. — Shall she come in? Were't
         good! —   95
      I think she stirs again. No. — What's best to do?
      If she come in, she'll sure speak to my wife.
      My wife! my wife! what wife! I have no wife.
      O, insupportable! O heavy hour!
      Methinks it should be now a huge eclipse   100
      Of sun and moon, and that th' affrighted globe
      Should yawn° at alteration.
EMILIA (*within*):   I do beseech you
      That I may speak with you, O good my lord!
OTHELLO: I had forgot thee. O, come in, Emilia.
      Soft, by and by. — Let me the curtains draw. — 105

[*Closes the bed-curtains.*]

      Where art thou?

[*Opens the door.*]
Enter Emilia.
                      What's the matter with thee now?
EMILIA: O my good lord, yonder's foul murder done!
OTHELLO: What? Now?
EMILIA: But now, my lord.
OTHELLO: It is the very error° of the moon.   110
      She comes more nearer earth than she was wont
      And makes men mad.
EMILIA: Cassio, my lord, hath killed a young Venetian
      Called Roderigo.
OTHELLO: Roderigo killed?
      And Cassio killed?
EMILIA: No, Cassio is not killed.   115
OTHELLO: Not Cassio killed? Then murder's out of
         tune,
      And sweet revenge grows harsh.
DESDEMONA: O, falsely, falsely murdered?

---

92. **By and by:** Just a moment (addressed to Emilia).
102. **yawn:** Open, as in an earthquake.   110. **error:** Straying
off course.

EMILIA: O, Lord!
    what cry is that?
OTHELLO: That? What?
120 EMILIA: Out and alas! that was my lady's voice.
    Help! help, ho! help! O lady, speak again!
    Sweet Desdemona! O sweet mistress, speak!
DESDEMONA: A guiltless death I die.
EMILIA: O, who hath done this deed?
125 DESDEMONA: Nobody — I myself. Farewell.
    Commend° me to my kind lord. O, farewell!

(*She dies.*)

OTHELLO: Why, how should she be murd'red?
EMILIA: Alas,
    who knows?
OTHELLO: You heard her say herself, it was not I.
EMILIA: She said so. I must needs report the truth.
130 OTHELLO: She's like a liar gone to burning hell!
    'Twas I that killed her.
EMILIA: O, the more angel she,
    And you the blacker devil!
OTHELLO: She turned to folly, and she was a whore.
EMILIA: Thou dost belie her, and thou art a devil.
OTHELLO: She was false as water.°
EMILIA: Thou art rash as fire
135   to say
    That she was false. O, she was heavenly true!
OTHELLO: Cassio did top her. Ask thy husband else.
    O, I were damned beneath all depth in hell
    But that I did proceed upon just grounds
140   To this extremity. Thy husband knew it all.
EMILIA: My husband?
OTHELLO: Thy husband.
EMILIA: That she was false to wedlock?
OTHELLO: Ay, with Cassio. Nay, had she been true,
145   If heaven would make me such another world
    Of one entire and perfect chrysolite,°
    I'ld not have sold her for it.
EMILIA: My husband?
OTHELLO: Ay 'twas he that told me first.
    An honest man he is, and hates the slime
    That sticks on filthy deeds.
150 EMILIA: My husband?
OTHELLO: What needs this iterance,° woman? I say thy
    husband.
EMILIA: O mistress, villainy hath made mocks with
    love!
    My husband say that she was false?
OTHELLO: He, woman.
    I say, thy husband. Dost understand the word?
155   My friend, thy husband; honest, honest Iago.
EMILIA: If he say so, may his pernicious soul
    Rot half a grain a day! he lies to th' heart.
    She was too fond of her most filthy bargain.
OTHELLO: Ha!

EMILIA: Do thy worst.   160
    This deed of thine is no more worthy heaven
    Than thou wast worthy her.
OTHELLO: Peace, you were best.
EMILIA: Thou hast not half the power to do me harm
    As I have to be hurt.° O gull! O dolt!
    As ignorant as dirt! thou hast done a deed —   165
    I care not for thy sword; I'll make thee known,
    Though I lost twenty lives. Help! help! Ho! help!
    The Moor hath killed my mistress! Murder!
    murder!

Enter Montano, Gratiano, Iago, and others.

MONTANO: What is the matter? How now, general?
EMILIA: O, are you come, Iago? You have done well,   170
    That men must lay their murders on your neck.
GRATIANO: What is the matter?
EMILIA: Disprove this villain, if thou be'st a man.
    He says thou told'st him that his wife was false.
    I know thou didst not; thou'rt not such a villain.   175
    Speak, for my heart is full.
IAGO: I told him what I thought, and told no more
    Than what he found himself was apt and true.
EMILIA: But did you ever tell him she was false?
IAGO: I did.   180
EMILIA: You told a lie, an odious damnèd lie!
    Upon my soul, a lie! a wicked lie!
    She false with Cassio? Did you say with Cassio?
IAGO: With Cassio, mistress. Go to, charm° your
    tongue.
EMILIA: I will not charm my tongue; I am bound to
    speak: 185
    My mistress here lies murdered in her bed —
ALL: O heavens forfend!
EMILIA: And your reports have set the murder on.
OTHELLO: Nay, stare not, masters. It is true indeed.
GRATIANO: 'Tis a strange truth.   190
MONTANO: O monstrous act!
EMILIA: Villainy, villainy, villainy!
    I think upon't — I think I smell't! — O villainy!
    I thought so then. — I'll kill myself for grief. —
    O villainy, villainy!
IAGO: What, are you mad? I charge you get you home.   195
EMILIA: Good gentlemen, let me have leave to speak.
    'Tis proper I obey him, but not now.
    Perchance, Iago, I will ne'er go home.
OTHELLO: O! O! O!   (*Falls on the bed.*)
EMILIA: Nay, lay thee down and roar!
    For thou hast killed the sweetest innocent   200
    That e'er did lift up eye.
OTHELLO: O, she was foul!

[*Rises.*]

    I scarce did know you, uncle. There lies your niece,
    Whose breath, indeed, these hands have newly
    stopped.

---

126. Commend: Remember.   **135. water:** (Which is yielding).
146. chrysolite: (Precious topaz).   **151. iterance:** Repetition.

164. to be hurt: To endure hurt.   **184. charm:** Cast a spell on.

I know this act shows° horrible and grim.
GRATIANO: Poor Desdemon! I am glad thy father's
205   dead.
Thy match was mortal to him, and pure grief
Shore his old thread in twain. Did he live now,
This sight would make him do a desperate turn;°
Yea, curse his better angel from his side,
210   And fall to reprobation.°
OTHELLO: 'Tis pitiful; but yet Iago knows
That she with Cassio hath the act of shame
A thousand times committed. Cassio confessed it;
And she did gratify° his amorous works
215   With that recognizance° and pledge of love
Which I first gave her. I saw it in his hand.
It was a handkerchief, an antique token
My father gave my mother.
EMILIA: O God! O heavenly God!
IAGO: Zounds, hold your peace!
220 EMILIA: 'Twill out, 'twill out! I peace?
No, I will speak as liberal as the north,°
Let heaven and men and devils, let them all,
All, all, cry shame against me, yet I'll speak.
IAGO: Be wise, and get you home.
EMILIA: I will not.

[*Iago draws and threatens Emilia.*]

GRATIANO: Fie!
225   Your sword upon a woman?
EMILIA: O thou dull Moor, that handkerchief thou
        speak'st of
I found by fortune, and did give my husband;
For often with a solemn earnestness —
More than indeed belonged to such a trifle —
He begged of me to steal't.
230 IAGO: Villainous whore!
EMILIA: She give it Cassio? No, alas, I found it,
And I did give't my husband.
IAGO: Filth, thou liest!
EMILIA: By heaven, I do not, I do not, gentlemen.
O murd'rous coxcomb! what should such a fool
Do with so good a wife?
235 OTHELLO: Are there no stones° in heaven
But what serves for the thunder? Precious villain!

The Moor runs at Iago [*but is disarmed by Montano*].
Iago kills his wife.

GRATIANO: The woman falls. Sure he hath killed his
        wife.
EMILIA: Ay, ay. O, lay me by my mistress' side.
                                        Exit Iago.
GRATIANO: He's gone, but his wife's killed.
MONTANO: 'Tis a notorious° villain. Take you this
240   weapon,

---

204. **shows:** Appears.   207. **turn:** Act.   209. **reprobation:** Rejection by God, damnation.   214. **gratify:** Reward.   215. **recognizance:** Token.   221. **liberal as the north:** Unchecked as the north wind blows.   235. **stones:** Bolts like those used for thunderbolts.   240. **notorious:** Notable.

Which I have here recovered from the Moor.
Come, guard the door without. Let him not pass,
But kill him rather. I'll after that same villain,
For 'tis a damnèd slave.

    Exit [*Montano, with all but Othello and Emilia*].

OTHELLO: I am not valiant neither;
But every puny whipster° gets my sword.   245
But why should honor outlive honesty?
Let it go all.
EMILIA: What did thy song bode, lady?
Hark, canst thou hear me? I will play the swan,
And die in music. [*Sings.*] "Willow, willow, willow."
Moor, she was chaste. She loved thee, cruel Moor: 250
So come my soul to bliss as I speak true.
So speaking as I think, alas, I die.

(*She dies.*)

OTHELLO: I have another weapon in this chamber;
It is a sword of Spain, the ice brook's° temper.
O, here it is. — Uncle, I must come forth.   255
GRATIANO (*within*): If thou attempt it, it will cost thee
        dear.
Thou hast no weapon, and perforce must suffer.
OTHELLO: Look in upon me then and speak with me,
Or, naked° as I am, I will assault thee.

[*Enter Gratiano.*]

GRATIANO: What is the matter?
OTHELLO: Behold, I have a weapon;   260
A better never did itself sustain
Upon a soldier's thigh. I have seen the day
That with this little arm and this good sword
I have made my way through more impediments
Than twenty times your stop.° But O vain boast!   265
Who can control his fate? 'Tis not so now.
Be not afraid, though you do see me weaponed.
Here is my journey's end, here is my butt,°
And very seamark° of my utmost sail:
Do you go back dismayed? 'Tis a lost° fear.   270
Man but a rush° against Othello's breast,
And he retires. Where should Othello go?
Now, how dost thou look now? O ill-starred
        wench!
Pale as thy smock! When we shall meet at compt,°
This look of thine will hurl my soul from heaven,   275
And fiends will snatch at it. Cold, cold, my girl?
Even like thy chastity.
O cursèd, cursèd slave! Whip me, ye devils,
From the possession of this heavenly sight!
Blow me about in winds! roast me in sulphur!   280

---

245. **puny whipster:** Whippersnapper.   254. **ice brook:** I.e., a Spanish blade, tempered in cold running water.   259. **naked:** Disarmed.   265. **stop:** Power to stop.   268. **butt:** Limit.   269. **seamark:** Beacon, destination.   270. **lost:** Wasted.   271. **Man but a rush:** Wield only a reed.   274. **compt:** Final accounting, Last Judgment.

Wash me in steep-down gulfs of liquid fire!
Oh Desdemon! dead Desdemon! dead! Oh! Oh!

Enter Lodovico, Montano, Iago [as prisoner], and Offi-
cers; Cassio in a chair.

LODOVICO: Where is this rash and most unfortunate
    man?
OTHELLO: That's he that was Othello. Here I am.
285 LODOVICO: Where is that viper? Bring the villain forth.
OTHELLO: I look down towards his feet° — but that's a
    fable.
    If that thou be'st a devil, I cannot kill thee.

[*Wounds Iago.*]

LODOVICO: Wrench his sword from him.

[*Othello is disarmed.*]

IAGO: I bleed, sir, but not killed.
OTHELLO: I am not sorry neither. I'ld have thee live;
290   For in my sense, 'tis happiness to die.
LODOVICO: O thou Othello that wert once so good,
    Fall'n in the practice° of a damnèd slave,
    What shall be said to thee?
OTHELLO: Why, anything;
    An honorable murderer, if you will;
295   For naught did I in hate, but all in honor.
LODOVICO: This wretch hath part confessed his
    villainy.
    Did you and he consent in° Cassio's death?
OTHELLO: Ay.
CASSIO: Dear general, I never gave you cause.
300 OTHELLO: I do believe it, and I ask your pardon.
    Will you, I pray, demand that demi-devil
    Why he hath thus ensnared my soul and body?
IAGO: Demand me nothing. What you know, you
    know.
    From this time forth I never will speak word.
LODOVICO: What, not to pray?
305 GRATIANO: Torments will ope your lips.
OTHELLO: Well, thou dost best.
LODOVICO: Sir, you shall understand what hath
    befall'n,
    Which, as I think, you know not. Here is a letter
    Found in the pocket of the slain Roderigo;
310   And here another. The one of them imports
    The death of Cassio to be undertook
    By Roderigo.
OTHELLO: O villain!
CASSIO: Most heathenish and most gross!
LODOVICO: Now here's another discontented paper
315   Found in the pocket too; and this, it seems,
    Roderigo mean t' have sent this damnèd villain;
    But that, belike, Iago in the nick°
    Came in and satisfied him.

OTHELLO: O thou pernicious caitiff! —
    How came you, Cassio, by that handkerchief
    That was my wife's?
CASSIO: I found it in my chamber;   320
    And he himself confessed but even now
    That there he dropped it for a special purpose
    Which wrought to his desire.
OTHELLO: O fool! fool! fool!
CASSIO: There is besides in Roderigo's letter,
    How he upbraids Iago that he made him   325
    Brave me upon the watch; whereon it came
    That I was cast;° and even but now he spake,
    After long seeming dead — Iago hurt him,
    Iago set him on.
LODOVICO: You must forsake this room and go with
    us.   330
    Your power and your command is taken off,
    And Cassio rules in Cyprus. For this slave,
    If there be any cunning cruelty
    That can torment him much and hold him long,
    It shall be his. You shall close prisoner rest   335
    Till that the nature of your fault be known
    To the Venetian state. Come, bring away.
OTHELLO: Soft you! a word or two before you go.
    I have done the state some service, and they
        know't.
    No more of that. I pray you, in your letters,   340
    When you shall these unlucky° deeds relate,
    Speak of me as I am. Nothing extenuate,
    Nor set down aught in malice. Then must you
        speak
    Of one that loved not wisely, but too well;
    Of one not easily jealous, but, being wrought,   345
    Perplexed° in the extreme; of one whose hand,
    Like the base Judean,° threw a pearl away
    Richer than all his tribe; of one whose subdued°
        eyes,
    Albeit unusèd to the melting mood,
    Drop tears as fast as the Arabian trees   350
    Their med'cinable gum. Set you down this.
    And say besides that in Aleppo once,
    Where a malignant and a turbaned Turk
    Beat a Venetian and traduced the state,
    I took by th' throat the circumcisèd dog   355
    And smote him — thus.

(*He stabs himself.*)

LODOVICO: O bloody period!°
GRATIANO: All that's spoke is marred.
OTHELLO: I kissed thee ere I killed thee. No way but
    this,
    Killing myself, to die upon a kiss.

(*He [falls upon the bed and] dies.*)

---

286. I . . . feet: I.e., to see if they are cloven, like the Devil's.
292. practice: Plot.   **297. consent in:** Agree upon.   **317. nick:**
Nick of time.

327. cast: Dismissed.   **341. unlucky:** Fatal.   **346. Perplexed:**
Distracted.   **347. Judean:** Judas Iscariot (?) (quarto reads "In-
dian").   **348. subdued:** I.e., conquered by grief.   **357. period:**
Ending.

CASSIO: This did I fear, but thought he had no
360 weapon;
 For he was great of heart.
LODOVICO [*to Iago*]: O Spartan dog,
 More fell° than anguish, hunger, or the sea!
 Look on the tragic loading of this bed.
 This is thy work. The object poisons sight;
365 Let it be hid.° Gratiano, keep the house,

And seize upon° the fortunes of the Moor,
For they succeed on you. To you, lord governor,
Remains the censure° of this hellish villain,
The time, the place, the torture. O, enforce it!
Myself will straight aboard, and to the state 370
This heavy act with heavy heart relate.

            Exeunt.

362. fell: Cruel. **365. Let it be hid:** I.e., draw the bed curtains.

366. seize upon: Take legal possession of. **368. censure:** Judicial sentence.

COMMENTARIES

The great Shakespeare critic A. C. Bradley examines Othello's character in a portion of his series of lectures on the play. His approach is to probe Othello's essential nature, beginning with the premise that Othello is not by nature jealous but that Iago makes him so. Virginia Mason Vaughan offers insights into the way in which one of the greatest nineteenth-century English actors prepared for the role and what he felt he had to trim from the text in order to satisfy midcentury audiences. John Holstrom's review of Laurence Olivier's singular performance in the newly founded Royal Shakespeare Company in 1964 is mixed. He praises Olivier but complains of the ensemble around him. This review touches on the ways in which even a memorable performance can be marred by a questionable production.

A. C. Bradley *(1851–1935)*
OTHELLO'S CHARACTER   *1904*

Among his distinguished lectures on Shakespearean tragedy, A. C. Bradley meditated on the essential nature of Othello. He sees him as a relatively simple man, especially in contrast to Iago, whom Bradley sees as more highly charged and luminous in the play. But what he sees in Othello is nobility, the same nobility that scores of theatergoers have seen on stages throughout the world.

The character of Othello is comparatively simple, but, as I have dwelt on the prominence of intrigue and accident in the play, it is desirable to show how essentially the success of Iago's plot is connected with this character. Othello's description of himself as

 one not easily jealous, but, being wrought,
Perplexed in the extreme,

is perfectly just. His tragedy lies in this — that his whole nature was indisposed to jealousy and yet was such that he was unusually open to deception and, if once wrought to passion, likely to act with little reflection, with no delay, and in the most decisive manner conceivable.

Let me first set aside a mistaken view. I do not mean the ridiculous notion that Othello was jealous by temperament, but the idea, which has some little plausibility, that the play is primarily a study of a noble barbarian, who has become a Christian and has imbibed some of the civilization of his employers, but who retains beneath the surface the savage passions of his Moorish blood and also the suspiciousness regarding female chastity common among Oriental peoples, and that the last three Acts depict the outburst of these original feelings through the thin crust of Venetian culture. It would take too long to discuss this idea,[1] and it would perhaps be useless to do so, for all arguments against it must end in an appeal to the reader's understanding of Shakespeare. If he thinks it is like Shakespeare to look at things in this manner; that he had a historical mind and occupied himself with problems of "Kulturgeschichte"; that he labored to make his Romans perfectly Roman, to give a correct view of the Britons in the days of Lear or Cymbeline, to portray in Hamlet a stage of the moral consciousness not yet reached by the people around him, the reader will also think this interpretation of *Othello* probable. To me it appears hopelessly un-Shakespearean. I could as easily believe that Chaucer meant the Wife of Bath for a study of the peculiarities of Somersetshire. I do not mean that Othello's race is a matter of no account. It has, as we shall presently see, its importance in the play. It makes a difference to our idea of him; it makes a difference to the action and catastrophe. But in regard to the essentials of his character it is not important; and if anyone had told Shakespeare that no Englishman would have acted like the Moor and had congratulated him on the accuracy of his racial psychology, I am sure he would have laughed.

Othello is, in one sense of the word, by far the most romantic figure among Shakespeare's heroes; and he is so partly from the strange life of war and adventure which he has lived from childhood. He does not belong to our world, and he seems to enter it we know not whence — almost as if from wonderland. There is something mysterious in his descent from men of royal siege; in his wanderings in vast deserts and among marvelous peoples; in his tales of magic handkerchiefs and prophetic Sibyls; in the sudden vague glimpses we get of numberless battles and sieges in which he has played the hero and has borne a charmed life; even in chance references to his baptism, his being sold to slavery, his sojourn in Aleppo.

And he is not merely a romantic figure; his own nature is romantic. He has not, indeed, the meditative or speculative imagination of Hamlet; but in the strictest sense of the word he is more poetic than Hamlet. Indeed, if one recalls Othello's most famous speeches — those that begin, "Her father loved me," "O now for ever," "Never, Iago," "Had it pleased Heaven," "It is the cause," "Behold, I have a weapon," "Soft you, a word or two before you go"— and if one places side by side with these speeches an equal number by any other hero, one will not doubt that Othello is the greatest poet of them all. There is the same poetry in his casual phrases — like "These nine moons wasted," "Keep up your bright swords, for the dew will rust them," "You chaste stars," "It is a sword of Spain, the ice-brook's

---

[1]The reader who is tempted by it should, however, first ask himself whether Othello does act like a barbarian or like a man who, though wrought almost to madness, does "all in honour."

temper," "It is the very error of the moon"— and in those brief expressions of intense feeling which ever since have been taken as the absolute expression, like

> If it were now to die,
> 'Twere now to be most happy; for, I fear,
> My soul hath her content so absolute
> That not another comfort like to this
> Succeeds in unknown fate,

or

> If she be false, O then heaven mocks itself,
> I'll not believe it;

or

> No, my heart is turned to stone; I strike it, and it hurts
>   my hand,

or

> But yet the pity of it, Iago! O Iago, the pity of it, Iago!

or

> O thou weed,
> Who are so lovely fair and smell'st so sweet
> That the sense aches at thee, would thou hadst ne'er been
>   born.

And this imagination, we feel, has accompanied his whole life. He has watched with a poet's eye the Arabian trees dropping their med'cinable gum, and the Indian throwing away his chance-found pearl; and has gazed in a fascinated dream at the Pontic sea rushing, never to return, to the Propontic and the Hellespont; and has felt as no other man ever felt (for he speaks of it as none other ever did) the poetry of the pride, pomp, and circumstance of glorious war.

So he comes before us, dark and grand, with a light upon him from the sun where he was born; but no longer young, and now grave, self-controlled, steeled by the experience of countless perils, hardships, and vicissitudes, at once simple and stately in bearing and in speech, a great man naturally modest but fully conscious of his worth, proud of his services to the State, unawed by dignitaries and unelated by honors, secure, it would seem, against all dangers from without and all rebellion from within. And he comes to have his life crowned with the final glory of love, a love as strange, adventurous and romantic as any passage of his eventful history, filling his heart with tenderness and his imagination with ecstasy. For there is no love, not that of Romeo in his youth, more steeped in imagination than Othello's.

The sources of danger in this character are revealed but too clearly by the story. In the first place, Othello's mind, for all its poetry, is very simple. He is not observant. His nature tends outward. He is quite free from introspection and is not given to reflection. Emotion excites his imagination, but it confuses and dulls his intellect. On this side he is the very opposite of Hamlet, with whom, however, he shares a great openness and trustfulness of nature. In addition, he has little experience of the corrupt products of civilized life and is ignorant of European women.

In the second place, for all his dignity and massive calm (and he has greater dignity than any other of Shakespeare's men), he is by nature full of the most vehement passion. Shakespeare emphasizes his self-control, not only by the wonderful pictures of the First Act, but by references to the past. Lodovico, amazed at his violence, exclaims:

> Is this the noble Moor whom our full Senate
> Call all in all sufficient? Is this the nature
> Whom passion could not shake? whose solid virtue
> The shot of accident nor dart of chance
> Could neither graze nor pierce?

Iago, who has here no motive for lying, asks:

> Can he be angry? I have seen the cannon
> When it hath blown his ranks into the air,
> And, like the devil, from his very arm
> Puffed his own brother — and can he be angry?[2]

This, and other aspects of his character, are best exhibited by a single line — one of Shakespeare's miracles — the words by which Othello silences in a moment the night brawl between his attendants and those of Brabantio:

> Keep up your bright swords, for the dew will rust them.

And the same self-control is strikingly shown where Othello endeavors to elicit some explanation of the fight between Cassio and Montano. Here, however, there occur ominous words, which make us feel how necessary was this self-control, and make us admire it the more:

> Now, by heaven,
> My blood begins my safer guides to rule,
> And passion, having my best judgment collied,
> Assays to lead the way.

We remember these words later, when the sun of reason is "collied," blackened and blotted out in total eclipse.

Lastly, Othello's nature is all of one piece. His trust, where he trusts, is absolute. Hesitation is almost impossible to him. He is extremely self-reliant, and decides and acts instantaneously. If stirred to indignation, as "in Aleppo once," he answers with one lightning stroke. Love, if he loves, must be to him the heaven where either he must live or bear no life. If such a passion as jealousy seizes him, it will swell into a well-nigh uncontrollable flood. He will press for immediate conviction or immediate relief. Convinced, he will act with the authority of a judge and the swiftness of a man in mortal pain. Undeceived, he will do like execution on himself.

This character is so noble, Othello's feelings and actions follow so inevitably from it and from the forces brought to bear on it, and his sufferings are so heartrending that he stirs, I believe, in most readers a passion of mingled love and pity which they feel for no other hero in Shakespeare and to which not even Mr. Swinburne can do more than justice. Yet there are some critics and not a few readers who cherish a grudge against him. They do not merely think that in the later stages of his temptation he showed a certain obtuseness and that, to speak pedantically, he acted with unjustifiable precipitance and violence; no one, I sup-

---

[2]For the actor, then, to represent him as violently angry when he cashiers Cassio is an utter mistake.

pose, denies that. But even when they admit that he was not of a jealous temper, they consider that he *was* "easily jealous"; they seem to think that it was inexcusable in him to feel any suspicion of his wife at all; and they blame him for never suspecting Iago or asking him for evidence. I refer to this attitude of mind chiefly in order to draw attention to certain points in the story. It comes partly from mere inattention (for Othello did suspect Iago and did ask him for evidence); partly from a misconstruction of the text which makes Othello appear jealous long before he really is so; and partly from failure to realize certain essential facts. I will begin with these.

(1) Othello, we have seen, was trustful and thorough in his trust. He put entire confidence in the honesty of Iago, who had not only been his companion in arms but, as he believed, had just proved his faithfulness in the matter of the marriage. This confidence was misplaced, and we happen to know it; but it was no sign of stupidity in Othello. For his opinion of Iago was the opinion of practically everyone who knew him: and that opinion was that Iago was before all things "honest," his very faults being those of excess in honesty. This being so, even if Othello had not been trustful and simple, it would have been quite unnatural in him to be unmoved by the warnings of so honest a friend, warnings offered with extreme reluctance and manifestly from a sense of a friend's duty.[3] *Any* husband would have been troubled by them.

(2) Iago does not bring these warnings to a husband who had lived with a wife for months and years and knew her like his sister or his bosom friend. Nor is there any ground in Othello's character for supposing that, if he had been such a man, he would have felt and acted as he does in the play. But he was newly married; in the circumstances he cannot have known much of Desdemona before his marriage; and further he was conscious of being under the spell of a feeling which can give glory to the truth but can also give it to a dream.

(3) This consciousness in any imaginative man is enough, in such circumstances, to destroy his confidence in his powers of perception. In Othello's case, after a long and most artful preparation, there now comes, to reinforce its effect, the suggestions that he is not an Italian, nor even a European; that he is totally ignorant of the thoughts and the customary morality of Venetian women;[4] that he had himself seen in Desdemona's deception of her father how perfect an actress she could be. As he listens in horror, for a moment at least the past is revealed to him in a new and dreadful light, and the ground seems to sink under his feet. These suggestions are followed by a tentative but hideous and humiliating insinuation of what his honest and much-experienced friend fears may be the true explanation of Desdemona's rejection of acceptable suitors and of her strange, and naturally temporary, preference for a black man. Here Iago goes too far. He sees something in Othello's face that frightens him, and he breaks off. Nor does this idea take any hold of Othello's mind. But it is not surprising that his utter powerlessness to repel it on the ground of knowledge of his wife, or even of that instinctive interpretation

---

[3]It is important to observe that, in his attempt to arrive at the facts about Cassio's drunken misdemeanor, Othello had just had an example of Iago's unwillingness to tell the whole truth where it must injure a friend. No wonder he feels in the temptation scene that "this honest creature doubtless Sees and knows more, much more, than he unfolds."

[4]To represent that Venetian women do not regard adultery so seriously as Othello does, and again that Othello would be wise to accept the situation like an Italian husband, is one of Iago's most artful and most maddening devices.

of character which is possible between persons of the same race,[5] should complete his misery, so that he feels he can bear no more, and abruptly dismisses his friend (III, iii, 238).

Now I repeat that *any* man situated as Othello was would have been disturbed by Iago's communications, and I add that many men would have been made wildly jealous. But up to this point, where Iago is dismissed, Othello, I must maintain, does not show jealousy. His confidence is shaken, he is confused and deeply troubled, he feels even horror; but he is not yet jealous in the proper sense of that word. In his soliloquy (III, iii, 258 ff.) the beginning of this passion may be traced; but it is only after an interval of solitude, when he has had time to dwell on the idea presented to him, and especially after statements of fact, not mere general grounds of suspicion, are offered, that the passion lays hold of him. Even then, however, and indeed to the very end, he is quite unlike the essentially jealous man, quite unlike Leontes. No doubt the thought of another man's possessing the woman he loves is intolerable to him; no doubt the sense of insult and the impulse of revenge are at times most violent; and these are the feelings of jealousy proper. But these are not the chief or the deepest source of Othello's suffering. It is the wreck of his faith and his love. It is the feeling,

> If she be false, oh then Heaven mocks itself;

the feeling,

> O Iago, the pity of it, Iago!

the feeling,

> But there where I have garner'd up my heart,
> Where either I must live, or bear no life;
> The fountain from the which my current runs,
> Or else dries up — to be discarded thence. . . .

You will find nothing like this in Leontes.

Up to this point, it appears to me, there is not a syllable to be said against Othello. But the play is a tragedy, and from this point we may abandon the ungrateful and undramatic task of awarding praise and blame. When Othello, after a brief interval, reenters (III, iii, 330), we see at once that the poison has been at work, and "burns like the mines of sulphur."

> Look where he comes! Not poppy, nor mandragora,
> Nor all the drowsy syrups of the world,
> Shall ever medicine thee to that sweet sleep
> Which thou owedst yesterday.

He is "on the rack," in an agony so unbearable that he cannot endure the sight of Iago. Anticipating the probability that Iago has spared him the whole truth, he feels that in that case his life is over and his "occupation gone" with all its glories. But he has not abandoned hope. The bare possibility that his friend is deliberately deceiv-

---

[5]If the reader has ever chanced to see an African violently excited, he may have been startled to observe how completely at a loss he was to interpret those bodily expressions of passion which in a fellow countryman he understands at once, and in a European foreigner with somewhat less certainty. The effect of difference in blood in increasing Othello's bewilderment regarding his wife is not sufficiently realized. The same effect has to be remembered in regard to Desdemona's mistakes in dealing with Othello in his anger.

ing him — though such a deception would be a thing so monstrously wicked that he can hardly conceive it credible — is a kind of hope. He furiously demands proof, ocular proof. And when he is compelled to see that he is demanding an impossibility he still demands evidence. He forces it from the unwilling witness, and hears the maddening tale of Cassio's dream. It is enough. And if it were not enough, has he not sometimes seen a handkerchief spotted with strawberries in his wife's hand? Yes, it was his first gift to her.

> I know not that; but such a handkerchief —
> I am sure it was your wife's — did I to-day
> See Cassio wipe his beard with.

"If it be that," he answers — but what need to test the fact? The "madness of revenge" is in his blood, and hesitation is a thing he never knew. He passes judgment and controls himself only to make his sentence a solemn vow.

The Othello of the Fourth Act is Othello in his fall. His fall is never complete, but he is much changed. Toward the close of the temptation scene he becomes at times most terrible, but his grandeur remains almost undiminished. Even in the following scene (III, iv), where he goes to test Desdemona in the matter of the handkerchief and receives a fatal confirmation of her guilt, our sympathy with him is hardly touched by any feeling of humiliation. But in the Fourth Act "Chaos has come." A slight interval of time may be admitted here. It is but slight; for it was necessary for Iago to hurry on, and terribly dangerous to leave a chance for a meeting of Cassio with Othello; and his insight into Othello's nature taught him that his plan was to deliver blow on blow, and never to allow his victim to recover from the confusion of the first shock. Still there is a slight interval; and when Othello reappears we see at a glance that he is a changed man. He is physically exhausted, and his mind is dazed. He sees everything blurred through a mist of blood and tears. He has actually forgotten the incident of the handkerchief and has to be reminded of it. When Iago, perceiving that he can now risk almost any lie, tells him that Cassio has confessed his guilt, Othello, the hero who has seemed to us only second to Coriolanus in physical power, trembles all over; he mutters disjointed words; a blackness suddenly intervenes between his eyes and the world; he takes it for the shuddering testimony of nature to the horror he has just heard, and he falls senseless to the ground. When he recovers it is to watch Cassio, as he imagines, laughing over his shame. It is an imposition so gross, and should have been one so perilous, that Iago would never have ventured it before. But he is safe now. The sight only adds to the confusion of intellect the madness of rage; and a ravenous thirst for revenge, contending with emotions of infinite longing and regret, conquers them. The delay till nightfall is torture to him. His self-control has wholly deserted him, and he strikes his wife in the presence of the Venetian envoy. He is so lost to all sense of reality that he never asks himself what will follow the deaths of Cassio and his wife. An ineradicable instinct of justice, rather than any last quiver of hope, leads him to question Emilia; but nothing could convince him now, and there follows the dreadful scene of accusation; and then, to allow us the relief of burning hatred and burning tears, the interview of Desdemona with Iago, and that last talk of hers with Emilia, and her last song.

But before the end there is again a change. The supposed death of Cassio (v, i) satiates the thirst for vengeance. The Othello who enters the bedchamber with the words,

> It is the cause, it is the cause, my soul,

is not the man of the Fourth Act. The deed he is bound to do is no murder, but a sacrifice. He is to save Desdemona from herself, not in hate but in honor; in honor, and also in love. His anger has passed; a boundless sorrow has taken its place; and

> this sorrow's heavenly:
> It strikes where it doth love.

Even when, at the sight of her apparent obduracy, and at the hearing of words which by a crowning fatality can only reconvince him of her guilt, these feelings give way to others, it is to righteous indignation they give way, not to rage; and, terribly painful as this scene is, there is almost nothing here to diminish the admiration and love which heighten pity. And pity itself vanishes, and love and admiration alone remain, in the majestic dignity and sovereign ascendancy of the close. Chaos has come and gone; and the Othello of the Council Chamber and the quay of Cyprus has returned or a greater and nobler Othello still. As he speaks those final words in which all the glory and agony of his life — long ago in India and Arabia and Aleppo, and afterward in Venice, and now in Cyprus — seem to pass before us, like the pictures that flash before the eyes of a drowning man, a triumphant scorn for the fetters of the flesh and the littleness of all the lives that must survive him sweeps our grief away, and when he dies upon a kiss the most painful of all tragedies leaves us for the moment free from pain, and exulting in the power of "love and man's unconquerable mind."

Virginia Mason Vaughan (b. 1947)
MACREADY'S OTHELLO   *1994*

In her discussion of Othello's *performance history, Virginia Mason Vaughan describes one of the greatest Shakespearean actors of the mid-nineteenth century. William Charles Macready (1793–1873) was born in England and performed in London and throughout the United States. His care in producing* Othello, *including his willingness to edit out sensitive lines, gives us an interesting insight into the history of the play's production.*

Alan Downer, Macready's biographer, describes the tragedian's acting methods: "In the study and rehearsal of a part, Macready searched for character traits which an audience would recognize as natural, and by the skillful use of pause, transition, and colloquialism strove to convey the poet's meaning."[1] One technique was the "Macready pause," a slight hesitation within the speech in imitation of a natural speaking voice. Macready used these pauses to make Othello seem more realistic. On 1 November 1836, he recorded: "I think I acted Othello well with considerable spirit, and more *pause* than I generally allow myself, which is an undoubted

---

[1]Alan Downer, *The Eminent Tragedian: William Charles Macready* (Cambridge: Harvard University Press, 1966), p. 80. See also Bertram Joseph, *The Tragic Actor* (London: Routledge and Kegan Paul, 1959), pp. 284–320, for a discussion of Macready's acting style and the traits of his competitors, including Vandenhoff, Phelps, and Kean.

improvement."[2] Again, on 7 November: "Acted Othello, not exactly well, but again derived great benefit from *taking time* between my sentences."[3] Macready also used specific stage business to achieve what he thought would be a more natural effect. Downer observes, for example, that "To further contribute to the reality of the senate scene in *Othello* he played with his back to the audience."[4]

The productions Macready mounted at Covent Garden and Drury Lane demonstrate his meticulousness over scenic design and costume. George Ellis prepared watercolor drawings of costumes and scenery from the Covent Garden *Othello* for Charles Kean; seven scenic drawings, now in the Folger Shakespeare Library,[5] show careful attention to detail. The first is a wash of the Rialto that was also used for *The Merchant of Venice,* complete with bridge, canal, gondola, and Renaissance buildings in the background. The second scene is the citadel of Famagusta on the isle of Cyprus. It consists of three layers: the front panel shows the castle wall and cannons pointing out to sea; the middle panel portrays a castle turret, while the back panel opens to a prospect across the harbor. The third scene is a gateway leading from outside the castle to the inside. The drunken revels of *Othello,* act II, scene III, would be staged before these gates. The fourth watercolor is an ornate chamber in the castle, suitable for the temptation scene, the fifth an antechamber in the castle, ornamented with carved scrolled walls. The sixth set is a piazza outside an Italian Renaissance building, flanked by columns. Last, of course, is the bedchamber. The bed, hidden in the center back alcove, is ornately decked with labial curtains. At first the bed's upstage location seems to marginalize Desdemona, but three sets of brightly colored curtains draped above lure the eye inward toward the recess. The entire set, in contrast to the grim action of the murder, is brightly colored in shades of blue, pink, and yellow.

Macready's elaborate scenery was symptomatic of his efforts to produce Shakespeare in historically accurate settings. Shattuck demonstrates the tragedian's meticulous attention to historical detail when he produced *King John.*[6] This concern was not confined to the history plays, however. For *Othello* accuracy meant realistic scenes from Renaissance Venice (the Rialto, bridge, canal, gondolas, and Doge's Palace) and Cyprus (the citadel at Famagusta). Though they were painted after the fact, these watercolors demonstrate the extravagant beauty of Macready's 1837 Covent Garden *Othello,* a beauty that set a high standard for subsequent spectacular, historically based productions.

Macready's quest for scenic harmony included detailed attention to costumes. For London productions no expense was spared. Watercolor sketches of the Covent Garden costumes[7] are just as detailed and colorful as the scenic designs. They too may have been used, where appropriate, in *The Merchant of Venice.* Brabantio wears a red robe trimmed with ermine over a black doublet. Gratiano, in

---

[2]William Charles Macready, *The Diaries of William Charles Macready,* ed. William Toynbee (London: Chapman and Hall, Ltd., 1912), v. 1, p. 354.

[3]Ibid., p. 357.

[4]Downer, *Eminent Tragedian,* p. 75.

[5]The promptbooks described below are listed in Charles H. Shattuck's *The Shakespeare Promptbooks: A Descriptive Catalogue* (Urbana: University of Illinois Press, 1965). This particular promptbook, Folger 14, is listed in Shattuck as no. 26 (p. 359).

[6]See Charles H. Shattuck, *William Charles Macready's King John* (Urbana: University of Illinois Press, 1962).

[7]Folger Promptbook 15, Shattuck 27. (See note 5 above.)

contrast, appears in a black robe with red doublet. Othello's red tunic is fringed with gold to match his gold cape. Iago is dressed in a buff doublet with a green vest and gold trim. He wears red hose and black shoes. Later, he changes to buff leggings and a blue jacket. Cassio is foppish. He sports a plumed hat, green vest, and a gold doublet slashed to show red beneath. Lodovico is more decorous in silver and blue, with hat, cape, doublet, and hose. Montano wears a long white gown trimmed in red with a gold sash. The Venetian guard appears in sixteenth-century armor, while servants are appareled in rough brown jackets and doublets. White lace signifies Desdemona's purity, whereas black (with a red underskirt) suggests Emilia's earthiness. Tissue of gold or silver bespeaks an exalted station.

Red, black, gold, white, and blue — the colors create that harmonious effect Macready so cherished. Othello's red aligned him with the Venetian Senators, figures of law and authority. Emilia's red petticoat picks up the color scheme, but her scarlet indicates easy virtue. Each scene is chromatically planned, even the bed curtains' labial folds — the shapes and colors, like the acting, should suggest the emotions represented onstage.

The grandeur of Macready's Covent Garden *Othello* is best conveyed by the Senate Council scene (I, iii). Macready's promptbook notes:

> The Senators are discov'd seated on an elevated platform, up the sides, and aX the back of the stage. Ten in Red Gowns- / including the Duke-Gratiano-and Brabantio / aX at back- Thirty- / including Lodovico / - in Black Gowns, with large open ermin'd sleeves, -at sides R & L. - The Duke's seat is slightly elevated above the others.- The Secretary is seated, - writing, and faces the duke.[8]

This scene was the culmination of Macready's search in *Othello* productions for historical accuracy; this was the Doge and his Council as he envisioned it from historical research and his own visits to Venice. Macready even covered the walls of the Doge's Hall with Titians and Tintorettos.[9] He was pleased with the result: his diary of 16 October 1837 exudes that "The Council of Forty was a scene of beautiful effect, one of the most real things I ever saw."[10]

Productions in the provinces and the United States could never be this elaborate, but traveling stars could carry their costumes with them; the Moor, at least, could be seen in appropriate splendor. Even through the swamps of Georgia, from Savannah to Mobile, Macready carted mammoth trunks of resplendent costumes so that he could represent his characters as he envisioned them.

Costumes aside, Macready's careful preparation was often wasted when he left London to play with provincial casts or journeyed to the backwoods of America. Although he was a difficult, egocentric man who often upstaged his fellow actors, as Kean had before him, one can sympathize with the meticulous actor faced with inadequate theatres and poorly prepared casts. In Liverpool, 31 January 1850, Macready found that "The Roderigo, Mr. Brown was *drunk*!"[11] Later that year in

[8]Folger Promptbook 13, Shattuck 25.

[9]Julie Hankey, Ed., *Othello* by William Shakespeare (Bristol: Bristol Classical Press, 1987), p. 153.

[10]William Charles Macready, *Macready's Reminiscences: and Selections from His Diaries and Letters*, ed. Sir Frederick Pollock (New York: Harper & Brothers, 1875), p. 416.

[11]Toynbee, *Diaries*, vol. II, p. 446.

Birmingham, Macready acted with an Othello who "actually *belaboured* [him] in the third act; it was so bad that at last [he] was obliged to resist the gentleman's 'corporal chastisement' and decline his shaking and pummelling!"[12] Perhaps such treatment was Macready's just punishment for rough handling of Desdemonas like Helena Faucit Martin. The wonder is that the perfectionist Macready could act at all with provincial and American casts too reluctant to rehearse and rather short on theatrical talent.

That Macready traveled from city to city, cast to cast, and performed Shakespeare's *Othello* night after night testifies to the uniformity of mid-nineteenth-century productions. As manager at Covent Garden and Drury Lane, Macready supervised his ideal *Othello*, a carefully designed performance in which scenery, costumes, blocking, and acting created a harmonious experience. In the provinces or outside New York and Philadelphia, the council scene might have two Senators instead of forty, but the blocking was substantially the same. So was the text.

A collation of the 1839 Macready acting edition with its predecessors — Mrs. Inchbald's (ca. 1808), Kemble's (1814), and Oxberry's (based on Edmund Kean's performances, 1819) — shows that Macready's Covent Garden *Othello* was somewhat more chaste and sensitive to the delicate feelings of his audiences than his predecessors'. Like Oxberry, but unlike Kemble and Inchbald, Macready's Iago makes no reference to "making the beast with two backs." Macready's Senate scene is by design much grander, requiring forty Senators rather than his predecessors' seven. Othello's cannibals and anthropophagi are quietly eliminated in keeping with the hero's dignity. On the Cyprus quay Macready drops Iago's reference to wives as "Players in your housewifery and housewives in your beds" (II, i, 111). Iago's observation that Othello "hath not yet made wanton the night with her . . ." (II, ii, 16) is also removed. Instead of "Happiness to their sheets!" Iago cries, "Happiness to them!" In the temptation scene, lines 463 to 467 are cut, whereas Inchbald and Kemble had retained them. Macready and Oxberry also root out the kisses from Cassio's dream. The major cuts from the eighteenth century — clown, Bianca, fit, willow song scene — persist. Macready's fastidiousness climaxes in act IV, scene ii, where he removes "Oh thou weed . . . That the sense aches at thee" (67–69) and "Was this fair paper . . . made to write whore upon" (71–72). He also substitutes the tame "one" for "strumpet" and "whore." In the next scene, Desdemona is not allowed to ask for her nightly apparel. Macready restores the original "Let me the curtains draw" (V, ii, 105), probably in reference to stage business. Hankey notes contemporary accounts of Macready's "thrilling effect" of thrusting his dark face through the curtains at Emilia's knock.[13] He closes the play — as Kean had done in performance — with Othello's last words.

Macready's purified text drops, in other words, all references to sheets, beds, going to bed, adultery, and sex. The bed behind half-closed curtains perhaps symbolizes the hidden sexuality underlying the play. While nothing remains in the revised language to offend a Victorian, the subject — adultery — was indeed salacious. Yet *Othello* was popular among all audiences, and no one apparently condemned the plot as immoral.

[12]Ibid., p. 463.
[13]Hankey, *Othello*, p. 317.

John Holstrom
GOING IT ALONE: A REVIEW OF OLIVIER'S OTHELLO   1964

Laurence Olivier has been considered one of the greatest Othellos of our time, but in this review John Holstrom finds fault with the production. He is careful to note that Olivier's portrayal of Othello is "a towering success," but he does so in the context of condemning most of the rest of the production. Holstrom makes us aware that for the play to work well, the cast must be balanced and equal to the measure of Othello himself.

There are differing opinions about foils. I don't mean those fencing things, or the wrappings of chocolate bars, but the setting of unobtrusive nonprecious metal into which a jewel is sunk, to shine the brighter against its dull background. This, in theatrical terms, was the view of those actor-managers (a dying if not dead race now) who surrounded themselves with a weak, untalented company so that they could shine out alone, without fear of distracting competition.

Others, however, believe that a precious stone is made more brilliant, not less, by being set in fine silver; others again have been made painfully aware that the effect of a great virtuoso performance on the stage is not heightened but cheapened by unworthy support from the rest of the cast. Acting isn't a finished form like plastic art. It has to be born again each time the curtain rises. The dynamism of a performance depends on intermeshing with a rhythm established by the lesser cogs; its character depends on relationships.

So I feel bitterly disappointed that when a theatrical jewel of great price — the long-awaited Olivier Othello, no less — finally comes our way, it should have been set in so feebly uninspired a production (by John Dexter, incredibly enough) and such a dreary, characterless cast that its power is lamed, its brilliance made to look suspect and its imaginative flights too often left to crash from their trapezes.

Sir Laurence has been quoted as saying, a few years back, that one of the reasons he hadn't attempted Othello was unwillingness to black up and sweat blood only to have the show stolen by some brilliant young fellow playing Iago. True enough, this can happen. Iago is infinitely the easier and more rewarding part, and it's rare (though it has been managed) for an actor not to be pretty striking in it. But Olivier is no fool. Having decided to do it, he wouldn't let vanity or insecurity betray him into doing an actor-manager on us, when *Othello* was at stake. This one knows. And yet the net result, at the National Theatre, has been as bad as if he had.

Essentially, make no mistake about it, his Othello is a towering success. Its lines are drawn as bravely and clearly as only a master can. This is a humorous, coolly intelligent Moor, quick to detect any false note, who could only be blinded to Iago's treachery by the deepest trust in him. He must lean on Iago with the absolute reliance many great officers have had in their serjeant-majors. Iago must therefore be a man with a different but entirely convincing mask for Othello, Cassio, Roderigo, Emilia, all the people he's intricately involved with. He must gaze into Othello's eyes with the passionate, worried devotion of a great hound. He must equally convince everyone else that he has their welfare at heart, come what may.

And at the National Theatre, what Iago do we get? We get a good little character actor called Frank Finlay, who has been puffed-up by the Royal Court claque into a thoroughly bad leading one. In Northern character parts, like Willie Mossop in *Hobson's Choice*, Finlay is admirable. As Stogumber in *Saint Joan* he was a pain. As Iago he is a national disaster, because he's giving no support at all to what would have been (but isn't) the greatest Othello of our day. Finlay's Iago is as nonexistent as Errol John's Othello was in the same building a year ago. Buff jerkined, he lopes busily about the stage with a constant flow of neat, overelaborate gesture. He orates with flexed eyeballs and tirelessly bared teeth, spitting out each word with equal emphasis, like a punch-drunk Methodist preacher who's past caring what, if anything, it means. It's as crude, boring, and perfunctory an Iago as we'll see for a while: and the tragedy is that it gives Olivier nothing to play against and thus makes him seem sometimes unconvincing, sometimes artificial.

For this Othello, a highly wrought conception, desperately needs support. Olivier starts at a low pitch, with slightly thickened voice, working lightly and gracefully towards the sentiment and later the troubled guts of the part. In the marvelous temptation scene, he instantly registers a flicker of unease about the vanishing Cassio, but defers actual seriousness till audaciously late in the scene, holding the most delicate balance between joking and credence, keeping Iago's insinuations at bay in a kind of ironic game. He is also a Christian Othello, with a cross on his chest, and it's only when his control snaps that he tears the cross off and prays ("Now by yond marble heaven") as a Mohammedan. The epileptic fit remains a threat, nearly recurring more than once after the actual swoon. The great Propontic speeches are half-chanted, almost like Grand Opera, and it's here most of all that Olivier, supported by no sort of grandeur or passion in the rest, seems overcalculated in his isolation. The end is touchingly and beautifully done, with a return to the earlier poise and tenderness.

It could have been great. With even an averagely good Iago it probably would have been. And with a decent production and a fine Iago — the best in recent memory have been Richard Burton's rock-solid beast and Leo McKern's magnificent creation wasted on poor Errol John last year — it would have been something to tell our grandchildren about. But when all's said, this is a first attempt, not a last. Olivier is in his prime. Burton and McKern are still around, and so is Vladek Sheybal, that marvellous Pole who in spite of his accent would probably be the best Iago of all. As for the National Theatre Company, only six months old, it's already time for a ruthless shake-up.

One word of praise to Maggie Smith for a Desdemona of considerable dignity and delicacy. Her face, perhaps, is too ineradicably sly, and the mournful little voice, so perfect in comedy, is sometimes a problem in tragedy. But she was sweetly serious, besides sporting a most wringable neck.

A CULTURAL CASEBOOK

The Issue of Race and Othello

Abdul El-Ouahed Ben Messasud, Moorish Ambassador to Queen Elizabeth I (reigned 1558–1603). Oil on panel. Artist unknown.

294

By the sixteenth century, Elizabethan England had already inherited the seeds of racial prejudice. Explorers and adventurers of the fourteenth and fifteenth centuries had written of distant, culturally exotic nations whose inhabitants were dark-skinned. In Shakespeare's time, enough Africans lived in London and in other large coastal towns that theater audiences would have had some contact with black people. Late in her reign, the strong presence of Africans in England provoked Queen Elizabeth to order some of them sent back to Africa. Understanding his times, Shakespeare knew that his audience would be prejudiced against Othello — just as certain characters in the play itself are prejudiced. He crafted his play to stimulate conflicting emotional responses in his audience — creating the black Othello as a noble, grand, and imposing figure whose flaw, jealousy, and his willingness to trust his white officer, Iago, combine to seal his fate. Playing with his audience's notion of good and evil and black and white, Shakespeare confronts Renaissance racism with irony.

Some early critics disputed whether Shakespeare had in mind a "tawny" Moor or a "black" Moor for the title character. While the nineteenth-century stage preferred a light-skinned Othello, twentieth-century versions preferred a black Othello, usually with a black actor playing the role. Some great Othellos have been performed by white actors with the reasoning that Shakespeare wrote the part for Richard Burbage, who was white and one of the greatest actors of his day. Today the role is usually reserved for black actors, with a number of outstanding performances by Moses Gunn, James Earl Jones, and others.

The documents compiled here help us to consider *Othello* in the context of racial prejudice, both in Shakespeare's time and our own. Sir John Mandeville's *Travels,* dating 1357, demonstrates that early reports about the existence of black civilizations had reached Europe. Ethiopians were known to the English and referred to as Moors. Around the time of the first performance of *Othello,* an Arab delegation in London drew attention with its exotic fashions and styles. By the time *Othello* was performed, the English audience would have understood from general knowledge and experience what a "dark-visaged" man — either from north or central Africa — would have looked like.

Sir John Mandeville attempted to explain the nature of both Egypt and neighboring Ethiopia. He maintained that the inhabitants had been turned black by the heat of the sun. Much later, Richard Eden translated a travel book by Peter Martyr written in 1530. The single paragraph included in this casebook indicates that blacks were already present in Quarequa, a mountainous region of Haiti and the Dominican Republic. Eden theorizes that these black inhabitants were the descendants of seafaring Africans who were blown off course and landed in the Caribbean.

A Muslim convert to Christianity, Leo Africanus (as he became known to Europeans) wrote *A Geographical Historie of Africa* in 1550. It was expanded and revised for an English audience by John Pory in 1600. The book was a popular treatise that answered the needs of the curious to learn about Africa. In a sometimes fanciful fashion, it describes regions and nations as well as peoples, customs, and religious practices.

In "Othello and Color Prejudice," G. K. Hunter, a distinguished modern Shakespeare scholar, asserts that "Shakespeare intended his hero to be a black man." Hunter clarifies this statement with reference to other Renaissance works and writers. Margaret Webster, who directed the great performance of Paul Robeson in *Othello* in 1943, discusses the question of race in the play from the perspective of the mid-twentieth century. Her focus is on Desdemona as much as on Othello. Peter Marks reviewed Patrick Stewart (of *Star Trek* fame) in a production that had an all-black cast except for Stewart's portrayal of Othello. Marks felt that the result "tends to take the racial issue off the table." Whether that is the case or not, we should attempt to know as much as we can about the prejudices and understandings of Shakespeare's time as well as those of our own in regard to *Othello*.

In addition to the material in this Casebook, we should refer to Ben Jonson's *Masque of Blackness*, which follows. It was commissioned by Queen Anne for the court of King James I and was performed the same year and in the same theater as *Othello*. In some ways Jonson's *Masque* can be seen as a commentary on the age and perhaps on *Othello*.

Sir John Mandeville (c. 1300–1372)
FROM MANDEVILLE'S TRAVELS   1357

TRANSLATED FROM THE FRENCH BY COTTON TITUS

Mandeville's Travels, *written in France in 1357, was one of the most popular travel books of the late Middle Ages and early Renaissance. Some of it is fantasy; some of it is gathered from the travels of many people. Othello's line concerning "men whose heads / Do grow beneath their shoulders" (I, III, 144–45) comes from this well-known book. The excerpts here point to contemporary views of Africans available to Shakespeare.*

And between Egypt and Nubia it hath well a twelve journeys of desert. And men of Nubia be Christian, but they be black as the Moors for great heat of the sun.

In Egypt there be five provinces; one that hight° Sa'id, that other that hight Damanhur, another Rosetta that is an isle in Nile, another Alexandria, and another the land of Damietta. That city was wont to be right strong, but it was twice won of the Christian men. And therefore after that the Saracens beat down the walls, and with the walls and the towers thereof the Saracens made another city more far from the sea and cleped it the New Damietta, so that now no man dwelleth at the rather town of Damietta. At that city of Damietta is one of the havens of Egypt. And at Alexandria is that other, that is a full strong city, but there is no water to drink but if it come by conduit from Nile that entereth into their cisterns; and whoso stopped that water from them, they might not endure there. In Egypt there be but few fortlets or castles because that the country is so strong of himself.

Note of a Marvel

At the deserts of Egypt was a worthy man that was an holy hermit,[1] and there met with him a monster; that is to say, a monster is a thing deformed against kind both of man or of beast or of anything else, and that is cleped° a monster. And this

---

hight: Is called.
[1]St. Anthony or St. Paul the Hermit.
cleped: Named.

monster that met with this holy hermit was as it had been a man that had two horns trenchant on his forehead, and he had a body like a man to the navel, and beneath he had the body like a goat. And the hermit asked him what he was, and the monster answered him and said he was a deadly creature such as God had formed and dwelled in those deserts in purchasing his sustenance; and besought the hermit that he would pray God for him, the which that came from Heaven for to save all mankind, and was born of a maiden, and suffered passion and death, as we well know, by whom we live and be. And yet is the head with the two horns of that monster at Alexandria for a marvel.

In Egypt is the city of Heliopolis, that is to say the city of the sun. In that city there is a temple made round after the shape of the Temple of Jerusalem. The priests of that temple have all their writings under the date of the fowl that is cleped Phoenix, and there is none but one in all the world. And he cometh to burn himself upon the altar of that temple at the end of five hundred year, for so long he liveth. And at the five hundred years' end the priests array their altar honestly and put thereupon spices and sulphur vif and other things that will burn lightly, and the bird Phoenix cometh and burneth himself to ashes. And the first day next after men find in the ashes a worm; and the second day next after men find a bird quick and perfect; and the third day next after he flieth his way. And so there is no more birds of that kind in all the world but it alone, and truly that is a great miracle of God. And men may well liken that bird unto God because that there is no God but one, and also that Our Lord arose from death to life the third day.[. . .]

Beside the land of Chaldea is the land of Amazonia, that is the land of Feminia. And in that realm is all women and no man, not as some men say that men may not live there but for because that the women will not suffer no men amongst them to be their sovereigns. For sometime there was a king in that country, and men married as in other countries. And so befell that the king had war with them of Scythia, the which king hight Scolopitus, that was slain in battle and all the good blood of his realm. And when the queen and all the other noble ladies saw that they were all widows, and that all the royal blood was lost, they armed them and as creatures out of wit they slew all the men of the country that were left, for they would that all the women were widows as the queen and they were.

And from that time hitherwards they never would suffer man to dwell amongst them longer than seven days and seven nights, nor that no child that were male should dwell amongst them longer than he were nourished and then sent to his father. And when they will have any company of man, then they draw them towards the lands marching next to them. And then they have their loves that use them, and they dwell with them an eight days or ten, and then go home again. And if they have any knave child, they keep it a certain time and then send it to the father when he can go alone and eat by himself, or else they slay it. And if it be a female, they do away that one pap with an hot iron. And if it be a woman of great lineage, they do away the left pap that they may the better bear a shield. And if it be a woman on foot, they do away the right pap for to shoot with bow Turkish, for they shoot well with bows.

In that land they have a queen that governeth all that land, and all they be obedient to her. And always they make their queen by election that is most worthy in arms, for they be right good warriors and orped° and wise, noble, and worthy. And they go often time insold to help of other kings in their wars for gold and silver as

orped: Valiant.

other soldiers do, and they maintain themselves right vigorously. This land of Amazonia is an isle all environed with the sea save in two places where be two entries. And beyond that water dwell the men that be their paramours and their loves, where they go to solace them when they will.

Beside Amazonia is the land of *terra Margine,* that is a great country and a full delectable. And for the goodness of the country King Alexander let first make there the city of Alexandria (and yet he made twelve cities of the same name), but that city is now cleped Seleucia.

And from that other coast of Chaldea toward the south is Ethiopia, a great country that stretcheth to the end of Egypt. Ethiopia is departed into two principal parts, and that is in the east part and in the meridional part, the which part meridional is cleped Mauretania. And the folk of that country be black enough and more black than in the other part, and they be cleped Moors. In that part is a well that in the day it is so cold that no man may drink thereof, and in the night it is so hot that no man may suffer his hand therein. And beyond that part toward the south to pass by the Sea Ocean is a great land and a great country, but men may not dwell there for the fervent burning of the sun, so is it passing hot in that country. In Ethiopia all the rivers and all the waters be troubled, and they be some deal salt for the great heat that is there.

And the folk of that country be lightly drunk and have but little appetite to meat. And they have commonly the flux of the womb, and they live not long. In Ethiopia be many diverse folk. And Ethiopia is cleped Cusis. In that country be folk that have but one foot, and they go so blithe that it is marvel, and the foot is so large that it shadoweth all the body against the sun when they will lie and rest them. In Ethiopia, when the children be young and little, they be all yellow, and when that they wax of age that yellowness turneth to be all black. In Ethiopia is the city of Savah and the land of the which one of the three kings that presented Our Lord in Bethlehem was king of.

Richard Eden (1521?–1576)
FROM *DECADES OF THE NEW WORLD*   1555

Around 1555, Richard Eden translated the work of Peter Martyr, written originally in 1530. Eden added his own material to Martyr's book and produced a popular "introduction" to the New World. In this excerpt he comments on black inhabitants of a mountainous region of Hispaniola (now Haiti and the Dominican Republic), whom he assumes arrived in the New World by accident.

There is a region not past two days journey distant from *Quarequa,* in which they found only black Moors: and those exceeding fierce and cruel. They suppose that in time past certain black moors sailed thither out of *Aethiopia* to rob: and that by shipwreck or some other chance, they were driven to those mountains. Th[e] inhabitants of *Quarequa* live in continual war and debate with these black men.

Leo Africanus (c. 1485–c. 1554)
and John Pory (1572–1635)

FROM *A GEOGRAPHICAL HISTORIE OF AFRICA*   1550, 1600

The travel accounts of Leo Africanus, born al-Hasan ibn Muhammad al-Wazzān Al-Zayyātī, were widely read in Elizabethan England. Most important in shaping the Elizabethans' impressions of Africans was his work, A Geographical Historie of Africa (1550), which was revised and expanded by another traveler, John Pory, in 1600. The first two excerpts that follow are by Pory, who emphasizes certain negative features of north African outlaws. Africanus, born in Granada, explains later in his account that he owes his birth to Africa, and balances the picture by stressing the civility, liberality, and fidelity of the Moors inhabiting the desert of Libya.

The People of Cafri, Part of the Lower Ethiopia

The people of this place called in the Arabian tongue Cafri, Cafres, or Cafates, that is to say, lawless or outlaws, are for the most part exceeding black of color, which very thing may be a sufficient argument, that the sun is not the sole or chief cause of their blackness; for in diverse other countries where the heat thereof is far more scorching and intolerable, there are tawny, brown, yellowish, ash-colored, and white people; so that the cause thereof seemeth rather to be of an hereditary quality transfused from the parents, than the intemperance of an hot climate, though it also may be some furtherance thereunto. The Hollanders in the year 1595, entering the harbor of Saint Bras, somewhat to the east of Cabo das Agulhas, had conversation and truck with some of these Cafres, whom they found to be a stout and valiant people, but very base and contemptible in their behavior and apparel, being clad in ox and sheeps skins, wrapped about their shoulders with the hairy sides inward, in form of a mantle. Their weapons are a kind of small slender darts or pikes, some whereof are headed with some kind of metal, the residue being unheaded, and hardened only at the points with fire. They cover their private parts with a sheeps tail, which is bound up before and behind with a girdle. Their home-beasts are, like those of Spaine, very well limbed and proportioned. Their sheep are great and fair, not having any wool on their backs, but a kind of harsh hair like goats. Other particulars by them observed, for brevitys sake, I omit.

The Kingdom of Damut

The kingdom of Damut (as *Sanutus* affirmeth) doth border upon the kingdom of Xoa, and is enclosed on either side with the lake of Barcena, and the land of Zanguebar. Howbeit others place Damut between the kingdoms of Vangue and Goiame toward the west, which opinion seemeth most probable. This country aboundeth with gold, ginger, grapes, corn, and beasts of all sorts. The slaves of this kingdom are much esteemed, and are commonly sold throughout all Arabia, Persia, and Egypt, where they prove most valiant soldiers. The greater part of the people of Damut are Gentiles, and the residue Christians, who have certain monasteries. In this kingdom is that exceeding high and dreadful mountain (having one narrow passage only to ascend by), whither the *Prete* sendeth his nobles which are convicted of any heinous crime, to suffer ignominious death with hunger and cold. About the fountains of Nilus some say, that there are Amazones or women-warriors, most valiant and redoubted, which use bows and arrows, and live under the government of a Queen: as likewise the people called Cafri or Cafates, being as black as pitch, and of a mighty stature, and (as some think) descended of the Jewes; but now they are idolators, and most deadly enemies to the Christians; for they make continual assaults upon the Abassins, despoiling them both of life and goods: but all the day-time they lie lurking in mountains, woods, and deep valleys.

The Manners and Customs of the African People, which Inhabit the Desert of Libya

The women of this nation be gross, corpulent, and of a swart complexion. They are fattest upon their breast and paps, but slender about the girdle-stead. Very civil they are, after their manner, both in speech and gestures: sometimes they will accept of a kiss; but whoso tempteth them farther, putteth his own life in hazard. For by reason of jealousy you may see them daily one to be the death and destruction of another, and that in such savage and brutish manner, that in this case they will show no compassion at all. And they seem to be more wise in this behalf than divers of our people for they will by no means match themselves unto an harlot. The liberality of this people hath at all times been exceeding great. And when any travelers may pass through their dry and desert territories, they will never repair to their tents, neither will they themselves travel upon the common highway. And if any caravan or multitude of merchants will pass those deserts, they are bound to pay certain custom unto the prince of the said people, namely, for every camels load a piece of cloth worth a ducat. Upon a time I remember that traveling in the company of certain merchants over the desert by them called Araoan, it was our chance there to meet with the prince of Zanaga; who, after he had received his due custom, invited the said company of merchants, for their recreation, to go and abide with him in his tents four or five days. Howbeit, because his tents were too far out of our way, and for that we should have wandered farther than we thought good, esteeming it more convenient for us to hold on our direct course, we refused his gentle offer, and for his courtesy gave him great thanks. But nor being satisfied therewith, he commanded that our camels should proceed on forward, but the merchants he carried along with him, and gave them very sumptuous entertainment of his place of abode. Where we were no sooner arrived, but this good prince caused camels of all kinds and ostriches, which he had hunted and taken by the way, to be killed for his household provision. Howbeit we requested him not to make such daily slaughters of his camels; affirming moreover, that we never used to eat the flesh of a geld camel, but when all other victuals failed us. Whereunto he answered, that he should deal uncivilly, if he welcomed so worthy and so seldom-seen guests with the killing of small cattle only. Wherefore he wished us to fall to such provision as was set before us. Here might you have seen great plenty of roasted and sodden flesh: their roasted ostriches were brought to the table in wicker platters, being seasoned with sundry kinds of herbs and spices. Their bread made of Mill and panicke was of a most savory and pleasant taste: and always at the end of dinner or supper we had plenty of dates and great store of milk served in. Yea, this bountiful and noble prince, that he might sufficiently show how welcome we were unto him, would together with his nobility always bear us company: howbeit we ever dined and supped apart by our selves. Moreover he caused certain religious and most learned men to come unto our banquet; who, all the time we remained with the said prince, used not to eat any bread at all, but fed only upon flesh and milk. Whereat we being somewhat amazed, the good prince gently told us, that they all were born in such places whereas no kind of grain would grow: howbeit that himself, for the entertainment of strangers, had great plenty of corn laid up in store. Wherefore he bad us to be of good cheer, saying that he would eat only of such things as his own native soil afforded: affirming moreover, that bread was yet in use among them at their feast of passover, and at other feasts also, whereupon they used to offer sacrifice. And thus we remained with him for the space of two days; all which time, what wonderful and magnificent cheer we had made us, would seem incredible to report. But the third day, being desirous to take our leave, the prince accompanied us to that place where we overtook our camels and company sent before. And this I dare most deeply take mine oath on, that we spent the said prince ten times more, than our custom which he received came to. We thought it not amiss here to set down this history, to declare in some sort the courtesy and liberality of the said nation. Neither could the prince aforesaid understand our language nor we his; but all our speech to and fro was made by an interpreter. And this which we have here recorded as touching this nation, is likewise to be understood of the other four nations above mentioned, which are dispersed over the residue of the Numidian deserts.

The Commendable Actions and Virtues of the Africans

Those Arabians which inhabit in Barbarie or upon the coast of the Mediterran sea, are greatly addicted unto the study of good arts and sciences: and those things which concern their law and religion are esteemed by them in the first place. Moreover they have been heretofore most studious of the Mathematics, of Philosophy, and of Astrology: but these arts (as it is aforesaid) were four hundred years ago, utterly destroyed and taken away by the chief professors of their law. The inhabitants of cities do most religiously observe and reverence those things which appertain unto their religion: yea they honor those doctors and priests, of whom they learn their law, as if they were petty-gods. Their Churches they frequent very diligently, to the end they may repeat certain prescript and formal prayers; most superstitiously persuading themselves that the same day wherein they make their prayers, it is not lawful for them to wash certain of their members, when as at other times they will wash their whole bodies. Whereof we will (by Gods help) discourse more at large in the second Book of this present treatise, when we shall fall into the mentioning of *Mahumet* and of his religion. Moreover those which inhabit Barbarie are of great cunning & dexterity for building & for mathematical inventions, which a man may easily conjecture by their artificial works. Most honest people they are, and destitute of all fraud and guile; not only embracing all simplicity and truth, but also practicing the same throughout the whole course of their lives: albeit certain Latin authors, which have written of the same regions, are far otherwise of opinion. Likewise they are most strong and valiant people, especially those which dwell upon the mountains. They keep their covenant most faithfully; insomuch that they had rather die than break promise. No nation in the world is so subject unto jealousy; for they will rather lease their lives, than put up any disgrace in the behalf of their women. So desirous they are of riches and honor, that therein no other people can go beyond them. They travel in a manner over the whole world to exercise traffic. For they are continually to be seen in Aegypt, in Aethiopia, in Arabia, Persia, India, and Turkie: and whithersoever they go, they are most honorably esteemed of: for none of them will possess any art, unless he hath attained unto great exactness and perfection therein. They have always been much delighted with all kind of civility and modest behavior: and it is accounted heinous among them for any man to utter in company, any bawdy or unseemly word. They have always in mind this sentence of a grave author; Give place to thy superior. If any youth in presence of his father, his uncle, or any other of his kindred, doth sing or talk aught of love matters, he is deemed to be worthy of grievous punishment. Whatsoever lad or youth there lighteth by chance into any company which discourseth of love, no sooner heareth nor understandeth what their talk tendeth unto, but immediately he withdraweth himself from among them. These are the things which we thought most worthy of relation as concerning the civility, humanity, and upright dealing of the Barbarians: let us now proceed unto the residue. Those Arabians which dwell in tents, that is to say, which bring up cattle, are of a more liberal and civil disposition: to wit, they are in their kind as devout, valiant, patient, courteous, hospitable, and as honest in life and conversation as any other people. They be most faithful observers of their word and promise; insomuch that the people, which before we said to dwell in the mountains, are greatly stirred up with emulation of their virtues. Howbeit the said mountainers, both for learning, for virtue, and for religion, are thought much inferior to the Numidians, albeit they have little or no knowledge at all in natural philosophy. They are reported likewise to be most skilful warriors, to be valiant, and exceeding lovers and practicers of all humanity. Also, the Moors and Arabians inhabiting Libya are somewhat civil of behavior, being plain dealers, void of dissimulation, favorable to strangers, and lovers of simplicity. Those which we before named white, or tawny Moors, are steadfast in friendship: as likewise, they indifferently and favorably esteem of other nations: and wholly endeavor themselves in this one thing, namely, that they may lead a most pleasant and jocund life. Moreover they maintain most learned professors of liberal arts, and such men are most devout in their religion. Neither is there any people in all Africa that lead a more happy and honorable life.

G. K. Hunter (b. 1920)
FROM "OTHELLO AND COLOR PREJUDICE"   1978

In attempting to determine Shakespeare's motives in portraying Othello as a black Moor, G. K. Hunter, a professor at Yale University, has examined the evidence suggesting the associations an Elizabethan audience would have made with the color black. In this excerpt he establishes the common color prejudice that would have been present in Shakespeare's audience and implies that Shakespeare consciously worked against it.

It is generally admitted today that Shakespeare was a practical man of the theater: however careless he may have been about maintaining consistency for the exact *reader* of his plays, he was not likely to introduce a theatrical novelty which would only puzzle his audience; it does not seem wise, therefore, to dismiss his theatrical innovations as if they were unintentional. The blackness of Othello is a case in point. Shakespeare largely modified the story he took over from Cinthio: he made a tragic hero out of Cinthio's passionate and bloody lover; he gave him a royal origin, a Christian baptism, a romantic *bravura* of manner, and, most impor-

[Read as the British Academy Shakespeare Lecture, 19 April 1967. First published in *The Proceedings of the British Academy*, liii (1967).]

tant of all, an orotund magnificence of diction. Yet, changing all this, he did not change his color and so produced a daring theatrical novelty — a black hero for a white community — a novelty which remains too daring for many recent theatrical audiences. Shakespeare cannot merely have carried over the color of Othello by being too lazy or too uninterested to meddle with it; for no actor, spending the time in "blacking-up," and hence no producer, could be indifferent to such an innovation, especially in that age, devoted to "imitation" and hostile to "originality." In fact, the repeated references to Othello's color in the play and the wider net of images of dark and light spread across the diction, show that Shakespeare was not only not unaware of the implication of his hero's color but was indeed intensely aware of it as one of the primary factors in his play.[1] I am therefore assuming in this lecture that the blackness of Othello has a theatrical purpose, and I intend to try to suggest what it was possible for that purpose to have been.

Shakespeare intended his hero to be a black man — that much I take for granted;[2] what is unknown is what the idea of a black man suggested to Shakespeare, and what reaction the appearance of a black man on the stage was calculated to produce. It is fairly certain, however, that some modern reactions are not likely to have been shared by the Elizabethans. The modern theater-going European intellectual, with a background of cultivated superiority to "color problems" in other continents, would often choose to regard Othello as a fellow man and to watch the story — which could so easily be reduced to its headline level: "sheltered white girl errs: said, 'Color does not matter'" — with a sense of freedom from such prejudices. But this lofty fair-mindedness may be too lofty for Shakespeare's play and not take the European any nearer the Othello of Shakespeare than the lady from Maryland quoted in the Furness New Variorum edition: "In studying the play of *Othello*, I have always *imagined* its hero a white man." Both views, that the color of Othello does not matter and that it matters too much to be tolerable, err, I suggest, by oversimplifying. Shakespeare was clearly deliberate in keeping Othello's color; and it is obvious that he counted on some positive audience reaction to this color; but it is equally obvious that he did not wish the audience to dismiss Othello as a stereotype.[. . .]

Modern rationalizations about "color" tend to be different from those of the Middle Ages and Renaissance. We are powerfully aware of the relativism of viewpoints; we distinguish easily between different racial cultures; and explicit arguments about the mingling of the races usually begin at the economic and social level and only move to questions of God's providence at the lunatic fringe.

The Elizabethans also had a powerful sense of the economic threat posed by the foreign groups they had daily contact with — Flemings or Frenchmen — but they had little or no continuous contact with "Moors" and no sense of economic threat from them. This did not mean, however, that they had no racial or color prejudice. They had, to start with, the basic common man's attitude that all foreigners are curious and inferior — the more foreign the more inferior, in the sense of the proverb quoted by Purchas: "Three Moors to a Portuguese; three Portuguese to an Englishman."[3] They had also the basic and ancient sense that black is the color of

[1] See R. B. Heilman, "More Fair Than Black: Light and Dark in *Othello*," *Essays in Criticism*, i (1951), 313–35.

[2] I ignore the many treatises devoted to proving that he was of tawny or sunburnt color. These are, however, very worthy of study, as documents of prejudice.[. . .]

[3] See M. P. Tilley, *A Dictionary of Proverbs* (1950), M. 1132.

sin and death, "the badge of hell, the hue of dungeons, and the school of night" (as Shakespeare himself says).[4] This supposition is found all over the world (even in darkest Africa)[5] from the earliest to the latest times; which suggests a response to the basic antinomy of day and night. Certainly in the West there is a continuous and documented cultural tradition depending on it.[6][. . .]

An extreme example of this status of the Moor appears in the report of the pageant for the baptism of Prince Henry in 1594. It had been arranged that a lion should pull the triumphal car; but the lion could not be used, so a Moor was substituted.[7]

Renaissance scepticism and the voyages of discovery might seem, at first sight, to have destroyed the ignorance on which such thoughtless equations of black men and devils depended. But this does not prove to have been so. The voyagers brought back some accurate reports of black and heathen; but they often saw, or said they saw, what they expected to see — the marvels of the East.[8] In any case the vocabulary at their disposal frustrated any attempt at scientific discrimination. The world was still seen largely, in terms of vocabulary, as a network of religious names. The word "Moor" had no clear racial status. Elizabethan authors describe "Moors" as existing all over the globe. We hear of "Mores of Malabar" from Spenser,[9] of Moors in Malacca from James Lancaster,[10] of Moors in Guinea from Eden,[11] of Moors in Ethiopia from Lodge,[12] of Moors in Fukien from Willes,[13] of Moors in America from Marlowe[14] and sundry others. There seem to be Moors everywhere; but only everywhere, we should note, in that outer circuit of non-Christian lands where the saving grace of Jerusalem is weakest in its whitening power. Throughout the Elizabethan period there seems to remain considerable confusion whether the Moor is a human being or a monster. In the "plat" of the perished play of *Tamar Cam* (1592) we are told of an entry of "Tartars, Geates, Amozins, Nagars, ollive cullord moores, Canniballs, Hermophrodites, Pigmies," etc. — a characteristic medley.[15] In *Volpone* we are given a list of the undesirables

---

[4]*Love's Labour's Lost*, IV, III, 250 f.

[5]See V. W. Turner, "Colour Classification in Ndembu Ritual," *Anthropological Approaches to the Study of Religion*, ed. M. Banton (1966); Arthur Leib, "The Mystical Significance of Colours in . . . Madagascar," *Folk-lore*, lvii (1946), 128–33; Joan Westcott, "The Sculpture and Myths of Eshu-Elegba, the Yoruba Trickster," *Africa*, xxxii (1962).

[6]See E. Hoffman-Krayer and H. Bächtold-Stäubli, *Handwörterbuch des deutschen Aberglaubens* [1927], s.v. Schwartz.

[7]See *A True Reportary of the Baptisme of Frederik Henry, Prince of Scotland* (1594) (S.T.C. 13163).

[8]See R. Wittkower, "Marvels of the East," *Journal of the Warburg and Courtauld Institutes*, v (1942), 159–97.[. . .]

[9]*Faerie Queene*, VI, VII, 43.

[10]R. Hakluyt, *Principal Navigations* (Glasgow, 1903–1905 edition), vi. 399.

[11]Peter Martyr Anglerius, tr. R. Eden, *The History of Travel* (1577), fl. 348v.

[12]*Works* (Hunterian Society), ii. 52.

[13]Hakluyt, vi. 321 (where it is quite clear that "Moorish" means "Mahomedan."

[14]*Doctor Faustus* (*Works*, ed. C. F. Tucker Brooke, p. 150). Compare the "black Indians" in A. Brewer's *The Lovesick King* (Bang's Materialien [1907], 952 f.) and in B. Googe's *The Popish Kingdom* (translated from H. Kirchmeyer) (1570) — 1880 ed., p. 39 — and the "African Indians" in *Sir Thomas Stukeley* (1596) — Tudor Facsimile Texts, 2169.

[15]*Henslowe Papers*, ed. W. W. Greg (1907), p. 148. Compare the "Negro-Tartars" in *Gesta Grayorum* (M.S.R. 46) and the "Negarian Tartars" (ibid. 52).

that Volpone has coupled with to produce his Fool, Dwarf, and Hermaphrodite. The supposed parents are described as

> beggars,
> Gipsies and Jews and black-moors.[16]

The geographical vagueness of these authors does not mean, however, that they are vague in their sense of an antithetical relationship between "Moors" (wherever they live) and civilized white Christians. The first meaning given to the word "Moor" in *O.E.D.* is "Mahomedan" (with examples up to 1629); but in many of the examples this seems to mean no more than "infidel," non-Christian. The pressure that defines the word is more negative than positive. Like *Barbarian* and *Gentile* (or *Wog*) it was a word for "people not like us,"[17] so signaled by color. The word *Gentile* itself had still the religious sense of *Pagan,* and the combined phrase "Moors and Gentiles" is used regularly to represent the religious gamut of non-Christian possibilities (see *O.E.D.* for examples). Similarly, *Barbary* was not simply a place in Africa, but also the unclearly located home of Barbarism, as in Chaucer (Franklin's Tale, 1451, Man of Law's Tale, 183).

I have suggested above that the discoveries of the voyagers contributed little to Renaissance scientific or nontheological explanations of the world. And this was particularly true of the problems raised by the black-skinned races. No scientific explanation of black skins had ever been achieved, though doctors had long disputed it. Lodovicus Caelius Rhodiginus in his *Lectionum Antiquarum libri XXX* (1620) can cite column after column of authorities; but all without conclusive answers. We hear among the latest reports of Africa collected in T. Astley's *New General Collection of Voyages* (1745) that the blackness of the Negro is "a Topic that has given Rise to numberless Conjectures and great Disputes among the Learned in Europe" (ii, 269). Sir Thomas Browne in three essays in his *Pseudodoxia Epidemica* (VI, x–xii) not only declared that the subject was "amply and satisfactorily discussed as we know by no man" but proceeded to remedy this by way of amplitude rather than satisfactoriness. The theological explanation was left in possession of the field. Adam and Eve, it was assumed, were white; it follows that the creation of the black races can only be ascribed to some subsequent *fiat*. The two favorite possibilities were the cursing of Cain and the cursing of Ham or Cham and his posterity — and sometimes these two were assumed to be different expressions of the same event; at least one might allege, with Sir Walter Ralegh, that "the sonnes of Cham did possesse the vices of the sonnes of Cain."[18] The Cham explanation had the great advantage that "the threefold world" of tradition could be described in terms of the three sons of Noah — Japhet having produced the Europeans, Shem the Asiatics, while the posterity of Ham occupied Africa, or, in a more sophisticated version, "the Meridionall or southern partes of the world both in Asia and Africa"[19] — sophisticated, we should notice, without altering the basic theological assumption that Cham's posterity were banished to the most uncomfortable part of the globe, and a foretaste of the Hell to come. This geographical

---

[16]Ben Jonson, *Volpone,* I, v, 44 f.
[17]So that "Wogs begin at Calais," etc.
[18]*The History of the World,* I, VI, 2.
[19]A. Willet, *Hexapla in Genesin* (1605), p. 119.

assumption fitted in with the wisdom that the etymological doctors had in the Middle Ages been able to glean from the name *Ham* — defined as "*Cham: calidus, et ipse ex praesagio futuri cognominatus est. Posteritas enim eius eam terrae partem possedit quae vicino sole calentior est.*"[20] When this is linked to the other point made in relation to the Cham story — that his posterity were cursed to be slaves[21] — one can see how conveniently and plausibly such a view fitted the facts and desires found in the early navigators. Azurara, the chronicler of Prince Henry the Navigator's voyages, tells us that it was natural to find blackamoors as the slaves of lighter skinned men:

> these blacks were Moors (i.e. Mahomedans) like the others, though their slaves, in accordance with ancient custom which I believe to have been because of the curse which, after the Deluge, Noah laid upon his son Cain [*sic*], cursing him in this way: that his race should be subject to all the other races in the world. And from his race these blacks are descended.[22]

The qualities of the "Moors" who appear on the Elizabethan stage are hardly at all affected by Elizabethan knowledge of real Moors from real geographical locations, and, given the literary modes available, this is hardly surprising. It is true that the first important Moor-role — that of Muly Hamet in Peele's *The Battle of Alcazar* (c. 1589) — tells the story of a real man (with whom Queen Elizabeth had a treaty) in a real historical situation. But the dramatic focus that Peele manages to give to his Moorish character is largely dependent on the devil and underworld associations he can suggest for him — making him call up "Fiends, Fairies, hags that fight in beds of steel" and causing him to show more acquaintance with the geography of hell than with that of Africa. Aaron in *Titus Andronicus* is liberated from even such slender ties as associate Muly Hamet with geography. Aaron is in the play as the representative of a world of generalized barbarism, which is Gothic in Tamora and Moorish in Aaron, and unfocused in both. The purpose of the play is served by a general opposition between Roman order and Barbarian disorder. Shakespeare has the doubtful distinction of making explicit here (perhaps for the first time in English literature) the projection of black wickedness in terms of negro sexuality. The relationship between Tamora and Aaron is meant, clearly enough, to shock our normal sensibilities and their black baby is present as an emblem of disorder. In this respect, as in most others, Eleazer in *Lust's Dominion* (c. 1600) — the third pre-Othello stage-Moor — is copied from Aaron. The location of this play (Spain) gives a historically plausible excuse to present the devil in his favorite human form —"that of a Negro or Moor," but does not really use the locale to establish any racial points.

These characters provide the dominant images that must have been present in the minds of Shakespeare's original audience when they entered the Globe to see a play called *The Moor of Venice* — an expectation of pagan devilry set against white Christian civilization — excessive civilization perhaps in Venice, but civilization at least "like us." Even those who knew Cinthio's story of the Moor of Venice could not have had very different expectations, which may be summed up from the

---

[20]Isidore of Seville, *Etymologiae*, VII, VI, 17. (*Patrologia Latina*, lxxxii, col. 276.)
[21]See St Ambrose, *Comment. in epist. ad Philippenses* (*P.L.* xvii, col. 432). [. . .]
[22]*Discovery and Conquest of Guinea* (Hakluyt Society, XCV [1896], 54).

story told by Bandello (III, xxi) in which a master beats his Moorish servant, and the servant in revenge rapes and murders his wife and children.[23] Bandello draws an illuminating moral:

> By this I intend it to appear that a man should not be served by this sort of slave; for they are seldom found faithful, and at best they are full of filth, unclean, and stink all the time like goats. But all this is as nothing put beside the savage cruelty that reigns in them.

It is in such terms that the play opens. We hear from men like us of a man not like us, of "his Moorship," "the Moor," "the thick-lips," "an old black ram," "a Barbary horse," "the devil," of "the gross clasps of a lascivious Moor." The sexual fear and disgust that lie behind so much racial prejudice are exposed for our derisive expectations to fasten upon them. And we are at this point bound to agree with these valuations, for no alternative view is revealed. There is, of course, a certain comic *brio* which helps to distance the whole situation, and neither Brabantio, nor Iago nor Roderigo can wholly command our identification. None the less we are drawn on to await the entry of a traditional Moor figure, the kind of person we came to the theatre expecting to find.

When the second scene begins, however, it is clear that Shakespeare is bent to ends other than the fulfilment of these expectations. The Iago/Roderigo relationship of I, i, is repeated in the Iago/Othello relationship of the opening of I, ii; but Othello's response to the real-seeming circumstance with which Iago lards his discourse is very different from the hungrily self-absorbed questionings of Roderigo. Othello draws on an inward certainty about himself, a radiant clarity about his own well-founded moral position. This is no "lascivious Moor," but a great Christian gentleman, against whom Iago's insinuations break like water against granite. Not only is Othello a Christian, moreover; he is the leader of Christendom in the last and highest sense in which Christendom existed as a viable entity, crusading against the "black pagans." He is to defend Cyprus against the Turk, "hellish horseleaches of Christian blood."[24] It was the fall of Cyprus which produced the alliance of Lepanto, and we should associate Othello with the emotion that Europe continued to feel — till well after the date of *Othello* — about that victory and about Don John of Austria.

Shakespeare has presented to us a traditional view of what Moors are like, i.e., gross, disgusting, inferior, carrying the symbol of their damnation on their skin; and has caught our overeasy assent to such assumptions in the grip of a guilt which associates us and our assent with the white man representative of such views in the play — Iago. Othello acquires the glamour of an innocent man that *we* have wronged, and an admiration stronger than he could have achieved by virtue plainly represented:

> . . . as these black masks
> Proclaim an enshield beauty ten times louder
> Than beauty could, displayed.

[23]M. Bandello, *Novelle*, Book III, novel xxi, derived from Pontanus (Opera, i, 25, b), and translated by F. Belleforest, *Histoires tragiques*. The story was apparently Englished in ballad form, in 1569, 1570, and again in 1624, 1675. See E. Hyder Rollins, "Analytical Index" (*Studies in Philology*, xxi [1924]), item 2542: "a strange petyful novell Dyscoursynge of a noble Lorde and his lady with thayre ij cheldren executed by a blacke morryon."

[24]Hakluyt, *Principal Navigations* (1903–5 ed.), V. 122.

(Is it an accident that Shakespeare wrote these lines from *Measure for Measure* in approximately the same year as he wrote *Othello*?) Iago is a "civilized" man; but where, for the "inferior" Othello, appearance and reality, statement and truth are linked indissolubly, civilization for Iago consists largely of a capacity to manipulate appearances and probabilities:

> For when my outward action doth demonstrate
> The native act and figure of my heart
> In compliment extern, 'tis not long after
> But I will wear my heart upon my sleeve
> For daws to peck at: I am not what I am.

Othello may be "the devil" in appearance: but it is the "fair" Iago who gives birth to the dark realities of sin and death in the play:

> It is engender'd. Hell and night
> Must bring this monstrous birth to the world's light

The relationship between these two is developed in terms of appearance and reality. Othello controls the reality of action; Iago the "appearance" of talk about action; Iago the Italian is isolated (even from his wife), envious, enigmatic (even to himself), self-centered; Othello the "extravagant and wheeling stranger" is surrounded and protected by a network of duties, obligations, esteems, pious to his father-in-law, deferential to his superiors, kind to his subordinates, loving to his wife. To sum up, assuming that *soul* is reality and *body* is appearance, we may say that Iago is the white man with the black soul while Othello is the black man with the white soul. Long before Blake's little black boy had said

> I am black, but oh my soul is white.
> White as an angel is the English child,
> But I am black as if bereaved of light.

and before Kipling's Gunga Din:

> An' for all 'is dirty 'ide
> 'E was white, clear white inside . . .
> You're a better man than I am, Gunga Din!

Othello had represented the guilty awareness of Europe that the "foreigner type" is only the type we do not know, whose foreignness vanishes when we have better acquaintance; that the prejudicial foreign appearance may conceal a vision of truth, as Brabantio is told:

> If virtue no delighted beauty lack
> Your son-in-law is far more fair than black.

This reality of fairness in Othello provides a principal function for Desdemona in the play. Her love is of a spiritual intensity, of a strong simplicity equal to that of Othello himself, and pierces without effort beyond appearance, into reality:

> I saw Othello's visage in his mind.

Her love is a daring act of faith, beyond reason or social propriety. Like Beauty in the fairytale she denies the beastly (or devilish) appearance to proclaim her allegiance to the invisible reality. And she does so throughout the play, even when the case for the appearance seems most strong and when Iago's power over appearances rides highest. Even when on the point of death at Othello's hands, she gives testimony to her faith (martyr in the true sense of the word):

> Commend me to my *kind* lord.

Othello is then a play which manipulates our sympathies, supposing that we will have brought to the theater a set of careless assumptions about "Moors." It assumes also that we will find it easy to abandon these as the play brings them into focus and identifies them with Iago, draws its elaborate distinction between the external appearance of devilishness and the inner reality.

Margaret Webster (1905–1972)
SHAKESPEARE WITHOUT TEARS   *1942*

> *Margaret Webster directed the notable Broadway performance of* Othello *with Paul Robeson in 1943–1944. In this excerpt from her memoirs, she comments on the question of race and its importance to the play. She focuses on Desdemona and her motives in marrying a black man whom her father could not accept. She connects this important detail to Othello's "acceptance of the possibility of Desdemona's infidelity."*

The question of Othello's race is of paramount importance to the play. There has been much controversy as to Shakespeare's intention. It is improbable that he troubled himself greatly with ethnological exactness. The Moor, to an Elizabethan, was a blackamoor, an African, an Ethiopian. Shakespeare's other Moor, Aaron, in *Titus Andronicus,* is specifically black; he has thick lips and a fleece of woolly hair. The Prince of Morocco in *The Merchant of Venice* bears "the shadowed livery of the burnished sun," and even Portia recoils from his "complexion" which he himself is at great pains to excuse.

Othello is repeatedly described, both by himself and others, as black; not pale beige, but black; and for a century and a half after the play's first presentation he was so represented on the stage. But after this the close consideration of nice minds began to discern something not quite ladylike about Desdemona's marrying a black man with thick lips. They cannot have been more horrified than Brabantio, her father, who thought that only witchcraft could have caused "nature so preposterously to err," or more convinced of the disastrous outcome of such a match than Iago, who looked upon it as nothing but a "frail vow between an erring Barbarian and a supersubtle Venetian," and declared, with his invincible cynicism, that "when she is sated with his body, she will find the error of her choice: She must have change; she must!"

It is very apparent, and vital to the play, that Othello himself was very conscious of these same considerations and quiveringly aware of what the judgment of the world would be upon his marriage. It is one of the most potent factors in his acceptance of the possibility of Desdemona's infidelity. And she herself loses much in the quality of her steadfastness and courage if it be supposed that she simply married against her father's wishes a man who chanced to be a little darker than his fellows, instead of daring a marriage which would cause universal condemnation among

Ron Canada as Iago and Patrick Stewart as Othello, in the Shakespeare Theater's 1997–1998 production of *Othello* in Washington, D.C., directed by Jude Kelly. In this version Stewart played Othello with an all-black cast.

the ladies of polite society. To scamp this consideration in the play is to deprive Othello of his greatest weakness, Desdemona of her highest strength, Iago of his skill and judgment, Emilia of a powerful factor in her behavior both to her master and her mistress, and Venice itself of an arrogance in toleration which was one of the principal hallmarks of its civilization — a civilization which frames, first and last, the soaring emotions of the play.

After these three tragedies, Shakespeare will never again take us into so passion-tossed a world, never set his actors to release themselves so fully from the normal restraints of polite behavior, never pound his audience into submission by the relentless power of words. He will give us a jealous man in Leontes, an ambitious one in Octavius, an embittered outcast in Timon, but it will not be the sacrificial jealousy of Othello, the haunted ambition of Macbeth, or the madness of Lear. Nothing that happens in the later plays will carry us beyond the sphere where reason is still a comfortable guide. Nor will man ever again cry with such anguish to the stars to shield him from the unbearable responsibility of the world he has fashioned. The theatre will revert to its normal self, its walls solid and comfortably bounding the two hours' traffic of make-believe. There will be plenty of technical problems to be faced. *Antony and Cleopatra* especially will call for a width and range of vision; many of the plays to come will need adroit and lavish handling. But never again will the hearts of players and audience be so swept with the mystery of life and the bitter release of death.

Peter Marks

REVIEW OF PATRICK STEWART AS OTHELLO   *1997*

Patrick Stewart is probably best known for his role as Jean-Luc Picard on Star Trek, *but before that he was with the Royal Shakespeare Company in England and has acted in many Shakespeare plays. This review finds him as a white Othello in an all-black production, so that the racial roles are reversed. Marks, surprisingly, finds that such an approach downplays the racial issues.*

In the past, white actors who played Othello inevitably became obsessed with makeup. "The whole thing will be in the lips and the color," Laurence Olivier observed in a 1964 *Life* magazine interview, in the midst of preparing his legendary portrayal. "I'll use just a little tiny touch of lake and a lot more brown and a little mauve."

The rules over the centuries for Caucasians contriving Othello's blackness were, by the standard of modern sensibilities, comically rigid: "A tawny tinge is now the color used for the gallant Moor," instructed an 1827 book on theater makeup. Today, of course, an Othello in blackface might justifiably be subject to catcalls. So is there any way a white performer can comfortably be cast in the part?

Patrick Stewart and the British director Jude Kelly have come upon one: eliminate the makeup altogether. In their kinetic, earth-toned, eye-filling production at the Shakespeare Theater here, Othello, played by Mr. Stewart, is white. The Venetians, from noble Cassio to twisted Iago to doomed Desdemona, are black. And in the race reversing, the company seeks to shatter stereotypes and remind playgoers of the endlessly adaptive nature of Shakespeare's exploration of otherness.

Thanks to some moving and polished performances by Teagle F. Bougere as Cassio, Franchelle Stewart Dorn as Emilia, Patrice Johnson as Desdemona, and, above all, to Mr. Stewart's captivating, devastatingly human portrayal, this *Othello* does not reveal itself as a curiosity but as a fascinating study of the fragile border between possessive love and obliterating paranoia.

Interestingly, the racial turning of the tables does not tilt the play toward ham-handed irony; rather, it tends to take the racial issue off the table. Though a few glaring casting problems, having more to do with technique than philosophy, deny the production the glowing mark of distinction it might have earned, the overall sensitivity and quality of the effort is ample justification for the risks its creators took.

The vigorous, sinewy Mr. Stewart, wearing a hoop earring and a serpentine tattoo on the back of his shaved head, is Ms. Kelly's chief insurance that her version never seems a mere trick. In this modern-dress production, she places him at the helm of a mercenary force that occupies Cyprus, rendered strikingly by Robert Innes Hopkins as a bomb-strafed fortress. (A romantic score by Michael Ward adds Italianate warmth.) The most controversial use of color in the play, however, may be in Mr. Hopkins's costumes: the Venetians' plum-colored fatigues (the Cypriots wear tangerine) make the actors look like members of a United Nations peacekeep-ing unit as outfitted by Banana Republic.

Othello himself is often played as a towering man of honor, a virtual stone figure on a pedestal. Untethered in other important ways from the role's history, Mr. Stewart finds in his Othello a charmed soldier of fortune more interested in making love than war. There is sigh-inducing passion in his poetic recall of how he wooed Desdemona with words. "She loved me for the dangers I had passed / And I loved her that she did pity them," he says, and it's abundantly clear in Mr. Stewart's rap-turous gaze that this is the conquest he most highly treasures.

The speech is delivered during an early scene in which Othello is engaged by Venice's noblemen to rout the Turks from Cyprus; it's also one of the moments in which the play's racial tensions are most apparent. Brabantio, Desdemona's father (Darrell Carey), opposes his daughter's secret marriage, and he makes his objec-tions plain.

In traditional productions, surrounded by a roomful of white faces, Othello seems a figure of strength and sympathy. But when Othello is a white military leader — what more recognizable authority figure exists in Western culture? — it's hard to feel particularly sorry for him. It's an instance in which race reversal does not jibe with an audience's sense of the way the world beyond the theater works.

More troublesome in this production, however, is the disappointingly wan battle of wills between Othello and his nemesis, Iago. The villainous underling who flatly announces, "I hate the Moor," is in some ways the play's most accessible character. He speaks to the audience constantly; we watch the drama unfold, in a sense, over his shoulder. Ms. Kelly's notion is an Iago who is a bitterly frustrated minor officer, passed over for promotions and even asked, humiliatingly, to carry Othello's luggage ashore.

But Ron Canada provides a dishearteningly wooden Iago, which robs his scenes with Mr. Stewart of their delicious cat-and-mouse aspect. The performance also unbalances Iago's encounters with Roderigo (Jimonn Cole), the jealous suitor he manipulates. Mr. Cole goes way over the top in his sniveling fool of a Roderigo, in what seems a vain attempt to energize his exchanges with Mr. Canada.

The tonic in this production comes in its portrayal of domestic disintegration. Ms. Johnson and Mr. Stewart have a winsome rapport that makes their marriage a true coupling, and until her fiery death scene, Ms. Dorn, as Iago's mate, conveys the dead-eyed complacency of a battered doormat. Mr. Stewart is never anything less than uncanny in his psychological portrait: it's like watching an autopsy on human feeling. The precise moment at which Iago first plants doubt about Desdemona's constancy registers on Mr. Stewart's intense features; you sense the tragic events to follow in the terrifying blink of his eye.

This fine actor, so magnetic a Prospero in George Wolfe's 1995 *Tempest*, seems to get better and better. Next time around, it might be even more rewarding to see his Iago.

Ben Jonson

Known primarily as a writer of comedies such as *Every Man in His Humor* (1598) and *Every Man out of His Humor* (1599) in the reign of Elizabeth I, Jonson's most interesting plays were performed during the reign (called the Jacobean period) of her successor, King James I. *Volpone* (1606) and *The Alchemist* (1610) stand today as Jonson's most often produced plays. Both are broad comedies: *Volpone* plays on the foxiness of a dying man who is anxious to see which of his heirs is worthy, and *The Alchemist* is a satire on the wiliness of con men who pretend to know how to transmute base metal into gold. All of these plays were highly regarded in Jacobean times. In addition to his comedies, Jonson's tragedies *Sejanus* (1603) and *Catiline* (1611) earned him the description of "best in tragedy" from a contemporary who maintained a diary devoted to his experiences in the theater.

Jonson led an exciting life. Born after his father died, he was placed in the Westminster School at the expense of its master, William Camden, author of the famous survey *Britannia*. There Jonson learned Latin and Greek but he himself said that instead of attending a university, he practiced his trade. Because Jonson's stepfather was a bricklayer, it has been assumed that Jonson learned that trade. He eventually grew tired of bricklaying and managed to get a job as an actor. In 1598, while a member of Philip Henslowe's theater, he killed a fellow actor in a brawl. He claimed self-defense and was granted "benefit of clergy," which was accorded those who could read and translate a Latin passage, but as punishment he carried a brand on his thumb from Tyburn, the place of execution and punishment, for the rest of his life.

For Jonson the stage was a way of making a living. He aspired to be a pure poet and was accorded great honor in his lifetime by other poets. But he could not, even with the patronage of important noblemen, eke out a sufficient living writing only poetry. Jonson was imprisoned in Elizabeth's reign for writing an offensive play, *The Isle of Dogs* (1597), and in the early years of King James's reign, which began on March 24, 1603, play writing continued to be dangerous. Toward the end of 1605, Jonson teamed with George Chapman and William Marston to write *Eastward Ho!*, a comedy that ridiculed the Scots (James I was a Scot). Jonson and Chapman were imprisoned, but Jonson eventually contacted enough important people to secure his release, probably in October, claiming that the few offensive lines had been written by Marston, who had fled London to avoid prison. Then in November the great Gunpowder Plot — remembered today with bonfires on November 5, Guy Fawkes Day — cast a dangerous shadow over him. Led by the Catholic conspirator Guy Fawkes, the Gunpowder Plot was a plan to kill the king, his advisors, and all members of the hierarchy of the Church and Parliament. Guy Fawkes's use of the pseudonym John Johnson, together with Jonson's conversion to Catholicism, may have resulted in the playwright's becoming a suspect. Luckily, he was well known in James's court and was able to demonstrate his loyalty and innocence.

For most of his life Jonson made his living by writing for the public stage, but he was by no means always successful. Although many of his plays are today regarded as among the most important of the late Renaissance, tastes changed during his lifetime, and by the end of his life he found himself no longer in vogue.

Jonson won considerable acclaim as a writer in the court of James I and Queen Anne. He composed entertainments and masques designed to be associated with important state occasions. The masque was a dramatic form that enjoyed great popularity for close to a century and a half. It was restricted to the entertainment and participation of royalty and courtiers. As its name implies, characters were sometimes masked to represent abstract ideas such as Blackness or Beauty or mythic characters such as Albion, an allegory for England itself.

Inigo Jones (1573–1652), brought to court by Queen Anne, collaborated with Jonson to make the Jacobean masque a dazzling spectacle. Jones was a painter and architect who had traveled abroad and returned to England with members of Anne's court when Anne ascended the British throne. He was responsible for designing costumes, scenery, special effects, and lighting. He introduced Italian theater machinery and techniques into his entertainments. The Jacobean masque was elaborate, sensational, and so enormously expensive that it is said to have contributed to the impoverishment of the crown inherited by James's successor, Charles I.

THE MASQUE OF BLACKNESS

Apparently dissatisfied with Samuel Daniel, the poet and writer who had produced the first masque for her court, Queen Anne turned to Ben Jonson and asked him to create a masque in which she and some of her court ladies could paint themselves black and pretend to be Moors. The source for her inspiration is unclear, but she may have encountered African emissaries in London or otherwise been aware of the presence of numerous Africans in London. During the later years of her reign, Queen Elizabeth felt there were too many black Africans in London and ordered them sent abroad. James does not seem to have followed her example.

The Masque of Blackness was the first of Ben Jonson's many masques. It was performed January 6, 1605, in the same theater and around the same time as *Othello*. Inigo Jones's machinery impressed the audience, which included foreign emissaries, such as the Venetian and Spanish ambassadors. Sir Dudley Carleton, present at the performance, was not pleased that the Queen and her attendants had painted themselves black. He feared that kissing the hands of the masquers might blacken his face. He may have been familiar with earlier royal entertainments in which black characters were represented with long black gloves and black cloth masks.

Jonson's opening description of the setting is extensive because in masques the costumes and imaginative figures took on great importance. But his text is also ingenious. Given the assignment to produce a masque for blackamoors, he invented the conceit that "the Ethiops were as fair / As other dames, now black with black despair." Hence, the narrative moves these figures toward recovering their original brightness by seeking a nation whose name ends in "-tania" and residing there for thirteen days. Their journey takes them to Mauretania, Lusitania, and Aquitania, but none of those nations can avail them. Finally, Britannia fulfills their desire, and the masque ends with the prospect of their remaining another twelve nights.

The daughters of Niger are described as beautiful women, all the more beautiful because of their black skin and hair, but in Jonson's masque they encounter a Eurocentric point of view expressed by "some few / Poor brainsick men" who convince them that they should be "fair." The word "fair" in Elizabethan English means primarily beautiful, but it also means light in color. The point of the masque is to emphasize the beauty of the daughters (who are played by the Queen and her attendants) and to restore them to their original fairness.

One important feature of the masque is the representation of figures in an allegorical fashion. In other words, Oceanus is not a psychologically real character but a figure who represents the ocean. Niger is the river, Aethiopia the nation. All the characters in the masque follow this pattern. When the Queen and her attendants dance (line 302), they assume allegorical identities. The Queen is Euphoris, or Happiness, and her symbol is a "golden tree laden with fruit." The dance that the Queen and her attendants perform is the highlight of the masque, and the courtiers who participated felt it to be a joyful and exciting occasion.

The Masque of Blackness, like all Jacobean masques, was a multimedia event, like a modern "happening." The lines of dialogue are carefully crafted, and the narrative suitably dramatic. But it is the music, the song, the dance, and the machinery of the setting — the rocking and moving seashell and the sudden appearances of characters — that make the masque successful and impressive. As far as we know, masques such as this were not performed more than once or twice, partly because of expense and partly because of the demand for novelty in a relatively small court.

The speaking characters were played by professional actors, but all the other roles were drawn from the court. That way the poetry could be heard and the drama maintained without stressing the courtiers, who would have had, with very few exceptions, no aspirations toward the stage.

The Masque of Blackness in Performance

Since the masque is preeminently a performance piece, we must credit the spectacle over the poetry and dialogue. Even Jonson, early in his collaboration, pays homage to Inigo Jones's innovations in the masque. Sir Dudley Carleton, who was present at the performance in the old banqueting house, had much to say about it. His comments help us imagine the scene:

On Twelfth-Day . . . at night, we had the Queen's masque in the Banqueting House, or rather her pageant. There was a great engine at the lower end of the room, which had motion, and in it were the images of sea horses, with other terrible fishes, which were ridden by Moors; the indecorum was, that there was all fish and no water. At the further end was a great shell in the form of a scallop, wherein were four seats; on

Inigo Jones, Costume for a Nymph, Daughter of Niger. Jonson described the masquers: "The attire of [the] *Masquers* was alike, in all, without difference: the colors, *azure,* and *silver*; (their hair thick, and curled upright in tresses, like *Pyramids*), but returned on the top with a scroll and antique dressing of feathers, and jewels interlaced with ropes of pearl. And, for the front, ear, neck, and wrists, the ornament was of the most choice and orient pearl; best setting off from the black."

the lowest sat the Queen with my lady Bedford; on the rest were placed the ladies . . . their apparel was rich, but too courtesan-like for such great ones. Instead of vizards, their faces, and arms up to elbows, were painted black, which was disguise sufficient, for they were hard to be known; *but it became them nothing so well as their own red and white, and you cannot imagine a more ugly sight than a troop of lean-cheeked Moors.* The Spanish and Venetian Ambassadors were both present, and sat by the King in state; at which Monsieur Beaumont [the French ambassador] quarrels so extremely that he saith the whole court is Spanish . . . the night's work was concluded with a banquet in the great chamber, which was so seriously assaulted that down went tables and trestles before one bit was touched.

Masques are occasionally performed today but in nothing like their original form. The costs for the *Masque of Blackness* exceeded £3,000, a fortune of hundreds of thousands of dollars in today's money.

Ben Jonson (1572–1637)

The Masque of Blackness

1605

List of Characters

Oceanus
Niger
Aethiopia
Tritons, Sea-Maids, Nymphs, the Daughters of
    Niger, *and* Oceaniae

    The honor and splendor of these spectacles was such in the performance as, could those hours have lasted, this of mine now had been a most unprofitable work. But, when it is the fate even of the greatest and most
5 absolute° births to need and borrow a life of posterity, little had been done to the study of magnificence° in these° if presently with the rage of the people, who, as a part of greatness, are privileged by custom to deface their carcases,° the spirits had also perished. In duty,
10 therefore, to that majesty who gave them their authority and grace, and, no less than the most royal of predecessors, deserves eminent celebration for these solemnities, I add this later hand to redeem them° as well from ignorance as envy, two common evils, the one of censure, the
15 other of oblivion.
    Pliny, Solinus, Ptolemy, and of late Leo the African, remember° unto us a river in Ethiopia famous by the name of Niger, of which the people were called *Nigritae,* now Negroes, and are the blackest nation of the world.
20 This river taketh spring out of a certain lake,° eastward, and after a long race falleth into the western ocean. Hence, because it was her majesty's will to have them° blackamores at first, the invention° was derived by me, and presented thus.

25   *First, for the scene, was drawn a Landtschap°* con-*sisting of small woods, and here and there a void place filled with huntings;° which falling,° an artificial sea was seen to shoot forth, as if it flowed to the land, raised with waves which seemed to move, and in some places*
30 *the billow to break, as imitating that orderly disorder which is common in nature. In front of this sea were placed six tritons in moving and sprightly actions, their*

upper parts human, save that their hairs were blue, as partaking of the sea color, their desinent° parts fish, mounted above their heads, and all varied in disposi-
35 *tion.° From their backs were borne out certain light pieces of taffeta as if carried by the wind, and their music made out of wreathed shells. Behind these a pair of sea-maids, for song, were as conspicuously seated; be-tween which two great sea-horses, as big as the life, put*
40 *forth themselves, the one mounting aloft and writhing his head from the other, which seemed to sink forwards (so intended for variation, and that the figure behind might come off better); upon their backs Oceanus and Niger were advanced.*
45   *Oceanus presented in a human form, the color of his flesh blue, and shadowed° with a robe of sea-green; his head grey and horned, as he is described by the ancients; his beard of the like mixed color. He was garlanded with algae, or sea-grass, and in his hand a trident.*
50   *Niger in form and color of an Ethiop, his hair and rare° beard curled, shadowed with a blue and bright mantle; his front,° neck and wrists adorned with pearl; and crowned with an artificial wreath of cane and paper-rush.°*
55   *These induced° the masquers, which were twelve nymphs, Negroes, and the daughters of Niger, attended by so many of the Oceaniae,° which were their light-bearers.*
60   *The masquers were placed in a great concave shell like mother of pearl, curiously° made to move on those waters and rise with the billow; the top thereof was stuck with a chevron of lights which, indented to the proportion of the shell, struck a glorious beam upon*
65 *them as they were seated one above another; so that they were all seen, but in an extravagant° order.*
    On sides of the shell did swim six huge sea-monsters, varied in their shape and dispositions,° bearing on their backs the twelve torch-bearers, who were planted there
70 *in several greces,° so as the backs of some were seen, some in purfle,° or side, others in face; and all having their lights burning out of whelks or murex shells.*
    The attire of the masquers was alike in all, without difference: the colors, azure and silver; their hair thick and curled upright in tresses, like pyramids, but returned
75

---

5. absolute: Perfect; here, noble. **6. magnificence:** According to Aristotle, the virtue of monarchs. **7. these:** I.e., masques. **7–9. people . . . carcases:** At the end of the masque, the audience was traditionally permitted to tear down the scenery and plunder the decorations. **13. them:** The "spirits" of line 9. **17. remember:** Mention. **20. lake:** Lake Chad. **22. them:** The masquers. **invention:** Device of the masque. **25. Landt-schap:** Landscape. **27. huntings:** Animals hunting their prey. **which falling:** The landscape-curtain was released from above, and fell to the floor in front of the stage to reveal the scene.

34. desinent: Terminal. **35–36. disposition:** Arrangement. **47. shadowed:** Covered. **52. rare:** Thin. **53. front:** Forehead. **55. paper-rush:** Papyrus. **56. induced:** Brought in. **58. Oce-aniae:** Sea nymphs, daughters of Oceanus. **61. curiously:** Art-fully. **66. extravagant:** (1) Unusual; (2) moving about in an extraordinary way. **68. dispositions:** Positions. **70. greces:** Steps. **71. purfle:** Profile.

on the top with a scroll and antique dressing of feathers
and jewels interlaced with ropes of pearl. And for the
front,° ear, neck and wrists, the ornament was of the
most choice and orient pearl, best setting off from the
80 *black.*

For the light-bearers, sea-green, waved about the
skirts with gold and silver; their hair loose and flowing,
garlanded with sea-grass, and that stuck with branches
of coral.

85 *These thus presented,° the scene behind seemed a*
vast sea, and united with this that flowed forth, from
the termination or horizon of which (being the level of
the state,° which was placed in the upper end of the
hall) was drawn, by the lines of perspective, the whole
90 *work shooting downwards from the eye; which deco-*
rum made it more conspicuous, and caught the eye afar
off with a wandering beauty. To which was added an
obscure and cloudy night-piece that made the whole set
off. So much for the bodily part, which was of Master
95 *Inigo Jones° his design and act.*

By this,° one of the tritons, with the two sea-maids,
began to sing to the others' loud music, their voices
being a tenor and two trebles.°

SONG:
　Sound, sound aloud
100 　The welcome of the orient flood
　Into the west;
　Fair Niger, son to great Oceanus,
　Now honored thus,
　With all his beauteous race,
105 　Who, though but black in face,
　Yet are they bright,
　And full of life and light,
　To prove that beauty best
　Which not the color but the feature°
110 　Assures unto the creature.
OCEANUS: Be silent now the ceremony's done,
　And Niger, say, how comes it, lovely son,
　That thou, the Ethiop's river, so far east,
　Art seen to fall into th'extremest west
115 　Of me, the king of floods, Oceanus,
　And in mine empire's heart salute me thus?
　My ceaseless current now amazèd stands
　To see thy labor through so many lands
　Mix thy fresh billow with my brackish stream,
120 　And in thy sweetness stretch thy diadem
　To these far distant and unequalled skies,
　This squarèd circle of celestial bodies.°
NIGER: Divine Oceanus, 'tis not strange at all
　That, since the immortal souls of creatures mortal

　Mix with their bodies, yet reserve forever   125
　A power of separation, I should sever
　My fresh streams from thy brackish, like things
　　fixed,
　Though with thy powerful saltness thus far mixed.
　Virtue, though chained to earth, will still live free,
　And hell itself must yield to industry.°   130
OCEANUS: But what's the end of thy herculean labors
　Extended to these calm and blessèd shores?
NIGER: To do a kind and careful father's part,
　In satisfying every pensive heart
　Of these my daughters, my most lovèd birth: 135
　Who, though they were the first formed dames of
　　earth,
　And in whose sparkling and refulgent eyes
　The glorious sun did still delight to rise;
　Though he — the best judge and most formal cause°
　Of all dames' beauties — in their firm hues draws   140
　Signs of his fervent'st love, and thereby shows
　That in their black° the perfect'st beauty grows,
　Since the fixed color of their curlèd hair,
　Which is the highest grace of dames most fair,
　No cares, no age can change, or there display   145
　The fearful tincture of abhorrèd grey,
　Since Death herself (herself being pale and blue)
　Can never alter their most faithful hue;
　All which are arguments to prove how far
　Their beauties conquer in great beauty's war,   150
　And more, how near divinity they be
　That stand from passion or decay so free.
　Yet since the fabulous voices of some few
　Poor brainsick men, styled poets here with you,
　Have with such envy of their graces sung   155
　The painted beauties other empires sprung,
　Letting their loose and wingèd fictions fly
　To infect all climates, yea, our purity;
　As of one Phaëton,° that fired the world,
　And that before his heedless flames were hurled   160
　About the globe, the Ethiops were as fair
　As other dames, now black with black despair;
　And in respect of their complexions changed,
　Are eachwhere since for luckless creatures ranged.
　Which when my daughters heard, as women are   165
　Most jealous of their beauties, fear and care
　Possessed them° whole; yea, and believing them,
　They wept such ceaseless tears into my stream
　That it hath thus far overflowed his shore
　To seek them patience, who have since e'ermore   170
　As the sun riseth charged his burning throne

---

78. **front:** Forehead.　85. **presented:** Having been presented.
87–88. **level . . . state:** Height of the royal throne.　95. **Inigo
Jones** (1573–1652): Architect and stage designer, Jonson's
collaborator throughout his career as court masque writer.
96. **this:** This time.　98. **trebles:** Sopranos.　109. **feature:**
Form.　122. **squarèd . . . bodies:** I.e., heavenly bodies perfectly transformed into an earthly realm.

130. *hell . . . industry:* From Horace, Odes I, iii, 36: "herculean effort overcame hell"; alluded to in the next line.
139. **formal cause:** Creator of the form or essence; Aristotelian
terminology.　142. **black:** Synonymous with ugly in Elizabethan English.　159. **Phaëton:** Son of Phoebus Apollo, the
sun god. He was allowed to drive the chariot of the sun, but
could not control the horses, and Zeus destroyed him lest he set
the world afire.　167. **them:** The poets. (Jonson)

With volleys of revilings, 'cause he shone
On their scorched cheeks with such intemperate
    fires,
And other dames made queens of all desires.
175 To frustrate which strange error oft I sought,
Though most in vain, against a settled thought
As women's are, till they confirmed at length
By miracle what I with so much strength
Of argument resisted; else they feigned:
180 For in the lake where their first spring they gained,
As they sat cooling their soft limbs one night,
Appeared a face all circumfused with light —
And sure they saw't, for Ethiops never dream —
Wherein they might decipher through the stream
185 These words:

That they a land must forthwith seek
Whose termination, of the Greek,
Sounds *-tania*; where bright Sol,° that heat
Their bloods, doth never rise or set,
190 But in his journey passeth by,
And leaves that climate of the sky
To comfort of a greater light,
Who forms all beauty with his sight.

In search of this have we three princedoms passed
195 That speak out *-tania* in their accents last;
Black Mauretania° first, and secondly
Swarth° Lusitania;° next we did descry
Rich Aquitania,° and yet cannot find
The place unto these longing nymphs designed.°
200 Instruct and aid me, great Oceanus:
What land is this that now appears to us?
OCEANUS: This land that lifts into the temperate air
His snowy cliff is Albion° the fair,
So called of Neptune's son, who ruleth here;
205 For whose dear guard, myself four thousand year,
Since old Deucalion's° days, have walked the round
About his empire, proud to see him crowned
Above my waves.

At this the moon was discovered in the upper part of
210 *the house, triumphant in a silver throne made in figure*
of a pyramis.° Her garments white and silver, the dress-
ing of her head antique, and crowned with a luminary,
or sphere of light, which striking on the clouds, and
heightened with silver, reflected as natural clouds do by
215 *the splendor of the moon. The heaven about her was*
vaulted with blue silk and set with stars of silver which
had in them their several lights burning. The sudden
sight of which made Niger to interrupt Oceanus with
this present° passion.

NIGER: O see, our silver star! 220
Whose pure, auspicious light greets us thus far!
Great Aethiopia,° goddess of our shore,
Since with particular worship we adore
Thy general brightness, let particular grace
Shine on my zealous daughters: show the place 225
Which long their longings urged their eyes to see.
Beautify them, which long have deified thee.
AETHIOPIA: Niger, be glad; resume thy native cheer.
Thy daughters' labors have their period° here,
And so thy errors.° I was that bright face 230
Reflected by the lake, in which thy race
Read mystic lines; which skill Pythagoras
First taught to men by a reverberate° glass.°
This blessèd isle doth with that *-tania* end,
Which there they saw inscribed, and shall extend 235
Wished satisfaction to their best desires.
Britannia, which the triple world° admires,
This isle hath now recovered for her name,°
Where reign those beauties that with so much fame
The sacred muses' sons have honorèd, 240
And from bright Hesperus° to Eos° spread.
With that great name Britannia, this blessed isle
Hath won her ancient dignity and style,°
A world divided from the world, and tried
The abstract of it in his general pride.° 245
For were the world with all his wealth a ring,
Britannia, whose new name° makes all tongues sing,
Might be a diamond worthy to enchase° it,
Ruled by a sun that to this height doth grace it,
Whose beams shine day and night, and are of force 250
To blanch an Ethiop, and revive a corse.°
His light sciential° is, and, past mere nature,
Can salve the rude defects of every creature.
Call forth thy honored daughters, then,
And let them, 'fore the Britain men, 255
Indent° the land with those pure traces°
They flow with in their native graces.
Invite them boldly to the shore;
Their beauties shall be scorched no more;
This sun is temperate, and refines 260
All things on which his radiance shines.

222. Aethiopia: The moon goddess. **229. period:** End.
230. errors: With a quibble on "wanderings." **233. reverberate:** Reflecting. **232–33. Pythagoras . . . glass:** Pythagoras
was supposedly able to reflect messages onto the moon by writing in blood on a mirror. **237. triple world:** Heaven, earth,
and the underworld. **238. recovered . . . name:** See line 247
and gloss. **241. Hesperus:** Evening, the west. **Eos:** Dawn,
the east. **243. style:** Characterization. **244–45. tried . . .
pride:** Experienced the ideal of it through England's own pride
in herself. "His" refers to England, despite "her" two lines earlier. **247. new name:** The name Great Britain was coined
when James VI of Scotland became king also of England and
Wales in 1604. It was not officially adopted, however, until
1707. **248. enchase:** Set in. **251. corse:** Corpse. **252. sci-
ential:** Endowed with the powers of science. **256. Indent:**
Leave footprints on. **traces:** Footsteps.

188. Sol: The sun. **196. Mauretania:** The land of the Moors,
including modern Morocco and part of Algeria. **197. Swarth:**
Swarthy. **Lusitania:** Portugal and western Spain.
198. Aquitania: Southwestern France. **199. designed:** Indicated. **203. Albion:** Traditional poetic name for England.
206. Deucalion: A Greek Noah, survivor of the universal flood.
211. pyramis: Pyramid. **219. present:** Immediate.

Here the tritons sounded, and they danced on shore,
every couple as they advanced severally presenting their
fans, in one of which were inscribed their mixed names,
265 *in the other a mute hieroglyphic expressing their mixed*
qualities. (Which manner of symbol I rather chose than
imprese,° as well for strangeness as relishing of antiq-
uity, and more applying to that original doctrine of
sculpture which the Egyptians are said first to have
270 *brought from the Ethiopians.)*

	The names	The symbols
The queen	*Euphoris°*	A golden tree° laden with fruit.
	1.	
Countess of Bedford	*Aglaia°*	
275 Lady Herbert	*Diaphane°*	The figure icosahedron° of crystal.
	2.	
Countess of Derby	*Eucampse°*	
Lady Rich	*Ocyte°*	A pair of naked feet in a river.°
	3.	
280 Countess of Suffolk	*Kathare°*	
Lady Bevill	*Notis°*	The salamander° simple.
	4.	
Lady Effingham	*Psychrote°*	
Lady Elizabeth 285 Howard	*Glycyte°*	A cloud full of rain,° dropping.
	5.	
Lady Susan de Vere	*Malacia°*	
Lady Wroth	*Baryte°*	An urn, sphered with wine.°
	6.	
Lady Walsingham	*Periphere°*	

290   The names of the Oceaniae were: *Doris, Petraea,*
Ocyrhoe, Cydippe, Glauce, Tyche, Beroe, Acaste, Clytia,
Ianthe, Lycoris, Plexaure.

267. **imprese:** Emblems.   272. *Euphoris:* Abundance.   **golden tree:** Symbol of fertility.   274. *Aglaia:* Splendor.   275. *Diaphane:* Transparent.   276. **icosahedron:** A twenty-sided figure symbolizing water.   277. *Eucampse:* Flexibility.   278. **Ocyte:** Swiftness.   279. **naked . . . river:** Symbolizing purity. 280. *Kathare:* Spotless.   281. *Notis:* Moisture.   **salamander:** Which is not harmed by fire and can extinguish it.   283. *Psychrote:* Coldness.   284. *Glycyte:* Sweetness.   284–85. **cloud . . . rain:** Symbolizing education.   286. *Malacia:* Delicacy. 287. *Baryte:* Weight.   287–88. **urn . . . wine:** Obscure, but the whole symbolizes the globe of earth.   289. *Periphere:* Revolving, circular.

Their own single dance ended, as they were about to
make choice of their men, one from the sea was heard to
call 'em with this charm, sung by a tenor voice.   295

SONG:
    Come away, come away,
    We grow jealous of your stay;
    If you do not stop your ear,
    We shall have more cause to fear
    Sirens of the land, than they   300
    To doubt the sirens of the sea.

Here they danced with their men several measures°
and corantos.° All which ended, they were again accited°
to sea with a song of two trebles,° whose cadences were
iterated by a double echo from several parts of the land.   305

SONG: Daughters of the subtle flood,
                        Do not let earth longer entertain you;
1ST ECHO: Let earth longer entertain you.
2ST ECHO: Longer entertain you.
                    'Tis to them enough of good   310
                    That you give this little hope to gain you.
1ST ECHO: Give this little hope to gain you.
2ND ECHO: Little hope to gain you.
                    If they love,
                        You shall quickly see;   315
                    For when to flight you move,
                    They'll follow you, the more you flee.
1ST ECHO: Follow you, the more you flee.
2ND ECHO: The more you flee.
                    If not, impute it each to other's matter;   320
                    They are but earth —
1ST ECHO: But earth,
2ND ECHO: Earth —
                        And what you vowed was water.
1ST ECHO: And what you vowed was water.   325
2ND ECHO: You vowed was water.
AETHIOPIA: Enough, bright nymphs, the night grows
                old,
    And we are grieved we cannot hold
    You longer light; but comfort take.
    Your father only to the lake   330
    Shall make return; yourselves, with feasts,
    Must here remain the Ocean's guests.
    Nor shall this veil the sun hath cast
    Above your blood more summers last;
    For which, you shall observe these rites: 335
    Thirteen times thrice, on thirteen nights
    (So often as I fill my sphere
    With glorious light throughout the year),
    You shall, when all things else do sleep
    Save your chaste thoughts, with reverence steep   340

302. *measures:* Slow dances.   303. *corantos:* Dances with a running or gliding step.   *accited:* Summoned.   304. *trebles:* Sopranos.

Your bodies in that purer brine
And wholesome dew called rosmarine;°
Then with that soft and gentler° foam,
Of which the ocean yet yields some,
345 Whereof bright Venus, beauty's queen,
Is said to have begotten been,
You shall your gentler limbs o'er-lave,
And for your pains perfection have;
So that, this night, the year gone round,°
350 You do again salute this ground,
And in the beams of yond' bright sun
Your faces dry, and all is done.

*At which, in a dance they returned to the sea, where
they took their shell, and with this full song went out.*

342. **rosmarine:** Sea dew.   343. **gentler:** Very gentle.   349. **year
. . . round:** The sequel, however, was not produced until 1608.

SONG:
Now Dian° with her burning face   355
    Declines apace,
    By which our waters know
    To ebb, that late did flow.
Back seas, back nymphs, but with a forward grace
    Keep, still, your reverence to the place;   360
And shout with joy of favor you have won
    In sight of Albion, Neptune's son.

*So ended the first masque, which, beside the singular
grace of music and dances, had that success in the nobility of performance as nothing needs to the illustration*   365
but the memory by whom it was personated.

355. **Dian:** The moon.

COMMENTARY

Eldred Jones (b. 1925)
AFRICA IN ENGLISH MASQUE AND PAGEANTRY   *1965*

In his book, Othello's Countrymen *(1965), Eldred Jones offers an extensive
review of the appearance of Africans in English entertainments. While the heyday
of the masque form is brief, it offered numerous opportunities to portray Africans
even before Ben Jonson's* Masque of Blackness. *What Jones demonstrates is that
the traditions and attitudes depicted in the masques were deeply ingrained in
English culture. Jonson relied on tradition as he developed his material.*

The English masque had only a short vogue. From its emergence as a distinct art
form with a name of its own, to its disappearance as a significant form, the period
stretches over less than a century and a half. Reckoning from the days when by the
combined efforts of Ben Jonson and Inigo Jones the masque rose to its final form,
the period shrinks to a little over three decades. But, from its earliest beginnings to
its disappearance, figures from Africa frequently contributed to the splendor and
strangeness of both the spectacle and the poetry of the masque. Like the form itself,
these African figures were at first vague and ill-defined, bearing little relevance to
any overall theme, and frequently having no connection with Africa except in
name. But later, as the masque took a settled form, they became more defined and
more deliberately related both to their supposed place of origin and to the themes
of the masques in which they appeared. For instance, figures which in the earliest

masques would have been described as "Moors" or "Blackamoors" appear in Jonson's *Masque of Blacknesse* as the "Daughters of Niger" against a background of both ancient and modern authorities: "Pliny, Solinus, Ptolemy, and of late Leo the African."

Whatever may have been the character or the strength of the stimulus which the English masque undoubtedly received from Renaissance Italy, certain of its features are to be found in activities which had been part of English life since medieval times. The dance was the nucleus around which the other features of the masque came to be established, and dancing, especially the dance called "Morisce" or "Morisco," had been an essential part of English medieval village festivals from earliest times. One of the customs associated with Morris dancing was the blackening of the faces of the participants. This tradition of blackening was also a feature of other popular activities in medieval England. The folk processions, the sword dance and the folk drama, all show an employment of the grotesque of which blackening was only one feature.

One of the most interesting characters in the medieval mummers play was the king of Egypt, who had a black face and who was accepted by tradition as the father of St. George. The devils in the mystery plays were also usually portrayed as black, and indeed some local traditions required all the participants in the mummers play to have black faces. The term "Moriscoe" (with its associations with "Moor" and "Morocco") and the king of Egypt also suggest a possible link between the English medieval dramatic tradition and Africa.

The practice of blackening was transferred to the more sophisticated court "disguisings" of the sixteenth century. In the earliest surviving description of a courtly festivity which involved blackening, the terms "Egipcians," "Moreskoes," and "blacke Moors" appear. In this masquelike performance in 1510, Henry VIII and the Earl of Essex had come in "appareled after Turkey fashion," while "the torchebearers were appareyled in Crymosyn satyne and grene, lyke Moreskoes, their faces blacke. . . ." Later in the same proceedings, six ladies also appeared "their heads rouled in plesauntes and typpers lyke the Egipcians, embroudered with gold. Their faces, neckes, armes and handes, covered with fyne plesaunce blacke . . . so that the same ladies seemed to be nigrost [sic] or blacke Mores." In this festivity, as in earlier entertainments of this kind, the black characters were merely decorative. The strangeness of their appearance had an exotic impact, and that was all that was required at that time. But it was this tradition which, continuing, made Queen Anne request Ben Jonson to make the characters in his masque of 1605 "Black-mores at first."

The Elizabethan outdoor pageant also frequently employed "Moors," and here again this use seems to have been linked with the use of grotesque characters in the medieval pageant. A king of Moors appeared in a pageant undertaken by the London drapers in 1522, and a surviving list of expenses in connection with it gives some indication of his function. The relevant entry records

> payment of 5s. to John Wakelyn, for playing the king of Moors, (the company finding him his apparell, his stage, and wyld fire).

Robert Withington, who notes this entry, draws the interesting conclusion that the "wyld fire" seems to connect the king of Moors here with the "wild man" or "green man" whose function in medieval pageantry was to clear a way through the crowd for the procession by using "wyld-fire" or fireworks. The king of Moors seems then to have crept into the later "procession" or "entertainment" as a grotesque character, to compel the crowds back by his strange appearance and his use of fireworks. (Individual items of the king's costume suggest that his appearance was spectacular: "the said king's girdle, his garland or turban of white feathers and black satin, sylver paper for his shoes, &c. .") In later outdoor pageants this crude function was refined so that the "Moor" or "king of Moors" appeared as a principal speaking character, often acting as the Presenter. In George Peele's pageant of 1585, for instance, the Presenter is described as "him that rid on a luzern before the Pageant, apparelled like a Moor." In Middleton's *Triumph of Truth* (1613) and Anthony Munday's *Chrysanaleia* (1616) similarly important functions were reserved for a Moor.

The popularity of Moors in masques can be judged by the number of references in surviving records either to masques specifically called masques of Moors, or to masques involving such characters, during the reigns of Edward VI, Elizabeth, and James I. The charges for a "Masque of Young Moors" given during Shrovetide 1547, in which King Edward took part, make very interesting reading, for they give illuminating information about the costuming of these characters. The blackening was effected through the use of black gloves, nether stockings, and face masks. These items are mentioned in the long list of charges: "To Rychard Lees of London mercer for viij yards d. of black vellett for gloves above thelbow for mores . . ."; "To hughe Eston the kynges hosyer for the makyng of xiiij peyres of nether stockes of lether black for mores"; a payment to "Nycholas modena straynger . . . for the trymyng Coloring and lyning of xvj vezars or maskes for moores." Some attempt was made to disguise the hair by giving the Moors "Cappes made with Cowrse budge." The elaborate costumes included "belles to hange at the skyrtes of the mores garments" and "dartes with brode heddes and ffethers of sylver. . . ." During the same reign, the accounts show that there was a masque involving Moors on 6 January 1551 and a masque of female Moors at Christmas 1551.

The accounts relating to the reign of Philip and Mary do not refer to any Moors in masques. In view of the apparent popularity of Moors in masques during Edward's reign, and the fact that a year after Elizabeth's accession they seem to have resumed their popularity and continued to hold it up to and during the reign of James I, this seems to indicate a significant temporary change of taste. One is led to speculate on whether portrayals of Moors were suspended out of deference to Philip, who, having had closer dealings with Moors, may have felt touchier on the subject than English monarchs.

Whatever the reasons were for the disappearance of Moors from masques during the reign of Philip and Mary, they reappeared in all their grandeur soon after Queen Elizabeth's accession. An inventory (dated 27 April 1560) of the wardrobe of the Office of the Revels refers to a masque of six Barbarians, and a masque of six Moors. The masque of Barbarians was performed on 1 January 1560, according to a note in the inventory, while the masque of Moors whose date is less certain is placed by E. K. Chambers on 29 January 1559.

There are no more references to masques involving African characters until 1579. (The records of the intervening years are either lost or are very incomplete.) But even this one masque referred to was not performed, although a Willyam Lyzard was paid "for patorns for the mores maske that should have served on Shrovetuesday." There are no other references to masques with Africans in Queen Elizabeth's reign.

Before we encounter our next Africans in masques, early in the reign of James I, a remarkable transformation had taken place. The masque had borrowed from the pageants and processions the use of poetry, and this new form had been employed by the gentlemen of the Inns of Court in their *Gesta Grayorum* (1595). Thus when the masque emerges under James I it emerges as a new form, a form worthy to engage the minds of serious poets. For a short while the English masque flourished as a serious art.

Queen Anne, who was to take a leading part in Ben Jonson's first court masque, expressed a wish "to have them [the masquers] Black-mores at first." This was not in itself a strange request. Now, however, more was involved than mere dressing-up. There had to be a poetic theme which would justify the introduction of black characters. It was therefore logical that Jonson should choose an African theme. His masquers thus emerged as "twelve Nymphs, Negro's, and the daughters of Niger . . ." since Negroes were "the blackest nation of the world." Niger himself was "in forme and colour of an Aethiope; his haire, and rare beard curled. . . ."

Around these characters Jonson weaves an ingenious story, using, whenever he so required, the fictions of the ancients to augment the fruits of his own imagination. The result is an engaging fable. The daughters of Niger had suddenly discovered, while reading Ovid, that they were not, after all, the most beautiful creatures in the world, and that their present color was the result of Phaeton's action:

> And, that, before his heedlesse flames were hurld
> About the Globe, the Aethiopes were as faire,
> As other Dames . . .

The now disillusioned and distracted girls cursed the sun for disfiguring them ("A custome of the Aethiopes, notable in Herod[otus] and Diod[orus] Sic[ulus]. See Plinie Nat. Hist. Lib. 5, cap. 8," adds a helpful Jonson) until they saw in a vision ("for Aethiopes never dreame") that they would recover their beauty if they traveled to a land with the termination "Tania." After passing through " 'blacke Mauritania, Swarth Lusitania and Rich Aquitania," they arrive in Britannia, the end of their quest. Here the beams of a "Sunne" (James),

> are of force
> To blanch an Aethiope, and revive a Cor's [sic].

All they had to do was to bathe thirteen nights in the ocean, and they would gain whiteness and beauty.

Jonson, once he had hit on the idea of black characters, wove both the poetry and, in so far as he controlled Inigo Jones, costume and scenery around them. The costumes and setting were carefully based on pale colors — silver and azure — with "jewells interlaced with ropes of pearle . . . best setting off from the black." The poetry is shot through with contrasts — light and darkness, black and white, death and life, the sun and the moon, and, by total implication, Africa and Europe. Niger's daughters for instance are thus described:

> Who, though but blacke in face,
> Yet, are they bright,
> And full of life and light.

In what must have been a *tour de force* in Elizabethan ears, Niger maintains that the black complexion is the most beautiful:

That, in their black, the prefectst beauty growes;
Since the fix't colour of their curled haire,
(Which is the highest grace of dames most faire)
No cares, no age can change; or there display
The fearefull tincture of abhorred *Gray*;
Since *Death* her selfe (her selfe being pale and blue)
Can never alter their most faithfull hiew.

Nothing as intricately harmonized as *The Masque of Blacknesse* had been attempted in the masque form before. It is a perfect blend of matter and manner; in it the extravagance which was germane to the masque is controlled by a disciplined imagination. This opinion was obviously not shared by Sir Dudley Carleton, whose comments on this presentation are preserved for us. Sir Dudley's criticisms of the scenery, that "there was all Fish and no Water," and of the apparel —"to light and Curtizan-light [sic] for such great ones"— show a literal rather than a literary mind. He, however, notes an interesting detail, namely that the masquers used paint (and not the usual velvet masks) to disguise their complexions:

Instead of Vizzards, their Faces and Arms up to the Elbows, were painted black, which was Disguise sufficient, for they were hard to be known; but it became them nothing so well as their red and white, and you cannot imagine a more ugly Sight, then a Troop of lean-cheek'd Moors.

The thirteen days promised in *The Masque of Blacknesse* ran into three years before the daughters of Niger, by then washed white, were to return to the stage in *The Masque of Beauty,* which was presented in 1608.

Late Seventeenth- and Eighteenth-Century Drama

The Restoration: Rebirth of Drama

Theater in England continued to thrive after Shakespeare's death, with a host of successful playwrights, including John Webster (1580?–1638?), Francis Beaumont (c. 1584–1616) and his collaborator John Fletcher (1579–1625), Philip Massinger (1583–1640), Thomas Middleton (1580–1627), John Ford (1586–c. 1655), and James Shirley (1596–1666). All these playwrights were busy working independently or in collaboration. Fletcher, chosen successor to Shakespeare at the Globe, furnished the theater with as many as four plays a year. But in 1642 long-standing religious and political conflicts between King Charles I and Parliament finally erupted into civil war, with the Parliament, under the influence of Puritanism, eventually winning.

The Puritans were religious extremists with narrow, specific values. They were essentially an emerging merchant class of well-to-do citizens who viewed the aristocracy as wastrels. Theater for them was associated with both the aristocracy and the low life. Theatergoing was synonymous with wasting time, the theaters were often a focus for immoral activity, and the neighborhoods around the theaters were as unsavory as any in England. Under the Puritan government, all theaters in England were closed for almost twenty years. When the new king, Charles II, was crowned in 1660, those that had not been converted to other uses had become completely outmoded.

As a young prince, Charles, with his mother and brother, had been sent to the Continent in the early stages of the civil war. When his father, Charles I, was beheaded, the future king and his family were in France, where they were in a position to see the remarkable achievements of French comedy and French classical tragedy. Charles II developed a taste for theater that accompanied him back to England. And when he returned in triumph to usher in the exciting and swashbuckling period known as the Restoration, he permitted favorites to build new theaters.

Theater on the Continent: Neoclassicism

Interaction among the leading European countries — England, Spain, and France — was sporadic at best in the seventeenth century because of intermittent wars among the nations, yet the development of theater in all three countries took similar turns throughout the early 1600s.

By the 1630s, the French were aware of Spanish achievements in the theater and Pierre Corneille (1606–1684), who emerged as France's leading playwright of the time, adapted a Spanish story by de Castro that became one of his most important plays, *Le Cid*.

By the time Charles II took up residence in France in the 1640s, the French had developed a suave, polished, and intellectually demanding approach to drama. Corneille and the neoclassicists were part of a large movement in European culture and the arts that tried to codify and emulate the achievement of the ancients. Qualities such as harmony, symmetry, balance in everything structural, and clear moral themes were most in evidence. Because NEOCLASSICISM valued thought over feeling, the thematic material in neoclassical drama was very important. That material was sometimes political, reflecting the values of Augustan Rome — 27 B.C. to A.D. 17 — when Caesar Augustus lived and when it was appropriate to think in terms of subordinating the self to the interests of the state. Neoclassical dramatists focused on honor, moral integrity, self-sacrifice, and heroic political subjects.

One school of critics held playwrights strictly to the Aristotelian concepts of the unities of time, place, character, and action. These "rules critics" demanded a perfect observance of the unities — that is, they wanted a play to have one plot, a single action that takes place in one day, and a single setting. In most cases the plays that satisfied them are now often thought of as static, cold, limited, and dull. Their perfection is seen today as rigid and emotionally icy.

Corneille's work did not please such critics, and they turned to a much younger competitor, Jean Racine (1639–1699), who brought the tradition of French tragedy to its fullest. Most of his plays are on classical subjects, beginning in 1667 with *Andromache*, continuing with *Britannicus* (1669), *Iphigenia* (1674), and *Mithridate* (1673), and ending in 1677 with his most famous and possibly best play, *Phaedra*.

Phaedra is a deeply passionate, moral play centering on the love of Phaedra for her stepson, Hippolytus. Venus is responsible for her incestuous love — which is the playwright's way of saying that Phaedra is impelled by the gods or by destiny, almost against her will.

The French stage, unlike the English, never substituted boys for female roles, and so plays such as *Phaedra* were opportunities for brilliant actresses. Phaedra, in particular, dominates the stage — she is a commanding and infinitely complex figure. It is no wonder that this play was a favorite of Sarah Bernhardt (1844–1923), one of France's greatest actresses.

French Comedy: Molière

At the same time that Racine commanded the tragic stage, Jean Baptiste Poquelin (1622–1673), known as Molière, began his dominance of the comic stage. He was aware of Racine's achievements and applauded them strongly. His career started with a small theater company that spent most of its time touring the countryside beyond Paris. When the company settled in Paris, its plays were influenced by some of the stock characters and situations of the commedia dell'arte, but they also began to reflect Molière's own genius for composition.

Seeing the company in 1658, King Louis XIV found it so much to his liking that he installed it in a theater and demanded to see more of its work. From that time on, Molière wrote, produced, and acted in one comedy after another, most of which have become part of the permanent repertoire of the French stage. Plays such as *The Misanthrope* (1666), *The Miser* (1669), *The Bourgeois Gentleman* (1670), *The Imaginary Invalid* (1673), and his satire on the theme of religious hypocrisy, *Tartuffe* (1669), are also staged all over the world.

Theater in England: Restoration Comedy of Manners

When the theaters reopened in England in the 1660s, they needed new plays. Times and tastes had changed, England had suffered enormous upheaval, and the Puritan-dominated, theater-darkened past was quickly undone. The new age wanted glitter, excitement, sensuality, and dramatic dazzle. Audiences wanted upbeat comedies that poked fun at the stuffed shirts of society and at old-fashioned institutions and fashions.

Several important physical changes took effect immediately. The new stages were in indoor theaters using artificial light. They could be operated year-round, and the price for seats varied according to location. The middle-priced seats were in the pit before the proscenium-arched stage (Figure 9). The first-level boxes against the walls were most expensive, while the lowest-priced seats were in the upper ranges of the balconies.

The new indoor theaters were generally adapted from spaces designed for courtly events. They were rectangular, often twice as long as they were wide, and usually lighted by candles in chandeliers. The proscenium frame around the stage appeared in the new theaters. Eventually, movable scenery and changeable painted backdrops helped the playwrights create their illusions, although some plays of the period could easily be performed on a bare stage.

Once English women were permitted to take part in theater, actresses appeared who commanded the stage immediately. The actresses of the period were bright, witty, and charming and were often the most important draw for seventeenth-century audiences. Nell Gwynne (1650–1687), one of the most famous actresses of her day and mistress to Charles II, became a legend of the English stage.

Among England's notable playwrights from 1660 through the eighteenth century were Aphra Behn (1640–1689), the first professional woman playwright on the English stage and author of *The Rover,* one of the most frequently performed plays of the period; William Wycherley (1640–1716), whose *The Plain Dealer,* indebted to Molière, and *The Country Wife* are regarded as his best work; William Congreve (1670–1729), whose *The Way of the World* is justly famous; and Richard Brinsley Sheridan (1751–1816), whose *School for Scandal* is still bright, lively, and engaging for modern audiences. Other important playwrights whose work is still performed are George Farquhar (1678–1707), especially known for *The Beaux Stratagem* (1707), John Gay (1685–1732), whose *Beggar's Opera* has been revived constantly since its first performance in 1728, and Oliver Goldsmith (1730–1774), author of *She Stoops to Conquer* (1773).

John Dryden (1631–1700), perhaps the most highly regarded English playwright from 1664 to 1677, collaborated in adaptations of Shakespeare's plays, but he became popular for his heroic dramas in rhymed verse: *The Indian Queen* (1664), its sequel *The Indian Emperor* (1665), *Tyrannick Love* (1669), and the two-part, ten-act *The Conquest of Granada* (1670). Montezuma is at the center of the first two plays; *Tyrannick Love* concerns the martyrdom

Figure 9. Conjectural reconstruction of an early Restoration theater. By Peter Kahn, Cornell University.

of St. Catherine by the Roman emperor, Maximin. *The Conquest of Granada* focuses on internal conflicts among the Moors fighting for survival in Spain. Almanzor, the main character, is considered one of Dryden's most accomplished creations. *Aureng-Zebe* (1675), his last effort in heroic rhymed drama, focuses on Aureng-Zebe, emperor of India and among the most rational and moral of his characters. Its plot and love complications are extremely dense and its mood somewhat melancholy. Today the heroic plays of the 1660s resemble high-style melodramas, but they were enormously popular in their time.

Dryden was also successful writing comedies such as *The Wild Gallant* (1663) and *The Rival Ladies* (1664). His tragicomedies were popular in his time and represent some of his most imaginative dramatic efforts. *Marriage à-la-Mode* (1672) is still highly regarded, especially for Dryden's songs. Among his experiments in opera is a version of Milton's *Paradise Lost* that he called *The State of Innocence and the Fall of Man* (1677) in which he rhymed some of Milton's blank verse. This work was never performed, although it remains a curiosity of the age. Dryden is also to be noted for his critical writing on drama, such as his famous *Of Dramatick Poesie* (1668) and *Of Heroick Plays* (1672), which laid down the theory behind his dramas and opened the questions of dramatic practice for examination.

Marriages of convenience are often the target of Restoration playwrights. The aristocratic attitude toward marriage usually centered on the union of "suitable" mates whose families were of the same social level and who were financially attractive to one another. Consequently, sometimes impoverished gentlemen of good name would seek out wealthy women and vice versa. The grounds for marriage were sometimes based on love but more often on financial or social convenience. As a result, the emotional expressions between marriage partners, as in Congreve's *The Way of the World*, are restricted and cautious. It is not until the end of the eighteenth century that the sentimental comedy appears, introducing recognizable emotional responses that appear to moderns as normal. Aristocratic attitudes toward marriage are evident in drama as late as the end of the nineteenth century, as in Oscar Wilde's *The Importance of Being Earnest*.

The English playwrights produced a wide range of comedy, drawing on their understanding of the audience's desire for bright, gay, and witty entertainment. The comedies of the period came to be known in the twentieth century as COMEDIES OF MANNERS because they reveal the foibles of the society that watched them. Society enjoyed laughing at itself. Although some of the English drama of the eighteenth century developed a moralistic tone and was often heavily classical, the earlier RESTORATION COMEDIES were less interested in reforming the society than in capitalizing on its faults.

Eighteenth-Century Drama

Eighteenth-century Europe absorbed much of the spirit of France and the French neoclassicists. England, like other European countries, began to see the effects of neoclassicism in the arts and literature. Emulation of classical art and classical values was common throughout Europe, and critics established standards of excellence in the arts to guarantee quality.

The most famous name in eighteenth-century English drama is David Garrick (1717–1779), the legendary actor and manager of the Drury Lane Theatre. The theaters, including his own, often reworked French drama and earlier English and Italian drama, but they began to develop a new SENTIMENTAL COMEDY to balance the neoclassical heroic tragedies of the period. It was a comedy in which the emotions of the audience were played on, manipulated, and exploited to arouse sympathy for the characters in the play.

Sentimental comedy flourished after 1720, but Colley Cibber (1671–1757) is sometimes credited with beginning the sentimental comedy with his *Love's Last Shift* (1696). The play centers on Loveless, who wanders from his marriage only to find that his wife has disguised herself as a prostitute to win him back. As in all sentimental comedies, what the audience most wants is what it gets: a certain amount of tears, a contrasting amount of laughter, and a happy ending. Cibber was especially well known as an actor for his portrayal of fops, his way of poking satiric fun at his own society and its pretensions.

Sir Richard Steele (1672–1729) wrote one of the best-known sentimental comedies, *The Conscious Lovers* (1722). Steele's coauthor of *The Spectator,* Joseph Addison (1672–1719), also distinguished himself with his contribution to the heroic tragedy of the age, the long neoclassical *Cato* (1713). It was considered to be the finest example of the moral heroic style. Today it is not a playable drama because the action is too slow, the speeches too long, and the theme too obscure, although it is a perfect model of what the age preferred in heroic tragedy. George Lillo (1693–1739) in *The London Merchant* (1731) produced a bourgeois tragedy in which the main character was from the middle class. It was one of the most frequently produced plays of its time.

The audiences at the time enjoyed bright, amusing comedies that often criticized wayward youth, overprotective parents, dishonest financial dealings, and social expectations. Their taste in tragedies veered toward a moralizing heroism that extolled the ideals of dedication to the values of the community and self-sacrifice on the part of the hero.

Late Seventeenth- and Eighteenth-Century Drama Timeline

DATE	THEATER	POLITICAL	SOCIAL/CULTURAL
1600–1700	**1606–1684:** French playwright Pierre Corneille, author of *Le Cid* (1636)	**1605:** Gun Powder Plot in London; execution of Guy Fawkes	**1608–1674:** John Milton, English author
	1622–1673: Molière (born John Baptiste Poquelin), French dramatist and actor, author of *The Misanthrope* (1666), *Tartuffe* (1667), and *The Learned Ladies* (1672)		**1610:** Galileo's first observations through a telescope
			1620: Voyage of the Mayflower
	c. 1634–1691: Sir George Etherege, author of *Love in a Tub* and *The Man of Mode* (1676)		**1631–1700:** John Dryden, English author and playwright
	1635–1710: Thomas Betterton, perhaps the Restoration's most important actor		
	1639–1699: Jean Baptiste Racine, French playwright, author of *Phaedre* (1677)		
	1640–1689: Aphra Behn, first professional woman playwright in the English theater, author of *The Rover* (1677–1680)	**1642:** Beginning of the English Civil War	
		1643: Louis XIV becomes king of France at age four.	
	1650–1687: Nell Gwynne, English actress and mistress of Charles II	**1649:** King Charles I of England is beheaded by Parliament.	
	1656: First use of Italianate scenery in England in a production of *The Siege of Rhodes*, designed by John Webb	**1655:** Oliver Cromwell prohibits Anglican church services and divides England into eleven districts governed by major-generals.	
	1658: Molière's troupe, the Illustre Théâtre, is invited to perform at the court of Louis XIV. The company is subsequently given permission to remain in Paris, as the Troupe de Monsieur, and allowed to use the Petit Bourbon for public performances.	**1658:** Cromwell dissolves Parliament.	
	1660: Theatrical activity resumes in London (after being halted in 1642) when Charles II issues patents to Thomas Killigrew and William Davenant. Women are permitted on the English stage for the first time.	**1660:** Restoration of the English monarchy and end of the Commonwealth. Charles II, son of the executed Charles I, is crowned.	**1660:** Dutch Boers settle on the Cape of Good Hope.
			1661–1731: Daniel Defoe, English author

DATE	THEATER	POLITICAL	SOCIAL/CULTURAL
1600–1700 (continued)	**1664:** Japanese playwright Fukui Yagozaemon writes *The Outcast's Revenge*, the first full-length kabuki play.	**1664:** The British annex New Amsterdam and rename it New York.	**1664–1666:** Isaac Newton (1642–1727), English mathematician and physicist, discovers the law of universal gravitation and begins to develop calculus.
	1670–1729: William Congreve, author of *Love for Love* (1695) and *The Way of the World* (1700)		**1665:** Plague devastates London.
	1680: The Comédie Française, the first national theater, opens in Paris.	**1682:** Louis XIV moves the French court to Versailles.	**1666:** Great Fire of London
		1682–1725: Peter the Great reigns as czar of Russia and calls for political and cultural reforms.	
	1695–1715: Proliferation of female playwrights in England. Thirty-seven new plays by women are produced on the London stage during this period by playwrights such as Mary Pix (1666–1706), Susanna Centlivre (c. 1670–1723), Mary Delarivière Manley (c. 1672–1724), and Catharine Trotter (1679–1749).	**1685:** Louis XIV revokes the Edict of Nantes, and persecution of the Huguenots (French Protestants) ensues.	**1685–1750:** J. S. Bach, German composer
		1688: William of Orange invades England with the encouragement of prominent Protestants, who fear James II's Catholicism. James flees to France and then England. William III and Mary II (daughter of James II) are crowned in 1689.	**1687:** Isaac Newton, English scientist, publishes *Mathematical Principles*.
			1688–1704: Alexander Pope, English poet
	1698: Jeremy Collier's *A Short View of the Immorality and Profaneness of the English Stage*, the most effective of several attacks on the theater published at the turn of the century	**1690:** An Irish uprising in favor of James II is suppressed by William III at the Battle of the Boyne.	**1692:** Salem witchcraft trials
		1697: The last remains of Mayan civilization destroyed by the Spanish.	**1694–1778:** François Marie Arouet de Voltaire, French author often described as the embodiment of the Enlightenment
1700–1800		**1703:** Peter the Great lays the foundation for St. Petersburg.	**1703–1758:** Jonathan Edwards, American theologian
	1707–1793: Carlo Goldoni, Italian playwright, author of *The Servant of Two Masters* (1743)	**1707:** The Act of Union unites Scotland and England, which become Great Britain.	**1709–1784:** Samuel Johnson, English literary critic, scholar, poet, and lexicographer
	1717–1779: David Garrick, greatest English actor of the eighteenth century and owner and manager of the Drury Lane Theatre in London	**1714:** The House of Hanover begins its rule with the accession of George I.	
		1715: Louis XIV, France's Sun King, dies.	
	1720–1806: Carlo Gozzi, Italian playwright, author of *King Stag* (1762) and *Turandot* (1762)		**1720:** First serialization of novels in newspapers
			1724: Emmanuel Kant, German metaphysic philosopher

DATE	THEATER	POLITICAL	SOCIAL/CULTURAL
1700–1800 (continued)	**1728:** John Gay (1685–1732) writes *The Beggar's Opera*, arguably the most popular English play of the eighteenth century.		**1726:** Jonathan Swift writes *Gulliver's Travels.*
	1729–1781: Gotthold Ephraim Lessing, Germany's first important playwright, author of *Minna von Barnhelm* (1767) and *Emilia Galotti* (1772)		**1732:** Covent Garden opera house opens in London.
			1732: Franz Josef Haydn, prolific Austrian composer
	1737: The Licensing Act in England prohibits the performance of any play not previously licensed by the Lord Chamberlain. A number of such laws regulating theatrical activity are enacted throughout the eighteenth century.	**1740:** Frederick the Great introduces freedom of press and worship in Prussia.	**1742:** Cotton factories are established in Birmingham and Northampton, England.
			1746–1828: Francisco de Goya, Spanish painter and political cartoonist
	1749–1832: Johann Wolfgang von Goethe, German writer. His early works include the play *Götz von Berlichingen* (1773) and the novel *The Sorrows of Young Werther* (1774).		**1751:** Dennis Diderot, French writer and philosopher, publishes the first volume of his *Encyclopédie.*
	1751–1816: Richard Brinsley Sheridan, playwright and statesman, author of *The School for Scandal* (1777)	**1756–1763:** Frederick begins the Seven Years War pitting Prussia and Great Britain against Russia, Austria, and France.	**1756–1791:** Wolfgang Amadeus Mozart, Austrian classical composer
			1757–1827: William Blake, Romantic poet and artist, author of *Songs of Innocence* and *Songs of Experience*
	1762: English actor-manager David Garrick prohibits audience members from sitting on the stage.	**1762:** Catherine the Great (b. 1729) becomes empress of Russia after overthrowing her husband, Peter III; she reigns until her death in 1796.	**1759–1797:** Mary Wollstonecraft, English writer and early feminist, author of *Vindication of the Rights of Woman* (1792)
		1763: The Treaty of Paris ends the Seven Years War. Prussia emerges as an important European power. France loses many colonial possessions.	**1762:** The Sorbonne library opens in Paris.
		1765: British Parliament passes the Stamp Act. Nine colonies draw up a declaration of rights and liberties.	
	c. 1769: Spectators are banned from sitting on the stage in Paris.	**1766:** Catherine the Great grants freedom of worship in Russia.	

Molière

Molière (1622–1673, born Jean Baptiste Poquelin) came from a family attached to the glittering court of King Louis XIV, the Sun King. His father had purchased an appointment to the king, and as a result the family was familiar with the exciting court life of Paris, although not on intimate terms with the courtiers who surrounded the king. Molière's father was a furnisher and upholsterer to the king; the family, while well-to-do and enjoying some power, was still apart from royalty and the privileged aristocracy.

Molière's education was exceptional. He went to Jesuit schools and spent more than five years at Collège de Clermont, which he left in 1641 having studied both the humanities and philosophy. His knowledge of philosophy was unusually deep, and his background in the classics was exceptionally strong. He also took a law degree in 1641 at Orléans, but never practiced. His father's dream was that his son should inherit his appointment as furnisher to the king, thereby guaranteeing himself a comfortable future.

That, however, was not to be. Instead of following the law, Molière decided at the last minute to abandon his secure future, change his name so as not to scandalize his family, and take up a career in the theater. He began by joining a company of actors run by the Béjart family. They established a theater based in Paris called the Illustre Théâtre. It was run by Madeleine Béjart, with whom Molière had a professional and personal relationship until she died in 1672. Eventually, Molière began writing plays but only after he had worked extensively as an actor.

The famed commedia dell'arte actor Tiberio Fiorillo, known as Scaramouche, was a close friend of Molière and perhaps responsible for Molière's choice of a career in theater. Scaramouche may have been part of the Illustre Théâtre, or he may have acted in it on occasion. Unfortunately, the Illustre Théâtre lasted only a year. It was one of several Parisian theatrical groups, and none of them prospered.

The company went bankrupt in 1644, and Molière, forced to leave Paris for about thirteen years, played in the provinces and remote towns. Before leaving Paris he had to be bailed out of debtors' prison. What was left of the Béjart group merged with another company on tour, and Molière became director of that company. During this time he suffered most of the indignities typical of the traveling life, including impoverishment.

In October 1658 Louis XIV saw Molière's troupe acting in one of his comedies at the Louvre. The royal court was so impressed with what it saw that the king gave him the use of a theater. Molière's work remained immensely popular and controversial. He acted in his own plays, produced his own plays, and wrote a succession of major works that are still favorites.

Because other companies envied his success and favor with the king, a number of "scandals" arose around some of his plays. The first play to invite controversy was *The School for Wives* (1662), in which Arnolphe reacts in horror

335

to the infidelities he sees in the wives all around him. He decides that his wife-to-be must be raised far from the world, where she will be ignorant of the way-ward lives of the Parisians. A man who intends to seduce her tells Arnolphe (not knowing who he is) how he will get her out of Arnolphe's grasp. The play is highly comic, but groups of theatergoers protested that it was immoral and scandalous. In response Molière wrote *Criticism of the School for Wives* (1663), in which the debate over the play is enacted.

One of Molière's most popular plays, *Tartuffe* (written in 1664), concerns a religious hypocrite who weasels his way into a noble household and then goes about trying to seduce its mistress. Molière envisioned the religious con man as his target in this play, and the name *Tartuffe* became shorthand for a religious hypocrite. The name still implies hypocrisy in France.

A French church group, the Society of the Holy Sacrament, thought it was being portrayed in the title role and protested that the play was immoral and offensive. The society's condemnation of the play effectively prevented it from being performed. Molière tried rewriting *Tartuffe,* but the society would not approve its production.

In 1669 the Society of the Holy Sacrament was dissolved in a restructuring of the French church, and *Tartuffe* was finally permitted to be played to large audiences. Theatergoers loved the play and found great amusement in the sly, lecherous rogue who completely beguiles Orgon, the man who thinks Tartuffe is a great saint and who introduces him into his household. In most modern productions Tartuffe is played broadly, almost as a caricature or a clown. Audiences find him amusing, scabrous, and irresistible. They usually find the play irresistible, as well, because it involves crafty maneuvering onstage and complicated deceptions.

Among Molière's other successes are *The Miser* (1668), *The Bourgeois Gentleman* (1670), and his final play, *The Imaginary Invalid* (1673). Molière had a bad cough for most of the last decade of his life, which onstage he often made to seem the cough of the character he was playing. But Molière was gen-uinely ill; he died on stage, playing the title role of *The Imaginary Invalid.*

THE MISANTHROPE

The Misanthrope (1666) in its own age was not the most successful of Molière's plays, but it has certainly been one of the most produced of all the plays in his canon. Typical of his work, it derives from a close and careful observation of French life and manners. Recently, English-language audiences have been able to savor this play in Richard Wilbur's superb translation, which catches the sharpness of the French wit and the elegance of the verse — both hallmarks of French seventeenth-century drama.

In one sense the play is based on the type of improbability that marks Greek New Comedy. It portrays the romance of two very different people, Alceste, the misanthrope who speaks his mind and brashly tells people what he thinks of them, and Célimène, the coquette who rarely says what she thinks but who enjoys the attention of many suitors. She enjoys society and her capacity to dominate it. Alceste cannot abide society and its superficialities. At the end of the play he resolves to leave it.

A revelation in the play is that while Alceste and Célimène are different on the surface, beneath the surface they are similar. They are both extreme types who behave extremely. Célimène carries coquetry to great lengths, leading on as many men as possible. Alceste is the epitome of a misanthrope, refusing to flatter people just to make them feel good. He says that he must tell the truth, and he does — even when it hurts, perhaps especially when it hurts. For him to fall in love with a coquette who must deceive those around her to keep herself at the center of attention is a wonderful comic irony. But beneath that irony lies the thought that Alceste himself may have flaws that are the opposite of Célimène's.

The ending of *The Misanthrope,* which avoids the marriage of the protagonists (a more typical ending of comedies), may have contributed to the disappointment of its initial audiences. Another comic playwright would have brought the two lovers together. But Molière chose a more complex and, for some, a less satisfying ending. While two secondary characters marry, the main characters — Alceste and Célimène — agree to disagree and decide to live separately after all. Molière leaves his audience simply hoping that the two will change their minds. But as the play ends, the audience has no real reason to expect that they will.

This is a very French drama. The society is elegant, formal, and mannered. Molière knows every character and reveals each one totally. The surface elegance of the verse is such that the manners of the society seem polished, artificial, and ritualistic without being especially deceptive. The deception in this play is not at the center of things nor does the play depend on mix-ups and misapprehensions for its success. This in itself gives us a rather intriguing hint about Molière's intentions. The theme of honesty is at the play's center, but it is no simple thing to decide, in a social situation such as these characters enjoy, exactly how honest honesty should be or when honesty is the best policy. Alceste has one view and Célimène has another.

Molière enjoys pitting the values of Célimène and Alceste against one another, but it is clear that he does not want to offer sweeping or simple solutions to their conflict. Instead, he is content to leave his audience thinking and wondering.

The Misanthrope in Performance

The first full production of *The Misanthrope* was on June 4, 1666, with Molière as Alceste and his wife as Célimène. Most of the players who joined them were aware that Alceste was modeled after Molière himself and that Molière was poking fun at himself and his marriage. Molière made the part more comical than serious. The French national theater, Comédie-Française, records some fifteen hundred performances of the play between 1680 and 1960, making it one of the most performed of all French comedies. Late in the eighteenth century, actors began playing Alceste as a serious character, as he is played today.

The first important American production in English was by Richard Mansfield, who acted the part of Alceste in New York in 1905. The reviews noted that "his embodiment of Alceste is vibrant with pain. . . . He smiles, but it is always the smile of bitterness." Richard Wilbur's verse translation played in the tiny Theatre East in New York in 1956 while the original rhymed French version with a French company played simultaneously at the Winter Garden on Broadway. Both productions were very successful. Wilbur's version has since played virtually all over America, with several productions in New York in the 1960s, 70s, and 80s. The West Side Repertory Theater performed it in modern black tie and tails in 1991, with James Jacobus as Alceste. *The Misanthrope* has also had innumerable college productions since Wilbur's translation, which has, at least in the United States, become the standard version.

Tony Harrison also translated the play for the British National Theatre in 1975 with Alec McCowan as Alceste and Diana Rigg as Célimène. Reviews were mixed, but the play was said to have "the brilliance of a tiara of diamonds."

Molière { Jean Baptiste Poquelin} (1622–1673)

THE MISANTHROPE   *1666*

TRANSLATED BY RICHARD WILBUR

Characters

ALCESTE, *in love with Célimène*
PHILINTE, *Alceste's friend*
ORONTE, *in love with Célimène*
CÉLIMÈNE, *Alceste's beloved*
ÉLIANTE, *Célimène's cousin*
ARSINOÉ, *a friend of Célimène's*
ACASTE
CLITANDRE } *Marquesses*
BASQUE, *Célimène's servant*
A GUARD *of the Marshalsea*
DUBOIS, *Alceste's valet*

The scene throughout is in Célimène's house at Paris.

ACT I • *Scene I* [*Philinte, Alceste.*]

PHILINTE: Now, what's got into you?
ALCESTE (*seated*):   Kindly leave me alone.
PHILINTE: Come, come, what is it? This lugubrious
    tone . . .
ALCESTE: Leave me, I said; you spoil my solitude.
PHILINTE: Oh, listen to me, now, and don't be rude.
ALCESTE: I choose to be rude, Sir, and to be hard of
5   hearing.
PHILINTE: These ugly moods of yours are not
    endearing;

Friends though we are, I really must insist . . .
ALCESTE (*abruptly rising*): Friends? Friends, you say?
    Well, cross me off your list.
I've been your friend till now, as you well know;
But after what I saw a moment ago   10
I tell you flatly that our ways must part.
I wish no place in a dishonest heart.
PHILINTE: Why, what have I done, Alceste? Is this quite
    just?
ALCESTE: My God, you ought to die of self-disgust.
I call your conduct inexcusable, Sir,   15
And every man of honor will concur.
I see you almost hug a man to death,
Exclaim for joy until you're out of breath,
And supplement these loving demonstrations
With endless offers, vows, and protestations;   20
Then when I ask you "Who was that?" I find
That you can barely bring his name to mind!
Once the man's back is turned, you cease to love
    him,
And speak with absolute indifference of him!
By God, I say it's base and scandalous   25
To falsify the heart's affections thus;
If I caught myself behaving in such a way,
I'd hang myself for shame, without delay.
PHILINTE: It hardly seems a hanging matter to me;
I hope that you will take it graciously   30
If I extend myself a slight reprieve,

And live a little longer, by your leave.
ALCESTE: How dare you joke about a crime so grave?
PHILINTE: What crime? How else are people to behave?
35 ALCESTE: I'd have them be sincere, and never part
    With any word that isn't from the heart.
PHILINTE: When someone greets us with a show of
    pleasure,
    It's but polite to give him equal measure,
    Return his love the best that we know how,
40   And trade him offer for offer, vow for vow.
ALCESTE: No, no, this formula you'd have me follow,
    However fashionable, is false and hollow,
    And I despise the frenzied operations
    Of all these barterers of protestations,
45   These lavishers of meaningless embraces
    These utterers of obliging commonplaces,
    Who court and flatter everyone on earth
    And praise the fool no less than the man of worth.
    Should you rejoice that someone fondles you,
50   Offers his love and service, swears to be true,
    And fills your ears with praises of your name,
    When to the first damned fop he'll say the same?
    No, no: no self-respecting heart would dream
    Of prizing so promiscuous an esteem;
55   However high the praise, there's nothing worse
    Than sharing honors with the universe.
    Esteem is founded on comparison:
    To honor all men is to honor none.
    Since you embrace this indiscriminate vice
60   Your friendship comes at far too cheap a price;
    I spurn the easy tribute of a heart
    Which will not set the worthy man apart:
    I choose, Sir, to be chosen; and in fine,
    The friend of mankind is no friend of mine.
65 PHILINTE: But in polite society, custom decrees
    That we show certain outward courtesies . . .
ALCESTE: Ah, no! we should condemn with all our
    force
    Such false and artificial intercourse.
    Let men behave like men; let them display
70   Their inmost hearts in everything they say;
    Let the heart speak, and let our sentiments
    Not mask themselves in silly compliments.
PHILINTE: In certain cases it would be uncouth
    And most absurd to speak the naked truth;
75   With all respect for your exalted notions,
    It's often best to veil one's true emotions.
    Wouldn't the social fabric come undone
    If we were wholly frank with everyone?
    Suppose you met with someone you couldn't bear;
80   Would you inform him of it then and there?
ALCESTE: Yes.
PHILINTE: Then you'd tell old Emilie it's pathetic
    The way she daubs her features with cosmetic
    And plays the gay coquette at sixty-four?
ALCESTE: I would.
PHILINTE: And you'd call Dorilas a bore,
85   And tell him every ear at court is lame
    From hearing him brag about his noble name?

ALCESTE: Precisely.
PHILINTE: Ah, you're joking.
ALCESTE: *Au contraire.*°
    In this regard there's none I'd choose to spare.
    All are corrupt; there's nothing to be seen
    In court or town but aggravates my spleen.°   90
    I fall into deep gloom and melancholy
    When I survey the scene of human folly,
    Finding on every hand base flattery,
    Injustice, fraud, self-interest, treachery. . . .
    Ah, it's too much; mankind has grown so base,   95
    I mean to break with the whole human race.
PHILINTE: This philosophic rage is a bit extreme;
    You've no idea how comical you seem;
    Indeed, we're like those brothers in the play
    Called *School for Husbands,*° one of whom was
    prey . . .   100
ALCESTE: Enough, now! None of your stupid similes.
PHILINTE: Then let's have no more tirades, if you
    please.
    The world won't change, whatever you say or do;
    And since plain speaking means so much to you,
    I'll tell you plainly that by being frank   105
    You've earned the reputation of a crank,
    And that you're thought ridiculous when you rage
    And rant against the manners of the age.
ALCESTE: So much the better; just what I wish to hear.
    No news could be more grateful to my ear.   110
    All men are so detestable in my eyes,
    I should be sorry if they thought me wise.
PHILINTE: Your hatred's very sweeping, is it not?
ALCESTE: Quite right: I hate the whole degraded lot.
PHILINTE: Must all poor human creatures be embraced,   115
    Without distinction, by your vast distaste?
    Even in these bad times, there are surely a few . . .
ALCESTE: No, I include all men in one dim view:
    Some men I hate for being rogues: the others
    I hate because they treat the rogues like brothers,   120
    And, lacking a virtuous scorn for what is vile,
    Receive the villain with a complaisant smile.
    Notice how tolerant people choose to be
    Toward that bold rascal who's at law with me.
    His social polish can't conceal his nature;   125
    One sees at once that he's a treacherous creature;
    No one could possibly be taken in
    By those soft speeches and that sugary grin.
    The whole world knows the shady means by
    which
    The low-brow's grown so powerful and rich,   130
    And risen to a rank so bright and high
    That virtue can but blush, and merit sigh.

87. *Au contraire:* On the contrary.   90. spleen: A body organ
thought to be the seat of melancholy, one of the four humors of
medieval physiology.   100. *School for Husbands:* A play by
Molière (1661) in which two brothers, Sganarelle and Ariste,
are guardians of two orphan girls. Sganarelle hopes to marry
one of the girls, Isabelle, but she frees herself by trickery from
his domineering ways and marries someone else.

Whenever his name comes up in conversation,
None will defend his wretched reputation;
135 Call him knave, liar, scoundrel, and all the rest,
Each head will nod, and no one will protest.
And yet his smirk is seen in every house,
He's greeted everywhere with smiles and bows,
And when there's any honor that can be got
140 By pulling strings, he'll get it, like as not.
My God! It chills my heart to see the ways
Men come to terms with evil nowadays
Sometimes, I swear, I'm moved to flee and find
Some desert land unfouled by humankind.
145 PHILINTE: Come, let's forget the follies of the times
And pardon mankind for its petty crimes;
Let's have an end of rantings and of railings,
And show some leniency toward human failings.
This world requires a pliant rectitude;
150 Too stern a virtue makes one stiff and rude;
Good sense views all extremes with detestation,
And bids us to be noble in moderation.
The rigid virtues of the ancient days
Are not for us; they jar with all our ways
155 And ask of us too lofty a perfection.
Wise men accept their times without objection,
And there's no greater folly, if you ask me,
Than trying to reform society.
Like you, I see each day a hundred and one
160 Unhandsome deeds that might be better done,
But still, for all the faults that meet my view,
I'm never known to storm and rave like you.
I take men as they are, or let them be,
And teach my soul to bear their frailty;
165 And whether in court or town, whatever the scene,
My phlegm's° as philosophic as your spleen.
ALCESTE: This phlegm which you so eloquently
commend,
Does nothing ever rile it up, my friend?
Suppose some man you trust should treacherously
170 Conspire to rob you of your property,
And do his best to wreck your reputation?
Wouldn't you feel a certain indignation?
PHILINTE: Why, no. These faults of which you so
complain
Are part of human nature, I maintain,
175 And it's no more a matter for disgust
That men are knavish, selfish and unjust,
Than that the vulture dines upon the dead,
And wolves are furious, and apes ill-bred.
ALCESTE: Shall I see myself betrayed, robbed, torn to
bits,
180 And not . . . Oh, let's be still and rest our wits.
Enough of reasoning, now. I've had my fill.
PHILINTE: Indeed, you would do well, Sir, to be still.
Rage less at your opponent, and give some thought
To how you'll win this lawsuit that he's brought.
185 ALCESTE: I assure you I'll do nothing of the sort.

166. **phlegm:** In medieval physiology, the humor thought to be
cold and moist and to cause sluggishness.

PHILINTE: Then who will plead your case before the
court?
ALCESTE: Reason and right and justice will plead for
me.
PHILINTE: Oh, Lord. What judges do you plan to see?
ALCESTE: Why, none. The justice of my cause is clear.
PHILINTE: Of course, man; but there's politics to
fear . . .   190
ALCESTE: No, I refuse to lift a hand. That's flat.
I'm either right, or wrong.
PHILINTE: Don't count on that.
ALCESTE: No, I'll do nothing.
PHILINTE: Your enemy's influence
Is great, you know . . .
ALCESTE: That makes no difference.
PHILINTE: It will; you'll see.
ALCESTE: Must honor bow to guile? 195
If so, I shall be proud to lose the trial.
PHILINTE: Oh, really . . .
ALCESTE: I'll discover by this case
Whether or not men are sufficiently base
And impudent and villainous and perverse
To do me wrong before the universe.   200
PHILINTE: What a man!
ALCESTE: Oh, I could wish, whatever the cost,
Just for the beauty of it, that my trial were lost.
PHILINTE: If people heard you talking so, Alceste,
They'd split their sides. Your name would be a jest.
ALCESTE: So much the worse for jesters.
PHILINTE: May I enquire 205
Whether this rectitude you so admire,
And these hard virtues you're enamored of
Are qualities of the lady whom you love?
It much surprises me that you, who seem
To view mankind with furious disesteem,   210
Have yet found something to enchant your eyes
Amidst a species which you so despise.
And what is more amazing, I'm afraid,
Is the most curious choice your heart has made.
The honest Éliante is fond of you,   215
Arsinoé, the prude, admires you too;
And yet your spirit's been perversely led
To choose the flighty Célimène instead,
Whose brittle malice and coquettish ways
So typify the manners of our days.   220
How is it that the traits you most abhor
Are bearable in this lady you adore?
Are you so blind with love that you can't find them?
Or do you contrive, in her case, not to mind them?
ALCESTE: My love for that young widow's not the kind 225
That can't perceive defects; no, I'm not blind.
I see her faults, despite my ardent love,
And all I see I fervently reprove.
And yet I'm weak; for all her falsity,
That woman knows the art of pleasing me,   230
And though I never cease complaining of her,
I swear I cannot manage not to love her.
Her charm outweighs her faults; I can but aim
To cleanse her spirit in my love's pure flame.

235 PHILINTE: That's no small task; I wish you all success.
        You think then that she loves you?
     ALCESTE: Heavens, yes!
        I wouldn't love her did she not love me.
     PHILINTE: Well, if her taste for you is plain to see,
        Why do these rivals cause you such despair?
240 ALCESTE: True love, Sir, is possessive, and cannot bear
        To share with all the world. I'm here today
        To tell her she must send that mob away.
     PHILINTE: If I were you, and had your choice to make,
        Éliante, her cousin, would be the one I'd take;
245   That honest heart, which cares for you alone,
        Would harmonize far better with your own.
     ALCESTE: True, true: each day my reason tells me so;
        But reason doesn't rule in love, you know.
     PHILINTE: I fear some bitter sorrow is in store;
250   This love . . .

Scene II [*Oronte, Alceste, Philinte.*]

     ORONTE (*to Alceste*): The servants told me at the door
        That Éliante and Célimène were out,
        But when I heard, dear Sir, that you were about,
        I came to say, without exaggeration,
  5   That I hold you in the vastest admiration,
        And that it's always been my dearest desire
        To be the friend of one I so admire.
        I hope to see my love of merit requited,
        And you and I in friendship's bond united.
 10   I'm sure you won't refuse — if I may be frank —
        A friend of my devotedness — and rank.

     (*During this speech of Oronte's Alceste is abstracted
     and seems unaware that he is being spoken to. He only
     breaks off his reverie when Oronte says:*)

        It was for you, if you please, that my words were
           intended.
     ALCESTE: For me, Sir?
     ORONTE: Yes, for you. You're not offended?
     ALCESTE: By no means. But this much surprises me . . .
 15   The honor comes most unexpectedly . . .
     ORONTE: My high regard should not astonish you;
        The whole world feels the same. It is your due.
     ALCESTE: Sir . . .
     ORONTE: Why, in all the State there isn't one
        Can match your merits; they shine, Sir, like the sun.
     ALCESTE: Sir . . .
 20 ORONTE: You are higher in my estimation
        Than all that's most illustrious in the nation.
     ALCESTE: Sir . . .
     ORONTE: If I lie, may heaven strike me dead!
        To show you that I mean what I have said,
        Permit me, Sir, to embrace you most sincerely,
 25   And swear that I will prize our friendship dearly.
        Give me your hand. And now, Sir, if you choose,
        We'll make our vows.
     ALCESTE: Sir . . .
     ORONTE: What! You refuse?

     ALCESTE: Sir, it's a very great honor you extend:
        But friendship is a sacred thing, my friend;
        It would be profanation to bestow   30
        The name of friend on one you hardly know.
        All parts are better played when well-rehearsed
        Let's put off friendship, and get acquainted first.
        We may discover it would be unwise
        To try to make our natures harmonize.   35
     ORONTE: By heaven! You're sagacious to the core;
        This speech has made me admire you even more.
        Let time, then, bring us closer day by day;
        Meanwhile, I shall be yours in every way.
        If, for example, there should be anything   40
        You wish at court, I'll mention it to the King.
        I have his ear, of course; it's quite well known
        That I am much in favor with the throne.
        In short, I am your servant. And now, dear friend,
        Since you have such fine judgment, I intend   45
        To please you, if I can, with a small sonnet
        I wrote not long ago. Please comment on it,
        And tell me whether I ought to publish it.
     ALCESTE: You must excuse me, Sir; I'm hardly fit
        To judge such matters.
     ORONTE: Why not?
     ALCESTE: I am. I fear,   50
        Inclined to be unfashionably sincere.
     ORONTE: Just what I ask; I'd take no satisfaction
        In anything but your sincere reaction.
        I beg you not to dream of being kind.
     ALCESTE: Since you desire it, Sir, I'll speak my mind.   55
     ORONTE: *Sonnet*. It's a sonnet. . . . *Hope.* . . . The
           poem's addressed
        To a lady who wakened hopes within my breast.
        Hope . . . this is not the pompous sort of thing,
        Just modest little verses, with a tender ring.
     ALCESTE: Well, we shall see.
     ORONTE: *Hope* . . . I'm anxious to hear 60
        Whether the style seems properly smooth and clear,
        And whether the choice of words is good or bad.
     ALCESTE: We'll see, we'll see.
     ORONTE: Perhaps I ought to add
        That it took me only a quarter-hour to write it.
     ALCESTE: The time's irrelevant, Sir: kindly recite it.   65
     ORONTE (*reading*): Hope comforts us awhile, 'tis true,
        Lulling our cares with careless laughter,
        And yet such joy is full of rue,
        My Phyllis, if nothing follows after.
     PHILINTE: I'm charmed by this already; the style's
           delightful.   70
     ALCESTE (*sotto voce,° to Philinte*): How can you say
           that? Why, the thing is frightful.
     ORONTE: Your fair face smiled on me awhile,
        But was it kindness so to enchant me?
        'Twould have been fairer not to smile,
        If hope was all you meant to grant me.   75
     PHILINTE: What a clever thought! How handsomely
           you phrase it!

71. [S.D.] *sotto voce:* In a soft voice or stage whisper.

ALCESTE (*sotto voce, to Philinte*): You know the thing
    is trash. How dare you praise it?
ORONTE: If it's to be my passion's fate
    Thus everlastingly to wait,
80   Then death will come to set me free:
    For death is fairer than the fair;
    Phyllis, to hope is to despair
    When one must hope eternally.
PHILINTE: The close is exquisite — full of feeling and
    grace.
ALCESTE (*sotto voce, aside*): Oh, blast the close; you'd
85   better close your face
    Before you send your lying soul to hell.
PHILINTE: I can't remember a poem I've liked so well.
ALCESTE (*sotto voce, aside*): Good Lord!
ORONTE (*to Philinte*):   I fear you're
    flattering me a bit.
PHILINTE: Oh, no!
ALCESTE (*sotto voce, aside*): What else d'you call it, you
    hypocrite?
ORONTE (*to Alceste*): But you, Sir, keep your promise
90   now: don't shrink
    From telling me sincerely what you think.
ALCESTE: Sir, these are delicate matters; we all desire
    To be told that we've the true poetic fire.
    But once, to one whose name I shall not mention
95   I said, regarding some verse of his invention,
    That gentlemen should rigorously control
    That itch to write which often afflicts the soul;
    That one should curb the heady inclination
    To publicize one's little avocation
100   And that in showing off one's works of art
    One often plays a very clownish part.
ORONTE: Are you suggesting in a devious way
    That I ought not . . .
ALCESTE: Oh, that I do not say.
    Further, I told him that no fault is worse
105   Than that of writing frigid, lifeless verse,
    And that the merest whisper of such a shame
    Suffices to destroy a man's good name.
ORONTE: D'you mean to say my sonnet's dull and
    trite?
ALCESTE: I don't say that. But I went on to cite
110   Numerous cases of once-respected men
    Who came to grief by taking up the pen.
ORONTE: And am I like them? Do I write so poorly?
ALCESTE: I don't say that. But I told this person, "Surely
    You're under no necessity to compose;
115   Why you should wish to publish, heaven knows.
    There's no excuse for printing tedious rot
    Unless one writes for bread, as you do not.
    Resist temptation, then, I beg of you;
    Conceal your pastimes from the public view;
120   And don't give up, on any provocation,
    Your present high and courtly reputation,
    To purchase at a greedy printer's shop
    The name of silly author and scribbling fop."
    These were the points I tried to make him see.

ORONTE: I sense that they are also aimed at me,   125
    But now — about my sonnet — I'd like to be told . . .
ALCESTE: Frankly, that sonnet should be pigeonholed.
    You've chosen the worst models to imitate.
    The style's unnatural. Let me illustrate:
    For example, Your fair face smiled on me awhile,   130
    Followed by, 'Twould have been fairer not to smile!
    Or this: such joy is full of rue;
    Or this: For death is fairer than the fair;
    Or, Phyllis, to hope is to despair
    When one must hope eternally!   135
    This artificial style, that's all the fashion,
    Has neither taste, nor honesty, nor passion;
    It's nothing but a sort of wordy play,
    And nature never spoke in such a way.
    What, in this shallow age, is not debased?   140
    Our fathers, though less refined, had better taste;
    I'd barter all that men admire today
    For one old love song I shall try to say:
    If the King had given me for my own
    Paris, his citadel,   145
    And I for that must leave alone
    Her whom I love so well,
    I'd say then to the Crown,
    Take back your glittering town;
    My darling is more fair, I swear,   150
    My darling is more fair.
    The rhyme's not rich, the style is rough and old,
    But don't you see that it's the purest gold
    Beside the tinsel nonsense now preferred,
    And that there's passion in its every word?   155
    If the King had given me for my own
    Paris, his citadel,
    And I for that must leave alone
    Her whom I love so well,
    I'd say then to the Crown,   160
    Take back your glittering town;
    My darling is more fair, I swear,
    My darling is more fair.
    There speaks a loving heart. (*To Philinte.*) You're
    laughing, eh?
    Laugh on, my precious wit. Whatever you say,   165
    I hold that song's worth all the bibelots°
    That people hail today with ah's and oh's.
ORONTE: And I maintain my sonnet's very good.
ALCESTE: It's not at all surprising that you should.
    You have your reasons; permit me to have mine   170
    For thinking that you cannot write a line.
ORONTE: Others have praised my sonnet to the skies.
ALCESTE: I lack their art of telling pleasant lies.
ORONTE: You seem to think you've got no end of wit.
ALCESTE: To praise your verse, I'd need still more of it.   175
ORONTE: I'm not in need of your approval, Sir.
ALCESTE: That's good; you couldn't have it if you were.
ORONTE: Come now, I'll lend you the subject of my
    sonnet;
    I'd like to see you try to improve upon it.

166. bibelots: Trinkets.

ALCESTE: I might, by chance, write something just as
180   shoddy;
    But then I wouldn't show it to everybody.
ORONTE: You're most opinionated and conceited.
ALCESTE: Go find your flatterers, and be better treated.
ORONTE: Look here, my little fellow, pray watch your
    tone.
ALCESTE: My great big fellow, you'd better watch your
185   own.
PHILINTE (*stepping between them*): Oh, please, please,
    gentlemen! This will never do.
ORONTE: The fault is mine, and I leave the field to you.
    I am your servant, Sir, in every way.
ALCESTE: And I, Sir, am your most abject valet.

Scene III [*Philinte, Alceste.*]

PHILINTE: Well, as you see, sincerity in excess
    Can get you into a very pretty mess;
    Oronte was hungry for appreciation. . . .
ALCESTE: Don't speak to me.
PHILINTE: What?
ALCESTE: No more conversation.
PHILINTE: Really, now . . .
ALCESTE: Leave me alone.
PHILINTE: If I . . .
5 ALCESTE: Out of my sight!
PHILINTE: But what . . .
ALCESTE: I won't listen.
PHILINTE: But . . .
ALCESTE: Silence!
PHILINTE: Now, it is polite . . .
ALCESTE: By heaven, I've had enough. Don't follow
    me.
PHILINTE: Ah, you're just joking. I'll keep you
    company.

ACT II • Scene I [*Alceste, Célimène.*]

ALCESTE: Shall I speak plainly, Madam? I confess
    Your conduct gives me infinite distress,
    And my resentment's grown too hot to smother.
    Soon, I foresee, we'll break with one another.
5   If I said otherwise, I should deceive you;
    Sooner or later, I shall be forced to leave you,
    And if I swore that we shall never part
    I should misread the omens of my heart.
CÉLIMÈNE: You kindly saw me home, it would appear,
10   So as to pour invectives in my ear.
ALCESTE: I've no desire to quarrel. But I deplore
    Your inability to shut the door
    On all these suitors who beset you so.
    There's what annoys me, if you care to know.
15 CÉLIMÈNE: Is it my fault that all these men pursue me?
    Am I to blame if they're attracted to me?
    And when they gently beg an audience,
    Ought I to take a stick and drive them hence?

ALCESTE: Madam, there's no necessity for a stick;
    A less responsive heart would do the trick.   20
    Of your attractiveness I don't complain;
    But those your charms attract, you then detain
    By a most melting and receptive manner,
    And so enlist their hearts beneath your banner.
    It's the agreeable hopes which you excite   25
    That keep these lovers round you day and night;
    Were they less liberally smiled upon,
    That sighing troop would very soon be gone.
    But tell me, Madam, why it is that lately
    This man Clitandre interests you so greatly?   30
    Because of what high merits do you deem
    Him worthy of the honor of your esteem?
    Is it that your admiring glances linger
    On the splendidly long nail of his little finger?
    Or do you share the general deep respect   35
    For the blond wig he chooses to affect?
    Are you in love with his embroidered hose?
    Do you adore his ribbons and his bows?
    Or is it that this paragon bewitches
    Your tasteful eye with his vast German breeches?   40
    Perhaps his giggle, or his falsetto voice,
    Makes him the latest gallant of your choice?
CÉLIMÈNE: You're much mistaken to resent him so.
    Why I put up with him you surely know:
    My lawsuit's very shortly to be tried,   45
    And I must have his influence on my side.
ALCESTE: Then lose your lawsuit, Madam, or let it
    drop;
    Don't torture me by humoring such a fop.
CÉLIMÈNE: You're jealous of the whole world, Sir.
ALCESTE: That's true,
    Since the whole world is well-received by you.   50
CÉLIMÈNE: That my good nature is so unconfined
    Should serve to pacify your jealous mind;
    Were I to smile on one, and scorn the rest,
    Then you might have some cause to be distressed.
ALCESTE: Well, if I mustn't be jealous, tell me, then,   55
    Just how I'm better treated than other men.
CÉLIMÈNE: You know you have my love. Will that not
    do?
ALCESTE: What proof have I that what you say is true?
CÉLIMÈNE: I would expect, Sir, that my having said it
    Might give the statement a sufficient credit.   60
ALCESTE: But how can I be sure that you don't tell
    The selfsame thing to other men as well?
CÉLIMÈNE: What a gallant speech! How flattering to
    me!
    What a sweet creature you make me out to be!
    Well then, to save you from the pangs of doubt,   65
    All that I've said I hereby cancel out;
    Now, none but yourself shall make a monkey of
    you:
    Are you content?
ALCESTE: Why, why am I doomed to love you?
    I swear that I shall bless the blissful hour
    When this poor heart's no longer in your power!   70
    I make no secret of it: I've done my best

To exorcise this passion from my breast
But thus far all in vain; it will not go;
It's for my sins that I must love you so.
CÉLIMÈNE: Your love for me is matchless, Sir; that's
75   clear.
ALCESTE: Indeed, in all the world it has no peer;
Words can't describe the nature of my passion,
And no man ever loved in such a fashion.
CÉLIMÈNE: Yes, it's a brand-new fashion, I agree:
80   You show your love by castigating me,
And all your speeches are enraged and rude.
I've never been so furiously wooed.
ALCESTE: Yet you could calm that fury, if you chose.
Come, shall we bring our quarrels to a close?
85   Let's speak with open hearts, then, and begin . . .

Scene II *[Célimène, Alceste, Basque.]*

CÉLIMÈNE: What is it?
BASQUE: Acaste is here.
CÉLIMÈNE: Well, send him in.

Scene III *[Célimène, Alceste.]*

ALCESTE: What! Shall we never be alone at all?
You're always ready to receive a call,
And you can't bear, for ten ticks of the clock,
Not to keep open house for all who knock.
5   CÉLIMÈNE: I couldn't refuse him: he'd be most put out.
ALCESTE: Surely that's not worth worrying about.
CÉLIMÈNE: Acaste would never forgive me if he guessed
That I consider him a dreadful pest.
ALCESTE: If he's a pest, why bother with him then?
10   CÉLIMÈNE: Heavens! One can't antagonize such men;
Why, they're the chartered gossips of the court,
And have a say in things of every sort.
One must receive them, and be full of charm;
They're no great help, but they can do you harm,
15   And though your influence be ever so great,
They're hardly the best people to alienate.
ALCESTE: I see, dear lady, that you could make a case
For putting up with the whole human race;
These friendships that you calculate so nicely . . .

Scene IV *[Alceste, Célimène, Basque.]*

BASQUE: Madam, Clitandre is here as well.
ALCESTE: Precisely.
CÉLIMÈNE: Where are you going?
ALCESTE: Elsewhere.
CÉLIMÈNE: Stay.
ALCESTE: No, no.
CÉLIMÈNE: Stay, Sir.
ALCESTE: I can't.
CÉLIMÈNE: I wish it.
ALCESTE: No, I must go.

I beg you, Madam, not to press the matter;
You know I have no taste for idle chatter.   5
CÉLIMÈNE: Stay. I command you.
ALCESTE: No, I cannot stay.
CÉLIMÈNE: Very well; you have my leave to go away.

Scene V *[Éliante, Philinte, Acaste, Clitandre, Alceste, Célimène, Basque.]*

ÉLIANTE (*to Célimène*): The Marquesses have kindly
    come to call.
Were they announced?
CÉLIMÈNE: Yes. Basque, bring chairs for all.

(*Basque provides the chairs and exits.*)

    (*To Alceste.*) You haven't gone?
ALCESTE: No; and I shan't depart
Till you decide who's foremost in your heart.
CÉLIMÈNE: Oh, hush.
ALCESTE: It's time to choose; take them, or me.   5
CÉLIMÈNE: You're mad.
ALCESTE: I'm not, as you shall shortly see.
CÉLIMÈNE: Oh?
ALCESTE: You'll decide.
CÉLIMÈNE: You're joking now, dear friend.
ALCESTE: No, no; you'll choose; my patience is at an
    end.
CLITANDRE: Madam, I come from court, where poor
    Cléonte
Behaved like a perfect fool, as is his wont.   10
Has he no friend to counsel him, I wonder,
And teach him less unerringly to blunder?
CÉLIMÈNE: It's true, the man's a most accomplished
    dunce;
His gauche behavior charms the eye at once;
And every time one sees him, on my word,   15
His manner's grown a trifle more absurd.
ACASTE: Speaking of dunces, I've just now conversed
With old Damon, who's one of the very worst;
I stood a lifetime in the broiling sun
Before his dreary monologue was done.   20
CÉLIMÈNE: Oh, he's a wondrous talker, and has the
    power
To tell you nothing hour after hour:
If, by mistake, he ever came to the point,
The shock would put his jawbone out of joint.
ÉLIANTE (*to Philinte*): The conversation takes its usual
    turn,   25
And all our dear friends' ears will shortly burn.
CLITANDRE: Timante's a character, Madam.
CÉLIMÈNE: Isn't he, though?
A man of mystery from top to toe,
Who moves about in a romantic mist
On secret missions which do not exist.   30
His talk is full of eyebrows and grimaces;
How tired one gets of his momentous faces;
He's always whispering something confidential

Which turns out to be quite inconsequential;
35　Nothing's too slight for him to mystify;
He even whispers when he says "good-by."
ACASTE: Tell us about Géralde.
CÉLIMÈNE:　　　　　　　　　That tiresome ass.
He mixes only with the titled class,
And fawns on dukes and princes, and is bored
40　With anyone who's not at least a lord.
The man's obsessed with rank, and his discourses
Are all of hounds and carriages and horses;
He uses Christian names with all the great,
And the word Milord, with him, is out of date.
45　CLITANDRE: He's very taken with Bélise, I hear.
CÉLIMÈNE: She is the dreariest company, poor dear.
Whenever she comes to call, I grope about
To find some topic which will draw her out,
But, owing to her dry and faint replies,
50　The conversation wilts, and droops, and dies.
In vain one hopes to animate her face
By mentioning the ultimate commonplace;
But sun or shower, even hail or frost
Are matters she can instantly exhaust.
55　Meanwhile her visit, painful though it is,
Drags on and on through mute eternities,
And though you ask the time, and yawn, and
　　　yawn,
She sits there like a stone and won't be gone.
ACASTE: Now for Adraste.
CÉLIMÈNE:　　　　　　　　Oh, that conceited elf
60　Has a gigantic passion for himself;
He rails against the court, and cannot bear it
That none will recognize his hidden merit;
All honors given to others give offense
To his imaginary excellence.
CLITANDRE: What about young Cléon? His house,
65　　they say,
Is full of the best society, night and day.
CÉLIMÈNE: His cook has made him popular, not he:
It's Cléon's table that people come to see.
ÉLIANTE: He gives a splendid dinner, you must admit.
70　CÉLIMÈNE: But must he serve himself along with it?
For my taste, he's a most insipid dish
Whose presence sours the wine and spoils the fish.
PHILINTE: Damis, his uncle is admired no end.
What's your opinion, Madam?
CÉLIMÈNE:　　　　　　　　　Why, he's my friend.
PHILINTE: He seems a decent fellow, and rather
75　　clever.
CÉLIMÈNE: He works too hard at cleverness,
　　however.
I hate to see him sweat and struggle so
To fill his conversation with *bons mots*.°
Since he's decided to become a wit
80　His taste's so pure that nothing pleases it;
He scolds at all the latest books and plays,
Thinking that wit must never stoop to praise,
That finding fault's a sign of intellect,

78. *bons mots:* Clever remarks, witticisms.

That all appreciation is abject,
And that by damning everything in sight　　　85
One shows oneself in a distinguished light.
He's scornful even of our conversations:
Their trivial nature sorely tries his patience;
He folds his arms, and stands above the battle,
And listens sadly to our childish prattle.　　90
ACASTE: Wonderful, Madam! You've hit him off
　　precisely.
CLITANDRE: No one can sketch a character so nicely.
ALCESTE: How bravely, Sirs, you cut and thrust
　　at all
These absent fools, till one by one they fall:
But let one come in sight, and you'll at once　95
Embrace the man you lately called a dunce,
Telling him in a tone sincere and fervent
How proud you are to be his humble servant.
CLITANDRE: Why pick on us? *Madame's* been speaking,
　　Sir.
And you should quarrel, if you must, with her.　100
ALCESTE: No, no, by God, the fault is yours,
　　because
You lead her on with laughter and applause,
And make her think that she's the more delightful
The more her talk is scandalous and spiteful.
Oh, she would stoop to malice far, far less　105
If no such claque approved her cleverness.
It's flatterers like you whose foolish praise
Nourishes all the vices of these days.
PHILINTE: But why protest when someone ridicules
Those you'd condemn, yourself, as knaves or
　　fools?　　　　　　　　　　　　　　　　110
CÉLIMÈNE: Why, Sir? Because he loves to make a
　　fuss.
You don't expect him to agree with us,
When there's an opportunity to express
His heaven-sent spirit of contrariness?
What other people think, he can't abide;　　115
Whatever they say, he's on the other side;
He lives in deadly terror of agreeing;
'Twould make him seem an ordinary being.
Indeed, he's so in love with contradiction,
He'll turn against his most profound conviction　120
And with a furious eloquence deplore it,
If only someone else is speaking for it.
ALCESTE: Go on, dear lady, mock me as you please;
You have your audience in ecstasies.
PHILINTE: But what she says is true: you have a way　125
Of bridling at whatever people say;
Whether they praise or blame, your angry spirit
Is equally unsatisfied to hear it.
ALCESTE: Men, Sir, are always wrong, and that's the
　　reason
That righteous anger's never out of season;　　130
All that I hear in all their conversation
Is flattering praise or reckless condemnation.
CÉLIMÈNE: But . . .
ALCESTE:　　　　　　No, no, Madam, I am forced to state
That you have pleasures which I deprecate,

135 And that these others, here, are much to blame
    For nourishing the faults which are your shame.
CLITANDRE: I shan't defend myself, Sir; but I vow
    I'd thought this lady faultless until now.
ACASTE: I see her charms and graces, which are many;
140 But as for faults, I've never noticed any.
ALCESTE: I see them, Sir; and rather than ignore them,
    I strenuously criticize her for them.
    The more one loves, the more one should object
    To every blemish, every least defect.
145 Were I this lady, I would soon get rid
    Of lovers who approved of all I did,
    And by their slack indulgence and applause
    Endorsed my follies and excused my flaws.
CÉLIMÈNE: If all hearts beat according to your
    measure,
150 The dawn of love would be the end of pleasure;
    And love would find its perfect consummation
    In ecstasies of rage and reprobation.
ÉLIANTE: Love, as a rule, affects men otherwise
    And lovers rarely love to criticize.
155 They see their lady as a charming blur,
    And find all things commendable in her.
    If she has any blemish, fault, or shame,
    They will redeem it by a pleasing name.
    The pale-faced lady's lily-white, perforce;
160 The swarthy one's a sweet brunette, of course;
    The spindly lady has a slender grace;
    The fat one has a most majestic pace;
    The plain one, with her dress in disarray
    They classify as *beauté négligée;*°
165 The hulking one's a goddess in their eyes,
    The dwarf, a concentrate of Paradise;
    The haughty lady has a noble mind;
    The mean one's witty, and the dull one's kind;
    The chatterbox has liveliness and verve,
170 The mute one has a virtuous reserve.
    So lovers manage, in their passion's cause,
    To love their ladies even for their flaws.
ALCESTE: But I still say . . .
CÉLIMÈNE   I think it would be nice
    To stroll around the gallery once or twice.
    What! You're not going, Sirs?
175 CLITANDRE AND ACASTE: No, Madam, no.
ALCESTE: You seem to be in terror lest they go.
    Do what you will, Sirs; leave, or linger on,
    But I shan't go till after you are gone.
ACASTE: I'm free to linger, unless I should perceive
180 *Madame* is tired, and wishes me to leave.
CLITANDRE: And as for me, I needn't go today
    Until the hour of the King's *coucher.*°
CÉLIMÈNE (to Alceste): You're joking, surely?
ALCESTE: Not in the
    least; we'll see
    Whether you'd rather part with them, or me.

---

164. *beauté négligée:* Slovenly beauty.   182. the King's *coucher:*
The King's bedtime, a ceremonial occasion.

Scene VI [*Alceste, Célimène, Éliante, Acaste,
Philinte, Clitandre, Basque.*]

BASQUE (*to Alceste*): Sir, there's a fellow here who bids
    me state
    That he must see you, and that it can't wait.
ALCESTE: Tell him that I have no such pressing affairs.
BASQUE: It's a long tailcoat that this fellow wears,
    With gold all over.
CÉLIMÈNE (*to Alceste*):   You'd best go down and see.
    Or — have him enter.   5

Scene VII [*Alceste, Célimène, Éliante, Acaste,
Philinte, Clitandre, Guard.*]

ALCESTE (*confronting the Guard*):   Well, what do you
    want with me?
    Come in. Sir.
GUARD: I've a word, Sir, for your ear.
ALCESTE: Speak it aloud, Sir; I shall strive to hear.
GUARD: The Marshals have instructed me to say
    You must report to them without delay.   5
ALCESTE: Who? Me, Sir?
GUARD: Yes, Sir; you.
ALCESTE: But what do they want?
PHILINTE (*to Alceste*): To scotch your silly quarrel with
    Oronte.
CÉLIMÈNE (*to Philinte*): What quarrel?
PHILINTE: Oronte and he have
    fallen out
    Over some verse he spoke his mind about;
    The Marshals wish to arbitrate the matter.   10
ALCESTE: Never shall I equivocate or flatter!
PHILINTE: You'd best obey their summons; come, let's
    go.
ALCESTE: How can they mend our quarrel, I'd like to
    know?
    Am I to make a cowardly retraction,
    And praise those jingles to his satisfaction?   15
    I'll not recant; I've judged that sonnet rightly.
    It's bad.
PHILINTE: But you might say so more politely . . .
ALCESTE: I'll not back down; his verses make me sick.
PHILINTE: If only you could be more politic!
    But come, let's go.
ALCESTE: I'll go, but I won't unsay   20
    A single word.
PHILINTE: Well, let's be on our way.
ALCESTE: Till I am ordered by my lord the King
    To praise that poem, I shall say the thing
    Is scandalous, by God, and that the poet
    Ought to be hanged for having the nerve to show it.   25

(*To Clitandre and Acaste, who are laughing.*)

    By heaven, Sirs, I really didn't know
    That I was being humorous.

Scene from the Williamstown Theatre Festival's 1973 production of *The Misanthrope*, directed by Austin Pendleton.

CÉLIMÈNE: Go, Sir, go;
  Settle your business.
ALCESTE: I shall, and when I'm through,
  I shall return to settle things with you.

ACT III • *Scene 1* [*Clitandre, Acaste.*]

CLITANDRE: Dear Marquess, how contented you
    appear;
  All things delight you, nothing mars your cheer.
  Can you, in perfect honesty, declare
  That you've a right to be so debonair?
5 ACASTE: By Jove, when I survey myself, I find
  No cause whatever for distress of mind.
  I'm young and rich; I can in modesty
  Lay claim to an exalted pedigree;
  And owing to my name and my condition
10   I shall not want for honors and position.
  Then as to courage, that most precious trait,
  I seem to have it, as was proved of late
  Upon the field of honor, where my bearing,
  They say, was very cool and rather daring.
15   I've wit, of course; and taste in such perfection
  That I can judge without the least reflection,

And at the theater, which is my delight,
Can make or break a play on opening night,
And lead the crowd in hisses or bravos,
And generally be known as one who knows.   20
I'm clever, handsome, gracefully polite;
My waist is small, my teeth are strong and white;
As for my dress, the world's astonished eyes
Assure me that I bear away the prize.
I find myself in favor everywhere,   25
Honored by men, and worshiped by the fair;
And since these things are so, it seems to me
I'm justified in my complacency.
CLITANDRE: Well, if so many ladies hold you dear,
  Why do you press a hopeless courtship here?   30
ACASTE: Hopeless, you say? I'm not the sort of fool
  That likes his ladies difficult and cool.
  Men who are awkward, shy, and peasantish
  May pine for heartless beauties, if they wish,
  Grovel before them, bear their cruelties,   35
  Woo them with tears and sighs and bended knees,
  And hope by dogged faithfulness to gain
  What their poor merits never could obtain.
  For men like me, however, it makes no sense
  To love on trust, and foot the whole expense.   40
  Whatever any lady's merits be,

I think, thank God, that I'm as choice as she;
That if my heart is kind enough to burn
For her, she owes me something in return;
45 And that in any proper love affair
The partners must invest an equal share.
CLITANDRE: You think, then, that our hostess favors
    you?
ACASTE: I've reason to believe that that is true.
CLITANDRE: How did you come to such a mad
    conclusion?
50   You're blind, dear fellow. This is sheer delusion.
ACASTE: All right, then: I'm deluded and I'm blind.
CLITANDRE: Whatever put the notion in your mind?
ACASTE: Delusion.
CLITANDRE: What persuades you that you're right?
ACASTE: I'm blind.
CLITANDRE: But have you any proofs to cite?
ACASTE: I tell you I'm deluded.
55 CLITANDRE: Have you, then,
    Received some secret pledge from Célimène?
ACASTE: Oh, no: she scorns me.
CLITANDRE: Tell me the truth, I beg.
ACASTE: She just can't bear me.
CLITANDRE: Ah, don't pull my leg.
    Tell me what hope she's given you, I pray.
60 ACASTE: I'm hopeless, and it's you who win the day.
    She hates me thoroughly, and I'm so vexed
    I mean to hang myself on Tuesday next.
CLITANDRE: Dear Marquess, let us have an armistice
    And make a treaty. What do you say to this?
65   If ever one of us can plainly prove
    That Célimène encourages his love,
    The other must abandon hope, and yield,
    And leave him in possession of the field.
ACASTE: Now, there's a bargain that appeals to me;
70   With all my heart, dear Marquess, I agree.
    But hush.

Scene II [*Célimène, Acaste, Clitandre.*]

CÉLIMÈNE: Still here?
CLITANDRE: 'Twas love that stayed our feet.
CÉLIMÈNE: I think I heard a carriage in the street.
    Whose is it? D'you know?

Scene III [*Célimène, Acaste, Clitandre, Basque.*]

BASQUE: Arsinoé is here, *Madame.*
CÉLIMÈNE: Arsinoé, you say? Oh, dear.
BASQUE: Éliante is entertaining her below.
CÉLIMÈNE: What brings the creature here, I'd like to
    know?
5 ACASTE: They say she's dreadfully prudish, but in fact
    I think her piety . . .
CÉLIMÈNE: It's all an act.
    At heart she's worldly, and her poor success
    In snaring men explains her prudishness.

It breaks her heart to see the beaux and gallants
Engrossed by other women's charms and talents, 10
And so she's always in a jealous rage
Against the faulty standards of the age.
She lets the world believe that she's a prude
To justify her loveless solitude,
And strives to put a brand of moral shame 15
On all the graces that she cannot claim.
But still she'd love a lover; and Alceste
Appears to be the one she'd love the best.
His visits here are poison to her pride;
She seems to think I've lured him from her side 20
And everywhere, at court or in the town,
The spiteful, envious woman runs me down.
In short, she's just as stupid as can be,
Vicious and arrogant in the last degree,
And . . . 25

Scene IV [*Arsinoé, Célimène, Clitandre, Acaste.*]

CÉLIMÈNE: Ah! What happy chance has brought you
    here?
    I've thought about you ever so much, my dear.
ARSINOÉ: I've come to tell you something you should
    know.
CÉLIMÈNE: How good of you to think of doing so!

(*Clitandre and Acaste go out, laughing.*)

Scene V [*Arsinoé, Célimène.*]

ARSINOÉ: It's just as well those gentlemen didn't tarry.
CÉLIMÈNE: Shall we sit down?
ARSINOÉ: That won't be necessary.
    Madam, the flame of friendship ought to burn
    Brightest in matters of the most concern,
    And as there's nothing which concerns us more 5
    Than honor, I have hastened to your door
    To bring you, as your friend, some information
    About the status of your reputation.
    I visited, last night, some virtuous folk,
    And, quite by chance, it was of you they spoke; 10
    There was, I fear, no tendency to praise
    Your light behavior and your dashing ways.
    The quantity of gentlemen you see
    And your by now notorious coquetry
    Were both so vehemently criticized 15
    By everyone, that I was much surprised.
    Of course, I needn't tell you where I stood;
    I came to your defense as best I could,
    Assured them you were harmless, and declared
    Your soul was absolutely unimpaired. 20
    But there are some things, you must realize,
    One can't excuse, however hard one tries,
    And I was forced at last into conceding
    That your behavior, Madam, is misleading,
    That it makes a bad impression, giving rise 25

To ugly gossip and obscene surmise,
And that if you were more *overtly* good,
You wouldn't be so much misunderstood.
Not that I think you've been unchaste — no! no!
30 The saints preserve me from a thought so low!
But mere good conscience never did suffice:
One must avoid the outward show of vice.
Madam, you're too intelligent, I'm sure,
To think my motives anything but pure
35 In offering you this counsel — which I do
Out of a zealous interest in you.
   CÉLIMÈNE: Madam, I haven't taken you amiss;
I'm very much obliged to you for this;
And I'll at once discharge the obligation
40 By telling you about *your* reputation.
You've been so friendly as to let me know
What certain people say of me, and so
I mean to follow your benign example
By offering you a somewhat similar sample.
45 The other day, I went to an affair
And found some most distinguished people there
Discussing piety, both false and true.
The conversation soon came round to you.
Alas! Your prudery and bustling zeal
50 Appeared to have a very slight appeal.
Your affectation of a grave demeanor,
Your endless talk of virtue and of honor,
The aptitude of your suspicious mind
For finding sin where there is none to find,
55 Your towering self-esteem, that pitying face
With which you contemplate the human race,
Your sermonizings and your sharp aspersions
On people's pure and innocent diversions —
All these were mentioned, Madam, and, in fact,
60 Were roundly and concertedly attacked.
"What good," they said, "are all these outward
     shows,
When everything belies her pious pose?
She prays incessantly, but then, they say,
She beats her maids and cheats them of their pay;
65 She shows her zeal in every holy place,
But still she's vain enough to paint her face;
She holds that naked statues are immoral,
But with a naked *man* she'd have no quarrel."
Of course, I said to everybody there
70 That they were being viciously unfair;
But still they were disposed to criticize you,
And all agreed that someone should advise you
To leave the morals of the world alone,
And worry rather more about your own.
They felt that one's self-knowledge should be
75   great
Before one thinks of setting others straight;
That one should learn the art of living well
Before one threatens other men with hell,
And that the Church is best equipped, no doubt,
80 To guide our souls and root our vices out.
Madam, you're too intelligent, I'm sure,
To think my motives anything but pure

In offering you this counsel — which I do
Out of a zealous interest in you.
ARSINOÉ: I dared not hope for gratitude, but I   85
Did not expect so acid a reply;
I judge, since you've been so extremely tart,
That my good counsel pierced you to the heart.
CÉLIMÈNE: Far from it, Madam. Indeed, it seems to me
We ought to trade advice more frequently.   90
One's vision of oneself is so defective
That it would be an excellent corrective.
If you are willing, Madam, let's arrange
Shortly to have another frank exchange
In which we'll tell each other, *entre nous,*°   95
What you've heard tell of me, and I of you.
ARSINOÉ: Oh, people never censure you, my dear;
It's me they criticize. Or so I hear.
CÉLIMÈNE: Madam, I think we either blame or praise
According to our taste and length of days.   100
There is a time of life for coquetry,
And there's a season, too, for prudery.
When all one's charms are gone, it is, I'm sure,
Good strategy to be devout and pure:
It makes one seem a little less forsaken.   105
Some day, perhaps, I'll take the road you've taken:
Time brings all things. But I have time aplenty,
And see no cause to be a prude at twenty.
ARSINOÉ: You give your age in such a gloating tone
That one would think I was an ancient crone;   110
We're not so far apart, in sober truth,
That you can mock me with a boast of youth!
Madam, you baffle me. I wish I knew
What moves you to provoke me as you do.
CÉLIMÈNE: For my part, Madam, I should like to know   115
Why you abuse me everywhere you go.
Is it my fault, dear lady, that your hand
Is not, alas, in very great demand?
If men admire me, if they pay me court
And daily make me offers of the sort   120
You'd dearly love to have them make to you,
How can I help it? What would you have me do?
If what you want is lovers, please feel free
To take as many as you can from me.
ARSINOÉ: Oh, come. D'you think the world is losing
     sleep   125
Over the flock of lovers which you keep,
Or that we find it difficult to guess
What price you pay for their devotedness?
Surely you don't expect us to suppose
Mere merit could attract so many beaux?   130
It's not your virtue that they're dazzled by;
Nor is it virtuous love for which they sigh.
You're fooling no one, Madam; the world's not
     blind;
There's many a lady heaven has designed
To call men's noblest, tenderest feelings out,   135
Who has no lovers dogging her about;
From which it's plain that lovers nowadays

95. *entre nous:* Between ourselves.

Must be acquired in bold and shameless ways,
And only pay one court for such reward
140   As modesty and virtue can't afford.
Then don't be quite so puffed up, if you please,
About your tawdry little victories;
Try, if you can, to be a shade less vain,
And treat the world with somewhat less disdain.
145   If one were envious of your amours,
One soon could have a following like yours;
Lovers are no great trouble to collect
If one prefers them to one's self-respect.
CÉLIMÈNE: Collect them then, my dear; I'd love to see
150   You demonstrate that charming theory;
Who knows, you might . . .
ARSINOÉ: Now, Madam, that will do;
It's time to end this trying interview.
My coach is late in coming to your door,
Or I'd have taken leave of you before.
CÉLIMÈNE: Oh, please don't feel that you must rush
155   away;
I'd be delighted, Madam, if you'd stay.
However, lest my conversation bore you,
Let me provide some better company for you;
This gentleman, who comes most apropos,
160   Will please you more than I could do, I know.

Scene VI [*Alceste, Célimène, Arsinoé.*]

CÉLIMÈNE: Alceste, I have a little note to write
Which simply must go out before tonight;
Please entertain *Madame*; I'm sure that she
Will overlook my incivility.

Scene VII [*Alceste, Arsinoé.*]

ARSINOÉ: Well, Sir, our hostess graciously contrives
For us to chat until my coach arrives;
And I shall be forever in her debt
For granting me this little *tête-à-tête*.°
5   We women very rightly give our hearts
To men of noble character and parts,
And your especial merits, dear Alceste
Have roused the deepest sympathy in my breast.
Oh, how I wish they had sufficient sense
10   At court, to recognize your excellence!
They wrong you greatly, Sir. How it must hurt you
Never to be rewarded for your virtue!
ALCESTE: Why, Madam, what cause have I to feel
          aggrieved?
What great and brilliant thing have I achieved?
15   What service have I rendered to the King
That I should look to him for anything?
ARSINOÉ: Not everyone who's honored by the State
Has done great services. A man must wait

4. *tête-à-tête:* French for "head-to-head," in private conversation.

Till time and fortune offer him the chance.
Your merit, Sir, is obvious at a glance,   20
And . . .
ALCESTE: Ah, forget my merit; I am not neglected.
The court, I think, can hardly be expected
To mine men's souls for merit, and unearth
Our hidden virtues and our secret worth.
ARSINOÉ: *Some* virtues, though, are far too bright to
          hide;   25
Yours are acknowledged, Sir, on every side.
Indeed, I've heard you warmly praised of late
By persons of considerable weight.
ALCESTE: This fawning age has praise for everyone,
And all distinctions, Madam, are undone.   30
All things have equal honor nowadays,
And no one should be gratified by praise.
To be admired, one only need exist,
And every lackey's on the honors list.
ARSINOÉ: I only wish, Sir, that you had your eye   35
On some position at court, however high;
You'd only have to hint at such a notion
For me to set the proper wheels in motion
I've certain friendships I'd be glad to use
To get you any office you might choose.   40
ALCESTE: Madam, I fear that any such ambition
Is wholly foreign to my disposition.
The soul God gave me isn't of the sort
That prospers in the weather of a court.
It's all too obvious that I don't possess   45
The virtues necessary for success.
My one great talent is for speaking plain;
I've never learned to flatter or to feign;
And anyone so stupidly sincere
Had best not seek a courtier's career.   50
Outside the court, I know, one must dispense
With honors, privilege, and influence;
But still one gains the right, foregoing these,
Not to be tortured by the wish to please.
One needn't live in dread of snubs and slights,   55
Nor praise the verse that every idiot writes,
Nor humor silly Marquesses, nor bestow
Politic sighs on Madam So-and-So.
ARSINOÉ: Forget the court, then; let the matter rest.
But I've another cause to be distressed   60
About your present situation, Sir.
It's to your love affair that I refer.
She whom you love, and who pretends to love you,
Is, I regret to say, unworthy of you.
ALCESTE: Why, Madam? Can you seriously intend   65
To make so grave a charge against your friend?
ARSINOÉ: Alas, I must. I've stood aside too long
And let that lady do you grievous wrong;
But now my debt to conscience shall be paid:
I tell you that your love has been betrayed.   70
ALCESTE: I thank you, Madam; you're extremely kind.
Such words are soothing to a lover's mind.
ARSINOÉ: Yes, though she *is* my friend, I say again
You're very much too good for Célimène.
She's wantonly misled you from the start.   75

ALCESTE: You may be right; who knows another's heart?
    But ask yourself if it's the part of charity
    To shake my soul with doubts of her sincerity.
ARSINOÉ: Well, if you'd rather be a dupe than doubt
    her,
80   That's your affair. I'll say no more about her.
ALCESTE: Madam, you know that doubt and vague
    suspicion
    Are painful to a man in my position;
    It's most unkind to worry me this way
    Unless you've some real proof of what you say.
85 ARSINOÉ: Sir, say no more: all doubts shall be removed,
    And all that I've been saying shall be proved.
    You've only to escort me home, and there
    We'll look into the heart of this affair.
    I've ocular evidence which will persuade you
80   Beyond a doubt, that Célimène's betrayed you.
    Then, if you're saddened by that revelation,
    Perhaps I can provide some consolation.

ACT IV • *Scene 1* [*Éliante, Philinte.*]

PHILINTE: Madam, he acted like a stubborn child
    I thought they never would be reconciled;
    In vain we reasoned, threatened, and appealed;
    He stood his ground and simply would not yield.
5   The Marshals, I feel sure have never heard
    An argument so splendidly absurd.
    "No, gentlemen," said he, "I'll not retract.
    His verse is bad: extremely bad, in fact.
    Surely it does the man no harm to know it.
10   Does it disgrace him, not to be a poet?
    A gentleman may be respected still,
    Whether he writes a sonnet well or ill.
    That I dislike his verse should not offend him;
    In all that touches honor, I commend him;
15   He's noble, brave, and virtuous — but I fear
    He can't in truth be called a sonneteer.
    I'll gladly praise his wardrobe; I'll endorse
    His dancing, or the way he sits a horse;
    But, gentlemen, I cannot praise his rhyme.
20   In fact, it ought to be a capital crime
    For anyone so sadly unendowed
    To write a sonnet, and read the thing aloud."
    At length he fell into a gentler mood
    And, striking a concessive attitude,
25   He paid Oronte the following courtesies:
    "Sir, I regret that I'm so hard to please,
    And I'm profoundly sorry that your lyric
    Failed to provoke me to a panegyric."°
    After these curious words, the two embraced
30   And then the hearing was adjourned — in haste.
ÉLIANTE: His conduct has been very singular lately;
    Still, I confess that I respect him greatly.
    The honesty in which he takes such pride
    Has — to my mind — its noble, heroic side.

28. panegyric: Elaborate praise.

    In this false age, such candor seems outrageous;   35
    But I could wish that it were more contagious.
PHILINTE: What most intrigues me in our friend Alceste
    Is the grand passion that rages in his breast.
    The sullen humors he's compounded of
    Should not, I think, dispose his heart to love;   40
    But since they do, it puzzles me still more
    That he should choose your cousin to adore.
ÉLIANTE: It does, indeed, belie the theory
    That love is born of gentle sympathy,
    And that the tender passion must be based   45
    On sweet accords of temper and of taste.
PHILINTE: Does she return his love, do you suppose?
ÉLIANTE: Ah, that's a difficult question, Sir. Who
    knows?
    How can we judge the truth of her devotion?
    Her heart's a stranger to its own emotion.
    Sometimes it thinks it loves, when no love's there;   50
    At other times it loves quite unaware.
PHILINTE: I rather think Alceste is in for more
    Distress and sorrow than he's bargained for;
    Were he of my mind, Madam, his affection   55
    Would turn in quite a different direction,
    And we would see him more responsive to
    The kind regard which he receives from you.
ÉLIANTE: Sir, I believe in frankness, and I'm inclined
    In matters of the heart, to speak my mind.   60
    I don't oppose his love for her; indeed,
    I hope with all my heart that he'll succeed,
    And were it in my power, I'd rejoice
    In giving him the lady of his choice.
    But if, as happens frequently enough   65
    In love affairs, he meets with a rebuff —
    If Célimène should grant some rival's suit —
    I'd gladly play the role of substitute;
    Nor would his tender speeches please me less
    Because they'd once been made without success.   70
PHILINTE: Well, Madam, as for me, I don't oppose
    Your hopes in this affair; and heaven knows
    That in my conversations with the man
    I plead your cause as often as I can.
    But if those two should marry, and so remove   75
    All chance that he will offer you his love,
    Then I'll declare my own, and hope to see
    Your gracious favor pass from him to me.
    In short, should you be cheated of Alceste,
    I'd be most happy to be second best.   80
ÉLIANTE: Philinte, you're teasing.
PHILINTE: Ah, Madam, never fear;
    No words of mine were ever so sincere
    And I shall live in fretful expectation
    Till I can make a fuller declaration.

Scene II [*Alceste, Éliante, Philinte.*]

ALCESTE: Avenge me, Madam! I must have satisfaction,
    Or this great wrong will drive me to distraction!
ÉLIANTE: Why, what's the matter? What's upset you so?

ALCESTE: Madam, I've had a mortal, mortal blow.
5   If Chaos repossessed the universe,
    I swear I'd not be shaken any worse.
    I'm ruined. . . . I can say no more. . . . My soul . . .
ÉLIANTE: Do try, Sir, to regain your self-control.
ALCESTE: Just heaven! Why were so much beauty and
    grace
10   Bestowed on one so vicious and so base?
ÉLIANTE: Once more, Sir, tell us
ALCESTE: My world has gone to wrack:
    I'm — I'm betrayed; she's stabbed me in the back:
    Yes, Célimène (who would have thought it of her?)
    Is false to me, and has another lover.
ÉLIANTE: Are you quite certain? Can you prove these
15   things?
PHILINTE: Lovers are prey to wild imaginings
    And jealous fancies. No doubt there's some
        mistake. . . .
ALCESTE: Mind your own business, Sir, for heaven's
    sake.
    (To Éliante.) Madam, I have the proof that you
        demand
20   Here in my pocket, penned by her own hand.
    Yes, all the shameful evidence one could want
    Lies in this letter written to Oronte —
    Oronte! whom I felt sure she couldn't love,
    And hardly bothered to be jealous of.
25 PHILINTE: Still, in a letter, appearances may deceive;
    This may not be so bad as you believe.
ALCESTE: Once more I beg you, Sir, to let me be;
    Tend to your own affairs; leave mine to me.
ÉLIANTE: Compose yourself; this anguish that you
    feel . . .
30 ALCESTE: Is something, Madam, you alone can heal.
    My outraged heart, beside itself with grief,
    Appeals to you for comfort and relief.
    Avenge me on your cousin, whose unjust
    And faithless nature has deceived my trust;
35   Avenge a crime your pure soul must detest.
ÉLIANTE: But how, Sir?
ALCESTE: Madam, this heart within my breast
    Is yours; pray take it; redeem my heart from her,
    And so avenge me on my torturer.
    Let her be punished by the fond emotion,
40   The ardent love, the bottomless devotion,
    The faithful worship which this heart of mine
    Will offer up to yours as to a shrine.
ÉLIANTE: You have my sympathy, Sir, in all you suffer;
    Nor do I scorn the noble heart you offer;
45   But I suspect you'll soon be mollified
    And this desire for vengeance will subside.
    When some belovèd hand has done us wrong
    We thirst for retribution — but not for long;
    However dark the deed that she's committed,
50   A lovely culprit's very soon acquitted.
    Nothing's so stormy as an injured lover,
    And yet no storm so quickly passes over.
ALCESTE: No, Madam, no — this is no lovers' spat;
    I'll not forgive her, it's gone too far for that;

My mind's made up; I'll kill myself before   55
I waste my hopes upon her any more.
Ah, here she is. My wrath intensifies.
I shall confront her with her tricks and lies,
And crush her utterly, and bring you then
A heart no longer slave to Célimène.   60

Scene III [Célimène, Alceste.]

ALCESTE (aside): Sweet heaven, help me to control my
    passion.
CÉLIMÈNE (aside): Oh, Lord. (To Alceste.) Why stand
    there staring in that fashion?
    And what d'you mean by those dramatic sighs,
    And that malignant glitter in your eyes?
ALCESTE: I mean that sins which cause the blood to
    freeze   5
    Look innocent beside your treacheries;
    That nothing Hell's or Heaven's wrath could do
    Ever produced so bad a thing as you.
CÉLIMÈNE: Your compliments were always sweet and
    pretty.
ALCESTE: Madam, it's not the moment to be witty.   10
    No, blush and hang your head; you've ample
        reason,
    Since I've the fullest evidence of your treason.
    Ah, this is what my sad heart prophesied;
    Now all my anxious fears are verified;
    My dark suspicion and my gloomy doubt   15
    Divined the truth, and now the truth is out.
    For all your trickery, I was not deceived;
    It was my bitter stars that I believed.
    But don't imagine that you'll go scot-free;
    You shan't misuse me with impunity.   20
    I know that love's irrational and blind;
    I know the heart's not subject to the mind,
    And can't be reasoned into beating faster;
    I know each soul is free to choose its master;
    Therefore had you but spoken from the heart,   25
    Rejecting my attention from the start,
    I'd have no grievance, or at any rate
    I could complain of nothing but my fate.
    Ah, but so falsely to encourage me —
    That was a treason and a treachery   30
    For which you cannot suffer too severely,
    And you shall pay for that behavior dearly.
    Yes, now I have no pity, not a shred;
    My temper's out of hand, I've lost my head
    Shocked by the knowledge of your double-
        dealings,   35
    My reason can't restrain my savage feelings;
    A righteous wrath deprives me of my senses,
    And I won't answer for the consequences.
CÉLIMÈNE: What does this outburst mean? Will you
    please explain?
    Have you, by any chance, gone quite insane?   40
ALCESTE: Yes, yes, I went insane the day I fell
    A victim to your black and fatal spell,

Thinking to meet with some sincerity
Among the treacherous charms that beckoned me.
CÉLIMÈNE: Pooh. Of what treachery can you
45   complain?
ALCESTE: How sly you are, how cleverly you feign!
But you'll not victimize me any more.
Look: here's a document you've seen before.
This evidence, which I acquired today,
50   Leaves you, I think, without a thing to say.
CÉLIMÈNE: Is this what sent you into such a fit?
ALCESTE: You should be blushing at the sight of it.
CÉLIMÈNE: Ought I to blush? I truly don't see why.
ALCESTE: Ah, now you're being bold as well as sly;
55   Since there's no signature, perhaps you'll claim . . .
CÉLIMÈNE: I wrote it, whether or not it bears my name.
ALCESTE: And you can view with equanimity
his proof of your disloyalty to me!
CÉLIMÈNE: Oh, don't be so outrageous and extreme.
60 ALCESTE: You take this matter lightly, it would seem.
Was it no wrong to me, no shame to you,
That you should send Oronte this *billet-doux*?°
CÉLIMÈNE: Oronte! Who said it was for him?
ALCESTE: Why, those
Who brought me this example of your prose.
65   But what's the difference? If you wrote the letter
To someone else, it pleases me no better.
My grievance and your guilt remain the same.
CÉLIMÈNE: But need you rage, and need I blush for
    shame,
If this was written to a *woman* friend?
70 ALCESTE: Ah! Most ingenious. I'm impressed no end;
And after that incredible evasion
Your guilt is clear. I need no more persuasion.
How dare you try so clumsy a deception?
D'you think I'm wholly wanting in perception?
75   Come, come, let's see how brazenly you'll try
To bolster up so palpable a lie:
Kindly construe this ardent closing section
As nothing more than sisterly affection!
Here, let me read it. Tell me, if you dare to,
That this is for a woman . . .
80 CÉLIMÈNE: I don't dare to.
What right have you to badger and berate me,
And so high-handedly interrogate me?
ALCESTE: Now, don't be angry; all I ask of you
Is that you justify a phrase or two . . .
85 CÉLIMÈNE: No, I shall not. I utterly refuse,
And you may take those phrases as you choose.
ALCESTE: Just show me how this letter could be meant
For a woman's eyes, and I shall be content.
CÉLIMÈNE: No, no, it's for Oronte; you're perfectly
    right.
90   I welcome his attentions with delight,
I prize his character and his intellect
And everything is just as you suspect.
Come, do your worst now; give your rage free rein;
But kindly cease to bicker and complain.

62. *billet-doux:* Love letter.

ALCESTE (*aside*): Good God! Could anything be more
    inhuman?   95
Was ever a heart so mangled by a woman?
When I complain of how she has betrayed me,
She bridles, and commences to upbraid me!
She tries my tortured patience to the limit;
She won't deny her guilt; she glories in it!   100
And yet my heart's too faint and cowardly
To break these chains of passion, and be free,
To scorn her as it should, and rise above
This unrewarded, mad, and bitter love.
(*To Célimène.*) Ah, traitress, in how confident a
    fashion   105
You take advantage of my helpless passion,
And use my weakness for your faithless charms
To make me once again throw down my arms!
But do at least deny this black transgression;
Take back that mocking and perverse confession;   110
Defend this letter and your innocence,
And I, poor fool, will aid in your defense.
Pretend, pretend, that you are just and true,
And I shall make myself believe in you.
CÉLIMÈNE: Oh, stop it. Don't be such a jealous dunce,   115
Or I shall leave off loving you at once.
Just why should I *pretend*? What could impel me
To stoop so low as that? And kindly tell me
Why, if I loved another, I shouldn't merely
Inform you of it, simply and sincerely!   120
I've told you where you stand, and that admission
Should altogether clear me of suspicion;
After so generous a guarantee
What right have you to harbor doubts of me?
Since women are (from natural reticence)   125
Reluctant to declare their sentiments,
And since the honor of our sex requires
That we conceal our amorous desires,
Ought any man for whom such laws are broken
To question what the oracle has spoken?   130
Should he not rather feel an obligation
To trust that most obliging declaration?
Enough, now. Your suspicions quite disgust me;
Why should I love a man who doesn't trust me?
I cannot understand why I continue,   135
Fool that I am, to take an interest in you.
I ought to choose a man less prone to doubt,
And give you something to be vexed about.
ALCESTE: Ah, what a poor enchanted fool I am;
These gentle words, no doubt, were all a sham,   140
But destiny requires me to entrust
My happiness to you, and so I must.
I'll love you to the bitter end, and see
How false and treacherous you dare to be.
CÉLIMÈNE: No, you don't really love me as you ought.   145
ALCESTE: I love you more than can be said or thought;
Indeed, I wish you were in such distress
That I might show my deep devotedness.
Yes, I could wish that you were wretchedly poor,
Unloved, uncherished, utterly obscure;   150
That fate had set you down upon the earth

Without possessions, rank, or gentle birth;
Then, by the offer of my heart, I might
Repair the great injustice of your plight;
155 I'd raise you from the dust, and proudly prove
The purity and vastness of my love.
CÉLIMÈNE: This is a strange benevolence indeed!
God grant that I may never be in need. . . .
Ah, here's Monsieur Dubois in quaint disguise.

Scene IV [*Célimène, Alceste, Dubois.*]

ALCESTE: Well, why this costume? Why those frightened
eyes?
What ails you?
DUBOIS: Well, Sir, things are most mysterious.
ALCESTE: What do you mean?
DUBOIS: I fear they're very serious.
ALCESTE: What?
DUBOIS: Shall I speak more loudly?
ALCESTE: Yes; speak out.
DUBOIS: Isn't there someone here, Sir?
5 ALCESTE: Speak, you lout!
Stop wasting time.
DUBOIS: Sir, we must slip away.
ALCESTE: How's that?
DUBOIS: We must decamp without delay.
ALCESTE: Explain yourself.
DUBOIS: I tell you we must fly.
ALCESTE: What for?
DUBOIS: We mustn't pause to say good-by.
ALCESTE: Now what d'you mean by all of this, you
10   clown?
DUBOIS: I mean, Sir, that we've got to leave this town.
ALCESTE: I'll tear you limb from limb and joint from
joint
If you don't come more quickly to the point.
DUBOIS: Well, Sir, today a man in a black suit,
15   Who wore a black and ugly scowl to boot,
Left us a document scrawled in such a hand
As even Satan couldn't understand.
It bears upon your lawsuit, I don't doubt;
But all hell's devils couldn't make it out.
20 ALCESTE: Well, well, go on. What then? I fail to see
How this event obliges us to flee.
DUBOIS: Well, Sir, an hour later, hardly more,
A gentleman who's often called before
Came looking for you in an anxious way.
25   Not finding you, he asked me to convey
(Knowing I could be trusted with the same)
The following message. . . . Now, what *was* his
name?
ALCESTE: Forget his name, you idiot. What did he say?
DUBOIS: Well, it was one of your friends, Sir, anyway.
30   He warned you to begone, and he suggested
That if you stay, you may well be arrested.
ALCESTE: What? Nothing more specific? Think, man,
think!
DUBOIS: No, Sir. He had me bring him pen and ink,

And dashed you off a letter which, I'm sure,
Will render things distinctly less obscure.   35
ALCESTE: Well — let me have it!
CÉLIMÈNE: What *is* this all about?
ALCESTE: God knows; but I have hopes of finding out.
How long am I to wait, you blitherer?
DUBOIS: (*after a protracted search for the letter*):
I must have left it on your table, Sir.
ALCESTE: I ought to . . .
CÉLIMÈNE: No, no, keep your self-control;   40
Go find out what's behind his rigmarole.
ALCESTE: It seems that fate, no matter what I do,
Has sworn that I may not converse with you;
But, Madam, pray permit your faithful lover
To try once more before the day is over.   45

ACT V • *Scene 1* [*Alceste, Philinte.*]

ALCESTE: No, it's too much. My mind's made up, I tell
you.
PHILINTE: Why should this blow, however hard,
compel you . . .
ALCESTE: No, no, don't waste your breath in argument;
Nothing you say will alter my intent;
This age is vile, and I've made up my mind   5
To have no further commerce with mankind.
Did not truth, honor, decency, and the laws
Oppose my enemy and approve my cause?
My claims were justified in all men's sight;
I put my trust in equity and right;   10
Yet, to my horror and the world's disgrace,
Justice is mocked, and I have lost my case!
A scoundrel whose dishonesty is notorious
Emerges from another lie victorious!
Honor and right condone his brazen fraud,   15
While rectitude and decency applaud!
Before his smirking face, the truth stands charmed,
And virtue conquered, and the law disarmed!
His crime is sanctioned by a court decree!
And not content with what he's done to me,   20
The dog now seeks to ruin me by stating
That I composed a book now circulating,
A book so wholly criminal and vicious
That even to speak its title is seditious!
Meanwhile Oronte, my rival, lends his credit   25
To the same libelous tale, and helps to spread it!
Oronte! a man of honor and of rank,
With whom I've been entirely fair and frank;
Who sought me out and forced me, willy-nilly,
To judge some verse I found extremely silly;   30
And who, because I properly refused
To flatter him, or see the truth abused,
Abets my enemy in a rotten slander!
There's the reward of honesty and candor!
The man will hate me to the end of time   35
For failing to commend his wretched rhyme!
And not this man alone, but all humanity
Do what they do from interest and vanity;

They prate of honor, truth, and righteousness,
40 But lie, betray, and swindle nonetheless.
Come then: man's villainy is too much to bear;
Let's leave this jungle and this jackal's lair.
Yes! treacherous and savage race of men,
You shall not look upon my face again.
45 PHILINTE: Oh, don't rush into exile prematurely;
Things aren't as dreadful as you make them, surely.
It's rather obvious, since you're still at large,
That people don't believe your enemy's charge.
Indeed, his tale's so patently untrue
50 That it may do more harm to him than you.
ALCESTE: Nothing could do that scoundrel any harm:
His frank corruption is his greatest charm,
And, far from hurting him, a further shame
Would only serve to magnify his name.
55 PHILINTE: In any case, his bald prevarication
Has done no injury to your reputation,
And you may feel secure in that regard.
As for your lawsuit, it should not be hard
To have the case reopened, and contest
This judgment . . .
60 ALCESTE: No, no, let the verdict rest.
Whatever cruel penalty it may bring,
I wouldn't have it changed for anything.
It shows the times' injustice with such clarity
That I shall pass it down to our posterity
65 As a great proof and signal demonstration
Of the black wickedness of this generation.
It may cost twenty thousand francs; but I
Shall pay their twenty thousand, and gain thereby
The right to storm and rage at human evil,
70 And send the race of mankind to the devil.
PHILINTE: Listen to me . . .
ALCESTE: Why? What can you possibly say?
Don't argue, Sir; your labor's thrown away.
Do you propose to offer lame excuses
For men's behavior and the times' abuses?
75 PHILINTE: No, all you say I'll readily concede:
This is a low, conniving age, indeed;
Nothing but trickery prospers nowadays,
And people ought to mend their shabby ways.
Yes, man's a beastly creature; but must we then
80 Abandon the society of men?
Here in the world, each human frailty
Provides occasion for philosophy,
And that is virtue's noblest exercise;
If honesty shone forth from all men's eyes,
85 If every heart were frank and kind and just,
What could our virtues do but gather dust
(Since their employment is to help us bear
The villainies of men without despair)?
A heart well-armed with virtue can endure . . .
90 ALCESTE: Sir, you're a matchless reasoner, to be sure;
Your words are fine and full of cogency;
But don't waste time and eloquence on me.
My reason bids me go, for my own good.
My tongue won't lie and flatter as it should;
95 God knows what frankness it might next commit,

And what I'd suffer on account of it.
Pray let me wait for Célimène's return
In peace and quiet. I shall shortly learn,
By her response to what I have in view,
Whether her love for me is feigned or true.   100
PHILINTE: Till then, let's visit Éliante upstairs.
ALCESTE: No, I am too weighed down with somber
cares.
Go to her, do; and leave me with my gloom
Here in the darkened corner of this room.
PHILINTE: Why, that's no sort of company, my friend;   105
I'll see if Éliante will not descend.

Scene II [*Célimène, Oronte, Alceste.*]

ORONTE: Yes, Madam, if you wish me to remain
Your true and ardent lover, you must deign
To give me some more positive assurance.
All this suspense is quite beyond endurance.
If your heart shares the sweet desires of mine,   5
Show me as much by some convincing sign;
And here's the sign I urgently suggest:
That you no longer tolerate Alceste,
But sacrifice him to my love, and sever
All your relations with the man forever.   10
CÉLIMÈNE: Why do you suddenly dislike him so?
You praised him to the skies not long ago.
ORONTE: Madam, that's not the point. I'm here to find
Which way your tender feelings are inclined.
Choose, if you please, between Alceste and me,   15
And I shall stay or go accordingly.
ALCESTE (*emerging from the corner*): Yes, Madam,
choose; this gentleman's demand
Is wholly just, and I support his stand.
I too am true and ardent; I too am here
To ask you that you make your feelings clear.   20
No more delays, now; no equivocation;
The time has come to make your declaration.
ORONTE: Sir, I've no wish in any way to be
An obstacle to your felicity.
ALCESTE: Sir, I've no wish to share her heart with you;   25
That may sound jealous, but at least it's true.
ORONTE: If, weighing us, she leans in your
direction . . .
ALCESTE: If she regards you with the least affection . . .
ORONTE: I swear I'll yield her to you there and then.
ALCESTE: I swear I'll never see her face again.   30
ORONTE: Now, Madam, tell us what we've come to
hear.
ALCESTE: Madam, speak openly and have no fear.
ORONTE: Just say which one is to remain your lover.
ALCESTE: Just name one name, and it will all be over.
ORONTE: What! Is it possible that you're undecided?   35
ALCESTE: What! Can your feelings possibly be divided?
CÉLIMÈNE: Enough: this inquisition's gone too far:
How utterly unreasonable you are!
Not that I couldn't make the choice with ease;
My heart has no conflicting sympathies   40

I know full well which one of you I favor,
And you'd not see me hesitate or waver.
But how can you expect me to reveal
So cruelly and bluntly what I feel?
45   I think it altogether too unpleasant
To choose between two men when both are present;
One's heart has means more subtle and more kind
Of letting its affections be divined,
Nor need one be uncharitably plain
50   To let a lover know he loves in vain.
ORONTE: No, no, speak plainly; I for one can stand it.
I beg you to be frank.
ALCESTE: And I demand it.
The simple truth is what I wish to know,
And there's no need for softening the blow.
55   You've made an art of pleasing everyone,
But now your days of coquetry are done:
You have no choice now, Madam, but to choose,
For I'll know what to think if you refuse;
I'll take your silence for a clear admission
60   That I'm entitled to my worst suspicion.
ORONTE: I thank you for this ultimatum, Sir.
And I may say I heartily concur.
CÉLIMÈNE: Really, this foolishness is very wearing:
Must you be so unjust and overbearing?
65   Haven't I told you why I must demur?
Ah, here's Éliante; I'll put the case to her.

Scene III [*Éliante, Philinte, Célimène, Oronte, Alceste.*]

CÉLIMÈNE: Cousin, I'm being persecuted here
By these two persons, who, it would appear,
Will not be satisfied till I confess
Which one I love the more, and which the less,
5   And tell the latter to his face that he
Is henceforth banished from my company.
Tell me, has ever such a thing been done?
ÉLIANTE: You'd best not turn to me; I'm not the one
To back you in a matter of this kind:
10   I'm all for those who frankly speak their mind.
ORONTE: Madam, you'll search in vain for a defender.
ALCESTE: You're beaten, Madam, and may as well
surrender.
ORONTE: Speak, speak, you must; and end this awful
strain.
ALCESTE: Or don't, and your position will be plain.
15   ORONTE: A single word will close this painful scene.
ALCESTE: But if you're silent, I'll know what you mean.

Scene IV [*Arsinoé, Célimène, Éliante, Alceste, Philinte, Acaste, Clitandre, Oronte.*]

ACASTE (*to Célimène*): Madam, with all due deference,
we two
Have come to pick a little bone with you.

CLITANDRE (*to Oronte and Alceste*): I'm glad you're
present, Sirs, as you'll soon learn,
Our business here is also your concern.
ARSINOÉ (*to Célimène*): Madam, I visit you so soon
again   5
Only because of these two gentlemen,
Who came to me indignant and aggrieved
About a crime too base to be believed.
Knowing your virtue, having such confidence in it,
I couldn't think you guilty for a minute,   10
In spite of all their telling evidence;
And, rising above our little difference
I've hastened here in friendship's name to see
You clear yourself of this great calumny.
ACASTE: Yes, Madam, let us see with what
composure   15
You'll manage to respond to this disclosure.
You lately sent Clitandre this tender note.
CLITANDRE: And this one, for Acaste, you also
wrote.
ACASTE (*to Oronte and Alceste*): You'll recognize this
writing, Sirs, I think;
The lady is so free with pen and ink   20
That you must know it all too well, I fear.
But listen: this is something you should hear.

"How absurd you are to condemn my lighteart-
edness in society, and to accuse me of being happiest
in the company of others. Nothing could be more   25
unjust; and if you do not come to me instantly and
beg pardon for saying such a thing, I shall never forgive you as long as I live. Our big bumbling friend the
Viscount . . ."

What a shame that he's not here.   30

"Our big bumbling friend the Viscount, whose
name stands first in your complaint, is hardly a man
to my taste; and ever since the day I watched him
spend three-quarters of an hour spitting into a well,
so as to make circles in the water, I have been unable 35
to think highly of him. As for the little Marquess . . ."

In all modesty, gentlemen, that is I.

"As for the little Marquess, who sat squeezing my
hand for such a long while yesterday, I find him in all 40
respects the most trifling creature alive; and the only
things of value about him are his cape and his sword.
As for the man with the green ribbons . . ."

(*To Alceste.*) It's your turn now, Sir.

"As for the man with the green ribbons, he   45
amuses me now and then with his bluntness and his
bearish ill-humor; but there are many times indeed
when I think him the greatest bore in the world. And
as for the sonneteer . . ."

50   (*To Oronte.*) Here's your helping.

        "And as for the sonneteer, who has taken it into
      his head to be witty, and insists on being an author in
      the teeth of opinion, I simply cannot be bothered to
      listen to him, and his prose wearies me quite as much
55   as his poetry. Be assured that I am not always so well-
      entertained as you suppose; that I long for your
      company, more than I dare to say, at all these enter-
      tainments to which people drag me; and that the
      presence of those one loves is the true and perfect
60   seasoning to all one's pleasures."

      CLITANDRE: And now for me.

        "Clitandre, whom you mention, and who so
      pesters me with his saccharine speeches, is the last
      man on earth for whom I could feel any affection. He
65   is quite mad to suppose that I love him, and so are
      you, to doubt that you are loved. Do come to your
      senses; exchange your suppositions for his; and visit
      me as often as possible, to help me bear the annoy-
      ance of his unwelcome attentions."

70   It's sweet character that these letters show,
      And what to call it, Madam, you well know.
      Enough. We're off to make the world acquainted
      With this sublime self-portrait that you've
           painted.
      ACASTE: Madam, I'll make you no farewell oration;
75   No, you're not worthy of my indignation.
      Far choicer hearts than yours, as you'll discover,
      Would like this little Marquess for a lover.

Scene V [*Célimène, Éliante, Arsinoé, Alceste, Oronte, Philinte.*]

ORONTE: So! After all those loving letters you
           wrote,
      You turn on me like this, and cut my throat!
      And your dissembling, faithless heart, I find,
      Has pledged itself by turns to all mankind!
5   How blind I've been! But now I clearly see;
      I thank you, Madam, for enlightening me.
      My heart is mine once more, and I'm content;
      The loss of it shall be your punishment.
      (*To Alceste.*) Sir, she is yours; I'll seek no more to
           stand
10   Between your wishes and this lady's hand.

Scene VI [*Célimène, Éliante, Arsinoé, Alceste, Philinte.*]

ARSINOÉ: (*to Célimène*): Madam, I'm forced to speak.
           I'm far too stirred
      To keep my counsel, after what I've heard.

I'm shocked and staggered by your want of morals.
It's not my way to mix in others' quarrels;   5
But really, when this fine and noble spirit,
This man of honor and surpassing merit,
Laid down the offering of his heart before you,
How *could* you . . .
ALCESTE: Madam, permit me, I implore you,
      To represent myself in this debate.   10
      Don't bother, please, to be my advocate.
      My heart, in any case, could not afford
      To give your services their due reward;
      And if I chose, for consolation's sake,
      Some other lady, 'twould not be you I'd take.
ARSINOÉ: What makes you think you could, Sir? And   15
           how dare you
      Imply that I've been trying to ensnare you?
      If you can for a moment entertain
      Such flattering fancies, you're extremely vain.
      I'm not so interested as you suppose   20
      In Célimène's discarded gigolos.
      Get rid of that absurd illusion, do.
      Women like me are not for such as you.
      Stay with this creature, to whom you're so
           attached;
      I've never seen two people better matched.

Scene VII [*Célimène, Éliante, Alceste, Philinte.*]

ALCESTE (*to Célimène*): Well, I've been still throughout
           this exposé,
      Till everyone but me has said his say.
      Come, have I shown sufficient self-restraint?
      And may I now . . .
CÉLIMÈNE: Yes, make your just complaint.   5
      Reproach me freely, call me what you will;
      You've every right to say I've used you ill.
      I've wronged you, I confess it; and in my shame
      I'll make no effort to escape the blame.
      The anger of those others I could despise;   10
      My guilt toward you I sadly recognize.
      Your wrath is wholly justified, I fear
      I know how culpable I must appear,
      I know all things bespeak my treachery,
      And that, in short, you've grounds for hating me.
      Do so; I give you leave.   15
ALCESTE: Ah, traitress — how,
      How should I cease to love you, even now?
      Though mind and will were passionately bent
      On hating you, my heart would not consent.
      (*To Éliante and Philinte.*) Be witness to my
           madness, both of you;   20
      See what infatuation drives one to;
      But wait; my folly's only just begun,
      And I shall prove to you before I'm done
      How strange the human heart is, and how far
      From rational we sorry creatures are.
      (*To Célimène.*) Woman, I'm willing to forget your   25
           shame,

And clothe your treacheries in a sweeter name;
I'll call them youthful errors, instead of crimes,
And lay the blame on these corrupting times.
My one condition is that you agree
30 To share my chosen fate, and fly with me
To that wild, trackless, solitary place
In which I shall forget the human race.
Only by such a course can you atone
For those atrocious letters; by that alone
35 Can you remove my present horror of you,
And make it possible for me to love you.
CÉLIMÈNE: What! *I* renounce the world at my young
      age,
And die of boredom in some hermitage?
ALCESTE: Ah, if you really loved me as you ought,
You wouldn't give the world a moment's
40   thought;
Must you have me, and all the world beside?
CÉLIMÈNE: Alas, at twenty one is terrified
Of solitude. I fear I lack the force
And depth of soul to take so stern a course.
45 But if my hand in marriage will content you,
Why, there's a plan which I might well consent to,
And . . .
ALCESTE: No, I detest you now. I could excuse
Everything else, but since you thus refuse
50 To love me wholly, as a wife should do,
And see the world in me, as I in you,
Go! I reject your hand, and disenthrall
My heart from your enchantments, once for all.

Scene VIII [*Éliante, Alceste, Philinte.*]

ALCESTE (*to Éliante*): Madam, your virtuous beauty
      has no peer;
Of all this world you only are sincere;
I've long esteemed you highly, as you know;
Permit me ever to esteem you so,
And if I do not now request your hand,   5
Forgive me, Madam, and try to understand.
I feel unworthy of it; I sense that fate
Does not intend me for the married state,
That I should do you wrong by offering you
My shattered heart's unhappy residue,   10
And that in short . . .
ÉLIANTE: Your argument's well taken:
Nor need you fear that I shall feel forsaken.
Were I to offer him this hand of mine,
Your friend Philinte, I think, would not decline.
PHILINTE: Ah, Madam, that's my heart's most
      cherished goal,   15
For which I'd gladly give my life and soul.
ALCESTE (*to Éliante and Philinte*): May you be true to
      all you now profess,
And so deserve unending happiness.
Meanwhile, betrayed and wronged in everything,
I'll flee this bitter world where vice is king,   20
And seek some spot unpeopled and apart
Where I'll be free to have an honest heart.
PHILINTE: Come, Madam, let's do everything we can
To change the mind of this unhappy man.

COMMENTARY

Lionel Gossman (*b. 1929*)
ALCESTE'S LOVE FOR CÉLIMÈNE   *1963*

What underlies Alceste's unlikely infatuation with Célimène? Gossman suggests that Alceste is playing to the very people of fashion whom he affects to look down on; consequently, he must conceal the real reasons for his love.

In reality, Alceste's love for Célimène is neither super-rational (above all reason and all explanation) nor irrational (below all reason and explanation). It is quite simply a peculiar and contradictory fascination which goes by the name of love in the vocabulary of the Alcestes of the world. It *can* be explained, and the explanation reveals that far from being the sincere and spontaneous being he says he is, Alceste is as calculating as anyone else.

It is precisely because Célimène is the most sought after and *worldly* of women (to all *appearances* the most unsuitable for Alceste) that he falls in love with her. It is not Célimène that Alceste loves or desires. She is irrelevant *as a person* to his "love." It is the world that he seeks to reach and possess through her. To have at his feet this woman whom all the world admires and courts would be to win the recognition of the world for himself. Alceste's love is entirely mediated by those very "gens à la mode"° for whom he so loudly protests his contempt. He "loves" Célimène because she has what he wants — the admiration of the world — and cannot admit he wants, without at the same time admitting that he is not the free, frank, and independent person he wants to be admired as. The object of his desire is thus also his unavowed rival, and this *for the very same reason* that she is the object of his desire. While he protests his love for Célimène, Alceste must therefore conceal the real reason for this love by affecting to deplore her participation in the "false" society of the *gens à la mode* and to despise her charms and her popularity. The final break with Célimène strikingly illustrates the ambiguity that characterizes Alceste's entire relationship with her from the beginning. Alceste calls on witnesses to observe how superior and disinterested his love is compared to the love of the elegant suitors who have abandoned Célimène, while at the same time he affirms before them his own contempt for it as unworthy of him:

> *Vous voyez* ce que peut une indigne tendresse,
> Et je vous fais tous deux *témoins* de ma foiblesse.
> Mais, à vous dire vrai, ce n'est pas encor tout,
> Et *vous allez me voir* la pousser jusqu'au bout,
> *Montrer* que c'est à tort que sages on nous nomme,
> Et que dans tous les coeurs il est toujours de l'homme.
> [V, VII, 19–24][1]

Having once proved how different his love is from that of Célimène's frivolous and calculating suitors, however, Alceste is only too quick to use her unwillingness to follow him to his desert as an excuse to drop her. Célimène without her suitors can have no attraction for Alceste.

Those who fall for Alceste's argument about the irrationality of passion are his dupes. Alceste cannot accept in the front rank of his own consciousness, or admit to others, that his whole life is pure posturing before others, that he who claims to be sincere and spontaneous is as preoccupied with the public as anybody and as mediated by it as those whom he charges with acting parts for others. Is he not, after all, the only person in the world who does not posture, whose emotions spring directly from the heart and who speaks nothing but what he really thinks and feels? Alceste uses the myth of the irrationality of passion to hide from others and from himself a character that is every bit as cold and ungenerous as the characters of those he criticizes for their coldness and lack of generosity.[. . .]

Alceste's life is in an important sense a life not of participation but of demonstration. This is one way in which he differs from the tragic heroes of Racine. The scandalous contradiction between the ideal and the real, between being and appearance, between the world of absolute values and the world of contingent opportunities is at the heart of seventeenth-century tragedy. There is never any danger, however, that Alceste will share in the somber destinies of Racine's heroes. His

---

"gens à la mode": Fashionable people.
[1]V, IV, 1751–56 of original text; italics added by Gossman.

world is far removed from theirs. He does not stake his destiny, as Junie or Andromaque or Monime° does, on living an authentic life in a world of inauthenticity. The inauthenticity of the world is not a menace to him; on the contrary, it is the very source of all his satisfactions. It provides the basis for his own superiority and he spends his time not in a real struggle to reach authenticity, but in endless efforts to have his superiority recognized by the very world of inauthenticity which he affects to detest. The absence of value in the world becomes, with Alceste, a matter for personal self-congratulation. Far from threatening his existence, the world of lies and deceit founds it. He exhausts himself in theatrical gestures, because all his wrestling with the ideal and the real, all his disgust with the world's falseness, however painfully experienced subjectively, is, objectively viewed, nothing but vain, ineffectual, and deeply inauthentic posturing. He does not really suffer because life is full of pretense and selfishness, because men have made their lives so vain and stupid. He suffers because he cannot bear to be like others and because others refuse him the adulation which he wants from them.[. . .]

Alceste acts the part of an absolute, but no one accepts his absoluteness: He loses his lawsuit, he fails to make Célimène submit to him, and he is laughed at by the world at large. He is an absolute in the world of his own conceptualizing alone, and thither he withdraws to decide for himself the fate of all his battles. The desert to which Alceste has always thought of withdrawing and to which he makes as if to withdraw at the end of the comedy is the world of his own mind. In it there is nothing to contradict his absoluteness, but there is unfortunately nothing to confirm it either. Alceste's difficulty is that his absoluteness can be experienced as real only with reference to others. Withdrawal to the desert cannot therefore be a final solution. It can only be an *act,* just as his rejection of Philinte at the beginning of the play was an act. This withdrawal requires an audience to watch it; and this hermit seeks not to escape but to be pursued. Alceste's withdrawal is simply a pose. And this is the very marrow of Molière's play. Alceste literally *joue la comédie.*° He is perpetually play-acting, whether we think of his passion for Célimène or of his passion for justice, and in this respect he resembles Molière's other comic heroes.

Junie . . . Andromaque . . . Monime: Characters in plays by Racine.
joue la comédie: Plays a sham part; play-acts.

Nineteenth-Century Drama through the Turn of the Century

Technical Innovations

Technically, theaters changed more during the period between 1800 and 1900 than in any comparable earlier period. The introduction of gas jets early in the century had a major effect. Now, light could be dimmed or raised as needed; the house could be gradually and entirely darkened. With gaslight onstage, selective lighting contributed to the emotional effect of plays and allowed actors to move deeper into the stage instead of playing important scenes on the apron. With the advent of elaborate scenery, as in the Drottningholm Theater in Sweden, lighting devices were often placed behind the proscenium pillars and scenery so that actors were more visible when they stood within the proscenium. The changes did not take place overnight, but as new theaters were built in the early nineteenth century (and as older theaters were refurbished) the apron shrank and the front doors leading to it disappeared. That change reinforced the nineteenth-century practice of treating the proscenium opening as the imaginary "fourth wall" of a room. The elaborate framing of Chicago's Auditorium (1889, Figure 10) allowed for complex lighting systems as well as the framing of the proscenium, which acts as a "window" into the dramatic action.

Numerous other technical innovations were introduced into the new theaters, such as London's Drury Lane Theatre, which was rebuilt in 1812. Highly sophisticated machinery lifted actors from below the stage, and flies or fly galleries above the stage permitted scene changes and other dramatic alterations and effects. The technical resources of the modern theaters in Europe were extraordinary by midcentury.

Romantic Drama

The architectural and lighting changes were complex and uneven, but they accompanied changes in styles of acting, styles of plays, and the content of plays. Early nineteenth-century English Romantic poets produced a variety of plays espousing a new philosophy of the individual, a philosophy of democracy, and a cry for personal liberation, but unfortunately their plays failed to capture the popular stage. William Wordsworth's *The Borderers* (1796–1797), concerning political struggles on the border between England and Scotland,

Figure 10. Elaborately decorated proscenium arch. Auditorium, Chicago, 1889.

was a failure. A recent production (1989) at Yale University revealed its static, declamatory nature. Even a play with an inherently dramatic subject such as *The Fall of Robespierre* (1794) by Robert Southey and Samuel Taylor Coleridge — concerning the violent excesses of the French Revolution of 1789 — could not stir popular audiences. John Keats wrote *Otho the Great* (1819) about a tenth-century dispute between brothers and a father and son. He hoped that the great actor and producer Edmund Kean would want to produce the play, but Kean declined. Percy Bysshe Shelley wrote *The Cenci* (1819) when he was in Italy, hoping it would be produced on the English stage, but it was banned by the censors. The style of Shelley's play has been compared with John Webster's *The Dutchess of Malfi* (1613); its themes include violent death and insanity. George Gordon, Lord Byron, wrote several plays that had admirers but were not successful. *Manfred* (1817) is a CLOSET DRAMA — a play meant to be read, not produced. It presents a powerful portrait of a brooding intellect that could, in some ways, be compared with Hamlet. Allardyce Nicoll, the British drama historian and critic, has said of this and other Romantic plays that "audiences and readers familiar with *Lear* and *Macbeth* and *Othello* could not be expected to feel a thrill of wonder and delight in the contemplation of works so closely akin to these in general aim and yet so far removed from them in freshness of imaginative power."

French and German Romantic dramatists were more successful than their English counterparts. Johann Wolfgang von Goethe (1749–1832), one of Germany's most important playwrights, produced a number of successful plays in the late eighteenth century. Then came his masterpiece, *Faust* (1808, 1832), in two parts, with a scope and grandeur of concept that challenged the theaters of his day. The play opens in heaven, with Mephistopheles presenting his plan for tempting Faust; Faust signs over his soul to Mephistopheles in return for one moment of perfect joy. Faust was willing to risk all in his efforts to live life to its fullest, and despite his sins he was admired as a hero. Faust's self-analytic individualism, marked by a love of excess and a capacity for deep feeling and frightening intensity, has fascinated the German mind ever since Goethe rediscovered him. His development of Faust as a psychologically complex character contrasts with Marlowe's version in *Doctor Faustus*.

Another important force in German theater was Johann Cristoph Friedrich von Schiller (1759–1805), whose early play *The Robbers* (1781) was written when he was twenty-two. This still-popular (and still-produced) play reminds English audiences of the legend of Robin Hood since its hero, Karl von Moor, is a robber admirable for his generosity and seriousness. His adversary is his evil brother, who dominates the castle, the emblem of local repressive political power. Schiller was a highly successful playwright throughout the late eighteenth century. In the early nineteenth century he produced several popular historical plays such as *Maria Stuart* (1800) on Scotland's Queen Mary, the ill-fated cousin of Queen Elizabeth I. *The Maid of Orleans* (1801) told the story of Joan of Arc, the French heroine who led her army to victory only to be burned at the stake to satisfy political and religious exigencies. Both plays evoke deep sympathy for their heroines and both have been noted for their sentimentality. His last play, *William Tell* (1804), like *The Robbers,* tells the story of a heroic individual's fight against the oppressive forces of an evil baron. Schiller made the story of William Tell universal, and his theatrical successes were soon known throughout Europe and the Americas.

In France, the Romantic tragedy held sway for some time in the 1830s. Victor Hugo (1802–1885) had a great success in *Hernani* (1830), although critics and writers who insisted on classical rules were so disturbed by its innovation that they made disturbances in the theater. They attended only to jeer the pardon of Hernani, an outlaw, by Don Carlos, king of Spain. At the end Hernani and Donna Sol, his loved one, drink a poison so as to die together because they could not live together. Alexandre Dumas (1802–1879), soon to be famous as a novelist, produced a number of successful, influential plays, among them *Henry III and His Court* (1829) and *The Tower of Nesle* (1832).

Melodrama

MELODRAMA developed in Germany and France in the mid- and late eighteenth century. The *melo* in *melodrama* means "song"; incidental music was a hallmark of melodrama. In England certain regulations separated Covent Garden, Drury Lane, and the Haymarket — the three "major" theaters with exclusive licenses to produce spoken drama — from the "minor" theaters, which had to produce musical plays such as burlettas, which resembled our comic operettas. Eventually, the minor theaters began to produce plays with spoken dialogue and accompanying music, heralding a new, popular style. Melodrama proved to be one of the most durable innovations of the late eighteenth century.

In Germany, August Friedrich Ferdinand von Kotzebue (1761–1819) and in France Guilbert de Pixérécourt (1773–1844), who coined the term *melodrama,* began developing the melodramatic play. Many of these dramas used background music that altered according to the mood of the scene, a tradition that continues in films and on television. Nineteenth-century melodramas featured familiar crises: the virtuous maiden fallen into the hands of an unscrupulous landlord; the father who, lamenting over a portrait of his dead wife, discovers that he is speaking to his — until then — lost daughter. Nineteenth-century melodramas had well-defined heroes, heroines, and villains. The plots were filled with surprises and unlikely twists designed to amaze and delight the audience. Most of the plays were explicitly sentimental, depending on a strong emotional appeal with clear-cut and relatively decisive endings.

Though not popular later on, the plays of Kotzebue and Pixérécourt pleased their contemporary audiences and helped establish melodrama as a dominant style for the first six decades of the nineteenth century. Kotzebue published thirty-six plays (twenty-two were produced) and enjoyed an immense popularity in England and the United States. Translated into several languages, his works influenced later popular playwrights, who admired his ability to invent and resolve complex plot situations. An example of the ending of *La-Peyrouse* (1798) may provide a taste of the mode. The hero, cast ashore on a desert island, falls in love with the "savage" Malvina. When he rejoins his wife, Adelaide, he is presented with the problem of what to do with Malvina. Here is the women's solution:

MALVINA (*turning affectionately, yet with trembling to Adelaide*): I have prayed for thee, and for myself — let us be sisters!

ADELAIDE: Sisters! (*She remains some moments lost in thought.*) Sisters! Sweet girl, you have awakened a consoling idea in my bosom! Yes, we will be sisters, and this man shall be our brother! Share him we cannot, nor can either possess him singly. (*With enthusiasm.*) We, the sisters, will inhabit one hut, he shall dwell in another. We will educate our children, he shall assist us both — by day we will make but one family, at night we will separate — how say you? will you consent? . . . (*Extending her arms to La-Peyrouse.*) A sisterly embrace!

In France Pixérécourt produced a similar and highly successful drama that pleased his audiences. Not everyone was pleased, however. Goethe resigned his office from the Weimar Court Theatre when Pixérécourt's *The Dog of Montargis* was produced in 1816 because he did not want to be associated with any play that had a dog as its hero.

Not all these plays have been forgotten. Alexandre Dumas's *La Dame aux camélias* (Camille) was a theatrical hit in 1852 and has remained popular ever since, inspiring the Verdi opera *La Traviata* (1853) and revivals and adaptations up to the present, including the British playwright Pam Gems's feminist version (1987), starring Kathleen Turner. Based on a woman Dumas knew in

Paris, it is the story of a wealthy young man who falls in love with a courtesan, Marguerite Gauthier. Like Angellica in *The Rover,* she has manipulated men throughout her life, but now she is truly in love with Armand. The young man's father opposes the match, but even he is moved by the majesty of their love. Eventually, the father faces Marguerite and convinces her that if she really loves his son, she will let him go since their union can bring nothing but harm to Armand. She then fabricates a contempt for Armand and dismisses him, broken-hearted. Later, after they have been separated and she has fallen deathly ill, Armand learns the truth and rushes to her. On her deathbed Armand professes his love as she dies in his arms.

In the United States, George Aiken produced another long-lasting and influential drama, *Uncle Tom's Cabin* (1852), based on Harriet Beecher Stowe's novel. Stowe, a prominent northern abolitionist, poured all her anger at slavery into her novel. Aiken's stage version played for three hundred nights in its first production and across the nation more than a quarter of a million times. Some of its characters — Uncle Tom, Little Eva, Sambo, Topsy, and Simon Legree — live on in the popular imagination, but despite the contemporary interest in Stowe and in this play, the paternalistic subtitle, "Life among the Lowly," marks its era.

The Well-Made Play

Early in the nineteenth century, a Frenchman with an unusual theatrical gift for pleasing popular audiences began a career that spanned fifty successful years. Eugène Scribe (1791–1861) may have produced as many as four or five hundred plays. He employed collaborators and mined novels and stories for his plots, producing tragedies, comedies, opera libretti, and vaudeville one-act pieces. He quickly determined that the plot held the attention of the audience and that rambling character studies were of lesser interest. Consequently, he developed a formula for dramatic action and made sure that all his works fit into it. The result was the creation of a "factory" for making plays. Among the elements of Scribe's formula were the following:

1. A careful exposition telling the audience what the situation is, usually including one or more secrets to be revealed later.
2. Surprises, such as letters to be opened at a critical moment and identities to be revealed later.
3. Suspense that builds steadily throughout the play, usually sustained by cliff-hanging situations and characters who miss each other by way of carefully timed entrances and exits. At critical moments, characters lose important papers or misplace identifying jewelry, for instance.
4. A CLIMAX late in the play when the secrets are revealed and the hero confronts his antagonists and succeeds.
5. A DENOUEMENT, the resolution of the drama when all the loose ends are drawn together and explanations are made that render all the action plausible.

It should be evident from this description that the WELL-MADE PLAY still thrives, not only on the stage but also in films and on television. Scribe's emphasis on plot was sensational for his time, and his success was unrivaled; however, none of his plays has survived in contemporary performance. Only one, *Adrienne*

Lecouvreur (1849), the story of a famous actress poisoned by a rival, is mentioned by critics as interesting because of its depth of characterization. Scribe was superficial and brilliant — a winning combination in theater at the time. He had numerous imitators and prepared the way for later developments in theater.

The Rise of Realism

Technical changes in theaters during the latter part of the nineteenth century continued at a rapid pace. When limelight was added to gas, the result was bright, intense lighting onstage; in the last decades of the century electric light heralded a new era in lighting design. Good lighting generally demanded detailed and authentic scenery; the dreamy light produced by gas often hid imperfections that were now impossible to disguise. The new Madison Square Theater (1879) in New York was built with elevators that allowed its stage, complete with detailed and realistic scenery as well as actors, to be raised into position. European theaters had developed similar capacities.

In the 1840s accurate period costumes began to be the norm for historical plays. In the Elizabethan theater, contemporary clothing had been worn onstage, but by the mid-1800s costume designers were researching historical periods and producing costumes that aimed at historical accuracy.

In addition to offering lifelike scenery, lighting, and costumes, the theaters of the latter part of the century also featured plays whose circumstances and language were recognizable, contemporary, and believable. Even the sentimental melodramas seemed more realistic than productions of *King Lear* or *Macbeth*, plays that were still popular. The work of Scribe, including his historical plays, used a relatively prosaic everyday language. The situations may not seem absolutely lifelike to our eyes, but in their day they prepared the way for realism.

Changes in philosophy also contributed to the development of a realistic drama. Émile Zola (1840–1902) preached a doctrine of NATURALISM, demanding that drama avoid the artificiality of convoluted plot and urging a drama of natural, lifelike action. He intended his work to help change social conditions in France. His naturalistic novel *Nana* (1880) focused on a courtesan whose life came to a terrifying end. The play *Thérèse Raquin* (1873), based on Zola's novel of the same name, told the story of a woman and her lover who murder her husband and then commit suicide out of a sense of mutual guilt. There are no twists, surprises, or even much suspense in the play. Zola's subjects seem to have been uniformly grim, and naturalism became associated with the darker side of life.

REALISM, which avoided mechanical "clockwork" plots with their artificially contrived conclusions, began in the later years of the eighteenth century (some scholars claim to see evidence of it even earlier, in the work of Middleton) and progressed steadily to the end of the nineteenth century. In the realistic plays of Henrik Ibsen (1828–1906) and August Strindberg (1849–1912), the details of the setting, the costuming, and the circumstances of the action were so fully realized as to convince audiences that they were listening in on life itself. (See Figure 11 for an example of a realistic stage setting.)

In England, Oscar Wilde (1854–1900), poet, novelist, and playwright, offered an alternative to both melodrama and realistic drama near the end of

Figure 11. Realistic setting in a 1941 production of Anton Chekhov's *The Cherry Orchard*.

the century. Wilde had spent much of his literary life promoting the philosophy of art for art's sake. He asserted that the pleasure of poetry was in its sounds, images, and thoughts. Poetry and drama did not serve religious, political, social, or even personal goals. For Wilde, art served itself. He was such a brilliant conversationalist that the Irish poet-playwright W. B. Yeats declared him the only person he ever heard who spoke complete, rounded sentences that sounded as if he had written and polished them the night before. His witticisms were often barbed and vicious but always incisive and perceptive. He became famous for his bright, witty comedies. *The Importance of Being Earnest* (1895), sometimes wrongly accused of being about nothing, is the most performed. It is an unsentimental, witty, and sometimes brittle comedy that dissects English upper-class attitudes that most of his audience would have taken for granted.

Wilde competed with numerous comic playwrights in England and abroad, such as the enormously successful Arthur Wing Pinero (1855–1934) and W. S. Gilbert (1836–1911) in England and Georges Feydeau (1862–1921) in France. None, though, could manage the unusual combination of wit and seriousness that marks Wilde's achievement. Another important competitor was also an Irish playwright, Bernard Shaw (1856–1950), whose plays were also comic and serious, such as *Arms and the Man* (1894), *You Never Can Tell* (1898), and *Pygmalion* (1913). But Shaw is probably best known for his plays of ideas — plays in which an underlying idea or principle drives the action — such as *Mrs. Warren's Profession* (1898), *Man and Superman* (1903), and *Major Barbara* (1905).

After a disappointing beginning as a playwright, Anton Chekhov (1860–1904) worked with the Moscow Arts Theatre under the directorship of Konstantin Stanislavski (1865–1938), one of the most influential figures in modern western drama. Stanislavski emphasized "inner realism" by having the actor become the character even in situations off stage by developing improvisational experiences to let the actor explore the character in situations other than those within the play. The Stanislavski Method helped the actor become the part, rather than just play the part. Chekhov and Stanislavski worked together to produce Chekhov's plays at a time when Chekhov felt himself a failure as a dramatist.

The first production of Chekhov's *The Seagull* (1896), his sixth major staged play, was a failure. Stanislavski convinced Chekhov to give it to his company to produce, resulting in an important triumph. Chekhov then reworked an earlier play into *Uncle Vanya* (1899) for Stanislavski and it, too, was a hit. *Three Sisters* (1901) was not successful in its first performances, but it later became known as one of Chekhov's finest works. His last play, *The Cherry Orchard* (1904), was put on by Stanislavski's company and has become one of the most important works of twentieth-century drama. Chekhov died of a heart attack soon after the play's first production. Today Chekhov's legacy continues, with all his major plays staged throughout the world in the latter half of the twentieth century. Thus one of the most important nineteenth-century writers led the way to new developments in twentieth-century drama that are still evident today on the stage as well as in films and on television. Modern treatments of Chekhov's plays include Michael Picardie's adaptation of *The Cherry Orchard* to South Africa and Brian Friel's adaptation to Ireland. Mustapha Matura's *Trinidad Sisters* (1988) moves *Three Sisters* to Trinidad, demonstrating in part the universal appeal of Chekhov's plays.

Nineteenth-Century Drama Timeline

DATE	THEATER	POLITICAL	SOCIAL/CULTURAL
1700–1800	**1759–1805:** Friedrich von Schiller, German playwright, author of *The Robbers* (1781) and *Maria Stuart* (1800)		
			1770–1827: Ludwig van Beethoven, German composer
	1761–1819: August Friedrich Ferdinand von Kotsebue, German playwright and one of the early developers of melodrama	**1775:** The American War of Independence begins at Concord, Massachusetts.	**1775–1817:** Jane Austen, English novelist
	1767–1787: *Sturm und Drang* period in German drama featuring the work of Goethe, Schiller, and others who rebelled against eighteenth-century rationalism	**1776:** The Declaration of Independence is signed. **1783:** Peace of Versailles: Britain recognizes the independence of the United States.	
	1773: The Swedish National Theater is established in Stockholm.	**1789:** French revolutionaries storm the Bastille as the French revolution sweeps over French society.	**1792–1822:** Percy Bysshe Shelley, English Romantic poet
	1773–1844: Guilbert de Pixérécourt, French playwright generally credited with originating the melodrama	**1793:** Louis XVI and his queen, Marie Antoinette, are guillotined. The reign of terror, a purge instituted by the revolutionary government of France, claims 35,000 lives in one year.	**1793:** Eli Whitney (1765–1825) invents the cotton gin. **1795:** British forces occupy the Cape of Good Hope. **1795–1821:** John Keats, English Romantic poet
	1791–1861: Eugène Scribe, French playwright, developer of the "well-made" play, author of *Adrienne Lecouvreur* (1849)	**1799:** Napoleon Bonaparte overthrows the Directory of France, the moderate government that replaced the government of terror.	**1798:** *Lyrical Ballads* is published by Wordsworth and Coleridge. **1799–1837:** Alexander Pushkin, Russian poet
1800–1900	**1806–1872:** Edwin Forrest, America's first great native-born actor	**1803:** The Louisiana Purchase doubles the area of the United States.	**1802–1885:** Victor Hugo, French novelist **1803–1882:** Ralph Waldo Emerson, American Transcendental philosopher, clergyman, and author
	1808 and 1832: German writer Johann Wolfgang von Goethe (1749–1832) produces his masterpiece, *Faust* (in two parts).	**1804:** Napoleon I (1769–1821) declares himself emperor of France. **1805:** Admiral Horatio Nelson's victory over Napoleon at Trafalgar establishes the supremacy of British naval forces.	**1805:** Gas lighting is introduced in Great Britain.
	1809–1852: Nikolai Gogol, Russian playwright, author of *The Inspector General* (1836)	**1811–1820:** The Regency period: George, Prince of Wales, acts as regent for George III, who was declared insane.	**1809–1852:** Louis Braille, French inventor of reading system for the blind
	1813–1837: Georg Büchner, German playwright, author of *Danton's Death* (1835) and *Woyzeck* (1836)	**1812:** The U.S. declares war on Britain. **1814:** Treaty of Ghent ends the War of 1812; Britain is defeated.	**1812–1870:** Charles Dickens, English novelist

DATE	THEATER	POLITICAL	SOCIAL/CULTURAL
1800–1900 (continued)	**1816:** Chestnut Street Theater in Philadelphia is the first theater to illuminate its stage with gas lighting.	**1815:** Napoleon is decisively defeated at the Battle of Waterloo.	**1816–1855:** Charlotte Bronte, English novelist
	1822–1890: Dion Boucicault, Irish American actor and writer of popular melodramas, among them *The Octoroon* (1859) and *The Colleen Bawn* (1860)	**1818:** Shaka ascends the Zulu throne in Southern Africa and initiates a period of military reform; he is assassinated in 1828.	**1817–1862:** Henry David Thoreau, American Transcendental writer and naturalist
	1828–1906: Henrik Ibsen, Norwegian playwright. Among his best-known works are *A Doll House* (1879) and *Hedda Gabler* (1890).	**1820:** Accession of George IV	**1820–1906:** Susan B. Anthony, American leader of the women's suffrage movement
		1820: The Missouri Compromise admits Maine as a free state and Missouri as a slave state.	**1821–1881:** Fyodor Dostoevsky, Russian novelist
	1830: *Hernani*, by the French novelist and playwright Victor Hugo (1802–1885), traditionally marks the beginning of French romanticism.	**1821:** Mexico declares its independence.	**1828–1910:** Leo Tolstoy, Russian novelist and philosopher
		1823: The Monroe Doctrine closes the American continent to European colonization.	**1830–1886:** Emily Dickinson, American poet
	1837: William Charles Macready (1793–1873), an English actor, is the first to use the limelight (or Drummond light), a prototype of the spotlight.		**1831:** William Lloyd Garrison (1805–1879), American abolitionist, founds the *Liberator*.
		1837: Queen Victoria begins her sixty-four-year reign in England.	**1833–1897:** Johannes Brahms, German composer
	1840–1902: Émile Zola, French writer and promoter of naturalism in literature. Among his works is the novel (also a play) *Thérèse Raquin* (1873).	**1839:** Beginning of the First opium War between England and China. The war ends in 1842 with the Treaty of Nanjing, which turns over Hong Kong to England and opens several Chinese ports to Western trade.	**1839:** Louis Daguerre (1789–1851) invents the daguerreotype, an early type of photograph.
			1840–1893: Peter Ilyich Tchaikovsky, Russian composer
			1843–1916: Henry James, American realist novelist
			1844: The telegraph is used for the first time.
			1845: Frederick Douglass (c. 1817–1895), African American abolitionist, publishes *Narrative of the Life of Frederick Douglass*.
			1845–1849: The great potato famine in Ireland kills nearly a million Irish; 1,600,000 immigrate to the United States.
	1849: The Astor Place Riot in New York is a result of the rivalry between the actors William Charles Macready and Edwin Forrest; twenty-two people are killed.	**1846–1848:** Mexican War over the United States' annexation of Texas. The Treaty of Guadalupe Hildago (1848) cedes Texas to the United States.	**1848:** The First U.S. Women's Rights Convention is held in Seneca Falls, N.Y.
			1848: California gold rush
	1849–1923: Sarah Bernhardt, French performer, perhaps the greatest actress of the nineteenth century		**1848:** Karl Marx, German political philosopher, writes *The Communist Manifesto*, with Friedrich Engels.
			1850: Tennyson succeeds Wordsworth as poet laureate of Great Britain.
	1849–1912: August Strindberg, Swedish playwright. Among his works are *Miss Julie* (1888) and *The Dream Play* (1902).	**1852:** Napoleon III declares himself emperor of France and rules until 1871.	**1851:** Herman Melville (1819–1891) publishes *Moby Dick*.
			1852: Harriet Beecher Stowe (1811–1896) publishes *Uncle Tom's Cabin*.

Nineteenth-Century Drama Timeline (continued)

DATE	THEATER	POLITICAL	SOCIAL/CULTURAL
1800–1900 (continued)	**1854–1900:** Oscar Wilde, English writer. His plays include *A Woman of No Importance* (1893) and *The Importance of Being Earnest* (1895).	**1857:** Czar Alexander II begins emancipation of serfs in Russia.	**1854–1856:** Scottish explorer David Livingstone crosses Africa.
	1856–1950: Bernard Shaw, Irish playwright. Among his works are *Mrs. Warren's Profession* (1898), *Major Barbara* (1905), and *Pygmalion* (1912).	**1860:** Abraham Lincoln is elected president. South Carolina secedes from the Union. **1861:** Italy is unified under Victor Emmanuel II. **1861–1865:** The Civil War is fought in the United States.	**1859:** Charles Darwin (1809–1882) publishes *On the Origin of Species by Natural Selection.*
	1860–1904: Anton Chekhov, Russian writer, author of *The Seagull* (1896) and *The Cherry Orchard* (1903)	**1862:** Otto von Bismarck is appointed prime minister of Prussia.	**1860s:** Louis Pasteur (1822–1895), French chemist, develops pasteurization.
	1870–1900: Golden Age of Peking (Beijing) Opera	**1865:** Abraham Lincoln is assassinated by the actor John Wilkes Booth at Ford's Theatre in Washington, D.C.	**1865–1939:** William Butler Yeats, Irish poet and playwright
	1871–1896: Gilbert and Sullivan write their comic operas, among them *H.M.S. Pinafore* (1878) and *The Pirates of Penzance* (1879).	**1869:** The Suez Canal opens. **1870–1871:** Franco-Prussian War	**1869:** The first transcontinental railroad in the United States is completed.
	1876: Opening of Richard Wagner's Festival Theater in Bayreuth, Germany. Among his works is the four-part *Der Ring des Nibelungen* (1853–1874).	**1871:** The German Empire is founded under Kaiser Wilhelm I. **1876:** At the Battle of the Little Bighorn, the Sioux defeat General George Custer's troops.	**1869–1959:** Frank Lloyd Wright, preeminent American architect **1876:** Alexander Graham Bell (1847–1922) invents the telephone. **1877:** Thomas Edison (1847–1931) invents the phonograph.
	1881: The Savoy Theatre is the first theater in London to be completely illuminated by electric light.	**1885:** The Congo becomes a personal possession of King Leopold II of Belgium.	**1879:** Thomas Edison invents the lightbulb.
	1887: Théâtre Libre is founded in Paris by André Antoine to pursue naturalism in subject matter and staging.	**1890:** The Battle of Wounded Knee ends the American Indians' wars of resistance; two hundred Indians are killed by the U.S. Army.	
	1890–1930: Vaudeville becomes one of the most popular forms of entertainment in the United States.	**1898:** The Spanish-American War. Cuban patriots demand independence and receive the military support of the United States. The 1898 Treaty of Paris gives Puerto Rico, Guam, the Philippines, and Cuba to the United States.	**1898–1976:** Paul Robeson, African American singer, actor, and civil rights activist
	1896: The first revolving stage is installed by Karl Lautenschlager at the Residenz Theater in Munich.		
	1898: The Moscow Art Theatre is founded under the direction of Konstantin Stanislavsky and Vladimir Nemirovich-Danchenko.	**1899–1902:** The Boer War (South African War) ends British supremacy in South Africa.	

Henrik Ibsen

Using the new style of realism, Henrik Ibsen (1828–1906) slowly and painfully became the most influential modern dramatist. Subjects that had been ignored on the stage became the center of his work. But his rise to fame was anything but direct. His family was extremely poor, and as a youth he worked in a drugstore in Grimstad, a seaport town in Norway. At seventeen he had an illegitimate child with a servant girl. At twenty-one he wrote his first play, in verse. In 1850, at the age of twenty-two, he left Grimstad for Oslo (then called Christiana) to become a student, but within a year he joined the new National Theater and stayed for six years, writing and directing.

In the 1850s he wrote numerous plays that did not bring him recognition: *St. John's Eve* (1853), *Lady Inger of Østraat* (1855), *Olaf Liljekrans* (1857),

Henrik Ibsen at age sixty-eight, six years after the first production of *Hedda Gabler*. He was the most influential playwright in Europe when this photograph was taken in 1896.

and *The Vikings at Helgeland* (1857). In the early 1860s, with a wife and daughter to support, he went through a period of serious self-doubt and despair, and his first play in five years, *Love's Comedy* (1862), was turned down for performance. Eventually, he got a job with the Christiana Theater and had a rare success with *The Pretenders* (1864), a historical play about thirteenth-century warriors vying for the vacant throne of Norway.

His breakthrough came with the publication in 1866 of the verse play *Brand,* which was written to be read and not performed. (It was first produced in 1885.) It is the portrait of a clergyman who takes the strictures of religion so seriously that he rejects the New Testament doctrine of love and accepts the Old Testament doctrine of the will of God. He destroys himself in the process and ends the play on a mountaintop in the Ice Church, facing an avalanche about to kill him. Out of the clouds comes the answer to his questions of whether love or will achieves salvation: "He is the God of Love." *Brand* made Ibsen famous. He followed it with another successful closet drama, *Peer Gynt* (1867), about a character, quite unlike Brand, who avoids the rigors of morality and ends up unable to know if he has been saved or condemned.

Despite these successes, Ibsen still struggled for recognition. It was not until 1877 that he had his first success in a play that experimented with the new realistic style of drama: *The Pillars of Society,* which probed behind the hypocrisies of Karsten Bernick, a merchant who prospers by all manner of double-dealing and betrayal of his relatives. Eventually, he admits his crimes but, instead of being punished, is welcomed back into society and is more successful than ever. This play gave Ibsen a reputation in Germany, where it was frequently performed, and prepared him for his great successes. *A Doll House* (1879), which he wrote in Italy, came two years later. It was more fully realistic in style than *The Pillars of Society* and, while immensely successful in Scandinavia, did not become widely known elsewhere for another ten years.

His next play, *Ghosts* (1881), was denounced violently because it dared to treat a subject that had been taboo on the stage: syphilis. *Ghosts* introduced a respectable family, the Alvings, who harbor the secret that the late father contracted the disease and passed it on to Oswald, his son. In addition, the theme of incest is suggested in the presence of Alving's illegitimate daughter, Regina, who falls in love with Oswald. This kind of material was so foreign to the late nineteenth-century stage that Ibsen was vilified and isolated by the literary community in Norway. He chose exile for a time in Rome, Amalfi, and Munich.

Ibsen's last years were filled with activity. He wrote some of his best-known plays in rapid succession: *An Enemy of the People* (1882), *The Wild Duck* (1884), *Hedda Gabler* (1890), *The Master Builder* (1892), and *John Gabriel Borkman* (1896). In 1891 he returned to live in Norway, where he died fifteen years later.

The most influential European dramatist in the late nineteenth century, Ibsen inspired emerging writers in the United States, Ireland, and many other nations. But his full influence was not felt until the early decades of the twentieth century, when other writers were able to spread the revolutionary doctrine that was implied in realism as practiced by Ibsen and Strindberg. Being direct, honest, and unsparing in treating character and theme became the normal mode of serious drama after Ibsen.

A DOLL HOUSE

Once Henrik Ibsen found his voice as a realist playwright, he began to develop plays centering on social problems and the problems of the individual struggling against the demands of society. In *A Doll House* (1879) he focused on the repression of women. It was a subject that deeply offended conservatives and was very much on the minds of progressive and liberal Scandinavians. It was therefore a rather daring theme. The play opens with the dutiful, eager wife Nora Helmer twittering like a lark and pattering like a squirrel pleasing her husband, Torvald. Helmer is consumed with propriety. As far as he is concerned, Nora is only a woman, an empty-headed ornament in a house designed to keep his life functioning smoothly.

Nora is portrayed as a macaroon-eating, sweet-toothed creature looking for ways to please her husband. When she reveals that she borrowed the money that took them to Italy for a year to save her husband's life, she shows us that she is made of much stronger stuff than anyone has given her credit for. Yet the manner in which she borrowed the money is technically criminal because she had to forge her father's signature, and she now finds herself at the mercy of the lender, Nils Krogstad.

From a modern perspective, Nora's action seems daring and imaginative rather than merely illegal and surreptitious. Torvald Helmer's moralistic position is to us essentially stifling. He condemns Nora's father for a similar failure

LEFT: For this 1906 production of Ibsen's *The Wild Duck*, the director, André Antoine, had the set constructed of Norwegian pine to achieve a high degree of realism. ABOVE: Edvard Munch's 1906 stage design for Max Reinhardt's production of Ibsen's *Ghosts* at the Kammerspiele in Berlin. Although *Ghosts* (1881) was written in Ibsen's realistic style, Munch's expressionistic lines and shadows seem to reflect the tendencies in Ibsen's late plays to move beyond realism to a more dreamlike structure.

to secure proper signatures, just as he condemns Nils Krogstad for doing the same. He condemns people for their crimes without considering their circumstances or motives. He is moralistic rather than moral.

The atmosphere of the Helmer household is oppressive. Everything is set up to amuse Torvald, and he lacks any awareness that other people might be his equal. Early in the play Ibsen establishes Nora's longings: she explains that to pay back her loan she has had to take in copying work, and rather than resent her labor, she observes that it made her feel wonderful, the way a man must feel. Ibsen said that his intention in the play was not primarily to promote the emancipation of women; it was to establish, as Ibsen's biographer Michael Meyer says, "that the primary duty of anyone was to find out who he or she really was and to become that person."

However, the play from the first was seen as addressing the problems of women, especially married women who were treated as their husbands' property. When the play was first performed, the slam of the door at Nora's leaving was much louder than it is today. It was shocking to late nineteenth-century society, which took Torvald Helmer's attitudes for granted. The first audiences probably were split in their opinions about Nora's actions. As Meyer reminds us, "No play had ever before contributed so momentously to the social debate, or been so widely and furiously discussed among people who were not normally interested in theatrical or even artistic matters." Although the critics in Copenhagen and England were very negative, the audiences were filled with curiosity and flocked to the theaters to see the play.

What the audiences saw was that once Nora is awakened, the kind of life Torvald imagines for her is death to Nora. Torvald cannot see how his self-absorbed concern and fear for his own social standing reveal his limitations and selfishness. Nora sees immediately the limits of his concern, and her only choice is to leave him so that she can grow morally and spiritually.

What she does and where she goes have been a matter of speculation since the play was first performed. Ibsen refused to encourage any specific conjecture. It is enough that she has the courage to leave. But the ending of the play bothered audiences as well as critics, and it was performed in Germany in 1880 with a happy ending that Ibsen himself wrote to forestall anyone else from doing so. The first German actress to play the part insisted that she would personally never leave her children and therefore would not do the play as written. In the revised version, instead of leaving, Nora is led to the door of her children's room and falls weeping as the curtain goes down. The so-called happy-ending version was played for a while in England and elsewhere. No one was satisfied with this ending, and eventually the play reverted to its original form.

Through the proscenium arch of the theater in Ibsen's day audiences were permitted to eavesdrop on themselves, since Ibsen clearly was analyzing their own mores. In a way the audience was looking at a dollhouse; but instead of containing miniature furniture and miniature people, it contained replicas of those watching. That very sense of intimacy, made possible by the late nineteenth-century theater, heightened the intensity of the play.

A Doll House in Performance

A Doll House was first produced in the Royal Theatre, Copenhagen, in December 1879. Despite its immediate success in Scandinavia and Germany, two years passed before the play appeared elsewhere and ten years before it appeared in England and America in a complete and accurate text. Further, the early German version (February 1880), with Hedwig Niemann-Raabe as Nora, had to be revised with a happy ending because the actress refused to play the original ending. Fortunately, the "happy ending," in which Nora does not leave home, was not successful and Niemann-Raabe eventually played the part as written. An adaptation, also with the happy ending, titled *The Child Wife,* was produced in Milwaukee in 1882. While the first professional London production of the play in 1889 found favor with the public, it was attacked in the press for being "unnatural, immoral and, in its concluding scene, essentially undramatic." Among other things, Ibsen was being condemned for not providing a vibrant plot.

Among the play's memorable performances was Ethel Barrymore's version in New York in 1905. Barrymore was praised for a brilliant interpretation of "the child wife." Ruth Gordon played the part to acclaim in 1937, as did Claire Bloom in 1971 on the stage and in 1973 in film. Jane Fonda played in Joseph Losey's film version of 1973. The Norwegian actress Liv Ullmann performed the role in Lincoln Center in 1975 and was praised as "the most enchanting," the "most honest" Nora that the critic Walter Kerr had seen. Other critics were less kind, but it was a successful run. One of the most riveting of modern productions starred Janet McTeer in Anthony Page's revival of *A Doll House.* This production began in London in 1997 and transferred to New York for a Broadway run the same year. Ben Brantley of the *New York Times* said of it, "Nothing can prepare you for the initial shock of Ms.

McTeer's performance, which transforms the passive Nora Helmer, Ibsen's childlike plaything of a wife, into an electric, even aggressive presence" revealing "previously hidden nuances in Ibsen's landmark work." This production was faithful to the production values of Ibsen's original, using an essentially Victorian-era setting with period costumes. Janet McTeer's energy transformed the play and gave Nora a new dimension that made the audience feel that she would do better than merely survive when she left her home. The play is performed regularly in college and regional theaters in the United States and elsewhere.

Henrik Ibsen (1828–1906)

A Doll House   *1879*

TRANSLATED BY ROLF FJELDE

The Characters

TORVALD HELMER, *a lawyer*
NORA, *his wife*
DR. RANK
MRS. LINDE
NILS KROGSTAD, *a bank clerk*
THE HELMERS' THREE SMALL CHILDREN
ANNE-MARIE, *their nurse*
HELENE, *a maid*
A DELIVERY BOY

The action takes place in Helmer's residence.

ACT I

(*A comfortable room, tastefully but not expensively furnished. A door to the right in the back wall leads to the entryway; another to the left leads to Helmer's study. Between these doors, a piano. Midway in the left-hand wall a door, and further back a window. Near the window a round table with an armchair and a small sofa. In the right-hand wall, toward the rear, a door, and nearer the foreground a porcelain stove with two armchairs and a rocking chair beside it. Between the stove and the side door, a small table. Engravings on the walls. An*

As Fjelde explains in his foreword to the translation, he does not use the possessive "A Doll's House" because "the house is not Nora's, as the possessive implies." Fjelde believes that Ibsen includes Torvald with Nora in the original title, "for the two of them at the play's opening are still posing like the little marzipan bride and groom atop the wedding cake."

étagère° with china figures and other small art objects; a small bookcase with richly bound books; the floor carpeted; a fire burning in the stove. It is a winter day.)

(*A bell rings in the entryway; shortly after we hear the door being unlocked. Nora comes into the room, humming happily to herself; she is wearing street clothes and carries an armload of packages, which she puts down on the table to the right. She has left the hall door open, and through it a Delivery Boy is seen holding a Christmas tree and a basket, which he gives to the Maid who let them in.*)

NORA: Hide the tree well, Helene. The children mustn't get a glimpse of it till this evening, after it's trimmed. (*To the Delivery Boy, taking out her purse.*) How much?
DELIVERY BOY: Fifty, ma'am.
NORA: There's a crown. No, keep the change. (*The Boy thanks her and leaves. Nora shuts the door. She laughs softly to herself while taking off her street things. Drawing a bag of macaroons from her pocket, she eats a couple, then steals over and listens at her husband's study door.*) Yes, he's home. (*Hums again as she moves to the table right.*)
HELMER (*from the study*): Is that my little lark twittering out there?
NORA (*busy opening some packages*): Yes, it is.
HELMER: Is that my squirrel rummaging around?
NORA: Yes!
HELMER: When did my squirrel get in?
NORA: Just now. (*Putting the macaroon bag in her pocket and wiping her mouth.*) Do come in, Torvald, and see what I've bought.

[S.D.] étagère: Cabinet with shelves.

HELMER: Can't be disturbed. (*After a moment he opens the door and peers in, pen in hand.*) Bought, you say? All that there? Has the little spendthrift been out throwing money around again?

NORA: Oh, but Torvald, this year we really should let ourselves go a bit. It's the first Christmas we haven't had to economize.

HELMER: But you know we can't go squandering.

NORA: Oh yes, Torvald, we can squander a little now. Can't we? Just a tiny, wee bit. Now that you've got a big salary and are going to make piles and piles of money.

HELMER: Yes — starting New Year's. But then it's a full three months till the raise comes through.

NORA: Pooh! We can borrow that long.

HELMER: Nora! (*Goes over and playfully takes her by the ear.*) Are your scatterbrains off again? What if today I borrowed a thousand crowns, and you squandered them over Christmas week, and then on New Year's Eve a roof tile fell on my head, and I lay there —

NORA (*putting her hand on his mouth*): Oh! Don't say such things!

HELMER: Yes, but what if it happened — then what?

NORA: If anything so awful happened, then it just wouldn't matter if I had debts or not.

HELMER: Well, but the people I'd borrowed from?

NORA: Them? Who cares about them! They're strangers.

HELMER: Nora, Nora, how like a woman! No, but seriously, Nora, you know what I think about that. No debts! Never borrow! Something of freedom's lost — and something of beauty, too — from a home that's founded on borrowing and debt. We've made a brave stand up to now, the two of us; and we'll go right on like that the little while we have to.

NORA (*going toward the stove*): Yes, whatever you say, Torvald.

HELMER (*following her*): Now, now, the little lark's wings mustn't droop. Come on, don't be a sulky squirrel. (*Taking out his wallet.*) Nora, guess what I have here.

NORA (*turning quickly*): Money!

HELMER: There, see. (*Hands her some notes.*) Good grief, I know how costs go up in a house at Christmastime.

NORA: Ten — twenty — thirty — forty. Oh, thank you, Torvald; I can manage no end on this.

HELMER: You really will have to.

NORA: Oh yes, I promise I will! But come here so I can show you everything I bought. And so cheap! Look, new clothes for Ivar here — and a sword. Here a horse and a trumpet for Bob. And a doll and a doll's bed here for Emmy; they're nothing much, but she'll tear them to bits in no time anyway. And here I have dress material and handkerchiefs for the maids. Old Anne-Marie really deserves something more.

HELMER: And what's in that package there?

NORA (*with a cry*): Torvald, no! You can't see that till tonight!

HELMER: I see. But tell me now, you little prodigal, what have you thought of for yourself?

NORA: For myself? Oh, I don't want anything at all.

HELMER: Of course you do. Tell me just what — within reason — you'd most like to have.

NORA: I honestly don't know. Oh, listen, Torvald —

HELMER: Well?

NORA (*fumbling at his coat buttons, without looking at him*): If you want to give me something, then maybe you could — you could —

HELMER: Come on, out with it.

NORA (*hurriedly*): You could give me money, Torvald. No more than you think you can spare; then one of these days I'll buy something with it.

HELMER: But Nora —

NORA: Oh, please, Torvald darling, do that! I beg you, please. Then I could hang the bills in pretty gilt paper on the Christmas tree. Wouldn't that be fun?

HELMER: What are those little birds called that always fly through their fortunes?

NORA: Oh yes, spendthrifts; I know all that. But let's do as I say, Torvald; then I'll have time to decide what I really need most. That's very sensible, isn't it?

HELMER (*smiling*): Yes, very — that is, if you actually hung onto the money I give you, and you actually used it to buy yourself something. But it goes for the house and for all sorts of foolish things, and then I only have to lay out some more.

NORA: Oh, but Torvald —

HELMER: Don't deny it, my dear little Nora. (*Putting his arm around her waist.*) Spendthrifts are sweet, but they use up a frightful amount of money. It's incredible what it costs a man to feed such birds.

NORA: Oh, how can you say that! Really, I save everything I can.

HELMER (*laughing*): Yes, that's the truth. Everything you can. But that's nothing at all.

NORA (*humming, with a smile of quiet satisfaction*): Hm, if you only knew what expenses we larks and squirrels have, Torvald.

HELMER: You're an odd little one. Exactly the way your father was. You're never at a loss for scaring up money; but the moment you have it, it runs right out through your fingers; you never know what you've done with it. Well, one takes you as you are. It's deep in your blood. Yes, these things are hereditary, Nora.

NORA: Ah, I could wish I'd inherited many of Papa's qualities.

HELMER: And I couldn't wish you anything but just what you are, my sweet little lark. But wait; it seems to me you have a very — what should I call it? — a very suspicious look today —

NORA: I do?

HELMER: You certainly do. Look me straight in the eye.

NORA (*looking at him*): Well?

HELMER (*shaking an admonitory finger*): Surely my sweet tooth hasn't been running riot in town today, has she?

NORA: No. Why do you imagine that?

HELMER: My sweet tooth really didn't make a little detour through the confectioner's?

NORA: No, I assure you, Torvald —

HELMER: Hasn't nibbled some pastry?

NORA: No, not at all.

HELMER: Not even munched a macaroon or two?

NORA: No, Torvald, I assure you, really —

HELMER: There, there now. Of course I'm only joking.

NORA (*going to the table, right*): You know I could never think of going against you.

HELMER: No, I understand that; and you *have* given me your word. (*Going over to her.*) Well, you keep your little Christmas secrets to yourself, Nora darling. I expect they'll come to light this evening, when the tree is lit.

NORA: Did you remember to ask Dr. Rank?

HELMER: No. But there's no need for that, it's assumed he'll be dining with us. All the same, I'll ask him when he stops by here this morning. I've ordered some fine wine. Nora, you can't imagine how I'm looking forward to this evening.

NORA: So am I. And what fun for the children, Torvald!

HELMER: Ah, it's so gratifying to know that one's gotten a safe, secure job, and with a comfortable salary. It's a great satisfaction, isn't it?

NORA: Oh, it's wonderful!

HELMER: Remember last Christmas? Three whole weeks before, you shut yourself in every evening till long after midnight, making flowers for the Christmas tree, and all the other decorations to surprise us. Ugh, that was the dullest time I've ever lived through.

NORA: It wasn't at all dull for me.

HELMER (*smiling*): But the outcome *was* pretty sorry, Nora.

NORA: Oh, don't tease me with that again. How could I help it that the cat came in and tore everything to shreds.

HELMER: No, poor thing, you certainly couldn't. You wanted so much to please us all, and that's what counts. But it's just as well that the hard times are past.

NORA: Yes, it's really wonderful.

HELMER: Now I don't have to sit here alone, boring myself, and you don't have to tire your precious eyes and your fair little delicate hands —

NORA (*clapping her hands*): No, is it really true, Torvald, I don't have to? Oh, how wonderfully lovely to hear! (*Taking his arm.*) Now I'll tell you just how I've thought we should plan things. Right after Christmas — (*The doorbell rings.*) Oh, the bell. (*Straightening the room up a bit.*) Somebody would have to come. What a bore!

HELMER: I'm not at home to visitors, don't forget.

MAID (*from the hall doorway*): Ma'am, a lady to see you —

NORA: All right, let her come in.

MAID (*to Helmer*): And the doctor's just come too.

HELMER: Did he go right to my study?

MAID: Yes, he did.

(*Helmer goes into his room. The Maid shows in Mrs. Linde, dressed in traveling clothes, and shuts the door after her.*)

MRS. LINDE (*in a dispirited and somewhat hesitant voice*): Hello, Nora.

NORA (*uncertain*): Hello —

MRS. LINDE: You don't recognize me.

NORA: No, I don't know — but wait, I think — (*Exclaiming.*) What! Kristine! Is it really you?

MRS. LINDE: Yes, it's me.

NORA: Kristine! To think I didn't recognize you. But then, how could I? (*More quietly.*) How you've changed, Kristine!

MRS. LINDE: Yes, no doubt I have. In nine — ten long years.

NORA: Is it so long since we met! Yes, it's all of that. Oh, these last eight years have been a happy time, believe me. And so now you've come in to town, too. Made the long trip in the winter. That took courage.

MRS. LINDE: I just got here by ship this morning.

NORA: To enjoy yourself over Christmas, of course. Oh, how lovely! Yes, enjoy ourselves, we'll do that. But take your coat off. You're not still cold? (*Helping her.*) There now, let's get cozy here by the stove. No, the easy chair there! I'll take the rocker here. (*Seizing her hands.*) Yes, now you have your old look again; it was only in that first moment. You're a bit more pale, Kristine — and maybe a bit thinner.

MRS. LINDE: And much, much older, Nora.

NORA: Yes, perhaps a bit older; a tiny, tiny bit; not much at all. (*Stopping short; suddenly serious.*) Oh, but thoughtless me, to sit here, chattering away. Sweet, good Kristine, can you forgive me?

MRS. LINDE: What do you mean, Nora?

NORA (*softly*): Poor Kristine, you've become a widow.

MRS. LINDE: Yes, three years ago.

NORA: Oh, I knew it, of course; I read it in the papers. Oh, Kristine, you must believe me; I often thought of writing you then, but I kept postponing it, and something always interfered.

MRS. LINDE: Nora dear, I understand completely.

NORA: No, it was awful of me, Kristine. You poor thing, how much you must have gone through. And he left you nothing?

MRS. LINDE: No.

NORA: And no children?

MRS. LINDE: No.

NORA: Nothing at all, then?

MRS. LINDE: Not even a sense of loss to feed on.

NORA (*looking incredulously at her*): But Kristine, how could that be?

MRS. LINDE (*smiling wearily and smoothing her hair*): Oh, sometimes it happens, Nora.

NORA: So completely alone. How terribly hard that must be for you. I have three lovely children. You can't see them now; they're out with the maid. But now you must tell me everything —

MRS. LINDE: No, no, no, tell me about yourself.

NORA: No, you begin. Today I don't want to be selfish. I want to think only of you today. But there is something I must tell you. Did you hear of the wonderful luck we had recently?

MRS. LINDE: No, what's that?

NORA: My husband's been made manager in the bank, just think!

MRS. LINDE: Your husband? How marvelous!

NORA: Isn't it? Being a lawyer is such an uncertain living, you know, especially if one won't touch any cases that aren't clean and decent. And of course Torvald would never do that, and I'm with him completely there. Oh, we're simply delighted, believe me! He'll join the bank right after New Year's and start getting a huge salary and lots of commissions. From now on we can live quite differently — just as we want. Oh, Kristine, I feel so light and happy! Won't it be lovely to have stacks of money and not a care in the world?

MRS. LINDE: Well, anyway, it would be lovely to have enough for necessities.

NORA: No, not just for necessities, but stacks and stacks of money!

MRS. LINDE (smiling): Nora, Nora, aren't you sensible yet? Back in school you were such a free spender.

NORA (with a quiet laugh): Yes, that's what Torvald still says. (Shaking her finger.) But "Nora, Nora" isn't as silly as you all think. Really, we've been in no position for me to go squandering. We've had to work, both of us.

MRS. LINDE: You too?

NORA: Yes, at odd jobs — needlework, crocheting, embroidery, and such — (casually) and other things too. You remember that Torvald left the department when we were married? There was no chance of promotion in his office, and of course he needed to earn more money. But that first year he drove himself terribly. He took on all kinds of extra work that kept him going morning and night. It wore him down, and then he fell deathly ill. The doctors said it was essential for him to travel south.

MRS. LINDE: Yes, didn't you spend a whole year in Italy?

NORA: That's right. It wasn't easy to get away, you know. Ivar had just been born. But of course we had to go. Oh, that was a beautiful trip, and it saved Torvald's life. But it cost a frightful sum, Kristine.

MRS. LINDE: I can well imagine.

NORA: Four thousand, eight hundred crowns it cost. That's really a lot of money.

MRS. LINDE: But it's lucky you had it when you needed it.

NORA: Well, as it was, we got it from Papa.

MRS. LINDE: I see. It was just about the time your father died.

NORA: Yes, just about then. And, you know, I couldn't make that trip out to nurse him. I had to stay here, expecting Ivar any moment, and with my poor sick Torvald to care for. Dearest Papa, I never saw him

again, Kristine. Oh, that was the worst time I've known in all my marriage.

MRS. LINDE: I know how you loved him. And then you went off to Italy?

NORA: Yes. We had the means now, and the doctors urged us. So we left a month after.

MRS. LINDE: And your husband came back completely cured?

NORA: Sound as a drum!

MRS. LINDE: But — the doctor?

NORA: Who?

MRS. LINDE: I thought the maid said he was a doctor, the man who came in with me.

NORA: Yes, that was Dr. Rank — but he's not making a sick call. He's our closest friend, and he stops by at least once a day. No, Torvald hasn't had a sick moment since, and the children are fit and strong, and I am, too. (Jumping up and clapping her hands.) Oh, dear God, Kristine, what a lovely thing to live and be happy! But how disgusting of me — I'm talking of nothing but my own affairs. (Sits on a stool close by Kristine, arms resting across her knees.) Oh, don't be angry with me! Tell me, is it really true that you weren't in love with your husband? Why did you marry him, then?

MRS. LINDE: My mother was still alive, but bedridden and helpless — and I had my two younger brothers to look after. In all conscience, I didn't think I could turn him down.

NORA: No, you were right there. But was he rich at the time?

MRS. LINDE: He was very well off, I'd say. But the business was shaky, Nora. When he died, it all fell apart, and nothing was left.

NORA: And then — ?

MRS. LINDE: Yes, so I had to scrape up a living with a little shop and a little teaching and whatever else I could find. The last three years have been like one endless workday without a rest for me. Now, it's over, Nora. My poor mother doesn't need me, for she's passed on. Nor the boys, either; they're working now and can take care of themselves.

NORA: How free you must feel —

MRS. LINDE: No — only unspeakably empty. Nothing to live for now. (Standing up anxiously.) That's why I couldn't take it any longer out in that desolate hole. Maybe here it'll be easier to find something to do and keep my mind occupied. If I could only be lucky enough to get a steady job, some office work —

NORA: Oh, but Kristine, that's so dreadfully tiring, and you already look so tired. It would be much better for you if you could go off to a bathing resort.

MRS. LINDE (going toward the window): I have no father to give me travel money, Nora.

NORA (rising): Oh, don't be angry with me.

MRS. LINDE (going to her): Nora dear, don't you be angry with me. The worst of my kind of situation is all the bitterness that's stored away. No one to work for, and yet you're always having to snap up your opportunities. You have to live; and so you grow self-ish. When you told me the happy change in your lot, do you know I was delighted less for your sakes than for mine?

NORA: How so? Oh, I see. You think maybe Torvald could do something for you.

MRS. LINDE: Yes, that's what I thought.

NORA: And he will, Kristine! Just leave it to me; I'll bring it up so delicately — find something attractive to humor him with. Oh, I'm so eager to help you.

MRS. LINDE: How very kind of you, Nora, to be so concerned over me — doubly kind, considering you really know so little of life's burdens yourself.

NORA: I — ? I know so little — ?

MRS. LINDE (*smiling*): Well, my heavens — a little needlework and such — Nora, you're just a child.

NORA (*tossing her head and pacing the floor*): You don't have to act so superior.

MRS. LINDE: Oh?

NORA: You're just like the others. You all think I'm incapable of anything serious —

MRS. LINDE: Come now —

NORA: That I've never had to face the raw world.

MRS. LINDE: Nora dear, you've just been telling me all your troubles.

NORA: Hm! Trivial! (*Quietly.*) I haven't told you the big thing.

MRS. LINDE: Big thing? What do you mean?

NORA: You look down on me so, Kristine, but you shouldn't. You're proud that you worked so long and hard for your mother.

MRS. LINDE: I don't look down on a soul. But it is true: I'm proud — and happy, too — to think it was given to me to make my mother's last days almost free of care.

NORA: And you're also proud thinking of what you've done for your brothers.

MRS. LINDE: I feel I've a right to be.

NORA: I agree. But listen to this, Kristine — I've also got something to be proud and happy for.

MRS. LINDE: I don't doubt it. But whatever do you mean?

NORA: Not so loud. What if Torvald heard! He mustn't, not for anything in the world. Nobody must know, Kristine. No one but you.

MRS. LINDE: But what is it, then?

NORA: Come here. (*Drawing her down beside her on the sofa.*) It's true — I've also got something to be proud and happy for. I'm the one who saved Torvald's life.

MRS. LINDE: Saved — ? Saved how?

NORA: I told you about the trip to Italy. Torvald never would have lived if he hadn't gone south —

MRS. LINDE: Of course; your father gave you the means —

NORA (*smiling*): That's what Torvald and all the rest think, but —

MRS. LINDE: But — ?

NORA: Papa didn't give us a pin. I was the one who raised the money.

MRS. LINDE: You? That whole amount?

NORA: Four thousand, eight hundred crowns. What do you say to that?

MRS. LINDE: But Nora, how was it possible? Did you win the lottery?

NORA (*disdainfully*): The lottery? Pooh! No art to that.

MRS. LINDE: But where did you get it from then?

NORA (*humming, with a mysterious smile*): Hmm, tra-la-la-la.

MRS. LINDE: Because you couldn't have borrowed it.

NORA: No? Why not?

MRS. LINDE: A wife can't borrow without her husband's consent.

NORA (*tossing her head*): Oh, but a wife with a little business sense, a wife who knows how to manage —

MRS. LINDE: Nora, I simply don't understand —

NORA: You don't have to. Whoever said I *borrowed* the money? I could have gotten it other ways. (*Throwing herself back on the sofa.*) I could have gotten it from some admirer or other. After all, a girl with my ravishing appeal —

MRS. LINDE: You lunatic.

NORA: I'll bet you're eaten up with curiosity, Kristine.

MRS. LINDE: Now listen here, Nora — you haven't done something indiscreet?

NORA (*sitting up again*): Is it indiscreet to save your husband's life?

MRS. LINDE: I think it's indiscreet that without his knowledge you —

NORA: But that's the point: He mustn't know! My Lord, can't you understand? He mustn't ever know the close call he had. It was to *me* the doctors came to say his life was in danger — that nothing could save him but a stay in the south. Didn't I try strategy then! I began talking about how lovely it would be for me to travel abroad like other young wives; I begged and I cried; I told him please to remember my condition, to be kind and indulge me; and then I dropped a hint that he could easily take out a loan. But at that, Kristine, he nearly exploded. He said I was frivolous, and it was his duty as man of the house not to indulge me in whims and fancies — as I think he called them. Aha, I thought, now you'll just have to be saved — and that's when I saw my chance.

MRS. LINDE: And your father never told Torvald the money wasn't from him?

NORA: No, never. Papa died right about then. I'd considered bringing him into my secret and begging him never to tell. But he was too sick at the time — and then, sadly, it didn't matter.

MRS. LINDE: And you've never confided in your husband since?

NORA: For heaven's sake, no! Are you serious? He's so strict on that subject. Besides — Torvald, with all his masculine pride — how painfully humiliating for him if he ever found out he was in debt to me. That would just ruin our relationship. Our beautiful, happy home would never be the same.

MRS. LINDE: Won't you ever tell him?

NORA (*thoughtfully, half smiling*): Yes — maybe some-time years from now, when I'm no longer so attractive. Don't laugh! I only mean when Torvald loves me less than now, when he stops enjoying my dancing and dressing up and reciting for him. Then it might be wise to have something in reserve — (*Breaking off.*) How ridiculous! That'll never happen — Well, Kristine, what do you think of my big secret? I'm capable of something too, hm? You can imagine, of course, how this thing hangs over me. It really hasn't been easy meeting the payments on time. In the business world there's what they call quarterly interest and what they call amortization, and these are always so terribly hard to manage. I've had to skimp a little here and there, wherever I could, you know. I could hardly spare anything from my house allowance, because Torvald has to live well. I couldn't let the children go poorly dressed; whatever I got for them, I felt I had to use up completely — the darlings!

MRS. LINDE: Poor Nora, so it had to come out of your own budget, then?

NORA: Yes, of course. But I was the one most responsible, too. Every time Torvald gave me money for new clothes and such, I never used more than half; always bought the simplest, cheapest outfits. It was a godsend that everything looks so well on me that Torvald never noticed. But it did weigh me down at times, Kristine. It *is* such a joy to wear fine things. You understand.

MRS. LINDE: Oh, of course.

NORA: And then I found other ways of making money. Last winter I was lucky enough to get a lot of copying to do. I locked myself in and sat writing every evening till late in the night. Ah, I was tired so often, dead tired. But still it was wonderful fun, sitting and working like that, earning money. It was almost like being a man.

MRS. LINDE: But how much have you paid off this way so far?

NORA: That's hard to say, exactly. These accounts, you know, aren't easy to figure. I only know that I've paid out all I could scrape together. Time and again I haven't known where to turn. (*Smiling.*) Then I'd sit here dreaming of a rich old gentleman who had fallen in love with me —

MRS. LINDE: What! Who is he?

NORA: Oh, really! And that he'd died, and when his will was opened, there in big letters it said, "All my fortune shall be paid over in cash, immediately, to that enchanting Mrs. Nora Helmer."

MRS. LINDE: But Nora dear — who *was* this gentleman?

NORA: Good grief, can't you understand? The old man never existed; that was only something I'd dream up time and again whenever I was at my wits' end for money. But it makes no difference now; the old fossil can go where he pleases for all I care; I don't need him or his will — because now I'm free. (*Jumping up.*) Oh, how lovely to think of that, Kristine! Care-free! To know you're carefree, utterly carefree; to be able to romp and play with the children, and to keep up a beautiful, charming home — everything just the way Torvald likes it! And think, spring is coming, with big blue skies. Maybe we can travel a little then. Maybe I'll see the ocean again. Oh yes, it *is* so marvelous to live and be happy!

(*The front doorbell rings.*)

MRS. LINDE (*rising*): There's the bell. It's probably best that I go.

NORA: No, stay. No one's expected. It must be for Torvald.

MAID (*from the hall doorway*): Excuse me, ma'am — there's a gentleman here to see Mr. Helmer, but I didn't know — since the doctor's with him —

NORA: Who is the gentleman?

KROGSTAD (*from the doorway*): It's me, Mrs. Helmer.

(*Mrs. Linde starts and turns away toward the window.*)

NORA (*stepping toward him, tense, her voice a whisper*): You? What is it? Why do you want to speak to my husband?

KROGSTAD: Bank business — after a fashion. I have a small job in the investment bank, and I hear now your husband is going to be our chief —

NORA: In other words, it's —

KROGSTAD: Just dry business, Mrs. Helmer. Nothing but that.

NORA: Yes, then please be good enough to step into the study. (*She nods indifferently as she sees him out by the hall door, then returns and begins stirring up the stove.*)

MRS. LINDE: Nora — who was that man?

NORA: That was a Mr. Krogstad — a lawyer.

MRS. LINDE: Then it really was him.

NORA: Do you know that person?

MRS. LINDE: I did once — many years ago. For a time he was a law clerk in our town.

NORA: Yes, he's been that.

MRS. LINDE: How he's changed.

NORA: I understand he had a very unhappy marriage.

MRS. LINDE: He's a widower now.

NORA: With a number of children. There now, it's burning. (*She closes the stove door and moves the rocker a bit to one side.*)

MRS. LINDE: They say he has a hand in all kinds of business.

NORA: Oh? That may be true; I wouldn't know. But let's not think about business. It's so dull.

(*Dr. Rank enters from Helmer's study.*)

RANK (*still in the doorway*): No, no, really — I don't want to intrude, I'd just as soon talk a little while with your wife. (*Shuts the door, then notices Mrs. Linde.*) Oh, beg pardon. I'm intruding here too.

NORA: No, not at all. (*Introducing him.*) Dr. Rank, Mrs. Linde.

RANK: Well now, that's a name much heard in this

house. I believe I passed the lady on the stairs as I came.

MRS. LINDE: Yes, I take the stairs very slowly. They're rather hard on me.

RANK: Uh-hm, some touch of internal weakness?

MRS. LINDE: More overexertion, I'd say.

RANK: Nothing else? Then you're probably here in town to rest up in a round of parties?

MRS. LINDE: I'm here to look for work.

RANK: Is that the best cure for overexertion?

MRS. LINDE: One has to live, Doctor.

RANK: Yes, there's a common prejudice to that effect.

NORA: Oh, come on, Dr. Rank — you really do want to live yourself.

RANK: Yes, I really do. Wretched as I am, I'll gladly prolong my torment indefinitely. All my patients feel like that. And it's quite the same, too, with the morally sick. Right at this moment there's one of those moral invalids in there with Helmer —

MRS. LINDE (*softly*): Ah!

NORA: Who do you mean?

RANK: Oh, it's a lawyer, Krogstad, a type you wouldn't know. His character is rotten to the root — but even he began chattering all-importantly about how he had to *live*.

NORA: Oh? What did he want to talk to Torvald about?

RANK: I really don't know. I only heard something about the bank.

NORA: I didn't know that Krog — that this man Krogstad had anything to do with the bank.

RANK: Yes, he's gotten some kind of berth down there. (*To Mrs. Linde.*) I don't know if you also have, in your neck of the woods, a type of person who scuttles about breathlessly, sniffing out hints of moral corruption, and then maneuvers his victim into some sort of key position where he can keep an eye on him. It's the healthy these days that are out in the cold.

MRS. LINDE: All the same, it's the sick who most need to be taken in.

RANK (*with a shrug*): Yes, there we have it. That's the concept that's turning society into a sanatorium.

(*Nora, lost in her thoughts, breaks out into quiet laughter and claps her hands.*)

RANK: Why do you laugh at that? Do you have any real idea of what society is?

NORA: What do I care about dreary old society? I was laughing at something quite different — something terribly funny. Tell me, Doctor — is everyone who works in the bank dependent now on Torvald?

RANK: Is that what you find so terribly funny?

NORA (*smiling and humming*): Never mind, never mind! (*Pacing the floor.*) Yes, that's really immensely amusing: that we — that Torvald has so much power now over all those people. (*Taking the bag out of her pocket.*) Dr. Rank, a little macaroon on that?

RANK: See here, macaroons! I thought they were contraband here.

NORA: Yes, but these are some that Kristine gave me.

MRS. LINDE: What? I — ?

NORA: Now, now, don't be afraid. You couldn't possibly know that Torvald had forbidden them. You see, he's worried they'll ruin my teeth. But hmp! Just this once! Isn't that so, Dr. Rank? Help yourself! (*Puts a macaroon in his mouth.*) And you too, Kristine. And I'll also have one, only a little one — or two, at the most. (*Walking about again.*) Now I'm really tremendously happy. Now's there's just one last thing in the world that I have an enormous desire to do.

RANK: Well! And what's that?

NORA: It's something I have such a consuming desire to say so Torvald could hear.

RANK: And why can't you say it?

NORA: I don't dare. It's quite shocking.

MRS. LINDE: Shocking?

RANK: Well, then it isn't advisable. But in front of us you certainly can. What do you have such a desire to say so Torvald could hear?

NORA: I have such a huge desire to say — to hell and be damned!

RANK: Are you crazy?

MRS. LINDE: My goodness, Nora!

RANK: Go on, say it. Here he is.

NORA (*hiding the macaroon bag*): Shh, shh, shh!

(*Helmer comes in from his study, hat in hand, overcoat over his arm.*)

NORA (*going toward him*): Well, Torvald dear, are you through with him?

HELMER: Yes, he just left.

NORA: Let me introduce you — this is Kristine, who's arrived here in town.

HELMER: Kristine — ? I'm sorry, but I don't know —

NORA: Mrs. Linde, Torvald dear. Mrs. Kristine Linde.

HELMER: Of course. A childhood friend of my wife's, no doubt?

MRS. LINDE: Yes, we knew each other in those days.

NORA: And just think, she made the long trip down here in order to talk with you.

HELMER: What's this?

MRS. LINDE: Well, not exactly —

NORA: You see, Kristine is remarkably clever in office work, and so she's terribly eager to come under a capable man's supervision and add more to what she already knows —

HELMER: Very wise, Mrs. Linde.

NORA: And then when she heard that you'd become a bank manager — the story was wired out to the papers — then she came in as fast as she could and — Really, Torvald, for my sake you can do a little something for Kristine, can't you?

HELMER: Yes, it's not at all impossible. Mrs. Linde, I suppose you're a widow?

MRS. LINDE: Yes.

HELMER: Any experience in office work?

MRS. LINDE: Yes, a good deal.

HELMER: Well, it's quite likely that I can make an opening for you —

NORA (*clapping her hands*): You see, you see!

HELMER: You've come at a lucky moment, Mrs. Linde.

MRS. LINDE: Oh, how can I thank you?

HELMER: Not necessary. (*Putting his overcoat on.*) But today you'll have to excuse me —

RANK: Wait, I'll go with you. (*He fetches his coat from the hall and warms it at the stove.*)

NORA: Don't stay out long, dear.

HELMER: An hour; no more.

NORA: Are you going too, Kristine?

MRS. LINDE (*putting on her winter garments*): Yes, I have to see about a room now.

HELMER: Then perhaps we can all walk together.

NORA (*helping her*): What a shame we're so cramped here, but it's quite impossible for us to —

MRS. LINDE: Oh, don't even think of it! Good-bye, Nora dear, and thanks for everything.

NORA: Good-bye for now. Of course you'll be back this evening. And you too, Dr. Rank. What? If you're well enough? Oh, you've got to be! Wrap up tight now.

(*In a ripple of small talk the company moves out into the hall; children's voices are heard outside on the steps.*)

NORA: There they are! There they are! (*She runs to open the door. The children come in with their nurse, Anne-Marie.*) Come in, come in! (*Bends down and kisses them.*) Oh, you darlings — ! Look at them, Kristine. Aren't they lovely!

RANK: No loitering in the draft here.

HELMER: Come, Mrs. Linde — this place is unbearable now for anyone but mothers.

(*Dr. Rank, Helmer, and Mrs. Linde go down the stairs. Anne-Marie goes into the living room with the children. Nora follows, after closing the hall door.*)

NORA: How fresh and strong you look. Oh, such red cheeks you have! Like apples and roses. (*The children interrupt her throughout the following.*) And it was so much fun? That's wonderful. Really? You pulled both Emmy and Bob on the sled? Imagine, all together! Yes, you're a clever boy, Ivar. Oh, let me hold her a bit, Anne-Marie. My sweet little doll baby! (*Takes the smallest from the nurse and dances with her.*) Yes, yes, Mama will dance with Bob as well. What? Did you throw snowballs? Oh, if I'd only been there! No, don't bother, Anne-Marie — I'll undress them myself. Oh yes, let me. It's such fun. Go in and rest; you look half frozen. There's hot coffee waiting for you on the stove. (*The nurse goes into the room to the left. Nora takes the children's winter things off, throwing them about, while the children talk to her all at once.*) Is that so? A big dog chased you? But it didn't bite? No, dogs never bite little, lovely doll babies. Don't peek in the packages, Ivar! What is it? Yes, wouldn't you like to know. No, no, it's an ugly something. Well? Shall we play? What shall we play? Hide-and-seek? Yes, let's play hide-and-seek. Bob must hide first. I must? Yes, let me hide first. (*Laughing and shouting, she and the chil-*

dren play in and out of the living room and the adjoining room to the right. At last Nora hides under the table. The children come storming in, search, but cannot find her, then hear her muffled laughter, dash over to the table, lift the cloth up and find her. Wild shouting. She creeps forward as if to scare them. More shouts. Meanwhile, a knock at the hall door; no one has noticed it. Now the door half opens, and Krogstad appears. He waits a moment; the game goes on.*)

KROGSTAD: Beg pardon, Mrs. Helmer —

NORA (*with a strangled cry, turning and scrambling to her knees*): Oh! What do you want?

KROGSTAD: Excuse me. The outer door was ajar; it must be someone forgot to shut it —

NORA (*rising*): My husband isn't home, Mr. Krogstad.

KROGSTAD: I know that.

NORA: Yes — then what do you want here?

KROGSTAD: A word with you.

NORA: With — ? (*To the children, quietly.*) Go in to Anne-Marie. What? No, the strange man won't hurt Mama. When he's gone, we'll play some more. (*She leads the children into the room to the left and shuts the door after them. Then, tense and nervous:*) You want to speak to me?

KROGSTAD: Yes, I want to.

NORA: Today? But it's not yet the first of the month —

KROGSTAD: No, it's Christmas Eve. It's going to be up to you how merry a Christmas you have.

NORA: What is it you want? Today I absolutely can't —

KROGSTAD: We won't talk about that till later. This is something else. You do have a moment to spare, I suppose?

NORA: Oh yes, of course — I do, except —

KROGSTAD: Good. I was sitting over at Olsen's Restaurant when I saw your husband go down the street —

NORA: Yes?

KROGSTAD: With a lady.

NORA: Yes. So?

KROGSTAD: If you'll pardon my asking: Wasn't that lady a Mrs. Linde?

NORA: Yes.

KROGSTAD: Just now come into town?

NORA: Yes, today.

KROGSTAD: She's a good friend of yours?

NORA: Yes, she is. But I don't see —

KROGSTAD: I also knew her once.

NORA: I'm aware of that.

KROGSTAD: Oh? You know all about it. I thought so. Well, then let me ask you short and sweet: Is Mrs. Linde getting a job in the bank?

NORA: What makes you think you can cross-examine me, Mr. Krogstad — you, one of my husband's employees? But since you ask, you might as well know — yes, Mrs. Linde's going to be taken on at the bank. And I'm the one who spoke for her Mr. Krogstad. Now you know.

KROGSTAD: So I guessed right.

NORA (*pacing up and down*): Oh, one does have a tiny

bit of influence, I should hope. Just because I am a woman, don't think it means that — When one has a subordinate position, Mr. Krogstad, one really ought to be careful about pushing somebody who — hm —

KROGSTAD: Who has influence?

NORA: That's right.

KROGSTAD (*in a different tone*): Mrs. Helmer, would you be good enough to use your influence on my behalf?

NORA: What? What do you mean?

KROGSTAD: Would you please make sure that I keep my subordinate position in the bank?

NORA: What does that mean? Who's thinking of taking away your position?

KROGSTAD: Oh, don't play the innocent with me. I'm quite aware that your friend would hardly relish the chance of running into me again; and I'm also aware now whom I can thank for being turned out.

NORA: But I promise you —

KROGSTAD: Yes, yes, yes, to the point: There's still time, and I'm advising you to use your influence to prevent it.

NORA: But Mr. Krogstad, I have absolutely no influence.

KROGSTAD: You haven't? I thought you were just saying —

NORA: You shouldn't take me so literally. I! How can you believe that I have any such influence over my husband?

KROGSTAD: Oh, I've known your husband from our student days. I don't think the great bank manager's more steadfast than any other married man.

NORA: You speak insolently about my husband, and I'll show you the door.

KROGSTAD: The lady has spirit.

NORA: I'm not afraid of you any longer. After New Year's, I'll soon be done with the whole business.

KROGSTAD: (*restraining himself*): Now listen to me, Mrs. Helmer. If necessary, I'll fight for my little job in the bank as if it were life itself.

NORA: Yes, so it seems.

KROGSTAD: It's not just a matter of income; that's the least of it. It's something else — All right, out with it! Look, this is the thing. You know, just like all the others, of course, that once, a good many years ago, I did something rather rash.

NORA: I've heard rumors to that effect.

KROGSTAD: The case never got into court; but all the same, every door was closed in my face from then on. So I took up those various activities you know about. I had to grab hold somewhere; and I dare say I haven't been among the worst. But now I want to drop all that. My boys are growing up. For their sakes, I'll have to win back as much respect as possible here in town. That job in the bank was like the first rung in my ladder. And now your husband wants to kick me right back down in the mud again.

NORA: But for heaven's sake, Mr. Krogstad, it's simply not in my power to help you.

KROGSTAD: That's because you haven't the will to — but I have the means to make you.

NORA: You certainly won't tell my husband that I owe you money?

KROGSTAD: Hm — what if I told him that?

NORA: That would be shameful of you. (*Nearly in tears.*) This secret — my joy and my pride — that he should learn it in such a crude and disgusting way — learn it from you. You'd expose me to the most horrible unpleasantness —

KROGSTAD: Only unpleasantness?

NORA (*vehemently*): But go on and try. It'll turn out the worse for you, because then my husband will really see what a crook you are, and then you'll never be able to hold your job.

KROGSTAD: I asked if it was just domestic unpleasantness you were afraid of?

NORA: If my husband finds out, then of course he'll pay what I owe at once, and then we'd be through with you for good.

KROGSTAD (*a step closer*): Listen, Mrs. Helmer — you've either got a very bad memory, or else no head at all for business. I'd better put you a little more in touch with the facts.

NORA: What do you mean?

KROGSTAD: When your husband was sick, you came to me for a loan of four thousand, eight hundred crowns.

NORA: Where else could I go?

KROGSTAD: I promised to get you that sum —

NORA: And you got it.

KROGSTAD: I promised to get you that sum, on certain conditions. You were so involved in your husband's illness, and so eager to finance your trip, that I guess you didn't think out all the details. It might just be a good idea to remind you. I promised you the money on the strength of a note I drew up.

NORA: Yes, and that I signed.

KROGSTAD: Right. But at the bottom I added some lines for your father to guarantee the loan. He was supposed to sign down there.

NORA: Supposed to? He did sign.

KROGSTAD: I left the date blank. In other words, your father would have dated his signature himself. Do you remember that?

NORA: Yes, I think —

KROGSTAD: Then I gave you the note for you to mail to your father. Isn't that so?

NORA: Yes.

KROGSTAD: And naturally you sent it at once — because only some five, six days later you brought me the note, properly signed. And with that, the money was yours.

NORA: Well, then; I've made my payments regularly, haven't I?

KROGSTAD: More or less. But — getting back to the point — those were hard times for you then, Mrs. Helmer.

NORA: Yes, they were.

KROGSTAD: Your father was very ill, I believe.

NORA: He was near the end.

KROGSTAD: He died soon after?

NORA: Yes.

KROGSTAD: Tell me, Mrs. Helmer, do you happen to recall the date of your father's death? The day of the month, I mean.

NORA: Papa died the twenty-ninth of September.

KROGSTAD: That's quite correct; I've already looked into that. And now we come to a curious thing — (*taking out a paper*) which I simply cannot comprehend.

NORA: Curious thing? I don't know —

KROGSTAD: This is the curious thing: that your father co-signed the note for your loan three days after his death.

NORA: How — ? I don't understand.

KROGSTAD: Your father died the twenty-ninth of September. But look. Here your father dated his signature October second. Isn't that curious, Mrs. Helmer? (*Nora is silent.*) Can you explain it to me? (*Nora remains silent.*) It's also remarkable that the words "October second" and the year aren't written in your father's hand, but rather in one that I think I know. Well, it's easy to understand. Your father forgot perhaps to date his signature, and then someone or other added it, a bit sloppily, before anyone knew of his death. There's nothing wrong in that. It all comes down to the signature. And there's no question about *that,* Mrs. Helmer. It really *was* your father who signed his own name here, wasn't it?

NORA (*after a short silence, throwing her head back and looking squarely at him*): No, it wasn't. *I* signed Papa's name.

TOP: Nora (Claire Bloom) is troubled as Helmer (Donald Madden) kisses her in Patrick Garland's 1971 production. RIGHT: Helmer, Nora, and Mrs. Linde (Patricia Elliott) discuss the possibility of finding a suitable job for Mrs. Linde in the bank. FAR RIGHT: Krogstad (Robert Gerringer) explains the seriousness of her actions to Nora.

KROGSTAD: Wait, now — are you fully aware that this is a dangerous confession?

NORA: Why? You'll soon get your money.

KROGSTAD: Let me ask you a question — why didn't you send the paper to your father?

NORA: That was impossible. Papa was so sick. If I'd asked him for his signature, I also would have had to tell him what the money was for. But I couldn't tell him, sick as he was, that my husband's life was in danger. That was just impossible.

KROGSTAD: Then it would have been better if you'd given up the trip abroad.

NORA: I couldn't possibly. The trip was to save my husband's life. I couldn't give that up.

KROGSTAD: But didn't you ever consider that this was a fraud against me?

NORA: I couldn't let myself be bothered by that. You weren't any concern of mine. I couldn't stand you, with all those cold complications you made, even though you knew how badly off my husband was.

KROGSTAD: Mrs. Helmer, obviously you haven't the vaguest idea of what you've involved yourself in. But I can tell you this: It was nothing more and nothing worse that I once did — and it wrecked my whole reputation.

NORA: You? Do you expect me to believe that you ever acted bravely to save your wife's life?

KROGSTAD: Laws don't inquire into motives.

NORA: Then they must be very poor laws.

KROGSTAD: Poor or not — if I introduce this paper in court, you'll be judged according to law.

NORA: This I refuse to believe. A daughter hasn't a right to protect her dying father from anxiety and care? A wife hasn't a right to save her husband's life? I don't know much about laws, but I'm sure that somewhere in the books these things are allowed. And you don't know anything about it — you who practice the law? You must be an awful lawyer, Mr. Krogstad.

KROGSTAD: Could be. But business — the kind of business we two are mixed up in — don't you think I know about that? All right. Do what you want now. But I'm telling you *this:* If I get shoved down a second time, you're going to keep me company. (*He bows and goes out through the hall.*)

NORA (*pensive for a moment, then tossing her head*): Oh, really! Trying to frighten me! I'm not so silly as all that. (*Begins gathering up the children's clothes, but soon stops.*) But — ? No, but that's impossible! I did it out of love.

THE CHILDREN (*in the doorway, left*): Mama, that strange man's gone out the door.

NORA: Yes, yes, I know it. But don't tell anyone about the strange man. Do you hear? Not even Papa!

THE CHILDREN: No, Mama. But now will you play again?

NORA: No, not now.

THE CHILDREN: Oh, but Mama, you promised.

NORA: Yes, but I can't now. Go inside; I have too much to do. Go in, go in, my sweet darlings. (*She herds them gently back in the room and shuts the door after them. Settling on the sofa, she takes up a piece of embroidery and makes some stitches, but soon stops abruptly.*) No! (*Throws the work aside, rises, goes to the hall door and calls out.*) Helene! Let me have the tree in here. (*Goes to the table, left, opens the table drawer, and stops again.*) No, but that's utterly impossible!

MAID (*with the Christmas tree*): Where should I put it, ma'am?

NORA: There. The middle of the floor.

MAID: Should I bring anything else?

NORA: No, thanks. I have what I need.

(*The Maid, who has set the tree down, goes out.*)

NORA (*absorbed in trimming the tree*): Candles here — and flowers here. That terrible creature! Talk, talk, talk! There's nothing to it at all. The tree's going to be lovely. I'll do anything to please you Torvald. I'll sing for you, dance for you —

(*Helmer comes in from the hall, with a sheaf of papers under his arm.*)

NORA: Oh! You're back so soon?

HELMER: Yes. Has anyone been here?

NORA: Here? No.

HELMER: That's odd. I saw Krogstad leaving the front door.

NORA: So? Oh yes, that's true. Krogstad was here a moment.

HELMER: Nora, I can see by your face that he's been here, begging you to put in a good word for him.

NORA: Yes.

HELMER: And it was supposed to seem like your own idea? You were to hide it from me that he'd been here. He asked you that, too, didn't he?

NORA: Yes, Torvald, but —

HELMER: Nora, Nora, and you could fall for that? Talk with that sort of person and promise him anything? And then in the bargain, tell me an untruth.

NORA: An untruth — ?

HELMER: Didn't you say that no one had been here? (*Wagging his finger.*) My little songbird must never do that again. A songbird needs a clean beak to warble with. No false notes. (*Putting his arm about her waist.*) That's the way it should be, isn't it? Yes, I'm sure of it. (*Releasing her.*) And so, enough of that. (*Sitting by the stove.*) Ah, how snug and cozy it is here. (*Leafing among his papers.*)

NORA (*busy with the tree, after a short pause*): Torvald!

HELMER: Yes.

NORA: I'm so much looking forward to the Stenborgs' costume party, day after tomorrow.

HELMER: And I can't wait to see what you'll surprise me with.

NORA: Oh, that stupid business!

HELMER: What?

NORA: I can't find anything that's right. Everything seems so ridiculous, so inane.

HELMER: So my little Nora's come to *that* recognition?

NORA (*going behind his chair, her arms resting on its back*): Are you very busy, Torvald?

HELMER: Oh —

NORA: What papers are those?

HELMER: Bank matters.

NORA: Already?

HELMER: I've gotten full authority from the retiring management to make all necessary changes in personnel and procedure. I'll need Christmas week for that. I want to have everything in order by New Year's.

NORA: So that was the reason this poor Krogstad —

HELMER: Hm.

NORA (*still leaning on the chair and slowly stroking the nape of his neck*): If you weren't so very busy, I would have asked you an enormous favor, Torvald.

HELMER: Let's hear. What is it?

NORA: You know, there isn't anyone who has your good taste — and I want so much to look well at the costume party. Torvald, couldn't you take over and decide what I should be and plan my costume?

HELMER: Ah, is my stubborn little creature calling for a lifeguard?

NORA: Yes, Torvald, I can't get anywhere without your help.

HELMER: All right — I'll think it over. We'll hit on something.

NORA: Oh, how sweet of you. (*Goes to the tree again. Pause.*) Aren't the red flowers pretty — ? But tell me, was it really such a crime that this Krogstad committed?

HELMER: Forgery. Do you have any idea what that means?

NORA: Couldn't he have done it out of need?

HELMER: Yes, or thoughtlessness, like so many others. I'm not so heartless that I'd condemn a man categorically for just one mistake.

NORA: No, of course not, Torvald!

HELMER: Plenty of men have redeemed themselves by openly confessing their crimes and taking their punishment.

NORA: Punishment — ?

HELMER: But now Krogstad didn't go that way. He got himself out by sharp practices, and that's the real cause of his moral breakdown.

NORA: Do you really think that would — ?

HELMER: Just imagine how a man with that sort of guilt in him has to lie and cheat and deceive on all sides, has to wear a mask even with the nearest and dearest he has, even with his own wife and children. And with the children, Nora — that's where it's most horrible.

NORA: Why?

HELMER: Because that kind of atmosphere of lies infects the whole life of a home. Every breath the children take in is filled with the germs of something degenerate.

NORA (*coming closer behind him*): Are you sure of that?

HELMER: Oh, I've seen it often enough as a lawyer. Almost everyone who goes bad early in life has a mother who's a chronic liar.

NORA: Why just — the mother?

HELMER: It's usually the mother's influence that's dominant, but the father's works in the same way, of course. Every lawyer is quite familiar with it. And still this Krogstad's been going home year in, year out, poisoning his own children with lies and pretense; that's why I call him morally lost. (*Reaching his hands out toward her.*) So my sweet little Nora must promise me never to plead his cause. Your hand on it. Come, come, what's this? Give me your hand. There, now. All settled. I can tell you it'd be impossible for me to work alongside of him. I literally feel physically revolted when I'm anywhere near such a person.

NORA (*withdraws her hand and goes to the other side of the Christmas tree*): How hot it is here! And I've got so much to do.

HELMER (*getting up and gathering his papers*): Yes, and I have to think about getting some of these read through before dinner. I'll think about your costume, too. And something to hang on the tree in gilt paper, I may even see about that. (*Putting his hand on her head.*) Oh you, my darling little songbird. (*He goes into his study and closes the door after him.*)

NORA (*softly, after a silence*): Oh, really! It isn't so. It's impossible. It must be impossible.

ANNE-MARIE (*in the doorway left*): The children are begging so hard to come in to Mama.

NORA: No, no, no, don't let them in to me! You stay with them, Anne-Marie.

ANNE-MARIE: Of course, ma'am. (*Closes the door.*)

NORA (*pale with terror*): Hurt my children — ! Poison my home? (*A moment's pause; then she tosses her head.*) That's not true. Never. Never in all the world.

ACT II

(*Same room. Beside the piano the Christmas tree now stands stripped of ornament, burned-down candle stubs on its ragged branches. Nora's street clothes lie on the sofa. Nora, alone in the room, moves restlessly about; at last she stops at the sofa and picks up her coat.*)

NORA (*dropping the coat again*): Someone's coming! (*Goes toward the door, listens.*) No — there's no one. Of course — nobody's coming today, Christmas Day — or tomorrow, either. But maybe — (*Opens the door and looks out.*) No, nothing in the mailbox. Quite empty. (*Coming forward.*) What nonsense! He won't do anything serious. Nothing terrible could happen. It's impossible. Why, I have three small children.

(*Anne-Marie, with a large carton, comes in from the room to the left.*)

ANNE-MARIE: Well, at last I found the box with the masquerade clothes.

NORA: Thanks. Put it on the table.

ANNE-MARIE (*does so*): But they're all pretty much of a mess.

NORA: Ahh! I'd love to rip them in a million pieces!

ANNE-MARIE: Oh, mercy, they can be fixed right up. Just a little patience.

NORA: Yes, I'll go get Mrs. Linde to help me.

ANNE-MARIE: Out again now? In this nasty weather? Miss Nora will catch cold — get sick.

NORA: Oh, worse things could happen — How are the children?

ANNE-MARIE: The poor mites are playing with their Christmas presents, but —

NORA: Do they ask for me much?

ANNE-MARIE: They're so used to having Mama around, you know.

NORA: Yes, but Anne-Marie, I *can't* be together with them as much as I was.

ANNE-MARIE: Well, small children get used to anything.

NORA: You think so? Do you think they'd forget their mother if she was gone for good?

ANNE-MARIE: Oh, mercy — gone for good!

NORA: Wait, tell me. Anne-Marie — I've wondered so often — how could you ever have the heart to give your child over to strangers?

ANNE-MARIE: But I had to, you know, to become little Nora's nurse.

NORA: Yes, but how could you *do* it?

ANNE-MARIE: When I could get such a good place? A girl who's poor and who's gotten in trouble is glad enough for that. Because that slippery fish, he didn't do a thing for me, you know.

NORA: But your daughter's surely forgotten you.

ANNE-MARIE: Oh, she certainly has not. She's written to me, both when she was confirmed and when she was married.

NORA (*clasping her about the neck*): You old Anne-Marie, you were a good mother for me when I was little.

ANNE-MARIE: Poor little Nora, with no other mother but me.

NORA: And if the babies didn't have one, then I know that you'd — What silly talk! (*Opening the carton.*) Go in to them. Now I'll have to — Tomorrow you can see how lovely I'll look.

ANNE-MARIE: Oh, there won't be anyone at the party as lovely as Miss Nora. (*She goes off into the room, left.*)

NORA (*begins unpacking the box, but soon throws it aside*): Oh, if I dared to go out. If only nobody would come. If only nothing would happen here while I'm out. What craziness — nobody's coming. Just don't think. This muff — needs a brushing. Beautiful gloves, beautiful gloves. Let it go. Let it go! One, two, three, four, five, six — (*With a cry.*) Oh, there they are! (*Poises to move toward the door, but remains irresolutely standing. Mrs. Linde enters from the hall, where she has removed her street clothes.*)

NORA: Oh, it's you, Kristine. There's no one else out there? How good that you've come.

MRS. LINDE: I hear you were up asking for me.

NORA: Yes, I just stopped by. There's something you really can help me with. Let's get settled on the sofa. Look, there's going to be a costume party tomorrow evening at the Stenborgs' right above us, and now Torvald wants me to go as a Neapolitan peasant girl and dance the tarantella that I learned in Capri.

MRS. LINDE: Really, are you giving a whole performance?

NORA: Torvald says yes, I should. See, here's the dress. Torvald had it made for me down there; but now it's all so tattered that I just don't know —

MRS. LINDE: Oh, we'll fix that up in no time. It's nothing more than the trimmings — they're a bit loose here and there. Needle and thread? Good, now we have what we need.

NORA: Oh, how sweet of you!

MRS. LINDE (*sewing*): So you'll be in disguise tomorrow, Nora. You know what? I'll stop by then for a moment and have a look at you all dressed up. But listen, I've absolutely forgotten to thank you for that pleasant evening yesterday.

NORA (*getting up and walking about*): I don't think it was as pleasant as usual yesterday. You should have come to town a bit sooner, Kristine — Yes, Torvald really knows how to give a home elegance and charm.

MRS. LINDE: And you do, too, if you ask me. You're not your father's daughter for nothing. But tell me, is Dr. Rank always so down in the mouth as yesterday?

NORA: No, that was quite an exception. But he goes around critically ill all the time — tuberculosis of the spine, poor man. You know, his father was a disgusting thing who kept mistresses and so on — and that's why the son's been sickly from birth.

MRS. LINDE (*lets her sewing fall to her lap*): But my dearest Nora, how do you know about such things?

NORA (*walking more jauntily*): Hmp! When you've had three children, then you've had a few visits from — from women who know something of medicine, and they tell you this and that.

MRS. LINDE (*resumes sewing; a short pause*): Does Dr. Rank come here every day?

NORA: Every blessed day. He's Torvald's best friend from childhood, and *my* good friend, too. Dr. Rank almost belongs to this house.

MRS. LINDE: But tell me — is he quite sincere? I mean, doesn't he rather enjoy flattering people?

NORA: Just the opposite. Why do you think that?

MRS. LINDE: When you introduced us yesterday, he was proclaiming that he'd often heard my name in this house; but later I noticed that your husband hadn't the slightest idea who I really was. So how could Dr. Rank — ?

NORA: But it's all true, Kristine. You see, Torvald loves me beyond words, and, as he puts it, he'd like to keep me all to himself. For a long time he'd almost be jealous if I even mentioned any of my old friends back home. So of course I dropped that. But with Dr. Rank I talk a lot about such things because he likes hearing about them.

MRS. LINDE: Now listen, Nora; in many ways you're still like a child. I'm a good deal older than you, with a little more experience. I'll tell you something: You ought to put an end to all this with Dr. Rank.

NORA: What should I put an end to?

MRS. LINDE: Both parts of it, I think. Yesterday you said something about a rich admirer who'd provide you with money —

NORA: Yes, one who doesn't exist — worse luck. So?

MRS. LINDE: Is Dr. Rank well off?

NORA: Yes, he is.

MRS. LINDE: With no dependents?

NORA: No, no one. But —

MRS. LINDE: And he's over here every day?

NORA: Yes, I told you that.

MRS. LINDE: How can a man of such refinement be so grasping?

NORA: I don't follow you at all.

MRS. LINDE: Now don't try to hide it, Nora. You think I can't guess who loaned you the forty-eight hundred crowns?

NORA: Are you out of your mind? How could you think such a thing! A friend of ours, who comes here every single day. What an intolerable situation that would have been!

MRS. LINDE: Then it really wasn't him.

NORA: No, absolutely not. It never even crossed my mind for a moment — And he had nothing to lend in those days; his inheritance came later.

MRS. LINDE: Well, I think that was a stroke of luck for you, Nora dear.

NORA: No, it never would have occurred to me to ask Dr. Rank — Still, I'm quite sure that if I had asked him —

MRS. LINDE: Which you won't, of course.

NORA: No, of course not. I can't see that I'd ever need to. But I'm quite positive that if I talked to Dr. Rank —

MRS. LINDE: Behind your husband's back?

NORA: I've got to clear up this other thing; *that's* also behind his back. I've *got* to clear it all up.

MRS. LINDE: Yes, I was saying that yesterday, but —

NORA (*pacing up and down*): A man handles these problems so much better than a woman —

MRS. LINDE: One's husband does, yes.

NORA: Nonsense. (*Stopping.*) When you pay everything you owe, then you get your note back, right?

MRS. LINDE: Yes, naturally.

NORA: And can rip it into a million pieces and burn it up — that filthy scrap of paper!

MRS. LINDE (*looking hard at her, laying her sewing aside, and rising slowly*): Nora, you're hiding something from me.

NORA: You can see it in my face?

MRS. LINDE: Something's happened to you since yesterday morning. Nora, what is it?

NORA (*hurrying toward her*): Kristine! (*Listening.*) Shh! Torvald's home. Look, go in with the children a while. Torvald can't bear all this snipping and stitching. Let Anne-Marie help you.

MRS. LINDE (*gathering up some of the things*): All right, but I'm not leaving here until we've talked this out. (*She disappears into the room, left, as Torvald enters from the hall.*)

NORA: Oh, how I've been waiting for you, Torvald dear.

HELMER: Was that the dressmaker?

NORA: No, that was Kristine. She's helping me fix up my costume. You know, it's going to be quite attractive.

HELMER: Yes, wasn't that a bright idea I had?

NORA: Brilliant! But then wasn't I good as well to give in to you?

HELMER: Good — because you give in to your husband's judgment? All right, you little goose, I know you didn't mean it like that. But I won't disturb you. You'll want to have a fitting, I suppose.

NORA: And you'll be working?

HELMER: Yes. (*Indicating a bundle of papers.*) See. I've been down to the bank. (*Starts toward his study.*)

NORA: Torvald.

HELMER (*stops*): Yes.

NORA: If your little squirrel begged you, with all her heart and soul, for something — ?

HELMER: What's that?

NORA: Then would you do it?

HELMER: First, naturally, I'd have to know what it was.

NORA: Your squirrel would scamper about and do tricks, if you'd only be sweet and give in.

HELMER: Out with it.

NORA: Your lark would be singing high and low in every room —

HELMER: Come on, she does that anyway.

NORA: I'd be a wood nymph and dance for you in the moonlight.

HELMER: Nora — don't tell me it's that same business from this morning?

NORA (*coming closer*): Yes, Torvald, I beg you, please!

HELMER: And you actually have the nerve to drag that up again?

NORA: Yes, yes, you've got to give in to me; you *have* to let Krogstad keep his job in the bank.

HELMER: My dear Nora, I've slated his job for Mrs. Linde.

NORA: That's awfully kind of you. But you could just fire another clerk instead of Krogstad.

HELMER: This is the most incredible stubbornness! Because you go and give an impulsive promise to speak up for him, I'm expected to —

NORA: That's not the reason, Torvald. It's for your own sake. That man does writing for the worst papers; you said it yourself. He could do you any amount of harm. I'm scared to death of him —

HELMER: Ah, I understand. It's the old memories haunting you.

NORA: What do you mean by that?

HELMER: Of course, you're thinking about your father.

NORA: Yes, all right. Just remember how those nasty gossips wrote in the papers about Papa and slandered him so cruelly. I think they'd have had him dismissed if the department hadn't sent you up to investigate, and if you hadn't been so kind and open-minded toward him.

HELMER: My dear Nora, there's a notable difference between your father and me. Your father's official career was hardly above reproach. But mine is; and I hope it'll stay that way as long as I hold my position.

NORA: Oh, who can ever tell what vicious minds can invent? We could be so snug and happy now in our quiet, carefree home — you and I and the children, Torvald! That's why I'm pleading with you so —

HELMER: And just by pleading for him you make it impossible for me to keep him on. It's already known at the bank that I'm firing Krogstad. What if it's rumored around now that the new bank manager was vetoed by his wife —

NORA: Yes, what then — ?

HELMER: Oh yes — as long as our little bundle of stubbornness gets her way — ! I should go and make myself ridiculous in front of the whole office — give people the idea I can be swayed by all kinds of outside pressure. Oh, you can bet I'd feel the effects of that soon enough! Besides — there's something that rules Krogstad right out at the bank as long as I'm the manager.

NORA: What's that?

HELMER: His moral failings I could maybe overlook if I had to —

NORA: Yes, Torvald, why not?

HELMER: And I hear he's quite efficient on the job. But he was a crony of mine back in my teens — one of those rash friendships that crop up again and again to embarrass you later in life. Well, I might as well say it straight out: We're on a first-name basis. And that tactless fool makes no effort at all to hide it in front of others. Quite the contrary — he thinks that entitles him to take a familiar air around me, and so every other second he comes booming out with his, "Yes, Torvald!" and "Sure thing, Torvald!" I tell you, it's been excruciating for me. He's out to make my place in the bank unbearable.

NORA: Torvald, you can't be serious about all this.

HELMER: Oh no? Why not?

NORA: Because these are such petty considerations.

HELMER: What are you saying? Petty? You think I'm petty!

NORA: No, just the opposite, Torvald dear. That's exactly why —

HELMER: Never mind. You call my motives petty; then I might as well be just that. Petty! All right! We'll put a stop to this for good. (*Goes to the hall door and calls.*) Helene!

NORA: What do you want?

HELMER (*searching among his papers*): A decision. (*The Maid comes in.*) Look here; take this letter; go out with it at once. Get hold of a messenger and have him deliver it. Quick now. It's already addressed. Wait, here's some money.

MAID: Yes, sir. (*She leaves with the letter.*)

HELMER (*straightening his papers*): There, now, little Miss Willful.

NORA (*breathlessly*): Torvald, what was that letter?

HELMER: Krogstad's notice.

NORA: Call it back, Torvald! There's still time. Oh, Torvald, call it back! Do it for my sake — for your sake, for the children's sake! Do you hear, Torvald; do it! You don't know how this can harm us.

HELMER: Too late.

NORA: Yes, too late.

HELMER: Nora, dear, I can forgive you this panic, even though basically you're insulting me. Yes, you are! Or isn't it an insult to think that *I* should be afraid of a courtroom hack's revenge? But I forgive you anyway, because this shows so beautifully how much you love me. (*Takes her in his arms.*) This is the way it should be, my darling Nora. Whatever comes, you'll see: When it really counts, I have strength and courage enough as a man to take on the whole weight myself.

NORA (*terrified*): What do you mean by that?

HELMER: The whole weight, I said.

NORA (*resolutely*): No, never in all the world.

HELMER: Good. So we'll share it, Nora, as man and wife. That's as it should be. (*Fondling her.*) Are you happy now? There, there, there — not these frightened dove's eyes. It's nothing at all but empty fantasies — Now you should run through your tarantella and practice your tambourine. I'll go to the inner office, and shut both doors, so I won't hear a thing; you can make all the noise you like. (*Turning in the doorway.*) And when Rank comes, just tell him where he can find me. (*He nods to her and goes with his papers into the study, closing the door.*)

NORA (*standing as though rooted, dazed with fright, in a whisper*): He really could do it. He will do it. He'll do it in spite of everything. No, not that, never, never! Anything but that! Escape! A way out — (*The doorbell rings.*) Dr. Rank! Anything but that! Anything, whatever it is! (*Her hands pass over her face, smoothing it; she pulls herself together, goes over and opens the hall door. Dr. Rank stands outside, hanging his fur coat up. During the following scene, it begins getting dark.*)

NORA: Hello, Dr. Rank. I recognized your ring. But you mustn't go in to Torvald yet; I believe he's working.

RANK: And you?

NORA: For you, I always have an hour to spare — you know that. (*He has entered, and she shuts the door after him.*)

RANK: Many thanks. I'll make use of these hours while I can.

NORA: What do you mean by that? While you can?

RANK: Does that disturb you?

NORA: Well, it's such an odd phrase. Is anything going to happen?

RANK: What's going to happen is what I've been expecting so long — but I honestly didn't think it would come so soon.

NORA (*gripping his arm*): What is it you've found out? Dr. Rank, you have to tell me!

RANK (*sitting by the stove*): It's all over with me. There's nothing to be done about it.

NORA (*breathing easier*): Is it you — then — ?

RANK: Who else? There's no point in lying to one's self. I'm the most miserable of all my patients, Mrs. Helmer. These past few days I've been auditing my internal accounts. Bankrupt! Within a month I'll probably be laid out and rotting in the churchyard.

NORA: Oh, what a horrible thing to say.

RANK: The thing itself is horrible. But the worst of it is all the other horror before it's over. There's only one final examination left; when I'm finished with that, I'll know about when my disintegration will begin. There's something I want to say. Helmer with his sen-

sitivity has such a sharp distaste for anything ugly. I don't want him near my sickroom.

NORA: Oh, but Dr. Rank —

RANK: I won't have him in there. Under no condition. I'll lock my door to him — As soon as I'm completely sure of the worst, I'll send you my calling card marked with a black cross, and you'll know then the wreck has started to come apart.

NORA: No, today you're completely unreasonable. And I wanted you so much to be in a really good humor.

RANK: With death up my sleeve? And then to suffer this way for somebody else's sins. Is there any justice in that? And in every single family, in some way or another, this inevitable retribution of nature goes on —

NORA (*her hands pressed over her ears*): Oh, stuff! Cheer up! Please — be gay!

RANK: Yes, I'd just as soon laugh at it all. My poor, innocent spine, serving time for my father's gay army days.

NORA (*by the table, left*): He was so infatuated with asparagus tips and pâté de foie gras, wasn't that it?

RANK: Yes — and with truffles.

NORA: Truffles, yes. And then with oysters, I suppose?

RANK: Yes, tons of oysters, naturally.

NORA: And then the port and champagne to go with it. It's so sad that all these delectable things have to strike at our bones.

RANK: Especially when they strike at the unhappy bones that never shared in the fun.

NORA: Ah, that's the saddest of all.

RANK (*looks searchingly at her*): Hm.

NORA (*after a moment*): Why did you smile?

RANK: No, it was you who laughed.

NORA: No, it was you who smiled, Dr. Rank!

RANK (*getting up*): You're even a bigger tease than I'd thought.

NORA: I'm full of wild ideas today.

RANK: That's obvious.

NORA (*putting both hands on his shoulders*): Dear, dear Dr. Rank, you'll never die for Torvald and me.

RANK: Oh, that loss you'll easily get over. Those who go away are soon forgotten.

NORA (*looks fearfully at him*): You believe that?

RANK: One makes new connections, and then —

NORA: Who makes new connections?

RANK: Both you and Torvald will when I'm gone. I'd say you're well under way already. What was that Mrs. Linde doing here last evening?

NORA: Oh, come — you can't be jealous of poor Kristine?

RANK: Oh yes, I am. She'll be my successor here in the house. When I'm down under, that woman will probably —

NORA: Shh! Not so loud. She's right in there.

RANK: Today as well. So you see.

NORA: Only to sew on my dress. Good gracious, how unreasonable you are. (*Sitting on the sofa.*) Be nice now, Dr. Rank. Tomorrow you'll see how beautifully

I'll dance; and you can imagine then that I'm dancing only for you — yes, and of course for Torvald, too — that's understood. (*Takes various items out of the carton.*) Dr. Rank, sit over here and I'll show you something.

RANK (*sitting*): What's that?

NORA: Look here. Look.

RANK: Silk stockings.

NORA: Flesh-colored. Aren't they lovely? Now it's so dark here, but tomorrow — No, no, no, just look at the feet. Oh well, you might as well look at the rest.

RANK: Hm —

NORA: Why do you look so critical? Don't you believe they'll fit?

RANK: I've never had any chance to form an opinion on that.

NORA (*glancing at him a moment*): Shame on you. (*Hits him lightly on the ear with the stockings.*) That's for you. (*Puts them away again.*)

RANK: And what other splendors am I going to see now?

NORA: Not the least bit more, because you've been naughty. (*She hunts a little and rummages among her things.*)

RANK (*after a short silence*): When I sit here together with you like this, completely easy and open, then I don't know — I simply can't imagine — whatever would have become of me if I'd never come into this house.

NORA (*smiling*): Yes, I really think you feel completely at ease with us.

RANK (*more quietly, staring straight ahead*): And then to have to go away from it all —

NORA: Nonsense, you're not going away.

RANK (*his voice unchanged*): — and not even be able to leave some poor show of gratitude behind, scarcely a fleeting regret — no more than a vacant place that anyone can fill.

NORA: And if I asked you now for — No —

RANK: For what?

NORA: For a great proof of your friendship —

RANK: Yes, yes?

NORA: No, I mean — for an exceptionally big favor —

RANK: Would you really, for once, make me so happy?

NORA: Oh, you haven't the vaguest idea what it is.

RANK: All right, then tell me.

NORA: No, but I can't, Dr. Rank — it's all out of reason. It's advice and help, too — and a favor —

RANK: So much the better. I can't fathom what you're hinting at. Just speak out. Don't you trust me?

NORA: Of course. More than anyone else. You're my best and truest friend, I'm sure. That's why I want to talk to you. All right, then, Dr. Rank: There's something you can help me prevent. You know how deeply, how inexpressibly dearly Torvald loves me; he'd never hesitate a second to give up his life for me.

RANK (*leaning close to her*): Nora — do you think he's the only one —

NORA (*with a slight start*): Who — ?

RANK: Who'd gladly give up his life for you.

NORA (*heavily*): I see.

RANK: I swore to myself you should know this before I'm gone. I'll never find a better chance. Yes, Nora, now you know. And also you know now that you can trust me beyond anyone else.

NORA (*rising, natural and calm*): Let me by.

RANK (*making room for her, but still sitting*): Nora —

NORA (*in the hall doorway*): Helene, bring the lamp in. (*Goes over to the stove.*) Ah, dear Dr. Rank, that was really mean of you.

RANK (*getting up*): That I've loved you just as deeply as somebody else? Was *that* mean?

NORA: No, but that you came out and told me. That was quite unnecessary —

RANK: What do you mean? Have you known — ?

(*The Maid comes in with the lamp, sets it on the table, and goes out again.*)

RANK: Nora — Mrs. Helmer — I'm asking you: Have you known about it?

NORA: Oh, how can I tell what I know or don't know? Really, I don't know what to say — Why did you have to be so clumsy, Dr. Rank! Everything was so good.

RANK: Well, in any case, you now have the knowledge that my body and soul are at your command. So won't you speak out?

NORA (*looking at him*): After that?

RANK: Please, just let me know what it is.

NORA: You can't know anything now.

RANK: I have to. You mustn't punish me like this. Give me the chance to do whatever is humanly possible for you.

NORA: Now there's nothing you can do for me. Besides, actually, I don't need any help. You'll see — it's only my fantasies. That's what it is. Of course! (*Sits in the rocker, looks at him, and smiles.*) What a nice one you are, Dr. Rank. Aren't you a little bit ashamed, now that the lamp is here?

RANK: No, not exactly. But perhaps I'd better go — for good?

NORA: No, you certainly can't do that. You must come here just as you always have. You know Torvald can't do without you.

RANK: Yes, but *you?*

NORA: You know how much I enjoy it when you're here.

RANK: That's precisely what threw me off. You're a mystery to me. So many times I've felt you'd almost rather be with me than with Helmer.

NORA: Yes — you see, there are some people that one loves most and other people that one would almost prefer being with.

RANK: Yes, there's something to that.

NORA: When I was back home, of course I loved Papa most. But I always thought it was so much fun when I could sneak down to the maids' quarters, because they never tried to improve me, and it was always so amusing, the way they talked to each other.

RANK: Aha, so it's their place that I've filled.

NORA (*jumping up and going to him*): Oh, dear, sweet Dr. Rank, that's not what I meant at all. But you can understand that with Torvald it's just the same as with Papa —

(*The Maid enters from the hall.*)

MAID: Ma'am — please! (*She whispers to Nora and hands her a calling card.*)

NORA (*glancing at the card*): Ah! (*Slips it into her pocket.*)

RANK: Anything wrong?

NORA: No, no, not at all. It's only some — it's my new dress —

RANK: Really? But — there's your dress.

NORA: Oh, that. But this is another one — I ordered it — Torvald mustn't know —

RANK: Ah, now we have the big secret.

NORA: That's right. Just go in with him — he's back in the inner study. Keep him there as long as —

RANK: Don't worry. He won't get away. (*Goes into the study.*)

NORA (*to the Maid*): And he's standing waiting in the kitchen?

MAID: Yes, he came up by the back stairs.

NORA: But didn't you tell him somebody was here?

MAID: Yes, but that didn't do any good.

NORA: He won't leave?

MAID: No, he won't go till he's talked with you, ma'am.

NORA: Let him come in, then — but quietly. Helene, don't breathe a word about this. It's a surprise for my husband.

MAID: Yes, yes, I understand — (*Goes out.*)

NORA: This horror — it's going to happen. No, no, no, it can't happen, it mustn't. (*She goes and bolts Helmer's door. The Maid opens the hall door for Krogstad and shuts it behind him. He is dressed for travel in a fur coat, boots, and a fur cap.*)

NORA (*going toward him*): Talk softly. My husband's home.

KROGSTAD: Well, good for him.

NORA: What do you want?

KROGSTAD: Some information.

NORA: Hurry up, then. What is it?

KROGSTAD: You know, of course, that I got my notice.

NORA: I couldn't prevent it, Mr. Krogstad. I fought for you to the bitter end, but nothing worked.

KROGSTAD: Does your husband's love for you run so thin? He knows everything I can expose you to, and all the same he dares to —

NORA: How can you imagine he knows anything about this?

KROGSTAD: Ah, no — I can't imagine it either, now. It's not at all like my fine Torvald Helmer to have so much guts —

NORA: Mr. Krogstad, I demand respect for my husband!

KROGSTAD: Why, of course — all due respect. But since the lady's keeping it so carefully hidden, may I presume to ask if you're also a bit better informed than yesterday about what you've actually done?

NORA: More than you ever could teach me.

KROGSTAD: Yes, I *am* such an awful lawyer.

NORA: What is it you want from me?

KROGSTAD: Just a glimpse of how you are, Mrs. Helmer. I've been thinking about you all day long. A cashier, a night-court scribbler, a — well, a type like me also has a little of what they call a heart, you know.

NORA: Then show it. Think of my children.

KROGSTAD: Did you or your husband ever think of mine? But never mind. I simply wanted to tell you that you don't need to take this thing too seriously. For the present, I'm not proceeding with any action.

NORA: Oh no, really! Well — I knew that.

KROGSTAD: Everything can be settled in a friendly spirit. It doesn't have to get around town at all; it can stay just among us three.

NORA: My husband must never know anything of this.

KROGSTAD: How can you manage that? Perhaps you can pay me the balance?

NORA: No, not right now.

KROGSTAD: Or you know some way of raising the money in a day or two?

NORA: No way that I'm willing to use.

KROGSTAD: Well, it wouldn't have done you any good, anyway. If you stood in front of me with a fistful of bills, you still couldn't buy your signature back.

NORA: Then tell me what you're going to do with it.

KROGSTAD: I'll just hold onto it — keep it on file. There's no outsider who'll even get wind of it. So if you've been thinking of taking some desperate step —

NORA: I have.

KROGSTAD: Been thinking of running away from home —

NORA: I have!

KROGSTAD: Or even of something worse —

NORA: How could you guess that?

KROGSTAD: You can drop those thoughts.

NORA: How could you guess I was thinking of *that*?

KROGSTAD: Most of us think about *that* at first. I thought about it too, but I discovered I hadn't the courage —

NORA (*lifelessly*): I don't either.

KROGSTAD (*relieved*): That's true, you haven't the courage? You too?

NORA: I don't have it — I don't have it.

KROGSTAD: It would be terribly stupid, anyway. After that first storm at home blows out, why, then — I have here in my pocket a letter for your husband —

NORA: Telling everything?

KROGSTAD: As charitably as possible.

NORA (*quickly*): He mustn't ever get that letter. Tear it up. I'll find some way to get money.

KROGSTAD: Beg pardon, Mrs. Helmer, but I think I just told you —

NORA: Oh, I don't mean the money I owe you. Let me know how much you want from my husband, and I'll manage it.

KROGSTAD: I don't want any money from your husband.

NORA: What do you want, then?

KROGSTAD: I'll tell you what. I want to recoup, Mrs. Helmer; I want to get on in the world — and there's where your husband can help me. For a year and a half I've kept myself clean of anything disreputable — all that time struggling with the worst conditions; but I was satisfied, working my way up step by step. Now I've been written right off, and I'm just not in the mood to come crawling back. I tell you, I want to move on. I want to get back in the bank — in a better position. Your husband can set up a job for me —

NORA: He'll never do that!

KROGSTAD: He'll do it. I know him. He won't dare breathe a word of protest. And once I'm in there together with him, you just wait and see! Inside of a year, I'll be the manager's right-hand man. It'll be Nils Krogstad, not Torvald Helmer, who runs the bank.

NORA: You'll never see the day!

KROGSTAD: Maybe you think you can —

NORA: I have the courage now — for *that*.

KROGSTAD: Oh, you don't scare me. A smart, spoiled lady like you —

NORA: You'll see; you'll see!

KROGSTAD: Under the ice, maybe? Down in the freezing, coal-black water? There, till you float up in the spring, ugly unrecognizable, with your hair falling out —

NORA: You don't frighten me.

KROGSTAD: Nor do you frighten me. One doesn't do these things, Mrs. Helmer. Besides what good would it be? I'd still have him safe in my pocket.

NORA: Afterwards? When I'm no longer — ?

KROGSTAD: Are you forgetting that *I'll* be in control then over your final reputation? (*Nora stands speechless, staring at him.*) Good; now I've warned you. Don't do anything stupid. When Helmer's read my letter, I'll be waiting for his reply. And bear in mind that it's your husband himself who's forced me back to my old ways. I'll never forgive him for that. Goodbye, Mrs. Helmer. (*He goes out through the hall.*)

NORA (*goes to the hall door, opens it a crack, and listens*): He's gone. Didn't leave the letter. Oh no, no, that's impossible too! (*Opening the door more and more.*) What's that? He's standing outside — not going downstairs. He's thinking it over? Maybe he'll — ? (*A letter falls in the mailbox; then Krog-*stad's footsteps are heard, dying away down a flight of stairs. Nora gives a muffled cry and runs over toward the sofa table. A short pause.) In the mailbox. (*Slips warily over to the hall door.*) It's lying there. Torvald, Torvald — now we're lost!

MRS. LINDE (*entering with the costume from the room, left*): There now, I can't see anything else to mend. Perhaps you'd like to try —

NORA (*in a hoarse whisper*): Kristine, come here.

MRS. LINDE (*tossing the dress on the sofa*): What's wrong? You look upset.

NORA: Come here. See that letter? There! Look — through the glass in the mailbox.

MRS. LINDE: Yes, yes, I see it.

NORA: That letter's from Krogstad —

MRS. LINDE: Nora — it's Krogstad who loaned you the money!

NORA: Yes, and now Torvald will find out everything.

MRS. LINDE: Believe me, Nora, it's best for both of you.

NORA: There's more you don't know. I forged a name.

MRS. LINDE: But for heaven's sake — ?

NORA: I only want to tell you that, Kristine, so that you can be my witness.

MRS. LINDE: Witness? Why should I — ?

NORA: If I should go out of my mind — it could easily happen —

MRS. LINDE: Nora!

NORA: Or anything else occurred — so I couldn't be present here —

MRS. LINDE: Nora, Nora, you aren't yourself at all!

NORA: And someone should try to take on the whole weight, all of the guilt, you follow me —

MRS. LINDE: Yes, of course, but why do you think — ?

NORA: Then you're the witness that it isn't true, Kristine. I'm very much myself; my mind right now is perfectly clear; and I'm telling you: Nobody else has known about this; I alone did everything. Remember that.

MRS. LINDE: I will. But I don't understand all this.

NORA: Oh, how could you ever understand it? It's the miracle now that's going to take place.

MRS. LINDE: The miracle?

NORA: Yes, the miracle. But it's so awful, Kristine. It mustn't take place, not for anything in the world.

MRS. LINDE: I'm going right over and talk with Krogstad.

NORA: Don't go near him; he'll do you some terrible harm!

MRS. LINDE: There was a time once when he'd gladly have done anything for me.

NORA: He?

MRS. LINDE: Where does he live?

NORA: Oh, how do I know? Yes. (*Searches in her pocket.*) Here's his card. But the letter, the letter — !

HELMER (*from the study, knocking on the door*): Nora!

NORA (*with a cry of fear*): Oh! What is it? What do you want?

HELMER: Now, now, don't be so frightened. We're not

coming in. You locked the door — are you trying on the dress?

NORA: Yes, I'm trying it. I'll look just beautiful, Torvald.

MRS. LINDE (*who has read the card*): He's living right around the corner.

NORA: Yes, but what's the use? We're lost. The letter's in the box.

MRS. LINDE: And your husband has the key?

NORA: Yes, always.

MRS. LINDE: Krogstad can ask for his letter back unread; he can find some excuse —

NORA: But it's just this time that Torvald usually —

MRS. LINDE: Stall him. Keep him in there. I'll be back as quick as I can. (*She hurries out through the hall entrance.*)

NORA (*goes to Helmer's door, opens it, and peers in*): Torvald!

HELMER (*from the inner study*): Well — does one dare set foot in one's own living room at last? Come on, Rank, now we'll get a look — (*In the doorway.*) But what's this?

NORA: What, Torvald dear?

HELMER: Rank had me expecting some grand masquerade.

RANK (*in the doorway*): That was my impression, but I must have been wrong.

NORA: No one can admire me in my splendor — not till tomorrow.

HELMER: But Nora dear, you look so exhausted. Have you practiced too hard?

NORA: No, I haven't practiced at all yet.

HELMER: You know, it's necessary —

NORA: Oh, it's absolutely necessary, Torvald. But I can't get anywhere without your help. I've forgotten the whole thing completely.

HELMER: Ah, we'll soon take care of that.

NORA: Yes, take care of me, Torvald, please! Promise me that? Oh, I'm so nervous. That big party — You must give up everything this evening for me. No business — don't even touch your pen. Yes? Dear Torvald, promise?

HELMER: It's a promise. Tonight I'm totally at your service — you little helpless thing. Hm — but first there's one thing I want to — (*Goes toward the hall door.*)

NORA: What are you looking for?

HELMER: Just to see if there's any mail.

NORA: No, no, don't do that, Torvald!

HELMER: Now what?

NORA: Torvald, please. There isn't any.

HELMER: Let me look, though. (*Starts out. Nora, at the piano, strikes the first notes of the tarantella. Helmer, at the door, stops.*) Aha!

NORA: I can't dance tomorrow if I don't practice with you.

HELMER (*going over to her*): Nora dear, are you really so frightened?

NORA: Yes, so terribly frightened. Let me practice right

now; there's still time before dinner. Oh, sit down and play for me, Torvald. Direct me. Teach me, the way you always have.

HELMER: Gladly, if it's what you want. (*Sits at the piano.*)

NORA (*snatches the tambourine up from the box, then a long, varicolored shawl, which she throws around herself, whereupon she springs forward and cries out*): Play for me now! Now I'll dance!

(*Helmer plays and Nora dances. Rank stands behind Helmer at the piano and looks on.*)

HELMER (*as he plays*): Slower. Slow down.

NORA: Can't change it.

HELMER: Not so violent, Nora!

NORA: Has to be just like this.

HELMER (*stopping*): No, no, that won't do at all.

NORA (*laughing and swinging her tambourine*): Isn't that what I told you?

RANK: Let me play for her.

HELMER (*getting up*): Yes, go on. I can teach her more easily then.

(*Rank sits at the piano and plays, Nora dances more and more wildly. Helmer has stationed himself by the stove and repeatedly gives her directions; she seems not to hear them; her hair loosens and falls over her shoulders; she does not notice, but goes on dancing. Mrs. Linde enters.*)

MRS. LINDE (*standing dumbfounded at the door*): Ah — !

NORA (*still dancing*): See what fun, Kristine!

HELMER: But Nora darling, you dance as if your life were at stake.

NORA: And it is.

HELMER: Rank, stop! This is pure madness. Stop it, I say!

(*Rank breaks off playing, and Nora halts abruptly.*)

HELMER (*going over to her*): I never would have believed it. You've forgotten everything I taught you.

NORA (*throwing away the tambourine*): You see for yourself.

HELMER: Well, there's certainly room for instruction here.

NORA: Yes, you see how important it is. You've got to teach me to the very last minute. Promise me that, Torvald?

HELMER: You can bet on it.

NORA: You mustn't, either today or tomorrow, think about anything else but me; you mustn't open any letters — or the mailbox —

HELMER: Ah, it's still the fear of that man —

NORA: Oh yes, yes, that too.

HELMER: Nora, it's written all over you — there's already a letter from him out there.

NORA: I don't know. I guess so. But you mustn't read such things now; there mustn't be anything ugly between us before it's all over.

RANK (*quietly to Helmer*): You shouldn't deny her.

HELMER (*putting his arm around her*): The child can have her way. But tomorrow night, after you've danced —

NORA: Then you'll be free.

MAID (*in the doorway, right*): Ma'am, dinner is served.

NORA: We'll be wanting champagne, Helene.

MAID: Very good, ma'am. (*Goes out.*)

HELMER: So — a regular banquet, hm?

NORA: Yes, a banquet — champagne till daybreak! (*Calling out.*) And some macaroons, Helene. Heaps of them — just this once.

HELMER (*taking her hands*): Now, now, now — no hysterics. Be my own little lark again.

NORA: Oh, I will soon enough. But go on in — and you, Dr. Rank. Kristine, help me put up my hair.

RANK (*whispering, as they go*): There's nothing wrong — really wrong, is there?

HELMER: Oh, of course not. It's nothing more than this childish anxiety I was telling you about. (*They go out, right.*)

NORA: Well?

MRS. LINDE: Left town.

NORA: I could see by your face.

MRS. LINDE: He'll be home tomorrow evening. I wrote him a note.

NORA: You shouldn't have. Don't try to stop anything now. After all, it's a wonderful joy, this waiting here for the miracle.

MRS. LINDE: What is it you're waiting for?

NORA: Oh, you can't understand that. Go in to them; I'll be along in a moment.

(*Mrs. Linde goes into the dining room. Nora stands a short while as if composing herself; then she looks at her watch.*)

NORA: Five. Seven hours to midnight. Twenty-four hours to the midnight after, and then the tarantella's done. Seven and twenty-four? Thirty-one hours to live.

HELMER (*in the doorway, right*): What's become of the little lark?

NORA (*going toward him with open arms*): Here's your lark!

ACT III

(*Same scene. The table, with chairs around it, has been moved to the center of the room. A lamp on the table is lit. The hall door stands open. Dance music drifts down from the floor above. Mrs. Linde sits at the table, absently paging through a book, trying to read, but apparently unable to focus her thoughts. Once or twice she pauses, tensely listening for a sound at the outer entrance.*)

MRS. LINDE (*glancing at her watch*): Not yet — and there's hardly any time left. If only he's not — (*Listening again.*) Ah, there it is. (*She goes out in the hall and cautiously opens the outer door. Quiet footsteps are heard on the stairs. She whispers.*) Come in. Nobody's here.

KROGSTAD (*in the doorway*): I found a note from you at home. What's back of all this?

MRS. LINDE: I just *had* to talk to you.

KROGSTAD: Oh? And it just *had* to be here in this house?

MRS. LINDE: At my place it was impossible; my room hasn't a private entrance. Come in, we're all alone. The maid's asleep, and the Helmers are at the dance upstairs.

KROGSTAD (*entering the room*): Well, well, the Helmers are dancing tonight? Really?

MRS. LINDE: Yes, why not?

KROGSTAD: How true — why not?

MRS. LINDE: All right, Krogstad, let's talk.

KROGSTAD: Do we two have anything more to talk about?

MRS. LINDE: We have a great deal to talk about.

KROGSTAD: I wouldn't have thought so.

MRS. LINDE: No, because you've never understood me, really.

KROGSTAD: Was there anything more to understand — except what's all too common in life? A calculating woman throws over a man the moment a better catch comes by.

MRS. LINDE: You think I'm so thoroughly calculating? You think I broke it off lightly?

KROGSTAD: Didn't you?

MRS. LINDE: Nils — is that what you really thought?

KROGSTAD: If you cared, then why did you write me the way you did?

MRS. LINDE: What else could I do? If I had to break off with you, then it was my job as well to root out everything you felt for me.

KROGSTAD (*wringing his hands*): So that was it. And this — all this, simply for money!

MRS. LINDE: Don't forget I had a helpless mother and two small brothers. We couldn't wait for you, Nils; you had such a long road ahead of you then.

KROGSTAD: That may be; but you still hadn't the right to abandon me for somebody else's sake.

MRS. LINDE: Yes — I don't know. So many, many times I've asked myself if I did have that right.

KROGSTAD (*more softly*): When I lost you, it was as if all the solid ground dissolved from under my feet. Look at me; I'm a half-drowned man now, hanging onto a wreck.

MRS. LINDE: Help may be near.

KROGSTAD: It was near — but then you came and blocked it off.

MRS. LINDE: Without my knowing it, Nils. Today for the first time I learned that it's you I'm replacing at the bank.

KROGSTAD: All right — I believe you. But now that you know, will you step aside?

MRS. LINDE: No, because that wouldn't benefit you in the slightest.

KROGSTAD: Not "benefit" me, hm! I'd step aside anyway.

MRS. LINDE: I've learned to be realistic. Life and hard, bitter necessity have taught me that.

KROGSTAD: And life's taught me never to trust fine phrases.

MRS. LINDE: Then life's taught you a very sound thing. But you do have to trust in actions, don't you?

KROGSTAD: What does that mean?

MRS. LINDE: You said you were hanging on like a half-drowned man to a wreck.

KROGSTAD: I've good reason to say that.

MRS. LINDE: I'm also like a half-drowned woman on a wreck. No one to suffer with; no one to care for.

KROGSTAD: You made your choice.

MRS. LINDE: There wasn't any choice then.

KROGSTAD: So — what of it?

MRS. LINDE: Nils, if only we two shipwrecked people could reach across to each other.

KROGSTAD: What are you saying?

MRS. LINDE: Two on one wreck are at least better off than each on his own.

KROGSTAD: Kristine!

MRS. LINDE: Why do you think I came into town?

KROGSTAD: Did you really have some thought of me?

MRS. LINDE: I have to work to go on living. All my born days, as long as I can remember, I've worked, and it's been my best and my only joy. But now I'm completely alone in the world; it frightens me to be so empty and lost. To work for yourself — there's no joy in that. Nils, give me something — someone to work for.

KROGSTAD: I don't believe all this. It's just some hysterical feminine urge to go out and make a noble sacrifice.

MRS. LINDE: Have you ever found me to be hysterical?

KROGSTAD: Can you honestly mean this? Tell me — do you know everything about my past?

MRS. LINDE: Yes.

KROGSTAD: And you know what they think I'm worth around here.

MRS. LINDE: From what you were saying before, it would seem that with me you could have been another person.

KROGSTAD: I'm positive of that.

MRS. LINDE: Couldn't it happen still?

KROGSTAD: Kristine — you're saying this in all seriousness? Yes, you are! I can see it in you. And do you really have the courage, then — ?

MRS. LINDE: I need to have someone to care for, and your children need a mother. We both need each other. Nils, I have faith that you're good at heart — I'll risk everything together with you.

KROGSTAD (*gripping her hands*): Kristine, thank you, thank you — Now I know I can win back a place in their eyes. Yes — but I forgot —

MRS. LINDE (*listening*): Shh! The tarantella. Go now! Go on!

KROGSTAD: Why? What is it?

MRS. LINDE: Hear the dance up there? When that's over, they'll be coming down.

KROGSTAD: Oh, then I'll go. But — it's all pointless. Of course, you don't know the move I made against the Helmers.

MRS. LINDE: Yes, Nils, I know.

KROGSTAD: And all the same, you have the courage to — ?

MRS. LINDE: I know how far despair can drive a man like you.

KROGSTAD: Oh, if I only could take it all back.

MRS. LINDE: You easily could — your letter's still lying in the mailbox.

KROGSTAD: Are you sure of that?

MRS. LINDE: Positive. But —

KROGSTAD (*looks at her searchingly*): Is that the meaning of it, then? You'll save your friend at any price. Tell me straight out. Is that it?

MRS. LINDE: Nils — anyone who's sold herself for somebody else once isn't going to do it again.

KROGSTAD: I'll demand my letter back.

MRS. LINDE: No, no.

KROGSTAD: Yes, of course. I'll stay here till Helmer comes down; I'll tell him to give me my letter again — that it only involves my dismissal — that he shouldn't read it —

MRS. LINDE: No, Nils, don't call the letter back.

KROGSTAD: But wasn't that exactly why you wrote me to come here?

MRS. LINDE: Yes, in that first panic. But it's been a whole day and night since then, and in that time I've seen such incredible things in this house. Helmer's got to learn everything; this dreadful secret has to be aired; those two have to come to a full understanding; all these lies and evasions can't go on.

KROGSTAD: Well, then, if you want to chance it. But at least there's one thing I can do, and do right away —

MRS. LINDE (*listening*): Go now, go, quick! The dance is over. We're not safe another second.

KROGSTAD: I'll wait for you downstairs.

MRS. LINDE: Yes, please do; take me home.

KROGSTAD: I can't believe it; I've never been so happy. (*He leaves by way of the outer door; the door between the room and the hall stays open.*)

MRS. LINDE (*straightening up a bit and getting together her street clothes*): How different now! How different! Someone to work for, to live for — a home to build. Well, it is worth the try! Oh, if they'd only come! (*Listening.*) Ah, there they are. Bundle up. (*She picks up her hat and coat. Nora's and Helmer's voices can be heard outside; a key turns in the lock, and Helmer brings Nora into the hall almost by force. She is wearing the Italian costume with a large black shawl about her; he has on evening dress, with a black domino open over it.*)

NORA (*struggling in the doorway*): No, no, no, not inside! I'm going up again. I don't want to leave so soon.

HELMER: But Nora dear —

NORA: Oh, I beg you, please, Torvald. From the bottom of my heart, *please* — only an hour more!

HELMER: Not a single minute, Nora darling. You know our agreement. Come on, in we go; you'll catch cold out here. (*In spite of her resistance, he gently draws her into the room.*)

MRS. LINDE: Good evening.

NORA: Kristine!

HELMER: Why, Mrs. Linde — are you here so late?

MRS. LINDE: Yes, I'm sorry, but I did want to see Nora in costume.

NORA: Have you been sitting here, waiting for me?

MRS. LINDE: Yes. I didn't come early enough; you were all upstairs; and then I thought I really couldn't leave without seeing you.

HELMER (*removing Nora's shawl*): Yes, take a good look. She's worth looking at, I can tell you that, Mrs. Linde. Isn't she lovely?

MRS. LINDE: Yes, I should say —

HELMER: A dream of loveliness, isn't she? That's what everyone thought at the party, too. But she's horribly stubborn — this sweet little thing. What's to be done with her? Can you imagine, I almost had to use force to pry her away.

NORA: Oh, Torvald, you're going to regret you didn't indulge me, even for just a half hour more.

HELMER: There, you see. She danced her tarantella and got a tumultuous hand — which was well earned, although the performance may have been a bit too naturalistic — I mean it rather overstepped the proprieties of art. But never mind — what's important is, she made a success, an overwhelming success. You think I could let her stay on after that and spoil the effect? Oh no; I took my lovely little Capri girl — my capricious little Capri girl, I should say — took her under my arm; one quick tour of the ballroom, a curtsy to every side, and then — as they say in novels — the beautiful vision disappeared. An exit should always be effective, Mrs. Linde, but that's what I can't get Nora to grasp. Phew, It's hot in here. (*Flings the domino on a chair and opens the door to his room.*) Why's it dark in here? Oh yes, of course. Excuse me. (*He goes in and lights a couple of candles.*)

NORA (*in a sharp, breathless whisper*): So?

MRS. LINDE (*quietly*): I talked with him.

NORA: And — ?

MRS. LINDE: Nora — you must tell your husband everything.

NORA (*dully*): I knew it.

MRS. LINDE: You've got nothing to fear from Krogstad, but you have to speak out.

NORA: I won't tell.

MRS. LINDE: Then the letter will.

NORA: Thanks, Kristine. I know now what's to be done. Shh!

HELMER (*reentering*): Well, then, Mrs. Linde — have you admired her?

MRS. LINDE: Yes, and now I'll say good night.

HELMER: Oh, come, so soon? Is this yours, this knitting?

MRS. LINDE: Yes, thanks. I nearly forgot it.

HELMER: Do you knit, then?

MRS. LINDE: Oh yes.

HELMER: You know what? You should embroider instead.

MRS. LINDE: Really? Why?

HELMER: Yes, because it's a lot prettier. See here, one holds the embroidery so, in the left hand, and then one guides the needle with the right — so — in an easy, sweeping curve — right?

MRS. LINDE: Yes, I guess that's —

HELMER: But, on the other hand, knitting — it can never be anything but ugly. Look, see here, the arms tucked in, the knitting needles going up and down — there's something Chinese about it. Ah, that was really a glorious champagne they served.

MRS. LINDE: Yes, good night, Nora, and don't be stubborn anymore.

HELMER: Well put, Mrs. Linde!

MRS. LINDE: Good night, Mr. Helmer.

HELMER (*accompanying her to the door*): Good night, good night. I hope you get home all right. I'd be very happy to — but you don't have far to go. Good night, good night. (*She leaves. He shuts the door after her and returns.*) There, now, at last we got her out the door. She's a deadly bore, that creature.

NORA: Aren't you pretty tired, Torvald?

HELMER: No, not a bit.

NORA: You're not sleepy?

HELMER: Not at all. On the contrary, I'm feeling quite exhilarated. But you? Yes, you really look tired and sleepy.

NORA: Yes, I'm very tired. Soon now I'll sleep.

HELMER: See! You see! I was right all along that we shouldn't stay longer.

NORA: Whatever you do is always right.

HELMER (*kissing her brow*): Now my little lark talks sense. Say, did you notice what a time Rank was having tonight?

NORA: Oh, was he? I didn't get to speak with him.

HELMER: I scarcely did either, but it's a long time since I've seen him in such high spirits. (*Gazes at her a moment, then comes nearer her.*) Hm — it's marvelous, though, to be back home again — to be completely alone with you. Oh, you bewitchingly lovely young woman!

NORA: Torvald, don't look at me like that!

HELMER: Can't I look at my richest treasure? At all that beauty that's mine, mine alone — completely and utterly.

NORA (*moving around to the other side of the table*): You mustn't talk to me that way tonight.

HELMER (*following her*): The tarantella is still in your blood. I can see — and it makes you even more enticing. Listen. The guests are beginning to go. (*Dropping his voice.*) Nora — it'll soon be quiet through this whole house.

NORA: Yes, I hope so.

HELMER: You do, don't you, my love? Do you realize — when I'm out at a party like this with you — do you know why I talk to you so little, and keep such a distance away; just send you a stolen look now and then — you know why I do it? It's because I'm imagining then that you're my secret darling, my secret young bride-to-be, and that no one suspects there's anything between us.

NORA: Yes, yes; oh, yes, I know you're always thinking of me.

HELMER: And then when we leave and I place the shawl over those fine young rounded shoulders — over that wonderful curving neck — then I pretend that you're my young bride, that we're just coming from the wedding, that for the first time I'm bringing you into my house — that for the first time I'm alone with you — completely alone with you, your trembling young beauty! All this evening I've longed for nothing but you. When I saw you turn and sway in the tarantella — my blood was pounding till I couldn't stand it — that's why I brought you down here so early —

NORA: Go away, Torvald! Leave me alone. I don't want all this.

HELMER: What do you mean? Nora, you're teasing me. You will, won't you? Aren't I your husband — ?

(*A knock at the outside door.*)

NORA (*startled*): What's that?

HELMER (*going toward the hall*): Who is it?

RANK (*outside*): It's me. May I come in a moment?

HELMER (*with quiet irritation*): Oh, what does he want now? (*Aloud.*) Hold on. (*Goes and opens the door.*) Oh, how nice that you didn't just pass us by!

RANK: I thought I heard your voice, and then I wanted so badly to have a look in. (*Lightly glancing about.*) Ah, me, these old familiar haunts. You have it snug and cozy in here, you two.

HELMER: You seemed to be having it pretty cozy upstairs, too.

RANK: Absolutely. Why shouldn't I? Why not take in everything in life? As much as you can, anyway, and as long as you can. The wine was superb —

HELMER: The champagne especially.

RANK: You noticed that too? It's amazing how much I could guzzle down.

NORA: Torvald also drank a lot of champagne this evening.

RANK: Oh?

NORA: Yes, and that always makes him so entertaining.

RANK: Well, why shouldn't one have a pleasant evening after a well-spent day?

HELMER: Well spent? I'm afraid I can't claim that.

RANK (*slapping him on the back*): But I can, you see!

NORA: Dr. Rank, you must have done some scientific research today.

RANK: Quite so.

HELMER: Come now — little Nora talking about scientific research!

NORA: And can I congratulate you on the results?

RANK: Indeed you may.

NORA: Then they were good?

RANK: The best possible for both doctor and patient — certainty.

NORA (*quickly and searchingly*): Certainty?

RANK: Complete certainty. So don't I owe myself a gay evening afterwards?

NORA: Yes, you're right, Dr. Rank.

HELMER: I'm with you — just so long as you don't have to suffer for it in the morning.

RANK: Well, one never gets something for nothing in life.

NORA: Dr. Rank — are you very fond of masquerade parties?

RANK: Yes, if there's a good array of odd disguises —

NORA: Tell me, what should we two go as at the next masquerade?

HELMER: You little featherhead — already thinking of the next!

RANK: We two? I'll tell you what: You must go as Charmed Life —

HELMER: Yes, but find a costume for that!

RANK: Your wife can appear just as she looks every day.

HELMER: That was nicely put. But don't you know what you're going to be?

RANK: Yes, Helmer, I've made up my mind.

HELMER: Well?

RANK: At the next masquerade I'm going to be invisible.

HELMER: That's a funny idea.

RANK: They say there's a hat — black, huge — have you never heard of the hat that makes you invisible? You put it on, and then no one on earth can see you.

HELMER (*suppressing a smile*): Ah, of course.

RANK: But I'm quite forgetting what I came for. Helmer, give me a cigar, one of the dark Havanas.

HELMER: With the greatest pleasure. (*Holds out his case.*)

RANK: Thanks. (*Takes one and cuts off the tip.*)

NORA (*striking a match*): Let me give you a light.

RANK: Thank you. (*She holds the match for him; he lights the cigar.*) And now good-bye.

HELMER: Good-bye, good-bye, old friend.

NORA: Sleep well, Doctor.

RANK: Thanks for that wish.

NORA: Wish me the same.

RANK: You? All right, if you like — Sleep well. And thanks for the light. (*He nods to them both and leaves.*)

HELMER (*his voice subdued*): He's been drinking heavily.

NORA (*absently*): Could be. (*Helmer takes his keys from his pocket and goes out in the hall.*) Torvald — what are you after?

HELMER: Got to empty the mailbox; it's nearly full. There won't be room for the morning papers.

NORA: Are you working tonight?

HELMER: You know I'm not. Why — what's this? Someone's been at the lock.

NORA: At the lock — ?

HELMER: Yes, I'm positive. What do you suppose — ? I can't imagine one of the maids — ? Here's a broken hairpin. Nora, it's yours —

NORA (*quickly*): Then it must be the children —

HELMER: You'd better break them of that. Hm, hm — well, opened it after all. (*Takes the contents out and calls into the kitchen.*) Helene! Helene, would you put out the lamp in the hall. (*He returns to the room, shutting the hall door, then displays the handful of mail.*) Look how it's piled up. (*Sorting through them.*) Now what's this?

NORA (*at the window*): The letter! Oh, Torvald, no!

HELMER: Two calling cards — from Rank.

NORA: From Dr. Rank?

HELMER (*examining them*): "Dr. Rank, Consulting Physician." They were on top. He must have dropped them in as he left.

NORA: Is there anything on them?

HELMER: There's a black cross over the name. See? That's a gruesome notion. He could almost be announcing his own death.

NORA: That's just what he's doing.

HELMER: What! You've heard something? Something he's told you?

NORA: Yes. That when those cards came, he'd be taking his leave of us. He'll shut himself in now and die.

HELMER: Ah, my poor friend! Of course I knew he wouldn't be here much longer. But so soon — And then to hide himself away like a wounded animal.

NORA: If it has to happen, then it's best it happens in silence — don't you think so, Torvald?

HELMER (*pacing up and down*): He's grown right into our lives. I simply can't imagine him gone. He with his suffering and loneliness — like a dark cloud setting off our sunlit happiness. Well, maybe it's best this way. For him, at least. (*Standing still.*) And maybe for us too, Nora. Now we're thrown back on each other, completely. (*Embracing her.*) Oh you, my darling wife, how can I hold you close enough? You know what, Nora — time and again I've wished you were in some terrible danger, just so I could stake my life and soul and everything, for your sake.

NORA (*tearing herself away, her voice firm and decisive*): Now you must read your mail, Torvald.

HELMER: No, no, not tonight. I want to stay with you, dearest.

NORA: With a dying friend on your mind?

HELMER: You're right. We've both had a shock. There's ugliness between us — these thoughts of death and corruption. We'll have to get free of them first. Until then — we'll stay apart.

NORA (*clinging about his neck*): Torvald — good night! Good night!

HELMER (*kissing her on the cheek*): Good night, little songbird. Sleep well, Nora. I'll be reading my mail now. (*He takes the letters into his room and shuts the door after him.*)

NORA (*with bewildered glances, groping about, seizing Helmer's domino, throwing it around her, and speaking in short, hoarse, broken whispers*): Never see him again. Never, never. (*Putting her shawl over her head.*) Never see the children either — them, too. Never, never. Oh, the freezing black water! The depths — down — Oh, I wish it were over — He has it now; he's reading it — now. Oh no, no, not yet. Torvald, good-bye, you and the children — (*She starts for the hall; as she does, Helmer throws open his door and stands with an open letter in his hand.*)

HELMER: Nora!

NORA (*screams*): Oh — !

HELMER: What is this? You know what's in this letter?

NORA: Yes, I know. Let me go! Let me out!

HELMER (*holding her back*): Where are you going?

NORA (*struggling to break loose*): You can't save me, Torvald!

HELMER (*slumping back*): True! Then it's true what he writes? How horrible! No, no, it's impossible — it can't be true.

NORA: It *is* true. I've loved you more than all this world.

HELMER: Ah, none of your slippery tricks.

NORA (*taking one step toward him*): Torvald — !

HELMER: What *is* this you've blundered into!

NORA: Just let me loose. You're not going to suffer for my sake. You're not going to take on my guilt.

HELMER: No more playacting. (*Locks the hall door.*) You stay right here and give me a reckoning. You understand what you've done? Answer! You understand?

NORA (*looking squarely at him, her face hardening*): Yes. I'm beginning to understand everything now.

HELMER (*striding about*): Oh, what an awful awakening! In all these eight years — she who was my pride and joy — a hypocrite, a liar — worse, worse — a criminal! How infinitely disgusting it all is! The shame! (*Nora says nothing and goes on looking straight at him. He stops in front of her.*) I should have suspected something of the kind. I should have known. All your father's flimsy values — Be still! All your father's flimsy values have come out in you. No religion, no morals, no sense of duty — Oh, how I'm punished for letting him off! I did it for your sake, and you repay me like this.

NORA: Yes, like this.

HELMER: Now you've wrecked all my happiness — ruined my whole future. Oh, it's awful to think of. I'm in a cheap little grafter's hands; he can do anything he wants with me, ask for anything, play with me like a puppet — and I can't breathe a word. I'll be swept down miserably into the depths on account of a featherbrained woman.

NORA: When I'm gone from this world, you'll be free.

HELMER: Oh, quit posing. Your father had a mess of those speeches too. What good would that ever do me if you were gone from this world, as you say? Not the slightest. He can still make the whole thing known; and if he does, I could be falsely suspected as your accomplice. They might even think that I was behind it — that I put you up to it. And all that I can thank you for — you that I've coddled the whole of our marriage. Can you see now what you've done to me?

NORA (*icily calm*): Yes.

HELMER: It's so incredible, I just can't grasp it. But we'll have to patch up whatever we can. Take off the shawl. I said, take it off! I've got to appease him somehow or other. The thing has to be hushed up at any cost. And as for you and me, it's got to seem like everything between us is just as it was — to the outside world, that is. You'll go right on living in this house, of course. But you can't be allowed to bring up the children; I don't dare trust you with them — Oh, to have to say this to someone I've loved so much! Well, that's done with. From now on happiness doesn't matter; all that matters is saving the bits and pieces, the appearance — (*The doorbell rings. Helmer starts.*) What's that? And so late. Maybe the worst — ? You think he'd — ? Hide, Nora! Say you're sick. (*Nora remains standing motionless. Helmer goes and opens the door.*)

MAID (*half dressed, in the hall*): A letter for Mrs. Helmer.

HELMER: I'll take it. (*Snatches the letter and shuts the door.*) Yes, it's from him. You don't get it; I'm reading it myself.

NORA: Then read it.

HELMER (*by the lamp*): I hardly dare. We may be ruined, you and I. But — I've got to know. (*Rips open the letter, skims through a few lines, glances at an enclosure, then cries out joyfully.*) Nora! (*Nora looks inquiringly at him.*) Nora! Wait — better check it again — Yes, yes, it's true. I'm saved. Nora, I'm saved!

NORA: And I?

HELMER: You too, of course. We're both saved, both of us. Look. He's sent back your note. He says he's sorry and ashamed — that a happy development in his life — oh, who cares what he says! Nora, we're saved! No one can hurt you. Oh, Nora, Nora — but first, this ugliness all has to go. Let me see — (*Takes a look at the note.*) No, I don't want to see it; I want the whole thing to fade like a dream. (*Tears the note and both letters to pieces, throws them into the stove and watches them burn.*) There — now there's nothing left — He wrote that since Christmas Eve you — Oh, they must have been three terrible days for you, Nora.

NORA: I fought a hard fight.

HELMER: And suffered pain and saw no escape but — No, we're not going to dwell on anything unpleasant. We'll just be grateful and keep on repeating: It's over now, it's over! You hear me, Nora? You don't seem to realize — it's over. What's it mean — that frozen look? Oh, poor little Nora, I understand. You

can't believe I've forgiven you. But I have, Nora; I swear I have. I know that what you did, you did out of love for me.

NORA: That's true.

HELMER: You loved me the way a wife ought to love her husband. It's simply the means that you couldn't judge. But you think I love you any the less for not knowing how to handle your affairs? No, no — just lean on me; I'll guide you and teach you. I wouldn't be a man if this feminine helplessness didn't make you twice as attractive to me. You mustn't mind those sharp words I said — that was all in the first confusion of thinking my world had collapsed. I've forgiven you, Nora; I swear I've forgiven you.

NORA: My thanks for your forgiveness. (*She goes out through the door, right.*)

HELMER: No, wait — (*Peers in.*) What are you doing in there?

NORA (*inside*): Getting out of my costume.

HELMER (*by the open door*): Yes, do that. Try to calm yourself and collect your thoughts again, my frightened little songbird. You can rest easy now; I've got wide wings to shelter you with. (*Walking about close by the door.*) How snug and nice our home is, Nora. You're safe here; I'll keep you like a hunted dove I've rescued out of a hawk's claws. I'll bring peace to your poor, shuddering heart. Gradually it'll happen, Nora; you'll see. Tomorrow all this will look different to you; then everything will be as it was. I won't have to go on repeating I forgive you; you'll feel it for yourself. How can you imagine I'd conceivably want to disown you — or even blame you in any way? Ah, you don't know a man's heart, Nora. For a man there's something indescribably sweet and satisfying in knowing he's forgiven his wife — and forgiven her out of a full and open heart. It's as if she belongs to him in two ways now: In a sense he's given her fresh into the world again, and she's become his wife and his child as well. From now on that's what you'll be to me — you little, bewildered, helpless thing. Don't be afraid of anything, Nora; just open your heart to me, and I'll be conscience and will to you both — (*Nora enters in her regular clothes.*) What's this? Not in bed? You've changed your dress?

NORA: Yes, Torvald, I've changed my dress.

HELMER: But why now, so late?

NORA: Tonight I'm not sleeping.

HELMER: But Nora dear —

NORA (*looking at her watch*): It's still not so very late. Sit down, Torvald; we have a lot to talk over. (*She sits at one side of the table.*)

HELMER: Nora — what is this? That hard expression —

NORA: Sit down. This'll take some time. I have a lot to say.

HELMER (*sitting at the table directly opposite her*): You worry me, Nora. And I don't understand you.

NORA: No, that's exactly it. You don't understand me. And I've never understood you either — until tonight. No, don't interrupt. You can just listen to what I say. We're closing out accounts, Torvald.

HELMER: How do you mean that?

NORA (*after a short pause*): Doesn't anything strike you about our sitting here like this?

HELMER: What's that?

NORA: We've been married now eight years. Doesn't it occur to you that this is the first time we two, you and I, man and wife, have ever talked seriously together?

HELMER: What do you mean — seriously?

NORA: In eight whole years — longer even — right from our first acquaintance, we've never exchanged a serious word on any serious thing.

HELMER: You mean I should constantly go and involve you in problems you couldn't possibly help me with?

NORA: I'm not talking of problems. I'm saying that we've never sat down seriously together and tried to get to the bottom of anything.

HELMER: But dearest, what good would that ever do you?

NORA: That's the point right there: You've never understood me. I've been wronged greatly, Torvald — first by Papa, and then by you.

HELMER: What! By us — the two people who've loved you more than anyone else?

NORA (*shaking her head*): You never loved me. You've thought it fun to be in love with me, that's all.

HELMER: Nora, what a thing to say!

NORA: Yes, it's true now, Torvald. When I lived at home with Papa, he told me all his opinions, so I had the same ones too; or if they were different I hid them, since he wouldn't have cared for that. He used to call me his doll-child, and he played with me the way I played with my dolls. Then I came into your house —

HELMER: How can you speak of our marriage like that?

NORA (*unperturbed*): I mean, then I went from Papa's hands into yours. You arranged everything to your own taste, and so I got the same taste as you — or I pretended to; I can't remember. I guess a little of both, first one, then the other. Now when I look back, it seems as if I'd lived here like a beggar — just from hand to mouth. I've lived by doing tricks for you, Torvald. But that's the way you wanted it. It's a great sin what you and Papa did to me. You're to blame that nothing's become of me.

HELMER: Nora, how unfair and ungrateful you are! Haven't you been happy here?

NORA: No, never. I thought so — but I never have.

HELMER: Not — not happy!

NORA: No, only lighthearted. And you've always been so kind to me. But our home's been nothing but a playpen. I've been your doll-wife here, just as at home I was Papa's doll-child. And in turn the children have been my dolls. I thought it was fun when you played with me, just as they thought it fun when I played with them. That's been our marriage, Torvald.

HELMER: There's some truth in what you're saying — under all the raving exaggeration. But it'll all be different after this. Playtime's over; now for the schooling.

NORA: Whose schooling — mine or the children's?

HELMER: Both yours and the children's, dearest.

NORA: Oh, Torvald, you're not the man to teach me to be a good wife to you.

HELMER: And you can say that?

NORA: And I — how am I equipped to bring up children?

HELMER: Nora!

NORA: Didn't you say a moment ago that that was no job to trust me with?

HELMER: In a flare of temper! Why fasten on that?

NORA: Yes, but you were so very right. I'm not up to the job. There's another job I have to do first. I have to try to educate myself. You can't help me with that. I've got to do it alone. And that's why I'm leaving you now.

HELMER (*jumping up*): What's that?

NORA: I have to stand completely alone, if I'm ever going to discover myself and the world out there. So I can't go on living with you.

HELMER: Nora, Nora!

NORA: I want to leave right away. Kristine should put me up for the night —

HELMER: You're insane! You've no right! I forbid you!

NORA: From here on, there's no use forbidding me anything. I'll take with me whatever is mine. I don't want a thing from you, either now or later.

HELMER: What kind of madness is this!

NORA: Tomorrow I'm going home — I mean, home where I came from. It'll be easier up there to find something to do.

HELMER: Oh, you blind, incompetent child!

NORA: I must learn to be competent, Torvald.

HELMER: Abandon your home, your husband, your children! And you're not even thinking what people will say.

NORA: I can't be concerned about that. I only know how essential this is.

HELMER: Oh, it's outrageous. So you'll run out like this on your most sacred vows.

NORA: What do you think are my most sacred vows?

HELMER: And I have to tell you that! Aren't they your duties to your husband and children?

NORA: I have other duties equally sacred.

HELMER: That isn't true. What duties are they?

NORA: Duties to myself.

HELMER: Before all else, you're a wife and a mother.

NORA: I don't believe in that anymore. I believe that before all else, I'm a human being, no less than you — or anyway, I ought to try to become one. I know the majority thinks you're right, Torvald, and plenty of books agree with you, too. But I can't go on believing what the majority says, or what's written in books. I have to think over these things myself and try to understand them.

HELMER: Why can't you understand your place in your own home? On a point like that, isn't there one everlasting guide you can turn to? Where's your religion?

NORA: Oh, Torvald, I'm really not sure what religion is.

HELMER: What — ?

NORA: I only know what the minister said when I was confirmed. He told me religion was this thing and that. When I get clear and away by myself, I'll go into that problem too. I'll see if what the minister said was right, or, in any case, if it's right for me.

HELMER: A young woman your age shouldn't talk like that. If religion can't move you, I can try to rouse your conscience. You do have some moral feeling? Or, tell me — has that gone too?

NORA: It's not easy to answer that, Torvald. I simply don't know. I'm all confused about these things. I just know I see them so differently from you. I find out for one thing, that the law's not at all what I'd thought — but I can't get it through my head that the law is fair. A woman hasn't a right to protect her dying father or save her husband's life! I can't believe that.

HELMER: You talk like a child. You don't know anything of the world you live in.

NORA: No, I don't. But now I'll begin to learn for myself. I'll try to discover who's right, the world or I.

HELMER: Nora, you're sick; you've got a fever. I almost think you're out of your head.

NORA: I've never felt more clearheaded and sure in my life.

HELMER: And — clearheaded and sure — you're leaving your husband and children?

NORA: Yes.

HELMER: Then there's only one possible reason.

NORA: What?

HELMER: You no longer love me.

NORA: No. That's exactly it.

HELMER: Nora! You can't be serious!

NORA: Oh, this is so hard, Torvald — you've been so kind to me always. But I can't help it. I don't love you anymore.

HELMER (*struggling for composure*): Are you also clearheaded and sure about that?

NORA: Yes, completely. That's why I can't go on staying here.

HELMER: Can you tell me what I did to lose your love?

NORA: Yes, I can tell you. It was this evening when the miraculous thing didn't come — then I knew you weren't the man I'd imagined.

HELMER: Be more explicit; I don't follow you.

NORA: I've waited now so patiently eight long years — for, my Lord, I know miracles don't come every day. Then this crisis broke over me, and such a certainty filled me: *Now* the miraculous event would occur. While Krogstad's letter was lying out there, I never for an instant dreamed that you could give in to his terms. I was so utterly sure you'd say to him: Go on, tell your tale to the whole wide world. And when he'd done that —

Janet McTeer as Nora Helmer in Anthony Page's production of *A Doll House* at the Belasco Theater on Broadway, 1997. McTeer's interpretation of the role electrified audiences who, according to Ben Brantley, found "previously hidden nuances in Ibsen's landmark work."

HELMER: Yes, what then? When I'd delivered my own wife into shame and disgrace — !

NORA: When he'd done that, I was so utterly sure that you'd step forward, take the blame on yourself and say: I am the guilty one.

HELMER: Nora — !

NORA: You're thinking I'd never accept such a sacrifice from you? No, of course not. But what good would my protests be against you? That was the miracle I was waiting for, in terror and hope. And to stave that off, I would have taken my life.

HELMER: I'd gladly work for you day and night, Nora — and take on pain and deprivation. But there's no one who gives up honor for love.

NORA: Millions of women have done just that.

HELMER: Oh, you think and talk like a silly child.

NORA: Perhaps. But you neither think nor talk like the man I could join myself to. When your big fright was over — and it wasn't from any threat against me, only for what might damage you — when all the danger was past, for you it was just as if nothing had happened. I was exactly the same, your little lark, your doll, that you'd have to handle with double care now that I'd turned out so brittle and frail. (*Gets up.*) Torvald — in that instant it dawned on me that for eight years I've been living here with a stranger, and that I'd even conceived three children — oh, I can't stand the thought of it! I could tear myself to bits.

HELMER (*heavily*): I see. There's a gulf that's opened between us — that's clear. Oh, but Nora, can't we bridge it somehow?

NORA: The way I am now, I'm no wife for you.

HELMER: I have the strength to make myself over.

NORA: Maybe — if your doll gets taken away.

HELMER: But to part! To part from you! No, Nora, no — I can't imagine it.

NORA (*going out, right*): All the more reason why it has to be. (*She reenters with her coat and a small overnight bag, which she puts on a chair by the table.*)

HELMER: Nora, Nora, not now! Wait till tomorrow.

NORA: I can't spend the night in a strange man's room.

HELMER: But couldn't we live here like brother and sister —

NORA: You know very well how long that would last. (*Throws her shawl about her.*) Good-bye, Torvald. I won't look in on the children. I know they're in better hands than mine. The way I am now, I'm no use to them.

HELMER: But someday, Nora — someday — ?

NORA: How can I tell? I haven't the least idea what'll become of me.

HELMER: But you're my wife, now and wherever you go.

NORA: Listen, Torvald — I've heard that when a wife deserts her husband's house just as I'm doing, then the law frees him from all responsibility. In any case, I'm freeing you from being responsible. Don't feel yourself bound, any more than I will. There has to be absolute freedom for us both. Here, take your ring back. Give me mine.

HELMER: That too?

NORA: That too.

HELMER: There it is.

NORA: Good. Well, now it's all over. I'm putting the keys here. The maids know all about keeping up the house — better than I do. Tomorrow, after I've left town, Kristine will stop by to pack up everything that's mine from home. I'd like those things shipped up to me.

HELMER: Over! All over! Nora, won't you ever think about me?

NORA: I'm sure I'll think of you often, and about the children and the house here.

HELMER: May I write you?

NORA: No — never. You're not to do that.

HELMER: Oh, but let me send you —

NORA: Nothing. Nothing.

HELMER: Or help you if you need it.

NORA: No. I accept nothing from strangers.

HELMER: Nora — can I never be more than a stranger to you?

NORA (*picking up the overnight bag*): Ah, Torvald — it would take the greatest miracle of all —

HELMER: Tell me the greatest miracle!

NORA: You and I both would have to transform ourselves to the point that — Oh, Torvald, I've stopped believing in miracles.

HELMER: But I'll believe. Tell me! Transform ourselves to the point that — ?

NORA: That our living together could be a true marriage. (*She goes out down the hall.*)

HELMER (*sinks down on a chair by the door, face buried in his hands*): Nora! Nora! (*Looking about and rising.*) Empty. She's gone. (*A sudden hope leaps in him.*) The greatest miracle — ?

(*From below, the sound of a door slamming shut.*)

COMMENTARIES

Ibsen wrote about his own work, both in his letters to producers and actors and in his notes describing the development of his plays. Such notes reveal his concern, his insights as he wrote the plays, and his motives. Sometimes what he says about the plays does not completely square with modern interpretations. On the other hand, he explains in his notes that the circumstances of women in modern society were much on his mind when he was working on *A Doll House*.

Ibsen's "Notes for the Modern Tragedy" is remarkable for suggesting a separate sensibility (spiritual law) for men and for women. His observations about the society in which women live — and in which Nora is confounded — sound as if they could have been written a century later than they were. When Bernard Shaw wrote his comments on *A Doll House*, the play was a popular shocker; Shaw's observations were designed to help audiences interpret the play's actions more carefully. He is one of the earliest critics of the play, and one must remember while reading Shaw that some productions of the play changed the ending to make it happy. Muriel C. Bradbrook's discussion of *A Doll House* focuses on the moral bankruptcy of Nora's situation, which is to say the situation of all wives of the period.

Henrik Ibsen (1828–1906)

NOTES FOR THE MODERN TRAGEDY   1878

TRANSLATED BY A. G. CHATER

Ibsen's first notes for A Doll House *were jotted down on October 19, 1878. They show that his thinking on the relations between men and women was considerably sophisticated and that the material for the play had been gestating. His comments indicate that the essentially male society he knew was one of his central concerns in the play.*

There are two kinds of spiritual law, two kinds of conscience, one in man and another, altogether different, in woman. They do not understand each other; but in practical life the woman is judged by man's law, as though she were not a woman but a man.

The wife in the play ends by having no idea of what is right or wrong; natural feeling on the one hand and belief in authority on the other have altogether bewildered her.

A woman cannot be herself in the society of the present day, which is an exclusively masculine society, with laws framed by men and with a judicial system that judges feminine conduct from a masculine point of view.

She has committed forgery, and she is proud of it; for she did it out of love for her husband, to save his life. But this husband with his commonplace principles of honor is on the side of the law and looks at the question from the masculine point of view.

Spiritual conflicts. Oppressed and bewildered by the belief in authority, she loses faith in her moral right and ability to bring up her children. Bitterness. A mother in modern society, like certain insects who go away and die when she has done her duty in the propagation of the race. Love of life, of home, of husband and children and family. Now and then a womanly shaking off of her thoughts. Sudden return of anxiety and terror. She must bear it all alone. The catastrophe approaches, inexorably, inevitably. Despair, conflict, and destruction.

(Krogstad has acted dishonorably and thereby become well-to-do; now his prosperity does not help him, he cannot recover his honor.)

Bernard Shaw (1856–1950)
A DOLL'S HOUSE   1891

One of the first English men of letters to pay close attention to Ibsen's work was Bernard Shaw. While beginning to write his own plays, Shaw also spent time in the theater as a critic. His landmark book The Quintessence of Ibsenism *(1891; rev. ed. 1913), in which this comment on A Doll House appears, is a thorough discussion not only of the individual plays that Ibsen had produced but also of their implication for future literature. Shaw saw the significance of the new realism and its implications for the audiences of the late nineteenth century. He saw, too, that Ibsen's brand of realism would have an effect on the beliefs of his audiences, that Ibsen's drama was a drama of important ideas. In the following excerpt Shaw is especially sensitive to the feminist issues that are at the heart of the play, and he pays close attention to Nora's character development.*

Unfortunately, *Pillars of Society*, as a propagandist play, is disabled by the circumstance that the hero, being a fraudulent hypocrite in the ordinary police-court sense of the phrase, would hardly be accepted as a typical pillar of society by the class he represents. Accordingly, Ibsen took care next time to make his idealist irreproachable from the standpoint of the ordinary idealist morality. In the famous *Doll's House*, the pillar of society who owns the doll is a model husband, father, and citizen. In his little household, with the three darling children and the affectionate little wife, all on the most loving terms with one another, we have the sweet home, the womanly woman, the happy family life of the idealist's dream. Mrs. Nora Helmer is happy in the belief that she has attained a valid realization of all these illusions; that she is an ideal wife and mother; and that Helmer is an ideal husband who would, if the necessity arose, give his life to save her reputation. A few simply contrived incidents disabuse her effectually on all these points. One of her earliest acts of devotion to her husband has been the secret raising of a sum of money to enable him to make a tour which was necessary to restore his health. As he would have broken down sooner than go into debt, she has had to persuade him that the money was a gift from her father. It was really obtained from a money-lender, who refused to make her the loan unless she induced her father to endorse the promissory note. This being impossible, as her father was dying at the time, she took the shortest way out of the difficulty by writing the name herself, to the entire satisfaction of the moneylender, who, though not at all duped, knew that forged bills are often the surest to be paid. Since then she has slaved in secret at scrivener's work until she has nearly paid off the debt.

At this point Helmer is made manager of the bank in which he is employed; and the moneylender, wishing to obtain a post there, uses the forged bill to force Nora to exert her influence with Helmer on his behalf. But she, having a hearty contempt for the man, cannot be persuaded by him that there was any harm in putting her father's name on the bill, and ridicules the suggestion that the law would not recognize that she was right under the circumstances. It is her husband's own contemptuous denunciation of a forgery formerly committed by the moneylender himself that destroys her self-satisfaction and opens her eyes to her ignorance of the serious business of the world to which her husband belongs: the world outside the home he shares with her. When he goes on to tell her that commercial dishonesty is generally to be traced to the influence of bad mothers, she begins to perceive that the happy way in which she plays with the children, and the care she takes to dress them nicely, are not sufficient to constitute her a fit person to train them. To redeem the forged bill, she resolves to borrow the balance due upon it from an intimate friend of the family. She has learnt to coax her husband into giving her what she asks by appealing to his affection for her: that is, by playing all sorts of pretty tricks until he is wheedled into an amorous humor. This plan she has adopted without thinking about it, instinctively taking the line of least resistance with him. And now she naturally takes the same line with her husband's friend. An unexpected declaration of love from him is the result; and it at once explains to her the real nature of the domestic influence she has been so proud of.

All her illusions about herself are now shattered. She sees herself as an ignorant and silly woman, a dangerous mother, and a wife kept for her husband's pleasure merely; but she clings all the harder to her illusion about him: he is still the ideal husband who would make any sacrifice to rescue her from ruin. She resolves to kill herself rather than allow him to destroy his own career by taking the forgery on himself to save her reputation. The final disillusion comes when he, instead of at once proposing to pursue this ideal line of conduct when he hears of the forgery, naturally enough flies into a vulgar rage and heaps invective on her for disgracing him. Then she sees that their whole family life has been a fiction: their home a mere doll's house in which they have been playing at ideal husband and father, wife and mother. So she leaves him then and there and goes out into the real world to find out its reality for herself, and to gain some position not fundamentally false, refusing to see her children again until she is fit to be in charge of them, or to live with him until she and he become capable of a more honorable relation to one another. He at first cannot understand what has happened, and flourishes the shattered ideals over her as if they were as potent as ever. He presents the course most agreeable to him — that of her staying at home and avoiding a scandal — as her duty to her husband, to her children, and to her religion; but the magic of these disguises is gone; and at last even he understands what has really happened, and sits down alone to wonder whether that more honorable relation can ever come to pass between them.

Muriel C. Bradbrook (1909–1993)
A Doll's House: Ibsen the Moralist   1948

In her important study of Ibsen, Ibsen: The Norwegian, *Muriel Bradbrook discusses all the important plays, but she reserves a special place for* A Doll House. *In her analysis she suggests that Nora slowly discovers the fundamental bankruptcy of her marriage. Bradbrook calls it "eight years' prostitution." She also shows the true extent of Torvald's possessiveness and immaturity. As Bradbrook says, the true moment of recognition — in the Greek tragic sense — occurs when Nora sees both herself and Torvald in their true nature. Bradbrook also helps us see the full implication of Nora's leaving her home. She can never hope again for the comforts she has enjoyed as Torvald's wife.*

Poor Nora, living by playing her tricks like a little pet animal, sensing how to manage Torvald by those pettinesses in his character she does not know she knows of, is too vulnerably sympathetic to find her life-work in reading John Stuart Mill. At the end she still does not understand the strange world in which she has done wrong by forging a signature. She does understand that she has lived by what Virginia Woolf called "the slow waterlogged sinking of her will into his." And this picture is built up for her and for us by the power of structural implication, a form of writing particularly suited to drama, where the latent possibilities of a long stretch of past time can be thrown into relief by a crisis. In *A Doll's House,* the past is not only lighted up by the present, as a transparency might be lit up with a lamp; the past is changed by the present so that it becomes a different thing. Nora's marriage becomes eight years' prostitution, as she gradually learns the true nature of her relations with Torvald and the true nature of Torvald's feelings for her.

In Act I, no less than six different episodes bring out the war that is secretly waged between his masculine dictatorship and her feminine wiles:

Her wheedling him for money with a simple transference: "Let us do as *you* suggest. . . ."

Her promise to Christine: "Just leave it to me: I will broach the matter very cleverly." She is evidently habituated to and aware of her own technique.

Her description of how she tried to coax Torvald into taking the holiday and how she was saving up the story of the bond "for when I am no longer as good-looking as I am now." She knows the precarious nature of her hold.

Her method of asking work for Christine by putting Christine also into a (completely bogus) position of worshiping subservience to Torvald.

Her boast to Krogstad about her influence. Whilst this may be a justifiable triumph over her tormentor, it is an unconscious betrayal of Torvald (witness his fury in Act II at the idea of being thought uxorious).

After this faceted exposition, the treatment grows much broader. Nora admits Torvald's jealousy: Yet she flirts with Rank, aware but not acknowledging the grounds of her control. The pressure of implication remains constant throughout: It is comparable with the effect of a dialect, coloring all that is said. To take a few lines at random from the dialogue of Nora and Rank in Act II:

> NORA (*putting her hand on his shoulder*): Dear, dear Dr. Rank! Death mustn't take you away from Torvald and me. [Nora is getting demonstrative as she senses Rank's responsiveness, and her hopes of obtaining a loan from him rise. Hence her warmth of feeling, purely seductive.]
>
> RANK: It is a loss you will easily recover from. Those who are gone away are soon forgotten. [Poor Rank is reminded by that "Torvald and me" how little he really counts to Nora.]
>
> NORA (*anxiously*): Do you believe that? [Rank has awakened her thoughts of what may happen if *she* has to go away.]

Her methods grow more desperate — the open appeal to Torvald to keep Krogstad and the frantic expedient of the tarantella. In the last act her fate is upon her; yet in spite of all her terror and Torvald's tipsy amorousness, she still believes in his chivalry and devotion. This extraordinary self-deception is perhaps the subtlest and most telling implication of all. Practice had left her theory unshaken: So when the crash comes, she cries, "I have been living with a strange man," yet it was but the kind of man her actions had always implied him to be. Her vanity had completely prevented her from recognizing what she was doing, even though she had become such an expert at doing it.

Torvald is more gradually revealed. In the first act he appears indulgent, perhaps a trifle inclined to nag about the macaroons and to preach, but virtually a more efficient David Copperfield curbing a rather better-trained Dora. In the second act, his resentment and his pleasure alike uncover the deeper bases of his dominance. His anger at the prospect of being thought under his wife's influence and his fury at the imputation of narrow-mindedness show that it is really based on his own cowardice, the need for something weaker to bully: This is confirmed when he gloats over Nora's panic as evidence of her love for him, and over her agitation in the tarantella ("you little helpless thing!"). His love of order and his fastidiousness, when joined to such qualities, betray a set personality; and the last act shows that he has neither control nor sympathy on the physical level. But he is no fool, and his integrity is not all cowardice. Doubtless, debt or forgery really was abhorrent to him.

The climax of the play comes when Nora sees Torvald and sees herself: It is an *anagnorisis,* a recognition. Her life is cored like an apple. For she has had no life apart from this. Behind the irrelevant program for self-education there stands a woman, pitifully inexperienced, numbed by emotional shock, but with a newfound will to face what has happened, to accept her bankruptcy, as, in a very different way, Peer Gynt had at last accepted his.

"Yes, I am beginning to understand. . . ." she says. "What you did," observes the now magnanimous Torvald, "you did out of love for me." "That is true," says Nora: And she calls him to a "settling of accounts," not in any spirit of hostility but in an attempt to organize vacancy. "I have made nothing of my life. . . . I must stand quite alone . . . it is necessary to me . . ." That is really the program. *Ainsi tout leur a craqué dans les mains.*°

The spare and laminated speech gains its effect by inference and riddle. But these are the characteristic virtues of Norse. Irony is its natural weapon. Ibsen was working with the grain of the language. It was no accident that it fell to a Norwegian to take that most finely tooled art, the drama, and bring it to a point and precision so nice that literally not a phrase is without its direct contribution to the structure. The unrelenting cohesion of *A Doll's House* is perhaps, like that of the *Oedipus the King,* too hard on the playgoer; he is allowed no relief. Nora cannot coo to her baby without saying: "My sweet little *baby doll!*" or play with her children without choosing, significantly, *Hide and Seek.* Ibsen will not allow the smallest action to escape from the psychopathology of everyday life. However, a play cannot be acted so that every moment is tense with significance, and, in practice, an actor, for the sake of light and shade, will probably slur some of Ibsen's points, deliberately or unconsciously. The tension between the characters is such that the slightest movement of one sets all the others quivering. But this is partly because they are seen with such detachment, like a clear-cut intaglio. The play is, above all, articulated.

That is not to say that it is the mere dissection of a problem. Perhaps Rank and Mrs. Linde would have been more subtly wrought into the action at a later date; but the tight control kept over Nora and Torvald does not mean that they can be exhausted by analysis or staled by custom. They are so far in advance of the characters of *Pillars of Society* that they are capable of the surprising yet inevitable development that marks the character conceived "in the round," the character that is, in Ibsen's phrase, fully "seen."

Consider, for example, Torvald's soliloquy whilst Nora is taking off her masquerade dress. It recalls at one moment Dickens's most unctuous hypocrites — "Here I will protect you like a hunted dove that I have saved from the claws of the hawk!"— at another Meredith's Willoughby Patterne° —"Only be frank and open with me and I will be both will and conscience to you"— yet from broadest caricature to sharpest analysis, it remains the self-glorified strut of the one character, the bank clerk in his pride, cousin to Peer Gynt, that typical Norwegian, and to Hjalmer Ekdal, the toiling breadwinner of the studio.

Whilst the Ibsenites might have conceded that Torvald is Art, they would probably have contended that Nora is Truth. Nora, however, is much more than a Revolting Wife. She is not a sour misanthropist or a fighting suffragette, but a lovely young woman who knows that she still holds her husband firmly infatuated after eight years of marriage. . . .

In leaving her husband Nora is seeking a fuller life as a human being. She is emancipating herself. Yet the seeking itself is also a renunciation, a kind of death — "I must stand alone." No less than Falk, or the hero of *On the Vidda,* she gives up something that has been her whole life. She is as broken as Torvald in the end: But she is a strong character and he is a weak one. In the "happy ending" which Ibsen reluctantly allowed to be used, it was the sight of the children that persuaded her to

Ainsi . . . mains: Thus everything has shattered in their hands.
Willoughby Patterne: The protagonist in George Meredith's novel *The Egoist* (1879), an arrogant aristocrat who lacks awareness of the needs and desires of the women in his life.

stay, and unless it is remembered that leaving Torvald means leaving the children, the full measure of Nora's decision cannot be taken. An actress gets her chance to make this point in the reply to Torvald's plea that Nora should stay for the children's sake.

It should be remembered, too, that the seriousness of the step she takes is lost on the present generation. She was putting herself outside society, inviting insult, destitution, and loneliness. She went out into a very dark night.

August Strindberg

The Swedish playwright August Strindberg (1849–1912) wrote fifty-eight plays, more than a dozen novels, and more than a hundred short stories, all collected now in fifty-five volumes. Much of the time he was producing this astonishing body of work, he was the victim of persistent paranoia, suffered the destruction of three marriages, and lived through a major nervous breakdown.

He was a man of enormous complexity whose work has traditionally been broken into two parts. The first comprises the work he wrote up to 1894, which includes *The Father* (1877), *Miss Julie* (1888), *The Creditors* (1889), and other naturalistic plays; the second comprises work he wrote after 1897, including *To Damascus* (1898–1901), *There Are Crimes and Crimes* (1899), *Easter,* and *The Dance of Death* (both 1901), *A Dream Play* (1902), and *Ghost Sonata* (1907). These are largely expressionist plays. EXPRESSIONISM disregarded the strict demands of naturalism to present a "slice of life" without artistic shaping of plot and resolution. Instead, expressionist drama used materials that resembled dreams — or nightmares — and focused on symbolic actions and a subjective interpretation of the world. Strindberg's later drama is often symbolic, taut, and psychological. His novel *Inferno* (1897) not only marks the transition between his early and late work; it gives this period of his life its name. Strindberg's *Inferno* period was a time of madness and paranoic behavior that virtually redirected his life for more than three years. During this time he was convinced that the secrets of life were wrapped in the occult, and his energies went into alchemical experiments and studies of cabalistic lore.

The first period of his dramatic career began with *Master Olof* (1872), a historical drama that he chose to write in prose, which he felt was a more natural medium than verse, the convention for such plays at the time. The play was turned down, and he rewrote it in verse in 1876. It was rejected for a second time by the Royal Dramatic Theater but was finally produced the following year. At that time, Strindberg recorded: "In 1877 Antoine opened his Théâtre Libre in Paris, and *Thérèse Raquin,* although nothing but an adapted novel, became the dominant model. It was the powerful theme and the concentrated form that showed innovation, although the unity of time was not yet observed, and curtain falls were retained. It was then I wrote my dramas: *Lady Julie, The Father,* and *Creditors.*" *Thérèse Raquin,* Émile Zola's naturalistic play, inspired Strindberg to move further toward his own interpretation of naturalism, which is perhaps most evident in *Miss Julie.* Strindberg was more subjective in his approach to naturalism, less scientific and deterministic, than Zola. Whereas Zola's approach might be described as "photographic" realism, Strindberg's was more selective and impressionistic but no less honest and true. He saw his characters operating out of "a whole series of deeply buried motives." They were not necessarily the product of their biology or their social circumstances, as the naturalists of Zola's stripe sometimes implied. Yet Strindberg saw clearly that class distinctions helped determine the behavior of many people. He seemed to accept the view that people were not created by their class but rather belonged to their class because of the kind of people they were. Strindberg probed deeply into the psychology of his characters, whose emotional lives, rather than outward social qualities, determined their actions.

Strindberg is often described as a woman-hater, a misogynist. For periods of his life he seems to have been misogynistic, but he was nonetheless extremely contradictory in both behavior and belief. There is no simple way to talk about Strindberg's attitude toward women. On the one hand, he is conventional in his thinking that women belong in the home. On the other hand, he married a highly successful actress, Siri von Essen. As he said in a letter in 1895, "Woman is to me the earth and all its glory, the bond that binds, and of all the evil the worst evil I have seen is the female sex." A decade later in *A Blue Book,* he wrote, "When I approach a woman as a lover, I look up to her, I see something of the mother in her, and this I respect. I assume a subordinate position, become childish and puerile and actually am subordinate, like most men. . . . I put her on a pedestal." As in many things, including his attitude toward dramatic techniques and style, Strindberg is a mass of contradictions and complexities of the sort sometimes associated with genius.

MISS JULIE

Miss Julie, the daughter of a count, and Jean, the count's valet, come from strikingly different social backgrounds. In ordinary circumstances, they might not have been on friendly terms, much less have become lovers, as they do. But the count is away, and Miss Julie and Jean are drawn into a sexual liaison marked by a struggle for dominance and control. Miss Julie's fiancé has been disposed of before the play begins because he refused to debase himself slavishly to her will. She is a free spirit, but her breeding is suspect because her mother, like her, took a lover and defied the count. Miss Julie's mother rebelled against her husband and punished him by burning their house down after the insurance expired. As further punishment and abasement, she humiliated the count by arranging to have her lover loan him the money to rebuild the house. Thus, Miss Julie's heritage is one of independence, rebellion, and unorthodoxy.

Under her mother's tutelage, Miss Julie was raised to manipulate men, but she cannot accept them totally. She also seems to feel a mixture of contempt for herself as a woman along with her contempt for men. In his preface to the play, Strindberg says that Julie is a modern "half-woman" "man-hater" who sells herself for honors of various kinds. (See the commentary on p. 432.)

The play has a mysterious quality. It takes place on Midsummer Eve, when lovers reveal themselves to one another and when almost anything can happen. In primitive fertility rites it was a time associated with sexual awakening. Kristine mentions that it is the feast of St. John and alludes to his beheading for spurning Salome's advances. Jean (French for John) in one tense moment of the play beheads Julie's pet bird as a sign of the violence pent up in him. This incident also foreshadows Miss Julie's death.

The fairy-tale quality that creeps into the play — as in *A Midsummer Night's Dream,* set on the same day — may seem out of place in a realistic drama, but it is profoundly compelling. It is also typical of Strindberg, who often uses symbolism to suggest a dream quality and deepen the significance of the action. (Dreams are a part of reality that modern playwrights have taken great pains to explore.)

The count himself, Julie's father, never appears in the play, but his presence is always ominous and intense, again much as in a fairy tale. Jean tells Miss Julie that he would willingly kill himself if the count were to order it. The cook, Kristine, like a witch, demands retribution because she was spurned by Jean, who once was her lover. Near the end of the play she prevents Julie and Jean from running away from the count by impounding the horses in the stable, thus wreaking her revenge on both of them.

Although Julie may be seen as the princess, Jean has very little claim to being Prince Charming of the play, especially since he has little strength of character. He feels superior to his station as a valet, and Strindberg in his preface refers to him as a nobleman. However, like Kristine, he is coarse beneath his outwardly polished appearance. His highest ambition is to be the proprietor of a first-class hotel, a prospect he wants to share with Julie.

One of the most striking passages in the play is the story Jean tells Julie almost reluctantly. He tries to explain to her what it feels like to be "down below," where she has never been. When he was a boy, he thought of the apple trees in her father's garden as part of the "Garden of Eden, guarded by angry angels." He entered this enchanted place with his mother to weed onions and wandered into the outhouse — a building like a Turkish pavilion whose function he could not guess. While he was exploring it, he heard someone coming and had to exit beneath the outhouse and hide himself under a pile of weeds and "wet dirt that stank." From his hiding place he saw Julie in a pink dress and white stockings. He rushed to the millpond and jumped in to wash the filth off himself. Ironically, only a few moments after he tells her this story, he calls her a whore, and she, in response, says, "Oh, God in heaven, end my wretched life! Take me away from the filth I'm sinking into! Save me! Save me!"

Miss Julie falls under the power of her lover and cannot redirect her life; she sinks deeper and deeper into "filth." She has few choices at the end of the play, and the conclusion to *Miss Julie* is swift. The contrast between the willfulness of Julie and the caution of Jean makes their situation especially desperate. When Julie leaves at the end of the play to seal her fate, we sense the terrible weight of their society's values. Those values are symbolized by the return of the count and the expectations he had of Julie's behavior while he was gone.

Miss Julie in Performance

The first planned professional production of *Miss Julie* was canceled at the last minute by censors in Copenhagen on March 1, 1889. Although the play was performed privately on March 14, 1889, in Copenhagen University's Students' Union, it was not performed professionally in Stockholm until 1906. Some important early productions of the play were in Paris in Antoine's distinguished Théâtre Libre in 1893 and in Berlin in Max Reinhardt's Kleine Theater in 1904. Reinhardt produced seventeen of Strindberg's plays and was one of his great champions. In 1907 Strindberg produced the play in his own Intimate Theatre in Stockholm, where it ran intermittently for 134 showings. He even arranged a special performance for Bernard Shaw. The first London production was in 1912, but since the 1930s it has been revived many times, with many distinguished actors in all three major roles.

Among the notable modern productions is the Old Vic's 1966 version directed by Michael Elliott, with Maggie Smith and Albert Finney starring. The Baxter Theatre of Johannesburg, South Africa, produced the play in 1985 with the black actor John Kani as Jean and the white Afrikaner actress Sandra Prinsloo as Julie. Some white audiences considered that casting as outrageous. The sensational Ingmar Bergman production at the Brooklyn Academy of Music in 1991 stretched the play to two hours and made it more of a domestic tragedy — as John Simon said, "more like us, more believable, and, therefore, more terrifying."

Filmed at least five times, *Miss Julie* has been televised as well. It is one of the most produced of modern plays.

August Strindberg (1849–1912)

MISS JULIE   1888

TRANSLATED BY HARRY G. CARLSON

Characters

MISS JULIE, *25 years old*
JEAN, *her father's valet, 30 years old*
KRISTINE, *her father's cook, 35 years old*

(*The action takes place in the Count's kitchen on midsummer eve.*)

Setting: (*A large kitchen, the ceiling and side walls of which are hidden by draperies. The rear wall runs diagonally from down left to up right. On the wall down left are two shelves with copper, iron, and pewter utensils; the shelves are lined with scalloped paper. Visible to the right is most of a set of large, arched glass doors, through which can be seen a fountain with a statue of Cupid, lilac bushes in bloom, and the tops of some Lombardy poplars. At down left is the corner of a large tiled stove; a portion of its hood is showing. At right, one end of the servants' white pine dining table juts out; several chairs stand around it. The stove is decorated with birch branches; juniper twigs are strewn on the floor. On the end of the table stands a large Japanese spice jar, filled with lilac blossoms. An ice box, a sink, and a washstand. Above the door is an old-fashioned bell on a spring; to the left of the door, the mouthpiece of a speaking tube is visible.*)

(*Kristine is frying something on the stove. She is wearing a light-colored cotton dress and an apron. Jean enters. He is wearing livery and carries a pair of high riding boots with spurs, which he puts down on the floor where they can be seen by the audience.*)

JEAN: Miss Julie's crazy again tonight; absolutely crazy!

KRISTINE: So you finally came back?

JEAN: I took the Count to the station and when I returned past the barn I stopped in for a dance. Who do I see but Miss Julie leading off the dance with the gamekeeper! But as soon as she saw me she rushed over to ask me for the next waltz. And she's been waltzing ever since — I've never seen anything like it. She's crazy!

KRISTINE: She always has been, but never as bad as the last two weeks since her engagement was broken off.

JEAN: Yes, I wonder what the real story was there. He was a gentleman, even if he wasn't rich. Ah! These people have such romantic ideas. (*Sits at the end of the table.*) Still, it's strange, isn't it? I mean that she'd rather stay home with the servants on midsummer eve instead of going with her father to visit relatives?

KRISTINE: She's probably embarrassed after that row with her fiancé.

JEAN: Probably! He gave a good account of himself, though. Do you know how it happened, Kristine? I saw it, you know, though I didn't let on I had.

KRISTINE: No! You saw it?

JEAN: Yes, I did. —— That evening they were out near the stable, and she was "training" him — as she called it. Do you know what she did? She made him jump over her riding crop, the way you'd teach a dog to jump. He jumped twice and she hit him each time. But the third time he grabbed the crop out of her hand, hit her with it across the cheek, and broke it in pieces. Then he left.

KRISTINE: So, that's what happened! I can't believe it!

JEAN: Yes, that's the way it went! —— What have you got for me that's tasty, Kristine?

KRISTINE (*serving him from the pan*): Oh, it's only a piece of kidney I cut from the veal roast.

JEAN (*smelling the food*): Beautiful! That's my favorite *délice*.° (*Feeling the plate.*) But you could have warmed the plate!

KRISTINE: You're fussier than the Count himself, once you start! (*She pulls his hair affectionately.*)

JEAN (*angry*): Stop it, leave my hair alone! You know I'm touchy about that.

KRISTINE: Now, now, it's only love, you know that. (*Jean eats. Kristine opens a bottle of beer.*)

JEAN: Beer? On midsummer eve? No thank you! I can do better than that. (*Opens a drawer in the table and takes out a bottle of red wine with yellow sealing wax.*) See that? Yellow seal! Give me a glass! A wine glass! I'm drinking this *pur*.°

KRISTINE (*returns to the stove and puts on a small saucepan*): God help the woman who gets you for a husband! What a fussbudget.

JEAN: Nonsense! You'd be damned lucky to get a man like me. It certainly hasn't done you any harm to have people call me your sweetheart. (*Tastes the wine.*) Good! Very good! Just needs a little warming. (*Warms the glass between his hands.*) We bought this in Dijon. Four francs a liter, not counting the cost of the bottle, or the customs duty. —— What are you cooking now? It stinks like hell!

KRISTINE: Oh, some slop Miss Julie wants to give Diana.

JEAN: Watch your language, Kristine. But why should you have to cook for that damn mutt on midsummer eve? Is she sick?

KRISTINE: Yes, she's sick! She sneaked out with the gate-keeper's dog — and now there's hell to pay. Miss Julie won't have it!

JEAN: Miss Julie has too much pride about some things and not enough about others, just like her mother was. The Countess was most at home in the kitchen and the cowsheds, but a *one*-horse carriage wasn't elegant enough for her. The cuffs of her blouse were dirty, but she had to have her coat of arms on her cuff-links. —— And Miss Julie won't take proper care of herself either. If you ask me, she just isn't refined. Just now, when she was dancing in the barn, she pulled the gamekeeper away from Anna and made him dance with her. *We* wouldn't behave like that, but that's what happens when aristocrats pretend they're common people — they get *common!* —— But she is quite a woman! Magnificent! What shoulders, and what — et cetera!

KRISTINE: Oh, don't overdo it! I've heard what Clara says, and she dresses her.

JEAN: Ha, Clara! You're all jealous of each other! I've been out riding with her. . . . And the way she dances!

KRISTINE: Listen, Jean! You're going to dance with me, when I'm finished here, aren't you?

JEAN: Of course I will.

KRISTINE: Promise?

JEAN: Promise? When I say I'll do something, I do it! By the way, the kidney was very good. (*Corks the bottle.*)

JULIE (*in the doorway to someone outside*): I'll be right back! You go ahead for now! (*Jean sneaks the bottle back into the table drawer and gets up respectfully. Miss Julie enters and crosses to Kristine by the stove.*) Well? Is it ready? (*Kristine indicates that Jean is present.*)

JEAN (*gallantly*): Are you ladies up to something secret?

JULIE (*flicking her handkerchief in his face*): None of your business!

JEAN: Hmm! I like the smell of violets!

JULIE (*coquettishly*): Shame on you! So you know about perfumes, too? You certainly know how to dance. Ah, ah! No peeking! Go away.

JEAN (*boldly but respectfully*): Are you brewing up a magic potion for midsummer eve? Something to prophesy by under a lucky star, so you'll catch a glimpse of your future husband!

JULIE (*caustically*): You'd need sharp eyes to see him! (*To Kristine.*) Pour out half a bottle and cork it well. —— — Come and dance a schottische° with me, Jean . . .

JEAN (*hesitating*): I don't want to be impolite to anyone, and I've already promised this dance to Kristine . . .

JULIE: Oh, she can have another one — can't you, Kristine? Won't you lend me Jean?

KRISTINE: It's not up to me, ma'am. (*To Jean.*) If the mistress is so generous, it wouldn't do for you to say no. Go on, Jean, and thank her for the honor.

JEAN: To be honest, and no offense intended, I wonder whether it's wise for you to dance twice running with the same partner, especially since these people are quick to jump to conclusions . . .

JULIE (*flaring up*): What's that? What sort of conclusions? What do you mean?

JEAN (*submissively*): If you don't understand, ma'am, I must speak more plainly. It doesn't look good to play favorites with your servants. . . .

---

délice: Delight.   *pur*: Pure; the first drink from the bottle.

schottische: A Scottish round dance resembling a polka.

JULIE: Play favorites! What an idea! I'm astonished! As mistress of the house, I honor your dance with my presence. And when I dance, I want to dance with someone who can lead, so I won't look ridiculous.

JEAN: As you order, ma'am! I'm at your service!

JULIE (*gently*): Don't take it as an order! On a night like this we're all just ordinary people having fun, so we'll forget about rank. Now, take my arm! ——— Don't worry, Kristine! I won't steal your sweetheart! (*Jean offers his arm and leads Miss Julie out.*)

Mime

(*The following should be played as if the actress playing Kristine were really alone. When she has to, she turns her back to the audience. She does not look toward them, nor does she hurry as if she were afraid they would grow impatient. Schottische music played on a fiddle sounds in the distance. Kristine hums along with the music. She clears the table, washes the dishes, dries them, and puts them away. She takes off her apron. From a table drawer she removes a small mirror and leans it against the bowl of lilacs on the table. She lights a candle, heats a hairpin over the flame, and uses it to set a curl on her forehead. She crosses to the door and listens, then returns to the table. She finds the handkerchief Miss Julie left behind, picks it up, and smells it. Then, preoccupied, she spreads it out, stretches it, smoothes out the wrinkles, and folds it into quarters, and so forth.*)

JEAN (*enters alone*): God, she really *is* crazy! What a way to dance! Everybody's laughing at her behind her back. What do you make of it, Kristine?

KRISTINE: Ah! It's that time of the month for her, and she always gets peculiar like that. Are you going to dance with me now?

JEAN: You're not mad at me, are you, for leaving . . . ?

KRISTINE: Of course not! ——— Why should I be, for a little thing like that? Besides, I know my place . . .

JEAN (*puts his arm around her waist*): You're a sensible girl, Kristine, and you'd make a good wife . . .

JULIE (*entering; uncomfortably surprised; with forced good humor*): What a charming escort — running away from his partner.

JEAN: On the contrary, Miss Julie. Don't you see how I rushed back to the partner I abandoned!

JULIE (*changing her tone*): You know, you're a superb dancer! ——— But why are you wearing livery on a holiday? Take it off at once!

JEAN: Then I must ask you to go outside for a moment. You see, my black coat is hanging over here . . . (*Gestures and crosses right.*)

JULIE: Are you embarrassed about changing your coat in front of me? Well, go in your room then. Either that or stay and I'll turn my back.

JEAN: With your permission, ma'am! (*He crosses right. His arm is visible as he changes his jacket.*)

JULIE (*to Kristine*): Tell me, Kristine — you two are so close — . Is Jean your fiancé?

KRISTINE: Fiancé? Yes, if you wish. We can call him that.

JULIE: What do you mean?

KRISTINE: You had a fiancé yourself, didn't you? So . . .

JULIE: Well, we were properly engaged . . .

KRISTINE: But nothing came of it, did it? (*Jean returns dressed in a frock coat and bowler hat.*)

JULIE: *Très gentil, monsieur Jean! Très gentil!*

JEAN: *Vous voulez plaisanter, madame!*

JULIE: *Et vous voulez parler français!*° Where did you learn that?

JEAN: In Switzerland, when I was wine steward in one of the biggest hotels in Lucerne!

JULIE: You look like a real gentleman in that coat! *Charmant!*° (*Sits at the table.*)

JEAN: Oh, you're flattering me!

JULIE (*offended*): Flattering you?

JEAN: My natural modesty forbids me to believe that you would really compliment someone like me, and so I took the liberty of assuming that you were exaggerating, which polite people call flattering.

JULIE: Where did you learn to talk like that? You must have been to the theater often.

JEAN: Of course. And I've done a lot of traveling.

JULIE: But you come from here, don't you?

JEAN: My father was a farmhand on the district attorney's estate nearby. I used to see you when you were little, but you never noticed me.

JULIE: No! Really?

JEAN: Sure. I remember one time especially . . . but I can't talk about that.

JULIE: Oh, come now! Why not? Just this once!

JEAN: No, I really couldn't, not now. Some other time, perhaps.

JULIE: Why some other time? What's so dangerous about now?

JEAN: It's not dangerous, but there are obstacles. ——— Her, for example. (*Indicating Kristine, who has fallen asleep in a chair by the stove.*)

JULIE: What a pleasant wife she'll make! She probably snores, too.

JEAN: No, she doesn't, but she talks in her sleep.

JULIE (*cynically*): How do *you* know?

JEAN (*audaciously*): I've heard her! (*Pause, during which they stare at each other.*)

JULIE: Why don't you sit down?

JEAN: I couldn't do that in your presence.

JULIE: But if I order you to?

JEAN: Then I'd obey.

JULIE: Sit down, then. ——— No, wait. Can you get me something to drink first?

JEAN: I don't know what we have in the ice box. I think there's only beer.

JULIE: Why do you say "only"? My tastes are so simple I

Très gentil . . . français!: Very pleasing, Mr. Jean! Very pleasing. You would trifle with me, madam! And you want to speak French!   *Charmant!:* Charming!

prefer beer to wine. (*Jean takes a bottle of beer from the ice box and opens it. He looks for a glass and a plate in the cupboard and serves her.*)

JEAN: Here you are, ma'am.

JULIE: Thank you. Won't you have something yourself?

JEAN: I'm not partial to beer, but if it's an order . . .

JULIE: An order? ——— Surely a gentleman can keep his lady company.

JEAN: You're right, of course. (*Opens a bottle and gets a glass.*)

JULIE: Now, drink to my health! (*He hesitates.*) What? A man of the world — and shy?

JEAN (*in mock romantic fashion, he kneels and raises his glass*): Skål to my mistress!

JULIE: Bravo! ——— Now kiss my shoe, to finish it properly. (*Jean hesitates, then boldly seizes her foot and kisses it lightly.*) Perfect! You should have been an actor.

JEAN (*rising*): That's enough now, Miss Julie! Someone might come in and see us.

JULIE: What of it?

JEAN: People talk, that's what! If you knew how their tongues were wagging just now at the dance, you'd . . .

JULIE: What were they saying? Tell me! ——— Sit down!

JEAN (*sits*): I don't want to hurt you, but they were saying things ——— suggestive things, that, that . . . well, you can figure it out for yourself! You're not a child. If a woman is seen drinking alone with a man — let alone a servant — at night — then . . .

JULIE: Then what? Besides, we're not alone. Kristine is here.

JEAN: Asleep!

JULIE: Then I'll wake her up. (*Rising.*) Kristine! Are you asleep? (*Kristine mumbles in her sleep.*)

JULIE: Kristine! ——— She certainly can sleep!

KRISTINE (*in her sleep*): The Count's boots are brushed — put the coffee on — right away, right away — uh, huh — oh!

JULIE (*grabbing Kristine's nose*): Will you wake up!

JEAN (*severely*): Leave her alone — let her sleep!

JULIE (*sharply*): What?

JEAN: Someone who's been standing over a stove all day has a right to be tired by now. Sleep should be respected . . .

JULIE (*changing her tone*): What a considerate thought — it does you credit — thank you! (*Offering her hand.*) Come outside and pick some lilacs for me! (*During the following, Kristine awakens and shambles sleepily off right to bed.*)

JEAN: Go with you?

JULIE: With me!

JEAN: We couldn't do that! Absolutely not!

JULIE: I don't understand. Surely you don't imagine . . .

JEAN: No, I don't, but the others might.

JULIE: What? That I've fallen in love with a servant?

JEAN: I'm not a conceited man, but such things happen — and for these people, nothing is sacred.

JULIE: I do believe you're an aristocrat!

JEAN: Yes, I am.

JULIE: And I'm stepping down . . .

JEAN: Don't step down, Miss Julie, take my advice. No one'll believe you stepped down voluntarily. People will always say you fell.

JULIE: I have a higher opinion of people than you. Come and see! ——— Come! (*She stares at him broodingly.*)

JEAN: You're very strange, do you know that?

JULIE: Perhaps! But so are you! ——— For that matter, everything is strange. Life, people, everything. Like floating scum, drifting on and on across the water, until it sinks down and down! That reminds me of a dream I have now and then. I've climbed up on top of a pillar. I sit there and see no way of getting down. I get dizzy when I look down, and I must get down, but I don't have the courage to jump. I can't hold on firmly, and I long to be able to fall, but I don't fall. And yet I'll have no peace until I get down, no rest unless I get down, down on the ground! And if I did get down to the ground, I'd want to be under the earth . . . Have you ever felt anything like that?

JEAN: No. I dream that I'm lying under a high tree in a dark forest. I want to get up, up on top, and look out over the bright landscape, where the sun is shining, and plunder the bird's nest up there, where the golden eggs lie. And I climb and climb, but the trunk's so thick and smooth, and it's so far to the first branch. But I know if I just reached that first branch, I'd go right to the top, like up a ladder. I haven't reached it yet, but I will, even if it's only in a dream!

JULIE: Here I am chattering with you about dreams. Come, let's go out! Just into the park! (*She offers him her arm, and they start to leave.*)

JEAN: We'll have to sleep on nine midsummer flowers, Miss Julie, to make our dreams come true! (*They turn at the door. Jean puts his hand to his eye.*)

JULIE: Did you get something in your eye?

JEAN: It's nothing — just a speck — it'll be gone in a minute.

JULIE: My sleeve must have brushed against you. Sit down and let me help you. (*She takes him by the arm and seats him. She tilts his head back and with the tip of a handkerchief tries to remove the speck.*) Sit still, absolutely still! (*She slaps his hand.*) Didn't you hear me? ——— Why, you're trembling; the big, strong man is trembling! (*Feels his biceps.*) What muscles you have!

JEAN (*warning*): Miss Julie!

JULIE: Yes, *monsieur* Jean.

JEAN: *Attention! Je ne suis qu'un homme!*°

JULIE: Will you sit still! ——— There! Now it's gone! Kiss my hand and thank me.

JEAN (*rising*): Miss Julie, listen to me! ——— Kristine has gone to bed! ——— Will you listen to me!

JULIE: Kiss my hand first!

Attention! Je ne suis qu'un homme!: Watch out! I am only a man!

JEAN: Listen to me!

JULIE: Kiss my hand first!

JEAN: All right, but you've only yourself to blame!

JULIE: For what?

JEAN: For what? Are you still a child at twenty-five? Don't you know that it's dangerous to play with fire?

JULIE: Not for me. I'm insured.

JEAN (*boldly*): No, you're not! But even if you were, there's combustible material close by.

JULIE: Meaning you?

JEAN: Yes! Not because it's me, but because I'm young ——

JULIE: And handsome — what incredible conceit! A Don Juan perhaps! Or a Joseph!° Yes, that's it, I do believe you're a Joseph!

JEAN: Do you?

JULIE: I'm almost afraid so. (*Jean boldly tries to put his arm around her waist and kiss her. She slaps his face.*) How dare you?

JEAN: Are you serious or joking?

JULIE: Serious.

JEAN: Then so was what just happened. You play games too seriously, and that's dangerous. Well, I'm tired of games. You'll excuse me if I get back to work. I haven't done the Count's boots yet and it's long past midnight.

JULIE: Put the boots down!

JEAN: No! It's the work I have to do. I never agreed to be your playmate, and never will. It's beneath me.

JULIE: You're proud.

JEAN: In certain ways, but not in others.

JULIE: Have you ever been in love?

JEAN: We don't use that word, but I've been fond of many girls, and once I was sick because I couldn't have the one I wanted. That's right, sick, like those princes in the Arabian Nights — who couldn't eat or drink because of love.

JULIE: Who was she? (*Jean is silent.*) Who was she?

JEAN: You can't force me to tell you that.

JULIE: But if I ask you as an equal, as a — friend! Who was she?

JEAN: You!

JULIE (*sits*): How amusing . . .

JEAN: Yes, if you like! It was ridiculous! —— You see, that was the story I didn't want to tell you earlier. Maybe I will now. Do you know how the world looks from down below? —— Of course you don't. Neither do hawks and falcons, whose backs we can't see because they're usually soaring up there above us. I grew up in a shack with seven brothers and sisters and a pig, in the middle of a wasteland, where there wasn't a single tree. But from our window I could see the tops of apple trees above the wall of your father's garden. That was the Garden of Eden, guarded by angry angels with flaming swords.

All the same, the other boys and I managed to find our way to the Tree of Life. —— Now you think I'm contemptible, I suppose.

JULIE: Oh, all boys steal apples.

JEAN: You say that, but you think I'm contemptible anyway. Oh well! One day I went into the Garden of Eden with my mother, to weed the onion beds. Near the vegetable garden was a small Turkish pavilion in the shadow of jasmine bushes and over-grown with honeysuckle. I had no idea what it was used for, but I'd never seen such a beautiful building. People went in and came out again, and one day the door was left open. I sneaked close and saw walls covered with pictures of kings and emperors, and red curtains with fringes at the windows — now you know the place I mean. I —— (*Breaks off a sprig of lilac and holds it in front of Miss Julie's nose.*) —— I'd never been inside the manor house, never seen anything except the church — but this was more beautiful. From then on, no matter where my thoughts wandered, they returned — there. And gradually I got a longing to experience, just once, the full pleasure of — *enfin*,° I sneaked in, saw, and marveled! But then I heard someone coming! There was only one exit for ladies and gentlemen, but for me there was another, and I had no choice but to take it! (*Miss Julie, who has taken the lilac sprig, lets it fall on the table.*) Afterwards, I started running. I crashed through a raspberry bush, flew over a strawberry patch, and came up onto the rose terrace. There I caught sight of a pink dress and a pair of white stockings — it was you. I crawled under a pile of weeds, and I mean under — under thistles that pricked me and wet dirt that stank. And I looked at you as you walked among the roses, and I thought: If it's true that a thief can enter heaven and be with the angels, then why can't a farm-hand's son here on God's earth enter the manor house garden and play with the Count's daughter?

JULIE (*romantically*): Do you think all poor children would have thought the way you did?

JEAN (*at first hesitant, then with conviction*): If *all* poor — yes — of course. Of course!

JULIE: It must be terrible to be poor!

JEAN (*with exaggerated suffering*): Oh, Miss Julie! Oh! —— A dog can lie on the Countess's sofa, a horse can have his nose patted by a young lady's hand, but a servant —— (*Changing his tone.*) —— oh, I know — now and then you find one with enough stuff in him to get ahead in the world, but how often? —— Anyhow, do you know what I did then? —— I jumped in the millstream with my clothes on, was pulled out, and got a beating. But the following Sunday, when my father and all the others went to my grandmother's, I arranged to stay home. I scrubbed myself with soap and water, put on my best clothes, and went to church so that I could see you! I saw you and returned home, determined to

---

Don Juan . . . Joseph: Don Juan in Spanish legend is a seducer of women; in Genesis, Joseph resists the advances of Potiphar's wife.

enfin: Finally.

die. But I wanted to die beautifully and pleasantly, without pain. And then I remembered that it was dangerous to sleep under an elder bush. We had a big one, and it was in full flower. I plundered its treasures and bedded down under them in the oat bin. Have you ever noticed how smooth oats are? — and soft to the touch, like human skin . . . ! Well, I shut the lid and closed my eyes. I fell asleep and woke up feeling very sick. But I didn't die, as you can see. What was I after? ——— I don't know. There was no hope of winning you, of course. ——— You were a symbol of the hopelessness of ever rising out of the class in which I was born.

JULIE: You're a charming storyteller. Did you ever go to school?

JEAN: A bit, but I've read lots of novels and been to the theater often. And then I've listened to people like you talk — that's where I learned most.

JULIE: Do you listen to what we say?

JEAN: Naturally! And I've heard plenty, too, driving the carriage or rowing the boat. Once I heard you and a friend . . .

JULIE: Oh? ——— What did you hear?

JEAN: I'd better not say. But I was surprised a little. I couldn't imagine where you learned such words. Maybe at bottom there isn't such a great difference between people as we think.

JULIE: Shame on you! We don't act like you when we're engaged.

JEAN (*staring at her*): Is that true? ——— You don't have to play innocent with me, Miss . . .

JULIE: The man I gave my love to was a swine.

JEAN: That's what you all say — afterwards.

JULIE: All?

JEAN: I think so. I know I've heard that phrase before, on similar occasions.

JULIE: What occasions?

JEAN: Like the one I'm talking about. The last time . . .

JULIE (*rising*): Quiet! I don't want to hear any more!

JEAN: That's interesting — that's what *she* said, too. Well, if you'll excuse me, I'm going to bed.

JULIE (*gently*): To bed? On midsummer eve?

JEAN: Yes! Dancing with the rabble out there doesn't amuse me much.

JULIE: Get the key to the boat and row me out on the lake. I want to see the sun come up.

JEAN: Is that wise?

JULIE: Are you worried about your reputation?

JEAN: Why not? Why should I risk looking ridiculous and getting fired without a reference, just when I'm trying to establish myself. Besides, I think I owe something to Kristine.

JULIE: So, now it's Kristine . . .

JEAN: Yes, but you, too. ——— Take my advice, go up and go to bed!

JULIE: Am I to obey you?

JEAN: Just this once — for your own good! Please! It's very late. Drowsiness makes people giddy and liable to lose their heads! Go to bed! Besides — unless I'm mistaken — I hear the others coming to look for me. And if they find us together, you'll be lost!

(*The Chorus approaches, singing.*)

The swineherd found his true love
a pretty girl so fair,
The swineherd found his true love
but let the girl beware.

For then he saw the princess
the princess on the golden hill,
but then saw the princess,
so much fairer still.

So the swineherd and the princess
they danced the whole night through,
and he forgot his first love,
to her he was untrue.

And when the long night ended,
and in the light of day, of day,
the dancing too was ended,
and the princess could not stay.

Then the swineherd lost his true love,
and the princess grieves him still,
and never more she'll wander
from atop the golden hill.

JULIE: I know all these people and I love them, just as they love me. Let them come in and you'll see.

JEAN: No, Miss Julie, they don't love you. They take your food, but they spit on it! Believe me! Listen to them, listen to what they're singing! ——— No. don't listen to them!

JULIE (*listening*): What are they singing?

JEAN: It's a dirty song! About you and me!

JULIE: Disgusting! Oh! How deceitful! ———

JEAN: The rabble is always cowardly! And in a battle like this, you don't fight; you can only run away!

JULIE: Run away? But where? We can't go out — or into Kristine's room.

JEAN: True. But there's my room. Necessity knows no rules. Besides, you can trust me. I'm your friend and I respect you.

JULIE: But suppose — suppose they look for you in there?

JEAN: I'll bolt the door, and if anyone tries to break in, I'll shoot! ——— Come! (*On his knees.*) Come!

JULIE (*urgently*): Promise me. . . ?

JEAN: I swear! (*Miss Julie runs off right. Jean hastens after her.*)

Ballet

(*Led by a fiddler, the servants and farm people enter, dressed festively, with flowers in their hats. On the table they place a small barrel of beer and a keg of schnapps, both garlanded. Glasses are brought out, and the drink-*

ing starts. A dance circle is formed and "The Swineherd and the Princess" is sung. When the dance is finished, everyone leaves, singing.)

(Miss Julie enters alone. She notices the mess in the kitchen, wrings her hands, then takes out her powder puff and powders her nose.)

JEAN *(enters, agitated)*: There, you see? And you heard them. We can't possibly stay here now, you know that.

JULIE: Yes, I know. But what can we do?

JEAN: Leave, travel, far away from here.

JULIE: Travel? Yes, but where?

JEAN: To Switzerland, to the Italian lakes. Have you ever been there?

JULIE: No. Is it beautiful?

JEAN: Oh, an eternal summer — oranges growing everywhere, laurel trees, always green . . .

JULIE: But what'll we do there?

JEAN: I'll open a hotel — with first-class service for first-class people.

JULIE: Hotel?

JEAN: That's the life, you know. Always new faces, new languages. No time to worry or be nervous. No hunting for something to do — there's always work to be done: bells ringing night and day, train whistles blowing, carriages coming and going, and all the while gold rolling into the till! That's the life!

JULIE: Yes, it sounds wonderful. But what'll I do?

JEAN: You'll be mistress of the house: the jewel in our crown! With your looks . . . and your manner — oh — success is guaranteed! It'll be wonderful! You'll sit in your office like a queen and push an electric button to set your slaves in motion. The guests will file past your throne and timidly lay their treasures before you. —— You have no idea how people tremble when they get their bill. —— I'll salt the bills° and you'll sweeten them with your prettiest smile. —— Let's get away from here — *(Takes a timetable out of his pocket.)* —— Right away, on the next train! —— We'll be in Malmö six-thirty tomorrow morning, Hamburg at eight-forty; from Frankfort to Basel will take a day, then on to Como by way of the St. Gotthard Tunnel, in, let's see, three days. Three days!

JULIE: That's all very well! But Jean — you must give me courage! —— Tell me you love me! Put your arms around me!

JEAN *(hesitating)*: I want to — but I don't dare. Not in this house, not again. I love you — never doubt that — you don't doubt it, do you, Miss Julie?

JULIE *(shy; very feminine)*: "Miss!"—— Call me Julie! There are no barriers between us anymore. Call me Julie!

JEAN *(tormented)*: I can't! There'll always be barriers between us as long as we stay in this house. —— There's the past and there's the Count. I've never met anyone I had such respect for. —— When I see his gloves lying on a chair, I feel small. —— When I

salt the bills: Inflate or pad the bills.

hear that bell up there ring, I jump like a skittish horse. —— And when I look at his boots standing there so stiff and proud, I feel like bowing! *(Kicking the boots.)* Superstitions and prejudices we learned as children — but they can easily be forgotten. If I can just get to another country, a republic, people will bow and scrape when they see my livery — *they'll* bow and scrape, you hear, not me! I wasn't born to cringe. I've got stuff in me, I've got character, and if I can only grab onto that first branch, you watch me climb! I'm a servant today, but next year I'll own my own hotel. In ten years I'll have enough to retire. Then I'll go to Rumania and be decorated. I could — mind you I said *could* — end up a count!

JULIE: Wonderful, wonderful!

JEAN: Ah, in Rumania you just buy your title, and so you'll be a countess after all. My countess!

JULIE: But I don't care about that — that's what I'm putting behind me! Show me you love me, otherwise — otherwise, what am I?

JEAN: I'll show you a thousand times — afterwards! Not here! And whatever you do, no emotional outbursts, or we'll both be lost! We must think this through coolly, like sensible people. *(He takes out a cigar, snips the end, and lights it.)* You sit there, and I'll sit here. We'll talk as if nothing happened.

JULIE *(desperately)*: Oh, my God! Have you no feelings?

JEAN: Me? No one has more feelings than I do, but I know how to control them.

JULIE: A little while ago you could kiss my shoe — and now!

JEAN *(harshly)*: Yes, but that was before. Now we have other things to think about.

JULIE: Don't speak harshly to me!

JEAN: I'm not — just sensibly! We've already done one foolish thing, let's not have any more. The Count could return any minute, and by then we've got to decide what to do with our lives. What do you think of my plans for the future? Do you approve?

JULIE: They sound reasonable enough. I have only one question: For such a big undertaking you need capital — do you have it?

JEAN *(chewing on the cigar)*: Me? Certainly! I have my professional expertise, my wide experience, and my knowledge of languages. That's capital enough, I should think!

JULIE: But all that won't even buy a train ticket.

JEAN: That's true. That's why I'm looking for a partner to advance me the money.

JULIE: Where will you find one quickly enough?

JEAN: That's up to you, if you want to come with me.

JULIE: But I can't; I have no money of my own. *(Pause.)*

JEAN: Then it's all off . . .

JULIE: And . . .

JEAN: Things stay as they are.

JULIE: Do you think I'm going to stay in this house as your lover? With all the servants pointing their fingers at me? Do you imagine I can face my father after this? No! Take me away from here, away from

Helen Mirren as Miss Julie in a 1971 production of Strindberg's play.

shame and dishonor ——— Oh, what have I done! My God, my God! (*She cries.*)

JEAN: Now, don't start that old song! ——— What have you done? The same as many others before you.

JULIE (*screaming convulsively*): And now you think I'm contemptible! ——— I'm falling, I'm falling!

JEAN: Fall down to my level and I'll lift you up again.

JULIE: What terrible power drew me to you? The attraction of the weak to the strong? The falling to the rising? Or was it love? Was this love? Do you know what love is?

JEAN: Me? What do you take me for? You don't think this was my first time, do you?

JULIE: The things you say, the thoughts you think!

JEAN: That's the way I was taught, and that's the way I am! Now don't get excited and don't play the grand lady, because we're in the same boat now! ——— Come on, Julie, I'll pour you a glass of something

special! (*He opens a drawer in the table, takes out a wine bottle, and fills two glasses already used.*)

JULIE: Where did you get that wine?

JEAN: From the cellar.

JULIE: My father's burgundy!

JEAN: That'll do for his son-in-law, won't it?

JULIE: And I drink beer! Beer!

JEAN: That only shows I have better taste.

JULIE: Thief!

JEAN: Planning to tell?

JULIE: Oh, oh! Accomplice of a common thief! Was I drunk? Have I been walking in a dream the whole evening? Midsummer eve! A time of innocent fun!

JEAN: Innocent, eh?

JULIE (*pacing back and forth*): Is there anyone on earth more miserable than I am at this moment?

JEAN: Why should you be? After such a conquest? Think of Kristine in there. Don't you think she has feelings, too?

JULIE: I thought so awhile ago, but not any more. No, a servant is a servant . . .

JEAN: And a whore is a whore!

JULIE (*on her knees, her hands clasped*): Oh, God in heaven, end my wretched life! Take me away from the filth I'm sinking into! Save me! Save me!

JEAN: I can't deny I feel sorry for you. When I lay in that onion bed and saw you in the rose garden, well . . . I'll be frank . . . I had the same dirty thoughts all boys have.

JULIE: And you wanted to die for me!

JEAN: In the oat bin? That was just talk.

JULIE: A lie, in other words!

JEAN (*beginning to feel sleepy*): More or less! I got the idea from a newspaper story about a chimney sweep who curled up in a firewood bin full of lilacs because he got a summons for not supporting his illegitimate child . . .

JULIE: So, that's what you're like . . .

JEAN: I had to think of something. And that's the kind of story women always go for.

JULIE: Swine!

JEAN: *Merde!*

JULIE: And now you've seen the hawk's back . . .

JEAN: Not exactly its *back* . . .

JULIE: And I was to be the first branch . . .

JEAN: But the branch was rotten . . .

JULIE: I was to be the sign on the hotel . . .

JEAN: And I the hotel . . .

JULIE: Sit at your desk, entice your customers, pad their bills . . .

JEAN: That I'd do myself . . .

JULIE: How can anyone be so thoroughly filthy?

JEAN: Better clean up then!

JULIE: You lackey, you menial, stand up, when I speak to you!

JEAN: Menial's strumpet, lackey's whore, shut up and get out of here! Who are you to lecture me on coarseness? None of my kind is ever as coarse as you were tonight. Do you think one of your maids would throw herself at a man the way you did? Have you ever seen any girl of my class offer herself like that? I've only seen it among animals and streetwalkers.

JULIE (*crushed*): You're right. Hit me, trample on me. I don't deserve any better. I'm worthless. But help me! If you see any way out of this, help me, Jean, please!

JEAN (*more gently*): I'd be lying if I didn't admit to a sense of triumph in all this, but do you think that a person like me would have dared even to look at someone like you if you hadn't invited it? I'm still amazed . . .

JULIE: And proud . . .

JEAN: Why not? Though I must say it was too easy to be really exciting.

JULIE: Go on, hit me, hit me harder!

JEAN (*rising*): No! Forgive me for what I've said! I don't hit a man when he's down, let alone a woman. I can't deny though, that I'm pleased to find out that what looked so dazzling to us from below was only tinsel, that the hawk's back was only gray, after all, that the lovely complexion was only powder, that those polished fingernails had black edges, and that a dirty handkerchief is still dirty, even if it smells of perfume . . . ! On the other hand, it hurts me to find out that what I was striving for wasn't finer, more substantial. It hurts me to see you sunk so low that you're inferior to your own cook. It hurts like watching flowers beaten down by autumn rains and turned into mud.

JULIE: You talk as if you were already above me.

JEAN: I am. You see, I could make you a countess, but you could never make me a count.

JULIE: But I'm the child of a count — something you could never be!

JEAN: That's true. But I could be the father of counts — if . . .

JULIE: But you're a thief. I'm not.

JEAN: There are worse things than being a thief! Besides, when I'm working in a house, I consider myself sort of a member of the family, like one of the children. And you don't call it stealing when a child snatches a berry off a full bush. (*His passion is aroused again.*) Miss Julie, you're a glorious woman, much too good for someone like me! You were drinking and you lost your head. Now you want to cover up your mistake by telling yourself that you love me! You don't. Maybe there was a physical attraction — but then your love is no better than mine. —— I could never be satisfied to be no more than an animal to you, and I could never arouse real love in you.

JULIE: Are you sure of that?

JEAN: You're suggesting it's possible —— Oh, I could fall in love with you, no doubt about it. You're beautiful, you're refined —— (*approaching and taking her hand*) —— cultured, lovable when you want to be, and once you start a fire in a man, it never goes out. (*Putting his arm around her waist.*) You're like hot, spicy wine, and one kiss from you . . . (*He tries to lead her out, but she slowly frees herself.*)

JULIE: Let me go!? —— You'll never win me like that.

JEAN: *How* then? —— Not like that? Not with caresses and pretty speeches. Not with plans about the future or rescue from disgrace! *How* then?

JULIE: How? How? I don't know! —— I have no idea! —— I detest you as I detest rats, but I can't escape from you.

JEAN: Escape with me!

JULIE (*pulling herself together*): Escape? Yes, we must escape! —— But I'm so tired. Give me a glass of wine? (*Jean pours the wine. She looks at her watch.*) But we must talk first. We still have a little time. (*She drains the glass, then holds it out for more.*)

JEAN: Don't drink so fast. It'll go to your head.

JULIE: What does it matter?

JEAN: What does it matter? It's vulgar to get drunk! What did you want to tell me?

JULIE: We must escape! But first we must talk, I mean I must talk. You've done all the talking up to now. You told about your life, now I want to tell about mine, so we'll know all about each other before we go off together.

JEAN: Just a minute! Forgive me! If you don't want to regret it afterwards, you'd better think twice before revealing any secrets about yourself.

JULIE: Aren't you my friend?

JEAN: Yes, sometimes! But don't rely on me.

JULIE: You're only saying that. —— Besides, everyone already knows my secrets. —— You see, my mother was a commoner — very humble background. She was brought up believing in social equality, women's rights, and all that. The idea of marriage repelled her. So, when my father proposed, she replied that she would never become his wife, but he could be her lover. He insisted that he didn't want the woman he loved to be less respected than he. But his passion ruled him, and when she explained that the world's respect meant nothing to her, he accepted her conditions.

But now his friends avoided him and his life was restricted to taking care of the estate, which couldn't satisfy him. I came into the world — against my mother's wishes, as far as I can understand. She wanted to bring me up as a child of nature, and, what's more, to learn everything a boy had to learn, so that I might be an example of how a woman can be as good as a man. I had to wear boy's clothes and learn to take care of horses, but I was never allowed in the cowshed. I had to groom and harness the horses and go hunting — and even had to watch them slaughter animals — that was disgusting! On the estate men were put on women's jobs and women on men's jobs — with the result that the property became run down and we became the laughingstock of the district. Finally, my father must have awakened from his trance because he rebelled and changed everything his way. My parents were then married quietly. Mother became ill — I don't know what illness it was — but she often had convulsions, hid in the attic and in the garden, and sometimes stayed out all night. Then came the great fire, which you've heard about. The house, the stables, and the cowshed all burned down, under very curious circumstances, suggesting arson, because the accident happened the day after the insurance had expired. The quarterly premium my father sent in was delayed because of a messenger's carelessness and didn't arrive in time. (*She fills her glass and drinks.*)

JEAN: Don't drink any more!

JULIE: Oh, what does it matter. ——— We were left penniless and had to sleep in the carriages. My father had no idea where to find money to rebuild the house because he had so slighted his old friends that they had forgotten him. Then my mother suggested that he borrow from a childhood friend of hers, a brick manufacturer who lived nearby. Father got the loan without having to pay interest, which surprised him. And that's how the estate was rebuilt. ——— (*Drinks again.*) Do you know who started the fire?

JEAN: The Countess, your mother.

JULIE: Do you know who the brick manufacturer was?

JEAN: Your mother's lover?

JULIE: Do you know whose money it was?

JEAN: Wait a moment — no, I don't.

JULIE: It was my mother's.

JEAN: You mean the Count's, unless they didn't sign an agreement when they were married.

JULIE: They didn't. ——— My mother had a small inheritance which she didn't want under my father's control, so she entrusted it to her — friend.

JEAN: Who stole it!

JULIE: Exactly! He kept it. ——— All this my father found out, but he couldn't bring it to court, couldn't repay his wife's lover, couldn't prove it was his wife's money! It was my mother's revenge for being forced into marriage against her will. It nearly drove him to suicide — there was a rumor that he tried with a pistol, but failed. So, he managed to live through it and my mother had to suffer for what she'd done. You can imagine that those were a terrible five years for me. I loved my father, but I sided with my mother because I didn't know the circumstances. I learned from her to hate men — you've heard how she hated the whole male sex — and I swore to her I'd never be a slave to any man.

JEAN: But you got engaged to that lawyer.

JULIE: In order to make him my slave.

JEAN: And he wasn't willing?

JULIE: He was willing, all right, but I wouldn't let him. I got tired of him.

JEAN: I saw it — out near the stable.

JULIE: What did you see?

JEAN: I saw — how he broke off the engagement.

JULIE: That's a lie! I was the one who broke it off. Has he said that he did? That swine . . .

JEAN: He was no swine, I'm sure. So, you hate men, Miss Julie?

JULIE: Yes! ——— Most of the time! But sometimes — when the weakness comes, when passion burns! Oh, God, will the fire never die out?

JEAN: Do you hate me, too?

JULIE: Immeasurably! I'd like to have you put to death, like an animal . . .

JEAN: I see — the penalty for bestiality — the woman gets two years at hard labor and the animal is put to death. Right?

JULIE: Exactly!

JEAN: But there's no prosecutor here — and no animal. So, what'll we do?

JULIE: Go away!

JEAN: To torment each other to death?

JULIE: No! To be happy for — two days, a week, as long as we can be happy, and then — die . . .

JEAN: Die? That's stupid! It's better to open a hotel!

JULIE (*without listening*): ——— on the shore of Lake Como, where the sun always shines, where the laurels are green at Christmas and the oranges glow.

JEAN: Lake Como is a rainy hole, and I never saw any oranges outside the stores. But tourists are attracted there because there are plenty of villas to be rented out to lovers, and that's a profitable business. ——— Do you know why? Because they sign a lease for six months — and then leave after three weeks!

JULIE (*naively*): Why after three weeks?

JEAN: They quarrel, of course! But they still have to pay the rent in full! And so you rent the villas out again. And that's the way it goes, time after time. There's never a shortage of love — even if it doesn't last long!

JULIE: You don't want to die with me?

JEAN: I don't want to die at all! For one thing, I like living, and for another, I think suicide is a crime against the Providence which gave us life.

JULIE: You believe in God? *You?*

JEAN: Of course I do. And I go to church every other Sunday. ——— To be honest, I'm tired of all this, and I'm going to bed.

JULIE: Are you? And do you think I can let it go at that? A man owes something to the woman he's shamed.

JEAN (*taking out his purse and throwing a silver coin on the table*): Here! I don't like owing anything to anybody.

JULIE (*pretending not to notice the insult*): Do you know what the law states . . .

JEAN: Unfortunately the law doesn't state any punishment for the woman who seduces a man!

JULIE (*as before*): Do you see any way out but to leave, get married, and then separate?

JEAN: Suppose I refuse such a *mésalliance*?°

JULIE: *Mésalliance* . . .

JEAN: Yes, for me! You see, I come from better stock than you. There's no arsonist in my family.

JULIE: How do you know?

JEAN: You can't prove otherwise. We don't keep charts

---

mésalliance: Misalliance or mismatch, especially regarding relative social status.

on our ancestors — there's just the police records! But I've read about your family. Do you know who the founder was? He was a miller who let the king sleep with his wife one night during the Danish War. I don't have any noble ancestors like that. I don't have any noble ancestors at all, but I could become one myself.

JULIE: This is what I get for opening my heart to someone unworthy, for giving my family's honor . . .

JEAN: Dishonor! —— Well, I told you so: When people drink, they talk, and talk is dangerous!

JULIE: Oh, how I regret it! —— How I regret it! —— If you at least loved me.

JEAN: For the last time —— what do you want? Shall I cry; shall I jump over your riding crop? Shall I kiss you and lure you off to Lake Como for three weeks, and then God knows what. . . ? What shall I do? What do you want? This is getting painfully embarrassing! But that's what happens when you stick your nose in women's business. Miss Julie! I see that you're unhappy. I know you're suffering, but I can't understand you. We don't have such romantic ideas; there's not this kind of hate between us. Love is a game we play when we get time off from work, but we don't have all day and night, like you. I think you're sick, really sick. Your mother was crazy, and her ideas have poisoned your life.

JULIE: Be kind to me. At least now you're talking like a human being.

JEAN: Be human yourself, then. You spit on me, and you won't let me wipe myself off ——

JULIE: Help me! Help me! Just tell me what to do, where to go!

JEAN: In God's name, if I only knew myself!

JULIE: I've been crazy, out of my mind, but isn't there any way out?

JEAN: Stay here and keep calm! No one knows anything!

JULIE: Impossible! The others know and Kristine knows.

JEAN: No they don't, and they'd never believe a thing like that!

JULIE (hesitantly): But — it could happen again!

JEAN: That's true!

JULIE: And then?

JEAN (frightened): Then? —— Why didn't I think about that? Yes, there is only one thing to do — get away from here! Right away! I can't come with you, then we'd be finished, so you'll have to go alone — away — anywhere!

JULIE: Alone? —— Where? —— I can't do that!

JEAN: You must! And before the Count gets back! If you stay, you know what'll happen. Once you make a mistake like this, you want to continue because the damage has already been done. . . . Then you get bolder and bolder — until finally you're caught! So leave! Later you can write to the Count and confess everything — except that it was me! He'll never guess who it was, and he's not going to be eager to find out, anyway.

JULIE: I'll go if you come with me.

JEAN: Are you out of your head? Miss Julie runs away with her servant! In two days it would be in the newspapers, and that's something your father would never live through.

JULIE: I can't go and I can't stay! Help me! I'm so tired, so terribly tired. —— Order me! Set me in motion — I can't think or act on my own . . .

JEAN: What miserable creatures you people are! You strut around with your noses in the air as if you were the lords of creation! All right, I'll order you. Go upstairs and get dressed! Get some money for the trip, and then come back down!

JULIE (in a half-whisper): Come up with me!

JEAN: To your room? —— Now you're crazy again! (Hesitates for a moment.) No! Go, at once! (Takes her hand to lead her out.)

JULIE (as she leaves): Speak kindly to me, Jean!

JEAN: An order always sounds unkind — now you know how it feels. (Jean, alone, sighs with relief. He sits at the table, takes out a notebook and pencil, and begins adding up figures, counting aloud as he works. He continues in dumb show until Kristine enters, dressed for church. She is carrying a white tie and shirt front.)

KRISTINE: Lord Jesus, what a mess! What have you been up to?

JEAN: Oh, Miss Julie dragged everybody in here. You mean you didn't hear anything? You must have been sleeping soundly.

KRISTINE: Like a log.

JEAN: And dressed for church already?

KRISTINE: Of course! You remember you promised to come with me to communion today!

JEAN: Oh, yes, that's right. —— And you brought my things. Come on, then! (He sits down. Kristine starts to put on his shirt front and tie. Pause. Jean begins sleepily.) What's the gospel text for today?

KRISTINE: On St. John's Day? — the beheading of John the Baptist, I should think!

JEAN: Ah, that'll be a long one, for sure. —— Hey, you're choking me! —— Oh, I'm sleepy, so sleepy!

KRISTINE: Yes, what have you been doing, up all night? Your face is absolutely green.

JEAN: I've been sitting here gabbing with Miss Julie.

KRISTINE: She has no idea what's proper, that one! (Pause.)

JEAN: You know, Kristine . . .

KRISTINE: What?

JEAN: It's really strange when you think about it. —— Her!

KRISTINE: What's so strange?

JEAN: Everything! (Pause.)

KRISTINE (looking at the half-empty glasses standing on the table): Have you been drinking together, too?

JEAN: Yes.

KRISTINE: Shame on you! —— Look me in the eye!

JEAN: Well?

KRISTINE: Is it possible? Is it possible?

JEAN (thinking it over for a moment): Yes, it is.

KRISTINE: Ugh! I never would have believed it! No, shame on you, shame!

JEAN: You're not jealous of her, are you?

KRISTINE: No, not of her! If it had been Clara or Sofie I'd have scratched your eyes out! ——— I don't know why, but that's the way I feel. ——— Oh, it's disgusting!

JEAN: Are you angry at her, then?

KRISTINE: No, at you! That was an awful thing to do, awful! Poor girl! ——— No, I don't care who knows it — I won't stay in a house where we can't respect the people we work for.

JEAN: Why should we respect them?

KRISTINE: You're so clever, you tell me! Do you want to wait on people who can't behave decently? Do you? You disgrace yourself that way, if you ask me.

JEAN: But it's a comfort to know they aren't any better than us.

KRISTINE: Not for me. If they're no better, what do we have to strive for to better ourselves. ——— And think of the Count! Think of him! As if he hasn't had enough misery in his life! Lord Jesus! No, I won't stay in this house any longer! ——— And it had to be with someone like you! If it had been that lawyer, if it had been a real gentleman . . .

JEAN: What do you mean?

KRISTINE: Oh, you're all right for what you are, but there are men and gentlemen, after all! ——— No, this business with Miss Julie I can never forget. She was so proud, so arrogant with men, you wouldn't have believed she could just go and give herself — and to someone like you! And she was going to have poor Diana shot for running after the gatekeepers' mutt! ——— Yes, I'm giving my notice, I mean it — I won't stay here any longer. On the twenty-fourth of October, I leave!

JEAN: And then?

KRISTINE: Well, since the subject has come up, it's about time you looked around for something since we're going to get married, in any case.

JEAN: Where am I going to look? I couldn't find a job like this if I was married.

KRISTINE: No, that's true. But you can find work as a porter or as a caretaker in some government office. The state doesn't pay much, I know, but it's secure, and there's a pension for the wife and children . . .

JEAN (grimacing): That's all very well, but it's a bit early for me to think about dying for a wife and children. My ambitions are a little higher than that.

KRISTINE: Your ambitions, yes! Well, you have obligations, too! Think about them!

JEAN: Don't start nagging me about obligations. I know what I have to do! (Listening for something outside.) Besides, this is something we have plenty of time to think over. Go and get ready for church.

KRISTINE: Who's that walking around up there?

JEAN: I don't know, unless it's Clara.

KRISTINE (going): You don't suppose it's the Count, who came home without us hearing him?

JEAN (frightened): The Count? No, I don't think so. He'd have rung.

KRISTINE (going): Well, God help us! I've never seen anything like this before. (The sun has risen and shines through the treetops in the park. The light shifts gradually until it slants in through the windows. Jean goes to the door and signals. Miss Julie enters, dressed in travel clothes and carrying a small bird cage, covered with a cloth, which she places on a chair.)

JULIE: I'm ready now.

JEAN: Shh! Kristine is awake.

JULIE (very nervous during the following): Does she suspect something?

JEAN: She doesn't know anything. But my God, you look awful!

JULIE: Why? How do I look?

JEAN: You're pale as a ghost and — excuse me, but your face is dirty.

JULIE: Let me wash up then. ——— (She goes to the basin and washes her hands and face.) Give me a towel! ——— Oh ——— the sun's coming up.

JEAN: Then the goblins will disappear.

JULIE: Yes, there must have been goblins out last night! ——— Jean, listen, come with me! I have some money now.

JEAN (hesitantly): Enough?

JULIE: Enough to start with. Come with me! I just can't travel alone on a day like this — midsummer day on a stuffy train — jammed in among crowds of people staring at me. Eternal delays at every station, while I'd wish I had wings. No, I can't, I can't! And then there'll be memories, memories of midsummer days when I was little. The church — decorated with birch leaves and lilacs; dinner at the big table with relatives and friends, the afternoons in the park, dancing, music, flowers, and games. Oh, no matter how far we travel, the memories will follow in the baggage car, with remorse and guilt!

JEAN: I'll go with you — but right away, before it's too late. Right this minute!

JULIE: Get dressed, then! (Picking up the bird cage.)

JEAN: But no baggage! It would give us away!

JULIE: No, nothing! Only what we can have in the compartment with us.

JEAN (has taken his hat): What've you got there? What is it?

JULIE: It's only my greenfinch. I couldn't leave her behind.

JEAN: What? Bring a bird cage with us? You're out of your head! Put it down!

JULIE: It's the only thing I'm taking from my home — the only living being that loves me, since Diana was unfaithful. Don't be cruel! Let me take her!

JEAN: Put the cage down, I said! ——— And don't talk so loudly — Kristine will hear us!

JULIE: No, I won't leave her in the hands of strangers! I'd rather you killed her.

JEAN: Bring the thing here, then, I'll cut its head off!

JULIE: Oh! But don't hurt her! Don't . . . no, I can't.

JEAN: Bring it here! I can!

JULIE (*taking the bird out of the cage and kissing it*): Oh, my little Serena, must you die and leave your mistress?

JEAN: Please don't make a scene! Your whole future is at stake! Hurry up! (*He snatches the bird from her, carries it over to the chopping block, and picks up a meat cleaver. Miss Julie turns away.*) You should have learned how to slaughter chickens instead of how to fire pistols. (*He chops off the bird's head.*) Then you wouldn't feel faint at the sight of blood.

JULIE (*screaming*): Kill me, too! Kill me! You, who can slaughter an innocent animal without blinking an eye! Oh, how I hate, how I detest you! There's blood between us now! I curse the moment I set eyes on you! I curse the moment I was conceived in my mother's womb!

JEAN: What good does cursing do? Let's go!

JULIE (*approaching the chopping block, as if drawn against her will*): No, I don't want to go yet. I can't . . . until I see . . . Shh! I hear a carriage ——— (*She listens, but her eyes never leave the cleaver and the chopping block.*) Do you think I can't stand the sight of blood? You think I'm so weak . . . Oh — I'd like to see your blood and your brains on a chopping block! ——— I'd like to see your whole sex swimming in a sea of blood, like my little bird . . . I think I could drink from your skull! I'd like to bathe my feet in your open chest and eat your heart roasted whole! ——— You think I'm weak. You think I love you because my womb craved your seed. You think I want to carry your spawn under my heart and nourish it with my blood — bear your child and take your name! By the way, what is your family name? I've never heard it. ——— Do you have one? I was to be Mrs. Bootblack — or Madame Pigsty. ——— You dog, who wears my collar, you lackey, who bears my coat of arms on your buttons — do I have to share you with my cook, compete with my own servant? Oh! Oh! Oh! ——— You think I'm a coward who wants to run away! No, now I'm staying — and let the storm break! My father will come home . . . to find his desk broken open . . . and his money gone! Then he'll ring — that bell . . . twice for his valet — and then he'll send for the police . . . and then I'll tell everything! Everything! Oh, what a relief it'll be to have it all end — if only it will end! ——— And then he'll have a stroke and die . . . That'll be the end of all of us — and there'll be peace . . . quiet . . . eternal rest! ——— And then our coat of arms will be broken against his coffin — the family title extinct — but the valet's line will go on in an orphanage . . . win laurels in the gutter, and end in jail!

JEAN: There's the blue blood talking! Very good, Miss Julie! Just don't let that miller out of the closet! (*Kristine enters, dressed for church, with a psalm-book in her hand.*)

JULIE (*rushing to Kristine and falling into her arms, as if seeking protection*): Help me, Kristine! Help me against this man!

KRISTINE (*unmoved and cold*): What a fine way to behave on a Sunday morning! (*Sees the chopping block.*) And look at this mess! ——— What does all this mean? Why all this screaming and carrying on?

JULIE: Kristine! You're a woman and my friend! Beware of this swine!

JEAN (*uncomfortable*): While you ladies discuss this, I'll go in and shave. (*Slips off right.*)

JULIE: You must listen to me so you'll understand!

KRISTINE: No, I could never understand such disgusting behavior! Where are you off to in your traveling clothes? ——— And he had his hat on. ——— Well? ——— Well? ———

JULIE: Listen to me, Kristine! Listen, and I'll tell you everything ———

KRISTINE: I don't want to hear it . . .

JULIE: But you must listen to me . . .

KRISTINE: What about? If it's about this silliness with Jean, I'm not interested, because it's none of my business. But if you're thinking of tricking him into running out, we'll soon put a stop to that!

JULIE (*extremely nervous*): Try to be calm now, Kristine, and listen to me! I can't stay here, and neither can Jean — so we must go away . . .

KRISTINE: Hm, hm!

JULIE (*brightening*): You see, I just had an idea ——— What if all three of us go — abroad — to Switzerland and start a hotel together? ——— I have money, you see — and Jean and I could run it — and I thought you, you could take care of the kitchen . . . Wouldn't that be wonderful? ——— Say yes! And come with us, and then everything will be settled! ——— Oh, do say yes! (*Embracing Kristine and patting her warmly.*)

KRISTINE (*coolly, thoughtfully*): Hm, hm!

JULIE (*presto tempo*):° You've never traveled, Kristine. ——— You must get out and see the world. You can't imagine how much fun it is to travel by train — always new faces — new countries. ——— And when we get to Hamburg, we'll stop off at the zoo — you'll like that. ——— and then we'll go to the theater and the opera — and when we get to Munich, dear, there we have museums, with Rubens and Raphael, the great painters, as you know. ——— You've heard of Munich, where King Ludwig lived — the king who went mad. ——— And then we'll see his castles — they're still there and they're like castles in fairy tales. ——— And from there it isn't far to Switzerland — and the Alps. ——— Imagine — the Alps have snow on them even in the middle of summer! ——— And oranges grow there and laurel trees that are green all year round ——— (*Jean can be seen in the wings right, sharpening his razor on a strop which he holds with his teeth and his left hand. He*

---

presto tempo: At a rapid pace.

listens to the conversation with satisfaction, nodding now and then in approval. Miss Julie continues tempo prestissimo.)° And then we'll start a hotel — and I'll be at the desk, while Jean greets the guests . . . does the shopping . . . writes letters. ———— You have no idea what a life it'll be — the train whistles blowing and the carriages arriving and the bells ringing in the rooms and down in the restaurant. ———— And I'll make out the bills — and I know how to salt them! . . . You'll never believe how timid travelers are when they have to pay their bills! ———— And you — you'll be in charge of the kitchen. ———— Naturally, you won't have to stand over the stove yourself. ———— And since you're going to be seen by people, you'll have to wear beautiful clothes. ———— And you, with your looks — no, I'm not flattering you — one fine day you'll grab yourself a husband! ———— You'll see! ———— A rich Englishman — they're so easy to ———— (*Slowing down.*) ———— catch — and then we'll get rich — and build ourselves a villa on Lake Como. ———— It's true it rains there a little now and then, but ———— (*Dully.*) ———— the sun has to shine sometimes — although it looks dark — and then . . . of course we could always come back home again ———— (*Pause.*) ———— here — or somewhere else ————

KRISTINE: Listen, Miss Julie, do you believe all this?

JULIE (*crushed*): Do I believe it?

KRISTINE: Yes!

JULIE (*wearily*): I don't know. I don't believe in anything anymore. (*She sinks down on the bench and cradles her head in her arms on the table.*) Nothing! Nothing at all!

KRISTINE (*turning right to where Jean is standing*): So, you thought you'd run out!

JEAN (*embarrassed; puts the razor on the table*): Run out? That's no way to put it. You hear Miss Julie's plan, and even if she is tired after being up all night, it's still a practical plan.

KRISTINE: Now you listen to me! Did you think I'd work as a cook for that . . .

JEAN (*sharply*): You watch what you say in front of your mistress! Do you understand?

KRISTINE: Mistress!

JEAN: Yes!

KRISTINE: Listen to him! Listen to him!

JEAN: Yes, you listen! It'd do you good to listen more and talk less! Miss Julie is your mistress. If you despise her, you have to despise yourself for the same reason!

KRISTINE: I've always had enough self-respect ————

JEAN: ———— to be able to despise other people!

KRISTINE: ———— to stop me from doing anything that's beneath me. You can't say that the Count's cook has been up to something with the groom or the swineherd! Can you?

JEAN: No, you were lucky enough to get hold of a gentleman!

KRISTINE: Yes, a gentleman who sells the Count's oats from the stable.

JEAN: You should talk — taking a commission from the grocer and bribes from the butcher.

KRISTINE: What?

JEAN: And you say you can't respect your employers any longer. You, you, you!

KRISTINE: Are you coming to church with me, now? You could use a good sermon after your fine deed!

JEAN: No, I'm not going to church today. You'll have to go alone and confess what you've been up to.

KRISTINE: Yes, I'll do that, and I'll bring back enough forgiveness for you, too. The Savior suffered and died on the Cross for all our sins, and if we go to Him with faith and a penitent heart, He takes all our sins on Himself.

JEAN: Even grocery sins?

JULIE: And do you believe that, Kristine?

KRISTINE: It's my living faith, as sure as I stand here. It's the faith I learned as a child, Miss Julie, and kept ever since. "Where sin abounded, grace did much more abound!"

JULIE: Oh, if I only had your faith. If only . . .

KRISTINE: Well, you see, we can't have it without God's special grace, and that isn't given to everyone ————

JULIE: Who is it given to then?

KRISTINE: That's the great secret of the workings of grace, Miss Julie, and God is no respecter of persons, for the last shall be the first . . .

JULIE: Then He does respect the last.

KRISTINE (*continuing*): . . . and it is easier for a camel to go through the eye of a needle, than for a rich man to enter the Kingdom of God. That's how it is, Miss Julie! Anyhow, I'm going now — alone, and on the way I'm going to tell the groom not to let any horses out, in case anyone wants to leave before the Count gets back! ———— Goodbye! (*Leaves.*)

JEAN: What a witch! ———— And all this because of a greenfinch!

JULIE (*dully*): Never mind the greenfinch! ———— Can you see any way out of this? Any end to it?

JEAN (*thinking*): No!

JULIE: What would you do in my place?

JEAN: In your place? Let's see — as a person of position, as a woman who had — fallen. I don't know — wait, now I know.

JULIE (*taking the razor and making a gesture*): You mean like this?

JEAN: Yes! But — understand — *I* wouldn't do it! That's the difference between us!

JULIE: Because you're a man and I'm a woman? What sort of difference is that?

JEAN: The usual difference — between a man and a woman.

JULIE (*with the razor in her hand*): I want to, but I can't! ———— My father couldn't either, the time he should have done it.

tempo prestissimo: At a very rapid pace.

JEAN: No, he shouldn't have! He had to revenge himself first.

JULIE: And now my mother is revenged again, through me.

JEAN: Didn't you ever love your father, Miss Julie?

JULIE: Oh yes, deeply, but I've hated him, too. I must have done so without realizing it! It was he who brought me up to despise my own sex, making me half woman, half man. Whose fault is what's happened? My father's, my mother's, my own? My own? I don't have anything that's my own. I don't have a single thought that I didn't get from my father, not an emotion that I didn't get from my mother, and this last idea — that all people are equal — I got that from my fiancé. ——— That's why I called him a swine! How can it be my fault? Shall I let Jesus take on the blame, the way Kristine does? ——— No, I'm too proud to do that and too sensible — thanks to my father's teachings. ——— And as for someone rich not going to heaven, that's a lie. But Kristine won't get in — how will she explain the money she has in the savings bank? Whose fault is it? ——— What does it matter whose fault it is? I'm still the one who has to bear the blame, face the consequences . . .

JEAN: Yes, but . . . (*The bell rings sharply twice. Miss Julie jumps up. Jean changes his coat.*) The Count is back! Do you suppose Kristine — (*He goes to the speaking tube, taps the lid, and listens.*)

JULIE: He's been to his desk!

JEAN: It's Jean, sir! (*Listening; the audience cannot hear the Count's voice.*) Yes, sir! (*Listening.*) Yes, sir! Right away! (*Listening.*) At once, sir! (*Listening.*) I see, in half an hour!

JULIE (*desperately frightened*): What did he say? Dear Lord, what did he say?

JEAN: He wants his boots and his coffee in half an hour.

JULIE: So, in half an hour! Oh, I'm so tired. I'm not able to do anything. I can't repent, can't run away, can't stay, can't live — can't die! Help me now! Order me, and I'll obey like a dog! Do me this last service, save my honor, save his name! You know what I *should* do, but don't have the will to . . . You will it, you order me to do it!

JEAN: I don't know why ——— but now I can't either ——— I don't understand. ——— It's as if this coat made it impossible for me to order you to do anything. ——— And now, since the Count spoke to me — I — I can't really explain it — but — ah, it's the damn lackey in me! ——— I think if the Count came down here now — and ordered me to cut my throat, I'd do it on the spot.

JULIE: Then pretend you're he, and I'm you! ——— You gave such a good performance before when you knelt at my feet. ——— You were a real nobleman. ——— Or — have you ever seen a hypnotist in the theater? (*Jean nods.*) He says to his subject: "Take the broom," and he takes it. He says: "Sweep," and he sweeps ———

JEAN: But the subject has to be asleep.

JULIE (*ecstatically*): I'm already asleep. ——— The whole room is like smoke around me . . . and you look like an iron stove . . . shaped like a man in black, with a tall hat — and your eyes glow like coals when the fire is dying — and your face is a white patch, like ashes ——— (*The sunlight has reached the floor and now shines on Jean.*) ——— it's so warm and good ——— (*She rubs her hands as if warming them before a fire.*) ——— and bright — and so peaceful!

JEAN (*taking the razor and putting it in her hand*): Here's the broom! Go now while it's bright — out to the barn — and . . . (*Whispers in her ear.*)

JULIE (*awake*): Thank you. I'm going now to rest! But just tell me — that those who are first can also receive the gift of grace. Say it, even if you don't believe it.

JEAN: The first? No, I can't ——— But wait — Miss Julie — now I know! You're no longer among the first — you're now among — the last!

JULIE: That's true. ——— I'm among the very last. I'm the last one of all! Oh! ——— But now I can't go! ——— Tell me once more to go!

JEAN: No, now I can't either! I can't!

JULIE: And the first shall be the last!

JEAN: Don't think, don't think! You're taking all my strength from me, making me a coward. ——— What was that? I thought the bell moved! ——— No! Shall we stuff paper in it? ——— To be so afraid of a bell! ——— But it isn't just a bell. ——— There's someone behind it — a hand sets it in motion — and something else sets the hand in motion. ——— Maybe if you cover your ears — cover your ears! But then it rings even louder! rings until someone answers. ——— And then it's too late! And then the police come — and — then — (*The bell rings twice loudly. Jean flinches, then straightens up.*) It's horrible! But there's no other way! ——— Go! (*Miss Julie walks firmly out through the door.*)

COMMENTARY

August Strindberg (1849–1912)
FROM THE PREFACE TO *MISS JULIE*   1888

TRANSLATED BY HARRY G. CARLSON

Strindberg's preface sets out his intentions in writing Miss Julie, *a play concerned with the problem of "social climbing or falling, of higher or lower, better or worse, man or woman." He discusses the struggle for dominance between Miss Julie and Jean, and characterizes Miss Julie as a woman forced to "wreak vengeance" on herself.*

Miss Julie is a modern character. Not that the man-hating half-woman has not existed in all ages but because now that she has been discovered, she has come out in the open to make herself heard. The half-woman is a type who pushes her way ahead, selling herself nowadays for power, decorations, honors, and diplomas, as formerly she used to do for money. The type implies a retrogressive step in evolution, an inferior species who cannot endure. Unfortunately, they are able to pass on their wretchedness; degenerate men seem unconsciously to choose their mates from among them. And so they breed, producing an indeterminate sex for whom life is a torture. Fortunately, the offspring go under either because they are out of harmony with reality or because their repressed instincts break out uncontrollably or because their hopes of achieving equality with men are crushed. The type is tragic, revealing the drama of a desperate struggle against Nature, tragic as the romantic heritage now being dissipated by naturalism, which has a contrary aim: happiness, and happiness belongs only to the strong and skillful species.

But Miss Julie is also: a relic of the old warrior nobility now giving way to a new nobility of nerve and intellect, a victim of her own flawed constitution, a victim of the discord caused in a family by a mother's "crime," a victim of the delusions and conditions of her age — and together these are the equivalent of the concept of Destiny, or Universal Law, of antiquity. Guilt has been abolished by the naturalist, along with God, but the consequences of an action — punishment, imprisonment or the fear of it — that he cannot erase, for the simple reason that they remain, whether he pronounces acquittal or not. Those who have been injured are not as kind and understanding as an unscathed outsider can afford to be. Even if her father felt constrained not to seek revenge, his daughter would wreak vengeance upon herself, as she does here, out of an innate or acquired sense of honor, which the upper classes inherit — from where? From barbarism, from the ancient Aryan home of the race, from medieval chivalry. It is a beautiful thing, but nowadays a hindrance to the survival of the race. It is the nobleman's harikari, which compels him to slit open his own stomach when someone insults him and which survives in a modified form in the duel, that privilege of the nobility. That is why Jean, the servant, lives, while Miss Julie cannot live without honor. The slave's advantage over the nobleman is that he lacks this fatal preoccupation with honor. But in all of us Aryans there is something of the nobleman, or a Don Quixote. And so we sympathize with the suicide, whose act means a loss of honor. We are noblemen enough to be pained when we see the mighty fallen and as superfluous as a corpse, yes, even if the fallen should rise again and make amends through an honorable act. The servant Jean is a race-founder, someone in whom the process of differentiation can be detected. Born the son of a tenant farmer, he has educated himself in the things a gentleman should know. He has been quick to learn, has finely developed senses (smell, taste, sight) and a feeling for what is beautiful. He is already moving up in the world and is not embarrassed about using other people's help. He is alienated from his fellow servants, despising them as parts of a past he has already put behind him. He fears and flees them because they know his secrets, pry into his intentions, envy his rise, and look forward eagerly to his fall. Hence his dual, indecisive nature, vacillating between sympathy for people in high social positions and hatred for those who currently occupy those positions. He is an aristocrat, as he himself says, has learned the secrets of good society, is polished on the surface but coarse beneath, wears a frock coat tastefully but without any guarantee that his body is clean.

He has respect for Miss Julie, but is afraid of Kristine because she knows his dangerous secrets. He is sufficiently callous not to let the night's events disturb his plans for the future. With both a slave's brutality and a master's lack of squeamishness, he can see blood without fainting and shake off misfortune easily. Consequently, he comes through the struggle unscathed and will probably end up an innkeeper. And even if *he* does not become a Rumanian count, his son will become a university student and possibly a county police commissioner. . . .

Apart from the fact that Jean is rising in the world, he is superior to Miss Julie because he is a man. Sexually, he is an aristocrat because of his masculine strength, his more keenly developed senses, and his capacity for taking the initiative. His sense of inferiority is mostly due to the social circumstances in which he happens to be living, and he can probably shed it along with his valet's jacket.

His slave mentality expresses itself in the fearful respect he has for the Count (the boots) and his religious superstition; but he respects the Count mainly as the occupant of the kind of high position to which he himself aspires; and the respect remains even after he has conquered the daughter of the house and seen how empty the lovely shell was.

I do not believe that love in any "higher" sense can exist between two people of such different natures, and so I have Miss Julie's love as something she fabricates in order to protect and excuse herself; and I have Jean suppose himself capable of loving her under other social circumstances. I think it is the same with love as with the hyacinth, which must take root in darkness *before* it can produce a sturdy flower. Here a flower shoots up, blooms, and goes to seed all at once, and that is why it dies so quickly.

Oscar Wilde

Oscar Fingal O'Flahertie Wills Wilde (1854–1900) was born to a famous eye surgeon who maintained a home in Dublin's most exclusive neighborhood. Wilde's mother, known by her literary name as Speranza, was noted for collecting Irish folk stories in the western hills in the late 1870s. Her work was important to later literature, but it was especially important for its timing, since most of the storytellers in Ireland were gone by the turn of the century.

Wilde was a brilliant classics scholar at Trinity College, Dublin, where his tutor was the legendary Mahaffy, who later traveled with him in France. After Trinity, he went to Magdalen College, Oxford, where he took a distinguished degree. Among his influences in Oxford was Slade Professor of Art John Ruskin, with whom Wilde had long walks and talks. Ruskin had published important books on northern Gothic art and on Italian art, especially the art of Venice. Art was one of Wilde's primary passions, especially decoration and the decorative arts. He agreed with Walter Pater, a contemporary art critic, that art must best serve the needs of art. He felt, for example, that poetry did not serve religious, political, social, or biographical goals. Its ends were aesthetic and its pleasures were in its sounds, images, and thoughts.

Partly because of his brilliance and partly because he was one of the age's greatest conversationalists, he was soon in the company of the famous and amusing people of his generation. Some of his conversational gift is apparent in his plays.

By his own admission, his life was marked by an overindulgence in sensuality: "What paradox was to me in the sphere of thought, perversity became to me in the sphere of passion." He married Constance Lloyd in 1884 and soon had two sons. But by 1891 he had already had several homosexual liaisons, one of which was to bring him to ruin. His relationship with the much younger Lord Alfred Douglas ended with Douglas's father, the marquis of Queensberry, publicly denouncing Wilde as a sodomite. Wilde sued for libel but lost. As a result, in 1895 he was tried for sodomy, convicted, and sentenced to two years' hard labor. Wilde's actions have been seen as self-destructive, but they are also consistent with his efforts to force society to examine its own hypocrisy. Unfortunately, his efforts in court and prison ruined him, and he died in exile in Paris three years after his release.

His best-known novel, *The Picture of Dorian Gray* (1890; expanded 1891), is the story of a young man whose sensual life eats away at him and eventually destroys him. The novel's failure led Wilde to try the stage, where he was a signal success. Remarkably, all his plays were written in the period between 1891 and his imprisonment in 1895. Most of his plays — *Salomé* (1891), *Lady Windermere's Fan* (1892), *A Woman of No Importance* (1893), *An Ideal Husband* (1895), and *The Importance of Being Earnest* (1895) — rank as witty, insightful, and sharp commentaries on the upper-class British society he knew best. They owe a great deal to eighteenth-century comedies, such as William Congreve's *The Way of the World*. But they also owe a great deal to English and European farces and comedies of his own time, many of which he seems to have studied closely. Unlike those plays — many have never been published and no longer exist — Wilde's are still funny and still seem pertinent even though the class he criticized has long vanished.

The Importance of Being Earnest was a remarkable success when it opened at St. James's Theatre on Valentine's Day 1895, but it closed in two months after fewer than one hundred performances when the scandal of Wilde's conviction became public. Wilde's reputation as playwright was made and broken in a matter of a few years, and it was not restored until after his death.

THE IMPORTANCE OF BEING EARNEST

The play was originally written in four acts, but because the producer requested it be cut, Wilde reworked it into three acts, agreeing that the excisions made the play stronger. Its subtitle, *A Trivial Comedy for Serious People,* has prompted commentators to think of the play as farcical fluff, a play about little or nothing that is nonetheless profoundly amusing. The *New York Times* commented after its first U.S. opening, "The thing is as slight in structure and as devoid of purpose as a paper balloon, but it is extraordinarily funny." Recent critics have challenged this view on the grounds that its subject matter centers on the questions of identity and reality. One current view is that its surfaces are slight but that beneath the surface is a commentary on a society that judges things only by appearance.

The primary characters are Algernon Moncrieff and Jack Worthing, young gentlemen of marriageable age. Among the women are Algernon's cousin Gwendolen Fairfax, who adores the name Ernest and is in love with Jack; Lady Bracknell, her mother; and Cecily Cardew, Jack's ward. Bunbury, referred to by Algernon, seems to be a character, but is instead an invention. He is a convenience for Algernon, a country friend whose illnesses Algernon uses to avoid social events he dislikes, such as Lady Bracknell's dinners. Jack, who lives in the country, has created a similar figure to help him escape to town — an imaginary brother Ernest. In town, Jack pretends to be Ernest; and all his town acquaintances, including Algernon and Gwendolen, know Jack by that name.

The similarities with Congreve's *The Way of the World* are striking. The question of marriage is central in both plays, and attitudes toward marriage in Wilde's social class are among the targets of his satire. When Lady Bracknell probes into Jack Worthing's background, she discovers the distressing news about his family "line": Jack is a foundling who had been left in a handbag in Victoria Station. His family "line" is the Brighton Line. Gwendolen could also have stepped from a Congreve comedy. She is determined to have Jack Worthing, and when he seems sluggish about proposing she prompts him, offering a critique of his proposal by telling him he seems inexperienced at it.

The play owes perhaps even more to the farces of the 1880s and 1890s and a great deal to the well-made play of Eugène Scribe and his successors. Critics often compare Wilde to Alexandre Dumas, the author of *La Dame aux camélias* (*Camille*), because both writers fashioned their plays with a considerable degree of artificiality, planting information in the first act that would prove the solution to problems in the last act. They also play with questions of identity, disguise, and revelation at the last minute in much the way Wilde does here when he reveals the identity of Ernest.

In melodramas and well-made plays, the revelation at the end was not that the potential husband had the right name so much as that he had the right background: he was an aristocrat and not the commoner he seemed to be. Wilde has fun with this convention and many others. In an instant, he ridicules the trick of revealing the hero to be "marriageable" because of his birth by emphasizing the triviality of a name. Yet names are of great importance (as Shakespeare tells us in *Romeo and Juliet*), and the earnestness implied in Ernest is one ingredient that helps Jack Worthing succeed.

Kerry Powell has demonstrated that almost every device in *The Importance of Being Earnest* was drawn from a contemporary farce or comedy. The device of the child lost in a piece of luggage was used in *The Lost Child* (1863), and *The Foundling* (1894) actually takes place in Brighton. The name Bunbury and the concept of "Bunburying" come from *The Godpapa* (1891). Even the device of baptism was used in *Crimes and Christening* (1891). Wilde was adept at taking the theater conventions his audience was most familiar with and using them to his own ends — to entertain his audience, but at the same time to help him put an extra edge on his satire.

The Importance of Being Earnest in Performance

After the first production closed down in 1895, the play was revived in London in 1898 and 1902, but an even more successful production in 1909 saw 324 performances. The benchmark for a truly successful play in those days seems to have been one hundred performances, and Wilde would have felt vindicated by the 1909 production, had he lived to see it. *The Importance of Being Earnest* has been produced so often in England and the United States that only a few productions can be taken into account here. The first New York production was in 1902. John Gielgud and Edith Evans played in the 1939 London production and then again in 1942. In 1947 Gielgud played in New York with Clifton Webb and Estelle Winwood. The reviews were especially strong, calling the play "as insolently monocled in manner and as killingly high-toned in language as mischievous tomfoolery can make it."

The play inspired at least five musicals between 1927 and 1984. The 1979 production at Stratford, Ontario, was called "a perfect play in a perfect production." An unsuccessful production by the Berlin Play Actors in 1987 used all men and relied on insights drawn from transvestite performers, but it was badly received. University productions of the play are fairly common, although, like the Yale Repertory production in 1986, they are not always able to pull off the comic demands of the play's exacting language. The original four-act version of the play, discovered in 1977 in the New York Public Library, was produced in Ohio in the John Carroll University's Marinello Theater in 1985. It was more a curiosity than a triumph. The 1993 production at the Aldwych in London received great praise for its dazzling sets that "matched Wilde's word pictures with bold stage pictures." Maggie Smith played Lady Bracknell.

The play is a witty tour de force of language. Its surfaces gleam, and the best productions play it straight.

Oscar Wilde (1854–1900)

THE IMPORTANCE OF BEING EARNEST   *1895*
A TRIVIAL COMEDY FOR SERIOUS PEOPLE

The Persons of the Play

JOHN WORTHING, J.P., *of the Manor House, Woolton, Hertfordshire*
ALGERNON MONCRIEFF, *his friend*
REV. CANON CHASUBLE, D.D., *rector of Woolton*
MERRIMAN, *butler to Mr. Worthing*
LANE, *Mr. Moncrieff's manservant*
LADY BRACKNELL
HON. GWENDOLEN FAIRFAX, *her daughter*
CECILY CARDEW, *John Worthing's ward*
MISS PRISM, *her governess*

The Scenes of the Play

Act I: *Algernon Moncrieff's Flat in Half Moon Street, W.*
Act II: *The Garden at the Manor House, Woolton*
Act III: *Morning Room at the Manor House, Woolton*

ACT I

(*Scene: Morning room in Algernon's flat in Half Moon Street. The room is luxuriously and artistically furnished. The sound of a piano is heard in the adjoining room. Lane is arranging afternoon tea on the table, and after the music has ceased, Algernon enters.*)

ALGERNON: Did you hear what I was playing, Lane?

LANE: I didn't think it polite to listen, sir.

ALGERNON: I'm sorry for that, for your sake. I don't play accurately — anyone can play accurately — but I play with wonderful expression. As far as the piano is concerned, sentiment is my forte. I keep science for Life.

LANE: Yes, sir.

ALGERNON: And, speaking of the science of Life, have you got the cucumber sandwiches cut for Lady Bracknell?

LANE: Yes, sir.   (*Hands them on a salver.*)

ALGERNON (*inspects them, takes two, and sits down on the sofa*): Oh! — by the way, Lane, I see from your book that on Thursday night, when Lord Shoreham and Mr. Worthing were dining with me, eight bottles of champagne are entered as having been consumed.

LANE: Yes, sir; eight bottles and a pint.

ALGERNON: Why is it that at a bachelor's establishment the servants invariably drink the champagne? I ask merely for information.

LANE: I attribute it to the superior quality of the wine, sir. I have often observed that in married households the champagne is rarely of a first-rate brand.

ALGERNON: Good heavens! Is marriage so demoralizing as that?

LANE: I believe it *is* a very pleasant state, sir. I have had very little experience of it myself up to the present. I have only been married once. That was in consequence of a misunderstanding between myself and a young person.

ALGERNON (*languidly*): I don't know that I am much interested in your family life, Lane.

LANE: No, sir; it is not a very interesting subject. I never think of it myself.

ALGERNON: Very natural, I am sure. That will do, Lane, thank you.

LANE: Thank you, sir.   (*Lane goes out.*)

ALGERNON: Lane's views on marriage seem somewhat lax. Really, if the lower orders don't set us a good example, what on earth is the use of them? They seem, as a class, to have absolutely no sense of moral responsibility.

(*Enter Lane.*)

LANE: Mr. Ernest Worthing.

(*Enter Jack. Lane goes out.*)

ALGERNON: How are you, my dear Ernest? What brings you up to town?

JACK: Oh, pleasure, pleasure! What else should bring one anywhere? Eating as usual, I see, Algy!

ALGERNON (*stiffly*): I believe it is customary in good society to take some slight refreshment at five o'clock. Where have you been since last Thursday?

JACK (*sitting down on the sofa*): In the country.

ALGERNON: What on earth do you do there?

JACK (*pulling off his gloves*): When one is in town one amuses oneself. When one is in the country one amuses other people. It is excessively boring.

ALGERNON: And who are the people you amuse?

JACK (*airily*): Oh, neighbors, neighbors.

ALGERNON: Got nice neighbors in your part of Shropshire?

JACK: Perfectly horrid! Never speak to one of them.

ALGERNON: How immensely you must amuse them! (*Goes over and takes sandwich.*) By the way, Shropshire is your county, is it not?

JACK: Eh? Shropshire? Yes, of course. Hallo! Why all these cups? Why cucumber sandwiches? Why such reckless extravagance in one so young? Who is coming to tea?

ALGERNON: Oh! merely Aunt Augusta and Gwendolen.

JACK: How perfectly delightful!

ALGERNON: Yes, that is all very well; but I am afraid Aunt Augusta won't quite approve of your being here.

JACK: May I ask why?

ALGERNON: My dear fellow, the way you flirt with Gwendolen is perfectly disgraceful. It is almost as bad as the way Gwendolen flirts with you.

JACK: I am in love with Gwendolen. I have come up to town expressly to propose to her.

ALGERNON: I thought you had come up for pleasure? — I call that business.

JACK: How utterly unromantic you are!

ALGERNON: I really don't see anything romantic in proposing. It is very romantic to be in love. But there is nothing romantic about a definite proposal. Why, one may be accepted. One usually is, I believe. Then the excitement is all over. The very essence of romance is uncertainty. If ever I get married, I'll certainly try to forget the fact.

JACK: I have no doubt about that, dear Algy. The Divorce Court was specially invented for people whose memories are so curiously constituted.

ALGERNON: Oh! there is no use speculating on that subject. Divorces are made in heaven — (*Jack puts out his hand to take a sandwich. Algernon at once interferes.*) Please don't touch the cucumber sandwiches. They are ordered specially for Aunt Augusta. (*Takes one and eats it.*)

JACK: Well, you have been eating them all the time.

ALGERNON: That is quite a different matter. She is my aunt. (*Takes plate from below.*) Have some bread and butter. The bread and butter is for Gwendolen. Gwendolen is devoted to bread and butter.

JACK (*advancing to table and helping himself*): And very good bread and butter it is too.

ALGERNON: Well, my dear fellow, you need not eat as if you were going to eat it all. You behave as if you were married to her already. You are not married to her already, and I don't think you ever will be.

JACK: Why on earth do you say that?

ALGERNON: Well, in the first place, girls never marry the men they flirt with. Girls don't think it right.

JACK: Oh, that is nonsense!

ALGERNON: It isn't. It is a great truth. It accounts for the extraordinary number of bachelors that one sees all over the place. In the second place, I don't give my consent.

JACK: Your consent!

ALGERNON: My dear fellow, Gwendolen is my first cousin. And before I allow you to marry her, you will have to clear up the whole question of Cecily.

(*Rings bell.*)

JACK: Cecily! What on earth do you mean? What do you mean, Algy, by Cecily? I don't know anyone of the name of Cecily.

(*Enter Lane.*)

ALGERNON: Bring me that cigarette case Mr. Worthing left in the smoking room the last time he dined here.

LANE: Yes, sir.   (*Lane goes out.*)

JACK: Do you mean to say you have had my cigarette case all this time? I wish to goodness you had let me know. I have been writing frantic letters to Scotland Yard about it. I was very nearly offering a large reward.

ALGERNON: Well, I wish you would offer one. I happen to be more than usually hard up.

JACK: There is no good offering a large reward now that the thing is found.

(*Enter Lane with the cigarette case on a salver. Algernon takes it at once. Lane goes out.*)

ALGERNON: I think that is rather mean of you, Ernest, I must say. (*Opens case and examines it.*) However, it makes no matter, for, now that I look at the inscription inside, I find that the thing isn't yours after all.

JACK: Of course it's mine. (*Moving to him.*) You have seen me with it a hundred times, and you have no right whatsoever to read what is written inside. It is a very ungentlemanly thing to read a private cigarette case.

ALGERNON: Oh! it is absurd to have a hard-and-fast rule about what one should read and what one shouldn't. More than half of modern culture depends on what one shouldn't read.

JACK: I am quite aware of the fact, and I don't propose to discuss modern culture. It isn't the sort of thing one should talk of in private. I simply want my cigarette case back.

ALGERNON: Yes; but this isn't your cigarette case. This cigarette case is a present from someone of the name of Cecily, and you said you didn't know anyone of that name.

JACK: Well, if you want to know, Cecily happens to be my aunt.

ALGERNON: Your aunt!

JACK: Yes. Charming old lady she is, too. Lives at Tunbridge Wells. Just give it back to me, Algy.

ALGERNON (*retreating to back of sofa*): But why does she call herself little Cecily if she is your aunt and lives at Tunbridge Wells? (*Reading.*) "From little Cecily with her fondest love."

JACK (*moving to sofa and kneeling upon it*): My dear fellow, what on earth is there in that? Some aunts are tall, some aunts are not tall. That is a matter that surely an aunt may be allowed to decide for herself. You seem to think that every aunt should be exactly like your aunt! That is absurd! For heaven's sake give me back my cigarette case.

(*Follows Algernon round the room.*)

ALGERNON: Yes. But why does your aunt call you her uncle? "From little Cecily, with her fondest love to her dear Uncle Jack." There is no objection, I admit, to an aunt being a small aunt, but why an aunt, no matter what her size may be, should call her own nephew her uncle, I can't quite make out. Besides, your name isn't Jack at all; it is Ernest.

JACK: It isn't Ernest; it's Jack.

ALGERNON: You have always told me it was Ernest. I have introduced you to everyone as Ernest. You answer to the name of Ernest. You look as if your name was Ernest. You are the most earnest looking person I ever saw in my life. It is perfectly absurd your saying that your name isn't Ernest. It's on your cards. Here is one of them (*taking it from case*) "Mr. Ernest Worthing, B.4, The Albany." I'll keep this as a proof that your name is Ernest if ever you attempt to deny it to me, or to Gwendolen, or to anyone else.

(*Puts the card in his pocket.*)

JACK: Well, my name is Ernest in town and Jack in the country, and the cigarette case was given to me in the country.

ALGERNON: Yes, but that does not account for the fact that your small Aunt Cecily, who lives at Tunbridge Wells, calls you her dear uncle. Come, old boy, you had much better have the thing out at once.

JACK: My dear Algy, you talk exactly as if you were a dentist. It is very vulgar to talk like a dentist when one isn't a dentist. It produces a false impression.

ALGERNON: Well, that is exactly what dentists always do. Now, go on! Tell me the whole thing. I may mention that I have always suspected you of being a confirmed and secret Bunburyist; and I am quite sure of it now.

JACK: Bunburyist? What on earth do you mean by a Bunburyist?

ALGERNON: I'll reveal to you the meaning of that incomparable expression as soon as you are kind enough to inform me why you are Ernest in town and Jack in the country.

JACK: Well, produce my cigarette case first.

ALGERNON: Here it is. (*Hands cigarette case.*) Now produce your explanation, and pray make it improbable. (*Sits on sofa.*)

JACK: My dear fellow, there is nothing improbable about my explanation at all. In fact it's perfectly ordinary. Old Mr. Thomas Cardew, who adopted me when I was a little boy, made me in his will guardian to his granddaughter, Miss Cecily Cardew. Cecily, who addresses me as her uncle from motives of respect that you could not possibly appreciate, lives at my place in the country under the charge of her admirable governess, Miss Prism.

ALGERNON: Where is that place in the country, by the way?

JACK: That is nothing to you, dear boy. You are not going to be invited — I may tell you candidly that the place is not in Shropshire.

ALGERNON: I suspected that, my dear fellow! I have Bunburyed all over Shropshire on two separate occasions. Now, go on. Why are you Ernest in town and Jack in the country?

JACK: My dear Algy, I don't know whether you will be able to understand my real motives. You are hardly serious enough. When one is placed in the position of guardian, one has to adopt a very high moral tone on all subjects. It's one's duty to do so. And as a high moral tone can hardly be said to conduce very much to either one's health or one's happiness, in order to get up to town I have always pretended to have a younger brother of the name of Ernest, who lives in the Albany, and gets into the most dreadful scrapes. That, my dear Algy, is the whole truth pure and simple.

ALGERNON: The truth is rarely pure and never simple. Modern life would be very tedious if it were either and modern literature a complete impossibility!

JACK: That wouldn't be at all a bad thing.

ALGERNON: Literary criticism is not your forte, my dear fellow. Don't try it. You should leave that to people who haven't been at a university. They do it so well in the daily papers. What you really are is a Bunburyist. I was quite right in saying you were a Bunburyist. You are one of the most advanced Bunburyists I know.

JACK: What on earth do you mean?

ALGERNON: You have invented a very useful younger brother called Ernest, in order that you may be able to come up to town as often as you like. I have invented an invaluable permanent invalid called Bunbury, in order that I may be able to go down into the country whenever I choose. Bunbury is perfectly invaluable. If it wasn't for Bunbury's extraordinary bad health, for instance, I wouldn't be able to dine with you at Willis's tonight, for I have been really engaged to Aunt Augusta for more than a week.

JACK: I haven't asked you to dine with me anywhere tonight.

ALGERNON: I know. You are absurdly careless about sending out invitations. It is very foolish of you. Nothing annoys people so much as not receiving invitations.

JACK: You had much better dine with your Aunt Augusta.

ALGERNON: I haven't the smallest intention of doing anything of the kind. To begin with, I dined there on Monday, and once a week is quite enough to dine with one's own relations. In the second place, whenever I do dine there I am always treated as a member of the family, and sent down with° either no woman at all, or two. In the third place, I know perfectly well whom she will place me next to, tonight. She will place me next Mary Farquhar, who always flirts with her own husband across the dinner table. That is not very pleasant. Indeed, it is not even decent — and that sort of thing is enormously on the increase. The amount of women in London who flirt with their own husbands is perfectly scandalous. It looks so bad. It is simply washing one's clean linen in public. Besides, now that I know you to be a confirmed Bunburyist I naturally want to talk to you about Bunburying. I want to tell you the rules.

JACK: I'm not a Bunburyist at all. If Gwendolen accepts me, I am going to kill my brother, indeed I think I'll kill him in any case. Cecily is a little too much interested in him. It is rather a bore. So I am going to get rid of Ernest. And I strongly advise you to do the same with Mr. — with your invalid friend who has the absurd name.

ALGERNON: Nothing will induce me to part with Bunbury, and if you ever get married, which seems to me extremely problematic, you will be very glad to know Bunbury. A man who marries without knowing Bunbury has a very tedious time of it.

JACK: That is nonsense. If I marry a charming girl like Gwendolen, and she is the only girl I ever saw in my life that I would marry, I certainly won't want to know Bunbury.

ALGERNON: Then your wife will. You don't seem to realize, that in married life three is company and two is none.

JACK (sententiously): That, my dear young friend, is the theory that the corrupt French drama has been propounding for the last fifty years.

ALGERNON: Yes; and that the happy English home has proved in half the time.

JACK: For heaven's sake, don't try to be cynical. It's perfectly easy to be cynical.

ALGERNON: My dear fellow, it isn't easy to be anything nowadays. There's such a lot of beastly competition about. (The sound of an electric bell is heard.) Ah! that must be Aunt Augusta. Only relatives, or creditors, ever ring in that Wagnerian° manner. Now, if I

sent down with: Assigned a woman to escort into the dining room for dinner.   Wagnerian: Referring to the operas of Richard Wagner (1813–1883), whose music was popularly thought to be loud.

get her out of the way for ten minutes, so that you can have an opportunity for proposing to Gwendolen, may I dine with you tonight at Willis's?

JACK: I suppose so, if you want to.

ALGERNON: Yes, but you must be serious about it. I hate people who are not serious about meals. It is so shallow of them.

(Enter Lane.)

LANE: Lady Bracknell and Miss Fairfax.

(Algernon goes forward to meet them. Enter Lady Bracknell and Gwendolen.)

LADY BRACKNELL: Good afternoon, dear Algernon, I hope you are behaving very well.

ALGERNON: I'm feeling very well, Aunt Augusta.

LADY BRACKNELL: That's not quite the same thing. In fact the two things rarely go together.

(Sees Jack and bows to him with icy coldness.)

ALGERNON (to Gwendolen): Dear me, you are smart!

GWENDOLEN: I am always smart! Aren't I, Mr. Worthing?

JACK: You're quite perfect, Miss Fairfax.

GWENDOLEN: Oh! I hope I am not that. It would leave no room for developments, and I intend to develop in many directions.

(Gwendolen and Jack sit down together in the corner.)

LADY BRACKNELL: I'm sorry if we are a little late Algernon, but I was obliged to call on dear Lady Harbury. I hadn't been there since her poor husband's death. I never saw a woman so altered; she looks quite twenty years younger. And now I'll have a cup of tea, and one of those nice cucumber sandwiches you promised me.

ALGERNON: Certainly, Aunt Augusta.
                                    (Goes over to tea table.)

LADY BRACKNELL: Won't you come and sit here, Gwendolen?

GWENDOLEN: Thanks, Mama, I'm quite comfortable where I am.

ALGERNON (picking up empty plate in horror): Good heavens! Lane! Why are there no cucumber sandwiches? I ordered them specially.

LANE (gravely): There were no cucumbers in the market this morning, sir. I went down twice.

ALGERNON: No cucumbers!

LANE: No, sir. Not even for ready money.

ALGERNON: That will do, Lane, thank you.

LANE: Thank you, sir.   (Goes out.)

ALGERNON: I am greatly distressed, Aunt Augusta, about there being no cucumbers, not even for ready money.

LADY BRACKNELL: It really makes no matter, Algernon. I had some crumpets with Lady Harbury, who seems to me to be living entirely for pleasure now.

ALGERNON: I hear her hair has turned quite gold from grief.

LADY BRACKNELL: It certainly has changed its color. From what cause I, of course, cannot say. (*Algernon crosses and hands tea.*) Thank you. I've quite a treat for you tonight, Algernon. I am going to send you down with Mary Farquhar. She is such a nice woman, and so attentive to her husband. It's delightful to watch them.

ALGERNON: I am afraid, Aunt Augusta, I shall have to give up the pleasure of dining with you tonight after all.

LADY BRACKNELL (*frowning*): I hope not, Algernon. It would put my table completely out. Your uncle would have to dine upstairs. Fortunately he is accustomed to that.

ALGERNON: It is a great bore, and, I need hardly say, a terrible disappointment to me, but the fact is I have just had a telegram to say that my poor friend Bunbury is very ill again. (*Exchanges glances with Jack.*) They seem to think I should be with him.

LADY BRACKNELL: It is very strange. This Mr. Bunbury seems to suffer from curiously bad health.

ALGERNON: Yes; poor Bunbury is a dreadful invalid.

LADY BRACKNELL: Well, I must say, Algernon, that I think it is high time that Mr. Bunbury made up his mind whether he was going to live or to die. This shilly-shallying with the question is absurd. Nor do I in any way approve of the modern sympathy with invalids. I consider it morbid. Illness of any kind is hardly a thing to be encouraged in others. Health is the primary duty of life. I am always telling that to your poor uncle, but he never seems to take much notice — as far as any improvement in his ailments goes. I should be much obliged if you would ask Mr. Bunbury, from me, to be kind enough not to have a relapse on Saturday, for I rely on you to arrange my music for me. It is my last reception, and one wants something that will encourage conversation, particularly at the end of the season when everyone has practically said whatever they had to say, which, in most cases, was probably not much.

ALGERNON: I'll speak to Bunbury, Aunt Augusta, if he is still conscious, and I think I can promise you he'll be all right by Saturday. Of course the music is a great difficulty. You see, if one plays good music, people don't listen, and if one plays bad music people don't talk. But I'll run over the program I've drawn out, if you will kindly come into the next room for a moment.

LADY BRACKNELL: Thank you, Algernon. It is very thoughtful of you. (*Rising, and following Algernon.*) I'm sure the program will be delightful, after a few expurgations. French songs I cannot possibly allow. People always seem to think that they are improper, and either look shocked, which is vulgar, or laugh, which is worse. But German sounds a thoroughly respectable language, and indeed, I believe is so. Gwendolen, you will accompany me.

GWENDOLEN: Certainly, Mama.

(*Lady Bracknell and Algernon go into the music room. Gwendolen remains behind.*)

JACK: Charming day it has been, Miss Fairfax.

GWENDOLEN: Pray don't talk to me about the weather Mr. Worthing. Whenever people talk to me about the weather, I always feel quite certain that they mean something else. And that makes me so nervous.

JACK: I do mean something else.

GWENDOLEN: I thought so. In fact, I am never wrong.

JACK: And I would like to be allowed to take advantage of Lady Bracknell's temporary absence —

GWENDOLEN: I would certainly advise you to do so. Mama has a way of coming back suddenly into a room that I have often had to speak to her about.

JACK (*nervously*): Miss Fairfax, ever since I met you I have admired you more than any girl — I have ever met since — I met you.

GWENDOLEN: Yes, I am quite aware of the fact. And I often wish that in public, at any rate, you had been more demonstrative. For me you have always had an irresistible fascination. Even before I met you I was far from indifferent to you. (*Jack looks at her in amazement.*) We live, as I hope you know Mr. Worthing, in an age of ideals. The fact is constantly mentioned in the more expensive monthly magazines, and has reached the provincial pulpits I am told: And my ideal has always been to love someone of the name of Ernest. There is something in that name that inspires absolute confidence. The moment Algernon first mentioned to me that he had a friend called Ernest, I knew I was destined to love you.

JACK: You really love me, Gwendolen?

GWENDOLEN: Passionately!

JACK: Darling! You don't know how happy you've made me.

GWENDOLEN: My own Ernest!

JACK: But you don't mean to say that you couldn't love me if my name wasn't Ernest?

GWENDOLEN: But your name is Ernest.

JACK: Yes, I know it is. But supposing it was something else? Do you mean to say you couldn't love me then?

GWENDOLEN (*glibly*): Ah! that is clearly a metaphysical speculation, and like most metaphysical speculations has very little reference at all to the actual facts of real life, as we know them.

JACK: Personally, darling, to speak quite candidly, I don't much care about the name of Ernest — I don't think the name suits me at all.

GWENDOLEN: It suits you perfectly. It is a divine name. It has a music of its own. It produces vibrations.

JACK: Well, really, Gwendolen, I must say that I think there are lots of other much nicer names. I think Jack, for instance, a charming name.

GWENDOLEN: Jack? — No, there is very little music in the name Jack, if any at all, indeed. It does not thrill. It produces absolutely no vibrations — I have known several Jacks, and they all, without exception, were more than usually plain. Besides, Jack is a notorious domesticity for John! And I pity any woman who is married to a man called John. She would probably never be allowed to know the entrancing pleasure of a single moment's solitude. The only really safe name is Ernest.

JACK: Gwendolen, I must get christened at once — I mean we must get married at once. There is no time to be lost.

GWENDOLEN: Married, Mr. Worthing?

JACK (*astounded*): Well — surely. You know that I love you, and you led me to believe, Miss Fairfax that you were not absolutely indifferent to me.

GWENDOLEN: I adore you. But you haven't proposed to me yet. Nothing has been said at all about marriage. The subject has not even been touched on.

JACK: Well — may I propose to you now?

GWENDOLEN: I think it would be an admirable opportunity. And to spare you any possible disappointment, Mr. Worthing, I think it only fair to tell you quite frankly beforehand that I am fully determined to accept you.

JACK: Gwendolen!

GWENDOLEN: Yes, Mr. Worthing, what have you got to say to me?

JACK: You know what I have got to say to you.

GWENDOLEN: Yes, but you don't say it.

JACK: Gwendolen, will you marry me?

(*Goes on his knees.*)

GWENDOLEN: Of course I will, darling. How long you have been about it! I am afraid you have had very little experience in how to propose.

JACK: My own one, I have never loved anyone in the world but you.

GWENDOLEN: Yes, but men often propose for practice. I know my brother Gerald does. All my girlfriends tell me so. What wonderfully blue eyes you have, Ernest! They are quite, quite blue. I hope you will always look at me just like that, especially when there are other people present.

(*Enter Lady Bracknell.*)

LADY BRACKNELL: Mr. Worthing! Rise, sir, from this semirecumbent posture. It is most indecorous.

GWENDOLEN: Mama! (*He tries to rise; she restrains him.*) I must beg you to retire. This is no place for you. Besides, Mr. Worthing has not quite finished yet.

LADY BRACKNELL: Finished what, may I ask?

GWENDOLEN: I am engaged to Mr. Worthing, Mama.

(*They rise together.*)

LADY BRACKNELL: Pardon me, you are not engaged to anyone. When you do become engaged to someone, I, or your father, should his health permit him, will inform you of the fact. An engagement should come on a young girl as a surprise, pleasant or unpleasant, as the case may be. It is hardly a matter that she could be allowed to arrange for herself — And now I have a few questions to put to you, Mr. Worthing. While I am making these inquiries, you, Gwendolen, will wait for me below in the carriage.

GWENDOLEN (*reproachfully*): Mama!

LADY BRACKNELL: In the carriage, Gwendolen! (*Gwendolen goes to the door. She and Jack blow kisses to each other behind Lady Bracknell's back. Lady Bracknell looks vaguely about as if she could not understand what the noise was. Finally turns round.*) Gwendolen, the carriage!

GWENDOLEN: Yes, Mama.

(*Goes out, looking back at Jack.*)

LADY BRACKNELL (*sitting down*): You can take a seat, Mr. Worthing.

(*Looks in her pocket for notebook and pencil.*)

JACK: Thank you, Lady Bracknell, I prefer standing.

LADY BRACKNELL (*pencil and notebook in hand*): I feel bound to tell you that you are not down on my list of eligible young men, although I have the same list as the dear Duchess of Bolton has. We work together, in fact. However, I am quite ready to enter your name, should your answers be what a really affectionate mother requires. Do you smoke?

JACK: Well, yes, I must admit I smoke.

LADY BRACKNELL: I am glad to hear it. A man should always have an occupation of some kind. There are far too many idle men in London as it is. How old are you?

JACK: Twenty-nine.

LADY BRACKNELL: A very good age to be married at. I have always been of opinion that a man who desires to get married should know either everything or nothing. Which do you know?

JACK (*after some hesitation*): I know nothing, Lady Bracknell.

LADY BRACKNELL: I am pleased to hear it. I do not approve of anything that tampers with natural ignorance. Ignorance is like a delicate exotic fruit; touch it and the bloom is gone. The whole theory of modern education is radically unsound. Fortunately in England, at any rate, education produces no effect whatsoever. If it did, it would prove a serious danger to the upper classes, and probably lead to acts of violence in Grosvenor Square. What is your income?

JACK: Between seven and eight thousand a year.

LADY BRACKNELL (*makes a note in her book*): In land, or in investments?

JACK: In investments, chiefly.

LADY BRACKNELL: That is satisfactory. What between the duties expected of one during one's lifetime, and the duties exacted from one after one's death, land has ceased to be either a profit or a pleasure. It gives one position, and prevents one from keeping it up. That's all that can be said about land.

JACK: I have a country house with some land, of course, attached to it, about fifteen hundred acres, I believe; but I don't depend on that for my real income. In fact, as far as I can make out, the poachers are the only people who make anything out of it.

LADY BRACKNELL: A country house! How many bedrooms? Well, that point can be cleared up afterwards. You have a town house, I hope? A girl with a simple, unspoiled nature, like Gwendolen, could hardly be expected to reside in the country.

JACK: Well, I own a house in Belgrave Square, but it is let by the year to Lady Bloxham. Of course, I can get it back whenever I like, at six months' notice.

LADY BRACKNELL: Lady Bloxham? I don't know her.

JACK: Oh, she goes about very little. She is a lady considerably advanced in years.

LADY BRACKNELL: Ah, nowadays that is no guarantee of respectability of character. What number in Belgrave Square?

JACK: 149.

LADY BRACKNELL (*shaking her head*): The unfashionable side. I thought there was something. However, that could easily be altered.

JACK: Do you mean the fashion, or the side?

LADY BRACKNELL (*sternly*): Both, if necessary, I presume. What are your politics?

JACK: Well, I am afraid I really have none. I am a Liberal Unionist.

LADY BRACKNELL: Oh, they count as Tories. They dine with us. Or come in the evening, at any rate. Now to minor matters. Are your parents living?

JACK: I have lost both my parents.

LADY BRACKNELL: Both? To lose one parent may be regarded as a misfortune — to lose *both* seems like carelessness. Who was your father? He was evidently a man of some wealth. Was he born in what the Radical papers call the purple of commerce, or did he rise from the ranks of the aristocracy?

JACK: I am afraid I really don't know. The fact is, Lady Bracknell, I said I had lost my parents. It would be nearer the truth to say that my parents seem to have lost me — I don't actually know who I am by birth. I was — well, I was found.

LADY BRACKNELL: Found!

JACK: The late Mr. Thomas Cardew, an old gentleman of a very charitable and kindly disposition, found me, and gave me the name of Worthing, because he happened to have a first-class ticket for Worthing in his pocket at the time. Worthing is a place in Sussex. It is a seaside resort.

LADY BRACKNELL: Where did the charitable gentleman who had a first-class ticket for this seaside resort find you?

JACK (*gravely*): In a handbag.

LADY BRACKNELL: A handbag?

JACK (*very seriously*): Yes, Lady Bracknell. I was in a handbag — a somewhat large, black leather handbag, with handles to it — an ordinary handbag in fact.

LADY BRACKNELL: In what locality did this Mr. James, or Thomas, Cardew come across this ordinary handbag?

JACK: In the cloakroom at Victoria Station. It was given to him in mistake for his own.

LADY BRACKNELL: The cloakroom at Victoria Station?

JACK: Yes. The Brighton line.

LADY BRACKNELL: The line is immaterial. Mr. Worthing, I confess I feel somewhat bewildered by what you have just told me. To be born, or at any rate bred, in a handbag, whether it had handles or not, seems to me to display a contempt for the ordinary decencies of family life that reminds one of the worst excesses of the French Revolution. And I presume you know what that unfortunate movement led to? As for the particular locality in which the handbag was found, a cloakroom at a railway station might serve to conceal a social indiscretion — has probably, indeed, been used for that purpose before now — but it could hardly be regarded as an assured basis for a recognized position in good society.

JACK: May I ask you then what you would advise me to do? I need hardly say I would do anything in the world to ensure Gwendolen's happiness.

LADY BRACKNELL: I would strongly advise you, Mr. Worthing, to try and acquire some relations as soon as possible, and to make a definite effort to produce at any rate one parent of either sex, before the season is quite over.

JACK: Well, I don't see how I could possibly manage to do that. I can produce the handbag at any moment. It is in my dressing room at home. I really think that should satisfy you, Lady Bracknell.

LADY BRACKNELL: Me, sir! What has it to do with me? You can hardly imagine that I and Lord Bracknell would dream of allowing our only daughter — a girl brought up with the utmost care — to marry into a cloakroom, and form an alliance with a parcel? Good morning, Mr. Worthing!

(*Lady Bracknell sweeps out in majestic indignation.*)

JACK: Good morning! (*Algernon, from the other room, strikes up the Wedding March. Jack looks perfectly furious, and goes to the door.*) For goodness' sake don't play that ghastly tune, Algy! How idiotic you are!

(*The music stops, and Algernon enters cheerily.*)

ALGERNON: Didn't it go off all right, old boy? You don't mean to say Gwendolen refused you? I know it is a way she has. She is always refusing people. I think it is most ill-natured of her.

JACK: Oh, Gwendolen is as right as a trivet. As far as she is concerned, we are engaged. Her mother is perfectly unbearable. Never met such a Gorgon° — I don't really know what a Gorgon is like, but I am quite sure that Lady Bracknell is one. In any case, she is a monster, without being a myth, which is rather unfair. I beg your pardon, Algy, I suppose I shouldn't talk about your own aunt in that way before you.

ALGERNON: My dear boy, I love hearing my relations abused. It is the only thing that makes me put up with them at all. Relations are simply a tedious pack of people, who haven't got the remotest knowledge

---

Gorgon: In Greek myth, one of three very ugly sisters who had, among other characteristics, serpents for hair.

of how to live, nor the smallest instinct about when to die.

JACK: Oh, that is nonsense!

ALGERNON: It isn't!

JACK: Well, I won't argue about the matter. You always want to argue about things.

ALGERNON: That is exactly what things were originally made for.

JACK: Upon my word, if I thought that, I'd shoot myself — (*A pause.*) You don't think there is any chance of Gwendolen becoming like her mother in about a hundred and fifty years, do you Algy?

ALGERNON: All women become like their mothers. That is their tragedy. No man does. That's his.

JACK: Is that clever?

ALGERNON: It is perfectly phrased! and quite as true as any observation in civilized life should be.

JACK: I am sick to death of cleverness. Everybody is clever nowadays. You can't go anywhere without meeting clever people. The thing has become an absolute public nuisance. I wish to goodness we had a few fools left.

ALGERNON: We have.

JACK: I should extremely like to meet them. What do they talk about?

ALGERNON: The fools? Oh! about the clever people, of course.

JACK: What fools!

ALGERNON: By the way, did you tell Gwendolen the truth about your being Ernest in town, and Jack in the country?

JACK (*in a very patronizing manner*): My dear fellow, the truth isn't quite the sort of thing one tells to a nice sweet refined girl. What extraordinary ideas you have about the way to behave to a woman!

ALGERNON: The only way to behave to a woman is to make love to her if she is pretty, and to someone else if she is plain.

JACK: Oh, that is nonsense.

ALGERNON: What about your brother? What about the profligate Ernest?

JACK: Oh, before the end of the week I shall have got rid of him. I'll say he died in Paris of apoplexy. Lots of people die of apoplexy, quite suddenly, don't they?

ALGERNON: Yes, but it's hereditary, my dear fellow. It's a sort of thing that runs in families. You had much better say a severe chill.

JACK: You are sure a severe chill isn't hereditary, or anything of that kind?

ALGERNON: Of course it isn't!

JACK: Very well, then. My poor brother Ernest is carried off suddenly in Paris, by a severe chill. That gets rid of him.

ALGERNON: But I thought you said that — Miss Cardew was a little too much interested in your poor brother Ernest? Won't she feel his loss a good deal?

JACK: Oh, that is all right. Cecily is not a silly romantic girl, I am glad to say. She has got a capital appetite,

goes long walks, and pays no attention at all to her lessons.

ALGERNON: I would rather like to see Cecily.

JACK: I will take very good care you never do. She is excessively pretty, and she is only just eighteen.

ALGERNON: Have you told Gwendolen yet that you have an excessively pretty ward who is only just eighteen?

JACK: Oh! one doesn't blurt these things out to people. Cecily and Gwendolen are perfectly certain to be extremely great friends. I'll bet you anything you like that half an hour after they have met, they will be calling each other sister.

ALGERNON: Women only do that when they have called each other a lot of other things first. Now, my dear boy, if we want to get a good table at Willis's, we really must go and dress. Do you know it is nearly seven?

JACK: (*irritably*): Oh! it always is nearly seven.

ALGERNON: Well, I'm hungry.

JACK: I never knew you when you weren't —

ALGERNON: What shall we do after dinner? Go to a theater?

JACK: Oh, no! I loathe listening.

ALGERNON: Well, let us go to the Club?

JACK: Oh, no! I hate talking.

ALGERNON: Well, we might trot round to the Empire° at ten?

JACK: Oh, no! I can't bear looking at things. It is so silly.

ALGERNON: Well, what shall we do?

JACK: Nothing!

ALGERNON: It is awfully hard work doing nothing. However, I don't mind hard work where there is no definite object of any kind.

(*Enter Lane.*)

LANE: Miss Fairfax.

(*Enter Gwendolen. Lane goes out.*)

ALGERNON: Gwendolen, upon my word!

GWENDOLEN: Algy, kindly turn your back. I have something very particular to say to Mr. Worthing.

ALGERNON: Really, Gwendolen, I don't think I can allow this at all.

GWENDOLEN: Algy, you always adopt a strictly immoral attitude towards life. You are not quite old enough to do that.

(*Algernon retires to the fireplace.*)

JACK: My own darling!

GWENDOLEN: Ernest, we may never be married. From the expression on Mama's face I fear we never shall. Few parents nowadays pay any regard to what their children say to them. The old-fashioned respect for the young is fast dying out. Whatever influence I ever had over Mama, I lost at the age of three. But although she may prevent us from becoming man and wife, and I may marry someone else, and marry often,

---

Empire: Empire Theatre, a London music hall that was also a rendezvous for prostitutes.

Scene from the Huntington Theatre Company's production of *The Importance of Being Earnest.*

nothing that she can possibly do can alter my eternal devotion to you.

JACK: Dear Gwendolen!

GWENDOLEN: The story of your romantic origin, as related to me by Mama, with unpleasing comments, has naturally stirred the deeper fibers of my nature. Your Christian name has an irresistible fascination. The simplicity of your character makes you exquisitely incomprehensible to me. Your town address at the Albany I have. What is your address in the country?

JACK: The Manor House, Woolton, Hertfordshire.

(*Algernon, who has been carefully listening, smiles to himself, and writes the address on his shirt cuff. Then picks up the Railway Guide.*)

GWENDOLEN: There is a good postal service, I suppose? It may be necessary to do something desperate. That of course will require serious consideration. I will communicate with you daily.

JACK: My own one!

GWENDOLEN: How long do you remain in town?

JACK: Till Monday.

GWENDOLEN: Good! Algy, you may turn round now.

ALGERNON: Thanks, I've turned round already.

GWENDOLEN: You may also ring the bell.

JACK: You will let me see you to your carriage, my own darling?

GWENDOLEN: Certainly.

JACK (*to Lane, who now enters*): I will see Miss Fairfax out.

LANE: Yes, sir.   (*Jack and Gwendolen go off.*)

(*Lane presents several letters on a salver to Algernon. It is to be surmised that they are bills, as Algernon, after looking at the envelopes, tears them up.*)

ALGERNON: A glass of sherry, Lane.

LANE: Yes, sir.

ALGERNON: Tomorrow, Lane, I'm going Bunburying.

LANE: Yes, sir.

ALGERNON: I shall probably not be back till Monday. You can put up my dress clothes, my smoking jacket, and all the Bunbury suits —

LANE: Yes, sir.   (*Handing sherry.*)

ALGERNON: I hope tomorrow will be a fine day, Lane.

LANE: It never is, sir.

ALGERNON: Lane, you're a perfect pessimist.

LANE: I do my best to give satisfaction, sir.

(*Enter Jack. Lane goes off.*)

JACK: There's a sensible, intellectual girl! the only girl I ever cared for in my life. (*Algernon is laughing immoderately.*) What on earth are you so amused at?

ALGERNON: Oh, I'm a little anxious about poor Bunbury, that is all.

JACK: If you don't take care, your friend Bunbury will get you into a serious scrape some day.

ALGERNON: I love scrapes. They are the only things that are never serious.

JACK: Oh, that's nonsense, Algy. You never talk anything but nonsense.

ALGERNON: Nobody ever does.

(*Jack looks indignantly at him, and leaves the room. Algernon lights a cigarette, reads his shirt cuff, and smiles.*)

ACT II

(*Scene: Garden at the Manor House. A flight of gray stone steps leads up to the house. The garden, an old-fashioned one, full of roses. Time of year, July. Basket chairs, and a table covered with books, are set under a large yew tree. Miss Prism discovered seated at the table. Cecily is at the back watering flowers.*)

MISS PRISM (*calling*): Cecily, Cecily! Surely such a utilitarian occupation as the watering of flowers is rather Moulton's duty than yours? Especially at a moment when intellectual pleasures await you. Your German grammar is on the table. Pray open it at page fifteen. We will repeat yesterday's lesson.

CECILY (*coming over very slowly*): But I don't like German. It isn't at all a becoming language. I know perfectly well that I look quite plain after my German lesson.

MISS PRISM: Child, you know how anxious your guardian is that you should improve yourself in every way. He laid particular stress on your German, as he was leaving for town yesterday. Indeed, he always lays stress on your German when he is leaving for town.

CECILY: Dear Uncle Jack is so very serious! Sometimes he is so serious that I think he cannot be quite well.

MISS PRISM (*drawing herself up*): Your guardian enjoys the best of health, and his gravity of demeanor is especially to be commended in one so comparatively young as he is. I know no one who has a higher sense of duty and responsibility.

CECILY: I suppose that is why he often looks a little bored when we three are together.

MISS PRISM: Cecily! I am surprised at you. Mr. Worthing has many troubles in his life. Idle merriment and triviality would be out of place in his conversation. You must remember his constant anxiety about that unfortunate young man his brother.

CECILY: I wish Uncle Jack would allow that unfortunate young man, his brother, to come down here sometimes. We might have a good influence over him, Miss Prism. I am sure you certainly would. You know German, and geology, and things of that kind influence a man very much.

(*Cecily begins to write in her diary.*)

MISS PRISM (*shaking her head*): I do not think that even I could produce any effect on a character that according to his own brother's admission is irretrievably weak and vacillating. Indeed I am not sure that I would desire to reclaim him. I am not in favor of this modern mania for turning bad people into good people at a moment's notice. As a man sows so let him reap. You must put away your diary, Cecily. I really don't see why you should keep a diary at all.

CECILY: I keep a diary in order to enter the wonderful secrets of my life. If I didn't write them down I should probably forget all about them.

MISS PRISM: Memory, my dear Cecily, is the diary that we all carry about with us.

CECILY: Yes, but it usually chronicles the things that have never happened, and couldn't possibly have happened. I believe that Memory is responsible for nearly all the three-volume novels that Mudie sends us.

MISS PRISM: Do not speak slightingly of the three-volume novel, Cecily. I wrote one myself in earlier days.

CECILY: Did you really, Miss Prism? How wonderfully clever you are! I hope it did not end happily? I don't like novels that end happily. They depress me so much.

MISS PRISM: The good ended happily, and the bad unhappily. That is what Fiction means.

CECILY: I suppose so. But it seems very unfair. And was your novel ever published?

MISS PRISM: Alas! no. The manuscript unfortunately was abandoned. I use the word in the sense of lost or mislaid. To your work, child, these speculations are profitless.

CECILY (*smiling*): But I see dear Dr. Chasuble coming up through the garden.

MISS PRISM (*rising and advancing*): Dr. Chasuble! This is indeed a pleasure.

(*Enter Canon Chasuble.*)

CHASUBLE: And how are we this morning? Miss Prism, you are, I trust, well?

CECILY: Miss Prism has just been complaining of a slight headache. I think it would do her so much good to have a short stroll with you in the park, Dr. Chasuble.

MISS PRISM: Cecily, I have not mentioned anything about a headache.

CECILY: No, dear Miss Prism, I know that, but I felt instinctively that you had a headache. Indeed I was thinking about that, and not about my German lesson, when the Rector came in.

CHASUBLE: I hope, Cecily, you are not inattentive.

CECILY: Oh, I am afraid I am.

CHASUBLE: That is strange. Were I fortunate enough to be Miss Prism's pupil, I would hang upon her lips.

(*Miss Prism glares.*) I spoke metaphorically. — My metaphor was drawn from bees. Ahem! Mr. Worthing, I suppose, has not returned from town yet?

MISS PRISM: We do not expect him till Monday afternoon.

CHASUBLE: Ah yes, he usually likes to spend his Sunday in London. He is not one of those whose sole aim is enjoyment, as, by all accounts, that unfortunate young man his brother seems to be. But I must not disturb Egeria° and her pupil any longer.

MISS PRISM: Egeria? My name is Laetitia, Doctor.

CHASUBLE (*bowing*): A classical allusion merely, drawn from the Pagan authors. I shall see you both no doubt at Evensong?

MISS PRISM: I think, dear Doctor, I will have a stroll with you. I find I have a headache after all, and a walk might do it good.

CHASUBLE: With pleasure, Miss Prism, with pleasure. We might go as far as the schools and back.

MISS PRISM: That would be delightful. Cecily, you will read your Political Economy in my absence. The chapter on the Fall of the Rupee° you may omit. It is somewhat too sensational. Even these metallic problems have their melodramatic side.

(*Goes down the garden with Dr. Chasuble.*)

CECILY (*picks up books and throws them back on table*): Horrid Political Economy! Horrid Geography! Horrid, horrid German!

(*Enter Merriman with a card on a salver.*)

MERRIMAN: Mr. Ernest Worthing has just driven over from the station. He has brought his luggage with him.

CECILY (*takes the card and reads it*): "Mr. Ernest Worthing, B.4, The Albany, W." Uncle Jack's brother! Did you tell him Mr. Worthing was in town?

MERRIMAN: Yes, Miss. He seemed very much disappointed. I mentioned that you and Miss Prism were in the garden. He said he was anxious to speak to you privately for a moment.

CECILY: Ask Mr. Ernest Worthing to come here. I suppose you had better talk to the housekeeper about a room for him.

MERRIMAN: Yes, Miss.   (*Merriman goes off.*)

CECILY: I have never met any really wicked person before. I feel rather frightened. I am so afraid he will look just like everyone else.

(*Enter Algernon, very gay and debonair.*)

He does!

ALGERNON (*raising his hat*): You are my little cousin Cecily, I'm sure.

CECILY: You are under some strange mistake. I am not little. In fact, I believe I am more than usually tall for my age (*Algernon is rather taken aback.*) But I am

your cousin Cecily. You, I see from your card, are Uncle Jack's brother, my cousin Ernest, my wicked cousin Ernest.

ALGERNON: Oh! I am not really wicked at all, Cousin Cecily. You mustn't think that I am wicked.

CECILY: If you are not, then you have certainly been deceiving us all in a very inexcusable manner. I hope you have not been leading a double life, pretending to be wicked and being really good all the time. That would be hypocrisy.

ALGERNON (*looks at her in amazement*): Oh! Of course I have been rather reckless.

CECILY: I am glad to hear it.

ALGERNON: In fact, now you mention the subject, I have been very bad in my own small way.

CECILY: I don't think you should be so proud of that, though I am sure it must have been very pleasant.

ALGERNON: It is much pleasanter being here with you.

CECILY: I can't understand how you are here at all. Uncle Jack won't be back till Monday afternoon.

ALGERNON: That is a great disappointment. I am obliged to go up by the first train on Monday morning. I have a business appointment that I am anxious — to miss.

CECILY: Couldn't you miss it anywhere but in London?

ALGERNON: No: the appointment is in London.

CECILY: Well, I know, of course, how important it is not to keep a business engagement, if one wants to retain any sense of the beauty of life, but still I think you had better wait till Uncle Jack arrives. I know he wants to speak to you about your emigrating.

ALGERNON: About my what?

CECILY: Your emigrating. He has gone up to buy your outfit.

ALGERNON: I certainly wouldn't let Jack buy my outfit. He has no taste in neckties at all.

CECILY: I don't think you will require neckties. Uncle Jack is sending you to Australia.

ALGERNON: Australia! I'd sooner die.

CECILY: Well, he said at dinner on Wednesday night, that you would have to choose between this world, the next world, and Australia.

ALGERNON: Oh, well! The accounts I have received of Australia and the next world are not particularly encouraging. This world is good enough for me, Cousin Cecily.

CECILY: Yes, but are you good enough for it?

ALGERNON: I'm afraid I'm not that. That is why I want you to reform me. You might make that your mission, if you don't mind, Cousin Cecily.

CECILY: I'm afraid I've no time, this afternoon.

ALGERNON: Well, would you mind my reforming myself this afternoon?

CECILY: It is rather quixotic° of you. But I think you should try.

ALGERNON: I will. I feel better already.

CECILY: You are looking a little worse.

Egeria: Roman goddess of water.   **Fall of the Rupee:** Reference to the Indian rupee, whose steady deflation between 1873 and 1893 caused the Indian governments finally to close the mints.

quixotic: Foolishly impractical, from the idealistic hero of Cervantes' *Don Quixote*.

ALGERNON: That is because I am hungry.

CECILY: How thoughtless of me. I should have remembered that when one is going to lead an entirely new life, one requires regular and wholesome meals. Won't you come in?

ALGERNON: Thank you. Might I have a buttonhole° first? I never have any appetite unless I have a buttonhole first.

CECILY: A Maréchal Niel?°

ALGERNON: No, I'd sooner have a pink rose.

CECILY: Why?   (Cuts a flower.)

ALGERNON: Because you are like a pink rose, Cousin Cecily.

CECILY: I don't think it can be right for you to talk to me like that. Miss Prism never says such things to me.

ALGERNON: Then Miss Prism is a shortsighted old lady. (Cecily puts the rose in his buttonhole.) You are the prettiest girl I ever saw.

CECILY: Miss Prism says that all good looks are a snare.

ALGERNON: They are a snare that every sensible man would like to be caught in.

CECILY: Oh! I don't think I would care to catch a sensible man. I shouldn't know what to talk to him about.

(They pass into the house. Miss Prism and Dr. Chasuble return.)

MISS PRISM: You are too much alone, dear Dr. Chasuble. You should get married. A misanthrope I can understand — a womanthrope, never!

CHASUBLE (with a scholar's shudder): Believe me, I do not deserve so neologistic a phrase. The precept as well as the practice of the Primitive Church was distinctly against matrimony.

MISS PRISM (sententiously): That is obviously the reason why the Primitive Church has not lasted up to the present day. And you do not seem to realize, dear Doctor, that by persistently remaining single, a man converts himself into a permanent public temptation. Men should be more careful; this very celibacy leads weaker vessels astray.

CHASUBLE: But is a man not equally attractive when married?

MISS PRISM: No married man is ever attractive except to his wife.

CHASUBLE: And often, I've been told, not even to her.

MISS PRISM: That depends on the intellectual sympathies of the woman. Maturity can always be depended on. Ripeness can be trusted. Young women are green. (Dr. Chasuble starts.) I spoke horticulturally. My metaphor was drawn from fruits. But where is Cecily?

CHASUBLE: Perhaps she followed us to the schools.

(Enter Jack slowly from the back of the garden. He is dressed in the deepest mourning, with crepe hatband and black gloves.)

MISS PRISM: Mr. Worthing!

CHASUBLE: Mr. Worthing?

buttonhole: Boutonniere.   Maréchal Niel: A yellow rose.

MISS PRISM: This is indeed a surprise. We did not look for you till Monday afternoon.

JACK (shakes Miss Prism's hand in a tragic manner): I have returned sooner than I expected. Dr. Chasuble, I hope you are well?

CHASUBLE: Dear Mr. Worthing, I trust this garb of woe does not betoken some terrible calamity?

JACK: My brother.

MISS PRISM: More shameful debts and extravagance?

CHASUBLE: Still leading his life of pleasure?

JACK (shaking his head): Dead!

CHASUBLE: Your brother Ernest dead?

JACK: Quite dead.

MISS PRISM: What a lesson for him! I trust he will profit by it.

CHASUBLE: Mr. Worthing, I offer you my sincere condolence. You have at least the consolation of knowing that you were always the most generous and forgiving of brothers.

JACK: Poor Ernest! He had many faults, but it is a sad, sad blow.

CHASUBLE: Very sad indeed. Were you with him at the end?

JACK: No. He died abroad, in Paris, in fact. I had a telegram last night from the manager of the Grand Hotel.

CHASUBLE: Was the cause of death mentioned?

JACK: A severe chill, it seems.

MISS PRISM: As a man sows, so shall he reap.

CHASUBLE (raising his hand): Charity, dear Miss Prism, charity! None of us are perfect. I myself am peculiarly susceptible to drafts. Will the interment take place here?

JACK: No. He seemed to have expressed a desire to be buried in Paris.

CHASUBLE: In Paris! (Shakes his head.) I fear that hardly points to any very serious state of mind at the last. You would no doubt wish me to make some slight allusion to this tragic domestic affliction next Sunday. (Jack presses his hand convulsively.) My sermon on the meaning of the manna in the wilderness can be adapted to almost any occasion, joyful, or, as in the present case, distressing. (All sigh.) I have preached it at harvest celebrations, christenings, confirmations, on days of humiliation and festal days. The last time I delivered it was in the Cathedral, as a charity sermon on behalf of the Society for the Prevention of Discontent among the Upper Orders. The Bishop, who was present, was much struck by some of the analogies I drew.

JACK: Ah! that reminds me, you mentioned christenings I think, Dr. Chasuble? I suppose you know how to christen all right? (Dr. Chasuble looks astounded.) I mean, of course, you are continually christening, aren't you?

MISS PRISM: It is, I regret to say, one of the Rector's most constant duties in this parish. I have often spoken to the poorer classes on the subject. But they don't seem to know what thrift is.

CHASUBLE: But is there any particular infant in whom you are interested, Mr. Worthing? Your brother was, I believe, unmarried, was he not?

JACK: Oh yes.

MISS PRISM (*bitterly*): People who live entirely for pleasure usually are.

JACK: But it is not for any child, dear Doctor. I am very fond of children. No! the fact is, I would like to be christened myself, this afternoon, if you have nothing better to do.

CHASUBLE: But surely, Mr. Worthing, you have been christened already?

JACK: I don't remember anything about it.

CHASUBLE: But have you any grave doubts on the subject?

JACK: I certainly intend to have. Of course I don't know if the thing would bother you in any way, or if you think I am a little too old now.

CHASUBLE: Not at all. The sprinkling, and, indeed, the immersion of adults is a perfectly canonical practice.

JACK: Immersion!

CHASUBLE: You need have no apprehensions. Sprinkling is all that is necessary, or indeed I think advisable. Our weather is so changeable. At what hour would you wish the ceremony performed?

JACK: Oh, I might trot round about five if that would suit you.

CHASUBLE: Perfectly, perfectly! In fact I have two similar ceremonies to perform at that time. A case of twins that occurred recently in one of the outlying cottages on your own estate. Poor Jenkins the carter, a most hardworking man.

JACK: Oh! I don't see much fun in being christened along with other babies. It would be childish. Would half-past five do?

CHASUBLE: Admirably! Admirably! (*Takes out watch.*) And now, dear Mr. Worthing, I will not intrude any longer into a house of sorrow. I would merely beg you not to be too much bowed down by grief. What seem to us bitter trials are often blessings in disguise.

MISS PRISM: This seems to me a blessing of an extremely obvious kind.

(*Enter Cecily from the house.*)

CECILY: Uncle Jack! Oh, I am pleased to see you back. But what horrid clothes you have got on! Do go and change them.

MISS PRISM: Cecily!

CHASUBLE: My child! my child!

(*Cecily goes towards Jack; he kisses her brow in a melancholy manner.*)

CECILY: What is the matter, Uncle Jack? Do look happy! You look as if you had toothache, and I have got such a surprise for you. Who do you think is in the dining room? Your brother!

JACK: Who?

CECILY: Your brother Ernest. He arrived about half an hour ago.

JACK: What nonsense! I haven't got a brother.

CECILY: Oh, don't say that. However badly he may have behaved to you in the past he is still your brother. You couldn't be so heartless as to disown him. I'll tell him to come out. And you will shake hands with him, won't you, Uncle Jack?

(*Runs back into the house.*)

CHASUBLE: These are very joyful tidings.

MISS PRISM: After we had all been resigned to his loss, his sudden return seems to me peculiarly distressing.

JACK: My brother is in the dining room? I don't know what it all means. I think it is perfectly absurd.

(*Enter Algernon and Cecily hand in hand. They come slowly up to Jack.*)

JACK: Good heavens!   (*Motions Algernon away.*)

ALGERNON: Brother John, I have come down from town to tell you that I am very sorry for all the trouble I have given you, and that I intend to lead a better life in the future.

(*Jack glares at him and does not take his hand.*)

CECILY: Uncle Jack, you are not going to refuse your own brother's hand?

JACK: Nothing will induce me to take his hand. I think his coming down here disgraceful. He knows perfectly well why.

CECILY: Uncle Jack, do be nice. There is some good in everyone. Ernest has just been telling me about his poor invalid friend Mr. Bunbury whom he goes to visit so often. And surely there must be much good in one who is kind to an invalid, and leaves the pleasures of London to sit by a bed of pain.

JACK: Oh! he has been talking about Bunbury has he?

CECILY: Yes, he has told me all about poor Mr. Bunbury, and his terrible state of health.

JACK: Bunbury! Well, I won't have him talk to you about Bunbury or about anything else. It is enough to drive one perfectly frantic.

ALGERNON: Of course I admit that the faults were all on my side. But I must say that I think that Brother John's coldness to me is peculiarly painful. I expected a more enthusiastic welcome, especially considering it is the first time I have come here.

CECILY: Uncle Jack, if you don't shake hands with Ernest I will never forgive you.

JACK: Never forgive me?

CECILY: Never, never, never!

JACK: Well, this is the last time I shall ever do it.

(*Shakes hands with Algernon and glares.*)

CHASUBLE: It's pleasant, is it not, to see so perfect a reconciliation? I think we might leave the two brothers together.

MISS PRISM: Cecily, you will come with us.

CECILY: Certainly, Miss Prism. My little task of reconciliation is over.

CHASUBLE: You have done a beautiful action today, dear child.

MISS PRISM: We must not be premature in our judgments.

CECILY: I feel very happy.   (*They all go off.*)

JACK: You young scoundrel, Algy, you must get out of this place as soon as possible. I don't allow any Bunburying here.

(*Enter Merriman.*)

MERRIMAN: I have put Mr. Ernest's things in the room next to yours, sir. I suppose that is all right?

JACK: What?

MERRIMAN: Mr. Ernest's luggage, sir. I have unpacked it and put it in the room next to your own.

JACK: His luggage?

MERRIMAN: Yes, sir. Three portmanteaus, a dressing case, two hatboxes, and a large luncheon basket.

ALGERNON: I am afraid I can't stay more than a week this time.

JACK: Merriman, order the dog cart at once. Mr. Ernest has been suddenly called back to town.

MERRIMAN: Yes, sir.   (*Goes back into the house.*)

ALGERNON: What a fearful liar you are, Jack. I have not been called back to town at all.

JACK: Yes, you have.

ALGERNON: I haven't heard anyone call me.

JACK: Your duty as a gentleman calls you back.

ALGERNON: My duty as a gentleman has never interfered with my pleasures in the smallest degree.

JACK: I can quite understand that.

ALGERNON: Well, Cecily is a darling.

JACK: You are not to talk of Miss Cardew like that. I don't like it.

ALGERNON: Well, I don't like your clothes. You look perfectly ridiculous in them. Why on earth don't you go up and change? It is perfectly childish to be in deep mourning for a man who is actually staying for a whole week in your house as a guest. I call it grotesque.

JACK: You are certainly not staying with me for a whole week as a guest or anything else. You have got to leave — by the four-five train.

ALGERNON: I certainly won't leave you so long as you are in mourning. It would be most unfriendly. If I were in mourning you would stay with me, I suppose. I should think it very unkind if you didn't.

JACK: Well, will you go if I change my clothes?

ALGERNON: Yes, if you are not too long. I never saw anybody take so long to dress, and with such little result.

JACK: Well, at any rate, that is better than being always overdressed as you are.

ALGERNON: If I am occasionally a little overdressed, I make up for it by being always immensely overeducated.

JACK: Your vanity is ridiculous, your conduct an outrage, and your presence in my garden utterly absurd. However, you have got to catch the four-five, and I hope you will have a pleasant journey back to town. This Bunburying, as you call it, has not been a great success for you.

(*Goes into the house.*)

ALGERNON: I think it has been a great success. I'm in love with Cecily, and that is everything.

(*Enter Cecily at the back of the garden. She picks up the can and begins to water the flowers.*)

But I must see her before I go, and make arrangements for another Bunbury. Ah, there she is.

CECILY: Oh, I merely came back to water the roses. I thought you were with Uncle Jack.

ALGERNON: He's gone to order the dog cart for me.

CECILY: Oh, is he going to take you for a nice drive?

ALGERNON: He's going to send me away.

CECILY: Then have we got to part?

ALGERNON: I am afraid so. It's a very painful parting.

CECILY: It is always painful to part from people whom one has known for a very brief space of time. The absence of old friends one can endure with equanimity. But even a momentary separation from anyone to whom one has just been introduced is almost unbearable.

ALGERNON: Thank you.

(*Enter Merriman.*)

MERRIMAN: The dog cart is at the door, sir.

(*Algernon looks appealingly at Cecily.*)

CECILY: It can wait, Merriman — for — five minutes.

MERRIMAN: Yes, miss.   (*Exit Merriman.*)

ALGERNON: I hope, Cecily, I shall not offend you if I state quite frankly and openly that you seem to me to be in every way the visible personification of absolute perfection.

CECILY: I think your frankness does you great credit, Ernest. If you will allow me I will copy your remarks into my diary.

(*Goes over to table and begins writing in diary.*)

ALGERNON: Do you really keep a diary? I'd give anything to look at it. May I?

CECILY: Oh no. (*Puts her hand over it.*) You see, it is simply a very young girl's record of her own thoughts and impressions, and consequently meant for publication. When it appears in volume form I hope you will order a copy. But pray, Ernest, don't stop. I delight in taking down from dictation. I have reached "absolute perfection." You can go on. I am quite ready for more.

ALGERNON (*somewhat taken aback*): Ahem! Ahem!

CECILY: Oh, don't cough, Ernest. When one is dictating one should speak fluently and not cough. Besides, I don't know how to spell a cough.

(*Writes as Algernon speaks.*)

ALGERNON (*speaking very rapidly*): Cecily, ever since I first looked upon your wonderful and incomparable beauty, I have dared to love you wildly, passionately, devotedly, hopelessly.

CECILY: I don't think that you should tell me that you love me wildly, passionately, devotedly, hopelessly. Hopelessly doesn't seem to make much sense, does it?

ALGERNON: Cecily!

(*Enter Merriman.*)

MERRIMAN: The dog cart is waiting, sir.

ALGERNON: Tell it to come round next week, at the same hour.

MERRIMAN (*looks at Cecily, who makes no sign*): Yes, sir.   (*Merriman retires.*)

CECILY: Uncle Jack would be very much annoyed if he knew you were staying on till next week, at the same hour.

ALGERNON: Oh, I don't care about Jack. I don't care for anybody in the whole world but you. I love you, Cecily. You will marry me, won't you?

CECILY: You silly boy! Of course. Why, we have been engaged for the last three months.

ALGERNON: For the last three months?

CECILY: Yes, it will be exactly three months on Thursday.

ALGERNON: But how did we become engaged?

CECILY: Well, ever since dear Uncle Jack first confessed to us that he had a younger brother who was very wicked and bad, you of course have formed the chief topic of conversation between myself and Miss Prism. And of course a man who is much talked about is always very attractive. One feels there must be something in him after all. I daresay it was foolish of me, but I fell in love with you, Ernest.

ALGERNON: Darling! And when was the engagement actually settled?

CECILY: On the 14th of February last. Worn out by your entire ignorance of my existence, I determined to end the matter one way or the other, and after a long struggle with myself I accepted you under this dear old tree here. The next day I bought this little ring in your name, and this is the little bangle with the true lovers' knot I promised you always to wear.

ALGERNON: Did I give you this? It's very pretty, isn't it?

CECILY: Yes, you've wonderfully good taste, Ernest. It's the excuse I've always given for your leading such a bad life. And this is the box in which I keep all your dear letters.

(*Kneels at table, opens box, and produces letters tied up with blue ribbon.*)

ALGERNON: My letters! But my own sweet Cecily, I have never written you any letters.

CECILY: You need hardly remind me of that, Ernest. I remember only too well that I was forced to write your letters for you. I wrote always three times a week, and sometimes oftener.

ALGERNON: Oh, do let me read them, Cecily!

CECILY: Oh, I couldn't possibly. They would make you far too conceited. (*Replaces box.*) The three you wrote me after I had broken off the engagement are so beautiful, and so badly spelled, that even now I can hardly read them without crying a little.

ALGERNON: But was our engagement ever broken off?

CECILY: Of course it was. On the 22nd of last March. You can see the entry if you like. (*Shows diary.*)

"Today I broke off my engagement with Ernest. I feel it is better to do so. The weather still continues charming."

ALGERNON: But why on earth did you break it off? What had I done? I had done nothing at all. Cecily, I am very much hurt indeed to hear you broke it off. Particularly when the weather was so charming.

CECILY: It would hardly have been a really serious engagement if it hadn't been broken off at least once. But I forgave you before the week was out.

ALGERNON (*crossing to her, and kneeling*): What a perfect angel you are, Cecily.

CECILY: You dear romantic boy. (*He kisses her; she puts her fingers through his hair.*) I hope your hair curls naturally, does it?

ALGERNON: Yes, darling, with a little help from others.

CECILY: I am so glad.

ALGERNON: You'll never break off our engagement again, Cecily?

CECILY: I don't think I could break it off now that I have actually met you. Besides, of course, there is the question of your name.

ALGERNON (*nervously*): Yes, of course.

CECILY: You must not laugh at me, darling, but it had always been a girlish dream of mine to love someone whose name was Ernest. (*Algernon rises, Cecily also.*) There is something in that name that seems to inspire absolute confidence. I pity any poor married woman whose husband is not called Ernest.

ALGERNON: But, my dear child, do you mean to say you could not love me if I had some other name?

CECILY: But what name?

ALGERNON: Oh, any name you like — Algernon — for instance —

CECILY: But I don't like the name of Algernon.

ALGERNON: Well, my own dear, sweet, loving little darling, I really can't see why you should object to the name of Algernon. It is not at all a bad name. In fact, it is rather an aristocratic name. Half of the chaps who get into the Bankruptcy Court are called Algernon. But seriously, Cecily — (*moving to her*) — if my name was Algy, couldn't you love me?

CECILY (*rising*): I might respect you, Ernest, I might admire your character, but I fear that I should not be able to give you my undivided attention.

ALGERNON: Ahem! Cecily! (*Picking up hat.*) Your Rector here is, I suppose, thoroughly experienced in the practice of all the rites and ceremonials of the Church?

CECILY: Oh yes. Dr. Chasuble is a most learned man. He has never written a single book, so you can imagine how much he knows.

ALGERNON: I must see him at once on a most important christening — I mean on most important business.

CECILY: Oh!

ALGERNON: I shan't be away more than half an hour.

CECILY: Considering that we have been engaged since February the 14th, and that I only met you today for the first time, I think it is rather hard that you should leave me for so long a period as half an hour. Couldn't you make it twenty minutes?

ALGERNON: I'll be back in no time.

(*Kisses her and rushes down the garden.*)

CECILY: What an impetuous boy he is! I like his hair so much. I must enter his proposal in my diary.

(*Enter Merriman.*)

MERRIMAN: A Miss Fairfax has just called to see Mr. Worthing. On very important business Miss Fairfax states.

CECILY: Isn't Mr. Worthing in his library?

MERRIMAN: Mr. Worthing went over in the direction of the Rectory some time ago.

CECILY: Pray ask the lady to come out here; Mr. Worthing is sure to be back soon. And you can bring tea.

MERRIMAN: Yes, miss.   (*Goes out.*)

CECILY: Miss Fairfax! I suppose one of the many good elderly women who are associated with Uncle Jack in some of his philanthropic work in London. I don't quite like women who are interested in philanthropic work. I think it is so forward of them.

(*Enter Merriman.*)

MERRIMAN: Miss Fairfax.

(*Enter Gwendolen. Exit Merriman.*)

CECILY (*advancing to meet her*): Pray let me introduce myself to you. My name is Cecily Cardew.

GWENDOLEN: Cecily Cardew? (*Moving to her and shaking hands.*) What a very sweet name! Something tells me that we are going to be great friends. I like you already more than I can say. My first impressions of people are never wrong.

CECILY: How nice of you to like me so much after we have known each other such a comparatively short time. Pray sit down.

GWENDOLEN (*still standing up*): I may call you Cecily, may I not?

CECILY: With pleasure!

GWENDOLEN: And you will always call me Gwendolen, won't you?

CECILY: If you wish.

GWENDOLEN: Then that is all quite settled, is it not?

CECILY: I hope so.

(*A pause. They both sit down together.*)

GWENDOLEN: Perhaps this might be a favorable opportunity for my mentioning who I am. My father is Lord Bracknell. You have never heard of Papa, I suppose?

CECILY: I don't think so.

GWENDOLEN: Outside the family circle, Papa, I am glad to say, is entirely unknown. I think that is quite as it should be. The home seems to me to be the proper sphere for the man. And certainly once a man begins to neglect his domestic duties he becomes painfully effeminate, does he not? And I don't like that. It makes men so very attractive. Cecily, Mama, whose views on education are remarkably strict, has brought me up to be extremely shortsighted; it is part of her system, so do you mind my looking at you through my glasses?

CECILY: Oh! not at all, Gwendolen. I am very fond of being looked at.

GWENDOLEN (*after examining Cecily carefully through a lorgnette*): You are here on a short visit I suppose?

CECILY: Oh no! I live here.

GWENDOLEN (*severely*): Really? Your mother, no doubt, or some female relative of advanced years, resides here also?

CECILY: Oh no! I have no mother, nor, in fact, any relations.

GWENDOLEN: Indeed?

CECILY: My dear guardian, with the assistance of Miss Prism, has the arduous task of looking after me.

GWENDOLEN: Your guardian?

CECILY: Yes, I am Mr. Worthing's ward.

GWENDOLEN: Oh! It is strange he never mentioned to me that he had a ward. How secretive of him! He grows more interesting hourly. I am not sure, however, that the news inspires me with feelings of unmixed delight. (*Rising and going to her.*) I am very fond of you, Cecily; I have liked you ever since I met you! But I am bound to state that now that I know that you are Mr. Worthing's ward, I cannot help expressing a wish you were — well just a little older than you seem to be — and not quite so very alluring in appearance. In fact, if I may speak candidly —

CECILY: Pray do! I think that whenever one has anything unpleasant to say, one should always be quite candid.

GWENDOLEN: Well, to speak with perfect candor, Cecily, I wish that you were fully forty-two, and more than usually plain for your age. Ernest has a strong upright nature. He is the very soul of truth and honor. Disloyalty would be as impossible to him as deception. But even men of the noblest possible moral character are extremely susceptible to the influence of the physical charms of others. Modern, no less than Ancient History, supplies us with many most painful examples of what I refer to. If it were not so, indeed, History would be quite unreadable.

CECILY: I beg your pardon, Gwendolen, did you say Ernest?

GWENDOLEN: Yes.

CECILY: Oh, but it is not Mr. Ernest Worthing who is my guardian. It is his brother — his elder brother.

GWENDOLEN (*sitting down again*): Ernest never mentioned to me that he had a brother.

CECILY: I am sorry to say they have not been on good terms for a long time.

GWENDOLEN: Ah! that accounts for it. And now that I think of it I have never heard any man mention his brother. The subject seems distasteful to most men. Cecily, you have lifted a load from my mind. I was growing almost anxious. It would have been terrible if any cloud had come across a friendship like ours, would it not? Of course you are quite, quite sure that it is not Mr. Ernest Worthing who is your guardian?

CECILY: Quite sure. (*A pause.*) In fact, I am going to be his.

GWENDOLEN (*inquiringly*): I beg your pardon?

CECILY (*rather shy and confidingly*): Dearest Gwendolen, there is no reason why I should make a secret of it to you. Our little county newspaper is sure to chronicle the fact next week. Mr. Ernest Worthing and I are engaged to be married.

GWENDOLEN (*quite politely, rising*): My darling Cecily, I think there must be some slight error. Mr. Ernest Worthing is engaged to me. The announcement will appear in the *Morning Post* on Saturday at the latest.

CECILY (*very politely, rising*): I am afraid you must be under some misconception. Ernest proposed to me exactly ten minutes ago.   (*Shows diary.*)

GWENDOLEN (*examines diary through her lorgnette carefully*): It is certainly very curious, for he asked me to be his wife yesterday afternoon at 5:30. If you would care to verify the incident, pray do so. (*Produces diary of her own.*) I never travel without my diary. One should always have something sensational to read in the train. I am so sorry, dear Cecily, if it is any disappointment to you, but I am afraid *I* have the prior claim.

CECILY: It would distress me more than I can tell you, dear Gwendolen, if it caused you any mental or physical anguish, but I feel bound to point out that since Ernest proposed to you he clearly has changed his mind.

GWENDOLEN (*meditatively*): If the poor fellow has been entrapped into any foolish promise I shall consider it my duty to rescue him at once, and with a firm hand.

CECILY (*thoughtfully and sadly*): Whatever unfortunate entanglement my dear boy may have got into, I will never reproach him with it after we are married.

GWENDOLEN: Do you allude to me, Miss Cardew, as an entanglement? You are presumptuous. On an occasion of this kind it becomes more than a moral duty to speak one's mind. It becomes a pleasure.

CECILY: Do you suggest, Miss Fairfax, that I entrapped Ernest into an engagement? How dare you? This is no time for wearing the shallow mask of manners. When I see a spade I call it a spade.

GWENDOLEN (*satirically*): I am glad to say that I have never seen a spade. It is obvious that our social spheres have been widely different.

(*Enter Merriman, followed by the Footman. He carries a salver, tablecloth, and plate stand. Cecily is about to retort. The presence of the servants exercises a restraining influence, under which both girls chafe.*)

MERRIMAN: Shall I lay tea here as usual, miss?

CECILY (*sternly, in a calm voice*): Yes, as usual.

(*Merriman begins to clear table and lay cloth. A long pause. Cecily and Gwendolen glare at each other.*)

GWENDOLEN: Are there many interesting walks in the vicinity, Miss Cardew?

CECILY: Oh! Yes! a great many. From the top of one of the hills quite close one can see five counties.

GWENDOLEN: Five counties! I don't think I should like that. I hate crowds.

CECILY (*sweetly*): I suppose that is why you live in town?

(*Gwendolen bites her lip, and beats her foot nervously with her parasol.*)

GWENDOLEN (*looking round*): Quite a well-kept garden this is, Miss Cardew.

CECILY: So glad you like it, Miss Fairfax.

GWENDOLEN: I had no idea there were any flowers in the country.

CECILY: Oh, flowers are as common here, Miss Fairfax, as people are in London.

GWENDOLEN: Personally I cannot understand how anybody manages to exist in the country, if anybody who is anybody does. The country always bores me to death.

CECILY: Ah! This is what the newspapers call agricultural depression, is it not? I believe the aristocracy are suffering very much from it just at present. It is almost an epidemic amongst them, I have been told. May I offer you some tea, Miss Fairfax?

GWENDOLEN (*with elaborate politeness*): Thank you. (*Aside.*) Detestable girl! But I require tea!

CECILY (*sweetly*): Sugar?

GWENDOLEN (*superciliously*): No, thank you. Sugar is not fashionable anymore.

(*Cecily looks angrily at her, takes up the tongs, and puts four lumps of sugar into the cup.*)

CECILY (*severely*): Cake or bread and butter?

GWENDOLEN (*in a bored manner*): Bread and butter, please. Cake is rarely seen at the best houses nowadays.

CECILY (*cuts a very large slice of cake, and puts it on the tray*): Hand that to Miss Fairfax.

(*Merriman does so, and goes out with Footman. Gwendolen drinks the tea and makes a grimace. Puts down cup at once, reaches out her hand to the bread and butter, looks at it, and finds it is cake. Rises in indignation.*)

GWENDOLEN: You have filled my tea with lumps of sugar, and though I asked most distinctly for bread and butter, you have given me cake. I am known for the gentleness of my disposition, and the extraordinary sweetness of my nature, but I warn you, Miss Cardew, you may go too far.

CECILY (*rising*): To save my poor, innocent, trusting boy from the machinations of any other girl there are no lengths to which I would not go.

GWENDOLEN: From the moment I saw you I distrusted you. I felt that you were false and deceitful. I am never deceived in such matters. My first impressions of people are invariably right.

CECILY: It seems to me, Miss Fairfax, that I am trespassing on your valuable time. No doubt you have many other calls of a similar character to make in the neighborhood.

(*Enter Jack.*)

GWENDOLEN (*catching sight of him*): Ernest! My own Ernest!

JACK: Gwendolen! Darling!   (*Offers to kiss her.*)

GWENDOLEN (*drawing back*): A moment! May I ask if you are engaged to be married to this young lady? (*Points to Cecily.*)

JACK (*laughing*): To dear little Cecily! Of course not! What could have put such an idea into your pretty little head?

GWENDOLEN: Thank you. You may!

                              (*Offers her cheek.*)

CECILY (*very sweetly*): I knew there must be some misunderstanding, Miss Fairfax. The gentleman whose arm is at present round your waist is my dear guardian, Mr. John Worthing.

GWENDOLEN: I beg your pardon?

CECILY: This is Uncle Jack.

GWENDOLEN (*receding*): Jack! Oh!

(*Enter Algernon.*)

CECILY: Here is Ernest.

ALGERNON (*goes straight over to Cecily without noticing anyone else*): My own love!

                              (*Offers to kiss her.*)

CECILY (*drawing back*): A moment, Ernest! May I ask you — are you engaged to be married to this young lady?

ALGERNON (*looking round*): To what young lady? Good heavens! Gwendolen!

CECILY: Yes! to good heavens, Gwendolen, I mean to Gwendolen.

ALGERNON (*laughing*): Of course not! What could have put such an idea into your pretty little head?

CECILY: Thank you. (*Presenting her cheek to be kissed.*) You may.   (*Algernon kisses her.*)

GWENDOLEN: I felt there was some slight error, Miss Cardew. The gentleman who is now embracing you is my cousin, Mr. Algernon Moncrieff.

CECILY (*breaking away from Algernon*): Algernon Moncrieff! Oh!

(*The two girls move towards each other and put their arms round each other's waists as if for protection.*)

CECILY: Are you called Algernon?

ALGERNON: I cannot deny it.

CECILY: Oh!

GWENDOLEN: Is your name really John?

JACK (*standing rather proudly*): I could deny it if I liked. I could deny anything if I liked. But my name certainly is John. It has been John for years.

CECILY (*to Gwendolen*): A gross deception has been practiced on both of us.

GWENDOLEN: My poor wounded Cecily!

CECILY: My sweet wronged Gwendolen!

GWENDOLEN (*slowly and seriously*): You will call me sister, will you not?

(*They embrace. Jack and Algernon groan and walk up and down.*)

CECILY (*rather brightly*): There is just one question I would like to be allowed to ask my guardian.

GWENDOLEN: An admirable idea! Mr. Worthing, there is just one question I would like to be permitted to put to you. Where is your brother Ernest? We are both engaged to be married to your brother Ernest, so it is a matter of some importance to us to know where your brother Ernest is at present.

JACK (*slowly and hesitatingly*): Gwendolen — Cecily — it is very painful for me to be forced to speak the truth. It is the first time in my life that I have ever been reduced to such a painful position, and I am really quite inexperienced in doing anything of the kind. However I will tell you quite frankly that I have no brother Ernest. I have no brother at all. I never had a brother in my life, and I certainly have not the smallest intention of ever having one in the future.

CECILY (*surprised*): No brother at all?

JACK (*cheerily*): None!

GWENDOLEN (*severely*): Had you never a brother of any kind?

JACK (*pleasantly*): Never. Not even of any kind.

GWENDOLEN: I am afraid it is quite clear, Cecily, that neither of us is engaged to be married to anyone.

CECILY: It is not a very pleasant position for a young girl suddenly to find herself in. Is it?

GWENDOLEN: Let us go into the house. They will hardly venture to come after us there.

CECILY: No, men are so cowardly, aren't they?

        (*They retire into the house with scornful looks.*)

JACK: This ghastly state of things is what you call Bunburying, I suppose?

ALGERNON: Yes, and a perfectly wonderful Bunbury it is. The most wonderful Bunbury I have ever had in my life.

JACK: Well, you've no right whatsoever to Bunbury here.

ALGERNON: That is absurd. One has a right to Bunbury anywhere one chooses. Every serious Bunburyist knows that.

JACK: Serious Bunburyist! Good heavens!

ALGERNON: Well, one must be serious about something, if one wants to have any amusement in life. I happen to be serious about Bunburying. What on earth you are serious about I haven't got the remotest idea. About everything, I should fancy. You have such an absolutely trivial nature.

JACK: Well, the only small satisfaction I have in the whole of this wretched business is that your friend Bunbury is quite exploded. You won't be able to run down to the country quite so often as you used to do, dear Algy. And a very good thing too.

ALGERNON: Your brother is a little off color, isn't he, dear Jack? You won't be able to disappear to London quite so frequently as your wicked custom was. And not a bad thing either.

JACK: As for your conduct towards Miss Cardew, I must say that your taking in a sweet, simple, innocent girl like that is quite inexcusable. To say nothing of the fact that she is my ward.

ALGERNON: I can see no possible defense at all for your deceiving a brilliant, clever, thoroughly experienced young lady like Miss Fairfax. To say nothing of the fact that she is my cousin.

JACK: I wanted to be engaged to Gwendolen, that is all. I love her.

ALGERNON: Well, I simply wanted to be engaged to Cecily. I adore her.

JACK: There is certainly no chance of your marrying Miss Cardew.

ALGERNON: I don't think there is much likelihood, Jack, of you and Miss Fairfax being united.

JACK: Well, that is no business of yours.

ALGERNON: If it was my business, I wouldn't talk about it. (*Begins to eat muffins.*) It is very vulgar to talk about one's business. Only people like stockbrokers do that, and then merely at dinner parties.

JACK: How you can sit there, calmly eating muffins when we are in this horrible trouble. I can't make out. You seem to me to be perfectly heartless.

ALGERNON: Well, I can't eat muffins in an agitated manner. The butter would probably get on my cuffs. One should always eat muffins quite calmly. It is the only way to eat them.

JACK: I say it's perfectly heartless your eating muffins at all, under the circumstances.

ALGERNON: When I am in trouble, eating is the only thing that consoles me. Indeed, when I am in really great trouble, as anyone who knows me intimately will tell you, I refuse everything except food and drink. At the present moment I am eating muffins because I am unhappy. Besides, I am particularly fond of muffins.   (*Rising.*)

JACK (*rising*): Well, that is no reason why you should eat them all in that greedy way.

(*Takes muffins from Algernon.*)

ALGERNON (*offering tea cake*): I wish you would have tea cake instead. I don't like tea cake.

JACK: Good heavens! I suppose a man may eat his own muffins in his own garden.

ALGERNON: But you have just said it was perfectly heartless to eat muffins.

JACK: I said it was perfectly heartless of you, under the circumstances. That is a very different thing.

ALGERNON: That may be, but the muffins are the same. (*He seizes the muffin dish from Jack.*)

JACK: Algy, I wish to goodness you would go.

ALGERNON: You can't possibly ask me to go without having some dinner. It's absurd. I never go without my dinner. No one ever does, except vegetarians and people like that. Besides I have just made arrangements with Dr. Chasuble to be christened at a quarter to six under the name of Ernest.

JACK: My dear fellow, the sooner you give up that nonsense the better. I made arrangements this morning with Dr. Chasuble to be christened myself at 5:30, and I naturally will take the name of Ernest. Gwendolen would wish it. We can't both be christened Ernest. It's absurd. Besides, I have a perfect right to be christened if I like. There is no evidence at all that I ever have been christened by anybody. I should think it extremely probable I never was, and so does Dr. Chasuble. It is entirely different in your case. You have been christened already.

ALGERNON: Yes, but I have not been christened for years.

JACK: Yes, but you have been christened. That is the important thing.

ALGERNON: Quite so. So I know my constitution can stand it. If you are not quite sure about your ever having been christened, I must say I think it rather dangerous your venturing on it now. It might make you very unwell. You can hardly have forgotten that someone very closely connected with you was very nearly carried off this week in Paris by a severe chill.

JACK: Yes, but you said yourself that a severe chill was not hereditary.

ALGERNON: It usen't to be, I know — but I daresay it is now. Science is always making wonderful improvements in things.

JACK (*picking up the muffin dish*): Oh, that is nonsense; you are always talking nonsense.

ALGERNON: Jack, you are at the muffins again! I wish you wouldn't. There are only two left. (*Takes them.*) I told you I was particularly fond of muffins.

JACK: But I hate tea cake.

ALGERNON: Why on earth then do you allow tea cake to be served up for your guests? What ideas you have of hospitality!

JACK: Algernon! I have already told you to go. I don't want you here. Why don't you go!

ALGERNON: I haven't quite finished my tea yet! and there is still one muffin left.

(*Jack groans, and sinks into a chair. Algernon still continues eating.*)

ACT III

(*Scene: Morning room at the Manor House. Gwendolen and Cecily are at the window, looking out into the garden.*)

GWENDOLEN: The fact that they did not follow us at once into the house, as anyone else would have done, seems to me to show that they have some sense of shame left.

CECILY: They have been eating muffins. That looks like repentance.

GWENDOLEN (*after a pause*): They don't seem to notice us at all. Couldn't you cough?

CECILY: But I haven't got a cough.

GWENDOLEN: They're looking at us. What effrontery!

CECILY: They're approaching. That's very forward of them.

GWENDOLEN: Let us preserve a dignified silence.

CECILY: Certainly. It's the only thing to do now.

(*Enter Jack followed by Algernon. They whistle some dreadful popular air from a British opera.*)

GWENDOLEN: This dignified silence seems to produce an unpleasant effect.

CECILY: A most distasteful one.

GWENDOLEN: But we will not be the first to speak.

CECILY: Certainly not.

GWENDOLEN: Mr. Worthing, I have something very particular to ask you. Much depends on your reply.

CECILY: Gwendolen, your common sense is invaluable. Mr. Moncrieff, kindly answer me the following question. Why did you pretend to be my guardian's brother?

ALGERNON: In order that I might have an opportunity of meeting you.

CECILY (*to Gwendolen*): That certainly seems a satisfactory explanation, does it not?

GWENDOLEN: Yes, dear, if you can believe him.

CECILY: I don't. But that does not affect the wonderful beauty of his answer.

GWENDOLEN: True. In matters of grave importance, style, not sincerity is the vital thing. Mr. Worthing, what explanation can you offer to me for pretending to have a brother? Was it in order that you might have an opportunity of coming up to town to see me as often as possible?

JACK: Can you doubt it, Miss Fairfax?

GWENDOLEN: I have the gravest doubts upon the subject. But I intend to crush them. This is not the moment for German skepticism. (*Moving to Cecily.*) Their explanations appear to be quite satisfactory, especially Mr. Worthing's. That seems to me to have the stamp of truth upon it.

CECILY: I am more than content with what Mr. Moncrieff said. His voice alone inspires one with absolute credulity.

GWENDOLEN: Then you think we should forgive them?

CECILY: Yes. I mean no.

GWENDOLEN: True! I had forgotten. There are principles at stake that one cannot surrender. Which of us should tell them? The task is not a pleasant one.

CECILY: Could we not both speak at the same time?

GWENDOLEN: An excellent idea! I nearly always speak at the same time as other people. Will you take the time from me?

CECILY: Certainly.

(*Gwendolyn beats time with uplifted finger.*)

GWENDOLEN and CECILY (*speaking together*): Your Christian names are still an insuperable barrier. That is all!

JACK and ALGERNON (*speaking together*): Our Christian names! Is that all? But we are going to be christened this afternoon.

GWENDOLEN (*to Jack*): For my sake you are prepared to do this terrible thing?

JACK: I am!

CECILY (*to Algernon*): To please me you are ready to face this fearful ordeal?

ALGERNON: I am!

GWENDOLEN: How absurd to talk of the equality of the sexes! Where questions of self-sacrifice are concerned, men are infinitely beyond us.

JACK: We are! (*Clasps hands with Algernon.*)

CECILY: They have moments of physical courage of which we women know absolutely nothing.

GWENDOLEN (*to Jack*): Darling!

ALGERNON (*to Cecily*): Darling!

(*They fall into each other's arms.*)

(*Enter Merriman. When he enters he coughs loudly, seeing the situation.*)

MERRIMAN: Ahem! Ahem! Lady Bracknell!

JACK: Good heavens!

(*Enter Lady Bracknell. The couples separate, in alarm. Exit Merriman.*)

LADY BRACKNELL: Gwendolen! What does this mean?

GWENDOLEN: Merely that I am engaged to be married to Mr. Worthing, Mama.

LADY BRACKNELL: Come here. Sit down. Sit down immediately. Hesitation of any kind is a sign of mental decay in the young, of physical weakness in the old. (*Turns to Jack.*) Apprised, sir, of my daughter's sudden flight by her trusty maid, whose confidence I purchased by means of a small coin, I followed her at once by a luggage train. Her unhappy father is, I am glad to say, under the impression that she is attending a more than usually lengthy lecture by the University Extension Scheme on the influence of a permanent income on thought. I do not propose to undeceive him. Indeed I have never undeceived him on any question. I would consider it wrong. But of course, you will clearly understand that all communication between yourself and my daughter must cease immediately from this moment. On this point, as indeed on all points, I am firm.

JACK: I am engaged to be married to Gwendolen, Lady Bracknell!

LADY BRACKNELL: You are nothing of the kind, sir. And now, as regards Algernon! — Algernon!

ALGERNON: Yes, Aunt Augusta.

LADY BRACKNELL: May I ask if it is in this house that your invalid friend Mr. Bunbury resides?

ALGERNON (*stammering*): Oh! No! Bunbury doesn't live here. Bunbury is somewhere else at present. In fact, Bunbury is dead.

LADY BRACKNELL: Dead! When did Mr. Bunbury die? His death must have been extremely sudden.

ALGERNON (*airily*): Oh! I killed Bunbury this afternoon. I mean poor Bunbury died this afternoon.

LADY BRACKNELL: What did he die of?

ALGERNON: Bunbury? Oh, he was quite exploded.

LADY BRACKNELL: Exploded! Was he the victim of a revolutionary outrage? I was not aware that Mr. Bunbury was interested in social legislation. If so, he is well punished for his morbidity.

ALGERNON: My dear Aunt Augusta, I mean he was found out! The doctors found out that Bunbury could not live, that is what I mean — so Bunbury died.

Eric Stoltz and Schuyler Grant propose a toast in the Irish Repertory Theatre's 1996 production of *The Importance of Being Earnest.*

LADY BRACKNELL: He seems to have had great confidence in the opinion of his physicians. I am glad, however, that he made up his mind at the last to some definite course of action, and acted under proper medical advice. And now that we have finally got rid of this Mr. Bunbury, may I ask, Mr. Worthing, who is that young person whose hand my nephew Algernon is now holding in what seems to me a peculiarly unnecessary manner?

JACK: That lady is Miss Cecily Cardew, my ward.

(*Lady Bracknell bows coldly to Cecily.*)

ALGERNON: I am engaged to be married to Cecily, Aunt Augusta.

LADY BRACKNELL: I beg your pardon?

CECILY: Mr. Moncrieff and I are engaged to be married, Lady Bracknell.

LADY BRACKNELL (*with a shiver, crossing to the sofa and sitting down*): I do not know whether there is anything peculiarly exciting in the air of this particular part of Hertfordshire, but the number of engagements that go on seems to me considerably above the proper average that statistics have laid down for our guidance. I think some preliminary inquiry on my part would not be out of place. Mr. Worthing, is Miss Cardew at all connected with any of the larger railway stations in London? I merely desire information. Until yesterday I had no idea that there were any families or persons whose origin was a Terminus.

(*Jack looks perfectly furious, but restrains himself.*)

JACK (*in a clear, cold voice*): Miss Cardew is the granddaughter of the late Mr. Thomas Cardew of 149, Belgrave Square, S.W.; Gervase Park, Dorking, Surrey; and the Sporran, Fifeshire, N.B.

LADY BRACKNELL: That sounds not unsatisfactory. Three addresses always inspire confidence, even in tradesmen. But what proof have I of their authenticity?

JACK: I have carefully preserved the Court Guides of the period. They are open to your inspection, Lady Bracknell.

LADY BRACKNELL (*grimly*): I have known strange errors in that publication.

JACK: Miss Cardew's family solicitors are Messrs. Markby, Markby, and Markby.

LADY BRACKNELL: Markby, Markby, and Markby? A firm of the very highest position in their profession. Indeed I am told that one of the Mr. Markbys is occasionally to be seen at dinner parties. So far I am satisfied.

JACK (*very irritably*): How extremely kind of you, Lady Bracknell! I have also in my possession, you will be pleased to hear, certificates of Miss Cardew's birth, baptism, whooping cough, registration, vaccination, confirmation, and the measles; both the German and the English variety.

LADY BRACKNELL: Ah! A life crowded with incident I see; though perhaps somewhat too exciting for a young girl. I am not myself in favor of premature experiences. (*Rises, looks at her watch.*) Gwendolen! the time approaches for our departure. We have not a moment to lose. As a matter of form, Mr. Worthing, I had better ask you if Miss Cardew has any little fortune?

JACK: Oh! about a hundred and thirty thousand pounds in the Funds. That is all. Good-bye, Lady Bracknell. So pleased to have seen you.

LADY BRACKNELL (*sitting down again*): A moment, Mr. Worthing. A hundred and thirty thousand pounds! And in the Funds! Miss Cardew seems to me a most attractive young lady, now that I look at her. Few girls of the present day have any really solid qualities, any of the qualities that last, and improve with time. We live, I regret to say, in an age of surfaces. (*To Cecily.*) Come over here, dear. (*Cecily goes across.*) Pretty child! your dress is sadly simple, and your hair seems almost as Nature might have left it. But we can soon alter all that. A thoroughly experienced French maid produces a really marvelous result in a very brief space of time. I remember recommending one to young Lady Lancing, and after three months her own husband did not know her.

JACK (*aside*): And after six months nobody knew her.

LADY BRACKNELL (*glares at Jack for a few moments. Then bends, with a practiced smile, to Cecily*): Kindly turn round, sweet child. (*Cecily turns completely round.*) No, the side view is what I want. (*Cecily presents her profile.*) Yes, quite as I expected. There are distinct social possibilities in your profile. The two weak points in our age are its want of principle and its want of profile. The chin a little higher, dear. Style largely depends on the way the chin is worn. They are worn very high, just at present. Algernon!

ALGERNON: Yes, Aunt Augusta!

LADY BRACKNELL: There are distinct social possibilities in Miss Cardew's profile.

ALGERNON: Cecily is the sweetest, dearest, prettiest girl in the whole world. And I don't care twopence about social possibilities.

LADY BRACKNELL: Never speak disrespectfully of Society, Algernon. Only people who can't get into it do that. (*To Cecily.*) Dear child, of course you know that Algernon has nothing but his debts to depend upon. But I do not approve of mercenary marriages. When I married Lord Bracknell I had no fortune of any kind. But I never dreamed for a moment of allowing that to stand in my way. Well, I suppose I must give my consent.

ALGERNON: Thank you, Aunt Augusta.

LADY BRACKNELL: Cecily, you may kiss me!

CECILY (*kisses her*): Thank you, Lady Bracknell.

LADY BRACKNELL: You may also address me as Aunt Augusta for the future.

CECILY: Thank you, Aunt Augusta.

LADY BRACKNELL: The marriage, I think, had better take place quite soon.

ALGERNON: Thank you, Aunt Augusta.

CECILY: Thank you, Aunt Augusta.

LADY BRACKNELL: To speak frankly, I am not in favor of long engagements. They give people the opportunity of finding out each other's character before marriage, which I think is never advisable.

JACK: I beg your pardon for interrupting you, Lady Bracknell, but this engagement is quite out of the question. I am Miss Cardew's guardian, and she cannot marry without my consent until she comes of age. That consent I absolutely decline to give.

LADY BRACKNELL: Upon what grounds may I ask? Algernon is an extremely, I may almost say an ostentatiously, eligible young man. He has nothing, but he looks everything. What more can one desire?

JACK: It pains me very much to have to speak frankly to you, Lady Bracknell, about your nephew, but the fact is that I do not approve at all of his moral character. I suspect him of being untruthful.

(*Algernon and Cecily look at him in indignant amazement.*)

LADY BRACKNELL: Untruthful! My nephew Algernon? Impossible! He is an Oxonian.°

JACK: I fear there can be no possible doubt about the matter. This afternoon, during my temporary absence in London on an important question of romance, he obtained admission to my house by means of the false pretense of being my brother. Under an assumed name he drank, I've just been informed by my butler, an entire pint bottle of my Perrier-Jouêt, Brut, '89; a wine I was specially reserving for myself. Continuing his disgraceful deception, he succeeded in the course of the afternoon in alienating the affections of my only ward. He subsequently stayed to tea, and devoured every single muffin. And what makes his conduct all the more heartless is, that he was perfectly well aware from the first that I have no brother, that I never had a brother, and that I don't intend to have a brother, not even of any kind. I distinctly told him so myself yesterday afternoon.

LADY BRACKNELL: Ahem! Mr. Worthing, after careful consideration I have decided entirely to overlook my nephew's conduct to you.

JACK: That is very generous of you, Lady Bracknell. My own decision, however, is unalterable. I decline to give my consent.

LADY BRACKNELL (*to Cecily*): Come here, sweet child. (*Cecily goes over.*) How old are you, dear?

CECILY: Well, I am really only eighteen, but I always admit to twenty when I go to evening parties.

Oxonian: Educated at Oxford University.

LADY BRACKNELL: You are perfectly right in making some slight alteration. Indeed, no woman should ever be quite accurate about her age. It looks so calculating — (*In a meditative manner.*) Eighteen but admitting to twenty at evening parties. Well, it will not be very long before you are of age and free from the restraints of tutelage. So I don't think your guardian's consent is, after all, a matter of any importance.

JACK: Pray excuse me, Lady Bracknell, for interrupting you again, but it is only fair to tell you that according to the terms of her grandfather's will Miss Cardew does not come legally of age till she is thirty-five.

LADY BRACKNELL: That does not seem to me to be a grave objection. Thirty-five is a very attractive age. London society is full of women of the very highest birth who have, of their own free choice, remained thirty-five for years. Lady Dumbleton is an instance in point. To my own knowledge she has been thirty-five ever since she arrived at the age of forty, which was many years ago now. I see no reason why our dear Cecily should not be even still more attractive at the age you mention than she is at present. There will be a large accumulation of property.

CECILY: Algy, could you wait for me till I was thirty-five?

ALGERNON: Of course I could, Cecily. You know I could.

CECILY: Yes, I felt it instinctively, but I couldn't wait all that time. I hate waiting even five minutes for anybody. It always makes me rather cross. I am not punctual myself, I know, but I do like punctuality in others, and waiting, even to be married, is quite out of the question.

ALGERNON: Then what is to be done, Cecily?

CECILY: I don't know, Mr. Moncrieff.

LADY BRACKNELL: My dear Mr. Worthing, as Miss Cardew states positively that she cannot wait till she is thirty-five — a remark which I am bound to say seems to me to show a somewhat impatient nature — I would beg of you to reconsider your decision.

JACK: But my dear Lady Bracknell, the matter is entirely in your own hands. The moment you consent to my marriage with Gwendolen, I will most gladly allow your nephew to form an alliance with my ward.

LADY BRACKNELL (*rising and drawing herself up*): You must be quite aware that what you propose is out of the question.

JACK: Then a passionate celibacy is all that any of us can look forward to.

LADY BRACKNELL: That is not the destiny I propose for Gwendolen. Algernon, of course, can choose for himself. (*Pulls out her watch.*) Come, dear; (*Gwendolen rises*) we have already missed five, if not six, trains. To miss any more might expose us to comment on the platform.

(*Enter Dr. Chasuble.*)

CHASUBLE: Everything is quite ready for the christenings.

LADY BRACKNELL: The christenings, sir! Is not that somewhat premature?

CHASUBLE (*looking rather puzzled, and pointing to Jack and Algernon*): Both these gentlemen have expressed a desire for immediate baptism.

LADY BRACKNELL: At their age? The idea is grotesque and irreligious! Algernon, I forbid you to be baptized. I will not hear of such excesses. Lord Bracknell would be highly displeased if he learned that that was the way in which you wasted your time and money.

CHASUBLE: Am I to understand then that there are to be no christenings at all this afternoon?

JACK: I don't think that, as things are now, it would be of much practical value to either of us, Dr. Chasuble.

CHASUBLE: I am grieved to hear such sentiments from you, Mr. Worthing. They savor of the heretical views of the Anabaptists,° views that I have completely refuted in four of my unpublished sermons. However, as your present mood seems to be one peculiarly secular, I will return to the church at once. Indeed, I have just been informed by the pew opener that for the last hour and a half Miss Prism has been waiting for me in the vestry.

LADY BRACKNELL (*starting*): Miss Prism! Did I hear you mention a Miss Prism?

CHASUBLE: Yes, Lady Bracknell. I am on my way to join her.

LADY BRACKNELL: Pray allow me to detain you for a moment. This matter may prove to be one of vital importance to Lord Bracknell and myself. Is this Miss Prism a female of repellent aspect, remotely connected with education?

CHASUBLE (*somewhat indignantly*): She is the most cultivated of ladies, and the very picture of respectability.

LADY BRACKNELL: It is obviously the same person. May I ask what position she holds in your household?

CHASUBLE (*severely*): I am a celibate, madam.

JACK (*interposing*): Miss Prism, Lady Bracknell, has been for the last three years Miss Cardew's esteemed governess and valued companion.

LADY BRACKNELL: In spite of what I hear of her, I must see her at once. Let her be sent for.

CHASUBLE (*looking off*): She approaches; she is nigh.

(*Enter Miss Prism hurriedly.*)

MISS PRISM: I was told you expected me in the vestry, dear Canon. I have been waiting for you there for an hour and three-quarters.

(*Catches sight of Lady Bracknell who has fixed her with a stony glare. Miss Prism grows pale and quails. She looks anxiously round as if desirous to escape.*)

LADY BRACKNELL (*in a severe, judicial voice*): Prism! (*Miss Prism bows her head in shame.*) Come here, Prism! (*Miss Prism approaches in a humble manner.*) Prism! Where is that baby? (*General consternation. The Canon starts back in horror. Algernon and Jack pretend to be anxious to shield Cecily and*

Anabaptists: A religious sect beginning in the sixteenth century and advocating adult baptism and church membership by adults only.

Gwendolen from hearing the details of a terrible public scandal.) Twenty-eight years ago, Prism, you left Lord Bracknell's house, Number 104, Upper Grosvenor Street, in charge of a perambulator that contained a baby, of the male sex. You never returned. A few weeks later, through the elaborate investigations of the Metropolitan police, the perambulator was discovered at midnight, standing by itself in a remote corner of Bayswater. It contained the manuscript of a three-volume novel of more than usually revolting sentimentality. (*Miss Prism starts in involuntary indignation.*) But the baby was not there! (*Everyone looks at Miss Prism.*) Prism! Where is that baby?   (*A pause.*)

MISS PRISM: Lady Bracknell, I admit with shame that I do not know. I only wish I did. The plain facts of the case are these. On the morning of the day you mention, a day that is forever branded on my memory, I prepared as usual to take the baby out in its perambulator. I had also with me a somewhat old, but capacious handbag in which I had intended to place the manuscript of a work of fiction that I had written during my few unoccupied hours. In a moment of mental abstraction, for which I never can forgive myself, I deposited the manuscript in the bassinette, and placed the baby in the handbag.

JACK (*who has been listening attentively*): But where did you deposit the handbag?

MISS PRISM: Do not ask me, Mr. Worthing.

JACK: Miss Prism, this is a matter of no small importance to me. I insist on knowing where you deposited the handbag that contained that infant.

MISS PRISM: I left it in the cloakroom of one of the larger railway stations in London.

JACK: What railway station?

MISS PRISM (*quite crushed*): Victoria. The Brighton line.
(*Sinks into a chair.*)

JACK: I must retire to my room for a moment. Gwendolen, wait here for me.

GWENDOLEN: If you are not too long, I will wait here for you all my life.

(*Exit Jack in great excitement.*)

CHASUBLE: What do you think this means, Lady Bracknell?

LADY BRACKNELL: I dare not even suspect, Dr. Chasuble. I need hardly tell you that in families of high position strange coincidences are not supposed to occur. They are hardly considered the thing.

(*Noises heard overhead as if someone was throwing trunks about. Everyone looks up.*)

CECILY: Uncle Jack seems strangely agitated.

CHASUBLE: Your guardian has a very emotional nature.

LADY BRACKNELL: This noise is extremely unpleasant. It sounds as if he was having an argument. I dislike arguments of any kind. They are always vulgar, and often convincing.

CHASUBLE (*looking up*): It has stopped now.

(*The noise is redoubled.*)

LADY BRACKNELL: I wish he would arrive at some conclusion.

GWENDOLEN: This suspense is terrible. I hope it will last.

(*Enter Jack with a handbag of black leather in his hand.*)

JACK (*rushing over to Miss Prism*): Is this the handbag, Miss Prism? Examine it carefully before you speak. The happiness of more than one life depends on your answer.

MISS PRISM (*calmly*): It seems to be mine. Yes, here is the injury it received through the upsetting of a Gower Street omnibus in younger and happier days. Here is the stain on the lining caused by the explosion of a temperance beverage, an incident that occurred at Leamington. And here, on the lock, are my initials. I had forgotten that in an extravagant mood I had had them placed there. The bag is undoubtedly mine. I am delighted to have it so unexpectedly restored to me. It has been a great inconvenience being without it all these years.

JACK (*in a pathetic voice*): Miss Prism, more is restored to you than this handbag. I was the baby you placed in it.

MISS PRISM (*amazed*): You?

JACK (*embracing her*): Yes — mother!

MISS PRISM (*recoiling in indignant astonishment*): Mr. Worthing! I am unmarried!

JACK: Unmarried! I do not deny that is a serious blow. But after all, who has the right to cast a stone against one who has suffered? Cannot repentance wipe out an act of folly? Why should there be one law for men, and another for women? Mother, I forgive you.
(*Tries to embrace her again.*)

MISS PRISM (*still more indignant*): Mr. Worthing, there is some error. (*Pointing to Lady Bracknell.*) There is the lady who can tell you who you really are.

JACK (*after a pause*): Lady Bracknell, I hate to seem inquisitive, but would you kindly inform me who I am?

LADY BRACKNELL: I am afraid that the news I have to give you will not altogether please you. You are the son of my poor sister, Mrs. Moncrieff, and consequently Algernon's elder brother.

JACK: Algy's elder brother! Then I have a brother after all. I knew I had a brother! I always said I had a brother! Cecily, — how could you have ever doubted that I had a brother. (*Seizes hold of Algernon.*) Dr. Chasuble, my unfortunate brother. Miss Prism, my unfortunate brother. Gwendolen, my unfortunate brother. Algy, you young scoundrel, you will have to treat me with more respect in the future. You have never behaved to me like a brother in all your life.

ALGERNON: Well, not till today, old boy, I admit. I did my best, however, though I was out of practice.
(*Shakes hands.*)

GWENDOLEN (*to Jack*): My own! But what own are you? What is your Christian name, now that you have become someone else?

JACK: Good heavens! — I had quite forgotten that point. Your decision on the subject of my name is irrevocable, I suppose?

GWENDOLEN: I never change, except in my affections.

CECILY: What a noble nature you have, Gwendolen!

JACK: Then the question had better be cleared up at once. Aunt Augusta, a moment. At the time when Miss Prism left me in the handbag, had I been christened already?

LADY BRACKNELL: Every luxury that money could buy, including christening, had been lavished upon you by your fond and doting parents.

JACK: Then I was christened! That is settled. Now, what name was I given? Let me know the worst.

LADY BRACKNELL: Being the eldest son you were naturally christened after your father.

JACK (*irritably*): Yes, but what was my father's Christian name?

LADY BRACKNELL (*meditatively*): I cannot at the present moment recall what the General's Christian name was. But I have no doubt he had one. He was eccentric, I admit. But only in later years. And that was the result of the Indian climate, and marriage, and indigestion, and other things of that kind.

JACK: Algy! Can't you recollect what our father's Christian name was?

ALGERNON: My dear boy, we were never even on speaking terms. He died before I was a year old.

JACK: His name would appear in the Army Lists of the period, I suppose, Aunt Augusta?

LADY BRACKNELL: The General was essentially a man of peace, except in his domestic life. But I have no doubt his name would appear in any military directory.

JACK: The Army Lists of the last forty years are here. These delightful records should have been my constant study. (*Rushes to bookcase and tears the books out.*) M. Generals — Mallam, Maxbohm, Magley, what ghastly names they have — Markby, Migsby, Mobbs, Moncrieff! Lieutenant 1840, Captain, Lieutenant-Colonel, Colonel, General 1869, Christian names, Ernest John. (*Puts book very quietly down and speaks quite calmly.*) I always told you, Gwendolen, my name was Ernest, didn't I? Well, it is Ernest after all. I mean it naturally is Ernest.

LADY BRACKNELL: Yes, I remember now that the General was called Ernest. I knew I had some particular reason for disliking the name.

GWENDOLEN: Ernest! My own Ernest! I felt from the first that you could have no other name!

JACK: Gwendolen, it is a terrible thing for a man to find out suddenly that all his life he has been speaking nothing but the truth. Can you forgive me?

GWENDOLEN: I can. For I feel that you are sure to change.

JACK: My own one!

CHASUBLE (*to Miss Prism*): Laetitia! (*Embraces her.*)

MISS PRISM (*enthusiastically*): Frederick! At last!

ALGERNON: Cecily! (*Embraces her.*) At last!

JACK: Gwendolen! (*Embraces her.*) At last!

LADY BRACKNELL: My nephew, you seem to be displaying signs of triviality.

JACK: On the contrary, Aunt Augusta, I've now realized for the first time in my life the vital Importance of Being Earnest.

COMMENTARIES

Peter Raby (*b. 1939*)
AN UNPUBLISHED LETTER FROM OSCAR WILDE
ON *THE IMPORTANCE OF BEING EARNEST*   1991

Peter Raby introduces an 1894 letter from Oscar Wilde describing the plot of the play to his friend George Alexander. Wilde was under enormous financial pressure at the time and was eager to have his play produced. What we see in this letter is the human, vulnerable side of a witty, ironic comic playwright.

The full text of Oscar Wilde's first version of *The Importance of Being Earnest* has been lost for many years. Wilde sent it to George Alexander in July 1894, before leaving for a two-month holiday with his family in Worthing. He was desperate for money. Every encounter with Lord Alfred Douglas cost him more: he was overdrawn at the bank, and, so he claims in the letter, he had to bear the expenses of his mother's household as well as his own

Wilde's output during 1894 was astonishing: he completed *An Ideal Husband,* wrote the contrasting *A Florentine Tragedy* and most of *La Sainte Courtisane,* and embarked on an entirely new genre in *Earnest.* The more tumultuous and complex his private life, the more productive he became. He was in frequent correspondence with a number of producers and managers during the course of the year: with John Hare and Lewis Waller over *An Ideal Husband,* with Charles Frohman and Albert Palmer in New York in connection with a number of properties, both existing and unwritten, and with Dion Boucicault, who was producing *Lady Windermere's Fan* in Australia. Frohman, who controlled the American rights to *Lady Windermere's Fan,* was negotiating for *An Ideal Husband.* The year before, he had invited Wilde to write him a new play, perhaps a "modern *School for Scandal* style of play"; Wilde's American agent, the "brilliant delightful" Elizabeth Marbury, wrote to Wilde in July from Paris with details of Frohman's latest offer, which included an option on his next modern comedy. Albert Palmer was also angling for a comedy "with no real serious interest."

Completed plays and royalties were no longer enough to keep Wilde's finances buoyant. He turned his gift for story-telling to advantage in the form of the scenario. Alexander, generous and approachable, and the producer of Wilde's first great theatrical success, *Lady Windermere's Fan,* had expressed an interest in the new comedy. Wilde seems to have dashed off the *Earnest* scenario more to secure a £150 advance than because he thought the play right for a romantic actor of modern and costume pieces. (In fact, having received the advance, he rapidly backpedalled, suggesting the piece was too farcical, and sending Alexander a more suitable scenario from Worthing, something "strong" and serious, which Frank Harris eventually turned into *Mr and Mrs Daventry.*)

There are many stages between the outline of *Earnest* and the script which was played at the St James's Theatre on February 14, 1895, while the Marquess of Queensberry prowled around the building, unable to gain admission, and when Wilde's world was on the point of disintegration. There are some manuscript pages in a notebook in the Clark Library, at the University of California in Los Angeles, containing notes and scraps of dialogue, for example:

> Beautiful name — Ernest, I couldn't love anybody who wasn't called Ernest —
> Oh! don't say that Gwendolen. It sounds perfectly heartless of you — why should love be dependent on the action of an irresponsible godfather. Is a man's whole fortune to depend on the font. I am told that there was a moment when my father contemplated calling me John —

Another fragment seems to encapsulate a sharply visualized image:

> Gwen: Leave the room, Mamma. This is no place for you.
> Duchess: Mr Worthing rise from this semi-recumbent posture — it is most unbefitting.

The future Lady Bracknell springs fully armed from that one phrase. Indeed, the women characters — Prism, Gwendolen, Duchess — are throughout more vividly delineated in these early phases.

From these fragments, the play grew into a four-act version, with a brace of butlers named after Wilde's publishers, a gardener, and an ominous solicitor. There followed a collection of names with geographical or personal associations: Lancing, Shoreham, Bracknell, Blaxam, Bunbury, Maxbohm, Cardew. (Cicely Cardew, daughter of friends of Wilde, was born in 1893; her uncle was a director of the London and South East Railway, and the Cardew engine hauled the evening boat-train to Newhaven.) By Christmas, the new play had been promised to Charles Wyndham. When Alexander found he had a failure on his hands in Henry James's *Guy Domville*, Wyndham agreed to concede his rights in *Earnest*, provided Wilde wrote him an original play before completing yet another for Alexander. Alexander persuaded Wilde to compress *Earnest* into three acts (which was the form of the original scenario he had been shown). Wilde resisted for a little, but trusted Alexander's judgment; the play, he told Ada Leverson, "must go like a pistol shot." Wilde wanted to attend rehearsals, as he had for his previous London openings, but Douglas, "so beautiful is his nature," declined. Instead, Wilde accompanied Douglas on a final Bunbury to Algeria, returning alone for the final rehearsals of this play.

The following letter was described in Sotheby's Sale Catalogue for July 1933, under item 608, one of a number of Wilde's letters to her husband sold by Lady Alexander. The catalogue provided a synopsis, and reproduced one section. The text is taken from papers at the Clark Library. These are typewritten copies of letters from Wilde to Alexander, marked for inclusion in A.E.W. Mason's study, *Sir George Alexander and the St James's Theatre*, which was published in 1935. Mason wrote to Vyvyan Holland's solicitors, asking for permission to print excerpts, and bracketing those passages he wished to include: these papers are, most probably, Mason's originals. Mason printed only brief extracts from the opening and the last two paragraphs, and his book is the source for the extract printed in Sir Rupen Hart-Davis's edition of Wilde's *Letters*. So far as I am aware, the full letter has not been published before. It is reproduced here by permission of Mr Merlin Holland and the Clark Library (the letter is © Merlin Holland):

16, Tite Street,
S.W.

My dear Aleck,

Thanks for your letter. There really is nothing more to tell you about the comedy beyond what I said already. I mean that the real charm of the play, if it is to have charm, must be in the dialogue. The plot is slight, but, I think, adequate.

Act I. Evening party. 10 p.m.

Lord Alfred Rufford's rooms in Mayfair. Arrives from country Bertram Ashton his friend: a man of 25 or 30 years of age: his great friend.

Rufford asks him about his life. He tells him that he has a ward, etc. very young and pretty. That in the country he has to be serious, etc. that he comes to town to enjoy himself, and has invented a fictitious younger brother of the name of George — to whom all his misdeeds are put down. Rufford is deeply interested about the ward.

Guests arrive: the Duchess of Selby and her daughter, Lady Maud Rufford, with whom the guardian is in love — fin-de-siècle talk, a lot of guests — the guardian proposes to Lady Maud on his knees — enter Duchess —

Lady Maud. "Mamma, this is no place for you."

Scene: Duchess enquires for *her son Lord Alfred Rufford:* servant comes in with note to say that Lord Alfred has been suddenly called away to the country. Lady Maud vows eternal fidelity to the guardian whom she only knows under the name of *George* Ashton.

(P.S. The disclosure of the guardian of his double life is occasioned by Lord Alfred saying to him "You left your handkerchief here the last time you were up" (or cigarette case). The guardian takes it — the Lord A. says but "why, dear George, is it marked Bertram — who is Bertram Ashton?" Guardian discloses plot.)

Act II

The guardian's home — pretty cottage. Mabel Harbord, his ward, and her governess, Miss Prism, Governess of course dragon of propriety. Talk about the profligate George: maid comes in to say "Mr. George Ashton." — governess protests against his admission. Mabel insists. Enter Lord Alfred. Falls in love with ward at once. He is reproached with his bad life, etc. Expressed great repentance. They go to garden.

Enter guardian: Mabel comes in: "I have a great surprise for you — your brother is here"— Guardian, of course, denies having a brother. Mabel says "You cannot disown your own brother, whatever he has done."— and brings in Lord Alfred. Scene: also scene between two men alone. Finally Lord Alfred arrested for debt contracted by guardian: guardian delighted. Mabel, however, makes him forgive his brother and pay up. Guardian looks over bills and scolds Lord Alfred for profligacy.

Miss Prism backs the guardian up. Guardian then orders his brother out of the house. Mabel intercedes, and brother remains. Miss Prism has designs on the guardian — matrimonial — she is 40 at least — she believes he is proposing to her and accepts him — his consternation.

Act III. Mabel and the false brother. He proposes, and is accepted.

When Mabel is alone, Lady Maud, who only knows the guardian under the name of George, arrives alone. She tells Mabel she is engaged to George — scene naturally. Mabel retires: enter George, he kisses his sister naturally. Enter Mabel and sees them. Explanations, of course. Mabel breaks off the match on the ground that there is nothing to reform in George: she only consented to marry him because she thought he was bad and wanted guidance — He promises to be a bad husband — so as to give her an opportunity of making him a better man; she is a little mollified.

Enter guardian: he is reproached also by Lady Maud for his respectable life in the country: a J.P.: a county-councillor: a churchwarden: a philanthropist: a good example. He appeals to his life in London: she is mollified, on condition that he never lives in the country: the country is demoralising: it makes you respectable. "The simple fare at the Savoy: the quiet life in Piccadilly: the solitude of Mayfair is what you need, etc."

Enter Duchess in pursuit of her daughter — objects to both matches. Miss Prism, who had in early days been governess to the Duchess, sets it all right, without intending to do so — everything ends happily.

Result   Curtain

Author called.

Cigarette called.

Manager called.

Royalties for a year for author.

Manager credited with writing the play. He consoles himself for the slander with bag of red gold.

Fireworks

Of course this scenario is open to alterations: the third act, after entrance of Duchess, will have to be elaborated: also, the local doctor, or clergyman, must be brought in, in the play, for Prism.

Well, I think an amusing thing with lots of fun and wit might be made. If you think so, too, and care to have the refusal of it — do let me know — and send me £150. If, when the play is finished, you think it too slight — not serious enough — of course you have the £150 back — I want to go away and write it — and it could be ready in October — as I have nothing else to do — and Palmer is anxious to have a play from me for the States "with no real serious interest"— just a comedy.

In the meanwhile, my dear Aleck, I am so pressed for money, that I don't know what to do. Of course I am extravagant, but a great deal of my worries comes from the fact that I have had for three years to keep up two establishments — my dear Mother's as well as my own — like many Irish ladies she never gets her jointure° paid — small though it is — and naturally it falls on me — this is of course *quite private* but for these years I have had two houses on my shoulders — and of course, am extravagant besides — you have always been a good wise friend to me — so think what you can do.

Kind regards to Mrs. Aleck.

Ever,

OSCAR

jointure: A widow's portion of her husband's estate.

Peter Raby (b. 1939)

THE ORIGINS OF *THE IMPORTANCE OF BEING EARNEST*   1994

In this article, Peter Raby provides some insight into the origins of the play. Wilde wrote quickly, using material that was about him — including names of towns such as Worthing for his characters — so that one has the impression he reflected his environment in his work. However, it is also plain that Wilde lived at such a level that he had considerable need for the money his new farcical comedy was to provide.

Wilde, as the negotiations with Alexander[1] reveal, was acutely conscious of embarking on a new field with this play, referring to it as "farcical comedy" and, to another correspondent, as "quite nonsensical." Its first working title was "The Guardian," and the manuscript notebook in the Clark Library, which also contains speeches for *A Woman of No Importance,* seems to be an attempt at expanding aspects of the first scenario. Even at this early stage, some of the key names had shifted — indeed, only Miss Prism, of all the named characters, retains the same name from scenario to first performance, which gives her an unexpectedly high profile within the play's development. Lady Maud Rufford has become Lady Gwendolen; her mother retains the rank of Duchess; more significantly, Bertram/George Ashton, repeatedly referred to as "Guardian" in the scenario, has been transformed into Mr. Worthing. The importance of his Christian name is now central:

LADY G: Beautiful name — Ernest. I couldn't love anybody who wasn't called Ernest —
Oh! don't say that Gwendolen. it sounds perfectly heartless of you — why shd. love be dependent on the action of an irresponsible godfather. Is a man's whole fortune to depend on the font. I am told there was a moment when my father contemplated calling me John —
How very cruel of him!
I could love you under any other name —
Could you love me if my name was Jane? or Maria?
Devotedly —
Then you have no sense of romance. Those are not names meant for moonlight.
cd. you not love me if my name was Geoffrey —
I might respect you, but love wd. be out of the question — Geoffrey! too straightforward. I cd forgive anything in my husband except passion for telling the truth. That wd. make married life unbearable.

The obsession with the name, and so with form, lies at the play's core, alongside the art of lying, which alone can make married life bearable. Two other quotations from these notes reinforce the theme. On the third page, detached from the dialogue, at an angle and underscored, is the phrase: "Mr. Bunbury — always ill —"; and on the fourth, the following resonant exchange, expanded from the scenario:

GWEN: Leave the room, Mamma. This is no place for you.
DUCHESS: Mr. Worthing rise from this semirecumbent posture — it is most unbefitting[2]

---

[1]George Alexander (1858–1918): English actor and manager of the St. James Theatre. He commissioned *Lady Windermere's Fan* from Wilde.
[2]AMS Notebook, William Andrews Clark Library, Los Angeles.

All the evidence points to Wilde constructing *The Importance of Being Earnest* with great rapidity and zest, incorporating material which lay conveniently at hand — names, incidents, circumstances — into an outline, and more crucially a tone and manner, which had already taken shape in his mind. The choice of the Sussex seaside resort of Worthing for the guardian's borrowed name follows his habit of incorporating place-names into the comedy he was composing (Hunstanton, Goring). Worthing was particularly apposite for a "serious," propertied Justice of the Peace, following the convention of English comedy of manners. Other neighboring seaside villages to surface in the final text are Lancing and Shoreham. The train journey which John Worthing's benefactor, Thomas Cardew, was about to embark on when he was mistakenly handed the black leather handbag was the very journey from Victoria Station on the Brighton line which Wilde would have taken with his family, who on this occasion included a "horrid ugly Swiss governess."[3]

Other names make links with contrasting aspects of Wilde's life. The guardian's great friend of the scenario was "Lord Alfred Rufford," a name Wilde had already used in the final version of *A Woman of No Importance*. This may have struck Wilde as too blatant a glance at Lord Alfred Douglas; Algernon Moncrieff, Scottish and aristocratic in sound, was more circumspect. (There are several Moncrieffs in the Army List of 1894, including one serving General, stationed in Dublin, of whom Wilde may have heard.) The Douglas connection remains through the character who moved from the Duchess of Selby via Lady Brancaster to Lady Bracknell, Bracknell being the Berkshire home of Douglas's mother, the Marchioness of Queensberry. Wilde's circle of homosexual friends is glanced at obliquely through a number of references. The name Ernest itself has been fully discussed in this context, most recently by Joseph Bristow.[4] "Lady Bloxham" commemorates Jack Bloxam, the editor of the *Chameleon,* in which Wilde's "Phrases and Philosophies for the Use of the Young" was published. B4 the Albany, Jack's London address, echoes the residence of Wilde's friend George Ives. There may, too, be another submerged reference, this time to Robbie Ross, in the name of Miss Cardew's family solicitors, "Markby, Markby, and Markby." There was, in fact, an old-established firm of London solicitors which incorporated the name of Markby. The firm had no dealings with Wilde, but Ross was friendly with one of the managing clerks and would call in to the office to see him. Wilde was not primarily creating a private reference but selecting brilliantly from a set of possibilities to create a particular resonance. Markby, Markby, and Markby conveys an air of respectability, indeed gentility, far removed from the less salubrious solicitors of the four-act version, Gribsby and Parker, in which "Gribsby" has the ring of a particularly ruthless, Dickensian kind of lawyer.

In one version, "Gribsby" had been "Hubbard." Wilde's meticulous care to achieve precisely the right name is recorded in an anecdote of Coulson Kernahan. Kernahan was correcting the proofs of *The Picture of Dorian Gray* and recalls Wilde cross-questioning him: "There's a picture framer — a mere tradesman — in my story, isn't there?" On hearing that he had called him Ashton, Wilde replied: "Ashton is a gentleman's name. And I've given it — God forgive me — to a tradesman!

---

[3]*Letters of Oscar Wilde,* ed. Rupert Hart-Davis (London, 1962), 360.
[4]*The Importance of Being Earnest and Related Writings,* ed. Joseph Bristow (London, 1992), 18–20.

It must be changed to Hubbard. Hubbard positively smells of the tradesman!"[5] Having hit on names which seemed especially apt, Wilde would use them repeatedly, at least, as with these two, in drafts. He would occasionally use a name as a private act of revenge. Max Beerbohm recorded that the names of Wilde's publishers, Lane and Matthews, with whom he was in dispute during the autumn of 1894, were both brought into service as manservant and butler, before Wilde relented at least in the case of Matthews, who became Merriman. There may, too, be a personal dimension to the Bunbury joke. Kerry Powell has drawn attention to the farce *Godpapa,* which included a character called Bunbury with an imaginary ailment.[6] Charles Brookfield was the coauthor of the farce and played Bunbury. Wilde disliked Brookfield, who had mocked him in the travesty *The Poet and the Puppets*: it would have given Wilde a particular pleasure to have infiltrated Brookfield surreptitiously into his own travesty and to have disposed of him so finally and satisfactorily.

Wilde's social ear was acute. The names of the two singleminded girls in his play are finely differentiated. Gwendolen Fairfax carries a certain weight and crisp urbanity, appropriate for Lady Bracknell's daughter, while Jack's ward, Cicely Cardew, has a musical lightness about it. Wilde was an undergraduate at Magdalen with two of the Cardew family. Miss Cecily Cardew was born in 1893, and Wilde reportedly promised, when staying with the Cardews at their country house, that he would name the heroine of his next play after her. (The Victorians would have pronounced "Cecily" as "Cicely," as was done in Nicholas Hytner's 1993 production at the Aldwych Theatre, London.) The Cardew connection may even have prompted Wilde's inventive use of the cloakroom at Victoria Station, for Christopher Baldock Cardew was a director of the London and South East Railway. On the other hand, it may simply have been a dimension of Wilde's genius to create artful fictions that uncannily but surreally echoed life.

Wilde's work is relentlessly self-referential. It also contrives to reflect, shadow, and finally subvert a wide range of contemporary plays. The parallels and motifs which Powell has set out in *Oscar Wilde and the Theatre of the 1890s* draw attention both to Wilde's affinities with an astonishing range of near-contemporary farce and to the specific example of Lestocq and Robson's *The Foundling,* which shared not only a number of common features with *The Importance of Being Earnest* but also a New York producer, Charles Frohman. *The Foundling* opened at Terry's on August 30, 1894. The time-scale is tight, and it cannot be established that Wilde saw a performance: he claimed he did not have the rail-fare to London before his luncheon at the Garrick with Alexander. The date on the typescript draft of Acts III and IV, September 19th, suggests completion some days before. The *Morning Post* of August 31, 1894, reported in its review that Dick Pennell, the hopeful bridegroom and Jack Worthing counterpart, is informed "that he is really a foundling, having been discovered, as a baby, in a bedroom of a hotel at Margate," whereupon Mrs Cotton, the girl's mother, declares that "he shall not be allowed to marry her daughter until he can satisfy her that his parentage is at least respectable." By the time Wilde had composed his first complete draft, he had an excellent opportu-

---

[5]Coulson Kernahan, *In Good Company: Some Personal Recollections of Swinburne, Lord Roberts, Watts-Dunton, Oscar Wilde, Edward Whymper, S. J. Stone and Stephen Philips* (London, 1917), 213.

[6]Kerry Powell, *Oscar Wilde and the Theatre of the 1890s* (Cambridge, 1990), 127.

nity to see *The Foundling* without traveling to London. One of the few communications from this period which can be dated precisely, a telegram to Ada Leverson, puts Wilde and Douglas in Worthing on September 22. On September 20, *The Foundling* was acted at the Brighton Theatre, Brighton being the actual setting of this seaside farce. A fortnight later, the more serious but near-farcical episode of Douglas's illness would be enacted at Brighton's Grand Hotel.

Wilde offered a brilliant and versatile synthesis of the genre of farcical comedy, as though he had been steeped in it all his life rather than coming to it as a new experiment. It is not an imitation but a subversion which at the same time develops it into a distinct and continuously surprising new form. The mood of hard-edged gaiety which infuses it is one which he was struggling to recapture in his own life. Telling Douglas about his luncheon with Gladys de Grey, with Reggie Lister and Aleck Yorke, he commented wistfully: "They want me to go to Paris with them on Thursday: they say one wears flannels and straw hats and dines in the Bois, but, of course, I have no money, as usual, and can't go."[7] This is the yearning of Ernest-in-town. But Wilde's earlier life was full of such impromptu outings, and a glance through some of the letters of his Oxford years reveals experiences which he seems to have drawn upon for the Bunbury-in-the-country scenes. Traveling to his uncle's Lincolnshire rectory, he accepted a lift from the station in a neighbor's dog-cart, and examined schools in geography and played lawn tennis, and argued with his uncle, who revenged himself "by preaching on Rome in the morning, and on humility in the evening";[8] and then, after the triumph of his First, he went to stay with Frank Miles at Bingham Rectory, where he played more lawn tennis, and ate strawberries, and where he found the four Miles daughters: "all very pretty indeed, one of them who is writing at the other side of the table quite lovely." The idyll, though, is not sufficiently like art or literature to be entirely perfect: "A wonderful garden with such white lilies and rose walks; only there are no serpents or apples it would be quite Paradise."[9] With *The Importance of Being Earnest,* Wilde constructed the glittering, uncompromising idyll of his last great fiction, with a full complement of apples and serpents.

In this artificially constructed world, at once like and unlike both farcical comedy and society, everyone invents what they desire, and everyone finally acquires it. Each character is resourcefully creative: diaries, three-volume novels, sermons, visiting cards, lists of eligible young men form the fabricated evidence which gives credibility to their fictions. Jack invents Ernest, Algernon impersonates him: Cecily and Gwendolen respond to the challenge, and the double fiction becomes reality, within the artificial world of the play. The emphasis on names, that apparently trivial pun which so irritated Sidney Grundy, turns out to be important after all. Form and style, not sincerity, are dominant, and, as Wilde predicted in his initial scenario, "everything ends happily." But the charm of the dialogue has all the practiced artifice of experience, and the serpent's irony makes itself felt in every phrase and cadence.

[7] *Letters of Oscar Wilde,* 358.
[8] *Letters of Oscar Wilde,* 14.
[9] *Letters of Oscar Wilde,* 16–17.

Anton Chekhov

Anton Chekhov (1860–1904) spent most of his childhood in relative poverty. His family managed to set up its household in Moscow after years spent in remote Taganrog, six hundred miles to the south. He studied medicine in Moscow and eventually took his degree. Though he practiced medicine most of his life, he said that if medicine was his wife, literature was his mistress. His earliest literary efforts were for the purpose of relieving his family's poverty, but it was not long before he earned more from writing than from medicine. By 1896 he had written more than three hundred short stories, most of them published in newspapers. Many of them are classics.

His first theatrical works, apart from his short farces, were not successful. *Ivanov* (1887–1889), rushed to production, was a failure, but its revised 1889 version, reflecting much of his personal life, was successful. *The Wood Demon* (1889), also a failure, helped Chekhov eventually produce his great plays: *The Seagull* (1896); *Uncle Vanya* (1897); *Three Sisters* (1901); and his last, *The Cherry Orchard* (1903). These plays essentially reshaped modern drama, creating a style that critic Richard Peace describes as a "subtle blend of naturalism and symbolism."

The Seagull attracted the attention of the Moscow Art Theatre. The play was not a success in its first production in 1896, but two years later it became one of the theater's triumphs. Konstantin Stanislavsky, the great Russian director and actor, played Trigorin, the lead character, but Chekhov felt that he was overacting. They often had disagreements about the playwright's work, but the Moscow Art Theatre supported Chekhov fully.

The surfaces of Chekhov's plays are so lifelike that at times one feels his dramatic purposes are submerged, and to an extent that is true. Chekhov is the master of the SUBTEXT, a technique in which the surface of the dialogue seems innocuous or meandering, but deeper meanings are implied. Madame Ranevskaya's musings about her childhood in act I of *The Cherry Orchard* contrast with the purposeful dialogue of Lopakhin. Her long speeches in act III talking about the "millstone" she loves in Paris are also meanderings, but they reveal an idealistic character doomed to suffer at the hands of a new generation of realists who have no time for her ramblings and sentimentalism.

Because Chekhov's subtexts are always present, to read his work requires close attention. One must constantly probe, analyze, ask what is implied by what is being said. Chekhov resists "explaining" his plays by having key characters give key thematic speeches. Instead, the meaning builds slowly. Our understanding of what a situation or circumstance finally means will change as we read and as we gather more understanding of the subtleties veiled by surfaces.

Chekhov's style is remarkable for its clarity; its surface is direct, simple, and effective. Even his short stories have a clear dramatic center, and the characters he chose to observe are exceptionally modern in that they are not heroes, not villains. The dramatic concept of a larger-than-life Oedipus or of *Hamlet*'s devilish Claudius is nowhere to be seen in his work. Chekhov's characters are limited, recognizable, and in many ways completely ordinary.

Chekhov's genius was in showing such characters' ambitions, pain, and successes. He was quite aware of important social changes taking place in Russia; the old aristocratic classes, who once owned serfs, were being reduced to a genteel impoverishment, while the children of former slaves were beginning to succeed in business and real estate ventures. Since Chekhov's grandfather had been a serf who bought his freedom in 1841, it is likely that Chekhov was especially supportive of such social change; we see evidence of that in his best plays.

THE CHERRY ORCHARD

The Cherry Orchard (1903), premiered on Chekhov's birthday, January 17, in 1904. The Moscow Art Theatre performance was directed by Konstantin Stanislavsky, an actor-director who pioneered a new method of realistic acting. (Stanislavsky is still read and admired the world over. His techniques were modified in the United States and form the basis of METHOD ACTING.) For the subtle effects that Chekhov wanted, however, he found Stanislavsky too stagey, flamboyant, and melodramatic. They argued hotly over what should happen in his plays, and often Stanislavsky prevailed.

One argument was over whether *The Cherry Orchard* was a tragedy. Chekhov steadfastly called it a comedy, but Stanislavsky saw the ruin of Madame Ranevskaya and the destruction of the cherry orchard as tragic. Chekhov perhaps saw it the same way, but he also considered its potential as the beginning of a new, more realistic life for Madame Ranevskaya and her brother Gayev. Their impracticality was an important cause of their having lost their wealth and estate.

How audiences interpret Lopakhin depends on how they view the ambition of the new class of businessmen whose zeal, work, and cleverness earn them the estates that previously they could have hoped only to work on. Social change is fueled by money, which replaces an inherited aristocracy with ambitious moneymakers who earn the power to force changes on the old, less flexible aristocrats. In Russia massive social change was eventually effected by revolution and the institution of communism. But *The Cherry Orchard* shows that change would have come to Russia in any event.

Perhaps Chekhov's peasant blood helped him see the play as more of a comedy than a tragedy, even though he portrays the characters with greater complexity than we might expect in comedy. Lopakhin is not a simple, unsympathetic character; Trofimov is not a simple dreamer. We need to look closely at what they do and why they do it. For example, when thinking about preserving the beauties of the cherry orchard, Trofimov reminds people that all of Russia is an orchard, that the world is filled with beautiful places. Such a view makes it difficult for him to feel nostalgia for aristocratic privilege.

Trofimov sounds a striking note about the practice of slavery in Russia. He tells Madame Ranevskaya and Gayev that they are living on credit, that they must repay debts to the Russian people. The cherry orchard is beautiful because each tree represents the soul of a serf. The beautiful class of people to which the impractical Madame Ranevskaya belongs owes its beauty and grace to the institution of slavery, and soon the note will be presented for payment. The sound of the breaking string in act I, repeated at the end of the play, is Chekhov's way of symbolizing the losses and changes represented in the play.

Madame Ranevskaya, however, cannot change. Her habits of mind are fully formed before the play begins; nothing that Lopakhin can say will help change her. Even though she knows she is dangerously in debt, she gives a gold coin to a beggar. *Noblesse oblige* — the duty of the upper class to help the poor — is still part of her ethos, even if it also involves her own ruin.

A sense of tragedy is apparent in Madame Ranevskaya's feelings and her helplessness. She seems incapable of transforming herself, no matter how much she may wish to change. We see her as a victim of fate, a fate that is formed by her expectations and training. But the play also contains comic and nonsensical moments, as, for example, in the byplay of Varya, Yasha, and Yepikhodov over a game of billiards in act III. In his letters Chekhov mentions that the play is happy and frivolous, "in places even a farce."

The Cherry Orchard in Performance

Since its first production in 1904, *The Cherry Orchard* has played to responsive audiences in Europe and abroad. It was produced in London in 1911, Berlin in 1919, and New York in 1923 (in Russian). Eva Le Gallienne produced it in New York in her English version in 1928. In 1968 she directed the play with Uta Hagen as Madame Ranevskaya. Tyrone Guthrie directed it at the Old Vic in 1933 and again in 1941. John Gielgud, Peggy Ashcroft, Judy Dench, and Dorothy Tutin performed in a powerful and well-reviewed version in London in 1961. When an all-black *Cherry Orchard* was produced by Joseph Papp in 1973, James Earl Jones was praised as a powerful Lopakhin.

Andrei Serban's 1977 production for Joseph Papp at Lincoln Center in New York was praised for its extraordinary stage effects. According to the reviewer at *Time* magazine,

> Serban's best images effectively magnify the play's conflict between the old order and the bright new world that is its doom: a frieze of peasants laboring beneath modern telegraph wires, a group of aristocrats watching the setting sun silhouette a factory on the horizon.

The American playwright Jean Claude van Italie has revised the text for contemporary audiences. His version, produced at the John Drew Theater of Guild Hall in East Hampton in July 1985, was directed by Elinor Renfield. Amanda Plummer played Anya and Joanna Merlin played Madame Ranevskaya. Peter Brook's 1987 New York production, with Brian Dennehy as a notable Lopakhin, had little scenery beyond a great number of Oriental rugs. It was played without intermissions at breakneck speed. *New York Times* critic Frank Rich said of it, "On this director's magic carpets, *The Cherry Orchard* flies." In 1997 Galina Volchek staged a Russian-language version in the Martin Beck Theater on Broadway. Critic Peter Marks said the play was "communicated vividly."

Anton Chekhov (1860–1904)

THE CHERRY ORCHARD   *1903*

TRANSLATED BY ANN DUNNIGAN

Characters

RANEVSKAYA, LYUBOV ANDREYEVNA, *a landowner*
ANYA, *her daughter, seventeen years old*
VARYA, *her adopted daughter, twenty-four years old*
GAYEV, LEONID ANDREYEVICH, *Madame Ranevskaya's brother*
LOPAKHIN, YERMOLAI ALEKSEYEVICH, *a merchant*
TROFIMOV, PYOTR SERGEYEVICH, *a student*
SEMYONOV-PISHCHIK, BORIS BORISOVICH, *a landowner*
CHARLOTTA IVANOVNA, *a governess*
YEPIKHODOV, SEMYON PANTELEYEVICH, *a clerk*
DUNYASHA, *a maid*
FIRS, *an old valet, eighty-seven years old*
YASHA, *a young footman*
A STRANGER
THE STATIONMASTER
A POST OFFICE CLERK
GUESTS, SERVANTS

The action takes place on Madame Ranevskaya's estate.

ACT I

(*A room that is still called the nursery. One of the doors leads into Anya's room. Dawn; the sun will soon rise. It is May, the cherry trees are in bloom, but it is cold in the orchard; there is a morning frost. The windows in the room are closed. Enter Dunyasha with a candle, and Lopakhin with a book in his hand.*)

LOPAKHIN: The train is in, thank God. What time is it?

DUNYASHA: Nearly two. (*Blows out the candle.*) It's already light.

LOPAKHIN: How late is the train, anyway? A couple of hours at least. (*Yawns and stretches.*) I'm a fine one! What a fool I've made of myself! Came here on purpose to meet them at the station, and then overslept. . . . Fell asleep in the chair. It's annoying. . . . You might have waked me.

DUNYASHA: I thought you had gone. (*Listens.*) They're coming now, I think!

LOPAKHIN (*listens*): No . . . they've got to get the luggage and one thing and another. (*Pause.*) Lyubov Andreyevna has lived abroad for five years, I don't know what she's like now. . . . She's a fine person. Sweet-tempered, simple. I remember when I was a boy of fifteen, my late father — he had a shop in the village then — gave me a punch in the face and made

my nose bleed. . . . We had come into the yard here for some reason or other, and he'd had a drop too much. Lyubov Andreyevna — I remember as if it were yesterday — still young, and so slender, led me to the washstand in this very room, the nursery. "Don't cry, little peasant," she said, "it will heal in time for your wedding. . . ." (*Pause.*) Little peasant . . . my father was a peasant, it's true, and here I am in a white waistcoat and tan shoes. Like a pig in a pastry shop. . . . I may be rich, I've made a lot of money, but if you think about it, analyze it, I'm a peasant through and through. (*Turning pages of the book.*) Here I've been reading this book, and I didn't understand a thing. Fell asleep over it. (*Pause.*)

DUNYASHA: The dogs didn't sleep all night: They can tell that their masters are coming.

LOPAKHIN: What's the matter with you, Dunyasha, you're so . . .

DUNYASHA: My hands are trembling. I'm going to faint.

LOPAKHIN: You're much too delicate, Dunyasha. You dress like a lady, and do your hair like one, too. It's not right. You should know your place.

(*Enter Yepikhodov with a bouquet, he wears a jacket and highly polished boots that squeak loudly. He drops the flowers as he comes in.*)

YEPIKHODOV (*picking up the flowers*): Here, the gardener sent these. He says you're to put them in the dining room. (*Hands the bouquet to Dunyasha.*)

LOPAKHIN: And bring me some kvas.°

DUNYASHA: Yes, sir. (*Goes out.*)

YEPIKHODOV: There's a frost this morning — three degrees — and the cherry trees are in bloom. I cannot approve of our climate. (*Sighs.*) I cannot. Our climate is not exactly conducive. And now, Yermolai Alekseyevich, permit me to append: The day before yesterday I bought myself a pair of boots, which, I venture to assure you, squeak so that it's quite infeasible. What should I grease them with?

LOPAKHIN: Leave me alone. You make me tired.

YEPIKHODOV: Every day some misfortune happens to me. But I don't complain, I'm used to it, I even smile.

(*Dunyasha enters, serves Lopakhin the kvas.*)

YEPIKHODOV: I'm going. (*Stumbles over a chair and upsets it.*) There! (*As if in triumph.*) Now you see, excuse the expression . . . the sort of circumstance,

---

kvas: A Russian beer.

incidentally. . . . It's really quite remarkable! (*Goes out.*)

DUNYASHA: You know, Yermolai Alekseyich, I have to confess that Yepikhodov has proposed to me.

LOPAKHIN: Ah!

DUNYASHA: And I simply don't know. . . . He's a quiet man, but sometimes, when he starts talking, you can't understand a thing he says. It's nice, and full of feeling, only it doesn't make sense. I sort of like him. He's madly in love with me. But he's an unlucky fellow: Every day something happens to him. They tease him about it around here; they call him Two-and-twenty Troubles.

LOPAKHIN (*listening*): I think I hear them coming . . .

DUNYASHA: They're coming! What's the matter with me? I'm cold all over.

LOPAKHIN: They're really coming. Let's go and meet them. Will she recognize me? It's five years since we've seen each other.

DUNYASHA (*agitated*): I'll faint this very minute . . . oh, I'm going to faint!

(*Two carriages are heard driving up to the house. Lopakhin and Dunyasha go out quickly. The stage is empty. There is a hubbub in the adjoining rooms. Firs hurriedly crosses the stage leaning on a stick. He has been to meet Lyubov Andreyevna and wears old fashioned livery and a high hat. He mutters something to himself, not a word of which can be understood. The noise offstage grows louder and louder. A voice: "Let's go through here. . . ." Enter Lyubov Andreyevna, Anya, Charlotta Ivanovna with a little dog on a chain, all in traveling dress; Varya wearing a coat and kerchief; Gayev, Semyonov-Pishchik, Lopakhin, Dunyasha with a bundle and parasol; servants with luggage — all walk through the room.*)

ANYA: Let's go this way. Do you remember, Mama, what room this is?

LYUBOV ANDREYEVNA: (*joyfully, through tears*): The nursery!

VARYA: How cold it is! My hands are numb. (*To Lyubov Andreyevna.*) Your rooms, both the white one and the violet one, are just as you left them, Mama.

LYUBOV ANDREYEVNA: The nursery . . . my dear, lovely nursery. . . . I used to sleep here when I was little. . . . (*Weeps.*) And now, like a child, I . . . (*Kisses her brother, Varya, then her brother again.*) Varya hasn't changed; she still looks like a nun. And I recognized Dunyasha. . . . (*Kisses Dunyasha.*)

GAYEV: The train was two hours late. How's that? What kind of management is that?

CHARLOTTA (*to Pishchik*): My dog even eats nuts.

PISHCHIK (*amazed*): Think of that now!

(*They all go out except Anya and Dunyasha.*)

DUNYASHA: We've been waiting and waiting for you. . . . (*Takes off Anya's coat and hat.*)

ANYA: I didn't sleep for four nights on the road . . . now I feel cold.

DUNYASHA: It was Lent when you went away, there was snow and frost then, but now? My darling! (*Laughs and kisses her.*) I've waited so long for you, my joy, my precious . . . I must tell you at once, I can't wait another minute. . . .

ANYA (*listlessly*): What now?

DUNYASHA: The clerk, Yepikhodov, proposed to me just after Easter.

ANYA: You always talk about the same thing. . . . (*Straightening her hair.*) I've lost all my hairpins. . . . (*She is so exhausted she can hardly stand.*)

DUNYASHA: I really don't know what to think. He loves me — he loves me so!

ANYA (*looking through the door into her room, tenderly*): My room, my windows . . . it's just as though I'd never been away. I am home! Tomorrow morning I'll get up and run into the orchard. . . . Oh, if I could only sleep! I didn't sleep during the entire journey, I was so tormented by anxiety.

DUNYASHA: Pyotr Sergeich arrived the day before yesterday.

ANYA (*joyfully*): Petya!

DUNYASHA: He's asleep in the bathhouse, he's staying there. "I'm afraid of being in the way," he said. (*Looks at her pocket watch.*) I ought to wake him up, but Varvara Mikhailovna told me not to. "Don't you wake him," she said.

(*Enter Varya with a bunch of keys at her waist.*)

VARYA: Dunyasha, coffee, quickly . . . Mama's asking for coffee.

DUNYASHA: This very minute. (*Goes out.*)

VARYA: Thank God, you've come! You're home again. (*Caressing her.*) My little darling has come back! My pretty one is here!

ANYA: I've been through so much.

VARYA: I can imagine!

ANYA: I left in Holy Week, it was cold then. Charlotta never stopped talking and doing her conjuring tricks the entire journey. Why did you saddle me with Charlotta?

VARYA: You couldn't have traveled alone, darling. At seventeen!

ANYA: When we arrived in Paris, it was cold, snowing. My French is awful. . . . Mama was living on the fifth floor, and when I got there, she had all sorts of Frenchmen and ladies with her, and an old priest with a little book, and it was full of smoke, dismal. Suddenly I felt sorry for Mama, so sorry. I took her head in my arms and held her close and couldn't let her go. Afterward she kept hugging me and crying. . . .

VARYA (*through her tears*): Don't talk about it, don't talk about it. . . .

ANYA: She had already sold her villa near Mentone, and she had nothing left, nothing. And I hadn't so much as a kopeck left, we barely managed to get there. But Mama doesn't understand! When we had dinner in a station restaurant, she always ordered the most expensive dishes and tipped each of the waiters a ruble. Charlotta is the same. And Yasha also ordered a dinner, it was simply awful. You know, Yasha is Mama's footman; we brought him with us.

VARYA: I saw the rogue.

ANYA: Well, how are things? Have you paid the interest?

VARYA: How could we?

ANYA: Oh, my God, my God!

VARYA: In August the estate will be put up for sale.

ANYA: My God!

(*Lopakhin peeps in at the door and moos like a cow.*)

LOPAKHIN: Moo-o-o! (*Disappears.*)

VARYA (*through her tears*): What I couldn't do to him! (*Shakes her fist.*)

ANYA (*embracing Varya, softly*): Varya, has he proposed to you? (*Varya shakes her head.*) But he loves you. . . . Why don't you come to an understanding, what are you waiting for?

VARYA: I don't think anything will ever come of it. He's too busy, he has no time for me . . . he doesn't even notice me. I've washed my hands of him, it makes me miserable to see him. . . . Everyone talks of our wedding, they all congratulate me, and actually there's nothing to it — it's all like a dream. . . . (*In a different tone.*) You have a brooch like a bee.

ANYA (*sadly*): Mama bought it. (*Goes into her own room; speaks gaily, like a child.*) In Paris I went up in a balloon!

VARYA: My darling is home! My pretty one has come back!

(*Dunyasha has come in with the coffeepot and prepares coffee.*)

VARYA (*stands at the door of Anya's room*): You know, darling, all day long I'm busy looking after the house, but I keep dreaming. If we could marry you to a rich man I'd be at peace. I could go into a hermitage, then to Kiev, to Moscow, and from one holy place to another. . . . I'd go on and on. What a blessing!

ANYA: The birds are singing in the orchard. What time is it?

VARYA: It must be after two. Time you were asleep, darling. (*Goes into Anya's room.*) What a blessing!

(*Yasha enters with a lap robe and a traveling bag.*)

YASHA (*crosses the stage mincingly*): May one go through here?

DUNYASHA: A person would hardly recognize you, Yasha. Your stay abroad has done wonders for you.

YASHA: Hm. . . . And who are you?

DUNYASHA: When you left here I was only that high — (*indicating with her hand*). I'm Dunyasha, Fyodor Kozoyedov's daughter. You don't remember?

YASHA: Hm. . . . A little cucumber! (*Looks around, then embraces her; she cries out and drops a saucer. He quickly goes out.*)

VARYA (*in a tone of annoyance, from the doorway*): What's going on here?

DUNYASHA (*tearfully*): I broke a saucer.

VARYA: That's good luck.

ANYA: We ought to prepare Mama: Petya is here. . . .

VARYA: I gave orders not to wake him.

ANYA (*pensively*): Six years ago Father died, and a month later brother Grisha drowned in the river . . . a pretty little seven-year-old boy. Mama couldn't bear it and went away . . . went without looking back. . . . (*Shudders.*) How I understand her, if she only knew! (*Pause.*) And Petya Trofimov was Grisha's tutor, he may remind her. . . .

(*Enter Firs wearing a jacket and a white waistcoat.*)

FIRS (*goes to the coffeepot, anxiously*): The mistress will have her coffee here. (*Puts on white gloves.*) Is the coffee ready? (*To Dunyasha, sternly.*) You! Where's the cream?

DUNYASHA: Oh, my goodness! (*Quickly goes out.*)

FIRS (*fussing over the coffeepot*): Ah, what an addlepate! (*Mutters to himself.*) They've come back from Paris. . . . The master used to go to Paris . . . by carriage. . . . (*Laughs.*)

VARYA: What is it, Firs?

FIRS: If you please? (*Joyfully.*) My mistress has come home! At last! Now I can die. . . . (*Weeps with joy.*)

(*Enter Lyubov Andreyevna, Gayev, and Semyonov-Pishchik, the last wearing a sleeveless peasant coat of fine cloth and full trousers. Gayev, as he comes in, goes through the motions of playing billiards.*)

LYUBOV ANDREYEVNA: How does it go? Let's see if I can remember . . . cue ball into the corner! Double the rail to center table.

GAYEV: Cut shot into the corner! There was a time, sister, when you and I used to sleep here in this very room, and now I'm fifty-one, strange as it may seem. . . .

LOPAKHIN: Yes, time passes.

GAYEV: How's that?

LOPAKHIN: Time, I say, passes.

GAYEV: It smells of patchouli here.

ANYA: I'm going to bed. Good night, Mama. (*Kisses her mother.*)

LYUBOV ANDREYEVNA: My precious child. (*Kisses her hands.*) Are you glad to be home? I still feel dazed.

ANYA: Good night, Uncle.

GAYEV (*kisses her face and hands*): God bless you. How like your mother you are! (*To his sister.*) At her age you were exactly like her, Lyuba.

(*Anya shakes hands with Lopakhin and Pishchik and goes out, closing the door after her.*)

LYUBOV ANDREYEVNA: She's exhausted.

PISHCHIK: Must have been a long journey.

VARYA: Well, gentlemen? It's after two, high time you were going.

LYUBOV ANDREYEVNA (*laughs*): You haven't changed, Varya. (*Draws Varya to her and kisses her.*) I'll just drink my coffee and then we'll all go. (*Firs places a cushion under her feet.*) Thank you, my dear. I've got used to coffee. I drink it day and night. Thanks, dear old man. (*Kisses him.*)

VARYA: I'd better see if all the luggage has been brought in.

LYUBOV ANDREYEVNA: Is this really me sitting here? (*Laughs.*) I feel like jumping about and waving my arms. (*Buries her face in her hands.*) What if it's only a dream! God knows I love my country, love it dearly. I couldn't look out the train window, I was crying so! (*Through tears.*) But I must drink my coffee. Thank you, Firs, thank you, my dear old friend. I'm so glad you're still alive.

FIRS: The day before yesterday.

GAYEV: He's hard of hearing.

LOPAKHIN: I must go now, I'm leaving for Kharkov about five o'clock. It's so annoying! I wanted to have a good look at you, and have a talk. You're as splendid as ever.

PISHCHIK (*breathing heavily*): Even more beautiful. . . . Dressed like a Parisienne. . . . There goes my wagon, all four wheels!

LOPAKHIN: Your brother here, Leonid Andreich, says I'm a boor, a moneygrubber, but I don't mind. Let him talk. All I want is that you should trust me as you used to, and that your wonderful, touching eyes should look at me as they did then. Merciful God! My father was one of your father's serfs, and your grandfather's, but you yourself did so much for me once, that I've forgotten all that and love you as if you were my own kin — more than my kin.

LYUBOV ANDREYEVNA: I can't sit still, I simply cannot. (*Jumps up and walks about the room in great excitement.*) I cannot bear this joy. . . . Laugh at me, I'm silly. . . . My dear little bookcase . . . (*kisses bookcase*) my little table . . .

GAYEV: Nurse died while you were away.

LYUBOV ANDREYEVNA (*sits down and drinks coffee*): Yes, God rest her soul. They wrote me.

GAYEV: And Anastasy is dead. Petrushka Kosoi left me and is now with the police inspector in town. (*Takes a box of hard candies from his pocket and begins to suck one.*)

PISHCHIK: My daughter, Dashenka . . . sends her regards . . .

LOPAKHIN: I wish I could tell you something very pleasant and cheering. (*Glances at his watch.*) I must go directly, there's no time to talk, but . . . well, I'll say it in a couple of words. As you know, the cherry orchard is to be sold to pay your debts. The auction is set for August twenty-second, but you need not worry, my dear, you can sleep in peace, there is a way out. This is my plan. Now, please listen! Your estate is only twenty versts° from town, the railway runs close by, and if the cherry orchard and the land along the river were cut up into lots and leased for summer cottages, you'd have, at the very least, an income of twenty-five thousand a year.

versts: A verst is approximately equal to a kilometer, a little more than half a mile.

GAYEV: Excuse me, what nonsense!

LYUBOV ANDREYEVNA: I don't quite understand you, Yermolai Alekseich.

LOPAKHIN: You will get, at the very least, twenty-five rubles a year for a two-and-a-half-acre lot, and if you advertise now, I guarantee you won't have a single plot of ground left by autumn, everything will be snapped up. In short, I congratulate you, you are saved. The site is splendid, the river is deep. Only, of course, the ground must be cleared . . . you must tear down all the old outbuildings, for instance, and this house, which is worthless, cut down the old cherry orchard —

LYUBOV ANDREYEVNA: Cut it down? Forgive me, my dear, but you don't know what you are talking about. If there is one thing in the whole province that is interesting, not to say remarkable, it's our cherry orchard.

LOPAKHIN: The only remarkable thing about this orchard is that it is very big. There's a crop of cherries every other year, and then you can't get rid of them, nobody buys them.

GAYEV: This orchard is even mentioned in the *Encyclopedia*.

LOPAKHIN (*glancing at his watch*): If we don't think of something and come to a decision, on the twenty-second of August the cherry orchard, and the entire estate, will be sold at auction. Make up your minds! There is no other way out, I swear to you. None whatsoever.

FIRS: In the old days, forty or fifty years ago, the cherries were dried, soaked, marinated, and made into jam, and they used to —

GAYEV: Be quiet, Firs.

FIRS: And they used to send cartloads of dried cherries to Moscow and Kharkov. And that brought in money! The dried cherries were soft and juicy in those days, sweet, fragrant. . . . They had a method then . . .

LYUBOV ANDREYEVNA: And what has become of that method now?

FIRS: Forgotten. Nobody remembers. . . .

PISHCHIK: How was it in Paris? What's it like there? Did you eat frogs?

LYUBOV ANDREYEVNA: I ate crocodiles.

PISHCHIK: Think of that now!

LOPAKHIN: There used to be only the gentry and the peasants living in the country, but now these summer people have appeared. All the towns, even the smallest ones, are surrounded by summer cottages. And it is safe to say that in another twenty years these people will multiply enormously. Now the summer resident only drinks tea on his porch, but it may well be that he'll take to cultivating his acre and then your cherry orchard will be a happy, rich, luxuriant —

GAYEV (*indignantly*): What nonsense!

(*Enter Varya and Yasha.*)

VARYA: There are two telegrams for you, Mama. (*Picks out a key and with a jingling sound opens an old-fashioned bookcase.*) Here they are.

LYUBOV ANDREYEVNA: From Paris. (*Tears up the telegrams without reading them.*) That's all over. . . .

GAYEV: Do you know, Lyuba, how old this bookcase is? A week ago I pulled out the bottom drawer, and what do I see? Some figures burnt into it. The bookcase was made exactly a hundred years ago. What do you think of that? Eh? We could have celebrated its jubilee. It's an inanimate object, but nevertheless, for all that, it's a bookcase.

PISHCHIK: A hundred years . . . think of that now!

GAYEV: Yes . . . that is something. . . . (*Feeling the bookcase.*) Dear, honored bookcase. I salute thy existence, which for over one hundred years has served the glorious ideals of goodness and justice; thy silent appeal to fruitful endeavor, unflagging in the course of a hundred years, tearfully sustaining through generations of our family, courage and faith in a better future, and fostering in us ideals of goodness and social consciousness. . . .

(*A pause.*)

LOPAKHIN: Yes . . .

LYUBOV ANDREYEVNA: You are the same as ever, Lyonya.

GAYEV (*somewhat embarrassed*): Carom into the corner, cut shot to center table.

LOPAKHIN (*looks at his watch*): Well, time for me to go.

YASHA (*hands medicine to Lyubov Andreyevna*): Perhaps you will take your pills now.

PISHCHIK: Don't take medicaments, dearest lady, they do neither harm nor good. Let me have them, honored lady. (*Takes the pillbox, shakes the pills into his hand, blows on them, puts them into his mouth and washes them down with kvas.*) There!

LYUBOV ANDREYEVNA (*alarmed*): Why, you must be mad!

PISHCHIK: I've taken all the pills.

LOPAKHIN: What a glutton!

(*Everyone laughs.*)

FIRS: The gentleman stayed with us during Holy Week . . . ate half a bucket of pickles. . . . (*Mumbles.*)

LYUBOV ANDREYEVNA: What is he saying?

VARYA: He's been muttering like that for three years now. We've grown used to it.

YASHA: He's in his dotage.

(*Charlotta Ivanovna, very thin, tightly laced, in a white dress with a lorgnette at her belt, crosses the stage.*)

LOPAKHIN: Forgive me, Charlotta Ivanovna, I haven't had a chance to say how do you do to you. (*Tries to kiss her hand.*)

CHARLOTTA (*pulls her hand away*): If I permit you to kiss my hand you'll be wanting to kiss my elbow next, then my shoulder.

LOPAKHIN: I have no luck today. (*Everyone laughs.*) Charlotta Ivanovna, show us a trick!

LYUBOV ANDREYEVNA: Charlotta, show us a trick!

CHARLOTTA: No. I want to sleep. (*Goes out.*)

LOPAKHIN: In three weeks we'll meet again. (*Kisses Lyubov Andreyevna's hand.*) Good-bye till then. Time to go. (*To Gayev.*) Good-bye. (*Kisses Pishchik.*) Good-bye. (*Shakes hands with Varya, then with Firs and Yasha.*) I don't feel like going. (*To Lyubov Andreyevna.*) If you make up your mind about the summer cottages and come to a decision, let me know; I'll get you a loan of fifty thousand or so. Think it over seriously.

VARYA (*angrily*): Oh, why don't you go!

LOPAKHIN: I'm going, I'm going. (*Goes out.*)

GAYEV: Boor. Oh, pardon. Varya's going to marry him, he's Varya's young man.

VARYA: Uncle dear, you talk too much.

LYUBOV ANDREYEVNA: Well, Varya, I shall be very glad. He's a good man.

PISHCHIK: A man, I must truly say . . . most worthy. . . . And my Dashenka . . . says, too, that . . . says all sorts of things. (*Snores but wakes up at once.*) In any case, honored lady, oblige me . . . a loan of two hundred and forty rubles . . . tomorrow the interest on my mortgage is due. . . .

VARYA (*in alarm*): We have nothing, nothing at all!

LYUBOV ANDREYEVNA: I really haven't any money.

PISHCHIK: It'll turn up. (*Laughs.*) I never lose hope. Just when I thought everything was lost, that I was done for, lo and behold — the railway line ran through my land . . . and they paid me for it. And before you know it, something else will turn up, if not today — tomorrow. . . . Dashenka will win two hundred thousand . . . she's got a lottery ticket.

LYUBOV ANDREYEVNA: The coffee is finished, we can go to bed.

FIRS (*brushing Gayev's clothes, admonishingly*): You've put on the wrong trousers again. What am I to do with you?

VARYA (*softly*): Anya's asleep. (*Quietly opens the window.*) The sun has risen, it's no longer cold. Look, Mama dear, what wonderful trees! Oh, Lord, the air! The starlings are singing!

GAYEV (*opens another window*): The orchard is all white. You haven't forgotten, Lyuba? That long avenue there that runs straight — straight as a stretched-out strap; it gleams on moonlight nights. Remember? You've not forgotten?

LYUBOV ANDREYEVNA (*looking out the window at the orchard*): Oh, my childhood, my innocence! I used to sleep in this nursery, I looked out from here into the orchard, happiness awoke with me each morning, it was just as it is now, nothing has changed. (*Laughing with joy.*) All, all white! Oh, my orchard! After the dark, rainy autumn and the cold winter, you are young again, full of happiness, the heavenly angels have not forsaken you. . . . If I could cast off this heavy stone weighing on my breast and shoulders, if I could forget my past!

GAYEV: Yes, and the orchard will be sold for our debts, strange as it may seem. . . .

LYUBOV ANDREYEVNA: Look, our dead mother walks in the orchard . . . in a white dress! (*Laughs with joy.*) It is she!

GAYEV: Where?

VARYA: God be with you, Mama dear.

LYUBOV ANDREYEVNA: There's no one there, I just imagined it. To the right, as you turn to the summerhouse, a slender white sapling is bent over . . . it looks like a woman.

(*Enter Trofimov wearing a shabby student's uniform and spectacles.*)

LYUBOV ANDREYEVNA: What a wonderful orchard! The white masses of blossoms, the blue sky —

TROFIMOV: Lyubov Andreyevna! (*She looks around at him.*) I only want to pay my respects, then I'll go at once. (*Kisses her hand ardently.*) I was told to wait until morning, but I hadn't the patience.

(*Lyubov Andreyevna looks at him, puzzled.*)

VARYA (*through tears*): This is Petya Trofimov.

TROFIMOV: Petya Trofimov, I was Grisha's tutor. . . . Can I have changed so much?

(*Lyubov Andreyevna embraces him, quietly weeping.*)

GAYEV (*embarrassed*): There, there, Lyuba.

VARYA (*crying*): Didn't I tell you, Petya, to wait till tomorrow?

LYUBOV ANDREYEVNA: My Grisha . . . my little boy . . . Grisha . . . my son. . . .

VARYA: What can we do, Mama dear? It's God's will.

TROFIMOV (*gently, through tears*): Don't, don't. . . .

LYUBOV ANDREYEVNA (*quietly weeping*): My little boy dead, drowned. . . . Why? Why, my friend? (*In a lower voice.*) Anya is sleeping in there, and I'm talking loudly . . . making all this noise. . . . But Petya, why do you look so bad? Why have you grown so old?

TROFIMOV: A peasant woman in the train called me a mangy gentleman.

LYUBOV ANDREYEVNA: You were just a boy then, a charming little student, and now your hair is thin — and spectacles! Is it possible you are still a student? (*Goes toward the door.*)

TROFIMOV: I shall probably be an eternal student.

LYUBOV ANDREYEVNA (*kisses her brother, then Varya*): Now, go to bed. . . . You've grown older too, Leonid.

PISHCHIK (*follows her*): Well, seems to be time to sleep. . . . Oh, my gout! I'm staying the night. Lyubov Andreyevna, my soul, tomorrow morning . . . two hundred and forty rubles. . . .

GAYEV: He keeps at it.

PISHCHIK: Two hundred and forty rubles . . . to pay the interest on my mortgage.

LYUBOV ANDREYEVNA: I have no money, my friend.

PISHCHIK: My dear, I'll pay it back. . . . It's a trifling sum.

LYUBOV ANDREYEVNA: Well, all right, Leonid will give it to you. . . . Give it to him, Leonid.

GAYEV: Me give it to him! . . . Hold out your pocket!

LYUBOV ANDREYEVNA: It can't be helped, give it to him. . . . He needs it. . . . He'll pay it back.

(*Lyubov Andreyevna, Trofimov, Pishchik, and Firs go out. Gayev, Varya, and Yasha remain.*)

GAYEV: My sister hasn't yet lost her habit of squandering money. (*To Yasha.*) Go away, my good fellow, you smell of the henhouse.

YASHA (*with a smirk*): And you, Leonid Andreyevich, are just the same as ever.

GAYEV: How's that? (*To Varya.*) What did he say?

VARYA: Your mother has come from the village; she's been sitting in the servants' room since yesterday, waiting to see you. . . .

YASHA: Let her wait, for God's sake!

VARYA: Aren't you ashamed?

YASHA: A lot I need her! She could have come tomorrow. (*Goes out.*)

VARYA: Mama's the same as ever, she hasn't changed a bit. She'd give away everything, if she could.

GAYEV: Yes. . . . (*A pause.*) If a great many remedies are suggested for a disease, it means that the disease is incurable. I keep thinking, racking my brains, I have many remedies, a great many, and that means in effect, that I have none. It would be good to receive a legacy from someone, good to marry our Anya to a very rich man, good to go to Yaroslav and try our luck with our aunt, the Countess. She is very, very rich, you know.

VARYA (*crying*): If only God would help us!

GAYEV: Stop bawling. Auntie's very rich, but she doesn't like us. In the first place, sister married a lawyer, not a nobleman . . . (*Anya appears in the doorway.*) She married beneath her, and it cannot be said that she has conducted herself very virtuously. She is good, kind, charming, and I love her dearly, but no matter how much you allow for extenuating circumstances, you must admit she leads a sinful life. You feel it in her slightest movement.

VARYA (*in a whisper*): Anya is standing in the doorway.

GAYEV: What? (*Pause.*) Funny, something got into my right eye . . . I can't see very well. And Thursday, when I was in the district court . . .

(*Anya enters.*)

VARYA: Why aren't you asleep, Anya?

ANYA: I can't get to sleep. I just can't.

GAYEV: My little one! (*Kisses Anya's face and hands.*) My child. . . . (*Through tears.*) You are not my niece, you are my angel, you are everything to me. Believe me, believe . . .

ANYA: I believe you, Uncle. Everyone loves you and respects you, but, Uncle dear, you must keep quiet, just keep quiet. What were you saying just now about my mother, about your own sister? What made you say that?

GAYEV: Yes, yes. . . . (*Covers his face with her hand.*) Really, it's awful! My God! God help me! And today I made a speech to the bookcase . . . so stupid! And it was only when I had finished that I realized it was stupid.

VARYA: It's true, Uncle dear, you ought to keep quiet. Just don't talk, that's all.

ANYA: If you could keep from talking, it would make things easier for you, too.

GAYEV: I'll be quiet. (*Kisses Anya's and Varya's hands.*) I'll be quiet. Only this is about business. On Thursday I was in the district court, well, a group of us gathered together and began talking about one thing and another, this and that, and it seems it might be possible to arrange a loan on a promissory note to pay the interest at the bank.

VARYA: If only God would help us!

GAYEV: On Tuesday I'll go and talk it over again. (*To Varya.*) Stop bawling. (*To Anya.*) Your mama will talk to Lopakhin; he, of course, will not refuse her. . . . And as soon as you've rested, you will go to Yaroslav to the Countess, your great-aunt. In that way we shall be working from three directions — and our business is in the hat. We'll pay the interest, I'm certain of it. . . . (*Puts a candy in his mouth.*) On my honor, I'll swear by anything you like, the estate shall not be sold. (*Excitedly.*) By my happiness, I swear it! Here's my hand on it, call me a worthless, dishonorable man if I let it come to auction! I swear by my whole being!

ANYA (*a calm mood returns to her, she is happy*): How good you are, Uncle, how clever! (*Embraces him.*) Now I am at peace! I'm at peace! I'm happy!

(*Enter Firs.*)

FIRS (*reproachfully*): Leonid Andreich, have you no fear of God? When are you going to bed?

GAYEV: Presently, presently. Go away, Firs. I'll . . . all right, I'll undress myself. Well, children, bye-bye. . . . Details tomorrow, and now go to sleep. (*Kisses Anya and Varya.*) I am a man of the eighties. . . . They don't think much of that period today, nevertheless, I can say that in the course of my life I have suffered not a little for my convictions. It is not for nothing that the peasant loves me. You have to know the peasant! You have to know from what —

ANYA: There you go again, Uncle!

VARYA: Uncle dear, do be quiet.

FIRS (*angrily*): Leonid Andreich!

GAYEV: I'm coming, I'm coming. . . . Go to bed. A clean double rail shot to center table. . . . (*Goes out; Firs hobbles after him.*)

ANYA: I'm at peace now. I would rather not go to Yaroslav, I don't like my great-aunt, but still, I'm at peace, thanks to Uncle. (*She sits down.*)

VARYA: We must get some sleep. I'm going now. Oh, something unpleasant happened while you were away. In the old servants' quarters, as you know, there are only the old people: Yefimushka, Polya, Yevstignei, and, of course, Karp. They began letting in all sorts of rogues to spend the night — I didn't say anything. But then I heard they'd been spreading a rumor that I'd given an order for them to be fed nothing but dried peas. Out of stinginess, you

see. . . . It was all Yevstignei's doing. . . . Very well, I think, if that's how it is, you just wait. I send for Yevstignei . . . (*yawning*) he comes. . . . "How is it, Yevstignei," I say, "that you could be such a fool. . . ." (*Looks at Anya.*) She's fallen asleep. (*Takes her by the arm.*) Come to your little bed. . . . Come along. (*Leading her.*) My little darling fell asleep. Come. . . . (*They go.*)

(*In the distance, beyond the orchard, a shepherd is playing on a reed pipe. Trofimov crosses the stage and, seeing Varya and Anya, stops.*)

VARYA: Sh! She's asleep . . . asleep. . . . Come along, darling.

ANYA (*softly, half-asleep*): I'm so tired. . . . Those bells . . . Uncle . . . dear . . . Mama and Uncle . . .

VARYA: Come, darling, come along. (*They go into Anya's room.*)

TROFIMOV (*deeply moved*): My sunshine! My spring!

ACT II

(*A meadow. An old, lopsided, long-abandoned little chapel; near it a well, large stones that apparently were once tombstones, and an old bench. A road to the Gayev manor house can be seen. On one side, where the cherry orchard begins, tall poplars loom. In the distance a row of telegraph poles, and far, far away, on the horizon, the faint outline of a large town, which is visible only in very fine, clear weather. The sun will soon set. Charlotta, Yasha, and Dunyasha are sitting on the bench; Yepikhodov stands near playing something sad on the guitar. They are all lost in thought. Charlotta wears an old forage cap; she has taken a gun from her shoulder and is adjusting the buckle on the sling.*)

CHARLOTTA (*reflectively*): I haven't got a real passport, I don't know how old I am, but it always seems to me that I'm quite young. When I was a little girl, my father and mother used to travel from one fair to another giving performances — very good ones. And I did the *salto mortale*° and all sorts of tricks. Then when Papa and Mama died, a German lady took me to live with her and began teaching me. Good. I grew up and became a governess. But where I come from and who I am — I do not know. . . . Who my parents were — perhaps they weren't even married — I don't know. (*Takes a cucumber out of her pocket and eats it.*) I don't know anything. (*Pause.*) One wants so much to talk, but there isn't anyone to talk to . . . I have no one.

YEPIKHODOV (*plays the guitar and sings*): "What care I for the clamorous world, what's friend or foe to me?". . . How pleasant it is to play a mandolin!

DUNYASHA: That's a guitar, not a mandolin. (*Looks at herself in a hand mirror and powders her face.*)

salto mortale: Somersault.

YEPIKHODOV: To a madman, in love, it is a mandolin. . . . (*Sings.*) "Would that the heart were warmed by the flame of requited love . . ."

(*Yasha joins in.*)

CHARLOTTA: How horribly these people sing! . . . Pfui! Like jackals!

DUNYASHA (*to Yasha*): Really, how fortunate to have been abroad!

YASHA: Yes, to be sure. I cannot but agree with you there. (*Yawns, then lights a cigar.*)

YEPIKHODOV: It stands to reason. Abroad everything has long since been fully constituted.

YASHA: Obviously.

YEPIKHODOV: I am a cultivated man, I read all sorts of remarkable books, but I am in no way able to make out my own inclinations, what it is I really want, whether, strictly speaking, to live or to shoot myself; nevertheless, I always carry a revolver on me. Here it is. (*Shows revolver.*)

CHARLOTTA: Finished. Now I'm going. (*Slings the gun over her shoulder.*) You're a very clever man, Yepikhodov, and quite terrifying; women must be mad about you. Brrr! (*Starts to go.*) These clever people are all so stupid, there's no one for me to talk to. . . . Alone, always alone, I have no one . . . and who I am, and why I am, nobody knows. . . . (*Goes out unhurriedly.*)

YEPIKHODOV: Strictly speaking, all else aside, I must state regarding myself, that fate treats me unmercifully, as a storm does a small ship. If, let us assume, I am mistaken, then why, to mention a single instance, do I wake up this morning, and there on my chest see a spider of terrifying magnitude? . . . Like that. (*Indicates with both hands.*) And likewise, I take up some kvas to quench my thirst, and there see something in the highest degree unseemly, like a cockroach. (*Pause.*) Have you read Buckle?° (*Pause.*) If I may trouble you, Avdotya Fedorovna, I should like to have a word or two with you.

DUNYASHA: Go ahead.

YEPIKHODOV: I prefer to speak with you alone. . . . (*Sighs.*)

DUNYASHA (*embarrassed*): Very well . . . only first bring me my little cape . . . you'll find it by the cupboard. . . . It's rather damp here. . . .

YEPIKHODOV: Certainly, ma'am . . . I'll fetch it, ma'am. . . . Now I know what to do with my revolver. . . . (*Takes the guitar and goes off playing it.*)

YASHA: Two-and-twenty Troubles! Between ourselves, a stupid fellow. (*Yawns.*)

DUNYASHA: God forbid that he should shoot himself. (*Pause.*) I've grown so anxious, I'm always worried. I was only a little girl when I was taken into the mas-

ter's house, and now I'm quite unused to the simple life, and my hands are white as can be, just like a lady's. I've become so delicate, so tender and ladylike, I'm afraid of everything. . . . Frightfully so. And, Yasha, if you deceive me, I just don't know what will become of my nerves.

YASHA (*kisses her*): You little cucumber! Of course, a girl should never forget herself. What I dislike above everything is when a girl doesn't conduct herself properly.

DUNYASHA: I'm passionately in love with you, you're educated, you can discuss anything. (*Pause.*)

YASHA (*yawns*): Yes. . . . As I see it, it's like this: If a girl loves somebody, that means she's immoral. (*Pause.*) Very pleasant smoking a cigar in the open air. . . . (*Listens.*) Someone's coming this way. . . . It's the masters. (*Dunyasha impulsively embraces him.*) You go home, as if you'd been to the river to bathe; take that path, otherwise they'll see you and suspect me of having a rendezvous with you. I can't endure that sort of thing.

DUNYASHA (*with a little cough*): My head is beginning to ache from your cigar. . . . (*Goes out.*)

(*Yasha remains, sitting near the chapel. Lyubov Andreyevna, Gayev, and Lopakhin enter.*)

LOPAKHIN: You must make up your mind once and for all — time won't stand still. The question, after all, is quite simple. Do you agree to lease the land for summer cottages or not? Answer in one word: Yes or no? Only one word!

LYUBOV ANDREYEVNA: Who is it that smokes those disgusting cigars out here? (*Sits down.*)

GAYEV: Now that the railway line is so near, it's made things convenient. (*Sits down.*) We went to town and had lunch . . . cue ball to the center! I feel like going to the house first and playing a game.

LYUBOV ANDREYEVNA: Later.

LOPAKHIN: Just one word! (*Imploringly.*) Do give me an answer!

GAYEV (*yawning*): How's that?

LYUBOV ANDREYEVNA (*looks into her purse*): Yesterday I had a lot of money, and today there's hardly any left. My poor Varya tries to economize by feeding everyone milk soup, and in the kitchen the old people get nothing but dried peas, while I squander money foolishly. . . . (*Drops the purse, scattering gold coins.*) There they go. . . . (*Vexed.*)

YASHA: Allow me, I'll pick them up in an instant. (*Picks up the money.*)

LYUBOV ANDREYEVNA: Please do, Yasha. And why did I go to town for lunch? . . . That miserable restaurant of yours with its music, and tablecloths smelling of soap. . . . Why drink so much, Lyonya? Why eat so much? Why talk so much? Today in the restaurant again you talked too much, and it was all so pointless. About the seventies, about the decadents. And to whom? Talking to waiters about the decadents!

LOPAKHIN: Yes.

GAYEV (*waving his hand*): I'm incorrigible, that's evi-

Buckle: Thomas Henry Buckle (1821–1862) was a radical historian who formulated a scientific basis for history emphasizing the interrelationship of climate, food production, population, and wealth.

dent. . . . (*Irritably to Yasha.*) Why do you keep twirling about in front of me?

YASHA (*laughs*): I can't help laughing when I hear your voice.

GAYEV (*to his sister*): Either he or I —

LYUBOV ANDREYEVNA: Go away, Yasha, run along.

YASHA (*hands Lyubov Andreyevna her purse*): I'm going, right away. (*Hardly able to contain his laughter.*) This very instant. . . . (*Goes out.*)

LOPAKHIN: That rich man, Deriganov, is prepared to buy the estate. They say he's coming to the auction himself.

LYUBOV ANDREYEVNA: Where did you hear that?

LOPAKHIN: That's what they're saying in town.

LYUBOV ANDREYEVNA: Our aunt in Yaroslav promised to send us something, but when and how much, no one knows.

LOPAKHIN: How much do you think she'll send? A hundred thousand? Two hundred?

LYUBOV ANDREYEVNA: Oh . . . ten or fifteen thousand, and we'll be thankful for that.

LOPAKHIN: Forgive me, but I have never seen such frivolous, such queer, unbusinesslike people as you, my friends. You are told in plain language that your estate is to be sold, and it's as though you don't understand it.

ABOVE: The spare set in Ron Daniel's 1993 production of *The Cherry Orchard* at the American Repertory Theatre highlights the characters' emotional isolation. RIGHT: Claire Bloom as Madame Ranevskaya.

LYUBOV ANDREYEVNA: But what are we to do? Tell us what to do.

LOPAKHIN: I tell you every day. Every day I say the same thing. Both the cherry orchard and the land must be leased for summer cottages, and it must be done now, as quickly as possible — the auction is close at hand. Try to understand! Once you definitely decide on the cottages, you can raise as much money as you like, and then you are saved.

LYUBOV ANDREYEVNA: Cottages, summer people — forgive me, but it's so vulgar.

GAYEV: I agree with you, absolutely.

LOPAKHIN: I'll either burst into tears, start shouting, or fall into a faint! I can't stand it! You've worn me out! (*To Gayev.*) You're an old woman!

GAYEV: How's that?

LOPAKHIN: An old woman! (*Starts to go.*)

LYUBOV ANDREYEVNA (*alarmed*): No, don't go, stay, my dear. I beg you. Perhaps we'll think of something!

LOPAKHIN: What is there to think of?

LYUBOV ANDREYEVNA: Don't go away, please. With you here it's more cheerful somehow. . . . (*Pause.*) I keep expecting something to happen, like the house caving in on us.

GAYEV (*in deep thought*): Double rail shot into the corner. . . . Cross table to the center. . . .

LYUBOV ANDREYEVNA: We have sinned so much. . . .

LOPAKHIN: What sins could you have —

GAYEV (*puts a candy into his mouth*): They say I've eaten up my entire fortune in candies. . . . (*Laughs.*)

LYUBOV ANDREYEVNA: Oh, my sins. . . . I've always squandered money recklessly, like a madwoman, and I married a man who did nothing but amass debts. My husband died from champagne — he drank terribly — then, to my sorrow, I fell in love with another man, lived with him, and just at that time — that was my first punishment, a blow on the head — my little boy was drowned . . . here in the river. And I went abroad, went away for good, never to return, never to see this river. . . . I closed my eyes and ran, beside myself, and *he* after me . . . callously, without pity. I bought a villa near Mentone, because he fell ill there, and for three years I had no rest, day or night. The sick man wore me out, my soul dried up. Then last year, when the villa was sold to pay my debts, I went to Paris, and there he stripped me of everything, and left me for another woman; I tried to poison myself. . . . So stupid, so shameful. . . . And suddenly I felt a longing for Russia, for my own country, for my little girl. . . . (*Wipes away her tears.*) Lord, Lord, be merciful, forgive my sins! Don't punish me anymore! (*Takes a telegram out of her pocket.*) This came today from Paris. . . . He asks my forgiveness, begs me to return. . . . (*Tears up telegram.*) Do I hear music? (*Listens.*)

GAYEV: That's our famous Jewish band. You remember, four violins, a flute, and double bass.

LYUBOV ANDREYEVNA: It's still in existence? We ought to send for them sometime and give a party.

LOPAKHIN (*listens*): I don't hear anything. . . . (*Sings softly.*) "The Germans, for pay, will turn Russians into Frenchmen, they say." (*Laughs.*) What a play I saw yesterday at the theater — very funny!

LYUBOV ANDREYEVNA: There was probably nothing funny about it. Instead of going to see plays you ought to look at yourselves a little more often. How drab your lives are, how full of futile talk!

LOPAKHIN: That's true. I must say, this life of ours is stupid. . . . (*Pause.*) My father was a peasant, an idiot; he understood nothing, taught me nothing; all he did was beat me when he was drunk, and always with a stick. As a matter of fact, I'm as big a blockhead and idiot as he was. I never learned anything, my handwriting's disgusting, I write like a pig — I'm ashamed to have people see it.

LYUBOV ANDREYEVNA: You ought to get married, my friend.

LOPAKHIN: Yes . . . that's true.

LYUBOV ANDREYEVNA: To our Varya. She's a nice girl.

LOPAKHIN: Yes.

LYUBOV ANDREYEVNA: She's a girl who comes from simple people, works all day long, but the main thing is she loves you. Besides, you've liked her for a long time now.

LOPAKHIN: Well? I've nothing against it. . . . She's a good girl. (*Pause.*)

GAYEV: I've been offered a place in the bank. Six thousand a year. . . . Have you heard?

LYUBOV ANDREYEVNA: How could you! You stay where you are. . . .

(*Firs enters carrying an overcoat.*)

FIRS (*to Gayev*): If you please, sir, put this on, it's damp.

GAYEV (*puts on the overcoat*): You're a pest, old man.

FIRS: Never mind. . . . You went off this morning without telling me. (*Looks him over.*)

LYUBOV ANDREYEVNA: How you have aged, Firs!

FIRS: What do you wish, madam?

LOPAKHIN: She says you've grown very old!

FIRS: I've lived a long time. They were arranging a marriage for me before your papa was born. . . . (*Laughs.*) I was already head footman when the emancipation came. At that time I wouldn't consent to my freedom, I stayed with the masters. . . . (*Pause.*) I remember, everyone was happy, but what they were happy about, they themselves didn't know.

LOPAKHIN: It was better in the old days. At least they flogged them.

FIRS (*not hearing*): Of course. The peasants kept to the masters, the masters kept to the peasants; but now they have all gone their own ways, you can't tell about anything.

GAYEV: Be quiet, Firs. Tomorrow I must go to town. I've been promised an introduction to a certain general who might let us have a loan.

LOPAKHIN: Nothing will come of it. And you can rest assured, you won't even pay the interest.

LYUBOV ANDREYEVNA: He's raving. There is no such general.

(*Enter Trofimov, Anya, and Varya.*)

GAYEV: Here come our young people.

ANYA: There's Mama.

LYUBOV ANDREYEVNA (*tenderly*): Come, come along, my darlings. (*Embraces Anya and Varya.*) If you only knew how I love you both! Sit here beside me — there, like that.

(*They all sit down.*)

LOPAKHIN: Our eternal student is always with the young ladies.

TROFIMOV: That's none of your business.

LOPAKHIN: He'll soon be fifty, but he's still a student.

TROFIMOV: Drop your stupid jokes.

LOPAKHIN: What are you so angry about, you queer fellow?

TROFIMOV: Just leave me alone.

LOPAKHIN (*laughs*): Let me ask you something: What do you make of me?

TROFIMOV: My idea of you, Yermolai Alekseich, is this: You're a rich man, you will soon be a millionaire. Just as the beast of prey, which devours everything that crosses its path, is necessary in the metabolic process, so are you necessary.

(*Everyone laughs.*)

VARYA: Petya, you'd better tell us something about the planets.

LYUBOV ANDREYEVNA: No, let's go on with yesterday's conversation.

TROFIMOV: What was it about?

GAYEV: About the proud man.

TROFIMOV: We talked a long time yesterday, but we didn't get anywhere. In the proud man, in your sense of the word, there's something mystical. And you may be right from your point of view, but if you look at it simply, without being abstruse, why even talk about pride? Is there any sense in it if, physiologically, man is poorly constructed, if, in the vast majority of cases, he is coarse, ignorant, and profoundly unhappy? We should stop admiring ourselves. We should just work, and that's all.

GAYEV: You die, anyway.

TROFIMOV: Who knows? And what does it mean — to die? It may be that man has a hundred senses, and at his death only the five that are known to us perish, and the other ninety-five go on living.

LYUBOV ANDREYEVNA: How clever you are, Petya!

LOPAKHIN (*ironically*): Terribly clever!

TROFIMOV: Mankind goes forward, perfecting its powers. Everything that is now unattainable will some day be comprehensible and within our grasp, only we must work, and help with all our might those who are seeking the truth. So far, among us here in Russia, only a very few work. The great majority of the intelligentsia that I know seek nothing, do nothing, and as yet are incapable of work. They call themselves the intelligentsia, yet they belittle their servants, treat the peasants like animals, are wretched students, never read anything serious, and do absolutely nothing; they only talk about science and know very little about art. They all look serious, have grim expressions, speak of weighty matters, and philosophize; and meanwhile anyone can see that the workers eat abominably, sleep without pillows, thirty or forty to a room, and everywhere there are bedbugs, stench, dampness, and immorality. . . . It's obvious that all our fine talk is merely to delude ourselves and others. Show me the day nurseries they are always talking about — and where are the reading rooms? They only write about them in novels, but in reality they don't exist. There is nothing but filth, vulgarity, asiaticism.° . . . I'm afraid of those very serious countenances, I don't like them, I'm afraid of serious conversations. We'd better to remain silent.

LOPAKHIN: You know, I get up before five in the morning, and I work from morning to night; now, I'm always handling money, my own and other people's, and I see what people around me are like. You have only to start doing something to find out how few honest, decent people there are. Sometimes, when I can't sleep, I think: "Lord, Thou gavest us vast forests, boundless fields, broad horizons, and living in their midst we ourselves ought truly to be giants. . . ."

LYUBOV ANDREYEVNA: Now you want giants! They're good only in fairy tales, otherwise they're frightening.

(*Yepikhodov crosses at the rear of the stage, playing the guitar.*)

LYUBOV ANDREYEVNA (*pensively*): There goes Yepikhodov . . .

ANYA (*pensively*): There goes Yepikhodov . . .

GAYEV: The sun has set, ladies and gentlemen.

TROFIMOV: Yes.

GAYEV (*in a low voice, as though reciting*): Oh, Nature, wondrous Nature, you shine with eternal radiance, beautiful and indifferent; you, whom we call mother, unite within yourself both life and death, giving life and taking it away. . . .

VARYA (*beseechingly*): Uncle dear!

ANYA: Uncle, you're doing it again!

TROFIMOV: You'd better cue ball into the center.

GAYEV: I'll be silent, silent.

(*All sit lost in thought. The silence is broken only by the subdued muttering of Firs. Suddenly a distant sound is heard, as if from the sky, like the sound of a snapped string mournfully dying away.*)

LYUBOV ANDREYEVNA: What was that?

LOPAKHIN: I don't know. Somewhere far off in a mine shaft a bucket's broken loose. But somewhere very far away.

GAYEV: It might be a bird of some sort . . . like a heron.

asiaticism: Trofimov, expressing a common prejudice of the time, refers to Asian apathy.

TROFIMOV: Or an owl . . .

LYUBOV ANDREYEVNA (*shudders*): It's unpleasant some-how. . . . (*Pause.*)

FIRS: The same thing happened before the troubles: An owl hooted and the samovar hissed continually.

GAYEV: Before what troubles?

FIRS: Before the emancipation.

LYUBOV ANDREYEVNA: Come along, my friends, let us go, evening is falling. (*To Anya.*) There are tears in your eyes — what is it, my little one?

(*Embraces her.*)

ANYA: It's all right, Mama. It's nothing.

TROFIMOV: Someone is coming.

(*A Stranger appears wearing a shabby white forage cap and an overcoat. He is slightly drunk.*)

STRANGER: Permit me to inquire, can I go straight through here to the station?

GAYEV: You can. Follow the road.

STRANGER: I am deeply grateful to you. (*Coughs.*) Splendid weather. . . . (*Reciting.*) "My brother, my suffering brother . . . come to the Volga, whose groans" . . . (*To Varya.*) Mademoiselle, will you oblige a hungry Russian with thirty kopecks?

(*Varya, frightened, cries out.*)

LOPAKHIN (*angrily*): There's a limit to everything.

LYUBOV ANDREYEVNA (*panic-stricken*): Here you are — take this. . . . (*Fumbles in her purse.*) I have no silver. . . . Never mind, here's a gold piece for you. . . .

STRANGER: I am deeply grateful to you. (*Goes off.*)

(*Laughter.*)

VARYA (*frightened*): I'm leaving . . . I'm leaving. . . . Oh, Mama, dear, there's nothing in the house for the servants to eat, and you give him a gold piece!

LYUBOV ANDREYEVNA: What's to be done with such a silly creature? When we get home I'll give you all I've got. Yermolai Alekseyevich, you'll lend me some more!

LOPAKHIN: At your service.

LYUBOV ANDREYEVNA: Come, my friends, it's time to go. Oh, Varya, we have definitely made a match for you. Congratulations!

VARYA (*through tears*): Mama, that's not something to joke about.

LOPAKHIN: "Aurelia, get thee to a nunnery . . ."°

GAYEV: Look, my hands are trembling: It's a long time since I've played a game of billiards.

LOPAKHIN: "Aurelia, O Nymph, in thy orisons, be all my sins remember'd!"

LYUBOV ANDREYEVNA: Let us go, my friends, it will soon be suppertime.

"Aurelia . . . nunnery": From Hamlet's famous line rejecting Ophelia (Lopakhin's next line is also from Shakespeare's *Hamlet*).

VARYA: He frightened me. My heart is simply pounding.

LOPAKHIN: Let me remind you, ladies and gentlemen: On the twenty-second of August the cherry orchard is to be sold. Think about that! — Think!

(*All go out except Trofimov and Anya.*)

ANYA (*laughs*): My thanks to the stranger for frightening Varya, now we are alone.

TROFIMOV: Varya is so afraid we might suddenly fall in love with each other that she hasn't left us alone for days. With her narrow mind she can't understand that we are above love. To avoid the petty and the illusory, which prevent our being free and happy — that is the aim and meaning of life. Forward! We are moving irresistibly toward the bright star that burns in the distance! Forward! Do not fall behind, friends!

ANYA (*clasping her hands*): How well you talk! (*Pause.*) It's marvelous here today!

TROFIMOV: Yes, the weather is wonderful.

ANYA: What have you done to me, Petya, that I no longer love the cherry orchard as I used to? I loved it so tenderly, it seemed to me there was no better place on earth than our orchard.

TROFIMOV: All Russia is our orchard. It is a great and beautiful land, and there are many wonderful places in it. (*Pause.*) Just think, Anya: Your grandfather, your great-grandfather, and all your ancestors were serf-owners, possessors of living souls. Don't you see that from every cherry tree, from every leaf and trunk, human beings are peering out at you? Don't you hear their voices? To possess living souls — that has corrupted all of you, those who lived before and you who are living now, so that your mother, you, your uncle, no longer perceive that you are living in debt, at someone else's expense, at the expense of those whom you wouldn't allow to cross your threshold. . . . We are at least two hundred years behind the times, we have as yet absolutely nothing, we have no definite attitude toward the past, we only philosophize, complain of boredom, or drink vodka. Yet it's quite clear that to begin to live we must first atone for the past, be done with it, and we can atone for it only by suffering, only by extraordinary, unceasing labor. Understand this, Anya.

ANYA: The house we live in hasn't really been ours for a long time, and I shall leave it, I give you my word.

TROFIMOV: If you have the keys of the household, throw them into the well and go. Be as free as the wind.

ANYA (*in ecstasy*): How well you put that!

TROFIMOV: Believe me, Anya, believe me! I am not yet thirty, I am young, still a student, but I have already been through so much! As soon as winter comes, I am hungry, sick, worried, poor as a beggar, and — where has not fate driven me! Where have I not been? And yet always, every minute of the day and night, my soul was filled with inexplicable premonitions. I have a premonition of happiness, Anya, I can see it . . .

ANYA: The moon is rising.

(*Yepikhodov is heard playing the same melancholy song on the guitar. The moon rises. Somewhere near the poplars Varya is looking for Anya and calling: "Anya, where are you?"*)

TROFIMOV: Yes, the moon is rising. (*Pause.*) There it is — happiness . . . it's coming, nearer and nearer, I can hear its footsteps. And if we do not see it, if we do not recognize it, what does it matter? Others will see it.

VARYA'S VOICE: Anya! Where are you?

TROFIMOV: That Varya again! (*Angrily.*) It's revolting!

ANYA: Well? Let's go down to the river. It's lovely there.

TROFIMOV: Come on. (*They go.*)

VARYA'S VOICE: Anya! Anya!

ACT III

(*The drawing room, separated by an arch from the ball-room. The chandelier is lighted. The Jewish band that was mentioned in act II is heard playing in the hall. It is evening. In the ballroom they are dancing a grand rond. The voice of Semyonov-Pishchik: "Promenade à une paire!"° They all enter the drawing room: Pishchik and Charlotta Ivanovna are the first couple, Trofimov and Lyubov Andreyevna the second, Anya and the Post-Office Clerk the third, Varya and the Stationmaster the fourth, etc. Varya, quietly weeping, dries her tears as she dances. Dunyasha is in the last couple. As they cross the drawing room Pishchik calls: "Grand rond, bal-ancez!" and "Les cavaliers à genoux et remercier vos dames!"° Firs, wearing a dress coat, brings in a tray with seltzer water. Pishchik and Trofimov come into the drawing room.*)

PISHCHIK: I'm a full-blooded man, I've already had two strokes, and dancing's hard work for me, but as they say, "If you run with the pack, you can bark or not, but at least wag your tail." At that, I'm as strong as a horse. My late father — quite a joker he was, God rest his soul — used to say, talking about our origins, that the ancient line of Semyonov-Pishchik was descended from the very horse that Caligula had seated in the Senate.° . . . (*Sits down.*) But the trouble is — no money! A hungry dog believes in nothing but meat. . . . (*Snores but wakes up at once.*) It's the same with me — I can think of nothing but money. . . .

TROFIMOV: You know, there really is something equine about your figure.

PISHCHIK: Well, a horse is a fine animal. . . . You can sell a horse.

(*There is the sound of a billiard game in the next room. Varya appears in the archway.*)

TROFIMOV (*teasing her*): Madame Lopakhina! Madame Lopakhina!

VARYA (*angrily*): Mangy gentleman!

TROFIMOV: Yes, I am a mangy gentleman, and proud of it!

VARYA (*reflecting bitterly*): Here we've hired musicians, and what are we going to pay them with? (*Goes out.*)

TROFIMOV (*to Pishchik*): If the energy you have ex-pended in the course of your life trying to find money to pay interest had gone into something else, ulti-mately, you might very well have turned the world upside down.

PISHCHIK: Nietzsche . . . the philosopher . . . the great-est, most renowned . . . a man of tremendous intel-lect . . . says in his works that it is possible to forge banknotes.

TROFIMOV: And have you read Nietzsche?

PISHCHIK: Well . . . Dashenka told me. I'm in such a state now that I'm just about ready for forging. . . . The day after tomorrow I have to pay three hundred and ten rubles . . . I've got a hundred and thirty. . . . (*Feels in his pocket, grows alarmed.*) The money is gone! I've lost the money! (*Tearfully.*) Where is my money? (*Joyfully.*) Here it is, inside the lining. . . . I'm all in a sweat. . . .

(*Lyubov Andreyevna and Charlotta Ivanovna come in.*)

LYUBOV ANDREYEVNA (*humming a* Lezginka):° Why does Leonid take so long? What is he doing in town? (*To Dunyasha.*) Dunyasha, offer the musicians some tea.

TROFIMOV: In all probability, the auction didn't take place.

LYUBOV ANDREYEVNA: It was the wrong time to have the musicians, the wrong time to give a dance. . . . Well, never mind. . . . (*Sits down and hums softly.*)

CHARLOTTA (*gives Pishchik a deck of cards*): Here's a deck of cards for you. Think of a card.

PISHCHIK: I've thought of one.

CHARLOTTA: Now shuffle the pack. Very good. And now, my dear Mr. Pishchik, hand it to me. *Ein, zwei, drei!°* Now look for it — it's in your side pocket.

PISHCHIK (*takes the card out of his side pocket*): The eight of spades — absolutely right! (*Amazed.*) Think of that, now!

CHARLOTTA (*holding the deck of cards in the palm of her hand, to Trofimov*): Quickly, tell me, which card is on top?

TROFIMOV: What? Well, the queen of spades.

CHARLOTTA: Right! (*To Pishchik.*) Now which card is on top?

PISHCHIK: The ace of hearts.

CHARLOTTA: Right! (*Claps her hands and the deck of cards disappears.*) What lovely weather we're having today! (*A mysterious feminine voice, which seems to come from under the floor, answers her: "Oh, yes,*

"Promenade à une paire!": French for "Walk in pairs!"
"Grand rond . . . dames!": Instructions in the dance: "Large circle!" and "Gentlemen, kneel down and thank your ladies!"
Caligula . . . Senate: Caligula (A.D. 12–41), a cavalry soldier, was Roman emperor (A.D. 37–41).

Lezginka: A lively Russian tune for a dance.   ***Ein, zwei, drei!:*** "One, two, three" (German).

splendid weather, madam.") You are so nice, you're my ideal. . . . (*The voice:* "*And I'm very fond of you, too, madam.*")

STATIONMASTER (*applauding*): Bravo, Madame Ventriloquist!

PISHCHIK (*amazed*): Think of that, now! Most enchanting Charlotta Ivanovna . . . I am simply in love with you. . . .

CHARLOTTA: In love? (*Shrugs her shoulders.*) Is it possible that you can love? *Guter Mensch, aber schlechter Musikant.*°

TROFIMOV (*claps Pishchik on the shoulder*): You old horse, you!

CHARLOTTA: Attention, please! One more trick. (*Takes a lap robe from a chair.*) Here's a very fine lap robe; I should like to sell it. (*Shakes it out.*) Doesn't anyone want to buy it?

PISHCHIK (*amazed*): Think of that, now!

CHARLOTTA: *Ein, zwei, drei!* (*Quickly raises the lap robe, behind it stands Anya, who curtsies, runs to her mother, embraces her, and runs back into the ballroom amid the general enthusiasm.*)

LYUBOV ANDREYEVNA (*applauding*): Bravo, bravo!

CHARLOTTA: Once again! *Ein, zwei, drei.* (*Raises the lap robe; behind it stands Varya, who bows.*)

PISHCHIK (*amazed*): Think of that, now!

CHARLOTTA: The end! (*Throws the robe at Pishchik, makes a curtsy, and runs out of the room.*)

PISHCHIK (*hurries after her*): The minx! . . . What a woman! What a woman! (*Goes out.*)

LYUBOV ANDREYEVNA: And Leonid still not here. What he is doing in town so long, I do not understand! It must be all over by now. Either the estate is sold, or the auction didn't take place — but why keep us in suspense so long!

VARYA (*trying to comfort her*): Uncle has bought it, I am certain of that.

TROFIMOV (*mockingly*): Yes.

VARYA: Great-aunt sent him power of attorney to buy it in her name and transfer the debt. She's doing it for Anya's sake. And I am sure, with God's help, Uncle will buy it.

LYUBOV ANDREYEVNA: Our great-aunt in Yaroslav sent fifteen thousand to buy the estate in her name — she doesn't trust us — but that's not even enough to pay the interest. (*Covers her face with her hands.*) Today my fate will be decided, my fate . . .

TROFIMOV (*teasing Varya*): Madame Lopakhina!

VARYA (*angrily*): Eternal student! Twice already you've been expelled from the university.

LYUBOV ANDREYEVNA: Why are you so cross, Varya? If he teases you about Lopakhin, what of it? Go ahead and marry Lopakhin if you want to. He's a nice man, he's interesting. And if you don't want to, don't. Nobody's forcing you, my pet.

VARYA: To be frank, Mama dear, I regard this matter seriously. He is a good man, I like him.

LYUBOV ANDREYEVNA: Then marry him. I don't know what you're waiting for!

VARYA: Mama, I can't propose to him myself. For the last two years everyone's been talking to me about him; everyone talks, but he is either silent or he jokes. I understand. He's getting rich, he's absorbed in business, he has no time for me. If I had some money, no matter how little, if it were only a hundred rubles, I'd drop everything and go far away. I'd go into a nunnery.

TROFIMOV: A blessing!

VARYA (*to Trofimov*): A student ought to be intelligent! (*In a gentle tone, tearfully.*) How homely you have grown, Petya, how old! (*To Lyubov Andreyevna, no longer crying.*) It's just that I cannot live without work, Mama. I must be doing something every minute.

(*Yasha enters.*)

YASHA (*barely able to suppress his laughter*): Yepikhodov has broken a billiard cue! (*Goes out.*)

VARYA: But why is Yepikhodov here? Who gave him permission to play billiards? I don't understand these people. . . . (*Goes out.*)

LYUBOV ANDREYEVNA: Don't tease her, Petya. You can see she's unhappy enough without that.

TROFIMOV: She's much too zealous, always meddling in other people's affairs. All summer long she's given Anya and me no peace — afraid a romance might develop. What business is it of hers? Besides, I've given no occasion for it, I am far removed from such banality. We are above love!

LYUBOV ANDREYEVNA: And I suppose I am beneath love. (*In great agitation.*) Why isn't Leonid here? If only I knew whether the estate had been sold or not! The disaster seems to me so incredible that I don't even know what to think, I'm lost. . . . I could scream this very instant . . . I could do something foolish. Save me, Petya. Talk to me, say something. . . .

TROFIMOV: Whether or not the estate is sold today — does it really matter? That's all done with long ago; there's no turning back, the path is overgrown. Be calm, my dear. One must not deceive oneself; at least once in one's life one ought to look the truth straight in the eye.

LYUBOV ANDREYEVNA: What truth? You can see where there is truth and where there isn't, but I seem to have lost my sight, I see nothing. You boldly settle all the important problems, but tell me, my dear boy, isn't it because you are young and have not yet had to suffer for a single one of your problems? You boldly look ahead, but isn't it because you neither see nor expect anything dreadful, since life is still hidden from your young eyes? You're bolder, more honest, deeper than we are, but think about it, be just a little bit magnanimous, and spare me. You see, I was born here, my mother and father lived here, and my grand-

Guter Mensch, aber schlechter Musikant: "Good man, but poor musician" (German).

father. I love this house, without the cherry orchard my life has no meaning for me, and if it must be sold, then sell me with the orchard. . . . (*Embraces Trofimov and kisses him on the forehead.*) And my son was drowned here. . . . (*Weeps.*) Have pity on me, you good, kind man.

TROFIMOV: You know I feel for you with all my heart.

LYUBOV ANDREYEVNA: But that should have been said differently, quite differently. . . . (*Takes out her handkerchief and a telegram falls to the floor.*) My heart is heavy today, you can't imagine. It's so noisy here, my soul quivers at every sound, I tremble all over, and yet I can't go to my room. When I am alone the silence frightens me. Don't condemn me, Petya . . . I love you as if you were my own. I would gladly let you marry Anya, I swear it, only you must study, my dear, you must get your degree. You do nothing, fate simply tosses you from place to place — it's so strange. . . . Isn't that true? Isn't it? And you must do something about your beard, to make it grow somehow. . . . (*Laughs.*) You're so funny!

TROFIMOV (*picks up the telegram*): I have no desire to be an Adonis.°

LYUBOV ANDREYEVNA: That's a telegram from Paris. I get them every day. One yesterday, one today. That wild man has fallen ill again, he's in trouble again. . . . He begs my forgiveness, implores me to come, and really, I ought to go to Paris to be near him. Your face is stern, Petya, but what can one do, my dear? What am I to do? He is ill, he's alone and unhappy, and who will look after him there, who will keep him from making mistakes, who will give him his medicine on time? And why hide it or keep silent, I love him, that's clear. I love him, love him. . . . It's a millstone round my neck, I'm sinking to the bottom with it, but I love that stone, I cannot live without it. (*Presses Trofimov's hand.*) Don't think badly of me, Petya, and don't say anything to me, don't say anything. . . .

TROFIMOV (*through tears*): For God's sake, forgive my frankness: You know that he robbed you!

LYUBOV ANDREYEVNA: No, no, no, you mustn't say such things! (*Covers her ears.*)

TROFIMOV: But he's a scoundrel! You're the only one who doesn't know it! He's a petty scoundrel, a nonentity —

LYUBOV ANDREYEVNA (*angry, but controlling herself*): You are twenty-six or twenty-seven years old, but you're still a schoolboy!

TROFIMOV: That may be!

LYUBOV ANDREYEVNA: You should be a man, at your age you ought to understand those who love. And you ought to be in love yourself. (*Angrily.*) Yes, yes! It's not purity with you, it's simply prudery, you're a ridiculous crank, a freak —

TROFIMOV (*horrified*): What is she saying!

LYUBOV ANDREYEVNA: I am above love! You're not above love, you're just an addlepate, as Firs would say. Not to have a mistress at your age!

TROFIMOV (*in horror*): This is awful! What is she saying! . . . (*Goes quickly toward the ballroom.*) This is awful . . . I can't . . . I won't stay here. . . . (*Goes out, but immediately returns.*) All is over between us! (*Goes out to the hall.*)

LYUBOV ANDREYEVNA (*calls after him*): Petya, wait! You absurd creature, I was joking! Petya!

(*In the hall there is the sound of someone running quickly downstairs and suddenly falling with a crash. Anya and Varya scream, but a moment later laughter is heard.*)

LYUBOV ANDREYEVNA: What was that?

(*Anya runs in.*)

ANYA (*laughing*): Petya fell down the stairs! (*Runs out.*)

LYUBOV ANDREYEVNA: What a funny boy that Petya is!

(*The Stationmaster stands in the middle of the ballroom and recites A. Tolstoy's° "The Sinner." Everyone listens to him, but he has no sooner spoken a few lines than the sound of a waltz is heard from the hall and the recitation is broken off. They all dance. Trofimov, Anya, Varya, and Lyubov Andreyevna come in from the hall.*)

LYUBOV ANDREYEVNA: Come, Petya . . . come, you pure soul . . . please, forgive me. . . . Let's dance. . . . (*They dance.*)

(*Anya and Varya dance. Firs comes in, puts his stick by the side door. Yasha also comes into the drawing room and watches the dancers.*)

YASHA: What is it, grandpa?

FIRS: I don't feel well. In the old days, we used to have generals, barons, admirals, dancing at our balls, but now we send for the post office clerk and the stationmaster, and even they are none too eager to come. Somehow I've grown weak. The late master, their grandfather, dosed everyone with sealing wax, no matter what ailed them. I've been taking sealing wax every day for twenty years or more, maybe that's what's kept me alive.

YASHA: You bore me, grandpa. (*Yawns.*) High time you croaked.

FIRS: Ah, you . . . addlepate! (*Mumbles.*)

(*Trofimov and Lyubov Andreyevna dance from the ballroom into the drawing room.*)

LYUBOV ANDREYEVNA: *Merci.* I'll sit down a while. (*Sits.*) I'm tired.

(*Anya comes in.*)

ANYA (*excitedly*): There was a man in the kitchen just now saying that the cherry orchard was sold today.

Adonis: From Greek myth, a beautiful young man.

A. Tolstoy: Aleksey Konstantinovich Tolstoy (1817–1875), Russian novelist, dramatist, and poet.

LYUBOV ANDREYEVNA: Sold to whom?

ANYA: He didn't say. He's gone. (*Dances with Trofimov; they go into the ballroom.*)

YASHA: That was just some old man babbling. A stranger.

FIRS: Leonid Andreich is not back yet, still hasn't come. And he's wearing the light, between-seasons overcoat; like enough he'll catch cold. Ah, when they're young they're green.

LYUBOV ANDREYEVNA: This is killing me. Yasha, go and find out who it was sold to.

YASHA: But that old man left long ago. (*Laughs.*)

LYUBOV ANDREYEVNA (*slightly annoyed*): Well, what are you laughing at? What are you so happy about?

YASHA: That Yepikhodov is very funny! Hopeless! Two-and-twenty Troubles.

LYUBOV ANDREYEVNA: Firs, if the estate is sold, where will you go?

FIRS: Wherever you tell me to go, I'll go.

LYUBOV ANDREYEVNA: Why do you look like that? Aren't you well? You ought to go to bed.

FIRS: Yes. . . . (*With a smirk.*) Go to bed, and without me who will serve, who will see to things? I'm the only one in the whole house.

YASHA (*to Lyubov Andreyevna*): Lyubov Andreyevna! Permit me to make a request, be so kind! If you go back to Paris again, do me the favor of taking me with you. It is positively impossible for me to stay here. (*Looking around, then in a low voice.*) There's no need to say it, you can see for yourself, it's an uncivilized country, the people have no morals, and the boredom! The food they give us in the kitchen is unmentionable, and besides, there's this Firs who keeps walking about mumbling all sorts of inappropriate things. Take me with you, be so kind!

(*Enter Pishchik.*)

PISHCHIK: May I have the pleasure of a waltz with you, fairest lady? (*Lyubov Andreyevna goes with him.*) I really must borrow a hundred and eighty rubles from you, my charmer . . . I really must. . . . (*Dancing.*) Just a hundred and eighty rubles. . . . (*They pass into the ballroom.*)

YASHA (*softly sings*): "Wilt thou know my soul's unrest . . ."

(*In the ballroom a figure in a gray top hat and checked trousers is jumping about, waving its arms; there are shouts of "Bravo, Charlotta Ivanovna!"*)

DUNYASHA (*stopping to powder her face*): The young mistress told me to dance — there are lots of gentlemen and not enough ladies — but dancing makes me dizzy, and my heart begins to thump. Firs Nikolayevich, the post office clerk just said something to me that took my breath away.

(*The music grows more subdued.*)

FIRS: What did he say to you?

DUNYASHA: "You," he said, "are like a flower."

YASHA (*yawns*): What ignorance. . . . (*Goes out.*)

DUNYASHA: Like a flower. . . . I'm such a delicate girl, I just adore tender words.

FIRS: You'll get your head turned.

(*Enter Yepikhodov.*)

YEPIKHODOV: Avdotya Fyodorovna, you are not desirous of seeing me. . . . I might almost be some sort of insect. (*Sighs.*) Ah, life!

DUNYASHA: What is it you want?

YEPIKHODOV: Indubitably, you may be right. (*Sighs.*) But, of course, if one looks at it from a point of view, then, if I may so express myself, and you will forgive my frankness, you have completely reduced me to a state of mind. I know my fate, every day some misfortune befalls me, but I have long since grown accustomed to that; I look upon my fate with a smile. But you gave me your word, and although I —

DUNYASHA: Please, we'll talk about it later, but leave me in peace now. Just now I'm dreaming. . . . (*Plays with her fan.*)

YEPIKHODOV: Every day a misfortune, and yet, if I may so express myself, I merely smile, I even laugh.

(*Varya enters from the ballroom.*)

VARYA: Are you still here, Semyon? What a disrespectful man you are, really! (*To Dunyasha.*) Run along, Dunyasha. (*To Yepikhodov.*) First you play billiards and break a cue, then you wander about the drawing room as though you were a guest.

YEPIKHODOV: You cannot, if I may so express myself, penalize me.

VARYA: I am not penalizing you, I'm telling you. You do nothing but wander from one place to another, and you don't do your work. We keep a clerk, but for what, I don't know.

YEPIKHODOV (*offended*): Whether I work, or wander about, or eat, or play billiards, these are matters to be discussed only by persons of discernment, and my elders.

VARYA: You dare say that to me! (*Flaring up.*) You dare? You mean to say I have no discernment? Get out of here! This instant!

YEPIKHODOV (*intimidated*): I beg you to express yourself in a more delicate manner.

VARYA (*beside herself*): Get out, this very instant! Get out! (*He goes to the door, she follows him.*) Two-and-twenty Troubles! Don't let me set eyes on you again!

YEPIKHODOV (*goes out, his voice is heard behind the door*): I shall lodge a complaint against you!

VARYA: Oh, you're coming back? (*Seizes the stick left near the door by Firs.*) Come, come on. . . . Come, I'll show you. . . . Ah, so you're coming, are you? Then take that — (*Swings the stick just as Lopakhin enters.*)

LOPAKHIN: Thank you kindly.

VARYA (*angrily and mockingly*): I beg your pardon.

LOPAKHIN: Not at all. I humbly thank you for your charming reception.

VARYA: Don't mention it. (*Walks away, then looks back and gently asks.*) I didn't hurt you, did I?

LOPAKHIN: No, it's nothing. A huge bump coming up, that's all.

(*Voices in the ballroom: "Lopakhin has come! Yermolai Alekseich!" Pishchik enters.*)

PISHCHIK: As I live and breathe! (*Kisses Lopakhin.*) There is a whiff of cognac about you, dear soul. And we've been making merry here, too.

(*Enter Lyubov Andreyevna.*)

LYUBOV ANDREYEVNA: Is that you, Yermolai Alekseich? What kept you so long? Where's Leonid?

LOPAKHIN: Leonid Andreich arrived with me, he's coming . . .

LYUBOV ANDREYEVNA (*agitated*): Well, what happened? Did the sale take place? Tell me!

LOPAKHIN (*embarrassed, fearing to reveal his joy*): The auction was over by four o'clock. . . . We missed the train, had to wait till half past nine. (*Sighing heavily.*) Ugh! My head is swimming. . . .

(*Enter Gayev; he carries his purchases in one hand and wipes away his tears with the other.*)

LYUBOV ANDREYEVNA: Lyonya, what happened? Well, Lyonya? (*Impatiently, through tears.*) Be quick, for God's sake!

GAYEV (*not answering her, simply waves his hand. To Firs, weeping*): Here, take these. . . . There's anchovies, Kerch herrings. . . . I haven't eaten anything all day. . . . What I have been through! (*The click of billiard balls is heard through the open door to the billiard room, and Yasha's voice: "Seven and eighteen!" Gayev's expression changes, he is no longer weeping.*) I'm terribly tired. Firs, help me change. (*Goes through the ballroom to his own room, followed by Firs.*)

PISHCHIK: What happened at the auction? Come on, tell us!

LYUBOV ANDREYEVNA: Is the cherry orchard sold?

LOPAKHIN: It's sold.

LYUBOV ANDREYEVNA: Who bought it?

LOPAKHIN: I bought it. (*Pause.*)

(*Lyubov Andreyevna is overcome; she would fall to the floor if it were not for the chair and table near which she stands. Varya takes the keys from her belt and throws them on the floor in the middle of the drawing room and goes out.*)

LOPAKHIN: I bought it! Kindly wait a moment, ladies and gentlemen, my head is swimming. I can't talk. . . . (*Laughs.*) We arrived at the auction, Deriganov was already there. Leonid Andreich had only fifteen thousand, and straight off Deriganov bid thirty thousand over and above the mortgage. I saw how the land lay, so I got into the fight and bid forty. He bid forty-five. I bid fifty-five. In other words, he kept raising it by five thousand, and I by ten. Well, it finally came to an end. I bid ninety thousand above the mortgage, and it was knocked down to me. The cherry orchard is now mine! Mine! (*Laughs uproariously.*) Lord! God in heaven! The cherry orchard is mine! Tell me I'm drunk, out of my mind, that I imagine it. . . . (*Stamps his feet.*) Don't laugh at me! If my father and my grandfather could only rise from their graves and see all that has happened, how their Yermolai, their beaten, half-literate Yermolai, who used to run about barefoot in winter, how that same Yermolai has bought an estate, the most beautiful estate in the whole world! I bought the estate where my father and grandfather were slaves, where they weren't even allowed in the kitchen. I'm asleep, this is just some dream of mine, it only seems to be. . . . It's the fruit of your imagination, hidden in the darkness of uncertainty. . . . (*Picks up the keys, smiling tenderly.*) She threw down the keys, wants to show that she's not mistress here anymore. . . . (*Jingles the keys.*) Well, no matter. (*The orchestra is heard tuning up.*) Hey, musicians, play, I want to hear you! Come on, everybody, and see how Yermolai Lopakhin will lay the ax to the cherry orchard, how the trees will fall to the ground! We're going to build summer cottages and our grandsons and great-grandsons will see a new life here. . . . Music! Strike up!

(*The orchestra plays. Lyubov Andreyevna sinks into a chair and weeps bitterly.*)

LOPAKHIN (*reproachfully*): Why didn't you listen to me, why? My poor friend, there's no turning back now. (*With tears.*) Oh, if only all this could be over quickly, if somehow our discordant, unhappy life could be changed!

PISHCHIK (*takes him by the arm; speaks in an undertone*): She's crying. Let's go into the ballroom, let her be alone. . . . Come on. . . . (*Leads him into the ballroom.*)

LOPAKHIN: What's happened? Musicians, play so I can hear you! Let everything be as I want it! (*Ironically.*) Here comes the new master, owner of the cherry orchard! (*Accidentally bumps into a little table, almost upsetting the candelabrum.*) I can pay for everything! (*Goes out with Pishchik.*)

(*There is no one left in either the drawing room or the ballroom except Lyubov Andreyevna, who sits huddled up and weeping bitterly. The music plays softly. Anya and Trofimov enter hurriedly. Anya goes to her mother and kneels before her. Trofimov remains in the doorway of the ballroom.*)

ANYA: Mama! . . . Mama, you're crying! Dear, kind, good Mama, my beautiful one, I love you . . . I bless you. The cherry orchard is sold, it's gone, that's true, true, but don't cry, Mama, life is still before you, you still have your good, pure soul. . . . Come with me, come, darling, we'll go away from here! . . . We'll plant a new orchard, more luxuriant than this one. You will see it and understand; and joy, quiet, deep joy, will sink into your soul, like the evening sun, and you will smile, Mama! Come, darling, let us go. . . .

ACT IV

(*The scene is the same as act I. There are neither curtains on the windows nor pictures on the walls, and only a little furniture piled up in one corner, as if for sale. There is a sense of emptiness. Near the outer door, at the rear of the stage, suitcases, traveling bags, etc., are piled up. Through the open door on the left the voices of Varya and Anya can be heard. Lopakhin stands waiting. Yasha is holding a tray with little glasses of champagne. In the hall, Yepikhodov is tying up a box. Offstage, at the rear, there is a hum of voices. It is the peasants who have come to say good-bye. Gayev's voice: "Thanks, brothers, thank you."*)

YASHA: The peasants have come to say good-bye. In my opinion, Yermolai Alekseich, peasants are good-natured, but they don't know much.

(*The hum subsides. Lyubov Andreyevna enters from the hall with Gayev. She is not crying, but she is pale, her face twitches, and she cannot speak.*)

GAYEV: You gave them your purse, Lyuba. That won't do! That won't do!

LYUBOV ANDREYEVNA: I couldn't help it! I couldn't help it! (*They both go out.*)

LOPAKHIN (*in the doorway, calls after them*): Please, do me the honor of having a little glass at parting. I didn't think of bringing champagne from town, and at the station I found only one bottle. Please! What's the matter, friends, don't you want any? (*Walks away from the door.*) If I'd known that, I wouldn't have bought it. Well, then I won't drink any either. (*Yasha carefully sets the tray down on a chair.*) At least you have a glass, Yasha.

YASHA: To those who are departing! Good luck! (*Drinks.*) This champagne is not the real stuff, I can assure you.

LOPAKHIN: Eight rubles a bottle. (*Pause.*) It's devilish cold in here.

YASHA: They didn't light the stoves today; it doesn't matter, since we're leaving. (*Laughs.*)

LOPAKHIN: Why are you laughing?

YASHA: Because I'm pleased.

LOPAKHIN: It's October, yet it's sunny and still outside, like summer. Good for building. (*Looks at his watch, then calls through the door.*) Bear in mind, ladies and gentlemen, only forty-six minutes till train time! That means leaving for the station in twenty minutes. Better hurry up!

(*Trofimov enters from outside wearing an overcoat.*)

TROFIMOV: Seems to me it's time to start. The carriages are at the door. What the devil has become of my rubbers? They're lost. (*Calls through the door.*) Anya, my rubbers are not here. I can't find them.

LOPAKHIN: I've got to go to Kharkov. I'm taking the same train you are. I'm going to spend the winter in Kharkov. I've been hanging around here with you, and I'm sick and tired of loafing. I can't live without work, I don't know what to do with my hands; they dangle in some strange way, as if they didn't belong to me.

TROFIMOV: We'll soon be gone, then you can take up your useful labors again.

LOPAKHIN: Here, have a little drink.

TROFIMOV: No, I don't want any.

LOPAKHIN: So you're off for Moscow?

TROFIMOV: Yes, I'll see them into town, and tomorrow I'll go to Moscow.

LOPAKHIN: Yes. . . . Well, I expect the professors haven't been giving any lectures: They're waiting for you to come!

TROFIMOV: That's none of your business.

LOPAKHIN: How many years is it you've been studying at the university?

TROFIMOV: Can't you think of something new? That's stale and flat. (*Looks for his rubbers.*) You know we'll probably never see each other again, so allow me to give you one piece of advice at parting: Don't wave your arms about! Get out of that habit — of arm-waving. And another thing, building cottages and counting on the summer residents in time becoming independent farmers — that's just another form of arm-waving. Well, when all's said and done, I'm fond of you anyway. You have fine, delicate fingers, like an artist; you have a fine delicate soul.

LOPAKHIN (*embraces him*): Good-bye, my dear fellow. Thank you for everything. Let me give you some money for the journey, if you need it.

TROFIMOV: What for? I don't need it.

LOPAKHIN: But you haven't any!

TROFIMOV: I have. Thank you. I got some money for a translation. Here it is in my pocket. (*Anxiously.*) But where are my rubbers?

VARYA (*from the next room*): Here, take the nasty things! (*Flings a pair of rubbers onto the stage.*)

TROFIMOV: What are you so cross about, Varya? Hm. . . . But these are not my rubbers.

LOPAKHIN: In the spring I sowed three thousand acres of poppies, and now I've made forty thousand rubles clear. And when my poppies were in bloom, what a picture it was! So, I'm telling you, I've made forty thousand, which means I'm offering you a loan because I can afford to. Why turn up your nose? I'm a peasant — I speak bluntly.

TROFIMOV: Your father was a peasant, mine was a pharmacist — which proves absolutely nothing. (*Lopakhin takes out his wallet.*) No, don't — even if you gave me two hundred thousand I wouldn't take it. I'm a free man. And everything that is valued so highly and held so dear by all of you, rich and poor alike, has not the slightest power over me — it's like a feather floating in the air. I can get along without you, I can pass you by, I'm strong and proud.

Mankind is advancing toward the highest truth, the highest happiness attainable on earth, and I am in the front ranks!

LOPAKHIN: Will you get there?

TROFIMOV: I'll get there. (*Pause.*) I'll either get there or I'll show others the way to get there.

(*The sound of axes chopping down trees is heard in the distance.*)

LOPAKHIN: Well, good-bye, my dear fellow. It's time to go. We turn up our noses at one another, but life goes on just the same. When I work for a long time without stopping, my mind is easier, and it seems to me that I, too, know why I exist. But how many there are in Russia, brother, who exist nobody knows why. Well, it doesn't matter, that's not what makes the wheels go round. They say Leonid Andreich has taken a position in the bank, six thousand a year. . . . Only, of course, he won't stick it out, he's too lazy. . . .

ANYA (*in the doorway*): Mama asks you not to start cutting down the cherry orchard until she's gone.

TROFIMOV: Yes, really, not to have had the tact . . . (*Goes out through the hall.*)

LOPAKHIN: Right away, right away. . . . Ach, what people. . . . (*Follows Trofimov out.*)

ANYA: Has Firs been taken to the hospital?

YASHA: I told them this morning. They must have taken him.

ANYA (*to Yepikhodov, who is crossing the room*): Semyon Panteleich, please find out if Firs has been taken to the hospital.

YASHA (*offended*): I told Yegor this morning. Why ask a dozen times?

YEPIKHODOV: It is my conclusive opinion that the venerable Firs is beyond repair; it's time he was gathered to his fathers. And I can only envy him. (*Puts a suitcase down on a hatbox and crushes it.*) There you are! Of course! I knew it! (*Goes out.*)

YASHA (*mockingly*): Two-and-twenty Troubles!

VARYA (*through the door*): Has Firs been taken to the hospital?

ANYA: Yes, he has.

VARYA: Then why didn't they take the letter to the doctor?

ANYA: We must send it on after them. . . . (*Goes out.*)

VARYA (*from the adjoining room*): Where is Yasha? Tell him his mother has come to say good-bye to him.

YASHA (*waves his hand*): They really try my patience.

(*Dunyasha has been fussing with the luggage; now that Yasha is alone she goes up to him.*)

DUNYASHA: You might give me one little look, Yasha. You're going away . . . leaving me. . . . (*Cries and throws herself on his neck.*)

YASHA: What's there to cry about? (*Drinks champagne.*) In six days I'll be in Paris again. Tomorrow we'll take the express, off we go, and that's the last you'll see of us. I can hardly believe it. *Vive la France!* This place is not for me, I can't live here. . . . It can't be helped.

I've had enough of this ignorance — I'm fed up with it. (*Drinks champagne.*) What are you crying for? Behave yourself properly, then you won't cry.

DUNYASHA (*looks into a small mirror and powders her face*): Send me a letter from Paris. You know, I loved you, Yasha, how I loved you! I'm such a tender creature, Yasha!

YASHA: Here they come. (*Busies himself with the luggage, humming softly.*)

(*Enter Lyubov Andreyevna, Gayev, Charlotta Ivanovna.*)

GAYEV: We ought to be leaving. There's not much time now. (*Looks at Yasha.*) Who smells of herring?

LYUBOV ANDREYEVNA: In about ten minutes we should be getting into the carriages. (*Glances around the room.*) Good-bye, dear house, old grandfather. Winter will pass, spring will come, and you will no longer be here, they will tear you down. How much these walls have seen! (*Kisses her daughter warmly.*) My treasure, you are radiant, your eyes are sparkling like two diamonds. Are you glad? Very?

ANYA: Very! A new life is beginning, Mama!

GAYEV (*cheerfully*): Yes, indeed, everything is all right now. Before the cherry orchard was sold we were all worried and miserable, but afterward, when the question was finally settled once and for all, everybody calmed down and felt quite cheerful. . . . I'm in a bank now, a financier . . . cue ball into the center . . . and you, Lyuba, say what you like, you look better, no doubt about it.

LYUBOV ANDREYEVNA: Yes. My nerves are better, that's true. (*Her hat and coat are handed to her.*) I sleep well. Carry out my things, Yasha, it's time. (*To Anya.*) My little girl, we shall see each other soon. . . . I shall go to Paris and live there on the money your great-aunt sent to buy the estate — long live Auntie! — but that money won't last long.

ANYA: You'll come back soon, Mama, soon . . . won't you? I'll study hard and pass my high school examinations, and then I can work and help you. We'll read all sorts of books together, Mama. . . . Won't we? (*Kisses her mother's hand.*) We'll read in the autumn evenings, we'll read lots of books, and a new and wonderful world will open up before us. . . . (*Dreaming.*) Mama, come back. . . .

LYUBOV ANDREYEVNA: I'll come, my precious. (*Embraces her.*)

(*Enter Lopakhin, Charlotta Ivanovna is softly humming a song.*)

GAYEV: Happy Charlotta: She's singing!

CHARLOTTA (*picks up a bundle and holds it like a baby in swaddling clothes*): Bye, baby, bye. . . . (*A baby's crying is heard, "Wah! Wah!"*) Be quiet, my darling, my dear little boy. ("*Wah! Wah!*") I'm so sorry for you! (*Throws the bundle down.*) You will find me a position, won't you? I can't go on like this.

LOPAKHIN: We'll find something, Charlotta Ivanovna, don't worry.

GAYEV: Everyone is leaving us, Varya's going away . . . all of a sudden nobody needs us.

CHARLOTTA: I have nowhere to go in town. I must go away. (*Hums.*) It doesn't matter . . .

(*Enter Pishchik.*)

LOPAKHIN: Nature's wonder!

PISHCHIK (*panting*): Ugh! Let me catch my breath. . . . I'm exhausted. . . . My esteemed friends. . . . Give me some water. . . .

GAYEV: After money, I suppose? Excuse me, I'm fleeing from temptation. . . . (*Goes out.*)

PISHCHIK: It's a long time since I've been to see you . . . fairest lady. . . . (*To Lopakhin*) So you're here. . . . Glad to see you, you intellectual giant. . . . Here . . . take it . . . four hundred rubles . . . I still owe you eight hundred and forty . . .

LOPAKHIN (*shrugs his shoulders in bewilderment*): I must be dreaming. . . . Where did you get it?

PISHCHIK: Wait . . . I'm hot. . . . A most extraordinary event. Some Englishmen came to my place and discovered some kind of white clay on my land. (*To Lyubov Andreyevna*) And four hundred for you . . . fairest, most wonderful lady. . . . (*Hands her the money.*) The rest later. (*Takes a drink of water.*) Just now a young man in the train was saying that a certain . . . great philosopher recommends jumping off roofs. . . . "Jump!" he says, and therein lies the whole problem. (*In amazement.*) Think of that, now! . . . Water!

LOPAKHIN: Who were those Englishmen?

PISHCHIK: I leased them the tract of land with the clay on it for twenty-four years. . . . And now, excuse me, I have no time . . . I must be trotting along . . . I'm going to Znoikov's . . . to Kardamanov's . . . I owe everybody. (*Drinks.*) Keep well . . . I'll drop in on Thursday . . .

LYUBOV ANDREYEVNA: We're just moving into town, and tomorrow I go abroad . . .

PISHCHIK: What? (*Alarmed.*) Why into town? That's why I see the furniture . . . suitcases. . . . Well, never mind. . . . (*Through tears.*) Never mind. . . . Men of the greatest intellect, those Englishmen. . . . Never mind. . . . Be happy . . . God will help you. . . . Never mind. . . . Everything in this world comes to an end. . . . (*Kisses Lyubov Andreyevna's hand.*) And should the news reach you that my end has come, just remember this old horse, and say: "There once lived a certain Semyonov-Pishchik, God rest his soul." . . . Splendid weather. . . . Yes. . . . (*Goes out greatly disconcerted, but immediately returns and speaks from the doorway.*) Dashenka sends her regards. (*Goes out.*)

LYUBOV ANDREYEVNA: Now we can go. I am leaving with two things on my mind. First — that Firs is sick. (*Looks at her watch.*) We still have about five minutes. . . .

ANYA: Mama, Firs has already been taken to the hospital. Yasha sent him there this morning.

LYUBOV ANDREYEVNA: My second concern is Varya. She's used to getting up early and working, and now, with no work to do, she's like a fish out of water. She's grown pale and thin, and cries all the time, poor girl. . . . (*Pauses.*) You know very well, Yermolai Alekseich, that I dreamed of marrying her to you, and everything pointed to your getting married. (*Whispers to Anya, who nods to Charlotta, and they both go out.*) She loves you, you are fond of her, and I don't know — I don't know why it is you seem to avoid each other. I can't understand it!

LOPAKHIN: To tell you the truth, I don't understand it myself. The whole thing is strange, somehow. . . . If there's still time, I'm ready right now. . . . Let's finish it up — and *basta,*° but without you I feel I'll never be able to propose to her.

LYUBOV ANDREYEVNA: Splendid! After all, it only takes a minute. I'll call her in at once.

LOPAKHIN: And we even have the champagne. (*Looks at the glasses.*) Empty! Somebody's already drunk it. (*Yasha coughs.*) That's what you call lapping it up.

LYUBOV ANDREYEVNA (*animatedly*): Splendid! We'll leave you. . . . Yasha, *allez!*° I'll call her. . . . (*At the door.*) Varya, leave everything and come here. Come! (*Goes out with Yasha.*)

LOPAKHIN (*looking at his watch*): Yes. . . . (*Pause.*)

(*Behind the door there is smothered laughter and whispering; finally Varya enters.*)

VARYA (*looking over the luggage for a long time*): Strange, I can't seem to find it . . .

LOPAKHIN: What are you looking for?

VARYA: I packed it myself, and I can't remember . . . (*Pause.*)

LOPAKHIN: Where are you going now, Varya Mikhailovna?

VARYA: I? To the Ragulins'. . . . I've agreed to go there to look after the house . . . as a sort of housekeeper.

LOPAKHIN: At Yashnevo? That would be about seventy versts from here. (*Pause.*) Well, life in this house has come to an end. . . .

VARYA (*examining the luggage*): Where can it be? . . . Perhaps I put it in the trunk. . . . Yes, life in this house has come to an end . . . there'll be no more . . .

LOPAKHIN: And I'm off for Kharkov . . . by the next train. I have a lot to do. I'm leaving Yepikhodov here . . . I've taken him on.

VARYA: Really!

LOPAKHIN: Last year at this time it was already snowing, if you remember, but now it's still and sunny. It's cold though. . . . About three degrees of frost.

VARYA: I haven't looked. (*Pause.*) And besides, our thermometer's broken. (*Pause.*)

(*A voice from the yard calls: "Yermolai Alekseich!"*)

LOPAKHIN (*as if he had been waiting for a long time for the call*): Coming! (*Goes out quickly.*)

basta: Italian for "enough."   *allez!*: French for "go!"

(*Varya sits on the floor, lays her head on a bundle of clothes, and quietly sobs. The door opens and Lyubov Andreyevna enters cautiously.*)

LYUBOV ANDREYEVNA: Well? (*Pause.*) We must be going.

VARYA (*no longer crying, dries her eyes*): Yes, it's time, Mama dear. I can get to the Ragulins' today, if only we don't miss the train.

LYUBOV ANDREYEVNA (*in the doorway*): Anya, put your things on!

(*Enter Anya, then Gayev and Charlotta Ivanovna. Gayev wears a warm overcoat with a hood. The servants and coachmen come in. Yepikhodov bustles about the luggage.*)

LYUBOV ANDREYEVNA: Now we can be on our way.

ANYA (*joyfully*): On our way!

GAYEV: My friends, my dear, cherished friends! Leaving this house forever, can I pass over in silence, can I refrain from giving utterance, as we say farewell, to those feelings that now fill my whole being —

ANYA (*imploringly*): Uncle!

VARYA: Uncle dear, don't!

GAYEV (*forlornly*): Double the rail off the white to center table . . . yellow into the side pocket. . . . I'll be quiet. . . .

(*Enter Trofimov, then Lopakhin.*)

TROFIMOV: Well, ladies and gentlemen, it's time to go!

LOPAKHIN: Yepikhodov, my coat!

LYUBOV ANDREYEVNA: I'll sit here just one more minute. It's as though I had never before seen what the walls of this house were like, what the ceilings were like, and now I look at them hungrily, with such tender love . . .

GAYEV: I remember when I was six years old, sitting on this windowsill on Whitsunday, watching my father going to church . . .

LYUBOV ANDREYEVNA: Have they taken all the things?

LOPAKHIN: Everything, I think. (*Puts on his overcoat.*) Yepikhodov, see that everything is in order.

YEPIKHODOV (*in a hoarse voice*): Rest assured, Yermolai Alekseich!

LOPAKHIN: What's the matter with your voice?

YEPIKHODOV: Just drank some water . . . must have swallowed something.

YASHA (*contemptuously*): What ignorance!

LYUBOV ANDREYEVNA: When we go — there won't be a soul left here. . . .

LOPAKHIN: Till spring.

VARYA (*pulls an umbrella out of a bundle as though she were going to hit someone; Lopakhin pretends to be frightened*): Why are you — I never thought of such a thing!

TROFIMOV: Ladies and gentlemen, let's get into the carriages — it's time now! The train will soon be in!

VARYA: Petya, there they are — your rubbers, by the suitcase. (*Tearfully.*) And what dirty old things they are!

TROFIMOV (*putting on his rubbers*): Let's go, ladies and gentlemen!

GAYEV (*extremely upset, afraid of bursting into tears*): The train . . . the station. . . . Cross table to the center, double the rail . . . on the white into the corner.

LYUBOV ANDREYEVNA: Let us go!

GAYEV: Are we all here? No one in there? (*Locks the side door on the left.*) There are some things stored in there, we must lock up. Let's go!

ANYA: Good-bye, house! Good-bye, old life!

TROFIMOV: Hail to the new life! (*Goes out with Anya.*)

(*Varya looks around the room and slowly goes out. Yasha and Charlotta with her dog go out.*)

LOPAKHIN: And so, till spring. Come along, my friends. . . . Till we meet! (*Goes out.*)

(*Lyubov Andreyevna and Gayev are left alone. As though they had been waiting for this, they fall onto each other's necks and break into quiet, restrained sobs, afraid of being heard.*)

GAYEV (*in despair*): My sister, my sister. . . .

LYUBOV ANDREYEVNA: Oh, my dear, sweet, lovely orchard! . . . My life, my youth, my happiness, good-bye! . . . Good-bye!

ANYA'S VOICE (*gaily calling*): Mama!

TROFIMOV'S VOICE (*gay and excited*): Aa-oo!

LYUBOV ANDREYEVNA: One last look at these walls, these windows. . . . Mother loved to walk about in this room. . . .

GAYEV: My sister, my sister!

ANYA'S VOICE: Mama!

TROFIMOV'S VOICE: Aa-oo!

LYUBOV ANDREYEVNA: We're coming! (*They go out.*)

(*The stage is empty. There is the sound of doors being locked, then of the carriages driving away. It grows quiet. In the stillness there is the dull thud of an ax on a tree, a forlorn, melancholy sound. Footsteps are heard. From the door on the right Firs appears. He is dressed as always in a jacket and white waistcoat, and wears slippers. He is ill.*)

FIRS (*goes to the door and tries the handle*): Locked. They have gone. . . . (*Sits down on the sofa.*) They've forgotten me. . . . Never mind. . . . I'll sit here awhile. . . . I expect Leonid Andreich hasn't put on his fur coat and has gone off in his overcoat. (*Sighs anxiously.*) And I didn't see to it. . . . When they're young, they're green! (*Mumbles something which cannot be understood.*) I'll lie down awhile. . . . There's no strength left in you, nothing's left, nothing. . . . Ach, you . . . addlepate! (*Lies motionless.*)

(*A distant sound is heard that seems to come from the sky, the sound of a snapped string mournfully dying away. A stillness falls, and nothing is heard but the thud of the ax on a tree far away in the orchard.*)

COMMENTARIES

Anton Chekhov (1860–1904)
FROM *LETTERS OF ANTON CHEKOV*   *1888–1903*

TRANSLATED BY MICHAEL HENRY HEIM WITH SIMON KARLINSKY

Chekhov, like Ibsen, was an inveterate letter writer. In letters to family members and colleagues, he spoke quite frankly about his hopes, expectations, and difficulties regarding his work. Chekhov's letters concerning his purpose as an artist and his play The Cherry Orchard *give us some insight into the anxieties and hopes that Chekhov had for his work. His awareness of the difficulties he faced in his writing helps us understand how his plays developed into complex and demanding works.*

October 4, 1888

The people I fear are those who look for tendentiousness between the lines and are determined to see me as either liberal or conservative. I am neither liberal, nor conservative, nor gradualist, nor monk, nor indifferentist. I should like to be a free artist and nothing else. That is why I cultivate no particular predilection for policemen, butchers, scientists, writers, or the younger generation. I look upon tags and labels as prejudices. My holy of holies is the human body, health, intelligence, talent, inspiration, love and the most absolute freedom imaginable, freedom from violence and lies.

November 25, 1892

Keep in mind that the writers we call eternal or simply good, the writers who intoxicate us, have one highly important trait in common: They are moving towards something definite and beckon you to follow, and you feel with your entire being, not only with your mind, that they have a certain goal, like the ghost of Hamlet's father, which had a motive for coming and stirring Hamlet's imagination. Depending on their caliber, some have immediate goals — the abolition of serfdom, the liberation of one's country, politics, beauty, or simply vodka . . . — while the goals of others are more remote — God, life after death, the happiness of mankind, etc. The best of them are realistic and describe life as it is, but because each line is saturated with the consciousness of its goal, you feel life as it should be in addition to life as it is, and you are captivated by it. But what about us? Us! We describe life as it is and stop dead right there. We wouldn't lift a hoof if you lit into us with a whip. We have neither immediate nor remote goals, and there is an emptiness in our souls. We have no politics, we don't believe in revolution, there is no God, we're not afraid of ghosts, and I personally am not even afraid of death or blindness. If you want nothing, hope for nothing, and fear nothing, you cannot be an artist.

To K. S. Stanislavsky°
Yalta. Oct. 30, 1903

When I was writing Lopakhin, I thought of it as a part for you. If for any reason you don't care for it, take the part of Gayev. Lopakhin is a merchant, of course, but he is a very decent person in every sense. He must behave with perfect decorum, like an educated man, with no petty ways or tricks of any sort, and it seemed to me this part, the central one of the play, would come out brilliantly in your hands. . . . In choosing an actor for the part you must remember that Varya, a serious and religious girl, is in love with Lopakhin; she wouldn't be in love with a mere money-grubber. . . .

To Vl. I. Nemirovich-Danchenko°
Yalta. Nov. 2, 1903

. . . Pishchik is a Russian, an old man, worn out by the gout, age, and satiety; stout, dressed in a sleeveless undercoat (à la Simov [an actor in the Moscow Art Theatre]), boots without heels. Lopakhin — a white waistcoat, yellow shoes; when walking, swings his arms, a broad stride, thinks deeply while walking, walks as if on a straight line. Hair not short, and therefore often throws back his head; while in thought he passes his hand through his beard, combing it from the back forward, i.e., from the neck toward the mouth. Trofimov, I think, is clear. Varya — black dress, wide belt.

Three years I spent writing "The Cherry Orchard," and for three years I have been telling you that it is necessary to invite an actress for the role of Lyubov Andreyevna. And now you see you are trying to solve a puzzle that won't work out.

To K. S. Alekseyev (Stanislavsky)
Yalta. Nov. 5, 1903

The house in the play is two-storied, a large one. But in the third act does it not speak of a stairway leading down? Nevertheless, this third act worries me. . . . N. has it that the third act takes place in "some kind of hotel"; . . . evidently I made an error in the play. The action does not pass in "some kind of hotel," but in a *drawing-room*. If I mention a hotel in the play, which I cannot now doubt, after Vl. Iv.'s [Nemirovich-Danchenko] letter, please telegraph me. We must correct it; we cannot issue it thus, with grave errors distorting its meaning.

The house must be large, solid; wooden (like Aksakov's, which, I think, S. T. Morozov has seen) or stone, it is all the same. It is very old and imposing; country residents do not take such houses; such houses are usually wrecked and the material employed for the construction of a country house. The furniture is ancient, stylish, solid; ruin and debt have not affected the surroundings.

When they buy such a house, they reason thus: it is cheaper and easier to build a new and smaller one than to repair this old one.

Your shepherd played well. That was most essential.

K. S. Stanislavsky: Konstantin Stanislavsky (1863–1938), director with the Moscow Art Theatre, which produced most of Chekhov's plays.
Vl. I. Nemirovich-Danchenko: Vladimir Ivanovich Nemirovich-Danchenko (1858–1943), novelist and codirector of the Moscow Art Theatre.

Maxim Gorky (1868–1936)

FROM *RECOLLECTIONS*   *1921*

TRANSLATED BY KATHERINE MANSFIELD

Alexei Maximovitch Pyeshkov changed his name to Maxim Gorky, which in Russian means "Maxim the Bitter." His childhood and early years gave him great reason for bitterness because he was raised by a brutal grandfather who regularly beat Maxim and his mother. Once, when Maxim was eight, he attacked his grandfather with a bread knife for beating his frail and sick mother. Gorky spent many years tramping through Russia and became a writer of the common people. He was introduced to the Moscow Art Theatre by Chekhov, and his first play, The Lower Depths *(1902), starred Chekhov's wife, Olga Knipper. It was a mercilessly realistic portrait of the homeless, impoverished castaways of Russian life. It established Gorky as a major dramatist, and after the Russian revolution he became the most revered of Soviet writers.*

Reading Anton Chekhov's stories, one feels oneself in a melancholy day of late autumn, when the air is transparent and the outline of naked trees, narrow houses, grayish people, is sharp. Everything is strange, lonely, motionless, helpless. The horizon, blue and empty, melts into the pale sky, and its breath is terribly cold upon the earth, which is covered with frozen mud. The author's mind, like the autumn sun, shows up in hard outline the monotonous roads, the crooked streets, the little squalid houses in which tiny, miserable people are stifled by boredom and laziness and fill the houses with an unintelligible, drowsy bustle. . . .

Here is the lachrymose Ranevskaya and the other owners of *The Cherry Orchard,* egotistical like children, with the flabbiness of senility. They missed the right moment for dying; they whine, seeing nothing of what is going on around them, understanding nothing, parasites without the power of again taking root in life. The wretched little student, Trofimov, speaks eloquently of the necessity of working — and does nothing but amuse himself, out of sheer boredom, with stupid mockery of Varya, who works ceaselessly for the good of idlers. . . .

There passes before one a long file of men and women, slaves of their love, of their stupidity and idleness, of their greed for the good things of life; there walk the slaves of the dark fear of life; they straggle anxiously along, filling life with incoherent words about the future, feeling that in the present there is no place for them.

At moments out of the gray mass of them one hears the sound of a shot: Ivanov [in *Ivanov*] or Treplev [in *The Seagull*] has guessed what he ought to do and has died.

Many of them have nice dreams of how pleasant life will be in three hundred years, but it occurs to none of them to ask themselves who will make life pleasant if we only dream.

In front of that dreary, gray crowd of helpless people there passed a great, wise, and observant man; he looked at all these dreary inhabitants of his country, and, with a sad smile, with a tone of gentle but deep reproach, with anguish in his face and in his heart, in a beautiful and sincere voice, he said to them:

"You live badly, my friends. It is shameful to live like that."

Virginia Woolf (1882–1941)
ON *THE CHERRY ORCHARD*   1920

Virginia Woolf was one of the most important experimental writers of fiction in the first half of the twentieth century. Her best-known works include Mrs. Dalloway *(1925),* To the Lighthouse *(1927),* Orlando *(1928),* A Room of One's Own *(1930), and* The Waves *(1931). But in addition to these landmark works, she wrote a huge number of essays and commentaries, not to mention letters that have now been gathered into five large volumes. Her insight into literature is always keen and original. Her approach, for instance, to a 1920 production of* The Cherry Orchard *is through language. She is naturally sensitive to careful use of language, and it is therefore important for her to observe that out of the apparently disjointed use of sentences comes extraordinary drama. She ends her commentary with an interesting comparison that delves into the realm of music — or, more properly, into an imaginative realm in which the theatergoers themselves are musical instruments.*

It is, as a rule, when a critic does not wish to commit himself or to trouble himself, that he refers to atmosphere. And, given time, something might be said in greater detail of the causes which produced this atmosphere — the strange dislocated sentences, each so erratic and yet cutting out the shape so firmly, of the realism, of the humor, of the artistic unity. But let the word atmosphere be taken literally to mean that Chekhov has contrived to shed over us a luminous vapor in which life appears as it is, without veils, transparent and visible to the depths. Long before the play was over, we seemed to have sunk below the surface of things and to be feeling our way among submerged but recognizable emotions. "I have no proper passport. I don't know how old I am; I always feel I am still young"— how the words go sounding on in one's mind — how the whole play resounds with such sentences, which reverberate, melt into each other, and pass far away out beyond everything! In short, if it is permissible to use such vague language, I do not know how better to describe the sensation at the end of *The Cherry Orchard*, than by saying that it sends one into the street feeling like a piano played upon at last, not in the middle only but all over the keyboard and with the lid left open so that the sound goes on.

John Corbin (1870–1959)
REVIEW OF *THE CHERRY ORCHARD*   1923

After brief praise for the Russian-language production of the Moscow Players, John Corbin's review centers itself entirely on an analysis of the play. Clearly, he sees the main characters as feckless and wasteful and has little sympathy for them. On the other hand, he sees in Lopakhin a man of industry and progress. His interpretation may well depend on the emphasis of the postrevolutionary Russian players, whose sympathies would certainly not have aligned with aristocrats.

The Moscow players proceeded last night from the lower depths of Gorky to the high comedy of Tchekhoff, revealing new artistic resources. Stanislavsky, Olga Knipper-Tchekhova, Moskvin, Leonidoff and half a dozen others entered with consummate ease into a rich variety of new characterizations. The stage management was less signal in its effects, but no less perfect. Yet for some reason *The Cherry Orchard* failed to stir the audience, even the Russian portion of it, as did *The Lower Depths* and even *Tsar Fyodor*.

This is a play of comedy values both high and light. The milleu is that of the ancient landed aristocracy, beautifully symbolized by an orchard of cherry trees in full bloom which surrounds the crumbling manor house. Quite obviously, these amiable folks have fallen away from the pristine vigor of their race.

The middle-aged brother and sister who live together are unconscious, irreclaimable spendthrifts, both of their shrinking purses and of their waning lives. With a little effort, one is made to feel, even with a modicum of mental concentration, calamity could be averted. But that is utterly beyond their vacuous and futile amiability; so their estate is sold over their heads and the leagues of gay cherry trees are felled to make way for suburban villas.

Beneath the graceful, easy-going surface of the play one feels rather than perceives a criticism on the Russia of two decades ago. Here is a woman of truly Slavic instability, passing with a single gesture from heartbreak to the gayety of a moment, from acutely maternal grief for an only child long dead to weak doting on a Parisian lover who is faithless to her and yet has power to hold her and batten on her bounty. Here is a man whose sentiment for the home of his ancestors breaks forth in fluent declaiming, quasi-poetic and quasi-philosophic, yet who cannot lift a finger to avert financial disaster.

In the entire cast only one person has normal human sense. Lopakhin is the son of a serf who has prospered in freedom. He is loyal enough to the old masters, dogging their footsteps with good advice. But in the end it is he who buys the estate and fells the cherry trees for the villas of an industrial population. It is as if Tchekhoff saw in the new middle class the hope of a disenchanted yet sounder and more progressive Russia. The war has halted that movement, but indications are not lacking that it is already resuming.

With such a theme developed by the subtly masterful act of Tchekhoff there is scope for comedy acting of the highest quality. It is more than likely that the company seized every opportunity and improved upon it. But to any one who does not understand Russian, judgment in such a matter is quite impossible. Where effects are to be achieved only by the subtlest intonation, the most delicate phrasing, it fares ill with those whose entire vocabulary is da, da.

As an example of the art of the most distinguished company that has visited our shores in modern memory, this production of *The Cherry Orchard* is abundantly worth seeing. The play in itself is of interest as the masterpiece of the man who, with Gorky, has touched the pinnacle of modern Russian comedy. But if some Moscovite should rise up and tell us that in any season our own stage produces casts as perfect and ensembles as finely studied in detail, it would be quite possible to believe him.

Peter Brook (b. 1925)
ON CHEKHOV

1987

Peter Brook has established himself as one of the most distinguished directors of recent years. He was educated at Oxford University and has been a director of the Royal Shakespeare Company in England. In 1987 he directed The Cherry Orchard *at the Brooklyn Academy of Music. Some of his thoughts as he prepared to direct the play are presented here, showing his awareness of Chekhov's "film sense" in a play that was written just as film was emerging as a popular form. He is also aware of Chekhov's personal vision of death and sees it expressed in the circumstances of the play.*

Chekhov always looked for what's natural; he wanted performances and productions to be as limpid as life itself. Chekhov's writing is extremely concentrated, employing a minimum of words; in a way, it is similar to Pinter or Beckett. As with them, it is construction that counts, rhythm, the purely theatrical poetry that comes not from beautiful words but from the right word at the right moment. In the theater, someone can say "yes" in such a way that the "yes" is no longer ordinary — it can become a beautiful word, because it is the perfect expression of what cannot be expressed in any other way. With Chekhov, periods, commas, points of suspension are all of a fundamental importance, as fundamental as the "pauses" precisely indicated by Beckett. If one fails to observe them, one loses the rhythm and tensions of the play. In Chekhov's work, the punctuation represents a series of coded messages which record characters' relationships and emotions, the moments at which ideas come together or follow their own course. The punctuation enables us to grasp what the words conceal.

Chekhov is like a perfect filmmaker. Instead of cutting from one image to another — perhaps from one place to another — he switches from one emotion to another just before it gets too heavy. At the precise moment when the spectator risks becoming too involved in a character, an unexpected situation cuts across: Nothing is stable. Chekhov portrays individuals and a society in a state of perpetual change, he is the dramatist of life's movement, simultaneously smiling and serious, amusing and bitter — completely free from the "music," the Slav "nostalgia" that Paris nightclubs still preserve. He often stated that his plays were comedies — this was the central issue of his conflict with Stanislavsky.

But it's wrong to conclude that *The Cherry Orchard* should be performed as a vaudeville. Chekhov is an infinitely detailed observer of the human comedy. As a doctor, he knew the meaning of certain kinds of behavior, how to discern what was essential, to expose what he diagnosed. Although he shows tenderness and an attentive sympathy, he never sentimentalizes. One doesn't imagine a doctor shedding tears over the illnesses of his patients. He learns how to balance compassion with distance.

In Chekhov's work, death is omnipresent — he knew it well — but there is nothing negative or unsavory in its presence. The awareness of death is balanced with a desire to live. His characters possess a sense of the present moment, and the need to taste it fully. As in great tragedies, one finds a harmony between life and death.

Chekhov died young, having traveled, written, and loved enormously, having taken part in the events of his day, in great schemes of social reform. He died shortly after asking for some champagne, and his coffin was transported in a wagon bearing the inscription "Fresh Oysters." His awareness of death, and of the precious moments that could be lived, endow his work with a sense of the relative: in other words, a viewpoint from which the tragic is always a bit absurd.

In Chekhov's work, each character has its own existence: not one of them resembles another, particularly in *The Cherry Orchard,* which presents a microcosm of the political tendencies of the time. There are those who believe in social transformations, others attached to a disappearing past. None of them can achieve satisfaction or plenitude, and seen from outside, their existences might well appear empty, senseless. But they all burn with intense desires. They are not disillusioned, quite the contrary: In their own ways, they are all searching for a better quality of life, emotionally and socially. Their drama is that society — the outside world — blocks their energy. The complexity of their behavior is not indicated in the words, it emerges from the mosaic construction of an infinite number of details. What is essential is to see that these are not plays about lethargic people. They are hypervital people in a lethargic world, forced to dramatize the minutest happening out of a passionate desire to live. They have not given up.

Drama in the Early and Mid-Twentieth Century

The realist tradition in drama had certain EXPRESSIONIST qualities evident in the symbolic actions in Strindberg's *Miss Julie* and the romantic fantasies of Hedda in *Hedda Gabler*. But the surfaces of the plays appear realistic, consisting of a sequence of events that we might imagine happening in real life. The subject matter is also in the tradition of naturalism because it is drawn from life and not beautified or toned down for the middle-class audience.

But in the early to mid-twentieth century realistic drama took a new turn, incorporating distortions of reality that border on the unreal or *surreal*. From the time of Anton Chekhov in 1903 to Samuel Beckett in the 1950s, drama exploited the possibilities of realism, antirealism, and the poetic expansion of expressionism.

The Heritage of Realism

In the late nineteenth century realism was often perceived as too severe for an audience that had loved melodrama. Realistic plays forced comfortable audiences to observe psychological and physical problems that their status as members of the middle class usually allowed them to avoid. Audiences often protested loudly at this painful experience.

The technique of realism could, however, be adapted for many different purposes, and eventually realism was reshaped to satisfy middle-class sensibilities by commercial playwrights, who produced popular, pleasant plays. By the 1920s in Europe and the 1930s in America, theatergoing audiences expected plays to be realistic. Even the light comedies dominating the commercial stage were in a more or less realistic mode. Anything that disturbed the illusion of realism was thought to be a flaw.

Reactions to the comfortable use of realistic techniques were numerous, especially after the First World War. One extreme reaction was that of DADAISM. Through the Dadaists' chief propagandist, Tristan Tzara (1896–1963), the group promoted an art that was essentially enigmatic and incoherent to the average person. That was its point. The Dadaists blamed World War I on sensible, middle-class people who were logical and well intentioned but never questioned convention. The brief plays that were performed in many Dadaist clubs in Europe often featured actors speaking simultaneously so that nothing they said could be understood. The purpose was to confound the normal expectations of theatergoers.

Other developments were also making it possible for playwrights to experiment and move away from a strict reliance on "comfortable" realism. By World War I motion pictures began to make melodramatic entertainment available to most people in the world. Even when films were silent, they relied on techniques that had been common on the nineteenth-century stage. Their growing domination of popular dramatic entertainment provided an outlet for the expectations of middle-class audiences and freed more imaginative playwrights to experiment and develop in different directions.

Realism and Myth

The incorporation of myth in drama offered new opportunities to expand the limits of realism. Sigmund Freud's theories of psychoanalysis at the turn of the century stimulated a new interest in myth and dreams as a psychological link between people. Freud studied Greek myths for clues to the psychic state of his patients, and he published a number of commentaries on Greek plays and on Shakespeare. (See the excerpt on pp. 71–74.) The psychologist Carl Jung, a follower of Freud who eventually split with him, helped give a powerful impetus to the interest in dreams and the symbolism of myth by suggesting that all members of a culture share an inborn knowledge of the basic myths of the culture. Jung postulated a collective unconscious, a repository of mythic material in the mind that all humans inherit as part of their birthright. This theory gave credence to the power of myth in everyday life; along with Freud's theories, it is one of the most important ideas empowering drama and other art forms in this century. Playwrights who used elements of myth in their plays produced a poetic form of realism that deals with a level of truth common to all humans.

Myth and Culture

Some non-European drama depends on interpretation of local myth in relation to the culture or cultures that produce it. Wole Soyinka's background as a Nigerian familiar with Yoruba culture and myth, along with his formal education in England, prepared him for a career that expanded the horizons of drama for both Nigerian and European audiences.

Soyinka's experimentation has spanned two traditions — modern European theater and modern ritual theater of the Yoruba people of Nigeria. Traditional Yoruba drama develops from religious celebrations and annual festivals and includes music and dance. Soyinka's plays, including *The Strong Breed*, concern themselves with African traditions and issues, but they often also explore mythic forces that link European and African cultures. His plays have been produced throughout the world and have demonstrated the universality of the community and the anxiety of the individual it sometimes breeds. Soyinka has also written critical studies on Yoruba tragedy and has interpreted, translated, and produced Greek tragedy.

Poetic Realism

The Abbey Theatre in Dublin, which functioned with distinction from the turn of the century, produced major works by John Millington Synge, W. B. Yeats, Sean O'Casey, and Lady Gregory. Lady Gregory's peasant plays concentrated on the charming, the amusing, and occasionally the grotesque. She tried to represent the dialect she heard in the west of Ireland, a dialect that was distinctive, poetic, and colorful. She also took advantage of local Irish myths and used some of them for her most powerful plays, such as *Dervorgilla* and *Grania,* both portraits of passionate women from Irish legend and myth.

John Millington Synge, like Lady Gregory, was interested in the twin forces of myth and peasant dialects. His plays are difficult to fit into a realist mold, although their surfaces are sometimes naturalistic. Some audiences reacted violently to his realistic portrayals of peasant life because they were unflattering. Synge's plays were sometimes directly connected with ancient Irish myth, as in *Deirdre of the Sorrows* (1910), which concerns a willful Irish princess who runs off with a young warrior and his brothers on the eve of her wedding to an old king. The story ends sadly for Deirdre, and she is regarded as a fated heroine, almost a Greek figure. Synge's most popular play, *The Playboy of the Western World,* a comedy with a few dark overtones, reveals his gift for emulating the Irish way of speaking English in Ireland's western county of Mayo. His creation of peasant dialogue remains one of his most important contributions to modern drama.

In the United States, Eugene O'Neill, influenced by Strindberg, experimented with realism, first by presenting stark, powerful plays that disturbed his audiences. *The Hairy Ape* (1922) portrayed a primitive coal stoker on a passenger liner who awakened base emotions in the more refined passengers. In *The Emperor Jones* (1921) O'Neill produced the first important American expressionist play. The shifting scenery, created by lighting, was dreamlike and at times frightening. The experience of the play reflected the frightening psychic experiences of the main character, Brutus Jones.

O'Neill also experimented with more poetic forms of realism. In *Desire under the Elms* (1924), he explores the myth of Phaedra — centering on her incestuous love for her husband's son — but sets it in rural New England on a rock-hard farm. In the tradition of realism, the play treats unpleasant themes: sons' distrust of their father and their dishonoring him, lust between a son and his stepmother, and the murder of a baby to "prove" love. But it is not simply realistic. Without its underpinning of myth, the play would be sordid, but the myth helps us see that fate operates even today, not in terms of messages from the gods but rather in terms of messages from our hearts and bodies. Lust is a force in nature that drives and destroys.

Meanwhile, in Fascist Spain, Federico García Lorca, also a poetic realist, was uncovering dark emotional centers of the psyche in his *House of Bernarda Alba* (1936), which explores erotic forces repressed and then set loose. Lorca was opposed to Fascism and was murdered by a Fascist agent. His plays reveal a bleakness of spirit that helps us imagine the darkness — moral and psychological — that enveloped Europe in the 1940s.

Social Realism

Ten years after *Desire under the Elms* enjoyed popularity, a taste for plays based on SOCIAL REALISM developed. This was realism with a political conscience. Because the world was in the throes of a depression that reduced many people to destitution and homelessness, drama began to aim at awakening governments to the consequences of unbridled capitalism and the depressions that freewheeling economies produced.

Plays like Jack Kirkland's *Tobacco Road* (1933), adapted from Erskine Caldwell's novel, presented a grim portrait of rural poverty in America. Sidney Kingsley's *Dead End* (1935) portrayed the life of virtually homeless boys on the Lower East Side of Manhattan. In the same year Maxwell Anderson produced a verse tragedy, *Winterset,* with gangsters and gangsterism at its core. Also in 1935 Clifford Odets produced *Waiting for Lefty,* an openly leftist labor drama. These plays' realist credentials lay primarily in their effort to show audiences portraits of life that might shock their middle-class sensibilities.

Realism and Expressionism

After Eugene O'Neill's experiments in combining myth and realism, later American dramatists looked for new ways to expand the resources of realism while retaining its power. The use of EXPRESSIONISM — often poetic in language and effect — was one solution that appealed to both Tennessee Williams and Arthur Miller. Expressionism developed in the first and second decades of the twentieth century. The movement began in Germany, and was influenced by some of Strindberg's work. Because expressionism takes many forms, there is no simple way to define the term except to see it as an alternative to realistic drama. Instead of having realistic sets, the stage may sometimes be barren or flooded with light or draped. Characters sometimes become symbolic; dialogue is often sharp, abrupt, enigmatic. The German theater saw its earliest developments in Frank Wedekind, whose first play, *Spring Awakening,* which explored sexual repression, abandoned a naturalistic style. His work influenced later German playwrights such as George Kaiser, Ernst Toller, Erwin Piscator, and Bertolt Brecht, whose *Three-Penny Opera* (1928) incorporated some of the hallmarks of expressionism, such as a music-hall atmosphere and broadly drawn characters.

Later American playwrights modified the characteristics of expressionism; they melded expressionist elements, such as fantastic sets and highly poetic diction, with a relatively realistic style. Tennessee Williams's *The Glass Menagerie* (1944) and Arthur Miller's *Death of a Salesman* (1949) both use expressionist techniques. Williams's poetic stage directions make clear that he is drawing on nonrealistic dramatic devices. He describes the scene as "memory and . . . therefore nonrealistic." He calls for an interior "rather dim and poetic," and he uses a character who also steps outside the staged action to serve as a narrator — one who "takes whatever license with dramatic convention as is convenient to his purposes." As the narrator tells his story, the walls of the building seem to melt away, revealing the inside of a house and the lives and fantasies of his mother and sister, both caught in their own distorted visions of life.

Arthur Miller's original image for *Death of a Salesman* was the inside of Willy Loman's mind; Jo Mielziner's expressionist set represented his idea as a cross-section of Loman's house. As the action in one room concluded, lights went up to begin action in another (Figure 12). This evocative staging influenced the production of numerous plays by later writers. In the original set, a scrim, or gauze screen, was painted with branches and leaves. When this scrim was lit from the front for memory scenes, the set was transformed to evoke an earlier time when the sons were boys.

Miller used expressionist techniques to create the hallucinatory sequences when Willy talks with Ben, the man who walked into the jungle poor and

Figure 12. Expressionistic setting in Arthur Miller's *Death of a Salesman*.

walked out a millionaire, and when Biff recalls seeing Willy with the woman in Boston.

While expressionism made some inroads in American theater, the techniques of realism persisted and developed. Lorraine Hansberry's *A Raisin in the Sun* (1959) uses basically realistic staging and dialogue to portray the difficulties of the members of one family in reaching for opportunity to overcome poverty. For Williams and Miller, expressionism offered a way to bring other worlds to bear on the staged action — the worlds of dream and fantasy. Hansberry does not use the expressionist techniques of Miller. Her only exotic touch is the visit of the African young man, Asagai, who offers a moment of cultural counterpoint. Hansberry's realism is essentially conservative.

Antirealism

SURREALISM (literally, "beyond realism") in the early twentieth century was based originally on an interpretation of experience not through the lucid mind of the waking person but through the mind of the dreamer, the unconscious mind that Freud described. Surrealism augmented or, for some playwrights, supplanted realism and became a means of distorting reality for emotional purposes.

When Pirandello's six characters come onstage looking for their author in *Six Characters in Search of an Author* (1921), no one believes that they are characters rather than actors. Pirandello's play is an examination of the realities we take for granted in drama. He turns the world of expectation in drama upside down. He reminds us that what we assume to be real is always questionable: we cannot be sure of anything; we must presume that things are true, and in some cases we must take them on faith.

Pirandello's philosophy dominated his stories, plays, and novels. His questioning of the certainty of human knowledge was designed to undermine his audience's faith in an absolute reality. Modern physicists have concurred with philosophers, ancient and modern, who question everyday reality. Pirandello was influenced by the modern theories of relativity that physicists were developing, and he found in them validation of his own attack on certainty.

Epic Theater

Bertolt Brecht (1898–1956) began writing plays just after World War I. He was a political dramatist who rejected the theater of his day, which valued the realistic "well-made play," in which all the parts fit perfectly together and function like a machine. His feeling was that such plays were too mechanical, like a "clockwork mouse."

Exploring the style of his predecessor Irwin Piscator, Brecht developed EPIC THEATER. The term implies a sequence of actions or episodes of the kind found in Homer's *Iliad*. In epic theater the sense of dramatic illusion is constantly voided by reminders from the stage that one is watching a play. Stark, harsh lighting, blank stages, placards announcing changes of scenes, bands playing music onstage, and long, discomfiting pauses make it impossible for an audience to become totally immersed in a realistic illusion. Brecht, offering a genuine alternative to realistic drama, wanted the audience to analyze the play's thematic content rather than to sit back and be entertained. He believed that realistic drama convinced audiences that the play's vision of reality described not just things as they are but things as they must be. Such drama, Brecht asserted, helped maintain the social problems that they portrayed by reinforcing, rather than challenging, their realities.

Brecht's *Mother Courage* (written in 1939 and produced in 1941) is an antiwar drama staged early in World War II. The use of song, an unreal setting, and an unusual historical perspective (the Thirty Years' War in the seventeenth century) help to achieve the "defamiliarization" that Brecht thought drama ought to produce in its audiences. The techniques of epic theater in *Galileo* and *The Good Woman of Setzuan* (1943) — a study of the immoralities that prosper under capitalism — were imitated by playwrights in the 1950s. Hardly a major play in that period is free of Brecht's influence.

Eugène Ionesco (1909–1994) is said to have been the first of the postwar absurdist dramatists, with his production of *The Bald Soprano* and *The Lesson* (both in 1951). Ionesco called them "anti-plays" because they avoided the normal causal relationship of actions and realistic expectations of conventional drama.

Absurdist Drama

The critic Martin Esslin coined the term THEATER OF THE ABSURD when describing the work of Samuel Beckett (1906–1989), the Irish playwright whose dramas often dispense with almost everything that makes the well-made play well made. Some of his plays have no actors onstage — amplified breathing is the only hint of human presence in one case. Some have little or no plot; others have no words. His theater is minimalist, offering a stage reality that seems cut to the bone, without the usual realistic devices of plot, character development, and intricate setting.

The theater of the absurd assumes that the world is meaningless, that meaning is a human concept, and that individuals must create significance and not rely on institutions or traditions to provide it. The absurdist movement grew out of EXISTENTIALISM, a postwar French philosophy demanding that the individual face the emptiness of the universe and create meaning in a life that has no essential meaning within itself. *Waiting for Godot* (1952) captured the modern imagination and established a landmark in absurdist drama.

In *Waiting for Godot* two tramps, Vladimir and Estragon, meet near a tree where they expect Godot to arrive to talk with them. The play has two acts that both end with a small boy explaining that Godot cannot come today but will come tomorrow. Godot is not coming, and the tramps who wait for Godot will wait forever. While they wait they entertain themselves with vaudeville routines and eventually are met by a rich man, Pozzo, and his slave, Lucky. Lucky, on the command "Think, pig," speaks in a stream of garbled phrases that evoke Western philosophy and religion but that remain meaningless. Pozzo and Lucky have no interest in joining Vladimir and Estragon in waiting for Godot. They leave the two alone, waiting — afraid to leave for fear of missing Godot, but uncertain that Godot will ever arrive.

Beckett seems to be saying that in an absurd world such gestures are necessary to create the sense of significance that people need to live. His characters' awareness of an audience and his refusal to create a drama in which an audience can "lose" itself in a comfortable surface of realistic illusion are all, in their own way, indebted to Brecht.

Beckett's *Krapp's Last Tape* (1958) places some extraordinary limitations on performance. Krapp is the only person onstage throughout the play, and his dialogues are with tapes of himself made many years before. The situation is absurd, but as Beckett reveals to us, the absurd has its own complexities, and situations such as Krapp's can sustain complex interpretations. Beckett expects his audience to analyze the drama, not merely be entertained.

The illusion of reality is shed almost entirely in *Endgame*. Hamm cannot move. His parents, both legless, are in trashcans onstage. Clov performs all the play's movement on a barren, cellarlike stage.

The great plays of this period reflect the values of the cultures from which they spring. They make comments on life in the modern world and question the values that the culture takes for granted. The drama of this part of the twentieth century is a drama of examination.

Early and Mid-Twentieth-Century Drama Timeline

DATE	THEATER	POLITICAL	SOCIAL/CULTURAL
1850–1900	**1854–1931:** David Belasco, American producer. Belasco uses pictorial realism in staging and creates "stars" on the New York stage. **1862–1928:** Adolphe Appia, influential Swiss designer **1871–1909:** John Millington Synge, Irish playwright, author of *Riders to the Sea* (1904) and *The Playboy of the Western World* (1907) **1872–1966:** Edward Gordon Craig, influential English theatrical designer **1873–1943:** Max Reinhardt, Austrian director, producer, and theorist **1880–1964:** Sean O'Casey, Irish playwright, author of *Juno and the Paycock* (1924) and *The Plough and the Stars* (1926) **1887–1954:** Robert Edmond Jones, revolutionary American scenic designer **1888–1953:** Eugene O'Neill, American playwright. Among his works are *Desire under the Elms* (1924), *Mourning Becomes Electra* (1931), and *Long Day's Journey into Night* (1939–1941). **1898–1956:** Bertolt Brecht, German playwright, author of *The Threepenny Opera* (1928), *Mother Courage* (1941), and *The Good Woman of Setzuan* (1943) **1898:** The Irish Literary Society is founded by William Butler Yeats (1865–1939) and Lady Augusta Gregory (1863–1935). The group leads the way in creating an indigenous Irish theater.		

Early and Mid-Twentieth-Century Drama Timeline *(continued)*

DATE	THEATER	POLITICAL	SOCIAL/CULTURAL
1900–1950	**1904:** The Abbey Theatre, evolved from the Irish Literary Society founded by Yeats and Lady Gregory, opens in Dublin. **1905–1984:** Lillian Hellman, American playwright, author of *The Children's Hour* (1934) and *The Little Foxes* (1939). Other important American female playwrights of the period include Rachel Crothers (1876–1958), Zona Gale (1874–1938), and Susan Glaspell (1876–1948). **1906–1989:** Samuel Beckett, Irish playwright who wrote some of his plays in French. Among his works are *Waiting for Godot* (1952) and *Endgame* (1957). **1911–1983:** Tennessee Williams, American playwright, author of *The Glass Menagerie* (1945), *A Streetcar Named Desire* (1947), and *Cat on a Hot Tin Roof* (1955) **1915:** Arthur Miller, American playwright, born. Among his works are *Death of a Salesman* (1949) and *The Crucible* (1953). **1915:** George Cram Cook, Eugene O'Neill, and Susan Glaspell found the Provincetown Players in Provincetown, Massachusetts. **1917:** J. L. Williams's *Why Marry?* receives the first Pulitzer Prize for drama. **1918:** Formation of the Theater Guild in New York City **1919:** Actors Equity Association is officially recognized as a union in the United States. **1920:** Théâtre National Populaire is founded in Paris.	**1900:** The Boxer Rebellion attempts to curtail Western commercial interests in China. **1901:** Queen Victoria of England dies and is succeeded by her son Edward VII. **1904–1905:** Russo-Japanese War. Russia is defeated, and Japan emerges as a world power. **1905:** The Sinn Fein party is founded in Dublin. **1912:** Sun Yat Sen is elected president of the Republic of China and founds the Kuomintang. **1914:** World War I begins with the assassination of Austrian Archduke Franz Ferdinand in Sarajevo. **1916:** The Easter Rising in Ireland is suppressed by the British. **1917:** The Russian Revolution overthrows the czar and establishes Bolshevik control under V. I. Lenin. **1919:** The Treaty of Versailles formally ends World War I. **1920:** The Nineteenth Amendment grants women the right to vote. **1921:** Southern Ireland becomes the independent Republic of Ireland.	**1900–1971:** Louis Armstrong, African American jazz trumpet player **1900:** Sigmund Freud (1856–1939) writes *The Interpretation of Dreams*. **1901:** Ragtime music becomes popular in the United States. **1903:** Wilbur and Orville Wright's first flight **1905:** The first movie theater in the United States opens in New York City. **1905–1914:** Over 10 million immigrants arrive in the United States. **1906:** An earthquake and subsequent fire ravage San Francisco. **1907:** Picasso's (1881–1973) *Les Demoiselles d'Avignon* is significant to cubism movement in art. **1908:** Henry Ford (1863–1947) designs the Model T. **1910:** W. E. B. DuBois (1868–1963), African American civil rights leader and author, establishes the NAACP. **1912:** The ocean liner *Titanic* sinks, killing 1,513 passengers. **1913:** Niels Bohr (1885–1962) formulates his theory of atomic structure. **1914:** The Panama Canal is completed. **1915:** D. W. Griffith's film *The Birth of a Nation* is released. **c. 1916:** Albert Einstein (1879–1955) formulates his theory of relativity. **1916:** Jazz music evolves in New Orleans, Chicago, and New York City. **1918:** Influenza epidemic kills 22 million people worldwide by 1922. **1919:** The Bauhaus, an influential school of art and architecture, is established by Walter Gropius in Germany. **1920:** Prohibition begins in the United States.

Early and Mid-Twentieth-Century Drama Timeline (continued)

DATE	THEATER	POLITICAL	SOCIAL/CULTURAL
1900–1950 (continued)	**1921:** Italian playwright Luigi Pirandello (1867–1936) writes *Six Characters in Search of an Author.*	**1921:** Ku Klux Klan activities become violent throughout southern United States.	
	1923–1924: Moscow Art Theater visits the United States for the first time.	**1921:** Sacco and Vanzetti, Italian anarchists, are sentenced to death in the United States.	**1922:** T. S. Eliot (1888–1965) publishes *The Waste Land.*
		1922: Fascist dictator Benito Mussolini gains power in Italy.	**1922:** James Joyce (1882–1941) publishes *Ulysses.*
			1923: George Gershwin (1898–1937) performs *Rhapsody in Blue.*
		1924–1972: J. Edgar Hoover, director of the Federal Bureau of Investigation	**1925:** F. Scott Fitzgerald (1896–1940) publishes *The Great Gatsby.*
		1925: Adolf Hitler reorganizes the Nazi Party and publishes volume 1 of *Mein Kampf.*	**1925:** Margaret Sanger (1883–1966) organizes the first international birth control conference.
	1927: Neil Simon born. His plays include *The Odd Couple* (1965), *Chapter Two* (1979), and *Biloxi Blues* (1984).	**1928:** The Kellogg-Briand Pact, outlawing war, is signed in Paris by 65 states.	**1920s:** Harlem Renaissance: African American literature, music, and art flourish in New York City. Langston Hughes (1902–1967), Zora Neale Hurston (1901–1960), Jean Toomer (1894–1967), and many others publish.
	1930–1965: Lorraine Hansberry, African American playwright, author of *A Raisin in the Sun* (1959)	**c. 1928:** Joseph Stalin comes to power in the Soviet Union.	**1925:** John T. Scopes, schoolteacher, is tried for violating a Tennessee law that prohibits the teaching of the theory of evolution.
	1930: María Irene Fornés, Cuban playwright, born. Among her works are *Fefu and Her Friends* (1977) and *The Conduct of Life* (1985).	**1929:** The U.S. stock market crash begins the Great Depression.	**1926:** Ernest Hemingway (1899–1961) publishes *The Sun Also Rises.*
	1931: The Group Theatre is founded by Harold Clurman, Cheryl Crawford, and Lee Strasberg and operates for ten years.	**1933:** New Deal economic reforms attempt to provide recovery from the Depression.	**1926:** Duke Ellington's (1899–1974) first records appear.
			1927: *The Jazz Singer* is the first "talkie" movie.
	1934: Wole Soyinka, Nigerian playwright, born. His works include *The Strong Breed* (1962) and *A Play of Giants* (1985).	**1933:** Adolf Hitler comes to power in Germany. German labor unions and political parties other than the Nazi are suppressed. Nazis erect their first concentration camp; persecution of Jews begins in Germany.	**1927:** Charles Lindbergh (1902–1974) makes the first solo nonstop transatlantic flight.
			1927: Virginia Woolf (1882–1941), English novelist, publishes *To the Lighthouse.*
	1934: Socialist realism is declared the official artistic policy in Soviet theater.	**1933:** Prohibition is repealed.	**1929:** William Faulkner (1897–1962) publishes *The Sound and the Fury.*
	1935: The American plays *Dead End* by Sidney Kingsley, *Winterset* by Maxwell Anderson, and *Waiting for Lefty* by Clifford Odets are produced.	**1935:** Roosevelt signs the U.S. Social Security Act.	**1931:** Robert Frost (1874–1963) wins the Pulitzer Prize for *Collected Poems.*
		1935: The Nuremberg laws in Nazi Germany deprive German Jews of their citizenship and civil rights.	**1931:** The Empire State Building in New York City is completed.
		1935–1936: Italy's conquest of Ethiopia	**1932:** Aldous Huxley (1894–1963) publishes *Brave New World.*
		1936: Chiang Kai-shek declares war on Japan.	

Early and Mid-Twentieth-Century Drama Timeline (continued)

DATE	THEATER	POLITICAL	SOCIAL/CULTURAL
1900–1950 (continued)	**1935–1939:** The Federal Theatre Project operates in the United States under the auspices of the Works Progress Administration.	**1936–1939:** Civil War in Spain results in Generalissimo Franco's consolidation of power.	**1937:** Amelia Earhart (1897–1937), the first woman to fly across the Atlantic, vanishes over the Pacific Ocean.
	1936: Federico García Lorca, Spanish playwright, writes *The House of Bernarda Alba.*	**1939:** England and France declare war on Germany and its allies.	**1938:** Joe Louis (1914–1981), African American heavyweight boxer, defeats German Max Schmeling.
	1937: Peter Stein, influential German director, born. Among his important productions are *Peer Gynt* (1971) and the *Oresteia* (1980).	**1939:** Germany invades Poland.	
		1940: Germany invades France.	
	1938: Antonín Artaud, French playwright and theorist, writes *The Theater and Its Double.*	**1941:** Japan attacks Pearl Harbor, and the United States enters World War II.	
		1942: Germany begins killing Jews and others in gas chambers.	
		1942: The U.S. Army interns Japanese Americans in prison camps.	**1943:** Penicillin is first used in the treatment of chronic diseases.
		1944: Allies liberate France.	**1940s:** The era of great musical theater begins in the United States, featuring the songs of Cole Porter (1891–1964), Richard Rodgers (1902–1979), and Oscar Hammerstein (1895–1960), among many others.
	1946: The Living Theatre is founded by Judith Malina and Julian Beck.	**1945:** The United States drops atomic bombs on Hiroshima and Nagazaki, Japan.	
		1945: Hitler commits suicide in Berlin, and Germany signs an unconditional surrender.	
		1946: Juan Perón is elected president of Argentina.	
	1947: The Actors Studio is founded in New York City by Robert Lewis, Elia Kazan, and Cheryl Crawford. Lee Strasberg assumes control by 1948.	**1947:** India proclaims independence and is divided into Pakistan and India.	**1947:** Jackie Robinson (1919–1972) becomes the first African American to sign a contract with a major baseball club.
		1948: The Republic of Israel is proclaimed by Jewish leaders in Palestine.	
	1947: Beginning of the regional theater movement in the United States. Margo Jones opens an arena theater in Dallas, Nina Vance founds the Alley Theatre in Houston, and the Arena Stage opens in 1949 in Washington, D.C.	**1948:** Indian leader Mahatma Gandhi is assassinated.	
		1949: Mao Zedong announces the establishment of the People's Republic of China.	
		1949: The North Atlantic Treaty Organization allies Canada, Western Europe, and the United States.	
	1949: The Berliner Ensemble is founded in East Berlin.	**1949:** The apartheid system is established in South Africa.	

Susan Glaspell

Susan Glaspell (1876–1948) is an important figure in early twentieth-century American drama. Through her influence, serious theater began to thrive in an environment used to musicals, sentimental comedies, and fashionable revivals. She was born in Davenport, Iowa, to Irish immigrant parents and grew up writing. After graduating from Drake University, she took a job as a reporter and by 1901 had become a full-time writer. Her first novel, *The Glory of the Conquered: The Story of a Great Love,* published in 1909, earned her enough to spend a year in Paris. *The Visioning,* which followed in 1911, was set on an army base and presented a less sentimentalized world than did her first book. She published her first collection of stories, *Lifted Masks,* in 1912. Her best novel, *Fidelity,* was published in 1915, after she had returned to the United States.

In 1908 Glaspell first met her future husband, George Cram (Jig) Cook, a traveled intellectual and Harvard graduate who was teaching at Iowa University. After the initial meeting, Cook eventually married someone else, but five years later was divorced. Following Glaspell's return from Europe in 1913, they were reintroduced by mutual friends; they now felt that they had been fated for each other. They settled on Cape Cod and, with Mary Heaton Vorse, founded the Provincetown Players. The theater company became a highly influential platform for a number of important American writers, such as Djuna Barnes, Edna Ferber, and Edna St. Vincent Millay. Eugene O'Neill, a prominent member of the Provincetown Players, played roles in Glaspell's works, including *Trifles* (1916). Her earliest play — first produced in her living room then moved to the Provincetown Playhouse — was *Suppressed Desires* (1915), a spoof on the rage for using Freudian theories to explain everyday life. In a letter to the New York *Times* (February 13, 1920) she said that the play "is having fun with the people who went off their heads about psychoanalysis — went 'bugs'— when this subject reached the first circle in New York to know of it."

Glaspell's one-act plays, including *Close the Book* (1917), *A Woman's Honor* (1918), and *Tickless Time* (1919), were collected in 1920. Her first full-length play, *Bernice* (1919), centered on interpreting the character of a dead woman. Its success led to another full-length play, *The Verge* (1921), about a woman who tries to make a new reality around herself and begins with creating new kinds of plants. Some critics saw the protagonist as an admirable new woman; others saw her as neurotic. *The Inheritors* (1921), also a full-length drama, focuses on the third-generation inheritors of a Midwestern college who clash because one family has liberal views and one has conservative views. Her last play, winner of the Pulitzer Prize, was *Alison's House* (1930), based on the life of Emily Dickinson. The latter part of Glaspell's life was spent writing fiction, concentrating on four novels set in the Midwest about the struggles of women to maintain their ideals and values.

Jig Cook, a writer himself, and a partner in many of Glaspell's ventures, spent the last two years of his life living in Delphi, Greece, in the manner of the peasants living on Mount Parnassus near the temple of Apollo. He died in 1924, and when Glaspell returned to the United States she wrote a memoir of their life together called *The Road to the Temple*. In 1925 she broke with the Provincetown Players, who had moved in directions she did not approve of under the directorship of Eugene O'Neill. O'Neill tried to mollify Glaspell, but she never accepted his use of the theater company she and her husband had cofounded. When she died in 1948, she and O'Neill were essentially unreconciled.

TRIFLES

Trifles (1916) was apparently written as a companion piece for Eugene O'Neill's first produced play, the one-act *Bound East for Cardiff*. The two were put together to make a complete evening presentation. In one sense *Trifles* is a murder mystery, but in another it is a critique of the gender-rigid attitudes of the officials whose responsibility it is to investigate the death of John Wright. Its main character, Minnie Foster Wright, is never presented, only described as a sweet woman who loved to sing when she was young but who married a man who slowly stifled her joy in living.

The setting of the play is a kitchen where the women, Mrs. Peters and Mrs. Hale, remain throughout the action. They examine the condition of the room and by extension, the condition of Minnie Foster Wright. The men, examining the crime scene, the upstairs bedroom, spend much of the time offstage. They feel that they are examining the important evidence; yet when they return with their findings, they are unable to understand what led to the death of John Wright, who to them seems quite a normal farmer.

The women, however, by examining the messy condition of the kitchen, the state of Minnie's preserves, and the quilt she was working on, begin to understand the motive behind Wright's murder. When they get to the dead body of the songbird Minnie had valued, they understand things in a way that the men cannot. The men observe that women are concerned with trifles, things of no importance. But the truth is that the women understand the fate of Minnie Foster Wright and John Wright in a way that would be almost impossible for the men, given their sense of what is significant and what is a trifle.

In many ways the play is a study of gender differences and the way men's expectations and their sense of reality can distort the truth and deform a woman's life. In 1917 Glaspell wrote a short story, using all the same material, called "A Jury of Her Peers," implying that the only peers of Minnie Foster Wright would be women like Mrs. Hale and Mrs. Peters. In 1917, however, women could not vote and in most states could not serve on juries.

Trifles in Performance

The original production included Eugene O'Neill among its cast members and received a positive response, but after Glaspell's death most of her work fell out of fashion. *Trifles* was neglected until the early 1960s, when feminist interest helped revive her plays. Teacher and writer Sylvan Barnet included the play in his drama anthology, helping to bring it to the attention of contemporary viewers. Now produced most often by school and college groups, the play enjoys considerable popularity.

Susan Glaspell (1882–1948)

TRIFLES

1916

Characters

GEORGE HENDERSON, *county attorney*
HENRY PETERS, *sheriff*
LEWIS HALE, *a neighboring farmer*
MRS. PETERS
MRS. HALE

Scene: *The kitchen in the now abandoned farmhouse of John Wright, a gloomy kitchen, and left without having been put in order — the walls covered with a faded wall paper. Down right is a door leading to the parlor. On the right wall above this door is a built-in kitchen cupboard with shelves in the upper portion and drawers below. In the rear wall at right, up two steps is a door opening onto stairs leading to the second floor. In the rear wall at left is a door to the shed and from there to the outside. Between these two doors is an old-fashioned black iron stove. Running along the left wall from the shed door is an old iron sink and sink shelf, in which is set a hand pump. Downstage of the sink is an uncurtained window. Near the window is an old wooden rocker. Center stage is an unpainted wooden kitchen table with straight chairs on either side. There is a small chair down right. Unwashed pans under the sink, a loaf of bread outside the breadbox, a dish towel on the table — other signs of incompleted work. At the rear the shed door opens and the Sheriff comes in followed by the County Attorney and Hale. The Sheriff and Hale are men in middle life, the County Attorney is a young man; all are much bundled up and go at once to the stove. They are followed by the two women — the Sheriff's wife, Mrs. Peters, first: she is a slight wiry woman, a thin nervous face. Mrs. Hale is larger and would ordinarily be called more comfortable looking, but she is disturbed now and looks fearfully about as she enters. The women have come in slowly, and stand close together near the door.*

COUNTY ATTORNEY (*at stove rubbing his hands*): This feels good. Come up to the fire, ladies.

MRS. PETERS (*after taking a step forward*): I'm not — cold.

SHERIFF (*unbuttoning his overcoat and stepping away from the stove to right of table as if to mark the beginning of official business*): Now, Mr. Hale, before we move things about, you explain to Mr. Henderson just what you saw when you came here yesterday morning.

COUNTY ATTORNEY (*crossing down to left of the table*): By the way, has anything been moved? Are things just as you left them yesterday?

SHERIFF (*looking about*): It's just about the same. When it dropped below zero last night I thought I'd better send Frank out this morning to make a fire for us — (*sits right of center table*) no use getting pneumonia with a big case on, but I told him not to touch anything except the stove — and you know Frank.

COUNTY ATTORNEY: Somebody should have been left here yesterday.

SHERIFF: Oh — yesterday. When I had to send Frank to Morris Center for that man who went crazy — I want you to know I had my hands full yesterday. I knew you could get back from Omaha by today and as long as I went over everything here myself ——

COUNTY ATTORNEY: Well, Mr. Hale, tell just what happened when you came here yesterday morning.

HALE (*crossing down to above table*): Harry and I had started to town with a load of potatoes. We came along the road from my place and as I got here I said, "I'm going to see if I can't get John Wright to go in with me on a party telephone." I spoke to Wright about it once before and he put me off, saying folks talked too much anyway, and all he asked was peace and quiet — I guess you know about how much he talked himself; but I thought maybe if I went to the house and talked about it before his wife, though I said to Harry that I didn't know as what his wife wanted made much difference to John ———

COUNTY ATTORNEY: Let's talk about that later, Mr. Hale. I do want to talk about that, but tell now just what happened when you got to the house.

HALE: I didn't hear or see anything; I knocked at the door, and still it was all quiet inside. I knew they must be up, it was past eight o'clock. So I knocked again, and I thought I heard someone say, "Come in." I wasn't sure, I'm not sure yet, but I opened the door — this door (*indicating the door by which the two women are still standing*) and there in that rocker — (*pointing to it*) sat Mrs. Wright. (*They all look at the rocker down left.*)

COUNTY ATTORNEY: What — was she doing?

HALE: She was rockin' back and forth. She had her apron in her hand and was kind of — pleating it.

COUNTY ATTORNEY: And how did she — look?

HALE: Well, she looked queer.

COUNTY ATTORNEY: How do you mean — queer?

HALE: Well, as if she didn't know what she was going to do next. And kind of done up.

COUNTY ATTORNEY (*takes out notebook and pencil and sits left of center table*): How did she seem to feel about your coming?

HALE: Why, I don't think she minded — one way or other. She didn't pay much attention. I said, "How do, Mrs. Wright, it's cold, ain't it?" And she said, "Is it?" — and went on kind of pleating at her apron. Well, I was surprised; she didn't ask me to come up to the stove, or to set down, but just sat there, not even looking at me, so I said, "I want to see John." And then she — laughed. I guess you would call it a laugh. I thought of Harry and the team outside, so I said a little sharp: "Can't I see John?" "No," she says, kind o' dull like. "Ain't he home?" says I. "Yes," says she, "he's home." "Then why can't I see him?" I asked her, out of patience. "'Cause he's dead," says she. "*Dead?*" says I. She just nodded her head, not getting a bit excited, but rockin' back and forth. "Why — where is he?" says I, not knowing what to say. She just pointed upstairs — like that. (*Himself pointing to the room above.*) I started for the stairs, with the idea of going up there. I walked from there to here — then I says, "Why, what did he die of?" "He died of a rope round his neck," says she, and just went on pleatin' at her apron. Well, I went out and called Harry. I thought I might — need help. We went upstairs and there he was lyin'———

COUNTY ATTORNEY: I think I'd rather have you go into that upstairs, where you can point it all out. Just go on now with the rest of the story.

HALE: Well, my first thought was to get that rope off. It looked . . . (*stops; his face twitches*) . . . but Harry, he went up to him, and he said, "No, he's dead all right, and we'd better not touch anything." So we went right back downstairs. She was still sitting that same way. "Has anybody been notified?" I asked. "No," says she, unconcerned. "Who did this, Mrs. Wright?" said Harry. He said it businesslike — and she stopped pleatin' of her apron. "I don't know," she says. "You don't *know?*" says Harry. "No," says she. "Weren't you sleepin' in the bed with him?" says Harry. "Yes," says she, "but I was on the inside." "Somebody slipped a rope round his head and strangled him and you didn't wake up?" says Harry. "I didn't wake up," she said after him. We must 'a' looked as if we didn't see how that could be, for after a minute she said, "I sleep sound." Harry was going to ask her more questions but I said maybe we ought to let her tell her story first to the coroner, or the sheriff, so Harry went fast as he could to Rivers' place, where there's a telephone.

COUNTY ATTORNEY: And what did Mrs. Wright do when she knew that you had gone for the coroner?

HALE: She moved from the rocker to that chair over there (*pointing to a small chair in the down right corner*) and just sat there with her hands held together and looking down. I got a feeling that I ought to make some conversation, so I said I had come in to see if John wanted to put in a telephone, and at that she started to laugh, and then she stopped and looked at me — scared. (*The County Attorney, who has had his notebook out, makes a note.*) I dunno, maybe it wasn't scared. I wouldn't like to say it was. Soon Harry got back, and then Dr. Lloyd came and you, Mr. Peters, and so I guess that's all I know that you don't.

COUNTY ATTORNEY (*rising and looking around*): I guess we'll go upstairs first — and then out to the barn and around there. (*To the Sheriff.*) You're convinced that there was nothing important here — nothing that would point to any motive?

SHERIFF: Nothing here but kitchen things. (*The County Attorney, after again looking around the kitchen, opens the door of a cupboard closet in right wall. He brings a small chair from right — gets on it and looks on a shelf. Pulls his hand away, sticky.*)

COUNTY ATTORNEY: Here's a nice mess. (*The women draw nearer up to center.*)

MRS. PETERS (*to the other woman*): Oh, her fruit; it did freeze. (*To the Lawyer.*) She worried about that when it turned so cold. She said the fire'd go out and her jars would break.

SHERIFF (*rises*): Well, can you beat the woman! Held for murder and worryin' about her preserves.

COUNTY ATTORNEY (*getting down from chair*): I guess before we're through she may have something more serious than preserves to worry about. (*Crosses down right center.*)

HALE: Well, women are used to worrying over trifles. (*The two women move a little closer together.*)

COUNTY ATTORNEY (*with the gallantry of a young politician*): And yet, for all their worries, what would we do without the ladies? (*The women do not unbend. He goes below the center table to the sink, takes a dipperful of water from the pail, and pouring it into a basin, washes his hands. While he is doing this the Sheriff and Hale cross to cupboard, which they inspect. The County Attorney starts to wipe his hands on the roller towel, turns it for a cleaner place.*) Dirty towels! (*Kicks his foot against the pans under the sink.*) Not much of a housekeeper, would you say, ladies?

MRS. HALE (*stiffly*): There's a great deal of work to be done on a farm.

COUNTY ATTORNEY: To be sure. And yet (*with a little bow to her*) I know there are some Dickson County farmhouses which do not have such roller towels. (*He gives it a pull to expose its full-length again.*)

MRS. HALE: Those towels get dirty awful quick. Men's hands aren't always clean as they might be.

COUNTY ATTORNEY: Ah, loyal to your sex, I see. But you and Mrs. Wright were neighbors. I suppose you were friends, too.

MRS. HALE (*shaking her head*): I've not seen much of her of late years. I've not been in this house — it's more than a year.

COUNTY ATTORNEY (*crossing to women up center*): And why was that? You didn't like her?

MRS. HALE: I liked her all well enough. Farmer's wives have their hands full, Mr. Henderson. And then ——

COUNTY ATTORNEY: Yes —— ?

MRS. HALE (*looking about*): It never seemed a very cheerful place.

COUNTY ATTORNEY: No — it's not cheerful. I shouldn't say she had the homemaking instinct.

MRS. HALE: Well, I don't know as Wright had, either.

COUNTY ATTORNEY: You mean that they didn't get on very well?

MRS. HALE: No, I don't mean anything. But I don't think a place'd be any cheerfuller for John Wright's being in it.

COUNTY ATTORNEY: I'd like to talk more of that a little later. I want to get the lay of things upstairs now. (*He goes past the women to up right where the steps lead to a stair door.*)

SHERIFF: I suppose anything Mrs. Peters does'll be all right. She was to take in some clothes for her, you know, and a few little things. We left in such a hurry yesterday.

COUNTY ATTORNEY: Yes, but I would like to see what you take, Mrs. Peters, and keep an eye out for anything that might be of use to us.

MRS. PETERS: Yes, Mr. Henderson. (*The men leave by up right door to stairs. The women listen to the men's steps on the stairs, then look about the kitchen.*)

MRS. HALE (*crossing left to sink*): I'd hate to have men coming into my kitchen, snooping around and criticizing. (*She arranges the pans under sink which the lawyer had shoved out of place.*)

MRS. PETERS: Of course it's no more than their duty. (*Crosses to cupboard up right.*)

MRS. HALE: Duty's all right, but I guess that deputy sheriff that came out to make the fire might have got a little of this on. (*Gives the roller towel a pull.*) Wish I'd though of that sooner. Seems mean to talk about her for not having things slicked up when she had to come away in such a hurry. (*Crosses right to Mrs. Peters at cupboard.*)

MRS. PETERS (*who has been looking through cupboard, lifts one end of towel that covers a pan*): She had bread set. (*Stands still.*)

MRS. HALE (*eyes fixed on a loaf of bread beside the breadbox, which is on a low shelf of the cupboard*): She was going to put this in there. (*Picks up loaf, abruptly drops it. In a manner of returning to familiar things.*) It's a shame about her fruit. I wonder if it's all gone. (*Gets up on chair and looks.*) I think there's some here that's all right, Mrs. Peters. Yes — here; (*holding it toward the window*) this is cherries, too. (*Looking again.*) I declare I believe that's the only one. (*Gets down, jar in hand. Goes to the sink and wipes it off on the outside.*) She'll feel awful bad after all her hard work in the hot weather. I remember the afternoon I put up my cherries last summer. (*She puts the jar on the big kitchen table, center of the room. With a sigh, is about to sit down in the rocking chair. Before she is seated realizes what chair it is; with a slow look at it, steps back. The chair which she has touched rocks back and forth. Mrs. Peters moves to center table and they both watch the chair rock for a moment or two.*)

MRS. PETERS (*shaking off the mood which the empty rocking chair has evoked. Now in a businesslike manner she speaks*): Well I must get those things from the front room closet. (*She goes to the door at the right but, after looking into the other room, steps back.*) You coming with me, Mrs. Hale? You could help me carry them. (*They go in the other room; reappear, Mrs. Peters carrying a dress, petticoat, and skirt, Mrs. Hale following with a pair of shoes.*) My, it's cold in there. (*She puts the clothes on the big table and hurries to the stove.*)

MRS. HALE (*right of center table examining the skirt*): Wright was close. I think maybe that's why she kept so much to herself. She didn't even belong to the Ladies' Aid. I suppose she felt she couldn't do her part, and then you don't enjoy things when you feel shabby. I heard she used to wear pretty clothes and be lively, when she was Minnie Foster, one of the town girls singing in the choir. But that — oh, that was thirty years ago. This all you want to take in?

MRS. PETERS: She said she wanted an apron. Funny thing to want, for there isn't much to get you dirty in jail, goodness knows. But I suppose just to make her feel more natural. (*Crosses to cupboard.*) She said they was in the top drawer in this cupboard. Yes, here. And then her little shawl that always hung behind the door. (*Opens stair door and looks.*) Yes, here it is. (*Quickly shuts door leading upstairs.*)

MRS. HALE (*abruptly moving toward her*): Mrs. Peters?

MRS. PETERS: Yes, Mrs. Hale? (*At up right door.*)

MRS. HALE: Do you think she did it?

MRS. PETERS (*in a frightened voice*): Oh, I don't know.

MRS. HALE: Well, I don't think she did. Asking for an apron and her little shawl. Worrying about her fruit.

MRS. PETERS (*starts to speak, glances up, where footsteps are heard in the room above. In a low voice*): Mr. Peters says it looks bad for her. Mr. Henderson is awful sarcastic in a speech and he'll make fun of her sayin' she didn't wake up.

MRS. HALE: Well, I guess John Wright didn't wake when they was slipping that rope under his neck.

MRS. PETERS (*crossing slowly to table and placing shawl and apron on table with other clothing*): No, it's strange. It must have been done awful crafty and still. They say it was such a — funny way to kill a man, rigging it all up like that.

MRS. HALE (*crossing to left of Mrs. Peters at table*): That's just what Mr. Hale said. There was a gun in the house. He says that's what he can't understand.

MRS. PETERS: Mr. Henderson said coming out that what was needed for the case was a motive: something to show anger, or — sudden feeling.

MRS. HALE (*who is standing by the table*): Well, I don't see any signs of anger around here. (*She puts her hand on the dish towel, which lies on the table, stands looking down at table, one-half of which is clean, the other half messy.*) It's wiped to here. (*Makes a move as if to finish work, then turns and looks at loaf of bread outside the breadbox. Drops towel. In that voice of coming back to familiar things.*) Wonder how they are finding things upstairs. (*Crossing below table to down right.*) I hope she had it a little more red-up° up there. You know, it seems kind of *sneaking*. Locking her up in town and then coming out here and trying to get her own house to turn against her!

MRS. PETERS: But, Mrs. Hale, the law is the law.

MRS. HALE: I s'pose 'tis. (*Unbuttoning her coat.*) Better loosen up your things, Mrs. Peters. You won't feel them when you go out. (*Mrs. Peters takes off her fur tippet, goes to hang it on chair back left of table, stands looking at the work basket on floor near down left window.*)

MRS. PETERS: She was piecing a quilt. (*She brings the large sewing basket to the center table and they look at the bright pieces, Mrs. Hale above the table and Mrs. Peters left of it.*)

MRS. HALE: It's a log cabin pattern. Pretty, isn't it? I wonder if she was goin' to quilt it or just knot it? (*Footsteps have been heard coming down the stairs. The Sheriff enters followed by Hale and the County Attorney.*)

SHERIFF: They wonder if she was going to quilt it or just knot it! (*The men laugh, the women look abashed.*)

COUNTY ATTORNEY (*rubbing his hands over the stove*): Frank's fire didn't do much up there, did it? Well, let's go out to the barn and get that cleared up. (*The men go outside by up left door.*)

---

red-up: (slang) Ready for company.

MRS. HALE (*resentfully*): I don't know as there's anything so strange, our takin' up our time with little things while we're waiting for them to get the evidence. (*She sits in chair right of table smoothing out a block with decision.*) I don't see as it's anything to laugh about.

MRS. PETERS (*apologetically*): Of course they've got awful important things on their minds. (*Pulls up a chair and joins Mrs. Hale at the left of the table.*)

MRS. HALE (*examining another block*): Mrs. Peters, look at this one. Here, this is the one she was working on, and look at the sewing! All the rest of it has been so nice and even. And look at this! It's all over the place! Why, it looks as if she didn't know what she was about! (*After she has said this they look at each other, then start to glance back at the door. After an instant Mrs. Hale has pulled at a knot and ripped the sewing.*)

MRS. PETERS: Oh, what are you doing, Mrs. Hale?

MRS. HALE (*mildly*): Just pulling out a stitch or two that's not sewed very good. (*Threading a needle.*) Bad sewing always made me fidgety.

MRS. PETERS (*with a glance at the door, nervously*): I don't think we ought to touch things.

MRS. HALE: I'll just finish up this end. (*Suddenly stopping and leaning forward.*) Mrs. Peters?

MRS. PETERS: Yes, Mrs. Hale?

MRS. HALE: What do you suppose she was so nervous about?

MRS. PETERS: Oh — I don't know. I don't know as she was nervous. I sometimes sew awful queer when I'm just tired. (*Mrs. Hale starts to say something, looks at Mrs. Peters, then goes on sewing.*) Well, I must get these things wrapped up. They may be through sooner than we think. (*Putting apron and other things together.*) I wonder where I can find a piece of paper, and string. (*Rises.*)

MRS. HALE: In that cupboard, maybe.

MRS. PETERS (*crosses right looking in cupboard*): Why, here's a bird-cage. (*Holds it up.*) Did she have a bird, Mrs. Hale?

MRS. HALE: Why, I don't know whether she did or not — I've not been here for so long. There was a man around last year selling canaries cheap, but I don't know as she took one; maybe she did. She used to sing real pretty herself.

MRS. PETERS (*glancing around*): Seems funny to think of a bird here. But she must have had one, or why would she have a cage? I wonder what happened to it?

MRS. HALE: I s'pose maybe the cat got it.

MRS. PETERS: No, she didn't have a cat. She's got that feeling some people have about cats — being afraid of them. My cat got in her room and she was real upset and asked me to take it out.

MRS. HALE: My sister Bessie was like that. Queer, ain't it?

MRS. PETERS (*examining the cage*): Why, look at this door. It's broke. One hinge is pulled apart. (*Takes a step down to Mrs. Hale's right.*)

MRS. HALE (*looking too*): Looks as if someone must have been rough with it.

MRS. PETERS: Why, yes. (*She brings the cage forward and puts it on the table.*)

MRS. HALE (*glancing toward up left door*): I wish if they're going to find any evidence they'd be about it. I don't like this place.

MRS. PETERS: But I'm awful glad you came with me, Mrs. Hale. It would be lonesome for me sitting here alone.

MRS. HALE: It would, wouldn't it? (*Dropping her sewing.*) But I tell you what I do wish, Mrs. Peters. I wish I had come over sometimes when *she* was here. I — (*looking around the room*) — wish I had.

MRS. PETERS: But of course you were awful busy, Mrs. Hale — your house and your children.

MRS. HALE (*rises and crosses left*): I could've come. I stayed away because it weren't cheerful — and that's why I ought to have come. I — (*looking out left window*) — I've never liked this place. Maybe it's because it's down in a hollow and you don't see the road. I dunno what it is, but it's a lonesome place and always was. I wish I had come over to see Minnie Foster sometimes. I can see now — (*Shakes her head.*)

MRS. PETERS (*left of table and above it*): Well, you mustn't reproach yourself, Mrs. Hale. Somehow we just don't see how it is with other folks until — something turns up.

MRS. HALE: Not having children makes less work — but it makes a quiet house, and Wright out to work all day, and no company when he did come in. (*Turning from window.*) Did you know John Wright, Mrs. Peters?

MRS. PETERS: Not to know him; I've seen him in town. They say he was a good man.

MRS. HALE: Yes — good; he didn't drink, and kept his word as well as most, I guess, and paid his debts. But he was a hard man, Mrs. Peters. Just to pass the time of day with him — (*Shivers.*) Like a raw wind that gets to the bone. (*Pauses, her eye falling on the cage.*) I should think she would 'a' wanted a bird. But what do you suppose went with it?

MRS. PETERS: I don't know, unless it got sick and died. (*She reaches over and swings the broken door, swings it again, both women watch it.*)

MRS. HALE: You weren't raised round here, were you? (*Mrs. Peters shakes her head.*) You didn't know — her?

MRS. PETERS: Not till they brought her yesterday.

MRS. HALE: She — come to think of it, she was kind of like a bird herself — real sweet and pretty, but kind of timid and — fluttery. How — she — did — change. (*Silence: then as if struck by a happy thought and relieved to get back to everyday things. Crosses right above Mrs. Peters to cupboard, replaces small chair used to stand on to its original place down right.*) Tell you what, Mrs. Peters, why don't you take the quilt in with you? It might take up her mind.

MRS. PETERS: Why, I think that's a real nice idea, Mrs.

Hale. There couldn't possibly be any objection to it could there? Now, just what would I take? I wonder if her patches are in here — and her things. (*They look in the sewing basket.*)

MRS. HALE (*crosses to right of table*): Here's some red. I expect this has got sewing things in it. (*Brings out a fancy box.*) What a pretty box. Looks like something somebody would give you. Maybe her scissors are in here. (*Opens box. Suddenly puts her hand to her nose.*) Why —— (*Mrs. Peters bends nearer, then turns her face away.*) There's something wrapped up in this piece of silk.

MRS. PETERS: Why, this isn't her scissors.

MRS. HALE (*lifting the silk*): Oh, Mrs. Peters — it's —— — (*Mrs. Peters bends closer.*)

MRS. PETERS: It's the bird.

MRS. HALE: But, Mrs. Peters — look at it! Its neck! Look at its neck! It's all — other side *to*.

MRS. PETERS: Somebody — wrung — its — neck. (*Their eyes meet. A look of growing comprehension, of horror. Steps are heard outside. Mrs. Hale slips box under quilt pieces, and sinks into her chair. Enter Sheriff and County Attorney. Mrs. Peters steps down left and stands looking out of window.*)

COUNTY ATTORNEY (*as one turning from serious things to little pleasantries*): Well, ladies, have you decided whether she was going to quilt it or knot it? (*Crosses to center above table.*)

MRS. PETERS: We think she was going to — knot it. (*Sheriff crosses to right of stove, lifts stove lid, and glances at fire, then stands warming hands at stove.*)

COUNTY ATTORNEY: Well, that's interesting, I'm sure. (*Seeing the bird-cage.*) Has the bird flown?

MRS. HALE (*putting more quilt pieces over the box*): We think the — cat got it.

COUNTY ATTORNEY (*preoccupied*): Is there a cat? (*Mrs. Hale glances in a quick covert way at Mrs. Peters.*)

MRS. PETERS (*turning from window takes a step in*): Well, not *now*. They're superstitious, you know. They leave.

COUNTY ATTORNEY (*to Sheriff Peters, continuing an interrupted conversation*): No sign at all of anyone having come from the outside. Their own rope. Now let's go up again and go over it piece by piece. (*They start upstairs.*) It would have to have been someone who knew just the —— (*Mrs. Peters sits down left of table. The two women sit there not looking at one another, but as if peering into something and at the same time holding back. When they talk now it is in the manner of feeling their way over strange ground, as if afraid of what they are saying, but as if they cannot help saying it.*)

MRS. HALE (*hesistatively and in hushed voice*): She liked the bird. She was going to bury it in that pretty box.

MRS. PETERS (*in a whisper*): When I was a girl — my kitten — there was a boy took a hatchet, and before my eyes — and before I could get there —— (*Covers her face an instant.*) If they hadn't held me back I would have — (*catches herself, looks upstairs where steps are heard, falters weakly*) — hurt him.

MRS. HALE (*with a slow look around her*): I wonder how it would seem never to have had any children around. (*Pause.*) No, Wright wouldn't like the bird — a thing that sang. She used to sing. He killed that, too.

MRS. PETERS (*moving uneasily*): We don't know who killed the bird.

MRS. HALE: I knew John Wright.

MRS. PETERS: It was an awful thing was done in this house that night, Mrs. Hale. Killing a man while he slept, slipping a rope around his neck that choked the life out of him.

MRS. HALE: His neck. Choked the life out of him. (*Her hand goes out and rests on the bird-cage.*)

MRS. PETERS (*with rising voice*): We don't know who killed him. We don't *know*.

MRS. HALE (*her own feelings not interrupted*): If there'd been years and years of nothing, then a bird to sing to you, it would be awful — still, after the bird was still.

MRS. PETERS (*something within her speaking*): I know what stillness is. When we homesteaded in Dakota, and my first baby died — after he was two years old, and me with no other then ——

MRS. HALE (*moving*): How soon do you suppose they'll be through looking for the evidence?

MRS. PETERS: I know what stillness is. (*Pulling herself back.*) The law has got to punish crimes, Mrs. Hale.

MRS. HALE (*not as if answering that*): I wish you'd seen Minnie Foster when she wore a white dress with blue ribbons and stood up there in the choir and sang. (*A look around the room.*) Oh, I *wish* I'd come over here once in a while! That was a crime! That was a crime! Who's going to punish that?

MRS. PETERS (*looking upstairs*): We mustn't — take on.

MRS. HALE: I might have known she needed help! I know how things can be — for women. I tell you, it's queer, Mrs. Peters. We live close together and we live far apart. We all go through the same things — it's all just a different kind of the same thing. (*Brushes her eyes, noticing the jar of fruit, reaches out for it.*) If I was you I wouldn't tell her her fruit was gone. Tell her it *ain't*. Tell her it's all right. Take this in to prove it to her. She — she may never know whether it was broke or not.

MRS. PETERS (*takes the jar, looks about for something to wrap it in; takes petticoat from the clothes brought from the other room, very nervously begins winding this around the jar. In a false voice*): My, it's a good thing the men couldn't hear us. Wouldn't they just laugh! Getting all stirred up over a little thing like a — dead canary. As if they could have anything to do with — with — wouldn't they *laugh*! (*The men are heard coming downstairs.*)

MRS. HALE (*under her breath*): Maybe they would — maybe they wouldn't.

COUNTY ATTORNEY: No, Peters, it's all perfectly clear except a reason for doing it. But you know juries when it comes to women. If there was some definite thing. (*Crosses slowly to above table. Sheriff crosses down right. Mrs. Hale and Mrs. Peters remain seated at either side of table.*) Something to show — something to make a story about — a thing that would connect up with this strange way of doing it —— (*The women's eyes meet for an instant. Enter Hale from outer door.*)

HALE (*remaining by door*): Well, I've got the team around. Pretty cold out there.

COUNTY ATTORNEY: I'm going to stay awhile by myself. (*To the Sheriff.*) You can send Frank out for me, can't you? I want to go over everything. I'm not satisfied that we can't do better.

SHERIFF: Do you want to see what Mrs. Peters is going to take in? (*The Lawyer picks up the apron, laughs.*)

COUNTY ATTORNEY: Oh, I guess they're not very dangerous things the ladies have picked out. (*Moves a few things about, disturbing the quilt pieces which cover the box. Steps back.*) No, Mrs. Peters doesn't need supervising. For that matter a sheriff's wife is married to the law. Ever think of it that way, Mrs. Peters?

MRS. PETERS: Not — just that way.

SHERIFF (*chuckling*): Married to the law. (*Moves to down right door to the other room.*) I just want you to come in here a minute, George. We ought to take a look at these windows.

COUNTY ATTORNEY (*scoffingly*): Oh, windows!

SHERIFF: We'll be right out, Mr. Hale. (*Hale goes outside. The Sheriff follows the County Attorney into the room. Then Mrs. Hale rises, hands tight together, looking intensely at Mrs. Peters, whose eyes make a slow turn, finally meeting Mrs. Hale's. A moment Mrs. Hale holds her, then her own eyes point the way to where the box is concealed. Suddenly Mrs. Peters throws back quilt pieces and tries to put the box in the bag she is carrying. It is too big. She opens box, starts to take bird out, cannot touch it, goes to pieces, stands there helpless. Sound of a knob turning in the other room. Mrs. Hale snatches the box and puts it in the pocket of her big coat. Enter County Attorney and Sheriff, who remains down right.*)

COUNTY ATTORNEY (*crosses to up left door facetiously*): Well, Henry, at least we found out that she was not going to quilt it. She was going to — what is it you call it, ladies?

MRS. HALE (*standing center below table facing front, her hand against her pocket*): We call it — knot it, Mr. Henderson.

COMMENTARY

Christine Dymkowski (b. 1950)

ON THE EDGE: THE PLAYS OF SUSAN GLASPELL   *1988*

Christine Dymkowski sees Trifles *as a play that occupies the edge — the marginalized space reserved for women. The male figures in the play assume that their interests are central to the murder investigation, whereas Glaspell demonstrates that the most significant issues in the investigation are on the edge of men's attention, where they can never see them.*

The paradoxically central nature of the edge informs Glaspell's theatrical methods and themes. Her first play, *Trifles* (1916), illustrates its use in several ways, the irony of the title already having been noted. The plot revolves around the visit to a farmhouse by County Attorney Henderson and Sheriff Peters to investigate the murder of John Wright; they are accompanied by the farmer who discovered the murder and, almost incidentally, by the farmer's and sheriff's wives. The men's assumption is that Minnie Wright, already in custody for the crime, has killed her husband, and they are there to search the house for clues to a motive. The audience undoubtedly sees them as protagonists at the start of the play.

The stage directions immediately call attention to the women's marginality: the men, "much bundled up" against the freezing cold, "go at once to the stove" in the Wrights' kitchen, while the women who follow them in do so "slowly, and stand close together near the door." The separateness of the female and male worlds is thus immediately established visually and then reinforced by the dialogue:

> MRS. PETERS (*to the other woman*): Oh, her fruit; it did freeze. (*To the Lawyer.*) She worried about that when it turned so cold. . . .
> SHERIFF: Well, can you beat the women [*sic*]! Held for murder and worryin' about her preserves.
> COUNTY ATTORNEY: I guess before we're through she may have something more serious than preserves to worry about.
> HALE: Well, women are used to worrying over trifles.
>
> (*The two women move a little closer together.*)

Not surprisingly, the women are relegated to the kitchen, while the men's attention turns to the rest of the house, particularly the bedroom where the crime was committed: "You're convinced that there was nothing important here — nothing that would point to any motive," Henderson asks Peters, and is assured that there is "Nothing here but kitchen things." However, while the men view the kitchen as marginal to their purpose, the drama stays centered there where the women are: contrary to expectation, it becomes the central focus of the play.

Ironically, it is the kitchen that holds the clues to the desperation and loneliness of Minnie's life and yields the women the answers for which the men search in vain; moreover, the understanding that they do reach goes beyond the mere solving of

520

the crime to a redefinition of what the crime was. Mrs. Hale blames herself for a failure of imagination: "Oh, I *wish* I'd come over here once in a while! That was a crime! That was a crime! Who's going to punish that? . . . I might have known she needed help! I know how things can be — for women. I tell you, it's queer, Mrs. Peters. We live close together and we live far apart. We all go through the same things — it's all just a different kind of the same thing." The empathy both women feel for Minnie leads them to suppress the evidence they have found, patiently enduring the men's condescension instead of competing with them on their own ground. Conventional moral values are overturned, just as the expected form of the murder mystery is ignored: the play differentiates between justice and law and shows that the traditional "solution" is no such thing.

Just as Glaspell sets the play in the seemingly marginal kitchen, she makes the absent Minnie Wright its focus, a tactic she was to use again in *Bernice* and *Alison's House*; although noted by critics, this use of an absent central character has not received much comment. It is yet another way in which Glaspell makes central the apparently marginal — indeed, in stage terms, the nonexistent.

Luigi Pirandello

Luigi Pirandello (1867–1936) was an Italian short-story writer and novelist, a secondary school teacher, and finally a playwright. His life was complicated by business failures that wiped out his personal income and threw his wife into a psychological depression that Pirandello quite bluntly described as madness. Out of his acquaintance with madness — he remained with his wife for fourteen years after she lost touch with reality — Pirandello claimed to have developed much of his attitude toward the shifting surfaces of appearances.

Pirandello's short stories and novels show the consistent pattern of his plays: a deep examination of what we know to be real and a questioning of our confidence in our beliefs. His novel *Shoot* (1915) questions the surfaces of cinema reality, which contemporary Italy had embraced with great enthusiasm. His relentless examination of the paradoxes of experience has given him a reputation for pessimism. He himself said, "I think of life as a very sad piece of buffoonery," and he insisted that people bear within them a deep need to deceive themselves "by creating a reality . . . which . . . is discovered to be vain and illusory."

As Pirandello was not a popular writer in Italy, much of his dramatic work was first performed abroad. But he did win the Nobel Prize for literature in 1934, an indication that his particular brand of modernism was indeed influential. At that time Pirandello was a member of the Fascist Party in Italy, although his participation was limited primarily to his work in the state-supported Art Theater of Rome, which he founded.

Pirandello's influence in modern theater resulted from his experimentation with the concept of realism that dominated drama from the time of Strindberg and Ibsen. The concept of the imaginary "fourth wall" of the stage through which the audience observed the action of characters in their living rooms had become the norm in theater. Pirandello, however, questioned all thought of norms by bringing the very idea of reality under philosophical scrutiny. His questioning helped playwrights around the world expand their approaches to theater in the early part of the twentieth century. Pirandello was one of the first, and one of the best, experimentalists.

SIX CHARACTERS IN SEARCH OF AN AUTHOR

Pirandello's play is part of a trilogy: *Six Characters in Search of an Author* (1921), *Each in His Own Way* (1924), and *Tonight We Improvise* (1930). These plays all examine the impossibility of knowing reality. There is no objective truth to know, Pirandello tells us, and what we think of as reality is totally subjective, something that each of us maintains independently of other people and that none of us can communicate. We are, in other words, apart, sealed into our own limited world.

These ideas were hardly novel. Playwrights had dealt with them before, even during the Elizabethan age, at a time when — because of the Protestant Reformation — the absolute systems of reality promoted by the Roman Catholic Church had crumbled. Pirandello's plays were also produced during a period — the 1920s — when his culture was uncertain, frightened, and still reeling in shock from the destruction of World War I. In this depressed time, Pirandello's audience saw in his work a reflection of their own dispirited, fearful selves.

In a sense, *Six Characters in Search of an Author* is about the relationship between art and life, and especially about the relationship between drama and life. The premise of the play is absurd. In the middle of a rehearsal of a Pirandello play, several characters appear and request that an author be present to cobble them into a play. The stage manager assumes that they are presenting themselves as actors to be in a play, but they explain that they are not actors. They are real characters. This implies a paradox that characters are independent of the actors who play them (we are used to the characters being only on paper). When they demand actors to represent them, we know that one limit of impossibility has been reached.

The characters who appear are, in a sense, types: a father, a mother, a stepdaughter, a son, two silent figures — the boy and the child — and, finally, a milliner, Madame Pace. They share the stage with the actors of the company who are rehearsing the Pirandello play *Mixing It Up*. The six characters have been abandoned by their creator, the author who has absconded, leaving them in search of a substitute. The stepdaughter, late in the play, surmises that their author abandoned them "in a fit of depression, of disgust for the ordinary theater as the public knows it and likes it."

Pirandello uses his characters and their situation to comment on the life of the theater in the 1920s, and he also uses them to begin a series of speculations on the relationship of a public to the actors they see in plays, the characters the actors play, and the authors who create them. To an extent, the relationship between an author and his or her characters always implies a metaphor for the relationship between a creator and all creation. It is tempting to think of Samuel Beckett years later in his *Waiting for Godot* imagining an "author" having abandoned his creations because they failed to satisfy him. The six characters — or creations — who invade the stage in Pirandello's play have a firm sense of themselves and their actions. They bring with them a story — as all characters in plays do — and they invite the manager to participate in their stories, just as characters invite audiences to become one with their narratives.

One of the more amusing scenes depicts the characters' reactions to seeing actors play their parts. Since they are "real" characters, they have the utmost authority in knowing how their parts should be played, and they end up laughing at the inept efforts of the actors in act II. When the manager disputes with them, wondering why they protest so vigorously, they explain that they want to make sure the truth is told. The truth: the concept seems so simple on the surface, but in the situation that Pirandello has conceived, it is loaded with complexities that the stage manager cannot fathom.

By the time the question of truth has been raised, the manager has begun to get a sense of the poignancy of the story that these characters have to tell. He has also begun to see that he must let them continue to tell their story — except that they are not telling it, they are living it. When the climax of their story is reached in the last moments of the play, the line between what is acted and what is lived onstage has become almost completely blurred. When the play ends, it is difficult to know what has truly occurred and what has truly been acted out.

Six Characters in Search of an Author has endured because it still rings true in its examination of the relationship between art and life, illusion and reality. The very word *illusion* is rejected by the characters — as characters they are part of the illusion of reality. They reject the thought that they are literature, asserting, "This is Life, this is passion!"

Six Characters in Search of an Author in Performance

The 1916 Italian production of *Six Characters in Search of an Author* established Pirandello as a dramatist of major importance. The first London production was in the Kingsway Theatre in March 1922. The reviews were positive, and the audiences, although at times puzzled, were responsive to what the *Christian Science Monitor* called "one of the freshest and most original productions seen for a long time." The first production in New York was directed by Brock Pemberton at the Princess Theater in October 1922 with the distinguished American actress Florence Eldridge as the stepdaughter. One newspaper critic said, "Pirandello turns a powerful microscope on the dramatist's mental workshop — the modus operandi of play production — and after having destroyed our illusion, like a prestidigitator who shows us how a trick is done, expects us to believe in him."

Pirandello directed the play in Italian in London in 1925, and despite the audience's general inability to understand the language, the New Oxford Theatre was filled for every night of its run. He brought the company to the United States after the British censor determined that the play was "unsuitable for English audiences" and closed the play in London. It was not officially licensed for performance in England again until 1928.

Revivals of the play have been numerous. Three productions in New York in the 1930s preceded revivals in 1948 and 1955. London saw productions in February 1932 and November 1950. By the 1930s audience confusion had simmered down, and in 1932 one London critic declared, "Repetition cannot dull the brilliance of the play's attack on theatrical shams." Sir Ralph Richardson performed in London's West End in 1963. In 1955, Tyrone Guthrie's Phoenix Theater used a translation and adaptation by Guthrie and Michael Wager. The production was not successful, although critics liked the translation. Robert Brustein received extraordinary praise for his American Repertory Theatre (ART) production in 1985. Instead of having the six characters interrupt a Pirandello play, they interrupt the rehearsal of a Molière play, *Sganarelle,* which has roots in Italian commedia dell'arte, and which had been a highly successful ART production. This self-reference — in Pirandellian fashion — helped to blur the line between the realities on and off the stage. Boston critic Kevin Kelly said of the performance, "Brustein immediately links the paradox in Pirandello's theme about reality in illusion / illusion in reality to . . . the pragmatic fantasy of theater itself."

Luigi Pirandello (1867–1936)

SIX CHARACTERS IN SEARCH OF AN AUTHOR   *1921*

A COMEDY IN THE MAKING

TRANSLATED BY EDWARD STORER

Characters of the Comedy in the Making

THE FATHER
THE MOTHER
THE STEPDAUGHTER
THE SON
THE BOY ⎱
THE CHILD ⎰ *do not speak*
MADAME PACE

Actors of the Company

THE MANAGER
LEADING LADY
LEADING MAN
SECOND LADY LEAD
L'INGÉNUE
JUVENILE LEAD
OTHER ACTORS AND ACTRESSES
PROPERTY MAN
PROMPTER
MACHINIST
MANAGER'S SECRETARY
DOOR-KEEPER
SCENE SHIFTERS

Scene: *Daytime. The stage of a theater.*

(**N.B.:** *The Comedy is without acts or scenes. The performance is interrupted once, without the curtain being lowered, when the Manager and the chief characters withdraw to arrange a scenario. A second interruption of the action takes place when, by mistake, the stage hands let the curtain down.*)

ACT I

(*The spectators will find the curtain raised and the stage as it usually is during the daytime. It will be half dark, and empty, so that from the beginning the public may have the impression of an impromptu performance.*)

(*Prompter's box and a small table and chair for the Manager.*)

(*Two other small tables and several chairs scattered about as during rehearsals.*)

(*The Actors and Actresses of the company enter from the back of the stage: first one, then another, then two together; nine or ten in all. They are about to rehearse a Pirandello play: Mixing It Up. Some of the company move off toward their dressing rooms. The Prompter, who has the "book" under his arm, is waiting for the Manager in order to begin the rehearsal.*)

(*The Actors and Actresses, some standing, some sitting, chat and smoke. One perhaps reads a paper; another cons his part.*)

(*Finally, the Manager enters and goes to the table prepared for him. His Secretary brings him his mail, through which he glances. The Prompter takes his seat, turns on a light, and opens the "book."*)

THE MANAGER (*throwing a letter down on the table*): I can't see. (*To Property Man.*) Let's have a little light, please!

PROPERTY MAN: Yes, sir, yes, at once. (*A light comes down on to the stage.*)

THE MANAGER (*clapping his hands*): Come along! Come along! Second act of "Mixing It Up." (*Sits down.*)

(*The Actors and Actresses go from the front of the stage to the wings, all except the three who are to begin the rehearsal.*)

THE PROMPTER (*reading the "book"*): "Leo Gala's house. A curious room serving as dining-room and study."

THE MANAGER (*to Property Man*): Fix up the old red room.

PROPERTY MAN (*noting it down*): Red set. All right!

THE PROMPTER (*continuing to read from the "book"*): "Table already laid and writing desk with books and papers. Bookshelves. Exit rear to Leo's bedroom. Exit left to kitchen. Principal exit to right."

THE MANAGER (*energetically*): Well, you understand: The principal exit over there; here, the kitchen. (*Turning to actor who is to play the part of Socrates.*) You make your entrances and exits here. (*To Property Man.*) The baize doors at the rear, and curtains.

PROPERTY MAN (*noting it down*): Right!

PROMPTER (*reading as before*): "When the curtain rises, Leo Gala, dressed in cook's cap and apron, is busy beating an egg in a cup. Philip, also dressed as a cook, is beating another egg. Guidi Venanzi is seated and listening."

LEADING MAN (*to Manager*): Excuse me, but must I absolutely wear a cook's cap?

THE MANAGER (*annoyed*): I imagine so. It says so there anyway. (*Pointing to the "book."*)

LEADING MAN: But it's ridiculous!

THE MANAGER (*jumping up in a rage*): Ridiculous? Ridiculous? Is it my fault if France won't send us any more good comedies, and we are reduced to putting on Pirandello's works, where nobody understands anything, and where the author plays the fool with us all? (*The Actors grin. The Manager goes to Leading Man and shouts.*) Yes sir, you put on the cook's cap and beat eggs. Do you suppose that with all this egg-beating business you are on an ordinary stage? Get that out of your head. You represent the shell of the eggs you are beating! (*Laughter and comments among the Actors.*) Silence! and listen to my explanations, please! (*To Leading Man.*) "The empty form of reason without the fullness of instinct, which is blind."— You stand for reason, your wife is instinct. It's a mixing up of the parts, according to which you

who act your own part become the puppet of yourself. Do you understand?

LEADING MAN: I'm hanged if I do.

THE MANAGER: Neither do I. But let's get on with it. It's sure to be a glorious failure anyway. (*Confidentially.*) But I say, please face three-quarters. Otherwise, what with the abstruseness of the dialogue, and the public that won't be able to hear you, the whole thing will go to hell. Come on! come on!

PROMPTER: Pardon sir, may I get into my box? There's a bit of a draft.

THE MANAGER: Yes, yes, of course!

(*At this point, the Door-Keeper has entered from the stage door and advances toward the Manager's table, taking off his braided cap. During this maneuver, the Six Characters enter, and stop by the door at back of stage, so that when the Door-Keeper is about to announce their coming to the Manager, they are already on the stage. A tenuous light surrounds them, almost as if irradiated by them — the faint breath of their fantastic reality.*)

(*This light will disappear when they come forward toward the actors. They preserve, however, something of the dream lightness in which they seem almost suspended; but this does not detract from the essential reality of their forms and expressions.*)

(*He who is known as the Father is a man of about 50: hair, reddish in color, thin at the temples; he is not bald, however, thick mustaches, falling over his still fresh mouth, which often opens in an empty and uncertain smile. He is fattish, pale; with an especially wide forehead. He has blue, oval-shaped eyes, very clear and piercing. Wears light trousers and a dark jacket. He is alternatively mellifluous and violent in his manner.*)

(*The Mother seems crushed and terrified as if by an intolerable weight of shame and abasement. She is dressed in modest black and wears a thick widow's veil of crepe. When she lifts this, she reveals a waxlike face. She always keeps her eyes downcast.*)

(*The Stepdaughter is dashing, almost impudent, beautiful. She wears mourning too, but with great elegance. She shows contempt for the timid half-frightened manner of the wretched Boy (14 years old, and also dressed in black); on the other hand, she displays a lively tenderness for her little sister, the Child (about four), who is dressed in white, with a black silk sash at the waist.*)

(*The Son (22) is tall, severe in his attitude of contempt for the Father, supercilious and indifferent to the Mother. He looks as if he had come on the stage against his will.*)

DOOR-KEEPER (*cap in hand*): Excuse me, sir . . .

THE MANAGER (*rudely*): Eh? What is it?

DOOR-KEEPER (*timidly*): These people are asking for you, sir.

THE MANAGER (*furious*): I am rehearsing, and you know perfectly well no one's allowed to come in during rehearsals! (*Turning to the Characters.*) Who are you, please? What do you want?

THE FATHER (*coming forward a little, followed by the*

others who seem embarrassed): As a matter of fact . . . we have come here in search of an author . . .

THE MANAGER (*half angry, half amazed*): An author? What author?

THE FATHER: Any author, sir.

THE MANAGER: But there's no author here. We are not rehearsing a new piece.

THE STEPDAUGHTER (*vivaciously*): So much the better, so much the better! We can be your new piece.

AN ACTOR (*coming forward from the others*): Oh, do you hear that?

THE FATHER (*to Stepdaughter*): Yes, but if the author isn't here . . . (*To Manager.*) unless you would be willing . . .

THE MANAGER: You are trying to be funny.

THE FATHER: No, for Heaven's sake, what are you saying? We bring you a drama, sir.

THE STEPDAUGHTER: We may be your fortune.

THE MANAGER: Will you oblige me by going away? We haven't time to waste with mad people.

THE FATHER (*mellifluously*): Oh sir, you know well that life is full of infinite absurdities, which, strangely enough, do not even need to appear plausible, since they are true.

THE MANAGER: What the devil is he talking about?

THE FATHER: I say that to reverse the ordinary process may well be considered a madness: that is, to create credible situations, in order that they may appear true. But permit me to observe that if this be madness, it is the sole *raison d'être*° of your profession, gentlemen. (*The Actors look hurt and perplexed.*)

THE MANAGER (*getting up and looking at him*): So our profession seems to you one worthy of madmen then?

THE FATHER: Well, to make seem true that which isn't true . . . without any need . . . for a joke as it were . . . Isn't that your mission, gentlemen: to give life to fantastic characters on the stage?

THE MANAGER (*interpreting the rising anger of the Company*): But I would beg you to believe, my dear sir, that the profession of the comedian is a noble one. If today, as things go, the playwrights give us stupid comedies to play and puppets to represent instead of men, remember we are proud to have given life to immortal works here on these very boards! (*The Actors, satisfied, applaud their Manager.*)

THE FATHER (*interrupting furiously*): Exactly, perfectly, to living beings more alive than those who breathe and wear clothes: beings less real perhaps, but truer! I agree with you entirely. (*The Actors look at one another in amazement.*)

THE MANAGER: But what do you mean? Before, you said . . .

THE FATHER: No, excuse me, I meant it for you, sir, who were crying out that you had no time to lose with madmen, while no one better than yourself knows that nature uses the instrument of human fantasy in order to pursue her high creative purpose.

raison d'être: French for "reason to exist."

THE MANAGER: Very well, — but where does all this take us?

THE FATHER: Nowhere! It is merely to show you that one is born to life in many forms, in many shapes, as tree, or as stone, as water, as butterfly, or as woman. So one may also be born a character in a play.

THE MANAGER (*with feigned comic dismay*): So you and these other friends of yours have been born characters?

THE FATHER: Exactly, and alive as you see! (*Manager and Actors burst out laughing.*)

THE FATHER (*hurt*): I am sorry you laugh, because we carry in us a drama, as you can guess from this woman here veiled in black.

THE MANAGER (*losing patience at last and almost indignant*): Oh, chuck it! Get away please! Clear out of here! (*To Property Man.*) For Heaven's sake, turn them out!

THE FATHER (*resisting*): No, no, look here, we . . .

THE MANAGER (*roaring*): We come here to work, you know.

LEADING ACTOR: One cannot let oneself be made such a fool of.

THE FATHER (*determined, coming forward*): I marvel at your incredulity, gentlemen. Are you not accustomed to see the characters created by an author spring to life in yourselves and face each other? Just because there is no "book" (*pointing to the Prompter's box*) which contains us, you refuse to believe . . .

THE STEPDAUGHTER (*advances toward Manager, smiling and coquettish*): Believe me, we are really six most interesting characters, sir; sidetracked however.

THE FATHER: Yes, that is the word! (*To Manager all at once.*) In the sense, that is, that the author who created us alive no longer wished, or was no longer able, materially to put us into a work of art. And this was a real crime, sir, because he who has had the luck to be born a character can laugh even at death. He cannot die. The man, the writer, the instrument of the creation will die, but his creation does not die. And to live for ever, it does not need to have extraordinary gifts or to be able to work wonders. Who was Sancho Panza? Who was Don Abbondio?° Yet they live eternally because — live germs as they were — they had the fortune to find a fecundating matrix, a fantasy which could raise and nourish them: make them live for ever!

THE MANAGER: That is quite all right. But what do you want here, all of you?

THE FATHER: We want to live.

THE MANAGER (*ironically*): For Eternity?

THE FATHER: No, sir, only for a moment . . . in you.

AN ACTOR: Just listen to him!

LEADING LADY: They want to live, in us . . . !

JUVENILE LEAD (*pointing to the Stepdaughter*): I've no objection, as far as that one is concerned!

Sancho Panza . . . Don Abbondio: Memorable characters in novels: the squire in Cervantes's *Don Quixote* and the priest in Manzoni's *I Promessi Sposi* (*The Betrothed*), respectively.

THE FATHER: Look here! look here! The comedy has to be made. (*To the Manager.*) But if you and your actors are willing, we can soon concert it among ourselves.

THE MANAGER (*annoyed*): But what do you want to concert? We don't go in for concerts here. Here we play dramas and comedies!

THE FATHER: Exactly! That is just why we have come to you.

THE MANAGER: And where is the "book"?

THE FATHER: It is in us! (*The Actors laugh.*) The drama is in us, and we are the drama. We are impatient to play it. Our inner passion drives us on to this.

THE STEPDAUGHTER (*disdainful, alluring, treacherous full of impudence*): My passion, sir! Ah, if you only knew! My passion for him! (*Points to the Father and makes a pretense of embracing him. Then she breaks out into a loud laugh.*)

THE FATHER (*angrily*): Behave yourself! And please don't laugh in that fashion.

THE STEPDAUGHTER: With your permission, gentlemen, I, who am a two months orphan, will show you how I can dance and sing. (*Sings and then dances Prenez garde à Tchou-Tchin-Tchou.*)

Les chinois sont un peuple malin,
De Shangaî à Pékin,
Ils ont mis des écriteaux partout:
Prenez garde à Tchou-Tchin-Tchou.°

ACTORS AND ACTRESSES: Bravo! Well done! Tip-top!

THE MANAGER: Silence! This isn't a café concert, you know! (*Turning to the Father in consternation.*) Is she mad?

THE FATHER: Mad? No, she's worse than mad.

THE STEPDAUGHTER (*to Manager*): Worse? Worse? Listen! Stage this drama for us at once! Then you will see that at a certain moment I . . . when this little darling here. . . . (*Takes the Child by the hand and leads her to the Manager.*) Isn't she a dear? (*Takes her up and kisses her.*) Darling! Darling! (*Puts her down again and adds feelingly.*) Well, when God suddenly takes this dear little child away from that poor mother there; and this imbecile here (*seizing hold of the Boy roughly and pushing him forward*) does the stupidest things, like the fool he is, you will see me run away. Yes, gentlemen, I shall be off. But the moment hasn't arrived yet. After what has taken place between him and me (*indicates the Father with a horrible wink*) I can't remain any longer in this society, to have to witness the anguish of this mother here for that fool. . . . (*Indicates the Son.*) Look at him! Look at him! See how indifferent, how frigid he is, because he is the legitimate son. He despises me, despises him (*pointing to the Boy*), despises this baby

Prenez . . . Tchou: This French popular song is an adaptation of "Chu-Chin-Chow," an old Broadway show tune. "The Chinese are a sly people; / From Shanghai to Peking, / They've stuck up warning signs; / Beware of Tchou-Tchin-Tchou." (The words are funnier in French because *chou* means "cabbage.")

here; because . . . we are bastards. (*Goes to the Mother and embraces her.*) And he doesn't want to recognize her as his mother — she who is the common mother of us all. He looks down upon her as if she were only the mother of us three bastards. Wretch! (*She says all this very rapidly, excitedly. At the word "bastards" she raises her voice, and almost spits out the final "Wretch!"*)

THE MOTHER (*to the Manager, in anguish*): In the name of these two little children, I beg you. . . . (*She grows faint and is about to fall.*) Oh God!

THE FATHER (*coming forward to support her as do some of the Actors*): Quick, a chair, a chair for this poor widow!

THE ACTORS: Is it true? Has she really fainted?

THE MANAGER: Quick, a chair! Here!

(*One of the Actors brings a chair, the others proffer assistance. The Mother tries to prevent the Father from lifting the veil which covers her face.*)

THE FATHER: Look at her! Look at her!

THE MOTHER: No, no; stop it please!

THE FATHER (*raising her veil*): Let them see you!

THE MOTHER (*rising and covering her face with her hands, in desperation*): I beg you, sir, to prevent this man from carrying out his plan which is loathsome to me.

THE MANAGER (*dumbfounded*): I don't understand at all. What is the situation? (*To the Father.*) Is this lady your wife?

THE FATHER: Yes, gentlemen: my wife!

THE MANAGER: But how can she be a widow if you are alive? (*The Actors find relief for their astonishment in a loud laugh.*)

THE FATHER: Don't laugh! Don't laugh like that, for Heaven's sake. Her drama lies just here in this: she has had a lover, a man who ought to be here.

THE MOTHER (*with a cry*): No! No!

THE STEPDAUGHTER: Fortunately for her, he is dead. Two months ago as I said. We are in mourning, as you see.

THE FATHER: He isn't here, you see, not because he is dead. He isn't here — look at her a moment and you will understand — because her drama isn't a drama of the love of two men for whom she was incapable of feeling anything except possibly a little gratitude — gratitude not for me but for the other. She isn't a woman, she is a mother, and her drama — powerful, sir, I assure you — lies, as a matter of fact, all in these four children she has had by two men.

THE MOTHER: I had them? Have you got the courage to say that I wanted them? (*To the Company.*) It was his doing. It was he who gave me that other man, who forced me to go away with him.

THE STEPDAUGHTER: It isn't true.

THE MOTHER (*startled*): Not true, isn't it?

THE STEPDAUGHTER: No, it isn't true, it just isn't true.

THE MOTHER: And what can you know about it?

THE STEPDAUGHTER: It isn't true. Don't believe it. (*To Manager.*) Do you know why she says so? For that fellow there. (*Indicates the Son.*) She tortures herself, destroys herself on account of the neglect of that son there, and she wants him to believe that if she abandoned him when he was only two years old, it was because he (*indicates the Father*) made her do so.

THE MOTHER (*vigorously*): He forced me to it, and I call God to witness it. (*To the Manager.*) Ask him (*indicates Husband*) if it isn't true. Let him speak. You (*to Daughter*) are not in a position to know anything about it.

THE STEPDAUGHTER: I know you lived in peace and happiness with my father while he lived. Can you deny it?

THE MOTHER: No, I don't deny it. . . .

THE STEPDAUGHTER: He was always full of affection and kindness for you. (*To the Boy, angrily.*) It's true, isn't it? Tell them! Why don't you speak, you little fool?

THE MOTHER: Leave the poor boy alone. Why do you want to make me appear ungrateful, daughter? I don't want to offend your father. I have answered him that I didn't abandon my house and my son through any fault of mine, nor from any wilful passion.

THE FATHER: It is true. It was my doing.

LEADING MAN (*to the Company*): What a spectacle!

LEADING LADY: We are the audience this time.

JUVENILE LEAD: For once, in a way.

THE MANAGER (*beginning to get really interested*): Let's hear them out. Listen!

THE SON: Oh yes, you're going to hear a fine bit now. He will talk to you of the Demon of Experiment.

THE FATHER: You are a cynical imbecile. I've told you so already a hundred times. (*To the Manager.*) He tries to make fun of me on account of this expression which I have found to excuse myself with.

THE SON (*with disgust*): Yes, phrases! phrases!

THE FATHER: Phrases! Isn't everyone consoled when faced with a trouble or fact he doesn't understand, by a word, some simple word, which tells us nothing and yet calms us?

THE STEPDAUGHTER: Even in the case of remorse. In fact, especially then.

THE FATHER: Remorse? No, that isn't true. I've done more than use words to quiet the remorse in me.

THE STEPDAUGHTER: Yes, there was a bit of money too. Yes, yes, a bit of money. There were the hundred lire he was about to offer me in payment, gentlemen. . . . (*Sensation of horror among the Actors.*)

THE SON (*to the Stepdaughter*): This is vile.

THE STEPDAUGHTER: Vile? There they were in a pale blue envelope on a little mahogany table in the back of Madame Pace's shop. You know Madame Pace — one of those ladies who attract poor girls of good family into their ateliers, under the pretext of their selling *robes et manteaux*.°

THE SON: And he thinks he has bought the right to tyrannize over us all with those hundred lire he was going to pay; but which, fortunately — note this, gentlemen — he had no chance of paying.

robes et manteaux: French for "dresses and capes."

THE STEPDAUGHTER: It was a near thing, though, you know! (*Laughs ironically.*)

THE MOTHER (*protesting*): Shame, my daughter, shame!

THE STEPDAUGHTER: Shame indeed! This is my revenge! I am dying to live that scene . . . The room . . . I see it . . . Here is the window with the mantles exposed, there the divan, the looking-glass, a screen, there in front of the window the little mahogany table with the blue envelope containing one hundred lire. I see it. I see it. I could take hold of it. . . . But you, gentlemen, you ought to turn your backs now: I am almost nude, you know. But I don't blush: I leave that to him. (*Indicating Father.*)

THE MANAGER: I don't understand this at all.

THE FATHER: Naturally enough. I would ask you, sir, to exercise your authority a little here, and let me speak before you believe all she is trying to blame me with. Let me explain.

THE STEPDAUGHTER: Ah yes, explain it in your own way.

THE FATHER: But don't you see that the whole trouble lies here? In words, words. Each one of us has within him a whole world of things, each man of us his own special world. And how can we ever come to an understanding if I put in the words I utter the sense and value of things as I see them; while you who listen to me must inevitably translate them according to the conception of things each one of you has within himself. We think we understand each other, but we never really do. Look here! This woman (*indicating the Mother*) takes all my pity for her as a specially ferocious form of cruelty.

THE MOTHER: But you drove me away.

THE FATHER: Do you hear her? I drove her away! She believes I really sent her away.

THE MOTHER: You know how to talk, and I don't but, believe me, sir (*to Manager*), after he had married me . . . who knows why? . . . I was a poor insignificant woman. . . .

THE FATHER: But, good Heavens! it was just for your humility that I married you. I loved this simplicity in you. (*He stops when he sees she makes signs to contradict him, opens his arms wide in sign of desperation, seeing how hopeless it is to make himself understood.*) You see she denies it. Her mental deafness, believe me, is phenomenal, the limit: (*touches his forehead*) deaf, deaf, mentally deaf! She has plenty of feeling. Oh yes, a good heart for the children; but the brain — deaf, to the point of desperation — !

THE STEPDAUGHTER: Yes, but ask him how his intelligence has helped us.

THE FATHER: If we could see all the evil that may spring from good, what should we do? (*At this point the Leading Lady, who is biting her lips with rage at seeing the Leading Man flirting with the Stepdaughter, comes forward and speaks to the Manager.*)

LEADING LADY: Excuse me, but are we going to rehearse today?

MANAGER: Of course, of course; but let's hear them out.

JUVENILE LEAD: This is something quite new.

L'INGÉNUE: Most interesting!

LEADING LADY: Yes, for the people who like that kind of thing. (*Casts a glance at Leading Man.*)

THE MANAGER (*to Father*): You must please explain yourself quite clearly. (*Sits down.*)

THE FATHER: Very well then: listen! I had in my service a poor man, a clerk, a secretary of mine, full of devotion, who became friends with her. (*Indicating the Mother.*) They understood one another, were kindred souls in fact, without, however, the least suspicion of any evil existing. They were incapable even of thinking of it.

THE STEPDAUGHTER: So he thought of it — for them!

THE FATHER: That's not true. I meant to do good to them — and to myself, I confess, at the same time. Things had come to the point that I could not say a word to either of them without their making a mute appeal, one to the other, with their eyes. I could see them silently asking each other how I was to be kept in countenance, how I was to be kept quiet. And this, believe me, was just about enough of itself to keep me in a constant rage, to exasperate me beyond measure.

THE MANAGER: And why didn't you send him away then — this secretary of yours?

THE FATHER: Precisely what I did, sir. And then I had to watch this poor woman drifting forlornly about the house like an animal without a master, like an animal one has taken in out of pity.

THE MOTHER: Ah yes. . . !

THE FATHER (*suddenly turning to the Mother*): It's true about the son anyway, isn't it?

THE MOTHER: He took my son away from me first of all.

THE FATHER: But not from cruelty. I did it so that he should grow up healthy and strong by living in the country.

THE STEPDAUGHTER (*pointing to him ironically*): As one can see.

THE FATHER (*quickly*): Is it my fault if he has grown up like this? I sent him to a wet nurse in the country, a peasant, as *she* did not seem to me strong enough, though she is of humble origin. That was, anyway, the reason I married her. Unpleasant all this may be, but how can it be helped? My mistake possibly, but there we are! All my life I have had these confounded aspirations towards a certain moral sanity. (*At this point the Stepdaughter bursts into a noisy laugh.*) Oh, stop it! Stop it! I can't stand it.

THE MANAGER: Yes, please stop it, for Heaven's sake.

THE STEPDAUGHTER: But imagine moral sanity from him, if you please — the client of certain ateliers like that of Madame Pace!

THE FATHER: Fool! That is the proof that I am a man! This seeming contradiction, gentlemen, is the strongest proof that I stand here a live man before you. Why, it is just for this very incongruity in my nature that I have had to suffer what I have. I could not live by the side of that woman (*indicating the Mother*) any longer; but not so much for the boredom she inspired me with as for the pity I felt for her.

THE MOTHER: And so he turned me out — .

THE FATHER: — well provided for! Yes, I sent her to that man, gentlemen . . . to let her go free of me.

THE MOTHER: And to free himself.

THE FATHER: Yes, I admit it. It was also a liberation for me. But great evil has come of it. I meant well when I did it, and I did it more for her sake than mine. I swear it. (*Crosses his arms on his chest; then turns suddenly to the Mother.*) Did I ever lose sight of you until that other man carried you off to another town, like the angry fool he was? And on account of my pure interest in you . . . my pure interest, I repeat, that had no base motive in it . . . I watched with the tenderest concern the new family that grew up around her. She can bear witness to this. (*Points to the Stepdaughter.*)

THE STEPDAUGHTER: Oh yes, that's true enough. When I was a kiddie so so high, you know, with plaits over my shoulders and knickers longer than my skirts, I used to see him waiting outside the school for me to come out. He came to see how I was growing up.

THE FATHER: This is infamous, shameful!

THE STEPDAUGHTER: No. Why?

THE FATHER: Infamous! infamous! (*Then excitedly to Manager, explaining.*) After she (*indicating the Mother*) went away, my house seemed suddenly empty. She was my incubus, but she filled my house. I was like a dazed fly alone in the empty rooms. This boy here (*indicating the Son*) was educated away from home, and when he came back, he seemed to me to be no more mine. With no mother to stand between him and me, he grew up entirely for himself, on his own, apart, with no tie of intellect or affection binding him to me. And then — strange but true — I was driven, by curiosity at first and then by some tender sentiment, towards her family, which had come into being through my will. The thought of her began gradually to fill up the emptiness I felt all around me. I wanted to know if she were happy in living out the simple daily duties of life. I wanted to think of her as fortunate and happy because far away from the complicated torments of my spirit. And so, to have proof of this, I used to watch that child coming out of school.

THE STEPDAUGHTER: Yes, yes. True. He used to follow me in the street and smiled at me, waved his hand, like this. I would look at him with interest, wondering who he might be. I told my mother, who guessed at once. (*The Mother agrees with a nod.*) Then she didn't want to send me to school for some days; and when I finally went back, there he was again — looking so ridiculous — with a paper parcel in his hands. He came close to me, caressed me, and drew out a fine straw hat from the parcel, with a bouquet of flowers — all for me!

THE MANAGER: A bit discursive this, you know!

THE SON (*contemptuously*): Literature! Literature!

Scene from the 1984 American
Repertory Theatre production of *Six
Characters in Search of an Author,*
directed by Robert Brustein.

THE FATHER: Literature indeed! This is life, this is passion!

THE MANAGER: It may be, but it won't act.

THE FATHER: I agree. This is only the part leading up. I don't suggest this should be staged. She (*pointing to the Stepdaughter*), as you see, is no longer the flapper with plaits down her back —

THE STEPDAUGHTER: — and knickers showing below the skirt!

THE FATHER: The drama is coming now, sir; something new, complex, most interesting.

THE STEPDAUGHTER: As soon as my father died . . .

THE FATHER: — there was absolute misery for them. They came back here, unknown to me. Through her stupidity! (*Pointing to the Mother.*) It is true she can barely write her own name; but she could anyhow have got her daughter to write to me that they were in need . . .

THE MOTHER: And how was I to divine all this sentiment in him?

THE FATHER: That is exactly your mistake, never to have guessed any of my sentiments.

THE MOTHER: After so many years apart, and all that had happened . . .

THE FATHER: Was it my fault if that fellow carried you away? It happened quite suddenly, for after he had obtained some job or other, I could find no trace of them; and so, not unnaturally, my interest in them dwindled. But the drama culminated unforeseen and violent on their return, when I was impelled by my miserable flesh that still lives. . . . Ah! what misery, what wretchedness is that of the man who is alone and disdains debasing *liaisons!* Not old enough to do without women, and not young enough to go and look for one without shame. Misery? It's worse than misery; it's a horror; for no woman can any longer give him love; and when a man feels this. . . . One ought to do without, you say? Yes, yes, I know. Each of us when he appears before his fellows is clothed in a certain dignity. But every man knows what unconfessable things pass within the secrecy of his own heart. One gives way to the temptation, only to rise from it again, afterwards, with a great eagerness to reestablish one's dignity, as if it were a tombstone to place on the grave of one's shame, and a monument to hide and sign the memory of our weaknesses. Everybody's in the same case. Some folks haven't the courage to say certain things, that's all!

THE STEPDAUGHTER: All appear to have the courage to do them though.

THE FATHER: Yes, but in secret. Therefore, you want more courage to say these things. Let a man but speak these things out, and folks at once label him a cynic. But it isn't true. He is like all the others, better indeed, because he isn't afraid to reveal with the light of the intelligence the red shame of human bestiality on which most men close their eyes so as not to see it.

Woman — for example, look at her case! She turns tantalizing inviting glances on you. You seize her. No sooner does she feel herself in your grasp than she closes her eyes. It is the sign of her mission, the sign by which she says to man: "Blind yourself, for I am blind."

THE STEPDAUGHTER: Sometimes she can close them no

more: when she no longer feels the need of hiding her shame to herself, but dry-eyed and dispassionately, sees only that of the man who has blinded himself without love. Oh, all these intellectual complications make me sick, disgust me — all this philosophy that uncovers the beast in man, and then seeks to save him, excuse him . . . I can't stand it, sir. When a man seeks to "simplify" life bestially, throwing aside every relic of humanity, every chaste aspiration, every pure feeling, all sense of ideality, duty, modesty, shame . . . then nothing is more revolting and nauseous than a certain kind of remorse — crocodiles' tears, that's what it is.

THE MANAGER: Let's come to the point. This is only discussion.

THE FATHER: Very good, sir! But a fact is like a sack which won't stand up when it's empty. In order that it may stand up, one has to put into it the reason and sentiment which have caused it to exist. I couldn't possibly know that after the death of that man, they had decided to return here, that they were in misery, and that she (*pointing to the Mother*) had gone to work as a modiste,° and at a shop of the type of that of Madame Pace.

THE STEPDAUGHTER: A real high-class modiste, you must know, gentlemen. In appearance, she works for the leaders of the best society; but she arranges matters so that these elegant ladies serve her purpose . . . without prejudice to other ladies who are . . . well . . . only so so.

THE MOTHER: You will believe me, gentlemen, that it never entered my mind that the old hag offered me work because she had her eye on my daughter.

THE STEPDAUGHTER: Poor mamma! Do you know, sir, what that woman did when I brought her back the work my mother had finished? She would point out to me that I had torn one of my frocks, and she would give it back to my mother to mend. It was I who paid for it, always I; while this poor creature here believed she was sacrificing herself for me and these two children here, sitting up at night sewing Madame Pace's robes.

THE MANAGER: And one day you met there . . .

THE STEPDAUGHTER: Him, him. Yes sir, an old client. There's a scene for you to play! Superb!

THE FATHER: She, the Mother arrived just then . . .

THE STEPDAUGHTER (*treacherously*): Almost in time!

THE FATHER (*crying out*): No, in time! in time! Fortunately I recognized her . . . in time. And I took them back home with me to my house. You can imagine now her position and mine; she, as you see her; and I who cannot look her in the face.

THE STEPDAUGHTER: Absurd! How can I possibly be expected — after that — to be a modest young miss, a fit person to go with his confounded aspirations for "a solid moral sanity"?

THE FATHER: For the drama lies all in this — in the con-

modiste: A person who makes fashionable clothing for women.

science that I have, that each one of us has. We believe this conscience to be a single thing, but it is many-sided. There is one for this person, and another for that. Diverse consciences. So we have this illusion of being one person for all, of having a personality that is unique in all our acts. But it isn't true. We perceive this when, tragically perhaps, in something we do, we are as it were, suspended, caught up in the air on a kind of hook. Then we perceive that all of us was not in that act, and that it would be an atrocious injustice to judge us by that action alone, as if all our existence were summed up in that one deed. Now do you understand the perfidy of this girl? She surprised me in a place, where she ought not to have known me, just as I could not exist for her; and she now seeks to attach to me a reality such as I could never suppose I should have to assume for her in a shameful and fleeting moment of my life. I feel this above all else. And the drama, you will see, acquires a tremendous value from this point. Then there is the position of the others . . . his. . . . (*Indicating the Son.*)

THE SON (*shrugging his shoulders scornfully*): Leave me alone! I don't come into this.

THE FATHER: What? You don't come into this?

THE SON: I've got nothing to do with it, and don't want to have; because you know well enough I wasn't made to be mixed up in all this with the rest of you.

THE STEPDAUGHTER: We are only vulgar folk! He is the fine gentleman. You may have noticed, Mr. Manager, that I fix him now and again with a look of scorn while he lowers his eyes — for he knows the evil he has done me.

THE SON (*scarcely looking at her*): I?

THE STEPDAUGHTER: You! you! I owe my life on the streets to you. Did you or did you not deny us, with your behavior, I won't say the intimacy of home, but even that mere hospitality which makes guests feel at their ease? We were intruders who had come to disturb the kingdom of your legitimacy. I should like to have you witness, Mr. Manager, certain scenes between him and me. He says I have tyrannized over everyone. But it was just his behavior which made me insist on the reason for which I had come into the house, — this reason he calls "vile"— into his house, with my mother who is his mother too. And I came as mistress of the house.

THE SON: It's easy for them to put me always in the wrong. But imagine, gentlemen, the position of a son, whose fate it is to see arrive one day at his home a young woman of impudent bearing, a young woman who inquires for his father, with whom who knows what business she has. This young man has then to witness her return bolder than ever, accompanied by that child there. He is obliged to watch her treat his father in an equivocal and confidential manner. She asks for money of him in a way that lets one suppose he must give it to her, *must,* do you understand, because he has every obligation to do so.

THE FATHER: But I have, as a matter of fact, this obligation. I owe it to your mother.

THE SON: How should I know? When had I ever seen or heard of her? One day there arrive with her (*indicating Stepdaughter*) that lad and this baby here. I am told: "This is *your* mother too, you know." I divine from her manner (*indicating Stepdaughter again*) why it is they have come home. I had rather not say what I feel and think about it. I shouldn't even care to confess to myself. No action can therefore be hoped for from me in this affair. Believe me, Mr. Manager, I am an "unrealized" character, dramatically speaking; and I find myself not at all at ease in their company. Leave me out of it, I beg you.

THE FATHER: What? It is just because you are so that . . .

THE SON: How do you know what I am like? When did you ever bother your head about me?

THE FATHER: I admit it. I admit it. But isn't that a situation in itself? This aloofness of yours which is so cruel to me and to your mother, who returns home and sees you almost for the first time grown up, who doesn't recognize you but knows you are her son. . . . (*Pointing out the Mother to the Manager.*) See, she's crying!

THE STEPDAUGHTER (*angrily, stamping her foot*): Like a fool!

THE FATHER (*indicating Stepdaughter*): She can't stand him, you know. (*Then referring again to the Son.*) He says he doesn't come into the affair, whereas he is really the hinge of the whole action. Look at that lad who is always clinging to his mother, frightened and humiliated. It is on account of this fellow here. Possibly his situation is the most painful of all. He feels himself a stranger more than the others. The poor little chap feels mortified, humiliated at being brought into a home out of charity as it were. (*In confidence.*) He is the image of his father. Hardly talks at all. Humble and quiet.

THE MANAGER: Oh, we'll cut him out. You've no notion what a nuisance boys are on the stage. . . .

THE FATHER: He disappears soon, you know. And the baby too. She is the first to vanish from the scene. The drama consists finally in this: when that mother reenters my house, her family born outside of it, and shall we say superimposed on the original, ends with the death of the little girl, the tragedy of the boy and the flight of the elder daughter. It cannot go on, because it is foreign to its surroundings. So after much torment, we three remain: I, the mother, that son. Then, owing to the disappearance of that extraneous family, we too find ourselves strange to one another. We find we are living in an atmosphere of mortal desolation which is the revenge, as he (*indicating Son*) scornfully said of the Demon of Experiment, that unfortunately hides in me. Thus, sir, you see when faith is lacking, it becomes impossible to create certain states of happiness, for we lack the necessary humility. Vaingloriously, we try to substitute ourselves for this faith, creating thus for the rest of the world a reality which we believe after their fashion, while, actually, it doesn't exist. For each one of us has his own reality to be respected before God, even when it is harmful to one's very self.

THE MANAGER: There is something in what you say. I assure you all this interests me very much. I begin to think there's the stuff for a drama in all this, and not a bad drama either.

THE STEPDAUGHTER (*coming forward*): When you've got a character like me . . .

THE FATHER (*shutting her up, all excited to learn the decision of the Manager*): You be quiet!

THE MANAGER (*reflecting, heedless of interruption*): It's new . . . hem . . . yes. . . .

THE FATHER: Absolutely new!

THE MANAGER: You've got a nerve though, I must say, to come here and fling it at me like this . . .

THE FATHER: You will understand, sir, born as we are for the stage . . .

THE MANAGER: Are you amateur actors then?

THE FATHER: No, I say born for the stage, because . . .

THE MANAGER: Oh, nonsense. You're an old hand, you know.

THE FATHER: No sir, no. We act that role for which we have been cast, that role which we are given in life. And in my own case, passion itself, as usually happens, becomes a trifle theatrical when it is exalted.

THE MANAGER: Well, well, that will do. But you see, without an author. . . . I could give you the address of an author if you like . . .

THE FATHER: No, no. Look here! You must be the author.

THE MANAGER: I? What are you talking about?

THE FATHER: Yes, you, you! Why not?

THE MANAGER: Because I have never been an author: that's why.

THE FATHER: Then why not turn author now? Everybody does it. You don't want any special qualities. Your task is made much easier by the fact that we are all here alive before you. . . .

THE MANAGER: It won't do.

THE FATHER: What? When you see us live our drama. . . .

THE MANAGER: Yes, that's all right. But you want someone to write it.

THE FATHER: No, no. Someone to take it down, possibly, while we play it, scene by scene! It will be enough to sketch it out at first, and then try it over.

THE MANAGER: Well . . . I am almost tempted. It's a bit of an idea. One might have a shot at it.

THE FATHER: Of course. You'll see what scenes will come out of it. I can give you one, at once . . .

THE MANAGER: By Jove, it tempts me. I'd like to have a go at it. Let's try it out. Come with me to my office. (*Turning to the Actors.*) You are at liberty for a bit, but don't step out of the theater for long. In a quarter of an hour, twenty minutes, all back here again! (*To the Father.*) We'll see what can be done. Who knows if we don't get something really extraordinary out of it?

THE FATHER: There's no doubt about it. They (*indicating the Characters*) had better come with us too, hadn't they ?

THE MANAGER: Yes, yes. Come on! come on! (*Moves away and then turning to the Actors.*) Be punctual, please! (*Manager and the Six Characters cross the stage and go off. The other Actors remain, looking at one another in astonishment.*)

LEADING MAN: Is he serious? What the devil does he want to do?

JUVENILE LEAD: This is rank madness.

THIRD ACTOR: Does he expect to knock up a drama in five minutes?

JUVENILE LEAD: Like the improvisers!

LEADING LADY: If he thinks I'm going to take part in a joke like this. . . .

JUVENILE LEAD: I'm out of it anyway.

FOURTH ACTOR: I should like to know who they are. (*Alludes to Characters.*)

THIRD ACTOR: What do you suppose? Madmen or rascals!

JUVENILE LEAD: And he takes them seriously!

L'INGÉNUE: Vanity! He fancies himself as an author now.

LEADING MAN: It's absolutely unheard of. If the stage has come to this . . . well I'm . . .

FIFTH ACTOR: It's rather a joke.

THIRD ACTOR: Well, we'll see what's going to happen next.

(*Thus talking, the Actors leave the stage, some going out by the little door at the back, others retiring to their dressing rooms.*)

(*The curtain remains up.*)

(*The action of the play is suspended for twenty minutes.*)

ACT II

(*The stage call-bells ring to warn the company that the play is about to begin again.*)

(*The Stepdaughter comes out of the Manager's office along with the Child and the Boy. As she comes out of the office, she cries: —*)

Nonsense! nonsense! Do it yourselves! I'm not going to mix myself up in this mess. (*Turning to the Child and coming quickly with her on to the stage.*) Come on, Rosetta, let's run!

(*The Boy follows them slowly, remaining a little behind and seeming perplexed.*)

THE STEPDAUGHTER (*stops, bends over the Child and takes the latter's face between her hands*): My little darling! You're frightened, aren't you? You don't know where we are, do you? (*Pretending to reply to a question of the Child.*) What is the stage? It's a place, baby, you know, where people play at being serious, a place where they act comedies. We've got to act a comedy now, dead serious, you know; and

you're in it also, little one. (*Embraces her, pressing the little head to her breast, and rocking the Child for a moment.*) Oh darling, darling, what a horrid comedy you've got to play! What a wretched part they've found for you! A garden . . . a fountain . . . look . . . just suppose, kiddie, it's here. Where, you say? Why, right here in the middle. It's all pretense you know. That's the trouble, my pet: it's all make-believe here. It's better to imagine it though, because if they fix it up for you, it'll only be painted cardboard, painted cardboard for the rockery, the water, the plants. . . . Ah, but I think a baby like this one would sooner have a make-believe fountain than a real one, so she could play with it. What a joke it'll be for the others! But for you, alas! not quite such a joke: you who are real, baby dear, and really play by a real fountain that is big and green and beautiful, with ever so many bamboos around it that are reflected in the water, and a whole lot of little ducks swimming about. . . . No, Rosetta, no, your mother doesn't bother about you on account of that wretch of a son there. I'm in the devil of a temper, and as for that lad. . . . (*Seizes Boy by the arm to force him to take one of his hands out of his pockets.*) What have you got there? What are you hiding? (*Pulls his hand out of his pocket, looks into it, and catches the glint of a revolver.*) Ah! where did you get this? (*The Boy, very pale in the face, looks at her, but does not answer.*) Idiot! If I'd been in your place, instead of killing myself, I'd have shot one of those two, or both of them: father and son.

(*The Father enters from the office, all excited from his work. The Manager follows him.*)

THE FATHER: Come on, come on dear! Come here for a minute! We've arranged everything. It's all fixed up.

THE MANAGER (*also excited*): If you please, young lady, there are one or two points to settle still. Will you come along?

THE STEPDAUGHTER (*following him toward the office*): Ouff! what's the good, if you've arranged everything.

(*The Father, Manager, and Stepdaughter go back into the office again [off] for a moment. At the same time, the Son, followed by the Mother, comes out.*)

THE SON (*looking at the three entering office*): Oh this is fine, fine! And to think I can't even get away!

(*The Mother attempts to look at him, but lowers her eyes immediately when he turns away from her. She then sits down. The Boy and the Child approach her. She casts a glance again at the Son, and speaks with humble tones, trying to draw him into conversation.*)

THE MOTHER: And isn't my punishment the worst of all? (*Then seeing from the Son's manner that he will not bother himself about her.*) My God! Why are you so cruel? Isn't it enough for one person to support all this torment? Must you then insist on others seeing it also?

THE SON (*half to himself, meaning the Mother to hear, however*): And they want to put it on the stage! If there was at least a reason for it! He thinks he has got at the meaning of it all. Just as if each one of us in every circumstance of life couldn't find his own explanation of it! (*Pauses.*) He complains he was discovered in a place where he ought not to have been seen, in a moment of his life which ought to have remained hidden and kept out of the reach of that convention which he has to maintain for other people. And what about my case? Haven't I had to reveal what no son ought ever to reveal: how father and mother live and are man and wife for themselves quite apart from that idea of father and mother which we give them? When this idea is revealed, our life is then linked at one point only to that man and that woman; and as such it should shame them, shouldn't it?

(*The Mother hides her face in her hands. From the dressing rooms and the little door at the back of the stage the Actors and Stage Manager return, followed by the Property Man and the Prompter. At the same moment, the Manager comes out of his office, accompanied by the Father and the Stepdaughter.*)

THE MANAGER: Come on, come on, ladies and gentlemen! Heh! you there, machinist!

MACHINIST: Yes sir?

THE MANAGER: Fix up the parlor with the floral decorations. Two wings and a drop with a door will do. Hurry up!

(*The Machinist runs off at once to prepare the scene and arranges it while the Manager talks with the Stage Manager, the Property Man, and the Prompter on matters of detail.*)

THE MANAGER (*to Property Man*): Just have a look, and see if there isn't a sofa or a divan in the wardrobe . . .

PROPERTY MAN: There's the green one.

THE STEPDAUGHTER: No no! Green won't do. It was yellow, ornamented with flowers — very large! and most comfortable!

PROPERTY MAN: There isn't one like that.

THE MANAGER: It doesn't matter. Use the one we've got.

THE STEPDAUGHTER: Doesn't matter? It's most important!

THE MANAGER: We're only trying it now. Please don't interfere. (*To Property Man.*) See if we've got a shop window — long and narrowish.

THE STEPDAUGHTER: And the little table! The little mahogany table for the pale blue envelope!

PROPERTY MAN (*to Manager*): There's that little gilt one.

THE MANAGER: That'll do fine.

THE FATHER: A mirror.

THE STEPDAUGHTER: And the screen! We must have a screen. Otherwise how can I manage?

PROPERTY MAN: That's all right, Miss. We've got any amount of them.

THE MANAGER (*to the Stepdaughter*): We want some clothes pegs too, don't we?

THE STEPDAUGHTER: Yes, several, several!

THE MANAGER: See how many we've got and bring them all.

PROPERTY MAN: All right!

(*The Property Man hurries off to obey his orders. While he is putting the things in their places, the Manager talks to the Prompter and then with the Characters and the Actors.*)

THE MANAGER (*to Prompter*): Take your seat. Look here: this is the outline of the scenes, act by act. (*Hands him some sheets of paper.*) And now I'm going to ask you to do something out of the ordinary.

PROMPTER: Take it down in shorthand?

THE MANAGER (*pleasantly surprised*): Exactly! Can you do shorthand?

PROMPTER: Yes, a little.

THE MANAGER: Good! (*Turning to a Stage Hand.*) Go and get some paper from my office, plenty, as much as you can find.

(*The Stage Hand goes off and soon returns with a handful of paper which he gives to the Prompter.*)

THE MANAGER (*to Prompter*): You follow the scenes as we play them, and try and get the points down, at any rate the most important ones. (*Then addressing the Actors.*) Clear the stage, ladies and gentlemen! Come over here (*pointing to the left*) and listen attentively.

LEADING LADY: But, excuse me, we . . .

THE MANAGER (*guessing her thought*): Don't worry! You won't have to improvise.

LEADING MAN: What have we to do then?

THE MANAGER: Nothing. For the moment you just watch and listen. Everybody will get his part written out afterwards. At present we're going to try the thing as best we can. They're going to act now.

THE FATHER (*as if fallen from the clouds into the confusion of the stage*): We? What do you mean, if you please, by a rehearsal?

THE MANAGER: A rehearsal for them. (*Points to the Actors.*)

THE FATHER: But since we are the characters . . .

THE MANAGER: All right: "characters" then, if you insist on calling yourselves such. But here, my dear sir, the characters don't act. Here the actors do the acting. The characters are there, in the "book" (*pointing toward Prompter's box*) — when there is a "book"!

THE FATHER: I won't contradict you; but excuse me, the actors aren't the characters. They want to be, they pretend to be, don't they? Now if these gentlemen here are fortunate enough to have us alive before them . . .

THE MANAGER: Oh, this is grand! You want to come before the public yourselves then?

THE FATHER: As we are. . . .

THE MANAGER: I can assure you it would be a magnificent spectacle!

LEADING MAN: What's the use of us here anyway then?

THE MANAGER: You're not going to pretend that you can

act? It makes me laugh! (*The Actors laugh.*) There, you see, they are laughing at the notion. But, by the way, I must cast the parts. That won't be difficult. They cast themselves. (*To the Second Lady Lead.*) You play the Mother. (*To the Father.*) We must find her a name.

THE FATHER: Amalia, sir.

THE MANAGER: But that is the real name of your wife. We don't want to call her by her real name.

THE FATHER: Why ever not, if it is her name? . . . Still, perhaps, if that lady must . . . (*Makes a slight motion of the hand to indicate the Second Lady Lead.*) I see this woman here (*means the Mother*) as Amalia. But do as you like. (*Gets more and more confused.*) I don't know what to say to you. Already, I begin to hear my own words ring false, as if they had another sound . . .

THE MANAGER: Don't you worry about it. It'll be our job to find the right tones. And as for her name, if you want her Amalia, Amalia it shall be; and if you don't like it, we'll find another! For the moment though, we'll call the characters in this way: (*To Juvenile Lead.*) You are the Son. (*To the Leading Lady.*) You naturally are the Stepdaughter. . . .

THE STEPDAUGHTER (*excitedly*): What? what? I, that woman there? (*Bursts out laughing.*)

THE MANAGER (*angry*): What is there to laugh at?

LEADING LADY (*indignant*): Nobody has ever dared to laugh at me. I insist on being treated with respect; otherwise I go away.

THE STEPDAUGHTER: No, no, excuse me . . . I am not laughing at you. . . .

THE MANAGER (*to Stepdaughter*): You ought to feel honored to be played by . . .

LEADING LADY (*at once, contemptuously*): "That woman there". . .

THE STEPDAUGHTER: But I wasn't speaking of you, you know. I was speaking of myself — whom I can't see at all in you! That is all. I don't know . . . but . . . you . . . aren't in the least like me. . . .

THE FATHER: True. Here's the point. Look here, sir, our temperaments, our souls. . . .

THE MANAGER: Temperament, soul, be hanged! Do you suppose the spirit of the piece is in you? Nothing of the kind!

THE FATHER: What, haven't we our own temperaments, our own souls?

THE MANAGER: Not at all. Your soul or whatever you like to call it takes shape here. The actors give body and form to it, voice and gesture. And my actors — I may tell you — have given expression to much more lofty material than this little drama of yours, which may or may not hold up on the stage. But if it does, the merit of it, believe me, will be due to my actors.

THE FATHER: I don't dare contradict you, sir, but, believe me, it is a terrible suffering for us who are as we are, with these bodies of ours, these features to see. . . .

THE MANAGER (*cutting him short and out of patience*):

Good heavens! The make-up will remedy all that, man, the make-up. . . .

THE FATHER: Maybe. But the voice, the gestures . . .

THE MANAGER: Now, look here! On the stage, you as yourself, cannot exist. The actor here acts you, and that's an end to it!

THE FATHER: I understand. And now I think I see why our author who conceived us as we are, all alive, didn't want to put us on the stage after all. I haven't the least desire to offend your actors. Far from it! But when I think that I am to be acted by . . . I don't know by whom. . . .

LEADING MAN (*on his dignity*): By me, if you've no objection!

THE FATHER (*humbly, mellifluously*): Honored, I assure you, sir. (*Bows.*) Still, I must say that try as this gentleman may, with all his good will and wonderful art, to absorb me into himself. . . .

LEADING MAN: Oh chuck it! "Wonderful art!" Withdraw that, please!

THE FATHER: The performance he will give, even doing his best with make-up to look like me. . . .

LEADING MAN: It will certainly be a bit difficult! (*The Actors laugh.*)

THE FATHER: Exactly! It will be difficult to act me as I really am. The effect will be rather — apart from the make-up — according as to how he supposes I am, as he senses me — if he does sense me — and not as I inside of myself feel myself to be. It seems to me then that account should be taken of this by everyone whose duty it may become to criticize us. . . .

THE MANAGER: Heavens! The man's starting to think about the critics now! Let them say what they like. It's up to us to put on the play if we can. (*Looking around.*) Come on! come on! Is the stage set? (*To the Actors and Characters.*) Stand back — stand back! Let me see, and don't let's lose any more time! (*To the Stepdaughter.*) Is it all right as it is now?

THE STEPDAUGHTER: Well, to tell the truth, I don't recognize the scene.

THE MANAGER: My dear lady, you can't possibly suppose that we can construct that shop of Madame Pace piece by piece here? (*To the Father.*) You said a white room with flowered wallpaper, didn't you?

THE FATHER: Yes.

THE MANAGER: Well then. We've got the furniture right more or less. Bring that little table a bit further forward. (*The Stage Hands obey the order. To Property Man.*) You go and find an envelope, if possible, a pale blue one; and give it to that gentleman. (*Indicates Father.*)

PROPERTY MAN: An ordinary envelope?

MANAGER AND FATHER: Yes, yes, an ordinary envelope.

PROPERTY MAN: At once, sir. (*Exit.*)

THE MANAGER: Ready, everyone! First scene — the Young Lady. (*The Leading Lady comes forward.*) No, no, you must wait. I meant her. (*Indicating the Stepdaughter.*) You just watch —

THE STEPDAUGHTER (*adding at once*): How I shall play it, how I shall live it! . . .

LEADING LADY (*offended*): I shall live it also, you may be sure, as soon as I begin!

THE MANAGER (*with his hands to his head*): Ladies and gentlemen, if you please! No more useless discussions! Scene I: the Young Lady with Madame Pace: Oh! (*Looks around as if lost.*) And this Madame Pace, where is she?

THE FATHER: She isn't with us, sir.

THE MANAGER: Then what the devil's to be done?

THE FATHER: But she is alive too.

THE MANAGER: Yes, but where is she?

THE FATHER: One minute. Let me speak! (*Turning to the Actresses.*) If these ladies would be so good as to give me their hats for a moment. . . .

THE ACTRESSES (*half surprised, half laughing, in chorus*): What? Why? Our hats? What does he say?

THE MANAGER: What are you going to do with the ladies' hats? (*The Actors laugh.*)

THE FATHER: Oh nothing. I just want to put them on these pegs for a moment. And one of the ladies will be so kind as to take off her mantle. . . .

THE ACTORS: Oh, what d'you think of that? Only the mantle? He must be mad.

SOME ACTRESSES: But why? Mantles as well?

THE FATHER: To hang them up here for a moment. Please be so kind, will you?

THE ACTRESSES (*taking off their hats, one or two also their cloaks, and going to hang them on the racks*): After all, why not? There you are! This is really funny. We've got to put them on show.

THE FATHER: Exactly; just like that, on show.

THE MANAGER: May we know why?

THE FATHER: I'll tell you. Who knows if, by arranging the stage for her, she does not come here herself, attracted by the very articles of her trade? (*Inviting the Actors to look toward the exit at back of stage.*) Look! Look!

(*The door at the back of stage opens and Madame Pace enters and takes a few steps forward. She is a fat, oldish woman with puffy oxygenated hair. She is rouged and powdered, dressed with a comical elegance in black silk. Round her waist is a long silver chain from which hangs a pair of scissors. The Stepdaughter runs over to her at once amid the stupor of the Actors.*)

THE STEPDAUGHTER (*turning toward her*): There she is! There she is!

THE FATHER (*radiant*): It's she! I said so, didn't I! There she is!

THE MANAGER (*conquering his surprise, and then becoming indignant*): What sort of a trick is this?

LEADING MAN (*almost at the same time*): What's going to happen next?

JUVENILE LEAD: Where does she come from?

L'INGÉNUE: They've been holding her in reserve, I guess.

LEADING LADY: A vulgar trick!

THE FATHER (*dominating the protests*): Excuse me, all of you! Why are you so anxious to destroy in the name of a vulgar, commonplace sense of truth, this reality which comes to birth attracted and formed by the magic of the stage itself, which has indeed more right to live here than you, since it is much truer than you — if you don't mind my saying so? Which is the actress among you who is to play Madame Pace? Well, here is Madame Pace herself. And you will allow, I fancy, that the actress who acts her will be less true than this woman here, who is herself in person. You see my daughter recognized her and went over to her at once. Now you're going to witness the scene!

(*But the scene between the Stepdaughter and Madame Pace has already begun despite the protest of the Actors and the reply of the Father. It has begun quietly, naturally, in a manner impossible for the stage. So when the Actors, called to attention by the Father, turn round and see Madame Pace, who has placed one hand under the Stepdaughter's chin to raise her head, they observe her at first with great attention, but hearing her speak in an unintelligible manner their interest begins to wane.*)

THE MANAGER: Well? well?

LEADING MAN: What does she say?

LEADING LADY: One can't hear a word.

JUVENILE LEAD: Louder! Louder please!

THE STEPDAUGHTER (*leaving Madame Pace, who smiles a Sphinx-like smile, and advancing toward the Actors*): Louder? Louder? What are you talking about? These aren't matters which can be shouted at the top of one's voice. If I have spoken them out loud, it was to shame him and have my revenge. (*Indicates Father.*) But for Madame it's quite a different matter.

THE MANAGER: Indeed? indeed? But here, you know people have got to make themselves heard, my dear. Even we who are on the stage can't hear you. What will it be when the public's in the theater? And anyway, you can very well speak up now among yourselves, since we shan't be present to listen to you as we are now. You've got to pretend to be alone in a room at the back of a shop where no one can hear you.

(*The Stepdaughter coquettishly and with a touch of malice makes a sign of disagreement two or three times with her finger.*)

THE MANAGER: What do you mean by no?

THE STEPDAUGHTER (*sotto voce,° mysteriously*): There's someone who will hear us if she (*indicating Madame Pace*) speaks out loud.

THE MANAGER (*in consternation*): What? Have you got someone else to spring on us now? (*The Actors burst out laughing.*)

THE FATHER: No, no sir. She is alluding to me. I've got to

---

sotto voce: In a soft voice or stage whisper.

be here — there behind that door, in waiting; and Madame Pace knows it. In fact, if you will allow me, I'll go there at once, so I can be quite ready. (*Moves away.*)

THE MANAGER (*stopping him*): No! wait! wait! We must observe the conventions of the theater. Before you are ready . . .

THE STEPDAUGHTER (*interrupting him*): No, get on with it at once! I'm just dying, I tell you, to act this scene. If he's ready, I'm more than ready.

THE MANAGER (*shouting*): But, my dear young lady, first of all, we must have the scene between you and this lady. . . . (*Indicates Madame Pace.*) Do you understand?

THE STEPDAUGHTER: Good Heavens! She's been telling me what you know already: that mama's work is badly done again, that the material's ruined; and that if I want her to continue to help us in our misery I must be patient. . . .

MADAME PACE (*coming forward with an air of great importance*): Yes indeed, sir, I no wanta take advantage of her, I no wanta be hard. . . .

(*Note: Madame Pace is supposed to talk in a jargon half Italian, half English.*)

THE MANAGER (*alarmed*): What? What? She talks like that? (*The Actors burst out laughing again.*)

THE STEPDAUGHTER (*also laughing*): Yes yes, that's the way she talks, half English, half Italian! Most comical it is!

MADAME PACE: Itta seem not verra polite gentlemen laugha atta me eeff I trya best speaka English.

THE MANAGER: *Diamine!*° Of course! Of course! Let her talk like that! Just what we want. Talk just like that, Madame, if you please! The effect will be certain. Exactly what was wanted to put a little comic relief into the crudity of the situation. Of course she talks like that! Magnificent!

THE STEPDAUGHTER: Magnificent? Certainly! When certain suggestions are made to one in language of that kind, the effect is certain, since it seems almost a joke. One feels inclined to laugh when one hears her talk about an "old signore" "who wanta talka nicely with you." Nice old signore, eh, Madame?

MADAME PACE: Not so old my dear, not so old! And even if you no like him, he won't make any scandal!

THE MOTHER (*jumping up amid the amazement and consternation of the Actors, who had not been noticing her. They move to restrain her*): You old devil! You murderess!

THE STEPDAUGHTER (*running over to calm her Mother*): Calm yourself, Mother, calm yourself! Please don't. . . .

THE FATHER (*going to her also at the same time*): Calm yourself! Don't get excited! Sit down now!

THE MOTHER: Well then, take that woman away out of my sight!

Diamine!: Italian for "Well, I'll be damned!"

THE STEPDAUGHTER (*to Manager*): It is impossible for my mother to remain here.

THE FATHER (*to Manager*): They can't be here together. And for this reason, you see: that woman there was not with us when we came. . . . If they are on together, the whole thing is given away inevitably, as you see.

THE MANAGER: It doesn't matter. This is only a first rough sketch — just to get an idea of the various points of the scene, even confusedly. . . . (*Turning to the Mother and leading her to her chair.*) Come along, my dear lady, sit down now, and let's get on with the scene. . . .

(*Meanwhile, the Stepdaughter, coming forward again, turns to Madame Pace.*)

THE STEPDAUGHTER: Come on, Madame, come on!

MADAME PACE (*offended*): No, no, *grazie.* I do not do anything witha your mother present.

THE STEPDAUGHTER: Nonsense! Introduce this "old signore" who wants to talk nicely to me. (*Addressing the Company imperiously.*) We've got to do this scene one way or another, haven't we? Come on! (*To Madame Pace.*) You can go!

MADAME PACE: Ah yes! I go'way! I go'way! Certainly! (*Exits furious.*)

THE STEPDAUGHTER (*to the Father*): Now you make your entry. No, you needn't go over there. Come here. Let's suppose you've already come in. Like that, yes! I'm here with bowed head, modest like. Come on! Out with your voice! Say "Good morning, Miss" in that peculiar tone, that special tone. . . .

THE MANAGER: Excuse me, but are you the Manager, or am I? (*To the Father, who looks undecided and perplexed.*) Get on with it, man! Go down there to the back of the stage. You needn't go off. Then come right forward here.

(*The Father does as he is told, looking troubled and perplexed at first. But as soon as he begins to move, the reality of the action affects him, and he begins to smile and to be more natural. The Actors watch intently.*)

THE MANAGER (*sotto voce, quickly to the Prompter in his box*): Ready! ready! Get ready to write now.

THE FATHER (*coming forward and speaking in a different tone*): Good afternoon, Miss!

THE STEPDAUGHTER (*head bowed down slightly, with restrained disgust*): Good afternoon!

THE FATHER (*looks under her hat which partly covers her face. Perceiving she is very young, he makes an exclamation, partly of surprise, partly of fear lest he compromise himself in a risky adventure*): Ah . . . but . . . ah . . . I say . . . this is not the first time that you have come here, is it?

THE STEPDAUGHTER (*modestly*): No sir.

THE FATHER: You've been here before, eh? (*Then seeing her nod agreement.*) More than once? (*Waits for her to answer, looks under her hat, smiles, and then says:*) Well then, there's no need to be so shy, is there? May I take off your hat?

THE STEPDAUGHTER (*anticipating him and with veiled disgust*): No sir . . . I'll do it myself. (*Takes it off quickly.*)

(*The Mother, who watches the progress of the scene with the Son and the other two children who cling to her, is on thorns; and follows with varying expressions of sorrow, indignation, anxiety, and horror the words and actions of the other two. From time to time she hides her face in her hands and sobs.*)

THE MOTHER: Oh, my God, my God!

THE FATHER (*playing his part with a touch of gallantry*): Give it to me! I'll put it down. (*Takes hat from her hands.*) But a dear little head like yours ought to have a smarter hat. Come and help me choose one from the stock, won't you?

L'INGÉNUE (*interrupting*): I say . . . those are our hats you know.

THE MANAGER (*furious*): Silence! silence! Don't try and be funny, if you please. . . . We're playing the scene now, I'd have you notice. (*To the Stepdaughter.*) Begin again, please!

THE STEPDAUGHTER (*continuing*): No thank you, sir.

THE FATHER: Oh, come now. Don't talk like that. You must take it. I shall be upset if you don't. There are some lovely little hats here; and then — Madame will be pleased. She expects it, anyway, you know.

THE STEPDAUGHTER: No, no! I couldn't wear it!

THE FATHER: Oh, you're thinking about what they'd say at home if they saw you come in with a new hat? My dear girl, there's always a way round these little matters, you know.

THE STEPDAUGHTER (*all keyed up*): No, it's not that. I couldn't wear it because I am . . . as you see . . . you might have noticed . . .

(*Showing her black dress.*)

THE FATHER: . . . in mourning! Of course: I beg your pardon: I'm frightfully sorry. . . .

THE STEPDAUGHTER (*forcing herself to conquer her indignation and nausea*): Stop! Stop! It's I who must thank you. There's no need for you to feel mortified or specially sorry. Don't think any more of what I've said. (*Tries to smile.*) I must forget that I am dressed so. . . .

THE MANAGER (*interrupting and turning to the Prompter*): Stop a minute! Stop! Don't write that down. Cut out that last bit. (*Then to the Father and Stepdaughter.*) Fine! it's going fine! (*To the Father only.*) And now you can go on as we arranged. (*To the Actors.*) Pretty good that scene, where he offers her the hat, eh?

THE STEPDAUGHTER: The best's coming now. Why can't we go on?

THE MANAGER: Have a little patience! (*To the Actors.*) Of course, it must be treated rather lightly.

LEADING MAN: Still, with a bit of go in it!

LEADING LADY: Of course! It's easy enough! (*To Leading Man.*) Shall you and I try it now?

LEADING MAN: Why, yes! I'll prepare my entrance. (*Exit in order to make his entrance.*)

THE MANAGER (*to Leading Lady*): See here! The scene between you and Madame Pace is finished. I'll have it written out properly after. You remain here . . . oh, where are you going?

LEADING LADY: One minute. I want to put my hat on again. (*Goes over to hatrack and puts her hat on her head.*)

THE MANAGER: Good! You stay here with your head bowed down a bit.

THE STEPDAUGHTER: But she isn't dressed in black.

LEADING LADY: But I shall be, and much more effectively than you.

THE MANAGER (*to Stepdaughter*): Be quiet please, and watch! You'll be able to learn something. (*Clapping his hands.*) Come on! come on! Entrance, please!

(*The door at rear of stage opens, and the Leading Man enters with the lively manner of an old gallant. The rendering of the scene by the Actors from the very first words is seen to be quite a different thing, though it has not in any way the air of a parody. Naturally, the Stepdaughter and the Father, not being able to recognize themselves in the Leading Lady and the Leading Man, who deliver their words in different tones and with a different psychology, express, sometimes with smiles, sometimes with gestures, the impression they receive.*)

LEADING MAN: Good afternoon, Miss . . .

THE FATHER (*at once unable to contain himself*): No! no!

(*The Stepdaughter, noticing the way the Leading Man enters, bursts out laughing.*)

THE MANAGER (*furious*): Silence! And you, please, just stop that laughing. If we go on like this, we shall never finish.

THE STEPDAUGHTER: Forgive me, sir but it's natural enough. This lady (*indicating Leading Lady*) stands there still; but if she is supposed to be me, I can assure you that if I heard anyone say "Good afternoon" in that manner and in that tone, I should burst out laughing as I did.

THE FATHER: Yes, yes, the manner, the tone . . .

THE MANAGER: Nonsense! Rubbish! Stand aside and let me see the action.

LEADING MAN: If I've got to represent an old fellow who's coming into a house of an equivocal character . . .

THE MANAGER: Don't listen to them, for Heaven's sake! Do it again! It goes fine. (*Waiting for the Actors to begin again.*) Well?

LEADING MAN: Good afternoon, Miss.

LEADING LADY: Good afternoon.

LEADING MAN (*imitating the gesture of the Father when he looked under the hat, and then expressing quite clearly first satisfaction and then fear*): Ah, but . . . I say . . . this is not the first time that you have come here, is it?

THE MANAGER: Good, but not quite so heavily. Like

this. (*Acts himself.*) "This isn't the first time that you have come here". . . (*To Leading Lady.*) And you say: "No, sir."

LEADING LADY: No, sir.

LEADING MAN: You've been here before, more than once.

THE MANAGER: No, no, stop! Let her nod "yes" first. "You've been here before, eh?" (*The Leading Lady lifts up her head slightly and closes her eyes as though in disgust. Then she inclines her head twice.*)

THE STEPDAUGHTER (*unable to contain herself*): Oh my God! (*Puts a hand to her mouth to prevent herself from laughing.*)

THE MANAGER (*turning round*): What's the matter?

THE STEPDAUGHTER: Nothing, nothing!

THE MANAGER (*to Leading Man*): Go on!

LEADING MAN: You've been here before, eh? Well then, there's no need to be so shy, is there? May I take off your hat?

(*The Leading Man says this last speech in such a tone and with such gestures that the Stepdaughter, though she has her hand to her mouth, cannot keep from laughing.*)

LEADING LADY (*indignant*): I'm not going to stop here to be made a fool of by that woman there.

LEADING MAN: Neither am I! I'm through with it!

THE MANAGER (*shouting to Stepdaughter*): Silence! for once and all, I tell you!

THE STEPDAUGHTER: Forgive me! forgive me!

THE MANAGER: You haven't any manners: that's what it is! You go too far.

THE FATHER (*endeavoring to intervene*): Yes, it's true, but excuse her . . .

THE MANAGER: Excuse what? It's absolutely disgusting.

THE FATHER: Yes, sir, but believe me, it has such a strange effect when . . .

THE MANAGER: Strange? Why strange? Where is it strange?

THE FATHER: No, sir; I admire your actors — this gentleman here, this lady; but they are certainly not us!

THE MANAGER: I should hope not. Evidently they cannot be you, if they are actors.

THE FATHER: Just so: actors! Both of them act our parts exceedingly well. But, believe me, it produces quite a different effect on us. They want to be us, but they aren't, all the same.

THE MANAGER: What is it then anyway?

THE FATHER: Something that is . . . that is theirs — and no longer ours . . .

THE MANAGER: But naturally, inevitably, I've told you so already.

THE FATHER: Yes, I understand . . . I understand . . .

THE MANAGER: Well then, let's have no more of it! (*Turning to the Actors.*) We'll have the rehearsals by ourselves, afterwards, in the ordinary way. I never could stand rehearsing with the author present. He's never satisfied! (*Turning to Father and Stepdaughter.*) Come on! Let's get on with it again; and try and see if you can't keep from laughing.

THE STEPDAUGHTER: Oh, I shan't laugh any more. There's a nice little bit coming from me now: you'll see.

THE MANAGER: Well then: when she says "Don't think any more of what I've said, I must forget, etc.," you (*addressing the Father*) come in sharp with "I understand"; and then you ask her . . .

THE STEPDAUGHTER (*interrupting*): What?

THE MANAGER: Why she is in mourning.

THE STEPDAUGHTER: Not at all! See here: when I told him that it was useless for me to be thinking about my wearing mourning, do you know how he answered me? "Ah well," he said, "then let's take off this little frock."

THE MANAGER: Great! Just what we want, to make a riot in the theater!

THE STEPDAUGHTER: But it's the truth!

THE MANAGER: What does that matter? Acting is our business here. Truth up to a certain point, but no further.

THE STEPDAUGHTER: What do you want to do then?

THE MANAGER: You'll see, you'll see! Leave it to me.

THE STEPDAUGHTER: No sir! What you want to do is to piece together a little romantic sentimental scene out of my disgust, out of all the reasons, each more cruel and viler than the other, why I am what I am. He is to ask me why I'm in mourning; and I'm to answer with tears in my eyes, that it is just two months since papa died. No sir, no! He's got to say to me, as he did say, "Well, let's take off this little dress at once." And I, with my two months' mourning in my heart, went there behind that screen, and with these fingers tingling with shame . . .

THE MANAGER (*running his hands through his hair*): For Heaven's sake! What are you saying?

THE STEPDAUGHTER (*crying out excitedly*): The truth! The truth!

THE MANAGER: It may be. I don't deny it, and I can understand all your horror; but you must surely see that you can't have this kind of thing on the stage. It won't go.

THE STEPDAUGHTER: Not possible, eh? Very well! I'm much obliged to you — but I'm off.

THE MANAGER: Now be reasonable! Don't lose your temper!

THE STEPDAUGHTER: I won't stop here! I won't! I can see you fixed it all up with him in your office. All this talk about what is possible for the stage . . . I understand! He wants to get at his complicated "cerebral drama," to have his famous remorses and torments acted; but I want to act my part, *my part!*

THE MANAGER (*annoyed, shaking his shoulders*): Ah! Just *your* part! But, if you will pardon me, there are other parts than yours: His (*indicating the Father*) and hers (*indicating the Mother*)! On the stage you can't have a character becoming too prominent and overshadowing all the others. The thing is to pack them all into a neat little framework and then act what is actable. I am aware of the fact that everyone has his own interior life which he wants very much to put forward. But the difficulty lies in this fact: to set out just so much as is necessary for the stage, taking the other characters into consideration, and at the same time hint at the unrevealed interior life of each. I am willing to admit, my dear young lady, that from your point of view it would be a fine idea if each character could tell the public all his troubles in a nice monologue or a regular one hour lecture. (*Good humoredly.*) You must restrain yourself, my dear, and in your own interest, too; because this fury of yours, this exaggerated disgust you show, may make a bad impression, you know. After you have confessed to me that there were others before him at Madame Pace's and more than once . . .

THE STEPDAUGHTER (*bowing her head, impressed*): It's true. But remember those others mean him for me all the same.

THE MANAGER (*not understanding*): What? The others? What do you mean?

THE STEPDAUGHTER: For one who has gone wrong, sir, he who was responsible for the first fault is responsible for all that follow. He is responsible for my faults, was, even before I was born. Look at him, and see if it isn't true!

THE MANAGER: Well, well! And does the weight of so much responsibility seem nothing to you? Give him a chance to act it, to get it over!

THE STEPDAUGHTER: How? How can he act all his "noble remorses," all his "moral torments," if you want to spare him the horror of being discovered one day — after he had asked her what he did ask her — in the arms of her, that already fallen woman, that child, sir, that child he used to watch come out of school? (*She is moved.*)

(*The Mother at this point is overcome with emotion and breaks out into a fit of crying. All are touched. A long pause.*)

THE STEPDAUGHTER (*as soon as the Mother becomes a little quieter, adds resolutely and gravely*): At present, we are unknown to the public. Tomorrow, you will act us as you wish, treating us in your own manner. But do you really want to see drama, do you want to see it flash out as it really did?

THE MANAGER: Of course! That's just what I do want, so I can use as much of it as is possible.

THE STEPDAUGHTER: Well then, ask that Mother there to leave us.

THE MOTHER (*changing her low plaint into a sharp cry*): No! No! Don't permit it, sir, don't permit it!

THE MANAGER: But it's only to try . . .

THE MOTHER: I can't bear it. I can't.

THE MANAGER: But since it has happened already . . . I don't understand!

THE MOTHER: It's taking place now. It happens all the time. My torment isn't a pretended one. I live and feel every minute of my torture. Those two children there — have you heard them speak? They can't speak anymore. They cling to me to keep my torment

actual and vivid for me. But for themselves, they do not exist, they aren't anymore. And she (*indicating the Stepdaughter*) has run away, she has left me, and is lost. If I now see her here before me, it is only to renew for me the tortures I have suffered for her too.

THE FATHER: The eternal moment! She (*indicating the Stepdaughter*) is here to catch me, fix me, and hold me eternally in the stocks for that one fleeting and shameful moment of my life. She can't give it up! And you, sir, cannot either fairly spare me . . .

THE MANAGER: I never said I didn't want to act it. It will form, as a matter of fact, the nucleus of the whole first act right up to her surprise. (*Indicates the Mother.*)

THE FATHER: Just so! This is my punishment: the passion in all of us that must culminate in her final cry.

THE STEPDAUGHTER: I can hear it still in my ears. It's driven me mad, that cry! — You can put me on as you like; it doesn't matter. Fully dressed, if you like — provided I have at least the arm bare; because, standing like this (*she goes close to the Father and leans her head on his breast*) with my head so, and my arms round his neck, I saw a vein pulsing in my arm here; and then, as if that live vein had awakened disgust in me, I closed my eyes like this, and let my head sink on his breast. (*Turning to the Mother.*) Cry out, mother! Cry out! (*Buries head in Father's breast, and with her shoulders raised as if to prevent her hearing the cry, adds in tones of intense emotion.*) Cry out as you did then!

THE MOTHER (*coming forward to separate them*): No! My daughter, my daughter! (*And after having pulled her away from him.*) You brute! you brute! She is my daughter! Don't you see she's my daughter?

THE MANAGER (*walking backward toward footlights*): Fine! fine! Damned good! And then, of course — curtain!

THE FATHER (*going toward him excitedly*): Yes, of course, because that's the way it really happened.

THE MANAGER (*convinced and pleased*): Oh, yes, no doubt about it. Curtain here, curtain!

(*At the reiterated cry of the Manager, the Machinist lets the curtain down, leaving the Manager and the Father in front of it before the footlights.*)

THE MANAGER: The darned idiot! I said "curtain" to show the act should end there, and he goes and lets it down in earnest. (*To the Father, while he pulls the curtain back to go on to the stage again.*) Yes, yes, it's all right. Effect certain! That's the right ending. I'll guarantee the first act at any rate.

ACT III

(*When the curtain goes up again, it is seen that the stage hands have shifted the bit of scenery used in the last part and have rigged up instead at the back of the stage a drop, with some trees, and one or two wings. A portion of a fountain basin is visible. The Mother is sitting on*) *the right with the two children by her side. The Son is on the same side, but away from the others. He seems bored, angry, and full of shame. The Father and the Stepdaughter are also seated toward the right front. On the other side (left) are the Actors, much in the positions they occupied before the curtain was lowered. Only the Manager is standing up in the middle of the stage, with his hand closed over his mouth, in the act of meditating.)*

THE MANAGER (*shaking his shoulders after a brief pause*): Ah yes: the second act! Leave it to me, leave it all to me as we arranged, and you'll see! It'll go fine!

THE STEPDAUGHTER: Our entry into his house (*indicates Father*) in spite of him . . . (*Indicates the Son.*)

THE MANAGER (*out of patience*): Leave it to me, I tell you!

THE STEPDAUGHTER: Do let it be clear, at any rate, that it is in spite of my wishes.

THE MOTHER (*from her corner, shaking her head*): For all the good that's come of it . . .

THE STEPDAUGHTER (*turning toward her quickly*): It doesn't matter. The more harm done us, the more remorse for him.

THE MANAGER (*impatiently*): I understand! Good Heavens! I understand! I'm taking it into account.

THE MOTHER (*supplicatingly*): I beg you, sir, to let it appear quite plain that for conscience' sake I did try in every way . . .

THE STEPDAUGHTER (*interrupting indignantly and continuing for the Mother*): . . . to pacify me, to dissuade me from spiting him. (*To Manager.*) Do as she wants: satisfy her, because it is true! I enjoy it immensely. Anyhow, as you can see, the meeker she is, the more she tries to get at his heart, the more distant and aloof does he become.

THE MANAGER: Are we going to begin this second act or not?

THE STEPDAUGHTER: I'm not going to talk any more now. But I must tell you this: you can't have the whole action take place in the garden, as you suggest. It isn't possible!

THE MANAGER: Why not?

THE STEPDAUGHTER: Because he (*indicates the Son again*) is always shut up alone in his room. And then there's all the part of that poor dazed-looking boy there which takes place indoors.

THE MANAGER: Maybe! On the other hand, you will understand — we can't change scenes three or four times in one act.

LEADING MAN: They used to once.

THE MANAGER: Yes, when the public was up to the level of that child there.

LEADING LADY: It makes the illusion easier.

THE FATHER (*irritated*): The illusion! For Heaven's sake, don't say illusion. Please don't use that word, which is particularly painful for . . .

THE MANAGER (*astounded*): And why, if you please?

THE FATHER: It's painful, cruel, really cruel; and you ought to understand that.

THE MANAGER: But why? What ought we to say then? The illusion, I tell you, sir, which we've got to create for the audience. . . .

THE LEADING MAN: With our acting.

THE MANAGER: The illusion of a reality.

THE FATHER: I understand; but you, perhaps, do not understand us. Forgive me! You see . . . here for you and your actors, the thing is only — and rightly so . . . a kind of game. . . .

THE LEADING LADY (*interrupting indignantly*): A game! We're not children here, if you please! We are serious actors.

THE FATHER: I don't deny it. What I mean is the game, or play, of your art, which has to give, as the gentleman says, a perfect illusion of reality.

THE MANAGER: Precisely — !

THE FATHER: Now, if you consider the fact that we (*indicates himself and the other five Characters*), as we are, have no other reality outside of this illusion. . . .

THE MANAGER (*astonished, looking at his Actors, who are also amazed*): And what does that mean?

THE FATHER (*after watching them for a moment with a wan smile*): As I say, sir, that which is a game of art for you is our sole reality. (*Brief pause. He goes a step or two nearer the Manager and adds.*) But not only for us, you know, by the way. Just you think it over well. (*Looks him in the eyes.*) Can you tell me who you are?

THE MANAGER (*perplexed, half-smiling*): What? Who am I? I am myself.

THE FATHER: And if I were to tell you that that isn't true, because you and I . . . ?

THE MANAGER: I should say you were mad — ! (*The Actors laugh.*)

THE FATHER: You're quite right to laugh: because we are all making believe here. (*To Manager.*) And you can therefore object that it's only for a joke that that gentleman there (*indicates the Leading Man*), who naturally is himself, has to be me, who am on the contrary myself — this thing you see here. You see I've caught you in a trap! (*The Actors laugh.*)

THE MANAGER (*annoyed*): But we've had all this over once before. Do you want to begin again?

THE FATHER: No, no! That wasn't my meaning! In fact, I should like to request you to abandon this game of art (*looking at the Leading Lady as if anticipating her*) which you are accustomed to play here with your actors, and to ask you seriously once again: who are you?

THE MANAGER (*astonished and irritated, turning to his Actors*): If this fellow here hasn't got a nerve! A man who calls himself a character comes and asks me who I am!

THE FATHER (*with dignity, but not offended*): A character, sir, may always ask a man who he is. Because a character has really a life of his own, marked with his especial characteristics; for which reason he is always "somebody." But a man — I'm not speaking of you now — may very well be "nobody."

THE MANAGER: Yes, but you are asking these questions of me, the boss, the manager! Do you understand?

THE FATHER: But only in order to know if you, as you really are now, see yourself as you once were with all the illusions that were yours then, with all the things both inside and outside of you as they seemed to you — as they were then indeed for you. Well, sir, if you think of all those illusions that mean nothing to you now, of all those things which don't even *seem* to you to exist anymore, while once they *were* for you, don't you feel that — I won't say these boards — but the very earth under your feet is sinking away from you when you reflect that in the same way this *you* as you feel it today — all this present reality of yours — is fated to seem a mere illusion to you tomorrow?

THE MANAGER (*without having understood much, but astonished by the specious argument*): Well, well! And where does all this take us anyway?

THE FATHER: Oh, nowhere! It's only to show you that if we (*indicating the Characters*) have no other reality beyond the illusion, you too must not count over-much on your reality as you feel it today, since, like that of yesterday, it may prove an illusion for you tomorrow.

THE MANAGER (*determining to make fun of him*): Ah, excellent! Then you'll be saying next that you, with this comedy of yours that you brought here to act, are truer and more real than I am.

THE FATHER (*with the greatest seriousness*): But of course, without doubt!

THE MANAGER: Ah, really?

THE FATHER: Why, I thought you'd understand that from the beginning.

THE MANAGER: More real than I?

THE FATHER: If your reality can change from one day to another. . . .

THE MANAGER: But everyone knows it can change. It is always changing, the same as anyone else's.

THE FATHER (*with a cry*): No, sir, not ours! Look here! That is the very difference! Our reality doesn't change: it can't change! It can't be other than what it is, because it is already fixed for ever. It's terrible. Ours is an immutable reality which should make you shudder when you approach us if you are really conscious of the fact that your reality is a mere transitory and fleeting illusion, taking this form today and that tomorrow, according to the conditions, according to your will, your sentiments, which in turn are controlled by an intellect that shows them to you today in one manner and tomorrow . . . who knows how? . . . Illusions of reality represented in this fatuous comedy of life that never ends, nor can ever end! Because if tomorrow it were to end . . . then why, all would be finished.

THE MANAGER: Oh for God's sake, will you *at least* finish with this philosophizing and let us try and shape this comedy which you yourself have brought me here? You argue and philosophize a bit too much, my dear sir. You know you seem to me almost, al-

most . . . (*Stops and looks him over from head to foot.*) Ah, by the way, I think you introduced yourself to me as a — what shall . . . we say — a "character," created by an author who did not afterward care to make a drama of his own creations.

THE FATHER: It is the simple truth, sir.

THE MANAGER: Nonsense! Cut that out, please! None of us believes it, because it isn't a thing, as you must recognize yourself, which one can believe seriously. If you want to know, it seems to me you are trying to imitate the manner of a certain author whom I heartily detest — I warn you — although I have unfortunately bound myself to put on one of his works. As a matter of fact, I was just starting to rehearse it, when you arrived. (*Turning to the Actors.*) And this is what we've gained — out of the frying-pan into the fire!

THE FATHER: I don't know to what author you may be alluding, but believe me I feel what I think; and I seem to be philosophizing only for those who do not think what they feel, because they blind themselves with their own sentiment. I know that for many people this self-blinding seems much more "human"; but the contrary is really true. For man never reasons so much and becomes so introspective as when he suffers, since he is anxious to get at the cause of his sufferings, to learn who has produced them, and whether it is just or unjust that he should have to bear them. On the other hand, when he is happy, he takes his happiness as it comes and doesn't analyze it, just as if happiness were his right. The animals suffer without reasoning about their sufferings. But take the case of a man who suffers and begins to reason about it. Oh no! it can't be allowed! Let him suffer like an animal, and then — ah yes, he is "human"!

THE MANAGER: Look here! Look here! You're off again, philosophizing worse than ever.

THE FATHER: Because I suffer, sir! I'm not philosophizing: I'm crying aloud the reason of my sufferings.

THE MANAGER (*makes brusque movement as he is taken with a new idea*): I should like to know if anyone has ever heard of a character who gets right out of his part and perorates and speechifies as you do. Have you ever heard of a case? I haven't.

THE FATHER: You have never met such a case, sir, because authors, as a rule, hide the labor of their creations. When the characters are really alive before their author, the latter does nothing but follow them in their action, in other words, in the situations which they suggest to him; and he has to will them the way they will themselves — for there's trouble if he doesn't. When a character is born, he acquires at once such an independence, even of his own author, that he can be imagined by everybody even in many other situations where the author never dreamed of placing him; and so he acquires for himself a meaning which the author never thought of giving him.

THE MANAGER: Yes, yes, I know this.

THE FATHER: What is there then to marvel at in us?

Imagine such a misfortune for characters as I have described to you: to be born of an author's fantasy, and be denied life by him; and then answer me if these characters left alive, and yet without life, weren't right in doing what they did do and are doing now, after they have attempted everything in their power to persuade him to give them their stage life. We've all tried him in turn, I, she (*indicating the Stepdaughter*) and she (*indicating the Mother*).

THE STEPDAUGHTER: It's true. I too have sought to tempt him, many, many times, when he has been sitting at his writing table, feeling a bit melancholy, at the twilight hour. He would sit in his armchair too lazy to switch on the light, and all the shadows that crept into his room were full of our presence coming to tempt him. (*As if she saw herself still there by the writing table, and was annoyed by the presence of the Actors.*) Oh, if you would only go away, go away and leave us alone — mother here with that son of hers — I with that child — that boy there always alone — and then I with him (*just hints at the Father*) — and then I alone, alone . . . in those shadows! (*Makes a sudden movement as if in the vision she has of herself illuminating those shadows she wanted to seize hold of herself.*) Ah! my life! my life! Oh, what scenes we proposed to him — and I tempted him more than any of the others!

THE FATHER: Maybe. But perhaps it was your fault that he refused to give us life: because you were too insistent, too troublesome.

THE STEPDAUGHTER: Nonsense! Didn't he make me so himself? (*Goes close to the Manager to tell him as if in confidence.*) In my opinion he abandoned us in a fit of depression, of disgust for the ordinary theater as the public knows it and likes it.

THE SON: Exactly what it was, sir; exactly that!

THE FATHER: Not at all! Don't believe it for a minute. Listen to me! You'll be doing quite right to modify, as you suggest, the excesses both of this girl here, who wants to do too much, and of this young man, who won't do anything at all.

THE SON: No, nothing!

THE MANAGER: You too get over the mark occasionally, my dear sir, if I may say so.

THE FATHER: I? When? Where?

THE MANAGER: Always! Continuously! Then there's this insistence of yours in trying to make us believe you are a character. And then too, you must really argue and philosophize less, you know, much less.

THE FATHER: Well, if you want to take away from me the possibility of representing the torment of my spirit which never gives me peace, you will be suppressing me: that's all. Every true man, sir, who is a little above the level of the beasts and plants does not live for the sake of living, without knowing how to live; but he lives so as to give a meaning and a value of his own to life. For me this is *everything*. I cannot give up this, just to represent a mere fact as she (*indicating the Stepdaughter*) wants. It's all very well for

her, since her "vendetta" lies in the "fact." I'm not going to do it. It destroys my *raison d'être*.

THE MANAGER: Your *raison d'être*! Oh, we're going ahead fine! First she starts off, and then you jump in. At this rate, we'll never finish.

THE FATHER: Now, don't be offended! Have it your own way — provided, however, that within the limits of the parts you assign us each one's sacrifice isn't too great.

THE MANAGER: You've got to understand that you can't go on arguing at your own pleasure. Drama is action, sir, action and not confounded philosophy.

THE FATHER: All right. I'll do just as much arguing and philosophizing as everybody does when he is considering his own torments.

THE MANAGER: If the drama permits! But for Heaven's sake, man, let's get along and come to the scene.

THE STEPDAUGHTER: It seems to me we've got too much action with our coming into his house. (*Indicating Father.*) You said, before, you couldn't change the scene every five minutes.

THE MANAGER: Of course not. What we've got to do is to combine and group up all the facts in one simultaneous, close-knit action. We can't have it as you want, with your little brother wandering like a ghost from room to room, hiding behind doors and meditating a project which — what did you say it did to him?

THE STEPDAUGHTER: Consumes him, sir, wastes him away!

THE MANAGER: Well, it may be. And then at the same time, you want the little girl there to be playing in the garden . . . one in the house, and the other in the garden; isn't that it?

THE STEPDAUGHTER: Yes, in the sun, in the sun! That is my only pleasure: to see her happy and careless in the garden after the misery and squalor of the horrible room where we all four slept together. And I had to sleep with her — I, do you understand? — with my vile contaminated body next to hers; with her holding me fast in her loving little arms. In the garden, whenever she spied me, she would run to take me by the hand. She didn't care for the big flowers, only the little ones; and she loved to show me them and pet me.

THE MANAGER: Well then, we'll have it in the garden. Everything shall happen in the garden; and we'll group the other scenes there. (*Calls a Stage Hand.*) Here, a backcloth with trees and something to do as a fountain basin. (*Turning round to look at the back of the stage.*) Ah, you've fixed it up. Good! (*To Stepdaughter.*) This is just to give an idea, of course. The Boy, instead of hiding behind the doors, will wander about here in the garden, hiding behind the trees. But it's going to be rather difficult to find a child to do that scene with you where she shows you the flowers. (*Turning to the Boy.*) Come forward a little, will you please? Let's try it now! Come along! come along! (*Then seeing him come shyly forward, full of fear and looking lost.*) It's a nice business, this lad here.

What's the matter with him? We'll have to give him a word or two to say. (*Goes close to him, puts a hand on his shoulders, and leads him behind one of the trees.*) Come on! come on! Let me see you a little! Hide here . . . yes, like that. Try and show your head just a little as if you were looking for someone. . . . (*Goes back to observe the effect, when the Boy at once goes through the action.*) Excellent! fine! (*Turning to Stepdaughter.*) Suppose the little girl there were to surprise him as he looks round, and run over to him, so we could give him a word or two to say?

THE STEPDAUGHTER: It's useless to hope he will speak, as long as that fellow there is here. . . . (*Indicates the Son.*) You must send him away first.

THE SON (*jumping up*): Delighted! Delighted! I don't ask for anything better. (*Begins to move away.*)

THE MANAGER (*at once stopping him*): No! No! Where are you going? Wait a bit!

(*The Mother gets up alarmed and terrified at the thought that he is really about to go away. Instinctively she lifts her arms to prevent him, without, however, leaving her seat.*)

THE SON (*to Manager, who stops him*): I've got nothing to do with this affair. Let me go, please! Let me go!

THE MANAGER: What do you mean by saying you've got nothing to do with this?

THE STEPDAUGHTER (*calmly, with irony*): Don't bother to stop him: he won't go away.

THE FATHER: He has to act the terrible scene in the garden with his mother.

THE SON (*suddenly resolute and with dignity*): I shall act nothing at all. I've said so from the very beginning. (*To the Manager.*) Let me go!

THE STEPDAUGHTER (*going over to the Manager*): Allow me? (*Puts down the Manager's arm which is restraining the Son.*) Well, go away then, if you want to! (*The Son looks at her with contempt and hatred. She laughs and says.*) You see, he can't, he can't go away! He is obliged to stay here, indissolubly bound to the chain. If I, who fly off when that happens which has to happen because I can't bear him — if I am still here and support that face and expression of his, you can well imagine that he is unable to move. He has to remain here, has to stop with that nice father of his, and that mother whose only son he is. (*Turning to the Mother.*) Come on, mother, come along! (*Turning to Manager to indicate her.*) You see, she was getting up to keep him back. (*To the Mother, beckoning her with her hand.*) Come on, come on! (*Then to Manager.*) You can imagine how little she wants to show these actors of yours what she really feels; but so eager is she to get near him that. . . . There, you see? She is willing to act her part. (*And in fact, the Mother approaches him; and as soon as the Stepdaughter has finished speaking, opens her arms to signify that she consents.*)

THE SON (*suddenly*): No! no! If I can't go away, then I'll stop here; but I repeat: I act nothing!

THE FATHER (*to Manager excitedly*): You can force him, sir.

THE SON: Nobody can force me.

THE FATHER: I can.

THE STEPDAUGHTER: Wait a minute, wait . . . First of all, the baby has to go to the fountain. . . . (*Runs to take the Child and leads her to the fountain.*)

THE MANAGER: Yes, yes of course; that's it. Both at the same time.

(*The Second Lady Lead and the Juvenile Lead at this point separate themselves from the group of Actors. One watches the Mother attentively; the other moves about studying the movements and manner of the Son whom he will have to act.*)

THE SON (*to Manager*): What do you mean by both at the same time? It isn't right. There was no scene between me and her. (*Indicates the Mother.*) Ask her how it was!

THE MOTHER: Yes, it's true. I had come into his room. . . .

THE SON: Into my room, do you understand? Nothing to do with the garden.

THE MANAGER: It doesn't matter. Haven't I told you we've got to group the action?

THE SON (*observing the Juvenile Lead studying him*): What do you want?

THE JUVENILE LEAD: Nothing! I was just looking at you.

THE SON (*turning toward the Second Lady Lead*): Ah! she's at it too: to re-act her part! (*Indicating the Mother.*)

THE MANAGER: Exactly! And it seems to me that you ought to be grateful to them for their interest.

THE SON: Yes, but haven't you yet perceived that it isn't possible to live in front of a mirror which not only freezes us with the image of ourselves, but throws our likeness back at us with a horrible grimace?

THE FATHER: That is true, absolutely true. You must see that.

THE MANAGER (*to Second Lady Lead and Juvenile Lead*): He's right! Move away from them!

THE SON: Do as you like. I'm out of this!

THE MANAGER: Be quiet, you, will you? And let me hear your mother! (*To Mother.*) You were saying you had entered. . . .

THE MOTHER: Yes, into his room, because I couldn't stand it any longer. I went to empty my heart to him of all the anguish that tortures me. . . . But as soon as he saw me come in. . . .

THE SON: Nothing happened! There was no scene. I went away, that's all! I don't care for scenes!

THE MOTHER: It's true, true. That's how it was.

THE MANAGER: Well now, we've got to do this bit between you and him. It's indispensable.

THE MOTHER: I'm ready . . . when you are ready. If you could only find a chance for me to tell him what I feel here in my heart.

THE FATHER (*going to Son in a great rage*): You'll do this for your mother, for your mother, do you understand?

THE SON (*quite determined*): I do nothing!

THE FATHER (*taking hold of him and shaking him*): For God's sake, do as I tell you! Don't you hear your mother asking you for a favor? Haven't you even got the guts to be a son?

THE SON (*taking hold of the Father*): No! No! And for God's sake stop it, or else.... (*General agitation. The Mother, frightened, tries to separate them.*)

THE MOTHER (*pleading*): Please! please!

THE FATHER (*not leaving hold of the Son*): You've got to obey, do you hear?

THE SON (*almost crying from rage*): What does it mean, this madness you've got? (*They separate.*) Have you no decency, that you insist on showing everyone our shame? I won't do it! I won't! And I stand for the will of our author in this. He didn't want to put us on the stage, after all!

THE MANAGER: Man alive! You came here . . .

THE SON (*indicating Father*): *He* did! I didn't!

THE MANAGER: Aren't you here now?

THE SON: It was his wish, and he dragged us along with him. He's told you not only the things that did happen, but also things that have never happened at all.

THE MANAGER: Well, tell me then what did happen. You went out of your room without saying a word?

THE SON: Without a word, so as to avoid a scene!

THE MANAGER: And then what did you do?

THE SON: Nothing . . . walking in the garden. . . . (*Hesitates for a moment with expression of gloom.*)

THE MANAGER (*coming closer to him, interested by his extraordinary reserve*): Well, well . . . walking in the garden. . . .

THE SON (*exasperated*): Why on earth do you insist? It's horrible!

(*The Mother trembles, sobs, and looks toward the fountain.*)

THE MANAGER (*slowly observing the glance and turning toward the Son with increasing apprehension*): The baby?

THE SON: There in the fountain. . . .

THE FATHER (*pointing with tender pity to the Mother*): She was following him at the moment. . . .

THE MANAGER (*to the Son anxiously*): And then you. . . .

THE SON: I ran over to her; I was jumping in to drag her out when I saw something that froze my blood . . . the boy standing stock still, with eyes like a madman's, watching his little drowned sister, in the fountain! (*The Stepdaughter bends over the fountain to hide the Child. She sobs.*) Then. . . . (*A revolver shot rings out behind the trees where the Boy is hidden.*)

THE MOTHER (*with a cry of terror runs over in that direction together with several of the Actors amid general confusion*): My son! My son! (*Then amid the cries and exclamations one hears her voice.*) Help! Help!

THE MANAGER (*pushing the Actors aside while they lift up the Boy and carry him off*): Is he really wounded?

SOME ACTORS: He's dead! dead!

OTHER ACTORS: No, no, it's only make-believe, it's only pretense!

THE FATHER (*with a terrible cry*): Pretense? Reality, sir, reality!

THE MANAGER: Pretense? Reality? To hell with it all! Never in my life has such a thing happened to me. I've lost a whole day over these people, a whole day!

COMMENTARY

John Corbin (1870–1959)

REVIEW OF *SIX CHARACTERS IN SEARCH OF AN AUTHOR*　　　1922

Corbin's review of the distinguished 1922 production of Six Characters in Search of an Author *reminds us how much the audiences loved the play. They stood clapping long after the last curtain. Florence Eldridge, who became famous for her role, is given relatively little attention here. Corbin instead focused his comments on the complexity of the play's comic premise.*

Philosophical fooling and shrewd criticism on the art of the theatre mingle in the Italian play which Brock Pemberton is presenting in translation at the Princess.

Imagine a playwright whose creative mind is haunted by six characters, the persons of a harrowing family drama, all urging insistently that they be given full and subtly shaded representation in the theatre. That is the normal condition of authentic creation; but as art consists in rigid elimination as well as in delicate emphasis, many of the aspirations of the six for self-expression have to be denied. Imagine next that the subject of their suffering is not sympathetic to the public, and that the only true and significant outcome is undramatic — not moving and inspiring, but static. That very often happens when a dramatist takes his real inspiration from life as it is actually lived, and in the supreme court of the manager's office he is nonsuited. There is no play.

But there are characters more live and vital than most of those that see the footlights. Imagine, finally, that these characters, still longing to live out their lives on the scene, go out in search of a more obliging author — and find a stage manager who has a company but no new play, only the stock stuff of a world somewhat deficient in new inspiration. Recognizing raw materials of interest and power, the enterprising business man undertakes to supply the place of the author. It seems to him a positive windfall to be relieved of that insistent and obnoxious incident of production. He will allow the six characters to live out their own lives while a secretary takes down the dialogue and his company stands by preparing to assume the parts. Magnificent!

Those who look upon ordinary rehearsals as a madhouse will receive illumination. Instead of a single author, long subdued in misery, the manager has his six orphans to contend with. The actors of his company, accustomed to have parts ruthlessly adapted to their personalities, are confronted each with a fury of unreason, demanding the absolute. For these characters, though the shadows of a dream, are "real" in the sense of being raw vitality unshaped to the necessities of art and the practical ends of the theatre. In the turmoil that ensues there is much satire on the foibles of player folk and managers and no little philosophy of dramatic art and dramatic criticism.

Margaret Wycherly is Mother in the roving dramatis personae and lends to the character genuine imagination and emotional power. Moffat Johnston is the garrulous father, eagerly philosophic and disquisitional. Florence Eldridge is the stepdaughter, overflowing with eager youth and charm. Throughout the production is able and highly competent. The audience last night, largely composed of folk of the theatre, rose to the novelty and humor of the idea and lingered long in applause after the brief three acts were over.

What the public will say to this rather slender and technical satire remains to be seen, but already it may be said that the season is indebted to Mr. Pemberton for one more exploration of strange fields and pastures new.

Eugene O'Neill

Eugene O'Neill (1888–1953) is a major figure in American drama. His enormous output is in the tradition of realism established by Strindberg and Ibsen, and his early plays, such as *Anna Christie* (1921), introduced Americans to the techniques of the great European realists. Realism for Americans was a move away from the sentimental comedies, the pathetic dramas, and the melodrama that dominated the American stage from before the Civil War to World War I. Some of O'Neill's plays, such as *Strange Interlude* (1928) and *Dynamo* (1929), were expressionist in style, demonstrating a considerable range. O'Neill rejected the kind of theater in which his father had thrived. James O'Neill had long been a stage star, traveling across the country in his production of *The Count of Monte Cristo,* which had made him rich but had also made him a prisoner of a single role.

Eugene O'Neill won the Pulitzer Prize for drama three times in the 1920s and the Nobel Prize for literature in 1936. Although not popular successes in his own day, his plays — including those published posthumously — are now mainstays of the American theater. Some of America's finest actors have taken a strong interest in his work, both producing his plays and acting in them on the stage and on television. From the 1950s to the 1990s, the late Colleen Dewhurst and Jason Robards, Jr., in particular, gave some magnificent performances and interpretations of O'Neill's work.

The young O'Neill was a romantic in the popular sense of the word. After a year at Princeton University, he began to travel on the sea. His jaunts took him to South America, and he once wound up virtually broke and without resources in Buenos Aires. When he returned to America, he studied for a year with George Pierce Baker, the most famous drama teacher of his day. Eventually, he took up residence in Provincetown, Massachusetts, where a group of people dedicated to theater — including the playwright Susan Glaspell — began to put on plays in their living rooms. When their audiences spilled over, the group created the Provincetown Playhouse, the theater in which many of O'Neill's earliest pieces were first performed.

The subjects of many of O'Neill's plays were not especially appealing to general theater audiences. Those who hoped for light comedy and a good laugh or light melodrama and a good cry found the intensity of his dark vision of the world to be overwhelming. They came for mere entertainment, and he was providing them with frightening visions of the soul's interior. The glum and painful surroundings of *Anna Christie* (1921) and the brutality of the lower-class coal stoker in *The Hairy Ape* (1922) were foreign to the comfortable middle-class audiences who supported commercial theater in America. They found O'Neill's characters to be haunted by family agonies, affections never given, ambitions never realized, pains never assuaged. Despite his remarkable abilities and the power of his drama, audiences often did not know what to make of him. To a large extent, his acceptance came on waves of shock, as had the acceptance of the Scandinavian realists.

O'Neill's early work is marked by a variety of experiments with theatrical effects and moods. He tried to use the primary influences of Greek drama in such plays as *Desire under the Elms* (1924), which has been described by critics as Greek tragedy, and *Mourning Becomes Electra* (1931), based on the *Oresteia,* which took three days to perform. But many of his early plays now seem dated and strange. His most impressive plays are his later work, such as *Ah, Wilderness!* (1933), *The Iceman Cometh* (1939), *Long Day's Journey into Night* (1939–1941), *A Moon for the Misbegotten* (1943), and *A Touch of the Poet* (1935–1942), which was performed posthumously in 1957.

DESIRE UNDER THE ELMS

Desire under the Elms (1924) is Eugene O'Neill's first effort at writing in the style of Greek tragedy. He did not follow the Greek tradition and choose a great figure of noble birth about whom the fates would unravel their mystery. Rather, he was deliberately democratic, choosing a New England farmer and his family as the protagonists of his drama. Just as fate animates a Greek tragedy, the emotional forces of jealousy, resentment, lust, and incestuous love animate *Desire under the Elms*.

O'Neill set his play on a typically rocky New England soil, which in many ways bears a striking resemblance to the rocky soil of Athens and the Greek coastline. The unyielding toughness of life on that land contrasts with the easy life to be made from gold mining in California. Ephraim Cabot, the seventy-five-year-old father, has been made hard and physically powerful by his work. He has just taken a third wife, the young and scheming Abbie. His youngest son, Eben, has decided to stay on the farm while his two other sons plan to go to California and put New England behind them.

The sense of having been dispossessed of his farm by his new stepmother drives Eben to hate Abbie, who has married the elder Cabot merely to inherit his farm. At first the sparring between Abbie and Eben is based on calculating self-interest, but eventually their feelings overpower them. Lust turns to love, and the son they produce is passed off as old Cabot's, although the townspeople have no illusion about whose child it is.

The farm itself is a powerful presence in the play. Whenever old Cabot thinks he should give up and follow the promise of easy money in California, he feels God's presence urging him to stay. God operates for Ephraim as the oracle in *Oedipus Rex* does, giving him a message that is painful but must be obeyed. The rocks on the farm are unforgiving, and so is the fate that Abbie and Eben face. Theirs is an impossible love; everything they do to prove their love condemns them even more. The forces of fate center on the farm. When the play opens, Eben says of it, "God! Purty!" When the play ends, the sheriff praises the farm and says he surely would like to own it, striking a clear note of irony: the agony of the play is rooted in lust — lust for the farm that parallels the lust between Abbie and Eben.

The play is haunted by the ghost of Eben's mother, whom Ephraim married primarily for her farm. Her ghost is exorcised only after the cycle of retribution has begun. Old Cabot has committed a crime against her, and now he must become the victim.

The language of the dialogue is that of New England in the mid-nineteenth century. Living in New England, O'Neill understood the ways and the language of its people. He seems to have imagined the "down-east" flavor of Maine in the language, and he has been careful to build the proper pronunciation into the dialogue. This folksy way of speaking helps emphasize the peasantlike qualities in these New England farmers. O'Neill's careful use of language is reminiscent of Synge's masterful representation of the Irish-English speech in *Playboy of the Western World*.

The language of O'Neill's characters has a rocky toughness at times. Characters are laconic — they often answer in a single word: "Ay-eh." Faithful to his vision of the simple speech of country folk, O'Neill avoids giving them elaborate poetic soliloquies. Instead, he shows how, despite their limited language, rural people feel profound emotions and act on them.

O'Neill carefully links Abbie with Queen Phaedra, who in Euripides' play *Hippolytus* and in Racine's seventeenth-century play *Phaedra* finds herself uncontrollably desiring her husband's son as a lover. Racine and Racine's audience could easily imagine such intense emotions overwhelming a noblewoman because they thought that nobility felt more intensely and lived more intensely than ordinary people. But O'Neill is trying to make his audience see that even unlettered farm people can feel as deeply as tragic heroes of any age do. The Cabots are victims of passion. They share their fate with the great families of the Greek tragedies.

Desire under the Elms in Performance

Desire under the Elms was first performed in Greenwich Village in 1924 under the auspices of the Provincetown Players. A year later it appeared on Broadway for thirty-six weeks, a long run for a tragedy. Its first reviewers were courteous but puzzled. They compared the play with earlier O'Neill works, remarking on its "tragic gloom and irony" and praising its language. At the Los Angeles production in 1926, the cast was arrested for "giving an obscene play." The sexual themes offended theatergoers in California, and even those who defended the play admitted that the text would be offensive to some members of the audience.

Because the English censor banned the play until 1938, its first European production was in Prague's National Theatre in 1925. Its Czech title translated as "The Farm under the Elms." The director used a highly stylized set influenced by the Moscow Art Theatre and later described as "a sort of two-storied wooded edifice . . . rather like a log cabin multiplied by four."

Other earlier European productions followed in Moscow in 1932, in Stockholm in 1933, and finally in London in 1940. The 1952 New York revival was not successful. The 1963 revival at the Circle in the Square in New York starred George C. Scott and his wife, Colleen Dewhurst. Jose Quintero, a notable interpreter of O'Neill, directed. Critics complained about "awkward" echoes of Greek tragedy while admitting that the play had an uncanny power despite its flaws. It ran for 380 performances.

The play has often been revived: in Boston in 1967; at the Berkshire Theater Festival in 1974; at the Roundabout Theater in New York, directed by Terry Schrieber, in 1984; and by numerous local theater groups. In 1978 Edward Thomas staged it at Connecticut College in New London as an opera. A creditable production, it emphasized the play's American folk qualities.

Eugene O'Neill (1888–1953)

DESIRE UNDER THE ELMS   *1924*

Characters

EPHRAIM CABOT
SIMEON ⎫
PETER ⎬ *his sons*
EBEN   ⎭
ABBIE PUTNAM
YOUNG GIRL, TWO FARMERS, *the* FIDDLER, *a* SHERIFF, *and other folk from the neighboring farms.*

(**Scene:** *The action of the entire play takes place in, and immediately outside of, the Cabot farmhouse in New England, in the year 1850. The south end of the house faces front to a stone wall with a wooden gate at center opening on a country road. The house is in good condition but in need of paint. Its walls are a sickly grayish, the green of the shutters faded. Two enormous elms are on each side of the house. They bend their trailing branches down over the roof. They appear to protect and at the same time subdue. There is a sinister maternity in their aspect, a crushing, jealous absorption. They have developed from their intimate contact with the life of man in the house an appalling humaneness. They brood oppressively over the house. They are like exhausted women resting their sagging breasts and hands and hair on its roof, and when it rains their tears trickle down monotonously and rot on the shingles.*

There is a path running from the gate around the right corner of the house to the front door. A narrow porch is on this side. The end wall facing us has two windows in its upper story, two larger ones on the floor below. The two upper are those of the father's bedroom and that of the brothers. On the left, ground floor, is the kitchen — on the right, the parlor, the shades of which are always drawn down.)

PART I • *Scene 1*

(*Exterior of the farmhouse. It is sunset of a day at the beginning of summer in the year 1850. There is no wind and everything is still. The sky above the roof is suffused with deep colors, the green of the elms glows, but the house is in shadow, seeming pale and washed out by contrast.*)

(*A door opens and Eben Cabot comes to the end of the porch and stands looking down the road to the right. He has a large bell in his hand and this he swings mechanically, awakening a deafening clangor. Then he puts his hands on his hips and stares up at the sky. He sighs with a puzzled awe and blurts out with halting appreciation.*)

EBEN: God! Purty! (*His eyes fall and he stares about him frowningly. He is twenty-five, tall and sinewy. His face is well formed, good-looking, but its expression is resentful and defensive. His defiant, dark eyes remind one of a wild animal's in captivity. Each day is a cage in which he finds himself trapped but inwardly unsubdued. There is a fierce repressed vitality about him. He has black hair, mustache, a thin curly trace of beard. He is dressed in rough farm clothes.*)

(*He spits on the ground with intense disgust, turns, and goes back into the house.*)

(*Simeon and Peter come in from their work in the fields. They are tall men, much older than their half-brother [Simeon is thirty-nine and Peter thirty-seven], built on a squarer, simpler model, fleshier in body, more bovine and homelier in face, shrewder and more practical. Their shoulders stoop a bit from years of farm work. They clump heavily along in their clumsy thick-soled* boots caked with earth. Their clothes, their faces, hands, bare arms, and throats are earth-stained. They smell of earth. They stand together for a moment in front of the house and, as if with the one impulse, stare dumbly up at the sky, leaning on their hoes. Their faces have a compressed, unresigned expression. As they look upward, this softens.)

SIMEON (grudgingly): Purty.

PETER: Ay-eh.

SIMEON (suddenly): Eighteen year ago.

PETER: What?

SIMEON: Jenn. My woman. She died.

PETER: I'd fergot.

SIMEON: I rec'lect — now an' agin. Makes it lonesome. She'd hair long's a hoss' tail — an' yeller like gold!

PETER: Waal — she's gone. (This with indifferent finality — then after a pause.) They's gold in the West, Sim.

SIMEON (still under the influence of sunset — vaguely): In the sky?

PETER: Waal — in a manner o' speakin' — that's the promise. (Growing excited.) Gold in the sky — in the West — Golden Gate — Californi-a! — Goldest West! — fields o' gold!

SIMEON (excited in his turn): Fortunes layin' just atop o' the ground waitin' t' be picked! Solomon's mines, they says! (For a moment they continue looking up at the sky — then their eyes drop.)

PETER (with sardonic bitterness): Here — it's stones atop o' the ground — stones atop o' stones — makin' stone walls — year atop o' year — him 'n' yew 'n' me 'n' then Eben — makin' stone walls fur him to fence us in!

SIMEON: We've wuked. Give our strength. Give our years. Plowed 'em under in the ground — (He stamps rebelliously.) — rottin' — makin' soil for his crops! (A pause.) Waal — the farm pays good for hereabouts.

PETER: If we plowed in Californi-a, they'd be lumps o' gold in the furrow!

SIMEON: Californi-a's t'other side o' earth, a'most. We got t' calc'late —

PETER (after a pause): 'Twould be hard fur me, too, to give up what we've 'arned here by our sweat. (A pause. Eben sticks his head out of the dining room window, listening.)

SIMEON: Ay-eh. (A pause.) Mebbe — he'll die soon.

PETER (doubtfully): Mebbe.

SIMEON: Mebbe — fur all we knows — he's dead now.

PETER: Ye'd need proof.

SIMEON: He's been gone two months — with no word.

PETER: Left us in the fields an evenin' like this. Hitched up an' druv off into the West. That's plum onnateral. He hadn't never been off this farm 'ceptin' t' the village in thirty year or more, not since he married Eben's maw. (A pause. Shrewdly.) I calc'late we might git him declared crazy by the court.

SIMEON: He skinned 'em too slick. He got the best o' all on 'em. They'd never b'lieve him crazy. (A pause.) We got t' wait — till he's underground.

EBEN (with a sardonic chuckle): Honor thy father! (They turn startled, and stare at him. He grins, then scowls.) I pray he's died. (They stare at him. He continues matter-of-factly.) Supper's ready.

SIMEON AND PETER (together): Ay-eh.

EBEN (gazing up at the sky): Sun's downin' purty.

SIMEON AND PETER (together): Ay-eh. They's gold in the West.

EBEN: Ay-eh. (Pointing.) Yonder atop o' the hill pasture, ye mean?

SIMEON AND PETER (together): In Californi-a!

EBEN: Hunh? (Stares at them indifferently for a second, then drawls.) Waal — supper's gittin' cold. (He turns back into kitchen.)

SIMEON (startled — smacks his lips): I air hungry!

PETER (sniffing): I smells bacon!

SIMEON (with hungry appreciation): Bacon's good!

PETER (in same tone): Bacon's bacon! (They turn, shouldering each other, their bodies bumping and rubbing together as they hurry clumsily to their food, like two friendly oxen toward their evening meal. They disappear around the right corner of house and can be heard entering the door.)

Scene II

(The color fades from the sky. Twilight begins. The interior of the kitchen is now visible. A pine table is at center, a cook-stove in the right rear corner, four rough wooden chairs, a tallow candle on the table. In the middle of the rear wall is fastened a big advertising poster with a ship in full sail and the word "California" in big letters. Kitchen utensils hang from nails. Everything is neat and in order but the atmosphere is of a men's camp kitchen rather than that of a home.)

(Places for three are laid. Eben takes boiled potatoes and bacon from the stove and puts them on the table, also a loaf of bread and a crock of water. Simeon and Peter shoulder in, slump down in their chairs without a word. Eben joins them. The three eat in silence for a moment, the two elder as naturally unrestrained as beasts of the field, Eben picking at his food without appetite, glancing at them with a tolerant dislike.)

SIMEON (suddenly turns to Eben): Looky here! Ye'd oughtn't t' said that, Eben.

PETER: 'Twa'n't righteous.

EBEN: What?

SIMEON: Ye prayed he'd died.

EBEN: Waal — don't yew pray it? (A pause.)

PETER: He's our Paw.

EBEN (violently): Not mine!

SIMEON (dryly): Ye'd not let no one else say that about yer Maw! Ha! (He gives one abrupt sardonic guffaw. Peter grins.)

EBEN (very pale): I meant — I hain't his'n — I hain't like him — he hain't me!

PETER (dryly): Wait till ye've growed his age!

EBEN (*intensely*): I'm Maw — every drop o' blood! (*A pause. They stare at him with indifferent curiosity.*)

PETER (*reminiscently*): She was good t' Sim 'n' me. A good Stepmaw's scurse.

SIMEON: She was good t' everyone.

EBEN (*greatly moved, gets to his feet and makes an awkward bow to each of them — stammering*): I be thankful t' ye. I'm her — her heir. (*He sits down in confusion.*)

PETER (*after a pause — judicially*): She was good even t' him.

EBEN (*fiercely*): An' fur thanks he killed her!

SIMEON (*after a pause*): No one never kills nobody. It's allus somethin'. That's the murderer.

EBEN: Didn't he slave Maw t' death?

PETER: He's slaved himself t' death. He's slaved Sim 'n' me 'n' yew t' death — on'y none o' us hain't died — yit.

SIMEON: It's somethin' — drivin' him — t' drive us!

EBEN (*vengefully*): Waal — I hold him t' jedgment! (*Then scornfully.*) Somethin'! What's somethin'?

SIMEON: Dunno.

EBEN (*sardonically*): What's drivin' yew to Californi-a, mebbe? (*They look at him in surprise.*) Oh, I've heerd ye! (*Then, after a pause.*) But ye'll never go t' the gold fields!

PETER (*assertively*): Mebbe!

EBEN: Whar'll ye git the money?

PETER: We kin walk. It's an a'mighty ways — Californi-a — but if yew was t' put all the steps we've walked on this farm end t' end we'd be in the moon!

EBEN: The Injuns'll skulp ye on the plains.

SIMEON (*with grim humor*): We'll mebbe make 'em pay a hair fur a hair!

EBEN (*decisively*): But t'aint that. Ye won't never go because ye'll wait here fur yer share o' the farm, thinkin' allus he'll die soon.

SIMEON (*after a pause*): We've a right.

PETER: Two-thirds belongs t'us.

EBEN (*jumping to his feet*): Ye've no right! She wa'n't yewr Maw! It was her farm! Didn't he steal it from her? She's dead. It's my farm.

SIMEON (*sardonically*): Tell that t' Paw — when he comes! I'll bet ye a dollar he'll laugh — fur once in his life. Ha! (*He laughs himself in one single mirthless bark.*)

PETER (*amused in turn, echoes his brother*): Ha!

SIMEON (*after a pause*): What've ye got held agin us, Eben? Year arter year it's skulked in yer eye — somethin'.

PETER: Ay-eh.

EBEN: Ay-eh. They's somethin'. (*Suddenly exploding.*) Why didn't ye never stand between him 'n' my Maw when he was slavin' her to her grave — t' pay her back fur the kindness she done t' yew? (*There is a long pause. They stare at him in surprise.*)

SIMEON: Waal — the stock'd got t' be watered.

PETER: 'R they was woodin' t' do.

SIMEON: 'R plowin'.

PETER: 'R hayin'.

SIMEON: 'R spreadin' manure.

PETER: 'R weedin'.

SIMEON: 'R prunin'.

PETER: 'R milkin'.

EBEN (*breaking in harshly*): An' makin' walls — stone atop o' stone — makin' walls till yer heart's a stone ye heft up out o' the way o' growth onto a stone wall t' wall in yer heart!

SIMEON (*matter-of-factly*): We never had no time t' meddle.

PETER (*to Eben*): Yew was fifteen afore yer Maw died — an' big fur yer age. Why didn't ye never do nothin'?

EBEN (*harshly*): They was chores t' do, wasn't they? (*A pause — then slowly.*) It was on'y arter she died I come to think o' it. Me cookin' — doin' her work — that made me know her, suffer her sufferin' — she'd come back t' help — come back t' bile potatoes — come back t' fry bacon — come back t' bake biscuits — come back all cramped up t' shake the fire, an' carry ashes, her eyes weepin' an' bloody with smoke an' cinders same's they used t' be. She still comes back — stands by the stove thar in the evenin' — she can't find it nateral sleepin' an' restin' in peace. She can't git used t' bein' free — even in her grave.

SIMEON: She never complained none.

EBEN: She'd got too tired. She'd got too used t' bein' too tired. That was what he done. (*With vengeful passion.*) An' sooner'r later, I'll meddle. I'll say the thin's I didn't say then t' him! I'll yell 'em at the top o' my lungs. I'll see t' it my Maw gits some rest an' sleep in her grave! (*He sits down again, relapsing into a brooding silence. They look at him with a queer indifferent curiosity.*)

PETER (*after a pause*): Whar in tarnation d'ye s'pose he went, Sim?

SIMEON: Dunno. He druv off in the buggy, all spick an' span, with the mare all breshed an' shiny, druv off clackin' his tongue an' wavin' his whip. I remember it right well. I was finishin' plowin', it was spring an' May an' sunset, an' gold in the West, an' he druv off into it. I yells "Whar ye goin', Paw?" an' he hauls up by the stone wall a jiffy. His old snake's eyes was glitterin' in the sun like he'd been drinkin' a jugful an' he says with a mule's grin: "Don't ye run away till I come back!"

PETER: Wonder if he knowed we was wantin' fur Californ-a?

SIMEON: Mebbe. I didn't say nothin' and he says, lookin' kinder queer an' sick: "I been hearin' the hens cluckin' an' the roosters crowin' all the durn day. I been listenin' the cows lowin' an' everythin' else kickin' up till I can't stand it no more. It's spring an' I'm feelin' damned," he says. "Damned like an old bare hickory tree fit on'y fur burnin'," he says. An' then I calc'late I must've looked a mite hopeful, fur he adds real spry and vicious: "But don't git no fool idee I'm dead. I've sworn t' live a hundred an' I'll do it, if on'y t' spite yer sinful greed! An' now I'm ridin' out t' learn God's message t' me in the spring, like the prophets done. An' yew git back t' yer plowin'," he says. An' he druv off singin' a hymn. I thought he was drunk — 'r I'd stopped him goin'.

EBEN (*scornfully*): No, ye wouldn't! Ye're scared o' him. He's stronger — inside — than both o' ye put together!

PETER (*sardonically*): An' yew — be yew Samson?°

EBEN: I'm gittin' stronger. I kin feel it growin' in me — growin' an' growin' — till it'll bust out — ! (*He gets up and puts on his coat and a hat. They watch him, gradually breaking into grins. Eben avoids their eyes sheepishly.*) I'm goin' out fur a spell — up the road.

PETER: T' the village.

SIMEON: T' see Minnie?

EBEN (*defiantly*): Ay-eh!

PETER (*jeeringly*): The Scarlet Woman!

SIMEON: Lust — that's what's growin' in ye!

EBEN: Waal — she's purty!

PETER: She's been purty fur twenty year.

SIMEON: A new coat o' paint'll make a heifer out of forty.

EBEN: She hain't forty!

PETER: If she hain't, she's teeterin' on the edge.

EBEN (*desperately*): What d'yew know —

PETER: All they is . . . Sim knew her — an' then me arter —

SIMEON: An' Paw kin tell yew somethin' too! He was fust!

EBEN: D'ye mean t' say he . . . ?

SIMEON (*with a grin*): Ay-eh! We air his heirs in everythin'!

EBEN (*intensely*): That's more to it! That grows on it! It'll bust soon! (*Then violently.*) I'll go smash my fist in her face! (*He pulls open the door in rear violently.*)

SIMEON (*with a wink at Peter — drawlingly*): Mebbe — but the night's wa'm — purty — by the time ye git thar mebbe ye'll kiss her instead!

PETER: Sart'n he will! (*They both roar with coarse laughter. Eben rushes out and slams the door — then the outside front door — comes around the corner of the house and stands still by the gate, staring up at the sky.*)

SIMEON (*looking after him*): Like his Paw.

PETER: Dead spit an' image!

SIMEON: Dog'll eat dog!

PETER: Ay-eh. (*Pause. With yearning.*) Mebbe a year from now we'll be in Californi-a.

SIMEON: Ay-eh. (*A pause. Both yawn.*) Let's git t'bed. (*He blows out the candle. They go out door in rear. Eben stretches his arms up to the sky — rebelliously.*)

EBEN: Waal — thar's a star, an' somewhar's they's him, an' here's me, an' thar's Min up the road — in the same night. What if I does kiss her? She's like t'night, she's soft 'n' wa'm, her eyes kin wink like a star, her

Samson: A biblical hero known for his great physical strength.

mouth's wa'm, her arms're wa'm, she smells like a wa'm plowed field, she's purty . . . Ay-eh! By God A'mighty she's purty, an' I don't give a damn how many sins she's sinned afore mine or who she's sinned 'em with, my sin's as purty as any one on 'em! (*He strides off down the road to the left.*)

Scene III

(*It is the pitch darkness just before dawn. Eben comes in from the left and goes around to the porch, feeling his way, chuckling bitterly and cursing half-aloud to himself.*)

EBEN: The cussed old miser! (*He can be heard going in the front door. There is a pause as he goes upstairs, then a loud knock on the bedroom door of the brothers.*) Wake up!

SIMEON (*startledly*): Who's thar?

EBEN (*Pushing open the door and coming in, a lighted candle in his hand. The bedroom of the brothers is revealed. Its ceiling is the sloping roof. They can stand upright only close to the center dividing wall of the upstairs. Simeon and Peter are in a double bed, front. Eben's cot is to the rear. Eben has a mixture of silly grin and vicious scowl on his face.*): I be!

PETER (*angrily*): What in hell's-fire. . . ?

EBEN: I got news fur ye! Ha! (*He gives one abrupt sardonic guffaw.*)

SIMEON (*angrily*): Couldn't ye hold it 'til we'd got our sleep?

EBEN: It's nigh sunup. (*Then explosively.*) He's gone an' married agen!

SIMEON AND PETER (*explosively*): Paw?

EBEN: Got himself hitched to a female 'bout thirty-five — an' purty, they says . . .

SIMEON (*aghast*): It's a durn lie!

PETER: Who says?

SIMEON: They been stringin' ye!

EBEN: Think I'm a dunce, do ye? The hull village says. The preacher from New Dover, he brung the news — told it t'our preacher — New Dover, that's whar the old loon got himself hitched — that's whar the woman lived —

PETER (*no longer doubting — stunned*): Waal . . . !

SIMEON (*the same*): Waal . . . !

EBEN (*sitting down on a bed — with vicious hatred*): Ain't he a devil out o' hell? It's jest t' spite us — the damned old mule!

PETER (*after a pause*): Everythin'll go t'her now.

SIMEON: Ay-eh. (*A pause — dully.*) Waal — if it's done —

PETER: It's done us. (*Pause — then persuasively.*) They's gold in the fields o' Californi-a, Sim. No good a-stayin' here now.

SIMEON: Jest what I was a-thinkin'. (*Then with decision.*) S'well fust's last! Let's light out and git this mornin'.

PETER: Suits me.

EBEN: Ye must like walkin'.

SIMEON (*sardonically*): If ye'd grow wings on us we'd fly thar!

EBEN: Ye'd like ridin' better — on a boat, wouldn't ye? (*Fumbles in his pocket and takes out a crumpled sheet of foolscap.*) Waal, if ye sign this ye kin ride on a boat. I've had it writ out an' ready in case ye'd ever go. It says fur three hundred dollars t' each ye agree yewr shares o' the farm is sold t' me. (*They look suspiciously at the paper. A pause.*)

SIMEON (*wonderingly*): But if he's hitched agen —

PETER: An' whar'd yew git that sum o' money, anyways?

EBEN (*cunningly*): I know whar it's hid. I been waitin' — Maw told me. She knew whar it lay fur years, but she was waitin' . . . It's her'n — the money he hoarded from her farm an' hid from Maw. It's my money by rights now.

PETER: Whar's it hid?

EBEN (*cunningly*): Whar yew won't never find it without me. Maw spied on him —'r she'd never knowed. (*A pause. They look at him suspiciously, and he at them.*) Waal, is it fa'r trade?

SIMEON: Dunno.

PETER: Dunno.

SIMEON (*looking at window*): Sky's grayin'.

PETER: Ye better start the fire, Eben.

SIMEON: An' fix some vittles.

EBEN: Ay-eh. (*Then with a forced jocular heartiness.*) I'll git ye a good one. If ye're startin' t' hoof it t' Californi-a ye'll need somethin' that'll stick t' yer ribs. (*He turns to the door, adding meaningly.*) But ye kin ride on a boat if ye'll swap. (*He stops at the door and pauses. They stare at him.*)

SIMEON (*suspiciously*): Whar was ye all night?

EBEN (*defiantly*): Up t' Min's. (*Then slowly.*) Walkin' thar, fust I felt 's if I'd kiss her; then I got a-thinkin' o' what ye'd said o' him an' her an' I says, I'll bust her nose fur that! Then I got t' the village an' heerd the news an' I got madder'n hell an' run all the way t' Min's not knowin' what I'd do — (*He pauses — then sheepishly but more defiantly.*) Waal — when I seen her, I didn't hit her — nor I didn't kiss her nuther — I begun t' beller like a calf an' cuss at the same time, I was so durn mad — an' she got scared — an' I jest grabbed holt an' tuk her! (*Proudly.*) Yes, sirree! I tuk her. She may've been his'n — an' your'n, too — but she's mine now!

SIMEON (*dryly*): In love, air yew?

EBEN (*with lofty scorn*): Love! I don't take no stock in sech slop!

PETER (*winking at Simeon*): Mebbe Eben's aimin' t' marry, too.

SIMEON: Min'd make a true faithful he'pmeet! (*They snicker.*)

EBEN: What do I care fur her —'ceptin' she's round an' wa'm? The p'int is she was his'n — an' now she b'longs t' me! (*He goes to the door — then turns — rebelliously.*) An' Min hain't sech a bad un. They's worse'n Min in the world, I'll bet ye! Wait'll we see this cow the Old Man's hitched t'! She'll beat Min, I got a notion! (*He starts to go out.*)

SIMEON (*suddenly*): Mebbe ye'll try t' make her your'n, too?

PETER: Ha! (*He gives a sardonic laugh of relish at this idea.*)

EBEN (*spitting with disgust*): Her — here — sleepin' with him — stealin' my Maw's farm! I'd as soon pet a skunk 'r kiss a snake! (*He goes out. The two stare after him suspiciously. A pause. They listen to his steps receding.*)

PETER: He's startin' the fire.

SIMEON: I'd like t' ride t' Californi-a — but —

PETER: Min might o' put some scheme in his head.

SIMEON: Mebbe it's all a lie 'bout Paw marryin'. We'd best wait an' see the bride.

PETER: An' don't sign nothin' till we does!

SIMEON: Nor till we've tested it's good money! (*Then with a grin.*) But if Paw's hitched we'd be sellin' Eben somethin' we'd never git nohow!

PETER: We'll wait an' see. (*Then with sudden vindictive anger.*) An' till he comes, let's yew 'n' me not wuk a lick, let Eben tend to thin's if he's a mind t', let's us jest sleep an' eat an' drink likker, an' let the hull damned farm go t' blazes!

SIMEON (*excitedly*): By God, we've 'arned a rest! We'll play rich fur a change. I hain't a-going to stir outa bed till breakfast's ready.

PETER: An' on the table!

SIMEON (*after a pause — thoughtfully*): What d'ye calc'late she'll be like — our new Maw? Like Eben thinks?

PETER: More'n likely.

SIMEON (*vindictively*): Waal — I hope she's a she-devil that'll make him wish he was dead an' livin' in the pit o' hell fur comfort!

PETER (*fervently*): Amen!

SIMEON (*imitating his father's voice*): "I'm ridin' out t' learn God's message t' me in the spring like the prophets done," he says. I'll bet right then an' thar he knew plumb well he was goin' whorin', the stinkin' old hypocrite!

Scene IV

(*Same as scene II — shows the interior of the kitchen with a lighted candle on table. It is gray dawn outside. Simeon and Peter are just finishing their breakfast. Eben sits before his plate of untouched food, brooding frowningly.*)

PETER (*glancing at him rather irritably*): Lookin' glum don't help none.

SIMEON (*sarcastically*): Sorrowin' over his lust o' the flesh!

PETER (*with a grin*): Was she yer fust?

EBEN (*angrily*): None o' yer business. (*A pause.*) I was thinkin' o' him. I got a notion he's gittin' near — I kin feel him comin' on like yew kin feel malaria chill afore it takes ye.

PETER: It's too early yet.

SIMEON: Dunno. He'd like t' catch us nappin' — jest t' have somethin' t' hoss us 'round over.

PETER (*Mechanically gets to his feet. Simeon does the same.*): Waal — let's git t'wuk. (*They both plod mechanically toward the door before they realize. Then they stop short.*)

SIMEON (*grinning*): Ye're a cussed fool, Pete — and I be wuss! Let him see we hain't wukin'! We don't give a durn!

PETER (*as they go back to the table*): Not a damned durn! It'll serve t' show him we're done with him. (*They sit down again. Eben stares from one to the other with surprise.*)

SIMEON (*grins at him*): We're aimin' t' start bein' lilies o' the field.

PETER: Nary a toil 'r spin 'r lick o' wuk do we put in!

SIMEON: Ye're sole owner — till he comes — that's what ye wanted. Waal, ye got t' be sole hand, too.

PETER: The cows air bellerin'. Ye better hustle at the milkin'.

EBEN (*with excited joy*): Ye mean ye'll sign the paper?

SIMEON (*dryly*): Mebbe.

PETER: Mebbe.

SIMEON: We're considerin'. (*Peremptorily.*) Ye better git t' wuk.

EBEN (*with queer excitement*): It's Maw's farm agen! It's my farm! Them's my cows! I'll milk my durn fingers off fur cows o' mine! (*He goes out door in rear, they stare after him indifferently.*)

SIMEON: Like his Paw.

PETER: Dead spit 'n' image!

SIMEON: Waal — let dog eat dog! (*Eben comes out of front door and around the corner of the house. The sky is beginning to grow flushed with sunrise. Eben stops by the gate and stares around him with glowing, possessive eyes. He takes in the whole farm with his embracing glance of desire.*)

EBEN: It's purty! It's damned purty! It's mine! (*He suddenly throws his head back boldly and glares with hard, defiant eyes at the sky.*) Mine, d'ye hear? Mine! (*He turns and walks quickly off left, rear, toward the barn. The two brothers light their pipes.*)

SIMEON (*putting his muddy boots up on the table, tilting back his chair, and puffing defiantly*): Waal — this air solid comfort — fur once.

PETER: Ay-eh. (*He follows suit. A pause. Unconsciously they both sigh.*)

SIMEON (*suddenly*): He never was much o' a hand at milkin', Eben wa'n't.

PETER (*with a snort*): His hands air like hoofs! (*A pause.*)

SIMEON: Reach down the jug thar! Let's take a swaller. I'm feelin' kind o' low.

PETER: Good idee! (*He does so — gets two glasses — they pour out drinks of whisky.*) Here's t' the gold in Californi-a!

SIMEON: An' luck t' find it! (*They drink — puff resolutely — sigh — take their feet down from the table.*)

PETER: Likker don't pear t' sot right.

SIMEON: We hain't used t' it this early. (*A pause. They become very restless.*)

PETER: Gittin' close in this kitchen.

SIMEON (*with immense relief*): Let's git a breath o' air. (*They arise briskly and go out rear — appear around house and stop by the gate. They stare up at the sky with a numbed appreciation.*)

PETER: Purty!

SIMEON: Ay-eh. Gold's t' the East now.

PETER: Sun's startin' with us fur the Golden West.

SIMEON (*staring around the farm, his compressed face tightened, unable to conceal his emotion*): Waal — it's our last mornin' — mebbe.

PETER (*the same*): Ay-eh.

SIMEON (*stamps his foot on the earth and addresses it desperately*): Waal — ye've thirty year o' me buried in ye — spread out over ye — blood an' bone an' sweat — rotted away — fertilizin' ye — richin' yer soul — prime manure, by God, that's what I been t' ye!

PETER: Ay-eh! An' me.

SIMEON: An' yew, Peter. (*He sighs — then spits.*) Waal — no use'n cryin' over spilt milk.

PETER: They's gold in the West — an' freedom, mebbe. We been slaves t' stone walls here.

SIMEON (*defiantly*): We hain't nobody's slaves from this out — nor nothin's slaves nuther. (*A pause — restlessly.*) Speaking o' milk, wonder how Eben's managin'?

PETER: I s'pose he's managin'.

SIMEON: Mebbe we'd ought t' help — this once.

PETER: Mebbe. The cows knows us.

SIMEON: An' likes us. They don't know him much.

PETER: An' the hosses, an' pigs, an' chickens. They don't know him much.

SIMEON: They knows us like brothers — an' likes us! (*Proudly.*) Hain't we raised 'em t' be fust-rate, number one prize stock?

PETER: We hain't — not no more.

SIMEON (*dully*): I was fergittin'. (*Then resignedly.*) Waal, let's go help Eben a spell an' git waked up.

PETER: Suits me. (*They are starting off down left, rear, for the barn when Eben appears from there hurrying toward them, his face excited.*)

EBEN (*breathlessly*): Waal — har they be! The old mule an' the bride! I seen 'em from the barn down below at the turnin'.

PETER: How could ye tell that far?

EBEN: Hain't I as far-sight as he's near-sight? Don't I know the mare 'n' buggy, an' two people settin' in it? Who else . . . ? An' I tell ye I kin feel 'em a'comin', too! (*He squirms as if he had the itch.*)

PETER (*beginning to be angry*): Waal — let him do his own unhitchin'!

SIMEON (*angry in his turn*): Let's hustle in an' git our

bundles an' be a-goin' as he's a-comin'. I don't want never t' step inside the door agen arter he's back. (*They both start back around the corner of the house. Eben follows them.*)

EBEN (*anxiously*): Will ye sign it afore ye go?

PETER: Let's see the color o' the old skinflint's money an' we'll sign. (*They disappear left. The two brothers clump upstairs to get their bundles. Eben appears in the kitchen, runs to window, peers out, comes back and pulls up a strip of flooring in under stove, takes out a canvas bag and puts it on table, then sets the floorboard back in place. The two brothers appear a moment after. They carry old carpetbags.*)

EBEN (*puts his hand on bag guardingly*): Have ye signed?

SIMEON (*shows paper in his hand*): Ay-eh. (*Greedily.*) Be that the money?

EBEN (*opens bag and pours out pile of twenty-dollar gold pieces*): Twenty-dollar pieces — thirty of 'em. Count 'em. (*Peter does so, arranging them in stacks of five, biting one or two to test them.*)

PETER: Six hundred. (*He puts them in bag and puts it inside his shirt carefully.*)

SIMEON (*handing paper to Eben*): Har ye be.

EBEN (*after a glance, folds it carefully and hides it under his shirt — gratefully*): Thank yew.

PETER: Thank yew fur the ride.

SIMEON: We'll send ye a lump o' gold fur Christmas. (*A pause. Eben stares at them and they at him.*)

PETER (*awkwardly*): Waal — we're a-goin'.

SIMEON: Comin' out t' the yard?

EBEN: No. I'm waitin' in here a spell. (*Another silence. The brothers edge awkwardly to door in rear — then turn and stand.*)

SIMEON: Waal — good-by.

PETER: Good-by.

EBEN: Good-by. (*They go out. He sits down at the table, faces the stove and pulls out the paper. He looks from it to the stove. His face, lighted up by the shaft of sunlight from the window, has an expression of trance. His lips move. The two brothers come out to the gate.*)

PETER (*looking off toward barn*): Thar he be — un-hitchin'.

SIMEON (*with a chuckle*): I'll bet ye he's riled!

PETER: An thar she be.

SIMEON: Let's wait 'n' see what our new Maw looks like.

PETER (*with a grin*): An' give him our partin' cuss!

SIMEON (*grinning*): I like raisin' fun. I feel light in my head an' feet.

PETER: Me, too. I feel like laffin' till I'd split up the middle.

SIMEON: Reckon it's the likker?

PETER: No. My feet feel itchin' t' walk an' walk — an' jump high over thin's — an'. . . .

SIMEON: Dance? (*A pause.*)

PETER (*puzzled*): It's plumb onnateral.

SIMEON (*a light coming over his face*): I calc'late it's 'cause school's out. It's holiday. Fur once we're free!

PETER (*dazedly*): Free?

SIMEON: The halter's broke — the harness is busted — the fence bars is down — the stone walls air crumblin' an' tumblin'! We'll be kickin' up an' tearin' away down the road!

PETER (*drawing a deep breath — oratorically*): Anybody that wants this stinkin' old rock-pile of a farm kin hev it. T'ain't our'n, no sirree!

SIMEON (*takes the gate off its hinges and puts it under his arm*): We harby 'bolishes shet gates, an' open gates, an' all gates, by thunder!

PETER: We'll take it with us fur luck an' let 'er sail free down some river.

SIMEON (*as a sound of voices comes from left, rear*): Har they comes! (*The two brothers congeal into two stiff, grim-visaged statues. Ephraim Cabot and Abbie Putnam come in. Cabot is seventy-five, tall and gaunt, with great, wiry, concentrated power, but stoop-shouldered from toil. His face is as hard as if it were hewn out of a boulder, yet there is a weakness in it, a petty pride in its own narrow strength. His eyes are small, close together, and extremely near-sighted, blinking continually in the effort to focus on objects, their stare having a straining, ingrowing quality. He is dressed in his dismal black Sunday suit. Abbie is thirty-five, buxom, full of vitality. Her round face is pretty but marred by its rather gross sensuality. There is strength and obstinacy in her jaw, a hard determination in her eyes, and about her whole personality the same unsettled, untamed, desperate quality which is so apparent in Eben.*)

CABOT (*as they enter — a queer strangled emotion in his dry cracking voice*): Har we be t' hum, Abbie.

ABBIE (*with lust for the word*): Hum! (*Her eyes gloating on the house without seeming to see the two stiff figures at the gate.*) It's purty — purty! I can't b'lieve it's r'ally mine.

CABOT (*sharply*): Yewr'n? Mine! (*He stares at her penetratingly. She stares back. He adds relentingly.*) Our'n — mebbe! It was lonesome too long. I was growin' old in the spring. A hum's got t' hev a woman.

ABBIE (*her voice taking possession*): A woman's got t' hev a hum!

CABOT (*nodding uncertainly*): Ay-eh. (*Then irritably.*) Whar be they? Ain't thar nobody about —'r wukin' —'r nothin'?

ABBIE (*Sees the brothers. She returns their stare of cold appraising contempt with interest — slowly.*): Thar's two men loafin' at the gate an' starin' at me like a couple o' strayed hogs.

CABOT (*straining his eyes*): I kin see 'em — but I can't make out. . . .

SIMEON: It's Simeon.

PETER: It's Peter.

CABOT (*exploding*): Why hain't ye wukin'?

SIMEON (*dryly*): We're waitin' t' welcome ye hum — yew an' the bride!

CABOT (*confusedly*): Huh? Waal — this be yer new Maw, boys. (*She stares at them and they at her.*)

SIMEON (*turns away and spits contemptuously*): I see her!

PETER (*spits also*): An I see her!

ABBIE (*with the conqueror's conscious superiority*): I'll go in an' look at *my* house. (*She goes slowly around to porch.*)

SIMEON (*with a snort*): *Her* house!

PETER (*calls after her*): Ye'll find Eben inside. Ye better not tell him it's *yewr* house.

ABBIE (*mouthing the name*): Eben. (*Then quietly.*) I'll tell Eben.

CABOT (*with a contemptuous sneer*): Ye needn't heed Eben. Eben's a dumb fool — like his Maw — soft an' simple!

SIMEON (*with his sardonic burst of laughter*): Ha! Eben's a chip o' yew — spit 'n' image — hard 'n' bitter's a hickory tree! Dog'll eat dog. He'll eat ye yet, old man!

CABOT (*commandingly*): Ye git t' wuk.

SIMEON (*as Abbie disappears in house — winks at Peter and says tauntingly*): So that thar's our new Maw, be it? Whar in hell did ye dig her up? (*He and Peter laugh.*)

PETER: Ha! Ye'd better turn her in the pen with the other sows. (*They laugh uproariously, slapping their thighs.*)

CABOT (*so amazed at their effrontery that he stutters in confusion*): Simeon! Peter! What's come over ye? Air ye drunk?

SIMEON: We're free, old man — free o' yew an' the hull damned farm! (*They grow more and more hilarious and excited.*)

PETER: An' we're startin' out fur the gold fields o' Californi-a!

SIMEON: Ye kin take this place an' burn it!

PETER: An' bury it — fur all we cares!

SIMEON: We're free, old man! (*He cuts a caper.*)

PETER: Free! (*He gives a kick in the air.*)

SIMEON (*in a frenzy*): Whoop!

PETER: Whoop! (*They do an absurd Indian war dance about the old man who is petrified between rage and the fear that they are insane.*)

SIMEON: We're free as Injuns! Lucky we don't skulp ye!

PETER: An' burn yer barn an' kill the stock!

SIMEON: An' rape yer new woman! Whoop! (*He and Peter stop their dance, holding their sides, rocking with wild laughter.*)

CABOT (*edging away*): Lust fur gold — fur the sinful, easy gold o' Californi-a! It's made ye mad!

SIMEON (*tauntingly*): Wouldn't ye like us to send ye back some sinful gold, ye old sinner?

PETER: They's gold besides what's in Californi-a! (*He retreats back beyond the vision of the old man and takes the bag of money and flaunts it in the air above his head, laughing.*)

SIMEON: And sinfuller, too!

PETER: We'll be voyagin' on the sea! Whoop! (*He leaps up and down.*)

SIMEON: Livin' free! Whoop! (*He leaps in turn.*)

CABOT (*suddenly roaring with rage*): My cuss on ye!

SIMEON: Take our'n in trade fur it! Whoop!

CABOT: I'll hev ye both chained up in the asylum!

PETER: Ye old skinflint! Good-by!

SIMEON: Ye old blood sucker! Good-by!

CABOT: Go afore I . . . !

PETER: Whoop! (*He picks a stone from the road. Simeon does the same.*)

SIMEON: Maw'll be in the parlor.

PETER: Ay-eh! One! Two!

CABOT (*frightened*): What air ye . . . ?

PETER: Three! (*They both throw, the stones hitting the parlor window with a crash of glass, tearing the shade.*)

SIMEON: Whoop!

PETER: Whoop!

CABOT (*in a fury now, rushing toward them*): If I kin lay hands on ye — I'll break yer bones fur ye! (*But they beat a capering retreat before him, Simeon with the gate still under his arm. Cabot comes back, panting with impotent rage. Their voices as they go off take up the song of the gold-seekers to the old tune of "Oh, Susannah!"*)

"I jumped aboard the Liza ship,
And traveled on the sea,
And every time I thought of home
I wished it wasn't me!
Oh! Californi-a,
That's the land fur me!
I'm off to Californi-a!
With my wash bowl on my knee."

(*In the meantime, the window of the upper bedroom on right is raised and Abbie sticks her head out. She looks down at Cabot — with a sigh of relief.*)

ABBIE: Waal — that's the last o' them two, hain't it? (*He doesn't answer. Then in possessive tones.*) This here's a nice bedroom, Ephraim. It's a r'al nice bed. Is it my room, Ephraim?

CABOT (*grimly — without looking up*): Our'n! (*She cannot control a grimace of aversion and pulls back her head slowly and shuts the window. A sudden horrible thought seems to enter Cabot's head.*) They been up to somethin'! Mebbe — mebbe they've pizened the stock —'r somethin'! (*He almost runs off down toward the barn. A moment later the kitchen door is slowly pushed open and Abbie enters. For a moment she stands looking at Eben. He does not notice her at first. Her eyes take him in penetratingly with a calculating appraisal of his strength as against hers. But under this her desire is dimly awakened by his youth and good looks. Suddenly he becomes conscious of her presence and looks up. Their eyes meet. He leaps to his feet, glowering at her speechlessly.*)

ABBIE (*in her most seductive tones which she uses all

through this scene): Be you — Eben? I'm Abbie — (*She laughs.*) I mean, I'm yer new Maw.

EBEN (*viciously*): No, damn ye!

ABBIE (*as if she hadn't heard — with a queer smile*): Yer Paw's spoke a lot o' yew. . . .

EBEN: Ha!

ABBIE: Ye mustn't mind him. He's an old man. (*A long pause. They stare at each other.*) I don't want t' pretend playin' Maw t' ye, Eben. (*Admiringly.*) Ye're too big an' too strong fur that. I want t' be frens with ye. Mebbe with me fur a fren ye'd find ye'd like livin' here better. I kin make it easy fur ye with him, mebbe. (*With a scornful sense of power.*) I calc'late I kin git him t' do most anythin' fur me.

EBEN (*with bitter scorn*): Ha! (*They stare again, Eben obscurely moved, physically attracted to her — in forced stilted tones.*) Yew kin go t' the devil!

ABBIE (*calmly*): If cussin' me does ye good, cuss all ye've a mind t'. I'm all prepared t' have ye agin me — at fust. I don't blame ye nuther. I'd feel the same at any stranger comin' t' take my Maw's place. (*He shudders. She is watching him carefully.*) Yew must've cared a lot fur yewr Maw, didn't ye? My Maw died afore I'd growed. I don't remember her none. (*A pause.*) But yew won't hate me long, Eben. I'm not the wust in the world — an' yew an' me've got a lot in common. I kin tell that by lookin' at ye. Waal — I've had a hard life, too — oceans o' trouble an' nuthin' but wuk fur reward. I was a orphan early an' had t' wuk fur others in other folks' hums. Then I married an' he turned out a drunken spreer an' so he had to wuk fur others an' me too agen in other folks' hums, an' the baby died, an' my husband got sick an' died too, an' I was glad sayin' now I'm free fur once, on'y I diskivered right away all I was free fur was t'wuk agen in other folks' hums, doin' other folks' wuk till I'd most give up hope o' ever doin' my own wuk in my own hum, an' then your Paw come . . . (*Cabot appears returning from the barn. He comes to the gate and looks down the road the brothers have gone. A faint strain of their retreating voices is heard: "Oh, Californi-a! That's the place for me." He stands glowering, his fist clenched, his face grim with rage.*)

EBEN (*fighting against his growing attraction and sympathy — harshly*): An' bought yew — like a harlot! (*She is stung and flushes angrily. She has been sincerely moved by the recital of her troubles. He adds furiously.*) An' the price he's payin' ye — this farm — was my Maw's, damn ye! — an' mine now!

ABBIE (*with a cool laugh of confidence*): Yewr'n? We'll see 'bout that! (*Then strongly.*) Waal — what if I did need a hum? What else'd I marry an old man like him fur?

EBEN (*maliciously*): I'll tell him ye said that!

ABBIE (*smiling*): I'll say ye're lyin' a-purpose — an' he'll drive ye off the place!

EBEN: Ye devil!

ABBIE (*defying him*): This be my farm — this be my hum — this be my kitchen — !

EBEN (*furiously, as if he were going to attack her*): Shut up, damn ye!

ABBIE (*walks up to him — a queer coarse expression of desire in her face and body — slowly*): An' upstairs — that be my bedroom — an' my bed! (*He stares into her eyes, terribly confused and torn. She adds softly.*) I hain't bad nor mean —'ceptin' fur an enemy — but I got t' fight fur what's due me out o' life, if I ever 'spect t' git it. (*Then putting her hand on his arm — seductively.*) Let's yew 'n' me be frens, Eben.

EBEN (*stupidly — as if hypnotized*): Ay-eh. (*Then furiously flinging off her arm.*) No, ye durned old witch! I hate ye! (*He rushes out the door.*)

ABBIE (*looks after him smiling satisfiedly — then half to herself, mouthing the word*): Eben's nice. (*She looks at the table, proudly.*) I'll wash up *my* dishes now. (*Eben appears outside, slamming the door behind him. He comes around corner, stops on seeing his father, and stands staring at him with hate.*)

CABOT (*raising his arms to heaven in the fury he can no longer control*): Lord God o' Hosts, smite the undutiful sons with Thy wust cuss!

EBEN (*breaking in violently*): Yew 'n' yewr God! Allus cussin' folks — allus naggin' 'em!

CABOT (*oblivious to him — summoningly*): God o' the old! God o' the lonesome!

EBEN (*mockingly*): Naggin' His sheep t' sin! T' hell with yewr God! (*Cabot turns. He and Eben glower at each other.*)

CABOT (*harshly*): So it's yew. I might've knowed it. (*Shaking his finger threateningly at him.*) Blasphemin' fool! (*Then quickly.*) Why hain't ye t' wuk?

EBEN: Why hain't yew? They've went. I can't wuk it all alone.

CABOT (*contemptuously*): Nor noways! I'm wuth ten o' ye yit, old's I be! Ye'll never be more'n half a man! (*Then, matter-of-factly.*) Waal — let's git t' the barn. (*They go. A last faint note of the "Californi-a" song is heard from the distance. Abbie is washing her dishes.*)

PART II • *Scene I*

(*The exterior of the farmhouse, as in part I — a hot Sunday afternoon two months later. Abbie, dressed in her best, is discovered sitting in a rocker at the end of the porch. She rocks listlessly, enervated by the heat, staring in front of her with bored, half-closed eyes.*)

(*Eben sticks his head out of his bedroom window. He looks around furtively and tries to see — or hear — if anyone is on the porch, but although he has been careful to make no noise, Abbie has sensed his movement. She stops rocking, her face grows animated and eager, she waits attentively. Eben seems to feel her presence, he scowls back his thoughts of her and spits with exaggerated disdain — then withdraws back into the room. Abbie waits, holding her breath as she listens with passionate eagerness for every sound within the house.*)

(*Eben comes out. Their eyes meet; his falter. He is confused, he turns away and slams the door resentfully. At this gesture, Abbie laughs tantalizingly, amused but at the same time piqued and irritated. He scowls, strides off the porch to the path and starts to walk past her to the road with a grand swagger of ignoring her existence. He is dressed in his store suit, spruced up, his face shines from soap and water. Abbie leans forward on her chair, her eyes hard and angry now, and, as he passes her, gives a sneering, taunting chuckle.*)

EBEN (*stung — turns on her furiously*): What air yew cacklin' 'bout?

ABBIE (*triumphant*): Yew!

EBEN: What about me?

ABBIE: Ye look all slicked up like a prize bull.

EBEN (*with a sneer*): Waal — ye hain't so durned purty yerself, be ye? (*They stare into each other's eyes, his held by hers in spite of himself, hers glowingly possessive. Their physical attraction becomes a palpable force quivering in the hot air.*)

ABBIE (*softly*): Ye don't mean that, Eben. Ye may think ye mean it, mebbe, but ye don't. Ye can't. It's agin nature, Eben. Ye been fightin' yer nature ever since the day I come — tryin' t' tell yerself I hain't purty t'ye. (*She laughs a low humid laugh without taking her eyes from his. A pause — her body squirms desirously — she murmurs languorously.*) Hain't the sun strong an' hot? Ye kin feel it burnin' into the earth — Nature — makin' thin's grow — bigger 'n' bigger — burnin' inside ye — makin' ye want t' grow — into somethin' else — till ye're jined with it — an' it's your'n — but it owns ye, too — ant makes ye grow bigger — like a tree — like them elums — (*She laughs again softly, holding his eyes. He takes a step toward her, compelled against his will.*) Nature'll beat ye, Eben. Ye might's well own up t' it fust 's last.

EBEN (*trying to break from her spell — confusedly*): If Paw'd hear ye goin' on. . . . (*Resentfully.*) But ye've made such a damned idjit out o' the old devil . . . ! (*Abbie laughs.*)

ABBIE: Waal — hain't it easier fur yew with him changed softer?

EBEN (*defiantly*): No. I'm fightin' him — fightin' yew — fightin' fur Maw's rights t' her hum! (*This breaks her spell for him. He glowers at her.*) An' I'm onto ye. Ye hain't foolin' me a mite. Ye're aimin' t' swaller up everythin' an' make it your'n. Waal, you'll find I'm a heap sight bigger hunk nor yew kin chew! (*He turns from her with a sneer.*)

ABBIE (*trying to regain her ascendancy — seductively*): Eben!

EBEN: Leave me be! (*He starts to walk away.*)

ABBIE (*more commandingly*): Eben!

EBEN (*stops — resentfully*): What d'ye want?

ABBIE (*trying to conceal a growing excitement*): Whar air ye goin'?

EBEN (*with malicious nonchalance*): Oh — up the road a spell.

ABBIE: T' the village?

EBEN (*airily*): Mebbe.

ABBIE (*excitedly*): T' see that Min, I s'pose?

EBEN: Mebbe.

ABBIE (*weakly*): What d'ye want t' waste time on her fur?

EBEN (*revenging himself now — grinning at her*): Ye can't beat Nature, didn't ye say? (*He laughs and again starts to walk away.*)

ABBIE (*bursting out*): An ugly old hake!

EBEN (*with a tantalizing sneer*): She's purtier'n yew be!

ABBIE: That every wuthless drunk in the country has. . . .

EBEN (*tauntingly*): Mebbe — but she's better'n yew. She owns up fa'r 'n' squar' t' her doin's.

ABBIE (*furiously*): Don't ye dare compare. . . .

EBEN: She don't go sneakin' an' stealin' — what's mine.

ABBIE (*savagely seizing on his weak point*): Your'n? Yew mean — my farm?

EBEN: I mean the farm yew sold yerself fur like any other old whore — my farm!

ABBIE (*stung — fiercely*): Ye'll never live t' see the day when even a stinkin' weed on it'll belong t' ye! (*Then in a scream.*) Git out o' my sight! Go on t' yer slut — disgracin' yer Paw 'n' me! I'll git yer Paw t' horse-whip ye off the place if I want t'! Ye're only livin' here 'cause I tolerate ye! Git along! I hate the sight o' ye! (*She stops, panting and glaring at him.*)

EBEN (*returning her glance in kind*): An' I hate the sight o' yew! (*He turns and strides off up the road. She follows his retreating figure with concentrated hate. Old Cabot appears coming up from the barn. The hard, grim expression of his face has changed. He seems in some queer way softened, mellowed. His eyes have taken on a strange, incongruous dreamy quality. Yet there is no hint of physical weakness about him — rather he looks more robust and younger. Abbie sees him and turns away quickly with unconcealed aversion. He comes slowly up to her.*)

CABOT (*mildly*): War yew an' Eben quarrelin' agen?

ABBIE (*shortly*): No.

CABOT: Ye was talkie' a'mighty loud. (*He sits down on the edge of porch.*)

ABBIE (*snappishly*): If ye heerd us they hain't no need askin' questions.

CABOT: I didn't hear what ye said.

ABBIE (*relieved*): Waal — it wa'n't nothin' t' speak on.

CABOT (*after a pause*): Eben's queer.

ABBIE (*bitterly*): He's the dead spit 'n' image o' yew!

CABOT (*queerly interested*): D'ye think so, Abbie? (*After a pause, ruminatingly.*) Me 'n' Eben's allus fit 'n' fit. I never could b'ar him noways. He's so thunderin' soft — like his Maw.

ABBIE (*scornfully*): Ay-eh! 'Bout as soft as yew be!

CABOT (*as if he hadn't heard*): Mebbe I been too hard on him.

ABBIE (*jeeringly*): Waal — ye're gittin' soft now — soft as slop! That's what Eben was sayin'.

CABOT (*his face instantly grim and ominous*): Eben was sayin'? Waal, he'd best not do nothin' t' try me 'r he'll soon diskiver. . . . (*A pause. She keeps her face turned away. His gradually softens. He stares up at the sky.*) Purty, hain't it?

ABBIE (*crossly*): I don't see nothin' purty.

CABOT: The sky. Feels like a wa'm field up thar.

ABBIE (*sarcastically*): Air yew aimin' t' buy up over the farm too? (*She snickers contemptuously.*)

CABOT (*strangely*): I'd like t' own my place up thar. (*A pause.*) I'm gittin' old, Abbie. I'm gittin' ripe on the bough. (*A pause. She stares at him mystified. He goes on.*) It's allus lonesome cold in the house — even when it's bilin' hot outside. Hain't yew noticed?

ABBIE: No.

CABOT: It's wa'm down t' the barn — nice smellin' an' warm — with the cows. (*A pause.*) Cows is queer.

ABBIE: Like yew?

CABOT: Like Eben. (*A pause.*) I'm gittin' t' feel resigned t' Eben — jest as I got t' feel 'bout his Maw. I'm gittin' t' learn to b'ar his softness — jest like her'n. I cal'c'late I c'd a'most take t' him — if he wa'n't sech a dumb fool! (*A pause.*) I s'pose it's old age a-creepin' in my bones.

ABBIE (*indifferently*): Waal — ye hain't dead yet.

CABOT (*roused*): No, I hain't, yew bet — not by a hell of a sight — I'm sound 'n' tough as hickory! (*Then moodily.*) But arter three score and ten the Lord warns ye t' prepare. (*A pause.*) That's why Eben's come in my head. Now that his cussed sinful brothers is gone their path t' hell, they's no one left but Eben.

ABBIE (*resentfully*): They's me, hain't they? (*Agitatedly.*) What's all this sudden likin' ye've tuk to Eben? Why don't ye say nothin' 'bout me? Hain't I yer lawful wife?

CABOT (*simply*): Ay-eh. Ye be. (*A pause — he stares at her desirously — his eyes grow avid — then with a sudden movement he seizes her hands and squeezes them, declaiming in a queer camp meeting preacher's tempo.*) Yew air my Rose o' Sharon! Behold, yew air fair; yer eyes air doves; yer lips air like scarlet; yer two breasts air like two fawns; yer navel be like a round goblet; yer belly be like a heap o' wheat. . . . (*He covers her hand with kisses. She does not seem to notice. She stares before her with hard angry eyes.*)

ABBIE (*jerking her hands away — harshly*): So ye're plannin' t' leave the farm t' Eben, air ye?

CABOT (*dazedly*): Leave . . . ? (*Then with resentful obstinacy.*) I hain't a-givin' it t' no one!

ABBIE (*remorselessly*): Ye can't take it with ye.

CABOT (*thinks a moment — then reluctantly*): No, I cal'c'late not. (*After a pause — with a strange passion.*) But if I could, I would, by the Eternal! 'R if I could, in my dyin' hour, I'd set it afire an' watch it burn — this house an' every ear o' corn an' every tree down t' the last blade o' hay! I'd sit an' know it was all a-dying with me an' no one else'd ever own what was mine, what I'd made out o' nothin' with my own sweat 'n' blood! (*A pause — then he adds with a queer affection.*) 'Ceptin' the cows. Them I'd turn free.

ABBIE (*harshly*): An' me?

CABOT (*with a queer smile*): Ye'd be turned free, too.

ABBIE (*furiously*): So that's the thanks I git fur marryin' ye — t' have ye change kind to Eben who hates ye, an' talk o' turnin' me out in the road.

CABOT (*hastily*): Abbie! Ye know I wa'n't. . . .

ABBIE (*vengefully*): Just let me tell ye a thing or two 'bout Eben! Whar's he gone? T' see that harlot, Min! I tried fur t' stop him. Disgracin' yew an' me — on the Sabbath, too!

CABOT (*rather guiltily*): He's a sinner — nateral-born. It's lust eatin' his heart.

ABBIE (*enraged beyond endurance — wildly vindictive*): An' his lust fur me! Kin ye find excuses fur that?

CABOT (*stares at her — after a dead pause*): Lust — fur yew?

ABBIE (*defiantly*): He was tryin' t' make love t' me — when ye heerd us quarrelin'.

CABOT (*stares at her — then a terrible expression of rage comes over his face — he springs to his feet shaking all over*): By the A'mighty God — I'll end him!

ABBIE (*frightened now for Eben*): No! Don't ye!

CABOT (*violently*): I'll git the shotgun an' blow his soft brains t' the top o' them elums!

ABBIE (*throwing her arms around him*): No, Ephraim!

CABOT (*pushing her away violently*): I will, by God!

ABBIE (*in a quieting tone*): Listen, Ephraim. 'Twa'n't nothin' bad — on'y a boy's foolin' — 'twa'n't meant serious — jest jokin' an' teasin'. . . .

CABOT: Then why did ye say — lust?

ABBIE: It must hev sounded wusser'n I meant. An' I was mad at thinkin' — ye'd leave him the farm.

CABOT (*quieter but still grim and cruel*): Waal then, I'll horsewhip him off the place if that much'll content ye.

ABBIE (*reaching out and taking his hand*): No. Don't think o' me! Ye mustn't drive him off. 'Tain't sensible. Who'll ye get to help ye on the farm? They's no one hereabouts.

CABOT (*considers this — then nodding his appreciation*): Ye got a head on ye. (*Then irritably.*) Waal, let him stay. (*He sits down on the edge of the porch. She sits beside him. He murmurs contemptuously.*) I oughtn't t' git riled so — at that 'ere fool calf. (*A pause.*) But har's the p'int. What son o' mine'll keep on here t' the farm — when the Lord does call me? Simeon an' Peter air gone t' hell — an' Eben's follerin' 'em.

ABBIE: They's me.

CABOT: Ye're on'y a woman.

ABBIE: I'm yewr wife.

CABOT: That hain't me. A son is me — my blood — mine. Mine ought t' git mine. An' then it's still mine — even though I be six foot under. D'ye see?

ABBIE (*giving him a look of hatred*): Ay-eh. I see. (*She becomes very thoughtful, her face growing shrewd, her eyes studying Cabot craftily.*)

CABOT: I'm gittin' old — ripe on the bough. (*Then with a sudden forced reassurance.*) Not but what I hain't a hard nut t' crack even yet — an' fur many a year t' come! By the Etarnal, I kin break most o' the young fellers' backs at any kind o' work any day o' the year!

ABBIE (*suddenly*): Mebbe the Lord'll give *us* a son.

CABOT (*turns and stares at her eagerly*): Ye mean — a son — t' me 'n' yew?

ABBIE (*with a cajoling smile*): Ye're a strong man yet, hain't ye? 'Tain't noways impossible, be it? We know that. Why d'ye stare so? Hain't ye never thought o' that afore? I been thinkin' o' it all along. Ay-eh — an' I been prayin' it'd happen, too.

CABOT (*his face growing full of joyous pride and a sort of religious ecstasy*): Ye been prayin', Abbie? — fur a son? — t' us?

ABBIE: Ay-eh. (*With a grim resolution.*) I want a son now.

CABOT (*excitedly clutching both of her hands in his*): It'd be the blessin' o' God, Abbie — the blessin' o' God A'mighty on me — in my old age — in my lonesomeness! They hain't nothin' I wouldn't do fur ye then, Abbie. Ye'd hev on'y t' ask it — anythin' ye'd a mind t'!

ABBIE (*interrupting*): Would ye will the farm t' me then — t' me an' it . . . ?

CABOT (*vehemently*): I'd do anythin' ye axed, I tell ye! I swar it! May I be everlastin' damned t' hell if I wouldn't! (*He sinks to his knees pulling her down with him. He trembles all over with the fervor of his hopes.*) Pray t' the Lord agen, Abbie. It's the Sabbath! I'll jine ye! Two prayers air better nor one. "An' God hearkened unto Rachel"! An' God hearkened unto Abbie! Pray, Abbie! Pray fur him to hearken! (*He bows his head, mumbling. She pretends to do likewise but gives him a side glance of scorn and triumph.*)

Scene II

(*About eight in the evening. The interior of the two bedrooms on the top floor is shown. Eben is sitting on the side of his bed in the room on the left. On account of the heat he has taken off everything but his undershirt and pants. His feet are bare. He faces front, brooding moodily, his chin propped on his hands, a desperate expression on his face.*)

(*In the other room Cabot and Abbie are sitting side by side on the edge of their bed, an old four-poster with feather mattress. He is in his nightshirt, she in her nightdress. He is still in the queer, excited mood into which the notion of a son has thrown him. Both rooms are lighted dimly and flickeringly by tallow candles.*)

CABOT: The farm needs a son.

ABBIE: I need a son.

CABOT: Ay-eh. Sometimes ye air the farm an' sometimes the farm be yew. That's why I clove t'ye in my lonesomeness. (*A pause. He pounds his knee with his fist.*) Me an' the farm has got t' beget a son!

ABBIE: Ye'd best go t' sleep. Ye're gittin' thin's all mixed.

CABOT (*with an impatient gesture*): No, I hain't. My mind's clear's a well. Ye don't know me, that's it. (*He stares hopelessly at the floor.*)

ABBIE (*indifferently*): Mebbe. (*In the next room Eben gets up and paces up and down distractedly. Abbie hears him. Her eyes fasten on the intervening wall with concentrated attention. Eben stops and stares. Their hot glances seem to meet through the wall. Unconsciously he stretches out his arms for her and she half rises. Then aware, he mutters a curse at himself and flings himself face downward on the bed, his clenched fists above his head, his face buried in the pillow. Abbie relaxes with a faint sigh but her eyes remain fixed on the wall; she listens with all her attention for some movement from Eben.*)

CABOT (*suddenly raises his head and looks at her — scornfully*): Will ye ever know me — 'r will any man 'r woman? (*Shaking his head.*) No. I calc'late wa'n't t' be. (*He turns away. Abbie looks at the wall. Then, evidently unable to keep silent about his thoughts, without looking at his wife, he puts out his hand and clutches her knee. She starts violently, looks at him, sees he is not watching her, concentrates again on the wall, and pays no attention to what he says.*) Listen, Abbie. When I come here fifty odd year ago — I was jest twenty an' the strongest an' hardest ye ever seen — ten times as strong an' fifty times as hard as Eben. Waal — this place was nothin' but fields o' stones. Folks laughed when I tuk it. They couldn't know what I knowed. When ye kin make corn sprout out o' stones, God's livin' in yew! They wa'n't strong enuf fur that! They reckoned God was easy. They laughed. They don't laugh no more. Some died hereabouts. Some went West an' died. They're all underground — fur follerin' arter an easy God. God hain't easy. (*He shakes his head slowly.*) An' I growed hard. Folks kept allus sayin' he's a hard man like 'twas sinful t' be hard, so's at last I said back at 'em: Waal then, by thunder, ye'll git me hard an' see how ye like it! (*Then suddenly.*) But I give in t' weakness once. 'Twas arter I'd been here two year. I got weak — despairful — they was so many stones. They was a party leavin', givin' up, goin' West. I jined 'em. We tracked on 'n' on. We come t' broad medders, plains, whar the soil was black an' rich as gold. Nary a stone. Easy. Ye'd on'y t' plow an' sow an' then set an' smoke yer pipe an' watch thin's grow. I could o' been a rich man — but somethin' in me fit me an' fit me — the voice o' God sayin': "This hain't wuth nothin' t' Me. Git ye back t' hum!" I got afeerd o' that voice an' I lit out back t' hum here, leavin' my claim an' crops t' whoever'd a mind t' take 'em. Ay-eh. I actoolly give up what was rightful mine! God's hard, not easy! God's in the stones! Build my church on a rock — out o' stones an' I'll be in them! That's what He meant t' Peter! (*He sighs heavily — a pause.*) Stones. I picked 'em up an' piled 'em into walls. Ye kin read the years of my life in them walls, every day a hefted stone, climbin' over the hills up and down, fencin' in the fields that was mine, whar I'd made thin's grow out o' nothin' — like the will o' God, like the servant o' His hand. It wa'n't easy. It was hard an' He made me hard fur it. (*He pauses.*) All the time I kept gittin' lonesomer. I tuk a wife. She bore Simeon an' Peter. She was a good woman. She wuked hard. We was married twenty year. She never knowed me. She helped but she never knowed what she was helpin'. I was allus lonesome. She died. After that it wa'n't so lonesome fur a spell. (*A pause.*) I lost count o' the years. I had no time t' fool away countin' 'em. Sim an' Peter helped. The farm growed. It was all mine! When I thought o' that I didn't feel lonesome. (*A pause.*) But ye can't hitch yer mind t' one thin' day an' night. I tuk another wife — Eben's Maw. Her folks was contestin' me at law over my deeds t' the farm — my farm! That's why Eben keeps a-talkin' his fool talk o' this bein' his Maw's farm. She bore Eben. She was purty — but soft. She tried t' be hard. She couldn't. She never knowed me nor nothin'. It was lonesomer 'n hell with her. After a matter o' sixteen odd years, she died. (*A pause.*) I lived with the boys. They hated me 'cause I was hard. I hated them 'cause they was soft. They coveted the farm without knowin' what it meant. It made me bitter 'n wormwood. It aged me — them coveting what I'd made fur mine. Then this spring the call come — the voice o' God cryin' in my wilderness, in my lonesomeness — t' go out an' seek an' find! (*Turning to her with strange passion.*) I sought ye an' I found ye! Yew air my Rose o' Sharon! Yer eyes air like.... (*She has turned a blank face, resentful eyes to his. He stares at her for a moment — then harshly.*) Air ye any the wiser fur all I've told ye?

ABBIE (*confusedly*): Mebbe.

CABOT (*pushing her away from him — angrily*): Ye don't know nothin' — nor never will. If ye don't hev a son t' redeem ye.... (*This in a tone of cold threat.*)

ABBIE (*resentfully*): I've prayed, hain't I?

CABOT (*bitterly*): Pray agen — fur understandin'!

ABBIE (*a veiled threat in her tone*): Ye'll have a son out o' me, I promise ye.

CABOT: How kin ye promise?

ABBIE: I got second-sight mebbe. I kin foretell. (*She gives a queer smile.*)

CABOT: I believe ye have. Ye give me the chills sometimes. (*He shivers.*) It's cold in this house. It's oneasy. They's thin's pokin' about in the dark — in the corners. (*He pulls on his trousers, tucking in his nightshirt, and pulls on his boots.*)

ABBIE (*surprised*): Whar air ye goin'?

CABOT (*queerly*): Down whar it's restful — whar it's warm — down t' the barn. (*Bitterly.*) I kin talk t' the cows. They know. They know the farm an' me. They'll give me peace. (*He turns to go out the door.*)

ABBIE (*a bit frightenedly*): Air ye ailin' tonight, Ephraim?

CABOT: Growin'. Growin' ripe on the bough. (*He turns and goes, his boots clumping down the stairs. Eben sits up with a start, listening. Abbie is conscious of his movement and stares at the wall. Cabot comes out of the house around the corner and stands by the gate, blinking at the sky. He stretches up his hands in a tortured gesture.*) God A'mighty, call from the dark! (*He listens as if expecting an answer. Then his arms drop, he shakes his head and plods off toward the barn. Eben and Abbie stare at each other through the wall. Eben sighs heavily and Abbie echoes it. Both become terribly nervous, uneasy. Finally Abbie gets up and listens, her ear to the wall. He acts as if he saw every move she was making, he becomes resolutely still. She seems driven into a decision — goes out the door in rear determinedly. His eyes follow her. Then as the door of his room is opened softly, he turns away, waits in an attitude of strained fixity. Abbie stands for a second staring at him, her eyes burning with desire. Then with a little cry she runs over and throws her arms about his neck, she pulls his head back and covers his mouth with kisses. At first, he submits dumbly; then he puts his arms about her neck and returns her kisses, but finally, suddenly aware of his hatred, he hurls her away from him, springing to his feet. They stand speechless and breathless, panting like two animals.*)

ABBIE (*at last — painfully*): Ye shouldn't, Eben — ye shouldn't — I'd make ye happy!

EBEN (*harshly*): I don't want t' be happy — from yew!

ABBIE (*helplessly*): Ye do, Eben! Ye do! Why d'ye lie?

EBEN (*viciously*): I don't take t'ye, I tell ye! I hate the sight o' ye!

ABBIE (*with an uncertain troubled laugh*): Waal, I kissed ye anyways — an' ye kissed back — yer lips was burnin' — ye can't lie 'bout that! (*Intensely.*) If ye don't care, why did ye kiss me back — why was yer lips burnin'?

EBEN (*wiping his mouth*): It was like pizen on 'em. (*Then tauntingly.*) When I kissed ye back, mebbe I thought 'twas someone else.

ABBIE (*wildly*): Min?

EBEN: Mebbe.

ABBIE (*torturedly*): Did ye go t' see her? Did ye r'ally go? I thought ye mightn't. Is that why ye throwed me off jest now?

EBEN (*sneeringly*): What if it be?

ABBIE (*raging*): Then ye're a dog, Eben Cabot!

EBEN (*threateningly*): Ye can't talk that way t' me!

ABBIE (*with a shrill laugh*): Can't I? Did ye think I was in love with ye — a weak thin' like yew? Not much! I on'y wanted ye fur a purpose o' my own — an' I'll hev ye fur it yet 'cause I'm stronger'n yew be!

EBEN (*resentfully*): I knowed well it was on'y part o' yer plan t' swaller everythin'!

ABBIE (*tauntingly*): Mebbe!

EBEN (*furious*): Git out o' my room!

ABBIE: This air my room an' ye're on'y hired help!

EBEN (*threateningly*): Git out afore I murder ye!

ABBIE (*quite confident now*): I hain't a mite afeerd. Ye want me, don't ye? Yes, ye do! An' yer Paw's son'll never kill what he wants! Look at yer eyes! They's

Abbie in the 1988 Pushkin Theatre (Moscow) production of *Desire under the Elms,* directed by Mark Lamos of the Hartford Stage Company.

lust fur me in 'em, burnin' 'em up! Look at yer lips now! They're tremblin' an' longin' t' kiss me, an' yer teeth t' bite! (*He is watching her now with a horrible fascination. She laughs a crazy triumphant laugh.*) I'm a-goin' t' make all o' this hum my hum! They's one room hain't mine yet, but it's a-goin' t' be tonight. I'm a-goin' down now an' light up! (*She makes him a mocking bow.*) Won't ye come courtin' me in the best parlor, Mister Cabot?

EBEN (*staring at her — horribly confused — dully*): Don't ye dare! It hain't been opened since Maw died an' was laid out thar! Don't ye . . . ! (*But her eyes are fixed on his so burningly that his will seems to wither before hers. He stands swaying toward her helplessly.*)

ABBIE (*holding his eyes and putting all her will into her words as she backs out the door*): I'll expect ye afore long, Eben.

EBEN (*Stares after her for a while, walking toward the door. A light appears in the parlor window. He murmurs.*): In the parlor? (*This seems to arouse connotations, for he comes back and puts on his white shirt, collar, half ties the tie mechanically, puts on coat, takes his hat, stands barefooted looking about*

him in bewilderment, mutters wonderingly.*) Maw! Whar air yew? (*Then goes slowly toward the door in rear.*)

Scene III

(*A few minutes later. The interior of the parlor is shown. A grim, repressed room like a tomb in which the family has been interred alive. Abbie sits on the edge of the horsehair sofa. She has lighted all the candles and the room is revealed in all its preserved ugliness. A change has come over the woman. She looks awed and frightened now, ready to run away.*)

(*The door is opened and Eben appears. His face wears an expression of obsessed confusion. He stands staring at her, his arms hanging disjointedly from his shoulders, his feet bare, his hat in his hand.*)

ABBIE (*after a pause — with a nervous, formal politeness*): Won't ye set?

EBEN (*dully*): Ay-eh. (*Mechanically he places his hat carefully on the floor near the door and sits stiffly beside her on the edge of the sofa. A pause. They both remain rigid, looking straight ahead with eyes full of fear.)*

ABBIE: When I fust come in — in the dark — they seemed somethin' here.

EBEN (*simply*): Maw.

ABBIE: I kin still feel — somethin'. . . .

EBEN: It's Maw.

ABBIE: At fust I was feered o' it. I wanted t' yell an' run. Now — since yew come — seems like it's growin' soft an' kind t' me. (*Addressing the air — queerly.*) Thank yew.

EBEN: Maw allus loved me.

ABBIE: Mebbe it knows I love yew, too. Mebbe that makes it kind t' me.

EBEN (*dully*): I dunno. I should think she'd hate ye.

ABBIE (*with certainty*): No. I kin feel it don't — not no more.

EBEN: Hate ye fur stealin' her place — here in her hum — settin' in her parlor whar she was laid — (*He suddenly stops, staring stupidly before him.*)

ABBIE: What is it, Eben?

EBEN (*in a whisper*): Seems like Maw didn't want me t' remind ye.

ABBIE (*excitedly*): I knowed, Eben! It's kind t' me! It don't b'ar me no grudges fur what I never knowed an' couldn't help!

EBEN: Maw b'ars him a grudge.

ABBIE: Waal, so does all o' us.

EBEN: Ay-eh. (*With passion.*) I does, by God!

ABBIE (*taking one of his hands in hers and patting it*): Thar! Don't git riled thinkin' o' him. Think o' yer Maw who's kind t' us. Tell me about yer Maw, Eben.

EBEN: They hain't nothin' much. She was kind. She was good.

ABBIE (*Putting one arm over his shoulder. He does not seem to notice — passionately.*): I'll be kind an' good t' ye!

EBEN: Sometimes she used t' sing fur me.

ABBIE: I'll sing fur ye!

EBEN: This was her hum. This was her farm.

ABBIE: This is my hum! This is my farm!

EBEN: He married her t' steal 'em. She was soft an' easy. He couldn't 'preciate her.

ABBIE: He can't 'preciate me!

EBEN: He murdered her with his hardness.

ABBIE: He's murderin' me!

EBEN: She died. (*A pause.*) Sometimes she used to sing fur me. (*He bursts into a fit of sobbing.*)

ABBIE (*both her arms around him — with wild passion*): I'll sing fur ye! I'll die fur ye! (*In spite of her overwhelming desire for him, there is a sincere maternal love in her manner and voice — a horribly frank mixture of lust and mother love.*) Don't cry, Eben! I'll take yer Maw's place! I'll be everythin' she was t' ye! Let me kiss ye, Eben! (*She pulls his head around. He makes a bewildered pretense of resistance. She is tender.*) Don't be afeered! I'll kiss ye pure, Eben — same 's if I was a Maw t' ye — an' ye kin kiss me back 's if yew was my son — my boy — sayin' good-night t' me! Kiss me, Eben. (*They kiss in restrained fashion. Then suddenly wild passion overcomes her. She kisses him lustfully again and again and he flings his arms about her and returns her kisses. Suddenly, as in the bedroom, he frees himself from her violently and springs to his feet. He is trembling all over, in a strange state of terror. Abbie strains her arms toward him with fierce pleading.*) Don't ye leave me, Eben! Can't ye see it hain't enuf — lovin' ye like a Maw — can't ye see it's got t' be that an' more — much more — a hundred times more — fur me t' be happy — fur yew t' be happy?

EBEN (*to the presence he feels in the room*): Maw! Maw! What d'ye want? What air ye tellin' me?

ABBIE: She's tellin' ye t' love me. She knows I love ye an' I'll be good t' ye. Can't ye feel it? Don't ye know? She's tellin' ye t' love me, Eben!

EBEN: Ay-eh. I feel — mebbe she — but — I can't figger out — why — when ye've stole her place — here in her hum — in the parlor whar she was —

ABBIE (*fiercely*): She knows I love ye!

EBEN (*his face suddenly lighting up with a fierce, triumphant grin*): I see it! I sees why. It's her vengeance on him — so's she kin rest quiet in her grave!

ABBIE (*wildly*): Vengeance o' God on the hull o' us! What d'we give a durn? I love ye, Eben! God knows I love ye! (*She stretches out her arms for him.*)

EBEN (*throws himself on his knees beside the sofa and grabs her in his arms — releasing all his pent-up passion*): An' I love ye, Abbie! — now I kin say it! I been dyin' fur want o' ye — every hour since ye come! I love ye! (*Their lips meet in a fierce, bruising kiss.*)

Scene IV

(*Exterior of the farmhouse. It is just dawn. The front door at right is opened and Eben comes out and walks around to the gate. He is dressed in his working clothes. He seems changed. His face wears a bold and confident expression, he is grinning to himself with evident satisfaction. As he gets near the gate, the window of the parlor is heard opening and the shutters are flung back and Abbie sticks her head out. Her hair tumbles over her shoulders in disarray, her face is flushed, she looks at Eben with tender, languorous eyes and calls softly.*)

ABBIE: Eben. (*As he turns — playfully.*) Jest one more kiss afore ye go. I'm goin' to miss ye fearful all day.

EBEN: An' me yew, ye kin bet! (*He goes to her. They kiss several times. He draws away, laughingly.*) Thar. That's enuf, hain't it? Ye won't hev none left fur next time.

ABBIE: I got a million o' 'em left fur yew! (*Then a bit anxiously.*) D'ye r'ally love me, Eben?

EBEN (*emphatically*): I like ye better'n any gal I ever knowed! That's gospel!

ABBIE: Likin' hain't lovin'.

EBEN: Waal then — I love ye. Now air yew satisfied?

ABBIE: Ay-eh, I be. (*She smiles at him adoringly.*)

EBEN: I better git t' the barn. The old critter's liable t' suspicion an' come sneakin' up.

ABBIE (*with a confident laugh*): Let him! I kin allus pull the wool over his eyes. I'm goin' t' leave the shutters open and let in the sun 'n' air. This room's been dead long enuf. Now it's goin' t' be my room!

EBEN (*frowning*): Ay-eh.

ABBIE (*hastily*): I meant — our room.

EBEN: Ay-eh.

ABBIE: We made it our'n last night, didn't we? We give it life — our lovin' did. (*A pause.*)

EBEN (*with a strange look*): Maw's gone back t' her grave. She kin sleep now.

ABBIE: May she rest in peace! (*Then tenderly rebuking.*) Ye oughtn't t' talk o' sad thin's — this mornin'.

EBEN: It jest come up in my mind o' itself.

ABBIE: Don't let it. (*He doesn't answer. She yawns.*) Waal, I'm a-goin' t' steal a wink o' sleep. I'll tell the Old Man I hain't feelin' pert. Let him git his own vittles.

EBEN: I see him comin' from the barn. Ye better look smart an' git upstairs.

ABBIE: Ay-eh. Good-by. Don't ferget me. (*She throws him a kiss. He grins — then squares his shoulders and awaits his father confidently. Cabot walks slowly up from the left, staring up at the sky with a vague face.*)

EBEN (*jovially*): Mornin', Paw. Star-gazin' in daylight?

CABOT: Purty, hain't it?

EBEN (*looking around him possessively*): It's a durned purty farm.

CABOT: I mean the sky.

EBEN (*grinning*): How d'ye know? Them eyes o' your'n can't see that fur. (*This tickles his humor and he slaps his thigh and laughs.*) Ho-ho! That's a good un!

CABOT (*grimly sarcastic*): Ye're feelin' right chipper, hain't ye? Whar'd ye steal the likker?

EBEN (*good-naturedly*): 'Tain't likker. Jest life. (*Suddenly holding out his hand — soberly.*) Yew 'n' me is quits. Let's shake hands.

CABOT (*suspiciously*): What's come over ye?

EBEN: Then don't. Mebbe it's jest as well. (*A moment's pause.*) What's come over me? (*Queerly.*) Didn't ye feel her passin' — goin' back t' her grave?

CABOT (*dully*): Who?

EBEN: Maw. She kin rest now an' sleep content. She's quit with ye.

CABOT (*confusedly*): I rested. I slept good — down with the cows. They know how t' sleep. They're teachin' me.

EBEN (*suddenly jovial again*): Good fur the cows! Waal — ye better git t' work.

CABOT (*grimly amused*): Air yew bossin' me, ye calf?

EBEN (*beginning to laugh*): Ay-eh! I'm bossin' yew! Ha-ha-ha! See how ye like it! Ha-ha-ha! I'm the prize rooster o' this roost. Ha-ha-ha! (*He goes off toward the barn laughing.*)

CABOT (*looks after him with scornful pity*): Soft-headed. Like his Maw. Dead spit 'n' image. No hope in him! (*He spits with contemptuous disgust.*) A born fool! (*Then matter-of-factly.*) Waal — I'm gittin' peckish. (*He goes toward door.*)

PART III • *Scene* I

(*A night in late spring the following year. The kitchen and the two bedrooms upstairs are shown. The two bedrooms are dimly lighted by a tallow candle in each. Eben is sitting on the side of the bed in his room, his chin propped on his fists, his face a study of the struggle he is making to understand his conflicting emotions. The noisy laughter and music from below where a kitchen dance is in progress annoy and distract him. He scowls at the floor.*)

(*In the next room a cradle stands beside the double bed.*)

(*In the kitchen all is festivity. The stove has been taken down to give more room to the dancers. The chairs, with wooden benches added, have been pushed back against the walls. On these are seated, squeezed in tight against one another, farmers and their wives and their young folks of both sexes from the neighboring farms. They are all chattering and laughing loudly. They evidently have some secret joke in common. There is no end of winking, of nudging, of meaning nods of the head toward Cabot who, in a state of extreme hilarious excitement increased by the amount he has drunk, is standing near the rear door where there is a small keg of whisky and serving drinks to all the men. In the left corner, front, dividing the attention with her husband, Abbie is sitting in a rocking chair, a shawl wrapped about her shoulders. She is very pale, her face is thin and drawn, her eyes are fixed anxiously on the open door in rear as if waiting for someone.*)

(*The musician is tuning up his fiddle, seated in the far right corner. He is a lanky young fellow with a long, weak face. His pale eyes blink incessantly and he grins about him slyly with a greedy malice.*)

ABBIE (*suddenly turning to a young girl on her right*): Whar's Eben?

YOUNG GIRL (*eyeing her scornfully*): I dunno, Mrs. Cabot. I hain't seen Eben in ages. (*Meaningly.*) Seems like he's spent most o' his time t' hum since yew come.

ABBIE (*vaguely*): I tuk his Maw's place.

YOUNG GIRL: Ay-eh. So I've heerd. (*She turns away to retail this bit of gossip to her mother sitting next to her. Abbie turns to her left to a big stoutish middle-aged man whose flushed face and starting eyes show the amount of "likker" he has consumed.*)

ABBIE: Ye hain't seen Eben, hev ye?

MAN: No, I hain't. (*Then he adds with a wink.*) If yew hain't, who would?

ABBIE: He's the best dancer in the county. He'd ought t' come an' dance.

MAN (*with a wink*): Mebbe he's doin' the dutiful an' walkin' the kid t' sleep. It's a boy, hain't it?

ABBIE (*nodding vaguely*): Ay-eh — born two weeks back — purty's a picter.

MAN: They all is — t' their Maws. (*Then in a whisper, with a nudge and a leer.*) Listen, Abbie — if ye ever git tired o' Eben, remember me! Don't fergit now! (*He looks at her uncomprehending face for a second — then grunts disgustedly.*) Waal — guess I'll likker agin. (*He goes over and joins Cabot who is arguing noisily with an old farmer over cows. They all drink.*)

ABBIE (*this time appealing to nobody in particular*): Wonder what Eben's a-doin'? (*Her remark is repeated down the line with many a guffaw and titter until it reaches the fiddler. He fastens his blinking eyes on Abbie.*)

FIDDLER (*raising his voice*): Bet I kin tell ye, Abbie, what Eben's a-doin'! He's down t' the church offerin' up prayers o' thanksgivin'. (*They all titter expectantly.*)

A MAN: What fur? (*Another titter.*)

FIDDLER: 'Cause unto him a — (*He hesitates just long enough.*) brother is born! (*A roar of laughter. They all look from Abbie to Cabot. She is oblivious, staring at the door. Cabot, although he hasn't heard the words, is irritated by the laughter and steps forward, glaring about him. There is an immediate silence.*)

CABOT: What're ye all bleatin' about — like a flock o' goats? Why don't ye dance, damn ye? I axed ye here t' dance — t' eat, drink an' be merry — an' thar ye set cacklin' like a lot o' wet hens with the pip! Ye've swilled my likker an' guzzled my vittles like hogs, hain't ye? Then dance fur me, can't ye? That's fa'r an' squar', hain't it? (*A grumble of resentment goes around but they are all evidently in too much awe of him to express it openly.*)

FIDDLER (*slyly*): We're waitin' fur Eben. (*A suppressed laugh.*)

CABOT (*with a fierce exultation*): T'hell with Eben! Eben's done fur now! I got a new son! (*His mood switching with drunken suddenness.*) But ye needn't t' laugh at Eben, none o' ye! He's my blood, if he be a dumb fool. He's better nor any o' yew! He kin do a day's work a'most up t' what I kin — an' that'd put any o' yew pore critters t' shame!

FIDDLER: An' he kin do a good night's work, too! (*A roar of laughter.*)

CABOT: Laugh, ye damn fools! Ye're right jist the same, Fiddler. He kin work day an' night too, like I kin, if need be!

OLD FARMER (*from behind the keg where he is weaving drunkenly back and forth — with great simplicity*): They hain't many t' touch ye, Ephraim — a son at seventy-six. That's a hard man fur ye! I be on'y sixty-eight an' I couldn't do it. (*A roar of laughter in which Cabot joins uproariously.*)

CABOT (*slapping him on the back*): I'm sorry fur ye, Hi. I'd never suspicion sech weakness from a boy like yew!

OLD FARMER: An' I never reckoned yew had it in ye nuther, Ephraim. (*There is another laugh.*)

CABOT (*suddenly grim*): I got a lot in me — a hell of a lot — folks don't know on. (*Turning to the fiddler.*) Fiddle 'er up, durn ye! Give 'em somethin' t' dance t'! What air ye, an ornament? Hain't this a celebration? Then grease yer elbow an' go it!

FIDDLER (*seizes a drink which the Old Farmer holds out to him and downs it*): Here goes! (*He starts to fiddle "Lady of the Lake." Four young fellows and four girls form in two lines and dance a square dance. The Fiddler shouts directions for the different movements, keeping his words in the rhythm of the music and interspersing them with jocular personal remarks to the dancers themselves. The people seated along the walls stamp their feet and clap their hands in unison. Cabot is especially active in this respect. Only Abbie remains apathetic, staring at the door as if she were alone in a silent room.*)

FIDDLER: Swing your partner t' the right! That's it, Jim! Give her a b'ar hug. Her Maw hain't lookin'. (*Laughter.*) Change partners! That suits ye, don't it, Essie, now ye got Reub afore ye? Look at her redden up, will ye? Waal, life is short an' so's love, as the feller says. (*Laughter.*)

CABOT (*excitedly, stamping his foot*): Go it, boys! Go it, gals!

FIDDLER (*with a wink at the others*): Ye're the spryest seventy-six ever I sees, Ephraim! Now if ye'd on'y good eyesight . . . ! (*Suppressed laughter. He gives Cabot no chance to retort but roars.*) Promenade! Ye're walkin' like a bride down the aisle, Sarah! Waal, while they's life they's allus hope, I've heerd tell. Swing your partner to the left! Gosh A'mighty, look at Johnny Cook high-steppin'! They hain't goin' t' be much strength left fur howin' in the corn lot t'morrow. (*Laughter.*)

CABOT: Go it! Go it! (*Then suddenly, unable to restrain himself any longer, he prances into the midst of the dancers, scattering them, waving his arms about wildly.*) Ye're all hoofs! Git out o' my road! Give me room! I'll show ye dancin'. Ye're all too soft! (*He pushes them roughly away. They crowd back toward the walls, muttering, looking at him resentfully.*)

FIDDLER (*jeeringly*): Go it, Ephraim! Go it! (*He starts "Pop, Goes the Weasel," increasing the tempo with every verse until at the end he is fiddling crazily as fast as he can go.*)

CABOT (*Starts to dance, which he does very well and with tremendous vigor. Then he begins to improvise, cuts incredibly grotesque capers, leaping up and cracking his heels together, prancing around in a circle with body bent in an Indian war dance, then suddenly straightening up and kicking as high as he can with both legs. He is like a monkey on a string. And all the while he intersperses his antics with shouts and derisive comments.*): Whoop! Here's dancin' fur ye! Whoop! See that! Seventy-six, if I'm a day! Hard as iron yet! Beatin' the young 'uns like I allus done! Look at me! I'd invite ye t' dance on my hundredth birthday on'y ye'll all be dead by then. Ye're a sickly generation! Yer hearts air pink, not red! Yer veins is full o' mud an' water! I be the on'y man in the county! Whoop! See that! I'm a Injun! I've killed Injuns in the West afore ye was born — an' skulped 'em too! They's a arrer wound on my backside I c'd show ye! The hull tribe chased me. I outrun 'em all — with the arrer stuck in me! An' I tuk vengeance on 'em. Ten eyes fur an eye, that was my motter! Whoop! Look at me! I kin kick the ceilin' off the room! Whoop!

FIDDLER (*stops playing — exhaustedly*): God A'mighty, I got enuf. Ye got the devil's strength in ye.

CABOT (*delightedly*): Did I beat yew, too? Waal, ye played smart. Hev a swig. (*He pours whisky for himself and Fiddler. They drink. The others watch Cabot silently with cold, hostile eyes. There is a dead pause. The Fiddler rests. Cabot leans against the keg, panting, glaring around him confusedly. In the room above, Eben gets to his feet and tiptoes out the door in rear, appearing a moment later in the other bedroom. He moves silently, even frightenedly, toward the cradle and stands there looking down at the baby. His face is as vague as his reactions are confused, but there is a trace of tenderness, of interested discovery. At the same moment that he reaches the cradle, Abbie seems to sense something. She gets up weakly and goes to Cabot.*)

ABBIE: I'm goin' up t' the baby.

CABOT (*with real solicitation*): Air ye able fur the stairs? D'ye want me t' help ye, Abbie?

ABBIE: No. I'm able. I'll be down agen soon.

CABOT: Don't ye git wore out! He needs ye, remember — our son does! (*He grins affectionately, patting her on the back. She shrinks from his touch.*)

ABBIE (*dully*): Don't — tech me. I'm goin' — up. (*She goes. Cabot looks after her. A whisper goes around the room. Cabot turns. It ceases. He wipes his forehead streaming with sweat. He is breathing pantingly.*)

CABOT: I'm a-goin' out t' git fresh air. I'm feelin' a mite dizzy. Fiddle up thar! Dance, all o' ye! Here's likker fur them as wants it. Enjoy yerselves. I'll be back. (*He goes, closing the door behind him.*)

FIDDLER (*sarcastically*): Don't hurry none on our account! (*A suppressed laugh. He imitates Abbie.*) Whar's Eben? (*More laughter.*)

A WOMAN (*loudly*): What's happened in this house is plain as the nose on yer face! (*Abbie appears in the doorway upstairs and stands looking in surprise and adoration at Eben who does not see her.*)

A MAN: Ssshh! He's li'ble t' be listenin' at the door. That'd be like him. (*Their voices die to an intensive whispering. Their faces are concentrated on this gossip. A noise as of dead leaves in the wind comes from the room. Cabot has come out from the porch and stands by the gate, leaning on it, staring at the sky blinkingly. Abbie comes across the room silently. Eben does not notice her until quite near.*)

EBEN (*starting*): Abbie!

ABBIE: Ssshh! (*She throws her arms around him. They kiss — then bend over the cradle together.*) Ain't he purty? — dead spit 'n' image o' yew!

EBEN (*pleased*): Air he? I can't tell none.

ABBIE: E-zactly like!

EBEN (*frowningly*): I don't like this. I don't like lettin' on what's mine's his'n. I been doin' that all my life. I'm gittin' t' the end o' b'arin' it!

ABBIE (*putting her finger on his lips*): We're doin' the best we kin. We got t' wait. Somethin's bound t' happen. (*She puts her arms around him.*) I got t' go back.

EBEN: I'm goin' out. I can't b'ar it with the fiddle playin' an' the laughin'.

ABBIE: Don't git feelin' low. I love ye, Eben. Kiss me. (*He kisses her. They remain in each other's arms.*)

CABOT (*at the gate, confusedly*): Even the music can't drive it out — somethin'. Ye kin feel it droppin' off the elums, climbin' up the roof, sneakin' down the chimney, pokin' in the corners! They's no peace in houses, they's no rest livin' with folks. Somethin's always livin' with ye. (*With a deep sigh.*) I'll go t' the barn an' rest a spell. (*He goes wearily toward the barn.*)

FIDDLER (*tuning up*): Let's celebrate the old skunk gittin' fooled! We kin have some fun now he's went. (*He starts to fiddle "Turkey in the Straw." There is real merriment now. The young folks get up to dance.*)

Scene II

(*A half hour later — exterior — Eben is standing by the gate looking up at the sky, an expression of dumb pain bewildered by itself on his face. Cabot appears, returning from the barn, walking wearily, his eyes on the ground. He sees Eben and his whole mood immediately changes. He becomes excited, a cruel, triumphant grin comes to his lips, he strides up and slaps Eben on the back. From within comes the whining of the fiddle and the noise of stamping feet and laughing voices.*)

CABOT: So har ye be!

EBEN (*startled, stares at him with hatred for a moment — then dully*): Ay-eh.

CABOT (*surveying him jeeringly*): Why hain't ye been in t' dance? They was all axin' fur ye.

EBEN: Let 'em ax!

CABOT: They's a hull passel o' purty gals.

EBEN: T' hell with 'em!

CABOT: Ye'd ought t' be marryin' one o' 'em soon.

EBEN: I hain't marryin' no one.

CABOT: Ye might 'arn a share o' a farm that way.

EBEN (*with a sneer*): Like yew did, ye mean? I hain't that kind.

CABOT (*stung*): Ye lie! 'Twas yer Maw's folks aimed t' steal my farm from me.

EBEN: Other folks don't say so. (*After a pause — defiantly.*) An' I got a farm, anyways!

CABOT (*derisively*): Whar?

EBEN (*stamps a foot on the ground*): Har!

CABOT (*throws his head back and laughs coarsely*): Ho-ho! Ye hev, hev ye? Waal, that's a good un!

EBEN (*controlling himself — grimly*): Ye'll see!

CABOT (*stares at him suspiciously, trying to make him out — a pause — then with scornful confidence*): Ay-eh. I'll see. So'll ye. It's ye that's blind — blind as a mole underground. (*Eben suddenly laughs, one short sardonic bark: "Ha." A pause. Cabot peers at him with renewed suspicion.*) What air ye hawin' 'bout? (*Eben turns away without answering. Cabot grows angry.*) God A'mighty, yew air a dumb dunce! They's nothin' in that thick skull o' your'n but noise — like a empty keg it be! (*Eben doesn't seem to hear. Cabot's rage grows.*) Yewr farm! God A'mighty! If ye wa'n't a born donkey ye'd know ye'll never own stick nor stone on it, specially now arter him bein' born. It's his'n, I tell ye — his'n arter I die — but I'll live a hundred jest t' fool ye all — an' he'll be growed then — yewr age a'most! (*Eben laughs again his sardonic "Ha." This drives Cabot into a fury.*) Ha? Ye think ye kin git 'round that someways, do ye? Waal, it'll be her'n, too — Abbie's — ye won't git 'round her — she knows yer tricks — she'll be too much fur ye — she wants the farm her'n — she was afeerd o' ye — she told me ye was sneakin' 'round tryin' t' make love t' her t' git her on yer side . . . ye . . . ye mad fool, ye! (*He raises his clenched fists threateningly.*)

EBEN (*is confronting him, choking with rage*): Ye lie, ye old skunk! Abbie never said no sech thing!

CABOT (*suddenly triumphant when he sees how shaken Eben is*): She did. An' I says, I'll blow his brains t' the top o' them elums — an' she says no that hain't sense, who'll ye git t' help ye on the farm in his place — an' then she says yew'n me ought t' have a son — I know we kin, she says — an' I says, if we do, ye kin have anythin' I've got ye've a mind t'. An' she says, I wants Eben cut off so's this farm'll be mine when ye die! (*With terrible gloating.*) An' that's what's happened, hain't it? An' the farm's her'n! An' the dust o' the road — that's you'rn! Ha! Now who's hawin'?

EBEN (*has been listening, petrified with grief and rage — suddenly laughs wildly and brokenly*): Ha-ha-ha! So that's her sneakin' game — all along! — like I suspicioned at fust — t' swaller it all — an' me, too . . . ! (*Madly.*) I'll murder her! (*He springs toward the porch but Cabot is quicker and gets in between.*)

CABOT: No, ye don't!

EBEN: Git out o' my road! (*He tries to throw Cabot aside. They grapple in what becomes immediately a murderous struggle. The old man's concentrated strength is too much for Eben. Cabot gets one hand on his throat and presses him back across the stone wall. At the same moment, Abbie comes out on the porch. With a stifled cry she runs toward them.*)

ABBIE: Eben! Ephraim! (*She tugs at the hand on Eben's throat.*) Let go, Ephraim! Ye're chokin' him!

CABOT (*Removes his hand and flings Eben sideways full length on the grass, gasping and choking. With a cry, Abbie kneels beside him, trying to take his head on her lap, but he pushes her away. Cabot stands looking down with fierce triumph.*): Ye needn't t've fret, Abbie, I wa'n't aimin' t' kill him. He hain't wuth hangin' fur — not by a hell of a sight! (*More and more triumphantly.*) Seventy-six an' him not thirty yit — an' look whar he be fur thinkin' his Paw was easy! No, by God, I hain't easy! An' him upstairs, I'll raise him t' be like me! (*He turns to leave them.*) I'm goin' in an' dance! — sing an' celebrate! (*He walks to the porch — then turns with a great grin.*) I don't calc'late it's left in him, but if he gits pesky, Abbie, ye jest sing out. I'll come a-runnin' an' by the Etarnal, I'll put him across my knee an' birch him! Ha-ha-ha! (*He goes into the house laughing. A moment later his loud "whoop" is heard.*)

ABBIE (*tenderly*): Eben. Air ye hurt? (*She tries to kiss him but he pushes her violently away and struggles to a sitting position.*)

EBEN (*gaspingly*): T'hell — with ye!

ABBIE (*not believing her ears*): It's me, Eben — Abbie — don't ye know me?

EBEN (*glowering at her with hatred*): Ay-eh — I know ye — now! (*He suddenly breaks down, sobbing weakly.*)

ABBIE (*fearfully*): Eben — what's happened t' ye — why did ye look at me 's if ye hated me?

EBEN (*violently, between sobs and gasps*): I do hate ye! Ye're a whore — a damn trickin' whore!

ABBIE (*shrinking back horrified*): Eben! Ye don't know what ye're sayin'!

EBEN (*scrambling to his feet and following her — accusingly*): Ye're nothin' but a stinkin' passel o' lies! Ye've been lyin' t' me every word ye spoke, day an' night, since we fust — done it. Ye've kept sayin' ye loved me. . . .

ABBIE (*frantically*): I do love ye! (*She takes his hand but he flings hers away.*)

EBEN (*unheeding*): Ye've made a fool o' me — a sick, dumb fool — a-purpose! Ye've been on'y playin' yer sneakin', stealin' game all along — gittin' me t' lie with ye so's ye'd hev a son he'd think was his'n, an' makin' him promise he'd give ye the farm and let me eat dust, if ye did git him a son! (*Staring at her with anguished, bewildered eyes.*) They must be a devil livin' in ye! T'ain't human t' be as bad as that be!

ABBIE (*stunned — dully*): He told yew . . . ?

EBEN: Hain't it true? It hain't no good in yew lyin'.

ABBIE (*pleadingly*): Eben, listen — ye must listen — it was long ago — afore we done nothin' — yew was scornin' me — goin' t' see Min — when I was lovin' ye — an' I said it t' him t' git vengeance on ye!

EBEN (*Unheedingly. With tortured passion.*): I wish ye was dead! I wish I was dead along with ye afore this come! (*Ragingly.*) But I'll git my vengeance too! I'll pray Maw t' come back t' help me — t' put her cuss on yew an' him!

ABBIE (*brokenly*): Don't ye, Eben! Don't ye! (*She throws herself on her knees before him, weeping.*) I didn't mean t' do bad t'ye! Fergive me, won't ye?

EBEN (*not seeming to hear her — fiercely*): I'll git squar' with the old skunk — an' yew! I'll tell him the truth 'bout the son he's so proud o'! Then I'll leave ye here t' pizen each other — with Maw comin' out o' her grave at nights — an' I'll go t' the gold fields o' Cali-forni-a whar Sim an' Peter be!

ABBIE (*terrified*): Ye won't — leave me? Ye can't!

EBEN (*with fierce determination*): I'm a-goin', I tell ye! I'll git rich thar an' come back an' fight him fur the farm he stole — an' I'll kick ye both out in the road — t' beg an' sleep in the woods — an' yer son along with ye — t' starve an' die! (*He is hysterical at the end.*)

ABBIE (*with a shudder — humbly*): He's yewr son, too, Eben.

EBEN (*torturedly*): I wish he never was born! I wish he'd die this minit! I wish I'd never sot eyes on him! It's him — yew havin' him — a-purpose t' steal — that's changed everythin'!

ABBIE (*gently*): Did ye believe I loved ye — afore he come?

EBEN: Aye-eh — like a dumb ox!

ABBIE: An' ye don't believe no more?

EBEN: B'lieve a lyin' thief! Ha!

ABBIE (*shudders — then humbly*): An' did ye r'ally love me afore?

EBEN (*brokenly*): Ay-eh — an' ye was trickin' me!

ABBIE: An' ye don't love me now!

EBEN (*violently*): I hate ye, I tell ye!

ABBIE: An' ye're truly goin' West — goin' t' leave me — all account o' him being born?

EBEN: I'm a-goin' in the mornin' — or may God strike me t' hell!

ABBIE (*after a pause — with a dreadful cold intensity — slowly*): If that's what his comin's done t' me — killin' yewr love — takin' yew away — my on'y joy — the on'y joy I ever knowed — like heaven t' me — purtier'n heaven — then I hate him, too, even if I be his Maw!

EBEN (*bitterly*): Lies! Ye love him! He'll steal the farm fur ye! (*Brokenly.*) But t'ain't the farm so much — not no more — it's yew foolin' me — gittin' me t' love ye — lyin' yew loved me — jest t' git a son t' steal!

ABBIE (*distractedly*): He won't steal! I'd kill him fust! I do love ye! I'll prove t' ye . . . !

EBEN (*harshly*): T'ain't no use lyin' no more. I'm deaf t' ye! (*He turns away.*) I hain't seein' ye agen. Good-by!

ABBIE (*pale with anguish*): Hain't ye even goin' t' kiss me — not once — arter all we loved?

EBEN (*in a hard voice*): I hain't wantin' t' kiss ye never agen! I'm wantin' t' forgit I ever sot eyes on ye!

ABBIE: Eben! — ye mustn't — wait a spell — I want t' tell ye. . . .

EBEN: I'm a-goin' in t' git drunk. I'm a-goin' t' dance.

ABBIE (*clinging to his arm — with passionate earnest-ness*): If I could make it —'s if he'd never come up between us — if I could prove t' ye I wa'n't schemin' t' steal from ye — so's everythin' could be jest the same with us, lovin' each other jest the same, kissin' an' happy the same's we've been happy afore he come — if I could do it — ye'd love me agen, wouldn't ye? Ye'd kiss me agen? Ye wouldn't never leave me, would ye?

EBEN (*moved*): I calc'late not. (*Then shaking her hand off his arm — with a bitter smile.*) But ye hain't God, be ye?

ABBIE (*exultantly*): Remember ye've promised! (*Then with strange intensity.*) Mebbe I kin take back one thin' God does!

EBEN (*peering at her*): Ye're gittin' cracked, hain't ye? (*Then going toward door.*) I'm a-goin' t' dance.

ABBIE (*calls after him intensely*): I'll prove t' ye! I'll prove I love ye better'n. . . . (*He goes in the door, not seeming to hear. She remains standing where she is, looking after him — then she finishes desperately.*) Better'n everythin' else in the world!

Scene III

(*Just before dawn in the morning — shows the kitchen and Cabot's bedroom. In the kitchen, by the light of a tallow candle on the table, Eben is sitting, his chin propped on his hands, his drawn face blank and expres-sionless. His carpetbag is on the floor beside him. In the bedroom, dimly lighted by a small whale-oil lamp, Cabot lies asleep. Abbie is bending over the cradle, lis-tening, her face full of terror yet with an undercurrent of desperate triumph. Suddenly, she breaks down and sobs, appears about to throw herself on her knees beside the cradle, but the old man turns restlessly, groaning in his sleep, and she controls herself, and, shrinking away from the cradle with a gesture of horror, backs swiftly toward the door in rear and goes out. A moment later she comes into the kitchen and, running to Eben, flings her arms about his neck and kisses him wildly. He hard-ens himself, he remains unmoved and cold, he keeps his eyes straight ahead.*)

ABBIE (*hysterically*): I done it, Eben! I told ye I'd do it! I've proved I love ye — better'n everythin' — so's ye can't never doubt me no more!

EBEN (*dully*): Whatever ye done, it hain't no good now.

ABBIE (*wildly*): Don't ye say that! Kiss me, Eben, won't ye? I need ye t' kiss me arter what I done! I need ye t' say ye love me!

EBEN (*kisses her without emotion — dully*): That's fur good-by. I'm a-goin' soon.

ABBIE: No! No! Ye won't go — not now!

EBEN (*going on with his own thoughts*): I been a-thinkin' — an' I hain't goin' t' tell Paw nothin'. I'll leave Maw t' take vengeance on ye. If I told him, the old skunk'd jest be stinkin' mean enuf to take it out on that baby. (*His voice showing emotion in spite of him.*) An' I don't want nothin' bad t' happen t' him.

He hain't t' blame fur yew. (*He adds with a certain queer pride.*) An' he looks like me! An' by God, he's mine! An' some day I'll be a-comin' back an' . . . !

ABBIE (*too absorbed in her own thoughts to listen to him — pleadingly*): They's no cause fur ye t' go now — they's no sense — it's all the same's it was — they's nothin' come b'tween us now — arter what I done!

EBEN (*Something in her voice arouses him. He stares at her a bit frightenedly.*): Ye look mad, Abbie. What did ye do?

ABBIE: I — I killed him, Eben.

EBEN (*amazed*): Ye killed him?

ABBIE (*dully*): Ay-eh.

EBEN (*recovering from his astonishment — savagely*): An' serves him right! But we got t' do somethin' quick t' make it look s'if the old skunk'd killed himself when he was drunk. We kin prove by 'em all how drunk he got.

ABBIE (*wildly*): No! No! Not him! (*Laughing distractedly.*) But that's what I ought t' done, hain't it? I oughter killed him instead! Why didn't ye tell me?

EBEN (*appalled*): Instead? What d'ye mean?

ABBIE: Not him.

EBEN (*his face grown ghastly*): Not — not that baby!

ABBIE (*dully*): Ay-eh!

EBEN (*falls to his knees as if he'd been struck — his voice trembling with horror*): Oh, God A'mighty! A'mighty God! Maw, whar was ye, why didn't ye stop her?

ABBIE (*simply*): She went back t' her grave that night we fust done it, remember? I hain't felt her about since. (*A pause. Eben hides his head in his hands, trembling all over as if he had the ague. She goes on dully.*) I left the piller over his little face. Then he killed himself. He stopped breathin'. (*She begins to weep softly.*)

EBEN (*rage beginning to mingle with grief*): He looked like me. He was mine, damn ye!

ABBIE (*slowly and brokenly*): I didn't want t' do it. I hated myself fur doin' it. I loved him. He was so purty — dead spit 'n' image o' yew. But I loved yew more — an' yew was goin' away — far off whar I'd never see ye agen, never kiss ye, never feel ye pressed agin me agen — an' ye said ye hated me fur havin' him — ye said ye hated him an' wished he was dead — ye said if it hain't been fur him comin' it'd be the same's afore between us.

EBEN (*unable to endure this, springs to his feet in a fury, threatening her, his twitching fingers seeming to reach out for her throat*): Ye lie! I never said — I never dreamed ye'd — I'd cut off my head afore I'd hurt his finger!

ABBIE (*piteously, sinking on her knees*): Eben, don't ye look at me like that — hatin' me — not after what I done fur ye — fur us — so's we could be happy agen —

EBEN (*furiously now*): Shut up, or I'll kill ye! I see yer game now — the same old sneakin' trick — ye're aimin' t' blame me fur the murder ye done!

ABBIE (*moaning — putting her hands over her ears*): Don't ye, Eben! Don't ye! (*She grasps his legs.*)

EBEN (*his mood suddenly changing to horror, shrinks away from her*): Don't ye tech me! Ye're pizen! How could ye — t' murder a pore little critter — Ye must've swapped yer soul t' hell! (*Suddenly raging.*) Ha! I kin see why ye done it! Not the lies ye jest told — but 'cause ye wanted t' steal agen — steal the last thin' ye'd left me — my part o' him — no, the hull o' him — ye saw he looked like me — ye knowed he was all mine — an' ye couldn't b'ar it — I know ye! Ye killed him fur bein' mine! (*All this has driven him almost insane. He makes a rush past her for the door — then turns — shaking both fists at her, violently.*) But I'll take vengeance now! I'll git the Sheriff! I'll tell him everythin'! Then I'll sing "I'm off to Californi-a!" an' go — gold — Golden Gate — gold sun — fields o' gold in the West! (*This last he half shouts, half croons incoherently, suddenly breaking off passionately.*) I'm a-goin' fur the Sheriff t' come an' git ye! I want ye tuk away, locked up from me! I can't stand t' luk at ye! Murderer an' thief 'r not, ye still tempt me! I'll give ye up t' the Sheriff! (*He turns and runs out, around the corner of house, panting and sobbing, and breaks into a swerving sprint down the road.*)

ABBIE (*struggling to her feet, runs to the door, calling after him*): I love ye, Eben! I love ye! (*She stops at the door weakly, swaying, about to fall.*) I don't care what ye do — if ye'll on'y love me agen — (*She falls limply to the floor in a faint.*)

Scene IV

(*About an hour later. Same as scene III. Shows the kitchen and Cabot's bedroom. It is after dawn. The sky is brilliant with the sunrise. In the kitchen, Abbie sits at the table, her body limp and exhausted, her head bowed down over her arms, her face hidden. Upstairs, Cabot is still asleep but awakens with a start. He looks toward the window and gives a snort of surprise and irritation — throws back the covers and begins hurriedly pulling on his clothes. Without looking behind him, he begins talking to Abbie whom he supposes beside him.*)

CABOT: Thunder 'n' lightin', Abbie! I hain't slept this late in fifty year! Looks 's if the sun was full riz a'most. Must've been the dancin' an' likker. Must be gittin' old. I hope Eben's t' wuk. Ye might've tuk the trouble t' rouse me, Abbie. (*He turns — sees no one there — surprised.*) Waal — whar air she? Gittin' vittles, I calc'late. (*He tiptoes to the cradle and peers down — proudly.*) Mornin', sonny. Purty's a picter! Sleepin' sound. He don't beller all night like most o' 'em. (*He goes quietly out the door in rear — a few moments later enters kitchen — sees Abbie — with satisfaction.*) So thar ye be. Ye got any vittles cooked?

ABBIE (*without moving*): No.

CABOT (*coming to her, almost sympathetically*): Ye feelin' sick?

ABBIE: No.

CABOT (*Pats her on shoulder. She shudders.*): Ye'd best lie down a spell. (*Half jocularly.*) Yer son'll be needin' ye soon. He'd ought t' wake up with a gnashin' appetite, the sound way he's sleepin'.

ABBIE (*shudders — then in a dead voice*): He hain't never goin' t' wake up.

CABOT (*jokingly*): Takes after me this mornin'. I hain't slept so late in . . .

ABBIE: He's dead.

CABOT (*stares at her — bewilderedly*): What. . . .

ABBIE: I killed him.

CABOT (*stepping back from her — aghast*): Air ye drunk —'r crazy —'r . . . ?

ABBIE (*suddenly lifts her head and turns on him — wildly*): I killed him, I tell ye! I smothered him. Go up an' see if ye don't b'lieve me!

(*Cabot stares at her a second, then bolts out the rear door, can be heard bounding up the stairs, and rushes into the bedroom and over to the cradle. Abbie has sunk back lifelessly into her former position. Cabot puts his hand down on the body in the crib. An expression of fear and horror comes over his face.*)

CABOT (*shrinking away — tremblingly*): God A'mighty! God A'mighty. (*He stumbles out the door — in a short while returns to the kitchen — comes to Abbie, the stunned expression still on his face — hoarsely.*) Why did ye do it? Why? (*As she doesn't answer, he grabs her violently by the shoulder and shakes her.*) I ax ye why ye done it! Ye'd better tell me 'r . . . !

ABBIE (*gives him a furious push which sends him staggering back and springs to her feet — with wild rage and hatred*): Don't ye dare tech me! What right hev ye t' question me 'bout him? He wa'n't yewr son! Think I'd have a son by yew? I'd die fust! I hate the sight o' ye an' allus did! It's yew I should've murdered, if I'd had good sense! I hate ye! I love Eben. I did from the fust. An' he was Eben's son — mine an' Eben's — not your'n!

CABOT (*stands looking at her dazedly — a pause — finding his words with an effort — dully*): That was it — what I felt — pokin' round the corners — while ye lied — holdin' yerself from me — sayin' ye'd already conceived — (*He lapses into crushed silence — then with a strange emotion.*) He's dead, sart'n. I felt his heart. Pore little critter! (*He blinks back one tear, wiping his sleeve across his nose.*)

ABBIE (*hysterically*): Don't ye! Don't ye! (*She sobs unrestrainedly.*)

CABOT (*with a concentrated effort that stiffens his body into a rigid line and hardens his face into a stony mask — through his teeth to himself*): I got t' be — like a stone — a rock o' jedgment! (*A pause. He gets complete control over himself — harshly.*) If he was Eben's, I be glad he air gone! An' mebbe I suspi-cioned it all along. I felt they was somethin' onnat-eral — somewhars — the house got so lonesome — an' cold — drivin' me down t' the barn — t' the beasts o' the field. . . . Ay-eh. I must've suspicioned — somethin'. Ye didn't fool me — not altogether, least-ways — I'm too old a bird — growin' ripe on the bough. . . . (*He becomes aware he is wandering, straightens again, looks at Abbie with a cruel grin.*) So ye'd liked t' hev murdered me 'steed o' him, would ye? Waal, I'll live to a hundred! I'll live t' see ye hung! I'll deliver ye up t' the jedgment o' God an' the law! I'll git the Sheriff now. (*Starts for the door.*)

ABBIE (*dully*): Ye needn't. Eben's gone fur him.

CABOT (*amazed*): Eben — gone fur the Sheriff?

ABBIE: Ay-eh.

CABOT: T' inform agen ye?

ABBIE: Ay-eh.

CABOT (*considers this — a pause — then in a hard voice*): Waal, I'm thankful fur him savin' me the trouble. I'll git t' wuk. (*He goes to the door — then turns — in a voice full of strange emotion.*) He'd ought t' been my son, Abbie. Ye'd ought t' loved me. I'm a man. If ye'd loved me, I'd never told no Sheriff on ye no matter what ye did, if they was t' brile me alive!

ABBIE (*defensively*): They's more to it nor yew know, makes him tell.

CABOT (*dryly*): Fur yewr sake, I hope they be. (*He goes out — comes around to the gate — stares up at the sky. His control relaxes. For a moment he is old and weary. He murmurs despairingly.*) God A'mighty, I be lonesomer'n ever! (*He hears running footsteps from the left, immediately is himself again. Eben runs in, panting exhaustedly, wild-eyed and mad looking. He lurches through the gate. Cabot grabs him by the shoulder. Eben stares at him dumbly.*) Did ye tell the Sheriff?

EBEN (*nodding stupidly*): Ay-eh.

CABOT (*gives him a push away that sends him sprawling — laughing with withering contempt*): Good fur ye! A prime chip o' yer Maw ye be! (*He goes toward the barn, laughing harshly. Eben scrambles to his feet. Suddenly Cabot turns — grimly threatening.*) Git off this farm when the Sheriff takes her — or, by God, he'll have t' come back an' git me fur murder, too! (*He stalks off. Eben does not appear to have heard him. He runs to the door and comes into the kitchen. Abbie looks up with a cry of anguished joy. Eben stumbles over and throws himself on his knees beside her sobbing brokenly.*)

EBEN: Fergive me!

ABBIE (*happily*): Eben! (*She kisses him and pulls his head over against her breast.*)

EBEN: I love ye! Fergive me!

ABBIE (*ecstatically*): I'd fergive ye all the sins in hell fur sayin' that! (*She kisses his head, pressing it to her with a fierce passion of possession.*)

EBEN (*brokenly*): But I told the Sheriff. He's comin' fur ye!

ABBIE: I kin b'ar what happens t' me — now!

EBEN: I woke him up. I told him. He says, wait 'til I git dressed. I was waiting. I got to thinkin' o' yew. I got to thinkin' how I'd loved ye. It hurt like somethin' was bustin' in my chest an' head. I got t' cryin'. I knowed sudden I loved ye yet, an' allus would love ye!

ABBIE (*caressing his hair — tenderly*): My boy, hain't ye?

EBEN: I begun t' run back. I cut across the fields an' through the woods. I thought ye might have time t' run away — with me — an' . . .

ABBIE (*shaking her head*): I got t' take my punishment — t' pay fur my sin.

EBEN: Then I want t' share it with ye.

ABBIE: Ye didn't do nothin'.

EBEN: I put it in yer head. I wisht he was dead! I as much as urged ye t' do it!

ABBIE: No. It was me alone!

EBEN: I'm as guilty as yew be! He was the child o' our sin.

ABBIE (*lifting her head as if defying God*): I don't repent that sin! I hain't askin' God t' fergive that!

EBEN: Nor me — but it led up t' the other — an' the murder ye did, ye did 'count o' me — an' it's my murder, too, I'll tell the Sheriff — an' if ye deny it, I'll say we planned it t'gether — an' they'll all b'lieve me, fur they suspicion everythin' we've done, an' it'll seem likely an' true to 'em. An' it is true — way down. I did help ye — somehow.

ABBIE (*laying her head on his — sobbing*): No! I don't want yew t' suffer!

EBEN: I got t' pay fur my part o' the sin! An' I'd suffer wuss leavin' ye, goin' West, thinkin' o' ye day an' night, bein' out when yew was in — (*lowering his voice*) 'r bein' alive when yew was dead. (*A pause.*) I want t' share with ye, Abbie, prison 'r death 'r hell 'r anythin'! (*He looks into her eyes and forces a trembling smile.*) If I'm sharin' with ye, I won't feel lonesome, leastways.

ABBIE (*weakly*): Eben! I won't let ye! I can't let ye!

EBEN (*kissing her — tenderly*): Ye can't he'p yerself. I got ye beat fur once!

ABBIE (*forcing a smile — adoringly*): I hain't beat — s'long's I got ye!

EBEN (*hears the sound of feet outside*): Ssshh! Listen! They've come t' take us!

ABBIE: No, it's him. Don't give him no chance to fight ye, Eben. Don't say nothin' — no matter what he says. An' I won't neither. (*It is Cabot. He comes up from the barn in a great state of excitement and strides into the house and then into the kitchen. Eben is kneeling beside Abbie, his arm around her, hers around him. They stare straight ahead.*)

CABOT (*Stares at them, his face hard. A long pause — vindictively.*): Ye make a slick pair o' murderin' turtle doves! Ye'd ought t' be both hung on the same limb an' left thar t' swing in the breeze an' rot — a warnin' t' old fools like me t' b'ar their lonesomeness alone — an' fur young fools like ye t' hobble their

lust. (*A pause. The excitement returns to his face, his eyes snap, he looks a bit crazy.*) I couldn't work today. I couldn't take no interest. T' hell with the farm! I'm leavin' it! I've turned the cows an' other stock loose! I've druv 'em into the woods whar they kin be free! By freein' 'em, I'm freein' myself! I'm quittin' here today! I'll set fire t' house an' barn an' watch 'em burn, an' I'll leave yer Maw t' haunt the ashes, an' I'll will the fields back t' God, so that nothin' human kin never touch 'em! I'll be a-goin' to Californi-a — t' jine Simeon an' Peter — true sons o' mine if they be dumb fools — an' the Cabots'll find Solomon's Mines t'gether! (*He suddenly cuts a mad caper.*) Whoop! What was the song they sung? "Oh, Californi-a! That's the land fur me." (*He sings this — then gets on his knees by the floorboard under which the money was hid.*) An' I'll sail thar on one o' the finest clippers I kin find! I've got the money! Pity ye didn't know whar this was hidden so's ye could steal. . . . (*He has pulled up the board. He stares — feels — stares again. A pause of dead silence. He slowly turns, slumping into a sitting position on the floor, his eyes like those of a dead fish, his face the sickly green of an attack of nausea. He swallows painfully several times — forces a weak smile at last.*) So — ye did steal it!

EBEN (*emotionlessly*): I swapped it t' Sim an' Peter fur their share o' the farm — t' pay their passage t' Californi-a.

CABOT (*with one sardonic*): Ha! (*He begins to recover. Gets slowly to his feet — strangely.*) I calc'late God give it to 'em — not yew! God's hard, not easy! Mebbe they's easy gold in the West but it hain't God's gold. It hain't fur me. I kin hear His voice warnin' me agen t' be hard an' stay on my farm. I kin see his hand usin' Eben t' steal t' keep me from weakness. I kin feel I be in the palm o' His hand, His fingers guidin' me. (*A pause — then he mutters sadly.*) It's a-goin' t' be lonesomer now than ever it war afore — an' I'm gittin' old, Lord — ripe on the bough. . . . (*Then stiffening.*) Waal — what d'ye want? God's lonesome, hain't He? God's hard an' lonesome! (*A pause. The Sheriff with two men comes up the road from the left. They move cautiously to the door. The Sheriff knocks on it with the butt of his pistol.*)

SHERIFF: Open in the name o' the law! (*They start.*)

CABOT: They've come fur ye. (*He goes to the rear door.*) Come in, Jim! (*The three men enter. Cabot meets them in doorway.*) Jest a minit, Jim. I got 'em safe here. (*The Sheriff nods. He and his companions remain in the doorway.*)

EBEN (*suddenly calls*): I lied this mornin', Jim. I helped her to do it. Ye kin take me, too.

ABBIE (*brokenly*): No!

CABOT: Take 'em both. (*He comes forward — stares at Eben with a trace of grudging admiration.*) Purty good — fur yew! Waal, I got t' round up the stock. Good-by.

EBEN: Good-by.

ABBIE: Good-by. (*Cabot turns and strides past the men — comes out and around the corner of the house, his shoulders squared, his face stony, and stalks grimly toward the barn. In the meantime the Sheriff and men have come into the room.*)
SHERIFF (*embarrassedly*): Waal — we'd best start.
ABBIE: Wait. (*Turns to Eben.*) I love ye, Eben.
EBEN: I love ye, Abbie. (*They kiss. The three men grin and shuffle embarrassedly. Eben takes Abbie's hand.*

They go out the door in rear, the men following, and come from the house, walking hand in hand to the gate. Eben stops there and points to the sunrise sky.) Sun's a-rizin'. Purty, hain't it?
ABBIE: Ay-eh. (*They both stand for a moment looking up raptly in attitudes strangely aloof and devout.*)
SHERIFF (*looking around at the farm enviously — to his companions*): It's a jim-dandy farm, no denyin'. Wished I owned it!

COMMENTARY

Stark Young (1881–1963)
REVIEW OF *DESIRE UNDER THE ELMS*   1924

Stark Young's sensitive review of this play contrasted with other reviewers. He saw the work as a significant advance for O'Neill and extensively discusses the drama in terms that reveal its importance. Young also gives particular praise to Walter Huston's performance and to the work's farmhouse setting. His final comments praise the writing in a specific scene "written with such poetry and terrible beauty as we rarely see in theatre."

Desire under the Elms, the first play by Eugene O'Neill to be produced since *Welded,* was presented last night at the Greenwich Village Theatre and proved to be as unlike that drama as it was unlike *The Hairy Ape* or *The Emperor Jones. Desire under the Elms* reverts in character to the earlier *Beyond the Horizon,* though it exhibits by comparison a fine progress in solidity and finish. It has less sentiment that this older piece and more passion; it is better written throughout; it has much tragic gloom and irony but a more mature conception and a more imaginative austerity.

Desire under the Elms is essentially a story of solitude, physical solitude, the solitude of the land, of men's dreams, of love, of life. The God behind the existence created on this New England farm is a harsh God, who is alone and is not understood. The minds of the people in this story are shaken and tinged with loneliness, with thwarted passion, with the trivial, the intense, the drab exaltation and denial of life. Underneath this solitude desire works, the redemption through love.

The children of old Cabot hate him. The youngest, the son of the second wife, remembers his dead mother, worked to death, and sees her about the place, risen from her grave. The father brings home a third wife. The two older sons go away to California; the younger stays and thinks to avenge his mother. In time he and the young wife come to love each other.

A son is born, which old Cabot thinks is to be heir to the farm, leaving the second wife's son adrift in the world. While a dance in honor of the newborn child goes on in the kitchen, the father and son quarrel outside; the son believes his father when he hears that the woman wanted a son only to cheat him out of the farm. He reviles her. To prove to him that it was the love of him and not the desire for the farm that had driven her to him, she kills the child. He runs off for the sheriff. The father turns the live stock loose in the woods and plans to go away, but when he finds the money gone from its hiding place, he believes that God another time has willed that he stand by the farm. The son returns from the sheriff's, he falls at the knees of the woman, takes part of the blame on himself, and they go away together to prison.

Robert Edmond Jones's setting for *Desire under the Elms* was profoundly dramatic. The end of a New England farmhouse with its overhanging elms was for all practical purposes built there on stage, with a wall of actual stone coming down to the footlights; a scene that was realistic but at the same time strangely and powerfully heightened in effect.

The general performance of the play was unusually adequate though not often on a level with the writing. Mary Morris, however, whose career as the fair Gertrude in *Fashion* last year was one of the flowers of the season's acting, played the wife in *Desire under the Elms* with a new and suppressed method that deepened at times into an admirable poignancy and a kind of grim, thin poetry that seemed the exact truth of her lines. Charles Ellis, though his work in earlier scenes was less successful or convincing, played with real poetry the passage where the boy is possessed with love for the woman and for his child. Walter Huston as the old man was everywhere trenchant, gaunt, fervid, harsh, as he should be in the part. In his ability to cover his gradations, to express the natural and convincing emotion, and to convey the harsh, inarticulate life embodied in this extraordinary portrait that Eugene O'Neill has drawn. Mr. Huston showed his talent and proved to be the best choice possible for the role.

The scene of *Desire under the Elms* that best illustrates the highest quality of the play is that in which we see the dance going on, the father outside the house, the young wife and her lover in the upstairs room in each other's arms beside the child's cradle, a scene written with such poetry and terrible beauty as we rarely see in the theatre, a scene that for these qualities of poetry, terror and at the same time unflinching realism rises above anything that Mr. O'Neill has written.

Bertolt Brecht

Among the most inventive and influential of modern playwrights, Bertolt Brecht (1898–1956) has left a legacy of important plays and theories about how those plays should be produced. Throughout most of his career he felt that drama should inform and awaken sensibilities, not just entertain or anesthetize an audience. Most of his plays concern philosophical and political issues, and some of them so threatened the Nazi regime that his works were burned publicly in Germany during the Third Reich.

At nineteen, Brecht worked as an orderly in a hospital during the last months of World War I. Seeing so much carnage and misery in the medical wards made him a lifelong pacifist. After the war he began writing plays while a student in Munich. His first successes in the Munich theater took the form of commentary on returned war veterans and on the questions of duty and heroism — which he treated negatively. His rejection of spiritual concepts was influenced by his readings of Hegel and the doctrines of Marx's dialectical materialism. Marx's theories predicted class struggles and based most social values in economic realities. Brecht eventually moved to Berlin, the theatrical center of Germany, and by 1926 was on his way to becoming a Communist.

Finding the political pressures in early Nazi Germany too frightening and dangerous for his writing, Brecht went into exile in 1933. He lived for a time in Scandinavia and later in the United States. After World War II Brecht and his wife returned to Berlin where, in 1949, he founded the Berliner Ensemble, which produced most of his later work. Brecht chose East Berlin as his home, in part because he felt his work could best be understood in a Communist setting. One irony is that his work has been even more widely appreciated and accepted in the West than in the former Communist eastern bloc.

Brecht wrote his most popular play in 1928, a musical in collaboration with the German composer Kurt Weill: *The Threepenny Opera*. The model for this play, the English writer John Gay's 1728 ballad opera *The Beggar's Opera*, provided Brecht with a perfect platform on which to comment satirically on the political and economic circumstances in Germany two hundred years after Gay wrote. The success of the Brecht-Weill collaboration — the work is still performed regularly — is due in part to Brecht's capacity to create appealing underworld characters such as Polly Peachum and Macheath, known as Mack the Knife. Brecht's wife, Helene Weigel, played Mrs. Peachum, the madam of the brothel in which the action takes place. Kurt Weill's second wife, Lotte Lenya, was an overnight sensation in the part of Jenny. She had a highly acclaimed reprise in New York almost twenty-five years later.

Brecht's most successful plays are *Galileo* (1938–1939), *Mother Courage* (1939), *The Good Woman of Setzuan* (1943), *The Private Lives of the Master Race* (1945), and *The Caucasian Chalk Circle* (1948). But these represent only a tiny fraction of a mass of work, including plays, poetry, criticism, and fiction.

His output is extraordinary in volume and quality. It includes plays borrowed not only from Gay but also from Sophocles, Molière, Gorky, Shakespeare, and John Webster, among others.

Brecht developed a number of theories regarding drama. He used the term *epic theater* to distinguish his own theater from traditional Aristotelian drama. Brecht expected his audience to observe critically, to draw conclusions, and to participate in an intellectual argument with the work at hand. The confrontational relationship he intended was designed to engage the audience in analyzing what they saw rather than in identifying with the main characters or in enjoying a wash of sentimentality or emotion.

One of the ways Brecht achieved his ends was by making the theatricality of the production's props, lights, sets, and equipment visible, thereby reminding the members of the audience that they were seeing a play. He used the term ALIENATION to define the effect he wanted his theater to have on an audience. He hoped that by alienating his audience from the drama he would keep them emotionally detached and intellectually alert. Brecht's theater was political. He saw a connection between an audience that could analyze theater critically and an audience that could analyze reality critically — and see that social, political, and economic conditions were not "natural" or fixed immutably but could (and should) be changed.

Brecht's theories produced interesting results and helped stimulate audiences that expected to be entertained by realistic or sentimental plays. His style spread rapidly throughout the world of theater, and it is still being used and developed by contemporary playwrights such as Heiner Müller and performers such as Pina Bausch.

MOTHER COURAGE

Since *Mother Courage* was first produced in 1941 in Zurich, it has become a classic of modern theater, performed successfully in the United States and most other Western countries. Brecht conceived of the drama as a powerful antiwar play. He set it in Germany during the Thirty Years' War, in which the German Protestants, supported by countries such as France, Denmark, and England, fought against the Hapsburg empire, which was allied with the Holy Roman Empire and the German Catholic princes. The war was actually a combination of many wars fought during the period of thirty years. It was bloody and seemingly interminable, devastating Germany's towns and citizenry as well as its agriculture and commerce. The armies fought to control territory, economic markets, and the religious differences between German Lutherans and Roman Catholics.

Brecht was not interested in the immediate causes underlying the Thirty Years' War. He was making a case against war entirely, regardless of its cause. To do this, he deliberately avoided making his play realistic. The stage setting is essentially barren; and the play is structured in scenes that are very intense but that avoid any sense of continuity of action. Audiences cannot become involved in unfolding action; they must always remain conscious of themselves as audience. Moreover, the lighting is high intensity, almost cruel at times, spotlighting the action in a way that is completely unnatural. In the early productions, Brecht included slide projections of the headings that accompany each of the twelve scenes so that the audience was always reminded of the presence of the playwright and the fact that they were seeing a play. These headings provided yet another break in the continuity of the action.

Although the printed text does not convey it, the play as Brecht produced it employed long silences, some of which were unsettling to the audience. When Swiss Cheese, Mother Courage's "honest" son, has a moment of rest in scene 3, he is in an intense ring of stage light as he comments on sitting in the sun in his shirtsleeves. He is relaxing for the last time, and the intensity of the light becomes an ironic device: it exposes him as a thief, and he is dragged off to his death as a result of having stolen the cash box from the regiment. Swiss Cheese has been corrupted by the war, just as virtually everyone is corrupted.

Mother Courage herself lives off the war by selling goods to the soldiers. She and her children haul their wagon across the battlefields with no concern for who is winning, who is losing, or even where they are. Her only ambition is to stock her wagon, sell her goods, and make sure she does not get stuck with any useless inventory. When the chaplain tells her that peace has broken out, she laments their condition because without war the family has no livelihood.

As Mother Courage continues to pull her wagon across field after field, she learns how to survive. But she also loses her children, one by one, to the war. Eilif, seduced into joining the army by a recruitment officer, is led into battle thinking that war is a heroic adventure. Swiss Cheese thinks he found a good deal in a paymaster's uniform. Both are wrong: there is no security in war, and they eventually perish.

Kattrin, the daughter, is likewise a victim of the violence of war. Having been violated by a Swedish soldier, she becomes mute. Near the end of the play she is treated violently again, and the terrible scar on her face leaves her unmarriageable. At the end Kattrin dies while sounding an alarm to give the sleeping town warning of an imminent attack.

Finally, Mother Courage is left alone. She picks up her wagon and finds that she can maneuver it herself. The play ends as she circles the stage, with everything around her consumed by war.

Brecht's stated intentions were somewhat thwarted by the reactions of the play's first audiences. They were struck by the power of Brecht's characterization of Mother Courage and treated her with immense sympathy. They saw her as an indomitable woman whose strength in the face of adversity was so great that she could not be overwhelmed. But Brecht intended the audience to analyze Mother Courage further and to see in her a reflection of society's wrong values. She conducts business on the field of battle, paying no attention to the moral question of war itself. She makes her living from the war but cannot see that it is the war that causes her anguish.

In response to the audiences' sympathetic reactions, Brecht revised the play, adding new lines to help audiences see the venality of Mother Courage's motives. But subsequent audiences have continued to treat her as a survivor —

almost a biblical figure. Brecht's German critics saw her as a model for one who endures all the terrors of war and yet remains a testament for the resilience of humankind. No matter how one decides to interpret her, Mother Courage remains one of the most unusual and haunting characters in modern drama.

Mother Courage in Performance

Brecht wrote *Mother Courage* in three months, beginning in September 1939, while he and Helene Weigel were in Sweden in exile from Nazi Germany. Its first production was on April 19, 1941, in Zurich, Switzerland, while Brecht waited in Sweden for entry papers to the United States. Brecht and Weigel returned to Europe after the war. In 1948 they went to East Berlin to work with a new theater group explicitly to produce *Mother Courage* with Helene Weigel in the title role in January 1949. In October 1950 Brecht directed Thérèsa Giehse as Courage in Munich. Other productions were staged in provincial German towns and in other European cities, such as Rotterdam and Paris, both in 1951.

Brecht's productions are sometimes regarded as "canonical," although contemporary directors often modify his original plans. He usually began the performance with a half-curtain and a four-person orchestra playing an overture. Next, an unseen record player played a song associated with Courage; as Courage came on stage, she sang the second verse of her song herself. The stage had only a CYCLORAMA, a large curved curtain used as a backdrop, and a circle marked on the floor. This defined the space that was Mother Courage's world, and various sets were placed on the circle to accommodate successive scenes. The circle itself was a revolving turntable on which the wagon moved, going essentially nowhere. Brecht used placards to indicate changes in time and place as well as to indicate events in the life of Mother Courage and her children. The lighting was generally bright, and the effect was lively and colorful.

Brecht was not widely produced in the West during the cold war, but Leon Epp directed *Mother Courage* at the Volkstheater in Vienna in 1963. In the same year Jerome Robbins produced the play at the Martin Beck Theatre on Broadway, with sets by Ming Cho Lee. Anne Bancroft played Mother Courage, and Zohra Lampert was Kattrin. The reviews praised Bancroft for achieving a "lonely magnificence" at the end of the play and maintained that Brecht produced a considerable emotional intensity despite his theoretical distaste for such effects.

The next year Joseph Slowik produced the play in the Goodman Theater in Chicago with a partial student cast and the distinguished Eugenie Leontovich as Mother Courage. In England *Mother Courage* was produced twice in the 1950s in London. In 1961 and 1965 it was produced by the Old Vic. Numerous local theaters put on the play in the late 1960s and 1970s. In 1980 Ntozake Shange adapted it for its second New York production and reset it in the period after the American Civil War; Gloria Foster and Morgan Freeman had the major roles. Frank Rich praised the acting and the energy of the play but feared that Brecht's original vision was altered almost beyond recognition: Mother Courage becomes "an innocent victim of an entire system," which is exactly what Brecht argued against.

The Royal Shakespeare Company produced the play in London in 1984 with Judi Dench as Courage and Zoë Wanamaker as Kattrin. Both received fine reviews, as did the production itself. Diana Rigg was Mother Courage in the production at the Olivier Theatre in London (November 1995–January 1996), which featured a new colloquial translation by the playwright David Hare and which reset the play in the period of World War I. Like all these productions, it maintained the circular set that Brecht had originally used and experimented with Brecht's theories of alienation and distancing. The success of these productions indicates the play's appeal for our time.

Bertolt Brecht (1898–1956)

MOTHER COURAGE AND HER CHILDREN   *1939*
A CHRONICLE OF THE THIRTY YEARS' WAR

TRANSLATED BY JOHN WILLETT

Characters

MOTHER COURAGE
KATTRIN, *her dumb daughter*
EILIF, *the elder son*
SWISS CHEESE, *the younger son*
THE RECRUITER
THE SERGEANT
THE COOK
THE GENERAL
THE CHAPLAIN
THE ARMOURER
YVETTE POTTER
THE MAN WITH THE PATCH
ANOTHER SERGEANT
THE ANCIENT COLONEL
A CLERK
A YOUNG SOLDIER
AN OLDER SOLDIER
A PEASANT
THE PEASANT'S WIFE
THE YOUNG MAN
THE OLD WOMAN
ANOTHER PEASANT
HIS WIFE
THE YOUNG PEASANT
THE ENSIGN
SOLDIERS
A VOICE

SCENE 1

(*Spring 1624. The Swedish Commander-in-Chief Count Oxenstierna is raising troops in Dalecarlia for the Polish campaign. The canteen woman Anna Fierling, known under the name of Mother Courage, loses one son.*)
(*Country road near a town.*)
(*A sergeant and a recruiter stand shivering.*)

RECRUITER: How can you muster a unit in a place like this? I've been thinking about suicide, sergeant. Here am I, got to find our commander four companies before the twelfth of the month, and people round here are so nasty I can't sleep nights. S'pose I get hold of some bloke and shut my eye to his pigeon chest and varicose veins, I get him proper drunk, he signs on the line, I'm just settling up, he goes for a piss, I follow him to the door because I smell a rat; bob's your uncle, he's off like a flea with the itch. No notion of word of honour, loyalty, faith, sense of duty. This place has shattered my confidence in the human race, sergeant.

SERGEANT: It's too long since they had a war here; stands to reason. Where's their sense of morality to come from? Peace — that's just a mess; takes a war to restore order. Peacetime, the human race runs wild. People and cattle get buggered about, who cares? Everyone eats just as he feels inclined, a hunk of cheese on top of his nice white bread, and a slice of fat on top of the cheese. How many young blokes and good horses in that town there, nobody knows; they never thought of counting. I been in places ain't seen a war for nigh seventy years: folks hadn't got names to them, couldn't tell one another apart. Takes a war to get proper nominal rolls and inventories — shoes in bundles and corn in bags, and man and beast properly numbered and carted off, cause it stands to reason: no order, no war.

RECRUITER: Too true.

SERGEANT: Same with all good things, it's a job to get a war going. But once it's blossomed out there's no holding it; folk start fighting shy of peace like punters what can't stop for fear of having to tot up what they lost. Before that it's war they're fighting shy of. It's something new to them.

RECRUITER: Hey, here's a cart coming. Two tarts with two young fellows. Stop her, sergeant. If this one's a flop I'm not standing around in your spring winds any longer, I can tell you.

(*Sound of a jew's-harp. Drawn by two young fellows, a covered cart rolls in. On it sit Mother Courage and her dumb daughter Kattrin.*)

MOTHER COURAGE: Morning, sergeant.

SERGEANT (*blocking the way*): Morning, all. And who are you?

MOTHER COURAGE: Business folk. (*Sings.*)

> You captains, tell the drums to slacken
> And give your infanteers a break:
> It's Mother Courage with her waggon
> Full of the finest boots they make.
> With crawling lice and looted cattle
> With lumbering guns and straggling kit —
> How can you flog them into battle
> Unless you get them boots that fit?
>> The new year's come. The watchmen shout.
>> The thaw sets in. The dead remain.
>> Whatever life has not died out
>> It staggers to its feet again.
>
> Captains, how can you make them face it —
> Marching to death without a brew?
> Courage has rum with which to lace it
> And boil their souls and bodies through.
> Their musket primed, their stomach hollow —
> Captains, your men don't look so well.
> So feed them up and let them follow
> While you command them into hell.
>> The new year's come. The watchmen shout.
>> The thaw sets in. The dead remain.
>> Wherever life has not died out
>> It staggers to its feet again.

SERGEANT: Halt! Who are you with, you trash?

THE ELDER SON: Second Finnish Regiment.

SERGEANT: Where's your papers?

MOTHER COURAGE: Papers?

THE YOUNGER SON: What, mean to say you don't know Mother Courage?

SERGEANT: Never heard of her. What's she called Courage for?

MOTHER COURAGE: Courage is the name they gave me because I was scared of going broke, sergeant, so I drove me cart right through the bombardment of Riga with fifty loaves of bread aboard. They were going mouldy, it was high time, hadn't any choice really.

SERGEANT: Don't be funny with me. Your papers.

MOTHER COURAGE (*pulling a bundle of papers from a tin box and climbing down off the cart*): That's all my papers, sergeant. You'll find a whole big missal from Altötting in Bavaria for wrapping gherkins in, and a road map of Moravia, the Lord knows when I'll ever get there, might as well chuck it away, and here's a stamped certificate that my horse hasn't got foot-and-mouth, only he's dead worse luck, cost fifteen florins he did — not me luckily. That enough paper for you?

SERGEANT: You pulling my leg? I'll knock that sauce out of you. S'pose you know you got to have a licence.

MOTHER COURAGE: Talk proper to me, do you mind, and don't you dare say I'm pulling your leg in front of my unsullied children, 'tain't decent, I got no time for you. My honest face, that's me licence with the Second Regiment, and if it's too difficult for you to read there's nowt I can do about it. Nobody's putting a stamp on that.

RECRUITER: Sergeant, methinks I smell insubordination in this individual. What's needed in our camp is obedience.

MOTHER COURAGE: Sausage, if you ask me.

SERGEANT: Name.

MOTHER COURAGE: Anna Fierling.

SERGEANT: You all called Fierling then?

MOTHER COURAGE: What'd you mean? It's me's called Fierling, not them.

SERGEANT: Aren't all this lot your children?

MOTHER COURAGE: You bet they are, but why should they all have to be called the same, eh? (*Pointing to her elder son.*) For instance, that one's called Eilif Nojocki — Why? his father always claimed he was called Kojocki or Mojocki or something. The boy remembers him clearly, except that the one he remembers was someone else, a Frenchie with a little beard. Aside from that he's got his father's wits; that man knew how to snitch a peasant's pants off his bum without him noticing. This way each of us has his own name, see.

SERGEANT: What, each one different?

MOTHER COURAGE: Don't tell me you ain't never come across that.

SERGEANT: So I s'pose he's a Chinaman? (*Pointing to the younger son.*)

MOTHER COURAGE: Wrong. Swiss.

SERGEANT: After the Frenchman?

MOTHER COURAGE: What Frenchman? I never heard tell of no Frenchman. You keep muddling things up, we'll be hanging around here till dark. A Swiss, but called Fejos, and the name has nowt to do with his father. He was called something quite different and was a fortifications engineer, only drunk all the time.

(*Swiss Cheese beams and nods; dumb Kattrin too is amused.*)

SERGEANT: How in hell can he be called Fejos?

MOTHER COURAGE: I don't like to be rude, sergeant, but

you ain't got much imagination, have you? Course he's called Fejos, because when he arrived I was with a Hungarian, very decent fellow, had terrible kidney trouble though he never touched a drop. The boy takes after him.

SERGEANT: But he wasn't his father . . .

MOTHER COURAGE: Took after him just the same. I call him Swiss Cheese. (*Pointing to her daughter.*) And that's Kattrin Haupt, she's half German.

SERGEANT: Nice family, I must say.

MOTHER COURAGE: Aye, me cart and me have seen the world.

SERGEANT: I'm writing all this down. (*He writes.*) And you're from Bamberg in Bavaria; how d'you come to be here?

MOTHER COURAGE: Can't wait till war chooses to visit Bamberg, can I?

RECRUITER (*to Eilif*): You two should be called Jacob Ox and Esau Ox, pulling the cart like that. I s'pose you never get out of harness?

EILIF: Ma, can I clobber him one? I wouldn't half like to.

MOTHER COURAGE: And I says you can't; just you stop where you are. And now two fine officers like you, I bet you could use a good pistol, or a belt buckle, yours is on its last legs, sergeant.

SERGEANT: I could use something else. Those boys are healthy as young birch trees, I observe: chests like barrels, solid leg muscles. So why are they dodging their military service, may I ask?

MOTHER COURAGE (*quickly*): Nowt doing, sergeant. Yours is no trade for my kids.

RECRUITER: But why not? There's good money in it, glory too. Flogging boots is women's work. (*To Eilif.*) Come here, let's see if you've muscles in you or if you're a chicken.

MOTHER COURAGE: He's a chicken. Give him a fierce look, he'll fall over.

RECRUITER: Killing a young bull that happens to be in his way. (*Wants to lead him off.*)

MOTHER COURAGE: Let him alone, will you? He's nowt for you folk.

RECRUITER: He was crudely offensive and talked about clobbering me. The two of us are going to step into that field and settle it man to man.

EILIF: Don't you worry, mum, I'll fix him.

MOTHER COURAGE: Stop there! You varmint! I know you, nowt but fights. There's a knife down his boot. A slasher, that's what he is.

RECRUITER: I'll draw it out of him like a milk-tooth. Come along, sonny.

MOTHER COURAGE: Sergeant, I'll tell the colonel. He'll have you both in irons. The lieutenant's going out with my daughter.

SERGEANT: No rough stuff, chum. (*To Mother Courage.*) What you got against military service? Wasn't his own father a soldier? Died a soldier's death, too? Said it yourself.

MOTHER COURAGE: He's nowt but a child. You want to take him off to slaughterhouse, I know you lot. They'll give you five florins for him.

RECRUITER: First he's going to get a smart cap and boots, eh?

EILIF: Not from you.

MOTHER COURAGE: Let's both go fishing, said angler to worm. (*To Swiss Cheese.*) Run off, call out they're trying to kidnap your brother. (*She pulls a knife.*) Go on, you kidnap him, just try. I'll slit you open, trash. I'll teach you to make war with him. We're doing an honest trade in ham and linen, and we're peaceable folk.

SERGEANT: Peaceable I don't think; look at your knife. You should be ashamed of yourself; put that knife away, you old harridan. A minute back you were admitting you live off the war, how else should you live, what from? But how's anyone to have war without soldiers?

MOTHER COURAGE: No need for it to be my kids.

SERGEANT: Oh, you'd like war to eat the pips but spit out the apple? It's to fatten up your kids, but you won't invest in it. Got to look after itself, eh? And you called Courage, fancy that. Scared of the war that keeps you going? Your sons aren't scared of it, I can see that.

EILIF: Take more than a war to scare me.

SERGEANT: And why? Look at me: has army life done all that badly by me? Joined up at seventeen.

MOTHER COURAGE: Still got to reach seventy.

SERGEANT: I don't mind waiting.

MOTHER COURAGE: Under the sod, eh?

SERGEANT: You trying to insult me, saying I'll die?

MOTHER COURAGE: S'pose it's true? S'pose I can see the mark's on you? S'pose you look like a corpse on leave to me? Eh?

SWISS CHEESE: She's got second sight, Mother has.

RECRUITER: Go ahead, tell the sergeant's fortune, might amuse him.

MOTHER COURAGE: Gimme helmet. (*He gives it to her.*)

SERGEANT: It don't mean a bloody sausage. Anything for a laugh though.

MOTHER COURAGE (*taking out a sheet of parchment and tearing it up*): Eilif, Swiss Cheese and Kattrin, may all of us be torn apart like this if we lets ourselves get too mixed up in the war. (*To the sergeant.*) Just for you I'm doing it for free. Black's for death. I'm putting a big black cross on this slip of paper.

SWISS CHEESE: Leaving the other one blank, see?

MOTHER COURAGE: Then I fold them across and shake them. All of us is jumbled together like this from our mother's womb, and now draw a slip and you'll know. (*The sergeant hesitates.*)

RECRUITER (*to Eilif*): I don't take just anybody, they all know I'm choosey, but you got the kind of fire I like to see.

SERGEANT (*fishing in the helmet*): Too silly. Load of eyewash.

SWISS CHEESE: Drawn a black cross, he has. Write him off.

RECRUITER: They're having you on; not everybody's name's on a bullet.

SERGEANT (*hoarsely*): You've put me in the shit.

MOTHER COURAGE: Did that yourself the day you became a soldier. Come along, let's move on now. 'Tain't every day we have a war, I got to get stirring.

SERGEANT: God damn it, you can't kid me. We're taking that bastard of yours for a soldier.

EILIF: Swiss Cheese'd like to be a soldier too.

MOTHER COURAGE: First I've heard of that. You'll have to draw too, all three of you. (*She goes to the rear to mark crosses on further slips.*)

RECRUITER (*to Eilif*): One of the things they say against us is that it's all holy-holy in the Swedish camp; but that's a malicious rumour to do us down. There's no hymn-singing but Sundays, just a single verse, and then only for those got voices.

MOTHER COURAGE (*coming back with the slips, which she drops into the sergeant's helmet*): Trying to get away from their ma, the devils, off to war like calves to salt-lick. But I'm making you draw lots, and that'll show you the world is no vale of joys with "Come along, son, we need a few more generals." Sergeant, I'm so scared they won't get through the war. Such dreadful characters, all three of them. (*She hands the helmet to Eilif.*) Hey, come on, fish out your slip. (*He fishes one out, unfolds it. She snatches it from him.*) There you are, it's a cross. Oh, wretched mother that I am, o pain-racked giver of birth! Shall he die? Aye, in the springtime of life he is doomed. If he becomes a soldier he shall bite the dust, it's plain to see. He is too foolhardy, like his dad was. And if he ain't sensible he'll go the way of all flesh, his slip proves it. (*Shouts at him.*) You going to be sensible?

EILIF: Why not?

MOTHER COURAGE: Sensible thing is stay with your mother, never mind if they poke fun at you and call you chicken, just you laugh.

RECRUITER: If you're pissing in your pants I'll make do with your brother.

MOTHER COURAGE: I told you laugh. Go on, laugh. Now you draw, Swiss Cheese. I'm not so scared on account you're honest. (*He fishes in the helmet.*) Oh, why look at your slip in that strange way? It's got to be a blank. There can't be any cross on it. Surely I'm not going to lose *you.* (*She takes the slip.*) A cross? What, you too? Is that because you're so simple, perhaps? O Swiss Cheese, you too will be sunk if you don't stay utterly honest all the while, like I taught you from childhood when you brought the change back from the baker's. Else you can't save yourself. Look, sergeant, that's a black cross, ain't it?

SERGEANT: A cross, that's right. Can't think how I come to get one. I always stay in the rear. (*To the recruiter.*) There's no catch. Her own family get it too.

SWISS CHEESE: I get it too. But I listen to what I'm told.

MOTHER COURAGE (*to Kattrin*): And now you're the only one I know's all right, you're a cross yourself; got a kind heart you have. (*Holds the helmet up to her on the cart, but takes the slip out herself.*) No, that's too much. That can't be right; must have made a mistake shuffling. Don't be too kind-hearted, Kattrin, you'll have to give it up, there's a cross above your path too. Lie doggo, girl, it can't be that hard once you're born dumb. Right, all of you know now. Look out for yourselves, you'll need to. And now up we get and on we go. (*She climbs on to the cart.*)

RECRUITER (*to the sergeant*): Do something.

SERGEANT: I don't feel very well.

RECRUITER: Must of caught a chill taking your helmet off in that wind. Involve her in a deal. (*Aloud.*) Might as well have a look at that belt-buckle, sergeant. After all, our friends here have to live by their business. Hey, you people, the sergeant wants to buy that belt-buckle.

MOTHER COURAGE: Half a florin. Two florins is what a belt like that's worth. (*Climbs down again.*)

SERGEANT: 'Tain't new. Let me get out of this damned wind and have a proper look at it. (*Goes behind the cart with the buckle.*)

MOTHER COURAGE: Ain't what I call windy.

SERGEANT: I s'pose it might be worth half a florin, it's silver.

MOTHER COURAGE (*joining him behind the cart*): It's six solid ounces.

RECRUITER (*to Eilif*): And then we men'll have one together. Got your bounty money here, come along. (*Eilif stands undecided.*)

MOTHER COURAGE: Half a florin it is.

SERGEANT: It beats me. I'm always at the rear. Sergeant's the safest job there is. You can send the others up front, cover themselves with glory. Me dinner hour's properly spoiled. Shan't be able to hold nowt down, I know.

MOTHER COURAGE: Mustn't let it prey on you so's you can't eat. Just stay at the rear. Here, take a swig of brandy, man. (*Gives him a drink.*)

RECRUITER (*has taken Eilif by the arm and is leading him away up stage*): Ten florins bounty money, then you're a gallant fellow fighting for the king and women'll be after you like flies. And you can clobber me for free for insulting you.

(*Exeunt both.°*)

(*Dumb Kattrin leans down from the cart and makes hoarse noises.*)

MOTHER COURAGE: All right, Kattrin, all right. Sergeant's just paying. (*Bites the half-florin.*) I got no faith in any kind of money. Burnt child, that's me, sergeant. This coin's good, though. And now let's get moving. Where's Eilif?

SWISS CHEESE: Went off with the recruiter.

MOTHER COURAGE (*stands quite still, then*): You simpleton. (*To Kattrin.*) 'Tain't your fault, you can't speak, I know.

SERGEANT: Could do with a swig yourself, ma. That's

Exeunt both: They both leave.

life. Plenty worse thing's than being a soldier. Want to live off war, but keep yourself and family out of it, eh?

MOTHER COURAGE: You'll have to help your brother pull now, Kattrin.

(*Brother and sister hitch themselves to the cart and start pulling. Mother Courage walks alongside. The cart rolls on.*)

SERGEANT (*looking after them*):
Like the war to nourish you?
Have to feed it something too.

SCENE 2

(*In the years 1625 and 1626 Mother Courage crosses Poland in the train of the Swedish armies. Before the fortress of Wallhof she meets her son again. Successful sale of a capon and heyday of her dashing son.*)
(*The general's tent.*)
(*Beside it, his kitchen. Thunder of cannon. The cook is arguing with Mother Courage, who wants to sell him a capon.*)

THE COOK: Sixty hellers for a miserable bird like that?

MOTHER COURAGE: Miserable bird? This fat brute? Mean to say some greedy old general — and watch your step if you got nowt for his dinner — can't afford sixty hellers for him?

THE COOK: I can get a dozen like that for ten hellers just down the road.

MOTHER COURAGE: What, a capon like this you can get just down the road? In time of siege, which means hunger that tears your guts. A rat you might get: "might" I say because they're all being gobbled up, five men spending best part of day chasing one hungry rat. Fifty hellers for a giant capon in time of siege!

THE COOK: But it ain't us having the siege, it's t'other side. We're conducting the siege, can't you get that in your head?

MOTHER COURAGE: But we got nowt to eat too, even worse than them in the town. Took it with them, didn't they? They're having a high old time, everyone says. And look at us! I been to the peasants, there's nowt there.

THE COOK: There's plenty. They're sitting on it.

MOTHER COURAGE (*triumphantly*): They ain't. They're bust, that's what they are. Just about starving. I saw some, were grubbing up roots from sheer hunger, licking their fingers after they boiled some old leather strap. That's way it is. And me got a capon here and supposed to take forty hellers for it.

THE COOK: Thirty, not forty. I said thirty.

MOTHER COURAGE: Here, this ain't just any old capon. It was such a gifted beast, I been told, it could only eat to music, had a military march of its own. It could count, it was that intelligent. And you say forty hellers is too much? General will make mincemeat of you if there's nowt on his table.

THE COOK: See what I'm doing? (*He takes a piece of beef and puts his knife to it.*) Here I got a bit of beef, I'm going to roast it. Make up your mind quick.

MOTHER COURAGE: Go on, roast it. It's last year's.

THE COOK: Last night's. That animal was still alive and kicking, I saw him myself.

MOTHER COURAGE: Alive and stinking, you mean.

THE COOK: I'll cook him five hours if need be. I'll just see if he's still tough. (*He cuts into it.*)

MOTHER COURAGE: Put plenty of pepper on it so his lordship the general don't smell the pong.

(*The general, a chaplain and Eilif enter the tent.*)

THE GENERAL (*slapping Eilif on the shoulder*): Now then, Eilif my son, into your general's tent with you and sit thou at my right hand. For you accomplished a deed of heroism, like a pious cavalier; and doing what you did for God, and in a war of religion at that, is something I commend in you most highly, you shall have a gold bracelet as soon as we've taken this town. Here we are, come to save their souls for them, and what do those insolent dung-encrusted yokels go and do? Drive their beef away from us. They stuff it into those priests of theirs all right, back and front, but you taught 'em manners, ha! So here's a pot of red wine for you, the two of us'll knock it back at one gulp. (*They do so.*) Piss all for the chaplain, the old bigot. And now, what would you like for dinner, my darling?

EILIF: A bit of meat, why not?

THE GENERAL: Cook! Meat!

THE COOK: And then he goes and brings guests when there's nowt there.

(*Mother Courage silences him so she can listen.*)

EILIF: Hungry job cutting down peasants.

MOTHER COURAGE: Jesus Christ, it's my Eilif.

THE COOK: Your what?

MOTHER COURAGE: My eldest boy. It's two years since I lost sight of him, they pinched him from me on the road, must think well of him if the general's asking him to dinner, and what kind of a dinner can you offer? Nowt. You heard what the visitor wishes to eat: meat. Take my tip, you settle for the capon, it'll be a florin.

THE GENERAL (*has sat down with Eilif, and bellows*): Food, Lamb, you foul cook, or I'll have your hide.

THE COOK: Give it over, dammit, this is blackmail.

MOTHER COURAGE: Didn't someone say it was a miserable bird?

THE COOK: Miserable; give it over, and a criminal price, fifty hellers.

MOTHER COURAGE: A florin, I said. For my eldest boy, the general's guest, no expense is too great for me.

THE COOK (*gives her the money*): You might at least pluck it while I see to the fire.

MOTHER COURAGE (*sits down to pluck the fowl*): He won't half be surprised to see me. He's my dashing clever son. Then I got a stupid one too, he's honest

Lotte Lenya as Mother Courage pulling her wagon in Brecht's 1979 Berliner Ensemble production of his play.

s'posed to come and pick them up. So I holds off and lets them drive their oxen together, reckoning they'd be better than me at finding 'em. I had my blokes slavering after the meat, cut their emergency rations even further for a couple of days till their mouths was watering at the least sound of any word beginning with "me-," like "measles" say.

THE GENERAL: Very clever of you.

EILIF: Possibly. The rest was a piece of cake. Except that the peasants had cudgels and outnumbered us three to one and made a murderous attack on us. Four of 'em shoved me into a thicket, knocked my sword from my hand and bawled out "Surrender!" What's the answer, I wondered; they're going to make mince-meat of me.

THE GENERAL: What did you do?

EILIF: I laughed.

THE GENERAL: You did what?

EILIF: Laughed. So we got talking. I put it on a business footing from the start, told them "Twenty florins a head's too much. I'll give you fifteen." As if I was meaning to pay. That threw them, and they began scratching their heads. In a flash I'd picked up my sword and was hacking 'em to pieces. Necessity's the mother of invention, eh, sir?

THE GENERAL: What is your view, pastor of souls?

THE CHAPLAIN: That phrase is not strictly speaking in the Bible, but when Our Lord turned the five loaves into five hundred there was no war on and he could tell people to love their neighbours as they'd had enough to eat. Today it's another story.

THE GENERAL (laughs): Quite another story. You can have a swig after all for that, you old Pharisee.° (To Eilif.) Hacked 'em to pieces, did you, so my gallant lads can get a proper bite to eat? What do the Scriptures say? "Whatsoever thou doest for the least of my brethren, thou doest for me." And what did you do for them? Got them a good square meal of beef, because they're not accustomed to mouldy bread, the old way was to fix a cold meal of rolls and wine in your helmet before you went out to fight for God.

EILIF: Aye, in a flash I'd picked up my sword and was hacking them to pieces.

THE GENERAL: You've the makings of a young Caesar. You ought to see the King.

EILIF: I have from a distance. He kind of glows. I'd like to model myself on him.

THE GENERAL: You've got something in common already. I appreciate soldiers like you, Eilif, men of courage. Somebody like that I treat as I would my own sort. (He leads him over to the map.) Have a look at the situation, Eilif; it's a long haul still.

MOTHER COURAGE (who has been listening and now angrily plucks the fowl): That must be a rotten general.

Pharisee: A member of a Jewish sect current in biblical days; the term is now commonly used to refer to a hypocritical, self-righteous person.

though. The girl's nowt. One good thing, she don't talk.

THE GENERAL: Drink up, my son, this is my best Falern-ian; only got a barrel or two left, but that's nothing to pay for a sign that there's still true faith to be found in my army. As for that shepherd of souls he can just look on, because all he does is preach, without the least idea how it's to be carried out. And now, my son Eilif, tell us more about the neat way you smashed those yokels and captured the twenty oxen. Let's hope they get here soon.

EILIF: A day or two at most.

MOTHER COURAGE: Thoughtful of our Eilif not to bring the oxen in till tomorrow, else you lot wouldn't have looked twice at my capon.

EILIF: Well, it was like this, see. I'd heard peasants had been driving the oxen they'd hidden, out of the forest into one particular wood, on the sly and mostly by night. That's where people from the town were

THE COOK: He's ravenous all right, but why rotten?

MOTHER COURAGE: Because he's got to have men of courage, that's why. If he knew how to plan a proper campaign what would he be needing men of courage for? Ordinary ones would do. It's always the same; whenever there's a load of special virtues around it means something stinks.

THE COOK: I thought it meant things is all right.

MOTHER COURAGE: No, that they stink. Look, s'pose some general or king is bone stupid and leads his men up shit creek, then those men've got to be fearless, there's another virtue for you. S'pose he's stingy and hires too few soldiers, then they got to be a crowd of Hercules's. And s'pose he's slapdash and don't give a bugger, then they got to be clever as monkeys else their number's up. Same way they got to show exceptional loyalty each time he gives them impossible jobs. Nowt but virtues no proper country and no decent king or general would ever need. In decent countries folk don't have to have virtues, the whole lot can be perfectly ordinary, average intelligence, and for all I know cowards.

THE GENERAL: I'll wager your father was a soldier.

EILIF: A great soldier, I been told. My mother warned me about it. There's a song I know.

THE GENERAL: Sing it to us. (*Roars.*) When's that dinner coming?

EILIF: It's called The Song of the Girl and the Soldier. (*He sings it, dancing a war dance with his sabre.*)

The guns blaze away, and the bay'nit'll slay
And the water can't hardly be colder.
What's the answer to ice? Keep off's my advice!
That's what the girl told the soldier.
Next thing the soldier, wiv' a round up the spout
Hears the band playing and gives a great shout:
Why, it's marching what makes you a soldier!
So it's down to the south and then northwards once
    more:
See him catching that bay'nit in his naked paw!
That's what his comrades done told her.

Oh, do not despise the advice of the wise
Learn wisdom from those that are older
And don't try for things that are out of your
    reach —
That's what the girl told the soldier.
Next thing the soldier, his bay'nit in place
Wades into the river and laughs in her face
Though the water comes up to his shoulder.
When the shingle roof glints in the light o' the
    moon
We'll be wiv' you again, not a moment too soon!
That's what his comrades done told her.

MOTHER COURAGE (*takes up the song in the kitchen, beating on a pot with her spoon*):

You'll go out like a light! And the sun'll take flight
For your courage just makes us feel colder.

Oh, that vanishing light! May God see that it's
    right! —
That's what the girl told the soldier.

EILIF: What's that?

MOTHER COURAGE (*continues singing*):

Next thing the soldier, his bay'nit in place
Was caught by the current and went down without
    trace
And the water couldn't hardly be colder.
Then the shingle roof froze in the light o' the
    moon
As both soldier and ice drifted down to their
    doom —
And d'you know what his comrades done told her?

He went out like a light. And the sunshine took
    flight
For his courage just made 'em feel colder.
Oh, do not despise the advice of the wise!
That's what the girl told the soldier.

THE GENERAL: The things they get up to in my kitchen these days.

EILIF (*Has gone into the kitchen. He flings his arms round his mother.*): Fancy seeing you again, ma! Where's the others?

MOTHER COURAGE (*in his arms*): Snug as a bug in a rug. They made Swiss Cheese paymaster of the Second Finnish; any road he'll stay out of fighting that way, I couldn't keep him out altogether.

EILIF: How's the old feet?

MOTHER COURAGE: Bit tricky getting me shoes on of a morning.

THE GENERAL (*has joined them*): So you're his mother, I hope you've got plenty more sons for me like this one.

EILIF: Ain't it my lucky day? You sitting out there in the kitchen, ma, hearing your son commended . . .

MOTHER COURAGE: You bet I heard. (*Slaps his face.*)

EILIF (*holding his cheek*): What's that for? Taking the oxen?

MOTHER COURAGE: No. Not surrendering when those four went for you and wanted to make mincemeat of you. Didn't I say you should look after yourself? You Finnish devil!

(*The general and the chaplain stand in the doorway laughing.*)

SCENE 3

(*Three years later Mother Courage is taken prisoner along with elements of a Finnish regiment. She manages to save her daughter, likewise her covered cart, but her honest son is killed.*)
(*Military camp.*)

(*Afternoon. A flagpole with the regimental pay. From her cart, festooned now with all kinds of goods, Mother Courage has stretched a washing line to a large cannon, across which she and Kattrin are folding the washing. She is bargaining at the same time with an armourer over a sack of shot. Swiss Cheese, now wearing a paymaster's uniform, is looking on. A comely person, Yvette Pottier, is sewing a gaily coloured hat, a glass of brandy before her. She is in her stockinged feet, having laid aside her red high-heeled boots.*)

THE ARMOURER: I'll let you have that shot for a couple of florins. It's cheap at the price, I got to have the money because the colonel's been boozing with his officers since two days back, and the drink's run out.

MOTHER COURAGE: That's troops' munitions. They catch me with that, I'm for court-martial. You crooks flog the shot, and troops got nowt to fire at enemy.

THE ARMOURER: Have a heart, can't you; you scratch my back and I'll scratch yours.

MOTHER COURAGE: I'm not taking army property. Not at that price.

THE ARMOURER: You can sell it on the q.t. tonight to the Fourth Regiment's armourer for five florins, eight even, if you let him have a receipt for twelve. He's right out of ammunition.

MOTHER COURAGE: Why not you do it?

THE ARMOURER: I don't trust him, he's a pal of mine.

MOTHER COURAGE (*takes the sack*): Gimme. (*To Kattrin.*) Take it away and pay him a florin and a half. (*The armourer protests.*) I said a florin and a half. (*Kattrin drags the sack upstage, the armourer following her. Mother Courage addresses Swiss Cheese.*) Here's your woollies, now look after them, it's October and autumn may set in any time. I ain't saying it's got to, cause I've learned nowt's got to come when you think it will, not even seasons of the year. But your regimental accounts got to add up right, come what may. Do they add up right?

SWISS CHEESE: Yes, mother.

MOTHER COURAGE: Don't you forget they made you paymaster cause you was honest, not dashing like your brother, and above all so stupid I bet you ain't even thought of clearing off with it, no not you. That's a big consolation to me. And don't lose those woollies.

SWISS CHEESE: No, mother, I'll put them under my mattress. (*Begins to go.*)

THE ARMOURER: I'll go along with you, paymaster.

MOTHER COURAGE: And don't you start learning him none of your tricks.

(*The armourer leaves with Swiss Cheese without any farewell gesture.*)

YVETTE (*waving to him*): No reason not to say goodbye, armourer.

MOTHER COURAGE (*to Yvette*): I don't like to see them together. He's wrong company for our Swiss Cheese. Oh well, war's off to a good start. Easily take four, five years before all countries are in. A bit of fore-sight, don't do nothing silly, and business'll flourish. Don't you know you ain't s'posed to drink before midday with your complaint?

YVETTE: Complaint, who says so, it's a libel.

MOTHER COURAGE: They all say so.

YVETTE: Because they're all telling lies, Mother Courage, and me at my wits' end cause they're all avoiding me like something the cat brought in thanks to those lies, what the hell am I remodelling my hat for? (*She throws it away.*) That's why I drink before midday. Never used to, gives you crows' feet, but now what the hell? All the Second Finnish know me. Ought to have stayed at home when my first fellow did me wrong. No good our sort being proud. Eat shit, that's what you got to do, or down you go.

MOTHER COURAGE: Now don't you start up again about that Pieter of yours and how it all happened, in front of my innocent daughter too.

YVETTE: She's the one should hear it, put her off love.

MOTHER COURAGE: Nobody can put 'em off that.

YVETTE: Then I'll go on, get it off my chest. It all starts with yours truly growing up in lovely Flanders, else I'd never of seen him and wouldn't be stuck here now in Poland, cause he was an army cook, fair-haired, a Dutchman but thin for once. Kattrin, watch out for the thin ones, only in those days I didn't know that, or that he'd got a girl already, or that they all called him Puffing Piet cause he never took his pipe out of his mouth when he was on the job, it meant that little to him. (*She sings the Song of Fraternisation.*)

When I was only sixteen
The foe came into our land.
He laid aside his sabre
And with a smile he took my hand.
After the May parade
The May light starts to fade.
The regiment dressed by the right
The drums were beaten, that's the drill.
The foe took us behind the hill
And fraternised all night.

There were so many foes then
But mine worked in the mess.
I loathed him in the daytime.
At night I loved him none the less.
After the May parade
The May light starts to fade.
The regiment dressed by the right
The drums were beaten, that's the drill.
The foe took us behind the hill
And fraternised all night.

The love which came upon me
Was wished on me by fate.
My friends could never grasp why
I found it hard to share their hate.
The fields were wet with dew
When sorrow first I knew.

The regiment dressed by the right
The drums were beaten, that's the drill.
And then the foe, my lover still
Went marching out of sight.

I followed him, fool that I was, but I never found him, and that was five years back. (*She walks unsteadily behind the cart.*)

MOTHER COURAGE: You left your hat here.

YVETTE: Anyone wants it can have it.

MOTHER COURAGE: Let that be a lesson, Kattrin. Don't you start anything with them soldiers. Love makes the world go round, I'm warning you. Even with fellows not in the army it's no bed of roses. He says he'd like to kiss the ground your feet walk on — reminds me, did you wash them yesterday? — and after that you're his skivvy. Be thankful you're dumb, then you can't contradict yourself and won't be wanting to bite your tongue off for speaking the truth; it's a godsend, being dumb is. And here comes the general's cook, now what's he after?

(*Enter the cook and the chaplain.*)

THE CHAPLAIN: I have a message for you from your son Eilif, and the cook has come along because you made such a profound impression on him.

THE COOK: I just came along to get a bit of air.

MOTHER COURAGE: That you can always do here if you behave yourself, and if you don't I can deal with you. What does he want? I got no spare cash.

THE CHAPLAIN: Actually I had a message for his brother the paymaster.

MOTHER COURAGE: He ain't here now nor anywhere else neither. He ain't his brother's paymaster. He's not to lead him into temptation nor be clever at his expense. (*Giving him money from the purse slung round her.*) Give him this, it's a sin, he's banking on mother's love and ought to be ashamed of himself.

THE COOK: Not for long, he'll have to be moving off with the regiment, might be to his death. Give him a bit extra, you'll be sorry later. You women are tough, then later on you're sorry. A little glass of brandy wouldn't have been a problem, but it wasn't offered and, who knows, a bloke may lie beneath the green sod and none of you people will ever be able to dig him up again.

THE CHAPLAIN: Don't give way to your feelings, cook. To fall in battle is a blessing, not an inconvenience, and why? It is a war of faith. None of your common wars but a special one, fought for the faith and therefore pleasing to God.

THE COOK: Very true. It's a war all right in one sense, what with requisitioning, murder and looting and the odd bit of rape thrown in, but different from all the other wars because it's a war of faith; stands to reason. But it's thirsty work at that, you must admit.

THE CHAPLAIN (*to Mother Courage, indicating the cook*): I tried to stop him, but he says he's taken a shine to you, you figure in his dreams.

THE COOK (*lighting a stumpy pipe*): Just want a glass of brandy from a fair hand, what harm in that? Only I'm groggy already cause the chaplain here's been telling such jokes all the way along you bet I'm still blushing.

MOTHER COURAGE: Him a clergyman too. I'd best give the pair of you a drink or you'll start making me immoral suggestions cause you've nowt else to do.

THE CHAPLAIN: Behold a temptation, said the court preacher, and fell. (*Turning back to look at Kattrin as he leaves.*) And who is this entrancing young person?

MOTHER COURAGE: That ain't an entrancing but a decent young person. (*The chaplain and the cook go behind the cart with Mother Courage. Kattrin looks after them, then walks away from her washing towards the hat. She picks it up and sits down, pulling the red boots towards her. Mother Courage can be heard in the background talking politics with the chaplain and the cook.*)

MOTHER COURAGE: Those Poles here in Poland had no business sticking their noses in. Right, our king moved in on them, horse and foot, but did they keep the peace? no, went and stuck their noses into their own affairs, they did, and fell on king just as he was quietly clearing off. They committed a breach of peace, that's what, so blood's on their own head.

THE CHAPLAIN: All our king minded about was freedom. The emperor had made slaves of them all, Poles and Germans alike, and the king had to liberate them.

THE COOK: Just what I say, your brandy's first rate, I weren't mistaken in your face, but talk of the king, it cost the king dear trying to give freedom to Germany, what with giving Sweden the salt tax, what cost the poor folk a bit, so I've heard, on top of which he had to have the Germans locked up and drawn and quartered cause they wanted to carry on slaving for the emperor. Course the king took a serious view when anybody didn't want to be free. He set out by just trying to protect Poland against bad people, particularly the emperor, then it started to become a habit till he ended up protecting the whole of Germany. They didn't half kick. So the poor old king's had nowt but trouble for all his kindness and expenses, and that's something he had to make up for by taxes of course, which caused bad blood, not that he'd let a little matter like that depress him. One thing he had on his side, God's word, that was a help. Because otherwise folk would of been saying he done it all for himself and to make a bit on the side. So he's always had a good conscience, which was the main point.

MOTHER COURAGE: Anyone can see you're no Swede or you wouldn't be talking that way about the Hero King.

THE CHAPLAIN: After all he provides the bread you eat.

THE COOK: I don't eat it, I bake it.

MOTHER COURAGE: They'll never beat him, and why, his men got faith in him. (*Seriously.*) To go by what the big shots say, they're waging war for almighty God and in the name of everything that's good and lovely. But look closer, they ain't so silly, they're waging it for what they can get. Else little folk like me wouldn't be in it at all.

THE COOK: That's the way it is.

THE CHAPLAIN: As a Dutchman you'd do better to glance at the flag above your head before venting your opinions here in Poland.

MOTHER COURAGE: All good Lutherans here. Prosit!°

(*Kattrin has put on Yvette's hat and begun strutting around in imitation of her way of walking.*)

(*Suddenly there is a noise of cannon fire and shooting. Drums. Mother Courage, the cook and the chaplain rush out from behind the cart, the two last-named still carrying their glasses. The armourer and another soldier run up to the cannon and try to push it away.*)

MOTHER COURAGE: What's happening? Wait till I've taken my washing down, you louts! (*She tries to rescue her washing.*)

THE ARMOURER: The Catholics! Broken through. Don't know if we'll get out of here. (*To the soldier.*) Get that gun shifted! (*Runs on.*)

THE COOK: God, I must find the general. Courage, I'll drop by in a day or two for another talk.

MOTHER COURAGE: Wait, you forgot your pipe.

THE COOK (*in the distance*): Keep it for me. I'll be needing it.

MOTHER COURAGE: Would happen just as we're making a bit of money.

THE CHAPLAIN: Ah well, I'll be going too. Indeed, if the enemy is so close as that it might be dangerous. Blessèd are the peacemakers is the motto in wartime. If only I had a cloak to cover me.

MOTHER COURAGE: I ain't lending no cloaks, not on your life. I been had too often.

THE CHAPLAIN: But my faith makes it particularly dangerous for me.

MOTHER COURAGE (*gets him a cloak*): Goes against my conscience, this does. Now you run along.

THE CHAPLAIN: Thank you, dear lady, that's very generous of you, but I think it might be wiser for me to remain seated here; it could arouse suspicion and bring the enemy down on me if I were seen to run.

MOTHER COURAGE (*to the soldier*): Leave it, you fool, who's going to pay you for that? I'll look after it for you, you're risking your neck.

THE SOLDIER (*running away*): You can tell 'em I tried.

MOTHER COURAGE: Cross my heart. (*Sees her daughter with the hat.*) What you doing with that strumpet's hat? Take that lid off, you gone crazy? And the enemy arriving any minute! (*Pulls the hat off Kattrin's head.*) Want 'em to pick you up and make a prostitute of you? And she's gone and put those boots on, whore of Babylon! Off with those boots! (*Tries to tug them off her.*) Jesus Christ, chaplain, gimme a hand, get those boots off her, I'll be right back. (*Runs to the cart.*)

Prosit!: Cheers!

YVETTE (*arrives, powdering her face*): Fancy that, the Catholics are coming. Where's my hat? Who's been kicking it around? I can't go about looking like this if the Catholics are coming. What'll they think of me? No mirror either. (*To the chaplain.*) How do I look? Too much powder?

THE CHAPLAIN: Exactly right.

YVETTE: And where are them red boots? (*Fails to find them as Kattrin hides her feet under her skirt.*) I left them here all right. Now I'll have to get to me tent barefoot. It's an outrage.

(*Exit.*)

(*Swiss Cheese runs in carrying in a small box.*)

MOTHER COURAGE (*Arrives with her hands full of ashes. To Kattrin.*): Here some ashes. (*To Swiss Cheese.*) What's that you're carrying?

SWISS CHEESE: Regimental cash box.

MOTHER COURAGE: Chuck it away. No more paymastering for you.

SWISS CHEESE: I'm responsible. (*He goes to the rear.*)

MOTHER COURAGE (*to the chaplain*): Take your clerical togs off, padre, or they'll spot you under that cloak. (*She rubs Kattrin's face with ash.*) Keep still, will you? There you are, a bit of muck and you'll be safe. What a disaster. Sentries were drunk. Hide your light under a bushel, it says. Take a soldier, specially a Catholic one, add a clean face, and there's your instant whore. For weeks they get nowt to eat, then soon as they manage to get it by looting they're falling on anything in skirts. That ought to do. Let's have a look. Not bad. Looks like you been grubbing in muckheap. Stop trembling. Nothing'll happen to you like that. (*To Swiss Cheese.*) Where d'you leave cash box?

SWISS CHEESE: Thought I'd put it in cart.

MOTHER COURAGE (*horrified*): What, my cart? Sheer criminal idiocy. Only take me eyes off you one instant. Hang us all three, they will.

SWISS CHEESE: I'll put it somewhere else then, or clear out with it.

MOTHER COURAGE: You sit on it, it's too late now.

THE CHAPLAIN (*who is changing his clothes downstage*): For heaven's sake, the flag!

MOTHER COURAGE (*hauls down the regimental flag*): Bozhe moi! I'd given up noticing it were there. Twenty-five years I've had it.

(*The thunder of cannon intensifies.*)

(*A morning three days later. The cannon has gone. Mother Courage, Kattrin, the chaplain and Swiss Cheese are sitting gloomily over a meal.*)

SWISS CHEESE: That's three days I been sitting around with nowt to do, and sergeant's always been kind to me but any moment now he'll start asking where's Swiss Cheese with the pay box?

MOTHER COURAGE: You thank your stars they ain't after you.

THE CHAPLAIN: What can I say? I can't even hold a service here, it might make trouble for me. Whosoever hath a full heart, his tongue runneth over, it says, but heaven help me if mine starts running over.

MOTHER COURAGE: That's how it goes. Here they sit, one with his faith and the other with his cash box. Dunno which is more dangerous.

THE CHAPLAIN: We are all of us in God's hands.

MOTHER COURAGE: Oh, I don't think it's as bad as that yet, though I must say I can't sleep nights. If it weren't for you, Swiss Cheese, things'd be easier. I think I got meself cleared. I told 'em I didn't hold with Antichrist, the Swedish one with horns on, and I'd observed left horn was a bit unserviceable. Half way through their interrogation I asked where I could get church candles not too dear. I knows the lingo cause Swiss Cheese's dad were Catholic, often used to make jokes about it, he did. They didn't believe me all that much, but they ain't got no regimental canteen lady. So they're winking an eye. Could turn out for the best, you know. We're prisoners, but same like fleas on dog.

THE CHAPLAIN: That's good milk. But we'll need to cut down our Swedish appetites a bit. After all, we've been defeated.

MOTHER COURAGE: Who's been defeated? Look, victory and defeat ain't bound to be same for the big shots up top as for them below, not by no means. Can be times the bottom lot find a defeat really pays them. Honour's lost, nowt else. I remember once up in Livonia our general took such a beating from enemy I got a horse off our baggage train in the confusion, pulled me cart seven months, he did, before we won and they checked up. As a rule you can say victory and defeat both come expensive to us ordinary folk. Best thing for us is when politics get bogged down solid. (*To Swiss Cheese.*) Eat up.

SWISS CHEESE: Got no appetite for it. What's sergeant to do when pay day comes round?

MOTHER COURAGE: They don't have pay days on a retreat.

SWISS CHEESE: It's their right, though. They needn't retreat if they don't get paid. Needn't stir a foot.

MOTHER COURAGE: Swiss Cheese, you're that conscientious it makes me quite nervous. I brought you up to be honest, you not being clever, but you got to know where to stop. Chaplain and me, we're off now to buy Catholic flag and some meat. Dunno anyone so good at sniffing meat, like sleepwalking it is, straight to target. I'd say he can pick out a good piece by the way his mouth starts watering. Well, thank goodness they're letting me go on trading. You don't ask tradespeople their faith but their prices. And Lutheran trousers keep cold out too.

THE CHAPLAIN: What did the mendicant say when he heard the Lutherans were going to turn everything in town and country topsy-turvy? "They'll always need beggars." (*Mother Courage disappears into the cart.*) So she's still worried about the cash box. So far they've taken us all for granted as part of the cart, but how long for?

SWISS CHEESE: I can get rid of it.

THE CHAPLAIN: That's almost more dangerous. Suppose you're seen. They have spies. Yesterday a fellow popped up out of the ditch in front of me just as I was relieving myself first thing. I was so scared I only just suppressed an ejaculatory prayer. That would have given me away all right. I think what they'd like best is to go sniffing people's excrement to see if they're Protestants. The spy was a little runt with a patch over one eye.

MOTHER COURAGE (*clambering out of the cart with a basket*): What have I found, you shameless creature? (*She holds up the red boots in triumph.*) Yvette's red high-heeled boots! Coolly went and pinched them, she did. Cause you put it in her head she was an enchanting young person. (*She lays them in the basket.*) I'm giving them back. Stealing Yvette's boots! She's wrecking herself for money. That's understandable. But you'd do it for nothing, for pleasure. What did I tell you: you're to wait till it's peace. No soldiers for you. You're not to start exhibiting yourself till it's peacetime.

THE CHAPLAIN: I don't find she exhibits herself.

MOTHER COURAGE: Too much for my liking. Let her be like a stone in Dalecarlia, where there's nowt else, so folk say "Can't see that cripple," that's how I'd lief have her. Then nowt'll happen to her. (*To Swiss Cheese.*) You leave that box where it is, d'you hear? And keep an eye on your sister, she needs it. The pair of you'll have me in grave yet. Sooner be minding a bagful of fleas.

(*She leaves with the chaplain. Kattrin clears away the dishes.*)

SWISS CHEESE: Won't be able to sit out in the sun in shirtsleeves much longer. (*Kattrin points at a tree.*) Aye, leaves turning yellow. (*Kattrin asks by gestures if he wants a drink.*) Don't want no drink. I'm thinking. (*Pause.*) Said she can't sleep. Best if I got rid of that box, found a good place for it. All right, let's have a glass. (*Kattrin goes behind the cart.*) I'll stuff it down the rat-hole by the river for the time being. Probably pick it up tonight before first light and take it to Regiment. How far can they have retreated in three days? Bet sergeant's surprised. I'm agreeably disappointed in you, Swiss Cheese, he'll say. I make you responsible for the cash, and you go and bring it back.

(*As Kattrin emerges from behind the cart with a full glass in her hand, two men confront her. One is a sergeant, the other doffs his hat to her. He has a patch over one eye.*)

THE MAN WITH THE PATCH: God be with you, mistress. Have you seen anyone round here from Second Finnish Regimental Headquarters?

(*Kattrin, badly frightened, runs downstage, spilling the brandy. The two men look at one another, then withdraw on seeing Swiss Cheese sitting there.*)

SWISS CHEESE (*interrupted in his thoughts*): You spilt half of it. What are those faces for? Jabbed yourself in eye? I don't get it. And I'll have to be off, I've thought it over, it's the only way. (*He gets up. She does everything possible to make him realise the danger. He only shrugs her off.*) Wish I knew what you're trying to say. Sure you mean well, poor creature, just can't get words out. What's it matter your spilling my brandy, I'll drink plenty more glasses yet, what's one more or less? (*He gets the box from the cart and takes it under his tunic.*) Be back in a moment. Don't hold me up now, or I'll be angry. I know you mean well. Too bad you can't speak.

(*As she tries to hold him back he kisses her and tears himself away. Exit. She is desperate, running hither and thither uttering little noises. The chaplain and Mother Courage return. Kattrin rushes to her mother.*)

MOTHER COURAGE: What's all this? Pull yourself together, love. They done something to you? Where's Swiss Cheese? Tell it me step by step, Kattrin. Mother understands you. What, so that bastard did take the box? I'll wrap it round his ears, the little hypocrite. Take your time and don't gabble, use your hands, I don't like it when you howl like a dog, what'll his reverence say? Makes him uncomfortable. What, a one-eyed man came along?

THE CHAPLAIN: That one-eyed man is a spy. Have they arrested Swiss Cheese? (*Kattrin shakes her head, shrugs her shoulders.*) We're done for.

MOTHER COURAGE (*fishes in her basket and brings out a Catholic flag, which the chaplain fixes to the mast*): Better hoist new flag.

THE CHAPLAIN (*bitterly*): All good Catholics here.

(*Voices are heard from the rear. The two men bring in Swiss Cheese.*)

SWISS CHEESE: Let me go, I got nowt. Don't twist my shoulder, I'm innocent.

SERGEANT: Here's where he came from. You know each other.

MOTHER COURAGE: Us? How?

SWISS CHEESE: I don't know her. Got no idea who she is, had nowt to do with them. I bought me dinner here, ten hellers it cost. You might have seen me sitting here, it was too salty.

SERGEANT: Who are you people, eh?

MOTHER COURAGE: We're law-abiding folk. That's right, he bought a dinner. Said it was too salty.

SERGEANT: Trying to pretend you don't know each other, that it?

MOTHER COURAGE: Why should I know him? Can't know everyone. I don't go asking 'em what they're called and are they a heretic; if he pays he ain't a heretic. You a heretic?

SWISS CHEESE: Go on.

THE CHAPLAIN: He sat there very properly, never opening his mouth except when eating. Then he had to.

SERGEANT: And who are you?

MOTHER COURAGE: He's just my potboy. Now I expect you gentlemen are thirsty, I'll get you a glass of brandy, you must be hot and tired with running.

SERGEANT: No brandy on duty. (*To Swiss Cheese.*) You were carrying something. Must have hidden it by the river. Was a bulge in your tunic when you left here.

MOTHER COURAGE: You sure it was him?

SWISS CHEESE: You must be thinking of someone else. I saw someone bounding off with a bulge in his tunic. I'm the wrong man.

MOTHER COURAGE: I'd say it was a misunderstanding too, such things happen. I'm a good judge of people, I'm Courage, you heard of me, everyone knows me, and I tell you that's an honest face he has.

SERGEANT: We're on the track of the Second Finnish Regiment's cash box. We got the description of the fellow responsible for it. Been trailing him two days. It's you.

SWISS CHEESE: It's not me.

SERGEANT: And you better cough it up, or you're a goner, you know. Where is it?

MOTHER COURAGE (*urgently*): Of course he'd give it over rather than be a goner. Right out he'd say: I got it, here it is, you're too strong. He ain't all that stupid. Speak up, stupid idiot, here's the sergeant giving you a chance.

SWISS CHEESE: S'pose I ain't got it.

SERGEANT: Then come along. We'll get it out of you. (*They lead him off.*)

MOTHER COURAGE (*calls after them*): He'd tell you. He's not that stupid. And don't you twist his shoulder! (*Runs after them.*)

(*Evening of the same day. The chaplain and dumb Kattrin are cleaning glasses and polishing knives.*)

THE CHAPLAIN: Cases like that, where somebody gets caught, are not unknown in religious history. It reminds me of the Passion of Our Lord and Saviour. There's an old song about that. (*He sings the Song of the Hours.°*)

In the first hour Jesus mild
Who had prayed since even
Was betrayed and led before
Pontius the heathen.

Pilate found him innocent
Free from fault and error
Therefore, having washed his hands
Sent him to King Herod.

In the third hour he was scourged
Stripped and clad in scarlet
And a plaited crown of thorns
Set upon his forehead.

Song of the Hours: Translated by Ralph Manheim.

On the Son of Man they spat
Mocked him and made merry.
Then the cross of death was brought
Given him to carry.

At the sixth hour with two thieves
To the cross they nailed him
And the people and the thieves
Mocked him and reviled him.

This is Jesus King of Jews
Cried they in derision
Till the sun withdrew its light
From that awful vision.

At the ninth hour Jesus wailed
Why hast thou me forsaken?
Soldiers brought him vinegar
Which he left untaken.

Then he yielded up the ghost
And the earth was shaken.
Rended was the temple's veil
And the saints were wakened.

Soldiers broke the two thieves' legs
As the night descended.
Thrust a spear in Jesus' side
When his life had ended.

Still they mocked, as from his wound
Flowed the blood and water
And blasphemed the Son of Man
With their cruel laughter.

MOTHER COURAGE (*entering excitedly*): It's touch and go. They say sergeant's open to reason though. Only we mustn't let on it's Swiss Cheese else they'll say we helped him. It's a matter of money, that's all. But where's money to come from? Hasn't Yvette been round? I ran into her, she's got her hooks on some colonel, maybe he'd buy her a canteen business.

THE CHAPLAIN: Do you really wish to sell?

MOTHER COURAGE: Where's money for sergeant to come from?

THE CHAPLAIN: What'll you live on, then?

MOTHER COURAGE: That's just it.

(*Yvette Pottier arrives with an extremely ancient colonel.*)

YVETTE (*embracing Mother Courage*): My dear Courage, fancy seeing you so soon. (*Whispers.*) He's not unwilling. (*Aloud.*) This is my good friend who advises me in business matters. I happened to hear you wanted to sell your cart on account of circumstances. I'll think it over.

MOTHER COURAGE: Pledge it, not sell, just not too much hurry, tain't every day you find a cart like this in wartime.

YVETTE (*disappointed*): Oh, pledge. I thought it was for sale. I'm not so sure I'm interested. (*To the colonel.*) How do you feel about it?

THE COLONEL: Just as you feel, pet.

MOTHER COURAGE: I'm only pledging it.

YVETTE: I thought you'd got to have the money.

MOTHER COURAGE (*firmly*): I got to have it, but sooner run myself ragged looking for a bidder than sell outright. And why? The cart's our livelihood. It's a chance for you, Yvette; who knows when you'll get another like it and have a special friend to advise you, am I right?

YVETTE: Yes, my friend thinks I should clinch it, but I'm not sure. If it's only a pledge . . . so you agree we ought to buy outright?

THE COLONEL: I agree, pet.

MOTHER COURAGE: Best look and see if you can find anything for sale then; maybe you will if you don't rush it, take your friend along with you, say a week or fortnight, might find something suits you.

YVETTE: Then let's go looking. I adore going around looking for things, I adore going around with you, Poldi, it's such fun, isn't it? No matter if it takes a fortnight. How soon would you pay the money back if you got it?

MOTHER COURAGE: I'd pay back in two weeks, maybe one.

YVETTE: I can't make up my mind, Poldi chéri, you advise me. (*Takes the colonel aside.*) She's got to sell, I know, no problem there. And there's that ensign, you know, the fair-haired one, he'd be glad to lend me the money. He's crazy about me, says there's someone I remind him of. What do you advise?

THE COLONEL: You steer clear of him. He's no good. He's only making use of you. I said I'd buy you something, didn't I, pussykins?

YVETTE: I oughtn't to let you. Of course if you think the ensign might try to take advantage . . . Poldi, I'll accept it from you.

THE COLONEL: That's how I feel too.

YVETTE: Is that your advice?

THE COLONEL: That is my advice.

YVETTE (*to Courage once more*): My friend's advice would be to accept. Make me out a receipt saying the cart's mine once two weeks are up, with all its contents, we'll check it now, I'll bring the two hundred florins later. (*To the colonel.*) You go back to the camp, I'll follow, I got to check it all and see there's nothing missing from my cart. (*She kisses him. He leaves. She climbs up on the cart.*) Not all that many boots, are there?

MOTHER COURAGE: Yvette, it's no time for checking your cart, s'posing it is yours. You promised you'd talk to sergeant about Swiss Cheese, there ain't a minute to lose, they say in an hour he'll be court-martialled.

YVETTE: Just let me count the shirts.

MOTHER COURAGE (*pulling her down by the skirt*): You bloody vampire. Swiss Cheese's life's at stake. And not a word about who's making the offer, for God's sake, pretend it's your friend, else we're all done for cause we looked after him.

YVETTE: I fixed to meet that one-eyed fellow in the copse, he should be there by now.

THE CHAPLAIN: It doesn't have to be the whole two hundred either, I'd go up to a hundred and fifty, that may be enough.

MOTHER COURAGE: Since when has it been your money? You kindly keep out of this. You'll get your hotpot all right, don't worry. Hurry up and don't haggle, it's life or death. (*Pushes Yvette off.*)

THE CHAPLAIN: Far be it from me to interfere, but what are we going to live on? You're saddled with a daughter who can't earn her keep.

MOTHER COURAGE: I'm counting on regimental cash box, Mr. Clever. They'll allow it as his expenses.

THE CHAPLAIN: But will she get the message right?

MOTHER COURAGE: It's her interest I should spend her two hundred so she gets the cart. She's set on that, God knows how long that colonel of hers'll last. Kattrin, polish the knives, there's the pumice. And you, stop hanging round like Jesus on Mount of Olives,° get moving, wash them glasses, we'll have fifty or more of cavalry in tonight and I don't want to hear a lot of "I'm not accustomed to having to run about, oh my poor feet, we never ran in church." Thank the Lord they're corruptible. After all, they ain't wolves, just humans out for money. Corruption in humans is same as compassion in God. Corruption's our only hope. Long as we have it there'll be lenient sentences and even an innocent man'll have a chance of being let off.

YVETTE (*comes in panting*): They'll do it for two hundred. But it's got to be quick. Soon be out of their hands. Best thing is I go right away to my colonel with the one-eyed man. He's admitted he had the box, they put the thumbscrews on him. But he chucked it in the river soon as he saw they were on his track. The box is a write-off. I'll go and get the money from my colonel, shall I?

MOTHER COURAGE: Box is a write-off? How'm I to pay back two hundred then?

YVETTE: Oh, you thought you'd get it from the box, did you? And I was to be Joe Soap I suppose? Better not count on that. You'll have to pay up if you want Swiss Cheese back, or would you sooner I dropped the whole thing so's you can keep your cart?

MOTHER COURAGE: That's something I didn't allow for. Don't worry, you'll get your cart, I've said goodbye to it, had it seventeen years, I have. I just need a moment to think, it's bit sudden, what'm I to do, two hundred's too much for me, pity you didn't beat 'em down. Must keep a bit back, else any Tom, Dick and Harry'll be able to shove me in ditch. Go and tell

Jesus on Mount of Olives: The Bible shows Jesus on the Mount of Olives when he preaches the Sermon on the Mount and when he prays in anguish before his betrayal by Peter.

them I'll pay hundred and twenty florins, else it's all off, either way I'm losing me cart.

YVETTE: They won't do it. That one-eyed man's impatient already, keeps looking over his shoulder, he's so worked up. Hadn't I best pay them the whole two hundred?

MOTHER COURAGE (*in despair*): I can't pay that. Thirty years I been working. She's twenty-five already, and no husband. I got her to think of too. Don't push me, I know what I'm doing. Say a hundred and twenty, or it's off.

YVETTE: It's up to you. (*Rushes off.*)

(*Without looking at either the chaplain or her daughter, Mother Courage sits down to help Kattrin polish knives.*)

MOTHER COURAGE: Don't smash them glasses, they ain't ours now. Watch what you're doing, you'll cut yourself. Swiss Cheese'll be back, I'll pay two hundred if it comes to the pinch. You'll get your brother, love. For eighty florins we could fill a pack with goods and start again. Plenty of folk has to make do.

THE CHAPLAIN: The Lord will provide, it says.

MOTHER COURAGE: See they're properly dry. (*She cleans knives in silence. Kattrin suddenly runs behind the cart, sobbing.*)

YVETTE (*comes running in*): They won't do it. I told you so. The one-eyed man wanted to leave right away, said there was no point. He says he's just waiting for the drum-roll; that means sentence has been pronounced. I offered a hundred and fifty. He didn't even blink. I had to convince him to stay there so's I could have another word with you.

MOTHER COURAGE: Tell him I'll pay the two hundred. Hurry! (*Yvette runs off. They sit in silence. The chaplain has stopped polishing the glasses.*) I reckon I bargained too long.

(*In the distance drumming is heard. The chaplain gets up and goes to the rear. Mother Courage remains seated. It grows dark. The drumming stops. It grows light once more. Mother Courage is sitting exactly as before.*)

YVETTE (*arrives, very pale*): Well, you got what you asked for, with your haggling and trying to keep your cart. Eleven bullets they gave him, that's all. You don't deserve I should bother any more about you. But I did hear they don't believe the box really is in the river. They've an idea it's here and anyhow that you're connected with him. They're going to bring him here, see if you gives yourself away when you sees him. Thought I'd better warn you so's you don't recognise him, else you'll all be for it. They're right on my heels, best tell you quick. Shall I keep Kattrin away? (*Mother Courage shakes her head.*) Does she know? She mayn't have heard the drumming or know what it meant.

MOTHER COURAGE: She knows. Get her.

(*Yvette fetches Kattrin, who goes to her mother and stands beside her. Mother Courage takes her hand. Two lansequenets come carrying a stretcher with something lying on it covered by a sheet. The sergeant marches beside them. They set down the stretcher.*)

SERGEANT: Here's somebody we dunno the name of. It's got to be listed, though, so everything's shipshape. He had a meal here. Have a look, see if you know him. (*He removes the sheet.*) Know him? (*Mother Courage shakes her head.*) What, never see him before he had that meal here? (*Mother Courage shakes her head.*) Pick him up. Chuck him in the pit. He's got nobody knows him. (*They carry him away.*)

SCENE 4

(*Mother Courage sings the Song of the Grand Capitulation.*)
(*Outside an officer's tent.*)
(*Mother Courage is waiting. A clerk looks out of the tent.*)

THE CLERK: I know you. You had a paymaster from the Lutherans with you, what was in hiding. I'd not complain if I were you.

MOTHER COURAGE: But I got a complaint to make. I'm innocent, would look as how I'd a bad conscience if I let this pass. Slashed everything in me cart to pieces with their sabres, they did, then wanted I should pay five taler fine for nowt, I tell you, nowt.

CLERK: Take my tip, better shut up. We're short of canteens, so we let you go on trading, specially if you got a bad conscience and pay a fine now and then.

MOTHER COURAGE: I got a complaint.

CLERK: Have it your own way. Then you must wait till the captain's free. (*Withdraws inside the tent.*)

YOUNG SOLDIER (*enters aggressively*): Bouque la Madonne! Where's that bleeding pig of a captain what's took my reward money to swig with his tarts? I'll do him.

OLDER SOLDIER (*running after him*): Shut up. They'll put you in irons.

YOUNG SOLDIER: Out of there, you thief! I'll slice you into pork chops, I will. Pocketing my prize money after I'd swum the river, only one in the whole squadron, and now I can't even buy meself a beer. I'm not standing for that. Come on out there so I can cut you up!

OLDER SOLDIER: Blessed Mother of God, he's asking for trouble.

MOTHER COURAGE: Is it some reward he weren't paid?

YOUNG SOLDIER: Lemme go, I'll slash you too while I'm at it.

OLDER SOLDIER: He rescued the colonel's horse and got no reward for it. He's young yet, still wet behind the ears.

MOTHER COURAGE: Let him go, he ain't a dog you got to chain up. Wanting your reward is good sound sense. Why be a hero otherwise?

YOUNG SOLDIER: So's he can sit in there and booze.

You're shit-scared, the lot of you. I done something special and I want my reward.

MOTHER COURAGE: Don't you shout at me, young fellow. Got me own worries, I have; any road you should spare your voice, be needing it when captain comes, else there he'll be and you too hoarse to make a sound, which'll make it hard for him to clap you in irons till you turn blue. People what shouts like that can't keep it up ever; half an hour, and they have to be rocked to sleep, they're so tired.

YOUNG SOLDIER: I ain't tired and to hell with sleep. I'm hungry. They make our bread from acorns and hemp-seed, and they even skimp on that. He's whoring away my reward and I'm hungry. I'll do him.

MOTHER COURAGE: Oh I see, you're hungry. Last year that general of yours ordered you all off roads and across fields so corn should be trampled flat; I could've got ten florins for a pair of boots s'pose I'd had boots and s'pose anyone'd been able to pay ten florins. Thought he'd be well away from that area this year, he did, but here he is, still there, and hunger is great. I see what you're angry about.

YOUNG SOLDIER: I won't have it, don't talk to me, it ain't fair and I'm not standing for that.

MOTHER COURAGE: And you're right; but how long? How long you not standing for unfairness? One hour, two hours? Didn't ask yourself that, did you, but it's the whole point, and why, once you're in irons it's too bad if you suddenly finds you can put up with unfairness after all.

YOUNG SOLDIER: What am I listening to you for, I'd like to know? Bouque la Madonne, where's that captain?

MOTHER COURAGE: You been listening to me because you knows it's like what I say, your anger has gone up in smoke already, it was just a short one and you needed a long one, but where you going to get it from?

YOUNG SOLDIER: Are you trying to tell me asking for my reward is wrong?

MOTHER COURAGE: Not a bit. I'm just telling you your anger ain't long enough, it's good for nowt, pity. If you'd a long one I'd be trying to prod you on. Cut him up, the swine, would be my advice to you in that case; but how about if you don't cut him up cause you feels your tail going between your legs? Then I'd look silly and captain'd take it out on me.

OLDER SOLDIER: You're perfectly right, he's just a bit crazy.

YOUNG SOLDIER: Very well, let's see if I don't cut him up. (*Draws his sword.*) When he arrives I'm going to cut him up.

CLERK (*looks out*): The captain'll be here in one minute. Sit down.

(*The young soldier sits down.*)

MOTHER COURAGE: He's sitting now. See, what did I say? You're sitting now. Ah, how well they know us, no one need tell 'em how to go about it. Sit down! and, bingo, we're sitting. And sitting and sedition don't mix. Don't try to stand up, you won't stand the way you was standing before. I shouldn't worry about what I think; I'm no better, not one moment. Bought up all our fighting spirit, they have. Eh? S'pose I kick back, might be bad for business. Let me tell you a thing or two about the Grand Capitulation. (*She sings the Song of the Grand Capitulation.*)

Back when I was young, I was brought to realise
What a very special person I must be
(Not just any old cottager's daughter, what with my
        looks and my talents and my urge towards
        Higher Things)
And insisted that my soup should have no hairs in it.
No one makes a sucker out of me!
(All or nothing, only the best is good enough, each
        man for himself, nobody's telling *me* what to do.)
Then I heard a tit
Chirp: Wait a bit!
        And you'll be marching with the band
        In step, responding to command
        And striking up your little dance:
        Now we advance.
        And now: parade, form square!
        Then men swear God's there —
        Not the faintest chance!

In no time at all anyone who looked could see
That I'd learned to take my medicine with good
        grace.
(Two kids on my hands and look at the price of
        bread, and things they expect of you!)
When they finally came to feel that they were
        through with me
They'd got me grovelling on my face.
(Takes all sorts to make a world, you scratch my
        back and I'll scratch yours, no good banging
        your head against a brick wall.)
Then I heard that tit
Chirp: Wait a bit!
        And you'll be marching with the band
        In step, responding to command
        And striking up your little dance:
        Now they advance.
        And now: parade, form square!
        Then men swear God's there —
        Not the faintest chance!

I've known people tried to storm the summits:
There's no star too bright or seems too far away.
(Dogged does it, where there's a will there's a way,
        by hook or by crook.)
As each peak disclosed fresh peaks to come, it's
Strange how much a plain straw hat could weigh.
(You have to cut your coat according to your cloth.)
Then I hear the tit
Chirp: Wait a bit!
        And they'll be marching with the band
        In step, responding to command

And striking up their little dance:
Now they advance.
And now: parade, form square!
Then men swear God's there —
Not the faintest chance!

MOTHER COURAGE (*to the young soldier*): That's why I reckon you should stay there with your sword drawn if you're truly set on it and your anger's big enough, because you got grounds, I agree, but if your anger's a short one best leave right away.

YOUNG SOLDIER: Oh stuff it. (*He staggers off with the older soldier following.*)

CLERK (*sticks his head out*): Captain's here now. You can make your complaint.

MOTHER COURAGE: I changed me mind. I ain't complaining.

(*Exit.*)

SCENE 5

(*Two years have gone by. The war is spreading to new areas. Ceaselessly on the move, Courage's little cart crosses Poland, Moravia, Bavaria, Italy then Bavaria again. 1631. Tilly's victory at Magdeburg costs Mother Courage four officers' shirts.*)

(*Mother Courage's cart has stopped in a badly shot-up village. Thin military music in the distance. Two soldiers at the bar being served by Kattrin and Mother Courage. One of them has a lady's fur coat over his shoulders.*)

MOTHER COURAGE: Can't pay, that it? No money, no schnapps. They give us victory parades, but catch them giving men their pay.

SOLDIER: I want my schnapps. I missed the looting. That double-crossing general only allowed an hour's looting in the town. He ain't an inhuman monster, he said. Town must of paid him.

THE CHAPLAIN (*stumbles in*): There are people still lying in that yard. The peasant's family. Somebody give me a hand. I need linen.

(*The second soldier goes off with him. Kattrin becomes very excited and tries to make her mother produce linen.*)

MOTHER COURAGE: I got none. All my bandages was sold to regiment. I ain't tearing up my officer's shirts for that lot.

CHAPLAIN (*calling back*): I need linen, I tell you.

MOTHER COURAGE (*blocking Kattrin's way into the cart by sitting on the step*): I'm giving nowt. They'll never pay, and why, nowt to pay with.

CHAPLAIN (*bending over a woman he has carried in*): Why d'you stay around during the gunfire?

PEASANT WOMAN (*feebly*): Farm.

MOTHER COURAGE: Catch them abandoning anything. But now I'm s'posed to foot the bill. I won't do it.

FIRST SOLDIER: Those are Protestants. What they have to be Protestants for?

MOTHER COURAGE: They ain't bothering about faith. They lost their farm.

SECOND SOLDIER: They're no Protestants. They're Catholics like us.

FIRST SOLDIER: No way of sorting 'em out in a bombardment.

A PEASANT (*brought in by the chaplain*): My arm's gone.

THE CHAPLAIN: Where's that linen?

MOTHER COURAGE: I can't give nowt. What with expenses, taxes, loan interest and bribes. (*Making guttural noises, Kattrin raises a plank and threatens her mother with it.*) You gone plain crazy? Put that plank away or I'll paste you one, you cow. I'm giving nowt, don't want to, got to think of meself. (*The chaplain lifts her off the steps and sets her on the ground, then starts pulling out shirts and tearing them into strips.*) My officers' shirts! Half a florin apiece! I'm ruined. (*From the house comes the cry of a child in pain.*)

THE PEASANT: The baby's in there still. (*Kattrin dashes in.*)

THE CHAPLAIN (*to the woman*): Don't move. They'll get it out.

MOTHER COURAGE: Stop her, roof may fall in.

THE CHAPLAIN: I'm not going back in there.

MOTHER COURAGE (*torn both ways*): Don't waste my precious linen.

(*Kattrin brings a baby out of the ruins.*)

MOTHER COURAGE: How nice, found another baby to cart around? Give it to its ma this instant, unless you'd have me fighting for hours to get it off you, like last time, d'you hear? (*To the second soldier.*) Don't stand there gawping, you go back and tell them cut out that music, we can see it's a victory with our own eyes. All your victories mean to me is losses.

THE CHAPLAIN (*tying a bandage*): Blood's coming through.

(*Kattrin is rocking the baby and making lullaby noises.*)

MOTHER COURAGE: Look at her, happy as a queen in all this misery; give it back at once, its mother's coming round. (*She catches the first soldier, who has been attacking the drinks and is trying to make off with one of the bottles.*) Psia krew! Thought you'd score another victory, you animal? Now pay.

FIRST SOLDIER: I got nowt.

MOTHER COURAGE (*pulling the fur coat off his back*): Then leave that coat, it's stolen any road.

THE CHAPLAIN: There's still someone under there.

SCENE 6

(*Outside the Bavarian town of Ingolstadt Courage participates in the funeral of the late Imperial commander Tilly. Discussions are held about war heroes and the war's duration. The chaplain complains that his talents are lying fallow, and dumb Kattrin gets the red boots. The year is 1632.*)

(*Inside a canteen tent.*)

(*It has a bar towards the rear. Rain. Sound of drums and Funeral music. The chaplain and the regimental clerk are playing a board game. Mother Courage and her daughter are stocktaking.*)

THE CHAPLAIN: Now the funeral procession will be moving off.

MOTHER COURAGE: Too bad about commander in chief — twenty-two pairs those socks — he fell by accident, they say. Mist over fields, that was the trouble. General had just been haranguing a regiment saying they must fight to last man and last round, he was riding back when mist made him lose direction so he was up front and a bullet got him in midst of battle — only four hurricane lamps left. (*A whistle from the rear. She goes to the bar.*) You scrimshankers, dodging your commander in chief's funeral, scandal I call it. (*Pours drinks.*)

THE CLERK: They should never of paid troops out before the funeral. Instead of going now they're all getting pissed.

THE CHAPLAIN (*to the clerk*): Aren't you supposed to go to the funeral?

THE CLERK: Dodged it cause of the rain.

MOTHER COURAGE: It's different with you, your uniform might get wet. I heard they wanted to toll bells for funeral as usual, except it turned out all churches had been blown to smithereens by his orders, so poor old commander in chief won't be hearing no bells as they let the coffin down. They're going to let off three salvoes instead to cheer things up — seventeen belts.

SHOUTS (*from the bar*): Hey, Missis, a brandy!

MOTHER COURAGE: Let's see your money. No, I ain't having you in my tent with your disgusting boots. You can drink outside, rain or no rain. (*To the clerk.*) I'm only letting in sergeants and up. Commander in chief had been having his worries, they say. S'posed to have been trouble with Second Regiment cause he stopped their pay, said it was a war of faith and they should do it for free. (*Funeral march. All look to the rear.*)

THE CHAPLAIN: Now they'll be filing past the noble corpse.

MOTHER COURAGE: Can't help feeling sorry for those generals and emperors, there they are maybe thinking they're doing something extra special what folk'll talk about in years to come, and earning a public monument, like conquering the world for instance, that's a fine ambition for a general, how's he to know any better? I mean, he plagues hisself to death, then it all breaks down on account of ordinary folk what just wants their beer and bit of a chat, nowt higher. Finest plans get bolloxed up by the pettiness of them as should be carrying them out, because emperors can't do nowt themselves, they just counts on soldiers and people to back 'em up whatever happens, am I right?

THE CHAPLAIN (*laughs*): Courage, you're right, aside

from the soldiers. They do their best. Give me that lot outside there, for instance, drinking their brandy in the rain, and I'd guarantee to make you one war after another for a hundred years if need be, and I'm no trained general.

MOTHER COURAGE: You don't think war might end, then?

THE CHAPLAIN: What, because the commander in chief's gone? Don't be childish. They're two a penny, no shortage of heroes.

MOTHER COURAGE: Ee, I'm not asking for fun of it, but because I'm thinking whether to stock up, prices are low now, but if war's going to end it's money down the drain.

THE CHAPLAIN: I realise it's a serious question. There've always been people going round saying "the war can't go on for ever." I tell you there's nothing to stop it going on for ever. Of course there can be a bit of a breathing space. The war may need to get its second wind, it may even have an accident so to speak. There's no guarantee against that; nothing's perfect on this earth of ours. A perfect war, the sort you might say couldn't be improved on, that's something we shall probably never see. It can suddenly come to a standstill for some quite unforeseen reason, you can't allow for everything. A slight case of negligence, and it's bogged down up to the axles. And then it's a matter of hauling the war out of the mud again. But emperor and kings and popes will come to its rescue. So on the whole it has nothing serious to worry about, and will live to a ripe old age.

A SOLDIER (sings at the bar):

> A schnapps, landlord, you're late!
> A soldier cannot wait
> To do his emperor's orders.

Make it a double, this is a holiday.

MOTHER COURAGE: S'pose I went by what you say . . .

THE CHAPLAIN: Think it out for yourself. What's to compete with the war?

THE SOLDIER (at the rear):

> Your breast, my girl, you're late!
> A soldier cannot wait
> To ride across the borders.

THE CLERK (unexpectedly): And what about peace? I'm from Bohemia and I'd like to go home some day.

THE CHAPLAIN: Would you indeed? Ah, peace. Where is the hole once the cheese has been eaten?

THE SOLDIER (at the rear):

> Lead trumps, my friend, you're late!
> A soldier cannot wait.
> His emperor needs him badly.

> Your blessing, priest, you're late!
> A soldier cannot wait.
> Must lay his life down gladly.

THE CLERK: In the long run lifes impossible if there's no peace.

THE CHAPLAIN: I'd say there's peace in war too; it has its peaceful moments. Because war satisfies all requirements, peaceable ones included, they're catered for, and it would simply fizzle out if they weren't. In war you can do a crap like in the depths of peacetime, then between one battle and the next you can have a beer, then even when you're moving up you can lay your head on your arms and have a bit of shuteye in the ditch, it's entirely possible. During a charge you can't play cards maybe, but nor can you in the depths of peacetime when you're ploughing, and after a victory there are various openings. You may get a leg blown off, then you start by making a lot of fuss as though it were serious, but afterwards you calm down or get given a schnapps, and you end up hopping around and the war's no worse off than before. And what's to stop you being fruitful and multiplying in the middle of all the butchery, behind a barn or something, in the long run you can't be held back from it, and then the war will have your progeny and can use them to carry on with. No, the war will always find an outlet, mark my words. Why should it ever stop?

(Kattrin has ceased working and is staring at the chaplain.)

MOTHER COURAGE: I'll buy fresh stock then. If you say so. (Kattrin suddenly flings a basket full of bottles to the ground and runs off.) Kattrin! (Laughs.) Damn me if she weren't waiting for peace. I promised her she'd get a husband soon as peace came. (Hurries after her.)

THE CLERK (standing up): I won. You been talking too much. Pay up.

MOTHER COURAGE (returning with Kattrin): Don't be silly, war'll go on a bit longer, and we'll make a bit more money, and peacetime'll be all the nicer for it. Now you go into town, that's ten minutes' walk at most, fetch things from Golden Lion, the expensive ones, we can fetch rest in cart later, it's all arranged, regimental clerk here will go with you. Nearly everybody's attending commander in chief's funeral, nowt can happen to you. Careful now, don't let them steal nowt, think of your dowry.

(Kattrin puts a cloth over her head and leaves with the clerk.)

THE CHAPLAIN: Is that all right to let her go with the clerk?

MOTHER COURAGE: She's not that pretty they'd want to ruin her.

THE CHAPLAIN: I admire the way you run your business and always win through. I see why they called you Courage.

MOTHER COURAGE: Poor folk got to have courage. Why, they're lost. Simply getting up in morning takes some doing in their situation. Or ploughing a field, and in a war at that. Mere fact they bring kids into world shows they got courage, cause there's no hope for them. They have to hang one another and slaughter one another, so just looking each other in face must call for courage. Being able to put up with emperor and pope shows supernatural courage, cause those two cost 'em their lives. (*She sits down, takes a little pipe from her purse and smokes.*) You might chop us a bit of kindling.

THE CHAPLAIN (*reluctantly removing his coat and preparing to chop up sticks*): I happen to be a pastor of souls, not a woodcutter.

MOTHER COURAGE: I got no soul, you see. Need firewood, though.

THE CHAPLAIN: Where's that stumpy pipe from?

MOTHER COURAGE: Just a pipe.

THE CHAPLAIN: What d'you mean, "just," it's a quite particular pipe, that.

MOTHER COURAGE: Aha?

THE CHAPLAIN: That stumpy pipe belongs to the Oxenstierna Regiment's cook.

MOTHER COURAGE: If you know that already why ask, Mr. Clever?

THE CHAPLAIN: Because I didn't know if you were aware what you're smoking. You might just have been rummaging around in your things, come across some old pipe or other, and used it out of sheer absence of mind.

MOTHER COURAGE: And why not?

THE CHAPLAIN: Because you didn't. You're smoking that deliberately.

MOTHER COURAGE: And why shouldn't I?

THE CHAPLAIN: Courage, I'm warning you. It's my duty. Probably you'll never clap eyes on the gentleman again, and that's no loss but your good fortune. He didn't make at all a reliable impression on me. Quite the opposite.

MOTHER COURAGE: Really? Nice fellow that.

THE CHAPLAIN: So he's what you would call a nice fellow? I wouldn't. Far be it from me to bear him the least ill-will, but nice is not what I would call him. More like one of those Don Juans, a slippery one. Have a look at that pipe if you don't believe me. You must admit it tells you a good deal about his character.

MOTHER COURAGE: Nowt that I can see. Worn out, I'd call it.

THE CHAPLAIN: Practically bitten through, you mean. A man of wrath. That is the pipe of an unscrupulous man of wrath; you must see that if you have any discrimination left.

MOTHER COURAGE: Don't chop my chopping block in two.

THE CHAPLAIN: I told you I'm not a woodcutter by trade. I studied to be a pastor of souls. My talent and abilities are being abused in this place, by manual labour. My God-given endowments are denied expression. It's a sin. You have never heard me preach. One sermon of mine can put a regiment in such a frame of mind it'll treat the enemy like a flock of sheep. Life to them is a smelly old foot cloth which they fling away in a vision of final victory. God has given me the gift of speech. I can preach so you'll lose all sense of sight and hearing.

MOTHER COURAGE: I don't wish to lose my sense of sight and hearing. Where'd that leave me?

THE CHAPLAIN: Courage, I have often thought that your dry way of talking conceals more than just a warm heart. You too are human and need warmth.

MOTHER COURAGE: Best way for us to get this tent warm is have plenty of firewood.

THE CHAPLAIN: Don't change the subject. Seriously, Courage, I sometimes ask myself what it would be like if our relationship were to become somewhat closer. I mean, given that the whirlwind of war has so strangely whirled us together.

MOTHER COURAGE: I'd say it was close enough. I cook meals for you and you run around and chop firewood for instance.

THE CHAPLAIN (*coming closer*): You know what I mean by closer; it's not a relationship founded on meals and wood-chopping and other such base necessities. Let your head speak, harden thyself not.

MOTHER COURAGE: Don't you come at me with that axe. That'd be too close a relationship.

THE CHAPLAIN: You shouldn't make a joke of it. I'm a serious person and I've thought about what I'm saying.

MOTHER COURAGE: Be sensible, padre. I like you. I don't want to row you. All I'm after is get myself and children through all this with my cart. I don't see it as mine, and I ain't in the mood for private affairs. Right now I'm taking a gamble, buying stores just when commander in chief's fallen and all the talk's of peace. Where d'you reckon you'd turn if I'm ruined? Don't know, do you? You chop us some kindling wood, then we can keep warm at night, that's quite something these times. What's this? (*She gets up. Enter Kattrin, out of breath, with a wound above her eye. She is carrying a variety of stuff: parcels, leather goods, a drum and so on.*)

MOTHER COURAGE: What happened, someone assault you? On way back? She was assaulted on her way back. Bet it was that trooper was getting drunk here. I shouldn't have let you go, love. Drop that stuff. Not too bad, just a flesh wound you got. I'll bandage it and in a week it'll be all right. Worse than wild beasts, they are. (*She ties up the wound.*)

THE CHAPLAIN: It's not them I blame. They never went raping back home. The fault lies with those that start wars, it brings humanity's lowest instincts to the surface.

MOTHER COURAGE: Calm down. Didn't clerk come back with you? That's because you're respectable, they don't bother. Wound ain't a deep one, won't leave no mark. There you are, all bandaged up. You'll get something, love, keep calm. Something I put aside for you, wait till you see. (*She delves into a*

sack and brings out Yvette's red high-heeled boots.)
Made you open your eyes, eh? Something you always
wanted. They're yours. Put 'em on quick, before I
change me mind. Won't leave no mark, and what if it
does? Ones I'm really sorry for's the ones they fancy.
Drag them around till they're worn out, they do.
Those they don't care for they leaves alive. I seen girls
before now had pretty faces, then in no time looking
fit to frighten a hyaena. Can't even go behind a bush
without risking trouble, horrible life they lead. Same
like with trees, straight well-shaped ones get chopped
down to make beams for houses and crooked ones
live happily ever after. So it's a stroke of luck for you
really. Them boots'll be all right, I greased them
before putting them away.

(*Kattrin leaves the boots where they are and crawls into
the cart.*)

THE CHAPLAIN: Let's hope she's not disfigured.
MOTHER COURAGE: She'll have a scar. No use her waiting for peacetime now.
THE CHAPLAIN: She didn't let them steal the things.
MOTHER COURAGE: Maybe I shouldn't have dinned that
into her so. Wish I knew what went on in that head
of hers. Just once she stayed out all night, once in all
those years. Afterwards she went around like before,
except she worked harder. Couldn't get her to tell
what had happened. Worried me quite a while, that
did. (*She collects the articles brought by Kattrin, and
sorts them angrily.*) That's war for you. Nice way to
get a living!

(*Sound of cannon fire.*)

THE CHAPLAIN: Now they'll be burying the commander
in chief. This is a historic moment.
MOTHER COURAGE: What I call a historic moment is
them bashing my daughter over the eye. She's half
wrecked already, won't get no husband now, and her
so crazy about kids; anyway, she's only dumb from
war, soldier stuffed something in her mouth when she
was little. As for Swiss Cheese I'll never see him again,
and where Eilif is God alone knows. War be damned.

SCENE 7

(*Mother Courage at the peak of her business career.*)
(*High road.*)
(*The chaplain, Mother Courage, and Kattrin are pulling
the cart, which is hung with new wares. Mother
Courage is wearing a necklace of silver coins.*)

MOTHER COURAGE: I won't have you folk spoiling my
war for me. I'm told it kills off the weak, but they're
write-off in peacetime too. And war gives its people a
better deal. (*She sings.*)

> And if you feel your forces fading
> You won't be there to share the fruits.

> But what is war but private trading
> That deals in blood instead of boots?

And what's the use of settling down? Them as does
are first to go. (*Sings.*)

> Some people think to live by looting
> The goods some others haven't got.
> You think it's just a line they're shooting
> Until you hear they have been shot.

> And some I saw dig six feet under
> In haste to lie down and pass out.
> Now they're at rest perhaps they wonder
> Just what was all their haste about.

(*They pull it further.*)

SCENE 8

(*The same year sees the death of the Swedish king Gus-
tavus Adolphus at the battle of Lützen. Peace threatens
to ruin Mother Courage's business. Courage's dashing
son performs one heroic deed too many and comes to a
sticky end.*)
(*Camp.*)
(*A summer morning. In front of the cart stand an old
woman and her son. The son carries a large sack of bedding.*)

MOTHER COURAGE'S VOICE (*from inside the cart*): Does
it need to be this ungodly hour?
THE YOUNG MAN: We walked twenty miles in the night
and got to be back today.
MOTHER COURAGE'S VOICE: What am I to do with bedding? Folk've got no houses.
THE YOUNG MAN: Best have a look first.
THE OLD WOMAN: This place is no good either. Come on.
THE YOUNG MAN: What, and have them sell the roof
over our head for taxes? She might pay three florins if
you throw in the bracelet. (*Bells start ringing.*) Listen,
mother.
VOICES (*from the rear*): Peace! Swedish king's been killed.
MOTHER COURAGE (*Sticks her head out of the cart. She
has not yet done her hair.*): What's that bell-ringing
about in mid-week?
THE CHAPLAIN (*crawling out from under the cart*):
What are they shouting? Peace?
MOTHER COURAGE: Don't tell me peace has broken out
just after I laid in new stock.
THE CHAPLAIN (*calling to the rear*): That true? Peace?
VOICES: Three weeks ago, they say, only no one told us.
THE CHAPLAIN (*to Courage*): What else would they be
ringing the bells for?
VOICES: A whole lot of Lutherans have driven into
town, they brought the news.
THE YOUNG MAN: Mother, it's peace. What's the matter?

(*The old woman has collapsed.*)

MOTHER COURAGE (*speaking into the cart*): Holy cow! Kattrin, peace! Put your black dress on, we're going to church. Least we can do for Swiss Cheese. Is it true, though?

THE YOUNG MAN: The people here say so. They've made peace. Can you get up? (*The old woman stands up dumbfounded.*) I'll get the saddlery going again. I promise. It'll all work out. Father will get his bedding back. Can you walk? (*To the chaplain.*) She came over queer. It's the news. She never thought there'd be peace again. Father always said so. We're going straight home. (*They go off.*)

MOTHER COURAGE'S VOICE: Give her a schnapps.

THE CHAPLAIN: They've already gone.

MOTHER COURAGE'S VOICE: What's up in camp?

THE CHAPLAIN: They're assembling. I'll go on over. Shouldn't I put on my clerical garb?

MOTHER COURAGE'S VOICE: Best check up before parading yourself as heretic. I'm glad about peace, never mind if I'm ruined. Any road I'll have got two of me children through the war. Be seeing Eilif again now.

THE CHAPLAIN: And who's that walking down the lines? Bless me, the army commander's cook.

THE COOK (*somewhat bedraggled and carrying a bundle*): What do I behold? The padre!

THE CHAPLAIN: Courage, we've got company.

(*Mother Courage clambers out.*)

THE COOK: I promised I'd drop over for a little talk soon as I had the time. I've not forgotten your brandy, Mrs. Fierling.

MOTHER COURAGE: Good grief, the general's cook! After all these years! Where's my eldest boy Eilif?

THE COOK: Hasn't he got here? He left before me, he was on his way to see you too.

THE CHAPLAIN: I shall don my clerical garb, just a moment.

(*Goes off behind the cart.*)

MOTHER COURAGE: Then he may be here any minute. (*Calls into the cart.*) Kattrin, Eilif's on his way. Get cook a glass of brandy, Kattrin! (*Kattrin does not appear.*) Drag your hair down over it, that's all right. Mr. Lamb's no stranger. (*Fetches the brandy herself.*) She don't like to come out, peace means nowt to her. Took too long coming, it did. They gave her a crack over one eye, you barely notice it now but she thinks folks are staring at her.

THE COOK: Ah yes. War. (*He and Mother Courage sit down.*)

MOTHER COURAGE: Cooky, you caught me at bad moment. I'm ruined.

THE COOK: What? That's hard.

MOTHER COURAGE: Peace'll wring my neck. I went and took chaplain's advice, laid in fresh stocks only t'other day. And now they're going to demobilise and I'll be left sitting on me wares.

THE COOK: What'd you want to go and listen to padre for? If I hadn't been in such a hurry that time, the Catholics arriving so quickly and all, I'd warned you against that man. All piss and wind, he is. So he's the authority around here, eh?

MOTHER COURAGE: He's been doing washing-up for me and helping pull.

THE COOK: Him pull! I bet he told you some of those jokes of his too, I know him, got a very unhealthy view of women, he has, all my good influence on him went for nowt. He ain't steady.

MOTHER COURAGE: You steady then?

THE COOK: Whatever else I ain't, I'm steady. Mud in your eye!

MOTHER COURAGE: Steady, that's nowt. I only had one steady fellow, thank God. Hardest I ever had to work in me life; he flogged the kids' blankets soon as autumn came, and he called me mouth-organ an unchristian instrument. Ask me, you ain't saying much for yourself admitting you're steady.

THE COOK: Still tough as nails, I see; but that's what I like about you.

MOTHER COURAGE: Now don't tell me you been dreaming of me nails.

THE COOK: Well, well, here we are, along with armistice bells and your brandy like what nobody else ever serves, it's famous, that is.

MOTHER COURAGE: I don't give two pins for your armistice bells just now. Can't see 'em handing out all the back pay what's owing, so where does that leave me with my famous brandy? Had your pay yet?

THE COOK (*hesitantly*): Not exactly. That's why we all shoved off. If that's how it is, I thought, I'll go and visit friends. So here I am sitting with you.

MOTHER COURAGE: Other words you got nowt.

THE COOK: High time they stopped that bloody clanging. Wouldn't mind getting into some sort of trade. I'm fed up being cook to that lot. I'm s'posed to rustle them up meals out of tree roots and old bootsoles, then they fling the hot soup in my face. Cook these days is a dog's life. Sooner do war service, only of course it's peacetime now. (*He sees the chaplain reappearing in his old garments.*) More about that later.

THE CHAPLAIN: It's still all right, only had a few moths in it.

THE COOK: Can't see why you bother. You won't get your old job back, who are you to inspire now to earn his pay honourably and lay down his life? What's more I got a bone to pick with you, cause you advised this lady to buy a lot of unnecessary goods saying war would go on for ever.

THE CHAPLAIN (*heatedly*): I'd like to know what concern that is of yours.

THE COOK: Because it's unscrupulous, that sort of thing is. How dare you meddle in other folks' business arrangements with your unwanted advice?

THE CHAPLAIN: Who's meddling? (*To Courage.*) I never knew this gentleman was such an intimate you had to account to him for everything.

MOTHER COURAGE: Keep your hair on, cook's only giving his personal opinion and you can't deny your war was a flop.

THE CHAPLAIN: You should not blaspheme against peace, Courage. You are a hyaena of the battlefield.

MOTHER COURAGE: I'm what?

THE COOK: If you're going to insult this lady you'll have to settle with me.

THE CHAPLAIN: It's not you I'm talking to. Your intentions are only too transparent. (*To Courage.*) But when I see you picking up peace betwixt your finger and your thumb like some dirty old snot-rag, then my humanity feels outraged; for then I see that you don't want peace but war, because you profit from it; in which case you shouldn't forget the ancient saying that whosoever sups with the devil needs a long spoon.

MOTHER COURAGE: I got no use for war, and war ain't got much use for me. But I'm not being called no hyaena, you and me's through.

THE CHAPLAIN: Then why grumble about peace when everybody's breathing sighs of relief? Because of some old junk in your cart?

MOTHER COURAGE: My goods ain't old junk but what I lives by, and you too up to now.

THE CHAPLAIN: Off war, in other words. Aha.

THE COOK (*to the chaplain*): You're old enough to know it's always a mistake offering advice. (*To Courage.*) Way things are, your best bet's to get rid of certain goods quick as you can before prices hit rock-bottom. Dress yourself and get moving, not a moment to lose.

MOTHER COURAGE: That ain't bad advice. I'll do that, I guess.

THE CHAPLAIN: Because cooky says it.

MOTHER COURAGE: Why couldn't you say it? He's right, I'd best go off to market. (*Goes inside the cart.*)

THE COOK: That's one to me, padre. You got no presence of mind. What you should of said was: what, me offer advice, all I done was discuss politics. Better not take me on. Cockfighting don't suit that get-up.

THE CHAPLAIN: If you don't stop your gob I'll murder you, get-up or no get-up.

THE COOK (*pulling off his boots and unwrapping his footcloths*): Pity the war made such a godless shit of you, else you'd easily get another parsonage now it's peacetime. Cooks won't be needed, there's nowt to cook, but faith goes on just the same, nowt changed in that direction.

THE CHAPLAIN: Mr. Lamb, I'm asking you not to elbow me out. Since I came down in the world I've become a better person. I couldn't preach to anyone now.

(*Enter Yvette Pottier in black, dressed up to the nines, carrying a cane. She is much older and fatter, and heavily powdered. She is followed by a manservant.*)

YVETTE: Hullo there, everybody. Is this Mother Courage's establishment?

THE CHAPLAIN: It is. And with whom have we the honour . . . ?

YVETTE: With the Countess Starhemberg, my good man. Where's Courage?

THE CHAPLAIN (*calls into the cart*): The Countess Starhemberg wishes to speak to you.

MOTHER COURAGE'S VOICE: Just coming.

YVETTE: It's Yvette.

MOTHER COURAGE'S VOICE: Oh, Yvette!

YVETTE: Come to see how you are. (*Sees the cook turn round aghast.*) Pieter!

THE COOK: Yvette!

YVETTE: Well I never! How d'you come to be here?

THE COOK: Got a lift.

THE CHAPLAIN: You know each other then? Intimately?

YVETTE: I should think so. (*She looks the cook over.*) Fat.

THE COOK: Not all that skinny yourself.

YVETTE: All the same I'm glad to see you, you shit. Gives me a chance to say what I think of you.

THE CHAPLAIN: You say it, in full; but don't start till Courage is out here.

MOTHER COURAGE (*coming out with all kinds of goods*): Yvette! (*They embrace.*) But what are you in mourning for?

YVETTE: Suits me, don't it? My husband the colonel died a few years back.

MOTHER COURAGE: That old fellow what nearly bought the cart?

YVETTE: His elder brother.

MOTHER COURAGE: Then you're sitting pretty. Nice to find somebody what's made it in this war.

YVETTE: Up and down and up again, that's the way it went.

MOTHER COURAGE: I'm not hearing a word against colonels, they make a mint of money.

THE CHAPLAIN: I would put my boots back on if I were you. (*To Yvette.*) You promised you would say what you think of the gentleman.

THE COOK: Don't kick up a stink here, Yvette.

MOTHER COURAGE: Yvette, this is a friend of mine.

YVETTE: That's old Puffing Piet.

THE COOK: Let's drop the nicknames. I'm called Lamb.

MOTHER COURAGE (*laughs*): Puffing Piet! Him as made all the women crazy! Here, I been looking after your pipe for you.

THE CHAPLAIN: Smoking it, too.

YVETTE: What luck I can warn you against him. Worst of the lot, he was, rampaging along the whole Flanders coastline. Got more girls in trouble than he has fingers.

THE COOK: That's all a long while ago. Tain't true anyhow.

YVETTE: Stand up when a lady brings you into the conversation! How I loved this man! All the time he had a little dark girl with bandy legs, got her in trouble too of course.

THE COOK: Got you into high society more like, far as I can see.

YVETTE: Shut your trap, you pathetic remnant! Better watch out for him, though; fellows like that are still dangerous even when on their last legs.

MOTHER COURAGE (*to Yvette*): Come along, got to get

rid of my stuff afore prices start dropping. You might be able to put a word in for me at regiment, with your connections. (*Calls into the cart.*) Kattrin, church is off, I'm going to market instead. When Eilif turns up, one of you give him a drink. (*Exit with Yvette.*)

YVETTE (*as she leaves*): Fancy a creature like that ever making me leave the straight and narrow path. Thank my lucky stars I managed to reach the top all the same. But I've cooked your goose, Puffing Piet, and that's something that'll be credited to me one day in the world to come.

THE CHAPLAIN: I would like to take as a text for our little talk "The mills of God grind slowly." Weren't you complaining about my jokes?

THE COOK: Dead out of luck, I am. It's like this, you see: I thought I might get a hot meal. Here am I starving, and now they'll be talking about me and she'll get quite a wrong picture. I think I'll clear out before she's back.

THE CHAPLAIN: I think so too.

THE COOK: Padre, I'm fed up already with this bloody peace. Human race has to go through fire and sword cause it's sinful from the cradle up. I wish I could be roasting a fat capon once again for the general, wherever he's got to, in mustard sauce with a carrot or two.

THE CHAPLAIN: Red cabbage. Red cabbage for a capon.

THE COOK: You're right, but carrots was what he had to have.

THE CHAPLAIN: No sense of what's fitting.

THE COOK: Not that it stopped you guzzling your share.

THE CHAPLAIN: With misgivings.

THE COOK: Anyway you must admit those were the days.

THE CHAPLAIN: I might admit it if pressed.

THE COOK: Now you've called her a hyaena your days here are finished. What you staring at?

THE CHAPLAIN: Eilif! (*Eilif arrives, followed by soldiers with pikes. His hands are fettered. His face is chalky-white.*) What's wrong?

EILIF: Where's mother?

THE CHAPLAIN: Gone into town.

EILIF: I heard she was around. They've allowed me to come and see her.

THE COOK (*to the soldiers*): What you doing with him?

A SOLDIER: Something not nice.

THE CHAPLAIN: What's he been up to?

THE SOLDIER: Broke into a peasant's place. The wife's dead.

THE CHAPLAIN: How could you do a thing like that?

EILIF: It's what I did last time, ain't it?

THE COOK: Aye, but it's peace now.

EILIF: Shut up. All right if I sit down till she comes?

THE SOLDIER: We've no time.

THE CHAPLAIN: In wartime they recommended him for that, sat him at the general's right hand. Dashing, it was, in those days. Any chance of a word with the provost-marshal?

THE SOLDIER: Wouldn't do no good. Taking some peasant's cattle, what's dashing about that?

THE COOK: Dumb, I call it.

EILIF: If I'd been dumb you'd of starved, clever bugger.

THE COOK: But as you were clever you're going to be shot.

THE CHAPLAIN: We'd better fetch Kattrin out anyhow.

EILIF: Sooner have a glass of schnapps, could do with that.

THE SOLDIER: No time, come along.

THE CHAPLAIN: And what shall we tell your mother?

EILIF: Tell her it wasn't any different, tell her it was the same thing. Or tell her nowt. (*The soldiers propel him away.*)

THE CHAPLAIN: I'll accompany you on your grievous journey.

EILIF: Don't need any bloody parsons.

THE CHAPLAIN: Wait and see. (*Follows him.*)

THE COOK (*calls after them*): I'll have to tell her, she'll want to see him.

THE CHAPLAIN: I wouldn't tell her anything. At most that he was here and will come again, maybe tomorrow. By then I'll be back and can break it to her. (*Hurries off.*)

(*The cook looks after him, shaking his head, then walks restlessly around. Finally he comes up to the cart.*)

THE COOK: Hoy! Don't you want to come out? I can understand you hiding away from peace. Like to do the same myself. Remember me, I'm general's cook? I was wondering if you'd a bit of something to eat while I wait for your mum. I don't half feel like a bit of pork, or bread even, just to fill the time. (*Peers inside.*) Head under blanket. (*Sound of gunfire off.*)

MOTHER COURAGE (*runs in, out of breath and with all her goods still*): Cooky, peacetime's over. War's been on again three days now. Heard news before selling me stuff, thank God. They're having a shooting match with Lutherans in town. We must get cart away at once. Kattrin, pack up! What you in the dumps for? What's wrong?

THE COOK: Nowt.

MOTHER COURAGE: Something is. I see it way you look.

THE COOK: Cause war's starting up again, I s'pose. Looks as if it'll be tomorrow night before I get next hot food inside me.

MOTHER COURAGE: You're lying, cooky.

THE COOK: Eilif was here. Had to leave almost at once, though.

MOTHER COURAGE: Was he now? Then we'll be seeing him on the march. I'm joining our side this time. How's he look?

THE COOK: Same as usual.

MOTHER COURAGE: Oh, he'll never change. Take more than war to steal him from me. Clever, he is. You going to help me get packed? (*Begins to pack up.*) What's his news? Still in general's good books? Say anything about his deeds of valour?

THE COOK (*glumly*): Repeated one of them, I'm told.

MOTHER COURAGE: Tell it me later, we got to move off. (*Kattrin appears.*) Kattrin, peacetime's finished now. We're moving on. (*To the cook.*) How about you?

THE COOK: Have to join up again.

MOTHER COURAGE: Why don't you . . . Where's padre?

THE COOK: Went into town with Eilif.

MOTHER COURAGE: Then you come along with us a way. Need somebody to help me.

THE COOK: That business with Yvette, you know . . .

MOTHER COURAGE: Done you no harm in my eyes. Opposite. Where there's smoke there's fire, they say. You coming along?

THE COOK: I won't say no.

MOTHER COURAGE: The Twelfth moved off already. Take the shaft. Here's a bit of bread. We must get round behind to Lutherans. Might even be seeing Eilif tonight. He's my favourite one. Short peace, wasn't it? Now we're off again. (*She sings as the cook and Kattrin harness themselves up.*)

> From Ulm to Metz, from Metz to Munich
> Courage will see the war gets fed.
> The war will show a well-filled tunic
> Given its daily shot of lead.
> But lead alone can hardly nourish
> It must have soldiers to subsist.
> It's you it needs to make it flourish.
> The war's still hungry. So enlist!

SCENE 9

(*It is the seventeenth year of the great war of faith. Germany has lost more than half her inhabitants. Those who survive the bloodbath are killed off by terrible epidemics. Once fertile areas are ravaged by famine, wolves roam the burnt-out towns. In autumn 1634 we find Courage in the Fichtelgebirge, off the main axis of the Swedish armies. The winter this year is early and harsh. Business is bad, so that there is nothing to do but beg. The cook gets a letter from Utrecht and is sent packing.*)
(*Outside a semi-dilapidated parsonage.*)
(*Grey morning in early winter. Gusts of wind. Mother Courage and the cook in shabby sheepskins, drawing the cart.*)

THE COOK: It's all dark, nobody up yet.

MOTHER COURAGE: Except it's parson's house. Have to crawl out of bed to ring bells. Then he'll have hot soup.

THE COOK: What from, when the whole village is burnt? We seen it.

MOTHER COURAGE: It's lived in, though, dog was barking.

THE COOK: S'pose parson's got, he'll give nowt.

MOTHER COURAGE: Maybe if we sing. . . .

THE COOK: I've had enough. (*Abruptly.*) Got a letter from Utrecht saying mother died of cholera and inn's mine. Here's letter if you don't believe me. No business of yours the way aunty goes on about my mode of existence, but have a look.

MOTHER COURAGE: (*Reads the letter.*) Lamb, I'm tired too of always being on the go. I feel like butcher's dog, dragging meat round customers and getting nowt off it. I got nowt left to sell, and folk got nowt left to buy nowt with. Saxony a fellow in rags tried landing me a stack of old books for two eggs, Württemberg they wanted to swap their plough for a titchy bag of salt. What's to plough for? Nowt growing no more, just brambles. In Pomerania villages are s'posed to have started in eating the younger kids, and nuns have been caught sticking folk up.

THE COOK: World's dying out.

MOTHER COURAGE: Sometimes I sees meself driving through hell with me cart selling brimstone, or across heaven with packed lunches for hungry souls. Give me my kids what's left, let's find some place they ain't shooting, and I'd like a few more years undisturbed.

THE COOK: You and me could get that inn going, Courage, think it over. Made up me mind in the night, I did: back to Utrecht with or without you, and starting today.

MOTHER COURAGE: Have to talk to Kattrin. That's a bit quick for me; I'm against making decisions all freezing cold and nowt inside you. Kattrin! (*Kattrin climbs out of the cart.*) Kattrin, got something to tell you. Cook and I want to go to Utrecht. He's been left an inn there. That'd be a settled place for you, let you meet a few people. Lots of 'em respect somebody mature, looks ain't everything. I'd like it too. I get on with cook. Say one thing for him, got a head for business. We'd have our meals for sure, not bad, eh? And your own bed too; like that, wouldn't you? Road's no life really. God knows how you might finish up. Lousy already, you are. Have to make up our minds, see, we could move with the Swedes, up north, they're somewhere up that way. (*She points to the left.*) Reckon that's fixed, Kattrin.

THE COOK: Anna, I got something private to say to you.

MOTHER COURAGE: Get back in cart, Kattrin.

(*Kattrin climbs back.*)

THE COOK: I had to interrupt, cause you don't understand, far as I can see. I didn't think there was need to say it, sticks out a mile. But if it don't, then let me tell you straight, no question of taking her along, not on your life. You get me, eh.

(*Kattrin sticks her head out of the cart behind them and listens.*)

MOTHER COURAGE: You mean I'm to leave Kattrin back here?

THE COOK: Use your imagination. Inn's got no room. It ain't one of the sort got three bar parlours. Put our backs in it we two'll get a living, but not three, no chance of that. She can keep cart.

MOTHER COURAGE: Thought she might find husband in Utrecht.

THE COOK: Go on, make me laugh. Find a husband, how? Dumb and that scar on top of it. And at her age?

MOTHER COURAGE: Don't talk so loud.

THE COOK: Loud or soft, no getting over facts. And that's another reason why I can't have her in the inn. Customers don't want to be looking at that all the time. Can't blame them.

MOTHER COURAGE: Shut your big mouth. I said not so loud.

THE COOK: Light's on in parson's house. We can try singing.

MOTHER COURAGE: Cooky, how's she to pull the cart on her own? War scares her. She'll never stand it. The dreams she must have . . . I hear her nights groaning. Mostly after a battle. What's she seeing in those dreams, I'd like to know. She's got a soft heart. Lately I found she'd got another hedgehog tucked away what we'd run over.

THE COOK: Inn's too small. (*Calls out.*) Ladies and gentlemen, domestic staff and other residents! We are now going to give you a song concerning Solomon, Julius Caesar and other famous personages what had bad luck. So's you can see we're respectable folk, which makes it difficult to carry on, particularly in winter. (*They sing.*)

> You saw sagacious Solomon
> You know what came of him.
> To him complexities seemed plain.
> He cursed the hour that gave birth to him
> And saw that everything was vain.
> How great and wise was Solomon!
> The world however didn't wait
> But soon observed what followed on.
> It's wisdom that had brought him to this state —
> How fortunate the man with none!

Yes, the virtues are dangerous stuff in this world, as this fine song proves, better not to have them and have a pleasant life and breakfast instead, hot soup for instance. Look at me: I haven't any but I'd like some. I'm a serving soldier but what good did my courage do me in all them battles, nowt, here I am starving and better have been shit-scared and stayed at home. For why?

> You saw courageous Caesar next
> You know what he became.
> They deified him in his life
> Then had him murdered just the same.
> And as they raised the fatal knife
> How loud he cried: You too, my son!
> The world however didn't wait
> But soon observed what followed on.
> It's courage that had brought him to that state.
> How fortunate the man with none!

(*Sotto voce.*) Don't even look out. (*Aloud.*) Ladies and gentlemen, domestic staff and other inmates! All right, you may say, gallantry never cooked a man's dinner, what about trying honesty? You can eat all you want then, or anyhow not stay sober. How about it?

> You heard of honest Socrates
> The man who never lied:
> They weren't so grateful as you'd think
> Instead the rulers fixed to have him tried
> And handed him the poisoned drink.
> How honest was the people's noble son!
> The world however didn't wait
> But soon observed what followed on.
> It's honesty that brought him to that state.
> How fortunate the man with none!

Ah yes, they say, be unselfish and share what you've got, but how about if you got nowt? It's all very well to say the do-gooders have a hard time, but you still got to have something. Aye, unselfishness is a rare virtue, cause it just don't pay.

> Saint Martin couldn't bear to see
> His fellows in distress.
> He met a poor man in the snow
> And shared his cloak with him, we know.
> Both of them therefore froze to death.
> His place in Heaven was surely won!
> The world however didn't wait
> But soon observed what followed on.
> Unselfishness had brought him to that state.
> How fortunate the man with none!

That's how it is with us. We're respectable folk, stick together, don't steal, don't murder, don't burn places down And all the time you might say we're sinking lower and lower, and it's true what the song says, and soup is few and far between, and if we weren't like this but thieves and murderers I dare say we'd be eating our fill. For virtues aren't their own reward, only wickednesses are, that's how the world goes and it didn't ought to.

> Here you can see respectable folk
> Keeping to God's own laws.
> So far he hasn't taken heed.
> You who sit safe and warm indoors
> Help to relieve our bitter need!
> How virtuously we had begun!
> The world however didn't wait
> But soon observed what followed on.
> It's fear of God that brought us to that state.
> How fortunate the man with none!

VOICE (*from above*): Hey, you there! Come on up! There's hot soup if you want.

MOTHER COURAGE: Lamb, me stomach won't stand nowt. 'Tain't that it ain't sensible, what you say, but is that your last word? We got on all right.

THE COOK: Last word. Think it over.

MOTHER COURAGE: I've nowt to think. I'm not leaving her here.

THE COOK: That's proper senseless, nothing I can do about it though. I'm not a brute, just the inn's a small one. So now we better get on up, or there'll be nowt here either and wasted time singing in the cold.

MOTHER COURAGE: I'll get Kattrin.

THE COOK: Better bring a bit back for her. Scare them if they sees three of us coming. (*Exeunt both.*)

(*Kattrin climbs out of the cart with a bundle. She looks around to see if the other two have gone. Then she takes an old pair of trousers of the cook's and a skirt of her mother's, and lays them side by side on one of the wheels, so that they are easily seen. She has finished and is picking up her bundle to go, when Mother Courage comes back from the house.*)

MOTHER COURAGE (*with a plate of soup*): Kattrin! Will you stop there? Kattrin! Where you off to with that bundle? Has devil himself taken you over? (*She examines the bundle.*) She's packed her things. You been listening? I told him nowt doing, Utrecht, his rotten inn, what'd we be up to there? You and me, inn's no place for us. Still plenty to be got out of war. (*She sees the trousers and the skirt.*) You're plain stupid. S'pose I'd seen that, and you gone away? (*She holds Kattrin back as she tries to break away.*) Don't you start thinking it's on your account I given him the push. It was cart, that's it. Catch me leaving my cart I'm used to, it ain't you, it's for cart. We'll go off in t'other direction, and we'll throw cook's stuff out so he finds it, silly man. (*She climbs in and throws out a few other articles in the direction of the trousers.*) There, he's out of our business now, and I ain't having nobody else in, ever. You and me'll carry on now. This winter will pass, same as all the others. Get hitched up, it looks like snow.

(*They both harness themselves to the cart, then wheel it round and drag it off. When the cook arrives he looks blankly at his kit.*)

SCENE 10

(*During the whole of 1635 Mother Courage and her daughter Kattrin travel over the highroads of central Germany, in the wake of the increasingly bedraggled armies.*)
(*High road.*)
(*Mother Courage and Kattrin are pulling the cart. They pass a peasant's house inside which there is a voice singing.*)

THE VOICE:

> The roses in our arbour
> Delight us with their show:
> They have such lovely flowers
> Repaying all our labour
> After the summer showers.
> Happy are those with gardens now:
> They have such lovely flowers.

> When winter winds are freezing
> As through the woods they blow
> Our home is warm and pleasing.
> We fixed the thatch above it
> With straw and moss we wove it.
> Happy are those with shelter now
> When winter winds are freezing.

(*Mother Courage and Kattrin pause to listen, then continue pulling.*)

SCENE 11

(*January 1636. The emperor's troops are threatening the Protestant town of Halle. The stone begins to speak. Mother Courage loses her daughter and trudges on alone. The war is a long way from being over.*)
(*The cart is standing, much the worse for wear, alongside a peasant's house with a huge thatched roof, backing on a wall of rock. It is night.*)
(*An ensign and three soldiers in heavy armour step out of the wood.*)

THE ENSIGN: I want no noise now. Anyone shouts, shove your pike into him.

FIRST SOLDIER: Have to knock them up, though, if we're to find a guide.

THE ENSIGN: Knocking sounds natural. Could be a cow bumping the stable wall.

(*The soldiers knock on the door of the house. The peasant's wife opens it. They stop her mouth. Two soldiers go in.*)

MAN'S VOICE (*within*): What is it?

(*The soldiers bring out the peasant and his son.*)

THE ENSIGN (*pointing at the cart, where Kattrin's head has appeared*): There's another one. (*A Soldier drags her out.*) Anyone else live here beside you lot?

THE PEASANTS: This is our son. And she's dumb. Her mother's gone into town to buy stuff. For their business, cause so many people's getting out and selling things cheap. They're just passing through. Canteen folk.

THE ENSIGN: I'm warning you, keep quiet, or if there's the least noise you get a pike across your nut. Now I want someone to come with us and show us the path to the town. (*Points to the young peasant.*) Here, you.

THE YOUNG PEASANT: I don't know no path.

SECOND SOLDIER (*grinning*): He don't know no path.

THE YOUNG PEASANT: I ain't helping Catholics.

THE ENSIGN (*to the second soldier*): Stick your pike in his ribs.

THE YOUNG PEASANT (*forced to his knees, with the pike threatening him*): I won't do it, not to save my life.

FIRST SOLDIER: I know what'll change his mind. (*Goes towards the stable.*) Two cows and an ox. Listen, you: if you're not reasonable I'll chop up your cattle.

THE YOUNG PEASANT: No, not that!

THE PEASANT'S WIFE (*weeps*): Please spare our cattle, captain, it'd be starving us to death.

THE ENSIGN: They're dead if he goes on being obstinate.

FIRST SOLDIER: I'm taking the ox first.

THE YOUNG PEASANT (*to his father*): Have I got to? (*The wife nods.*) Right.

THE PEASANT'S WIFE: And thank you kindly, captain, for sparing us, for ever and ever, Amen.

(*The peasant stops his wife from further expressions of gratitude.*)

FIRST SOLDIER: I knew the ox was what they minded about most, was I right?

(*Guided by the young peasant, the ensign and his men continue on their way.*)

THE PEASANT: What are they up to, I'd like to know. Nowt good.

THE PEASANT'S WIFE: Perhaps they're just scouting. What you doing?

THE PEASANT (*putting a ladder against the roof and climbing up it*): Seeing if they're on their own. (*From the top.*) Something moving in the wood. Can see something down by the quarry. And there are men in armour in the clearing. And a gun. That's at least a regiment. God's mercy on the town and everyone in it!

THE PEASANT'S WIFE: Any lights in the town?

THE PEASANT: No. They'll all be asleep. (*Climbs down.*) If those people get in they'll butcher the lot.

THE PEASANT'S WIFE: Sentries're bound to spot them first.

THE PEASANT: Sentry in the tower up the hill must have been killed, or he'd have blown his bugle.

THE PEASANT'S WIFE: If only there were more of us.

THE PEASANT: Just you and me and that cripple.

THE PEASANT'S WIFE: Nowt we can do, you'd say. . . .

THE PEASANT: Nowt.

THE PEASANT'S WIFE: Can't possibly run down there in the blackness.

THE PEASANT: Whole hillside's crawling with 'em. We could give a signal.

THE PEASANT'S WIFE: What, and have them butcher us too?

THE PEASANT: You're right, nowt we can do.

THE PEASANT'S WIFE (*to Kattrin*): Pray, poor creature, pray! Nowt we can do to stop bloodshed. You can't talk, maybe, but at least you can pray. He'll hear you if no one else can. I'll help you. (*All kneel, Kattrin behind the two peasants.*) Our Father, which art in Heaven, hear Thou our prayer, let not the town be destroyed with all what's in it sound asleep and suspecting nowt. Arouse Thou them that they may get up and go to the walls and see how the enemy approacheth with picks and guns in the blackness across fields below the slope. (*Turning to Kattrin.*) Guard Thou our mother and ensure that the watch-man sleepeth not but wakes up, or it will be too late. Succour our brother-in-law also, he is inside there with his four children, spare Thou them, they are innocent and know nowt. (*To Kattrin, who gives a groan.*) One of them's not two yet, the eldest's seven. (*Kattrin stands up distractedly.*) Our Father, hear us, for only Thou canst help; we look to be doomed, for why, we are weak and have no pike and nowt and can risk nowt and are in Thy hand along with our cattle and all the farm, and same with the town, it too is in Thy hand and the enemy is before the walls in great strength.

(*Unobserved, Kattrin has slipped away to the cart and taken from it something which she hides beneath her apron; then she climbs up the ladder on to the stable roof.*)

THE PEASANT'S WIFE: Forget not the children, what are in danger, the littlest ones especially, the old folk what can't move, and every living creature.

THE PEASANT: And forgive us our trespasses as we forgive them that trespass against us. Amen.

(*Sitting on the roof, Kattrin begins to beat the drum which she has pulled out from under her apron.*)

THE PEASANT'S WIFE: Jesus Christ, what's she doing?

THE PEASANT: She's out of her mind.

THE PEASANT'S WIFE: Quick, get her down.

(*The peasant hurries to the ladder, but Kattrin pulls it up on to the roof.*)

THE PEASANT'S WIFE: She'll do us in.

THE PEASANT: Stop drumming at once, you cripple!

THE PEASANT'S WIFE: Bringing the Catholics down on us!

THE PEASANT (*looking for stones to throw*): I'll stone you.

THE PEASANT'S WIFE: Where's your feelings? Where's your heart? We're done for if they come down on us. Slit our throats, they will.

(*Kattrin stares into the distance towards the town and carries on drumming.*)

THE PEASANT'S WIFE (*to her husband*): I told you we shouldn't have allowed those vagabonds on to farm. What do they care if our last cows are taken?

THE ENSIGN (*runs in with his soldiers and the young peasant*): I'll cut you to ribbons, all of you!

THE PEASANT'S WIFE: Please, sir, it's not our fault, we couldn't help it. It was her sneaked up there. A foreigner.

THE ENSIGN: Where's the ladder?

THE PEASANT: There.

THE ENSIGN (*calls up*): I order you, throw that drum down.

(*Kattrin goes on drumming.*)

THE ENSIGN: You're all in this together. It'll be the end of you.

THE PEASANT: They been cutting pine trees in that wood. How about if we got one of the trunks and poked her off. . . .

FIRST SOLDIER (*to the ensign*): Permission to make a suggestion, sir! (*He whispers something in the ensign's ear.*) Listen, we got a suggestion could help you. Get down off there and come into town with us right away. Show us which your mother is and we'll see she ain't harmed.

(*Kattrin goes on drumming.*)

THE ENSIGN (*pushes him roughly aside*): She doesn't trust you; with a mug like yours it's not surprising. (*Calls up.*) Suppose I gave you my word? I can give my word of honour as an officer.

(*Kattrin drums harder.*)

THE ENSIGN: Is nothing sacred to her?

THE YOUNG PEASANT: There's more than her mother involved, sir.

FIRST SOLDIER: This can't go on much longer. They're bound to hear in the town.

THE ENSIGN: We'll have somehow to make a noise that's louder than her drumming. What can we make a noise with?

FIRST SOLDIER: Thought we weren't s'posed to make no noise.

THE ENSIGN: A harmless one, you fool. A peaceful one.

THE PEASANT: I could chop wood with my axe.

THE ENSIGN: Good: you chop. (*The peasant fetches his axe and attacks a tree-trunk.*) Chop harder! Harder! You're chopping for your life.

(*Kattrin has been listening, drumming less loudly the while. She now looks wildly round, and goes on drumming.*)

THE ENSIGN: Not loud enough. (*To the first soldier.*) You chop too.

THE PEASANT: Only got the one axe. (*Stops chopping.*)

THE ENSIGN: We'll have to set the farm on fire. Smoke her out, that's it.

THE PEASANT: It wouldn't help, captain. If the townspeople see a fire here they'll know what's up.

(*Kattrin has again been listening as she drums. At this point she laughs.*)

THE ENSIGN: Look at her laughing at us. I'm not having that. I'll shoot her down, and damn the consequences. Fetch the harquebus.

(*Three soldiers hurry off. Kattrin goes on drumming.*)

THE PEASANT'S WIFE: I got it, captain. That's their cart. If we smash it up she'll stop. Cart's all they got.

THE ENSIGN (*to the young peasant*): Smash it up. (*Calls up.*) We're going to smash up your cart if you don't stop drumming. (*The young peasant gives the cart a few feeble blows.*)

THE PEASANT'S WIFE: Stop it, you animal!

(*Desperately looking towards the cart, Kattrin emits pitiful noises. But she goes on drumming.*)

THE ENSIGN: Where are those clodhoppers with the harquebus?

FIRST SOLDIER: Can't have heard nowt in town yet, else we'd be hearing their guns.

THE ENSIGN (*calls up*): They can't hear you at all. And now we're going to shoot you down. For the last time: throw down that drum!

THE YOUNG PEASANT (*suddenly flings away his plank*): Go on drumming! Or they'll all be killed! Go on, go on. . . .

(*The soldier knocks him down and beats him with his pike. Kattrin starts to cry, but she goes on drumming.*)

THE PEASANT'S WIFE: Don't strike his back! For God's sake, you're beating him to death!

(*The soldiers hurry in with the harquebus.*)

SECOND SOLDIER: Colonel's frothing at the mouth, sir. We're all for court-martial.

THE ENSIGN: Set it up! Set it up! (*Calls up while the gun is being erected.*) For the very last time: stop drumming! (*Kattrin, in tears, drums as loud as she can.*) Fire! (*The soldiers fire. Kattrin is hit, gives a few more drumbeats and then slowly crumples.*)

THE ENSIGN: That's the end of that.

(*But Kattrin's last drumbeats are taken up by the town's cannon. In the distance can be heard a confused noise of tocsins and gunfire.*)

FIRST SOLDIER: She's made it.

SCENE 12

(*Before first light. Sound of the fifes and drums of troops marching off into the distance.*)

(*In front of the cart Mother Courage is squatting by her daughter. The peasant family are standing near her.*)

THE PEASANTS (*with hostility*): You must go, missis. There's only one more regiment behind that one. You can't go on your own.

MOTHER COURAGE: I think she's going to sleep. (*She sings.*)

> Lullaby baby
> What's that in the hay?
> Neighbours' kids grizzle
> But my kids are gay.
> Neighbours' are in tatters
> And you're dressed in lawn
> Cut down from the raiment an
> Angel has worn.
> Neighbours' kids go hungry
> And you shall eat cake
> Suppose it's too crumbly

You've only to speak.
Lullaby baby
What's that in the hay?
The one lies in Poland
The other — who can say?

Better if you'd not told her nowt about your brother-in-law's kids.

THE PEASANT: If you'd not gone into town to get your cut it might never of happened.

MOTHER COURAGE: Now she's asleep.

THE PEASANT'S WIFE: She ain't asleep. Can't you see she's passed over?

THE PEASANT: And it's high time you got away yourself. There are wolves around and, what's worse, marauders.

MOTHER COURAGE: Aye.

(*She goes and gets a tarpaulin to cover the dead girl with.*)

THE PEASANT'S WIFE: Ain't you got nobody else? What you could go to?

MOTHER COURAGE: Aye, one left. Eilif.

THE PEASANT (*as Mother Courage covers the dead girl*): Best look for him, then. We'll mind her, see she gets proper burial. Don't you worry about that.

MOTHER COURAGE: Here's money for expenses.

(*She counts out coins into the peasant's hands. The peasant and his son shake hands with her and carry Kattrin away.*)

THE PEASANT'S WIFE (*as she leaves*): I'd hurry.

MOTHER COURAGE (*harnessing herself to the cart*): Hope I can pull cart all right by meself. Be all right, nowt much inside it. Got to get back in business again.

(*Another regiment with its fifes and drums marches past in the background.*)

MOTHER COURAGE (*tugging the cart*): Take me along! (*Singing is heard from offstage.*)

With all its luck and all its danger
The war is dragging on a bit
Another hundred years or longer
The common man won't benefit.
Filthy his food, no soap to shave him
The regiment steals half his pay.
But still a miracle may save him:
Tomorrow is another day!
   The new year's come. The watchmen shout.
   The thaw sets in. The dead remain.
   Wherever life has not died out
   It staggers to its feet again.

COMMENTARIES

Bertolt Brecht (1898–1956)

THE ALIENATION EFFECT   1964

TRANSLATED BY JOHN WILLETT

In this short description, Brecht explains some of his theories of staging and acting. His alienation effect reminds the audience that the characters on stage are dramatic constructs, not real people suffering real emotions. As he explains, the A-effect is the opposite of traditional acting, which is designed to produce an empathy between actor and audience. The A-effect rejects that empathy.

What follows represents an attempt to describe a technique of acting which was applied in certain theaters with a view to taking the incidents portrayed and alienating them from the spectator. The aim of this technique, known as the alienation effect, was to make the spectator adopt an attitude of inquiry and criticism in his approach to the incident. The means were artistic.

The first condition for the A-effect's application to this end is that stage and auditorium must be purged of everything "magical" and that no "hypnotic tensions" should be set up. This ruled out any attempt to make the stage convey the flavor of a particular place (a room at evening, a road in the autumn), or to create atmosphere by relaxing the tempo of the conversation. The audience was not "worked up" by a display of temperament or "swept away" by acting with tautened muscles; in short, no attempt was made to put it in a trance and give it the illusion of watching an ordinary unrehearsed event. As will be seen presently, the audience's tendency to plunge into such illusions has to be checked by specific artistic means.

The first condition for the achievement of the A-effect is that the actor must invest what he has to show with a definite gest of showing. It is of course necessary to drop the assumption that there is a fourth wall cutting the audience off from the stage and the consequent illusion that the stage action is taking place in reality and without an audience. That being so, it is possible for the actor in principle to address the audience directly.

It is well known that contact between audience and stage is normally made on the basis of empathy. Conventional actors devote their efforts so exclusively to bringing about this psychological operation that they may be said to see it as the principal aim of their art. Our introductory remarks will already have made it clear that the technique which produces an A-effect is the exact opposite of that which aims at empathy. The actor applying it is bound not to try to bring about the empathy operation.

Yet in his efforts to reproduce particular characters and show their behavior he need not renounce the means of empathy entirely. He uses these means just as any normal person with no particular acting talent would use them if he wanted to portray someone else, i.e., show how he behaves. This showing of other people's behavior happens time and again in ordinary life (witnesses of an accident demonstrating to newcomers how the victim behaved, a facetious person imitating a friend's walk, etc.), without those involved making the least effort to subject their spectators to an illusion. At the same time they do feel their way into their characters' skins with a view to acquiring their characteristics.

As has already been said, the actor too will make use of this psychological operation. But whereas the usual practice in acting is to execute it during the actual performance, in the hope of stimulating the spectator into a similar operation, he will achieve it only at an earlier stage, at some time during rehearsals.

To safeguard against an unduly "impulsive," frictionless and uncritical creation of characters and incidents, more reading rehearsals can be held than usual. The actor should refrain from living himself into the part prematurely in any way, and should go on functioning as long as possible as a reader (which does not mean a reader-aloud). An important step is memorizing one's first impressions.

When reading his part the actor's attitude should be one of a man who is astounded and contradicts. Not only the occurrence of the incidents, as he reads about them, but the conduct of the man he is playing, as he experiences it, must be weighed up by him and their peculiarities understood; none can be taken as given, as something that "was bound to turn out that way," that was "only to be expected from a character like that." Before memorizing the words he must memorize what he felt astounded at and where he felt impelled to contradict. For these are dynamic forces that he must preserve in creating his performance.

When he appears on the stage, besides what he actually is doing he will at all essential points discover, specify, imply what he is not doing; that is to say he will act in such a way that the alternative emerges as clearly as possible, that his acting allows the other possibilities to be inferred and only represents one out of the possible variants. He will say for instance "You'll pay for that," and not say "I forgive you." He detests his children; it is not the case that he loves them. He moves down stage left and not up stage right. Whatever he doesn't do must be contained and conserved in what he does. In this way every sentence and every gesture signifies a decision; the character remains under observation and is tested. The technical term for this procedure is "fixing the 'not . . . but.'"

The actor does not allow himself to become completely transformed on the stage into the character he is portraying. He is not Lear, Harpagon, Schweik; he shows them. He reproduces their remarks as authentically as he can; he puts forward their way of behaving to the best of his abilities and knowledge of men; but he never tries to persuade himself (and thereby others) that this amounts to a complete transformation. Actors will know what it means if I say that a typical kind of acting without this complete transformation takes place when a producer or colleague shows one how to play a particular passage. It is not his own part, so he is not completely transformed; he underlines the technical aspect and retains the attitude of someone just making suggestions.

Once the idea of total transformation is abandoned the actor speaks his part not as if he were improvising it himself but like a quotation. At the same time he obviously has to render all the quotation's overtones, the remark's full human and concrete shape; similarly the gesture he makes must have the full substance of a human gesture even though it now represents a copy.

Given this absence of total transformation in the acting there are three aids which may help to alienate the actions and remarks of the characters being portrayed:

1. Transposition into the third person.
2. Transposition into the past.
3. Speaking the stage directions out loud.

Using the third person and the past tense allows the actor to adopt the right attitude of detachment. In addition he will look for stage directions and remarks that comment on his lines, and speak them aloud at rehearsal ("He stood up and exclaimed angrily, not having eaten: . . . ," or "He had never been told so before, and didn't know if it was true or not," or "He smiled, and said with forced nonchalance: . . ."). Speaking the stage directions out loud in the third person results in a clash between two tones of voice, alienating the second of them, the text proper. This style of acting is further alienated by taking place on the stage after having already been outlined and announced in words. Transposing it into the past gives the speaker a standpoint from which he can look back at his sentence. The sentence too is thereby alienated without the speaker adopting an unreal point of view; unlike the spectator, he has read the play right through and is better placed to judge the sentence in accordance with the ending, with its consequences, than the former, who knows less and is more of a stranger to the sentence.

This composite process leads to an alienation of the text in the rehearsals which generally persists in the performance too. The directness of the relationship with the audience allows and indeed forces the actual speech delivery to be varied in accordance with the greater or smaller significance attaching to the sentences. Take the case of witnesses addressing a court. The underlinings, the characters' insistence on their remarks, must be developed as a piece of effective virtuosity. If the actor turns to the audience it must be a whole-hearted turn rather than the asides and soliloquizing technique of the old-fashioned theater. To get the full A-effect from the poetic medium the actor should start at rehearsal by paraphrasing the verse's content in vulgar prose, possibly accompanying this by the gestures designed for the verse. A daring and beautiful handling of verbal media will alienate the text. (Prose can be alienated by translation into the actor's native dialect.)

Gesture will be dealt with below, but it can at once be said that everything to do with the emotions has to be externalized; that is to say, it must be developed into a gesture. The actor has to find a sensibly perceptible outward expression for his character's emotions, preferably some action that gives away what is going on inside him. The emotion in question must be brought out, must lose all its restrictions so that it can be treated on a big scale. Special elegance, power and grace of gesture bring about the A-effect.

A masterly use of gesture can be seen in Chinese acting. The Chinese actor achieves the A-effect by being seen to observe his own movements.

Whatever the actor offers in the way of gesture, verse structure, etc., must be finished and bear the hallmarks of something rehearsed and rounded-off. The impression to be given is one of ease, which is at the same time one of difficulties overcome. The actor must make it possible for the audience to take his own art, his mastery of technique, lightly too. He puts an incident before the spectator with perfection and as he thinks it really happened or might have happened. He does not conceal the fact that he has rehearsed it, any more than an acrobat conceals his training, and he emphasizes that it is his own (actor's) account, view, version of the incident.

Because he doesn't identify himself with him he can pick a definite attitude to adopt towards the character whom he portrays, can show what he thinks of him and invite the spectator, who is likewise not asked to identify himself, to criticize the character portrayed.

The attitude which he adopts is a socially critical one. In his exposition of the incidents and in his characterization of the person he tries to bring out those features which come within society's sphere. In this way his performance becomes a discussion (about social conditions) with the audience he is addressing. He prompts the spectator to justify or abolish these conditions according to what class he belongs to.

The object of the A-effect is to alienate the social gest underlying every incident. By social gest is meant the mimetic and gestural expression of the social relationships prevailing between people of a given period.

It helps to formulate the incident for society, and to put it across in such a way that society is given the key, if titles are thought up for the scenes. These titles must have a historical quality.

This brings us to a crucial technical device: historicization.

The actor must play the incidents as historical ones. Historical incidents are unique, transitory incidents associated with particular periods. The conduct of the persons involved in them is not fixed and "universally human"; it includes elements that have been or may be overtaken by the course of history, and is subject to criticism from the immediately following period's point of view. The conduct of those born before us is alienated[1] from us by an incessant evolution.

It is up to the actor to treat present-day events and modes of behavior with the same detachment as the historian adopts with regard to those of the past. He must alienate these characters and incidents from us.

Characters and incidents from ordinary life, from our immediate surroundings, being familiar, strike us as more or less natural. Alienating them helps to make them seem remarkable to us. Science has carefully developed a technique of getting irritated with the everyday, "self-evident," universally accepted occurrence, and there is no reason why this infinitely useful attitude should not be taken over by art. It is an attitude which arose in science as a result of the growth in human productive powers. In art the same motive applies.

As for the emotions, the experimental use of the A-effect in the epic theater's German productions indicated that this way of acting too can stimulate them, though possibly a different class of emotion is involved from those of the orthodox theater. A critical attitude on the audience's part is a thoroughly artistic one. Nor does the actual practice of the A-effect seem anything like so unnatural as its description. Of course it is a way of acting that his nothing to do with stylization as commonly practiced. The main advantage of the epic theater with its A-effect, intended purely to show the world in such a way that it becomes manageable, is precisely its quality of being natural and earthly, its humor and its renunciation of all the mystical elements that have stuck to the orthodox theater from the old days.

[1]*Entfremdet.*

Bertolt Brecht (1898–1956)

NOTES FOR *MOTHER COURAGE,* SCENE 12   1949

TRANSLATED BY ERIC BENTLEY AND HUGO SCHMIDT

Brecht produced booklets for some of his work that supply a great deal of background information that does not appear in the text of the plays. Brecht's manner of producing his plays were important to him. While he did not expect every successive production to adhere strictly to the standards he established in commentaries such as this, he hoped his intentions would be substantially respected.

Twelfth Scene
Courage Moves On

The peasants have to convince Courage that Kattrin is dead. Kattrin's lullaby. Mother Courage pays for Kattrin's funeral and receives the expressions of sympathy of the peasants. Mother Courage harnesses herself to her empty covered wagon. Still hoping to get back into business, she follows the tattered army.

Basic Arrangement

The wagon stands on the empty stage. Mother Courage holds dead Kattrin's head in her lap. The peasants stand at the foot of the dead girl, huddled together and hostile. Courage talks as if her daughter were only sleeping, and deliberately overhears the reproach of the peasants that she was to blame for Kattrin's death.

Kattrin's lullaby. The mother's face is bent low over the face of the daughter. The song does not conciliate those who listen.

Mother Courage pays for Kattrin's funeral and receives expressions of sympathy from the peasants. After she has realized that her last child is dead, Courage gets up laboriously and hobbles around the corpse (right), along the footlights, behind the wagon. She returns with a tent cloth, and answers over her shoulder the peasant's question whether she had no one to turn to: "Oh yes, one. Eilif." And places the cloth over the body, with her back toward the footlights. At the head of the corpse, she pulls the cloth all the way over the face, then again takes her place behind the corpse. The peasant and his son shake hands with her and bow ceremoniously before carrying the body out (to the right). The peasant woman, too, shakes hands with Courage, walks to the right and stops once more, undecided. The two women exchange a few words, then the peasant woman exits.

Mother Courage harnesses herself to her empty covered wagon. Still hoping to get back into business, she follows the tattered army. Slowly, the old woman walks to the wagon, rolls up the rope which Dumb Kattrin had been pulling to this point, takes a stick, looks at it, slips it through the sling of the second rope, tucks the stick under her arm, and starts pulling. The turntable begins to move, and Courage circles the stage once. The curtain closes when she is upstage right for the second time.

The Peasants	The attitude of the peasants toward Courage is hostile. She got them into difficulties, and they will be saddled with her if she does not catch up with the regiments. Besides, she is to blame for the accident herself, in their opinion. And moreover the canteen woman is not part of the resident population, and now, in time of war, she belongs to the fleecers, cutthroats, and marauders in the wake of the armies. When they condole with her by shaking her hand, they merely follow custom.
The Bow	During this entire scene, Weigel, as Courage, showed an almost animal indifference. All the more beautiful was the deep bow that she made when the body was carried away.
The Lullaby	The lullaby must be sung without sentimentality and without the desire to arouse sentimentality. Otherwise, its significance does not get across. The thought that is the basis of this song is a murderous one: the child of this mother was supposed to be better off than other children of other mothers. Through a slight stress on the "you," Weigel revealed the treacherous hope of Courage to get her child, and perhaps only hers, through the war alive. The child to whom the most common things were denied was promised the uncommon.
Paying for the Funeral	Even when paying for the funeral, Weigel gave another hint at the character of Courage. She fished a few coins from her leather purse, put one back, and gave the rest to the peasant. The overpowering impression she gave of having been destroyed was not in the least diminished by this.
The Last Verse	While Courage slowly harnessed herself to her wagon, the last verse of her song was sung from the box in which the band had been placed. It expresses one more time her undestroyed hope to get something out of war anyway. It becomes more impressive in that it does not aim at the illusion that the song is actually sung by army units moving past in the distance.

Giehse in the Role
of Courage

When covering up the body, Giehse put her head under the cloth, looking at her daughter one more time, before finally dropping it over her face.

Before she began pulling away her covered wagon — another beautiful variant — she looked into the distance, to figure out where to go, and before she started pulling, she blew her nose with her index finger.

Take Your Time

At the end of the play it is necessary that one see the wagon roll away. Naturally, the audience gets the idea when the wagon starts. If the movement is extended, a moment of irritation arises ("that's long enough, now"). If it is prolonged even further, deeper understanding sets in.

Pulling the Wagon in the
Last Scene

For the 12th scene, farm house and stable with roof (of the 11th scene) were cleared away, and only the wagon and Dumb Kattrin's body were left. The act of dragging the wagon off — the large letters "Saxony" were pulled up (out of sight) when the music begins — took place on a completely empty stage: whereby one remembered the setting of the first scene. Courage and her wagon moved in a complete circle on the revolving stage. She passed the footlights once more. As usual, the stage was bathed in light.

Discoveries of the Realists

Wherein lies the effectiveness of Weigel's gesture when she mechanically puts one coin back into her purse, after having fished her money out, as she hands the peasant the funeral money for dead Kattrin? She shows that this tradeswoman, in all her grief, does not completely forget to count, since money is so hard to come by. And she shows this as a discovery about human nature that is shaped by certain conditions. This little feature has the power and the suddenness of a discovery. The art of the realists consists of digging out the truth from under the rubble of the evident, of connecting the particular with the general, of pinning down the unique within the larger process.

A Change of Text

After "I'll manage, there isn't much in it now," Courage added, in the Munich and then also in the Berlin production: "I must start up again in business."

Mother Courage Learns
Nothing

In the last scene, Weigel's Courage appeared like an eighty-year-old woman. And she comprehends nothing. She reacts only to the statements that are connected with war, such as that one must not remain behind. She overhears the crude reproach of the peasants that Kattrin's death was her fault.

Courage's inability to learn from the unproductiveness of war was a prophecy in the year 1938 when the play was written. At the Berlin production in 1948 the desire was voiced that Courage should at least come to a realization in the play. To make it possible for the spectator to get something out of this realistic play, i.e., to make the spectator learn a lesson, theaters have to arrive at an acting style that does not seek an identification of the spectator with the protagonist.

Judging on the basis of reports of spectators and newspaper reviews, the Zurich world premiere — although artistically on a high level — presented only the image of war as a natural catastrophe and an inevitable fate, and thereby it underscored to the middle-class spectator in the orchestra his own indestructibility, his ability to survive. But even to the likewise middle-class Courage, the decision "Join in or don't join in" was always left open in the play. The production, it seems, must also have presented Courage's business dealings, profiteering, willingness to take risks, as quite natural, "eternally human" behavior, so that she had no other choice. Today, it is true, the man of the middle class can no longer stay out of war, as Courage could have. To him, a production of the play can probably teach nothing but a real hatred of war, and a certain insight into the fact that the big deals of which war consists are not made by the little people. In that sense, the play is more of a lesson than reality is, because here in the play the situation of war is more of an experimental situation, made for the sake of insights. I.e., the spectator attains the attitude of a student — as long as the acting style is correct. The part of the audience that belongs to the proletariat, i.e., the class that actually can struggle against and overcome war, should be given insight into the connection between business and war (again provided the acting style is correct): the proletariat as a class can do away with war by doing away with capitalism. Of course, as far as the proletarian part of the audience is concerned, one must also take into consideration the fact that this class is busy drawing its own conclusions — inside as well as outside the theater.

The Epic Element

The Epic element was certainly visible in the production at the Deutsches Theater — in the arrangement, in the presentation of the characters, in the minute execution of details, and in the pacing of the entire play. Also, contradictory elements were not eliminated but stressed, and the parts, visible as such, made a convincing whole. However, the goal of Epic Theater was not reached. Much became clear, but clarification was in the end absent. Only in a few recasting-rehearsals did it clearly emerge, for then the actors were only "pretending," i.e., they only showed to the newly added colleague the positions and intonations, and then the whole thing received that preciously loose, unlabored, non-urgent element that incites the spectator to have his own independent thoughts and feelings.

That the production did not have an Epic foundation was never remarked, however: which was probably the reason the actors did not dare provide one.

Concerning the Notes Themselves

We hope that the present notes, offering various explanations and inventions essential to the production of a play, will not have an air of spurious seriousness. It is admittedly hard to establish the lightness and casualness that are of the essence of theater. The arts, even when they are instructive, are forms of amusement.

Tennessee Williams

Tennessee Williams pausing on the set of *Night of the Iguana* at London's Savoy Theatre in 1965.

Tennessee Williams (1911–1983) was one of a handful of post–World War II American playwrights to achieve an international reputation. He was born Thomas Lanier Williams in Columbus, Mississippi, the son of a traveling shoe salesman who eventually moved the family to a dark and dreary tenement in St. Louis. A precocious child, Williams was given a typewriter by his mother when he was eleven years old. The instrument helped him create fantasy worlds that seemed more real, more important to him than the dark and sometimes threatening world in which he lived. His parents, expecting a third child, bought a house whose gloominess depressed virtually everyone in it. His mother and father found themselves arguing, and his sister, Rose, took refuge from the real world by closeting herself with a collection of glass animals.

Both Rose and Tennessee responded badly to their environment, and both had breakdowns. Tennessee was so ill that he suffered a partial paralysis of his legs, a disorder that made him a victim of bullies at school and a disappointment to his father at home. He could never participate in sports and was always somewhat frail; however, he was very advanced intellectually and published his first story when he was sixteen.

His education was sporadic. He attended the University of Missouri but, failing ROTC because of his physical limitations, soon dropped out to work in a shoe company. He then went to Washington University in St. Louis but dropped out again. Finally, he earned a bachelor's degree in playwriting at the State University of Iowa when he was twenty-four. During this time he was writing plays, some of which were produced at Washington University. Two years after he graduated, the Theatre Guild produced his first commercial play, *Battle of Angels* (1940), in Boston. It was such a distinct failure that he feared his fledgling career was stunted, but he kept writing and managed to live for a few years on foundation grants. It was not until the production of *The Glass Menagerie* (1944 in Chicago, 1945 in New York) that he achieved the kind of notice he knew he deserved. His first real success, the play was given the New York Drama Critics' Circle Award, the sign of his having achieved a measure of professional recognition and financial independence.

After trying several jobs, including an unsuccessful attempt at screenwriting, he had no more worries about work after *The Glass Menagerie* ran on Broadway for 561 performances. In 1947 his second success, *A Streetcar Named Desire,* starring the then unknown Marlon Brando, was an even bigger box-office smash. It ran for 855 performances and won the Pulitzer Prize. By the time Tennessee Williams was thirty-six, he was regarded as one of the most important playwrights in America.

Williams followed these successes with a number of plays that were not all as well received as his first works. *Summer and Smoke* (1948), *The Rose Tattoo* (1951), and *Camino Real* (1953) were met with measured enthusiasm from the public, although the critics thought highly of Williams's work. These plays were followed by the saga of a southern family, *Cat on a Hot Tin Roof,* which won all the major drama prizes in 1955, including the Pulitzer.

Williams's energy was unfailing in the next several years. He authored a screenplay, *Baby Doll,* with the legendary director Elia Kazan, in 1956. In 1958 he wrote a one-act play, *Suddenly Last Summer,* and in 1959 *Sweet Bird of Youth.* Some of his later plays are *The Night of the Iguana* (1961), *The Milk Train Doesn't Stop Here Anymore* (1963), and *Small Craft Warnings* (1972). He also wrote a novel and several volumes of short stories, establishing himself as an important writer in many genres. His sudden death in 1983 was a blow to the theater world.

THE GLASS MENAGERIE

Tennessee Williams has often been accused of exorcising his family demons in his plays and of therefore sometimes cloaking events in a personal symbolism that is impossible for an audience to penetrate totally. *The Glass Menagerie* (1944) certainly derives from his personal experience growing up in St. Louis in a tenement, the setting for the play. The characters are drawn from his own family, particularly the character Laura, who is based on his sister. But the symbolism in the play is not so obscure as to give an audience special difficulty.

In a way Williams thought of the play as a tribute to his sister, Rose. Rose's depressions were so severe that eventually she received a lobotomy, which rendered her more passive and more hopeless than before. The operation did not achieve anything positive, and Williams felt somewhat responsible because he had not urged the family to refuse the treatment.

In the play Amanda Wingfield is obsessed with finding gentlemen callers and a suitable career for her daughter, Laura, who walks with a slight limp and is exceedingly shy. Amanda lives in a world of imagination, endlessly retelling stories about a glorious past filled with suitors she could have had before she married. Amanda bullies Laura, whose only defense is to bury herself in her own fantasy world of spun-glass animals. Tom, the son and narrator of the play, is also a victim of Amanda's bullying, but he is more independent and better able to withstand her assaults.

Both children are great disappointments to Amanda. Tom is aloof, indolent, something like his father who is present only in his picture on the wall. Laura calls herself a cripple and has no self-esteem or hope for a future such as the one her mother conceives for her. Laura's shyness is almost uncontrollable. It has ruined any hope of a business career, to Amanda's intense distress. When Tom brings home Jim, and his sister recognizes him as a boy she admired from afar in high school, Laura is nearly too shy to come to the dinner table. And when it becomes clear that Jim is not the gentleman caller of Amanda's dreams, Amanda and Laura are left to face reality or to continue living in their fantasy worlds.

Amanda confronts Tom at the end of the play and asserts that he "live[s] in a dream" and "manufacture[s] illusions." She could be speaking about any character in the play, including Jim, who lives according to popular illusions about self-fulfillment. But the Wingfields in particular pay dearly for their illusions, perhaps Laura more than anyone because of her mother's inability to relinquish intense but unrealistic hopes for her daughter.

Williams's written presentation of the play provides more insights than usual for a reading audience. His stage directions are elaborate, poetic, and exceptionally evocative. Through Tom, as narrator, he says that the play is not realistic but rather is a memory play, an enactment of moments in Tom's memory.

Williams specifies a setting that is almost dreamlike, using Brechtian devices such as the visual images and screen legends flashed at appropriate moments. He uses music to establish a mood or stimulate an association. Because modern productions rarely follow Williams's directions, the dreamlike quality is sometimes lost. In fact, ironically, modern productions of this play are often realistic rather than symbolic, although they usually maintain the mood that Williams hoped to achieve.

The Glass Menagerie in Performance

The first production of *The Glass Menagerie* opened in Chicago on December 26, 1944, during World War II. Audiences were not drawn to it at first, but the critics' positive reviews began to attract people to the theater. In March 1945, when it was playing to full houses, the play transferred to New York and began a run of 561 performances. It won the Drama Critics' Circle Award as the best American play of the 1944–1945 season. Two road companies then toured the play around the country. The first London performance, in the large and distinguished Theatre Royal in Haymarket in July 1948, was directed by John Gielgud and starred Helen Hayes as Amanda Wingfield. A film version followed in 1950.

Revivals of the play have been both numerous and successful. Laurette Taylor, who played Amanda in the original New York production, set a standard with her interpretation of Williams's poetic language. Maureen Stapleton, whose more vigorous approach contrasted sharply with Taylor's, took the role in the 1965 production in the Brooks Atkinson Theater in New York. The critic Howard Taubman said, "Maureen Stapleton does not cause one to forget Miss Taylor. . . . Through the magic of her own sensitivity, she gives Amanda a strong, binding thread of sadness and tenderness." Katharine Hepburn's first television performance was as Amanda in 1973. "She gives a brilliant, multi-faceted performance that is surely the acting tour de force of the year," said Percy Shain. Jessica Tandy performed the role in 1983 at the Eugene O'Neill Theater in New York, with Amanda Plummer as Laura. *New York Times* critic Frank Rich declared, "This Amanda is tough, and even her most comic badgerings leave a bitter aftertaste." The British director of that production, John Dexter, used some of the flash cards that Williams specified in the original published version but that had been omitted from previous productions. They flashed important speeches on the scrim during the performance.

Joanne Woodward played Amanda in the 1986 revival at the Long Wharf Theater in New Haven in a version that had been performed at the Williamstown Theatre Festival in 1982. Treat Williams was the son, James Naughton was the suitor, and the Long Wharf production was impressively dreamlike and powerful. Woodward's husband, Paul Newman, directed this version in the 1987 film of the play.

Tennessee Williams (*1911–1983*)

THE GLASS MENAGERIE   1944

nobody, not even the rain, has such small hands — E. E. CUMMINGS

Production Notes by Tennessee Williams

Being a "memory play," *The Glass Menagerie* can be presented with unusual freedom of convention. Because of its considerably delicate or tenuous material, atmospheric touches and subtleties of direction play a particularly important part. Expressionism and all other unconventional techniques in drama have only one valid aim, and this is a closer approach to truth. When a play employs unconventional techniques, it is not, or certainly shouldn't be, trying to escape its responsibility of dealing with reality, or interpreting experience, but is actually or should be attempting to find a closer approach, or more penetrating and vivid expression of things as they are. The straight realistic play with its genuine frigidaire and authentic ice cubes, its characters that speak exactly as its audience speaks, corresponds to the academic landscape and has the same virtue of a photographic likeness. Everyone should know nowadays the unimportance of the photographic in art: that truth, life, or reality is an organic thing which the poetic imagination can represent or suggest, in essence, only through transformation, through changing into other forms than those which were merely present in appearance.

These remarks are not meant as a preface only to this particular play. They have to do with a conception of a new, plastic theatre which must take the place of the exhausted theatre of realistic conventions if the theatre is to resume vitality as a part of our culture.

The Screen Device. There is *only one important difference between the original and acting version of the play* and that is the *omission* in the latter of the device which I tentatively included in my *original* script. This device was the use of a screen on which were projected magic-lantern slides bearing images or titles. I do not regret the omission of this device from the present Broadway production. The extraordinary power of Miss Taylor's performance made it suitable to have the utmost simplicity in the physical production. But I think it may be interesting to some readers to see how this device was conceived. So I am putting it into the published manuscript. These images and legends, projected from behind, were cast on a section of wall between the front-room and dining-room areas, which should be indistinguishable from the rest when not in use.

The purpose of this will probably be apparent. It is to give accent to certain values in each scene. Each scene contains a particular point (or several) which is structurally the most important. In an episodic play, such as this, the basic structure or narrative line may be obscured from the audience; the effect may seem fragmentary rather than architectural. This may not be the fault of the play so much as a lack of attention in the audience. The legend or image upon the screen will strengthen the effect of what is merely allusion in the writing and allow the primary point to be made more simply and lightly than if the entire responsibility were on the spoken lines. Aside from this structural value, I think the screen will have a definite emotional appeal, less definable but just as important. An imaginative producer or director may invent many other uses for this device than those

indicated in the present script. In fact the possibilities of the device seem much larger to me than the instance of this play can possibly utilize.

The Music. Another extra-literary accent in this play is provided by the use of music. A single recurring tune, "The Glass Menagerie," is used to give emotional emphasis to suitable passages. This tune is like circus music, not when you are on the grounds or in the immediate vicinity of the parade, but when you are at some distance and very likely thinking of something else. It seems under those circumstances to continue almost interminably and it weaves in and out of your preoccupied consciousness; then it is the lightest, most delicate music in the world and perhaps the saddest. It expresses the surface vivacity of life with the underlying strain of immutable and inexpressible sorrow. When you look at a piece of delicately spun glass you think of two things: how beautiful it is and how easily it can be broken. Both of those ideas should be woven into the recurring tune, which dips in and out of the play as if it were carried on a wind that changes. It serves as a thread of connection and allusion between the narrator with his separate point in time and space and the subject of his story. Between each episode it returns as reference to the emotion, nostalgia, which is the first condition of the play. It is primarily Laura's music and therefore comes out most clearly when the play focuses upon her and the lovely fragility of glass which is her image.

The Lighting. The lighting in the play is not realistic. In keeping with the atmosphere of memory, the stage is dim. Shafts of light are focused on selected areas or actors, sometimes in contradistinction to what is the apparent center. For instance, in the quarrel scene between Tom and Amanda, in which Laura has no active part, the clearest pool of light is on her figure. This is also true of the supper scene, when her silent figure on the sofa should remain the visual center. The light upon Laura should be distinct from the others, having a peculiar pristine clarity such as light used in early religious portraits of female saints or madonnas. A certain correspondence to light in religious paintings, such as El Greco's, where the figures are radiant in atmosphere that is relatively dusky, could be effectively used throughout the play. (It will also permit a more effective use of the screen.) A free, imaginative use of light can be of enormous value in giving a mobile, plastic quality to plays of a more or less static nature.

Characters

AMANDA WINGFIELD, *the mother. A little woman of great but confused vitality clinging frantically to another time and place. Her characterization must be carefully created, not copied from type. She is not paranoiac, but her life is paranoia. There is much to admire in Amanda, and as much to love and pity as there is to laugh at. Certainly she has endurance and a kind of heroism, and though her foolishness makes her unwittingly cruel at times, there is tenderness in her slight person.*

LAURA WINGFIELD, *her daughter. Amanda, having failed to establish contact with reality, continues to live vitally in her illusions, but Laura's situation is even graver. A childhood illness has left her crippled, one leg slightly shorter than the other, and held in a brace. This defect need not be more than suggested on the stage. Stemming from this, Laura's separation increases till she is like a piece of her own glass collection, too exquisitely fragile to move from the shelf.*

TOM WINGFIELD, *her son. And the narrator of the play. A poet with a job in a warehouse. His nature is not remorseless, but to escape from a trap he has to act without pity.*

JIM O'CONNOR, *the gentleman caller. A nice, ordinary, young man.*

Scene: *An alley in St. Louis.*
Part I: *Preparation for a Gentleman Caller.*
Part II: *The Gentleman Calls.*
Time: *Now and the Past.*

SCENE 1

(*The Wingfield apartment is in the rear of the building, one of those vast hive-like conglomerations of cellular living-units that flower as warty growths in overcrowded urban centers of lower middle-class population and are symptomatic of the impulse of this largest and fundamentally enslaved section of American society to avoid fluidity and differentiation and to exist and function as one interfused mass of automatism.*)

(*The apartment faces an alley and is entered by a fire escape, a structure whose name is a touch of accidental poetic truth, for all of these huge buildings are always burning with the slow and implacable fires of human desperation. The fire escape is included in the set — that is, the landing of it and steps descending from it.*)

(*The scene is memory and is therefore nonrealistic. Memory takes a lot of poetic license. It omits some details; others are exaggerated, according to the emotional value of the articles it touches, for memory is seated predominantly in the heart. The interior is therefore rather dim and poetic.*)

(*At the rise of the curtain, the audience is faced with the dark, grim rear wall of the Wingfield tenement. This building, which runs parallel to the footlights, is flanked on both sides by dark, narrow alleys which run into murky canyons of tangled clotheslines, garbage cans, and the sinister latticework of neighboring fire escapes. It is up and down these side alleys that exterior entrances and exits are made, during the play. At the end of Tom's opening commentary, the dark tenement wall slowly reveals (by means of a transparency) the interior of the ground floor Wingfield apartment.*)

(*Downstage is the living room, which also serves as a sleeping room for Laura, the sofa unfolding to make her bed. Upstage, center, and divided by a wide arch or second proscenium with transparent faded portieres (or second curtain), is the dining room. In an old-fashioned what-not in the living room are seen scores of transparent glass animals. A blown-up photograph of the father hangs on the wall of the living room, facing the audience, to the left of the archway. It is the face of a very handsome young man in a doughboy's First World War cap. He is gallantly smiling, ineluctably smiling, as if to say, "I will be smiling forever."*)

(*The audience hears and sees the opening scene in the dining room through both the transparent fourth wall of the building and the transparent gauze portieres of the dining-room arch. It is during this revealing scene that the fourth wall slowly ascends, out of sight. This transparent exterior wall is not brought down again until the very end of the play, during Tom's final speech.*)

(*The narrator is an undisguised convention of the play. He takes whatever license with dramatic convention as is convenient to his purposes.*)

(*Tom enters dressed as a merchant sailor from alley, stage left, and strolls across the front of the stage to the fire escape. There he stops and lights a cigarette. He addresses the audience.*)

TOM: Yes, I have tricks in my pocket, I have things up my sleeve. But I am the opposite of a stage magician. He gives you illusion that has the appearance of truth. I give you truth in the pleasant disguise of illusion. To begin with, I turn back time. I reverse it to that quaint period, the thirties, when the huge middle class of America was matriculating in a school for the blind. Their eyes had failed them, or they had failed their eyes, and so they were having their fingers pressed forcibly down on the fiery Braille alphabet of a dissolving economy. In Spain there was revolution. Here there was only shouting and confusion. In Spain there was Guernica. Here there were disturbances of labor, sometimes pretty violent, in otherwise peaceful cities such as Chicago, Cleveland, Saint Louis. . . . This is the social background of the play.

(*Music.*)

The play is memory. Being a memory play, it is dimly lighted, it is sentimental, it is not realistic. In memory everything seems to happen to music. That explains the fiddle in the wings. I am the narrator of the play, and also a character in it. The other characters are my mother, Amanda, my sister, Laura, and a gentleman caller who appears in the final scenes. He is the most realistic character in the play, being an emissary from a world of reality that we were somehow set apart from. But since I have a poet's weakness for symbols, I am using this character also as a symbol; he is the long delayed but always expected something that we live for. There is a fifth character in the play who doesn't appear except in this larger-than-life photograph over the mantel. This is our father who left us a long time ago. He was a telephone man who fell in love with long distances; he gave up his job with the telephone company and skipped the light fantastic out of town . . . The last we heard of him was a picture postcard from Mazatlan, on the Pacific coast of Mexico, containing a message of two words —"Hello — Good-bye!" and no address. I think the rest of the play will explain itself. . . .

(*Amanda's voice becomes audible through the portieres.*)
(*Legend on Screen: "Où Sont les Neiges."*)°
(*He divides the portieres and enters the upstage area.*)
(*Amanda and Laura are seated at a drop-leaf table. Eating is indicated by gestures without food or utensils. Amanda faces the audience. Tom and Laura are seated in profile.*)
(*The interior has lit up softly and through the scrim we see Amanda and Laura seated at the table in the upstage area.*)

AMANDA (*calling*): Tom?
TOM: Yes, Mother.
AMANDA: We can't say grace until you come to the table!
TOM: Coming, Mother. (*He bows slightly and withdraws, reappearing a few moments later in his place at the table.*)
AMANDA (*to her son*): Honey, don't *push* with your *fingers*. If you have to push with something, the thing to push with is a crust of bread. And chew — chew! Animals have sections in their stomachs which enable them to digest food without mastication, but human beings are supposed to chew their food before they swallow it down. Eat food leisurely, son, and really enjoy it. A well-cooked meal has lots of delicate flavors that have to be held in the mouth for appreciation. So chew your food and give your salivary glands a chance to function!

(*Tom deliberately lays his imaginary fork down and pushes his chair back from the table.*)

TOM: I haven't enjoyed one bite of this dinner because of your constant directions on how to eat it. It's you

Où Sont les Neiges: Where are the snows [of yesteryear].

that makes me rush through meals with your hawk-like attention to every bite I take. Sickening — spoils my appetite — all this discussion of animals' secretion — salivary glands — mastication!
AMANDA (*lightly*): Temperament like a Metropolitan° star! (*He rises and crosses downstage.*) You're not excused from the table.
TOM: I'm getting a cigarette.
AMANDA: You smoke too much.

(*Laura rises.*)

LAURA: I'll bring in the blancmange.

(*He remains standing with his cigarette by the portieres during the following.*)

AMANDA (*rising*): No, sister, no, sister — you be the lady this time and I'll be the darky.
LAURA: I'm already up.
AMANDA: Resume your seat, little sister — I want you to stay fresh and pretty — for gentlemen callers!
LAURA: I'm not expecting any gentlemen callers.
AMANDA (*crossing out to kitchenette. Airily*): Sometimes they come when they are least expected! Why, I remember one Sunday afternoon in Blue Mountain — (*Enters kitchenette.*)
TOM: I know what's coming!
LAURA: Yes. But let her tell it.
TOM: Again?
LAURA: She loves to tell it.

(*Amanda returns with bowl of dessert.*)

AMANDA: One Sunday afternoon in Blue Mountain — your mother received — *seventeen!* — gentlemen callers! Why, sometimes there weren't chairs enough to accommodate them all. We had to send the nigger over to bring in folding chairs from the parish house.
TOM (*remaining at portieres*): How did you entertain those gentlemen callers?
AMANDA: I understood the art of conversation!
TOM: I bet you could talk.
AMANDA: Girls in those days *knew* how to talk, I can tell you.
TOM: Yes?

(*Image: Amanda as a girl on a porch greeting callers.*)

AMANDA: They knew how to entertain their gentlemen callers. It wasn't enough for a girl to be possessed of a pretty face and a graceful figure — although I wasn't slighted in either respect. She also needed to have a nimble wit and a tongue to meet all occasions.
TOM: What did you talk about?
AMANDA: Things of importance going on in the world! Never anything coarse or common or vulgar. (*She addresses Tom as though he were seated in the vacant chair at the table though he remains by portieres. He plays this scene as though he held the book.*) My callers were gentlemen — all! Among my

Metropolitan: The Metropolitan Opera in New York City.

callers were some of the most prominent young planters of the Mississippi Delta — planters and sons of planters!

(*Tom motions for music and a spot of light on Amanda.*)
(*Her eyes lift, her face glows, her voice becomes rich and elegiac.*)
(*Screen legend: "Où Sont les Neiges."*)

There was young Champ Laughlin who later became vice-president of the Delta Planters Bank. Hadley Stevenson who was drowned in Moon Lake and left his widow one hundred and fifty thousand in Government bonds. There were the Cutrere brothers, Wesley and Bates. Bates was one of my bright particular beaux! He got in a quarrel with that wild Wainright boy. They shot it out on the floor of Moon Lake Casino. Bates was shot through the stomach. Died in the ambulance on his way to Memphis. His widow was also well-provided for, came into eight or ten thousand acres, that's all. She married him on the rebound — never loved her — carried my picture on him the night he died! And there was that boy that every girl in the Delta had set her cap for! That beautiful, brilliant young Fitzhugh boy from Greene County!

TOM: What did he leave his widow?

AMANDA: He never married! Gracious, you talk as though all of my old admirers had turned up their toes to the daisies!

TOM: Isn't this the first you mentioned that still survives?

AMANDA: That Fitzhugh boy went North and made a fortune — came to be known as the Wolf of Wall Street! He had the Midas touch, whatever he touched turned to gold! And I could have been Mrs. Duncan J. Fitzhugh, mind you! But — I picked your *father*!

LAURA (*rising*): Mother, let me clear the table.

AMANDA: No, dear, you go in front and study your typewriter chart. Or practice your shorthand a little. Stay fresh and pretty! — It's almost time for our gentlemen callers to start arriving. (*She flounces girlishly toward the kitchenette.*) How many do you suppose we're going to entertain this afternoon?

(*Tom throws down the paper and jumps up with a groan.*)

LAURA (*alone in the dining room*): I don't believe we're going to receive any, Mother.

AMANDA (*reappearing, airily*): What? No one — not one? You must be joking! (*Laura nervously echoes her laugh. She slips in a fugitive manner through the half-open portieres and draws them gently behind her. A shaft of very clear light is thrown on her face against the faded tapestry of the curtains. Music: "The Glass Menagerie" under faintly. Lightly.*) Not one gentleman caller? It can't be true! There must be a flood, there must have been a tornado!

LAURA: It isn't a flood, it's not a tornado, Mother. I'm just not popular like you were in Blue Mountain. . . .
(*Tom utters another groan. Laura glances at him*

with a faint, apologetic smile. Her voice catching a little.*) Mother's afraid I'm going to be an old maid.

(*The scene dims out with "Glass Menagerie" music.*)

SCENE 2

(*"Laura, Haven't You Ever Liked Some Boy?"*)
(*On the dark stage the screen is lighted with the image of blue roses.*)
(*Gradually Laura's figure becomes apparent and the screen goes out.*)
(*The music subsides.*)
(*Laura is seated in the delicate ivory chair at the small clawfoot table.*)
(*She wears a dress of soft violet material for a kimono — her hair tied back from her forehead with a ribbon.*)
(*She is washing and polishing her collection of glass.*)
(*Amanda appears on the fire escape steps. At the sound of her ascent, Laura catches her breath, thrusts the bowl of ornaments away and seats herself stiffly before the diagram of the typewriter keyboard as though it held her spellbound. Something has happened to Amanda. It is written in her face as she climbs to the landing: a look that is grim and hopeless and a little absurd.*)
(*She has on one of those cheap or imitation velvety-looking cloth coats with imitation fur collar. Her hat is five or six years old, one of those dreadful cloche hats that were worn in the late twenties, and she is clasping an enormous black patent-leather pocketbook with nickel clasp and initials. This is her full-dress outfit, the one she usually wears to the D.A.R.°*)
(*Before entering she looks through the door.*)
(*She purses her lips, opens her eyes wide, rolls them upward and shakes her head.*)
(*Then she slowly lets herself in the door. Seeing her mother's expression Laura touches her lips with a nervous gesture.*)

LAURA: Hello, Mother, I was — (*She makes a nervous gesture toward the chart on the wall. Amanda leans against the shut door and stares at Laura with a martyred look.*)

AMANDA: Deception? Deception? (*She slowly removes her hat and gloves, continuing the swift suffering stare. She lets the hat and gloves fall on the floor — a bit of acting.*)

LAURA (*shakily*): How was the D.A.R. meeting? (*Amanda slowly opens her purse and removes a dainty white handkerchief which she shakes out delicately and delicately touches to her lips and nostrils.*) Didn't you go to the D.A.R. meeting, Mother?

D.A.R.: Daughters of the American Revolution, a patriotic organization for women whose ancestors were involved in the American Revolutionary War.

AMANDA (*faintly, almost inaudibly*): — No. — No. (*Then more forcibly*). I did not have the strength — to go to the D.A.R. In fact, I did not have the courage! I wanted to find a hole in the ground and hide myself in it forever! (*She crosses slowly to the wall and removes the diagram of the typewriter keyboard. She holds it in front of her for a second, staring at it sweetly and sorrowfully — then bites her lips and tears it in two pieces.*)

LAURA (*faintly*): Why did you do that, Mother? (*Amanda repeats the same procedure with the chart of the Gregg Alphabet.*) Why are you —

AMANDA: Why? Why? How old are you, Laura?

LAURA: Mother, you know my age.

AMANDA: I thought that you were an adult; it seems that I was mistaken. (*She crosses slowly to the sofa and sinks down and stares at Laura.*)

LAURA: Please don't stare at me, Mother.

(*Amanda closes her eyes and lowers her head. Count ten.*)

AMANDA: What are we going to do, what is going to become of us, what is the future?

(*Count ten.*)

LAURA: Has something happened, Mother? (*Amanda draws a long breath and takes out the handkerchief again. Dabbing process.*) Mother, has — something happened?

AMANDA: I'll be all right in a minute. I'm just bewildered — (*Count five.*) — by life. . . .

LAURA: Mother, I wish that you would tell me what's happened.

AMANDA: As you know, I was supposed to be inducted into my office at the D.A.R. this afternoon. (*Image: a swarm of typewriters.*) But I stopped off at Rubicam's Business College to speak to your teachers about your having a cold and ask them what progress they thought you were making down there.

LAURA: Oh. . . .

AMANDA: I went to the typing instructor and introduced myself as your mother. She didn't know who you were. Wingfield, she said. We don't have any such student enrolled at the school! I assured her she did, that you had been going to classes since early in January. "I wonder," she said, "if you could be talking about that terribly shy little girl who dropped out of school after only a few days' attendance?" "No," I said, "Laura, my daughter, has been going to school every day for the past six weeks!" "Excuse me," she said. She took the attendance book out and there was your name, unmistakably printed, and all the dates you were absent until they decided that you had dropped out of school. I still said, "No, there must have been some mistake! There must have been some mix-up in the records!" And she said, "No — I remember her perfectly now. Her hands shook so that she couldn't hit the right keys! The first time we gave a speed test, she broke down completely — was sick at the stomach and almost had to be carried into the wash-room! After that morning she never showed up any more. We phoned the house but never got any answer"— while I was working at Famous and Barr, I suppose, demonstrating those — Oh! I felt so weak I could barely keep on my feet. I had to sit down while they got me a glass of water! Fifty dollars' tuition, all of our plans — my hopes and ambitions for you — just gone up the spout, just gone up the spout like that. (*Laura draws a long breath and gets awkwardly to her feet. She crosses to the victrola and winds it up.*) What are you doing?

LAURA: Oh! (*She releases the handle and returns to her seat.*)

AMANDA: Laura, where have you been going when you've gone out pretending that you were going to business college?

LAURA: I've just been going out walking.

AMANDA: That's not true.

LAURA: It is. I just went walking.

AMANDA: Walking? Walking? In winter? Deliberately courting pneumonia in that light coat? Where did you walk to, Laura?

LAURA: All sorts of places — mostly in the park.

AMANDA: Even after you'd started catching that cold?

LAURA: It was the lesser of two evils, Mother. (*Image: winter scene in park.*) I couldn't go back up. I — threw up — on the floor!

AMANDA: From half past seven till after five every day you mean to tell me you walked around in the park, because you wanted to make me think that you were still going to Rubicam's Business College?

LAURA: It wasn't as bad as it sounds. I went inside places to get warmed up.

AMANDA: Inside where?

LAURA: I went in the art museum and the bird houses at the Zoo. I visited the penguins every day! Sometimes I did without lunch and went to the movies. Lately I've been spending most of my afternoons in the Jewel-box, that big glass house where they raise the tropical flowers.

AMANDA: You did all this to deceive me, just for the deception? (*Laura looks down.*) Why?

LAURA: Mother, when you're disappointed, you get that awful suffering look on your face, like the picture of Jesus' mother in the museum!

AMANDA: Hush!

LAURA: I couldn't face it.

(*Pause. A whisper of strings.*)
(*Legend: "The Crust of Humility."*)

AMANDA (*hopelessly fingering the huge pocketbook*): So what are we going to do the rest of our lives? Stay home and watch the parades go by? Amuse ourselves with the glass menagerie, darling? Eternally play those worn-out phonograph records your father left as a painful reminder of him? We won't have a business career — we've given that up because it gave us nervous indigestion! (*Laughs wearily.*) What is there left but dependency all our lives? I know so well what becomes of unmarried women who aren't prepared to occupy a position. I've seen such pitiful cases in the South — barely tolerated spinsters living upon the grudging patronage of sister's husband or brother's wife! — stuck away in some little mousetrap of a room — encouraged by one in-law to visit another — little birdlike women without any nest — eating the crust of humility all their life! Is that the future that we've mapped out for ourselves? I swear it's the only alternative I can think of! It isn't a very pleasant alternative, is it? Of course — some girls do *marry.* (*Laura twists her hands nervously.*) Haven't you ever liked some boy?

LAURA: Yes. I liked one once. (*Rises.*) I came across his picture a while ago.

AMANDA (*with some interest*): He gave you his picture?

LAURA: No, it's in the yearbook.

AMANDA (*disappointed*): Oh — a high-school boy.

(*Screen image: Jim as high school hero bearing a silver cup.*)

LAURA: Yes. His name was Jim. (*Laura lifts the heavy annual from the clawfoot table.*) Here he is in *The Pirates of Penzance.*

AMANDA (*absently*): The what?

LAURA: The operetta the senior class put on. He had a wonderful voice and we sat across the aisle from each other Mondays, Wednesdays, and Fridays in the Aud. Here he is with the silver cup for debating! See his grin?

AMANDA (*absently*): He must have had a jolly disposition.

LAURA: He used to call me — Blue Roses.

(*Image: blue roses.*)

AMANDA: Why did he call you such a name as that?

LAURA: When I had that attack of pleurosis — he asked me what was the matter when I came back. I said pleurosis — he thought that I said Blue Roses! So that's what he always called me after that. Whenever he saw me, he'd holler, "Hello, Blue Roses!" I didn't care for the girl that he went out with. Emily Meisenbach. Emily was the best-dressed girl at Soldan. She never struck me, though, as being sincere . . . It says in the Personal Section — they're engaged. That's — six years ago! They must be married by now.

AMANDA: Girls that aren't cut out for business careers usually wind up married to some nice man. (*Gets up with a spark of revival.*) Sister, that's what you'll do!

(*Laura utters a startled, doubtful laugh. She reaches quickly for a piece of glass.*)

LAURA: But, Mother —

AMANDA: Yes? (*Crossing to photograph.*)

LAURA (*in a tone of frightened apology*): I'm — crippled!

(*Image: screen.*)

AMANDA: Nonsense! Laura, I've told you never, never to use that word. Why, you're not crippled, you just have a little defect — hardly noticeable, even! When people have some slight disadvantage like that, they cultivate other things to make up for it — develop charm — and vivacity — and — *charm!* That's all you have to do! (*She turns again to the photograph.*) One thing your father had *plenty of* — was *charm!*

(*Tom motions to the fiddle in the wings.*)
(*The scene fades out with music.*)

SCENE 3

(*Legend on screen: "After the Fiasco —"*)
(*Tom speaks from the fire escape landing.*)

TOM: After the fiasco at Rubicam's Business College, the idea of getting a gentleman caller for Laura began to play a more important part in Mother's calculations. It became an obsession. Like some archetype of the universal unconscious, the image of the gentleman caller haunted our small apartment. . . . (*Image: young man at door with flowers.*) An evening at home rarely passed without some allusion to this image, this specter, this hope. . . . Even when he wasn't mentioned, his presence hung in Mother's preoccupied look and in my sister's frightened, apologetic manner — hung like a sentence passed upon the Wingfields! Mother was a woman of action as well as words. She began to take logical steps in the planned direction. Late that winter and in the early spring — realizing that extra money would be needed to properly feather the nest and plume the bird — she conducted a vigorous campaign on the telephone, roping in subscribers to one of those magazines for matrons called *The Home-maker's Companion,* the type of journal that features the serialized sublimations of ladies of letters who think in terms of delicate cuplike breasts, slim, tapering waists, rich, creamy thighs, eyes like wood smoke in autumn, fingers that soothe and caress like strains of music, bodies as powerful as Etruscan sculpture.

(*Screen image: glamor magazine cover.*)
(*Amanda enters with phone on long extension cord. She is spotted in the dim stage.*)

AMANDA: Ida Scott? This is Amanda Wingfield! We *missed* you at the D.A.R. last Monday! I said to myself: She's probably suffering with that sinus condition! How is that sinus condition? Horrors! Heaven have mercy! — You're a Christian martyr, yes, that's what you are, a Christian martyr! Well I just now happened to notice that your subscription to the *Companion*'s about to expire! Yes, it expires with the next issue, honey! — just when that wonderful new serial by Bessie Mae Hopper is getting off to such an exciting start. Oh, honey, it's something that you can't miss! You remember how *Gone with the Wind* took everybody by storm? You simply couldn't go out if you hadn't read it. All everybody *talked* was Scarlett O'Hara. Well, this is a book that critics already compare to *Gone with the Wind.* It's the *Gone with the Wind* of the post–World War generation! — What? — Burning? — Oh, honey, don't let them burn, go take a look in the oven and I'll hold the wire! Heavens — I think she's hung up!

(*Dim out.*)

(*Legend on screen: "You Think I'm in Love with Continental Shoemakers?"*)

(*Before the stage is lighted, the violent voices of Tom and Amanda are heard.*)

(*They are quarreling behind the portieres. In front of them stands Laura with clenched hands and panicky expression.*)

(*A clear pool of light on her figure throughout this scene.*)

TOM: What in Christ's name am I —

AMANDA (*shrilly*): Don't you use that —

TOM: Supposed to do!

AMANDA: Expression! Not in my —

TOM: Ohhh!

AMANDA: Presence! Have you gone out of your senses?

TOM: I have, that's true, *driven* out!

AMANDA: What is the matter with you, you — big — big — IDIOT!

TOM: Look — I've got *no thing*, no single thing —

AMANDA: Lower your voice!

TOM: In my life here that I can call my OWN! Everything is —

AMANDA: Stop that shouting!

TOM: Yesterday you confiscated my books! You had the nerve to —

AMANDA: I took that horrible novel back to the library — yes! That hideous book by that insane Mr. Lawrence. (*Tom laughs wildly.*) I cannot control the output of diseased minds or people who cater to them — (*Tom laughs still more wildly.*) BUT I WON'T ALLOW SUCH FILTH BROUGHT INTO MY HOUSE! No, no, no, no, no!

TOM: House, house! Who pays rent on it, who makes a slave of himself to —

AMANDA (*fairly screeching*): Don't you DARE to —

TOM: No, no, I mustn't say things! *I've* got to just —

AMANDA: Let me tell you —

TOM: I don't want to hear any more! (*He tears the portieres open. The upstage area is lit with a turgid smoky red glow.*)

(*Amanda's hair is in metal curlers and she wears a very old bathrobe, much too large for her slight figure, a relic of the faithless Mr. Wingfield.*)

(*An upright typewriter and a wild disarray of manuscripts are on the dropleaf table. The quarrel was probably precipitated by Amanda's interruption of his creative labor. A chair lying overthrown on the floor.*)

(*Their gesticulating shadows are cast on the ceiling by the fiery glow.*)

AMANDA: You *will* hear more, you —

TOM: No, I won't hear more, I'm going out!

AMANDA: You come right back in —

TOM: Out, out out! Because I'm —

AMANDA: Come back here, Tom Wingfield! I'm not through talking to you!

TOM: Oh, go —

LAURA (*desperately*): Tom!

AMANDA: You're going to listen, and no more insolence from you! I'm at the end of my patience! (*He comes back toward her.*)

TOM: What do you think I'm at? Aren't I supposed to have any patience to reach the end of, Mother? I know, I know. It seems unimportant to you, what I'm *doing* — what I *want* to do — having a little *difference* between them! You don't think that —

AMANDA: I think you've been doing things that you're ashamed of. That's why you act like this. I don't believe that you go every night to the movies. Nobody goes to the movies night after night. Nobody in their right minds goes to the movies as often as you pretend to. People don't go to the movies at nearly midnight, and movies don't let out at two A.M. Come in stumbling. Muttering to yourself like a maniac! You get three hours' sleep and then go to work. Oh, I can picture the way you're doing down there. Moping, doping, because you're in no condition.

TOM (*wildly*): No, I'm in no condition!

AMANDA: What right have you got to jeopardize your job? Jeopardize the security of us all? How do you think we'd manage if you were —

TOM: Listen! You think I'm crazy *about* the *warehouse?* (*He bends fiercely toward her slight figure.*) You think I'm in love with the Continental Shoemakers? You think I want to spend fifty-five *years* down there in that — *celotex interior!* with — *fluorescent* — *tubes!* Look! I'd rather somebody picked up a crowbar and battered out my brains — than go back mornings! I *go!* Every time you come in yelling that God damn *"Rise and Shine!" "Rise and Shine!"* I say to myself, *"How lucky dead people are!"* But I get up. I *go!* For sixty-five dollars a month I give up all that I dream of doing and being *ever!* And you say self — *self's* all I ever think of. Why, listen, if self is what I thought of, Mother, I'd be where he is — GONE! (*Pointing to father's picture.*) As far as the system of transportation reaches! (*He starts past her. She grabs his arm.*) Don't grab at me, Mother!

AMANDA: Where are you going?

TOM: I'm going to the *movies!*

AMANDA: I don't believe that lie!

TOM (*Crouching toward her, overtowering her tiny figure. She backs away, gasping.*): I'm going to opium dens! Yes, opium dens, dens of vice and criminals' hangouts, Mother. I've joined the Hogan gang, I'm a hired assassin, I carry a tommy-gun in a violin case! I run a string of cathouses in the Valley! They call me Killer, Killer Wingfield, I'm leading a double life, a simple, honest warehouse worker by day, by night, a dynamic *czar* of the *underworld, Mother.* I go to gambling casinos, I spin away fortunes on the roulette table! I wear a patch over one eye and a false mustache, sometimes I put on green whiskers. On those occasions they call me — *El Diablo!* Oh, I could tell you things to make you sleepless! My enemies plan to dynamite this place. They're going to blow us all skyhigh some night! I'll be glad, very happy, and so will you! You'll go up, up on a broomstick, over Blue Mountain with seventeen gentlemen callers! You ugly — babbling old — *witch.* . . . (*He goes through a series of violent, clumsy movements, seizing his overcoat, lunging to the door, pulling it fiercely open. The women watch him, aghast. His arm catches in the sleeve of the coat as he struggles to pull it on. For a moment he is pinioned by the bulky garment. With an outraged groan he tears the coat off again, splitting the shoulders of it, and hurls it across the room. It strikes against the shelf of Laura's glass collection, there is a tinkle of shattering glass. Laura cries out as if wounded.*)

(*Music legend: "The Glass Menagerie."*)

LAURA (*shrilly*): My glass! — menagerie. . . . (*She covers her face and turns away.*)

(*But Amanda is still stunned and stupefied by the "ugly witch" so that she barely notices this occurrence. Now she recovers her speech.*)

AMANDA (*in an awful voice*): I won't speak to you — until you apologize! (*She crosses through portieres and draws them together behind her. Tom is left with Laura. Laura clings weakly to the mantel with her face averted. Tom stares at her stupidly for a moment. Then he crosses to shelf. Drops awkwardly to his knees to collect the fallen glass, glancing at Laura as if he would speak but couldn't.*)

(*"The Glass Menagerie" steals in as the scene dims out.*)

SCENE 4

(*The interior is dark. Faint light in the alley.*)

(*A deep-voiced bell in a church is tolling the hour of five as the scene commences.*)

(*Tom appears at the top of the alley. After each solemn boom of the bell in the tower, he shakes a little noisemaker or rattle as if to express the tiny spasm of man in contrast to the sustained power and dignity of the Almighty. This and the unsteadiness of his advance make it evident that he has been drinking.*)

(*As he climbs the few steps to the fire escape landing light steals up inside. Laura appears in nightdress, observing Tom's empty bed in the front room.*)

(*Tom fishes in his pockets for the door key, removing a motley assortment of articles in the search, including a perfect shower of movie ticket stubs and an empty bottle. At last he finds the key, but just as he is about to*

insert it, it slips from his fingers. He strikes a match and crouches below the door.*)

TOM (*bitterly*): One crack — and it falls through!

(*Laura opens the door.*)

LAURA: Tom! Tom, what are you doing?
TOM: Looking for a door key.
LAURA: Where have you been all this time?
TOM: I have been to the movies.
LAURA: All this time at the movies?
TOM: There was a very long program. There was a Garbo picture and a Mickey Mouse and a travelogue and a newsreel and a preview of coming attractions. And there was an organ solo and a collection for the milk fund — simultaneously — which ended up in a terrible fight between a fat lady and an usher!
LAURA (*innocently*): Did you have to stay through everything?
TOM: Of course! And, oh, I forgot! There was a big stage show! The headliner on this stage show was Malvolio the Magician. He performed wonderful tricks, many of them, such as pouring water back and forth between pitchers. First it turned to wine and then it turned to beer and then it turned to whiskey. I know it was whiskey it finally turned into because he needed somebody to come up out of the audience to help him, and I came up — both shows! It was Kentucky Straight Bourbon. A very generous fellow, he gave souvenirs. (*He pulls from his back pocket a shimmering rainbow-colored scarf.*) He gave me this. This is his magic scarf. You can have it, Laura. You wave it over a canary cage and you get a bowl of goldfish. You wave it over the goldfish bowl and they fly away canaries. . . . But the wonderfullest trick of all was the coffin trick. We nailed him into a coffin and he got out of the coffin without removing one nail. (*He has come inside.*) There is a trick that would come in handy for me — get me out of this 2 by 4 situation! (*Flops onto bed and starts removing shoes.*)
LAURA: Tom — Shhh!
TOM: What you shushing me for?
LAURA: You'll wake up Mother.
TOM: Goody, goody! Pay 'er back for all those "Rise an' Shines." (*Lies down, groaning.*) You know it don't take much intelligence to get yourself into a nailed-up coffin, Laura. But who in hell ever got himself out of one without removing one nail?

(*As if in answer, the father's grinning photograph lights up.*)

(*Scene dims out.*)

(*Immediately following: The church bell is heard striking six. At the sixth stroke the alarm clock goes off in Amanda's room, and after a few moments we hear her calling: "Rise and Shine! Rise and Shine! Laura, go tell your brother to rise and shine!"*)

TOM (*sitting up slowly*): I'll rise — but I won't shine.

(*The light increases.*)

AMANDA: Laura, tell your brother his coffee is ready.

(*Laura slips into front room.*)

LAURA: Tom! it's nearly seven. Don't make Mother nervous. (*He stares at her stupidly. Beseechingly.*) Tom, speak to Mother this morning. Make up with her, apologize, speak to her!

TOM: She won't to me. It's her that started not speaking.

LAURA: If you just say you're sorry she'll start speaking.

TOM: Her not speaking — is that such a tragedy?

LAURA: Please — please!

AMANDA (*calling from kitchenette*): Laura, are you going to do what I asked you to do, or do I have to get dressed and go out myself?

LAURA: Going, going — soon as I get on my coat! (*She pulls on a shapeless felt hat with nervous, jerky movement, pleadingly glancing at Tom. Rushes awkwardly for coat. The coat is one of Amanda's, inaccurately made over, the sleeves too short for Laura.*) Butter and what else?

AMANDA (*entering upstage*): Just butter. Tell them to charge it.

LAURA: Mother, they make such faces when I do that.

AMANDA: Sticks and stones may break my bones, but the expression on Mr. Garfinkel's face won't harm us! Tell your brother his coffee is getting cold.

LAURA (*at door*): Do what I asked you, will you, will you, Tom?

(*He looks sullenly away.*)

AMANDA: Laura, go now or just don't go at all!

LAURA (*rushing out*): Going — going! (*A second later she cries out. Tom springs up and crosses to the door. Amanda rushes anxiously in. Tom opens the door.*)

TOM: Laura?

LAURA: I'm all right. I slipped, but I'm all right.

AMANDA (*peering anxiously after her*): If anyone breaks a leg on those fire escape steps, the landlord ought to be sued for every cent he possesses! (*She shuts door. Remembers she isn't speaking and returns to other room.*)

(*As Tom enters listlessly for his coffee, she turns her back to him and stands rigidly facing the window on the gloomy gray vault of the areaway. Its light on her face with its aged but childish features is cruelly sharp, satirical as a Daumier print.*)

(*Music under: "Ave Maria."*)

(*Tom glances sheepishly but sullenly at her averted figure and slumps at the table. The coffee is scalding hot; he sips it and gasps and spits it back in the cup. At his gasp, Amanda catches her breath and half turns. Then catches herself and turns back to window.*)

(*Tom blows on his coffee, glancing sidewise at his mother. She clears her throat. Tom clears his. He starts to rise. Sinks back down again, scratches his head, clears his throat again. Amanda coughs. Tom raises his cup in both hands to blow on it, his eyes staring over the rim of it at his mother for several moments. Then he slowly sets the cup down and awkwardly and hesitantly rises from the chair.*)

TOM (*hoarsely*): Mother. I — I apologize. Mother. (*Amanda draws a quick, shuddering breath. Her face works grotesquely. She breaks into childlike tears.*) I'm sorry for what I said, for everything that I said, I didn't mean it.

AMANDA (*sobbingly*): My devotion has made me a witch and so I make myself hateful to my children!

TOM: *No*, you *don't*.

AMANDA: I worry so much, don't sleep, it makes me nervous!

TOM (*gently*): I understand that.

AMANDA: I've had to put up a solitary battle all these years. But you're my right-hand bower! Don't fall down, don't fail!

TOM (*gently*): I try, Mother.

AMANDA (*with great enthusiasm*): Try and you will SUCCEED! (*The notion makes her breathless.*) Why, you — you're just *full* of natural endowments! Both of my children — they're *unusual* children! Don't you think I know it? I'm so — *proud!* Happy and — feel I've — so much to be thankful for but — Promise me one thing, son!

TOM: What, Mother?

AMANDA: Promise, son, you'll — never be a drunkard!

LEFT: Laurette Taylor as Amanda in the original 1944 production of *The Glass Menagerie*. RIGHT: Julie Haydon as Laura. ABOVE: Jo Mielziner's drawing of the set for the original production of *The Glass Menagerie*.

TOM (*turns to her grinning*): I will never be a drunkard, Mother.

AMANDA: That's what frightened me so, that you'd be drinking! Eat a bowl of Purina!

TOM: Just coffee, Mother.

AMANDA: Shredded wheat biscuit?

TOM: No, no, Mother, just coffee.

AMANDA: You can't put in a day's work on an empty stomach. You've got ten minutes — don't gulp! Drinking too-hot liquids makes cancer of the stomach. . . . Put cream in.

TOM: No, thank you.

AMANDA: To cool it.

TOM: No! No, thank you, I want it black.

AMANDA: I know, but it's not good for you. We have to do all that we can to build ourselves up. In these trying times we live in, all that we have to cling to is — each other. . . . That's why it's so important to — Tom, I — I sent out your sister so I could discuss something with you. If you hadn't spoken I would have spoken to you. (*Sits down.*)

TOM (*gently*): What is it, Mother, that you want to discuss?

AMANDA: *Laura!*

(*Tom puts his cup down slowly.*)
(*Legend on screen: "Laura."*)
(*Music: "The Glass Menagerie."*)

TOM: — Oh. — Laura . . .

AMANDA (*touching his sleeve*): You know how Laura is. So quiet but — still water runs deep! She notices things and I think she — broods about them. (*Tom looks up.*) A few days ago I came in and she was crying.

TOM: What about?

AMANDA: You.

TOM: Me?

AMANDA: She has an idea that you're not happy here.

TOM: What gave her that idea?

AMANDA: What gives her any idea? However, you do act strangely. I — I'm not criticizing, understand *that!* I know your ambitions do not lie in the warehouse, that like everybody in the whole wide world — you've had to — make sacrifices, but — Tom — Tom — life's not easy, it calls for — Spartan endurance! There's so many things in my heart that I cannot describe to you! I've never told you but I — *loved your father. . . .*

TOM (*gently*): I know that, Mother.

AMANDA: And you — when I see you taking after his ways! Staying out late — and — well, you *had* been drinking the night you were in that — terrifying condition! Laura says that you hate the apartment and that you go out nights to get away from it! Is that true, Tom?

TOM: No. You say there's so much in your heart that you can't describe to me. That's true of me, too. There's so much in my heart that I can't describe to *you!* So let's respect each other's —

AMANDA: But, why — *why,* Tom — are you always so *restless?* Where do you go to, nights?

TOM: I — go to the movies.

AMANDA: Why do you go to the movies so much, Tom?

TOM: I go to the movies because — I like adventure. Adventure is something I don't have much of at work, so I go to the movies.

AMANDA: But, Tom, you go to the movies *entirely* too *much!*

TOM: I like a lot of adventure.

(*Amanda looks baffled, then hurt. As the familiar inquisition resumes he becomes hard and impatient again. Amanda slips back into her querulous attitude toward him.*)
(*Image on screen: sailing vessel with Jolly Roger.°*)

AMANDA: Most young men find adventure in their careers.

TOM: Then most young men are not employed in a warehouse.

AMANDA: The world is full of young men employed in warehouses and offices and factories.

TOM: Do all of them find adventure in their careers?

AMANDA: They do or they do without it! Not everybody has a craze for adventure.

TOM: Man is by instinct a lover, a hunter, a fighter, and none of those instincts are given much play at the warehouse!

AMANDA: Man is by instinct! Don't quote instinct to me! Instinct is something that people have got away from! It belongs to animals! Christian adults don't want it!

TOM: What do Christian adults want, then, Mother?

AMANDA: Superior things! Things of the mind and the spirit! Only animals have to satisfy instincts! Surely your aims are somewhat higher than theirs! Than monkeys — pigs —

TOM: I reckon they're not.

AMANDA: You're joking. However, that isn't what I wanted to discuss.

TOM (*rising*): I haven't much time.

AMANDA (*pushing his shoulders*): Sit down.

TOM: You want me to punch in red at the warehouse, Mother?

AMANDA: You have five minutes. I want to talk about Laura.

(*Legend: "Plans and Provisions."*)

TOM: All right! What about Laura?

AMANDA: We have to be making plans and provisions for her. She's older than you, two years, and nothing has happened. She just drifts along doing nothing. It frightens me terribly how she just drifts along.

TOM: I guess she's the type that people call home girls.

AMANDA: There's no such type, and if there is, it's a pity! That is unless the home is hers, with a husband!

Jolly Roger: The black flag with white skull and crossbones used by pirates.

TOM: What?

AMANDA: Oh, I can see the handwriting on the wall as plain as I see the nose in front of my face! It's terrifying! More and more you remind me of your father! He was out all hours without explanation — Then *left! Good-bye!* And me with a bag to hold. I saw that letter you got from the Merchant Marine. I know what you're dreaming of. I'm not standing here blindfolded. Very well, then. Then *do* it! But not till there's somebody to take your place.

TOM: What do you mean?

AMANDA: I mean that as soon as Laura has got somebody to take care of her, married, a home of her own, independent — why, then you'll be free to go wherever you please, on land, on sea, whichever way the wind blows you! But until that time you've got to look out for your sister. I don't say me because I'm old and don't matter! I say for your sister because she's young and dependent. I put her in business college — a dismal failure! Frightened her so it made her sick to her stomach. I took her over to the Young People's League at the church. Another fiasco. She spoke to nobody, nobody spoke to her. Now all she does is fool with those pieces of glass and play those worn-out records. What kind of a life is that for a girl to lead!

TOM: What can I do about it?

AMANDA: Overcome selfishness! Self, self, self is all that you ever think of! (*Tom springs up and crosses to get his coat. It is ugly and bulky. He pulls on a cap with earmuffs.*) Where is your muffler? Put your wool muffler on! (*He snatches it angrily from the closet and tosses it around his neck and pulls both ends tight.*) Tom! I haven't said what I had in mind to ask you.

TOM: I'm too late to —

AMANDA (*Catching his arms — very importunately. Then shyly*): Down at the warehouse, aren't there some — nice young men?

TOM: No!

AMANDA: There *must* be — *some* . . .

TOM: Mother —

(*Gesture.*)

AMANDA: Find out one that's clean-living — doesn't drink and — ask him out for sister!

TOM: What?

AMANDA: For *sister!* To *meet!* Get *acquainted!*

TOM (*stamping to door*): Oh, my *go-osh!*

AMANDA: Will you? (*He opens door. Imploringly.*) Will you? (*He starts down.*) Will you? *Will* you, dear?

TOM (*calling back*): YES!

(*Amanda closes the door hesitantly and with a troubled but faintly hopeful expression.*)
    (*Screen image: glamor magazine cover.*)
    (*Spot° Amanda at phone.*)

AMANDA: Ella Cartwright? This is Amanda Wingfield! How are you, honey? How is that kidney condition?

Spot: Spotlight.

(*Count five.*) Horrors! (*Count five.*) You're a Christian martyr, yes, honey, that's what you are, a Christian martyr! Well, I just happened to notice in my little red book that your subscription to the *Companion* has just run out! I knew that you wouldn't want to miss out on the wonderful serial starting in this new issue. It's by Bessie Mae Hopper, the first thing she's written since *Honeymoon for Three.* Wasn't that a strange and interesting story? Well, this one is even lovelier, I believe. It has a sophisticated society background. It's all about the horsey set on Long Island!

(*Fade out.*)

SCENE 5

(*Legend on screen "Annunciation." Fade with music.*)
    (*It is early dusk of a spring evening. Supper has just been finished in the Wingfield apartment. Amanda and Laura in light colored dresses are removing dishes from the table, in the upstage area, which is shadowy, their movements formalized almost as a dance or ritual, their moving forms as pale and silent as moths.*)
    (*Tom, in white shirt and trousers, rises from the table and crosses toward the fire escape.*)

AMANDA (*as he passes her*): Son, will you do me a favor?

TOM: What?

AMANDA: Comb your hair! You look so pretty when your hair is combed! (*Tom slouches on sofa with evening paper. Enormous caption "Franco Triumphs."*) There is only one respect in which I would like you to emulate your father.

TOM: What respect is that?

AMANDA: The care he always took of his appearance. He never allowed himself to look untidy. (*He throws down the paper and crosses to fire escape.*) Where are you going?

TOM: I'm going out to smoke.

AMANDA: You smoke too much. A pack a day at fifteen cents a pack. How much would that amount to in a month? Thirty times fifteen is how much, Tom? Figure it out and you will be astounded at what you could save. Enough to give you a night school course in accounting at Washington U! Just think what a wonderful thing that would be for you, son!

(*Tom is unmoved by the thought.*)

TOM: I'd rather smoke. (*He steps out on landing, letting the screen door slam.*)

AMANDA (*sharply*): I know! That's the tragedy of it. . . . (*Alone, she turns to look at her husband's picture.*)

(*Dance music: "All the World is Waiting for the Sunrise!"*)

TOM (*to the audience*): Across the alley from us was the Paradise Dance Hall. On evenings in spring the windows and doors were open and the music came outdoors. Sometimes the lights were turned out except for a large glass sphere that hung from the ceiling. It would turn slowly about and filter the dusk with delicate rainbow colors. Then the orchestra played a waltz or a tango, something that had a slow and sensuous rhythm. Couples would come outside, to the relative privacy of the alley. You could see them kissing behind ash-pits and telephone poles. This was the compensation for lives that passed like mine, without any change or adventure. Adventure and change were imminent in this year. They were waiting around the corner for all these kids. Suspended in the mist over Berchtesgaden, caught in the folds of Chamberlain's umbrella — In Spain there was Guernica!° But here there was only hot swing music and liquor, dance halls, bars, and movies, and sex that hung in the gloom like a chandelier and flooded the world with brief, deceptive rainbows. . . . All the world was waiting for bombardments!

(*Amanda turns from the picture and comes outside.*)

AMANDA (*sighing*): A fire escape landing's a poor excuse for a porch. (*She spreads a newspaper on a step and sits down, gracefully and demurely as if she were settling into a swing on a Mississippi veranda.*) What are you looking at?

TOM: The moon.

AMANDA: Is there a moon this evening?

TOM: It's rising over Garfinkel's Delicatessen.

AMANDA: So it is! A little silver slipper of a moon. Have you made a wish on it yet?

TOM: Um-hum.

AMANDA: What did you wish for?

TOM: That's a secret.

AMANDA: A secret, huh? Well, I won't tell mine either. I will be just as mysterious as you.

TOM: I bet I can guess what yours is.

AMANDA: Is my head so transparent?

TOM: You're not a sphinx.

AMANDA: No, I don't have secrets. I'll tell you what I wished for on the moon. Success and happiness for my precious children! I wish for that whenever there's a moon, and when there isn't a moon, I wish for it, too.

TOM: I thought perhaps you wished for a gentleman caller.

AMANDA: Why do you say that?

TOM: Don't you remember asking me to fetch one?

AMANDA: I remember suggesting that it would be nice for your sister if you brought home some nice young man from the warehouse. I think I've made that suggestion more than once.

Berchtesgaden . . . Chamberlain . . . Guernica: All references to the approaches of World War II in Europe. Berchtesgaden was Hitler's summer home; Neville Chamberlain was the prime minister of England who signed the Munich Pact, which was regarded as a capitulation to Hitler; and the Spanish town Guernica was destroyed by German bombs during the Spanish Civil War in the late 1930s.

TOM: Yes, you have made it repeatedly.

AMANDA: Well?

TOM: We are going to have one.

AMANDA: *What?*

TOM: A gentleman caller!

(*The annunciation is celebrated with music.*)
    (*Amanda rises.*)
    (*Image on screen: caller with bouquet.*)

AMANDA: You mean you have asked some nice young man to come over?

TOM: Yep. I've asked him to dinner.

AMANDA: You really did?

TOM: I did!

AMANDA: You did, and did he — *accept?*

TOM: He did!

AMANDA: Well, well — well, well! That's — lovely!

TOM: I thought that you would be pleased.

AMANDA: It's definite, then?

TOM: Very definite.

AMANDA: Soon?

TOM: Very soon.

AMANDA: For heaven's sake, stop putting on and tell me some things, will you?

TOM: What things do you want me to tell you?

AMANDA: *Naturally* I would like to know when he's *coming!*

TOM: He's coming tomorrow.

AMANDA: *Tomorrow?*

TOM: Yep. Tomorrow.

AMANDA: But, Tom!

TOM: Yes, Mother?

AMANDA: Tomorrow gives me no time!

TOM: Time for what?

AMANDA: Preparations! Why didn't you phone me at once, as soon as you asked him, the minute that he accepted? Then, don't you see, I could have been getting ready!

TOM: You don't have to make any fuss.

AMANDA: Oh, Tom, Tom, Tom, of course I have to make a fuss! I want things nice, not sloppy! Not thrown together. I'll certainly have to do some fast thinking, won't I?

TOM: I don't see why you have to think at all.

AMANDA: You just don't know. We can't have a gentleman caller in a pigsty! All my wedding silver has to be polished, the monogrammed table linen ought to be laundered! The windows have to be washed and fresh curtains put up. And how about clothes? We have to *wear* something, don't we?

TOM: Mother, this boy is no one to make a fuss over!

AMANDA: Do you realize he's the first young man we've introduced to your sister? It's terrible, dreadful, disgraceful that poor little sister has never received a single gentleman caller! Tom, come inside! (*She opens the screen door.*)

TOM: What for?

AMANDA: I want to ask you some things.

TOM: If you're going to make such a fuss, I'll call it off, I'll tell him not to come.

AMANDA: You certainly won't do anything of the kind. Nothing offends people worse than broken engagements. It simply means I'll have to work like a Turk! We won't be brilliant, but we'll pass inspection. Come on inside. (*Tom follows, groaning.*) Sit down.

TOM: Any particular place you would like me to sit?

AMANDA: Thank heavens I've got that new sofa! I'm also making payments on a floor lamp I'll have sent out! And put the chintz covers on, they'll brighten things up! Of course I'd hoped to have these walls repapered. . . . What is the young man's name?

TOM: His name is O'Connor.

AMANDA: That, of course, means fish — tomorrow is Friday!° I'll have that salmon loaf — with Durkee's dressing! What does he do? He works at the warehouse?

TOM: Of course! How else would I —

AMANDA: Tom, he — doesn't drink?

TOM: Why do you ask me that?

AMANDA: Your father *did!*

TOM: Don't get started on that!

AMANDA: He *does* drink, then?

TOM: Not that I know of!

AMANDA: Make sure, be certain! The last thing I want for my daughter's a boy who drinks!

TOM: Aren't you being a little premature? Mr. O'Connor has not yet appeared on the scene!

AMANDA: But will tomorrow. To meet your sister, and what do I know about his character? Nothing! Old maids are better off than wives of drunkards!

TOM: Oh, my God!

AMANDA: Be still!

TOM (*leaning forward to whisper*): Lots of fellows meet girls whom they don't marry!

AMANDA: Oh, talk sensibly, Tom — and don't be sarcastic! (*She has gotten a hairbrush.*)

TOM: What are you doing?

AMANDA: I'm brushing that cowlick down! What is this young man's position at the warehouse?

TOM (*submitting grimly to the brush and the interrogation*): This young man's position is that of a shipping clerk, Mother.

AMANDA: Sounds to me like a fairly responsible job, the sort of a job *you* would be in if you just had more *get-up*. What is his salary? Have you got any idea.

TOM: I would judge it to be approximately eighty-five dollars a month.

AMANDA: Well — not princely, but —

TOM: Twenty more than I make.

AMANDA: Yes, how well I know! But for a family man, eighty-five dollars a month is not much more than you can just get by on. . . .

TOM: Yes, but Mr. O'Connor is not a family man.

fish . . . Friday: Until the 1960s Catholics were prohibited from eating meat on Fridays.

AMANDA: He might be, mightn't he? Some time in the future?

TOM: I see. Plans and provisions.

AMANDA: You are the only young man that I know of who ignores the fact that the future becomes the present, the present the past, and the past turns into everlasting regret if you don't plan for it!

TOM: I will think that over and see what I can make of it.

AMANDA: Don't be supercilious with your mother! Tell me some more about this — what do you call him?

TOM: James D. O'Connor. The D. is for Delaney.

AMANDA: Irish on *both* sides! *Gracious!* And doesn't drink?

TOM: Shall I call him up and ask him right this minute?

AMANDA: The only way to find out about those things is to make discreet inquiries at the proper moment. When I was a girl in Blue Mountain and it was suspected that a young man drank, the girl whose attentions he had been receiving, if any girl *was,* would sometimes speak to the minister of his church, or rather her father would if her father was living, and sort of feel him out on the young man's character. That is the way such things are discreetly handled to keep a young woman from making a tragic mistake!

TOM: Then how did you happen to make a tragic mistake?

AMANDA: That innocent look of your father's had everyone fooled! He *smiled* — the world was *enchanted!* No girl can do worse than put herself at the mercy of a handsome appearance! I hope that Mr. O'Connor is not too good-looking.

TOM: No, he's not too good-looking. He's covered with freckles and hasn't too much of a nose.

AMANDA: He's not right-down homely, though?

TOM: Not right-down homely. Just medium homely, I'd say.

AMANDA: Character's what to look for in a man.

TOM: That's what I've always said, Mother.

AMANDA: You've never said anything of the kind and I suspect you would never give it a thought.

TOM: Don't be suspicious of me.

AMANDA: At least I hope he's the type that's up and coming.

TOM: I think he really goes in for self-improvement.

AMANDA: What reason have you to think so?

TOM: He goes to night school.

AMANDA (*beaming*): Splendid! What does he do, I mean study?

TOM: Radio engineering and public speaking!

AMANDA: Then he has visions of being advanced in the world! Any young man who studies public speaking is aiming to have an executive job some day! And radio engineering? A thing for the future! Both of these facts are very illuminating. Those are the sort of things that a mother should know concerning any young man who comes to call on her daughter. Seriously or — not.

TOM: One little warning. He doesn't know about Laura.

I didn't let on that we had dark ulterior motives. I just said, why don't you come have dinner with us? He said okay and that was the whole conversation.

AMANDA: I bet it was! You're eloquent as an oyster. However, he'll know about Laura when he gets here. When he sees how lovely and sweet and pretty she is, he'll thank his lucky stars he was asked to dinner.

TOM: Mother, you mustn't expect too much of Laura.

AMANDA: What do you mean?

TOM: Laura seems all those things to you and me because she's ours and we love her. We don't even notice she's crippled anymore.

AMANDA: Don't say crippled! You know that I never allow that word to be used!

TOM: But face facts, Mother. She is and — that's not all —

AMANDA: What do you mean not all?

TOM: Laura is very different from other girls.

AMANDA: I think the difference is all to her advantage.

TOM: Not quite all — in the eyes of others — strangers — she's terribly shy and lives in a world of her own and those things make her seem a little peculiar to people outside the house.

AMANDA: Don't say peculiar.

TOM: Face the facts. She is.

(*The dance-hall music changes to a tango that has a minor and somewhat ominous tone.*)

AMANDA: In what way is she peculiar — may I ask?

TOM (*gently*): She lives in a world of her own — a world of — little glass ornaments, Mother. . . . (*Gets up. Amanda remains holding brush, looking at him, troubled.*) She plays old phonograph records and — that's about all — (*He glances at himself in the mirror and crosses to door.*)

AMANDA (*sharply*): Where are you going?

TOM: I'm going to the movies. (*Out screen door.*)

AMANDA: Not to the movies, every night to the movies! (*Follows quickly to screen door.*) I don't believe you always go to the movies! (*He is gone. Amanda looks worriedly after him for a moment. Then vitality and optimism return and she turns from the door. Crossing to portieres.*) Laura! Laura! (*Laura answers from kitchenette.*)

LAURA: Yes, Mother.

AMANDA: Let those dishes go and come in front! (*Laura appears with dish towel. Gaily.*) Laura, come here and make a wish on the moon!

LAURA (*entering*): Moon — moon?

AMANDA: A little silver slipper of a moon. Look over your left shoulder, Laura, and make a wish! (*Laura looks faintly puzzled as if called out of sleep. Amanda seizes her shoulders and turns her at an angle by the door.*) Now! Now, darling, *wish!*

LAURA: What shall I wish for, Mother?

AMANDA (*her voice trembling and her eyes suddenly filling with tears*): Happiness! Good Fortune!

(*The violin rises and the stage dims out.*)

SCENE 6

(*Image: high school hero.*)

TOM: And so the following evening I brought Jim home to dinner. I had known Jim slightly in high school. In high school Jim was a hero. He had tremendous Irish good nature and vitality with the scrubbed and polished look of white chinaware. He seemed to move in a continual spotlight. He was a star in basketball, captain of the debating club, president of the senior class and the glee club and he sang the male lead in the annual light operas. He was always running or bounding, never just walking. He seemed always at the point of defeating the law of gravity. He was shooting with such velocity through his adolescence — that you would logically expect him to arrive at nothing short of the White House by the time he was thirty. But Jim apparently ran into more interference after his graduation from Soldan. His speed had definitely slowed. Six years after he left high school he was holding a job that wasn't much better than mine.

(*Image: clerk.*)

He was the only one at the warehouse with whom I was on friendly terms. I was valuable to him as someone who could remember his former glory, who had seen him win basketball games and the silver cup in debating. He knew of my secret practice of retiring to a cabinet of the washroom to work on poems when business was slack in the warehouse. He called me Shakespeare. And while the other boys in the warehouse regarded me with suspicious hostility, Jim took a humorous attitude toward me. Gradually his attitude affected the others, their hostility wore off and they also began to smile at me as people smile at an oddly fashioned dog who trots across their path at some distance.

I knew that Jim and Laura had known each other at Soldan, and I had heard Laura speak admiringly of his voice. I didn't know if Jim remembered her or not. In high school Laura had been as unobtrusive as Jim had been astonishing. If he did remember Laura, it was not as my sister, for when I asked him to dinner, he grinned and said, "You know, Shakespeare, I never thought of you as having folks!"

He was about to discover that I did. . . .

(*Light up stage.*)

(*Legend on screen: "The Accent of a Coming Foot."*)

(*Friday evening. It is about five o'clock of a late spring evening which comes "scattering poems in the sky."*)

(*A delicate lemony light is in the Wingfield apartment.*)

(*Amanda has worked like a Turk in preparation for the gentleman caller. The results are astonishing. The new floor lamp with its rose-silk shade is in place, a colored paper lantern conceals the broken light fixture in the ceiling, new billowing white curtains are at the windows, chintz covers are on chairs and sofa, a pair of new sofa pillows make their initial appearance.*)

(*Open boxes and tissue paper are scattered on the floor.*)

(*Laura stands in the middle with lifted arms while Amanda crouches before her, adjusting the hem of the new dress, devout and ritualistic. The dress is colored and designed by memory. The arrangement of Laura's hair is changed; it is softer and more becoming. A fragile, unearthly prettiness has come out in Laura: she is like a piece of translucent glass touched by light, given a momentary radiance, not actual, not lasting.*)

AMANDA (*impatiently*): Why are you trembling?
LAURA: Mother, you've made me so nervous!
AMANDA: How have I made you nervous?
LAURA: By all this fuss! You make it seem so important!
AMANDA: I don't understand you, Laura. You couldn't be satisfied with just sitting home, and yet whenever I try to arrange something for you, you seem to resist it. (*She gets up.*) Now take a look at yourself. No, wait! Wait just a moment — I have an idea!
LAURA: What is it now?

(*Amanda produces two powder puffs which she wraps in handkerchiefs and stuffs in Laura's bosom.*)

LAURA: Mother, what are you doing?
AMANDA: They call them "Gay Deceivers"!
LAURA: I won't wear them!
AMANDA: You will!
LAURA: Why should I?
AMANDA: Because, to be painfully honest, your chest is flat.
LAURA: You make it seem like we were setting a trap.
AMANDA: All pretty girls are a trap, a pretty trap, and men expect them to be. (*Legend: "A Pretty Trap."*) Now look at yourself, young lady. This is the prettiest you will ever be! I've got to fix myself now! You're going to be surprised by your mother's appearance! (*She crosses through portieres, humming gaily.*)

(*Laura moves slowly to the long mirror and stares solemnly at herself.*)

(*A wind blows the white curtains inward in a slow, graceful motion and with a faint, sorrowful sighing.*)

AMANDA (*offstage*): It isn't dark enough yet. (*She turns slowly before the mirror with a troubled look.*)

(*Legend on screen: "This Is My Sister: Celebrate Her with Strings!" Music.*)

AMANDA (*laughing, off*): I'm going to show you something. I'm going to make a spectacular appearance!
LAURA: What is it, Mother?
AMANDA: Possess your soul in patience — you will see! Something I've resurrected from that old trunk! Styles haven't changed so terribly much after all. . . . (*She parts the portieres.*) Now just look at your mother! (*She wears a girlish frock of yellowed voile with a blue silk sash. She carries a bunch of jonquils — the legend of her youth is nearly revived.*

Feverishly.) This is the dress in which I led the cotillion. Won the cakewalk twice at Sunset Hill, wore one spring to the Governor's ball in Jackson! See how I sashayed around the ballroom, Laura? (*She raises her skirt and does a mincing step around the room.*) I wore it on Sundays for my gentlemen callers! I had it on the day I met your father — I had malaria fever all that spring. The change of climate from East Tennessee to the Delta — weakened resistance — I had a little temperature all the time — not enough to be serious — just enough to make me restless and giddy! Invitations poured in — parties all over the Delta! — "Stay in bed," said Mother, "you have fever!" — but I just wouldn't. — I took quinine but kept on going, going! — Evenings, dances! — Afternoons, long, long rides! Picnics — lovely! — So lovely, that country in May. — All lacy with dogwood, literally flooded with jonquils! — That was the spring I had the craze for jonquils. Jonquils became an absolute obsession. Mother said, "Honey, there's no more room for jonquils." And still I kept on bringing in more jonquils. Whenever, wherever I saw them, I'd say, "Stop! Stop! I see jonquils!" I made the young men help me gather the jonquils! It was a joke, Amanda and her jonquils! Finally there were no more vases to hold them, every available space was filled with jonquils. No vases to hold them? All right, I'll hold them myself! And then I — (*She stops in front of the picture. Music.*) met your father! Malaria fever and jonquils and then — this — boy. . . . (*She switches on the rose-colored lamp.*) I hope they get here before it starts to rain. (*She crosses upstage and places the jonquils in bowl on table.*) I gave your brother a little extra change so he and Mr. O'Connor could take the service car home.
LAURA (*with altered look*): What did you say his name was?
AMANDA: O'Connor.
LAURA: What is his first name?
AMANDA: I don't remember. Oh, yes, I do. It was — Jim!

(*Laura sways slightly and catches hold of a chair.*)
(*Legend on screen: "Not Jim!"*)

LAURA (*faintly*): Not — Jim!
AMANDA: Yes, that was it, it was Jim! I've never known a Jim that wasn't nice!

(*Music: ominous.*)

LAURA: Are you sure his name is Jim O'Connor?
AMANDA: Yes. Why?
LAURA: Is he the one that Tom used to know in high school?
AMANDA: He didn't say so. I think he just got to know him at the warehouse.
LAURA: There was a Jim O'Connor we both knew in high school — (*Then, with effort.*) If that is the one that Tom is bringing to dinner — you'll have to excuse me, I won't come to the table.

AMANDA: What sort of nonsense is this?

LAURA: You asked me once if I'd ever liked a boy. Don't you remember I showed you this boy's picture?

AMANDA: You mean the boy you showed me in the year-book?

LAURA: Yes, that boy.

AMANDA: Laura, Laura, were you in love with that boy?

LAURA: I don't know, Mother. All I know is I couldn't sit at the table if it was him!

AMANDA: It won't be him! It isn't the least bit likely. But whether it is or not, you will come to the table. You will not be excused.

LAURA: I'll have to be, Mother.

AMANDA: I don't intend to humor your silliness, Laura. I've had too much from you and your brother, both! So just sit down and compose yourself till they come. Tom has forgotten his key so you'll have to let them in, when they arrive.

LAURA (*panicky*): Oh, Mother — *you* answer the door!

AMANDA (*lightly*): I'll be in the kitchen — busy!

LAURA: Oh, Mother, please answer the door, don't make me do it!

AMANDA (*crossing into kitchenette*): I've got to fix the dressing for the salmon. Fuss, fuss — silliness! — over a gentleman caller!

(*Door swings shut. Laura is left alone.*)

(*Legend: "Terror!"*)

(*She utters a low moan and turns off the lamp — sits stiffly on the edge of the sofa, knotting her fingers together.*)

(*Legend on screen: "The Opening of a Door!"*)

(*Tom and Jim appear on the fire escape steps and climb to landing. Hearing their approach, Laura rises with a panicky gesture. She retreats to the portieres.*)

(*The doorbell. Laura catches her breath and touches her throat. Low drums.*)

AMANDA (*calling*): Laura, sweetheart! The door!

(*Laura stares at it without moving.*)

JIM: I think we just beat the rain.

TOM: Uh-huh. (*He rings again, nervously. Jim whistles and fishes for a cigarette.*)

AMANDA (*very, very gaily*): Laura, that is your brother and Mr. O'Connor! Will you let them in, darling?

(*Laura crosses toward kitchenette door.*)

LAURA (*breathlessly*): Mother — you go to the door!

(*Amanda steps out of kitchenette and stares furiously at Laura. She points imperiously at the door.*)

LAURA: Please, please!

AMANDA (*in a fierce whisper*): What is the matter with
 you, you silly thing?

LAURA (*desperately*): Please, you answer it, *please!*

AMANDA: I told you I wasn't going to humor you,
 Laura. Why have you chosen this moment to lose
 your mind?

LAURA: Please, please, please, you go!

AMANDA: You'll have to go to the door because I can't!

LAURA (*despairingly*): I can't either!

AMANDA: *Why?*

LAURA: I'm *sick!*

AMANDA: I'm sick, too — of your nonsense! Why can't
 you and your brother be normal people? Fantastic
 whims and behavior! (*Tom gives a long ring.*) Preposterous goings on! Can you give me one reason —
 (*Calls out lyrically.*) COMING! JUST ONE SECOND! —

why should you be afraid to open a door? Now you
 answer it, Laura!

LAURA: Oh, oh, oh . . . (*She returns through the portieres.
 Darts to the victrola and winds it frantically and turns
 it on.*)

AMANDA: Laura Wingfield, you march right to that door!

LAURA: Yes — yes, Mother!

(*A faraway, scratchy rendition of "Dardanella" softens
the air and gives her strength to move through it. She
slips to the door and draws it cautiously open.*)
 (*Tom enters with the caller, Jim O'Connor.*)

TOM: Laura, this is Jim. Jim, this is my sister, Laura.

JIM (*stepping inside*): I didn't know that Shakespeare
 had a sister!

LAURA (*retreating stiff and trembling from the door*):
 How — how do you do?

JIM (*heartily extending his hand*): Okay!

(*Laura touches it hesitantly with hers.*)

JIM: Your hand's *cold*, Laura!

LAURA: Yes, well — I've been playing the victrola. . . .

JIM: Must have been playing classical music on it! You ought to play a little hot swing music to warm you up!

LAURA: Excuse me — I haven't finished playing the victrola. . . .

(*She turns awkwardly and hurries into the front room. She pauses a second by the victrola. Then catches her breath and darts through the portieres like a frightened deer.*)

JIM (*grinning*): What was the matter?

TOM: Oh — with Laura? Laura is — terribly shy.

JIM: Shy, huh? It's unusual to meet a shy girl nowadays. I don't believe you ever mentioned you had a sister.

TOM: Well, now you know. I have one. Here is the *Post Dispatch*. You want a piece of it?

JIM: Uh-huh.

TOM: What piece? The comics?

JIM: Sports! (*Glances at it.*) Ole Dizzy Dean is on his bad behavior.

TOM (*disinterest*): Yeah? (*Lights cigarette and crosses back to fire escape door.*)

JIM: Where are *you* going?

TOM: I'm going out on the terrace.

JIM (*goes after him*): You know, Shakespeare — I'm going to sell you a bill of goods!

TOM: What goods?

JIM: A course I'm taking.

TOM: Huh?

JIM: In public speaking! You and me, we're not the warehouse type.

TOM: Thanks — that's good news. But what has public speaking got to do with it?

JIM: It fits you for — executive positions!

TOM: Awww.

JIM: I tell you it's done a helluva lot for me.

(*Image: executive at desk.*)

TOM: In what respect?

JIM: In every! Ask yourself what is the difference between you an' me and men in the office down front? Brains? — No! — Ability? — No! Then what? Just one little thing —

TOM: What is that one little thing?

JIM: Primarily it amounts to — social poise! Being able to square up to people and hold your own on any social level!

AMANDA (*offstage*): Tom?

TOM: Yes, Mother?

AMANDA: Is that you and Mr. O'Connor?

TOM: Yes, Mother.

AMANDA: Well, you just make yourselves comfortable in there.

TOM: Yes, Mother.

AMANDA: Ask Mr. O'Connor if he would like to wash his hands.

JIM: Aw, — no — no — thank you — I took care of that at the warehouse. Tom —

TOM: Yes?

JIM: Mr. Mendoza was speaking to me about you.

TOM: Favorably?

JIM: What do you think?

TOM: Well —

JIM: You're going to be out of a job if you don't wake up.

TOM: I am waking up —

JIM: You show no signs.

TOM: The signs are interior.

(*Image on screen: the sailing vessel with Jolly Roger again.*)

TOM: I'm planning to change. (*He leans over the rail speaking with quiet exhilaration. The incandescent marquees and signs of the first-run movie houses light his face from across the alley. He looks like a voyager.*) I'm right at the point of committing myself to a future that doesn't include the warehouse and Mr. Mendoza or even a night school course in public speaking.

JIM: What are you gassing about?

TOM: I'm tired of the movies.

JIM: Movies!

TOM: Yes, movies! Look at them — (*A wave toward the marvels of Grand Avenue.*) All of those glamorous people — having adventures — hogging it all, gobbling the whole thing up! You know what happens? People go to the *movies* instead of *moving*! Hollywood characters are supposed to have all the adventures for everybody in America, while everybody in America sits in a dark room and watches them have them! Yes, until there's a war. That's when adventure becomes available to the masses! *Everyone's* dish, not only Gable's! Then the people in the dark room come out of the dark room to have some adventures themselves — Goody, goody! — It's our turn now, to go to the South Sea Island — to make a safari — to be exotic, far-off! — But I'm not patient. I don't want to wait till then. I'm tired of the *movies* and I am *about* to *move*!

JIM (*incredulously*): Move?

TOM: Yes.

JIM: When?

TOM: Soon!

JIM: Where? Where?

(*Theme three music seems to answer the question, while Tom thinks it over. He searches among his pockets.*)

TOM: I'm starting to boil inside. I know I seem dreamy, but inside — well, I'm boiling! Whenever I pick up a shoe, I shudder a little thinking how short life is and what I am doing! — Whatever that means. I know it doesn't mean shoes — except as something to wear on a traveler's feet! (*Finds paper.*) Look —

JIM: What?

TOM: I'm a member.

JIM (*reading*): The Union of Merchant Seamen.

TOM: I paid my dues this month, instead of the light bill.

JIM: You will regret it when they turn the lights off.

TOM: I won't be here.

JIM: How about your mother?

TOM: I'm like my father. The bastard son of a bastard! See how he grins? And he's been absent going on sixteen years!

JIM: You're just talking, you drip. How does your mother feel about it?

TOM: Shhh! — Here comes Mother! Mother is not acquainted with my plans!

AMANDA (*enters portieres*): Where are you all?

TOM: On the terrace, Mother.

(*They start inside. She advances to them. Tom is distinctly shocked at her appearance. Even Jim blinks a little. He is making his first contact with girlish Southern vivacity and in spite of the night school course in public speaking is somewhat thrown off the beam by the unexpected outlay of social charm.*)

(*Certain responses are attempted by Jim but are swept aside by Amanda's gay laughter and chatter. Tom is embarrassed but after the first shock Jim reacts very warmly. Grins and chuckles, is altogether won over.*)

(*Image: Amanda as a girl.*)

AMANDA (*coyly smiling, shaking her girlish ringlets*): Well, well, well, so this is Mr. O'Connor. Introductions entirely unnecessary. I've heard so much about you from my boy. I finally said to him, Tom — good gracious! — why don't you bring this paragon to supper? I'd like to meet this nice young man at the warehouse! — Instead of just hearing him sing your praises so much! I don't know why my son is so standoffish — that's not Southern behavior! Let's sit down and — I think we could stand a little more air in here! Tom, leave the door open. I felt a nice fresh breeze a moment ago. Where has it gone to? Mmm, so warm already! And not quite summer, even. We're going to burn up when summer really gets started. However, we're having — we're having a very light supper. I think light things are better fo' this time of year. The same as light clothes are. Light clothes an' light food are what warm weather calls fo'. You know our blood gets so thick during th' winter — it takes a while fo' us to *adjust* ou'selves! — when the season changes . . . It's come so quick this year. I wasn't prepared. All of a sudden — heavens! Already summer! — I ran to the trunk an' pulled out this light dress — Terribly old! Historical almost! But feels so good — so good an' co-ol, y'know. . . .

TOM: Mother —

AMANDA: Yes, honey?

TOM: How about — supper?

AMANDA: Honey, you go ask Sister if supper is ready! You know that Sister is in full charge of supper! Tell

her you hungry boys are waiting for it. (*To Jim.*) Have you met Laura?

JIM: She —

AMANDA: Let you in? Oh, good, you've met already! It's rare for a girl as sweet an' pretty as Laura to be domestic! But Laura is, thank heavens, not only pretty but also very domestic. I'm not at all. I never was a bit. I never could make a thing but angel food cake. Well, in the South we had so many servants. Gone, gone, gone. All vestiges of gracious living! Gone completely! I wasn't prepared for what the future brought me. All of my gentlemen callers were sons of planters and so of course I assumed that I would be married to one and raise my family on a large piece of land with plenty of servants. But man proposes — and woman accepts the proposal! — To vary that old, old saying a little bit — I married no planter! I married a man who worked for the telephone company! — That gallantly smiling gentleman over there! (*Points to the picture.*) A telephone man who — fell in love with long distance! — Now he travels and I don't even know where! — But what am I going on for about my — tribulations! Tell me yours — I hope you don't have any! Tom?

TOM (*returning*): Yes, Mother?

AMANDA: Is supper nearly ready?

TOM: It looks to me like supper is on the table.

AMANDA: Let me look — (*She rises prettily and looks through portieres.*) Oh, lovely! — But where is Sister?

TOM: Laura is not feeling well and she says that she thinks she'd better not come to the table.

AMANDA: What? — Nonsense! — Laura? Oh, Laura!

LAURA (*offstage, faintly*): Yes, Mother.

AMANDA: You really must come to the table. We won't be seated until you come to the table! Come in, Mr. O'Connor. You sit over there, and I'll — Laura? Laura Wingfield! You're keeping us waiting, honey! We can't say grace until you come to the table!

(*The back door is pushed weakly open and Laura comes in. She is obviously quite faint, her lips trembling, her eyes wide and staring. She moves unsteadily toward the table.*)

(*Legend: "Terror!"*)

(*Outside a summer storm is coming abruptly. The white curtains billow inward at the windows and there is a sorrowful murmur and deep blue dusk.*)

(*Laura suddenly stumbles — she catches at a chair with a faint moan.*)

TOM: Laura!

AMANDA: Laura! (*There is a clap of thunder.*) (*Legend: "Ah!"*) (*Despairingly.*) Why, Laura, you *are* sick, darling! Tom, help your sister into the living room, dear! Sit in the living room, Laura — rest on the sofa. Well! (*To the gentleman caller.*) Standing over the hot stove made her ill! — I told her that it was just too warm this evening, but — (*Tom comes back in. Laura is on the sofa.*) Is Laura all right now?

TOM: Yes.

AMANDA: What *is* that? Rain? A nice cool rain has come up! (*She gives the gentleman caller a frightened look.*) I think we may — have grace — now . . . (*Tom looks at her stupidly.*) Tom, honey — you say grace!

TOM: Oh . . . "For these and all thy mercies —" (*They bow their heads, Amanda stealing a nervous glance at Jim. In the living room Laura, stretched on the sofa, clenches her hand to her lips, to hold back a shuddering sob.*) God's Holy Name be praised —

(*The scene dims out.*)

SCENE 7

(*A Souvenir*)

(*Half an hour later. Dinner is just being finished in the upstage area which is concealed by the drawn portieres.*)

(*As the curtain rises Laura is still huddled upon the sofa, her feet drawn under her, her head resting on a pale blue pillow, her eyes wide and mysteriously watchful. The new floor lamp with its shade of rose-colored silk gives a soft, becoming light to her face, bringing out the fragile, unearthly prettiness which usually escapes attention. There is a steady murmur of rain, but it is slackening and stops soon after the scene begins; the air outside becomes pale and luminous as the moon breaks out.*)

(*A moment after the curtain rises, the lights in both rooms flicker and go out.*)

JIM: Hey, there, Mr. Light Bulb!

(*Amanda laughs nervously.*)
(*Legend: "Suspension of a Public Service."*)

AMANDA: Where was Moses when the lights went out? Ha-ha. Do you know the answer to that one, Mr. O'Connor?

JIM: No, Ma'am, what's the answer?

AMANDA: In the dark! (*Jim laughs appreciably.*) Everybody sit still. I'll light the candles. Isn't it lucky we have them on the table? Where's a match? Which of you gentlemen can provide a match?

JIM: Here.

AMANDA: Thank you, sir.

JIM: Not at all, Ma'am!

AMANDA: I guess the fuse has burnt out. Mr. O'Connor, can you tell a burnt-out fuse? I know I can't and Tom is a total loss when it comes to mechanics. (*Sound: getting up: voices recede a little to kitchenette.*) Oh, be careful you don't bump into something. We don't want our gentleman caller to break his neck. Now wouldn't that be a fine howdy-do?

JIM: Ha-ha! Where is the fuse box?

AMANDA: Right here next to the stove. Can you see anything?

JIM: Just a minute.

AMANDA: Isn't electricity a mysterious thing? Wasn't it Benjamin Franklin who tied a key to a kite? We live in such a mysterious universe, don't we? Some people say that science clears up all the mysteries for us. In my opinion it only creates more! Have you found it yet?

JIM: No, Ma'am. All these fuses look okay to me.

AMANDA: Tom!

TOM: Yes, Mother?

AMANDA: That light bill I gave you several days ago. The one I told you we got the notices about?

TOM: Oh. — Yeah.

(*Legend: "Ha!"*)

AMANDA: You didn't neglect to pay it by any chance?

TOM: Why, I —

AMANDA: Didn't! I might have known it!

JIM: Shakespeare probably wrote a poem on that light bill, Mrs. Wingfield.

AMANDA: I might have known better than to trust him with it! There's such a high price for negligence in this world!

JIM: Maybe the poem will win a ten-dollar prize.

AMANDA: We'll just have to spend the remainder of the evening in the nineteenth century, before Mr. Edison made the Mazda lamp!

JIM: Candlelight is my favorite kind of light.

AMANDA: That shows you're romantic! But that's no excuse for Tom. Well, we got through dinner. Very considerate of them to let us get through dinner before they plunged us into everlasting darkness, wasn't it, Mr. O'Connor?

JIM: Ha-ha!

AMANDA: Tom, as a penalty for your carelessness you can help me with the dishes.

JIM: Let me give you a hand.

AMANDA: Indeed you will not!

JIM: I ought to be good for something.

AMANDA: Good for something? (*Her tone is rhapsodic.*) *You*? Why, Mr. O'Connor, nobody, *nobody's* given me this much entertainment in years — as you have!

JIM: Aw, now, Mrs. Wingfield!

AMANDA: I'm not exaggerating, not one bit! But Sister is all by her lonesome. You go keep her company in the parlor! I'll give you this lovely old candelabrum that used to be on the altar at the church of the Heavenly Rest. It was melted a little out of shape when the church burnt down. Lightning struck it one spring. Gypsy Jones was holding a revival at the time and he intimated that the church was destroyed because the Episcopalians gave card parties.

JIM: Ha-ha.

AMANDA: And how about coaxing Sister to drink a little wine? I think it would be good for her! Can you carry both at once?

JIM: Sure. I'm Superman!

AMANDA: Now, Thomas, get into this apron!

(*The door of kitchenette swings closed on Amanda's gay laughter; the flickering light approaches the portieres.*)

(*Laura sits up nervously as he enters. Her speech at first is low and breathless from the almost intolerable strain of being alone with a stranger.*)

(*The legend: "I Don't Suppose You Remember Me at All!"*)

(*In her first speeches in this scene, before Jim's warmth overcomes her paralyzing shyness, Laura's voice is thin and breathless as though she has just run up a steep flight of stairs.*)

(*Jim's attitude is gently humorous. In playing this scene it should be stressed that while the incident is apparently unimportant, it is to Laura the climax of her secret life.*)

JIM: Hello, there, Laura.

LAURA (*faintly*): Hello. (*She clears her throat.*)

JIM: How are you feeling now? Better?

LAURA: Yes. Yes, thank you.

JIM: This is for you. A little dandelion wine. (*He extends it toward her with extravagant gallantry.*)

LAURA: Thank you.

JIM: Drink it — but don't get drunk! (*He laughs heartily. Laura takes the glass uncertainly; laughs shyly.*) Where shall I set the candles?

LAURA: Oh — oh, anywhere . . .

JIM: How about here on the floor? Any objections?

LAURA: No.

JIM: I'll spread a newspaper under to catch the drippings. I like to sit on the floor. Mind if I do?

LAURA: Oh, no.

JIM: Give me a pillow?

LAURA: What?

JIM: A pillow!

LAURA: Oh . . . (*Hands him one quickly.*)

JIM: How about you? Don't you like to sit on the floor?

LAURA: Oh — yes.

JIM: Why don't you, then?

LAURA: I — will.

JIM: Take a pillow! (*Laura does. Sits on the other side of the candelabrum. Jim crosses his legs and smiles engagingly at her.*) I can't hardly see you sitting way over there.

LAURA: I can — see you.

JIM: I know, but that's not fair, I'm in the limelight. (*Laura moves her pillow closer.*) Good! Now I can see you! Comfortable?

LAURA: Yes.

JIM: So am I. Comfortable as a cow. Will you have some gum?

LAURA: No, thank you.

JIM: I think that I will indulge, with your permission. (*Musingly unwraps it and holds it up.*) Think of the fortune made by the guy that invented the first piece of chewing gum. Amazing, huh? The Wrigley Building is one of the sights of Chicago. — I saw it summer before last when I went up to the Century of Progress. Did you take in the Century of Progress?

LAURA: No, I didn't.

JIM: Well, it was quite a wonderful exposition. What impressed me most was the Hall of Science. Gives you an idea of what the future will be in America, even more wonderful than the present time is!

(*Pause. Smiling at her.*) Your brother tells me you're shy. Is that right, Laura?

LAURA: I — don't know.

JIM: I judge you to be an old-fashioned type of girl. Well, I think that's a pretty good type to be. Hope you don't think I'm being too personal — do you?

LAURA (*hastily, out of embarrassment*): I believe I *will* take a piece of gum, if you — don't mind. (*Clearing her throat.*) Mr. O'Connor, have you — kept up with your singing?

JIM: Singing? Me?

LAURA: Yes. I remember what a beautiful voice you had.

JIM: When did you hear me sing?

(*Voice offstage in the pause.*)

VOICE: (*offstage*): O blow, ye winds, heigh-ho,
    A-roving I will go!
        I'm off to my love
        With a boxing glove —
    Ten thousand miles away!

JIM: You say you've heard me sing?

LAURA: Oh, yes! Yes, very often . . . I — don't suppose you remember me — at all?

JIM (*smiling doubtfully*): You know I have an idea I've seen you before. I had that idea soon as you opened the door. It seemed almost like I was about to remember your name. But the name that I started to call you — wasn't a name! And so I stopped myself before I said it.

LAURA: Wasn't it — Blue Roses?

JIM (*Springs up. Grinning.*): Blue Roses! My gosh, yes — Blue Roses! That's what I had on my tongue when you opened the door! Isn't it funny what tricks your memory plays? I didn't connect you with the high school somehow or other. But that's where it was; it was high school. I didn't even know you were Shakespeare's sister! Gosh, I'm sorry.

LAURA: I didn't expect you to. You — barely knew me!

JIM: But we did have a speaking acquaintance, huh?

LAURA: Yes, we — spoke to each other.

JIM: When did you recognize me?

LAURA: Oh, right away!

JIM: Soon as I came in the door?

LAURA: When I heard your name I thought it was probably you. I knew that Tom used to know you a little in high school. So when you came in the door — Well, then I was — sure.

JIM: Why didn't you *say* something, then?

LAURA (*breathlessly*): I didn't know what to say, I was — too surprised!

JIM: For goodness' sakes! You know, this sure is funny!

LAURA: Yes! Yes, isn't it, though . . .

JIM: Didn't we have a class in something together?

LAURA: Yes, we did.

JIM: What class was that?

LAURA: It was — singing — Chorus!

JIM: Aw!

LAURA: I sat across the aisle from you in the Aud.

JIM: Aw.

LAURA: Mondays, Wednesdays, and Fridays.

JIM: Now I remember — you always came in late.

LAURA: Yes, it was so hard for me, getting upstairs. I had that brace on my leg — it clumped so loud!

JIM: I never heard any clumping.

LAURA (*wincing at the recollection*): To me it sounded like — thunder!

JIM: Well, well, well, I never even noticed.

LAURA: And everybody was seated before I came in. I had to walk in front of all those people. My seat was in the back row. I had to go clumping all the way up the aisle with everyone watching!

JIM: You shouldn't have been self-conscious.

LAURA: I know, but I was. It was always such a relief when the singing started.

JIM: Aw, yes, I've placed you now! I used to call you Blue Roses. How was it that I got started calling you that?

LAURA: I was out of school a little while with pleurosis. When I came back you asked me what was the matter. I said I had pleurosis — you thought I said Blue Roses. That's what you always called me after that!

JIM: I hope you didn't mind.

LAURA: Oh, no — I liked it. You see, I wasn't acquainted with many — people. . . .

JIM: As I remember you sort of stuck by yourself.

LAURA: I — I — never had much luck at — making friends.

JIM: I don't see why you wouldn't.

LAURA: Well, I — started out badly.

JIM: You mean being —

LAURA: Yes, it sort of — stood between me —

JIM: You shouldn't have let it!

LAURA: I know, but it did, and —

JIM: You were shy with people!

LAURA: I tried not to be but never could —

JIM: Overcome it?

LAURA: No, I — I never could!

JIM: I guess being shy is something you have to work out of kind of gradually.

LAURA (*sorrowfully*): Yes — I guess it —

JIM: Takes time!

LAURA: Yes —

JIM: People are not so dreadful when you know them. That's what you have to remember! And everybody has problems, not just you, but practically everybody has got some problems. You think of yourself as having the only problems, as being the only one who is disappointed. But just look around you and you will see lots of people as disappointed as you are. For instance, I hoped when I was going to high school that I would be further along at this time, six years later, than I am now — You remember that wonderful write-up I had in *The Torch*?

LAURA: Yes! (*She rises and crosses to table.*)

JIM: It said I was bound to succeed in anything I went into! (*Laura returns with the annual.*) Holy Jeez! *The Torch!* (*He accepts it reverently. They smile across it with mutual wonder. Laura crouches beside him and*

they begin to turn through it. Laura's shyness is dissolving in his warmth.)

LAURA: Here you are in *Pirates of Penzance*!

JIM (*wistfully*): I sang the baritone lead in that operetta.

LAURA (*rapidly*): So — *beautifully*!

JIM (*protesting*): Aw —

LAURA: Yes, yes — beautifully — beautifully!

JIM: You heard me?

LAURA: All three times!

JIM: No!

LAURA: Yes!

JIM: All three performances?

LAURA (*looking down*): Yes.

JIM: Why?

LAURA: I — wanted to ask you to — autograph my program.

JIM: Why didn't you ask me to?

LAURA: You were always surrounded by your own friends so much that I never had a chance to.

JIM: You should have just —

LAURA: Well, I — thought you might think I was —

JIM: Thought I might think you was — what?

LAURA: Oh —

JIM (*with reflective relish*): I was beleaguered by females in those days.

LAURA: You were terribly popular!

JIM: Yeah —

LAURA: You had such a — friendly way —

JIM: I was spoiled in high school.

LAURA: Everybody — liked you!

JIM: Including you?

LAURA: I — yes, I — I did, too — (*She gently closes the book in her lap.*)

JIM: Well, well, well! — Give me that program, Laura. (*She hands it to him. He signs it with a flourish.*) There you are — better late than never!

LAURA: Oh, I — what a — surprise!

JIM: My signature isn't worth very much right now. But some day — maybe — it will increase in value! Being disappointed is one thing and being discouraged is something else. I am disappointed but I am not discouraged. I'm twenty-three years old. How old are you?

LAURA: I'll be twenty-four in June.

JIM: That's not old age!

LAURA: No, but —

JIM: You finished high school?

LAURA (*with difficulty*): I didn't go back.

JIM: You mean you dropped out?

LAURA: I made bad grades in my final examinations. (*She rises and replaces the book and the program. Her voice strained.*) How is — Emily Meisenbach getting along?

JIM: Oh, that kraut-head!

LAURA: Why do you call her that?

JIM: That's what she was.

LAURA: You're not still — going with her?

JIM: I never see her.

LAURA: It said in the Personal Section that you were — engaged!

JIM: I know, but I wasn't impressed by that — propaganda!

LAURA: It wasn't — the truth?

JIM: Only in Emily's optimistic opinion!

LAURA: Oh —

(*Legend: "What Have You Done since High School?"*)

(*Jim lights a cigarette and leans indolently back on his elbows smiling at Laura with a warmth and charm which lights her inwardly with altar candles. She remains by the table and turns in her hands a piece of glass to cover her tumult.*)

JIM (*after several reflective puffs on a cigarette*): What have you done since high school? (*She seems not to hear him.*) Huh? (*Laura looks up.*) I said what have you done since high school, Laura?

LAURA: Nothing much.

JIM: You must have been doing something these six long years.

LAURA: Yes.

JIM: Well, then, such as what?

LAURA: I took a business course at business college —

JIM: How did that work out?

LAURA: Well, not very — well — I had to drop out, it gave me — indigestion —

(*Jim laughs gently.*)

JIM: What are you doing now?

LAURA: I don't do anything — much. Oh, please don't think I sit around doing nothing! My glass collection takes up a good deal of my time. Glass is something you have to take good care of.

JIM: What did you say — about glass?

LAURA: Collection I said — I have one — (*She clears her throat and turns away again, acutely shy.*)

JIM (*abruptly*): You know what I judge to be the trouble with you? Inferiority complex! Know what that is? That's what they call it when someone low-rates himself! I understand it because I had it, too. Although my case was not so aggravated as yours seems to be. I had it until I took up public speaking, developed my voice, and learned that I had an aptitude for science. Before that time I never thought of myself as being outstanding in any way whatsoever! Now I've never made a regular study of it, but I have a friend who says I can analyze people better than doctors that make a profession of it. I don't claim that to be necessarily true, but I can sure guess a person's psychology, Laura! (*Takes out his gum.*) Excuse me, Laura. I always take it out when the flavor is gone. I'll use this scrap of paper to wrap it in. I know how it is to get it stuck on a shoe. Yep — that's what I judge to be your principal trouble. A lack of confidence in yourself as a person. You don't have the proper amount of faith in yourself. I'm basing that fact on a number of your remarks and also on certain observations I've made.

For instance that clumping you thought was so awful in high school. You say that you even dreaded to walk into class. You see what you did? You dropped out of school, you gave up an education because of a clump, which as far as I know was practically nonexistent! A little physical defect is what you have. Hardly noticeable even! Magnified thousands of times by imagination! You know what my strong advice to you is? Think of yourself as *superior* in some way!

LAURA: In what way would I think?

JIM: Why, man alive, Laura! Just look about you a little. What do you see? A world full of common people! All of 'em born and all of 'em going to die! Which of them has one-tenth of your good points! Or mine! Or anyone else's, as far as that goes — Gosh! Everybody excels in some one thing. Some in many! (*Unconsciously glances at himself in the mirror.*) All you've got to do is discover in what! Take me, for instance. (*He adjusts his tie at the mirror.*) My interest happens to lie in electro-dynamics. I'm taking a course in radio engineering at night school, Laura, on top of a fairly responsible job at the warehouse. I'm taking that course and studying public speaking.

LAURA: Ohhhh.

JIM: Because I believe in the future of television! (*Turning back to her.*) I wish to be ready to go up right along with it. Therefore I'm planning to get in on the ground floor. In fact, I've already made the right connections and all that remains is for the industry itself to get under way! Full steam — (*His eyes are starry.*) Knowledge — Zzzzzp! Money — Zzzzzzp! — Power! That's the cycle democracy is built on! (*His attitude is convincingly dynamic. Laura stares at him, even her shyness eclipsed in her absolute wonder. He suddenly grins.*) I guess you think I think a lot of myself!

LAURA: No — o-o-o, I —

JIM: Now how about you? Isn't there something you take more interest in than anything else?

LAURA: Well, I do — as I said — have my — glass collection —

(*A peal of girlish laughter from the kitchen.*)

JIM: I'm not right sure I know what you're talking about. What kind of glass is it?

LAURA: Little articles of it, they're ornaments mostly! Most of them are little animals made out of glass, the tiniest little animals in the world. Mother calls them a glass menagerie! Here's an example of one, if you'd like to see it! This one is one of the oldest. It's nearly thirteen. (*He stretches out his hand.*) (*Music: "The Glass Menagerie."*) Oh, be careful — if you breathe, it breaks!

JIM: I'd better not take it. I'm pretty clumsy with things.

LAURA: Go on, I trust you with him! (*Places it in his palm.*) There now — you're holding him gently! Hold him over the light, he loves the light! You see how the light shines through him?

JIM: It sure does shine!

LAURA: I shouldn't be partial, but he is my favorite one.

JIM: What kind of a thing is this one supposed to be?

LAURA: Haven't you noticed the single horn on his forehead?

JIM: A unicorn, huh?

LAURA: Mmm-hmmm!

JIM: Unicorns, aren't they extinct in the modern world?

LAURA: I know!

JIM: Poor little fellow, he must feel sort of lonesome.

LAURA (*smiling*): Well, if he does he doesn't complain about it. He stays on a shelf with some horses that don't have horns and all of them seem to get along nicely together.

JIM: How do you know?

LAURA (*lightly*): I haven't heard any arguments among them!

JIM (*grinning*): No arguments, huh? Well, that's a pretty good sign! Where shall I set him?

LAURA: Put him on the table. They all like a change of scenery once in a while!

JIM (*stretching*): Well, well, well, well — Look how big my shadow is when I stretch!

LAURA: Oh, oh, yes — it stretches across the ceiling!

JIM (*crossing to door*): I think it's stopped raining. (*Opens fire escape door.*) Where does the music come from?

LAURA: From the Paradise Dance Hall across the alley.

JIM: How about cutting the rug a little, Miss Wingfield?

LAURA: Oh, I —

JIM: Or is your program filled up? Let me have a look at it. (*Grasps imaginary card.*) Why, every dance is taken! I'll just have to scratch some out. (*Waltz music: "La Golondrina."*) Ahhh, a waltz! (*He executes some sweeping turns by himself then holds his arms toward Laura.*)

LAURA (*breathlessly*): I — can't dance!

JIM: There you go, that inferiority stuff!

LAURA: I've never danced in my life!

JIM: Come on, try!

LAURA: Oh, but I'd step on you!

JIM: I'm not made out of glass.

LAURA: How — how — how do we start?

JIM: Just leave it to me. You hold your arms out a little.

LAURA: Like this?

JIM: A little bit higher. Right. Now don't tighten up, that's the main thing about it — relax.

LAURA (*laughing breathlessly*): It's hard not to.

JIM: Okay.

LAURA: I'm afraid you can't budge me.

JIM: What do you bet I can't? (*He swings her into motion.*)

LAURA: Goodness, yes, you can!

JIM: Let yourself go, now, Laura, just let yourself go.

LAURA: I'm —

JIM: Come on!

LAURA: Trying!

JIM: Not so stiff — Easy does it!

LAURA: I know but I'm —

JIM: Loosen th' backbone! There now, that's a lot better.

LAURA: Am I?

JIM: Lots, lots better! (*He moves her about the room in a clumsy waltz.*)

LAURA: Oh, my!

JIM: Ha-ha!

LAURA: Oh, my goodness!

JIM: Ha-ha-ha! (*They suddenly bump into the table. Jim stops.*) What did we hit on?

LAURA: Table.

JIM: Did something fall off it? I think —

LAURA: Yes.

JIM: I hope that it wasn't the little glass horse with the horn!

LAURA: Yes.

JIM: Aw, aw, aw. Is it broken?

LAURA: Now it is just like all the other horses.

JIM: It's lost its —

LAURA: Horn! It doesn't matter. Maybe it's a blessing in disguise.

JIM: You'll never forgive me. I bet that that was your favorite piece of glass.

LAURA: I don't have favorites much. It's no tragedy, Freckles. Glass breaks so easily. No matter how careful you are. The traffic jars the shelves and things fall off them.

JIM: Still I'm awfully sorry that I was the cause.

LAURA (*smiling*): I'll just imagine he had an operation. The horn was removed to make him feel less — freakish! (*They both laugh.*) Now he will feel more at home with the other horses, the ones that don't have horns . . .

JIM: Ha-ha, that's very funny! (*Suddenly serious.*) I'm glad to see that you have a sense of humor. You know — you're — well — very different! Surprisingly different from anyone else I know! (*His voice becomes soft and hesitant with a genuine feeling.*) Do you mind me telling you that? (*Laura is abashed beyond speech.*) I mean it in a nice way . . . (*Laura nods shyly, looking away.*) You make me feel sort of — I don't know how to put it! I'm usually pretty good at expressing things, but — This is something that I don't know how to say! (*Laura touches her throat and clears it — turns the broken unicorn in her hands.*) (*Even softer.*) Has anyone ever told you that you were pretty? (*Pause: Music.*) (*Laura looks up slowly, with wonder, and shakes her head.*) Well, you are! In a very different way from anyone else. And all the nicer because of the difference, too. (*His voice becomes low and husky. Laura turns away, nearly faint with the novelty of her emotions.*) I wish that you were my sister. I'd teach you to have some confidence in yourself. The different people are not like other people, but being different is nothing to be ashamed of. Because other people are not such wonderful people. They're one hundred times one thousand. You're one times one! They walk all over the earth. You just stay here. They're common as — weeds, but — you — well, you're — *Blue Roses!*

(*Image on screen: blue roses.*)
  (*Music changes.*)

LAURA: But blue is wrong for — roses . . .
JIM: It's right for you — You're — pretty!
LAURA: In what respect am I pretty?
JIM: In all respects — believe me! Your eyes — your hair — are pretty! Your hands are pretty! (*He catches hold of her hand.*) You think I'm making this up because I'm invited to dinner and have to be nice. Oh, I could do that! I could put on an act for you, Laura, and say lots of things without being very sincere. But this time I am. I'm talking to you sincerely. I happened to notice you had this inferiority complex that keeps you from feeling comfortable with people. Somebody needs to build your confidence up and make you proud instead of shy and turning away and — blushing — Somebody ought to — Ought to — *kiss* you, Laura! (*His hand slips slowly up her arm to her shoulder.*) (*Music swells tumultuously.*) (*He suddenly turns her about and kisses her on the lips. When he releases her Laura sinks on the sofa with a bright, dazed look. Jim backs away and fishes in his pocket for a cigarette.*) (*Legend on screen: "Souvenir."*) Stumble-john! (*He lights the cigarette, avoiding her look. There is a peal of girlish laughter from Amanda in the kitchen. Laura slowly raises and opens her hand. It still contains the little broken glass animal. She looks at it with a tender, bewildered expression.*) Stumble-john! I shouldn't have done that — That was way off the beam. You don't smoke, do you? (*She looks up, smiling, not hearing the question. He sits beside her a little gingerly. She looks at him speechlessly — waiting. He coughs decorously and moves a little farther aside as he considers the situation and senses her feelings, dimly, with perturbation. Gently.*) Would you — care for a — mint? (*She doesn't seem to hear him but her look grows brighter even.*) Peppermint — Life Saver? My pocket's a regular drugstore — wherever I go . . . (*He pops a mint in his mouth. Then gulps and decides to make a clean breast of it. He speaks slowly and gingerly.*) Laura, you know, if I had a sister like you, I'd do the same thing as Tom. I'd bring out fellows and — introduce her to them. The right type of boys of a type to — appreciate her. Only — well — he made a mistake about me. Maybe I've got no call to be saying this. That may not have been the idea in having me over. But what if it was? There's nothing wrong about that. The only trouble is that in my case — I'm not in a situation to — do the right thing. I can't take down your number and say I'll phone. I can't call up next week and — ask for a date. I thought I had better explain the situation in case you misunderstood it and — hurt your feelings. . . . (*Pause. Slowly, very slowly, Laura's look changes, her eyes returning slowly from his to the ornament in her palm.*)

(*Amanda utters another gay laugh in the kitchen.*)

LAURA (*faintly*): You — won't — call again?
JIM: No, Laura, I can't. (*He rises from the sofa.*) As I was just explaining, I've — got strings on me, Laura, I've — been going steady! I go out all the time with a girl named Betty. She's a home-girl like you, and Catholic, and Irish, and in a great many ways we — get along fine. I met her last summer on a moonlight boat trip up the river to Alton, on the *Majestic.* Well — right away from the start it was — love! (*Legend: Love!*) (*Laura sways slightly forward and grips the arm of the sofa. He fails to notice, now enrapt in his own comfortable being.*) Being in love has made a new man of me! (*Leaning stiffly forward, clutching the arm of the sofa, Laura struggles visibly with her storm. But Jim is oblivious, she is a long way off.*) The power of love is really pretty tremendous! Love is something that — changes the whole world, Laura! (*The storm abates a little and Laura leans back. He notices her again.*) It happened that Betty's aunt took sick, she got a wire and had to go to Centralia. So Tom — when he asked me to dinner — I naturally just accepted the invitation, not knowing that you — that he — that I — (*He stops awkwardly.*) Huh — I'm a stumble-john! (*He flops back on the sofa. The holy candles in the altar of Laura's face have been snuffed out! There is a look of almost infinite desolation. Jim glances at her uneasily.*) I wish that you would — say something. (*She bites her lip which was trembling and then bravely smiles. She opens her hand again on the broken glass ornament. Then she gently takes his hand and raises it level with her own. She carefully places the unicorn in the palm of his hand, then pushes his fingers closed upon it.*) What are you — doing that for? You want me to have him? — Laura? (*She nods.*) What for?
LAURA: A — souvenir . . .

(*She rises unsteadily and crouches beside the victrola to wind it up.*)

(*Legend on screen: "Things Have a Way of Turning out so Badly."*)

(*Or Image: "Gentleman Caller Waving Goodbye! — Gaily."*)

(*At this moment Amanda rushes brightly back in the front room. She bears a pitcher of fruit punch in an old-fashioned cut-glass pitcher and a plate of macaroons. The plate has a gold border and poppies painted on it.*)

AMANDA: Well, well, well! Isn't the air delightful after the shower? I've made you children a little liquid refreshment. (*Turns gaily to the gentleman caller.*) Jim, do you know that song about lemonade?
"Lemonade, lemonade
    Made in the shade and stirred with a spade —
    Good enough for any old maid!"
JIM (*uneasily*): Ha-ha! No — I never heard it.
AMANDA: Why, Laura! You look so serious!
JIM: We were having a serious conversation.
AMANDA: Good! Now you're better acquainted!

JIM (*uncertainly*): Ha-ha! Yes.

AMANDA: You modern young people are much more serious-minded than my generation. I was so gay as a girl!

JIM: You haven't changed, Mrs. Wingfield.

AMANDA: Tonight I'm rejuvenated! The gaiety of the occasion, Mr. O'Connor! (*She tosses her head with a peal of laughter. Spills lemonade.*) Oooo! I'm baptizing myself!

JIM: Here — let me —

AMANDA (*setting the pitcher down*): There now. I discovered we had some maraschino cherries. I dumped them in, juice and all!

JIM: You shouldn't have gone to that trouble, Mrs. Wingfield.

AMANDA: Trouble, trouble? Why it was loads of fun! Didn't you hear me cutting up in the kitchen? I bet your ears were burning! I told Tom how out-done with him I was for keeping you to himself so long a time! He should have brought you over much, much sooner! Well, now that you've found your way, I want you to be a very frequent caller! Not just occasional but all the time. Oh, we're going to have a lot of gay times together! I see them coming! Mmm, just breathe that air! So fresh, and the moon's so pretty! I'll skip back out — I know where my place is when young folks are having a — serious conversation!

JIM: Oh, don't go out, Mrs. Wingfield. The fact of the matter is I've got to be going.

AMANDA: Going, now? You're joking! Why, it's only the shank of the evening, Mr. O'Connor!

JIM: Well, you know how it is.

AMANDA: You mean you're a young workingman and have to keep workingmen's hours. We'll let you off early tonight. But only on the condition that next time you stay later. What's the best night for you? Isn't Saturday night the best night for you workingmen?

JIM: I have a couple of time clocks to punch, Mrs. Wingfield. One at morning, another one at night!

AMANDA: My, but you *are* ambitious! You work at night, too?

JIM: No, Ma'am, not work but — Betty! (*He crosses deliberately to pick up his hat. The band at the Paradise Dance Hall goes into a tender waltz.*)

AMANDA: Betty? Betty? Who's — Betty! (*There is an ominous cracking sound in the sky.*)

JIM: Oh, just a girl. The girl I go steady with! (*He smiles charmingly. The sky falls.*)

(*Legend: "The Sky Falls."*)

AMANDA (*a long-drawn exhalation*): Ohhhh . . . Is it a serious romance, Mr. O'Connor?

JIM: We're going to be married the second Sunday in June.

AMANDA: Ohhhh — how nice! Tom didn't mention that you were engaged to be married.

JIM: The cat's not out of the bag at the warehouse yet. You know how they are. They call you Romeo and stuff like that. (*He stops at the oval mirror to put on his hat. He carefully shapes the brim and the crown*

to give a discreetly dashing effect.) It's been a wonderful evening, Mrs. Wingfield. I guess this is what they mean by Southern hospitality.

AMANDA: It really wasn't anything at all.

JIM: I hope it don't seem like I'm rushing off. But I promised Betty I'd pick her up at the Wabash depot, an' by the time I get my jalopy down there her train'll be in. Some women are pretty upset if you keep 'em waiting.

AMANDA: Yes, I know — The tyranny of women! (*Extends her hand.*) Good-bye, Mr. O'Connor. I wish you luck — and happiness — and success! All three of them, and so does Laura! — Don't you, Laura?

LAURA: Yes!

JIM (*taking her hand*): Good-bye, Laura. I'm certainly going to treasure that souvenir. And don't you forget the good advice I gave you. (*Raises his voice to a cheery shout.*) So long, Shakespeare! Thanks again, ladies — Good night!

(*He grins and ducks jauntily out.*)

(*Still bravely grimacing, Amanda closes the door on the gentleman caller. Then she turns back to the room with a puzzled expression. She and Laura don't dare to face each other. Laura crouches beside the victrola to wind it.*)

AMANDA (*faintly*): Things have a way of turning out so badly. I don't believe that I would play the victrola. Well, well — well — Our gentleman caller was engaged to be married! Tom!

TOM (*from back*): Yes, Mother?

AMANDA: Come in here a minute. I want to tell you something awfully funny.

TOM (*enters with macaroon and a glass of the lemonade*): Has the gentleman caller gotten away already?

AMANDA: The gentleman caller has made an early departure. What a wonderful joke you played on us!

TOM: How do you mean?

AMANDA: You didn't mention that he was engaged to be married.

TOM: Jim? Engaged?

AMANDA: That's what he just informed us.

TOM: I'll be jiggered! I didn't know about that.

AMANDA: That seems very peculiar.

TOM: What's peculiar about it?

AMANDA: Didn't you call him your best friend down at the warehouse?

TOM: He is, but how did I know?

AMANDA: It seems extremely peculiar that you wouldn't know your best friend was going to be married!

TOM: The warehouse is where I work, not where I know things about people!

AMANDA: You don't know things anywhere! You live in a dream; you manufacture illusions! (*He crosses to door.*) Where are you going?

TOM: I'm going to the movies.

AMANDA: That's right, now that you've had us make such fools of ourselves. The effort, the preparations, all the expense! The new floor lamp, the rug, the clothes for Laura! All for what? To entertain some other girl's fiancé! Go to the movies, go! Don't think about us, a mother deserted, an unmarried sister who's crippled and has no job! Don't let anything interfere with your selfish pleasure! Just go, go, go — to the movies!

TOM: All right, I will! The more you shout about my selfishness to me the quicker I'll go, and I won't go to the movies!

AMANDA: Go, then! Then go to the moon — you selfish dreamer!

(*Tom smashes his glass on the floor. He plunges out on the fire escape, slamming the door. Laura screams — cut by door.*)

(*Dance hall music up. Tom goes to the rail and grips it desperately, lifting his face in the chill white moonlight penetrating the narrow abyss of the alley.*)

(*Legend on screen: "And so Good-bye . . ."*)

(*Tom's closing speech is timed with the interior pantomime. The interior scene is played as though viewed through soundproof glass. Amanda appears to be making a comforting speech to Laura who is huddled upon the sofa. Now that we cannot hear the mother's speech, her silliness is gone and she has dignity and tragic beauty. Laura's dark hair hides her face until at the end of the speech she lifts it to smile at her mother. Amanda's gestures are slow and graceful, almost dancelike, as she comforts the daughter. At the end of her speech she glances a moment at the father's picture — then withdraws through the portieres. At close of Tom's speech, Laura blows out the candles, ending the play.*)

TOM: I didn't go to the moon, I went much further — for time is the longest distance between two places — Not long after that I was fired for writing a poem on the lid of a shoebox. I left Saint Louis. I descended the steps of this fire escape for a last time and followed, from then on, in my father's footsteps, attempting to find in motion what was lost in space — I traveled around a great deal. The cities swept about me like dead leaves, leaves that were brightly colored but torn away from the branches. I would have stopped, but I was pursued by something. It always came upon me unawares, taking me altogether by surprise. Perhaps it was a familiar bit of music. Perhaps it was only a piece of transparent glass — Perhaps I am walking along a street at night, in some strange city, before I have found companions. I pass the lighted window of a shop where perfume is sold. The window is filled with pieces of colored glass, tiny transparent bottles in delicate colors, like bits of a shattered rainbow. Then all at once my sister touches my shoulder. I turn around and look into her eyes . . . Oh, Laura, Laura, I tried to leave you behind me, but I am more faithful than I intended to be! I reach for a cigarette, I cross the street, I run into the movies or a bar, I buy a drink, I speak to the nearest stranger — anything that can blow your candles out! (*Laura bends over the candles.*) — for nowadays the world is lit by lightning! Blow out your candles, Laura — and so good-bye. . . .

(*She blows the candles out.*)
(*The scene dissolves.*)

COMMENTARIES

Tennessee Williams is a fascinating figure in American drama. He was a forceful personality who charmed his friends and the public alike, although his life was often filled with uncertainties and unresolved problems. Some of his best work derived from his private agonies. His work was taken seriously almost from the first, and a body of criticism has developed around it, including biographies, personal reminiscences of collaborators, critical commentaries, and scholarship.

In the *New York Times* review of *The Glass Menagerie* (included here as a commentary), Lewis Nichols describes Laurette Taylor's performance as Amanda as "completely perfect." Donald Spoto, who wrote *The Kindness of Strangers: The Life of Tennessee Williams* (1985), says that Taylor, a powerful actress whose career had seemed finished when the part was offered to her, almost refused the role at first. But her interpretation established a point of reference to which later actresses had to pay homage. Spoto helps us understand the power of collaboration between actor and playwright that sometimes helps both expand their understanding of the work.

Benjamin Nelson explains that "*The Glass Menagerie* exhibits several of Williams's weaknesses as well as his strengths as a playwright." He discusses Williams's characterizations, especially of Laura and Amanda. He also points to "poetic passages" in the play that he feels are weaknesses. Ultimately, Nelson poses an interesting dramatic question: Is the play a tragedy? The search for an answer to this question involves a full consideration of the play's strengths and weaknesses, its success or failure.

Lewis Nichols (1903–1982)
REVIEW OF *THE GLASS MENAGERIE*   1945

Lewis Nichols's review of the New York premiere of The Glass Menagerie *focused on the stellar performance of Laurette Taylor, who played the Mother. Nichols also points out the quality of Williams's writing and his ear for "faintly sardonic dialogue." He saw the play as a superb vehicle for sublime acting.*

The theatre opened its Easter basket the night before and found it a particularly rich one. Preceded by warm and tender reports from Chicago, *The Glass Menagerie* opened at the Playhouse on Saturday, and immediately it was clear that for once the advance notes were not in error. Tennessee Williams's simple play forms the framework for some of the finest acting to be seen in many a day. "Memorable" is an overworked word, but that is the only one to describe Laurette Taylor's performance. March left the theatre like a lioness.

Miss Taylor's picture of a blowsy, impoverished woman who is living on memories of a flower-scented Southern past is completely perfect. It combines qualities of humor and human understanding. The Mother of the play is an amusing figure and a pathetic one. Aged, with two children, living in an apartment off an alley in St. Louis, she recalls her past glories, her seventeen suitors, the old and better life. She is a bit of a scold, a bit of a snob; her finery has worn threadbare, but she has kept it for occasions of state. Miss Taylor makes her a person known by any other name to everyone in her audience. That is art.

In the story the Mother is trying to do the best she can for her children. The son works in a warehouse, although he wants to go to far places. The daughter, a cripple, never has been able to finish school. She is shy, she spends her time collecting glass animals — the title comes from this — and playing old phonograph records. The Mother thinks it is time she is getting married, but there has never been a Gentleman Caller at the house. Finally the son brings home another man from the warehouse and out comes the finery and the heavy if bent candlestick. Even the Gentleman Caller fails. He is engaged to another girl.

Mr. Williams's play is not all of the same caliber. A strict perfectionist could easily find a good many flaws. There are some unconnected odds and ends which have little to do with the story: Snatches of talk about the war, bits of psychology, occasional moments of rather flowery writing. But Mr. Williams has a real ear for faintly sardonic dialogue, unexpected phrases and an affection for his characters.

Miss Taylor takes these many good passages and makes them sing. She plays softly and part of the time seems to be mumbling — a mumble that can be heard at the top of the gallery. Her accents, like the author's phrases, are unexpected, her gestures are vague and fluttery. There is no doubt she was a Southern belle; there is no doubt she is a great actress.

Eddie Dowling, who is coproducer, and, with Margo Jones, codirector, has the double job of narrator and the player of The Son. The narration is like that of *Our Town* and *I Remember Mama* and it probably is not essential to *The Glass Menagerie*. In the play itself Mr. Dowling gives his quiet, easy performance. Julie Haydon, very ethereal and slight, is good as the daughter, as is Anthony Ross as the Gentleman Caller. The Caller had been the hero in high school, but he, too, had been unsuccessful. Jo Mielziner's setting fits the play, as does Paul Bowles's music. In fact, everything fits. *The Glass Menagerie*, like spring, is a pleasure to have in the neighborhood.

Donald Spoto (b. 1941)
LAURETTE TAYLOR IN *THE GLASS MENAGERIE*   1985

Before the part of Amanda Wingfield was offered to her, Laurette Taylor had thought her career as an actress was over. Donald Spoto, the biographer of Tennessee Williams, gives us a vision of how persistence and devotion to someone of genuine talent produced a legend in American acting.

That month [December 1944], the details moved together swiftly. [Actor-producer-director Eddie] Dowling, who had directed actress Julie Haydon in *The Time of Your Life*,° convinced her that (although she was thirty-four) she would be credible as the lame, fragile Laura, a character at least a decade younger. She, in turn, took the play to her friend and mentor (later her husband), the formidable critic George Jean Nathan, whose approval she felt obligatory. At the same time, the forty-nine-year-old Dowling announced — without a smile — that he would play young (twentyish) Tom, the shoe-warehouse clerk and aspiring poet; for the role of the gentleman caller, Anthony Ross was hired. The remaining role to be cast was Amanda Wingfield — the "little woman of great but confused vitality," as Williams described her in the play, "clinging frantically to another time and place." The role demanded not mere competence, but the nuances of dramatic greatness. Nathan suggested Laurette Taylor. Dowling and [Audrey] Wood [Williams's agent] and Williams saw his wisdom; they also panicked.

Laurette Taylor, then sixty, had been up to the 1930s one of the great ladies of the American stage. Those who had seen her in *Peg O'My Heart* (in 1912) or *The Furies* (in 1928) or *Outward Bound* (in 1938) knew her gifts. But for almost ten years she had herself become a woman of great but confused vitality, and a confirmed alcoholic.

At that time, Taylor was living in sad withdrawal from the theater, at a hotel on East 60th Street, where she was daily attended by a drama student named Eloise

The Time of Your Life: A play (1939) by William Saroyan.

Sheldon. In return for acting lessons, the young woman cared for the practical details of Taylor's life and offered devoted companionship. The play reached Taylor by the circuitous route of Wood to Dowling to Haydon to Nathan to Sheldon to Taylor. It also bore a new title — *The Glass Menagerie.*

"Of course her first reaction was to turn it down," Eloise Sheldon Armen recalled years later; "she thought her career was over. But we prevailed on her to see that no one could bring this character to life the way she could." At last, with the loving encouragement of Eloise —"a small flame," as Laurette Taylor's daughter appreciatively wrote of the young student, "guiding [Taylor] back to the paths of everyday life"— she accepted the part. She did not, however, stop drinking, nor did she seem to give much attention to memorizing lines before or during rehearsals.

In November, Dowling (with, Williams insisted, Margo Jones as codirector) began rehearsals in New York prior to a scheduled Chicago tryout at the end of December. Terrified that something like the history of *Battle of Angels* would be repeated — not because of the new play's content (which could not have been more different) but because he no longer believed the play was anything but "rather dull, too nice"— Williams fled New York for St. Louis. There he was interviewed on his life and work and hopes by the drama critic of the *Star-Times,* a man named William Inge. The resulting article was full of inaccuracies, half-truths, and Williams's typical alterations of personal history; the resulting friendship was much more intense and dramatic.

But Audrey and Dowling would not allow Williams to be an absentee author, and in December he was summoned to Chicago. The situation, he quickly realized, was as bleak as the fierce winter that had already descended.

First of all, Laurette Taylor — with only a week remaining before the December 26 premiere — attended the final rehearsals in what can only be called an alcoholic stupor, barely summarizing the dialogue and so broadly defining the woman's Southern accent and character that, as Williams wrote . . . , she made the play sound like the Aunt Jemima Pancake Hour. In addition, Jo Mielziner's stage designs were being followed with great difficulty, and the music Williams had commissioned from his old acquaintance Paul Bowles sounded harsh through the theater's crude sound system. Luggage had not arrived; a winter storm raged; the Civic Theatre was inconvenient to Chicago's main theater district; there was no budget for advertising or publicity; and everyone in the company (except Eddie Dowling and Julie Haydon) — cast, crew, author — submerged the fear of failure in strong drink. Margo Jones, Williams wrote . . . , was like a scoutmaster leading a wayward and desperate troop to their doom.

As late as Christmas Eve, the lines of the play had been neither "frozen" (fixed by the producer and playwright to be performed as written) nor completely memorized. Laurette Taylor managed only a martini mumble, Dowling was demanding rewrites, and the cast was stumbling into props and one another. "Mr. Dowling," Williams said quietly that night, "art is experience remembered in tranquillity. And I find no tranquillity in Chicago."

The night after Christmas, *The Glass Menagerie* was somehow performed for a small, diffident audience. By the afternoon of the twenty-seventh, the box office had taken in only four hundred dollars, and the producers prepared a closing notice. But then Audrey telephoned them to read two brief reviews: Critic Claudia

Cassidy, writing in the *Chicago Daily Tribune,* said the play had "the stamina of success . . . [it] knows people and how they tick. . . . If it is your play, as it is mine, it reaches out . . . and you are caught in its spell." And Ashton Stevens, in the *Herald American,* said *The Glass Menagerie* "has the courage of true poetry couched in colloquial prose."

Before the end of that day, the mayor of Chicago, at the urging of the Civic Theatre's management, authorized a fifty-percent ticket subsidy for municipal employees. On the third night, Laurette Taylor was not simply discharging a half-formed role, she was creating a legend, she had begun to draw a more wonderful portrait than anyone could have imagined — not Eddie Dowling (who resented the critics' subsequent raves about her), not Tennessee Williams nor Audrey Wood, not anyone connected with the play.

"Actually," according to the playwright, "she directed many of the scenes, particularly the ones between mother and daughter, and she did a top-notch job. She was continually working on her part, putting in little things and taking them out — almost every night in Chicago there was something new, but she never disturbed the central characterization. Everything she did was absolutely in character."

The closing notice was removed — not, however, because box-office business dramatically improved, but because Claudia Cassidy and Ashton Stevens had been championing the play, returning almost nightly and telling and writing about it almost daily. "It gripped players and audiences alike," Cassidy wrote on January 7, 1945, "and created one of those rare evenings in the theater that make 'stagestruck' an honorable word." By the middle of the month, no tickets were available. In an unusual example of journalistic salvation, a play was for once not lost but kept alive because of critical support.

Benjamin Nelson
PROBLEMS IN *THE GLASS MENAGERIE*   *1961*

Benjamin Nelson's analysis of Williams's play recognizes the power of the circumstances portrayed in the play. Nelson is concerned, however, that the characters, especially Laura, are not as fully and carefully drawn as they need to be to make the play truly powerful. He also criticizes Williams for creating a universe that "does not allow tragedy."

The Glass Menagerie exhibits several of Williams's weaknesses as well as his strengths as a playwright. The great strength of the play is of course the delicate, sympathetic, yet objective creation of meaningful people in a meaningful situation. Williams has caught a decisive and desperate moment in the lives of four individuals and given it illumination and a sense of deep meaning — no small feat for any writer.

His characterizations are not equally realized. He has been unable to create Laura on more than a single dimension, while Amanda is overwhelming in her multifaceted delineation. On a more technical level the play manifests a doubt on the part of its author toward the power of the written word. As a backdrop for *The*

Glass Menagerie, Williams originally wished to use a screen to register emotions and present images from the past, present, and future. For example, when Jim O'Connor confesses to the family that he is going steady with another girl, the legend on the screen is to read, "The Sky Falls." Fortunately, [actor-director] Eddie Dowling deleted these touches of the poet from his production, but the play still abounds with a number of pretentious statements on the part of Tom as Narrator.

I assume that the final scene between Amanda and Laura is played in pantomime because Williams wished to portray Amanda's dignity through her gestures and her daughter's reaction rather than through the mother's speech, which during the course of the drama has been either shrill, simpering, or saucy. But in relegating this scene to background silence while Tom makes a self-conscious statement about drifting like a dead leaf "attempting to find in motion what was lost in space," he has substituted a painfully pretentious narration for what could have been an intense and luminous moment between the two women.

Again, on the credit side of the author, his play presents genuine situation, motivation, and, as Joseph Wood Krutch has noted, "a hard substantial core of shrewd observation and deft, economical characterization." But Mr. Krutch also noted that "this hard core is enveloped in a fuzzy haze of pretentious, sentimental, pseudopoetic verbiage."[1] In *The Glass Menagerie,* the strained lyricism runs parallel with dialogue that is fresh, alive, and highly characteristic, particularly in the speech of Amanda. This dialogue fortunately dominates the proceedings, but the excess of self-conscious "poetical" passages is quite apparent and is a fault of which Williams is to be guilty in much of his later work.

But the great weakness of *The Glass Menagerie* does not lie in its author's artistic or technical deficiencies. The weakness lies at the core of the play and evolves out of what is to become the playwright's hardening philosophical commitment. We can begin to comprehend this when we ask ourselves whether or not *The Glass Menagerie* is a tragedy. It presents a tragic situation and characters who, despite their moodiness and foolishness and self-deception, possess a sense of the tragic. With the possible exception of Laura, they are intensely genuine and the destruction of their dreams and aspirations bears the illusion of great importance. But the play is not a tragedy. The universe of *The Glass Menagerie* does not allow tragedy.

Everyone in the play is a failure and in the course of their drama they all perish a little. Amanda, the most heroic of the quartet, is pitiful but not tragic because from the outset she is doomed to failure despite her desperate struggle to right things. None of these people are given the opportunity to triumph against a fate which is as malignant as it is implacable. Their struggle is a rear-guard action against life, a continuous retreat. This retreat may be moving, pathetic, melodramatic, or boisterous, but it is always a withdrawal. After all, what is the world outside the glass menagerie?

> There was only hot swing music and liquor, dance halls, bars, and movies, and sex that hung in the gloom like a chandelier and flooded the world with brief, deceptive rainbows. . . . All the world was waiting for bombardments! (p. 632)

The world outside the Wingfield apartment is a world of illusions, also, even more deceptive and destructive than those held by Amanda and Laura. It is the world of *Stairs to the Roof* and this time the escape is not to a new star but into the

---

[1]Joseph Wood Krutch, *The Nation* 14 April 1945:24.

individual and personal illusions fostered by each of the characters as his private defense against destruction. Jim waits for the day when his "zzzzzp!" will at last disperse his fear and uncertainty; Laura creates her own sparkling, cold world which gives the illusion of warmth but is as eternal in its unreality as the glass from which it is composed; Amanda strikes out with all her power against her fate by clinging to the past as to a shield; and Tom, recognizing the plight of his family, can do no more than drift away from them, rudderless, frightened, and never really as far from Amanda and Laura as he knows he should be.

Not one of these individuals can cope with his situation. They struggle and their hopes and the destruction of these hopes possess a sense of great importance because Williams has created genuine people in an intensely genuine situation, but they lack the completeness to truly cope with their dilemma. They are not responsible for what has happened to them and they are much too helpless to do more than delay the inevitable. And destruction is inevitable because it is implicit in the universe of Tennessee Williams.

> For the sins of the world are really only its partialities, and these are what sufferings must atone for. . . . The nature of man is full of such makeshift arrangements, devised by himself to cover his incompletion. He feels a part of himself to be like a missing wall or a room left unfurnished and he tries as well as he can to make up for it. The use of imagination, resorting to dreams or the loftier purpose of art, is a mask he devises to cover his incompletion. Or violence such as a war, between two men or among a number of nations, is also a blind and senseless compensation for that which is not yet formed in human nature. Then there is still another compensation. This one is found in the principle of atonement, the surrender of self to violent treatment by others with the idea of thereby cleansing one's self of his guilt.[2]

This statement emanates from the core of Williams's thought and is perhaps his most illuminating commentary about himself and his work. It represents a philosophy, or let us say an attitude toward man in his universe, which is to manifest itself in all his work. It is taken from his short story, "Desire and the Black Masseur," which deals with the final compensation cited in the above quotation: purification through violence. In this tale, a man atones for what the author feels is a cosmic fragmentation and guilt by allowing — and actually furthering — his destruction by a cannibal. In *Battle of Angels* and *The Purification,* we find this same kind of violent cleansing.

The Glass Menagerie is a far cry from any of these works; it is the most nonviolent drama written by Williams. Nevertheless it adheres to the belief set forth in the short story. The underlying belief in *The Glass Menagerie* is that there is very little, if any, reason for living. Man is by nature incomplete because his universe is fragmented. There is nothing to be done about this condition because nothing *can* be done about it. Human guilt becomes a corollary of universal guilt and man's life is an atonement for the human condition. In each character in *The Glass Menagerie* there is a part "like a missing wall or a room left unfurnished and he tries as well as he can to make up for it." The mask devised by Laura and Amanda and Tom and Jim is "the use of imagination, resorting to dreams." The Wingfields are broken, fragmented people because "the sins of the world are really only its partialities." They are really not at all responsible for their condition, and thus are in no way able to cope with it. They are trapped in a determined universe. Without some kind

---

[2]Williams, "Desire and the Black Masseur," *One Arm and Other Stories* (New York, 1948), 85.

of responsibility on the part of the protagonist there is opportunity neither for tragic elevation nor tragic fall. The Wingfields were doomed the moment they were born. At best their struggles will allow them to survive . . . for a time. They will never be allowed to triumph. Thus their struggles, their hopes, and even their eventual destruction can never move far beyond pathos. The beauty and magic of *The Glass Menagerie* is that this pathos is genuine, objective, and deeply moving.

Arthur Miller

Arthur Miller (b. 1915) has been the dean of American playwrights since the opening of *Death of a Salesman* in 1949. His steady output as a writer and a playwright began with his first publications after college in 1939, when he worked in the New York Federal Theatre Project, a branch of the Works Progress Administration (WPA), Franklin D. Roosevelt's huge Depression-era effort to put Americans back to work.

Miller, the son of a Jewish immigrant, was born and raised during his early years in the Harlem section of Manhattan and later in Brooklyn after his father's business failed. In high school Miller thought of himself more as an athlete than as a student, and he had trouble getting teachers' recommendations for college. After considerable struggle and waiting, he entered the University of Michigan, where his talent as a playwright emerged under the tutelage of Kenneth Rowe, his playwriting professor. His undergraduate plays won important university awards, and he became noticed by the Theatre Guild, a highly respected theater founded to present excellent plays (not necessarily commercial successes). His career was under way.

From 1939 to 1947 Miller wrote radio plays, screenplays, articles, stories, and a novel. His work covered a wide range of material, much of it growing out of his childhood memories of a tightly knit and somewhat eccentric family that provided him with a large gallery of characters. But he also dealt with political issues and problems of anti-Semitism, which was widespread in the 1930s and 1940s. Miller's political concerns have been a constant presence in his work since his earliest writings.

All My Sons (1947) was his first successful play. It ran on Broadway for three hundred performances, a remarkable record for a serious drama. The story centers on a man who knowingly produces defective parts for airplanes and then blames the subsequent crashes on his business partner, who is ruined and imprisoned. When the guilty man's son finds out the truth, he confronts his father and rebukes him. Ultimately, the man realizes not only that he has lost his son because of his deceit but that the dead pilots were also "all my sons." The play won the New York Drama Critics' Circle Award.

Miller's next play, *Death of a Salesman* (1949), was written in six weeks. Focusing on the American ideal of business success, its conclusions were a challenge to standard American business values. Willy Loman, first performed by Lee J. Cobb, was intended to be a warning for Americans in the postwar period of the cost of growing wealth and affluence.

Miller's next play, *The Crucible* (1953), portrayed witch-hunts of seventeenth-century New England, but most people recognized the subtext: it was about contemporary anti-Communist witch-hunts. In the late 1940s and early 1950s the House Un-American Activities Committee (HUAC) held hearings to uncover suspected Communists in all areas of American life, particularly the arts. Many writers, artists, and performers came under close, often unfair, scrutiny by HUAC for their own political views and allegiances and were often asked to testify against their friends. Many were blacklisted (prevented from working in commercial theaters and movie companies), some were imprisoned for not testifying at others' trials, and some had their reputations and careers destroyed.

Arthur Miller was fearless in facing down HUAC, and he was convicted of contempt of court for not testifying against his friends. For a time he too was blacklisted, but his contempt citation was reversed, and he was not imprisoned. Given his personal political stance during this dangerous time, it is not a surprise to find that he usually chooses to write about matters of social concern.

In the 1990s Miller became the darling of the London stage while at the same time being somewhat neglected in the United States. One full-scale play, *Broken Glass* (1994), played in regional theater before going to a brief run on Broadway and then a longer run in London's West End. The play concerns a woman who becomes paralyzed in response to *Kristallnacht* (night of crystal), a night of violent rampages against Jews and Jewish property that resulted in 91 Jewish dead, hundreds injured, and 7,500 businesses and 177 synagogues gutted. After November 9, 1938, it was clear that Jews were no longer safe in Hitler's Germany. The subject of the play is intense, significant, and still timely.

The Ride Down Mount Morgan had its premiere in London in 1991; it then took seven years to open in New York in 1998. Its protagonist, Lyman Felt, played by Patrick Stewart in New York, was conceived as a Reaganite go-getter of the late 1980s: economically rapacious, sexually voracious, and amoral. When Felt's Porsche crashes on a ride down Mount Morgan, his two wives discover one another at the hospital. The play proceeds, examining the ethical values that permit Felt to live as he does. George Wolfe produced the play at the Joseph Papp Public Theatre. The Broadway production opened at the Ambassador Theater in April 2000, again with Patrick Stewart. The play was nominated for a Tony Award.

DEATH OF A SALESMAN

Death of a Salesman (1949) was a hit from its first performances and has remained at the center of modern American drama ever since. It has been successful in China, where there were no salesmen, and in Europe, where many salesmen dominate certain industries. Everywhere this play has touched the hearts and minds of its audiences. Its success is a phenomenon of American drama.

The play was first performed in an experimental environment. Miller had originally conceived of a model of a man's head as the stage setting. He has said: "The first image that occurred to me which was to result in *Death of a*

Salesman was of an enormous face the height of the proscenium arch which would appear and then open up, and we would see the inside of a man's head. In fact, *The Inside of His Head* was the first title." This technique was not used, but when Miller worked with the director and producer of the first production, he helped develop a setting that became a model for the "American style" in drama. The multilevel set permitted the play to shift from Willy Loman and his wife, Linda, having a conversation in their kitchen to their son's bedroom on the second level of the house. The set permitted portions of the stage to be reserved for Willy's visions of his brother, Ben, and for scenes outside the house such as Willy's interlude with the woman in Boston.

In a way, the setup of the stage respected Miller's original plan, but instead of portraying a cross-section of Willy's head, it presented a metaphor for a cross-section of his life. The audience was not looking in on just a living room, as in the nineteenth-century Ibsenist approach, but on an entire house and an entire life.

Using a cross-section of a house as a metaphor was an especially important device in this play because of the play's allusions to Greek tragedy. The great Greek tragedies usually portray the destruction of a house — such as the house of Atreus — in which "house" stands for a whole family, not a building. When Shakespeare's Hamlet dies, for example, his entire line dies with him. The death in *Death of a Salesman* implies the destruction of a family holding certain beliefs that have been wrong from the start.

The life of the salesman has given Willy a sense of dignity and worth, and he imagines that the modern world has corrupted that sense by robbing salesmen of the value of their personality. He thinks that the modern world has failed him, but he is wrong. His original belief — that what counts is not *what* you know but *whom* you know and how well you are liked — lies at the heart of his failure. When the play opens, he already has failed at the traveling salesman's job because he can no longer drive to his assigned territory. He cannot sell what he needs to sell.

Willy has inculcated his beliefs in his sons, Happy and Biff, and both are as ineffectual as their father. Willy doted on Biff and encouraged him to become a high school football star at the expense of his studies. But when Biff cannot pass an important course, and his plans to make up the work are subverted by his disillusionment in his father, his dreams of a college football career vanish. He cannot change and recover from this defeat. Happy, like his father, builds castles in the air and assumes somehow that he will be successful, though he has nothing to back himself up with. He wants the glory — and he spends time in fanciful imaginings, as Willy does — but he cannot do the basic work that makes it possible to achieve glory. Ironically, it is the "anemic" Bernard — who studies hard, stresses personal honesty and diligence, and never brags — who is successful.

Linda supports Willy's illusions, allowing him to be a fraud by sharing — or pretending to believe — in his dream. Willy has permitted himself to feel that integrity, honesty, and fidelity are not as important as being well liked.

The play ends with Willy still unable to face the deceptions he has perpetuated. He commits suicide, believing that his sons will be able to follow in his footsteps and succeed where he did not; he thinks that his insurance money will save the house and the family. What he does not realize is that his sons are no more capable than he is. They have been corrupted by his thinking, his values, his beliefs. And they cannot solve the problems that overwhelmed him.

Death of a Salesman has been given a privileged position in American drama because it is a modern tragedy. Aristotle felt that only characters of noble birth could be tragic heroes, but Miller confounds this theory, as Eugene O'Neill did, by showing the human integrity in even the most humble characters. Miller's Willy Loman is not a peasant, nor is he noble. In fact, Miller took a frightening risk in producing a figure that we find hard to like. Willy wants to be well liked, but as an audience we find it difficult to like a person who whines, complains, and accepts petty immorality as a normal way of life. Despite his character, we are awed by his fate.

One Chinese commentator said, after the Chinese production, that China is filled with such dreamers as Willy. Certainly America has been filled with them. Willy stands as an aspect of our culture, commercial and otherwise, that is at the center of our reflection of ourselves. Perhaps we react so strongly to Willy because we are afraid that we might easily become a Willy Loman if we are not vigilant about our moral views, our psychological well-being, and the limits of our commitment to success. Willy Loman has mesmerized audiences in America in many different economic circumstances: prosperity, recession, rapid growth, and cautious development. No matter what those circumstances, we have looked at the play as if looking in a mirror. What we have seen has always involved us, although it has not always made us pleased with ourselves.

Death of a Salesman in Performance

Death of a Salesman opened on Broadway on February 10, 1949, and won virtually every prize available for drama, including the Pulitzer Prize and the New York Drama Critics' Circle Award for best play. It ran on Broadway for an incredible 742 performances. Elia Kazan, director, was instrumental in establishing the play's innovative staging. Lee J. Cobb was cast as Willy, Mildred Dunnock as Linda, Arthur Kennedy as Biff, and Cameron Mitchell as Happy. The London production in July 1949, with Paul Muni as Willy and Kevin McCarthy as Biff, lasted 204 performances. Robert Coleman said of the New York production: "An explosion of emotional dynamite was set off last evening in the Morosco [Theater]. . . . In fashioning *Death of a Salesman* for them, author Arthur Miller and director Elia Kazan have collaborated on as exciting and devastating a theatrical blast as the nerves of modern playgoers can stand." Of Cobb, Howard Barnes said, "Cobb contributes a mammoth and magnificent portrayal of the central character. In his hands the salesman's frustration and final suicide are a matter of tremendous import."

An all-black production was directed by Lee Sankowich in Baltimore in 1972. Miller, in the audience on that production's opening night, commented that the play had been well received in "many countries and cultures" and that the Baltimore production further underscored the universality of the play. George C. Scott was praised for the power of his performance as Willy in New York's Circle in the Square production in 1975. A Chinese production directed by Arthur Miller was enormously successful in the 1980s. In the most celebrated revival of the play Dustin Hoffman portrayed Willy, John Malkovich played Biff, and Michael Rudman directed at the Broadhurst Theatre in New York in 1984. The critic Benedict Nightingale said of that production: "Somewhere at the core of him [Willy] an elaborate battle is being fought between dishonesty and honesty, glitter and substance, appearance and reality, between the promises or supposed promises of society and the claims of the self, between what Willy professes to value and what, perhaps without knowing it, he actually does value." In 1985 Dustin Hoffman brought his production of Miller's play to television, where it was viewed by an estimated twenty-five million people.

On February 10, 1999, exactly fifty years to the day from its original opening, the play's most recent production opened with Brian Dennehy as Willy Loman. The production was conceived in Chicago by the Goodman Theater Company, and in its revival Dennehy was praised by critics and theater-goers alike for presenting a powerful portrayal of Willy Loman for a new generation. Critics praised the timelessness of the drama — ultimately crowning it as an American classic.

Arthur Miller (b. 1915)

Death of a Salesman   *1949*
CERTAIN PRIVATE CONVERSATIONS IN TWO ACTS AND A REQUIEM

Characters

WILLY LOMAN	UNCLE BEN
LINDA	HOWARD WAGNER
BIFF	JENNY
HAPPY	STANLEY
BERNARD	MISS FORSYTHE
THE WOMAN	LETTA
CHARLEY	

The action takes place in Willy Loman's house and yard and in various places he visits in the New York and Boston of today.

(Throughout the play, in the stage directions, left and right mean stage left and stage right.)

ACT I

(A melody is heard, played upon a flute. It is small and fine, telling of grass and trees and the horizon. The curtain rises.)

*(Before us is the Salesman's house. We are aware of towering, angular shapes behind it, surrounding it on all sides. Only the blue light of the sky falls upon the house and forestage; the surrounding area shows an angry glow of orange. As more light appears, we see a solid vault of apartment houses around the small, fragile-*seeming home. An air of the dream clings to the place, a dream rising out of reality. The kitchen at center seems actual enough, for there is a kitchen table with three chairs, and a refrigerator. But no other fixtures are seen. At the back of the kitchen there is a draped entrance, which leads to the living room. To the right of the kitchen, on a level raised two feet, is a bedroom furnished only with a brass bedstead and a straight chair. On a shelf over the bed a silver athletic trophy stands. A window opens onto the apartment house at the side.)*

(Behind the kitchen, on a level raised six and a half feet, is the boys' bedroom, at present barely visible. Two beds are dimly seen, and at the back of the room a dormer window. [This bedroom is above the unseen living room.] At the left a stairway curves up to it from the kitchen.)

(The entire setting is wholly or, in some places, partially transparent. The roofline of the house is one-dimensional; under and over it we see the apartment buildings. Before the house lies an apron, curving beyond the forestage into the orchestra. This forward area serves as the back yard as well as the locale of all Willy's imaginings and of his city scenes. Whenever the action is in the present the actors observe the imaginary wall-lines, entering the house only through its door at the left. But in the scenes of the past these boundaries are broken, and characters enter or leave a room by stepping "through" a wall onto the forestage.)

(*From the right, Willy Loman, the Salesman, enters, carrying two large sample cases. The flute plays on. He hears but is not aware of it. He is past sixty years of age, dressed quietly. Even as he crosses the stage to the doorway of the house, his exhaustion is apparent. He unlocks the door, comes into the kitchen, and thankfully lets his burden down, feeling the soreness of his palms. A word-sigh escapes his lips — it might be "Oh, boy, oh, boy." He closes the door then carries his cases out into the living room, through the draped kitchen doorway.*)

(*Linda, his wife, has stirred in her bed at the right. She gets out and puts on a robe, listening. Most often jovial, she has developed an iron repression of her exceptions to Willy's behavior — she more than loves him, she admires him, as though his mercurial nature, his temper, his massive dreams and little cruelties, served her only as sharp reminders of the turbulent longings within him, longings which she shares but lacks the temperament to utter and follow to their end.*)

LINDA (*hearing Willy outside the bedroom, calls with some trepidation*): Willy!

WILLY: It's all right. I came back.

LINDA: Why? What happened? (*Slight pause.*) Did something happen, Willy?

WILLY: No, nothing happened.

LINDA: You didn't smash the car, did you?

WILLY (*with casual irritation*): I said nothing happened. Didn't you hear me?

LINDA: Don't you feel well?

WILLY: I'm tired to the death. (*The flute has faded away. He sits on the bed beside her, a little numb.*) I couldn't make it. I just couldn't make it, Linda.

LINDA (*very carefully, delicately*): Where were you all day? You look terrible.

WILLY: I got as far as a little above Yonkers. I stopped for a cup of coffee. Maybe it was the coffee.

LINDA: What?

WILLY (*after a pause*): I suddenly couldn't drive anymore. The car kept going off onto the shoulder, y'know?

LINDA (*helpfully*): Oh. Maybe it was the steering again. I don't think Angelo knows the Studebaker.

WILLY: No, it's me, it's me. Suddenly I realize I'm goin' sixty miles an hour and I don't remember the last five minutes. I'm — I can't seem to — keep my mind to it.

LINDA: Maybe it's your glasses. You never went for your new glasses.

WILLY: No, I see everything. I came back ten miles an hour. It took me nearly four hours from Yonkers.

LINDA (*resigned*): Well, you'll just have to take a rest, Willy, you can't continue this way.

WILLY: I just got back from Florida.

LINDA: But you didn't rest your mind. Your mind is overactive, and the mind is what counts, dear.

WILLY: I'll start out in the morning. Maybe I'll feel better in the morning. (*She is taking off his shoes.*) These goddam arch supports are killing me.

LINDA: Take an aspirin. Should I get you an aspirin? It'll soothe you.

WILLY (*with wonder*): I was driving along, you understand? And I was fine. I was even observing the scenery. You can imagine, me looking at scenery, on the road every week of my life. But it's so beautiful up there, Linda, the trees are so thick, and the sun is warm. I opened the windshield and just let the warm air bathe over me. And then all of a sudden I'm goin' off the road! I'm tellin' ya, I absolutely forgot I was driving. If I'd've gone the other way over the white line I might've killed somebody. So I went on again — and five minutes later I'm dreamin' again, and I nearly — (*He presses two fingers against his eyes.*) I have such thoughts, I have such strange thoughts.

LINDA: Willy, dear. Talk to them again. There's no reason why you can't work in New York.

WILLY: They don't need me in New York. I'm the New England man. I'm vital in New England.

LINDA: But you're sixty years old. They can't expect you to keep traveling every week.

WILLY: I'll have to send a wire to Portland. I'm supposed to see Brown and Morrison tomorrow morning at ten o'clock to show the line. Goddammit, I could sell them! (*He starts putting on his jacket.*)

LINDA (*taking the jacket from him*): Why don't you go down to the place tomorrow and tell Howard you've simply got to work in New York? You're too accommodating, dear.

WILLY: If old man Wagner was alive I'd a been in charge of New York now! That man was a prince, he was a masterful man. But that boy of his, that Howard, he don't appreciate. When I went north the first time, the Wagner Company didn't know where New England was!

LINDA: Why don't you tell those things to Howard, dear?

WILLY (*encouraged*): I will, I definitely will. Is there any cheese?

LINDA: I'll make you a sandwich.

WILLY: No, go to sleep. I'll take some milk. I'll be up right away. The boys in?

LINDA: They're sleeping. Happy took Biff on a date tonight.

WILLY (*interested*): That so?

LINDA: It was so nice to see them shaving together, one behind the other, in the bathroom. And going out together. You notice? The whole house smells of shaving lotion.

WILLY: Figure it out. Work a lifetime to pay off a house. You finally own it, and there's nobody to live in it.

LINDA: Well, dear, life is a casting off. It's always that way.

WILLY: No, no, some people — some people accomplish something. Did Biff say anything after I went this morning?

LINDA: You shouldn't have criticized him, Willy, especially after he just got off the train. You mustn't lose your temper with him.

WILLY: When the hell did I lose my temper? I simply asked him if he was making any money. Is that a criticism?

LINDA: But, dear, how could he make any money?

WILLY (*worried and angered*): There's such an undercurrent in him. He became a moody man. Did he apologize when I left this morning?

LINDA: He was crestfallen, Willy. You know how he admires you. I think if he finds himself, then you'll both be happier and not fight any more.

WILLY: How can he find himself on a farm? Is that a life? A farmhand? In the beginning, when he was young, I thought, well, a young man, it's good for him to tramp around, take a lot of different jobs. But it's more than ten years now and he has yet to make thirty-five dollars a week!

LINDA: He's finding himself, Willy.

WILLY: Not finding yourself at the age of thirty-four is a disgrace!

LINDA: Shh!

WILLY: The trouble is he's lazy, goddammit!

LINDA: Willy, please!

WILLY: Biff is a lazy bum!

LINDA: They're sleeping. Get something to eat. Go on down.

WILLY: Why did he come home? I would like to know what brought him home.

LINDA: I don't know. I think he's still lost, Willy. I think he's very lost.

WILLY: Biff Loman is lost. In the greatest country in the world a young man with such — personal attractiveness, gets lost. And such a hard worker. There's one thing about Biff — he's not lazy.

LINDA: Never.

WILLY (*with pity and resolve*): I'll see him in the morning; I'll have a nice talk with him. I'll get him a job selling. He could be big in no time. My God! Remember how they used to follow him around in high school? When he smiled at one of them their faces lit up. When he walked down the street . . . (*He loses himself in reminiscences.*)

LINDA (*trying to bring him out of it*): Willy, dear, I got a new kind of American-type cheese today. It's whipped.

WILLY: Why do you get American when I like Swiss?

LINDA: I just thought you'd like a change —

WILLY: I don't want a change! I want Swiss cheese. Why am I always being contradicted?

LINDA (*with a covering laugh*): I thought it would be a surprise.

WILLY: Why don't you open a window in here, for God's sake?

LINDA (*with infinite patience*): They're all open, dear.

WILLY: The way they boxed us in here. Bricks and windows, windows and bricks.

LINDA: We should've bought the land next door.

WILLY: The street is lined with cars. There's not a breath of fresh air in the neighborhood. The grass don't grow anymore, you can't raise a carrot in the back yard. They should've had a law against apartment houses. Remember those two beautiful elm trees out there? When I and Biff hung the swing between them?

LINDA: Yeah, like being a million miles from the city.

WILLY: They should've arrested the builder for cutting those down. They massacred the neighborhood. (*Lost.*) More and more I think of those days, Linda. This time of year it was lilac and wisteria. And then the peonies would come out, and the daffodils. What fragrance in this room!

LINDA: Well, after all, people had to move somewhere.

WILLY: No, there's more people now.

LINDA: I don't think there's more people. I think —

WILLY: There's more people! That's what's ruining this country! Population is getting out of control. The competition is maddening! Smell the stink from that apartment house! And another one on the other side . . . How can they whip cheese?

(*On Willy's last line, Biff and Happy raise themselves up in their beds, listening.*)

LINDA: Go down, try it. And be quiet.

WILLY (*turning to Linda, guiltily*): You're not worried about me, are you, sweetheart?

BIFF: What's the matter?

HAPPY: Listen!

LINDA: You've got too much on the ball to worry about.

WILLY: You're my foundation and my support, Linda.

LINDA: Just try to relax, dear. You make mountains out of molehills.

WILLY: I won't fight with him any more. If he wants to go back to Texas, let him go.

LINDA: He'll find his way.

WILLY: Sure. Certain men just don't get started till later in life. Like Thomas Edison, I think. Or B. F. Goodrich. One of them was deaf. (*He starts for the bedroom doorway.*) I'll put my money on Biff.

LINDA: And Willy — if it's warm Sunday we'll drive in the country. And we'll open the windshield, and take lunch.

WILLY: No, the windshields don't open on the new cars.

LINDA: But you opened it today.

WILLY: Me? I didn't. (*He stops.*) Now isn't that peculiar! Isn't that a remarkable — (*He breaks off in amazement and fright as the flute is heard distantly.*)

LINDA: What, darling?

WILLY: That is the most remarkable thing.

LINDA: What, dear?

WILLY: I was thinking of the Chevvy. (*Slight pause.*) Nineteen twenty-eight . . . when I had that red Chevvy — (*Breaks off.*) That funny? I coulda sworn I was driving that Chevvy today.

LINDA: Well, that's nothing. Something must've reminded you.

WILLY: Remarkable. Ts. Remember those days? The way Biff used to simonize that car? The dealer refused to believe there was eighty thousand miles on it. (*He shakes his head.*) Heh! (*To Linda.*) Close your eyes, I'll be right up. (*He walks out of the bedroom.*)

HAPPY (*to Biff*): Jesus, maybe he smashed up the car again!

LINDA (*calling after Willy*): Be careful on the stairs, dear! The cheese is on the middle shelf! (*She turns, goes over to the bed, takes his jacket, and goes out of the bedroom.*)

(*Light has risen on the boys' room. Unseen, Willy is heard talking to himself, "Eighty thousand miles," and a little laugh. Biff gets out of bed, comes downstage a bit, and stands attentively. Biff is two years older than his brother Happy, well built, but in these days bears a worn air and seems less self-assured. He has succeeded less, and his dreams are stronger and less acceptable than Happy's. Happy is tall, powerfully made. Sexuality is like a visible color on him, or a scent that many women have discovered. He, like his brother, is lost, but in a different way, for he has never allowed himself to turn his face toward defeat and is thus more confused and hard-skinned, although seemingly more content.*)

HAPPY (*getting out of bed*): He's going to get his license taken away if he keeps that up. I'm getting nervous about him, y'know, Biff?

BIFF: His eyes are going.

HAPPY: No, I've driven with him. He sees all right. He just doesn't keep his mind on it. I drove into the city with him last week. He stops at a green light and then it turns red and he goes. (*He laughs.*)

BIFF: Maybe he's color-blind.

HAPPY: Pop? Why he's got the finest eye for color in the business. You know that.

BIFF (*sitting down on his bed*): I'm going to sleep.

HAPPY: You're not still sour on Dad, are you, Biff?

BIFF: He's all right, I guess.

WILLY (*underneath them, in the living room*): Yes, sir, eighty thousand miles — eighty-two thousand!

BIFF: You smoking?

HAPPY (*holding out a pack of cigarettes*): Want one?

BIFF (*taking a cigarette*): I can never sleep when I smell it.

WILLY: What a simonizing job, heh!

HAPPY (*with deep sentiment*): Funny, Biff, y'know? Us sleeping in here again? The old beds. (*He pats his bed affectionately.*) All the talk that went across those two beds, huh? Our whole lives.

BIFF: Yeah. Lotta dreams and plans.

HAPPY (*with a deep and masculine laugh*): About five hundred women would like to know what was said in this room.

(*They share a soft laugh.*)

BIFF: Remember that big Betsy something — what the hell was her name — over on Bushwick Avenue?

HAPPY (*combing his hair*): With the collie dog!

BIFF: That's the one. I got you in there, remember?

HAPPY: Yeah, that was my first time — I think. Boy, there was a pig. (*They laugh, almost crudely.*) You taught me everything I know about women. Don't forget that.

BIFF: I bet you forgot how bashful you used to be. Especially with girls.

HAPPY: Oh, I still am, Biff.

BIFF: Oh, go on.

HAPPY: I just control it, that's all. I think I got less bashful and you got more so. What happened, Biff? Where's the old humor, the old confidence? (*He shakes Biff's knee. Biff gets up and moves restlessly about the room.*) What's the matter?

BIFF: Why does Dad mock me all the time?

HAPPY: He's not mocking you, he —

BIFF: Everything I say there's a twist of mockery on his face. I can't get near him.

HAPPY: He just wants you to make good, that's all. I wanted to talk to you about Dad for a long time, Biff. Something's — happening to him. He — talks to himself.

BIFF: I noticed that this morning. But he always mumbled.

HAPPY: But not so noticeable. It got so embarrassing I sent him to Florida. And you know something? Most of the time he's talking to you.

BIFF: What's he say about me?

HAPPY: I can't make it out.

BIFF: What's he say about me?

HAPPY: I think the fact that you're not settled, that you're still kind of up in the air . . .

BIFF: There's one or two other things depressing him, Happy.

HAPPY: What do you mean?

BIFF: Never mind. Just don't lay it all to me.

HAPPY: But I think if you just got started — I mean — is there any future for you out there?

BIFF: I tell ya, Hap, I don't know what the future is. I don't know — what I'm supposed to want.

HAPPY: What do you mean?

BIFF: Well, I spent six or seven years after high school trying to work myself up. Shipping clerk, salesman, business of one kind or another. And it's a measly manner of existence. To get on that subway on the hot mornings in summer. To devote your whole life to keeping stock, or making phone calls, or selling or buying. To suffer fifty weeks of the year for the sake of a two-week vacation, when all you really desire is to be outdoors, with your shirt off. And always to have to get ahead of the next fella. And still — that's how you build a future.

HAPPY: Well, you really enjoy it on a farm? Are you content out there?

BIFF (*with rising agitation*): Hap, I've had twenty or thirty different kinds of jobs since I left home before the war, and it always turns out the same. I just realized it lately. In Nebraska when I herded cattle, and the Dakotas, and Arizona, and now in Texas. It's why I came home now, I guess, because I realized it. This farm I work on, it's spring there now, see? And they've got about fifteen new colts. There's nothing more inspiring or — beautiful than the sight of a mare and a new colt. And it's cool there now, see?

Texas is cool now, and it's spring. And whenever spring comes to where I am, I suddenly get the feeling, my God, I'm not gettin' anywhere! What the hell am I doing, playing around with horses, twenty-eight dollars a week! I'm thirty-four years old, I oughta be makin' my future. That's when I come running home. And now, I get here, and I don't know what to do with myself. (*After a pause.*) I've always made a point of not wasting my life, and every time I come back here I know that all I've done is to waste my life.

HAPPY: You're a poet, you know that, Biff? You're a — you're an idealist!

BIFF: No, I'm mixed up very bad. Maybe I oughta get married. Maybe I oughta get stuck into something. Maybe that's my trouble. I'm like a boy. I'm not married, I'm not in business, I just — I'm like a boy. Are you content, Hap? You're a success, aren't you? Are you content?

HAPPY: Hell, no!

BIFF: Why? You're making money, aren't you?

HAPPY (*moving about with energy, expressiveness*): All I can do now is wait for the merchandise manager to die. And suppose I get to be merchandise manager? He's a good friend of mine, and he just built a terrific estate on Long Island. And he lived there about two months and sold it, and now he's building another one. He can't enjoy it once it's finished. And I know that's just what I would do. I don't know what the hell I'm workin' for. Sometimes I sit in my apartment — all alone. And I think of the rent I'm paying. And it's crazy. But then, it's what I always wanted. My own apartment, a car, and plenty of women. And still, goddammit, I'm lonely.

BIFF (*with enthusiasm*): Listen, why don't you come out West with me?

HAPPY: You and I, heh?

BIFF: Sure, maybe we could buy a ranch. Raise cattle, use our muscles. Men built like we are should be working out in the open.

HAPPY (*avidly*): The Loman Brothers, heh?

BIFF (*with vast affection*): Sure, we'd be known all over the counties!

HAPPY (*enthralled*): That's what I dream about, Biff. Sometimes I want to just rip my clothes off in the middle of the store and outbox that goddam merchandise manager. I mean I can outbox, outrun and outlift anybody in that store, and I have to take orders from those common, petty sons-of-bitches till I can't stand it anymore.

BIFF: I'm tellin' you, kid, if you were with me I'd be happy out there.

HAPPY (*enthused*): See, Biff, everybody around me is so false that I'm constantly lowering my ideals . . .

BIFF: Baby, together we'd stand up for one another, we'd have someone to trust.

HAPPY: If I were around you —

BIFF: Hap, the trouble is we weren't brought up to grub for money. I don't know how to do it.

HAPPY: Neither can I!

BIFF: Then let's go!

HAPPY: The only thing is — what can you make out there?

BIFF: But look at your friend. Builds an estate and then hasn't the peace of mind to live in it.

HAPPY: Yeah, but when he walks into the store the waves part in front of him. That's fifty-two thousand dollars a year coming through the revolving door, and I got more in my pinky finger than he's got in his head.

BIFF: Yeah, but you just said —

HAPPY: I gotta show some of those pompous, self-important executives over there that Hap Loman can make the grade. I want to walk into the store the way he walks in. Then I'll go with you, Biff. We'll be together yet, I swear. But take those two we had tonight. Now weren't they gorgeous creatures?

BIFF: Yeah, yeah, most gorgeous I've had in years.

HAPPY: I get that any time I want, Biff. Whenever I feel disgusted. The only trouble is, it gets like bowling or something. I just keep knockin' them over and it doesn't mean anything. You still run around a lot?

BIFF: Naa. I'd like to find a girl — steady, somebody with substance.

HAPPY: That's what I long for.

BIFF: Go on! You'd never come home.

HAPPY: I would! Somebody with character, with resistance! Like Mom, y'know? You're gonna call me a bastard when I tell you this. That girl Charlotte I was with tonight is engaged to be married in five weeks. (*He tries on his new hat.*)

BIFF: No kiddin'!

HAPPY: Sure, the guy's in line for the vice-presidency of the store. I don't know what gets into me, maybe I just have an overdeveloped sense of competition or something, but I went and ruined her, and furthermore I can't get rid of her. And he's the third executive I've done that to. Isn't that a crummy characteristic? And to top it all, I go to their weddings! (*Indignantly, but laughing.*) Like I'm not supposed to take bribes. Manufacturers offer me a hundred-dollar bill now and then to throw an order their way. You know how honest I am, but it's like this girl, see. I hate myself for it. Because I don't want the girl, and, still, I take it and — I love it!

BIFF: Let's go to sleep.

HAPPY: I guess we didn't settle anything, heh?

BIFF: I just got one idea that I think I'm going to try.

HAPPY: What's that?

BIFF: Remember Bill Oliver?

HAPPY: Sure, Oliver is very big now. You want to work for him again?

BIFF: No, but when I quit he said something to me. He put his arm on my shoulder, and he said, "Biff, if you ever need anything, come to me."

HAPPY: I remember that. That sounds good.

BIFF: I think I'll go to see him. If I could get ten thousand or even seven or eight thousand dollars I could buy a beautiful ranch.

HAPPY: I bet he'd back you. 'Cause he thought highly of you, Biff. I mean, they all do. You're well liked, Biff. That's why I say to come back here, and we both have the apartment. And I'm tellin' you, Biff, any babe you want . . .

BIFF: No, with a ranch I could do the work I like and still be something. I just wonder though. I wonder if Oliver still thinks I stole that carton of basketballs.

HAPPY: Oh, he probably forgot that long ago. It's almost ten years. You're too sensitive. Anyway, he didn't really fire you.

BIFF: Well, I think he was going to. I think that's why I quit. I was never sure whether he knew or not. I know he thought the world of me, though. I was the only one he'd let lock up the place.

WILLY (below): You gonna wash the engine, Biff?

HAPPY: Shh!

(*Biff looks at Happy, who is gazing down, listening. Willy is mumbling in the parlor.*)

HAPPY: You hear that?

(*They listen. Willy laughs warmly.*)

BIFF (growing angry): Doesn't he know Mom can hear that?

WILLY: Don't get your sweater dirty, Biff!

(*A look of pain crosses Biff's face.*)

HAPPY: Isn't that terrible? Don't leave again, will you? You'll find a job here. You gotta stick around. I don't know what to do about him, it's getting embarrassing.

WILLY: What a simonizing job!

BIFF: Mom's hearing that!

WILLY: No kiddin', Biff, you got a date? Wonderful!

HAPPY: Go on to sleep. But talk to him in the morning, will you?

BIFF (reluctantly getting into bed): With her in the house. Brother!

HAPPY (getting into bed): I wish you'd have a good talk with him.

(*The light on their room begins to fade.*)

BIFF (to himself in bed): That selfish, stupid . . .

HAPPY: Sh . . . Sleep, Biff.

(*Their light is out. Well before they have finished speaking, Willy's form is dimly seen below in the darkened kitchen. He opens the refrigerator, searches in there, and takes out a bottle of milk. The apartment houses are fading out, and the entire house and surroundings become covered with leaves. Music insinuates itself as the leaves appear.*)

WILLY: Just wanna be careful with those girls, Biff, that's all. Don't make any promises. No promises of any kind. Because a girl, y'know, they always believe what you tell 'em, and you're very young, Biff, you're too young to be talking seriously to girls.

(*Light rises on the kitchen. Willy, talking, shuts the refrigerator door and comes downstage to the kitchen table. He pours milk into a glass. He is totally immersed in himself, smiling faintly.*)

WILLY: Too young entirely, Biff. You want to watch your schooling first. Then when you're all set, there'll be plenty of girls for a boy like you. (*He smiles broadly at a kitchen chair.*) That so? The girls pay for you? (*He laughs.*) Boy, you must really be makin' a hit.

(*Willy is gradually addressing — physically — a point offstage, speaking through the wall of the kitchen, and his voice has been rising in volume to that of a normal conversation.*)

WILLY: I been wondering why you polish the car so careful. Ha! Don't leave the hubcaps, boys. Get the chamois to the hubcaps. Happy, use newspaper on the windows, it's the easiest thing. Show him how to do it, Biff! You see, Happy? Pad it up, use it like a pad. That's it, that's it, good work. You're doin' all right, Hap. (*He pauses, then nods in approbation for a few seconds, then looks upward.*) Biff, first thing we gotta do when we get time is clip that big branch over the house. Afraid it's gonna fall in a storm and hit the roof. Tell you what. We get a rope and sling her around, and then we climb up there with a couple of saws and take her down. Soon as you finish the car, boys, I wanna see ye. I got a surprise for you, boys.

BIFF (offstage): Whatta ya got, Dad?

WILLY: No, you finish first. Never leave a job till you're finished — remember that. (*Looking toward the "big trees."*) Biff, up in Albany I saw a beautiful hammock. I think I'll buy it next trip, and we'll hang it right between those two elms. Wouldn't that be something? Just swingin' there under those branches. Boy, that would be . . .

(*Young Biff and Young Happy appear from the direction Willy was addressing. Happy carries rags and a pail of water. Biff, wearing a sweater with a block "S," carries a football.*)

BIFF (pointing in the direction of the car offstage): How's that, Pop, professional?

WILLY: Terrific. Terrific job, boys. Good work, Biff.

HAPPY: Where's the surprise, Pop?

WILLY: In the back seat of the car.

HAPPY: Boy! (*He runs off.*)

BIFF: What is it, Dad? Tell me, what'd you buy?

WILLY (laughing, cuffs him): Never mind, something I want you to have.

BIFF (turns and starts off): What is it, Hap?

HAPPY (offstage): It's a punching bag!

BIFF: Oh, Pop!

WILLY: It's got Gene Tunney's signature on it!

(*Happy runs onstage with a punching bag.*)

BIFF: Gee, how'd you know we wanted a punching bag?

Biff (Kevin Anderson), Willy (Brian Dennehy), and Happy (Ted Koch) in a bright moment in Robert Falls's 1999 Broadway revival of *Death of a Salesman*.

WILLY: Well, it's the finest thing for the timing.

HAPPY (*lies down on his back and pedals with his feet*): I'm losing weight, you notice, Pop?

WILLY (*to Happy*): Jumping rope is good too.

BIFF: Did you see the new football I got?

WILLY (*examining the ball*): Where'd you get a new ball?

BIFF: The coach told me to practice my passing.

WILLY: That so? And he gave you the ball, heh?

BIFF: Well, I borrowed it from the locker room. (*He laughs confidentially.*)

WILLY (*laughing with him at the theft*): I want you to return that.

HAPPY: I told you he wouldn't like it!

BIFF (*angrily*): Well, I'm bringing it back!

WILLY (*stopping the incipient argument, to Happy*): Sure, he's gotta practice with a regulation ball, doesn't he? (*To Biff.*) Coach'll probably congratulate you on your initiative!

BIFF: Oh, he keeps congratulating my initiative all the time, Pop.

WILLY: That's because he likes you. If somebody else took that ball there'd be an uproar. So what's the report, boys, what's the report?

BIFF: Where'd you go this time, Dad? Gee we were lonesome for you.

WILLY (*pleased, puts an arm around each boy and they come down to the apron*): Lonesome, heh?

BIFF: Missed you every minute.

WILLY: Don't say? Tell you a secret, boys. Don't breathe it to a soul. Someday I'll have my own business, and I'll never have to leave home anymore.

HAPPY: Like Uncle Charley, heh?

WILLY: Bigger than Uncle Charley! Because Charley is not — liked. He's liked, but he's not — well liked.

BIFF: Where'd you go this time, Dad?

WILLY: Well, I got on the road, and I went north to Providence. Met the Mayor.

BIFF: The Mayor of Providence!

WILLY: He was sitting in the hotel lobby.

BIFF: What'd he say?

WILLY: He said, "Morning!" And I said, "You got a fine city here, Mayor." And then he had coffee with me. And then I went to Waterbury. Waterbury is a fine city. Big clock city, the famous Waterbury clock. Sold a nice bill there. And then Boston — Boston is the cradle of the Revolution. A fine city. And a couple of other towns in Mass., and on to Portland and Bangor and straight home!

BIFF: Gee, I'd love to go with you sometime, Dad.

WILLY: Soon as summer comes.

HAPPY: Promise?

WILLY: You and Hap and I, and I'll show you all the towns. America is full of beautiful towns and fine, upstanding people. And they know me, boys, they know me up and down New England. The finest people. And when I bring you fellas up, there'll be open sesame for all of us, 'cause one thing, boys: I have friends. I can park my car in any street in New England, and the cops protect it like their own. This summer, heh?

BIFF AND HAPPY (*together*): Yeah! You bet!

WILLY: We'll take our bathing suits.

HAPPY: We'll carry your bags, Pop!

WILLY: Oh, won't that be something! Me comin' into the Boston stores with you boys carryin' my bags. What a sensation!

(*Biff is prancing around, practicing passing the ball.*)

WILLY: You nervous, Biff, about the game?

BIFF: Not if you're gonna be there.

WILLY: What do they say about you in school, now that they made you captain?

HAPPY: There's a crowd of girls behind him every time the classes change.

BIFF (*taking Willy's hand*): This Saturday, Pop, this Saturday — just for you, I'm going to break through for a touchdown.

HAPPY: You're supposed to pass.

BIFF: I'm takin' one play for Pop. You watch me, Pop, and when I take off my helmet, that means I'm breakin' out. Then you watch me crash through that line!

WILLY (*kisses Biff*): Oh, wait'll I tell this in Boston!

(*Bernard enters in knickers. He is younger than Biff, earnest and loyal, a worried boy.*)

BERNARD: Biff, where are you? You're supposed to study with me today.

WILLY: Hey, looka Bernard. What're you lookin' so anemic about, Bernard?

BERNARD: He's gotta study, Uncle Willy. He's got Regents next week.

HAPPY (*tauntingly, spinning Bernard around*): Let's box, Bernard!

BERNARD: Biff! (*He gets away from Happy.*) Listen, Biff, I heard Mr. Birnbaum say that if you don't start studyin' math he's gonna flunk you, and you won't graduate. I heard him!

WILLY: You better study with him, Biff. Go ahead now.

BERNARD: I heard him!

BIFF: Oh, Pop, you didn't see my sneakers! (*He holds up a foot for Willy to look at.*)

WILLY: Hey, that's a beautiful job of printing!

BERNARD (*wiping his glasses*): Just because he printed University of Virginia on his sneakers doesn't mean they've got to graduate him, Uncle Willy!

WILLY (*angrily*): What're you talking about? With scholarships to three universities they're gonna flunk him?

BERNARD: But I heard Mr. Birnbaum say —

WILLY: Don't be a pest, Bernard! (*To his boys.*) What an anemic!

BERNARD: Okay, I'm waiting for you in my house, Biff.

(*Bernard goes off. The Lomans laugh.*)

WILLY: Bernard is not well liked, is he?

BIFF: He's liked, but he's not well liked.

HAPPY: That's right, Pop.

WILLY: That's just what I mean. Bernard can get the best marks in school, y'understand, but when he gets out in the business world, y'understand, you are going to be five times ahead of him. That's why I thank Almighty God you're both built like Adonises. Because the man who makes an appearance in the business world, the man who creates personal interest, is the man who gets ahead. Be liked and you will never want. You take me, for instance. I never have to wait in line to see a buyer. "Willy Loman is here!" That's all they have to know, and I go right through.

BIFF: Did you knock them dead, Pop?

WILLY: Knocked 'em cold in Providence, slaughtered 'em in Boston.

HAPPY (*on his back, pedaling again*): I'm losing weight, you notice, Pop?

(*Linda enters as of old, a ribbon in her hair, carrying a basket of washing.*)

LINDA (*with youthful energy*): Hello, dear!

WILLY: Sweetheart!

LINDA: How'd the Chevvy run?

WILLY: Chevrolet, Linda, is the greatest car ever built. (*To the boys.*) Since when do you let your mother carry wash up the stairs?

BIFF: Grab hold there, boy!

HAPPY: Where to, Mom?

LINDA: Hang them up on the line. And you better go down to your friends, Biff. The cellar is full of boys. They don't know what to do with themselves.

BIFF: Ah, when Pop comes home they can wait!

WILLY (*laughs appreciatively*): You better go down and tell them what to do, Biff.

BIFF: I think I'll have them sweep out the furnace room.

WILLY: Good work, Biff.

BIFF (*goes through wall-line of kitchen to doorway at back and calls down*): Fellas! Everybody sweep out the furnace room! I'll be right down!

VOICES: All right! Okay, Biff.

BIFF: George and Sam and Frank, come out back! We're hangin' up the wash! Come on, Hap, on the double! (*He and Happy carry out the basket.*)

LINDA: The way they obey him!

WILLY: Well, that's training, the training. I'm tellin' you,

I was sellin' thousands and thousands, but I had to come home.

LINDA: Oh, the whole block'll be at that game. Did you sell anything?

WILLY: I did five hundred gross in Providence and seven hundred gross in Boston.

LINDA: No! Wait a minute, I've got a pencil. (*She pulls pencil and paper out of her apron pocket.*) That makes your commission . . . Two hundred — my God! Two hundred and twelve dollars!

WILLY: Well, I didn't figure it yet, but . . .

LINDA: How much did you do?

WILLY: Well, I — I did — about a hundred and eighty gross in Providence. Well, no — it came to — roughly two hundred gross on the whole trip.

LINDA (*without hesitation*): Two hundred gross. That's . . . (*She figures.*)

WILLY: The trouble was that three of the stores were half-closed for inventory in Boston. Otherwise I woulda broke records.

LINDA: Well, it makes seventy dollars and some pennies. That's very good.

WILLY: What do we owe?

LINDA: Well, on the first there's sixteen dollars on the refrigerator —

WILLY: Why sixteen?

LINDA: Well, the fan belt broke, so it was a dollar eighty.

WILLY: But it's brand new.

LINDA: Well, the man said that's the way it is. Till they work themselves in, y'know.

(*They move through the wall-line into the kitchen.*)

WILLY: I hope we didn't get stuck on that machine.

LINDA: They got the biggest ads of any of them!

WILLY: I know, it's a fine machine. What else?

LINDA: Well, there's nine-sixty for the washing machine. And for the vacuum cleaner there's three and a half due on the fifteenth. Then the roof, you got twenty-one dollars remaining.

WILLY: It don't leak, does it?

LINDA: No, they did a wonderful job. Then you owe Frank for the carburetor.

WILLY: I'm not going to pay that man! That goddam Chevrolet, they ought to prohibit the manufacture of that car!

LINDA: Well, you owe him three and a half. And odds and ends, comes to around a hundred and twenty dollars by the fifteenth.

WILLY: A hundred and twenty dollars! My God, if business don't pick up I don't know what I'm gonna do!

LINDA: Well, next week you'll do better.

WILLY: Oh, I'll knock 'em dead next week. I'll go to Hartford. I'm very well liked in Hartford. You know, the trouble is, Linda, people don't seem to take to me.

(*They move onto the forestage.*)

LINDA: Oh, don't be foolish.

WILLY: I know it when I walk in. They seem to laugh at me.

LINDA: Why? Why would they laugh at you? Don't talk that way, Willy.

(*Willy moves to the edge of the stage. Linda goes into the kitchen and starts to darn stockings.*)

WILLY: I don't know the reason for it, but they just pass me by. I'm not noticed.

LINDA: But you're doing wonderful, dear. You're making seventy to a hundred dollars a week.

WILLY: But I gotta be at it ten, twelve hours a day. Other men — I don't know — they do it easier. I don't know why — I can't stop myself — I talk too much. A man oughta come in with a few words. One thing about Charley. He's a man of few words, and they respect him.

LINDA: You don't talk too much, you're just lively.

WILLY (*smiling*): Well, I figure, what the hell, life is short, a couple of jokes. (*To himself.*) I joke too much! (*The smile goes.*)

LINDA: Why? You're —

WILLY: I'm fat. I'm very — foolish to look at, Linda. I didn't tell you, but Christmas time I happened to be calling on F. H. Stewarts, and a salesman I know, as I was going in to see the buyer I heard him say something about — walrus. And I — I cracked him right across the face. I won't take that. I simply will not take that. But they do laugh at me. I know that.

LINDA: Darling . . .

WILLY: I gotta overcome it. I know I gotta overcome it. I'm not dressing to advantage, maybe.

LINDA: Willy, darling, you're the handsomest man in the world —

WILLY: Oh, no, Linda.

LINDA: To me you are. (*Slight pause.*) The handsomest.

(*From the darkness is heard the laughter of a woman. Willy doesn't turn to it, but it continues through Linda's lines.*)

LINDA: And the boys, Willy. Few men are idolized by their children the way you are.

(*Music is heard as behind a scrim, to the left of the house, The Woman, dimly seen, is dressing.*)

WILLY (*with great feeling*): You're the best there is, Linda, you're a pal, you know that? On the road — on the road I want to grab you sometimes and just kiss the life outa you.

(*The laughter is loud now, and he moves into a brightening area at the left, where The Woman has come from behind the scrim and is standing, putting on her hat, looking into a "mirror" and laughing.*)

WILLY: 'Cause I get so lonely — especially when business is bad and there's nobody to talk to. I get the feeling that I'll never sell anything again, that I won't make a living for you, or a business, a business for the boys. (*He talks through The Woman's subsiding laughter; The Woman primps at the "mirror."*) There's so much I want to make for —

THE WOMAN: Me? You didn't make me, Willy. I picked you.

WILLY (*pleased*): You picked me?

THE WOMAN (*who is quite proper-looking, Willy's age*): I did. I've been sitting at that desk watching all the salesmen go by, day in, day out. But you've got such a sense of humor, and we do have such a good time together, don't we?

WILLY: Sure, sure. (*He takes her in his arms.*) Why do you have to go now?

THE WOMAN: It's two o'clock . . .

WILLY: No, come on in! (*He pulls her.*)

THE WOMAN: . . . my sisters'll be scandalized. When'll you be back?

WILLY: Oh, two weeks about. Will you come up again?

THE WOMAN: Sure thing. You do make me laugh. It's good for me. (*She squeezes his arm, kisses him.*) And I think you're a wonderful man.

WILLY: You picked me, heh?

THE WOMAN: Sure. Because you're so sweet. And such a kidder.

WILLY: Well, I'll see you next time I'm in Boston.

THE WOMAN: I'll put you right through to the buyers.

WILLY (*slapping her bottom*): Right. Well, bottoms up!

THE WOMAN (*slaps him gently and laughs*): You just kill me, Willy. (*He suddenly grabs her and kisses her roughly.*) You kill me. And thanks for the stockings. I love a lot of stockings. Well, good night.

WILLY: Good night. And keep your pores open!

THE WOMAN: Oh, Willy!

(*The Woman bursts out laughing, and Linda's laughter blends in. The Woman disappears into the dark. Now the area at the kitchen table brightens. Linda is sitting where she was at the kitchen table, but now is mending a pair of her silk stockings.*)

LINDA: You are, Willy. The handsomest man. You've got no reason to feel that —

WILLY (*coming out of The Woman's dimming area and going over to Linda*): I'll make it all up to you, Linda, I'll —

LINDA: There's nothing to make up, dear. You're doing fine, better than —

WILLY (*noticing her mending*): What's that?

LINDA: Just mending my stockings. They're so expensive —

WILLY (*angrily, taking them from her*): I won't have you mending stockings in this house! Now throw them out!

(*Linda puts the stockings in her pocket.*)

BERNARD (*entering on the run*): Where is he? If he doesn't study!

WILLY (*moving to the forestage, with great agitation*): You'll give him the answers!

BERNARD: I do, but I can't on a Regents! That's a state exam! They're liable to arrest me!

WILLY: Where is he? I'll whip him, I'll whip him!

LINDA: And he'd better give back that football, Willy, it's not nice.

WILLY: Biff! Where is he? Why is he taking everything?

LINDA: He's too rough with the girls, Willy. All the mothers are afraid of him!

WILLY: I'll whip him!

BERNARD: He's driving the car without a license!

(*The Woman's laugh is heard.*)

WILLY: Shut up!

LINDA: All the mothers —

WILLY: Shut up!

BERNARD (*backing quietly away and out*): Mr. Birnbaum says he's stuck up.

WILLY: Get outa here!

BERNARD: If he doesn't buckle down he'll flunk math! (*He goes off.*)

LINDA: He's right, Willy, you've gotta —

WILLY (*exploding at her*): There's nothing the matter with him! You want him to be a worm like Bernard? He's got spirit, personality . . .

(*As he speaks, Linda, almost in tears, exits into the living room. Willy is alone in the kitchen, wilting and staring. The leaves are gone. It is night again, and the apartment houses look down from behind.*)

WILLY: Loaded with it. Loaded! What is he stealing? He's giving it back, isn't he? Why is he stealing? What did I tell him? I never in my life told him anything but decent things.

(*Happy in pajamas has come down the stairs; Willy suddenly becomes aware of Happy's presence.*)

HAPPY: Let's go now, come on.

WILLY (*sitting down at the kitchen table*): Huh! Why did she have to wax the floors herself? Everytime she waxes the floors she keels over. She knows that!

HAPPY: Shh! Take it easy. What brought you back tonight?

WILLY: I got an awful scare. Nearly hit a kid in Yonkers. God! Why didn't I go to Alaska with my brother Ben that time! Ben! That man was a genius, that man was success incarnate! What a mistake! He begged me to go.

HAPPY: Well, there's no use in —

WILLY: You guys! There was a man started with the clothes on his back and ended up with diamond mines!

HAPPY: Boy, someday I'd like to know how he did it.

WILLY: What's the mystery? The man knew what he wanted and went out and got it! Walked into a jungle, and comes out, the age of twenty-one, and he's rich! The world is an oyster, but you don't crack it open on a mattress!

HAPPY: Pop, I told you I'm gonna retire you for life.

WILLY: You'll retire me for life on seventy goddam dollars a week? And your women and your car and your apartment, and you'll retire me for life! Christ's sake,

I couldn't get past Yonkers today! Where are you guys, where are you? The woods are burning! I can't drive a car!

(*Charley has appeared in the doorway. He is a large man, slow of speech, laconic, immovable. In all he says, despite what he says, there is pity, and, now, trepidation. He has a robe over pajamas, slippers on his feet. He enters the kitchen.*)

CHARLEY: Everything all right?

HAPPY: Yeah, Charley, everything's . . .

WILLY: What's the matter?

CHARLEY: I heard some noise. I thought something happened. Can't we do something about the walls? You sneeze in here, and in my house hats blow off.

HAPPY: Let's go to bed, Dad. Come on.

(*Charley signals to Happy to go.*)

WILLY: You go ahead, I'm not tired at the moment.

HAPPY (*to Willy*): Take it easy, huh? (*He exits.*)

WILLY: What're you doin' up?

CHARLEY (*sitting down at the kitchen table opposite Willy*): Couldn't sleep good. I had a heartburn.

WILLY: Well, you don't know how to eat.

CHARLEY: I eat with my mouth.

WILLY: No, you're ignorant. You gotta know about vitamins and things like that.

CHARLEY: Come on, let's shoot. Tire you out a little.

WILLY (*hesitantly*): All right. You got cards?

CHARLEY (*taking a deck from his pocket*): Yeah, I got them. Someplace. What is it with those vitamins?

WILLY (*dealing*): They build up your bones. Chemistry.

CHARLEY: Yeah, but there's no bones in a heartburn.

WILLY: What are you talkin' about? Do you know the first thing about it?

CHARLEY: Don't get insulted.

WILLY: Don't talk about something you don't know anything about.

(*They are playing. Pause.*)

CHARLEY: What're you doin' home?

WILLY: A little trouble with the car.

CHARLEY: Oh. (*Pause.*) I'd like to take a trip to California.

WILLY: Don't say.

CHARLEY: You want a job?

WILLY: I got a job, I told you that. (*After a slight pause.*) What the hell are you offering me a job for?

CHARLEY: Don't get insulted.

WILLY: Don't insult me.

CHARLEY: I don't see no sense in it. You don't have to go on this way.

WILLY: I got a good job. (*Slight pause.*) What do you keep comin' in here for?

CHARLEY: You want me to go?

WILLY (*after a pause, withering*): I can't understand it. He's going back to Texas again. What the hell is that?

CHARLEY: Let him go.

WILLY: I got nothin' to give him, Charley, I'm clean, I'm clean.

CHARLEY: He won't starve. None a them starve. Forget about him.

WILLY: Then what have I got to remember?

CHARLEY: You take it too hard. To hell with it. When a deposit bottle is broken you don't get your nickel back.

WILLY: That's easy enough for you to say.

CHARLEY: That ain't easy for me to say.

WILLY: Did you see the ceiling I put up in the living room?

CHARLEY: Yeah, that's a piece of work. To put up a ceiling is a mystery to me. How do you do it?

WILLY: What's the difference?

CHARLEY: Well, talk about it.

WILLY: You gonna put up a ceiling?

CHARLEY: How could I put up a ceiling?

WILLY: Then what the hell are you bothering me for?

CHARLEY: You're insulted again.

WILLY: A man who can't handle tools is not a man. You're disgusting.

CHARLEY: Don't call me disgusting, Willy.

(*Uncle Ben, carrying a valise and an umbrella, enters the forestage from around the right corner of the house. He is a stolid man, in his sixties, with a mustache and an authoritative air. He is utterly certain of his destiny, and there is an aura of far places about him. He enters exactly as Willy speaks.*)

WILLY: I'm getting awfully tired, Ben.

(*Ben's music is heard. Ben looks around at everything.*)

CHARLEY: Good, keep playing; you'll sleep better. Did you call me Ben?

(*Ben looks at his watch.*)

WILLY: That's funny. For a second there you reminded me of my brother Ben.

BEN: I only have a few minutes. (*He strolls, inspecting the place. Willy and Charley continue playing.*)

CHARLEY: You never heard from him again, heh? Since that time?

WILLY: Didn't Linda tell you? Couple of weeks ago we got a letter from his wife in Africa. He died.

CHARLEY: That so.

BEN (*chuckling*): So this is Brooklyn, eh?

CHARLEY: Maybe you're in for some of his money.

WILLY: Naa, he had seven sons. There's just one opportunity I had with that man . . .

BEN: I must make a train, William. There are several properties I'm looking at in Alaska.

WILLY: Sure, sure! If I'd gone with him to Alaska that time, everything would've been totally different.

CHARLIE: Go on, you'd froze to death up there.

WILLY: What're you talking about?

BEN: Opportunity is tremendous in Alaska, William. Surprised you're not up there.

WILLY: Sure, tremendous.

CHARLEY: Heh?

WILLY: There was the only man I ever met who knew the answers.

CHARLEY: Who?

BEN: How are you all?

WILLY (*taking a pot, smiling*): Fine, fine.

CHARLEY: Pretty sharp tonight.

BEN: Is Mother living with you?

WILLY: No, she died a long time ago.

CHARLEY: Who?

BEN: That's too bad. Fine specimen of a lady, Mother.

WILLY (*to Charley*): Heh?

BEN: I'd hoped to see the old girl.

CHARLEY: Who died?

BEN: Heard anything from Father, have you?

WILLY (*unnerved*): What do you mean, who died?

CHARLEY (*taking a pot*): What're you talkin' about?

BEN (*looking at his watch*): William, it's half-past eight!

WILLY (*as though to dispel his confusion he angrily stops Charley's hand*): That's my build!

CHARLEY: I put the ace —

WILLY: If you don't know how to play the game I'm not gonna throw my money away on you!

CHARLEY (*rising*): It was my ace, for God's sake!

WILLY: I'm through, I'm through!

BEN: When did Mother die?

WILLY: Long ago. Since the beginning you never knew how to play cards.

CHARLEY (*picks up the cards and goes to the door*): All right! Next time I'll bring a deck with five aces.

WILLY: I don't play that kind of game!

CHARLEY (*turning to him*): You ought to be ashamed of yourself!

WILLY: Yeah?

CHARLEY: Yeah! (*He goes out.*)

WILLY (*slamming the door after him*): Ignoramus!

BEN (*as Willy comes toward him through the wall-line of the kitchen*): So you're William.

WILLY (*shaking Ben's hand*): Ben! I've been waiting for you so long! What's the answer? How did you do it?

BEN: Oh, there's a story in that.

(*Linda enters the forestage, as of old, carrying the wash basket.*)

LINDA: Is this Ben?

BEN (*gallantly*): How do you do, my dear.

LINDA: Where've you been all these years? Willy's always wondered why you —

WILLY (*pulling Ben away from her impatiently*): Where is Dad? Didn't you follow him? How did you get started?

BEN: Well, I don't know how much you remember.

WILLY: Well, I was just a baby, of course, only three or four years old —

BEN: Three years and eleven months.

WILLY: What a memory, Ben!

BEN: I have many enterprises, William, and I have never kept books.

WILLY: I remember I was sitting under the wagon in — was it Nebraska?

BEN: It was South Dakota, and I gave you a bunch of wild flowers.

WILLY: I remember you walking away down some open road.

BEN (*laughing*): I was going to find Father in Alaska.

WILLY: Where is he?

BEN: At that age I had a very faulty view of geography, William. I discovered after a few days that I was heading due south, so instead of Alaska, I ended up in Africa.

LINDA: Africa!

WILLY: The Gold Coast!

BEN: Principally diamond mines.

LINDA: Diamond mines!

BEN: Yes, my dear. But I've only a few minutes —

WILLY: No! Boys! Boys! (*Young Biff and Happy appear.*) Listen to this. This is your Uncle Ben, a great man! Tell my boys, Ben!

BEN: Why, boys, when I was seventeen I walked into the jungle, and when I was twenty-one I walked out. (*He laughs.*) And by God I was rich.

WILLY (*to the boys*): You see what I been talking about? The greatest things can happen!

BEN (*glancing at his watch*): I have an appointment in Ketchikan Tuesday week.

WILLY: No, Ben! Please tell about Dad. I want my boys to hear. I want them to know the kind of stock they spring from. All I remember is a man with a big beard, and I was in Mamma's lap, sitting around a fire, and some kind of high music.

BEN: His flute. He played the flute.

WILLY: Sure, the flute, that's right!

(*New music is heard, a high, rollicking tune.*)

BEN: Father was a very great and a very wild-hearted man. We would start in Boston, and he'd toss the whole family into the wagon, and then he'd drive the team right across the country; through Ohio, and Indiana, Michigan, Illinois, and all the Western states. And we'd stop in the towns and sell the flutes that he'd made on the way. Great inventor Father. With one gadget he made more in a week than a man like you could make in a lifetime.

WILLY: That's just the way I'm bringing them up, Ben — rugged, well liked, all-around.

BEN: Yeah? (*To Biff.*) Hit that, boy — hard as you can. (*He pounds his stomach.*)

BIFF: Oh, no, sir!

BEN (*taking boxing stance*): Come on, get to me! (*He laughs.*)

WILLY: Go to it, Biff! Go ahead, show him!

BIFF: Okay! (*He cocks his fists and starts in.*)

LINDA (*to Willy*): Why must he fight, dear?

BEN (*sparring with Biff*): Good boy! Good boy!

WILLY: How's that, Ben, heh?

HAPPY: Give him the left, Biff!

LINDA: Why are you fighting?

BEN: Good boy! (*Suddenly comes in, trips Biff, and stands over him, the point of his umbrella poised over Biff's eye.*)

LINDA: Look out, Biff!

BIFF: Gee!

BEN (*patting Biff's knee*): Never fight fair with a stranger, boy. You'll never get out of the jungle that way. (*Taking Linda's hand and bowing.*) It was an honor and a pleasure to meet you, Linda.

LINDA (*withdrawing her hand coldly, frightened*): Have a nice — trip.

BEN (*to Willy*): And good luck with your — what do you do?

WILLY: Selling.

BEN: Yes. Well . . . (*He raises his hand in farewell to all.*)

WILLY: No, Ben, I don't want you to think . . . (*He takes Ben's arm to show him.*) It's Brooklyn, I know, but we hunt too.

BEN: Really, now.

WILLY: Oh, sure, there's snakes and rabbits and — that's why I moved out here. Why, Biff can fell any one of these trees in no time! Boys! Go right over to where they're building the apartment house and get some sand. We're gonna rebuild the entire front stoop right now! Watch this, Ben!

BIFF: Yes, sir! On the double, Hap!

HAPPY (*as he and Biff run off*): I lost weight, Pop, you notice?

(*Charley enters in knickers, even before the boys are gone.*)

CHARLEY: Listen, if they steal any more from that building, the watchman'll put the cops on them!

LINDA (*to Willy*): Don't let Biff . . .

(*Ben laughs lustily.*)

WILLY: You shoulda seen the lumber they brought home last week. At least a dozen six-by-tens worth all kinds a money.

CHARLEY: Listen, if that watchman —

WILLY: I gave them hell, understand. But I got a couple of fearless characters there.

CHARLEY: Willy, the jails are full of fearless characters.

BEN (*clapping Willy on the back, with a laugh at Charley*): And the stock exchange, friend!

WILLY (*joining in Ben's laughter*): Where are the rest of your pants?

CHARLEY: My wife bought them.

WILLY: Now all you need is a golf club and you can go upstairs and go to sleep. (*To Ben.*) Great athlete! Between him and his son Bernard they can't hammer a nail!

BERNARD (*rushing in*): The watchman's chasing Biff!

WILLY (*angrily*): Shut up! He's not stealing anything!

LINDA (*alarmed, hurrying off left*): Where is he? Biff, dear! (*She exits.*)

WILLY (*moving toward the left, away from Ben*): There's nothing wrong. What's the matter with you?

BEN: Nervy boy. Good!

WILLY (*laughing*): Oh, nerves of iron, that Biff!

CHARLEY: Don't know what it is. My New England man comes back and he's bleedin', they murdered him up there.

WILLY: It's contacts, Charley, I got important contacts!

CHARLEY (*sarcastically*): Glad to hear it, Willy. Come in later, we'll shoot a little casino. I'll take some of your Portland money. (*He laughs at Willy and exits.*)

WILLY (*turning to Ben*): Business is bad, it's murderous. But not for me, of course.

BEN: I'll stop by on my way back to Africa.

WILLY (*longingly*): Can't you stay a few days? You're just what I need, Ben, because I — I have a fine position here, but I — well, Dad left when I was such a baby and I never had a chance to talk to him and I still feel — kind of temporary about myself.

BEN: I'll be late for my train.

(*They are at opposite ends of the stage.*)

WILLY: Ben, my boys — can't we talk? They'd go into the jaws of hell for me, see, but I —

BEN: William, you're being first-rate with your boys. Outstanding, manly chaps!

WILLY (*hanging on to his words*): Oh, Ben, that's good to hear! Because sometimes I'm afraid that I'm not teaching them the right kind of — Ben, how should I teach them?

BEN (*giving great weight to each word, and with a certain vicious audacity*): William, when I walked into the jungle, I was seventeen. When I walked out I was twenty-one. And, by God, I was rich! (*He goes off into darkness around the right corner of the house.*)

WILLY: . . . was rich! That's just the spirit I want to imbue them with! To walk into a jungle! I was right! I was right! I was right!

(*Ben is gone, but Willy is still speaking to him as Linda, in nightgown and robe, enters the kitchen, glances around for Willy, then goes to the door of the house, looks out and sees him. Comes down to his left. He looks at her.*)

LINDA: Willy, dear? Willy?

WILLY: I was right!

LINDA: Did you have some cheese? (*He can't answer.*) It's very late, darling. Come to bed, heh?

WILLY (*looking straight up*): Gotta break your neck to see a star in this yard.

LINDA: You coming in?

WILLY: Whatever happened to that diamond watch fob? Remember? When Ben came from Africa that time? Didn't he give me a watch fob with a diamond in it?

LINDA: You pawned it, dear. Twelve, thirteen years ago. For Biff's radio correspondence course.

WILLY: Gee, that was a beautiful thing. I'll take a walk.

LINDA: But you're in your slippers.

WILLY (*starting to go around the house at the left*): I was right! I was! (*Half to Linda, as he goes, shaking his head.*) What a man! There was a man worth talking to. I was right!

LINDA (*calling after Willy*): But in your slippers, Willy!

(*Willy is almost gone when Biff, in his pajamas, comes down the stairs and enters the kitchen.*)

BIFF: What is he doing out there?

LINDA: Sh!

BIFF: God Almighty, Mom, how long has he been doing this?

LINDA: Don't, he'll hear you.

BIFF: What the hell is the matter with him?

LINDA: It'll pass by morning.

BIFF: Shouldn't we do anything?

LINDA: Oh, my dear, you should do a lot of things, but there's nothing to do, so go to sleep.

(*Happy comes down the stair and sits on the steps.*)

HAPPY: I never heard him so loud, Mom.

LINDA: Well, come around more often, you'll hear him. (*She sits down at the table and mends the lining of Willy's jacket.*)

BIFF: Why didn't you ever write me about this, Mom?

LINDA: How would I write to you? For over three months you had no address.

BIFF: I was on the move. But you know I thought of you all the time. You know that, don't you, pal?

LINDA: I know, dear, I know. But he likes to have a letter. Just to know that there's still a possibility for better things.

BIFF: He's not like this all the time, is he?

LINDA: It's when you come home he's always the worst.

BIFF: When I come home?

LINDA: When you write you're coming, he's all smiles and talks about the future, and — he's just wonderful. And then the closer you seem to come, the more shaky he gets, and then, by the time you get here, he's arguing, and he seems angry at you. I think it's just that maybe he can't bring himself to — to open up to you. Why are you so hateful to each other? Why is that?

BIFF (*evasively*): I'm not hateful, Mom.

LINDA: But you no sooner come in the door than you're fighting!

BIFF: I don't know why. I mean to change. I'm tryin', Mom, you understand?

LINDA: Are you home to stay now?

BIFF: I don't know. I want to look around, see what's goin'.

LINDA: Biff, you can't look around all your life, can you?

BIFF: I just can't take hold, Mom. I can't take hold of some kind of a life.

LINDA: Biff, a man is not a bird, to come and go with the springtime.

BIFF: Your hair . . . (*He touches her hair.*) Your hair got so gray.

LINDA: Oh, it's been gray since you were in high school. I just stopped dyeing it, that's all.

BIFF: Dye it again, will ye? I don't want my pal looking old. (*He smiles.*)

LINDA: You're such a boy! You think you can go away for a year and . . . You've got to get it into your head now that one day you'll knock on this door and there'll be strange people here —

BIFF: What are you talking about? You're not even sixty, Mom.

LINDA: But what about your father?

BIFF (*lamely*): Well, I meant him too.

HAPPY: He admires Pop.

LINDA: Biff, dear, if you don't have any feeling for him, then you can't have any feeling for me.

BIFF: Sure I can, Mom.

LINDA: No. You can't just come to see me, because I love him. (*With a threat, but only a threat, of tears.*) He's the dearest man in the world to me, and I won't have anyone making him feel unwanted and low and blue. You've got to make up your mind now, darling, there's no leeway any more. Either he's your father and you pay him that respect, or else you're not to come here. I know he's not easy to get along with — nobody knows that better than me — but . . .

WILLY (*from the left, with a laugh*): Hey, hey, Biffo!

BIFF (*starting to go out after Willy*): What the hell is the matter with him? (*Happy stops him.*)

LINDA: Don't — don't go near him!

BIFF: Stop making excuses for him! He always, always wiped the floor with you. Never had an ounce of respect for you.

HAPPY: He's always had respect for —

BIFF: What the hell do you know about it?

HAPPY (*surlily*): Just don't call him crazy!

BIFF: He's got no character — Charley wouldn't do this. Not in his own house — spewing out that vomit from his mind.

HAPPY: Charley never had to cope with what he's got to.

BIFF: People are worse off than Willy Loman. Believe me, I've seen them!

LINDA: Then make Charley your father, Biff. You can't do that, can you? I don't say he's a great man. Willy Loman never made a lot of money. His name was never in the paper. He's not the finest character that ever lived. But he's a human being, and a terrible thing is happening to him. So attention must be paid. He's not to be allowed to fall into his grave like an old dog. Attention, attention must be finally paid to such a person. You called him crazy —

BIFF: I didn't mean —

LINDA: No, a lot of people think he's lost his — balance. But you don't have to be very smart to know what his trouble is. The man is exhausted.

HAPPY: Sure!

LINDA: A small man can be just as exhausted as a great man. He works for a company thirty-six years this March, opens up unheard-of territories to their trademark, and now in his old age they take his salary away.

HAPPY (*indignantly*): I didn't know that, Mom.

LINDA: You never asked, my dear! Now that you get your spending money someplace else you don't trouble your mind with him.

HAPPY: But I gave you money last —

LINDA: Christmas time, fifty dollars! To fix the hot water it cost ninety-seven fifty! For five weeks he's been on straight commission, like a beginner, an unknown!

BIFF: Those ungrateful bastards!

LINDA: Are they any worse than his sons? When he brought them business, when he was young, they were glad to see him. But now his old friends, the old buyers that loved him so and always found some order to hand him in a pinch — they're all dead, retired. He used to be able to make six, seven calls a day in Boston. Now he takes his valises out of the car and puts them back and takes them out again and he's exhausted. Instead of walking he talks now. He drives seven hundred miles, and when he gets there no one knows him anymore, no one welcomes him. And what goes through a man's mind, driving seven hundred miles home without having earned a cent? Why shouldn't he talk to himself? Why? When he has to go to Charley and borrow fifty dollars a week and pretend to me that it's his pay? How long can that go on? How long? You see what I'm sitting here and waiting for? And you tell me he has no character? The man who never worked a day but for your benefit? When does he get the medal for that? Is this his reward — to turn around at the age of sixty-three and find his sons, who he loved better than his life, one a philandering bum —

HAPPY: Mom!

LINDA: That's all you are, my baby! (*To Biff.*) And you! What happened to the love you had for him? You were such pals! How you used to talk to him on the phone every night! How lonely he was till he could come home to you!

BIFF: All right, Mom. I'll live here in my room, and I'll get a job. I'll keep away from him, that's all.

LINDA: No, Biff. You can't stay here and fight all the time.

BIFF: He threw me out of this house, remember that.

LINDA: Why did he do that? I never knew why.

BIFF: Because I know he's a fake and he doesn't like anybody around who knows!

LINDA: Why a fake? In what way? What do you mean?

BIFF: Just don't lay it all at my feet. It's between me and him — that's all I have to say. I'll chip in from now on. He'll settle for half my pay check. He'll be all right. I'm going to bed. (*He starts for the stairs.*)

LINDA: He won't be all right.

BIFF (*turning on the stairs, furiously*): I hate this city and I'll stay here. Now what do you want?

LINDA: He's dying, Biff.

(*Happy turns quickly to her, shocked.*)

BIFF (*after a pause*): Why is he dying?

LINDA: He's been trying to kill himself.

BIFF (*with great horror*): How?

LINDA: I live from day to day.

BIFF: What're you talking about?

LINDA: Remember I wrote you that he smashed up the car again? In February?

BIFF: Well?

LINDA: The insurance inspector came. He said that they have evidence. That all these accidents in the last year — weren't — weren't — accidents.

HAPPY: How can they tell that? That's a lie.

LINDA: It seems there's a woman . . . (*She takes a breath as*)

BIFF (*sharply but contained*): ⎱ What woman?

LINDA (*simultaneously*): ⎰ . . . and this woman . . .

LINDA: What?

BIFF: Nothing. Go ahead.

LINDA: What did you say?

BIFF: Nothing. I just said what woman?

HAPPY: What about her?

LINDA: Well, it seems she was walking down the road and saw his car. She says that he wasn't driving fast at all, and that he didn't skid. She says he came to that little bridge, and then deliberately smashed into the railing, and it was only the shallowness of the water that saved him.

BIFF: Oh, no, he probably just fell asleep again.

LINDA: I don't think he fell asleep.

BIFF: Why not?

LINDA: Last month . . . (*With great difficulty.*) Oh, boys, it's so hard to say a thing like this! He's just a big stupid man to you, but I tell you there's more good in him than in many other people. (*She chokes, wipes her eyes.*) I was looking for a fuse. The lights blew out, and I went down the cellar. And behind the fuse box — it happened to fall out — was a length of rubber pipe — just short.

HAPPY: No kidding!

LINDA: There's a little attachment on the end of it. I knew right away. And sure enough, on the bottom of the water heater there's a new little nipple on the gas pipe.

HAPPY (*angrily*): That — jerk.

BIFF: Did you have it taken off?

LINDA: I'm — I'm ashamed to. How can I mention it to him? Every day I go down and take away that little rubber pipe. But, when he comes home, I put it back where it was. How can I insult him that way? I don't know what to do. I live from day to day, boys. I tell you, I know every thought in his mind. It sounds so old-fashioned and silly, but I tell you he put his whole life into you and you've turned your backs on him. (*She is bent over in the chair, weeping, her face in her hands.*) Biff, I swear to God! Biff, his life is in your hands!

HAPPY (*to Biff*): How do you like that damned fool!

BIFF (*kissing her*): All right, pal, all right. It's all settled now. I've been remiss. I know that, Mom. But now I'll stay, and I swear to you, I'll apply myself. (*Kneeling in front of her, in a fever of self-reproach.*) It's just — you see, Mom, I don't fit in business. Not that I won't try. I'll try, and I'll make good.

HAPPY: Sure you will. The trouble with you in business was you never tried to please people.

BIFF: I know, I —

HAPPY: Like when you worked for Harrison's. Bob Harrison said you were tops, and then you go and do some damn fool thing like whistling whole songs in the elevator like a comedian.

BIFF (*against Happy*): So what? I like to whistle sometimes.

HAPPY: You don't raise a guy to a responsible job who whistles in the elevator!

LINDA: Well, don't argue about it now.

HAPPY: Like when you'd go off and swim in the middle of the day instead of taking the line around.

BIFF (*his resentment rising*): Well, don't you run off? You take off sometimes, don't you? On a nice summer day?

HAPPY: Yeah, but I cover myself!

LINDA: Boys!

HAPPY: If I'm going to take a fade the boss can call any number where I'm supposed to be and they'll swear to him that I just left. I'll tell you something that I hate to say, Biff, but in the business world some of them think you're crazy.

BIFF (*angered*): Screw the business world!

HAPPY: All right, screw it! Great, but cover yourself!

LINDA: Hap, Hap!

BIFF: I don't care what they think! They've laughed at Dad for years, and you know why? Because we don't belong in this nuthouse of a city! We should be mixing cement on some open plain, or — or carpenters. A carpenter is allowed to whistle!

(*Willy walks in from the entrance of the house, at left.*)

WILLY: Even your grandfather was better than a carpenter. (*Pause. They watch him.*) You never grew up. Bernard does not whistle in the elevator, I assure you.

BIFF (*as though to laugh Willy out of it*): Yeah, but you do, Pop.

WILLY: I never in my life whistled in an elevator! And who in the business world thinks I'm crazy?

BIFF: I didn't mean it like that, Pop. Now don't make a whole thing out of it, will ye?

WILLY: Go back to the West! Be a carpenter, a cowboy, enjoy yourself!

LINDA: Willy, he was just saying —

WILLY: I heard what he said!

HAPPY (*trying to quiet Willy*): Hey, Pop, come on now . . .

WILLY (*continuing over Happy's line*): They laugh at me, heh? Go to Filene's, go to the Hub, go to Slattery's, Boston. Call out the name Willy Loman and see what happens! Big shot!

BIFF: All right, Pop.

WILLY: Big!

BIFF: All right!

WILLY: Why do you always insult me?

BIFF: I didn't say a word. (*To Linda.*) Did I say a word?

LINDA: He didn't say anything, Willy.

WILLY (*going to the doorway of the living room*): All right, good night, good night.

LINDA: Willy, dear, he just decided . . .

WILLY (*to Biff*): If you get tired hanging around tomorrow, paint the ceiling I put up in the living room.

BIFF: I'm leaving early tomorrow.

HAPPY: He's going to see Bill Oliver, Pop.

WILLY (*interestedly*): Oliver? For what?

BIFF (*with reserve, but trying, trying*): He always said he'd stake me. I'd like to go into business, so maybe I can take him up on it.

LINDA: Isn't that wonderful?

WILLY: Don't interrupt. What's wonderful about it? There's fifty men in the City of New York who'd stake him. (*To Biff.*) Sporting goods?

BIFF: I guess so. I know something about it and —

WILLY: He knows something about it! You know sporting goods better than Spalding, for God's sake! How much is he giving you?

BIFF: I don't know, I didn't even see him yet, but —

WILLY: Then what're you talkin' about?

BIFF (*getting angry*): Well, all I said was I'm gonna see him, that's all!

WILLY (*turning away*): Ah, you're counting your chickens again.

BIFF (*starting left for the stairs*): Oh, Jesus, I'm going to sleep!

WILLY (*calling after him*): Don't curse in this house!

BIFF (*turning*): Since when did you get so clean?

HAPPY (*trying to stop them*): Wait a . . .

WILLY: Don't use that language to me! I won't have it!

HAPPY (*grabbing Biff, shouts*): Wait a minute! I got an idea. I got a feasible idea. Come here, Biff, let's talk this over now, let's talk some sense here. When I was down in Florida last time, I thought of a great idea to sell sporting goods. It just came back to me. You and I, Biff — we have a line, the Loman Line. We train a couple of weeks, and put on a couple of exhibitions, see?

WILLY: That's an idea!

HAPPY: Wait! We form two basketball teams, see? Two water polo teams. We play each other. It's a million dollars' worth of publicity. Two brothers, see? The Loman Brothers. Displays in the Royal Palms — all the hotels. And banners over the ring and the basketball court: "Loman Brothers." Baby, we could sell sporting goods!

WILLY: That is a one-million-dollar idea!

LINDA: Marvelous!

BIFF: I'm in great shape as far as that's concerned.

HAPPY: And the beauty of it is, Biff, it wouldn't be like a business. We'd be out playin' ball again . . .

BIFF (*enthused*): Yeah, that's . . .

WILLY: Million-dollar . . .

HAPPY: And you wouldn't get fed up with it, Biff. It'd be the family again. There'd be the old honor, and comradeship, and if you wanted to go off for a swim or somethin' — well, you'd do it! Without some smart cooky gettin' up ahead of you!

WILLY: Lick the world! You guys together could absolutely lick the civilized world.

BIFF: I'll see Oliver tomorrow. Hap, if we could work that out . . .

LINDA: Maybe things are beginning to —

WILLY (*wildly enthused, to Linda*): Stop interrupting! (*To Biff.*) But don't wear sport jacket and slacks when you see Oliver.

BIFF: No, I'll —

WILLY: A business suit, and talk as little as possible, and don't crack any jokes.

BIFF: He did like me. Always liked me.

LINDA: He loved you!

WILLY (*to Linda*): Will you stop! (*To Biff.*) Walk in very serious. You are not applying for a boy's job. Money is to pass. Be quiet, fine, and serious. Everybody likes a kidder, but nobody lends him money.

HAPPY: I'll try to get some myself, Biff. I'm sure I can.

WILLY: I see great things for you kids, I think your troubles are over. But remember, start big and you'll end big. Ask for fifteen. How much you gonna ask for?

BIFF: Gee, I don't know —

WILLY: And don't say "Gee." "Gee" is a boy's word. A man walking in for fifteen thousand dollars does not say "Gee!"

BIFF: Ten, I think, would be top though.

WILLY: Don't be so modest. You always started too low. Walk in with a big laugh. Don't look worried. Start off with a couple of your good stories to lighten things up. It's not what you say, it's how you say it — because personality always wins the day.

LINDA: Oliver always thought the highest of him —

WILLY: Will you let me talk?

BIFF: Don't yell at her, Pop, will ye?

WILLY (*angrily*): I was talking, wasn't I?

BIFF: I don't like you yelling at her all the time, and I'm tellin' you, that's all.

WILLY: What're you, takin' over this house?

LINDA: Willy —

WILLY (*turning to her*): Don't take his side all the time, goddammit!

BIFF (*furiously*): Stop yelling at her!

WILLY (*suddenly pulling on his cheek, beaten down, guilt ridden*): Give my best to Bill Oliver — he may remember me. (*He exits through the living room doorway.*)

LINDA (*her voice subdued*): What'd you have to start that for? (*Biff turns away.*) You see how sweet he was as soon as you talked hopefully? (*She goes over to Biff.*) Come up and say good night to him. Don't let him go to bed that way.

HAPPY: Come on, Biff, let's buck him up.

LINDA: Please, dear. Just say good night. It takes so little to make him happy. Come. (*She goes through the living room doorway, calling upstairs from within the living room.*) Your pajamas are hanging in the bathroom, Willy!

HAPPY (*looking toward where Linda went out*): What a woman! They broke the mold when they made her. You know that, Biff?

BIFF: He's off salary. My God, working on commission!

HAPPY: Well, let's face it: he's no hot-shot selling man. Except that sometimes, you have to admit, he's a sweet personality.

BIFF (*deciding*): Lend me ten bucks, will ye? I want to buy some new ties.

HAPPY: I'll take you to a place I know. Beautiful stuff. Wear one of my striped shirts tomorrow.

BIFF: She got gray. Mom got awful old. Gee, I'm gonna go in to Oliver tomorrow and knock him for a —

HAPPY: Come on up. Tell that to Dad. Let's give him a whirl. Come on.

BIFF (*steamed up*): You know, with ten thousand bucks, boy!

HAPPY (*as they go into the living room*): That's the talk, Biff, that's the first time I've heard the old confidence out of you! (*From within the living room, fading off.*) You're gonna live with me, kid, and any babe you want just say the word . . . (*The last lines are hardly heard. They are mounting the stairs to their parents' bedroom.*)

LINDA (*entering her bedroom and addressing Willy, who is in the bathroom. She is straightening the bed for him.*): Can you do anything about the shower? It drips.

WILLY (*from the bathroom*): All of a sudden everything falls to pieces. Goddam plumbing, oughta be sued, those people. I hardly finished putting it in and the thing . . . (*His words rumble off.*)

LINDA: I'm just wondering if Oliver will remember him. You think he might?

WILLY (*coming out of the bathroom in his pajamas*): Remember him? What's the matter with you, you crazy? If he'd've stayed with Oliver he'd be on top by now! Wait'll Oliver gets a look at him. You don't know the average caliber any more. The average young man today — (*he is getting into bed*) — is got a caliber of zero. Greatest thing in the world for him was to bum around.

(*Biff and Happy enter the bedroom. Slight pause.*)

WILLY (*stops short, looking at Biff*): Glad to hear it, boy.

HAPPY: He wanted to say good night to you, sport.

WILLY (*to Biff*): Yeah. Knock him dead, boy. What'd you want to tell me?

BIFF: Just take it easy, Pop. Good night. (*He turns to go.*)

WILLY (*unable to resist*): And if anything falls off the desk while you're talking to him — like a package or something — don't you pick it up. They have office boys for that.

LINDA: I'll make a big breakfast —

WILLY: Will you let me finish? (*To Biff.*) Tell him you were in the business in the West. Not farm work.

BIFF: All right, Dad.

LINDA: I think everything —

WILLY (*going right through her speech*): And don't undersell yourself. No less than fifteen thousand dollars.

BIFF (*unable to bear him*): Okay. Good night, Mom. (*He starts moving.*)

WILLY: Because you got a greatness in you, Biff, remember that. You got all kinds of greatness . . . (*He lies back, exhausted. Biff walks out.*)

LINDA (*calling after Biff*): Sleep well, darling!

HAPPY: I'm gonna get married, Mom. I wanted to tell you.

LINDA: Go to sleep, dear.

HAPPY (*going*): I just wanted to tell you.

WILLY: Keep up the good work. (*Happy exits.*) God . . . remember that Ebbets Field game? The championship of the city?

LINDA: Just rest. Should I sing to you?

WILLY: Yeah. Sing to me. (*Linda hums a soft lullaby.*) When that team came out — he was the tallest, remember?

LINDA: Oh, yes. And in gold.

(*Biff enters the darkened kitchen, takes a cigarette, and leaves the house. He comes downstage into a golden pool of light. He smokes, staring at the night.*)

WILLY: Like a young god. Hercules — something like that. And the sun, the sun all around him. Remember how he waved to me? Right up from the field, with the representatives of three colleges standing by? And the buyers I brought, and the cheers when he came out — Loman, Loman, Loman! God Almighty, he'll be great yet. A star like that, magnificent, can never really fade away!

(*The light on Willy is fading. The gas heater begins to glow through the kitchen wall, near the stairs, a blue flame beneath red coils.*)

LINDA (*timidly*): Willy dear, what has he got against you?

WILLY: I'm so tired. Don't talk anymore.

(*Biff slowly returns to the kitchen. He stops, stares toward the heater.*)

LINDA: Will you ask Howard to let you work in New York?

WILLY: First thing in the morning. Everything'll be all right.

(*Biff reaches behind the heater and draws out a length of rubber tubing. He is horrified and turns his head toward Willy's room, still dimly lit, from which the strains of Linda's desperate but monotonous humming rise.*)

WILLY (*staring through the window into the moonlight*): Gee, look at the moon moving between the buildings!

(*Biff wraps the tubing around his hand and quickly goes up the stairs.*)

ACT II

(*Music is heard, gay and bright. The curtain rises as the music fades away. Willy, in shirt sleeves is sitting at the kitchen table, sipping coffee, his hat in his lap. Linda is piling his cup when she can.*)

WILLY: Wonderful coffee. Meal in itself.

LINDA: Can I make you some eggs?

WILLY: No. Take a breath.

LINDA: You look so rested, dear.

WILLY: I slept like a dead one. First time in months. Imagine, sleeping till ten on a Tuesday morning. Boys left nice and early, heh?

LINDA: They were out of here by eight o'clock.

WILLY: Good work!

LINDA: It was so thrilling to see them leaving together. I can't get over the shaving lotion in this house!

WILLY (*smiling*): Mmm —

LINDA: Biff was very changed this morning. His whole attitude seemed to be hopeful. He couldn't wait to get downtown to see Oliver.

WILLY: He's heading for a change. There's no question, there simply are certain men that take longer to get — solidified. How did he dress?

LINDA: His blue suit. He's so handsome in that suit. He could be a — anything in that suit!

(*Willy gets up from the table. Linda holds his jacket for him.*)

WILLY: There's no question, no question at all. Gee, on the way home tonight I'd like to buy some seeds.

LINDA (*laughing*): That'd be wonderful. But not enough sun gets back there. Nothing'll grow any more.

WILLY: You wait, kid, before it's all over we're gonna get a little place out in the country, and I'll raise some vegetables, a couple of chickens . . .

LINDA: You'll do it yet, dear.

(*Willy walks out of his jacket. Linda follows him.*)

WILLY: And they'll get married, and come for a weekend. I'd build a little guest house. 'Cause I got so many fine tools, all I'd need would be a little lumber and some peace of mind.

LINDA (*joyfully*): I sewed the lining . . .

WILLY: I could build two guest houses, so they'd both come. Did he decide how much he's going to ask Oliver for?

LINDA (*getting him into the jacket*): He didn't mention it, but I imagine ten or fifteen thousand. You going to talk to Howard today?

WILLY: Yeah. I'll put it to him straight and simple. He'll just have to take me off the road.

LINDA: And Willy, don't forget to ask for a little advance, because we've got the insurance premium. It's the grace period now.

WILLY: That's a hundred . . . ?

LINDA: A hundred and eight, sixty-eight. Because we're a little short again.

WILLY: Why are we short?

LINDA: Well, you had the motor job on the car . . .

WILLY: That goddam Studebaker!

LINDA: And you got one more payment on the refrigerator . . .

WILLY: But it just broke again!

LINDA: Well, it's old, dear.

WILLY: I told you we should've bought a well-advertised machine. Charley bought a General Electric and it's twenty years old and it's still good, that son-of-a-bitch.

LINDA: But, Willy —

WILLY: Whoever heard of a Hastings refrigerator? Once in my life I would like to own something outright before it's broken! I'm always in a race with the junkyard! I just finished paying for the car and it's on its last legs. The refrigerator consumes belts like a goddamn maniac. They time those things. They time them so when you finally paid for them, they're used up.

LINDA (*buttoning up his jacket as he unbuttons it*): All told, about two hundred dollars would carry us, dear. But that includes the last payment on the mortgage. After this payment, Willy, the house belongs to us.

WILLY: It's twenty-five years!

LINDA: Biff was nine years old when we bought it.

WILLY: Well, that's a great thing. To weather a twenty-five year mortgage is —

LINDA: It's an accomplishment.

WILLY: All the cement, the lumber, the reconstruction I put in this house! There ain't a crack to be found in it anymore.

LINDA: Well, it served its purpose.

WILLY: What purpose? Some stranger'll come along, move in, and that's that. If only Biff would take this house, and raise a family . . . (*He starts to go.*) Good-by, I'm late.

LINDA (*suddenly remembering*): Oh, I forgot! You're supposed to meet them for dinner.

WILLY: Me?

LINDA: At Frank's Chop House on Forty-eighth near Sixth Avenue.

WILLY: Is that so! How about you?

LINDA: No, just the three of you. They're gonna blow you to a big meal!

WILLY: Don't say! Who thought of that?

LINDA: Biff came to me this morning, Willy, and he said, "Tell Dad, we want to blow him to a big meal." Be there six o'clock. You and your two boys are going to have dinner.

WILLY: Gee whiz! That's really somethin'. I'm gonna knock Howard for a loop, kid. I'll get an advance, and I'll come home with a New York job. Goddammit, now I'm gonna do it!

LINDA: Oh, that's the spirit, Willy!

WILLY: I will never get behind a wheel the rest of my life!

LINDA: It's changing, Willy, I can feel it changing!

WILLY: Beyond a question. G'by, I'm late. (*He starts to go again.*)

LINDA (*calling after him as she runs to the kitchen table for a handkerchief*): You got your glasses?

WILLY (*feels for them, then comes back in*): Yeah, yeah, got my glasses.

LINDA (*giving him the handkerchief*): And a handkerchief.

WILLY: Yeah, handkerchief.

LINDA: And your saccharine?

WILLY: Yeah, my saccharine.

LINDA: Be careful on the subway stairs.

(*She kisses him, and a silk stocking is seen hanging from her hand. Willy notices it.*)

WILLY: Will you stop mending stockings? At least while I'm in the house. It gets me nervous. I can't tell you. Please.

(*Linda hides the stocking in her hand as she follows Willy across the forestage in front of the house.*)

LINDA: Remember, Frank's Chop House.

WILLY (*passing the apron*): Maybe beets would grow out there.

LINDA (*laughing*): But you tried so many times.

WILLY: Yeah. Well, don't work hard today. (*He disappears around the right corner of the house.*)

LINDA: Be careful!

(*As Willy vanishes, Linda waves to him. Suddenly the phone rings. She runs across the stage and into the kitchen and lifts it.*)

LINDA: Hello? Oh, Biff! I'm so glad you called, I just . . . Yes, sure, I just told him. Yes, he'll be there for dinner at six o'clock, I didn't forget. Listen, I was just dying to tell you. You know that little rubber pipe I told you about? That he connected to the gas heater? I finally decided to go down the cellar this morning and take it away and destroy it. But it's gone! Imagine? He took it away himself, it isn't there! (*She listens.*) When? Oh, then you took it. Oh — nothing, it's just that I'd hoped he'd taken it away himself. Oh, I'm not worried, darling, because this morning he left in such high spirits, it was like the old days! I'm not afraid any more. Did Mr. Oliver see you? . . . Well, you wait there then. And make a nice impression on him, darling. Just don't perspire too much before you see him. And have a nice time with Dad. He may have big news too! . . . That's right, a New York job. And be sweet to him tonight, dear. Be loving to him. Because he's only a little boat looking for a harbor. (*She is trembling with sorrow and joy.*) Oh, that's wonderful, Biff, you'll save his life. Thanks, darling. Just put your arm around him when he comes into the restaurant. Give him a smile. That's the boy . . . Good-by, dear. . . . You got your comb? . . . That's fine. Good-by, Biff dear.

(*In the middle of her speech, Howard Wagner, thirty-six, wheels in a small typewriter table on which is a wire-recording machine and proceeds to plug it in. This is on the left forestage. Light slowly fades on Linda as it rises on Howard. Howard is intent on threading the machine and only glances over his shoulder as Willy appears.*)

WILLY: Pst! Pst!

HOWARD: Hello, Willy, come in.

WILLY: Like to have a little talk with you, Howard.

HOWARD: Sorry to keep you waiting. I'll be with you in a minute.

WILLY: What's that, Howard?

HOWARD: Didn't you ever see one of these? Wire recorder.

WILLY: Oh. Can we talk a minute?

HOWARD: Records things. Just got delivery yesterday. Been driving me crazy, the most terrific machine I ever saw in my life. I was up all night with it.

WILLY: What do you do with it?

HOWARD: I bought it for dictation, but you can do anything with it. Listen to this. I had it home last night. Listen to what I picked up. The first one is my daughter. Get this. (*He flicks the switch and "Roll out the Barrel" is heard being whistled.*) Listen to that kid whistle.

WILLY: That is lifelike, isn't it?

HOWARD: Seven years old. Get that tone.

WILLY: Ts, ts. Like to ask a little favor if you . . .

(*The whistling breaks off, and the voice of Howard's daughter is heard.*)

HIS DAUGHTER: Now you, Daddy.

HOWARD: She's crazy for me! (*Again the same song is whistled.*) That's me! Ha! (*He winks.*)

WILLY: You're very good!

(*The whistling breaks off again. The machine runs silent for a moment.*)

HOWARD: Sh! Get this now, this is my son.

HIS SON: "The capital of Alabama is Montgomery; the capital of Arizona is Phoenix; the capital of Arkansas is Little Rock; the capital of California is Sacramento . . ." (*and on, and on.*)

HOWARD (*holding up five fingers*): Five years old, Willy!

WILLY: He'll make an announcer some day!

HIS SON (*continuing*): "The capital . . ."

HOWARD: Get that — alphabetical order! (*The machine breaks off suddenly.*) Wait a minute. The maid kicked the plug out.

WILLY: It certainly is a —

HOWARD: Sh, for God's sake!

HIS SON: "It's nine o'clock, Bulova watch time. So I have to go to sleep."

WILLY: That really is —

HOWARD: Wait a minute! The next is my wife.

(*They wait.*)

HOWARD'S VOICE: "Go on, say something." (*Pause.*) "Well, you gonna talk?"

HIS WIFE: "I can't think of anything."

HOWARD'S VOICE: "Well, talk — it's turning."

HIS WIFE (*shyly, beaten*): "Hello." (*Silence.*) "Oh, Howard, I can't talk into this . . ."

HOWARD (*snapping the machine off*): That was my wife.

WILLY: That is a wonderful machine. Can we —

HOWARD: I tell you, Willy, I'm gonna take my camera, and my bandsaw, and all my hobbies, and out they

go. This is the most fascinating relaxation I ever found.

WILLY: I think I'll get one myself.

HOWARD: Sure, they're only a hundred and a half. You can't do without it. Supposing you wanna hear Jack Benny, see? But you can't be at home at that hour. So you tell the maid to turn the radio on when Jack Benny comes on, and this automatically goes on with the radio . . .

WILLY: And when you come home you . . .

HOWARD: You can come home twelve o'clock, one o'clock, any time you like, and you get yourself a Coke and sit yourself down, throw the switch, and there's Jack Benny's program in the middle of the night!

WILLY: I'm definitely going to get one. Because lots of times I'm on the road, and I think to myself, what I must be missing on the radio!

HOWARD: Don't you have a radio in the car?

WILLY: Well, yeah, but who ever thinks of turning it on?

HOWARD: Say, aren't you supposed to be in Boston?

WILLY: That's what I want to talk to you about, Howard. You got a minute? (*He draws a chair in from the wing.*)

HOWARD: What happened? What're you doing here?

WILLY: Well . . .

HOWARD: You didn't crack up again, did you?

WILLY: Oh, no. No . . .

HOWARD: Geez, you had me worried there for a minute. What's the trouble?

WILLY: Well, tell you the truth, Howard. I've come to the decision that I'd rather not travel anymore.

HOWARD: Not travel! Well, what'll you do?

WILLY: Remember, Christmas time, when you had the party here? You said you'd try to think of some spot for me here in town.

HOWARD: With us?

WILLY: Well, sure.

HOWARD: Oh, yeah, yeah. I remember. Well, I couldn't think of anything for you, Willy.

WILLY: I tell ya, Howard. The kids are all grown up, y'know. I don't need much anymore. If I could take home — well, sixty-five dollars a week, I could swing it.

HOWARD: Yeah, but Willy, see I —

WILLY: I tell ya why, Howard. Speaking frankly and between the two of us, y'know — I'm just a little tired.

HOWARD: Oh, I could understand that, Willy. But you're a road man, Willy, and we do a road business. We've only got a half-dozen salesmen on the floor here.

WILLY: God knows, Howard, I never asked a favor of any man. But I was with the firm when your father used to carry you in here in his arms.

HOWARD: I know that, Willy, but —

WILLY: Your father came to me the day you were born and asked me what I thought of the name Howard, may he rest in peace.

HOWARD: I appreciate that, Willy, but there just is no

spot here for you. If I had a spot I'd slam you right in, but I just don't have a single solitary spot.

(*He looks for his lighter. Willy has picked it up and gives it to him. Pause.*)

WILLY (*with increasing anger*): Howard, all I need to set my table is fifty dollars a week.

HOWARD: But where am I going to put you, kid?

WILLY: Look, it isn't a question of whether I can sell merchandise, is it?

HOWARD: No, but it's business, kid, and everybody's gotta pull his own weight.

WILLY (*desperately*): Just let me tell you a story, Howard —

HOWARD: 'Cause you gotta admit, business is business.

WILLY (*angrily*): Business is definitely business, but just listen for a minute. You don't understand this. When I was a boy — eighteen, nineteen — I was already on the road. And there was a question in my mind as to whether selling had a future for me. Because in those days I had a yearning to go to Alaska. See, there were three gold strikes in one month in Alaska, and I felt like going out. Just for the ride, you might say.

HOWARD (*barely interested*): Don't say.

WILLY: Oh, yeah, my father lived many years in Alaska. He was an adventurous man. We've got quite a little streak of self-reliance in our family. I thought I'd go out with my older brother and try to locate him, and maybe settle in the North with the old man. And I was almost decided to go, when I met a salesman in the Parker House. His name was Dave Singleman. And he was eighty-four years old, and he'd drummed merchandise in thirty-one states. And old Dave, he'd go up to his room, y'understand, put on his green velvet slippers — I'll never forget — and pick up his phone and call the buyers, and without ever leaving his room, at the age of eighty-four, he made his living. And when I saw that, I realized that selling was the greatest career a man could want. 'Cause what could be more satisfying than to be able to go, at the age of eighty-four, into twenty or thirty different cities, and pick up a phone, and be remembered and loved and helped by so many different people? Do you know? When he died — and by the way he died the death of a salesman, in his green velvet slippers in the smoker of the New York, New Haven and Hartford, going into Boston — when he died, hundreds of salesmen and buyers were at his funeral. Things were sad on a lotta trains for months after that. (*He stands up. Howard has not looked at him.*) In those days there was personality in it, Howard. There was respect and comradeship, and gratitude in it. Today, it's all cut and dried, and there's no chance for bringing friendship to bear — or personality. You see what I mean? They don't know me any more.

HOWARD (*moving away, to the right*): That's just the thing, Willy.

WILLY: If I had forty dollars a week — that's all I'd need. Forty dollars, Howard.

HOWARD: Kid, I can't take blood from a stone, I —

WILLY (*desperation is on him now*): Howard, the year Al Smith was nominated, your father came to me and —

HOWARD (*starting to go off*): I've got to see some people, kid.

WILLY (*stopping him*): I'm talking about your father! There were promises made across this desk! You mustn't tell me you've got people to see — I put thirty-four years into this firm, Howard, and now I can't pay my insurance! You can't eat the orange and throw the peel away — a man is not a piece of fruit! (*After a pause.*) Now pay attention. Your father — in 1928 I had a big year. I averaged a hundred and seventy dollars a week in commissions.

HOWARD (*impatiently*): Now, Willy, you never averaged —

WILLY (*banging his hand on the desk*): I averaged a hundred and seventy dollars a week in the year of 1928! And your father came to me — or rather I was in the office here — it was right over this desk — and he put his hand on my shoulder —

HOWARD (*getting up*): You'll have to excuse me, Willy, I gotta see some people. Pull yourself together. (*Going out.*) I'll be back in a little while.

(*On Howard's exit, the light on his chair grows very bright and strange.*)

WILLY: Pull myself together! What the hell did I say to him? My God, I was yelling at him! How could I? (*Willy breaks off, staring at the light, which occupies the chair, animating it. He approaches this chair, standing across the desk from it.*) Frank, Frank, don't you remember what you told me that time? How you put your hand on my shoulder, and Frank . . . (*He leans on the desk and as he speaks the dead man's name he accidentally switches on the recorder, and instantly*)

HOWARD'S SON: ". . . of New York is Albany. The capital of Ohio is Cincinnati, the capital of Rhode Island is . . ." (*The recitation continues.*)

WILLY (*leaping away with fright, shouting*): Ha! Howard! Howard! Howard!

HOWARD (*rushing in*): What happened?

WILLY (*pointing at the machine, which continues nasally, childishly, with the capital cities*): Shut it off! Shut it off!

HOWARD (*pulling the plug out*): Look, Willy . . .

WILLY (*pressing his hands to his eyes*): I gotta get myself some coffee. I'll get some coffee . . .

(*Willy starts to walk out. Howard stops him.*)

HOWARD (*rolling up the cord*): Willy, look . . .

WILLY: I'll go to Boston.

HOWARD: Willy, you can't go to Boston for us.

WILLY: Why can't I go?

HOWARD: I don't want you to represent us. I've been meaning to tell you for a long time now.

WILLY: Howard, are you firing me?

HOWARD: I think you need a good long rest, Willy.

WILLY: Howard —

HOWARD: And when you feel better, come back, and we'll see if we can work something out.

WILLY: But I gotta earn money, Howard. I'm in no position to —

HOWARD: Where are your sons? Why don't your sons give you a hand?

WILLY: They're working on a very big deal.

HOWARD: This is no time for false pride, Willy. You go to your sons and you tell them that you're tired. You've got two great boys, haven't you?

WILLY: Oh, no question, no question, but in the meantime . . .

HOWARD: Then that's that, heh?

WILLY: All right, I'll go to Boston tomorrow.

HOWARD: No, no.

WILLY: I can't throw myself on my sons. I'm not a cripple!

HOWARD: Look, kid, I'm busy this morning.

WILLY (*grasping Howard's arm*): Howard, you've got to let me go to Boston!

HOWARD (*hard, keeping himself under control*): I've got a line of people to see this morning. Sit down, take five minutes, and pull yourself together, and then go home, will ya? I need the office, Willy. (*He starts to go, turns, remembering the recorder, starts to push off the table holding the recorder.*) Oh, yeah. Whenever you can this week, stop by and drop off the samples. You'll feel better, Willy, and then come back and we'll talk. Pull yourself together, kid, there's people outside.

(*Howard exits, pushing the table off left. Willy stares into space, exhausted. Now the music is heard — Ben's music — first distantly, then closer, closer. As Willy speaks, Ben enters from the right. He carries valise and umbrella.*)

WILLY: Oh, Ben, how did you do it? What is the answer? Did you wind up the Alaska deal already?

BEN: Doesn't take much time if you know what you're doing. Just a short business trip. Boarding ship in an hour. Wanted to say good-by.

WILLY: Ben, I've got to talk to you.

BEN (*glancing at his watch*): Haven't the time, William.

WILLY (*crossing the apron to Ben*): Ben, nothing's working out. I don't know what to do.

BEN: Now, look here, William. I've bought timberland in Alaska and I need a man to look after things for me.

WILLY: God, timberland! Me and my boys in those grand outdoors!

BEN: You've a new continent at your doorstep, William. Get out of these cities, they're full of talk and time payments and courts of law. Screw on your fists and you can fight for a fortune up there.

WILLY: Yes, yes! Linda, Linda!

(*Linda enters as of old, with the wash.*)

LINDA: Oh, you're back?

BEN: I haven't much time.

WILLY: No, wait! Linda, he's got a proposition for me in Alaska.

LINDA: But you've got — (*To Ben.*) He's got a beautiful job here.

WILLY: But in Alaska, kid, I could —

LINDA: You're doing well enough, Willy!

BEN (*to Linda*): Enough for what, my dear?

LINDA (*frightened of Ben and angry at him*): Don't say those things to him! Enough to be happy right here, right now. (*To Willy, while Ben laughs.*) Why must everybody conquer the world? You're well liked, and the boys love you, and someday — (*To Ben*) — why, old man Wagner told him just the other day that if he keeps it up he'll be a member of the firm, didn't he, Willy?

WILLY: Sure, sure. I am building something with this firm, Ben, and if a man is building something he must be on the right track, mustn't he?

BEN: What are you building? Lay your hand on it. Where is it?

WILLY (*hesitantly*): That's true, Linda, there's nothing.

LINDA: Why? (*To Ben.*) There's a man eighty-four years old —

WILLY: That's right, Ben, that's right. When I look at that man I say, what is there to worry about?

BEN: Bah!

WILLY: It's true, Ben. All he has to do is go into any city, pick up the phone, and he's making his living and you know why?

BEN (*picking up his valise*): I've got to go.

WILLY (*holding Ben back*): Look at this boy!

(*Biff, in his high school sweater, enters carrying suitcase. Happy carries Biff's shoulder guards, gold helmet, and football pants.*)

WILLY: Without a penny to his name, three great universities are begging for him, and from there the sky's the limit, because it's not what you do, Ben. It's who you know and the smile on your face! It's contacts, Ben, contacts! The whole wealth of Alaska passes over the lunch table at the Commodore Hotel, and that's the wonder, the wonder of this country, that a man can end with diamonds here on the basis of being liked! (*He turns to Biff.*) And that's why when you get out on that field today it's important. Because thousands of people will be rooting for you and loving you. (*To Ben, who has again begun to leave.*) And Ben! when he walks into a business office his name will sound out like a bell and all the doors will open to him! I've seen it, Ben, I've seen it a thousand times! You can't feel it with your hand like timber, but it's there!

BEN: Good-by, William.

WILLY: Ben, am I right? Don't you think I'm right? I value your advice.

BEN: There's a new continent at your doorstep, William. You could walk out rich. Rich! (*He is gone.*)

WILLY: We'll do it here, Ben! You hear me? We're gonna do it here!

(*Young Bernard rushes in. The gay music of the Boys is heard.*)

BERNARD: Oh, gee, I was afraid you left already!
WILLY: Why? What time is it?
BERNARD: It's half-past one!
WILLY: Well, come on, everybody! Ebbets Field next stop! Where's the pennants? (*He rushes through the wall-line of the kitchen and out into the living room.*)
LINDA (*to Biff*): Did you pack fresh underwear?
BIFF (*who has been limbering up*): I want to go!
BERNARD: Biff, I'm carrying your helmet, ain't I?
HAPPY: No, I'm carrying the helmet.
BERNARD: Oh, Biff, you promised me.
HAPPY: I'm carrying the helmet.
BERNARD: How am I going to get in the locker room?
LINDA: Let him carry the shoulder guards. (*She puts her coat and hat on in the kitchen.*)
BERNARD: Can I, Biff? 'Cause I told everybody I'm going to be in the locker room.
HAPPY: In Ebbets Field it's the clubhouse.
BERNARD: I meant the clubhouse. Biff!
HAPPY: Biff!
BIFF (*grandly, after a slight pause*): Let him carry the shoulder guards.
HAPPY (*as he gives Bernard the shoulder guards*): Stay close to us now.

(*Willy rushes in with the pennants.*)

WILLY (*handing them out*): Everybody wave when Biff comes out on the field. (*Happy and Bernard run off.*) You set now, boy?

(*The music has died away.*)

BIFF: Ready to go, Pop. Every muscle is ready.
WILLY (*at the edge of the apron*): You realize what this means?
BIFF: That's right, Pop.
WILLY (*feeling Biff's muscles*): You're comin' home this afternoon captain of the All-Scholastic Championship Team of the City of New York.
BIFF: I got it, Pop. And remember, pal, when I take off my helmet, that touchdown is for you.
WILLY: Let's go! (*He is starting out, with his arm around Biff, when Charley enters, as of old, in knickers.*) I got no room for you, Charley.
CHARLEY: Room? For what?
WILLY: In the car.
CHARLEY: You goin' for a ride? I wanted to shoot some casino.
WILLY (*furiously*): Casino! (*Incredulously.*) Don't you realize what today is?
LINDA: Oh, he knows, Willy. He's just kidding you.
WILLY: That's nothing to kid about!
CHARLEY: No, Linda, what's goin' on?
LINDA: He's playing in Ebbets Field.
CHARLEY: Baseball in this weather?
WILLY: Don't talk to him. Come on, come on! (*He is pushing them out.*)

CHARLEY: Wait a minute, didn't you hear the news?
WILLY: What?
CHARLEY: Don't you listen to the radio? Ebbets Field just blew up.
WILLY: You go to hell! (*Charley laughs. Pushing them out.*) Come on, come on! We're late.
CHARLEY (*as they go*): Knock a homer, Biff, knock a homer!
WILLY (*the last to leave, turning to Charley*): I don't think that was funny, Charley. This is the greatest day of his life.
CHARLEY: Willy, when are you going to grow up?
WILLY: Yeah, heh? When this game is over, Charley, you'll be laughing out of the other side of your face. They'll be calling him another Red Grange. Twenty-five thousand a year.
CHARLEY (*kidding*): Is that so?
WILLY: Yeah, that's so.
CHARLEY: Well, then, I'm sorry, Willy. But tell me something.
WILLY: What?
CHARLEY: Who is Red Grange?
WILLY: Put up your hands. Goddam you, put up your hands!

(*Charley, chuckling, shakes his head and walks away, around the left corner of the stage. Willy follows him. The music rises to a mocking frenzy.*)

WILLY: Who the hell do you think you are, better than everybody else? You don't know everything, you big, ignorant, stupid . . . Put up your hands!

(*Light rises, on the right side of the forestage, on a small table in the reception room of Charley's office. Traffic sounds are heard. Bernard, now mature, sits whistling to himself. A pair of tennis rackets and an overnight bag are on the floor beside him.*)

WILLY (*offstage*): What are you walking away for? Don't walk away! If you're going to say something say it to my face! I know you laugh at me behind my back. You'll laugh out of the other side of your goddam face after this game. Touchdown! Touchdown! Eighty thousand people! Touchdown! Right between the goal posts.

(*Bernard is a quiet, earnest, but self-assured young man. Willy's voice is coming from right upstage now. Bernard lowers his feet off the table and listens. Jenny, his father's secretary, enters.*)

JENNY (*distressed*): Say, Bernard, will you go out in the hall?
BERNARD: What is that noise? Who is it?
JENNY: Mr. Loman. He just got off the elevator.
BERNARD (*getting up*): Who's he arguing with?
JENNY: Nobody. There's nobody with him. I can't deal with him anymore, and your father gets all upset everytime he comes. I've got a lot of typing to do, and your father's waiting to sign it. Will you see him?
WILLY (*entering*): Touchdown! Touch — (*He sees

Jenny.) Jenny, Jenny, good to see you. How're ya? Workin'? Or still honest?

JENNY: Fine. How've you been feeling?

WILLY: Not much any more, Jenny. Ha, ha! (*He is surprised to see the rackets.*)

BERNARD: Hello, Uncle Willy.

WILLY (*almost shocked*): Bernard! Well, look who's here! (*He comes quickly, guiltily, to Bernard and warmly shakes his hand.*)

BERNARD: How are you? Good to see you.

WILLY: What are you doing here?

BERNARD: Oh, just stopped by to see Pop. Get off my feet till my train leaves. I'm going to Washington in a few minutes.

WILLY: Is he in?

BERNARD: Yes, he's in his office with the accountant. Sit down.

WILLY (*sitting down*): What're you going to do in Washington?

BERNARD: Oh, just a case I've got there, Willy.

WILLY: That so? (*Indicating the rackets.*) You going to play tennis there?

BERNARD: I'm staying with a friend who's got a court.

WILLY: Don't say. His own tennis court. Must be fine people, I bet.

BERNARD: They are, very nice. Dad tells me Biff's in town.

WILLY (*with a big smile*): Yeah, Biff's in. Working on a very big deal, Bernard.

BERNARD: What's Biff doing?

WILLY: Well, he's been doing very big things in the West. But he decided to establish himself here. Very big. We're having dinner. Did I hear your wife had a boy?

BERNARD: That's right. Our second.

WILLY: Two boys! What do you know!

BERNARD: What kind of a deal has Biff got?

WILLY: Well, Bill Oliver — very big sporting-goods man — he wants Biff very badly. Called him in from the West. Long distance, carte blanche, special deliveries. Your friends have their own private tennis court?

BERNARD: You still with the old firm, Willy?

WILLY (*after a pause*): I'm — I'm overjoyed to see how you made the grade, Bernard, overjoyed. It's an encouraging thing to see a young man really — really — Looks very good for Biff — very — (*He breaks off, then.*) Bernard — (*He is so full of emotion, he breaks off again.*)

BERNARD: What is it, Willy?

WILLY (*small and alone*): What — what's the secret?

BERNARD: What secret?

WILLY: How — how did you? Why didn't he ever catch on?

BERNARD: I wouldn't know that, Willy.

WILLY (*confidentially, desperately*): You were his friend, his boyhood friend. There's something I don't understand about it. His life ended after that Ebbets Field game. From the age of seventeen nothing good ever happened to him.

BERNARD: He never trained himself for anything.

WILLY: But he did, he did. After high school he took so many correspondence courses. Radio mechanics; television; God knows what, and never made the slightest mark.

BERNARD (*taking off his glasses*): Willy, do you want to talk candidly?

WILLY (*rising, faces Bernard*): I regard you as a very brilliant man, Bernard. I value your advice.

BERNARD: Oh, the hell with the advice, Willy. I couldn't advise you. There's just one thing I've always wanted to ask you. When he was supposed to graduate, and the math teacher flunked him —

WILLY: Oh, that son-of-a-bitch ruined his life.

BERNARD: Yeah, but, Willy, all he had to do was go to summer school and make up that subject.

WILLY: That's right, that's right.

BERNARD: Did you tell him not to go to summer school?

WILLY: Me? I begged him to go. I ordered him to go!

BERNARD: Then why wouldn't he go?

WILLY: Why? Why! Bernard, that question has been trailing me like a ghost for the last fifteen years. He flunked the subject, and laid down and died like a hammer hit him!

BERNARD: Take it easy, kid.

WILLY: Let me talk to you — I got nobody to talk to. Bernard, Bernard, was it my fault? Y'see? It keeps going around in my mind, maybe I did something to him. I got nothing to give him.

BERNARD: Don't take it so hard.

WILLY: Why did he lay down? What is the story there? You were his friend!

BERNARD: Willy, I remember, it was June, and our grades came out. And he'd flunked math.

WILLY: That son-of-a-bitch!

BERNARD: No, it wasn't right then. Biff just got very angry, I remember, and he was ready to enroll in summer school.

WILLY (*surprised*): He was?

BERNARD: He wasn't beaten by it at all. But then, Willy, he disappeared from the block for almost a month. And I got the idea that he'd gone up to New England to see you. Did he have a talk with you then?

(*Willy stares in silence.*)

BERNARD: Willy?

WILLY (*with a strong edge of resentment in his voice*): Yeah, he came to Boston. What about it?

BERNARD: Well, just that when he came back — I'll never forget this, it always mystifies me. Because I'd thought so well of Biff, even though he'd always taken advantage of me. I loved him, Willy, y'know? And he came back after that month and took his sneakers — remember those sneakers with "University of Virginia" printed on them? He was so proud of those, wore them every day. And he took them down in the cellar, and burned them up in the furnace. We had a fist fight. It lasted at least half an hour. Just the two of us, punching each other down the cellar, and crying right through it. I've often thought of how strange it was that I knew he'd given up his life. What happened in Boston, Willy?

(*Willy looks at him as at an intruder.*)

BERNARD: I just bring it up because you asked me.

WILLY (*angrily*): Nothing. What do you mean, "What happened?" What's that got to do with anything?

BERNARD: Well, don't get sore.

WILLY: What are you trying to do, blame it on me? If a boy lays down is that my fault?

BERNARD: Now, Willy, don't get —

WILLY: Well, don't — don't talk to me that way! What does that mean, "What happened?"

(*Charley enters. He is in his vest, and he carries a bottle of bourbon.*)

CHARLEY: Hey, you're going to miss that train. (*He waves the bottle.*)

BERNARD: Yeah, I'm going. (*He takes the bottle.*) Thanks, Pop. (*He picks up his rackets and bag.*) Good-by, Willy, and don't worry about it. You know, "If at first you don't succeed . . ."

WILLY: Yes, I believe in that.

BERNARD: But sometimes, Willy, it's better for a man just to walk away.

WILLY: Walk away?

BERNARD: That's right.

WILLY: But if you can't walk away?

BERNARD (*after a slight pause*): I guess that's when it's tough. (*Extending his hand.*) Good-by, Willy.

WILLY (*shaking Bernard's hand*): Good-by, boy.

CHARLEY (*an arm on Bernard's shoulder*): How do you like this kid? Gonna argue a case in front of the Supreme Court.

BERNARD (*protesting*): Pop!

WILLY (*genuinely shocked, pained, and happy*): No! The Supreme Court!

BERNARD: I gotta run. 'By, Dad!

CHARLEY: Knock 'em dead, Bernard!

(*Bernard goes off.*)

WILLY (*as Charley takes out his wallet*): The Supreme Court! And he didn't even mention it!

CHARLEY (*counting out money on the desk*): He don't have to — he's gonna do it.

WILLY: And you never told him what to do, did you? You never took any interest in him.

CHARLEY: My salvation is that I never took any interest in anything. There's some money — fifty dollars. I got an accountant inside.

WILLY: Charley, look . . . (*With difficulty.*) I got my insurance to pay. If you can manage it — I need a hundred and ten dollars.

(*Charley doesn't reply for a moment; merely stops moving.*)

WILLY: I'd draw it from my bank but Linda would know, and I . . .

CHARLEY: Sit down, Willy.

WILLY (*moving toward the chair*): I'm keeping an account of everything, remember. I'll pay every penny back. (*He sits.*)

CHARLEY: Now listen to me, Willy.

WILLY: I want you to know I appreciate . . .

CHARLEY (*sitting down on the table*): Willy, what're you doin'? What the hell is goin' on in your head?

WILLY: Why? I'm simply . . .

CHARLEY: I offered you a job. You make fifty dollars a week. And I won't send you on the road.

WILLY: I've got a job.

CHARLEY: Without pay? What kind of a job is a job without pay? (*He rises.*) Now, look, kid, enough is enough. I'm no genius but I know when I'm being insulted.

WILLY: Insulted!

CHARLEY: Why don't you want to work for me?

WILLY: What's the matter with you? I've got a job.

CHARLEY: Then what're you walkin' in here every week for?

WILLY (*getting up*): Well, if you don't want me to walk in here —

CHARLEY: I'm offering you a job.

WILLY: I don't want your goddam job!

CHARLEY: When the hell are you going to grow up?

WILLY (*furiously*): You big ignoramus, if you say that to me again I'll rap you one! I don't care how big you are! (*He's ready to fight.*)

(*Pause.*)

CHARLEY (*kindly, going to him*): How much do you need, Willy?

WILLY: Charley, I'm strapped. I'm strapped. I don't know what to do. I was just fired.

CHARLEY: Howard fired you?

WILLY: That snotnose. Imagine that? I named him. I named him Howard.

CHARLEY: Willy, when're you gonna realize that them things don't mean anything? You named him Howard, but you can't sell that. The only thing you got in this world is what you can sell. And the funny thing is that you're a salesman, and you don't know that.

WILLY: I've always tried to think otherwise, I guess. I always felt that if a man was impressive, and well liked, that nothing —

CHARLEY: Why must everybody like you? Who liked J. P. Morgan?° Was he impressive? In a Turkish bath he'd look like a butcher. But with his pockets on he was very well liked. Now listen, Willy, I know you don't like me, and nobody can say I'm in love with you, but I'll give you a job because — just for the hell of it, put it that way. Now what do you say?

WILLY: I — I just can't work for you, Charley.

CHARLEY: What're you, jealous of me?

WILLY: I can't work for you, that's all, don't ask me why.

J. P. **Morgan:** (1837–1913), wealthy financier and art collector whose money was made chiefly in banking, railroads, and steel.

CHARLEY (*angered, takes out more bills*): You been jealous of me all your life, you dammed fool! Here, pay your insurance. (*He puts the money in Willy's hand.*)

WILLY: I'm keeping strict accounts.

CHARLEY: I've got some work to do. Take care of yourself. And pay your insurance.

WILLY (*moving to the right*): Funny, y'know? After all the highways, and the trains, and the appointments, and the years, you end up worth more dead than alive.

CHARLEY: Willy, nobody's worth nothin' dead. (*After a slight pause.*) Did you hear what I said?

(*Willy stands still, dreaming.*)

CHARLEY: Willy!

WILLY: Apologize to Bernard for me when you see him. I didn't mean to argue with him. He's a fine boy. They're all fine boys, and they'll end up big — all of them. Someday they'll all play tennis together. Wish me luck, Charley. He saw Bill Oliver today.

CHARLEY: Good luck.

WILLY (*on the verge of tears*): Charley, you're the only friend I got. Isn't that a remarkable thing? (*He goes out.*)

CHARLEY: Jesus!

(*Charley stares after him a moment and follows. All light blacks out. Suddenly raucous music is heard, and a red glow rises behind the screen at right. Stanley, a young waiter, appears, carrying a table, followed by Happy, who is carrying two chairs.*)

STANLEY (*putting the table down*): That's all right, Mr. Loman, I can handle it myself. (*He turns and takes the chairs from Happy and places them at the table.*)

HAPPY (*glancing around*): Oh, this is better.

STANLEY: Sure, in the front there you're in the middle of all kinds of noise. Whenever you got a party, Mr. Loman, you just tell me and I'll put you back here. Y'know, there's a lotta people they don't like it private, because when they go out they like to see a lotta action around them because they're sick and tired to stay in the house by theirself. But I know you, you ain't from Hackensack. You know what I mean?

HAPPY (*sitting down*): So how's it coming, Stanley?

STANLEY: Ah, it's a dog life. I only wish during the war they'd a took me in the Army. I coulda been dead by now.

HAPPY: My brother's back, Stanley.

STANLEY: Oh, he come back, heh? From the Far West.

HAPPY: Yeah, big cattle man, my brother, so treat him right. And my father's coming too.

STANLEY: Oh, your father too!

HAPPY: You got a couple of nice lobsters?

STANLEY: Hundred percent, big.

HAPPY: I want them with the claws.

STANLEY: Don't worry, I don't give you no mice. (*Happy laughs.*) How about some wine? It'll put a head on the meal.

HAPPY: No. You remember, Stanley, that recipe I brought you from overseas? With the champagne in it?

STANLEY: Oh, yeah, sure. I still got it tacked up yet in the kitchen. But that'll have to cost a buck apiece anyways.

HAPPY: That's all right.

STANLEY: What'd you, hit a number or somethin'?

HAPPY: No, it's a little celebration. My brother is — I think he pulled off a big deal today. I think we're going into business together.

STANLEY: Great! That's the best for you. Because a family business, you know what I mean? — that's the best.

HAPPY: That's what I think.

STANLEY: 'Cause what's the difference? Somebody steals? It's in the family. Know what I mean? (*Sotto voce.*°) Like this bartender here. The boss is goin' crazy what kinda leak he's got in the cash register. You put it in but it don't come out.

HAPPY (*raising his head*): Sh!

STANLEY: What?

HAPPY: You notice I wasn't lookin' right or left, was I?

STANLEY: No.

HAPPY: And my eyes are closed.

STANLEY: So what's the — ?

HAPPY: Strudel's comin'.

STANLEY (*catching on, looks around*): Ah, no, there's no —

(*He breaks off as a furred, lavishly dressed girl enters and sits at the next table. Both follow her with their eyes.*)

STANLEY: Geez, how'd ya know?

HAPPY: I got radar or something. (*Staring directly at her profile.*) Oooooooo . . . Stanley.

STANLEY: I think that's for you, Mr. Loman.

HAPPY: Look at that mouth. Oh, God. And the binoculars.

STANLEY: Geez, you got a life, Mr. Loman.

HAPPY: Wait on her.

STANLEY (*going to the girl's table*): Would you like a menu, ma'am?

GIRL: I'm expecting someone, but I'd like a —

HAPPY: Why don't you bring her — excuse me, miss, do you mind? I sell champagne, and I'd like you to try my brand. Bring her a champagne, Stanley.

GIRL: That's awfully nice of you.

HAPPY: Don't mention it. It's all company money. (*He laughs.*)

GIRL: That's a charming product to be selling, isn't it?

HAPPY: Oh, gets to be like everything else. Selling is selling, y'know.

GIRL: I suppose.

HAPPY: You don't happen to sell, do you?

GIRL: No, I don't sell.

HAPPY: Would you object to a compliment from a stranger? You ought to be on a magazine cover.

GIRL (*looking at him a little archly*): I have been.

(*Stanley comes in with a glass of champagne.*)

Sotto voce: In a soft voice or stage whisper.

HAPPY: What'd I say before, Stanley? You see? She's a cover girl.

STANLEY: Oh, I could see, I could see.

HAPPY (*to the Girl*): What magazine?

GIRL: Oh, a lot of them. (*She takes the drink.*) Thank you.

HAPPY: You know what they say in France, don't you? "Champagne is the drink of the complexion" — Hya, Biff!

(*Biff has entered and sits with Happy.*)

BIFF: Hello, kid. Sorry I'm late.

HAPPY: I just got here. Uh, Miss — ?

GIRL: Forsythe.

HAPPY: Miss Forsythe, this is my brother.

BIFF: Is Dad here?

HAPPY: His name is Biff. You might've heard of him. Great football player.

GIRL: Really? What team?

HAPPY: Are you familiar with football?

GIRL: No, I'm afraid I'm not.

HAPPY: Biff is quarterback with the New York Giants.

GIRL: Well, that is nice, isn't it? (*She drinks.*)

HAPPY: Good health.

GIRL: I'm happy to meet you.

HAPPY: That's my name. Hap. It's really Harold, but at West Point they called me Happy.

GIRL (*now really impressed*): Oh, I see. How do you do? (*She turns her profile.*)

BIFF: Isn't Dad coming?

HAPPY: You want her?

BIFF: Oh, I could never make that.

HAPPY: I remember the time that idea would never come into your head. Where's the old confidence Biff?

BIFF: I just saw Oliver —

HAPPY: Wait a minute. I've got to see that old confidence again. Do you want her? She's on call.

BIFF: Oh, no. (*He turns to look at the Girl.*)

HAPPY: I'm telling you. Watch this. (*Turning to the Girl*): Honey? (*She turns to him.*) Are you busy?

GIRL: Well, I am . . . but I could make a phone call.

HAPPY: Do that, will you, honey? And see if you can get a friend. We'll be here for a while. Biff is one of the greatest football players in the country.

GIRL (*standing up*): Well, I'm certainly happy to meet you.

HAPPY: Come back soon.

GIRL: I'll try.

HAPPY: Don't try, honey, try hard.

(*The Girl exits. Stanley follows, shaking his head in bewildered admiration.*)

HAPPY: Isn't that a shame now? A beautiful girl like that? That's why I can't get married. There's not a good woman in a thousand. New York is loaded with them, kid!

BIFF: Hap, look —

HAPPY: I told you she was on call!

BIFF (*strangely unnerved*): Cut it out, will ya? I want to say something to you.

HAPPY: Did you see Oliver?

BIFF: I saw him all right. Now look, I want to tell Dad a couple of things and I want you to help me.

HAPPY: What? Is he going to back you?

BIFF: Are you crazy? You're out of your goddam head, you know that?

HAPPY: Why? What happened?

BIFF (*breathlessly*): I did a terrible thing today, Hap. It's been the strangest day I ever went through. I'm all numb, I swear.

HAPPY: You mean he wouldn't see you?

BIFF: Well, I waited six hours for him, see? All day. Kept sending my name in. Even tried to date his secretary so she'd get me to him, but no soap.

HAPPY: Because you're not showin' the old confidence Biff. He remembered you, didn't he?

BIFF (*stopping Happy with a gesture*): Finally, about five o'clock, he comes out. Didn't remember who I was or anything. I felt like such an idiot, Hap.

HAPPY: Did you tell him my Florida idea?

BIFF: He walked away. I saw him for one minute. I got so mad I could've torn the walls down! How the hell did I ever get the idea I was a salesman there? I even believed myself that I'd been a salesman for him! And then he gave me one look and — I realized what a ridiculous lie my whole life has been! We've been talking in a dream for fifteen years. I was a shipping clerk.

HAPPY: What'd you do?

BIFF (*with great tension and wonder*): Well, he left, see. And the secretary went out. I was all alone in the waiting room. I don't know what came over me, Hap. The next thing I know I'm in his office — paneled walls, everything. I can't explain it. I — Hap, I took his fountain pen.

HAPPY: Geez, did he catch you?

BIFF: I ran out. I ran down all eleven flights. I ran and ran and ran.

HAPPY: That was an awful dumb — what'd you do that for?

BIFF (*agonized*): I don't know, I just — wanted to take something, I don't know. You gotta help me, Hap. I'm gonna tell Pop.

HAPPY: You crazy? What for?

BIFF: Hap, he's got to understand that I'm not the man somebody lends that kind of money to. He thinks I've been spiting him all these years and it's eating him up.

HAPPY: That's just it. You tell him something nice.

BIFF: I can't.

HAPPY: Say you got a lunch date with Oliver tomorrow.

BIFF: So what do I do tomorrow?

HAPPY: You leave the house tomorrow and come back at night and say Oliver is thinking it over. And he thinks it over for a couple of weeks, and gradually it fades away and nobody's the worse.

BIFF: But it'll go on forever!

HAPPY: Dad is never so happy as when he's looking forward to something!

(*Willy enters.*)

HAPPY: Hello, scout!

WILLY: Gee, I haven't been here in years!

(*Stanley has followed Willy in and sets a chair for him. Stanley starts off but Happy stops him.*)

HAPPY: Stanley!

(*Stanley stands by, waiting for an order.*)

BIFF (*going to Willy with guilt, as to an invalid*): Sit down, Pop. You want a drink?

WILLY: Sure, I don't mind.

BIFF: Let's get a load on.

WILLY: You look worried.

BIFF: N-no. (*To Stanley.*) Scotch all around. Make it doubles.

STANLEY: Doubles, right. (*He goes.*)

WILLY: You had a couple already, didn't you?

BIFF: Just a couple, yeah.

WILLY: Well, what happened, boy? (*Nodding affirmatively, with a smile.*) Everything go all right?

BIFF (*takes a breath, then reaches out and grasps Willy's hand*): Pal . . . (*He is smiling bravely, and Willy is smiling too.*) I had an experience today.

HAPPY: Terrific, Pop.

WILLY: That so? What happened?

BIFF (*high, slightly alcoholic, above the earth*): I'm going to tell you everything from first to last. It's been a strange day. (*Silence. He looks around, composes himself as best he can, but his breath keeps breaking the rhythm of his voice.*) I had to wait quite a while for him, and —

WILLY: Oliver?

BIFF: Yeah, Oliver. All day, as a matter of cold fact. And a lot of — instances — facts, Pop, facts about my life came back to me. Who was it, Pop? Who ever said I was a salesman with Oliver?

WILLY: Well, you were.

BIFF: No, Dad, I was a shipping clerk.

WILLY: But you were practically —

BIFF (*with determination*): Dad, I don't know who said it first, but I was never a salesman for Bill Oliver.

WILLY: What're you talking about?

BIFF: Let's hold on to the facts tonight, Pop. We're not going to get anywhere bullin' around. I was a shipping clerk.

WILLY (*angrily*): All right, now listen to me —

BIFF: Why don't you let me finish?

WILLY: I'm not interested in stories about the past or any crap of that kind because the woods are burning, boys, you understand? There's a big blaze going on all around. I was fired today.

BIFF (*shocked*): How could you be?

WILLY: I was fired, and I'm looking for a little good news to tell your mother, because the woman has waited and the woman has suffered. The gist of it is that I haven't got a story left in my head, Biff. So

don't give me a lecture about facts and aspects. I am not interested. Now what've you got to say to me?

(*Stanley enters with three drinks. They wait until he leaves.*)

WILLY: Did you see Oliver?

BIFF: Jesus, Dad!

WILLY: You mean you didn't go up there?

HAPPY: Sure he went up there.

BIFF: I did. I — saw him. How could they fire you?

WILLY (*on the edge of his chair*): What kind of a welcome did he give you?

BIFF: He won't even let you work on commission?

WILLY: I'm out! (*Driving.*) So tell me, he gave you a warm welcome?

HAPPY: Sure, Pop, sure!

BIFF (*driven*): Well, it was kind of —

WILLY: I was wondering if he'd remember you. (*To Happy.*) Imagine, man doesn't see him for ten, twelve years and gives him that kind of a welcome!

HAPPY: Damn right!

BIFF (*trying to return to the offensive*): Pop, look —

WILLY: You know why he remembered you, don't you? Because you impressed him in those days.

BIFF: Let's talk quietly and get this down to the facts, huh?

WILLY (*as though Biff had been interrupting*): Well, what happened? It's great news, Biff. Did he take you into his office or'd you talk in the waiting room?

BIFF: Well, he came in, see, and —

WILLY (*with a big smile*): What'd he say? Betcha he threw his arm around you.

BIFF: Well, he kinda —

WILLY: He's a fine man. (*To Happy.*) Very hard man to see, y'know.

HAPPY (*agreeing*): Oh, I know.

WILLY (*to Biff*): Is that where you had the drinks?

BIFF: Yeah, he gave me a couple of — no, no!

HAPPY (*cutting in*): He told him my Florida idea.

WILLY: Don't interrupt. (*To Biff.*) How'd he react to the Florida idea?

BIFF: Dad, will you give me a minute to explain?

WILLY: I've been waiting for you to explain since I sat down here! What happened? He took you into his office and what?

BIFF: Well — I talked. And — and he listened, see.

WILLY: Famous for the way he listens, y'know. What was his answer?

BIFF: His answer was — (*He breaks off, suddenly angry.*) Dad, you're not letting me tell you what I want to tell you!

WILLY (*accusing, angered*): You didn't see him, did you?

BIFF: I did see him!

WILLY: What'd you insult him or something? You insulted him, didn't you?

BIFF: Listen, will you let me out of it, will you just let me out of it!

HAPPY: What the hell!

WILLY: Tell me what happened!

BIFF (*to Happy*): I can't talk to him!

(*A single trumpet note jars the ear. The light of green leaves stains the house, which holds the air of night and a dream. Young Bernard enters and knocks on the door of the house.*)

YOUNG BERNARD (*frantically*): Mrs. Loman, Mrs. Loman!

HAPPY: Tell him what happened!

BIFF (*to Happy*): Shut up and leave me alone!

WILLY: No, no! You had to go and flunk math!

BIFF: What math? What're you talking about?

YOUNG BERNARD: Mrs. Loman, Mrs. Loman!

(*Linda appears in the house, as of old.*)

WILLY (*wildly*): Math, math, math!

BIFF: Take it easy, Pop!

YOUNG BERNARD: Mrs. Loman!

WILLY (*furiously*): If you hadn't flunked you'd've been set by now!

BIFF: Now, look, I'm gonna tell you what happened, and you're going to listen to me.

YOUNG BERNARD: Mrs. Loman!

BIFF: I waited six hours —

HAPPY: What the hell are you saying?

BIFF: I kept sending in my name but he wouldn't see me. So finally he . . . (*He continues unheard as light fades low on the restaurant.*)

YOUNG BERNARD: Biff flunked math!

LINDA: No!

YOUNG BERNARD: Birnbaum flunked him! They won't graduate him!

LINDA: But they have to. He's gotta go to the university. Where is he? Biff! Biff!

YOUNG BERNARD: No, he left. He went to Grand Central.

LINDA: Grand — You mean he went to Boston!

YOUNG BERNARD: Is Uncle Willy in Boston?

LINDA: Oh, maybe Willy can talk to the teacher. Oh, the poor, poor boy!

(*Light on house area snaps out.*)

BIFF (*at the table, now audible, holding up a gold fountain pen*): . . . so I'm washed up with Oliver, you understand? Are you listening to me?

WILLY (*at a loss*): Yeah, sure. If you hadn't flunked —

BIFF: Flunked what? What're you talking about?

WILLY: Don't blame everything on me! I didn't flunk math — you did! What pen?

HAPPY: That was awful dumb, Biff, a pen like that is worth —

WILLY (*seeing the pen for the first time*): You took Oliver's pen?

BIFF (*weakening*): Dad, I just explained it to you.

WILLY: You stole Bill Oliver's fountain pen!

BIFF: I didn't exactly steal it! That's just what I've been explaining to you!

HAPPY: He had it in his hand and just then Oliver walked in, so he got nervous and stuck it in his pocket!

WILLY: My God, Biff!

BIFF: I never intended to do it, Dad!

OPERATOR'S VOICE: Standish Arms, good evening!

WILLY (*shouting*): I'm not in my room!

BIFF (*frightened*): Dad, what's the matter? (*He and Happy stand up.*)

OPERATOR: Ringing Mr. Loman for you!

WILLY: I'm not there, stop it!

BIFF (*horrified, gets down on one knee before Willy*): Dad, I'll make good, I'll make good. (*Willy tries to get to his feet. Biff holds him down.*) Sit down now.

WILLY: No, you're no good, you're no good for anything.

BIFF: I am, Dad, I'll find something else, you understand? Now don't worry about anything. (*He holds up Willy's face.*) Talk to me, Dad.

OPERATOR: Mr. Loman does not answer. Shall I page him?

WILLY (*attempting to stand, as though to rush and silence the Operator*): No, no, no!

HAPPY: He'll strike something, Pop.

WILLY: No, no . . .

BIFF (*desperately, standing over Willy*): Pop, listen! Listen to me! I'm telling you something good. Oliver talked to his partner about the Florida idea. You listening? He — he talked to his partner, and he came to me . . . I'm going to be all right, you hear? Dad, listen to me, he said it was just a question of the amount!

WILLY: Then you . . . got it?

HAPPY: He's gonna be terrific, Pop!

WILLY (*trying to stand*): Then you got it, haven't you? You got it! You got it!

BIFF (*agonized, holds Willy down*): No, no. Look, Pop. I'm supposed to have lunch with them tomorrow. I'm just telling you this so you'll know that I can still make an impression, Pop. And I'll make good somewhere, but I can't go tomorrow, see?

WILLY: Why not? You simply —

BIFF: But the pen, Pop!

WILLY: You give it to him and tell him it was an oversight!

HAPPY: Sure, have lunch tomorrow!

BIFF: I can't say that —

WILLY: You were doing a crossword puzzle and accidentally used his pen!

BIFF: Listen, kid, I took those balls years ago, now I walk in with his fountain pen? That clinches it, don't you see? I can't face him like that! I'll try elsewhere.

PAGE'S VOICE: Paging Mr. Loman!

WILLY: Don't you want to be anything?

BIFF: Pop, how can I go back?

WILLY: You don't want to be anything, is that what's behind it?

BIFF (*now angry at Willy for not crediting his sympathy*): Don't take it that way! You think it was easy walking into that office after what I'd done to him? A team of horses couldn't have dragged me back to Bill Oliver!

WILLY: Then why'd you go?

BIFF: Why did I go? Why did I go! Look at you! Look at what's become of you!

(*Off left, The Woman laughs.*)

WILLY: Biff, you're going to go to that lunch tomorrow, or —

BIFF: I can't go. I've got no appointment!

HAPPY: Biff, for . . . !

WILLY: Are you spiting me?

BIFF: Don't take it that way! Goddammit!

WILLY (*strikes Biff and falters away from the table*): You rotten little louse! Are you spiting me?

THE WOMAN: Someone's at the door, Willy!

BIFF: I'm no good, can't you see what I am?

HAPPY (*separating them*): Hey, you're in a restaurant! Now cut it out, both of you! (*The girls enter.*) Hello, girls, sit down.

(*The Woman laughs, off left.*)

MISS FORSYTHE: I guess we might as well. This is Letta.

THE WOMAN: Willy, are you going to wake up?

BIFF (*ignoring Willy*): How're ya, miss, sit down. What do you drink?

MISS FORSYTHE: Letta might not be able to stay long.

LETTA: I gotta get up very early tomorrow. I got jury duty. I'm so excited! Were you fellows ever on a jury?

BIFF: No, but I been in front of them! (*The girls laugh.*) This is my father.

LETTA: Isn't he cute? Sit down with us, Pop.

HAPPY: Sit him down, Biff!

BIFF (*going to him*): Come on, slugger, drink us under the table. To hell with it! Come on, sit down, pal.

(*On Biff's last insistence, Willy is about to sit.*)

THE WOMAN (*now urgently*): Willy, are you going to answer the door!

(*The Woman's call pulls Willy back. He starts right, befuddled.*)

BIFF: Hey, where are you going?

WILLY: Open the door.

BIFF: The door?

WILLY: The washroom . . . the door . . . where's the door?

BIFF (*leading Willy to the left*): Just go straight down.

(*Willy moves left.*)

THE WOMAN: Willy, Willy, are you going to get up, get up, get up, get up?

(*Willy exits left.*)

LETTA: I think it's sweet you bring your daddy along.

MISS FORSYTHE: Oh, he isn't really your father!

BIFF (*at left, turning to her resentfully*): Miss Forsythe, you've just seen a prince walk by. A fine, troubled prince. A hard-working, unappreciated prince. A pal, you understand? A good companion. Always for his boys.

LETTA: That's so sweet.

HAPPY: Well, girls, what's the program? We're wasting time. Come on, Biff. Gather round. Where would you like to go?

BIFF: Why don't you do something for him?

HAPPY: Me!

BIFF: Don't you give a damn for him, Hap?

HAPPY: What're you talking about? I'm the one who —

BIFF: I sense it, you don't give a good goddam about him. (*He takes the rolled-up hose from his pocket and puts it on the table in front of Happy.*) Look what I found in the cellar, for Christ's sake. How can you bear to let it go on?

HAPPY: Me? Who goes away? Who runs off and —

BIFF: Yeah, but he doesn't mean anything to you. You could help him — I can't! Don't you understand what I'm talking about? He's going to kill himself, don't you know that?

HAPPY: Don't I know it! Me!

BIFF: Hap, help him! Jesus . . . help him . . . Help me, help me, I can't bear to look at his face! (*Ready to weep, he hurries out, up right.*)

HAPPY (*starting after him*): Where are you going?

MISS FORSYTHE: What's he so mad about?

HAPPY: Come on, girls, we'll catch up with him.

MISS FORSYTHE (*as Happy pushes her out*): Say, I don't like that temper of his!

HAPPY: He's just a little overstrung, he'll be all right!

WILLY (*off left, as The Woman laughs*): Don't answer! Don't answer!

LETTA: Don't you want to tell your father —

HAPPY: No, that's not my father. He's just a guy. Come on, we'll catch Biff, and, honey, we're going to paint this town! Stanley, where's the check! Hey, Stanley!

(*They exit. Stanley looks toward left.*)

STANLEY (*calling to Happy indignantly*): Mr. Loman! Mr. Loman!

(*Stanley picks up a chair and follows them off. Knocking is heard off left. The Woman enters, laughing. Willy follows her. She is in a black slip; he is buttoning his shirt. Raw, sensuous music accompanies their speech.*)

WILLY: Will you stop laughing? Will you stop?

THE WOMAN: Aren't you going to answer the door? He'll wake the whole hotel.

WILLY: I'm not expecting anybody.

THE WOMAN: Whyn't you have another drink, honey, and stop being so damn self-centered?

WILLY: I'm so lonely.

THE WOMAN: You know you ruined me, Willy? From now on, whenever you come to the office, I'll see that you go right through to the buyers. No waiting at my desk anymore, Willy. You ruined me.

WILLY: That's nice of you to say that.

THE WOMAN: Gee, you are self-centered! Why so sad?

You are the saddest, self-centeredest soul I ever did see-saw. (*She laughs. He kisses her.*) Come on inside, drummer boy. It's silly to be dressing in the middle of the night. (*As knocking is heard.*) Aren't you going to answer the door?

WILLY: They're knocking on the wrong door.

THE WOMAN: But I felt the knocking. And he heard us talking in here. Maybe the hotel's on fire!

WILLY (*his terror rising*): It's a mistake.

THE WOMAN: Then tell him to go away!

WILLY: There's nobody there.

THE WOMAN: It's getting on my nerves, Willy. There's somebody standing out there and it's getting on my nerves!

WILLY (*pushing her away from him*): All right, stay in the bathroom here, and don't come out. I think there's a law in Massachusetts about it, so don't come out. It may be that new room clerk. He looked very mean. So don't come out. It's a mistake, there's no fire.

(*The knocking is heard again. He takes a few steps away from her, and she vanishes into the wing. The light follows him, and now he is facing Young Biff, who carries a suitcase. Biff steps toward him. The music is gone.*)

BIFF: Why didn't you answer?

WILLY: Biff! What are you doing in Boston?

BIFF: Why didn't you answer? I've been knocking for five minutes, I called you on the phone —

WILLY: I just heard you. I was in the bathroom and had the door shut. Did anything happen home?

BIFF: Dad — I let you down.

WILLY: What do you mean?

BIFF: Dad . . .

WILLY: Biffo, what's this about? (*Putting his arm around Biff.*) Come on, let's go downstairs and get you a malted.

BIFF: Dad, I flunked math.

WILLY: Not for the term?

BIFF: The term. I haven't got enough credits to graduate.

WILLY: You mean to say Bernard wouldn't give you the answers?

BIFF: He did, he tried, but I only got a sixty-one.

WILLY: And they wouldn't give you four points?

BIFF: Birnbaum refused absolutely. I begged him, Pop, but he won't give me those points. You gotta talk to him before they close the school. Because if he saw the kind of man you are, and you just talked to him in your way, I'm sure he'd come through for me. The class came right before practice, see, and I didn't go enough. Would you talk to him? He'd like you, Pop. You know the way you could talk.

WILLY: You're on. We'll drive right back.

BIFF: Oh, Dad, good work! I'm sure he'll change it for you!

WILLY: Go downstairs and tell the clerk I'm checkin' out. Go right down.

BIFF: Yes, sir! See, the reason he hates me, Pop — one day he was late for class so I got up at the blackboard and imitated him. I crossed my eyes and talked with a lithp.

WILLY (*laughing*): You did? The kids like it?

BIFF: They nearly died laughing!

WILLY: Yeah? What'd you do?

BIFF: The thquare root of thixthy twee is . . . (*Willy bursts out laughing; Biff joins.*) And in the middle of it he walked in!

(*Willy laughs and The Woman joins in offstage.*)

WILLY (*without hesitation*): Hurry downstairs and —

BIFF: Somebody in there?

WILLY: No, that was next door.

(*The Woman laughs offstage.*)

BIFF: Somebody got in your bathroom!

WILLY: No, it's the next room, there's a party —

THE WOMAN (*enters, laughing. She lisps this.*): Can I come in? There's something in the bathtub, Willy, and it's moving!

(*Willy looks at Biff, who is staring open-mouthed and horrified at The Woman.*)

WILLY: Ah — you better go back to your room. They must be finished painting by now. They're painting her room so I let her take a shower here. Go back, go back . . . (*He pushes her.*)

THE WOMAN (*resisting*): But I've got to get dressed, Willy, I can't —

WILLY: Get out of here! Go back, go back . . . (*Suddenly striving for the ordinary.*) This is Miss Francis, Biff, she's a buyer. They're painting her room. Go back, Miss Francis, go back . . .

THE WOMAN: But my clothes, I can't go out naked in the hall!

WILLY (*pushing her offstage*): Get outa here! Go back, go back!

(*Biff slowly sits down on his suitcase as the argument continues offstage.*)

THE WOMAN: Where's my stockings? You promised me stockings, Willy!

WILLY: I have no stockings here!

THE WOMAN: You had two boxes of size nine sheers for me, and I want them!

WILLY: Here, for God's sake, will you get outa here!

THE WOMAN (*enters holding a box of stockings*): I just hope there's nobody in the hall. That's all I hope. (*To Biff.*) Are you football or baseball?

BIFF: Football.

THE WOMAN (*angry, humiliated*): That's me too. G'night. (*She snatches her clothes from Willy, and walks out.*)

WILLY (*after a pause*): Well, better get going. I want to get to the school first thing in the morning. Get my suits out of the closet. I'll get my valise. (*Biff doesn't move.*) What's the matter! (*Biff remains motionless, tears falling.*) She's a buyer. Buys for J. H. Simmons. She lives down the hall — they're painting. You don't imagine — (*He breaks off. After a pause.*) Now listen, pal, she's just a buyer. She sees merchandise in her room and they have to keep it looking just so . . . (*Pause. Assuming command.*) All right, get my suits. (*Biff doesn't move.*) Now stop crying and do as I say. I gave you an order. Biff, I gave you an order! Is that what you do when I give you an order? How dare you cry! (*Putting his arm around Biff.*) Now look, Biff, when you grow up you'll understand about these things. You mustn't — you mustn't overemphasize a thing like this. I'll see Birnbaum first thing in the morning.

BIFF: Never mind.

WILLY (*getting down beside Biff*): Never mind! He's going to give you those points. I'll see to it.

BIFF: He wouldn't listen to you.

WILLY: He certainly will listen to me. You need those points for the U. of Virginia.

BIFF: I'm not going there.

WILLY: Heh? If I can't get him to change that mark you'll make it up in summer school. You've got all summer to —

BIFF (*his weeping breaking from him*): Dad . . .

WILLY (*infected by it*): Oh, my boy . . .

BIFF: Dad . . .

WILLY: She's nothing to me, Biff. I was lonely, I was terribly lonely.

BIFF: You — you gave her Mama's stockings! (*His tears break through and he rises to go.*)

WILLY (*grabbing for Biff*): I gave you an order!

BIFF: Don't touch me, you — liar!

WILLY: Apologize for that!

BIFF: You fake! You phony little fake! You fake! (*Overcome, he turns quickly and weeping fully goes out with his suitcase. Willy is left on the floor on his knees.*)

WILLY: I gave you an order! Biff, come back here or I'll beat you! Come back here! I'll whip you!

(*Stanley comes quickly in from the right and stands in front of Willy.*)

WILLY (*shouts at Stanley*): I gave you an order . . .

STANLEY: Hey, let's pick it up, pick it up, Mr. Loman. (*He helps Willy to his feet.*) Your boys left with the chippies. They said they'll see you home.

(*A second waiter watches some distance away.*)

WILLY: But we were supposed to have dinner together.

(*Music is heard, Willy's theme.*)

STANLEY: Can you make it?

WILLY: I'll — sure, I can make it. (*Suddenly concerned about his clothes.*) Do I — I look all right?

STANLEY: Sure, you look all right. (*He flicks a speck off Willy's lapel.*)

WILLY: Here — here's a dollar.

STANLEY: Oh, your son paid me. It's all right.

WILLY (*putting it in Stanley's hand*): No, take it. You're a good boy.

STANLEY: Oh, no, you don't have to . . .

WILLY: Here — here's some more, I don't need it any-

more. (*After a slight pause.*) Tell me — is there a seed store in the neighborhood?

STANLEY: Seeds? You mean like to plant?

(*As Willy turns, Stanley slips the money back into his jacket pocket.*)

WILLY: Yes. Carrots, peas . . .

STANLEY: Well, there's hardware stores on Sixth Avenue, but it may be too late now.

WILLY (*anxiously*): Oh, I'd better hurry. I've got to get some seeds. (*He starts off to the right.*) I've got to get some seeds, right away. Nothing's planted. I don't have a thing in the ground.

(*Willy hurries out as the light goes down. Stanley moves over to the right after him, watches him off. The other waiter has been staring at Willy.*)

STANLEY (*to the waiter*): Well, whatta you looking at?

(*The waiter picks up the chairs and moves off right. Stanley takes the table and follows him. The light fades on this area. There is a long pause, the sound of the flute coming over. The light gradually rises on the kitchen, which is empty. Happy appears at the door of the house, followed by Biff. Happy is carrying a large bunch of long-stemmed roses. He enters the kitchen, looks around for Linda. Not seeing her, he turns to Biff, who is just outside the house door, and makes a gesture with his hands, indicating "Not here, I guess." He looks into the living room and freezes. Inside, Linda, unseen, is seated, Willy's coat on her lap. She rises ominously and quietly and moves toward Happy, who backs up into the kitchen, afraid.*)

HAPPY: Hey, what're you doing up? (*Linda says nothing but moves toward him implacably.*) Where's Pop? (*He keeps backing to the right, and now Linda is in full view in the doorway to the living room.*) Is he sleeping?

LINDA: Where were you?

HAPPY (*trying to laugh it off*): We met two girls, Mom, very fine types. Here, we brought you some flowers. (*Offering them to her.*) Put them in your room, Ma.

(*She knocks them to the floor at Biff's feet. He has now come inside and closed the door behind him. She stares at Biff, silent.*)

HAPPY: Now what'd you do that for? Mom, I want you to have some flowers —

LINDA (*cutting Happy off, violently to Biff*): Don't you care whether he lives or dies?

HAPPY (*going to the stairs*): Come upstairs, Biff.

BIFF (*with a flare of disgust, to Happy*): Go away from me! (*To Linda.*) What do you mean, lives or dies? Nobody's dying around here, pal.

LINDA: Get out of my sight! Get out of here!

BIFF: I wanna see the boss.

LINDA: You're not going near him!

BIFF: Where is he? (*He moves into the living room and Linda follows.*)

LINDA (*shouting after Biff*): You invite him for dinner. He looks forward to it all day — (*Biff appears in his parents' bedroom, looks around, and exits*) — and then you desert him there. There's no stranger you'd do that to!

HAPPY: Why? He had a swell time with us. Listen, when I — (*Linda comes back into the kitchen*) — desert him I hope I don't outlive the day!

LINDA: Get out of here!

HAPPY: Now look, Mom . . .

LINDA: Did you have to go to women tonight? You and your lousy rotten whores!

(*Biff reenters the kitchen.*)

HAPPY: Mom, all we did was follow Biff around trying to cheer him up! (*To Biff.*) Boy, what a night you gave me!

LINDA: Get out of here, both of you, and don't come back! I don't want you tormenting him any more. Go on now, get your things together! (*To Biff.*) You can sleep in his apartment. (*She starts to pick up the flowers and stops herself.*) Pick up this stuff, I'm not your maid anymore. Pick it up, you bum, you!

(*Happy turns his back to her in refusal. Biff slowly moves over and gets down on his knees, picking up the flowers.*)

LINDA: You're a pair of animals! Not one, not another living soul would have had the cruelty to walk out on that man in a restaurant!

BIFF (*not looking at her*): Is that what he said?

LINDA: He didn't have to say anything. He was so humiliated he nearly limped when he came in.

HAPPY: But, Mom, he had a great time with us —

BIFF (*cutting him off violently*): Shut up!

(*Without another word, Happy goes upstairs.*)

LINDA: You! You didn't even go in to see if he was all right!

BIFF (*still on the floor in front of Linda, the flowers in his hand; with self-loathing*): No. Didn't. Didn't do a damned thing. How do you like that, heh? Left him babbling in a toilet.

LINDA: You louse. You . . .

BIFF: Now you hit it on the nose! (*He gets up, throws the flowers in the wastebasket.*) The scum of the earth, and you're looking at him!

LINDA: Get out of here!

BIFF: I gotta talk to the boss, Mom. Where is he?

LINDA: You're not going near him. Get out of this house!

BIFF (*with absolute assurance, determination*): No. We're gonna have an abrupt conversation, him and me.

LINDA: You're not talking to him.

(*Hammering is heard from outside the house, off right. Biff turns toward the noise.*)

LINDA (*suddenly pleading*): Will you please leave him alone?

BIFF: What's he doing out there?

LINDA: He's planting the garden!

BIFF (*quietly*): Now? Oh, my God!

(*Biff moves outside, Linda following. The light dies down on them and comes up on the center of the apron as Willy walks into it. He is carrying a flashlight, a hoe, and a handful of seed packets. He raps the top of the hoe sharply to fix it firmly, and then moves to the left, measuring off the distance with his foot. He holds the flashlight to look at the seed packets, reading off the instructions. He is in the blue of night.*)

WILLY: Carrots . . . quarter-inch apart. Rows . . . one-foot rows. (*He measures it off.*) One foot. (*He puts down a package and measures off.*) Beets. (*He puts down another package and measures again.*) Lettuce. (*He reads the package, puts it down.*) One foot — (*He breaks off as Ben appears at the right and moves slowly down to him.*) What a proposition, ts, ts. Terrific, terrific. 'Cause she's suffered, Ben, the woman has suffered. You understand me? A man can't go out the way he came in, Ben, a man has got to add up to something. You can't, you can't — (*Ben moves toward him as though to interrupt.*) You gotta consider, now. Don't answer so quick. Remember, it's a guaranteed twenty-thousand-dollar proposition. Now look, Ben, I want you to go through the ins and outs of this thing with me. I've got nobody to talk to, Ben, and the woman has suffered, you hear me?

BEN (*standing still, considering*): What's the proposition?

WILLY: It's twenty thousand dollars on the barrelhead. Guaranteed, gilt-edged, you understand?

BEN: You don't want to make a fool of yourself. They might not honor the policy.

WILLY: How can they dare refuse? Didn't I work like a coolie to meet every premium on the nose? And now they don't pay off? Impossible!

BEN: It's called a cowardly thing, William.

WILLY: Why? Does it take more guts to stand here the rest of my life ringing up a zero?

BEN (*yielding*): That's a point, William. (*He moves, thinking, turns.*) And twenty thousand — that is something one can feel with the hand, it is there.

WILLY (*now assured, with rising power*): Oh, Ben, that's the whole beauty of it! I see it like a diamond, shining in the dark, hard and rough, that I can pick up and touch in my hand. Not like — like an appointment! This would not be another damned-fool appointment, Ben, and it changes all the aspects. Because he thinks I'm nothing, see, and so he spites me. But the funeral — (*Straightening up.*) Ben, that funeral will be massive! They'll come from Maine, Massachusetts, Vermont, New Hampshire! All the old-timers with the strange license plates — that boy will be thunderstruck, Ben, because he never realized — I am known! Rhode Island, New York, New Jersey — I am known, Ben and he'll see it with his eyes once and for all. He'll see what I am, Ben! He's in for a shock, that boy!

BEN (*coming down to the edge of the garden*): He'll call you a coward.

WILLY (*suddenly fearful*): No, that would be terrible.

BEN: Yes. And a damned fool.

WILLY: No, no, he mustn't, I won't have that! (*He is broken and desperate.*)

BEN: He'll hate you, William.

(*The gay music of the Boys is heard.*)

WILLY: Oh, Ben, how do we get back to all the great times? Used to be so full of light, and comradeship, the sleigh-riding in winter, and the ruddiness on his cheeks. And always some kind of good news coming up, always something nice coming up ahead. And never even let me carry the valises in the house, and simonizing, simonizing that little red car! Why, why can't I give him something and not have him hate me?

BEN: Let me think about it. (*He glances at his watch.*) I still have a little time. Remarkable proposition, but you've got to be sure you're not making a fool of yourself.

(*Ben drifts off upstage and goes out of sight. Biff comes down from the left.*)

WILLY (*suddenly conscious of Biff, turns and looks up at him, then begins picking up the packages of seeds in confusion*): Where the hell is that seed? (*Indignantly.*) You can't see nothing out here! They boxed in the whole goddam neighborhood!

BIFF: There are people all around here. Don't you realize that?

WILLY: I'm busy. Don't bother me.

BIFF (*taking the hoe from Willy*): I'm saying good-by to you, Pop. (*Willy looks at him, silent, unable to move.*) I'm not coming back any more.

WILLY: You're not going to see Oliver tomorrow?

BIFF: I've got no appointment, Dad.

WILLY: He put his arm around you, and you've got no appointment?

BIFF: Pop, get this now, will you? Everytime I've left it's been a fight that sent me out of here. Today I realized something about myself and I tried to explain it to you and I — I think I'm just not smart enough to make any sense out of it for you. To hell with whose fault it is or anything like that. (*He takes Willy's arm.*) Let's just wrap it up, heh? Come on in, we'll tell Mom. (*He gently tries to pull Willy to left.*)

WILLY (*frozen, immobile, with guilt in his voice*): No, I don't want to see her.

BIFF: Come on! (*He pulls again, and Willy tries to pull away.*)

WILLY (*highly nervous*): No, no, I don't want to see her.

BIFF (*tries to look into Willy's face, as if to find the answer there*): Why don't you want to see her?

WILLY (*more harshly now*): Don't bother me, will you?

BIFF: What do you mean, you don't want to see her? You don't want them calling you yellow, do you? This isn't your fault; it's me, I'm a bum. Now come

inside! (*Willy strains to get away.*) Did you hear what I said to you?

(*Willy pulls away and quickly goes by himself into the house. Biff follows.*)

LINDA (*to Willy*): Did you plant, dear?

BIFF (*at the door, to Linda*): All right, we had it out. I'm going and I'm not writing any more.

LINDA (*going to Willy in the kitchen*): I think that's the best way, dear. 'Cause there's no use drawing it out, you'll just never get along.

(*Willy doesn't respond.*)

BIFF: People ask where I am and what I'm doing, you don't know, and you don't care. That way it'll be off your mind and you can start brightening up again. All right? That clears it, doesn't it? (*Willy is silent, and Biff goes to him.*) You gonna wish me luck, scout? (*He extends his hand.*) What do you say?

LINDA: Shake his hand, Willy.

WILLY (*turning to her, seething with hurt*): There's no necessity to mention the pen at all, y'know.

BIFF (*gently*): I've got no appointment, Dad.

WILLY (*erupting fiercely*): He put his arm around . . . ?

BIFF: Dad, you're never going to see what I am, so what's the use of arguing? If I strike oil I'll send you a check. Meantime forget I'm alive.

WILLY (*to Linda*): Spite, see?

BIFF: Shake hands, Dad.

WILLY: Not my hand.

BIFF: I was hoping not to go this way.

WILLY: Well, this is the way you're going. Good-by.

(*Biff looks at him a moment, then turns sharply and goes to the stairs.*)

WILLY (*stops him with*): May you rot in hell if you leave this house!

BIFF (*turning*): Exactly what is it that you want from me?

WILLY: I want you to know, on the train, in the mountains, in the valleys, wherever you go, that you cut down your life for spite!

BIFF: No, no.

WILLY: Spite, spite, is the word of your undoing! And when you're down and out, remember what did it. When you're rotting somewhere beside the railroad tracks, remember, and don't you dare blame it on me!

BIFF: I'm not blaming it on you!

WILLY: I won't take the rap for this, you hear?

(*Happy comes down the stairs and stands on the bottom step, watching.*)

BIFF: That's just what I'm telling you!

WILLY (*sinking into a chair at a table, with full accusation*): You're trying to put a knife in me — don't think I don't know what you're doing!

BIFF: All right, phony! Then let's lay it on the line. (*He whips the rubber tube out of his pocket and puts it on the table.*)

Dustin Hoffman as Willy Loman in the 1985 film version of *Death of a Salesman*.

HAPPY: You crazy . . .

LINDA: Biff! (*She moves to grab the hose, but Biff holds it down with his hand.*)

BIFF: Leave it there! Don't move it!

WILLY (*not looking at it*): What is that?

BIFF: You know goddam well what that is.

WILLY (*caged, wanting to escape*): I never saw that.

BIFF: You saw it. The mice didn't bring it into the cellar! What is this supposed to do, make a hero out of you? This supposed to make me sorry for you?

WILLY: Never heard of it.

BIFF: There'll be no pity for you, you hear it? No pity!

WILLY (*to Linda*): You hear the spite!

BIFF: No, you're going to hear the truth — what you are and what I am!

LINDA: Stop it!

WILLY: Spite!

HAPPY (*coming down toward Biff*): You cut it now!

BIFF (*to Happy*): The man don't know who we are! The man is gonna know! (*To Willy.*) We never told the truth for ten minutes in this house!

HAPPY: We always told the truth!

BIFF (*turning on him*): You big blow, are you the assistant buyer? You're one of the two assistants to the assistant, aren't you?

HAPPY: Well, I'm practically . . .

BIFF: You're practically full of it! We all are! and I'm through with it. (*To Willy.*) Now hear this, Willy, this is me.

WILLY: I know you!

BIFF: You know why I had no address for three months? I stole a suit in Kansas City and I was in jail. (*To Linda, who is sobbing.*) Stop crying. I'm through with it.

(*Linda turns away from them, her hands covering her face.*)

WILLY: I suppose that's my fault!

BIFF: I stole myself out of every good job since high school!

WILLY: And whose fault is that?

BIFF: And I never got anywhere because you blew me so full of hot air I could never stand taking orders from anybody! That's whose fault it is!

WILLY: I hear that!

LINDA: Don't, Biff!

BIFF: It's goddam time you heard that! I had to be boss big shot in two weeks, and I'm through with it!

WILLY: Then hang yourself! For spite, hang yourself!

BIFF: No! Nobody's hanging himself, Willy! I ran down eleven flights with a pen in my hand today. And suddenly I stopped, you hear me? And in the middle of that office building, do you hear this? I stopped in the middle of that building and I saw — the sky. I saw the things that I love in this world. The work and the food and time to sit and smoke. And I looked at the pen and said to myself, what the hell am I grabbing this for? Why am I trying to become what I don't want to be? What am I doing in an office, making a contemptuous begging fool of myself, when all I want is out there, waiting for me the minute I say I know who I am! Why can't I say that, Willy? (*He tries to make Willy face him, but Willy pulls away and moves to the left.*)

WILLY (*with hatred, threateningly*): The door of your life is wide open!

BIFF: Pop! I'm a dime a dozen, and so are you!

WILLY (*turning on him now in an uncontrolled outburst*): I am not a dime a dozen! I am Willy Loman, and you are Biff Loman!

(*Biff starts for Willy, but is blocked by Happy. In his fury, Biff seems on the verge of attacking his father.*)

BIFF: I am not a leader of men, Willy, and neither are you. You were never anything but a hard-working drummer who landed in the ash can like all the rest of them! I'm one dollar an hour, Willy! I tried seven states and couldn't raise it. A buck an hour! Do you gather my meaning? I'm not bringing home any prizes any more, and you're going to stop waiting for me to bring them home!

WILLY (*directly to Biff*): You vengeful, spiteful mutt!

(*Biff breaks from Happy. Willy, in fright, starts up the stairs. Biff grabs him.*)

BIFF (*at the peak of his fury*): Pop, I'm nothing! I'm nothing, Pop. Can't you understand that? There's no spite in it any more. I'm just what I am, that's all.

(*Biff's fury has spent itself and he breaks down, sobbing, holding on to Willy, who dumbly fumbles for Biff's face.*)

WILLY (*astonished*): What're you doing? What're you doing? (*To Linda.*) Why is he crying?

BIFF (*crying, broken*): Will you let me go, for Christ's sake? Will you take that phony dream and burn it before something happens? (*Struggling to contain himself he pulls away and moves to the stairs.*) I'll go in the morning. Put him — put him to bed. (*Exhausted, Biff moves up the stairs to his room.*)

WILLY (*after a long pause, astonished, elevated*): Isn't that — isn't that remarkable? Biff — he likes me!

LINDA: He loves you, Willy!

HAPPY (*deeply moved*): Always did, Pop.

WILLY: Oh, Biff! (*Staring wildly.*) He cried! Cried to me. (*He is choking with his love, and now cries out his promise.*) That boy — that boy is going to be magnificent!

(*Ben appears in the light just outside the kitchen.*)

BEN: Yes, outstanding, with twenty thousand behind him.

LINDA (*sensing the racing of his mind, fearfully, carefully*): Now come to bed, Willy. It's all settled now.

WILLY (*finding it difficult not to rush out of the house*): Yes, we'll sleep. Come on. Go to sleep, Hap.

BEN: And it does take a great kind of a man to crack the jungle.

(*In accents of dread, Ben's idyllic music starts up.*)

HAPPY (*his arm around Linda*): I'm getting married, Pop, don't forget it. I'm changing everything. I'm gonna run that department before the year is up. You'll see, Mom. (*He kisses her.*)

BEN: The jungle is dark but full of diamonds, Willy.

(*Willy turns, moves, listening to Ben.*)

LINDA: Be good. You're both good boys, just act that way, that's all.

HAPPY: 'Night, Pop. (*He goes upstairs.*)

LINDA (*to Willy*): Come, dear.

BEN (*with greater force*): One must go in to fetch a diamond out.

WILLY (*to Linda, as he moves slowly along the edge of kitchen, toward the door*): I just want to get settled down, Linda. Let me sit alone for a little.

LINDA (*almost uttering her fear*): I want you upstairs.

WILLY (*taking her in his arms*): In a few minutes, Linda. I couldn't sleep right now. Go on, you look awful tired. (*He kisses her.*)

BEN: Not like an appointment at all. A diamond is rough and hard to the touch.

WILLY: Go on now. I'll be right up.

LINDA: I think this is the only way, Willy.

WILLY: Sure, it's the best thing.

BEN: Best thing!

WILLY: The only way. Everything is gonna be — go on, kid, get to bed. You look so tired.

LINDA: Come right up.

WILLY: Two minutes.

(*Linda goes into the living room, then reappears in her bedroom. Willy moves just outside the kitchen door.*)

Biff (Kevin Anderson) and Willy (Brian Dennehy) try to console one another in Robert Falls's 1999 production of *Death of a Salesman.*

WILLY: Loves me. (*Wonderingly.*) Always loved me. Isn't that a remarkable thing? Ben, he'll worship me for it!

BEN (*with promise*): It's dark there, but full of diamonds.

WILLY: Can you imagine that magnificence with twenty thousand dollars in his pocket?

LINDA (*calling from her room*): Willy! Come up!

WILLY (*calling into the kitchen*): Yes! yes. Coming! It's very smart, you realize that, don't you, sweetheart? Even Ben sees it. I gotta go, baby. 'By! 'By! (*Going over to Ben, almost dancing.*) Imagine? When the mail comes he'll be ahead of Bernard again!

BEN: A perfect proposition all around.

WILLY: Did you see how he cried to me? Oh, if I could kiss him, Ben!

BEN: Time, William, time!

WILLY: Oh, Ben, I always knew one way or another we were gonna make it, Biff and I!

BEN (*looking at his watch*): The boat. We'll be late. (*He moves slowly off into the darkness.*)

WILLY (*elegiacally, turning to the house*): Now when you kick off, boy, I want a seventy-yard boot, and get right down the field under the ball, and when you hit, hit low and hit hard, because it's important, boy. (*He swings around and faces the audience.*) There's all kinds of important people in the stands, and the first thing you know . . . (*Suddenly realizing he is alone.*) Ben! Ben, where do I . . . ? (*He makes a sudden movement of search.*) Ben, how do I . . . ?

LINDA (*calling*): Willy, you coming up?

WILLY (*uttering a gasp of fear, whirling about as if to quiet her*): Sh! (*He turns around as if to find his way; sounds, faces, voices, seem to be swarming in upon him and he flicks at them, crying, Sh! Sh! Suddenly music, faint and high, stops him. It rises in intensity, almost to an unbearable scream. He goes up and down on his toes, and rushes off around the house.*) Shhh!

LINDA: Willy?

(*There is no answer. Linda waits. Biff gets up off his bed. He is still in his clothes. Happy sits up. Biff stands listening.*)

LINDA (*with real fear*): Willy, answer me! Willy!

(*There is the sound of a car starting and moving away at full speed.*)

LINDA: No!

BIFF (*rushing down the stairs*): Pop!

(*As the car speeds off, the music crashes down in a frenzy of sound, which becomes the soft pulsation of a single cello string. Biff slowly returns to his bedroom. He and Happy gravely don their jackets. Linda slowly walks out of her room. The music has developed into a dead march. The leaves of day are appearing over everything. Charley and Bernard, somberly dressed, appear and knock on the kitchen door. Biff and Happy slowly descend the stairs to the kitchen as Charley and Bernard enter. All stop a moment when Linda, in clothes of mourning, bearing a little bunch of roses, comes through the draped doorway into the kitchen. She goes to Charley and takes his arm. Now all move toward the audience, through the wall-line of the kitchen. At the limit of the apron, Linda lays down the flowers, kneels, and sits back on her heels. All stare down at the grave.*)

REQUIEM

CHARLEY: It's getting dark, Linda.

(*Linda doesn't react. She stares at the grave.*)

BIFF: How about it, Mom? Better get some rest, heh? They'll be closing the gate soon.

(*Linda makes no move. Pause.*)

HAPPY (*deeply angered*): He had no right to do that. There was no necessity for it. We would've helped him.

CHARLEY (*grunting*): Hmmm.

BIFF: Come along, Mom.

LINDA: Why didn't anybody come?

CHARLEY: It was a very nice funeral.

LINDA: But where are all the people he knew? Maybe they blame him.

CHARLEY: Naa. It's a rough world, Linda. They wouldn't blame him.

LINDA: I can't understand it. At this time especially. First time in thirty-five years we were just about free and clear. He only needed a little salary. He was even finished with the dentist.

CHARLEY: No man only needs a little salary.

LINDA: I can't understand it.

BIFF: There were a lot of nice days. When he'd come home from a trip; or on Sundays, making the stoop; finishing the cellar; putting on the new porch; when he built the extra bathroom; and put up the garage. You know something, Charley, there's more of him in that front stoop than in all the sales he ever made.

CHARLEY: Yeah. He was a happy man with a batch of cement.

LINDA: He was so wonderful with his hands.

BIFF: He had the wrong dreams. All, all, wrong.

HAPPY (*almost ready to fight Biff*): Don't say that!

BIFF: He never knew who he was.

CHARLEY (*stopping Happy's movement and reply. To Biff*): Nobody dast blame this man. You don't understand: Willy was a salesman. And for a salesman, there is no rock bottom to the life. He don't put a bolt to a nut, he don't tell you the law or give you medicine. He's a man way out there in the blue, riding on a smile and a shoeshine. And when they start not smiling back — that's an earthquake. And then you get yourself a couple of spots on your hat, and you're finished. Nobody dast blame this man. A salesman is got to dream, boy. It comes with the territory.

BIFF: Charley, the man didn't know who he was.

HAPPY (*infuriated*): Don't say that!

BIFF: Why don't you come with me, Happy?

HAPPY: I'm not licked that easily. I'm staying right in this city, and I'm gonna beat this racket! (*He looks at Biff, his chin set.*) The Loman Brothers!

BIFF: I know who I am, kid.

HAPPY: All right, boy. I'm gonna show you and everybody else that Willy Loman did not die in vain. He had a good dream. It's the only dream you can have — to come out number-one man. He fought it out here, and this is where I'm gonna win it for him.

BIFF (*with a hopeless glance at Happy, bends toward his mother*): Let's go, Mom.

LINDA: I'll be with you in a minute. Go on, Charley. (*He hesitates.*) I want to, just for a minute. I never had a chance to say good-by.

(*Charley moves away, followed by Happy. Biff remains a slight distance up and left of Linda. She sits there, summoning herself. The flute begins, not far away, playing behind her speech.*)

LINDA: Forgive me, dear. I can't cry. I don't know what it is, but I can't cry. I don't understand it. Why did you ever do that? Help me, Willy, I can't cry. It seems to me that you're just on another trip. I keep expecting you. Willy, dear, I can't cry. Why did you do it? I search and search and I search, and I can't understand it, Willy. I made the last payment on the house today. Today, dear. And there'll be nobody home. (*A sob rises in her throat.*) We're free and clear. (*Sobbing more fully, released.*) We're free. (*Biff comes slowly toward her.*) We're free . . . We're free . . .

(*Biff lifts her to her feet and moves out up right with her in his arms. Linda sobs quietly. Bernard and Charley come together and follow them, followed by Happy. Only the music of the flute is left on the darkening stage as over the house the hard towers of the apartment buildings rise into sharp focus, and the curtain falls.*)

COMMENTARIES

Arthur Miller (b. 1915)
IN MEMORIAM   *1932*

"In Memoriam," a short story about a salesman written in 1932 when Arthur Miller was seventeen, was published in 1995 after it was discovered in the Arthur Miller Archive at the University of Texas's Harry Ransom library. A note on the manuscript indicates that the real Schoenzeit threw himself in front of an elevated railway train the day after the incident the story records. While not providing the model for Death of a Salesman, *the story reminds us that Miller had experience with men like Willy Loman.*

Sitting here now, thinking of him, he seems to be a romantic figure, but really he wasn't. Yet I couldn't venture to call him "commonplace." I never knew him intimately, yet I feel as though I knew him more closely, more thoroughly, than I know myself. His was a salesman's profession, if one may describe such dignified slavery as a profession, and though he tried to interest himself in his work he never became entirely molded into the pot of that business. His emotions were displayed at the wrong times always, and he never quite knew when to laugh. Perhaps, if I may say so, he never was complete. He had lost something vital. There was an air of quiet solitude, of cryptic wondering about both him and his name.

Although he was ever simply and immaculately dressed, I always imagined he had been dressed by someone else.

When I first heard his name, I wondered if he hadn't forgotten some other and had merely been called this by men. His last name was Schoenzeit; the first I never learned, but it had to be Alfred. He always seemed to need that name. Especially when he sat at the small glass-topped table in my father's showroom, slowly perusing the columns of the *Times,* with tears of perspiration dotting the reddened ridge that his gray felt hat had made around his head. The shined, bulgy-toed shoes placed flatly and it seemed carefully on the carpet, his overcoat folded neatly on a chair, the bow of his tie stuck so perfectly into the crevice of a starched, rounded collar completed a setting where I am sure he never belonged.

Schoenzeit, as everyone called him, often was gay. I might add "happy," but of the last I shall never be sure. He laughed as superciliously as any of the others when someone was the object of a quip. But these occasions were rare and never lasted, as far as he was concerned. Always he returned to his fogged manner, and after the joke had faded from his mind the light which seemed to brighten his countenance, too, disappeared, and he was once more enigmatic and incomprehensible.

I had, on several occasions, been alone with him, and may truthfully say I deeply pitied such a dejected soul. At one time it was necessary for him to go to the Bronx to interview a large retail drygoods store, and I was instructed to carry his samples. It was late spring, the sky was cloudless and blue, a yellow sun was slowly warming the cool morning air, and the usual city hurriers were plying their trade.

I had six coats in my arms, holding them against my chest, while he walked, leaning very slightly forward, by my side. His feet must have hurt him, for he pointed them outward, laying them flat on the ground at every step. When walking, he seemed to be striving against a stiff wind, his eyebrows peaked together, forming tiny creases at the bridge of his nose. His hat, placed straight on his head, shaded his eyes, which gazed seekingly ahead.

It was necessary to walk from Eighth to Third Avenue in order to reach the Elevated, and he offered many times to rest. I must have looked tired, because he turned to me once and laughed, saying in his cracked yet resonant baritone, "Hard work, eh, kid? Some business . . ." Of course, I didn't admit my weariness, and pitching my head to one side, raising my eyebrows and smiling, assured him that I was enjoying it as much as he was.

In due time, we approached the El, and about a block away he slowly and lightly touched my arm and, still looking ahead, he asked, "Arthur, do you get paid from the firm for carfare?" He said this in a low tone, as though he were trying to hide his point until it was absolutely necessary to take the plunge.

I thought for a moment and answered, "Well, whenever I have to go anywhere out of walking distance I am given money to ride, but I have no standing allowance for such purposes." He seemed to falter, and flushed a trifle before answering, and for a second I felt both rage and pity for this decrepit soul, who, it seemed, aged many years as he turned to me. I knew then that he felt as though his life were ended, that he was merely being pushed by outside forces. And though his body went on as before, the soul inside had crumpled and broken beyond repair.

He was asking me now for carfare. I knew he would rather have been pulled apart by a tiger, but he was asking me for carfare, a nickel to hold out to a corpulent, uninterested machine for his fare. My heart bled for him at that moment, and as we mounted the long stairway to the trains I realized that as low and shakingly embarrassed as I felt, his senses were that much more tormented and destroyed. And I marvelled at his poise under the circumstances. The coats were warm now against me, and I was thankful to God himself for this refuge for my gawky body which, with the expression of my eyes, must reveal to him my sensations.

I tried as best I could to make this situation seem as if it were common-place — I who had carried samples for so many salesmen. And when we reached the turnstile, I balanced my burden on one knee while I dipped my free hand into my pocket. Behind my throat, I cursed myself for not having the change. I turned from him in order to get the nickels required, and when I lifted my eyes to his figure I prayed, until my temples seemed to burst, for his salvation. At that moment, he looked so broken, so dejected and lost that I hastily lowered my gaze. He appeared to me then, as he stood there at the turnstile, like a small dog who has messed in the house, standing now, after his beating, waiting for his master to open the door to the back yard.

During the entire ride uptown, we two spoke but sparingly. The bright streets below changed constantly as we racketed past, and the windows of the houses facing the trains offered a haven for my confused and weary imagination.

He sold nothing that day and was profusely maltreated by the attending force at the buying office who, by virtue of their superior intelligence and ties to match, were vindicated even when they were consciously adding to the vicissitudes of a seller's life.

On the return trip, Alfred, as I subconsciously called him, became more voluble and questioned me as to my ambitions and my occupations in my leisure time.

Upon hearing that I owned an old car, he immediately became interested and spoke a little less haltingly than was his wont. From constant rebuff, he was loath to venture an opinion, and often embarrassed us both by ending a bountiful conversation unexpectedly.

He accompanied me to my father's place and, placing his hand on the small of my back, patted me lightly, and said with a faint smile, "Thanks, Arthur — and I'll . . . see you tomorrow."

With that farewell, he was off into the crowd, and his restless body faded slowly into the dark overcoats of unknowns as it willingly shrank from my sight.

I never saw him again and had forgotten him entirely when I heard of his death.

"Schoenzeit is dead," and my only recollection of that second when I heard those words is a slow exhaling of my breath and a cool, soft, glowing smile within my soul.

Arthur Miller (b. 1915)
TRAGEDY AND THE COMMON MAN   1949

One of the curious debates that arose around Death of a Salesman *was the question of whether it was a genuine tragedy. One of the requirements for traditional tragedy is that the hero be of noble birth. Miller countered that notion with a clear statement of modern purpose regarding tragedy.*

In this age few tragedies are written. It has often been held that the lack is due to a paucity of heroes among us, or else that modern man has had the blood drawn out of his organs of belief by the skepticism of science, and the heroic attack on life cannot feed on an attitude of reserve and circumspection. For one reason or another, we are often held to be below tragedy — or tragedy above us. The inevitable conclusion is, of course, that the tragic mode is archaic, fit only for the very highly placed, the kings or the kingly, and where this admission is not made in so many words it is most often implied.

I believe that the common man is as apt a subject for tragedy in its highest sense as kings were. On the face of it this ought to be obvious in the light of modern psychiatry, which bases its analysis upon classic formulations, such as the Oedipus and Orestes complexes, for instance, which were enacted by royal beings, but which apply to everyone in similar emotional situations.

More simply, when the question of tragedy in art is not at issue, we never hesitate to attribute to the well-placed and the exalted the very same mental processes as the lowly. And finally, if the exaltation of tragic action were truly a property of the high-bred character alone, it is inconceivable that the mass of mankind should cherish tragedy above all other forms, let alone be capable of understanding it.

As a general rule, to which there may be exceptions unknown to me, I think the tragic feeling is evoked in us when we are in the presence of a character who is ready to lay down his life, if need be, to secure one thing — his sense of personal dignity. From Orestes to Hamlet, Medea to Macbeth, the underlying struggle is that of the individual attempting to gain his "rightful" position in his society.

Sometimes he is one who has been displaced from it, sometimes one who seeks to attain it for the first time, but the fateful wound from which the inevitable events spiral is the wound of indignity, and its dominant force is indignation. Tragedy, then, is the consequence of a man's total compulsion to evaluate himself justly.

In the sense of having been initiated by the hero himself, the tale always reveals what has been called his "tragic flaw," a failing that is not peculiar to grand or elevated characters. Nor is it necessarily a weakness. The flaw, or crack in the character, is really nothing — and need be nothing — but his inherent unwillingness to remain passive in the face of what he conceives to be a challenge to his dignity, his image of his rightful status. Only the passive, only those who accept their lot without active retaliation, are "flawless." Most of us are in that category.

But there are among us today, as there always have been, those who act against the scheme of things that degrades them, and in the process of action everything we have accepted out of fear or insensitivity or ignorance is shaken before us and examined, and from this total onslaught by an individual against the seemingly stable cosmos surrounding us — from this total examination of the "unchangeable" environment — comes the terror and the fear that is classically associated with tragedy.

More important, from this total questioning of what has previously been unquestioned, we learn. And such a process is not beyond the common man. In revolutions around the world, these past thirty years, he has demonstrated again and again this inner dynamic of all tragedy.

Insistence upon the rank of the tragic hero, or the so-called nobility of his character, is really but a clinging to the outward forms of tragedy. If rank or nobility of character was indispensable, then it would follow that the problems of those with rank were the particular problems of tragedy. But surely the right of one monarch to capture the domain from another no longer raises our passions, nor are our concepts of justice what they were to the mind of an Elizabethan king.

The quality in such plays that does shake us, however, derives from the underlying fear of being displaced, the disaster inherent in being torn away from our chosen image of what and who we are in this world. Among us today this fear is as strong, and perhaps stronger, than it ever was. In fact, it is the common man who knows this fear best.

Now, if it is true that tragedy is the consequence of a man's total compulsion to evaluate himself justly, his destruction in the attempt posits a wrong or an evil in his environment. And this is precisely the morality of tragedy and its lesson. The discovery of the moral law, which is what the enlightenment of tragedy consists of, is not the discovery of some abstract or metaphysical quantity.

The tragic right is a condition of life, a condition in which the human personality is able to flower and realize itself. The wrong is the condition which suppresses man, perverts the flowing out of his love and creative instinct. Tragedy enlightens — and it must, in that it points the heroic finger at the enemy of man's freedom. The thrust for freedom is the quality in tragedy which exalts. The revolutionary questioning of the stable environment is what terrifies. In no way is the common man debarred from such thoughts or such actions.

Seen in this light, our lack of tragedy may be partially accounted for by the turn which modern literature has taken toward the purely psychiatric view of life, or the purely sociological. If all our miseries, our indignities, are born and bred within our minds, then all action, let alone the heroic action, is obviously impossible.

And if society alone is responsible for the cramping of our lives, then the protagonist must needs be so pure and faultless as to force us to deny his validity as a character. From neither of these views can tragedy derive, simply because neither represents a balanced concept of life. Above all else, tragedy requires the finest appreciation by the writer of cause and effect.

No tragedy can therefore come about when its author fears to question absolutely everything, when he regards any institution, habit, or custom as being either everlasting, immutable, or inevitable. In the tragic view the need of man to wholly realize himself is the only fixed star, and whatever it is that hedges his nature and lowers it is ripe for attack and examination. Which is not to say that tragedy must preach revolution.

The Greeks could probe the very heavenly origin of their ways and return to confirm the rightness of laws. And Job could face God in anger, demanding his right, and end in submission. But for a moment everything is in suspension, nothing is accepted, and in this stretching and tearing apart of the cosmos, in the very action of so doing, the character gains "size," the tragic stature which is spuriously attached to the royal or the highborn in our minds. The commonest of men may take on that stature to the extent of his willingness to throw all he has into the contest, the battle to secure his rightful place in his world.

There is a misconception of tragedy with which I have been struck in review after review, and in many conversations with writers and readers alike. It is the idea that tragedy is of necessity allied to pessimism. Even the dictionary says nothing more about the word than that it means a story with a sad or unhappy ending. This impression is so firmly fixed that I almost hesitate to claim that in truth tragedy implies more optimism in its author than does comedy, and that its final result ought to be the reinforcement of the onlooker's brightest opinions of the human animal.

For, if it is true to say that in essence the tragic hero is intent upon claiming his whole due as a personality, and if this struggle must be total and without reservation, then it automatically demonstrates the indestructible will of man to achieve his humanity.

The possibility of victory must be there in tragedy. Where pathos rules, where pathos is finally derived, a character has fought a battle he could not possibly have won. The pathetic is achieved when the protagonist is, by virtue of his witlessness, his insensitivity, or the very air he gives off, incapable of grappling with a much superior force.

Pathos truly is the mode for the pessimist. But tragedy requires a nicer balance between what is possible and what is impossible. And it is curious, although edifying, that the plays we revere, century after century, are the tragedies. In them, and in them alone, lies the belief — optimistic, if you will — in the perfectibility of man.

It is time, I think, that we who are without kings, took up this bright thread of our history and followed it to the only place it can possibly lead in our time — the heart and spirit of the average man.

Michiko Kakutani (b. 1955)
A Salesman Who Transcends Time   *1999*

Brian Dennehy revived Death of a Salesman *fifty years after its premiere and discovered that the audiences were as deeply moved in 1999 as they were in 1949. Michiko Kakutani perceives the center of interest in the play shifting in this new production to emphasize the relationship of a father with his sons. Kakutani notes that despite the play's flaws, its larger issues of love between father and son and longings for immortality have taken on even more significance.*

A half century after its premiere, *Death of a Salesman* has become an American classic — a perennial produced around the world, from Baltimore to Beijing, and routinely taught in high school English classes and mounted in community theaters. The play has become an institution, part of the accepted theater canon, and today even boasts its own Web site (www.deathofasalesman.com), where, in an ironic twist on its central theme, you will be able to purchase souvenirs.

With the opening on Wednesday of the Goodman Theater's new production of *Salesman* at the Eugene O'Neill Theatre on Broadway — fifty years to the day from the play's 1949 world premiere — it is clear that many of the debates that attended the original opening have long since become obsolete. We no longer question whether a play about a little man (a "low-man," as opposed to a king or powerful ruler) can be called a tragedy, just as we no longer question the ethnicity of the play's hero, the Jewishness or non-Jewishness of his locution.

At the same time, however, other debates persist. While *Salesman* opened to — and has continued to enjoy — enormous popular success, both the play and its author have maintained a less than stellar reputation among many highbrow critics. *Salesman* has been debunked as a didactic commentary on the bankruptcy of the American dream of success, while Mr. Miller has been dismissed as an epigone of Ibsenism, a preachy, pompous, and, yes, portentous writer who belongs, like Clifford Odets and Lillian Hellman, to a middlebrow, premodernist past. In retrospect, it is an overly simplistic judgment — especially when it comes to *Salesman,* Mr. Miller's most famous, most enduring, and in many ways most anomalous play.

Oddly enough, Mr. Miller's own ponderous pronouncements have tended to reinforce the perception of his work as an outmoded form of social realism. In one 1950 essay, he argued that *Death of a Salesman* — which chronicles the last day in the life of a salesman named Willy Loman, who has lost his job and, he fears, the love of his son Biff — is "the tragedy of a man who did believe that he alone was not meeting the qualifications laid down for mankind by those clean-shaven frontiersmen who inhabit the peaks of broadcasting and advertising offices."

Willy the failed salesman and willful suicide, Mr. Miller suggested in his own autobiography, represents the fate of a true believer in America's false dream of success: "This pseudo life that thought to touch the clouds by standing on top of a refrigerator, waving a paid-up mortgage at the moon, victorious at last." His singleminded pursuit of success has blinded him to the love of his own family, robbed him of his sense of self, and left him to subsist on a diet of illusions.

In contrast to Eugene O'Neill, who declared that he was "interested only in the relation of man and God," Mr. Miller has implied that the tragedy in his own work springs from the relation between man and the conditions that suppress him and pervert "the flowing out of his love and creative instinct." The playwright's own unhappy experiences during the Depression and the 1950s, when he was convicted of contempt of Congress for refusing to name names before the House Un-American Activities Committee, persuaded him, he has said, that politics "determines the exteriors of your personality," and he remained convinced, he once stated, that all serious plays ultimately address a single question: "How may a man make of the outside world a home?"

Truly great work, he declared in a 1958 interview, is "that work which will show at one and the same time the power and force of the human will working with and against the force of society upon it."

Yet in Robert Falls's darkly hued new staging from Chicago, *Death of a Salesman* seems less a social drama about what Harold Clurman called "the breakdown of the whole concept of salesmanship inherent in our society" than a fierce portrait of a father and son, caught in a fatal embrace of love and resentment and guilt. And Brian Dennehy's Willy Loman seems less a man, in Mr. Miller's words, who "embodies in himself some of the most terrible conflicts running through the streets of America today" than a perpetual adolescent caught in the dizzying gap between reality and his own expectations. This Willy Loman, like Dustin Hoffman's in 1984 on Broadway, may not be a tragic figure — to the last moment, self-awareness continues to elude him — but like Kierkegaard's "unhappiest man," he is a touching one, subsisting on past memory and future hope. His dilemmas are more psychological than sociological, more existential than environmental.

The play's structure, too, seems a far cry from the rough-hewn carpentry often associated with Mr. Miller's work. There is a dreamlike quality to *Salesman,* an expressionistic invocation of shifting moods and time frames that helps conceal the creaky stage machinery apparent in so many other Miller plays from *All My Sons* (1947) to *Broken Glass* (1994).

Certainly *Salesman,* too, has its problems: a paint-by-numbers Freudianism, a conveniently withheld secret that overshadows the second act, and supporting characters who are little more than cardboard cutouts. As written, Willy's long-suffering wife, Linda, is basically a doormat — a passive accomplice in her husband's denial, what we would today call an enabler. And Willy's successful brother, Ben — who walked into the jungle at seventeen, and walked out at twenty-one a rich man with diamonds in his pockets — remains a transparent symbol of rough and ready capitalism, a Horatio Alger joke.

These flaws, however, are subsumed by the play's visceral and deeply affecting portrait of father and son: Willy, intent for years on passing on to his son his own tarnished dreams; and Biff, finally shorn of those illusions, intent on making his father face the hard facts of his existence. The play limns Willy's fears of losing Biff's love and his own longings for immortality — his desire not just to be liked, but to be well liked — and it immerses the audience in Willy's conflicted, contradictory state of mind. In fact, Mr. Miller once noted that his original title for *Salesman* was "The Inside of His Head."

The play was constructed on the premise that Willy, in his growing panic and confusion, sees time not as a continuum but as a simultaneity of moments past and present. In the play's confessional structure, current anxieties fade into remembered guilts, and dreams and regrets blur and overlap — a structure not dissimilar to the narrative strategy adopted by Mr. Miller in his own 1987 autobiography, *Timebends.* The play, Mr. Miller wrote in that book, was meant to "cut through time like a knife through a layer cake or a road through a mountain revealing its geologic layers."

In later works like *After the Fall* (1964) and *The Price* (1968), Mr. Miller would again try to focus on his characters' inner lives, but never again with such urgency and skill as in *Salesman*. His other better-known plays would remain rooted in more topical concerns and feature characters who are more clearly symbols than flesh-and-blood human beings. *All My Sons* (1947) depicts a businessman — read greedy capitalist — covering up his role in the manufacture of defective parts that doomed twenty-one Air Force planes during World War II. *The Crucible* (1953) uses the Salem witch hunts of the late 1600s as a metaphor for the Communist witch hunts of the 1950s. *A View from the Bridge* (1955) examines the costs of McCarthy-era betrayal through its portrait of a longshoreman who rats on two illegal immigrants. *The American Clock* (1980), inspired by Studs Terkel's *Hard Times*, attempts to provide a panoramic portrait of the Depression. And *The Ride Down Mount Morgan* (1991) casts a cold eye on the rampant selfishness of the Reagan era. All too often in these works, Mr. Miller's efforts to "prove the theme" result in sanctimonious speechifying, message-driven melodramatics and two-dimensional characters who come across as illustrations of one or more social ills.

In recent years, the most successful productions of these works have played down the political, polemic aspects of the texts, to reveal their psychological subtext, the bedrock emotions of sexual passion and familial love, betrayal and guilt that lurk beneath the sociology. Last year, the Roundabout Theater Company's highly acclaimed production of *A View from the Bridge* shrugged off the play's McCarthy-era echoes to focus on the hero's secret obsession with his wife's teenage niece and the psychosexual drives that lead him to commit a shocking act of betrayal. Nicholas Hytner's dazzling 1996 movie version of *The Crucible* similarly stripped away that play's McCarthy-era moorings: by firmly grounding the story in the particulars of seventeenth-century Salem, the film uncovered the story's primal drama, its fascination with the consequences of lying and deception and sexual repression.

The success of such productions underscores the current renaissance that Mr. Miller has been enjoying — not just in England, where his work has found a ready audience among theatergoers reared, since the heyday of anti-Thatcherism, on politically committed playwriting, but also here in the States, where the Signature Theater Company recently completed a yearlong retrospective of his plays in New York.

What accounts for Mr. Miller's continuing appeal? Perhaps some of the very aspects of his work that seem so old-fashioned — his moral seriousness and fondness for mythic intonations (inspired by his favorite works, the Bible and Greek tragedies) — are refreshing anomalies in this age of relentless irony and cynicism.

In a day when the avant-garde has insistently purveyed a vision of a fractured, fragmented world, Mr. Miller's assumption that "life has meaning" appeals to our vestigial belief (or hope) that the dots *can* be connected, that a pattern *can* be found in the carpet. And in a day when the arts are increasingly becoming a form of entertainment, when the commercial theater has increasingly given us slice-of-life dramas, brittle satires, and glitzy theme-park musicals, his efforts, however ham-handed, to address the large questions of right and wrong suggest that the theater still matters, that it can still provide a venue for intellectual debate.

Indeed, his plays attest to his own belief that works of art can "change the consciousness of people and their estimate of who they are and what they stand for."

Brenda Murphy (b. 1950)
DEATH OF A SALESMAN: THE DESIGN PROCESS   *1995*

Brenda Murphy examines the process by which the design for the set began to take shape. The distinguished set designer Jo Mielziner was presented with a highly novel concept in the action of the play, and his solution has spawned many imitations. His solution was to concentrate on the salesman's house, presenting it in a dramatic cross-section.

While the casting proceeded, the biggest unanswered question about the script, the design concept, was being addressed. On September 24, Jo Mielziner received a call from Kermit Bloomgarden asking whether he could come straight over and talk to him about "something very interesting." After learning that Kazan hoped to begin rehearsal of the play in two weeks, Mielziner left the meeting with the *Salesman* script to read. During that afternoon and evening, Mielziner began to understand the difficulty of the job he was faced with: "It was not only that there were so many different scenic locations but that the action demanded instantaneous time changes from the present to the past and back again. Actors playing a contemporaneous scene suddenly went back fifteen years in exactly the same setting — the Salesman's house."

As he looked for a design solution to the many changes in scene and time demanded by the script, Mielziner hit on the concept that was to become the key to the production:

> The most important visual symbol in the play — the real background of the story — was the Salesman's house. Therefore, why should that house not be the main set, with all the other scenes — the corner of a graveyard, a hotel room in Boston, the corner of a business office, a lawyer's consultation room, and so on — played on a forestage? If I designed these little scenes in segments and fragments, with easily moved props and fluid lighting effects, I might be able, without ever lowering the curtain, to achieve the easy flow that the author dearly wanted.

The problem was that developing this design scheme would require more than the two weeks that remained before rehearsals were scheduled to begin. Miller would have to make substantial revisions in the script to change blackouts at the end of each scene to instantaneous scene changes, and Kazan would have to reconceive the whole production. What's more, if the play's opening was delayed, the pre-Broadway theatre bookings and the New York opening would have to be canceled and rescheduled. Mielziner asked for a meeting with Bloomgarden, Miller, and Kazan for that afternoon.

A long discussion followed Mielziner's presentation of his ideas on September 25. In the end, the aesthetic advantages of the single-set design scheme built around the material symbol of the house were determined to far outweigh the difficulties:

> To Arthur Miller, a design scheme allowing him as author to blend scenes at will without even the shortest break for physical changes was a significant decision. To Kazan, with his strong sense of movement, stimulated by his already proven genius as a film director, the scheme would permit use of some of the best cinematic techniques.

In the end, it was decided to postpone the start of rehearsals until the end of December and the New York opening until 10 February, allowing enough time for

Miller's revisions and Kazan's rethinking of the direction as well as for the development of the design. Kazan was to consider Mielziner's "concept of a house standing like a specter behind all the scenes of the play, always present as it might be always present in Willy's mind, wherever his travels take him, even behind the office he visits, even behind the Boston hotel room and above his grave plot," the "single most critically important contribution and the key to the way [he] directed the play." Eloquently described by Miller on the opening pages of the published play, it has served the same purpose for millions of readers who have never seen a production of *Death of a Salesman.*

Mielziner set to work immediately to realize his ideas scenically. He made a number of rough sketches over the next few days, along with a ground plan of the stage, and worked on a breakdown of the script, which gave a page reference for each key scene and a notation of the needed lighting, scenery, props, and elevations. On September 28, he flew to Boston, where Kazan was rehearsing the pre-Broadway previews for *Love Life,* and went over his ideas at a breakfast meeting, leaving his director "after a brief hour with about ninety-percent approval." During the next week, Mielziner made about twenty black-and-white sketches representing the scenic design of the whole production and set his assistants to work on translating his sketches into an accurate floor plan and building a scale model of the set. When he met on October 4 with Bloomgarden, Kazan, and Miller, the designer had "a group of ground plans and sketches that . . . solved the major puzzles and were at least indications of the right style" for the production.

Mielziner's set was the culmination of a style of design he had been developing in his productions of Tennessee Williams's plays. In *The Glass Menagerie, A Streetcar Named Desire,* and *Summer and Smoke,* he had combined translucent scenery, expert lighting effects, and sets that went, as the eye traveled upward, from drab realistic interiors to light, delicate frameworks that were mere suggestions of buildings. The result was a style that was beginning to be recognized as his signature and that signaled to audiences a subjective realism in the play that juxtaposed ostensibly objective reality with a character's fantasy as easily as the scenery juxtaposed realism with symbolic abstraction.

Mielziner's *Salesman* set developed from his careful reading of the dialogue and the brief descriptive note that Miller had given him. Miller's note read: "[The house] had once been surrounded by open country, but it was now hemmed in with apartment houses. Trees that used to shade the house against the open sky and hot summer sun now were for the most part dead or dying." In the dialogue, Mielziner had underlined the lines "Boxed us in here"; "Bricks and windows, windows and bricks"; and "beautiful elm trees out there." From these visual suggestions, he conceived a tri-level set for the house, with Willy and Linda's bedroom on the lower floor, at stage right, one step up from the kitchen, which, at center stage, formed the largest playing space. On the far left of the kitchen were steps leading up to the boys' bedroom, above and behind the kitchen. All three rooms could be seen simultaneously. Although there was no wall between the parents' bedroom and the kitchen, the rear wall of each room was hung with translucent backdrops stenciled with "wallpaper" patterns. The lower floor also contained a bed, several chairs, a table, a telephone stand, and a refrigerator. Mielziner's original sketches also showed the hot water heater in the kitchen, but it was eventually hidden behind a curtain because it had become intrusive.

Rising above the lower floor there were only the skeletal rafters representing the gabled roof line and a platform holding the boys' beds and a chest. Behind the house was a translucent backdrop with two trees, the outline of the roof, and the boys' dormer window painted on the facing side. On the back were painted the outlines of bare, rectangular buildings with rectangular windows. When lit from the front with a soft golden light, the backdrop showed the Lomans' house as it used to be, a small but brave structure rising with hope and light to the sky. When lit from the back with a threatening reddish glow, it showed the house in the play's present, its fragile skeleton threatened by the huge, glowering apartment buildings.

On October 4, the main design problems that remained were lack of room for movement on the stage and transitions in time. The lack of room was solved only on December 8, when Kazan convinced Bloomgarden to take eleven seats out of the first row (at a cost of $323.40 per week in receipts) in order to extend the forestage. One of the biggest transition problems was getting Biff and Hap from the scene in their bedroom dressed in pajamas to the immediately following scene in which they appear to Willy in the kitchen as they were in the past, dressed in football uniforms. To manage this without closing the curtain or blacking the stage out, Mielziner had elevators built into the boys' beds so the actors could be moved unnoticed from one scene to the other. In order to give them time for a costume change, Miller expanded Willy's monologue about polishing the car by several minutes.

As the autumn progressed, Mielziner confronted the questions of lighting and props. Arthur Miller remembers that Mielziner and lighting expert Eddie Kook together "once worked an entire afternoon lighting a chair." The chair was the one that Willy addresses as if it were his old boss Frank Wagner in Howard's office, reminding him of the promises he had made. As Willy speaks to it, "the chair must become alive, quite as though his old boss were in it as he addresses him." Miller marveled that, "rather than being lit, the chair subtly seemed to begin emanating light" in the production. To achieve this effect, all of the surrounding lights on the stage had to be dimmed imperceptibly, rather than bringing up the spotlight on the chair, which would produce an effect too obvious to the audience.

This effect, and the attention that Mielziner and Kook gave to it, provide a good illustration of the designer's attitude toward the lighting of *Death of a Salesman*. Always a designer who made full artistic use of the scenic expression of lighting, Mielziner had decided that lighting was the key to *Salesman*'s time shifts. He decided to signify the passage of time on stage by creating two environments for the house through the lighting. When the set was first revealed, the audience saw the muslin backdrop lit from behind to show the oppressive apartment houses towering over the fragile house. When the scene shifted to the past, the lights behind the backdrop were dimmed out, and the buildings faded out as soft amber light and images of green leaves were projected onto the backdrop from a number of projection units that were carefully placed backstage, throughout the auditorium, and on the balcony. Mielziner felt that this visual symbol of the spring leaves, "liberating the house from the oppression of the surrounding structures and giving the stage a feeling of the free outdoors," was an "integral part of the Salesman's life story and had to be an easily recognized symbol of the springtime of that life." Combined with the music provided by Alex North, this lighting change would bring the audience effectively into the past along with Willy as each daydream began.

The painstaking work involved in the lighting of the original *Death of a Salesman* is almost inconceivable in these days of computerized stage lighting. Each of the 141 lighting units on the eight pipe battens above the stage had to be carefully hung and angled, and each light cue individually adjusted and marked up so that it could be re-created manually during each performance. It took three days for the hanging and angling, and another twenty-hour-day to set the approximately 150 light cues when the production was moved into the theater. In addition to the projection units, Mielziner had also persuaded Bloomgarden of the necessity of two special follow-spots, which could be manipulated to produce particular effects. Because their fine adjustments needed careful attention, each of these lights required a trained technician for its operation throughout the performance, a significant expense. Mielziner used the projection units to address spatial as well as temporal difficulties. He and Kazan had agreed early on that the most minimal of visual suggestions would suffice in creating the sets for the scenes to be played on the forestage — the Boston hotel room, the restaurant, and Howard's and Charley's offices. He created the hotel room by projecting a seedy wallpaper design from the theater balcony onto a section of the trellis at the side of the house. With the rest of the stage dimmed, this was enough to evoke the environment where Biff is disillusioned when he surprises Willy with The Woman.

This suggestiveness went along with the minimalism that Mielziner and Kazan had agreed on in the props. A few objects, such as the beds, the chairs, and the table, were required by the action on the stage. Most of the props, such as the refrigerator, the hot water heater, Willy's sample cases, the silk stockings, the rubber tubing, the hoe and seeds, and the gold fountain pen, served a necessary function but also took on a symbolic resonance. Kazan and Mielziner also agreed on several props which served primarily as material signifiers for the audience of some theme in the play, such as Biff's football trophy on a shelf over Willy's bed and a deflated football in the boys' room. The fact that props were kept to a minimum, with no attempt at realism, helped to foreground the few objects that did appear, encouraging the audience to perceive their symbolic significance.

Throughout the production process, the impulse was toward greater abstraction and symbolism, less realism. A good example is the Requiem scene, in which the original plan was to have a gravestone rise from a trick trapdoor in the forestage. Mielziner persuaded Kazan to use a simple bouquet of flowers to signify the grave instead, using a projection of autumn leaves to complete the symbolic statement of death in opposition to the life and hope suggested by the spring leaves in the daydream scenes. What made the production's style unique, however, was the juxtaposition of the abstract and poetic with the real and prosaic. The props that were introduced into the abstract suggestiveness of the set were authentic, battered objects that the Lomans might very well have owned. The kitchen table was covered with a cloth painted with an "oilcloth" design. The refrigerator was a careful reproduction of a typical model from the 1929 Sears Roebuck catalogue. It was vital to the production's aesthetic that these objects signify a specific time, place, class, and way of life in juxtaposition with the insistent visions in Willy's mind, and that they resonate with symbolic significance in the context of the play as a total experience.

Samuel Beckett

Samuel Beckett (1906–1989) was born in Dublin to an upper-middle-class Protestant family. After a privileged education at the Portora Royal School, he went to Trinity College, Dublin, where he studied French and Italian. He was an exceptionally good student and, in 1928 after graduation, taught English at the École Normale Supérieure in Paris.

Beckett early on straddled two literary cultures: Irish and Anglo-Irish. Most of the literary energy in Ireland in the 1920s and 1930s was split between the essentially conservative Anglo-Irish Protestants, such as William Butler Yeats and Lady Gregory, and the more avant-garde Catholics, such as James Joyce, with whom Beckett formed an enduring personal and literary friendship in Paris. Although much younger than Joyce, Beckett developed a close artistic sympathy with him. Beckett's first published work (1929) was one of the earliest critical essays on Joyce's most radical literary composition, the not-yet-published *Finnegans Wake*.

When he was first in France, Beckett's reading of French philosophers, especially Descartes, exerted a strong influence on his work. Beckett's earliest writings appeared in Eugene Jolas's avant-garde literary journal *transition,* which put him in the center of Parisian literary activity in the late 1920s. After 1930, his series of short stories published under the title *More Pricks Than Kicks* (1934) established him as an important writer. After settling in Paris in 1937, Beckett wrote the novel *Murphy* (1938), on a recognizably Irish theme of economic impoverishment, alienation, and inward meditation and spiritual complexity.

When World War II began in 1939, Beckett took up the cause of the French Resistance. After his activity caught the eye of the Gestapo, for two years he lay low in unoccupied France by working as a farmhand and also writing another novel, *Watt* (written in 1944 but published in 1953). After the war he took up residence again in Paris and began writing most of his work in French. His greatest novels were written in the five years after the war, and they are often referred to as his trilogy: *Molloy, Malone Dies,* and *The Unnamable.* These three novels are about men who have become disaffected with society and who have strange and compelling urgencies to be alone and to follow exacting and repetitive patterns of behavior. In a sense, they are archetypes of the kinds of protagonists that Beckett created in most of his work.

Beckett's first published play, *Waiting for Godot* (1952), was produced in Paris (1953), in London (1955), and in Miami (1956). From the first, its repetitive, whimsical, and sometimes nonsensical style established the play as a major postwar statement. In a barren setting, Vladimir and Estragon, two tramps who echo the comic vision of Charlie Chaplin, wait for Godot to come. They amuse themselves by doing vaudeville routines, but their loneliness and isolation are painfully apparent to the audience. Godot has promised to come, and as they wait, Vladimir and Estragon speculate on whether or not Godot will come.

The comic moments in the play, along with the enigma of Vladimir and Estragon's fruitless waiting, combined to capture the imagination of audiences and the press. They saw the play as a modern statement about the condition of humankind, although there was never any agreement on just what the statement was. Godot sends a boy to say that he will indeed come, but when the play ends, he has not arrived. The implication seems to be that he will never arrive. Most audiences saw Godot as a metaphor for God. Despite the critics' constant inquiries, Beckett never confirmed the view that Godot was God and kept Godot's identity open-ended.

The play itself was open-ended, as Beckett had hoped, and therefore could be interpreted in many ways. One was to see the play as a commentary on the futility of religion; another was to suggest that the play underscored the loneliness of humankind in an empty universe; yet a third implied that it was up to individuals, represented by the hapless Vladimir and Estragon, to shape the significance of their own lives, and their waiting represented that effort.

Many of the themes in *Waiting for Godot* are apparent in Beckett's later plays. The radio play *All That Fall* (1957) was followed by the very successful *Krapp's Last Tape* (1958). Also in 1957, *Endgame,* a play on the themes of the end of the world, was produced, followed in 1961 by *Happy Days.* Beckett experimented with minimalist approaches to drama, exemplified in *Act without Words I* and *Act without Words II,* both mime plays. Other plays experiment with minimalism in setting, props, and — in the mime plays — even words.

Beckett's plays reveal the deep influence of French postwar philosophers, such as Albert Camus and Jean-Paul Sartre, both existentialists. Their philosophy declares that people are not essentially good, bad, kind, or anything else but are what they make of themselves. Beckett's adaptation of existentialism sometimes borders on pessimism because his vision seems to negate many of the consolations of religious and secular philosophy. His style is antirealist, but the search for beliefs that are reasonable and plausible in a fundamentally absurd world, and the plight of individuals who must make their own meanings is central to most of his work.

Beckett's view of the world is not cheerful. But his vision is consistent, honest, and sympathetic to the persistence of his characters, who endure even in the face of apparent defeat. The significance of Beckett's achievements was recognized in 1969 when he was awarded the Nobel Prize for literature.

ENDGAME

The title of this play derives from the game of chess, which has three different strategies to mark the opening, the middle game, and the endgame. The strategy of the endgame is based on the protection of the king and depends on very few pieces being left on the board — the king and sometimes a rook and a pawn. The moves in the endgame are always restricted, often repetitive, and limited by the fact that the king, if it can move at all, cannot move more than one space at a time. In Beckett's *Endgame* Hamm is the king and the central character in the drama; however, he cannot move or even stand by himself. His parents, Nagg and Nell, stuck immobile in ashcans, resemble rooks, who protect the king by controlling spaces forward, backward, and side to side but have little reason themselves to move. Clov, who most closely resembles a pawn, cannot sit down and is the only character in the play who can move. He is also the only means by which Hamm can move. Beckett has described Hamm as "a king in the chess game lost from the start."

World politics in 1957, when the play was written, were dominated by the threat of nuclear war and the possible extinction of the human race. The circumstances of *Endgame* suggest that the play portrays a version of the end of the world. Clov's description of the world outside the window implies desolation and grief. At one point as Clov looks out the window, Hamm tells him to use his "glass," his telescope, and to report back to him. Clov says all is "Zero," and Hamm asks, "All is what?" "In a word?" says Clov. "Is that what you want to know?" And in a moment he reports his one word: "Corpsed."

Unlike Hamm and Clov, who seem rooted only in the present, Nagg and Nell have a past. They remember rowing on Lake Como on an April afternoon after they were engaged. It was a moment in which Nell remembers she was happy. But they also remember the day they crashed on their tandem bicycle and lost their legs. Nagg recalls it was in the Ardennes forest on the road to Sedan. Beckett is alluding to the French forest at Ardennes, site of the most appalling and murderous fighting in World War I, and to the French town of Sedan, the place where Napoleon III surrendered to the Germans in a battle during the Franco-Prussian war.

Ruby Cohn and other critics have noted that the characters' names echo associations with hammers and nails: Nell is a homophone for *nail*; Hamm is a shortened form of *hammer*; Nagg is from the German *nagel,* for *nail*; and Clov is from the French *clou,* also for *nail.* The characters thus seem to be equipped to rebuild their society, but they refuse to do so. By using English, French, and German versions of *nail*, Beckett involves the principal combatants of modern European wars.

Some critics have observed that Beckett's drama often focuses on elements of play. Plays are play; life is play. In chess an endgame is played. In Beckett's drama characters' actions seem to be performed as if they were part of a game. Clov exercises great precision, for example, in placing Hamm exactly where he wishes to be. When Clov has done the rounds and moved Hamm's chair back to its position, Hamm says, "I feel a little too far to the left. Now I feel a little too far to the right." In a game of chess it would matter if he were too far to the left or right. In an endgame the king might move to one square and then move back again and again. The movements of Hamm and Clov are repetitious and meaningful only within the "system" of the drama and its space, just as all moves in an endgame are meaningful only within the "system" of the game of chess. Clov continually enters and exits with his ladder and looks out the windows, only to find that nothing has changed. He picks up the lids of Nagg and Nell's ashcans and replaces them several times. He pushes Hamm's chair along the wall, making minute adjustments, for no apparent reason, when he returns the chair to the center of the room. His moves are part of an endgame, and *Endgame* is a play.

Beckett critic Ted Estess has said that "in Beckett's literature 'existence is play,'" implying a form of absurdity of the kind Martin Esslin talks about in his discussion of theater of the absurd. (See the commentary on p. 740.) The absurd implies a nonmeaning, such as the meaningless movements of Hamm by Clov. The meaning of those moves is in the action itself, which strikes those in the audience as absurd. Beckett's use of the absurd helps him move away from the well-made play with its clearly marked beginning, middle, and end. In the process he pokes fun at that concept by embedding the end in the beginning of *Endgame*. As the lights go up and Clov removes the sheets from the ashcans and from Hamm in his chair, he intones to the audience: "Finished." The audience is meant to feel this irony. It is the endgame when the action — and the play — are expected to stop, but as Hamm says: "The end is in the beginning and yet you go on."

Endgame in Performance

Endgame was first produced in 1957. The year before, *Waiting for Godot* had been produced in Miami and New York, establishing Beckett as an important figure in modern absurdist drama. *Endgame,* his next major play, satisfied the critics but baffled the public. The first London production was in French, at the Royal Court Theatre, which was known for producing experimental plays. Roger Blin directed. The first Paris production began three weeks later, April 26, 1957, in the Studio des Champs-Élysées. The New York production, directed by Beckett's friend and interpreter Alan Schneider, opened on January 28, 1958. A number of important revivals of the play have attested to its continuing power. In 1964 *Endgame* was produced at The Royal Shakespeare Company's Aldwych Theatre. Beckett himself directed the play at the Schiller Theatre in Berlin in September 1967. In the 1970 Open Theater Production at the Loeb Theater in Cambridge, Massachusetts, Joseph Chaikin as Hamm created a richly nuanced performance:

> Joseph Chaikin as the chairbound Hamm throws an eerie light over the play. . . . He is sensual, domineering, crafty, and infinitely tender; he prattles and tells macabre stories and his dominion over the dwindling lives of his family is like the last hoarse gasp of King Lear over the strangled body of Cordelia.   (Samuel Hirsch, *Herald Traveler,* Boston, May 13, 1970)

Andre Gregory directed the play at the Manhattan Project in 1973. Clive Barnes noted the unusual staging of this production:

> Mr. Gregory has built himself a strange, bullring of a theater. It is hexagonal, and the audience is on two levels. The audience is placed in cubicles — each holding four chairs. Each cubicle is insulated from the stage and from the world by chicken wire. (*New York Times,* February 9, 1973)

The Royal Court played it in English during its Beckett Festival in 1976. Beckett directed the play again in London at the Young Vic in January 1980 and then in Chicago's Goodman Theater with the San Quentin Workshop in September 1980. In 1984 JoAnn Akalaitis staged a controversial *Endgame* at the American Repertory Theatre in Cambridge, Massachusetts. She set the play in a burned-out subway tunnel and commissioned an eerie musical score by minimalist composer Philip Glass. Grove Press, Beckett's representative, complained that the production disregarded "the playwright's sparse, rigorous scenic demands" and added uncalled-for music. As one critic noted, Akalaitis had "simply, vividly visualized and auralized *Endgame*'s nuclear-holocaustal implications, at the expense of its chess and theatrical imagery" (Carolyn Clay, *Boston Phoenix*, December 18, 1984). The production was allowed to continue after the American Repertory Theatre agreed to include a program insert, signed by Beckett, "decrying the interpretation."

Samuel Beckett (1906–1989)

ENDGAME
A PLAY IN ONE ACT

1957

The Characters

NAGG   HAMM
NELL   CLOV

(*Bare interior.*)
  (*Gray light.*)
  (*Left and right back, high up, two small windows, curtains drawn.*)
  (*Front right, a door. Hanging near door, its face to wall, a picture.*)
  (*Front left, touching each other, covered with an old sheet, two ashbins.°*)
  (*Center, in an armchair on castors, covered with an old sheet, Hamm.*)
  (*Motionless by the door, his eyes fixed on Hamm, Clov. Very red face.*)
  (*Brief tableau.*)

(*Clov goes and stands under window left. Stiff, staggering walk. He looks up at window left. He turns and looks at window right. He goes and stands under window right. He looks up at window right. He turns and looks at window left. He goes out, comes back immediately with a small stepladder, carries it over and sets it down under window left, gets up on it, draws back curtain. He gets down, takes six steps (for example) towards window right, goes back for ladder, carries it over and sets it down under window right, gets up on it, draws back curtain. He gets down, takes three steps towards window left, goes back for ladder, carries it over and sets it down under window left, gets up on it, looks out of window. Brief laugh. He gets down, takes one step towards window right, goes back for ladder, carries it over and sets it down under window right, gets*

ashbins: trash cans.

up on it, looks out of window. Brief laugh. He gets down, goes with ladder towards ashbins, halts, turns, carries back ladder and sets it down under window right, goes to ashbins, removes sheet covering them, folds it over his arm. He raises one lid, stoops and looks into bin. Brief laugh. He closes lid. Same with other bin. He goes to Hamm, removes sheet covering him, folds it over his arm. In a dressing gown, a stiff toque° on his head, a large bloodstained handkerchief over his face, a whistle hanging from his neck, a rug over his knees, thick socks on his feet, Hamm seems to be asleep. Clov looks over him. Brief laugh. He goes to door, halts, turns towards auditorium.)

CLOV (*fixed gaze, tonelessly*): Finished, it's finished, nearly finished, it must be nearly finished.

(*Pause.*)

  Grain upon grain, one by one, and one day, suddenly, there's a heap, a little heap, the impossible heap.

(*Pause.*)

  I can't be punished anymore.

(*Pause.*)

  I'll go now to my kitchen, ten feet by ten feet by ten feet, and wait for him to whistle me.

(*Pause.*)

  Nice dimensions, nice proportions, I'll lean on the table, and look at the wall, and wait for him to whistle me.

(*He remains a moment motionless, then goes out. He comes back immediately, goes to window right, takes up*

toque: A small, brimless, close-fitting hat.

the ladder and carries it out. Pause. Hamm stirs. He yawns under the handkerchief. He removes the handkerchief from his face. Very red face. Black glasses.)

HAMM: Me — (*he yawns*) — to play.

(*He holds the handkerchief spread out before him.*)

Old stancher!°

(*He takes off his glasses, wipes his eyes, his face, the glasses, puts them on again, folds the handkerchief and puts it back neatly in the breast pocket of his dressing gown. He clears his throat, joins the tips of his fingers.*)

Can there be misery — (*he yawns*) — loftier than mine? No doubt. Formerly. But now?

(*Pause.*)

My father?

(*Pause.*)

My mother?

(*Pause.*)

My . . . dog?

(*Pause.*)

Oh I am willing to believe they suffer as much as such creatures can suffer. But does that mean their sufferings equal mine? No doubt.

(*Pause.*)

No, all is a — (*he yawns*) — bsolute, (*proudly*) the bigger a man is the fuller he is.

(*Pause. Gloomily.*)

And the emptier.

(*He sniffs.*)

Clov!

(*Pause.*)

No, alone.

(*Pause.*)

What dreams! Those forests!

(*Pause.*)

Enough, it's time it ended, in the shelter too.

(*Pause.*)

And yet I hesitate, I hesitate to . . . to end. Yes there it is, it's time it ended and yet I hesitate to — (*he yawns*) — to end.

(*Yawns.*)

God, I'm tired, I'd be better off in bed.

(*He whistles. Enter Clov immediately. He halts beside the chair.*)

You pollute the air!

---

stancher: Item that stops, or stanches, the flow of blood.

(*Pause.*)

Get me ready, I'm going to bed.

CLOV: I've just got you up.

HAMM: And what of it?

CLOV: I can't be getting you up and putting you to bed every five minutes, I have things to do.

(*Pause.*)

HAMM: Did you ever see my eyes?

CLOV: No.

HAMM: Did you never have the curiosity, while I was sleeping, to take off my glasses and look at my eyes?

CLOV: Pulling back the lids?

(*Pause.*)

No.

HAMM: One of these days I'll show them to you.

(*Pause.*)

It seems they've gone all white.

(*Pause.*)

What time is it?

CLOV: The same as usual.

HAMM (*gesture towards window right*): Have you looked?

CLOV: Yes.

HAMM: Well?

CLOV: Zero.

HAMM: It'd need to rain.

CLOV: It won't rain.

(*Pause.*)

HAMM: Apart from that, how do you feel?

CLOV: I don't complain.

HAMM: You feel normal?

CLOV (*irritably*): I tell you I don't complain.

HAMM: I feel a little queer.

(*Pause.*)

Clov!

CLOV: Yes.

HAMM: Have you not had enough?

CLOV: Yes!

(*Pause.*)

Of what?

HAMM: Of this . . . this . . . thing.

CLOV: I always had.

(*Pause.*)

Not you?

HAMM (*gloomily*): Then there's no reason for it to change.

CLOV: It may end.

(*Pause.*)

All life long the same questions, the same answers.

HAMM: Get me ready.

(*Clov does not move.*)

Go and get the sheet.

(*Clov does not move.*)

Clov!

CLOV: Yes.

HAMM: I'll give you nothing more to eat.

CLOV: Then we'll die.

HAMM: I'll give you just enough to keep you from dying. You'll be hungry all the time.

CLOV: Then we won't die.

(*Pause.*)

I'll go and get the sheet.

(*He goes towards the door.*)

HAMM: No!

(*Clov halts.*)

I'll give you one biscuit per day.

(*Pause.*)

One and a half.

(*Pause.*)

Why do you stay with me?

CLOV: Why do you keep me?

HAMM: There's no one else.

CLOV: There's nowhere else.

(*Pause.*)

HAMM: You're leaving me all the same.

CLOV: I'm trying.

HAMM: You don't love me.

CLOV: No.

HAMM: You loved me once.

CLOV: Once!

HAMM: I've made you suffer too much.

(*Pause.*)

Haven't I?

CLOV: It's not that.

HAMM (*shocked*): I haven't made you suffer too much?

CLOV: Yes!

HAMM (*relieved*): Ah you gave me a fright!

(*Pause. Coldly.*)

Forgive me.

(*Pause. Louder.*)

I said, Forgive me.

CLOV: I heard you.

(*Pause.*)

Have you bled?

HAMM: Less.

(*Pause.*)

Is it not time for my painkiller?

CLOV: No.

(*Pause.*)

HAMM: How are your eyes?

CLOV: Bad.

HAMM: How are your legs?

CLOV: Bad.

HAMM: But you can move.

CLOV: Yes.

HAMM (*violently*): Then move!

(*Clov goes to back wall, leans against it with his forehead and hands.*)

Where are you?

CLOV: Here.

HAMM: Come back!

(*Clov returns to his place beside the chair.*)

Where are you?

CLOV: Here.

HAMM: Why don't you kill me?

CLOV: I don't know the combination of the cupboard.

(*Pause.*)

HAMM: Go and get two bicycle wheels.

CLOV: There are no more bicycle wheels.

HAMM: What have you done with your bicycle?

CLOV: I never had a bicycle.

HAMM: The thing is impossible.

CLOV: When there were still bicycles I wept to have one. I crawled at your feet. You told me to go to hell. Now there are none.

HAMM: And your rounds? When you inspected my paupers. Always on foot?

CLOV: Sometimes on horse.

(*The lid of one of the bins lifts and the hands of Nagg appear, gripping the rim. Then his head emerges. Nightcap. Very white face. Nagg yawns, then listens.*)

I'll leave you, I have things to do.

HAMM: In your kitchen?

CLOV: Yes.

HAMM: Outside of here it's death.

(*Pause.*)

All right, be off.

(*Exit Clov. Pause.*)

We're getting on.

NAGG: Me pap!

HAMM: Accursed progenitor!

NAGG: Me pap!

HAMM: The old folks at home! No decency left! Guzzle, guzzle, that's all they think of.

(*He whistles. Enter Clov. He halts beside the chair.*)

Well! I thought you were leaving me.

CLOV: Oh not just yet, not just yet.

NAGG: Me pap!
HAMM: Give him his pap.
CLOV: There's no more pap.
HAMM (*to Nagg*): Do you hear that? There's no more pap. You'll never get any more pap.
NAGG: I want me pap!
HAMM: Give him a biscuit.

(*Exit Clov.*)

Accursed fornicator! How are your stumps?
NAGG: Never mind me stumps.

(*Enter Clov with biscuit.*)

CLOV: I'm back again, with the biscuit.

(*He gives biscuit to Nagg who fingers it, sniffs it.*)

NAGG (*plaintively*): What is it?
CLOV: Spratt's medium.
NAGG (*as before*): It's hard! I can't!
HAMM: Bottle him!

(*Clov pushes Nagg back into the bin, closes the lid.*)

CLOV (*returning to his place beside the chair*): If age but knew!
HAMM: Sit on him!
CLOV: I can't sit.
HAMM: True. And I can't stand.
CLOV: So it is.
HAMM: Every man his speciality.

(*Pause.*)

No phone calls?

(*Pause.*)

Don't we laugh?
CLOV (*after reflection*): I don't feel like it.
HAMM (*after reflection*): Nor I.

(*Pause.*)

Clov!
CLOV: Yes.
HAMM: Nature has forgotten us.
CLOV: There's no more nature.
HAMM: No more nature! You exaggerate.
CLOV: In the vicinity.
HAMM: But we breathe, we change! We lose our hair, our teeth! Our bloom! Our ideals!
CLOV: Then she hasn't forgotten us.
HAMM: But you say there is none.
CLOV (*sadly*): No one that ever lived ever thought so crooked as we.
HAMM: We do what we can.
CLOV: We shouldn't.

(*Pause.*)

HAMM: You're a bit of all right, aren't you?
CLOV: A smithereen.

(*Pause.*)

HAMM: This is slow work.

(*Pause.*)

Is it not time for my painkiller?
CLOV: No.

(*Pause.*)

I'll leave you, I have things to do.
HAMM: In your kitchen?
CLOV: Yes.
HAMM: What, I'd like to know.
CLOV: I look at the wall.
HAMM: The wall! And what do you see on your wall? Mene, mene?° Naked bodies?
CLOV: I see my light dying.
HAMM: Your light dying! Listen to that! Well, it can die just as well here, *your* light. Take a look at me and then come back and tell me what you think of *your* light.

(*Pause.*)

CLOV: You shouldn't speak to me like that.

(*Pause.*)

HAMM (*coldly*): Forgive me.

(*Pause. Louder.*)

I said, Forgive me.
CLOV: I heard you.

(*The lid of Nagg's bin lifts. His hands appear, gripping the rim. Then his head emerges. In his mouth the biscuit. He listens.*)

HAMM: Did your seeds come up?
CLOV: No.
HAMM: Did you scratch round them to see if they had sprouted?
CLOV: They haven't sprouted.
HAMM: Perhaps it's still too early.
CLOV: If they were going to sprout they would have sprouted.

(*Violently.*)

They'll never sprout!

(*Pause. Nagg takes biscuit in his hand.*)

HAMM: This is not much fun.

(*Pause.*)

But that's always the way at the end of the day, isn't it, Clov?
CLOV: Always.
HAMM: It's the end of the day like any other day, isn't it, Clov?
CLOV: Looks like it.

Mene, mene: The handwriting on the wall in Daniel 5:25 indicating the end of King Belshazzar's reign: "MENE, MENE, TEKEL, and PARSIN."

(*Pause.*)

HAMM (*anguished*): What's happening, what's happening?

CLOV: Something is taking its course.

(*Pause.*)

HAMM: All right, be off.

(*He leans back in his chair, remains motionless. Clov does not move, heaves a great groaning sigh. Hamm sits up.*)

I thought I told you to be off.

CLOV: I'm trying.

(*He goes to door, halts.*)

Ever since I was whelped.

(*Exit Clov.*)

HAMM: We're getting on.

(*He leans back in his chair, remains motionless. Nagg knocks on the lid of the other bin. Pause. He knocks harder. The lid lifts and the hands of Nell appear, gripping the rim. Then her head emerges. Lace cap. Very white face.*)

NELL: What is it, my pet?

(*Pause.*)

Time for love?

NAGG: Were you asleep?

NELL: Oh no!

NAGG: Kiss me.

NELL: We can't.

NAGG: Try.

(*Their heads strain towards each other, fail to meet, fall apart again.*)

NELL: Why this farce, day after day?

(*Pause.*)

NAGG: I've lost me tooth.

NELL: When?

NAGG: I had it yesterday.

NELL (*elegiac*): Ah yesterday!

(*They turn painfully towards each other.*)

NAGG: Can you see me?

NELL: Hardly. And you?

NAGG: What?

NELL: Can you see me?

NAGG: Hardly.

NELL: So much the better, so much the better.

NAGG: Don't say that.

(*Pause.*)

Our sight has failed.

NELL: Yes.

(*Pause. They turn away from each other.*)

NAGG: Can you hear me?

NELL: Yes. And you?

NAGG: Yes.

(*Pause.*)

Our hearing hasn't failed.

NELL: Our what?

NAGG: Our hearing.

NELL: No.

(*Pause.*)

Have you anything else to say to me?

NAGG: Do you remember —

NELL: No.

NAGG: When we crashed on our tandem and lost our shanks.

(*They laugh heartily.*)

NELL: It was in the Ardennes.

(*They laugh less heartily.*)

NAGG: On the road to Sedan.

(*They laugh still less heartily.*)

Are you cold?

NELL: Yes, perished. And you?

NAGG:

(*Pause.*)

I'm freezing.

(*Pause.*)

Do you want to go in?

NELL: Yes.

NAGG: Then go in.

(*Nell does not move.*)

Why don't you go in?

NELL: I don't know.

(*Pause.*)

NAGG: Has he changed your sawdust?

NELL: It isn't sawdust.

(*Pause. Wearily.*)

Can you not be a little accurate, Nagg?

NAGG: Your sand then. It's not important.

NELL: It is important.

(*Pause.*)

NAGG: It was sawdust once.

NELL: Once!

NAGG: And now it's sand.

(*Pause.*)

From the shore.

(*Pause. Impatiently.*)

Now it's sand he fetches from the shore.

NELL: Now it's sand.
NAGG: Has he changed yours?
NELL: No.
NAGG: Nor mine.

(*Pause.*)

I won't have it!

(*Pause. Holding up the biscuit.*)

Do you want a bit?
NELL: No.

(*Pause.*)

Of what?
NAGG: Biscuit. I've kept you half.

(*He looks at the biscuit. Proudly.*)

Three quarters. For you. Here.

(*He proffers the biscuit.*)

No?

(*Pause.*)

Do you not feel well?
HAMM (*wearily*): Quiet, quiet, you're keeping me awake.

(*Pause.*)

Talk softer.

(*Pause.*)

If I could sleep I might make love. I'd go into the woods. My eyes would see . . . the sky, the earth. I'd run, run, they wouldn't catch me.

(*Pause.*)

Nature!

(*Pause.*)

There's something dripping in my head.

(*Pause.*)

A heart, a heart in my head.

(*Pause.*)

NAGG (*soft*): Do you hear him? A heart in his head!

(*He chuckles cautiously.*)

NELL: One mustn't laugh at those things, Nagg. Why must you always laugh at them?
NAGG: Not so loud!
NELL (*without lowering her voice*): Nothing is funnier than unhappiness, I grant you that. But —
NAGG (*shocked*): Oh!
NELL: Yes, yes, it's the most comical thing in the world. And we laugh, we laugh, with a will, in the beginning. But it's always the same thing. Yes, it's like the funny story we have heard too often, we still find it funny, but we don't laugh anymore.

(*Pause.*)

Have you anything else to say to me?

NAGG: No.
NELL: Are you quite sure?

(*Pause.*)

Then I'll leave you.
NAGG: Do you not want your biscuit?

(*Pause.*)

I'll keep it for you.

(*Pause.*)

I thought you were going to leave me.
NELL: I am going to leave you.
NAGG: Could you give me a scratch before you go?
NELL: No.

(*Pause.*)

Where?
NAGG: In the back.
NELL: No.

(*Pause.*)

Rub yourself against the rim.
NAGG: It's lower down. In the hollow.
NELL: What hollow?
NAGG: The hollow!

(*Pause.*)

Could you not?

(*Pause.*)

Yesterday you scratched me there.
NELL (*elegiac*): Ah yesterday!
NAGG: Could you not?

(*Pause.*)

Would you like me to scratch you?

(*Pause.*)

Are you crying again?
NELL: I was trying.

(*Pause.*)

HAMM: Perhaps it's a little vein.

(*Pause.*)

NAGG: What was that he said?
NELL: Perhaps it's a little vein.
NAGG: What does that mean?

(*Pause.*)

That means nothing.

(*Pause.*)

Will I tell you the story of the tailor?
NELL: No.

(*Pause.*)

What for?

NAGG: To cheer you up.
NELL: It's not funny.
NAGG: It always made you laugh.

(*Pause.*)

The first time I thought you'd die.
NELL: It was on Lake Como.

(*Pause.*)

One April afternoon.

(*Pause.*)

Can you believe it?
NAGG: What?
NELL: That we once went out rowing on Lake Como.

(*Pause.*)

One April afternoon.
NAGG: We had got engaged the day before.
NELL: Engaged!
NAGG: You were in such fits that we capsized. By rights we should have been drowned.
NELL: It was because I felt happy.
NAGG (*indignant*): It was not, it was not, it was my story and nothing else. Happy! Don't you laugh at it still? Every time I tell it. Happy!
NELL: It was deep, deep. And you could see down to the bottom. So white. So clean.
NAGG: Let me tell it again.

(*Raconteur's voice.*)

An Englishman, needing a pair of striped trousers in a hurry for the New Year festivities, goes to his tailor who takes his measurements.

(*Tailor's voice.*)

"That's the lot, come back in four days, I'll have it ready." Good. Four days later.

(*Tailor's voice.*)

"So sorry, come back in a week, I've made a mess of the seat." Good, that's all right, a neat seat can be very ticklish. A week later.

(*Tailor's voice.*)

"Frightfully sorry, come back in ten days, I've made a hash of the crotch." Good, can't be helped, a snug crotch is always a teaser. Ten days later.

(*Tailor's voice.*)

"Dreadfully sorry, come back in a fortnight, I've made a balls of the fly." Good, at a pinch, a smart fly is a stiff proposition.

(*Pause. Normal voice.*)

I never told it worse.

(*Pause. Gloomy.*)

I tell this story worse and worse.

(*Pause. Raconteur's voice.*)

Well, to make it short, the bluebells are blowing and he ballockses the buttonholes.

(*Customer's voice.*)

"God damn you to hell, Sir, no, it's indecent, there are limits! In six days, do you hear me, six days, God made the world. Yes Sir, no less Sir, the WORLD! And you are not bloody well capable of making me a pair of trousers in three months!"

(*Tailor's voice, scandalized.*)

"But my dear Sir, my dear Sir, look — (*disdainful gesture, disgustedly*) — at the world — (*pause*) and look — (*loving gesture, proudly*) — at my TROUSERS!"

(*Pause. He looks at Nell who has remained impassive, her eyes unseeing, breaks into a high forced laugh, cuts it short, pokes his head towards Nell, launches his laugh again.*)

HAMM: Silence!

(*Nagg starts, cuts short his laugh.*)

NELL: You could see down to the bottom.
HAMM (*exasperated*): Have you not finished? Will you never finish?

(*With sudden fury.*)

Will this never finish?

(*Nagg disappears into his bin, closes the lid behind him. Nell does not move. Frenziedly.*)

My kingdom for a nightman!

(*He whistles. Enter Clov.*)

Clear away this muck! Chuck it in the sea!

(*Clov goes to bins, halts.*)

NELL: So white.
HAMM: What? What's she blathering about?

(*Clov stoops, takes Nell's hand, feels her pulse.*)

NELL (*to Clov*): Desert!

(*Clov lets go her hand, pushes her back in the bin, closes the lid.*)

CLOV (*returning to his place beside the chair*): She has no pulse.
HAMM: What was she driveling about?
CLOV: She told me to go away, into the desert.
HAMM: Damn busybody! Is that all?
CLOV: No.
HAMM: What else?
CLOV: I didn't understand.
HAMM: Have you bottled her?
CLOV: Yes.
HAMM: Are they both bottled?

CLOV: Yes.
HAMM: Screw down the lids.

(*Clov goes towards door.*)

Time enough.

(*Clov halts.*)

My anger subsides, I'd like to pee.
CLOV (*with alacrity*): I'll go and get the catheter.

(*He goes towards door.*)

HAMM: Time enough.

(*Clov halts.*)

Give me my painkiller.
CLOV: It's too soon.

(*Pause.*)

It's too soon on top of your tonic, it wouldn't act.
HAMM: In the morning they brace you up and in the evening they calm you down. Unless it's the other way round.

(*Pause.*)

That old doctor, he's dead naturally?
CLOV: He wasn't old.
HAMM: But he's dead?
CLOV: Naturally.

(*Pause.*)

You ask *me* that?

(*Pause.*)

HAMM: Take me for a little turn.

(*Clov goes behind the chair and pushes it forward.*)

Not too fast!

(*Clov pushes chair.*)

Right round the world!

(*Clov pushes chair.*)

Hug the walls, then back to the center again.

(*Clov pushes chair.*)

I was right in the center, wasn't I?
CLOV (*pushing*): Yes.
HAMM: We'd need a proper wheelchair. With big wheels. Bicycle wheels!

(*Pause.*)

Are you hugging?
CLOV (*pushing*): Yes.
HAMM (*groping for wall*): It's a lie! Why do you lie to me?
CLOV (*bearing closer to wall*): There! There!
HAMM: Stop!

(*Clov stops chair close to back wall. Hamm lays his hand against wall.*)

Old wall!

(*Pause.*)

Beyond is the . . . other hell.

(*Pause. Violently.*)

Closer! Closer! Up against!
CLOV: Take away your hand.

(*Hamm withdraws his hand. Clov rams chair against wall.*)

There!

(*Hamm leans towards wall, applies his ear to it.*)

HAMM: Do you hear?

(*He strikes the wall with his knuckles.*)

Do you hear? Hollow bricks!

(*He strikes again.*)

All that's hollow!

(*Pause. He straightens up. Violently.*)

That's enough. Back!
CLOV: We haven't done the round.
HAMM: Back to my place!

(*Clov pushes chair back to center.*)

Is that my place?
CLOV: Yes, that's your place.
HAMM: Am I right in the center?
CLOV: I'll measure it.
HAMM: More or less! More or less!
CLOV (*moving chair slightly*): There!
HAMM: I'm more or less in the center?
CLOV: I'd say so.
HAMM: You'd say so! Put me right in the center!
CLOV: I'll go and get the tape.
HAMM: Roughly! Roughly!

(*Clov moves chair slightly.*)

Bang in the center!
CLOV: There!

(*Pause.*)

HAMM: I feel a little too far to the left.

(*Clov moves chair slightly.*)

Now I feel a little too far to the right.

(*Clov moves chair slightly.*)

I feel a little too far forward.

(*Clov moves chair slightly.*)

Now I feel a little too far back.

(*Clov moves chair slightly.*)

Don't stay there (*i.e., behind the chair*), you give me the shivers.

(*Clov returns to his place beside the chair.*)

CLOV: If I could kill him I'd die happy.

(*Pause.*)

HAMM: What's the weather like?
CLOV: As usual.
HAMM: Look at the earth.
CLOV: I've looked.
HAMM: With the glass?
CLOV: No need of the glass.
HAMM: Look at it with the glass.
CLOV: I'll go and get the glass.

(*Exit Clov.*)

HAMM: No need of the glass!

(*Enter Clov with telescope.*)

CLOV: I'm back again, with the glass.

(*He goes to window right, looks up at it.*)

I need the steps.
HAMM: Why? Have you shrunk?

(*Exit Clov with telescope.*)

I don't like that, I don't like that.

(*Enter Clov with ladder, but without telescope.*)

CLOV: I'm back again, with the steps.

(*He sets down ladder under window right, gets up on it, realizes he has not the telescope, gets down.*)

I need the glass.

(*He goes towards door.*)

HAMM (*violently*): But you have the glass!
CLOV (*halting, violently*): No, I haven't the glass!

(*Exit Clov.*)

HAMM: This is deadly.

(*Enter Clov with telescope. He goes towards ladder.*)

CLOV: Things are livening up.

(*He gets up on ladder, raises the telescope, lets it fall.*)

I did it on purpose.

(*He gets down, picks up the telescope, turns it on auditorium.*)

I see . . . a multitude . . . in transports . . . of joy.

(*Pause.*)

That's what I call a magnifier.

(*He lowers the telescope, turns towards Hamm.*)

Well? Don't we laugh?
HAMM (*after reflection*): I don't.
CLOV (*after reflection*): Nor I.

(*He gets up on ladder, turns the telescope on the without.*)

Let's see.

(*He looks, moving the telescope.*)

Zero . . . (*he looks*) . . . zero . . . (*he looks*) . . . and zero.
HAMM: Nothing stirs. All is —
CLOV: Zer —
HAMM (*violently*): Wait till you're spoken to!

(*Normal voice.*)

All is . . . all is . . . all is what?

(*Violently.*)

All is what?
CLOV: What all is? In a word? Is that what you want to know? Just a moment.

(*He turns the telescope on the without, looks, lowers the telescope, turns towards Hamm.*)

Corpsed.

(*Pause.*)

Well? Content?
HAMM: Look at the sea.
CLOV: It's the same.
HAMM: Look at the ocean!

(*Clov gets down, takes a few steps towards window left, goes back for ladder, carries it over and sets it down under window left, gets up on it, turns the telescope on the without, looks at length. He starts, lowers the telescope, examines it, turns it again on the without.*)

CLOV: Never seen anything like that!
HAMM (*anxious*): What? A sail? A fin? Smoke?
CLOV (*looking*): The light is sunk.
HAMM (*relieved*): Pah! We all knew that.
CLOV (*looking*): There was a bit left.
HAMM: The base.
CLOV (*looking*): Yes.
HAMM: And now?
CLOV (*looking*): All gone.
HAMM: No gulls?
CLOV (*looking*): Gulls!
HAMM: And the horizon? Nothing on the horizon?
CLOV (*lowering the telescope, turning towards Hamm, exasperated*): What in God's name could there be on the horizon?

(*Pause.*)

HAMM: The waves, how are the waves?
CLOV: The waves?

(*He turns the telescope on the waves.*)

Lead.
HAMM: And the sun?
CLOV (*looking*): Zero.
HAMM: But it should be sinking. Look again.
CLOV (*looking*): Damn the sun.
HAMM: Is it night already then?
CLOV (*looking*): No.

HAMM: Then what is it?
CLOV (*looking*): Gray.

(*Lowering the telescope, turning towards Hamm, louder.*)

.   Gray!

(*Pause. Still louder.*)

    GRRAY!

(*Pause. He gets down, approaches Hamm from behind, whispers in his ear.*)

HAMM (*starting*): Gray! Did I hear you say gray?
CLOV: Light black. From pole to pole.
HAMM: You exaggerate.

(*Pause.*)

    Don't stay there, you give me the shivers.

(*Clov returns to his place beside the chair.*)

CLOV: Why this farce, day after day?
HAMM: Routine. One never knows.

(*Pause.*)

    Last night I saw inside my breast. There was a big sore.
CLOV: Pah! You saw your heart.
HAMM: No, it was living.

(*Pause. Anguished.*)

    Clov!
CLOV: Yes.
HAMM: What's happening?
CLOV: Something is taking its course.

(*Pause.*)

HAMM: Clov!
CLOV (*impatiently*): What is it?
HAMM: We're not beginning to . . . to . . . mean something?

RIGHT: Hamm (Alvin Epstein), seated, and Clov (Peter Evans) in the 1984 Harold Clurman Theatre production of *Endgame,* directed by Alvin Epstein. FAR RIGHT: Nell (Alice Drummond), Nagg (James Greene), Hamm, and Clov.

CLOV: Mean something! You and I, mean something!

(*Brief laugh.*)

Ah that's a good one!

HAMM: I wonder.

(*Pause.*)

Imagine if a rational being came back to earth, wouldn't he be liable to get ideas into his head if he observed us long enough.

(*Voice of rational being.*)

Ah, good, now I see what it is, yes, now I understand what they're at!

(*Clov starts, drops the telescope and begins to scratch his belly with both hands. Normal voice.*)

And without going so far as that, we ourselves . . . (*with emotion*) . . . we ourselves . . . at certain moments . . .

(*Vehemently.*)

To think perhaps it won't all have been for nothing!

CLOV (*anguished, scratching himself*): I have a flea!

HAMM: A flea! Are there still fleas?

CLOV: On me there's one.

(*Scratching.*)

Unless it's a crablouse.

HAMM (*very perturbed*): But humanity might start from there all over again! Catch him, for the love of God!

CLOV: I'll go and get the powder.

(*Exit Clov.*)

HAMM: A flea! This is awful! What a day!

(*Enter Clov with a sprinkling tin.*)

CLOV: I'm back again, with the insecticide.

HAMM: Let him have it!

(*Clov loosens the top of his trousers, pulls it forward and shakes powder into the aperture. He stoops, looks, waits, starts, frenziedly shakes more powder, stoops, looks, waits.*)

CLOV: The bastard!

HAMM: Did you get him?

CLOV: Looks like it.

(*He drops the tin and adjusts his trousers.*)

Unless he's laying doggo.°

HAMM: Laying! Lying you mean. Unless he's *lying* doggo.

CLOV: Ah? One says lying? One doesn't say laying?

HAMM: Use your head, can't you. If he was laying we'd be bitched.

CLOV: Ah.

(*Pause.*)

What about that pee?

HAMM: I'm having it.

CLOV: Ah that's the spirit, that's the spirit!

(*Pause.*)

HAMM (*with ardor*): Let's go from here, the two of us! South! You can make a raft and the currents will carry us away, far away, to other . . . mammals!

CLOV: God forbid!

HAMM: Alone, I'll embark alone! Get working on that raft immediately. Tomorrow I'll be gone forever.

CLOV (*hastening towards door*): I'll start straight away.

HAMM: Wait!

(*Clov halts.*)

Will there be sharks, do you think?

CLOV: Sharks? I don't know. If there are there will be.

(*He goes towards door.*)

HAMM: Wait!

(*Clov halts.*)

Is it not yet time for my painkiller?

CLOV (*violently*): No!

(*He goes towards door.*)

HAMM: Wait!

(*Clov halts.*)

How are your eyes?

CLOV: Bad.

HAMM: But you can see.

CLOV: All I want.

HAMM: How are your legs

CLOV: Bad.

HAMM: But you can walk.

CLOV: I come . . . and go.

HAMM: In my house.

(*Pause. With prophetic relish.*)

One day you'll be blind, like me. You'll be sitting there, a speck in the void, in the dark, forever, like me.

(*Pause.*)

One day you'll say to yourself, I'm tired, I'll sit down,

doggo: In hiding.

and you'll go and sit down. Then you'll say, I'm hungry, I'll get up and get something to eat. But you won't get up. You'll say, I shouldn't have sat down, but since I have I'll sit on a little longer, then I'll get up and get something to eat. But you won't get up and you won't get anything to eat.

(*Pause.*)

You'll look at the wall a while, then you'll say, I'll close my eyes, perhaps have a little sleep, after that I'll feel better, and you'll close them. And when you open them again there'll be no wall anymore.

(*Pause.*)

Infinite emptiness will be all around you, all the resurrected dead of all the ages wouldn't fill it, and there you'll be like a little bit of grit in the middle of the steppe.

(*Pause.*)

Yes, one day you'll know what it is, you'll be like me, except that you won't have anyone with you, because you won't have had pity on anyone and because there won't be anyone left to have pity on.

(*Pause.*)

CLOV: It's not certain.

(*Pause.*)

And there's one thing you forget.

HAMM: Ah?

CLOV: I can't sit down.

HAMM (*impatiently*): Well you'll lie down then, what the hell! Or you'll come to a standstill, simply stop and stand still, the way you are now. One day you'll say, I'm tired, I'll stop. What does the attitude matter?

(*Pause.*)

CLOV: So you all want me to leave you.

HAMM: Naturally.

CLOV: Then I'll leave you.

HAMM: You can't leave us.

CLOV: Then I won't leave you.

(*Pause.*)

HAMM: Why don't you finish us?

(*Pause.*)

I'll tell you the combination of the cupboard if you promise to finish me.

CLOV: I couldn't finish you.

HAMM: Then you won't finish me.

(*Pause.*)

CLOV: I'll leave you, I have things to do.

HAMM: Do you remember when you came here?

CLOV: No. Too small, you told me.

HAMM: Do you remember your father?

CLOV (*wearily*): Same answer.

(*Pause.*)

You've asked me these questions millions of times.
HAMM: I love the old questions.

(*With fervor.*)

Ah the old questions, the old answers, there's nothing like them!

(*Pause.*)

It was I was a father to you.
CLOV: Yes.

(*He looks at Hamm fixedly.*)

You were that to me.
HAMM: My house a home for you.
CLOV: Yes.

(*He looks about him.*)

This was that for me.
HAMM (*proudly*): But for me (*gesture towards himself*), no father. But for Hamm (*gesture towards surroundings*), no home.

(*Pause.*)

CLOV: I'll leave you.
HAMM: Did you ever think of one thmg?
CLOV: Never.
HAMM: That here we're down in a hole.

(*Pause.*)

But beyond the hills? Eh? Perhaps it's still green. Eh?

(*Pause.*)

Flora! Pomona!

(*Ecstatically.*)

Ceres!°

(*Pause.*)

Perhaps you won't need to go very far.
CLOV: I can't go very far.

(*Pause.*)

I'll leave you.
HAMM: Is my dog ready?
CLOV: He lacks a leg.
HAMM: Is he silky?
CLOV: He's a kind of Pomeranian.
HAMM: Go and get him.
CLOV: He lacks a leg.
HAMM: Go and get him!

(*Exit Clov.*)

We're getting on.

Flora . . . Ceres: Three Roman goddesses — Flora, of flowers; Pomona, of fruit; Ceres, of agriculture.

(*Enter Clov holding by one of its three legs a black toy dog.*)

CLOV: Your dogs are here.

(*He hands the dog to Hamm who feels it, fondles it.*)

HAMM: He's white, isn't he?
CLOV: Nearly.
HAMM: What do you mean, nearly? Is he white or isn't he?
CLOV: He isn't.

(*Pause.*)

HAMM: You've forgotten the sex.
CLOV (*vexed*): But he isn't finished. The sex goes on at the end.

(*Pause.*)

HAMM: You haven't put on his ribbon.
CLOV (*angrily*): But he isn't finished, I tell you! First you finish your dog and then you put on his ribbon!

(*Pause.*)

HAMM: Can he stand?
CLOV: I don't know.
HAMM: Try.

(*He hands the dog to Clov who places it on the ground.*)

Well?
CLOV: Wait!

(*He squats down and tries to get the dog to stand on its three legs, fails, lets it go. The dog falls on its side.*)

HAMM (*impatiently*): Well?
CLOV: He's standing.
HAMM (*groping for the dog*): Where? Where is he?

(*Clov holds up the dog in a standing position.*)

CLOV: There.

(*He takes Hamm's hand and guides it towards the dog's head.*)

HAMM (*his hand on the dog's head*): Is he gazing at me?
CLOV: Yes.
HAMM (*proudly*): As if he were asking me to take him for a walk?
CLOV: If you like.
HAMM (*as before*): Or as if he were begging me for a bone.

(*He withdraws his hand.*)

Leave him like that, standing there imploring me.

(*Clov straightens up. The dog falls on its side.*)

CLOV: I'll leave you.
HAMM: Have you had your visions?
CLOV: Less.
HAMM: Is Mother Pegg's light on?
CLOV: Light! How could anyone's light be on?
HAMM: Extinguished!

CLOV: Naturally it's extinguished. If it's not on it's extinguished.

HAMM: No, I mean Mother Pegg.

CLOV: But naturally she's extinguished!

(*Pause.*)

What's the matter with you today?

HAMM: I'm taking my course.

(*Pause.*)

Is she buried?

CLOV: Buried! Who would have buried her?

HAMM: You.

CLOV: Me! Haven't I enough to do without burying people?

HAMM: But you'll bury me.

CLOV: No I won't bury you.

(*Pause.*)

HAMM: She was bonny once, like a flower of the field.

(*With reminiscent leer.*)

And a great one for the men!

CLOV: We too were bonny — once. It's a rare thing not to have been bonny — once.

(*Pause.*)

HAMM: Go and get the gaff.

(*Clov goes to door, halts.*)

CLOV: Do this, do that, and I do it. I never refuse. Why?

HAMM: You're not able to.

CLOV: Soon I won't do it anymore.

HAMM: You won't be able to anymore.

(*Exit Clov.*)

Ah the creatures, the creatures, everything has to be explained to them.

(*Enter Clov with gaff.*)

CLOV: Here's your gaff. Stick it up.

(*He gives the gaff to Hamm who, wielding it like a punt-pole,° tries to move his chair.*)

HAMM: Did I move?

CLOV: No.

(*Hamm throws down the gaff.*)

HAMM: Go and get the oilcan.

CLOV: What for?

HAMM: To oil the casters.

CLOV: I oiled them yesterday.

HAMM: Yesterday! What does that mean? Yesterday!

CLOV (*violently*): That means that bloody awful day, long ago, before this bloody awful day. I use the

---

puntpole: A pole used to propel a punt, a flat-bottomed boat, through the water.

---

words you taught me. If they don't mean anything anymore, teach me others. Or let me be silent.

(*Pause.*)

HAMM: I once knew a madman who thought the end of the world had come. He was a painter — and engraver. I had a great fondness for him. I used to go and see him, in the asylum. I'd take him by the hand and drag him to the window. Look! There! All that rising corn! And there! Look! The sails of the herring fleet! All that loveliness!

(*Pause.*)

He'd snatch away his hand and go back into his corner. Appalled. All he had seen was ashes.

(*Pause.*)

He alone had been spared.

(*Pause.*)

Forgotten.

(*Pause.*)

It appears the case is . . . was not so . . . so unusual.

CLOV: A madman? When was that?

HAMM: Oh way back, way back, you weren't in the land of the living.

CLOV: God be with the days!

(*Pause. Hamm raises his toque.*)

HAMM: I had a great fondness for him.

(*Pause. He puts on his toque again.*)

He was a painter — and engraver.

CLOV: There are so many terrible things.

HAMM: No, no, there are not so many now.

(*Pause.*)

Clov!

CLOV: Yes.

HAMM: Do you not think this has gone on long enough?

CLOV: Yes!

(*Pause.*)

What?

HAMM: This . . . this . . . thing.

CLOV: I've always thought so.

(*Pause.*)

You not?

HAMM (*gloomily*): Then it's a day like any other day.

CLOV: As long as it lasts.

(*Pause.*)

All life long the same inanities.

HAMM: I can't leave you.

CLOV: I know. And you can't follow me.

(*Pause.*)

HAMM: If you leave me how shall I know?
CLOV (*briskly*): Well you simply whistle me and if I don't come running it means I've left you.

(*Pause.*)

HAMM: You won't come and kiss me good-bye?
CLOV: Oh I shouldn't think so.

(*Pause.*)

HAMM: But you might be merely dead in your kitchen.
CLOV: The result would be the same.
HAMM: Yes, but how would I know, if you were merely dead in your kitchen?
CLOV: Well . . . sooner or later I'd start to stink.
HAMM: You stink already. The whole place stinks of corpses.
CLOV: The whole universe.
HAMM (*angrily*): To hell with the universe.

(*Pause.*)

Think of something.
CLOV: What?
HAMM: An idea, have an idea.

(*Angrily.*)

A bright idea!
CLOV: Ah good.

(*He starts pacing to and fro, his eyes fixed on the ground, his hands behind his back. He halts.*)

The pains in my legs! It's unbelievable! Soon I won't be able to think anymore.
HAMM: You won't be able to leave me.

(*Clov resumes his pacing.*)

What are you doing?
CLOV: Having an idea.

(*He paces.*)

Ah!

(*He halts.*)

HAMM: What a brain!

(*Pause.*)

Well?
CLOV: Wait!

(*He meditates. Not very convinced.*)

Yes . . .

(*Pause. More convinced.*)

Yes!

(*He raises his head.*)

I have it! I set the alarm.

(*Pause.*)

HAMM: This is perhaps not one of my bright days, but frankly —

CLOV: You whistle me. I don't come. The alarm rings. I'm gone. It doesn't ring. I'm dead.

(*Pause.*)

HAMM: Is it working?

(*Pause. Impatiently.*)

The alarm, is it working?
CLOV: Why wouldn't it be working?
HAMM: Because it's worked too much.
CLOV: But it's hardly worked at all.
HAMM (*angrily*): Then because it's worked too little!
CLOV: I'll go and see.

(*Exit Clov. Brief ring of alarm off. Enter Clov with alarm clock. He holds it against Hamm's ear and releases alarm. They listen to it ringing to the end. Pause.*)

Fit to wake the dead! Did you hear it?
HAMM: Vaguely.
CLOV: The end is terrific!
HAMM: I prefer the middle.

(*Pause.*)

Is it not time for my painkiller?
CLOV: No!

(*He goes to door, turns.*)

I'll leave you.
HAMM: It's time for my story. Do you want to listen to my story?
CLOV: No.
HAMM: Ask my father if he wants to listen to my story.

(*Clov goes to bins, raises the lid of Nagg's, stoops, looks into it. Pause. He straightens up.*)

CLOV: He's asleep.
HAMM: Wake him.

(*Clov stoops, wakes Nagg with the alarm. Unintelligible words. Clov straightens up.*)

CLOV: He doesn't want to listen to your story.
HAMM: I'll give him a bonbon.

(*Clov stoops. As before.*)

CLOV: He wants a sugarplum.
HAMM: He'll get a sugarplum.

(*Clov stoops. As before.*)

CLOV: It's a deal.

(*He goes towards door. Nagg's hands appear, gripping the rim. Then the head emerges. Clov reaches door, turns.*)

Do you believe in the life to come?
HAMM: Mine was always that.

(*Exit Clov.*)

Got him that time!

NAGG: I'm listening.
HAMM: Scoundrel! Why did you engender me?
NAGG: I didn't know.
HAMM: What? What didn't you know?
NAGG: That it'd be you.

(*Pause.*)

You'll give me a sugarplum?
HAMM: After the audition.
NAGG: You swear?
HAMM: Yes.
NAGG: On what?
HAMM: My honor.

(*Pause. They laugh heartily.*)

NAGG: Two.
HAMM: One.
NAGG: One for me and one for —
HAMM: One! Silence!

(*Pause.*)

Where was I?

(*Pause. Gloomily.*)

It's finished, we're finished.

(*Pause.*)

Nearly finished.

(*Pause.*)

There'll be no more speech.

(*Pause.*)

Something dripping in my head, ever since the fontanelles.°

(*Stifled hilarity of Nagg.*)

Splash, splash, always on the same spot.

(*Pause.*)

Perhaps it's a little vein.

(*Pause.*)

A little artery.

(*Pause. More animated.*)

Enough of that, it's story time, where was I?

(*Pause. Narrative tone.*)

The man came crawling towards me, on his belly. Pale, wonderfully pale and thin, he seemed on the point of —

(*Pause. Normal tone.*)

No, I've done that bit.

(*Pause. Narrative tone.*)

since the fontanelles: Since soft membranes linked the incompletely developed skull bones in his infant head.

I calmly filled my pipe — the meerschaum, lit it with . . . let us say a vesta,° drew a few puffs. Aah!

(*Pause.*)

Well, what is it *you* want?

(*Pause.*)

It was an extraordinarily bitter day, I remember, zero by the thermometer. But considering it was Christmas Eve there was nothing . . . extraordinary about that. Seasonable weather, for once in a way.

(*Pause.*)

Well, what ill wind blows you my way? He raised his face to me, black with mingled dirt and tears.

(*Pause. Normal tone.*)

That should do it.

(*Narrative tone.*)

No no, don't look at me, don't look at me. He dropped his eyes and mumbled something, apologies I presume.

(*Pause.*)

I'm a busy man, you know, the final touches, before the festivities, you know what it is.

(*Pause. Forcibly.*)

Come on now, what is the object of this invasion?

(*Pause.*)

It was a glorious bright day, I remember, fifty by the heliometer,° but already the sun was sinking down into the . . . down among the dead.

(*Normal tone.*)

Nicely put, that.

(*Narrative tone.*)

Come on now, come on, present your petition and let me resume my labors.

(*Pause. Normal tone.*)

There's English for you. Ah well . . .

(*Narrative tone.*)

It was then he took the plunge. It's my little one, he said. Tsstss, a little one, that's bad. My little boy, he said, as if the sex mattered. Where did he come from? He named the hole. A good half-day, on horse. What are you insinuating? That the place is still inhabited? No, no, not a soul, except himself and the child — assuming he existed. Good. I inquired about the situation at Kov, beyond the gulf. Not a sinner. Good.

vesta: Wooden match.
heliometer: A telescope for measuring the apparent diameter of the sun.

And you expect me to believe you have left your little one back there, all alone, and alive into the bargain? Come now!

(*Pause.*)

It was a howling wild day, I remember, a hundred by the anemometer.° The wind was tearing up the dead pines and sweeping them . . . away.

(*Pause. Normal tone.*)

A bit feeble, that.

(*Narrative tone.*)

Come on, man, speak up, what is you want from me, I have to put up my holly.

(*Pause.*)

Well to make it short it finally transpired that what he wanted from me was . . . bread for his brat? Bread? But I have no bread, it doesn't agree with me. Good. Then perhaps a little corn?

(*Pause. Normal tone.*)

That should do it.

(*Narrative tone.*)

Corn, yes, I have corn, it's true, in my granaries. But use your head. I give you some corn, a pound, a pound and a half, you bring it back to your child and you make him — if he's still alive — a nice pot of porridge, (*Nagg reacts*) a nice pot and a half of porridge, full of nourishment. Good. The colors come back into his little cheeks — perhaps. And then?

(*Pause.*)

I lost patience.

(*Violently.*)

Use your head, can't you, use your head, you're on earth, there's no cure for that!

(*Pause.*)

It was an exceedingly dry day, I remember, zero by the hygrometer.° Ideal weather, for my lumbago.

(*Pause. Violently.*)

But what in God's name do you imagine? That the earth will awake in spring? That the rivers and seas will run with fish again? That there's manna in heaven still for imbeciles like you?

(*Pause.*)

Gradually I cooled down, sufficiently at least to ask him how long he had taken on the way. Three whole days. Good. In what condition he had left the child. Deep in sleep.

anemometer: An instrument for measuring wind speed.
hygrometer: Device for measuring humidity.

(*Forcibly.*)

But deep in what sleep, deep in what sleep already?

(*Pause.*)

Well to make it short I finally offered to take him into my service. He had touched a chord. And then I imagined already that I wasn't much longer for this world.

(*He laughs. Pause.*)

Well?

(*Pause.*)

Well? Here if you were careful you might die a nice natural death, in peace and comfort.

(*Pause.*)

Well?

(*Pause.*)

In the end he asked me would I consent to take in the child as well — if he were still alive.

(*Pause.*)

It was the moment I was waiting for.

(*Pause.*)

Would I consent to take in the child . . .

(*Pause.*)

I can see him still, down on his knees, his hands flat on the ground, glaring at me with his mad eyes, in defiance of my wishes.

(*Pause. Normal tone.*)

I'll soon have finished with this story.

(*Pause.*)

Unless I bring in other characters.

(*Pause.*)

But where would I find them?

(*Pause.*)

Where would I look for them?

(*Pause. He whistles. Enter Clov.*)

Let us pray to God.
NAGG: Me sugarplum!
CLOV: There's a rat in the kitchen!
HAMM: A rat! Are there still rats?
CLOV: In the kitchen there's one.
HAMM: And you haven't exterminated him?
CLOV: Half. You disturbed us.
HAMM: He can't get away?
CLOV: No.
HAMM: You'll finish him later. Let us pray to God.
CLOV: Again!
NAGG: Me sugarplum!

HAMM: God first!

(*Pause.*)

Are you right?

CLOV (*resigned*): Off we go.

HAMM (*to Nagg*): And you?

NAGG (*clasping his hands, closing his eyes, in a gabble*): Our Father which art —

HAMM: Silence! In silence! Where are your manners?

(*Pause.*)

Off we go.

(*Attitudes of prayer. Silence. Abandoning his attitude, discouraged.*)

Well?

CLOV (*abandoning his attitude*): What a hope! And you?

HAMM: Sweet damn all!

(*To Nagg.*)

And you?

NAGG: Wait!

(*Pause. Abandoning his attitude.*)

Nothing doing!

HAMM: The bastard! He doesn't exist!

CLOV: Not yet.

NAGG: Me sugarplum!

HAMM: There are no more sugarplums!

(*Pause.*)

NAGG: It's natural. After all I'm your father. It's true if it hadn't been me it would have been someone else. But that's no excuse.

(*Pause.*)

Turkish Delight,° for example, which no longer exists, we all know that, there is nothing in the world I love more. And one day I'll ask you for some, in return for a kindness, and you'll promise it to me. One must live with the times.

(*Pause.*)

Whom did you call when you were a tiny boy, and were frightened, in the dark? Your mother? No. Me. We let you cry. Then we moved you out of earshot, so that we might sleep in peace.

(*Pause.*)

I was asleep, as happy as a king, and you woke me up to have me listen to you. It wasn't indispensable, you didn't really need to have me listen to you.

(*Pause.*)

I hope the day will come when you'll really need to have me listen to you, and need to hear my voice, any voice.

Turkish Delight: Gummy candy.

(*Pause.*)

Yes, I hope I'll live till then, to hear you calling me like when you were a tiny boy, and were frightened, in the dark, and I was your only hope.

(*Pause. Nagg knocks on lid of Nell's bin. Pause.*)

Nell!

(*Pause. He knocks louder. Pause. Louder.*)

Nell!

(*Pause. Nagg sinks back into his bin, closes the lid behind him. Pause.*)

HAMM: Our revels now are ended.

(*He gropes for the dog.*)

The dog's gone.

CLOV: He's not a real dog, he can't go.

HAMM (*groping*): He's not there.

CLOV: He's lain down.

HAMM: Give him up to me.

(*Clov picks up the dog and gives it to Hamm. Hamm holds it in his arms. Pause. Hamm throws away the dog.*)

Dirty brute!

(*Clov begins to pick up the objects lying on the ground.*)

What are you doing?

CLOV: Putting things in order.

(*He straightens up. Fervently.*)

I'm going to clear everything away!

(*He starts picking up again.*)

HAMM: Order!

CLOV (*straightening up*): I love order. It's my dream. A world where all would be silent and still and each thing in its last place, under the last dust.

(*He starts picking up again.*)

HAMM (*exasperated*): What in God's name do you think you are doing?

CLOV (*straightening up*): I'm doing my best to create a little order.

HAMM: Drop it!

(*Clov drops the objects he has picked up.*)

CLOV: After all, there or elsewhere.

(*He goes towards door.*)

HAMM (*irritably*): What's wrong with your feet?

CLOV: My feet?

HAMM: Tramp! Tramp!

CLOV: I must have put on my boots.

HAMM: Your slippers were hurting you?

(*Pause.*)

CLOV: I'll leave you.

HAMM: No!

CLOV: What is there to keep me here?
HAMM: The dialogue.

(*Pause.*)

I've got on with my story.

(*Pause.*)

I've got on with it well.

(*Pause. Irritably.*)

Ask me where I've got to.
CLOV: Oh, by the way, your story?
HAMM (*surprised*): What story?
CLOV: The one you've been telling yourself all your days.
HAMM: Ah you mean my chronicle?
CLOV: That's the one.

(*Pause.*)

HAMM (*angrily*): Keep going, can't you, keep going!
CLOV: You've got on with it, I hope.
HAMM (*modestly*): Oh not very far, not very far.

(*He sighs.*)

There are days like that, one isn't inspired.

(*Pause.*)

Nothing you can do about it, just wait for it to come.

(*Pause.*)

No forcing, no forcing, it's fatal.

(*Pause.*)

I've got on with it a little all the same.

(*Pause.*)

Technique, you know.

(*Pause. Irritably.*)

I say I've got on with it a little all the same.
CLOV (*admiringly*): Well I never! In spite of everything you were able to get on with it!
HAMM (*modestly*): Oh not very far, you know, not very far, but nevertheless, better than nothing.
CLOV: Better than nothing! Is it possible?
HAMM: I'll tell you how it goes. He comes crawling on his belly —
CLOV: Who?
HAMM: What?
CLOV: Who do you mean, he?
HAMM: Who do I mean! Yet another.
CLOV: Ah him! I wasn't sure.
HAMM: Crawling on his belly, whining for bread for his brat. He's offered a job as gardener. Before —

(*Clov bursts out laughing.*)

What is there so funny about that?
CLOV: A job as gardener!
HAMM: Is that what tickles you?

CLOV: It must be that.
HAMM: It wouldn't be the bread?
CLOV: Or the brat.

(*Pause.*)

HAMM: The whole thing is comical, I grant you that. What about having a good guffaw the two of us together?
CLOV (*after reflection*): I couldn't guffaw again today.
HAMM (*after reflection*): Nor I.

(*Pause.*)

I continue then. Before accepting with gratitude he asks if he may have his little boy with him.
CLOV: What age?
HAMM: Oh tiny.
CLOV: He would have climbed the trees.
HAMM: All the little odd jobs.
CLOV: And then he would have grown up.
HAMM: Very likely.

(*Pause.*)

CLOV: Keep going, can't you, keep going!
HAMM: That's all. I stopped there.

(*Pause.*)

CLOV: Do you see how it goes on.
HAMM: More or less.
CLOV: Will it not soon be the end?
HAMM: I m afraid it will.
CLOV: Pah! You'll make up another.
HAMM: I don't know.

(*Pause.*)

I feel rather drained.

(*Pause.*)

The prolonged creative effort.

(*Pause.*)

If I could drag myself down to the sea! I'd make a pillow of sand for my head and the tide would come.
CLOV: There's no more tide.

(*Pause.*)

HAMM: Go and see is she dead.

(*Clov goes to bins, raises the lid of Nell's, stoops, looks into it. Pause.*)

CLOV: Looks like it.

(*He closes the lid, straightens up. Hamm raises his toque. Pause. He puts it on again.*)

HAMM (*with his hand to his toque*): And Nagg?

(*Clov raises lid of Nagg's bin, stoops, looks into it. Pause.*)

CLOV: Doesn't look like it.

(*He closes the lid, straightens up.*)

HAMM (*letting go his toque*): What's he doing?

(*Clov raises lid of Nagg's bin, stoops, looks into it. Pause.*)

CLOV: He's crying.

(*He closes lid, straightens up.*)

HAMM: Then he's living.

(*Pause.*)

> Did you ever have an instant of happiness?

CLOV: Not to my knowledge.

(*Pause.*)

HAMM: Bring me under the window.

(*Clov goes towards chair.*)

> I want to feel the light on my face.

(*Clov pushes chair.*)

> Do you remember, in the beginning, when you took me for a turn? You used to hold the chair too high. At every step you nearly tipped me out.

(*With senile quaver.*)

> Ah great fun, we had, the two of us, great fun.

(*Gloomily.*)

> And then we got into the way of it.

(*Clov stops the chair under window right.*)

> There already?

(*Pause. He tilts back his head.*)

> Is it light?

CLOV: It isn't dark.

HAMM (*angrily*): I'm asking you is it light.

CLOV: Yes.

(*Pause.*)

HAMM: The curtain isn't closed?

CLOV: No.

HAMM: What window is it?

CLOV: The earth.

HAMM: I knew it!

(*Angrily.*)

> But there's no light there! The other!

(*Clov pushes chair towards window left.*)

> The earth!

(*Clov stops the chair under window left. Hamm tilts back his head.*)

> That's what I call light!

(*Pause.*)

> Feels like a ray of sunshine.

(*Pause.*)

> No?

CLOV: No.

HAMM: It isn't a ray of sunshine I feel on my face?

CLOV: No.

(*Pause.*)

HAMM: Am I very white?

(*Pause. Angrily.*)

> I'm asking you am I very white!

CLOV: Not more so than usual.

(*Pause.*)

HAMM: Open the window.

CLOV: What for?

HAMM: I want to hear the sea.

CLOV: You wouldn't hear it.

HAMM: Even if you opened the window?

CLOV: No.

HAMM: Then it's not worthwhile opening it?

CLOV: No.

HAMM (*violently*): Then open it!

(*Clov gets up on the ladder, opens the window. Pause.*)

> Have you opened it?

CLOV: Yes.

(*Pause.*)

HAMM: You swear you've opened it?

CLOV: Yes.

(*Pause.*)

HAMM: Well . . . !

(*Pause.*)

> It must be very calm.

(*Pause. Violently.*)

> I'm asking you is it very calm!

CLOV: Yes.

HAMM: It's because there are no more navigators.

(*Pause.*)

> You haven't much conversation all of a sudden. Do you not feel well?

CLOV: I'm cold.

HAMM: What month are we?

(*Pause.*)

> Close the window, we're going back.

(*Clov closes the window, gets down, pushes the chair back to its place, remains standing behind it, head bowed.*)

> Don't stay there, you give me the shivers!

(*Clov returns to his place beside the chair.*)

RIGHT: Clov (John Bottoms) and Hamm (Ben Halley, Jr.), seated, in the 1984 American Repertory Theatre production of *Endgame,* directed by JoAnne Akalaitis. BELOW: Hamm and Clov.

Father!

(*Pause. Louder.*)

Father!

(*Pause.*)

Go and see did he hear me.

(*Clov goes to Nagg's bin, raises the lid, stoops. Unintelligible words. Clov straightens up.*)

CLOV: Yes.
HAMM: Both times?

(*Clov stoops. As before.*)

CLOV: Once only.
HAMM: The first time or the second?

(*Clov stoops. As before.*)

CLOV: He doesn't know.
HAMM: It must have been the second.
CLOV: We'll never know.

(*He closes lid.*)

HAMM: Is he still crying?
CLOV: No.
HAMM: The dead go fast.

(*Pause.*)

What's he doing?
CLOV: Sucking his biscuit.
HAMM: Life goes on.

(*Clov returns to his place beside the chair.*)

Give me a rug,° I'm freezing.
CLOV: There are no more rugs.

(*Pause.*)

HAMM: Kiss me.

(*Pause.*)

Will you not kiss me?
CLOV: No.
HAMM: On the forehead.
CLOV: I won't kiss you anywhere.

(*Pause.*)

HAMM (*holding out his hand*): Give me your hand at
    least.

(*Pause.*)

Will you not give me your hand?
CLOV: I won't touch you.

(*Pause.*)

HAMM: Give me the dog.

(*Clov looks round for the dog.*)

rug: A small blanket to cover the lap, legs, and feet.

No!
CLOV: Do you not want your dog?
HAMM: No.
CLOV: Then I'll leave you.
HAMM (*head bowed, absently*): That's right.

(*Clov goes to door, turns.*)

CLOV: If I don't kill that rat he'll die.
HAMM (*as before*): That's right.

(*Exit Clov. Pause.*)

Me to play.

(*He takes out his handkerchief, unfolds it, holds it
spread out before him.*)

We're getting on.

(*Pause.*)

You weep, and weep, for nothing, so as not to laugh,
and little by little . . . you begin to grieve.

(*He folds the handkerchief, puts it back in his pocket,
raises his head.*)

All those I might have helped.

(*Pause.*)

Helped!

(*Pause.*)

Saved.

(*Pause.*)

Saved!

(*Pause.*)

The place was crawling with them!

(*Pause. Violently.*)

Use your head, can't you, use your head, you're on
earth, there's no cure for that!

(*Pause.*)

Get out of here and love one another! Lick your
neighbor as yourself!

(*Pause. Calmer.*)

When it wasn't bread they wanted it was crumpets.

(*Pause. Violently.*)

Out of my sight and back to your petting parties!

(*Pause.*)

All that, all that!

(*Pause.*)

Not even a real dog!

(*Calmer.*)

The end is in the beginning and yet you go on.

(*Pause.*)

Perhaps I could go on with my story, end it and begin another.

(*Pause.*)

Perhaps I could throw myself out on the floor.

(*He pushes himself painfully off his seat, falls back again.*)

Dig my nails into the cracks and drag myself forward with my fingers.

(*Pause.*)

It will be the end and there I'll be, wondering what can have brought it on and wondering what can have . . . (*he hesitates*) . . . why it was so long coming.

(*Pause.*)

There I'll be, in the old shelter, alone against the silence and . . . (*he hesitates*) . . . the stillness. If I can hold my peace, and sit quiet, it will be all over with sound, and motion, all over and done with.

(*Pause.*)

I'll have called my father and I'll have called my . . . (*he hesitates*) . . . my son. And even twice, or three times, in case they shouldn't have heard me, the first time, or the second.

(*Pause.*)

I'll say to myself, He'll come back.

(*Pause.*)

And then?

(*Pause.*)

And then?

(*Pause.*)

He couldn't, he has gone too far.

(*Pause.*)

And then?

(*Pause. Very agitated.*)

All kinds of fantasies! That I'm being watched! A rat! Steps! Breath held and then . . .

(*He breathes out.*)

Then babble, babble, words, like the solitary child who turns himself into children, two, three, so as to be together, and whisper together, in the dark.

(*Pause.*)

Moment upon moment, pattering down, like the millet grains of . . . (*he hesitates*) . . . that old Greek, and all life long you wait for that to mount up to a life.

(*Pause. He opens his mouth to continue, renounces.*)

Ah let's get it over!

(*He whistles. Enter Clov with alarm clock. He halts beside the chair.*)

What? Neither gone nor dead?

CLOV: In spirit only.

HAMM: Which?

CLOV: Both.

HAMM: Gone from me you'd be dead.

CLOV: And vice versa.

HAMM: Outside of here it's death!

(*Pause.*)

And the rat?

CLOV: He's got away.

HAMM: He can't go far.

(*Pause. Anxious.*)

Eh?

CLOV: He doesn't need to go far.

(*Pause.*)

HAMM: Is it not time for my painkiller?

CLOV: Yes.

HAMM: Ah! At last! Give it to me! Quick!

(*Pause.*)

CLOV: There's no more painkiller.

(*Pause.*)

HAMM (*appalled*): Good . . . !

(*Pause.*)

No more painkiller!

CLOV: No more painkiller. You'll never get any more painkiller.

(*Pause.*)

HAMM: But the little round box. It was full!

CLOV: Yes. But now it's empty.

(*Pause. Clov starts to move about the room. He is looking for a place to put down the alarm clock.*)

HAMM (*soft*): What'll I do?

(*Pause. In a scream.*)

What'll I do?

(*Clov sees the picture, takes it down, stands it on the floor with its face to the wall, hangs up the alarm clock in its place.*)

What are you doing?

CLOV: Winding up.

HAMM: Look at the earth.

CLOV: Again!

HAMM: Since it's calling to you.

CLOV: Is your throat sore?

(*Pause.*)

Would you like a lozenge?

(*Pause.*)

No.

(*Pause.*)

Pity.

(*Clov goes, humming, towards window right, halts before it, looks up at it.*)

HAMM: Don't sing.

CLOV (*turning towards Hamm*): One hasn't the right to sing anymore?

HAMM: No.

CLOV: Then how can it end?

HAMM: You want it to end?

CLOV: I want to sing.

HAMM: I can't prevent you.

(*Pause. Clov turns towards window right.*)

CLOV: What did I do with that steps?

(*He looks around for ladder.*)

You didn't see that steps?

(*He sees it.*)

Ah, about time.

(*He goes towards window left.*)

Sometimes I wonder if I'm in my right mind. Then it passes over and I'm as lucid as before.

(*He gets up on ladder, looks out of window.*)

Christ, she's under water!

(*He looks.*)

How can that be?

(*He pokes forward his head, his hand above his eyes.*)

It hasn't rained.

(*He wipes the pane, looks. Pause.*)

Ah what a fool I am! I'm on the wrong side!

(*He gets down, takes a few steps towards window right.*)

Under water!

(*He goes back for ladder.*)

What a fool I am!

(*He carries ladder towards window right.*)

Sometimes I wonder if I'm in my right senses. Then it passes off and I'm as intelligent as ever.

(*He sets down ladder under window right, gets up on it, looks out of window. He turns towards Hamm.*)

Any particular sector you fancy? Or merely the whole thing?

HAMM: Whole thing.

CLOV: The general effect? Just a moment.

(*He looks out of window. Pause.*)

HAMM: Clov.

CLOV (*absorbed*): Mmm.

HAMM: Do you know what it is?

CLOV (*as before*): Mmm.

HAMM: I was never there.

(*Pause.*)

Clov!

CLOV (*turning towards Hamm, exasperated*): What is it?

HAMM: I was never there.

CLOV: Lucky for you.

(*He looks out of window.*)

HAMM: Absent, always. It all happened without me. I don't know what's happened.

(*Pause.*)

Do you know what's happened?

(*Pause.*)

Clov!

CLOV (*turning towards Hamm, exasperated*): Do you want me to look at this muckheap, yes or no?

HAMM: Answer me first.

CLOV: What?

HAMM: Do you know what's happened?

CLOV: When? Where?

HAMM (*violently*): When! What's happened? Use your head, can't you! What has happened?

CLOV: What for Christ's sake does it matter?

(*He looks out of window.*)

HAMM: I don't know.

(*Pause. Clov turns towards Hamm.*)

CLOV (*harshly*): When old Mother Pegg asked you for oil for her lamp and you told her to get out to hell, you knew what was happening then, no?

(*Pause.*)

You know what she died of, Mother Pegg? Of darkness.

HAMM (*feebly*): I hadn't any.

CLOV (*as before*): Yes, you had.

(*Pause.*)

HAMM: Have you the glass?

CLOV: No, it's clear enough as it is.

HAMM: Go and get it.

(*Pause. Clov casts up his eyes, brandishes his fists. He loses balance, clutches on to the ladder. He starts to get down, halts.*)

CLOV: There's one thing I'll never understand.

(*He gets down.*)

Why I always obey you. Can you explain that to me?

HAMM: No. . . . Perhaps it's compassion.

(*Pause.*)

A kind of great compassion.

(*Pause.*)

Oh you won't find it easy, you won't find it easy.

(*Pause. Clov begins to move about the room in search of the telescope.*)

CLOV: I'm tired of our goings on, very tired.

(*He searches.*)

You're not sitting on it?

(*He moves the chair, looks at the place where it stood, resumes his search.*)

HAMM (*anguished*): Don't leave me there!

(*Angrily Clov restores the chair to its place.*)

Am I right in the center?

CLOV: You'd need a microscope to find this —

(*He sees the telescope.*)

Ah, about time.

(*He picks up the telescope, gets up on the ladder, turns the telescope on the without.*)

HAMM: Give me the dog.

CLOV (*looking*): Quiet!

HAMM (*angrily*): Give me the dog!

(*Clov drops the telescope, clasps his hands to his head. Pause. He gets down precipitately, looks for the dog, sees it, picks it up, hastens towards Hamm and strikes him violently on the head with the dog.*)

CLOV: There's your dog for you!

(*The dog falls to the ground. Pause.*)

HAMM: He hit me!

CLOV: You drive me mad, I'm mad!

HAMM: If you must hit me, hit me with the axe.

(*Pause.*)

Or with the gaff, hit me with the gaff. Not with the dog. With the gaff. Or with the axe.

(*Clov picks up the dog and gives it to Hamm who takes it in his arms.*)

CLOV (*imploringly*): Let's stop playing!

HAMM: Never!

(*Pause.*)

Put me in my coffin.

CLOV: There are no more coffins.

HAMM: Then let it end!

(*Clov goes towards ladder.*)

With a bang!

(*Clov gets up on ladder, gets down again, looks for telescope, sees it, picks it up, gets up ladder, raises telescope.*)

Of darkness! And me? Did anyone ever have pity on me?

CLOV (*lowering the telescope, turning towards Hamm*): What?

(*Pause.*)

Is it me you're referring to?

HAMM (*angrily*): An aside, ape! Did you never hear an aside before?

(*Pause.*)

I'm warming up for my last soliloquy.

CLOV: I warn you. I'm going to look at this filth since it's an order. But it's the last time.

(*He turns the telescope on the without.*)

Let's see.

(*He moves the telescope.*)

Nothing . . . nothing . . . good . . . good . . . nothing . . . goo —

(*He starts, lowers the telescope, examines it, turns it again on the without. Pause.*)

Bad luck to it!

HAMM: More complications!

(*Clov gets down.*)

Not an underplot, I trust.

(*Clov moves ladder nearer window, gets up on it, turns telescope on the without.*)

CLOV (*dismayed*): Looks like a small boy!

HAMM (*sarcastic*): A small . . . boy!

CLOV: I'll go and see.

(*He gets down, drops the telescope, goes towards door, turns.*)

I'll take the gaff.

(*He looks for the gaff, sees it, picks it up, hastens towards door.*)

HAMM: No!

(*Clov halts.*)

CLOV: No? A potential procreator?

HAMM: If he exists he'll die there or he'll come here. And if he doesn't . . .

(*Pause.*)

CLOV: You don't believe me? You think I'm inventing?

(*Pause.*)

HAMM: It's the end, Clov, we've come to the end. I don't need you anymore.

(*Pause.*)

CLOV: Lucky for you.

(*He goes towards door.*)

HAMM: Leave me the gaff.

(*Clov gives him the gaff, goes towards door, halts, looks at alarm clock, takes it down, looks round for a better place to put it, goes to bins, puts it on lid of Nagg's bin. Pause.*)

CLOV: I'll leave you.

(*He goes towards door.*)

HAMM: Before you go . . .

(*Clov halts near door.*)

. . . say something.

CLOV: There is nothing to say.

HAMM: A few words . . . to ponder . . . in my heart.

CLOV: Your heart!

HAMM: Yes.

(*Pause. Forcibly.*)

Yes!

(*Pause.*)

With the rest, in the end, the shadows, the murmurs, all the trouble, to end up with.

(*Pause.*)

Clov. . . . He never spoke to me. Then, in the end, before he went, without my having asked him, he spoke to me. He said . . .

CLOV (*despairingly*): Ah . . . !

HAMM: Something . . . from your heart.

CLOV: My heart!

HAMM: A few words . . . from your heart.

(*Pause.*)

CLOV (*fixed gaze, tonelessly, towards auditorium*): They said to me, That's love, yes, yes, not a doubt, now you see how —

HAMM: Articulate!

CLOV (*as before*): How easy it is. They said to me, That's friendship, yes, yes, no question, you've found it. They said to me, Here's the place, stop, raise your head and look at all that beauty. That order! They said to me, Come now, you're not a brute beast, think upon these things and you'll see how all becomes clear. And simple! They said to me, What skilled attention they get, all these dying of their wounds.

HAMM: Enough!

CLOV (*as before*): I say to myself — sometimes, Clov, you must learn to suffer better than that if you want them to weary of punishing you — one day. I say to myself — sometimes, Clov, you must be there better than that if you want them to let you go — one day. But I feel too old, and too far, to form new habits. Good, it'll never end, I'll never go.

(*Pause.*)

Then one day, suddenly, it ends, it changes, I don't understand, it dies, or it's me, I don't understand, that either. I ask the words that remain — sleeping, waking, morning, evening. They have nothing to say.

(*Pause.*)

I open the door of the cell and go. I am so bowed I only see my feet, if I open my eyes, and between my legs a little trail of black dust. I say to myself that the earth is extinguished, though I never saw it lit.

(*Pause.*)

It's easy going.

(*Pause.*)

When I fall I'll weep for happiness.

(*Pause. He goes towards door.*)

HAMM: Clov!

(*Clov halts, without turning.*)

Nothing.

(*Clov moves on.*)

Clov!

(*Clov halts, without turning.*)

CLOV: This is what we call making an exit.

HAMM: I'm obliged to you, Clov. For your services.

CLOV (*turning, sharply*): Ah pardon, it's I am obliged to you.

HAMM: It's we are obliged to each other.

(*Pause. Clov goes towards door.*)

One thing more.

(*Clov halts.*)

A last favor.

(*Exit Clov.*)

Cover me with the sheet.

(*Long pause.*)

No? Good.

(*Pause.*)

Me to play.

(*Pause. Wearily.*)

Old endgame lost of old, play and lose and have done with losing.

(*Pause. More animated.*)

Let me see.

(*Pause.*)

Ah yes!

(*He tries to move the chair, using the gaff as before. Enter Clov, dressed for the road. Panama hat, tweed coat, raincoat over his arm, umbrella, bag. He halts by the door and stands there, impassive and motionless, his eyes fixed on Hamm, till the end. Hamm gives up.*)

Good.

(*Pause.*)

Discard.

(*He throws away the gaff, makes to throw away the dog, thinks better of it.*)

Take it easy.

(*Pause.*)

And now?

(*Pause.*)

Raise hat.

(*He raises his toque.*)

Peace to our . . . arses.

(*Pause.*)

And put on again.

(*He puts on his toque.*)

Deuce.

(*Pause. He takes off his glasses.*)

Wipe.

(*He takes out his handkerchief and, without unfolding it, wipes his glasses.*)

And put on again.

(*He puts on his glasses, puts back the handkerchief in his pocket.*)

We're coming. A few more squirms like that and I'll call.

(*Pause.*)

A little poetry.

(*Pause.*)

You prayed —

(*Pause. He corrects himself.*)

You CRIED for night; it comes —

(*Pause. He corrects himself.*)

It FALLS: now cry in darkness.

(*He repeats, chanting.*)

You cried for night; it falls: now cry in darkness.

(*Pause.*)

Nicely put, that.

(*Pause.*)

And now?

(*Pause.*)

Moments for nothing, now as always, time was never and time is over, reckoning closed and story ended.

(*Pause. Narrative tone.*)

If he could have his child with him. . . .

(*Pause.*)

It was the moment I was waiting for.

(*Pause.*)

You don't want to abandon him? You want him to bloom while you are withering? Be there to solace your last million last moments?

(*Pause.*)

He doesn't realize, all he knows is hunger, and cold, and death to crown it all. But you! You ought to know what the earth is like, nowadays. Oh I put him before his responsibilities!

(*Pause. Normal tone.*)

Well, there we are, there I am, that's enough.

(*He raises the whistle to his lips, hesitates, drops it. Pause.*)

Yes, truly!

(*He whistles. Pause. Louder. Pause.*)

Good.

(*Pause.*)

Father!

(*Pause. Louder.*)

Father!

(*Pause.*)

Good.

(*Pause.*)

We're coming.

(*Pause.*)

And to end up with?

(*Pause.*)

Discard.

(*He throws away the dog. He tears the whistle from his neck.*)

With my compliments.

(*He throws whistle towards auditorium. Pause. He sniffs. Soft.*)

Clov!

(*Long pause.*)

No? Good.

(*He takes out the handkerchief.*)

Since that's the way we're playing it . . . (*he unfolds handkerchief*) . . . let's play it that way . . . (*he unfolds*) . . . and speak no more about it . . . (*he finishes unfolding*) . . . speak no more.

(*He holds handkerchief spread out before him.*)

Old stancher!

(*Pause.*)

You . . . remain.

(*Pause. He covers his face with handkerchief, lowers his arms to armrests, remains motionless.*)

(*Brief tableau.*)

COMMENTARIES

Martin Esslin (*b. 1918*)
THE THEATER OF THE ABSURD   *1961*

Martin Esslin is a drama critic whose work has had wide currency. He was the first to write extensively about the theater of the absurd, a term that has come to describe the plays of Samuel Beckett and a number of other post–World War II playwrights such as Eugène Ionesco and Harold Pinter. The question of what use playwrights make of the absurd and why it is an appropriate term to reflect the achievement of Beckett is explored briefly in this excerpt.

The Theater of the Absurd shows the world as an incomprehensible place. The spectators see the happenings on the stage entirely from the outside, without ever understanding the full meaning of these strange patterns of events, as newly arrived visitors might watch life in a country of which they have not yet mastered the language. The confrontation of the audience with characters and happenings which they are not quite able to comprehend makes it impossible for them to share the aspirations and emotions depicted in the play. Brecht's famous *Verfremdungseffekt* (alienation effect), the inhibition of any identification between spectator and actor, which Brecht could never successfully achieve in his own highly rational theater, really comes into its own in the Theater of the Absurd. It is impossible to identify oneself with characters one does not understand or whose motives remain a closed book, and so the distance between the public and the happenings on the stage can be maintained. Emotional identification with the characters is replaced by a puzzled, critical attention. For while the happenings on the stage are absurd, they yet remain recognizable as somehow related to real life with *its* absurdity, so that eventually the spectators are brought face to face with the irrational side of their existence. Thus, the absurd and fantastic goings-on of the Theater of the Absurd will, in the end, be found to reveal the irrationality of the human condition and the illusion of what we thought was its apparent logical structure.

If the dialogue in these plays consists of meaningless clichés and the mechanical, circular repetition of stereotyped phrases — how many meaningless clichés and stereotyped phrases do we use in our day-to-day conversation? If the characters change their personality halfway through the action, how consistent and truly integrated are the people we meet in our real life? And if people in these plays appear as mere marionettes, helpless puppets without any will of their own, passively at the mercy of blind fate and meaningless circumstance, do we, in fact, in our overorganized world, still possess any genuine initiative or power to decide our own destiny? The spectators of the Theater of the Absurd are thus confronted with a grotesquely heightened picture of their own world: a world without faith, meaning, and genuine freedom of will. In this sense, the Theater of the Absurd is the true theater of our time.

The theater of most previous epochs reflected an accepted moral order, a world whose aims and objectives were clearly present to the minds of all its public, whether it was the audience of the medieval mystery plays with their solidly accepted faith in the Christian world order or the audience of the drama of Ibsen, Shaw, or Hauptmann with their unquestioned belief in evolution and progress. To such audiences, right and wrong were never in doubt, nor did they question the then accepted goals of human endeavor. Our own time, at least in the Western world, wholly lacks such a generally accepted and completely integrated world picture. The decline of religious faith, the destruction of the belief in automatic social and biological progress, the discovery of vast areas of irrational and unconscious forces within the human psyche, the loss of a sense of control over rational human development in an age of totalitarianism and weapons of mass destruction, have all contributed to the erosion of the basis for a dramatic convention in which the action proceeds within a fixed and self-evident framework of generally accepted values. Faced with the vacuum left by the destruction of a universally accepted and unified set of beliefs, most serious playwrights have felt the need to fit their work into the frame of values and objectives expressed in one of the contemporary ideologies: Marxism, psychoanalysis, aestheticism, or nature worship. But these, in the eyes of a writer like Adamov, are nothing but superficial rationalizations which try to hide the depth of man's predicament, his loneliness and his anxiety. Or, as Ionesco puts it:

> As far as I am concerned, I believe sincerely in the poverty of the poor, I deplore it; it is real; it can become a subject for the theatre; I also believe in the anxieties and serious troubles the rich may suffer from; but it is neither in the misery of the former nor in the melancholia of the latter, that I, for one, find my dramatic subject matter. Theatre is for me the outward projection onto the stage of an inner world; it is in my dreams, in my anxieties, in my obscure desires, in my internal contradictions that I, for one, reserve for myself the right of finding my dramatic subject matter. As I am not alone in the world, as each of us, in the depth of his being, is at the same time part and parcel of all others, my dreams, my desires, my anxieties, my obsessions do not belong to me alone. They form part of an ancestral heritage, a very ancient storehouse which is a portion of the common property of all mankind. It is this, which, transcending their outward diversity, reunites all human beings and constitutes our profound common patrimony, the universal language.[1]

In other words, the commonly acceptable framework of beliefs and values of former epochs which has now been shattered is to be replaced by the community of dreams and desires of a collective unconscious. And, to quote Ionesco again:

> . . . the new dramatist is one . . . who tries to link up with what is most ancient: new language and subject matter in a dramatic structure which aims at being clearer, more stripped of inessentials and more purely theatrical; the rejection of traditionalism to rediscover

[1] Eugène Ionesco, "L'Impromptu de l'Alma," *Théâtre* II (Paris, 1958).

tradition; a synthesis of knowledge and invention, of the real and imaginary, of the particular and the universal, or as they say now, of the individual and the collective. . . . By expressing my deepest obsessions, I express my deepest humanity. I become one with all others, spontaneously, over and above all the barriers of caste and different psychologies. I express my solitude and become one with all other solitudes.[2]

What is the tradition with which the Theater of the Absurd — at first sight the most revolutionary and radically new movement — is trying to link itself? It is in fact a very ancient and a very rich tradition, nourished from many and varied sources: the verbal exuberance and extravagant inventions of Rabelais, the age-old clowning of the Roman mimes and the Italian Commedia dell'Arte, the knock-about humor of circus clowns like Grock; the wild, archetypal symbolism of English nonsense verse, the baroque horror of Jacobean dramatists like Webster or Tourneur, the harsh, incisive, and often brutal tones of the German drama of Grabbe, Büchner, Kleist, and Wedekind with its delirious language and grotesque inventiveness; and the Nordic paranoia of the dreams and persecution fantasies of Strindberg.

[2]Ionesco, "The Avant-Garde Theatre," *World Theatre* 8.3 (Autumn 1959).

Sidney Homan (b. 1938)
THE ENDING OF ENDGAME   1984

Sidney Homan's book Beckett's Theaters: Interpretations for Performance *concentrates on the production of Beckett's plays. His discussion of* Endgame *focuses on the performance aspects of movement in the final moments of the play. The question of death is central to the question of* Endgame.

Despite its seeming chaos on the surface, Hamm's last speech, that string of short phrases and snatches of dialogue much like that of Winnie in *Happy Days,* provides the most sustained insight into his playwright's mentality. In the words of the Unnamable,° it is the "end of the joke," the aesthetic painkiller if you will, as handy as that literal painkiller in the cupboard was not. Unseen, except by us, Clov constitutes the onstage audience of one. The speech itself is surely meant to contrast with Hamm's opening dialogue: This time Hamm is not discovered but rather constitutes *all* the stage, at least as far as he knows, and the speech is about endings rather than beginnings. The proper verbal constructions, in terms of his opening lines, would be something akin to "Me to play having played." No fear of mere "reveling" here.

Hamm's speech seems to be madness without matter. As with the scattered fragments in the closing lines of Eliot's *The Waste Land,* however, there is here an order and a depth of reference below the surface. Clov is absent, though he stands impassive upstage. The sheet with which he "discovered" Hamm at the opening is now useless. In a larger sense, Hamm has been revealed, the play itself representing his disclosure as a symbol. The removal of the sheet itself is thereby the stimulus for an aesthetic revelation. He is now moving toward the purely symbolic, and the chess metaphor comes to the fore, chess itself a symbolic enactment of literal battles and

---

Unnamable: Narrator of *The Unnamable* (1958), third in a trilogy of novels by Beckett.

armies: "Me to play" and "Old endgame." Indeed, Hamm is moving toward the same sense of completeness found by Mr. Endon in *Murphy*. The King, the central piece, is now immobile at the center of the board, the word for both the theater and the field of chess pieces. Then "discard" the last life-support; the gaff is thrown away, though the dog, symbol of Hamm's artifice, is retained.

We see the artist now attempting to document the moment before human extinction. It is the process toward that movement, and not the actual event itself, defining the limits of our earthly inquiry.

Like Shakespeare, Beckett does not depict a hereafter. We may speculate on what will happen to Lear — can a pagan go to any sort of heaven? — but the Renaissance playwright, like the modern one, is content to show him approaching the end, promised or otherwise. There is a farewell here to the audience, obscene to be sure, and with that salute an identification with us as Hamm uses the plural possessive "our." The "You" who wants poetry, or the efficacy of prayer, or night to come is also the "you" that, in an absurdist or relative world, must cry in darkness. Again, we all die alone. Hamm's aesthetic consciousness, like that of the narrator in *Cascando*,° is now most acute: "Nicely put, that."

If relativity, both in terms of time itself and the mutability of all human things, relentlessly moves on, Hamm, now enveloped in his story, is about to make time run, to echo the Renaissance poet Marvell. The time is "over, reckoning closed and story ended." The wish for extinction, however, cannot hold as the life force, the final reference to the father and his starving son, is sounded. Hamm cannot shake off that memory. An invasion of his world, the story irritates the aesthetic fiber he has so closely woven. It is another world, with a past, with characters, and involving those issues of life and the sustenance of life that Hamm has otherwise so assiduously blocked out in his bomb shelter, in his circumscribed, lonely, inner world. The "Oh I put him before his responsibilities" sounds as much neurotic as convincing. Then with a *calm* — again, one of Beckett's favorite words — returning, Hamm reverses himself in the recognition that he is not alone, that he is part and parcel of all humanity, including us, including the fictive, or seemingly fictive father and his son: "Well, there we are, there I am, that's enough." This is something "truly," though the aesthetic inner world is itself in flux, only a momentary stay against reality, and yet Hamm will now be able to sustain this playwright-actor's posture at least until the end.

He approaches death with the same sense of "knowing" his story that several modern biblical scholars have attributed to Christ, an "actor" who plays the parts of a visitor to earth, prophet, crucified savior, and risen spirit. We approach now the closest thing to transcendence in Beckett, undercut, of course, by the fact that Hamm "*remains motionless*" as the curtain closes (he can no more leave his stage than Vladimir and Estragon can leave theirs). The dog is discarded, the last vestige of his creation; and then in a brilliant gesture he throws the whistle toward us, the audience — the "*auditorium.*" Though the isolation is illusory — again, Clov is backstage, visible to us if not to Hamm — for Hamm it is a convincing illusion. He is approaching the nonbeing sought by Nell in her vision of a silent, white ocean bottom, an empty world where nothingness is a fact, not a conceit, where we can cease to be like those talkative "political" artists who, in giving form to nothing,

Cascando: Beckett's radio play for voice and music (1962), first broadcast in English by the BBC in 1964.

are bound to fail. In essence, Hamm is trying to give up the last hold on life, even if that "life" be the illusory existence of the stage world.

The transcendence itself is aborted. However much he would later cut away at the time scheme or the plot or the place of his plays (witness *Breath*), Beckett cannot present us with nothing: "Nothing" itself can be spoken of but not enacted. A bare stage is only a bare stage and not a play. Here Beckett is like Emily Dickinson in "I heard a fly buzz when I died," as she tries poetically to cross the thin boundary line between life and death and is frustrated in that attempt when a fly intervenes between her eyes and the "light." Beckett is trying to go to the nonstate, if I may put it that way, of nonbeing. That is the way Hamm would "play it," so that he could "speak no more about it." I repeat his wish: "Speak no more." He seeks here not the failure of words, the very possibility that unnerves Winnie. Nor will he use words anymore to define nonbeing.

Now, without words and with the major character free of the tension in seeking physical life or death, we move to the level of mime. Our audience surrogate, the silent Clov, now sees Hamm hold the bloodied handkerchief before him and then cover his face. Two phrases act as glosses to the action. One is the descriptive "Old stancher," lest an audience member fail to identify properly the symbol, Hamm's Greek-like mask that is the physical correlative for his misery, for his suffering than which no one's is greater, as he reminds us early in the play. In effect, Hamm, like the figures in Greek myths, has passed through earthly existence and literally become a star. He has won his right to be a symbol, a symbol sustained by the play, a symbol that now wordlessly compresses all that he means, or has meant. This wretched piece of a costume, in effect, now equals the entire play. In Beckett, truly, the last shall be first. One also thinks of the handkerchief worn by Keaton in *Film,* and that used by Willie in *Happy Days,* though neither was so developed, nor so perfect a symbol of suffering.

The other phrase, a tantalizing one, is the closing "You . . . remain." Initially, it appears simply an appositive for "Old stancher," but I also take it as a reference to the audience. That is, Hamm has now *realized* his role; he has been elevated to a symbol. Our task has now just begun; we must leave the theater, refreshed by Beckett's mirror world, and must encounter the suffering anew. Outside of here it is hell, as the Beckett characters are fond of saying. We remain; we are the "mutes or audience" of the act to which Hamlet refers (V, ii, 338).

The play closes beyond words, as Hamm covers his face with the handkerchief and, like the Auditor in *Not I,* lowers his arms and in a mockery of mime and its movements stops on the stage direction to remain *"motionless."* Initiated by language, the play ends in silence, the *"Brief tableau,"* like that called for by Beckett in *The Unnamable. Curtain.* It will also start again; as Winnie observes, even if the glass breaks, it will be there whole tomorrow. Tomorrow the handkerchief will revert to the old sheet covering Hamm, that, with the bloodstained handkerchief, will in turn be removed, discovering another potential tragic hero — or "figure," if "hero" sounds too affirmative for some readers. The uncovering will allow theatrical life to flow again, the act of artistic creation, the long creative process to which Hamm himself refers, the informing of a vision and the production of a symbol — a symbol that, at the end, will remain with us, only to be undone the next day, the next performance. Curtain.[. . .]

Lorraine Hansberry

Lorraine Hansberry (1930–1965), like John Millington Synge, died tragically young. Her loss to the American stage is incalculable; her successes were only beginning, and at her death she seemed on the verge of a remarkable career.

Hansberry grew up in a middle-class black family in Chicago. Her father, who was successful in real estate, founded one of the first banks for blacks in Chicago. However, he spent much of his life vainly trying to find a way to make a decent life for himself and his family in America. He eventually gave up on the United States, and, when he died in 1945, he was scouting for a place in Mexico where he could move his family to live comfortably.

Lorraine Hansberry went to college after her father died, and her first ambition was to become a visual artist. She attended the Art Institute of Chicago and numerous other schools before moving to New York. Once there, she became interested in some drama groups and soon married the playwright Howard Nemiroff. She began writing, sharing parts of her first play with friends in her own living room. They helped raise money to stage the play and, with black director Lloyd Richards and little-known Sidney Poitier as Walter Lee Younger, *A Raisin in the Sun* (1959) thrust her into the drama spotlight.

In 1959, only twenty-nine years old, Hansberry was the most promising woman writing for the American stage. She was also the first black American to win the New York Drama Critics' Circle Award for the best play of the year. She died of cancer the day her second produced play, *The Sign in Sidney Brustein's Window*, closed. She had finished a third play, *Les Blancs*, which was brought to Broadway by Nemiroff in 1970. Neither of her other plays was as popular as *Raisin*, but the two later plays demonstrate a deepening concern for and understanding of some of the key issues of racial and sexual politics that interested her throughout her career.

The Sign in Sidney Brustein's Window's hero is a Jewish intellectual in the 1950s in Greenwich Village. Feeling that all the radical struggle of the 1930s has been lost, he agitates for personal involvement, for emotional and intellectual action. This idealistic play anticipates the political agitation in the United States during the mid-1960s and early 1970s. *Les Blancs* takes as its central character a black African intellectual, Tshembe, and explores his relationship to both Europe and Africa. In his uneasiness with both cultures he discovers that he cannot live outside his own history. *Les Blancs* reveals some of Hansberry's deep interest in Pan-Africanism and the search for a personal heritage.

A posthumous work was put together by Howard Nemiroff from Hansberry's notes, letters, and early writings. Titled *To Be Young, Gifted, and Black* (1971), it has helped solidify her achievements. Although we will never know just how Hansberry's career would have developed had she lived, her gifts were so remarkable that we can only lament that she is not writing for the stage today.

A RAISIN IN THE SUN

When produced on Broadway in 1959, *A Raisin in the Sun* was somewhat prophetic. Lorraine Hansberry's themes of blacks pressing forward with legitimate demands and expressing interest in their African heritage were to become primary themes of black culture in the 1960s, 1970s, and, indeed, to this day. The title of her play is from a poem by Langston Hughes, one of the poets of the Harlem Renaissance. It warns of the social explosions that might occur if society permits blacks to remain unequal and unfree.

The work appeared at the beginning of renewed political activity on the part of African Americans; it reveals its historical position in the use of the word *Negro,* which black activists rejected in the 1960s as an enslaving euphemism. This play illustrates the American dream as it is felt not just by African Americans but by all Americans: if you work hard, save your money, are honorable, and hope, then you can one day buy your own home and have the kind of space and privacy that permit people to live with dignity. Yet this very theme has plagued the play from the beginning: its apparent emphasis on middle-class, bourgeois values. On the surface, it seems to celebrate a mild form of consumerism — the desire for the house in the suburbs with the TV set inside to anesthetize its occupants. Hansberry was shocked when such criticisms, from black critics as well as white, were leveled against the play. She had written it very carefully to explore just those issues but in a context that demonstrated that black families' needs paralleled white families' while also having a different dimension that most white families could not understand.

Hansberry was quick to admit that Walter Lee Younger was affected by the same craziness influencing all Americans who lusted after possessions and the power they might confer. Walter wants to take his father's insurance money to buy a liquor store in partnership with a con man. Lena Younger argues against her son's plan as a profanation of her husband's memory as well as an abuse of the American dream: she believes that the product of a liquor store will further poison the community. What she wants is not a consumer product but the emblem of identity and security that she feels her family deserves.

Hansberry is painfully honest in this play. Walter Lee's weaknesses are recognizable. His male chauvinistic behavior undoes him. He is caught up in the old, failing pattern of male dominance over women. But none of the women in his life will tolerate his behavior. Hansberry also admits the social distinctions among African Americans. George Murchison is a young man from a wealthy black family, and when Beneatha tells Lena that she will not marry George, she says, "The only people in the world who are more snobbish than rich white people are rich colored people." Beneatha's desire to be a doctor is obviously not rooted in consumerism any more than in the middle-class need to be comfortable and rich.

The confusion brought to the family by a native African, Asagai, is realistically portrayed. In the early days of the Pan-African movement in the 1960s, blacks were often bemused by the way Africans presented themselves. Interest in Africa on the part of the American blacks was distorted by Tarzan movies and *National Geographic* articles, none of which presented black Africans as role models. Therefore, the adjustment to black African pride — while made swiftly — was not without difficulties. The Youngers are presented as no more sophisticated about black Africans than the rest of black society would be.

The dignity of the Younger family finally triumphs. When Walter Lee stands up for himself, he is asserting not macho domination but black manhood — a manhood that needs no domination over women. He is expressing not a desire for a big house — as he had done when he reflected on the possessions of his rich employer — but a desire to demonstrate to members of the Clybourne Park Improvement Association that the Youngers are their social equals and that they have a right to live wherever they choose.

A Raisin in the Sun in Performance

Lloyd Richards directed the first production at the Ethel Barrymore Theater in New York on March 11, 1959. The play won major prizes, and Sidney Poitier as a passionate Walter Lee Younger was a signal success. *New York Times* critic Brooks Atkinson said, "Since the performance is also honest and since Sidney Poitier is a candid actor, *A Raisin in the Sun* has vigor as well as veracity and is likely to destroy the complacency of any one who sees it." Critics were astonished that a first play could have the sophistication and depth they saw onstage.

The Theater Guild staged the play in 1960 in Boston with a different cast but the production received similar reviews. The film version, with most of the New York cast, was directed by Daniel Petrie in 1961. A revival in Chicago in 1983 at the Art Institute of Chicago — Hansberry's alma mater — was not altogether successful, but critics felt the text held up well. The Chicago revival, like the 1985 Merrimack Repertory Theater revival in Lowell, Massachusetts, demonstrated only that the play needs strong actors to have the desired impact. A twenty-fifth anniversary production was directed by Lloyd Richards at the Yale Repertory Theatre in 1983. This production was taken to New York in 1986 and enjoyed a successful run. The setting was a realistic interior, emphasizing the play's realistic style. Critic Mel Gussow felt the revival demonstrated that the play is "an enduring work of contemporary theater." The production also revealed that Hansberry's language had not become dated, nor had the social issues of the play become any less critical and important for the lapse of twenty-five years. Like the proletarian plays of Sean O'Casey, who inspired Lorraine Hansberry, this play continues to move us because its problems are serious and still remain.

Lorraine Hansberry (1930–1965)

A Raisin in the Sun

1959

Harlem (A Dream Deferred)

What happens to a dream deferred?

> Does it dry up
> like a raisin in the sun?
> Or fester like a sore —
> And then run?
> Does it stink like rotten meat?

Or crust and sugar over —
like a syrupy sweet?

Maybe it just sags
like a heavy load.

Or does it explode?   — LANGSTON HUGHES

Characters

RUTH YOUNGER
TRAVIS YOUNGER
WALTER LEE YOUNGER (brother)
BENEATHA YOUNGER
LENA YOUNGER (Mama)
JOSEPH ASAGAI
GEORGE MURCHISON
MRS. JOHNSON
KARL LINDNER
BOBO
MOVING MEN

The action of the play is set in Chicago's Southside, sometime between World War II and the present.

Act I
Scene I: Friday morning.
Scene II: The following morning.

Act II
Scene I: Later, the same day.
Scene II: Friday night, a few weeks later.
Scene III: Moving day, one week later.

Act III
An hour later.

ACT I • Scene I

(The Younger living room would be a comfortable and well-ordered room if it were not for a number of inde-structible contradictions to this state of being. Its furnishings are typical and undistinguished and their primary feature now is that they have clearly had to accommodate the living of too many people for too many years — and they are tired. Still, we can see that at some time, a time probably no longer remembered by the family [except perhaps for Mama], the furnishings

of this room were actually selected with care and love and even hope — and brought to this apartment and arranged with taste and pride.)

(That was a long time ago. Now the once loved pattern of the couch upholstery has to fight to show itself from under acres of crocheted doilies and couch covers which have themselves finally come to be more important than the upholstery. And here a table or a chair has been moved to disguise the worn places in the carpet; but the carpet has fought back by showing its weariness, with depressing uniformity, elsewhere on its surface.)

(Weariness has, in fact, won in this room. Everything has been polished, washed, sat on, used, scrubbed too often. All pretenses but living itself have long since vanished from the very atmosphere of this room.)

(Moreover, a section of this room, for it is not really a room unto itself, though the landlord's lease would make it seem so, slopes backward to provide a small kitchen area, where the family prepares the meals that are eaten in the living room proper, which must also serve as dining room. The single window that has been provided for these "two" rooms is located in this kitchen area. The sole natural light the family may enjoy in the course of a day is only that which fights its way through this little window.)

(At left, a door leads to a bedroom which is shared by Mama and her daughter, Beneatha. At right, opposite, is a second room [which in the beginning of the life of this apartment was probably a breakfast room] which serves as a bedroom for Walter and his wife, Ruth.)

(Time: Sometime between World War II and the present.)

(Place: Chicago's Southside.)

(At rise: It is morning dark in the living room. Travis is asleep on the make-down bed at center. An alarm clock sounds from within the bedroom at right, and presently Ruth enters from that room and closes the door behind her. She crosses sleepily toward the window. As she passes her sleeping son she reaches down and shakes him a little. At the window she raises the shade and a dusky Southside morning light comes in feebly. She fills a pot with water and puts it on to boil. She *calls to the boy, between yawns, in a slightly muffled voice.*)

(*Ruth is about thirty. We can see that she was a pretty girl, even exceptionally so, but now it is apparent that life has been little that she expected, and disappointment has already begun to hang in her face. In a few years, before thirty-five even, she will be known among her people as a "settled woman.")*

(*She crosses to her son and gives him a good, final, rousing shake.*)

RUTH: Come on now, boy, it's seven thirty! (*Her son sits up at last, in a stupor of sleepiness.*) I say hurry up, Travis! You ain't the only person in the world got to use a bathroom! (*The child, a sturdy, handsome little boy of ten or eleven, drags himself out of the bed and almost blindly takes his towels and "today's clothes" from drawers and a closet and goes out to the bathroom, which is in an outside hall and which is shared by another family or families on the same floor. Ruth crosses to the bedroom door at right and opens it and calls in to her husband.*) Walter Lee! . . . It's after seven thirty! Lemme see you do some waking up in there now! (*She waits.*) You better get up from there, man! It's after seven thirty I tell you. (*She waits again.*) All right, you just go ahead and lay there and next thing you know Travis be finished and Mr. Johnson'll be in there and you'll be fussing and cussing round here like a madman! And be late too! (*She waits, at the end of patience.*) Walter Lee — it's time for you to GET UP!

(*She waits another second and then starts to go into the bedroom, but is apparently satisfied that her husband has begun to get up. She stops, pulls the door to, and returns to the kitchen area. She wipes her face with a moist cloth and runs her fingers through her sleep-disheveled hair in a vain effort and ties an apron around her housecoat. The bedroom door at right opens and her husband stands in the doorway in his pajamas, which are rumpled and mismated. He is a lean, intense young man in his middle thirties, inclined to quick nervous movements and erratic speech habits — and always in his voice there is a quality of indictment.*)

WALTER: Is he out yet?

RUTH: What you mean *out*? He ain't hardly got in there good yet.

WALTER (*wandering in, still more oriented to sleep than to a new day*): Well, what was you doing all that yelling for if I can't even get in there yet? (*Stopping and thinking.*) Check coming today?

RUTH: They *said* Saturday and this is just Friday and I hopes to God you ain't going to get up here first thing this morning and start talking to me 'bout no money — 'cause I 'bout don't want to hear it.

WALTER: Something the matter with you this morning?

RUTH: No — I'm just sleepy as the devil. What kind of eggs you want?

WALTER: Not scrambled. (*Ruth starts to scramble eggs.*)

Paper come? (*Ruth points impatiently to the rolled up Tribune on the table, and he gets it and spreads it out and vaguely reads the front page.*) Set off another bomb yesterday.

RUTH (*maximum indifference*): Did they?

WALTER (*looking up*): What's the matter with you?

RUTH: Ain't nothing the matter with me. And don't keep asking me that this morning.

WALTER: Ain't nobody bothering you. (*Reading the news of the day absently again.*) Say Colonel McCormick is sick.

RUTH (*affecting tea-party interest*): Is he now? Poor thing.

WALTER (*sighing and looking at his watch*): Oh, me. (*He waits.*) Now what is that boy doing in that bathroom all this time? He just going to have to start getting up earlier. I can't be being late to work on account of him fooling around in there.

RUTH (*turning on him*): Oh, no he ain't going to be getting up no earlier no such thing! It ain't his fault that he can't get to bed no earlier nights 'cause he got a bunch of crazy good-for-nothing clowns sitting up running their mouths in what is supposed to be his bedroom after ten o'clock at night . . .

WALTER: That's what you mad about, ain't it? The things I want to talk about with my friends just couldn't be important in your mind, could they?

(*He rises and finds a cigarette in her handbag on the table and crosses to the little window and looks out, smoking and deeply enjoying this first one.*)

RUTH (*almost matter of factly, a complaint too automatic to deserve emphasis*): Why you always got to smoke before you eat in the morning?

WALTER (*at the window*): Just look at 'em down there . . . Running and racing to work . . . (*He turns and faces his wife and watches her a moment at the stove, and then, suddenly.*) You look young this morning, baby.

RUTH (*indifferently*): Yeah?

WALTER: Just for a second — stirring them eggs. Just for a second it was — you looked real young again. (*He reaches for her; she crosses away. Then, drily.*) It's gone now — you look like yourself again!

RUTH: Man, if you don't shut up and leave me alone.

WALTER (*looking out to the street again*): First thing a man ought to learn in life is not to make love to no colored woman first thing in the morning. You all some eeeevil people at eight o'clock in the morning.

(*Travis appears in the hall doorway, almost fully dressed and quite wide awake now, his towels and pajamas across his shoulders. He opens the door and signals for his father to make the bathroom in a hurry.*)

TRAVIS (*watching the bathroom*): Daddy, come on!

(*Walter gets his bathroom utensils and flies out to the bathroom.*)

RUTH: Sit down and have your breakfast, Travis.

TRAVIS: Mama, this is Friday. (*Gleefully.*) Check coming tomorrow, huh?

RUTH: You get your mind off money and eat your breakfast.

TRAVIS (*eating*): This is the morning we supposed to bring the fifty cents to school.

RUTH: Well, I ain't got no fifty cents this morning.

TRAVIS: Teacher say we have to.

RUTH: I don't care what teacher say. I ain't got it. Eat your breakfast, Travis.

TRAVIS: I *am* eating.

RUTH: Hush up now and just eat!

(*The boy gives her an exasperated look for her lack of understanding and eats grudgingly.*)

TRAVIS: You think Grandmama would have it?

RUTH: No! And I want you to stop asking your grandmother for money, you hear me?

TRAVIS (*outraged*): Gaaaleee! I don't ask her, she just gimme it sometimes!

RUTH: Travis Willard Younger — I got too much on me this morning to be —

TRAVIS: Maybe Daddy —

RUTH: Travis!

(*The boy hushes abruptly. They are both quiet and tense for several seconds.*)

TRAVIS (*presently*): Could I maybe go carry some groceries in front of the supermarket for a little while after school then?

RUTH: Just hush, I said. (*Travis jabs his spoon into his cereal bowl viciously and rests his head in anger upon his fists.*) If you through eating, you can get over there and make up your bed.

(*The boy obeys stiffly and crosses the room, almost mechanically, to the bed and more or less folds the bedding into a heap, then angrily gets his books and cap.*)

TRAVIS (*sulking and standing apart from her unnaturally*): I'm gone.

RUTH (*looking up from the stove to inspect him automatically*): Come here. (*He crosses to her and she studies his head.*) If you don't take this comb and fix this here head, you better! (*Travis puts down his books with a great sigh of oppression and crosses to the mirror. His mother mutters under her breath about his "slubbornness."*) 'Bout to march out of here with that head looking just like chickens slept in it! I just don't know where you get your slubborn ways . . . And get your jacket, too. Looks chilly out this morning.

TRAVIS (*with conspicuously brushed hair and jacket*): I'm gone.

RUTH: Get carfare and milk money — (*waving one finger*) — and not a single penny for no caps, you hear me?

TRAVIS (*with sullen politeness*): Yes'm.

(*He turns in outrage to leave. His mother watches after him as in his frustration he approaches the door almost comically. When she speaks to him, her voice has become a very gentle tease.*)

RUTH (*mocking; as she thinks he would say it*): Oh, Mama makes me so mad sometimes, I don't know what to do! (*She waits and continues to his back as he stands stock-still in front of the door.*) I wouldn't kiss that woman good-bye for nothing in this world this morning! (*The boy finally turns around and rolls his eyes at her, knowing the mood has changed and he is vindicated; he does not, however, move toward her yet.*) Not for nothing in this world! (*She finally laughs aloud at him and holds out her arms to him and we see that it is a way between them, very old and practiced. He crosses to her and allows her to embrace him warmly but keeps his face fixed with masculine rigidity. She holds him back from her presently and looks at him and runs her fingers over the features of his face. With utter gentleness —*) Now — whose little old angry man are you?

TRAVIS (*the masculinity and gruffness start to fade at last*): Aw gaalee — Mama . . .

RUTH (*mimicking*): Aw — gaaaaalleeeee, Mama! (*She pushes him, with rough playfulness and finality, toward the door.*) Get on out of here or you going to be late.

TRAVIS (*in the face of love, new aggressiveness*): Mama, could I *please* go carry groceries?

RUTH: Honey, it's starting to get so cold evenings.

WALTER (*coming in from the bathroom and drawing a make-believe gun from a make-believe holster and shooting at his son*): What is it he wants to do?

RUTH: Go carry groceries after school at the supermarket.

WALTER: Well, let him go . . .

TRAVIS (*quickly, to the ally*): I *have* to — she won't gimme the fifty cents . . .

WALTER (*to his wife only*): Why not?

RUTH (*simply, and with flavor*): 'Cause we don't have it.

WALTER (*to Ruth only*): What you tell the boy things like that for? (*Reaching down into his pants with a rather important gesture.*) Here, son —

(*He hands the boy the coin, but his eyes are directed to his wife's. Travis takes the money happily.*)

TRAVIS: Thanks, Daddy.

(*He starts out. Ruth watches both of them with murder in her eyes. Walter stands and stares back at her with defiance and suddenly reaches into his pocket again on an afterthought.*)

WALTER (*without even looking at his son, still staring hard at his wife*): In fact, here's another fifty cents . . . Buy yourself some fruit today — or take a taxicab to school or something!

TRAVIS: Whoopee —

(*He leaps up and clasps his father around the middle with his legs, and they face each other in mutual appreciation; slowly Walter Lee peeks around the boy to*) catch the violent rays from his wife's eyes and draws his head back as if shot.)

WALTER: You better get down now — and get to school, man.

TRAVIS (at the door): O.K. Good-bye.

(He exits.)

WALTER (after him, pointing with pride): That's my boy. (She looks at him in disgust and turns back to her work.) You know what I was thinking 'bout in the bathroom this morning?

RUTH: No.

WALTER: How come you always try to be so pleasant!

RUTH: What is there to be pleasant 'bout!

WALTER: You want to know what I was thinking 'bout in the bathroom or not!

RUTH: I know what you thinking 'bout.

WALTER (ignoring her): 'Bout what me and Willy Harris was talking about last night.

RUTH (immediately — a refrain): Willy Harris is a good-for-nothing loudmouth.

WALTER: Anybody who talks to me has got to be a good-for-nothing loudmouth, ain't he? And what you know about who is just a good-for-nothing loudmouth? Charlie Atkins was just a "good-for-nothing loud-mouth" too, wasn't he! When he wanted me to go in the dry-cleaning business with him. And now — he's grossing a hundred thousand a year. A hundred thousand dollars a year! You still call *him* a loudmouth!

RUTH (bitterly): Oh, Walter Lee . . .

(She folds her head on her arms over the table.)

WALTER (rising and coming to her and standing over her): You tired, ain't you? Tired of everything. Me, the boy, the way we live — this beat-up hole — everything. Ain't you? (She doesn't look up, doesn't answer.) So tired — moaning and groaning all the time, but you wouldn't do nothing to help, would you? You couldn't be on my side that long for nothing, could you?

RUTH: Walter, please leave me alone.

WALTER: A man needs for a woman to back him up . . .

RUTH: Walter —

WALTER: Mama would listen to you. You know she listen to you more than she do me and Bennie. She think more of you. All you have to do is just sit down with her when you drinking your coffee one morning and talking 'bout things like you do and — (He sits down beside her and demonstrates graphically what he thinks her methods and tone should be.) — you just sip your coffee, see, and say easy like that you been thinking 'bout that deal Walter Lee is so interested in, 'bout the store and all, and sip some more coffee, like what you saying ain't really that important to you — And the next thing you know, she be listening good and asking you questions and when I come home — I can tell her the details. This ain't no fly-by-night proposition, baby. I mean we figured it out, me and Willy and Bobo.

RUTH (with a frown): Bobo?

WALTER: Yeah. You see, this little liquor store we got in mind cost seventy-five thousand and we figured the initial investment on the place be 'bout thirty thousand, see. That be ten thousand each. Course, there's a couple of hundred you got to pay so's you don't spend your life just waiting for them clowns to let your license get approved —

RUTH: You mean graft?

WALTER (frowning impatiently): Don't call it that. See there, that just goes to show you what women understand about the world. Baby, don't *nothing* happen for you in this world 'less you pay *somebody* off!

RUTH: Walter, leave me alone! (She raises her head and stares at him vigorously — then says, more quietly.) *Eat* your eggs, they gonna be cold.

WALTER (straightening up from her and looking off): That's it. There you are. Man say to his woman: I got me a dream. His woman say: Eat your eggs. (Sadly, but gaining in power.) Man say: I got to take hold of this here world, baby! And a woman will say: Eat your eggs and go to work. (Passionately now.) Man say: I got to change my life, I'm choking to death, baby! And his woman say — (in utter anguish as he brings his fists down on his thighs) — Your eggs is getting cold!

RUTH (softly): Walter, that ain't none of our money.

WALTER (not listening at all or even looking at her): This morning, I was lookin' in the mirror and thinking about it . . . I'm thirty-five years old; I been married eleven years and I got a boy who sleeps in the living room — (very, very quietly) — and all I got to give him is stories about how rich white people live . . .

RUTH: Eat your eggs, Walter.

WALTER (slams the table and jumps up): — DAMN MY EGGS — DAMN ALL THE EGGS THAT EVER WAS!

RUTH: Then go to work.

WALTER (looking up at her): See — I'm trying to talk to you 'bout myself — (shaking his head with the repetition) — and all you can say is eat them eggs and go to work.

RUTH (wearily): Honey, you never say nothing new. I listen to you every day, every night and every morning, and you never say nothing new. (Shrugging.) So you would rather *be* Mr. Arnold than be his chauffeur. So — I would *rather* be living in Buckingham Palace.

WALTER: That is just what is wrong with the colored woman in this world . . . Don't understand about building their men up and making 'em feel like they somebody. Like they can do something.

RUTH (drily, but to hurt): There *are* colored men who do things.

WALTER: No thanks to the colored woman.

RUTH: Well, being a colored woman, I guess I can't help myself none.

(She rises and gets the ironing board and sets it up and attacks a huge pile of rough-dried clothes, sprinkling them in preparation for the ironing and then rolling them into tight fat balls.)

WALTER (*mumbling*): We one group of men tied to a race of women with small minds!

(*His sister Beneatha enters. She is about twenty, as slim and intense as her brother. She is not as pretty as her sister-in-law, but her lean, almost intellectual face has a handsomeness of its own. She wears a bright red flannel nightie, and her thick hair stands wildly about her head. Her speech is a mixture of many things; it is different from the rest of the family's insofar as education has permeated her sense of English — and perhaps the Midwest rather than the South has finally — at last — won out in her inflection; but not altogether, because over all of it is a soft slurring and transformed use of vowels which is the decided influence of the Southside. She passes through the room without looking at either Ruth or Walter and goes to the outside door and looks, a little blindly, out to the bathroom. She sees that it has been lost to the Johnsons. She closes the door with a sleepy vengeance and crosses to the table and sits down a little defeated.*)

BENEATHA: I am going to start timing those people.

WALTER: You should get up earlier.

BENEATHA (*Her face in her hands. She is still fighting the urge to go back to bed.*): Really — would you suggest dawn? Where's the paper?

WALTER (*pushing the paper across the table to her as he studies her almost clinically, as though he has never seen her before*): You a horrible-looking chick at this hour.

BENEATHA (*drily*): Good morning, everybody.

WALTER (*senselessly*): How is school coming?

BENEATHA (*in the same spirit*): Lovely. Lovely. And you know, biology is the greatest. (*Looking up at him.*) I dissected something that looked just like you yesterday.

WALTER: I just wondered if you've made up your mind and everything.

BENEATHA (*gaining in sharpness and impatience*): And what did I answer yesterday morning — and the day before that?

RUTH (*from the ironing board, like someone disinterested and old*): Don't be so nasty, Bennie.

BENEATHA (*still to her brother*): And the day before that and the day before that!

WALTER (*defensively*): I'm interested in you. Something wrong with that? Ain't many girls who decide —

WALTER AND BENEATHA (*in unison*): — "to be a doctor."

(*Silence.*)

WALTER: Have we figured out yet just exactly how much medical school is going to cost?

RUTH: Walter Lee, why don't you leave that girl alone and get out of here to work?

BENEATHA (*exits to the bathroom and bangs on the door*): Come on out of there, please!

(*She comes back into the room.*)

WALTER (*looking at his sister intently*): You know the check is coming tomorrow.

BENEATHA (*turning on him with a sharpness all her own*): That money belongs to Mama, Walter, and it's for her to decide how she wants to use it. I don't care if she wants to buy a house or a rocketship or just nail it up somewhere and look at it. It's hers. Not ours — *hers*.

WALTER (*bitterly*): Now ain't that fine! You just got your mother's interest at heart, ain't you, girl? You such a nice girl — but if Mama got that money she can always take a few thousand and help you through school too — can't she?

BENEATHA: I have never asked anyone around here to do anything for me!

WALTER: No! And the line between asking and just accepting when the time comes is big and wide — ain't it!

BENEATHA (*with fury*): What do you want from me, Brother — that I quit school or just drop dead, which!

WALTER: I don't want nothing but for you to stop acting holy 'round here. Me and Ruth done made some sacrifices for you — why can't you do something for the family?

RUTH: Walter, don't be dragging me in it.

WALTER: You are in it — Don't you get up and go work in somebody's kitchen for the last three years to help put clothes on her back?

RUTH: Oh, Walter — that's not fair . . .

WALTER: It ain't that nobody expects you to get on your knees and say thank you, Brother; thank you, Ruth; thank you, Mama — and thank you, Travis, for wearing the same pair of shoes for two semesters —

BENEATHA (*dropping to her knees*): Well — I *do* — all right? — thank everybody! And forgive me for ever wanting to be anything at all! (*Pursuing him on her knees across the floor.*) FORGIVE ME, FORGIVE ME, FORGIVE ME!

RUTH: Please stop it! Your mama'll hear you.

WALTER: Who the hell told you you had to be a doctor? If you so crazy 'bout messing 'round with sick people — then go be a nurse like other women — or just get married and be quiet . . .

BENEATHA: Well — you finally got it said . . . It took you three years but you finally got it said. Walter, give up; leave me alone — it's Mama's money.

WALTER: *He was my father, too!*

BENEATHA: So what? He was mine, too — and Travis' grandfather — but the insurance money belongs to Mama. Picking on me is not going to make her give it to you to invest in any liquor stores — (*under breath, dropping into a chair*) — and I for one say, God bless Mama for that!

WALTER (*to Ruth*): See — did you hear? Did you hear!

RUTH: Honey, please go to work.

WALTER: Nobody in this house is ever going to understand me.

BENEATHA: Because you're a nut.

Ester Rolle as Lena Younger comforts
her daughter-in-law Ruth in the
Huntington Theatre Company's 1994
production of *A Raisin in the Sun.*
Also in the scene are Marguerite
Hannah as Ruth and B. W. Gonzalez
as Beneatha.

WALTER: Who's a nut?

BENEATHA: You — you are a nut. Thee is mad, boy.

WALTER (*looking at his wife and his sister from the door, very sadly*): The world's most backward race of people, and that's a fact.

BENEATHA (*turning slowly in her chair*): And then there are all those prophets who would lead us out of the wilderness — (*Walter slams out of the house.*) — into the swamps!

RUTH: Bennie, why you always gotta be pickin' on your brother? Can't you be a little sweeter sometimes? (*Door opens. Walter walks in. He fumbles with his cap, starts to speak, clears throat, looks everywhere but at Ruth. Finally.*)

WALTER (*to Ruth*): I need some money for carfare.

RUTH (*looks at him, then warms; teasing, but tenderly*): Fifty cents? (*She goes to her bag and gets money.*) Here — take a taxi!

(*Walter exits. Mama enters. She is a woman in her early sixties, full-bodied and strong. She is one of those women of a certain grace and beauty who wear it so unobtrusively that it takes a while to notice. Her dark brown face is surrounded by the total whiteness of her hair, and, being a woman who has adjusted to many things in life and overcome many more, her face is full of strength. She has, we can see, wit and faith of a kind that keep her eyes lit and full of interest and expectancy. She is, in a word, a beautiful woman. Her bearing is perhaps most like the noble bearing of the women of the Hereros of Southwest Africa — rather as if she imagines that as she walks she still bears a basket or a vessel upon her head. Her speech, on the other hand, is as careless as her carriage is precise — she is inclined to slur everything — but her voice is perhaps not so much quiet as simply soft.*)

MAMA: Who that 'round here slamming doors at this hour?

(*She crosses through the room, goes to the window, opens it, and brings in a feeble little plant growing doggedly in a small pot on the window sill. She feels the dirt and puts it back out.*)

RUTH: That was Walter Lee. He and Bennie was at it again.

MAMA: My children and they tempers. Lord, if this little old plant don't get more sun than it's been getting it ain't never going to see spring again. (*She turns from the window.*) What's the matter with you this morning, Ruth? You looks right peaked. You aiming to iron all them things? Leave some for me. I'll get to 'em this afternoon. Bennie honey, it's too drafty for you to be sitting 'round half dressed. Where's your robe?

BENEATHA: In the cleaners.

MAMA: Well, go get mine and put it on.

BENEATHA: I'm not cold, Mama, honest.

MAMA: I know — but you so thin . . .

BENEATHA (*irritably*): Mama, I'm not cold.

MAMA (*seeing the make-down bed as Travis has left it*): Lord have mercy, look at that poor bed. Bless his heart — he tries, don't he?

(*She moves to the bed Travis has sloppily made up.*)

RUTH: No — he don't half try at all 'cause he knows you going to come along behind him and fix everything. That's just how come he don't know how to do nothing right now — you done spoiled that boy so.

MAMA (*folding bedding*): Well — he's a little boy. Ain't supposed to know 'bout housekeeping. My baby, that's what he is. What you fix for his breakfast this morning?

RUTH (*angrily*): I feed my son, Lena!

MAMA: I ain't meddling — (*Under breath; busybodyish.*) I just noticed all last week he had cold cereal, and when it starts getting this chilly in the fall a child ought to have some hot grits or something when he goes out in the cold —

RUTH (*furious*): I gave him hot oats — is that all right!

MAMA: I ain't meddling. (*Pause.*) Put a lot of nice butter on it? (*Ruth shoots her an angry look and does not reply.*) He likes lots of butter.

RUTH (*exasperated*): Lena —

MAMA (*To Beneatha. Mama is inclined to wander conversationally sometimes.*): What was you and your brother fussing 'bout this morning?

BENEATHA: It's not important, Mama.

(*She gets up and goes to look out at the bathroom, which is apparently free, and she picks up her towels and rushes out.*)

MAMA: What was they fighting about?

RUTH: Now you know as well as I do.

MAMA (*shaking her head*): Brother still worrying hisself sick about that money?

RUTH: You know he is.

MAMA: You had breakfast?

RUTH: Some coffee.

MAMA: Girl, you better start eating and looking after yourself better. You almost thin as Travis.

RUTH: Lena —

MAMA: Un-hunh?

RUTH: What are you going to do with it?

MAMA: Now don't you start, child. It's too early in the morning to be talking about money. It ain't Christian.

RUTH: It's just that he got his heart set on that store —

MAMA: You mean that liquor store that Willy Harris want him to invest in?

RUTH: Yes —

MAMA: We ain't no business people, Ruth. We just plain working folks.

RUTH: Ain't nobody business people till they go into business. Walter Lee say colored people ain't never going to start getting ahead till they start gambling on some different kinds of things in the world — investments and things.

MAMA: What done got into you, girl? Walter Lee done finally sold you on investing.

RUTH: No. Mama, something is happening between Walter and me. I don't know what it is — but he needs something — something I can't give him anymore. He needs this chance, Lena.

MAMA (*frowning deeply*): But liquor, honey —

RUTH: Well — like Walter say — I spec people going to always be drinking themselves some liquor.

MAMA: Well — whether they drinks it or not ain't none of my business. But whether I go into business selling it to 'em *is*, and I don't want that on my ledger this late in life. (*Stopping suddenly and studying her daughter-in-law.*) Ruth Younger, what's the matter with you today? You look like you could fall over right there.

RUTH: I'm tired.

MAMA: Then you better stay home from work today.

RUTH: I can't stay home. She'd be calling up the agency and screaming at them, "My girl didn't come in today — send me somebody! My girl didn't come in!" Oh, she just have a fit . . .

MAMA: Well, let her have it. I'll just call her up and say you got the flu —

RUTH (*laughing*): Why the flu?

MAMA: 'Cause it sounds respectable to 'em. Something white people get, too. They know 'bout the flu. Otherwise they think you been cut up or something when you tell 'em you sick.

RUTH: I got to go in. We need the money.

MAMA: Somebody would of thought my children done all but starved to death the way they talk about money here late. Child, we got a great big old check coming tomorrow.

RUTH (*sincerely, but also self-righteously*): Now that's your money. It ain't got nothing to do with me. We all feel like that — Walter and Bennie and me — even Travis.

MAMA (*thoughtfully, and suddenly very far away*): Ten thousand dollars.

RUTH: Sure is wonderful.

MAMA: Ten thousand dollars.

RUTH: You know what you should do, Miss Lena? You should take yourself a trip somewhere. To Europe or South America or someplace —

MAMA (*throwing up her hands at the thought*): Oh, child!

RUTH: I'm serious. Just pack up and leave! Go on away and enjoy yourself some. Forget about the family and have yourself a ball for once in your life —

MAMA (*drily*): You sound like I'm just about ready to die. Who'd go with me? What I look like wandering 'round Europe by myself?

RUTH: Shoot — these here rich white women do it all the time. They don't think nothing of packing up they suitcases and piling on one of them big steamships and — swoosh! — they gone, child.

MAMA: Something always told me I wasn't no rich white woman.

RUTH: Well — what are you going to do with it then?

MAMA: I ain't rightly decided. (*Thinking. She speaks now with emphasis.*) Some of it got to be put away for Beneatha and her schoolin' — and ain't nothing going to touch that part of it. Nothing. (*She waits several seconds, trying to make up her mind about something, and looks at Ruth a little tentatively before going on.*) Been thinking that we maybe could meet the notes on a little old two-story somewhere, with a yard where Travis could play in the summertime, if we use part of the insurance for a down payment and everybody kind of pitch in. I could maybe take on a little day work again, few days a week —

RUTH (*studying her mother-in-law furtively and concentrating on her ironing, anxious to encourage without seeming to*): Well, Lord knows, we've put enough rent into this here rat trap to pay for four houses by now . . .

MAMA (*looking up at the words "rat trap" and then looking around and leaning back and sighing — in a suddenly reflective mood —*): "Rat trap" — yes, that's all it is. (*Smiling.*) I remember just as well the day me and Big Walter moved in here. Hadn't been married but two weeks and wasn't planning on living here no more than a year. (*She shakes her head at the dissolved dream.*) We was going to set away, little by little, don't you know, and buy a little place out in Morgan Park. We had even picked out the house. (*Chuckling a little.*) Looks right dumpy today. But Lord, child, you should know, all the dreams I had 'bout buying that house and fixing it up and making me a little garden in the back — (*She waits and stops smiling.*) And didn't none of it happen.

(*Dropping her hands in a futile gesture.*)

RUTH (*keeps her head down, ironing*): Yes, life can be a barrel of disappointments, sometimes.

MAMA: Honey, Big Walter would come in here some nights back then and slump down on that couch there and just look at the rug, and look at me and look at the rug and then back at me — and I'd know he was down then . . . really down. (*After a second very long and thoughtful pause; she is seeing back to times that only she can see.*) And then, Lord, when I lost that baby — little Claude — I almost thought I was going to lose Big Walter too. Oh, that man grieved hisself! He was one man to love his children.

RUTH: Ain't nothin' can tear at you like losin' your baby.

MAMA: I guess that's how come that man finally worked hisself to death like he done. Like he was fighting his own war with this here world that took his baby from him.

RUTH: He sure was a fine man, all right. I always liked Mr. Younger.

MAMA: Crazy 'bout his children! God knows there was plenty wrong with Walter Younger — hard-headed, mean, kind of wild with women — plenty wrong with him. But he sure loved his children. Always wanted them to have something — be something. That's where Brother gets all these notions, I reckon. Big Walter used to say, he'd get right wet in the eyes sometimes, lean his head back with the water standing in his eyes and say, "Seem like God didn't see fit to give the black man nothing but dreams — but He did give us children to make them dreams seem worthwhile." (*She smiles.*) He could talk like that, don't you know.

RUTH: Yes, he sure could. He was a good man, Mr. Younger.

MAMA: Yes, a fine man — just couldn't never catch up with his dreams, that's all.

(*Beneatha comes in, brushing her hair and looking up to the ceiling, where the sound of a vacuum cleaner has started up.*)

BENEATHA: What could be so dirty on that woman's rugs that she has to vacuum them every single day?

RUTH: I wish certain young women 'round here who I could name would take inspiration about certain rugs in a certain apartment I could also mention.

BENEATHA (*shrugging*): How much cleaning can a house need, for Christ's sakes.

MAMA (*not liking the Lord's name used thus*): Bennie!

RUTH: Just listen to her — just listen!

BENEATHA: Oh, God!

MAMA: If you use the Lord's name just one more time —

BENEATHA (*a bit of a whine*): Oh, Mama —

RUTH: Fresh — just fresh as salt, this girl!

BENEATHA (*drily*): Well — if the salt loses its savor —

MAMA: Now that will do. I just ain't going to have you 'round here reciting the scriptures in vain — you hear me?

BENEATHA: How did I manage to get on everybody's wrong side by just walking into a room?

RUTH: If you weren't so fresh —

BENEATHA: Ruth, I'm twenty years old.

MAMA: What time you be home from school today?

BENEATHA: Kind of late. (*With enthusiasm.*) Madeline is going to start my guitar lessons today.

(*Mama and Ruth look up with the same expression.*)

MAMA: Your *what* kind of lessons?

BENEATHA: Guitar.

RUTH: Oh, Father!

MAMA: How come you done taken it in your mind to learn to play the guitar?

BENEATHA: I just want to, that's all.

MAMA (*smiling*): Lord, child, don't you know what to do with yourself? How long it going to be before you get tired of this now — like you got tired of that little play-acting group you joined last year? (*Looking at Ruth.*) And what was it the year before that?

RUTH: The horseback-riding club for which she bought that fifty-five-dollar riding habit that's been hanging in the closet ever since!

MAMA (*to Beneatha*): Why you got to flit so from one thing to another, baby?

BENEATHA (*sharply*): I just want to learn to play the guitar. Is there anything wrong with that?

MAMA: Ain't nobody trying to stop you. I just wonders sometimes why you has to flit so from one thing to another all the time. You ain't never done nothing with all that camera equipment you brought home —

BENEATHA: I don't flit! I — I experiment with different forms of expression —

RUTH: Like riding a horse?

BENEATHA: — People have to express themselves one way or another.

MAMA: What is it you want to express?

BENEATHA (*angrily*): Me! (*Mama and Ruth look at each other and burst into raucous laughter.*) Don't worry — I don't expect you to understand.

MAMA (*to change the subject*): Who you going out with tomorrow night?

BENEATHA (*with displeasure*): George Murchison again.

MAMA (*pleased*): Oh — you getting a little sweet on him?

RUTH: You ask me, this child ain't sweet on nobody but herself — (*Under breath.*) Express herself!

(*They laugh.*)

BENEATHA: Oh — I like George all right, Mama. I mean I like him enough to go out with him and stuff, but —

RUTH (*for devilment*): What does *and stuff* mean?

BENEATHA: Mind your own business.

MAMA: Stop picking at her now, Ruth. (*She chuckles — then a suspicious sudden look at her daughter as she turns in her chair for emphasis.*) What DOES it mean?

BENEATHA (*wearily*): Oh, I just mean I couldn't ever really be serious about George. He's — he's so shallow.

RUTH: Shallow — what do you mean he's shallow? He's *Rich!*

MAMA: Hush, Ruth.

BENEATHA: I know he's rich. He knows he's rich, too.

RUTH: Well — what other qualities a man got to have to satisfy you, little girl?

BENEATHA: You wouldn't even begin to understand. Anybody who married Walter could not possibly understand.

MAMA (*outraged*): What kind of way is that to talk about your brother?

BENEATHA: Brother is a flip — let's face it.

MAMA (*to Ruth, helplessly*): What's a flip?

RUTH (*glad to add kindling*): She's saying he's crazy.

BENEATHA: Not crazy. Brother isn't really crazy yet — he — he's an elaborate neurotic.

MAMA: Hush your mouth!

BENEATHA: As for George. Well. George looks good — he's got a beautiful car and he takes me to nice places and, as my sister-in-law says, he is probably the richest boy I will ever get to know and I even like him sometimes — but if the Youngers are sitting around waiting to see if their little Bennie is going to tie up the family with the Murchisons, they are wasting their time.

RUTH: You mean you wouldn't marry George Murchison if he asked you someday? That pretty, rich thing? Honey, I knew you was odd —

BENEATHA: No I would not marry him if all I felt for him was what I feel now. Besides, George's family wouldn't really like it.

MAMA: Why not?

BENEATHA: Oh, Mama — The Murchisons are honest-to-God-real-*live*-rich colored people, and the only people in the world who are more snobbish than rich white people are rich colored people. I thought everybody knew that. I've met Mrs. Murchison. She's a scene!

MAMA: You must not dislike people 'cause they well off, honey.

BENEATHA: Why not? It makes just as much sense as disliking people 'cause they are poor, and lots of people do that.

RUTH (*A wisdom-of-the-ages manner. To Mama.*): Well, she'll get over some of this —

BENEATHA: Get over it? What are you talking about, Ruth? Listen, I'm going to be a doctor. I'm not worried about who I'm going to marry yet — if I ever get married.

MAMA AND RUTH: *If!*

MAMA: Now, Bennie —

BENEATHA: Oh, I probably will . . . but first I'm going to be a doctor, and George, for one, still thinks that's pretty funny. I couldn't be bothered with that. I am going to be a doctor and everybody around here better understand that!

MAMA (*kindly*): 'Course you going to be a doctor, honey, God willing.

BENEATHA (*drily*): God hasn't got a thing to do with it.

MAMA: Beneatha — that just wasn't necessary.

BENEATHA: Well — neither is God. I get sick of hearing about God.

MAMA: Beneatha!

BENEATHA: I mean it! I'm just tired of hearing about God all the time. What has He got to do with anything? Does he pay tuition?

MAMA: You 'bout to get your fresh little jaw slapped!

RUTH: That's just what she needs, all right!

BENEATHA: Why? Why can't I say what I want to around here, like everybody else?

MAMA: It don't sound nice for a young girl to say things like that — you wasn't brought up that way. Me and your father went to trouble to get you and Brother to church every Sunday.

BENEATHA: Mama, you don't understand. It's all a matter of ideas, and God is just one idea I don't accept. It's not important. I am not going out and be immoral or commit crimes because I don't believe in God. I don't even think about it. It's just that I get tired of Him getting credit for all the things the human race achieves through its own stubborn effort. There simply is no blasted God — there is only man and it is *he* who makes miracles!

(*Mama absorbs this speech, studies her daughter and rises slowly and crosses to Beneatha and slaps her powerfully across the face. After, there is only silence and the daughter drops her eyes from her mother's face, and Mama is very tall before her.*)

MAMA: Now — you say after me, in my mother's house there is still God. (*There is a long pause and Beneatha stares at the floor wordlessly. Mama repeats the phrase with precision and cool emotion.*) In my mother's house there is still God.

BENEATHA: In my mother's house there is still God.

(*A long pause.*)

MAMA (*Walking away from Beneatha, too disturbed for triumphant posture. Stopping and turning back to her daughter.*): There are some ideas we ain't going to have in this house. Not long as I am at the head of this family.

BENEATHA: Yes, ma'am.

(*Mama walks out of the room.*)

RUTH (*almost gently, with profound understanding*): You think you a woman, Bennie — but you still a little girl. What you did was childish — so you got treated like a child.

BENEATHA: I see. (*Quietly.*) I also see that everybody thinks it's all right for Mama to be a tyrant. But all the tyranny in the world will never put a God in the heavens!

(*She picks up her books and goes out. Pause.*)

RUTH (*goes to Mama's door*): She said she was sorry.

MAMA (*coming out, going to her plant*): They frightens me, Ruth. My children.

RUTH: You got good children, Lena. They just a little off sometimes — but they're good.

MAMA: No — there's something come down between me and them that don't let us understand each other and I don't know what it is. One done almost lost his mind thinking 'bout money all the time and the other done commence to talk about things I can't seem to understand in no form or fashion. What is it that's changing, Ruth.

RUTH (*soothingly, older than her years*): Now . . . you taking it all too seriously. You just got strong-willed children and it takes a strong woman like you to keep 'em in hand.

MAMA (*looking at her plant and sprinkling a little water on it*): They spirited all right, my children. Got to admit they got spirit — Bennie and Walter. Like this little old plant that ain't never had enough sunshine or nothing — and look at it . . .

(*She has her back to Ruth, who has had to stop ironing and lean against something and put the back of her hand to her forehead.*)

RUTH (*trying to keep Mama from noticing*): You . . . sure . . . loves that little old thing, don't you? . . .

MAMA: Well, I always wanted me a garden like I used to see sometimes at the back of the houses down home. This plant is close as I ever got to having one. (*She looks out of the window as she replaces the plant.*) Lord, ain't nothing as dreary as the view from this window on a dreary day, is there? Why ain't you singing this morning, Ruth? Sing that "No Ways Tired." That song always lifts me up so — (*She turns at last to see that Ruth has slipped quietly to the floor, in a state of semiconsciousness.*) Ruth! Ruth honey — what's the matter with you . . . Ruth!

Scene II

(*It is the following morning; a Saturday morning, and house cleaning is in progress at the Youngers'. Furniture has been shoved hither and yon and Mama is giving the kitchen-area walls a washing down. Beneatha, in dungarees, with a handkerchief tied around her face, is spraying insecticide into the cracks in the walls. As they work, the radio is on and a Southside disk jockey program is inappropriately filling the house with a rather exotic saxophone blues. Travis, the sole idle one, is leaning on his arms, looking out of the window.*)

TRAVIS: Grandmama, that stuff Bennie is using smells awful. Can I go downstairs, please?

MAMA: Did you get all them chores done already? I ain't seen you doing much.

TRAVIS: Yes'm — finished early. Where did Mama go this morning?

MAMA (*looking at Beneatha*): She had to go on a little errand.

(*The phone rings. Beneatha runs to answer it and reaches it before Walter, who has entered from bedroom.*)

TRAVIS: Where?

MAMA: To tend to her business.

BENEATHA: Haylo . . . (*Disappointed.*) Yes, he is. (*She tosses the phone to Walter, who barely catches it.*) It's Willie Harris again.

WALTER (*as privately as possible under Mama's gaze*): Hello, Willie. Did you get the papers from the lawyer? . . . No, not yet. I told you the mailman doesn't get here till ten-thirty . . . No, I'll come there . . . Yeah! Right away. (*He hangs up and goes for his coat.*)

BENEATHA: Brother, where did Ruth go?

WALTER (*as he exits*): How should I know!

TRAVIS: Aw come on, Grandma. Can I go outside?

MAMA: Oh, I guess so. You stay right in front of the house, though, and keep a good lookout for the postman.

TRAVIS: Yes'm. (*He darts into bedroom for stickball and bat, reenters, and sees Beneatha on her knees spraying under sofa with behind upraised. He edges closer to the target, takes aim, and lets her have it. She screams.*) Leave them poor little cockroaches alone, they ain't bothering you none! (*He runs as she swings the spraygun at him viciously and playfully.*) Grandma! Grandma!

MAMA: Look out there, girl, before you be spilling some of that stuff on that child!

TRAVIS (*safely behind the bastion of Mama*): That's right — look out, now! (*He exits.*)

BENEATHA (*drily*): I can't imagine that it would hurt him — it has never hurt the roaches.

MAMA: Well, little boys' hides ain't as tough as South-side roaches. You better get over there behind the bureau. I seen one marching out of there like Napoleon yesterday.

BENEATHA: There's really only one way to get rid of them, Mama —

MAMA: How?

BENEATHA: Set fire to this building! Mama, where did Ruth go?

MAMA (*looking at her with meaning*): To the doctor, I think.

BENEATHA: The doctor? What's the matter? (*They exchange glances.*) You don't think —

MAMA (*with her sense of drama*): Now I ain't saying what I think. But I ain't never been wrong 'bout a woman neither.

(*The phone rings.*)

BENEATHA (*at the phone*): Hay-lo . . . (*Pause, and a moment of recognition.*) Well — when did you get back! . . . And how was it? . . . Of course I've missed you — in my way . . . This morning? No . . . house cleaning and all that and Mama hates it if I let people come over when the house is like this . . . You *have?* Well, that's different . . . What is it — Oh, what the hell, come on over . . . Right, see you then. *Arrivederci.*

(*She hangs up.*)

MAMA (*who has listened vigorously, as is her habit*): Who is that you inviting over here with this house looking like this? You ain't got the pride you was born with!

BENEATHA: Asagai doesn't care how houses look, Mama — he's an intellectual.

MAMA: *Who?*

BENEATHA: Asagai — Joseph Asagai. He's an African boy I met on campus. He's been studying in Canada all summer.

MAMA: What's his name?

BENEATHA: Asagai, Joseph. Ah-sah-guy . . . He's from Nigeria.

MAMA: Oh, that's the little country that was founded by slaves way back . . .

BENEATHA: No, Mama — that's Liberia.

MAMA: I don't think I never met no African before.

BENEATHA: Well, do me a favor and don't ask him a whole lot of ignorant questions about Africans. I mean, do they wear clothes and all that —

MAMA: Well, now, I guess if you think we so ignorant 'round here maybe you shouldn't bring your friends here —

BENEATHA: It's just that people ask such crazy things. All anyone seems to know about when it comes to Africa is Tarzan —

MAMA (*indignantly*): Why should I know anything about Africa?

BENEATHA: Why do you give money at church for the missionary work?

MAMA: Well, that's to help save people.

BENEATHA: You mean save them from *heathenism* —

MAMA (*innocently*): Yes.

BENEATHA: I'm afraid they need more salvation from the British and the French.

(*Ruth comes in forlornly and pulls off her coat with dejection. They both turn to look at her.*)

RUTH (*dispiritedly*): Well, I guess from all the happy faces — everybody knows.

BENEATHA: You pregnant?

MAMA: Lord have mercy, I sure hope it's a little old girl. Travis ought to have a sister.

(*Beneatha and Ruth give her a hopeless look for this grandmotherly enthusiasm.*)

BENEATHA: How far along are you?

RUTH: Two months.

BENEATHA: Did you mean to? I mean did you plan it or was it an accident?

MAMA: What do you know about planning or not planning?

BENEATHA: Oh, Mama.

RUTH (*wearily*): She's twenty years old, Lena.

BENEATHA: Did you plan it, Ruth?

RUTH: Mind your own business.

BENEATHA: It is my business — where is he going to live, on the *roof?* (*There is silence following the remark as the three women react to the sense of it.*) Gee — I didn't mean that, Ruth, honest. Gee, I don't feel like that at all. I — I think it is wonderful.

RUTH (*dully*): Wonderful.

BENEATHA: Yes — really.

MAMA (*looking at Ruth, worried*): Doctor say everything going to be all right?

RUTH (*far away*): Yes — she says everything is going to be fine . . .

MAMA (*immediately suspicious*): "She" — What doctor you went to?

(*Ruth folds over, near hysteria.*)

MAMA (*worriedly hovering over Ruth*): Ruth honey — what's the matter with you — you sick?

(*Ruth has her fists clenched on her thighs and is fighting hard to suppress a scream that seems to be rising in her.*)

BENEATHA: What's the matter with her, Mama?

MAMA (*working her fingers in Ruth's shoulders to relax her*): She be all right. Women gets right depressed sometimes when they get her way. (*Speaking softly, expertly, rapidly.*) Now you just relax. That's right . . . just lean back, don't think 'bout nothing at all . . . nothing at all —

RUTH: I'm all right . . .

(*The glassy-eyed look melts and then she collapses into a fit of heavy sobbing. The bell rings.*)

BENEATHA: Oh, my God — that must be Asagai.

MAMA (*to Ruth*): Come on now, honey. You need to lie down and rest awhile . . . then have some nice hot food.

(*They exit, Ruth's weight on her mother-in-law. Beneatha, herself profoundly disturbed, opens the door to admit a rather dramatic-looking young man with a large package.*)

ASAGAI: Hello, Alaiyo —

BENEATHA (*holding the door open and regarding him with pleasure*): Hello . . . (*Long pause.*) Well — come in. And please excuse everything. My mother was very upset about my letting anyone come here with the place like this.

ASAGAI (*coming into the room*): You look disturbed too . . . Is something wrong?

BENEATHA (*still at the door, absently*): Yes . . . we've all got acute ghetto-itus. (*She smiles and comes toward him, finding a cigarette and sitting.*) So — sit down! No! Wait! (*She whips the spraygun off sofa where she had left it and puts the cushions back. At last perches on arm of sofa. He sits.*) So, how was Canada?

ASAGAI (*a sophisticate*): Canadian.

BENEATHA (*looking at him*): Asagai, I'm very glad you are back.

ASAGAI (*looking back at her in turn*): Are you really?

BENEATHA: Yes — very.

ASAGAI: Why? — you were quite glad when I went away. What happened?

BENEATHA: You went away.

ASAGAI: Ahhhhhhhh.

BENEATHA: Before — you wanted to be so serious before there was time.

ASAGAI: How much time must there be before one knows what one feels?

BENEATHA (*Stalling this particular conversation. Her hands pressed together, in a deliberately childish gesture.*): What did you bring me?

ASAGAI (*handing her the package*): Open it and see.

BENEATHA (*eagerly opening the package and drawing out some records and the colorful robes of a Nigerian woman*): Oh, Asagai! . . . You got them for me! . . . How beautiful . . . and the records too! (*She lifts out the robes and runs to the mirror with them and holds the drapery up in front of herself.*)

ASAGAI (*coming to her at the mirror*): I shall have to teach you how to drape it properly. (*He flings the material about her for the moment and stands back to look at her.*) Ah — Oh-pay-gay-day, oh-gbah-mu-shay. (*A Yoruba exclamation for admiration.*) You wear it well . . . very well . . . mutilated hair and all.

BENEATHA (*turning suddenly*): My hair — what's wrong with my hair?

ASAGAI (*shrugging*): Were you born with it like that?

BENEATHA (*reaching up to touch it*): No . . . of course not.

(*She looks back to the mirror, disturbed.*)

ASAGAI (*smiling*): How then?

BENEATHA: You know perfectly well how . . . as crinkly as yours . . . that's how.

ASAGAI: And it is ugly to you that way?

BENEATHA (*quickly*): Oh, no — not ugly . . . (*More slowly, apologetically.*) But it's so hard to manage when it's, well — raw.

ASAGAI: And so to accommodate that — you mutilate it every week?

BENEATHA: It's not mutilation!

ASAGAI (*laughing aloud at her seriousness*): Oh . . . please! I am only teasing you because you are so very serious about these things. (*He stands back from her and folds his arms across his chest as he watches her pulling at her hair and frowning in the mirror.*) Do you remember the first time you met me at school? . . . (*He laughs.*) You came up to me and you said — and I thought you were the most serious little thing I had ever seen — you said: (*He imitates her.*) "Mr. Asagai — I want very much to talk with you. About Africa. You see, Mr. Asagai, I am looking for my *identity!*"

(*He laughs.*)

BENEATHA (*turning to him, not laughing*): Yes —

(*Her face is quizzical, profoundly disturbed.*)

ASAGAI (*still teasing and reaching out and taking her face in his hands and turning her profile to him*): Well . . . it is true that this is not so much a profile of a Hollywood queen as perhaps a queen of the Nile — (*A mock dismissal of the importance of the question*.) But what does it matter? Assimilationism is so popular in your country.

BENEATHA (*wheeling, passionately, sharply*): I am not an assimilationist!

ASAGAI (*the protest hangs in the room for a moment and Asagai studies her, his laughter fading*): Such a serious one. (*There is a pause*.) So — you like the robes? You must take excellent care of them — they are from my sister's personal wardrobe.

BENEATHA (*with incredulity*): You — you sent all the way home — for me?

ASAGAI (*with charm*): For you — I would do much more . . . Well, that is what I came for. I must go.

BENEATHA: Will you call me Monday?

ASAGAI: Yes . . . We have a great deal to talk about. I mean about identity and time and all that.

BENEATHA: Time?

ASAGAI: Yes. About how much time one needs to know what one feels.

BENEATHA: You see! You never understood that there is more than one kind of feeling which can exist between a man and a woman — or, at least, there should be.

ASAGAI (*shaking his head negatively but gently*): No. Between a man and a woman there need be only one kind of feeling. I have that for you . . . Now even . . . right this moment . . .

BENEATHA: I know — and by itself — it won't do. I can find that anywhere.

ASAGAI: For a woman it should be enough.

BENEATHA: I know — because that's what it says in all the novels that men write. But it isn't. Go ahead and laugh — but I'm not interested in being someone's little episode in America or — (*with feminine vengeance*) — one of them! (*Asagai has burst into laughter again*.) That's funny as hell, huh!

ASAGAI: It's just that every American girl I have known has said that to me. White — black — in this you are all the same. And the same speech, too!

BENEATHA (*angrily*): Yuk, yuk, yuk!

ASAGAI: It's how you can be sure that the world's most liberated women are not liberated at all. You all talk about it too much!

(*Mama enters and is immediately all social charm because of the presence of a guest*.)

BENEATHA: Oh — Mama — this is Mr. Asagai.

MAMA: How do you do?

ASAGAI (*total politeness to an elder*): How do you do, Mrs. Younger. Please forgive me for coming at such an outrageous hour on a Saturday.

MAMA: Well, you are quite welcome. I just hope you understand that our house don't always look like this. (*Chatterish*.) You must come again. I would love to hear all about — (*not sure of the name*) — your country. I think it's so sad the way our American Negroes don't know nothing about Africa 'cept Tarzan and all that. And all that money they pour into these churches when they ought to be helping

you people over there drive out them French and Englishmen done taken away your land.

(*The mother flashes a slightly superior look at her daughter upon completion of the recitation*.)

ASAGAI (*taken aback by this sudden and acutely unrelated expression of sympathy*): Yes . . . yes . . .

MAMA (*smiling at him suddenly and relaxing and looking him over*): How many miles is it from here to where you come from?

ASAGAI: Many thousands.

MAMA (*looking at him as she would Walter*): I bet you don't half look after yourself, being away from your mama either. I spec you better come 'round here from time to time to get yourself some decent home-cooked meals . . .

ASAGAI (*moved*): Thank you. Thank you very much. (*They are all quiet, then —*) Well . . . I must go. I will call you Monday, Alaiyo.

MAMA: What's that he call you?

ASAGAI: Oh — "Alaiyo." I hope you don't mind. It is what you would call a nickname, I think. It is a Yoruba word. I am a Yoruba.

MAMA (*looking at Beneatha*): I — I thought he was from — (*Uncertain*.)

ASAGAI (*understanding*): Nigeria is my country. Yoruba is my tribal origin —

BENEATHA: You didn't tell us what Alaiyo means . . . for all I know, you might be calling me Little Idiot or something . . .

ASAGAI: Well . . . let me see . . . I do not know how just to explain it . . . The sense of a thing can be so different when it changes languages.

BENEATHA: You're evading.

ASAGAI: No — really it is difficult . . . (*Thinking*.) It means . . . it means One for Whom Bread — Food — Is Not Enough. (*He looks at her*.) Is that all right?

BENEATHA (*understanding, softly*): Thank you.

MAMA (*looking from one to the other and not understanding any of it*): Well . . . that's nice . . . You must come see us again — Mr. ——

ASAGAI: Ah-sah-guy . . .

MAMA: Yes . . . Do come again.

ASAGAI: Good-bye.

(*He exits*.)

MAMA (*after him*): Lord, that's a pretty thing just went out here! (*Insinuatingly, to her daughter*.) Yes, I guess I see why we done commence to get so interested in Africa 'round here. Missionaries my aunt Jenny!

(*She exits*.)

BENEATHA: Oh, Mama! . . .

(*She picks up the Nigerian dress and holds it up to her in front of the mirror again. She sets the headdress on haphazardly and then notices her hair again and clutches at it and then replaces the headdress and frowns at herself. Then she starts to wriggle in front of the mirror as she thinks a Nigerian woman might. Travis enters and stands regarding her.*)

TRAVIS: What's the matter, girl, you cracking up?
BENEATHA: Shut up.

(*She pulls the headdress off and looks at herself in the mirror and clutches at her hair again and squinches her eyes as if trying to imagine something. Then, suddenly, she gets her raincoat and kerchief and hurriedly prepares for going out.*)

MAMA (*coming back into the room*): She's resting now. Travis, baby, run next door and ask Miss Johnson to please let me have a little kitchen cleanser. This here can is empty as Jacob's kettle.
TRAVIS: I just came in.
MAMA: Do as you told. (*He exits and she looks at her daughter.*) Where you going?
BENEATHA (*halting at the door*): To become a queen of the Nile!

(*She exits in a breathless blaze of glory. Ruth appears in the bedroom doorway.*)

MAMA: Who told you to get up?
RUTH: Ain't nothing wrong with me to be lying in no bed for. Where did Bennie go?
MAMA (*drumming her fingers*): Far as I could make out — to Egypt. (*Ruth just looks at her.*) What time is it getting to?
RUTH: Ten twenty. And the mailman going to ring that bell this morning just like he done every morning for the last umpteen years.

(*Travis comes in with the cleanser can.*)

TRAVIS: She say to tell you that she don't have much.
MAMA (*angrily*): Lord, some people I could name sure is tight-fisted! (*Directing her grandson.*) Mark two cans of cleanser down on the list there. If she that hard up for kitchen cleanser, I sure don't want to forget to get her none!
RUTH: Lena — maybe the woman is just short on cleanser —
MAMA (*not listening*): — Much baking powder as she done borrowed from me all these years, she could of done gone into the baking business!

(*The bell sounds suddenly and sharply and all three are stunned — serious and silent — mid-speech. In spite of all the other conversations and distractions of the morning, this is what they have been waiting for, even Travis, who looks helplessly from his mother to his grandmother. Ruth is the first to come to life again.*)

RUTH (*to Travis*): Get down them steps, boy!

(*Travis snaps to life and flies out to get the mail.*)

MAMA (*her eyes wide, her hand to her breast*): You mean it done really come?
RUTH (*excited*): Oh, Miss Lena!
MAMA (*collecting herself*): Well . . . I don't know what

we all so excited about 'round here for. We known it was coming for months.
RUTH: That's a whole lot different from having it come and being able to hold it in your hands . . . a piece of paper worth ten thousand dollars . . . (*Travis bursts back into the room. He holds the envelope high above his head, like a little dancer, his face is radiant and he is breathless. He moves to his grandmother with sudden slow ceremony and puts the envelope into her hands. She accepts it, and then merely holds it and looks at it.*) Come on! Open it . . . Lord have mercy, I wish Walter Lee was here!
TRAVIS: Open it, Grandmama!
MAMA (*staring at it*): Now you all be quiet. It's just a check.
RUTH: Open it . . .
MAMA (*still staring at it*): Now don't act silly . . . We ain't never been no people to act silly 'bout no money —
RUTH (*swiftly*): We ain't never had none before — OPEN IT!

(*Mama finally makes a good strong tear and pulls out the thin blue slice of paper and inspects it closely. The boy and his mother study it raptly over Mama's shoulders.*)

MAMA: Travis! (*She is counting off with doubt.*) Is that the right number of zeros.
TRAVIS: Yes'm . . . ten thousand dollars. Gaalee, Grandmama, you rich.
MAMA (*She holds the check away from her, still looking at it. Slowly her face sobers into a mask of unhappiness.*): Ten thousand dollars. (*She hands it to Ruth.*) Put it away somewhere, Ruth. (*She does not look at Ruth; her eyes seem to be seeing something somewhere very far off.*) Ten thousand dollars they give you. Ten thousand dollars.
TRAVIS (*to his mother, sincerely*): What's the matter with Grandmama — don't she want to be rich?
RUTH (*distractedly*): You go on out and play now, baby. (*Travis exits. Mama starts wiping dishes absently, humming intently to herself. Ruth turns to her, with kind exasperation.*) You've gone and got yourself upset.
MAMA (*not looking at her*): I spec if it wasn't for you all . . . I would just put that money away or give it to the church or something.
RUTH: Now what kind of talk is that. Mr. Younger would just be plain mad if he could hear you talking foolish like that.
MAMA (*stopping and staring off*): Yes . . . he sure would. (*Sighing.*) We got enough to do with that money, all right. (*She halts then, and turns and looks at her daughter-in-law hard; Ruth avoids her eyes and Mama wipes her hands with finality and starts to speak firmly to Ruth.*) Where did you go today, girl?
RUTH: To the doctor.
MAMA (*impatiently*): Now, Ruth . . . you know better than that. Old Doctor Jones is strange enough in his

way but there ain't nothing 'bout him make somebody slip and call him "she" — like you done this
morning.

RUTH: Well, that's what happened — my tongue slipped.

MAMA: You went to see that woman, didn't you?

RUTH (*defensively, giving herself away*): What woman
you talking about?

MAMA (*angrily*): That woman who —

(*Walter enters in great excitement.*)

WALTER: Did it come?

MAMA (*quietly*): Can't you give people a Christian
greeting before you start asking about money?

WALTER (*to Ruth*): Did it come? (*Ruth unfolds the
check and lays it quietly before him, watching him
intently with thoughts of her own. Walter sits down
and grasps it close and counts off the zeros.*) Ten
thousand dollars — (*He turns suddenly, frantically
to his mother and draws some papers out of his
breast pocket.*) Mama — look. Old Willy Harris put
everything on paper —

MAMA: Son — I think you ought to talk to your wife . . .
I'll go on out and leave you alone if you want —

WALTER: I can talk to her later — Mama, look —

MAMA: Son —

WALTER: WILL SOMEBODY PLEASE LISTEN TO ME TODAY!

MAMA (*quietly*): I don't 'low no yellin' in this house,
Walter Lee, and you know it — (*Walter stares at them
in frustration and starts to speak several times.*) And
there ain't going to be no investing in no liquor stores.

WALTER: But, Mama, you ain't even looked at it.

MAMA: I don't aim to have to speak on that again.

(*A long pause.*)

WALTER: You ain't looked at it and you don't aim to
have to speak on that again? You ain't even looked at
it and *you* have decided — (*Crumpling his papers.*)
Well, *you* tell that to my boy tonight when you put
him to sleep on the living room couch . . . (*Turning
to Mama and speaking directly to her.*) Yeah — and
tell it to my wife, Mama, tomorrow when she has to
go out of here to look after somebody else's kids.
And tell it to *me*, Mama, every time we need a new
pair of curtains and I have to watch *you* go out and
work in somebody's kitchen. Yeah, you tell me then!

(*Walter starts out.*)

RUTH: Where you going?

WALTER: I'm going out!

RUTH: Where?

WALTER: Just out of this house somewhere —

RUTH (*getting her coat*): I'll come too.

WALTER: I don't want you to come!

RUTH: I got something to talk to you about, Walter.

WALTER: That's too bad.

MAMA (*still quietly*): Walter Lee — (*She waits and he
finally turns and looks at her.*) Sit down.

WALTER: I'm a grown man, Mama.

MAMA: Ain't nobody said you wasn't grown. But you

still in my house and my presence. And as long as you
are — you'll talk to your wife civil. Now sit down.

RUTH (*suddenly*): Oh, let him go on out and drink himself to death! He makes me sick to my stomach! (*She
flings her coat against him and exits to bedroom.*)

WALTER (*violently flinging the coat after her*): And you
turn mine too, baby! (*The door slams behind her.*)
That was my biggest mistake —

MAMA (*still quietly*): Walter, what is the matter with
you?

WALTER: Matter with me? Ain't nothing the matter with
me!

MAMA: Yes there is. Something eating you up like a
crazy man. Something more than me not giving you
this money. The past few years I been watching it
happen to you. You get all nervous acting and kind
of wild in the eyes — (*Walter jumps up impatiently
at her words.*) I said sit there now, I'm talking to you!

WALTER: Mama — I don't need no nagging at me today.

MAMA: Seem like you getting to a place where you
always tied up in some kind of knot about something. But if anybody ask you 'bout it you just yell at
'em and bust out the house and go out and drink
somewheres. Walter Lee, people can't live with that.
Ruth's a good, patient girl in her way — but you getting to be too much. Boy, don't make the mistake of
driving that girl away from you.

WALTER: Why — what she do for me?

MAMA: She loves you.

WALTER: Mama — I'm going out. I want to go off
somewhere and be by myself for a while.

MAMA: I'm sorry 'bout your liquor store, son. It just
wasn't the thing for us to do. That's what I want to
tell you about —

WALTER: I got to go out, Mama —

(*He rises.*)

MAMA: It's dangerous, son.

WALTER: What's dangerous?

MAMA: When a man goes outside his home to look for
peace.

WALTER (*beseechingly*): Then why can't there never be
no peace in this house then?

MAMA: You done found it in some other house?

WALTER: No — there ain't no woman! Why do women
always think there's a woman somewhere when a
man gets restless. (*Picks up the check.*) Do you know
what this money means to me? Do you know what
this money can do for us? (*Puts it back.*) Mama —
Mama — I want so many things . . .

MAMA: Yes, son —

WALTER: I want so many things that they are driving me
kind of crazy . . . Mama — look at me.

MAMA: I'm looking at you. You a good-looking boy.
You got a job, a nice wife, a fine boy and —

WALTER: A job. (*Looks at her.*) Mama, a job? I open and
close car doors all day long. I drive a man around in
his limousine and I say, "Yes, sir, no, sir; very good,
sir; shall I take the Drive, sir?" Mama, that ain't no

kind of job . . . that ain't nothing at all. (*Very quietly.*) Mama, I don't know if I can make you understand.

MAMA: Understand what, baby?

WALTER (*quietly*): Sometimes it's like I can see the future stretched out in front of me — just plain as day. The future, Mama. Hanging over there at the edge of my days. Just waiting for me — a big, looming blank space — full of *nothing*. Just waiting for *me*. But it don't have to be. (*Pause. Kneeling beside her chair.*) Mama — sometimes when I'm downtown and I pass them cool, quiet-looking restaurants where them white boys are sitting back and talking 'bout things . . . sitting there turning deals worth millions of dollars . . . sometimes I see guys don't look much older than me —

MAMA: Son — how come you talk so much 'bout money?

WALTER (*with immense passion*): Because it is life, Mama!

MAMA (*quietly*): Oh — (*Very quietly.*) So now it's life. Money is life. Once upon a time freedom used to be life — now it's money. I guess the world really do change . . .

WALTER: No — it was always money, Mama. We just didn't know about it.

MAMA: No . . . something has changed. (*She looks at him.*) You something new, boy. In my time we was worried about not being lynched and getting to the North if we could and how to stay alive and still have a pinch of dignity too . . . Now here come you and Beneatha — talking 'bout things we ain't never even thought about hardly, me and your daddy. You ain't satisfied or proud of nothing we done. I mean that you had a home, that we kept you out of trouble till you was grown, that you don't have to ride to work on the back of nobody's streetcar — You my children — but how different we done become.

WALTER (*A long beat. He pats her hand and gets up.*): You just don't understand, Mama, you just don't understand.

MAMA: Son — do you know your wife is expecting another baby? (*Walter stands, stunned, and absorbs what his mother has said.*) That's what she wanted to talk to you about. (*Walter sinks down into a chair.*) This ain't for me to be telling — but you ought to know. (*She waits.*) I think Ruth is thinking 'bout getting rid of that child.

WALTER (*slowly understanding*): — No — no — Ruth wouldn't do that.

MAMA: When the world gets ugly enough — a woman will do anything for her family. *The part that's already living.*

WALTER: You don't know Ruth, Mama, if you think she would do that.

(*Ruth opens the bedroom door and stands there a little limp.*)

RUTH (*beaten*): Yes I would too, Walter. (*Pause.*) I gave her a five-dollar down payment.

(*There is total silence as the man stares at his wife and the mother stares at her son.*)

MAMA (*presently*): Well — (*Tightly.*) Well — son, I'm waiting to hear you say something . . . (*She waits.*) I'm waiting to hear how you be your father's son. Be the man he was . . . (*Pause. The silence shouts.*) Your wife says she going to destroy your child. And I'm waiting to hear you talk like him and say we a people who give children life, not who destroys them — (*She rises.*) I'm waiting to see you stand up and look like your daddy and say we done give up one baby to poverty and that we ain't going to give up nary another one . . . I'm waiting.

WALTER: Ruth — (*He can say nothing.*)

MAMA: If you a son of mine, tell her! (*Walter picks up his keys and his coat and walks out. She continues, bitterly.*) You . . . you are a disgrace to your father's memory. Somebody get me my hat!

ACT II • Scene I

(*Time: Later the same day.*)

(*At rise: Ruth is ironing again. She has the radio going. Presently Beneatha's bedroom door opens and Ruth's mouth falls and she puts down the iron in fascination.*)

RUTH: What have we got on tonight!

BENEATHA (*emerging grandly from the doorway so that we can see her thoroughly robed in the costume Asagai brought*): You are looking at what a well dressed Nigerian woman wears — (*She parades for Ruth, her hair completely hidden by the headdress; she is coquettishly fanning herself with an ornate oriental fan, mistakenly more like Butterfly° than any Nigerian that ever was.*) Isn't it beautiful? (*She promenades to the radio and, with an arrogant flourish, turns off the good loud blues that is playing.*) Enough of this assimilationist junk! (*Ruth follows her with her eyes as she goes to the phonograph and puts on a record and turns and waits ceremoniously for the music to come up. Then, with a shout —*) OCOMOGOSIAY!

(*Ruth jumps. The music comes up, a lovely Nigerian melody. Beneatha listens, enraptured, her eyes far away — "back to the past." She begins to dance. Ruth is dumfounded.*)

RUTH: What kind of dance is that?

BENEATHA: A folk dance.

RUTH (*Pearl Bailey*): What kind of folks do that, honey?

BENEATHA: It's from Nigeria. It's a dance of welcome.

RUTH: Who you welcoming?

BENEATHA: The men back to the village.

RUTH: Where they been?

BENEATHA: How should I know — out hunting or something. Anyway, they are coming back now . . .

Butterfly: Madame Butterfly, the title character in the opera by Puccini, set in Japan.

RUTH: Well, that's good.

BENEATHA (*with the record*): *Alundi, alundi*
Alundi alunya
Jop pu a jeepua
Ang gu soooooooooo

Ai yai yue . . .
Ayehaye — alundi . . .

(*Walter comes in during this performance; he has obviously been drinking. He leans against the door heavily and watches his sister, at first with distaste. Then his eyes look off — "back to the past" — as he lifts both his fists to the roof, screaming.*)

WALTER: YEAH . . . AND ETHIOPIA STRETCH FORTH HER HANDS AGAIN! . . .

RUTH (*drily, looking at him*): Yes — and Africa sure is claiming her own tonight. (*She gives them both up and starts ironing again.*)

WALTER (*all in a drunken, dramatic shout*): Shut up! . . . I'm digging them drums . . . them drums move me! . . . (*He makes his weaving way to his wife's face and leans in close to her.*) In my *heart of hearts* — (*he thumps his chest*) — I am much warrior!

RUTH (*without even looking up*): In your heart of hearts you are much drunkard.

WALTER (*coming away from her and starting to wander around the room, shouting*): Me and Jomo . . . (*Intently, in his sister's face. She has stopped dancing to watch him in this unknown mood.*) That's my man, Kenyatta. (*Shouting and thumping his chest.*) FLAMING SPEAR! HOT DAMN! (*He is suddenly in possession of an imaginary spear and actively spearing enemies all over the room.*) OCOMOGOSIAY . . .

BENEATHA (*to encourage Walter, thoroughly caught up with this side of him*): OCOMOGOSIAY, FLAMING SPEAR!

WALTER: THE LION IS WAKING . . . OWIMOWEH! (*He pulls his shirt open and leaps up on the table and gestures with his spear.*)

BENEATHA: OWIMOWEH!

WALTER (*On the table, very far gone, his eyes pure glass sheets. He sees what we cannot, that he is a leader of his people, a great chief, a descendant of Chaka, and that the hour to march has come.*): Listen, my black brothers —

BENEATHA: OCOMOGOSIAY!

WALTER: — Do you hear the waters rushing against the shores of the coastlands —

BENEATHA: OCOMOGOSIAY!

WALTER: — Do you hear the screeching of the cocks in yonder hills beyond where the chiefs meet in council for the coming of the mighty war —

BENEATHA: OCOMOGOSIAY!

(*And now the lighting shifts subtly to suggest the world of Walter's imagination, and the mood shifts from pure comedy. It is the inner Walter speaking: the Southside chauffeur has assumed an unexpected majesty.*)

WALTER: — Do you hear the beating of the wings of the birds flying low over the mountains and the low places of our land —

BENEATHA: OCOMOGOSIAY!

WALTER: — Do you hear the singing of the women singing the war songs of our fathers to the babies in the great houses? Singing the sweet war songs! (*The doorbell rings.*) OH, DO YOU HEAR, MY BLACK BROTHERS!

BENEATHA (*completely gone*): We hear you, Flaming Spear —

(*Ruth shuts off the phonograph and opens the door. George Murchison enters.*)

WALTER: Telling us to prepare for the GREATNESS OF THE TIME! (*Lights back to normal. He turns and sees George.*) Black Brother!

(*He extends his hand for the fraternal clasp.*)

GEORGE: Black Brother, hell!

RUTH (*having had enough, and embarrassed for the family*): Beneatha, you got company — what's the matter with you? Walter Lee Younger, get down off that table and stop acting like a fool . . .

(*Walter comes down off the table suddenly and makes a quick exit to the bathroom.*)

RUTH: He's had a little to drink . . . I don't know what her excuse is.

GEORGE (*to Beneatha*): Look honey, we're going *to* the theater — we're not going to be *in* it . . . so go change, huh?

(*Beneatha looks at him and slowly, ceremoniously, lifts her hands and pulls off the headdress. Her hair is close-cropped and unstraightened. George freezes mid-sentence and Ruth's eyes all but fall out of her head.*)

GEORGE: What in the name of —

RUTH (*touching Beneatha's hair*): Girl, you done lost your natural mind? Look at your head!

GEORGE: What have you done to your head — I mean your hair!

BENEATHA: Nothing — except cut it off.

RUTH: Now that's the truth — it's what ain't been done to it! You expect this boy to go out with you with your head all nappy like that?

BENEATHA (*looking at George*): That's up to George. If he's ashamed of his heritage —

GEORGE: Oh, don't be so proud of yourself, Bennie — just because you look eccentric.

BENEATHA: How can something that's natural be eccentric?

GEORGE: That's what being eccentric means — being natural. Get dressed.

BENEATHA: I don't like that, George.

RUTH: Why must you and your brother make an argument out of everything people say?

BENEATHA: Because I hate assimilationist Negroes!

RUTH: Will somebody please tell me what assimila-whoever means!

GEORGE: Oh, it's just a college girl's way of calling people Uncle Toms — but that isn't what it means at all.

RUTH: Well, what does it mean?

BENEATHA (*cutting George off and staring at him as she replies to Ruth*): It means someone who is willing to give up his own culture and submerge himself completely in the dominant, and in this case *oppressive* culture!

GEORGE: Oh, dear, dear, dear! Here we go! A lecture on the African past! On our Great West African Heritage! In one second we will hear all about the great Ashanti empires; the great Songhay civilizations; and the great sculpture of Bénin — and then some poetry in the Bantu — and the whole monologue will end with the word *heritage*! (*Nastily.*) Let's face it, baby, your heritage is nothing but a bunch of raggedy-assed spirituals and some grass huts!

BENEATHA: GRASS HUTS! (*Ruth crosses to her and forcibly pushes her toward the bedroom.*) See there . . . you are standing there in your splendid ignorance talking about people who were the first to smelt iron on the face of the earth! (*Ruth is pushing her through the door.*) The Ashanti were performing surgical operations when the English — (*Ruth pulls the door to, with Beneatha on the other side, and smiles graciously at George. Beneatha opens the door and shouts the end of the sentence defiantly at George*) — were still tatooing themselves with blue dragons! (*She goes back inside.*)

RUTH: Have a seat, George. (*They both sit. Ruth folds her hands rather primly on her lap, determined to demonstrate the civilization of the family.*) Warm, ain't it? I mean for September. (*Pause.*) Just like they always say about Chicago weather: If it's too hot or cold for you, just wait a minute and it'll change. (*She smiles happily at this cliché of clichés.*) Everybody say it's got to do with them bombs and things they keep setting off. (*Pause.*) Would you like a nice cold beer?

GEORGE: No, thank you. I don't care for beer. (*He looks at his watch.*) I hope she hurries up.

RUTH: What time is the show?

GEORGE: It's an eight-thirty curtain. That's just Chicago, though. In New York standard curtain time is eight forty.

(*He is rather proud of this knowledge.*)

RUTH (*properly appreciating it*): You get to New York a lot?

GEORGE (*offhand*): Few times a year.

RUTH: Oh — that's nice. I've never been to New York.

(*Walter enters. We feel he has relieved himself, but the edge of unreality is still with him.*)

WALTER: New York ain't got nothing Chicago ain't. Just a bunch of hustling people all squeezed up together — being "Eastern."

(*He turns his face into a screw of displeasure.*)

GEORGE: Oh — you've been?

WALTER: *Plenty* of times.

RUTH (*shocked at the lie*): Walter Lee Younger!

WALTER (*staring her down*): Plenty! (*Pause.*) What we got to drink in this house? Why don't you offer this man some refreshment. (*To George.*) They don't know how to entertain people in this house, man.

GEORGE: Thank you — I don't really care for anything.

WALTER (*feeling his head; sobriety coming*): Where's Mama?

RUTH: She ain't come back yet.

WALTER (*looking Murchison over from head to toe, scrutinizing his carefully casual tweed sports jacket over cashmere V-neck sweater over soft eyelet shirt and tie, and soft slacks, finished off with white buck-skin shoes*): Why all you college boys wear them faggoty-looking white shoes?

RUTH: Walter Lee!

(*George Murchison ignores the remark.*)

WALTER (*to Ruth*): Well, they look crazy as hell — white shoes, cold as it is.

RUTH (*crushed*): You have to excuse him —

WALTER: No he don't! Excuse me for what? What you always excusing me for! I'll excuse myself when I needs to be excused! (*A pause.*) They look as funny as them black knee socks Beneatha wears out of here all the time.

RUTH: It's the college *style*, Walter.

WALTER: Style, hell. She looks like she got burnt legs or something!

RUTH: Oh, Walter —

WALTER (*an irritable mimic*): Oh, Walter! Oh, Walter! (*To Murchison.*) How's your old man making out? I understand you all going to buy that big hotel on the Drive? (*He finds a beer in the refrigerator, wanders over to Murchison, sipping and wiping his lips with the back of his hand, and straddling a chair backward to talk to the other man.*) Shrewd move. Your old man is all right, man. (*Tapping his head and half winking for emphasis.*) I mean he knows how to operate. I mean he thinks *big*, you know what I mean, I mean for a *home*, you know? But I think he's kind of running out of ideas now. I'd like to talk to him. Listen, man, I got some plans that could turn this city upside down. I mean think like he does. *Big*. Invest big, gamble big, hell, lose *big* if you have to, you know what I mean. It's hard to find a man on this whole Southside who understands my kind of thinking — you dig? (*He scrutinizes Murchison again, drinks his beer, squints his eyes, and leans in close, confidential, man to man.*) Me and you ought to sit down and talk sometimes, man. Man, I got me some ideas . . .

MURCHISON (*with boredom*): Yeah — sometimes we'll have to do that, Walter.

WALTER (*understanding the indifference, and offended*): Yeah — well, when you get the time, man. I know you a busy little boy.

RUTH: Walter, please —

WALTER (*bitterly, hurt*): I know ain't nothing in this world as busy as you colored college boys with your fraternity pins and white shoes . . .

RUTH (*covering her face with humiliation*): Oh, Walter Lee —

WALTER: I see you all all the time — with the books tucked under your arms — going to your (*British A — a mimic*) "clahsses." And for what! What the hell you learning over there? Filling up your heads — (*counting off on his fingers*) — with the sociology and the psychology — but they teaching you how to be a man? How to take over and run the world? They teaching you how to run a rubber plantation or a steel mill? Naw — just to talk proper and read books and wear them faggoty-looking white shoes . . .

GEORGE (*looking at him with distaste, a little above it all*): You're all wacked up with bitterness, man.

WALTER (*intently, almost quietly, between the teeth, glaring at the boy*): And you — ain't you bitter, man? Ain't you just about had it yet? Don't you see no stars gleaming that you can't reach out and grab? You happy? — You contented son-of-a-bitch — you happy? You got it made? Bitter? Man, I'm a volcano. Bitter? Here I am a giant — surrounded by ants! Ants who can't even understand what it is the giant is talking about.

RUTH (*passionately and suddenly*): Oh, Walter — ain't you with nobody!

WALTER (*violently*): No! 'Cause ain't nobody with me! Not even my own mother!

RUTH: Walter, that's a terrible thing to say!

(*Beneatha enters, dressed for the evening in a cocktail dress and earrings, hair natural.*)

GEORGE: Well — hey — (*Crosses to Beneatha; thoughtful, with emphasis, since this is a reversal.*) You look great!

WALTER (*seeing his sister's hair for the first time*): What's the matter with your head?

BENEATHA (*tired of the jokes now*): I cut it off, Brother.

WALTER (*coming close to inspect it and walking around her*): Well, I'll be damned. So that's what they mean by the African bush . . .

BENEATHA: Ha ha. Let's go, George.

GEORGE (*looking at her*): You know something? I like it. It's sharp. I mean it really is. (*Helps her into her wrap.*)

RUTH: Yes — I think so, too. (*She goes to the mirror and starts to clutch at her hair.*)

WALTER: Oh no! You leave yours alone, baby. You might turn out to have a pin-shaped head or something!

BENEATHA: See you all later.

RUTH: Have a nice time.

GEORGE: Thanks. Good night. (*Half out the door, he reopens it. To Walter.*) Good night, Prometheus!°

Prometheus: Defiantly inventive Titan who stole fire from the gods and gave it to humans.

(*Beneatha and George exit.*)

WALTER (*to Ruth*): Who is Prometheus?

RUTH: I don't know. Don't worry about it.

WALTER (*in fury, pointing after George*): See there — they get to a point where they can't insult you man to man — they got to go talk about something ain't nobody never heard of!

RUTH: How do you know it was an insult? (*To humor him.*) Maybe Prometheus is a nice fellow.

WALTER: Prometheus! I bet there ain't even no such thing! I bet that simple-minded clown —

RUTH: Walter —

(*She stops what she is doing and looks at him.*)

WALTER (*yelling*): Don't start!

RUTH: Start what?

WALTER: Your nagging! Where was I? Who was I with? How much money did I spend?

RUTH (*plaintively*): Walter Lee — why don't we just try to talk about it . . .

WALTER (*not listening*): I been out talking with people who understand me. People who care about the things I got on my mind.

RUTH (*wearily*): I guess that means people like Willy Harris.

WALTER: Yes, people like Willy Harris.

RUTH (*with a sudden flash of impatience*): Why don't you all just hurry up and go into the banking business and stop talking about it!

WALTER: Why? You want to know why? 'Cause we all tied up in a race of people that don't know how to do nothing but moan, pray, and have babies!

(*The line is too bitter even for him and he looks at her and sits down.*)

RUTH: Oh, Walter . . . (*Softly.*) Honey, why can't you stop fighting me?

WALTER (*without thinking*): Who's fighting you? Who even cares about you?

(*This line begins the retardation of his mood.*)

RUTH: Well — (*She waits a long time, and then with resignation starts to put away her things.*) I guess I might as well go on to bed . . . (*More or less to herself.*) I don't know where we lost it . . . but we have . . . (*Then, to him.*) I — I'm sorry about this new baby, Walter. I guess maybe I better go on and do what I started . . . I guess I just didn't realize how bad things was with us . . . I guess I just didn't really realize — (*She starts out to the bedroom and stops.*) You want some hot milk?

WALTER: Hot milk?

RUTH: Yes — hot milk.

WALTER: Why hot milk?

RUTH: 'Cause after all that liquor you come home with you ought to have something hot in your stomach.

WALTER: I don't want no milk.

RUTH: You want some coffee then?

WALTER: No, I don't want no coffee. I don't want nothing hot to drink. (*Almost plaintively.*) Why you always trying to give me something to eat?

RUTH (*standing and looking at him helplessly*): What else can I give you, Walter Lee Younger?

(*She stands and looks at him and presently turns to go out again. He lifts his head and watches her going away from him in a new mood which began to emerge when he asked her "Who cares about you?"*)

WALTER: It's been rough, ain't it, baby? (*She hears and stops but does not turn around and he continues to her back.*) I guess between two people there ain't never as much understood as folks generally thinks there is. I mean like between me and you — (*She turns to face him.*) How we gets to the place where we scared to talk softness to each other. (*He waits, thinking hard himself.*) Why you think it got to be like that? (*He is thoughtful, almost as a child would be.*) Ruth, what is it gets into people ought to be close?

RUTH: I don't know, honey. I think about it a lot.

WALTER: On account of you and me, you mean? The way things are with us. The way something done come down between us.

RUTH: There ain't so much between us, Walter . . . Not when you come to me and try to talk to me. Try to be with me . . . a little even.

WALTER (*total honesty*): Sometimes . . . sometimes . . . I don't even know how to try.

RUTH: Walter —

WALTER: Yes?

RUTH (*coming to him, gently and with misgiving, but coming to him*): Honey . . . life don't have to be like this. I mean sometimes people can do things so that things are better . . . You remember how we used to talk when Travis was born . . . about the way we were going to live . . . the kind of house . . . (*She is stroking his head.*) Well, it's all starting to slip away from us . . .

(*He turns her to him and they look at each other and kiss, tenderly and hungrily. The door opens and Mama enters — Walter breaks away and jumps up. A beat.*)

WALTER: Mama, where have you been?

MAMA: My — them steps is longer than they used to be. Whew! (*She sits down and ignores him.*) How you feeling this evening, Ruth?

(*Ruth shrugs, disturbed at having been interrupted and watching her husband knowingly.*)

WALTER: Mama, where have you been all day?

MAMA (*still ignoring him and leaning on the table and changing to more comfortable shoes*): Where's Travis?

RUTH: I let him go out earlier and he ain't come back yet. Boy, is he going to get it!

WALTER: Mama!

MAMA (*as if she has heard him for the first time*): Yes, son?

WALTER: Where did you go this afternoon?

MAMA: I went downtown to tend to some business that I had to tend to.

WALTER: What kind of business?

MAMA: You know better than to question me like a child, Brother.

WALTER (*rising and bending over the table*): Where were you, Mama? (*Bringing his fists down and shouting.*) Mama, you didn't go do something with that insurance money, something crazy?

(*The front door opens slowly, interrupting him, and Travis peeks his head in, less than hopefully.*)

TRAVIS (*to his mother*): Mama, I —

RUTH: "Mama I" nothing! You're going to get it, boy! Get on in that bedroom and get yourself ready!

TRAVIS: But I —

MAMA: Why don't you all never let the child explain himself.

RUTH: Keep out of it now, Lena.

(*Mama clamps her lips together, and Ruth advances toward her son menacingly.*)

RUTH: A thousand times I have told you not to go off like that —

MAMA (*holding out her arms to her grandson*): Well — at least let me tell him something. I want him to be the first one to hear . . . Come here, Travis. (*The boy obeys, gladly.*) Travis — (*she takes him by the shoulder and looks into his face*) — you know that money we got in the mail this morning?

TRAVIS: Yes'm —

MAMA: Well — what you think your grandmama gone and done with that money?

TRAVIS: I don't know, Grandmama.

MAMA (*putting her finger on his nose for emphasis*): She went out and she bought you a house! (*The explosion comes from Walter at the end of the revelation and he jumps up and turns away from all of them in a fury. Mama continues, to Travis.*) You glad about the house? It's going to be yours when you get to be a man.

TRAVIS: Yeah — I always wanted to live in a house.

MAMA: All right, gimme some sugar then — (*Travis puts his arms around her neck as she watches her son over the boy's shoulder. Then, to Travis, after the embrace.*) Now when you say your prayers tonight, you thank God and your grandfather — 'cause it was him who give you the house — in his way.

RUTH (*taking the boy from Mama and pushing him toward the bedroom*): Now you get out of here and get ready for your beating.

TRAVIS: Aw, Mama —

RUTH: Get on in there — (*Closing the door behind him and turning radiantly to her mother-in-law.*) So you went and did it!

MAMA (*quietly, looking at her son with pain*): Yes, I did.

RUTH (*raising both arms classically*): PRAISE GOD! (*Looks at Walter a moment, who says nothing. She* crosses rapidly to her husband.) Please, honey — let me be glad . . . you be glad too. (*She has laid her hands on his shoulders, but he shakes himself free of her roughly, without turning to face her.*) Oh, Walter . . . a home . . . *a home.* (*She comes back to Mama.*) Well — where is it? How big is it? How much it going to cost?

MAMA: Well —

RUTH: When we moving?

MAMA (*smiling at her*): First of the month.

RUTH (*throwing back her head with jubilance*): *Praise God!*

MAMA (*tentatively, still looking at her son's back turned against her and Ruth*): It's — it's a nice house too . . . (*She cannot help speaking directly to him. An imploring quality in her voice, her manner, makes her almost like a girl now.*) Three bedrooms — nice big one for you and Ruth . . . Me and Beneatha still have to share our room, but Travis have one of his own and (*with difficulty*) I figure if the — new baby — is a boy, we could get one of them double-decker outfits . . . And there's a yard with a little patch of dirt where I could maybe get to grow me a few flowers . . . And a nice big basement . . .

RUTH: Walter honey, be glad —

MAMA (*still to his back, fingering things on the table*): 'Course I don't want to make it sound fancier than it is . . . It's just a plain little old house — but it's made good and solid — and it will be *ours.* Walter Lee — it makes a difference in a man when he can walk on floors that belong to *him* . . .

RUTH: Where is it?

MAMA (*frightened at this telling*): Well — well — it's out there in Clybourne Park —

(*Ruth's radiance fades abruptly, and Walter finally turns slowly to face his mother with incredulity and hostility.*)

RUTH: Where?

MAMA (*matter-of-factly*): Four o six Clybourne Street, Clybourne Park.

RUTH: Clybourne Park? Mama, there ain't no colored people living in Clybourne Park.

MAMA (*almost idiotically*): Well, I guess there's going to be some now.

WALTER (*bitterly*): So that's the peace and comfort you went out and bought for us today!

MAMA (*raising her eyes to meet his finally*): Son — I just tried to find the nicest place for the least amount of money for my family.

RUTH (*trying to recover from the shock*): Well — well — 'course I ain't one never been 'fraid of no crackers,° mind you — but — well, wasn't there no other houses nowhere?

MAMA: Them houses they put up for colored in them areas way out all seem to cost twice as much as other houses. I did the best I could.

crackers: White people, often used to refer disparagingly to poor whites.

RUTH (*struck senseless with the news, in its various degrees of goodness and trouble, she sits a moment, her fists propping her chin in thought, and then she starts to rise, bringing her fists down with vigor, the radiance spreading from cheek to cheek again*): Well — well — All I can say is — if this is my time in life — MY TIME — to say good-bye — (*and she builds with momentum as she starts to circle the room with an exuberant, almost tearfully happy release*) — to these Goddamned cracking walls! — (*she pounds the walls*) — and these marching roaches! — (*she wipes at an imaginary army of marching roaches*) — and this cramped little closet which ain't now or never was no kitchen! . . . then I say it loud and good, HALLELUJAH! AND GOOD-BYE MISERY . . . I DON'T NEVER WANT TO SEE YOUR UGLY FACE AGAIN! (*She laughs joyously, having practically destroyed the apartment, and flings her arms up and lets them come down happily, slowly, reflectively, over her abdomen, aware for the first time perhaps that the life therein pulses with happiness and not despair.*) Lena?

MAMA (*moved, watching her happiness*): Yes, honey?

RUTH (*looking off*): Is there — is there a whole lot of sunlight?

MAMA (*understanding*): Yes, child, there's a whole lot of sunlight.

(*Long pause.*)

RUTH (*collecting herself and going to the door of the room Travis is in*): Well — I guess I better see 'bout Travis. (*To Mama.*) Lord, I sure don't feel like whipping nobody today!

(*She exits.*)

MAMA (*the mother and son are left alone now and the mother waits a long time, considering deeply, before she speaks*): Son — you — you understand what I done, don't you? (*Walter is silent and sullen.*) I — I just seen my family falling apart today . . . just falling to pieces in front of my eyes . . . We couldn't of gone on like we was today. We was going backwards 'stead of forwards — talking 'bout killing babies and wishing each other was dead . . . When it gets like that in life — you just got to do something different, push on out and do something bigger . . . (*She waits.*) I wish you say something, son . . . I wish you'd say how deep inside you you think I done the right thing —

WALTER (*crossing slowly to his bedroom door and finally turning there and speaking measuredly*): What you need me to say you done right for? *You* the head of this family. You run our lives like you want to. It was your money and you did what you wanted with it. So what you need for me to say it was all right for? (*Bitterly, to hurt her as deeply as he knows is possible.*) So you butchered up a dream of mine — you — who always talking 'bout your children's dreams . . .

MAMA: Walter Lee —

(*He just closes the door behind him. Mama sits alone, thinking heavily.*)

Scene II

(*Time: Friday night. A few weeks later.*)

(*At rise: Packing crates mark the intention of the family to move. Beneatha and George come in, presumably from an evening out again.*)

GEORGE: O.K. . . . O.K., whatever you say . . . (*They both sit on the couch. He tries to kiss her. She moves away.*) Look, we've had a nice evening; let's not spoil it, huh? . . .

(*He again turns her head and tries to nuzzle in and she turns away from him, not with distaste but with momentary lack of interest; in a mood to pursue what they were talking about.*)

BENEATHA: I'm *trying* to talk to you.

GEORGE: We always talk.

BENEATHA: Yes — and I love to talk.

GEORGE (*exasperated; rising*): I know it and I don't mind it sometimes . . . I want you to cut it out, see — The moody stuff, I mean. I don't like it. You're a nice-looking girl . . . all over. That's all you need, honey, forget the atmosphere. Guys aren't going to go for the atmosphere — they're going to go for what they see. Be glad for that. Drop the Garbo routine. It doesn't go with you. As for myself, I want a nice — (*groping*) — simple (*thoughtfully*) — sophisticated girl . . . not a poet — O.K.?

(*He starts to kiss her, she rebuffs him again, and he jumps up.*)

BENEATHA: Why are you angry, George?

GEORGE: Because this is stupid! I don't go out with you to discuss the nature of "quiet desperation" or to hear all about your thoughts — because the world will go on thinking what it thinks regardless —

BENEATHA: Then why read books? Why go to school?

GEORGE (*with artificial patience, counting on his fingers*): It's simple. You read books — to learn facts — to get grades — to pass the course — to get a degree. That's all — it has nothing to do with thoughts.

(*A long pause.*)

BENEATHA: I see. (*He starts to sit.*) Good night, George.

(*George looks at her a little oddly and starts to exit. He meets Mama coming in.*)

GEORGE: Oh — hello, Mrs. Younger.

MAMA: Hello, George, how you feeling?

GEORGE: Fine — fine, how are you?

MAMA: Oh, a little tired. You know them steps can get you after a day's work. You all have a nice time tonight?

GEORGE: Yes — a fine time. A fine time.

MAMA: Well, good night.

GEORGE: Good night. (*He exits. Mama closes the door behind her.*)

MAMA: Hello, honey. What you sitting like that for?

BENEATHA: I'm just sitting.

MAMA: Didn't you have a nice time?

BENEATHA: No.

MAMA: No? What's the matter?

BENEATHA: Mama, George is a fool — honest. (*She rises.*)

MAMA (*Hustling around unloading the packages she has entered with. She stops.*): Is he, baby?

BENEATHA: Yes.

(*Beneatha makes up Travis's bed as she talks.*)

MAMA: You sure?

BENEATHA: Yes.

MAMA: Well — I guess you better not waste your time with no fools.

(*Beneatha looks up at her mother, watching her put groceries in the refrigerator. Finally she gathers up her things and starts into the bedroom. At the door she stops and looks back at her mother.*)

BENEATHA: Mama —

MAMA: Yes, baby —

BENEATHA: Thank you.

MAMA: For what?

BENEATHA: For understanding me this time.

(*She exits quickly and the mother stands, smiling a little, looking at the place where Beneatha just stood. Ruth enters.*)

RUTH: Now don't you fool with any of this stuff, Lena —

MAMA: Oh, I just thought I'd sort a few things out. Is Brother here?

RUTH: Yes.

MAMA (*with concern*): Is he —

RUTH (*reading her eyes*): Yes.

(*Mama is silent and someone knocks on the door. Mama and Ruth exchange weary and knowing glances and Ruth opens it to admit the neighbor, Mrs. Johnson,° who is a rather squeaky wide-eyed lady of no particular age, with a newspaper under her arm.*)

MAMA (*changing her expression to acute delight and a ringing cheerful greeting*): Oh — hello there, Johnson.

JOHNSON (*this is a woman who decided long ago to be enthusiastic about EVERYTHING in life and she is inclined to wave her wrist vigorously at the height of her exclamatory comments*): Hello there, yourself! H'you this evening, Ruth?

RUTH (*not much of a deceptive type*): Fine, Mis' Johnson, h'you?

JOHNSON: Fine. (*Reaching out quickly, playfully, and patting Ruth's stomach.*) Ain't you starting to poke out none yet! (*She mugs with delight at the overfamiliar remark and her eyes dart around looking at the crates and packing preparation; Mama's face is a cold sheet of endurance.*) Oh, ain't we getting ready round here, though! Yessir! Lookathere! I'm telling

---

Mrs. Johnson: This character and the scene of her visit were cut from the original production and early editions of the play.

you the Youngers is really getting ready to "move on up a little higher!" — Bless God!

MAMA (*a little drily, doubting the total sincerity of the Blesser*): Bless God.

JOHNSON: He's good, ain't He?

MAMA: Oh yes, He's good.

JOHNSON: I mean sometimes He works in mysterious ways . . . but He works, don't He!

MAMA (*the same*): Yes, he does.

JOHNSON: I'm just sooooo happy for y'all. And this here child — (*about Ruth*) looks like she could just pop open with happiness, don't she. Where's all the rest of the family?

MAMA: Bennie's gone to bed —

JOHNSON: Ain't no . . . (*the implication is pregnancy*) sickness done hit you — I hope . . . ?

MAMA: No — she just tired. She was out this evening.

JOHNSON (*all is a coo, an emphatic coo*): Aw — ain't that lovely. She still going out with the little Murchison boy?

MAMA (*drily*): Ummmm huh.

JOHNSON: That's lovely. You sure got lovely children, Younger. Me and Isaiah talks all the time 'bout what fine children you was blessed with. We sure do.

MAMA: Ruth, give Mis' Johnson a piece of sweet potato pie and some milk.

JOHNSON: Oh honey, I can't stay hardly a minute — I just dropped in to see if there was anything I could do. (*Accepting the food easily.*) I guess y'all seen the news what's all over the colored paper this week . . .

MAMA: No — didn't get mine yet this week.

JOHNSON (*lifting her head and blinking with the spirit of catastrophe*): You mean you ain't read 'bout them colored people that was bombed out their place out there?

(*Ruth straightens with concern and takes the paper and reads it. Johnson notices her and feeds commentary.*)

JOHNSON: Ain't it something how bad these here white folks is getting here in Chicago! Lord, getting so you think you right down in Mississippi! (*With a tremendous and rather insincere sense of melodrama.*) 'Course I thinks it's wonderful how our folks keeps on pushing out. You hear some of these Negroes round here talking 'bout how they don't go where they ain't wanted and all that — but not me, honey! (*This is a lie.*) Wilhemenia Othella Johnson goes anywhere, any time she feels like it! (*With head movement for emphasis.*) Yes I do! Why if we left it up to these here crackers the poor niggers wouldn't have nothing — (*She clasps her hand over her mouth.*) Oh, I always forgets you don't 'low that word in your house.

MAMA (*quietly, looking at her*): No — I don't 'low it.

JOHNSON (*vigorously again*): Me neither! I was just telling Isaiah yesterday when he come using it in front of me — I said, "Isaiah, it's just like Mis' Younger says all the time —"

MAMA: Don't you want some more pie?

JOHNSON: No — no thank you; this was lovely. I got to get on over home and have my midnight coffee. I hear some people say it don't let them sleep but I finds I can't close my eyes right lessen I done had that laaaast cup of coffee . . . (*She waits. A beat. Undaunted.*) My Good-night coffee, I calls it!

MAMA (*with much eye-rolling and communication between herself and Ruth*): Ruth, why don't you give Mis' Johnson some coffee.

(*Ruth gives Mama an unpleasant look for her kindness.*)

JOHNSON (*accepting the coffee*): Where's Brother tonight?

MAMA: He's lying down.

JOHNSON: Mmmmmmm, he sure gets his beauty rest, don't he? Good-looking man. Sure is a good-looking man! (*Reaching out to pat Ruth's stomach again.*) I guess that's how come we keep on having babies around here. (*She winks at Mama.*) One thing 'bout Brother, he always know how to have a *good* time. And sooooooo ambitious! I bet it was his idea y'all moving out to Clybourne Park. Lord — I bet this time next month y'all's names will have been in the papers plenty — (*Holding up her hands to mark off each word of the headline she can see in front of her.*) "NEGROS INVADE CLYBOURNE PARK — BOMBED!"

MAMA (*she and Ruth look at the woman in amazement*): We ain't exactly moving out there to get bombed.

JOHNSON: Oh, honey — you know I'm praying to God every day that don't nothing like that happen! But you have to think of life like it is — and these here Chicago peckerwoods is some baaaad peckerwoods.

MAMA (*wearily*): We done thought about all that Mis' Johnson.

(*Beneatha comes out of the bedroom in her robe and passes through to the bathroom. Mrs. Johnson turns.*)

JOHNSON: Hello there, Bennie!

BENEATHA (*crisply*): Hello, Mrs. Johnson.

JOHNSON: How is school?

BENEATHA (*crisply*): Fine, thank you. (*She goes out.*)

JOHNSON (*insulted*): Getting so she don't have much to say to nobody.

MAMA: The child was on her way to the bathroom.

JOHNSON: I know — but sometimes she act like ain't got time to pass the time of day with nobody ain't been to college. Oh — I ain't criticizing her none. It's just — you know how some of our young people gets when they get a little education. (*Mama and Ruth say nothing, just look at her.*) Yes — well. Well, I guess I better get on home. (*Unmoving.*) 'Course I can understand how she must be proud and everything — being the only one in the family to make something of herself. I know just being a chauffeur ain't never satisfied Brother none. He shouldn't feel like that, though. Ain't nothing wrong with being a chauffeur.

MAMA: There's plenty wrong with it.

JOHNSON: What?

MAMA: Plenty. My husband always said being any kind of a servant wasn't a fit thing for a man to have to be. He always said a man's hands was made to make things, or to turn the earth with — not to drive nobody's car for 'em — or — (*she looks at her own hands*) carry they slop jars. And my boy is just like him — he wasn't meant to wait on nobody.

JOHNSON (*rising, somewhat offended*): Mmmmmmm- mmm. The Youngers is too much for me! (*She looks around.*) You sure one proud-acting bunch of col- ored folks. Well — I always thinks like Booker T. Washington said that time — "Education has spoiled many a good plow hand" —

MAMA: Is that what old Booker T. said?

JOHNSON: He sure did.

MAMA: Well, it sounds just like him. The fool.

JOHNSON (*indignantly*): Well — he was one of our great men.

MAMA: Who said so?

JOHNSON (*nonplussed*): You know, me and you ain't never agreed about some things, Lena Younger. I guess I better be going —

RUTH (*quickly*): Good night.

JOHNSON: Good night. Oh — (*Thrusting it at her.*) You can keep the paper! (*With a trill.*) 'Night.

MAMA: Good night, Mis' Johnson.

(*Mrs. Johnson exits.*)

RUTH: If ignorance was gold . . .

MAMA: Shush. Don't talk about folks behind their backs.

RUTH: You do.

MAMA: I'm old and corrupted. (*Beneatha enters.*) You was rude to Mis' Johnson, Beneatha, and I don't like it at all.

BENEATHA (*at her door*): Mama, if there are two things we, as a people, have got to overcome, one is the Klu Klux Klan — and the other is Mrs. Johnson. (*She exits.*)

MAMA: Smart aleck.

(*The phone rings.*)

RUTH: I'll get it.

MAMA: Lord, ain't this a popular place tonight.

RUTH (*at the phone*): Hello — Just a minute. (*Goes to door.*) Walter, it's Mrs. Arnold. (*Waits. Goes back to the phone. Tense.*) Hello. Yes, this is his wife speak- ing . . . He's lying down now. Yes . . . well, he'll be in tomorrow. He's been very sick. Yes — I know we should have called, but we were so sure he'd be able to come in today. Yes — yes, I'm very sorry. Yes . . . Thank you very much. (*She hangs up. Walter is standing in the doorway of the bedroom behind her.*) That was Mrs. Arnold.

WALTER (*indifferently*): Was it?

RUTH: She said if you don't come in tomorrow that they are getting a new man . . .

WALTER: Ain't that sad — ain't that crying sad.

RUTH: She said Mr. Arnold has had to take a cab for

three days . . . Walter, you ain't been to work for three days! (*This is a revelation to her.*) Where you been, Walter Lee Younger? (*Walter looks at her and starts to laugh.*) You're going to lose your job.

WALTER: That's right . . . (*He turns on the radio.*)

RUTH: Oh, Walter, and with your mother working like a dog every day —

(*A steamy, deep blues pours into the room.*)

WALTER: That's sad too — Everything is sad.

MAMA: What you been doing for these three days, son?

WALTER: Mama — you don't know all the things a man what got leisure can find to do in this city . . . What's this — Friday night? Well — Wednesday I borrowed Willy Harris's car and I went for a drive . . . just me and myself and I drove and drove . . . Way out . . . way past South Chicago, and I parked the car and I sat and looked at the steel mills all day long. I just sat in the car and looked at them big black chimneys for hours. Then I drove back and I went to the Green Hat. (*Pause.*) And Thursday — Thursday I borrowed the car again and I got in it and I pointed it the other way and I drove the other way — for hours — way, way up to Wisconsin, and I looked at the farms. I just drove and looked at the farms. Then I drove back and I went to the Green Hat. (*Pause.*) And today — today I didn't get the car. Today I just walked. All over the Southside. And I looked at the Negroes and they looked at me and finally I just sat down on the curb at Thirty-ninth and South Parkway and I just sat there and watched the Negroes go by. And then I went to the Green Hat. You all sad? You all depressed? And you know where I am going right now —

(*Ruth goes out quietly.*)

MAMA: Oh, Big Walter, is this the harvest of our days?

WALTER: You know what I like about the Green Hat? I like this little cat they got there who blows a sax . . . He blows. He talks to me. He ain't but 'bout five feet tall and he's got a conked head and his eyes is always closed and he's all music —

MAMA (*rising and getting some papers out of her hand- bag*): Walter —

WALTER: And there's this other guy who plays the piano . . . and they got a sound. I mean they can work on some music . . . They got the best little combo in the world in the Green Hat . . . You can just sit there and drink and listen to them three men play and you realize that don't nothing matter worth a damn, but just being there —

MAMA: I've helped do it to you, haven't I, son? Walter I been wrong.

WALTER: Naw — you ain't never been wrong about nothing, Mama.

MAMA: Listen to me, now. I say I been wrong, son. That I been doing to you what the rest of the world been doing to you. (*She turns off the radio.*) Walter — (*She stops and he looks up slowly at her and she meets his eyes pleadingly.*) What you ain't never understood is that I ain't got nothing, don't own nothing, ain't never really wanted nothing that wasn't for you. There ain't nothing as precious to me . . . There ain't nothing worth holding on to, money, dreams, nothing else — if it means — if it means it's going to destroy my boy. (*She takes an envelope out of her handbag and puts it in front of him and he watches her without speaking or moving.*) I paid the man thirty-five hundred dollars down on the house. That leaves sixty-five hundred dollars. Monday morning I want you to take this money and take three thousand dollars and put it in a savings account for Beneatha's medical schooling. The rest you put in a checking account — with your name on it. And from now on any penny that come out of it or that go in it is for you to look after. For you to decide. (*She drops her hands a little helplessly.*) It ain't much, but it's all I got in the world and I'm putting it in your hands. I'm telling you to be the head of this family from now on like you supposed to be.

WALTER (*stares at the money*): You trust me like that, Mama?

MAMA: I ain't never stop trusting you. Like I ain't never stop loving you.

(*She goes out, and Walter sits looking at the money on the table. Finally, in a decisive gesture, he gets up and, in mingled joy and desperation, picks up the money. At the same moment, Travis enters for bed.*)

TRAVIS: What's the matter, Daddy? You drunk?

WALTER (*sweetly, more sweetly than we have ever known him*): No, Daddy ain't drunk. Daddy ain't going to never be drunk again . . .

TRAVIS: Well, good night, Daddy.

(*The father has come from behind the couch and leans over, embracing his son.*)

WALTER: Son, I feel like talking to you tonight.

TRAVIS: About what?

WALTER: Oh, about a lot of things. About you and what kind of man you going to be when you grow up. . . . Son — son, what do you want to be when you grow up?

TRAVIS: A bus driver.

WALTER (*laughing a little*): A what? Man, that ain't nothing to want to be!

TRAVIS: Why not?

WALTER: 'Cause, man — it ain't big enough — you know what I mean.

TRAVIS: I don't know then. I can't make up my mind. Sometimes Mama asks me that too. And sometimes when I tell her I just want to be like you — she says she don't want me to be like that and sometimes she says she does. . . .

WALTER (*gathering him up in his arms*): You know what, Travis? In seven years you going to be seventeen years old. And things is going to be very different with us in seven years Travis. . . . One day when you are seventeen I'll come home — home from my office downtown somewhere —

TRAVIS: You don't work in no office, Daddy.

WALTER: No — but after tonight. After what your daddy gonna do tonight, there's going to be offices — a whole lot of offices. . . .

TRAVIS: What you gonna do tonight, Daddy?

WALTER: You wouldn't understand yet, son, but your daddy's gonna make a transaction . . . a business transaction that's going to change our lives. . . . That's how come one day when you 'bout seventeen years old I'll come home and I'll be pretty tired, you know what I mean, after a day of conferences and secretaries getting things wrong the way they do . . . 'cause an executive's life is hell man — (*The more he talks the farther away he gets.*) And I'll pull the car up on the driveway . . . just a plain black Chrysler, I think, with white walls — no — black tires. More elegant. Rich people don't have to be flashy . . . though I'll have to get something a little sportier for Ruth — maybe a Cadillac convertible to do her shopping in. . . . And I'll come up the steps to the house and the gardener will be clipping away at the hedges and he'll say, "Good evening, Mr. Younger." And I'll say, "Hello, Jefferson, how are you this evening?" And I'll go inside and Ruth will come downstairs and meet me at the door and we'll kiss each other and she'll take my arm and we'll go up to your room to see you sitting on the floor with the catalogues of all the great schools in America around you. . . . All the great schools in the world! And — and I'll say, all right son — it's your seventeenth birthday, what is it you've decided? . . . Just tell me where you want to go to school and you'll *go*. Just tell me, what it is you want to be — and you'll *be* it. . . . Whatever you want to be — Yessir! (*He holds his arms open for Travis.*) You just name it, son . . . (*Travis leaps into them*) and I hand you the world!

(*Walter's voice has risen in pitch and hysterical promise and on the last line he lifts Travis high.*)

Scene III

(*Time: Saturday, moving day, one week later.*)

(*Before the curtain rises, Ruth's voice, a strident, dramatic church alto, cuts through the silence.*)

(*It is, in the darkness, a triumphant surge, a penetrating statement of expectation: "Oh, Lord, I don't feel no ways tired! Children, oh, glory hallelujah!"*)

(*As the curtain rises we see that Ruth is alone in the living room, finishing up the family's packing. It is moving day. She is nailing crates and tying cartons. Beneatha enters, carrying a guitar case, and watches her exuberant sister-in-law.*)

RUTH: Hey!

BENEATHA (*putting away the case*): Hi.

RUTH (*pointing at a package*): Honey — look in that

package there and see what I found on sale this morning at the South Center. (*Ruth gets up and moves to the package and draws out some curtains.*) Lookahere — hand-turned hems!

BENEATHA: How do you know the window size out there?

RUTH (*who hadn't thought of that*): Oh — Well, they bound to fit something in the whole house. Anyhow, they was too good a bargain to pass up. (*Ruth slaps her head, suddenly remembering something.*) Oh, Bennie — I meant to put a special note on that carton over there. That's your mama's good china and she wants 'em to be very careful with it.

BENEATHA: I'll do it.

(*Beneatha finds a piece of paper and starts to draw large letters on it.*)

RUTH: You know what I'm going to do soon as I get in that new house?

BENEATHA: What?

RUTH: Honey — I'm going to run me a tub of water up to here . . . (*With her fingers practically up to her nostrils.*) And I'm going to get in it — and I am going to sit . . . and sit . . . and sit in that hot water and the first person who knocks to tell *me* to hurry up and come out —

BENEATHA: Gets shot at sunrise.

RUTH (*laughing happily*): You said it, sister! (*Noticing how large Beneatha is absent-mindedly making the note.*) Honey, they ain't going to read that from no airplane.

BENEATHA (*laughing herself*): I guess I always think things have more emphasis if they are big, somehow.

RUTH (*looking up at her and smiling*): You and your brother seem to have that as a philosophy of life. Lord, that man — done changed so 'round here. You know — you know what we did last night? Me and Walter Lee?

BENEATHA: What?

RUTH (*smiling to herself*): We went to the movies. (*Looking at Beneatha to see if she understands.*) We went to the movies. You know the last time me and Walter went to the movies together?

BENEATHA: No.

RUTH: Me neither. That's how long it been. (*Smiling again.*) But we went last night. The picture wasn't much good, but that didn't seem to matter. We went — and we held hands.

BENEATHA: Oh, Lord!

RUTH: We held hands — and you know what?

BENEATHA: What?

RUTH: When we come out of the show it was late and dark and all the stores and things was closed up . . . and it was kind of chilly and there wasn't many people on the streets . . . and we was still holding hands, me and Walter.

BENEATHA: You're killing me.

(*Walter enters with a large package. His happiness is deep in him; he cannot keep still with his newfound exu-*

berance. He is singing and wiggling and snapping his fingers. He puts his package in a corner and puts a phonograph record which he has brought in with him, on the record player. As the music, soulful and sensuous, comes up he dances over to Ruth and tries to get her to dance with him. She gives in at last to his raunchiness and in a fit of giggling allows herself to be drawn into his mood. They dip and she melts into his arms in a classic, body-melding "slow drag."*)

BENEATHA (*regarding them a long time as they dance, then drawing in her breath for a deeply exaggerated comment which she does not particularly mean*): Talk about — olddddddddddd — fashionedddddddd — Negroes!

WALTER (*stopping momentarily*): What kind of Negroes?

(*He says this in fun. He is not angry with her today, nor with anyone. He starts to dance with his wife again.*)

BENEATHA: Old-fashioned.

WALTER (*as he dances with Ruth*): You know, when these *New Negroes* have their convention — (*pointing at his sister*) — that is going to be the chairman of the Committee on Unending Agitation. (*He goes on dancing, then stops.*) Race, race, race! . . . Girl, I do believe you are the first person in the history of the entire human race to successfully brainwash yourself. (*Beneatha breaks up and he goes on dancing. He stops again, enjoying his tease.*) Damn, even the N double A C P takes a holiday sometimes! (*Beneatha and Ruth laugh. He dances with Ruth some more and starts to laugh and stops and pantomimes someone over an operating table.*) I can just see that chick someday looking down at some poor cat on an operating table and before she starts to slice him, she says . . . (*pulling his sleeves back maliciously*) "By the way, what are your views on civil rights down there? . . ."

(*He laughs at her again and starts to dance happily. The bell sounds.*)

BENEATHA: Sticks and stones may break my bones but . . . words will never hurt me!

(*Beneatha goes to the door and opens it as Walter and Ruth go on with the clowning. Beneatha is somewhat surprised to see a quiet-looking middle-aged white man in a business suit holding his hat and a briefcase in his hand and consulting a small piece of paper.*)

MAN: Uh — how do you do, miss. I am looking for a Mrs. — (*he looks at the slip of paper*) Mrs. Lena Younger? (*He stops short, struck dumb at the sight of the oblivious Walter and Ruth.*)

BENEATHA (*smoothing her hair with slight embarrassment*): Oh — yes, that's my mother. Excuse me. (*She closes the door and turns to quiet the other two.*) Ruth! Brother! (*Enunciating precisely but soundlessly: "There's a white man at the door!" They stop dancing, Ruth cuts off the phonograph, Beneatha opens the door. The man casts a curious quick glance at all of them.*) Uh — come in please.

MAN (*coming in*): Thank you.

BENEATHA: My mother isn't here just now. Is it business?

MAN: Yes . . . well, of a sort.

WALTER (*freely, the Man of the House*): Have a seat. I'm Mrs. Younger's son. I look after most of her business matters.

(*Ruth and Beneatha exchange amused glances.*)

MAN (*regarding Walter, and sitting*): Well — My name is Karl Lindner . . .

WALTER (*stretching out his hand*): Walter Younger. This is my wife — (*Ruth nods politely*) — and my sister.

LINDNER: How do you do.

WALTER (*amiably, as he sits himself easily on a chair, leaning forward on his knees with interest and looking expectantly into the newcomer's face*): What can we do for you, Mr. Lindner!

LINDNER (*some minor shuffling of the hat and briefcase on his knees*): Well — I am a representative of the Clybourne Park Improvement Association —

WALTER (*pointing*): Why don't you sit your things on the floor?

LINDNER: Oh — yes. Thank you. (*He slides the briefcase and hat under the chair.*) And as I was saying — I am from the Clybourne Park Improvement Association and we have had it brought to our attention at the last meeting that you people — or at least your mother — has bought a piece of residential property at — (*he digs for the slip of paper again*) — four o six Clybourne Street . . .

WALTER: That's right. Care for something to drink? Ruth, get Mr. Lindner a beer.

LINDNER (*upset for some reason*): Oh — no, really. I mean thank you very much, but no thank you.

RUTH: (*innocently*): Some coffee?

LINDNER: Thank you, nothing at all.

(*Beneatha is watching the man carefully.*)

LINDNER: Well, I don't know how much you folks know about our organization. (*He is a gentle man; thoughtful and somewhat labored in his manner.*) It is one of these community organizations set up to look after — oh, you know, things like block upkeep and special projects and we also have what we call our New Neighbors Orientation Committee . . .

BENEATHA (*drily*): Yes — and what do they do?

LINDNER (*turning a little to her and then returning the main force to Walter*): Well — it's what you might call a sort of welcoming committee, I guess. I mean they, we — I'm the chairman of the committee — go around and see the new people who move into the neighborhood and sort of give them the lowdown on the way we do things out in Clybourne Park.

BENEATHA (*with appreciation of the two meanings, which escape Ruth and Walter*): Un-huh.

LINDNER: And we also have the category of what the association calls — (*he looks elsewhere*) — uh — special community problems . . .

BENEATHA: Yes — and what are some of those?

WALTER: Girl, let the man talk.

LINDNER (*with understated relief*): Thank you. I would sort of like to explain this thing in my own way. I mean I want to explain to you in a certain way.

WALTER: Go ahead.

LINDNER: Yes. Well. I'm going to try to get right to the point. I'm sure we'll all appreciate that in the long run.

BENEATHA: Yes.

WALTER: Be still now!

LINDNER: Well —

RUTH (*still innocently*): Would you like another chair — you don't look comfortable.

LINDNER (*more frustrated than annoyed*): No, thank you very much. Please. Well — to get right to the point I — (*a great breath, and he is off at last*) I am sure you people must be aware of some of the incidents which have happened in various parts of the city when colored people have moved into certain areas — (*Beneatha exhales heavily and starts tossing a piece of fruit up and down in the air.*) Well — because we have what I think is going to be a unique type of organization in American community life — not only do we deplore that kind of thing — but we are trying to do something about it. (*Beneatha stops tossing and turns with a new and quizzical interest to the man.*) We feel — (*gaining confidence in his mission because of the interest in the faces of the people he is talking to*) — we feel that most of the trouble in this world, when you come right down to it — (*he hits his knee for emphasis*) — most of the trouble exists because people just don't sit down and talk to each other.

RUTH (*nodding as she might in church, pleased with the remark*): You can say that again, mister.

LINDNER (*more encouraged by such affirmation*): That we don't try hard enough in this world to understand the other fellow's problem. The other guy's point of view.

RUTH: Now that's right.

(*Beneatha and Walter merely watch and listen with genuine interest.*)

LINDNER: Yes — that's the way we feel out in Clybourne Park. And that's why I was elected to come here this afternoon and talk to you people. Friendly like, you know, the way people should talk to each other and see if we couldn't find some way to work this thing out. As I say, the whole business is a matter of *caring* about the other fellow. Anybody can see that you are a nice family of folks, hard-working and honest I'm sure. (*Beneatha frowns slightly, quizzically, her head tilted regarding him.*) Today everybody knows what it means to be on the outside of *something*. And of course, there is always somebody who is out to take advantage of people who don't always understand.

WALTER: What do you mean?

LINDNER: Well — you see our community is made up of people who've worked hard as the dickens for years to build up that little community. They're not rich and fancy people; just hard-working, honest people who don't really have much but those little homes and a dream of the kind of community they want to raise their children in. Now, I don't say we are perfect and there is a lot wrong in some of the things they want. But you've got to admit that a man, right or wrong, has the right to want to have the neighborhood he lives in a certain kind of way. And at the moment the overwhelming majority of our people out there feel that people get along better, take more of a common interest in the life of the community, when they share a common background. I want you to believe me when I tell you that race prejudice simply doesn't enter into it. It is a matter of the people of Clybourne Park believing, rightly or wrongly, as I say, that for the happiness of all concerned that our Negro families are happier when they live in their *own* communities.

BENEATHA (*with a grand and bitter gesture*): This, friends, is the Welcoming Committee!

WALTER (*dumfounded, looking at Lindner*): Is this what you came marching all the way over here to tell us?

LINDNER: Well, now we've been having a fine conversation. I hope you'll hear me all the way through.

WALTER (*tightly*): Go ahead, man.

LINDNER: You see — in the face of all the things I have said, we are prepared to make your family a very generous offer . . .

BENEATHA: Thirty pieces and not a coin less!

WALTER: Yeah!

LINDNER (*putting on his glasses and drawing a form out of the briefcase*): Our association is prepared, through the collective effort of our people, to buy the house from you at a financial gain to your family.

RUTH: Lord have mercy, ain't this the living gall!

WALTER: All right, you through?

LINDNER: Well, I want to give you the exact terms of the financial arrangement —

WALTER: We don't want to hear no exact terms of no arrangements. I want to know if you got any more to tell us 'bout getting together?

LINDNER (*taking off his glasses*): Well — I don't suppose that you feel . . .

WALTER: Never mind how I feel — you got any more to say 'bout how people ought to sit down and talk to each other? . . . Get out of my house, man.

(*He turns his back and walks to the door.*)

LINDNER (*looking around at the hostile faces and reaching and assembling his hat and briefcase*): Well — I don't understand why you people are reacting this way. What do you think you are going to gain by moving into a neighborhood where you just aren't wanted and where some elements — well — people can get awful worked up when they feel that their whole way of life and everything they've ever worked for is threatened.

WALTER: Get out.

LINDNER (*at the door, holding a small card*): Well — I'm sorry it went like this.

WALTER: Get out.

LINDNER (*almost sadly regarding Walter*): You just can't force people to change their hearts, son.

(*He turns and puts his card on a table and exits. Walter pushes the door to with stinging hatred, and stands looking at it. Ruth just sits and Beneatha just stands. They say nothing. Mama and Travis enter.*)

MAMA: Well — this all the packing got done since I left out of here this morning. I testify before God that my children got all the energy of the *dead!* What time the moving men due?

BENEATHA: Four o'clock. You had a caller, Mama.

(*She is smiling, teasingly.*)

MAMA: Sure enough — who?

BENEATHA (*her arms folded saucily*): The Welcoming Committee.

(*Walter and Ruth giggle.*)

MAMA (*innocently*): Who?

BENEATHA: The Welcoming Committee. They said they're sure going to be glad to see you when you get there.

WALTER (*devilishly*): Yeah, they said they can't hardly wait to see your face.

(*Laughter.*)

MAMA (*sensing their facetiousness*): What's the matter with you all?

WALTER: Ain't nothing the matter with us. We just telling you 'bout the gentleman who came to see you this afternoon. From the Clybourne Park Improvement Association.

MAMA: What he want?

RUTH (*in the same mood as Beneatha and Walter*): To welcome you, honey.

WALTER: He said they can't hardly wait. He said the one thing they don't have, that they just *dying* to have out there is a fine family of fine colored people! (*To Ruth and Beneatha.*) Ain't that right!

RUTH (*mockingly*): Yeah! He left his card —

BENEATHA (*handing card to Mama*): In case.

(*Mama reads and throws it on the floor — understanding and looking off as she draws her chair up to the table on which she has put her plant and some sticks and some cord.*)

MAMA: Father, give us strength. (*Knowingly — and without fun.*) Did he threaten us?

BENEATHA: Oh — Mama — they don't do it like that anymore. He talked Brotherhood. He said everybody ought to learn how to sit down and hate each other with good Christian fellowship.

(*She and Walter shake hands to ridicule the remark.*)

MAMA (*sadly*): Lord, protect us . . .
RUTH: You should hear the money those folks raised to buy the house from us. All we paid and then some.
BENEATHA: What they think we going to do — eat 'em?
RUTH: No, honey, marry 'em.
MAMA (*shaking her head*): Lord, Lord, Lord . . .
RUTH: Well — that's the way the crackers crumble. (*A beat.*) Joke.
BENEATHA (*laughingly noticing what her mother is doing*): Mama, what are you doing?
MAMA: Fixing my plant so it won't get hurt none on the way . . .
BENEATHA: Mama, you going to take *that* to the new house?
MAMA: Un-huh —
BENEATHA: That raggedy-looking old thing?
MAMA (*stopping and looking at her*): It expresses ME!
RUTH (*with delight, to Beneatha*): So there, Miss Thing!

(*Walter comes to Mama suddenly and bends down behind her and squeezes her in his arms with all his strength. She is overwhelmed by the suddenness of it and, though delighted, her manner is like that of Ruth and Travis.*)

MAMA: Look out now, boy! You make me mess up my thing here!
WALTER (*his face lit, he slips down on his knees beside her, his arms still about her*): Mama . . . you know what it means to climb up in the chariot.
MAMA (*gruffly, very happy*): Get on away from me now . . .
RUTH (*near the gift-wrapped package, trying to catch Walter's eye*): Psst —
WALTER: What the old song say, Mama . . .
RUTH: Walter — Now?

(*She is pointing at the package.*)

WALTER (*speaking the lines, sweetly, playfully, in his mother's face*): I got wings . . . you got wings . . .
All God's Children got wings . . .
MAMA: Boy — get out of my face and do some work . . .
WALTER: When I get to heaven gonna put on my wings, Gonna fly all over God's heaven . . .
BENEATHA (*teasingly, from across the room*): Everybody talking 'bout heaven ain't going there!
WALTER (*to Ruth, who is carrying the box across to them*): I don't know, you think we ought to give her that . . . Seems to me she ain't been very appreciative around here.
MAMA (*eyeing the box, which is obviously a gift*): What is that?
WALTER (*taking it from Ruth and putting it on the table in front of Mama*): Well — what you all think? Should we give it to her?

RUTH: Oh — she was pretty good today.
MAMA: I'll good you —

(*She turns her eyes to the box again.*)

BENEATHA: Open it, Mama.

(*She stands up, looks at it, turns, and looks at all of them, and then presses her hands together and does not open the package.*)

WALTER (*sweetly*): Open it, Mama. It's for you. (*Mama looks in his eyes. It is the first present in her life without its being Christmas. Slowly she opens her package and lifts out, one by one, a brand-new sparkling set of gardening tools. Walter continues, prodding.*) Ruth made up the note — read it . . .
MAMA (*picking up the card and adjusting her glasses*): "To our own Mrs. Miniver — Love from Brother, Ruth and Beneatha." Ain't that lovely . . .
TRAVIS (*tugging at his father's sleeve*): Daddy, can I give her mine now?
WALTER: All right, son. (*Travis flies to get his gift.*)
MAMA: Now I don't have to use my knives and forks no more . . .
WALTER: Travis didn't want to go in with the rest of us, Mama. He got his own. (*Somewhat amused.*) We don't know what it is . . .
TRAVIS (*racing back in the room with a large hatbox and putting it in front of his grandmother*): Here!
MAMA: Lord have mercy, baby. You done gone and bought your grandmother a hat?
TRAVIS (*very proud*): Open it!

(*She does and lifts out an elaborate, but very elaborate, wide gardening hat, and all the adults break up at the sight of it.*)

RUTH: Travis, honey, what is that?
TRAVIS (*who thinks it is beautiful and appropriate*): It's a gardening hat! Like the ladies always have on in the magazines when they work in their gardens.
BENEATHA (*giggling fiercely*): Travis — we were trying to make Mama Mrs. Miniver — not Scarlett O'Hara!
MAMA (*indignantly*): What's the matter with you all! This here is a beautiful hat! (*Absurdly.*) I always wanted me one just like it!

(*She pops it on her head to prove it to her grandson, and the hat is ludicrous and considerably oversized.*)

RUTH: Hot dog! Go, Mama!
WALTER (*doubled over with laughter*): I'm sorry, Mama — but you look like you ready to go out and chop you some cotton sure enough!

(*They all laugh except Mama, out of deference to Travis's feelings.*)

MAMA (*gathering the boy up to her*): Bless your heart — this is the prettiest hat I ever owned — (*Walter, Ruth, and Beneatha chime in — noisily, festively, and insincerely congratulating Travis on his gift.*) What are we all standing around here for? We ain't finished packin' yet. Bennie, you ain't packed one book.

(*The bell rings.*)

BENEATHA: That couldn't be the movers . . . it's not hardly two good yet —

(*Beneatha goes into her room. Mama starts for door.*)

WALTER (*turning, stiffening*): Wait — wait — I'll get it.

(*He stands and looks at the door.*)

MAMA: You expecting company, son?
WALTER (*just looking at the door*): Yeah — yeah . . .

(*Mama looks at Ruth, and they exchange innocent and unfrightened glances.*)

MAMA (*not understanding*): Well, let them in, son.
BENEATHA (*from her room*): We need some more string.
MAMA: Travis — you run to the hardware and get me some string cord.

(*Mama goes out and Walter turns and looks at Ruth. Travis goes to a dish for money.*)

RUTH: Why don't you answer the door, man?
WALTER (*suddenly bounding across the floor to embrace her*): 'Cause sometimes it hard to let the future begin! (*Stooping down in her face.*)
I got wings! You got wings!
All God's children got wings!
(*He crosses to the door and throws it open. Standing there is a very slight little man in a not too prosperous business suit and with haunted frightened eyes and a hat pulled down tightly, brim up, around his forehead. Travis passes between the men and exits. Walter leans deep in the man's face, still in his jubilance.*) When I get to heaven gonna put on my wings, Gonna fly all over God's heaven . . . (*The little man just stares at him.*) Heaven — (*Suddenly he stops and looks past the little man into the empty hallway.*) Where's Willy, man?
BOBO: He ain't with me.
WALTER (*not disturbed*): Oh — come on in. You know my wife.
BOBO (*dumbly, taking off his hat*): Yes — h'you, Miss Ruth.
RUTH (*quietly, a mood apart from her husband already, seeing Bobo*): Hello, Bobo.
WALTER: You right on time today . . . Right on time. That's the way! (*He slaps Bobo on his back.*) Sit down . . . lemme hear.

(*Ruth stands stiffly and quietly in back of them, as though somehow she senses death, her eyes fixed on her husband.*)

BOBO (*his frightened eyes on the floor, his hat in his hands*): Could I please get a drink of water, before I tell you about it, Walter Lee?

(*Walter does not take his eyes off the man. Ruth goes blindly to the tap and gets a glass of water and brings it to Bobo.*)

WALTER: There ain't nothing wrong, is there?
BOBO: Lemme tell you —
WALTER: Man — didn't nothing go wrong?
BOBO: Lemme tell you — Walter Lee. (*Looking at Ruth and talking to her more than to Walter.*) You know how it was. I got to tell you how it was. I mean first I got to tell you how it was all the way . . . I mean about the money I put in, Walter Lee . . .
WALTER (*with taut agitation now*): What about the money you put in?
BOBO: Well — it wasn't much as we told you — me and Willy — (*He stops.*) I'm sorry, Walter. I got a bad feeling about it. I got a real bad feeling about it . . .
WALTER: Man, what you telling me about all this for? . . . Tell me what happened in Springfield . . .
BOBO: Springfield.
RUTH (*like a dead woman*): What was supposed to happen in Springfield?
BOBO (*to her*): This deal that me and Walter went into with Willy — Me and Willy was going to go down to Springfield and spread some money 'round so's we wouldn't have to wait so long for the liquor license . . . That's what we were going to do. Everybody said that was the way you had to do, you understand, Miss Ruth?
WALTER: Man — what happened down there?
BOBO (*a pitiful man, near tears*): I'm trying to tell you, Walter.
WALTER (*screaming at him suddenly*): THEN TELL ME, GODDAMMIT . . . WHAT'S THE MATTER WITH YOU?
BOBO: Man . . . I didn't go to no Springfield, yesterday.
WALTER (*halted, life hanging in the moment*): Why not?
BOBO (*the long way, the hard way to tell*): 'Cause I didn't have no reasons to . . .
WALTER: Man, what are you talking about!
BOBO: I'm talking about the fact that when I got to the train station yesterday morning — eight o'clock like we planned . . . Man — *Willy didn't never show up.*
WALTER: Why . . . where was he . . . where is he?
BOBO: That's what I'm trying to tell you . . . I don't know . . . I waited six hours . . . I called his house . . . and I waited . . . six hours . . . I waited in that train station six hours . . . (*Breaking into tears.*) That was all the extra money I had in the world . . . (*Looking up at Walter with the tears running down his face.*) Man, *Willy is gone.*
WALTER: Gone, what you mean Willy is gone? Gone where? You mean he went by himself. You mean he went off to Springfield by himself — to take care of getting the license — (*Turns and looks anxiously at Ruth.*) You mean maybe he didn't want too many people in on the business down there? (*Looks to Ruth again, as before.*) You know Willy got his own ways. (*Looks back to Bobo.*) Maybe you was late

yesterday and he just went on down there without you. Maybe — maybe — he's been callin' you at home tryin' to tell you what happened or something. Maybe — maybe — he just got sick. He's somewhere — he's got to be somewhere. We just got to find him — me and you got to find him. (*Grabs Bobo senselessly by the collar and starts to shake him.*) We got to!

BOBO (*in sudden angry, frightened agony*): What's the matter with you, Walter! *When a cat take off with your money he don't leave you no road maps!*

WALTER (*turning madly, as though he is looking for Willy in the very room*): Willy! . . . Willy . . . don't do it . . . Please don't do it . . . Man, not with that money . . . Man, please, not with that money . . . Oh, God . . . Don't let it be true . . . (*He is wandering around, crying out for Willy and looking for him or perhaps for help from God.*) Man . . . I trusted you . . . Man, I put my life in your hands . . . (*He starts to crumple down on the floor as Ruth just covers her face in horror. Mama opens the door and comes into the room, with Beneatha behind her.*) Man . . . (*He starts to pound the floor with his fists, sobbing wildly.*) THAT MONEY IS MADE OUT MY FATHER'S FLESH ——

BOBO (*standing over him helplessly*): I'm sorry, Walter . . . (*Only Walter's sobs reply. Bobo puts on his hat.*) I had my life staked on this deal, too . . .

(*He exits.*)

MAMA (*to Walter*): Son — (*She goes to him, bends down to him, talks to his bent head.*) Son . . . Is it gone? Son, I gave you sixty-five hundred dollars. Is it gone? All of it? Beneatha's money too?

WALTER (*lifting his head slowly*): Mama . . . I never . . . went to the bank at all . . .

MAMA (*not wanting to believe him*): You mean . . . your sister's school money . . . you used that too . . . Walter? . . .

WALTER: Yessss! All of it . . . It's all gone . . .

(*There is total silence. Ruth stands with her face covered with her hands; Beneatha leans forlornly against a wall, fingering a piece of red ribbon from the mother's gift. Mama stops and looks at her son without recognition and then, quite without thinking about it, starts to beat him senselessly in the face. Beneatha goes to them and stops it.*)

BENEATHA: Mama!

(*Mama stops and looks at both of her children and rises slowly and wanders vaguely, aimlessly away from them.*)

MAMA: I seen . . . him . . . night after night . . . come in . . . and look at that rug . . . and then look at me . . . the red showing in his eyes . . . the veins moving in his head . . . I seen him grow thin and old before he was forty . . . working and working and working like somebody's old horse . . . killing him-

self . . . and you — you give it all away in a day — (*She raises her arms to strike him again.*)

BENEATHA: Mama —

MAMA: Oh, God . . . (*She looks up to Him.*) Look down here — and show me the strength.

BENEATHA: Mama —

MAMA (*folding over*): Strength . . .

BENEATHA (*plaintively*): Mama . . .

MAMA: Strength!

ACT III

(*An hour later.*)

(*At curtain, there is a sullen light of gloom in the living room, gray light not unlike that which began the first scene of act I. At left we can see Walter within his room, alone with himself. He is stretched out on the bed, his shirt out and open, his arms under his head. He does not smoke, he does not cry out, he merely lies there, looking up at the ceiling, much as if he were alone in the world.*)

(*In the living room Beneatha sits at the table, still surrounded by the now almost ominous packing crates. She sits looking off. We feel that this is a mood struck perhaps an hour before, and it lingers now, full of the empty sound of profound disappointment. We see on a line from her brother's bedroom the sameness of their attitudes. Presently the bell rings and Beneatha rises without ambition or interest in answering. It is Asagai, smiling broadly, striding into the room with energy and happy expectation and conversation.*)

ASAGAI: I came over . . . I had some free time. I thought I might help with the packing. Ah, I like the look of packing crates! A household in preparation for a journey! It depresses some people . . . but for me . . . it is another feeling. Something full of the flow of life, do you understand? Movement, progress . . . It makes me think of Africa.

BENEATHA: Africa!

ASAGAI: What kind of a mood is this? Have I told you how deeply you move me?

BENEATHA: He gave away the money, Asagai . . .

ASAGAI: Who gave away what money?

BENEATHA: The insurance money. My brother gave it away.

ASAGAI: Gave it away?

BENEATHA: He made an investment! With a man even Travis wouldn't have trusted with his most worn-out marbles.

ASAGAI: And it's gone?

BENEATHA: Gone!

ASAGAI: I'm very sorry . . . And you, now?

BENEATHA: Me? . . . Me? . . . Me, I'm nothing . . . Me. When I was very small . . . we used to take our sleds out in the wintertime and the only hills we had were the ice-covered stone steps of some houses down the street. And we used to fill them in with snow and

make them smooth and slide down them all day . . .
and it was very dangerous, you know . . . far too
steep . . . and sure enough one day a kid named
Rufus came down too fast and hit the sidewalk and
we saw his face just split open right there in front of
us . . . And I remember standing there looking at his
bloody open face thinking that was the end of Rufus.
But the ambulance came and they took him to the
hospital and they fixed the broken bones and they
sewed it all up . . . and the next time I saw Rufus he
just had a little line down the middle of his face . . . I
never got over that . . .

ASAGAI: What?

BENEATHA: That that was what one person could do for
another, fix him up — sew up the problem, make him
all right again. That was the most marvelous thing in
the world . . . I wanted to do that. I always thought it
was the one concrete thing in the world that a human
being could do. Fix up the sick, you know — and
make them whole again. This was truly being
God . . .

ASAGAI: You wanted to be God?

BENEATHA: No — I wanted to cure. It used to be so
important to me. I wanted to cure. It used to matter. I
used to care. I mean about people and how their bodies hurt . . .

ASAGAI: And you've stopped caring?

BENEATHA: Yes — I think so.

ASAGAI: Why?

BENEATHA (bitterly): Because it doesn't seem deep
enough, close enough to what ails mankind! It was a
child's way of seeing things — or an idealist's.

ASAGAI: Children see things very well sometimes — and
idealists even better.

BENEATHA: I know that's what you think. Because you
are still where I left off. You with all your talk and
dreams about Africa! You still think you can patch
up the world. Cure the Great Sore of Colonialism —
(loftily, mocking it) with the Penicillin of Independence —!

ASAGAI: Yes!

BENEATHA: Independence and then what? What about
all the crooks and thieves and just plain idiots who
will come into power and steal and plunder the same
as before — only now they will be black and do it in
the name of the new Independence — WHAT ABOUT
THEM?!

ASAGAI: That will be the problem for another time. First
we must get there.

BENEATHA: And where does it end?

ASAGAI: End? Who even spoke of an end? To life? To
living?

BENEATHA: An end to misery! To stupidity! Don't you
see there isn't any real progress, Asagai, there is only
one large circle that we march in, around and
around, each of us with our own little picture in
front of us — our own little mirage that we think is
the future.

ASAGAI: That is the mistake.

BENEATHA: What?

ASAGAI: What you just said — about the circle. It isn't a
circle — it is simply a long line — as in geometry,
you know, one that reaches into infinity. And because
we cannot see the end — we also cannot see how it
changes. And it is very odd but those who see the
changes — who dream, who will not give up — are
called idealists . . . and those who see only the
circle — we call them the "realists"!

BENEATHA: Asagai, while I was sleeping in that bed in
there, people went out and took the future right out
of my hands! And nobody asked me, nobody con-
sulted me — they just went out and changed my life!

ASAGAI: Was it your money?

BENEATHA: What?

ASAGAI: Was it your money he gave away?

BENEATHA: It belonged to all of us.

ASAGAI: But did you earn it? Would you have had it at
all if your father had not died?

BENEATHA: No.

ASAGAI: Then isn't there something wrong in a house —
in a world — where all dreams, good or bad, must
depend on the death of a man? I never thought to see
you like this, Alaiyo. You! Your brother made a mistake and you are grateful to him so that now you can
give up the ailing human race on account of it! You
talk about what good is struggle, what good is anything! Where are we all going and why are we bothering!

BENEATHA: AND YOU CANNOT ANSWER IT!

ASAGAI (shouting over her): I LIVE THE ANSWER! (Pause.)
In my village at home it is the exceptional man who
can even read a newspaper . . . or who ever sees a
book at all. I will go home and much of what I will
have to say will seem strange to the people of my village. But I will teach and work and things will happen, slowly and swiftly. At times it will seem that
nothing changes at all . . . and then again the sudden
dramatic events which make history leap into the
future. And then quiet again. Retrogression even.
Guns, murder, revolution. And I even will have
moments when I wonder if the quiet was not better
than all that death and hatred. But I will look about
my village at the illiteracy and disease and ignorance
and I will not wonder long. And perhaps . . . perhaps
I will be a great man . . . I mean perhaps I will hold
on to the substance of truth and find my way always
with the right course . . . and perhaps for it I will be
butchered in my bed some night by the servants of
empire . . .

BENEATHA: The martyr!

ASAGAI (he smiles): . . . or perhaps I shall live to be a
very old man, respected and esteemed in my new
nation . . . And perhaps I shall hold office and this is
what I'm trying to tell you, Alaiyo: Perhaps the
things I believe now for my country will be wrong
and outmoded, and I will not understand and do terrible things to have things my way or merely to keep
my power. Don't you see that there will be young

men and women — not British soldiers then, but my own black countrymen — to step out of the shadows some evening and slit my then useless throat? Don't you see they have always been there . . . that they always will be. And that such a thing as my own death will be an advance? They who might kill me even . . . actually replenish all that I was.

BENEATHA: Oh, Asagai, I know all that.

ASAGAI: Good! Then stop moaning and groaning and tell me what you plan to do.

BENEATHA: Do?

ASAGAI: I have a bit of a suggestion.

BENEATHA: What?

ASAGAI (*rather quietly for him*): That when it is all over — that you come home with me —

BENEATHA (*staring at him and crossing away with exasperation*): Oh — Asagai — at this moment you decide to be romantic!

ASAGAI (*quickly understanding the misunderstanding*): My dear, young creature of the New World — I do not mean across the city — I mean across the ocean: home — to Africa.

BENEATHA (*slowly understanding and turning to him with murmured amazement*): To Africa?

ASAGAI: Yes! . . . (*Smiling and lifting his arms playfully.*) Three hundred years later the African Prince rose up out of the seas and swept the maiden back across the middle passage over which her ancestors had come —

BENEATHA (*unable to play*): To — to Nigeria?

ASAGAI: Nigeria. Home. (*Coming to her with genuine romantic flippancy.*) I will show you our mountains and our stars; and give you cool drinks from gourds and teach you the old songs and the ways of our people — and, in time, we will pretend that — (*very softly*) — you have only been away for a day. Say that you'll come — (*He swings her around and takes her full in his arms in a kiss which proceeds to passion.*)

BENEATHA (*pulling away suddenly*): You're getting me all mixed up —

ASAGAI: Why?

BENEATHA: Too many things — too many things have happened today. I must sit down and think. I don't know what I feel about anything right this minute.

(*She promptly sits down and props her chin on her fist.*)

ASAGAI (*charmed*): All right, I shall leave you. No — don't get up. (*Touching her, gently, sweetly.*) Just sit awhile and think . . . Never be afraid to sit awhile and think. (*He goes to door and looks at her.*) How often I have looked at you and said, "Ah — so this is what the New World hath finally wrought . . ."

(*He exits. Beneatha sits on alone. Presently Walter enters from his room and starts to rummage through things, feverishly looking for something. She looks up and turns in her seat.*)

BENEATHA (*hissingly*): Yes — just look at what the New World hath wrought! . . . Just look! (*She gestures with bitter disgust.*) There he is! *Monsieur le petit bourgeois noir*° — himself! There he is — Symbol of a Rising Class! Entrepreneur! Titan° of the system! (*Walter ignores her completely and continues frantically and destructively looking for something and hurling things to floor and tearing things out of their place in his search. Beneatha ignores the eccentricity of his actions and goes on with the monologue of insult.*) Did you dream of yachts on Lake Michigan, Brother? Did you see yourself on that Great Day sitting down at the Conference Table, surrounded by all the mighty bald-headed men in America? All halted, waiting, breathless, waiting for your pronouncements on industry? Waiting for you — Chairman of the Board! (*Walter finds what he is looking for — a small piece of white paper — and pushes it in his pocket and puts on his coat and rushes out without ever having looked at her. She shouts after him.*) I look at you and I see the final triumph of stupidity in the world!

(*The door slams and she returns to just sitting again. Ruth comes quickly out of Mama's room.*)

RUTH: Who was that?

BENEATHA: Your husband.

RUTH: Where did he go?

BENEATHA: Who knows — maybe he has an appointment at U.S. Steel.

RUTH (*anxiously, with frightened eyes*): You didn't say nothing bad to him, did you?

BENEATHA: Bad? Say anything bad to him? No — I told him he was a sweet boy and full of dreams and everything is strictly peachy keen, as the ofay° kids say!

(*Mama enters from her bedroom. She is lost, vague, trying to catch hold, to make some sense of her former command of the world, but it still eludes her. A sense of waste overwhelms her gait; a measure of apology rides on her shoulders. She goes to her plant, which has remained on the table, looks at it, picks it up and takes it to the window sill and sits it outside, and she stands and looks at it a long moment. Then she closes the window, straightens her body with effort, and turns around to her children.*)

MAMA: Well — ain't it a mess in here, though? (*A false cheerfulness, a beginning of something.*) I guess we all better stop moping around and get some work done. All this unpacking and everything we got to do. (*Ruth raises her head slowly in response to the sense of the line; and Beneatha in similar manner turns very slowly to look at her mother.*) One of you all better call the moving people and tell 'em not to come.

RUTH: Tell 'em not to come?

MAMA: Of course, baby. Ain't no need in 'em coming all the way here and having to go back. They charges for that too. (*She sits down, fingers to her brow, think-*

Monsieur . . . noir: Mr. Black Lower Middle Class.
Titan: Person of great power; originally, a god.
ofay: White person, usually used disparagingly.

ing.) Lord, ever since I was a little girl, I always remembers people saying, "Lena — Lena Eggleston, you aims too high all the time. You needs to slow down and see life a little more like it is. Just slow down some." That's what they always used to say down home — "Lord, that Lena Eggleston is a high-minded thing. She'll get her due one day!"

RUTH: No, Lena . . .

MAMA: Me and Big Walter just didn't never learn right.

RUTH: Lena, no! We gotta go. Bennie — tell her . . . (*She rises and crosses to Beneatha with her arms outstretched. Beneatha doesn't respond.*) Tell her we can still move . . . the notes ain't but a hundred and twenty-five a month. We got four grown people in this house — we can work . . .

MAMA (*to herself*): Just aimed too high all the time —

RUTH (*turning and going to Mama fast — the words pouring out with urgency and desperation*): Lena — I'll work . . . I'll work twenty hours a day in all the kitchens in Chicago . . . I'll strap my baby on my back if I have to and scrub all the floors in America and wash all the sheets in America if I have to — but we got to MOVE! We got to get OUT OF HERE!!

(*Mama reaches out absently and pats Ruth's hand.*)

MAMA: No — I sees things differently now. Been thinking 'bout some of the things we could do to fix this place up some. I seen a second-hand bureau over on Maxwell Street just the other day that could fit right there. (*She points to where the new furniture might go. Ruth wanders away from her.*) Would need some new handles on it and then a little varnish and it look like something brand new. And — we can put up them new curtains in the kitchen . . . Why this place be looking fine. Cheer us all up so that we forget trouble ever come . . . (*To Ruth.*) And you could get some nice screens to put up in your room round the baby's bassinet . . . (*She looks at both of them, pleadingly.*) Sometimes you just got to know when to give up some things . . . and hold on to what you got. . . .

(*Walter enters from the outside, looking spent and leaning against the door, his coat hanging from him.*)

MAMA: Where you been, son?

WALTER (*breathing hard*): Made a call.

MAMA: To who, son?

WALTER: To The Man. (*He heads for his room.*) MAMA: What man, baby?

WALTER (*stops in the door*): The Man, Mama. Don't you know who The Man is?

RUTH: Walter Lee?

WALTER: *The Man.* Like the guys in the streets say — The Man. Captain Boss — Mistuh Charley . . . Old Cap'n Please Mr. Bossman . . .

BENEATHA (*suddenly*): Lindner!

WALTER: That's right! That's good. I told him to come right over.

BENEATHA (*fiercely, understanding*): For what? What do you want to see him for!

WALTER (*looking at his sister*): We going to do business with him.

MAMA: What you talking 'bout, son?

WALTER: Talking 'bout life, Mama. You all always telling me to see life like it is. Well — I laid in there on my back today . . . and I figured it out. Life just like it is. Who gets and who don't get. (*He sits down with his coat on and laughs.*) Mama, you know it's all divided up. Life is. Sure enough. Between the takers and the "tooken." (*He laughs.*) I've figured it out finally. (*He looks around at them.*) Yeah. Some of us always getting "tooken." (*He laughs.*) People like Willy Harris, they don't never get "tooken." And you know why the rest of us do? 'Cause we all mixed up. Mixed up bad. We get to looking 'round for the right and the wrong; and we worry about it and cry about it and stay up nights trying to figure out 'bout the wrong and the right of things all the time . . . And all the time, man, them takers is out there operating, just taking and taking. Willy Harris? Shoot — Willy Harris don't even count. He don't even count in the big scheme of things. But I'll say one thing for old Willy Harris . . . he's taught me something. He's taught me to keep my eye on what counts in this world. Yeah — (*Shouting out a little.*) Thanks, Willy!

RUTH: What did you call that man for, Walter Lee?

WALTER: Called him to tell him to come on over to the show. Gonna put on a show for the man. Just what he wants to see. You see, Mama, the man came here today and he told us that them people out there where you want us to move — well they so upset they willing to pay us *not* to move! (*He laughs again.*) And — and oh, Mama — you would of been proud of the way me and Ruth and Bennie acted. We told him to get out . . . Lord have mercy! We told the man to get out! Oh, we was some proud folks this afternoon, yeah. (*He lights a cigarette.*) We were still full of that old-time stuff . . .

RUTH (*coming toward him slowly*): You talking 'bout taking them people's money to keep us from moving in that house?

WALTER: I ain't just talking 'bout it, baby — I'm telling you that's what's going to happen!

BENEATHA: Oh, God! Where is the bottom! Where is the real honest-to-God bottom so he can't go any farther!

WALTER: See — that's the old stuff. You and that boy that was here today. You all want everybody to carry a flag and a spear and sing some marching songs, huh? You wanna spend your life looking into things and trying to find the right and the wrong part, huh? Yeah. You know what's going to happen to that boy someday — he'll find himself sitting in a dungeon, locked in forever — and the takers will have the key! Forget it, baby! There ain't no causes — there ain't nothing but taking in this world, and he who takes most is smartest — and it don't make a damn bit of difference *how.*

MAMA: You making something inside me cry, son. Some awful pain inside me.

WALTER: Don't cry, Mama. Understand. That white man is going to walk in that door able to write checks for more money than we ever had. It's important to him and I'm going to help him . . . I'm going to put on the show, Mama.

MAMA: Son — I come from five generations of people who was slaves and sharecroppers — but ain't nobody in my family never let nobody pay 'em no money that was a way of telling us we wasn't fit to walk the earth. We ain't never been that poor. (*Raising her eyes and looking at him.*) We ain't never been that — dead inside.

BENEATHA: Well — we are dead now. All the talk about dreams and sunlight that goes on in this house. It's all dead now.

WALTER: What's the matter with you all! I didn't make this world! It was give to me this way! Hell, yes, I want me some yachts someday! Yes, I want to hang some real pearls 'round my wife's neck. Ain't she supposed to wear no pearls? Somebody tell me — tell me, who decides which women is suppose to wear pearls in this world. I tell you I am a *man* — and I think my wife should wear some pearls in this world!

(*This last line hangs a good while and Walter begins to move about the room. The word "Man" has penetrated his consciousness; he mumbles it to himself repeatedly between strange agitated pauses as he moves about.*)

MAMA: Baby, how you going to feel on the inside?

WALTER: Fine! . . . Going to feel fine . . . a man . . .

MAMA: You won't have nothing left then, Walter Lee.

WALTER (*coming to her*): I'm going to feel fine, Mama. I'm going to look that son-of-a-bitch in the eyes and say — (*he falters*) — and say, "All right, Mr. Lindner — (*he falters even more*) — that's *your* neighborhood out there! You got the right to keep it like you want! You got the right to have it like you want! Just write the check and — the house is yours." And — and I am going to say — (*His voice almost breaks.*) "And you — you people just put the money in my hand and you won't have to live next to this bunch of stinking niggers! . . ." (*He straightens up and moves away from his mother, walking around the room.*) And maybe — maybe I'll just get down on my black knees . . . (*He does so; Ruth and Bennie and Mama watch him in frozen horror.*) "Captain, Mistuh, Bossman — (*Groveling and grinning and wringing his hands in profoundly anguished imitation of the slow-witted movie stereotype.*) A-hee-hee-hee! Oh, yassuh boss! Yasssssuh! Great white — (*voice breaking, he forces himself to go on*) — Father, just gi' ussen de money, fo' God's sake, and we's — we's ain't gwine come out deh and dirty up yo' white folks neighborhood . . ." (*He breaks down completely.*) And I'll feel fine! Fine! FINE! (*He gets up and goes into the bedroom.*)

BENEATHA: That is not a man. That is nothing but a toothless rat.

MAMA: Yes — death done come in this here house. (*She is nodding, slowly, reflectively.*) Done come walking in my house on the lips of my children. You what supposed to be my beginning again. You — what supposed to be my harvest. (*To Beneatha.*) You — you mourning your brother?

BENEATHA: He's no brother of mine.

MAMA: What you say?

BENEATHA: I said that that individual in that room is no brother of mine.

MAMA: That's what I thought you said. You feeling like you better than he is today? (*Beneatha does not answer.*) Yes? What you tell him a minute ago? That he wasn't a man? Yes? You give him up for me? You done wrote his epitaph too — like the rest of the world? Well, who give you the privilege?

BENEATHA: Be on my side for once! You saw what he just did, Mama! You saw him — down on his knees. Wasn't it you who taught me to despise any man who would do that? Do what he's going to do?

MAMA: Yes — I taught you that. Me and your daddy. But I thought I taught you something else too . . . I thought I taught you to love him.

BENEATHA: Love him? There is nothing left to love.

MAMA: There is *always* something left to love. And if you ain't learned that, you ain't learned nothing. (*Looking at her.*) Have you cried for that boy today? I don't mean for yourself and for the family 'cause we lost the money. I mean for him: what he been through and what it done to him. Child, when do you think is the time to love somebody the most? When they done good and made things easy for everybody? Well then, you ain't through learning — because that ain't the time at all. It's when he's at his lowest and can't believe in hisself 'cause the world done whipped him so! When you starts measuring somebody, measure him right, child, measure him right. Make sure you done taken into account what hills and valleys he come through before he got to wherever he is.

(*Travis bursts into the room at the end of the speech, leaving the door open.*)

TRAVIS: Grandmama — the moving men are downstairs! The truck just pulled up.

MAMA (*turning and looking at him*): Are they, baby? They downstairs?

(*She sighs and sits. Lindner appears in the doorway. He peers in and knocks lightly, to gain attention, and comes in. All turn to look at him.*)

LINDNER (*hat and briefcase in hand*): Uh — hello . . .

(*Ruth crosses mechanically to the bedroom door and opens it and lets it swing open freely and slowly as the lights come up on Walter within, still in his coat, sitting at the far corner of the room. He looks up and out through the room to Lindner.*)

RUTH: He's here.

(*A long minute passes and Walter slowly gets up.*)

LINDNER (*coming to the table with efficiency, putting his briefcase on the table and starting to unfold papers and unscrew fountain pens*): Well, I certainly was glad to hear from you people. (*Walter has begun the trek out of the room, slowly and awkwardly, rather like a small boy, passing the back of his sleeve across his mouth from time to time.*) Life can really be so much simpler than people let it be most of the time. Well — with whom do I negotiate? You, Mrs. Younger, or your son here? (*Mama sits with her hands folded on her lap and her eyes closed as Walter advances. Travis goes closer to Lindner and looks at the papers curiously.*) Just some official papers, sonny.

RUTH: Travis, you go downstairs —

MAMA (*opening her eyes and looking into Walter's*): No. Travis, you stay right here. And you make him understand what you doing, Walter Lee. You teach him good. Like Willy Harris taught you. You show where our five generations done come to. (*Walter looks from her to the boy, who grins at him innocently.*) Go ahead, son — (*She folds her hands and closes her eyes.*) Go ahead.

WALTER (*at last crosses to Lindner, who is reviewing the contract*): Well, Mr. Lindner. (*Beneatha turns away.*) We called you — (*there is a profound, simple groping quality in his speech*) — because, well, me and my family (*he looks around and shifts from one foot to the other*) Well — we are very plain people . . .

LINDNER: Yes —

WALTER: I mean — I have worked as a chauffeur most of my life — and my wife here, she does domestic work in people's kitchens. So does my mother. I mean — we are plain people . . .

LINDNER: Yes, Mr. Younger —

WALTER (*really like a small boy, looking down at his shoes and then up at the man*): And — uh — well, my father, well, he was a laborer most of his life. . . .

LINDNER (*absolutely confused*): Uh, yes — yes, I understand. (*He turns back to the contract.*)

WALTER (*a beat; staring at him*): And my father — (*With sudden intensity.*) My father almost *beat a man to death* once because this man called him a bad name or something, you know what I mean?

LINDNER (*looking up, frozen*): No, no, I'm afraid I don't —

WALTER (*A beat. The tension hangs; then Walter steps back from it.*): Yeah. Well — what I mean is that we come from people who had a lot of *pride*. I mean — we are very proud people. And that's my sister over there and she's going to be a doctor — and we are very proud —

LINDNER: Well — I am sure that is very nice, but —

WALTER: What I am telling you is that we called you over here to tell you that we are very proud and that this — (*Signaling to Travis.*) Travis, come here. (*Travis crosses and Walter draws him before him facing the man.*) This is my son, and he makes the sixth generation of our family in this country. And we have all thought about your offer —

LINDNER: Well, good . . . good —

WALTER: And we have decided to move into our house because my father — my father — he earned it for us brick by brick. (*Mama has her eyes closed and is rocking back and forth as though she were in church, with her head nodding the Amen yes.*) We don't want to make no trouble for nobody or fight no causes, and we will try to be good neighbors. And that's *all* we got to say about that. (*He looks the man absolutely in the eyes.*) We don't want your money. (*He turns and walks away.*)

LINDNER (*looking around at all of them*): I take it then — that you have decided to occupy . . .

BENEATHA: That's what the man said.

LINDNER (*to Mama in her reverie*): Then I would like to appeal to you, Mrs. Younger. You are older and wiser and understand things better I am sure . . .

MAMA: I am afraid you don't understand. My son said we was going to move and there ain't nothing left for me to say. (*Briskly.*) You know how these young folks is nowadays, mister. Can't do a thing with 'em! (*As he opens his mouth, she rises.*) Goodbye.

LINDNER (*folding up his materials*): Well — if you are that final about it . . . there is nothing left for me to say. (*He finishes, almost ignored by the family, who are concentrating on Walter Lee. At the door Lindner halts and looks around.*) I sure hope you people know what you're getting into.

(*He shakes his head and exits.*)

RUTH (*looking around and coming to life*): Well, for God's sake — if the moving men are here — LET'S GET THE HELL OUT OF HERE!

MAMA (*into action*): Ain't it the truth! Look at all this here mess. Ruth, put Travis's good jacket on him . . . Walter Lee, fix your tie and tuck your shirt in, you look like somebody's hoodlum! Lord have mercy, where is my plant? (*She flies to get it amid the general bustling of the family, who are deliberately trying to ignore the nobility of the past moment.*) You all start on down . . . Travis child, don't go empty-handed . . . Ruth, where did I put that box with my skillets in it? I want to be in charge of it myself . . . I'm going to make us the biggest dinner we ever ate tonight . . . Beneatha, what's the matter with them stockings? Pull them things up, girl . . .

(*The family starts to file out as two moving men appear and begin to carry out the heavier pieces of furniture, bumping into the family as they move about.*)

BENEATHA: Mama, Asagai asked me to marry him today and go to Africa —

MAMA (*in the middle of her getting-ready activity*): He did? You ain't old enough to marry nobody — (*Seeing the moving men lifting one of her chairs precariously.*) Darling, that ain't no bale of cotton, please handle it so we can sit in it again! I had that chair twenty-five years . . .

(*The movers sigh with exasperation and go on with their work.*)

BENEATHA (*girlishly and unreasonably trying to pursue the conversation*): To go to Africa, Mama — be a doctor in Africa . . .

MAMA (*distracted*): Yes, baby —

WALTER: *Africa!* What he want you to go to Africa for?

BENEATHA: To practice there . . .

WALTER: Girl, if you don't get all them silly ideas out your head! You better marry yourself a man with some loot . . .

BENEATHA (*angrily, precisely as in the first scene of the play*): What have you got to do with who I marry!

WALTER: Plenty. Now I think George Murchison —

BENEATHA: *George Murchison!* I wouldn't marry him if he was Adam and I was Eve!

(*Walter and Beneatha go out yelling at each other vigorously and the anger is loud and real till their voices diminish. Ruth stands at the door and turns to Mama and smiles knowingly.*)

MAMA (*fixing her hat at last*): Yeah — they something all right, my children . . .

RUTH: Yeah — they're something. Let's go, Lena.

MAMA (*stalling, starting to look around at the house*): Yes — I'm coming. Ruth —

RUTH: Yes?

MAMA (*quietly, woman to woman*): He finally come into his manhood today, didn't he? Kind of like a rainbow after the rain . . .

RUTH (*biting her lip lest her own pride explode in front of Mama*): Yes, Lena.

(*Walter's voice calls for them raucously.*)

WALTER (*offstage*): Y'all come on! These people charges by the hour you know!

MAMA (*waving Ruth out vaguely*): All right, honey — go on down. I be down directly.

(*Ruth hesitates, then exits. Mama stands, at last alone in the living room, her plant on the table before her as the lights start to come down. She looks around at all the walls and ceilings and suddenly, despite herself, while the children call below, a great heaving thing rises in her and she puts her fist to her mouth to stifle it, takes a final desperate look, pulls her coat about her, pats her hat, and goes out. The lights dim down. The door opens and she comes back in, grabs her plant, and goes out for the last time.*)

COMMENTARY

Brooks Atkinson (1894–1984)
REVIEW OF *A RAISIN IN THE SUN*   1959

It is clear from this review that Atkinson felt the "craftsmanship" of the play could have been more polished, but it is also clear that he was struck by the honesty of the entire enterprise. His praise for Sidney Poitier, who played Walter Lee Younger, and his praise for the director Lloyd Richards emphasize the eloquence and directness of their work.

In *A Raisin in the Sun*, which opened at the Ethel Barrymore last evening, Lorraine Hansberry touched on some serious problems. No doubt, her feelings about them are as strong as any one's.

But she has not tipped her play to prove one thing or another. The play is honest. She has told the inner as well as the outer truth about a Negro family in the southside of Chicago at the present time. Since the performance is also honest and since Sidney Poitier is a candid actor, *A Raisin in the Sun* has vigor as well as veracity and is likely to destroy the complacency of any one who sees it.

The family consists of a firm-minded widow, her daughter, her restless son and his wife and son. The mother has brought up her family in a tenement that is small, battered but personable. All the mother wants is that her children adhere to the code of honor and self-respect that she inherited from her parents.

The son is dreaming of success in a business deal. And the daughter, who is race-conscious, wants to become a physician and heal the wounds of her people. After a long delay the widow receives $10,000 as the premium on her husband's life insurance. The money projects the family into a series of situations that test their individual characters.

What the situations are does not matter at the moment. For *A Raisin in the Sun* is a play about human beings who want, on the one hand, to preserve their family pride and, on the other hand, to break out of the poverty that seems to be their fate. Not having any axe to grind, Miss Hansberry has a wide range of topics to write about — some of them hilarious, some of them painful in the extreme.

You might, in fact, regard *A Raisin in the Sun* as a Negro *The Cherry Orchard*. Although the social scale of the characters is different, the knowledge of how character is controlled by environment is much the same, and the alternation of humor and pathos is similar.

If there are occasional crudities in the craftsmanship, they are redeemed by the honesty of the writing. And also by the rousing honesty of the stage work. For Lloyd Richards has selected an admirable cast and directed a bold and stirring performance.

Mr. Poitier is a remarkable actor with enormous power that is always under control. Cast as the restless son, he vividly communicates the tumult of a high-strung young man. He is as eloquent when he has nothing to say as when he has a pungent line to speak. He can convey devious processes of thought as graphically as he can clown and dance.

As the matriarch, Claudia McNeil gives a heroic performance. Although the character is simple, Miss McNeil gives it nobility of spirit. Diana Sands's amusing portrait of the overintellectualized daughter; Ivan Dixon's quiet, sagacious student from Nigeria; Ruby Dee's young wife burdened with problems; Louis Gossett's supercilious suitor; John Fiedler's timid white man, who speaks sanctimonious platitudes — bring variety and excitement to a first-rate performance.

All the crises and comic sequences take place inside Ralph Alswang's set, which depicts both the poverty and the taste of the family. Like the play, it is honest. That is Miss Hansberry's personal contribution to an explosive situation in which simple honesty is the most difficult thing in the world. And also the most illuminating.

Contemporary Drama

Experimentation

The experimentation in drama that flourished in the first half of the twentieth century has continued in contemporary drama. In fact, the achievements of Tennessee Williams, Arthur Miller, Samuel Beckett, and other midcentury playwrights encouraged later playwrights to experiment more daringly with mixing media such as film, video, opera, rock, and other music with live actors. Mixed-media approaches are still options for playwrights at the beginning of the twenty-first century, but most contemporary plays celebrated by critics and audiences have been relatively traditional. They build on the achievement of nineteenth-century realism and twentieth-century expressionism.

Harold Pinter's distinctive style, developed in the late 1950s and early 1960s, is connected with some of the absurdist experiments in drama. His dialogue is acerbic, repetitive, sometimes apparently aimless. However, he is able to produce intense emotional situations, such as that in *The Dumb Waiter* (1957), in which two "hit men" wait for instructions in a basement room. *The Caretaker* (1959) and *The Homecoming* (1965), his first commercial successes, established him as a major figure in modern theater. He has also been a screenwriter for such films as *The Quiller Memorandum* (1966), *The French Lieutenant's Woman* (1981), and *The Handmaid's Tale* (1990). His experiments with time and sequence in his full-length play *Betrayal* (1978), for which he also wrote the screenplay, have inspired other playwrights, such as Paula Vogel, to experiment with the backward movement of action.

Most of the interesting late twentieth-century experimental theater was done in groups such as Richard Schechner's Performance Group, which created what Schechner called ENVIRONMENTAL THEATER in New York City in the late 1960s, and Jerzy Grotowski's Polish Laboratory Theatre in Wroclaw, Poland, during the same period. Ensembles like the Bread and Puppet Theatre, San Francisco Mime Troupe, and Luis Valdez's El Teatro Campesino on the West Coast combined a radical political message with theatrical experimentation. The work of these groups is effective primarily at the level of performance; their texts are not representative of their impact on audiences.

Theater of Cruelty

The ensembles of the 1960s and 1970s were strongly influenced by the work of Antonin Artaud (1896–1948), French actor, director, and a theorist of theater. In creating what came to be known as the THEATER OF CRUELTY, he insisted on removing the comforting distance between actors and audience. Thus the audience was involved in a direct, virtually physical fashion with the dramatic action. Artaud designed theater to be a total experience — a sensational spectacle that did not depend on coherent plot or development. He concentrated on what he called a total theater that emphasized movement, gesture, music, sound, light, and other nonverbal elements to intensify the experience.

Artaud's manifestos collected in a work called *The Theater and Its Double* (1938) inspired some of the most important twentieth-century theater practitioners, including Peter Brook and Robert Wilson, among others. Artaud's notion of a "serious" theater is at the root of his influence:

> Our long habit of seeking diversion has made us forget the idea of a serious theater, which, overturning all our preconceptions, inspires us with the fiery magnetism of its images and acts upon us like a spiritual therapeutics whose touch can never be forgotten.
>
> Everything that acts is a cruelty. It is upon this idea of extreme action, pushed beyond all limits, that theater must be rebuilt.

Artaud compared the theater artist he envisioned to a victim "burnt at the stake, signaling through the flames."

Environmental Theater

Richard Schechner's most famous production, based on Euripides' *The Bacchae,* was *Dionysus in 69* (1968), in which Pentheus is torn to pieces in an impassioned frenzy. Part of the point of Schechner's production was to inspire the audience so much that they would take to the stage, becoming indistinguishable from the actors. *Dionysus in 69* was an effort to draw on the same spiritual energies tapped by Greek drama by connecting with the feasts of Dionysus, god of wine and ecstasy. The play was a spontaneous and partly improvised performance piece rather than a text meant to be read. At one point the audience and actors disrobed in a simulation of a Greek religious orgy and Schechner's goal of involving audience and actors in a pagan ritual was realized night after night during the run.

In a similar way Julian Beck and Judith Malina's Living Theatre maintained a special relationship with the audience. Beck's plays were designed to break down the absolutes of dramatic space and audience space by having the actors roam through the audience and interact apparently at random with audience members. *Paradise Now* (1968) is his best-known play. Like Schechner's *Dionysus in 69*, it was essentially a performance piece. Certain segments were improvised; therefore, as a reading text, it has relatively little power.

"Poor Theater"

Jerzy Grotowski called his work "poor theater" because it was meant to contrast with the "rich theater" of the commercial stage, with its expensive lighting, decorated stages, rich costumes, numerous props, and elaborate settings. Grotowski's Laboratory Theatre, begun in 1959, relied on preexisting texts but interpreted them broadly through a total reconception of their meaning. For example, Grotowski's *Akropolis* (1962; revised frequently from 1963 to 1975) adapted an older Polish drama by Stanislaw Wyspiański (1904) and reset it in modern times in Auschwitz with the actors, dressed in ragged sackcloth prison uniforms, looking wretched and starving. At the end of the play the prisoners follow a headless puppet-corpse, Christ, into an afterlife. They march in an eerie ritual procession offstage into the waiting prison camp ovens.

Grotowski's theater has been influential worldwide. When the Polish government clamped down on the Solidarity° movement in the late 1970s, Grotowski left Poland. After 1970 Grotowski shifted his focus from public performances to small, intense group workshops and to the ritual performances of cultures from all over the world. The first phase of his work with the Laboratory Theatre has remained the most influential. One of his actors, Richard Cieslak, traveled widely training people in Grotowski's methods.

Theater of Images

Robert Wilson experimented in the 1970s, 1980s, and 1990s with repetitive narratives that sometimes take eight hours to perform. His multimedia dramas involve huge casts and ordinarily cover an immense historic range (Figure 13). One of his most extraordinary successes was *Einstein on the Beach* (1976), an opera written in collaboration with composer Philip Glass. Eight hours long, it was originally produced in a conventional theater, but it uses dramatic techniques that involve extensive patterns of repetition, the creation of enigmatic and evocative images, and characters who are cartoonlike caricatures of historical people. The overall effect is hypnotic; one of the points of Wilson's work seems to be to induce a trancelike state in his audience. One of his multimedia productions, *CIVIL warS* (1983), continued to develop this concept of massive theater that transcends conventional dramatic boundaries. In 1994 Wilson produced a monologue version of *Hamlet* that received some acclaim.

Gay and Lesbian Theater and Other New Ensembles

Some of the most energetic theater of the late twentieth century came from groups that were excluded for long periods from representation in mainstream theater. Gay, lesbian, African American, Hispanic American, and Native American groups have been virtually ignored by commercial theater and as a result have formed their own collectives and groups.

One reason for the development of gay theater in the United States and Great Britain in the 1960s was the decriminalization of homosexuality beginning in 1967 in Boston. Depiction of homosexual love onstage waited even longer, until the Gay Workshop's plays in London beginning in 1976. The first openly gay play was Mart Crowley's *The Boys in the Band* (1968), a popular success produced just after the repeal of a New York law prohibiting homosexuality from being represented on stage.

The Ridiculous Theatrical Company, founded by Charles Ludlam (1940–1987) in 1969, produced a formidable body of work rooted in the experiences of the homosexual community of New York. Its influence spread to many parts of the world. One of Ludlam's catchphrases was "plays without the stink of art." His plays were often ridiculously funny. *Bluebeard* (1970), for example, focused on creating a third gender by inventing a third genital. *Camille* (1973), starring Ludlam himself in the title role, hilariously spoofed not only Dumas's play but most of the "Hallmark card" conventions about romantic love. A gifted female impersonator, Ludlam played Hedda Gabler at the American Ibsen Theatre in Pittsburgh. Under the direction of Ludlam's partner, Everett Quinton, the Ridiculous Theatrical Company continues to produce Ludlam's plays as well as new plays in his tradition.

Solidarity: A labor organizing movement in Communist Poland led by Lech Walesa.

Figure 13. Multimedia effects in Robert Wilson's *CIVIL warS*.

Many of the most-praised recent plays have addressed the issues of AIDS and its ravaging of the gay community. Harvey Fierstein's *Torch Song Trilogy* (1982) was named best play of the year and appeared several years later on television. *As Is* by William M. Hoffman (1985) has been described by Don Shewey as the "best gay play anyone has written on AIDS yet." Tony Kushner dazzled New York with *Angels in America Part One: Millennium Approaches* (1992) and *Part Two: Perestroika* (1992). This two-part drama approached the problems of gay life in America both on a personal and a public, political level. The plays are called a "fantasia" and use a free-form, nonrealistic style of presentation.

Lesbian theatrical groups have sprung up in the United States and Great Britain. They often merge with women's theater groups and address issues such as male violence, societal restrictions on women, and women's opportunities. A number of important collectives, such as the Rhode Island Women's Theater and At the Foot of the Mountain in Minneapolis, treated general women's issues in the 1970s. Groups such as Medusa's Revenge (founded 1976) and

Atlanta's Red Dyke Theater (1974) centered more on lesbian experience. These last two groups disbanded after a few years of successful productions. Megan Terry's Omaha Magic Theater, founded with Joanne Schmidman, has been a long-lasting theater focusing on women's issues. Other groups such as Spider-woman, consisting of three Native American sisters, and the highly successful Split Britches consider Cafe WOW in New York's East Village to be the home of lesbian theater. Gay and lesbian theater groups have often been concerned with erasing stereotypes while also celebrating gay and lesbian lifestyles. Plays that once played only to gay and lesbian audiences — such as Martin Sherman's (b. 1938) *Bent* (1977) and Larry Kramer's (b. 1936) *The Normal Heart* (1985) — are now shown in theaters worldwide.

Other important women playwrights have made their mark in contemporary theater, with plays such as María Irene Fornés's *Fefu and Her Friends* (1977), a sprawling play featuring women in roles traditionally reserved for men. It has become a cult classic, with many productions in regional theaters. Her *The Conduct of Life* (1985) is a cruel parody of macho values in a Latin American dictatorship. It won an Obie Award for best play of the year. Caryl Churchill has been a dominant figure in British drama since the first production of *Cloud Nine* (1979), a drama that critiques colonialism and gender stereotyping. *Top Girls* (1982) is one of her most successful plays. It centers on an employment agency for women but has as its premise the introduction of famous women from the past of several cultures. It is a powerful feminist statement. *Fen* (1983), *Serious Money* (1987), and *The Skriker* (1994) have solidified her reputation as an experimental, powerful dramatist. Marsha Norman's *Getting Out* (1977), *'night Mother* (1982), and *The Secret Garden* (1991) have been produced to considerable acclaim. Norman has become an important presence in American drama. Emily Mann's *Execution of Justice* (1983) centers on the trial of Dan White, who murdered Harvey Milk, San Francisco's first openly gay mayor. Anne Devlin's *Ourselves Alone* (1986); Lynn Siefert's *Coyote Ugly* (1986); Tina Howe's *Painting Churches* (1982); and Suzan-Lori Parks's *The Death of the Last Black Man in the Whole Entire World* (1990), *The America Play* (1993), *Venus* (1996), and *In the Blood* (1999) have all added stature to the position of women in contemporary theater.

Through the 1970s, 1980s, and 1990s numerous black theatrical groups developed in many parts of the world. An important Afro-Caribbean theater group was formed in the Keskidee Center in North London, with Edgar White (b. 1947) as one of its directors. White's plays are often centered in Caribbean mystical experiences, including Rastafarianism. *The Nine Night* (1983), produced in London, focuses on a Jamaican funeral tradition designed to help the deceased enter the gates of heaven.

Experiments with Theater Space

Drama around the world has developed alternatives to the proscenium theater. Theater in the round, which seats audiences on all sides of the actors, has been exceptionally powerful for certain plays. Peter Weiss's *Persecution and Assassination of Jean-Paul Marat as Performed by the Inmates of the Asylum of Charenton under the Direction of the Marquis de Sade* (1964) was especially effective in this format. Other theatrical experiments explored the power of spaces one would not have thought appropriate for drama. For example, Wladimir Pereira Cardoso designed an elaborate welded-steel set for a production of Jean Genet's *The Balcony* in the Ruth Escobar Theater in São Paulo, Brazil. The set was a huge suspended cone in which people sat looking inward while the actors were suspended in the spherical space before them. The production was first staged in 1969 and was seen through 1971 and most of 1972 by many thousands of people. The set was constructed of eighty tons of iron assembled like a trellis and requiring 500,000 welds. The entire insides of the theater were torn out to accommodate the new set. The audience of 250 was seated on circular platforms and the actors moved through the space on ramps, on suspended cables, and on moving platforms. The same theater produced *The Voyage,* an adaptation of an epic poem, *The Lusiads,* about the origin of Portuguese people. That set used open welded platforms suggesting ships' decks. In Dubrovnik, Yugoslavia, a replica of Columbus's *Santa Maria* — built much larger than the original — was used to stage Miroslav Krleza's expressionist play *Christopher Columbus,* written in 1917. The ship was docked in Dubrovnik Harbor for the performances.

Richard Foreman's Ontological-Hysteric Theatre performs in a loft in New York City with all audience members facing in the same direction. This is not fundamentally different from the traditional proscenium theater, but the open loft space and the visible movements of actors offstage create a new relationship to the action. Foreman's work, such as *Sophia = (Wisdom)* (1970 and later), which has been performed in many parts, has none of the usually accepted narrative clues to its action. However, it aims to explore hitherto hidden aspects of experience, such as sexual taboos and unorthodox relationships. The relationship of the author to the performance is also experimental in his theater, since he directs his actors, often using a loud buzzer, as if they were extensions of his will. His work, begun in the 1960s, has continued to this day. He collaborated in the staging of Suzan-Lori Parks's *Venus* (1996).

Experimentation within the Tradition

Much of the powerful and lasting drama of the 1980s and 1990s has been achieved in a proscenium theater, using traditional methods of DRAMATURGY, the craft or techniques of dramatic composition. Contemporary dramatists are by no means shy of experimentation, but they are also sensitive to the continuing resources of the traditional stage as it was conceived by Chekhov and Ibsen and Miller. Marsha Norman, who wrote *'night, Mother,* has said that her plays are "wildly traditional. I'm a purist about structure. Plays are like plane rides. You [the audience] buy the ticket and you have to get where the ticket takes you. Or else you've been had."

Sam Shepard, one of the most prolific modern playwrights, experiments with his material, much of which premiered in small theaters in Greenwich Village, such as the La Mama Experimental Theater Club. But his most widely known plays, among them *Buried Child* (1978), are produced easily on conventional stages. Shepard's work is wide-ranging and challenging. His language is coarse, a representation of the way he has heard people speak, and the violence he portrays onstage is strong enough to alienate many in the audience. Shepard, important as he is, has not found a popular commercial audience for his plays. At root, his work is always experimental.

Athol Fugard, a South African, writes powerful plays that also work well on conventional proscenium stages. Like Shepard's, his subject matter is not the kind that permits an audience to sit back relaxed and appreciate the drama with a sense of detachment. Instead, the plays usually disturb audiences. His primary subject matter is the devastation — for blacks and whites — caused by apartheid in South Africa. Fugard's work with black actors in South Africa produced a vital experimental theater out of which his best early work grew.

Fugard's *The Blood Knot* (1961) and *Boesman and Lena* (1969), part of a trilogy on South Africa, are based on the theme of racial discrimination. But other plays, such as *A Lesson from Aloes* (1978) and *My Children! My Africa!* (1989), are involved with problems of individuals in relation to their political world. Fugard is in many ways a traditional playwright, except for his subject matter. His characters are thoroughly developed, but with great economy. In *"MASTER HAROLD". . . and the boys*, for example, we are given a deep understanding of Hally and Sam, whose relationship, past, present, and future, is the center of the play. Fugard is not writing the well-made play, any more than the other contemporary playwrights in this collection are. There is nothing "mechanical" in Fugard's work but rather a sense of organic growth, of actions arising from perceptible conditions and historical circumstances. These contribute to the sense of integrity that his plays communicate.

Some of Caryl Churchill's plays, emphasizing themes of socialism, colonialism, and feminism, were developed in workshops and collaborations with actors and directors. When writing a play, she experiments early in the first stages by spending time in the environments her plays depict. When she worked on *Top Girls* (1982), she came up with the idea of setting the action in an employment agency after she had talked with many people whose lives are wrapped up in business. For *Serious Money* (1987), she and the group developing the play spent time at the London Stock Exchange, absorbing the atmosphere of frenetic buying and selling.

Though she claims to be a traditionalist, Marsha Norman has written experimental plays. Her first success, *Getting Out* (1977), portrays the same character at two periods in her life — as an adolescent and as an adult — on separate parts of the stage at the same time. The effect is startling, but the structure of the play is clear and simple: Arlene is trying to start life over after leaving prison, while Arlie, her younger, rebellious self, is still with her, commenting on what she is doing. The play ends with a reconciliation of the two parts of the character.

Norman's *'night, Mother* is another traditionally structured play. It respects the Aristotelian unities of time, place, and action, and it is confrontational. Thelma and her daughter, Jessie, are in a power struggle over Jessie's right to commit suicide. The technique is naturalistic, and the play's subject matter, as in the plays of Strindberg and Ibsen, is discomforting to its contemporary audiences.

August Wilson has been working on a series of ten plays on the subject of black life in modern America. So far he has written eight of those plays, and each of the first four won the New York Drama Critics' Circle Award for best play of the year. All of Wilson's plays have explored the way the heritage of blacks enables them to live intelligently in the present, with understanding and dignity. People in his plays have lost touch with the past and, for that reason, risk a loss of self-understanding. Wilson's plays also show the pain endured by blacks in an America that is supposed to be the land of opportunity. Like

Arthur Miller in *Death of a Salesman* and Lorraine Hansberry in *A Raisin in the Sun,* Wilson explores the nature and consequences of the American dream, especially for those effectively excluded from this dream. Blacks' frustration, exploitation, and suffering are presented in Wilson's powerful characters, such as Troy Maxson in *Fences* (1985). Troy is a garbage collector who was a star baseball player at a time when blacks could play only in their own leagues. (The major leagues were exclusively white until 1947, when Jackie Robinson joined the Brooklyn Dodgers and the game began to be integrated.) The play centers on Maxson's anger, his pride for his family, and his concerns for his son's growing up into a world in which he must empower himself to achieve what he most wants for himself. Cory, Troy's son, does not see the same kind of discrimination and has not felt the unfairness that was Troy's primary experience in growing up. Showing the world as Troy Maxson sees it is one of the functions of the play.

Wilson's plays have a naturalistic surface, but they also allude to the supernatural, as in *The Piano Lesson* (1990). Some of the roots of this tradition are in the black church and some in African religion, a source shared by Soyinka and Wilson, among others.

Among the current playwrights, David Henry Hwang has been active in writing for both stage and film. His work has often centered on Chinese Americans and the problems they encounter in their experiences in the United States. Hwang has sensitized audiences to subjects about which playwrights had hitherto been silent. His first success, *FOB* (1980), focused on how new immigrants were viewed by Chinese Americans who had already assimilated. The play's title is an acronym for "fresh off the boat." Hwang's most successful play, *M. Butterfly* (1987), is about a romance between a French diplomat and a transvestite Chinese opera singer.

David Mamet responds to a social situation in *Oleanna* (1992). The characters, a male college professor and a female student, at first adopt an ordinary teacher-student relationship; eventually, though, that relationship alters. Mamet explores questions of power and issues of sexual harassment. As the lines he draws shift back and forth, the audience never knows exactly how clear the lines are meant to be. The issues in the play are thus subject to a number of different interpretations.

Tony Kushner's two-part drama *Angels in America: Millennium Approaches* (1992) and *Perestroika* (1992) explores issues in modern American history, with an emphasis on religion, politics, and a variety of hysterias. The plays explore homophobia, red-baiting politics, and the impact of AIDS on contemporary society. The open, dynamic structure of the play is enormously powerful. The entire drama lasts six and a half hours and has been seen not only in San Francisco, where it opened, but also in New York, London, other European cities, and regional theaters throughout the United States.

In the late 1990s women and young men made important contributions to theater. José Rivera (b. 1955) presented two plays that drew on the tradition of magical realism that is prominent in Latin American fiction. *Marisol* (1992) and *Cloud Tectonics* (1995) are visually and emotionally impressive pieces that work counter to the Ibsenist tradition of realism. As especially theatrical pieces, they give the director a considerable degree of freedom in staging. Yasmina Reza (b. 1959) had major success in France, England, the United States, and many other nations with her award-winning comedy *"Art,"* which raises unexpected questions about taste and friendship. Martin McDonagh (b. 1970) startled the London theater scene with his Leenane trilogy: *The Beauty Queen of Leenane* (1996), *A Skull in Connemara* (1997), and *The Lonesome West* (1997). The three plays and his *The Cripple of Inishmaan* (1996) were produced at the same time in London, a record for a twenty-seven-year-old playwright. Paula Vogel (b. 1951) created a portrait of an adolescent girl, Li'l Bit, involved with an incestuous Uncle Peck in *How I Learned to Drive* (1997). The play won the Pulitzer Prize that year and established her as one of the most important American playwrights. The works of these playwrights demonstrate the vitality and energy that sustains drama in the first years of the twenty-first century.

Contemporary Drama Timeline

DATE	THEATER	POLITICAL	SOCIAL/CULTURAL
1950–present	**1951:** Anna Deavere Smith, African American playwright and actress, born. Among her works are *Fires in the Mirror* (1991) and *Twilight: Los Angeles, 1992* (1994).	**1950:** U.S. Senator Joseph McCarthy begins his war on Communism by investigating the alleged "un-American activities" of hundreds of U.S. citizens.	**1950:** Simone de Beauvoir (1908–1986), French author, publishes *The Second Sex*.
		1951: The USSR explodes its first atomic bomb.	
		1953: Joseph Stalin dies.	**1952:** Ralph Ellison (1914–1994), African American novelist, publishes *Invisible Man*.
	1954: Joseph Papp founds the New York Shakespeare festival.	**1954:** *Brown v. Board of Education* finds school segregation unconstitutional.	**1954:** Elvis Presley (1935–1977) makes his first recording at Sun Studios.
		1954: Senator Joseph McCarthy's witch hunt for Communist infiltration in the United States ends.	
	1956: John Osborne's *Look Back in Anger* is produced in London.	**1955:** Communist Eastern European allies sign the Warsaw Pact.	
	1956: Tony Kushner, American playwright, born. He is best known for the plays *Angels in America, Parts 1 and 2* (1992).	**1955:** Montgomery, Alabama, bus boycott	**1957:** Jack Kerouac (1922–1969) publishes *On the Road*.
	1959: Jerzy Grotowski establishes the Laboratory Theater in Poland. In 1968 he publishes *Towards a Poor Theatre*.	**1958:** Fidel Castro begins total war against Batista in Cuba; in 1959 he becomes premier.	
	1960s: Off-Off-Broadway flourishes with the formation of such groups as Café Cino (1958), La Mama ETC (1962), the Open Theatre (1963), and the Performance Group (1967).	**1958–1969:** Charles de Gaulle is president of France.	
		1960: The Belgian Congo is granted independence.	
	1961: Peter Schumann founds the Bread and Puppet Theatre, an influential political ensemble, in the United States.	**1961:** The Berlin Wall blocks immigration to and from East and West Germany.	
		1962: The cold war reaches one of its tensest moments when the United States confronts the USSR over Soviet nuclear missile bases in Cuba.	**1962:** James Watson and Francis Crick share the Nobel Prize for defining the 3-D molecular structure of DNA.
	1963: The National Theatre is established in London under the direction of Laurence Olivier.		**1962:** Cesar Chavez (1927–1993) organizes California migrant farm workers.
	1964: Ariane Mnouchkine forms the Théâtre du Soleil in France.	**1962:** The first U.S. combat troops are sent to fight in South Vietnam.	**1962:** Alexander Solzhenitsyn's *One Day in the Life of Ivan Denisovich* describes life in the Soviet gulag.
	1964: Peter Brook's production of Peter Weiss's *Marat/Sade* opens at the Royal Shakespeare Company.	**1963:** President John F. Kennedy is assassinated in Dallas.	**1964:** The Beatles appear on the *Ed Sullivan Show*.
		1965: Malcolm X is assassinated in New York.	**1965:** The National Endowment for the Arts is established by the U.S. government.

DATE	THEATER	POLITICAL	SOCIAL/CULTURAL
1950–present (continued)	**1968:** The Negro Ensemble Company is established in the United States under the direction of Douglas Turner Ward.	**1967:** In the Six-Day War, Israel responds to Arab provocation by capturing territory from Egypt, Syria, and Jordan.	**1966:** The National Organization for Women (NOW) is established to end discrimination against women.
	1968: The Living Theatre produces its highly influential experimental work, *Paradise Now.*	**1967:** Thurgood Marshall (1908–1993) is the first African American appointed to the U.S. Supreme Court.	**1967:** Dr. Christiaan N. Barnard performs the world's first human heart transplant operation in South Africa.
	1968: Theatrical censorship, in place since the Licensing Act of 1737, is finally abolished in England.	**1968:** The American civil rights leader Martin Luther King Jr. is assassinated.	
	1968: *Hair!,* the first rock musical, hits Broadway; it is followed by *Jesus Christ Superstar* in 1971.	**1968:** Students demonstrate throughout France.	**1969:** U.S. astronaut Neil Armstrong walks on the moon.
	1968: The Performance Group produces *Dionysus in 69* under the direction of Richard Schechner.	**1970–1975:** Civil war is fought in Cambodia; Communist leader Pol Pot takes power in 1975 and begins genocidal campaign.	**1969:** New York City police raid the Stonewall Inn, and the resulting three-day protest becomes a symbol for the emerging gay rights movement.
	1970: Peter Brook's acclaimed production of *A Midsummer Night's Dream* opens at the Royal Shakespeare Company.	**1972:** U.S. President Richard Nixon and Soviet leader Leonid Breshnev sign the Strategic Arms Limitation Treaty (SALT).	
		1972: Philippine President Ferdinand Marcos declares martial law and assumes dictatorial powers.	
		1973: In *Roe v. Wade,* the U.S. Supreme Court legalizes abortion.	
		1973: U.S. troops are withdrawn from Vietnam.	
		1974: President Nixon resigns from office as a result of the Watergate scandal.	
	1975: Michael Bennett's musical *A Chorus Line* opens on Broadway and runs until 1990.	**1975:** The Spanish dictator Francisco Franco dies.	
		1976: The Chinese Communist leader Mao Zedong dies. Deng Xiaoping emerges as the new Chinese leader in 1978.	**1976:** The Episcopal Church approves the ordination of women to be priests and bishops.
		1976: Waves of violence against apartheid in Cape Town, Soweto, and Johannesburg, South Africa	

Contemporary Drama Timeline (continued)

DATE	THEATER	POLITICAL	SOCIAL/CULTURAL
1950–present (continued)	**1978:** Harold Pinter's *Betrayal* premiers at the National Theatre in London.		
	1979: Stephen Sondheim's *Sweeney Todd* opens on Broadway. Other musicals by the prolific composer include *Sunday in the Park with George* (1984), *Into the Woods* (1987), and *Passion* (1995).	**1979:** After the overthrow of Shah Mohammad Reza Pahlevi, the Ayatollah Khomeini establishes the Islamic Republic of Iran.	
	1980: Sam Shephard's *True West* premieres.	**1980:** The Iran-Iraq War begins when Iraq invades Iran; the war lasts for eight years.	
		1981: General Idi Amin begins his eight-year reign of terror in Uganda.	**1981:** Sandra Day O'Connor becomes the first woman appointed to the U.S. Supreme Court.
	1982: Athol Fugard's *"MASTER HAROLD"... and the boys* premieres at the Yale Repertory Theatre.	**1981:** Egyptian leader Anwar Sadat is assassinated by Muslim extremists.	**1981:** IBM markets its first personal computer.
	1982: Caryl Churchill's *Cloud Nine* premieres.		**1982:** Wisconsin becomes the first state to protect gays and lesbians under civil rights legislation.
	1983: Marsha Norman's *'night, Mother* opens at New York's Golden Theater and wins the Pulitzer Prize.		
	1985: August Wilson's *Fences* premieres at the Yale Repertory Theatre and wins the Pulitzer Prize in 1987.	**1985:** Mikhail Gorbachev becomes the leader of the Soviet Union and institutes a policy of *glasnost* (openness).	
			1986: In *Bowers v. Hardwick*, the U.S. Supreme Court upholds the constitutionality of the Georgia state law against sodomy.
	1987: The immensely popular Broadway adaptation of Victor Hugo's *Les Misérables* opens.	**1989:** A student demonstration in Beijing's Tiananmen Square results in bloodshed.	**1986:** The U.S. space shuttle *Challenger* explodes seconds after liftoff, killing all seven on board.
		1989: Communism crumbles in Eastern Europe, and the Berlin Wall is torn down.	
	1990s: In a proliferation of Shakespeare on film, new versions of *Hamlet, Henry V, Much Ado about Nothing, Othello,* and *Richard III* are released.	**1990:** Iraq invades Kuwait, which leads to the Gulf War in 1991.	**1990:** Octavio Paz, Mexican poet, receives the Nobel Prize for literature.
		1990: East and West Germany reunite after 45 years of separation.	**1990:** The National Endowment for the Arts is attacked when controversial awards are publicized.
		1990: The South African nationalist leader Nelson Mandela is released from prison.	

Contemporary Drama Timeline (continued)

DATE	THEATER	POLITICAL	SOCIAL/CULTURAL
1950–present (continued)		**1990–1991:** South Africa repeals its apartheid laws.	
		1991: The Soviet Union collapses. U.S. President Bush officially recognizes the twelve new countries created as a result.	
	1992: David Mamet's *Oleanna* premiers off-Broadway and runs for over 250 performances.	**1991:** Yugoslavia dissolves. Croatia, Slovenia, Bosnia-Herzegovina, and Macedonia declare independence, and bitter fighting ensues for several years.	**1993:** Toni Morrison (b. 1931), African American novelist, is awarded the Nobel Prize for literature.
		1994: Nelson Mandela (b. 1918) is elected the first black president of South Africa after that nation's first multiracial elections.	**mid-1990s:** *Internet* and *World Wide Web* become household words.
		1994: Chechnya declares independence from Russia; Russian troops invade the republic in 1994 and again in 1999.	
	1996: Jonathan Larson's *Rent,* a musical based on Puccini's *La Bohème,* wins the Pulitzer Prize.	**1995:** The Israeli leader Yitzhak Rabin is assassinated.	**1995:** Shannon Faulkner is the first woman to be admitted to the Citadel military academy.
	1997: Martin McDonagh, at age 27, has four plays running simultaneously in London.	**1997:** Hong Kong is returned to China after 156 years as a British colony.	**1995:** The National Endowment for the Arts budget is slashed by the newly elected Republican Congress. The Public Broadcasting Corporation and the National Endowment for the Humanities also come under fire.
	1998: Paula Vogel's play *How I Learned to Drive* wins the Pulitzer Prize.	**1998:** Asian nations face dramatic recession after economic booms of the 1980s and early 1990s.	
	1998: Yasmina Reza's *"Art"* wins a Tony Award for best play.	**1999:** Congress impeaches President Clinton for his improper conduct in the White House, but the president remains in office.	**1996:** In *Rome v. Evans,* the U.S. Supreme Court rules that the equal protection clause of the Constitution applies to lesbians and gay men.
		1999: U.N. troops keep a tentative peace between ethnic Albanians and Serbian Albanians in Kosovo.	**1997:** Scottish scientist Ian Wilmot clones a sheep.
		1999: The United States transfers Panama Canal to Panama.	
		1999: After East Timor votes for independence from Indonesia, the Indonesia militia occupy East Timor.	
		2000: Boris Yeltsin resigns as president of Russia.	

Athol Fugard

Athol Fugard (b. 1932) was an actor before becoming a playwright. Fugard's wife, the actress Sheila Meiring, stimulated his interest in theater, and in 1956 he began working with a theater group called the Serpent Company in Cape Town, South Africa. The group included both black and white actors at a time when racial mixing was illegal and went on to make a notable contribution to world drama.

Fugard, who is white, met Zakes Mokae, a black musician and actor, in the early days of the Serpent players, and the two collaborated on several works. Mokae has said that the tradition in Africa was not so much for a solitary playwright to compose a work that others would act out as it was for people to develop a communal approach to drama, crafting a dramatic piece through their interaction. To some extent, Fugard in his early efforts did just that. He worked with actors, watched the developments among them, and then shaped the drama accordingly.

In 1960 he began to write a two-person play called *The Blood Knot* while he was in England trying to establish a theater group there. This play was part of a trilogy called *The Family,* with *Hello and Goodbye* (1965) and *Boesman and Lena* (1969). *The Blood Knot* was given its first performance in Dorkay House in Johannesburg late in 1961. As Fugard has said, the entire production, which starred Fugard and Mokae, was put together so quickly that the government never had time to stop it. The play is about two brothers, one black, the other light-skinned enough to pass for white. It is exceptionally powerful, and in the play's first performances in Johannesburg, it was a sensation. It toured South Africa and had a revival in New Haven and in New York in 1984 and 1985.

While they toured South Africa, Fugard and Mokae were victims of the country's apartheid policies. They could not travel in the same train car: Fugard went first class, and Mokae had to go in special cars for blacks. After *The Blood Knot*'s success the government passed laws making it all but impossible for black and white actors to work together on the stage, but that policy has now changed.

Fugard has had a considerable number of plays produced in New York and London in recent years. *Sizwe Banzi Is Dead* (1972), written with John Kani and Winston Ntshona, is about a man who exchanges identity with a corpse as a way of avoiding the racial laws of South Africa; it was well received. *The Island* (1975), also written with Kani and Ntshona, starred the latter two black actors, who have become associated with Fugard and his work. They portray prisoners who, while putting on *Antigone,* become immersed in the political themes of the play, seeing it as an example of the political repression they experience in their own lives.

His plays *A Lesson from Aloes* (1978) and *The Road to Mecca* (1984) were successful in their first American productions at the Yale Repertory Theatre and on Broadway. Fugard's works are not always concerned with racial problems, but they usually center on political issues and the stress that individuals feel in trying to be themselves in an intolerant society.

The situation in South Africa has improved since *"MASTER HAROLD" . . . and the boys* was first produced in 1982. Apartheid has been abolished, and the government is in the hands of the African National Congress. The shift has been more successful than white South Africans expected, although political tensions still exist. Fugard's attachment and commitment to South Africa remain deep and lifelong. He has been criticized by black writers for dealing with themes they feel belong to them, while also being criticized by whites for his sympathies toward blacks. In the new South Africa some of these problems have begun to sort themselves out. Fugard's latest play, *Valley Song* (1996), produced at London's Royal Court Theatre, explores the problems and the promise of the new South Africa.

"MASTER HAROLD" . . . AND THE BOYS

Athol Fugard has said that *"MASTER HAROLD" . . . and the boys* (1982) is a very personal play in which he exorcises personal guilt (Fugard's entire name is Athol Harold Lannigan Fugard). As a white South African he has written numerous plays that represent the racial circumstances of life in that troubled nation. This play has won international distinction and has made a reputation for its stars, especially Zakes Mokae, with whom Fugard has worked for more than thirty years.

Hally reveals throughout the play (which is set in 1950) that he is more attached emotionally to Sam, the black waiter who has befriended him, than he is even to his own parents, owners of the restaurant. His attitude toward his father is complicated by his father's alcoholism and confinement. At that time in South Africa even such an alcoholic was considered automatically superior to a black man such as Sam, who is intelligent, quick, thoughtful, and generous. When Hally reveals his anxiety about his father, Sam warns him that it is dishonorable to treat one's father the way he does, but Sam's presumption in admonishing Hally triggers Hally's mean outburst toward him.

Zakes Mokae, who created the role of Sam in the first performance of the play at the Yale Repertory Theatre, has commented extensively about his role and the character of Sam. He has observed that some black audience members called out during a performance that he should beat Hally up the minute Hally demands that Sam call him Master Harold. But other black audience members spoke with him after the performance and agreed that, because Sam had never taken that kind of stand against Harold or his father, he was getting what he deserved. Mokae himself has pointed out that Sam is probably not living in

Port Elizabeth legally and that to have taken action, even if he wanted to, would have ended with his removal from the town into exile.

Zakes Mokae understands the character from his perspective as a black South African, and he realizes Sam's limits. But he has said that in his version of the play Sam would give Hally a beating and "suffer the consequences." He points out, however, that he is an urban South African, unlike Sam, and his attitude is quite different from anything that Sam would have understood. As an urban black, Mokae could not have been sent into exile, although he could certainly have been punished, for beating a white boy.

On the question of whether the play made a positive contribution to white-black relations in South Africa, Mokae feels that a play cannot change people's minds. Audiences were not likely to seek to change the government of South Africa simply because they had seen a play. But at the same time, he feels that it was productive to talk about the apartheid and racial distrust in South Africa.

Unfortunately, the government of South Africa decided that the play was too inflammatory for performance in its country, and it was banned briefly from performance in Johannesburg and other theatrical centers in South Africa. This suggests that while Zakes Mokae did not feel that one play would have much impact on injustices in South Africa, it is likely that the government feared otherwise.

In an important way, *"MASTER HAROLD"* . . . *and the boys* is a personal statement by Fugard that establishes the extent to which apartheid damages even a person sympathetic to black rights. It is astonishing in retrospect to think, as his interviewer, Heinrich von Staden, once said, that Hally could grow up to be Athol himself. If this is true, then it is also true that the play is hopeful.

One sign of hope is that the violence in the play is restrained. Sam does not beat Hally for humiliating him, although he probably would like to. And no one in the play makes a move to be physically threatening to Sam. However faint, these are signs of hope. And as Zakes Mokae has said about the situation in his homeland, "One is always optimistic. It can't go on forever." He was right. On June 5, 1991, Parliament abandoned apartheid, and South Africa had a new beginning.

"MASTER HAROLD" . . . *and the boys* in Performance

The world premiere of *"MASTER HAROLD"* . . . *and the boys* was at the Yale Repertory Theatre in March 1982. Fugard himself directed the play, with Zakes Mokae as Sam, Danny Glover as Willie, and Željko Ivanek as Hally. It was the first of his plays to premiere outside South Africa. Fugard chose New Haven in part because the play's setting was so personal that he feared it might disturb his brother and sister if it were produced first in South Africa. The setting was a bright tea room — a restaurant that serves light meals — interpreted to look like the tea room Fugard's mother actually ran in Port Elizabeth when he was a child. The space was open, the walls a whitish hue, everything simple and plain in decoration.

New York Times critic Frank Rich reviewed the premiere, saying, "*'MASTER HAROLD'* . . . *and the boys* is only an anecdote, really, and it's often as warm and musical as the men's dance. But somewhere along the way it rises up and breaks over the audience like a storm." Alan Stern of the *Boston Phoenix* linked the play with Greek tragedy:

> One reason for the play's potency is that, as in Greek tragedy, the events seem preordained — they're the by-product of social forces and human nature. Even as he spits in Sam's face, Hally realizes the magnitude of his action, that he is the one who will be harmed by it. And yet he can't help himself. Power corrupts, and in a society that sanctions the domination of one man — or set of men — over another, all relationships, even the promising ones, are poisoned.

Zakes Mokae and Danny Glover starred in the Broadway production in May 1982. After a brief period in which it was banned, the play was produced in Johannesburg, South Africa, in March 1983 with a South African cast. Joseph Lelyveld, in the *New York Times,* said of that production: "Athol Fugard's confessional drama about a white adolescent's initiation in the uses of racial power has come home to South Africa, and it left its multiracial audience . . . visibly shaken and stunned. . . . Many, blacks and whites, were crying."

The play was televised in 1984 with Matthew Broderick as Hally. It has had revivals in 1985 by the Trinity Repertory Company in Providence, in 1986 by the Boston Shakespeare Company in Boston, and in 1987 at the American Stage Festival in Milford, New Hampshire. These productions, although without Fugard's direction and without a "star" cast, had the same effect on their audiences as the major productions in New York and Johannesburg. Clifford Gallo in the *Boston Globe* called the American Stage production "a devastating look at the loss of racial innocence in a nation where political and social inequality are the norm."

Athol Fugard (*b. 1932*)
"MASTER HAROLD" . . . AND THE BOYS   *1982*

Characters

WILLIE
SAM
HALLY

(*The St. George's Park Tea Room on a wet and windy Port Elizabeth afternoon.*)

(*Tables and chairs have been cleared and are stacked on one side except for one which stands apart with a single chair. On this table a knife, fork, spoon and side plate in anticipation of a simple meal, together with a pile of comic books.*)

(*Other elements: a serving counter with a few stale cakes under glass and a not very impressive display of sweets, cigarettes and cool drinks, etc.; a few cardboard advertising handouts — Cadbury's Chocolate, Coca-Cola — and a blackboard on which an untrained hand has chalked up the prices of Tea, Coffee, Scones, Milkshakes — all flavors — and Cool Drinks; a few sad ferns in pots; a telephone; an old-style jukebox.*)

(*There is an entrance on one side and an exit into a kitchen on the other.*)

(*Leaning on the solitary table, his head cupped in one hand as he pages through one of the comic books, is Sam. A black man in his mid-forties. He wears the white coat of a waiter. Behind him on his knees, mopping down the floor with a bucket of water and a rag, is Willie. Also black and about the same age as Sam. He has his sleeves and trousers rolled up.*)

(*The year: 1950.*)

WILLIE (*singing as he works*): "She was scandalizin'
     my name,
   She took my money

She called me honey
But she was scandalizin' my name.
Called it love but was playin' a game. . . ."

(*He gets up and moves the bucket. Stands thinking for a moment, then, raising his arms to hold an imaginary partner, he launches into an intricate ballroom dance step. Although a mildly comic figure, he reveals a reasonable degree of accomplishment.*)

Hey, Sam.

(*Sam, absorbed in the comic book, does not respond.*)

Hey, Boet° Sam!

(*Sam looks up.*)

I'm getting it. The quickstep. Look now and tell me. (*He repeats the step.*) Well?

SAM (*encouragingly*): Show me again.

WILLIE: Okay, count for me.

SAM: Ready?

WILLIE: Ready.

SAM: Five, six, seven, eight. . . . (*Willie starts to dance.*) A-n-d one two three four . . . and one two three four. . . . (*Ad libbing as Willie dances.*) Your shoulders, Willie . . . your shoulders! Don't look down! Look happy, Willie! Relax, Willie!

WILLIE (*desperate but still dancing*): I am relax.

SAM: No, you're not.

WILLIE (*he falters*): Ag no man, Sam! Mustn't talk. You make me make mistakes.

SAM: But you're stiff.

WILLIE: Yesterday I'm not straight . . . today I'm too stiff!

SAM: Well, you are. You asked me and I'm telling you.

WILLIE: Where?

SAM: Everywhere. Try to glide through it.

WILLIE: Glide?

SAM: Ja, make it smooth. And give it more style. It must look like you're enjoying yourself.

WILLIE (*emphatically*): I wasn't.

SAM: Exactly.

WILLIE: How can I enjoy myself? Not straight, too stiff and now it's also glide, give it more style, make it smooth. . . . Haai! Is hard to remember all those things, Boet Sam.

SAM: That's your trouble. You're trying too hard.

WILLIE: I try hard because it *is* hard.

SAM: But don't let me see it. The secret is to make it look easy. Ballroom must look happy, Willie, not like hard work. It must. . . . Ja! . . . it must look like romance.

WILLIE: Now another one! What's romance?

SAM: Love story with happy ending. A handsome man in tails, and in his arms, smiling at him, a beautiful lady in evening dress!

WILLIE: Fred Astaire, Ginger Rogers.

SAM: You got it. Tapdance or ballroom, it's the same. Romance. In two weeks' time when the judges look

°Boet: Brother.

at you and Hilda, they must see a man and a woman who are dancing their way to a happy ending. What I saw was you holding her like you were frightened she was going to run away.

WILLIE: Ja! Because that is what she wants to do! I got no romance left for Hilda anymore, Boet Sam.

SAM: Then pretend. When you put your arms around Hilda, imagine she is Ginger Rogers.

WILLIE: With no teeth? You try.

SAM: Well, just remember, there's only two weeks left.

WILLIE: I know, I know! (*To the jukebox.*) I do it better with music. You got sixpence for Sarah Vaughan?

SAM: That's a slow foxtrot. You're practicing the quickstep.

WILLIE: I'll practice slow foxtrot.

SAM (*shaking his head*): It's your turn to put money in the jukebox.

WILLIE: I only got bus fare to go home. (*He returns disconsolately to his work.*) Love story and happy ending! She's doing it all right, Boet Sam, but is not me she's giving happy endings. Fuckin' whore! Three nights now she doesn't come practice. I wind up gramophone, I get record ready and I sit and wait. What happens? Nothing. Ten o'clock I start dancing with my pillow. You try and practice romance by yourself, Boet Sam. Struesgod, she doesn't come tonight I take back my dress and ballroom shoes and I find me new partner. Size twenty-six. Shoes size seven. And now she's also making trouble for me with the baby again. Reports me to Child Wellfed, that I'm not giving her money. She lies! Every week I am giving her money for milk. And how do I know is my baby? Only his hair looks like me. She's fucking around all the time I turn my back. Hilda Samuels is a bitch! (*Pause.*) Hey, Sam!

SAM: Ja.

WILLIE: You listening?

SAM: Ja.

WILLIE: So what you say?

SAM: About Hilda?

WILLIE: Ja.

SAM: When did you last give her a hiding?

WILLIE (*reluctantly*): Sunday night.

SAM: And today is Thursday.

WILLIE (*he knows what's coming*): Okay.

SAM: Hiding on Sunday night, then Monday, Tuesday, and Wednesday she doesn't come to practice . . . and you are asking me why?

WILLIE: I said okay, Boet Sam!

SAM: You hit her too much. One day she's going to leave you for good.

WILLIE: So? She makes me the hell-in too much.

SAM (*emphasizing his point*): *Too* much and *too* hard. You had the same trouble with Eunice.

WILLIE: Because she also make the hell-in, Boet Sam. She never got the steps right. Even the waltz.

SAM: Beating her up every time she makes a mistake in the waltz? (*Shaking his head.*) No, Willie! That takes the pleasure out of ballroom dancing.

WILLIE: Hilda is not too bad with the waltz, Boet Sam. Is the quickstep where the trouble starts.

SAM (*teasing him gently*): How's your pillow with the quickstep?

WILLIE (*ignoring the tease*): Good! And why? Because it got no legs. That's her trouble. She can't move them quick enough, Boet Sam. I start the record and before halfway Count Basie is already winning. Only time we catch up with him is when gramophone runs down. (*Sam laughs.*) Haaikona, Boet Sam, is not funny.

SAM (*snapping his fingers*): I got it! Give her a handicap.

WILLIE: What's that?

SAM: Give her a ten-second start and then let Count Basie go. Then I put my money on her. Hot favorite in the Ballroom Stakes: Hilda Samuels ridden by Willie Malopo.

WILLIE (*turning away*): I'm not talking to you no more.

SAM (*relenting*): Sorry, Willie. . . .

WILLIE: It's finish between us.

SAM: Okay, okay . . . I'll stop.

WILLIE: You can also fuck off.

SAM: Willie, listen! I want to help you!

WILLIE: No more jokes?

SAM: I promise.

WILLIE: Okay. Help me.

SAM (*his turn to hold an imaginary partner*): Look and learn. Feet together. Back straight. Body relaxed. Right hand placed gently in the small of her back and wait for the music. Don't start worrying about making mistakes or the judges or the other competitors. It's just you, Hilda and the music, and you're going to have a good time. What Count Basie do you play?

WILLIE: "You the cream in my coffee, you the salt in my stew."

SAM: Right. Give it to me in strict tempo.

WILLIE: Ready?

SAM: Ready.

WILLIE: A-n-d . . . (*Singing.*)
    "You the cream in my coffee.
    You the salt in my stew.
    You will always be my necessity.
    I'd be lost without you. . . ." (*etc.*)

(*Sam launches into the quickstep. He is obviously a much more accomplished dancer than Willie. Hally enters. A seventeen-year-old white boy. Wet raincoat and school case. He stops and watches Sam. The demonstration comes to an end with a flourish. Applause from Hally and Willie.*)

HALLY: Bravo! No question about it. First place goes to Mr. Sam Semela.

WILLIE (*in total agreement*): You was gliding with style, Boet Sam.

HALLY (*cheerfully*): How's it, chaps?

SAM: Okay, Hally.

WILLIE (*springing to attention like a soldier and saluting*): At your service, Master Harold!

HALLY: Not long to the big event, hey!

SAM: Two weeks.

HALLY: You nervous?

SAM: No.

HALLY: Think you stand a chance?

SAM: Let's just say I'm ready to go out there and dance.

HALLY: It looked like it. What about you, Willie?

(*Willie groans.*)

    What's the matter?

SAM: He's got leg trouble.

HALLY (*innocently*): Oh, sorry to hear that, Willie.

WILLIE: Boet Sam! You promised. (*Willie returns to his work.*)

(*Hally deposits his school case and takes off his raincoat. His clothes are a little neglected and untidy: black blazer with school badge, gray flannel trousers in need of an ironing, khaki shirt and tie, black shoes. Sam has fetched a towel for Hally to dry his hair.*)

HALLY: God, what a lousy bloody day. It's coming down cats and dogs out there. Bad for business, chaps. . . . (*Conspiratorial whisper.*) . . . but it also means we're in for a nice quiet afternoon.

SAM: You can speak loud. Your Mom's not here.

HALLY: Out shopping?

SAM: No. The hospital.

HALLY: But it's Thursday. There's no visiting on Thursday afternoons. Is my Dad okay?

SAM: Sounds like it. In fact, I think he's going home.

HALLY (*stopped short by Sam's remark*): What do you mean?

SAM: The hospital phoned.

HALLY: To say what?

SAM: I don't know. I just heard your Mom talking.

HALLY: So what makes you say he's going home?

SAM: It sounded as if they were telling her to come and fetch him.

(*Hally thinks about what Sam has said for a few seconds.*)

HALLY: When did she leave?

SAM: About an hour ago. She said she would phone you. Want to eat?

(*Hally doesn't respond.*)

    Hally, want your lunch?

HALLY: I suppose so. (*His mood has changed.*) What's on the menu? . . . as if I don't know.

SAM: Soup, followed by meat pie and gravy.

HALLY: Today's?

SAM: No.

HALLY: And the soup?

SAM: Nourishing pea soup.

HALLY: Just the soup. (*The pile of comic books on the table.*) And these?

SAM: For your Dad. Mr. Kempston brought them.

HALLY: You haven't been reading them, have you?

SAM: Just looking.

HALLY (*examining the comics*): Jungle Jim . . . Batman

and Robin . . . Tarzan . . . God, what rubbish! Mental pollution. Take them away.

(*Sam exits waltzing into the kitchen. Hally turns to Willie.*)

HALLY: Did you hear my Mom talking on the telephone, Willie?

WILLIE: No, Master Hally. I was at the back.

HALLY: And she didn't say anything to you before she left?

WILLIE: She said I must clean the floors.

HALLY: I mean about my Dad.

WILLIE: She didn't say nothing to me about him, Master Hally.

HALLY (*with conviction*): No! It can't be. They said he needed at least another three weeks of treatment. Sam's definitely made a mistake. (*Rummages through his school case, finds a book and settles down at the table to read.*) So, Willie!

WILLIE: Yes, Master Hally! Schooling okay today?

HALLY: Yes, okay. . . . (*He thinks about it.*) . . . No, not really. Ag, what's the difference? I don't care. And Sam says you've got problems.

WILLIE: Big problems.

HALLY: Which leg is sore?

(*Willie groans.*)

Both legs.

WILLIE: There is nothing wrong with my legs. Sam is just making jokes.

HALLY: So then you *will* be in the competition.

WILLIE: Only if I can find a partner.

HALLY: But what about Hilda?

SAM (*returning with a bowl of soup*): She's the one who's got trouble with her legs.

HALLY: What sort of trouble, Willie?

SAM: From the way he describes it, I think the lady has gone a bit lame.

HALLY: Good God! Have you taken her to see a doctor?

SAM: I think a vet would be better.

HALLY: What do you mean?

SAM: What do you call it again when a racehorse goes very fast?

HALLY: Gallop?

SAM: That's it!

WILLIE: Boet Sam!

National Theatre of London's 1983 production of *"MASTER HAROLD" . . . and the boys* with (l. to r.) Ramolao Makene as Willie, Duart Sylwain as Hally, and John Kani as Sam.

HALLY: "A gallop down the homestretch to the winning post." But what's that got to do with Hilda?
SAM: Count Basie always gets there first.

(*Willie lets fly with his slop rag. It misses Sam and hits Hally.*)

HALLY (*furious*): For Christ's sake, Willie! What the hell do you think you're doing?
WILLIE: Sorry, Master Hally, but it's him. . . .
HALLY: Act your bloody age! (*Hurls the rag back at Willie.*) Cut out the nonsense now and get on with your work. And you too, Sam. Stop fooling around.

(*Sam moves away.*)

No. Hang on. I haven't finished! Tell me exactly what my Mom said.
SAM: I have. "When Hally comes, tell him I've gone to the hospital and I'll phone him."
HALLY: She didn't say anything about taking my Dad home?
SAM: No. It's just that when she was talking on the phone. . . .
HALLY (*interrupting him*): No, Sam. They can't be discharging him. She would have said so if they were. In any case, we saw him last night and he wasn't in good shape at all. Staff nurse even said there was talk about taking more X-rays. And now suddenly today he's better? If anything, it sounds more like a bad turn to me . . . which I sincerely hope it isn't. Hang on . . . how long ago did you say she left?
SAM: Just before two . . . (*His wrist watch.*) . . . hour and a half.
HALLY: I know how to settle it. (*Behind the counter to the telephone. Talking as he dials.*) Let's give her ten minutes to get to the hospital, ten minutes to load him up, another ten, at the most, to get home, and another ten to get him inside. Forty minutes. They should have been home for at least half an hour already. (*Pause — he waits with the receiver to his ear.*) No reply, chaps. And you know why? Because she's at his bedside in hospital helping him pull through a bad turn. You definitely heard wrong.
SAM: Okay.

(*As far as Hally is concerned, the matter is settled. He returns to his table, sits down, and divides his attention between the book and his soup. Sam is at his school case and picks up a textbook.*)

Modern Graded Mathematics for Standards Nine and Ten. (*Opens it at random and laughs at something he sees.*) Who is this supposed to be?
HALLY: Old fart-face Prentice.
SAM: Teacher?
HALLY: Thinks he is. And believe me, that is not a bad likeness.
SAM: Has he seen it?
HALLY: Yes.
SAM: What did he say?

HALLY: Tried to be clever, as usual. Said I was no Leonardo da Vinci and that bad art had to be punished. So, six of the best, and his are bloody good.
SAM: On your bum?
HALLY: Where else? The days when I got them on my hands are gone forever, Sam.
SAM: With your trousers down!
HALLY: No. He's not quite that barbaric.
SAM: That's the way they do it in jail.
HALLY (*flicker of morbid interest*): Really?
SAM: Ja. When the magistrate sentences you to "strokes with a light cane."
HALLY: Go on.
SAM: They make you lie down on a bench. One policeman pulls down your trousers and holds your ankles, another one pulls your shirt over your head and holds your arms. . . .
HALLY: Thank you! That's enough.
SAM: . . . and the one that gives you the strokes talks to you gently and for a long time between each one. (*He laughs.*)
HALLY: I've heard enough, Sam! Jesus! It's a bloody awful world when you come to think of it. People can be real bastards.
SAM: That's the way it is, Hally.
HALLY: It doesn't *have* to be that way. There is something called progress, you know. We don't exactly burn people at the stake anymore.
SAM: Like Joan of Arc.
HALLY: Correct. If she was captured today, she'd be given a fair trial.
SAM: And then the death sentence.
HALLY (*a world-weary sigh*): I know, I know! I oscillate between hope and despair for this world as well, Sam. But things will change, you wait and see. One day somebody is going to get up and give history a kick up the backside and get it going again.
SAM: Like who?
HALLY (*after thought*): They're called social reformers. Every age, Sam, has got its social reformer. My history book is full of them.
SAM: So where's ours?
HALLY: Good question. And I hate to say it, but the answer is: I don't know. Maybe he hasn't even been born yet. Or is still only a babe in arms at his mother's breast. God, what a thought.
SAM: So we just go on waiting.
HALLY: Ja, looks like it. (*Back to his soup and the book.*)
SAM (*reading from the textbook*): "Introduction: In some mathematical problems only the magnitude. . . ." (*He mispronounces the word "magnitude."*)
HALLY (*correcting him without looking up*): Magnitude.
SAM: What's it mean?
HALLY: How big it is. The size of the thing.
SAM (*reading*): ". . . magnitude of the quantities is of importance. In other problems we need to know whether these quantities are negative or positive. For example, whether there is a debit or credit bank balance . . ."

HALLY: Whether you're broke or not.

SAM: ". . . whether the temperature is above or below Zero. . . ."

HALLY: Naught degrees. Cheerful state of affairs! No cash and you're freezing to death. Mathematics won't get you out of that one.

SAM: "All these quantities are called . . ." (*spelling the word*) . . . s-c-a-l. . . .

HALLY: Scalars.

SAM: Scalars! (*Shaking his head with a laugh.*) You understand all that?

HALLY (*turning a page*): No. And I don't intend to try.

SAM: So what happens when the exams come?

HALLY: Failing a maths exam isn't the end of the world, Sam. How many times have I told you that examination results don't measure intelligence?

SAM: I would say about as many times as you've failed one of them.

HALLY (*mirthlessly*): Ha, ha, ha.

SAM (*simultaneously*): Ha, ha, ha.

HALLY: Just remember Winston Churchill didn't do particularly well at school.

SAM: You've also told me that one many times.

HALLY: Well, it just so happens to be the truth.

SAM (*enjoying the word*): Magnitude! Magnitude! Show me how to use it.

HALLY (*after thought*): An intrepid social reformer will not be daunted by the magnitude of the task he has undertaken.

SAM (*impressed*): Couple of jaw-breakers in there!

HALLY: I gave you three for the price of one. Intrepid, daunted, and magnitude. I did that once in an exam. Put five of the words I had to explain in one sentence. It was half a page long.

SAM: Well, I'll put my money on you in the English exam.

HALLY: Piece of cake. Eighty percent without even trying.

SAM (*another textbook from Hally's case*): And history?

HALLY: So-so. I'll scrape through. In the fifties if I'm lucky.

SAM: You didn't do too badly last year.

HALLY: Because we had World War One. That at least has some action. You try to find that in the South African Parliamentary system.

SAM (*reading from the history textbook*): "Napoleon and the principle of equality." Hey! This sounds interesting. "After concluding peace with Britain in 1802, Napoleon used a brief period of calm to insti-tute . . ."

HALLY: Introduce.

SAM: ". . . many reforms. Napoleon regarded all people as equal before the law and wanted them to have equal opportunities for advancement. All ves-ti-ges of the feu-dal sys-tem with its oppression of the poor were abol-ished." Vestiges, feudal system, and abolished. I'm all right on oppression.

HALLY: I'm thinking. He swept away . . . abol-ished . . . the last remains . . . vestiges . . . of the bad old days . . . feudal system.

SAM: Ha! There's the social reformer we're waiting for. He sounds like a man of some magnitude.

HALLY: I'm not so sure about that. It's a damn good title for a book, though. A man of magnitude!

SAM: He sounds pretty big to me, Hally.

HALLY: Don't confuse historical significance with greatness. But maybe I'm being a bit prejudiced. Have a look in there and you'll see he's two chapters long. And hell! . . . has he only got dates, Sam, all of which you've got to remember! This campaign and that campaign, and then, because of all the fighting, the next thing is we get Peace Treaties all over the place. And what's the end of the story? Battle of Waterloo, which he loses. Wasn't worth it. No, I don't know about him as a man of magnitude.

SAM: Then who would you say was?

HALLY: To answer that, we need a definition of greatness, and I suppose that would be somebody who . . . somebody who benefited all mankind.

SAM: Right. But like who?

HALLY (*he speaks with total conviction*): Charles Darwin. Remember him? That big book from the library. *The Origin of the Species.*

SAM: Him?

HALLY: Yes. For his Theory of Evolution.

SAM: You didn't finish it.

HALLY: I ran out of time. I didn't finish it because my two weeks was up. But I'm going to take it out again after I've digested what I read. It's safe. I've hidden it away in the Theology section. Nobody ever goes in there. And anyway who are you to talk? You hardly even looked at it.

SAM: I tried. I looked at the chapters in the beginning and I saw one called "The Struggle for an Existence." Ah ha, I thought. At last! But what did I get? Something called the mistiltoe which needs the apple tree and there's too many seeds and all are going to die except one . . . ! No, Hally.

HALLY (*intellectually outraged*): What do you mean, No! The poor man had to start somewhere. For God's sake, Sam, he revolutionized science. Now we know.

SAM: What?

HALLY: Where we come from and what it all means.

SAM: And that's a benefit to mankind? Anyway, I still don't believe it.

HALLY: God, you're impossible. I showed it to you in black and white.

SAM: Doesn't mean I got to believe it.

HALLY: It's the likes of you that kept the Inquisition in business. It's called bigotry. Anyway, that's my man of magnitude. Charles Darwin! Who's yours?

SAM (*without hesitation*): Abraham Lincoln.

HALLY: I might have guessed as much. Don't get sentimental, Sam. You've never been a slave, you know. And anyway we freed your ancestors here in South

Africa long before the Americans. But if you want to thank somebody on their behalf, do it to Mr. William Wilberforce.° Come on. Try again. I want a real genius.

(*Now enjoying himself, and so is Sam. Hally goes behind the counter and helps himself to a chocolate.*)

SAM: William Shakespeare.

HALLY (*no enthusiasm*): Oh. So you're also one of them, are you? You're basing that opinion on only one play, you know. You've only read my *Julius Caesar* and even I don't understand half of what they're talking about. They should do what they did with the old Bible: bring the language up to date.

SAM: That's all you've got. It's also the only one *you've* read.

HALLY: I know. I admit it. That's why I suggest we reserve our judgment until we've checked up on a few others. I've got a feeling, though, that by the end of this year one is going to be enough for me, and I can give you the names of twenty-nine other chaps in the Standard Nine class of the Port Elizabeth Technical College who feel the same. But if you want him, you can have him. My turn now. (*Pacing.*) This is a damned good exercise, you know! It started off looking like a simple question and here it's got us really probing into the intellectual heritage of our civilization.

SAM: So who is it going to be?

HALLY: My next man . . . and he gets the title on two scores: social reform and literary genius . . . is Leo Nikolaevich Tolstoy.

SAM: That Russian.

HALLY: Correct. Remember the picture of him I showed you?

SAM: With the long beard.

HALLY (*trying to look like Tolstoy*): And those burning, visionary eyes. My God, the face of a social prophet if ever I saw one! And remember my words when I showed it to you? Here's a *man*, Sam!

SAM: Those were words, Hally.

HALLY: Not many intellectuals are prepared to shovel manure with the peasants and then go home and write a "little book" called *War and Peace*. Incidentally, Sam, he was somebody else who, to quote, ". . . did not distinguish himself scholastically."

SAM: Meaning?

HALLY: He was also no good at school.

SAM: Like you and Winston Churchill.

HALLY (*mirthlessly*): Ha, ha, ha.

SAM (*simultaneously*): Ha, ha, ha.

HALLY: Don't get clever, Sam. That man freed his serfs of his own free will.

SAM: No argument. He was a somebody, all right. I accept him.

Mr. William Wilberforce: (1759–1833), British statesman who supported a bill outlawing the slave trade and suppressing slavery in the British Empire.

HALLY: I'm sure Count Tolstoy will be very pleased to hear that. Your turn. Shoot. (*Another chocolate from behind the counter.*) I'm waiting, Sam.

SAM: I've got him.

HALLY: Good. Submit your candidate for examination.

SAM: Jesus.

HALLY (*stopped dead in his tracks*): Who?

SAM: Jesus Christ.

HALLY: Oh, come on, Sam!

SAM: The Messiah.

HALLY: Ja, but still . . . No, Sam. Don't let's get started on religion. We'll just spend the whole afternoon arguing again. Suppose I turn around and say Mohammed?

SAM: All right.

HALLY: You can't have them both on the same list!

SAM: Why not? You like Mohammed, I like Jesus.

HALLY: I *don't* like Mohammed. I never have. I was merely being hypothetical. As far as I'm concerned, the Koran is as bad as the Bible. No. Religion is out! I'm not going to waste my time again arguing with you about the existence of God. You know perfectly well I'm an atheist . . . and I've got homework to do.

SAM: Okay, I take him back.

HALLY: You've got time for one more name.

SAM (*after thought*): I've got one I know we'll agree on. A simple straightforward great Man of Magnitude . . . and no arguments. And *he* really *did* benefit all mankind.

HALLY: I wonder. After your last contribution I'm beginning to doubt whether anything in the way of an intellectual agreement is possible between the two of us. Who is he?

SAM: Guess.

HALLY: Socrates? Alexandre Dumas? Karl Marx, Dostoevsky? Nietzsche?

(*Sam shakes his head after each name.*)

Give me a clue.

SAM: The letter *P* is important. . . .

HALLY: Plato!

SAM: . . . and his name begins with an *F*.

HALLY: I've got it. Freud and Psychology.

SAM: No. I didn't understand him.

HALLY: That makes two of us.

SAM: Think of moldy apricot jam.

HALLY (*after a delighted laugh*): Penicillin and Sir Alexander Fleming! And the title of the book: *The Microbe Hunters*. (*Delighted.*) Splendid, Sam! Splendid. For once we are in total agreement. The major breakthrough in medical science in the Twentieth Century. If it wasn't for him, we might have lost the Second World War. It's deeply gratifying, Sam, to know that I haven't been wasting my time in talking to you. (*Strutting around proudly.*) Tolstoy may have educated his peasants, but I've educated you.

SAM: Standard Four to Standard Nine.

HALLY: Have we been at it as long as that?

SAM: Yep. And my first lesson was geography.

HALLY (*intrigued*): Really? I don't remember.

SAM: My room there at the back of the old Jubilee Boarding House. I had just started working for your Mom. Little boy in short trousers walks in one afternoon and asks me seriously: "Sam, do you want to see South Africa?" Hey man! Sure I wanted to see South Africa!

HALLY: Was that me?

SAM: . . . So the next thing I'm looking at a map you had just done for homework. It was your first one and you were very proud of yourself.

HALLY: Go on.

SAM: Then came my first lesson. "Repeat after me, Sam: Gold in the Transvaal, mealies in the Free State, sugar in Natal, and grapes in the Cape." I still know it!

HALLY: Well, I'll be buggered. So that's how it all started.

SAM: And your next map was one with all the rivers and the mountains they came from. The Orange the Vaal, the Limpopo, the Zambezi. . . .

HALLY: You've got a phenomenal memory!

SAM: You should be grateful. That is why you started passing your exams. You tried to be better than me.

(*They laugh together. Willie is attracted by the laughter and joins them.*)

HALLY: The old Jubilee Boarding House. Sixteen rooms with board and lodging, rent in advance and one week's notice. I haven't thought about it for donkey's years . . . and I don't think that's an accident. God, was I glad when we sold it and moved out. Those years are not remembered as the happiest ones of an unhappy childhood.

WILLIE (*knocking on the table and trying to imitate a woman's voice*): "Hally, are you there?"

HALLY: Who's that supposed to be?

WILLIE: "What you doing in there, Hally? Come out at once!"

HALLY (*to Sam*): What's he talking about?

SAM: Don't you remember?

WILLIE: "Sam, Willie . . . is he in there with you boys?"

SAM: Hiding away in our room when your mother was looking for you.

HALLY (*another good laugh*): Of course! I used to crawl and hide under your bed! But finish the story, Willie. Then what used to happen? You chaps would give the game away by telling her I was in there with you. So much for friendship.

SAM: We couldn't lie to her. She knew.

HALLY: Which meant I got another rowing for hanging around the "servants' quarters." I think I spent more time in there with you chaps than anywhere else in that dump. And do you blame me? Nothing but bloody misery wherever you went. Somebody was always complaining about the food, or my mother was having a fight with Micky Nash because she'd caught her with a petty officer in her room. Maud Meiring was another one. Remember those two?

They were prostitutes, you know. Soldiers and sailors from the troopships. Bottom fell out of the business when the war ended. God, the flotsam and jetsam that life washed up on our shores! No joking, if it wasn't for your room, I would have been the first certified ten-year-old in medical history. Ja, the memories are coming back now. Walking home from school and thinking: "What can I do this afternoon?" Try out a few ideas, but sooner or later I'd end up in there with you fellows. I bet you I could still find my way to your room with my eyes closed. (*He does exactly that.*) Down the corridor . . . telephone on the right, which my Mom keeps locked because somebody is using it on the sly and not paying . . . past the kitchen and unappetizing cooking smells . . . around the corner into the backyard, hold my breath again because there are more smells coming when I pass your lavatory, then into that little passageway, first door on the right and into your room. How's that?

SAM: Good. But, as usual, you forgot to knock.

HALLY: Like that time I barged in and caught you and Cynthia . . . at it. Remember? God, was I embarrassed! I didn't know what was going on at first.

SAM: Ja, that taught you a lesson.

HALLY: And about a lot more than knocking on doors, I'll have you know, and I don't mean geography either. Hell, Sam, couldn't you have waited until it was dark?

SAM: No.

HALLY: Was it that urgent?

SAM: Yes, and if you don't believe me, wait until your time comes.

HALLY: No, thank you. I am not interested in girls. (*Back to his memories. . . . Using a few chairs he recreates the room as he lists the items.*) A gray little room with a cold cement floor. Your bed against that wall . . . and I now know why the mattress sags so much! . . . Willie's bed . . . it's propped up on bricks because one leg is broken . . . that wobbly little table with the washbasin and jug of water . . . Yes! . . . stuck to the wall above it are some pin-up pictures from magazines. Joe Louis. . . .

WILLIE: Brown Bomber. World Title. (*Boxing pose.*) Three rounds and knockout.

HALLY: Against who?

SAM: Max Schmeling.

HALLY: Correct. I can also remember Fred Astaire and Ginger Rogers, and Rita Hayworth in a bathing costume which always made me hot and bothered when I looked at it. Under Willie's bed is an old suitcase with all his clothes in a mess, which is why I never hide there. Your things are neat and tidy in a trunk next to your bed, and on it there is a picture of you and Cynthia in your ballroom clothes, your first silver cup for third place in a competition and an old radio which doesn't work anymore. Have I left out anything?

SAM: No.

HALLY: Right, so much for the stage directions. Now the characters. (*Sam and Willie move to their appropriate positions in the bedroom.*) Willie is in bed, under his blankets with his clothes on, complaining nonstop about something, but we can't make out a word of what he's saying because he's got his head under the blankets as well. You're on your bed trimming your toenails with a knife — not a very edifying sight — and as for me. . . . What am I doing?

SAM: You're sitting on the floor giving Willie a lecture about being a good loser while you get the checkerboard and pieces ready for a game. Then you go to Willie's bed, pull off the blankets and make him play with you first because you know you're going to win, and that gives you the second game with me.

HALLY: And you certainly were a bad loser, Willie!

WILLIE: Haai!

HALLY: Wasn't he, Sam? And so slow! A game with you almost took the whole afternoon. Thank God I gave up trying to teach you how to play chess.

WILLIE: You and Sam cheated.

HALLY: I never saw Sam cheat, and mine were mostly the mistakes of youth.

WILLIE: Then how is it you two was always winning?

HALLY: Have you ever considered the possibility, Willie, that it was because we were better than you?

WILLIE: Every time better?

HALLY: Not every time. There were occasions when we deliberately let you win a game so that you would stop sulking and go on playing with us. Sam used to wink at me when you weren't looking to show me it was time to let you win.

WILLIE: So then you two didn't play fair.

HALLY: It was for your benefit, Mr. Malopo, which is more than being fair. It was an act of self-sacrifice. (*To Sam.*) But you know what my best memory is, don't you?

SAM: No.

HALLY: Come on, guess. If your memory is so good, you must remember it as well.

SAM: We got up to a lot of tricks in there, Hally.

HALLY: This one was special, Sam.

SAM: I'm listening.

HALLY: It started off looking like another of those useless nothing-to-do afternoons. I'd already been down to Main Street looking for adventure, but nothing had happened. I didn't feel like climbing trees in the Donkin Park or pretending I was a private eye and following a stranger . . . so as usual: See what's cooking in Sam's room. This time it was you on the floor. You had two thin pieces of wood and you were smoothing them down with a knife. It didn't look particularly interesting, but when I asked you what you were doing, you just said, "Wait and see, Hally. Wait . . . and see". . . in that secret sort of way of yours, so I knew there was a surprise coming. You teased me, you bugger, by being deliberately slow and not answering my questions!

(*Sam laughs.*)

And whistling while you worked away! God, it was infuriating! I could have brained you! It was only when you tied them together in a cross and put that down on the brown paper that I realized what you were doing. "Sam is making a kite?" And when I asked you and you said, "Yes". . . ! (*Shaking his head with disbelief.*) The sheer audacity of it took my breath away. I mean, seriously, what the hell does a black man know about flying a kite? I'll be honest with you, Sam, I had no hopes for it. If you think I was excited and happy, you got another guess coming. In fact, I was shit-scared that we were going to make fools of ourselves. When we left the boarding house to go up onto the hill, I was praying quietly that there wouldn't be any other kids around to laugh at us.

SAM (*enjoying the memory as much as Hally*): Ja, I could see that.

HALLY: I made it obvious, did I?

SAM: Ja. You refused to carry it.

HALLY: Do you blame me? Can you remember what the poor thing looked like? Tomato-box wood and brown paper! Flour and water for glue! Two of my mother's old stockings for a tail, and then all those bits and pieces of string you made me tie together so that we could fly it! Hell, no, that was now only asking for a miracle to happen.

SAM: Then the big argument when I told you to hold the string and run with it when I let go.

HALLY: I was prepared to run, all right, but straight back to the boarding house.

SAM (*knowing what's coming*): So what happened?

HALLY: Come on, Sam, you remember as well as I do.

SAM: I want to hear it from you.

(*Hally pauses. He wants to be as accurate as possible.*)

HALLY: You went a little distance from me down the hill, you held it up ready to let it go. . . . "This is it," I thought. "Like everything else in my life, here comes another fiasco." Then you shouted, "Go, Hally!" and I started to run. (*Another pause.*) I don't know how to describe it, Sam. Ja! The miracle happened! I was running, waiting for it to crash to the ground, but instead suddenly there was something alive behind me at the end of the string, tugging at it as if it wanted to be free. I looked back . . . (*Shakes his head.*) . . . I still can't believe my eyes. It was flying! Looping around and trying to climb even higher into the sky. You shouted to me to let it have more string. I did, until there was none left and I was just holding that piece of wood we had tied it to. You came up and joined me. You were laughing.

SAM: So were you. And shouting, "It works, Sam! We've done it!"

HALLY: And we had! I was so proud of us! It was the most splendid thing I had ever seen. I wished there were hundreds of kids around to watch us. The part that scared me, though, was when you showed me how to make it dive down to the ground and then just when it was on the point of crashing, swoop up again!

SAM: You didn't want to try yourself.

HALLY: Of course not! I would have been suicidal if anything had happened to it. Watching you do it made me nervous enough. I was quite happy just to see it up there with its tail fluttering behind it. You left me after that, didn't you? You explained how to get it down, we tied it to the bench so that I could sit and watch it, and you went away. I wanted you to stay, you know. I was a little scared of having to look after it by myself.

SAM (*quietly*): I had work to do, Hally.

HALLY: It was sort of sad bringing it down, Sam. And it looked sad again when it was lying there on the ground. Like something that had lost its soul. Just tomato-box wood, brown paper and two of my mother's old stockings! But, hell, I'll never forget that first moment when I saw it up there. I had a stiff neck the next day from looking up so much.

(*Sam laughs. Hally turns to him with a question he never thought of asking before.*)

Why did you make that kite, Sam?

SAM (*evenly*): I can't remember.

HALLY: Truly?

SAM: Too long ago, Hally.

HALLY: Ja, I suppose it was. It's time for another one, you know.

SAM: Why do you say that?

HALLY: Because it feels like that. Wouldn't be a good day to fly it, though.

SAM: No. You can't fly kites on rainy days.

HALLY (*He studies Sam. Their memories have made him conscious of the man's presence in his life.*): How old are you, Sam?

SAM: Two score and five.

HALLY: Strange, isn't it?

SAM: What?

HALLY: Me and you.

SAM: What's strange about it?

HALLY: Little white boy in short trousers and a black man old enough to be his father flying a kite. It's not every day you see that.

SAM: But why strange? Because the one is white and the other black?

HALLY: I don't know. Would have been just as strange, I suppose, if it had been me and my Dad . . . cripple man and a little boy! Nope! There's no chance of me flying a kite without it being strange. (*Simple statement of fact — no self-pity.*) There's a nice little short story there. "The Kite-Flyers." But we'd have to find a twist in the ending.

SAM: Twist?

HALLY: Yes. Something unexpected. The way it ended with us was too straightforward . . . me on the bench and you going back to work. There's no drama in that.

WILLIE: And me?

HALLY: You?

WILLIE: Yes me.

HALLY: You want to get into the story as well, do you? I got it! Change the title: "Afternoons in Sam's Room". . . expand it and tell all the stories. It's on its way to being a novel. Our days in the old Jubilee. Sad in a way that they're over. I almost wish we were still in that little room.

SAM: We're still together.

HALLY: That's true. It's just that life felt the right size in there . . . not too big and not too small. Wasn't so hard to work up a bit of courage. It's got so bloody complicated since then.

(*The telephone rings. Sam answers it.*)

SAM: St. George's Park Tea Room . . . Hello, Madam . . . Yes, Madam, he's here. . . . Hally, it's your mother.

HALLY: Where is she phoning from?

SAM: Sounds like the hospital. It's a public telephone.

HALLY (*relieved*): You see! I told you. (*The telephone.*) Hello, Mom . . . Yes . . . Yes no fine. Everything's under control here. How's things with poor old Dad? . . . Has he had a bad turn? . . . What? . . . Oh, God! . . . Yes, Sam told me, but I was sure he'd made a mistake. But what's this all about, Mom? He didn't look at all good last night. How can he get better so quickly? . . . Then very obviously you must say no. Be firm with him. You're the boss. . . . You know what it's going to be like if he comes home. . . . Well then, don't blame me when I fail my exams at the end of the year. . . . Yes! How am I expected to be fresh for school when I spend half the night massaging his gammy leg? . . . So am I! . . . So tell him a white lie. Say Dr. Colley wants more X-rays of his stump. Or bribe him. We'll sneak in double tots of brandy in future. . . . What? . . . Order him to get back into bed at once! If he's going to behave like a child, treat him like one. . . . All right, Mom! I was just trying to . . . I'm sorry. . . . I said I'm sorry. . . . Quick, give me your number. I'll phone you back. (*He hangs up and waits a few seconds.*) Here we go again! (*He dials.*) I'm sorry, Mom. . . . Okay. . . . But now listen to me carefully. All it needs is for you to put your foot down. Don't take no for an answer. . . . Did you hear me? And whatever you do, don't discuss it with him. . . . Because I'm frightened you'll give in to him. . . . Yes, Sam gave me lunch. . . . I ate all of it! . . . No, Mom not a soul. It's still raining here. . . . Right, I'll tell them. I'll just do some homework and then lock up. . . . But remember now, Mom. Don't listen to anything he says. And phone me back and let me know what happens. . . . Okay. Bye, Mom. (*He hangs up. The men are staring at him.*) My Mom says that when you're finished with the floors you must do the windows. (*Pause.*) Don't misunderstand me, chaps. All I want is for him to get better. And if he was, I'd be the first person to say: "Bring him home." But he's not, and we can't give him the medical care and attention he needs at home. That's what hospitals are there for. (*Brusquely.*) So don't just stand there! Get on with it!

(*Sam clears Hally's table.*)

You heard right. My Dad wants to go home.

SAM: Is he better?

HALLY (*sharply*): No! How the hell can he be better when last night he was groaning with pain? This is not an age of miracles!

SAM: Then he should stay in hospital.

HALLY (*seething with irritation and frustration*): Tell me something I don't know, Sam. What the hell do you think I was saying to my Mom? All I can say is fuck-it-all.

SAM: I'm sure he'll listen to your Mom.

HALLY: You don't know what she's up against. He's already packed his shaving kit and pajamas and is sitting on his bed with his crutches, dressed and ready to go. I know him when he gets in that mood. If she tries to reason with him, we've had it. She's no match for him when it comes to a battle of words. He'll tie her up in knots. (*Trying to hide his true feelings.*)

SAM: I suppose it gets lonely for him in there.

HALLY: With all the patients and nurses around? Regular visits from the Salvation Army? Balls! It's ten times worse for him at home. I'm at school and my mother is here in the business all day.

SAM: He's at least got you at night.

HALLY (*before he can stop himself*): And we've got him! Please! I don't want to talk about it anymore. (*Unpacks his school case, slamming down books on the table.*) Life is just a plain bloody mess, that's all. And people are fools.

SAM: Come on, Hally.

HALLY: Yes, they are! They bloody well deserve what they get.

SAM: Then don't complain.

HALLY: Don't try to be clever, Sam. It doesn't suit you. Anybody who thinks there's nothing wrong with this world needs to have his head examined. Just when things are going along all right, without fail someone or something will come along and spoil everything. Somebody should write that down as a fundamental law of the Universe. The principle of perpetual disappointment. If there is a God who created this world, he should scrap it and try again.

SAM: All right, Hally, all right. What you got for homework?

HALLY: Bullshit, as usual. (*Opens an exercise book and reads.*) "Write five hundred words describing an annual event of cultural or historical significance."

SAM: That should be easy enough for you.

HALLY: And also plain bloody boring. You know what

he wants, don't you? One of their useless old ceremonies. The commemoration of the landing of the 1820 Settlers, or if it's going to be culture, Carols by Candlelight every Christmas.

SAM: It's an impressive sight. Make a good description, Hally. All those candles glowing in the dark and the people singing hymns.

HALLY: And it's called religious hysteria. (*Intense irritation.*) Please, Sam! Just leave me alone and let me get on with it. I'm not in the mood for games this afternoon. And remember my Mom's orders . . . you're to help Willie with the windows. Come on now, I don't want any more nonsense in here.

SAM: Okay, Hally, okay.

(*Hally settles down to his homework; determined preparations . . . pen, ruler, exercise book, dictionary, another cake . . . all of which will lead to nothing.*)

(*Sam waltzes over to Willie and starts to replace tables and chairs. He practices a ballroom step while doing so. Willie watches. When Sam is finished, Willie tries.*)

Good! But just a little bit quicker on the turn and only move in to her after she's crossed over. What about this one?

(*Another step. When Sam is finished, Willie again has a go.*)

Much better. See what happens when you just relax and enjoy yourself? Remember that in two weeks' time and you'll be all right.

WILLIE: But I haven't got partner, Boet Sam.

SAM: Maybe Hilda will turn up tonight.

WILLIE: No, Boet Sam. (*Reluctantly.*) I gave her a good hiding.

SAM: You mean a bad one.

WILLIE: Good bad one.

SAM: Then you mustn't complain either. Now you pay the price for losing your temper.

WILLIE: I also pay two pounds ten shilling entrance fee.

SAM: They'll refund you if you withdraw now.

WILLIE (*appalled*): You mean, don't dance?

SAM: Yes.

WILLIE: No! I wait too long and I practice too hard. If I find me new partner, you think I can be ready in two weeks? I ask Madam for my leave now and we practice every day.

SAM: Quickstep nonstop for two weeks. World record, Willie, but you'll be mad at the end.

WILLIE: No jokes, Boet Sam.

SAM: I'm not joking.

WILLIE: So then what?

SAM: Find Hilda. Say you're sorry and promise you won't beat her again.

WILLIE: No.

SAM: Then withdraw. Try again next year.

WILLIE: No.

SAM: Then I give up.

WILLIE: Haaikona, Boet Sam, you can't.

SAM: What do you mean, I can't? I'm telling you: I give up.

WILLIE (*adamant*): No! (*Accusingly.*) It was you who start me ballroom dancing.

SAM: So?

WILLIE: Before that I use to be happy. And is you and Miriam who bring me to Hilda and say here's partner for you.

SAM: What are you saying, Willie?

WILLIE: You!

SAM: But me what? To blame?

WILLIE: Yes.

SAM: Willie . . . ? (*Bursts into laughter.*)

WILLIE: And now all you do is make jokes at me. You wait. When Miriam leaves you is my turn to laugh. Ha! Ha! Ha!

SAM (*he can't take Willie seriously any longer*): She can leave me tonight! I know what to do. (*Bowing before an imaginary partner.*) May I have the pleasure? (*He dances and sings.*)
"Just a fellow with his pillow . . .
Dancin' like a willow . . .
In an autumn breeze. . . ."

WILLIE: There you go again!

(*Sam goes on dancing and singing.*)

Boet Sam!

SAM: There's the answer to your problem! Judges' announcement in two weeks' time: "Ladies and gentlemen, the winner in the open section . . . Mr. Willie Malopo and his pillow!"

(*This is too much for a now really angry Willie. He goes for Sam, but the latter is too quick for him and puts Hally's table between the two of them.*)

HALLY (*exploding*): For Christ's sake, you two!

WILLIE (*still trying to get at Sam*): I donner you, Sam! Struesgod!

SAM (*still laughing*): Sorry, Willie . . . Sorry. . . .

HALLY: Sam! Willie! (*Grabs his ruler and gives Willie a vicious whack on the bum.*) How the hell am I supposed to concentrate with the two of you behaving like bloody children!

WILLIE: Hit him too!

HALLY: Shut up, Willie.

WILLIE: He started jokes again.

HALLY: Get back to your work. You too, Sam. (*His ruler.*) Do you want another one, Willie?

(*Sam and Willie return to their work. Hally uses the opportunity to escape from his unsuccessful attempt at homework. He struts around like a little despot, ruler in hand, giving vent to his anger and frustration.*)

Suppose a customer had walked in then? Or the Park Superintendent. And seen the two of you behaving like a pair of hooligans. That would have been the end of my mother's license, you know. And your jobs? Well, this is the end of it. From now on there will be no more of your ballroom nonsense in here.

This is a business establishment, not a bloody New Brighton dancing school. I've been far too lenient with the two of you. (*Behind the counter for a green cool drink and a dollop of ice cream. He keeps up his tirade as he prepares it.*) But what really makes me bitter is that I allow you chaps a little freedom in here when business is bad and what do you do with it? The foxtrot! Specially you, Sam. There's more to life than trotting around a dance floor and I thought at least you knew it.

SAM: It's a harmless pleasure, Hally. It doesn't hurt anybody.

HALLY: It's also a rather simple one, you know.

SAM: You reckon so? Have you ever tried?

HALLY: Of course not.

SAM: Why don't you? Now.

HALLY: What do you mean? Me dance?

SAM: Yes. I'll show you a simple step — the waltz — then you try it.

HALLY: What will that prove?

SAM: That it might not be as easy as you think.

HALLY: I didn't say it was easy. I said it was simple — like in simple-minded, meaning mentally retarded. You can't exactly say it challenges the intellect.

SAM: It does other things.

HALLY: Such as?

SAM: Make people happy.

HALLY (*the glass in his hand*): So do American cream sodas with ice cream. For God's sake, Sam, you're not asking me to take ballroom dancing serious, are you?

SAM: Yes.

HALLY (*sigh of defeat*): Oh, well, so much for trying to give you a decent education. I've obviously achieved nothing.

SAM: You still haven't told me what's wrong with admiring something that's beautiful and then trying to do it yourself.

HALLY: Nothing. But we happen to be talking about a foxtrot, not a thing of beauty.

SAM: But that is just what I'm saying. If you were to see two champions doing, two masters of the art . . . !

HALLY: Oh God, I give up. So now it's also art!

SAM: Ja.

HALLY: There's a limit, Sam. Don't confuse art and entertainment.

SAM: So then what is art?

HALLY: You want a definition?

SAM: Ja.

HALLY (*He realizes he has got to be careful. He gives the matter a lot of thought before answering.*): Philosophers have been trying to do that for centuries. What is Art? What is Life? But basically I suppose it's . . . the giving of meaning to matter.

SAM: Nothing to do with beautiful?

HALLY: It goes beyond that. It's the giving of form to the formless.

SAM: Ja, well, maybe it's not art, then. But I still say it's beautiful.

HALLY: I'm sure the word you mean to use is entertaining.

SAM (*adamant*): No. Beautiful. And if you want proof come along to the Centenary Hall in New Brighton in two weeks' time.

(*The mention of the Centenary Hall draws Willie over to them.*)

HALLY: What for? I've seen the two of you prancing around in here often enough.

SAM (*he laughs*): This isn't the real thing, Hally. We're just playing around in here.

HALLY: So? I can use my imagination.

SAM: And what do you get?

HALLY: A lot of people dancing around and having a so-called good time.

SAM: That all?

HALLY: Well, basically it is that, surely.

SAM: No, it isn't. Your imagination hasn't helped you at all. There's a lot more to it than that. We're getting ready for the championships, Hally, not just another dance. There's going to be a lot of people, all right, and they're going to have a good time, but they'll only be spectators, sitting around and watching. It's just the competitors out there on the dance floor. Party decorations and fancy lights all around the walls! The ladies in beautiful evening dresses!

HALLY: My mother's got one of those, Sam, and, quite frankly, it's an embarrassment every time she wears it.

SAM (*undeterred*): Your imagination left out the excitement.

(*Hally scoffs.*)

Oh, yes. The finalists are not going to be out there just to have a good time. One of those couples will be the 1950 Eastern Province Champions. And your imagination left out the music.

WILLIE: Mr. Elijah Gladman Guzana and his Orchestral Jazzonions.

SAM: The sound of the big band, Hally. Trombone, trumpet, tenor and alto sax. And then, finally, your imagination also left out the climax of the evening when the dancing is finished, the judges have stopped whispering among themselves and the Master of Ceremonies collects their scorecards and goes up onto the stage to announce the winners.

HALLY: All right. So you make it sound like a bit of a do. It's an occasion. Satisfied?

SAM (*victory*): So you admit that!

HALLY: Emotionally yes, intellectually no.

SAM: Well, I don't know what you mean by that, all I'm telling you is that it is going to be *the* event of the year in New Brighton. It's been sold out for two weeks already. There's only standing room left. We've got competitors coming from Kingwilliamstown, East London, Port Alfred.

(*Hally starts pacing thoughtfully.*)

HALLY: Tell me a bit more.

SAM: I thought you weren't interested . . . intellectually.

HALLY (*mysteriously*): I've got my reasons.

SAM: What do you want to know?

HALLY: It takes place every year?

SAM: Yes. But only every third year in New Brighton. It's East London's turn to have the championships next year.

HALLY: Which, I suppose, makes it an even more significant event.

SAM: Ah ha! We're getting somewhere. Our "occasion" is now a "significant event."

HALLY: I wonder.

SAM: What?

HALLY: I wonder if I would get away with it.

SAM: But what?

HALLY (*to the table and his exercise book*): "Write five hundred words describing an annual event of cultural or historical significance." Would I be stretching poetic license a little too far if I called your ballroom championships a cultural event?

SAM: You mean . . . ?

HALLY: You think we could get five hundred words out of it, Sam?

SAM: Victor Sylvester has written a whole book on ballroom dancing.

WILLIE: You going to write about it, Master Hally?

HALLY: Yes, gentlemen, that is precisely what I am considering doing. Old Doc Bromely — he's my English teacher — is going to argue with me, of course. He doesn't like natives. But I'll point out to him that in strict anthropological terms the culture of a primitive black society includes its dancing and singing. To put my thesis in a nutshell: The war-dance has been replaced by the waltz. But it still amounts to the same thing: the release of primitive emotions through movement. Shall we give it a go?

SAM: I'm ready.

WILLIE: Me also.

HALLY: Ha! This will teach the old bugger a lesson. (*Decision taken.*) Right. Let's get ourselves organized. (*This means another cake on the table. He sits.*) I think you've given me enough general atmosphere, Sam, but to build the tension and suspense I need facts. (*Pencil poised.*)

WILLIE: Give him facts, Boet Sam.

HALLY: What you called the climax . . . how many finalists?

SAM: Six couples.

HALLY (*making notes*): Go on. Give me the picture.

SAM: Spectators seated right around the hall. (*Willie becomes a spectator.*)

HALLY: . . . and it's a full house.

SAM: At one end, on the stage, Gladman and his Orchestral Jazzonions. At the other end is a long table with the three judges. The six finalists go onto the dance floor and take up their positions. When they are ready and the spectators have settled down, the Master of Ceremonies goes to the microphone. To start with, he makes some jokes to get people laughing. . . .

HALLY: Good touch. (*As he writes.*) ". . . creating a relaxed atmosphere which will change to one of tension and drama as the climax is approached."

SAM (*onto a chair to act out the M.C.*): "Ladies and gentlemen, we come now to the great moment you have all been waiting for this evening. . . . The finals of the 1950 Eastern Province Open Ballroom Dancing Championships. But first let me introduce the finalists! Mr. and Mrs. Welcome Tchabalala from Kingwilliamstown . . ."

WILLIE (*he applauds after every name*): Is when the people clap their hands and whistle and make a lot of noise, Master Hally.

SAM: "Mr. Mulligan Njikelane and Miss Nomhle Nkonyeni of Grahamstown; Mr. and Mrs. Norman Nchinga from Port Alfred; Mr. Fats Bokolane and Miss Dina Plaatjies from East London; Mr. Sipho Dugu and Mrs. Mable Magada from Peddie; and from New Brighton our very own Mr. Willie Malopo and Miss Hilda Samuels."

(*Willie can't believe his ears. He abandons his role as spectator and scrambles into position as a finalist.*)

WILLIE: Relaxed and ready to romance!

SAM: The applause dies down. When everybody is silent, Gladman lifts up his sax, nods at the Orchestral Jazzonions. . . .

WILLIE: Play the jukebox please, Boet Sam!

SAM: I also only got bus fare, Willie.

HALLY: Hold it, everybody. (*Heads for the cash register behind the counter.*) How much is in the till, Sam?

SAM: Three shillings. Hally . . . Your Mom counted it before she left.

(*Hally hesitates.*)

HALLY: Sorry, Willie. You know how she carried on the last time I did it. We'll just have to pool our combined imaginations and hope for the best. (*Returns to the table.*) Back to work. How are the points scored, Sam?

SAM: Maximum of ten points each for individual style, deportment, rhythm, and general appearance.

WILLIE: Must I start?

HALLY: Hold it for a second, Willie. And penalties?

SAM: For what?

HALLY: For doing something wrong. Say you stumble or bump into somebody . . . do they take off any points?

SAM (*aghast*): Hally . . . !

HALLY: When you're dancing. If you and your partner collide into another couple.

(*Hally can get no further. Sam has collapsed with laughter. He explains to Willie.*)

SAM: If me and Miriam bump into you and Hilda. . . .

(*Willie joins him in another good laugh.*)

Hally, Hally . . . !

HALLY (*perplexed*): Why? What did I say?

SAM: There's no collisions out there, Hally. Nobody trips or stumbles or bumps into anybody else. That's what that moment is all about. To be one of those finalists on that dance floor is like . . . like being in a dream about a world in which accidents don't happen.

HALLY (*genuinely moved by Sam's image*): Jesus, Sam! That's beautiful!

WILLIE (*can endure waiting no longer*): I'm starting!

(*Willie dances while Sam talks.*)

SAM: Of course it is. That's what I've been trying to say to you all afternoon. And it's beautiful because that is what we want life to be like. But instead, like you said, Hally, we're bumping into each other all the time. Look at the three of us this afternoon: I've bumped into Willie, the two of us have bumped into you, you've bumped into your mother, she bumping into your Dad. . . . None of us knows the steps and there's no music playing. And it doesn't stop with us. The whole world is doing it all the time. Open a newspaper and what do you read? America has bumped into Russia, England is bumping into India, rich man bumps into poor man. Those are big collisions, Hally. They make for a lot of bruises. People get hurt in all that bumping, and we're sick and tired of it now. It's been going on for too long. Are we never going to get it right? . . . Learn to dance life like champions instead of always being just a bunch of beginners at it?

HALLY (*deep and sincere admiration of the man*): You've got a vision, Sam!

SAM: Not just me. What I'm saying to you is that everybody's got it. That's why there's only standing room left for the Centenary Hall in two weeks' time. For as long as the music lasts, we are going to see six couples get it right, the way we want life to be.

HALLY: But is that the best we can do, Sam . . . watch six finalists dreaming about the way it should be?

SAM: I don't know. But it starts with that. Without the dream we won't know what we're going for. And anyway I reckon there are a few people who have got past just dreaming about it and are trying for something real. Remember that thing we read once in the paper about the Mahatma Gandhi? Going without food to stop those riots in India?

HALLY: You're right. He certainly was trying to teach people to get the steps right.

SAM: And the Pope.

HALLY: Yes, he's another one. Our old General Smuts° as well, you know. He's also out there dancing. You know, Sam, when you come to think of it, that's what the United Nations boils down to . . . a dancing school for politicians!

General Smuts: (1870–1950), South African statesman who fought the British in the Boer War in 1899, was instrumental in forming the Union of South Africa in 1910, and was active in the creation of the United Nations.

SAM: And let's hope they learn.

HALLY (*a little surge of hope*): You're right. We mustn't despair. Maybe there's some hope for mankind after all. Keep it up, Willie. (*Back to his table with determination.*) This is a lot bigger than I thought. So what have we got? Yes, our title: "A World Without Collisions."

SAM: That sounds good! "A World Without Collisions."

HALLY: Subtitle: "Global Politics on the Dance Floor." No. A bit too heavy, hey? What about "Ballroom Dancing as a Political Vision"?

(*The telephone rings. Sam answers it.*)

SAM: St. George's Park Tea Room . . . Yes, Madam . . . Hally, it's your Mom.

HALLY (*back to reality*): Oh, God, yes! I'd forgotten all about that. Shit! Remember my words, Sam? Just when you're enjoying yourself, someone or something will come along and wreck everything.

SAM: You haven't heard what she's got to say yet.

HALLY: Public telephone?

SAM: No.

HALLY: Does she sound happy or unhappy?

SAM: I couldn't tell. (*Pause.*) She's waiting, Hally.

HALLY (*to the telephone*): Hello, Mom . . . No, everything is okay here. Just doing my homework. . . . What's your news? . . . You've what? . . . (*Pause. He takes the receiver away from his ear for a few seconds. In the course of Hally's telephone conversation, Sam and Willie discreetly position the stacked tables and chairs. Hally places the receiver back to his ear.*) Yes, I'm still here. Oh, well, I give up now. Why did you do it, Mom? . . . Well, I just hope you know what you've let us in for. . . . (*Loudly.*) I said I hope you know what you've let us in for! It's the end of the peace and quiet we've been having. (*Softly.*) Where is he? (*Normal voice.*) He can't hear us from in there. But for God's sake, Mom, what happened? I told you to be firm with him. . . . Then you and the nurses should have held him down, taken his crutches away. . . . I know only too well he's my father! . . . I'm not being disrespectful, but I'm sick and tired of emptying stinking chamber pots full of phlegm and piss. . . . Yes, I do! When you're not there, he asks *me* to do it. . . . If you really want to know the truth, that's why I've got no appetite for my food. . . . Yes! There's a lot of things you don't know about. For your information, I still haven't got that science textbook I need. And you know why? He borrowed the money you gave me for it. . . . Because I didn't want to start another fight between you two. . . . He says that every time. . . . All right, Mom! (*Viciously.*) Then just remember to start hiding your bag away again, because he'll be at your purse before long for money for booze. And when he's well enough to come down here, you better keep an eye on the till as well, because that is also going to develop a leak. . . . Then don't complain to me when he starts his old tricks. . . . Yes, you do. I get it from

you on one side and from him on the other, and it makes life hell for me. I'm not going to be the peacemaker anymore. I'm warning you now: when the two of you start fighting again, I'm leaving home. . . . Mom, if you start crying, I'm going to put down the receiver. . . . Okay. . . . (*Lowering his voice to a vicious whisper.*) Okay, Mom. I heard you. (*Desperate.*) No. . . . Because I don't want to. I'll see him when I get home! Mom! . . . (*Pause. When he speaks again, his tone changes completely. It is not simply pretense. We sense a genuine emotional conflict.*) Welcome home, chum! . . . What's that? . . . Don't be silly, Dad. You being home is just about the best news in the world. . . . I bet you are. Bloody depressing there with everybody going on about their ailments, hey! . . . How you feeling? . . . Good. . . . Here as well, pal. Coming down cats and dogs. . . . That's right. Just the day for a kip° and a toss in your old Uncle Ned. . . . Everything's just hunky-dory on my side, Dad. . . . Well, to start with, there's a nice pile of comics for you on the counter. . . . Yes, old Kemple brought them in. *Batman and Robin, Submariner* . . . just your cup of tea. . . . I will. . . . Yes, we'll spin a few yarns tonight. . . . Okay, chum, see you in a little while. . . . No, I promise. I'll come straight home. . . . (*Pause — his mother comes back on the phone.*) Mom? Okay. I'll lock up now. . . . What? . . . Oh, the brandy . . . Yes, I'll remember! . . . I'll put it in my suitcase now, for God's sake. I know well enough what will happen if he doesn't get it. . . . (*Places a bottle of brandy on the counter.*) I *was* kind to him, Mom. I didn't say anything nasty! . . . All right. Bye. (*End of telephone conversation. A desolate Hally doesn't move. A strained silence.*)

SAM (*quietly*): That sounded like a bad bump, Hally.

HALLY (*Having a hard time controlling his emotions. He speaks carefully.*): Mind your own business, Sam.

SAM: Sorry. I wasn't trying to interfere. Shall we carry on? Hally? (*He indicates the exercise book. No response from Hally.*)

WILLIE (*also trying*): Tell him about when they give out the cups, Boet Sam.

SAM: Ja! That's another big moment. The presentation of the cups after the winners have been announced. You've got to put that in.

(*Still no response from Hally.*)

WILLIE: A big silver one, Master Hally, called floating trophy for the champions.

SAM: We always invite some big-shot personality to hand them over. Guest of honor this year is going to be His Holiness Bishop Jabulani of the All African Free Zionist Church.

(*Hally gets up abruptly, goes to his table, and tears up the page he was writing on.*)

HALLY: So much for a bloody world without collisions.

kip: Nap.

SAM: Too bad. It was on its way to being a good composition.

HALLY: Let's stop bullshitting ourselves, Sam.

SAM: Have we been doing that?

HALLY: Yes! That's what all our talk about a decent world has been . . . just so much bullshit.

SAM: We did say it was still only a dream.

HALLY: And a bloody useless one at that. Life's a fuckup and it's never going to change.

SAM: Ja, maybe that's true.

HALLY: There's no maybe about it. It's a blunt and brutal fact. All we've done this afternoon is waste our time.

SAM: Not if we'd got your homework done.

HALLY: I don't give a shit about my homework, so, for Christ's sake, just shut up about it. (*Slamming books viciously into his school case.*) Hurry up now and finish your work. I want to lock up and get out of here. (*Pause.*) And then go where? Home-sweet-fucking-home. Jesus, I hate that word.

(*Hally goes to the counter to put the brandy bottle and comics in his school case. After a moment's hesitation, he smashes the bottle of brandy. He abandons all further attempts to hide his feelings. Sam and Willie work away as unobtrusively as possible.*)

Do you want to know what is really wrong with your lovely little dream, Sam? It's not just that we are all bad dancers. That does happen to be perfectly true, but there's more to it than just that. You left out the cripples.

SAM: Hally!

HALLY (*now totally reckless*): Ja! Can't leave them out, Sam. That's why we always end up on our backsides on the dance floor. They're also out there dancing . . . like a bunch of broken spiders trying to do the quickstep! (*An ugly attempt at laughter.*) When you come to think of it, it's a bloody comical sight. I mean, it's bad enough on two legs . . . but one and a pair of crutches! Hell, no, Sam. That's guaranteed to turn that dance floor into a shambles. Why you shaking your head? Picture it, man. For once this afternoon let's use our imaginations sensibly.

SAM: Be careful, Hally.

HALLY: Of what? The truth? I seem to be the only one around here who is prepared to face it. We've had the pretty dream, it's time now to wake up and have a good long look at the way things really are. Nobody knows the steps, there's no music, the cripples are also out there tripping up everybody and trying to get into the act, and it's all called the All-Comers-How-to-Make-a-Fuckup-of-Life Championships. (*Another ugly laugh.*) Hang on, Sam! The best bit is still coming. Do you know what the winner's trophy is? A beautiful big chamber pot with roses on the side, and it's full to the brim with piss. And guess who I think is going to be this year's winner.

SAM (*almost shouting*): Stop now!

HALLY (*suddenly appalled by how far he has gone*): Why?

SAM: Hally? It's your father you're talking about.

HALLY: So?

SAM: Do you know what you've been saying?

(*Hally can't answer. He is rigid with shame. Sam speaks to him sternly.*)

No, Hally, you mustn't do it. Take back those words and ask for forgiveness! It's a terrible sin for a son to mock his father with jokes like that. You'll be punished if you carry on. Your father is your father, even if he is a . . . cripple man.

WILLIE: Yes, Master Hally. Is true what Sam say.

SAM: I understand how you are feeling, Hally, but even so. . . .

HALLY: No, you don't!

SAM: I think I do.

HALLY: And I'm telling you you don't. Nobody does. (*Speaking carefully as his shame turns to rage at Sam.*) It's your turn to be careful, Sam. Very careful! You're treading on dangerous ground. Leave me and my father alone.

SAM: I'm not the one who's been saying things about him.

HALLY: What goes on between me and my Dad is none of your business!

SAM: Then don't tell me about it. If that's all you've got to say about him, I don't want to hear.

(*For a moment Hally is at loss for a response.*)

HALLY: Just get on with your bloody work and shut up.

SAM: Swearing at me won't help you.

HALLY: Yes, it does! Mind your own fucking business and shut up!

SAM: Okay. If that's the way you want it, I'll stop trying.

(*He turns away. This infuriates Hally even more.*)

HALLY: Good. Because what you've been trying to do is meddle in something you know nothing about. All that concerns you in here, Sam, is to try and do what you get paid for — keep the place clean and serve the customers. In plain words, just get on with your job. My mother is right. She's always warning me about allowing you to get too familiar. Well, this time you've gone too far. It's going to stop right now.

(*No response from Sam.*)

You're only a servant in here, and don't forget it.

(*Still no response. Hally is trying hard to get one.*)

And as far as my father is concerned, all you need to remember is that he is your boss.

SAM (*needled at last*): No, he isn't. I get paid by your mother.

HALLY: Don't argue with me, Sam!

SAM: Then don't say he's my boss.

HALLY: He's a white man and that's good enough for you.

SAM: I'll try to forget you said that.

HALLY: Don't! Because you won't be doing me a favor if you do. I'm telling you to remember it.

(*A pause. Sam pulls himself together and makes one last effort.*)

SAM: Hally, Hally . . . ! Come on now. Let's stop before it's too late. You're right. We *are* on dangerous ground. If we're not careful, somebody is going to get hurt.

HALLY: It won't be me.

SAM: Don't be so sure.

HALLY: I don't know what you're talking about, Sam.

SAM: Yes, you do.

HALLY (*furious*): Jesus, I wish you would stop trying to tell me what I do and what I don't know.

(*Sam gives up. He turns to Willie.*)

SAM: Let's finish up.

HALLY: Don't turn your back on me! I haven't finished talking.

(*He grabs Sam by the arm and tries to make him turn around. Sam reacts with a flash of anger.*)

SAM: Don't do that, Hally! (*Facing the boy.*) All right, I'm listening. Well? What do you want to say to me?

HALLY (*pause as Hally looks for something to say*): To begin with, why don't you also start calling me Master Harold, like Willie.

SAM: Do you mean that?

HALLY: Why the hell do you think I said it?

SAM: And if I don't?

HALLY: You might just lose your job.

SAM (*quietly and very carefully*): If you make me say it once, I'll never call you anything else again.

HALLY: So? (*The boy confronts the man.*) Is that meant to be a threat?

SAM: Just telling you what will happen if you make me do that. You must decide what it means to you.

HALLY: Well, I have. It's good news. Because that is exactly what Master Harold wants from now on. Think of it as a little lesson in respect, Sam, that's long overdue, and I hope you remember it as well as you do your geography. I can tell you now that somebody who will be glad to hear I've finally given it to you will be my Dad. Yes! He agrees with my Mom. He's always going on about it as well. "You must teach the boys to show you more respect, my son."

SAM: So now you can stop complaining about going home. Everybody is going to be happy tonight.

HALLY: That's perfectly correct. You see, you mustn't get the wrong idea about me and my Dad, Sam. We also have our good times together. Some bloody good laughs. He's got a marvelous sense of humor. Want to know what our favorite joke is? He gives out a big groan, you see, and says: "It's not fair, is it, Hally?" Then I have to ask: "What, chum?" And then he says: "A nigger's arse" . . . and we both have a good laugh.

(*The men stare at him with disbelief.*)

What's the matter, Willie? Don't you catch the joke? You always were a bit slow on the uptake. It's what is called a pun. You see, fair means both light in color and to be just and decent. (*He turns to Sam.*) I thought *you* would catch it, Sam.

SAM: Oh ja, I catch it all right.

HALLY: But it doesn't appeal to your sense of humor.

SAM: Do you really laugh?

HALLY: Of course.

SAM: To please him? Make him feel good?

HALLY: No, for heavens sake! I laugh because I think it's a bloody good joke.

SAM: You're really trying hard to be ugly, aren't you? And why drag poor old Willie into it? He's done nothing to you except show you the respect you want so badly. That's also not being fair, you know . . . and I mean just or decent.

WILLIE: It's all right, Sam. Leave it now.

SAM: It's me you're after. You should just have said "Sam's arse". . . because that's the one you're trying to kick. Anyway, how do you know it's not fair? You've never seen it. Do you want to? (*He drops his trousers and underpants and presents his backside for Hally's inspection.*) Have a good look. A real Basuto arse . . . which is about as nigger as they can come. Satisfied? (*Trousers up.*) Now you can make your Dad even happier when you go home tonight. Tell him I showed you my arse and he is quite right. It's not fair. And if it will give him an even better laugh next time, I'll also let *him* have a look. Come, Willie, let's finish up and go.

(*Sam and Willie start to tidy up the tea room. Hally doesn't move. He waits for a moment when Sam passes him.*)

HALLY (*quietly*): Sam . . .

(*Sam stops and looks expectantly at the boy. Hally spits in his face. A long and heartfelt groan from Willie. For a few seconds Sam doesn't move.*)

SAM (*taking out a handkerchief and wiping his face*): It's all right, Willie.

(*To Hally.*)

Ja, well, you've done it . . . Master Harold. Yes, I'll start calling you that from now on. It won't be difficult anymore. You've hurt yourself, Master Harold. I saw it coming. I warned you, but you wouldn't listen. You've just hurt yourself *bad*. And you're a coward, Master Harold. The face you should be spitting in is your father's . . . but you used mine, because you think you're safe inside your fair skin . . . and this time I don't mean just or decent. (*Pause, then moving violently toward Hally.*) Should I hit him, Willie?

WILLIE (*stopping Sam*): No, Boet Sam.

SAM (*violently*): Why not?

WILLIE: It won't help, Boet Sam.

SAM: I don't want to help! I want to hurt him.

WILLIE: You also hurt yourself.

SAM: And if he had done it to you, Willie?

WILLIE: Me? Spit at me like I was a dog? (*A thought*

that had not occurred to him before. He looks at Hally.) Ja. Then I want to hit him. I want to hit him hard!

(*A dangerous few seconds as the men stand staring at the boy. Willie turns away, shaking his head.*)

But maybe all I do is go cry at the back. He's little boy, Boet Sam. Little *white* boy. Long trousers now, but he's still little boy.

SAM (*his violence ebbing away into defeat as quickly as it flooded*): You're right. So go on, then: groan again, Willie. You do it better than me. (*To Hally.*) You don't know all of what you've just done ... Master Harold. It's not just that you've made me feel dirtier than I've ever been in my life ... I mean, how do I wash off yours and your father's filth? ... I've also failed. A long time ago I promised myself I was going to try and do something, but you've just shown me ... Master Harold ... that I've failed. (*Pause.*) I've also got a memory of a little white boy when he was still wearing short trousers and a black man, but they're not flying a kite. It was the old Jubilee days, after dinner one night. I was in my room. You came in and just stood against the wall, looking down at the ground, and only after I'd asked you what you wanted, what was wrong, I don't know how many times, did you speak and even then so softly I almost didn't hear you. "Sam, please help me to go and fetch my Dad." Remember? He was dead drunk on the floor of the Central Hotel Bar. They'd phoned for your Mom, but you were the only one at home. And do you remember how we did it? You went in first by yourself to ask permission for me to go into the bar. Then I loaded him onto my back like a baby and carried him back to the boarding house with you following behind carrying his crutches. (*Shaking his head as he remembers.*) A crowded Main Street with all the people watching a little white boy following his drunk father on a nigger's back! I felt for that little boy ... Master Harold. I felt for him. After that we still had to clean him up, remember? He'd messed in his trousers, so we had to clean him up and get him into bed.

HALLY (*great pain*): I love him, Sam.

SAM: I know you do. That's why I tried to stop you from saying these things about him. It would have been so simple if you could have just despised him for being a weak man. But he's your father. You love him and you're ashamed of him. You're ashamed of so much! ... And now that's going to include yourself. That was the promise I made to myself: to try and stop that happening. (*Pause.*) After we got him to bed you came back with me to my room and sat in a corner and carried on just looking down at the ground. And for days after that! You hadn't done anything wrong, but you went around as if you owed the world an apology for being alive. I didn't like seeing that! That's not the way a boy grows up to be a man! ... But the one person who should have been

teaching you what that means was the cause of your shame. If you really want to know, that's why I made you that kite. I wanted you to look up, be proud of something, of yourself ... (*bitter smile at the memory*) ... and you certainly were that when I left you with it up there on the hill. Oh, ja ... something else! ... If you ever do write it as a short story, there *was* a twist in our ending. I couldn't sit down there and stay with you. It was a "Whites Only" bench. You were too young, too excited to notice then. But not anymore. If you're not careful ... Master Harold ... you're going to be sitting up there by yourself for a long time to come, and there won't be a kite in the sky. (*Sam has got nothing more to say. He exits into the kitchen, taking off his waiter's jacket.*)

WILLIE: Is bad. Is all bad in here now.

HALLY (*books into his school case, raincoat on*): Willie ... (*It is difficult to speak.*) Will you lock up for me and look after the keys?

WILLIE: Okay.

(*Sam returns. Hally goes behind the counter and collects the few coins in the cash register. As he starts to leave. ...*)

SAM: Don't forget the comic books.

(*Hally returns to the counter and puts them in his case. He starts to leave again.*)

SAM (*to the retreating back of the boy*): Stop ... Hally. ...

(*Hally stops, but doesn't turn to face him.*)

Hally ... I've got no right to tell you what being a man means if I don't behave like one myself, and I'm not doing so well at that this afternoon. Should we try again, Hally?

HALLY: Try what?

SAM: Fly another kite, I suppose. It worked once, and this time I need it as much as you do.

HALLY: It's still raining, Sam. You can't fly kites on rainy days, remember.

SAM: So what do we do? Hope for better weather tomorrow?

HALLY (*helpless gesture*): I don't know. I don't know anything anymore.

SAM: You sure of that, Hally? Because it would be pretty hopeless if that was true. It would mean nothing has been learnt in here this afternoon, and there was a hell of a lot of teaching going on ... one way or the other. But anyway, I don't believe you. I reckon there's one thing you know. You don't *have* to sit up there by yourself. You know what that bench means now, and you can leave it any time you choose. All you've got to do is stand up and walk away from it.

(*Hally leaves. Willie goes up quietly to Sam.*)

WILLIE: Is okay, Boet Sam. You see. Is ... (*he can't find any better words*) ... is going to be okay tomorrow. (*Changing his tone.*) Hey, Boet Sam! (*He is trying hard.*) You right. I think about it and you right. Tonight I find Hilda and say sorry. And make promise I won't beat her no more. You hear me, Boet Sam?

SAM: I hear you, Willie.

WILLIE: And when we practice I relax and romance with her from beginning to end. Nonstop! You watch! Two weeks' time: "First prize for promising newcomers: Mr. Willie Malopo and Miss Hilda Samuels." (*Sudden impulse.*) To hell with it! I walk home. (*He goes to the jukebox, puts in a coin and selects a record. The machine comes to life in the gray twilight, blushing its way through a spectrum of soft, romantic colors.*) How did you say it, Boet Sam? Let's dream. (*Willie sways with the music and gestures for Sam to dance.*)

(*Sarah Vaughan sings.*)

"Little man you're crying,
I know why you're blue,
Someone took your kiddy car away;
Better go to sleep now,
Little man you've had a busy day." (*etc., etc.*)
You lead. I follow.

(*The men dance together.*)

"Johnny won your marbles,
Tell you what we'll do;
Dad will get you new ones right away;
Better go to sleep now,
Little man you've had a busy day."

COMMENTARIES

Heinrich von Staden (*b. 1939*)
INTERVIEW WITH ATHOL FUGARD   1982

When "MASTER HAROLD" . . . and the boys was first produced at the Yale Repertory Theatre, Athol Fugard had the chance to respond to some questions about its significance to him. He revealed that the play was deeply personal and that through it he had been able to exorcise a demon that had haunted him for some time. In this interview Fugard details his involvement with South African drama and black actors in South Africa. He also comments on the extent to which censorship and other political pressures in South Africa made it difficult for his work to be produced in his own country.

von Staden: The bombs of fiction — Athol, aren't they more explosive than TNT?

Fugard: I'd like to believe that. You understand I've got to be careful about that one. I've got to be careful about flattering myself about the potency of the one area of activity which I've got, which is theater and being a writer.

von Staden: How often have there been productions of your plays for nonsegregated audiences in South Africa?

Fugard: I've had to change my tactics in terms of that over the years. At a period when the policy on segregated audiences in South Africa was rigid and very strictly enforced, I had to make a decision whether to take on an act of silence, just be silent because I couldn't go into a theater that was decent in my terms, or whether to take on the compromising circumstances of segregated audiences simply because I felt that if a play has got something to say, at least say it. And there were years when I decided to do the latter. I did perform before segregated audiences. In a sense I regret that decision now. I think I might possibly have looked after myself — and maybe the situation — better by not accepting that compromise. But I did.

von Staden: But do you think you had a genuine choice at that time?

Fugard: I had a choice between silence or being heard.

von Staden: Let me ask you along similar lines, when you are writing a play or a novel like *Tsotsi,* do you sense constraints on the way you are writing in view of the fact that certain things are anathema to the government, also in fiction?

Fugard: I would like to believe that I have operated at the table at which I sit and write, that I have operated totally without self-censorship. Maybe some awareness of what is possible and is not possible has operated subconsciously and is deciding choices I make in terms of what I favor. I think it may be pertinent to the conversation we are having, that *"MASTER HAROLD" . . . and the boys* is the first play of mine in twenty-four years of writing that will have its premiere outside of South Africa. And one of the reasons why I'm doing that this time is that there are elements in *"MASTER HAROLD" . . . and the boys* that might have run into censorship problems. [. . .]

von Staden: Here you are, a person who, critics say, has achieved exceptional insight into human nature, and you never obtained a university degree. What institutions, what processes do you think contributed most to the insights you have?

Fugard: Well, I think to be a South African is in a way to be at a university that teaches you about that. The South African experience is certainly one in which, if you're prepared to keep your eyes open and look, you're going to see a lot of suffering. But then, in terms of personal specifics, I suppose for me there was a very, very important relationship, a friendship, with a black man in what I suppose is any person's most formative and definitive years, the age between eleven, ten up until the age of twenty-one. It was a black man in Port Elizabeth, and my play *"MASTER HAROLD" . . . and the boys* reflects something of that friendship, tries to talk about it, look at it. I left South Africa, hitchhiked through the African continent, ended up as a sailor on a ship which, apart from the officers and engineers, had a totally nonwhite, had a totally black crew, and I was a sailor in a totally black crew. There was that, I think I can't nail down any one specific traumatic incident as being totally decisive. But I could be certain that *"MASTER HAROLD" . . . and the boys* deals with one specific moment which I'm trying to exorcise out of my soul.

von Staden: In all of your plays and in the novel you always have a South African setting. Yet your plays and your novels, though so rooted in the specifics of the South African situation, seem to have a tremendous appeal to audiences that are largely ignorant of the situation there. To what do you ascribe that?

Fugard: You take a chance. As a storyteller one year ago, I took a chance [. . .] I realized that it was finally time to deal with the story of a seventeen-year-old boy and his friendship with two black men. And it's a gamble. There's no formula. There is no way that you can make or decide or guarantee before the event that that story is going to resonate outside of its specific context. You just take a bloody chance.

Athol Fugard (b. 1932)
FROM NOTEBOOKS 1960–1977   1983

Like most playwrights, Athol Fugard is a journal writer. In his notebooks he has written scraps of memory that have special meaning to him. In one entry for March 1961, long before he began to write "MASTER HAROLD" . . . and the boys (1982), he describes one of his childhood memories. It concerns the real-life Sam, and it reveals — very painfully — exactly what the personal crime was that his play deals with. His gesture of contempt for the man who was like a grandfather to him became a demon that had to be exorcised.

Sam Semela — Basuto — with the family fifteen years. Meeting him again when he visited Mom set off string of memories.

The kite which he produced for me one day during those early years when Mom ran the Jubilee Hotel and he was a waiter there. He had made it himself: brown paper, its ribs fashioned from thin strips of tomato-box plank which he had smoothed down, a paste of flour and water for glue. I was surprised and bewildered that he had made it for me.

I vaguely recall shyly "haunting" the servants' quarters in the well of the hotel — cold, cement-gray world — the pungent mystery of the dark little rooms — a world I didn't understand. Frightened to enter any of the rooms. Sam, broad-faced, broader based — he smelled of woodsmoke. The "kaffir smell" of South Africa is the smell of poverty — woodsmoke and sweat.

Later, when he worked for her at the Park café, Mom gave him the sack: ". . . he became careless. He came late for work. His work went to hell. He didn't seem to care no more." I was about thirteen and served behind the counter while he waited on table.

Realize now he was the most significant — the only — friend of my boyhood years. On terrible windy days when no one came to swim or walk in the park, we would sit together and talk. Or I was reading — Introductions to Eastern Philosophy or Plato and Socrates — and when I had finished he would take the book back to New Brighton.

Can't remember now what precipitated it, but one day there was a rare quarrel between Sam and myself. In a truculent silence we closed the café, Sam set off home to New Brighton on foot and I followed a few minutes later on my bike. I saw him walking ahead of me and, coming out of a spasm of acute loneliness, as I rode up behind him I called his name, he turned in mid-stride to look back and, as I cycled past, I spat in his face. Don't suppose I will ever deal with the shame that overwhelmed me the second after I had done that.

Now he is thin. We had a long talk. He told about the old woman ("Ma") whom he and his wife have taken in to look after their house while he goes to work — he teaches ballroom dancing. "Ma" insists on behaving like a domestic — making Sam feel guilty and embarrassed. She brings him an early morning cup of coffee. Sam: "No, Ma, you mustn't, man." Ma: "I must." Sam: "Look, Ma, if I want it, I can make it." Ma: "No, I must."

Occasionally, when she is doing something, Sam feels like a cup of tea but is too embarrassed to ask her, and daren't make one for himself. Similarly, with his washing. After three days or a week away in other towns, giving dancing lessons, he comes back with underclothes that are very dirty. He is too shy to give them out to be washed so washes them himself. When Ma sees this she goes and complains to Sam's wife that he doesn't trust her, that it's all wrong for him to do the washing.

Of tsotsis,° he said: "They grab a old man, stick him with a knife, and ransack him. And so he must go to hospital and his kids is starving with hungry." Of others: "He's got some little moneys. So he is facing starvation for the weekend."

Of township snobs, he says there are the educational ones: "If you haven't been to the big school, like Fort Hare, what you say isn't true." And the money ones: "If you aren't selling shops or got a business or a big car, man, you're nothing."

Sam's incredible theory about the likeness of those "with the true seed of love." Starts with Plato and Socrates — they were round. "Man is being shrinking all the time. An Abe Lincoln, him too, taller, but that's because man is shrinking." Basically, those with the true seed of love look the same —"It's in the eyes."

He spoke admiringly of one man, a black lawyer in East London, an educated man — university background — who was utterly without snobbery, looking down on no one — any man, educated or ignorant, rich or poor, was another *man* to him, another human being, to be respected, taken seriously, to be talked to, listened to.

"They" won't allow Sam any longer to earn a living as a dancing teacher. "You must get a job!" One of his fellow teachers was forced to work at Fraser's Quarries.

tsotis: Gang members.

August Wilson

August Wilson was born in Pittsburgh in 1945, the son of a white father who never lived with his family and a black mother who had come from North Carolina to a Pittsburgh slum, where she worked to keep her family together. Wilson's early childhood was spent in an environment very similar to that of his play *Fences,* and Troy Maxson seems to be patterned somewhat on Wilson's stepfather.

Wilson's writing is rooted to a large extent in music, specifically the blues. As a poet, writing over several years, Wilson found himself interested in the speech patterns and rhythms that were familiar to him from black neighborhoods, but the value of those patterns became clearer to him when he grew older and moved from Pittsburgh to Minneapolis. From a distance, he was able to see more clearly what had attracted him to the language and to begin to use the language more fully in his work.

In the 1960s and 1970s Wilson became involved in the civil rights movement and began to describe himself as a black nationalist, a term he has said he feels comfortable with. He began writing plays in the 1960s in Pittsburgh and then took a job in St. Paul writing dramatic skits for the Science Museum of Minnesota. He founded the Playwrights Center in Minneapolis and began writing a play, *Jitney,* about a gypsy cab station, which was first produced in 1982 and which was staged in New York in April 2000 in a revised version at the Second Stage Theater. *Fullerton Street,* about Pittsburgh, was another play written in this early period. Wilson's first commercial success, *Ma Rainey's Black Bottom,* eventually premiered at the Yale Repertory Theatre in 1984 and then went to Broadway, where it enjoyed 275 performances and won the New York Drama Critics' Circle Award.

Ma Rainey's Black Bottom was the first of a planned sequence of ten plays based on the black American experience. As Wilson said, "I think the black Americans have the most dramatic story of all mankind to tell." The concept of such a vast project echoes O'Neill's projected group of eleven plays based on the Irish-American experience. (Unfortunately, O'Neill destroyed all but *A Touch of the Poet* in his series.) Wilson's project, however, is ongoing and intense and so far has produced some of the most successful plays in the recent American theater.

Ma Rainey is about the legendary black blues singer who preceded Bessie Smith and Billie Holiday. The play is about the way in which she was exploited by white managers and recording executives and the way in which she knowingly dealt with her exploitation. In the cast of the play are several black musicians in the backup band. Levee, the trumpet player, has a dream of leading his own band and establishing himself as an important jazz musician. But he is haunted by memories of seeing his mother raped by a gang of white men when he was a boy. He wants to "improve" the session he's playing by making the old jazz tune "Black Bottom" swing in the new jazz style, but Ma Rainey keeps him in tow and demands that they play the tune in the old way. Levee finally cracks under the pressure, and the play ends painfully.

Fences opened at the Yale Repertory Theatre in 1985 and in New York in early 1987, where it won the Pulitzer Prize as well as the New York Drama Critics' Circle Award. This long-running success established Wilson firmly as an important writer. *Joe Turner's Come and Gone* opened at the Yale Repertory Theatre in late 1986 and moved to New York in early 1988, where it too has been hailed as an important play, winning its author the New York Drama Critics' Circle Award. Set in a rooming house in Pittsburgh in 1911, *Joe Turner* is a study of the children of former slaves. They have come north to find work, and some of them have been found by the legendary bounty hunter Joe Turner. As a study of a people in transition, the play is a quiet masterpiece. It incorporates a number of important African traditions, especially religious rituals of healing as performed by Bynum, the "bone man," a seer and a medicine man. In this play and others, Wilson makes a special effort to highlight the elements of African heritage that white society strips away from blacks.

The next play in Wilson's projected series, *The Piano Lesson,* which premiered at the Yale Repertory Theatre in 1987, also portrays the complexity of black attitudes toward the past and black heritage. The piano represents two kinds of culture: the white culture that produced the musical instrument and the black culture, in the form of Papa Boy Willie, who carved into it images from black Africa. The central question in the play is whether Boy Willie should sell the piano and use the money for a down payment on land and therefore on the future. Or should he follow his sister Berniece's advice and keep it because it is too precious to sell? The conflict is deep and the play ultimately focuses on a profound moment of spiritual exorcism. How one exorcises the past — how one lives with it or without it — is a central theme in Wilson's work.

The next play, *Two Trains Running,* is set in 1969, in the decade that saw the Vietnam War, racial and political riots, and the assassinations of John and Robert Kennedy, Malcolm X, and Martin Luther King Jr. The play premiered at the Yale Repertory Theatre in 1990 and opened on Broadway at the Walter Kerr Theater in April 1992, directed by Lloyd Richards. The characters remain in Memphis Lee's diner — scheduled for demolition — throughout the play. The two trains in the title are heading to Africa and to the old South, but the characters are immobile and seem indifferent to both of them. Wilson moved away from the careful structure of the well-made play in this work and produced an open-ended conclusion, leaving the racial and philosophical tensions unresolved.

Seven Guitars (1996) takes place in a backyard in Pittsburgh in 1948 on the eve of the landmark boxing match between Joe Louis and "Jersey" Joe Walcott. The play focuses on a blues musician, Floyd Barton, who hopes to regain his lost love, put his band back together, and move to Chicago to make his second recording. *Seven Guitars* emphasizes the blues, especially in its long first act, with Barton's friends gathered in his backyard to mourn his death and the loss of his talent. People did much the same when Joe Louis, the "Brown Bomber," lost his fight, a loss that punctuated the end of an era. The second act focuses on Hedley, a West Indian boarder, whom critic Margo Jefferson describes as "half madman and half prophet." Hedley recites a litany of racial injustices and gives voice to a torrent of wrongs. Hedley's voice is a counterpoint to the blues; he gives us a powerful range of responses to the condition of being black in Pittsburgh in the late 1940s.

Wilson's most recent play in the series is set in 1985. *King Hedley II* (1999) picks up some of the characters of *Seven Guitars,* including the character Hedley, and develops further the experience of living in the Hill District of Pittsburgh. Wilson describes *King Hedley II* as focusing on "the breakdown of the black community's extended-family structure." The sequence of the plays detailing the African American experience for each decade of the century needs only the first and last decades' coverage. Wilson now lives primarily in Seattle, but he returned to his hometown for the December 1999 premiere of *King Hedley II,* the first play produced in the new O'Reilly Theater by the Pittsburgh Public Theater. It moved in March 2000 to the Seattle Repertory Theater.

FENCES

Fences (1985), like most of August Wilson's recent plays, was directed by Lloyd Richards, who also directed the first production of Lorraine Hansberry's *A Raisin in the Sun.* Richards was, until 1991, the dean of the School of Drama at Yale University and ran the Yale Repertory Theatre, where he directed all of the plays Wilson has written in his projected ten-play cycle about black American life.

Fences presents a slice of life in a black tenement in Pittsburgh in the 1950s. Its main character, Troy Maxson, is a garbage collector who has taken great pride in keeping his family together and providing for them. When the play opens, he and his friend Bono are talking about Troy's challenge to the company and the union about blacks' ability to do the same "easy" work that whites do. Troy's rebellion and frustration set the tone of the entire play: he is looking for his rights, and, at age fifty-three, he has missed many opportunities to get what he deserves.

Troy's struggle for fairness becomes virtually mythic as he describes his wrestling with death during a bout with pneumonia in 1941. He describes a three-day struggle in which he eventually overcame his foe. Troy — a good baseball player who was relegated to the Negro leagues — sees death as nothing but a fastball, and he could always deal with a fastball. Both Bono and Troy's wife, Rose, show an intense admiration for him as he describes his ordeal.

The father-son relationship that begins to take a central role in the drama is complicated by strong feelings of pride and independence on both sides. Troy's son Cory wants to play football, and Troy wants him to work on the fence he's mending. Cory's youthful enthusiasm probably echoes Troy's own youthful innocence, but Troy resents it in Cory, seeing it as partly responsible for his own predicament. Cory cannot see his father's point of view and feels that he is exempt from the kind of prejudice his father suffered.

The agony of the father-son relationship, their misperceptions of each other, persist through the play. Rose's capacity to cope with the deepest of Troy's anxieties — his fear of death — is one of her most important achievements in the play. At the end of the play Rose demands that Cory give Troy the respect he deserves, although Cory's anger and inexperience make it all but impossible for him to see his father as anything other than an oppressor. Cory feels that he must say no to his father once, but Rose will not let him deny his father. When the play ends with Gabe's fantastic ritualistic dance, the audience feels a sense of closure, of spiritual finish.

Fences in Performance

Like many of America's best plays, *Fences* began in a workshop production. Its first version was performed in a reading without full production — no sets, no full lighting, actors working "on book" instead of fully memorizing the play — in the summer of 1983 at the Eugene O'Neill Center in Waterford, Connecticut. This early version was four hours long.

Once Wilson found the focus of his play, it premiered in 1985 at the Yale Repertory Theatre in New Haven. Lloyd Richards, then dean of Yale Drama School, directed this as well as the New York production. The New York opening on March 27, 1987, starred Mary Alice, James Earl Jones, and Ray Anranha, the cast from New Haven. Frank Rich in the *New York Times* praised James Earl Jones, congratulating him on finding "what may be the best role of his career." He also said, "*Fences* leaves no doubt that Mr. Wilson is a major writer, combining a poet's ear for vernacular with a robust sense of humor (political and sexual), a sure instinct for crackling dramatic incident and a passionate commitment to a great subject."

From the first, *Fences* was recognized as an important play. It won four Tony Awards: best play, best actor, best supporting actress, and best director. It also won the New York Drama Critics' Circle Award for best play. Before the New York production, it had traveled to Chicago, San Francisco, and Seattle. It has been performed numerous times since, with the 1990 Stage West production in Springfield, Massachusetts, among the most recent. A film version of the play is scheduled for release in 2000.

August Wilson (b. 1946)

FENCES

1987

Characters

TROY MAXSON
JIM BONO, *Troy's friend*
ROSE, *Troy's wife*
LYONS, *Troy's oldest son by previous marriage*
GABRIEL, *Troy's brother*
CORY, *Troy and Rose's son*
RAYNELL, *Troy's daughter*

Setting: *The setting is the yard which fronts the only entrance to the Maxson household, an ancient two-story brick house set back off a small alley in a big-city neighborhood. The entrance to the house is gained by two or three steps leading to a wooden porch badly in need of paint.*

A relatively recent addition to the house and running its full width, the porch lacks congruence. It is a sturdy porch with a flat roof. One or two chairs of dubious value sit at one end where the kitchen window opens onto the porch. An old-fashioned icebox stands silent guard at the opposite end.

The yard is a small dirt yard, partially fenced, except for the last scene, with a wooden sawhorse, a pile of lumber, and other fence-building equipment set off to the side. Opposite is a tree from which hangs a ball made of rags. A baseball bat leans against the tree. Two oil drums serve as garbage receptacles and sit near the house at right to complete the setting.

The Play: *Near the turn of the century, the destitute of Europe sprang on the city with tenacious claws and an honest and solid dream. The city devoured them. They swelled its belly until it burst into a thousand furnaces and sewing machines, a thousand butcher shops and bakers' ovens, a thousand churches and hospitals and funeral parlors and money-lenders. The city grew. It nourished itself and offered each man a partnership limited only by his talent, his guile, and his willingness and capacity for hard work. For the immigrants of Europe, a dream dared and won true.*

The descendants of African slaves were offered no such welcome or participation. They came from places called the Carolinas and the Virginias, Georgia, Alabama, Mississippi, and Tennessee. They came strong, eager, searching. The city rejected them and they fled and settled along the riverbanks and under bridges in shallow, ramshackle houses made of sticks and tarpaper. They collected rags and wood. They sold the use of their muscles and their bodies. They cleaned houses and washed clothes, they shined shoes, and in quiet desperation and vengeful pride, they stole, and lived in pursuit of their own dream. That they could breathe free, finally, and stand to meet life with the force of dignity and whatever eloquence the heart could call upon.

By 1957, the hard-won victories of the European immigrants had solidified the industrial might of America. War had been confronted and won with new energies that used loyalty and patriotism as its fuel. Life was rich, full, and flourishing. The Milwaukee Braves won the World Series, and the hot winds of change that would make the sixties a turbulent, racing, dangerous, and provocative decade had not yet begun to blow full.

ACT I • *Scene I*

(It is 1957. Troy and Bono enter the yard, engaged in conversation. Troy is fifty-three years old, a large man with thick, heavy hands; it is this largeness that he strives to fill out and make an accommodation with. Together with his blackness, his largeness informs his sensibilities and the choices he has made in his life.)

(Of the two men, Bono is obviously the follower. His commitment to their friendship of thirty-odd years is rooted in his admiration of Troy's honesty, capacity for hard work, and his strength, which Bono seeks to emulate.)

(It is Friday night, payday, and the one night of the week the two men engage in a ritual of talk and drink. Troy is usually the most talkative and at times he can be crude and almost vulgar, though he is capable of rising to profound heights of expression. The men carry lunch buckets and wear or carry burlap aprons and are dressed in clothes suitable to their jobs as garbage collectors.)

BONO: Troy, you ought to stop that lying!
TROY: I ain't lying! The nigger had a watermelon this big.

(He indicates with his hands.)

Talking about . . . "What watermelon, Mr. Rand?" I liked to fell out! "What watermelon, Mr. Rand?" . . . And it sitting there big as life.
BONO: What did Mr. Rand say?
TROY: Ain't said nothing. Figure if the nigger too dumb to know he carrying a watermelon, he wasn't gonna get much sense out of him. Trying to hide that great big old watermelon under his coat. Afraid to let the white man see him carry it home.

BONO: I'm like you . . . I ain't got no time for them kind of people.

TROY: Now what he look like getting mad cause he see the man from the union talking to Mr. Rand?

BONO: He come to me talking about . . ."Maxson gonna get us fired." I told him to get away from me with that. He walked away from me calling you a troublemaker. What Mr. Rand say?

TROY: Ain't said nothing. He told me to go down the Commissioner's office next Friday. They called me down there to see them.

BONO: Well, as long as you got your complaint filed, they can't fire you. That's what one of them white fellows tell me.

TROY: I ain't worried about them firing me. They gonna fire me cause I asked a question? That's all I did. I went to Mr. Rand and asked him, "Why? Why you got the white mens driving and the colored lifting?" Told him "what's the matter, don't I count? You think only white fellows got sense enough to drive a truck. That ain't no paper job! Hell, anybody can drive a truck. How come you got all whites driving and the colored lifting?" He told me "take it to the union." Well, hell, that's what I done! Now they wanna come up with this pack of lies.

BONO: I told Brownie if the man come and ask him any questions . . . just tell the truth! It ain't nothing but something they done trumped up on you cause you filed a complaint on them.

TROY: Brownie don't understand nothing. All I want them to do is change the job description. Give everybody a chance to drive the truck. Brownie can't see that. He ain't got that much sense.

BONO: How you figure he be making out with that gal be up at Taylors' all the time . . . that Alberta gal?

TROY: Same as you and me. Getting just as much as we is. Which is to say nothing.

BONO: It is, huh? I figure you doing a little better than me . . . and I ain't saying what I'm doing.

TROY: Aw, nigger, look here . . . I know you. If you had got anywhere near that gal, twenty minutes later you be looking to tell somebody. And the first one you gonna tell . . . that you gonna want to brag to . . . is gonna be me.

BONO: I ain't saying that. I see where you be eyeing her.

TROY: I eye all the women. I don't miss nothing. Don't never let nobody tell you Troy Maxson don't eye the women.

BONO: You been doing more than eyeing her. You done bought her a drink or two.

TROY: Hell yeah, I bought her a drink! What that mean? I bought you one, too. What that mean cause I buy her a drink? I'm just being polite.

BONO: It's all right to buy her one drink. That's what you call being polite. But when you wanna be buying two or three . . . that's what you call eyeing her.

TROY: Look here, as long as you known me . . . you ever known me to chase after women?

BONO: Hell yeah! Long as I done known you. You forgetting I knew you when.

TROY: Naw, I'm talking about since I been married to Rose?

BONO: Oh, not since you been married to Rose. Now, that's the truth, there. I can say that.

TROY: All right then! Case closed.

BONO: I see you be walking up around Alberta's house. You supposed to be at Taylors' and you be walking up around there.

TROY: What you watching where I'm walking for? I ain't watching after you.

BONO: I seen you walking around there more than once.

TROY: Hell, you liable to see me walking anywhere! That don't mean nothing cause you see me walking around there.

BONO: Where she come from anyway? She just kinda showed up one day.

TROY: Tallahassee. You can look at her and tell she one of them Florida gals. They got some big healthy women down there. Grow them right up out the ground. Got a little bit of Indian in her. Most of them niggers down in Florida got some Indian in them.

BONO: I don't know about that Indian part. But she damn sure big and healthy. Woman wear some big stockings. Got them great big old legs and hips as wide as the Mississippi River.

TROY: Legs don't mean nothing. You don't do nothing but push them out of the way. But them hips cushion the ride!

BONO: Troy, you ain't got no sense.

TROY: It's the truth! Like you riding on Goodyears!

(*Rose enters from the house. She is ten years younger than Troy, her devotion to him stems from her recognition of the possibilities of her life without him: a succession of abusive men and their babies, a life of partying and running the streets, the Church, or aloneness with its attendant pain and frustration. She recognizes Troy's spirit as a fine and illuminating one and she either ignores or forgives his faults, only some of which she recognizes. Though she doesn't drink, her presence is an integral part of the Friday night rituals. She alternates between the porch and the kitchen, where supper preparations are under way.*)

ROSE: What you all out here getting into?

TROY: What you worried about what we getting into for? This is men talk, woman.

ROSE: What I care what you all talking about? Bono, you gonna stay for supper?

BONO: No, I thank you, Rose. But Lucille say she cooking up a pot of pigfeet.

TROY: Pigfeet! Hell, I'm going home with you! Might even stay the night if you got some pigfeet. You got something in there to top them pigfeet, Rose?

ROSE: I'm cooking up some chicken. I got some chicken and collard greens.

TROY: Well, go on back in the house and let me and

Bono finish what we was talking about. This is men talk. I got some talk for you later. You know what kind of talk I mean. You go on and powder it up.

ROSE: Troy Maxson, don't you start that now!

TROY (*puts his arm around her*): Aw, woman . . . come here. Look here, Bono . . . when I met this woman . . . I got out that place, say, "Hitch up my pony, saddle up my mare . . . there's a woman out there for me somewhere. I looked here. Looked there. Saw Rose and latched on to her." I latched on to her and told her — I'm gonna tell you the truth — I told her, "Baby, I don't wanna marry, I just wanna be your man." Rose told me . . . tell him what you told me, Rose.

ROSE: I told him if he wasn't the marrying kind, then move out the way so the marrying kind could find me.

TROY: That's what she told me. "Nigger, you in my way. You blocking the view! Move out the way so I can find me a husband." I thought it over two or three days. Come back —

ROSE: Ain't no two or three days nothing. You was back the same night.

TROY: Come back, told her . . . "Okay, baby . . . but I'm gonna buy me a banty rooster and put him out there in the backyard . . . and when he see a stranger come, he'll flap his wings and crow . . ." Look here, Bono, I could watch the front door by myself . . . it was that back door I was worried about.

ROSE: Troy, you ought not talk like that. Troy ain't doing nothing but telling a lie.

TROY: Only thing is . . . when we first got married . . . forget the rooster . . . we ain't had no yard!

BONO: I hear you tell it. Me and Lucille was staying down there on Logan Street. Had two rooms with the outhouse in the back. I ain't mind the outhouse none. But when that goddamn wind blow through there in the winter . . . that's what I'm talking about! To this day I wonder why in the hell I ever stayed down there for six long years. But see, I didn't know I could do no better. I thought only white folks had inside toilets and things.

ROSE: There's a lot of people don't know they can do no better than they doing now. That's just something you got to learn. A lot of folks still shop at Bella's.

TROY: Ain't nothing wrong with shopping at Bella's. She got fresh food.

ROSE: I ain't said nothing about if she got fresh food. I'm talking about what she charge. She charge ten cents more than the A&P.

TROY: The A&P ain't never done nothing for me. I spends my money where I'm treated right. I go down to Bella, say, "I need a loaf of bread, I'll pay you Friday." She give it to me. What sense that make when I got money to go and spend it somewhere else and ignore the person who done right by me? That ain't in the Bible.

ROSE: We ain't talking about what's in the Bible. What sense it make to shop there when she overcharge?

TROY: You shop where you want to. I'll do my shopping where the people been good to me.

ROSE: Well, I don't think it's right for her to overcharge. That's all I was saying.

BONO: Look here . . . I got to get on. Lucille going be raising all kind of hell.

TROY: Where you going, nigger? We ain't finished this pint. Come here, finish this pint.

BONO: Well, hell, I am . . . if you ever turn the bottle loose.

TROY (*hands him the bottle*): The only thing I say about the A&P is I'm glad Cory got that job down there. Help him take care of his school clothes and things. Gabe done moved out and things getting tight around here. He got that job. . . . He can start to look out for himself.

ROSE: Cory done went and got recruited by a college football team.

TROY: I told that boy about that football stuff. The white man ain't gonna let him get nowhere with that football. I told him when he first come to me with it. Now you come telling me he done went and got more tied up in it. He ought to go and get recruited in how to fix cars or something where he can make a living.

ROSE: He ain't talking about making no living playing football. It's just something the boys in school do. They gonna send a recruiter by to talk to you. He'll tell you he ain't talking about making no living playing football. It's a honor to be recruited.

TROY: It ain't gonna get him nowhere. Bono'll tell you that.

BONO: If he be like you in the sports . . . he's gonna be all right. Ain't but two men ever played baseball as good as you. That's Babe Ruth and Josh Gibson.° Them's the only two men ever hit more home runs than you.

TROY: What it ever get me? Ain't got a pot to piss in or a window to throw it out of.

ROSE: Times have changed since you was playing baseball, Troy. That was before the war. Times have changed a lot since then.

TROY: How in hell they done changed?

ROSE: They got lots of colored boys playing ball now. Baseball and football.

BONO: You right about that, Rose. Times have changed, Troy. You just come along too early.

TROY: There ought not never have been no time called too early! Now you take that fellow . . . what's that fellow they had playing right field for the Yankees back then? You know who I'm talking about, Bono. Used to play right field for the Yankees.

ROSE: Selkirk?

TROY: Selkirk! That's it! Man batting .269, understand? .269. What kind of sense that make? I was hitting .432 with thirty-seven home runs! Man batting .269 and playing right field for the Yankees! I saw Josh Gibson's daughter yesterday. She walking around

---

Josh Gibson: (1911–1947), powerful black baseball player known in the 1930s as the Babe Ruth of the Negro leagues.

with raggedy shoes on her feet. Now I bet you Selkirk's daughter ain't walking around with raggedy shoes on her feet! I bet you that!

ROSE: They got a lot of colored baseball players now. Jackie Robinson was the first. Folks had to wait for Jackie Robinson.

TROY: I done seen a hundred niggers play baseball better than Jackie Robinson. Hell, I know some teams Jackie Robinson couldn't even make! What you talking about Jackie Robinson. Jackie Robinson wasn't nobody. I'm talking about if you could play ball then they ought to have let you play. Don't care what color you were. Come telling me I come along too early. If you could play . . . then they ought to have let you play.

(*Troy takes a long drink from the bottle.*)

ROSE: You gonna drink yourself to death. You don't need to be drinking like that.

TROY: Death ain't nothing. I done seen him. Done wrassled with him. You can't tell me nothing about death. Death ain't nothing but a fastball on the outside corner. And you know what I'll do to that! Lookee here, Bono . . . am I lying? You get one of them fastballs, about waist high, over the outside corner of the plate where you can get the meat of the bat on it . . . and good god! You can kiss it goodbye. Now, am I lying?

BONO: Naw, you telling the truth there. I seen you do it.

TROY: If I'm lying . . . that 450 feet worth of lying!

(*Pause.*)

That's all death is to me. A fastball on the outside corner.

ROSE: I don't know why you want to get on talking about death.

TROY: Ain't nothing wrong with talking about death. That's part of life. Everybody gonna die. You gonna die, I'm gonna die. Bono's gonna die. Hell, we all gonna die.

ROSE: But you ain't got to talk about it. I don't like to talk about it.

TROY: You the one brought it up. Me and Bono was talking about baseball . . . you tell me I'm gonna drink myself to death. Ain't that right, Bono? You know I don't drink this but one night out of the week. That's Friday night. I'm gonna drink just enough to where I can handle it. Then I cuts it loose. I leave it alone. So don't you worry about me drinking myself to death. 'Cause I ain't worried about Death. I done seen him. I done wrestled with him.

Look here, Bono . . . I looked up one day and Death was marching straight at me. Like Soldiers on Parade! The Army of Death was marching straight at me. The middle of July, 1941. It got real cold just like it be winter. It seem like Death himself reached out and touched me on the shoulder. He touch me just like I touch you. I got cold as ice and Death standing there grinning at me.

ROSE: Troy, why don't you hush that talk.

TROY: I say . . . What you want, Mr. Death? You be wanting me? You done brought your army to be getting me? I looked him dead in the eye. I wasn't fearing nothing. I was ready to tangle. Just like I'm ready to tangle now. The Bible say be ever vigilant. That's why I don't get but so drunk. I got to keep watch.

ROSE: Troy was right down there in Mercy Hospital. You remember he had pneumonia? Laying there with a fever talking plumb out of his head.

TROY: Death standing there staring at me . . . carrying that sickle in his hand. Finally he say, "You want bound over for another year?" See, just like that . . . "You want bound over for another year?" I told him, "Bound over hell! Let's settle this now!"

It seem like he kinda fell back when I said that, and all the cold went out of me. I reached down and grabbed that sickle and threw it just as far as I could throw it . . . and me and him commenced to wrestling.

We wrestled for three days and three nights. I can't say where I found the strength from. Every time it seemed like he was gonna get the best of me, I'd reach way down deep inside myself and find the strength to do him one better.

ROSE: Every time Troy tell that story he find different ways to tell it. Different things to make up about it.

TROY: I ain't making up nothing. I'm telling you the facts of what happened. I wrestled with Death for three days and three nights and I'm standing here to tell you about it.

(*Pause.*)

All right. At the end of the third night we done weakened each other to where we can't hardly move. Death stood up, throwed on his robe . . . had him a white robe with a hood on it. He throwed on that robe and went off to look for his sickle. Say, "I'll be back." Just like that. "I'll be back." I told him, say, "Yeah, but . . . you gonna have to find me!" I wasn't no fool. I wan't going looking for him. Death ain't nothing to play with. And I know he's gonna get me. I know I got to join his army . . . his camp followers. But as long as I keep my strength and see him coming . . . as long as I keep up my vigilance . . . he's gonna have to fight to get me. I ain't going easy.

BONO: Well, look here, since you got to keep up your vigilance . . . let me have the bottle.

TROY: Aw hell, I shouldn't have told you that part. I should have left out that part.

ROSE: Troy be talking that stuff and half the time don't even know what he be talking about.

TROY: Bono know me better than that.

BONO: That's right. I know you. I know you got some Uncle Remus° in your blood. You got more stories than the devil got sinners.

Uncle Remus: Black storyteller who recounts traditional African American tales in the book by Joel Chandler Harris.

TROY: Aw hell, I done seen him too! Done talked with the devil.

ROSE: Troy, don't nobody wanna be hearing all that stuff.

(*Lyons enters the yard from the street. Thirty-four years old, Troy's son by a previous marriage, he sports a neatly trimmed goatee, sport coat, white shirt, tieless and buttoned at the collar. Though he fancies himself a musician, he is more caught up in the rituals and "idea" of being a musician than in the actual practice of the music. He has come to borrow money from Troy, and while he knows he will be successful, he is uncertain as to what extent his lifestyle will be held up to scrutiny and ridicule.*)

LYONS: Hey, Pop.

TROY: What you come "Hey, Popping" me for?

LYONS: How you doing, Rose?

(*He kisses her.*)

Mr. Bono. How you doing?

BONO: Hey, Lyons . . . how you been?

TROY: He must have been doing all right. I ain't seen him around here last week.

ROSE: Troy, leave your boy alone. He come by to see you and you wanna start all that nonsense.

TROY: I ain't bothering Lyons.

(*Offers him the bottle.*)

Here . . . get you a drink. We got an understanding. I know why he come by to see me and he know I know.

LYONS: Come on, Pop . . . I just stopped by to say hi . . . see how you was doing.

TROY: You ain't stopped by yesterday.

ROSE You gonna stay for supper, Lyons? I got some chicken cooking in the oven.

LYONS: No, Rose . . . thanks. I was just in the neighborhood and thought I'd stop by for a minute.

TROY: You was in the neighborhood all right, nigger. You telling the truth there. You was in the neighborhood cause it's my payday.

LYONS: Well, hell, since you mentioned it . . . let me have ten dollars.

TROY: I'll be damned! I'll die and go to hell and play blackjack with the devil before I give you ten dollars.

BONO: That's what I wanna know about . . . that devil you done seen.

LYONS: What . . . Pop done seen the devil? You too much, Pops.

TROY: Yeah, I done seen him. Talked to him too!

ROSE: You ain't seen no devil. I done told you that man ain't had nothing to do with the devil. Anything you can't understand, you want to call it the devil.

TROY: Look here, Bono . . . I went down to see Hertzberger about some furniture. Got three rooms for two-ninety-eight. That what it say on the radio. "Three rooms . . . two-ninety-eight." Even made up a little song about it. Go down there . . . man tell me I can't get no credit. I'm working every day and can't get no credit. What to do? I got an empty house with some raggedy furniture in it. Cory ain't got no bed. He's sleeping on a pile of rags on the floor. Working every day and can't get no credit. Come back here — Rose'll tell you — madder than hell. Sit down . . . try to figure what I'm gonna do. Come a knock on the door. Ain't been living here but three days. Who know I'm here? Open the door . . . devil standing there bigger than life. White fellow . . . got on good clothes and everything. Standing there with a clipboard in his hand. I ain't had to say nothing. First words come out of his mouth was . . . "I understand you need some furniture and can't get no credit." I liked to fell over. He say, "I'll give you all the credit you want, but you got to pay the interest on it." I told him, "Give me three rooms worth and charge whatever you want." Next day a truck pulled up here and two men unloaded them three rooms. Man what drove the truck give me a book. Say send ten dollars, first of every month to the address in the book and everything will be all right. Say if I miss a payment the devil was coming back and it'll be hell to pay. That was fifteen years ago. To this day . . . the first of the month I send my ten dollars, Rose'll tell you.

ROSE: Troy lying.

TROY: I ain't never seen that man since. Now you tell me who else that could have been but the devil? I ain't sold my soul or nothing like that, you understand. Naw, I wouldn't have truck with the devil about nothing like that. I got my furniture and pays my ten dollars the first of the month just like clockwork.

BONO: How long you say you been paying this ten dollars a month?

TROY: Fifteen years!

BONO: Hell, ain't you finished paying for it yet? How much the man done charged you.

TROY: Ah hell, I done paid for it. I done paid for it ten times over! The fact is I'm scared to stop paying it.

ROSE: Troy lying. We got that furniture from Mr. Glickman. He ain't paying no ten dollars a month to nobody.

TROY: Aw hell, woman. Bono know I ain't that big a fool.

LYONS: I was just getting ready to say . . . I know where there's a bridge for sale.

TROY: Look here, I'll tell you this . . . it don't matter to me if he was the devil. It don't matter if the devil give credit. Somebody has got to give it.

ROSE: It ought to matter. You going around talking about having truck with the devil . . . God's the one you gonna have to answer to. He's the one gonna be at the Judgment.

LYONS: Yeah, well, look here, Pop . . . let me have that ten dollars. I'll give it back to you. Bonnie got a job working at the hospital.

TROY: What I tell you, Bono? The only time I see this nigger is when he wants something. That's the only time I see him.

LYONS: Come on, Pop, Mr. Bono don't want to hear all that. Let me have the ten dollars. I told you Bonnie working.

TROY: What that mean to me? "Bonnie working." I don't care if she working. Go ask her for the ten dollars if she working. Talking about "Bonnie working." Why ain't you working?

LYONS: Aw, Pop, you know I can't find no decent job. Where am I gonna get a job at? You know I can't get no job.

TROY: I told you I know some people down there. I can get you on the rubbish if you want to work. I told you that the last time you came by here asking me for something.

LYONS: Naw, Pop . . . thanks. That ain't for me. I don't wanna be carrying nobody's rubbish. I don't wanna be punching nobody's time clock.

TROY: What's the matter, you too good to carry people's rubbish? Where you think that ten dollars you talking about come from? I'm just supposed to haul people's rubbish and give my money to you cause you too lazy to work. You too lazy to work and wanna know why you ain't got what I got.

ROSE: What hospital Bonnie working at? Mercy?

LYONS: She's down at Passavant working in the laundry.

TROY: I ain't got nothing as it is. I give you that ten dollars and I got to eat beans the rest of the week. Naw . . . you ain't getting no ten dollars here.

LYONS: You ain't got to be eating no beans. I don't know why you wanna say that.

TROY: I ain't got no extra money. Gabe done moved over to Miss Pearl's paying her the rent and things done got tight around here. I can't afford to be giving you every payday.

LYONS: I ain't asked you to give me nothing. I asked you to loan me ten dollars. I know you got ten dollars.

TROY: Yeah, I got it. You know why I got it? Cause I don't throw my money away out there in the streets. You living the fast life . . . wanna be a musician . . . running around in them clubs and things . . . then, you learn to take care of yourself. You ain't gonna find me going and asking nobody for nothing. I done spent too many years without.

LYONS: You and me is two different people, Pop.

TROY: I done learned my mistake and learned to do what's right by it. You still trying to get something for nothing. Life don't owe you nothing. You owe it to yourself. Ask Bono. He'll tell you I'm right.

LYONS: You got your way of dealing with the world . . . I got mine. The only thing that matters to me is the music.

TROY: Yeah, I can see that! It don't matter how you gonna eat . . . where your next dollar is coming from. You telling the truth there.

LYONS: I know I got to eat. But I got to live too. I need something that gonna help me to get out of the bed in the morning. Make me feel like I belong in the world. I don't bother nobody. I just stay with my music cause that's the only way I can find to live in the world. Otherwise there ain't no telling what I might do. Now I don't come criticizing you and how you live. I just come by to ask you for ten dollars. I don't wanna hear all that about how I live.

TROY: Boy, your mamma did a hell of a job raising you.

LYONS: You can't change me, Pop. I'm thirty-four years old. If you wanted to change me, you should have been there when I was growing up. I come by to see you . . . ask for ten dollars and you want to talk about how I was raised. You don't know nothing about how I was raised.

ROSE: Let the boy have ten dollars, Troy.

TROY (to Lyons): What the hell you looking at me for? I ain't got no ten dollars. You know what I do with my money.

(To Rose.)

Give him ten dollars if you want him to have it.

ROSE: I will. Just as soon as you turn it loose.

TROY (handing Rose the money): There it is. Seventy-six dollars and forty-two cents. You see this, Bono? Now, I ain't gonna get but six of that back.

ROSE: You ought to stop telling that lie. Here, Lyons. (She hands him the money.)

LYONS: Thanks, Rose. Look . . . I got to run . . . I'll see you later.

TROY: Wait a minute. You gonna say, "thanks, Rose" and ain't gonna look to see where she got that ten dollars from? See how they do me, Bono?

LYONS: I know she got it from you, Pop. Thanks. I'll give it back to you.

TROY: There he go telling another lie. Time I see that ten dollars . . . he'll be owing me thirty more.

LYONS: See you, Mr. Bono.

BONO: Take care, Lyons!

LYONS: Thanks, Pop. I'll see you again.

(Lyons exits the yard.)

TROY: I don't know why he don't go and get him a decent job and take care of that woman he got.

BONO: He'll be all right, Troy. The boy is still young.

TROY: The boy is thirty-four years old.

ROSE: Let's not get off into all that.

BONO: Look here . . . I got to be going. I got to be getting on. Lucille gonna be waiting.

TROY (puts his arm around Rose): See this woman, Bono? I love this woman. I love this woman so much it hurts. I love her so much . . . I done run out of ways of loving her. So I got to go back to basics. Don't you come by my house Monday morning talking about time to go to work . . . 'cause I'm still gonna be stroking!

ROSE: Troy! Stop it now!

BONO: I ain't paying him no mind, Rose. That ain't nothing but gin-talk. Go on, Troy. I'll see you Monday.

TROY: Don't you come by my house, nigger! I done told you what I'm gonna be doing.

(The lights go down to black.)

Scene II

(*The lights come up on Rose hanging up clothes. She hums and sings softly to herself. It is the following morning.*)

ROSE (*sings*): Jesus, be a fence all around me every day
    Jesus, I want you to protect me as I travel on my
      way.
    Jesus, be a fence all around me every day.

(*Troy enters from the house.*)

    Jesus, I want you to protect me
    As I travel on my way.
    (*To Troy.*) 'Morning. You ready for breakfast? I can fix it soon as I finish hanging up these clothes.
TROY: I got the coffee on. That'll be all right. I'll just drink some of that this morning.
ROSE: That 651 hit yesterday. That's the second time this month. Miss Pearl hit for a dollar . . . seem like those that need the least always get lucky. Poor folks can't get nothing.
TROY: Them numbers don't know nobody. I don't know why you fool with them. You and Lyons both.
ROSE: It's something to do.
TROY: You ain't doing nothing but throwing your money away.
ROSE: Troy, you know I don't play foolishly. I just play a nickel here and a nickel there.
TROY: That's two nickels you done thrown away.
ROSE: Now I hit sometimes . . . that makes up for it. It always comes in handy when I do hit. I don't hear you complaining then.
TROY: I ain't complaining now. I just say it's foolish. Trying to guess out of six hundred ways which way the number gonna come. If I had all the money niggers, these Negroes, throw away on numbers for one week — just one week — I'd be a rich man.
ROSE: Well, you wishing and calling it foolish ain't gonna stop folks from playing numbers. That's one thing for sure. Besides . . . some good things come from playing numbers. Look where Pope done bought him that restaurant off of numbers.
TROY: I can't stand niggers like that. Man ain't had two dimes to rub together. He walking around with his shoes all run over bumming money for cigarettes. All right. Got lucky there and hit the numbers . . .
ROSE: Troy, I know all about it.
TROY: Had good sense, I'll say that for him. He ain't throwed his money away. I seen niggers hit the numbers and go through two thousand dollars in four days. Man bought him that restaurant down there . . . fixed it up real nice . . . and then didn't want nobody to come in it! A Negro go in there and can't get no kind of service. I seen a white fellow come in there and order a bowl of stew. Pope picked all the meat out the pot for him. Man ain't had nothing but a bowl of meat! Negro come behind him and ain't got nothing but the potatoes and carrots. Talk-

ing about what numbers do for people, you picked a wrong example. Ain't done nothing but make a worser fool out of him than he was before.
ROSE: Troy, you ought to stop worrying about what happened at work yesterday.
TROY: I ain't worried. Just told me to be down there at the Commissioner's office on Friday. Everybody think they gonna fire me. I ain't worried about them firing me. You ain't got to worry about that.

(*Pause.*)

    Where's Cory? Cory in the house? (*Calls.*) Cory?
ROSE: He gone out.
TROY: Out, huh? He gone out 'cause he know I want him to help me with this fence. I know how he is. That boy scared of work.

(*Gabriel enters. He comes halfway down the alley and, hearing Troy's voice, stops.*)

TROY (*continues*): He ain't done a lick of work in his life.
ROSE: He had to go to football practice. Coach wanted them to get in a little extra practice before the season start.
TROY: I got his practice . . . running out of here before he get his chores done.
ROSE: Troy, what is wrong with you this morning? Don't nothing set right with you. Go on back in there and go to bed . . . get up on the other side.
TROY: Why something got to be wrong with me? I ain't said nothing wrong with me.
ROSE: You got something to say about everything. First it's the numbers . . . then it's the way the man runs his restaurant . . . then you done got on Cory. What's it gonna be next? Take a look up there and see if the weather suits you . . . or is it gonna be how you gonna put up the fence with the clothes hanging in the yard.
TROY: You hit the nail on the head then.
ROSE: I know you like I know the back of my hand. Go on in there and get you some coffee . . . see if that straighten you up. 'Cause you ain't right this morning.

(*Troy starts into the house and sees Gabriel. Gabriel starts singing. Troy's brother, he is seven years younger than Troy. Injured in World War II, he has a metal plate in his head. He carries an old trumpet tied around his waist and believes with every fiber of his being that he is the Archangel Gabriel. He carries a chipped basket with an assortment of discarded fruits and vegetables he has picked up in the strip district and which he attempts to sell.*)

GABRIEL (*singing*): Yes, ma'am, I got plums
    You ask me how I sell them
    Oh ten cents apiece
    Three for a quarter
    Come and buy now
    'Cause I'm here today
    And tomorrow I'll be gone

(*Gabriel enters.*)

Hey, Rose!

ROSE: How you doing, Gabe?

GABRIEL: There's Troy . . . Hey, Troy!

TROY: Hey, Gabe.

(*Exit into kitchen.*)

ROSE (*to Gabriel*): What you got there?

GABRIEL: You know what I got, Rose. I got fruits and vegetables.

ROSE (*looking in basket*): Where's all these plums you talking about?

GABRIEL: I ain't got no plums today, Rose. I was just singing that. Have some tomorrow. Put me in a big order for plums. Have enough plums tomorrow for St. Peter and everybody.

(*Troy reenters from kitchen, crosses to steps.*)
(*To Rose.*)

Troy's mad at me.

TROY: I ain't mad at you. What I got to be mad at you about? You ain't done nothing to me.

GABRIEL: I just moved over to Miss Pearl's to keep out from in your way. I ain't mean no harm by it.

TROY: Who said anything about that? I ain't said anything about that.

GABRIEL: You ain't mad at me, is you?

TROY: Naw . . . I ain't mad at you, Gabe. If I was mad at you I'd tell you about it.

GABRIEL: Got me two rooms. In the basement. Got my own door too. Wanna see my key?

(*He holds up a key.*)

That's my own key! Ain't nobody else got a key like that. That's my key! My two rooms!

TROY: Well, that's good, Gabe. You got your own key . . . that's good.

ROSE: You hungry, Gabe? I was just fixing to cook Troy his breakfast.

GABRIEL: I'll take some biscuits. You got some biscuits? Did you know when I was in heaven . . . every morning me and St. Peter would sit down by the gate and eat some big fat biscuits? Oh, yeah! We had us a good time. We'd sit there and eat us them biscuits and then St. Peter would go off to sleep and tell me to wake him up when it's time to open the gates for the judgment.

ROSE: Well, come on . . . I'll make up a batch of biscuits.

(*Rose exits into the house.*)

GABRIEL: Troy . . . St. Peter got your name in the book. I seen it. It say . . . Troy Maxson. I say . . . I know him! He got the same name like what I got. That's my brother!

TROY: How many times you gonna tell me that, Gabe?

GABRIEL: Ain't got my name in the book. Don't have to have my name. I done died and went to heaven. He got your name though. One morning St. Peter was looking at his book . . . marking it up for the judgment . . . and he let me see your name. Got it in there under M. Got Rose's name . . . I ain't seen it like I seen yours . . . but I know it's in there. He got a great big book. Got everybody's name what was ever been born. That's what he told me. But I seen your name. Seen it with my own eyes.

TROY: Go on in the house there. Rose going to fix you something to eat.

GABRIEL: Oh, I ain't hungry. I done had breakfast with Aunt Jemimah. She come by and cooked me up a whole mess of flapjacks. Remember how we used to eat them flapjacks?

TROY: Go on in the house and get you something to eat now.

GABRIEL: I got to go sell my plums. I done sold some tomatoes. Got me two quarters. Wanna see?

(*He shows Troy his quarters.*)

I'm gonna save them and buy me a new horn so St. Peter can hear me when it's time to open the gates.

(*Gabriel stops suddenly. Listens.*)

Hear that? That's the hellhounds. I got to chase them out of here. Go on get out of here! Get out!

(*Gabriel exits singing.*)

Better get ready for the judgment
Better get ready for the judgment
My Lord is coming down

(*Rose enters from the house.*)

TROY: He gone off somewhere.

GABRIEL (*offstage*): Better get ready for the judgment
Better get ready for the judgment morning
Better get ready for the judgment
My God is coming down

ROSE: He ain't eating right. Miss Pearl say she can't get him to eat nothing.

TROY: What you want me to do about it, Rose? I done did everything I can for the man. I can't make him get well. Man got half his head blown away . . . what you expect?

ROSE: Seem like something ought to be done to help him.

TROY: Man don't bother nobody. He just mixed up from that metal plate he got in his head. Ain't no sense for him to go back into the hospital.

ROSE: Least he be eating right. They can help him take care of himself.

TROY: Don't nobody wanna be locked up, Rose. What you wanna lock him up for? Man go over there and fight the war . . . messin' around with them Japs, get half his head blown off . . . and they give him a lousy three thousand dollars. And I had to swoop down on that.

ROSE: Is you fixing to go into that again?

TROY: That's the only way I got a roof over my head . . . cause of that metal plate.

ROSE: Ain't no sense you blaming yourself for nothing. Gabe wasn't in no condition to manage that money. You done what was right by him. Can't nobody say you ain't done what was right by him. Look how long you took care of him . . . till he wanted to have his own place and moved over there with Miss Pearl.

TROY: That ain't what I'm saying, woman! I'm just stating the facts. If my brother didn't have that metal plate in his head . . . I wouldn't have a pot to piss in or a window to throw it out of. And I'm fifty-three years old. Now see if you can understand that!

(*Troy gets up from the porch and starts to exit the yard.*)

ROSE: Where you going off to? You been running out of here every Saturday for weeks. I thought you was gonna work on this fence?

TROY: I'm gonna walk down to Taylors'. Listen to the ball game. I'll be back in a bit. I'll work on it when I get back.

(*He exits the yard. The lights go to black.*)

Scene III

(*The lights come up on the yard. It is four hours later. Rose is taking down the clothes from the line. Cory enters carrying his football equipment.*)

ROSE: Your daddy like to had a fit with you running out of here this morning without doing your chores.

CORY: I told you I had to go to practice.

ROSE: He say you were supposed to help him with this fence.

CORY: He been saying that the last four or five Saturdays, and then he don't never do nothing but go down to Taylors'. Did you tell him about the recruiter?

ROSE: Yeah, I told him.

CORY: What he say?

ROSE: He ain't said nothing too much. You get in there and get started on your chores before he gets back. Go on and scrub down them steps before he gets back here hollering and carrying on.

CORY: I'm hungry. What you got to eat, Mama?

ROSE: Go on and get started on your chores. I got some meat loaf in there. Go on and make you a sandwich . . . and don't leave no mess in there.

(*Cory exits into the house. Rose continues to take down the clothes. Troy enters the yard and sneaks up and grabs her from behind.*)

Troy! Go on, now. You liked to scared me to death. What was the score of the game? Lucille had me on the phone and I couldn't keep up with it.

TROY: What I care about the game? Come here, woman. (*He tries to kiss her.*)

ROSE: I thought you went down Taylors' to listen to the game. Go on, Troy! You supposed to be putting up this fence.

TROY (*attempting to kiss her again*): I'll put it up when I finish with what is at hand.

ROSE: Go on, Troy. I ain't studying you.

TROY (*chasing after her*): I'm studying you . . . fixing to do my homework!

ROSE: Troy, you better leave me alone.

TROY: Where's Cory? That boy brought his butt home yet?

ROSE: He's in the house doing his chores.

TROY (*calling*): Cory! Get your butt out here, boy!

(*Rose exits into the house with the laundry. Troy goes over to the pile of wood, picks up a board, and starts sawing. Cory enters from the house.*)

TROY: You just now coming in here from leaving this morning?

CORY: Yeah, I had to go to football practice.

TROY: Yeah, what?

CORY: Yessir.

TROY: I ain't but two seconds off you noway. The garbage sitting in there overflowing . . . you ain't done none of your chores . . . and you come in here talking about "Yeah."

CORY: I was just getting ready to do my chores now, Pop . . .

TROY: Your first chore is to help me with this fence on Saturday. Everything else come after that. Now get that saw and cut them boards.

(*Cory takes the saw and begins cutting the boards. Troy continues working. There is a long pause.*)

CORY: Hey, Pop . . . why don't you buy a TV?

TROY: What I want with a TV? What I want one of them for?

CORY: Everybody got one. Earl, Ba Bra . . . Jesse!

TROY: I ain't asked you who had one. I say what I want with one?

CORY: So you can watch it. They got lots of things on TV. Baseball games and everything. We could watch the World Series.

TROY: Yeah . . . and how much this TV cost?

CORY: I don't know. They got them on sale for around two hundred dollars.

TROY: Two hundred dollars, huh?

CORY: That ain't that much, Pop.

TROY: Naw, it's just two hundred dollars. See that roof you got over your head at night? Let me tell you something about that roof. It's been over ten years since that roof was last tarred. See now . . . the snow come this winter and sit up there on that roof like it is . . . and it's gonna seep inside. It's just gonna be a little bit . . . ain't gonna hardly notice it. Then the next thing you know, it's gonna be leaking all over the house. Then the wood rot from all that water and you gonna need a whole new roof. Now, how much you think it cost to get that roof tarred?

CORY: I don't know.

TROY: Two hundred and sixty-four dollars . . . cash money. While you thinking about a TV, I got to be thinking about the roof . . . and whatever else go

ABOVE LEFT: Lynn Thigpen and James Earl Jones in the 1987 production of *Fences*. ABOVE: James Earl Jones as Troy Maxson in *Fences*. RIGHT: Jones and Courtney Vance as his son Cory.

wrong around here. Now if you had two hundred dollars, what would you do . . . fix the roof or buy a TV?

CORY: I'd buy a TV. Then when the roof started to leak . . . when it needed fixing . . . I'd fix it.

TROY: Where you gonna get the money from? You done spent it for a TV. You gonna sit up and watch the water run all over your brand new TV.

CORY: Aw, Pop. You got money. I know you do.

TROY: Where I got it at, huh?

CORY: You got it in the bank.

TROY: You wanna see my bankbook? You wanna see that seventy-three dollars and twenty-two cents I got sitting up in there.

CORY: You ain't got to pay for it all at one time. You can put a down payment on it and carry it on home with you.

TROY: Not me. I ain't gonna owe nobody nothing if I can help it. Miss a payment and they come and snatch it right out your house. Then what you got? Now, soon as I get two hundred dollars clear, then I'll buy a TV. Right now, as soon as I get two hundred and sixty-four dollars, I'm gonna have this roof tarred.

CORY: Aw . . . Pop!

TROY: You go on and get you two hundred dollars and buy one if ya want it. I got better things to do with my money.

CORY: I can't get no two hundred dollars. I ain't never seen two hundred dollars.

TROY: I'll tell you what . . . you get you a hundred dollars and I'll put the other hundred with it.

CORY: All right, I'm gonna show you.

TROY: You gonna show me how you can cut them boards right now.

(*Cory begins to cut the boards. There is a long pause.*)

CORY: The Pirates won today. That makes five in a row.

TROY: I ain't thinking about the Pirates. Got an all-white team. Got that boy . . . that Puerto Rican boy . . . Clemente. Don't even half-play him. That boy could be something if they give him a chance. Play him one day and sit him on the bench the next.

CORY: He gets a lot of chances to play.

TROY: I'm talking about playing regular. Playing every day so you can get your timing. That's what I'm talking about.

CORY: They got some white guys on the team that don't play every day. You can't play everybody at the same time.

TROY: If they got a white fellow sitting on the bench . . . you can bet your last dollar he can't play! The colored guy got to be twice as good before he get on the team. That's why I don't want you to get all tied up in them sports. Man on the team and what it get him? They got colored on the team and don't use them. Same as not having them. All them teams the same.

CORY: The Braves got Hank Aaron and Wes Covington. Hank Aaron hit two home runs today. That makes forty-three.

TROY: Hank Aaron ain't nobody. That's what you supposed to do. That's how you supposed to play the game. Ain't nothing to it. It's just a matter of timing . . . getting the right follow-through. Hell, I can hit forty-three home runs right now!

CORY: Not off no major-league pitching, you couldn't.

TROY: We had better pitching in the Negro leagues. I hit seven home runs off of Satchel Paige.° You can't get no better than that!

CORY: Sandy Koufax. He's leading the league in strike-outs.

TROY: I ain't thinking of no Sandy Koufax.

CORY: You got Warren Spahn and Lew Burdette. I bet you couldn't hit no home runs off of Warren Spahn.

TROY: I'm through with it now. You go on and cut them boards.

(*Pause.*)

Your mama tell me you done got recruited by a college football team? Is that right?

CORY: Yeah. Coach Zellman say the recruiter gonna be coming by to talk to you. Get you to sign the permission papers.

TROY: I thought you supposed to be working down there at the A&P. Ain't you suppose to be working down there after school?

CORY: Mr. Stawicki say he gonna hold my job for me until after the football season. Say starting next week I can work weekends.

TROY: I thought we had an understanding about this football stuff? You suppose to keep up with your chores and hold that job down at the A&P. Ain't been around here all day on a Saturday. Ain't none of your chores done . . . and now you telling me you done quit your job.

CORY: I'm gonna be working weekends.

TROY: You damn right you are! And ain't no need for nobody coming around here to talk to me about signing nothing.

CORY: Hey, Pop . . . you can't do that. He's coming all the way from North Carolina.

TROY: I don't care where he coming from. The white man ain't gonna let you get nowhere with that football noway. You go on and get your book-learning so you can work yourself up in that A&P or learn how to fix cars or build houses or something, get you a trade. That way you have something can't nobody take away from you. You go on and learn how to put your hands to some good use. Besides hauling people's garbage.

CORY: I get good grades, Pop. That's why the recruiter wants to talk with you. You got to keep up your grades to get recruited. This way I'll be going to college. I'll get a chance . . .

TROY: First you gonna get your butt down there to the A&P and get your job back.

Satchel Paige: (1906–1982), legendary black pitcher in the Negro leagues.

CORY: Mr. Stawicki done already hired somebody else 'cause I told him I was playing football.

TROY: You a bigger fool than I thought . . . to let somebody take away your job so you can play some football. Where you gonna get your money to take out your girlfriend and whatnot? What kind of foolishness is that to let somebody take away your job?

CORY: I'm still gonna be working weekends.

TROY: Naw . . . naw. You getting your butt out of here and finding you another job.

CORY: Come on, Pop! I got to practice. I can't work after school and play football too. The team needs me. That's what Coach Zellman say . . .

TROY: I don't care what nobody else say. I'm the boss . . . you understand? I'm the boss around here. I do the only saying what counts.

CORY: Come on, Pop!

TROY: I asked you . . . did you understand?

CORY: Yeah . . .

TROY: What?!

CORY: Yessir.

TROY: You go on down there to that A&P and see if you can get your job back. If you can't do both . . . then you quit the football team. You've got to take the crookeds with the straights.

CORY: Yessir.

(*Pause.*)

Can I ask you a question?

TROY: What the hell you wanna ask me? Mr. Stawicki the one you got the questions for.

CORY: How come you ain't never liked me?

TROY: Liked you? Who the hell say I got to like you? What law is there say I got to like you? Wanna stand up in my face and ask a damn fool-ass question like that. Talking about liking somebody. Come here, boy, when I talk to you.

(*Cory comes over to where Troy is working. He stands slouched over and Troy shoves him on his shoulder.*)

Straighten up, goddammit! I asked you a question . . . what law is there say I got to like you?

CORY: None.

TROY: Well, all right then! Don't you eat every day?

(*Pause.*)

Answer me when I talk to you! Don't you eat every day?

CORY: Yeah.

TROY: Nigger, as long as you in my house, you put that sir on the end of it when you talk to me!

CORY: Yes . . . sir.

TROY: You eat every day.

CORY: Yessir!

TROY: Got a roof over your head.

CORY: Yessir!

TROY: Got clothes on your back.

CORY: Yessir.

TROY: Why you think that is?

CORY: Cause of you.

TROY: Ah, hell I know it's 'cause of me . . . but why do you think that is?

CORY (*hesitant*): Cause you like me.

TROY: Like you? I go out of here every morning . . . bust my butt . . . putting up with them crackers° every day . . . cause I like you? You about the biggest fool I ever saw.

(*Pause.*)

It's my job. It's my responsibility! You understand that? A man got to take care of his family. You live in my house . . . sleep you behind on my bedclothes . . . fill you belly up with my food . . . cause you my son. You my flesh and blood. Not 'cause I like you! Cause it's my duty to take care of you. I owe a responsibility to you! Let's get this straight right here . . . before it go along any further . . . I ain't got to like you. Mr. Rand don't give me my money come payday cause he likes me. He gives me cause he owe me. I done give you everything I had to give you. I gave you your life! Me and your mama worked that out between us. And liking your black ass wasn't part of the bargain. Don't you try and go through life worrying about if somebody like you or not. You best be making sure they doing right by you. You understand what I'm saying, boy?

CORY: Yessir.

TROY: Then get the hell out of my face, and get on down to that A&P.

(*Rose has been standing behind the screen door for much of the scene. She enters as Cory exits.*)

ROSE: Why don't you let the boy go ahead and play football, Troy? Ain't no harm in that. He's just trying to be like you with the sports.

TROY: I don't want him to be like me! I want him to move as far away from my life as he can get. You the only decent thing that ever happened to me. I wish him that. But I don't wish him a thing else from my life. I decided seventeen years ago that boy wasn't getting involved in no sports. Not after what they did to me in the sports.

ROSE: Troy, why don't you admit you was too old to play in the major leagues? For once . . . why don't you admit that?

TROY: What do you mean too old? Don't come telling me I was too old. I just wasn't the right color. Hell, I'm fifty-three years old and can do better than Selkirk's .269 right now!

ROSE: How's was you gonna play ball when you were over forty? Sometimes I can't get no sense out of you.

TROY: I got good sense, woman. I got sense enough not to let my boy get hurt over playing no sports. You been mothering that boy too much. Worried about if people like him.

---

crackers: White people (derogatory).

ROSE: Everything that boy do . . . he do for you. He wants you to say "Good job, son." That's all.

TROY: Rose, I ain't got time for that. He's alive. He's healthy. He's got to make his own way. I made mine. Ain't nobody gonna hold his hand when he get out there in that world.

ROSE: Times have changed from when you was young, Troy. People change. The world's changing around you and you can't even see it.

TROY (*slow, methodical*): Woman . . . I do the best I can do. I come in here every Friday. I carry a sack of potatoes and a bucket of lard. You all line up at the door with your hands out. I give you the lint from my pockets. I give you my sweat and my blood. I ain't got no tears. I done spent them. We go upstairs in that room at night . . . and I fall down on you and try to blast a hole into forever. I get up Monday morning . . . find my lunch on the table. I go out. Make my way. Find my strength to carry me through to the next Friday.

(*Pause.*)

That's all I got, Rose. That's all I got to give. I can't give nothing else.

(*Troy exits into the house. The lights go down to black.*)

Scene IV

(*It is Friday. Two weeks later. Cory starts out of the house with his football equipment. The phone rings.*)

CORY (*calling*): I got it!

(*He answers the phone and stands in the screen door talking.*)

Hello? Hey, Jesse. Naw . . . I was just getting ready to leave now.

ROSE (*calling*): Cory!

CORY: I told you, man, them spikes is all tore up. You can use them if you want, but they ain't no good. Earl got some spikes.

ROSE (*calling*): Cory!

CORY (*calling to Rose*): Mam? I'm talking to Jesse.

(*Into phone.*)

When she say that? (*Pause.*) Aw, you lying, man. I'm gonna tell her you said that.

ROSE (*calling*): Cory, don't you go nowhere!

CORY: I got to go to the game, Ma!

(*Into the phone.*)

Yeah, hey, look, I'll talk to you later. Yeah, I'll meet you over Earl's house. Later. Bye, Ma.

(*Cory exits the house and starts out the yard.*)

ROSE: Cory, where you going off to? You got that stuff all pulled out and thrown all over your room.

CORY (*in the yard*): I was looking for my spikes. Jesse wanted to borrow my spikes.

ROSE: Get up there and get that cleaned up before your daddy get back in here.

CORY: I got to go to the game! I'll clean it up *when I get back*.

(*Cory exits.*)

ROSE: That's all he need to do is see that room all messed up.

(*Rose exits into the house. Troy and Bono enter the yard. Troy is dressed in clothes other than his work clothes.*)

BONO: He told him the same thing he told you. Take it to the union.

TROY: Brownie ain't got that much sense. Man wasn't thinking about nothing. He wait until I confront them on it . . . then he wanna come crying seniority.

(*Calls.*)

Hey, Rose!

BONO: I wish I could have seen Mr. Rand's face when he told you.

TROY: He couldn't get it out of his mouth! Liked to bit his tongue! When they called me down there to the Commissioner's office . . . he thought they was gonna fire me. Like everybody else.

BONO: I didn't think they was gonna fire you. I thought they was gonna put you on the warning paper.

TROY: Hey, Rose!

(*To Bono.*)

Yeah, Mr. Rand like to bit his tongue.

(*Troy breaks the seal on the bottle, takes a drink, and hands it to Bono.*)

BONO: I see you run right down to Taylors' and told that Alberta gal.

TROY (*calling*): Hey, Rose! (*To Bono.*) I told everybody. Hey, Rose! I went down there to cash my check.

ROSE (*entering from the house*): Hush all that hollering, man! I know you out here. What they say down there at the Commissioner's office?

TROY: You supposed to come when I call you, woman. Bono'll tell you that.

(*To Bono.*)

Don't Lucille come when you call her?

ROSE: Man, hush your mouth. I ain't no dog . . . talk about "come when you call me."

TROY (*puts his arm around Rose*): You hear this Bono? I had me an old dog used to get uppity like that. You say, "C'mere, Blue!" . . . and he just lay there and look at you. End up getting a stick and chasing him away trying to make him come.

ROSE: I ain't studying you and your dog. I remember you used to sing that old song.

TROY (*he sings*): Hear it ring! Hear it ring! I had a dog his name was Blue.

ROSE: Don't nobody wanna hear you sing that old song.

TROY (*sings*): You know Blue was mighty true.

ROSE: Used to have Cory running around here singing that song.

BONO: Hell, I remember that song myself.

TROY (*sings*): You know Blue was a good old dog.
Blue treed a possum in a hollow log.
That was my daddy's song. My daddy made up that song.

ROSE: I don't care who made it up. Don't nobody wanna hear you sing it.

TROY (*makes a song like calling a dog*): Come here, woman.

ROSE: You come in here carrying on, I reckon they ain't fired you. What they say down there at the Commissioner's office?

TROY: Look here, Rose . . . Mr. Rand called me into his office today when I got back from talking to them people down there . . . it come from up top . . . he called me in and told me they was making me a driver.

ROSE: Troy, you kidding!

TROY: No I ain't. Ask Bono.

ROSE: Well, that's great, Troy. Now you don't have to hassle them people no more.

(*Lyons enters from the street.*)

TROY: Aw hell, I wasn't looking to see you today. I thought you was in jail. Got it all over the front page of the *Courier* about them raiding Sefus' place . . . where you be hanging out with all them thugs.

LYONS: Hey, Pop . . . that ain't got nothing to do with me. I don't go down there gambling. I go down there to sit in with the band. I ain't got nothing to do with the gambling part. They got some good music down there.

TROY: They got some rogues . . . is what they got.

LYONS: How you been, Mr. Bono? Hi, Rose.

BONO: I see where you playing down at the Crawford Grill tonight.

ROSE: How come you ain't brought Bonnie like I told you. You should have brought Bonnie with you, she ain't been over in a month of Sundays.

LYONS: I was just in the neighborhood . . . thought I'd stop by.

TROY: Here he come . . .

BONO: Your daddy got a promotion on the rubbish. He's gonna be the first colored driver. Ain't got to do nothing but sit up there and read the paper like them white fellows.

LYONS: Hey, Pop . . . if you knew how to read you'd be all right.

BONO: Naw . . . naw . . . you mean if the nigger knew how to *drive* he'd be all right. Been fighting with them people about driving and ain't even got a license. Mr. Rand know you ain't got no driver's license?

TROY: Driving ain't nothing. All you do is point the truck where you want it to go. Driving ain't nothing.

BONO: Do Mr. Rand know you ain't got no driver's license? That's what I'm talking about. I ain't asked if driving was easy. I asked if Mr. Rand know you ain't got no driver's license.

TROY: He ain't got to know. The man ain't got to know my business. Time he find out, I have two or three driver's licenses.

LYONS (*going into his pocket*): Say, look here, Pop . . .

TROY: I knew it was coming. Didn't I tell you, Bono? I know what kind of "Look here, Pop" that was. The nigger fixing to ask me for some money. It's Friday night. It's my payday. All them rogues down there on the avenue . . . the ones that ain't in jail . . . and Lyons is hopping in his shoes to get down there with them.

LYONS: See, Pop . . . if you give somebody else a chance to talk sometime, you'd see that I was fixing to pay you back your ten dollars like I told you. Here . . . I told you I'd pay you when Bonnie got paid.

TROY: Naw . . . you go ahead and keep that ten dollars. Put it in the bank. The next time you feel like you wanna come by here and ask me for something . . . you go on down there and get that.

LYONS: Here's your ten dollars, Pop. I told you I don't want you to give me nothing. I just wanted to borrow ten dollars.

TROY: Naw . . . you go on and keep that for the next time you want to ask me.

LYONS: Come on, Pop . . . here go your ten dollars.

ROSE: Why don't you go on and let the boy pay you back, Troy?

LYONS: Here you go, Rose. If you don't take it I'm gonna have to hear about it for the next six months.

(*He hands her the money.*)

ROSE: You can hand yours over here too, Troy.

TROY: You see this, Bono. You see how they do me.

BONO: Yeah, Lucille do me the same way.

(*Gabriel is heard singing offstage. He enters.*)

GABRIEL: Better get ready for the Judgment! Better get ready for . . . Hey! . . . Hey! . . . There's Troy's boy!

LYONS: How are you doing, Uncle Gabe?

GABRIEL: Lyons . . . The King of the Jungle! Rose . . . hey, Rose. Got a flower for you.

(*He takes a rose from his pocket.*)

Picked it myself. That's the same rose like you is!

ROSE: That's right nice of you, Gabe.

LYONS: What you been doing, Uncle Gabe?

GABRIEL: Oh, I been chasing hellhounds and waiting on the time to tell St. Peter to open the gates.

LYONS: You been chasing hellhounds, huh? Well . . . you doing the right thing, Uncle Gabe. Somebody got to chase them.

GABRIEL: Oh, yeah . . . I know it. The devil's strong.

The devil ain't no pushover. Hellhounds snipping at everybody's heels. But I got my trumpet waiting on the judgment time.

LYONS: Waiting on the Battle of Armageddon, huh?

GABRIEL: Ain't gonna be too much of a battle when God get to waving that Judgment sword. But the people's gonna have a hell of a time trying to get into heaven if them gates ain't open.

LYONS (*putting his arm around Gabriel*): You hear this, Pop. Uncle Gabe, you all right!

GABRIEL (*laughing with Lyons*): Lyons! King of the Jungle.

ROSE: You gonna stay for supper, Gabe. Want me to fix you a plate?

GABRIEL: I'll take a sandwich, Rose. Don't want no plate. Just wanna eat with my hands. I'll take a sandwich.

ROSE: How about you, Lyons? You staying? Got some short ribs cooking.

LYONS: Naw, I won't eat nothing till after we finished playing.

(*Pause.*)

You ought to come down and listen to me play, Pop.

TROY: I don't like that Chinese music. All that noise.

ROSE: Go on in the house and wash up, Gabe . . . I'll fix you a sandwich.

GABRIEL (*to Lyons, as he exits*): Troy's mad at me.

LYONS: What you mad at Uncle Gabe for, Pop.

ROSE: He thinks Troy's mad at him cause he moved over to Miss Pearl's.

TROY: I ain't mad at the man. He can live where he want to live at.

LYONS: What he move over there for? Miss Pearl don't like nobody.

ROSE: She don't mind him none. She treats him real nice. She just don't allow all that singing.

TROY: She don't mind that rent he be paying . . . that's what she don't mind.

ROSE: Troy, I ain't going through that with you no more. He's over there cause he want to have his own place. He can come and go as he please.

TROY: Hell, he could come and go as he please here. I wasn't stopping him. I ain't put no rules on him.

ROSE: It ain't the same thing, Troy. And you know it.

(*Gabriel comes to the door.*)

Now, that's the last I wanna hear about that. I don't wanna hear nothing else about Gabe and Miss Pearl. And next week . . .

GABRIEL: I'm ready for my sandwich, Rose.

ROSE: And next week . . . when that recruiter come from that school . . . I want you to sign that paper and go on and let Cory play football. Then that'll be the last I have to hear about that.

TROY (*to Rose as she exits into the house*): I ain't thinking about Cory nothing.

LYONS: What . . . Cory got recruited? What school he going to?

TROY: That boy walking around here smelling his piss . . . thinking he's grown. Thinking he's gonna do what he want, irrespective of what I say. Look here, Bono . . . I left the Commissioner's office and went down to the A&P . . . that boy ain't working down there. He lying to me. Telling me he got his job back . . . telling me he working weekends . . . telling me he working after school . . . Mr. Stawicki tell me he ain't working down there at all!

LYONS: Cory just growing up. He's just busting at the seams trying to fill out your shoes.

TROY: I don't care what he's doing. When he get to the point where he wanna disobey me . . . then it's time for him to move on. Bono'll tell you that. I bet he ain't never disobeyed his daddy without paying the consequences.

BONO: I ain't never had a chance. My daddy came on through . . . but I ain't never knew him to see him . . . or what he had on his mind or where he went. Just moving on through. Searching out the New Land. That's what the old folks used to call it. See a fellow moving around from place to place . . . woman to woman . . . called it searching out the New Land. I can't say if he ever found it. I come along, didn't want no kids. Didn't know if I was gonna be in one place long enough to fix on them right as their daddy. I figured I was going searching too. As it turned out I been hooked up with Lucille near about as long as your daddy been with Rose. Going on sixteen years.

TROY: Sometimes I wish I hadn't known my daddy. He ain't cared nothing about no kids. A kid to him wasn't nothing. All he wanted was for you to learn how to walk so he could start you to working. When it come time for eating . . . he ate first. If there was anything left over, that's what you got. Man would sit down and eat two chickens and give you the wing.

LYONS: You ought to stop that, Pop. Everybody feed their kids. No matter how hard times is . . . everybody care about their kids. Make sure they have something to eat.

TROY: The only thing my daddy cared about was getting them bales of cotton in to Mr. Lubin. That's the only thing that mattered to him. Sometimes I used to wonder why he was living. Wonder why the devil hadn't come and got him. "Get them bales of cotton in to Mr. Lubin" and find out he owe him money . . .

LYONS: He should have just went on and left when he saw he couldn't get nowhere. That's what I would have done.

TROY: How he gonna leave with eleven kids? And where he gonna go? He ain't knew how to do nothing but farm. No, he was trapped and I think he knew it. But I'll say this for him . . . he felt a responsibility toward us. Maybe he ain't treated us the way I felt he should have . . . but without that responsibility he could have walked off and left us . . . made his own way.

BONO: A lot of them did. Back in those days what you

talking about . . . they walk out their front door and just take on down one road or another and keep on walking.

LYONS: There you go! That's what I'm talking about.

BONO: Just keep on walking till you come to something else. Ain't you never heard of nobody having the walking blues? Well, that's what you call it when you just take off like that.

TROY: My daddy ain't had them walking blues! What you talking about? He stayed right there with his family. But he was just as evil as he could be. My mama couldn't stand him. Couldn't stand that evilness. She run off when I was about eight. She sneaked off one night after he had gone to sleep. Told me she was coming back for me. I ain't never seen her no more. All his women run off and left him. He wasn't good for nobody.

When my turn come to head out, I was fourteen and got to sniffing around Joe Canewell's daughter. Had us an old mule we called Greyboy. My daddy sent me out to do some plowing and I tied up Greyboy and went to fooling around with Joe Canewell's daughter. We done found us a nice little spot, got real cozy with each other. She about thirteen and we done figured we was grown anyway . . . so we down there enjoying ourselves . . . ain't thinking about nothing. We didn't know Greyboy had got loose and wandered back to the house and my daddy was looking for me. We down there by the creek enjoying ourselves when my daddy come up on us. Surprised us. He had them leather straps off the mule and commenced to whupping me like there was no tomorrow. I jumped up, mad and embarrassed. I was scared of my daddy. When he commenced to whupping on me . . . quite naturally I run to get out of the way.

(*Pause.*)

Now I thought he was mad cause I ain't done my work. But I see where he was chasing me off so he could have the gal for himself. When I see what the matter of it was, I lost all fear of my daddy. Right there is where I become a man . . . at fourteen years of age.

(*Pause.*)

Now it was my turn to run him off. I picked up them same reins that he had used on me. I picked up them reins and commenced to whupping on him. The gal jumped up and run off . . . and when my daddy turned to face me, I could see why the devil had never come to get him . . . cause he was the devil himself. I don't know what happened. When I woke up, I was laying right there by the creek, and Blue . . . this old dog we had . . . was licking my face. I thought I was blind. I couldn't see nothing. Both my eyes were swollen shut. I layed there and cried. I didn't know what I was gonna do. The only thing I knew was the time had come for me to leave my daddy's house.

And right there the world suddenly got big. And it was a long time before I could cut it down to where I could handle it.

Part of that cutting down was when I got to the place where I could feel him kicking in my blood and knew that the only thing that separated us was the matter of a few years.

(*Gabriel enters from the house with a sandwich.*)

LYONS: What you got there, Uncle Gabe?

GABRIEL: Got me a ham sandwich. Rose gave me a ham sandwich.

TROY: I don't know what happened to him. I done lost touch with everybody except Gabriel. But I hope he's dead. I hope he found some peace.

LYONS: That's a heavy story, Pop. I didn't know you left home when you was fourteen.

TROY: And didn't know nothing. The only part of the world I knew was the forty-two acres of Mr. Lubin's land. That's all I knew about life.

LYONS: Fourteen's kinda young to be out on your own. (*Phone rings.*) I don't even think I was ready to be out on my own at fourteen. I don't know what I would have done.

TROY: I got up from the creek and walked on down to Mobile. I was through with farming. Figured I could do better in the city. So I walked the two hundred miles to Mobile.

LYONS: Wait a minute . . . you ain't walked no two hundred miles, Pop. Ain't nobody gonna walk no two hundred miles. You talking about some walking there.

BONO: That's the only way you got anywhere back in them days.

LYONS: Shhh. Damn if I wouldn't have hitched a ride with somebody!

TROY: Who you gonna hitch it with? They ain't had no cars and things like they got now. We talking about 1918.

ROSE (*entering*): What you all out here getting into?

TROY (*to Rose*): I'm telling Lyons how good he got it. He don't know nothing about this I'm talking.

ROSE: Lyons, that was Bonnie on the phone. She say you supposed to pick her up.

LYONS: Yeah, okay, Rose.

TROY: I walked on down to Mobile and hitched up with some of them fellows that was heading this way. Got up here and found out . . . not only couldn't you get a job . . . you couldn't find no place to live. I thought I was in freedom. Shhh. Colored folks living down there on the riverbanks in whatever kind of shelter they could find for themselves. Right down there under the Brady Street Bridge. Living in shacks made of sticks and tarpaper. Messed around there and went from bad to worse. Started stealing. First it was food. Then I figured, hell, if I steal money I can buy me some food. Buy me some shoes too! One thing led to another. Met your mama. I was young and anxious to be a man. Met your mama and had you. What I do that for? Now I got to worry about feeding you and her. Got to steal three times as much. Went out one day looking for somebody to rob . . . that's what I was, a robber. I'll tell you the truth. I'm ashamed of it today. But it's the truth. Went to rob this fellow . . . pulled out my knife . . . and he pulled out a gun. Shot me in the chest. It felt just like somebody had taken a hot branding iron and laid it on me. When he shot me I jumped at him with my knife. They told me I killed him and they put me in the penitentiary and locked me up for fifteen years. That's where I met Bono. That's where I learned how to play baseball. Got out that place and your mama had taken you and went on to make life without me. Fifteen years was a long time for her to wait. But that fifteen years cured me of that robbing stuff. Rose'll tell you. She asked me when I met her if I had gotten all that foolishness out of my system. And I told her, "Baby, it's you and baseball all what count with me." You hear me, Bono? I meant it too. She say "Which one comes first?" I told her, "Baby, ain't no doubt it's baseball . . . but you stick and get old with me and we'll both outlive this baseball." Am I right, Rose? And it's true.

ROSE: Man, hush your mouth. You ain't said no such thing. Talking about, "Baby, you know you'll always be number one with me." That's what you was talking.

TROY: You hear that, Bono. That's why I love her.

BONO: Rose'll keep you straight. You get off the track, she'll straighten you up.

ROSE: Lyons, you better get on up and get Bonnie. She waiting on you.

LYONS (gets up to go): Hey, Pop, why don't you come on down to the Grill and hear me play?

TROY: I ain't going down there. I'm too old to be sitting around in them clubs.

BONO: You got to be good to play down at the Grill.

LYONS: Come on, Pop . . .

TROY: I got to get up in the morning.

LYONS: You ain't got to stay long.

TROY: Naw, I'm gonna get my supper and go on to bed.

LYONS: Well, I got to go. I'll see you again.

TROY: Don't you come around my house on my payday.

ROSE: Pick up the phone and let somebody know you coming. And bring Bonnie with you. You know I'm always glad to see her.

LYONS: Yeah, I'll do that, Rose. You take care now. See you, Pop. See you, Mr. Bono. See you, Uncle Gabe.

GABRIEL: Lyons! King of the Jungle!

(Lyons exits.)

TROY: Is supper ready, woman? Me and you got some business to take care of. I'm gonna tear it up too.

ROSE: Troy, I done told you now!

TROY (puts his arm around Bono): Aw hell, woman . . .

this is Bono. Bono like family. I done known this nigger since . . . how long I done know you?

BONO: It's been a long time.

TROY: I done known this nigger since Skippy was a pup. Me and him done been through some times.

BONO: You sure right about that.

TROY: Hell, I done know him longer than I known you. And we still standing shoulder to shoulder. Hey, look here, Bono . . . a man can't ask for no more than that.

(Drinks to him.)

I love you, nigger.

BONO: Hell, I love you too . . . but I got to get home see my woman. You got yours in hand. I got to go get mine.

(Bono starts to exit as Cory enters the yard, dressed in his football uniform. He gives Troy a hard, uncompromising look.)

CORY: What you do that for, Pop?

(He throws his helmet down in the direction of Troy.)

ROSE: What's the matter? Cory . . . what's the matter?

CORY: Papa done went up to the school and told Coach Zellman I can't play football no more. Wouldn't even let me play the game. Told him to tell the recruiter not to come.

ROSE: Troy . . .

TROY: What you Troying me for. Yeah, I did it. And the boy know why I did it.

CORY: Why you wanna do that to me? That was the one chance I had.

ROSE: Ain't nothing wrong with Cory playing football, Troy.

TROY: The boy lied to me. I told the nigger if he wanna play football . . . to keep up his chores and hold down that job at the A&P. That was the conditions. Stopped down there to see Mr. Stawicki . . .

CORY: I can't work after school during the football season, Pop! I tried to tell you that Mr. Stawicki's holding my job for me. You don't never want to listen to nobody. And then you wanna go and do this to me!

TROY: I ain't done nothing to you. You done it to yourself.

CORY: Just cause you didn't have a chance! You just scared I'm gonna be better than you, that's all.

TROY: Come here.

ROSE: Troy . . .

(Cory reluctantly crosses over to Troy.)

TROY: All right! See. You done made a mistake.

CORY: I didn't even do nothing!

TROY: I'm gonna tell you what your mistake was. See . . . you swung at the ball and didn't hit it. That's strike one. See, you in the batter's box now. You swung and you missed. That's strike one. Don't you strike out!

(Lights fade to black.)

ACT II • *Scene I*

(*The following morning. Cory is at the tree hitting the ball with the bat. He tries to mimic Troy, but his swing is awkward, less sure. Rose enters from the house.*)

ROSE: Cory, I want you to help me with this cupboard.

CORY: I ain't quitting the team. I don't care what Poppa say.

ROSE: I'll talk to him when he gets back. He had to go see about your Uncle Gabe. The police done arrested him. Say he was disturbing the peace. He'll be back directly. Come on in here and help me clean out the top of this cupboard.

(*Cory exits into the house. Rose sees Troy and Bono coming down the alley.*)

Troy . . . what they say down there?

TROY: Ain't said nothing. I give them fifty dollars and they let him go. I'll talk to you about it. Where's Cory.

ROSE: He's in there helping me clean out these cupboards.

TROY: Tell him to get his butt out here.

(*Troy and Bono go over to the pile of wood. Bono picks up the saw and begins sawing.*)

TROY (*to Bono*): All they want is the money. That makes six or seven times I done went down there and got him. See me coming they stick out their *hands*.

BONO: Yeah. I know what you mean. That's all they care about . . . that money. They don't care about what's right.

(*Pause.*)

Nigger, why you got to go and get some hard wood? You ain't doing nothing but building a little old fence. Get you some soft pine wood. That's all you need.

TROY: I know what I'm doing. This is outside wood. You put pine wood inside the house. Pine wood is inside wood. This here is outside wood. Now you tell me where the fence is gonna be?

BONO: You don't need this wood. You can put it up with pine wood and it'll stand as long as you gonna be here looking at it.

TROY: How you know how long I'm gonna be here, nigger? Hell, I might just live forever. Live longer than old man Horsely.

BONO: That's what Magee used to say.

TROY: Magee's a damn fool. Now you tell me who you ever heard of gonna pull their own teeth with a pair of rusty pliers.

BONO: The old folks . . . my granddaddy used to pull his teeth with pliers. They ain't had no dentists for the colored folks back then.

TROY: Get clean pliers! You understand? Clean pliers! Sterilize them! Besides we ain't living back then. All Magee had to do was walk over to Doc Goldblum's.

BONO: I see where you and that Tallahassee gal . . . that Alberta . . . I see where you all done got tight.

TROY: What you mean "got tight"?

BONO: I see where you be laughing and joking with her all the time.

TROY: I laughs and jokes with all of them, Bono. You know me.

BONO: That ain't the kind of laughing and joking I'm talking about.

(*Cory enters from the house.*)

CORY: How you doing, Mr. Bono?

TROY: Cory? Get that saw from Bono and cut some wood. He talking about the wood's too hard to cut. Stand back there, Jim, and let that young boy show you how it's done.

BONO: He's sure welcome to it.

(*Cory takes the saw and begins to cut the wood.*)

Whew-e-e! Look at that. Big old strong boy. Look like Joe Louis. Hell, must be getting old the way I'm watching that boy whip through that wood.

CORY: I don't see why Mama want a fence around the yard noways.

TROY: Damn if I know either. What the hell she keeping out with it? She ain't got nothing nobody want.

BONO: Some people build fences to keep people out . . . and other people build fences to keep people in. Rose wants to hold on to you all. She loves you.

TROY: Hell, nigger, I don't need nobody to tell me my wife loves me, Cory . . . go on in the house and see if you can find that other saw.

CORY: Where's it at?

TROY: I said find it! Look for it till you find it!

(*Cory exits into the house.*)

What's that supposed to mean? Wanna keep us in?

BONO: Troy . . . I done known you seem like damn near my whole life. You and Rose both. I done know both of you all for a long time. I remember when you met Rose. When you was hitting them baseball out the park. A lot of them old gals was after you then. You had the pick of the litter. When you picked Rose, I was happy for you. That was the first time I knew you had any sense. I said . . . My man Troy knows what he's doing . . . I'm gonna follow this nigger . . . he might take me somewhere. I been following you too. I done learned a whole heap of things about life watching you. I done learned how to tell where the shit lies. How to tell it from the alfalfa. You done learned me a lot of things. You showed me how to not make the same mistakes . . . to take life as it comes along and keep putting one foot in front of the other.

(*Pause.*)

Rose a good woman, Troy.

TROY: Hell, nigger, I know she a good woman. I been

married to her for eighteen years. What you got on your mind, Bono?

BONO: I just say she a good woman. Just like I say anything. I ain't got to have nothing on my mind.

TROY: You just gonna say she a good woman and leave it hanging out there like that? Why you telling me she a good woman?

BONO: She loves you, Troy. Rose loves you.

TROY: You saying I don't measure up. That's what you trying to say. I don't measure up cause I'm seeing this other gal. I know what you trying to say.

BONO: I know what Rose means to you, Troy. I'm just trying to say I don't want to see you mess up.

TROY: Yeah, I appreciate that, Bono. If you was messing around on Lucille I'd be telling you the same thing.

BONO: Well, that's all I got to say. I just say that because I love you both.

TROY: Hell, you know me . . . I wasn't out there looking for nothing. You can't find a better woman than Rose. I know that. But seems like this woman just stuck onto me where I can't shake her loose. I done wrestled with it, tried to throw her off me . . . but she just stuck on tighter. Now she's stuck on for good.

BONO: You's in control . . . that's what you tell me all the time. You responsible for what you do.

TROY: I ain't ducking the responsibility of it. As long as it sets right in my heart . . . then I'm okay. Cause that's all I listen to. It'll tell me right from wrong every time. And I ain't talking about doing Rose no bad turn. I love Rose. She done carried me a long ways and I love and respect her for that.

BONO: I know you do. That's why I don't want to see you hurt her. But what you gonna do when she find out? What you got then? If you try and juggle both of them . . . sooner or later you gonna drop one of them. That's common sense.

TROY: Yeah, I hear what you saying, Bono. I been trying to figure a way to work it out.

BONO: Work it out right, Troy. I don't want to be getting all up between you and Rose's business . . . but work it so it come out right.

TROY: Ah hell, I get all up between you and Lucille's business. When you gonna get that woman that refrigerator she been wanting? Don't tell me you ain't got no money now. I know who your banker is. Mellon don't need that money bad as Lucille want that refrigerator. I'll tell you that.

BONO: Tell you what I'll do . . . when you finish building this fence for Rose . . . I'll buy Lucille that refrigerator.

TROY: You done stuck your foot in your mouth now!

(*Troy grabs up a board and begins to saw. Bono starts to walk out the yard.*)

Hey, nigger . . . where you going?

BONO: I'm going home. I know you don't expect me to help you now. I'm protecting my money. I wanna see you put that fence up by yourself. That's what I want to see. You'll be here another six months without me.

TROY: Nigger, you ain't right.

BONO: When it comes to my money . . . I'm right as fireworks on the Fourth of July.

TROY: All right, we gonna see now. You better get out your bankbook.

(*Bono exits, and Troy continues to work. Rose enters from the house.*)

ROSE: What they say down there? What's happening with Gabe?

TROY: I went down there and got him out. Cost me fifty dollars. Say he was disturbing the peace. Judge set up a hearing for him in three weeks. Say to show cause why he shouldn't be recommitted.

ROSE: What was he doing that cause them to arrest him?

TROY: Some kids was teasing him and he run them off home. Say he was howling and carrying on. Some folks seen him and called the police. That's all it was.

ROSE: Well, what's you say? What'd you tell the judge?

TROY: Told him I'd look after him. It didn't make no sense to recommit the man. He stuck out his big greasy palm and told me to give him fifty dollars and take him on home.

ROSE: Where's he at now? Where'd he go off to?

TROY: He's gone on about his business. He don't need nobody to hold his hand.

ROSE: Well, I don't know. Seem like that would be the best place for him if they did put him into the hospital. I know what you're gonna say. But that's what I think would be best.

TROY: The man done had his life ruined fighting for what? And they wanna take and lock him up. Let him be free. He don't bother nobody.

ROSE: Well, everybody got their own way of looking at it I guess. Come on and get your lunch. I got a bowl of lima beans and some cornbread in the oven. Come on get something to eat. Ain't no sense you fretting over Gabe.

(*Rose turns to go into the house.*)

TROY: Rose . . . got something to tell you.

ROSE: Well, come on . . . wait till I get this food on the table.

TROY: Rose!

(*She stops and turns around.*)

I don't know how to say this.

(*Pause.*)

I can't explain it none. It just sort of grows on you till it gets out of hand. It starts out like a little bush . . . and the next thing you know it's a whole forest.

ROSE: Troy . . . what is you talking about?

TROY: I'm talking, woman, let me talk. I'm trying to find a way to tell you . . . I'm gonna be a daddy. I'm gonna be somebody's daddy.

ROSE: Troy . . . you're not telling me this? You're gonna be . . . what?

TROY: Rose . . . now . . . see . . .

ROSE: You telling me you gonna be somebody's daddy? You telling your *wife* this?

(*Gabriel enters from the street. He carries a rose in his hand.*)

GABRIEL: Hey, Troy! Hey, Rose!

ROSE: I have to wait eighteen years to hear something like this.

GABRIEL: Hey, Rose . . . I got a flower for you.

(*He hands it to her.*)

That's a rose. Same rose like you is.

ROSE: Thanks, Gabe.

GABRIEL: Troy, you ain't mad at me is you? Them bad mens come and put me away. You ain't mad at me is you?

TROY: Naw, Gabe, I ain't mad at you.

ROSE: Eighteen years and you wanna come with this.

GABRIEL (*takes a quarter out of his pocket*): See what I got? Got a brand new quarter.

TROY: Rose . . . it's just . . .

ROSE: Ain't nothing you can say, Troy. Ain't no way of explaining that.

GABRIEL: Fellow that give me this quarter had a whole mess of them. I'm gonna keep this quarter till it stop shining.

ROSE: Gabe, go on in the house there. I got some watermelon in the frigidaire. Go on and get you a piece.

GABRIEL: Say, Rose . . . you know I was chasing hellhounds and them bad mens come and get me and take me away. Troy helped me. He come down there and told them they better let me go before he beat them up. Yeah, he did!

ROSE: You go on and get you a piece of watermelon, Gabe. Them bad mens is gone now.

GABRIEL: Okay, Rose . . . gonna get me some watermelon. The kind with the stripes on it.

(*Gabriel exits into the house.*)

ROSE: Why, Troy? Why? After all these years to come dragging this in to me now. It don't make no sense at your age. I could have expected this ten or fifteen years ago, but not now.

TROY: Age ain't got nothing to do with it, Rose.

ROSE: I done tried to be everything a wife should be. Everything a wife could be. Been married eighteen years and I got to live to see the day you tell me you been seeing another woman and done fathered a child by her. And you know I ain't never wanted no half nothing in my family. My whole family is half. Everybody got different fathers and mothers . . . my two sisters and my brother. Can't hardly tell who's who. Can't never sit down and talk about Papa and Mama. It's your papa and your mama and my papa and my mama . . .

TROY: Rose . . . stop it now.

ROSE: I ain't never wanted that for none of my children. And now you wanna drag your behind in here and tell me something like this.

TROY: You ought to know. It's time for you to know.

ROSE: Well, I don't want to know, goddamn it!

TROY: I can't just make it go away. It's done now. I can't wish the circumstance of the thing away.

ROSE: And you don't want to either. Maybe you want to wish me and my boy away. Maybe that's what you want? Well, you can't wish us away. I've got eighteen years of my life invested in you. You ought to have stayed upstairs in my bed where you belong.

TROY: Rose . . . now listen to me . . . we can get a handle on this thing. We can talk this out . . . come to an understanding.

ROSE: All of a sudden it's "we." Where was "we" at when you was down there rolling around with some godforsaken woman? "We" should have come to an understanding before you started making a damn fool of yourself. You're a day late and a dollar short when it comes to an understanding with me.

TROY: It's just . . . She gives me a different idea . . . a different understanding about myself. I can step out of this house and get away from the pressures and problems . . . be a different man. I ain't got to wonder how I'm gonna pay the bills or get the roof fixed. I can just be a part of myself that I ain't never been.

ROSE: What I want to know . . . is do you plan to continue seeing her. That's all you can say to me.

TROY: I can sit up in her house and laugh. Do you understand what I'm saying. I can laugh out loud . . . and it feels good. It reaches all the way down to the bottom of my shoes.

(*Pause.*)

Rose, I can't give that up.

ROSE: Maybe you ought to go on and stay down there with her . . . if she's a better woman than me.

TROY: It ain't about nobody being a better woman or nothing. Rose, you ain't the blame. A man couldn't ask for no woman to be a better wife than you've been. I'm responsible for it. I done locked myself into a pattern trying to take care of you all that I forgot about myself.

ROSE: What the hell was I there for? That was my job, not somebody else's.

TROY: Rose, I done tried all my life to live decent . . . to live a clean . . . hard . . . useful life. I tried to be a good husband to you. In every way I knew how. Maybe I come into the world backwards, I don't know. But . . . you born with two strikes on you before you come to the plate. You got to guard it closely . . . always looking for the curve ball on the inside corner. You can't afford to let none get past you. You can't afford a call strike. If you going down . . . you going down swinging. Everything lined up against you. What you gonna do. I fooled them, Rose. I bunted. When I found you and Cory and a halfway decent job . . . I was safe. Couldn't nothing touch me. I wasn't gonna strike out no more. I wasn't going back to the penitentiary. I wasn't gonna lay in the streets with a bottle of wine. I was safe. I had me a family. A job. I wasn't gonna get that last strike. I was on first looking for one of them boys to knock me in. To get me home.

ROSE: You should have stayed in my bed, Troy.

TROY: Then when I saw that gal . . . she firmed up my backbone. And I got to thinking that if I tried . . . I just might be able to steal second. Do you understand after eighteen years I wanted to steal second.

ROSE: You should have held me tight. You should have grabbed me and held on.

TROY: I stood on first base for eighteen years and I thought . . . well, goddamn it . . . go on for it!

ROSE: We're not talking about baseball! We're talking about you going off to lay in bed with another woman . . . and then bring it home to me. That's what we're talking about. We ain't talking about no baseball.

TROY: Rose, you're not listening to me. I'm trying the best I can to explain it to you. It's not easy for me to admit that I been standing in the same place for eighteen years.

ROSE: I been standing with you! I been right here with you, Troy. I got a life too. I gave eighteen years of my life to stand in the same spot with you. Don't you think I ever wanted other things? Don't you think I had dreams and hopes? What about my life? What about me. Don't you think it ever crossed my mind to want to know other men? That I wanted to lay up somewhere and forget about my responsibilities? That I wanted someone to make me laugh so I could feel good? You not the only one who's got wants and needs. But I held on to you, Troy. I took all my feelings, my wants and needs, my dreams . . . and I buried them inside you. I planted a seed and watched and prayed over it. I planted myself inside you and waited to bloom. And it didn't take me no eighteen years to find out the soil was hard and rocky and it wasn't never gonna bloom.

But I held on to you, Troy. I held you tighter. You was my husband. I owed you everything I had. Every part of me I could find to give you. And upstairs in that room . . . with the darkness falling in on me . . . I gave everything I had to try and erase the doubt that you wasn't the finest man in the world. And wherever you was going . . . I wanted to be there with you. Cause you was my husband. Cause that's the only way I was gonna survive as your wife. You always talking about what you give . . . and what you don't have to give. But you take too. You take . . . and don't even know nobody's giving!

(*Rose turns to exit into the house; Troy grabs her arm.*)

TROY: You say I take and don't give!

ROSE: Troy! You're hurting me!

TROY: You say I take and don't give.

ROSE: Troy . . . you're hurting my arm! Let go!

TROY: I done give you everything I got. Don't you tell that lie on me.

ROSE: Troy!

TROY: Don't you tell that lie on me!

(*Cory enters from the house.*)

CORY: Mama!

ROSE: Troy. You're hurting me.

TROY: Don't you tell me about no taking and giving.

(*Cory comes up behind Troy and grabs him. Troy, surprised, is thrown off balance just as Cory throws a glancing blow that catches him on the chest and knocks him down. Troy is stunned, as is Cory.*)

ROSE: Troy. Troy. No!

(*Troy gets to his feet and starts at Cory.*)

Troy . . . no. Please! Troy!

(*Rose pulls on Troy to hold him back. Troy stops himself.*)

TROY (*to Cory*): All right. That's strike two. You stay away from around me, boy. Don't you strike out. You living with a full count. Don't you strike out.

(*Troy exits out the yard as the lights go down.*)

Scene II

(*It is six months later, early afternoon. Troy enters from the house and starts to exit the yard. Rose enters from the house.*)

ROSE: Troy, I want to talk to you.

TROY: All of a sudden, after all this time, you want to talk to me, huh? You ain't wanted to talk to me for months. You ain't wanted to talk to me last night. You ain't wanted no part of me then. What you wanna talk to me about now?

ROSE: Tomorrow's Friday.

TROY: I know what day tomorrow is. You think I don't know tomorrow's Friday? My whole life I ain't done nothing but look to see Friday coming and you got to tell me it's Friday.

ROSE: I want to know if you're coming home.

TROY: I always come home, Rose. You know that. There ain't never been a night I ain't come home.

ROSE: That ain't what I mean . . . and you know it. I want to know if you're coming straight home after work.

TROY: I figure I'd cash my check . . . hang out at Taylors' with the boys . . . maybe play a game of checkers . . .

ROSE: Troy, I can't live like this. I won't live like this. You livin' on borrowed time with me. It's been going on six months now you ain't been coming home.

TROY: I be here every night. Every night of the year. That's 365 days.

ROSE: I want you to come home tomorrow after work.

TROY: Rose . . . I don't mess up my pay. You know that now. I take my pay and I give it to you. I don't have no money but what you give me back. I just want to have a little time to myself . . . a little time to enjoy life.

ROSE: What about me? When's my time to enjoy life?

TROY: I don't know what to tell you, Rose. I'm doing the best I can.

ROSE: You ain't been home from work but time enough to change your clothes and run out . . . and you wanna call that the best you can do?

TROY: I'm going over to the hospital to see Alberta. She went into the hospital this afternoon. Look like she might have the baby early. I won't be gone long.

ROSE: Well, you ought to know. They went over to Miss Pearl's and got Gabe today. She said you told them to go ahead and lock him up.

TROY: I ain't said no such thing. Whoever told you that is telling a lie. Pearl ain't doing nothing but telling a big fat lie.

ROSE: She ain't had to tell me. I read it on the papers.

TROY: I ain't told them nothing of the kind.

ROSE: I saw it right there on the papers.

TROY: What it say, huh?

ROSE: It said you told them to take him.

TROY: Then they screwed that up, just the way they screw up everything. I ain't worried about what they got on the paper.

ROSE: Say the government send part of his check to the hospital and the other part to you.

TROY: I ain't got nothing to do with that if that's the way it works. I ain't made up the rules about how it work.

ROSE: You did Gabe just like you did Cory. You wouldn't sign the paper for Cory . . . but you signed for Gabe. You signed that paper.

(The telephone is heard ringing inside the house.)

TROY: I told you I ain't signed nothing, woman! The only thing I signed was the release form. Hell, I can't read, I don't know what they had on that paper! I ain't signed nothing about sending Gabe away.

ROSE: I said send him to the hospital . . . you said let him be free . . . now you done went down there and signed him to the hospital for half his money. You went back on yourself, Troy. You gonna have to answer for that.

TROY: See now . . . you been over there talking to Miss Pearl. She done got mad cause she ain't getting Gabe's rent money. That's all it is. She's liable to say anything.

ROSE: Troy, I seen where you signed the paper.

TROY: You ain't seen nothing I signed. What she doing got papers on my brother anyway? Miss Pearl telling a big fat lie. And I'm gonna tell her about it too! You ain't seen nothing I signed. Say . . . you ain't seen nothing I signed.

(Rose exits into the house to answer the telephone. Presently she returns.)

ROSE: Troy . . . that was the hospital. Alberta had the baby.

TROY: What she have? What is it?

ROSE: It's a girl.

TROY: I better get on down to the hospital to see her.

ROSE: Troy . . .

TROY: Rose . . . I got to go see her now. That's only right . . . what's the matter . . . the baby's all right, ain't it?

ROSE: Alberta died having the baby.

TROY: Died . . . you say she's dead? Alberta's dead?

ROSE: They said they done all they could. They couldn't do nothing for her.

TROY: The baby? How's the baby?

ROSE: They say it's healthy. I wonder who's gonna bury her.

TROY: She had family, Rose. She wasn't living in the world by herself.

ROSE: I know she wasn't living in the world by herself.

TROY: Next thing you gonna want to know if she had any insurance.

ROSE: Troy, you ain't got to talk like that.

TROY: That's the first thing that jumped out your mouth. "Who's gonna bury her?" Like I'm fixing to take on that task for myself.

ROSE: I am your wife. Don't push me away.

TROY: I ain't pushing nobody away. Just give me some space. That's all. Just give me some room to breathe.

(Rose exits into the house. Troy walks about the yard.)

TROY (*with a quiet rage that threatens to consume him*): All right . . . Mr. Death. See now . . . I'm gonna tell you what I'm gonna do. I'm gonna take and build me a fence around this yard. See? I'm gonna build me a fence around what belongs to me. And then I want you to stay on the other side. See? You stay over there until you're ready for me. Then you come on. Bring your army. Bring your sickle. Bring your wrestling clothes. I ain't gonna fall down on my vigilance this time. You ain't gonna sneak up on me no more. When you ready for me . . . when the top of your list say Troy Maxson . . . that's when you come around here. You come up and knock on the front door. Ain't nobody else got nothing to do with this. This is between you and me. Man to man. You stay on the other side of that fence until you ready for me. Then you come up and knock on the front door. Anytime you want. I'll be ready for you.

(The lights go down to black.)

Scene III

(The lights come up on the porch. It is late evening three days later. Rose sits listening to the ball game waiting for Troy. The final out of the game is made and Rose switches off the radio. Troy enters the yard carrying an infant wrapped in blankets. He stands back from the house and calls.)

(*Rose enters and stands on the porch. There is a long, awkward silence, the weight of which grows heavier with each passing second.*)

TROY: Rose . . . I'm standing here with my daughter in my arms. She ain't but a wee bittie little old thing. She don't know nothing about grownups' business. She innocent . . . and she ain't got no mama.

ROSE: What you telling me for, Troy?

(*She turns and exits into the house.*)

TROY: Well . . . I guess we'll just sit out here on the porch.

(*He sits down on the porch. There is an awkward indelicateness about the way he handles the baby. His largeness engulfs and seems to swallow it. He speaks loud enough for Rose to hear.*)

A man's got to do what's right for him. I ain't sorry for nothing I done. It felt right in my heart.

(*To the baby.*)

What you smiling at? Your daddy's a big man. Got these great big old hands. But sometimes he's scared. And right now your daddy's scared cause we sitting out here and ain't got no home. Oh, I been homeless before. I ain't had no little baby with me. But I been homeless. You just be out on the road by your lonesome and you see one of them trains coming and you just kinda go like this . . .

(*He sings as a lullaby.*)

Please, Mr. Engineer let a man ride the line
Please, Mr. Engineer let a man ride the line
I ain't got no ticket please let me ride the blinds

(*Rose enters from the house. Troy hearing her steps behind him, stands and faces her.*)

She's my daughter, Rose. My own flesh and blood. I can't deny her no more than I can deny them boys.

(*Pause.*)

You and them boys is my family. You and them and this child is all I got in the world. So I guess what I'm saying is . . . I'd appreciate it if you'd help me take care of her.

ROSE: Okay, Troy . . . you're right. I'll take care of your baby for you . . . cause . . . like you say . . . she's innocent . . . and you can't visit the sins of the father upon the child. A motherless child has got a hard time.

(*She takes the baby from him.*)

From right now . . . this child got a mother. But you a womanless man.

(*Rose turns and exits into the house with the baby. Lights go down to black.*)

Scene IV

(*It is two months later. Lyons enters from the street. He knocks on the door and calls.*)

LYONS: Hey, Rose! (*Pause.*) Rose!

ROSE (*from inside the house*): Stop that yelling. You gonna wake up Raynell. I just got her to sleep.

LYONS: I just stopped by to pay Papa this twenty dollars I owe him. Where's Papa at?

ROSE: He should be here in a minute. I'm getting ready to go down to the church. Sit down and wait on him.

LYONS: I got to go pick up Bonnie over her mother's house.

ROSE: Well, sit it down there on the table. He'll get it.

LYONS (*enters the house and sets the money on the table*): Tell Papa I said thanks. I'll see you again.

ROSE: All right, Lyons. We'll see you.

(*Lyons starts to exit as Cory enters.*)

CORY: Hey, Lyons.

LYONS: What's happening, Cory. Say man, I'm sorry I missed your graduation. You know I had a gig and couldn't get away. Otherwise, I would have been there, man. So what you doing?

CORY: I'm trying to find a job.

LYONS: Yeah I know how that go, man. It's rough out here. Jobs are scarce.

CORY: Yeah, I know.

LYONS: Look here, I got to run. Talk to Papa . . . he know some people. He'll be able to help get you a job. Talk to him . . . see what he say.

CORY: Yeah . . . all right, Lyons.

LYONS: You take care. I'll talk to you soon. We'll find some time to talk.

(*Lyons exits the yard. Cory wanders over to the tree, picks up the bat, and assumes a batting stance. He studies an imaginary pitcher and swings. Dissatisfied with the result, he tries again. Troy enters. They eye each other for a beat. Cory puts the bat down and exits the yard. Troy starts into the house as Rose exits with Raynell. She is carrying a cake.*)

TROY: I'm coming in and everybody's going out.

ROSE: I'm taking this cake down to the church for the bake sale. Lyons was by to see you. He stopped by to pay you your twenty dollars. It's laying in there on the table.

TROY (*going into his pocket*): Well . . . here go this money.

ROSE: Put it in there on the table, Troy. I'll get it.

TROY: What time you coming back?

ROSE: Ain't no use in you studying me. It don't matter what time I come back.

TROY: I just asked you a question, woman. What's the matter . . . can't I ask you a question?

ROSE: Troy, I don't want to go into it. Your dinner's in there on the stove. All you got to do is heat it up. And don't you be eating the rest of them cakes in there.

I'm coming back for them. We having a bake sale at the church tomorrow.

(*Rose exits the yard. Troy sits down on the steps, takes a pint bottle from his pocket, opens it, and drinks. He begins to sing.*)

TROY: Hear it ring! Hear it ring!
  Had an old dog his name was Blue
  You know Blue was mighty true
  You know Blue as a good old dog
  Blue trees a possum in a hollow log
  You know from that he was a good old dog

(*Bono enters the yard.*)

BONO: Hey, Troy.

TROY: Hey, what's happening, Bono?

BONO: I just thought I'd stop by to see you.

TROY: What you stop by and see me for? You ain't stopped by in a month of Sundays. Hell, I must owe you money or something.

BONO: Since you got your promotion I can't keep up with you. Used to see you every day. Now I don't even know what route you working.

TROY: They keep switching me around. Got me out in Greentree now . . . hauling white folks' garbage.

BONO: Greentree, huh? You lucky, at least you ain't got to be lifting them barrels. Damn if they ain't getting heavier. I'm gonna put in my two years and call it quits.

TROY: I'm thinking about retiring myself.

BONO: You got it easy. You can *drive* for another five years.

TROY: It ain't the same, Bono. It ain't like working the back of the truck. Ain't got nobody to talk to . . . feel like you working by yourself. Naw, I'm thinking about retiring. How's Lucille?

BONO: She all right. Her arthritis get to acting up on her sometime. Saw Rose on my way in. She going down to the church, huh?

TROY: Yeah, she took up going down there. All them preachers looking for somebody to fatten their pockets.

(*Pause.*)

  Got some gin here.

BONO: Naw, thanks. I just stopped by to say hello.

TROY: Hell, nigger . . . you can take a drink. I ain't never known you to say no to a drink. You ain't got to work tomorrow.

BONO: I just stopped by. I'm fixing to go over to Skinner's. We got us a domino game going over his house every Friday.

TROY: Nigger, you can't play no dominoes. I used to whup you four games out of five.

BONO: Well, that learned me. I'm getting better.

TROY: Yeah? Well, that's all right.

BONO: Look here . . . I got to be getting on. Stop by sometime, huh?

TROY: Yeah, I'll do that, Bono. Lucille told Rose you bought her a new refrigerator.

BONO: Yeah, Rose told Lucille you had finally built your fence . . . so I figured we'd call it even.

TROY: I knew you would.

BONO: Yeah . . . okay. I'll be talking to you.

TROY: Yeah, take care, Bono. Good to see you. I'm gonna stop over.

BONO: Yeah. Okay, Troy.

(*Bono exits. Troy drinks from the bottle.*)

TROY: Old Blue died and I dig his grave
  Let him down with a golden chain
  Every night when I hear old Blue bark
  I know Blue treed a possum in Noah's Ark.
  Hear it ring! Hear it ring!

(*Cory enters the yard. They eye each other for a beat. Troy is sitting in the middle of the steps. Cory walks over.*)

CORY: I got to get by.

TROY: Say what? What's you say?

CORY: You in my way. I got to get by.

TROY: You got to get by where? This is my house. Bought and paid for. In full. Took me fifteen years. And if you wanna go in my house and I'm sitting on the steps . . . you say excuse me. Like your mama taught you.

CORY: Come on, Pop . . . I got to get by.

(*Cory starts to maneuver his way past Troy. Troy grabs his leg and shoves him back.*)

TROY: You just gonna walk over top of me?

CORY: I live here too!

TROY (*advancing toward him*): You just gonna walk over top of me in my own house?

CORY: I ain't scared of you.

TROY: I ain't asked if you was scared of me. I asked you if you was fixing to walk over top of me in my own house? That's the question. You ain't gonna say excuse me? You just gonna walk over top of me?

CORY: If you wanna put it like that.

TROY: How else am I gonna put it?

CORY: I was walking by you to go into the house cause you sitting on the steps drunk, singing to yourself. You can put it like that.

TROY: Without saying excuse me???

(*Cory doesn't respond.*)

  I asked you a question. Without saying excuse me???

CORY: I ain't got to say excuse me to you. You don't count around here no more.

TROY: Oh, I see . . . I don't count around here no more. You ain't got to say excuse me to your daddy. All of a sudden you done got so grown that your daddy don't count around here no more . . . Around here in his own house and yard that he done paid for with the sweat of his brow. You done got so grown to where you gonna take over. You gonna take over my house. Is that right? You gonna wear my pants. You gonna go in there and stretch out on my bed. You ain't got to say excuse me cause I don't count around here no more. Is that right?

CORY: That's right. You always talking this dumb stuff. Now, why don't you just get out my way.

TROY: I guess you got someplace to sleep and something to put in your belly. You got that, huh? You got that? That's what you need. You got that, huh?

CORY: You don't know what I got. You ain't got to worry about what I got.

TROY: You right! You one hundred percent right! I done spent the last seventeen years worrying about what you got. Now it's your turn, see? I'll tell you what to do. You grown . . . we done established that. You a man. Now, let's see you act like one. Turn your behind around and walk out this yard. And when you get out there in the alley . . . you can forget about this house. See? 'Cause this is my house. You go on and be a man and get your own house. You can forget about this. 'Cause this is mine. You go on and get yours 'cause I'm through with doing for you.

CORY: You talking about what you did for me . . . what'd you ever give me?

TROY: Them feet and bones! That pumping heart, nigger! I give you more than anybody else is ever gonna give you.

CORY: You ain't never gave me nothing! You ain't never done nothing but hold me back. Afraid I was gonna be better than you. All you ever did was try and make me scared of you. I used to tremble every time you called my name. Every time I heard your footsteps in the house. Wondering all the time . . . what's Papa gonna say if I do this? . . . What's he gonna say if I do that? . . . What's Papa gonna say if I turn on the radio? And Mama, too . . . she tries . . . but she's scared of you.

TROY: You leave your mama out of this. She ain't got nothing to do with this.

CORY: I don't know how she stand you . . . after what you did to her.

TROY: I told you to leave your mama out of this!

(*He advances toward Cory.*)

CORY: What you gonna do . . . give me a whupping? You can't whup me no more. You're too old. You just an old man.

TROY (*shoves him on his shoulder*): Nigger! That's what you are. You just another nigger on the street to me!

CORY: You crazy! You know that?

TROY: Go on now! You got the devil in you. Get on away from me!

CORY: You just a crazy old man . . . talking about I got the devil in me.

TROY: Yeah, I'm crazy! If you don't get on the other side of that yard . . . I'm gonna show you how crazy I am! Go on . . . get the hell out of my yard.

CORY: It ain't your yard. You took Uncle Gabe's money he got from the army to buy this house and then you put him out.

TROY (*Troy advances on Cory*): Get your black ass out of my yard!

(*Troy's advance backs Cory up against the tree. Cory grabs up the bat.*)

CORY: I ain't going nowhere! Come on . . . put me out! I ain't scared of you.

TROY: That's my bat!

CORY: Come on!

TROY: Put my bat down!

CORY: Come on, put me out.

(*Cory swings at Troy, who backs across the yard.*)

What's the matter? You so bad . . . put me out!

(*Troy advances toward Cory.*)

CORY (*backing up*): Come on! Come on!

TROY: You're gonna have to use it! You wanna draw that bat back on me . . . you're gonna have to use it.

CORY: Come on! . . . Come on!

(*Cory swings the bat at Troy a second time. He misses. Troy continues to advance toward him.*)

TROY: You're gonna have to kill me! You wanna draw that bat back on me. You're gonna have to kill me.

(*Cory, backed up against the tree, can go no farther. Troy taunts him. He sticks out his head and offers him a target.*)

Come on! Come on!

(*Cory is unable to swing the bat. Troy grabs it.*)

TROY: Then I'll show you.

(*Cory and Troy struggle over the bat. The struggle is fierce and fully engaged. Troy ultimately is the stronger and takes the bat from Cory and stands over him ready to swing. He stops himself.*)

Go on and get away from around my house.

(*Cory, stung by his defeat, picks himself up, walks slowly out of the yard and up the alley.*)

CORY: Tell Mama I'll be back for my things.

TROY: They'll be on the other side of that fence.

(*Cory exits.*)

TROY: I can't taste nothing. Helluljah! I can't taste nothing no more. (*Troy assumes a batting posture and begins to taunt Death, the fastball on the outside corner.*) Come on! It's between you and me now! Come on! Anytime you want! Come on! I be ready for you . . . but I ain't gonna be easy.

(*The lights go down on the scene.*)

Scene V

(*The time is 1965. The lights come up in the yard. It is the morning of Troy's funeral. A funeral plaque with a light hangs beside the door. There is a small garden plot off to the side. There is noise and activity in the house as Rose, Gabriel, and Bono have gathered. The door opens and Raynell, seven years old, enters dressed in a flannel nightgown. She crosses to the garden and pokes around with a stick. Rose calls from the house.*)

ROSE: Raynell!
RAYNELL: Mam?
ROSE: What you doing out there?
RAYNELL: Nothing.

(*Rose comes to the door.*)

ROSE: Girl, get in here and get dressed. What you doing?
RAYNELL: Seeing if my garden growed.
ROSE: I told you it ain't gonna grow overnight. You got to wait.
RAYNELL: It don't look like it never gonna grow. Dag!
ROSE: I told you a watched pot never boils. Get in here and get dressed.
RAYNELL: This ain't even no pot, Mama.
ROSE: You just have to give it a chance. It'll grow. Now you come on and do what I told you. We got to be getting ready. This ain't no morning to be playing around. You hear me?
RAYNELL: Yes, mam.

(*Rose exits into the house. Raynell continues to poke at her garden with a stick. Cory enters. He is dressed in a Marine corporal's uniform, and carries a duffel bag. His posture is that of a military man, and his speech has a clipped sternness.*)

CORY (*to Raynell*): Hi.

(*Pause.*)

   I bet your name is Raynell.
RAYNELL: Uh huh.
CORY: Is your mama home?

(*Raynell runs up on the porch and calls through the screen door.*)

RAYNELL: Mama . . . there's some man out here. Mama?

(*Rose comes to the door.*)

ROSE: Cory? Lord have mercy! Look here, you all!

(*Rose and Cory embrace in a tearful reunion as Bono and Lyons enter from the house dressed in funeral clothes.*)

BONO: Aw, looka here . . .
ROSE: Done got all grown up!
CORY: Don't cry, Mama. What you crying about?
ROSE: I'm just so glad you made it.
CORY: Hey Lyons. How you doing, Mr. Bono.

(*Lyons goes to embrace Cory.*)

LYONS: Look at you, man. Look at you. Don't he look good, Rose. Got them Corporal stripes.
ROSE: What took you so long.
CORY: You know how the Marines are, Mama. They got to get all their paperwork straight before they let you do anything.
ROSE: Well, I'm sure glad you made it. They let Lyons come. Your Uncle Gabe's still in the hospital. They don't know if they gonna let him out or not. I just talked to them a little while ago.
LYONS: A Corporal in the United States Marines.
BONO: Your daddy knew you had it in you. He used to tell me all the time.
LYONS: Don't he look good, Mr. Bono?
BONO: Yeah, he remind me of Troy when I first met him.

(*Pause.*)

   Say, Rose, Lucille's down at the church with the choir. I'm gonna go down and get the pallbearers lined up. I'll be back to get you all.
ROSE: Thanks, Jim.
CORY: See you, Mr. Bono.
LYONS (*with his arm around Raynell*): Cory . . . look at Raynell. Ain't she precious? She gonna break a whole lot of hearts.
ROSE: Raynell, come and say hello to your brother. This is your brother, Cory. You remember Cory.
RAYNELL: No, Mam.
CORY: She don't remember me, Mama.
ROSE: Well, we talk about you. She heard us talk about you. (*To Raynell.*) This is your brother, Cory. Come on and say hello.
RAYNELL: Hi.
CORY: Hi. So you're Raynell. Mama told me a lot about you.
ROSE: You all come on into the house and let me fix you some breakfast. Keep up your strength.
CORY: I ain't hungry, Mama.
LYONS: You can fix me something, Rose. I'll be in there in a minute.
ROSE: Cory, you sure you don't want nothing. I know they ain't feeding you right.
CORY: No, Mama . . . thanks. I don't feel like eating. I'll get something later.
ROSE: Raynell . . . get on upstairs and get that dress on like I told you.

(*Rose and Raynell exit into the house.*)

LYONS: So . . . I hear you thinking about getting married.
CORY: Yeah, I done found the right one, Lyons. It's about time.
LYONS: Me and Bonnie been split up about four years now. About the time Papa retired. I guess she just got tired of all them changes I was putting her through.

(*Pause.*)

I always knew you was gonna make something out yourself. Your head was always in the right direction. So . . . you gonna stay in . . . make it a career . . . put in your twenty years?

CORY: I don't know. I got six already, I think that's enough.

LYONS: Stick with Uncle Sam and retire early. Ain't nothing out here. I guess Rose told you what happened with me. They got me down the workhouse. I thought I was being slick cashing other people's checks.

CORY: How much time you doing?

LYONS: They give me three years. I got that beat now. I ain't got but nine more months. It ain't so bad. You learn to deal with it like anything else. You got to take the crookeds with the straights. That's what Papa used to say. He used to say that when he struck out. I seen him strike out three times in a row . . . and the next time up he hit the ball over the grandstand. Right out there in Homestead Field. He wasn't satisfied hitting in the seats . . . he want to hit it over everything! After the game he had two hundred people standing around waiting to shake his hand. You got to take the crookeds with the straights. Yeah, Papa was something else.

CORY: You still playing?

LYONS: Cory . . . you know I'm gonna do that. There's some fellows down there we got us a band . . . we gonna try and stay together when we get out . . . but yeah, I'm still playing. It still helps me to get out of bed in the morning. As long as it do that I'm gonna be right there playing and trying to make some sense out of it.

ROSE (calling): Lyons, I got these eggs in the pan.

LYONS: Let me go on and get these eggs, man. Get ready to go bury Papa.

(Pause.)

How you doing? You doing all right?

(Cory nods. Lyons touches him on the shoulder and they share a moment of silent grief. Lyons exits into the house. Cory wanders about the yard. Raynell enters.)

RAYNELL: Hi.

CORY: Hi.

RAYNELL: Did you used to sleep in my room?

CORY: Yeah . . . that used to be my room.

RAYNELL: That's what Papa call it. "Cory's room." It got your football in the closet.

(Rose comes to the door.)

ROSE: Raynell, get in there and get them good shoes on.

RAYNELL: Mama, can't I wear these. Them other one hurt my feet.

ROSE: Well, they just gonna have to hurt your feet for a while. You ain't said they hurt your feet when you went down to the store and got them.

RAYNELL: They didn't hurt then. My feet done got bigger.

ROSE: Don't you give me no backtalk now. You get in there and get them shoes on.

(Raynell exits into the house.)

Ain't too much changed. He still got that piece of rag tied to that tree. He was out here swinging that bat. I was just ready to go back in the house. He swung that bat and then he just fell over. Seem like he swung it and stood there with this grin on his face . . . and then he just fell over. They carried him on down to the hospital, but I knew there wasn't no need . . . why don't you come on in the house?

CORY: Mama . . . I got something to tell you. I don't know how to tell you this . . . but I've got to tell you . . . I'm not going to Papa's funeral.

ROSE: Boy, hush your mouth. That's your daddy you talking about. I don't want hear that kind of talk this morning. I done raised you to come to this? You standing there all healthy and grown talking about you ain't going to your daddy's funeral?

CORY: Mama . . . listen . . .

ROSE: I don't want to hear it, Cory. You just get that thought out of your head.

CORY: I can't drag Papa with me everywhere I go. I've got to say no to him. One time in my life I've got to say no.

ROSE: Don't nobody have to listen to nothing like that. I know you and your daddy ain't seen eye to eye, but I ain't got to listen to that kind of talk this morning. Whatever was between you and your daddy . . . the time has come to put it aside. Just take it and set it over there on the shelf and forget about it. Disrespecting your daddy ain't gonna make you a man, Cory. You got to find a way to come to that on your own. Not going to your daddy's funeral ain't gonna make you a man.

CORY: The whole time I was growing up . . . living in his house . . . Papa was like a shadow that followed you everywhere. It weighed on you and sunk into your flesh. It would wrap around you and lay there until you couldn't tell which one was you anymore. That shadow digging in your flesh. Trying to crawl in. Trying to live through you. Everywhere I looked, Troy Maxson was staring back at me . . . hiding under the bed . . . in the closet. I'm just saying I've got to find a way to get rid of that shadow, Mama.

ROSE: You just like him. You got him in you good.

CORY: Don't tell me that, Mama.

ROSE: You Troy Maxson all over again.

CORY: I don't want to be Troy Maxson. I want to be me.

ROSE: You can't be nobody but who you are, Cory. That shadow wasn't nothing but you growing into yourself. You either got to grow into it or cut it down to fit you. But that's all you got to make life with. That's all you got to measure yourself against that world out there. Your daddy wanted you to be everything he wasn't . . . and at the same time he tried to make you into everything he was. I don't know if he was right or wrong . . . but I do know he meant to do more good than he meant to do harm. He wasn't always right. Sometimes when he touched he bruised. And sometimes when he took me in his arms he cut.

When I first met your daddy I thought . . . Here is a man I can lay down with and make a baby. That's the first thing I thought when I seen him. I was thirty years old and had done seen my share of men. But when he walked up to me and said "I can dance a waltz that'll make you dizzy," I thought, Rose Lee, here is a man that you can open yourself up to and be filled to bursting. Here is a man that can fill all them empty spaces you been tipping around the edges of. One of them empty spaces was being somebody's mother.

I married your daddy and settled down to cooking his supper and keeping clean sheets on the bed. When your daddy walked through the house he was so big he filled it up. That was my first mistake. Not to make him leave some room for me. For my part in the matter. But at that time I wanted that. I wanted a house that I could sing in. And that's what your daddy gave me. I didn't know to keep up his strength I had to give up little pieces of mine. I did that. I took on his life as mine and mixed up the pieces so that you couldn't hardly tell which was which anymore. It was my life and I didn't have to live it like that. But that's what life offered me in the way of being a woman and I took it. I grabbed hold of it with both hands.

By the time Raynell came into the house, me and your daddy had done lost touch with one another. I didn't want to make my blessing off of nobody's misfortune . . . but I took on to Raynell like she was all them babies I had wanted and never had.

(*The phone rings.*)

Like I'd been blessed to relive a part of my life. And if the Lord see fit to keep up my strength . . . I'm gonna do her just like your daddy did you . . . I'm gonna give her the best of what's in me.

RAYNELL (*entering, still with her old shoes*): Mama . . . Reverend Tollivier on the phone.

(*Rose exits into the house.*)

RAYNELL: Hi.
CORY: Hi.
RAYNELL: You in the Army or the Marines?
CORY: Marines.
RAYNELL: Papa said it was the Army. Did you know Blue?
CORY: Blue? Who's Blue?
RAYNELL: Papa's dog what he sing about all the time.
CORY (*singing*): Hear it ring! Hear it ring!
I had a dog his name was Blue
You know Blue was mighty true
You know Blue was a good old dog
Blue treed a possum in a hollow log
You know from that he was a good old dog.
Hear it ring! Hear it ring!

(*Raynell joins in singing.*)

CORY AND RAYNELL: Blue treed a possum out on a limb
Blue looked at me and I looked at him
Grabbed that possum and put him in a sack
Blue stayed there till I came back
Old Blue's feets was big and round
Never allowed a possum to touch the ground.

Old Blue died and I dug his grave
I dug his grave with a silver spade
Let him down with a golden chain
And every night I call his name
Go on Blue, you good dog you
Go on Blue, you good dog you

RAYNELL: Blue laid down and died like a man
Blue laid down and died . . .
BOTH: Blue laid down and died like a man
Now he's treeing possums in the Promised Land
I'm gonna tell you this to let you know
Blue's gone where the good dogs go
When I hear old Blue bark
When I hear old Blue bark
Blue treed a possum in Noah's Ark
Blue treed a possum in Noah's Ark.

(*Rose comes to the screen door.*)

ROSE: Cory, we gonna be ready to go in a minute.
CORY (*to Raynell*): You go on in the house and change them shoes like Mama told you so we can go to Papa's funeral.
RAYNELL: Okay, I'll be back.

(*Raynell exits into the house. Cory gets up and crosses over to the tree. Rose stands in the screen door watching him. Gabriel enters from the alley.*)

GABRIEL (*calling*): Hey, Rose!
ROSE: Gabe?
GABRIEL: I'm here, Rose. Hey Rose, I'm here!

(*Rose enters from the house.*)

ROSE: Lord . . . Look here, Lyons!
LYONS: See, I told you, Rose . . . I told you they'd let him come.
CORY: How you doing, Uncle Gabe?
LYONS: How you doing, Uncle Gabe?
GABRIEL: Hey, Rose. It's time. It's time to tell St. Peter to open the gates. Troy, you ready? You ready, Troy. I'm gonna tell St. Peter to open the gates. You get ready now.

(*Gabriel, with great fanfare, braces himself to blow. The trumpet is without a mouthpiece. He puts the end of it into his mouth and blows with great force, like a man who has been waiting some twenty-odd years for this single moment. No sound comes out of the trumpet. He braces himself and blows again with the same result. A third time he blows. There is a weight of impossible description that falls away and leaves him bare and exposed to a frightful realization. It is a trauma that a sane and normal mind would be unable to withstand. He begins to dance. A slow, strange dance, eerie and life-giving. A dance of atavistic signature and ritual. Lyons attempts to embrace him. Gabriel pushes Lyons away. He begins to howl in what is an attempt at song, or per-* *haps a song turning back into itself in an attempt at speech. He finishes his dance and the gates of heaven stand open as wide as God's closet.)*

That's the way that go!

COMMENTARIES

David Savran (b. 1950)
INTERVIEW WITH AUGUST WILSON   1987

August Wilson is interested not only in the characters in his plays but also in their political circumstances. One of his primary efforts has been to help strip away the black male stereotypes so that his audiences can see his people as he sees them. In this interview he discusses the social conditions of African Americans and the relationship between Troy Maxson and his son Cory. Wilson's views about their relationship may be surprising, since he interprets it in a way that differs from many of the critics' interpretations.

Savran: In reading *Fences,* I came to view Troy more and more critically as the play progressed, sharing Rose's point of view. We see that Troy has been crippled by his father. That's being replayed in Troy's relationship with Cory. Do you think there's a way out of that cycle?

Wilson: Surely. First of all, we're all like our parents. The things we are taught early in life, how to respond to the world, our sense of morality — everything, we get from them. Now you can take that legacy and do with it anything you want to do. It's in your hands. Cory is Troy's son. How can he be Troy's son without sharing Troy's values? I was trying to get at why Troy made the choices he made, how they have influenced his values and how he attempts to pass those along to his son. Each generation gives the succeeding generation what they think they need. One question in the play is "Are the tools we are given sufficient to compete in a world that is different from the one our parents knew?" I think they are — it's just that we have to do different things with the tools. That's all Troy has to give. Troy's flaw is that he does not recognize that the world was changing. That's because he spent fifteen years in a penitentiary.

As African-Americans, we should demand to participate in society as Africans. That's the way out of the vicious cycle of poverty and neglect that exists in 1987 in America, where you have a huge percentage of blacks living in the equivalent of South African townships, in housing projects. No one is inviting these people to participate in society. Look at the poverty levels — $8,500 for a family of four, if you have $8,501 you're not counted. Those statistics would go up enormously if we had an honest assessment of the cost of living in America. I don't know how anybody can support a family of four on $8,500. What I'm saying is that 85 or 90 percent of blacks in America are living in abject poverty and, for the most part, are crowded into what amount to concentration camps. The situation for blacks in America is worse than it was forty years ago. Some sociologists will tell you about the tremendous progress we've made. They didn't put me out when I walked in the door. And you can always point to someone who works on Wall Street, or is a doctor. But they don't count in the larger scheme of things.

Savran: Do you have any idea how these political changes could take place?

Wilson: I'm not sure. I know that blacks must be allowed their cultural differences. I think the process of assimilation to white American society was a big mistake. We don't want to be like you. Blacks living in housing projects are isolated from the society, for the most part — living as they choose, as Africans. Only they don't realize the value in what they're doing because they have accepted their victimization. They've marked themselves as victims. Once they recognize that, they can begin to move through society in a different manner, from a stronger position, and claim what is theirs.

Savran: A project of yours is to point up what happens when oppression is internalized.

Wilson: Yes, transfer of aggression to the wrong target. I think it's interesting that the two roads open to blacks for "full participation" are entertainment and sports. *Ma Rainey* and *Fences,* and I didn't plan it that way. I don't think that they're the correct roads. I think Troy's right. Now with the benefit of historical perspective, I can say that the athletic scholarship was actually a way of exploiting. Now you've got two million kids who think they're going to play in the NBA. In the sixties the universities made a lot of money off of athletics. You had kids playing for free who, by and large, were not getting educated, were taking courses in basketweaving. Some of them could barely read.

Savran: Troy may be right about that issue, but it seems that he has passed on certain destructive traits in spite of himself. Take the hostility between father and son.

Wilson: I think every generation says to the previous generation: you're in my way, I've got to get by. The father-son conflict is actually a normal generational conflict that happens all the time.

Savran: So it's a healthy and a good thing?

Wilson: Oh, sure. Troy is seeing this boy walk around, smelling his piss. Two men cannot live in the same household. Troy would have been tremendously disappointed if Cory had not challenged him. Troy knows that this boy has to go out and do battle with that world: "So I had best prepare him because I know that's a harsh, cruel place out there. But that's going to be easy compared to what he's getting here. Ain't nobody gonna whip your ass like I'm gonna whip it." He has a tremendous love for the kid. But he's not going to say, "I love you," he's going to demonstrate it. He's carrying garbage for seventeen years just for the kid. The only world Troy knows is the one that he made. Cory's going to go on to find another one, he's going to arrive at the same place as Troy. I think one of the most important lines in the play is when Troy is talking about his father: "I got to the place where I could feel him kicking in my blood and knew that the only thing that separated us was the matter of a few years."

Hopefully, Cory will do things a bit differently with his son. For Troy, sports was not the way to go, the white man wouldn't let him get away with that. "Get you a job, with your hands, something that nobody can take away from you." The idea of school — he doesn't know what that is. That's for white folks. Very few blacks had paperwork jobs. But if you knew how to fix cars, you could always make some money. That's what Troy wants for Cory. There aren't many people who ever jumped up in Troy's face. So he's proud of the kid at the same time that he expresses a hurt that all men feel. You got to cut your kid loose at some point. There's that sense of loss and separation. You find out how Troy left his father's house and you see how Cory leaves his house. I suspect with Cory it will repeat with some differences and maybe, after five or six generations, they'll find a different way to do it.

Savran: Where Cory ends up is very ambiguous, as a marine in 1965.

Wilson: Yes. For the average black kid on the street, that was an alternative. You went into the army because you could learn how to do something. I can remember my parents talking about the son of some friends: "He's in the navy. He *did* something"— as opposed to standing on the street corner, shooting drugs, drinking wine, and robbing stores. Lyons says to Cory, "I always knew you were going to make something out of yourself." It really wounds me. He's a corporal in the marines. For blacks, that is a sense of accomplishment. Therein lies one of the tragedies of blacks in America. Cory says, "I don't know. I put in six years. That's enough." Anyone who goes into the army and makes a career out of it is a loser. They sit there and are nurtured by the army and they don't have to confront life. Then they get out of the army and find there's nothing to do. They didn't learn any skills. And if they did, they can't find a job. Four months later, they're shooting dope. In the sixties a whole bunch of blacks went over, fought and died in the Vietnam War. The survivors came back to the same street corners and found out nothing had changed. They still couldn't get a job.

At the end of *Fences* every person, with the exception of Raynell, is institutionalized. Rose is in a church. Lyons is in a penitentiary. Gabriel's in a mental hospital and Cory's in the marines. The only free person is the girl, Troy's daughter, the hope for the future. That was conscious on my part because in '57 that's what I saw. Blacks have relied on institutions which are really foreign — except for the black church, which has been our saving grace. I have some problems with it but I recognize it as a central social organization and sometimes an economic organization for the black community. I would like to see blacks develop their own institutions that respond to their needs.

Frank Rich (b. 1949)
REVIEW OF *FENCES*   1987

Frank Rich, the New York Times *critic, reviews* Fences *in context with August Wilson's other plays. Rich criticizes the old-fashioned structure of the plot, which he characterizes as "clunky," but he also admits that the play is "gripping," especially in the second act. Rich focuses on the struggle between father and son, which he sees as meaningful to "theatergoers from all kinds of families."*

To hear his wife tell it, Troy Maxson, the middle-aged Pittsburgh sanitation worker at the center of *Fences*, is "so big" that he fills up his tenement house just by walking through it. Needless to say, that description could also apply to James Earl Jones, the actor who has found what may be the best role of his career in August Wilson's new play, at the 46th Street Theater. But the remarkable stature of the character — and of the performance — is not a matter of sheer size. If Mr. Jones's Troy is a mountainous man prone to tyrannical eruptions of rage, he is also a dignified, delicate figure capable of cradling a tiny baby, of pleading gravely to his wife for understanding, of standing still to stare death unflinchingly in the eye. A black man, a free man, a descendant of slaves, a menial laborer, a father, a husband, a lover — Mr. Jones's Troy embraces all the contradictions of being black and male and American in his time.

That time is 1957 — three decades after the period of Mr. Wilson's previous and extraordinary *Ma Rainey's Black Bottom*. For blacks like Troy in the industrial North of *Fences*, social and economic equality is more a legal principle than a reality: the Maxson's slum neighborhood, a panorama of grimy brick and smokestack-blighted sky in James D. Sandefur's eloquent design, is a cauldron of busted promises, waiting to boil over. The conflagration is still a decade away — the streetlights burn like the first sparks of distant insurrection — so Mr. Wilson writes about the pain of an extended family lost in the wilderness of de facto segregation and barren hope.

It speaks of the power of the play — and of the cast assembled by the director, Lloyd Richards — that Mr. Jones's patriarch doesn't devour the rest of *Fences* so much as become the life force that at once nurtures and stunts the characters who share his blood. The strongest countervailing player is his wife, Rose, luminously acted by Mary Alice. Rose is a quiet woman who, as she says, "planted herself" in the "hard and rocky" soil of her husband. But she never bloomed: marriage brought frustration and betrayal in equal measure with affection.

Even so, Ms. Alice's performance emphasizes strength over self-pity, open anger over festering bitterness. The actress finds the spiritual quotient in the acceptance that accompanies Rose's love for a scarred, profoundly complicated man. It's rare to find a marriage of any sort presented on stage with such balance — let alone one in which the husband has fathered children by three different women. Mr. Wilson grants both partners the right to want to escape the responsibilities of their domestic drudgery while affirming their respective claims to forgiveness.

The other primary relationship of *Fences* is that of Troy to his son Cory (Courtney B. Vance) — a promising 17-year-old football player being courted by a college recruiter. Troy himself was once a baseball player in the Negro Leagues — early enough to hit homers off Satchel Paige, too early to benefit from Jackie Robinson's breakthrough — and his bitter, long-ago disappointment leads him to decree a different future for his son. But while Troy wants Cory to settle for a workhorse trade guaranteeing a weekly paycheck, the boy resists. The younger Maxson is somehow convinced that the dreams of his black generation need not end in the city's mean alleys with the carting of white men's garbage.

The struggle between father and son over conflicting visions of black identity, aspirations and values is the play's narrative fulcrum, and a paradigm of violent divisions that would later tear apart a society. As written, the conflict is also a didactic one, reminiscent of old-fashioned plays, black and white, about disputes between first-generation American parents and their rebellious children.

In *Ma Rainey* — set at a blues recording session — Mr. Wilson's characters were firecrackers exploding in a bottle, pursuing jagged theatrical riffs reflective of their music and of their intimacy with the Afro-American experience that gave birth to that music. The relative tameness of *Fences* — with its laboriously worked-out titular metaphor, its slow-fused Act I exposition — is as much an expression of its period as its predecessor was of the hotter 20s. Intentionally or not — and perhaps to the satisfaction of those who found the more esthetically daring *Ma Rainey* too "plotless"— Mr. Wilson invokes the clunkier dramaturgy of Odets, Miller and Hansberry on this occasion.

Such formulaic theatrical tidiness, while exasperating at times, proves a minor price for the gripping second act (strengthened since the play's Yale debut in 1985) and for the scattered virtuoso passages throughout. Like *Ma Rainey* and the latest Wilson work seen at Yale (*Joe Turner's Come and Gone,* also promised for New York), *Fences* leaves no doubt that Mr. Wilson is a major writer, combining a poet's ear for vernacular with a robust sense of humor (political and sexual), a sure instinct for crackling dramatic incident and a passionate commitment to a great subject.

Mr. Wilson continues to see history as fully as he sees his characters. In one scene, Troy and his oldest friend (played with brimming warmth by Ray Aranha) weave an autobiographical "talking blues"— a front-porch storytelling jaunt from the antebellum plantation through the pre-industrial urban South, jail and northward migration. *Fences* is pointedly bracketed by two disparate wars that swallowed up black manhood, and, as always with Mr. Wilson, is as keenly cognizant of its characters' bonds to Africa, however muted here, as their bondage to white America. One hears the cadences of a centuries-old heritage in Mr. Jones's efforts to shout down the devil. It is a frayed scrap of timeless blues singing, unpretty but unquenchable, that proves the over-powering cathartic link among the disparate branches of the Maxson family tree.

Under the exemplary guidance of Mr. Richards — whose staging falters only in the awkward scene transitions — the entire cast is impressive, including Frankie R. Faison in the problematic (but finally devastating) role of a brain-damaged, horn-playing uncle named Gabriel, and Charles Brown, as a Maxson son who falls into the sociological crack separating the play's two principal generations. As Cory, Courtney B. Vance is not only formidable in challenging Mr. Jones to a psychological (and sometimes physical) kill-or-be-killed battle for supremacy but also seems to grow into Troy's vocal timbre and visage by the final scene. Like most sons, Mr. Vance just can't elude "the shadow" of his father, no matter how hard he tries. Such is the long shadow Mr. Jones's father casts in *Fences* that theatergoers from all kinds of families may find him impossible to escape.

Yasmina Reza

Yasmina Reza (b. 1959) studied at Paris X University and later at the Jacques Lecoq Drama School. She began working as an actress in France and appeared in numerous plays by contemporary authors as well as plays by Molière, Marivaux, and Sacha Guitry. In 1987 she wrote *Conversations after a Burial* for performance in France and won the prestigious Molière Award for best author as well as many other awards. Following its performance in France, the play was produced in translation in Europe and South America.

Reza's French translation of Steven Berkoff's adaptation of Franz Kafka's novel *Metamorphosis* for performance by Roman Polanski was nominated for the 1988 Molière Award for translation. *Winter Crossing* (1990), her second play, won the 1990 Molière Award for best fringe production that year. *"Art"* premiered in Berlin and opened in Paris in 1994, where it won the Molière Award for best author, best play, and best production. It also won prizes in London for best comedy and in Germany for best foreign play. *The Unexpected Man* (1995) was produced in London, France, and several other European countries. It was revived in 1998 by the Royal Shakespeare Company at the Barbican in London. It has also played in New York.

In addition to playwriting, Yasmina Reza has also been engaged in screenwriting, with two recent films shown in Europe: *See You Tomorrow* and *Lulu Kreutz's Picnic*. Her novel, *Hammerklavier*, was published in 1997.

"ART"

"Art" is only partly about art. Essentially it is a play about three men who have been friends for fifteen years. Serge is a successful dermatologist who has bought an expensive painting by a painter named Antrios. It is a white painting with almost indistinguishable diagonal lines, and it cost two hundred thousand francs (close to fifty thousand dollars). Serge is a thoughtful man, knowledgeable about art and modernism. His friend Marc hates the painting. Marc is an aeronautical engineer who values his intellectual superiority and expects others to acknowledge it. Their friend Yvan is a man in therapy on the eve of a complicated but unavoidable marriage. Yvan is less sure of himself than Serge or Marc but has a touching emotional life that causes him to cry when stressed. He is not a successful man. He has been "in" textiles for years and recently began to work for his wife-to-be's uncle in stationery. The painting Serge has bought becomes a wedge that begins to pry apart the friendship.

"*Art*" is a study of close relationships and the dynamics that underlie them. Marc reveals at one point that he has always enjoyed playing mentor to Serge and pointing Serge in the direction of new interests and experiences. Marc's taste in painting is sharply realistic, as we learn from seeing his "Flemish"-style landscape of Carcasonne, and he resents Serge's independence as measured by his purchase of a nonrepresentative painting. Meanwhile, a third painting hangs on Yvan's wall and is described as a "daub," with no further details. For Marc, Yvan is something of a joker, and Yvan sees himself in the role of the joker. Yet Yvan is so deeply interested in learning about himself that he sees a therapist, Finkelzohn, who gives him some interesting advice: "If I'm who I am because I'm who I am and you're who you are because you're who you are, then I'm who I am and you're who you are. If, on the other hand, I'm who I am because you're who you are, and if you're who you are because I'm who I am, then I'm not who I am and you're not who you are." The implication is that people see each other as they wish to rather than as they really are. "*Art*" raises the question of what one knows about one's closest friends just as it raises the question of what one knows about art or values.

One important issue in the play concerns Serge's, Marc's, and Yvan's relationships with women. Yvan has the most interesting and lengthy speeches about the women in his life. Catherine, his wife-to-be, controls the wedding invitations. As a result, his detested stepmother's name will be on the invitations, and therefore his own mother wants her name removed. Serge has a wife from whom he is separated, and Marc's relationship with Paula has never really pleased Serge. In the course of the drama, the tensions aroused by these relationships begin to clarify the pressures on the men's relationships with each other.

"*Art*" is a comedy, and in performance it is often extremely funny. There is laughter in the play as well as tears. Audiences have found it moving, but most of all comic. A careful study of the play reveals much that is serious in the play, but it has some broadly humorous moments, and none are more amusing than the reactions of Marc and Yvan to Serge's painting.

"*Art*" in Performance

"*Art*" has been performed in more than twenty countries and almost as many languages. It has proved to be a durable comedy in whatever language it is played in. It premiered in Berlin, and in 1994 it opened in Paris. In 1996 it was produced in London's West End, the equivalent of New York's Broadway, and one newspaper declared it "the perfect West End play." It won the Evening Standard Award for best comedy in 1996 and the Laurence Olivier Award for best comedy in 1997. It was produced in Broadway's Royale Theatre and won the Tony Award for best play in 1998. The cast for the play in English varied throughout its run. In London Tom Courtenay, Ken Stott, and Albert Finney opened the play, and later Stacey Keach, George Wendt, and David Dukes continued. In New York, Alan Alda opened the play, and later Judd Hirsch, George Wendt, and Joe Morton took over. The cast was always important, but the play itself seems to have worked independently of the stars who have played in it.

The set and lighting were spare in the New York production. Before the lights came up the audience saw the back of the canvas, hung at the stage apron, facing into the stage space. Later, Serge holds up the painting for the audience and the actors to contemplate. The settings for Marc's and Yvan's apartments were essentially unchanged except for the substitution of Yvan's "daub" and Marc's landscape. The simplicity of the set and lighting and the effectiveness of the simple substitution of paintings helped to maintain a focus on the significance of the text and the action of the drama.

Yasmina Reza (b. 1959)

"Art"

1994

TRANSLATED BY CHRISTOPHER HAMPTON

Characters

MARC
SERGE
YVAN

Scene: *The main room of a flat.*
> *A single set. As stripped-down and neutral as possible.*
> *The scenes unfold, successively, at Serge's, Yvan's, and Marc's.*
> *Nothing changes, except for the painting on the wall.*

(*Marc, alone.*)

MARC: My friend Serge has bought a painting. It's a canvas about five foot by four: white. The background is white and if you screw up your eyes, you can make out some fine white diagonal lines.
> Serge is one of my oldest friends.
> He's done very well for himself, he's a dermatologist and he's keen on *art*.
> On Monday, I went to see the painting; Serge had actually got hold of it on the Saturday, but he'd been lusting after it for several months.
> This white painting with white lines.

(*At Serge's.*)
> (*At floor level, a white canvas with fine white diagonal scars. Serge looks at his painting, thrilled. Marc looks at the painting. Serge looks at Marc looking at the painting.*)
> (*Long silence: from both of them, a whole range of wordless emotions.*)

MARC: Expensive?
SERGE: Two hundred thousand.
MARC: Two hundred thousand?
SERGE: Huntingdon would take if off my hands for two hundred and twenty.
MARC: Who's that?
SERGE: Huntingdon?

MARC: Never heard of him.
SERGE: Huntingdon! The Huntingdon Gallery!
MARC: The Huntingdon Gallery would take it off your hands for two hundred and twenty?
SERGE: No, not the Gallery. Him. Huntingdon himself. For his own collection.
MARC: Then why didn't Huntingdon buy it?
SERGE: It's important for them to sell to private clients. That's how the market circulates.
MARC: Mm hm. . . .
SERGE: Well?
MARC: . . .
SERGE: You're not in the right place. Look at it from this angle.
> Can you see the lines?
MARC: What's the name of the . . . ?
SERGE: Painter. Antrios.
MARC: Well-known?
SERGE: Very. Very!

(*Pause.*)

MARC: Serge, you haven't bought this painting for two hundred thousand francs?
SERGE: You don't understand, that's what it costs. It's an Antrios.
MARC: You haven't bought this painting for two hundred thousand francs?
SERGE: I might have known you'd miss the point.
MARC: You paid two hundred thousand francs for this shit?

(*Serge, as if alone.*)

SERGE: My friend Marc's an intelligent enough fellow, I've always valued our relationship, he has a good job, he's an aeronautical engineer, but he's one of those new-style intellectuals, who are not only enemies of modernism, but seem to take some sort of incomprehensible pride in running it down. . . .

In recent years these nostalgia-merchants have become quite breathtakingly arrogant.

(*Same pair. Same place. Same painting.*)
(*Pause.*)

SERGE: What do you mean, "this shit"?

MARC: Serge, where's your sense of humor? Why aren't you laughing? . . . It's fantastic, you buying this painting.

(*Marc laughs. Serge remains stony.*)

SERGE: I don't care how fantastic you think it is, I don't mind if you laugh, but I would like to know what you mean by "this shit."

MARC: You're taking the piss!°

SERGE: No, I'm not. By whose standards is it shit? If you call something shit, you need to have some criterion to judge it by.

MARC: Who are you talking to? Who do you think you're talking to? Hello! . . .

SERGE: You have no interest whatsoever in contemporary painting, you never have had. This is a field about which you know absolutely nothing, so how can you assert that any given object, which conforms to laws you don't understand, is shit?

MARC: Because it is. It's shit. I'm sorry.

(*Serge, alone.*)

SERGE: He doesn't like the painting.
    Fine. . . .
    But there was no warmth in the way he reacted.
    No attempt.
    No warmth when he dismissed it out of hand.
    Just that vile, pretentious laugh.
    A real know-all laugh.
    I hated that laugh.

(*Marc, alone.*)

MARC: It's a complete mystery to me, Serge buying this painting. It's unsettled me, it's filled me with some indefinable unease.
    When I left this place, I had to take three capsules of Gelsemium 9X which Paula recommended — Gelsemium or Ignatia,° she said, Gelsemium or Ignatia, which do you prefer, I mean, how the hell should I know? — because I couldn't begin to understand how Serge, my friend, could have bought that picture.
    Two hundred thousand francs!
    He's comfortably off, but he's hardly rolling in money.
    Comfortable, no more, just comfortable. And he spends two hundred grand on a white painting.
    I must go and see Yvan, he's a friend of ours, I have to discuss this with Yvan. Mind you, Yvan's a very tolerant bloke, which of course, when it comes to relationships, is the worst thing you can be.

---

taking the piss: You're getting irritated.
Gelsemium or Ignatia: Herbal remedies.

Yvan's very tolerant because he couldn't care less. If Yvan tolerates the fact that Serge has spent two hundred grand on some piece of white shit, it's because he couldn't care less about Serge.
    Obviously.

(*At Yvan's.*)
(*On the wall, some daub.*)
(*Yvan is on all fours with his back to us. He seems to be looking for something underneath a piece of furniture. As he does so, he turns to introduce himself.*)

YVAN: I'm Yvan.
    I'm a bit tense at the moment, because, having spent my life in textiles, I've just found a new job as a sales agent for a wholesale stationery business.
    People like me. My professional life has always been a failure and I'm getting married in a couple of weeks. She's a lovely intelligent girl from a good family.

(*Marc enters. Yvan has resumed his search and has his back to him.*)

MARC: What are you doing?

YVAN: I'm looking for the top of my pen.

(*Time passes.*)

MARC: All right, that's enough.

YVAN: I had it five minutes ago.

MARC: It doesn't matter.

YVAN: Yes, it does.

(*Marc gets down on his knees to help him look. Both of them spend some time looking. Marc straightens up.*)

MARC: Stop it. Buy another one.

YVAN: It's a felt-tip, they're special, they'll write on any surface. . . . It's just infuriating. Objects, I can't tell you how much they infuriate me. I had it in my hand five minutes ago.

MARC: Are you going to live here?

YVAN: Do you think it's suitable for a young couple?

MARC: Young couple! Ha, ha. . . .

YVAN: Try not to laugh like that in front of Catherine.

MARC: How's the stationery business?

YVAN: All right. I'm learning.

MARC: You've lost weight.

YVAN: A bit. I'm pissed off about that top. It'll all dry up. Sit down.

MARC: If you go on looking for that top, I'm leaving.

YVAN: OK, I'll stop. You want something to drink?

MARC: A Perrier, if you have one.
    Have you seen Serge lately?

YVAN: No. Have you?

MARC: Yesterday.

YVAN: Is he well?

MARC: Very.
    He's just bought a painting.

YVAN: Oh yes?

MARC: Mm.

YVAN: Nice?

MARC: White.

YVAN: White?

MARC: White.

Imagine a canvas about five foot by four . . . with a white background . . . completely white in fact . . . with fine white diagonal stripes . . . you know . . . and maybe another horizontal white line, towards the bottom. . . .

YVAN: How can you see them?

MARC: What?

YVAN: These white lines. If the background's white, how can you see the lines?

MARC: You just do. Because I suppose the lines are slightly grey, or vice versa, or anyway there are degrees of white! There's more than one kind of white!

YVAN: Don't get upset. Why are you getting upset?

MARC: You immediately start quibbling. Why can't you let me finish?

YVAN: All right. Go on.

MARC: Right. So, you have an idea of what the painting looks like.

YVAN: I think so, yes.

RIGHT: Alan Alda as Marc studying Serge's painting and Victor Garber as Serge admiring it in Yasmina Reza's *"Art"* at Broadway's Royale Theatre in 1998. BELOW: Yvan (Alfred Molina), Serge (Victor Garber), and Marc (Alan Alda) consider the painting in *"Art"* at Broadway's Royale Theatre in 1998.

MARC: Now you have to guess how much Serge paid for it.

YVAN: Who's the painter?

MARC: Antrios. Have you heard of him?

YVAN: No. Is he fashionable?

MARC: I knew you were going to ask me that!

YVAN: Well, it's logical. . . .

MARC: No, it isn't logical. . . .

YVAN: Of course it's logical, you ask me to guess the price, you know very well the price depends on how fashionable the painter might be. . . .

MARC: I'm not asking you to apply a whole set of critical standards, I'm not asking you for a professional valuation, I'm asking you what you, Yvan, would give for a white painting tarted up with a few off-white stripes.

YVAN: Bugger all.

MARC: Right. And what about Serge? Pick a figure at random.

YVAN: Ten thousand francs.

MARC: Ha!

YVAN: Fifty thousand.

MARC: Ha!

YVAN: A hundred thousand.

MARC: Keep going.

YVAN: A hundred and fifty? Two hundred?!

MARC: Two hundred. Two hundred grand.

YVAN: No!

MARC: Yes.

YVAN: Two hundred grand?

MARC: Two hundred grand.

YVAN: Has he gone crazy?

MARC: Looks like it.

(*Slight pause.*)

YVAN: All the same. . . .

MARC: What do you mean, all the same?

YVAN: If it makes him happy . . . he can afford it. . . .

MARC: So that's what you think, is it?

YVAN: Why? What do you think?

MARC: You don't understand the seriousness of this, do you?

YVAN: Er . . . no.

MARC: It's strange how you're missing the basic point of this story. All you can see is externals. You don't understand the seriousness of it.

YVAN: What is the seriousness of it?

MARC: Don't you understand what this means?

YVAN: Would you like a cashew nut?

MARC: Don't you see that suddenly, in some grotesque way, Serge fancies himself as a "collector."

YVAN: Well . . .

MARC: From now on, our friend Serge is one of the great connoisseurs.

YVAN: Bollocks.°

MARC: Well of course it's bollocks. You can't buy your way in that cheap. But that's what *he* thinks.

YVAN: Oh, I see.

Bollocks: Balls.

MARC: Doesn't that upset you?

YVAN: No. Not if it makes him happy.

MARC: If it makes him happy. What's that supposed to mean?

What sort of a philosophy is that, if it makes him happy?

YVAN: As long as it's not doing any harm to anyone else. . . .

MARC: But it is. It's doing harm to me! I'm disturbed, I'm disturbed, more than that, I'm hurt, yes, I am, I'm fond of Serge, and to see him let himself be ripped off and lose every ounce of discernment through sheer snobbery. . . .

YVAN: I don't know why you're so surprised. He's always haunted galleries in the most absurd way, he's always been an exhibition freak.

MARC: He's always been a freak, but a freak with a sense of humor. You see, basically, what really upsets me is that you can't have a laugh with him any more.

YVAN: I'm sure you can.

MARC: You can't!

YVAN: Have you tried?

MARC: Of course I've tried. I laughed. Heartily. What do you think I did? He didn't crack a smile.

Mind you, two hundred grand, I suppose it might be hard to see the funny side.

YVAN: Yes.

(*They laugh.*)

I'll make him laugh.

MARC: I'd be amazed. Any more nuts?

YVAN: He'll laugh, you just wait.

(*At Serge's.*)
(*Serge is with Yvan. The painting isn't there.*)

SERGE: . . . and you get on with the in-laws?

YVAN: Wonderfully. As far as they're concerned, I'm some berk tottering from one dodgy job to another and now I'm groping my way into the world of vellum. . . . This thing on my hand, what is it?

(*Serge examines it.*)

Is it serious?

SERGE: No.

YVAN: Oh, good. How are things?

SERGE: Nothing. Lot of work. Exhausted.

It's nice to see you. You never phone.

YVAN: I don't like to disturb you.

SERGE: You're joking. You just speak to my secretary and I'll call you back right away.

YVAN: I suppose so.

Your place gets more and more monastic. . . .

(*Serge laughs.*)

SERGE: Yes!

Seen Marc recently?

YVAN: Not recently, no.

Have you?

SERGE: Two or three days ago.

YVAN: Is he all right?

SERGE: Yes. More or less.

YVAN: Oh?

SERGE: No, he's all right.

YVAN: I talked to him on the phone last week, he seemed all right.

SERGE: Well, he is. He's all right.

YVAN: You seemed to be implying he wasn't all right.

SERGE: On the contrary, I said, he was all right.

YVAN: More or less, you said.

SERGE: Yes, more or less. More or less all right.

(*Long silence. Yvan wanders around the room.*)

YVAN: You been out? Seen anything?

SERGE: No. I can't afford to go out.

YVAN: Oh?

SERGE (*cheerfully*): I'm ruined.

YVAN: Oh?

SERGE: You want to see something special? Would you like to?

YVAN: Of course I would. Show me.

(*Serge exits and returns with the Antrios, which he turns round and sets down in front of Yvan.*

Yvan looks at the painting and, strangely enough, doesn't manage the hearty laugh he'd predicted.

A long pause, while Yvan studies the painting and Serge studies Yvan.)

Oh, yes. Yes, yes.

SERGE: Antrios.

YVAN: Yes, yes.

SERGE: It's a seventies Antrios. Worth mentioning. He's going through a similar phase now, but this one's from the seventies.

YVAN: Yes, yes.
   Expensive?

SERGE: In absolute terms, yes. In fact, no.
   You like it?

YVAN: Oh, yes, yes, yes.

SERGE: Plain.

YVAN: Plain, yes . . . Yes . . . And at the same time . . .

SERGE: Magnetic.

YVAN: Mm . . . yes . . .

SERGE: You don't really get the resonance just at the moment.

YVAN: Well, a bit . . .

SERGE: No, you don't. You have to come back in the middle of the day. That resonance you get from something monochromatic, it doesn't really happen under artificial light.

YVAN: Mm hm.

SERGE: Not that it is actually monochromatic.

YVAN: No! . . . How much was it?

SERGE: Two hundred thousand.

YVAN: Very reasonable.

SERGE: Very.

(*Silence. Suddenly Serge bursts out laughing, immediately followed by Yvan. Both of them roar with laughter.*)

   Crazy, or what?

YVAN: Crazy!

SERGE: Two hundred grand!

(*Hearty laughter. They stop. They look at each other. They start again. Then stop.*
   They've calmed down.)

SERGE: You know Marc's seen this painting.

YVAN: Oh?

SERGE: Devastated.

YVAN: Oh?

SERGE: He told me it was shit. A completely inappropriate description.

YVAN: Absolutely.

SERGE: You can't call this shit.

YVAN: No.

SERGE: You can say, I don't get it, I can't grasp it, you can't say "it's shit."

YVAN: You've seen his place.

SERGE: Nothing to see.
   It's like yours, it's . . . what I mean is, you couldn't care less.

YVAN: His taste is classical, he likes things classical, what do you expect. . . .

SERGE: He started in with this sardonic laugh. . . . Not a trace of charm. . . . Not a trace of humor.

YVAN: You know Marc is moody, there's nothing new about that. . . .

SERGE: He has no sense of humor. With you, I can laugh. With him, I'm like a block of ice.

YVAN: It's true he's a bit gloomy at the moment.

SERGE: I don't blame him for not responding to this painting, he hasn't the training, there's a whole apprenticeship you have to go through, which he hasn't, either because he's never wanted to or because he has no particular instinct for it, none of that matters, no, what I blame him for is his tone of voice, his complacency, his tactlessness.
   I blame him for his insensitivity. I don't blame him for not being interested in modern Art, I couldn't give a toss about that, I like him for other reasons. . . .

YVAN: And he likes you!

SERGE: No, no, no, no, I felt it the other day, a kind of . . . a kind of condescension . . . contempt with a really bitter edge. . . .

YVAN: No, surely not!

SERGE: Oh, yes! Don't keep trying to smooth things over. Where d'you get this urge to be the great reconciler of the human race? Why don't you admit that Marc is atrophying? If he hasn't already atrophied.

(*Silence.*)

(*At Marc's.*)
   (*On the wall, a figurative painting: a landscape seen through a window.*)

YVAN: We had a laugh.

MARC: You had a laugh?

YVAN: We had a laugh. Both of us. We had a laugh. I promise you on Catherine's life, we had a good laugh, both of us, together.

MARC: You told him it was shit and you had a good laugh.

YVAN: No, I didn't tell him it was shit, we laughed spontaneously.

MARC: You arrived, you looked at the painting and you laughed. And then he laughed.

YVAN: Yes. If you like. We talked a bit, then it was more or less as you described.

MARC: A genuine laugh, was it?

YVAN: Perfectly genuine.

MARC: Well, then, I've made a mistake. Good. I'm really pleased to hear it.

YVAN: It was even better than you think. It was Serge who laughed first.

MARC: It was Serge who laughed first. . . .

YVAN: Yes.

MARC: He laughed first and you joined in.

YVAN: Yes.

MARC: But what made him laugh?

YVAN: He laughed because he sensed I was about to laugh. If you like, he laughed to put me at my ease.

MARC: It doesn't count if he laughed first.
    If he laughed first, it was to defuse your laughter.
    It means it wasn't a genuine laugh.

YVAN: It was a genuine laugh.

MARC: It may have been a genuine laugh, but it wasn't for the right reason.

YVAN: What is the right reason? I'm confused.

MARC: He wasn't laughing because his painting is ridiculous, you and he weren't laughing for the same reasons, you were laughing at the painting and he was laughing to ingratiate himself, to put himself on your wavelength, to show you that on top of being an aesthete who can spend more on a painting than you earn in a year, he's still your same old subversive mate who likes a good laugh.

YVAN: Mm hm . . .

(*A brief silence.*)

    You know . . .

MARC: Yes. . . .

YVAN: This is going to amaze you. . . .

MARC: Go on. . . .

YVAN: I didn't like the painting . . . but I didn't actually hate it.

MARC: Well, of course. You can't hate what's invisible, you can't hate nothing.

YVAN: No, no, it has something. . . .

MARC: What do you mean?

YVAN: It has something. It's not nothing.

MARC: You're joking.

YVAN: I'm not as harsh as you. It's a work of art, there's a system behind it.

MARC: A system?

YVAN: A system.

MARC: What system?

YVAN: It's the completion of a journey. . . .

MARC: Ha, ha, ha!

YVAN: It wasn't painted by accident, it's a work of art which stakes its claim as part of a trajectory. . . .

MARC: Ha, ha, ha!

YVAN: All right, laugh.

MARC: You're parroting out all Serge's nonsense. From him, it's heart-breaking, from you it's just comical!

YVAN: You know, Marc, this complacency, you want to watch out for it. You're getting bitter, it's not very attractive.

MARC: Good. The older I get, the more offensive I hope to become.

YVAN: Great.

MARC: A system!

YVAN: You're impossible to talk to.

MARC: There's a system behind it! . . . You look at this piece of shit, but never mind, never mind, there's a system behind it! . . . You reckon there's a system behind this landscape? (*He indicates the painting on his wall.*) . . . No, uh? Too evocative. Too expressive. Everything's on the canvas! No scope for a system! . . .

YVAN: I'm glad you're enjoying yourself.

MARC: Yvan, look, speak for yourself. Describe your feelings to me.

YVAN: I felt a resonance.

MARC: You felt a resonance? . . .

YVAN: You're denying that I'm capable of appreciating this painting on my own account.

MARC: Of course I am.

YVAN: Well, why?

MARC: Because I know you. Because apart from your disastrous indulgence, you're quite sane.

YVAN: I wish I could say the same for you.

MARC: Yvan, look me in the eye.

YVAN: I'm looking at you.

MARC: Were you moved by Serge's painting?

YVAN: No.

MARC: Answer me this. You're getting married tomorrow and you and Catherine get this painting as a wedding present. Does it make you happy? . . .
    Does it make you happy? . . .

(*Yvan, alone.*)

YVAN: Of course it doesn't make me happy.
    It doesn't make me happy, but, generally speaking, I'm not the sort of person who can say I'm happy, just like that.
    I'm trying to . . . I'm trying to think of an occasion when I could have said yes, I'm happy. . . . Are you happy to be getting married, my mother stupidly asked me one day, are you at least happy to be getting married? . . . Why wouldn't I be, mother?
    What do you mean, why wouldn't I be? You're either happy or you're not happy, what's why wouldn't I be got to do with it? . . .

(*Serge, alone.*)

SERGE: As far as I'm concerned, it's not white.

When I say as far as I'm concerned, I mean objectively.

Objectively speaking, it's not white.

It has a white background, with a whole range of greys. . . .

There's even some red in it.

You could say it's very pale.

I wouldn't like it if it was white.

Marc thinks it's white . . . that's his limit. . . .

Marc thinks it's white because he's got hung up on the idea that it's white.

Unlike Yvan. Yvan can see it isn't white.

Marc can think what he likes, what do I care?

(Marc, alone.)

MARC: Obviously I should have taken the Ignatia.

Why do I have to be so categorical?

What possible difference can it make to me, if Serge lets himself be taken in by modern Art?

I mean, it is a serious matter. But I could have found some other way to put it to him.

I could have taken a less aggressive tone.

Even if it makes me physically ill that my best friend has bought a white painting, all the same I ought to avoid attacking him about it.

I ought to be nice to him.

From now on, I'm on my best behavior.

(At Serge's.)

SERGE: Feel like a laugh?

MARC: Go on.

SERGE: Yvan liked the Antrios.

MARC: Where is it? . . .

SERGE: You want another look?

MARC: Fetch it out.

SERGE: I knew you'd come round to it! . . .

(He exits and returns with the painting. A moment of contemplation.)

Yvan got the hang of it. Right away.

MARC: Mm.

SERGE: All right, listen, it's just a picture, we don't have to get bogged down with it, life's too short. . . . By the way, have you read this? *(He picks up* De Vita Beata *by Seneca° and throws it on to the low table just in front of Marc.)* Read it, it's a masterpiece.

(Marc picks up the book, opens it and leafs through it.)

Incredibly modern. Read that, you don't need to read anything else. What with the office, the hospital, Françoise, who's now decreed that I'm to see the children every weekend — which is something new for

De Vita Beata *by Seneca*: *On the Good Life,* a philosophical work by Lucius Seneca (4? B.C.–A.D. 65), a Roman philosopher, political leader, and author of tragedies. For Seneca, as for other Stoics, virtue and reason are the basis for a good life, which should be led simply and in accordance with nature.

Françoise, the notion that children need a father — I don't have time to read any more, I'm obliged to go straight for the essentials.

MARC: . . . As in the painting . . . Where you've ingeniously eliminated form and color. Those old chestnuts.

SERGE: Yes . . . Although I'm still capable of appreciating more figurative work. Like your Flemish job. Very restful.

MARC: What's Flemish about it? It's a view of Carcassonne.

SERGE: Yes, but I mean . . . it's slightly Flemish in style . . . the window, the view, the . . . in any case, it's very pretty.

MARC: It's not worth anything, you know that.

SERGE: What difference does that make? . . . Anyway, in a few years God knows if the Antrios will be worth anything! . . .

MARC: . . . You know, I've been thinking. I've been thinking and I've changed my mind. The other day, driving across Paris, I was thinking about you and I said to myself: isn't there, deep down, something really poetic about what Serge has done? . . . Isn't surrendering to this incoherent urge to buy in fact an authentically poetic impulse?

SERGE: You're very conciliatory today. Unrecognizable. What's this bland, submissive tone of voice? It doesn't suit you at all, by the way.

MARC: No, no, I'm trying to explain, I'm apologizing.

SERGE: Apologizing? What for?

MARC: I'm too thin-skinned, I'm too highly strung, I overreact. . . . You could say, I lack judgment.

SERGE: Read Seneca.

MARC: That's it. See, for instance, you say "read Seneca" and I could easily have got annoyed. I'm quite capable of being really annoyed by your saying to me, in the course of our conversation, "read Seneca." Which is absurd!

SERGE: No. It's not absurd.

MARC: Really?

SERGE: No, because you thought you could identify . . .

MARC: I didn't say I *was* annoyed. . . .

SERGE: You said you could easily . . .

MARC: Yes, yes. I could easily. . . .

SERGE: Get annoyed, and I understand that. Because when I said "read Seneca," you thought you could identify a kind of superiority. You tell me you lack judgment and my answer is "read Seneca," well, it's obnoxious!

MARC: It is, rather.

SERGE: Having said that, it's true you lack judgment, because I didn't say "read Seneca," I said "read Seneca!"

MARC: You're right. You're right.

SERGE: The fact of the matter is, you've quite simply lost your sense of humor.

MARC: Probably.

SERGE: You've lost your sense of humor, Marc. You really have lost your sense of humor, old chap. When I was talking to Yvan the other day, we agreed you'd lost your sense of humor. Where the hell is he? He's incapable of being on time, it's infuriating! We'll miss the beginning!

MARC: . . . Yvan thinks I've lost my sense of humor? . . .

SERGE: Yvan agrees with me that recently you've somewhat lost your sense of humor.

MARC: The last time you saw each other, Yvan said he liked your painting very much and I'd lost my sense of humor. . . .

SERGE: Oh, yes, that, yes, the painting, really, very much. And he meant it. . . . What's that you're eating?

MARC: Ignatia.

SERGE: Oh, you believe in homeopathy now?

MARC: I don't believe in anything.

SERGE: Didn't you think Yvan had lost a lot of weight?

MARC: So's she.

SERGE: It's the wedding, eating away at them.

MARC: Yes.

(*They laugh.*)

SERGE: How's Paula?

MARC: All right. (*He indicates the Antrios.*) Where are you going to put it?

SERGE: Haven't decided. There. Or there? . . . Too ostentatious.

MARC: Are you going to have it framed?

(*Serge laughs discreetly.*)

SERGE: No! . . . No, no. . . .

MARC: Why not?

SERGE: It's not supposed to be framed.

MARC: Is that right?

SERGE: The artist doesn't want it to be. It mustn't be interrupted. It's already in its setting. (*He signals Marc over to examine the edge.*) Look . . . you see . . .

MARC: What is it, Elastoplast?

SERGE: No, it's a kind of Kraft paper. . . . Made up by the artist.

MARC: It's funny the way you say "the artist."

SERGE: What else am I supposed to say?

MARC: You say "the artist" when you could say "the painter" or . . . whatever his name is . . . Antrios. . . .

SERGE: So?

MARC: But you say "the artist," as if he's a sort of . . . well, anyway, doesn't matter. What are we seeing? Let's try and see something with a bit of substance for once.

SERGE: It's eight o'clock. Everything will have started. I can't imagine how this man, who has nothing whatsoever to do — am I right? — manages to be late every single time. Where the fuck is he?

MARC: Let's just have dinner.

SERGE: All right. It's five past eight. We said we'd meet between seven and half-past. . . . What d'you mean, the way I say "the artist"?

MARC: Nothing. I was going to say something stupid.

SERGE: Well, go on.

MARC: You say "the artist" as if . . . as if he's some unattainable being. The artist . . . some sort of god. . . .

(*Serge laughs.*)

SERGE: Well, for me, he is a god! You don't think I'd have forked out a fortune for a mere mortal! . . .

MARC: I see.

SERGE: I went to the Pompidou on Monday, you know how many Antrioses they have at the Pompidou? . . . Three! Three Antrioses! . . . At the Pompidou!

MARC: Amazing.

SERGE: And mine's as good as any of them! If not better! . . .

Listen, I have a suggestion, let's give Yvan exactly three more minutes and then bugger off. I've found a very good new place. Lyonnaise.

MARC: Why are you so jumpy?

SERGE: I'm not jumpy.

MARC: Yes, you are jumpy.

SERGE: I am not jumpy, well, I am, I'm jumpy because this slackness is intolerable, this inability to practice any kind of self-discipline!

MARC: The fact is, I'm getting on your nerves and you're taking it out on poor Yvan.

SERGE: What do you mean, poor Yvan, are you taking the piss? You're not getting on my nerves, why should you be getting on my nerves?

SERGE: He is getting on my nerves. It's true.

He's getting on my nerves.

It's this ingratiating tone of voice. A little smile behind every word.

It's as if he's forcing himself to be pleasant.

Don't be pleasant, whatever you do, don't be pleasant!

Could it be buying the Antrios? . . . Could buying the Antrios have triggered off this feeling of constraint between us?

Buying something . . . without his backing? . . .

Well, bugger his backing! Bugger your backing, Marc!

MARC: Could it be the Antrios, buying the Antrios?

No —

It started some time ago. . . .

To be precise, it started on the day we were discussing some work of art and you uttered, quite seriously, the word *deconstruction*.

It wasn't so much the word *deconstruction* which upset me, it was the air of solemnity you imbued it with.

You said, humorlessly, unapologetically, without a trace of irony, the word *deconstruction*, you, my friend.

I wasn't sure how best to deal with the situation, so I made this throwaway remark, I said I think I must be getting intolerant in my old age, and you answered, who do you think you are? What makes you so high and mighty? . . .

What gives you the right to set yourself apart, Serge answered in the bloodiest possible way. And quite unexpectedly.

You're just Marc, what makes you think you're so special?

That day, I should have punched him in the mouth.

And when he was lying there on the ground, half-dead, I should have said to him, you're supposed to be my friend, what sort of a friend are you, Serge, if you don't think your friends are special?

(*At Serge's.*)
(*Marc and Serge, as we left them.*)

MARC: Lyonnaise, did you say? Bit heavy, isn't it? Bit fatty, all those sausages. . . . What do you think?

(*The doorbell rings.*)

SERGE: Twelve minutes past eight.

(*Serge goes to open the door to Yvan. Yvan walks into the room, already talking.*)

YVAN: So, a crisis, insoluble problem, major crisis, both stepmothers want their names on the wedding invitation. Catherine adores her stepmother, who more or less brought her up, she wants her name on the invitation, she wants it and her stepmother is not anticipating, which is understandable, since the mother is dead, not appearing next to Catherine's father, whereas my stepmother, whom I detest, it's out of the question her name should appear on the invitation, but my father won't have his name on it if hers isn't, unless Catherine's stepmother's is left off, which is completely unacceptable, I suggested none of the parents' names should be on it, after all we're not adolescents, we can announce our wedding and invite people ourselves, so Catherine screamed her head off, arguing that would be a slap in the face for her parents who were paying through the nose for the reception, and particularly for her stepmother, who's gone to so much trouble when she isn't even her daughter and I finally let myself be persuaded, totally against my better judgment, because she wore me down, I finally agreed that my stepmother, whom I detest, who's a complete bitch, will have her name on the invitation, so I telephoned my mother to warn her, mother, I said, I've done everything I can to avoid this, but we have absolutely no choice, Yvonne's name has to be on the invitation, she said, if Yvonne's name is on the invitation, take mine off it, mother, I said, please, I beg you, don't make things even more difficult, and she said, how dare you suggest my name is left to float around the card on its own, as if I was some abandoned woman, below Yvonne, who'll be clamped on to your father's surname, like a limpet, I said to her, mother, I have friends waiting for me, I'm going to hang up and we'll discuss all this tomorrow after a good night's sleep, she said, why is it I'm always an afterthought, what are you talking about, mother, you're not always an afterthought, of course I am and when you say don't make things even more difficult, what you mean is, everything's already been decided, everything's been organized without me, everything's been cooked up behind my back, good old Huguette, she'll agree to anything and all this, she said — to put the old tin lid on it — in aid of an event, the importance of which I'm having some trouble grasping, mother, I have friends waiting for me, that's right, there's always something better to do, anything's more important than I am, good-bye and she hung up, Catherine, who was next to me, but who hadn't heard her side of the conversation, said, what did she say, I said, she doesn't want her name on the invitation with Yvonne, which is understandable, I'm not talking about that, what was it she said about the wedding, nothing, you're lying, I'm not, Cathy, I promise you, she just doesn't want her name on the invitation with Yvonne, call her back and tell her when your son's getting married, you rise above your vanity, you could say the same thing to your stepmother, that's got nothing to do with it, Catherine shouted, it's me, I'm the one who's insisting her name's on it, it's not her, poor thing, she's tact personified, if she had any idea of the problem this is causing, she'd be down on her knees, begging for her name to be taken off the invitation, now call your mother, so I called her again, by now I'm in shreds, Catherine's listening on the extension, Yvan, my mother says, up to now you've conducted your affairs in the most chaotic way imaginable and just because, out of the blue, you've decided to embark on matrimony, I find myself obliged to spend all afternoon and evening with your father, a man I haven't seen for seventeen years and to whom I was not expecting to have to reveal my hip-size and my puffy cheeks, not to mention Yvonne who incidentally, I may tell you, according to Félix Perolari, has now taken up bridge — my mother also plays bridge — I can see none of this can be helped, but on the invitation, the one item everyone is going to receive and examine, I insist on making a solo appearance, Catherine, listening on the extension, shakes her head and screws up her face in disgust, mother, I say, why are you so selfish, I'm not selfish, I'm not selfish, Yvan, you're not going to start as well, you're not going to be like Mme Roméro this morning and tell me I have a heart of stone, that everybody in our family has a heart of stone, that's what Mme Roméro said this morning when I refused to raise her wages — she's gone completely mad, by the way — to sixty francs an hour tax-free, she had the gall to say everyone in the family had a heart of stone, when she knows very well about poor André's pacemaker, you haven't even bothered to drop him a line, yes, that's right, very funny, everything's a joke to you, it's not me who's the selfish one, Yvan, you've still got a lot to learn about life, off you go, my boy, go on, go on, go and see your precious friends. . . .

(*Silence.*)

SERGE: Then what? . . .

YVAN: Then nothing. Nothing's been resolved. I hung up. Minidrama with Catherine. Cut short, because I was late.

MARC: Why do you let yourself be buggered around by all these women?

YVAN: Why do I let myself be buggered around, I don't know! They're all insane.

SERGE: You've lost weight.

YVAN: Of course I have. Half a stone. Purely through stress.

MARC: Read Seneca. . . .

YVAN: *De Vita Beata,* Just what I need!
   What's he suggest?

MARC: It's a masterpiece.

YVAN: Oh?

SERGE: He hasn't read it.

YVAN: Oh.

MARC: No, but Serge just told me it was a masterpiece.

SERGE: I said it was a masterpiece because it is a masterpiece.

MARC: Quite.

SERGE: It is a masterpiece.

MARC: Why are you getting annoyed?

SERGE: You seem to be insinuating I use the word *masterpiece* at the slightest excuse.

MARC: Not at all. . . .

SERGE: You said the word in a kind of sarcastic way. . . .

MARC: Not at all!

SERGE: Yes, yes, the word *masterpiece* in a kind of . . .

MARC: Is he crazy? Not at all! . . . However, when you used the word, you qualified it by saying "incredibly modern."

SERGE: Yes. So?

MARC: You said "incredibly modern," as if modern was the highest compliment you could give. As if, when describing something, you couldn't think of anything more admirable, more profoundly admirable, than modern.

SERGE: So?

MARC: So nothing.
   And please note I made no mention of the word *incredibly.* . . . Incredibly modern!

SERGE: You're really needling me today.

MARC: No, I'm not . . .

YVAN: You're not going to quarrel all evening, that would just about finish me!

SERGE: You don't think it's extraordinary that a man who wrote nearly two thousand years ago should still be bang up to date?

MARC: No. Of course not. That's the definition of a classic.

SERGE: You're just playing with words.

YVAN: So, what are we going to do? I suppose the cinema's up the spout, sorry. Shall we eat?

MARC: Serge tells me you're very taken with his painting.

YVAN: Yes . . . I am quite . . . taken with it, yes. . . .
   You're not, I gather.

MARC: No.
   Let's go and eat. Serge knows a tasty spot. Lyonnaise.

SERGE: You think the food's too fatty.

MARC: I think the food's a bit on the fatty side, but I don't mind giving it a whirl.

SERGE: No, if you think the food's too fatty, we'll find somewhere else.

MARC: No, I don't mind giving it a whirl.

SERGE: We'll go to the restaurant if you think you'll like it. If not, we won't.
   (*To Yvan.*) You like Lyonnaise food?

YVAN: I'll do whatever you like.

MARC: He'll do whatever you like. Whatever you like, he'll always do.

YVAN: What's the matter with you? You're both behaving very strangely.

SERGE: He's right, you might once in a while have an opinion of your own.

YVAN: Listen, if you think you're going to use me as a coconut shy, I'm out of here! I've put up with enough today.

MARC: Where's your sense of humor, Yvan?

YVAN: What?

MARC: Where's your sense of humor, old chap?

YVAN: Where's my sense of humor? I don't see anything to laugh at. Where's my sense of humor, are you trying to be funny?

MARC: I think recently you've somewhat lost your sense of humor. You want to watch out, believe me!

YVAN: What's the matter with you?

MARC: Don't you think recently I've also somewhat lost my sense of humor?

YVAN: Oh, I see!

SERGE: All right, that's enough, let's make a decision. Tell you the truth, I'm not even hungry.

YVAN: You're both really sinister this evening.

SERGE: You want my opinion about your women problems?

YVAN: Go on.

SERGE: In my view, the most hysterical of them all is Catherine. By far.

MARC: No question.

SERGE: And if you're already letting yourself be buggered around by her, you're in for a hideous future.

YVAN: What can I do?

MARC: Cancel it.

YVAN: Cancel the wedding?

SERGE: He's right.

YVAN: But I can't, are you crazy?

MARC: Why not?

YVAN: Well, because I can't, that's all! It's all arranged. I've only been working at the stationery business for a month. . . .

MARC: What's that got to do with it?

YVAN: It's her uncle's stationery business, he had absolutely no need to take on anyone, least of all someone who's only ever worked in textiles.

SERGE: You must do what you like. I've told you what I think.

YVAN: I'm sorry, Serge, I don't mean to be rude, but you're not necessarily the person I'd come to for matrimonial advice. You can't claim to have been a great success in that field. . . .

SERGE: Precisely.

YVAN: I can't back out of the wedding. I know Catherine is hysterical but she has her good points. There are certain crucial qualities you need when you're marrying someone like me. . . . (*He indicates the Antrios.*) Where are you going to put it?

SERGE: I don't know yet.

YVAN: Why don't you put it there?

SERGE: Because there, it'd be wiped out by the sunlight.

YVAN: Oh, yes.

I thought of you today at the shop, we ran off five hundred posters by this bloke who paints white flowers, totally white, on a white background.

SERGE: The Antrios is not white.

YVAN: No, of course not. I was just saying.

MARC: You think this painting is not white, Yvan?

YVAN: Not entirely, no. . . .

MARC: Ah. Then what color is it?

YVAN: Various colors. . . . There's yellow, there's grey, some slightly ochrish lines.

MARC: And you're moved by these colors?

YVAN: Yes . . . I'm moved by these colors.

MARC: You have no substance, Yvan. You're flabby, you're an amoeba.

SERGE: Why are you attacking Yvan like this?

MARC: Because he's a little arse-licker, he's obsequious, dazzled by money, dazzled by what he believes to be culture, and as you know culture is something I absolutely piss on.

(*Brief silence.*)

SERGE: . . . What's got into you?

MARC (*to Yvan*): How could you, Yvan? . . . And in front of me. In front of me, Yvan.

YVAN: What d'you mean, in front of you? . . . What d'you mean, in front of you?

I find these colors touching. Yes. If it's all the same to you.

Stop wanting to control everything.

MARC: How could you say, in front of me, that you find these colors touching?

YVAN: Because it's the truth.

MARC: The truth? You find these colors touching?

YVAN: Yes. I find these colors touching.

MARC: You find these colors touching, Yvan?!

SERGE: He finds these colors touching! He's perfectly entitled to!

MARC: No, he's not entitled to.

SERGE: What do you mean, he's not entitled to?

MARC: He's not entitled to.

YVAN: I'm not entitled to? . . .

MARC: No.

SERGE: Why is he not entitled to? I don't think you're very well, perhaps you ought to go and see someone.

MARC: He's not entitled to say he finds these colors touching, because he doesn't.

YVAN: I don't find these colors touching?

MARC: There are no colors. You can't see them. And you don't find them touching.

YVAN: Speak for yourself!

MARC: This is really demeaning, Yvan! . . .

SERGE: Who do you think you are, Marc? . . .

Who are you to legislate? You don't like anything, you despise everyone. You take pride in not being a man of your time. . . .

MARC: What's that supposed to mean, a man of my time?

YVAN: Right. I'm off.

SERGE: Where are you going?

YVAN: I'm off. I don't see why I have to put up with your tantrums.

SERGE: Don't go! You're not going to start taking offense, are you? . . . If you go, you're giving in to him.

(*Yvan stands there, hesitating, caught between two possibilities.*)

A man of his time is a man who lives in his own time.

MARC: Balls. How can a man live in any other time but his own? Answer me that.

SERGE: A man of his time is someone of whom it can be said in twenty years' or in a hundred years' time, he was representative of his era.

MARC: Hm.

To what end?

SERGE: What do you mean, to what end?

MARC: What use is it to me if one day somebody says, I was representative of my era?

SERGE: Listen, old fruit, we're not talking about you, if you can imagine such a thing! We don't give a fuck about you! A man of his time, I'm trying to explain to you, like most people you admire, is someone who makes some contribution to the human race. . . . A man of his time doesn't assume the history of Art has come to an end with a pseudo-Flemish view of Cavaillon. . . .

MARC: Carcassonne.

SERGE: Same thing. A man of his time plays his part in the fundamental dynamic of evolution. . . .

MARC: And that's a good thing, in your view.

SERGE: It's not good or bad, why do you always have to moralize, it's just the way things are.

MARC: And you, for example, you play your part in the fundamental dynamic of evolution.

SERGE: I do.

MARC: What about Yvan? . . .

YVAN: Surely not. What sort of part can an amoeba play?

SERGE: In his way, Yvan is a man of his time.

MARC: How can you tell? Not from that daub hanging over his mantelpiece!

YVAN: That is not a daub!

SERGE: It is a daub.

YVAN: It is not!

SERGE: What's the difference? Yvan represents a certain way of life, a way of thinking which is completely modern. And so do you. I'm sorry, but you're a typical man of your time. And in fact, the harder you try not to be, the more you are.

MARC: Well, that's all right then. So what's the problem?

SERGE: There's no problem, except for you, because you take pride in your desire to shut yourself off from humanity. And you'll never manage it. It's like you're in a quicksand, the more you struggle to get out of it, the deeper you sink. Now apologize to Yvan.

MARC: Yvan is a coward.

(*At this point, Yvan makes his decision, and exits in a rush.*)

(*Slight pause.*)

SERGE: Well done.

(*Silence.*)

MARC: It wasn't a good idea to meet this evening . . . was it? . . . I'd better go as well. . . .

SERGE: Maybe. . . .

MARC: Right.

SERGE: You're the coward . . . attacking someone who's incapable of defending himself . . . as you well know.

MARC: You're right . . . you're right and when you put it like that, it makes me feel even worse . . . the thing is, all of a sudden, I can't understand, I have no idea what Yvan and I have in common. . . . I have no idea what my relationship with him consists of.

SERGE: Yvan's always been as he is.

MARC: No. He used to be eccentric, kind of absurd . . . he was always unstable, but his eccentricity was disarming. . . .

SERGE: What about me?

MARC: What about you?

SERGE: Have you any idea what you and I have in common? . . .

MARC: That's a question that could take us down a very long road. . . .

SERGE: Lead on.

(*Short silence.*)

MARC: . . . I'm sorry I upset Yvan.

SERGE: Ah! At last you've said something approximately human. . . . What makes it worse is that the daub he has hanging over his mantelpiece was I'm afraid painted by his father.

MARC: Was it? Shit.

SERGE: Yes. . . .

MARC: But you said . . .

SERGE: Yes, yes, but I remembered as soon as I'd said it.

MARC: Oh, shit. . . .

SERGE: Mm. . . .

(*Slight pause.*)

(*The doorbell rings. Serge goes to answer it. Yvan enters immediately, talking as he arrives, as before.*)

YVAN: Yvan returns! The lift was full, I plunged off down the stairs, clattering all the way down thinking, a coward, an amoeba, no substance, I thought I'll come back with a gun and blow his head off, then he'll see how flabby and obsequious I am, I got to the ground floor and I said to myself, listen, mate, you haven't been in therapy for six years to finish up shooting your best friend and you haven't been in therapy for six years without learning that some deep malaise must lie behind his insane aggression, so I relaunch myself, telling myself as I mount the penitential stair, this is a cry for help. I have to help Marc if it's the last thing I do. . . . In fact the other day I discussed you both with Finkelzohn. . . .

SERGE: You discussed us with Finkelzohn?

YVAN: I discuss everything with Finkelzohn.

SERGE: And why exactly were you discussing us?

MARC: I forbid you to discuss me with that arsehole.

YVAN: You're in no position to forbid me anything.

SERGE: Why were you discussing us?

YVAN: I knew your relationship was under strain and I wanted Finkelzohn to explain. . . .

SERGE: And what did the bastard say?

YVAN: He said something rather amusing. . . .

MARC: They're allowed to give their opinions?

YVAN: No, they never give their opinions, but this time he did give his opinion, he even made a gesture and he never makes a gesture, he's always rigid, I sometimes say to him, for God's sake, move about a bit! . . .

SERGE: All right, what did he say?

MARC: Who gives a fuck what he said?

SERGE: What did he say?

MARC: What possible interest could we have in what he said?

SERGE: I want to know what the bastard said, all right? Shit!

(*Yvan reaches into his jacket pocket.*)

YVAN: You want to know? . . .

(*He fetches out a piece of folded paper.*)

MARC: You took notes?

YVAN (*unfolding it*): I wrote it down because it was complicated. . . . Shall I read it to you?

SERGE: Go on.

YVAN: . . . "If I'm who I am because I'm who I am and you're who you are because you're who you are, then I'm who I am and you're who you are. If, on the other hand, I'm who I am because you're who you are, and if you're who you are because I'm who I am, then I'm not who I am and you're not who you are. . . ."

You see why I had to write it down.

(*Short silence.*)

MARC: How much do you pay this man?

YVAN: Four hundred francs a session, twice a week.

MARC: Great.

SERGE: And in cash. I found something out, they don't allow you to pay by check. Freud said you have to feel the banknotes as they slip through your fingers.

MARC: What a lucky man you are, to be getting the benefit of this fellow's experience.

SERGE: Absolutely! . . . We'd really appreciate it if you'd copy that out for us.

MARC: Yes. It's bound to come in handy.

(*Yvan carefully refolds the piece of paper.*)

YVAN: You're wrong. It's very profound.

MARC: If it's because of him you've come back to turn the other cheek, you should be grateful to him. He's turned you into a pudding, but you're happy, that's all that counts.

YVAN (*to Serge*): And all this because he doesn't want to believe I like your Antrios.

SERGE: I don't give a fuck what you think of it. Either of you.

YVAN: The more I see it, the more I like it, honestly.

SERGE: Let's stop talking about the painting, shall we; once and for all. I have no interest in discussing it further.

MARC: Why are you so touchy?

SERGE: I am not touchy, Marc. You've told us what you think. Fine. The subject is closed.

MARC: You're getting upset.

SERGE: I am not getting upset. I'm exhausted.

MARC: See, if you're touchy about it, it means you're too caught up in other people's opinions.

SERGE: I'm exhausted, Marc. This is completely pointless. . . . To tell you the truth, I'm quite close to getting bored with the pair of you.

YVAN: Let's go and eat.

SERGE: You go, why don't you go off together?

YVAN: No! It's so rare the three of us are together.

SERGE: Just as well, by the look of it.

YVAN: I don't understand what's going on. Can't we just calm down? There's no reason to insult each other, especially over a painting.

SERGE: You realize all this "calm down" and behaving like the vicar is just adding fuel to the fire! Is this something new?

YVAN: I will not be undermined.

MARC: This is most impressive. Perhaps I should go to Finkelzohn! . . .

YVAN: You can't. There are no vacancies.
    What's that you're eating?

MARC: Gelsemium.

YVAN: I've given in to the logic of events, marriage, children, death. Stationery. What can go wrong?

(*Moved by a sudden impulse, Serge picks up the Antrios and takes it back where he found it, in the next room. He returns immediately.*)

MARC: We're not worthy to look at it. . . .

SERGE: Exactly.

MARC: Or are you afraid, if it stays in my presence, you'll finish up looking at it through my eyes? . . .

SERGE: No. You know what Paul Valéry° says? And I'd go quite a bit further.

MARC: I don't give a fuck what Paul Valéry says.

SERGE: You've gone off Paul Valéry?

MARC: Don't quote Paul Valéry at me.

SERGE: But you used to love Paul Valéry.

MARC: I don't give a fuck what Paul Valéry says.

SERGE: But I discovered him through you. You're the one who put me on to Paul Valéry.

MARC: Don't quote Paul Valéry at me, I don't give a fuck what Paul Valéry says.

SERGE: What do you give a fuck about?

MARC: I give a fuck about you buying that painting.
    I give a fuck about you spending two hundred grand on that piece of shit.

YVAN: Don't start again, Marc!

SERGE: I'm going to tell you what I give a fuck about — since everyone is coming clean — I give a fuck about your sniggering and insinuations, your suggestion that I also think this picture is a grotesque joke. You've denied that I could feel a genuine attachment to it. You've tried to set up some kind of loathsome complicity between us. And that's what's made me feel, Marc, to repeat your expression, that we have less and less in common recently, your perpetual display of suspicion.

MARC: It's true I can't imagine you genuinely loving that painting.

YVAN: But why?

MARC: Because I love Serge and I can't love the Serge who's capable of buying that painting.

SERGE: Why do you say, buying, why don't you say, loving?

MARC: Because I can't say loving, I can't believe loving.

SERGE: So why would I buy it, if I didn't love it?

MARC: That's the nub of the question.

SERGE (*to Yvan*): See how smug he is! All I'm doing is teasing him, and his answer is this serenely pompous heavy hint! . . . (*To Marc.*) And it never crossed your mind for a second, however improbable it might seem, that I might really love it and that your vicious, inflexible opinions and your disgusting assumption of complicity might be hurtful to me?

MARC: No.

SERGE: When you asked me what I thought of Paula — a girl who once spent an entire dinner party maintaining Elhers-Danlos syndrome° could be cured homeopathically — did I say I found her ugly, repellent, and charmless? I could have done.

MARC: Is that what you think of Paula?

SERGE: What's your theory?

Paul Valéry: (1871–1945), French poet, regarded by many as the greatest French writer of the twentieth century.

Elhers-Danlos syndrome: A group of connective-tissue disorders that cause fragile skin and unstable joints.

YVAN: No, of course he doesn't think that! You couldn't possibly think that of Paula!

MARC: Answer me.

SERGE: You see the effect you can have!

MARC: Do you think what you just said about Paula?

SERGE: Worse, actually.

YVAN: No!

MARC: Worse, Serge? Worse than repellent? Will you explain how someone can be worse than repellent?

SERGE: Aha! When it's something that concerns you personally, I see words can bite a little deeper! . . .

MARC: Serge, will you explain how someone can be worse than repellent? . . .

SERGE: No need to take that frosty tone. Perhaps it's — let me try and answer you — perhaps it's the way she waves away cigarette smoke.

MARC: The way she waves away cigarette smoke. . . .

SERGE: Yes. The way she waves away cigarette smoke. What appears to you a gesture of no significance, what you think of as a harmless gesture is in fact the opposite, and the way she waves away cigarette smoke sits right at the heart of her repellentness.

MARC: You're speaking to me of Paula, the woman who shares my life, in these intolerable terms, because you disapprove of her method of waving away cigarette smoke? . . .

SERGE: That's right. Her method of waving away cigarette smoke condemns her out of hand.

MARC: Serge, before I completely lose control, you'd better explain yourself. This is very serious, what you're doing.

SERGE: A normal woman would say, I'm sorry, I find the smoke a bit uncomfortable, would you mind moving your ashtray, but not her, she doesn't deign to speak, she describes her contempt in the air with this calculated gesture, wearily malicious, this hand movement she imagines is imperceptible, the implication of which is to say, go on, smoke, smoke, it's pathetic but what's the point of calling attention to it, which means you can't tell if it's you or your cigarette that's getting up her nose.

YVAN: You're exaggerating!

SERGE: You notice he doesn't say I'm wrong, he says I'm exaggerating, but he doesn't say I'm wrong. Her method of waving away cigarette smoke reveals a cold, condescending, and narrow-minded nature. Just what you're in the process of acquiring yourself. It's a shame, Marc, it's a real shame you've taken up with such a life-denying woman. . . .

YVAN: Paula is not life-denying! . . .

MARC: Take back everything you've just said, Serge.

SERGE: No.

YVAN: Yes, you must!

MARC: Take back what you've just said. . . .

YVAN: Take it back, take it back! This is ridiculous!

MARC: Serge, for the last time, I demand you take back what you've just said.

SERGE: In my view, the two of you are an aberration. A pair of fossils.

(*Marc throws himself at Serge. Yvan rushes forward to get between them.*)

MARC (*to Yvan*): Get off! . . .

SERGE (*to Yvan*): Mind your own business! . . .

(*A kind of bizarre struggle ensues, very short, which ends with a blow mistakenly landing on Yvan.*)

YVAN: Oh, shit! . . . Oh, shit! . . .

SERGE: Show me, show me. . . .

(*Yvan is groaning. More than is necessary, it would seem.*)

Come on, show me! . . . That's all right. . . . it's nothing. . . . Wait a minute. . . .

(*He goes out and comes back with a compress.*)

There you are, hold that on it for a while.

YVAN: . . . You're complete freaks, both of you. Two normal men gone completely insane!

SERGE: Don't get excited.

YVAN: That really hurt! . . . If I find out you've burst my eardrum! . . .

SERGE: Of course not.

YVAN: How do you know? You're not ear, nose, and throat! . . . Two old friends, educated people! . . .

SERGE: Go on, calm down.

YVAN: You can't demolish someone because you don't like her method of waving away cigarette smoke! . . .

SERGE: Yes, you can.

YVAN: But it doesn't make any sense!

SERGE: What do you know about sense?

YVAN: That's right, attack me, keep attacking me! . . . I could be hemorrhaging internally, I've just seen a mouse running past! . . .

SERGE: It's a rat.

YVAN: A rat?

SERGE: He comes and goes.

YVAN: You have a rat?!

SERGE: Don't take the compress away, leave it where it is.

YVAN: What's the matter with you? . . . What's happened between you? Something must have happened for you to go this demented.

SERGE: I've bought a work of art which makes Marc uncomfortable.

YVAN: You're starting again! . . . You're in a downward spiral, both of you, you can't stop yourselves. . . . It's like me and Yvonne. The most pathological relationship you can imagine!

SERGE: Who's Yvonne?

YVAN: My stepmother!

SERGE: It's a long time since you mentioned her.

(*Brief silence.*)

MARC: Why didn't you tell me right away what you thought about Paula?

SERGE: I didn't want to upset you.

MARC: No, no, no. . . .

SERGE: What do you mean, no, no, no? . . .

MARC: No.

When I asked you what you thought of Paula, what you said was: she's a perfect match for you.

SERGE: Yes. . . .

MARC: Which sounded quite positive, coming from you.

SERGE: Sure. . . .

MARC: Given the state you were in at the time.

SERGE: All right, what are you trying to prove?

MARC: But today, your assessment of Paula, or in other words me, is far harsher.

SERGE: . . . I don't understand.

MARC: Of course you understand.

SERGE: I don't.

MARC: Since I can no longer support you in your frenzied, though recent, craving for novelty, I've become "condescending," "narrow-minded,". . ."fossilized.". . .

YVAN: I'm in agony! It's like a corkscrew drilling through my brain!

SERGE: Have a drop of brandy.

YVAN: What do you think? . . . If something's shaken loose in my brain, don't you think alcohol's a bit of a risk?

SERGE: Would you like an aspirin?

YVAN: I'm not sure aspirin agrees with me. . . .

SERGE: Then what the hell do you want?

YVAN: Don't worry about me. Carry on with your preposterous conversation, don't pay any attention to me.

MARC: Easier said than done.

YVAN: You might squeeze out a drop of compassion. But no.

SERGE: I don't mind your spending time with Paula. I don't resent you being with Paula.

MARC: You've no reason to resent it.

SERGE: But you . . . you resent me . . . well, I was about to say, for being with the Antrios!

MARC: Yes!

SERGE: I'm missing something here.

MARC: I didn't replace you with Paula.

SERGE: Are you saying, I replaced you with the Antrios?

MARC: Yes.

SERGE: . . . I replaced you with the Antrios?

MARC: Yes. With the Antrios . . . and all it implies.

SERGE (to Yvan): Do you understand what he's talking about?

YVAN: I couldn't care less, you're both insane.

MARC: In my time, you'd never have bought that picture.

SERGE: What's that supposed to mean, in your time?

MARC: The time you made a distinction between me and other people, when you judged things by my standards.

SERGE: Was there such a time?

MARC: That's just cruel. And petty.

SERGE: No, I assure you, I'm staggered.

MARC: And if Yvan hadn't turned into such a sponge, he'd back me up.

YVAN: Go on, that's right, I've told you, it's water off a duck's back.

MARC (to Serge): There was a time you were proud to be my friend. . . . You congratulated yourself on my peculiarity, on my taste for standing apart. You enjoyed exhibiting me untamed to your circle, you, whose life was so normal. I was your alibi. But . . . eventually, I suppose, that sort of affection dries up. . . . Belatedly, you claim your independence.

SERGE: "Belatedly" is nice.

MARC: But I detest your independence. Its violence. You've abandoned me. I've been betrayed. As far as I'm concerned, you're a traitor.

(Silence.)

SERGE (to Yvan): . . . If I understand correctly, he was my mentor! . . .

(Yvan doesn't respond. Marc stares at him contemptuously. Slight pause.)

. . . And if I loved you as my mentor . . . what was the nature of your feelings?

MARC: You can guess.

SERGE: Yes, yes, but I want to hear you say it.

MARC: . . . I enjoyed your admiration. I was flattered. I was always grateful to you for thinking of me as a man apart. I even thought being a man apart was a somehow superior condition, until one day you pointed out to me that it wasn't.

SERGE: This is very alarming.

MARC: It's the truth.

SERGE: What a disaster . . . !

MARC: Yes, what a disaster!

SERGE: What a disaster!

MARC: Especially for me. . . . Whereas you've found a new family. Your penchant for idolatry has unearthed new objects of worship. The Artist! . . . *Deconstruction!*

(Short silence.)

YVAN: What is deconstruction? . . .

MARC: You don't know about deconstruction? . . . Ask Serge, he's very much on top of the subject. . . . (To Serge.) To convince me some ridiculous artwork is comprehensible, you pick a phrase from *Builders' Weekly.* . . . Oh, you're smiling! You see, when you smile like that, I think there's still some hope, like an idiot. . . .

YVAN: Why don't you make up? And let's spend an enjoyable evening, all this is ludicrous!

MARC: . . . It's my fault. We haven't seen much of one another recently. I've been away and you started mixing with the great and the good . . . the Ropses . . . the Desprez-Couderts . . . that dentist, Guy Hallié . . . he's the one who . . .

SERGE: No, no, no, no, not at all, he's from another world, he only likes conceptual Art. . . .

MARC: It's all the same thing.

SERGE: No, it's not all the same thing.

MARC: You see, more evidence of how I let you slip away . . . now when we talk we can't even make ourselves understood.

SERGE: I had no idea whatsoever — really, it's come as a complete surprise — the extent to which I was under your influence and in your control.

MARC: Not in my control, as it turns out. . . . You should never leave your friends unchaperoned. Your friends need to be chaperoned, otherwise they'll get away. . . .

Look at poor Yvan, whose chaotic behavior used to delight us, we've allowed him to become this timid stationer. . . . Practically married. . . . He brought us his originality and now he's making every effort to piss it away.

SERGE: Us! He brought us! Do you realize what you're saying? Everything has to revolve around you! Why can't you learn to love people for themselves, Marc?

MARC: What does that mean, for themselves?

SERGE: For what they are.

MARC: But what are they?! What are they?! . . .

Apart from my faith in them? . . .

I'm desperate to find a friend who has some kind of prior existence. So far, I've had no luck. I've had to mold you. . . . But you see, it never works. There comes a day when your creature has dinner with the Desprez-Couderts and, to confirm his new status, goes off and buys a white painting.

(*Silence.*)

SERGE: So here we are at the end of a fifteen-year friendship. . . .

MARC: Yes. . . .

YVAN: Pathetic. . . .

MARC: You see, if we'd only managed to have a normal discussion, that is, if I'd have been able to put my point of view without losing my temper. . . .

SERGE: Well? . . .

MARC: Nothing. . . .

SERGE: Yes. Go on. Why can't we exchange one single dispassionate word?

MARC: . . . I don't believe in the values which dominate contemporary Art. The rule of novelty. The rule of surprise.

Surprise is dead meat, Serge. No sooner conceived than dead.

SERGE: All right. So?

MARC: That's all.

Except that my appeal to you has always been my surprise value.

SERGE: What are you talking about?

MARC: A surprise which has lasted quite some time, I'll admit.

YVAN: Finkelzohn is a genius.

I told you he'd understood the whole thing!

MARC: I'd prefer it if you stopped refereeing, Yvan, and stopped imagining you're not fully implicated in this conversation.

YVAN: You want to implicate me, I refuse, what's it to do with me? I've already got a burst eardrum, you work things out for yourselves!

MARC: Perhaps he does have a burst eardrum. I hit him very hard.

(*Serge sniggers.*)

SERGE: Please, stop boasting.

MARC: See, Yvan, what I can't bear about you at the moment — quite apart from what I've already told you — is your urge to put Serge and me on the same level. You would like us to be equal. To indulge your cowardice. Talking on an equal footing, equal the way you thought of us when we were friends. But we never were equal, Yvan. You have to choose.

YVAN: I have chosen.

MARC: Excellent.

SERGE: I don't need a supporter.

MARC: You're not going to turn the poor boy down?

YVAN: Why do we see each other, if we hate each other? It's obvious we do hate each other! Or rather, I don't hate you, but you hate each other! And you hate me! So why do we see each other? . . . I was looking forward to a relaxing evening after a ridiculously fraught week, meeting my two best friends, going to the cinema, having a laugh, getting away from all these dramas. . . .

SERGE: Are you aware that you've talked about nothing but yourself?

YVAN: Well, who are you talking about? Everybody talks about themselves!

SERGE: You fuck up our evening, you . . .

YVAN: I fuck up your evening? . . .

SERGE: Yes.

YVAN: I fuck up your evening?! I?! I fuck up your evening?!

MARC: All right, don't get excited!

YVAN: You're saying it's me who's fucked up your evening?! . . .

SERGE: How many more times are you going to say it?

YVAN: Just answer the question, are you saying it's me who's fucked up your evening?! . . .

MARC: You arrive three-quarters of an hour late, you don't apologize, you deluge us with your domestic woes. . . .

SERGE: And your inertia, your sheer neutral spectator's inertia has lured Marc and me into the worst excesses.

YVAN: You as well! You're starting as well?

SERGE: Yes, because on this subject I'm entirely in agreement with him. You create the conditions of conflict.

MARC: You've been piping up with this finicky, subservient voice of reason ever since you arrived, it's intolerable.

YVAN: You know I could burst into tears. . . . I could start crying right now. . . . I'm very close to tears.

MARC: Cry.

SERGE: Cry.

YVAN: Cry! You're telling me to cry!

MARC: You've every reason to cry, you're marrying a gorgon, you're losing your two best friends. . . .

YVAN: That's it then, is it, it's all over!

MARC: You said it yourself, what's the point of seeing each other, if we hate each other?

YVAN: What about my wedding?! You're my witnesses, remember?
SERGE: Find someone else.
YVAN: I can't! You're on the invitation!
MARC: You can choose someone else at the last minute.
YVAN: You're not allowed to!
SERGE: Of course you are!
YVAN: You're not! . . .
MARC: Don't panic, we'll come.
SERGE: But what you ought to do is cancel the wedding.
MARC: He's right.
YVAN: Oh, shit! What have I ever done to you? Shit!

(*He bursts into tears.*)
(*Time passes.*)

It's brutal what you're doing! You could have had your fight after the 12th, but no, you're determined to ruin my wedding, a wedding which is already a catastrophe, which has made me lose half a stone and now you're completely buggering it up! The only two people whose presence guaranteed some spark of satisfaction are determined to destroy one another, just my luck! . . . (*To Marc.*) You think I like packs of filofax paper or rolls of sellotape, you think any normal man wakes up one day desperate to sell expandable document wallets? . . . What am I supposed to do? I pissed around for forty years, I made you laugh, oh, yes, wonderful, I made all my friends laugh their heads off playing the fool, but come the evening, who was left solitary as a rat? Who crawled back into his hole every evening all on his own? This buffoon, dying of loneliness, who'd switch on anything that talks and who does he find on the answering machine? His mother. His mother. And his mother.

(*A short silence.*)

MARC: Don't get yourself in such a state.
YVAN: Don't get yourself in such a state! Who got me in this state in the first place? Look at me — I don't have your refined sensibilities. I'm a lightweight. I have no opinions.
MARC: Calm down. . . .
YVAN: Don't tell me to calm down! What possible reason do I have to calm down, are you trying to drive me demented, telling me to calm down? Calm down's the worst thing you can say to someone who's lost his calm! I'm not like you, I don't want to be an authority figure, I don't want to be a point of reference, I don't want to be self-sufficient, I just want to be your friend Yvan the joker! Yvan the joker!

(*Silence.*)

SERGE: Could we try to steer clear of pathos? . . .
YVAN: I've finished.
Haven't you got any nibbles? Anything, just to stop from passing out.
SERGE: I have some olives.
YVAN: Hand them over.

(*Serge reaches for a little bowl of olives and hands it to him.*)

SERGE (*to Marc*): Want some?

(*Marc nods. Yvan hands him the bowl. They eat olives.*)

YVAN: Is there somewhere to put the . . .
SERGE: Yes.

(*He fetches a saucer and puts it on the table. Pause.*)

YVAN (*still eating olives*): . . . To think we've reached these extremes. . . . Apocalypse because of a white square. . . .
SERGE: It is not white.
YVAN: A piece of white shit! . . .

(*He's seized by uncontrollable laughter.*)

That's what it is, a piece of white shit! . . . Let's face it, mate. . . . What you've bought is insane! . . .

(*Marc laughs, caught up by Yvan's extravagance. Serge leaves the room. He returns immediately with the Antrios.*)

SERGE: Do you have one of your famous felt-tips? . . .
YVAN: What for? . . . You're not going to draw on the painting.
SERGE: Do you or don't you?
YVAN: Just a minute. . . . (*He goes through the pockets of his jacket.*) Yes. . . . A blue one. . . .
SERGE: Give it to me.

(*Yvan hands the felt-tip to Serge.*)
(*Serge takes the felt-tip, pulls the top off it, examines the tip for a moment, puts the top back on.*)
(*He looks up at Marc and throws him the felt-tip. Marc catches it.*)
(*Slight pause.*)

(*To Marc.*) Go on.

(*Silence.*)

Go on!

(*Marc approaches the painting. . . .
He looks at Serge. . . .
Then he takes the top off the felt-tip.*)

YVAN: You're not going to do it! . . .

(*Marc is looking at Serge.*)

SERGE: Come on.
YVAN: You're raving mad, both of you!

(*Marc leans towards the painting.
Under Yvan's horrified gaze, he draws the felt-tip along one of the diagonal scars. Serge remains impassive.
Then, carefully, on this slope, Marc draws a little skier with a woolly hat.
When he's finished, he straightens up and contemplates his work.*)
(*Serge remains adamantine.*)
(*Yvan is as if turned to stone.*)
(*Silence.*)

SERGE: Well, I'm starving.
    Shall we eat?

(*Marc tries a smile. He puts the top back on and play-fully throws the pen to Yvan, who catches it.*)

(*At Serge's.*)

    (*At the back, hanging on the wall, the Antrios. Stand-ing in front of the canvas, Marc is holding a basin of water, into which Serge is dipping a little piece of cloth. Marc has rolled up his sleeves and Serge is wearing a little builder's apron which is too short for him. Round about are various cleaning products, bottles of white spirit and stain remover, rags and sponges. Moving very delicately, Serge puts the finishing touch to the cleaning of the painting.*)

    (*The Antrios is as white as ever. Marc puts down the basin and looks at the painting. Serge turns to Yvan, who's sitting off to one side. Yvan nods approvingly. Serge steps back and contemplates the picture in his turn.*)

    (*Silence.*)

YVAN (*as if alone, speaking in a slightly muffled voice*): . . . The day after the wedding, at the Mont-parnasse cemetery, Catherine put her wedding bou-quet and a little bag of sugared almonds on her mother's grave. I slipped away to cry behind a monument and in the evening, thinking again about this touching tribute, I started silently sobbing in my bed. I absolutely must speak to Finkelzohn about my tendency to cry, I cry all the time, it's not normal for someone my age. It started, or at least clearly revealed itself at Serge's, the evening of the white painting. After Serge, in an act of pure madness, had demonstrated to Marc that he cared more about him than he did about his painting, we went and had dinner, chez Emile. Over dinner, Serge and Marc took the decision to try to rebuild a relationship destroyed by word and deed. At a certain moment, one of them used the expression "trial period" and I burst into tears.

    This expression, "trial period," applied to our friendship, set off in me an uncontrollable and ridicu-lous convulsion.

    In fact I can no longer bear any kind of rational argument, nothing formative in the world, nothing great or beautiful in the world has ever been born of rational argument.

(*Pause.*)

(*Serge dries his hands. He goes to empty the basin of water then puts away all the cleaning products, until there's no sign left of domestic activity. Once again he looks at his painting. Then he turns and advances towards the audience.*)

SERGE: When Marc and I succeeded in obliterating the skier, with the aid of Swiss soap with added ox gall, recommended by Paula, I looked at the Antrios and turned to Marc:
    "Did you know ink from felt-tips was washable?"
    "No," Marc said. . . ."No . . . did you?"
    "No," I said, very fast, lying. I came within an inch of saying, yes, I did know. But how could I have launched our trial period with such a disappointing admission? . . . On the other hand, was it right to start with a lie? . . . A lie! Let's be reasonable. Why am I so absurdly virtuous? Why does my relationship with Marc have to be so complicated? . . .

(*Gradually, the light begins to narrow down on the Antrios. Marc approaches the painting.*)

MARC: Under the white clouds, the snow is falling.
    You can't see the white clouds, or the snow.
    Or the cold, or the white glow of the earth.
    A solitary man glides downhill on his skis.
    The snow is falling.
    It falls until the man disappears back into the landscape.
    My friend Serge, who's one of my oldest friends, has bought a painting.
    It's a canvas about five foot by four.
    It represents a man who moves across a space and disappears.

COMMENTARY

Louis Menand (b. 1952)
WHAT IS "ART"?   *1998*

Yasmina Reza's play is not really about art in the sense that Louis Menand considers in this discussion of the play and of modern avant-garde art. However, for those in the audience concerned about matters aesthetic and haunted by the issues that center on an abstract white-on-white painting, Menand's commentary is extremely useful. He examines the issues in the play in the context of modern art.

Yasmina Reza's one-act play *"Art,"* which opens here this winter, is about a white-on-white abstract painting that nearly ruins a friendship among three men. A character named Serge buys the painting for an extravagant sum; his friend Marc, invited to admire the new purchase, pronounces it "shit"; the third friend, Yvan, who has no aesthetic views (or is happy to see equal merit in both views), is made wretched by the subsequent bickering, to which most of the play's ninety minutes are devoted.

By far the most interesting thing about *"Art"* is its popularity. It premiered in Berlin and in 1994 opened in Paris, where it ran for eighteen months at the Comédie des Champs-Élysées and won the Molière Award for best play, best production, and best author. Sean Connery's wife, Micheline, saw the French production and persuaded her husband to bring the play to London, where, with Connery as coproducer, in a translation by Christopher Hampton, and starring Albert Finney and Tom Courtenay, it opened in 1996 and was a big hit all over again.

As the quotation marks in the title signal, the play basically sides with Marc, the character who thinks that his friend's notion of "art" is ridiculous. Still, it suggests, Marc is taking his outrage a shade too seriously, since, as phony as the painting probably is, there's no point in spoiling a friendship over it. This is evidently a view that suits the audience that has made *"Art"* an international success. When I saw the play in London last fall, the audience laughed earnestly at every one of Marc's rather blunt and obvious gibes but gasped in horror when, toward the end of the play, he defaced the painting with a felt-tip pen. They agreed that the canvas had no aesthetic merit, but they felt that its market value ought to be respected.

What's odd about the play is the notion that a white-on-white canvas represents the latest refinement in avant-garde pretension. White-on-white canvases were the latest refinement in avant-garde pretension forty years ago. And monochrome art didn't represent a sneer at aesthetic values. It represented the culmination of aestheticism, the final distillation of the idea of painting as painting. The fictional Serge has invested in one of the prime artifacts of an era that the real-life, present-day avant-garde is in boisterous reaction against. The tacky "representational" landscape that hangs in Marc's living room is a lot more plausibly postmodern than his friend's Greenbergian antique.

What does seem right about *"Art,"* though, is how inarticulate the characters become when they attempt to justify their reactions to Serge's painting ("shit" is perhaps not the critical *mot juste* for an all-white canvas) and how quickly the disagreement turns personal. This is, at bottom, what the audiences are probably responding to. They've been in these situations themselves, and, although the relationships in the play are not very convincing — it's hard to understand how these three guys ever got to be friends in the first place, so the damage to their friendship is somewhat lacking in poignancy — the spectacle of a disagreement about art devolving into a bitter spat about personalities carries a certain low-level shock of recognition.

The incoherence and inconclusiveness of the aesthetic arguments in *"Art"* strike a chord because people have lost any clear sense of what a coherent and conclusive aesthetic argument would look like. This is not the result of dumbing down; it's the result of smartening up. It derives from the view that aesthetic arguments are really only ex-post-facto justifications for art that people happen to like, and this seems to have become the advanced view on the subject.

Last fall when the *Times* asked seventeen "art-world participants and observers" the question "What is art?," all the experts gave the same answer. They said that the question has no answer. The art historians Thomas McEvilley ("It seems pretty clear by now that more or less anything can be designated as art") and Robert Rosenblum ("By now the idea of defining art is so remote I don't think anyone would dare to do it"), William Rubin, of the Museum of Modern Art ("There is no single definition of art"), Philippe de Montebello, of the Metropolitan Museum of Art ("There's no consensus about anything today"), Arthur Danto, a philosopher and the art critic of *The Nation* ("You can't say something's art or not art anymore. That's all finished"), and Peter Hoekstra, a Republican congressman from Michigan, who is a leading opponent of the National Endowment for the Arts ("Art is whatever people want to perceive it to be"), all agreed. There can be no definition of art because art is just whatever people say it is.

The triumph of the consensus of no consensus should be gratifying to Arthur Danto, who has been trying since 1984 to explain why it is no longer possible, by referring to the way it looks, to distinguish something that is a work of art from something that is not. His argument, eloquently summed up in his most recent book, *After the End of Art,* is that after Andy Warhol exhibited simulacra of Brillo boxes (actually of shipping cartons for Brillo boxes), in 1964, anything could be art. With *Brillo Box,* the history of art came to an end. There was no longer a master narrative dictating what form works of art should take next, since having a particular form no longer determined whether a thing was a work of art.

People in London who last fall walked from the theater where *"Art"* was playing across Piccadilly Circus to the Royal Academy of Arts could see realized, in an exhibition, from the Saatchi Collection, called "Sensation," the polymorphous vision that must have been dancing in Danto's head when he introduced his theory back in 1984: snapshots, videos, abstract paintings, figurative paintings, found objects, installations, and the dead animals of Damien Hirst. A characteristic piece — *Self,* by Marc Quinn — is listed in the catalogue as having been rendered in the following media: blood, stainless steel, Perspex, and refrigeration equipment. Chris Ofili's works on linen were executed in oil paint, polyester resin, map pins, and elephant dung. If Serge had a Lucite box containing the head of a cow crawling with maggots on display in his living room (which is the substance of a piece by Hirst entitled *A Thousand Years*), "*Art*" would seem a lot more up to date.

Danto still believes that art has essential qualities; he just doesn't think that those qualities reside in its appearance. But it's easy to slip from the recognition that anything could be art to the position that art is an arbitrary category: Danto calls his conception of posthistorical art "pluralist," meaning that all forms of expression are now permitted; and one reason so many of the people in the *Times* survey echo his view is that pluralism is the ascendant philosophy of the day. Nobody wants to get caught asserting that one type of art is inherently better than another — not even Congressman Hoekstra. Pluralist talk about tastes and values is everywhere. The belief that we should never fall into the grip of a single belief has us firmly in its grip.

Pluralism is an admirable point of view, but it wouldn't be much use if it prevented people from judging anything. The way to do the right pluralist thing today, therefore, seems to involve the following decorum: you do not criticize someone else's tastes or values by saying they are inferior, perverted, uncivilized, or "not art." That kind of talk is invidious, and suggests that you are applying standards you imagine to be impersonal. Instead, you say, "I don't happen to like it," and you are absolved of chauvinism. You are also absolved of attending to any reasons you should like it. When liking is all, disliking is enough.

If you are a pro-arts person, of course, you're supposed to keep your dislikes to yourself (which is why the audience for "*Art*" disapproves of Marc's antics, even though they sympathize with his exasperation). One of the pieces in the "Sensation" exhibition in London was a large clock — *A Bigger Clock,* by Darren Almond. Every sixty seconds, it emitted a tremendous reverberating noise, like the amplified sound of a prison door slamming shut. The piece was mounted in the lobby, where the tickets and the catalogues were sold. I bought my catalogue from a young guy who looked like the kind of fairly hip young guy you would expect to find selling catalogues in a gallery. I asked him if listening to this amplified sound of a prison door slamming shut every sixty seconds all day might possibly get a little — well, old. He gave me a look that said, "If I could get my hands on the guy who made that thing, I would personally strangle the bastard." But all he actually said was "A little."

In dispensing with a single definition of art, we are liberating ourselves less completely than we imagine. The regime of "no definition" is just as dictatorial as every previous regime. A pluralist consensus demands a pluralist art. When the official art-world position is that art can look like anything, you get the kind of art on display in the "Sensation" show — that is, art that looks the way art would look if art could look like anything. As long as "art" is a term that confers value on an object (and there's no reason to have the term at all if it doesn't), people will mean something by it, whether or not they are willing to say so to the *Times*. There is no exit from concepts.

For the artists themselves, philosophical definitions are usually secondary anyway. As easily persuaded of his own significance as he was, Warhol probably didn't think he was bringing the history of art to an end. He had a much more parochial ambition in mind: he wanted to succeed Jackson Pollock as the American art king. *POPism,* his brilliantly catty memoir of the demise of the genius-driven, Abstract Expressionist, macho New York art world of the fifties, has a story that's so close to the story of *"Art"* it's hard to believe Reza doesn't know it. One day around 1960, Warhol drops in on his friend Emile de Antonio, who owns one of Frank Stella's early black paintings, and finds him distraught. A neighbor had seen the Stella on the wall, de Antonio recounts, and asked what it was. When he told her it was a painting, she burst out laughing: *That* was a painting? And she walked over and poured a bottle of whiskey on it, completely ruining it. Just then, the phone rings and, coincidentally, it's Stella. De Antonio describes ruefully what has just happened to his painting. Stella tells him not to worry. He'll make him another one just like it.

Paula Vogel

Paula Vogel (b. 1951) came from a working-class family and knew she would have to make it on her own if she made it at all. For her, that knowledge was essentially the best inheritance she could have had. Her early years were marred by her parents' divorce and the loss of a father whom she came to know only in later years when her closest sibling, Carl, was dying of AIDS. Her earliest efforts in playwriting also met with rejection. After losing her scholarship to Bryn Mawr College and when she devoted herself to dramatic literature, she graduated from Catholic University in Washington and then was turned down by the Yale School of Drama. Her earliest plays were also turned down by the Eugene O'Neill National Playwright's Conference. In retrospect, she feels that these were good things because they made her learn her craft in a difficult — and original — way, which led eventually to her winning the Pulitzer Prize for *How I Learned to Drive*.

Vogel's earliest exposure to theater was in Washington, D.C. She talks about having "stumbled into drama class" when she was a sophomore in high school and beginning to find her way in theater. Her high school drama teacher was gay, and she feels he must have realized that she was herself a lesbian. She resisted taking acting roles — although she coached other students — and spent her years in high school as a stage manager. As a young playwright she found other friends who were trying to write, and they gathered together to read each other's work. They occasionally did exercises, some of which became useful teaching tools for Vogel at Brown University. For example, they wrote complete plays in forty-eight hours as a way of getting the essentials down as quickly as possible. Some of her earliest work had its origin in these experiments, including a version of *How I Learned to Drive*.

Some of her plays have startling images, such as a bizarre Groucho-Marx-like doctor treating a dying AIDS patient in *The Baltimore Waltz* (Obie Award for best play 1992), a play about the death of her beloved brother Carl, who had begun a professional career as an English professor but switched to being a librarian. He was gay, and homophobia, according to Vogel, hurt him more than the disease that killed him. Her plays are famous for scatological humor, jokes about the body, and extremely plain talk.

Among her early plays is one about lesbians who parent several little boys: *And Baby Makes Seven* (1984) — a daring excursion into territory that few playwrights have explored. Another early play, *The Oldest Profession* (1988), treats older prostitutes. *Hot 'n' Throbbing* (1994) examines the effect of theater on its characters. *The Mineola Twins* (1996) was written before *How I Learned to Drive* but was produced later, in 1999. Vogel thinks of this play as a comedy and something of a contrast to *How I Learned to Drive*, which is, if not a tragedy, certainly serious in nature. Yet it too has moments of genuine comedy.

Currently, Paula Vogel is preparing screenplays for two of her theater pieces: *The Oldest Profession* and *How I Learned to Drive*.

HOW I LEARNED TO DRIVE

How I Learned to Drive was first produced in New York off-Broadway in 1997. It won not only the Pulitzer Prize but the New York Drama Critics' Circle, Drama Desk, and Obie awards for best play of the year. It is published in a volume with *The Mineola Twins* called *The Mammary Plays*. Vogel explains that large-busted women remained an emblem for her in the construction of both plays. As a feminist, Vogel is interested in our fetishization of women's bodies, and both these plays move toward revealing the way the culture, both men and women, regard women's bodies, even while praising their minds.

All the characters in Li'l Bit's family are named in an unusual way. Li'l Bit explains, "In my family, if we call someone 'Big Papa,' it's not because he's tall. In my family, folks tend to get nicknamed for their genitalia. Uncle Peck, for example. My mamma's adage was 'the titless wonder.' Even Li'l Bit was named after she was physically examined at birth. Uncle Peck, married to Li'l Bit's mother's sister Mary, is not a blood relation — a fact he constantly stresses to Li'l Bit — and he tells her he has loved her since she was small enough to hold in his hand. Even Big Papa chases Grandma around the house: it's an unusual and curious family.

The play is about sexual molestation — but about many other things, too. It is about families, about growing up, about becoming independent, and most of all about being a survivor. In a interview with Arthur Holmberg, Vogel has said, "My play dramatizes the gifts we receive from people who hurt us." When asked what gift Li'l Bit received, she responded, "She received the gift of how to survive." Vogel uses learning to drive as a complex metaphor for sexual initiation. At the same time, the metaphor examines what a man expects from a close relationship with a woman and what a woman expects from a close relationship with a man. Uncle Peck is careful never to hurt Li'l Bit and always reminds her that he doesn't want her to do anything she doesn't wish to do. But at the same time, Uncle Peck "has a way" with adolescent girls, as his wife tells us. He listens to Li'l Bit and becomes her confidante, patiently waiting for her to accept him on his own terms.

Although he is a predator, Uncle Peck is not necessarily a villain in the play. He takes advantage of Li'l Bit starting at age eleven and continues until she is eighteen and in college. For Vogel, part of the learning process for Li'l Bit is, as Vogel has said, becoming "an adult looking at and understanding her complicity." Then the next step is self-forgiveness. This step is essential to moving forward in her life.

How I Learned to Drive in Performance

The Vineyard Theatre in New York City produced the play in February 1997 and moved it to the large Century Theater in April. It was reviewed warmly and received positively by audiences, eventually winning Vogel the Pulitzer Prize for drama for 1997. The play relies on an interesting device, the Greek Chorus, a character who speaks in the voice of characters alluded to but not present, such as Li'l Bit's mother, grandmother, grandfather, and aunt. Vogel also wanted to have slides shown at critical moments, such as the scene in which Uncle Peck is taking photographs of Li'l Bit and in the scene in which Uncle Peck rhapsodizes over 1950s automobiles. Not all directors use the slides. For example, they were not used in the original New York production. Vogel's method of writing, like that of many playwrights, is to respond to the actors' interpretation of lines during rehearsal and rewriting. *How I Learned to Drive* benefited from that method.

In 1998 *How I Learned to Drive* had twenty-six regional productions and was the most produced play in America. More than thirty more productions are scheduled abroad.

Paula Vogel (b. 1951)

HOW I LEARNED TO DRIVE

1997

Characters

LI'L BIT, *A woman who ages forty-something to eleven years old.*

PECK, *Attractive man in his forties. Despite a few problems, he should be played by an actor one might cast in the role of Atticus in* To Kill A Mockingbird.

THE GREEK CHORUS, *If possible, these three members should be able to sing three-part harmony.*

    MALE GREEK CHORUS, *Plays Grandfather, Waiter, High School Boys. Thirties — forties.*
    FEMALE GREEK CHORUS, *Plays Mother, Aunt Mary, High School Girls. Thirty–fifty.*
    TEENAGE GREEK CHORUS, *Plays Grandmother, High School Girls, and the voice of eleven-year-old Li'l Bit. Note on the casting of this actor: I would strongly recommend casting a young woman who is "of legal age," that is, twenty-one to twenty-five years old, who can look as close to eleven as possible. The contrast with the other cast members will help. If the actor is too young, the audience may feel uncomfortable.*

(*As the house lights dim, a Voice announces:*)

Safety First — You and Driver Education.

(*Then the sound of a key turning the ignition of a car. Li'l Bit steps into a spotlight on the stage; "well-endowed," she is a softer-looking woman in the present time than she was at seventeen.*)

LI'L BIT: Sometimes to tell a secret, you first have to teach a lesson. We're going to start our lesson tonight on an early, warm summer evening.

In a parking lot overlooking the Beltsville Agricultural Farms in suburban Maryland.

Less than a mile away, the crumbling concrete of U.S. One wends its way past one-room revival churches, the porno drive-in, and boarded up motels with For Sale signs tumbling down.

Like I said, it's a warm summer evening.

Here on the land the Department of Agriculture owns, the smell of sleeping farm animal is thick on the air. The smells of clover and hay mix in with the smells of the leather dashboard. You can still imagine how Maryland used to be, before the malls took over. This countryside was once dotted with farmhouses — from their porches you could have witnessed the Civil War raging in the front fields.

Oh yes. There's a moon over Maryland tonight, that spills into the car where I sit beside a man old enough to be — did I mention how still the night is? Damp soil and tranquil air. It's the kind of night that makes a middle-aged man with a mortgage feel like a country boy again.

It's 1969. And I am very old, very cynical of the world, and I know it all. In short, I am seventeen years old, parking off a dark lane with a married man on an early summer night.

(*Lights up on two chairs facing front — or a Buick Riviera, if you will. Waiting patiently, with a smile on his face, Peck sits sniffing the night air. Li'l Bit climbs in beside him, seventeen years old and tense. Throughout the following, the two sit facing directly front. They do not touch.* *Their bodies remain passive. Only their facial expressions emote.*)

PECK: Ummm. I love the smell of your hair.

LI'L BIT: Uh-huh.

PECK: Oh, Lord. Ummmm. (*Beat.*) A man could die happy like this.

LI'L BIT: Well, *don't.*

PECK: What shampoo is this?

LI'L BIT: Herbal Essence.

PECK: Herbal Essence. I'm gonna buy me some. Herbal Essence. And when I'm all alone in the house, I'm going to get into the bathtub, and uncap the bottle and —

LI'L BIT: — Be good.

PECK: What?

LI'L BIT: Stop being . . . bad.

PECK: What did you think I was going to say? What do you think I'm going to do with the shampoo?

LI'L BIT: I don't want to know. I don't want to hear it.

PECK: I'm going to wash my hair. That's all.

LI'L BIT: Oh.

PECK: What did you think I was going to do?

LI'L BIT: Nothing . . . I don't know. Something . . . nasty.

PECK: With shampoo? Lord, gal — your mind!

LI'L BIT: And whose fault is it?

PECK: Not mine. I've got the mind of a boy scout.

LI'L BIT: Right. A horny boy scout.

PECK: Boy scouts are always horny. What do you think the first Merit Badge is for?

LI'L BIT: There. You're going to be nasty again.

PECK: Oh, no. I'm good. Very good.

LI'L BIT: It's getting late.

PECK: Don't change the subject. I was talking about how good I am. (*Beat.*) Are you ever gonna let me show you how good I am?

LI'L BIT: Don't go over the line now.

PECK: I won't. I'm not gonna do anything you don't want me to do.

LI'L BIT: That's right.

PECK: And I've been good all week.

LI'L BIT: You have?

PECK: Yes. All week. Not a single drink.

LI'L BIT: Good boy.

PECK: Do I get a reward? For not drinking?

LI'L BIT: A small one. It's getting late.

PECK: Just let me undo you. I'll do you back up.

LI'L BIT: All right. But be quick about it.

(*Peck pantomimes undoing Li'l Bit's brassiere with one hand.*)

You know, that's amazing. The way you can undo the hooks through my blouse with one hand.

PECK: Years of practice.

LI'L BIT: You would make an incredible brain surgeon with that dexterity.

PECK: I'll bet Clyde — what's the name of the boy taking you to the prom?

LI'L BIT: Claude Souders.

PECK: Claude Souders. I'll bet it takes him two hands, lights on, and you helping him on to get to first base.

LI'L BIT: Maybe.

(*Beat.*)

PECK: Can I . . . kiss them? Please?

LI'L BIT: I don't know.

PECK: Don't make a grown man beg.

LI'L BIT: Just one kiss.

PECK: I'm going to lift your blouse.

LI'L BIT: It's a little cold.

(*Peck laughs gently.*)

PECK: That's not why you're shivering.

(*They sit, perfectly still, for a long moment of silence. Peck makes gentle, concentric circles with his thumbs in the air in front of him.*)

How does that feel?

(*Li'l Bit closes her eyes, carefully keeps her voice calm:*)

LI'L BIT: It's . . . okay.

(*Sacred music, organ music or a boy's choir swells beneath the following.*)

PECK: I tell you, you can keep all the cathedrals of Europe. Just give me a second with these — these celestial orbs —

(*Peck bows his head as if praying. But he is kissing her nipple. Li'l Bit, eyes still closed, rears back her head on the leather Buick car seat.*)

LI'L BIT: Uncle Peck — we've got to go. I've got graduation rehearsal at school tomorrow morning. And you should get on home to Aunt Mary —

PECK: — All right, Li'l Bit.

LI'L BIT: — *Don't* call me that no more. (*Calmer.*) Any more. I'm a big girl now, Uncle Peck. As you know.

(*Li'l Bit pantomimes refastening her bra behind her back.*)

PECK: That you are. Going on eighteen. Kittens will turn into cats. (*Sighs.*) I live all week long for these few minutes with you — you know that?

LI'L BIT: I'll drive.

(*A Voice cuts in with:*)

Idling in the Neutral Gear.

(*Sound of car revving cuts off the sacred music; Li'l Bit, now an adult, rises out of the car and comes to us.*)

LI'L BIT: In most families, relatives get names like "Junior," or "Brother," or "Bubba." In my family, if we call someone "Big Papa," it's not because he's tall. In my family, folks tend to get nicknamed for their genitalia. Uncle Peck, for example. My mama's adage was "the titless wonder," and my cousin Bobby got branded for life as "B.B."

(*In unison with Greek Chorus:*)

LI'L BIT: For blue balls.   GREEK CHORUS: For blue balls.

FEMALE GREEK CHORUS (*as Mother*): And of course, we were so excited to have a baby girl that when the nurse brought you in and said, "It's a girl! It's a baby girl!" I just had to see for myself. So we whipped your diapers down and parted your chubby little legs — and right between your legs there was —

(*Peck has come over during the above and chimes along:*)

PECK: Just a little bit.   GREEK CHORUS: Just a little bit.

FEMALE GREEK CHORUS (*as Mother*): And when you were born, you were so tiny that you fit in Uncle Peck's outstretched hand.

(*Peck stretches his hand out.*)

PECK: Now that's a fact. I held you, one day old, right in this hand.

(*A traffic signal is projected of a bicycle in a circle with a diagonal red slash.*)

LI'L BIT: Even with my family background, I was sixteen or so before I realized that pedophilia did not mean people who loved to bicycle . . . .

(*A Voice intrudes:*)

Driving in First Gear.

LI'L BIT: 1969. A typical family dinner.

FEMALE GREEK CHORUS (*as Mother*): Look, Grandma. Li'l Bit's getting to be as big in the bust as you are.

LI'L BIT: Mother! Could we please change the subject?

TEENAGE GREEK CHORUS (*as Grandmother*): Well, I hope you are buying her some decent bras. I never had a decent bra, growing up in the Depression, and now my shoulders are just crippled — crippled from the weight hanging on my shoulders — the dents from my bra straps are big enough to put your finger in. — Here, let me show you —

(*As Grandmother starts to open her blouse:*)

LI'L BIT: Grandma! Please don't undress at the dinner table.

PECK: I thought the entertainment came *after* the dinner.

LI'L BIT (*to the audience*): This is how it always starts. My grandfather, Big Papa, will chime in next with —

MALE GREEK CHORUS (*as Grandfather*): Yup. If Li'l Bit gets any bigger, we're gonna haveta buy her a wheelbarrow to carry in front of her —

LI'L BIT: — Damn it —

PECK: — How about those Redskins on Sunday, Big Papa?

LI'L BIT (*to the audience*): The only sport Big Papa followed was chasing Grandma around the house —

MALE GREEK CHORUS (*as Grandfather*): — Or we could write to Kate Smith. Ask her for somma her used brassieres she don't want anymore — she could maybe give to Li'l Bit here —

LI'L BIT: — I can't stand it. I can't.

PECK: Now, honey, that's just their way —

FEMALE GREEK CHORUS (*as Mother*): I tell you, Grandma, Li'l Bit's at that age. She's so sensitive, you can't say boo —

LI'L BIT: I'd like some privacy, that's all. Okay? Some goddamn privacy —

PECK: — Well, at least she didn't use the savior's name —

LI'L BIT (*to the audience*): And Big Papa wouldn't let a dead dog lie. No sirree.

MALE GREEK CHORUS (*as Grandfather*): Well, she'd better stop being so sensitive. 'Cause five minutes before Li'l Bit turns the corner, her tits turn first —

LI'L BIT (*starting to rise from the table*): — That's it. That's it.

PECK: Li'l Bit, you can't let him get to you. Then he wins.

LI'L BIT: I hate him. *Hate* him.

PECK: That's fine. But hate him and eat a good dinner at the same time.

(*Li'l Bit calms down and sits with perfect dignity.*)

LI'L BIT: The gumbo is really good, Grandma.

MALE GREEK CHORUS (*as Grandfather*): A'course, Li'l Bit's got a big surprise coming for her when she goes to that fancy college this fall —

PECK: Big Papa — let it go.

MALE GREEK CHORUS (*as Grandfather*): What does she need a college degree for? She's got all the credentials she'll need on her chest —

LI'L BIT: — Maybe I want to learn things. Read. Rise above my cracker° background —

PECK: — Whoa, now, Li'l Bit —

MALE GREEK CHORUS (*as Grandfather*): What kind of things do you want to read?

LI'L BIT: There's a whole semester course, for example, on Shakespeare —

(*Greek Chorus, as Grandfather, laughs until he weeps.*)

MALE GREEK CHORUS (*as Grandfather*): Shakespeare. That's a good one. Shakespeare is really going to help you in life.

PECK: I think it's wonderful. And on scholarship!

MALE GREEK CHORUS (*as Grandfather*): How is Shakespeare going to help her lie on her back in the dark?

(*Li'l Bit is on her feet.*)

LI'L BIT: You're getting old, Big Papa. You are going to die — very very soon. Maybe even *tonight*. And when you get to heaven, God's going to be a beautiful

---

cracker: A derogatory term for a poor, Southern, white person.

black woman in a long white robe. She's gonna look at your chart and say: Uh-oh. Fornication. Dog-ugly mean with blood relatives. Oh. Uh-oh. Voted for George Wallace. Well, one last chance: If you can name the play, all will be forgiven. And then she'll quote: "The quality of mercy is not strained." Your answer? Oh, too bad — *Merchant of Venice:* Act IV, Scene iii. And then she'll send your ass to fry in hell with all the other crackers. Excuse me, please.

(*To the audience.*) And as I left the house, I would always hear Big Papa say:

MALE GREEK CHORUS (*as Grandfather*): Lucy, your daughter's got a mouth on her. Well, no sense in wasting good gumbo. Pass me her plate, Mama.

LI'L BIT: And Aunt Mary would come up to Uncle Peck:

FEMALE GREEK CHORUS (*as Aunt Mary*): Peck, go after her, will you? You're the only one she'll listen to when she gets like this.

PECK: She just needs to cool off.

FEMALE GREEK CHORUS (*as Aunt Mary*): Please, honey — Grandma's been on her feet cooking all day.

PECK: All right.

LI'L BIT: And as he left the room, Aunt Mary would say:

FEMALE GREEK CHORUS (*as Aunt Mary*): Peck's so good with them when they get to be this age.

(*Li'l Bit has stormed to another part of the stage, her back turned, weeping with a teenage fury. Peck, cautiously, as if stalking a deer, comes to her. She turns away even more. He waits a bit.*)

PECK: I don't suppose you're talking to family. (*No response.*) Does it help that I'm in-law?

LI'L BIT: Don't you dare make fun of this.

PECK: I'm not. There's nothing funny about this. (*Beat.*) Although I'll bet when Big Papa is about to meet his maker, he'll remember *The Merchant of Venice.*

LI'L BIT: I've got to get away from here.

PECK: You're going away. Soon. Here, take this.

(*Peck hands her his folded handkerchief. Li'l Bit uses it, noisily. Hands it back. Without her seeing, he reverently puts it back.*)

LI'L BIT: I hate this family.

PECK: Your grandfather's ignorant. And you're right — he's going to die soon. But he's family. Family is . . . family.

LI'L BIT: Grown-ups are always saying that. Family.

PECK: Well, when you get a little older, you'll see what we're saying.

LI'L BIT: Uh-huh. So family is another acquired taste, like French kissing?

PECK: Come again?

LI'L BIT: You know, at first it really grosses you out, but in time you grow to like it?

PECK: Girl, you are . . . a handful.

LI'L BIT: Uncle Peck — you have the keys to your car?

PECK: Where do you want to go?

LI'L BIT: Just up the road.

PECK: I'll come with you.

LI'L BIT: No — please? I just need to . . . to drive for a little bit. Alone.

(*Peck tosses her the keys.*)

PECK: When can I see you alone again?

LI'L BIT: Tonight.

(*Li'l Bit crosses to center stage while the lights dim around her. A Voice directs:*)

Shifting Forward from First to Second Gear.

LI'L BIT: There were a lot of rumors about why I got kicked out of that fancy school in 1970. Some say I got caught with a man in my room. Some say as a kid on scholarship I fooled around with a rich man's daughter.

(*Li'l Bit smiles innocently at the audience.*) I'm not talking.

But the real truth was I had a constant companion in my dorm room — who was less than discreet. Canadian V.O. A fifth a day.

1970. A Nixon recession. I slept on the floors of friends who were out of work themselves. Took factory work when I could find it. A string of dead-end jobs that didn't last very long.

What I did, most nights, was cruise the Beltway and the back roads of Maryland, where there was still country, past the battlefields and farm houses. Racing in a 1965 Mustang — and as long as I had gasoline for my car and whiskey for me, the nights would pass. Full tanked, I would speed past the churches and the trees on the bend, thinking just one notch of the steering wheel would be all it would take, and yet some . . . reflex took over. My hands on the wheel in the nine and three o'clock position — I never so much as got a ticket. He taught me well.

(*A Voice announces:*)

You and the Reverse Gear.

LI'L BIT: Back up. 1968. On the Eastern Shore. A celebration dinner.

(*Li'l Bit joins Peck at a table in a restaurant.*)

PECK: Feeling better, missy?

LI'L BIT: The bathroom's really amazing here, Uncle Peck! They have these little soaps — instead of borax or something — and they're in the shape of shells.

PECK: I'll have to take a trip to the gentleman's room just to see.

LI'L BIT: How did you know about this place?

PECK: This inn is famous on the Eastern Shore — it's been open since the seventeenth century. And I know how you like history. . . .

(*Li'l Bit is shy and pleased.*)

Lı'ʟ Bıт: It's great.

Pᴇᴄᴋ: And you've just done your first, legal, long-distance drive. You must be hungry.

Lı'ʟ Bıт: I'm starved.

Pᴇᴄᴋ: I would suggest a dozen oysters to start, and the crab imperial. . . . (*Li'l Bit is genuinely agog.*) You might be interested to know the town history. When the British sailed up this very river in the dead of night — see outside where I'm pointing? — they were going to bombard the heck out of this town. But the town fathers were ready for them. They crept up all the trees with lanterns so that the British would think they saw the town lights and they aimed their cannons too high. And that's why the inn is still here for business today.

Lı'ʟ Bıт: That's a great story.

Pᴇᴄᴋ (*casually*): Would you like to start with a cocktail?

Lı'ʟ Bıт: You're not . . . you're not going to start drinking, are you, Uncle Peck?

Pᴇᴄᴋ: Not me. I told you, as long as you're with me, I'll never drink. I asked you if *you'd* like a cocktail before dinner. It's nice to have a little something with the oysters.

Lı'ʟ Bıт: But . . . I'm not . . . legal. We could get arrested. Uncle Peck, they'll never believe I'm twenty-one!

Pᴇᴄᴋ: So? Today we celebrate your driver's license — on the first try. This establishment reminds me a lot of places back home.

Lı'ʟ Bıт: What does that mean?

Pᴇᴄᴋ: In South Carolina, like here on the Eastern Shore, they're . . . (*Searches for the right euphemism.*) . . . "European." Not so puritanical. And very understanding if gentlemen wish to escort very attractive young ladies who might want a before-dinner cocktail. If you want one, I'll order one.

Lı'ʟ Bıт: Well — sure. Just . . . one.

(*The Female Greek Chorus appears in a spot.*)

Fᴇᴍᴀʟᴇ Gʀᴇᴇᴋ Cʜᴏʀᴜs (*as Mother*): A Mother's Guide to Social Drinking:

A lady never gets sloppy — she may, however, get tipsy and a little gay.

Never drink on an empty stomach. Avail yourself of the bread basket and generous portions of butter. *Slather* the butter on your bread.

Sip your drink, slowly, let the beverage linger in your mouth — interspersed with interesting, fascinating conversation. Sip, never . . . slurp or gulp. Your glass should always be three-quarters full when his glass is empty.

Stay away from *ladies'* drinks: drinks like pink ladies, slow gin fizzes, piña coladas, mai tais, planters punch, white Russians, black Russians, red Russians, melon balls, blue balls, hummingbirds, hemorrhages, and hurricanes. In short, avoid anything with sugar, or anything with an umbrella. Get your vitamin C from *fruit*. Don't order anything with Voodoo or Vixen in the title or sexual positions in the name like Dead Man Screw or the Missionary. (*She sort of titters.*)

Believe me, they are lethal. . . . I think you were conceived after one of those.

Drink, instead, like a man: straight up or on the rocks, with plenty of water in between.

Oh, yes. And never mix your drinks. Stay with one all night long, like the man you came in with: bourbon, gin, or tequila till dawn, damn the torpedoes, full speed ahead!

(*As the Female Greek Chorus retreats, the Male Greek Chorus approaches the table as a Waiter.*)

Mᴀʟᴇ Gʀᴇᴇᴋ Cʜᴏʀᴜs (*as Waiter*): I hope you all are having a pleasant evening. Is there something I can bring you, sir, before you order?

(*Li'l Bit waits in anxious fear. Carefully, Uncle Peck says with command:*)

Pᴇᴄᴋ: I'll have a plain iced tea. The lady would like a drink, I believe.

(*The Male Greek Chorus does a double take; there is a moment when Uncle Peck and he are in silent communication.*)

Mᴀʟᴇ Gʀᴇᴇᴋ Cʜᴏʀᴜs (*as Waiter*): Very good. What would the . . . lady like?

Lı'ʟ Bıт (*a bit flushed*): Is there . . . is there any sugar in a martini?

Pᴇᴄᴋ: None that I know of.

Lı'ʟ Bıт: That's what I'd like then — a dry martini. And could we maybe have some bread?

Pᴇᴄᴋ: A drink fit for a woman of the world. — Please bring the lady a dry martini, be generous with the olives, straight up.

(*The Male Greek Chorus anticipates a* large *tip.*)

Mᴀʟᴇ Gʀᴇᴇᴋ Cʜᴏʀᴜs (*as Waiter*): Right away. Very good, sir.

(*The Male Greek Chorus returns with an empty martini glass which he puts in front of Li'l Bit.*)

Pᴇᴄᴋ: Your glass is empty. Another martini, madam?

Lı'ʟ Bıт: Yes, thank you.

(*Peck signals the Male Greek Chorus, who nods.*)

So why did you leave South Carolina, Uncle Peck?

Pᴇᴄᴋ: I was stationed in D.C. after the war, and decided to stay. Go North, Young Man, someone might have said.

Lı'ʟ Bıт: What did you do in the service anyway?

Pᴇᴄᴋ (*suddenly taciturn*): I . . . I did just this and that. Nothing heroic or spectacular.

Lı'ʟ Bıт: But did you see fighting? Or go to Europe?

Pᴇᴄᴋ: I served in the Pacific Theater. It's really nothing interesting to talk about.

Lı'ʟ Bıт: It is to me. (*The Waiter has brought another*

empty glass.) Oh, goody. I love the color of the swizzle sticks. What were we talking about?

PECK: Swizzle sticks.

LI'L BIT: Do you ever think of going back?

PECK: To the Marines?

LI'L BIT: No — to South Carolina.

PECK: Well, we do go back. To visit.

LI'L BIT: No, I mean to live.

PECK: Not very likely. I think it's better if my mother doesn't have a daily reminder of her disappointment.

LI'L BIT: Are these floorboards slanted?

PECK: Yes, the floor is very slanted. I think this is the original floor.

LI'L BIT: Oh, good.

(*The Female Greek Chorus as Mother enters swaying a little, a little past tipsy.*)

FEMALE GREEK CHORUS (*as Mother*): Don't leave your drink unattended when you visit the ladies' room. There is such a thing as white slavery; the modus operandi is to spike an unsuspecting young girl's drink with a "mickey" when she's left the room to powder her nose.

But if you feel you have had more than your sufficiency in liquor, do go to the ladies' room — often. Pop your head out of doors for a refreshing breath of the night air. If you must, wet your face and head with tap water. Don't be afraid to dunk your head if necessary. A wet woman is still less conspicuous than a drunk woman.

(*The Female Greek Chorus stumbles a little; conspiratorially.*) When in the course of human events it becomes necessary, go to a corner stall and insert the index and middle finger down the throat almost to the epiglottis. Divulge your stomach contents by such persuasion, and then wait a few moments before rejoining your beau waiting for you at your table.

Oh, no. Don't be shy or embarrassed. In the very best of establishments, there's always one or two debutantes crouched in the corner stalls, their beaded purses tossed willy-nilly, sounding like cats in heat, heaving up the contents of their stomachs.

(*The Female Greek Chorus begins to wander off.*) I wonder what is it they do in the men's rooms. . . .

LI'L BIT: So why is your mother disappointed in you, Uncle Peck?

LI'L BIT: Every mother in Horry County has Great Expectations.

LI'L BIT: — Could I have another mar-ti-ni, please?

PECK: I think this is your last one.

(*Peck signals the Waiter. The Waiter looks at Li'l Bit and shakes his head no. Peck raises his eyebrow, raises his finger to indicate one more, and then rubs his fingers together. It looks like a secret code. The Waiter sighs, shakes his head sadly, and brings over another empty martini glass. He glares at Peck.*)

LI'L BIT: The name of the county where you grew up is "Horry?" (*Li'l Bit, plastered, begins to laugh. Then*

she stops.) I think your mother should be proud of you.

(*Peck signals for the check.*)

PECK: Well, missy, she wanted me to do — to *be* everything my father was not. She wanted me to amount to something.

LI'L BIT: But you have! You've amounted a lot. . . .

PECK: I'm just a very ordinary man.

(*The Waiter has brought the check and waits. Peck draws out a large bill and hands it to the Waiter. Li'l Bit is in the soppy stage.*)

LI'L BIT: I'll bet your mother loves you, Uncle Peck.

(*Peck freezes a bit. To Male Greek Chorus as Waiter:*)

PECK: Thank you. The service was exceptional. Please keep the change.

MALE GREEK CHORUS (*as Waiter, in a tone that could freeze*): Thank you, sir. Will you be needing any help?

PECK: I think we can manage, thank you.

(*Just then, the Female Greek Chorus as Mother lurches on stage; the Male Greek Chorus as Waiter escorts her off as she delivers:*)

FEMALE GREEK CHORUS (*as Mother*): Thanks to judicious planning and several trips to the ladies' loo, your mother once out-drank an entire regiment of British officers on a good-will visit to Washington! Every last man of them! Milquetoasts! How'd they ever kick Hitler's cahones, huh? No match for an American lady — I could drink every man in here under the table.

(*She delivers one last crucial hint before she is gently "bounced."*)

As a last resort, when going out for an evening on the town, be sure to wear a skin-tight girdle — so tight that only a surgical knife or acetylene torch can get it off you — so that if you do pass out in the arms of your escort, he'll end up with rubber burns on his fingers before he can steal your virtue —

(*A Voice punctures the interlude with:*)

Vehicle Failure.
Even with careful maintenance and preventive operation of your automobile, it is all too common for us to experience an unexpected breakdown. If you are driving at any speed when a breakdown occurs, you must slow down and guide the automobile to the side of the road.

(*Peck is slowly propping up Li'l Bit as they work their way to his car in the parking lot of the inn.*)

PECK: How are you doing, missy?

LI'L BIT: It's so far to the car, Uncle Peck. Like the lanterns in the trees the British fired on. . . .

(*Li'l Bit stumbles. Peck swoops her up in his arms.*)

PECK: Okay, I think we're going to take a more direct route.

(*Li'l Bit closes her eyes.*)

Dizzy?

(*She nods her head.*)

Don't look at the ground. Almost there — do you feel sick to your stomach?

(*Li'l Bit nods. They reach the "car." Peck gently deposits her on the front seat.*)

Just settle here a little while until things stop spinning.

(*Li'l Bit opens her eyes.*)

LI'L BIT: What are we doing?
PECK: We're just going to sit here until your tummy settles down.
LI'L BIT: It's such nice upholst'ry —
PECK: Think you can go for a ride, now?
LI'L BIT: Where are you taking me?
PECK: Home.
LI'L BIT: You're not taking me — upstairs? There's no room at the inn? (*Li'l Bit giggles.*)
PECK: Do you want to go upstairs?

(*Li'l Bit doesn't answer.*)

Or home?
LI'L BIT: — This isn't right, Uncle Peck.
PECK: What isn't right?
LI'L BIT: What we're doing. It's wrong. It's very wrong.
PECK: What are we doing?

(*Li'l Bit does not answer.*)

We're just going out to dinner.
LI'L BIT: You know. It's not nice to Aunt Mary.
PECK: You let me be the judge of what's nice and not nice to my wife.

(*Beat.*)

LI'L BIT: Now you're mad.
PECK: I'm not mad. It's just that I thought you . . . understood me, Li'l Bit. I think you're the only one who does.
LI'L BIT: Someone will get hurt.
PECK: Have I forced you to do anything?

(*There is a long pause as Li'l Bit tries to get sober enough to think this through.*)

LI'L BIT: . . . I guess not.
PECK: We are just enjoying each other's company. I've told you, nothing is going to happen between us until you want it to. Do you know that?
LI'L BIT: Yes.
PECK: Nothing is going to happen until you want it. (*A second more, with Peck staring ahead at the river while seated at the wheel of his car. Then, softly:*) Do you want something to happen?

(*Peck reaches over and strokes her face, very gently. Li'l Bit softens, reaches for him, and buries her head in his neck. Then she kisses him. Then she moves away, dizzy again.*)

LI'L BIT: . . . I don't know.

(*Peck smiles; this has been good news for him — it hasn't been a "no."*)

PECK: Then I'll wait. I'm a very patient man. I've been waiting for a long time. I don't mind waiting.
LI'L BIT: Someone is going to get hurt.
PECK: No one is going to get hurt. (*Li'l Bit closes her eyes.*) Are you feeling sick?
LI'L BIT: Sleepy.

(*Carefully, Peck props Li'l Bit up on the seat.*)

PECK: Stay here a second.
LI'L BIT: Where're you going?
PECK: I'm getting something from the back seat.
LI'L BIT (*scared; too loud*): What? What are you going to do?

(*Peck reappears in the front seat with a lap rug.*)

PECK: Shhh. (*Peck covers Li'l Bit. She calms down.*) There. Think you can sleep?

(*Li'l Bit nods. She slides over to rest on his shoulder. With a look of happiness, Peck turns the ignition key. Beat. Peck leaves Li'l Bit sleeping in the car and strolls down to the audience. Wagner's* Flying Dutchman *comes up faintly.*) (*A Voice interjects:*)

Idling in the Neutral Gear.

TEENAGE GREEK CHORUS: Uncle Peck Teaches Cousin Bobby How to Fish.
PECK: I get back once or twice a year — supposedly to visit Mama and the family, but the real truth is to fish. I miss this the most of all. There's a smell in the Low Country — where the swamp and fresh inlet join the saltwater — a scent of sand and cypress, that I haven't found anywhere yet.

I don't say this very often up North because it will just play into the stereotype everyone has, but I will tell you: I didn't wear shoes in the summertime until I was sixteen. It's unnatural down here to pen up your feet in leather. Go ahead — take 'em off. Let yourself breathe — it really will make you feel better.

We're going to aim for some pompano today — and I have to tell you, they're a very shy, mercurial fish. Takes patience, and psychology. You have to believe it doesn't matter if you catch one or not.

Sky's pretty spectacular — there's some beer in the cooler next to the crab salad I packed, so help yourself if you get hungry. Are you hungry? Thirsty? Holler if you are.

Okay. You don't want to lean over the bridge like that — pompano feed in shallow water, and you don't want to get too close — they're frisky and shy little things — wait, check your line. Yep, something's been munching while we were talking.

Okay, look: We take the sand flea and you take the hook like this — right through his little sand flea rump. Sand fleas should always keep their backs to the wall. Okay. Cast it in, like I showed you. That's great! I can taste that pompano now, sautéed with some pecans and butter, a little bourbon — now — let it lie on the bottom — now, reel, jerk, reel, jerk —

Look — look at your line. There's something calling, all right. Okay, tip the rod up — not too sharp — hook it — all right, now easy, reel and then rest — let it play. And reel — play it out, that's right — really good! I can't believe it! It's a pompano. — Good work! Way to go! You are an official fisherman now. Pompano are hard to catch. We are going to have a delicious little —

What? Well, I don't know how much pain a fish feels — you can't think of that. Oh, no, don't cry, come on now, it's just a fish — the other guys are going to see you. — No, no, you're just real sensitive, and I think that's wonderful at your age — look, do you want me to cut it free? You do?

Okay, hand me those pliers — look — I'm cutting the hook — okay? And we're just going to drop it in — no I'm not mad. It's just for fun, okay? There — it's going to swim back to its lady friend and tell her what a terrible day it had and she's going to stroke him with her fins until he feels better, and then they'll do something alone together that will make them both feel good and sleepy. . . .

(*Peck bends down, very earnest.*) I don't want you to feel ashamed about crying. I'm not going to tell anyone, okay? I can keep secrets. You know, men cry all the time. They just don't tell anybody, and they don't let anybody catch them. There's nothing you could do that would make me feel ashamed of you. Do you know that? Okay. (*Peck straightens up, smiles.*)

Do you want to pack up and call it a day? I tell you what — I think I can still remember — there's a really neat tree house where I used to stay for days. I think it's still here — it was the last time I looked. But it's a secret place — you can't tell anybody we've gone there — least of all your mom or your sisters. — This is something special just between you and me. Sound good? We'll climb up there and have a beer and some crab salad — okay, B.B.? Bobby? Robert. . . .

(*Li'l Bit sits at a kitchen table with the two Female Greek Chorus members.*)

LI'L BIT (*to the audience*): Three women, three generations, sit at the kitchen table.

On Men, Sex, and Women: Part I:

FEMALE GREEK CHORUS (*as Mother*): Men only want one thing.

LI'L BIT (*wide-eyed*): But what? What is it they want?

FEMALE GREEK CHORUS (*as Mother*): And once they have it, they lose all interest. So Don't Give It to Them.

TEENAGE GREEK CHORUS (*as Grandmother*): I never had the luxury of the rhythm method. Your grandfather is just a big bull. A big bull. Every morning, every evening.

FEMALE GREEK CHORUS (*as Mother, whispers to Li'l Bit*): And he used to come home for lunch every day.

LI'L BIT: My god, Grandma!

TEENAGE GREEK CHORUS (*as Grandmother*): Your grandfather only cares that I do two things: have the table set and the bed turned down.

FEMALE GREEK CHORUS (*as Mother*): And in all that time, Mother, you never have experienced — ?

LI'L BIT (*to the audience*): — Now my grandmother believed in all the sacraments of the church, to the day she died. She believed in Santa Claus and the Easter Bunny until she was fifteen. But she didn't believe in —

TEENAGE GREEK CHORUS (*as Grandmother*): — Orgasm! That's just something you and Mary have made up! I don't believe you.

FEMALE GREEK CHORUS (*as Mother*): Mother, it happens to women all the time —

TEENAGE GREEK CHORUS (*as Grandmother*): — Oh, now you're going to tell me about the G force!

LI'L BIT: No, Grandma, I think that's astronauts —

FEMALE GREEK CHORUS (*as Mother*): Well, Mama, after all, you were a child bride when Big Papa came and got you — you were a married woman and you still believed in Santa Claus.

TEENAGE GREEK CHORUS (*as Grandmother*): It was legal, what Daddy and I did! I was fourteen and in those days, fourteen was a grown-up woman —

(*Big Papa shuffles in the kitchen for a cookie.*)

MALE GREEK CHORUS (*as Grandfather*): — Oh, now we're off on Grandma and the Rape of the Sa-bean Women!

TEENAGE GREEK CHORUS (*as Grandmother*): Well, you were the one in such a big hurry —

MALE GREEK CHORUS (*as Grandfather to Li'l Bit*): — I picked your grandmother out of that herd of sisters just like a lion chooses the gazelle — the plump, slow, flaky gazelle dawdling at the edge of the herd — your sisters were too smart and too fast and too scrawny —

LI'L BIT (*to the audience*): — The family story is that when Big Papa came for Grandma, my Aunt Lily was waiting for him with a broom — and she beat him over the head all the way down the stairs as he was carrying out Grandma's hope chest —

MALE GREEK CHORUS (*as Grandfather*): — And they were *mean*. 'Specially Lily.

FEMALE GREEK CHORUS (*as Mother*): Well, you were robbing the baby of the family!

TEENAGE GREEK CHORUS (*as Grandmother*): I still keep a broom handy in the kitchen! And I know how to use it! So get your hand out of the cookie jar and don't you spoil your appetite for dinner — out of the kitchen!

(*Male Greek Chorus as Grandfather leaves chuckling with a cookie.*)

FEMALE GREEK CHORUS (*as Mother*): Just one thing a married woman needs to know how to use — the rolling pin or the broom. I prefer a heavy, cast-iron fry pan — they're great on a man's head, no matter how thick the skull is.

TEENAGE GREEK CHORUS (*as Grandmother*): Yes, sir, your father is ruled by only two bosses! Mr. Gut and Mr. Peter! And sometimes, first thing in the morning, Mr. Sphincter Muscle!

FEMALE GREEK CHORUS (*as Mother*): It's true. Men are like children. Just like little boys.

TEENAGE GREEK CHORUS (*as Grandmother*): Men are bulls! Big bulls!

(*The Greek Chorus is getting aroused.*)

FEMALE GREEK CHORUS (*as Mother*): They'd still be crouched on their haunches over a fire in a cave if we hadn't cleaned them up!

TEENAGE GREEK CHORUS (*as Grandmother, flushed*): Coming in smelling of sweat —

FEMALE GREEK CHORUS (*as Mother*): — Looking at those naughty pictures like boys in a dime store with a dollar in their pockets!

TEENAGE GREEK CHORUS (*as Grandmother; raucous*): No matter to them what they smell like! They've got to have it, right then, on the spot, right there! Nasty! —

FEMALE GREEK CHORUS (*as Mother*): — Vulgar!

TEENAGE GREEK CHORUS (*as Grandmother*): Primitive! —

FEMALE GREEK CHORUS (*as Mother*): — Hot! —

LI'L BIT: And just about then, Big Papa would shuffle in with —

MALE GREEK CHORUS (*as Grandfather*): — What are you all cackling about in here?

TEENAGE GREEK CHORUS (*as Grandmother*): Stay out of the kitchen! This is just for girls!

(*As Grandfather leaves:*)

MALE GREEK CHORUS (*as Grandfather*): Lucy, you'd better not be filling Mama's head with sex! Every time you and Mary come over and start in about sex, when I ask a simple question like, "What time is dinner going to be ready?," Mama snaps my head off!

TEENAGE GREEK CHORUS (*as Grandmother*): Dinner will be ready when I'm good and ready! Stay out of this kitchen!

(*Li'l Bit steps out.*)

(*A Voice directs:*)

When Making a Left Turn, You Must Downshift While Going Forward.

LI'L BIT: 1979. A long bus trip to Upstate New York. I settled in to read, when a young man sat beside me.

MALE GREEK CHORUS (*as Young Man; voice cracking*): "What are you reading?"

LI'L BIT: He asked. His voice broke into that miserable equivalent of vocal acne, not quite falsetto and not tenor, either. I glanced a side view. He was appealing in an odd way, huge ears at a defiant angle springing forward at ninety degrees. He must have been shaving, because his face, with a peach sheen, was speckled with nicks and styptic. "I have a class tomorrow," I told him.

MALE GREEK CHORUS (*as Young Man*): "You're taking a class?"

LI'L BIT: "I'm teaching a class." He concentrated on lowering his voice.

MALE GREEK CHORUS (*as Young Man*): "I'm a senior. Walt Whitman High."

LI'L BIT: The light was fading outside, so perhaps he was — with a very high voice.

I felt his "interest" quicken. Five steps ahead of the hopes in his head, I slowed down, waited, pretended surprise, acted at listening, all the while knowing we would get off the bus, he would just then seem to think to ask me to dinner, he would chivalrously insist on walking me home, he would continue to converse in the street until I would casually invite him up to my room — and — I was only into the second moment of conversation and I could see the whole evening before me.

And dramaturgically speaking, after the faltering and slightly comical "first act," there was the very briefest of intermissions, and an extremely capable and forceful and *sustained* second act. And after the second act climax and a gentle denouement — before the post-play discussion — I lay on my back in the dark and I thought about you, Uncle Peck. Oh. Oh — this is the allure. Being older. Being the first. Being the translator, the teacher, the epicure, the already jaded. This is how the giver gets taken.

(*Li'l Bit changes her tone.*) On Men, Sex, and Women: Part II:

(*Li'l Bit steps back into the scene as a fifteen-year-old, gawky and quiet, as the gazelle at the edge of the herd.*)

TEENAGE GREEK CHORUS (*as Grandmother, to Li'l Bit*): You're being mighty quiet, missy. Cat Got Your Tongue?

LI'L BIT: I'm just listening. Just thinking.

TEENAGE GREEK CHORUS (*as Grandmother*): Oh, yes, Little Miss Radar Ears? Soaking it all in? Little Miss Sponge? Penny for your thoughts?

(*Li'l Bit hesitates to ask but she really wants to know.*)

LI'L BIT: Does it — when you do it — you know, theoretically when I do it and I haven't done it before — I mean — does it hurt?

FEMALE GREEK CHORUS (*as Mother*): Does what hurt, honey?

LI'L BIT: When a . . . when a girl does it for the first time — with a man — does it hurt?

TEENAGE GREEK CHORUS (*as Grandmother; horrified*): *That's* what you're thinking about?

FEMALE GREEK CHORUS (*as Mother, calm*): Well, just a little bit. Like a pinch. And there's a little blood.

TEENAGE GREEK CHORUS (*as Grandmother*): Don't tell her that! She's too young to be thinking those things!

FEMALE GREEK CHORUS (*as Mother*): Well, if she doesn't find out from me, where is she going to find out? In the street?

TEENAGE GREEK CHORUS (*as Grandmother*): Tell her it hurts! It's agony! You think you're going to die! Especially if you do it before marriage!

FEMALE GREEK CHORUS (*as Mother*): Mama! I'm going to tell her the truth! Unlike you, you left me and Mary completely in the dark with fairy tales and told us to go to the priest! What does an eighty-year-old priest know about lovemaking with girls!

LI'L BIT (*getting upset*): It's not fair!

FEMALE GREEK CHORUS (*as Mother*): Now, see, she's getting upset — you're scaring her.

TEENAGE GREEK CHORUS (*as Grandmother*): Good! Let her be good and scared! It hurts! You bleed like a stuck pig! And you lay there and say, "Why, O Lord, have you forsaken me?!"

LI'L BIT: It's not fair! Why does everything have to hurt for girls? Why is there always blood?

FEMALE GREEK CHORUS (*as Mother*): It's not a lot of blood — and it feels wonderful after the pain subsides. . . .

TEENAGE GREEK CHORUS (*as Grandmother*): You're encouraging her to just go out and find out with the first drugstore joe who buys her a milkshake!

FEMALE GREEK CHORUS (*as Mother*): Don't be scared. It won't hurt you — if the man you go to bed with really loves you. It's important that he loves you.

TEENAGE GREEK CHORUS (*as Grandmother*): — Why don't you just go out and rent a motel room for her, Lucy?

FEMALE GREEK CHORUS (*as Mother*): I believe in telling my daughter the truth! We have a very close relationship! I want her to be able to ask me anything — I'm not scaring her with stories about Eve's sin and snakes crawling on their bellies for eternity and women bearing children in mortal pain —

Tim Crowe as Uncle Peck and Annie Sullivan as Li'l Bit in the Trinity Repertory Theater's production of *How I Learned to Drive*.

TEENAGE GREEK CHORUS (*as Grandmother*): — If she stops and thinks before she takes her knickers off, maybe someone in this family will finish high school!

(*Li'l Bit knows what is about to happen and starts to retreat from the scene at this point.*)

FEMALE GREEK CHORUS (*as Mother*): Mother! If you and Daddy had helped me — I wouldn't have had to marry that — that no-good-son-of-a —

TEENAGE GREEK CHORUS (*as Grandmother*): — He was good enough for you on a full moon! I hold you responsible!

FEMALE GREEK CHORUS (*as Mother*): — You could have helped me! You could have told me something about the facts of life!

TEENAGE GREEK CHORUS (*as Grandmother*): — I told you what my mother told me! A girl with her skirt up can outrun a man with his pants down!

(*The Male Greek Chorus enters the fray; Li'l Bit edges farther downstage.*)

FEMALE GREEK CHORUS (*as Mother*): And when I turned to you for a little help, all I got afterwards was —

MALE GREEK CHORUS (*as Grandfather*): You Made Your Bed; Now Lie On It!

(*The Greek Chorus freezes, mouths open, argumentatively.*)

LI'L BIT (*to the audience*): Oh, please! I still can't bear to listen to it, after all these years —

(*The Male Greek Chorus "unfreezes," but out of his open mouth, as if to his surprise, comes a bass refrain from a Motown song.*)

MALE GREEK CHORUS: "Do-Bee-Do-Wah!"

(*The Female Greek Chorus member is also surprised; but she, too, unfreezes.*)

FEMALE GREEK CHORUS: "Shoo-doo-be-doo-be-doo; shoo-doo-be-doo-be-doo."

(*The Male and Female Greek Chorus members continue with their harmony, until the Teenage member of the Chorus starts in with Motown lyrics such as "Dedicated to the One I Love," or "In the Still of the Night," or "Hold Me" — any Sam Cooke will do. The three modulate down into three-part harmony, softly, until they are submerged by the actual recording playing over the radio in the car in which Uncle Peck sits in the driver's seat, waiting. Li'l Bit sits in the passenger's seat.*)

LI'L BIT: Ahh. That's better.

(*Uncle Peck reaches over and turns the volume down; to Li'l Bit:*)

PECK: How can you hear yourself think?

(*Li'l Bit does not answer.*)

(*A Voice insinuates itself in the pause:*)

Before You Drive.
Always check under your car for obstructions — broken bottles, fallen tree branches, and the bodies of small children. Each year hundreds of children are crushed beneath the wheels of unwary drivers in their own driveways. Children depend on you to watch them.

(*Pause.*)

(*The Voice continues:*)

You and the Reverse Gear.

(*In the following section, it would be nice to have slides of erotic photographs of women and cars: women posed over the hood; women draped along the sideboards; women with water hoses spraying the car; and the actress playing Li'l Bit with a Bel Air or any 1950s car one can find for the finale.*)

LI'L BIT: 1967. In a parking lot of the Beltsville Agricultural Farms. The Initiation into a Boy's First Love.

PECK (*with a soft look on his face*): Of course, my favorite car will always be the '56 Bel Air Sports Coupe. Chevy sold more '55s, but the '56! — a V-8 with Corvette option, 225 horsepower; went from zero to sixty miles per hour in 8.9 seconds.

LI'L BIT (*to the audience*): Long after a mother's tits, but before a woman's breasts:

PECK: Super-Turbo-Fire! What a Power Pack — mechanical lifters, twin four-barrel carbs, lightweight valves, dual exhausts —

LI'L BIT (*to the audience*): After the milk but before the beer:

PECK: A specific intake manifold, higher-lift camshaft, and the tightest squeeze Chevy had ever made —

LI'L BIT (*to the audience*): Long after he's squeezed down the birth canal but before he's pushed his way back in: The boy falls in love with the thing that bears his weight with speed.

PECK: I want you to know your automobile inside and out. — Are you there? Li'l Bit?

(*Slides end here.*)

LI'L BIT: — What?

PECK: You're drifting. I need you to concentrate.

LI'L BIT: Sorry.

PECK: Okay. Get into the driver's seat. (*Li'l Bit does.*) Okay. Now. Show me what you're going to do before you start the car.

(*Li'l Bit sits, with her hands in her lap. She starts to giggle.*)

LI'L BIT: I don't know, Uncle Peck.

PECK: Now, come on. What's the first thing you're going to adjust?

LI'L BIT: My bra strap? —

PECK: — Li'l Bit. What's the most important thing to have control of on the inside of the car?

LI'L BIT: That's easy. The radio. I tune the radio from Mama's old fart tunes to —

(*Li'l Bit turns the radio up so we can hear a 1960s tune. With surprising firmness, Peck commands:*)

PECK: — Radio off. Right now. (*Li'l Bit turns the radio off.*) When you are driving your car, with your license, you can fiddle with the stations all you want. But when you are driving with a learner's permit in my car, I want all your attention to be on the road.

LI'L BIT: Yes, sir.

PECK: Okay. Now the seat — forward and up. (*Li'l Bit pushes it forward.*) Do you want a cushion?

LI'L BIT: No — I'm good.

PECK: You should be able to reach all the switches and controls. Your feet should be able to push the accelerator, brake and clutch all the way down. Can you do that?

LI'L BIT: Yes.

PECK: Okay, the side mirrors. You want to be able to see just a bit of the right side of the car in the right mirror — can you?

LI'L BIT: Turn it out more.

PECK: Okay. How's that?

LI'L BIT: A little more. . . . Okay, that's good.

PECK: Now the left — again, you want to be able to see behind you — but the left lane — adjust it until you feel comfortable. (*Li'l Bit does so.*) Next. I want you to check the rearview mirror. Angle it so you have a clear vision of the back. (*Li'l Bit does so.*) Okay. Lock your door. Make sure all the doors are locked.

LI'L BIT (*making a joke of it*): But then I'm locked in with you.

PECK: Don't fool.

LI'L BIT: All right. We're locked in.

PECK: We'll deal with the air vents and defroster later. I'm teaching you on a manual — once you learn manual, you can drive anything. I want you to be able to drive any car, any machine. Manual gives you *control*. In ice, if your brakes fail, if you need more power — okay? It's a little harder at first, but then it becomes like breathing. Now. Put your hands on the wheel. I never want to see you driving with one hand. Always two hands. (*Li'l Bit hesitates.*) What? What is it now?

LI'L BIT: If I put my hands on the wheel — how do I defend myself?

PECK (*softly*): Now listen. Listen up close. We're not going to fool around with this. This is serious business. I will never touch you when you are driving a car. Understand?

LI'L BIT: Okay.

PECK: Hands on the nine o'clock and three o'clock position gives you maximum control and turn.

(*Peck goes silent for a while. Li'l Bit waits for more instruction.*)

Okay. Just relax and listen to me, Li'l Bit, okay? I want you to lift your hands for a second and look at them.

(*Li'l Bit feels a bit silly, but does it.*)

Those are your two hands. When you are driving, your life is in your own two hands. Understand?

(*Li'l Bit nods.*)

I don't have any sons. You're the nearest to a son I'll ever have — and I want to give you something. Something that really matters to me.

There's something about driving — when you're in control of the car, just you and the machine and the road — that nobody can take from you. A power. I feel more myself in my car than anywhere else. And that's what I want to give to you.

There's a lot of assholes out there. Crazy men, arrogant idiots, drunks, angry kids, geezers who are blind — and you have to be ready for them. I want to teach you to drive like a man.

LI'L BIT: What does that mean?

PECK: Men are taught to drive with confidence — with aggression. The road belongs to them. They drive defensively — always looking out for the other guy. Women tend to be polite — to hesitate. And that can be fatal.

You're going to learn to think what the other guy is going to do before he does it. If there's an accident, and ten cars pile up, and people get killed, you're the one who's gonna steer through it, put your foot on the gas if you have to, and be the only one to walk away. I don't know how long you or I are going to live, but we're for damned sure not going to die in a car.

So if you're going to drive with me, I want you to take this very seriously.

LI'L BIT: I will, Uncle Peck. I want you to teach me to drive.

PECK: Good. You're going to pass your test on the first try. Perfect score. Before the next four weeks are over, you're going to know this baby inside and out. Treat her with respect.

LI'L BIT: Why is it a "she?"

PECK: Good question. It doesn't have to be a "she" — but when you close your eyes and think of someone who responds to your touch — someone who performs just for you and gives you what you ask for — I guess I always see a "she." You can call her what you like.

LI'L BIT (*to the audience*): I closed my eyes — and decided not to change the gender.

(*A Voice:*)

Defensive driving involves defending yourself from hazardous and sudden changes in your automotive environment. By thinking ahead, the defensive driver can adjust to weather, road conditions, and road kill. Good defensive driving involves mental and physical preparation. Are you prepared?

(*Another Voice chimes in:*)

You and the Reverse Gear.

LI'L BIT: 1966. The Anthropology of the Female Body in Ninth Grade — Or A Walk Down Mammary Lane.

(*Throughout the following, there is occasional rhythmic beeping, like a transmitter signaling. Li'l Bit is aware of it, but can't figure out where it is coming from. No one else seems to hear it.*)

MALE GREEK CHORUS: In the hallway of Francis Scott Key Middle School.

(*A bell rings; the Greek Chorus is changing classes and meets in the hall, conspiratorially.*)

TEENAGE GREEK CHORUS: She's coming!

(*Li'l Bit enters the scene; the Male Greek Chorus member has a sudden, violent sneezing and lethal allergy attack.*)

FEMALE GREEK CHORUS: Jerome? Jerome? Are you all right?
MALE GREEK CHORUS: I — don't — know. I can't breathe — get Li'l Bit —
TEENAGE GREEK CHORUS: — He needs oxygen!
FEMALE GREEK CHORUS: — Can you help us here?
LI'L BIT: What's wrong? Do you want me to get the school nurse —

(*The Male Greek Chorus member wheezes, grabs his throat and sniffs at Li'l Bit's chest, which is beeping away.*)

MALE GREEK CHORUS: No — it's okay — I only get this way when I'm around an allergy trigger —
LI'L BIT: Golly. What are you allergic to?
MALE GREEK CHORUS (*with a sudden grab of her breast*): Foam rubber.

(*The Greek Chorus members break up with hilarity; Jerome leaps away from Li'l Bit's kicking rage with agility; as he retreats:*)

LI'L BIT: Jerome! Creep! Cretin! Cro-Magnon!
TEENAGE GREEK CHORUS: Rage is not attractive in a girl.
FEMALE GREEK CHORUS: Really. Get a Sense of Humor.

(*A Voice echoes:*)

Good defensive driving involves mental and physical preparation. Were You Prepared?

FEMALE GREEK CHORUS: Gym Class: In the showers.

(*The sudden sound of water; the Female Greek Chorus members and Li'l Bit, while fully clothed, drape towels across their fronts, miming nudity. They stand, hesitate, at an imaginary shower's edge.*)

LI'L BIT: Water looks hot.
FEMALE GREEK CHORUS: Yesss. . . .

(*Female Greek Chorus members are not going to make the first move. One dips a tentative toe under the water, clutching the towel around her.*)

LI'L BIT: Well, I guess we'd better shower and get out of here.
FEMALE GREEK CHORUS: Yep. You go ahead. I'm still cooling off.
LI'L BIT: Okay. — Sally? Are you gonna shower?
TEENAGE GREEK CHORUS: After you —

(*Li'l Bit takes a deep breath for courage, drops the towel and plunges in: The two Female Greek Chorus members look at Li'l Bit in the all together, laugh, gasp and high-five each other.*)

TEENAGE GREEK CHORUS: Oh my god! Can you believe —
FEMALE GREEK CHORUS: Told you! It's not foam rubber! I win! Jerome owes me fifty cents!

(*A Voice editorializes:*)

Were You Prepared?

(*Li'l Bit tries to cover up; she is exposed, as suddenly 1960s Motown fills the room and we segue into:*)

FEMALE GREEK CHORUS: The Sock Hop.

(*Li'l Bit stands up against the wall with her female classmates. Teenage Greek Chorus is mesmerized by the music and just sways alone, lip-synching the lyrics.*)

LI'L BIT: I don't know. Maybe it's just me — but — do you ever feel like you're just a walking Mary Jane joke?
FEMALE GREEK CHORUS: I don't know what you mean.
LI'L BIT: You haven't heard the Mary Jane jokes? (*Female Greek Chorus member shakes her head no.*) Okay. "Little Mary Jane is walking through the woods, when all of a sudden this man who was hiding behind a tree *jumps* out, *rips* open Mary Jane's blouse, and *plunges* his hands on her breasts. And Little Mary Jane just laughed and laughed because she knew her money was in her shoes."

(*Li'l Bit laughs; the Female Greek Chorus does not.*)

FEMALE GREEK CHORUS: You're weird.

(*In another space, in a strange light, Uncle Peck stands and stares at Li'l Bit's body. He is setting up a tripod, but he just stands, appreciative, watching her.*)

LI'L BIT: Well, don't you ever feel . . . self-conscious? Like you're being looked at all the time?

FEMALE GREEK CHORUS: That's not a problem for me. — Oh — look — Greg's coming over to ask you to dance.

(*Teenage Creek Chorus becomes attentive, flustered. Male Greek Chorus member, as Greg, bends slightly as a very short young man, whose head is at Li'l Bit's chest level. Ardent, sincere, and socially inept, Greg will become a successful gynecologist.*)

TEENAGE GREEK CHORUS (*softly*): Hi, Greg.

(*Greg does not hear. He is intent on only one thing.*)

MALE GREEK CHORUS (*as Greg, to Li'l Bit*): Good Evening. Would you care to dance?

LI'L BIT (*gently*): Thank you very much, Greg — but I'm going to sit this one out.

MALE GREEK CHORUS (*as Greg*): Oh. Okay. I'll try my luck later.

(*He disappears.*)

TEENAGE GREEK CHORUS: Oohhh.

(*Li'l Bit relaxes. Then she tenses, aware of Peck's gaze.*)

FEMALE GREEK CHORUS: Take pity on him. Someone should.

LI'L BIT: But he's so short.

TEENAGE GREEK CHORUS: He can't help it.

LI'L BIT: But his head comes up to (*Li'l Bit gestures*) here. And I think he asks me on the fast dances so he can watch me — you know — jiggle.

FEMALE GREEK CHORUS: I wish I had your problems.

(*The tune changes; Greg is across the room in a flash.*)

MALE GREEK CHORUS (*as Greg*): Evening again. May I ask you for the honor of a spin on the floor?

LI'L BIT: I'm . . . very complimented, Greg. But I . . . I just don't do fast dances.

MALE GREEK CHORUS (*as Greg*): Oh. No problem. That's okay.

(*He disappears. Teenage Greek Chorus watches him go.*)

TEENAGE GREEK CHORUS: That is just so — *sad.*

(*Li'l Bit becomes aware of Peck waiting.*)

FEMALE GREEK CHORUS: You know, you should take it as a compliment that the guys want to watch you jiggle. They're guys. That's what they're supposed to do.

LI'L BIT: I guess you're right. But sometimes I feel like these alien life forces, these two mounds of flesh have grafted themselves onto my chest, and they're using me until they can "propagate" and take over the world and they'll just keep growing, with a mind of their own until I collapse under their weight and they suck all the nourishment out of my body and I finally just waste away while they get bigger and bigger and — (*Li'l Bit's classmates are just staring at her in disbelief.*)

FEMALE GREEK CHORUS: — You are the strangest girl I have ever met.

(*Li'l Bit's trying to joke but feels on the verge of tears.*)

LI'L BIT: Or maybe someone's implanted radio transmitters in my chest at a frequency I can't hear, that girls can't detect, but they're sending out these signals to men who get mesmerized, like sirens, calling them to dash themselves on these "rocks" —

(*Just then, the music segues into a slow dance, perhaps a Beach Boys tune like "Little Surfer," but over the music there's a rhythmic, hypnotic beeping transmitted, which both Greg and Peck hear. Li'l Bit hears it too, and in horror she stares at her chest. She, too, is almost hypnotized. In a trance, Greg responds to the signals and is called to her side — actully, her front. Like a zombie, he stands in front of her, his eyes planted on her two orbs.*)

MALE GREEK CHORUS (*as Greg*): This one's a slow dance. I hope your dance card isn't . . . filled?

(*Li'l Bit is aware of Peck; but the signals are calling her to him. The signals are no longer transmitters, but an electromagnetic force, pulling Li'l Bit to his side, where he again waits for her to join him. She must get away from the dance floor.*)

LI'L BIT: Greg — you really are a nice boy. But I don't like to dance.

MALE GREEK CHORUS (*as Greg*): That's okay. We don't have to move or anything. I could just hold you and we could just *sway* a little —

LI'L BIT: — No! I'm sorry — but I think I have to leave; I hear someone calling me —

(*Li'l Bit starts across the dance floor, leaving Greg behind. The beeping stops. The lights change, although the music does not. As Li'l Bit talks to the audience, she continues to change and prepare for the coming session. She should be wearing a tight tank top or a sheer blouse and very tight pants. To the audience:*)

In every man's home some small room, some zone in his house, is set aside. It might be the attic, or the study, or a den. And there's an invisible sign as if from the old treehouse: Girls Keep Out. Here, away from female eyes, lace doilies and crochet, he keeps his manly toys: the Vargas pinups, the tackle. A scent of tobacco and WD-40. (*She inhales deeply.*) A dash of his Bay Rum. Ahhh . . . (*Li'l Bit savors it for just a moment more.*) Here he keeps his secrets: a violin or saxophone, drum set or darkroom, and the stacks of *Playboy.* (*In a whisper.*) Here, in my aunt's home, it was the basement. Uncle Peck's turf.

(*A Voice commands:*)

You and the Reverse Gear.

LI'L BIT: 1965. The Photo Shoot.

(*Li'l Bit steps into the scene as a nervous but curious thirteen-year-old. Music, from the previous scene, continues to play, changing into something like Roy Orbison later — something seductive with a beat. Peck fiddles, all business, with his camera. As in the driving lesson, he is all competency and concentration. Li'l Bit stands awkwardly. He looks through the Leica camera on the tripod, adjusts the back lighting, etc.*)

PECK: Are you cold? The lights should heat up some in a few minutes —

LI'L BIT: — Aunt Mary is?

PECK: At the National Theatre matinee. With your mother. We have time.

LI'L BIT: But — what if —

PECK: — And so what if they return? I told them you and I were going to be working with my camera. They won't come down.

(*Li'l Bit is quiet, apprehensive.*)

Look, are you sure you want to do this?

LI'L BIT: I said I'd do it. But —

PECK: — I know. You've drawn the line.

LI'L BIT (*reassured*): That's right. No frontal nudity.

PECK: Good heavens, girl, where did you pick that up?

LI'L BIT (*defensive*): I read.

(*Peck tries not to laugh.*)

PECK: And I read *Playboy* for the interviews. Okay. Let's try some different music.

(*Peck goes to an expensive reel-to-reel and forwards. Something like "Sweet Dreams" begins to play.*)

LI'L BIT: I didn't know you listened to this.

PECK: I'm not dead, you know, I try to keep up. Do you like this song?

(*Li'l Bit nods with pleasure.*)

Good. Now listen — at professional photo shoots, they always play music for the models. Okay? I want you to just enjoy the music. Listen to it with your body, and just — respond.

LI'L BIT: Respond to the music with my . . . body?

PECK: Right. Almost like dancing. Here — let's get you on the stool, first. (*Peck comes over and helps her up.*)

LI'L BIT: But nothing showing —

(*Peck firmly, with his large capable hands, brushes back her hair, angles her face. Li'l Bit turns to him like a plant to the sun.*)

PECK: Nothing showing. Just a peek.

(*He holds her by the shoulders, looking at her critically. Then he unbuttons her blouse to the midpoint, and runs his hands over the flesh of her exposed sternum, arranging the fabric, just touching her. Deliberately, calmly.*

Asexually. *Li'l Bit quiets, sits perfectly still, and closes her eyes.*)

Okay?

LI'L BIT: Yes.

(*Peck goes back to his camera.*)

PECK: I'm going to keep talking to you. Listen without responding to what I'm saying; you want to *listen* to the music. Sway, move just your torso or your head — I've got to check the light meter.

LI'L BIT: But — you'll be watching.

PECK: No — I'm not here — just my voice. Pretend you're in your room all alone on a Friday night with your mirror — and the music feels good — just move for me, Li'l Bit —

(*Li'l Bit closes her eyes. At first self-conscious; then she gets more into the music and begins to sway. We hear the camera start to whir. Throughout the shoot, there can be a slide montage of actual shots of the actor playing Li'l Bit — interspersed with other models à la* Playboy, *Calvin Klein, and Victoriana/Lewis Carroll's Alice Liddell.*)

That's it. That looks great. Okay. Just keep doing that. Lift your head up a bit more, good, good, just keep moving, that a girl — you're a very beautiful young woman. Do you know that?

(*Li'l Bit looks up, blushes. Peck shoots the camera. The audience should see this shot on the screen.*)

LI'L BIT: No. I don't know that.

PECK: Listen to the music.

(*Li'l Bit closes her eyes again.*)

Well you are. For a thirteen-year-old, you have a body a twenty-year-old woman would die for.

LI'L BIT: The boys in school don't think so.

PECK: The boys in school are little Neanderthals in short pants. You're ten years ahead of them in maturity; it's gonna take a while for them to catch up.

(*Peck clicks another shot; we see a faint smile on Li'l Bit on the screen.*)

Girls turn into women long before boys turn into men.

LI'L BIT: Why is that?

PECK: I don't know, Li'l Bit. But it's a blessing for men.

(*Li'l Bit turns silent.*)

Keep moving. Try arching your back on the stool, hands behind you, and throw your head back.

(*The slide shows a* Playboy *model in this pose.*)

Oohh, great. That one was great. Turn your head away, same position. (*Whir.*) Beautiful.

(*Li'l Bit looks at him a bit defiantly.*)

LI'L BIT: I think Aunt Mary is beautiful.

(*Peck stands still.*)

PECK: My wife is a very beautiful woman. Her beauty doesn't cancel yours out. (*More casually; he returns to the camera.*) All the women in your family are beautiful. In fact, I think all women are. You're not listening to the music. (*Peck shoots some more film in silence.*) All right, turn your head to the left. Good. Now take the back of your right hand and put it on your right cheek — your elbow angled up — now slowly, slowly, stroke your cheek, draw back your hair with the back of your hand. (*Another classic* Playboy *or* Vargas.) Good. One hand above and behind your head; stretch your body; smile. (*Another pose.*) Li'l Bit. I want you to think of something that makes you laugh —

LI'L BIT: I can't think of anything.

PECK: Okay. Think of Big Papa chasing Grandma around the living room.

(*Li'l Bit lifts her head and laughs. Click. We should see this shot.*)

Good. Both hands behind your head. Great! Hold that. (*From behind his camera.*) You're doing great work. If we keep this up, in five years we'll have a really professional portfolio.

(*Li'l Bit stops.*)

LI'L BIT: What do you mean in five years?

PECK: You can't submit work to *Playboy* until you're eighteen. —

(*Peck continues to shoot; he knows he's made a mistake.*)

LI'L BIT: — Wait a minute. You're joking, aren't you, Uncle Peck?

PECK: Heck, no. You can't get into *Playboy* unless you're the very best. And you are the very best.

LI'L BIT: I would never do that!

(*Peck stops shooting. He turns off the music.*)

PECK: Why? There's nothing wrong with *Playboy* — it's a very classy maga —

LI'L BIT (*more upset*): But I thought you said I should go to college!

PECK: Wait — Li'l Bit — it's nothing like that. Very respectable women model for *Playboy* — actresses with major careers — women in college — there's an Ivy League issue every —

LI'L BIT: — I'm never doing anything like that! You'd show other people these — other *men* — what I'm doing. — Why would you do that?! Any *boy* around here could just pick up, just go into The Stop & Go and *buy* — Why would you ever want to — to share —

PECK: — Whoa, whoa. Just stop a second and listen to me. Li'l Bit. Listen. There's nothing wrong in what we're doing. I'm very proud of you. I think you have a wonderful body and an even more wonderful mind. And of course I want other people to *appreciate* it. It's not anything shameful.

LI'L BIT (*hurt*): But this is something — that I'm only doing for you. This is something — that you said was just between us.

PECK: It is. And if that's how you feel, five years from now, it will remain that way. Okay? I know you're not going to do anything you don't feel like doing. (*He walks back to the camera.*) Do you want to stop now? I've got just a few more shots on this roll —

LI'L BIT: I don't want anyone seeing this.

PECK: I swear to you. No one will. I'll treasure this — that you're doing this only for me.

(*Li'l Bit, still shaken, sits on the stool. She closes her eyes.*)

Li'l Bit? Open your eyes and look at me.

(*Li'l Bit shakes her head no.*)

Come on. Just open your eyes, honey.

LI'L BIT: If I look at you — if I look at the camera: You're gonna know what I'm thinking. You'll see right through me —

PECK: — No, I won't. I want you to look at me. All right, then. I just want you to listen. Li'l Bit.

(*She waits.*)

I love you.

(*Li'l Bit opens her eyes; she is startled. Peck captures the shot. On the screen we see right through her. Peck says softly.*)

Do you know that?

(*Li'l Bit nods her head yes.*)

I have loved you every day since the day you were born.

LI'L BIT: Yes.

(*Li'l Bit and Peck just look at each other. Beat. Beneath the shot of herself on the screen, Li'l Bit, still looking at her uncle, begins to unbutton her blouse.*

A neutral Voice cuts off the above scene with:)

Implied Consent.
As an individual operating a motor vehicle in the state of Maryland, you must abide by "Implied Consent." If you do not consent to take the blood alcohol content test, there may be severe penalties: a suspension of license, a fine, community service, and a possible jail *sentence.*

(*The Voice shifts tone:*)

Idling in the Neutral Gear.

MALE GREEK CHORUS (*announcing*): Aunt Mary on behalf of her husband.

(*Female Greek Chorus checks her appearance, and with dignity comes to the front of the stage and sits down to talk to the audience.*)

FEMALE GREEK CHORUS (*as Aunt Mary*): My husband was such a good man — is. Is such a good man. Every night, he does the dishes. The second he comes home, he's taking out the garbage, or doing yard work, lifting the heavy things I can't. Everyone in the neighborhood borrows Peck — it's true — women with husbands of their own, men who just don't have Peck's abilities — there's always a knock on our door for a jump start on cold mornings, when anyone needs a ride, or help shoveling the sidewalk — I look out, and there Peck is, without a coat, pitching in.

I know I'm lucky. The man works from dawn to dusk. And the overtime he does every year — my poor sister. She sits every Christmas when I come to dinner with a new stole, or diamonds, or with the tickets to Bermuda.

I know he has troubles. And we don't talk about them. I wonder, sometimes, what happened to him during the war. The men who fought World War II didn't have "rap sessions" to talk about their feelings. Men in his generation were expected to be quiet about it and get on with their lives. And sometimes I can feel him just fighting the trouble — whatever has burrowed deeper than the scar tissue — and we don't talk about it. I know he's having a bad spell because he comes looking for me in the house, and just hangs around me until it passes. And I keep my banter light — I discuss a new recipe, or sales, or gossip — because I think domesticity can be a balm for men when they're lost. We sit in the house and listen to the peace of the clock ticking in his well-ordered living room, until it passes.

(*Sharply.*) I'm not a fool. I know what's going on. I wish you could feel how hard Peck fights against it — he's swimming against the tide, and what he needs is to see me on the shore, believing in him, knowing he won't go under, he won't give up —

And I want to say this about my niece. She's a sly one, that one is. She knows exactly what she's doing; she's twisted Peck around her little finger and thinks it's all a big secret. Yet another one who's borrowing my husband until it doesn't suit her anymore.

Well. I'm counting the days until she goes away to school. And she manipulates someone else. And then he'll come back again, and sit in the kitchen while I bake, or beside me on the sofa when I sew in the evenings. I'm a very patient woman. But I'd like my husband back.

I am counting the days.

(*A Voice repeats:*)

You and the Reverse Gear.

MALE GREEK CHORUS: Li'l Bit's Thirteenth Christmas. Uncle Peck Does the Dishes. Christmas 1964.

(*Peck stands in a dress shirt and tie, nice pants, with an apron. He is washing dishes. He's in a mood we haven't seen. Quiet, brooding. Li'l Bit watches him a moment before seeking him out.*)

LI'L BIT: Uncle Peck?

(*He does not answer. He continues to work on the pots.*)

I didn't know where you'd gone to.

(*He nods. She takes this as a sign to come in.*)

Don't you want to sit with us for a while?
PECK: No. I'd rather do the dishes.

(*Pause. Li'l Bit watches him.*)

LI'L BIT: You're the only man I know who does dishes.

(*Peck says nothing.*)

I think it's really nice.
PECK: My wife has been on her feet all day. So's your grandmother and your mother.
LI'L BIT: I know. (*Beat.*) Do you want some help?
PECK: No. (*He softens a bit towards her.*) You can help by just talking to me.
LI'L BIT: Big Papa never does the dishes. I think it's nice.
PECK: I think men should be nice to women. Women are always working for us. There's nothing particularly manly in wolfing down food and then sitting around in a stupor while the women clean up.
LI'L BIT: That looks like a really neat camera that Aunt Mary got you.
PECK: It is. It's a very nice one.

(*Pause, as Peck works on the dishes and some demon that Li'l Bit intuits.*)

LI'L BIT: Did Big Papa hurt your feelings?
PECK (*tired*): What? Oh, no — it doesn't hurt me. Family is family. I'd rather have him picking on me than — I don't pay him any mind, Li'l Bit.
LI'L BIT: Are you angry with us?
PECK: No, Li'l Bit. I'm not angry.

(*Another pause.*)

LI'L BIT: We missed you at Thanksgiving. . . . I did. I missed you.
PECK: Well, there were . . . "things" going on. I didn't want to spoil anyone's Thanksgiving.
LI'L BIT: Uncle Peck? (*Very carefully.*) Please don't drink anymore tonight.
PECK: I'm not . . . overdoing it.
LI'L BIT: I know. (*Beat.*) Why do you drink so much?

(*Peck stops and thinks, carefully.*)

PECK: Well, Li'l Bit — let me explain it this way. There are some people who have a . . . a "fire" in the belly. I think they go to work on Wall Street or they run for office. And then there are people who have a "fire" in their heads — and they become writers or scientists or historians. (*He smiles a little at her.*) You. You've got a "fire" in the head. And then there are people like me.

LI'L BIT: Where do you have . . . a fire?

PECK: I have a fire in my heart. And sometimes the drinking helps.

LI'L BIT: There's got to be other things that can help.

PECK: I suppose there are.

LI'L BIT: Does it help — to talk to me?

PECK: Yes. It does. (*Quiet.*) I don't get to see you very much.

LI'L BIT: I know. (*Li'l Bit thinks.*) You could talk to me more.

PECK: Oh?

LI'L BIT: I could make a deal with you, Uncle Peck.

PECK: I'm listening.

LI'L BIT: We could meet and talk — once a week. You could just store up whatever's bothering you during the week — and then we could talk.

PECK: Would you like that?

LI'L BIT: As long as you don't drink. I'd meet you somewhere for lunch or for a walk — on the weekends — as long as you stop drinking. And we could talk about whatever you want.

PECK: You would do that for me?

LI'L BIT: I don't think I'd want Mom to know. Or Aunt Mary. I wouldn't want them to think —

PECK: — No. It would just be us talking.

LI'L BIT: I'll tell Mom I'm going to a girlfriend's. To study. Mom doesn't get home until six, so you can call me after school and tell me where to meet you.

PECK: You get home at four?

LI'L BIT: We can meet once a week. But only in public. You've got to let me — draw the line. And once it's drawn, you mustn't cross it.

PECK: Understood.

LI'L BIT: Would that help?

(*Peck is very moved.*)

PECK: Yes. Very much.

LI'L BIT: I'm going to join the others in the living room now. (*Li'l Bit turns to go.*)

PECK: Merry Christmas, Li'l Bit.

(*Li'l Bit bestows a very warm smile on him.*)

LI'L BIT: Merry Christmas, Uncle Peck.

(*A Voice dictates:*)

Shifting Forward from Second to Third Gear.

(*The Male and Female Greek Chorus members come forward.*)

MALE GREEK CHORUS: 1969. Days and Gifts: A Countdown:

FEMALE GREEK CHORUS: A note. "September 3, 1969. Li'l Bit: You've only been away two days and it feels like months. Hope your dorm room is cozy. I'm sending you this tape cassette — it's a new model — so you'll have some music in your room. Also that music you're reading about for class — *Carmina Burana.* Hope you enjoy. Only ninety days to go! — Peck."

MALE GREEK CHORUS: September 22. A bouquet of roses. A note: "Miss you like crazy. Sixty-nine days . . ."

TEENAGE GREEK CHORUS: September 25. A box of chocolates. A card: "Don't worry about the weight gain. You still look great. Got a post office box — write to me there. Sixty-six days. — Love, your candy man."

MALE GREEK CHORUS: October 16. A note: "Am trying to get through the Jane Austen you're reading — *Emma* — here's a book in return: *Liaisons Dangereuses.* Hope you're saving time for me." Scrawled in the margin the number: "47."

FEMALE GREEK CHORUS: November 16. "Sixteen days to go! — Hope you like the perfume. — Having a hard time reaching you on the dorm phone. You must be in the library a lot. Won't you think about me getting you your own phone so we can talk?"

TEENAGE GREEK CHORUS: November 18. "Li'l Bit — got a package returned to the P.O. Box. Have you changed dorms? Call me at work or write to the P.O. Am still on the wagon. Waiting to see you. Only two weeks more!"

MALE GREEK CHORUS: November 23. A letter. "Li'l Bit. So disappointed you couldn't come home for the turkey. Sending you some money for a nice dinner out — nine days and counting!"

GREEK CHORUS (*in unison*): November 25th. A letter:

LI'L BIT: "Dear Uncle Peck: I am sending this to you at work. Don't come up next weekend for my birthday. I will not be here —"

(*A Voice directs:*)

Shifting Forward from Third to Fourth Gear.

MALE GREEK CHORUS: December 10, 1969. A hotel room. Philadelphia. There is no moon tonight.

(*Peck sits on the side of the bed while Li'l Bit paces. He can't believe she's in his room, but there's a desperate edge to his happiness. Li'l Bit is furious, edgy. There is a bottle of champagne in an ice bucket in a very nice hotel room.*)

PECK: Why don't you sit?

LI'L BIT: I don't want to. — What's the champagne for?

PECK: I thought we might toast your birthday —

LI'L BIT: — I am so pissed off at you, Uncle Peck.

PECK: Why?

LI'L BIT: I mean, are you crazy?

PECK: What did I do?

LI'L BIT: You scared the holy crap out of me — sending me that stuff in the mail —

PECK: — They were gifts! I just wanted to give you some little perks your first semester —

LI'L BIT: — Well, what the hell were those numbers all about! Forty-four days to go — only two more weeks. — And then just numbers — 69 — 68 — 67 — like some serial killer!

PECK: Li'l Bit! Whoa! This is me you're talking to — I was just trying to pick up your spirits, trying to celebrate your birthday.

LI'L BIT: My *eighteenth* birthday. I'm not a child, Uncle Peck. You were counting down to my eighteenth birthday.

PECK: So?

LI'L BIT: So? So statutory rape is not in effect when a young woman turns eighteen. And you and I both know it.

(*Peck is walking on ice.*)

PECK: I think you misunderstand.

LI'L BIT: I think I understand all too well. I know what you want to do five steps ahead of you doing it. Defensive Driving 101.

PECK: Then why did you suggest we meet here instead of the restaurant?

LI'L BIT: I don't want to have this conversation in public.

PECK: Fine. Fine. We have a lot to talk about.

LI'L BIT: Yeah. We do.
(*Li'l Bit doesn't want to do what she has to do.*)
Could I . . . have some of that champagne?

PECK: Of course, madam! (*Peck makes a big show of it.*) Let me do the honors. I wasn't sure which you might prefer — Taittingers or Veuve Clicquot — so I thought we'd start out with an old standard — Perrier Jouet. (*The bottle is popped.*)
Quick — Li'l Bit — your glass! (*Uncle Peck fills Li'l Bit's glass. He puts the bottle back in the ice and goes for a can of ginger ale.*) Let me get some of this ginger ale — my bubbly — and toast you.

(*He turns and sees that Li'l Bit has not waited for him.*)

LI'L BIT: Oh — sorry, Uncle Peck. Let me have another.

(*Peck fills her glass and reaches for his ginger ale; she stops him.*)

Uncle Peck — maybe you should join me in the champagne.

PECK: You want me — to drink?

LI'L BIT: It's not polite to let a lady drink alone.

PECK: Well, missy, if you insist. . . . (*Peck hesitates.*) — Just one. It's been a while. (*Peck fills another flute for himself.*) There. I'd like to propose a toast to you and your birthday! (*Peck sips it tentatively.*) I'm not used to this anymore.

LI'L BIT: You don't have anywhere to go tonight, do you?

(*Peck hopes this is a good sign.*)

PECK: I'm all yours. — God, it's good to see you! I've gotten so used to . . . to . . . talking to you in my head. I'm used to seeing you every week — there's so much — I don't quite know where to begin. How's school, Li'l Bit?

LI'L BIT: I — it's hard. Uncle Peck. Harder than I thought it would be. I'm in the middle of exams and papers and — I don't know.

PECK: You'll pull through. You always do.

LI'L BIT: Maybe. I . . . might be flunking out.

PECK: You always think the worst, Li'l Bit, but when the going gets tough —

(*Li'l Bit shrugs and pours herself another glass.*)

— Hey, honey, go easy on that stuff, okay?

LI'L BIT: Is it very expensive?

PECK: Only the best for you. But the cost doesn't matter — champagne should be "sipped."

(*Li'l Bit is quiet.*)

Look — if you're in trouble in school — you can always come back home for a while.

LI'L BIT: No — (*Li'l Bit tries not to be so harsh.*) — Thanks, Uncle Peck, but I'll figure some way out of this.

PECK: You're supposed to get in scrapes, your first year away from home.

LI'L BIT: Right. How's Aunt Mary?

PECK: She's fine. (*Pause.*) Well — how about the new car?

LI'L BIT: It's real nice. What is it, again?

PECK: It's a Cadillac El Dorado.

LI'L BIT: Oh. Well, I'm real happy for you, Uncle Peck.

PECK: I got it for you.

LI'L BIT: What?

PECK: I always wanted to get a Cadillac — but I thought, Peck, wait until Li'l Bit's old enough — and thought maybe you'd like to drive it, too.

LI'L BIT (*confused*): Why would I want to drive your car?

PECK: Just because it's the best — I want you to have the best.

(*They are running out of "gas"; small talk.*)

LI'L BIT: Listen, Uncle Peck, I don't know how to begin this, but —	PECK: I have been thinking of how to say this in my head, over and over —

PECK: Sorry.

LI'L BIT: You first.

PECK: Well, your going away — has just made me realize how much I miss you. Talking to you and being alone with you. I've really come to depend on you, Li'l Bit. And it's been so hard to get in touch with you lately — the distance and — and you're never in when I call — I guess you've been living in the library —

LI'L BIT: — No — the problem is, I haven't been in the library —

PECK: — Well, it doesn't matter — I hope you've been missing me as much.

LI'L BIT: Uncle Peck — I've been thinking a lot about this — and I came here tonight to tell you that — I'm not doing very well. I'm getting very confused — I can't concentrate on my work — and now that I'm away — I've been going over and over it in my mind — and I don't want us to "see" each other anymore. Other than with the rest of the family.

PECK (*quiet*): Are you seeing other men?

LI'L BIT (*getting agitated*): I — no, that's not the reason — I — well, yes, I am seeing other — listen, it's not really anybody's business!

PECK: Are you in love with anyone else?

LI'L BIT: That's not what this is about.

PECK: Li'l Bit — you're scared. Your mother and your grandparents have filled your head with all kinds of nonsense about men — I hear them working on you all the time — and you're scared. It won't hurt you — if the man you go to bed with really loves you. (*Li'l Bit is scared. She starts to tremble.*) And I have loved you since the day I held you in my hand. And I think everyone's just gotten you frightened to death about something that is just like breathing —

LI'L BIT: Oh, my god — (*She takes a breath.*) I can't see you anymore, Uncle Peck.

(*Peck downs the rest of his champagne.*)

PECK: Li'l Bit. Listen. Listen. Open your eyes and look at me. Come on. Just open your eyes, honey. (*Li'l Bit, eyes squeezed shut, refuses.*) All right then. I just want you to listen. Li'l Bit — I'm going to ask you just this once. Of your own free will. Just lie down on the bed with me — our clothes on — just lie down with me, a man and a woman . . . and let's . . . hold one another. Nothing else. Before you say anything else. I want the chance to . . . hold you. Because sometimes the body knows things that the mind isn't listening to . . . and after I've held you, then I want you to tell me what you feel.

LI'L BIT: You'll just . . . hold me?

PECK: Yes. And then you can tell me what you're feeling.

(*Li'l Bit — half wanting to run, half wanting to get it over with, half wanting to be held by him:*)

LI'L BIT: Yes. All right. Just hold. Nothing else.

(*Peck lies down on the bed and holds his arms out to her. Li'l Bit lies beside him, putting her head on his chest. He looks as if he's trying to soak her into his pores by osmosis. He strokes her hair, and she lies very still. The Male Greek Chorus member and the Female Greek Chorus member as Aunt Mary come into the room.*)

MALE GREEK CHORUS: Recipe for a Southern Boy:

FEMALE GREEK CHORUS (*as Aunt Mary*): A drawl of molasses in the way he speaks.

MALE GREEK CHORUS: A gumbo of red and brown mixed in the cream of his skin.

(*While Peck lies, his eyes closed, Li'l Bit rises in the bed and responds to her aunt.*)

LI'L BIT: Warm brown eyes —

FEMALE GREEK CHORUS (*as Aunt Mary*): Bedroom eyes —

MALE GREEK CHORUS: A dash of Southern Baptist Fire and Brimstone —

LI'L BIT: A curl of Elvis on his forehead —

FEMALE GREEK CHORUS (*as Aunt Mary*): A splash of Bay Rum —

MALE GREEK CHORUS: A closely shaven beard that he razors just for you —

FEMALE GREEK CHORUS (*as Aunt Mary*): Large hands — rough hands —

LI'L BIT: Warm hands —

MALE GREEK CHORUS: The steel of the military in his walk —

LI'L BIT: The slouch of the fishing skiff in his walk —

MALE GREEK CHORUS: Neatly pressed khakis —

FEMALE GREEK CHORUS (*as Aunt Mary*): And under the wide leather of the belt —

LI'L BIT: Sweat of cypress and sand —

MALE GREEK CHORUS: Neatly pressed khakis —

LI'L BIT: His heart beating Dixie —

FEMALE GREEK CHORUS (*as Aunt Mary*): The whisper of the zipper — you could reach out with your hand and —

LI'L BIT: His mouth —

FEMALE GREEK CHORUS (*as Aunt Mary*): You could just reach out and —

LI'L BIT: Hold him in your hand —

FEMALE GREEK CHORUS (*as Aunt Mary*): And his mouth —

(*Li'l Bit rises above her uncle and looks at his mouth; she starts to lower herself to kiss him — and wrenches herself free. She gets up from the bed.*)

LI'L BIT: — I've got to get back.

PECK: Wait — Li'l Bit. Did you . . . feel nothing?

LI'L BIT (*lying*): No. Nothing.

PECK: Do you — do you think of me?

(*The Greek Chorus whispers:*)

FEMALE GREEK CHORUS: Khakis —

MALE GREEK CHORUS: Bay Rum —

FEMALE GREEK CHORUS: The whisper of the —

LI'L BIT: — No.

(*Peck, in a rush, trembling, gets something out of his pocket.*)

PECK: I'm forty-five. That's not old for a man. And I haven't been able to do anything else but think of you. I can't concentrate on my work — Li'l Bit. You've got to — I want you to think about what I am about to ask you.

LI'L BIT: I'm listening.

(*Peck opens a small ring box.*)

PECK: I want you to be my wife.

LI'L BIT: This isn't happening.

PECK: I'll tell Mary I want a divorce. We're not blood-related. It would be legal —

LI'L BIT: — What have you been thinking! You are married to my aunt, Uncle Peck. She's my family. You

Mary-Louise Parker as Li'l Bit and David Morse as Uncle Peck in *How I Learned to Drive* in 1997 at the Vineyard Theatre, New York City.

have — you have gone way over the line. Family is family.

(*Quickly, Li'l Bit flies through the room, gets her coat.*) I'm leaving. Now. I am not seeing you. Again.

(*Peck lies down on the bed for a moment, trying to absorb the terrible news. For a moment, he almost curls into a fetal position.*)

I'm not coming home for Christmas. You should go home to Aunt Mary. Go home now, Uncle Peck.

(*Peck gets control, and sits, rigid.*)

Uncle Peck? — I'm sorry but I have to go.

(*Pause.*)

Are you all right?

(*With a discipline that comes from being told that boys don't cry, Peck stands upright.*)

PECK: I'm fine. I just think — I need a real drink.

(*The Male Greek Chorus has become a bartender. At a small counter, he is lining up shots for Peck. As Li'l Bit narrates, we see Peck sitting, carefully and calmly downing shot glasses.*)

LI'L BIT (*to the audience*): I never saw him again. I stayed away from Christmas and Thanksgiving for years after.

It took my uncle seven years to drink himself to

death. First he lost his job, then his wife, and finally his driver's license. He retreated to his house, and had his bottles delivered.

(*Peck stands, and puts his hands in front of him — almost like Superman flying.*)

One night he tried to go downstairs to the basement — and he flew down the steep basement stairs. My aunt came by weekly to put food on the porch, and she noticed the mail and the papers stacked up, uncollected.

They found him at the bottom of the stairs. Just steps away from his dark room.

Now that I'm old enough, there are some questions I would have liked to have asked him. Who did it to you, Uncle Peck? How old were you? Were you eleven?

(*Peck moves to the driver's seat of the car and waits.*)

Sometimes I think of my uncle as a kind of Flying Dutchman. In the opera, the Dutchman is doomed to wander the sea; but every seven years he can come ashore, and if he finds a maiden who will love him of her own free will — he will be released.

And I see Uncle Peck in my mind, in his Chevy '56, a spirit driving up and down the back roads of Carolina — looking for a young girl who, of her own free will, will love him. Release him.

(*A Voice states:*)

You and the Reverse Gear.

LI'L BIT: The summer of 1962. On Men, Sex, and Women: Part III:

(*Li'l Bit steps, as an eleven-year-old, into:*)

FEMALE GREEK CHORUS (*as Mother*): It is out of the question. End of Discussion.

LI'L BIT: But why?

FEMALE GREEK CHORUS (*as Mother*): Li'l Bit — we are not discussing this. I said no.

LI'L BIT: But I could spend an extra week at the beach! You're not telling me why!

FEMALE GREEK CHORUS (*as Mother*): Your uncle pays entirely too much attention to you.

LI'L BIT: He listens to me when I talk. And — and he talks to me. He teaches me about things. Mama — he knows an awful lot.

FEMALE GREEK CHORUS (*as Mother*): He's a small town hick who's learned how to mix drinks from Hugh Hefner.

LI'L BIT: Who's Hugh Hefner?

(*Beat.*)

FEMALE GREEK CHORUS (*as Mother*): I am not letting an eleven-year-old girl spend seven hours alone in the car with a man. . . . I don't like the way your uncle looks at you.

LI'L BIT: For god's sake, mother! Just because you've gone through a bad time with my father — you think every man is evil!

FEMALE GREEK CHORUS (*as Mother*): Oh no, Li'l Bit — not all men. . . . We . . . we just haven't been very lucky with the men in our family.

LI'L BIT: Just because you lost your husband — I still deserve a chance at having a father! Someone! A man who will look out for me! Don't I get a chance?

FEMALE GREEK CHORUS (*as Mother*): I will feel terrible if something happens.

LI'L BIT: Mother! It's in your head! Nothing will happen! I can take care of myself. And I can certainly handle Uncle Peck.

FEMALE GREEK CHORUS (*as Mother*): All right. But I'm warning you — if anything happens, I hold you responsible.

(*Li'l Bit moves out of this scene and toward the car.*)

LI'L BIT: 1962. On the Back Roads of Carolina: The First Driving Lesson.

(*The Teenage Greek Chorus member stands apart on stage. She will speak all of Li'l Bit's lines. Li'l Bit sits beside Peck in the front seat. She looks at him closely, remembering.*)

PECK: Li'l Bit? Are you getting tired?

TEENAGE GREEK CHORUS: A little.

PECK: It's a long drive. But we're making really good time. We can take the back road from here and see . . . a little scenery. Say — I've got an idea — (*Peck checks his rearview mirror.*)

TEENAGE GREEK CHORUS: Are we stopping, Uncle Peck?

PECK: There's no traffic here. Do you want to drive?

TEENAGE GREEK CHORUS: I can't drive.

PECK: It's easy. I'll show you how. I started driving when I was your age. Don't you want to? —

TEENAGE GREEK CHORUS: — But it's against the law at my age!

PECK: And that's why you can't tell anyone I'm letting you do this —

TEENAGE GREEK CHORUS: — But — I can't reach the pedals.

PECK: You can sit in my lap and steer. I'll push the pedals for you. Did your father ever let you drive his car?

TEENAGE GREEK CHORUS: No way.

PECK: Want to try?

TEENAGE GREEK CHORUS: Okay. (*Li'l Bit moves into Peck's lap. She leans against him, closing her eyes.*)

PECK: You're just a little thing, aren't you? Okay — now think of the wheel as a big clock — I want you to put your right hand on the clock where three o'clock would be; and your left hand on the nine —

(*Li'l Bit puts one hand to Peck's face, to stroke him. Then, she takes the wheel.*)

TEENAGE GREEK CHORUS: Am I doing it right?

PECK: That's right. Now, whatever you do, don't let go of the wheel. You tell me whether to go faster or slower —

TEENAGE GREEK CHORUS: Not so fast, Uncle Peck!

PECK: Li'l Bit — I need you to watch the road —

(*Peck puts his hands on Li'l Bit's breasts. She relaxes against him, silent, accepting his touch.*)

TEENAGE GREEK CHORUS: Uncle Peck — what are you doing?

PECK: Keep driving. (*He slips his hands under her blouse.*)

TEENAGE GREEK CHORUS: Uncle Peck — please don't do this —

PECK: — Just a moment longer . . . (*Peck tenses against Li'l Bit.*)

TEENAGE GREEK CHORUS (*trying not to cry*): This isn't happening.

(*Peck tenses more, sharply. He buries his face in Li'l Bit's neck, and moans softly. The Teenage Greek Chorus exits, and Li'l Bit steps out of the car. Peck, too, disappears.*)

(*A Voice reflects:*)

Driving in Today's World.

LI'L BIT: That day was the last day I lived in my body. I retreated above the neck, and I've lived inside the "fire" in my head ever since.

    And now that seems like a long, long time ago. When we were both very young.

And before you know it, I'll be thirty-five. That's getting up there for a woman. And I find myself believing in things that a younger self vowed never to believe in. Things like family and forgiveness.

I know I'm lucky. Although I still have never known what it feels like to jog or dance. Any thing that . . . "jiggles." I do like to watch people on the dance floor, or out on the running paths, just jiggling away. And I say — good for them. (*Li'l Bit moves to the car with pleasure.*)

The nearest sensation I feel — of flight in the body — I guess I feel when I'm driving. On a day like today. It's five A.M. The radio says it's going to be clear and crisp. I've got five hundred miles of highway ahead of me — and some back roads too. I filled the tank last night, and had the oil checked. Checked the tires, too. You've got to treat her . . . with respect.

First thing I do is: Check under the car. To see if any two year olds or household cats have crawled beneath, and strategically placed their skulls behind my back tires. (*Li'l Bit crouches.*)

Nope. Then I get in the car. (*Li'l Bit does so.*)

I lock the doors. And turn the key. Then I adjust the most important control on the dashboard — the radio — (*Li'l Bit turns the radio on: We hear all of the Greek Chorus overlapping, and static:*)

FEMALE GREEK CHORUS (*overlapping*): — "You were so tiny you fit in his hand —"

MALE GREEK CHORUS (*overlapping*): — "How is Shakespeare gonna help her lie on her back in the —"

TEENAGE GREEK CHORUS (*overlapping*): — "Am I doing it right?"

(*Li'l Bit fine-tunes the radio station. A song like "Dedicated to the One I Love" or Orbison's "Sweet Dreams" comes on, and cuts off the Greek Chorus.*)

LI'L BIT: Ahh . . . (*Beat.*) I adjust my seat. Fasten my seat belt. Then I check the right side mirror — check the left side. (*She does.*) Finally, I adjust the rearview mirror.

(*As Li'l Bit adjusts the rearview mirror, a faint light strikes the spirit of Uncle Peck, who is sitting in the back seat of the car. She sees him in the mirror. She smiles at him, and he nods at her. They are happy to be going for a long ride together. Li'l Bit slips the car into first gear; to the audience:*)

And then — I floor it.

(*Sound of a car taking off. Blackout.*)

COMMENTARIES

Caridad Svich (b. 1963) *and Peter Franklin* (b. 1951)
COAST TO COAST WITH PAULA VOGEL   1999

Caridad Svich of the Dramatists Guild interviewed Paula Vogel in Los Angeles in 1999, and a few days later Vogel's literary agent, Peter Franklin, continued the interview in New York. The result is an intimate view of the way in which Paula Vogel works and how she developed into the playwright she has become.

Los Angeles

Caridad Svich: My initial question is: how do you sustain your focus when you're working? *How I Learned to Drive* has had such extraordinary success, and well deserved, but you still have to write that next play. How do you keep yourself in line, on track?

Paula Vogel: I've been very lucky. I didn't come from a family with trust funds. I was lucky in that. I was also lucky that I wasn't accepted into Yale School of Drama. All along, I knew that there was not family money and that I knew no one in the arts. If I was to make it in this world, I would have to do the writing on top of at least forty hours a week or more of work. In my twenties and early thirties, when I was struggling in New York, I was working sixty hours a week and writing plays.

No one in my circle of friends was being produced, so we all got together as a group. There was Mac Wellman, Jeff Jones, Y York, and maybe Connie Congdon. We dared each other to write a play in forty-eight hours. Mac wrote this brilliant play called *Cleveland*. I wrote *Heirlooms*, which actually contains many of the seeds of *How I Learned to Drive*, and then I promptly put the play in a drawer and forgot about it. I became convinced that it was appropriate to do your first draft, if not in forty-eight hours, then in a week or two, because theater is a time-oriented form.

When I got my job at Brown University, I thought, "We're going to call it The Great American Play Bakeoff." Every year, we would do these bakeoffs at Brown, and something very interesting always happened. Because they had permission to play, the forty-eight-hour bakeoff plays actually contained the seeds of what would become major works.

The Mineola Twins is on its seventeenth draft, but I did the first draft in maybe three or four weeks. The first draft of *How I Learned to Drive* was written in two weeks. You can rewrite a play for the rest of your life, but for that first draft, you put the pedal to the metal. Yes, it may be underwritten, but that rush to get to the end gives the play energy.

So in terms of focus, the key is to give yourself the permission to play and the confinement of less time rather than more time to release your creativity. When we first started our bakeoffs, we thought, once upon a time, Racine and Corneille met over coffee and said to each other, "I dare you to do a Phèdre play." That sense of writing in community is very interesting to me. I don't think playwrights write in isolation. I think we're writing to our peer group. The more great art there is, the more we all can be great.

Svich: The idea of community is so important. In Los Angeles, it's hard to establish those communities, simply because of geography, but it can happen. I wonder how you view the work of other artists, particularly young artists.

Vogel: I think about this all the time. It's not a matter of needing new plays and new artists. We are blessed with a critical mass. We need new producers, new models of production. It's no longer "Let's write a play" but "Let's make a theater."

Of course, by the time you build a theater, it's already outmoded. By the time you raise the money, the next generation is writing something that's antithetical to that space. So it's important that institutions create opportunities for the next generation. The question is: can larger institutions accept the oedipal principle? That's something Molly Smith told me many years ago. When we were in our twenties, she formed Perseverance Theater, which is my favorite theater in the country. Molly was very frustrated, because she kept knocking on doors, and everyone said, "Go away, kid." She told me, "As we age as artists, we become the king. Then there come the king-slayers."

So the question is: how do we say, "Come through the door. Here's my breast, Oedipus. Come through the door. Your art is antithetical to everything I stand for, and isn't that wonderful? That's how it should be." Great artistic directors do this. Great institutional theaters do this. It's not just making plays. It's making new structures for collaborations among playwrights, directors, and actors.

Svich: I admire your continued excitement and passion for the younger voices. When I was in London, I heard you talk at Donmar Warehouse about decadent art and naïve art, which I found fascinating. I wonder if you could encapsulate some of those ideas for those who weren't there.

Vogel: That comes from Bert States, my mentor. He said, "Every art movement goes through three stages: naïve, sophisticated, and decadent." The naïve stage is the first time something is done. For example, at some point, someone said, "What if a guy steps out from the chorus? What if three people step out of the chorus?" Suddenly, it's a new game called "drama." After a while, you say, "Yeah, yeah, three guys and a chorus. I get it. So what?" Then you go into a sophisticated stage, where everyone has seen a drama. You become very refined in your devices, and you hide all the raw edges. Then, after you've seen two thousand dramas, you get to the decadent stage. You go to the theater and say, "This better be good. Tell me something I've never seen before. Surprise me." At that point, you are in the decadent stage, which is almost a return to the naïve stage. We again expose the devices. It's raw. We again play with the form, break down the walls, and dismantle the scenery. It's the difference among Aeschylus as naïve, Sophocles as sophisticated, and Euripedes as decadent. Let's go a step further.

In the first five minutes of a play, the audience is naïve. They don't know what the rules of the game are yet. By midway, they're sophisticated. They know the vocabulary. Then comes that great moment when you pull the rug out from under them. You deconstruct the play and expose the devices in a decadent mode. I know a play works when, while the audience runs through their computer brains of the two thousand plays they've seen and tries to calculate where the play is going, the emotion grabs them by the throat and they forget about all the other plays they've seen. I'm excited by younger artists, because they dismantle my assumptions. They dismantle the dramaturgy I've spent twenty years trying to formulate. It's a kick in the pants! [. . .]

New York

Peter Franklin: I'm very excited to be doing this. I've had many conversations with Paula Vogel but never one like this. I've been privileged to represent her work for a number of years now. Aside from being one of the most extraordinary writing talents in the world, she also happens to be one of the great people in the world, so this is a double pleasure for me. I want to begin with a question I've always wanted to ask you, Paula, but never have. If you see things going off-track in a production, how do you address them?

Paula Vogel: Very quickly. (*Laughter.*) On the first day of rehearsal, you usually get a sense if things are going in a different direction. I don't mean in a different direction from what you had visualized but in a direction that may be counterproductive to the play. On the first day, I often discover a difference of opinion that delights me, a different vision that's thrilling, but if something goes off-track, I talk to the director. However, I don't necessarily do it directly. I don't necessarily say, "This is what I want." I tell jokes. I have meals with them. I just spend a lot of time with the director. In the beginning, we talk about anything *but* the play, so the director gets a sense of my rhythm, my humor, and my take on the world. I don't want to threaten their autonomy or vision. It's not until much later in the process that we talk directly about the play. I believe in sending roses first.

Franklin: So it's an intuitive process?

Vogel: Yes. Anne Bogart was very crucial in teaching me how to talk to directors. I realize it's a mistake to answer questions directly. It's sometimes best to say, "I don't think I can answer that." If something is off-track, I'm comfortable saying, "That's a fascinating impulse. It will cause problems in act two, but if you want to go out on that limb now, that's great." However, it's not necessary to have a synthesis of ideas. On *Baltimore Waltz*, Anne called me and said, "We're at the hospital looking at lounge furniture." I said, "Anne, why are you at the hospital?" "We're looking at lounge furniture." "*Baltimore Waltz* takes place on this huge bed. I wrote it for this huge bed." "That's wonderful, but that's not the vision I have. I promise you won't miss the bed." At that point, a little voice in my head said, "Shut up, Vogel. You're talking to Anne Bogart!" (*Laughter.*) Anne said, "I promise I'll give you beds, but not *one* bed." The more she talked, the more I thought, "I'm not a smart director. I don't have that genius. Give it up."

Similarly, when Mark Brokaw and I talked about *How I Learned to Drive*, he said, "No slides." I had slides in my script, but he said, "I don't see slides." He told me why. He had a very clear vision. When you talk to directors and actors, you can see the passion in their face, hear it in their voice. I don't want to dampen that enthusiasm. So I told Mark, "Fine, no slides." I will give up an early battle, so that when there's something sacred in the script, I can keep it inviolable. The other reason is that I find words very cheap. Theater isn't all about words. It isn't about the text. Theater is created in the gaps between the text and the performers and the audience. I'm just the ghostwriter, not really the author. [. . .]

Q: I have a question about another subject, a nuts-and-bolts question. I read an interview with you in the *Dramatists Guild Quarterly*, where you mentioned that *How I Learned to Drive* has a circular structure. Could you talk a little more about that?

Vogel: Recently, I've been doing weeklong "boot camps" and one-day playwriting workshops. In a nutshell, I talk about plot, character, language, and plasticity. I break down the six basic plot forms. Of course, no play is purely written in one form. You play with the different forms.

Number one is the syllogistic plot. It's cause and effect — A causes B causes C causes D, then "Boom!" There's an explosion. For example, *Oedipus* or the middle plays of Ibsen. It's actually the hardest structure for me. *How I Learned to Drive* is actually written in reverse syllogistic plot — copied from Pinter's *Betrayal*. There is cause and effect, but you go backward. Number two is the epic or associative plot. There are many different names for it, but A makes B happen, then there's a song and dance, then F makes G happen, then there's a patter song, and then it all comes home. It's Shakespeare and Brecht. For example, in "The Scottish Play," after Duncan's assassination, you don't see the immediate aftermath. You see a drunken porter in the following scene. It's always moving forward, but there's no direct cause and effect from one scene to the next. I wrote *The Mineola Twins* in associative form.

Number three is the circular plot. For example, *Waiting for Godot*. You end and begin the play at the same instance. Number four is the pattern plot. In every scene, a pattern is repeated. For example, David Mamet's *Duck Variations*. There are two guys on a bench talking about ducks in just about every single scene. I wrote *Oldest Profession*, in which there are five prostitutes, then four, then three, then two. You begin to see a pattern. It's also *Same Time, Next Year* and *La Ronde*.

Number five is the conventional plot. We know the rules of the game before we go to the theater. It's the murder mystery, the Broadway musical, the detective story — even the wedding, as in *Tony 'n' Tina's Wedding*. Number six is what I call the "synthetic fragment" plot. My students [at Brown University] do it effortlessly, but it's very hard for me to do. For example, Heiner Mueller, the German playwright who wrote *Hamletmachine*. Time no longer goes forward. All time is onstage simultaneously.

In "boot camp" I ask people to take *Hamlet* and write six plot synopses in all six different forms. I've seen astonishing, amazing *Hamlet* plays. When you start to play with these things, with a syllogistic plot or a circular plot, you start to become aware of how to design your own plot structure, and it's fun. The greatest plot structure I've ever seen is in Tom Stoppard's *Artist Descending a Staircase*. It is sheer genius. I keep saying to myself, "One of these days, I don't know when, I'm going to do a playwriting book," but it would be an anti-playwriting playwriting book. Every time I read a playwriting book, I think, "That sounds good," but then I think, "Now, how do I break all the rules I just read?"

Franklin: Any other questions?

Q: What's your writing process like? Does it depend on the play?

Vogel: I've never been a morning writer or written in any regular block of time. I'm a binge writer. However, I think for a long, long time before I sit down and write. In the "boot camp" and at Brown, I make my students write a play in forty-eight hours. I don't write plays in forty-eight hours anymore, but I write in two or three weeks. I need that momentum. I push on to finish that first draft, even if I underwrite the play. I can always go back and fill in spots later.

As you know, we writers are always juggling a rewrite of one play with a first draft of another with a screenplay. I design a different soundtrack for every project, so I almost drool like a Pavlovian dog. When I hear "Dedicated to the One I Love" or Roy Orbison, I'm in the world of *How I Learned to Drive*. If I hear Teresa Brewer, I know I'm doing rewrites on *Mineola Twins*. Janet Jackson's "Nasty" is *Hot 'n' Throbbing*. It's very specific. Nobody can live with me when I'm writing, because I make tape loops that repeat and repeat. I'll shut myself away and listen to these tape loops for the two to three weeks. The other thing I do is use a specific font and format for each play. Screenwriting books tell us there's a standard format, but that's deadly. I take one look at the page, and I'm in the world of the play. It helps me program myself. I do rewrites in the blank hours between my chores, doing the dishes and all that. That gives me all the rewriting time I need. So that's my process.

Franklin: Is writing for the screen different for you than writing for the stage?

Vogel: With a screenplay, you have less control of the result, but you can envision things that you can't do on stage. It's extraordinary how you can play with images in film. It can be a superbly surrealistic medium, though only independents or Europeans really use it in a surrealistic way. Writing screenplays, I start to think, "Now, how would I do that on stage?" It increases my stage vocabulary. For example, *How I Learned to Drive* started with a screenplay image. I saw a woman driving someplace in the Arizona desert. She adjusts her rearview mirror, and a dead man materializes in the back seat.

There's a fabulous writer named John Jeserun. I saw something he did at La MaMa° about fifteen years ago. It began with a man lying on the floor, just watching the curling smoke from a cigarette standing upright on the floor in front of him. A woman's voice offstage said, "John, why are you lying on the floor?" There was a quick blackout. Then you saw the actor lying "on the floor," but standing upright gazing straight out at the audience. The woman's voice again said, "John, why are

---

La MaMa: La MaMa Experimental Theater Club, New York.

you lying on the floor?" The actor was lying against a Plexiglas sheet, which you couldn't see, with the cigarette pasted above his head as if the camera created the floor's POV. It created the most cinematic cut. It was mesmerizing and exciting. There's a whole host of writers that have a different kind of muscle and sinew, who are using a kind of cinematic vocabulary.

Q: When do you finish writing? If you see something that you're not happy with after a play is produced or published, will you change it?

Vogel: I see a couple of things that I'm not happy with, even now, in *How I Learned to Drive*. I don't think I've ever told you this, Peter. I wanted to put in a dance between Peck and Li'l Bit. I didn't, and I'm sorry about that. I miss it. I've actually told a couple of directors who've done it. It's not in the printed version, but I think, "Well, that's the way that goes."

Franklin: After the opening in London, I told Paula, "I'm hearing things in this play I don't even remember." She said, "Well, I put some things back in!" (*Laughter.*)

Vogel: It's true! I feel it's a mistake not to do rewrites during rehearsals of a first production. It's a mistake not to use those particular actors to full advantage. You should tailor a role for an actor who has your play for the first time. Though it may not have been your original intention, what she or he does is going to become "universal." In rehearsal for *How I Learned to Drive*, I'd be thinking, "Mary-Louise [Parker] doesn't need all those words. She doesn't need all those transitions." So I cut a lot. I'd be thinking, "We already know that. Skip over it." One or two times, she said, "I need a little more stage time here," and I put in lines. I really tailored it, so there was a logic and a rhythm in that first production. I'm not a perfectionist, but I do keep rewriting. This summer, I'm going back to *Hot 'n' Throbbing* and doing a major rewrite for a possible production. I literally haven't looked at the script for maybe four or five years. It was published, but I knew I messed up the ending. After I finished *How I Learned to Drive*, I realized how to fix it. That often happens. Your next play teaches you how to work on your previous play.

David Savran (*b. 1950*)
PAULA VOGEL   *1999*

    David Savran, Paula Vogel's colleague in the English Department at Brown University, is well known for his series of interviews with contemporary playwrights. His interview with Paula Vogel appears in his book The Playwright's Voice *(1999), but this excerpt is his review of Vogel's career and precedes the interview itself. His observations describe in an economical fashion the special features of her work.*

    In her playwriting classes, Paula Vogel always asks her students to write the impossible: a play with a dog as protagonist, a play that cannot be staged, a play that dramatizes the end of the world in five pages. And while these provocative exercises stretch students' imaginations in remarkable ways, they also inadvertently reveal much about Vogel's own playwriting. For all her plays endeavor to stage the impossible. They defy traditional theater logic, subtly calling conventions into question or, in some cases, pushing them well past their limits. What other playwright would dare memorialize her brother in a play filled with fart jokes and riotous sex, whose medical authority, a cross between Dr. Strangelove and Groucho Marx, ends up drinking his own piss? What other feminist would dare write so many jokes about tits?

For a Vogel play is never simply a politely dramatized fiction, it is always a meditation on the theater itself — on role-playing, on the socially sanctioned scripts from which characters diverge at their peril, and on a theatrical tradition that has punished women who don't remain quiet, passive and demure. Take, for example, *The Mineola Twins* (1996), which plays deliriously and chillingly with the age-old farcical convention of using one virtuosic actor (and a battery of wigs) to play two startlingly dissimilar identical twins. Or *Hot 'n' Throbbing* (1994), which transforms a theater into a living room and a living room into a theater in order to dramatize the fatal consequences of stage directions gone out of control. Or her Pulitzer Prize–winning *How I Learned to Drive* (1997), which does far more than explain the effects of sexual predation on a young girl; it literally splits her into two — a body and a voice — in order to represent the radical alienation from Self that results from having been molested.

In *How I Learned to Drive*, Vogel turns the theater itself into a vehicle for memory, using first gear to move forward in time and reverse to move backwards. By reenacting the driving lessons given her by her Uncle Peck, Li'l Bit remembers her strangely — and literally — intoxicating sexual initiation. For there is no question but that her uncle's seduction has caused her to retreat "above the neck." At the same time, Peck, that most charming of pedophiles and himself a victim of abuse, is the only member of her family who makes a real effort to understand, nurture, and help her grow up. For *How I Learned to Drive* is the story not only of Li'l Bit's molestation. It is also a slyly subversive dramatization of how a girl — perhaps any girl — becomes an adult.

At the beginning of the play, Li'l Bit remembers the suburban Maryland of her youth, completely absorbed in the touch, smell, and taste of a "warm summer evening." These sensory perceptions connect her to the past, to the land and to her own body as she renders herself miraculously whole again through the power of memory. But as Li'l Bit knows all too well — and any adult will tell you — this primordial wholeness cannot last, and the remainder of the play shows her being taken for a drive that will lead her into another realm, one dominated by the senses of sight and hearing. For if touch, smell, and taste are the tokens of intimacy and wholeness, then sight and hearing are undeniably the most objectifying of the senses; they introduce a radical separation between subject and object. This is perhaps why the very center of the play is a photo shoot, for it is in this scene that Li'l Bit most graphically becomes an object for Uncle Peck and, more ominously, for herself as well. Yet this sequence is so effective theatrically because it tacitly recognizes that sight and hearing are also the senses, by no mere coincidence, upon which theater depends. It demonstrates that the theater, like the photo shoot, will always produce figures who are subjected to the scrutiny of voyeuristic spectators (or lascivious uncles). Li'l Bit, in other words, suddenly discovers that she has become an actor in a drama that has been scripted for her by an exploitative, if well-meaning spectator who is, in turn, the product of a society that values women for their allure. Yet *How I Learned to Drive* is no more an indictment of theater than it is of eroticism. For it is precisely the theater that gives Li'l Bit the time and the place to remember, that is, to reconstruct herself, to put herself back together. In learning to drive, the play shows us, Li'l Bit learns how to desire, how to use the theater, and the act of self-presentation, to put herself quite literally in the driver's seat.

In *How I Learned to Drive*, Li'l Bit is literally haunted by the unquiet spirit of her Uncle Peck in the same way that Anna in *The Baltimore Waltz* (1992) — and Vogel herself — is haunted by the spirit of her dead brother, Carl. For in attempting to remember, Vogel's theater calls up ghosts, figures lighter than air yet heavy with the past. It is obsessed with commemorating what has been lost, while understanding that loss always pays a kind of dividend that is experienced both on a personal and cultural level. For Vogel's ghosts always materialize at the place where memory turns into history, the particular into the universal. Thus, *Baltimore Waltz* becomes an exhilarating tribute and love letter not only to Carl, but to everyone who has died of AIDS, in the same way that *Drive*, by staging Li'l Bit's singular journey, dramatizes the relentless process by which we are each being produced as the subjects and objects of our own dramas.

For all their precision in documenting the act of remembering, Vogel's plays are perhaps unique in the way that they locate memory in the body. For it is far more than her punning sensibility that inspires her to title her most recent collection *The Mammary Plays* (TCG, 1998). Summoning up the "full-figured gal" of TV-commercial fame, both *Drive* and *The Mineola Twins* simultaneously exploit and critique the cliché of this "stacked" femme fatale. Both tacitly acknowledge that female bodies are steeped in history, that "sometimes the body," as Uncle Peck puts it, "knows things that the mind isn't listening to." And like her other plays, they are intent on listening to and reclaiming that lost, forgotten history. For as a feminist writer, Vogel not only attends to the deeply contradictory representations of women in our culture, but also delineates female characters who are prepared to use their physical charms (if need be) to wrest control of their lives. From the sprightly geriatric prostitutes of *The Oldest Profession* (1988) who have seized the means of production; to Myra, Mineola's answer to Patricia Hearst and Patricia Ireland; to the lesbian parents of three imaginary little boys in *And Baby Makes Seven* (1984); Vogel's women are themselves playwrights who attempt to write their way out of difficult situations and script more creative, bountiful lives. Like Vogel herself, they are committed to redressing a history of oppression by rewriting the scenes they have been handed. By so turning her female characters (and her students!) into playwrights of no mean accomplishments, she suggests that although a triumphal feminist theater seems an impossibility in our time, one may nonetheless endeavor to stage that impossibility, along with the glittering promises it holds.

Jill Dolan (b. 1957)
REVIEW OF *HOW I LEARNED TO DRIVE*   1997

Jill Dolan reviewed the Vineyard Theatre production of How I Learned to Drive *and examines the ways in which Paula Vogel establishes sympathy for Uncle Peck despite revealing him as a pedophile. Dolan sees sexuality as unstable and a matter of exploration in the drama, especially on Li'l Bit's part. In the process of commenting on the play Dolan gives us useful insights into the staging of the drama.*

Playwright Paula Vogel tends to select sensitive, difficult, fraught issues to theatricalize, and to spin them with a dramaturgy that's at once creative, highly imaginative, and brutally honest. In *How I Learned to Drive* — which won the 1997 Drama Desk Award for Best Play and several Obie Awards — Vogel's conceits remain personal, political, and highly theatrical. In a nonlinear narrative, Li'l Bit (Mary Louise Parker) tries to understand her relationship with her Uncle Peck (David Morse), whose driving lessons taught her as much about gender relations and her own sexuality as they did about the proper use of rearview mirrors, gearshifts, and turn signals.

Driving becomes the action that evokes Li'l Bit's memories; driving metaphors chart Li'l Bit's growth into automotive mastery and sexual mystery, punctuating the play's movement back and forth in time. Sitting in straight-backed chairs on a nearly bare set, Morse and Parker evoke the car rides that shape and intertwine their lives. Mark Brokaw's crisp, unsparing direction allows them to craft the scene with gesture and light, leaving the production unencumbered by more than minimal props and set pieces. The sparse set is framed by a map of Baltimore in the 1950s and 1960s, when the play's first memories occur. The geographical snippets, covered with interstates, route numbers, town names, and zip codes that move in and out of sight, remind spectators how difficult it is to truly map the territory of relationships, sexuality, and desire.

Vogel's choice to remember Li'l Bit and Peck's relationship nonchronologically illustrates its complexity, and allows the playwright to build sympathy for a man who might otherwise be despised and dismissed as a child molester. As played with affable gentility and gentleness by Morse, Peck is charming, kind, and sympathetic, a man driven toward children by his own demons but attentive to Li'l Bit's adolescent needs in ways that are never violent, paternalistic, or condescending. Peck takes the young woman seriously, and she takes great pleasure from believing that she helps him emotionally. Vogel paints their relationship as flirtatious and sexual, but also as a careful balance of power between Peck's adult desires and Li'l Bit's inchoate, exploratory impulses. Parker's lithe, erotic performance captures in subtle gestures and in postures weighted with ambivalence and desire the pleasure Li'l Bit takes in the power of saying no while her body urges her to say yes. The attraction between them becomes more urgent and mutual as the play progresses, along with Li'l Bit's knowledge that the relationship is not right. Li'l Bit's isolation in the face of strong emotions she can not understand is palpable; Parker's virtuosic performance illustrates the nuances of Li'l Bit's desire and loathing for a man who taught her so much and could finally give her so little.

Vogel builds the relationship in scenes sculpted with spare efficiency by Brokaw that crystallize moments of trust, disappointment, longing, and desire. When Peck's loneliness grips him, a very young Li'l Bit offers solace with weekly outings that are as much about companionship as they come to be about sex or driving lessons. Later, Peck photographs Li'l Bit in his basement studio, and although it's clear his motives are not pure, the experience instills in Li'l Bit a sense of her own allure, a glimpse of a budding sexuality that's powerful to her in a family life in which she is otherwise naive and powerless. Peck takes her to dinner at a sophisticated restaurant out of town when she passes her driving test. Under the disapproving eye of a sanctimonious waiter, Li'l Bit drinks martinis while one of the female chorus relates how to stay safe sexually while leaving the shores of sobriety in masculine company.

These interventions are delivered with wry and empathetic clarity directly to the audience by a three-actor chorus that shifts agilely through roles as family members and other commentators. The actors transform precisely and pointedly, with help from iconic costume pieces like glasses or scarves, into those who either deny or judge the relationship. Brokaw directs them on a nearly empty set, using chairs and the occasional table to evoke the car, the restaurant, the basement photo studio. The physical performances his actors achieve imaginatively flesh out the edges of this searing portrait.

How I Learned to Drive is only "about" incest after the scene of Li'l Bit's first molestation scene, when Li'l Bit asks the audience rhetorically, "How old were you when someone did this to you?" The moment is startling, because although the audience has witnessed Peck in an early scene prepare to molest a little boy (the boy is imagined and Morse elegantly, chillingly mimes the actions), the play has been about more than incest. Through Parker's and Morse's multilayered performances, power and danger are always present, but so are moments of understanding and mutuality.

Parker and Morse are empathetic and moving, and Johanna Day, Kerry O'Malley, and Michael Showalter, as the chorus, present tight economical sketches of Li'l Bit's family and the social characters with whom Bit and Peck interact. Vogel's wry, insightful humor captures the pain and awkward pleasure of growing into social awareness and understanding. Vogel's play is about forgiveness and family, about the instability of sexuality, about the unpredictable ways in which we learn who we are, how we desire, and how our growth is built on loss.

Writing about Drama

Why Write about Drama?

The act of writing involves making a commitment to ideas, and that commitment helps clarify your thinking. Your writing forces you to examine the details, the elements of a play that might otherwise pass unnoticed, and it helps you develop creative interpretations that enrich your appreciation of the plays you read. Besides deepening your own understanding, your writing can contribute to that of your peers and readers, as the commentaries in this book are meant to do.

Since every reader of plays has a unique experience and background, every reader can contribute something to the experience and awareness of others. You will see things that others do not. You will interpret things in a way that others will not. Naturally, every reader's aim is to respect the text, but it is not reasonable to think that there is only one way to interpret a text. Nor is it reasonable to think that only a few people can give "correct" interpretations. One of the most interesting aspects of writing about drama is that it is usually preceded by discussion, through which a range of possible interpretations begins to appear. When you start to write, you commit yourself to working with certain ideas, and you begin to deepen your thinking about those ideas as you write.

Conventions in Writing Criticism about Drama

Ordinarily, when you are asked to write about a play, you are expected to produce a critical and analytical study. A critical essay will go beyond any subjective experience and include a discussion of what the play achieves and how it does so. If you have a choice, you should choose a play that you admire and enjoy. If you have special background material on that play, such as a playbill or newspaper article, or if you have seen a production, these aids will be especially useful to you in writing.

For a critical study you will need to go far beyond retelling the events of the play. You may have to describe what you feel happens in a given scene or moment in a play, but simply rewriting the plot of the play in your own words does not constitute an interpretation. A critical reading of the play demands that you isolate evidence and comment on it. For example, you may want to quote passages of dialogue or stage direction to point out an idea that plays a key role in the drama. When you do so, quote in moderation. A critical essay that is merely a string of quotations linked together with a small amount of your commentary will not suffice. Further, make sure that the quotations you use are illustrations of your point; explain clearly their importance to your discussion.

Approaches to Criticism

Many critical approaches are available to the reader of drama. One approach might emphasize the response of audience members or readers, recognizing that the audience brings a great deal to the play even before the action begins. The audience's or reader's previous experience with drama influences expectations about what will happen on stage and about how the central characters will behave. Personal and cultural biases also influence how an audience member reacts to the unfolding drama. Reader response criticism pays close attention to these responses and to what causes them.

Another critical approach might treat the play as the coherent work of a playwright who intends the audience to perceive certain meanings in the play. This approach assumes that a careful analysis, or close reading, of the play will reveal the author's meanings. Either approach can lead to engaging essays on drama. In the pages that follow, you will find directions on how to pay attention to your responses as an audience member or reader and advice about how to read a play with close attention to dialogue, images, and patterns of action.

Reader Response Criticism

Response criticism depends on a full experience of the text — a good understanding of its meaning as well as of its conventions of staging and performance.

Your responses to various elements of the drama, whether to the characters, the setting, the theme, or the dialogue, may change and grow as you see a play or read it through. You might have a very different reaction to a play during a second reading or viewing of it. Keeping a careful record of your responses as you read is a first step in response criticism.

There is, however, a big difference between recording your responses and examining them. Douglas Atkins of the University of Kansas speaks not only of reader response in criticism but of reader responsibility, by which he means that readers have the responsibility to respond on more than a superficial level when they read drama. This book helps you reach deeper critical levels because you can read each play in light of the history of drama. The book also gives you important background material and commentary from the playwrights and from professional critics. Reading such criticism helps you understand what the critic's role is and what a critic can say about drama.

Reading drama in a historical perspective is important because it can highlight similarities between plays of different eras. Anyone who has read *Oedipus Rex* and *Antigone* will be better prepared to respond to *Hamlet*. In addition to the history and criticism of drama presented in this book, the variety of style, subject matter, and scope of the plays gives you the opportunity to read and respond to a broad range of drama. The more plays you read carefully, the better you will become at responding to drama and writing about it.

When you write response criticism, keep these guidelines in mind:

1. As you read, make note of the important effects the text has on you. Annotate in the margins moments that are especially effective. Do you find yourself alarmed, disturbed, sympathetic, or unsympathetic to a character? Do you sense suspense, or are you confused about what is happening? Do you feel personally involved with the action, or is it very distant? Do you find the situation funny? What overall response do you find yourself giving the play?

2. By analyzing the following two elements of your response, establish why the play had the effects you observe. Do you think it would have those effects on others? Have you observed that it does?

First, determine what it is about the play that causes you to have the response you do. Is it the structure of the play, the way the characters behave, their talk? Is it an unusual use of language, allusions to literature you know (or don't know)? Is the society portrayed especially familiar (or especially unfamiliar) to you? What does the author seem to expect the audience to know before the play begins?

Second, determine what it is about you, the reader, that causes you to respond as you do. Were you prepared for the dramatic conventions of the play, in terms of its genre as tragedy, comedy, tragicomedy or in terms of its place in the history of drama? How does your preparation affect your response? Did you have difficulty interpreting the language of the play because of unfamiliarity? Are you especially responsive to certain kinds of plays because of familiarity?

3. What do your responses to the play tell you about your own limitations, your own expertise, your own values, and your own attitudes toward social behavior, uses of language, and your sense of what is "normal"? Be sure to be willing to face your limitations as well as your strengths.[1]

Reader response criticism is flexible and useful in the way it allows you to explore possible interpretations of a text. Everyone is capable of responding to drama and everyone's response will differ depending on his or her preparation and background.

Close Reading

Analyzing a play by close reading means examining the text in detail, looking for patterns that might not be evident with a less attentive approach to the text. Annotation is the key to close reading, since the critic's job is to keep track of elements in the play that, innocent though they may seem alone, imply a greater significance when seen together.

Close reading implies rereading, since you do not know the first time through a text just what will be meaningful as the play unfolds, and you will want to read it again to confirm and deepen your impressions. You will usually make only a few discoveries the first time through. However, it is important to annotate the text even the first time you read it.

[1] Adapted from Kathleen McCormick, "Theory in the Reader: Bleich, Holland, and Beyond," *College English* 47 (1985): 838.

In annotating a play try following these guidelines:

1. Underline all the speeches and images you think are important. Look for dialogue that you think reveals the play's themes, the true nature of the characters, and the position of the playwright.

2. Watch for repetition of imagery (such as the garden and weed imagery in *Hamlet*) and keep track of it through annotation. Do the same for repeated ideas in the dialogue and for repeated comments on government or religion or psychology. Such repetitions will reveal their importance to the playwright.

3. Color-code or number-code various patterns in the text; then gather them either in photocopies or in lists for examination before you begin to plan your essay.

Criticism that uses the techniques of close reading pays very careful attention to the elements of drama — plot, characterization, setting, dialogue (use of language), movement, and theme — which were discussed earlier in relation to Lady Gregory's *The Rising of the Moon*. As you read a play, keep track of its chief elements because often they will give you useful ideas for your paper. You may find it helpful to refer to the earlier discussion of the elements in *The Rising of the Moon* since a short critical essay about that play is presented here (pp. 925–27).

Annotating the special use of any of the elements will help you decide how important they are and whether a close study of them can contribute to an interesting interpretation of the play. You may not want to discuss all the elements in an essay, or if you do, only one may be truly dominant, but you should be aware of them in any play you write about.

From Prewriting to Final Draft: A Sample Essay on *The Rising of the Moon*

Most good writing results from good planning. When you write criticism about drama, consider these important stages:

1. When possible, choose a play that you enjoy.
2. Annotate the play very carefully.
3. Spend time prewriting.
4. Write a good first draft, then revise for content, organization, style, and mechanics.

The essay on Lady Gregory's *The Rising of the Moon* at the end of this section involved several stages of writing. First, the writer read and annotated the play. In the process of doing so, she noticed the unusual stage direction beginning the play, *Moonlight,* and noticed also that when the two policemen leave the Sergeant, they take the lantern, but the Sergeant reminds them that it is very lonely waiting there "with nothing but the moon." Second, she used the stage directions regarding moonlight to guide her in several important techniques of prewriting, including brainstorming, clustering, freewriting, drafting a trial thesis, and outlining.

The first stage, brainstorming, involved listing ideas, words, or phrases suggested by reading the play. The idea of moonlight and the moon recurred often. Then the writer practiced clustering: beginning with *moon,* a key term developed from brainstorming, then radiating from it all the associations that naturally suggested themselves.

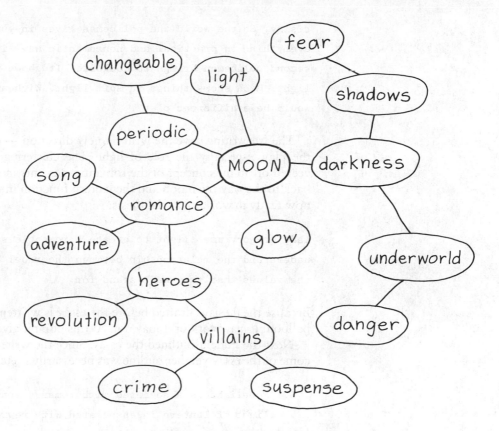

Next the student chose the term *romance* because it had generated a number of responses, and she performed a freewriting exercise around that term. Freewriting is a technique in which a writer takes four or five minutes to write whatever comes to mind. The technique is designed to be done quickly so the conscious censor has to be turned off. Anything you write in freewriting may be useful because you may produce ideas you did not know you had.

The following passage is part of the freewriting exercise the student wrote using *romance* as a key term. The passage is also an example of invisible writing because the writing was done on a computer and the writer turned off the monitor so that she could not censor or erase what she was writing. The writer could only go forward, as fast as possible.

```
The setting of the play is completely romantic. In a lot of ways
the play wouldn't work in a different setting. When you think
about it the moon in the title is what makes all the action
possible. Moon associated with darkness, underworld, world of
fairies, so the moon is what makes all the action possible. Moon
makes Sergeant look at things differently. The moon is the rebel
moon--that's what title means. Rebel moon is rising, always
```

```
rising. So the world the policeman lives in--sun lights up
everything in practical and nonromantic way--is like lantern that
second policeman brings to dockside. It shows things in a harsh
light. Moon shows things in soft light. Without the moon there
would be a different play.
```

The freewriting gave the writer a new direction — discussing the setting of the play, especially the role of light. The clustering began with the moon, veered off to the concept of the romantic elements in the play, and then came back to the way the moon and the lantern function in the play. The writer was now ready to work up a trial thesis:

```
Lady Gregory uses light to create a romantic setting that helps us
understand the relationship between the rebel and the Sergeant and
the values that they each stand for.
```

Because the thesis is drafted before the essay is written, the thesis is like a trial balloon. It may work or it may not. At this point it gives the writer direction.

Next the student outlined the essay. Since the writer did not know the outcome of the essay yet, her outline was necessarily sketchy:

```
  I.  Moonlight is associated with romance and rebellion; harsh
      light of lantern is associated with repressiveness of
      police.
      A.  Rebel is associated with romance.
      B.  Sergeant is associated with practicality and the
          law.
 II.  Without the lantern the Sergeant is under the influence
      of the romantic moon and the rebel.
      A.  Sergeant feels resentment about his job.
      B.  Rebel sings forbidden song and Sergeant reveals his
          former sympathies.
      C.  Sergeant admits he was romantic when young.
III.  Sergeant must choose between moon and lantern.
      A.  Sergeant seems ready to arrest rebel.
      B.  When police return with lantern the Sergeant sends
          them away.
      C.  Rebel escapes and Sergeant remains in moonlight.
```

The prewriting strategies of brainstorming, clustering, freewriting, drafting a thesis, and outlining helped the student generate ideas and material for her first draft. After writing this draft, she revised it carefully for organization, clarity of ideas, expression, punctuation, and format. What follows is her final draft.

Andrea James

Professor Jacobus

English 233

19 October

The Use of Light in The Rising of the Moon

Lady Gregory uses light imagery in The Rising of the Moon to contrast rebellion and repressiveness. Her initial stage direction is basic: Moonlight. She suggests some of the values associated with moonlight, such as rebellion and romance, caution and secrecy, daring exploits, and even the underworld. All these are set against the policemen, who are governed not by the moon, which casts shadows and makes the world look magical, but by the lantern, which casts a harsh light that even the Sergeant eventually rejects.

The ballad singer, the rebel, is associated with romance from the start: "Dark hair--dark eyes, smooth face. . . . There isn't another man in Ireland would have broken jail the way he did" (27-28). He is dark, handsome, and recklessly brave. The Sergeant, by contrast, is a practical man, no romantic. He sees that he might have a chance to arrest the rebel and gain the reward for his capture if he stays right on the quay, a likely place for the rebel to escape from. But he unknowingly spoils his chances by refusing to keep the lantern the policemen offer. He tells the policemen, "You can take the lantern. Don't be too long now. It's very lonesome here with nothing but the moon" (28). What he does not realize is that with the lantern as his guiding light, he will behave like a proper Sergeant. But with the moon to guide him, he will side with the rebel.

It takes only a few minutes for the rebel to show up on the scene. At first, the Sergeant is very tough and abrupt with the rebel, who is disguised as "Jimmy Walsh, a ballad singer." The rebel tells the Sergeant that he is a traveler, that he is from Ennis, and that he has been to Cork. Unlike the Sergeant, who has stayed in one place and is a family man, the ballad singer appears to be a romantic figure, in the sense that he follows his mind to go where he wants to, sings what he wants to, and does what he wants to.

When the ballad singer begins singing, the Sergeant reacts badly, telling the singer, "Stop that noise" (28). Maybe he is

envious of the ballad singer's freedom. When the Sergeant tries
to make the rebel leave, the rebel instead begins telling stories
about the man the Sergeant is looking for. He reminds the Sergeant of deeds done that would frighten anyone. "It was after
the time of the attack on the police barrack at Kilmallock. . . .
Moonlight . . . just like this" (29). The moonlight of the tale
and the moonlight of the setting combine to add mystery and
suspense to the situation.

The effect of the rebel's talk--and of the moonlight--is to
make the Sergeant feel sorry for himself in a thankless job. "It's
little we get but abuse from the people, and no choice but to obey
our orders," he says bitterly while sitting on the barrel sharing
a pipe with the singer (29). When the rebel sings an illegal song,
the Sergeant corrects a few words, revealing his former sympathies
with the people. The rebel realizes this, telling the Sergeant,
"It was with the people you were, and not with the law you were,
when you were a young man" (30). The Sergeant admits that when he
was young he too was a romantic, but now that he is older he is
practical and law-abiding: "Well, if I was foolish then, that
time's gone. . . . I have my duties and I know them" (30).

Pulled by his past and his present, the Sergeant is suddenly
forced to choose when the ballad singer's signal to his friend
reveals the singer's identity to the Sergeant. He must decide
whether his heart is with the world of moonlight or the world of
the lantern. He seizes the rebel's hat and wig and seems about to
arrest him when the policemen, with their lantern, come back. The
Sergeant orders the policemen back to the station, and they offer
to leave the lantern with him. But the Sergeant refuses. We know
that he will not turn the rebel in. He has chosen the world of
moonlight, of the rebel.

Before they leave the policemen try to make the world of the
lantern seem the right choice. Policeman B says:

> Well, I thought it might be a comfort to you. I often
> think when I have it in my hand and can be flashing it
> about into every dark corner (doing so) that it's the
> same as being beside the fire at home, and the bits of
> bogwood blazing up now and again. (Flashes it about, now
> on the barrel, now on Sergeant.) (31)

The Sergeant reacts furiously and tells them to get out--"yourselves and your lantern!"

The play ends with the Sergeant giving the hat and wig back to the rebel, obviously having chosen the side of the people. When the rebel leaves, the Sergeant wonders if he himself was crazy for losing his chance at the reward. But as the curtain goes down, the Sergeant is still in the moonlight.

How to Write a Review

What Is the Purpose of a Review?

A review is more than a critical essay because it covers the actual performance of a play. As a reviewer you write after digesting an evening's entertainment and observing how actors and a director present a production for your enjoyment. Your responsibility is to respond both to the production and to the text of the play; thus, you will discuss the quality of the acting, the effectiveness of the setting, the interpretation of the text, and the power of the direction.

Reviews of plays ordinarily appear in daily newspapers or in weekly or semiweekly publications timely enough to help a prospective playgoer decide on whether to see the play. Considering the cost of tickets in contemporary theater, the best reviewers can perform a valuable service by letting readers know what they feel is most worth seeing. Regular reviewers, such as Frank Rich and Vincent Canby in the *New York Times,* John Simon in *Newsweek,* and John Lahr in *The New Yorker,* develop their own following because playgoers know from experience whether they can rely on these reviewers' judgments.

Another purpose of theater reviews is to set a standard to which producers aspire. Criticism can promote excellence because experienced and demanding critics force producers of drama to maintain high standards. The power of theater critics in major cities is legendary: more than a few plays have closed prematurely after savage reviews in London, New York, Chicago, and elsewhere. Knowing that they risk close examination by knowledgeable reviewers convinces writers, directors, actors, and producers to do their best.

What You Need to Write a Good Review

The best reviewers ordinarily bring three qualities to their work: experience in the theater, a knowledge of theatrical history, and a sensitivity to dramatic production. Some reviewers have had experience onstage as actors or as production assistants. They are familiar with the process of preparing a play for the stage and in some cases may actually have written for the stage. Reviewers without such experience have, instead, spent hours in the theater watching plays; their rich experience of seeing a variety of plays enables them to make useful comparisons.

Knowledge of the basics of theater history is fundamental equipment for a good reviewer. New plays that borrow from the traditions of the Greek chorus, or plays that emulate medieval pageants or nineteenth-century melodrama need reviewers who understand their sources. Suzan-Lori Parks, for example, admits responding to the influence of Bertolt Brecht and Samuel Beckett. While expecting her audience to recognize some of that influence, she knows that her reviewers will spot most or all of it. This book is structured around the history of drama so that readers will better understand drama's roots and evolution. In that sense this book is an aid in helping a theater enthusiast to become a competent reviewer.

Besides knowing the history of drama, the reviewer needs also to be extremely well read. Some reviewers, for example, have not had the opportunity to see all of Shakespeare's plays, but a good reviewer will have read most of them and can refer to them as necessary. The same will be true of the plays of Bernard Shaw, as many have not been produced in the last dozen years or so. In the case of contemporary playwrights, it is common for a reviewer to refer to the playwright's earlier work to put the current production in a useful context. A knowledgeable reviewer knows not only the history of theater but also the work of other playwrights that may be relevant to the play under review.

Most of us have enough sensitivity to dramatic productions to write adequate reviews. The most sensitive reviewers will pay close attention to the suitability of the acting almost as a matter of first importance, especially if the play is well known. Most contemporary reviews single out actors and comment on their performance in some detail. Reviewers usually know the work of the most busy actors, and in some cases they will make comparisons with earlier roles. They will also indicate whether the actor has developed further as an artist or has perhaps walked mechanically through the part. The reviewer's sensitivity to individual actors is developed in part from past experience and therefore from having a benchmark against which to match a performance. Curiosity about an actor's performance sometimes drives a review, as in Peter Marks's examination of Patrick Stewart's acting in *Othello* (p. 311), which was the main focus of his essay on the play.

Obviously, neither Peter Marks nor any other reviewer is going to review *Othello* with an eye toward telling us that it is a good or bad play; the history of criticism has already done that. The reviewer of *Othello*, like the reviewer of any of Shakespeare's great plays, will aim to tell us about the quality of the acting or the effectiveness of the setting, as in Clive Barnes's review of *A Midsummer Night's Dream* (p. 233). Being sensitive to the effective use of lighting, props, costumes, and stage design is essential for any reviewer, but it is probably even more essential for a reviewer of classic theater.

Preparing to Review a Classic Play

If you have the opportunity to review a play that is well established — like most of the plays in this collection — you need special preparation. Besides having read the text before seeing the play, you need to imagine how the play should be staged. Once you understand what the play is about and what its implications may be, you then need to consult reviews or descriptions of early productions. You may do so by referring to the index of any major newspaper or to *New York Theatre Critics' Reviews,* which includes multiple reviews of important productions over the years. The point is simply to come to the experience of the drama as a fully informed viewer. Knowing how the play has been staged in the past will help you see the innovations and special interpretation of the current production.

Preparing to Review a New Play

Sometime you may have the opportunity to review a new play — one that playgoers, including the reviewers, have not had the chance to read in advance. In that case you need to pay special attention to the text, taking notes when necessary, to follow the development of the drama's ideas and issues. You are still responsible for commenting on the acting and the production, but in the case of a new play, your responsibility shifts to preparing the prospective audience to understand and respond to the play. They will need to know what the play is about, how it presents the primary issues in the drama, and what is at stake. You may need to tell something of the plot, but always with an eye toward not giving too much away, especially if the play involves suspense. Ask yourself how much the reader needs to know to decide whether to see the play.

Reviewers of new plays usually include a special commentary on a new or relatively unknown playwright. The most important information here would be any previous work of the playwright. The best reviewers will have seen that work and are prepared to relate it to the new play at hand. Reviewers of August Wilson, for example, spent time in the late 1980s establishing his credentials as a playwright. Now, when a new play of his is produced, reviewers usually attempt to describe how the new play fits into the growing body of his work. Since Wilson is in the process of writing a series of plays on African American life centering on specific decades of this century, the reviewer does the reader a service by explaining how a new play fits into his overall scheme.

Guidelines for Writing Reviews

Good reviewers approach the job of writing reviews from many different angles. Some of the reviews in this book begin with a generalization on the theme. Some begin with a personal observation about the play at hand or a personal experience in the theater. Others begin with a note on the background of the playwright, the actors, or the director. There is no one way to write a review, but the following suggestions can help you to structure your reaction.

1. If you are reviewing a professionally produced play, request a press kit from the theater. These kits usually include a great deal of information that could interest readers.

2. In your review provide any necessary background on a playwright who is contemporary or relatively unknown. The press kit should contain some information; if not, the program may do so. Check with the press representative or with the box office manager to see if the playwright is in the house and, before the play begins, ask to arrange an interview.

Sample Reviews

You can learn a great deal from some of the reviews in this book. Frank Rich's review of August Wilson's *Fences* (1987) is exemplary in many ways. Because the play was completely unknown to his readers, Frank Rich takes special care to discuss the details of the play's narrative and to comment on Wilson's other work, much of which may not be familiar to his audience. Rich carefully establishes the time period of the play, 1957, and the neighborhood in which it is set. He then goes on to examine the "mountainous" stature of Troy Maxson, played by James Earl Jones in what Rich feels may be one of his best roles. The struggle between Troy, the one-time player in the Negro baseball leagues, and his son, who is being courted by college football coaches, is central to the drama, and Rich helps us understand its import and its relevance to life in general, not just the play.

Rich reviews each of the main actors: James Earl Jones, Courtney Vance, Mary Alice, and Ray Aranha, clarifying the strength of their work. However, Rich also qualifies his praise of the play by suggesting that Wilson's earlier play, *Ma Rainey's Black Bottom*, is "more aesthetically daring." Yet that does not stop him from approving the power of Wilson's use of the "talking blues," and

"Mr. Jones's efforts to shout down the devil." Rich ends with a useful comment on Lloyd Richards's direction and the dominant struggle, both psychological and physical, between father and son that ends the play. Rich leaves the reader with no question about the importance of going to see *Fences*.

Analysis of any of the other reviews in this book will show variations on the structure of Barnes and Rich. When you write your own review, be sure to set up a checklist based on the one that follows here:

Author and title of play

What the play is about

The play's main issues

Actors

Setting

Description of the action

Direction

Theater and dates of performance

Your recommendation

Take the list to the theater with you and keep your notes on it. When you begin writing your review look at some of the tips in this discussion and some of the reviews elsewhere in this book. Your review should provide your readers a valuable service.

Glossary of Dramatic Terms

Act. A major division in the action of a play. Most plays from the Elizabethan era until the nineteenth century were divided into five acts by the playwrights or by later editors. In the nineteenth century many writers began to write four-act plays. Today one-, two-, and three-act plays are most common.

Action. What happens in a play; the events that make up the **plot**.

Agon. The Greek word for "contest." In Greek tragedy the *agon* was often a formal debate in which the **chorus** divided and took the sides of the disputants.

Alienation effect. In his **epic theater**, Bertolt Brecht (1898–1956) tried to make the familiar unfamiliar (or to alienate it) to show the audience that familiar, seemingly "natural," and therefore unalterable social conditions could be changed. Different devices achieved the alienation effect by calling attention to the theater as theater — stage lights brought in front of the curtain, musicians put onstage instead of hidden in an orchestra pit, placards indicating scene changes and interrupting the linear flow of the action, actors distancing themselves from their characters to invite the audience to analyze and criticize the characters instead of empathizing with them. These alienating devices prevented the audience from losing itself in the illusion of reality. (See **epic theater**.)

Allegory. A literary work that is coherent on at least two levels simultaneously: a literal level consisting of recognizable characters and events and an allegorical level in which the literal characters and events represent moral, political, religious, or other ideas and meanings.

Anagnorisis. Greek term for a character's discovery or recognition of someone or something previously unknown. *Anagnorisis* often paves the way for a reversal of fortune (see *peripeteia*). An example in *Oedipus Rex* is Oedipus's discovery of his true identity.

Antagonist. A character or force in conflict with the **protagonist**. The antagonist is often another character but may also be an intangible force such as nature or society. The dramatic conflict can also take the form of a struggle with the protagonist's own character.

Anticlimax. See **plot**.

Antimasque. See **masque**.

Antistrophe. The second of the three parts of the verse ode sung by the **chorus** in Greek drama. While singing the **strophe** the chorus moves in a dance rhythm from right to left; during the antistrophe it moves from left to right back to its original position. The third part, the **epode**, was sung standing still.

Apron stage. The apron is the part of the stage extending in front of the **proscenium arch**. A stage is an apron stage if all or most of it is in front of any framing structures. The Elizabethan stage, which the audience surrounded on three sides, is an example of an apron stage.

Arena stage. A stage surrounded on all sides by the audience, actors make exits and entrances through the aisles. Usually used in **theater in the round**.

Arras. A curtain hung at the back of the Elizabethan playhouse to partition off an alcove or booth. The curtain could be pulled back to reveal a room or a cave.

Aside. A short speech made by a character to the audience which, by **convention**, the other characters onstage cannot hear.

Atellan farce. Broad and sometimes coarse popular humor indigenous to the town of Atella in Italy. By the third century B.C., the Romans had imported the Atellan farce, which they continued to modify and develop.

Blank verse. An unrhymed verse form often used in writing drama. Blank verse is composed of ten-syllable lines accented on the second, fourth, sixth eighth, and tenth syllables (**iambic pentameter**).

Bombast. A loud, pompous speech whose inflated diction is disproportionate to the subject matter it expresses.

Bourgeois drama. Drama that treats middle-class subject matter or characters rather than the lives of the rich and powerful.

Braggart soldier. A **stock character** in comedy who is usually cowardly, parasitical, pompous, and easily victimized by practical jokers. Sir John Falstaff in Shakespeare's *Henry IV* (parts 1, 2) is an example of this type.

Burla (plural, *burle*). Jests or practical jokes that were part of the comic **stage business** in the **commedia dell'arte.**

Buskin. A thick-soled boot possibly worn by Greek tragedians to increase their stature. Later called a *cothornus.*

Catastrophe. See **plot.**

Catharsis. The feeling of emotional purgation or release that, according to Aristotle, an audience should feel after watching a tragedy.

Ceremonial drama. Egyptian passion play about the god Osiris.

Character. Any person appearing in a drama or narrative.

> **Stock character.** A stereotypical character type whose behavior, qualities, or beliefs conform to familiar dramatic **conventions,** such as the clever servant or the **braggart soldier.** (Also called *type character.*)

Chiton. Greek tunic worn by Roman actors.

Choregos. An influential citizen chosen to pay for the training and costuming of the **chorus** in Greek drama competitions. He probably also paid for the musicians and met other financial production demands not paid for by the state.

Chorus. A masked group that sang and danced in Greek tragedy. The chorus usually chanted in unison, offering advice and commentary on the action but rarely participating. See also **strophe, antistrophe,** and **epode.**

City Dionysia. See **Dionysus.**

Climax. See **plot.**

Closet drama. A drama, usually in verse, meant for reading rather than for performance. Hrosvitha's *Dulcitius,* Percy Bysshe Shelley's *Prometheus Unbound,* and John Milton's *Samson Agonistes* are examples.

Comedy. A type of drama intended to interest and amuse rather than to concern the audience deeply. Although characters experience various discomfitures, the audience feels confident that they will overcome their ill fortune and find happiness at the end.

> **Comedy of humors.** Form of comedy developed by Ben Jonson in the seventeenth century in which characters' actions are determined by the preponderance in their systems of one of the four bodily fluids or humors — blood, phlegm, choler (yellow bile), and melancholy (black bile). Characters' dispositions are exaggerated and stereotyped; common types are the melancholic and the belligerent bully.

> **Comedy of manners.** Realistic, often satiric comedy concerned with the manners and conventions of high society. Usually refers to the Restoration comedies of late seventeenth-century England, which feature witty dialogue or **repartee.** An example is William Congreve's *The Way of the World.*

> **Drawing room comedy.** A type of comedy of manners concerned with life in polite society. The action generally takes place in a drawing room.

> **Farce.** A short dramatic work that depends on exaggerated, improbable situations, incongruities, coarse wit, and horseplay for its comic effect.

> **High comedy.** Comedy that appeals to the intellect, often focusing on the pretensions, foolishness, and incongruity of human behavior. **Comedy of manners** with its witty dialogue is a type of high comedy.

> **Low comedy.** Comedy that lacks the intellectual appeal of **high comedy,** depending instead on boisterous buffoonery, "gags," and jokes for its comic effect.

> **Middle Comedy.** This transitional Greek style of comedy extended from 375 to about 330 B.C. It marks a change, especially in language, which grew less formal and closer to the way people spoke. Little evidence of Middle Comedy exists, but from suriviving statuettes we can surmise that costumes on stage resembled what Athenians actually wore on the street.

> **New Comedy.** Emerging between the fourth and third centuries B.C. in ancient Greece, New Comedy replaced the farcical **Old Comedy.** New Comedy, usually associated with Menander, is witty and intellectually engaging; it is often thought of as the first **high comedy.**

> **Old Comedy.** Greek comedy of the fifth century B.C. that uses bawdy farce to attack satirically social, religious, and political institutions. Old Comedy is usually associated with Aristophanes.

> **Sentimental comedy.** Comedy populated by stereotypical virtuous **protagonists** and villainous **antagonists** that resolves the domestic trials of middle-class people in a pat, happy ending.

> **Slapstick.** **Low comedy** that involves little plot or character development but consists of physical horseplay or practical jokes.

Comic relief. The use of humorous characters, speeches, or scenes in an otherwise serious or tragic drama.

Commedia dell'arte. Italian **low comedy** dating from around the mid-sixteenth century in which professional actors playing **stock characters** improvised dialogue to fit a given **scenario.**

Complication. See **plot.**

Conflict. See **plot.**

Convention. Any feature of a literary work that has become standardized over time, such as the **aside** or the **stock character.** Often refers to an unrealistic device (such as Danish characters speaking English in *Hamlet*) that the audience tacitly agrees to accept.

Coryphaeus. See *koryphaios.*

Cosmic irony. See **irony.**

Cothurnes. See **buskin.**

Craft play. Medieval sacred drama based on Old and New Testament stories. Craft plays were performed outside the church by members of a particular trade guild, and their subject matter often reflected the guild's trade. The fisherman's guild, for example, might present the story of Noah and the flood.

Crisis. Same as **climax.** See **plot.**

Cycle. A group of medieval **mystery plays** written in the vernacular (the language in common use rather than Latin) for performance outside the church. Cycles, each of which treated biblical stories from creation through the last judgment, are named after the town in which they were produced. Most extant mystery plays are from the York, Chester, Wakefield (Towneley), and N-Town cycles.

Decorum. A quality that exists when the style of a work is appropriate to the speaker, the occasion, and the subject matter. Kings should speak in a "high style" and clowns in a "low style," according to many Renaissance authors. Decorum was a guiding critical principle in **neoclassicism.**

Defamiliarization effect (*Verfremdungseffkt*). See **alienation effect.**

Denouement. See **plot.**

Deus ex machina. Latin for "a god out of a machine." In Greek drama, a mechanical device called a *mechane* could lower "gods" onto the stage to solve the seemingly unsolvable problems of mortal characters. Also used to describe a playwright's use of a forced or improbable solution to plot complications — for example, the discovery of a lost will or inheritance that will pay off the evil landlord.

Dialogue. Spoken interchange or conversation between two or more characters. Also see **soliloquy.**

Diction. A playwright's choice of words or the match between language and subject matter. Also refers collectively to an actor's phrasing, enunciation, and manner of speaking.

Dionysus. Greek nature god of wine, mystic revelry, and irrational impulse. Greek tragedy probably sprang from dramatized ritual choral celebrations in his honor.

City Dionysia. (Also called Great or Greater Dionysia.) The most important of the four Athenian festivals in honor of Dionysus. This spring festival sponsored the first tragedy competitions; comedy was associated with the winter festival, the Lenaea.

Director. The person responsible for a play's interpretation and staging and for the guidance of the actors.

Disguising. Medieval entertainment featuring a masked procession of actors performing short plays in pantomime; probably the origin of the court **masque.**

Dithyramb. Ancient Greek choral hymn sung and danced to honor **Dionysus;** originally divided into an improvised story sung by a choral leader and a traditional refrain sung by the **chorus.** Believed by some to be the origin of Greek tragedy.

Domestic tragedy. A serious play usually focusing on the family and depicting the fall of a middle-class **protagonist** rather than of a powerful or noble hero. Also called *bourgeois tragedy.* An example is Arthur Miller's *Death of a Salesman,* which traces the emotional collapse and eventual suicide of Willy Loman, a traveling salesman.

Double plot. See **plot.**

Drama. A play written in prose or verse that tells a story through **dialogue** and actions performed by actors impersonating the characters of the story.

Dramatic illusion. The illusion of reality created by drama and accepted by the audience for the duration of the play.

Dramatic irony. See **irony.**

Dramatist. The author of a play; playwright.

Dramaturge. One who represents the playwright and guides the production. In some cases, the dramaturge researches different aspects of the production or earlier productions of the play.

Dramaturgy. The art of writing plays.

Drawing room comedy. See **comedy.**

Empathy. The sense of feeling *with* a character. (Distinct from sympathy, which is feeling *for* a character.)

Ensemble acting. Performance by a group of actors, usually members of a **repertory** company, in which the integrated acting of all members is emphasized over individual star performances. The famous nineteenth-century director Konstantin Stanislavsky promoted this type of acting in the Moscow Art Theatre.

Environmental theater. A term used by Richard Schechner, director of the Performance Group in the late 1960s and early 1970s, to describe his work and the work of other theater companies, including the Bread and Puppet Theatre, Open Theatre, and Living Theatre. He also used the term to describe the indigenous theater of Africa and Asia. Environmental theater occupies the whole of a performance space; it is not confined to a stage separated from the audience. Action can take place in and around the audience, and audience members are often encouraged to participate in the theater event.

Epic theater. A type of theater first associated with German director Erwin Piscator (1893–1966). Bertolt Brecht (1898–1956) used the term to distinguish his own theater from the "dramatic" theater that created the illusion of reality and invited the audience to identify and empathize with the characters. Brecht criticized the dramatic theater for encouraging the audience to believe that social conditions were "natural" and therefore unalterable. According to Brecht, the theater should show human beings as dependent on certain political and economic factors and at the same time as capable of altering them. "The spectator is given the chance to criticize human behavior from a social point of view, and the scene is played as a piece of history," he wrote. Epic theater calls attention to itself as theater, bringing the stage lights in front of the curtain and interrupting the linear flow of the action to help the audience analyze the action and characters onstage. (See **alienation effect.**)

Epilogue. A final speech added to the end of a play. An example is Puck's "If we shadows have offended . . ." speech that ends Shakespeare's *A Midsummer Night's Dream*.

Epitasis. Ancient term for the **rising action** of a **plot.** (See also **plot.**)

Epode. The third of three parts of the verse ode sung by the **chorus** in a Greek drama. The epode follows the **strophe** and **antistrophe.**

Exodos. The concluding scene, which includes the exit of all characters and the **chorus,** of a Greek drama.

Exposition. See **plot.**

Expressionism. Early twentieth-century literary movement in Germany that posited that art should represent powerful emotional states and moods. Expressionists abandon **realism** and **verisimilitude,** producing distorted, nightmarish images of the individual unconscious.

Falling action. See **plot.**

Farce. See **comedy.**

First Folio. The first collected edition of thirty-six of Shakespeare's plays, collected by two of his fellow actors and published posthumously in 1623.

Foil. A character who, through difference or similarity, brings out a particular aspect of another character. Laertes, reacting to the death of his father, acts as a foil for Hamlet.

Foreshadowing. Ominous hints of events to come that help to create an air of suspense in a drama.

Frons scaena. The elaborately decorated facade of the *scaena* or stage house used in presenting Roman drama. (Also called *scaena frons.*)

Hamartia. An error or wrong act through which the fortunes of the **protagonist** are reversed in a tragedy.

High comedy. See **comedy.**

History play. A drama set in a time other than that in which it was written. The term usually refers to Elizabethan drama, such as Shakespeare's Henry plays, that draws its plots from English historical materials such as Holinshed's *Chronicles*.

Hubris (or *hybris*). Excessive pride or ambition. In ancient Greek tragedy hubris often causes the **protagonist's** fall.

Humor character. A stereotyped character in the **comedy of humors** (see **comedy**). Clever plots often play on the character's personality distortions (caused by an imbalance of humors), revealing his or her absurdity.

Iambic pentameter. A poetic meter that divides a line into five parts (or feet), each part containing an unaccented syllable followed by an accented syllable. The line "When I consider everything that grows" is an example of iambic pentameter verse.

Imitation. See *mimesis*.

Impressionism. A highly personal style of writing in which the author presents characters, scenes, or moods as they appear to him or her at a particular moment rather than striving for an objectively realistic description.

Interlude. A short play, usually either farcical or moralistic, performed between the courses of a feast or between the acts of a longer play. The interlude thrived during the late fifteenth and early sixteenth centuries in England.

Irony. The use of words to suggest a meaning that is the opposite of the literal meaning, as in "I can't wait to take the exam." Irony is present in a literary work that gives expression to contradictory attitudes or impulses to entertain ambiguity or to maintain detachment.

Cosmic irony. Irony present when destiny or the gods seem to be in favor of the **protagonist** but are actually engineering his or her downfall. (Same as *irony of fate*.)

Dramatic irony. Irony present when the outcome of an event or situation is the opposite of what a character expects.

Tragic irony. Irony that exists when a character's lack of complete knowledge or understanding (which the audience possesses) results in his or her fall or has tragic consequences for loved ones. An example from *Oedipus Rex* is Oedipus's declaration that he will stop at nothing to banish King Laios's murderer, whom the audience knows to be Oedipus himself.

Jongleur. Early medieval French musical entertainer who recited lyrics, ballads, and stories. Forerunner of the minstrel.

Koryphaios. The leader of the **chorus** in Greek drama.

Kothurnus. See **buskin.**

Lazzo (plural, *lazzi*). Comic routines or **stage business** associated with the stock situations and characters of the Italian **commedia dell'arte.** A scenario might, for example, call for the *lazzo* of fear.

Liturgical drama. Short dramatized sections of the medieval church service. Some scholars believe that these playlets evolved into the vernacular **mystery plays,** which were performed outside the church by lay people.

Low comedy. See **comedy.**

Mansion. Scenic structures used in medieval drama to indicate the locale or scene of the action. Mansions were areas inside the church used for performing liturgical drama; later more elaborate structures were built on pageant wagons to present **mystery plays** outside the church.

Mask. A covering used to disguise or ornament the face; used by actors in Greek drama and revived in the later **commedia dell'arte** and court **masque** to heighten dramatic effect.

Masque (also *mask*). A short but elaborately staged court drama, often mythological and allegorical, principally acted and danced by masked courtiers. (Professional actors often performed the major speaking and singing roles.) Popular in England during the late sixteenth and early seventeenth centuries, masques were often commissioned to honor a particular person or occasion. Ben Jonson was the most important masque writer; the genre's most elaborate sets and costumes were designed by Jonson's occasional partner Inigo Jones.

   Antimasque. A parody of the court **masque** developed by Ben Jonson featuring broad humor, grotesque characters, and ludicrous actions.

Melodrama. A suspenseful play filled with situations that appeal to the audience's emotions. Justice triumphs in a happy ending: the good characters (completely virtuous) are rewarded and the bad characters (thoroughly villainous) are punished.

Method acting. A naturalistic technique of acting developed by the Russian director Konstantin Stanislavsky and adapted for American actors by Lee Strasberg, among others. The Method actor identifies with the **character** he or she portrays and experiences the emotions called for by the play in an effort to render the character with emotional **verisimilitude.**

Middle Comedy. See **comedy.**

Mimesis. The Greek word for "imitation." Aristotle used the term to define the role of art as an imitation of an action.

Miracle play. A type of medieval sacred drama that depicts the lives of saints, focusing especially on the miracles performed by saints.

Mise-en-scène. The stage setting of a play, including the use of scenery, props, and stage movement.

Moira. Greek word for "fate."

Morality play. Didactic late medieval drama (flourishing in England c. 1400–1550) that uses **allegory** to dramatize some aspects of the Christian moral life. Abstract qualities or entities such as Virtue, Vice, Good Deeds, Knowledge, and Death are cast as characters who discuss with the **protagonist** issues related to salvation and the afterlife. *Everyman* is an example.

Motivation. The reasons for a character's actions in a drama. For drama to be effective, the audience must believe that a character's actions are justified and plausible given what they know about him or her.

Mouth of hell. A stage prop in medieval drama suggesting the entrance to hell. Often in the shape of an open-mouthed monster's head, the mouth of hell was positioned over a smoke-and-fire-belching pit in the stage that appeared to swallow up sinners.

Mystery play. A sacred medieval play dramatizing biblical events such as the creation, the fall of Adam and Eve, and Christ's birth and resurrection. The genre probably evolved from **liturgical drama;** mystery plays were often incorporated into larger **cycles** of plays.

Naturalism. Literary philosophy popularized during the nineteenth century that casts art's role as the scientifically accurate reflection of a "slice of life." Naturalism is aligned with the belief that each person is a product of heredity and environment driven by internal and external forces beyond his or her control. August Strindberg's *Miss Julie*, with its focus on reality's sordidness and humankind's powerlessness, draws on naturalism.

Neoclassicism. A movement in sixteenth-century Italy and seventeenth-century France to revive and emulate classical attitudes toward art based on principles of order, harmony, unity, restrained wit, and **decorum.** The neoclassical movement in France gave rise to a corresponding movement in England during the late seventeenth and eighteenth centuries.

New Comedy. See **comedy.**

Ode. A dignified Greek three-part song sung by the **chorus** in Greek drama. The parts are the **strophe,** the **antistrophe,** and the **epode.**

Old Comedy. See **comedy.**

Orchestra. Literally the "dancing place"; the circular stage where the Greek **chorus** performed.

Pageant. A movable stage or wagon (often called a pageant wagon) on which a set was built for the performance of medieval drama. The term can also refer to the spectacle itself.

Pallium. Long white cloak or mantle worn by Greek actors or Romans in Greek-based plays.

Pantomime. Silent acting using facial expression, body movement, and gesture to convey the plot and the characters' feelings.

Parodos. The often stately entrance song of the **chorus** in Greek drama. The term also refers to the aisles (plural, *paradoi*) on either side of the orchestra by which the chorus entered the Greek theater.

Pastoral drama. A dramatic form glorifying shepherds and rural life in an idealized natural setting; usually implies a negative comparison to urban life.

Pathos. The quality of evoking pity.

Peripeteia. A reversal of fortune, for better or worse, for the **protagonist**. Used especially to describe the main character's fall in Greek tragedy.

Performance art. A mid-twentieth-century form that often mixes media: music, video, film, opera, dance, and spoken text. It was originally defined in terms of artists using a live production for dramatic effect. However, it has widened to include performances that cross defined dramatic "boundaries." Dancers Martha Clarke and Pina Bausch, musicians such as Laurie Anderson, and experimental directors such as Richard Foreman have been identified as performance artists.

Phallus. An appendage meant to suggest the penis added to the front of blatantly comic male characters' costumes in some Greek comedy; associated chiefly with the Greek **satyr play.**

Play. A literary genre whose plot is usually presented dramatically by actors portraying characters before an audience.

Play-within-the-play. A brief secondary drama presented to or by the characters of a play that reflects or comments on the larger work. An example is the Pyramus and Thisby episode in Shakespeare's *A Midsummer Night's Dream.*

Plot. The events of a play or narrative. The sequence and relative importance a **dramatist** assigns to these events.

   Anticlimax. An unexpectedly trivial or significant conclusion to a series of significant events; an unsatisfying resolution that often occurs in place of a conventional **climax.**

   Catastrophe. The outcome or conclusion of a play; usually applied specifically to tragedy. (**Denouement** is a parallel term applied to both comedy and tragedy.)

   Climax. The turning point in a drama's action, preceded by the **rising action** and followed by the **falling action.** Same as **crisis.**

   Complication. The part of the plot preceding the **climax** that establishes the entanglements to be untangled in the **denouement.** Part of the **rising action.**

   Conflict. The struggle between the **protagonist** and the **antagonist** that propels the **rising action** of the plot and is resolved in the **denouement.**

   Denouement. The "unknotting" of the plot's **complication**; the resolution of a drama's action. See **catastrophe.**

   Double plot. A dramatic structure in which two related plots function simultaneously.

   Exposition. The presentation of essential information, especially about events that have occurred prior to the first scene of a play. The exposition appears early in the play and initiates the **rising action.**

   Falling action. The events of the plot following the **climax** and ending in the **catastrophe** or resolution.

   Rising action. The events of the plot leading up to the **climax.**

   Subplot. A secondary plot intertwined with the main plot, often reflecting or commenting on the main plot.

   Underplot. Same as **subplot.**

Problem play. A drama that argues a point or presents a problem (usually a social problem). Ibsen is a notable writer of problem plays.

Prologos. In Greek drama, an introductory scene for actor or actors that precedes the entrance of the **chorus.** This **convention** has evolved into the modern dramatic introductory monologue or **prologue.**

Prologue. A preface or introduction preceding the play proper.

Proscaena. The space in front of the *scaena* in a Roman theater.

Proscenium arch. An arched structure over the front of the stage from which a curtain often hangs. The arch frames the action onstage and separates the audience from the action.

Proskenion. The playing space in front of the *skene* or scene house in Greek drama.

Protagonist. The main character in a drama. This character is usually the most interesting and sympathetic and is the person involved in the **conflict** driving the **plot.**

Protasis. Classical term for the introductory act or **exposition** of a drama.

Psychomachia. Psychological struggle; a war of souls.

Quem Quaeritis **trope.** A brief dramatized section of the medieval church's Easter liturgy. The oldest extant **trope** and the probable origin of liturgical drama, it enacts the visit of the three Marys to Christ's empty tomb (*quem quaeritis* means "whom do you seek?" in Latin).

Rising action. See **plot.**

Realism. The literary philosophy holding that art should accurately reproduce an image of life. Avoiding the use of dramatic **conventions** such as asides and soliloquies, it depicts ordinary people in ordinary situations. Ibsen's *A Doll House* is an example of realism in drama.

Recognition. See *anagnorisis.*

Repartee. Witty and pointed verbal exchanges usually found in the **comedy of manners.**

Repertory. A theater company or group of actors that presents a set of plays alternately throughout a season. The term also refers to the set of plays itself.

Restoration comedy. A type of **comedy of manners** that developed in England in the late seventeenth century. Often features **repartee** in the service of complex romantic plots. William Congreve's *The Way of the World* is an example.

Revenge tragedy. Sensational tragedy popularized during the Elizabethan age that is notable for bloody plots involving such elements as murder, ghosts, insanity, and crimes of lust.

Reversal. See *peripeteia.*

Riposte. A quick or sharp reply; similar to **repartee.**

Rising action. See **plot.**

Ritual. Repeated formalized or ceremonial practices, many of which have their roots in primitive cultures. Certain theorists hold that primitive ritual evolved into drama.

Satire. A work that makes fun of a social institution or human foible, often in an intellectually sophisticated way, to persuade the audience to share the author's views. Molière's *The Misanthrope* contains social satire.

Satyr play. A comic play performed after the tragic trilogy in Greek tragedy competitions. The satyr play provided **comic relief** and was usually a farcical, boisterous treatment of mythological material.

Scaena. The stage house in Roman drama; the facade of the *scaena* (called the *frons scaena*) was often elaborately ornamented.

Scenario. The plot outline around which professional actors of the **commedia dell'arte** improvised their plays. Most scenarios specified the action's sequence and the entrances of the main characters.

Scene. Division of an **act** in a drama. By traditional definition a scene has no major shift in place or time frame, and it is performed by a static group of actors onstage (in French drama, if an actor enters or exits, the group is altered and the scene, technically, should change). The term also refers to the physical surroundings or locale in which a play's action is set.

Scenery. The backdrop and set (furniture and so on) onstage that suggest to the audience the surroundings in which a play's **action** takes place.

Scenography. Painting of backdrops and hangings.

Senecan tragedy. Tragic drama modeled on plays written by Seneca. The genre usually has five acts and features a chorus; it is notable for its thematic concern with bloodshed, revenge, and unnatural crimes. (See also **revenge tragedy.**)

Sentimental. Refers to tender emotions in excess of what the situation calls for.

Setting. All details of time, location, and environment relating to a play.

Skene. The building or scene house in the Greek theater that probably began as a dressing room and eventually was incorporated into the action as part of the scenery.

Slapstick. See **comedy.**

Slice of life. See **naturalism.**

Social problem play. Same as **problem play.**

Sock. Derived from the Latin *soccus,* the term refers to a light slipper or sock worn by Roman comic actors.

Soliloquy. A speech in which an actor, usually alone onstage, utters his or her thoughts aloud, revealing personal feelings. Hamlet's "To be, or not to be" speech is an example.

Spectacle. In Aristotle's terms, the costumes and scenery in a drama — the elements that appeal to the eye.

Stage business. Minor physical action, including an actor's posture and facial expression, and the use of props, all of which make up a particular interpretation of a character.

Stichomythia. Dialogue in which two speakers engage in a verbal duel in alternating lines.

Stock character. See **character.**

Strophe. The first of three parts of the verse **ode** sung by the Greek **chorus.** While singing the strophe the chorus moves in a dancelike pattern from right to left. See also **antistrophe** and **epode.**

Subplot. See **plot.**

Subtext. A level of meaning implicit in or underlying the surface meaning of a text.

Surrealism. A literary movement flourishing in France during the early twentieth century that valued the unwilled expression of the unconscious (usually as revealed in dreams) over a rendering of "reality" structured by the conscious mind.

Suspense. The sense of tension aroused by an audience's uncertainty about the resolution of dramatic conflicts.

Suspension of disbelief. An audience's willingness to accept the world of the drama as reality during the course of a play.

Symbolism. A literary device in which an object, event, or action is used to suggest a meaning beyond its literal meaning. The guns in *Hedda Gabler* have a symbolic function.

Theater. The building in which a play is performed. Also used to refer to drama as an art form.

Theater in the round. The presentation of a play on an **arena stage** surrounded by the audience.

Theater of the absurd. A type of twentieth-century drama presenting the human condition as meaningless, absurd, and illogical. An example of the genre is Samuel Beckett's *Waiting for Godot.*

Theater of cruelty. A type of drama created by Antonin Artaud in the 1930s that uses shock techniques to expose the audience's primitive obsessions with cruelty and sexuality. The purpose was to overwhelm spectators' rational minds, leading them to understand and even participate in the cycle of cruelty and ritual purgation dramatized in the performance.

Three unities. Aristotle noted that a play's action usually occurs in one day or a little more and that the plot should reveal clearly ordered actions and incidents moving toward the plot's resolution. Later scholars and critics, especially those in the neoclassical tradition, interpreted Aristotle's ideas as rules (unity of time and unity of action) and added a third, unity of place (a play's action should occur in a single locale).

Thrust stage. A stage extending beyond the **proscenium arch,** usually surrounded on three sides by the audience.

Tiring house. From "attiring house," the backstage space in Elizabethan public theaters used for storage and as a dressing room. The term also refers to the changing space beneath the medieval pageant wagon.

Total theater. A concept of the theater as an experience synthesizing all the expressive arts including music, dance, lighting, and so on.

Tragedy. Serious drama in which a **protagonist,** traditionally of noble position, suffers a series of unhappy events culminating in a **catastrophe** such as death or spiritual breakdown. Shakespeare's *Hamlet,* which ends with the prince's death, is an example of Elizabethan tragedy.

Tragicomedy. A play that combines elements of tragedy and comedy. Chekhov's *The Cherry Orchard* is an example. Tragicomedies often include a serious plot in which the expected tragic **catastrophe** is replaced by a happy ending.

Trope. Interpolation into or expansion of an existing medieval liturgical text. These expansions, such as the *Quem Quaeritis* trope, gave rise to **liturgical drama.**

Type character. See **character.**

Underplot. See **plot.**

Unity. The sense that the events of a play and the actions of the characters follow one another naturally to form one complete action. Unity is present when characters' behavior seems **motivated** and the work is perceived to be a connected artistic whole. See also **three unities.**

Verfremdungseffkt. German term coined by Bertolt Brecht to mean "alienation." See also **alienation effect.**

Verisimilitude. The degree to which a dramatic representation approximates an appearance of reality.

Well-made play. Drama that relies for effect on the suspense generated by its logical, cleverly constructed plot rather than on characterization. Plots often involve a withheld secret, a battle of wits between hero and villain, and a resolution in which the secret is revealed and the **protagonist** saved. The plays of Eugène Scribe (1791–1861) have defined the type.

Selected Bibliography

Selected References for Periods of Drama

GREEK DRAMA

Aylen, Leo. *The Greek Theater*. Rutherford: Fairleigh Dickinson UP, 1985.

Bieber, Margaret. *The History of the Greek and Roman Theater*. 2nd ed. Princeton: Princeton UP, 1961.

Easterling, P. E., ed. *The Cambridge Companion to Greek Tragedy*. Cambridge: Cambridge UP, 1997.

Green, John R. *Theatre in Ancient Greek Society*. New York: Routledge, 1994.

Hamilton, Edith. *The Greek Way*. New York: Norton, 1983.

Hartigan, Karelisa V. *Greek Tragedy on the American Stage: Ancient Drama in the Commercial Theater 1882–1994*. New York: Greenwood, 1995.

Havelock, Eric. "The Double Vision of Greek Tragedy." Hudson Review 37 (1984): 244–70.

Kitto, H. D. F. *Form and Meaning in Drama: A Study of Six Greek Plays and of Hamlet*. 2nd ed. New York: Barnes, 1968.

———. *Greek Tragedy: A Literary Study*. 3rd ed. London: Methuen, 1966.

Knox, Bernard M. *Word and Action: Essays on the Ancient Theater*. Baltimore: Johns Hopkins UP, 1979.

Mills, Sophie. *Theseus, Tragedy, and the Athenian Empire*. Oxford: Oxford UP, 1997.

Pickard-Cambridge, Arthur W. *Dramatic Festivals of Athens*. 2nd ed. Revised by John Gould and D. M. Lewis. Oxford: Clarendon, 1962.

Silk, M. S., ed. *Tragedy and the Tragic: Greek Theatre and Beyond*. Oxford: Clarendon, 1996.

Steiner, George. *The Death of Tragedy*. New York: Knopf, 1961.

Taplin, Oliver. *Greek Tragedy in Action*. Berkeley: U of California P, 1978.

Taylor, David. *The Greek and Roman Stage*. Bristol: Bristol Classical, 1999.

Trendall, A. D., and T. B. L. Webster. *Illustrations of Greek Drama*. London: Phaidon, 1971.

Vickers, Brian. *Towards Greek Tragedy: Drama, Myth, Society*. London: Longman, 1973.

Walcot, Peter. *Greek Drama in Its Theatrical and Social Context*. Cardiff: U of Wales P, 1976.

Walton, Michael J. *Living Greek Theater: A Handbook of Classical Performance and Modern Production*. New York: Greenwood, 1987.

Webster, T. B. L. *Greek Theater Production*. 2nd ed. London: Methuen, 1970.

Winkler, John J., and Froma I. Zeitlin. *Nothing to Do with Dionysus? Athenian Drama in Its Social Context*. Princeton: Princeton UP, 1990.

Wise, Jennifer. *Dionysus Writes: The Invention of Theatre in Ancient Greece*. Ithaca: Cornell UP, 1998.

Zinman, Toby. "Still Dangerous after All These Years: Now's Your Chance to Get Reacquainted with Greek Tragedy's High-and-Mighty Heroines." *American Theatre* 16.3 (1999): 18–21, 62–63.

ROMAN DRAMA

Beare, William. *The Roman Stage*. 3rd ed. London: Methuen, 1969.

Bieber, Margaret. *The History of the Greek and Roman Theater*. 2nd ed. Princeton: Princeton UP, 1961.

Dodwell, Charles R. *Anglo-Saxon Gestures and the Roman Stage*. New York: Cambridge UP, 1999.

Duckworth, George E. *The Nature of Roman Comedy: A Study in Popular Entertainment*. Princeton: Princeton UP, 1952.

Grant, M. D. "Plautus and Seneca: Acting in Nero's Rome." *Greece and Rome* 46.1 (1999): 27–33.

Hunter, R. L. *The New Comedy of Greece and Rome*. New York: Cambridge UP, 1985.

Kenney, E. J., ed. *The Cambridge History of Classical Literature*. 2 vols. New York: Cambridge UP, 1982.

Konstan, David. *Roman Comedy*. Ithaca: Cornell UP, 1983.

Reinheimer, David A. "The Roman Actor, Censorship, and Dramatic Autonomy." *Studies in English Literature 1500–1900* 38.2 (1998): 317–32.

Segal, Erich. *Roman Laughter*. Cambridge: Harvard UP, 1968.

Wiles, David. *The Masks of Menander: Sign and Meaning in Greek and Roman Performances*. New York: Cambridge UP, 1991.

Wiseman, Timothy P. *Roman Drama and Roman History*. Exeter: University of Exeter Press, 1998.

MEDIEVAL DRAMA

Bevington, David, ed. *Medieval Drama*. Boston: Houghton, 1975.

Briscoe, Marianne G., and John C. Coldewey. *Contexts for Early English Drama*. Bloomington: Indiana UP, 1989.

Chambers, Edmund K. *English Literature at the Close of the Middle Ages*. Oxford: Clarendon, 1945.

——. *The Medieval Stage*. 2 vols. London: Oxford UP, 1967.

Cox, John D., and David S. Kastan, eds. *A New History of Early English Drama*. New York: Columbia UP, 1997.

Craig, Hardin. *English Religious Drama of the Middle Ages*. 2nd ed. Westport, CT: Greenwood, 1978.

Davidson, Clifford, et al., eds. *Drama in the Middle Ages*. New York: AMS, 1982.

——. *Material Culture and Medieval Drama*. Kalamazoo: Medieval Institute, 1999.

Dillon, Janette. *Language and Stage in Medieval and Renaissance England*. Cambridge: Cambridge UP, 1998.

Elliott, John R. *Playing God: Medieval Mysteries on the Modern Stage*. Toronto: U Toronto P, 1989.

Enders, Jody. *The Medieval Theater of Cruelty: Rhetoric, Memory, Violence*. Ithaca: Cornell UP, 1999.

Gassner, John, ed. *Medieval and Tudor Drama*. New York: Bantam, 1971.

Hardison, O. B., Jr. *Christian Rite and Christian Drama in the Middle Ages: Essays in the Origin and Early History of Modern Drama*. Baltimore: Johns Hopkins UP, 1965.

Spinrad, Phoebe. *The Summons of Death on the Medieval and Renaissance English Stage*. Columbus: Ohio State UP, 1987.

Vince, Ronald W. *Ancient and Medieval Theatre: A Historiographical Handbook*. Westport: Greenwood, 1984.

Wickham, Glynne. *The Medieval Theatre*. 3rd ed. New York: Cambridge UP, 1987.

Woolf, Rosemary. *The English Mystery Plays*. Berkeley: U of California P, 1972.

Wright, Stephen, K. "The Betrayer's Art: Translating Medieval Drama for Modern Readers." *Research Opportunities in Renaissance Drama* 35 (1996): 85–96.

RENAISSANCE DRAMA

Adams, John C. *The Globe Playhouse*. 2nd ed. New York: Barnes, 1961.

Altman, Joel B. *The Tudor Play of Mind: Rhetorical Inquiry and the Development of Elizabethan Drama*. Berkeley: U of California P, 1978.

Axton, Richard. *European Drama of the Early Middle Ages*. London: Hutchinson, 1974.

Bevington, David. *From Mankind to Marlowe: Growth of Structure in the Popular Drama of Tudor England*. Cambridge: Harvard UP, 1962.

Bradbrook, Muriel C. *The Growth and Structure of Elizabethan Comedy*. London: Chatto, 1955.

Braunmuller, A. R., and Michael Hathaway. *The Cambridge Companion to Renaissance Drama*. New York: Cambridge UP, 1990.

Bush, Douglas. *The Renaissance and English Humanism*. Toronto: U of Toronto P, 1939.

Bushnell, Rebecca W. *Tragedies of Tyrants: Political Thought and Theater in the English Renaissance*. Ithaca: Cornell UP, 1990.

Cairns, Christopher, ed. *The Renaissance Theatre: Texts, Performance, Design*. Aldershot, UK: Ashgate, 1999.

Cartwright, Kent. *Theatre and Humanism: English Drama in the Sixteenth Century*. Cambridge: Cambridge UP, 1999.

Cerasano, S. P., and Marion Wynne-Davies, eds. *Readings in Renaissance Women's Drama: Criticism, History, and Performance, 1594–1998*. London: Routledge, 1998.

Chambers, E. K. *The Elizabethan Stage*. 4 vols. Oxford: Clarendon, 1923.

Coyle, Martin. "*Hamlet*, Gertrude and the Ghost: The Punishment of Women in Renaissance Drama." *Q/W/E/R/T/Y* 6 (1996): 29–38.

Farnham, W. *The Medieval Heritage of Elizabethan Tragedy*. Berkeley: U of California P, 1936.

Findaly, Alison. *A Feminist Perspective on Renaissance Drama*. Oxford: Blackwell Publishers, 1999.

Fumerton, Patricia, and Simon Hunt, eds. *Renaissance Culture and the Everyday*. Philadelphia: U of Philadelphia P, 1999.

Happe, Peter. *English Drama Before Shakespeare*. London: Longman, 1999.

Hussey, Maurice. *The World of Shakespeare and His Contemporaries: A Visual Approach*. New York: Viking, 1972.

Kernodle, George. *From Art to Theatre: Form and Convention in the Renaissance*. Chicago: U of Chicago P, 1944.

Lea, Kathleen M. *Italian Popular Comedy: A Study of the Commedia dell'Arte, 1560–1620*. 2 vols. Oxford: Clarendon, 1934.

Leggatt, Alexander. *Introduction to English Renaissance Comedy*. Manchester: Manchester UP, 1999.

Leinwand, Theodore B. *Theatre, Finance, and Society in Early Modern England*. Cambridge: Cambridge UP, 1999.

Loomba, Ania. *Gender, Race, and Renaissance Drama.* New York: Manchester UP, 1989.

Marcus, Leah S. *Unediting the Renaissance: Shakespeare, Marlowe, Milton.* London: Routledge, 1996.

Masten, Jeffrey, and Wendy Wall. *Renaissance Drama.* Evanston: Northwestern UP, 1999.

McLuskie, Kathleen. *Renaissance Dramatists.* Atlantic Highlands: Humanities International, 1989.

Nicoll, Allardyce. *The World of Harlequin.* Cambridge: Cambridge UP, 1963.

Rose, Mary Beth. *The Expense of Spirit: Love and Sexuality in English Renaissance Drama.* Ithaca: Cornell UP, 1988.

Rose, Mary Beth, ed. *Renaissance Dramatic Culture.* Evanston: Northwestern UP, 1998.

Tetzell, Kurt von Rosador. "The Power of Magic: From Endimion to *The Tempest.*" Shakespeare Survey 43 (1991): 1–13.

Waith, Eugene M. *Patterns and Perspectives in English Renaissance Drama.* Newark: U of Delaware P, 1988.

Welsford, Enid. *The Court Masque.* Cambridge: Cambridge UP, 1927.

White, Martin. *Renaissance Drama in Action: An Introduction to Aspects of Theatre Practice and Performance.* London: Routledge, 1998.

Wind, Edgar. *Pagan Mysteries in the Renaissance.* New Haven: Yale UP, 1958.

Woodbridge, Linda. *Woman and the English Renaissance: Literature and the Nature of Womankind, 1540–1620.* Urbana: U of Illinois P, 1984.

Yates, Frances A. *Theatre of the World.* Chicago: U of Chicago P, 1969.

LATE SEVENTEENTH- AND EIGHTEENTH-CENTURY DRAMA

Barber, Charles L. *The Idea of Honour in the English Drama, 1591–1700.* Stockholm: Göteborg, 1957.

Cox, Jeffrey N. *In the Shadows of Romance.* Athens: Ohio UP, 1987.

Grene, Nicholas. *Shakespeare, Jonson, Molière: The Comic Contract.* Totowa: Barnes, 1980.

Holland, Norman N. *The First Modern Comedies: The Significance of Etherege, Wycherley, and Congreve.* Cambridge: Harvard UP, 1959.

Hume, Robert. *The Rakish Stage: Studies in English Drama, 1660–1800.* Carbondale: Southern Illinois UP, 1983.

Kaplan, Deborah. "Representing the Nation: Restoration Comedies on the Early Twentieth-Century London Stage." *Theatre Survey* 36.2 (1995): 37–61.

Loftis, John, ed. *Restoration Drama.* New York: Oxford UP, 1966.

Lynch, Kathleen M. *The Social Mode of Restoration Comedy.* New York: Farrar, 1975.

Marshall, Geoffrey. *Restoration Serious Drama.* Norman: U of Oklahoma P, 1975.

McMillin, Scott, ed. *Restoration and Eighteenth-Century Comedy.* 2nd ed. New York: Norton, 1997.

Nicoll, Allardyce. *A History of Restoration Drama, 1600–1700.* New York: Cambridge UP, 1923.

Owen, Susan J. *Restoration Theatre and Crisis.* Oxford: Clarendon P, 1996.

Peters, Julie Stone. " 'Things Govern'd by Words': Late Seventeenth-Century Comedy and the Reformers." English Studies 68 (1987): 142–53.

Powell, Jocelyn. *Restoration Theatre Production.* Boston: Routledge, 1984.

Price, Cecil. *Theatre in the Age of Garrick.* Oxford: Oxford UP, 1973.

Richards, K. R., ed. *Essays on the Eighteenth Century English Stage.* London: Methuen, 1972.

Rothstein, Eric. *The Designs of Carolean Comedy.* Carbondale: Southern Illinois UP, 1988.

Stynan, J. L. *Restoration Comedy in Performance.* New York: Cambridge UP, 1986.

Turnell, Martin. *The Classical Movement: Studies in Corneille, Molière, and Racine.* New York: New Directions, 1948.

NINETEENTH-CENTURY DRAMA THROUGH THE TURN OF THE CENTURY

Bank, Rosemarie K. *Theatre Culture in America, 1825–1860.* Cambridge Studies in American Theatre and Drama. Cambridge: Cambridge UP, 1997.

Bentley, Eric. *The Playwright as Thinker: A Study of Drama in Modern Times.* New York: Harcourt, 1967.

Bogard, Travis, ed. *Modern Drama: Essays in Criticism.* New York: Oxford UP, 1965.

Booth, Michael. *English Melodrama.* London: Jenkins, 1965.

Brustein, Robert. *The Theatre of Revolt.* Boston: Little, 1964.

Cole, Toby, ed. *Playwrights on Playwriting: The Meaning and Making of Modern Drama from Ibsen to Ionesco.* New York: Hill, 1960.

Detsi-Diamanti, Zoe. *Early American Women Dramatists, 1775–1860.* Garland Studies in American Popular History and Culture. New York: Garland, 1998.

Driver, Tom Faw. *Romantic Quest and Modern Query: A History of the Modern Theatre.* New York: Delacorte, 1970.

Finney, Gail. *Women in Modern Drama: Freud, Feminism, and European Theater at the Turn of the Century.* Ithaca: Cornell UP, 1989.

Fisher, Judith L., and Stephen Watt, eds. *When They Weren't Doing Shakespeare: Essays on Nineteenth-Century British and American Theatre.* Athens: U of Georgia P, 1989.

Gilman, Richard. *The Making of Modern Drama: A Study of Buchner, Ibsen, Strindberg, Chekhov, Pirandello, Brecht, Beckett, Handke.* New York: Farrar, 1974.

Jewett, William. *Fatal Autonomy: Romantic Drama and the Rhetoric of Agency.* Ithaca: Cornell UP, 1997.

Krasner, David. *Resistance, Parody, and Double*

Consciousness in African American Theatre, 1895–1910. Basingstoke: Macmillan, 1997.

Newey, Katharine. "Melodrama and Metatheatre: Theatricality in the Nineteenth Century Theatre." *Journal of Dramatic Theory and Criticism* 11.2 (1997): 85–100.

Marker, Fredrick J., and Christopher Innes, eds. *Modernism in European Drama: Ibsen, Strindberg, Pirandello, Beckett.* Toronto: U of Toronto P, 1998.

Quinsey, Katherine M., ed. *Broken Boundaries: Women and Feminism in Restoration Drama.* Lexington: U of Kentucky P, 1996.

Riis, Thomas. "Opera and the Operatic, Drama and the Melodramatic: What Was the State of Things in Nineteenth-Century America?" *Nineteenth Century Theatre* 23.1–2 (1995): 76–89.

Stynan, J. L. *Modern Drama in Theory and Practice.* 3 vols. New York: Cambridge UP, 1980.

Valency, Maurice Jacques. *The Flower and the Castle: An Introduction to Modern Drama.* New York: Schocken, 1982.

Whitaker, Thomas R. *Fields of Play in Modern Drama.* Princeton: Princeton UP, 1977.

Williams, Raymond. *Drama from Ibsen to Eliot.* New York: Oxford UP, 1953.

DRAMA IN THE EARLY AND MID-TWENTIETH CENTURY

Artaud, Antonin. *The Theatre and Its Double.* Trans. Mary C. Richards. New York: Grove, 1958.

Bentley, Eric. *The Theatre of Commitment and Other Essays on Drama in Our Society.* New York: Atheneum, 1967.

Blau, Herbert, *The Impossible Theatre: A Manifesto.* New York: Macmillan, 1964.

Bogard, Travis, and William I. Oliver, eds. *Modern Drama: Essays in Criticism.* New York: Oxford UP, 1965.

Booth, Michael R., and Joel H. Kaplan, eds. *The Edwardian Theatre: Essays on Performance and the Stage.* Cambridge: Cambridge UP, 1996.

Bordman, Gerald Martin. *American Theatre: A Chronicle of Comedy and Drama, 1930–1969.* New York: Oxford UP, 1996.

Brater, Enoch, and Ruby Cohn, eds. *Around the Absurd: Essays on Modern and Postmodern Drama.* Ann Arbor: U of Michigan P, 1990.

Brockett, Oscar G. *History of the Theatre.* 5th ed. Boston: Allyn, 1987.

Brook, Peter. *The Empty Space.* New York: Avon, 1968.

Cohn, Ruby. *From Desire to Godot: Pocket Theater of Postwar Paris.* Berkeley: U of California P, 1987.

Davidson, Clifford, C. J. Gianakaris, and John H. Stroupe, eds. *Drama in the Twentieth Century: Comparative and Critical Essays.* New York: AMS, 1984.

Demastes, William W., and Katherine E. Kelly. *British Playwrights, 1880–1956: A Research and Production Sourcebook.* Westport, CT: Greenwood, 1996.

Esslin, Martin. *The Theatre of the Absurd.* Woodstock, NY: Overlook, 1973.

Fearnow, Mark. *The American Stage and the Great Depression: A Cultural History of the Grotesque.* Cambridge Studies in American Theatre and Drama. Cambridge: Cambridge UP, 1997.

Gassner, John. *Theatre at the Crossroads.* New York: Holt, 1960.

Goldberg, RosaLee. *Performance: Live Art 1909 to the Present.* New York: Abrams, 1979.

Hebel, Udo J. "Early American Women Playwrights (1916–1930) and the Remapping of Twentieth-Century American Drama." *Arbeiten aus Anglistik und Amerikanistik* 21.2 (1996): 267–86.

Kernan, Alvin B., ed. *The Modern American Theater: A Collection of Critical Essays.* Englewood Cliffs: Prentice, 1967.

Kirby, Michael. *A Formalist Theatre.* Philadelphia: U of Pennsylvania P, 1987.

Mason, Jeffrey D., and Ellen Gainer, eds. *Performing America: Cultural Nationalism in American Theater.* Ann Arbor: U of Michigan P, 1999.

Miller, Jordan Yale. *American Drama between the Wars: A Critical History.* Twayne's Critical History of American Drama. Boston: Twayne, 1997.

Murray, Christopher. "Modern Drama from Ibsen to Fugard." *Moderna Sprak* 88.1 (1994): 98–100.

Orr, John. *Tragic Drama and Modern Society: Studies in Social and Literary Theory of Drama from 1870 to the Present.* New York: Macmillan, 1981.

Piscator, Erwin. *The Political Theatre: A History, 1914–1929.* Trans. Hugh Rorrison. London: Eyre Methuen, 1980.

Roose-Evans, James. *Experimental Theatre: From Stanislavsky to Today.* 2nd ed. London: Studio Vista, 1973.

Smith, Wendy. *Real Life Drama: The Group Theatre and America, 1931–1940.* New York: Knopf, 1990.

Szilassy, Zolt N. *American Theater of the 1960s.* Carbondale: U of Illinois P, 1986.

CONTEMPORARY DRAMA

Andreach, Robert J. *Creating Self in the Contemporary American Theatre.* Carbondale: Southern Illinois UP, 1998.

Betsko, Kathleen, and Rachel Koenig. *Interviews with Contemporary Women Playwrights.* New York: Beech Tree, 1987.

Bigsby, Christopher W. E. *Contemporary American Playwrights.* Cambridge: Cambridge UP, 1999.

Blau, Herbert. *Eye of Prey: Subversions of the Postmodern.* Bloomington: Indiana UP, 1987.

Blumenthal, Eileen. *Joseph Chaikin: Exploring at the Boundaries of Theatre.* New York: Cambridge UP, 1984.

Brecht, Stefan. *The Theatre of Visions: Robert Wilson.* Frankfurt am Main: Suhrkamp, 1978.

Carpenter, Charles A. *Modern Drama: Scholarship and*

Criticism, 1981–1990: An International Bibliography. Toronto: U of Toronto P, 1997.

Cheney, Sheldon. *New Movement in the Theatre.* Westport, CT: Greenwood, 1971.

Coen, Stephanie. "No Comparisons." *American Theatre* 11.6 (1994): 26.

DiGaetani, John L. "David Ives." *Interviews with Contemporary Playwrights.* Ed. John L. DiGaetani. New York: Greenwood, 1991. 183–90.

Dobrez, Livio A. C. *The Existential and Its Exits: Literary and Philosophical Perspectives on the Works of Beckett, Ionesco, Genet, and Pinter.* New York: St. Martin's, 1986.

Grotowski, Jerzy. *Towards a Poor Theatre.* New York: Simon, 1968.

Hart, Lynda, ed. *Making a Spectacle: Feminist Essays on Contemporary Women's Theatre.* Ann Arbor: U of Michigan P, 1989.

Hayman, Ronald. *Theatre and Anti-Theatre: New Movements since Beckett.* New York: Oxford UP, 1979.

Heilpern, John. *How Good Is David Mamet Anyway? Writings on Theatre and Why It Matters.* New York: Routledge, 1999.

Hill, Errol, ed. *The Theatre of Black Americans.* 2 vols. Englewood Cliffs: Prentice, 1980.

Inverso, MaryBeth. *The Gothic Impulse in Contemporary Drama.* Ann Arbor: U of Michigan P, 1990.

Marranca, Bonnie, ed. *The Theatre of Images.* New York: Drama Book Specialists, 1977.

McDonough, Carla J. *Staging Masculinity: Male Identity in Contemporary American Drama.* Jefferson, NC: McFarland, 1997.

Orr, John. *Tragicomedy and Contemporary Culture: Play and Performance from Beckett to Shepard.* Ann Arbor: U of Michigan P, 1990.

Parker, Dorothy. *Essays on Modern American Drama: Williams, Miller, Albee, and Shepard.* Toronto: U of Toronto P, 1987.

Peacock, D. Keith. *Thatcher's Theatre: British Theatre and Drama in the Eighties.* Contributions in Drama and Theatre Studies 88. Westport, CT: Greenwood, 1999.

Roudané, Matthew Charles. *American Drama since 1960: A Critical History.* New York: Twayne, 1997.

Savran, David. *In Their Own Words: Contemporary American Playwrights.* New York: Theatre Communications Group, 1988.

Schechner, Richard. *Environmental Theater.* New York: Hawthorn, 1973.

Sinfield, Alan. *Out on Stage: Lesbian and Gay Theatre in the Twentieth Century.* New Haven: Yale UP, 1999.

Smith, Iris. "Authors in America: Tony Kushner, Arthur Miller, and Anna Deveare Smith." *Centennial Review* 40.1 (1996): 125–42.

Watt, Stephen. *Postmodern Drama: Reading the Contemporary Stage.* Ann Arbor: U of Michigan P, 1998.

Wellworth, George E. *The Theater of Protest and Paradox.* New York: New York UP, 1971.

Selected References for Playwrights and Plays

ARISTOPHANES

Colvin, Stephen. *Dialect in Aristophanes and the Politics of Language in Ancient Greek Literature.* Oxford: Clarendon, 1999.

Dane, Joseph A. *Parody: Critical Concepts versus Literary Practices, Aristophanes to Sterne.* Norman: U of Oklahoma P, 1988.

Deardon, C. W. *The Stage of Aristophanes.* London: Athlone, 1976.

Dover, K. J. *Aristophanic Comedy.* Berkeley: U of California P, 1972.

Forrest, W. G. "Aristophanes' *Lysistrata.*" *Classical Quarterly* 45.1 (1995): 240–41.

Harriott, Rosemary. *Aristophanes: Poet and Dramatist.* Baltimore: Johns Hopkins UP, 1986.

Henderson, Jeffrey. *Aristophanes' Lysistrata.* New York: Oxford UP, 1987.

Matz, D. "Ensuring That the Flea Wears Wax Slippers When Teaching Aristophanes and a One-Person Reenactment of a Choral Entry from *Lysistrata* in the Classroom." *Classical Journal* 87.1 (1991): 55–58.

McLeish, Kenneth. *The Theatre of Aristophanes.* New York: Taplinger, 1980.

Murray, Gilbert. *Aristophanes.* Oxford: Clarendon, 1933.

Reckford, Kenneth. *Aristophanes' Old-and-New Comedy.* Chapel Hill: U of North Carolina P, 1987.

Russo, Carlo Ferdinando. *Aristophanes: An Author for the Stage.* London: Routledge, 1997.

Segal, Erich, ed. *Oxford Readings in Aristophanes.* Oxford: Oxford UP, 1996.

Ussher, Robert Glenn. *Aristophanes.* New York: Oxford UP, 1979.

SAMUEL BECKETT

Andonian, Cathleen Culotta, ed. *The Critical Response to Samuel Beckett.* Westport, CT: Greenwood, 1998.

Astro, Alan. *Understanding Beckett.* Columbia: U of South Carolina P, 1990.

Athanason, Arthur N. Endgame: *The Ashbin Play.* New York: Twayne, 1993.

Begam, Richard. *Samuel Beckett and the End of Modernity.* Stanford: Stanford UP, 1996.

Beja, Morris, S. E. Gontarski, and Pierre Astier, eds. *Samuel Beckett: Humanistic Perspectives.* Columbus: Ohio State UP, 1983.

Ben-Zvi, Linda, ed. *Women in Beckett: Performance and Critical Perspectives.* Urbana: U of Illinois P, 1990.

Bloom, Harold. *Samuel Beckett's* Endgame. New York: Chelsea, 1988.

Brater, Enoch, ed. *Beckett at 80: Beckett in Context.* New York: Oxford UP, 1986.

————. *Why Beckett: With 122 Illustrations.* New York: Thames, 1989.

Bryden, Mary. "The Sacrificial Victim of Beckett's *Endgame.*" *Literature and Theology* 4.2 (1990): 219–25.

Buning, Marius, and Lois Oppenheim, eds. *Beckett in the 1990s.* Amsterdam: Rodopi, 1993.

Burkman, Katherine. *Myth and Ritual in the Plays of Samuel Beckett.* Rutherford: Fairleigh Dickinson UP, 1987.

Butler, Lance S., and Robin J. Davis, eds. *Rethinking Beckett: A Collection of Critical Essays.* New York: St. Martin's, 1990.

Cohn, Ruby. *Just Play: Beckett's Theater.* Princeton: Princeton UP, 1980.

————, ed. *Samuel Beckett: A Collection of Criticism.* New York: McGraw, 1975.

Connor, Steven, ed. *Gender in Transition:* Waiting for Godot *and* Endgame. New York: St. Martin's, 1992.

Cronin, Anthony. *Samuel Beckett: The Last Modernist.* New York. Harper, 1997.

Dearlove, J. E. *Accommodating the Chaos: Samuel Beckett's Nonrelational Art.* Durham: Duke UP, 1982.

Doll, Mary Aswell. *Beckett and Myth: An Archetypal Approach.* Syracuse: Syracuse UP, 1988.

Esslin, Martin, ed. *Samuel Beckett: A Collection of Critical Essays.* Englewood Cliffs: Prentice, 1965.

Fletcher, Beryl S., et al. *A Student's Guide to the Plays of Samuel Beckett.* 2nd ed. Boston: Faber, 1985.

Fletcher, John. *Beckett: The Playwright.* New York: Hill, 1985.

Gidal, Peter. *Understanding Beckett.* New York: St. Martin's, 1986.

Gontarski, S. E. *On Beckett: Essays and Criticism.* New York: Grove, 1986.

Gordon, Lois G. *The World of Samuel Beckett.* New Haven: Yale UP, 1996.

Kenner, Hugh. *A Reader's Guide to Samuel Beckett.* New York: Farrar, 1973.

Knowlson, James. *Damned to Fame: The Life of Samuel Beckett.* London: Bloomsbury, 1997.

Kumar, K. Jeevan. "The Chess Metaphor in Samuel Beckett's *Endgame.*" *Modern Drama* 40 (1997): 540–52.

Lawley, Paul. "Adoption in *Endgame.*" *Modern Drama* 31 (1988): 529–35.

Lyons, Charles R. *Samuel Beckett.* New York: Grove, 1983.

Popovic, Poll. "Beckett's *Endgame* as a Bond of Dependency." *European Studies Journal* 11.1 (1994): 35–47.

Rosen, Steven J. *Samuel Beckett and the Pessimistic Tradition.* New Brunswick: Rutgers UP, 1976.

Smith, Joseph H., ed. *The World of Samuel Beckett.* Baltimore: Johns Hopkins UP, 1991.

Tassi, Marguerite. "Shakespeare and Beckett Revisited: A Phenomenology of Theatre." *Comparative Drama* 31 (1997): 248–76.

Uhlmann, Anthony. *Beckett and Poststructuralism.* Cambridge: Cambridge UP, 1999.

Worth, Katharine. *Samuel Beckett's Theatre: Life-Journeys.* Oxford: Clarendon, 1999.

BERTOLT BRECHT

Bai, Ronnie. "Dances with Mei Lanfang: Brecht and the Alienation Effect." *Comparative Drama* 32 (1998): 389–433.

Bail, Henry, and Carol Martin, eds. *Bertolt Brecht: A Critical Anthology.* London: Routledge, 1999.

Beckley, Richard. "Brecht: The Reality and the Ideal." *Gestus* 2.1 (1986): 37–46.

Bodek, Richard. *Proletarian Performance in Weimar Berlin: Agitprop, Chorus, and Brecht.* Columbia: Camden House, 1997.

Brecht, Bertolt. *Brecht on Theatre: The Development of an Aesthetic.* Ed. and trans. John Willett. New York: Hill, 1964.

Brown, Russell E. *Intimacy and Intimidation: Three Essays on Bertolt Brecht.* Stuttgart: Steiner, 1990.

Bryant-Bertail, Sarah. "Women, Space, Ideology: Mutter Courage und Ihre Kinder." *The Brecht Yearbook* 12 (1983): 43–61.

Cima, Gay Gibson, Maarten Van Dijk, Liz Diamond, et al. "Brecht/'Brecht': A Symposium." *Theater* 25.2 (1994): 24–41.

Demetz, Peter, ed. *Brecht: A Collection of Critical Essays.* Englewood Cliffs: Prentice, 1962.

Docherty, Brian, ed. *Twentieth-Century European Drama.* New York: St. Martin's, 1994.

Eddershaw, Margaret. *Performing Brecht.* New York: Routledge, 1996.

Esslin, Martin. *Brecht: The Man and His Works.* Garden City: Doubleday, 1971.

Ewen, Frederick. *Bertolt Brecht: His Life, His Art and His Times.* New York: Citadel, 1967.

Fuegi, John. *Bertolt Brecht: Chaos, According to Plan.* New York: Cambridge UP, 1987.

————. *Brecht and Company: Sex, Politics, and the Making of Modern Drama.* New York: Grove, 1994.

Giles, Steve, and Rodney Livingstone, eds. *Bertolt Brecht: Centenary Essays.* Amsterdam: Rodopi, 1998.

Gleitman, Claire. "All in the Family: *Mother Courage* and the Ideology in the Gestus." *Comparative Drama* 25.2 (1991): 147–67.

Gray, Ronald. *Bertolt Brecht.* New York: Grove, 1967.

Harrington, R. "*Mother Courage and Her Children.*" *Appalachian Journal* 24.2 (1997): 141–43.

Hill, Claude. *Bertolt Brecht.* New York: Twayne, 1975.

Jameson, Fredric. *Brecht and Method.* London: Verso, 1998.

Kleber, Pia, and Colin Visser, eds. *Re-Interpreting Brecht: His Influence on Contemporary Drama and Film.* Cambridge: Cambridge UP, 1990.

Mews, Siegfried, ed. *A Bertolt Brecht Reference Companion.* Westport, CT: Greenwood, 1997.

————, comp. *Critical Essays on Bertolt Brecht.* Boston: Hall, 1989.

Munk, Erika, ed. "On Brecht." *Theater* 25.2 (1994): 9–55.

Potter, Robert. "Writing *Mother Courage.*" *The Brecht Yearbook* 24 (1999): 14–23.

Rouse, John. "Brecht and the Contradictory Actor." *Theatre Journal* 36.1 (1984): 25–41.

Schoeps, Karl Heinz. *Bertolt Brecht: Life, Work, and Criticism.* Fredericton: York, 1989.

Silberman, Marc. "A Postmodernized Brecht?" *Theatre Journal* 45.1 (1993): 1–19.

Spalter, Max. *Brecht's Tradition.* Baltimore: Johns Hopkins UP, 1967.

Speirs, Ronald. *Bertolt Brecht.* New York: St. Martin's, 1987.

Stern, Guy. "Enriching *Mother Courage.*" *Communications from the International Brecht Society* 25.1 (1996): 60–68.

Thomson, Peter, and Glendyr Sachs, eds. *The Cambridge Companion to Brecht.* Cambridge: Cambridge UP, 1994.

Tian, Min. "Alienation-Effect for Whom? Brecht's (Mis)interpretation of the Classical Chinese Theatre." *Asian Theatre Journal* 14.2 (1997): 200–22.

Willet, John. *Brecht in Context: Comparative Approaches.* 2nd ed. London: Methuen, 1998.

————. *The Theatre of Bertolt Brecht.* New York, 1959.

Willits, Ross D. "The Through-line of Meaning in *Mother Courage* and Brecht." *Text and Presentation.* Ed. Karelisa Hartigan. Lanham, MD: UP of America, 1989.

ANTON CHEKHOV

Baldwin, James. "Chekhov, the Rediscovery of Realism: Michel Saint-Denis' Productions of *Three Sisters* and *The Cherry Orchard.*" *Theatre Notebook* 53.2 (1999): 96–115.

Barricelli, Jean-Pierre, ed. *Chekhov's Great Plays: A Critical Anthology.* New York: New York UP, 1981.

Clayton, J. Douglas, ed. *Chekhov Then and Now: The Reception of Chekhov in World Culture.* New York: Peter Lang, 1997.

Eekman, Thomas A. *Critical Essays on Anton Chekhov.* Boston: Hall, 1989.

Emeljanow, Victor. *Chekhov: The Critical Heritage.* Boston: Routledge, 1981.

Hingley, Ronald. *Chekhov: A Biographical and Critical Study.* New York: Barnes, 1966.

Jackson, Robert Louis. *Chekhov: A Collection of Critical Essays.* Englewood Cliffs: Prentice, 1967.

Karlinsky, Simon, and Michael Heim, eds. *Anton Chekhov's Life and Thought: Selected Letters and Commentary.* Berkeley: U of California P, 1975.

Magarshak, David. *Chekhov the Dramatist.* New York: Hill, 1960.

Meister, Charles. *Chekhov Criticism 1880 through 1986.* New York: McFarland, 1988.

Peace, Richard. *Chekhov: A Study of the Four Major Plays.* New Haven: Yale UP, 1983.

Rayfield, Donald. *Anton Chekhov: A Life.* London: Harper, 1997.

————. *Understanding Chekhov: A Critical Study of Chekhov's Prose and Drama.* Bristol: Bristol Classical, 1999.

Russell, Robert, and Andrew Barratt, eds. *Russian Theatre in the Age of Modernism.* New York: St. Martin's, 1990.

Senderovich, Savely. "*The Cherry Orchard:* Chekhov's Last Testament." *Russian Literature* 35 (1994): 223–42.

Senelick, Laurence. *The Chekhov Theatre: A Century of Plays in Performance.* Cambridge: Cambridge UP, 1999.

Stanislavsky, Konstantin. *My Life in Art.* New York: Routledge Chapman and Hall, 1924.

Stynan, J. L. *Chekhov in Performance.* Cambridge: Cambridge UP, 1971.

Toumanova, Princess Nina Andronikova. *Anton Chekhov: The Voice of Twilight Russia.* New York: Columbia UP, 1960.

Tulloch, John, Tom Burvill, and Andrew Hood. "Reinhabiting *The Cherry Orchard:* Class and History in Performing Chekhov." *New Theatre Quarterly* 13 (1997): 318–28.

Valency, Maurice. *The Breaking String: The Plays of Anton Chekhov.* New York: Oxford UP, 1966.

Welleck, Rene, and Nonna D. Welleck, eds. *Chekhov: New Perspectives.* Englewood Cliffs: Prentice, 1984.

Williams, Lee J. *Anton Chekhov, the Iconoclast.* Scranton: U of Scranton P, 1989.

EVERYMAN

Bevington, David M. *From Mankind to Marlowe: Growth of Structure in the Popular Drama of Tudor England.* Cambridge: Harvard UP, 1962.

Cawley, A. C. *Everyman.* Manchester: Manchester UP, 1977.

————, ed. Everyman *and Medieval Miracle Plays.* New York: Dutton, 1977.

Cunningham, John. "Comedic and Liturgical Restoration in *Everyman.*" *Drama in the Middle Ages: Comparative and Critical Essays.* Second Series. Ed. Clifford Davidson and John H. Stroupe. New York: AMS, 1990.

Garner, Stanton B., Jr. "Theatricality in Mankind and Everyman." *Studies in Philology* 84.3 (1987): 272–85.

Gilman, Donald, ed. Everyman *and Company: Essays on the Theme and Structure of the European Moral Play.* New York: AMS, 1989.

Pietropoli, Cecilia. "Towards a New *Everyman:* Medieval Drama as a Link between Classical and

Renaissance Comedy." *International Conference on Aspects of European Medieval Drama*. 2 vols. Camerino: University degli Studi di Camerino, 1996.

Spinrad, Phoebe S. "The Last Temptation of *Everyman*." *Philological Quarterly* 64.2 (1985): 185–94.

Staub, August W., and Michael J. Hussey. "Saints and Cyborgs: Mystical Performance Spaces (Re)visioned." *Journal of Dramatic Theory and Criticism* 13.1 (1998): 177–82.

Tanner, Ron. "Humor in *Everyman* and the Middle English Morality Play." *Philological Quarterly* 70 (1991): 149–61.

White, D. Jerry. *Early English Drama:* Everyman *to 1580, A Reference Guide*. Boston: Hall, 1986.

ATHOL FUGARD

Barbera, Jack. "Athol Fugard Issue." *Twentieth-Century Literature* 39.4 (1993).

Benson, Mary. *Athol Fugard and Barney Simon: Bare Stage, A Few Props, Great Theatre*. Randburg, S. Africa: Ravan, 1997.

———. "Keeping an Appointment with the Future: The Theatre of Athol Fugard." *Theatre Quarterly* 7 (1977–78): 77–83.

Daymond, M. J., J. A. Jacobs, and Margaret Lenta, eds. *Momentum: On Recent South African Writing*. Pietermaritzburg: U of Natal P, 1984.

Durbach, Errol. " 'MASTER HAROLD'. . . and the boys: Athol Fugard and the Psychopathology of Apartheid." *Modern Drama* 30.4 (1987): 505–13.

Fugard, Athol. "Fugard on Actors, Actors on Fugard." *Theatre Quarterly* 7 (1977–78): 83–7.

———. "Fugard on Fugard." *Yale Theatre* 1 (Winter 1973): 41–54.

———. "Letter from Athol Fugard." *Classic* 1 (1966): 78–80.

———. *Notebooks 1960–1977*. New York: Knopf, 1983.

Gray, Stephen, ed. *Athol Fugard*. Southern Africa Literature Series 1. Johannesburg: McGraw, 1982.

Heywood, Christopher. *Aspects of South African Literature*. London: Heinemann, 1976.

Hoegberg, David. E. " '*Master Harold*' and the Bard: Education and Succession in Fugard and Shakespeare." *Comparative Drama* 29.4 (1996): 415–35.

Jordan, John O. "Life in the Theatre: Politics and Romance in 'MASTER HAROLD'. . . and the boys." *Twentieth-Century Literature* 39.4 (1993): 461–72.

Kavanagh, Robert Mshengu. *Theatre and Cultural Struggle in South Africa*. London: Zed, 1985.

Post, Robert M. "Racism in Athol Fugard's 'MASTER HAROLD'. . . and the boys." *World Literature Written in English* 30.1 (1990): 97–102.

Seidenspinner, Margarete. *Exploring the Labyrinth: Athol Fugard's Approach to South African Drama*. Essen: Verlag Die Blaue Eule, 1986.

Sutton, Brian. "Fugard's '*Master Harold*' . . . and the boys." *Explicator* 54.2 (1996): 120–23.

Vandenbrouke, Russell. *Truths the Hand Can Touch: The Theatre of Athol Fugard*. New York: Theatre Communications Group, 1985.

Walder, Dennis. *Athol Fugard*. New York: Grove, 1985.

Weales, Gerald. "Fugard Masters the Code." *Twentieth-Century Literature* 39.4 (1993): 503–16.

Wertheim, Albert. "Ballroom Dancing, Kites and Politics: Athol Fugard's '*MASTER HAROLD*' . . . and the boys." *SPAN* 30 (1990): 141–55.

———. "Triangles of Race: Athol Fugard's *Master Harold . . . and the Boys* and Paul Slabolepszy's *Saturday Night at the Palace*." *Commonwealth Essays and Studies* 20.1 (1997): 86–95.

SUSAN GLASPELL

Ben-Zvi, Linda. " 'Murder, She Wrote': The Genesis of Susan Glaspell's *Trifles*." *Theatre Journal* 44.2 (1992): 141–62.

———, ed. *Susan Glaspell: Essays on Her Theater and Fiction*. Ann Arbor: U of Michigan P, 1995.

———. "Susan Glaspell's Contributions to Contemporary Women Playwrights." *Feminine Focus: The New Women Playwrights*. Ed. Enoch Brater and Ruby Cohn. Oxford: Oxford UP, 1989.

Dymkowski, Christine. "On the Edge: The Plays of Susan Glaspell." *Modern Drama* 31.1 (1988): 91–105.

Kattwinkel, Susan. "Absence as a Site for Debate: Modern Feminism and Victorianism in the Plays of Susan Glaspell." *New England Theatre Journal* 7 (1996): 37–55.

Larabee, Ann E. " 'Meeting the Outside Face to Face': Susan Glaspell, Djuna Barnes, and O'Neill's *The Emperor Jones*." *Modern American Drama: The Female Canon*. Ed. June Schlueter. Rutherford: Fairleigh Dickinson UP, 1990. 77–85.

Mael, Phyllis. "*Trifles*: The Path to Sisterhood." *Literature-Film Quarterly* 17.4 (1989): 281–84.

Makowsky, Veronica. *Susan Glaspell's Century of American Women: A Critical Interpretation of Her Work*. New York: Oxford UP, 1993.

Mustazza, Leonard. "Generic Translation and Thematic Shift in Susan Glaspell's *Trifles* and 'A Jury of Her Peers.' " *Studies in Short Fiction* 26.4 (1989): 489–96.

Noe, Marcia. "Region as Metaphor in the Plays of Susan Glaspell." *Western Illinois Regional Studies* 4.1 (1981): 77–85.

———. "Reconfiguring the Subject/Recuperating Realism: Susan Glaspell's Unseen Woman." *American Drama* 4.2 (1995): 36–54.

Oziebolo, Barbara. "Rebellion and Rejection: The Plays of Susan Glaspell." *Modern American Drama: The Female Canon*. Ed. June Schlueter. Rutherford: Fairleigh Dickinson UP, 1990.

Ozieblo, Barbara. "Susan Glaspell." *American Drama*. Ed. Clive Bloom. New York: St. Martin's, 1995. 6–20.

Papke, Mary E. *Susan Glaspell: A Research and Production Sourcebook*. Westport, CT: Greenwood, 1993.
Russell, Judith K. "Glaspell's *Trifles*." *Explicator* 55.2 (1997): 88–90.

LADY GREGORY (ISABELLA AUGUSTA GREGORY)

Adams, Hazard. *Lady Gregory*. Lewisburg: Bucknell UP, 1973.
Conlon, John J. "Shaw, Lady Gregory and the Abbey: A Correspondence and A Record." *English Literature in Transition 1880–1920*. 40.3 (1997): 345–47.
Coxhead, Elizabeth. *Lady Gregory: A Literary Portrait*. New York: Harcourt, 1961.
Gregory, Lady. *Lady Gregory's Diaries, 1892–1902*. New York: Oxford UP, 1996.
———. *Lady Gregory's Journals, 1910–1930*. New York: Oxford UP, 1978.
———. *Our Irish Theatre*. Gerrards Cross: Smythe, 1972.
Kiberg, Declan. *Inventing Ireland: The Literature of the Modern Nation*. London: Vintage, 1996.
Kohfeldt, Mary Lou. *Lady Gregory: The Woman Behind the Irish Renaissance*. New York: Atheneum, 1985.
Kopper, E. A., Jr. "Lady Gregory's *The Rising of the Moon*." *Explicator* 47 (1989): 29–31.
Lenox-Conyngham, Melosina. *Diaries of Ireland: An Anthology, 1590–1987*. Dublin: Lilliput, 1998.
Maxwell, D. E. S. *A Critical History of Modern Irish Drama: 1891 1980*. New York: Cambridge UP, 1984.
O'Connor, Ulick. *All the Olympians*. New York: Atheneum, 1984.
Owens, C'il'n D., and Joan N. Radner. *Irish Drama: 1900–1980*. Washington: Catholic U of America P, 1990.
Saddlemyer, Ann. *In Defense of Lady Gregory, Playwright*. Dublin: Dolmen, 1966.
———. *Lady Gregory, Fifty Years After*. Totowa: Barnes, 1987.

LORRAINE HANSBERRY

Ashley, Leonard R. "Lorraine Hansberry and the Great Black Way." *Modern American Drama: The Female Canon*. Ed. June Schlueter. Rutherford: Fairleigh Dickinson UP, 1990. 151–60.
Carter, Steven R. *Hansberry's Drama: Commitment and Complexity*. Urbana: U of Illinois P, 1991.
Cheney, Anne. *Lorraine Hansberry*. Boston: Twayne, 1984.
Freedman, Morris. *American Drama in Social Context*. Carbondale: Southern Illinois UP, 1971.
Keyssar, Helene. "Rites and Responsibilities: The Drama of Black American Women." *The New Women Playwrights*. Ed. Enoch Brater and Ruby Cohn. Oxford: Oxford UP, 1989. 226–40.

Kodat, Catherine Gunther. "Confusion in a Dream Deferred: Context and Culture in Teaching *A Raisin in the Sun*." *Studies in the Literary Imagination* 31.1 (1998): 149–64.
Leeson, Richard M. *Lorraine Hansberry: A Research and Production Sourcebook*. Westport, CT: Greenwood, 1997.
McKelly, James C. "Hymns of Sedition: Portraits of the Artist in Contemporary African-American Drama." *Arizona Quarterly* 48.1 (1992): 87–107.
Scheader, Catherine. *Lorraine Hansberry: Playwright and Voice of Justice*. Springfield, NJ: Enslow, 1998.
———. *They Found a Way: Lorraine Hansberry*. Chicago: Children's, 1978.
Schlueter, June, ed. *Modern American Drama: The Female Canon*. Rutherford: Fairleigh Dickinson UP, 1990.
Seaton, Sandra. "*A Raisin in the Sun*: A Study in Afro-American Culture." *Midwestern Miscellany* 20 (1992): 40–49.
Sinnott, Susan. *Lorraine Hansberry: Award-Winning Playwright and Civil Rights Activist*. Berkeley: Conari P, 1999.
Washington, J. Charles. "*A Raisin in the Sun* Revisited." *Black American Literature Forum* 22.1 (1988): 109–24.
Weales, Gerald. "Lorraine Hansberry." *Contemporary Dramatists*. Ed. D. L. Kirkpatrick. 4th ed. Chicago: St. James, 1988. 653–54.
Wilkerson, Margaret B. "Excavating Our History: The Importance of Biographies of Women of Color." *Black American Forum* 24.1 (1990): 73–84.
Williams, Mance. *Black Theatre in the 1960s and 1970s*. Westport: Greenwood, 1985.

HROSVITHA

Carlson, Marvin. "Impassive Bodies: Hrotsvit Stages Martyrdom." *Theatre Journal* 50.4 (1998): 473–87.
Schmitt, Miriam. "Hrotsvit: Medieval Playwright." *Medieval Women Monastics: Wisdom's Wellsprings*. Ed. Miriam Schmitt and Linda Kulzer. Collegeville, MN: Liturgical Press, 1996.
Wilson, Katharine M. *Hrotsvit of Gandersheim: The Ethics of Authorial Stance*. New York: Brill, 1988.
———. *Hrotsvit of Gandersheim: Rara Avis in Saxonia? A Collection of Essays*. Ann Arbor: MARC, 1987.
Zeydel, Edwin H. "Hrotsvit von Gandersheim and the Eternal Womanly." *Studies in the German Drama: A Festschrift in Honor of Walter Silz*. Chapel Hill: U of North Carolina P, 1974. 1–14.

HENRIK IBSEN

Ackerman, Gretchen P. *Ibsen and the English Stage, 1889–1903*. New York: Garland, 1987.
Chamberlain, John S. *Ibsen: The Open Vision*. London: Athlone, 1982.

Egan, Michael, ed. *Ibsen: The Critical Heritage*. London: Routledge, 1972.

Ferguson, Robert. *Henrik Ibsen: A New Biography*. London, R. Cohen, 1996.

Fjelde, Rolf, ed. *Ibsen: A Collection of Critical Essays*. Englewood Cliffs: Prentice, 1965.

Gaskell, Ronald. *Drama and Reality: The European Theatre since Ibsen*. London: Routledge, 1972.

Goldman, Michael. *Ibsen: The Dramaturgy of Fear*. New York: Columbia UP, 1999.

Lebowitz, Naomi. *Ibsen and the Great World*. Baton Rouge: Louisiana UP, 1990.

Marker, Frederick J. *Ibsen's Lively Art: A Performance Study of the Major Plays*. New York: Cambridge UP, 1989.

McFarlane, James, ed. *Discussions of Henrik Ibsen*. Boston: Heath, 1962.

Meyer, Michael, *Henrik Ibsen: A Biography*. 3 vols. Garden City: Doubleday, 1971.

Noreng, Harald, et al., eds. *Contemporary Approaches to Ibsen*. Oslo: Universitetsforlaget, 1977.

Northam, John. *Ibsen: A Critical Study*. Cambridge: Cambridge UP, 1973.

Shaw, Bernard. *The Quintessence of Ibsenism*. New York: Hill, 1957.

Shepherd-Barr, Kirsten. *Ibsen and Early Modernist Theatre, 1890–1900*. Westport, CT: Greenwood, 1997.

Theoharis, Theoharis Constantine. *Ibsen's Drama: Right Action and Tragic Joy*. New York: St. Martin's, 1996.

Thomas, David. *Henrik Ibsen*. New York: Grove, 1984.

A Doll House

Andreas-Salomé, Lou. *Ibsen's Heroines*. Ed. and trans. Siegfried Mandel. Austrian/German Culture Series. Redding Ridge, CT: Black Swan, 1985.

Bradbrook, M. C. "*A Doll's House* and the Unweaving of the Web." *Women and Literature, 1779–1982*. Vol. 2. Totowa: Barnes, 1982. 81–92. 2 vols.

Drake, David B. "Ibsen's *A Doll House*." *Explicator* 53.1 (1994): 32–34.

Durbach, Errol. A Doll's House: *Ibsen's Myth of Transformation*. Boston: Twayne, 1991.

Ibsen, Henrik. "*Doll's House*" [Ibsen's notes on *A Doll House*]. *Playwrights on Playwriting*. Ed. Toby Cole. New York: Hill, 1960. 151–54.

Mitchell, Hayley R. *Readings on* A Doll's House. San Diego: Greenhaven, 1999.

Sprinchorn, E. M. "Ibsen and the Actors." *Ibsen and the Theatre*. Ed. Errol Durbach. New York: New York UP, 1980. 118–30.

Tornqvist, Egil. "Comparative Performance Semiotics: The End of Ibsen's *A Doll House*." Theatre Research International 19.2 (1994): 156–164.

BEN JONSON

Butler, Martin, ed. *Re-presenting Ben Jonson: Text, History, Performance*. New York: St. Martin's, 1999.

Floyd-Wilson, Mary. "Temperature, Temperance, and Racial Difference in Ben Jonson's *The Masque of Blackness.*" *English Literary Renaissance* 28.2 (1998): 183–209.

Hirsh, James, ed. *New Perspectives on Ben Jonson*. Madison, NJ: Fairleigh Dickinson UP, 1997.

Orgel, Stephen. *Marginal Jonson*. Cambridge: Cambridge UP, 1998.

Sanders, Julie. *Ben Jonson's Theatrical Republics*. Basingstoke: Macmillan, 1998.

———, ed., with Kate Chedgzoy and Susan Wiseman. *Refashioning Ben Jonson: Gender, Politics, and the Jonsonian Canon*. New York: St. Martin's, 1998.

Summers, Claude J. *Ben Jonson Revised*. New York: Twayne, 1999.

Watson, Robert N. *Critical Essays on Ben Jonson*. New York: Hall, 1997.

ARTHUR MILLER

Anderson, M. C. "*Death of a Salesman*: A Consideration of Willy Loman's Role in Twentieth-Century Tragedy." *CRUX* 20.2 (1986): 25–29.

Babcock, Granger. " 'What's the Secret?': Willy Loman as Desiring Machine." *American Drama* 2.1 (1992): 59–83.

Balakian, Jan. "Arthur Miller." *Speaking on Stage: Interviews with Contemporary American Playwrights*. Ed. Philip C. Kolin and Colby H. Kullman. Tuscaloosa: U of Alabama P, 1996. 40–57.

Bigsby, Christopher W. E. *Arthur Miller*. Cambridge Companions to Literature. Cambridge: Cambridge UP, 1997.

Bloom, Harold. *Arthur Miller*. Philadelphia: Chelsea, 1999.

———, ed. *Arthur Miller's* Death of a Salesman. New York: Chelsea, 1988.

———. *Willy Loman*. New York: Chelsea, 1990.

Brucher, Richard T. "Willy Loman and the Soul of a New Machine: Technology and the Common Man." *Journal of American Studies* 17.3 (1983): 325–36.

Carson, Neil. *Arthur Miller*. London: Macmillan; 1982.

Centola, Steven R. "Family Values in *Death of a Salesman*." *College Language Association Journal* 37.1 (1993): 29–41.

Corrigan, Robert W., ed. *Arthur Miller: A Collection of Critical Essays*. Englewood Cliffs: Prentice, 1969.

Goldstein, Laurence, ed. "Aurthur Miller." *Michigan Quarterly Review* 37.4 [Special Issue] (1998).

Griffin, Alice. *Understanding Arthur Miller*. Columbia: U of South Carolina P, 1996.

Hadomi, Leah. "Fantasy and Reality: Dramatic Rhythm in *Death of a Salesman*." *Modern Drama* 31.2 (1988): 157–74.

Harder, Harry. "*Death of a Salesman*: An American Classic." *Censored Books: Critical Viewpoints*. Ed. Nicholas J. Karolides, Lee Burress, and John M. Kean. Metuchen, NJ: Scarecrow, 1993.

Hayman, Ronald. *Arthur Miller*. New York: Ungar, 1972.

Huftel, Sheila. *Arthur Miller: The Burning Glass*. New York: Citadel, 1965.

Jenckes, Norma, ed. "Arthur Miller." *American Drama* 6.1 [Special Issue] (1996).

Koon, Helene Wickham. *Twentieth Century Interpretations of Death of a Salesman*. Englewood Cliffs: Prentice, 1983.

Martin, Robert A., ed. *Arthur Miller: New Perspectives*. Englewood Cliffs: Prentice, 1982.

———. "The Nature of Tragedy in Arthur Miller's *Death of a Salesman*." *South Atlantic Review* 61.4 (1996): 97–106.

Miller, Arthur. *Collected Plays*. New York: Viking, 1957.

———. *The Theater Essays of Arthur Miller*. Ed. and intro. Robert A. Martin. New York: Viking, 1978.

———. *Timebends: A Life*. New York: Grove, 1987.

Murphy, Brenda. "Arthur Miller: Revisioning Realism." *Realism and the American Dramatic Tradition*. Ed. William W. Demastes. Tuscaloosa: U of Alabama P, 1996. 189–202.

Roudane, Matthew C., ed. *Conversations with Arthur Miller*. Jackson: UP of Mississippi, 1987.

Schlueter, June, and James K. Flanagan. *Arthur Miller*. New York: Ungar, 1987.

Schockley, John S. "*Death of a Salesman* and American Leadership: Life Imitates Art." *Journal of American Culture* 17.2 (1994): 49–56.

Siebold, Thomas, ed. *Readings on Arthur Miller*. San Diego: Greenhaven, 1997.

———, ed. *Readings on Death of a Salesman*. San Diego: Greenhaven, 1999.

Stanton, Kay. "Women and the American Dream of *Death of a Salesman*." *Feminist Rereadings of Modern American Drama*. Ed. June Schlueter. Rutherford: Fairleigh Dickinson UP, 1989.

MOLIÈRE (JEAN BAPTISTE POQUELIN)

Bermel, Albert. *Molière's Theatrical Bounty: A New View of the Plays*. Carbondale: Southern Illinois UP, 1990.

Edney, David. "Molière in North America: Problems of Translation and Adaptation." *Modern Drama* 41.1 (1998): 60–76.

Gaines, James F., and Michael S. Koppisch eds. *Approaches to Teaching Molière's Tartuffe and Other Plays*. New York: Modern Language Association of America, 1995.

———. *Molière's Theater*. Columbus: Ohio State UP, 1984.

Gaston Hall, H. "Molière's Roles Written for Himself." *Australian Journal of French Studies* 33 (1996): 414–27.

Gross, Nathan. *From Gesture to Idea: Esthetics and Ethics in Molière's Comedy*. New York: Columbia UP, 1982.

Guicharnaud, Jacques. *Molière: A Collection of Critical Essays*. Englewood Cliffs: Prentice, 1964.

Hall, H. Gaston. *Comedy in Context: Essays on Molière*. Jackson: UP of Mississippi, 1984.

Jagendorf, Zvi. *The Happy End of Comedy: Jonson, Molière, and Shakespeare*. Newark: U of Delaware P, 1984.

Knutson, Harold C. *The Triumph of Wit: Molière and Restoration Comedy*. Columbus: Ohio State UP, 1988.

Lalande, Roxanne Decker. *Intruders in the Play World: The Dynamics of Gender in Molière's Comedies*. Madison, NJ: Fairleigh Dickinson UP, 1996.

Molière. *Tartuffe: Comedy in Five Acts*. Trans. Richard Wilbur. New York: Harcourt, 1963.

Spingler, Michael, ed. *Molière Today*. Amsterdam: Harwood, 1997.

Walker, Hallam. *Molière*. Rev. ed. Boston: Twayne, 1990.

EUGENE O'NEILL

Ahuja, Chaman. *Tragedy, Modern Temper, and O'Neill*. Atlantic Highlands: Humanities, 1984.

Berlin, Normand. *Eugene O'Neill*. New York: Grove, 1987.

Black, Stephen A. *Eugene O'Neill: Beyond Mourning and Tragedy*. New Haven: Yale UP, 1999.

Bogard, Travis. *Contour in Time: The Plays of Eugene O'Neill*. New York: Oxford UP, 1988.

Cargill, Oscar, N. Bryllion Fagan, and William J. Fisher, eds. *O'Neill and His Plays: Four Decades of Criticism*. New York: New York UP, 1961.

Cunningham, Frank R. "Eugene O'Neill and Reality in America." *Realism and the American Dramatic Tradition*. Ed. William W. Demastes. Tuscaloosa: U of Alabama P, 1996.

Fleche, Anne. *Mimetic Disillusion: Eugene O'Neill, Tennessee Williams, and U.S. Dramatic Realism*. Tuscaloosa: U of Alabama P, 1997.

Floyd, Virginia. *The Plays of Eugene O'Neill: A New Assessment*. New York: Ungar, 1985.

Frenz, Horst, and Susan Tuck, eds. *Eugene O'Neill's Critics: Voices from Abroad*. Boulder: netLibrary, 1999.

Gallup, Donald. *Eugene O'Neill and His Eleven-Play Cycle: "A Tale of Possessors Self-Possessed."* New Haven: Yale UP, 1998.

Gassner, John, ed. *O'Neill: A Collection of Critical Essays*. Englewood Cliffs: Prentice, 1964.

Leech, Clifford. *Eugene O'Neill*. New York: Grove, 1963.

Manheim, Michael, ed. *Eugene O'Neill*. Cambridge Companions to Literature. Cambridge: Cambridge UP, 1998.

Maufort, Marc, ed. *Eugene O'Neill and the Emergence of American Drama*. Atlanta: Rodopi, 1989.

Miller, Jordan Yale. *Eugene O'Neill and American Criticism: A Bibliographical Checklist*. 2nd ed. Hamden: Anchor, 1973.

Moorton, Richard F., Jr. *Eugene O'Neill's Century: Centennial Views on America's Foremost Critic*. New York: Greenwood, 1991.

Mottram, Eric. "Eugene O'Neill." *American Drama*. Ed. Clive Bloom. New York: St. Martin's, 1995. 21–45.

O'Neill, Eugene. *Long Day's Journey into Night*. New Haven: Yale UP, 1956.

———. *The Plays of Eugene O'Neill*. 3 vols. New York: Modern Library, 1982.

Pacheco, Gilda. "The Female Image in Eugene O'Neill's *Desire under the Elms* and *A Moon for the Misbegotten*." *Revista de Filologia y Linguistica de la Universidad de Costa Rica* 21.1 (1995): 55–63.

Pfister, Joel. *Staging Depth: Eugene O'Neill and the Politics of Psychological Discourse*. Boulder: netLibrary, 1999.

Porter, Laurin. *The Banished Prince: Time, Memory, and Ritual in the Late Plays of Eugene O'Neill*. Ann Arbor: UMI Research, 1988.

Ranald, Margaret Loftus. *The Eugene O'Neill Companion*. Westport, CT: Greenwood, 1984.

Siebold, Thomas. *Readings on Eugene O'Neill*. San Diego: Greenhaven, 1998.

Wainscott, Ronald Harold. *Staging O'Neill: The Experimental Years, 1920–1934*. New Haven: Yale UP, 1988.

Luigi Pirandello

Bassabesem, Fiora A. *Understanding Luigi Pirandello*. Columbia: U of South Carolina P, 1997.

Bassnett, Susan. *File on Pirandello*. London: Methuen, 1989.

Bassnett-McGuire, Susan. *Luigi Pirandello*. New York: Grove, 1983.

Bentley, Eric. *The Pirandello Commentaries*. Evanston: Northwestern UP, 1986.

Biasin, Gian-Paolo, and Manuela Giere, eds. *Luigi Pirandello: Contemporary Perspectives*. Toronto: U of Toronto P, 1999.

Bloom, Harold. *Luigi Pirandello*. New York: Chelsea, 1989.

Büdel, Oscar. *Pirandello*. New York: Hillary, 1969.

Caesar, Ann. *Characters and Authors in Luigi Pirandello*. Oxford: Clarendon, 1998.

Cambon, Glauco, ed. *Pirandello: A Collection of Critical Essays*. Englewood Cliffs: Prentice, 1967.

Caputi, Anthony. *Pirandello and the Crisis of Modern Consciousness*. Urbana: U of Illinois P, 1988.

Dashwood, Julie R. *Luigi Pirandello: The Theatre of Paradox*. Lewiston: Mellen, 1996.

Guidice, Gaspare. *Pirandello: A Biography*. Trans. Alastair Hamilton. New York: Oxford UP, 1975.

Hornby, Richard. "Three Modern Playwrights (Pirandello, Strindberg, Chekhov)." *Seewanee Review* 105 (1997): 595–99.

Mariani, Umberto. "The 'Pirandellian' Character." *Canadian Journal of Italian Studies* 12.38–39 (1989): 1–9.

Mazzaro, Jerome. "Pirandello's *Sei Personaggi* and Expressive Form." *Comparative Drama* 30 (1996–97): 503–24.

Oliver, Roger W. *Dreams of Passion: The Theater of Luigi Pirandello*. New York: New York UP, 1979.

Paolucci, Anne. *Pirandello's Theater*. Carbondale: Southern Illinois UP, 1974.

Pirandello, Luigi. *Naked Masks, Five Plays*. Ed. Eric Bentley. New York: Dutton, 1952.

———. *Short Stories*. Ed. and trans. Frederick May. New York: Oxford UP, 1965.

Ragusa, Olga. "Comparative Perspectives on Pirandello." *Atenea* 8.1 (1988): 19–36.

Starkie, Walter. *Luigi Pirandello, 1867–1936*. 3rd ed. Berkeley: U of California P, 1965.

Stone, Jennifer. *Pirandello's Naked Prompt: The Structure of Repetition in Modernism*. Ravenna: Longo Editore, 1989.

Plautus

Anderson, William Scovil. *Barbarian Play: Plautus' Roman Comedy*. Toronto: University of Toronto Press, 1996.

Moore, Timothy J. *The Theater of Plautus: Playing to the Audience*. Austin: U of Texas P, 1999.

Segal, Erich. *Roman Laughter: The Comedy of Plautus*. New York: Oxford UP, 1987.

Slater, Niall W. *Plautus in Performance: The Theater of the Mind*. Princeton: Princeton UP, 1985.

Yasmina Reza

Danto, Arthur C. " '*Art*,' from France to the U.S." *Nation* 29 June 1998: 28–31.

Seneca

Fairweather, Janet. *Seneca the Elder*. New York: Cambridge UP, 1981.

Stewart, J. "Challenging Prescriptions for Discourse: Seneca's Use of Paradox and Psymoron." *Mosaic* 30.1 (1997): 1–17.

Tarrant, R. J. *Seneca's* Thyestes. Atlanta: Scholars, 1985.

William Shakespeare

List of Plays

Comedies

The Comedy of Errors, 1592–94
The Taming of the Shrew, 1593–94
The Two Gentlemen of Verona, 1594
Love's Labor's Lost, 1594–95
A Midsummer Night's Dream, 1595–96
The Merchant of Venice, 1596–97
The Merry Wives of Windsor, 1597
Much Ado about Nothing, 1598–99
As You Like It, 1599
Twelfth Night, or What You Will, 1601–02
All's Well That Ends Well, 1602–03
Measure for Measure, 1604

Histories
Henry the Sixth, Part One, 1589–90
Henry the Sixth, Part Two, 1590–91
Henry the Sixth, Part Three, 1590–91
Richard the Third, 1592–93
King John, 1594–96
Richard the Second, 1595
Henry the Fourth, Part One, 1596–97
Henry the Fourth, Part Two, 1598
Henry the Fifth, 1599
Henry the Eighth, 1612–13

Tragedies
The Tragedy of Titus Andronicus, 1593
The Tragedy of Romeo and Juliet, 1595–96
The Tragedy of Julius Caesar, 1599
The Tragedy of Hamlet, 1600–01
The History of Troilus and Cressida, 1601–02
The Tragedy of Othello, the Moor of Venice, 1604
The Tragedy of King Lear, 1605
The Tragedy of Macbeth, 1606
The Tragedy of Antony and Cleopatra, 1606
The Tragedy of Coriolanus, 1607
The Life of Timon of Athens, 1607

Romances
Pericles, Prince of Tyre, 1607–08
Cymbeline, 1609–10
The Winter's Tale, 1610–11
The Tempest, 1611
Two Noble Kinsmen, 1613

Bamber, Linda. *Comic Women, Tragic Men: A Study of Gender and Genre in Shakespeare*. Stanford: Stanford UP, 1982.

Barber, C. L. *Shakespeare's Festive Comedy*. Princeton: Princeton UP, 1968.

Bloom, Harold. *Shakespeare: The Invention of the Human*. London: Fourth Estate, 1999.

Bradley, A. C. *Shakespearean Tragedy*. New York: Meridian, 1955.

Bullough, Geoffrey, ed. *Narrative and Dramatic Sources of Shakespeare*. 8 vols. New York: Columbia UP, 1957–75.

Chute, Marchette. *Shakespeare of London*. New York: Dutton, 1949.

Doran, Madeleine. *Shakespeare's Dramatic Language*. Madison: U of Wisconsin P, 1976.

Drakakis, John, ed. *Alternative Shakespeares*. New York: Methuen, 1985.

Dusinberre, Juliet. *Shakespeare and the Nature of Women*. 2nd. ed. New York: St. Martin's, 1996.

Dutton, Richard. *Shakespeare: A Literary Life*. New York: St. Martin's, 1989.

Eagleton, Terry. *William Shakespeare*. New York: Blackwell, 1986.

Erikson, Peter. *Rewriting Shakespeare, Rewriting Ourselves*. Berkeley: U of California P, 1991.

Frye, Northrop. *On Shakespeare*. New Haven: Yale UP, 1986.

Goddard, Harold C. *The Meaning of Shakespeare*. Chicago: U of Chicago P, 1951.

Grady, Hugh. *The Modernist Shakespeare: Critical Texts in a Material World*. New York: Oxford UP, 1991.

Granville-Barker, H. *Prefaces to Shakespeare*. Princeton: Princeton UP, 1946.

Greene, G., et al., eds. *The Women's Part: Feminist Criticism of Shakespeare*. Urbana: U of Illinois P, 1980.

Honan, Park. *Shakespeare: A Life*. Oxford: Oxford UP, 2000.

Hyland, Peter. *An Introduction to Shakespeare: The Dramatist in His Context*. Houndmills, UK: Macmillan, 1996.

Ioppolo, Grace. *Revising Shakespeare*. Cambridge: Harvard UP, 1991.

Jacobus, Lee. *Shakespeare and the Dialectic of Certainty*. New York: St. Martin's Press, 1992.

Jardine, Lisa. *Still Harping on Daughters: Women and Drama in the Age of Shakespeare*. Totowa: Barnes, 1983.

Kermode, Frank, ed. *Four Centuries of Shakespearean Criticism*. New York: Avon, 1974.

Kiernan, Pauline. *Shakespeare's Theory of Drama*. Cambridge: Cambridge UP, 1998.

Kiernan, Ryan, ed. *Shakespeare: Texts and Contexts*. New York: St. Martin's, 1999.

Kott, Jan. *Shakespeare Our Contemporary*. New York: Norton, 1974.

McDonald, Russ. *The Bedford Companion to Shakespeare: An Introduction with Documents*. Boston: Bedford, 1996.

Meagher, John C. *Shakespeare's Shakespeare: How the Plays Were Made*. New York: Continuum, 1997.

Orgel, Stephen and Sean Keilen. *Shakespeare in the Theatre*. Shakespeare: The Critical Complex 8. New York: Garland, 1999.

Righter, Anne. *Shakespeare and the Idea of the Play*. London: Chatto, 1962.

Schoenbaum, Samuel. *William Shakespeare: A Documentary Life*. New York: Oxford UP, 1975.

Schwartz, Murray M., and Coppelia Kahn, eds. *Representing Shakespeare: New Psychoanalytic Essays*. Baltimore: Johns Hopkins UP, 1981.

Scott, Michael. *Shakespeare and the Modern Dramatist*. New York: St. Martin's, 1989.

Shakespeare Quarterly. Annual Bibliography.

Shakespeare Survey 9.

Shellard, Dominic. *William Shakespeare*. The British Library Writers' Lives. New York: Oxford UP, 1998.

Wells, Stanley W., ed. *Shakespeare and Language*. Cambridge: Cambridge UP, 1997.

———, ed. *Shakespeare in the Theatre: An Anthology of Criticism*. Oxford: Clarendon, 1997.

———. *Shakespeare: The Poet and His Plays*. London: Methuen, 1997.

A Midsummer Night's Dream

Bloom, Harold, ed. *William Shakespeare's* A Midsummer Night's Dream. New York: Chelsea, 1987.

Brown, John Russell. *Shakespeare and His Comedies.* London: Methuen, 1968.

Fleissner, Robert F. "Shakespeare's *A Midsummer Night's Dream.*" *Explicator* 55.2 (1997): 72–73.

Garber, Marjorie. *Dream in Shakespeare: From Metaphor to Metamorphosis.* New Haven: Yale UP, 1974.

Girard, Rene. "Myth and Ritual in Shakespeare: *A Midsummer Night's Dream.*" *Textual Strategies: Perspectives in Post-Structuralist Criticism.* Ithaca: Cornell UP, 1979.

Griffiths, Trevor R., ed. *A Midsummer Night's Dream.* Shakespeare in Production. Cambridge: Cambridge UP, 1996.

Hawkes, Terrence. *A Midsummer Night's Dream.* New Casebooks. New York: St. Martin's, 1996.

Hendricks, Margo. "Obscured by Dreams, Race, Empire, and Shakespeare's *A Midsummer Night's Dream.*" *Shakespeare Quarterly* 47.1 (1996): 37–60.

Kehler, Dorothea, ed. A Midsummer Night's Dream: *Critical Essays.* New York: Garland, 1998.

Latham, Minor White. *The Elizabethan Fairies: The Fairies of Folklore and the Fairies of Shakespeare.* New York: Columbia UP, 1930.

Legatt, Alexander. A Midsummer Night's Dream: *Shakespeare's Comedy of Love.* London: Methuen, 1974.

Montrose, Louis Adrian. "'Shaping Fantasies': Figurations of Gender and Power in Elizabethan Culture." *Representations* 1.2 (1983): 61–94.

Paster, Gail Kern and Skiles Howard, eds. A Midsummer Night's Dream: *Texts and Contexts.* Boston: Bedford, 1999.

Shelbourne, David. *The Making of* A Midsummer Night's Dream. London: Methuen, 1982.

Wiles, David. "The Carnivalesque in *A Midsummer Night's Dream.*" *Shakespeare and Carnival: After Bakhtin.* Ed. Ronald Knowles. New York: St. Martin's, 1998. 61–82.

Young. David P. *Something of Great Constancy: The Art of* A Midsummmer Night's Dream. New Haven: Yale UP, 1966.

Othello

Bernard, J. "Theatricality and Textuality: The Example of *Othello.*" *New Literary History* 26 (1995): 931–49.

Ghazoul, Ferial J. The Arabization of *Othello.*" *Comparative Literature* 50.1 (1998): 1–31.

Hadfield, Andrew. "Race in *Othello*: The 'History and Description of Africa' and the Black Legend." *Notes and Queries* 45 (1998): 336–38.

Hogan, Patrick C. "*Othello,* Racism, and Despair." *College Language Association Journal* 41 (1998): 431–51.

Honigmann, E. A. J. *The Texts of* Othello *and Shakespearean Revision.* London: Routledge, 1996.

Pechter, Edward. Othello *and Interpretive Traditions.* Iowa City: U of Iowa P, 1999.

Widmayer, M. "Brabantio and Othello." *English Studies* 77.2 (1996): 113–26.

Xiaojing, Zhou. "Othello's Color in Shakespeare's Tragedy." *College Language Association Journal* 41 (1998): 335–48.

SOPHOCLES

List of Plays

(Sophocles wrote in the fifth century B.C. The exact dates for his plays are unknown.)

Oedipus Rex
Antigone
Oedipus at Colonus
Philoctetes
Ajax
Trachiniae
Elektra
Ichneutai
Aleadae

Bloom, Harold, ed. *Sophocles.* New York: Chelsea, 1990.

———, ed. *Sophocles' Oedipus Plays:* Oedipus the King, Oedipus at Colonus, *and* Antigone. Bloom's Notes. Broomhall, PA: Chelsea, 1999.

Bowra, Sir Maurice. *Sophoclean Tragedy.* Oxford: Clarendon, 1944.

Burton, Reginald William Boteler. *The Chorus in Sophocles' Tragedies.* New York: Oxford UP, 1980.

Bushnell, Rebecca. *Prophesying Tragedy: Sign and Voice in Sophocles' Theban Plays.* Ithaca: Cornell UP, 1988.

Buxton, R. G. A. *Sophocles.* New York: Clarendon, 1984.

Gardiner, Cynthia P. *The Sophoclean Chorus: A Study of Character and Function.* Iowa City: U of Iowa P, 1987.

Hogan, James C. *A Commentary on the Plays of Sophocles.* Boulder: netLibrary, 1999.

Kitto, H. D. F. *Sophocles: Dramatist and Philosopher.* London: Oxford UP, 1958.

Knox, Bernard M. *Sophocles at Thebes: Sophocles' Tragic Hero and His Time.* New York: Norton, 1971.

Reinhardt, Karl. *Sophokles.* Trans. D. Harvey and H. Harvey. New York: Barnes, 1978.

Scodel, Ruth. *Sophocles.* Boston: Twayne, 1984.

Segal, Charles. *Tragedy and Civilization: An Interpretation of Sophocles.* Cambridge: Harvard UP, 1981.

Waldock, A. J. A. *Sophocles the Dramatist.* Cambridge: Cambridge UP, 1951.

Wiles, David. *The Masks of Menander: Sign and Meaning in Greek and Roman Performances.* Cambridge: Cambridge UP, 1991.

Winnington-Ingram, R. P. *Sophocles: An Interpretation.* New York: Cambridge UP, 1980.

Woodard, T. M, ed. *Sophocles: A Collection of Critical Essays.* Englewood Cliffs: Prentice, 1966.

Antigone

Brown, Andrew. *A New Companion to Greek Tragedy.* Totowa: Barnes, 1983.

Chanter, Tina. "Tragic Discolations: Antigone's Modern Theatrics." *Differences: A Journal of Feminist Cultural Studies* 10.1 (1998): 75–97.

Goheen, R. F. *The Imagery of Sophocles'* Antigone: *A Study of Poetic Language and Structure.* Princeton: Princeton UP, 1951.

Linforth, I. M. *Antigone and Creon.* Berkeley: U of California P, 1961.

"Review: *Antigone.*" *Theatre Record* 18.6 (1998): 320–21.

Steiner, George. *Antigones.* New York: Clarendon, 1984.

Oedipus Rex

Bloom, Harold. *Sophocles'* Oedipus Rex. New York: Chelsea, 1988.

Cameron, Alister. *The Identity of Oedipus the King: Five Essays on the "Oedipus Tyrannus."* New York: New York UP, 1968.

Edmonds, Lowell. *Oedipus: The Ancient Legend and Its Later Analogues.* Baltimore: Johns Hopkins UP, 1985.

Fergusson, Francis. *The Idea of a Theater.* Princeton: Princeton UP, 1949.

———. "*Oedipus Rex*: The Tragic Rhythm of Action." *Ritual and Myth: Robertson Smith, Farzer, Hooke, and Harrison.* Ed. Robert A. Segal. New York: Garland, 1996. 67–95.

O'Brien, M. J., ed. *Twentieth Century Interpretations of Oedipus Rex.* Englewood Cliffs: Prentice, 1968.

Rudnytsky, Peter L. *Freud and Oedipus.* New York: Columbia UP, 1987.

Tonelli, Franco. "Sophocles' *Oedipus* and the Tale of the Theatre." *Speculum Artium Series* 12. Ravenna: Longo Editore, 1983.

Verhoeff, Han, and Harly Sonne. "Does Oedipus Have His Complex?" *Style* 18.3 (1984): 261–83.

AUGUST STRINDBERG

Carlson, Harry Gilbert. *Out of Inferno: Strindberg's Reawakening as an Artist.* Seattle: U of Washington P, 1996.

———. *Strindberg and the Poetry of Myth.* Berkeley: U of California P, 1982.

Chaudhuri, U. "Private Part: Sex, Class, and Stage Space in *Miss Julie.*" *Theatre Journal* 45.3 (1993): 317–32.

Franchuk, E. S. "Symbolism in *Miss Julie.*" *Theatre Research International* 18 (1993): 11–15.

Lally, M. L. K. "Strindberg's *Miss Julie.*" *Explicator* 48.3 (1990): 196–98.

Lucas, F. L. *The Drama of Ibsen and Strindberg.* London: Cassell, 1962.

Meidal, Bjorn. "A Strindberg Forgery: Carl Ohman's August Strindberg and the Origin of Scenic Expressionism." *Scandinavica* 34.1 (1995): 61–69.

Parker, Brian. "Strindberg's *Miss Julie* and the Legend of Salome." *Modern Drama* 32 (1989): 469–84.

Reinert, Otto, ed. *Strindberg: A Collection of Critical Essays.* Englewood Cliffs: Prentice, 1971.

Robinson, Michael. "August Strindberg: His True Life?" *Scandinavica* 28.2 (1989): 185–91.

———. *Studies in Strindberg.* Norwich, Eng.: Norvik, 1998.

Shideler, Ross. "The Absent Authority: From Darwin to Nora and Julie." *Space and Boundaries in Literature.* Proceedings of the Twelfth Congress of the International Comparative Literature Association. Ed. Roger Bauer and Donwe Fokkema. Munich: Iudicium, 1990.

Sprinchorn, Evert. *Strindberg as Dramatist.* New Haven: Yale UP, 1982.

Steene, Birgitta. *The Greatest Fire: A Study of August Strindberg.* Carbondale: Southern Illinois UP, 1973.

Stockenstrom, Goran, ed. *Strindberg's Dramaturgy.* Minneapolis: U of Minnesota P, 1988.

Tornqvist, Egil. Strindberg's *"Miss Julie"*: A Play and Its Transpositions. Norwich, Eng.: Norvik, 1988.

TERENCE

Forehand, Walter. *Terence.* Boston: Twayne, 1985.

Goldberg, Sander M. *Understanding Terence.* Princeton: Princeton UP, 1986.

PAULA VOGEL

Parker, Mary-Louise. "Paula Vogel." *Bomb* 61 (1997): 44–49.

Sova, Kathy. "Time to Laugh." *American Theatre* 14.2 (1997): 24.

OSCAR WILDE

Beckson, Karl E. *The Oscar Wilde Encyclopedia.* New York: AMS, 1998.

Bloom, Harold. *Oscar Wilde's* The Importance of Being Earnest. New York: Chelsea, 1988.

Byrne, Patrick. *The Wildes of Merrion Square: The Family of Oscar Wilde.* New York: Staples, 1953.

Calloway, Stephen. *Oscar Wilde: An Exquisite Life.* London: Orion Media, 1999.

Cohen, Ed. "Writing Gone Wild: Homoerotic Desire in the Closet of Representation." *PMLA* 102 (1987): 801–13.

Cohen, Philip K. *The Moral Vision of Oscar Wilde.* Rutherford: Fairleigh Dickinson UP, 1978.

Danson, Lawrence. *Wilde's Intentions. The Artist in His Criticism.* Oxford: Clarendon, 1997.

Ellmann, Richard. *Oscar Wilde.* New York: Knopf, 1988.

———. *Oscar Wilde: A Collection of Critical Essays.* Englewood Cliffs: Prentice, 1969.

Eltis, Sos. *Revisiting Wilde: Society and Subversion in the Plays of Oscar Wilde.* Oxford: Clarendon, 1996.

Erikson, Donald. *Oscar Wilde.* Boston: Twayne, 1977.

Gagnier, Regenia. *Idylls of the Marketplace: Oscar Wilde and the Victorian Public.* Stanford: Stanford UP, 1986.

Haley, Bruce. "Wilde's 'Decadence' and the Positivist Tradition." *Victorian Studies* 28 (1985): 215–29.

Hart-Davis, Rupert, ed. *Letters of Oscar Wilde.* New York: Harcourt, 1962.

———. *More Letters of Oscar Wilde.* New York: Vanguard, 1985.

Hodge, James H. *Famous Trials.* Baltimore: Penguin, 1963.

Mackie, W. Craven. "Bunburry Pure and Simple." *Modern Drama* 41.2 (1998): 327–30.

McCormack, Jerusha Hull, ed. *Wilde the Irishman.* New Haven: Yale UP, 1998.

Mikhail, E. H. *Oscar Wilde: Interviews and Recollections.* New York: Barnes, 1979.

Miller, Robert Keith. *Oscar Wilde.* New York: Ungar, 1982.

Poznar, Walter. "Life and Play in Wilde's *The Importance of Being Earnest.*" *Midwest Quarterly* 30.4 (1989): 515–28.

Raby, Peter, ed. *The Cambridge Companion to Oscar Wilde.* Cambridge: Cambridge UP, 1997.

———. "The Origins of *The Importance of Being Earnest.*" *Modern Drama* 37.1 (1994): 139–47.

San Juan, Epifanio. *The Art of Oscar Wilde.* Princeton: Princeton UP, 1963.

Smith, Philip E., and Michael S. Heffland, eds. *Oscar Wilde's Oxford Notebooks.* New York: Oxford UP, 1989.

Sullivan, Kevin. *Oscar Wilde.* Columbia Essays on Modern Writers 64. New York: Columbia UP, 1972.

Varty, Anne. *A Preface to Oscar Wilde.* Preface Books. London: Longman, 1998.

Weintraub, Stanley. *The Literary Criticism of Oscar Wilde.* Lincoln: U of Nebraska P, 1968.

Wilde, Oscar. *The Complete Works.* New York: Doubleday, 1923.

———. *The Plays of Oscar Wilde.* New York: Random, 1980.

TENNESSEE WILLIAMS

Aisbong, Emmanuel B. *Tennessee Williams: The Tragic Tension.* Elms Court: Stockwell, 1978.

Boxill, Roger. *Tennessee Williams.* New York: St. Martin's, 1987.

Bruhm, Steven. "Blackmailed by Sex: Tennessee Williams and the Economics of Desire." *Modern Drama* 34.4 (1991): 528–37.

Cranell, George W., ed. *The Critical Response to Tennessee Williams.* Westport, CT: Greenwood, 1996.

Devlin, Albert J., ed. *Conversations with Tennessee Williams.* Jackson: UP of Mississippi, 1986.

Donahue, Francis. *The Dramatic World of Tennessee Williams.* New York: Ungar, 1964.

Falk, Signi Lenea. *Tennessee Williams.* 2nd ed. Boston: Twayne, 1978.

Griffin, Alice. *Understanding Tennessee Williams.* Columbia: U of South Carolina P, 1995.

Hayman, Ronald. *Tennessee Williams: Everyone Else Is an Audience.* New Haven: Yale UP, 1993.

Koprince, Susan. "Tennessee Williams's Unseen Characters." *Southern Quarterly* 33.1 (1994): 87–95.

Leavitt, Richard Freeman, ed. *The World of Tennessee Williams.* New York: Putnam's, 1978.

Leverich, Lyle. *Tom: The Unknown Tennessee Williams.* London: Scepter, 1996.

Martin, Robert A., ed. *Critical Essays on Tennessee Williams.* New York: Hall, 1997.

Parker, R. B., ed. The Glass Menagerie: *A Collection of Critical Essays.* Englewood Cliffs: Prentice, 1983.

Roudané, Matthew Charles, ed. *The Cambridge Companion to Tennessee Williams.* Cambridge: Cambridge UP, 1997.

Sarotte, Georges-Michel. "Fluidity and Differentiation in Three Plays by Tennessee Williams: *The Glass Menagerie, A Streetcar Named Desire,* and *Cat on a Hot Tin Roof.*" *Staging Difference: Cultural Pluralism in American Theatre and Drama.* Ed. Marc Maufort. New York: Peter Lang, 1995. 141–56.

Savran, David. "'By coming suddenly into a room that I thought was empty': Mapping the Closet with Tennessee Williams." *Studies in the Literary Imagination* 24.2 (1991): 57–74.

———. *Communists, Cowboys and Queers: The Politics of Masculinity in the Work of Arthur Miller and Tennessee Williams.* Minneapolis: U of Minnesota P, 1992.

Spoto, Donald. *The Kindness of Strangers: The Life of Tennessee Williams.* Boston: Little, 1985.

Stanton, Stephen, ed. *Tennessee Williams: A Collection of Critical Essays.* Englewood Cliffs: Prentice, 1977.

Thompson, Judith. *Tennessee Williams' Plays: Memory, Myth, and Symbol.* New York: Lang, 1987.

Wilhelmi, Nancy O. "The Language of Power and Powerlessness: Verbal Combat in the Plays of Tennessee Williams." *The Text and Beyond: Essays in Literary Linguistics.* Ed. Cynthia Goldin-Bernstein. Tuscaloosa: U of Alabama P, 1994.

Williams, Dakin, with Shepherd Mead. *Tennessee Williams: An Intimate Biography.* New York: Arbor, 1983.

Williams, Tennessee. *Memoirs.* Garden City: Doubleday, 1975

The Glass Menagerie

Bloom, Harold. *Tennessee Williams's* The Glass Menagerie. New York: Chelsea, 1988.

Cardullo, Bert. "The Blue Rose of St. Louis: Laura, Romanticism, and *The Glass Menagerie.*" *Tennessee Williams Annual Review* (1998).

Greiff, Louis K. "Fathers, Daughters, and Spiritual Sisters: Marsha Norman's *'night, Mother* and Tennessee Williams's *The Glass Menagerie.*" *Text and Performance Quarterly* 9.3 (1989): 224–28.

Jones, John H. "The Missing Link: The Father in *The Glass Menagerie.*" *Notes on Mississippi Writers* 20.1 (1988): 29–38.

Kolin, Philip C. "The Black and Multi-Racial Productions of Tennessee Williams's *The Glass Menagerie.*" *Journal of Dramatic Theory and Criticism* 9.2 (1995): 96–128.

Levy, Eric P. "Through Soundproof Glass: The Prison of Self-Consciousness in *The Glass Menagerie.*" *Modern Drama* 36.4 (1993): 529–37.

Parker, R. B. "The Circle Closed: A Psychological Reading of *The Glass Menagerie* and the Two Character Play." *Modern Drama* 28 (1985): 517–34.

Presley, Delma Eugene. The Glass Menagerie: *An American Memory.* Boston: Twayne, 1990.

Reynolds, James. "The Failure of Technology in *The Glass Menagerie.*" *Modern Drama* 34.4 (1991): 522–27.

Siebold, Thomas., ed. *Readings on* The Glass Menagerie. San Diego: Greenhaven, 1998.

Smith, William Jay. "Tom: The Making of *The Glass Menagerie.*" *The New Criterion* 14 (1996): 72–77.

Thierfelder, William R. "Williams's *The Glass Menagerie.*" *Explicator* 48.4 (1990): 284–85.

Usui, Masami. "'A World of Her Own' in Tennessee Williams's *The Glass Menagerie.*" *Studies in Culture and the Humanities* 1 (1992): 21–37.

AUGUST WILSON

Arthur, Thomas H. "Looking for My Relatives: The Political Implications of 'Family' in Selected Works of Athol Fugard and August Wilson." *South African Theatre Journal* 6.2 (1992): 5–16.

Bogumil, Mary L. *Understanding August Wilson.* Columbia: U of South Carolina P, 1999.

DiGaetani, John L. *A Search for a Postmodern Theater: Interviews with Contemporary Playwrights.* New York: Greenwood, 1991.

Freedman, Samuel G. "A Voice from the Streets." *New York Times Magazine* 15 Mar. 1987: 33+.

———. "Wilson's New *Fences* Nurtures a Partnership." *New York Times* 5 May 1985, sec. I: 80.

Gerard, Jeremy. "Waterford to Broadway: Well-Traveled *Fences.*" *New York Times* 9 April 1987, sec. 3: 21.

Henderson, Heather. "Building Fences: An Interview with Mary Alice and James Earl Jones." *Yale Theater* 12 (Summer/Fall 1985): 67–70.

Herrington, Joan. *I Ain't Sorry for Nothin' I Done: August Wilson's Process of Playwrighting.* New York: Limelight, 1998.

Kelley, Kevin. "August Wilson an Heir to O'Neill." *Boston Globe* 24 Jan. 1988: A1+.

Lyons, B. "An Interview with August Wilson." *Contemporary Literature* 40.1 (1999): 1–21.

Nadel, Alan, ed. *May All Your Fences Have Gates: Essays on the Drama of August Wilson.* Iowa City: U of Iowa P, 1994.

Pereira, Kim. *August Wilson and the African American Odyssey.* Urbana: U of Illinois P, 1995.

Plum, Jay. "Blues, History and the Dramaturgy of August Wilson." *African American Review* 27.4 (1993): 561–67.

Rich, Frank. "Theater: Family Ties in Wilson's *Fences.*" *New York Times* 27 Mar. 1987, sec. II: 1.

Shannon, Sandra, "Blues, History, and Dramaturgy: An Interview with August Wilson." *African American Review* 27.4 (1993): 539–59.

———. "Conversing with the Past: Joe Turner's Come and Gone and *The Piano Lesson.*" *CEA Magazine* 4.1 (1991): 33–42.

Sterling, E. "Protecting Home: Patriarchal Authority in August Wilson's *Fences.*" *Essays in Theatre-Etudes Theatrales* 17.1 (1996): 53–62.

Wang, Qun. *An In-Depth Study of the Major Plays of African American Playwright August Wilson: Vernacularizing the Blues on Stage.* Lewiston: Mellen, 1999.

Wessling, J. H. "Wilson's *Fences.*" *Explicator* 57.2 (1999): 123–27.

Selected List of Film, Video, and Audiocassette Resources

The following list of audiovisual resources supplements the teaching of plays in *The Bedford Introduction to Drama*. The resources are listed alphabetically by playwright.

The films and videos marked with an asterisk (*) are available for rental from member institutions of the Consortium of College and University Media Centers. For further information, consult Media Sources: Consortium of College and University Media Centers, 1st ed. on CD-ROM.

Many of the videos are available for rental from local video outlets. Others are available through a distributor. Check the Directory of Distributors following this list for information.

ANONYMOUS

Anonymous, *Everyman.* 25 minutes, color, 1971. 16 mm film. Abridged by H. Frances Clark. Distributed by Coronet/MTI Film & Video.

Anonymous, *Everyman.* 53 minutes, color, 1991. VHS. Produced in conjunction with medieval literature scholar Holward Schless of Columbia University. Authentically staged in period costume. Distributed by Insight Media.

ARISTOPHANES

Aristophanes, *Lysistrata.* 97 minutes, color, 1987. VHS, Beta. A contemporary adaptation, shot on location at the Acropolis. In Greek with English subtitles. Distributed by New York Film Annex.

SAMUEL BECKETT

Samuel Beckett, *Endgame.* 92 minutes, color, 1989. Part of the "Literature in the Modern World" series. Starring Norman Beaton, Stephen Rea, and Kate Binchy. Distributed by the Roland Collection.

Samuel Beckett, *Endgame.* 96 minutes, color, 1992. Starring Bud Thorpe, Rick Cluchey, and Teresita Garcia Suro. Distributed by Smithsonian Institution Press.

Samuel Beckett, *Endgame.* 96 minutes, color, 1992. VHS. Samuel Beckett's work as presented by the University of Maryland in Collaboration with PBS. Distributed by Insight Media.

Samuel Beckett. 80 minutes, color, 1989. Beta, VHS, 3/4″ U-matic cassette. An autobiographical portrait of Beckett's artistic life through his work. Distributed by Films for the Humanities and Sciences.

BERTOLT BRECHT

Bertolt Brecht. 55 minutes, color, 1989. VHS, 3/4″ U-matic cassette. A biographical portrait of Brecht through his works. Distributed by Films for the Humanities and Sciences.

Gisela May: Reflections on the Theater of Brecht. 30 minutes, color, 1979. Beta, VHS, 1/2″ open reel (EIAJ), 3/4″ U-matic cassette, 2″ quadraplex open reel. Gisela May of the Berliner Ensemble performs excerpts from Brecht's plays. Distributed by Camera Three Productions Inc. and Creative Arts Television Archive.

ANTON CHEKHOV

Anton Chekhov. 30 minutes, color and b/w, 1996. VHS. A documentary filmed where Chekhov lived and worked. Part of the Great Authors series. Distributed by Kultur.

Anton Chekhov, *The Cherry Orchard.* 3 audiocassettes. Translated by Leonid Kipnis and performed by Jessica Tandy and Hume Cronyn. Distributed by Caedmon/Harper Audio.

Anton Chekhov, *The Cherry Orchard, Part I: Chekhov, Innovator of Modern Drama.* 21 minutes, color and b/w, 1968. Beta, VHS, 3/4″ U-matic cassette, 16-mm film. Important scenes with discussion led by Norris Houghton. Distributed by Encyclopaedia Britannica Educational Corp.

Anton Chekhov, *The Cherry Orchard, Part II: Comedy or Tragedy?* 21 minutes, color and b/w, 1967. Beta, VHS, 3/4″ U-matic cassette, 16-mm film. Important scenes with discussion led by Norris Houghton. Covers Chekhov's technique of dramatization of interior actions and examines the notion of subtext. Distributed by Encyclopaedia Britannica Educational Corp.

Anton Chekhov: A Writer's Life.. 37 minutes, b/w, 1974. VHS, 3/4″ U-matic cassette. A biographical portrait of the playwright. Distributed by Films for the Humanities and Sciences.

Chekhov. 1080 minutes, 1989. 12 audiocassettes. By Henri Troyat, read by Wolfram Kandinsky. A biography of the writer. Distributed by Books on Tape, Inc.

Chekhov: Humanity's Advocate. 46 minutes, 1968. Audiocassette. By Ernest J. Simmons. Explores various facets of Chekhov's works and his artistic principals. Classics of Russian Literature Series. Distributed by Audio-Forum.

ATHOL FUGARD

Athol Fugard, *"MASTER HAROLD" . . . and the boys.* 90 minutes, color, 1984. Beta, VHS. With Matthew Broderick. Directed by Michael Lindsay-Hogg. A made-for-cable production. Distributed by Warner Home Video, Inc.

LORRAINE HANSBERRY

Lorraine Hansberry: The Black Experience in the Creation of Drama. 35 minutes, color, 1975. Beta, VHS, 3/4″ U-matic cassette. With Sidney Poitier, Ruby Dee, and Al Freeman, Jr. Narrated by Claudia McNeil. A profile of the playwright's life and work. Distributed by Films for the Humanities and Sciences.

Lorraine Hansberry Speaks Out: Art and the Black Revolution. Audiocassette. By Lorraine Hansberry, edited by Robert Nemiroff. Distributed by Caedmon/HarperAudio.

A Raisin in the Sun. 128 minutes, b/w, 1961. Beta, VHS. With Sidney Poitier, Claudia McNeil and Ruby Dee. Directed by Daniel Petrie. Distributed by Columbia Tristar.

A Raisin in the Sun. 171 minutes, color, 1989. Beta, VHS. With Danny Glover, Esther Rolle, and Starletta DuPois. Directed by Bill Duke. An American Playhouse made-for-television production. Distributed by Chuck Fries Productions.

A Raisin in the Sun. 141 minutes. 2 audiocassettes. Dramatization performed by Ossie Davis and Ruby Dee. Distributed by Caedmon/Harper Audio.

To Be Young, Gifted, and Black. 90 minutes, color, 1981. Beta, VHS, 1/2″ open reel (EIAJ), 3/4″ U-matic cassette, 16-mm film. With Ruby Dee, Al Freeman, Jr., Claudia McNeil, Barbara Barrie, Lauren Jones, Roy Scheider, and Blythe Danner. A play about the life of Lorraine Hansberry. Distributed by Monterey Home Video.

HENRIK IBSEN

A Doll's House. 180 minutes, 1993. 3 audiocassettes. Read by Flo Gibson. Distributed by Audio Book Contractors.

A Doll's House, Part I: The Distinction of Illusion. 34 minutes, color, 1968. Beta, VHS, 3/4″ U-matic cassette, 16-mm film. Norris Houghton discusses the subsurface tensions in the play. Distributed by Encyclopaedia Britannica Educational Corp.

A Doll's House, Part II: Ibsen's Themes. 29 minutes, color, 1968. Beta, VHS, 3/4″ U-matic cassette, 16-mm film. Norris Houghton examines the case of characters and the themes in the play. Distributed by Encyclopaedia Britannica Educational Corp.

Henrik Ibsen, *A Doll's House.* 89 minutes, b/w, 1959. Beta, VHS, 3/4″ U-matic cassette. With Julie Harris, Christopher Plummer, Jason Robards, Hume Cronyn, Eileen Heckart, and Richard Thomas. An original television production. Distributed by MGM/UA Entertainment.

Henrik Ibsen, *A Doll's House.* 98 minutes, color, 1973. VHS, 16-mm film. With Jane Fonda, Edward Fox, and Trevor Howard. Screenplay by Christopher Hampton. Distributed by Prism Entertainment.

Henrik Ibsen, *A Doll's House.* 39 minutes, color, 1977. VHS. With Claire Bloom, Anthony Hopkins, and Ralph Richardson. Distributed by AIMS Media.

Ibsen's Life and Times, Part I: Youth and Self-Imposed Exile. 28 minutes, color. VHS. The conflict between individual and society is illustratd in scenes from *Ghosts*, featuring Beatrice Straight as Mrs. Alving. Includes a biographical segment on the playwright. Distributed by Insight Media.

Ibsen's Life and Times, Part II: The Later Years. 24 minutes, color. VHS. Includes scenes from *The Master Builder* and *Lady from the Sea*, emphasizing the realism in Ibsen's plays. A biographical segment includes on-location footage. Distributed by Insight Media.

FEDERICO GARCÍA LORCA

Federico García Lorca: El Balcon Abierto. 90 minutes, color. VHS, 3/4″ U-matic cassette. In Spanish. An examination of García Lorca's work, life, and violent death. Distributed by Films for the Humanities and Sciences.

Lorca: A Murder in Granada. 55 minutes, 1983. VHS, 3/4″ U-matic cassette. In Spanish and English. The authoritative film biography of García Lorca. Distributed by Films for the Humanities and Sciences.

CHRISTOPHER MARLOWE

Christopher Marlowe, *Doctor Faustus*. 93 minutes, 1968. VHS, Beta. Adaptation of Marlowe's classic. With Richard Burton and Elizabeth Taylor. Directed by Richard Burton and Neville Coghill. Distributed by Columbia Tristar Home Video.

ARTHUR MILLER

Death of a Salesman. 135 minutes, color, 1985. Beta, VHS. With Dustin Hoffman, John Malkovich, Charles Durning, and Stephen Lang. Directed by Volker Schlondorff. A made-for-television adaptation of the play. Distributed by Facets Multimedia and Warner Home Video.

Arthur Miller, *Death of a Salesman*. 2 audiocassettes. Performed by Lee J. Cobb and Mildred Dunnock. Distributed by Caedmon/Harper Audio.

Arthur Miller, *Death of a Salesman*. 44 minutes, 1986. Audiocassette. Dramatization performed by Paul Douglas. Distributed by Sounddeluxe Audio Publishing.

Private Conversations on the Set of Death of a Salesman. 82 minutes, color, 1985. Beta, VHS. With Arthur Miller, Dustin Hoffman, Volker Schlondorff, and John Malkovich. This PBS documentary presents heated discussion between actor, director, and playwright. Various interpretations of the play emerge and viewers gain insight into how each part contributed to the final production. Distributed by Video Learning Library.

MOLIÈRE

Molière, *Le Misanthrope*. 52 minutes, color, 1975. VHS. With Cyril Ritchard, Edward Petherbridge, and Neil Stacy. Distributed by Films for the Humanities and Sciences.

Molière, *Le Misanthrope*. 140 minutes, color, 1986. VHS, 3/4″ U-matic cassette. In French with English subtitles. Distributed by Films for the Humanities and Sciences.

Molière, *Le Misanthrope*. 89 minutes. 2 audiocassettes. With Richard Easton. Distributed by Caedmon.

Molière, *Le Misanthrope*. 104 minutes. 2 audiocassettes. Recorded live as part of L.A. Theater Works' The Play's the Thing series of performance productions. Distributed by L.A. Theater Works.

EUGENE O'NEILL

Eugene O'Neill. 30 minutes, b/w and color, 1996. VHS. A commentary on the author's life. Part of the Famous Authors series. Distributed by Kultur.

Eugene O'Neill, *Desire under the Elms*. 111 minutes, b/w, 1958. Beta, VHS, LaserDisc. Starring Anthony Perkins, Burl Ives, and Sophia Loren. Directed by

Delbert Mann. Distributed by Paramount Home Video.

LUIGI PIRANDELLO

Luigi Pirandello, *Six Characters in Search of an Author*. 52 minutes, color, 1976. VHS, 3/4″ U-matic cassette. Joseph Heller discusses the boundaries between reality and fiction. Distributed by Films for the Humanities and Sciences.

Luigi Pirandello, *Six Characters in Search of an Author*. 60 minutes, color, 1978. VHS, 3/4″ U-matic cassette. Hosted by Jose Ferrer. As an accompaniment to the play, Ossie Davis discusses Pirandello's work in the theater. Distributed by RMI Media Production, Inc.

Luigi Pirandello, *Six Characters in Search of an Author*. 96 minutes, b/w, 1998. A BBC Production featuring John Hurt, Brian Cox, and Tara Fitzgerald. Distributed by Films for the Humanities and Sciences.

WILLIAM SHAKESPEARE

A Midsummer Night's Dream

A Midsummer Night's Dream. 120 minutes. 2 audiocassettes. Performed by Robert Helpmann and Moira Shearer. An Old Vic production. Distributed by Durkin Hayes Publishing.

William Shakespeare, *A Midsummer Night's Dream*. 118 minutes, b/w, 1935. VHS. With James Cagney, Mickey Rooney, Olivia DeHaviland, and Dick Powell. Distributed by Critics' Choice.

William Shakespeare, *A Midsummer Night's Dream*. 111 minutes, b/w, 1963. Beta, VHS, 3/4″ U-matic cassette. With Patrick Allen, Eira Heath, Cyril Luckham, Tony Bateman, and Jill Bennett. A live BBC-TV performance, with Mendelsohn's incidental music. Distributed by Video Yesteryear.

William Shakespeare, *A Midsummer Night's Dream*. 120 minutes, 1968. VHS. With Diana Rigg and David Warner. Directed by Peter Hall. A Royal Shakespeare Company performance. Distributed by Critics' Choice.

William Shakespeare, *A Midsummer Night's Dream*. 120 minutes, color, 1982. Beta, VHS. With Helen Mirren, Peter McEnery, and Brian Glover. Distributed by Filmic Archives.

William Shakespeare, *A Midsummer Night's Dream*. 165 minutes, color, 1983. Beta, VHS, 3/4″ U-matic cassette. With William Hurt and Michelle Shay. A lively interpretation by Joseph Papp. Distributed by Films for the Humanities and Sciences.

William Shakespeare, *A Midsummer Night's Dream*. 194 minutes, color, 1987. VHS. With Ileana Cotrubas, James Bowman, and Curt Appelgren. Directed by Peter Hall. A performance of the Benjamin Britten opera, taped at the Glyndebourne Festival Opera. Distributed by Critics' Choice.

William Shakespeare, *A Midsummer Night's Dream.* 115 minutes, color, 1999. VHS, DVD. Starring Kevin Kline, Michelle Pfeiffer, Calista Flockhart, and Stanley Tucci. Distributed by Twentieth Century Fox.

William Shakespeare, *A Midsummer Night's Dream.* 2 audio compact discs. Dramatization performed by Paul Scofield and Joy Parker. With an introductory essay by scholar Harold Bloom. Distributed by Caedmon/Harper Audio.

Othello

Otello. 146 minutes, color, 1997. VHS. With Placido Domingo, Kiri Te Kanawa, and Sergei Leiferkus. Opera by Giuseppe Verdi. Conducted by Georg Solti. Production at the Royal Opera House, Covent Garden, London. Distributed by Public Media/Home Vision.

William Shakespeare, *Othello.* 92 minutes, b/w, 1952. VHS, laser disc. Directed by Orson Welles. The original version as it appeared in the 1952 Cannes Film Festival. Distributed by Voyager.

William Shakespeare, *Othello.* 208 minutes, color, 1982. VHS. With Bob Hoskins and Anthony Hopkins. Distributed by Ambrose Video Publishing, Inc.

William Shakespeare, *Othello.* 90 minutes, color, 1993. Various actors perform key scenes as scholars provide commentary. Distributed by the Video Catalog.

William Shakespeare, *Othello.* 124 minutes, color, 1995, VHS. With Laurence Fishburne, Kenneth Branagh, and Irene Jacob. Distributed by Castle Rock Entertainment.

William Shakespeare, *Othello.* 2 audiocassettes. Performed by Cyril Cusack and Alan Bates. Distributed by Caedmon/Harper Audio.

General

The Life and Times of William Shakespeare 1: The Historical Setting. 25 minutes, color, 1978. VHS. An overview of Elizabethan England. Distributed by the University of Wyoming Audio-Visual Services.

The Life and Times of William Shakespeare 2: English Drama. 20 minutes, color, 1978. VHS. History of drama from the Greeks to that of Shakespeare's time. Distributed by the University of Wyoming Audio-Visual Services.

The Life and Times of William Shakespeare 3: Stratford Years. 18 minutes, color, 1978. VHS. Deals with Shakespeare's early life. Distributed by the University of Wyoming Audio-Visual Services.

The Life and Times of William Shakespeare 4: London Years. 33 minutes, color, 1978. VHS. A history of the center of the English-speaking world. Distributed by the University of Wyoming Audio-Visual Services.

Shakespeare and the Globe. 31 minutes, color, 1985. VHS, 3/4" U-matic cassette. A survey of Shakespeare's life, work, and cultural milieu. Distributed by Films for the Humanities and Sciences.

Shakespeare and His Stage. 47 minutes, color, 1975. VHS, 16-mm film. Provides a montage of Shakespearean background, including scenes from Hamlet and the preparation of various actors for the role. Distributed by Films for the Humanities and Sciences.

Shakespeare's Heritage. 29 minutes, color, 1988. 16-mm film. Narrated by Anthony Quayle. Explores Stratford and the life of the playwright. Distributed by Encyclopaedia Britannica Educational Corp.

Shakespeare's Theater. 13 minutes, color, 1946. 16-mm film. Re-creates the experience of going to a play at the Globe Theatre in Shakespeare's time. Distributed by the Indiana University Instructional Support Services.

Shakespeare's Theater: The Globe Playhouse. 18 minutes, b/w, 1953. VHS. Provides a model of the Globe Theater and a discussion of the original staging of some of Shakespeare's plays. Distributed by the University of California Extension Media Center.

The Two Traditions. 50 minutes, color, 1983. VHS. Deals with the problem of overcoming barriers of time and culture to make Shakespeare relevant today. Examples from *Hamlet, Coriolanus, The Merchant of Venice,* and *Othello.* Part of the Playing Shakespeare Series. Distributed by Films for the Humanities and Sciences.

Understanding Shakespeare: His Sources. 20 minutes, color, 1972. Beta, VHS, 3/4" U-matic cassette, 16-mm film, other formats by special arrangement. Examines how Shakespeare's plays grew out of sources available to him, and how he enhanced the material with his own imagination. Distributed by Coronet/MTI Film & Video.

SOPHOCLES

Antigone

Antigone: Rites of Passion. 85 minutes, color, 1992. VHS. With Amy Greenfield, Bertram Ross, and Janet Eilber. Director by Amy Greenfield. A retelling of Sophocles' tragedy through action, dance, and rock music. Distributed by Mystic Fire Video.

Antigone. 2 audiocassettes. Dramatization of the Fitts and Fitzgerald translation. Performed by Dorothy Tutin and Max Adrian. Distributed by Caedmon/Harper Audio.

Sophocles, *Antigone.* 88 minutes, b/w, 1962. VHS. With Irene Papas. Directed by George Tzavellas. In Greek with English subtitles. Distributed by Ivy Video.

Sophocles, *Antigone.* 120 minutes, 1987. VHS, 3/4" U-matic cassette. With Juliet Stevenson, John Shrapnel, and John Gielgud. Staged version. Distributed by Films for the Humanities and Sciences.

Sophocles, *Antigone.* 58 minutes, color, 1994. VHS. With Seymour Simon. Distributed by RMI Media Productions.

Oedipus

Oedipus Rex: Age of Sophocles, I. 31 minutes, color and b/w, 1959. Beta, VHS, 3/4″ U-matic cassette, 16-mm film. Discusses Greek civilization, the classic Greek theater, and the theme of man's fundamental nature. Distributed by Encyclopaedia Britannica Educational Corp.

Oedipus Rex: The Character of Oedipus, II. 31 minutes, color and b/w, 1959. Beta, VHS, 3/4″ U-matic cassette, 16-mm film. Debates whether Oedipus's trouble is a result of character flaws or of fate. Distributed by Encyclopaedia Britannica Educational Corp.

Oedipus Rex: Man and God, III. 30 minutes, color and b/w, 1959. Beta, VHS, 3/4″ U-matic cassette, 16-mm film. Deals with the idea that Oedipus, although a worldly ruler, cannot overcome the gods and his destiny. Distributed by Encyclopaedia Britannica Educational Corp.

Oedipus Rex: Recovery of Oedipus, IV. 30 minutes, color and b/w, 1959. Beta, VHS, 3/4″ U-matic cassette, 16-mm film. Deals with man's existence in between God and beast. Distributed by Encyclopaedia Britannica Educational Corp.

Sophocles, *Oedipus Rex.* 20 minutes, color, 1957. Beta, VHS, 3/4″ U-matic cassette. Sophocles' play, presented in a signed version for the deaf. Distributed by Gallaudet University Library.

Sophocles, *Oedipus Rex.* 87 minutes, color, 1957. VHS, 16-mm film. With Douglas Campbell, Douglas Rain, Eric House, and Eleanor Stuart. Based on William Yeats's translation. Directed by Tyrone Guthrie. Contained and highly structured rendering by the Stratford (Ontario) Festival Players. Distributed by Water Bearer Films.

Sophocles, *Oedipus the King.* 97 minutes, color, 1967. VHS. With Donald Sutherland, Christopher Plummer, Lilli Palmer, Orson Welles, Cyril Cusack, Richard Johnson, and Roger Livesey. Directed by Philip Saville. Simplified film version of the play, filmed in Greece using an old amphitheater to serve as the background for much of the action. Distributed by Crossroads Video.

Sophocles, *Oedipus the King.* 45 minutes, color, 1975. Beta, VHS, 3/4″ U-matic cassette, 16-mm film. With Anthony Quayle, James Mason, Claire Bloom, and Ian Richardson. A production by the Athens Classical Theatre Company, with an English soundtrack. Distributed by Films for the Humanities and Sciences.

Sophocles, *Oedipus the King.* 120 minutes, color, 1987. VHS. With John Gielgud, Michael Pennington, and Claire Bloom. Distributed by Films for the Humanities and Sciences.

Sophocles, *Oedipus Rex.* 2 audiocassettes. Translated by William Butler Yeats. Performed by Douglas Campbell and Eric House. Dramatization. Distributed by Caedmon/Harper Audio.

Sophocles, *Oedipus at Colonus.* 120 minutes, color, 1987. Beta, VHS, 3/4″ U-matic cassette. With Anthony Quayle, Juliet Stevenson, and Kenneth Haigh. Staged version. Distributed by Films for the Humanities and Sciences.

Sophocles: The Theban Plays. 360 minutes, color, 1986. 3 videocassettes, VHS, 3/4″ U-matic cassette. Distributed by Films for the Humanities and Sciences.

AUGUST STRINDBERG

August Strindberg, *Miss Julie.* 90 minutes, b/w, 1950. VHS. Starring Anita Bjork and Ulf Palme. Directed by Alf Sjoberg. Distributed by Public Media/Home Vision.

August Strindberg, *Miss Julie.* 105 minutes, color, 1972. VHS. With Helen Mirren. A production of the Royal Shakespeare Company. Distributed by MasterVision.

August Strindberg, *Miss Julie.* 60 minutes, color, 1978. Beta, VHS, 3/4″ U-matic cassette. Ancillary materials available. With Patrick Stewart and Lisa Harrow. Hosted by Jose Ferrer. Opens with the rehearsal of a crucial scene and closes with a full-dress production of the play. In between, the actors show different ways of interpreting a scene. Distributed by Films, Inc.

August Strindberg, *Miss Julie.* 100 minutes, color, 1997. VHS. Directed by Michael Simpson. Distributed by Films for the Humanities and Sciences.

OSCAR WILDE

Oscar Wilde, *The Importance of Being Earnest.* 95 minutes, color, 1952. Beta, VHS. With Michael Redgrave, Edith Evans, Margaret Rutherford, Michael Dennison, and Joan Greenwood. Directed by Anthony Asquith. Staged version. Distributed by Paramount Home Video.

Oscar Wilde, *The Importance of Being Earnest.* 2 audiocassettes. Performed by Lynn Redgrave and Gladys Cooper. Distributed by Caedmon/Harper Audio.

Oscar Wilde: Spendthrift of Genius. 60 minutes, color, 1989. VHS. A portrait of this multitalented author. Distributed by Films for the Humanities and Sciences.

TENNESSEE WILLIAMS

The Glass Menagerie

The Glass Menagerie. 134 minutes, color, 1987. Beta, VHS. With Joanne Woodward, Karen Allen, John Malkovich, and James Naughton. Directed by Paul Newman. See local retailer.

Tennessee Williams, *The Glass Menagerie.* 2 audiocassettes. Performed by Montgomery Clift and Julie Harris. Distributed by Caedmon/Harper Audio.

Tennessee Williams, *Tennessee Williams Reads "The Glass Menagerie" and Others.* Audiocassette. Read by Tennessee Williams. Includes *The Glass Menagerie* (opening monologue and closing scene); "Cried the Fox"; "The Eyes"; "The Summer Belvedere"; "Some Poems Meant for Music"; "Little Horse"; "Which Is My Little Boy"; "Little One"; "Gold-Tooth Blues"; "Kitchen-Door Blues"; "Heavenly Grass"; and "The Yellow Bird." Distributed by Caedmon/Harper Audio.

The Glass Menagerie. Audiocassette. Read by Tennessee Williams. Includes "The Yellow Bird" (short story) and poems. Distributed by the American Audio Prose Library.

General

In the Country of Tennessee Williams. 30 minutes, color, 1977. Beta, VHS, 1/2" reel, 3/4" U-matic cassette, 2" Quad. A one-act play about how Williams developed as a writer. Distributed by the New York State Education Department.

General Resources

Black Theatre: The Making of a Movement. 113 minutes, color, VHS, 1978. A look at black theater born from the Civil Rights movement of the 1950s, 1960s, and 1970s. Recollections from Ossie Davis, James Earl Jones, Amiri Baraka, and Ntozake Shange. Distributed by California Newsreel.

A Day at the Globe. 30 minutes, color. VHS. Starts with a brief overview of early drama and of seventeenth-century England, then discusses the Globe Theater, using still images. Explains how actors, artisans, and other company members prepared for performances and presents dramatic readings, period costumes, music, and sound effects in order to help students envision how Shakespearean drama actually looked. Distributed by Insight Media.

Drama Comes of Age. 30 minutes, b/w, 1957. 16-mm film. Discusses the Shakespearean theater and neoclassic drama. Demonstrates early realism with a scene from *Hedda Gabler.* Distributed by the Indiana University Instructional Support Services.

Drama: How It Began. 30 minutes, b/w, 1957. 16-mm film. Discusses the early beginnings of the theater. Explains the techniques of the Greek theater and how playwriting developed. Illustrates the chorus technique with a scene from *Oedipus the King.* Distributed by the Indiana University Instructional Support Services.

The Elizabethan Age. 30 minutes, color. VHS. A discussion of the resurgence of enthusiasm for the arts and letters that swept seventeenth-century England. Uses original sources. Distributed by Insight Media.

Greek Tragedy. Audiocassette. Works of Euripides and Sophocles, Performed by Katina Paxinou and Alexis Minotis. Distributed by Caedmon/Harper Audio.

The Theatre in Ancient Greece. 26 minutes, color, 1989. Beta, VHS, 3/4" U-matic cassette. Program explores ancient theatre design, the origins or tragedy, the audience, the comparative roles of the writer/director and actors, and the use of landscape in many plays. Examines the theaters of Herodus, Atticus, Epidauros, Corinth, and numerous others. Distributed by Films for the Humanities and Sciences.

Directory of Distributors

AIMS Multimedia, 9710 DeSoto Avenue, Chatsworth, CA 91311-4409, (818) 773-4300, (800) 367-2467

Ambrose Video Publishing Inc., 28 West 44th Street, New York, NY 10036, (212) 768-7373, (800) 526-4663

American Audio Prose Library, PO Box 842, Crestland Avenue, Columbia, MO 65205, (573) 443-0361, (800) 447-2275

Annenberg/CPB, 901 E Street NW, Washington, DC 20004, (202) 879-9600

Applause Productions, 85-A Fernwood Lane, Roslyn, NY 11576, (516) 365-1259, (800) 253-5351

Audio Book Contractors, PO Box 40115, Washington, DC 20016, (202) 363-3429.

Audio-Forum, Jeffrey Norton Publishers, 96 Broad Street, Guilford, CT 06437, (203) 453-9794, (800) 243-1234

Books on Tape, Inc., PO Box 7900, Newport Beach, CA 92658, (800) 626-3333

Caedmon/Harper Audio, PO Box 588, Dunmore, PA 18512, (717) 343-4761, (800) 242-7737, (800) 982-4377 (in Pennsylvania)

California Newsreel, 149 Ninth Street, Suite 420, San Francisco, CA 94103, (415) 621-6196, (800) 621-6196

Camera Three Productions and Creative Arts Television Archive, Box 739, Kent, CT 06757, (860) 868-1771

Castle Rock Entertainment. See local retailers.

CBS/FOX Video. See local retailers.

Chuck Fries Productions, 6922 Hollywood Boulevard, Los Angeles, CA 90028, (323) 466-2266

Columbia Tristar Home Video. See local retailers.

Coronet/MTI Film & Video, 2349 Chaffee Drive, St. Louis, MO 63146, (314) 569-0211, (800) 221-1274

Crossroads Video, 15 Buckminster Lane, Manhasset, NY 11030, (516) 365-3715, (800) 548-5757

Durkin Hayes Publishing, 2221 Niagara Falls Boulevard, Niagara Falls, NY 14304, (716) 731-9177, (800) 962-5200

Encyclopaedia Britannica Educational Corporation, 310 South Michigan Avenue, Chicago, IL 60604, (312) 347-7900, (800) 621-3900

Facets Multimedia Inc., 1517 West Fullerton Avenue, Chicago, IL 60614, (773) 281-9075 (800) 331-6197

Filmic Archives, The Cinema Center, Botsford, CT 06404 (203) 261-1920

Films for the Humanities and Sciences, PO Box 2053, Princeton, NJ 08543-2053, (609) 275-1400, (800) 257-5126

Gallaudet University Library, Gallaudet Media Distribution, 800 Florida Avenue NE, Washington, DC 20002, (202) 651-5579, (202) 651-5440

Hallmark Home Entertainment. See local retailers.

Image Entertainment, 9333 Oso Avenue, Chatsworth, CA 91311

Indiana University Instructional Support Services, Franklin Hall, Room 0001, Bloomington, IN 47405-5901, (812) 855-2853

Insight Media, 2162 Broadway, New York, NY 10024, (212) 721-6316

Ivy Video, PO Box 18376, Asheville, NC 28814, (828) 285-9995, (800) 669-4057

Kultur, 195 Highway #36, West Long Branch, NJ 07764, (732) 229-0066, (800) 4-KULTUR

MasterVision, 969 Park Avenue, New York, NY 10028, (212) 879-0448

MGM/UA. See local retailers.

Monterey Home Video, 566 St. Charles Drive, Thousand Oaks, CA 91360, (805) 494-7199, (800) 424-2593

Mystic Fire Video, PO Box 422, Prince Street Station, New York, NY 10012, (212) 941-0999

National Broadcasting Company, 30 Rockefeller Plaza, New York, NY 10112, (212) 664-4444

National Public Radio, Audience Services, 635 Massachusetts Avenue NW, Washington, DC 20001, (202) 414-3232

New York Film Annex, 1618 West 4th Street, Brooklyn, NY 11223, (718) 382-8868

New York State Education Department, Media Distribution Network, Room 7-C-CEC, Empire State Plaza, Albany, NY 12230, (518) 474-3168

Paramount Home Video. See local retailers.

PBS Video, 1320 Braddock Place, Alexandria, VA 22314, (800) 344-3337

Prism Entertainment, 1888 Century Park East, Suite 350, Los Angeles, CA 90067, (310) 277-3270

Public Media/Home Vision, 4411 North Ravenswood Avenue, Chicago, IL 60640, (773) 878-2600, (800) 826-3456

RMI Media Productions, Inc., 1365 Winchester, Olathe, KS, 66061, (913) 768-1696, (800) 745-5480

The Roland Collection, 22D Hollywood Avenue, Hohokus, NJ 07423, (201) 251-8200, (800) 59-ROLAND

Smithsonian Institution Press, 470 L'Enfante Plaza, Suite 7100, Washington, DC 20650, (202) 287-3738

Sounddeluxe, Box H, Novato City, CA 94949, (800) 227-2020

Time-Life Video and Television, 1450 East Parham Road, Richmond, VA 23280, (800) 621-7026

Twentieth Century Fox Film Corporation. See local retailers.

Universal Studios Home Video. See local retailers.

University of California Extension Media Center, 2000 Center Street, Suite 400, Berkeley, CA 94704, (510) 642-0460

University of Wyoming Audio-Visual Services, Box 3273, Laramie, WY 82071, (307) 766-3184

Video Artists International, 109 Wheeler Avenue, Pleasantville, NY 10570, (914) 769-3691, (800) 477-7146

The Video Catalog Company, Inc., 561 Broadway, New York, NY 10012, (212) 334-0340

Video Learning Library, 15838 North 62 Street, Suite 101, Scottsdale, AZ 85254, (602) 596-9970, (800) 383-8811

Video Yesteryear, Box C, Sandy Hook, CT 06482, (800) 243-0987

Voyager, 424 35 Avenue, Seattle, WA 98122, (206) 323-1112

Warner Home Video. See local retailers.

Water Bearer Films, 48 West 21st Street, Suite 301, New York, NY 10010, (212) 242-8686, (800) 551-8304

Acknowledgments
(continued from p. ii)

Photo: A sculptural bust of Sophocles in marble. Museo Capitolino, Rome, Italy. Photo: CORBIS/Gianni Dagli Orti (p. 40).

Oedipus Rex from *Sophocles: The Oedipus Cycle, An English Version* by Dudley Fitts and Robert Fitzgerald, copyright 1949 by Harcourt, Inc. and renewed 1977 by Cornelia Fitts and Robert Fitzgerald. Reprinted by permission of the publisher. Photos: Henry S. Kranzler, all rights reserved (pp. 48–49); Museum for Gesaltung Zurich (p. 49); © Dr. Jaromir Svoboda (p. 50); Act One, Ltd./Michael Paul (p. 59).

"Poetics: Comedy and Epic and Tragedy" by Aristotle, from *Poetics*, translated by Gerald F. Else (1967). Reprinted by permission of The University of Michigan Press.

Excerpt from "The Structural Study of Myth" by Claude Levi-Strauss. Reprinted from *The Bibliographical and Special Series* of the American Folklore Society, Vol. 5 (1955).

Antigone from *Sophocles: The Oedipus Cycle, An English Version* by Dudley Fitts and Robert Fitzgerald, copyright 1939 by Harcourt, Inc. and renewed 1967 by Dudley Fitts and Robert Fitzgerald. Reprinted by permission of the publisher. CAUTION: All rights, including professional, amateur, motion picture, recitation, lecturing, performance, public reading, radio broadcasting, and television, are strictly reserved. Inquiries on all rights should be addressed to Harcourt Brace and Company, Permissions Department, Orlando, FL 32887-6777. Photos: © Martha Swope (pp. 81–82, 86–87).

"Emotion and Meaning in Greek Tragedy," excerpt from *Greek Tragedy in Action* by Oliver Taplin (Routledge). Reprinted by permission of International Thomson Publishing Services.

Excerpt from *Antigone* by Jean Anouilh, adapted and translated by Lewis Galantière. Copyright 1946 by Random House, Inc. and renewed 1974 by Lewis Galantière. Reprinted by permission of Random House, Inc.

Lysistrata: An English Version from *Aristophanes: Four Comedies* by Dudley Fitts, copyright 1954 by Harcourt, Inc. and renewed 1982 by Cornelia Fitts, Daniel H. Fitts, and Deborah W. Fitts. Reprinted by permission of the publisher. CAUTION: Professionals and amateurs are hereby warned that all titles included in this volume, being fully protected under the copyright laws of the United States of America, Canada, the British Empire, and all other countries which are signatories to the Universal Copyright Convention and the International Copyright Union, are subject to royalty. All rights, including professional, amateur, motion picture, recitation, lecturing, public reading, radio broadcasting, television and the rights of translation into foreign languages, are strictly reserved. Inquiries on professional rights should be addressed to Lucy Kroll Agency, 390 West End Avenue, New York, NY 10024. Inquiries on all other rights should be addressed to Harcourt Brace and Company, Permissions Department, Orlando, Florida 32887-6777. Photo: © Donald Cooper/PHOTOSTAGE (p. 123).

Review of *Lysistrata* by Brooks Atkinson. Copyright © 1930 by The New York Times Company. Reprinted by permission.

Roman Drama

Figure 3. The ancient Theater of Sabratha, in Sabratha, Libya. CORBIS/Roger Wood.

Figure 4. Theater of Marcellus from *The History of Greek and Roman Theater* by Margarete Bieber. Copyright 1939, 1961 by Princeton University Press. Fig. 641 after Peruzzi; redrawn by Mrs. Wadhams. Reprinted by permission of Princeton University Press.

Excerpt from *The Twin Menaechmi* from *Six Plays of Plautus* by Plautus, translated by Lionel Casson. Translation copyright © 1963 by Lionel Casson. Reprinted by permission of Doubleday, a division of Random House, Inc.

Excerpt from *The Brothers* from *The Mother-In-Law* by Terence from *Comedies of Terence*, translated by Robert Graves. Reprinted by permission of A. P. Watt Ltd. on behalf of The Trustees of the Robert Graves Copyright Trust.

Excerpt from *Theyestes* by Seneca from *The Complete Roman Drama* by George E. Duckworth. Copyright 1942 and renewed 1970 by Random House, Inc. Reprinted by permission of Random House, Inc.

Medieval Drama

Figure 5. Pageant wagon from *Early English Stages 1300 to 1660* by Glynne William Gladstone Wickham. Reprinted by permission of Columbia University Press and Routledge & Kegan Paul Ltd.

Dulcitius by Hrotsvitha copyright © 1989. From *The Plays of Hrosvit of Gandersheim*, Vol. 51, Series B, translated by Kathrina M. Wilson. Reproduced by permission of Taylor & Francis/Garland Publishing, http://www.taylorandfrancis.com.

"Reading Hrosvit's Tormented Bodies" excerpted from "Impassive Bodies: Hrotsvit Stages Martyrdom" by Marla Carlson. *Theatre Journal* 50 (December 1998). © The Johns Hopkins University Press. Reprinted by permission.

"Re-viewing Hrosvit" excerpted from "Re-viewing Hrosvit" by Sue Ellen Case. *Theatre Journal* 35 (December 1983). © The Johns Hopkins University Press. Reprinted by permission.

Everyman edited by A. C. Cawley reprinted from the *Everyman's Library* edition, 1974, with footnotes by A. C. Cawley, by permission of David Campbell Publishers Ltd. Photo: Act One, Ltd./Michael Paul (p. 177).

Renaissance Drama

Figure 6. Teatro Olimpico in Vicenza, Italy, Alinari/Art Resource New York.

Figure 7. Perspective setting designed by Peruzzi, Scala/Art Resource New York.

Figure 8. C. Walter Hodges, diagram of the Globe Theatre from *The Globe Restored*, published by Oxford University Press. © 1968 by C. Walter Hodges. Reprinted by permission of Oxford University Press.

Photo: Image of William Shakespeare included on the First Folio. Reprinted by permission of The Folger Shakespeare Library (p. 192).

A Midsummer Night's Dream by William Shakespeare from *The Complete Works of Shakespeare*, 4th edition, by David Bevington. © 1997 by Addision-Wesley Educational Publishers, Inc. Reprinted by permission. Photos: Richard M. Feldman (pp. 206–07); Mario Tursi © 1999 Twentieth Century Fox Film Corporation. Monarchy Enterprises B.V. and Regency Entertainment (USA), Inc. (p. 207); © Martha Swope (pp. 216–17); Osterreichisches Theatermuseum (p. 220).

"Masque Elements in *A Midsummer Night's Dream*" by Enid Welsford from *The Court Masque* by Enid Welsford. Cambridge: Cambridge University Press; New York: The Macmillan Company, 1927. Reprinted by permission of Cambridge University Press.

"On *A Midsummer Night's Dream*" by Linda Bamber. Reprinted from *Comic Women, Tragic Men: A Study of Gender and Genre in Shakespeare* by Linda Bamber with the permission of the publishers, Stanford University Press. Copyright © 1982 by the Board of Trustees of the Leland Stanford Junior University.

"The Play Is the Message . . ." by Peter Brook from *The Shifting Point* by Peter Brook. Copyright © 1987 by Peter Brook. Reprinted by permission of HarperCollins Publishers, Inc.

Review of *A Midsummer Night's Dream* by Clive Barnes. Copyright © 1970 by The New York Times Company. Reprinted by permission.

Othello by William Shakespeare, text and notes by Gerald Eades Bentley (Penguin Books, revised edition, 1970). © Penguin Books, Inc. 1958, 1970. Reprinted by permission of Penguin Books Ltd. Photos: Harvard Theatre Collection (p. 250); T. Charles Erickson Photography (p. 250); Rolf Konow © Castle Rock Entertainment (p. 260); Special Collections and University Archives, Rutgers University Libraries (p. 269).

Casebook Photos: Portrait of Abdul El-Ouahed Ben Messasud. Oil on panel. Artist unknown. University of Birmingham Collections (p. 294); The Shakespeare Theatre's 1997–98 production of *Othello*. Photo: Carol Rosegg (p. 310).

"Macready's Othello" from *Othello: A Contextual History* by Virginia Mason Vaughan. Copyright © 1994. Reprinted by permission of Cambridge University Press.

"Going It Alone: A Review of Olivier's Othello" by John Holstrom from *Plays and Players* (June 1964). *Theater Magazine*. Reprinted by permission of Duke University Press.

Excerpt from *Mandeville's Travels* by Sir John Mandeville, 1357. Edited by M.C. Seymour. Copyright © 1968. Reprinted by permission of Oxford University Press.

Excerpt from "*Othello* and Colour Prejudice" by G. K. Hunter from *Dramatic Identities and Cultural Tradition: Studies in Shakespeare and His Contemporaries* by G. K. Hunter, © 1978. Reprinted by permission of Rowman & Littlefield Publishers, Inc.

Review of Patrick Stewart's Othello by Peter Marks. Copyright © 1997 by The New York Times Company. Reprinted by permission.

The Masque of Blackness by Ben Jonson, from *Ben Jonson: The Complete Masques,* edited by Stephen Orgel. Copyright © 1969 by Yale University. Reprinted by permission of Yale University Press. Photo: Devonshire Collection, Chatsworth (p. 316).

"Africa in English Masque and Pageantry" by Eldred Jones from *Othello's Countrymen* by Eldred Jones. Copyright © 1965. Reprinted by permission of Oxford University Press.

Late Seventeenth- and Eighteenth-Century Drama

Figure 9. Early Restoration Theater, illustration by Peter Kahn. From *The Frolicks; or, The Lawyer Cheated* by Elizabeth Polwhele, edited by Judith Milhous and Robert D. Hume, Cornell University Press, 1977. Used by permission of the publisher, Cornell University Press.

The Misanthrope by Molière, translated by Richard Wilbur, copyright © 1955 and renewed 1983 by Richard Wilbur, reprinted by permission of Harcourt Brace & Company. CAUTION: Professionals and amateurs are hereby warned that this translation, being fully protected under the copyright laws of the United States, the British Commonwealth, the Dominion of Canada, and all other countries which are signatories to the Universal Copyright Convention, is subject to royalty. All rights, including professional, amateur, motion picture, recitation, lecturing, public reading, radio broadcasting, and television, are strictly reserved. Particular emphasis is laid on the question of readings, permission for which must be secured from the author's agent in writing. Inquiries on professional rights should be addressed to Mr. Gilbert Parker, William Morris Agency, 1350 Avenue of the Americas, New York, NY 10019. Inquiries on all other rights should be addressed to Harcourt Brace and Company, Permissions Department, Orlando, FL 32887-6777. The amateur acting rights of *The Misanthrope* are controlled exclusively by the Dramatists Play Service, Inc., 440 Park Avenue South, New York, NY 10016. No amateur performance of the play may be given without obtaining in advance the written permission of the Dramatists Play Service, Inc. and paying the requisite fee. Photo: Courtesy of the Williamstown Theatre Festival. Photo by Michael C. Durling (p. 347).

"Alceste's Love for Célimène," excerpt from *Men and Masks: A Study of Molière* by Lionel Gossman. Reprinted by permission of Johns Hopkins University Press. Copyright © 1963.

Nineteenth-Century Drama to the Turn of the Century

Figure 10. Auditorium, Chicago, 1889. Photo: Henrich Blessing. Courtesy of the Auditorium Theatre Council.

Figure 11. Realistic setting in Anton Chekhov's *The Cherry Orchard*, Harvard Theatre Collection.

Photos: Henrik Ibsen (c. 1896), CORBIS/Bettmann (p. 372); Realistic stage setting of Ibsen's *The Wild Duck*, Bibliothèque de l'Arsenal, Paris (p. 374); Edvard Munch's stage design for Ibsen's *Ghosts*, Munch Museum, Oslo Photo: Munch Museum (p. 375).

A Doll House from *The Complete Major Prose Plays of Henrik Ibsen* by Henrik Ibsen, translated by Rolf Fjelde, Translation copyright © 1965, 1970, 1978, by Rolf Fjelde. Used by permission of Dutton Signet, a division of Penguin Putnam Inc. Photos: © 1992 Martha Swope (pp. 386–87); Donald Cooper/PHOTOSTAGE (pp. 394–95); Sara Krulwich/NYT Pictures (p. 405).

"*A Doll's House*: Ibsen the Moralist" by Muriel C. Bradbrook from *Ibsen the Norwegian* by Muriel C. Bradbrook. Reprinted by permission of Random Century.

Miss Julie by August Strindberg, and excerpt from the Preface to *Miss Julie* from *Strindberg: Five Plays,* Harry Carlson, editor and translator. Copyright © 1983 The Regents of the University of California. Reprinted by permission of the University of California Press. Photo: © Donald Cooper/PHOTOSTAGE (p. 424).

The Importance of Being Earnest. Photos: © Richard Feldman (p. 445); Carol Rosegg (p. 457).

"An Unpublished Letter from Oscar Wilde on *The Importance of Being Earnest*" from "The Making of *The Importance of Being Earnest*" by Peter Raby. *Times Literary Supplement* No. 4629, December 1991. Reprinted by permission of Peter Raby. Oscar Wilde's letter to George Alexander is reprinted by permission of Merlin Holland.

The Cherry Orchard by Anton Chekhov from *The Major Plays of Anton Chekhov* by Anton Chekhov, translated by Ann Dunnigan. Translation copyright © 1964 by Ann Dunnigan. Used by permission of New American Library, a division of Penguin Books USA Inc. Photos: © Richard Feldman (p. 481).

"From Chekhov's Letters," two letters from *Letters of Anton Chekhov* translated by Michael Henry Heim with Simon Karlinsky. Copyright © 1973 by Harper & Row Publishers, Inc. Reprinted by permission of HarperCollins Publishers, Inc.

Excerpt from "Recollections" by Maxim Gorky from *Reminiscences of Tolstoy, Chekhov and Andreyev* by Maxim Gorky. Reprinted by permission of Random Century.

Review of *The Cherry Orchard* by John Corbin. Copyright © 1923 by The New York Times Company. Reprinted by permission.

"On Chekhov" by Peter Brook from *The Shifting Point* by Peter Brook. Copyright © 1987 by Peter Brook. Reprinted by permission of HarperCollins Publishers, Inc.

Drama in the Early and Mid-Twentieth Century

Figure 12. Expressionistic setting in Arthur Miller's *Death of a Salesman*, the Billy Rose Theatre Collection of New York Public Library for the Performing Arts/Astor, Lenox, and Tilden Foundations.

"On the Edge: The Plays of Susan Glaspell" by Christine Dymkowski from *Modern Drama* 31 (March 1988). Reprinted by permission of the University of Toronto Press.

Six Characters in Search of an Author copyright 1922 by E. P. Dutton. Renewed 1950 in the names of Stefano, Fausto, and Lietta Pirandello from *Naked Masks: Five Plays by Luigi Pirandello,* edited by Eric Bentley. Translation copyright 1922, 1952 by E. P. Dutton. Renewed 1950 in the names of Stefano, Fausto, and Lietta Pirandello. Introduction copyright 1952, © renewed 1980 by Eric Bentley. Used by permission of Dutton Signet, a division of Penguin Books USA Inc. Photo: © Richard Feldman (p. 531).

Desire under the Elms by Eugene O'Neill. Copyright 1924 and renewed 1952 by Eugene O'Neill. Reprinted from *The Plays of Eugene O'Neill* by Eugene O'Neill by permission of Random House, Inc. Photo: T. Charles Erickson Photography (p. 564).

Review of *Desire under the Elms* by Stark Young. Copyright © 1924 by The New York Times Company. Reprinted by permission.

Mother Courage and Her Children by Bertolt Brecht. Copyright © 1940 by Arvid Englind Teaterforlag, a.b., renewed June 1967 by Stefan S. Brecht; copyright © 1949 by Suhrkamp Verlag, Frankfurt am Main. Translation copyright © 1980 Stefan S. Brecht. Reprinted from *Mother Courage and Her Children* by Bertolt Brecht, published by Arcade Publishing Inc., New York, New York. Photo: Photofest (p. 585).

"The Alienation Effect" by Bertolt Brecht, translated by John Willett from *Brecht on Theatre,* edited and translated by John Willett. Copyright © 1964. Hill and Wang. Reprinted by permission of Farrar, Straus and Giroux.

"Notes for *Mother Courage*" by Bertolt Brecht from *Directors on Directing,* edited by Toby Cole and Helen Krich Chinoy. Copyright © 1963. Reprinted by permission of Prentice-Hall, Inc.

Photo: Tennessee Williams on the set of *Night of the Iguana* at the Savoy Theatre in 1965. CORBUS/Hulton Deutsch Collection.

The Glass Menagerie by Tennessee Williams Copyright 1945 by Tennessee Williams and Edwina D. Williams and renewed 1973 by Tennessee Williams. Reprinted by permission of Random House, Inc. Photos: The Billy Rose Theatre Collection of the New York Public Library for the Performing Arts/Astor, Lenox, and Tilden Foundations (pp. 628–29); Estate of Jo Mielziner, used by permission (p. 629); Joan Marcus/Arena Stage (p. 636–37).

Review of *The Glass Menagerie* by Lewis Nichols. Copyright © 1945 by The New York Times Company. Reprinted by permission.

"Laurette Taylor in *The Glass Menagerie*," excerpt from *The Kindness of Strangers: The Life of Tennessee Williams* by Donald Spoto. Copyright © 1985 by Donald Spoto. Reprinted by permission of Little, Brown and Company.

"Problems in *The Glass Menagerie*" by Benjamin Nelson. Excerpt from *Tennessee Williams: The Man and His Work* by Benjamin Nelson (New York: 1961). Reprinted by permission of the author.

Death of a Salesman by Arthur Miller. Copyright 1949, renewed © 1977 by Arthur Miller. All rights reserved. Used by permission of Viking Penguin, a division of Penguin Putnam Inc. Photos of the Goodman Theatre production of *Death of a Salesman* by Eric Y. Exit (pp. 665, 695); Photofest (p. 693).

"In Memoriam" by Arthur Miller is reprinted by permission of the author and International Creative Management, Inc. Copyright © 1995 by Arthur Miller. First appeared in *The New Yorker*.

"Tragedy and the Common Man," excerpt from *The Theatre Essays of Arthur Miller* by Arthur Miller, edited by Robert A. Martin. Copyright 1949, renewed © 1977 by Arthur Miller. Used by permission of Viking Penguin, a division of Penguin Putnam Inc.

"A Salesman Who Transcends Time" by Michiko Kakutani. Copyright © 1999 by The New York Times Company. Reprinted by permission.

"*Death of a Salesman*: The Design Process" from *Miller: Death of a Salesman* by Brenda Murphy. Copyright © 1995. Reprinted by permission of Cambridge University Press.

Endgame by Samuel Beckett. Copyright © 1958 by Grove Press, Inc.; copyright renewed © 1986 by Samuel Beckett. Used by permission of Grove Press, Inc. Photos: © 1992 Martha Swope (pp. 722–23); Richard M. Feldman (p. 733).

Excerpt from *The Theatre of the Absurd* by Martin Esslin. Reprinted by permission of the author.

"The Ending of *Endgame*," excerpt from *Beckett's Theaters: Interpretations for Performance* by Sidney Homan (Bucknell University Press). Reprinted by permission of Associated University Presses.

A Raisin in the Sun by Lorraine Hansberry. Copyright © 1958 by Robert Nemiroff. Copyright © 1959, 1966, 1984 by Robert Nemiroff, as an unpublished work. Copyright © 1959, 1966, 1984 by Robert Nemiroff. Reprinted by permission of Random House, Inc.

"Dream Deferred" ("Harlem") by Langston Hughes from *The Panther and the Lash* by Langston Hughes. Copyright 1951 by Langston Hughes. Reprinted by permission of Alfred A. Knopf, Inc.

Review of *A Raisin in the Sun* by Brooks Atkinson. Copyright © 1959 by The New York Times Company. Reprinted by permission. Photo: © Richard Feldman (p. 753).

Contemporary Drama

Figure 13. Multimedia effects in Robert Wilson's *CIVIL warS*, Richard M. Feldman.

"*Master Harold*" . . . *and the Boys* by Athol Fugard. Copyright © 1982 by Athol Fugard. Reprinted by permission of Alfred A. Knopf, Inc. Photo: © Donald Cooper/PHOTOSTAGE (p. 805).

"Interview with Athol Fugard" by Heinrich von Staden from *Theater* (Yale), Vol. 14, No. 1, Winter 1982. Reprinted by permission of the author.

Excerpt from *Notebooks 1960–1977* by Athol Fugard. Copyright © 1983 by Athol Fugard. Reprinted by permission of Alfred A. Knopf, Inc.

Fences by August Wilson. Copyright © 1986 August Wilson. Used by permission of Dutton Signet, a division of Penguin Putnam Inc. Photos: © Photofest (pp. 836–37).

Excerpt from an interview with August Wilson by David Savran from *In Their Own Words*. Reprinted by permission of Theatre Communications Group.

Review of *Fences* by Frank Rich ("Theatre: Family Ties in Wilson's '*Fences*'"). Copyright © 1987 by The New York Times Company. Reprinted by permission.

"*Art*" by Yasmina Reza, translated by Christopher Hampton. Copyright © 1994 by Yasmina Reza. Translation copyright © Yasmina Reza and Christopher Hampton, 1996. First published in 1996 by Faber & Faber Ltd. Reprinted by permission of the publisher. Photos: © Joan Marcus (p. 865).

"What Is '*Art*'?" by Louis Menand from *The New Yorker* 73 (February 9, 1998). Reprinted by permission of the author.

How I Learned to Drive by Paula Vogel from *The Mammary Plays* © 1998 by Paula Vogel. Reprinted by permission of Theatre Communications Group, Inc. Photos: T. Charles Erickson Photography (p. 896); Carol Rosegg (p. 907).

"Coast to Coast with Paula Vogel" by Caridad Svich and Peter Franklin from *The Dramatist* (July/August 1999). Reprinted by permission of the Dramatists Guild Inc.

"Paula Vogel" by David Savran from *The Playwright's Voice: American Dramatists on Memory, Writing and the Politics of Culture* by David Savran. Copyright © 1999 by David Savran. Reprinted by permission of Theatre Communications Group, Inc.

Review of *How I Learned to Drive* by Jill Dolan from *Theatre Journal* 50 (March 1998). Copyright © The Johns Hopkins University Press. Reprinted by permission.